"I just finished my A+ Certification class and had my first class of Network+ tonight. I couldn't help but notice that my teachers would get stumped on a question and always refer to this book as the 'almighty' to find the answer."

Chip Tomashek, Renton, Washington

"Your coverage, explanation, and writing style are the best in the business. I have the 11th and 12th Editions and would not part with them for twice the price I paid."

Ken Duge, Skidmore, Texas

"*Upgrading and Repairing PCs* has provided me with the fullest education I've ever received from a single book."

Michael D. Anderson, IT Coordinator, Taliesin Preservation

"When this treasure trove is not in use (hardly), it occupies a place of honour on my shelves next to J.R.R. Tolkien's works. Technicians and geeks everywhere shall sing the praises."

Andre Pretorius, Johannesburg, South Africa

"The book is brilliant. I suddenly seem to be addicted to finding out as much as I can about computers."

Roy Forrest, Lancashire, England

"You have the most exhaustive textbook on the planet! I have read your PC repair books from the 6th Edition to the present."

Gene Fowler, Corona, New York

"*Scott Mueller's Upgrading and Repairing PCs* is to the PC as Horowitz and Hill's *The Art of Electronics* is to electronics. By making this comparison, I don't think I can give Scott's book higher praise!"

Greg Parker, Ph.D., Professor of Photonics, University of Southampton, England

UPGRADING AND REPAIRING PCs,

16th Edition

Scott Mueller

800 East 96th Street
Indianapolis, Indiana 46240

Contents at a Glance

Upgrading and Repairing PCs, 16th Edition

Copyright © 2005 by Que Publishing

International Standard Book Number: 0-7897-3173-8
0-7897-3308-0
0-7897-3210-6

Library of Congress Catalog Card Number: 2004100886

Printed in the United States of America

First Printing: September 2004

07   06   05   04   4   3

Trademarks

Warning and Disclaimer

Bulk Sales

Que offers excellent discounts on this book when ordered in quantity for bulk purchases or special sales. For more information, please contact

U.S. Corporate and Government Sales
1-800-382-3419
corpsales@pearsontechgroup.com

For sales outside the U.S., please contact

International Sales
international@pearsoned.com

Associate Publisher
Greg Wiegand

Executive Editor
Rick Kughen

Acquisitions Editor
Todd Green

Development Editor
Todd Brakke

Managing Editor
Charlotte Clapp

Project Editors
Tonya Simpson
Tricia Liebig

Production Editor
Megan Wade

Indexer
Erika Millen

Proofreader
Jessica McCarty

Technical Editor
Mark Reddin

Publishing Coordinator
Sharry Lee Gregory

Multimedia Developer
Dan Scherf

Interior Designer
Anne Jones

Cover Designer
Anne Jones

Page Layout
Stacey DeRome

Graphics
Tammy Graham
Laura Robbins

Cover Photography
Mark Madeo
Future Network USA

DVD Production
Lynn Mueller

Contents

11 Floppy Disk Storage   685

12 High-Capacity Removable Storage   705

13 Optical Storage   737

16 Audio Hardware   941

17 I/O Interfaces from Serial and Parallel to IEEE 1394 and USB   981

To Emerson:

"The real test for any choice is having to make the same choice again, knowing full well what it might cost." —The Oracle

About the Author

Scott Mueller is president of Mueller Technical Research (MTR), an international research and corporate training firm. Since 1982, MTR has produced the industry's most in-depth, accurate, and effective seminars, books, articles, videos, and FAQs covering PC hardware and data recovery. MTR maintains a client list that includes Fortune 500 companies, the U.S. and foreign governments, major software and hardware corporations, as well as PC enthusiasts and entrepreneurs. His seminars have been presented to several thousands of PC support professionals throughout the world.

Scott personally teaches seminars nationwide covering all aspects of PC hardware (including troubleshooting, maintenance, repair, and upgrade), A+ Certification, and data recovery/forensics. He has a knack for making technical topics not only understandable, but entertaining as well; his classes are never boring! If you have 10 or more people to train, Scott can design and present a custom seminar for your organization.

Although he has taught classes virtually nonstop since 1982, Scott is best known as the author of the longest running, most popular, and most comprehensive PC hardware book in the world, *Upgrading and Repairing PCs*, which has not only been produced in more than 16 editions, but has also become the core of an entire series of books.

Scott has authored many books over the last 20+ years, including *Upgrading and Repairing PCs*, 1st through 16th and Academic editions; *Upgrading and Repairing Laptops*; *Upgrading and Repairing PCs: A+ Certification Study Guide*, 1st and 2nd editions; *Upgrading and Repairing PCs Technician's Portable Reference*, 1st and 2nd editions; *Upgrading and Repairing PCs Field Guide*; *Upgrading and Repairing PCs Quick Reference*; *Upgrading and Repairing PCs, Linux Edition*; *Killer PC Utilities*; *The IBM PS/2 Handbook*; and *Que's Guide to Data Recovery*.

Scott has produced several video training packages covering PC hardware, including a 6-hour, CD-based seminar titled *Upgrading and Repairing PCs Training Course: A Digital Seminar from Scott Mueller*. This course is ideal for those who cannot afford to bring Scott in-house.

Scott has also produced other videos over the years, including *Upgrading and Repairing PCs Video: 12th Edition; Your PC: The Inside Story*; as well as 2 hours of free video training that were included in each of the 10th, 12th, 13th, 14th, 15th, and 16th editions of *Upgrading and Repairing PCs*, as well as the new *Upgrading and Repairing Laptops* book. Scott has always included unique video segments with his books, rather than using the same clips every year. Many people have collected each of the older editions just to get the unique video training segments included with them.

Contact MTR directly if you have a unique book, article, or video project in mind, or if you want Scott to conduct a custom PC troubleshooting, repair, maintenance, upgrade, or data-recovery seminar tailored for your organization:

Mueller Technical Research
3700 Grayhawk Drive
Algonquin, IL 60102-6325
(847) 854-6794
(847) 854-6795 Fax
Internet: scottmueller@compuserve.com
Web: http://www.upgradingandrepairingpcs.com
             http://www.m-tr.com

Scott's premiere work, *Upgrading and Repairing PCs*, has sold well over 2 million copies, making it by far the most popular and longest-running PC hardware book on the market today. Scott has been featured in *Forbes* magazine and has written several articles for *Maximum PC* magazine, several newsletters, and the *Upgrading and Repairing PCs* Web site.

Scott has recently completed two new works, *Upgrading and Repairing Laptops* and *Upgrading and Repairing PCs Video Training Course*.

If you have suggestions for the next version of this book, any comments about the book in general, or new book or article topics you would like to see covered, send them to Scott via email at scottmueller@compuserve.com or visit www.upgradingandrepairingpcs.com and click the Ask Scott button.

When he is not working on PC-related books or on the road teaching seminars, Scott can usually be found in the garage working on several vehicular projects. He is currently working on a custom 1999 Harley-Davidson FLHRCI Road King Classic and a modified 1998 5.9L (360ci) Grand Cherokee—a hot rod 4×4.

Contributors and Technical Editors

Mark Edward Soper is president of Select Systems and Associates, Inc., a technical writing and training organization.

Mark has taught computer troubleshooting and other technical subjects to thousands of students from Maine to Hawaii since 1992. He is an A+ Certified hardware technician and a Microsoft Certified Professional. He has been writing technical documents since the mid-1980s and has contributed to several other Que books, including *Upgrading and Repairing PCs*, 11th, 12th, 13th, 14th, and 15th editions; *Upgrading and Repairing Networks, Second Edition*; and *Special Edition Using Microsoft Windows Millennium Edition*. Mark coauthored *Upgrading and Repairing PCs, Technician's Portable Reference*; *Upgrading and Repairing PCs Field Guide*; and *Upgrading and Repairing PCs: A+ Study Certification Guide, Second Edition*. He is the author of *The Complete Idiot's Guide to High-Speed Internet Connections*, *PC Help Desk in a Book*, and *Absolute Beginner's Guide to Cable Internet Connections* and is coauthor of *TechTV's Upgrading Your PC*.

Mark has been writing for major computer magazines since 1990, with more than 125 articles in publications such as *SmartComputing*, *PCNovice*, *PCNovice Guides*, and the *PCNovice Learning Series*. His early work was published in *WordPerfect Magazine*, *The WordPerfectionist*, and *PCToday*. Many of Mark's articles are available in back issues or electronically via the World Wide Web at www.smartcomputing.com. Select Systems maintains a subject index of all Mark's articles at http://www.selectsystems.com.

Mark welcomes comments at mesoper@selectsystems.com.

Mark Reddin is a Microsoft Certified Systems Engineer (MCSE) and A+ Certified PC technician. While a tyro, he enjoyed tinkering with computers during the time of the early Commodore and Atari systems (with all those wonderful games). Mark delved more seriously into computer technology during his undergraduate studies at Ball State University and has since been involved in the industry in various capacities. His experience with computers and networks has ranged from consulting to owning and operating a sales and repair shop. Additionally, he has been involved with numerous Que publications over the last few years, offering technical verification and development.

Acknowledgments

The new 16th edition continues the long tradition of making this the most accurate, in-depth, and up-to-date book of its kind on the market. This new edition is the product of a great deal of additional research and development over the previous editions. Several people have helped me with both the research and production of this book. I would like to thank the following people:

First, a very special thanks to my wife and partner, Lynn. Over the last few years, she has returned to school full-time, in addition to helping run our business. She recently graduated with full honors (congratulations!), receiving a degree in multimedia and Web design. She used her creative and technical skills to shoot and produce the video that is included with this book. I'm extremely proud of her for all I've seen her accomplish in the last few years. The dedication she has shown to her work has been inspiring.

Thanks to Lisa Carlson of Mueller Technical Research for helping with product research and office management. She has fantastic organizational skills that have been a tremendous help in managing all the information that comes into and goes out of this office.

I must give a special thanks to Rick Kughen at Que. Rick is the number one person responsible for taking what I submit and turning it into a finished book. His office is like a shrine to *Upgrading and Repairing PCs*, sporting a complete (and very rare) collection of every single edition since the first. His attention to detail is amazing, and he genuinely cares about both the book and my readers, often going far above and beyond the call of duty when it comes to customer service and support. Rick is always pushing to add extra value to the book and is constantly coming up with ways to improve the overall product.

Thanks also go to my new editor Todd Green. Although he is new to this book, he is a veteran in the publishing business and has been instrumental in helping to move this book through to completion.

I'd also like to thank Todd Brakke for doing the development editing for this edition. His excellent tips and suggestions really help to keep the material concise and up-to-date. I'd also like to thank the other editors, illustrators, designers, and technicians at Que who work so hard to complete the finished product and get this book out the door! They are a wonderful team that produces clearly the best computer books on the market. I am happy and proud to be closely associated with all the people at Que.

I would like to say thanks also to my publisher Greg Wiegand, who has stood behind all the *Upgrading and Repairing* book and video projects and is willing to take the risks in developing new versions like *Upgrading and Repairing Laptops*.

All the people at Que make me feel as if we are on the same team, and they are just as dedicated as I am to producing the best books possible.

I would also like to say thanks to Mark Soper, who has added expertise in areas that I might tend to neglect. Also thanks to Mark Reddin, who has become the primary technical editor for this book and who is not only extremely diligent in verifying details, but who also makes numerous suggestions about additional coverage, all of which are greatly appreciated. His input has been extremely important in helping me to ensure the highest level of technical accuracy and depth of coverage.

Special thanks go to Chris Beahan, who helped immensely in proofreading the text. Thanks also to all the other readers who emailed me with suggestions concerning this book; I welcome all your comments and even your criticisms. I take them seriously and apply them to the continuous improvement of this book. I especially enjoy answering the many questions you send me; your questions help me understand areas of the book that might need to be clarified and point out additional coverage that should be added. Interaction with my readers is the primary force that helps maintain this book as the most up-to-date and relevant work available *anywhere* on the subject of PC hardware.

Thanks to Tim Tavano, Carter Martin, Rob Luck, Andrew Puglise, and Zack Hall for helping out with the video shoot; we couldn't have done it without your assistance. Thanks to Doug Dodson and Bob Roark of PC Power and Cooling for supplying some very "cool" equipment for the video, as well. Finally, I would like to thank the thousands of people who have attended my seminars; you might not realize how much I learn from each of you and all your questions!

Many of my all-night writing raves are fueled by a variety of possibly less-than-nutritious (but very tasty and loaded with energy) food and beverage. In particular, this edition was fueled by many pounds of Starbucks coffee processed via a killer Capresso automatic coffee/espresso machine (utter nirvana for an addicted coffee drinker like me), cases of Coke Classic (no Pepsi allowed—gotta have the burn!), Red Bull and AMP energy drinks, Trolli Brite Crawler Eggs, and Pearson's Salted NutRolls. For special occasions when I really needed a boost, I enjoyed a couple of bottles of Skeleteens Brain Wash, the ultimate energy drink. Why, that covers the three major workaholic nerd/geek food groups right there: caffeine, sugar, and salt!

Tell Us What You Think!

As the reader of this book, *you* are our most important critic and commentator. We value your opinion and want to know what we're doing right, what we could do better, what areas you'd like to see us publish in, and any other words of wisdom you're willing to pass our way.

As an associate publisher for Que, I welcome your comments. You can email or write me directly to let me know what you did or didn't like about this book—as well as what we can do to make our books better.

Please note that I cannot help you with technical problems related to the topic of this book. We do have a User Services group, however, where I will forward specific technical questions related to the book.

When you write, please be sure to include this book's title and author as well as your name, email address, and phone number. I will carefully review your comments and share them with the author and editors who worked on the book.

Email: feedback@quepublishing.com

Mail: Greg Wiegand
         Associate Publisher
         Que Publishing
         800 East 96th Street
         Indianapolis, IN 46240 USA

For more information about this book or another Que title, visit our Web site at www.quepublishing.com. Type the ISBN (excluding hyphens) or the title of a book in the Search field to find the page you're looking for.

Introduction

Welcome to *Upgrading and Repairing PCs, 16th Edition*. Since debuting as the first book of its kind on the market in 1988, no other book on PC hardware has matched the depth and quality of the information found in this tome. The 16th edition continues *Upgrading and Repairing PCs'* role as not only the best-selling book of its type, but also the most comprehensive and complete PC hardware reference available. This book examines PCs in depth, outlines the differences among them, and presents options for configuring each system.

More than just a minor revision, the 16th edition of *Upgrading and Repairing PCs* contains hundreds of pages of new, revised, and reworked content. The PC industry is moving faster than ever, and this book is the most accurate, complete, in-depth, and up-to-date book of its kind on the market today.

I wrote this book for people who want to upgrade, repair, maintain, and troubleshoot computers or for those enthusiasts who want to know more about PC hardware. This book covers the full gamut of PC-compatible systems from the oldest 8-bit machines to the latest in high-end 64-bit multigigahertz speed PC-based workstations. If you need to know about everything from the original PC to the latest in PC technology on the market today, this book and the accompanying information-packed disc is definitely for you.

This book covers state-of-the-art hardware and accessories that make the most modern personal computers easier, faster, and more productive to use. Inside these pages you will find in-depth coverage of every PC processor from the original 8088 to the latest Pentium 4 Prescott and Athlon 64/64 FX.

Upgrading and Repairing PCs also doesn't ignore the less glamorous PC components. Every part of your PC plays a critical role in its stability and performance. Over the course of this book's 1,500+ pages, you'll find out exactly why your motherboard's chipset might just be the most important part of your PC and what can go wrong when you settle for a run-of-the-mill power supply that can't get enough juice to that monster processor you just bought. You'll also find in-depth coverage of technologies such as new form factors (including BTX, DDR, and DDR2 SDRAM), graphics and audio cards, AGP, PCI and PCI Express, flat-panel displays, DVD+/-RW drives, Serial ATA, USB 2.0, FireWire, and high-capacity removable storage—it's all in here, right down to the guts-level analysis of your mouse and keyboard.

New in the 16th Edition

Many of you who are reading this have purchased one or more of the previous editions. Based on your letters, emails, and other correspondence, I know that, as much as you value each new edition, you want to know what new information I'm bringing you. So, here is a short list of the major improvements to this edition:

■ In addition to the hundreds of pages of detail we have on every PC processor, including all those from Intel and AMD, this year we've added even more. Intel has moved to 90-nanometer chip production with the Prescott version of the Pentium 4, which has further unleashed the technology's extreme potential. AMD is making the first forays into 64-bit computing on the desktop with the Athlon 64 and 64 FX, using architectures previously limited only to servers. There are new sockets, new chipsets, and new motherboards designed to support these chips. You'll also find the straight dope on Intel's new processor numbering scheme.

■ Intel's newer Pentium 4 processors have Hyper-threading (HT) technology, which makes a single processor function more like two processors running simultaneously. The new Prescott versions also have a deeper 31-stage pipeline. You'll find out whether your system has what it takes to support the HT technology processors and how the deeper pipeline affects performance and clock speeds. You'll also get information about higher bus speeds, new types of memory, and more.

- Newer chipsets use dual-channel DDR memory, which uses two banks simultaneously to match the speed of the processor bus, eliminating a bottleneck and optimizing performance. The latest type of memory is DDR2 memory, supported by the newest chipsets and boards. In Chapter 6, "Memory," I not only expand my content on memory technologies, but also explain the benefits of the newer designs.

- An all-new chapter on system modifications, or *mods*, details the technology that controls the clock speed of your system and how it can be modified to make it faster by overclocking. Because more speed invariably means more heat, extreme cooling technologies are covered and the latest designs for cooling your PC are discussed. A simple modification is detailed that you can use to add the latest cooling technology to an existing system. Upgrading your chassis to include front-panel-mounted connectors for USB, FireWire, and other ports is detailed as well.

- Many changes are coming for PC chassis and motherboards, especially in the area of cooling. The ATX form factor has been the most popular form factor since 1996, but a new form factor called BTX is on the horizon. Chapter 4, "Motherboards and Buses," has all the details on the new BTX form factor, including detailed information about the reasons behind the change and how the change will affect the chassis, processor cooling, and more. New bus slots called PCI Express are also making it onto the motherboard, and Chapter 4 includes detailed information about these new slots as well.

- Interested in turning your PC into a hot rod game machine? Read my coverage of audio, video, and Internet connectivity for the lowdown on supercharging your PC. Inside you'll find new coverage of the latest video cards from NVIDIA (6800 series) and ATI (X800 series).

- As always, we have more new, high-quality technical illustrations. Every year we add, modify, and generally improve on the hundreds of figures in this book. These new and revised illustrations provide more technical detail, helping you understand difficult topics or showing you exactly how to complete a task.

- Just like last year, you'll find a DVD-ROM or CD-ROM (depending on the version) plastered to the inside back cover of this book. On it you'll find all the usual stand-bys, such as the Technical Reference and complete electronic versions of prior editions. Rather than recycle the same video clips from edition to edition as many of my competitors do, I've always included unique video clips for each new edition, and the 16th is no exception. I've included 2 hours of new video with this edition.

As with every edition, I've done as much research and homework as humanly possible to ensure that this volume is the most consistent and up-do-date text on PC hardware you're going to find in a book.

Book Objectives

Upgrading and Repairing PCs focuses on several objectives. The primary objective is to help you learn how to maintain, upgrade, and repair your PC system. To that end, *Upgrading and Repairing PCs* helps you fully understand the family of computers that has grown from the original IBM PC, including all PC-compatible systems. This book discusses all areas of system improvement, such as motherboards, processors, memory, and even case and power-supply improvements. The book discusses proper system and component care, specifies the most failure-prone items in various PC systems, and tells you how to locate and identify a failing component. You'll learn about powerful diagnostics hardware and software that enable a system to help you determine the cause of a problem and how to repair it.

PCs are moving forward rapidly in power and capabilities. Processor performance increases with every new chip design. *Upgrading and Repairing PCs* helps you gain an understanding of all the processors used in PC-compatible computer systems.

This book covers the important differences between major system architectures from the original Industry Standard Architecture (ISA) to the latest in AGP and PCI Express interface standards. *Upgrading and Repairing PCs* covers each of these system architectures and their adapter boards to help you make decisions about which type of system you want to buy in the future and to help you upgrade and troubleshoot such systems.

The amount of storage space available to modern PCs is increasing geometrically. *Upgrading and Repairing PCs* covers storage options ranging from larger, faster hard drives to state-of-the-art storage devices. In addition, it provides detailed information on upgrading and troubleshooting system RAM.

When you finish reading this book, you should have the knowledge to upgrade, troubleshoot, and repair almost any system and component.

Is This Book for You?

If you want to know more about PCs, then this book is most definitely for you!

Upgrading and Repairing PCs is designed for people who want a thorough understanding of PC hardware and how their PC systems work. Each section fully explains common and not-so-common problems, what causes problems, and how to handle problems when they arise. You will gain, for example, an understanding of disk configuration and interfacing that can improve your diagnostics and troubleshooting skills. You'll develop a feel for what goes on in a system so you can rely on your own judgment and observations and not some table of canned troubleshooting steps.

Upgrading and Repairing PCs is written for people who will select, install, configure, maintain, and repair systems they or their companies use. To accomplish these tasks, you need a level of knowledge much higher than that of an average system user. You must know exactly which tool to use for a task and how to use the tool correctly. This book can help you achieve this level of knowledge.

Scott has taught millions of people to upgrade and build PCs. Some of his students are computer experts, and some are computer novices. But they all have one thing in common: They believe Scott's book changed their lives. Scott can teach anyone.

Chapter-by-Chapter Breakdown

This book is organized into chapters that cover the components of a PC system. A few chapters serve to introduce or expand in an area not specifically component related, but most parts in the PC have a dedicated chapter or section, which will aid you in finding the information you want. Also note that the index has been improved greatly over previous editions, which will further aid in finding information in a book of this size.

Chapters 1 and 2 of this book serve primarily as an introduction. Chapter 1, "Development of the PC," begins with an introduction to the development of the original IBM PC and PC-compatibles. This chapter incorporates some of the historical events that led to the development of the microprocessor and the PC. Chapter 2, "PC Components, Features, and System Design," provides information about the various types of systems you encounter and what separates one type of system from another, including the types of system buses that differentiate systems. Chapter 2 also provides an overview of the types of PC systems that help build a foundation of knowledge essential for the remainder of the book, and it offers some insight as to how the PC market is driven and where components and technologies are sourced.

Chapter 3, "Microprocessor Types and Specifications," includes detailed coverage of Intel's Pentium 4 (Prescott, Northwood, and Willamette), Pentium III, Pentium II, Celeron, Xeon, and earlier central processing unit (CPU) chips. There's also new and extended coverage on AMD's line of high-performance Athlon 64/64 FX and Athlon XP processors as well as the Athlon, Duron, and K6 series. Because the processor is one of the most important parts of a PC, this book features more extensive and updated processor coverage than ever before. I dig deeply into the latest processor-upgrade socket and slot specifications, including coverage of Sockets 754, 939, and 940 for the Athlon 64/64 FX; Socket 423, Socket 478, and Socket T (LGA775) for the Pentium 4; Socket A (462) for AMD Athlon XP; and older sockets and slots such as Socket 7, Socket 370, Slot 1, and Slot A. Chapter 3 also tells you how to spot a re-marked processor. These are processors that have been modified by unscrupulous resellers to run faster than their rated speeds. These chips are then sold to the consumer as faster processors. I show you how to spot and avoid fakes.

Chapter 4, "Motherboards and Buses," covers the motherboard, chipsets, motherboard components, and system buses in detail. This chapter contains discussions of motherboard form factors, including specifications on everything from Baby-AT to the various ATX and new BTX standards. A chipset can either make a good PC better or choke the life out of an otherwise high-speed CPU. I cover the latest chipsets for current processor families, including chipsets from Intel, AMD, VIA, NVIDIA, SiS, ALi, and more. This chapter also covers special bus architectures and devices, such as high-speed Peripheral Component Interconnect (PCI), including PCI Express, and Accelerated Graphics Port (AGP), including AGP 8x. Everything from the specifications of the latest chipsets to the proper spacing of holes on an ATX or BTX motherboard can be found here.

Chapter 5, "BIOS," has a detailed discussion of the system BIOS, including types, features, and upgrades. This has grown from a section of a chapter to a complete chapter, with more information on this subject than ever before. Also included is updated coverage of the BIOS, with detailed information about BIOS setup utilities, Flash upgradable BIOSs, and Plug and Play BIOS.

See the exhaustive list of BIOS codes and error messages included on the accompanying disc. They're all printable, so be sure to print the codes for your BIOS in case you need them later.

Chapter 6, "Memory," provides a detailed discussion of PC memory, including the latest in cache and main memory specifications. Next to the processor and motherboard, the system memory is one of the most important parts of a PC. It's also one of the most difficult things to understand because it is somewhat intangible and how it works is not always obvious. If you're confused about the difference between system memory and cache memory; L1 cache and L2 cache; external and integrated on-die L2 cache; SIMMs, DIMMs, and RIMMs; SDRAM versus DDR SDRAM versus RDRAM; 60-nanosecond EDO versus PC133 versus PC3200 and the new DDR2 memory, this is the chapter that can answer your questions. So, before you attempt to upgrade your PC with Fast Page mode EDO SIMMs—rather than with PC3200 DDR SDRAM DIMMs—be sure you read this chapter.

Chapter 7, "The ATA/IDE Interface," provides a detailed discussion of ATA/IDE, including types and specifications. This covers the Ultra-ATA modes that allow 133MBps operation and why they won't increase your PC's performance much. There's also more new content on Serial ATA, the technology that is beginning to replace the parallel ATA we have been using for the last 16 years.

Chapter 8, "The SCSI Interface," discusses SCSI, including the new Serial Attached SCSI (SAS) standard that is related to Serial ATA. This chapter covers the new low-voltage differential signaling used by some of the higher-speed devices on the market, as well as the latest information on cables, terminators, and SCSI configurations. This chapter also includes the latest on UltraSCSI.

Chapter 9, "Magnetic Storage Principles," details the inner workings of magnetic storage devices such as disk and tape drives. Regardless of whether you understood electromagnetism in high school science, this chapter breaks down these difficult concepts and presents them in a way that will change the way you think about data and drives.

Chapter 10, "Hard Disk Storage," breaks down how data is stored to your drives and how it is retrieved when you double-click a file.

Chapter 11, "Floppy Disk Storage," takes an inside view of the venerable floppy disk drive. You learn how to properly connect these drives as well as how information is written to a floppy.

Chapter 12, "High-Capacity Removable Storage," covers removable storage drives, such as SuperDisk (LS-120), Iomega Zip, Jaz, and Click! drives, as well as provides all-new coverage of magnetic tape drives.

Chapter 13, "Optical Storage," covers optical drives and storage using CD and DVD technology, including CD recorders, rewritable CDs, and other optical technologies. This chapter includes detailed steps and advice for avoiding buffer underruns, creating bootable CDs, burning music CDs, and selecting the most reliable media. There's even extensive coverage of DVD, with everything you need to know to understand the differences between DVD-R, DVD-RAM, DVD-RW, and DVD+RW. This chapter also tells you which of these the drive you buy needs to have support for.

Chapter 14, "Physical Drive Installation and Configuration," covers how to install drives of all types in a PC system. You learn how to format and partition hard drives after they are installed.

Chapter 15, "Video Hardware," covers everything there is to know about video cards and displays. Learn about how both CRT and flat-panel monitors work and which is best suited for you. If you're a gamer or multimedia buff, you'll want to read about choosing the right 3D graphics accelerator. The leading technologies are compared, and I help you choose the right card.

Chapter 16, "Audio Hardware," covers sound and sound-related devices, including sound boards and speaker systems. Quality audio has become an increasingly important part of any good PC, and in this chapter I help you learn which features to look for in an audio card and which types of audio cards are suited to your needs. I even offer advice that can optimize your system's audio performance for gaming, listening to CDs, and recording and playing MP3 music files.

Chapter 17, "I/O Interfaces from Serial and Parallel to IEEE 1394 and USB," covers the standard serial and parallel ports still found in most systems, as well as newer technology such as USB and FireWire (IEEE 1394/i.LINK). I also cover the latest developments in USB 2.0, USB On-The-Go, and the new FireWire 800.

Chapter 18, "Input Devices," covers keyboards, pointing devices, and game ports used to communicate with a PC. I also discuss wireless mice and keyboards.

Chapter 19, "Internet Connectivity," compares high-speed connectivity methods that have come to the home desktop, including DSL, cable modems, and satellite.

Chapter 20, "Local Area Networking," covers setting up an Ethernet network in your home or small office. I show you how to install NICs, make your own Ethernet cables, and set up Windows networking services.

Chapter 21, "Power Supply and Chassis/Case," is a detailed investigation of the power supply, which still remains the primary cause of PC system problems and failures. When you buy a new PC, this undervalued component is the one most likely to be skimped on, which helps explain why it's the source of so many problems often attributed to Windows, memory, and several other components. You'll also find detailed specifications on the power connectors found in systems from AT to ATX. They're not all built equal, and making the wrong connections can be dangerous to you and your PC.

Chapter 22, "Building or Upgrading Systems," is where I show you how to select the parts you'll need for your upgrade or to build a PC from scratch. Then, I walk you step by step through the process. This chapter is loaded with professional photos that help you follow along.

Chapter 23, "Extreme Modifications: Overclocking, Cooling, and Chassis Upgrades," covers the technology that controls the speed of your system and how to safely run the system faster than the basic specifications call for, or *overclock* it. A detailed examination of system cooling is also found here, from air cooling, to liquid cooling, and even refrigeration. The latest chassis upgrades to improve cooling are also discussed, and a simple modification is detailed that can dramatically improve the cooling in existing systems for less than $10. Finally, many new motherboards have connections for front-panel I/O, and this chapter details options for adding front-panel I/O connections to existing systems.

Chapter 24, "PC Diagnostics, Testing, and Maintenance," covers diagnostic and testing tools and procedures. This chapter also adds more information on general PC troubleshooting and problem determination. Here, I show you what the prepared PC technician has in his toolkit. I also show you a few tools you might have never seen or used before.

Chapter 25, "File Systems and Data Recovery," covers file systems and data recovery procedures. If you're a Windows XP user deciding whether to switch to NTFS, or if you're not sure whether you should upgrade from FAT16 to FAT32, you should read this chapter. If you can't access your drive because of a corrupted master boot record (MBR) or volume boot record (VBR), you'll find information you can use to recover these sectors and regain access to your valuable data.

The 16th Edition DVD-ROM

The 16th edition of *Upgrading and Repairing PCs* includes a DVD-ROM or CD-ROM that contains as much valuable content as you'll find in the pages of this book.

Video

Whether you purchased the DVD-ROM or CD-ROM edition of this book, you're still going to have access to all-new professional-grade video (the DVD will play in your standalone DVD player, too). The CD-ROM version has just a tad less of it because of the reduced space. On the DVD you'll find

- *Building a PC from Scratch.* This segment describes the task of building a PC from scratch in detail. It includes a discussion of all the components you need, the tools you need to build the system, and all the steps required to assemble a fully functional system. If you've never built your own PC before, this video will take you through all the steps and guide you through the entire process. Whether you are building an Intel or AMD processor–based system, you'll find this very enlightening and informative. Even if you don't want to build a complete system yourself, the installation procedures shown here can be applied to any system upgrade, such as upgrading motherboards, processors, memory, power supplies, drives, and more. This information is useful when troubleshooting a system as well, because in many cases you have to disassemble and reassemble all or part of the system to troubleshoot a problem.

- *OS and Driver Installation.* Part of building or upgrading a system includes partitioning and formatting the hard drive, as well as installing the operating system and drivers. Unfortunately, this is where many people have problems—for example, not knowing which drivers to install first or in which order they should be installed. In this segment, I detail all the steps needed to install Windows XP, the device drivers, and even the Windows updates on a new system. This can also be used when reloading an existing system or when upgrading the operating system from an older OS to the latest version of XP.

If you enjoy these video segments and want to see more, a full 6-hour video with many more segments like these is available in Scott's *Upgrading and Repairing PCs Video Training Course!* The video training course packs in a total of 6 hours of live video training similar to Scott's world-renowned 4-day seminars. For more information on the *Upgrading and Repairing PCs Video Training Course*, please visit www.upgradingandrepairingpcs.com. If you have any comments on these videos or are interested in an in-depth, hands-on seminar featuring all these topics and more, please contact Scott directly via scottmueller@compuserve.com.

Searchable Databases

On the accompanying disc you'll find detailed specifications for thousands of hard drives in this comprehensive Hard Drive Specifications Database.

Complementing that is a detailed list of technology vendors. The Vendor List is a searchable database of key industry contacts, searchable by name or keyword. This is crucial contact information that no hardware maven should be without!

Technical Reference

The Technical Reference is a PDF repository of material that has appeared in previous editions of *Upgrading and Repairing PCs* but has been moved to the disc to make room for coverage of new technologies. The disc, combined with the printed content of the book, makes *Upgrading and Repairing PCs* far more than 2,000 pages long!

Its contents include a detailed listing of BIOS codes and legacy coverage from earlier editions of the book. It's included on the disc in printable PDF format.

Upgrading and Repairing PCs Bookshelf

PDF versions of the 10th, 11th, 12th, 13th, 14th, and 15th editions of *Upgrading and Repairing PCs* are included on the DVD!

Scott's Web Site— upgradingandrepairingpcs.com

Don't miss my book Web site at www.upgradingandrepairingpcs.com! Here, you'll find a cache of helpful material to go along with the book you're holding. I've loaded this site with tons of material, from video clips to monthly book updates. I use this spot to keep you updated throughout the year on major changes in the PC hardware industry. Each month, I write new articles covering new technologies released after this book was printed. These articles are archived so you can refer to them anytime.

I also use this site to post your reader questions and my answers. The Frequently Asked Questions (FAQ) is a tremendous resource because you benefit from the hundreds of reader emails I answer each month. Log on and post a question. I endeavor to answer each and every email personally.

You'll also find exclusive video clips available nowhere else!

I also use this site to tell you about some of the other fantastic *Upgrading and Repairing PCs* products I work on, including

- *Upgrading and Repairing Laptops*
- *Upgrading and Repairing PCs, Video Training Course* from Que and Prentice Hall (see the advertisement in the back of this book for ordering details)
- *Upgrading and Repairing Networks*

Laptops have become the largest growing segment of PCs, and my new book *Upgrading and Repairing Laptops* covers these systems in great detail. If you want to know as much about laptop and notebook systems as you do about desktop PCs, you need *Upgrading and Repairing Laptops*. Be sure to check the upgradingandrepairingpcs.com Web site for more information on all my latest books, videos, articles, FAQs, and more!

A Personal Note

When asked which was his favorite Corvette, Dave McLellan, former manager of the Corvette platform at General Motors, always said, "Next year's model." Now with the new 16th edition, next year's model has just become this year's model, until next year that is....

I believe this book is absolutely the best book of its kind on the market, and that is due in large part to the extensive feedback I have received from both my seminar attendees and book readers. I am so grateful to everyone who has helped me with this book over the last 16 years as well as all the loyal readers who have been reading this book, many of you since the first edition was published. I have had personal contact with many thousands of you in the seminars I have been teaching since 1982, and I enjoy your comments and even your criticisms tremendously. Using this book in a teaching environment has been a major factor in its development. Some of you might be interested to know that I originally began writing this book in early 1985; back then it was self-published and used exclusively in my PC hardware seminars before being professionally published by Que in 1988. In one way or another, I have been writing and rewriting this book for more than 20 years! In the more than 16 years since it was professionally published, *Upgrading and Repairing PCs* has proven to be not only the first but also the most comprehensive and yet approachable and easy-to-understand book of its kind. With the new 16th edition, it is even better than ever. Your comments, suggestions, and support have helped this book to become the best PC hardware book on the market. I look forward to hearing your comments after you see this exciting new edition.

Scott

CHAPTER 1

Development of the PC

Computer History—Before Personal Computers

Many discoveries and inventions have directly and indirectly contributed to the development of the personal computer as we know it today. Examining a few important developmental landmarks can help bring the entire picture into focus.

The first computers of any kind were simple calculators. Even these evolved from mechanical devices to electronic digital devices.

Timeline

The following is a timeline of some significant events in computer history. It is not meant to be complete, just a representation of some of the major landmarks in computer development:

1617   John Napier creates "Napier's Bones," wooden or ivory rods used for calculating.

1642   Blaise Pascal introduces the Pascaline digital adding machine.

1822   Charles Babbage introduces the Difference Engine and later the Analytical Engine, a true general-purpose computing machine.

1906   Lee De Forest patents the vacuum tube triode, used as an electronic switch in the first electronic computers.

1936   Alan Turing publishes "On Computable Numbers," a paper in which he conceives an imaginary computer called the Turing Machine, considered one of the foundations of modern computing. Turing later worked on breaking the German Enigma code.

1937   John V. Atanasoff begins work on the Atanasoff-Berry Computer (ABC), which would later be officially credited as the first electronic computer.

1943   Thomas (Tommy) Flowers develops the Colossus, a secret British code-breaking computer designed to decode secret messages encrypted by the German Enigma cipher machines.

1945   John von Neumann writes "First Draft of a Report on the EDVAC," in which he outlines the architecture of the modern stored-program computer.

1946   ENIAC is introduced, an electronic computing machine built by John Mauchly and J. Presper Eckert.

1947   On December 23, William Shockley, Walter Brattain, and John Bardeen successfully test the point-contact transistor, setting off the semiconductor revolution.

1949   Maurice Wilkes assembles the EDSAC, the first practical stored-program computer, at Cambridge University.

1950   Engineering Research Associates of Minneapolis builds the ERA 1101, one of the first commercially produced computers.

1952   The UNIVAC I delivered to the U.S. Census Bureau is the first commercial computer to attract widespread public attention.

1953   IBM ships its first electronic computer, the 701.

1954   A silicon-based junction transistor, perfected by Gordon Teal of Texas Instruments, Inc., brings a tremendous reduction in costs.

1954   The IBM 650 magnetic drum calculator establishes itself as the first mass-produced computer, with the company selling 450 in one year.

1955   Bell Laboratories announces the first fully transistorized computer, TRADIC.

1956   MIT researchers build the TX-0, the first general-purpose, programmable computer built with transistors.

1956   The era of magnetic disk storage dawns with IBM's shipment of a 305 RAMAC to Zellerbach Paper in San Francisco.

1958   Jack Kilby creates the first integrated circuit at Texas Instruments to prove that resistors and capacitors can exist on the same piece of semiconductor material.

1959   IBM's 7000 series mainframes are the company's first transistorized computers.

1959   Robert Noyce's practical integrated circuit, invented at Fairchild Camera and Instrument Corp., allows printing of conducting channels directly on the silicon surface.

1960   Bell Labs designs its Dataphone, the first commercial modem, specifically for converting digital computer data to analog signals for transmission across its long-distance network.

1960   The precursor to the minicomputer, DEC's PDP-1, sells for $120,000.

1961   According to *Datamation* magazine, IBM has an 81.2% share of the computer market in 1961, the year in which it introduces the 1400 series.

1964   CDC's 6600 supercomputer, designed by Seymour Cray, performs up to three million instructions per second—a processing speed three times faster than that of its closest competitor, the IBM Stretch.

1964   IBM announces System/360, a family of six mutually compatible computers and 40 peripherals that can work together.

1964   Online transaction processing makes its debut in IBM's SABRE reservation system, set up for American Airlines.

1965   Digital Equipment Corp. introduces the PDP-8, the first commercially successful minicomputer.

1966   Hewlett-Packard enters the general-purpose computer business with its HP-2115 for computation, offering a computational power formerly found only in much larger computers.

1969   The root of what is to become the Internet begins when the Department of Defense establishes four nodes on the ARPAnet: two at University of California campuses (one at Santa Barbara and one at Los Angeles) and one each at SRI International and the University of Utah.

1971   A team at IBM's San Jose Laboratories invents the 8" floppy disk.

1971   The first advertisement for a microprocessor, the Intel 4004, appears in *Electronic News*.

1971   The Kenbak-1, one of the first personal computers, advertises for $750 in *Scientific American*.

1972   Hewlett-Packard announces the HP-35 as "a fast, extremely accurate electronic slide rule" with a solid-state memory similar to that of a computer.

1972   Intel's 8008 microprocessor makes its debut.

1972   Steve Wozniak builds his "blue box," a tone generator to make free phone calls.

1973   Robert Metcalfe devises the Ethernet method of network connection at the Xerox Palo Alto Research Center.

1973   The Micral is the earliest commercial, non-kit personal computer based on a microprocessor, the Intel 8008.

1973   The TV Typewriter, designed by Don Lancaster, provides the first display of alphanumeric information on an ordinary television set.

1974   Researchers at the Xerox Palo Alto Research Center design the Alto, the first workstation with a built-in mouse for input.

1974   Scelbi advertises its 8H computer, the first commercially advertised U.S. computer based on a microprocessor, Intel's 8008.

1975   Telenet, the first commercial packet-switching network and civilian equivalent of ARPAnet, is born.

1975   The January edition of *Popular Electronics* features the Altair 8800, which is based on Intel's 8080 microprocessor, on its cover.

1975   The visual display module (VDM) prototype, designed by Lee Felsenstein, marks the first implementation of a memory-mapped alphanumeric video display for personal computers.

1976   Steve Wozniak designs the Apple I, a single-board computer.

1976   The 5 1/4" flexible disk drive and disk are introduced by Shugart Associates.

1976   The Cray I makes its name as the first commercially successful vector processor.

1977   Tandy Radio Shack introduces the TRS-80.

1977   Apple Computer introduces the Apple II.

1977   Commodore introduces the PET (Personal Electronic Transactor).

1978   The VAX 11/780 from Digital Equipment Corp. features the capability to address up to 4.3GB of virtual memory, providing hundreds of times the capacity of most minicomputers.

1979   Motorola introduces the 68000 microprocessor.

1980   John Shoch, at the Xerox Palo Alto Research Center, invents the computer "worm," a short program that searches a network for idle processors.

1980   Seagate Technology creates the first hard disk drive for microcomputers, the ST-506.

1980   The first optical data storage disk has 60 times the capacity of a 5 1/4" floppy disk.

1981   Xerox introduces the Star, the first personal computer with a graphical user interface (GUI).

1981   Adam Osborne completes the first portable computer, the Osborne I, which weighs 24 lbs. and costs $1,795.

1981   IBM introduces its PC, igniting a fast growth of the personal computer market. The IBM PC is the grandfather of all modern PCs.

1981   Sony introduces and ships the first 3 1/2" floppy drives and disks.

1981   Philips and Sony introduce the CD-DA (compact disc digital audio) format.

1982   Sony is the first with a CD player on the market.

1983   Apple introduces its Lisa, which incorporates a GUI that's very similar to the one first introduced on the Xerox Star.

1983   Compaq Computer Corp. introduces its first PC clone that uses the same software as the IBM PC.

1984   Apple Computer launches the Macintosh, the first successful mouse-driven computer with a GUI, with a single $1.5 million commercial during the 1984 Super Bowl.

1984   IBM releases the PC-AT (PC Advanced Technology), three times faster than original PCs and based on the Intel 286 chip. The AT introduces the 16-bit ISA bus and is the computer on which all modern PCs are based.

1985   Philips introduces the first CD-ROM drive.

1986   Compaq announces the Deskpro 386, the first computer on the market to use what was then Intel's new 386 chip.

1987   IBM introduces its PS/2 machines, which make the 3 1/2" floppy disk drive and VGA video standard for PCs. The PS/2 also introduces the MicroChannel Architecture (MCA) bus, the first plug-and-play bus for PCs.

1988   Apple cofounder Steve Jobs, who left Apple to form his own company, unveils the NeXT.

1988   Compaq and other PC-clone makers develop Enhanced Industry Standard Architecture (EISA), which unlike MicroChannel retains backward compatibility with the existing ISA bus.

1988   Robert Morris's worm floods the ARPAnet. The 23-year-old Morris, the son of a computer security expert for the National Security Agency, sends a nondestructive worm through the Internet, causing problems for about 6,000 of the 60,000 hosts linked to the network.

1989   Intel releases the 486 (P4) microprocessor, which contains more than one million transistors. Intel also introduces 486 motherboard chipsets.

1990   The World Wide Web (WWW) is born when Tim Berners-Lee, a researcher at CERN—the high-energy physics laboratory in Geneva—develops Hypertext Markup Language (HTML).

1993   Intel releases the Pentium (P5) processor. Intel shifts from numbers to names for its chips after it learns it's impossible to trademark a number. Intel also releases motherboard chipsets and, for the first time, complete motherboards as well.

1995   Intel releases the Pentium Pro processor, the first in the P6 processor family.

1995   Microsoft releases Windows 95, the first mainstream 32-bit operating system, in a huge rollout.

1997   Intel releases the Pentium II processor, essentially a Pentium Pro with MMX instructions added.

1997   AMD introduces the K6, which is compatible with the Intel P5 (Pentium).

1998   Microsoft releases Windows 98.

1998   Intel releases the Celeron, a low-cost version of the Pentium II processor. Initial versions have no cache, but within a few months Intel introduces versions with a smaller but faster L2 cache.

1999   Intel releases the Pentium III, essentially a Pentium II with SSE (Streaming SIMD Extensions) added.

1999   AMD introduces the Athlon.

1999   The IEEE officially approves the 5GHz band 802.11a 54Mbps and 2.4GHZ band 802.11b 11Mbps wireless networking standards. The Wi-Fi Alliance is formed to certify 802.11b products, ensuring interoperability.

2000   The first 802.11b Wi-Fi–certified products are introduced, and wireless networking rapidly builds momentum.

2000   Microsoft releases Windows Me (Millennium Edition) and Windows 2000.

2000   Both Intel and AMD introduce processors running at 1GHz.

2000   AMD introduces the Duron, a low-cost Athlon with reduced L2 cache.

2000   Intel introduces the Pentium 4, the latest processor in the Intel Architecture 32-bit (IA-32) family.

2001   Intel releases the Itanium processor, its first 64-bit (IA-64) processor for PCs.

2001   The industry celebrates the 20th anniversary of the release of the original IBM PC.

2001   Intel introduces the first 2GHz processor, a version of the Pentium 4. It took the industry 28 1/2 years to go from 108KHz to 1GHz, but only 18 months to go from 1GHz to 2GHz.

2001   Microsoft releases Windows XP Home and Professional, for the first time merging the consumer (9x/Me) and business (NT/2000) operating system lines under the same code base (an extension of Windows 2000).

2001   Atheros introduces the first 802.11a 54Mbps high-speed wireless chips, allowing 802.11a products to finally reach the market.

2002   Intel releases the first 3GHz-class processor, a 3.06GHz version of the Pentium 4. This processor also introduces Intel's Hyper-Threading (HT) technology (which enables a single processor to work with two application threads at the same time) to desktop computing.

2003   Intel releases the Pentium M, a processor designed specifically for mobile systems, offering extremely low power consumption that results in dramatically increased battery life while still offering relatively high performance. The Pentium M becomes the cornerstone of Intel's Centrino brand.

2003   AMD releases the Athlon 64, the first 64-bit processor targeted at the mainstream consumer and business markets.

2003   The IEEE officially approves the 802.11g 54Mbps high-speed wireless networking standard, which uses the same 2.4GHz band as (and is backward-compatible with) 802.11b. 802.11g products reach the market quickly, some even before the official standard is approved.

2004   Intel introduces a version of the Pentium 4 codenamed Prescott, the first PC processor built on 90-nanometer technology.

2004   Intel introduces EM64T (Extended Memory 64 Technology), which is a 64-bit extension to Intel's IA-32 architecture. EM64T is software-compatible with and targeted at the same market as the AMD Athlon 64, and is not compatible with the 64-bit Itanium.

Mechanical Calculators

One of the earliest calculating devices on record is the abacus, which has been known and widely used for more than 2,000 years. The abacus is a simple wooden rack holding parallel rods on which beads are strung. When these beads are manipulated back and forth according to certain rules, several types of arithmetic operations can be performed.

Math with standard Arabic numbers found its way to Europe in the eighth and ninth centuries. In the early 1600s, a man named Charles Napier (the inventor of logarithms) developed a series of rods (later called Napier's Bones) that could be used to assist with numeric multiplication.

Blaise Pascal is usually credited with building the first digital calculating machine in 1642. It could perform the addition of numbers entered on dials and was intended to help his father, who was a tax collector. Then in 1671, Gottfried Wilhelm von Leibniz invented a calculator that was finally built in 1694. His calculating machine could not only add, but by successive adding and shifting, it could also multiply.

In 1820, Charles Xavier Thomas developed the first commercially successful mechanical calculator that could not only add but also subtract, multiply, and divide. After that, a succession of ever-improving mechanical calculators created by various other inventors followed.

The First Mechanical Computer

Charles Babbage, a mathematics professor in Cambridge, England, is considered by many to be the father of computers because of his two great inventions—each a different type of mechanical computing engine.

The Difference Engine, as he called it, was conceived in 1812 and solved polynomial equations by the method of differences. By 1822, he had built a small working model of his Difference Engine for demonstration purposes. With financial help from the British government, Babbage started construction of a full-scale model in 1823. It was intended to be steam-powered and fully automatic, and it would even print the resulting tables.

Babbage continued work on it for 10 years, but by 1833 he had lost interest because he now had an idea for an even better machine, something he described as a general-purpose, fully program-controlled, automatic mechanical digital computer. Babbage called his new machine an Analytical Engine. The plans for the Analytical Engine specified a parallel decimal computer operating on numbers (words) of 50 decimal digits and with a storage capacity (memory) of 1,000 such numbers. Built-in operations were to include everything that a modern general-purpose computer would need, even the all-important conditional function, which would allow instructions to be executed in an order depending on certain conditions, not just in numerical sequence. In modern computer languages, this conditional capability is manifested in the IF statement. The Analytical Engine was also intended to use punched cards, which would control or program the machine. The machine was to operate automatically by steam power and would require only one attendant.

The Analytical Engine is regarded as the first real predecessor to a modern computer because it had all the elements of what is considered a computer today. These included the following:

- *An input device*. Using an idea similar to the looms used in textile mills at the time, a form of punched cards supplied the input.
- *A control unit*. A barrel-shaped section with many slats and studs was used to control or program the processor.
- *A processor (or calculator)*. A computing engine containing hundreds of axles and thousands of gears about 10 feet tall.
- *Storage*. A unit containing more axles and gears that could hold 1,000 50-digit numbers.
- *An output device*. Plates designed to fit in a printing press that were used to print the final results.

Alas, this potential first computer was never actually completed because of the problems in machining all the precision gears and mechanisms required. The tooling of the day was simply not good enough.

An interesting side note is that the punched card idea first proposed by Babbage finally came to fruition in 1890. That year a competition was held for a better method to tabulate the U.S. Census information, and Herman Hollerith, a Census Department employee, came up with the idea for punched cards. Without these cards, department employees had estimated the census data would take years to tabulate; with these cards they were able to finish in about six weeks. Hollerith went on to found the Tabulating Machine Company, which later became known as IBM.

IBM and other companies at the time developed a series of improved punch-card systems. These systems were constructed of electromechanical devices, such as relays and motors. Such systems included features to automatically feed in a specified number of cards from a "read-in" station; perform operations, such as addition, multiplication, and sorting; and feed out cards punched with results. These punched-card computing machines could process 50 250 cards per minute, with each card holding up to 80-digit numbers. The punched cards not only provided a means of input and output, but they also served as a form of memory storage. Punched-card machines did the bulk of the world's computing for more than 50 years and gave many of the early computer companies their starts.

Electronic Computers

A physicist named John V. Atanasoff (with associate Clifford Berry) is credited with creating the first true digital electronic computer during 1937–1942, while working at Iowa State University. The Atanasoff-Berry Computer (called the ABC) was the first to use modern digital switching techniques and vacuum tubes as switches, and it introduced the concepts of binary arithmetic and logic circuits. This was made legally official on October 19, 1973, when following a lengthy court trial, U.S. Federal Judge Earl R. Larson voided the ENIAC patent of Eckert and Mauchly and named Atanasoff as the inventor of the first electronic digital computer.

Military needs during World War II caused a great thrust forward in the evolution of computers. In 1943, Tommy Flowers completed a secret British code-breaking computer called Colossus, which was used to decode German secret messages. Unfortunately, that work went largely uncredited because Colossus was kept secret until many years after the war.

Besides code-breaking, systems were needed to calculate weapons trajectory and other military functions. In 1946, John P. Eckert, John W. Mauchly, and their associates at the Moore School of Electrical Engineering at the University of Pennsylvania built the first large-scale electronic computer for the military. This machine became known as ENIAC, the Electrical Numerical Integrator and Calculator. It operated on 10-digit numbers and could multiply two such numbers at the rate of 300 products per second by finding the value of each product from a multiplication table stored in its memory. ENIAC was about 1,000 times faster than the previous generation of electromechanical relay computers.

ENIAC used approximately 18,000 vacuum tubes, occupied 1,800 square feet (167 square meters) of floor space, and consumed around 180,000 watts of electrical power. Punched cards served as the input and output; registers served as adders and also as quick-access read/write storage.

The executable instructions composing a given program were created via specified wiring and switches that controlled the flow of computations through the machine. As such, ENIAC had to be rewired and switched for each program to be run.

Although Eckert and Mauchly were originally given a patent for the electronic computer, it was later voided and the patent awarded to John Atanasoff for creating the Atanasoff-Berry Computer.

Earlier in 1945, the mathematician John von Neumann demonstrated that a computer could have a very simple, fixed physical structure and yet be capable of executing any kind of computation effectively by means of proper programmed control without the need for any changes in hardware.

In other words, you could change the program without rewiring the system. The *stored-program technique*, as von Neumann's ideas are known, became fundamental for future generations of high-speed digital computers and has become universally adopted.

The first generation of modern programmed electronic computers to take advantage of these improvements appeared in 1947. This group of machines included EDVAC and UNIVAC, the first commercially available computers. These computers included, for the first time, the use of true random access memory (RAM) for storing parts of the program and data that is needed quickly. Typically, they were programmed directly in machine language, although by the mid-1950s progress had been made in several aspects of advanced programming. The standout of the era is the UNIVAC (Universal Automatic Computer), which was the first true general-purpose computer designed for both alphabetical and numerical uses. This made the UNIVAC a standard for business, not just science and the military.

Modern Computers

From UNIVAC to the present, computer evolution has moved very rapidly. The first-generation computers were known for using vacuum tubes in their construction. The generation to follow would use the much smaller and more efficient transistor.

From Tubes to Transistors

Any modern digital computer is largely a collection of electronic switches. These switches are used to represent and control the routing of data elements called *binary digits* (or *bits*). Because of the on or off nature of the binary information and signal routing the computer uses, an efficient electronic switch was required. The first electronic computers used vacuum tubes as switches, and although the tubes worked, they had many problems.

The type of tube used in early computers was called a *triode* and was invented by Lee De Forest in 1906 (see Figure 1.1). It consists of a cathode and a plate, separated by a control grid, suspended in a glass vacuum tube. The cathode is heated by a red-hot electric filament, which causes it to emit electrons that are attracted to the plate. The control grid in the middle can control this flow of electrons. By making it negative, the electrons are repelled back to the cathode; by making it positive, they are attracted toward the plate. Thus, by controlling the grid current, you can control the on/off output of the plate.

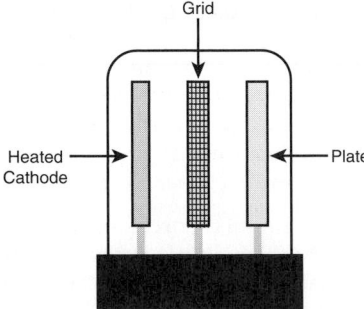

Figure 1.1   Triode Vacuum Tube.

Unfortunately, the tube was inefficient as a switch. It consumed a great deal of electrical power and gave off enormous heat—a significant problem in the earlier systems. Primarily because of the heat they generated, tubes were notoriously unreliable—in larger systems, one failed every couple of hours or so.

The invention of the transistor, or semiconductor, was one of the most important developments leading to the personal computer revolution. The transistor was first invented in 1947 and announced in

1948 by Bell Laboratory engineers John Bardeen and Walter Brattain. Bell associate William Shockley invented the junction transistor a few months later, and all three jointly shared the Nobel Prize in Physics in 1956 for inventing the transistor. The transistor, which essentially functions as a solid-state electronic switch, replaced the less-suitable vacuum tube. Because the transistor was so much smaller and consumed significantly less power, a computer system built with transistors was also much smaller, faster, and more efficient than a computer system built with vacuum tubes.

Transistors are made primarily from the elements silicon and germanium, with certain impurities added. Depending on the impurities added—its electron content—the material becomes known as either N-Type (negative) or P-Type (positive). Both types are conductors, allowing electricity to flow in either direction. However, when the two types are joined, a barrier is formed where they meet that allows current to flow in only one direction when a voltage is present in the right polarity. This is why they are typically called *semiconductors*.

A transistor is made by placing two P-N junctions back to back. They are made by sandwiching a thin wafer of one type of semiconductor material between two wafers of the other type. If the wafer in between is made from P-type material, the transistor is designated an NPN. If the wafer in between is N-type, the transistor is designated PNP.

In an NPN transistor, the N-type semiconductor material on one side of the wafer is called the *emitter* (or *source*) and is normally connected to a negative current (see Figure 1.2). The P-type material in the center is called the *base*, and the N-type material on the other side of the base is called the *collector* (or *drain*).

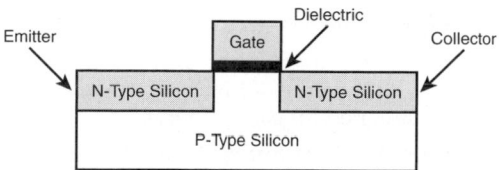

Figure 1.2 NPN transistor.

An NPN transistor compares to a triode tube such that the emitter is equivalent to the cathode, the base is equivalent to the grid, and the collector is equivalent to the plate. By controlling the current at the base, you can control the flow of current between the emitter and collector.

Compared to the tube, the transistor is much more efficient as a switch and can be miniaturized to microscopic scale. In June 2001, Intel researchers unveiled the world's smallest and fastest silicon transistors, only 20 nanometers (billionths of a meter) in size. These are expected to appear in PC processors in the year 2007, which will have one billion transistors running at speeds of 20GHz! By comparison, in 2003 the AMD Athlon 64 had more than 105.9 million transistors, and the Pentium 4 Extreme Edition had more than 178 million transistors.

The conversion from tubes to transistors began the trend toward miniaturization that continues to this day. Today's small laptop (or palmtop) PC and even Tablet PC systems, which run on batteries, have more computing power than many earlier systems that filled rooms and consumed huge amounts of electrical power.

Although vacuum tubes have been replaced in virtually all consumer applications by transistors and integrated circuits, they remain popular for high-end audio applications because they produce a warmer and richer sound than transistors do. Because computers are increasingly used for audio processing and playback, Acer's Aopen division has released a motherboard (the AX4B-533 Tube) that uses a dual-triode tube along with a special noise-reduction design to produce excellent music playback.

Integrated Circuits

The third generation of modern computers is known for using integrated circuits instead of individual transistors. In 1959, engineers at Texas Instruments invented the *integrated circuit (IC)*, a semiconductor circuit that contains more than one transistor on the same base (or substrate material) and connects the transistors without wires. The first IC contained only six transistors. By comparison, the Intel Pentium Pro microprocessor used in many of today's high-end systems has more than 5.5 million transistors, and the integral cache built into some of these chips contains as many as an additional 32 million transistors! Today, many ICs have transistor counts in the multimillion range.

The First Microprocessor

Intel was founded on July 18, 1968, by Robert Noyce, Gordon Moore, and Andrew Grove. They had a specific goal: to make semiconductor memory practical and affordable. This was not a given at the time, considering that silicon chip-based memory was at least 100 times more expensive than the magnetic core memory commonly used in those days. At the time, semiconductor memory was going for about a dollar a bit, whereas core memory was about a penny a bit. Noyce said, "All we had to do was reduce the cost by a factor of a hundred; then we'd have the market; and that's basically what we did."

By 1970, Intel was known as a successful memory chip company, having introduced a 1Kb memory chip much larger than anything else available at the time. (1Kb equals 1,024 bits, and a byte equals 8 bits. This chip, therefore, stored only 128 bytes—not much by today's standards.) Known as the 1103 dynamic random access memory (DRAM), it became the world's largest-selling semiconductor device by the end of the following year. By this time, Intel had also grown from the core founders and a handful of others to more than 100 employees.

Because of Intel's success in memory chip manufacturing and design, Japanese manufacturer Busicom asked Intel to design a set of chips for a family of high-performance programmable calculators. At the time, all logic chips were custom designed for each application or product. Because most chips had to be custom designed specific to a particular application, no one chip could have any widespread usage.

Busicom's original design for its calculator called for at least 12 custom chips. Intel engineer Ted Hoff rejected the unwieldy proposal and instead designed a single-chip, general-purpose logic device that retrieved its application instructions from semiconductor memory. As the core of a four-chip set, a program could control this central processing unit and essentially tailor its function to the task at hand. The chip was generic in nature, meaning it could function in designs other than calculators. Previous designs were hard-wired for one purpose, with built-in instructions; this chip would read a variable set of instructions from memory, which would control the function of the chip. The idea was to design, on a single chip, almost an entire computing device that could perform various functions, depending on which instructions it was given.

There was one problem with the new chip: Busicom owned the rights to it. Hoff and others knew that the product had almost limitless application, bringing intelligence to a host of "dumb" machines. They urged Intel to repurchase the rights to the product. While Intel founders Gordon Moore and Robert Noyce championed the new chip, others within the company were concerned that the product would distract Intel from its main focus—making memory. They were finally convinced by the fact that every four-chip microcomputer set included two memory chips. As the director of marketing at the time recalled, "Originally, I think we saw it as a way to sell more memories, and we were willing to make the investment on that basis."

Intel offered to return Busicom's $60,000 investment in exchange for the rights to the product. Struggling with financial troubles, the Japanese company agreed. Nobody else in the industry at the time, even at Intel, realized the significance of this deal. Of course, it paved the way for Intel's future in processors. The result was the 1971 introduction of the 4-bit Intel 4004 microcomputer set (the term *microprocessor* was not coined until later). Smaller than a thumbnail and packing 2,300 transistors with 10-micron (millionth of a meter) spacing, the $200 chip delivered as much computing power as one of the first electronic computers, ENIAC. By comparison, ENIAC relied on 18,000 vacuum tubes packed into 3,000 cubic feet (85 cubic meters) when it was built in 1946. The 4004 ran at 108KHz (just over one tenth of 1MHz) and executed 60,000 operations in 1 second—primitive by today's standards, but a major breakthrough at the time.

Intel introduced the 8008 microcomputer in 1972, which processed 8 bits of information at a time, twice as much as the original chip. By 1981, Intel's microprocessor family had grown to include the 16-bit 8086 and the 8-bit 8088 processors. These two chips garnered an unprecedented 2,500 design wins in a single year. Among those designs was a product from IBM that was to become the first PC.

Note

The term *PC* defines a type of personal computer using Intel architecture processors and loosely based on the original IBM PC, XT, and AT designs. Other types of personal computers existed before the PC, but what we call PCs today have dominated the market since they were first introduced in 1981.

In 1982, Intel introduced the 286 chip. With 134,000 transistors, it provided about three times the performance of other 16-bit processors of the time. Featuring on-chip memory management, the 286 also offered software compatibility with its predecessors. This revolutionary chip was first used in IBM's benchmark PC-AT, the system upon which all modern PCs are based.

In 1985 came the Intel 386 processor. With a new 32-bit architecture and 275,000 transistors, the chip could perform more than five million instructions every second (MIPS). Compaq's DESKPRO 386 was the first PC based on the new microprocessor.

Next out of the gate was the Intel 486 processor in 1989. The 486 had 1.2 million transistors and the first built-in math coprocessor. It was some 50 times faster than the original 4004, equaling the performance of some mainframe computers.

Then, in 1993, Intel introduced the first P5 family (586) processor, called the Pentium, setting new performance standards with up to five times the performance of the Intel 486 processor. The Pentium processor used 3.1 million transistors to perform up to 90 MIPS—now up to about 1,500 times the speed of the original 4004.

Note

Intel's change from using numbers (386/486) to names (Pentium/Pentium Pro) for its processors was based on the fact that it could not secure a registered trademark on a number and therefore could not prevent its competitors from using those same numbers on clone chip designs.

The first processor in the P6 (686) family, called the Pentium Pro processor, was introduced in 1995. With 5.5 million transistors, it was the first to be packaged with a second die containing high-speed L2 memory cache to accelerate performance.

Intel revised the original P6 (686/Pentium Pro) and introduced the Pentium II processor in May 1997. Pentium II processors had 7.5 million transistors packed into a cartridge rather than a conventional chip, allowing them to attach the L2 cache chips directly on the module. The Pentium II family was augmented in April 1998, with both the low-cost Celeron processor for basic PCs and the high-end Pentium II Xeon processor for servers and workstations. Intel followed with the Pentium III in 1999, essentially a Pentium II with Streaming SIMD Extensions (SSE) added.

Around the time the Pentium was establishing its dominance, AMD acquired NexGen, who had been working on its Nx686 processor. AMD incorporated that design along with a Pentium interface into what would be called the AMD K6. The K6 was both hardware and software compatible with the Pentium, meaning it plugged into the same Socket 7 and could run the same programs. As Intel dropped its Pentium in favor of the Pentium II and III, AMD continued making faster versions of the K6 and made huge inroads in the low-end PC market.

During 1998, Intel became the first to integrate L2 cache directly on the processor die (running at the full speed of the processor core), dramatically increasing performance. This was first done on the second-generation Celeron processor (based on the Pentium II core), as well as the Pentium IIPE (performance-enhanced) chip used only in notebook systems. The first high-end desktop PC chip with on-die full-core speed L2 cache was the second-generation (Coppermine core) Pentium III introduced in late 1999. After this, all the major processor manufacturers also integrated the L2 cache on the processor die, a trend that continues today.

AMD introduced the Athlon in 1999 to compete with Intel head to head in the high-end desktop PC market. The Athlon became very successful, and it seemed for the first time that Intel had some real competition in the higher-end systems. In hindsight the success of the Athlon might be easy to see, but at the time they were introduced, their success was anything but assured. Unlike the previous K6 chips, which were both hardware- and software-compatible with Intel processors, the Athlon was only software-compatible and required a motherboard with an Athlon supporting chipset and processor socket.

The year 2000 saw both companies introduce more new chips to the market. AMD premiered both its Athlon Thunderbird and Duron processors. The Duron is essentially an Athlon with a smaller L2 cache designed for lower-cost systems, whereas the Thunderbird uses a more integrated on-die cache to ratchet up the Athlon's performance. The Duron is a lower-cost chip primarily targeted as competition for Intel's lower-cost Celeron processors.

Intel introduced the Pentium 4 in late 2000, the latest processor in the Intel Architecture 32-bit (IA-32) family. It also announced the Itanium processor (code named Merced), which is the first IA-64 (Intel Architecture-64 bit) processor. Itanium is Intel's first processor with 64-bit instructions and is opening a whole new category of operating systems and applications while still remaining backward compatible with 32-bit software.

2000 also saw another significant milestone written into the history books when both Intel and AMD crossed the 1GHz barrier, a speed that many thought could never be accomplished.

▶▶ See "Intel Itanium and Itanium 2," p. 189.

In 2001, Intel introduced a Pentium 4 version running at 2GHz, the first PC processor to achieve that speed. AMD also introduced the Athlon XP, based on its newer Palomino core, as well as the Athlon MP, designed for multiprocessor server systems. During 2001, both AMD and Intel continued to increase the speed of their chips and enhance the existing Pentium III/Celeron, Pentium 4, and Athlon/Duron processors.

In 2002, Intel released a Pentium 4 version running at 3.06GHz, the first PC processor to achieve that speed. This and subsequent 3GHz+ processors feature Intel's hyper-threading (HT) technology, which turns the processor into a virtual dual-processor configuration. By running two application threads at the same time, HT-enabled processors can perform tasks at speeds 25%–40% faster than non-HT-enabled processors can. HT technology is also compatible with Windows XP Home Edition, which doesn't support dual-processor motherboards.

In 2003, AMD released its first 64-bit processor: the Athlon 64 (previously code named ClawHammer or K8). Unlike Intel's first 64-bit processors, the server-oriented Itanium and Itanium 2, which are optimized for a new 64-bit architecture and are relatively slow at running 32-bit x86 instructions used by conventional processors, the Athlon 64 is a 64-bit extension of the x86 family typified by the Athlon, Pentium 4, and earlier processors. Thus, the Athlon 64 runs 32-bit software as quickly as it runs 64-bit software. Intel followed with the Pentium 4 Extreme Edition, the first consumer-level processor that incorporated L3 cache. The whopping 2MB of cache added greatly to the transistor count as well as performance.

History of the PC

The fourth and current generation of the modern computer includes those that incorporate micro-processors in their designs. Of course, part of this fourth generation of computers is the personal computer, which itself was made possible by the advent of low-cost microprocessors and memory.

Birth of the Personal Computer

In 1973, some of the first microcomputer kits based on the 8008 chip were developed. These kits were little more than demonstration tools and didn't do much except blink lights. In April 1974, Intel introduced the 8080 microprocessor, which was 10 times faster than the earlier 8008 chip and addressed 64KB of memory. This was the breakthrough the personal computer industry had been waiting for.

A company called MITS introduced the Altair kit in a cover story in the January 1975 issue of *Popular Electronics*. The Altair kit, considered the first personal computer, included an 8080 processor, a power supply, a front panel with a large number of lights, and 256 bytes (not kilobytes) of memory. The kit sold for $395 and had to be assembled. Assembly back then meant you got out your soldering iron to actually finish the circuit boards, not like today where you can assemble a system of premade components with nothing more than a screwdriver.

Note

Micro Instrumentation and Telemetry Systems was the original name of the company founded in 1969 by Ed Roberts and several associates to manufacture and sell instruments and transmitters for model rockets. Ed Roberts became the sole owner in the early 1970s, after which he designed the Altair. By January 1975, when the Altair was introduced, the company was called MITS, Inc., which then stood for nothing more than the name of the company. In 1977, Roberts sold MITS to Pertec, moved to Georgia, went to medical school, and is now a practicing physician!

The Altair included an open architecture system bus called the S-100 bus because it had 100 pins per slot. The open architecture meant that anybody could develop boards to fit in these slots and interface to the system. This prompted various add-ons and peripherals from numerous aftermarket companies. The new processor inspired software companies to write programs, including the CP/M (control program for microprocessors) operating system and the first version of the Microsoft BASIC (beginners all-purpose symbolic instruction code) programming language.

IBM introduced what can be called its first personal computer in 1975. The Model 5100 had 16KB of memory, a built-in 16-line–by–64-character display, a built-in BASIC language interpreter, and a built-in DC-300 cartridge tape drive for storage. The system's $9,000 price placed it out of the mainstream personal computer marketplace, which was dominated by experimenters (affectionately referred to as *hackers*) who built low-cost kits ($500 or so) as a hobby. Obviously, the IBM system was not in competition for this low-cost market and did not sell as well by comparison.

The Model 5100 was succeeded by the 5110 and 5120 before IBM introduced what we know as the IBM Personal Computer (Model 5150). Although the 5100 series preceded the IBM PC, the older systems and the 5150 IBM PC had nothing in common. The PC that IBM turned out was more closely related to the IBM System/23 DataMaster, an office computer system introduced in 1980. In fact, many of the engineers who developed the IBM PC had originally worked on the DataMaster.

In 1976, a new company called Apple Computer introduced the Apple I, which originally sold for $666.66. The selling price was an arbitrary number selected by one of Apple's cofounders, Steve Jobs. This system consisted of a main circuit board screwed to a piece of plywood; a case and power supply were not included. Only a few of these computers were made, and they reportedly have sold to collectors for more than $20,000. The Apple II, introduced in 1977, helped set the standard for nearly all the important microcomputers to follow, including the IBM PC.

The microcomputer world was dominated in 1980 by two types of computer systems. One type, the Apple II, claimed a large following of loyal users and a gigantic software base that was growing at a fantastic rate. The other type, CP/M systems, consisted not of a single system but of all the many systems that evolved from the original MITS Altair. These systems were compatible with one another and were distinguished by their use of the CP/M operating system and expansion slots, which followed the S-100 standard. All these systems were built by a variety of companies and sold under various names. For the most part, however, these systems used the same software and plug-in hardware. It is interesting to note that none of these systems was PC compatible or Macintosh compatible, the two primary standards in place today.

A new competitor looming on the horizon was able to see that to be successful, a personal computer needed to have an open architecture, slots for expansion, a modular design, and healthy support from both hardware and software companies other than the original manufacturer of the system. This competitor turned out to be IBM, which was quite surprising at the time because IBM was not known for systems with these open-architecture attributes! IBM, in essence, became more like the early Apple, and Apple itself became like everybody expected IBM to be. The open architecture of the forthcoming IBM PC and the closed architecture of the forthcoming Macintosh caused a complete turnaround in the industry.

The IBM Personal Computer

At the end of 1980, IBM decided to truly compete in the rapidly growing low-cost personal computer market. The company established the Entry Systems Division, located in Boca Raton, Florida, to develop the new system. The division was located intentionally far away from IBM's main headquarters in New York, or any other IBM facilities, so that this new division would be able to operate independently as a separate unit. This small group consisted of 12 engineers and designers under the direction of Don Estridge and was charged with developing IBM's first real PC. (IBM considered the previous 5100 system, developed in 1975, to be an intelligent programmable terminal rather than a genuine computer, even though it truly was a computer.) Nearly all these engineers had come to the new division from the System/23 DataMaster project, which was a small office computer system introduced in 1980 and was the direct predecessor of the IBM PC.

Much of the PC's design was influenced by the DataMaster design. In the DataMaster's single-piece design, the display and keyboard were integrated into the unit. Because these features were limiting, they became external units on the PC, although the PC keyboard layout and electrical designs were copied from the DataMaster.

Several other parts of the IBM PC system also were copied from the DataMaster, including the expansion bus (or input/output slots), which included not only the same physical 62-pin connector, but also almost identical pin specifications. This copying of the bus design was possible because the PC used the same interrupt controller as the DataMaster and a similar direct memory access (DMA) controller. Also, expansion cards already designed for the DataMaster could easily be redesigned to function in the PC.

The DataMaster used an Intel 8085 CPU, which had a 64KB address limit and an 8-bit internal and external data bus. This arrangement prompted the PC design team to use the Intel 8088 CPU, which offered a much larger (1MB) memory address limit and an internal 16-bit data bus, but only an 8-bit external data bus. The 8-bit external data bus and similar instruction set enabled the 8088 to be easily interfaced into the earlier DataMaster designs.

IBM brought its system from idea to delivery of functioning systems in one year by using existing designs and purchasing as many components as possible from outside vendors. The Entry Systems Division was granted autonomy from IBM's other divisions and could tap resources outside the company, rather than go through the bureaucratic procedures that required exclusive use of IBM resources. IBM contracted out the PC's languages and operating system to a small company named Microsoft. That decision was the major factor in establishing Microsoft as the dominant force in PC software today.

Note

It is interesting to note that IBM had originally contacted Digital Research (the company that created CP/M, then the most popular personal computer operating system) to have it develop an operating system for the new IBM PC. However, Digital was leery of working with IBM and especially balked at the nondisclosure agreement IBM wanted Digital to sign. Microsoft jumped on the opportunity left open by Digital Research and, consequently, has become one of the largest software companies in the world. IBM's use of outside vendors in developing the PC was an open invitation for the aftermarket to jump in and support the system—and it did.

On August 12, 1981, a new standard was established in the microcomputer industry with the debut of the IBM PC. Since then, hundreds of millions of PC-compatible systems have been sold, as the original PC has grown into an enormous family of computers and peripherals. More software has been written for this computer family than for any other system on the market.

The PC Industry More Than 20 Years Later

In the more than 20 years since the original IBM PC was introduced, many changes have occurred. The IBM-compatible computer, for example, advanced from a 4.77MHz 8088-based system to 3GHz or faster Pentium 4–based systems—about 20,000 times faster than the original IBM PC (in actual processing speed, not just clock speed). The original PC had only one or two single-sided floppy drives that stored 160KB each using DOS 1.0, whereas modern systems easily can have 200GB (200 billion bytes) or more of hard disk storage.

A rule of thumb in the computer industry (called Moore's Law, originally set forth by Intel cofounder Gordon Moore) is that available processor performance and disk-storage capacity doubles every one and a half to two years, give or take.

Since the beginning of the PC industry, this pattern has held steady and, if anything, seems to be accelerating.

Moore's Law

In 1965, Gordon Moore was preparing a speech about the growth trends in computer memory and made an interesting observation. When he began to graph the data, he realized a striking trend existed. Each new chip contained roughly twice as much capacity as its predecessor, and each chip was released within 18–24 months of the previous chip. If this trend continued, he reasoned, computing power would rise exponentially over relatively brief periods of time.

Moore's observation, now known as Moore's Law, described a trend that has continued to this day and is still remarkably accurate. It was found to not only describe memory chips, but also accurately describe the growth of processor power and disk drive storage capacity. It has become the basis for many industry performance forecasts. As an example, in 30 years the number of transistors on a processor chip increased more than 18,000 times, from 2,300 transistors on the 4004 processor in 1971 to more than 140 million transistors on the Pentium III Xeon processor in May 2000. By 2007, Intel expects to release processors with one billion transistors running at 20GHz speeds.

In addition to performance and storage capacity, another major change since the original IBM PC was introduced is that IBM is not the only manufacturer of PC-compatible systems. IBM originated the PC-compatible standard, of course, but today it no longer sets the standards for the system it originated. More often than not, new standards in the PC industry are developed by companies and organizations other than IBM.

Today, it is Intel, Microsoft, and to an extent AMD who are primarily responsible for developing and extending the PC hardware and software standards. Some have even taken to calling PCs "Wintel" systems, owing to the dominance of the first two companies. Although AMD originally produced

Intel processors under license and later produced low-cost, pin-compatible counterparts to Intel's 486 and Pentium processors (AMD 486, K5/K6), starting with the Athlon, AMD has created completely unique processors that have been worthy rivals to Intel's Pentium II, III, and 4 models.

In more recent years, Intel, Microsoft, and AMD have carried the evolution of the PC forward. The introduction of hardware standards such as the Peripheral Component Interconnect (PCI) bus, Accelerated Graphics Port (AGP) bus, ATX and NLX motherboard form factors, processor socket and slot interfaces, and numerous others show that Intel is really pushing PC hardware design these days. Intel is also responsible for the motherboard chipsets used to support these features, enabling its newest processors to be immediately available in systems. AMD also makes chipsets for its own processors, but AMD chipsets have acted primarily as reference designs for other vendors to improve upon. Consequently, AMD-based systems often offer much more aggressive customization features than Intel-based systems at a lower cost. In a similar fashion, Microsoft is pushing the software side of things with the continual evolution of the Windows operating system as well as applications such as the Office suite. Both Intel and Microsoft continue to capitalize on the widespread popularity of the Internet, multimedia, and other types of rich media. Such uses as interactive gaming, DVD editing, broadband Internet access, and photo-quality printing are giving more and more people important reasons to use a PC. Even though recent sales have leveled off from the explosive growth of the mid-to-late 1990s, the reality is that most people who want to use a PC for a business or recreational task have one. Today, literally hundreds of system manufacturers follow the collective PC standard and produce computers that are fully PC compatible. In addition, thousands of peripheral manufacturers produce components that expand and enhance PC-compatible systems.

PC-compatible systems have thrived not only because compatible hardware can be assembled easily, but also because the primary operating system was available not from IBM but from a third party (Microsoft). The core of the system software is the basic input/output system (BIOS), and this was also available from third-party companies, such as AMI, Phoenix, and others. This situation enabled other manufacturers to license the operating system and BIOS software and sell their own compatible systems. The fact that DOS borrowed the functionality and user interface from both CP/M and Unix probably had a lot to do with the amount of software that became available. Later, with the success of Windows, even more reasons would exist for software developers to write programs for PC-compatible systems.

One reason Apple Macintosh systems never enjoyed the extreme success of PC systems is that Apple controls all the primary systems software (BIOS and OS) and, with one short-lived exception, has refused to license it to other companies for use in compatible systems.

After years of declining market share, Apple seemed to recognize that refusing to license its operating system was a flawed stance and in the mid-1990s licensed its software to third-party manufacturers such as Power Computing. After a short time, though, Apple canceled its licensing agreements with other manufacturers. Because Apple remains essentially a closed system, other companies cannot develop compatible machines, meaning Apple-compatible systems are available from only one source: Apple. Although the development of low-cost models such as the iMac and Apple's continued popularity with educators and artists have helped Apple maintain and modestly increase its market share, Apple will never effectively compete with the PC-compatible juggernaut because of its closed-system approach. It is fortunate for the computing public as a whole that IBM created a more open and extendible standard, which today finds systems being offered by hundreds of companies in thousands of configurations. This type of competition among manufacturers and vendors of PC-compatible systems is the reason such systems offer so much performance and so many capabilities for the money.

The PC continues to thrive and prosper, and new technology continues to be integrated into these systems, enabling them to grow with the times. These systems offer a high value for the money and have plenty of software available to run on them. It's a safe bet that PC-compatible systems will dominate the personal computer marketplace for the next 20 years.

CHAPTER 2

PC Components, Features, and System Design

What Is a PC?

I normally ask the question, "What exactly is a PC?" when I begin one of my PC hardware seminars. Of course, most people immediately answer that PC stands for *personal computer*, which in fact it does. They might then continue by defining a personal computer as any small computer system purchased and used by an individual. Unfortunately, that definition is not nearly precise or accurate enough for our purposes. I agree that a PC is a personal computer, but not all personal computers are PCs. For example, an Apple Macintosh system is clearly a personal computer, but nobody I know would call a Mac a PC, least of all Mac users! For the true definition of what a PC is, you must look deeper.

Calling something a PC implies that it is something much more specific than just any personal computer. One thing it implies is a family relation to the original IBM PC from 1981. In fact, I'll go so far as to say that IBM literally *invented* the type of computer we call a PC today; that is, IBM designed and created the very first one, and IBM originally defined and set all the standards that made the PC distinctive from other personal computers. Note that it is very clear in my mind—as well as in the historical record—that IBM did *not* invent the personal computer. (Most recognize the historical origins of the personal computer in the MITS Altair, introduced in 1975.) So, IBM did not invent the personal computer, but it did invent what today we call the PC. Some people might take this definition a step further and define a PC as any personal computer that is "IBM compatible." In fact, many years back, PCs were called either IBM compatibles or IBM clones, in essence paying homage to the origins of the PC at IBM.

The reality today is that although IBM clearly designed and created the first PC in 1981 and controlled the development and evolution of the PC standard for several years thereafter, IBM is no longer in control of the PC standard; that is, it does not dictate what makes up a PC today. IBM lost control of the PC standard in 1987 when it introduced its PS/2 line of systems. Up until then, other companies that were producing PCs literally copied IBM's systems right down to the chips; connectors; and even the shapes (form factors) of the boards, cases, and power supplies. After 1987, IBM abandoned many of the standards it created in the first place. That's why for many years now I have refrained from using the designation "IBM compatible" when referring to PCs.

If a PC is no longer an IBM-compatible system, what is it? The real question seems to be, "Who is in control of the PC standard today?" That question is best broken down into two parts. First, who is in control of PC software? Second, who is in control of PC hardware?

Who Controls PC Software?

Most of the people in my seminars don't even hesitate for a split second when I ask this question; they immediately respond, "Microsoft!" I don't think there is any argument with that answer. Microsoft clearly controls the operating systems used on PCs, which have migrated from the original MS-DOS to Windows 3.1/95/98/Me, Windows NT/2000, and now Windows XP.

Microsoft has effectively used its control of the PC operating system as leverage to also control other types of PC software, such as utilities and applications. For example, many utility programs originally offered by independent companies, such as disk caching, disk compression, file defragmentation, file structure repair, and even simple applications such as calculator and notepad programs, are now bundled in (included with) Windows. Microsoft has even bundled more comprehensive applications such as Web browsers, ensuring an automatic installed base for these applications—much to the dismay of companies who produce competing versions. Microsoft has also leveraged its control of the operating system to integrate its own networking software and applications suites more seamlessly into the operating system than others. That's why it now dominates most of the PC software universe, from operating systems to networking software to utilities, from word processors to database programs to spreadsheets.

In the early days of the PC, when IBM was clearly in control of the PC hardware standard, it hired Microsoft to provide most of the core software for the PC. IBM developed the hardware, wrote the basic input/output system (BIOS), and then hired Microsoft to develop the disk operating system

(DOS), as well as several other programs and utilities for the PC. In what was later viewed as perhaps the most costly business mistake in history, IBM failed to secure exclusive rights to the DOS it had contracted from Microsoft, either by purchasing it outright or by an exclusive license agreement. Instead, IBM licensed it nonexclusively, which subsequently allowed Microsoft to sell the same MS-DOS code it developed for IBM to any other company that was interested. Early PC cloners such as Compaq eagerly licensed this same operating system code, and suddenly consumers could purchase the same basic MS-DOS operating system with several different company names on the box. In retrospect, that single contractual error made Microsoft into the dominant software company it is today and subsequently caused IBM to lose control of the very PC standard it had created.

As a writer myself (of words, not software), I can appreciate what an incredible oversight this was. Imagine that a book publisher comes up with a great idea for a very popular book and then contracts with and subsequently pays an author to write it. Then, by virtue of a poorly written contract, the author discovers that he can legally sell the very same book (perhaps with a different title) to all the competitors of the original publisher. Of course, no publisher I know would allow this to happen; yet that is exactly what IBM allowed Microsoft to do back in 1981. By virtue of its deal with Microsoft, IBM had essentially lost control of the software it commissioned for its new PC from day one.

It is interesting to note that in the PC business, software enjoys copyright protection, whereas hardware can be protected only by patents, which are difficult, time-consuming, and expensive to get and which also expire after 17 years. To patent something requires that it be a unique and substantially new design. This made it impossible to patent most aspects of the IBM PC because it was designed using previously existing parts that anybody could purchase off the shelf! In fact, most of the important parts for the original PC came from Intel, such as the 8088 processor, 8284 clock generator, 8253/54 timer, 8259 interrupt controller, 8237 DMA (direct memory access) controller, 8255 peripheral interface, and 8288 bus controller. These chips made up the heart and soul of the original PC motherboard.

Because the design of the original PC was not wholly patentable, anybody could duplicate the hardware of the IBM PC. All she had to do was purchase the same chips from the same manufacturers and suppliers IBM used and design a new motherboard with a similar circuit. Seemingly as if to aid in this, IBM even published complete schematic diagrams of its motherboards and all its adapter cards in very detailed and easily available technical reference manuals. I have several of these early IBM manuals and still refer to them from time to time for specific component-level PC design information. In fact, I still recommend these original manuals to anybody who wants to delve deeply into PC hardware design.

The difficult part of copying the IBM PC was the software, which is protected by copyright law. Phoenix Software (today known as Phoenix Technologies) was among the first to develop a legal way around this problem, which enabled it to functionally duplicate (but not exactly copy) software such as the BIOS. The *BIOS* is defined as the core set of control software that drives the hardware devices in the system directly. These types of programs are normally called *device drivers*, so in essence, the BIOS is a collection of all the core device drivers used to operate and control the system hardware. The *operating system* (such as DOS or Windows) uses the drivers in the BIOS to control and communicate with the various hardware and peripherals in the system.

▶▶ See Chapter 5, "BIOS," p. 397.

Phoenix's method for legally duplicating the IBM PC BIOS was an ingenious form of reverse-engineering. It hired two teams of software engineers, the second of which had to be specially screened to consist only of people who had never before seen or studied the IBM BIOS code. The first team did study the IBM BIOS and wrote as complete a description of what it did as possible. The second team read the description written by the first team and set out to write from scratch a new BIOS that did everything the first team described. The end result was a new BIOS written from scratch with code that, although not identical to IBM's, had exactly the same functionality.

Phoenix called this a "clean room" approach to reverse-engineering software, and it can escape any legal attack. Because IBM's original PC BIOS consisted of only 8KB of code and had limited functionality, duplicating it through the clean room approach was not very difficult nor time-consuming. As the IBM BIOS evolved, Phoenix—as well as the other BIOS companies—found that keeping up with any changes IBM made was relatively easy. Discounting the power on self test (POST) or BIOS Setup program (used for configuring the system) portion of the BIOS, most motherboard BIOSs, even today, have only about 32KB–128KB of active code. Today, Phoenix and American Megatrends (AMI) are the leading developers of BIOS software for PC system and motherboard manufacturers. A third major producer of BIOS software, Award Software, is owned by Phoenix Technologies, which continues to sell Award BIOS–based products.

After the hardware and BIOS of the IBM PC were duplicated, all that was necessary to produce a fully IBM-compatible system was DOS. Reverse-engineering DOS, even with the clean room approach, would have been a daunting task because DOS is much larger than the BIOS and consists of many more programs and functions. Also, the operating system has evolved and changed more often than the BIOS, which by comparison has remained relatively constant. This means that the only way to get DOS on an IBM compatible was to license it. This is where Microsoft came in. Because IBM (who hired Microsoft to write DOS in the first place) did not ensure that Microsoft signed an exclusive license agreement, Microsoft was free to sell the same DOS it designed for IBM to anybody else who wanted it. With a licensed copy of MS-DOS, the last piece was in place and the floodgates were open for IBM-compatible systems to be produced whether IBM liked it or not.

In retrospect, this is exactly why there are no clones or compatibles of the Apple Macintosh system. It is not that Mac systems can't be duplicated; in fact, Mac hardware is fairly simple and easy to produce using off-the-shelf parts. The real problem is that Apple owns the Mac OS as well as the BIOS, and because Apple has seen fit not to license them, no other company can sell an Apple-compatible system. Also, note that the Mac BIOS and OS are very tightly integrated; the Mac BIOS is very large and complex, and it is essentially a part of the OS, unlike the much simpler and more easily duplicated BIOS found on PCs. The greater complexity and integration has allowed both the Mac BIOS and OS to escape any clean-room duplication efforts. This means that without Apple's blessing (in the form of licensing), no Mac clones are likely ever to exist.

It might be interesting to note that during 1996–1997, an effort was made by the more liberated thinkers at Apple to license its BIOS/OS combination, and several Mac-compatible machines were developed, produced, and sold. Companies such as Sony, Power Computing, Radius, and even Motorola invested millions of dollars in developing these systems, but shortly after these first Mac clones were sold, Apple rudely canceled all licensing! This was apparently the result of an edict from Steve Jobs, who had been hired back to run the company and who was one of the original architects of the closed-box, proprietary-design Macintosh system in the first place. By canceling these licenses, Apple has virtually guaranteed that its systems will never be a mainstream success. Along with its smaller market share come much higher system costs, fewer available software applications, and fewer hardware upgrades as compared to PCs. The proprietary design also means that major repair or upgrade components, such as motherboards, power supplies, and cases, are available only from Apple at very high prices and upgrades of these components are usually not cost effective.

I often think that if Apple had a different view and had licensed its OS and BIOS early on, this book might be called *Upgrading and Repairing Macs* instead!

Who Controls PC Hardware?

Although it is clear that Microsoft has always controlled PC software by virtue of its control over the PC operating system, what about the hardware? It is easy to see that IBM controlled the PC hardware standard up through 1987. After all, IBM invented the core PC motherboard design; the original expansion bus slot architecture (8/16-bit ISA bus); serial and parallel port implementations; video card design through VGA and XGA standards; floppy and hard disk interface and controller implementations; power supply designs; keyboard interfaces and designs; mouse interface; and even the physical shapes (form factors) of everything from the motherboard to the expansion cards, power supplies, and system chassis. All these pre-1987 IBM PC, XT, and AT system design features are still influencing modern systems today.

But to me the real question is which company has been responsible for creating and inventing newer and more recent PC hardware designs, interfaces, and standards? When I ask people that question, I normally see some hesitation in their responses—some people say Microsoft (but it controls the software, not the hardware), and some say Compaq or Dell, or they name a few other big-name system manufacturers. Only a few surmise the correct answer—Intel.

I can see why many people don't immediately realize this; I mean, how many people actually own an Intel-brand PC? No, not just one that says "Intel inside" on it (which refers only to the system having an Intel processor), but a system that was designed and built by, or even purchased through, Intel. Believe it or not, I think that many—if not most—people today do have Intel PCs!

Certainly this does not mean that consumers have purchased their systems from Intel because Intel does not sell complete PCs to end users. You can't currently order a system from Intel, nor can you purchase an Intel-brand system from somebody else. What I am talking about is the motherboard. In my opinion, the single most important part in a PC system is the motherboard, and I'd say that whoever made your motherboard would be considered the manufacturer of your system. Even back when IBM was the major supplier of PCs, it primarily made the motherboard and contracted out the other components of the system (power supply, disk drives, and so on) to others.

▶▶   See "Motherboards and Buses," p. 201.

Many of the top-selling system manufacturers do design and make their own motherboards. According to *Computer Reseller News* magazine, the top desktop systems manufacturers for the last several years have consistently been names such as HP, Compaq (now owned by HP), and IBM. These companies, for the most part, do design and manufacture their own motherboards, as well as many other system components. In some cases, they even design their own chips and chipset components for their own boards. Although sales are high for these individual companies, a larger overall segment of the market is what those in the industry call the *white-box* systems.

White-box is the term used by the industry to refer to what would otherwise be called *generic* PCs—that is, PCs assembled from a collection of industry-standard, commercially available components. The white-box designation comes from the fact that historically most of the chassis used by this type of system have been white (or ivory or beige).

The great thing about white-box systems is that they use industry-standard components that are interchangeable. This interchangeability is the key to future upgrades and repairs because it ensures that a plethora of replacement parts will be available to choose from and will interchange. For many years, I have recommended avoiding proprietary systems and recommended more industry-standard white-box systems instead.

Companies selling white-box systems do not really manufacture the systems; they assemble them. That is, they purchase commercially available motherboards, cases, power supplies, disk drives, peripherals, and so on, and assemble and market everything together as complete systems. Dell, Gateway, and Micron (now MPC) are some of the larger white-box system assemblers today, but hundreds more could be listed. In overall total volume, this ends up being the largest segment of the PC marketplace today. What is interesting about white-box systems is that, with very few exceptions, you and I can purchase the same motherboards and other components any of the white-box manufacturers can (although we would probably pay more than they do because of the volume discounts they receive). We can assemble a virtually identical white-box system from scratch ourselves, but that is a story for Chapter 22, "Building or Upgrading Systems."

Note that some of these white-box companies have incredible sales—for example, Dell has taken the top PC sales spot from Compaq (now HP), who had held it for many years. Gateway and the other white-box system builders are not far behind.

The point of all this is, of course, that if Dell, Gateway, MPC, and others do not manufacture their own motherboards, who does? You guessed it—Intel. Not only do those specific companies mainly use Intel motherboards, if you check around, you'll find today that many of the systems in the white-box market come with Intel motherboards. The only place Intel doesn't have a presence is the AMD-based systems designed to support Athlon-branded processors.

Although this is an extreme case, one review of 10 systems in *Computer Shopper* magazine listed 8 out of the 10 systems evaluated as having Intel motherboards. In fact, those 8 used the exact same Intel motherboard. Therefore, those systems differed only in the cosmetics of the exterior case assemblies and by which peripheral components, such as video card, disk drives, keyboard, and so on, were selected. The funny thing was that many of the peripheral items were identical among the systems as well. Before you compare preassembled systems from different manufacturers, be sure to get a listing of which parts they are using; you might be surprised to see how similar the systems on the market at any given time can be.

Although Intel still dominates motherboard sales, that dominance has faltered somewhat from a few years back. Because of Intel's focus on Rambus memory during the early Pentium 4 days, many of the lower-cost system builders switched to alternative products. Also, most of Intel's boards are designed to make overclocking either impossible or extremely difficult, so "hotrod" system builders typically choose non-Intel boards.

AMD, on the other hand, manufactures processors and chipsets but not complete motherboards. For that, AMD relies on a number of other motherboard manufacturers to make boards designed to accept AMD processors. These boards use either the AMD chipsets or other chipsets made by third-party companies specifically to support AMD processors. The same motherboard companies making boards for AMD processor–based systems also make motherboards for Intel processor–based systems, in essence competing directly with Intel's own motherboards.

▶▶   See "Chipsets," p. 239.

How did Intel come to dominate the interior of our PCs? Intel has been the dominant PC processor supplier since IBM chose the Intel 8088 CPU in the original IBM PC in 1981. By controlling the processor, Intel naturally controlled the chips necessary to integrate its processors into system designs. This naturally led Intel into the chipset business. It started its chipset business in 1989 with the 82350 Extended Industry Standard Architecture (EISA) chipset, and by 1993 it had become—along with the debut of the Pentium processor—the largest-volume major motherboard chipset supplier. Now I imagine Intel sitting there, thinking that it makes the processor and all the other chips necessary to produce a motherboard, so why not just eliminate the middleman and make the entire motherboard, too? The answer to this, and a real turning point in the industry, came about in 1994 when Intel became the largest-volume motherboard manufacturer in the world. And Intel has remained solidly on top ever since. It doesn't just lead in this category by any small margin; in fact, during 1997, Intel made more motherboards than the next eight largest motherboard manufacturers combined, with sales of more than 30 million boards, worth more than $3.6 billion! Note that this figure does not include processors or chipsets—only the boards themselves. These boards end up in the various system assembler brand PCs you and I buy, meaning that most of us are now essentially purchasing Intel-manufactured systems, no matter who actually wielded the screwdriver.

Intel controls the PC hardware standard because it controls the PC motherboard. It not only makes the vast majority of motherboards being used in systems today, but it also supplies the vast majority of processors and motherboard chipsets to other motherboard manufacturers.

Intel also has had a hand in setting several recent PC hardware standards, such as the following:

- PCI (Peripheral Component Interconnect) local bus interface
- PCI Express (originally known as 3GIO), the interface elected by the PCI Special Interest Group (PCI SIG) to replace PCI as a high-performance bus for future PCs
- Accelerated Graphics Port (AGP) interface for high-performance video cards
- ATX motherboard form factor (and variations such as MicroATX and FlexATX), which, beginning in 1996–1997, replaced the (somewhat long-in-the-tooth) IBM-designed Baby-AT form factor that had been used since the early 1980s

- NLX motherboard form factor to replace the proprietary and limited LPX design used by many lower-cost systems, which finally brought motherboard upgradability to those systems
- Desktop Management Interface (DMI) for monitoring system hardware functions
- Dynamic Power Management Architecture (DPMA) and Advanced Power Management (APM) standards for managing power use in the PC

Intel dominates not only the PC, but the entire semiconductor industry. According to the sales figures compiled by iSuppli.com, Intel has more than two and a half times the sales of the next closest semiconductor company (Samsung) and about nine times the sales of competitor AMD (see Table 2.1).

Table 2.1   Top 30 Semiconductor Companies Ranked by 2002 Semiconductor Sales

Supplier	2002 Rank	2002 Sales	2001 Rank	2001 Sales	2000 Rank	2000 Sales
Intel	1	$23.47	1	$23.54	1	$30.21
Samsung	2	$9.18	4	$6.14	4	$8.94
STMicro	3	$6.31	3	$6.36	6	$7.89
TI	4	$6.20	5	$6.05	3	$9.20
Toshiba	5	$6.19	2	$6.54	2	$10.43
Infineon	6	$5.36	8	$4.56	8	$6.74
NEC	7	$5.26	6	$5.30	5	$8.20
Motorola	8	$4.73	7	$4.83	7	$7.71
Philips	9	$4.36	9	$4.41	9	$6.27
Hitachi	10	$4.05	10	$4.24	12	$5.69
Mitsubishi	11	$3.62	11	$3.87	11	$5.79
IBM	12	$3.39	14	$3.56	18	$3.99
Matsushita	13	$3.28	16	$3.01	17	$4.33
Fujitsu	14	$3.24	13	$3.73	15	$5.01
Micron	15	$3.22	18	$2.45	10	$6.26
AMD	16	$2.61	12	$3.79	16	$4.38
Hynix	17	$2.57	19	$2.34	14	$5.10
Sony	18	$2.50	17	$2.47	20	$3.29
Rohm	19	$2.39	21	$2.21	23	$3.06
Sharp	20	$2.36	20	$3.36	19	$3.33
Sanyo	21	$2.10	22	$2.03	21	$3.28
Agere	22	$2.03	15	$3.14	13	$5.10
Analog Devices	23	$1.94	23	$1.93	24	$2.74
Qualcomm	24	$1.85	28	$1.39	37	$1.22
NVIDIA	25	$1.80	30	$1.29	51	$0.71
Agilent	26	$1.60	24	$1.53	27	$2.31
National	27	$1.57	26	$1.51	25	$2.36
LSI Logic	28	$1.51	25	$1.56	26	$2.34
Fairchild	29	$1.35	29	$1.34	31	$1.68
Atmel	30	$1.21	27	$1.48	29	$2.01

*Dollars in millions

As you can see by these figures, it is no wonder that a popular industry news Web site called The Register (http://www.theregister.co.uk) uses the term "Chipzilla" when referring to the industry giant.

Whoever controls the operating system controls the software for the PC, and whoever controls the processor—and therefore the motherboard—controls the hardware. Because Microsoft and Intel together seem to control software and hardware in the PC today, it is no surprise the modern PC is often called a "Wintel" system.

PC Design Guides

Even though Intel controls PC hardware, Microsoft recognizes its power over the PC from the operating system perspective and has been collaborating with Intel. Together, they have released a series of documents called the "PC *xx* Design Guides" (where *xx* designates the year) as a set of standard specifications to guide both hardware and software developers who are creating products that work with Windows. The requirements in these guides are part of Microsoft's "Designed for Windows" logo requirement. In other words, if you produce either a hardware or software product and you want the official "Designed for Windows" logo to be on your box, your product must meet the PC *xx* minimum requirements.

Following are the documents that have been produced in this series:

- "Hardware Design Guide for Microsoft Windows 95"
- "Hardware Design Guide Supplement for PC 95"
- "PC 97 Hardware Design Guide"
- "PC 98 System Design Guide"
- "PC 99 System Design Guide"
- "PC 2000 System Design Guide"
- "PC 2001 System Design Guide"

These documents are available for download from the PC Design Guides Web site (http://www.pcdesguide.org), as well as the Microsoft Web site (http://www.microsoft.com/whdc/hwdev/platform/pcdesign/desguide/pcguides.mspx).

These system-design guides present information for engineers who design and build personal computers, expansion cards, and peripheral devices that are to be used with Windows 9x/Me, NT/2000, and XP operating systems. The requirements and recommendations in these guides form the basis for the requirements of the "Designed for Windows" logo program for hardware Microsoft sponsors.

These guides include requirements for basic (desktop and mobile) systems, workstations, and even entertainment PCs. They also address Plug and Play device configuration and power management in PC systems; requirements for universal serial bus (USB) and IEEE-1394; and new devices supported under Windows, including new graphics and video device capabilities, DVD, scanners and digital cameras, and other devices.

Note

These guides do not mean anything directly for the end user; instead, they are meant to be guides for PC manufacturers to design and build their systems. As such, they are guides or recommendations, and they do not have to be followed to the letter. In some ways, they are a market-control tool for Intel and Microsoft to further wield their influence over PC hardware and software. In reality, the market often dictates that some of these recommendations are disregarded, which is one reason they continue to evolve with new versions year after year.

The PC 2001 System Design Guide is the most recent comprehensive design guide produced by Microsoft and Intel. These companies now produce individual whitepapers and other resources for this purpose. For updated system design information, see the following Web sites:

- The Microsoft Windows Platform Design – Overview site at
  http://www.microsoft.com/whdc/hwdev/platform/default.mspx
- The Intel developer Web site at http://developer.intel.com

System Types

PCs can be broken down into many categories. I like to break them down in two ways—by the type of software they can run and by the motherboard host bus, or processor bus design and width. Because this book concentrates mainly on hardware, let's look at that first.

When a processor reads data, the data moves into the processor via the processor's external data bus connection. The processor's data bus is directly connected to the processor host bus on the motherboard. The processor data bus or host bus is also sometimes referred to as the *local bus* because it is local to the processor that is connected directly to it. Any other devices connected to the host bus essentially appear as if they are directly connected to the processor as well. If the processor has a 32-bit data bus, the motherboard must be wired to have a 32-bit processor host bus. This means the system can move 32 bits of data into or out of the processor in a single cycle.

▶▶ See "Data I/O Bus," p. 46.

Different processors have different data bus widths, and the motherboards designed to accept them require a processor host bus with a matching width. Table 2.2 lists all the Intel and major Intel-compatible processors, their data bus widths, and their internal register sizes.

Table 2.2 Intel and Intel-Compatible Processors and Their Data Bus/Register Widths

Processor	Data Bus Width	Register Size
8088	8-bit	16-bit
8086	16-bit	16-bit
286	16-bit	16-bit
386SX	16-bit	32-bit
386DX	32-bit	32-bit
486/AMD-5x86	32-bit	32-bit
Pentium/AMD-K6	64-bit	32-bit
Pentium Pro/Celeron/II/III	64-bit	32-bit
AMD Duron/Athlon/Athlon XP	64-bit	32-bit
Pentium 4	64-bit	32-bit
Itanium	64-bit	64-bit
AMD Athlon 64	64-bit	64-bit

A common misconception arises in discussions of processor widths. Although the Pentium and newer processors all have 64-bit data bus widths, their internal registers are only 32 bits wide, and they process 32-bit commands and instructions. The Intel Itanium and AMD Athlon 64 are the first Intel-compatible processors to have 64-bit internal registers. Thus, from a software point of view, all chips from the 386 to the Athlon/Duron and Celeron/Pentium 4 have 32-bit registers and execute 32-bit instructions. From the electronic or physical perspective, these 32-bit, software-capable processors have been available in physical forms with 16-bit (386SX), 32-bit (386DX and 486), and 64-bit

(Pentium and beyond) data bus widths. The data bus width is the major factor in motherboard and memory system design because it dictates how many bits move in and out of the chip in one cycle.

▶▶   See "Internal Registers (Internal Data Bus)," p. 48.

The Itanium processor has a new Intel architecture 64-bit (IA-64) instruction set, but it can also process the same 32-bit instructions as processors ranging from the 386 through the Pentium 4. The Athlon 64 has a new x86-compatible 64-bit architecture but is designed to use 32-bit instructions written for normal Intel or compatible x86 processors as efficiently as a normal Athlon XP or comparable processor would.

▶▶   See "Processor Specifications," p. 41.

Referring to Table 2.2, you can see that all Pentium and newer systems have a 64-bit processor bus. Pentium processors, whether they are the original Pentium, Pentium MMX, Pentium Pro, or even the Pentium II/III or 4, all have 64-bit data buses, as do comparable processors from AMD (K6 family, Athlon, Duron, Athlon XP, and Athlon 64).

As you can see from Table 2.2, systems can be broken down into the following hardware categories:

- 8-bit
- 16-bit
- 32-bit
- 64-bit

What is interesting is that besides the bus width, the 16- through 64-bit systems are remarkably similar in basic design and architecture. The older 8-bit systems are very different, however. This gives us two basic system types, or classes, of hardware:

- 8-bit (PC/XT-class) systems
- 16/32/64-bit (AT-class) systems

In this verbiage, PC stands for personal computer; XT stands for an extended PC; and AT stands for an advanced-technology PC. The terms *PC*, *XT*, and *AT*, as they are used here, are taken from the original IBM systems of those names. The XT was a PC system that included a hard disk for storage in addition to the floppy drives found in the basic PC system. These systems had an 8-bit 8088 processor and an 8-bit Industry Standard Architecture (ISA) bus for system expansion. The *bus* is the name given to expansion slots in which additional plug-in circuit boards can be installed. The 8-bit designation comes from the fact that the ISA bus found in the PC/XT class systems can send and receive only 8 bits of data in a single cycle. The data in an 8-bit bus is sent along eight wires simultaneously, in parallel.

▶▶   See "The ISA Bus," p. 350.

16-bit and greater systems are said to be AT-class, which indicates that they follow certain standards and that they follow the basic design first set forth in the original IBM AT system. AT is the designation IBM applied to systems that first included more advanced 16-bit (and later, 32- and 64-bit) processors and expansion slots. AT-class systems must have a processor that is compatible with Intel 286 or higher processors (including the 386, 486, Pentium, Pentium Pro, Pentium II, Pentium III, Pentium 4, and Pentium M processors), and they must have a 16-bit or greater system bus. The system bus architecture is central to the AT system design, along with the basic memory architecture, interrupt request (IRQ), direct memory access (DMA), and I/O port address design. All AT-class systems are similar in the way these resources are allocated and how they function.

The first AT-class systems had a 16-bit version of the ISA bus, which is an extension of the original 8-bit ISA bus found in the PC/XT-class systems. Eventually, several expansion slot or bus designs were developed for AT-class systems, including the following:

- 16-bit ISA/AT bus
- 16-bit PC Card (PCMCIA) bus
- 16/32-bit Extended ISA (EISA) bus

- 16/32-bit PS/2 Micro Channel Architecture (MCA) bus

- 32-bit VESA Local (VL) bus

- 32/64-bit Peripheral Component Interconnect (PCI) bus

- 32-bit CardBus (PCMCIA) bus

- PCI Express bus

- ExpressCard bus

- 32-bit Accelerated Graphics Port (AGP) bus

A system with any of these types of expansion slots is by definition an AT-class system, regardless of the actual Intel or Intel-compatible processor that is used. AT-type systems with 386 or higher processors have special capabilities not found in the first generation of 286-based ATs. These distinct capabilities are in the areas of memory addressing, memory management, and possible 32- or 64-bit wide access to data. Most systems with 386DX or higher chips also have 32-bit bus architectures to take full advantage of the 32-bit data transfer capabilities of the processor.

Until recently, PC systems continued to incorporate a 16-bit ISA slot for backward-compatibility and lower-function adapters. However, in virtually all motherboards today, ISA slots have been completely replaced by PCI slots along with an AGP slot (a specialized expansion slot design) available in most systems (except for a few entry-level models with integrated video) for high-performance graphics. In addition, most portable systems use PC Card (PCMCIA) and CardBus slots in the portable unit and PCI slots in optional docking stations.

Chapter 4, "Motherboards and Buses," contains in-depth information on these and other PC system buses, including technical information such as pinouts, performance specifications, and bus operation and theory.

Table 2.3 summarizes the primary differences between the older 8-bit (PC/XT) systems and modern AT systems. This information distinguishes between these systems and includes all IBM and compatible models.

Table 2.3 Differences Between PC/XT and AT Systems

System Attributes	(8-Bit) PC/XT Type	(16/32/64-Bit) AT Type
Supported processors	All x86 or x88	286 or higher
Processor modes	Real	Real/Protected/Virtual Real
Software supported	16-bit only	16- or 32-bit
Bus slot width	8-bit	16/32/64-bit
Slot type	ISA only	ISA, EISA, MCA, PC Card, CardBus, ExpressCard, VL-Bus, PCI, PCI Express, and AGP
Hardware interrupts	8 (6 usable)	16 (11 usable)
DMA channels	4 (3 usable)	8 (7 usable)
Maximum RAM	1MB	16MB/4GB or more
Floppy controller speed	250Kbps	250/300/500/1,000 Kbps
Standard boot drive	360KB or 720KB	1.2MB/1.44MB/2.88MB
Keyboard interface	Unidirectional	Bidirectional
CMOS memory/clock	None standard	MC146818-compatible
Serial-port UART	8250B	16450/16550A or greater

The easiest way to identify a PC/XT (8-bit) system is by the 8-bit ISA expansion slots. No matter which processor or other features the system has, if all the slots are 8-bit ISA, the system is a PC/XT. AT (16-bit plus) systems can be similarly identified—they have 16-bit or greater slots of any type. These can be ISA, EISA, MCA, PC Card (formerly PCMCIA), CardBus, VL-Bus, or PCI. Any system using the new high-speed serial buses such as PCI Express or ExpressCard also qualifies as an AT-class system. Using this information, you can properly categorize virtually any system as a PC/XT type or an AT type. No PC/XT type (8-bit) systems have been manufactured for many years. Unless you are in a computer museum, virtually every system you encounter today is based on the AT-type design.

System Components

A modern PC is both simple and complicated. It is simple in the sense that over the years, many of the components used to construct a system have become integrated with other components into fewer and fewer actual parts. It is complicated in the sense that each part in a modern system performs many more functions than did the same types of parts in older systems.

This section briefly examines all the components and peripherals in a modern PC system. Each item is discussed further in later chapters.

The components and peripherals necessary to assemble a basic modern PC system are listed in Table 2.4.

Table 2.4   Basic PC Components

Component	Description
Motherboard	The motherboard is the core of the system. It really is the PC; everything else is connected to it, and it controls everything in the system. Motherboards are covered in detail in Chapter 4.
Processor	The processor is often thought of as the "engine" of the computer. It's also called the CPU (central processing unit). Processors are covered in detail in Chapter 3, "Microprocessor Types and Specifications."
Memory (RAM)	The system memory is often called RAM (for random access memory). This is the primary memory, which holds all the programs and data the processor is using at a given time. Memory is discussed in Chapter 6, "Memory."
Case/chassis	The case is the frame or chassis that houses the motherboard, power supply, disk drives, adapter cards, and any other physical components in the system. The case is covered in detail in Chapter 21, "Power Supply and Chassis/Case."
Power supply	The power supply feeds electrical power to every single part in the PC. The power supply is covered in detail in Chapter 21.
Floppy drive	The floppy drive is a simple, inexpensive, low-capacity, removable-media, magnetic-storage device. Many recent systems use other types of removable magnetic or USB-based flash memory devices instead of floppy drives for removable storage. Floppy drives are covered in detail in Chapter 11, "Floppy Disk Storage," and other removable-media drives are covered in Chapter 12, "High-Capacity Removable Storage."
Hard drive	The hard disk is the primary archival storage memory for the system. Hard disk drives are also discussed in Chapter 10, "Hard Disk Storage."
CD or DVD drive	CD (compact disc) and DVD (digital versatile disc) drives are relatively high-capacity, removable media, optical drives; many recent systems include a rewriteable CD (CD-RW) along with or combined with a DVD-ROM drive. These drives are covered in detail in Chapter 13, "Optical Storage."
Keyboard	The keyboard is the primary device on a PC that is used by a human to communicate with and control a system. Keyboards are covered in Chapter 18, "Input Devices."
Mouse	Although many types of pointing devices are on the market today, the first and most popular device for this purpose is the mouse. The mouse and other pointing devices are discussed in Chapter 18.
Video card*	The video card controls the information you see on the monitor. Video cards are covered in detail in Chapter 15, "Video Hardware."
Monitor	Monitors are covered in Chapter 15.
Sound card*	It enables the PC to generate complex sounds. Sound cards and speakers are discussed in detail in Chapter 16, "Audio Hardware."
Modem*	Most prebuilt PCs ship with a modem (generally an internal modem). Modems and other Internet-connectivity devices and methods are covered in Chapter 19, "Internet Connectivity."

Components marked with an * may be integrated into the motherboard on many recent systems, particularly entry-level systems.

CHAPTER 3

Microprocessor Types and Specifications

Pre-PC Microprocessor History

The brain or engine of the PC is the *processor* (sometimes called *microprocessor*), or *central processing unit (CPU)*. The CPU performs the system's calculating and processing. The processor is often the most expensive single component in the system (although graphics card pricing now surpasses it in some cases); in higher-end systems it can cost up to four or more times more than the motherboard it plugs into. Intel is generally credited with creating the first microprocessor in 1971 with the introduction of a chip called the 4004. Today Intel still has control over the processor market, at least for PC systems. This means that all PC-compatible systems use either Intel processors or Intel-compatible processors from a handful of competitors (such as AMD or VIA/Cyrix).

Intel's dominance in the processor market hadn't always been assured. Although Intel is generally credited with inventing the processor and introducing the first one on the market, by the late 1970s the two most popular processors for personal computers were *not* from Intel (although one was a clone of an Intel processor). Personal computers of that time primarily used the Z-80 by Zilog and the 6502 by MOS Technologies. The Z-80 was noted for being an improved and less expensive clone of the Intel 8080 processor, similar to the way companies such as AMD, VIA/Cyrix, IDT, and Rise Technologies have cloned Intel's Pentium processors. In the Z-80 case, though, the clone had become far more popular than the original. Some might argue that AMD has achieved that type of status over the past year, but even though they have made significant gains, Intel still controls the PC processor market.

Back then I had a system containing both of those processors, consisting of a 1MHz (yes, that's *1*, as in one megahertz!) 6502-based Apple II system with a Microsoft Softcard (Z-80 card) plugged into one of the slots. The Softcard contained a 2MHz Z-80 processor. This enabled me to run software for both processors on the one system. The Z-80 was used in systems of the late 1970s and early 1980s that ran the CP/M operating system, whereas the 6502 was best known for its use in the early Apple I and II computers (before the Mac).

The fate of both Intel and Microsoft was dramatically changed in 1981 when IBM introduced the IBM PC, which was based on a 4.77MHz Intel 8088 processor running the Microsoft Disk Operating System (MS-DOS) 1.0. Since that fateful decision was made to use an Intel processor in the first PC, subsequent PC-compatible systems have used a series of Intel or Intel-compatible processors, with each new one capable of running the software of the processor before it—from the 8088 to the current Pentium 4/III/Celeron and Athlon/Athlon XP. The following sections cover the various types of processor chips that have been used in personal computers since the first PC was introduced almost two decades ago. These sections provide a great deal of technical detail about these chips and explain why one type of CPU chip can do more work than another in a given period of time.

Microprocessors from 1971 to the Present

It is interesting to note that the microprocessor had existed for only 10 years prior to the creation of the PC! Intel invented the microprocessor in 1971; the PC was created by IBM in 1981. Now more than 20 years later, we are still using systems based more or less on the design of that first PC. The processors powering our PCs today are still backward compatible in many ways with the 8088 that IBM selected for the first PC in 1981.

November 15, 2001 marked the 30th anniversary of the microprocessor, and in those 30 years processor speed has increased more than 18,500 times (from 0.108MHz to 2GHz). The story of the development of the first microprocessor, the Intel 4004, can be read in Chapter 1, "Development of the PC." The 4004 was introduced on November 15, 1971 and originally ran at a clock speed of 108KHz (108,000 cycles per second, or just over one-tenth a megahertz). The 4004 contained 2,300 transistors and was built on a 10-micron process. This means that each line, trace, or transistor could be spaced about 10 microns (millionths of a meter) apart. Data was transferred 4 bits at a time, and the maximum addressable memory was only 640 bytes. The 4004 was designed for use in a calculator but proved to be useful for many other functions because of its inherent programmability. For example, the 4004 was used in traffic light controllers, blood analyzers, and even in the NASA Pioneer 10 deep space probe!

In April 1972, Intel released the 8008 processor, which originally ran at a clock speed of 200KHz (0.2MHz). The 8008 processor contained 3,500 transistors and was built on the same 10-micron process as the previous processor. The big change in the 8008 was that it had an 8-bit data bus, which meant it could move data 8 bits at a time—twice as much as the previous chip. It could also address more memory, up to 16KB. This chip was primarily used in dumb terminals and general-purpose calculators.

The next chip in the lineup was the 8080, introduced in April 1974, running at a clock rate of 2MHz. Due mostly to the faster clock rate, the 8080 processor had 10 times the performance of the 8008. The 8080 chip contained 6,000 transistors and was built on a 6-micron process. Similar to the previous chip, the 8080 had an 8-bit data bus, so it could transfer 8 bits of data at a time. The 8080 could address up to 64KB of memory, significantly more than the previous chip.

It was the 8080 that helped start the PC revolution because this was the processor chip used in what is generally regarded as the first personal computer, the Altair 8800. The CP/M operating system was written for the 8080 chip, and Microsoft was founded and delivered its first product: Microsoft BASIC for the Altair. These initial tools provided the foundation for a revolution in software because thousands of programs were written to run on this platform.

In fact, the 8080 became so popular that it was cloned. A company called Zilog formed in late 1975, joined by several ex-Intel 8080 engineers. In July 1976, it released the Z-80 processor, which was a vastly improved version of the 8080. It was not pin compatible but instead combined functions such as the memory interface and RAM refresh circuitry, which enabled cheaper and simpler systems to be designed. The Z-80 also incorporated a superset of 8080 instructions, meaning it could run all 8080 programs. It also included new instructions and new internal registers, so software designed for the Z-80 would not necessarily run on the older 8080. The Z-80 ran initially at 2.5MHz (later versions ran up to 10MHz) and contained 8,500 transistors. The Z-80 could access 64KB of memory.

RadioShack selected the Z-80 for the TRS-80 Model 1, its first PC. The chip also was the first to be used by many pioneering systems, including the Osborne and Kaypro machines. Other companies followed, and soon the Z-80 was the standard processor for systems running the CP/M operating system and the popular software of the day.

Intel released the 8085, its follow-up to the 8080, in March 1976. Even though it predated the Z-80 by several months, it never achieved the popularity of the Z-80 in personal computer systems. It was popular as an embedded controller, finding use in scales and other computerized equipment. The 8085 ran at 5MHz and contained 6,500 transistors. It was built on a 3-micron process and incorporated an 8-bit data bus.

Along different architectural lines, MOS Technologies introduced the 6502 in 1976. This chip was designed by several ex-Motorola engineers who had worked on Motorola's first processor, the 6800. The 6502 was an 8-bit processor like the 8080, but it sold for around $25, whereas the 8080 cost about $300 when it was introduced. The price appealed to Steve Wozniak, who placed the chip in his Apple I and Apple II designs. The chip was also used in systems by Commodore and other system manufacturers. The 6502 and its successors were also used in game consoles, including the original Nintendo Entertainment System (NES) among others. Motorola went on to create the 68000 series, which became the basis for the Apple Macintosh line of computers. Today those systems use the PowerPC chip, also by Motorola and a successor to the 68000 series.

All these previous chips set the stage for the first PC processors. Intel introduced the 8086 in June 1978. The 8086 chip brought with it the original x86 instruction set that is still present in current x86-compatible chips such as the Pentium 4 and AMD Athlon. A dramatic improvement over the previous chips, the 8086 was a full 16-bit design with 16-bit internal registers and a 16-bit data bus. This meant that it could work on 16-bit numbers and data internally and also transfer 16 bits at a time in and out of the chip. The 8086 contained 29,000 transistors and initially ran at up to 5MHz. The chip also used 20-bit addressing, so it could directly address up to 1MB of memory. Although not directly backward compatible with the 8080, the 8086 instructions and language were very similar and enabled older programs to quickly be ported over to run. This later proved important to help jump-start the PC software revolution with recycled CP/M (8080) software.

Although the 8086 was a great chip, it was expensive at the time and more importantly required expensive 16-bit board designs and infrastructure to support it. To help bring costs down, in 1979 Intel released what some called a *crippled* version of the 8086 called the 8088. The 8088 processor used the same internal core as the 8086, had the same 16-bit registers, and could address the same 1MB of memory, but the external data bus was reduced to 8 bits. This enabled support chips from the older 8-bit 8085 to be used, and far less expensive boards and systems could be made. These reasons are why IBM chose the 8088 instead of the 8086 for the first PC.

This decision would affect history in several ways. The 8088 was fully software compatible with the 8086, so it could run 16-bit software. Also, because the instruction set was very similar to the previous 8085 and 8080, programs written for those older chips could be quickly and easily modified to run. This enabled a large library of programs to be quickly released for the IBM PC, thus helping it become a success. The overwhelming blockbuster success of the IBM PC left in its wake the legacy of requiring backward compatibility with it. To maintain the momentum, Intel has pretty much been forced to maintain backward compatibility with the 8088/8086 in most of the processors it has released since then.

To date, backward compatibility has been maintained, but innovating and adding new features has still been possible. One major change in processors was the move from the 16-bit internal architecture of the 286 and earlier processors to the 32-bit internal architecture of the 386 and later chips, which Intel calls IA-32 (Intel Architecture, 32-bit). Intel's 32-bit architecture dates to 1985, and it took a full 10 years for both a partial 32-bit mainstream OS (Windows 95) as well as a full 32-bit OS requiring 32-bit drivers (Windows NT) to surface, and another 6 years for the mainstream to shift to a fully 32-bit environment for the OS and drivers (Windows XP). That's a total of 16 years from the release of 32-bit computing hardware to the full adoption of 32-bit computing in the mainstream with supporting software. I'm sure you can appreciate that 16 years is a lifetime in technology.

Now we are poised for another major architectural jump, as Intel and AMD have introduced 64-bit extensions to the standard 32-bit Intel architecture. Intel had introduced the IA-64 (Intel Architecture, 64-bit) in the form of the Itanium and Itanium 2 processors several years earlier, but this standard was something completely new and not an extension of the existing 32-bit technology. IA-64 was first announced in 1994 as a CPU development project with Intel and HP (codenamed Merced), and the first technical details were made available in October 1997. The result was the IA-64 architecture and Itanium chip, which was officially released in 2001.

Unfortunately, the IA-64 architecture is not an extension of IA-32 but is instead a whole new and completely different architecture. This is fine for non-PC environments such as servers (for which IA-64 was designed), but the PC market has always hinged on backward compatibility. Even though emulating IA-32 within IA-64 is possible, such emulation and support is slow.

AMD seized this opportunity to develop 64-bit extensions to IA-32, which it calls AMD64 and which is also called x86-64. Intel has now introduced its own set of 64-bit extensions, which it calls EM64T or IA-32e mode. As it turns out, the Intel extensions are almost identical to the AMD extensions, meaning they should be software compatible. It seems for the first time that Intel has actually followed AMD in the development of PC architecture.

Of course, what we need to make all this work is a 64-bit operating system and, more importantly, 64-bit drivers for all of our hardware to work under that OS. It will be important to keep all the memory size, software, and driver issues in mind when considering the transition from 32-bit to 64-bit technology. It might not take 16 years for 64-bit computing to become mainstream, but it won't happen overnight either.

PCs have certainly come a long way. The original 8088 processor used in the first PC contained 29,000 transistors and ran at 4.77MHz. The AMD Athlon 64 and Athlon 64 FX include 106 million transistors, the Pentium 4 580 (Prescott core) runs at 4GHz and has 125 million transistors, and the Extreme Edition Pentium 4 versions have even more due to their integrated L3 cache. Transistor count and cache sizes are expected to rise even more in the future.

Although it is technically not a PC processor, Intel's Itanium 2 (Madison core) gives a glimpse at where things are going for the processor in the PC on your desk. The Itanium 2 incorporates up to 6MB of integrated L3 cache and has an incredible 410 million transistors on a 374 sq.mm (over 19.3mm square) die using 0.13-micron technology. This establishes new records for transistor count as well as the amount of on-die cache. Future processor models with one billion transistors or more are in development. Intel has also released processors running at speeds up to and beyond 4GHz, and AMD is not very far behind. And the progress doesn't stop there because, according to Moore's Law, processing speed and transistor counts are doubling every 1.5–2 years.

Processor Specifications

Many confusing specifications often are quoted in discussions of processors. The following sections discuss some of these specifications, including the data bus, address bus, and speed. The next section includes a table that lists the specifications of virtually all PC processors.

Processors can be identified by two main parameters: how wide they are and how fast they are. The speed of a processor is a fairly simple concept. Speed is counted in megahertz (MHz) and gigahertz (GHz), which means millions and billions, respectively, of cycles per second—and faster is better! The width of a processor is a little more complicated to discuss because three main specifications in a processor are expressed in width. They are

- Data (I/O) bus
- Address bus
- Internal registers

Note that the processor data bus is also called the front side bus (FSB), processor side bus (PSB), or just CPU bus. All these terms refer to the bus that is between the CPU and the main chipset component (North Bridge or Memory Controller Hub). Intel uses the FSB or PSB terminology, whereas AMD uses only FSB. Personally I usually just like to say "CPU bus" in conversation or when speaking during my training seminars because that is the least confusing of the terms while also being completely accurate.

The number of bits a processor is designated can be confusing. All modern processors have 64-bit data buses; however, that does not mean they are classified as 64-bit processors. Processors such as the Pentium 4 and Athlon XP are 32-bit processors because their internal registers are 32 bits wide, although their data I/O buses are 64 bits wide and their address buses are 36 bits wide (both wider than their predecessors, the Pentium and K6 processors). The Itanium series and the AMD Opteron and Athlon 64 are 64-bit processors because their internal registers are 64 bits wide.

First, I'll present some tables describing the differences in specifications between all the PC processors; then the following sections will explain the width and other specifications in more detail. Refer to these tables as you read about the various processor specifications, and the information in the tables will become clearer.

Tables 3.1–3.4 list the Intel processors, AMD processors, and alternative processors from other manufacturers.

Table 3.1   Intel Processor Specifications

Processor	Process (Micron)	Clock Multiplier	Voltage	Internal Register Size	Data Bus Width	Max. Memory	L1 Cache
8088	3.0	1x	5V	16-bit	8-bit	1MB	—
8086	3.0	1x	5V	16-bit	16-bit	1MB	—
286	1.5	1x	5V	16-bit	16-bit	16MB	—
386SX	1.5, 1.0	1x	5V	32-bit	16-bit	16MB	—
386SL	1.0	1x	3.3V	32-bit	16-bit	16MB	0KB[1]
386DX	1.5, 1.0	1x	5V	32-bit	32-bit	4GB	—
486SX	1.0, 0.8	1x	5V	32-bit	32-bit	4GB	8KB
486SX2	0.8	2x	5V	32-bit	32-bit	4GB	8KB
487SX	1.0	1x	5V	32-bit	32-bit	4GB	8KB
486DX	1.0, 0.8	1x	5V	32-bit	32-bit	4GB	8KB
486SL[2]	0.8	1x	3.3V	32-bit	32-bit	4GB	8KB
486DX2	0.8	2x	5V	32-bit	32-bit	4GB	8KB
486DX4	0.6	2x+	3.3V	32-bit	32-bit	4GB	16KB
486 Pentium OD	0.6	2.5x	5V	32-bit	32-bit	4GB	2x16KB
Pentium 60/66	0.8	1x	5V	32-bit	64-bit	4GB	2x8KB
Pentium 75-200	0.6, 0.35	1.5x+	3.3V–3.5V	32-bit	64-bit	4GB	2x8KB
Pentium MMX	0.35, 0.25	1.5x+	1.8V–2.8V	32-bit	64-bit	4GB	2x16KB
Pentium Pro	0.35	2x+	3.3V	32-bit	64-bit	64GB	2x8KB
Pentium II (Klamath)	0.35	3.5x+	2.8V	32-bit	64-bit	64GB	2x16KB
Pentium II (Deschutes)	0.35	3.5x+	2.0V	32-bit	64-bit	64GB	2x16KB
Pentium II PE (Dixon)	0.25	3.5x+	1.6V	32-bit	64-bit	64GB	2x16KB
Celeron (Covington)	0.25	3.5x+	1.8V–2.8V	32-bit	64-bit	64GB	2x16KB
Celeron A (Mendocino)	0.25	3.5x+	1.5V–2V	32-bit	64-bit	64GB	2x16KB
Celeron III (Coppermine)	0.18	4.5x+	1.5–1.75V	32-bit	64-bit	64GB	2x16KB
Celeron III (Tualatin)	0.13	9x+	1.5V	32-bit	64-bit	64GB	2x16KB
Pentium III (Katmai)	0.25	4x+	2.0–2.05V	32-bit	64-bit	64GB	2x16KB
Pentium III (Coppermine)	0.18	4x+	1.6–1.75V	32-bit	64-bit	64GB	2x16KB
Pentium III (Tualatin)	0.13	8.5x+	1.45V	32-bit	64-bit	64GB	2x16KB
Celeron 4 (Willamette)	0.18	4.25x+	1.6V	32-bit	64-bit	64GB	2x16KB
Pentium 4 (Willamette)	0.18	3x+	1.7V	32-bit	64-bit	64GB	12+8KB
Pentium 4A (Northwood)	0.13	4x+	1.3V	32-bit	64-bit	64GB	12+8KB
Pentium 4EE (Prestonia)	0.13	8x+	1.5V	32-bit	64-bit	64GB	12+8KB
Pentium 4E (Prescott)	0.09	8x+	1.3V	32-bit	64-bit	64GB	12+16KB
Pentium M (Banias)	0.13	2.25x+	0.8–1.5V	32-bit	64-bit	64GB	2x32KB
Pentium M (Dothan)	0.13	4.25x+	1–1.3V	32-bit	64-bit	64GB	2x32KB

L2 Cache	L3 Cache	L2/L3 Cache Speed	Multimedia Instructions	No. of Transistors	Date Introduced
—	—	—	—	29,000	June '79
—	—	—	—	29,000	June '78
—	—	—	—	134,000	Feb. '82
—	—	Bus	—	275,000	June '88
—	—	Bus	—	855,000	Oct. '90
—	—	Bus	—	275,000	Oct. '85
—	—	Bus	—	1.185M	Apr. '91
—	—	Bus	—	1.185M	Apr. '94
—	—	Bus	—	1.2M	Apr. '91
—	—	Bus	—	1.2M	Apr. '89
—	—	Bus	—	1.4M	Nov. '92
—	—	Bus	—	1.2M	Mar. '92
—	—	Bus	—	1.6M	Feb. '94
—	—	Bus	—	3.1M	Jan. '95
—	—	Bus	—	3.1M	Mar. '93
—	—	Bus	—	3.3M	Mar. '94
—	—	Bus	MMX	4.5M	Jan. '97
256KB, 512KB, 1MB	—	Core[3]	—	5.5M	Nov. '95
512KB	—	1/2 core	MMX	7.5M	May '97
512KB	—	1/2 core	MMX	7.5M	May '97
256KB	—	Core	MMX	27.4M	Jan. '99
0KB	—	—	MMX	7.5M	Apr. '98
128KB	—	Core	MMX	19M	Aug. '98
128KB	—	Core	SSE	28.1M[4]	Feb. '00
256KB	—	Core	SSE	44M[5]	Oct. '01
512KB	—	1/2 core	SSE	9.5M	Feb. '99
256KB	—	Core	SSE	28.1M	Oct. '99
512KB	—	Core	SSE	44M	June '01
128KB	—	Core	SSE2	42M[6]	May '02
256KB	—	Core	SSE2	42M	Nov. '00
512KB	—	Core	SSE2	55M	Jan. '02
512KB	2GB	Core	SSE2	178M	Nov. '03
1MB	—	Core	SSE3	125M	Feb. '04
1MB	—	Core	SSE2	77M	Mar. '03
2MB	—	Core	SSE2	144M	May '04

Table 3.2   AMD Processor Specifications

Processor	Process (Microns)	CPU Clock	Voltage	Internal Register Size	Data Bus Width	Max. Memory
AMD K5	0.35	1.5x+	3.5V	32-bit	64-bit	4GB
AMD K6	0.35	2.5x+	2.2–3.2V	32-bit	64-bit	4GB
AMD K6-2	0.25	2.5x+	1.9–2.4V	32-bit	64-bit	4GB
AMD K6-3	0.25	3.5x+	1.8–2.4V	32-bit	64-bit	4GB
AMD Athlon	0.25	5x+	1.6–1.8V	32-bit	64-bit	4GB
AMD Duron	0.18	5x+	1.5–1.8V	32-bit	64-bit	4GB
AMD Athlon (Thunderbird)	0.18	5x+	1.5–1.8V	32-bit	64-bit	4GB
AMD Athlon XP (Palomino)	0.18	5x+	1.5–1.8V	32-bit	64-bit	4GB
AMD Athlon XP (Thoroughbred)	0.13	5x+	1.5–1.8V	32-bit	64-bit	4GB
AMD Athlon XP (Barton)	0.13	5.5x+	1.65V	32-bit	64-bit	4GB
AMD 64 (ClawHammer)	0.13	5.5x+	1.5V	64-bit	64-bit	1TB
AMD 64 FX (SledgeHammer)	0.13	5.5x+	1.5V	64-bit	128-bit	1TB

1. *The 386SL contains an integral-cache controller, but the cache memory must be provided outside the chip.*

2. *Intel later marketed SL Enhanced versions of the SX, DX, and DX2 processors. These processors were available in both 5V and 3.3V versions and included power management capabilities.*

Table 3.3   Intel/AMD Server/Workstation Processor Specifications

Processor	Process (Micron)	Clock Multiplier	Voltage	Internal Register Size	Data Bus Width	Max. Memory
Pentium II Xeon (Deschutes)	0.25	4x+	2.8V	32-bit	64-bit	64GB
Pentium III Xeon (Tanner)	0.25	5x+	2.0V	32-bit	64-bit	64GB
Pentium IIIE Xeon (Cascades)	0.18	4.5x+	1.65V	32-bit	64-bit	64GB
Xeon (Foster)	0.18	3.5x+	1.75V	32-bit	64-bit	64GB
Xeon (Prestonia)	0.13	4.5x+	1.5V	32-bit	64-bit	64GB
Itanium (Merced)	0.18	3x+	1.6V	64-bit	64-bit	16TB
Itanium 2 (McKinley)	0.18	3x+	1.6V	64-bit	128-bit	16TB
Itanium 2 (Madison)	0.13	3x+	1.6V	64-bit	128-bit	16TB
AMD Athlon MP (Palomino)	0.18	5x+	1.5–1.8V	32-bit	64-bit	4GB
AMD Athlon MP (Thoroughbred)	0.13	5x+	1.5–1.8V	32-bit	64-bit	4GB
AMD Athlon MP (Barton)	0.13	5.5x+	1.65V	32-bit	64-bit	4GB
AMD Opteron (SledgeHammer)	0.13	3.5x+	1.55V	64-bit	128-bit	1TB

L1 Cache	L2 Cache	L3 Cache	L2/L3 Cache Speed	Multimedia Instructions	No. of Transistors	Date Introduced
16+8KB	—	—	Bus	—	4.3M	March '96
2x32KB	—	—	Bus	MMX	8.8M	April '97
2x32KB	—	—	Bus	3DNow!	9.3M	May '98
2x32KB	256KB	—	Core	3DNow!	21.3M	Feb. '99
2x64KB	512KB	—	1/2–1/3 core	Enh. 3DNow!	22M	June '99
2x64KB	64KB	—	Core[3]	Enh. 3DNow!	25M	June '00
2x64KB	256KB	—	Core	Enh. 3DNow!	37M	June '00
2x64KB	256KB	—	Core	3DNow! Pro	37.5M	Oct. '01
2x64KB	256KB	—	Core	3DNow! Pro	37.2M	June '02
2x64KB	512KB	—	Core	3DNow! Pro	54.3M	Feb. '03
2x64KB	1MB	—	Core	3DNow! Pro	105.9M	Sept. '03
2x64KB	1MB	—	Core	3DNow! Pro	105.9M	Sept. '03

3. *L2 cache runs at full-core speed but is contained in a separate chip die.*
4. *128KB functional L2 cache (256KB total, 128KB disabled) uses the same die as the Pentium IIIE.*

5. *256KB functional L2 cache (512KB total, 256KB disabled) uses the same die as the Pentium IIIB.*
6. *128KB functional L2 cache (256KB total, 128KB disabled) uses the same die as the Pentium 4.*

L1 Cache	L2 Cache	L3 Cache	L2/L3 Cache Speed	Multimedia Instructions	No. of Transistors	Date Introduced
2x16KB	512KB, 1MB, 2MB	—	Core[1]	MMX	7.5M	June '98
2x16KB	512KB, 1MB, 2MB	—	Core[1]	SSE	9.5M	Mar. '99
2x16KB	256KB, 1MB, 2MB	—	Core	SSE	28.1M, 84M, 140M	Oct. '99, May '00
12+8KB	256KB	—	Core	SSE2	42M	May '01
12+8KB	512KB	0MB, 1MB, 2MB	Core	SSE2	169M	Jan. '02
2x16KB	96KB[2]	2MB, 4MB	Core	MMX	25M	May '01
2x16KB	256KB	1.5MB, 3MB	Core	MMX	221M	July '02
2x16KB	256KB	1.5MB, 6MB	Core	MMX	410M	June '03
2x64KB	256KB	—	Core	3DNow! Pro	37.5M	June '01
2x64KB	256KB	—	Core	3DNow! Pro	37.2M	Aug. '02
2x64KB	512KB	—	Core	3DNow! Pro	54.3M	May. '03
2x64KB	1MB	—	Core	3DNow! Pro	105.9M	Apr. '03

Table 3.4   Cyrix, NexGen, IDT, Rise, and VIA Processor Specifications

Processor	CPU Clock	Voltage	Internal Register Size	Data Bus Width	Max. Memory	L1 Cache
Cyrix 6x86	2x+	2.5–3.5V	32-bit	64-bit	4GB	16KB
Cyrix 6x86MX/MII	2x+	2.2–2.9V	32-bit	64-bit	4GB	64KB
Cyrix III	2.5x+	2.2V	32-bit	64-bit	4GB	64KB
NexGen Nx586	2x	4V	32-bit	64-bit	4GB	2x16KB
IDT Winchip	3x+	3.3–3.5V	32-bit	64-bit	4GB	2x32KB
IDT Winchip2/2A	2.33x+	3.3–3.5V	32-bit	64-bit	4GB	2x32KB
Rise mP6	2x+	2.8V	32-bit	64-bit	4GB	2x8KB
VIA C3[3]	6x+	1.6V	32-bit	64-bit	4GB	64KB
VIA C3[4]	6x+	1.35V	32-bit	64-bit	4GB	64KB
VIA C3[5]	5.5x+	1.35V	32-bit	64-bit	4GB	64KB
VIA C3[6]	7.5x+	1.4V	32-bit	64-bit	4GB	64KB

1. L2 cache runs at full-core speed but is contained in a separate chip die.

2. The Itanium also includes an additional 2MB (150M transistors) or 4MB (300M transistors) of integrated on-cartridge L3 cache running at full-core speed.

Data I/O Bus

Perhaps the most important features of a processor are the speed and width of its external data bus. This defines the rate at which data can be moved into or out of the processor.

The processor bus discussed most often is the external data bus—the bundle of wires (or pins) used to send and receive data. The more signals that can be sent at the same time, the more data can be transmitted in a specified interval and, therefore, the faster (and wider) the bus. A wider data bus is like having a highway with more lanes, which enables greater throughput.

Data in a computer is sent as digital information consisting of a time interval in which a single wire carries 3.3V or 5V to signal a 1 data bit or 0V to signal a 0 data bit. The more wires you have, the more individual bits you can send in the same time interval. All modern processors from the original Pentium through the latest Pentium 4, Athlon XP, Athlon 64, and even the Itanium and Itanium 2 have a 64-bit (8-byte) wide data bus. Therefore, they can transfer 64 bits of data at a time to and from the motherboard chipset or system memory.

A good way to understand this flow of information is to consider a highway and the traffic it carries. If a highway has only one lane for each direction of travel, only one car at a time can move in a certain direction. If you want to increase traffic flow, you can add another lane so that twice as many cars pass in a specified time. You can think of an 8-bit chip as being a single-lane highway because 1 byte flows through at a time. (1 byte equals 8 individual bits.) The 16-bit chip, with 2 bytes flowing at a time, resembles a two-lane highway. You might have four lanes in each direction to move a large number of automobiles; this structure corresponds to a 32-bit data bus, which has the capability to move 4 bytes of information at a time. Taking this further, a 64-bit data bus is like having an 8-lane highway moving data in and out of the chip.

Another ramification of the data bus in a chip is that the width of the data bus also defines the size of a bank of memory. So, a processor with a 32-bit data bus (such as the 486) reads and writes memory 32 bits at a time, whereas processors with a 64-bit data bus (most current processors) read and write memory 64 bits at a time.

In 486 class systems, because standard 72-pin single inline memory modules (SIMMs) are only 32 bits wide, they must be installed one at a time in most 486 class systems. When used in 64-bit Pentium class systems,

L2 Cache	L3 Cache	L2/L3 Cache Speed	Multimedia Instructions	No. of Transistors	Date Introduced
—	—	Bus	—	3M	Feb. '96
—	—	Bus	MMX	6.5M	May '97
256KB	—	Core[1]	3DNow!	22M	Feb. '00
—	—	Bus	—	3.5M	Mar. '94
—	—	Bus	MMX	5.4M	Oct. '97
—	—	Bus	3DNow!	5.9M	Sep. '98
—	—	Bus	MMX	3.6M	Oct. '98
128KB	—	Bus	MMX, 3DNow!	15.2M	Mar. '01
128KB	—	Bus	MMX, 3DNow!	15.4M	Mar. '01
128KB	—	Bus	MMX, 3DNow!	15.5M	Sep. '01
128KB	—	Bus	MMX, 3DNow!	20.5M	Jan. '02

3. *Samuel 2 core (improved version of Cyrix III core).*
4. *Ezra core.*
5. *Ezra-T core.*
6. *Nehemiah core.*

they must be installed two at a time. The current module standard, dual inline memory modules (DIMMs), are 64 bits wide. So, they are normally installed one at a time, unless the system is designed or configured for dual-channel memory. Dual-channel memory reads and writes two banks simultaneously, which means two DIMMs must be installed at a time. To improve memory performance, most future chipsets will support and eventually require that DIMM memory modules be installed in identical pairs.

The Rambus inline memory modules (RIMMs) used in some Pentium III and 4 systems are somewhat of an anomaly because they play by a different set of rules. They are typically only 16 or 32 bits wide. Depending on the module type and chipset, they are either used individually or in pairs.

▶▶ See "Memory Banks," p. 496.

Address Bus

The address bus is the set of wires that carries the addressing information used to describe the memory location to which the data is being sent or from which the data is being retrieved. As with the data bus, each wire in an address bus carries a single bit of information. This single bit is a single digit in the address. The more wires (digits) used in calculating these addresses, the greater the total number of address locations. The size (or width) of the address bus indicates the maximum amount of RAM a chip can address.

The highway analogy in the "Data I/O Bus" section can be used to show how the address bus fits in. If the data bus is the highway and the size of the data bus is equivalent to the number of lanes, the address bus relates to the house number or street address. The size of the address bus is equivalent to the number of digits in the house address number. For example, if you live on a street in which the address is limited to a two-digit (base 10) number, no more than 100 distinct addresses (00–99) can exist for that street (10^2). Add another digit, and the number of available addresses increases to 1,000 (000–999), or 10^3.

Computers use the binary (base 2) numbering system, so a two-digit number provides only four unique addresses (00, 01, 10, and 11), calculated as 2^2. A three-digit number provides only eight addresses (000–111), which is 2^3. For example, the 8086 and 8088 processors use a 20-bit address bus that calculates as a maximum of 2^{20} or 1,048,576 bytes (1MB) of address locations. Table 3.5 describes the memory-addressing capabilities of processors.

Table 3.5   Processor Physical Memory-Addressing Capabilities

Processor Family	Address Bus	Bytes	Kilobytes (KB)	Megabytes (MB)	Gigabytes (GB)	Terabytes (TB)
8088; 8086	20-bit	1,048,576	1,024	1	—	—
286; 386SX	24-bit	16,777,216	16,384	16	—	—
386DX; 486; Pentium	32-bit	4,294,967,296	4,194,304	4,096	4	—
K6; Duron; Athlon; Athlon XP	32-bit	4,294,967,296	4,194,304	4,096	4	—
Celeron; Pentium Pro; Pentium II; Pentium III; Pentium 4	36-bit	68,719,476,736	67,108,864	65,536	64	—
Athlon 64; Athlon 64 FX; Opteron	40-bit	1,099,511,627,776	1,073,741,824	1,048,576	1024	1
Itanium; Itanium 2	44-bit	17,592,186,044,416	17,179,869,184	16,777,216	16,384	16

Note: The terms kilobytes (KB), megabytes (MB), and terabytes (TB) are used here and throughout this chapter by convention; however, technically they should in the future be represented as kibibytes (KiB), gibibytes (GiB), and tebibytes (TiB). See www.iec.ch/zone/si/si_bytes.htm *for more information.*

The data bus and address bus are independent, and chip designers can use whatever size they want for each. Usually, however, chips with larger data buses have larger address buses. The sizes of the buses can provide important information about a chip's relative power, measured in two important ways. The size of the data bus is an indication of the chip's information-moving capability, and the size of the address bus tells you how much memory the chip can handle.

Internal Registers (Internal Data Bus)

The size of the internal registers indicates how much information the processor can operate on at one time and how it moves data around internally within the chip. This is sometimes also referred to as the *internal data bus*. A *register* is a holding cell within the processor; for example, the processor can add numbers in two different registers, storing the result in a third register. The register size determines the size of data on which the processor can operate. The register size also describes the type of software or commands and instructions a chip can run. That is, processors with 32-bit internal registers can run 32-bit instructions that are processing 32-bit chunks of data, but processors with 16-bit registers can't. Most advanced processors today—chips from the 386 to the Pentium 4—use 32-bit internal registers and can therefore run the same 32-bit operating systems and software. The Itanium and Athlon 64 processors have 64-bit internal registers, which require new operating systems and software to fully be utilized.

Some very old processors have an internal data bus (made up of data paths and storage units called registers) that is larger than the external data bus. The 8088 and 386SX are examples of this structure. Each chip has an internal data bus twice the width of the external bus. These designs, which sometimes are called *hybrid designs*, usually are low-cost versions of a "pure" chip. The 386SX, for example, can pass data around internally with a full 32-bit register size; for communications with the outside world, however, the chip is restricted to a 16-bit-wide data path. This design enabled a systems designer to build a lower-cost motherboard with a 16-bit bus design and still maintain software and instruction set compatibility with the full 32-bit 386. However, both the 8088 and the 386SX had lower performance than the 8086 and 386DX processors at the same speeds.

Internal registers often are larger than the data bus, which means the chip requires two cycles to fill a register before the register can be operated on. For example, both the 386SX and 386DX have internal 32-bit registers, but the 386SX must "inhale" twice (figuratively) to fill them, whereas the 386DX can do the job in one "breath." The same thing would happen when the data is passed from the registers back out to the system bus.

The Pentium is an example of this type of design. All Pentiums have a 64-bit data bus and 32-bit registers—a structure that might seem to be a problem until you understand that the Pentium has two internal 32-bit pipelines for processing information. In many ways, the Pentium is like two 32-bit chips in one. The 64-bit data bus provides for very efficient filling of these multiple registers. Multiple pipelines are called *superscalar* architecture, which was introduced with the Pentium processor.

▶▶ See "Pentium Processors," p. 125.

More advanced sixth- and seventh-generation processors from Intel and AMD have as many as six internal pipelines for executing instructions. Although some of these internal pipes are dedicated to special functions, these processors can execute multiple operations in one clock cycle.

Processor Modes

All Intel and Intel-compatible 32-bit processors (from the 386 on up) can run in several modes. Processor modes refer to the various operating environments and affect the instructions and capabilities of the chip. The processor mode controls how the processor sees and manages the system memory and the tasks that use it.

The three main modes of operation with several submodes are as follows:

- Real mode (16-bit software)
- IA-32 mode:
  - Protected mode (32-bit software)
  - Virtual real mode (16-bit programs within a 32-bit environment)
- IA-32e 64-bit extension mode (also called AMD64, x86-64, or EM64T):
  - 64-bit mode (64-bit software)
  - Compatibility mode (32-bit software)

Table 3.6 summarizes the processor modes.

Table 3.6   Processor Modes

Mode	Submode	OS Required	Software	Memory Address Size	Default Operand Size	Register Width
Real	—	16-bit	16-bit	24-bit	16-bit	16-bit
IA-32	Protected	32-bit	32-bit	32-bit	32-bit	32/16-bit
	Virtual real	32-bit	16-bit	24-bit	16-bit	16-bit
IA-32e	64-bit	64-bit	64-bit	64-bit	32-bit	64-bit
	Compatibility	64-bit	32-bit	32-bit	32-bit	32/16-bit

Real Mode

Real mode is sometimes called 8086 mode because it is based on the 8086 and 8088 processors. The original IBM PC included an 8088 processor that could execute 16-bit instructions using 16-bit internal registers and could address only 1MB of memory using 20 address lines. All original PC software was created to work with this chip and was designed around the 16-bit instruction set and 1MB memory model. For example, DOS and all DOS software, Windows 1.x through 3.x, and all Windows 1.x through 3.x applications are written using 16-bit instructions. These 16-bit operating systems and applications are designed to run on an original 8088 processor.

◄◄   See "Internal Registers (Internal Data Bus)," p. 48.

◄◄   See "Address Bus," p. 47.

Later processors such as the 286 could also run the same 16-bit instructions as the original 8088, but much faster. In other words, the 286 was fully compatible with the original 8088 and could run all 16-bit software just the same as an 8088, but, of course, that software would run faster. The 16-bit instruction mode of the 8088 and 286 processors has become known as *real mode*. All software running in real mode must use only 16-bit instructions and live within the 20-bit (1MB) memory architecture it supports. Software of this type is usually single-tasking—only one program can run at a time. No built-in protection exists to keep one program from overwriting another program or even the operating system in memory, so if more than one program is running, one of them could bring the entire system to a crashing halt.

IA-32 Mode (32-Bit)

Then came the 386, which was the PC industry's first 32-bit processor. This chip could run an entirely new 32-bit instruction set. To take full advantage of the 32-bit instruction set, a 32-bit operating system and a 32-bit application were required. This new 32-bit mode was referred to as *protected mode*, which alludes to the fact that software programs running in that mode are protected from overwriting one another in memory. Such protection helps make the system much more crash-proof because an errant program can't very easily damage other programs or the operating system. In addition, a crashed program can be terminated while the rest of the system continues to run unaffected.

Knowing that new operating systems and applications—which take advantage of the 32-bit protected mode—would take some time to develop, Intel wisely built a backward compatible real mode into the 386. That enabled it to run unmodified 16-bit operating systems and applications. It ran them quite well—much more quickly than any previous chip. For most people, that was enough. They did not necessarily want any new 32-bit software; they just wanted their existing 16-bit software to run more quickly. Unfortunately, that meant the chip was never running in the 32-bit protected mode, and all the features of that capability were being ignored.

When a high-powered processor such as a Pentium 4 is running DOS (real mode), it acts like a "Turbo 8088." Turbo 8088 means the processor has the advantage of speed in running any 16-bit programs; it otherwise can use only the 16-bit instructions and access memory within the same 1MB memory map of the original 8088. Therefore, if you have a 256MB Pentium 4 or Athlon system running Windows 3.x or DOS, you are effectively using only the first megabyte of memory, leaving the other 255MB largely unused!

New operating systems and applications that ran in the 32-bit protected mode of the modern processors were needed. Being stubborn, we resisted all the initial attempts at getting switched over to a 32-bit environment. It seems that as a user community, we are very resistant to change and would be content with our older software running faster rather than adopting new software with new features. I'll be the first one to admit that I was one of those stubborn users myself!

Because of this resistance, true 32-bit operating systems such as Unix or variants (such as Linux), OS/2, and even Windows NT/2000 or XP have taken a long time in getting a mainstream share in the PC marketplace. Windows XP is the first full 32-bit OS that has become a true mainstream product, and that is primarily because Microsoft has coerced us in that direction with Windows 95, 98, and Me (which are mixed 16-/32-bit systems). Windows 3.x was the last full 16-bit operating system. In fact, it was not really considered a complete operating system because it ran on top of DOS.

The Itanium processor family and the AMD Opteron add 64-bit native capability to the table for servers, whereas the AMD Athlon 64 provides this capability for desktop computers. Both processors run all the existing 32-bit software, but to fully take advantage of the processor, a 64-bit OS and applications are required. Microsoft has released 64-bit versions of Windows XP, and several companies have released 64-bit applications for networking and workstation use.

Note

The Intel Itanium family and the AMD Athlon 64/Opteron use different 64-bit architectures. Thus, 64-bit software written for one will not work on the other without being recompiled by the software vendor. This means that software written specifically for the Intel 64-bit architecture will not run on the AMD 64-bit processors and vice versa.

IA-32 Virtual Real Mode

The key to the backward compatibility of the Windows 32-bit environment is the third mode in the processor: virtual real mode. *Virtual real* is essentially a virtual real mode 16-bit environment that runs inside 32-bit protected mode. When you run a DOS prompt window inside Windows, you have created a virtual real mode session. Because protected mode enables true multitasking, you can actually have several real mode sessions running, each with its own software running on a virtual PC. These can all run simultaneously, even while other 32-bit applications are running.

Note that any program running in a virtual real mode window can access up to only 1MB of memory, which that program will believe is the first and only megabyte of memory in the system. In other words, if you run a DOS application in a virtual real window, it will have a 640KB limitation on memory usage. That is because there is only 1MB of total RAM in a 16-bit environment and the upper 384KB is reserved for system use. The virtual real window fully emulates an 8088 environment, so that aside from speed, the software runs as if it were on an original real mode-only PC. Each virtual machine gets its own 1MB address space, an image of the real hardware BIOS routines, and emulation of all other registers and features found in real mode.

Virtual real mode is used when you use a DOS window to run a DOS or Windows 3.x 16-bit program. When you start a DOS application, Windows creates a virtual DOS machine under which it can run.

One interesting thing to note is that all Intel and Intel-compatible (such as AMD and Cyrix) processors power up in real mode. If you load a 32-bit operating system, it automatically switches the processor into 32-bit mode and takes control from there.

It's also important to note that some 16-bit (DOS and Windows 3.x) applications misbehave in a 32-bit environment, which means they do things that even virtual real mode does not support. Diagnostics software is a perfect example of this. Such software does not run properly in a real-mode (virtual real) window under Windows. In that case, you can still run your Pentium 4 in the original no-frills real mode by either booting to a DOS floppy or, in the case of Windows 9x (excluding Me), interrupting the boot process and commanding the system to boot plain DOS. This is accomplished on Windows 9x systems by pressing the F8 key when you see the prompt Starting Windows... on the screen or immediately after the beep when the power on self test (POST) is completed. In the latter case, it helps to press the F8 key multiple times because getting the timing just right is difficult and Windows 9x looks for the key only during a short two-second time window.

If successful, you will then see the Startup menu. You can select one of the command-prompt choices that tell the system to boot plain 16-bit real mode DOS. The choice of Safe Mode Command Prompt is best if you are going to run true hardware diagnostics, which do not normally run in protected mode and should be run with a minimum of drivers and other software loaded.

Even though Windows Me is based on Windows 98, Microsoft removed the DOS Startup menu option in an attempt to further wean us from any 16-bit operation. Windows NT, 2000, and XP also lack the capability to start up DOS in this manner. For these operating systems, you need a startup disk (CD or floppy), which you can use to boot the system in real mode. Generally, you would do this to perform certain maintenance procedures, such as running hardware diagnostics or doing direct disk sector editing.

Although real mode is used by 16-bit DOS and "standard" DOS applications, special programs are available that "extend" DOS and allow access to extended memory (over 1MB). These are sometimes called *DOS extenders* and usually are included as part of any DOS or Windows 3.x software that uses them. The protocol that describes how to make DOS work in protected mode is called DOS protected mode interface (DPMI).

DPMI was used by Windows 3.x to access extended memory for use with Windows 3.x applications. It allowed these programs to use more memory even though they were still 16-bit programs. DOS extenders are especially popular in DOS games because they enable them to access much more of the system memory than the standard 1MB most real mode programs can address. These DOS extenders work by switching the processor in and out of real mode. In the case of those that run under Windows, they use the DPMI interface built into Windows, enabling them to share a portion of the system's extended memory.

Another exception in real mode is that the first 64KB of extended memory is actually accessible to the PC in real mode, despite the fact that it's not supposed to be possible. This is the result of a bug in the original IBM AT with respect to the 21st memory address line, known as A20 (A0 is the first address line). By manipulating the A20 line, real-mode software can gain access to the first 64KB of extended memory—the first 64KB of memory past the first megabyte. This area of memory is called the *high memory area (HMA)*.

IA-32e 64-Bit Extension Mode (AMD64, x86-64, EM64T)

64-bit extension mode is an enhancement to the IA-32 architecture originally designed by AMD and later adopted by Intel. Processors with 64-bit extension technology can run in real (8086) mode, IA-32 mode, or IA-32e mode. IA-32 mode enables the processor to run in protected mode and virtual real mode. IA-32e mode allows the processor to run in 64-bit mode and compatibility mode, which means you can run both 64-bit and 32-bit applications simultaneously. IA-32e mode includes two submodes:

- *64-bit mode.* Enables a 64-bit operating system to run 64-bit applications
- *Compatibility mode.* Enables a 64-bit operating system to run most existing 32-bit software

IA-32e 64-bit mode is enabled by loading a 64-bit operating system and is used by 64-bit applications. In the 64-bit submode, the following new features are available:

- 64-bit linear memory addressing
- Physical memory support beyond 4GB (limited by the specific processor)
- Eight new general-purpose registers (GPRs)
- Eight new registers for streaming SIMD extensions (MMX, SSE, SSE2, and SSE3)
- 64-bit-wide GPRs and instruction pointers

IE-32e compatibility mode enables 32-bit and 16-bit applications to run under a 64-bit operating system. Unfortunately, legacy 16-bit programs that run in virtual real mode (that is, DOS programs) are not supported and will not run, which is likely to be the biggest problem for many users. Similar to 64-bit mode, compatibility mode is enabled by the operating system on an individual code basis, which means 64-bit applications running in 64-bit mode can operate simultaneously with 32-bit applications running in compatibility mode.

What we need to make all this work is a 64-bit operating system and, more importantly, 64-bit drivers for all our hardware to work under that OS. A 64-bit OS already exists in two versions:

- Windows XP 64-bit Edition for Itanium
- Windows XP 64-bit Edition for 64-bit Extended Systems

Of those, the first is for IA-64 processors, such as Itanium and Itanium 2, and has been available in a released production version since 2001. The latter is for IA-32 processors with 64-bit extensions, such as the Athlon 64, Opteron, and future Xeon and Pentium processors supporting 64-bit extensions, and was released in a production version in the last half of 2004.

The differences between Windows XP 32-bit and 64-bit versions are shown in Table 3.7.

Table 3.7   Windows XP 32-Bit Versus 64-Bit

Address Space	Windows XP 32-Bit	Windows XP 64-Bit
Physical memory	4GB	32TB
Virtual memory	4GB	16TB
Paging file	16TB	512TB
Paged pool	470MB	128GB
Non-paged pool	256MB	128GB
System cache	1GB	1TB

The major difference between 32-bit and 64-bit Windows XP is memory support, specifically breaking the 4GB barrier found in 32-bit Windows systems. Windows XP 32-bit supports up to 4GB of physical or virtual memory, with up to 2GB of dedicated memory per process. Windows XP 64-bit Edition supports up to 32GB of physical memory and up to 16TB of virtual memory. Support for more memory means applications can preload more data into either physical or virtual memory, which the processor can access much more quickly. If you need more than 4GB of RAM, 64-bit systems and 64-bit Windows are required.

Windows XP 64-bit runs 32-bit Windows applications with no problems, but it does not run DOS applications or other programs that run in virtual real mode. Also, drivers are another big problem. 32-bit processes cannot load 64-bit dynamic link libraries (DLLs), and 64 bit processes cannot load 32-bit DLLs. This essentially means that, for all the devices you have connected to your system, you need both 32-bit and 64-bit drivers for them to work. Acquiring 64-bit drivers for older devices or devices that are no longer supported can be difficult or impossible. Even for new devices, it can be a couple of years before manufacturers provide 64-bit drivers as a standard feature.

You should keep all the memory size, software, and driver issues in mind when considering the transition from 32-bit to 64-bit technology. The transition from 32-bit hardware to mainstream 32-bit computing took 16 years. As I've already stated, it might not take 16 years for 64-bit computing to become mainstream, but it will most likely take at least a few years.

Processor Speed Ratings

A common misunderstanding about processors is their different speed ratings. This section covers processor speed in general and then provides more specific information about Intel, AMD, and VIA/Cyrix processors.

A computer system's clock speed is measured as a frequency, usually expressed as a number of cycles per second. A crystal oscillator controls clock speeds using a sliver of quartz sometimes contained in what looks like a small tin container. Newer systems include the oscillator circuitry in the motherboard chipset, so it might not be a visible separate component on newer boards. As voltage is applied to the quartz, it begins to vibrate (oscillate) at a harmonic rate dictated by the shape and size of the crystal (sliver). The oscillations emanate from the crystal in the form of a current that alternates at the harmonic rate of the crystal. This alternating current is the clock signal that forms the time base on which the computer operates. A typical computer system runs millions of these cycles per second, so speed is measured in megahertz. (One hertz is equal to one cycle per second.) An alternating current signal is like a sine wave, with the time between the peaks of each wave defining the frequency (see Figure 3.1).

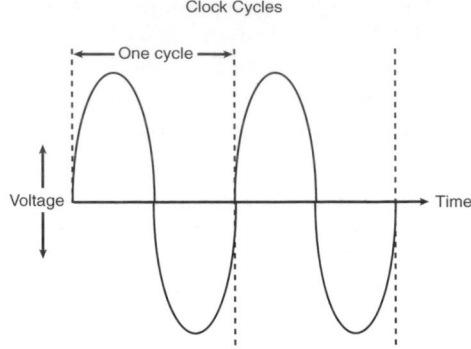

Figure 3.1   Alternating current signal showing clock cycle timing.

Note

The hertz was named for the German physicist Heinrich Rudolf Hertz. In 1885, Hertz confirmed the electromagnetic theory, which states that light is a form of electromagnetic radiation and is propagated as waves.

A single cycle is the smallest element of time for the processor. Every action requires at least one cycle and usually multiple cycles. To transfer data to and from memory, for example, a modern processor such as the Pentium 4 needs a minimum of three cycles to set up the first memory transfer and then only a single cycle per transfer for the next three to six consecutive transfers. The extra cycles on the first transfer typically are called *wait states*. A wait state is a clock tick in which nothing happens. This ensures that the processor isn't getting ahead of the rest of the computer.

▶▶   See "SIMMs, DIMMs, and RIMMs," p. 477.

The time required to execute instructions also varies:

- *8086 and 8088.* The original 8086 and 8088 processors take an average of 12 cycles to execute a single instruction.

- *286 and 386.* The 286 and 386 processors improve this rate to about 4.5 cycles per instruction.

- *486.* The 486 and most other fourth-generation Intel-compatible processors, such as the AMD 5x86, drop the rate further, to about 2 cycles per instruction.

- *Pentium, K6 series.* The Pentium architecture and other fifth-generation Intel-compatible processors, such as those from AMD and Cyrix, include twin instruction pipelines and other improvements that provide for operation at one or two instructions per cycle.

- *Pentium Pro, Pentium II/III/4/Celeron, and Athlon/Athlon XP/Duron.* These P6 and P7 (sixth- and seventh-generation) processors can execute as many as three or more instructions per cycle.

Different instruction execution times (in cycles) make comparing systems based purely on clock speed or number of cycles per second difficult. How can two processors that run at the same clock rate perform differently with one running "faster" than the other? The answer is simple: efficiency.

The main reason the 486 was considered fast relative to a 386 is that it executes twice as many instructions in the same number of cycles. The same thing is true for a Pentium; it executes about twice as many instructions in a given number of cycles as a 486. Therefore, given the same clock speed, a Pentium is twice as fast as a 486, and consequently a 133MHz 486 class processor (such as the AMD 5x86-133) is not even as fast as a 75MHz Pentium! That is because Pentium megahertz are "worth" about double what 486 megahertz are worth in terms of instructions completed per cycle.

The Pentium II and III are about 50% faster than an equivalent Pentium at a given clock speed because they can execute about that many more instructions in the same number of cycles.

Unfortunately, after the Pentium III, it becomes much more difficult to compare processors on clock speed alone. This is because the different internal architectures make some processors more efficient than others, but these same efficiency differences result in circuitry that is capable of running at different maximum speeds. The less efficient the circuit, the higher the clock speed it can attain, and vice versa.

Comparing relative processor performance, you can see that a 1GHz Pentium III is about equal to a (theoretical) 1.5GHz Pentium, which is about equal to a 3GHz 486, which is about equal to a 6GHz 386 or 286, which is about equal to a 12GHz 8088. The original PC's 8088 ran at only 4.77MHz; today, we have systems that are comparatively at least 2,500 times faster! As you can see, you must be careful in comparing systems based on pure MHz alone because many other factors affect system performance.

Evaluating CPU performance can be tricky. CPUs with different internal architectures do things differently and can be relatively faster at certain things and slower at others. To fairly compare various CPUs at different clock speeds, Intel has devised a specific series of benchmarks called the *iCOMP* *(Intel Comparative Microprocessor Performance) index* that can be run against processors to produce a relative gauge of performance. The iCOMP index benchmark has been updated twice and released in original iCOMP, iCOMP 2.0, and now iCOMP 3.0 versions.

Table 3.8 shows the relative power, or iCOMP 2.0 index, for several processors.

Note

Note that this reflects the most recent iCOMP index. Intel uses other benchmarks for the Pentium 4.

Table 3.8   Intel iCOMP 2.0 Index Ratings

Processor	iCOMP 2.0 Index	Processor	iCOMP 2.0 Index
Pentium 75	67	Pentium Pro 200	220
Pentium 100	90	Celeron 300	226
Pentium 120	100	Pentium II 233	267
Pentium 133	111	Celeron 300A	296
Pentium 150	114	Pentium II 266	303
Pentium 166	127	Celeron 333	318
Pentium 200	142	Pentium II 300	332
Pentium-MMX 166	160	Pentium II OverDrive 300	351
Pentium Pro 150	168	Pentium II 333	366
Pentium-MMX 200	182	Pentium II 350	386
Pentium Pro 180	197	Pentium II OverDrive 333	387
Pentium-MMX 233	203	Pentium II 400	440
Celeron 266	213	Pentium II 450	483

The iCOMP 2.0 index is derived from several independent benchmarks and is a stable indication of relative processor performance. The benchmarks balance integer with floating-point and multimedia performance.

When Intel developed the Pentium III, it discontinued the iCOMP 2.0 index and released the iCOMP 3.0 index. iCOMP 3.0 is an updated benchmark that incorporates an increasing use of 3D, multimedia, and Internet technology and software, as well as the increasing use of rich data streams and computer-intensive applications, including 3D, multimedia, and Internet technology. iCOMP 3.0 combines six benchmarks: WinTune 98 Advanced CPU Integer test, CPUmark 99, 3D WinBench 99-3D Lighting and Transformation Test, MultimediaMark 99, Jmark 2.0 Processor Test, and WinBench 99-FPU WinMark. These newer benchmarks take advantage of the SSE (Streaming SIMD Extensions), additional graphics and sound instructions built into the PIII. Without taking advantage of these new instructions, the PIII would benchmark at about the same speed as a PII at the same clock rate.

Table 3.9 shows the iCOMP Index 3.0 ratings for Pentium II and III processors.

Table 3.9   Intel iCOMP 3.0 Ratings

Processor	iCOMP 3.0 Index	Processor	iCOMP 3.0 Index
Pentium II 350	1000	Pentium III 650	2270
Pentium II 450	1240	Pentium III 700	2420
Pentium III 450	1500	Pentium III 750	2540
Pentium III 500	1650	Pentium III 800	2690
Pentium III 550	1780	Pentium III 866	2890
Pentium III 600	1930	Pentium III 1000	3280
Pentium III 600E	2110		

Intel and AMD currently rate their latest processors using the commercially available BAPCo SYSmark 2002 and 2004 benchmark suites. The ratings for the various processors under the 2002 and 2004 benchmark suites are shown in Tables 3.10 and 3.11.

Table 3.10   SYSmark 2002 Scores for Various Processors

CPU	Clock	SYSmark 2002 Rating	CPU	Clock	SYSmark 2002 Rating
Pentium 4 Extreme Edition	3.2GHz	362	AMD Athlon XP	1.72GHz	195
Pentium 4	3.2GHz	344	Pentium 4	1.9GHz	192
Pentium 4	3.0GHz	328	Pentium 4	1.8GHz	187
Pentium 4	3.06GHz	324	Pentium 4	1.7GHz	178
Pentium 4	2.8GHz	312	Pentium 4	1.6GHz	171
Pentium 4	2.6GHz	295	AMD Athlon XP	1.67GHz	171
Pentium 4	2.67GHz	285	Pentium 4	1.5GHz	162
Pentium 4	2.53GHz	273	AMD Athlon XP	1.53GHz	149
Pentium 4	2.4GHz	264	Pentium III	1.2GHz	108
Pentium 4	2.26GHz	252	Pentium III	1.3GHz	104
Pentium 4	2.2GHz	238	Pentium III	1.13GHz	100
Pentium 4	2.0GHz	222	Pentium III	1.0GHz	92

Table 3.11   SYSmark 2004 Scores for Various Processors

CPU	Clock	SYSmark 2004 Rating	CPU	Clock	SYSmark 2004 Rating
Intel Pentium 4EE	3.4GHz	225	AMD Athlon XP 3200+	2.2GHz	163
Intel Pentium 4E	3.4GHz	218	Intel Pentium 4C	2.4GHz	153
Intel Pentium 4EE	3.2GHz	215	AMD Athlon XP 2800+	2.25GHz	151
AMD Athlon FX-53	2.4GHz	213	AMD Athlon XP 2700i	2.18GHz	148
Intel Pentium 4C	3.4GHz	212	Intel Pentium 4B	2.8GHz	144
Intel Pentium 4E	3.2GHz	204	AMD Athlon XP 2600+	2.08GHz	144
AMD Athlon FX-51	2.2GHz	200	AMD Athlon XP 2400+	2.0GHz	133
AMD Athlon 64 3400+	2.2GHz	195	Intel Pentium 4B	2.4GHz	130
AMD Athlon 64 3200+	2.2GHz	194	Intel Celeron	2.8GHz	117
Intel Pentium 4C	3.0GHz	193	Intel Celeron	2.7GHz	115
Intel Pentium 4E	2.8GHz	182	AMD Athlon XP 1800+	1.53GHz	111
AMD Athlon 64 3200+	2.0GHz	180	Intel Celeron	2.5GHz	110
AMD Athlon 64 3000+	2.0GHz	178	Intel Celeron	2.4GHz	104
Intel Pentium 4C	2.8GHz	174	Intel Pentium 4A	2.0GHz	104
AMD Athlon 64 2800+	1.8GHz	164	Intel Pentium III	1.0GHz	64

SYSmark 2002 and 2004 are commercially available application-based benchmarks that reflect the normal usage of business users employing modern Internet content creation and Microsoft Office applications. However, it is important to note that the scores listed here are produced by complete systems and are affected by things such as the specific version of the processor, the motherboard and chipset used, the amount and type of memory installed, the speed of the hard disk, and other factors. For complete disclosure of the other factors resulting in the given scores, see the BAPCo Web site.

SYSmark 2002 incorporates the following applications, which it uses for testing:

■ *Internet Content Creation.* Includes Adobe Photoshop 6.01, Premiere 6.0, Microsoft Windows Media Encoder 7.1, Macromedia Dreamweaver 4, and Flash 5

■ *Office Productivity.* Includes Microsoft Word 2002, Excel 2002, PowerPoint 2002, Outlook 2002, Access 2002, Netscape Communicator 6.0, Dragon NaturallySpeaking Preferred v.5, WinZip 8.0, and McAfee VirusScan 5.13

SYSmark 2004 incorporates the following applications, which it uses for testing:

■ *Internet Content Creation.* Includes Adobe After Effects 5.5, Adobe Photoshop 7.01, Adobe Premiere 6.5, Discreet 3ds max 5.1, Macromedia Dreamweaver MX, Macromedia Flash MX, Microsoft Windows Media Encoder 9 Series, Network Associates McAfee VirusScan 7.0, and WinZip Computing WinZip 8.1

■ *Office Productivity.* Includes Adobe Acrobat 5.0.5, Microsoft Access 2002, Microsoft Excel 2002, Microsoft Internet Explorer 6, Microsoft Outlook 2002, Microsoft PowerPoint 2002, Microsoft Word 2002, Network Associates McAfee VirusScan 7.0, ScanSoft Dragon Naturally Speaking 6 Preferred, and WinZip Computing WinZip 8.1

SYSmark runs various scripts to do actual work using these applications and is used by many companies for testing and comparing PC systems and components. It is a much more modern and real-world benchmark than the iCOMP benchmark Intel previously used, and because it is available to anybody, the results can be independently verified. SYSmark 2002 and 2004 can be purchased from BAPCo at www.bapco.com.

Processor Speeds and Markings Versus Motherboard Speed

Another confusing factor when comparing processor performance is that virtually all modern processors since the 486DX2 run at some multiple of the motherboard speed. For example, a Pentium 4 2.53GHz chip runs at a multiple of 19/4 (4.75x) times the motherboard speed of 533MHz, whereas an AMD Athlon XP 2800+ using the latest Barton core (2.083GHz) runs at 75/12 (6.25x) times the motherboard speed of 333MHz. Up until early 1998, most motherboards ran at 66MHz or less. Starting in April 1998, Intel released both processors and motherboard chipsets designed to run at 100MHz.

By late 1999, chipsets and motherboards running at 133MHz became available to support the newer Pentium III processors. At that time, AMD Athlon motherboards and chipsets were introduced running a 100MHz clock but using a double transfer technique for an effective 200MHz data rate between the Athlon processor and the main chipset North Bridge chip.

In 2000 and 2001, processor bus speeds advanced further to 266MHz for the AMD Athlon and Intel Itanium and 400MHz to 533MHz for the Pentium 4. In 2002, the AMD Athlon XP processors began to support a processor bus speed of 333MHz. In 2003, Intel introduced the first Pentium 4 processors that supported a processor bus speed of 800MHz. Typically, the speed of the CPU bus is selected to match whatever memory types Intel and AMD want to support. Most of the modern CPU bus speeds are based on the speeds of the CPU as well as the available SDRAM, DDR SDRAM, and RDRAM memory. Note that the processor bus speed of Pentium 4 processors is not directly equivalent to a particular memory speed.

Note

See Chapter 4, "Motherboards and Buses," for more information on chipsets and bus speeds.

You can set the motherboard speed and multiplier setting via jumpers or another configuration mechanism (such as BIOS setup) on the motherboard. Modern systems use a variable-frequency synthesizer circuit usually found in the main motherboard chipset to control the motherboard and CPU speed. Most Pentium motherboards have three or four speed settings. The processors used today are available in a variety of versions that run at different frequencies based on a given motherboard speed. For example, most of the Pentium chips run at a speed that is some multiple of the true motherboard speed. For example, Pentium-class processors and motherboards run at the speeds shown in Table 3.12.

Note

For information on specific AMD, Cyrix, or VIA processors, see their respective sections later in this chapter.

Table 3.12   Intel Processor and Motherboard Speeds

CPU Type	CPU Speed (MHz)	CPU Clock Multiplier	Motherboard Speed (MHz)
Pentium	75	1.5x	50
Pentium	60	1x	60
Pentium	90	1.5x	60
Pentium	120	2x	60
Pentium	150	2.5x	60
Pentium/Pentium Pro	180	3x	60
Pentium	66	1x	66

Table 3.12   Continued

CPU Type	CPU Speed (MHz)	CPU Clock Multiplier	Motherboard Speed (MHz)
Pentium	100	1.5x	66
Pentium	133	2x	66
Pentium/Pentium Pro	166	2.5x	66
Pentium/Pentium Pro	200	3x	66
Pentium/Pentium II	233	3.5x	66
Pentium(Mobile)/Pentium II/Celeron	266	4x	66
Pentium II/Celeron	300	4.5x	66
Pentium II/Celeron	333	5x	66
Pentium II/Celeron	366	5.5x	66
Celeron	400	6x	66
Celeron	433	6.5x	66
Celeron	466	7x	66
Celeron	500	7.5x	66
Celeron	533	8x	66
Celeron	566	8.5x	66
Celeron	600	9x	66
Celeron	633	9.5x	66
Celeron	667	10x	66
Celeron	700	10.5x	66
Celeron	733	11x	66
Celeron	766	11.5x	66
Pentium II	350	3.5x	100
Pentium II	400	4x	100
Pentium II/III	450	4.5x	100
Pentium III	500	5x	100
Pentium III	550	5.5x	100
Pentium III	600	6x	100
Pentium III	650	6.5x	100
Pentium III	700	7x	100
Pentium III	750	7.5x	100
Pentium III/Celeron	800	8x	100
Pentium III/Celeron	850	8.5x	100
Pentium III/Celeron	900	9x	100
Pentium III/Celeron	950	9.5x	100
Pentium III/Celeron	1000	10x	100
Pentium III/Celeron	1100	11x	100
Pentium III/Celeron	1200	12x	100
Pentium III/Celeron	1300	13x	100
Pentium III/Celeron	1400	14x	100
Pentium III	533	4x	133
Pentium III	600	4.5x	133
Pentium III	667	5x	133
Pentium III	733	5.5x	133
Pentium III	800	6x	133
Pentium III	866	6.5x	133
Pentium III	933	7x	133

Table 3.12   Continued

CPU Type	CPU Speed (MHz)	CPU Clock Multiplier	Motherboard Speed (MHz)
Pentium III	1000	7.5x	133
Pentium III	1066	8x	133
Pentium III	1133	8.5x	133
Pentium III	1200	9x	133
Pentium III	1266	9.5x	133
Pentium III	1333	10x	133
Pentium III	1400	10.5x	133
Pentium 4	1300	3.25x	400
Pentium 4	1400	3.5x	400
Pentium 4	1500	3.75x	400
Pentium 4	1600	4x	400
Pentium 4/Celeron	1700	4.25x	400
Pentium 4	1800	4.5x	400
Pentium 4	1900	4.75x	400
Pentium 4	2000	5x	400
Pentium 4	2200	5.5x	400
Pentium 4	2400	6x	400
Pentium 4	2266	4.25x	533
Pentium 4	2400	4.5x	533
Pentium 4	2500	6.25X	400
Pentium 4	2533	4.75x	533
Pentium 4	2600	6.5x	400
Pentium 4	2660	5x	533
Pentium 4	2800	5.25x	533
Pentium 4	3060	5.75x	533
Pentium 4	3200	4x	800
Pentium 4	3400	4.25x	800
Itanium	733	2.75x	266
Itanium	800	3x	266
Itanium 2	1000	2.5x	400

If all other variables are equal—including the type of processor, the number of wait states (empty cycles) added to different types of memory accesses, and the width of the data bus—you can compare two systems by their respective clock rates. However, the construction and design of the memory controller (contained in the motherboard chipset) as well as the type and amount of memory installed can have an enormous effect on a system's final execution speed.

In building a processor, a manufacturer tests it at various speeds, temperatures, and pressures. After the processor is tested, it receives a stamp indicating the maximum safe speed at which the unit will operate under the wide variation of temperatures and pressures encountered in normal operation. These ratings are clearly marked on the processor package.

Cyrix Processor Speeds

Cyrix/IBM/VIA 6x86 processors—which were designed to compete with the Intel Pentium, early Pentium II, and AMD K5 and K6 series of processors—used a PR (performance rating) scale that was not equal to the true clock speed in megahertz. For example, the Cyrix 6x86MX/MII-PR366 actually runs at only 250MHz (2.5×100MHz). This is a little misleading—you must set up the motherboard as if a

250MHz processor were being installed, instead of the 366MHz you might suspect. Unfortunately, this led people to believe these systems were faster than they really were.

Table 3.13 shows the relationship between the Cyrix 6x86, 6x86MX, and M-II P-Ratings versus the actual chip speeds in MHz.

Table 3.13   Cyrix P-Ratings Versus Actual Chip Speeds in MHz

CPU Type	P-Rating	Actual CPU Speed (MHz)	Clock Multiplier	Motherboard Speed (MHz)
6x86	PR90	80	2x	40
6x86	PR120	100	2x	50
6x86	PR133	110	2x	55
6x86	PR150	120	2x	60
6x86	PR166	133	2x	66
6x86	PR200	150	2x	75
6x86MX	PR133	100	2x	50
6x86MX	PR133	110	2x	55
6x86MX	PR150	120	2x	60
6x86MX	PR150	125	2.5x	50
6x86MX	PR166	133	2x	66
6x86MX	PR166	137.5	2.5x	55
6x86MX	PR166	150	3x	50
6x86MX	PR166	150	2.5x	60
6x86MX	PR200	150	2x	75
6x86MX	PR200	165	3x	55
6x86MX	PR200	166	2.5x	66
6x86MX	PR200	180	3x	60
6x86MX	PR233	166	2x	83
6x86MX	PR233	187.5	2.5x	75
6x86MX	PR233	200	3x	66
6x86MX	PR266	207.5	2.5x	83
6x86MX	PR266	225	3x	75
6x86MX	PR266	233	3.5x	66
M-II	PR300	225	3x	75
M-II	PR300	233	3.5x	66
M-II	PR333	250	3x	83
M-II	PR366	250	2.5x	100
M-II	PR400	285	3x	95
M-II	PR433	300	3x	100
Cyrix III	PR433	350	3.5x	100
Cyrix III	PR466	366	3x	122
Cyrix III	PR500	400	3x	133
Cyrix III	PR533	433	3.5x	124
Cyrix III	PR533	450	4.5x	100

Note that a given P-Rating can mean several different actual CPU speeds—for example, a Cyrix 6x86MX-PR200 might actually be running at 150MHz, 165MHz, 166MHz, or 180MHz, but *not* at 200MHz.

This P-Rating was supposed to indicate speed in relation to an Intel Pentium processor, but the processor being compared to in this case is the original non-MMX, small L1 cache version running on an older motherboard platform with an older chipset and slower technology memory. The P-Rating did not compare well against the Celeron, Pentium II, or Pentium III processors. In other words, the MII-PR366 really ran at only 250MHz and compared well against Intel processors running at closer to that speed, making the ratings somewhat misleading.

AMD Processor Speeds

AMD's Athlon XP processors are excellent performers and have several notable features, but they unfortunately bring with them a resurrection of the infamous Cyrix/AMD performance rating. This is a simulated MHz number that does not indicate the actual speed of the chip but instead indicates an estimate of the relative MHz of a first-generation Intel Pentium 4 that would be approximately equal in performance. If this sounds confusing, that's because it is!

Table 3.14 shows the P-Rating and actual speeds of the AMD K5, K6, Athlon, Athlon XP, and Duron processors.

Table 3.14   AMD P-Ratings Versus Actual Chip Speeds in MHz

CPU Type	P-Rating	Actual CPU Speed (MHz)	Clock Multiplier	Motherboard Speed (MHz)
K5	75	75	1.5x	50
K5	90	90	1.5x	60
K5	100	100	1.5x	66
K5	120	90	1.5x	60
K5	133	100	1.5x	66
K5	166	116	1.75x	66
K6	166	166	2.5x	66
K6	200	200	3x	66
K6	233	233	3.5x	66
K6	266	266	4x	66
K6	300	300	4.5x	66
K6-2	233	233	3.5x	66
K6-2	266	266	4x	66
K6-2	300	300	4.5x	66
K6-2	300	300	3x	100
K6-2	333	333	5x	66
K6-2	333	333	3.5x	95
K6-2	350	350	3.5x	100
K6-2	366	366	5.5x	66
K6-2	380	380	4x	95
K6-2	400	400	6x	66
K6-2	400	400	4x	100
K6-2	450	450	4.5x	100
K6-2	475	475	5x	95
K6-2	500	500	5x	100
K6-2	533	533	5.5x	97
K6-2	550	550	5.5x	100
K6-3	400	400	4x	100
K6-3	450	450	4.5x	100
Athlon	500	500	2.5x	200
Athlon	550	550	2.75x	200
Athlon/Duron	600	600	3x	200

Table 3.14   Continued

CPU Type	P-Rating	Actual CPU Speed (MHz)	Clock Multiplier	Motherboard Speed (MHz)
Athlon/Duron	650	650	3.25x	200
Athlon/Duron	700	700	3.5x	200
Athlon/Duron	750	750	3.75x	200
Athlon/Duron	800	800	4x	200
Athlon/Duron	850	850	4.25x	200
Athlon/Duron	900	900	4.5x	200
Athlon/Duron	950	950	4.75x	200
Athlon/Duron	1000	1000	5x	200
Athlon/Duron	1100	1100	5.5x	200
Athlon/Duron	1200	1200	6x	200
Athlon/Duron	1300	1300	6.5x	200
Athlon/Duron	1400	1400	7x	200
Athlon	1000	1000	3.75x	266
Athlon	1133	1133	4.25x	266
Athlon	1200	1200	4.5x	266
Athlon	1333	1333	5x	266
Athlon	1400	1400	5.25x	266
Athlon XP	1500+	1333	5x	266
Athlon XP	1600+	1400	5.25x	266
Athlon XP	1700+	1466	5.5x	266
Athlon XP	1800+	1533	5.75x	266
Athlon XP	1900+	1600	6x	266
Athlon XP	2000+	1666	6.25x	266
Athlon XP	2100+	1733	6.5x	266
Athlon XP	2200+	1800	6.75x	266
Athlon XP	2400+	2000	7.5x	266
Athlon XP	2500+*	1833	5.5x	333
Athlon XP	2600+	2083	6.25x	333
Athlon XP	2600+	2133	8x	266
Athlon XP	2700+	2167	6.5x	333
Athlon XP	2800+*	2083	6.25x	333
Athlon XP	2800+	2250	6.75x	333
Athlon XP	3000+*	2167	6.5x	333
Athlon XP	3200+*	2333	7x	333

Note that the 200MHz and 266MHz bus speeds in the Athlon/Duron use 100MHz and 133MHz clock signals and two transfers per cycle for double the effective rate. Some motherboards refer to the CPU bus speed by the half-speed 100MHz or 133MHz clock and therefore use twice the clock multiplier settings shown here.

*These processors use the Barton core, which uses a larger 512KB cache instead of other Athlon XP models' 256KB cache to improve performance.

AMD's performance tests show that the 1.8GHz Athlon runs at the same "performance level" as a theoretical 2.2GHz Pentium 4, so it calls the chip an Athlon XP 2200+, assigning the 2200+ number as a designation of performance relative to Pentium 4MHz. This type of marketing, where a chip is assigned a number indicating a relative—rather than a true—speed rating, has been tried before with limited success. In some cases it left a bad impression with customers who felt that they were deceived when they found out the true MHz rating of the chips and systems they had purchased.

I liken the performance numbers AMD is using to the wind chill factor often used by weather reporters in the winter. There is of course the *real* temperature, and then there is the so-called wind chill factor, which is an estimated rating of how cold it "feels." The model numbers AMD uses with the new Athlon XP are like a "speed factor," which is supposed to tell you how fast the processor "feels" compared to a Pentium 4. (However, AMD does insist its performance rating numbers are not meant to be directly associated with the Pentium 4.)

AMD's marketing problem is real: How do you market a chip that performs faster than your rival when both are running at the same clock speed? An AMD Athlon XP with an actual clock speed of 2GHz is significantly faster than a 2GHz Pentium 4 and in fact performs about equal to a 2.4GHz Pentium 4 (hence, AMD calls this model the Athlon XP 2400+). This apparent disparity in performance is because the P4 uses a different architecture that utilizes a deeper instruction pipeline with more stages. The Pentium 4 has a 20-stage pipeline, which compares to a 10-stage pipeline in the Athlon and a 10-stage pipeline in the Pentium III/Celeron (see Table 3.15).

Table 3.15   Number of Pipelines per CPU

Processor	Pipeline Depth	Processor	Pipeline Depth
Pentium III	10-stage	Athlon 64/64 FX	12-stage
Pentium M	10-stage	Pentium 4	20-stage
Athlon/XP	10-stage	Pentium 4 Prescott	31-stage

A deeper pipeline effectively breaks instructions down into smaller microsteps, which allows overall higher clock rates to be achieved using the same silicon technology. However, it also means that overall fewer instructions can be executed in a single cycle as compared with the Athlon (or Pentium III). This is because, if a branch prediction or speculative execution step fails (which happens fairly frequently inside the processor as it attempts to line up instructions in advance), the entire pipeline has to be flushed and refilled. Thus, if you compared an Athlon to a Pentium III to a Pentium 4 all running at the same clock speed, the Athlon and Pentium III would both beat the Pentium 4 running typical benchmarks because they would execute more instructions in the same number of cycles.

Although this would sound bad for the Pentium 4, it really isn't. In fact, it is part of the design. Intel's reasoning is that even though the deeper pipeline might be 30% less efficient overall, it more than makes up for this by allowing at least 50% greater clock speeds than the Athlon or Pentium III with shorter pipelines. The deeper 20- or 31-stage pipeline in the P4 architecture enables significantly higher clock speeds to be achieved using the same silicon die process as other chips. As an example, the Athlon XP and Pentium 4 were originally made using the same 0.18-micron process (which describes the line width of components etched on the chips). The P4's 20-stage pipeline enabled the 0.18-micron die process to result in chips running up to 2.0GHz, whereas the same process achieves only 1.73GHz in the 10-stage Athlon XP and only 1.13GHz in the 10-stage Pentium III/Celeron. Using the newer 0.13-micron process, the Pentium 4 currently runs up to 3.4GHz and the Athlon XP tops out at 2.2GHz (3200+ model) in the same introduction timeframe. Even though the Pentium 4 executes fewer instructions in each cycle, the overall higher cycling speeds make up for the loss of efficiency. So, for the initial crop of Athlon XP and Pentium 4 processors, in the end, higher clock speed versus more efficient processing effectively cancel each other out.

Many systems display the clock speed of the processor during the initial boot cycle. Windows XP also displays the CPU clock speed on the General tab of the System Properties sheet. AMD would prefer that systems no longer indicate processor speed directly. In fact, *AMD does not recommend or validate motherboards using the Athlon XP if they display the processor's actual clock speed.* In the future, the curious will need to use a third-party program such as SiSoft Sandra or the Intel Frequency ID Utility to find out the true clock speed of their processors after it is installed.

Note

If you want to determine the designed clock speed for any type of Athlon processor (the actual clock speed could vary according to motherboard overclocking, underclocking, or power management clock speed adjustments), go to AMD's Web site and download the Data Sheet for the processor model you are interested in. You will find a table in each data sheet that lists the actual MHz (divide by 1,000 for the GHz) for each model. The latest Athlon XPs are Model 10, and earlier models are Model 8 and Model 6.

One thing is clear in all of this confusion: Raw MHz (or GHz) is not always a good way to compare chips, and generating pseudo-MHz numbers can only make things more confusing for the uninitiated. Even Intel is now moving away from using clock speed as its primary marketing designation. It still notes the speeds of its chips, but it is adding a new model number to the later Pentium 4 and Celeron processors to indicate a relative difference between them. This relative difference is based not just on speed, but also on architectural and other differences.

Overclocking

In some systems, the processor speed can be set higher than the rating on the chip; this is called *overclocking* the chip. In many cases, you can get away with a certain amount of overclocking because Intel, AMD, and others often build safety margins into their ratings. So, a chip rated for, say, 800MHz might in fact run at 900MHz or more but instead be down-rated to allow for a greater margin of reliability. By overclocking, you are using this margin and running the chip closer to its true maximum speed. I don't normally recommend overclocking for a novice, but if you are comfortable playing with your system settings, and you can afford and are capable of dealing with any potential consequences, overclocking might enable you to get 10%–20% or more performance from your system.

Overclocking Pitfalls

If you are intent on overclocking, there are several issues to consider. One is that most Intel processors since the Pentium II are multiplier-locked before they are shipped out. Therefore, the chip ignores any changes to the multiplier setting on the motherboard. Actually, both Intel and AMD lock the multipliers on most of their newer processors, but the AMD processors use solder bridges on top of the chip that can be manipulated if you are careful and somewhat mechanically inclined. Although originally done to prevent re-markers from fraudulently relabeling processors (creating "counterfeit" chips), this has impacted the computing performance enthusiast, leaving tweaking the motherboard bus speed as the only easy way (or in some cases, the only way possible) to achieve a clock speed higher than standard.

You can run into problems increasing motherboard bus speed, as well. Most older Intel motherboards, for example, simply don't support clock speeds other than the standard 66MHz, 100MHz, 133MHz, 400MHz, 533MHz or 800MHz settings. Newer Intel boards have a "burn-in" feature that allows you to increase the default processor bus speed (and also the speed of the processor core) by up to 4%. That is relatively mild, but easily achievable with most chips you might have. Most other brands of motherboards allow changing the bus speeds by even greater amounts.

Even if you could trick the processor into accepting a different clock multiplier setting, the jump from 66MHz to 100MHz or from 100MHz to 133MHz is a large one, and many processors will not make that much of a jump reliably. For example, a Pentium III 800E runs at a 100MHz bus speed with an 8x multiplier. Bumping the motherboard speed to 133MHz causes the processor to try to run at 8×133, or 1066MHz. It is not certain that the chip would run reliably at that speed. Likewise, a Celeron 600E runs at 9×66MHz. Raising the bus speed to 100MHz causes the chip to try and run at 9×100MHz, or 900MHz, another potentially unsuccessful change.

A board that supports intermediate speed settings and allows the settings to be changed in smaller increments is necessary. This is because a given chip is generally overclockable by a certain percentage. The smaller the steps you can take when increasing speed, the more likely that you'll be able to come close to the actual maximum speed of the chip without going over. For example, the Asus P3V4X motherboard supports frontside bus speed settings of 66MHz, 75MHz, 83MHz, 90MHz, 95MHz, 100MHz, 103MHz, 105MHz, 110MHz, 112MHz, 115MHz, 120MHz, 124MHz, 133MHz, 140MHz, and 150MHz. By setting the 800MHz Pentium IIIE to increments above 100MHz, you'd have the following:

Multiplier (Fixed)	Bus Speed	Processor Speed
8x	100MHz	800MHz
8x	103MHz	824MHz
8x	105MHz	840MHz
8x	110MHz	880MHz
8x	112MHz	896MHz
8x	115MHz	920MHz
8x	120MHz	960MHz
8x	124MHz	992MHz
8x	133MHz	1066MHz

Likewise, using this motherboard with a Celeron 600, you could try settings above the standard 66MHz bus speed as follows:

Multiplier (Fixed)	Bus Speed	Processor Speed
9x	66MHz	600MHz
9x	75MHz	675MHz
9x	83MHz	747MHz
9x	90MHz	810MHz
9x	95MHz	855MHz
9x	100MHz	900MHz

Typically, a 10%–20% increase is successful, so with this motherboard, you are likely to get your processor running 100MHz or faster than it was originally designed for.

An issue when it comes to increasing CPU bus speeds is that the other buses in the system will typically be similarly affected. Thus, if you increase the CPU bus speed by 10%, you might also be increasing the PCI or AGP bus by the same amount, and your video, network, or other cards might not be able to keep up. This is something that varies from board to board, so you have to consider each example as a potentially unique case.

Overclocking Socket A Processors

The AMD Athlon and Duron processors in the FC-PGA (flip-chip pin grid array) format, which plugs into Socket A, have special solder bridges on the top face of the chip that can be modified to change or remove the lock from the internal multiplier on the chip. This can increase the speed of the chip without changing the motherboard bus speed, thus affecting other buses or cards.

The selected multiplier is set or locked by very small solder connections between solder dots (contacts) on the surface of the chip. You can completely unlock the chip by bridging or disconnecting the appropriate dots. Unfortunately, it is somewhat difficult to add or remove these bridges; you usually have to mask off the particular bridge you want to create and, rather than dripping solder onto it, literally paint the bridge with silver or copper paint. For example, you can use the special copper paint sold in small vials at any auto parts store for repairing the window defogger grids. The real problem is that the contacts are very small, and if you bridge to adjacent rather than opposite contacts, you can render the chip nonfunctional. An Xacto knife or razor blade can be used to remove the bridges if desired. If you are not careful, you can easily damage a processor worth several hundred dollars. If you are leery of making such changes, you should try bus overclocking instead because this is done in the BIOS Setup and can easily be changed or undone without any mechanical changes to the chip.

CPU Voltage Settings

Another trick used by overclockers is playing with the voltage settings for the CPU. All modern CPU sockets and slots, including Slot 1, Slot A, Socket 8, Socket 370, Socket 423, Socket 478, and Socket A, have automatic voltage detection. With this detection, the system detects and sets the correct voltage by reading certain pins on the processor. Some motherboards, such as those made by Intel, do not allow any manual changes to these settings. Other motherboards, such as the Asus P3V4X mentioned earlier, allow you to tweak the voltage settings from the automatic setting up or down by tenths of a volt. Some experimenters have found that by either increasing or decreasing voltage slightly from the standard, a higher speed of overclock can be achieved with the system remaining stable.

My recommendation is to be careful when playing with voltages because you can damage the chip in this manner. Even without changing voltage, overclocking with an adjustable bus speed motherboard is very easy and fairly rewarding. I do recommend you make sure you are using a high-quality board, good memory, and especially a good system chassis with additional cooling fans and a heavy-duty power supply. See Chapter 21, "Power Supply and Chassis/Case," for more information on upgrading power supplies and chassis. Especially when overclocking, it is essential that the system components and the CPU remain properly cooled. Going a little bit overboard on the processor heatsink and adding extra cooling fans to the case never hurts and in many cases helps a great deal when hotrodding a system in this manner.

Note

One good source of online overclocking information is located at `http://www.tomshardware.com`. It includes, among other things, fairly thorough overclocking FAQs and an ongoing survey of users who have successfully (and sometimes unsuccessfully) overclocked their CPUs. Note that many of the newer Intel processors incorporate fixed bus multiplier ratios that effectively prevent or certainly reduce the ability to overclock. Unfortunately, this can be overridden with a simple hardware fix, and many counterfeit processor vendors are selling re-marked (overclocked) chips.

Cache Memory

As processor core speeds increased, memory speeds could not keep up. How could you run a processor faster than the memory from which you feed it without having performance suffer terribly? The answer was cache. In its simplest terms, *cache memory* is a high-speed memory buffer that temporarily stores data the processor needs, allowing the processor to retrieve that data faster than if it came from main memory. But there is one additional feature of a cache over a simple buffer, and that is intelligence. A cache is a buffer with a brain.

A buffer holds random data, usually on a first in, first out, or first in, last out basis. A cache, on the other hand, holds the data the processor is most likely to need in advance of it actually being needed. This enables the processor to continue working at either full speed or close to it without having to wait for the data to be retrieved from slower main memory. Cache memory is usually made up of static RAM (SRAM) memory integrated into the processor die, although older systems with cache also used chips installed on the motherboard.

▶▶ See "Cache Memory: SRAM," p. 461.

Two levels of processor/memory cache are used in a modern PC, called Level 1 (L1) and Level 2 (L2) (some server processors such as the Itanium series from Intel also have Level 3 cache). These caches and how they function are described in the following sections.

Internal Level 1 Cache

All modern processors starting with the 486 family include an integrated L1 cache and controller. The integrated L1 cache size varies from processor to processor, starting at 8KB for the original 486DX and now up to 32KB, 64KB, or more in the latest processors.

To understand the importance of cache, you need to know the relative speeds of processors and memory. The problem with this is that processor speed usually is expressed in MHz or GHz (millions or billions of cycles per second), whereas memory speeds are often expressed in nanoseconds (billionths of a second per cycle). Most newer types of memory express the speed in either MHz or in megabyte per second (MBps) bandwidth (throughput).

Both are really time- or frequency-based measurements, and a chart comparing them can be found in Table 6.3 in Chapter 6, "Memory." In this table, you will note that a 233MHz processor equates to 4.3-nanosecond cycling, which means you would need 4ns memory to keep pace with a 200MHz CPU. Also note that the motherboard of a 233MHz system typically runs at 66MHz, which corresponds to a speed of 15ns per cycle and requires 15ns memory to keep pace. Finally, note that 60ns main memory (common on many Pentium-class systems) equates to a clock speed of approximately 16MHz. So, a typical Pentium 233 system has a processor running at 233MHz (4.3ns per cycle), a motherboard running at 66MHz (15ns per cycle), and main memory running at 16MHz (60ns per cycle). This might seem like a rather dated example, but in a moment, you will see that the figures listed here make it easy for me to explain how cache memory works.

Because L1 cache is always built into the processor die, it runs at the full-core speed of the processor internally. By full-core speed, I mean this cache runs at the higher clock multiplied internal processor speed rather than the external motherboard speed. This cache basically is an area of very fast memory built into the processor and is used to hold some of the current working set of code and data. Cache memory can be accessed with no wait states because it is running at the same speed as the processor core.

Using cache memory reduces a traditional system bottleneck because system RAM is almost always much slower than the CPU; the performance difference between memory and CPU speed has become especially large in recent systems. Using cache memory prevents the processor from having to wait for code and data from much slower main memory, therefore improving performance. Without the L1 cache, a processor would frequently be forced to wait until system memory caught up.

Cache is even more important in modern processors because it is often the only memory in the entire system that can truly keep up with the chip. Most modern processors are clock multiplied, which means they are running at a speed that is really a multiple of the motherboard into which they are plugged. The Pentium 4 2.8GHz, for example, runs at a multiple of 5.25 times the true motherboard speed of 533MHz. The main memory is one half this speed (266MHz) because the Pentium 4 uses a quad-pumped memory bus. Because the main memory is plugged into the motherboard, it can run only at 266MHz maximum. The only 2.8GHz memory in such a system is the L1 and L2 caches built into the processor core. In this example, the Pentium 4 2.8GHz processor has 20KB of integrated L1 cache (8KB data cache and 12KB execution trace cache) and 512KB of L2, all running at the full speed of the processor core.

▶▶   See "Memory Module Speed," p. 497.

If the data the processor wants is already in the internal cache, the CPU does not have to wait. If the data is not in the cache, the CPU must fetch it from the Level 2 cache or (in less sophisticated system designs) from the system bus, meaning main memory directly.

How Cache Works

To learn how the L1 cache works, consider the following analogy.

This story involves a person (in this case you) eating food to act as the processor requesting and operating on data from memory. The kitchen where the food is prepared is the main memory (SIMM/DIMM) RAM. The cache controller is the waiter, and the L1 cache is the table at which you are seated.

Okay, here's the story. Say you start to eat at a particular restaurant every day at the same time. You come in, sit down, and order a hot dog. To keep this story proportionately accurate, let's say you normally eat at the rate of one bite (byte? <g>) every four seconds (233MHz = about 4ns cycling). It also takes 60 seconds for the kitchen to produce any given item that you order (60ns main memory).

So, when you first arrive, you sit down, order a hot dog, and you have to wait for 60 seconds for the food to be produced before you can begin eating. After the waiter brings the food, you start eating at your normal rate. Pretty quickly you finish the hot dog, so you call the waiter over and order a hamburger. Again you wait 60 seconds while the hamburger is being produced. When it arrives, you again begin eating at full speed. After you finish the hamburger, you order a plate of fries. Again you wait, and after it is delivered 60 seconds later, you eat it at full speed. Finally, you decide to finish the meal and order cheesecake for dessert. After another 60-second wait, you can eat cheesecake at full speed. Your overall eating experience consists of mostly a lot of waiting, followed by short bursts of actual eating at full speed.

After coming into the restaurant for two consecutive nights at exactly 6 p.m. and ordering the same items in the same order each time, on the third night the waiter begins to think, "I know this guy is going to be here at 6 p.m., order a hot dog, a hamburger, fries, and then cheesecake. Why don't I have these items prepared in advance and surprise him? Maybe I'll get a big tip." So you enter the restaurant and order a hot dog, and the waiter immediately puts it on your plate, with no waiting! You then proceed to finish the hot dog and right as you are about to request the hamburger, the waiter deposits one on your plate. The rest of the meal continues in the same fashion, and you eat the entire meal, taking a bite every four seconds, and never have to wait for the kitchen to prepare the food. Your overall eating experience this time consists of all eating, with no waiting for the food to be prepared, due primarily to the intelligence and thoughtfulness of your waiter.

This analogy exactly describes the function of the L1 cache in the processor. The L1 cache itself is the table that can contain one or more plates of food. Without a waiter, the space on the table is a simple food buffer. When stocked, you can eat until the buffer is empty, but nobody seems to be intelligently refilling it. The waiter is the cache controller who takes action and adds the intelligence to decide which dishes are to be placed on the table in advance of your needing them. Like the real cache controller, he uses his skills to literally guess which food you will require next, and if and when he guesses right, you never have to wait.

Let's now say on the fourth night you arrive exactly on time and start off with the usual hot dog. The waiter, by now really feeling confident, has the hot dog already prepared when you arrive, so there is no waiting.

Just as you finish the hot dog, and right as he is placing a hamburger on your plate, you say "Gee, I'd really like a bratwurst now; I didn't actually order this hamburger." The waiter guessed wrong, and the consequence is that this time you have to wait the full 60 seconds as the kitchen prepares your brat. This is known as a *cache miss*, in which the cache controller did not correctly fill the cache with the data the processor actually needed next. The result is waiting, or in the case of a sample 233MHz Pentium system, the system essentially throttles back to 16MHz (RAM speed) whenever a cache miss occurs.

According to Intel, the L1 cache in most of its processors has approximately a 90% hit ratio (some processors, such as the Pentium 4, are slightly higher). This means that the cache has the correct data 90% of the time, and consequently the processor runs at full speed—233MHz in this example—90% of the time. However, 10% of the time the cache controller guesses wrong and the data has to be retrieved out of the significantly slower main memory, meaning the processor has to wait. This essentially throttles the system back to RAM speed, which in this example was 60ns or 16MHz.

In this analogy, the processor was 14 times faster than the main memory. Memory speeds have increased from 16MHz (60ns) to 333MHz (3.0ns) or faster in the latest systems, but processor speeds have also risen to 3GHz and beyond, so even in the latest systems, memory is still 7.5 or more times *slower* than the processor. Cache is what makes up the difference.

The main feature of L1 cache is that it has always been integrated into the processor core, where it runs at the same speed as the core. This, combined with the hit ratio of 90% or greater, makes L1 cache very important for system performance.

Level 2 Cache

To mitigate the dramatic slowdown every time an L1 cache miss occurs, a secondary (L2) cache is employed.

Using the restaurant analogy I used to explain L1 cache in the previous section, I'll equate the L2 cache to a cart of additional food items placed strategically in the restaurant such that the waiter can retrieve food from the cart in only 15 seconds (versus 60 seconds from the kitchen). In an actual Pentium class (Socket 7) system, the L2 cache is mounted on the motherboard, which means it runs at motherboard speed—66MHz, or 15ns in this example. Now, if you ask for an item the waiter did not bring in advance to your table, instead of making the long trek back to the kitchen to retrieve the food and bring it back to you 60 seconds later, he can first check the cart where he has placed additional items. If the requested item is there, he will return with it in only 15 seconds. The net effect in the real system is that instead of slowing down from 233MHz to 16MHz waiting for the data to come from the 60ns main memory, the data can instead be retrieved from the 15ns (66MHz) L2 cache. The effect is that the system slows down from 233MHz to 66MHz.

Newer processors have integrated L2 cache that runs at the same speed as the processor core, which is also the same speed as the L1 cache. For the analogy to describe these newer chips, the waiter would simply place the cart right next to the table you were seated at in the restaurant. Then, if the food you desired wasn't on the table (L1 cache miss), it would merely take a longer reach over to the adjacent L2 cache (the cart, in this analogy) rather than a 15-second walk to the kitchen as with the older designs.

Cache Performance and Design

Just as with the L1 cache, most L2 caches have a hit ratio also in the 90% range; therefore, if you look at the system as a whole, 90% of the time it will be running at full speed (233MHz in this example) by retrieving data out of the L1 cache. Ten percent of the time it will slow down to retrieve the data from the L2 cache. Ninety percent of the time the processor goes to the L2 cache, the data will be in the L2, and 10% of that time it will have to go to the slow main memory to get the data because of an L2 cache miss. So, by combining both caches, our sample system runs at full processor speed 90% of the time (233MHz in this case), at motherboard speed 9% (90% of 10%) of the time (66MHz in this case), and at RAM speed about 1% (10% of 10%) of the time (16MHz in this case). You can clearly see the importance of both the L1 and L2 caches; without them the system uses main memory more often, which is significantly slower than the processor.

This brings up other interesting points. If you could spend money doubling the performance of either the main memory (RAM) or the L2 cache, which would you improve? Considering that main memory is used directly only about 1% of the time, if you doubled performance there, you would double the speed of your system only 1% of the time! That doesn't sound like enough of an improvement to justify much expense. On the other hand, if you doubled L2 cache performance, you would be doubling system performance 9% of the time, a much greater improvement overall. I'd much rather improve L2 than RAM performance.

The processor and system designers at Intel and AMD know this and have devised methods of improving the performance of L2 cache. In Pentium (P5) class systems, the L2 cache usually was found on the motherboard and had to therefore run at motherboard speed. Intel made the first dramatic improvement by migrating the L2 cache from the motherboard directly into the processor and initially running it at the same speed as the main processor. The cache chips were made by Intel and mounted next to the main processor die in a single chip housing. This proved too expensive, so with the Pentium II, Intel began using cache chips from third-party suppliers such as Sony, Toshiba, NEC, Samsung, and others. Because these were supplied as complete packaged chips and not raw die, Intel mounted them on a circuit board alongside the processor. This is why the Pentium II was designed as a cartridge rather than what looked like a chip.

One problem was the speed of the available third-party cache chips. The fastest ones on the market were 3ns or higher, meaning 333MHz or less in speed. Because the processor was being driven in speed above that, in the Pentium II and initial Pentium III processors Intel had to run the L2 cache at half the processor speed because that is all the commercially available cache memory could handle. AMD followed suit with the Athlon processor, which had to drop L2 cache speed even further in some models to two-fifths or one-third the main CPU speed to keep the cache memory speed less than the 333MHz commercially available chips.

Then a breakthrough occurred, which first appeared in Celeron processors 300A and above. These had 128KB of L2 cache, but no external chips were used. Instead, the L2 cache had been integrated directly into the processor core just like the L1. Consequently, both the L1 and L2 caches now would run at full processor speed, and more importantly scale up in speed as the processor speeds increased in the future. In the newer Pentium III, as well as all the Xeon and Celeron processors, the L2 cache runs at full processor core speed, which means there is no waiting or slowing down after an L1 cache miss. AMD also achieved full-core speed on-die cache in its later Athlon and Duron chips. Using on-die cache improves performance dramatically because 9% of the time the system would be using the L2, it would now remain at full speed instead of slowing down to one-half or less the processor speed or, even worse, slow down to motherboard speed as in Socket 7 designs. Another benefit of on-die L2 cache is cost, which is less because now fewer parts are involved.

Let's revisit the restaurant analogy using a modern Pentium 4 2GHz. You would now be taking a bite every half second (2GHz = 0.5ns cycling). The L1 cache would also be running at that speed, so you could eat anything on your table at that same rate (the table = L1 cache). The real jump in speed comes when you want something that isn't already on the table (L1 cache miss), in which case the waiter reaches over to the cart (which is now directly adjacent to the table) and nine out of ten times is able to find the food you want in only one-half second (L2 speed = 2GHz or 0.5ns cycling). In this more modern system, you would run at 2GHz 99% of the time (L1 and L2 hit ratios combined) and slow down to RAM speed (wait for the kitchen) only 1% of the time as before. With faster memory running at 400MHz (2.5ns), you would have to wait only 2.5 seconds for the food to come from the kitchen. If only restaurant performance would increase at the same rate processor performance has!

Cache Organization

You know that cache stores copies of data from various main memory addresses. Because the cache cannot hold copies of the data from all the addresses in main memory simultaneously, there has to be a way to know which addresses are currently copied into the cache so that, if we need data from those addresses, it can be read from the cache rather than from the main memory. This function is performed by Tag RAM, which is additional memory in the cache that holds an index of the addresses that are copied into the cache. Each line of cache memory has a corresponding address tag that stores the main memory address of the data currently copied into that particular cache line. If data from a particular main memory address is needed, the cache controller can quickly search the address tags to see whether the requested address is currently being stored in the cache (a hit) or not (a miss). If the data is there, it can be read from the faster cache; if it isn't, it has to be read from the much slower main memory.

Various ways of organizing or mapping the tags affect how cache works. A cache can be mapped as fully associative, direct-mapped, or set associative.

In a fully associative mapped cache, when a request is made for data from a specific main memory address, the address is compared against all the address tag entries in the cache tag RAM. If the requested main memory address is found in the tag (a *hit*), the corresponding location in the cache is returned. If the requested address is not found in the address tag entries, a *miss* occurs and the data must be retrieved from the main memory address instead of the cache.

In a direct-mapped cache, specific main memory addresses are preassigned to specific line locations in the cache where they will be stored. Therefore, the tag RAM can use fewer bits because when you know which main memory address you want, only one address tag needs to be checked and each tag needs to store only the possible addresses a given line can contain. This also results in faster operation because only one tag address needs to be checked for a given memory address.

A set associative cache is a modified direct-mapped cache. A direct-mapped cache has only one set of memory associations, meaning a given memory address can be mapped into (or associated with) only a specific given cache line location. A two-way set associative cache has two sets, so that a given memory location can be in one of two locations. A four-way set associative cache can store a given memory address into four different cache line locations (or sets). By increasing the set associativity, the chance of finding a value increases; however, it takes a little longer because more tag addresses must be checked when searching for a specific location in the cache. In essence, each set in an n-way set associative cache is a subcache that has associations with each main memory address. As the number of subcaches or sets increases, eventually the cache becomes fully associative—a situation in which any memory address can be stored in any cache line location. In that case, an n-way set associative cache is a compromise between a fully associative cache and a direct-mapped cache.

In general, a direct-mapped cache is the fastest at locating and retrieving data from the cache because it has to look at only one specific tag address for a given memory address. However, it also results in more misses overall than the other designs. A fully associative cache offers the highest hit ratio but is the slowest at locating and retrieving the data because it has many more address tags to check through. An n-way set associative cache is a compromise between optimizing cache speed and hit ratio, but the more associativity there is, the more hardware (tag bits, comparator circuits, and so on) is required, making the cache more expensive. Obviously, cache design is a series of tradeoffs, and what works best in one instance might not work best in another. Multitasking environments such as Windows are good examples of environments in which the processor needs to operate on different areas of memory simultaneously and in which an n-way cache can improve performance.

The organization of the cache memory in the 486 and MMX Pentium family is called a *four-way set associative cache*, which means that the cache memory is split into four blocks. Each block also is organized as 128 or 256 lines of 16 bytes each. The following table shows the associativity of various processor L1 and L2 caches.

Processor	L1 Cache Associativity	L2 Cache Associativity
486	Four-way	Not in CPU
Pentium (non-MMX)	Two-way	Not in CPU
Pentium MMX	Four-way	Not in CPU
Pentium Pro/II/III	Four-way	Four-way (off-die)
Pentium III/4	Four-way	Eight-way (on-die)

The contents of the cache must always be in sync with the contents of main memory to ensure that the processor is working with current data. For this reason, the internal cache in the 486 family is a *write-through* cache. Write-through means that when the processor writes information out to the cache, that information is automatically written through to main memory as well.

By comparison, the Pentium and later chips have an internal write-back cache, which means that both reads and writes are cached, further improving performance. Even though the internal 486 cache is write-through, the system can employ an external write-back cache for increased performance. In addition, the 486 can buffer up to 4 bytes before actually storing the data in RAM, improving efficiency in case the memory bus is busy.

Another feature of improved cache designs is that they are nonblocking. This is a technique for reducing or hiding memory delays by exploiting the overlap of processor operations with data accesses. A *nonblocking* cache enables program execution to proceed concurrently with cache misses as long as certain dependency constraints are observed. In other words, the cache can handle a cache miss much better and enable the processor to continue doing something nondependent on the missing data.

The cache controller built into the processor also is responsible for watching the memory bus when alternative processors, known as *bus masters*, are in control of the system. This process of watching the bus is referred to as *bus snooping*. If a bus master device writes to an area of memory that also is stored in the processor cache currently, the cache contents and memory no longer agree. The cache controller then marks this data as invalid and reloads the cache during the next memory access, preserving the integrity of the system.

All PC processor designs that support cache memory include a feature known as a translation lookaside buffer (TLB) to improve recovery from cache misses. The TLB is a table inside the processor that stores information about the location of recently accessed memory addresses. The TLB speeds up the translation of virtual addresses to physical memory addresses. To improve TLB performance, several recent processors have increased the number of entries in the TLB, as AMD did when it moved from the Athlon Thunderbird core to the Palomino core. Pentium 4 processors that support HT Technology have a separate instruction TLB (iTLB) for each virtual processor thread.

▶▶ See "Hyper-Threading Technology," p. 79.

As clock speeds increase, cycle time decreases. Newer systems don't use cache on the motherboard any longer because the faster DDR-SDRAM or RDRAM used in modern Pentium 4/Celeron or Athlon systems can keep up with the motherboard speed. Modern processors all integrate the L2 cache into the processor die just like the L1 cache. This enables the L2 to run at full-core speed because it is now a part of the core. Cache speed is always more important than size. The rule is that a smaller but faster cache is always better than a slower but bigger cache. Table 3.16 illustrates the need for and function of L1 (internal) and L2 (external) caches in modern systems.

Table 3.16   CPU Speeds Relative to Cache, RAM, and Motherboard

CPU Type	Pentium	Pentium Pro	Pentium II
CPU speed	233MHz	200MHz	450MHz
L1 cache speed	4.3ns (233MHz)	5.0ns (200MHz)	2.2ns (450MHz)
L1 cache size	16K	32K	32K
L2 cache type	onboard	on-chip	on-chip
L2 speed ratio	2/7	1/1	1/2
L2 cache speed	15ns (66MHz)	5ns (200MHz)	4.4ns (225MHz)
L2 cache size	varies[1]	256KB[2]	512KB
CPU bus speed	66MHz	66MHz	100MHz
Memory bus speed	60ns (16MHz)	60ns (16MHz)	10ns (100MHz)
CPU Type	**AMD K6-2**	**AMD K6-3**	**Pentium III**
CPU speed	550MHz	450MHz	1.4GHz
L1 cache speed	1.8ns (550MHz)	2.2ns (450MHz)	0.71ns (1.4GHz)
L1 cache size	64K	64K	32K
L2 cache type	onboard	on-die	on-die
L2 speed ratio	2/11	1/1	1/1
L2 cache speed	10ns (100MHz)	2.2ns (450MHz)	0.71ns (1.4GHz)
L2 cache size	varies[1]	256KB	512KB
CPU bus speed	100MHz	100MHz	133MHz
Memory bus speed	10ns (100MHz)	10ns (100MHz)	7.5ns (133MHz)

Table 3.16   Continued

CPU Type	Athlon XP	Athlon 64	Pentium 4
CPU speed	2.2GHz	2.4GHz	4.0GHz
L1 cache speed	0.45ns (2.2GHz)	0.42ns (2.4GHz)	0.25ns (4.0GHz)
L1 cache size	128K	128K	28K
L2 cache type	on-die	on-die	on-die
L2 speed ratio	1/1	1/1	1/1
L2 cache speed	0.45ns (2.2GHz)	0.42ns (2.4GHz)	0.25ns (4.0GHz)
L2 cache size	512KB	1024KB	1024KB
CPU bus speed	400MHz	400MHz	800MHz
Memory bus speed	2.5ns (400MHz)	2.5ns (400MHz)	2.5ns (400MHz)[3]

1. *The L2 cache is on the motherboard, and the amount depends on which board is chosen and how much is installed.*

2. *The Pentium Pro was also available with 512KB and 1024KB L2 cache.*

3. *Dual-channel memory uses two banks simultaneously, doubling the throughput.*

As you can see, having two levels of cache between the very fast CPU and the much slower main memory helps minimize any wait states the processor might have to endure, especially those with the on-die L2. This enables the processor to keep working closer to its true speed.

Processor Features

As new processors are introduced, new features are continually added to their architectures to help improve everything from performance in specific types of applications to the reliability of the CPU as a whole. The next few sections take a look at some of these technologies, including System Management Mode (SMM), Superscalar Execution, MMX, SSE, 3DNow!, and HT Technology.

SMM (Power Management)

Spurred on primarily by the goal of putting faster and more powerful processors in laptop computers, Intel has created power-management circuitry. This circuitry enables processors to conserve energy use and lengthen battery life. This was introduced initially in the Intel 486SL processor, which is an enhanced version of the 486DX processor. Subsequently, the power-management features were universalized and incorporated into all 75MHz and faster Pentium and later processors. This feature set is called SMM, which stands for *system management mode*.

SMM circuitry is integrated into the physical chip but operates independently to control the processor's power use based on its activity level. It enables the user to specify time intervals after which the CPU will be partially or fully powered down. It also supports the Suspend/Resume feature that allows for instant power on and power off, used mostly with laptop PCs. These settings are typically controlled via system BIOS settings.

Superscalar Execution

The fifth-generation Pentium and newer processors feature multiple internal instruction execution pipelines, which enable them to execute multiple instructions at the same time. The 486 and all preceding chips can perform only a single instruction at a time. Intel calls the capability to execute more than one instruction at a time *superscalar* technology. This technology provides additional performance compared with the 486.

▶▶   See "Pentium Processors," p. 125.

Superscalar architecture usually is associated with high-output Reduced Instruction Set Computer (RISC) chips. A RISC chip has a less complicated instruction set with fewer and simpler instructions. Although each instruction accomplishes less, overall the clock speed can be higher, which can usually increase performance. The Pentium is one of the first Complex Instruction Set Computer (CISC) chips to be considered superscalar. A CISC chip uses a richer, fuller-featured instruction set, which has more complicated instructions. As an example, say you wanted to instruct a robot to screw in a light bulb. Using CISC instructions, you would say

1. Pick up the bulb.
2. Insert it into the socket.
3. Rotate clockwise until tight.

Using RISC instructions, you would say something more along the lines of

1. Lower hand.
2. Grasp bulb.
3. Raise hand.
4. Insert bulb into socket.
5. Rotate clockwise one turn.
6. Is bulb tight? If not, repeat step 5.
7. End.

Overall, many more RISC instructions are required to do the job because each instruction is simpler (reduced) and does less. The advantage is that there are fewer overall commands the robot (or processor) has to deal with and it can execute the individual commands more quickly, and thus in many cases execute the complete task (or program) more quickly as well. The debate goes on whether RISC or CISC is really better, but in reality there is no such thing as a pure RISC or CISC chip—it is all just a matter of definition, and the lines are somewhat arbitrary.

Intel and compatible processors have generally been regarded as CISC chips, although the fifth- and sixth-generation versions have many RISC attributes and internally break CISC instructions down into RISC versions.

MMX Technology

MMX technology was originally named for multimedia extensions, or matrix math extensions, depending on whom you ask. Intel officially states that it is actually not an abbreviation and stands for nothing other than the letters MMX (not being an abbreviation was apparently required so that the letters could be trademarked); however, the internal origins are probably one of the preceding. MMX technology was introduced in the later fifth-generation Pentium processors as a kind of add-on that improves video compression/decompression, image manipulation, encryption, and I/O processing—all of which are used in a variety of today's software.

MMX consists of two main processor architectural improvements. The first is very basic; all MMX chips have a larger internal L1 cache than their non-MMX counterparts. This improves the performance of any and all software running on the chip, regardless of whether it actually uses the MMX-specific instructions.

The other part of MMX is that it extends the processor instruction set with 57 new commands or instructions, as well as a new instruction capability called single instruction, multiple data (SIMD).

Modern multimedia and communication applications often use repetitive loops that, while occupying 10% or less of the overall application code, can account for up to 90% of the execution time. SIMD enables one instruction to perform the same function on multiple pieces of data, similar to a teacher telling an entire class to "sit down," rather than addressing each student one at a time. SIMD enables the chip to reduce processor-intensive loops common with video, audio, graphics, and animation.

Intel also added 57 new instructions specifically designed to manipulate and process video, audio, and graphical data more efficiently. These instructions are oriented to the *highly parallel* and often repetitive sequences frequently found in multimedia operations. *Highly parallel* refers to the fact that the same processing is done on many data points, such as when modifying a graphic image. The main drawbacks to MMX were that it worked only on integer values and used the floating-point unit for processing, so time was lost when a shift to floating-point operations was necessary. These drawbacks were corrected in the additions to MMX from Intel and AMD.

Intel licensed the MMX capabilities to competitors such as AMD and Cyrix, who were then able to upgrade their own Intel-compatible processors with MMX technology.

SSE, SSE2, and SSE3

In February 1999, Intel introduced the Pentium III processor and included in that processor an update to MMX called Streaming SIMD Extensions (SSE). These were also called Katmai New Instructions (KNI) up until their debut because they were originally included on the Katmai processor, which was the codename for the Pentium III. The Celeron 533A and faster Celeron processors based on the Pentium III core also support SSE instructions. The earlier Pentium II and Celeron 533 and lower (based on the Pentium II core) do not support SSE.

SSE includes 70 new instructions for graphics and sound processing over what MMX provided. SSE is similar to MMX; in fact, besides being called KNI, SSE was also called MMX-2 by some before it was released. In addition to adding more MMX style instructions, the SSE instructions allow for floating-point calculations and now use a separate unit within the processor instead of sharing the standard floating-point unit as MMX did.

SSE2 was introduced in November 2000, along with the Pentium 4 processor, and adds 144 additional SIMD instructions. SSE2 also includes all the previous MMX and SSE instructions.

SSE3 was introduced in February 2004, along with the Pentium 4 Prescott processor, and adds 13 new SIMD instructions to improve complex math, graphics, video encoding, and thread synchronization. SSE3 also includes all the previous MMX, SSE, and SSE2 instructions.

The Streaming SIMD Extensions consist of new instructions, including SIMD floating-point, additional SIMD integer, and cacheability control instructions. Some of the technologies that benefit from the Streaming SIMD Extensions include advanced imaging, 3D video, streaming audio and video (DVD playback), and speech-recognition applications. The benefits of SSE include the following:

- Higher resolution and higher quality image viewing and manipulation for graphics software
- High-quality audio, MPEG2 video, and simultaneous MPEG2 encoding and decoding for multimedia applications
- Reduced CPU utilization for speech recognition, as well as higher accuracy and faster response times when running speech-recognition software

The SSEx instructions are particularly useful with MPEG2 decoding, which is the standard scheme used on DVD video discs. SSE-equipped processors should therefore be more capable of performing MPEG2 decoding in software at full speed without requiring an additional hardware MPEG2 decoder card. SSE-equipped processors are much better and faster than previous processors when it comes to speech recognition, as well.

One of the main benefits of SSE over plain MMX is that it supports single-precision floating-point SIMD operations, which have posed a bottleneck in the 3D graphics processing. Just as with plain MMX, SIMD enables multiple operations to be performed per processor instruction. Specifically, SSE supports up to four floating-point operations per cycle; that is, a single instruction can operate on four pieces of data simultaneously. SSE floating-point instructions can be mixed with MMX instructions with no performance penalties. SSE also supports data *prefetching*, which is a mechanism for reading data into the cache before it is actually called for.

Note that for any of the SSE instructions to be beneficial, they must be encoded in the software you are using, so SSE-aware applications must be used to see the benefits. Most software companies writing graphics- and sound-related software today have updated those applications to be SSE aware and use the features of SSE. For example, high-powered graphics applications such as Adobe Photoshop support SSE instructions for higher performance on processors equipped with SSE. Microsoft includes support for SSE in its DirectX 6.1 and later video and sound drivers, which are included with Windows 98 Second Edition, Windows Me, Windows NT 4.0 (with service pack 5 or later), Windows 2000, and Windows XP.

SSE is an extension to MMX; SSE2 is an extension to SSE; and SSE3 is an extension to SSE2. Therefore, processors that support SSE3 also support the SSE2 instructions, processors that support SSE2 also support SSE, and processors that support SSE also support the original MMX instructions. This means that standard MMX-enabled applications run as they did on MMX-only processors.

3DNow!, Enhanced 3DNow!, and Professional 3DNow!

3DNow! technology was originally introduced as AMD's alternative to the SSE instructions in the Intel processors. Actually, 3DNow! was first introduced in the K6 series before Intel released SSE in the Pentium III, and then AMD added Enhanced 3DNow! to the Athlon and Duron processors. The latest version, Professional 3DNow!, was introduced in the first Athlon XP processors. AMD licensed MMX from Intel, and all its K6 series, Athlon, Duron, and later processors include full MMX instruction support. Not wanting to additionally license the SSE instructions being developed by Intel, AMD first came up with a different set of extensions beyond MMX called 3DNow!. Introduced in May 1998 in the K6-2 processor and enhanced when the Athlon was introduced in June 1999, 3DNow!, and Enhanced 3DNow! are sets of instructions that extend the multimedia capabilities of the AMD chips beyond MMX. This enables greater performance for 3D graphics, multimedia, and other floating-point-intensive PC applications.

3DNow! technology is a set of 21 instructions that uses SIMD techniques to operate on arrays of data rather than single elements. Enhanced 3DNow! adds 24 more instructions (19 SSE and 5 DSP/communications instructions) to the original 21 for a total of 45 new instructions. Positioned as an extension to MMX technology, 3DNow! is similar to the SSE found in the Pentium III and Celeron processors from Intel. According to AMD, 3DNow! provides approximately the same level of improvement to MMX as did SSE, but in fewer instructions with less complexity. Although similar in capability, they are not compatible at the instruction level, so software specifically written to support SSE does not support 3DNow!, and vice versa. The latest version of 3DNow!, 3DNow! Professional, adds 51 SSE commands to 3DNow! Enhanced, meaning that 3DNow! Professional now supports all SSE commands, meaning that AMD chips now essentially have SSE capability. Unfortunately, AMD includes SSE2 only on the Athlon 64, Athlon 64FX, and Opteron 64-bit processors.

Just as with SSE, 3DNow! also supports single precision floating-point SIMD operations and enables up to four floating-point operations per cycle. 3DNow! floating-point instructions can be mixed with MMX instructions with no performance penalties. 3DNow! also supports data prefetching.

Also like SSE, 3DNow! is well supported by software, including Windows 9x, Windows NT 4.0, and all newer Microsoft operating systems. 3DNow!-specific support is no longer a big issue if you are using an Athlon XP or Athlon 64 processor because they now fully support SSE through their support of 3DNow! Professional.

Dynamic Execution

First used in the P6 or sixth-generation processors, dynamic execution enables the processor to execute more instructions on parallel, so tasks are completed more quickly. This technology innovation is comprised of three main elements:

■ *Multiple branch prediction.* Predicts the flow of the program through several branches

■ *Dataflow analysis.* Schedules instructions to be executed when ready, independent of their order in the original program

■ *Speculative execution.* Increases the rate of execution by looking ahead of the program counter and executing instructions that are likely to be necessary

Branch Prediction

Branch prediction is a feature formerly found only in high-end mainframe processors. It enables the processor to keep the instruction pipeline full while running at a high rate of speed. A special fetch/decode unit in the processor uses a highly optimized branch prediction algorithm to predict the direction and outcome of the instructions being executed through multiple levels of branches, calls, and returns. It is similar to a chess player working out multiple strategies in advance of game play by predicting the opponent's strategy several moves into the future. By predicting the instruction outcome in advance, the instructions can be executed with no waiting.

Dataflow Analysis

Dataflow analysis studies the flow of data through the processor to detect any opportunities for out-of-order instruction execution. A special dispatch/execute unit in the processor monitors many instructions and can execute these instructions in an order that optimizes the use of the multiple superscalar execution units. The resulting out-of-order execution of instructions can keep the execution units busy even when cache misses and other data-dependent instructions might otherwise hold things up.

Speculative Execution

Speculative execution is the processor's capability to execute instructions in advance of the actual program counter. The processor's dispatch/execute unit uses dataflow analysis to execute all available instructions in the instruction pool and store the results in temporary registers. A retirement unit then searches the instruction pool for completed instructions that are no longer data dependent on other instructions to run or which have unresolved branch predictions. If any such completed instructions are found, the results are committed to memory by the retirement unit or the appropriate standard Intel architecture in the order they were originally issued. They are then retired from the pool.

Dynamic execution essentially removes the constraint and dependency on linear instruction sequencing. By promoting out-of-order instruction execution, it can keep the instruction units working rather than waiting for data from memory. Even though instructions can be predicted and executed out of order, the results are committed in the original order so as not to disrupt or change program flow. This enables the P6 to run existing Intel architecture software exactly as the P5 (Pentium) and previous processors did—just a whole lot more quickly!

Dual Independent Bus Architecture

The Dual Independent Bus (DIB) architecture was first implemented in the sixth-generation processors from Intel and AMD. DIB was created to improve processor bus bandwidth and performance. Having two (dual) independent data I/O buses enables the processor to access data from either of its buses simultaneously and in parallel, rather than in a singular sequential manner (as in a single-bus system). The main (often called front-side) processor bus is the interface between the processor and the motherboard or chipset. The second (back-side) bus in a processor with DIB is used for the L2 cache, enabling it to run at much greater speeds than if it were to share the main processor bus.

Two buses make up the DIB architecture: the L2 cache bus and the main CPU bus, often called FSB (front-side bus). The P6 class processors from the Pentium Pro to the Celeron, Pentium II/III/4, and Athlon/Duron processors can use both buses simultaneously, eliminating a bottleneck there. The dual bus architecture enables the L2 cache of the newer processors to run at full speed inside the processor core on an independent bus, leaving the main CPU bus (FSB) to handle normal data flowing in and out of the chip. The two buses run at different speeds. The front-side bus or main CPU bus is coupled to the speed of the motherboard, whereas the back-side or L2 cache bus is coupled to the speed of the processor core. As the frequency of processors increases, so does the speed of the L2 cache.

The key to implementing DIB was to move the L2 cache memory off the motherboard and into the processor package. L1 cache always has been a direct part of the processor die, but L2 was larger and originally had to be external. By moving the L2 cache into the processor, the L2 cache could run at speeds more like the L1 cache, much faster than the motherboard or processor bus.

DIB also enables the system bus to perform multiple simultaneous transactions (instead of singular sequential transactions), accelerating the flow of information within the system and boosting performance. Overall, DIB architecture offers up to three times the bandwidth performance over a single-bus architecture processor.

Hyper-Threading Technology

Computers with two or more physical processors have long had a performance advantage over single-processor computers when the operating system supported multiple processors, as is the case with Windows NT 4.0, 2000, XP Professional, and Linux. However, dual-processor motherboards and systems have always been more expensive than otherwise-comparable single processor systems, and upgrading a dual-processor-capable system to dual-processor status can be difficult with only one processor because of the need to match processor speeds and specifications. However, Intel's new Hyper-Threading (HT) Technology allows a single processor to handle two independent sets of instructions at the same time. In essence, HT Technology converts a single physical processor into two virtual processors.

Intel originally introduced HT Technology in its line of Xeon processors for servers in March 2002. HT Technology enables multiprocessor servers to act as if they had twice as many processors installed. HT Technology was introduced on Xeon workstation-class processors with a 533MHz system bus and later found its way into PC processors, with the Pentium 4 3.06GHz processor in November 2002. HT Technology is also present in all Pentium 4 processors with 800MHz CPU bus speed (2.4GHz up through 3.4GHz).

How Hyper-Threading Works

Internally, an HT-enabled processor has two sets of general-purpose registers, control registers, and other architecture components, but both logical processors share the same cache, execution units, and buses. During operations, each logical processor handles a single thread (see Figure 3.2).

Although the sharing of some processor components means that the overall speed of an HT-enabled system isn't as high as a true dual-processor system would be, speed increases of 25% or more are possible when multiple applications or a single multithreaded application is being run.

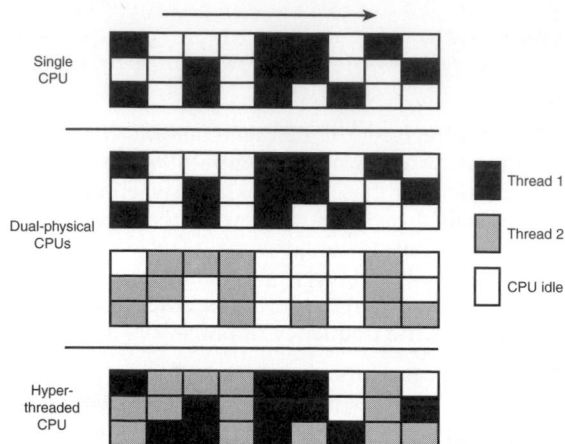

Figure 3.2   A processor with HT Technology enabled can fill otherwise-idle time with a second process, improving multitasking and performance of multithreading single applications.

Hyper-Threading Requirements

The first HT-enabled processor is the Intel Pentium 4 3.06GHz. All 3.06GHz and faster Pentium 4 models support HT Technology, as do all processors 2.4GHz and faster that use the 800MHz bus. However, an HT-enabled P4 processor by itself can't bring the benefits of HT Technology to your system. You also need the following:

- *A compatible motherboard (chipset).* It might need a BIOS upgrade.

- *BIOS support to enable/disable HT Technology.* If your operating system doesn't support HT Technology, you should disable this feature.

- *A compatible operating system such as Windows XP Home or Professional Editions.* When hyper-threading is enabled on these operating systems, the Device Manager shows two processors.

Intel's newer chipsets for the Pentium 4 support HT Technology; see the listing in Chapter 4 for details. However, if your motherboard or computer was released before HT Technology was introduced, you will need a BIOS upgrade from the motherboard or system vendor to be able to use HT Technology. Although Windows NT 4.0 and Windows 2000 are designed to use multiple physical processors, HT Technology requires specific operating system optimizations to work correctly. Linux distributions based on kernel 2.4.18 and higher also support HT Technology.

Processor Manufacturing

Processors are manufactured primarily from silicon, the second most common element on the planet (only the element oxygen is more common). Silicon is the primary ingredient in beach sand; however, in that form it isn't pure enough to be used in chips.

The manner in which silicon is formed into chips is a lengthy process that starts by growing pure silicon crystals via what is called the Czochralski method (named after the inventor of the process). In this method, electric arc furnaces transform the raw materials (primarily quartz rock that is mined) into metallurgical-grade silicon. Then to further weed out impurities, the silicon is converted to a liquid, distilled, and then redeposited in the form of semiconductor-grade rods, which are 99.999999% pure. These rods are then mechanically broken up into chunks and packed into quartz crucibles, which are loaded into electric crystal pulling ovens. There the silicon chunks are melted at more than 2,500° Fahrenheit. To prevent impurities, the ovens usually are mounted on very thick concrete cubes—often on a suspension to prevent any vibration, which would damage the crystal as it forms.

After the silicon is melted, a small seed crystal is inserted into the molten silicon and slowly rotated (see Figure 3.3). As the seed is pulled out of the molten silicon, some of the silicon sticks to the seed and hardens in the same crystal structure as the seed. By carefully controlling the pulling speed (10–40 millimeters per hour) and temperature (approximately 2,500°F), the crystal grows with a narrow neck that then widens into the full desired diameter. Depending on the chips being made, each ingot is 200mm (approximately 8") or 300mm (12") in diameter and more than 5 feet long, weighing hundreds of pounds.

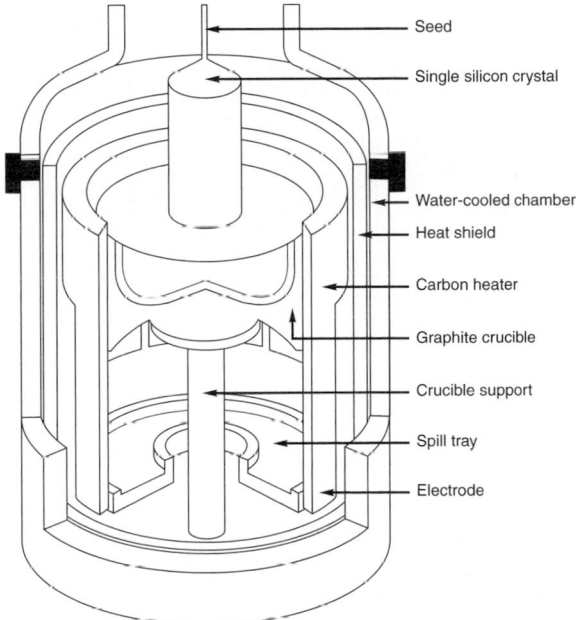

Seed

Single silicon crystal

Water-cooled chamber

Heat shield

Carbon heater

Graphite crucible

Crucible support

Spill tray

Electrode

Figure 3.3   Growing a pure silicon ingot in a high-pressure, high-temperature oven.

The ingot is then ground into a perfect 200mm- (8") or 300mm-diameter (12") cylinder, with a small, flat cut on one side for positioning accuracy and handling. Each ingot is then cut with a high-precision diamond saw into more than a thousand circular wafers, each less than a millimeter thick (see Figure 3.4). Each wafer is then polished to a mirror-smooth surface.

Chips are manufactured from the wafers using a process called *photolithography*. Through this photographic process, transistors and circuit and signal pathways are created in semiconductors by depositing different layers of various materials on the chip, one after the other. Where two specific circuits intersect, a transistor or switch can be formed.

The photolithographic process starts when an insulating layer of silicon dioxide is grown on the wafer through a vapor deposition process. Then a coating of photoresist material is applied, and an image of that layer of the chip is projected through a mask onto the now light-sensitive surface.

Doping is the term used to describe chemical impurities added to silicon (which is naturally a nonconductor), creating a material with semiconductor properties. The projector uses a specially created mask, which is essentially a negative of that layer of the chip etched in chrome on a quartz plate. Modern processors have 20 or more layers of material deposited and partially etched away (each requiring a mask) and up to six or more layers of metal interconnects.

As the light passes through a mask, the light is focused on the wafer surface, exposing the photoresist with the image of that layer of the chip. Each individual chip image is called a *die*. A device called a *stepper* then moves the wafer over a little bit, and the same mask is used to imprint another chip die immediately next to the previous one. After the entire wafer is imprinted with a layer of material and photoresist, a caustic solution washes away the areas where the light struck the photoresist, leaving the mask imprints of the individual chip circuit elements and pathways. Then, another layer of semiconductor material is deposited on the wafer with more photoresist on top, and the next mask is used to expose and then etch the next layer of circuitry. Using this method, the layers and components of each chip are built one on top of the other until the chips are completed.

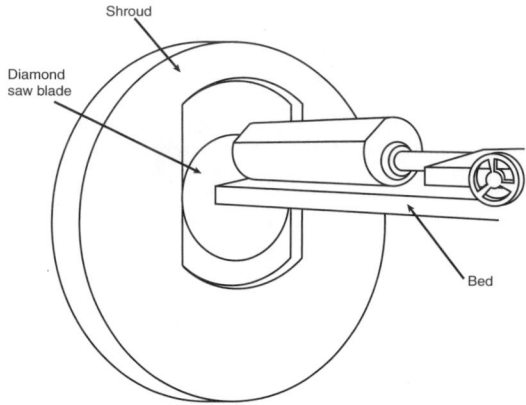

Figure 3.4   Slicing a silicon ingot into wafers with a diamond saw.

Some of the masks are used to add the *metallization* layers, which are the metal interconnects used to tie all the individual transistors and other components together. Most chips use aluminum interconnects, although during 2002 many moved to copper. The first commercial PC processor chip to use copper was the 0.18-micron Athlon made in AMD's Dresden fab, and Intel has shifted the Pentium 4 to copper with the 0.13-micron Northwood version (see Figure 3.5). Copper is a better conductor than aluminum and allows smaller interconnects with less resistance, meaning smaller and faster chips can be made. The reason copper hadn't been used until recently is that there were difficult corrosion problems to overcome during the manufacturing process that were not as much of a problem with aluminum. Now that these problems have been solved, more and more chips will be fabricated with copper interconnects.

Note

The Pentium III and Celeron chips with the "coppermine" (codename for the 0.18-micron die used in those chips) die used aluminum and not copper metal interconnects as many people assume. In fact, the chip name had nothing to do with metal; the codename instead came from the Coppermine River in the Northwest Territory of Canada. Intel has long had a fondness for using codenames based on rivers (and sometimes, other geological features), especially those in the northwest region of the North American continent. For example, an older version of the Pentium III (0.25-micron die) was codenamed Katmai, after an Alaskan river. Intel codenames read like the travel itinerary of a whitewater rafting enthusiast: Deerfield, Foster, Northwood, Tualatin, Gallatin, McKinley, and Madison are all rivers in Oregon, California, Alaska, Montana, and—in the case of Deerfield—Massachusetts and Vermont.

A completed circular wafer has as many chips imprinted on it as can possibly fit. Because each chip usually is square or rectangular, there are some unused portions at the edges of the wafer, but every attempt is made to use every square millimeter of surface.

The industry is going through several transitions in chip manufacturing. The trend in the industry is to use both larger wafers and a smaller chip die process. *Process* refers to the size and spacing of the individual circuits and transistors on the chip. In late 2001 and into 2002, chip manufacturing processes began moving from the 0.18-micron to the 0.13-micron process, the metal interconnects on the die began moving from aluminum to copper, and wafers began moving from 200mm (8") to 300mm (12") in diameter. The larger 300mm wafers alone enable more than double the number of chips to be made, compared to the 200mm used previously. The smaller 0.13-micron process enables more transistors to be incorporated into the die while maintaining a reasonable die size and allowing for a sufficient yield. This means the trend for incorporating more and more cache within the die will continue, and transistor counts will rise to 1 billion per chip or more by 2010.

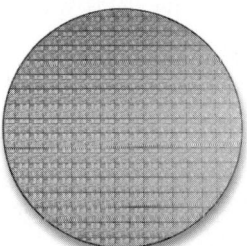

Figure 3.5   200mm wafer of the 0.13-micron Pentium 4 processors.

As an example of how this can affect a particular chip, let's look at the Pentium 4. The standard wafer size used in the industry for many years was 200mm in diameter, or just under 8". This results in a wafer of about 31,416 square millimeters in area. The first version of the Pentium 4 with the Willamette core used a 0.18-micron process with aluminum interconnects on a die that was 217 square millimeters in area, had 42 million transistors, and was made on 200mm wafers. Therefore, up to 145 of these chips could fit on a 200mm (8") wafer.

The newer Pentium 4 processors with the Northwood core use a smaller 0.13-micron process with copper interconnects on a die that is 131 square millimeters in area with 55 million transistors. Northwood has double the on-die L2 cache (512KB) as compared to Willamette, which is why the transistor count is significantly higher. Even with the higher transistor count, the smaller 0.13-micron process results in a die that is more than 60% smaller, allowing up to 240 chips to fit on the same 200mm (8") wafer that could hold only 145 Willamette die.

Starting in early 2002, Intel began producing Northwood on the larger 300mm wafers, which have a sur-face area of 70,686 square millimeters. These wafers have 2.25 times the surface area of the smaller 200mm wafers, enabling more than double the number of chips to be produced per wafer. In the case of the Pentium 4 Northwood, up to 540 chip dies fit on a 300mm wafer. By combining the smaller die with the larger wafer, Pentium 4 production has increased by more than 3.7 times since the chip was first introduced. This is one reason newer chips are often more plentiful and less expensive than older ones.

In 2004, the industry began moving to the 90-nanometer (0.09-micron) process, allowing even smaller and faster chips to be made. In 2007, we'll see a move toward a 65-nanometer process, and we'll see a 45-nanometer process in 2010. These advancements in process will allow 1 billion transistors per chip in 2010! All these will still be made on 300mm wafers because the next wafer transition isn't expected until 2013, when a transition to 450mm wafers is being considered. Table 3.17 lists the CPU process transitions.

Table 3.17   Past, Current, and Future CPU Process Transitions

Date:	1989	1991	1993	1995	1997	1999	2001	2004	2007	2010	2013	2016
Process (micron):	1.0	0.8	0.5	0.35	0.25	0.18	0.13	0.09	0.065	0.045	0.032	0.022
Process (nm):	1000	800	500	350	250	180	130	90	65	45	32	22

Note that not all the chips on each wafer will be good, especially as a new production line starts. As the manufacturing process for a given chip or production line is perfected, more and more of the chips will be good. The ratio of good to bad chips on a wafer is called the *yield*. Yields well under 50% are common when a new chip starts production; however, by the end of a given chip's life, the yields are normally in the 90% range. Most chip manufacturers guard their yield figures and are very secretive about them because knowledge of yield problems can give their competitors an edge. A low yield causes problems both in the cost per chip and in delivery delays to their customers. If a company has specific knowledge of competitors' improving yields, it can set prices or schedule production to get higher market share at a critical point.

After a wafer is complete, a special fixture tests each of the chips on the wafer and marks the bad ones to be separated out later. The chips are then cut from the wafer using either a high-powered laser or diamond saw.

After being cut from the wafers, the individual dies are then retested, packaged, and retested again. The packaging process is also referred to as *bonding* because the die is placed into a chip housing in which a special machine bonds fine gold wires between the die and the pins on the chip. The package is the container for the chip die, and it essentially seals it from the environment.

After the chips are bonded and packaged, final testing is done to determine both proper function and rated speed. Different chips in the same batch often run at different speeds. Special test fixtures run each chip at different pressures, temperatures, and speeds, looking for the point at which the chip stops working. At this point, the maximum successful speed is noted and the final chips are sorted into bins with those that tested at a similar speed. For example, the Pentium 4 2.0A, 2.2, 2.26, 2.4, and 2.53GHz are all exactly the same chip made using the same die. They were sorted at the end of the manufacturing cycle by speed.

One interesting thing about this is that as a manufacturer gains more experience and perfects a particular chip assembly line, the yield of the higher-speed versions goes way up. So, of all the chips produced from a single wafer, perhaps more than 75% of them check out at the highest speed and only 25% or less run at the lower speeds. The paradox is that Intel often sells a lot more of the lower-priced, lower-speed chips, so it just dips into the bin of faster ones, labels them as slower chips, and sells them that way. People began discovering that many of the lower-rated chips actually ran at speeds much higher than they were rated, and the business of overclocking was born.

Processor Re-marking

An interesting problem then arose: Unscrupulous vendors began re-marking slower chips and reselling them as if they were faster. Often the price between the same chip at different speed grades can be substantial—in the hundreds of dollars—so by changing a few numbers on the chip, the potential profits can be huge. Because most of the Intel and AMD processors are produced with a generous safety margin—that is, they typically run well past their rated speeds—the re-marked chips would seem to work fine in most cases. Of course, in many cases they wouldn't work fine, and the system would end up crashing or locking up periodically.

At first, the re-marked chips were just a case of rubbing off the original numbers and restamping with new official-looking numbers. These were easy to detect, though. Re-markers then resorted to manufacturing completely new processor housings, especially for the plastic-encased Slot 1 and Slot A processors from Intel and AMD. Although it might seem to be a huge bother to make a custom plastic case and swap it with the existing case, because the profits can be huge, criminals find it very lucrative. This type of re-marking is a form of organized crime and isn't just some kid in his basement with sandpaper and a rubber stamp.

Intel and AMD have seen fit to put a stop to some of the re-marking by building overclock protection in the form of a multiplier lock into most of their newer chips. This is usually done in the bonding or cartridge manufacturing process, where the chips are intentionally altered so they won't run at any speeds higher than they are rated. Usually this involves changing the bus frequency (BF) pins or traces on the chip, which control the internal multipliers the chip uses. Even so, enterprising individuals have found ways to run their motherboards at bus speeds higher than normal, so even though the chip won't allow a higher multiplier, you can still run it at a speed higher than it was designed for.

Be Wary of PII and PIII Slot 1 Overclocking Fraud

If you're still interested in purchasing Slot 1 processors, note that unscrupulous individuals have devised a small logic cir-cuit that bypasses the multiplier lock, enabling the chip to run at higher multipliers. This small circuit can be hidden in the PII or PIII cartridge, and then the chip can be re-marked or relabeled to falsely indicate it is a higher-speed version. This type of chip re-marking fraud is far more common in the industry than people want to believe. In fact, if you purchase your system or processor from a local computer flea market show, you have an excellent chance of getting a re-marked chip. I recommend purchasing processors only from more reputable direct distributors or dealers. You can contact Intel, AMD, or VIA for a list of them.

The real problem with the overclock protection as implemented by Intel and AMD is that the profes-sional counterfeiter has often been able to figure out a way around it by modifying the chip physi-cally. Socketed processors are much more immune to these re-marking attempts, but it is still possible, particularly because the evidence can be hidden under a heatsink. To protect yourself from purchasing a fraudulent chip, verify the specification numbers and serial numbers with Intel and AMD before you purchase. Also beware where you buy your hardware. Purchasing over online auction sites can be extremely dangerous because defrauding the purchaser is so easy. Also, traveling computer show/flea market arenas can be a hotbed of this type of activity. Finally, I recommend purchasing only "boxed" or retail-packaged versions of the Intel and AMD processors, rather than the raw OEM versions. The boxed versions are shrink-wrapped and contain a high-quality heatsink, documentation, and a 3-year warranty with the manufacturer.

Fraudulent computer components are not limited to processors. I have seen fake memory (SIMMs/DIMMs), fake mice, fake video cards, fake SCSI cards, fake cache memory, counterfeit operat-ing systems and applications, and even fake motherboards. The hardware that is faked usually works but is of inferior quality to the type it is purporting to be. For example, one of the most highly coun-terfeited pieces of hardware at one time was the Microsoft mouse. They originally sold for $35 whole-sale, yet I could purchase cheap mice from overseas manufacturers for as little as $2.32 each. It didn't take somebody long to realize that if they made the $2 mouse look like a $35 Microsoft mouse, they could sell it for $20 and people would think they were getting a genuine article for a bargain, while the thieves ran off with a substantial profit.

PGA Chip Packaging

Variations on the pin grid array (PGA) chip packaging have been the most commonly used chip pack-ages over the years. They were used starting with the 286 processor in the 1980s and are still used today for Pentium and Pentium Pro processors. PGA takes its name from the fact that the chip has a grid-like array of pins on the bottom of the package. PGA chips are inserted into sockets, which are often of a zero insertion force (ZIF) design. A ZIF socket has a lever to allow for easy installation and removal of the chip.

Most Pentium processors use a variation on the regular PGA called staggered pin grid array (SPGA), in which the pins are staggered on the underside of the chip rather than in standard rows and columns. This was done to move the pins closer together and decrease the overall size of the chip when a large number of pins is required. Figure 3.6 shows a Pentium Pro that uses the dual-pattern SPGA (on the right) next to an older Pentium 66 that uses the regular PGA. Note that the right half of the Pentium Pro shown here has additional pins staggered among the other rows and columns.

Figure 3.6   PGA on Pentium 66 (left) and dual-pattern SPGA on Pentium Pro (right).

Older PGA variations had the processor die mounted in a cavity underneath the substrate, with the top surface facing up if you turned the chip upside down. The die was then wire-bonded to the chip package with hundreds of tiny gold wires connecting the connections at the edge of the chip with the internal connections in the package. After the wire bonding, the cavity was sealed with a metal cover. This was an expensive and time-consuming method of producing chips, so cheaper and more efficient packaging methods were designed.

Most modern processors are built on a form of flip-chip pin grid array (FC-PGA) packaging. This type still plugs into a PGA socket, but the package itself is dramatically simplified. With FC-PGA, the raw silicon die is mounted face down on the top of the chip substrate, and instead of wire bonding, the connections are made with tiny solder bumps around the perimeter of the die. The edge is then sealed with a fillet of epoxy. With the original versions of FC-PGA, you could see the backside of the raw die sitting on the chip.

Unfortunately, there were some problems with attaching the heatsink to an FC-PGA chip. The heatsink sat on the top of the die, which acted as a pedestal. If you pressed down on one side of the heatsink excessively during the installation process (such as when you were attaching the clip), you risked cracking the silicon die and destroying the chip. This was especially a problem as heatsinks became larger and heavier and the force applied by the clip became greater.

AMD decreased the risk of damage by adding rubber spacers to each corner of the chip substrate, thus preventing the heatsink from tilting excessively during installation. Still, these bumpers could compress, and it was all too easy to crack the die. The Athlon XP currently uses FC-PGA with spacers at each corner of the substrate, and some aftermarket vendors sell specially designed shims that help provide additional protection. The Athlon 64 uses a different heatsink design, which attaches the heatsink to a clip. The clip is then screwed to the motherboard, which helps prevent damage to the processor.

Intel revised its packaging with a newer FC-PGA2 version used in the newer Pentium III and all Pentium 4 processors. This incorporates an integrated protective metal cap called a heat spreader that sits on top of the die, enabling larger and heavier heatsinks to be installed without any potential damage to the processor core. Ironically, the first processor for PCs to use a heat spreader was made by AMD (the K6 family).

Future packaging directions are headed toward what is called BBUL (bumpless build-up layer) packaging. This will embed the die completely in the package; in fact, the package layers will be built up around and on top of the die, fully encapsulating it within the package. This will embed the chip die and allow for a full flat surface for attaching the heatsink, as well as shorter internal interconnections within the package.

Single Edge Contact and Single Edge Processor Packaging

Intel and AMD used cartridge- or board-based packaging for some of their processors from 1997 through 2000. This packaging was called single edge contact cartridge (SECC) or single edge processor package (SEPP) and consisted of the CPU and optional separate L2 cache chips mounted on a circuit board that looked similar to an oversized memory module and that plugged into a slot. In some cases, the boards were covered with a plastic cartridge cover.

The SEC cartridge is an innovative—if a bit unwieldy—package design that incorporates the back-side bus and L2 cache internally. It was used as a cost-effective method for integrating L2 cache into the processor before it was feasible to include the cache directly inside the processor die.

A less expensive version of the SEC is called the single edge processor (SEP) package. The SEP package is basically the same circuit board containing processor and (optional) cache, but without the fancy plastic cover. This was used mainly by the lower-cost early Celeron processors. The SEP package plugs directly into the same Slot 1 connector used by the standard Pentium II or III. Four holes on the board enable the heatsink to be installed.

Slot 1, as shown in Figure 3.7, is the connection to the motherboard and has 242 pins. AMD used the same physical slot but rotated it 180° and called it Slot A. The SEC cartridge or SEP processor is plugged into the slot and secured with a processor-retention mechanism, which is a bracket that holds it in place. There also might be a retention mechanism or support for the processor heatsink. Figure 3.8 shows the parts of the cover that make up the SEC package. Note the large thermal plate used to aid in dissipating the heat from this processor. The SEP package is shown in Figure 3.9.

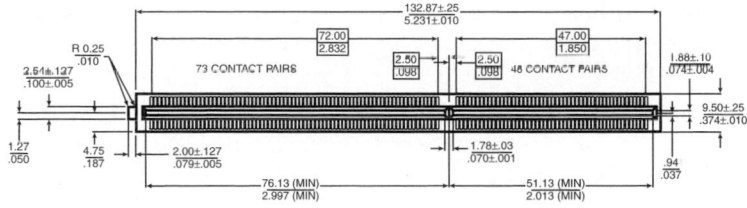

Figure 3.7   Pentium II Processor Slot 1 dimensions (metric/English).

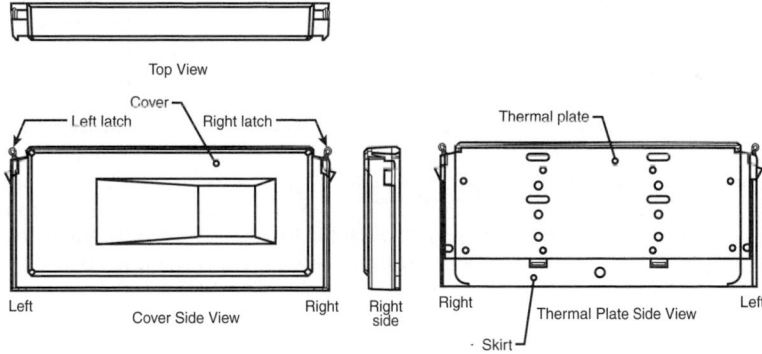

Figure 3.8   Pentium II Processor SEC package parts.

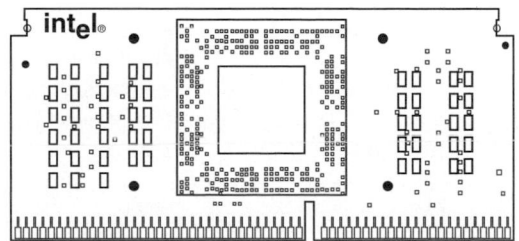

Figure 3.9   Celeron Processor SEP package front-side view.

With the Pentium III, Intel introduced a variation on the SEC packaging called single edge contact cartridge version 2 (SECC2). This new package covered only one side of the processor board with plastic and enables the heatsink to directly attach to the chip on the other side. This more direct thermal interface allowed for better cooling, and the overall lighter package was cheaper to manufacture. A newer Universal Retention System, consisting of a plastic upright stand, was required to hold the SECC2 package chip in place on the board. The Universal Retention System also worked with the older SEC package as used on most Pentium II processors, as well as the SEP package used on the slot-based Celeron processors. This made it the ideal retention mechanism for all Slot 1–based processors. AMD Athlon Slot A processors used the same retention mechanisms as Intel. Figure 3.10 shows the SECC2 package.

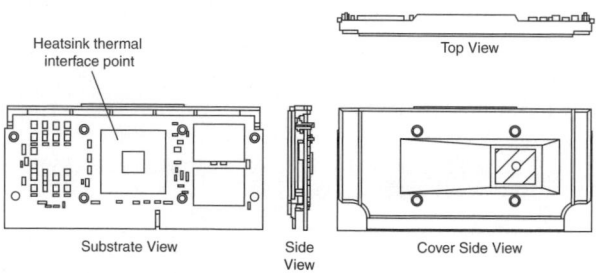

Figure 3.10   SECC2 packaging used in newer Pentium II and III processors.

The main reason for switching to the SEC and SEP packages in the first place was to be able to move the L2 cache memory off the motherboard and onto the processor in an economical and scalable way. This was necessary because, at the time, it was not feasible to incorporate the cache directly into the CPU core die. After building the L2 directly into the CPU die became possible, the cartridge and slot packaging were unnecessary. Because virtually all modern processors incorporate the L2 cache on-die, the processor packaging has gone back to the PGA socket form.

Processor Socket and Slot Types

Intel and AMD have created a set of socket and slot designs for their processors. Each socket or slot is designed to support a different range of original and upgrade processors. Table 3.18 shows the designations for the various 486 and newer processor sockets/slots and lists the chips designed to plug into them.

Table 3.18   CPU Socket and Slot Types and Specifications

Chip Class	Socket	Pins	Layout	Voltage	Supported Processors	Introduced
Intel/AMD 486 class	Socket 1	169	17×17 PGA	5V	486 SX/SX2, DX/DX2, DX4 OD	Apr. '89
	Socket 2	238	19×19 PGA	5V	486 SX/SX2, DX/DX2, DX4 OD, 486 Pentium OD	Mar. '92
	Socket 3	237	19×19 PGA	5V/3.3V	486 SX/SX2, DX/DX2, DX4, 486 Pentium OD, AMD 5x86	Feb. '94
	Socket 6[1]	235	19×19 PGA	3.3V	486 DX4, 486 Pentium OD	Feb. '94
Intel/AMD 586 (Pentium) class	Socket 4	273	21×21 PGA	5V	Pentium 60/66, OD	Mar. '93
	Socket 5	320	37×37 SPGA	3.3V/3.5V	Pentium 75-133, OD	Mar. '94
	Socket 7	321	37×37 SPGA	VRM	Pentium 75-233+, MMX, OD, AMD K5/K6, Cyrix M1/II	June '95

Table 3.18   Continued

Chip Class	Socket	Pins	Layout	Voltage	Supported Processors	Introduced
Intel 686 (Pentium II/III) class	Socket 8	387	Dual-pattern SPGA	Auto VRM	Pentium Pro, OD	Nov. '95
	Slot 1 (SC242)	242	Slot	Auto VRM	Pentium II/III, Celeron SECC	May '97
	Socket 370	370	37¥37 SPGA	Auto VRM	Celeron/Pentium III PPGA/ FC-PGA	Nov. '98
Intel Pentium 4 class	Socket 423	423	39×39 SPGA	Auto VRM	Pentium 4 FC-PGA	Nov. '00
	Socket 478	478	26×26 mPGA	Auto VRM	Pentium 4/Celeron FC-PGA2	Oct. '01
	Socket T (LGA775)	775	30×33 LGA	Auto VRM	Pentium 4/Celeron LGA775	June '04
AMD K7 class	Slot A	242	Slot	Auto VRM	AMD Athlon SECC	June '99
	Socket A (462)	462	37×37 SPGA	Auto VRM	AMD Athlon/Athlon XP/ Duron PGA/FC-PGA	June '00
AMD K8 class	Socket 754	754	29×29 mPGA	Auto VRM	AMD Athlon 64	Sep. '03
	Socket 939	939	31×31 mPGA	Auto VRM	AMD Athlon 64 v.2	June '04
	Socket 940	940	31×31 mPGA	Auto VRM	AMD Athlon 64FX, Opteron	Apr. '03
Intel/AMD server and workstation class	Slot 2 (SC330)	330	Slot	Auto VRM	Pentium II/III Xeon	Apr. '98
	Socket 603	603	31×25 mPGA	Auto VRM	Xeon (P4)	May '01
	Socket 604	604	31×25 mPGA	Auto VRM	Xeon (P4)	Oct. '03
	Socket PAC418	418	38×22	Auto VRM split SPGA	Itanium	May '01
	Socket PAC611	611	25×28	Auto VRM mPGA	Itanium 2	July '02
	Socket 940	940	31×31 mPGA	Auto VRM	AMD Athlon 64FX, Opteron	Apr. '03

1. Socket 6 was never actually implemented in any systems.
FC-PGA = Flip-chip pin grid array
FC-PGA2 = FC-PGA with an Integrated Heat Spreader (IHS)
OD = OverDrive (retail upgrade processors)
PAC = Pin array cartridge
PGA = Pin grid array
PPGA = Plastic pin grid array
SC242 = Slot connector, 242 pins

SC330 = Slot connector, 330 pins
SECC = Single edge contact cartridge
SPGA = Staggered pin grid array
mPGA = Micro pin grid array
VRM = Voltage regulator module with variable voltage output determined by module type or manual jumpers
Auto VRM = Voltage regulator module with automatic voltage selection determined by processor Voltage ID (VID) pins

Sockets 1, 2, 3, and 6 are 486 processor sockets and are shown together in Figure 3.11 so you can see the overall size comparisons and pin arrangements between these sockets. Sockets 4, 5, 7, and 8 are Pentium and Pentium Pro processor sockets and are shown together in Figure 3.12 so you can see the overall size comparisons and pin arrangements between these sockets. More detailed drawings of each socket are included throughout the remainder of this section with thorough descriptions of the sockets.

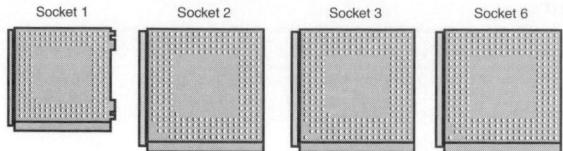

Figure 3.11   486 processor sockets.

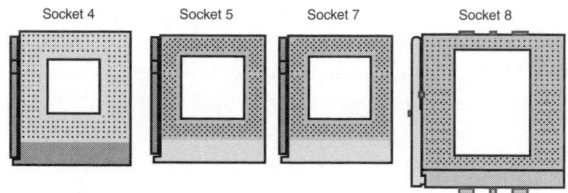

Figure 3.12   Pentium and Pentium Pro processor sockets.

Zero Insertion Force

When the Socket 1 specification was created, manufacturers realized that if users were going to upgrade processors, they had to make the process easier. The socket manufacturers found that 100 lbs. of insertion force is required to install a chip in a standard 169-pin screw Socket 1 motherboard. With this much force involved, you easily could damage either the chip or the socket during removal or reinstallation. Because of this, some motherboard manufacturers began using low insertion force (LIF) sockets, which required only 60 lbs. of insertion force for a 169-pin chip. With the LIF or standard socket, I usually advise removing the motherboard—that way you can support the board from behind when you insert the chip. Pressing down on the motherboard with 60–100 lbs. of force can crack the board if it is not supported properly. A special tool is also required to remove a chip from one of these sockets. As you can imagine, even the low insertion force was relative, and a better solution was needed if the average person was ever going to replace his CPU.

Manufacturers began using ZIF sockets in Socket 1 designs, and all processor sockets from Socket 2 and higher have been of the ZIF design. ZIF is required for all the higher-density sockets because the insertion force would simply be too great otherwise. ZIF sockets almost eliminate the risk involved in installing or removing a processor because no insertion force is necessary to install the chip and no tool is needed to extract one. Most ZIF sockets are handle-actuated: You lift the handle, drop the chip into the socket, and then close the handle. This design makes installing or removing a processor an easy task.

Socket 1

The original OverDrive socket, now officially called Socket 1, is a 169-pin PGA socket. Motherboards that have this socket can support any of the 486SX, DX, and DX2 processors and the DX2/OverDrive versions. This type of socket is found on most 486 systems that originally were designed for OverDrive upgrades. Figure 3.13 shows the pinout of Socket 1.

The original DX processor draws a maximum 0.9 amps of 5V power in 33MHz form (4.5 watts) and a maximum 1 amp in 50MHz form (5 watts). The DX2 processor, or OverDrive processor, draws a maximum 1.2 amps at 66MHz (6 watts). This minor increase in power requires only a passive heatsink consisting of aluminum fins that are glued to the processor with thermal transfer epoxy. Passive heatsinks don't have any mechanical components like fans. Heatsinks with fans or other devices that use power are called *active* heatsinks. OverDrive processors rated at 40MHz or less do not have heatsinks.

Socket 2

When the DX2 processor was released, Intel was already working on the new Pentium processor. The company wanted to offer a 32-bit, scaled-down version of the Pentium as an upgrade for systems that originally came with a DX2 processor. Rather than just increasing the clock rate, Intel created an all-new chip with enhanced capabilities derived from the Pentium.

The chip, called the Pentium OverDrive processor, plugs into a processor socket with the Socket 2 or Socket 3 design. These sockets hold any 486 SX, DX, or DX2 processor, as well as the Pentium OverDrive. Because this chip is essentially a 32-bit version of the (normally 64-bit) Pentium chip, many have taken to calling it a Pentium-SX. It was available in 25/63MHz and 33/83MHz versions. The first number indicates the base motherboard speed; the second number indicates the actual operating speed of the Pentium OverDrive chip. As you can see, it is a clock-multiplied chip that runs at 2.5 times the motherboard speed. Figure 3.14 shows the pinout configuration of the official Socket 2 design.

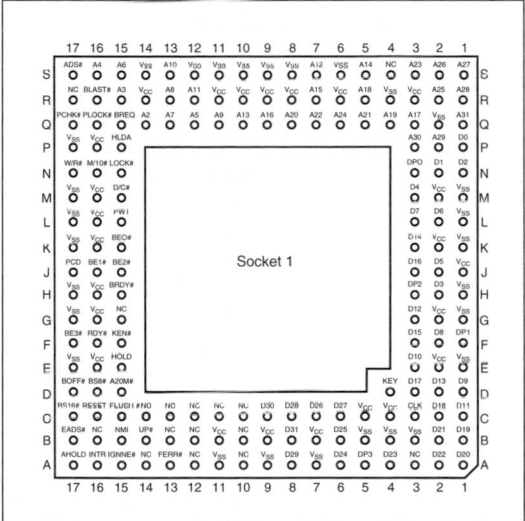

Figure 3.13   Intel Socket 1 pinout.

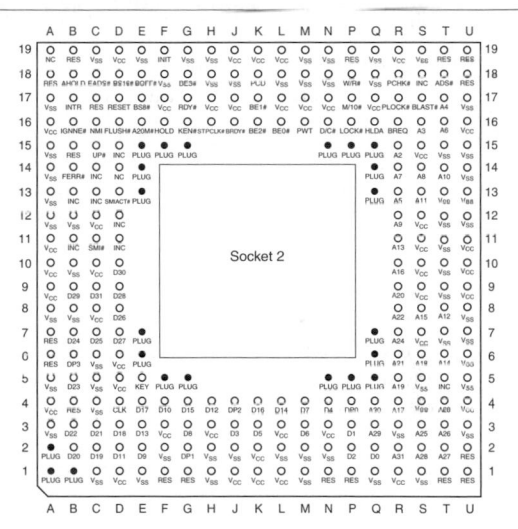

Figure 3.14   238-pin Intel Socket 2 configuration.

Notice that although the new chip for Socket 2 is called Pentium OverDrive, it is not a full-scale (64-bit) Pentium. Intel released the design of Socket 2 a little prematurely and found that the chip ran too hot for many systems. The company solved this problem by adding a special active heatsink to the Pentium OverDrive processor. This active heatsink is a combination of a standard heatsink and a built-in electric fan. Unlike the aftermarket glue-on or clip-on fans for processors that you might have seen, this one actually draws 5V power directly from the socket to drive the fan. No external connection to disk drive cables or the power supply is required. The fan/heatsink assembly clips and plugs directly into the processor and provides for easy replacement if the fan fails.

Another requirement of the active heatsink is additional clearance—no obstructions for an area about 1.4" off the base of the existing socket to allow for heatsink clearance. The Pentium OverDrive upgrade is difficult or impossible in systems that were not designed with this feature.

Another problem with this particular upgrade is power consumption. The 5V Pentium OverDrive processor draws up to 2.5 amps at 5V (including the fan) or 12.5 watts, which is more than double the 1.2 amps (6 watts) drawn by the DX2 66 processor.

Socket 3

Because of problems with the original Socket 2 specification and the enormous heat the 5V version of the Pentium OverDrive processor generates, Intel came up with an improved design. The new processor is the same as the previous Pentium OverDrive processor, except that it runs on 3.3V and draws a maximum 3.0 amps of 3.3V (9.9 watts) and 0.2 amp of 5V (1 watt) to run the fan—a total of 10.9 watts. This configuration provides a slight margin over the 5V version of this processor. The fan is easy to remove from the OverDrive processor for replacement, should it ever fail.

Intel had to create a new socket to support both the DX4 processor, which runs on 3.3V, and the 3.3V Pentium OverDrive processor. In addition to the new 3.3V chips, this new socket supports the older 5V SX, DX, DX2, and even the 5V Pentium OverDrive chip. The design, called Socket 3, is the most flexible upgradeable 486 design. Figure 3.15 shows the pinout specification of Socket 3.

Notice that Socket 3 has one additional pin and several others plugged in compared with Socket 2. Socket 3 provides for better keying, which prevents an end user from accidentally installing the processor in an improper orientation. However, one serious problem exists: This socket can't automatically determine the type of voltage that is provided to it. You will likely find a jumper on the motherboard near the socket to enable selecting 5V or 3.3V operation.

Caution

Because this jumper must be manually set, a user could install a 3.3V processor in this socket when it is configured for 5V operation. This installation instantly destroys the chip when the system is powered on. So, it is up to the end user to ensure that this socket is properly configured for voltage, depending on which type of processor is installed. If the jumper is set in 3.3V configuration and a 5V processor is installed, no harm will occur, but the system will not operate properly unless the jumper is reset for 5V.

Socket 4

Socket 4 is a 273-pin socket designed for the original Pentium processors. The original Pentium 60MHz and 66MHz version processors had 273 pins and plugged into Socket 4. It is a 5V-only socket because all the original Pentium processors run on 5V. This socket accepts the original Pentium 60MHz or 66MHz processor and the OverDrive processor. Figure 3.16 shows the pinout specification of Socket 4.

Somewhat amazingly, the original Pentium 66MHz processor consumes up to 3.2 amps of 5V power (16 watts), not including power for a standard active heatsink (fan). The 66MHz OverDrive processor that replaced it consumes a maximum 2.7 amps (13.5 watts), including about 1 watt to drive the fan. Even the original 60MHz Pentium processor consumes up to 2.91 amps at 5V (14.55 watts). It might seem strange that the replacement processor, which is twice as fast, consumes less power than the original, but this has to do with the manufacturing processes used for the original and OverDrive processors.

Although both processors run on 5V, the original Pentium processor was created with a circuit size of 0.8 micron, making that processor much more power-hungry than the 0.6-micron circuits used in the OverDrive and the other Pentium processors. Shrinking the circuit size is one of the best ways to decrease power consumption. Although the OverDrive processor for Pentium-based systems draws less power than the original processor, additional clearance might have to be allowed for the active heatsink assembly that is mounted on top. As in other OverDrive processors with built-in fans, the power to run the fan is drawn directly from the chip socket, so no separate power-supply connection is required. Also, the fan is easy to replace should it ever fail.

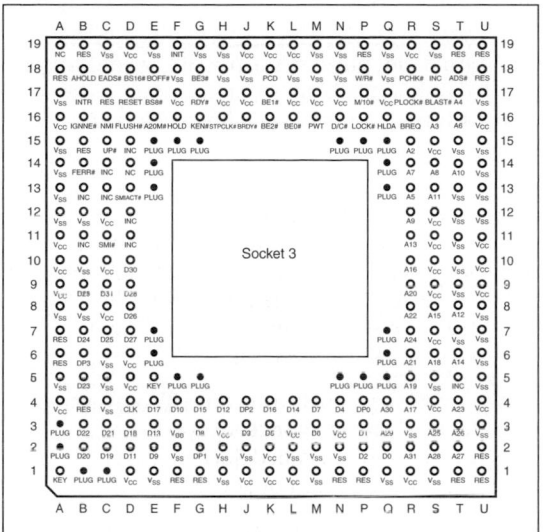

Figure 3.15 237-pin Intel Socket 3 configuration.

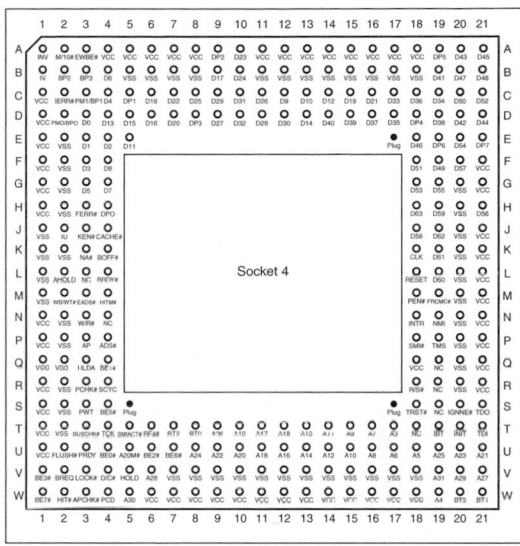

Figure 3.16 273-pin Intel Socket 4 configuration.

Socket 5

When Intel redesigned the Pentium processor to run at 75MHz, 90MHz, and 100MHz, the company went to a 0.6-micron manufacturing process and 3.3V operation. This change resulted in lower power consumption: only 3.25 amps at 3.3V (10.725 watts). Therefore, the 100MHz Pentium processor used far less power than even the original 60MHz version. This resulted in lower power consumption and enabled the extremely high clock rates without overheating.

The Pentium 75 and higher processors actually have 296 pins, although they plug into the official Intel Socket 5 design, which calls for a total of 320 pins. The additional pins are used by the Pentium OverDrive for Pentium processors. This socket has the 320 pins configured in a staggered PGA, in which the individual pins are staggered for tighter clearance.

Several OverDrive processors for existing Pentiums were available. These usually were later design chips with integral voltage regulators to enable operating on the higher voltages the older chips originally required. Intel no longer sells these; however, companies such as Evergreen and PowerLeap do still sell upgrade chips for older systems. Figure 3.17 shows the standard pinout for Socket 5.

The Pentium OverDrive for Pentium processors has an active heatsink (fan) assembly that draws power directly from the chip socket. The chip requires a maximum 4.33 amps of 3.3V to run the chip (14.289 watts) and 0.2 amp of 5V power to run the fan (one watt), which results in a total power consumption of 15.289 watts. This is less power than the original 66MHz Pentium processor requires, yet it runs a chip that is as much as four times faster!

Socket 6

The last 486 socket was designed for the 486 DX4 and the 486 Pentium OverDrive processor. Socket 6 was intended as a slightly redesigned version of Socket 3 and had an additional 2 pins plugged for proper chip keying. Socket 6 has 235 pins and accepts only 3.3V 486 or OverDrive processors. Although Intel went to the trouble of designing this socket, it never was built or implemented in any systems. Motherboard manufacturers instead stuck with Socket 3.

Socket 7 (and Super7)

Socket 7 is essentially the same as Socket 5 with one additional key pin in the opposite inside corner of the existing key pin. Socket 7, therefore, has 321 pins total in a 37×37 SPGA arrangement. The real difference with Socket 7 is not with the socket itself, but with the companion voltage regulator module (VRM) circuitry on the motherboard that must accompany it.

The VRM is either a small circuit board or a group of circuitry embedded in the motherboard that supplies the proper voltage level and regulation of power to the processor.

The main reason for the VRM is that Intel and AMD wanted to drop the voltages the processors would use from the 3.3V or 5V supplied to the motherboard by the power supply. Rather than require custom power supplies for different processors, the VRM converts the 3.3V or 5V to the proper voltage for the particular CPU you are using. Intel released different versions of the Pentium and Pentium-MMX processors that ran on 3.3V (called VR), 3.465V (called VRE), or 2.8V. Equivalent processors from AMD, Cyrix, and others used voltages from 3.3V to 1.8V. Because of the variety of voltages that might be required to support different processors, most motherboard manufacturers started including VRM sockets or building adaptable VRMs into their Pentium motherboards.

Figure 3.18 shows the Socket 7 pinout.

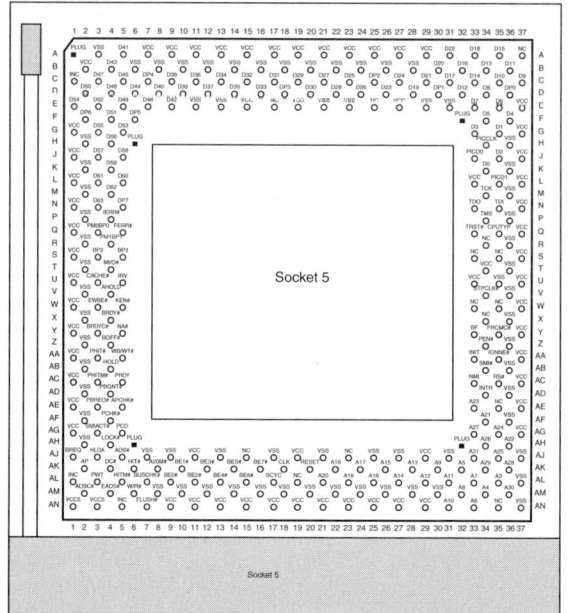

Figure 3.17　320-pin Intel Socket 5 configuration.

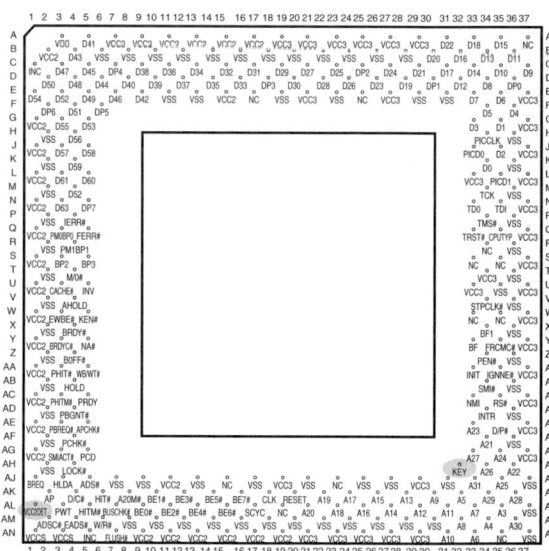

Figure 3.18　Socket 7 (Pentium) pinout (top view).

AMD, along with Cyrix and several chipset manufacturers, pioneered an improvement or extension to the Intel Socket 7 design called Super Socket 7 (or Super7), taking it from 66MHz to 95MHz and 100MHz. This enabled faster Socket 7–type systems to be made, supporting processors up to 500MHz, which are nearly as fast as some of the newer Slot 1– and Socket 370–type systems using Intel processors. Super7 systems also have support for the AGP video bus, as well as Ultra DMA hard disk controllers and advanced power management.

Major third-party chipset suppliers—including Acer Laboratories, Inc. (ALi); VIA Technologies; and Silicon Integrated Systems (SiS)—all released chipsets for Super7 boards. Most of the major motherboard manufacturers made Super7 boards in both Baby-AT and ATX form factors.

Socket 8

Socket 8 is a special SPGA socket featuring a whopping 387 pins! This was specifically designed for the Pentium Pro processor with the integrated L2 cache. The additional pins are to enable the chipset to control the L2 cache integrated in the same package as the processor. Figure 3.19 shows the Socket 8 pinout.

Socket 370 (PGA-370)

In November 1998, Intel introduced a new socket for P6 class processors. The socket was called Socket 370 or PGA-370 because it has 370 pins and originally was designed for lower-cost PGA versions of the Celeron and Pentium III processors. Socket 370 was originally designed to directly compete in the lower-end system market along with the Super7 platform supported by AMD and Cyrix. However, Intel later used it for the Pentium III processor. Initially all the Celeron and Pentium III processors were made in SECC or SEPP format. These are essentially circuit boards containing the processor and separate L2 cache chips on a small board that plugs into the motherboard via Slot 1. This type of design was necessary when the L2 cache chips were made a part of the processor but were not directly integrated into the processor die. Intel did make a multiple-die chip package for the Pentium Pro, but this proved to be a very expensive way to package the chip, and a board with separate chips was cheaper, which is why the Pentium II looks different from the Pentium Pro.

Starting with the Celeron 300A processor introduced in August 1998, Intel began combining the L2 cache directly on the processor die; it was no longer in separate chips. With the cache fully integrated into the die, there was no longer a need for a board-mounted processor. Because it costs more to make a Slot 1 board or cartridge-type processor instead of a socketed type, Intel moved back to the socket design to reduce the manufacturing cost—especially with the Celeron, which at that time was competing on the low end with Socket 7 chips from AMD and Cyrix.

The Socket 370 (PGA-370) pinout is shown in Figure 3.20.

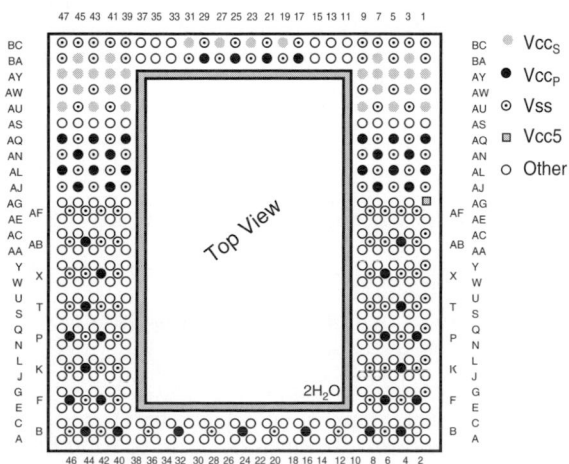

Figure 3.19 Socket 8 (Pentium Pro) pinout showing power pin locations.

Figure 3.20 Socket 370 (PGA-370) Pentium III/ Celeron pinout (top view).

The Celeron was gradually shifted over to PGA-370, although for a time both were available. All Celeron processors at 333MHz and lower were available only in the Slot 1 version. Celeron processors from 366MHz to 433MHz were available in both Slot 1 and Socket 370 versions; all Celeron processors from 466MHz and up through 1.4GHz are available only in the Socket 370 version.

Starting in October 1999, Intel also introduced Pentium III processors with integrated cache that plug into Socket 370. These use a packaging called flip chip pin grid array (FC-PGA), in which the raw die is mounted on the substrate upside down. The slot version of the Pentium III was more expensive and no longer necessary because of the on-die L2 cache.

Note that because of some voltage changes and one pin change, many original Socket 370 motherboards do not accept the later FC-PGA Socket 370 versions of the Pentium III and Celeron. Pentium III processors in the FC-PGA form have two RESET pins and require VRM 8.4 specifications. Prior motherboards designed only for the older versions of the Celeron are referred to as *legacy motherboards*, and the newer motherboards supporting the second RESET pin and VRM 8.4 specification are referred to as *flexible motherboards*. Contact your motherboard or system manufacturer for information to see whether your socket is the flexible version. Some motherboards, such as the Intel CA810, do support the VRM 8.4 specifications and supply proper voltage, but without Vtt support the Pentium III processor in the FC-PGA package will be held in RESET#. The last versions of the Pentium III and Celeron III use the Tualatin core design, which also requires a revised socket to operate. Motherboards that can handle Tualatin-core processors are known as *Tualatin-ready* and use different chipsets from those not designed to work with the Tualatin-core processor. Companies that sell upgrade processors offer products that enable you to install a Tualatin-core Pentium III or Celeron III processor into a motherboard that lacks built-in Tualatin support.

Installing a Pentium III processor in the FC-PGA package into an older motherboard is unlikely to damage the motherboard. However, the processor itself could be damaged. Pentium III processors in the 0.18-micron process operate at either 1.60V or 1.65V, whereas the Intel Celeron processors operate at 2.00V. The motherboard could be damaged if the motherboard BIOS fails to recognize the voltage identification of the processor. Contact your PC or motherboard manufacturer before installation to ensure compatibility.

A motherboard with a Slot 1 can be designed to accept almost any Celeron, Pentium II, or Pentium III processor. To use the socketed Celerons and Pentium III processors, several manufacturers have made available a low-cost slot-to-socket adapter sometimes called a *slot-ket*. This is essentially a Slot 1 board containing only a Socket 370, which enables you to use a PGA processor in any Slot 1 board. A typical slot-ket adapter is shown in the "Celeron" section later in this chapter.

▶▶   See "Celeron," p. 150.

Socket 423

Socket 423 is a ZIF-type socket introduced in November 2000 for the original Pentium 4. Figure 3.21 shows Socket 423.

Socket 423 supports a 400MHz processor bus, which connects the processor to the Memory Controller Hub (MCH), which is the main part of the motherboard chipset and similar to the North Bridge in earlier chipsets. Pentium 4 processors up to 2GHz were available for Socket 423; all faster versions require Socket 478 instead.

Socket 423 uses a unique heatsink mounting method that requires standoffs attached either to the chassis or to a special plate that mounts underneath the motherboard. This was designed to support the weight of the larger heatsinks required for the Pentium 4. Because of this, many Socket 423 motherboards require a special chassis that has the necessary additional standoffs installed. Fortunately, the need for these standoffs was eliminated with the newer Socket 478 for Pentium 4 processors.

The processor uses five voltage ID (VID) pins to signal the VRM built into the motherboard to deliver the correct voltage for the particular CPU you install. This makes the voltage selection completely automatic and foolproof. Most Pentium 4 processors for Socket 423 require 1.7V. A small triangular mark indicates the pin-1 corner for proper orientation of the chip.

Socket 478

Socket 478 is a ZIF-type socket for the Pentium 4 and Celeron 4 (Celerons based on the Pentium 4 core) introduced in October 2001. It was specially designed to support additional pins for future Pentium 4 processors and speeds over 2GHz. The heatsink mounting is different from the previous Socket 423, allowing larger heatsinks to be attached to the CPU. Figure 3.22 shows Socket 478.

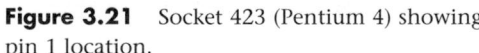

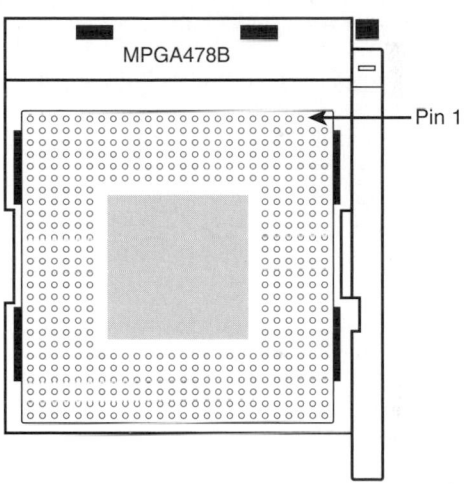

Figure 3.21   Socket 423 (Pentium 4) showing pin 1 location.

Figure 3.22   Socket 478 (Pentium 4) showing pin 1 location.

Socket 478 supports a 400MHz, 533MHz, or 800MHz processor bus that connects the processor to the memory controller hub (MCH), which is the main part of the motherboard chipset.

Socket 478 uses a new heatsink attachment method that clips the heatsink directly to the motherboard, and not the CPU socket or chassis (as with Socket 423). Therefore, any standard chassis can be used, and the special standoffs used by Socket 423 boards are not required. The new heatsink attachment allows for a much greater clamping load between the heatsink and processor, which aids cooling.

Socket 478 processors use five VID pins to signal the VRM built into the motherboard to deliver the correct voltage for the particular CPU you install. This makes the voltage selection completely automatic and foolproof. A small triangular mark indicates the pin-1 corner for proper orientation of the chip.

Socket A (Socket 462)

AMD introduced Socket A, also called Socket 462, in June 2000 to support the PGA versions of the Athlon and Duron processors. It is designed as a replacement for Slot A used by the original Athlon processor. Because the Athlon has now moved to incorporate L2 cache on-die, and the new low cost Duron is available only in an on-die cache version, there was no longer a need for the expensive cartridge packaging the original Athlon processors used.

Socket A has 462 pins and 11 plugs oriented in an SPGA form (see Figure 3.23). Socket A has the same physical dimensions and layout as Socket 370; however, the location and placement of the plugs prevent Socket 370 processors from being inserted. Socket A supports 31 voltage levels from 1.100V to 1.850V in 0.025V increments, controlled by the VID0-VID4 pins on the processor. The automatic voltage regulator module circuitry typically is embedded on the motherboard.

There are 11 total plugged holes, including 2 of the outside pin holes at A1 and AN1. These are used to allow for keying to force the proper orientation of the processor in the socket. The pinout of Socket A is shown in Figure 3.24.

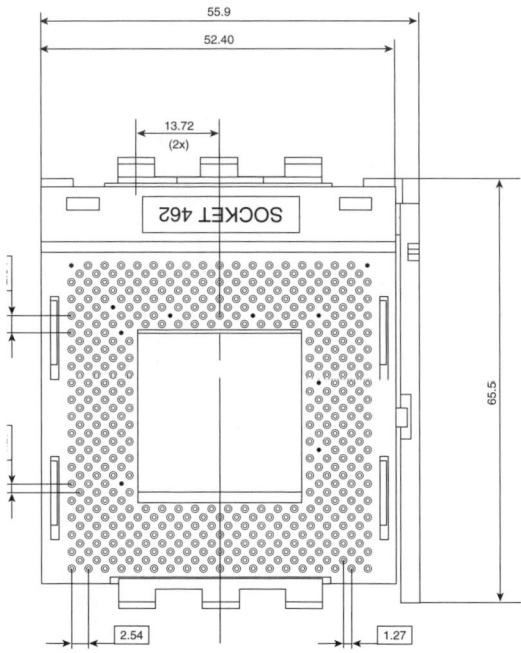

Figure 3.23   Socket A (Socket 462) Athlon/
Duron layout.

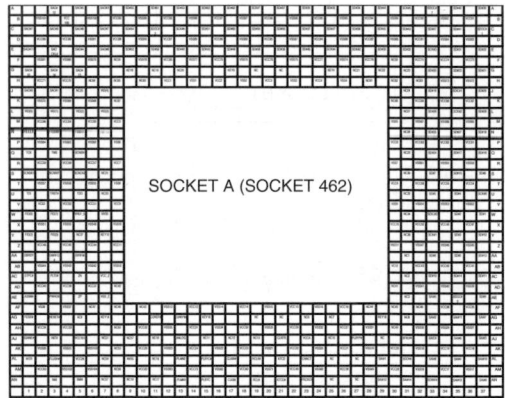

Figure 3.24   Socket A (Socket 462) Athlon/Duron pinout (top view).

After the introduction of Socket A, AMD moved all Athlon (including all Athlon XP) processors to this form factor, phasing out Slot A. In addition, for a time AMD also sold a reduced L2 cache version of the Athlon called the Duron in this form factor. The Athlon 64 uses a different processor socket called Socket 754.

Caution

Just because a chip can plug into a socket doesn't mean it will work. The newer Athlon XP processors require different voltages, BIOS, and chipset support than earlier Socket A Athlon and Duron processors. As always, make sure your motherboard supports the processor you intend to install.

Socket 603

Socket 603 is used with the Intel Xeon processor in DP (dual processor) and MP (multiple processor) configurations. These are typically used in motherboards designed for use in network file servers. Figure 3.25 shows Socket 603.

Socket 754

Socket 754 is used with the new AMD Athlon 64 processor Socket 754 version, which is AMD's first 64-bit processor for desktop computers. This socket supports single-channel unbuffered DDR SDRAM. Figure 3.26 shows an overhead view of this socket.

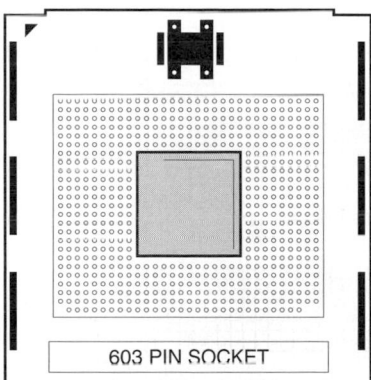

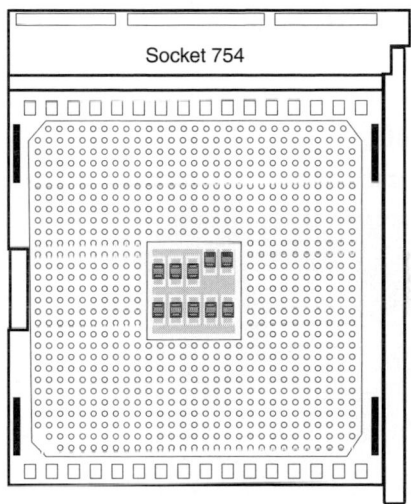

Figure 3.25   Socket 603 is used by the Intel Xeon processor.

Figure 3.26   Socket 754. The large cutout corner at the lower left indicates pin 1.

Socket 939 and 940

Socket 939 is used with the Socket 939 versions of the AMD Athlon 64 and 64 FX (see Figure 3.27). Motherboards using this socket support conventional unbuffered DDR SDRAM modules in either single- or dual-channel mode, rather than the server-oriented (more expensive) registered modules required by Socket 940 motherboards. Sockets 939 and 940 have different pin arrangements and processors for each and are not interchangeable.

Socket 940 is used with the Socket 940 version of the AMD Athlon 64 FX, as well as all AMD Opteron processors (see Figure 3.28). Motherboards using this socket support only registered DDR SDRAM modules in dual-channel mode. Because the pin arrangement is different, Socket 939 processors do not work in Socket 940, and vice versa.

Socket T

Socket T (LGA775) is used by the latest versions of the Intel Pentium 4 Prescott processor. The first-generation Prescott processors used Socket 478. Socket T is unique in that it uses a land grid array format, so the pins are on the socket, rather than the processor. The first LGA processors were the Pentium II and Celeron processors in 1997; in those processors LGA packaging was used for the chip mounted on the Slot-1 cartridge.

LGA uses gold pads (called *lands*) on the bottom of the substrate to replace the pins used in PGA packages. In socketed form, it allows for much greater clamping forces and therefore greater stability and improved thermal transfer (better cooling). LGA is really just a recycled version of what was previously called LCC (leadless chip carrier) packaging. This was used way back on the 286 processor in

'84, which had gold lands around the edge only (there were far fewer pins back then). In other ways LGA is simply a modified version of ball grid array (BGA), with gold lands replacing the solder balls, making it more suitable for socketed (rather than soldered) applications. The early LCC packages were ceramic, whereas the first Pentium II LGA packages were plastic, with the package soldered to a cartridge substrate. These days (and for the future) the LGA package is organic and directly socketed instead. On a technical level, the Pentium 4 LGA chips combine several packaging technologies that have all been used in the past, including organic land grid array (OLGA) for the substrate and controlled collapse chip connection (C4) flip-chip for the actual processor die.

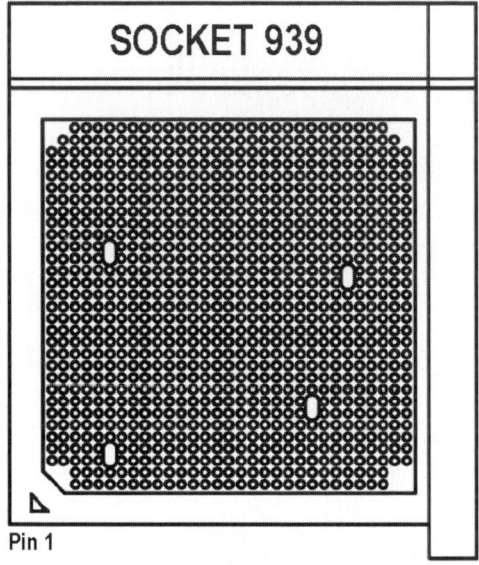
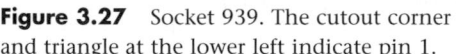

Figure 3.27 Socket 939. The cutout corner and triangle at the lower left indicate pin 1.

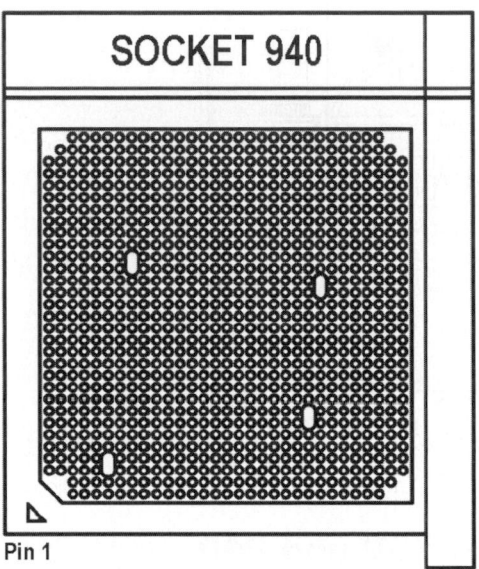

Figure 3.28 Socket 940. The cutout corner and triangle at the lower left indicate pin 1.

Processor Slots

After introducing the Pentium Pro with its integrated L2 cache, Intel discovered that the physical package it chose was very costly to produce. Intel was looking for a way to easily integrate cache and possibly other components into a processor package, and it came up with a cartridge or board design as the best way to do this. To accept its new cartridges, Intel designed two types of slots that could be used on motherboards.

Slot 1 is a 242-pin slot designed to accept Pentium II, Pentium III, and most Celeron processors. Slot 2, on the other hand, is a more sophisticated 330-pin slot designed for the Pentium II Xeon and Pentium III Xeon processors, which are primarily for workstations and servers. Besides the extra pins, the biggest difference between Slot 1 and Slot 2 is the fact that Slot 2 was designed to host up to four-way or more processing in a single board. Slot 1 allows only single or dual processing functionality.

Note that Slot 2 is also called SC330, which stands for slot connector with 330 pins. Intel later discovered less-expensive ways to integrate L2 cache into the processor core and no longer produces Slot 1 or Slot 2 processors. Both Slot 1 and Slot 2 processors are now obsolete, and many systems using these processors have been retired or upgraded with socket-based motherboards.

Slot 1 (SC242)

Slot 1, also called SC242 (slot connector 242 pins), is used by the SEC design that is used with the cartridge-type Pentium II/III and Celeron processors (see Figure 3.29).

◄◄ See "Single Edge Contact and Single Edge Processor Packaging," p. 86.

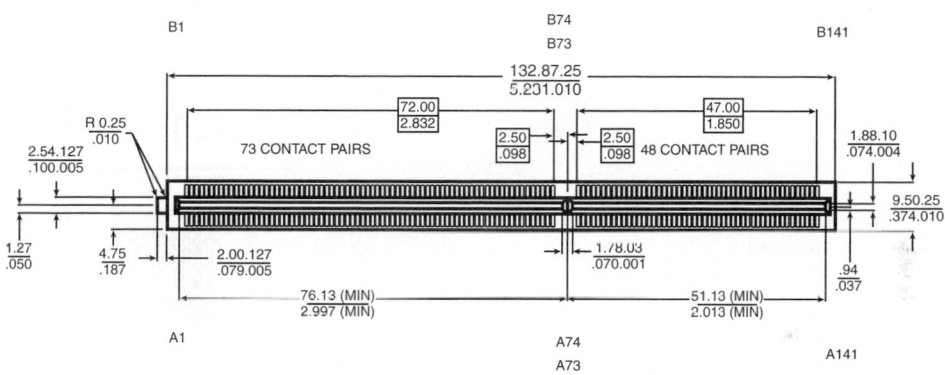

Figure 3.29 Slot 1 connector dimensions and pin layout.

Slot 2 (SC330)

Slot 2, otherwise called SC330 (slot connector 330 pins), is used on high-end motherboards that support the Pentium II and III Xeon processors. Figure 3.30 shows the Slot 2 connector.

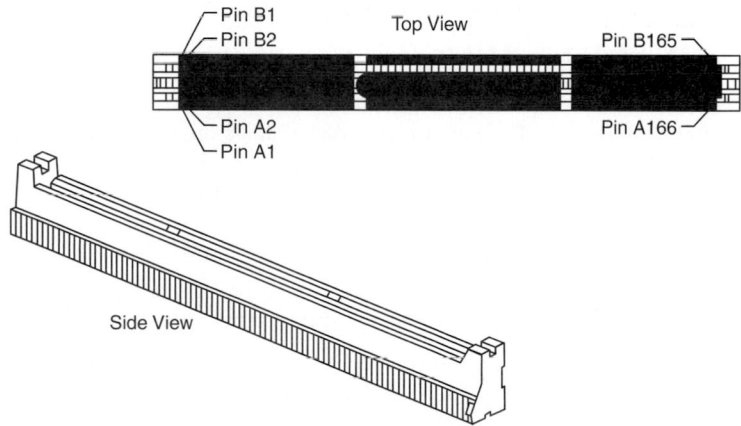

Figure 3.30 Slot 2 (SC330) connector dimensions and pin layout.

The Pentium II Xeon and Pentium III Xeon processors are designed in a cartridge similar to, but larger than, that used for the standard Pentium II/III. Figure 3.31 shows the Xeon cartridge.

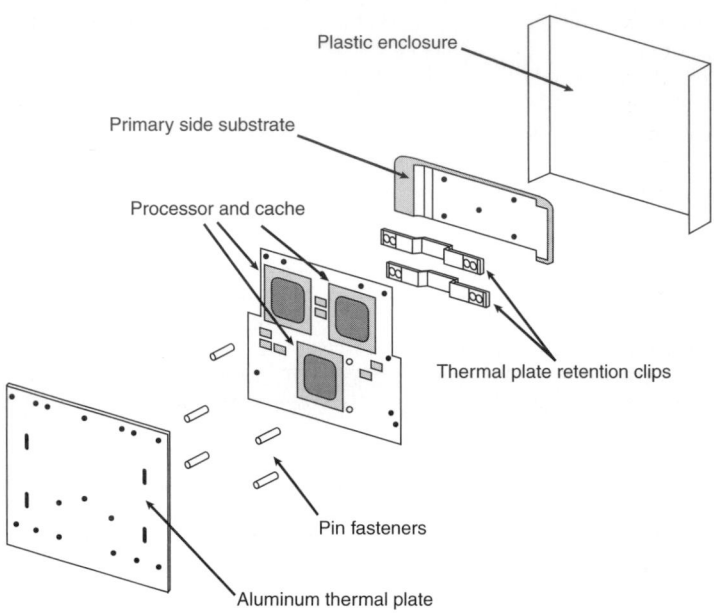

Figure 3.31   Pentium II/III Xeon cartridge.

Slot 2 motherboards were used in higher-end systems such as workstations or servers based on the Pentium II Xeon or Pentium III Xeon. These versions of the Xeon differ from the standard Pentium II and slot-based Pentium III mainly by virtue of having full-core speed L2 cache, and in some versions more of it. The additional pins allow for additional signals needed by multiple processors.

CPU Operating Voltages

One trend that is clear to anybody who has been following processor design is that the operating voltages have gotten lower and lower. The benefits of lower voltage are threefold. The most obvious is that with lower voltage comes lower overall power consumption. By consuming less power, the system is less expensive to run, but more importantly for portable or mobile systems, it runs much longer on existing battery technology. The emphasis on battery operation has driven many of the advances in lowering processor voltage because this has a great effect on battery life.

The second major benefit is that with less voltage and therefore less power consumption, less heat is produced. Processors that run cooler can be packed into systems more tightly and last longer.

The third major benefit is that a processor running cooler on less power can be made to run faster. Lowering the voltage has been one of the key factors in enabling the clock rates of processors to go higher and higher. This is because the lower the voltage, the shorter the time needed to change a signal from low to high.

Until the release of the mobile Pentium and both desktop and mobile Pentium MMX, most processors used a single voltage level to power both the core as well as run the input/output circuits. Originally, most processors ran both the core and I/O circuits at 5V, which was later reduced to 3.5V or 3.3V to lower power consumption. When a single voltage is used for both the internal processor core power as well as the external processor bus and I/O signals, the processor is said to have a single or unified power plane design.

When originally designing a version of the Pentium processor for mobile or portable computers, Intel came up with a scheme to dramatically reduce the power consumption while still remaining compatible with the existing 3.3V chipsets, bus logic, memory, and other components. The result was a dual-plane or split-plane power design in which the processor core ran off a lower voltage while the I/O circuits remained at 3.3V. This originally was called voltage reduction technology (VRT) and first debuted in the Mobile Pentium processors released in 1996. Later, this dual-plane power design also appeared in desktop processors such as the Pentium MMX, which used 2.8V to power the core and 3.3V for the I/O circuits. Now most recent processors, whether for mobile or desktop use, feature a dual-plane power design. Some of the more recent Mobile Pentium II processors run on as little as 1.6V for the core while still maintaining compatibility with 3.3V components for I/O.

Knowing the processor voltage requirements is not a big issue with Socket 8, Socket 370, Socket 478, Socket A, Socket 604, Socket 754, Socket 940, Pentium Pro (Socket 8), or Pentium II (Slot 1 or Slot 2) processors because these sockets and slots have special VID pins the processor uses to signal to the motherboard the exact voltage requirements. This enables the voltage regulators built into the motherboard to be automatically set to the correct voltage levels by merely installing the processor.

Unfortunately, this automatic voltage setting feature was not available on Super7, Socket 7, and earlier motherboard and processor designs. Therefore, you usually must set jumpers or otherwise configure the motherboard according to the voltage requirements of the processor you are installing. Pentium (Socket 4, 5, or 7) processors have run on a number of voltages, but the most recent MMX versions all use 2.8V—except for mobile Pentium processors, which are as low as 1.8V. Table 3.19 lists the voltage settings used by Intel Pentium (non-MMX) Socket 7 processors that use a single power plane and a dual power plane. A single power plane means that both the CPU core and the I/O pins run at the same voltage, whereas a dual power plane means that the core and I/O voltage values are different.

Table 3.19   Socket 7 Single- and Dual-Plane Processor Voltages

Voltage Setting	Processor	Core Voltage	I/O Voltage	Voltage Planes
VRE (3.5V)	Intel Pentium	3.5V	3.5V	Single
STD (3.3V)	Intel Pentium	3.3V	3.3V	Single
MMX (2.8V)	Intel MMX Pentium	2.8V	3.3V	Dual
VRE (3.5V)	AMD K5	3.5V	3.5V	Single
3.2V	AMD-K6	3.2V	3.3V	Dual
2.9V	AMD-K6	2.9V	3.3V	Dual
2.4V	AMD-K6-2/K6-3	2.4V	3.3V	Dual
2.2V	AMD-K6/K6-2	2.2V	3.3V	Dual
VRE (3.5V)	Cyrix 6x86	3.5V	3.5V	Single
2.9V	Cyrix 6x86MX/M-II	2.9V	3.3V	Dual
MMX (2.8V)	Cyrix 6x86L	2.8V	3.3V	Dual
2.45V	Cyrix 6x86LV	2.45V	3.3V	Dual

Generally, the acceptable range is plus or minus 5% from the nominal intended setting.

Most Socket 7 and later Pentium motherboards supply several voltages (such as 2.5V, 2.7V, 2.8V, and 2.9V) for compatibility with future devices. A voltage regulator built into the motherboard converts the power supply voltage into the various levels the processor core requires. Check the documentation for your motherboard and processor to find the appropriate settings.

The Pentium Pro and Pentium II processors were the first to automatically determine their voltage settings by controlling the motherboard-based voltage regulator through built-in VID pins. Those are explained in more detail later in this chapter.

▶▶   See "Pentium Pro Processors," p. 136.

▶▶   See "Pentium II Processors," p. 140.

Note that on the STD or VRE settings, the core and I/O voltages are the same; these are single-plane voltage settings. Any time a voltage other than STD or VRE is set, the motherboard defaults to a dual-plane voltage setting where the core voltage can be specifically set, while the I/O voltage remains constant at 3.3V no matter what.

Socket 5 was designed to supply only STD or VRE settings, so any processor that can work at those settings can work in Socket 5 as well as Socket 7. Older Socket 4 designs can supply only 5V, and they have a completely different pinout (fewer pins overall), so using a processor designed for Socket 7 or Socket 5 in Socket 4 is not possible.

Most Socket 7 and later Pentium motherboards supply several voltages (such as 2.2V, 2.4V, 2.5V, 2.7V, 2.8V, and 2.9V as well as the older STD or VRE settings) for compatibility with many processors. A voltage regulator built into the motherboard converts the power supply voltage into the various levels required by the processor core. Check the documentation for your motherboard and processor to find the appropriate settings.

Starting with the Pentium Pro, all newer processors (Celeron, Pentium II/III/4, AMD Athlon, Duron, Athlon XP, and Athlon 64) automatically determine their voltage settings by controlling the motherboard-based voltage regulator. That's done through built-in VID pins.

For hotrodding purposes, many newer motherboards for these processors have override settings that allow for manual voltage adjustment if desired. Many people have found that when attempting to overclock a processor, increasing the voltage by a tenth of a volt or so often helps. Of course, this increases the heat output of the processor and must be accounted for with adequate heatsinking and case cooling.

Heat and Cooling Problems

Heat can be a problem in any high-performance system. The higher-speed processors consume more power and therefore generate more heat. The processor is usually the single most power-hungry chip in a system, and in most situations, the fan inside your computer case is incapable of handling the load without some help.

To ensure a constant flow of air and more consistent performance, most processors include some form of heatsink, which is designed to draw heat away from the processor. Additionally, most heatsinks incorporate fans so they don't have to rely on the airflow within the system. Heatsinks with fans are referred to as *active* heatsinks (see Figure 3.32). Active heatsinks have a power connection. Older ones often used a spare disk drive power connector, but most recent heatsinks plug in to dedicated heatsink power connections found on the newer motherboards.

Processor cooling, including heatsinks, is covered in detail in Chapter 23, "Extreme Modifications: Overclocking, Cooling, Chassis, and Lighting."

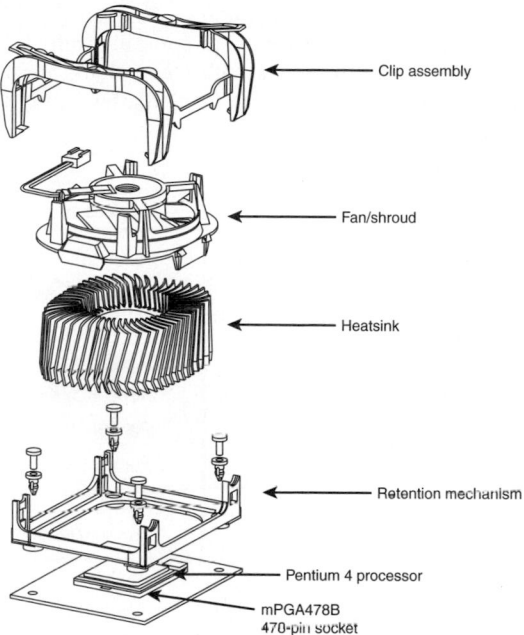

Clip assembly

Fan/shroud

Heatsink

Retention mechanism

Pentium 4 processor

mPGA478B
470-pin socket

Figure 3.32 Active heatsink suitable for a Pentium 4 processor using Socket 478.

Math Coprocessors (Floating-Point Units)

Th is section covers the floating-point unit (FPU) contained in the processor, which was formerly a separate external math coprocessor in the 386 and older chips. Older central processing units designed by Intel (and cloned by other companies) used an external math coprocessor chip. However, when Intel introduced the 486DX, it included a built-in math coprocessor, and every processor built by Intel (and AMD and Cyrix, for that matter) since then includes a math coprocessor. Coprocessors provide hardware for floating-point math, which otherwise would create an excessive drain on the main CPU. Math chips speed your computer's operation only when you are running software designed to take advantage of the coprocessor. All the subsequent fifth- and sixth-generation Intel and compatible processors (such as those from AMD and Cyrix) have featured an integrated floating-point unit.

Math chips (as coprocessors sometimes are called) can perform high-level mathematical operations—long division, trigonometric functions, roots, and logarithms, for example—at 10–100 times the speed of the corresponding main processor. The operations performed by the math chip are all operations that make use of noninteger numbers (numbers that contain digits after the decimal point). The need to process numbers in which the decimal is not always the last character leads to the term *floating point* because the decimal (point) can move (float), depending on the operation. The integer units in the primary CPU work with integer numbers, so they perform addition, subtraction, and multiplication operations. The primary CPU is designed to handle such computations; these operations are not offloaded to the math chip.

The instruction set of the math chip is different from that of the primary CPU. A program must detect the existence of the coprocessor and then execute instructions written explicitly for that coprocessor; otherwise, the math coprocessor draws power and does nothing else. Fortunately, most modern programs that can benefit from the use of the coprocessor correctly detect and use the coprocessor. These programs usually are math intensive: spreadsheet programs, database applications, statistical programs, and graphics programs, such as computer-aided design (CAD) software. Word processing programs do not benefit from a math chip and therefore are not designed to use one. Table 3.20 summarizes the coprocessors available for the Intel family of processors.

Table 3.20   Math Coprocessor Summary

Processor	Coprocessor	Processor	Coprocessor
8086	8087	486DX2	Built-in FPU
8088	8087	486DX4/5x86	Built-in FPU
286	287	Intel Pentium/Pentium MMX	Built-in FPU
386SX	387SX	Cyrix 6x86/MI/MII	Built-in FPU
386DX	387DX	AMD K5/K6/Athlon/Duron	Built-in FPU
486SX	487SX, DX2/OverDrive[1]	Pentium II/III/Celeron/Xeon	Built-in FPU
487SX[1]	Built-in FPU	Pentium II	Built-in FPU
486SX2	DX2/OverDrive[2]	Athlon 64	Built-in FPU
486DX	Built-in FPU	Itanium/Itanium II	Built-in FPU

FPU = Floating-point unit

1. The 487SX chip is a modified pinout 486DX chip with the math coprocessor enabled. When you plug in a 487SX chip, it disables the 486SX main processor and takes over all processing.

2. The DX2/OverDrive is equivalent to the SX2 with the addition of a functional FPU.

Although virtually all processors since the 486 series have built-in floating-point units, they vary in performance. Historically, the Intel processor FPUs have dramatically outperformed those from AMD and Cyrix, although AMD and Cyrix are achieving performance parity in their newer offerings.

Within each of the original 8087 group, the maximum speed of the math chips varies. A suffix digit after the main number, as shown in Table 3.21, indicates the maximum speed at which a system can run a math chip.

Table 3.21   Maximum Math Chip Speeds

Part	Speed	Part	Speed
8087	5MHz	287	6MHz
8087-3	5MHz	287-6	6MHz
8087-2	8MHz	287-8	8MHz
8087-1	10MHz	287-10	10MHz

The 387 math coprocessors and the 486 or 487 and Pentium processors always indicate their maximum speed ratings in MHz in the part number suffix. A 486DX2-66, for example, is rated to run at 66MHz. Some processors incorporate clock multiplication, which means they can run at different speeds compared with the rest of the system.

Most systems that use the 386 or earlier processors are socketed for a math coprocessor as an option, but they do not include a coprocessor as standard equipment. A few systems on the market at that time didn't even have a socket for the coprocessor because of cost and size considerations. These systems were usually low-cost or portable systems, such as older laptops, the IBM PS/1, and the PCjr. For more specific information about math coprocessors, see the discussions of the specific chips—8087, 287, 387, and 487SX—in the later sections. Table 3.22 shows the specifications of the various math coprocessors.

Table 3.22   Older Intel Math Coprocessor Specifications

Name	Power Consumption	Case Minimum Temperature	Case Maximum Temperature	No. of Transistors	Date Introduced
8087	3 watts	0°C, 32°F	85°C, 185°F	45,000	1980
287	3 watts	0°C, 32°F	85°C, 185°F	45,000	1982
287XL	1.5 watts	0°C, 32°F	85°C, 185°F	40,000	1990
387SX	1.5 watts	0°C, 32°F	85°C, 185°F	120,000	1988
387DX	1.5 watts	0°C, 32°F	85°C, 185°F	120,000	1987

Most often, you can learn which CPU and math coprocessor are installed in a particular system by checking the markings on the chip.

Processor Bugs

Processor manufacturers use specialized equipment to test their own processors, but you have to settle for a little less. The best processor-testing device to which you have access is a system that you know is functional; you then can use the diagnostics available from various utility software companies or your system manufacturer to test the motherboard and processor functions.

Perhaps the most infamous of these bugs is the floating-point division math bug in the early Pentium processors. This and a few other bugs are discussed in detail later in this chapter.

Because the processor is the brain of a system, most systems don't function with a defective processor. If a system seems to have a dead motherboard, try replacing the processor with one from a functioning motherboard that uses the same CPU chip. You might find that the processor in the original board is the culprit. If the system continues to play dead, however, the problem is elsewhere, most likely in the motherboard, memory, or power supply. See the chapters that cover those parts of the system for more information on troubleshooting those components. I must say that in all my years of troubleshooting and repairing PCs, I have rarely encountered defective processors.

A few system problems are built in at the factory, although these bugs or design defects are rare. By learning to recognize these problems, you can avoid unnecessary repairs or replacements. Each processor section describes several known defects in that generation of processors, such as the infamous floating-point error in the Pentium. For more information on these bugs and defects, see the following sections, and check with the processor manufacturer for updates.

Processor Update Feature

All processors can contain design defects or errors. Many times, the effects of any given bug can be avoided by implementing hardware or software workarounds. Intel documents these bugs and workarounds well for its processors in its processor Specification Update manual; this manual is available from Intel's Web site. Most of the other processor manufacturers also have bulletins or tips on their Web sites listing any problems or special fixes or patches for their chips.

Previously, the only way to fix a processor bug was to work around it or replace the chip with one that had the bug fixed. Now, a new feature built into the Intel P6 and P7 processors, including the Pentium Pro through Pentium III, Celeron, and Pentium 4, can allow many bugs to be fixed by altering the *microcode* in the processor. Microcode is essentially a set of instructions and tables in the processor that control how the processor operates. These processors incorporate a new feature called *reprogrammable microcode*, which enables certain types of bugs to be worked around via microcode updates. The microcode updates reside in the motherboard ROM BIOS and are loaded into the processor by the motherboard BIOS during the POST. Each time the system is rebooted, the fix code is reloaded, ensuring that it will have the bug fix installed anytime the processor is operating.

The updated microcode for a given processor is provided by Intel to the motherboard manufacturer so it can incorporate the microcode into the flash ROM BIOS for the board. This is one reason it is important to install the most recent motherboard BIOS anytime you install a new processor. If your processor is newer than your motherboard ROM BIOS code, it probably doesn't include updated microcode to support your processor. In that case, you should visit the Web site of your motherboard manufacturer so you can download and install the latest BIOS update for your motherboard.

Processor Codenames

Intel, AMD, and Cyrix have always used codenames when talking about future processors. The codenames usually are not supposed to become public, but they typically do. They can often be found in online and print news and magazine articles talking about future-generation processors. Sometimes, they even appear in motherboard manuals because the manuals are written before the processors are officially introduced. Table 3.23 lists processor codenames for reference purposes.

Table 3.23   Processor Codenames

AMD Codename	Description
X5	5x86-133 [Socket 3]
SSA5	K5 (original PR75-PR100) [Socket 5, 7]
5k86	K5 (newer PR120-PR200) [Socket 7]
K6	Original AMD K6 core; canceled
NX686	NexGen K6 core; became the K6 [Socket 7]
Little Foot	0.25μm K6 [Socket 7]
Chompers	K6-2 [Socket 7, Super7]
Sharptooth	K6-3 [Super7]
Argon	Formerly K7
K7	Athlon [Slot A]
K75	0.18μm Athlon [Slot A]
K76	0.18μm Athlon (copper interconnects) [Slot A]
K8	Athlon 64
Thunderbird	Athlon [Slot A, Socket A]
Mustang	Athlon w/large L2; canceled
Corvette	Former mobile Athlon (now Palomino)
Palomino	0.18μm Athlon XP/MP, Mobile Athlon 4 [Socket A]
Thoroughbred	0.13μm Athlon XP/MP [Socket A]
Barton	0.13μm Athlon XP/MP w/512K L2 [Socket A]
Spitfire	Duron [Socket A]
Camaro	Former Morgan
Morgan	Mobile Duron and Model 7 Duron [Socket A]
Appaloosa	0.13μm Morgan [Socket A]
ClawHammer	Athlon 64 (64-bit CPU) [Socket 754]
ClawHammer DP	Early name for Opteron DP [Socket 940]
San Diego	0.09μ Athlon 64
Odessa	0.09μ mobile Athlon 64
SledgeHammer	Opteron w/large L2 [Socket 940]

Table 3.23   Continued

VIA/Cyrix Codename	Description
M6	486DX [Socket 1, 2, 3]
M7	486DX2/DX4 [Socket 3]
M9	5x86 [Socket 3]
M1sc	5x86 [Socket 3]
Chili	5x86 project
M1	6x86 (3.3V/3.52V) [Socket 7]
M1L	6x86L (2.8V) [Socket 7]
M1R	6x86 on IBM 5M process
M2	6x86MX/M-II [Socket 7, Super7]
Cayenne	MXi and Gobi
Jedi	Former Joshua (before Gobi)
Gobi	Former Joshua
Joshua	Former Cyrix III (canceled)
MXi	Proprietary integrated CPU
Jalapeno	Former Mojave
Mojave	M3 [Socket 370]
Serrano	M4
C5	Samuel (Winchip-4)
C5B	0.15μm Samuel 2
C5C	0.13μm Ezra
C5M	Ezra-T
C5N	Ezra-T (copper interconnects)
Samuel	C3 [Socket 370]
Samuel 2	0.15μm C3 [Socket 370]
Ezra	0.13μm C3 [Socket 370]
Ezra-T	Ezra 1.25V [Socket 370]
C5X	Nehemiah
C5XL	Nehemiah (low power, small L2)
C5YL	Esther
Nehemiah	C3 [Socket 370] with encryption
Esther	C4 [Socket 370]
CZA	0.10μm Socket 478 CPU
Matthew	Proprietary integrated CPU
Intel Codename	**Description**
P23	486SX [Socket 1, 2, 3]
P23S	486SX SL-enhanced [Socket 1, 2, 3]
P23N	487SX (coprocessor) [Socket 1]
P4	486DX [Socket 1, 2, 3]
P4S	486DX SL-enhanced [Socket 1, 2, 3]
P24	486DX2 [Socket 1, 2, 3]

Table 3.23   Continued

Intel Codename	Description
P24S	486DX2 SL-enhanced [Socket 1, 2, 3]
P24D	486DX2 (write-back cache) [Socket 3]
P24C	486DX4 [Socket 3]
P23T	486DXODP (486 OverDrive) [Socket 3]
P4T	486DXODPR (486 OverDrive) [Socket 1, 2, 3]
P24T	PODP5V (Pentium OverDrive) [Socket 2, 3]
P24CT	Pentium OverDrive 3.3V [Socket 2, 3]
P5	Pentium 60/66MHz [Socket 4]
P5T	Pentium OverDrive 120/133MHz [Socket 4]
P54C	Pentium 75MHz–120MHz [Socket 5, 7]
P54CQS	Pentium 120MHz–133MHz [Socket 5, 7]
P54CS	Pentium 120MHz–200MHz [Socket 7]
P54CT(A)	Pentium OverDrive [Socket 5, 7]
P55C	Pentium MMX [Socket 7]
P54CTB	Pentium OverDrive MMX [Socket 5, 7]
Tillamook	Mobile Pentium MMX [Mobile Module]
P6	Pentium Pro [Socket 8]
P6T	Pentium II OverDrive [Socket 8]
Klamath	0.35µm Pentium II [Slot 1]
Deschutes	0.25µm Pentium II [Slot 1]
Drake	0.25µm Pentium II Xeon [Slot 2]
Tonga	Mobile Pentium II
Covington	Celeron (cacheless Pentium II) [Slot 1]
Mendocino	0.25µm Celeron w/128KB on-die L2 [Slot 1, Socket 370]
Dixon	Mobile Pentium II w/256KB on-die L2
Katmai	0.25µm Pentium III w/SSE [Slot 1]
Tanner	0.25µm Pentium III Xeon w/SSE [Slot 2]
Coppermine	0.18µm Pentium III w/on-die L2 [Slot 1, Socket 370]
Tualatin	0.13µm Pentium III [Socket 370]
Coppermine-T	0.18µm Pentium III w/Tualatin voltage [Socket 370]
Cascades	0.18µm Pentium III Xeon [Slot 2]
Coppermine-128	0.18µm Celeron w/128KB L2 [Socket 370]
Timna	Mobile Celeron w/DRAM controller; canceled
P68	Willamette
Willamette	0.18µm Pentium 4 [Socket 423, 478]
Northwood	0.13µm Pentium 4 [Socket 478]
Prescott	90nm Pentium 4 [Socket 478 and LGA-775]
Banias	130nm Pentium M w/1MB L2
Foster	Xeon DP [Socket 603]
Foster MP	Xeon MP [Socket 603]

Table 3.23   Continued

Intel Codename	Description
Prestonia	0.13μm Xeon DP [Socket 603]
Gallatin	0.13μm Xeon MP [Socket 603]
Nocona	0.09μm Xeon [Socket 603]
Dothan	90nm Pentium M w/2MB L2
P7	Former Merced (Itanium)
Merced	Itanium [PAC 418]
McKinley	Itanium 2 w/3MB on-die L3 [PAC 418]
Madison	0.13μm Itanium 2
Deerfield	Low-cost Madison
Montecito	0.09μm Madison
Shavano	Future Itanium family chip

Note that the codenames and information listed in these tables are used before the processor is officially introduced. After a chip is introduced, the codename is dropped and the chip is thereafter referred to by the marketing name used at the time of the introduction. Because many of these names refer to chips that are not yet officially released, the names or specifications might change. For chipset codenames, see Chapter 4.

Intel-Compatible Processors (AMD and Cyrix)

Several companies—mainly AMD and Cyrix—have developed processors that are compatible with Intel processors. These chips are fully Intel compatible, so they emulate every processor instruction in the Intel chips. Many of the chips are also pin compatible, which means that they can be used in any system designed to accept an Intel processor; others require a custom motherboard design. Any hardware or software that works on Intel-based PCs will work on PCs made with these third-party CPU chips. A number of companies currently offer Intel-compatible chips, and some of the most popular ones are discussed here.

AMD Processors

Advanced Micro Devices (AMD) has become a major player in the Pentium-compatible chip market with its own line of Intel-compatible processors. AMD ran into trouble with Intel several years ago because its 486-clone chips used actual Intel microcode. These differences have been settled, and AMD now has a cross-license agreement with Intel. In 1996, AMD finalized a deal to absorb NexGen, another maker of Intel-compatible CPUs. NexGen had been working on a chip it called the Nx686, which was renamed the K6 and introduced by AMD. AMD refined the design in the form of the K6-2 and K6-3. Its more recent chips, called the Athlon XP and Duron, are designed similarly to the Pentium III/4 and Celeron that have used both a similar but not identical slot and socket design. The newer AMD Athlon and Duron processors as well as the Athlon XP are designed to use Socket A, also called Socket 462. The newest AMD processor, the Athlon 64, is the first 64-bit processor designed for desktop computers. It uses the new Socket 754.

For a summary of the AMD processors, see Table 3.2 earlier in this chapter.

Cyrix

Cyrix was purchased by National Semiconductor in November 1997 and by VIA Technologies in 1999. Prior to that, it had been a fabless company, meaning it had no chip-manufacturing capability. All the Cyrix chips were manufactured for Cyrix first by Texas Instruments and then mainly by IBM up through the end of 1998. Starting in 1999, National Semiconductor took over manufacturing of the Cyrix processors. More recently, National has been purchased by VIA Technologies.

All Cyrix chips were manufactured by other companies such as IBM (who also marketed some of the 6x86 chips under its own name), National Semiconductor, and now VIA Technologies. See Table 3.2 earlier in this chapter, which summarizes the Cyrix and VIA processors.

P1 (086) First-Generation Processors

The first generation of processors represents the series of chips from Intel that were found in the first PCs. IBM, as the architect of the PC at the time, chose Intel processors and support chips to build the PC motherboard, setting a standard that would hold for many subsequent processor generations to come.

8088 and 8086 Processors

Intel introduced the 8086 back in June 1978. The 8086 was one of the first 16-bit processor chips on the market; at the time, virtually all other processors were 8-bit designs. The 8086 had 16-bit internal registers and could run a new class of software using 16-bit instructions. It also had a 16-bit external data path, so it could transfer data to memory 16 bits at a time.

The address bus was 20 bits wide, which enabled the 8086 to address a full 1MB (2^{20}) of memory. This was in stark contrast to most other chips of that time that had 8-bit internal registers, an 8-bit external data bus, and a 16-bit address bus allowing a maximum of only 64KB of RAM (2^{16}).

Unfortunately, most of the personal computer world at the time was using 8-bit processors, which ran 8-bit CP/M (Control Program for Microprocessors) operating systems and software. The board and circuit designs at the time were largely 8-bit, as well. Building a full 16-bit motherboard and memory system was costly, pricing such a computer out of the market.

The cost was high because the 8086 needed a 16-bit data bus rather than a less expensive 8-bit bus. Systems available at that time were 8-bit, and slow sales of the 8086 indicated to Intel that people weren't willing to pay for the extra performance of the full 16-bit design. In response, Intel introduced a kind of crippled version of the 8086, called the 8088. The 8088 essentially deleted 8 of the 16 bits on the data bus, making the 8088 an 8-bit chip as far as data input and output were concerned. However, because it retained the full 16-bit internal registers and the 20-bit address bus, the 8088 ran 16-bit software and was capable of addressing a full 1MB of RAM.

For these reasons, IBM selected the 8-bit 8088 chip for the original IBM PC. Years later, IBM was criticized for using the 8-bit 8088 instead of the 16-bit 8086. In retrospect, it was a very wise decision. IBM even covered up the physical design in its ads, which at the time indicated its new PC had a "high-speed 16-bit microprocessor." IBM could say that because the 8088 still ran the same powerful 16-bit software the 8086 ran, just a little more slowly. In fact, programmers universally thought of the 8088 as a 16-bit chip because there was virtually no way a program could distinguish an 8088 from an 8086. This enabled IBM to deliver a PC capable of running a new generation of 16-bit software, while retaining a much less expensive 8-bit design for the hardware. Because of this, the IBM PC was actually priced less at its introduction than the most popular PC of the time, the Apple II. For the trivia buffs out there, the IBM PC listed for $1,265 and included only 16KB of RAM, whereas a similarly configured Apple II cost $1,355.

Even though the 8088 was introduced in June 1979, the original IBM PC that used the processor did not appear until August 1981. Back then, a significant lag time often occurred between the introduction of a new processor and systems that incorporated it. That is unlike today, when new processors and systems using them often are released on the same day.

The 8088 in the IBM PC ran at 4.77MHz; the average instruction on the 8088 took 12 cycles to complete.

Computer users sometimes wonder why a 640KB conventional-memory barrier exists if the 8088 chip can address 1MB of memory. The conventional-memory barrier exists because IBM reserved 384KB of the upper portion of the 1024KB (1MB) address space of the 8088 for use by adapter cards and system BIOS. The lower 640KB is the conventional memory in which DOS and software applications execute.

80186 and 80188 Processors

After Intel produced the 8086 and 8088 chips, it created versions of these chips with some of the required support components integrated within the processor.

The relationship between the 80186 and 80188 is the same as that of the 8086 and 8088; the 80188 is essentially an 8-bit interface version of the 80186. The advantage of the 80186 and 80188 is that they combine on a single chip 15–20 of the 8086–8088 series system components—a fact that can greatly reduce the number of components in a computer design. The 80186 and 80188 chips were used for highly intelligent peripheral adapter cards of that age, such as network adapters.

8087 Coprocessor

The math coprocessor or floating-point unit that was paired with the 8086 chip was called the 8087 numeric data processor (NDP), the math coprocessor, or simply the math chip. The 8087 is designed to perform high-level math operations at many times the speed of the main processor. The primary advantage of using this chip is the increased execution speed in number-crunching programs, such as spreadsheet applications.

P2 (286) Second-Generation Processors

The second generation of PC processors allowed for a great leap in system speed and processing efficiency. With these chips we went from moving 8 bits of data around to moving 16 bits at a time. The following section details the second-generation PC processor, the 286.

286 Processors

The Intel 80286 (normally abbreviated as 286) processor did not suffer from the compatibility problems that damned the 80186 and 80188. The 286 chip, first introduced in 1982, is the CPU behind the original IBM PC AT (Advanced Technology). Other computer makers manufactured what came to be known as IBM clones, with many of these manufacturers calling their systems AT-compatible or AT-class computers.

When IBM developed the AT, it selected the 286 as the basis for the new system because the chip provided compatibility with the 8088 used in the PC and the XT. Therefore, software written for those chips should run on the 286. The 286 chip is many times faster than the 8088 used in the XT, and at the time it offered a major performance boost to PCs used in businesses. The processing speed, or throughput, of the original AT (which ran at 6MHz) is five times greater than that of the PC running at 4.77MHz. The die for the 286 is shown in Figure 3.33.

286 systems are faster than their predecessors for several reasons. The main reason is that 286 processors are much more efficient in executing instructions. An average instruction takes 12 clock cycles on the 8086 or 8088, but takes an average of only 4.5 cycles on the 286 processor. Additionally, the 286 chip can handle up to 16 bits of data at a time through an external data bus twice the size of the 8088.

The 286 chip has two modes of operation: real mode and protected mode. The two modes are distinct enough to make the 286 resemble two chips in one. In real mode, a 286 acts essentially the same as an 8086 chip and is fully *object-code compatible* with the 8086 and 8088. (A processor with object-code compatibility can run programs written for another processor without modification and execute every system instruction in the same manner.)

In the protected mode of operation, the 286 was truly something new. In this mode, a program designed to take advantage of the chip's capabilities believes that it has access to 1GB of memory (including virtual memory). The 286 chip, however, can address only 16MB of hardware memory. A significant failing of the 286 chip is that it cannot switch from protected mode to real mode without a hardware reset (a warm reboot) of the system. (It can, however, switch from real mode to protected mode without a reset.) A major improvement of the 386 over the 286 is that software can switch the 386 from real mode to protected mode, and vice versa. See the section "Processor Modes," earlier in this chapter for more information.

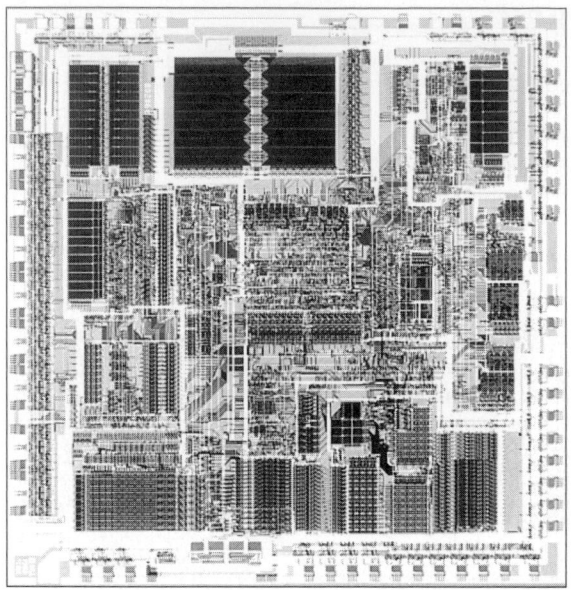

Figure 3.33 286 Processor die. *Photograph used by permission of Intel Corporation.*

Only a small amount of software that took advantage of the 286 chip was sold until Windows 3.0 offered standard mode for 286 compatibility; by that time, the hottest-selling chip was the 386. Still, the 286 was Intel's first attempt to produce a CPU chip that supported multitasking, in which multiple programs run at the same time.

80287 Coprocessor

The 80287, internally, is the same math chip as the 8087, although the pins used to plug them into the motherboard are different. Both the 80287 and the 8087 operate as though they are identical.

In most systems, the 80286 internally divides the system clock by 2 to derive the processor clock. The 80287 internally divides the system-clock frequency by 3. For this reason, most AT-type computers run the 80287 at one-third the system clock rate, which also is two-thirds the clock speed of the 80286. Because the 286 and 287 chips are asynchronous, the interface between the 286 and 287 chips is not as efficient as with the 8088 and 8087.

P3 (386) Third-Generation Processors

The third generation represents perhaps the most significant change in processors since the first PC. The big deal was the migration from processors that handled 16-bit operations to true 32-bit chips. The third-generation processors were so far ahead of their time, it took fully 10 years before 32-bit operating systems and software became mainstream, and by that time the third-generation chips had become a memory. The following section details the third-generation processors.

386 Processors

The Intel 80386 (usually abbreviated as 386) caused quite a stir in the PC industry because of the vastly improved performance it brought to the personal computer. Compared with 8088 and 286 systems, the 386 chip offered greater performance in almost all areas of operation.

The 386 is a full 32-bit processor optimized for high-speed operation and multitasking operating systems. Intel introduced the chip in 1985, but the 386 appeared in the first systems in late 1986 and early 1987. The Compaq Deskpro 386 and systems made by several other manufacturers introduced the chip; somewhat later, IBM used the chip in its PS/2 Model 80.

The 386 can execute the real-mode instructions of an 8086 or 8088, but in fewer clock cycles. The 386 was as efficient as the 286 in executing instructions—the average instruction took about 4.5 clock cycles. In raw performance, therefore, the 286 and 386 actually seemed to be at almost equal clock rates. The 386 offered greater performance in other ways, mainly because of additional software capability (modes) and a greatly enhanced memory management unit (MMU). The die for the 386 is shown in Figure 3.34.

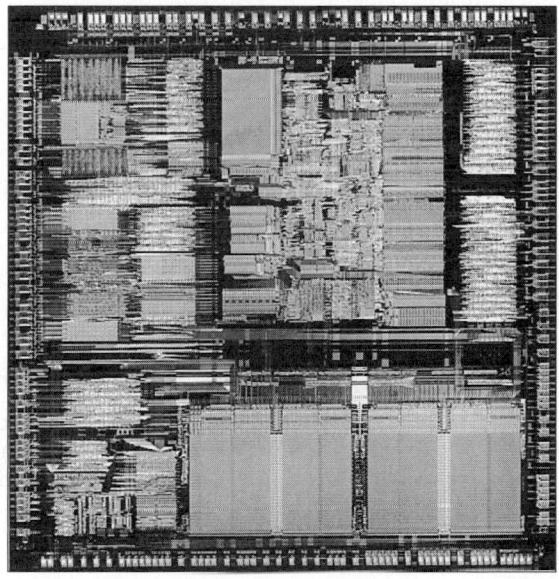

Figure 3.34 386 processor die. *Photograph used by permission of Intel Corporation.*

The 386 can switch to and from protected mode under software control without a system reset—a capability that makes using protected mode more practical. In addition, the 386 includes a new mode, called virtual real mode, which enables several real-mode sessions to run simultaneously under protected mode.

The protected mode of the 386 is fully compatible with the protected mode of the 286. The protected mode for both chips often is called their native mode of operation because these chips are designed for advanced operating systems such as Windows NT/2000/XP, which run only in protected mode. Intel extended the memory-addressing capabilities of 386 protected mode with a new MMU that provided advanced memory paging and program switching. These features were extensions of the 286 type of MMU, so the 386 remained fully compatible with the 286 at the system-code level.

The 386 chip's virtual real mode was also new. In virtual real mode, the processor could run with hardware memory protection while simulating an 8086's real-mode operation. Multiple copies of DOS and other operating systems, therefore, could run simultaneously on this processor, each in a protected area of memory. If the programs in one segment crashed, the rest of the system was protected.

Numerous variations of the 386 chip exist, some of which are less powerful and some of which are less power hungry. The following sections cover the members of the 386-chip family and their differences.

386DX Processors

The 386DX chip was the first of the 386 family members that Intel introduced. The 386 is a full 32-bit processor with 32-bit internal registers, a 32-bit internal data bus, and a 32-bit external data bus. The 386 contains 275,000 transistors in a very large scale integration (VLSI) circuit. The chip comes in a 132-pin package and draws approximately 400 milliamperes (ma), which is less power than even the 8086 requires. The 386 has a smaller power requirement because it is made of Complementary Metal-Oxide Semi-conductor (CMOS) materials. The CMOS design enables devices to consume extremely low levels of power.

The Intel 386 chip was available in clock speeds ranging from 16MHz–33MHz; other manufacturers, primarily AMD and Cyrix, offered comparable versions with speeds up to 40MHz.

The 386DX can address 4GB of physical memory. Its built-in virtual memory manager enables software designed to take advantage of enormous amounts of memory to act as though a system has 64TB of memory. (A terabyte, or TB, is 1,099,511,627,776 bytes of memory, or about 1000GB.)

386SX Processors

The 386SX was designed for systems designers looking for 386 capabilities at 286 system prices. Similar to the 286, the 386SX is restricted to only 16 bits when communicating with other system components, such as memory. Internally, however, the 386SX is identical to the DX chip; the 386SX has 32-bit internal registers and can therefore run 32-bit software. The 386SX uses a 24-bit memory-addressing scheme like that of the 286, rather than the full 32-bit memory address bus of the standard 386. The 386SX, therefore, can address a maximum 16MB of physical memory rather than the 4GB of physical memory the 386DX can address. Before it was discontinued, the 386SX was available in clock speeds ranging from 16MHz to 33MHz.

The 386SX signaled the end of the 286 because of the 386SX chip's superior MMU and the addition of the virtual real mode. Under a software manager such as Windows or OS/2, the 386SX can run numerous DOS programs at the same time. The capability to run 386-specific software is another important advantage of the 386SX over any 286 or older design. For example, Windows 3.1 runs nearly as well on a 386SX as it does on a 386DX.

386SL Processors

The 386SL is another variation on the 386 chip. This low-power CPU had the same capabilities as the 386SX, but it was designed for laptop systems in which low power consumption was necessary. The SL chips offered special power-management features that were important to systems that ran on batteries. The SL chip also offered several sleep modes to conserve power.

The chip included an extended architecture that contained a System Management Interrupt (SMI), which provided access to the power-management features. Also included in the SL chip was special support for LIM (Lotus Intel Microsoft) expanded memory functions and a cache controller. The cache controller was designed to control a 16KB–64KB external processor cache.

These extra functions account for the higher transistor count in the SL chips (855,000) compared with even the 386DX processor (275,000). The 386SL was available in 25MHz clock speed.

Intel offered a companion to the 386SL chip for laptops called the 82360SL I/O subsystem. The 82360SL provided many common peripheral functions, such as serial and parallel ports, a direct memory access (DMA) controller, an interrupt controller, and power-management logic for the 386SL processor. This chip subsystem worked with the processor to provide an ideal solution for the small size and low power-consumption requirements of portable and laptop systems.

80387 Coprocessor

Although the 80387 chips ran asynchronously, 386 systems were designed so that the math chip ran at the same clock speed as the main CPU. Unlike the 80287 coprocessor, which was merely an 8087 with different pins to plug into the AT motherboard, the 80387 coprocessor was a high-performance math chip specifically designed to work with the 386.

All 387 chips used a low power-consumption CMOS design. The 387 coprocessor had two basic designs: the 387DX coprocessor, which was designed to work with the 386DX processor, and the 387SX coprocessor, which was designed to work with the 386SX, SL, or SLC processor.

Intel originally offered several speeds for the 387DX coprocessor. But when the company designed the 33MHz version, a smaller mask was required to reduce the lengths of the signal pathways in the chip. This increased the performance of the chip by roughly 20%.

Note

Because Intel lagged in developing the 387 coprocessor, some early 386 systems were designed with a socket for a 287 coprocessor. Performance levels associated with that union, however, leave much to be desired.

Installing a 387DX is easy, but you must be careful to orient the chip in its socket properly; otherwise, the chip will be destroyed. The most common cause of burned pins on the 387DX is incorrect installation. In many systems, the 387DX was oriented differently from other large chips. Follow the manufacturer's installation instructions carefully to avoid damaging the 387DX; Intel's warranty does not cover chips that are installed incorrectly.

Several manufacturers developed their own versions of the Intel 387 coprocessors, some of which were touted as being faster than the original Intel chips. The general compatibility record of these chips was very good.

P4 (486) Fourth-Generation Processors

The third generation had been a large change from the previous generations of processors. With the fourth generation, more refinement than complete redesign was accomplished. Even so, Intel, AMD, and others managed to literally double processor performance with their fourth-generation processors. The following section defines the fourth-generation processors from Intel, AMD, and others.

486 Processors

In the race for more speed, the Intel 80486 (normally abbreviated as 486) was another major leap forward. The additional power available in the 486 fueled tremendous growth in the software industry. Tens of millions of copies of Windows, and millions of copies of OS/2, have been sold largely because the 486 finally made the GUI of Windows and OS/2 a realistic option for people who work on their computers every day.

Four main features make a given 486 processor roughly twice as fast as an equivalent MHz 386 chip. These features are

- *Reduced instruction-execution time.* A single instruction in the 486 takes an average of only two clock cycles to complete, compared with an average of more than four cycles on the 386. Clock-multiplied versions, such as the DX2 and DX4, further reduced this to about two cycles per instruction.

- *Internal (Level 1) cache.* The built-in cache has a hit ratio of 90%–95%, which describes how often zero-wait-state read operations occur. External caches can improve this ratio further.

- *Burst-mode memory cycles.* A standard 32-bit (4-byte) memory transfer takes two clock cycles. After a standard 32-bit transfer, more data up to the next 12 bytes (or three transfers) can be transferred with only one cycle used for each 32-bit (4-byte) transfer. Thus, up to 16 bytes of contiguous, sequential memory data can be transferred in as little as five cycles instead of eight cycles or more. This effect can be even greater when the transfers are only 8 bits or 16 bits each.

- *Built-in (synchronous) enhanced math coprocessor (some versions).* The math coprocessor runs synchronously with the main processor and executes math instructions in fewer cycles than previous designs did. On average, the math coprocessor built into the DX-series chips provides two to three times greater math performance than an external 387 chip.

The 486 chip is about twice as fast as the 386, so a 386DX-40 is about as fast as a 486SX-20. This made the 486 a much more desirable option, primarily because it could more easily be upgraded to a DX2 or DX4 processor at a later time. You can see why the arrival of the 486 rapidly killed off the 386 in the marketplace.

Most of the 486 chips were offered in a variety of maximum speed ratings, varying from 16MHz up to 133MHz. Additionally, 486 processors have slight differences in overall pin configurations. The DX, DX2, and SX processors have a virtually identical 168-pin configuration, whereas the OverDrive chips have either the standard 168-pin configuration or a specially modified 169-pin OverDrive (sometimes also called 487SX) configuration. If your motherboard has two sockets, the primary one likely supports the standard 168-pin configuration, and the secondary (OverDrive) socket supports the 169-pin OverDrive configuration. Most of the later 486-based motherboards with a single ZIF socket support any of the 486 processors except the DX4. The DX4 is different because it requires 3.3V to operate instead of 5V, like most other chips up to that time.

A processor rated for a given speed always functions at any of the lower speeds. A 100MHz-rated 486DX4 chip, for example, runs at 75MHz if it is plugged into a 25MHz motherboard. Note that the DX2/OverDrive processors operate internally at two times the motherboard clock rate, whereas the DX4 processors operate at two, two-and-one-half, or three times the motherboard clock rate. Table 3.24 shows the various speed combinations that can result from using the DX2 or DX4 processors with different motherboard clock speeds.

Table 3.24   Intel DX2 and DX4 Operating Speeds Versus CPU Bus (Motherboard) Clock Speeds

CPU Bus Speed	DX2/DX4 Speed (2× Mode)	DX4 Speed (2.5× Mode)	DX4 Speed (3× Mode)
16MHz	32MHz	40MHz	48MHz
20MHz	40MHz	50MHz	60MHz
25MHz	50MHz	63MHz	75MHz
33MHz	66MHz	83MHz	100MHz
40MHz	80MHz	100MHz	120MHz
50MHz	100MHz	n/a	n/a

The internal multiplier of the DX4 processor is controlled by the CLKMUL (clock multiplier) signal at pin R-17 (Socket 1) or S-18 (Socket 2, 3, or 6). In most cases, one or two jumpers will be on the board near the processor socket to control the settings for these pins. The motherboard documentation should cover these settings if they can be changed.

One interesting capability here is to run the DX4-100 chip in a doubled mode with a 50MHz motherboard speed. This gives you a very fast memory bus, along with the same 100MHz processor speed, as if you were running the chip in a 33/100MHz tripled mode.

Many VL-Bus motherboards can run the VL-Bus slots in a buffered mode, add wait states, or even selectively change the clock only for the VL-Bus slots to keep them compatible. In most cases, they don't run properly at 50MHz. Consult your motherboard—or even better, your chipset documentation—to see how your board is set up.

Caution

When upgrading an existing system, you should be sure that your socket supports the chip you are installing. This was especially true when putting a DX4 processor in an older system. In that scenario, you needed some type of adapter to regulate the voltage down to 3.3V. Putting the DX4 in a 5V socket destroys the chip! See the earlier section on processor sockets for more information.

486DX Processors

The original Intel 486DX processor was introduced on April 10, 1989, and systems using this chip first appeared during 1990. The first chips had a maximum speed rating of 25MHz; later versions of the 486DX were available in 33MHz- and 50MHz-rated versions. The 486DX originally was available only in a 5V, 168-pin PGA version, but later became available in 5V, 196-pin plastic quad flat pack (PQFP) and 3.3V, 208-pin small quad flat pack (SQFP). These latter form factors were available in SL enhanced versions, which were intended primarily for portable or laptop applications in which saving power is important.

Two main features separate the 486 processor from its predecessors:

- The 486DX integrates functions such as the math coprocessor, cache controller, and cache memory into the chip.

- The 486 also was designed with easy installation and upgradeability in mind; double-speed OverDrive upgrades were available for most systems.

The 486DX processor is fabricated with low-power CMOS technology. The chip has a 32-bit internal register size, a 32-bit external data bus, and a 32-bit address bus. These dimensions are equal to those of the 386DX processor. The internal register size is where the "32-bit" designation used in advertisements comes from. The 486DX chip contains 1.2 million transistors on a piece of silicon no larger than your thumbnail. This figure is more than four times the number of components on 386 processors and should give you a good indication of the 486 chip's relative power. The die for the 486 is shown in Figure 3.35.

Figure 3.35 486 processor die. *Photograph used by permission of Intel Corporation.*

The standard 486DX contains a processing unit, floating-point unit (math coprocessor), memory-management unit, and cache controller with 8KB of internal-cache RAM. Due to the internal cache and a more efficient internal processing unit, the 486 family of processors can execute individual instructions in an average of only 2 processor cycles. Compare this figure with the 286 and 386 families, both of which execute an average 4.5 cycles per instruction. Compare it also with the original 8086 and 8088 processors, which execute an average 12 cycles per instruction. At a given clock rate (MHz), therefore, a 486 processor is roughly twice as efficient as a 386 processor; a 16MHz 486SX is roughly equal to a 33MHz 386DX system; and a 20MHz 486SX is equal to a 40MHz 386DX system. Any of the faster 486s are way beyond the 386 in performance.

The 486 is fully instruction-set–compatible with previous Intel processors, such as the 386, but offers several additional instructions (most of which have to do with controlling the internal cache).

Similar to the 386DX, the 486 can address 4GB of physical memory and manage as much as 64TB of virtual memory. The 486 fully supports the three operating modes introduced in the 386: real mode, protected mode, and virtual real mode:

- *Real mode.* In this mode, the 486 (similar to the 386) runs unmodified 8086-type software.

- *Protected mode.* In this mode, the 486 (similar to the 386) offers sophisticated memory paging and program switching.

- *Virtual real mode.* In this mode, the 486 (similar to the 386) can run multiple copies of DOS or other operating systems while simulating an 8086's real-mode operation. Under an operating system such as Windows or OS/2, therefore, both 16-bit and 32-bit programs can run simultaneously on this processor with hardware memory protection. If one program crashes, the rest of the system is protected, and you can reboot the blown portion through various means, depending on the operating software.

The 486DX series has a built-in math coprocessor that sometimes is called an MCP (math coprocessor) or FPU. This series is unlike previous Intel CPU chips, which required you to add a math coprocessor if you needed faster calculations for complex mathematics. The FPU in the 486DX series is 100% software-compatible with the external 387 math coprocessor used with the 386, but it delivers more than twice the performance. It runs in synchronization with the main processor and executes most instructions in half as many cycles as the 386.

486SL

The 486SL was a short-lived, standalone chip. The SL enhancements and features became available in virtually all the 486 processors (SX, DX, and DX2) in what are called SL enhanced versions. SL enhancement refers to a special design that incorporates special power-saving features.

The SL enhanced chips originally were designed to be installed in laptop or notebook systems that run on batteries, but they found their way into desktop systems, as well. The SL-enhanced chips featured special power-management techniques, such as sleep mode and clock throttling, to reduce power consumption when necessary. These chips were available in 3.3V versions, as well.

Intel designed a power-management architecture called system management mode (SMM). This mode of operation is totally isolated and independent from other CPU hardware and software. SMM provides hardware resources such as timers, registers, and other I/O logic that can control and power down mobile-computer components without interfering with any of the other system resources. SMM executes in a dedicated memory space called system management memory, which is not visible and does not interfere with operating system and application software. SMM has an interrupt called system management interrupt (SMI), which services power-management events and is independent from—and a higher priority than—any of the other interrupts.

SMM provides power management with flexibility and security that were not available previously. For example, an SMI occurs when an application program tries to access a peripheral device that is powered down for battery savings, which powers up the peripheral device and re-executes the I/O instruction automatically.

Intel also designed a feature called Suspend/Resume in the SL processor. The system manufacturer can use this feature to provide the portable computer user with instant on-and-off capability. An SL system typically can resume (instant on) in 1 second from the suspend state (instant off) to exactly where it left off. You do not need to reboot, load the operating system, or load the applications and their data. Instead, simply push the Suspend/Resume button and the system is ready to go.

The SL CPU was designed to consume almost no power in the suspend state. This feature means that the system can stay in the suspend state possibly for weeks and yet start up instantly right where it left off. An SL system can keep working data in normal RAM memory safe for a long time while it is in the suspend state, but saving to a disk still is prudent.

486SX

The 486SX, introduced in April 1991, was designed to be sold as a lower-cost version of the 486. The 486SX is virtually identical to the full DX processor, but the chip does not incorporate the FPU or math coprocessor portion.

As you read earlier in this chapter, the 386SX was a scaled-down (some people would say crippled) 16-bit version of the full-blown 32-bit 386DX. The 386SX even had a completely different pinout and was not interchangeable with the more powerful DX version. The 486SX, however, is a different story. The 486SX is, in fact, a full-blown 32-bit 486 processor that is basically pin compatible with the DX. A few pin functions are different or rearranged, but each pin fits into the same socket.

The 486SX chip is more a marketing quirk than new technology. Early versions of the 486SX chip actually were DX chips that showed defects in the math-coprocessor section. Instead of being scrapped, the chips were packaged with the FPU section disabled and sold as SX chips. This arrangement lasted for only a short time; thereafter, SX chips got their own mask, which is different from the DX mask. (A *mask* is the photographic blueprint of the processor and is used to etch the intricate signal pathways into a silicon chip.) The transistor count dropped to 1.185 million (from 1.2 million) to reflect this new mask.

The 486SX was available in 16MHz-, 20MHz-, 25MHz-, and 33MHz-rated speeds, and a 486 SX/2 was also available that ran at up to 50MHz or 66MHz. The 486SX typically comes in a 168-pin version, although other surface-mount versions are available in SL-enhanced models.

Despite what Intel's marketing and sales information implies, no technical provision exists for adding a separate math coprocessor to a 486SX system; neither was a separate math coprocessor chip ever available to plug in. Instead, Intel wanted you to add a new 486 processor with a built-in math unit and disable the SX CPU that already was on the motherboard. If this situation sounds confusing, read on because this topic brings you to the most important aspect of 486 design: upgradeability.

487SX

The 487SX math coprocessor, as Intel calls it, really is a complete 25MHz 486DX CPU with an extra pin added and some other pins rearranged. When the 487SX is installed in the extra socket provided in a 486SX CPU-based system, the 487SX turns off the existing 486SX via a new signal on one of the pins. The extra key pin actually carries no signal itself and exists only to prevent improper orientation when the chip is installed in a socket.

The 487SX takes over all CPU functions from the 486SX and also provides math coprocessor functionality in the system. At first glance, this setup seems rather strange and wasteful, so perhaps further explanation is in order. Fortunately, the 487SX turned out to be a stopgap measure while Intel prepared its real surprise: the OverDrive processor. The DX2/OverDrive speed-doubling chips, which are designed for the 487SX 169-pin socket, have the same pinout as the 487SX. These upgrade chips are installed in exactly the same way as the 487SX; therefore, any system that supports the 487SX also supports the DX2/OverDrive chips.

Although in most cases you can upgrade a system by removing the 486SX CPU and replacing it with a 487SX (or even a DX or DX2/OverDrive), Intel originally discouraged this procedure. Instead, Intel recommended that PC manufacturers include a dedicated upgrade (OverDrive) socket in their systems because several risks were involved in removing the original CPU from a standard socket. (The following section elaborates on those risks.) Now Intel recommends—or even insists on—the use of a single processor socket of a ZIF design, which makes upgrading an easy task physically.

◄◄ See "Zero Insertion Force," p. 90.

DX2/OverDrive and DX4 Processors

On March 3, 1992, Intel introduced the DX2 speed-doubling processors. On May 26, 1992, Intel announced that the DX2 processors also would be available in a retail version called OverDrive. Originally, the OverDrive versions of the DX2 were available only in 169-pin versions, which meant that they could be used only with 486SX systems that had sockets configured to support the rearranged pin configuration.

On September 14, 1992, Intel introduced 168-pin OverDrive versions for upgrading 486DX systems. These processors could be added to existing 486 (SX or DX) systems as an upgrade, even if those systems did not support the 169-pin configuration. When you use this processor as an upgrade, you install the new chip in your system, which subsequently runs twice as fast.

The DX2/OverDrive processors run internally at twice the clock rate of the host system. If the motherboard clock is 25MHz, for example, the DX2/OverDrive chip runs internally at 50MHz; likewise, if the motherboard is a 33MHz design, the DX2/OverDrive runs at 66MHz. The DX2/OverDrive speed doubling has no effect on the rest of the system; all components on the motherboard run the same as they do with a standard 486 processor. Therefore, you do not have to change other components (such as memory) to accommodate the double-speed chip. The DX2/OverDrive chips have been available in several speeds. Three speed-rated versions have been offered:

- 40MHz DX2/OverDrive for 16MHz or 20MHz systems
- 50MHz DX2/OverDrive for 25MHz systems
- 66MHz DX2/OverDrive for 33MHz systems

Notice that these ratings indicate the maximum speed at which the chip is capable of running. You could use a 66MHz-rated chip in place of the 50MHz- or 40MHz-rated parts with no problem, although the chip will run only at the slower speeds. The actual speed of the chip is double the motherboard clock frequency. When the 40MHz DX2/OverDrive chip is installed in a 16MHz 486SX system, for example, the chip functions only at 32MHz—exactly double the motherboard speed. Intel originally stated that no 100MHz DX2/OverDrive chip would be available for 50MHz systems—which technically has not been true because the DX4 could be set to run in a clock-doubled mode and used in a 50MHz motherboard (see the discussion of the DX4 processor in this section).

The only part of the DX2 chip that doesn't run at double speed is the bus interface unit, a region of the chip that handles I/O between the CPU and the outside world. By translating between the differing internal and external clock speeds, the bus interface unit makes speed doubling transparent to the rest of the system. The DX2 appears to the rest of the system to be a regular 486DX chip, but one that seems to execute instructions twice as fast.

DX2/OverDrive chips are based on the 0.8-micron circuit technology that was first used in the 50MHz 486DX. The DX2 contains 1.2 million transistors in a three-layer form. The internal 8KB cache, integer, and floating-point units all run at double speed. External communication with the PC runs at normal speed to maintain compatibility.

Besides upgrading existing systems, one of the best parts of the DX2 concept was the fact that system designers could introduce very fast systems by using cheaper motherboard designs, rather than the more costly designs that would support a straight high-speed clock. Therefore, a 50MHz 486DX2 system was much less expensive than a straight 50MHz 486DX system. The system board in a 486DX-50 system operates at a true 50MHz. The 486DX2 CPU in a 486DX2-50 system operates internally at 50MHz, but the motherboard operates at only 25MHz.

You might be thinking that a true 50MHz DX processor–based system still would be faster than a speed-doubled 25MHz system, and this generally is true. But, the differences in speed actually are very slight—a real testament to the integration of the 486 processor and especially to the cache design.

When the processor has to go to system memory for data or instructions, for example, it must do so at the slower motherboard operating frequency (such as 25MHz). Because the 8KB internal cache of the 486DX2 has a hit rate of 90%–95%, however, the CPU must access system memory only 5%–10% of the time for memory reads. Therefore, the performance of the DX2 system can come very close to that of a true 50MHz DX system and cost much less. Even though the motherboard runs at only 33.33MHz, a system with a DX2 66MHz processor ends up being faster than a true 50MHz DX system, especially if the DX2 system has a good L2 cache.

Many 486 motherboard designs also include a secondary cache that is external to the cache integrated into the 486 chip. This external cache allows for much faster access when the 486 chip calls for external-memory access. The size of this external cache can vary anywhere from 16KB to 512KB or more. When you add a DX2 processor, an external cache is even more important for achieving the greatest perfor-mance gain. This cache greatly reduces the wait states the processor must add when writing to system memory or when a read causes an internal cache miss. For this reason, some systems perform better with the DX2/OverDrive processors than others, usually depending on the size and efficiency of the external-memory cache system on the motherboard. Systems that have no external cache still enjoy a near-doubling of CPU performance, but operations that involve a great deal of memory access are slower.

This brings us to the DX4 processor. Although the standard DX4 technically was not sold as a retail part, it could be purchased from several vendors, along with the 3.3V voltage adapter needed to install the chip in a 5V socket. These adapters have jumpers that enable you to select the DX4 clock multi-plier and set it to 2x, 2.5x, or 3x mode. In a 50MHz DX system, you could install a DX4/voltage-regulator combination set in 2x mode for a motherboard speed of 50MHz and a processor speed of 100MHz! Although you might not be able to take advantage of certain VL-Bus adapter cards, you will have one of the fastest 486-class PCs available.

Intel also sold a special DX4 OverDrive processor that included a built-in voltage regulator and heatsink that are specifically designed for the retail market. The DX4 OverDrive chip is essentially the same as the standard 3.3V DX4 with the main exception that it runs on 5V because it includes an on-chip regulator. Also, the DX4 OverDrive chip runs only in the tripled speed mode, and not the 2x or 2.5x modes of the standard DX4 processor.

Note

Intel has discontinued all 486 and DX2/DX4/OverDrive processors, including the so-called Pentium OverDrive processor.

Pentium OverDrive for 486SX2 and DX2 Systems

The Pentium OverDrive Processor became available in 1995. An OverDrive chip for 486DX4 systems had been planned, but poor marketplace performance of the SX2/DX2 chip resulted in it never seeing the light of day. One thing to keep in mind about the 486 Pentium OverDrive chip is that although it is intended primarily for SX2 and DX2 systems, it should work in any upgradeable 486SX or DX sys-tem that has a Socket 2 or Socket 3. If in doubt, check Intel's online upgrade guide for compatibility.

The Pentium OverDrive processor is designed for systems that have a processor socket that follows the Intel Socket 2 specification. This processor also works in systems that have a Socket 3 design, although you should ensure that the voltage is set for 5V rather than 3.3V. The Pentium OverDrive chip includes a 32KB internal L1 cache and the same superscalar (multiple instruction path) architecture of the real Pentium chip. Besides a 32-bit Pentium core, these processors feature increased clock-speed operation due to inter-nal clock multiplication and incorporate an internal write-back cache (standard with the Pentium). If the motherboard supports the write-back cache function, increased performance is realized. Unfortunately, most motherboards, especially older ones with the Socket 2 design, support only write-through cache.

Most tests of these OverDrive chips show them to be only slightly ahead of the DX4-100 and behind the DX4-120 and true Pentium 60, 66, or 75. Based on the relative affordability of low-end "real" Pentiums (in their day), it was hard not to justify making the step up to a Pentium system.

AMD 486 (5x86)

AMD made a line of 486-compatible chips that installed into standard 486 motherboards. In fact, AMD made the fastest 486 processor available, which it called the Am5x86(TM)-P75. The name was a little misleading because the 5x86 part made some people think that this was a fifth-generation Pentium-type processor. In reality, it was a fast clock-multiplied (4x clock) 486 that ran at four times the speed of the 33MHz 486 motherboard you plugged it into.

The 5x86 offered high-performance features such as a unified 16KB write-back cache and 133MHz core clock speed; it was approximately comparable to a Pentium 75, which is why it was denoted with a P-75 in the part number. It was the ideal choice for cost-effective 486 upgrades, where changing the motherboard is difficult or impossible.

Not all 486 motherboards support the 5x86. The best way to verify that your motherboard supports the chip is by checking with the documentation that came with the board. Look for keywords such as "Am5X86," "AMD-X5," "clock-quadrupled," "133MHz," or other similar wording. Another good way to determine whether your motherboard supports the AMD 5x86 is to look for it in the listed models on AMD's Web site.

There are a few things to note when installing a 5x86 processor into a 486 motherboard:

- *The operating voltage for the 5x86 is 3.45V +/- 0.15V.* Not all motherboards have this setting, but most that incorporate a Socket 3 design should. If your 486 motherboard is a Socket 1 or 2 design, you cannot use the 5x86 processor directly. The 3.45V processor does not operate in a 5V socket and can be damaged. To convert a 5V motherboard to 3.45V, processors with adapters could be purchased from several vendors, such as Kingston, PowerLeap, and Evergreen. These companies and others sold the 5x86 complete with a voltage regulator adapter attached in an easy-to-install package. These versions are ideal for older 486 motherboards that don't have a Socket 3 design and might still be available in the surplus or closeout market. If not, you can create your own upgrade kit with a processor, voltage adapter, and heatsink/fan.

- *It is generally better to purchase a new motherboard, processor, and RAM than to buy one of these adapters.* Buying a new motherboard is also better than using an adapter because the older BIOS might not understand the requirements of the processor as far as speed is concerned. BIOS updates often are required with older boards.

- *Most Socket 3 motherboards have jumpers, enabling you to set the voltage manually.* Some boards don't have jumpers, but have voltage autodetect instead. These systems check the VOLDET pin (pin S4) on the microprocessor when the system is powered on.

- *The VOLDET pin is tied to ground (Vss) internally to the microprocessor.* If you cannot find any jumpers for setting voltage, you can check the motherboard as follows: Switch the PC off, remove the microprocessor, connect pin S4 to a Vss pin on the ZIF socket, power on, and check any Vcc pin with a voltmeter. This should read 3.45 ([pm] 0.15) volts. See the previous section on CPU sockets for the pinout.

- *The 5x86 requires a 33MHz motherboard speed, so be sure the board is set to that frequency.* The 5x86 operates at an internal speed of 133MHz. Therefore, the jumpers must be set for "clock-quadrupled" or "4x clock" mode. By setting the jumpers correctly on the motherboard, the CLKMUL pin (pin R17) on the processor will be connected to ground (Vss). If there is no 4x clock setting, the standard DX2 2x clock setting should work.

- *Some motherboards have jumpers that configure the internal cache in either write-back (WB) or write-through (WT) mode.* They do this by pulling the WB/WT pin (pin B13) on the microprocessor to logic High (Vcc) for WB or ground (Vss) for WT. For best performance, configure your system in WB mode; however, reset the cache to WT mode if problems running applications occur or the floppy drive doesn't work right (DMA conflicts).

- *The 5x86 runs hot, so a heatsink is required.* It normally must have a fan, and most upgrade kits included a fan.

In addition to the 5x86, the AMD-enhanced 486 product line included 80MHz; 100MHz; and 120MHz CPUs. These are the A80486DX2-80SV8B (40MHz×2), A80486DX4-100SV8B (33MHz×3), and A80486DX4-120SV8B (40MHz×3).

Cyrix/TI 486

The Cyrix 486DX2/DX4 processors were available in 100MHz, 80MHz, 75MHz, 66MHz, and 50MHz versions. Similar to the AMD 486 chips, the Cyrix versions are fully compatible with Intel's 486 processors and work in most 486 motherboards.

The Cx486DX2/DX4 incorporates an 8KB write-back cache, an integrated floating-point unit, advanced power management, and SMM, and was available in 3.3V versions.

Note

TI originally made all the Cyrix-designed 486 processors, and under the agreement it also sold them under the TI name. They are essentially the same as the Cyrix chips.

P5 (586) Fifth-Generation Processors

After the fourth-generation chips such as the 486, Intel and other chip manufacturers went back to the drawing board to come up with new architectures and features that they would later incorporate into what they called fifth-generation chips. This section defines the fifth-generation processors from Intel, AMD, and others.

Pentium Processors

On October 19, 1992, Intel announced that the fifth generation of its compatible microprocessor line (codenamed P5) would be named the Pentium processor rather than the 586, as everybody had assumed. Calling the new chip the 586 would have been natural, but Intel discovered that it could not trademark a number designation, and the company wanted to prevent other manufacturers from using the same name for any clone chips they might develop. The actual Pentium chip shipped on March 22, 1993. Systems that used these chips were only a few months behind.

The Pentium is fully compatible with previous Intel processors, but it differs from them in many ways. At least one of these differences is revolutionary: The Pentium features twin data pipelines, which enable it to execute two instructions at the same time. The 486 and all preceding chips can perform only a single instruction at a time. Intel calls the capability to execute two instructions at the same time superscalar technology. This technology provides additional performance compared with the 486.

With superscalar technology, the Pentium can execute many instructions at a rate of two instructions per cycle. Superscalar architecture usually is associated with high-output RISC chips. The Pentium is one of the first CISC chips to be considered superscalar. The Pentium is almost like having two 486 chips under the hood. Table 3.25 shows the Pentium processor specifications.

Table 3.25   Pentium Processor Specifications

Introduced	March 22, 1993 (first generation); March 7, 1994 (second generation)
Maximum rated speeds	60/66MHz (first generation); 75/90/100/120/133/150/166/200MHz (second generation)
CPU clock multiplier	1x (first generation); 1.5x–3x (second generation)
Register size	32-bit
External data bus	64-bit
Memory address bus	32-bit
Maximum memory	4GB
Integral-cache size	8KB code; 8KB data

Table 3.25   Continued

Integral-cache type	Two-way set associative; write-back data
Burst-mode transfers	Yes
Number of transistors	3.1 million (first generation); 3.3 million (second generation)
Circuit size	0.8 micron (60/66MHz); 0.6 micron (75MHz–100MHz); 0.35 micron (120MHz and up)
External package	273-pin PGA; 296-pin SPGA; tape carrier
Math coprocessor	Built-in FPU
Power management	SMM; enhanced in second generation
Operating voltage	5V (first generation); 3.465V, 3.3V, 3.1V, 2.9V (second generation)

PGA = Pin grid array
SPGA = Staggered pin grid array

The two instruction pipelines within the chip are called the u- and v-pipes. The *u-pipe*, which is the primary pipe, can execute all integer and floating-point instructions. The *v-pipe* is a secondary pipe that can execute only simple integer instructions and certain floating-point instructions. The process of operating on two instructions simultaneously in the different pipes is called *pairing*. Not all sequentially executing instructions can be paired, and when pairing is not possible, only the u-pipe is used. To optimize the Pentium's efficiency, you can recompile software to enable more instructions to be paired.

The Pentium processor has a branch target buffer (BTB), which employs a technique called branch prediction. It minimizes stalls in one or more of the pipes caused by delays in fetching instructions that branch to nonlinear memory locations. The BTB attempts to predict whether a program branch will be taken and then fetches the appropriate instructions. The use of branch prediction enables the Pentium to keep both pipelines operating at full speed. Figure 3.36 shows the internal architecture of the Pentium processor.

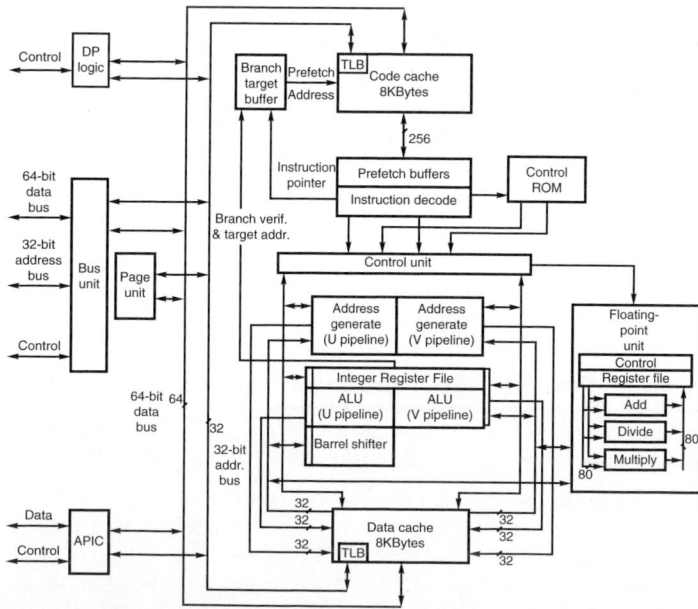

Figure 3.36   Pentium processor internal architecture.

The Pentium has a 32-bit address bus width, giving it the same 4GB memory-addressing capabilities as the 386DX and 486 processors. But the Pentium expands the data bus to 64 bits, which means it can move twice as much data into or out of the CPU, compared with a 486 of the same clock speed. The 64-bit data bus requires that system memory be accessed 64 bits wide, so each bank of memory is 64 bits.

On most motherboards, memory is installed via SIMMs or DIMMs. SIMMs are available in 8-bit-wide and 32-bit-wide versions, whereas DIMMs are 64 bits wide. In addition, versions are available with additional bits for parity or error correcting code (ECC) data. Most Pentium systems use the 32-bit-wide SIMMs—two of these SIMMs per bank of memory. Most Pentium motherboards have at least four of these 32-bit SIMM sockets, providing for a total of two banks of memory. Later Pentium systems and most Pentium II systems still in use today use DIMMs, which are 64 bits wide—just like the processor's external data bus, so only one DIMM is used per bank. This makes installing or upgrading memory much easier because DIMMs can go in one at a time and don't have to be matched up in pairs.

▶▶   See "SIMMs, DIMMs, and RIMMs," p. 477, and "Memory Banks," p. 496.

Even though the Pentium has a 64-bit data bus that transfers information 64 bits at a time into and out of the processor, the Pentium has only 32-bit internal registers. As instructions are being processed internally, they are broken down into 32-bit instructions and data elements and processed in much the same way as in the 486. Some people thought that Intel was misleading them by calling the Pentium a 64-bit processor, but 64-bit transfers do indeed take place. Internally, however, the Pentium has 32-bit registers that are fully compatible with the 486.

The Pentium has two separate internal 8KB caches, compared with a single 8KB or 16KB cache in the 486. The cache-controller circuitry and the cache memory are embedded in the CPU chip. The cache mirrors the information in normal RAM by keeping a copy of the data and code from different memory locations. The Pentium cache also can hold information to be written to memory when the load on the CPU and other system components is less. (The 486 makes all memory writes immediately.)

The separate code and data caches are organized in a two-way set associative fashion, with each set split into lines of 32 bytes each. Each cache has a dedicated translation lookaside buffer (TLB) that translates linear addresses to physical addresses. You can configure the data cache as write-back or write-through on a line-by-line basis. When you use the write-back capability, the cache can store write operations and reads, further improving performance over read-only write-through mode. Using write-back mode results in less activity between the CPU and system memory—an important improvement because CPU access to system memory is a bottleneck on fast systems. The code cache is an inherently write-protected cache because it contains only execution instructions and not data, which is updated. Because burst cycles are used, the cache data can be read or written very quickly.

Systems based on the Pentium can benefit greatly from secondary processor caches (L2), which usually consist of up to 512KB or more of extremely fast (15ns or less) SRAM chips. When the CPU fetches data that is not already available in its internal processor (L1) cache, wait states slow the CPU. If the data already is in the secondary processor cache, however, the CPU can go ahead with its work without pausing for wait states.

The Pentium uses a Bipolar Complementary Metal-Oxide Semiconductor (BiCMOS) process and super-scalar architecture to achieve the high level of performance expected from the chip. BiCMOS adds about 10% to the complexity of the chip design, but adds about 30%–35% better performance without a size or power penalty.

All 75MHz and faster Pentium processors are SL enhanced—they incorporate the SMM to provide full control of power-management features, which helps reduce power consumption. The second-generation Pentium processors (75MHz and faster) incorporate a more advanced form of SMM that includes processor clock control. This enables you to throttle the processor up or down to control power use. You can even stop the clock with these more advanced Pentium processors, putting the processor in a state of suspension that requires very little power. The second-generation Pentium processors run on 3.3V power (instead of 5V), reducing power requirements and heat generation even further.

Many Pentium motherboards supply either 3.465V or 3.3V. The 3.465V setting is called VRE (voltage reduced extended) by Intel and is required by some versions of the Pentium, particularly some of the 100MHz versions. The standard 3.3V setting is called STD (standard), which most of the second-generation Pentiums use. STD voltage means anything in a range from 3.135V to 3.465V with 3.3V nominal. Additionally, a special 3.3V setting called VR (voltage reduced) reduces the range from 3.300V to 3.465V with 3.38V nominal. Some of the processors require this narrower specification, which most motherboards provide. Here is a summary:

Voltage Specification	Nominal	Tolerance	Minimum	Maximum
STD (standard)	3.30V	±0.165	3.135V	3.465V
VR (voltage reduced)	3.38V	±0.083	3.300V	3.465V
VRE (VR extended)	3.50V	±0.100	3.400V	3.600V

For even lower power consumption, Intel introduced special Pentium processors with voltage reduction technology in the 75 to 266MHz family; the processors were intended for mobile computer applications. They did not use a conventional chip package and were instead mounted using a new format called tape carrier packaging (TCP). The tape carrier packaging does not encase the chip in ceramic or plastic as with a conventional chip package, but instead covers the actual processor die directly with a thin, protective plastic coating. The entire processor is less than 1mm thick, or about half the thickness of a dime, and weighs less than 1 gram. They were sold to system manufacturers in a roll that looks very much like a filmstrip.

The TCP processor is directly affixed (soldered) to the motherboard by a special machine, resulting in a smaller package, lower height, better thermal transfer, and lower power consumption. Special solder plugs on the circuit board located directly under the processor draw heat away and provide better cooling in the tight confines of a typical notebook or laptop system—no cooling fans are required. For more information on mobile processors and systems, see the chapter "Portable PCs" included on the disc accompanying this book.

The Pentium, like the 486, contains an internal math coprocessor or FPU. The FPU in the Pentium was rewritten to perform significantly better than the FPU in the 486 yet still be fully compatible with the 486 and 387 math coprocessors. The Pentium FPU is estimated to be two to as much as ten times faster than the FPU in the 486. In addition, the two standard instruction pipelines in the Pentium provide two units to handle standard integer math. (The math coprocessor handles only more complex calculations.) Other processors, such as the 486, have only a single-standard execution pipe and one integer math unit. Interestingly, the Pentium FPU contains a flaw that received widespread publicity. See the discussion in the section "Pentium Defects," later in this chapter.

First-Generation Pentium Processor

The Pentium has been offered in three basic designs, each with several versions. The first-generation design, which is no longer available, came in 60MHz and 66MHz processor speeds. This design used a 273-pin PGA form factor and ran on 5V power. In this design, the processor ran at the same speed as the motherboard—in other words, a 1x clock was used.

The first-generation Pentium was created through a 0.8-micron BiCMOS process. Unfortunately, this process, combined with the 3.1 million transistor count, resulted in a die that was overly large and complicated to manufacture. As a result, reduced yields kept the chip in short supply; Intel could not make them fast enough. The 0.8-micron process was criticized by other manufacturers, including Motorola and IBM, which had been using 0.6-micron technology for their most advanced chips. The huge die and 5V operating voltage caused the 66MHz versions to consume up to an incredible 3.2 amps or 16 watts of power, resulting in a tremendous amount of heat and problems in some systems that did not employ conservative design techniques. Fortunately, adding a fan to the processor solved most cooling problems, as long as the fan kept running.

Much of the criticism leveled at Intel for the first-generation Pentium was justified. Some people realized that the first-generation design was just that; they knew that new Pentium versions, made in a more advanced manufacturing process, were coming. Many of those people advised against purchasing any Pentium system until the second-generation version became available.

Tip

A cardinal rule of computing is never buy the first generation of any processor. Although you can wait forever because something better always will be on the horizon, a little waiting is worthwhile in many cases.

Those who purchased first-generation Pentiums still had a way out, however. As with previous 486 systems, Intel released OverDrive upgrade chips that effectively doubled the processor speed of the Pentium 60 or 66. These are a single-chip upgrade, meaning they replace the existing CPU. Because subsequent Pentiums are incompatible with the Pentium 60/66 Socket 4 arrangement, these OverDrive chips and comparable upgrades available from some third-party sources were the only way to upgrade an existing first-generation Pentium without replacing the motherboard.

Generally, it was better to consider a complete motherboard replacement, which would accept a newer design processor that would potentially be many times faster, than to upgrade using just an OverDrive processor, that might only be twice as fast.

Second-Generation Pentium Processor

Intel announced the second-generation Pentium on March 7, 1994. This new processor was introduced in 90MHz and 100MHz versions, with a 75MHz version not far behind. Eventually, 120MHz, 133MHz, 150MHz, 166MHz, and 200MHz versions were also introduced. The second-generation Pentium uses 0.6-micron (75/90/100MHz) BiCMOS technology to shrink the die and reduce power consumption. The newer, faster 120MHz (and higher) second-generation versions incorporate an even smaller die built on a 0.35-micron BiCMOS process. These smaller dies are not changed from the 0.6-micron versions; they are basically a photographic reduction of the P54C die. The die for the Pentium is shown in Figure 3.37. Additionally, these new processors run on 3.3V power. The 100MHz version consumes a maximum of 3.25 amps of 3.3V power, which equals only 10.725 watts. Further up the scale, the 150MHz chip uses 3.5 amps of 3.3V power (11.6 watts); the 166MHz unit draws 4.4 amps (14.5 watts); and the 200MHz processor uses 4.7 amps (15.5 watts).

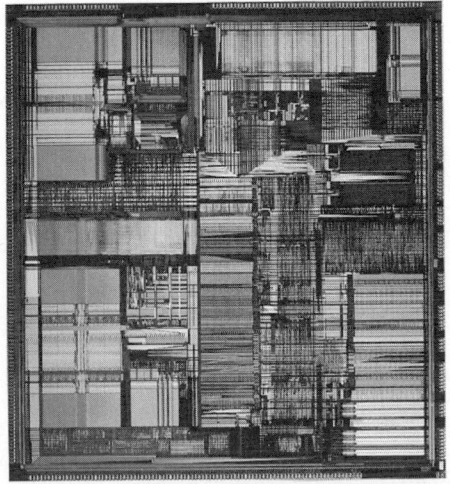

Figure 3.37   Pentium processor die. *Photograph used by permission of Intel Corporation.*

The second-generation Pentium processors come in a 296-pin SPGA form factor that is physically incompatible with the first-generation versions. The only way to upgrade from the first generation to the second is to replace the motherboard. The second-generation Pentium processors also have 3.3 million transistors—more than the earlier chips. The extra transistors exist because additional clock-control SL enhancements were added, along with an on-chip advanced programmable interrupt controller (APIC) and dual-processor interface.

The APIC and dual-processor interfaces are responsible for orchestrating dual-processor configurations in which two second-generation Pentium chips can process on the same motherboard simultaneously. Many of the Pentium motherboards designed for file servers come with dual Socket 7 specification sockets, which fully support the multiprocessing capability of the new chips. Software support for what usually is called symmetric multiprocessing (SMP) is being integrated into operating systems such as Windows NT and OS/2.

The second-generation Pentium processors use clock-multiplier circuitry to run the processor at speeds faster than the bus. The 150MHz Pentium processor, for example, can run at 2.5 times the bus frequency, which normally is 60MHz. The 200MHz Pentium processor can run at a 3x clock in a system using a 66MHz bus speed.

Virtually all Pentium motherboards had three speed settings: 50MHz, 60MHz, and 66MHz. Pentium chips were available with a variety of internal clock multipliers that caused the processor to operate at various multiples of these motherboard speeds. Refer to Table 3.7 for a list of the speeds of Pentium processors and motherboards.

The core-to-bus frequency ratio or clock multiplier is controlled in a Pentium processor by two pins on the chip labeled BF1 and BF2. Table 3.26 shows how the state of the BFx pins affects the clock multiplication in the Pentium processor.

Table 3.26   Pentium BFx Pins and Clock Multipliers

BF1	BF2	Clock Multiplier	Bus Speed (MHz)	Core Speed (MHz)
0	1	3x	66	200
0	1	3x	60	180
0	1	3x	50	150
0	0	2.5x	66	166
0	0	2.5x	60	150
0	0	2.5x	50	125
1	0	2x/4x	66	133/266[1]
1	0	2x	60	120
1	0	2x	50	100
1	1	1.5x/3.5x	66	100/233[1]
1	1	1.5x	60	90
1	1	1.5x	50	75

1. The 233MHz and 266MHz processors have modified the 1.5x and 2x multipliers to 3.5x and 4x, respectively.

Not all chips support all the bus frequency (BF) pins or combinations of settings. In other words, some of the Pentium processors operate only at specific combinations of these settings or might even be fixed at one particular setting. Many of the later Pentium motherboards included jumpers or switches that enabled you to control the BF pins and, therefore, alter the clock-multiplier ratio within the chip. In theory, you could run a 75MHz-rated Pentium chip at 133MHz by changing jumpers on the motherboard. This is called overclocking and is discussed in the section "Overclocking," earlier in this chapter. What Intel has done to discourage overclockers in its most recent Pentiums is discussed near the end of the "Processor Manufacturing" section of this chapter.

Intel also offered a single-chip OverDrive upgrade for second-generation Pentiums. These OverDrive chips are fixed at a 3x multiplier; they replace the existing Socket 5 or 7 CPU, increase processor speed up to 200MHz (with a 66MHz motherboard speed), and add MMX capability. Simply stated, a Pentium 100, 133, or 166 system equipped with the OverDrive chip has a processor speed of 200MHz. Perhaps the best feature of these Pentium OverDrive chips is that they incorporate MMX technology. MMX provides greatly enhanced performance while running the multimedia applications that are so popular today.

If you have a Socket 7 motherboard, you might not need the special OverDrive versions of the Pentium processor that have built-in voltage regulators. Instead, you can purchase a standard Pentium or Pentium-compatible chip and replace the existing processor with it. You must be sure to set the multiplier and voltage settings so that they are correct for the new processor.

Pentium-MMX Processors

A third generation of Pentium processors (codenamed P55C) was released in January 1997, and incorporates what Intel calls MMX technology into the second-generation Pentium design (see Figure 3.38). These Pentium-MMX processors are available in clock rates of 66/166MHz, 66/200MHz, and 66/233MHz and in a mobile-only version, which is 66/266MHz. The MMX processors have a lot in common with other second-generation Pentiums, including superscalar architecture, multiprocessor support, on-chip local APIC controller, and power-management features. New features include a pipelined MMX unit, 16KB code, write-back cache (versus 8KB in earlier Pentiums), and 4.5 million transistors. Pentium-MMX chips are produced on an enhanced 0.35-micron CMOS silicon process that allows for a lower 2.8V voltage level. The newer mobile 233MHz and 266MHz processors are built on a 0.25-micron process and run on only 1.8V. With this newer technology, the 266 processor actually uses less power than the non-MMX 133.

Figure 3.38   Pentium MMX. The left side shows the underside of the chip with the cover plate removed exposing the processor die. *Photograph used by permission of Intel Corporation.*

To use the Pentium-MMX, the motherboard must be capable of supplying the lower (2.8V or less) voltage these processors use. To enable a more universal motherboard solution with respect to these changing voltages, Intel has come up with the Socket 7 with VRM. The VRM is a socketed module that plugs in next to the processor and supplies the correct voltage. Because the module is easily replaced, reconfiguring a motherboard to support any of the voltages required by the newer Pentium processors is easy.

Of course, lower voltage is nice, but MMX is what this chip is really all about. MMX incorporates a process Intel calls single instruction multiple data (SIMD), which enables one instruction to perform the same function on many pieces of data. Fifty-seven new instructions designed specifically to handle video, audio, and graphics data have been added to the chip.

To add maximum upgradeability to the MMX Pentiums, a Pentium motherboard needs 321-pin processor sockets that fully meet the Intel Socket 7 specification. These also would include the VRM socket. If you have dual sockets, you can add a second Pentium processor to take advantage of SMP support in operating systems that support this feature.

Pentium Defects

Probably the most famous processor bug in history is the now legendary flaw in the Pentium FPU. It has often been called the FDIV bug because it affects primarily the FDIV (floating-point divide) instruction, although several other instructions that use division are also affected. Intel officially refers to this problem as Errata No. 23, titled "Slight precision loss for floating-point divides on specific operand pairs." The bug has been fixed in the D1 or later steppings of the 60/66MHz Pentium processors, as well as the B5 and later steppings of the 75/90/100MHz processors. The 120MHz and higher processors are manufactured from later steppings, which do not include this problem. Tables listing all the variations of Pentium processors and steppings and how to identify them appear later in this chapter.

This bug caused a tremendous fervor when it first was reported on the Internet by a mathematician in October 1994. Within a few days, news of the defect had spread nationwide, and even people who did not have computers had heard about it. The Pentium incorrectly performed floating-point division calculations with certain number combinations, with errors anywhere from the third digit on up.

By the time the bug was publicly discovered outside of Intel, the company had already incorporated the fix into the next stepping of both the 60/66MHz and the 75/90/100MHz Pentium processor, along with the other corrections Intel had made.

After the bug was made public and Intel admitted to already knowing about it, a fury erupted. As people began checking their spreadsheets and other math calculations, many discovered they had also encountered this problem and did not know it. Others who had not encountered the problem had their faith in the core of their PCs very shaken. People had come to put so much trust in the PC that they had a hard time coming to terms with the fact that it might not even be capable of doing math correctly!

One interesting result of the fervor surrounding this defect is that people are less likely to implicitly trust their PCs and are therefore doing more testing and evaluating of important results. The bottom line is that if your information and calculations are important enough, you should implement some results tests. Several math programs were found to have problems. For example, a bug was discovered in the yield function of Excel 5.0 that some were attributing to the Pentium processor. In this case, the problem turned out to be the software (which has been corrected in versions 5.0c and later).

Intel finally decided that in the best interest of the consumer and its public image, it would begin a lifetime replacement warranty on the affected processors. Therefore, if you ever encounter one of the Pentium processors with the Errata 23 floating-point bug, Intel will replace the processor with an equivalent one without this problem. Usually, all you have to do is call Intel and ask for the replacement. It will ship you a new part matching the ratings of the one you are replacing in an overnight shipping box. The replacement is free, including all shipping charges. You merely remove your old processor, replace it with the new one, and put the old one back in the box. Then you call the overnight service, who picks it up and sends it back. Intel will take a credit card number when you first call for the replacement only to ensure that the original defective chip is returned. As long as it gets the original CPU back within a specified amount of time, there will be no charges to you. Intel has indicated that these defective processors will be destroyed and will not be remarketed or resold in another form.

Testing for the FPU Bug

Testing a Pentium for this bug is relatively easy. All you have to do is execute one of the test division cases cited here and see whether your answer compares to the correct result.

The division calculation can be done in a spreadsheet (such as Lotus 1-2-3, Microsoft Excel, or any other), the Microsoft Windows built-in calculator, or any other calculating program that uses the FPU. Make sure that for the purposes of this test the FPU has not been disabled. That typically requires some special command or setting specific to the application and, of course, ensures that the test comes out correct, regardless of whether the chip is flawed.

The most severe Pentium floating-point errors occur as early as the third significant digit of the result. Here is an example of one of the more severe instances of the problem:

> 962,306,957,033 / 11,010,046 = 87,402.6282027341 (correct answer)
>
> 962,306,957,033 / 11,010,046 = 87,399.5805831329 (flawed Pentium)

Note

Note that your particular calculator program might not show the answer to the number of digits shown here. Most spreadsheet programs limit displayed results to 13 or 15 significant digits.

As you can see in the previous case, the error turns up in the third most significant digit of the result. In an examination of more than 5,000 integer pairs in the 5- to 15-digit range found to produce Pentium floating-point division errors, errors beginning in the sixth significant digit were the most likely to occur.

Several workarounds are available for this bug, but they extract a performance penalty. Because Intel has agreed to replace any Pentium processor with this flaw under a lifetime warranty replacement program, the best workaround is a free replacement!

Power Management Bugs

Starting with the second-generation Pentium processors, Intel added functions that enable these CPUs to be installed in energy-efficient systems. These are usually called *Energy Star systems* because they meet the specifications imposed by the EPA Energy Star program, but they are also unofficially called *green PCs* by many users.

Unfortunately, there have been several bugs with respect to these functions, causing them to either fail or be disabled. These bugs are in some of the functions in the power-management capabilities accessed through SMM. These problems are applicable only to the second-generation 75/90/100MHz processors because the first-generation 60/66MHz processors do not have SMM or power-management capabilities, and all higher-speed (120MHz and up) processors have the bugs fixed.

Most of the problems are related to the STPCLK# pin and the HALT instruction. If this condition is invoked by the chipset, the system will hang. For most systems, the only workaround for this problem is to disable the power-saving modes, such as suspend or sleep. Unfortunately, this means that your green PC won't be so green anymore! The best way to repair the problem is to replace the processor with a later stepping version that does not have the bug. These bugs affect the B1 stepping version of the 75/90/100MHz Pentiums, and they were fixed in the B3 and later stepping versions.

Pentium Processor Models and Steppings

We know that like software, no processor is truly ever perfect. From time to time, the manufacturers gather up what problems they have found and put into production a new stepping, which consists of a new set of masks that incorporate the corrections. Each subsequent stepping is better and more refined than the previous ones. Although no microprocessor is ever perfect, they come closer to perfection with each stepping. In the life of a typical microprocessor, a manufacturer might go through half a dozen or more such steppings.

See *Upgrading and Repairing PCs, Tenth Anniversary Edition,* which is included on the disc, for tables showing the Pentium processor steppings and revisions. This information is also available online from Intel via its Web site.

To determine the specifications of a given processor, you must look up the S-spec number in the table of processor specifications. To find your S-spec number, you have to read it off the chip directly. It can be found printed on both the top and bottom of the chip. If your heatsink is glued on, remove the chip and heatsink from the socket as a unit and read the numbers from the bottom of the chip. Then, you can look up the S-spec number in the Specification Guide Intel publishes (via its Web site); it tells you the specifications of that particular processor. Intel is introducing new chips all the time, so visit its Web site and search for the Pentium processor "Quick Reference Guide" in the developer portion of its site. There you will find a complete listing of all current processor specifications by S-spec number.

One interesting item to note is that several subtly different voltages are required by different Pentium processors. Table 3.27 summarizes the various processors and their required voltages.

Table 3.27   Pentium Processor Voltages

Model	Stepping	Voltage Spec.	Voltage Range
1	—	Std.	4.75V–5.25V
1	—	5V1	4.90V–5.25V
1	—	5V2	4.90V–5.40V
1	—	5V3	5.15V–5.40V
2+	B1-B5	Std.	3.135V–3.465V
2+	C2+	Std.	3.135V–3.600V
2+	—	VR	3.300V–3.465V
2+	B1-B5	VRE	3.45V–3.60V
2+	C2+	VRE	3.40V–3.60V
4+	—	MMX	2.70V–2.90V
4	3	Mobile	2.285V–2.665V
4	3	Mobile	2.10V–2.34V
8	1	Mobile	1.850V–2.150V
8	1	Mobile	1.665V–1.935V

Many of the newer Pentium motherboards have jumpers that allow for adjustments to the different voltage ranges. If you are having problems with a particular processor, it might not be matched correctly to your motherboard voltage output.

If you are purchasing an older, used Pentium system today, I recommend using only Model 2 (second-generation) or later version processors that are available in 75MHz or faster speeds. You should definitely get stepping C2 or later. Virtually all the important bugs and problems were fixed in the C2 and later releases. The newer Pentium processors have no serious bugs to worry about.

AMD-K5

The AMD-K5 is a Pentium-compatible processor developed by AMD and available as the PR75, PR90, PR100, PR120, PR133, PR166, and PR200. Because it is designed to be physically and functionally compatible, any motherboard that properly supports the Intel Pentium should support the AMD-K5. However, a BIOS upgrade might be required to properly recognize the AMD-K5. The K5 has the following features:

- 16KB instruction cache, 8KB write-back data cache
- Dynamic execution—branch prediction with speculative execution
- Five-stage, RISC-like pipeline with six parallel functional units

■ High-performance floating-point unit

■ Pin-selectable clock multiples of 1.5x, 1.75x, and 2x

The K5 is sold under the P-Rating system, which means that the number on the chip does not indicate true clock speed, only apparent speed when running certain applications.

Note that the actual clock speeds of several of these processors are not the same as their apparent rated speeds. For example, the PR-166 version actually runs at only 117 true MHz. Sometimes this can confuse the system BIOS, which might report the true speed rather than the P-Rating, which compares the chip against an Intel Pentium of that speed. AMD's assertion is that because of architecture enhancements over the Pentium, they do not need to run the same clock frequency to achieve that same performance. Even with such improvements, AMD marketed the K5 as a fifth-generation processor, just like the Pentium.

The AMD-K5 operates at 3.52V (VRE setting). Some older motherboards default to 3.3V, which is below specification for the K5 and could cause erratic operation. Because of the relatively low clock speeds and compatibility issues some users experienced with the K5, AMD replaced it with the K6 family of processors.

Intel P6 (686) Sixth-Generation Processors

The P6 (686) processors represent a new generation with features not found in the previous generation units. The P6 processor family began when the Pentium Pro was released in November 1995. Since then, Intel has released many other P6 chips, all using the same basic P6 core processor as the Pentium Pro. Table 3.28 shows the variations in the P6 family of processors.

Table 3.28   Intel P6 Processor Variations

Pentium Pro	Original P6 processor, includes 256KB, 512KB, or 1MB of full-core speed L2 cache
Pentium II	P6 with 512KB of half-core speed L2 cache
Pentium II Xeon	P6 with 512KB, 1MB, or 2MB of full-core speed L2 cache
Celeron	P6 with no L2 cache
Celeron-A	P6 with 128KB of on-die full-core speed L2 cache
Pentium III	P6 with SSE (MMX2), 512KB of half-core speed L2 cache
Pentium IIPE	P6 with 256KB of full-core speed L2 cache
Pentium IIIE	P6 with SSE (MMX2) plus 256KB or 512KB of full-core speed L2 cache
Pentium III Xeon	P6 with SSE (MMX2), 512KB, 1MB, or 2MB of full-core speed L2 cache

The main new feature in the fifth-generation Pentium processors was the superscalar architecture, in which two instruction execution units could execute instructions simultaneously in parallel. Later fifth-generation chips also added MMX technology to the mix, as well. So then what did Intel add in the sixth generation to justify calling it a whole new generation of chip? Besides many minor improvements, the real key features of all sixth-generation processors are Dynamic Execution and the Dual Independent Bus (DIB) architecture, plus a greatly improved superscalar design.

Dynamic Execution

Dynamic execution enables the processor to execute more instructions on parallel, so tasks are completed more quickly. This technology innovation is comprised of three main elements:

■ *Multiple branch prediction.* Predict the flow of the program through several branches

■ *Dataflow analysis.* Schedules instructions to be executed when ready, independent of their order in the original program

■ *Speculative execution.* Increases the rate of execution by looking ahead of the program counter and executing instructions that are likely to be necessary

Dual Independent Bus

The other main P6 architecture feature is known as the Dual Independent Bus. This refers to the fact that the processor has two data buses: one for the system (motherboard) and the other just for cache. This enables the cache memory to run at speeds previously not possible.

Other Sixth-Generation Improvements

Finally, the P6 architecture upgrades the superscalar architecture of the P5 processors by adding more instruction execution units and by breaking down the instructions into special micro-ops. This is where the CISC instructions are broken down into more RISC commands. The RISC-level commands are smaller and easier for the parallel instruction units to execute more efficiently. With this design, Intel has brought the benefits of a RISC processor—high-speed dedicated instruction execution—to the CISC world. Note that the P5 had only two instruction units, whereas the P6 has at least six separate dedicated instruction units. It is said to be three-way superscalar because the multiple instruction units can execute up to three instructions in one cycle.

Other improvements in efficiency also are included in the P6 architecture: built-in multiprocessor support, enhanced error detection and correction circuitry, and optimization for 32-bit software.

Rather than just being a faster Pentium, the Pentium Pro, Pentium II/III, and other sixth-generation processors have many feature and architectural improvements. The core of the chip is very RISC-like, whereas the external instruction interface is classic Intel CISC. By breaking down the CISC instructions into several RISC instructions and running them down parallel execution pipelines, the overall performance is increased.

Compared to a Pentium at the same clock speed, the P6 processors are faster—as long as you're running 32-bit software. The P6 Dynamic Execution is optimized for performance primarily when running 32-bit software, such as Windows NT. If you are using 16-bit software, such as Windows 95 or 98 (which still operate part time in a 16-bit environment) and most older applications, the P6 does not provide as marked a performance improvement over similarly speed-rated Pentium and Pentium-MMX processors. That's because the Dynamic Execution capability is not fully exploited. Because of this, Windows NT/2000/XP often are regarded as the most desirable operating systems for use with Pentium Pro/II/III/Celeron processors. Although this is not exactly true (a Pentium Pro/II/III/Celeron runs fine under Windows 95/98), Windows NT/2000/XP does take better advantage of the P6's capabilities.

Note that it is really not so much the operating system but which applications you use. Software developers can take steps to gain the full advantages of the sixth-generation processors. This includes using modern compilers that can improve performance for all current Intel processors, writing 32-bit code where possible, and making code as predictable as possible to take advantage of the processor's Dynamic Execution multiple branch prediction capabilities.

Pentium Pro Processors

Intel's successor to the Pentium is called the Pentium Pro. The Pentium Pro was the first chip in the P6 or sixth-generation processor family. It was introduced in November 1995 and became widely available in 1996. The chip is a 387-pin unit that resides in Socket 8, so it is not pin compatible with earlier Pentiums. The new chip is unique among processors because it is constructed in a multichip module (MCM) physical format, which Intel calls a dual cavity PGA package. Inside the 387-pin chip carrier are two dies. One contains the actual Pentium Pro processor (shown in Figure 3.39), and the other contains a 256KB (the Pentium Pro with 256KB cache is shown in Figure 3.40), 512KB, or 1MB L2 cache. The processor die contains 5.5 million transistors, the 256KB cache die contains 15.5 million transistors, and the 512KB cache die(s) have 31 million transistors each—for a potential total of nearly 68 million transistors in a Pentium Pro with 1MB of internal cache! A Pentium Pro with 1MB cache has two 512KB cache die and a standard P6 processor die (see Figure 3.41).

Figure 3.39   Pentium Pro processor die. *Photograph used by permission of Intel Corporation.*

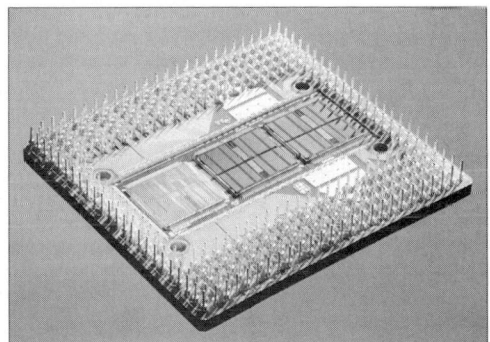

Figure 3.40   Pentium Pro processor with 256KB L2 cache (the cache is on the left side of the processor die). *Photograph used by permission of Intel Corporation.*

Figure 3.41   Pentium Pro processor with 1MB L2 cache (the cache is in the center and right portions of the die). *Photograph used by permission of Intel Corporation.*

The main processor die includes a 16KB split L1 cache with an 8KB two-way set associative cache for primary instructions and an 8KB four-way set associative cache for data.

Another sixth-generation processor feature found in the Pentium Pro is the DIB architecture, which addresses the memory bandwidth limitations of previous-generation processor architectures. Two buses make up the DIB architecture: the L2 cache bus (contained entirely within the processor package) and the processor-to-main memory system bus. The speed of the dedicated L2 cache bus on the Pentium Pro is equal to the full-core speed of the processor. This was accomplished by embedding the cache chips directly into the Pentium Pro package. The DIB processor bus architecture addresses processor-to-memory bus bandwidth limitations. It offers up to three times the performance bandwidth of the single-bus, "Socket 7" generation processors, such as the Pentium.

Table 3.29 shows Pentium Pro processor specifications, and Table 3.30 shows the specifications for each model within the Pentium Pro family because many variations exist from model to model.

Table 3.29   Pentium Pro Family Processor Specifications

Introduced	November 1995
Maximum rated speeds	150MHz, 166MHz, 180MHz, 200MHz
CPU clock	2x, 2.5x, 3x, 3.5x, 4x
Internal registers	32-bit
External data bus	64-bit
Memory address bus	36-bit
Addressable memory	64GB
Virtual memory	64TB
Integral L1 cache size	8KB code, 8KB data (16KB total)
Integrated L2 cache bus	64-bit, full-core speed
Socket/Slot	Socket 8
Physical package	387-pin dual cavity PGA
Package dimensions	2.46 (6.25cm)×2.66 (6.76cm)
Math coprocessor	Built-in FPU
Power management	SMM
Operating voltage	3.1V or 3.3V

Table 3.30   Pentium Pro Processor Specifications by Processor Model

Pentium Pro Processor (200MHz) with 1MB Integrated Level 2 Cache	
Introduction date	August 18, 1997
Clock speeds	200MHz (66MHz×3)
Number of transistors	5.5 million (0.35-micron process), plus 62 million in 1MB L2 cache (0.35-micron)
Cache memory	8K×2 (16KB) L1, 1MB core-speed L2
Die size	0.552" per side (14.0mm)
Pentium Pro Processor (166/180/200MHz)	
Introduction date	November 1, 1995
Clock speeds	200MHz (66MHz×3), 180MHz (60MHz×3), 166MHz (66MHz×2.5)
Number of transistors	5.5 million (0.35-micron process), plus 15.5 million in 256KB L2 cache (0.6-micron), or 31 million in 512KB L2 cache (0.35-micron)
Cache memory	8K×2 (16KB) L1, 256KB or 512KB core-speed L2
Die size	0.552" per side (14.0mm)
Pentium Pro Processor (150MHz)	
Introduction date	November 1, 1995
Clock speeds	150MHz (60MHz×2.5)
Number of transistors	5.5 million (0.6-micron process), plus 15.5 million in 256KB L2 cache (0.6-micron)
Cache memory	8K×2 (16KB) L1, 256KB core-speed L2
Die size	0.691" per side (17.6mm)

Performance comparisons on the iCOMP 2.0 Index rate a classic Pentium 200MHz at 142, whereas a Pentium Pro 200MHz scores an impressive 220. Just for comparison, note that a Pentium MMX 200MHz falls right about in the middle in regards to performance at 182. Keep in mind that using a Pentium Pro with any 16-bit software applications nullifies much of the performance gain shown by the iCOMP 2.0 rating.

Similar to the Pentium before it, the Pentium Pro runs clock multiplied on a 66MHz motherboard. The following table lists speeds for Pentium Pro processors and motherboards:

CPU Type/Speed	CPU Clock	Motherboard Speed
Pentium Pro 150	2.5x	60
Pentium Pro 166	2.5x	66
Pentium Pro 180	3x	60
Pentium Pro 200	3x	66

The integrated L2 cache is one of the really outstanding features of the Pentium Pro. By building the L2 cache into the CPU and getting it off the motherboard, the Pentium Pro can now run the cache at full processor speed rather than the slower 60MHz or 66MHz motherboard bus speed. In fact, the L2 cache features its own internal 64-bit back-side bus, which does not share time with the external 64-bit front-side bus used by the CPU. The internal registers and data paths are still 32-bit, as with the Pentium. By building the L2 cache into the system, motherboards can be cheaper because they no longer require separate cache memory. Some boards might still try to include cache memory in their designs, but the general consensus is that L3 cache (as it would be called) would offer less improvement with the Pentium Pro than with the Pentium.

One of the features of the built-in L2 cache is that multiprocessing is greatly improved. Rather than just SMP, as with the Pentium, the Pentium Pro supports a new type of multiprocessor configuration called the Multiprocessor Specification (MPS 1.1). The Pentium Pro with MPS enables configurations of up to four processors running together. Unlike other multiprocessor configurations, the Pentium Pro avoids cache coherency problems because each chip maintains a separate L1 and L2 cache internally.

Pentium Pro–based motherboards are pretty much exclusively PCI and ISA bus-based, and Intel has produced its own chipsets for these motherboards. Because of the greater cooling and space requirements, Intel designed the new ATX motherboard form factor to better support the Pentium Pro and other future processors, such as the Pentium II/III/4. Even so, the Pentium Pro can be found in all types of motherboard designs; ATX is not mandatory.

▶▶ See "Motherboard Form Factors," p. 202, and "Sixth-Generation (P6 Pentium Pro/Pentium II Class) Chipsets," p. 254.

The Pentium Pro system manufacturers were tempted to stick with the Baby-AT form factor. The big problem with the standard Baby-AT form factor is keeping the CPU properly cooled. The massive Pentium Pro processor consumes more than 25 watts and generates an appreciable amount of heat.

Four special VID pins are on the Pentium Pro processor. These pins can be used to support automatic selection of power supply voltage. Therefore, a Pentium Pro motherboard does not have voltage regulator jumper settings like most Pentium boards, which greatly eases the setup and integration of a Pentium Pro system. These pins are not actually signals, but are either an open circuit in the package or a short circuit to voltage. The sequence of opens and shorts defines the voltage the processor requires. In addition to allowing for automatic voltage settings, this feature was designed to support voltage specification variations on future Pentium Pro processors. The VID pins are named VID0 through VID3, and the definition of these pins is shown in Table 3.31. A 1 in this table refers to an open pin, and a 0 refers to a short to ground. The voltage regulators on the motherboard should supply the requested voltage or disable itself.

Table 3.31 Pentium Pro Voltage Identification Definition

VID [3:0]	Voltage Setting	VID [3:0]	Voltage Setting	VID [3:0]	Voltage Setting	VID [3:0]	Voltage Setting
0000	3.5	1000	2.7	0100	3.1	1100	2.3
0001	3.4	1001	2.6	0101	3.0	1101	2.2
0010	3.3	1010	2.5	0110	2.9	1110	2.1
0011	3.2	1011	2.4	0111	2.8	1111	No CPU present

Most Pentium Pro processors run at 3.3V, but a few run at 3.1V. Note that the 1111 (or all opens) ID can be used to detect the absence of a processor in a given socket.

The Pentium Pro never did become very popular on the desktop, but it did find a niche in file-server applications primarily because of the full-core speed high-capacity internal L2 cache. For a time, Intel offered an OverDrive upgrade processor for the Pentium Pro, but it no longer offers any OverDrive processors. PowerLeap offers several upgrades for Pentium Pro that use 700MHz-class Celeron PPGA processors in an adapter.

Pentium II Processors

Intel revealed the Pentium II in May 1997. Prior to its official unveiling, the Pentium II processor was popularly referred to by its codename, Klamath, and was surrounded by much speculation throughout the industry. The Pentium II is essentially the same sixth-generation processor as the Pentium Pro, with MMX technology added (which included double the L1 cache and 57 new MMX instructions); however, there are a few twists to the design. The Pentium II processor die is shown in Figure 3.42.

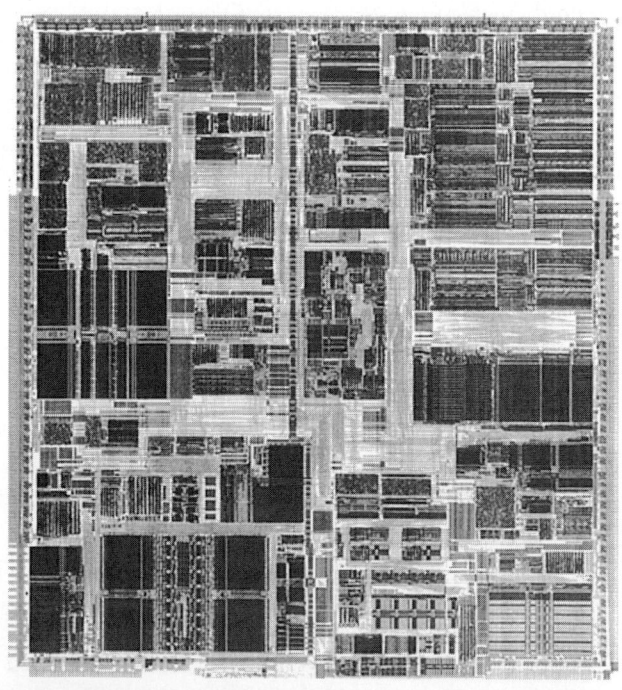

Figure 3.42 Pentium II Processor die. *Photograph used by permission of Intel Corporation.*

From a physical standpoint, it was a big departure from previous processors. Abandoning the chip in a socket approach used by virtually all processors up until this point, the Pentium II chip is characterized by its SEC cartridge design. The processor, along with several L2 cache chips, is mounted on a small circuit board (much like an oversized-memory SIMM) as shown in Figure 3.43, and the circuit board is then sealed in a metal and plastic cartridge. The cartridge is then plugged into the motherboard through an edge connector called Slot 1, which looks very much like an adapter card slot.

Figure 3.43   Pentium II processor board (normally found inside the SEC cartridge). *Photograph used by permission of Intel Corporation.*

The two variations on these cartridges are called SECC (single edge contact cartridge) and SECC2. Figure 3.44 shows a diagram of the SECC package; Figure 3.45 shows the SECC2 package.

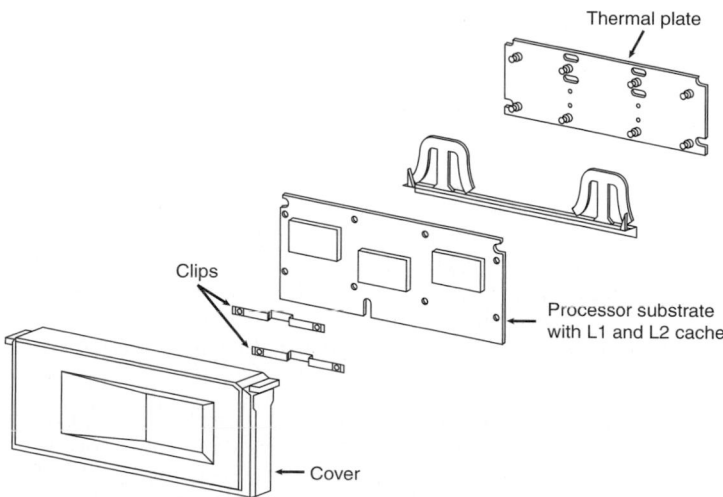

Figure 3.44   SECC components showing an enclosed processor board.

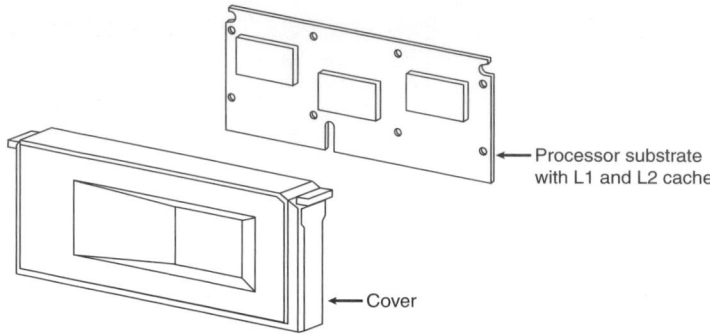

Processor substrate
with L1 and L2 cache

Cover

Figure 3.45 SECC, rev. 2 components showing a half-enclosed processor board.

As you can see from these figures, the SECC2 version is cheaper to make because it uses fewer overall parts. It also allows for a more direct heatsink attachment to the processor for better cooling. Intel transitioned from SECC to SECC2 in the beginning of 1999; all later PII chips, and the Slot 1 PIII chips that followed, use the improved SECC2 design.

By using separate chips mounted on a circuit board, Intel could build the Pentium II much less expensively than the multiple die within a package used in the Pentium Pro. Intel could also use cache chips from other manufacturers and more easily vary the amount of cache in future processors compared to the Pentium Pro design.

Intel has offered Pentium II processors with the following speeds:

CPU Type/Speed	CPU Clock	Motherboard Speed
Pentium II 233MHz	3.5x	66MHz
Pentium II 266MHz	4x	66MHz
Pentium II 300MHz	4.5x	66MHz
Pentium II 333MHz	5x	66MHz
Pentium II 350MHz	3.5x	100MHz
Pentium II 400MHz	4x	100MHz
Pentium II 450MHz	4.5x	100MHz

The Pentium II processor core has 7.5 million transistors and is based on Intel's advanced P6 architecture. The Pentium II started out using a 0.35-micron process technology, although the 333MHz and faster Pentium IIs are based on 0.25-micron technology. This enables a smaller die, allowing increased core frequencies and reduced power consumption. At 333MHz, the Pentium II processor delivers a 75%–150% performance boost, compared to the 233MHz Pentium processor with MMX technology, and approximately 50% more performance on multimedia benchmarks. As shown earlier in Table 3.3, the iCOMP 2.0 Index rating for the Pentium II 266MHz chip is more than twice as fast as a classic Pentium 200MHz.

Aside from speed, the best way to think of the Pentium II is as a Pentium Pro with MMX technology instructions and a slightly modified cache design. It has the same multiprocessor scalability as the Pentium Pro, as well as the integrated L2 cache. The 57 new multimedia-related instructions carried over from the MMX processors and the capability to process repetitive loop commands more efficiently are included as well. Also included as a part of the MMX upgrade is double the internal L1 cache from the Pentium Pro (from 16KB total to 32KB total in the Pentium II).

Maximum power usage for the Pentium II is shown in the following table:

Core Speed	Power Draw	Process	Voltage
450MHz	27.1w	0.25-micron	2.0V
400MHz	24.3w	0.25-micron	2.0V
350MHz	21.5w	0.25-micron	2.0V
333MHz	23.7w	0.25-micron	2.0V
300MHz	43.0w	0.35-micron	2.8V
266MHz	38.2w	0.35-micron	2.8V
233MHz	34.8w	0.35-micron	2.8V

You can see that the highest speed 450MHz version of the Pentium II actually uses less power than the slowest original 233MHz version! This was accomplished by using the smaller 0.25-micron process and running the processor on a lower voltage of only 2.0V. Pentium III and subsequent processors used even smaller processes and lower voltages to continue this trend.

The Pentium II includes Dynamic Execution, which describes unique performance-enhancing developments by Intel and was first introduced in the Pentium Pro processor. Major features of Dynamic Execution include multiple branch prediction, which speeds execution by predicting the flow of the program through several branches; dataflow analysis, which analyzes and modifies the program order to execute instructions when ready; and speculative execution, which looks ahead of the program counter and executes instruction that are likely to be needed. The Pentium II processor expands on these capabilities in sophisticated and powerful new ways to deliver even greater performance gains.

Similar to the Pentium Pro, the Pentium II also includes DIB architecture. The term *Dual Independent Bus* comes from the existence of two independent buses on the Pentium II processor—the L2 cache bus and the processor–to–main-memory system bus. The Pentium II processor can use both buses simultaneously, thus getting as much as twice as much data in and out of the Pentium II processor as a single-bus architecture processor. The DIB architecture enables the L2 cache of the 333MHz Pentium II processor to run 2 1/2 times as fast as the L2 cache of Pentium processors. As the frequency of future Pentium II processors increases, so will the speed of the L2 cache. Also, the pipelined system bus enables simultaneous parallel transactions instead of singular sequential transactions. Together, these DIB architecture improvements offer up to three times the bandwidth performance over a single-bus architecture as with the regular Pentium.

Table 3.32 shows the general Pentium II processor specifications. Table 3.33 shows the specifications that vary by model.

Table 3.32   Pentium II General Processor Specifications

Bus speeds	66MHz, 100MHz
CPU clock multiplier	3.5x, 4x, 4.5x, 5x
CPU speeds	233MHz, 266MHz, 300MHz, 333MHz, 350MHz, 400MHz, 450MHz
Cache memory	16K×2 (32KB) L1, 512KB 1/2-speed L2
Internal registers	32-bit
External data bus	64-bit system bus w/ ECC; 64-bit cache bus w/ optional ECC
Memory address bus	36-bit
Addressable memory	64GB
Virtual memory	64TB
Physical package	Single edge contact cartridge (S.E), 242 pins
Package dimensions	5.505" (13.98cm) × 2.473" (6.28cm) × 0.647" (1.64cm)
Math coprocessor	Built-in FPU
Power management	SMM

Table 3.33   Pentium II Specifications by Model

Pentium II MMX Processor (350MHz, 400MHz, and 450MHz)

Introduction date	April 15, 1998
Clock speeds	350MHz (100MHz×3.5), 400MHz (100MHz×4), and 450MHz (100MHz×4.5)
iCOMP Index 2.0 rating	386 (350MHz), 440 (400MHz), and 483 (450MHz)
Number of transistors	7.5 million (0.25-micron process), plus 31 million in 512KB L2 cache
Cacheable RAM	4GB
Operating voltage	2.0V
Slot	Slot 1
Die size	0.400" per side (10.2mm)

Mobile Pentium II Processor (266MHz, 300MHz, 333MHz, and 366MHz)

Introduction date	January 25, 1999
Clock speeds	266MHz, 300MHz, 333MHz, and 366MHz
Number of transistors	27.4 million (0.25-micron process), 256KB on-die L2 cache
Ball grid array (BGA)	Number of balls = 615
Dimensions	Width = 31mm; length = 35mm
Core voltage	1.6 volts
Thermal design power ranges by frequency	366MHz = 9.5 watts; 333MHz = 8.6 watts; 300MHz = 7.7 watts; 266MHz = 7.0 watts

Pentium II MMX Processor (333MHz)

Introduction date	January 26, 1998
Clock speed	333MHz (66MHz×5)
iCOMP Index 2.0 rating	366
Number of transistors	7.5 million (0.25-micron process), plus 31 million in 512KB L2 cache
Cacheable RAM	512MB
Operating voltage	2.0V
Slot	Slot 1
Die size	0.400" per side (10.2mm)

Pentium II MMX Processor (300MHz)

Introduction date	May 7, 1997
Clock speed	300MHz (66MHz×4.5)
iCOMP Index 2.0 rating	332
Number of transistors	7.5 million (0.35-micron process), plus 31 million in 512KB L2 cache
Cacheable RAM	512MB
Die size	0.560" per side (14.2mm)

Pentium II MMX Processor (266MHz)

Introduction date	May 7, 1997
Clock speed	266MHz (66MHz×4)
iCOMP Index 2.0 rating	303
Number of transistors	7.5 million (0.35-micron process), plus 31 million in 512KB L2 cache

Table 3.33   Continued

Pentium II MMX Processor (266MHz)	
Cacheable RAM	512MB
Slot	Slot 1
Die size	0.560" per side (14.2mm)
Pentium II MMX Processor (233MHz)	
Introduction date	May 7, 1997
Clock speed	233MHz (66MHz×3.5)
iCOMP Index 2.0 rating	267
Number of transistors	7.5 million (0.35-micron process), plus 31 million in 512KB L2 cache
Cacheable RAM	512MB
Slot	Slot 1
Die size	0.560" per side (14.2mm)

The L1 cache always runs at full-core speeds because it is mounted directly on the processor die. The L2 cache in the Pentium II normally runs at half-core speed, which saves money and allows for less expensive cache chips to be used. For example, in a 333MHz Pentium II, the L1 cache runs at a full 333MHz, whereas the L2 cache runs at 167MHz. Even though the L2 cache is not at full-core speed as it was with the Pentium Pro, this is still far superior to having cache memory on the motherboard running at the 66MHz motherboard speed of most Socket 7 Pentium designs. Intel claims that the DIB architecture in the Pentium II enables up to three times the bandwidth of normal single-bus processors, such as the original Pentium.

By removing the cache from the processor's internal package and using external chips mounted on a substrate and encased in the cartridge design, Intel can now use more cost-effective cache chips and more easily scale the processor up to higher speeds. The Pentium Pro was limited in speed to 200MHz, largely due to the inability to find affordable cache memory that runs any faster. By running the cache memory at half-core speed, the Pentium II can run up to 400MHz while still using 200MHz-rated cache chips. To offset the half-core speed cache used in the Pentium II, Intel doubled the basic amount of integrated L2 cache from 256KB standard in the Pro to 512KB standard in the Pentium II.

Note that the tag RAM included in the L2 cache enables up to 512MB of main memory to be cacheable in PII processors from 233MHz to 333MHz. The 350MHz, 400MHz, and faster versions include an enhanced tag-RAM that allows up to 4GB of main memory to be cacheable. This is very important if you ever plan on adding more than 512MB of memory. In that case, you would definitely want the 350MHz or faster version; otherwise, memory performance would suffer.

The system bus of the Pentium II provides "glueless" support for up to two processors. This enables low-cost, two-way multiprocessing on the L2 cache bus. These system buses are designed especially for servers or other mission-critical system use where reliability and data integrity are important. All Pentium IIs also include parity-protected address/request and response system bus signals with a retry mechanism for high data integrity and reliability.

To install the Pentium II in a system, a special processor-retention mechanism is required. This consists of a mechanical support that attaches to the motherboard and secures the Pentium II processor in Slot 1 to prevent shock and vibration damage. Retention mechanisms should be provided by the motherboard manufacturer. (For example, the Intel Boxed AL440FX and DK440LX motherboards included a retention mechanism, plus other important system integration components.)

The Pentium II can generate a significant amount of heat that must be dissipated. This is accomplished by installing a heatsink on the processor. Many of the Pentium II processors use an active heatsink that incorporates a fan. Unlike heatsink fans for previous Intel boxed processors, the Pentium II fans draw power from a three-pin power header on the motherboard. Most motherboards provide several fan connectors to supply this power.

Special heatsink supports are necessary to furnish mechanical support between the fan heatsink and support holes on the motherboard. Normally, a plastic support is inserted into the heatsink holes in the motherboard next to the CPU, before installing the CPU/heatsink package. Most fan heatsinks have two components: a fan in a plastic shroud and a metal heatsink. The heatsink is attached to the processor's thermal plate and should not be removed. The fan can be removed and replaced if necessary—for example, if it has failed. Figure 3.46 shows the SEC assembly with fan, power connectors, mechanical supports, and the slot and support holes on the motherboard.

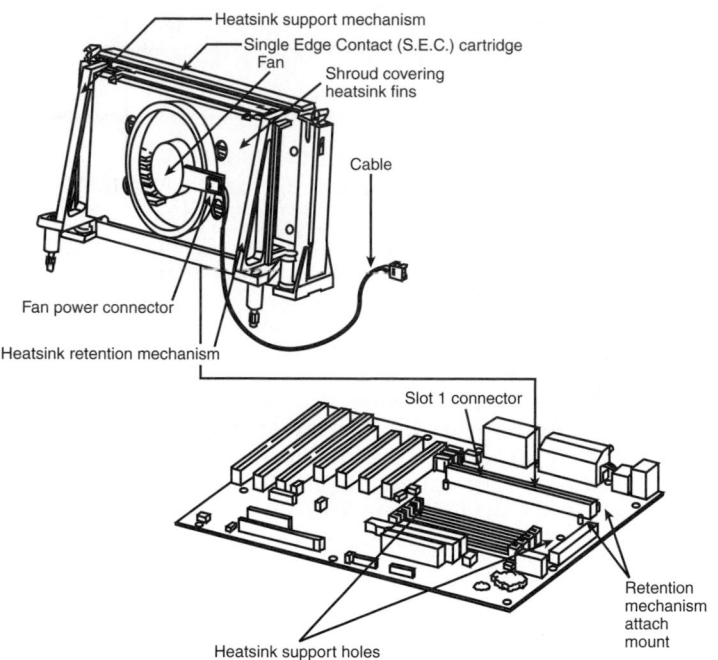

Figure 3.46 Pentium II/III processor and heatsink assembly.

The following tables show the specifications unique to certain versions of the Pentium II processor.

To identify exactly which Pentium II processor you have and what its capabilities are, look at the specification number printed on the SEC cartridge. You will find the specification number in the dynamic mark area on the top of the processor module. See Figure 3.47 to locate these markings.

After you have located the specification number (actually, it is an alphanumeric code), you can look it up in Table 3.34 to see exactly which processor you have.

For example, a specification number of SL2KA identifies the processor as a Pentium II 333MHz running on a 66MHz system bus, with an ECC L2 cache, and indicates that this processor runs on only 2.0V. The stepping is also identified, and by looking in the "Pentium II Specification Update Manual" published by Intel, you could figure out exactly which bugs were fixed in that revision.

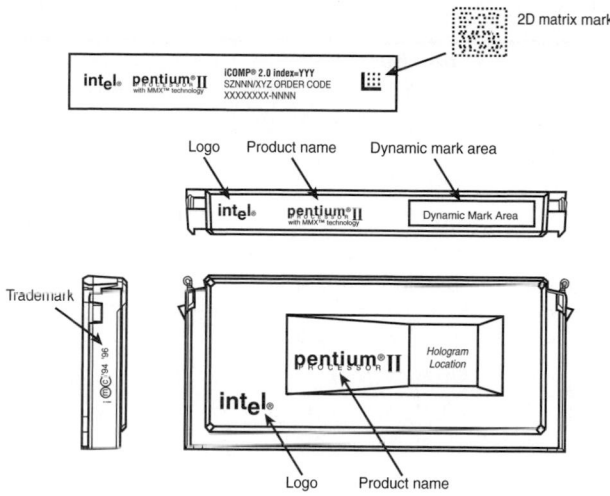

Figure 3.47   Pentium II/III SECC.

Table 3.34   Basic Pentium II Processor Identification Information

S-spec	Core Stepping	CPUID	Core/Bus Speed (MHz)	L2 Cache Size (KB)	L2 Cache Type	CPU Package	Notes (see footnotes)
SL264	C0	0633h	233/66	512	non-ECC	SECC 3.00	5
SL265	C0	0633h	266/66	512	non-ECC	SECC 3.00	5
SL268	C0	0633h	233/66	512	ECC	SECC 3.00	5
SL269	C0	0633h	266/66	512	ECC	SECC 3.00	5
SL28K	C0	0633h	233/66	512	non-ECC	SECC 3.00	1, 3, 5
SL28L	C0	0633h	266/66	512	non-ECC	SECC 3.00	1, 3, 5
SL28R	C0	0633h	300/66	512	ECC	SECC 3.00	5
SL2MZ	C0	0633h	300/66	512	ECC	SECC 3.00	1, 5
SL2HA	C1	0634h	300/66	512	ECC	SECC 3.00	5
SL2HC	C1	0634h	266/66	512	non-ECC	SECC 3.00	5
SL2HD	C1	0634h	233/66	512	non-ECC	SECC 3.00	5
SL2HE	C1	0634h	266/66	512	ECC	SECC 3.00	5
SL2HF	C1	0634h	233/66	512	ECC	SECC 3.00	5
SL2QA	C1	0634h	233/66	512	non-ECC	SECC 3.00	1, 3, 5
SL2QB	C1	0634h	266/66	512	non-ECC	SECC 3.00	1, 3, 5
SL2QC	C1	0634h	300/66	512	ECC	SECC 3.00	1, 5
SL2KA	dA0	0650h	333/66	512	ECC	SECC 3.00	5
SL2QF	dA0	0650h	333/66	512	ECC	SECC 3.00	1
SL2K9	dA0	0650h	266/66	512	ECC	SECC 3.00	
SL35V	dA1	0651h	300/66	512	ECC	SECC 3.00	1, 2
SL2QH	dA1	0651h	333/66	512	ECC	SECC 3.00	1, 2
SL2S5	dA1	0651h	333/66	512	ECC	SECC 3.00	2, 5
SL2ZP	dA1	0651h	333/66	512	ECC	SECC 3.00	2, 5
SL2ZQ	dA1	0651h	350/100	512	ECC	SECC 3.00	2, 5

Table 3.34 Continued

S-spec	Core Stepping	CPUID	Core/Bus Speed (MHz)	L2 Cache Size (KB)	L2 Cache Type	CPU Package	Notes (see footnotes)
SL2S6	dA1	0651h	350/100	512	ECC	SECC 3.00	2, 5
SL2S7	dA1	0651h	400/100	512	ECC	SECC 3.00	2, 5
SL2SF	dA1	0651h	350/100	512	ECC	SECC 3.00	1, 2
SL2SH	dA1	0651h	400/100	512	ECC	SECC 3.00	1, 2
SL2VY	dA1	0651h	300/66	512	ECC	SECC 3.00	1, 2
SL33D	dB0	0652h	266/66	512	ECC	SECC 3.00	1, 2, 5
SL2YK	dB0	0652h	300/66	512	ECC	SECC 3.00	1, 2, 5
SL2WZ	dB0	0652h	350/100	512	ECC	SECC 3.00	1, 2, 5
SL2YM	dB0	0652h	400/100	512	ECC	SECC 3.00	1, 2, 5
SL37G	dB0	0652h	400/100	512	ECC	SECC2 OLGA	1, 2, 4
SL2WB	dB0	0652h	450/100	512	ECC	SECC 3.00	1, 2, 5
SL37H	dB0	0652h	450/100	512	ECC	SECC2 OLGA	1, 2
SL2W7	dB0	0652h	266/66	512	ECC	SECC 2.00	2, 5
SL2W8	dB0	0652h	300/66	512	ECC	SECC 3.00	2, 5
SL2TV	dB0	0652h	333/66	512	ECC	SECC 3.00	2, 5
SL2U3	dB0	0652h	350/100	512	ECC	SECC 3.00	2, 5
SL2U4	dB0	0652h	350/100	512	ECC	SECC 3.00	2, 5
SL2U5	dB0	0652h	400/100	512	ECC	SECC 3.00	2, 5
SL2U6	dB0	0652h	400/100	512	ECC	SECC 3.00	2, 5
SL2U7	dB0	0652h	450/100	512	ECC	SECC 3.00	2, 5
SL356	dB0	0652h	350/100	512	ECC	SECC2 PLGA	2, 5
SL357	dB0	0652h	400/100	512	ECC	SECC2 OLGA	2, 5
SL358	dB0	0652h	450/100	512	ECC	SECC2 OLGA	2, 5
SL37F	dB0	0652h	350/100	512	ECC	SECC2 PLGA	1, 2, 5
SL3FN	dB0	0652h	350/100	512	ECC	SECC2 OLGA	2, 5
SL3EE	dB0	0652h	400/100	512	ECC	SECC2 PLGA	2, 5
SL3F9	dB0	0652h	400/100	512	ECC	SECC2 PLGA	1, 2
SL38M	dB1	0653h	350/100	512	ECC	SECC 3.00	1, 2, 5
SL38N	dB1	0653h	400/100	512	ECC	SECC 3.00	1, 2, 5
SL36U	dB1	0653h	350/100	512	ECC	SECC 3.00	2, 5
SL38Z	dB1	0653h	400/100	512	ECC	SECC 3.00	2, 5
SL3D5	dB1	0653h	400/100	512	ECC	SECC2 OLGA	1, 2

CPUID = The internal ID returned by the CPUID instruction

ECC = Error correcting code

OLGA = Organic land grid array

PLGA = Plastic land grid array

SECC = Single edge contact cartridge

SECC2 = Single edge contact cartridge revision 2

1. This is a boxed Pentium II processor with an attached fan heatsink.

2. These processors have an enhanced L2 cache, which can cache up to 4GB of main memory. Other standard PII processors can cache only up to 512MB of main memory.

3. These boxed processors might have packaging that incorrectly indicates ECC support in the L2 cache.

4. This is a boxed Pentium II OverDrive processor with an attached fan heatsink, designed for upgrading Pentium Pro (Socket 8) systems.

5. These parts operate only at the specified clock multiplier frequency ratio at which they were manufactured. They can be overclocked only by increasing the bus speed.

The two variations of the SECC2 cartridge vary by the type of processor core package on the board. The plastic land grid array (PLGA) is the older type of packaging used in previous SECC cartridges and was eventually phased out. A newer organic land grid array (OLGA), which is a processor core package that is smaller and easier to manufacture, took its place. It also enabled better thermal transfer between the processor die and the heatsink, which was attached directly to the top of the OLGA chip package. Figure 3.48 shows the open back side (where the heatsink would be attached) of SECC2 processors with PLGA and OLGA cores.

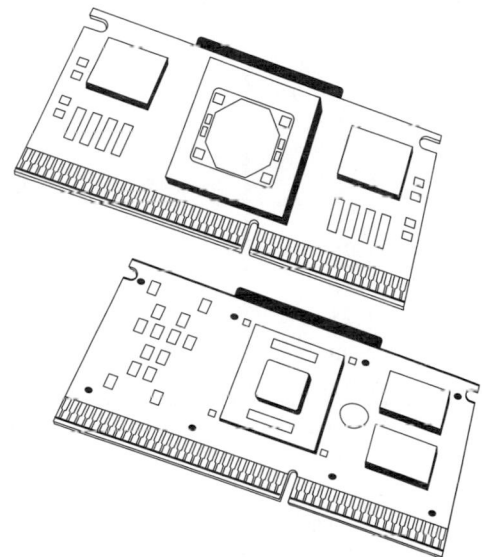

Figure 3.48   SECC2 processors with PLGA (top) and OLGA (bottom) cores.

Pentium II motherboards have an onboard voltage regulator circuit designed to power the CPU. Some Pentium II processors run at several different voltages, so the regulator must be set to supply the correct voltage for the specific processor you are installing. As with the Pentium Pro and unlike the older Pentium, no jumpers or switches must be set; the voltage setting is handled completely automatically through the VID pins on the processor cartridge. Table 3.35 shows the relationship between the pins and the selected voltage.

To ensure the system is ready for all Pentium II processor variations, the values in **bold** must be supported. Most Pentium II processors run at 2.8V, with some newer ones at 2.0V.

The Pentium II Mobile Module is a Pentium II for notebooks that includes the North Bridge of the high-performance 440BX chipset. This is the first chipset on the market that allows 100MHz processor bus operation, although that is currently not supported in the mobile versions. The 440BX chipset was released at the same time as the 350MHz and 400MHz versions of the Pentium II.

Newer variations on the Pentium II include the Pentium IIPE, which is a mobile version that includes 256KB of L2 cache directly integrated into the die. Therefore, it runs at full-core speed, making it faster than the desktop Pentium II because the desktop chips use half-speed L2 cache.

Table 3.35   Pentium II/III/Celeron Voltage ID Pin Definitions

VID4	VID3	VID2	VID1	VID0	Voltage	VID4	VID3	VID2	VID1	VID0	Voltage
0	1	1	1	1	1.30	1	1	1	1	1	**No Core**
0	1	1	1	0	1.35	1	1	1	1	0	**2.1**
0	1	1	0	1	1.40	1	1	1	0	1	**2.2**
0	1	1	0	0	1.45	1	1	1	0	0	**2.3**
0	1	0	1	1	1.50	1	1	0	1	1	**2.4**
0	1	0	1	0	1.55	1	1	0	1	0	**2.5**
0	1	0	0	1	1.60	1	1	0	0	1	**2.6**
0	1	0	0	0	1.65	1	1	0	0	0	**2.7**
0	0	1	1	1	1.70	1	0	1	1	1	**2.8**
0	0	1	1	0	1.75	1	0	1	1	0	2.9
0	0	1	0	1	**1.80**	1	0	1	0	1	3.0
0	0	1	0	0	**1.85**	1	0	1	0	0	3.1
0	0	0	1	1	**1.90**	1	0	0	1	1	3.2
0	0	0	1	0	**1.95**	1	0	0	1	0	3.3
0	0	0	0	1	**2.00**	1	0	0	0	1	3.4
0	0	0	0	0	**2.05**	1	0	0	0	0	3.5

0 = Processor pin connected to Vss.   *VID0–VID3 used on Socket 370.*   *VID0–VID4 used on Slot 1.*
1 = Open on processor.   *Socket 370 supports 1.30–2.05V settings only.*   *Slot 1 supports 1.30–3.5V settings.*

Celeron

The Celeron processor is a chameleon. It was originally a P6 with the same processor core as the Pentium II in the original two versions; later it came with the same core as the PIII; and more recently it uses the Pentium 4 core. It is designed mainly for lower-cost PCs.

Most of the features for the Celeron are the same as the Pentium II, III, or 4 because it uses the same internal processor cores. The main differences are in packaging, L2 cache amount, and CPU bus speed.

The first version of the Celeron was available in a package called the single edge processor package (SEPP or SEP package). The SEP package is basically the same Slot 1 design as the SECC used in the Pentium II/III, with the exception of the fancy plastic cartridge cover. This cover is deleted in the Celeron, making it cheaper to produce and sell. Essentially, the original Celeron used the same circuit board as is inside the Pentium II package.

◄◄   See "Single Edge Contact and Single Edge Processor Packaging," p. 86.

Even without the plastic covers, the Slot 1 packaging was more expensive than it should have been. This was largely due to the processor retention mechanisms (stands) required to secure the processor into Slot 1 on the motherboard, as well as the larger and more complicated heatsinks required. This, plus competition from the lower-end Socket 7 systems using primarily AMD processors, led Intel to introduce the Celeron in a socketed form. The socket is called PGA-370 or Socket 370 because it has 370 pins. The processor package designed for this socket is called the plastic pin grid array (PPGA) package (see Figure 3.49) or flip chip PGA (FC-PGA). Both the PPGA and FC-PGA packages plug into the 370 pin socket and allow for lower-cost, lower-profile, and smaller systems because of the less expensive processor retention and cooling requirements of the socketed processor.

◄◄   See "Socket 370 (PGA-370)," p. 95.

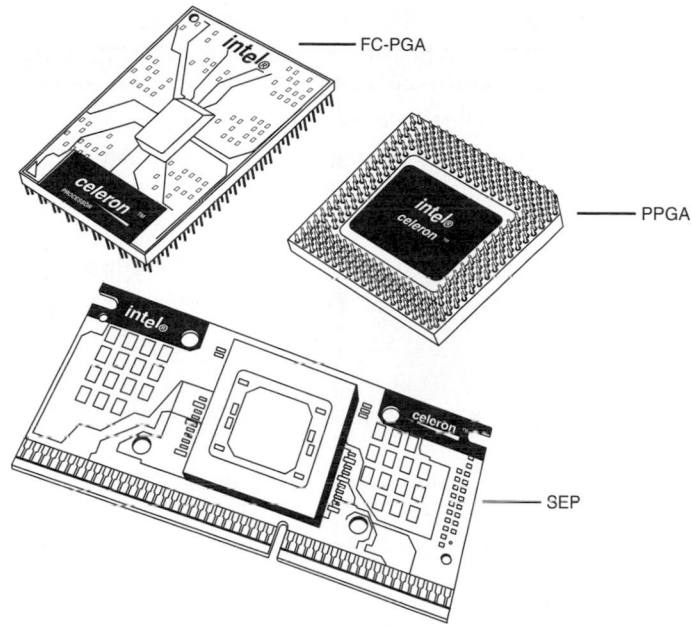

Figure 3.49   Celeron processors in the FC-PGA, PPGA, and SEP packages.

All Celeron processors at 433MHz and lower have been available in the SEPP that plugs into the 242-contact slot connector (Slot 1). The 300MHz and higher versions also are available in the PPGA package. This means that the 300MHz to 433MHz have been available in both packages, whereas the 466MHz and higher-speed versions are available only in the PPGA. The fastest Celeron processor for Socket 370 runs at 1.4GHz; faster Celerons use Socket 478 and are based on the Pentium 4 design.

Motherboards that include Socket 370 can accept the PGA versions of both the Celeron and Pentium III in most cases. If you want to use a Socket 370 version of the Celeron in a Slot 1 motherboard, slot-to-socket adapters (usually called slot-kets) are available for about $10–$20 that plug into Slot 1 and incorporate a Socket 370 on the card. Figure 3.50 shows a typical slot-ket adapter.

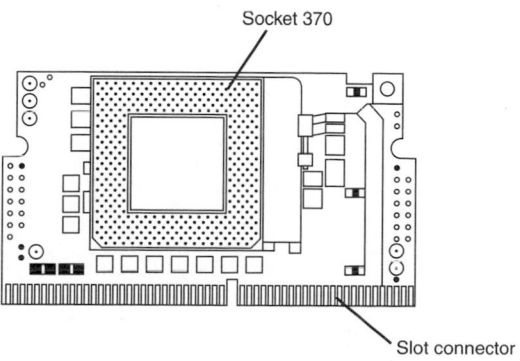

Figure 3.50   Slot-ket adapter for installing PPGA processors in Slot 1 motherboards.

Highlights of the Celeron include the following:

- Available at 300MHz (300A) and higher core frequencies with 128KB on-die L2 cache; 300MHz and 266MHz core frequencies without L2 cache

- L2 cache supports up to 4GB RAM address range and ECC

- Uses same P6 core processor as the Pentium II (266MHz through 533MHz) and now the Pentium III (533A MHz and higher) and Pentium 4 (1.7GHz and higher)

- Dynamic execution microarchitecture

- Operates on a 66MHz, 100MHz, or 400MHz CPU bus depending on the version

- Specifically designed for lower-cost value PC systems

- Includes MMX technology; Celeron 533A and higher include SSE; Celeron 1.7GHz and higher include SSE2

- More cost-effective packaging technology, including SEP, PPGA, and FC-PGA or FC-PGA2 packages

- Integrated L1 and L2 cache on most models, with amount and type depending on the version; typically, the Celeron has half the L2 cache of the processor core it is patterned after

- Integrated thermal diode for temperature monitoring

The Intel Celeron processors from the 300A and higher include integrated 128KB L2 cache. The core for the 300A through 533MHz versions that are based on the Pentium II core include 19 million transistors because of the addition of the integrated 128KB L2 cache. The 533A and faster versions are based on the Pentium III core and incorporate 28.1 million transistors. The 1.7GHz and faster versions are based on the Pentium 4 core with 42 million transistors. The Pentium III and Pentium 4–based versions actually have 256KB of L2 cache on the die; however, 128KB is disabled, leaving 128KB of functional L2 cache. This was done because it was cheaper for Intel to simply make the Celeron using the same die as the Pentium III or 4 and just disable part of the cache on the Celeron versions, rather than coming up with a unique die for the newer Celerons. The Pentium III–based Celeron processors also support the SSE in addition to MMX instructions, whereas the Pentium 4–based versions support SSE2 instructions. The older Celerons based on the Pentium II core support only MMX.

All the Celerons in SEPP and PPGA form are manufactured using the 0.25-micron process, whereas those in FC-PGA and FC-PGA2 form are made using an even better 0.18-micron process. The smaller process reduces processor heat and enables higher speeds.

What Exactly Is a Celeron?

The name *Celeron* is the general name Intel has used for its economy line of processors going all the way back to the Pentium II. In short, a *Celeron* is a Pentium II, Pentium III, or Pentium 4 processor with some features reduced or removed. Celerons are basically designed as less-expensive, stripped-down, economy versions of Intel's main processors. Although the specific details have varied over the years, Celerons have normally differed from Intel's Pentium II, Pentium III, or current Pentium 4 processors in the following ways:

- Lower CPU clock speeds
- Lower CPU bus speeds
- Smaller L2 cache

These differences have made Celeron processors less powerful than the particular Pentium II/III/4 they are based on, but these differences also make Celeron processors and Celeron-based systems less expensive. If you're looking for a low-cost system that's "Intel inside," a Celeron-based system is one way to get there.

A Brief Celeron History

The original Celerons were economy versions of the Intel Pentium II processor. Intel figured that by taking a Pentium II and deleting the separate L2 cache chips mounted inside the processor cartridge (and also deleting the cosmetic cover), it could create a "new" processor that was basically just a slower version of the Pentium II. As such, the first 266MHz and 300MHz Celeron models didn't include any L2 cache. Unfortunately, this proved to have far too great a crippling effect on performance, so starting with the 300A versions, the Celeron received 128KB of on-die full-speed L2 cache, which was actually faster and more advanced than the 512KB of half-speed cache used in the Pentium II it was based on! In fact, the Celeron was the first PC processor to receive on-die L2 cache. It wasn't until the Coppermine version of the Pentium III appeared that on-die L2 cache migrated to Intel's main processors.

Needless to say, this caused a lot of confusion in the marketplace about the Celeron. Considering that the Celeron started out as a "crippled" Pentium II and then was revised so as to actually be superior in some ways to the Pentium II on which it was based (all the while selling for less), many didn't know just where the Celeron stood in terms of performance. Fortunately, the crippling lack of L2 cache existed only in the earliest Celeron versions; all of those at speeds greater than 300MHz have on-die full-speed L2 cache.

The earliest Celerons from 266MHz up through 400MHz were produced in a SEPP design that physically looked like a circuit board and that was designed to fit into Slot 1. This is the same slot the Pentium II used, meaning the Celeron SEPP plugged into any Pentium II Slot-1 motherboard. As the Celeron continued to develop, the form factor was changed to correspond with changes in the Pentium II-, III-, and 4-class processors from which it was adapted. Starting with the 300A processor (300MHz Celeron with 128KB of on-die Level 2 cache), Celerons were produced in a PPGA package using the Socket 370 interface. This socket, with differences in voltage, was later used for most versions of the Pentium III. Celerons using Socket 370 range in speed from 300MHz all the way up to 1.4GHz. Along the way, the packaging changed from PPGA to FC-PGA and FC-PGA2. The latter added a metal heat spreader on top of the die offering better protection for the fragile die.

The latest Celerons are based on Pentium 4 processors. They are produced in an FC-PGA2 package that fits into the same Socket 478 that recent Pentium 4 processors use; the Celeron was never produced in the short-lived Socket 423 form factor the original Pentium 4 processors used.

As this very brief history shows, the name *Celeron* has never meant anything more specific than a reduced-performance version of Intel's current mainstream processor. Before you can decide whether a particular Celeron processor is a suitable choice, you need to know what its features are and especially on which processor it is based. At least eight discrete variations of the Celeron processor exist, which are detailed in Table 3.36.

Table 3.36   Celeron CPU Variations

Celeron Version	Based On	Codename	Process (Micron)	L2 Cache (KB)	Multimedia Support
Celeron	Pentium II Deschutes	Covington	0.25	0	MMX
Celeron A	Pentium II Deschutes	Mendocino	0.25	128	MMX
Celeron A-PGA	Pentium II Deschutes	Mendocino	0.25	128	MMX
Celeron III	Pentium III Coppermine	Coppermine-128	0.18	128	SSE
Celeron IIIA	Pentium III Tualatin	Tualatin-256	0.13	256	SSE
Celeron 4	Pentium 4 Willamette	Willamette-128	0.18	128	SSE2
Celeron 4A	Pentium 4 Northwood	Northwood-128	0.13	128	SSE2
Celeron D	Pentium 4 Prescott	Prescott-256	0.09	256	SSE3

All Celeron III below 800MHz use the 66MHz CPU bus; all Celeron III from 800MHz through 1.1GHz use the 100MHz bus.

SEPP = Single edge processor package

FC-PGA = Flip chip pin grid array

FC-PGA2 = FC-PGA with added heat spreader

MMX = Multimedia extensions; 57 additional instructions for graphics and sound processing

SSE = Streaming SIMD (single instruction multiple data) extensions; MMX plus 70 additional instructions for graphics and sound processing

Figure 3.51 shows the various Celeron package types.

Celeron/Celeron A SEPP (Slot-1)

Celeron 4 FC-PGA2 (Socket 478)

Celeron A-PGA PPGA (Socket 370)

Celeron IIIA FC-PGA2 (Socket 370)

Figure 3.51   Processors released under the Celeron brand. *Photos courtesy of Intel.*

As you can see, there is a wide range of what is called a Celeron, and you could consider the Celeron as a family of different core processor models in several package variations.

The following sections discuss the differences between these Celeron processors.

Physical Interface	Package	CPU Bus Speed	Min. Speed	Max. Speed
Slot-1	SEPP	66MHz	266MHz	300MHz
Slot-1	SEPP	66MHz	300AMHz	433MHz
Socket 370	PPGA	66MHz	300AMHz	533MHz
Socket 370	FC-PGA	66/100MHz*	533AMHz	1.1GHz
Socket 370	FC PGA2	100MHz	900MHz	1.4GHz
Socket 478	FC-PGA2	400MHz	1.7GHz	1.8GHz
Socket 478	FC-PGA2	400MHz	2.0GHz	2.8GHz
Socket 478/Socket T (LGA775)	FC-PGA2	533MHz	2.53GHz	3.2GHz

SSE2 = Streaming SIMD extensions 2; SSE plus 144 additional instructions for graphics and sound processing
The "Celeron Version" names listed here are not official; I made them up as a way to clearly identify the different Celeron processors.
The Celeron 4A version is not out yet, but it will be introduced during the third quarter of 2004.
Minimum and maximum speeds indicate the slowest and fastest rated speeds of each variation offered.

Socket 370 Versus Socket 478 Celerons

Although both Socket 370 and Socket 478 processors bear the name Celeron, enormous differences in internal design exist between Celeron processors in these form factors. These differences directly relate to which Intel Pentium-class processor a particular Celeron processor is based on.

Socket 370 Celerons are based on various versions of the Pentium II and Pentium III architecture, whereas Socket 478 Celerons are based on the Pentium 4 architecture. This discussion focuses on the Celeron IIIA, Celeron 4, and Celeron 4A versions because the previous versions have been discontinued.

Intel offers Celeron IIIA versions for new Socket 370 motherboards in speeds from 900MHz to 1.4GHz, Celeron 4 versions for Socket 478 motherboards in speeds from 1.7GHz to 1.8GHz, and faster Celeron 4A models in speeds from 2.0GHz to 2.8GHz. It also offers new Prescott-based Celeron D models in both Socket 478 and Socket T (LGA775) versions in speeds from 2.53GHz to 3.2GHz.

What are the differences in these processors, other than clock speed?

■ All Celeron IIIA Celerons have a CPU bus (sometimes called front-side-bus [FSB]) speed of 100MHz, whereas all Socket 478 Celerons have a CPU bus speed of 400MHz.

■ Celeron IIIA versions based on the Pentium III Tualatin core have 256KB of L2 cache, whereas those based on the earlier Pentium III Coppermine core or Pentium II Deschutes core have 128KB of L2 cache. All current Socket 478 Celerons based on the Pentium 4 Willamette core have 128KB of L2 cache, and newer versions based on the Northwood core also will have 128KB of L2 cache.

How Tualatin, Willamette, and Northwood Improve the Celeron

Compared to Celerons based on the previous Pentium III Coppermine core, Tualatin-based Celerons have the following differences:

- Larger L2 memory cache (256KB versus 128KB)
- Improved L2 cache design for better performance
- FC-PGA2 packaging, which includes a metal heat spreader over the fragile CPU core to protect it when attaching a heatsink

However, these improvements come at a cost in compatibility. Like the Tualatin-core versions of the Pentium III, Celerons based on the Tualatin core don't work in motherboards designed for older Pentium III or Celeron chips. Socket 370 is physically the same, but the Tualatin core redefines 10 pins in the socket, which require corresponding changes in the chipset and motherboard. So, if you're looking for a way to speed up an older Celeron by installing a Tualatin-core Celeron IIIA, make sure the motherboard is Tualatin-ready. Also note that Tualatin-core Celerons use the FC-PGA2 packaging, which includes a heat spreader on top of the CPU die. This requires a compatible heatsink.

Because of the variations in packaging, which require different heatsink solutions, I normally recommend only purchasing boxed versions of the processors, which include a compatible high-quality heatsink in the box. That way, you are assured of having the proper heatsink, clips, thermal interface material, and other items necessary for the chip to operate properly and safely in your system. The boxed processors also feature a three-year warranty direct with Intel, which is not available with raw or OEM processors.

The more recent Celeron 4 processors are designed to provide a low-cost alternative to users of Socket 478 and Socket T (LGA775) motherboards (the form factor used by recent and current Pentium 4 processors). Socket 478 Celerons currently use the Willamette core found in the original Pentium 4, but newer Celeron 4A versions use the Northwood core and the Celeron D models use the Prescott core found in most Pentium 4 models. The only difference between the latest Celeron processors and the Pentium 4 models on which they are based is that the Celeron versions have less L2 cache and run at lower bus speeds when compared to the corresponding Pentium 4 version. Compared to earlier Pentium III–based Celerons, the Pentium 4–based Celerons have the following improvements:

- Faster clock speeds (up to 3.2GHz and climbing).
- 400MHz or 533MHz CPU bus for data and memory transfers up to 4.266GBps (depending on the memory used on the motherboard).
- Support for SSE2 instructions, which include the SSE instructions found in the Pentium III–based Celerons plus 144 additional instructions for graphics and sound processing. Celeron D models support SSE3, which includes 13 additional instructions over SSE2.
- Deeper 20-stage or 31-stage (Celeron D) internal pipeline.
- 256-bit wide L2 cache.
- All other Pentium 4 architectural features.

Celerons have less cache than the Pentium 4 processors on which they are based. Even though the Celeron processors have less cache, the improvements in the cache architecture and CPU and bus speeds allow them to outperform previous-generation processors that might have even more cache. Celeron 4A CPUs have 256KB of L2 and perform even better than the current Celeron 4.

All the newer Celeron chips use Intel's FC-PGA2 design. This design adds a metal heat spreader to the top of the processor to improve heat transfer to the heatsink. This integrated heat spreader also prevents physical damage to the CPU during the processor and heatsink installation. Think of it as a metal protective cap over the CPU die.

Because Intel has offered Celerons in many distinctive variations, it's easy to get confused as to which is which, or which is available at a specific speed. By reading the spec number off a particular chip and looking up the number on the Intel developer Web site (`developer.intel.com`), you can find out the exact specification including socket type, voltage, stepping, cache size, and other information about the chip.

Pentium III

The Pentium III processor, shown in Figure 3.52, was first released in February 1999 and introduced several new features to the P6 family. It is essentially the same core as a Pentium II with the addition of SSE instructions and integrated on-die L2 cache in the later versions. SSE consists of 70 new instructions that dramatically enhance the performance and possibilities of advanced imaging, 3D, streaming audio, video, and speech-recognition applications.

Figure 3.52   Pentium III processor in SECC2 (Slot 1) and FC-PGA (Socket 370) packages.

Originally based on Intel's advanced 0.25-micron CMOS process technology, the PIII core started out with more than 9.5 million transistors. In late 1999, Intel shifted to a 0.18-micron process die (code-named Coppermine) and added 256KB of on-die L2 cache, which brought the transistor count to 28.1 million. The latest version of the Pentium III (codenamed Tualatin) uses a 0.13-micron process and has 44 million transistors; motherboards made before the Tualatin-core versions of the Pentium III generally do not support this processor because of logical pinout changes. The Pentium III also became available in speeds from 450MHz through 1.4GHz, as well as server versions with larger or faster cache called Xeon. The Pentium III also incorporates advanced features such as a 32KB L1 cache and either half-core speed 512KB L2 cache or full-core speed on-die 256KB or 512KB L2 with cacheability for up to 4GB of addressable memory space. The PIII also can be used in dual-processing systems with up to 64GB of physical memory. A self-reportable processor serial number gives security, authentication, and system management applications a powerful new tool for identifying individual systems. Because of privacy concerns when the processor was released, you can disable this feature in the system BIOS on most systems that use the Pentium III or Celeron III processors.

Pentium III processors were first made available in Intel's SECC2 form factor, which replaced the more expensive older SEC packaging. The SECC2 package covers only one side of the chip and allows for better heatsink attachment and less overall weight. Architectural features of the Pentium III processor include

- *Streaming SIMD extensions.* Seventy new instructions for dramatically faster processing and improved imaging, 3D streaming audio and video, Web access, speech recognition, new user interfaces, and other graphics and sound-rich applications.

- *Intel processor serial number.* The processor serial number serves as an electronic serial number for the processor and, by extension, its system or user. This feature can be enabled or disabled as desired in the BIOS Setup. The serial number enables the system/user to be identified by company internal networks and applications. The processor serial number can be used in applications that benefit from stronger forms of system and user identification, such as:

  - *Applications using security capabilities.* Managed access to new Internet content and services; electronic document exchange.

  - *Manageability applications.* Asset management; remote system load and configuration.

Although the initial release of Pentium III processors was made in the improved SECC2 packaging, Intel later switched to the FC-PGA package, which is even less expensive to produce and enables a more direct attachment of the heatsink to the processor core for better cooling. The FC-PGA version plugs into Socket 370 but can be used in Slot 1 with a slot-ket adapter.

All Pentium III processors have either 512KB or 256KB of L2 cache, which runs at either half-core or full-core speed. Pentium III Xeon versions have 512KB, 1MB, or 2MB of L2 cache that runs at full-core speed. The Pentium III Xeon is a more expensive version of the Pentium III designed for servers and workstations. All PIII processor L2 caches can cache up to 4GB of addressable memory space and include ECC capability.

Pentium III processors can be identified by their markings, which are found on the top edge of the processor cartridge. Figure 3.53 shows the format and meaning of the markings.

Table 3.37 shows variations of the Pentium III, indicated by the S-specification number.

Table 3.37   Intel Pentium III Processor Variations

Speed (MHz)	Bus Speed (MHz)	Multiplier	Boxed CPU S-spec	OEM CPU S-spec	Stepping	CPUID	L2 Cache
450	100	4.5x	SL3CC	SL364	kB0	0672	512K
450	100	4.5x	SL37C	SL35D	kC0	0673	512K
500	100	5x	SL3CD	SL365	kB0	0672	512K
500	100	5x	SL365	SL365	kB0	0672	512K
500	100	5x	SL37D	SL35E	kC0	0673	512K
500E	100	5x	SL3R2	SL3Q9	cA2	0681	256K
500E	100	5x	SL45R	SL444	cB0	0683	256K
533B	133	4x	SL3E9	SL3BN	kC0	0673	512K
533EB	133	4x	SL3SX	SL3N6	cA2	0681	256K
533EB	133	4x	SL3VA	SL3VF	cA2	0681	256K
533EB	133	4x	SL44W	SL3XG	cB0	0683	256K
533EB	133	4x	SL45S	SL3XS	cB0	0683	256K
550	100	5.5x	SL3FJ	SL3F7	kC0	0673	512K
550E	100	5.5x	SL3R3	SL3QA	cA2	0681	256K
550E	100	5.5x	SL3V5	SL3N7	cA2	0681	256K
550E	100	5.5x	SL44X	SL3XH	cB0	0683	256K
550E	100	5.5x	SL45T	N/A	cB0	0683	256K
600	100	6x	SL3JT	SL3JM	kC0	0673	512K
600E	100	6x	SL3NA	SL3H6	cA2	0681	256K
600E	100	6x	SL3NL	SL3VH	cA2	0681	256K
600E	100	6x	SL44Y	SL43E	cB0	0683	256K
600E	100	6x	SL45U	SL3XU	cB0	0683	256K
600E	100	6x	n/a	SL4CM	cC0	0686	256K
600E	100	6x	n/a	SL4C7	cC0	0686	256K
600B	133	4.5x	SL3JU	SL3JP	kC0	0673	512K
600EB	133	4.5x	SL3NB	SL3H7	cA2	0681	256K

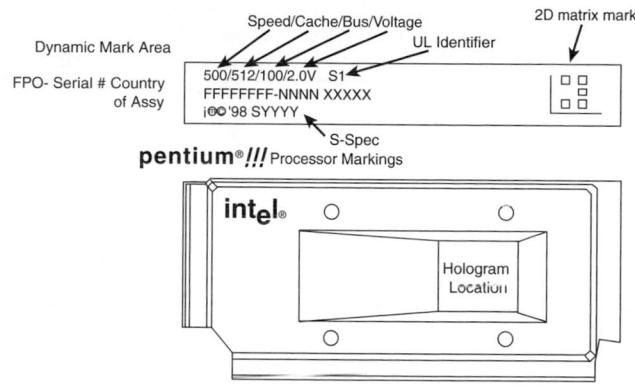

Figure 3.53   Pentium III processor markings.

L2 Speed	Max. Temp. (C)	Voltage	Max. Power (W)	Process (Microns)	Transistors	Package
225	90	2.00	25.3	0.25	9.5M	SECC2
225	90	2.00	25.3	0.25	9.5M	SECC2
250	90	2.00	28.0	0.25	9.5M	SECC2
250	90	2.00	28.0	0.25	9.5M	SECC2
250	90	2.00	28.0	0.25	9.5M	SECC2
500	85	1.60	13.2	0.18	28.1M	FC-PGA
500	85	1.60	13.2	0.18	28.1M	FC-PGA
267	90	2.05	29.7	0.25	9.5M	SECC2
533	85	1.65	14.0	0.18	28.1M	SECC2
533	85	1.65	14.0	0.18	28.1M	FC-PGA
533	85	1.65	14.0	0.18	28.1M	SECC2
533	85	1.65	14.0	0.18	28.1M	FC-PGA
275	80	2.00	30.8	0.25	9.5M	SECC2
550	85	1.60	14.5	0.18	28.1M	FC-PGA
550	85	1.60	14.5	0.18	28.1M	SECC2
550	85	1.60	14.5	0.18	28.1M	SECC2
550	85	1.60	14.5	0.18	28.1M	FC-PGA
300	85	2.00	34.5	0.25	9.5M	SECC2
600	82	1.65	15.8	0.18	28.1M	SECC2
600	82	1.65	15.8	0.18	28.1M	FC-PGA
600	82	1.65	15.8	0.18	28.1M	SECC2
600	82	1.65	15.8	0.18	28.1M	FC-PGA
600	82	1.7	15.8	0.18	28.1M	FC-PGA
600	82	1.7	15.8	0.18	28.1M	SECC2
300	85	2.05	34.5	0.25	9.5M	SECC2
600	82	1.65	15.8	0.18	28.1M	SECC2

Table 3.37   Continued

Speed (MHz)	Bus Speed (MHz)	Multiplier	Boxed CPU S-spec	OEM CPU S-spec	Stepping	CPUID	L2 Cache
600EB	133	4.5x	SL3VB	SL3VG	cA2	0681	256K
600EB	133	4.5x	SL44Z	SL3XJ	cB0	0683	256K
600EB	133	4.5x	SL45V	SL3XT	cB0	0683	256K
600EB	133	4.5x	SL4CL	SL4CL	cC0	0686	256K
600EB	133	4.5x	n/a	SL46C	cC0	0686	256K
650	100	6.5x	SL3NR	SL3KV	cA2	0681	256K
650	100	6.5x	SL3NM	SL3VJ	cA20	681	256K
650	100	6.5x	SL452	SL3XK	cB0	0683	256K
650	100	6.5x	SL45W	SL3XV	cB0	0683	256K
650	100	6.5x	n/a	SL4CK	cC0	0686	256K
650	100	6.5x	n/a	SL4C5	cC0	0686	256K
667	133	5x	SL3ND	SL3KW	cA2	0681	256K
667	133	5x	SL3T2	SL3VK	cA2	0681	256K
667	133	5x	SL453	SL3XL	cB0	0683	256K
667	133	5x	SL45X	SL3XW	cB0	0683	256K
667	133	5x	n/a	SL4CJ	cC0	0686	256K
667	133	5x	n/a	SL4C4	cC0	0686	256K
700	100	7x	SL3SY	SL3S9	cA2	0681	256K
700	100	7x	SL3T3	SL3VL	cA2	0681	256K
700	100	7x	SL454	SL453	cB0	0683	256K
700	100	7x	SL45Y	SL3XX	cB0	0683	256K
700	100	7x	SL4M7	SL4CH	cC0	0686	256K
700	100	7x	n/a	SL4C3	cC0	0686	256K
733	133	5.5x	SL3SZ	SL3SB	cA2	0681	256K
733	133	5.5x	SL3T4	SL3VM	cA2	0681	256K
733	133	5.5x	SL455	SL3XN	cB0	0683	256K
733	133	5.5x	SL45Z	SL3XY	cB0	0683	256K
733	133	5.5x	SL4M8	SL4CG	cC0	0686	256K
733	133	5.5x	SL4KD	SL4C2	cC0	0686	256K
733	133	5.5x	SL4FQ	SL4CX	cC0	0686	256K
750	100	7.5x	SL3V6	SL3WC	cA2	0681	256K
750	100	7.5x	SL3VC	SL3VN	cA2	0681	256K
750	100	7.5x	SL456	SL3XP	cB0	0683	256K
750	100	7.5x	SL462	SL3XZ	cB0	0683	256K
750	100	7.5x	SL4M9	SL4CF	cC0	0686	256K
750	100	7.5x	SL4KE	SL4BZ	cC0	0686	256K
800	100	8x	SL457	SL3XR	cB0	0683	256K
800	100	8x	SL463	SL3Y3	cB0	0683	256K
800	100	8x	SL4MA	SL4CE	cC0	0686	256K
800	100	8x	SL4KF	SL4BY	cC0	0686	256K
800EB	133	6x	SL458	SL3XQ	cB0	0683	256K
800EB	133	6x	SL464	SL3Y2	cB0	0683	256K

L2 Speed	Max. Temp. (C)	Voltage	Max. Power (W)	Process (Microns)	Transistors	Package
600	82	1.65	15.8	0.18	28.1M	FC-PGA
600	82	1.65	15.8	0.18	28.1M	SECC2
600	82	1.65	15.8	0.18	28.1M	FC-PGA
600	82	1.7	15.8	0.18	28.1M	FC-PGA
600	82	1.7	15.8	0.18	28.1M	SECC2
650	82	1.65	17.0	0.18	28.1M	SECC2
650	82	1.65	17.0	0.18	28.1M	FC-PGA
650	82	1.65	17.0	0.18	28.1M	SECC2
650	82	1.65	17.0	0.18	28.1M	FC-PGA
650	82	1.7	17.0	0.18	28.1M	FC-PGA
650	82	1.7	17.0	0.18	28.1M	SECC2
667	82	1.65	17.5	0.18	28.1M	SECC2
667	82	1.65	17.5	0.18	28.1M	FC-PGA
667	82	1.65	17.5	0.18	28.1M	SECC2
667	82	1.65	17.5	0.18	28.1M	FC-PGA
667	82	1.7	17.5	0.18	28.1M	FC-PGA
667	82	1.7	17.5	0.18	28.1M	SECC2
700	80	1.65	18.3	0.18	28.1M	SECC2
700	80	1.65	18.3	0.18	28.1M	FC-PGA
700	80	1.65	18.3	0.18	28.1M	SECC2
700	80	1.65	18.3	0.18	28.1M	FC-PGA
700	80	1.7	18.3	0.18	28.1M	FC-PGA
700	80	1.7	18.3	0.18	28.1M	SECC2
733	80	1.65	19.1	0.18	28.1M	SECC2
733	80	1.65	19.1	0.18	28.1M	FC-PGA
733	80	1.65	19.1	0.18	28.1M	SECC2
733	80	1.65	19.1	0.18	28.1M	FC-PGA
733	80	1.7	19.1	0.18	28.1M	FC-PGA
733	80	1.7	19.1	0.18	28.1M	SECC2
733	80	1.7	19.1	0.18	28.1M	SECC2
750	80	1.65	19.5	0.18	28.1M	SECC2
750	80	1.65	19.5	0.18	28.1M	FC-PGA
750	80	1.65	19.5	0.18	28.1M	SECC2
750	80	1.65	19.5	0.18	28.1M	FC-PGA
750	80	1.7	19.5	0.18	28.1M	FC-PGA
750	80	1.7	19.5	0.18	28.1M	SECC2
800	80	1.65	20.8	0.18	28.1M	SECC2
800	80	1.65	20.8	0.18	28.1M	FC-PGA
800	80	1.7	20.8	0.18	28.1M	FC-PGA
800	80	1.7	20.8	0.18	28.1M	SECC2
800	80	1.65	20.8	0.18	28.1M	SECC2
800	80	1.65	20.8	0.18	28.1M	FC-PGA

Table 3.37   Continued

Speed (MHz)	Bus Speed (MHz)	Multiplier	Boxed CPU S-spec	OEM CPU S-spec	Stepping	CPUID	L2 Cache
800EB	133	6x	SL4MB	SL4CD	cC0	0686	256K
800EB	133	6x	SL4G7	SL4XQ	cC0	0686	256K
800EB	133	6x	SL4KG	SL4BX	cC0	0686	256K
850	100	8.5x	SL47M	SL43F	cB0	0683	256K
850	100	8.5x	SL49G	SL43H	cB0	0683	256K
850	100	8.5x	SL4MC	SL4CC	cC0	0686	256K
850	100	8.5x	SL4KH	SL4BW	cC0	0686	256K
866	133	6.5x	SL47N	SL43G	cB0	0683	256K
866	133	6.5x	SL49H	SL43J	cB0	0683	256K
866	133	6.5x	SL4MD	SL4CB	cC0	0686	256K
866	133	6.5x	SL4KJ	SL4BV	cC0	0686	256K
866	133	6.5x	SL5B5	SL5QE	cD0	068A	256K
900	100	9x	n/a	SL4SD	cC0	0686	256K
933	133	7x	SL47Q	SL448	cB0	0683	256K
933	133	7x	SL49J	SL44J	cB0	0683	256K
933	133	7x	SL4ME	SL4C9	cC0	0686	256K
933	133	7x	SL4KK	SL4BT	cC0	0686	256K
933	133	7x	n/a	SL5QF	cD0	068A	256K
1000B	133	7.5x	SL4FP	SL48S	cB0	0683	256K
1000B	133	7.5x	SL4C8	SL4C8	cC0	0686	256K
1000B	133	7.5x	SL4MF	n/a	cC0	0686	256K
1000	100	10x	SL4BR	SL4BR	cC0	0686	256K
1000	100	10x	SL4KL	N/a	cC0	0686	256K
1000B	133	7.5x	SL4BS	SL4BS	cC0	0686	256K
1000B	100	10x	n/a	SL5QV	cD0	068A	256K
1000B	133	7.5x	SL5DV	N/a	cD0	068A	256K
1000B	133	7.5x	SL5B3	SL5B3	cD0	068A	256K
1000B	133	7.5x	SL52R	SL52R	cD0	068A	256K
1000B	133	7.5x	SL5FQ	n/a	cD0	068A	256K
1100	100	11x	n/a	SL5QW	cD0	068A	256K
1133	133	8.5x	SL5LT	n/a	tA1	06B1	256K
1133	133	8.5x	SL5GQ	SL5GQ	tA1	06B1	256K
1133-S	133	8.5x	SL5LV	n/a	tA1	06B1	512K
1133-S	133	8.5x	SL5PU	SL5PU	tA1	06B1	512K
1200	133	9x	SL5GN	SL5GN	tA1	06B1	256K
1200	133	9x	SL5PM	n/a	tA1	06B1	256K
1266-S	133	9.5x	SL5LW	SL5QL	tA1	06B1	512K
1333	133	10x	n/a	SL5VX	tA1	06B1	256K
1400-S	133	10.5x	SL657	SL5XL	tA1	06B1	512K

CPUID = The internal ID returned by the CPUID instruction   FC-PGA = Flip-chip pin grid array
ECC = Error correcting code   FC-PGA2 = Flip-chip pin grid array revision 2

L2 Speed	Max. Temp. (C)	Voltage	Max. Power (W)	Process (Microns)	Transistors	Package
800	80	1.7	20.8	0.18	28.1M	FC-PGA
800	80	1.7	20.8	0.18	28.1M	SECC2
800	80	1.7	20.8	0.18	28.1M	SECC2
850	80	1.65	22.5	0.18	28.1M	SECC2
850	80	1.65	22.5	0.18	28.1M	FC-PGA
850	80	1.7	22.5	0.18	28.1M	FC-PGA
850	80	1.7	22.5	0.18	28.1M	SECC2
866	80	1.65	22.9	0.18	28.1M	SECC2
866	80	1.65	22.9	0.18	28.1M	FC-PGA
866	80	1.7	22.5	0.18	28.1M	FC PGA
866	80	1.7	22.5	0.18	28.1M	SECC2
866	80	1.75	26.1	0.18	28.1M	FC-PGA
900	75	1.7	23.2	0.18	28.1M	FC-PGA
933	75	1.7	25.5	0.18	28.1M	SECC2
933	75	1.7	24.5	0.18	28.1M	FC-PGA
933	75	1.7	24.5	0.18	28.1M	FC-PGA
933	75	1.7	25.5	0.18	28.1M	SECC2
933	77	1.75	27.3	0.18	28.1M	FC-PGA
1000	70	1.7	26.1	0.18	28.1M	SECC2
1000	70	1.7	26.1	0.18	28.1M	FC-PGA
1000	70	1.7	26.1	0.18	28.1M	FC-PGA
1000	70	1.7	26.1	0.18	28.1M	SECC2
1000	70	1.7	26.1	0.18	28.1M	SECC2
1000	70	1.7	26.1	0.18	28.1M	SECC2
1000	75	1.75	29.0	0.18	28.1M	FC-PGA
1000	75	1.75	29.0	0.18	28.1M	FC-PGA
1000	75	1.75	29.0	0.18	28.1M	FC-PGA
1000	75	1.75	29.0	0.18	28.1M	FC-PGA
1000	75	1.75	29.0	0.18	28.1M	FC-PGA
1100	77	1.75	33.0	0.18	28.1M	FC-PGA
1133	69	1.475	29.1	0.13	44M	FC-PGA2
1133	69	1.475	29.1	0.13	44M	FC-PGA2
1133	69	1.45	27.9	0.13	44M	FC-PGA2
1133	69	1.45	27.9	0.13	44M	FC-PGA2
1200	69	1.475	29.9	0.13	44M	FC-PGA2
1200	69	1.475	29.9	0.13	44M	FC-PGA2
1266	69	1.45	29.5	0.13	44M	FC-PGA2
1333	69	1.475	29.9	0.13	44M	FC-PGA2
1400	69	1.45	29.9	0.13	44M	FC-PGA2

SECC = *Single edge contact cartridge*
SECC2 = *Single edge contact cartridge revision 2*

Pentium III processors are all clock multiplier locked. This is a means to prevent processor fraud and over-clocking by making the processor work only at a given clock multiplier. Unfortunately, this feature can be bypassed by making modifications to the processor under the cartridge cover, and unscrupulous individuals have been selling lower-speed processors re-marked as higher speeds. It pays to purchase your systems or processors from direct Intel distributors or high-end dealers who do not engage in these practices.

Pentium II/III Xeon

The Pentium II and III processors are available in special high-end versions called Pentium II Xeon and Pentium III Xeon processors (Intel now uses the term *Xeon* by itself to refer to Xeon processors based on the Pentium 4). Originally introduced in June 1998 in Pentium II versions, later Pentium III versions were introduced in March 1999. These differ from the standard Pentium II and III in three ways: packaging, cache size, and cache speed.

Pentium II/III Xeon processors use a larger SEC cartridge than the standard PII/III processors, mainly to house a larger internal board with more cache memory.

Besides the larger package, the Xeon processors also include more L2 cache. They were produced in three variations, with 512KB, 1MB, or 2MB of L2 cache.

Even more significant than the size of the cache is its speed. All the cache in the Xeon processors run at the full-core speed. This is difficult to do considering that the cache chips are separate chips on the board; up until recently they were not integrated into the processor die. The original Pentium II Xeon processors had 7.5 million transistors in the main processor die, whereas the later Pentium III Xeon came with 9.5 million. When the Pentium III versions with on-die cache were released, the transistor count went up to 28.1 million transistors in the 256KB cache version, 84 million transistors in the 1MB cache version, and a whopping 140 million transistors in the latest 2MB cache version, setting an industry record at the time. The high transistor counts are due to the on-die L2 cache, which is very transistor intensive. The L2 cache in all Pentium II and III Xeon processors has a full 64GB RAM address range and supports ECC.

Later versions of the Xeon processor were designed for Socket 370, and even newer versions based on the Pentium 4 are designed for Socket 603 and Socket 604.

Other Sixth-Generation Processors

Besides Intel, many other manufacturers have produced P6-type processors, but often with a difference. Most of them were designed to interface with P5 class motherboards for the lower-end markets. AMD later offered up the Athlon and Duron processors, which were true sixth-generation designs using their own proprietary connections to the system.

This section examines the various sixth-generation processors from manufacturers other than Intel.

NexGen Nx586

NexGen was founded by Thampy Thomas, who hired some of the people formerly involved with the 486 and Pentium processors at Intel. At NexGen, developers created the Nx586, a processor that was functionally the same as the Pentium but not pin compatible. As such, it was always supplied with a motherboard; in fact, it was usually soldered in. NexGen did not manufacture the chips or the motherboards they came in; for that it hired IBM Microelectronics. Later NexGen was bought by AMD, right before it was ready to introduce the Nx686—a greatly improved design by Greg Favor and a true competitor for the Pentium. AMD took the Nx686 design and combined it with a Pentium electrical interface to create a drop-in Pentium-compatible chip called the K6, which actually outperformed the original from Intel.

The Nx586 had all the standard fifth-generation processor features, such as superscalar execution with two internal pipelines and a high-performance integral L1 cache with separate code and data caches. One advantage is that the Nx586 includes separate 16KB instruction and 16KB data caches compared to 8KB each for the Pentium. These caches keep key instruction and data close to the processing engines to increase overall system performance.

The Nx586 also includes branch prediction capabilities, which are one of the hallmarks of a sixth-generation processor. Branch prediction means the processor has internal functions to predict program flow to optimize the instruction execution.

The Nx586 processor also featured a RISC core. A translation unit dynamically translates x86 instructions into RISC86 instructions. These RISC86 instructions were designed specifically with direct support for the x86 architecture while obeying RISC performance principles. They are thus simpler and easier to execute than the complex x86 instructions. This type of capability is another feature normally found only in P6 class processors.

The Nx586 was discontinued after the merger with AMD, which then took the design for the successor Nx686 and released it as the AMD-K6.

AMD-K6 Series

The AMD-K6 processor is a high-performance sixth-generation processor that is physically installable in a P5 (Pentium) motherboard. It essentially was designed for AMD by NexGen and was first known as the Nx686. The NexGen version never appeared because it was purchased by AMD before the chip was due to be released. The AMD-K6 delivers performance levels somewhere between the Pentium and Pentium II processor as a result of its unique hybrid design. Because it is designed to install in Socket 7, which is a fifth-generation processor socket and motherboard design, it can't quite perform as a true sixth-generation chip because the Socket 7 architecture severely limits cache and memory performance. However, with this processor, AMD gave Intel a lot of competition in the low- to mid-range market, where the Pentium was still popular.

The K6 processor contains an industry-standard, high-performance implementation of the new multimedia instruction set, enabling a high level of multimedia performance. The K6-2 introduced an upgrade to MMX that AMD calls 3DNow!, which adds even more graphics and sound instructions. AMD designed the K6 processor to fit the low-cost, high-volume Socket 7 infrastructure. Initially, it used AMD's 0.35-micron, five-metal layer process technology; more recent variations used the 0.25-micron processor to increase production quantities because of reduced die size, as well as to decrease power consumption.

AMD-K6 processor technical features include:

- Sixth-generation internal design, fifth-generation external interface
- Internal RISC core, translates x86 to RISC instructions
- Superscalar parallel execution units (seven)
- Dynamic execution
- Branch prediction
- Speculative execution
- Large 64KB L1 cache (32KB instruction cache plus 32KB write-back dual-ported data cache)
- Built-in floating-point unit
- Industry-standard MMX instruction support
- System Management Mode
- Ceramic pin grid array (CPGA) Socket 7 design
- Manufactured using 0.35-micron and 0.25-micron, five-layer designs

The K6-2 adds the following:

- Higher clock speeds
- Higher bus speeds of up to 100MHz (Super7 motherboards)
- 3DNow!; 21 new graphics and sound processing instructions

The K6-3 adds the following:

- 256KB of on-die full-core speed L2 cache

The addition of the full-speed L2 cache in the K6-3 was significant. It enables the K6 series to fully compete with the Intel Pentium II processors and the Celeron processors based on the Pentium II. The 3DNow! capability added in the K6-2/3 was also exploited by newer graphics programs, making these processors ideal for lower-cost gaming systems.

The AMD-K6 processor architecture is fully x86 binary code compatible, which means it runs all Intel software, including MMX instructions. To make up for the lower L2 cache performance of the Socket 7 design, AMD beefed up the internal L1 cache to 64KB total, twice the size of the Pentium II or III. This, plus the dynamic execution capability, enabled the K6 to outperform the Pentium and come close to the Pentium II and III in performance for a given clock rate. The K6-3 was even better with the addition of full-core speed L2 cache; however, this processor ran very hot and was discontinued after a relatively brief period.

Both the AMD-K5 and AMD-K6 processors are Socket 7 bus compatible. However, certain modifications might be necessary for proper voltage setting and BIOS revisions. To ensure reliable operation of the AMD-K6 processor, the motherboard must meet specific voltage requirements.

The AMD processors have specific voltage requirements. Most older split-voltage motherboards default to 2.8V Core/3.3V I/O, which is below specification for the AMD-K6 and could cause erratic operation. To work properly, the motherboard must have Socket 7 with a dual-plane voltage regulator supplying 2.9V or 3.2V (233MHz) to the CPU core voltage (Vcc2) and 3.3V for the I/O (Vcc3). The voltage regulator must be capable of supplying up to 7.5A (9.5A for the 233MHz) to the processor. When used with a 200MHz or slower processor, the voltage regulator must maintain the core voltage within 145mV of nominal (2.9V+/–145mV). When used with a 233MHz processor, the voltage regulator must maintain the core voltage within 100mV of nominal (3.2V+/–100mV).

If the motherboard has a poorly designed voltage regulator that cannot maintain this performance, unreliable operation can result. If the CPU voltage exceeds the absolute maximum voltage range, the processor can be permanently damaged. Also note that the K6 can run hot. Make sure your heatsink is securely fitted to the processor and that the thermally conductive grease or pad is properly applied.

The motherboard must have an AMD-K6 processor-ready BIOS with support for the K6 built in. Award has that support in its March 1, 1997 or later BIOS; AMI had K6 support in any of its BIOSs with CPU Module 3.31 or later; and Phoenix supports the K6 in version 4.0, release 6.0, or release 5.1 with build dates of 4/7/97 or later.

Because these specifications can be fairly complicated, AMD keeps a list of motherboards that have been verified to work with the AMD-K6 processor on its Web site. All the motherboards on that list have been tested to work properly with the AMD-K6. So, unless these requirements can be verified elsewhere, it is recommended that you use only a motherboard from that list with the AMD-K6 processor.

The multiplier, bus speed, and voltage settings for the K6 are shown in Table 3.38. You can identify which AMD-K6 you have by looking at the markings on this chip, as shown in Figure 3.54.

Table 3.38   AMD-K6 Processor Speeds and Voltages

Processor	Core Speed	Clock Multiplier	Bus Speed	Core Voltage	I/O Voltage
K6-3	450MHz	4.5x	100MHz	2.4V	3.3V
K6-3	400MHz	4x	100MHz	2.4V	3.3V
K6-2	475MHz	5x	95MHz	2.4V	3.3V
K6-2	450MHz	4.5x	100MHz	2.4V	3.3V
K6-2	400MHz	4x	100MHz	2.2V	3.3V
K6-2	380MHz	4x	95MHz	2.2V	3.3V
K6-2	366MHz	5.5x	66MHz	2.2V	3.3V
K6-2	350MHz	3.5x	100MHz	2.2V	3.3V
K6-2	333MHz	3.5x	95MHz	2.2V	3.3V
K6-2	333MHz	5.0x	66MHz	2.2V	3.3V
K6-2	300MHz	3x	100MHz	2.2V	3.3V
K6-2	300MHz	4.5x	66MHz	2.2V	3.3V

Table 3.38   Continued

Processor	Core Speed	Clock Multiplier	Bus Speed	Core Voltage	I/O Voltage
K6-2	266MHz	4x	66MHz	2.2V	3.3V
K6	300MHz	4.5x	66MHz	2.2V	3.45V
K6	266MHz	4x	66MHz	2.2V	3.3V
K6	233MHz	3.5x	66MHz	3.2V	3.3V
K6	200MHz	3x	66MHz	2.9V	3.3V
K6	166MHz	2.5x	66MHz	2.9V	3.3V

Figure 3.54   AMD Athlon processor for Slot A (cartridge form factor).

Older motherboards achieve the 3.5x setting by setting jumpers for 1.5x. The 1.5x setting for older motherboards equates to a 3.5x setting for the AMD-K6 and newer Intel parts. Getting the 4x and higher setting requires a motherboard that controls three BF pins, including BF2. Older motherboards can control only two BF pins. The settings for the multipliers are shown in Table 3.39.

Table 3.39   AMD-K6 Multiplier Settings

Multiplier Setting	BF0	BF1	BF2	Multiplier Setting	BF0	BF1	BF2
2.5x	Low	Low	High	4.5x	Low	Low	Low
3x	High	Low	High	5x	High	Low	Low
3.5x	High	High	High	5.5x	High	High	Low
4x	Low	High	Low				

These settings usually are controlled by jumpers on the motherboard. Consult your motherboard documentation to see where they are and how to set them for the proper multiplier and bus speed settings.

Unlike Cyrix and some of the other Intel competitors, AMD is a manufacturer and a designer. Therefore, it designs and builds its chips in its own fabs. Similar to Intel, AMD has migrated to 0.25-micron process technology and beyond (the AMD Athlon XP is built on a 0.13-micron process). The original K6 has 8.8 million transistors and is built on a 0.35-micron, five-layer process. The die is 12.7mm on each side, or about 162 square mm. The K6-3 uses a 0.25-micron process and incorporates 21.3 million transistors on a die only 10.9mm on each side, or about 118 square mm.

Because of its performance and compatibility with the Socket 7 interface, the K6 series is often looked at as an excellent processor upgrade for motherboards using older Pentium or Pentium MMX processors. Although they do work in Socket 7, the AMD-K6 processors have different voltage and bus speed requirements from the Intel processors. Before attempting any upgrades, you should check the board documentation or contact the manufacturer to see whether your board meets the necessary requirements. In some cases, a BIOS upgrade also is necessary.

AMD Athlon, Duron, and Athlon XP

The Athlon is AMD's successor to the K6 series (refer to Figure 3.60). The Athlon is a whole new chip from the ground up and does not interface via the Socket 7 or Super7 sockets like its previous chips. In the initial Athlon versions, AMD used a cartridge design, called Slot A, almost exactly like that of the Intel Pentium II and III. This was due to the fact that the original Athlons used 512KB of external L2 cache, which was mounted on the processor cartridge board. The external cache ran at one-half core, two-fifths core, or one-third core depending on which speed processor you had. In June 2000, AMD introduced a revised version of the Athlon (codenamed Thunderbird) that incorporates 256KB of L2 cache directly on the processor die. This on-die cache runs at full-core speed and eliminates a bottleneck in the original Athlon systems. Along with the change to on-die L2 cache, the Athlon was also introduced in a PGA or chip Socket A version, which replaced the Slot A cartridge version. The most recent Athlon version, called the Athlon XP, has several enhancements such as 3DNow! Professional instructions, which also include the Intel SSE instructions. The latest Athlon XP models have also returned to the use of 512KB L2 cache, but this time at full processor speed.

Although the Slot A cartridge looks a lot like the Intel Slot 1, and the Socket A looks like Intel's Socket 370, the pinouts are completely different and the AMD chips do not work in the same motherboards as the Intel chips. This was by design because AMD was looking for ways to improve its chip architecture and distance itself from Intel. Special blocked pins in either socket or slot design prevent accidentally installing the chip in the wrong orientation or wrong slot. Figure 3.55 shows the Athlon in the Slot A cartridge. Socket A versions of the Athlon closely resemble the Duron.

Figure 3.55 AMD Athlon XP 0.13-micron processor for Socket A (PGA form factor).

Table 3.40   AMD Athlon Slot A Cartridge Processor Information

Part Number	Model	Speed (MHz)	Bus Speed (MHz)	Multiplier	L2 Cache
AMD-K7500MTR51B	Model 1	500	100x2	5x	512KB
AMD-K7550MTR51B	Model 1	550	100x2	5.5x	512KB
AMD-K7600MTR51B	Model 1	600	100x2	6x	512KB
AMD-K7650MTR51B	Model 1	650	100x2	6.5x	512KB
AMD-K7700MTR51B	Model 1	700	100x2	7x	512KB
AMD-K7550MTR51B	Model 2	550	100x2	5.5x	512KB
AMD-K7600MTR51B	Model 2	600	100x2	6x	512KB
AMD-K7650MTR51B	Model 2	650	100x2	6.5x	512KB
AMD-K7700MTR51B	Model 2	700	100x2	7x	512KB
AMD-K7750MTR52B	Model 2	750	100x2	7.5x	512KB
AMD-K7800MPR52B	Model 2	800	100x2	8x	512KB
AMD-K7850MPR52B	Model 2	850	100x2	8.5x	512KB
AMD-K7900MNR53B	Model 2	900	100x2	9x	512KB
AMD-K7950MNR53B	Model 2	950	100x2	9.5x	512KB

The Athlon is available in speeds from 500MHz up to 1.4GHz and uses a 200MHz or 266MHz processor (front-side) bus called the EV6 to connect to the motherboard North Bridge chip as well as other processors. Licensed from Digital Equipment, the EV6 bus is the same as that used for the Alpha 21264 processor, now owned by Compaq. The EV6 bus uses a clock speed of 100MHz or 133MHz but double-clocks the data, transferring data twice per cycle, for a cycling speed of 200MHz or 266MHz. Because the bus is 8 bytes (64 bits) wide, this results in a throughput of 8 bytes times 200MHz/266MHz, which amounts to 1.6GBps or 2.1GBps. This bus is ideal for supporting PC1600 or PC2100 DDR memory, which also runs at those speeds. The AMD bus design eliminates a potential bottleneck between the chipset and processor and enables more efficient transfers compared to other processors. The use of the EV6 bus is one of the primary reasons the Athlon and Duron chips perform so well.

The Athlon has a very large 128KB of L1 cache on the processor die and one-half, two-fifths, or one-third core speed 512KB L2 cache in the cartridge in the older versions; 256KB of full-core speed cache in Socket A Athlon and most Athlon XP models; and 512KB of full-core speed cache in the latest Athlon XP models. All PGA socket A versions have the full-speed cache. The Athlon also has support for MMX and the Enhanced 3DNow! instructions, which are 45 new instructions designed to support graphics and sound processing. 3DNow! is very similar to Intel's SSE in design and intent, but the specific instructions are different and require software support. The Athlon XP adds the Intel SSE instructions, which it calls 3DNow! Professional. Fortunately, most companies producing graphics software have decided to support the 3DNow! instructions along with the Intel SSE instructions, with only a few exceptions.

The initial production of the Athlon used 0.25-micron technology, with newer and faster versions being made on 0.18-micron and 0.13-micron processes. The latest versions are even built using copper metal technology, a first in the PC processor business. Eventually all other processors will follow because copper connects allow for lower power consumption and faster operation.

Table 3.40 shows detailed information on the Slot A version of the Athlon processor.

In most benchmarks the AMD Athlon compares as equal, if not superior, to the Intel Pentium III. AMD beat Intel to the 1GHz mark by introducing its 1GHz Athlon two days before Intel introduced the 1GHz Pentium III.

Table 3.41 shows information on the PGA or Socket A version of the AMD Athlon processor. All Socket A processors are Model 4.

L2 Speed (MHz)	Voltage	Max. Power (W)	Process (Microns)	Transistors	Introduced
250	1.60V	42W	0.25	22M	Jun. 1999
275	1.60V	46W	0.25	22M	Jun. 1999
300	1.60V	50W	0.25	22M	Jun. 1999
325	1.60V	54W	0.25	22M	Aug. 1999
350	1.60V	50W	0.25	22M	Oct. 1999
275	1.60V	31W	0.18	22M	Nov. 1999
300	1.60V	34W	0.18	22M	Nov. 1999
325	1.60V	36W	0.18	22M	Nov. 1999
350	1.60V	39W	0.18	22M	Nov. 1999
300	1.60V	40W	0.18	22M	Nov. 1999
320	1.70V	48W	0.18	22M	Jan. 2000
340	1.70V	50W	0.18	22M	Feb. 2000
300	1.80V	60W	0.18	22M	Mar. 2000
317	1.80V	62W	0.18	22M	Mar. 2000

Table 3.40   Continued

Part Number	Model	Speed (MHz)	Bus Speed (MHz)	Multiplier	L2 Cache
AMD-K7100MNR53B	Model 2	1000	100x2	10x	512KB
AMD-A0650MPR24B	Model 4	650	100x2	6.5x	256KB
AMD-A0700MPR24B	Model 4	700	100x2	7x	256KB
AMD-A0750MPR24B	Model 4	750	100x2	7.5x	256KB
AMD-A0800MPR24B	Model 4	800	100x2	8x	256KB
AMD-A0850MPR24B	Model 4	850	100x2	8.5x	256KB
AMD-A0900MMR24B	Model 4	900	100x2	9x	256KB
AMD-A0950MMR24B	Model 4	950	100x2	9.5x	256KB
AMD-A1000MMR24B	Model 4	1000	100x2	10x	256KB

Table 3.41   AMD Athlon PGA (Socket A) Processor Information

Speed (MHz)	Bus Speed (MHz)	Multiplier	L2 Cache	L2 Speed (MHz)
650	200	3.25x	256KB	650
700	200	3.5x	256KB	700
750	200	3.25x	256KB	750
800	200	4x	256KB	800
850	200	4.25x	256KB	850
900	200	4.5x	256KB	900
950	200	4.75x	256KB	950
1000	200	5x	256KB	1000
1000	266	3.75x	256KB	1000
1100	200	5.5x	256KB	1100
1133	266	4.25x	256KB	1133
1200	200	6x	256KB	1200
1200	266	4.5x	256KB	1200
1300	200	6.5x	256KB	1300
1333	266	5x	256KB	1333
1400	266	5.5x	256KB	1400

AMD Duron

The AMD Duron processor (originally code named Spitfire) was announced in June 2000 and is a derivative of the AMD Athlon processor in the same fashion as the Celeron is a derivative of the Pentium II and III. Basically, the Duron is an Athlon with less L2 cache; all other capabilities are essentially the same. It is designed to be a lower-cost version with less cache but only slightly less performance. In keeping with the low-cost theme, Duron contains 64KB on-die L2 cache and is designed for Socket A, a socket version of the Athlon Slot A (see Figure 3.56). Except for the Duron markings, the Duron is almost identical externally to the Socket A versions of the original Athlon.

Essentially, the Duron was designed to compete against the Intel Celeron in the low-cost PC market, just as the Athlon was designed to compete in the higher-end Pentium III market. The Duron has

L2 Speed (MHz)	Voltage	Max. Power (W)	Process (Microns)	Transistors	Introduced
333	1.80V	65W	0.18	22M	Mar. 2000
650	1.70V	36.1W	0.18	37M	Jun. 2000
700	1.70V	38.3W	0.18	37M	Jun. 2000
750	1.70V	40.4W	0.18	37M	Jun. 2000
800	1.70V	42.6W	0.18	37M	Jun. 2000
850	1.70V	44.8W	0.18	37M	Jun. 2000
900	1.75V	49.7W	0.18	37M	Jun. 2000
950	1.75V	52.0W	0.18	37M	Jun. 2000
1000	1.75V	54.3W	0.18	37M	Jun. 2000

Voltage	Max. Power (W)	Process (Microns)	Transistors
1.75V	38.5W	0.18	37M
1.75V	40.3W	0.18	37M
1.75V	43.8W	0.18	37M
1.75V	45.5W	0.18	37M
1.75V	47.3W	0.18	37M
1.75V	50.8W	0.18	37M
1.75V	52.5W	0.18	37M
1.75V	54.3W	0.18	37M
1.75V	54.3W	0.18	37M
1.75V	59.5W	0.18	37M
1.75V	63.0W	0.18	37M
1.75V	66.5W	0.18	37M
1.75V	66.5W	0.18	37M
1.75V	68.3W	0.18	37M
1.75V	70.0W	0.18	37M
1.75V	72.0W	0.18	37M

since been discontinued, but most systems that use the Duron processor can use AMD Athlon or, in some cases Athlon XP, processors as an upgrade.

Because the Duron processor is derived from the Athlon core, it includes the Athlon 200MHz front-side system bus (interface to the chipset) as well as enhanced 3DNow! instructions in Model 3. Model 7 processors include 3DNow! Professional instructions (which include a full implementation of SSE instructions).

Table 3.42 shows information on the PGA or Socket A version of the AMD Duron processor. Durons that require 1.6V are Model 3 processors, whereas those that require 1.75V are Model 7 processors. The Model 7 version was originally code named Morgan.

Figure 3.56 AMD Duron processor.

Table 3.42 AMD Duron Processor Information

Speed (MHz)	Bus Speed (MHz)	L2 Cache	Voltage	Max. Power (W)	Process (Microns)	Transistors
550	200	64KB	1.6V	25.3W	0.18	25M
600	200	64KB	1.6V	27.4W	0.18	25M
650	200	64KB	1.6V	29.4W	0.18	25M
700	200	64KB	1.6V	31.4W	0.18	25M
750	200	64KB	1.6V	33.4W	0.18	25M
800	200	64KB	1.6V	35.4W	0.18	25M
850	200	64KB	1.6V	37.4W	0.18	25M
900	200	64KB	1.6V	39.5W	0.18	25M
900	200	64KB	1.75V	42.7W	0.18	25.2M
950	200	64KB	1.6V	41.5W	0.18	25M
950	200	64KB	1.75V	44.4W	0.18	25.2M
1000	200	64KB	1.75V	46.1W	0.18	25.2M
1100	200	64KB	1.75V	50.3W	0.18	25.2M
1200	200	64KB	1.75V	54.7W	0.18	25.2M
1300	200	64KB	1.75V	60.0W	0.18	25.2M
1400	266	64KB	1.5V	45.5W	0.13	37.2M
1600	266	64KB	1.5V	48.0W	0.13	37.2M
1800	266	64KB	1.5V	53.0W	0.13	37.2M

AMD Athlon XP

As mentioned earlier, the newest version of the Athlon is called the Athlon XP. This is basically an improved version of the previous Athlon, with improvements in the instruction set so it can execute Intel SSE instructions and a new marketing scheme that directly competes with the Pentium 4. The latest Athlon XP models have also adopted a larger (512KB) full-speed on-die cache.

AMD uses the term "QuantiSpeed" (a marketing term, not a technical term) to refer to the architecture of the Athlon XP. AMD defines this as including the following:

■ *A nine-issue superscalar, fully pipelined microarchitecture.* This provides more pathways for instructions to be sent into the execution sections of the CPU and includes three floating-point execution units, three integer units, and three address calculation units.

■ *A superscalar, fully pipelined floating-point calculation unit.* This provides faster operations per clock cycle and cures a long-time deficiency of AMD processors versus Intel processors.

■ *A hardware data prefetch.* This gathers the data needed from system memory and places it in the processor's Level 1 cache to save time.

■ *Improved translation look-aside buffers (TLBs).* These enable the storage of data where the processor can access it more quickly without duplication or stalling for lack of fresh information.

These design improvements wring more work out of each clock cycle, enabling a "slower" Athlon XP to beat a "faster" Pentium 4 processor in doing actual work (and play).

The first models of the Athlon XP used the Palomino core, which is also shared by the Athlon 4 mobile (laptop) processor. Later models have used the Thoroughbred core, which was later revised to improve thermal characteristics. The different Thoroughbred cores are sometimes referred to as Thoroughbred-A and Thoroughbred-B. The latest Athlon XP processors use a new core with 512KB on-die full-speed L2 cache known as Barton. Additional features include

■ 3DNow! Professional multimedia instructions (adding compatibility with the 70 additional SSE instructions in the Pentium III but not the 144 additional SSE2 instructions in the Pentium 4)

■ 266MHz or 333MHz FSB

■ 128KB Level 1 and 256KB or 512KB on-die Level 2 memory caches running at full CPU speed

■ Copper interconnects (instead of aluminum) for more electrical efficiency and less heat

Also new to the Athlon XP is the use of a thinner, lighter organic chip packaging compound similar to that used by recent Intel processors. Figure 3.57 shows the latest Athlon XP processors that use the Barton core.

Figure 3.57   AMD Athlon XP 0.13-micron processor with 512KB of L2 cache for Socket A (PGA form factor). *Photo courtesy of Advanced Micro Devices, Inc.*

This packaging allows for a more efficient layout of electrical components. The latest versions of the Athlon XP are made using a new 0.13-micron die process that results in a chip with a smaller die that uses less power, generates less heat, and is capable of running faster as compared to the previous models. The newest 0.13-micron versions of the Athlon XP run at actual clock speeds exceeding 2GHz. Table 3.43 provides detailed information about the Athlon XP.

Table 3.43   AMD Athlon XP Processor Information

P-Rating	Actual Speed (MHz)	Bus Speed (MHz)	Multiplier	L2 Cache	Voltage	Max. Power (W)	Process (Microns)	Transistors
1500+[1]	1333	266	5x	256KB	1.75V	60.0W	0.18	37.5
1600+[1]	1400	266	5.25x	256KB	1.75V	62.8W	0.18	37.5
1700+[1]	1467	266	5.5x	256KB	1.75V	64.0W	0.18	37.5
1800+[1]	1533	266	5.75x	256KB	1.75V	66.0W	0.18	37.5
1900+[1]	1600	266	6x	256KB	1.75V	68.0W	0.18	37.5
2000+[1]	1667	266	6.25x	256KB	1.75V	70.0W	0.18	37.5
2100+[1]	1733	266	6.5x	256KB	1.75V	72.0W	0.18	37.5
1700+[2]	1467	266	5.5x	256KB	1.5V	49.4W	0.13	37.2
1700+[3]	1467	266	5.5x	256KB	1.6V	59.8W	0.13	37.2
1800+[2]	1533	266	5.75x	256KB	1.5V	51.0W	0.13	37.2
1800+[3]	1533	266	5.75x	256KB	1.6V	59.8W	0.13	37.2
1900+[2]	1600	266	6x	256KB	1.5V	52.5W	0.13	37.2
2000+[2]	1667	266	6.25x	256KB	1.6V	60.3W	0.13	37.2
2000+[3]	1667	266	6.25x	256KB	1.6V	61.3W	0.13	37.2
2100+[2]	1733	266	6.5x	256KB	1.6V	62.1W	0.13	37.2
2100+[3]	1733	266	6.5x	256KB	1.6V	62.1W	0.13	37.2
2200+[2]	1800	266	6.75x	256KB	1.65V	67.9W	0.13	37.2
2200+[3]	1800	266	6.75x	256KB	1.6V	62.8W	0.13	37.2
2400+[3]	2000	266	7.5x	256KB	1.65V	68.3W	0.13	37.2
2500+[5]	1833	333	5.5x	512KB	1.65V	68.3W	0.13	54.3
2600+[3]	2133	266	8x	256KB	1.65V	68.3W	0.13	37.2
2600+[4]	2083	333	6.25x	256KB	1.65V	68.3W	0.13	37.2
2700+[4]	2167	333	6.5x	2167	1.65V	68.3W	0.13	37.2
2800+[5]	2083	333	6.25x	2083	1.65V	68.3W	0.13	54.3
3000+[5]	2167	333	6.5x	2167	1.65V	74.3W	0.13	54.3
3000+[5]	2100	400	5.25x	512KB	1.65V	68.3W	0.13	54.3
3200+[5]	2200	400	5.5x	512KB	1.65V	76.8W	0.13	54.3

1. *Model 6 Athlon XP (Palomino)*
2. *Model 8 Athlon XP CPUID 680 (Thoroughbred)*
3. *Model 8 Athlon XP CPUID 681 (Thoroughbred)*
4. *Model 8 Athlon XP with 333MHz FSB (Thoroughbred)*
5. *Model 10 Athlon XP (Barton)*

Athlon MP

The Athlon MP is AMD's first processor designed for multiprocessor support. Thus, it can be used in servers and workstations that demand multiprocessor support. The Athlon MP comes in the following three versions, which are similar to various Athlon and Athlon XP models:

- *Model 6 (1GHz, 1.2GHz)*. This model is similar to the Athlon Model 4.
- *Model 6 OPGA (1500+ through 2100+)*. This model is similar to the Athlon XP Model 6.
- *Model 8 (2000+, 2200+, 2400+, 2600+)*. This model is similar to the Athlon XP Model 8.
- *Model 10 (2500+, 2800+, 3000+)*. This model is similar to the Athlon XP Model 8, but with 512KB of L2 cache.

All Athlon MP processors use the same Socket A interface used by later models of the Athlon and all Duron and Athlon XP processors.

For more details about the Athlon MP, see the AMD Web site.

Cyrix/IBM 6x86 (M1) and 6x86MX (MII)

The Cyrix 6x86 processor family consists of the now-discontinued 6x86 and the newer 6x86MX processors. They are similar to the AMD-K5 and K6 in that they offer sixth-generation internal designs in a fifth-generation P5 Pentium-compatible Socket 7 exterior.

The Cyrix 6x86 and 6x86MX (renamed MII) processors incorporate two optimized superpipelined integer units and an on-chip floating-point unit. These processors include the dynamic execution capability that is the hallmark of a sixth-generation CPU design. This includes branch prediction and speculative execution.

The 6x86MX/MII processor is compatible with MMX technology to run MMX games and multimedia software. With its enhanced memory-management unit, a 64KB internal cache, and other advanced architectural features, the 6x86MX processor achieves higher performance and offers better value than competitive processors.

Features and benefits of the 6x86 processors include

- *Superscalar architecture.* Two pipelines to execute multiple instructions in parallel
- *Branch prediction.* Predicts with high accuracy the next instructions needed
- *Speculative execution.* Enables the pipelines to continuously execute instructions following a branch without stalling the pipelines
- *Out-of-order completion.* Lets the faster instruction exit the pipeline out of order, saving processing time without disrupting program flow

The 6x86 incorporates two caches: a 16KB dual-ported unified cache and a 256-byte instruction line cache. The unified cache is supplemented with a small, quarter-K-size, high-speed, fully associative instruction line cache. The improved 6x86MX design quadruples the internal cache size to 64KB, which significantly improves performance.

The 6x86MX also includes the 57 MMX instructions that speed up the processing of certain computing-intensive loops found in multimedia and communication applications.

All 6x86 processors feature support for SMM. This provides an interrupt that can be used for system power management or software transparent emulation of I/O peripherals. Additionally, the 6x86 supports a hardware interface that enables the CPU to be placed into a low-power suspend mode.

The 6x86 is compatible with x86 software and all popular x86 operating systems, including Windows 95/98/Me, Windows NT/2000, OS/2, DOS, Solaris, and Unix. Additionally, the 6x86 processor has been certified Windows 95 compatible by Microsoft.

As with the AMD-K6, there are some unique motherboard and BIOS requirements for the 6x86 processors. The 6x86 processor has been discontinued since Cyrix was absorbed into VIA, but the 6x86MX (MII) design is still sold and supported by VIA. Check motherboard compatibility with the 6x86MX or MII processors before integrating one into an existing Socket 7/Super7 system. A BIOS update might be necessary in some cases. When installing or configuring a system with the 6x86 processors, you have to set the correct motherboard bus speed and multiplier settings. The Cyrix processors are numbered based on a P-Rating scale, which is not the same as the true megahertz clock speed of the processor.

See the section "Cyrix Processor Speeds," earlier in this chapter, for the correct and true speed settings for the Cyrix 6x86 processors.

Note that because of the use of the P-Rating system, the actual speed of the chip is not the same number at which it is advertised. For example, the 6x86MX-PR300 is not a 300MHz chip; it actually runs at only 263MHz or 266MHz, depending on exactly how the motherboard bus speed and CPU clock multipliers are set. Cyrix says it runs as fast as a 300MHz Pentium, hence the P-Rating. Personally, I wish it would label the chip at the correct speed and then say that it runs faster than a Pentium at the same speed.

To install the 6x86 processors in a motherboard, you also must set the correct voltage. Normally, the markings on top of the chip indicate which voltage setting is appropriate. Various versions of the 6x86 run at 3.52V (use VRE setting), 3.3V (VR setting), or 2.8V (MMX) settings. The MMX versions use the standard split-plane 2.8V core 3.3V I/O settings.

The Cyrix MII is now sold by VIA Technologies.

VIA C3

The VIA C3 was originally known as the VIA Cyrix III and was designed to fit into the same Socket 370 used by the Pentium III and Celeron III. The initial versions of the C3, code named Joshua and Samuel, had 128KB L1 cache but didn't contain any L2 cache. As a consequence, they had much lower performance than similar 500MHz-class processors. The original Cyrix III/C3, code named Joshua, was developed by former Cyrix engineers after VIA bought Cyrix in late 1998, but the Samuel and subsequent versions are based on the Centaur Winchip (VIA purchased Centaur in 1999). The Samuel was built with a .18-micron process, whereas the Samuel 2 is a development of the Samuel with 64KB of L2 cache on board and is built on a .15-micron process. The Ezra core was the first .13-micron process C3 processor, but it, like previous C3 processors, was not compatible with Tualatin (late Pentium III-compatible) motherboards. The Ezra-T core was the first C3 to reach 1GHz and the first to support Tualatin motherboards. The latest C3 uses the Nehemiah core and features clock speeds over 1GHz and built-in encryption. C3 models feature 100MHz FSB (750MHz and 900MHz models) or 133MHz FSB (733MHz, 800MHz, 866MHz, 933MHz, and higher).

The C3 is fully software compatible with other x86 processors, including Pentium III and Celeron, but its microarchitecture is designed to enhance the performance of most frequently used instructions while reducing the performance of seldom-used instructions. This design feature significantly reduces the die size needed for C3 processors, but it also reduces performance in multimedia and graphics operations. By reducing the die size, the C3 in its Nehemiah version offers typical power consumption of only 11.25 watts, making it the coolest running processor available for Socket 370 applications.

Because of its low power consumption, cool operation, and relatively low performance compared to the Intel Celeron, the C3 processor should be considered primarily for computing appliances, set-top boxes, and portable computers in which small size and low power/cooling requirements (rather than performance) are paramount.

The C3 is also available in an enhanced ball grid array (EBGA) package called the E-series. E-series C3 processors are used for permanent installation on motherboards such as the Mini-ITX ultra-compact form factor designs also produced by VIA.

For more details about various versions of the C3, refer to Table 3.2 or the VIA Technologies Web site.

Intel Pentium 4 (Seventh-Generation) Processors

The Pentium 4 was introduced in November 2000 and represented a new generation in processors (see Figure 3.58). If this one had a number instead of a name, it might be called the 786 because it represents a generation beyond the previous 686 class processors. Three main variations on the Pentium 4 have been released, based on the processor die and architecture. They are called the Willamette, Northwood, and Prescott. The processor dies are shown in Figure 3.59.

Figure 3.58   Pentium 4 FC-PGA2 processor.

The main technical details for the Pentium 4 include

- Speeds range from 1.3GHz to 4GHz and beyond.
- 42 million transistors, 0.18-micron process, 217 sq. mm die (Willamette).
- 55 million transistors, 0.13-micron process, 131 sq. mm die (Northwood).
- 125 million transistors, 0.09-micron process, 112 sq. mm die (Prescott).
- Software compatible with previous Intel 32-bit processors.
- Processor (front-side) bus runs at 400MHz, 533MHz, or 800MHz.
- Arithmetic logic units (ALUs) run at twice the processor core frequency.
- Hyper-pipelined (20-stage or 31-stage) technology.
- Hyper-threading technology support in all 2.4GHz and faster processors running an 800MHz bus and all 3.06GHz and faster processors running a 533MHz bus.
- Very deep out-of-order instruction execution.
- Enhanced branch prediction.
- 8KB or 16KB L1 cache plus 12K micro-op execution trace cache.
- 256KB, 512KB, or 1MB of on-die, full-core speed 256-bit-wide L2 cache with eight-way associativity.
- L2 cache can handle up to 4GB RAM and supports ECC.
- 2MB of on-die, full-speed L3 cache (Extreme Edition).
- SSE2—SSE plus 144 new instructions for graphics and sound processing (Willamette and Northwood).
- SSE3—SSE2 plus 13 new instructions for graphics and sound processing (Prescott).
- Enhanced floating-point unit.
- Multiple low-power states.

Intel abandoned Roman numerals for a standard Arabic numeral 4 designation. Internally, the Pentium 4 introduces a new architecture Intel calls NetBurst microarchitecture, which is a marketing term and not a technical term. Intel uses NetBurst to describe hyper-pipelined technology, a rapid execution engine, a high-speed (400MHz, 533MHz, or 800MHz) system bus, and an execution trace cache. The hyper-pipelined technology doubles or triples the instruction pipeline depth as compared to the Pentium III (or Athlon/Athlon 64), meaning more and smaller steps are required to execute instructions. Even though this might seem less efficient, it enables much higher clock speeds to be more easily attained. The rapid execution engine enables the two integer arithmetic logic units (ALUs) to run at twice the processor core frequency, which means instructions can execute in half a clock cycle. The 400MHz/533MHz/800MHz system bus is a quad-pumped bus running off a 100MHz/133MHz/200MHz system clock transferring data four times per clock cycle. The execution trace cache is a high-performance Level 1 cache that stores approximately 12k decoded micro-operations. This removes the instruction decoder from the main execution pipeline, increasing performance.

 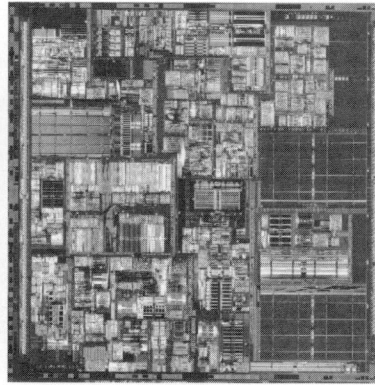 

Figure 3.59 The CPU dies for the Pentium 4 CPU based on the Willamette, Northwood, and Prescott cores.

Of these, the high-speed processor bus is most notable. Technically speaking, the processor bus is a 100MHz, 133MHz, or 200MHz quad-pumped bus that transfers four times per cycle (4x), for a 400MHz, 533MHz, or 800MHz effective rate. Because the bus is 64 bits (8 bytes) wide, this results in a throughput rate of 3200MBps, 4266MBps, or 6400MBps.

Table 3.44 shows how this transfer rate compares to dual-channel RDRAM and DDR SDRAM.

Table 3.44   Pentium 4 Processor Bus and RDRAM Speed Comparison

Pentium 4 Processor Bus Speed	Throughput (Processor Bus×8)	Dual-channel RIMM Throughput	Dual-channel DDR DIMM Throughput
400MHz	3200MBps	3200MBps	3200MBps
533MHz	4266MBps	4266MBps	4266MBps
800MHz	6400MBps	6400MBps	6400MBps

As you can see from Table 3.44, the throughput of the Pentium 4's processor bus is an exact match for the most common types of RDRAM and DDR SDRAM memory. The use of dual-channel memory means that modules must be added in matched pairs. Dual banks of PC1600, PC2100, or PC3200 DDR SDRAM are less expensive than equivalent RDRAM solutions, which is why virtually all newer chipsets— including the 865 (Springdale) and 875 (Canterwood)—support DDR SDRAM only for the Pentium 4.

In the new 20-stage or 31-stage pipelined internal architecture, individual instructions are broken down into many more substages, making this almost like a RISC processor. Unfortunately, this can add to the number of cycles taken to execute instructions if they are not optimized for this processor. Early benchmarks running existing software showed that existing Pentium III or AMD Athlon processors could easily keep pace with or even exceed the Pentium 4 in specific tasks; however, this is changing now that applications are being recompiled to work smoothly with the Pentium 4's deep pipelined architecture.

Another important architectural advantage is hyper-threading technology, which can be found in all Pentium 4 2.4GHz and faster processors running an 800MHz bus and all 3.06GHz and faster processors running a 533MHz bus. Hyper-threading enables a single processor to run two threads simultaneously, thereby acting as if it were two processors instead of one. For more information on hyper-threading technology, see the section "Hyper-Threading Technology," earlier in this chapter.

The Pentium 4 initially used Socket 423, which has 423 pins in a 39x39 SPGA arrangement. Later versions used Socket 478; recent versions use Socket T (LGA775), which has additional pins for future and faster variations of the chip. The Celeron was never designed to work in Socket 423, but Celeron versions are available for Socket 478 and Socket T (LGA775), allowing for lower-cost systems compatible with the Pentium 4. Voltage selection is made via an automatic voltage regulator module installed on the motherboard and wired to the socket.

Pentium 4 Extreme Edition

In November 2003, Intel introduced the Extreme Edition of the Pentium 4, which is notable for being the first desktop PC processor to incorporate L3 cache. The Extreme Edition (or Pentium 4EE) is basically a revamped version of the Prestonia core Xeon workstation/server processor, which has used L3 cache since November 2002. The Pentium 4EE has 2MB of L3 cache, which increases the transistor count to 178 million transistors and makes the die significantly larger than the standard Pentium 4. Because of the large die based on the 130-nanometer process, this chip is expensive to produce and the extremely high selling price reflects that. The Extreme Edition is targeted toward the gaming market, where people are willing to spend extra money for additional performance. The additional cache doesn't help standard business applications as well as it helps power-hungry 3D games.

Although the L3 cache found in the Pentium 4 Extreme Edition is unique today, in the future many processors will likely incorporate L3 cache as they strive for more and more performance and take advantage of industry reductions in process size. Expect to see an Extreme Edition of the Pentium 4 based on the Prescott core in 2005.

Memory Requirements

Pentium 4–based motherboards use either RDRAM or DDR SDRAM memory, depending on the chipset; however, most use DDR SDRAM. The RDRAM boards use the same Rambus RDRAM RIMM modules introduced for use with some of the chipsets used in Pentium III motherboards; however, the dual RDRAM channels the Pentium 4 uses require you to install pairs of identical modules (called RIMMs). Pentium 4 motherboards that use RDRAM accept either one or two pairs of RIMMs. Both pairs of memory must be the same speed, but need not be the same size.

Whereas most initial Pentium 4 motherboard chipsets supported only RDRAM memory, most newer chipsets are available that support more standard memory, such as SDRAM or DDR SDRAM. Since Intel's contract with RAMBUS expired in 2001, DDR SDRAM has become Intel's preferred memory type for mainstream systems.

Power Supply Issues

The Pentium 4 requires a lot of electrical power, and because of this, most Pentium 4 motherboards use a new design voltage regulator module that is powered from 12V instead of 3.3V or 5V, as with previous designs. By using the 12V power, more 3.3V and 5V power is available to run the rest of the system, and the overall current draw is greatly reduced with the higher voltage as a source. PC power supplies generate a more than adequate supply of 12V power, but the ATX motherboard and power supply design originally allotted only one pin for 12V power (each pin is rated for only 6 amps), so additional 12V lines were necessary to carry this power to the motherboard.

The fix appears in the form of a third power connector, called the ATX12V connector. This new connector is used in addition to the standard 20-pin ATX power supply connector and 6-pin auxiliary (3.3/5V) connector. Fortunately, the power supply itself won't need a redesign; there is more than enough 12V power available from the drive connectors. To utilize this, companies such as PC Power and Cooling sell an inexpensive ($8) adapter that converts a standard Molex-type drive power connector to the ATX12V connector. Typically, a 300-watt (the minimum recommended) or larger power supply has more than adequate levels of 12V power for both the drives and the ATX12V connector.

Table 3.45   Pentium 4 Processor Information

CPU Speed (GHz)	Bus Speed (MHz)	Bus Speed (GBps)	HT Support	Boxed S-spec	OEM S-spec	Stepping	CPUID
1.30	400	3.2	No	SL4QD	SL4SF	B2	0F07h
1.30	400	3.2	No	SL4SF	SL4SF	B2	0F07h
1.30	400	3.2	No	SL5GC	SL5FW	C1	0F0Ah
1.40	400	3.2	No	SL4SC	SL4SG	B2	0F07h
1.40	400	3.2	No	SL4SG	SL4SG	B2	0F07h
1.40	400	3.2	No	SL4X2	SL4WS	C1	0F0Ah
1.40	400	3.2	No	SL5N7	SL59U	C1	0F0Ah
1.40	400	3.2	No	SL59U	SL59U	C1	0F0Ah
1.40	400	3.2	No	SL5UE	SL5TG	D0	0F12h
1.40	400	3.2	No	SL5TG	SL5TG	D0	0F12h
1.50	400	3.2	No	SL4TY	SL4SH	B2	0F07h
1.50	400	3.2	No	SL4SH	SL4SH	B2	0F07h
1.50	400	3.2	No	SL4X3	SL4WT	C1	0F0Ah
1.50	400	3.2	No	SL4WT	SL4WT	C1	0F0Ah
1.50	400	3.2	No	SL5TN	SL5SX	D0	0F12h
1.50	400	3.2	No	SL5N8	SL59V	C1	0F0Ah
1.50	400	3.2	No	SL5UF	SL5TJ	D0	0F12h
1.50	400	3.2	No	SL5TJ	SL5TJ	D0	0F12h
1.50	400	3.2	No	SL62Y	SL62Y	D0	0F12h
1.60	400	3.2	No	SL4X4	SL4WU	C1	0F0Ah
1.60	400	3.2	No	SL5UL	SL5VL	D0	0F12h
1.60	400	3.2	No	SL5VL	SL5VL	D0	0F12h
1.60	400	3.2	No	SL5UW	SL5US	C1	0F0Ah
1.60	400	3.2	No	SL5UJ	SL5VH	D0	0F12h
1.60	400	3.2	No	SL5VH	SL5VH	D0	0F12h
1.60	400	3.2	No	SL6BC	SL679	E0	0F13h
1.60	400	3.2	No	SL679	SL679	E0	0F13h
1.60A	400	3.2	No	SL668	SL668	B0	0F24h
1.70	400	3.2	No	SL57V	SL57W	C1	0F0Ah
1.70	400	3.2	No	SL57W	SL57W	C1	0F0Ah
1.70	400	3.2	No	SL5TP	SL5SY	D0	0F12h
1.70	400	3.2	No	SL5N9	SL59X	C1	0F0Ah

If your power supply is less than the 300-watt minimum recommended, you need to purchase a replacement; some vendors now sell an off-the-shelf ATX12V ready model or one that uses the adapter mentioned previously.

The various Pentium 4 versions, including thermal and power specifications, are shown in Table 3.45.

L2 Cache	L3 Cache	Max. Temp	Max. Power	Socket	Process	Transistors
256K	0K	69°C	48.9W	423	180nm	42M
256K	0K	69°C	48.9W	423	180nm	42M
256K	0K	70°C	51.6W	423	180nm	42M
256K	0K	70°C	51.8W	423	180nm	42M
256K	0K	70°C	51.8W	423	180nm	42M
256K	0K	72°C	54.7W	423	180nm	42M
256K	0K	72°C	55.3W	478	180nm	42M
256K	0K	72°C	55.3W	478	180nm	42M
256K	0K	72°C	55.3W	478	180nm	42M
256K	0K	72°C	55.3W	478	180nm	42M
256K	0K	72°C	54.7W	423	180nm	42M
256K	0K	72°C	54.7W	423	180nm	42M
256K	0K	73°C	57.8W	423	180nm	42M
256K	0K	73°C	57.8W	423	180nm	42M
256K	0K	73°C	57.8W	423	180nm	42M
256K	0K	73°C	57.9W	478	180nm	42M
256K	0K	73°C	57.9W	478	180nm	42M
256K	0K	73°C	57.9W	478	180nm	42M
256K	0K	71°C	62.9W	478	180nm	42M
256K	0K	75°C	61.0W	423	180nm	42M
256K	0K	75°C	61.0W	423	180nm	42M
256K	0K	75°C	61.0W	423	180nm	42M
256K	0K	75°C	60.8W	478	180nm	42M
256K	0K	75°C	60.8W	478	180nm	42M
256K	0K	75°C	60.8W	478	180nm	42M
256K	0K	75°C	60.8W	478	180nm	42M
256K	0K	75°C	60.8W	478	180nm	42M
512K	0K	66°C	46.8W	478	130nm	55M
256K	0K	76°C	64.0W	423	180nm	42M
256K	0K	76°C	64.0W	423	180nm	42M
256K	0K	76°C	64.0W	423	180nm	42M
256K	0K	76°C	63.5W	478	180nm	42M

Table 3.45 Continued

CPU Speed (GHz)	Bus Speed (MHz)	Bus Speed (GBps)	HT Support	Boxed S-spec	OEM S-spec	Stepping	CPUID
1.70	400	3.2	No	SL5UG	SL5TK	D0	0F12h
1.70	400	3.2	No	SL5TK	SL5TK	D0	0F12h
1.70	400	3.2	No	SL62Z	SL62Z	D0	0F12h
1.70	400	3.2	No	SL6BD	SL67A	E0	0F13h
1.70	400	3.2	No	SL67A	SL67A	E0	0F13h
1.80	400	3.2	No	SL4X5	SL4WV	C1	0F0Ah
1.80	400	3.2	No	SL5UM	SL5VM	D0	0F12h
1.80	400	3.2	No	SL5VM	SL5VM	D0	0F12h
1.80	400	3.2	No	SL5UV	SL5UT	C1	0F0Ah
1.80	400	3.2	No	SL5UK	SL5VJ	D0	0F12h
1.80	400	3.2	No	SL5VJ	SL5VJ	D0	0F12h
1.80	400	3.2	No	SL6BE	SL67B	E0	0F13h
1.80	400	3.2	No	SL67B	SL67B	E0	0F13h
1.80A	400	3.2	No	SL63X	SL62P	B0	0F24h
1.80A	400	3.2	No	SL62P	SL62P	B0	0F24h
1.80A	400	3.2	No	SL68Q	SL66Q	B0	0F24h
1.80A	400	3.2	No	SL66Q	SL66Q	B0	0F24h
1.90	400	3.2	No	SL5WH	SL5VN	D0	0F12h
1.90	400	3.2	No	SL5VN	SL5VN	D0	0F12h
1.90	400	3.2	No	SL5WG	SL5VK	D0	0F12h
1.90	400	3.2	No	SL5VK	SL5VK	D0	0F12h
1.90	400	3.2	No	SL6BF	SL67C	E0	0F13h
1.90	400	3.2	No	SL67C	SL67C	E0	0F13h
2.0	400	3.2	No	SL5TQ	SL5SZ	D0	0F12h
2.0	400	3.2	No	SL5UH	SL5TL	D0	0F12h
2.0	400	3.2	No	SL5TL	SL5TL	D0	0F12h
2.0A	400	3.2	No	SL5ZT	SL5YR	B0	0F24h
2.0A	400	3.2	No	SL5YR	SL5YR	B0	0F24h
2.0A	400	3.2	No	SL68R	SL66R	B0	0F24h
2.0A	400	3.2	No	SL66R	SL66R	B0	0F24h
2.0A	400	3.2	No	SL6E7	SL6GQ	C1	0F27h
2.0A	400	3.2	No	SL6GQ	SL6GQ	C1	0F27h
2.0A	400	3.2	No	SL6QM	SL6PK	D1	0F29h
2.20	400	3.2	No	SL5ZU	SL5YS	B0	0F24h
2.20	400	3.2	No	SL5YS	SL5YS	B0	0F24h
2.20	400	3.2	No	SL68S	SL66S	B0	0F24h
2.20	400	3.2	No	SL66S	SL66S	B0	0F24h
2.20	400	3.2	No	SL6E8	SL6GR	C1	0F27h

L2 Cache	L3 Cache	Max. Temp	Max. Power	Socket	Process	Transistors
256K	0K	76°C	63.5W	478	180nm	42M
256K	0K	76°C	63.5W	478	180nm	42M
256K	0K	73°C	67.7W	478	180nm	42M
256K	0K	73°C	67.7W	478	180nm	42M
256K	0K	73°C	67.7W	478	180nm	42M
256K	0K	78°C	66.7W	423	180nm	42M
256K	0K	78°C	66.7W	423	180nm	42M
256K	0K	78°C	66.7W	423	180nm	42M
256K	0K	77°C	66.1W	478	180nm	42M
256K	0K	77°C	66.1W	478	180nm	42M
256K	0K	77°C	66.1W	478	180nm	42M
256K	0K	77°C	66.1W	478	180nm	42M
256K	0K	77°C	66.1W	478	180nm	42M
512K	0K	67°C	49.6W	478	130nm	55M
512K	0K	67°C	49.6W	478	130nm	55M
512K	0K	67°C	49.6W	478	130nm	55M
512K	0K	67°C	49.6W	478	130nm	55M
256K	0K	73°C	69.2W	423	180nm	42M
256K	0K	73°C	69.2W	423	180nm	42M
256K	0K	75°C	72.8W	478	180nm	42M
256K	0K	75°C	72.8W	478	180nm	42M
256K	0K	75°C	72.8W	478	180nm	42M
256K	0K	75°C	72.8W	478	180nm	42M
256K	0K	74°C	71.8W	423	180nm	42M
256K	0K	76°C	75.3W	478	180nm	42M
256K	0K	76°C	75.3W	478	180nm	42M
512K	0K	68°C	52.4W	478	130nm	55M
512K	0K	68°C	52.4W	478	130nm	55M
512K	0K	68°C	52.4W	478	130nm	55M
512K	0K	68°C	52.4W	478	130nm	55M
512K	0K	69°C	54.3W	478	130nm	55M
512K	0K	69°C	54.3W	478	130nm	55M
512K	0K	74°C	54.3W	478	130nm	55M
512K	0K	69°C	55.1W	478	130nm	55M
512K	0K	69°C	55.1W	478	130nm	55M
512K	0K	69°C	55.1W	478	130nm	55M
512K	0K	69°C	55.1W	478	130nm	55M
512K	0K	70°C	57.1W	478	130nm	55M

Table 3.45   Continued

CPU Speed (GHz)	Bus Speed (MHz)	Bus Speed (GBps)	HT Support	Boxed S-spec	OEM S-spec	Stepping	CPUID
2.20	400	3.2	No	SL6GR	SL6GR	C1	0F27h
2.20	400	3.2	No	SL6QN	SL6PL	D1	0F29h
2.26	533	4.3	No	SL683	SL67Y	B0	0F24h
2.26	533	4.3	No	SL67Y	SL67Y	B0	0F24h
2.26	533	4.3	No	SL6ET	SL6D6	B0	0F24h
2.26	533	4.3	No	SL6EE	SL6DU	C1	0F27h
2.26	533	4.3	No	SL6DU	SL6DU	C1	0F27h
2.26	533	4.3	No	SL6Q7	SL6PB	D1	0F29h
2.40	400	3.2	No	SL67R	SL65R	B0	0F24h
2.40	400	3.2	No	SL65R	SL65R	B0	0F24h
2.40	400	3.2	No	SL68T	SL66T	B0	0F24h
2.40	400	3.2	No	SL66T	SL66T	B0	0F24h
2.40	400	3.2	No	SL6E9	SL6GS	C1	0F27h
2.40	400	3.2	No	SL6GS	SL6GS	C1	0F27h
2.40A	533	4.3	No	SL7E8	SL7E8	C0	0F33h
2.40B	533	4.3	No	SL684	SL67Z	B0	0F24h
2.40B	533	4.3	No	SL67Z	SL67Z	B0	0F24h
2.40B	533	4.3	No	SL6EU	SL6D7	B0	0F24h
2.40B	533	4.3	No	SL6EF	SL6DV	C1	0F27h
2.40B	533	4.3	No	SL6DV	SL6DV	C1	0F27h
2.40B	533	4.3	No	SL6QP	SL6PM	D1	0F29h
2.40C	800	6.4	Yes	SL6WR	SL6WF	D1	0F29h
2.40C	800	6.4	Yes	SL6Z3	SL6Z3	M0	0F25h
2.50	400	3.2	No	SL6EB	SL6GT	C1	0F27h
2.50	400	3.2	No	SL6GT	SL6GT	C1	0F27h
2.50	400	3.2	No	SL6QQ	SL6QQ	D1	0F29h
2.53	533	4.3	No	SL685	SL682	B0	0F24h
2.53	533	4.3	No	SL682	SL682	B0	0F24h
2.53	533	4.3	No	SL6EV	SL6D8	B0	0F24h
2.53	533	4.3	No	SL6EG	SL6DW	C1	0F27h
2.53	533	4.3	No	SL6DW	SL6DW	C1	0F27h
2.53	533	4.3	No	SL6Q9	SL6PD	D1	0F29h
2.60	400	3.2	No	SL6HB	SL6GU	C1	0F27h
2.60	400	3.2	No	SL6GU	SL6GU	C1	0F27h
2.60	400	3.2	No	SL6QR	SL6QR	D1	0F29h
2.60B	533	4.3	No	SL6S3	SL6S3	C1	0F27h
2.60B	533	4.3	No	SL6QA	SL6PE	D1	0F29h
2.60C	800	6.4	Yes	SL6WS	SL6WH	D1	0F29h

L2 Cache	L3 Cache	Max. Temp	Max. Power	Socket	Process	Transistors
512K	0K	70°C	57.1W	478	130nm	55M
512K	0K	70°C	57.1W	478	130nm	55M
512K	0K	70°C	56.0W	478	130nm	55M
512K	0K	70°C	56.0W	478	130nm	55M
512K	0K	70°C	56.0W	478	130nm	55M
512K	0K	70°C	58.0W	478	130nm	55M
512K	0K	70°C	58.0W	478	130nm	55M
512K	0K	70°C	58.0W	478	130nm	55M
512K	0K	70°C	57.8W	478	130nm	55M
512K	0K	70°C	57.8W	478	130nm	55M
512K	0K	70°C	57.8W	478	130nm	55M
512K	0K	70°C	57.8W	478	130nm	55M
512K	0K	71°C	59.8W	478	130nm	55M
512K	0K	71°C	59.8W	478	130nm	55M
1M	0K	69°C	89.0W	478	90nm	125M
512K	0K	70°C	57.8W	478	130nm	55M
512K	0K	70°C	57.8W	478	130nm	55M
512K	0K	70°C	57.8W	478	130nm	55M
512K	0K	71°C	59.8W	478	130nm	55M
512K	0K	71°C	59.8W	478	130nm	55M
512K	0K	74°C	66.2W	478	130nm	55M
512K	0K	74°C	66.2W	478	130nm	55M
512K	0K	72°C	74.5W	478	130nm	55M
512K	0K	72°C	61.0W	478	130nm	55M
512K	0K	72°C	61.0W	478	130nm	55M
512K	0K	72°C	61.0W	478	130nm	55M
512K	0K	71°C	59.3W	478	130nm	55M
512K	0K	71°C	59.3W	478	130nm	55M
512K	0K	71°C	59.3W	478	130nm	55M
512K	0K	72°C	61.5W	478	130nm	55M
512K	0K	72°C	61.5W	478	130nm	55M
512K	0K	72°C	61.5W	478	130nm	55M
512K	0K	72°C	62.6W	478	130nm	55M
512K	0K	72°C	62.6W	478	130nm	55M
512K	0K	75°C	69.0W	478	130nm	55M
512K	0K	74°C	66.1W	478	130nm	55M
512K	0K	74°C	66.1W	478	130nm	55M
512K	0K	74°C	66.1W	478	130nm	55M

Table 3.45   Continued

CPU Speed (GHz)	Bus Speed (MHz)	Bus Speed (GBps)	HT Support	Boxed S-spec	OEM S-spec	Stepping	CPUID
2.60C	800	6.4	Yes	SL78X	N/A	D1	0F29h
2.80	533	4.3	No	SL6K6	SL6HL	C1	0F27h
2.80	533	4.3	No	SL6HL	SL6HL	C1	0F27h
2.80	533	4.3	No	SL6SL	SL6S4	C1	0F27h
2.80	533	4.3	No	SL6S4	SL6S4	C1	0F27h
2.80	533	4.3	No	SL6QB	SL6PF	D1	0F29h
2.80A	533	4.3	No	SL7D8	SL7D8	C0	0F33h
2.80C	800	6.4	Yes	SL6WT	SL6WJ	D1	0F29h
2.80C	800	6.4	Yes	SL78Y	N/A	D1	0F29h
2.80C	800	6.4	Yes	SL6Z5	N/A	M0	0F25h
2.80E	800	6.4	Yes	SL79K	SL79K	C0	0F33h
3.0	800	6.4	Yes	SL6WU	SL6WK	D1	0F29h
3.0	800	6.4	Yes	SL78Z	N/A	D1	0F29h
3.0	800	6.4	Yes	SL7BK	N/A	M0	0F25h
3.0E	800	6.4	Yes	SL79L	SL79L	C0	0F33h
3.06	533	4.3	Yes	SL6K7	SL6JJ	C1	0F27h
3.06	533	4.3	Yes	SL6JJ	SL6JJ	C1	0F27h
3.06	533	4.3	Yes	SL6SM	SL6S5	C1	0F27h
3.06	533	4.3	Yes	SL6S5	SL6S5	C1	0F27h
3.06	533	4.3	Yes	SL6QC	SL6PG	D1	0F29h
3.20	800	6.4	Yes	SL6WE	SL6WG	D1	0F29h
3.20	800	6.4	Yes	SL792	N/A	D1	0F29h
3.2EE	800	6.4	Yes	SL7AA	SL7AA	M0	0F25h
3.20E	800	6.4	Yes	SL7B8	SL7B8	C0	0F33h
3.40	800	6.4	Yes	SL793	SL793	D1	0F29h
3.4EE	800	6.4	Yes	SL7CH	SL7CH	M0	0F25h
3.40E	800	6.4	Yes	SL7AJ	SL7AJ	C0	0F33h

HT = Hyper-Threading technology   *90nm = Prescott core*
180nm = Willamette core   **Processor supports multiple core voltages, so these values vary.*
130nm = Northwood core

Cooling a high-wattage unit such as the Pentium 4 requires a large active heatsink. These heavy (sometimes more than 1 lb.) heatsinks can damage a CPU or destroy a motherboard when subjected to vibration or shock, especially during shipping. To prevent this, Intel's specifications for Socket 423 added four standoffs to the ATX chassis design flanking the Socket 423 to support the heatsink retention brackets. These standoffs enabled the chassis to support the weight of the heatsink instead of depending on the motherboard, as with older designs. Vendors also used other means to reinforce the CPU location without requiring a direct chassis attachment. For example, Asus's P4T motherboard was supplied with a metal reinforcing plate to enable off-the-shelf ATX cases to work with the motherboard.

Socket 478 systems do not require any special standoffs or reinforcement plates; instead they use a unique scheme in which the CPU heatsink attaches directly to the motherboard rather than to the

L2 Cache	L3 Cache	Max. Temp	Max. Power	Socket	Process	Transistors
512K	0K	74°C	66.1W	478	130nm	55M
512K	0K	75°C	68.4W	478	130nm	55M
512K	0K	75°C	68.4W	478	130nm	55M
512K	0K	75°C	68.4W	478	130nm	55M
512K	0K	75°C	68.4W	478	130nm	55M
512K	0K	75°C	69.7W	478	130nm	55M
1M	0K	69°C	89.0W	478	90nm	125M
512K	0K	75°C	69.7W	478	130nm	55M
512K	0K	75°C	69.7W	478	130nm	55M
512k	0K	73°C	76.0W	478	130nm	55M
1M	0K	69°C	89.0W	478	90nm	125M
512K	0K	70°C	81.9W	478	130nm	55M
512K	0K	70°C	81.9W	478	130nm	55M
512k	0K	66°C	82.0W	478	130nm	55M
1M	0K	69°C	89.0W	478	90nm	125M
512K	0K	69°C	81.8W	478	130nm	55M
512K	0K	69°C	81.8W	478	130nm	55M
512K	0K	69°C	81.8W	478	130nm	55M
512K	0K	69°C	81.8W	478	130nm	55M
512K	0K	69°C	81.8W	478	130nm	55M
512K	0K	70°C	82.0W	478	130nm	55M
512K	0K	70°C	82.0W	478	130nm	55M
512K	2M	64°C	92.1W	478	130nm	178M
1M	0K	73°C	103.0W	478	90nm	125M
512K	0K	70°C	89.0W	478	130nm	55M
512K	2M	68°C	102.9W	478	130nm	178M
1M	0K	73°C	103.0W	478	90nm	125M

CPU socket or chassis. Motherboards with Socket 478 can be installed into any ATX chassis—no special standoffs are required.

Pentium 4 processors use special heatsinks that, as noted previously, have different designs. If you purchase the shrink-wrapped or "boxed" processor, you get an Intel-specified high-quality heatsink in the box with the process. In addition, you get a 3-year warranty with Intel, making the boxed version ideal for upgraders and system builders.

Because of the included heatsink and warranty, I highly recommend purchasing only boxed processors instead of raw OEM processors for upgrades or building a new system.

Intel Processor Model Numbers

Most people associate clock speed with the processor, and Intel has always used the raw clock speed of its processors to market them. This has led many people to believe that faster-speed processors always result in faster or better systems, but that is not always the case. Processor architectures have a major effect on the performance of a processor, and it is entirely possible that a slower clock speed processor can handily outperform a faster one when running actual programs or doing real work. Unfortunately, this message is hard to convey when the main attribute used to market a chip is its raw clock speed.

AMD has long been marketing its chips with model numbers, which in this case do relate to speed—but not directly. Intel has now decided to go the model number route, but its model numbering scheme is distinctly different from AMD's. Whereas AMD uses model numbers that equate to "Pentium 4 equivalent" speed, Intel has decided to use a BMW-esque numbering scheme, with 7xx models as the top of the line, 5xx models as the mainstream, and 3xx models on the low end.

When creating the specific model number for a chip, Intel takes into account not only the raw clock speed of the chip, but also the internal architecture, cache sizes, bus speeds, and other features. In general, the higher the number, the more feature-rich the processor. In addition, within each series, the higher numbers are generally faster chips.

Examples of the model numbers currently assigned are shown in Table 3.46.

Table 3.46   Intel Processor Model Numbers and Meanings

Processor	Model No.	Clock Speed	Bus Speed	L2 Cache	Hyper-Threading
Pentium M	755	2.0GHz	400MHz	2MB	No
	745	1.8GHz	400MHz	2MB	No
	735	1.7GHz	400MHz	2MB	No
Pentium 4	720	3.73GHz	1066MHz	2MB	Yes
	580	4.0GHz	800MHz	1MB	Yes
	570	3.8GHz	800MHz	1MB	Yes
	560	3.6GHz	800MHz	1MB	Yes
	550	3.4GHz	800MHz	1MB	Yes
	540	3.2GHz	800MHz	1MB	Yes
	530	3.0GHz	800MHz	1MB	Yes
	520	2.8GHz	800MHz	1MB	Yes
Celeron D	350	3.2GHz	533MHz	256KB	No
	345	3.06GHz	533MHz	256KB	No
	340	2.93GHz	533MHz	256KB	No
	335	2.80GHz	533MHz	256KB	No
	330	2.66GHz	533MHz	256KB	No
	325	2.53GHz	533MHz	256KB	No

Note that not all 7xx chips are faster than 5xx chips, and not all 5xx chips are faster than 3xx chips. The model numbers are not strictly comparisons of speed and certainly don't pertain to speed comparisons outside the model line. For example, using the BMW automobile analogy from which these numbers seem to be derived, some 3-series cars are faster than some 5-series cars, and some 5-series cars are faster than some 7-series cars. However, as you go up in the series numbers, the higher-numbered series generally have more features or are premium models. Although not the most powerful chip it offers, Intel considers the Pentium M mobile processor a full-featured "executive-type" chip and the Celeron more of a "bargain-type" chip. Within the series, the model numbers do give somewhat of an indication of speed, in that a Pentium 4 580 is faster than a Pentium 4 570, and so on.

It will be interesting to see how these model numbers play out in the marketplace. I can say one thing, though—I wouldn't purchase either an Intel or an AMD chip without knowing what the *real* or true clock speeds are, as well as knowing the cache sizes and other features in the chip. The model numbers don't strictly tell that and are useful only for a rough comparison.

Beyond the Pentium 4

The Pentium 4 architecture is reaching the end of the line with the current Prescott die. Beyond that, simply using a smaller process and adding more features seems to have a diminishing return on the investment. Based on the current architecture, power consumption and heat generation are skyrocketing, and a new approach is necessary. Intel has learned a lot from the work it did on the Pentium M laptop processor, which was based mostly on the Pentium III design with some extremely creative power management tricks added. Many rumors are swirling around about the future, but Intel has made several things clear: Its future desktop processors will use many of the power conservation lessons learned from its mobile processors, such as the Pentium M, and future chips might use multiple cores. The latter is somewhat surprising—rather than creating new chip architectures, the best approach to increasing performance is simply to combine multiple processors into a single chip. Hyper-threading technology was actually the beginning of this, and one could have foretold the future by studying that alone. As more and more software is being designed to work using multiple threads of execution, having a hyper-threaded or multiple-core processor makes perfect sense. It might be a year or so before processors with multiple cores are introduced, but it seems as if that will be a natural extension of the existing hyper-threading technology.

Eighth-Generation (64-Bit Register) Processors

As of 2001, it had been about 15 years since PCs had begun to support 32-bit processors (all processors from the 80386 up through the Intel Pentium 4 and AMD Athlon XP). However, in 2001, Intel introduced the first 64-bit processor for servers—the Itanium—followed in 2002 by the improved Itanium 2. In 2003, AMD introduced the first 64-bit processor for desktop computers—the Athlon 64—followed by its first 64-bit server processor, the Opteron. The following sections discuss the major features of these processors and the different approaches taken by Intel and AMD to bring 64-bit computing to the PC server and desktop.

Intel Itanium and Itanium 2

Introduced on May 29, 2001, the Itanium was the first processor in Intel's IA-64 (Intel Architecture 64-bit) product family, and it incorporated innovative performance-enhancing architecture techniques, such as prediction and speculation. It and its newer sibling, the Itanium 2 (introduced in June 2002), are the highest-end processors from Intel and are designed mainly for the server market.

If Intel was still using numbers to designate its processors, the Itanium family might be called the 886 because the Itanium and Itanium 2 are the eighth-generation processors in the Intel family, and they represent the most significant processor architecture advancement since the 386.

Intel's IA-64 product family is designed to expand the capabilities of the Intel architecture to address the high-performance server and workstation market segments.

As with previous new processor introductions, the Itanium and Itanium 2 are not designed to replace the Pentium 4 or III. They feature an all-new design that is initially expensive and is found only in the highest-end systems such as file servers or workstations.

The Itanium's technical details are listed in Table 3.47.

Table 3.47   Intel Itanium and Itanium 2 Technical Details

Processor	Processor Speed	L2 Cache	L3 Cache Size	FSB Speed	Memory Bus Width	Bandwidth	Number of Transistors
Itanium	733MHz 800MHz	96KB	2MB[1] or 4MB[1]	266MHz	64-bit	2.1GBps	25 million (core) 150 or 300 million (cache)
Itanium 2	900MHz 1GHz	256KB	3MB[2]	400MHz	128-bit	6.4GBps	221 million
Itanium 2	1.4GHz 1.5GHz	256KB	6MB[2]	400MHz	128-bit	6.4GBps	410 million

1. On-cartridge, full-speed unified 128-bit wide
2. On-die, full-speed unified 128-bit wide

As noted in Table 3.47, the Itanium and Itanium 2 are the first Intel processors with three levels of integrated cache. Even though a few previous system designs featured L3 cache, the L3 cache was located on the motherboard and was therefore much slower. By building L3 cache in to the cartridge (Itanium) or on the processor die (Itanium 2), all three cache levels run at the full processor speed.

The following features apply to both Itanium and Itanium 2 processors:

- 16TB (terabytes) physical memory addressing (44-bit address bus).
- Full 32-bit instruction compatibility in hardware.
- EPIC (explicitly parallel instruction computing) technology, which enables up to 20 operations per cycle.
- Two integer and two memory units that can execute four instructions per clock.
- Two FMAC (floating-point multiply accumulate) units with 82-bit operands.
- Each FMAC unit is capable of executing two floating-point operations per clock.
- Two additional MMX units are capable of executing two single-precision FP operations each.
- A total of eight single-precision FP operations can be executed every cycle.
- 128 integer registers, 128 floating-point registers, 8 branch registers, 64 predicate registers.

The Itanium 2 also features

- 400MHz CPU Bus (versus 266MHz for Itanium)
- 128-bit-wide CPU Bus (versus 64-bit-wide for Itanium)

Intel and Hewlett-Packard began jointly working on the Itanium processor in 1994. In October 1997, more than three years after they first disclosed their plan to work together on a new microprocessor architecture, Intel and HP officially announced some of the new processor's technical details.

Itanium is the first microprocessor based on the Intel architecture-64 (IA-64) specification, which is also supported by Itanium 2. IA-64 is a completely different processor design that uses Very Long Instruction Words (VLIW), instruction prediction, branch elimination, speculative loading, and other advanced processes for enhancing parallelism from program code. The Itanium series features elements of both CISC and RISC design.

The Itanium series incorporates a new architecture Intel calls explicitly parallel instruction computing (EPIC), which enables the processor to execute *parallel instructions*—several instructions at the same time. In the Itanium and Itanium 2, three instructions can be encoded in one 128-bit word, so that each instruction has a few more bits than today's 32-bit instructions. The extra bits let the chip address more registers and tell the processor which instructions to execute in parallel. This approach simplifies the design of processors with many parallel-execution units and should let them run at higher clock rates. In other words, besides being capable of executing several instructions in parallel within the chip, the Itanium can be linked to other Itanium chips in a parallel processing environment. The Itanium 2 also supports parallel processing.

Besides having new features and running a completely new 64-bit instruction set, Itanium and Itanium 2 feature full backward compatibility with the current 32-bit Intel x86 software. In this way, they support 64-bit instructions while retaining full compatibility with today's 32-bit applications. Full backward compatibility means it will run all existing applications as well as any new 64-bit applications. Unfortunately, because this is not the native mode for the processor, performance is not as good when executing 32-bit instructions as it is in the Pentium 4 and earlier chips.

To use the IA-64 instructions, programs must be recompiled for the new instruction set. This is similar to what happened in 1985, when Intel introduced the 386, the first 32-bit PC processor. The 386 gave us a platform for an advanced 32-bit operating system that tapped this new power. To ensure immediate acceptance, the 386 and future 32-bit processors still ran 16-bit code. To take advantage of the 32-bit capability first found in the 386, new software would have to be written. Unfortunately, software evolves much more slowly than hardware. It took Microsoft a full 10 years after the 386 debuted to release Windows 95, the first mainstream 32-bit operating system for Intel processors.

That won't happen with the Itanium and Itanium 2, which already have support from four operating systems, including Microsoft Windows (XP 64-bit Edition and 64-bit Windows Advanced Server Limited Edition 2002), Linux (from four distributor companies: Red Hat, SuSE, Caldera, and Turbo Linux), and two Unix versions (Hewlett-Packard's HP-UX and IBM's AIX).

Despite the immediate OS support, it will likely take several years before the mainstream software market shifts to 64-bit operating systems and software. The installed base of 32-bit processors is simply too great. The backward compatible 32-bit mode of the Itanium family enables them to run 32-bit software because 32-bit instructions are handled directly in the hardware rather than through software emulation. Still, this does not perform as well as a native 32-bit chip.

Itanium and Itanium 2 were initially based on 0.18-micron technology; however, current versions of the Itanium 2 are based on 0.13-micron, allowing for higher speeds and larger caches.

Itaniums come in a new package called the pin array cartridge (PAC). This cartridge includes L3 cache and plugs into a PAC418 (418-pin for Itanium) or PAC611 (611-pin for Itanium 2) socket on the motherboard and not a slot. The package is about the size of a standard index card, weighs about 6oz. (170g), and has an alloy metal on its base to dissipate the heat (see Figure 3.60). Itanium has clips on its sides, enabling four of them to be hung from a motherboard, both below and above.

The first Itanium 2 was codenamed McKinley and officially introduced in June 2002. The current version uses the 0.13-micron Madison core, which has a whopping 410 million transistors and up to 6MB of on-die L3 cache. Because the Itanium 2 has a significantly higher CPU bus bandwidth (6.4GBps), higher clock speeds, larger caches, and a processor FSB twice as wide (128 bits) as the original Itanium, the Itanium 2 is significantly faster in overall processing. The Itanium 2 integrates all three levels of cache inside the processor die, so a cartridge is unnecessary (see Figure 3.61). The Itanium and Itanium 2 are not interchangeable and are supported by different sockets and chipsets.

Itanium Cartridge Features

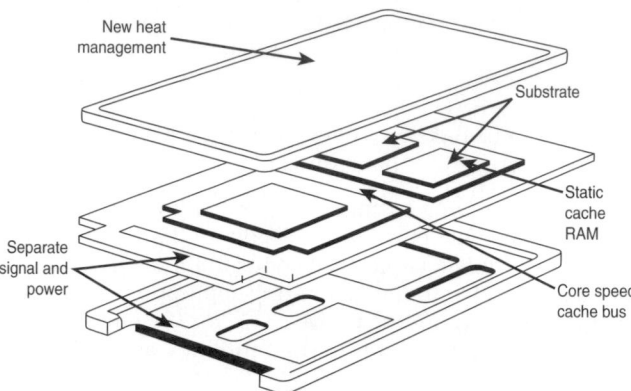

Figure 3.60   The Itanium's pin array cartridge.

Figure 3.61   The Itanium 2 is a more compact design than the original Itanium. *Photograph used by permission of Intel Corporation.*

AMD Athlon 64 and 64 FX

The AMD Athlon 64 and 64 FX, introduced in September 2003, are the first 64-bit processors for desktop (and not server) computers. Originally code named ClawHammer, the Athlon 64 and 64 FX are the desktop element of AMD's 64-bit processor family, which also includes the Opteron (code named SledgeHammer) server processor. The Athlon 64 and 64 FX (shown in Figure 3.62) are essentially Opteron chips but are designed for single-processor systems, and in some cases have decreased cache or memory bandwidth capabilities.

Besides support for 64-bit instructions, the biggest difference between the Athlon 64 and 64 FX and other processors is the fact that their memory controller is built in. The memory controller is normally part of the motherboard chipset North Bridge or memory controller hub, but with the Athlon 64 and 64 FX, the memory controller is now built in to the processor. This means that the typical CPU bus architecture is different with these chips. In a conventional design, the processor talks to the chipset North Bridge, which then talks to the memory and all other components in the system.

Because the Athlon 64 and 64 FX have integrated memory controllers, they talk to memory directly, and also talk to the North Bridge for other system communications. Separating the memory traffic from the CPU bus allows for greatly improved performance not only in memory transfers, but also in CPU bus transfers. The main difference in the Athlon 64 and 64 FX is in the different configurations of cache sizes and memory bus widths.

Figure 3.62 AMD Athlon 64 FX (Socket 940 version). *Photo courtesy of AMD.*

The major features of the Athlon 64 and 64 FX design include

- Speeds ranging from 1.8GHz to 2.4GHz and beyond
- 105.9 million transistors, 0.13-micron process, 193 sq. mm die
- 12-stage pipeline
- Single- or dual-channel 72-bit (64-bit plus ECC support) memory interface integrated into the processor (instead of the North Bridge or MCP, as in other recent chipsets)
- 128KB L1 cache
- 512KB or 1MB of on-die full-speed L2 cache
- Actual clock speeds of 1.6GHz–2.4GHz or faster
- Support for IA-32e (also called AMD64, x86-64, or EM64T) 64-bit extension technology (extends 32-bit x86 architecture)
- 3.2GBps or 4GBps Hypertransport link to chipset North Bridge
- Addressable memory size up to 1TB, greatly exceeding the 4GB or 64GB limit imposed by 32-bit processors
- SSE2 (SSE plus 144 new instructions for graphics and sound processing)
- Multiple low-power states

Although AMD has been criticized by many, including me, for its confusing performance-rating processor names in the Athlon XP series, AMD also uses this naming scheme with the Athlon 64. As I suggest with the Athlon XP, you should look at the actual performance of the processor with the applications you use most to determine whether the Athlon 64 is right for you and which model is best suited to your needs. The integrated memory bus in the Athlon 64 means that the Athlon 64 connects to memory more directly than any 32-bit chip and makes North Bridge design simpler. AMD offers its own chipsets for the Athlon 64, but most Athlon 64 motherboards and systems use third-party chipsets from the same vendors that now produce Athlon XP chipsets. See Chapter 4 for details.

The various models and features of the Athlon 64 and 64 FX are summed up in Tables 3.48 and 3.49.

Table 3.48 Athlon 64 Processor Information

Part Number	Model Number	CPU Speed	Bus Speed (GBps)	CPUID
ADA2800AEP4AX	2800+	1.8GHz	3.2	0FC0h
ADA3000AEP4AP	3000+	2.0GHz	3.2	0F48h
ADA3000AEP4AR	3000+	2.0GHz	3.2	0F4Ah
ADA3000AEP4AX	3000+	2.0GHz	3.2	0FC0h
ADA3200AEP5AP	3200+	2.0GHz	3.2	0F48h
ADA3200AEP5AR	3200+	2.0GHz	3.2	0F4Ah
ADA3200AEP4AX	3200+	2.2GHz	3.2	0FC0h
ADA3400AEP5AP	3400+	2.2GHz	3.2	0F48h
ADA3400AEP5AR	3400+	2.2GHz	3.2	0F4Ah
ADA3500DEP4AW	3500+	2.2GHz	4.0	0FF0h
ADA3700AEP5AR	3700+	2.4GHz	3.2	0F4Ah
ADA3800DEP4AW	3800+	2.4GHz	4.0	0FF0h

Table 3.49 Athlon 64 FX Processor Information

Part Number	Model Number	CPU Speed	Bus Speed (GBps)	CPUID
ADAFX51CEP5AK	FX-51	2.2GHz	3.2	0F58h
ADAFX51CEP5AT	FX-51	2.2GHz	3.2	0F5Ah
ADAFX53CEP5AT	FX-53	2.4GHz	3.2	0F5Ah
ADAFX53DEP5AS	FX-53	2.4GHz	4.0	0F7Ah

The Athlon 64 and 64 FX are available in three socket versions (see Table 3.50). The Athlon 64 is available in Socket 754 and Socket 939 versions, whereas the 64 FX is available in Socket 939 and Socket 940 versions. Socket 754 supports only a single-channel memory bus, whereas Sockets 939 and 940 both support dual-channel memory for double the memory bandwidth. Socket 939 also supports faster and cheaper unbuffered DDR SDRAM DIMMs; Socket 940 supports slower and more expensive registered DIMMs. Because of this, you should avoid any Socket 940 processors or motherboards because they require registered modules that are both slower and more expensive than unbuffered types. Socket 754 versions of the Athlon 64 are also designed to use more affordable unbuffered modules, but only in single-channel mode.

Table 3.50 AMD Athlon 64 and 64 FX Socket and Memory Types

Socket	Processor	Channels	Type
754	Athlon 64	Single-channel	Unbuffered
939	Athlon 64 Athlon 64 FX	Dual-channel	Unbuffered
940	Athlon 64 FX	Dual-channel	Registered

L2 Cache	Max. Temp	Voltage	Power	Socket	Process	Transistors
512K	70°C	1.5V	89W	754	130nm	105.9M
512K	70°C	1.5V	89W	754	130nm	105.9M
512K	70°C	1.5V	89W	754	130nm	105.9M
512K	70°C	1.5V	89W	754	130nm	105.9M
1M	70°C	1.5V	89W	754	130nm	105.9M
1M	70°C	1.5V	89W	754	130nm	105.9M
512K	70°C	1.5V	89W	754	130nm	105.9M
1M	70°C	1.5V	89W	754	130nm	105.9M
1M	70°C	1.5V	89W	754	130nm	105.9M
512K	70°C	1.5V	89W	939	130nm	105.9M
1M	70°C	1.5V	89W	754	130nm	105.9M
512K	70°C	1.5V	89W	939	130nm	105.9M

L2 Cache	Max. Temp	Voltage	Power	Socket	Process	Transistors
1M	70°C	1.5V	89W	940	130nm	105.9M
1M	70°C	1.5V	89W	940	130nm	105.9M
1M	70°C	1.5V	89W	940	130nm	105.9M
1M	70°C	1.5V	89W	939	130nm	105.9M

The Athlon 64 essentially comes in two versions: a Socket 754 version that has only a single-channel memory bus and an improved Socket 939 version that has a dual-channel memory bus. The Athlon 64 FX is also available in two versions: a Socket 940 version that uses expensive (and slower) registered memory and an improved Socket 939 version that uses unbuffered memory. The Socket 939 versions of the Athlon 64 and 64 FX are essentially the same chip, differing only in the amount of L2 cache included. For example, the Athlon 64 3800+ and Athlon 64 FX-53 both run at 2.4GHz and run dual-channel memory. The only difference is that the 3800+ has only 512KB of L2 cache whereas the FX-53 has 1MB of L2. Because the 64 and 64 FX chips are essentially the same, you need to read the fine print to determine the minor differences in configuration.

The Athlon 64 and 64 FX can draw up to 89W or more of power, which is high but still somewhat less than the more power-hungry Pentium 4 processors. As with the Pentium 4, motherboards for the Athlon 64 and 64 FX require the ATX12V connector to provide adequate 12V power to run the processor voltage regulator module.

The initial version of the Athlon 64 is built on a 0.13-micron (130-nanometer) process (see Figure 3.63). The second version—code named San Diego (desktop version) and Odessa (portable version)—is due in 2004 and will be AMD's first processor to use the .09-micron process.

Figure 3.63   AMD Athlon 64 die (130-nanometer process, 106 million transistors, 193 sq. mm). *Photo courtesy of AMD.*

AMD Opteron

The AMD Opteron is the workstation and server counterpart to the AMD Athlon 64, supporting the same x86-64 architecture as the Athlon 64. The Opteron was introduced in the spring of 2003.

The following are the major features of the Opteron:

- 128KB L1 cache
- 1MB L2 cache
- Initial clock speeds of 1.8GHz–2GHz
- Three 3.2MBps Hypertransport links to chipset
- Socket 940

- Integrated memory controller
- 128-bit plus ECC dual-channel memory bus
- Maximum addressable memory of 1 terabyte (40-bit physical) and 256 terabytes (48-bit virtual)
- x86-64 architecture

Unlike the Itanium series, which has been supported primarily by Intel chipsets, the Opteron has broad third-party chipset support from companies such as VIA, SiS, ALi, NVIDIA, and ATI (just like the Athlon 64 does).

Processor Upgrades

Since the 486, processor upgrades have been relatively easy for most systems. With the 486 and later processors, Intel designed in the capability to upgrade by designing standard sockets that would take a variety of processors. Thus, if you have a motherboard with Socket 3, you can put virtually any 486 processor in it; if you have a Socket 7 motherboard, it should be capable of accepting virtually any Pentium processor (or Socket 7–based third-party processor). This trend has continued to the present, with most motherboards being designed to handle a range of processors in the same family (Pentium III/Celeron III, Athlon/Duron/Athlon XP, Pentium 4/Celeron 4, and so forth).

To maximize your motherboard, you can almost always upgrade to the fastest processor your particular board will support. Because of the varieties of processor sockets and slots—not to mention voltages, speeds, and other potential areas of incompatibility—you should consult with your motherboard manufacturer to see whether a higher-speed processor will work in your board. Usually, that can be determined by the type of socket or slot on the motherboard, but other things such as the voltage regulator and BIOS can be deciding factors as well.

For example, if your motherboard uses Socket 370, you might be able to upgrade to the fastest 1.4GHz version of the Pentium III. Before purchasing a new CPU, you should verify that the motherboard has proper bus speed, voltage settings, and ROM BIOS support for the new chip.

Caution

If you are trying to upgrade the processor in a low-cost micro-ATX system from a company such as HP, you might have very few processor upgrade options. This is because many of the motherboards in low-cost computers don't provide much in the way of adjustments for clock speed or voltage.

If you are unable to install a faster processor directly into your system, a variety of third-party solutions are available, including adapters that can help first-generation Socket 423 Pentium 4 motherboards use Socket 478 processors, faster Socket 370 processors for older Slot 1 motherboards, and so on. Rather than purchasing processors and adapters separately, I usually recommend you purchase them together in a module from companies such as Evergreen or PowerLeap (see the Vendor List on the disc).

Upgrading the processor can, in some cases, double the performance of a system. However, if you already have the fastest processor that will fit a particular socket, you need to consider other alternatives. In that case, you really should look into a complete motherboard change, which would let you upgrade to a Pentium 4, Athlon XP, or Athlon 64 processor at the same time. If your chassis design is not proprietary and your system uses an industry-standard ATX motherboard design, I normally recommend changing the motherboard and processor rather than trying to find an upgrade processor that will work with your existing board.

OverDrive Processors

Intel at one time offered special OverDrive processors for upgrading systems. Often these were repackaged versions of the standard processors, sometimes including necessary voltage regulators and fans. Unfortunately, they frequently were overpriced, even when compared against purchasing a complete new motherboard and processor. They have all been withdrawn, and Intel has not announced any new versions. I don't recommend the OverDrive processors unless the deal is too good to pass up.

Processor Benchmarks

People love to know how fast (or slow) their computers are. We have always been interested in speed; it is human nature. To help us with this quest, various benchmark test programs can be used to measure different aspects of processor and system performance. Although no single numerical measurement can completely describe the performance of a complex device such as a processor or a complete PC, benchmarks can be useful tools for comparing different components and systems.

However, the only truly accurate way to measure your system's performance is to test the system using the actual software applications you use. Although you think you might be testing one component of a system, often other parts of the system can have an effect. It is inaccurate to compare systems with different processors, for example, if they also have different amounts or types of memory, different hard disks, video cards, and so on. All these things and more will skew the test results.

Benchmarks can typically be divided into two types: component or system tests. *Component* benchmarks measure the performance of specific parts of a computer system, such as a processor, hard disk, video card, or CD-ROM drive, whereas system benchmarks typically measure the performance of the entire computer system running a given application or test suite.

Benchmarks are, at most, only one kind of information you can use during the upgrading or purchasing process. You are best served by testing the system using your own set of software operating systems and applications and in the configuration you will be running.

Several companies specialize in benchmark tests and software. The following table lists the companies and the benchmarks they are known for. You can contact these companies via the information in the Vendor List on the disc.

Company	Benchmarks Published	Benchmark Type
Futuremark (formerly MadOnion.com)	SysMark PCMark Pro 3DMark	System System 3D graphics
Lionbridge (Veritest)	Winstone	System
(*PC Magazine* benchmarks)	WinBench CD WinBench NetBench WebBench	System CD/DVD drives Network Web server
Business Applications Performance Corporation (BAPCo)	MobileMark	Notebook battery life
Standard Performance Evaluation Corporation	SPECint SPECfp	Processor Integer Processor Floating-Point
SiSoftware	Sandra	System, memory, processor, multimedia

Processor Troubleshooting Techniques

Processors are normally very reliable. Most PC problems are with other devices, but if you suspect the processor, there are some steps you can take to troubleshoot it. The easiest thing to do is to replace the microprocessor with a known-good spare. If the problem goes away, the original processor is defective. If the problem persists, the problem is likely elsewhere.

Table 3.51 provides a general troubleshooting checklist for processor-related PC problems.

Table 3.51   Troubleshooting Processor-Related Problems

Problem Identification	Possible Cause	Resolution
System is dead, no cursor, no beeps, no fan.	Power cord failure.	Plug in or replace power cord. Power cords can fail even though they look fine.
	Power supply failure.	Replace the power supply. Use a known-good spare for testing.
	Motherboard failure.	Replace motherboard. Use a known-good spare for testing.
	Memory failure.	Remove all memory except 1 bank and retest. If the system still won't boot replace bank 1.
System is dead, no beeps, or locks up before POST begins.	All components either not installed or incorrectly installed.	Check all peripherals, especially memory and graphics adapter. Reseat all boards and socketed components.
System beeps on startup, fan is running, no cursor on screen.	Improperly seated or failing graphics adapter.	Reseat or replace graphics adapter. Use known-good spare for testing.
System powers up, fan is running, no beep or cursor.	Processor not properly installed.	Reseat or remove/reinstall processor and heatsink.

Table 3.51 Continued

Problem Identification	Possible Cause	Resolution
Locks up during or shortly after POST.	Poor heat dissipation.	Check CPU heatsink/fan; replace if necessary, use one with higher capacity.
	Improper voltage settings.	Set motherboard for proper core processor voltage.
	Wrong motherboard bus speed.	Set motherboard for proper speed.
	Wrong CPU clock multiplier.	Jumper motherboard for proper clock multiplier.
Improper CPU identification during POST.	Old BIOS.	Update BIOS from manufacturer.
	Board not configured properly.	Check manual and jumper board accordingly to proper bus and multiplier settings.
System won't start after new processor is installed.	Processor not properly installed.	Reseat or remove/reinstall processor and heatsink.
	BIOS doesn't support new processor.	Update BIOS from system or motherboard manufacturer.
	Motherboard can't use new processor.	Verify motherboard support.
Operating system will not boot.	Poor heat dissipation.	Check CPU fan; replace if necessary; it might need a higher-capacity heatsink or heatsink/fan on the North Bridge chip.
	Improper voltage settings.	Jumper motherboard for proper core voltage.
	Wrong motherboard bus speed.	Jumper motherboard for proper speed.
	Wrong CPU clock multiplier.	Jumper motherboard for proper clock multiplier.
	Applications will not install or run.	Improper drivers or incompatible hardware; update drivers and check for compatibility issues.
System appears to work, but no video is displayed.	Monitor turned off or failed.	Check monitor and power to monitor. Replace with known-good spare for testing.

If during the POST the processor is not identified correctly, your motherboard settings might be incorrect or your BIOS might need to be updated. Check that the motherboard is jumpered or configured correctly for your processor, and make sure you have the latest BIOS for your motherboard.

If the system seems to run erratically after it warms up, try setting the processor to a lower speed setting. If the problem goes away, the processor might be defective or overclocked.

Many hardware problems are really software problems in disguise. Be sure you have the latest BIOS for your motherboard, as well as the latest drivers for all your peripherals. Also, it helps to use the latest version of your given operating system because there usually will be fewer problems.

CHAPTER 4

Motherboards and Buses

Motherboard Form Factors

Without a doubt, the most important component in a PC system is the main board or motherboard. Some companies refer to the motherboard as a system board or planar. The terms *motherboard*, *main board*, *system board*, and *planar* are interchangeable, although I prefer the *motherboard* designation. This chapter examines the various types of motherboards available and those components typically contained on the motherboard and motherboard interface connectors.

Several common form factors are used for PC motherboards. The *form factor* refers to the physical dimensions (size and shape) as well as certain connector, screw hole, and other positions that dictate into which type of case the board will fit. Some are true standards (meaning that all boards with that form factor are interchangeable), whereas others are not standardized enough to allow for inter-changeability. Unfortunately, these nonstandard form factors preclude any easy upgrade or inexpensive replacement, which generally means they should be avoided. The more commonly known PC motherboard form factors include the following:

Obsolete Form Factors

- Baby-AT
- Full-size AT
- LPX (semiproprietary)
- WTX (no longer in production)
- ITX (FlexATX variation, never produced)

Modern Form Factors

- BTX
- microBTX
- picoBTX
- ATX
- microATX
- flexATX
- Mini-ITX (FlexATX variation)
- NLX

All Others

- Fully proprietary designs (certain Compaq, Packard Bell, Hewlett-Packard, notebook/portable systems, and so on)

Motherboards have evolved over the years from the original Baby-AT form factor boards used in the original IBM PC and XT to the current BTX and ATX boards used in most full-size desktop and tower systems. ATX has a number of variants, including microATX (which is a smaller version of the ATX form factor used in the smaller systems) and FlexATX (an even smaller version for the lowest-cost home PCs). The newest form factor, BTX, relocates major components to improve system cooling and incorporates a thermal module. BTX also has smaller microBTX and picoBTX variations. Another small form factor called Mini-ITX is also available; it's really just a minimum-size version of FlexATX designed for very small systems. NLX is designed for corporate desktop–type systems; WTX was designed for workstations and medium-duty servers, but never became popular. Table 4.1 shows the modern industry-standard form factors and their recommended uses.

Table 4.1 Common Industry-Standard Motherboard Form Factors

Form Factor	Use	Max. Slots
BTX	New-generation tower and desktop systems; likely to be the most common form factor from 2005 and beyond; supports high-end systems	7
microBTX	Smaller version of BTX; used in new-generation mid-range systems; fits the microBTX or BTX chassis	4
picoBTX	Smallest version of BTX; used in low-end small form factor, entertainment, or appliance systems; fits the picoBTX, microBTX, or BTX chassis	1
ATX	Standard tower and desktop systems; most common form factor from mid-1996 through 2004; supports high-end systems	7

Table 4.1   Continued

Form Factor	Use	Max. Slots
Mini-ATX	A slightly smaller version of ATX that fits the ATX chassis; many ATX motherboards are sold as Mini-ATX motherboards	6
microATX	Smaller version of ATX; used in mid-range systems; fits the microATX or ATX chassis	4
FlexATX	Smallest version of ATX; used in low-end small form factor, entertainment, or appliance systems; fits the FlexATX, microATX, or ATX chassis	3
Mini-ITX	Minimum-size FlexATX version; used in set-top boxes and compact/small form factor systems; highly integrated with one PCI expansion slot; fits in the Mini-ITX, FlexATX, microATX, or ATX chassis	1
NLX	Corporate slim desktop or mini-tower systems; fast and easy serviceability; slots on riser card	Varies

Although the Baby-AT, Full-size AT, and LPX boards were once popular, they have been replaced by more modern and interchangeable form factors. The modern form factors are true standards that provide improved interchangeability within each type. This means one brand of ATX boards can interchange with other brand ATX boards, BTX with other BTX, and so on. The additional features found on these boards as compared to the obsolete form factors, combined with true interchangeability, has made the migration to these newer form factors quick and easy. Today I recommend purchasing only systems with one of the modern industry-standard form factors. Each of these form factors, however, is discussed in more detail in the following sections.

Anything that does not fit into one of the industry-standard form factors should be considered proprietary. Unless there are special circumstances, I do not recommend purchasing systems with proprietary board designs. They will be virtually impossible to upgrade and very expensive to repair later because the motherboard, case, and often power supply will not be interchangeable with other models. I call proprietary form factor systems "disposable" PCs because that's what you must normally do with them when they are too slow or need repair out of warranty.

Caution

"Disposable" PCs might be more common than ever. Some estimate that as much as 60% of all PCs sold today are disposable models, not so much because of the motherboards used, but because of the tiny power supplies and cramped micro-tower cases that are favored on most retail-market PCs today. Although low-cost PCs using small chassis and power supplies are theoretically more upgradeable than past disposable type systems, you'll still hit the wall over time if you need more than three expansion slots or want to use more than two or three internal drives. Because mini-tower systems are so cramped and limited, I consider them to be almost as disposable as the LPX systems they have largely replaced.

You also need to watch out for systems that only appear to meet industry standards, such as certain Dell computer models built from 1996 to the present—especially the XPS line of systems. These computers often use rewired versions of the ATX power supply (or even some that are completely nonstandard in size and shape) and modified motherboard power connectors, which makes both components completely incompatible with standard motherboards and power supplies. In some of the systems, the power supply has a completely proprietary shape as well and the motherboards are not fully standard ATX either. If you want to upgrade the power supply, you must use a special Dell-compatible power supply. And if you want to upgrade the motherboard (assuming you can find one that fits), you must buy a standard power supply to match. The best alternative is to replace the motherboard, power supply, and possibly the case with industry-standard components simultaneously. For more details about how to determine whether your Dell computer uses nonstandard power connectors, see Chapter 21, "Power Supply and Chassis/Case."

If you want to have a truly upgradeable system, insist on systems that use ATX or BTX motherboards in a mid-tower or larger case with at least five drive bays.

PC and XT

The first popular PC motherboard was, of course, the original IBM PC released in August 1981. Figure 4.1 shows how this board looked. IBM followed the PC with the XT motherboard in March 1983, which had the same size and shape as the PC board but had eight slots instead of five. Both the IBM PC and XT motherboards were 9"×13" in size. Also, the slots were spaced 0.8" apart in the XT instead of 1" apart as in the PC (see Figure 4.2). The XT also eliminated the little-used cassette port in the back, which was supposed to be used to save BASIC programs on cassette tape instead of the much more expensive (at the time) floppy drive.

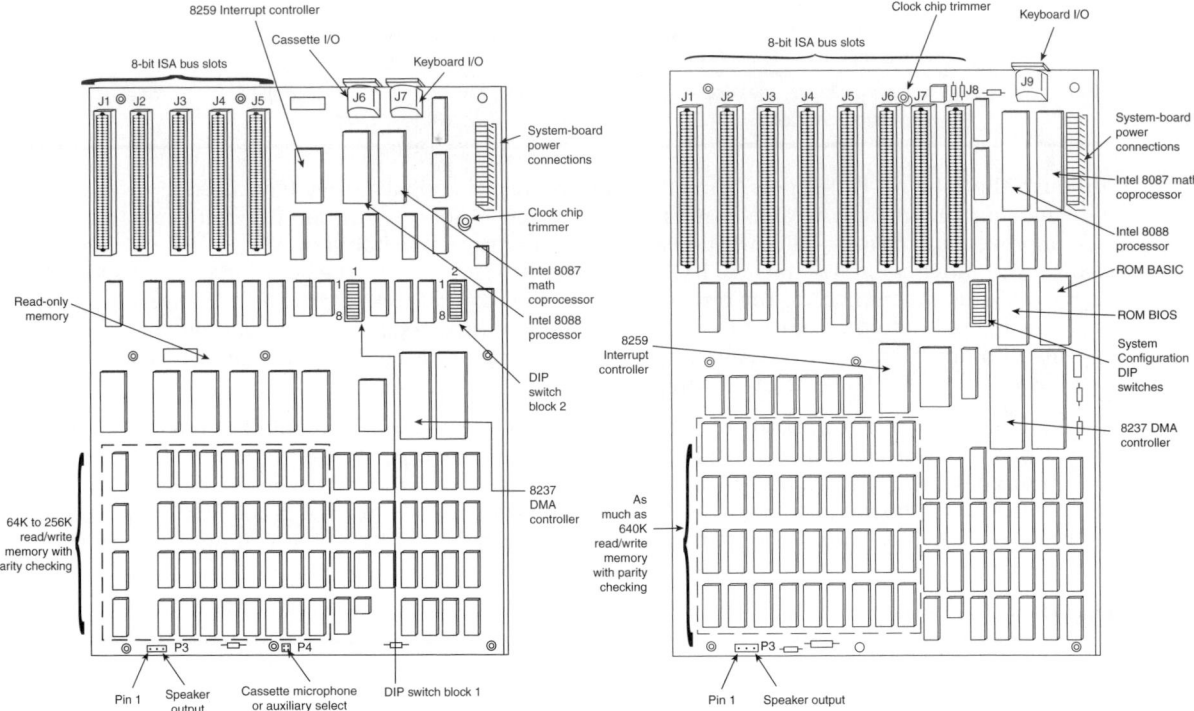

Figure 4.1   IBM PC motherboard (circa 1981).   **Figure 4.2**   IBM PC-XT motherboard (circa 1983).

Note

The Technical Reference section of the disc accompanying this book contains detailed information on the PC (5150) and XT (5160). All the information there is printable.

The minor differences in the slot positions and the deleted cassette connector on the back required a minor redesign of the case. In essence, the XT was a mildly enhanced PC, with a motherboard that was the same overall size and shape, used the same processor, and came in a case that was identical except for slot bracketry and the lack of a hole for the cassette port. Eventually, the XT motherboard design became very popular, and many other PC motherboard manufacturers of the day copied IBM's XT design and produced similar boards.

Full-Size AT

The full-size AT motherboard form factor matches the original IBM AT motherboard design. This allows for a very large board of up to 12" wide by 13.8" deep. The full-size AT board first debuted in August 1984, when IBM introduced the Personal Computer AT (advanced technology). To accommodate the 16-bit 286 processor and all the necessary support components at the time, IBM needed more room than the original PC/XT-sized boards could provide. So for the AT, IBM increased the size of the motherboard but retained the same screw hole and connector positions of the XT design. To accomplish this, IBM essentially started with a PC/XT-sized board and extended it in two directions (see Figure 4.3).

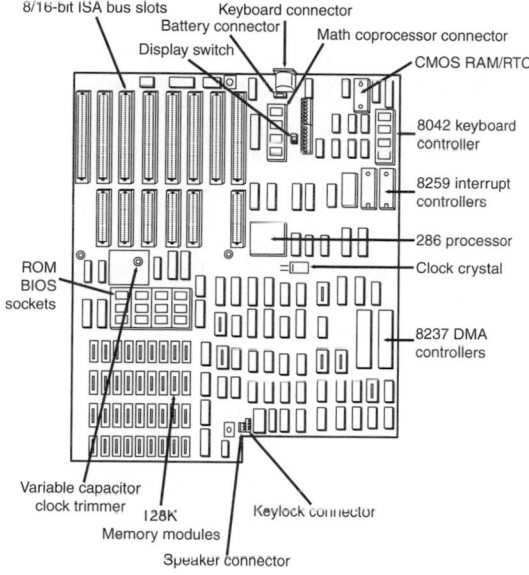

Figure 4.3 IBM AT motherboard (circa 1984).

Note

The Technical Reference section of the disc enclosed with this book contains detailed coverage of the AT and the XT Model 286.

A little more than a year after being introduced, the appearance of chipsets and other circuit consolidation allowed the same motherboard functionality to be built using fewer chips, so the board was redesigned to make it slightly smaller. Then, it was redesigned again as IBM shrank the board down to XT-size in a system it called the XT-286 (introduced in September 1986). The XT-286 board was virtually identical in size and shape to the original XT, a form factor which would later be known as Baby-AT.

The keyboard connector and slot connectors in the full-size AT boards still conformed to the same specific placement requirements to fit the holes in the XT cases already in use, but a larger case was still required to fit the larger board. Because of the larger size of the board, a full-size AT motherboard only fits into full-size AT desktop or tower cases. Because these motherboards do not fit into the smaller Baby-AT or mini-tower cases, and because of advances in component miniaturization, they are no longer being produced by most motherboard manufacturers—except in some cases for dual processor server applications.

The important thing to note about the full-size AT systems is that you can always replace a full-size AT motherboard with a Baby-AT (or XT-size) board, but the opposite is not true unless the case is large enough to accommodate the full-size AT design.

Baby-AT

After IBM released the AT in August 1984, component consolidation allowed subsequent systems to be designed using far fewer chips and requiring much less in the way of motherboard real estate. Therefore, all the additional circuits on the 16-bit AT motherboard could fit into boards using the smaller XT form factor.

IBM was one of the first to use the smaller boards when it introduced a system called the XT-286 in September 1986. Unfortunately the "XT" designation in the name of that system caused a lot of confusion, and many people did not want to buy a system they thought used older and slower technology. Sales of the XT-286 were dismal. By this time, other companies had also developed XT-size AT class systems. However, they decided that rather than calling these boards XT-size, which seemed to make people think they were 8-bit designs, they would refer to them as "Baby-AT" designs. The intention was to make people understand that these new boards had AT technology in a smaller form factor and were not souped-up versions of older technology as was seemingly implied by IBM's XT-286 moniker.

Thus, the Baby-AT form factor is essentially the same form factor as the original IBM XT motherboard. The only difference is a slight modification in one of the screw hole positions to fit into an AT-style case. These motherboards also have specific placement of the keyboard and slot connectors to match the holes in the case. Note that virtually all full-size AT and Baby-AT motherboards use the standard 5-pin DIN type connector for the keyboard. Baby-AT motherboards can be used to replace full-size AT motherboards and will fit into several case designs. Because of its flexibility, from 1983 into early 1996, the Baby-AT form factor was the most popular motherboard type. Starting in mid-1996, Baby-AT was replaced by the superior ATX motherboard design, which is not directly interchangeable. Most systems sold since 1996 have used the improved ATX, microATX, or NLX design, and Baby-AT is getting harder and harder to come by (surplus computer hardware outlets are your best bet for Baby-AT). Figure 4.5 shows the onboard features and layout of a late-model Baby-AT motherboard. Older Baby-AT motherboards have the same general layout but lack advanced features, such as USB connectors, DIMM memory sockets, and the AGP slot.

Any case that accepts a full-size AT motherboard will also accept a Baby-AT design. PC motherboards using the Baby-AT design have been manufactured to use virtually any processor from the original 8088 to the Pentium III or Athlon, although the pickings are slim where the newer processors are concerned. As such, systems with Baby-AT motherboards were the original upgradeable systems. Because any Baby-AT motherboard can be replaced with any other Baby-AT motherboard, this is an interchangeable design. Even though the Baby-AT design (shown in Figure 4.4) is now obsolete, ATX carries on its philosophy of interchangeability. Figure 4.5 shows a more modern Baby-AT motherboard, which includes USB compatibility, SIMM and DIMM sockets, and even a supplemental ATX power supply connection.

The easiest way to identify a Baby-AT form factor system without opening it is to look at the rear of the case. In a Baby-AT motherboard, the cards plug directly into the board at a 90° angle; in other words, the slots in the case for the cards are perpendicular to the motherboard. Also, the Baby-AT motherboard has only one visible connector directly attached to the board, which is the keyboard connector. Typically, this connector is the full-size 5-pin DIN type connector, although some Baby-AT systems use the smaller 6-pin mini-DIN connector (sometimes called a PS/2 type connector) and might even have a mouse connector. All other connectors are mounted on the case or on card edge brackets and are attached to the motherboard via cables. The keyboard connector is visible through an appropriately placed hole in the case.

▶▶   See "Keyboard/Mouse Interface Connectors," p. 1031.

Baby-AT boards all conform to specific widths and screw hole, slot, and keyboard connector locations, but one thing that can vary is the length of the board. Versions have been built that are smaller than the full 9"×13" size; these are often called mini-AT, micro-AT, or even things such as 2/3-Baby or 1/2-Baby. Even though they might not be the full size, they still bolt directly into the same case as a standard Baby-AT board and can be used as a direct replacement for one.

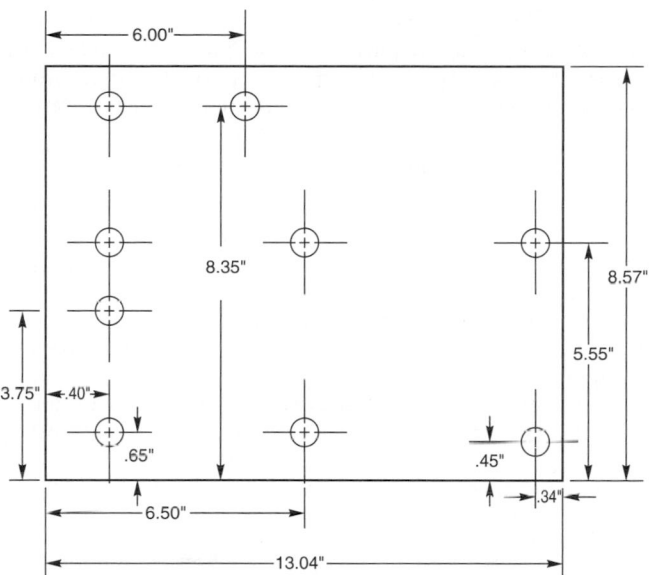

Figure 4.4   Baby-AT motherboard form factor dimensions.

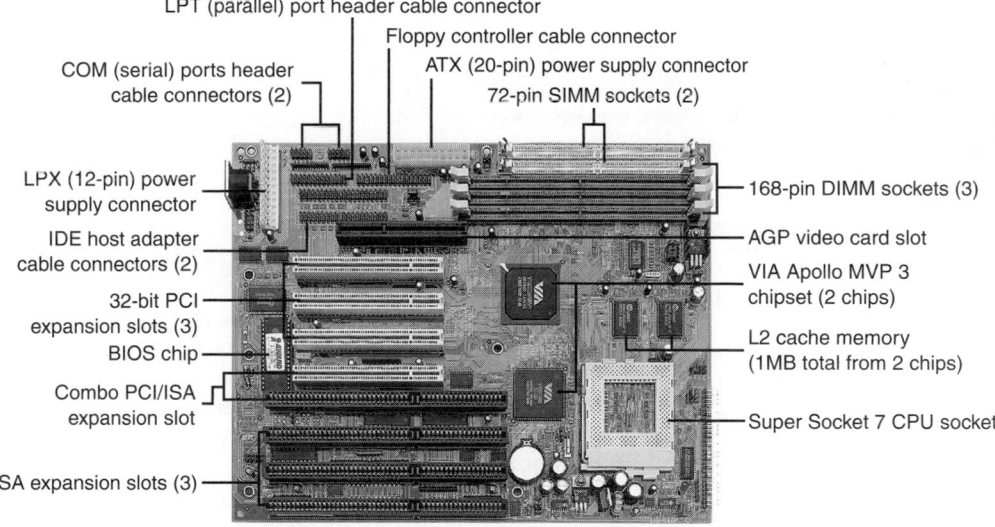

Figure 4.5   A late-model Baby-AT motherboard, the Tyan Trinity 100AT (S1590). *Photo courtesy of Tyan Computer Corporation.*

LPX

The LPX and mini-LPX form factor boards were a semiproprietary design that Western Digital originally developed in 1987 for some of its motherboards. The *LP* in LPX stands for Low Profile, which is so named because these boards incorporate slots that are parallel to the main board, enabling the expansion cards to install sideways. This allows for a slim or low-profile case design and overall a smaller system than the Baby-AT.

Although Western Digital no longer produces PC motherboards, the form factor lives on, and many other motherboard manufacturers have duplicated the design. Unfortunately, because the specifications were never laid out in exact detail—especially with regard to the bus riser card portion of the design— these boards are termed semiproprietary and are not interchangeable between manufacturers. Some vendors, such as IBM and HP, for example, have built LPX systems that use a T-shaped riser card that allows expansion cards to be mounted at the normal 90° angle to the motherboard but still above the motherboard. This lack of standardization means that if you have a system with an LPX board, in most cases you can't replace the motherboard with a different LPX board later. You essentially have a system you can't upgrade or repair by replacing the motherboard with something better. In other words, you have what I call a disposable PC, something I would not normally recommend that anybody purchase.

Most people were not aware of the semiproprietary nature of the design of these boards, and they were extremely popular in what I call "retail store" PCs from the late 1980s through the late 1990s. This would include primarily Compaq and Packard Bell systems, as well as many others who used this form factor in their lower-cost systems. These boards were most often used in low-profile or Slimline case systems but were found in tower cases, too. These were often lower-cost systems such as those sold at retail electronics superstores. Although scarce even in retail chains today, because of their proprietary nature, I recommend staying away from any system that uses an LPX motherboard.

Purchasing LPX Motherboards

Normally, I would never recommend upgrading an LPX system—they simply aren't worth the expense. However, a few vendors do sell LPX motherboards, so if it's absolutely necessary, an upgrade might be possible. The problem is the riser card, which is typically sold separately from the motherboard itself. It is up to you to figure out which riser card will work in your existing case, and often, if you choose the wrong riser card, you're stuck with it.

If you must locate LPX-compatible products, try these Web sites and vendors:

- Unicorn Computers (Taiwan): `www.unicorn-computer.com.tw`
- Hong Faith America (Taiwan): `america.hongfaith.com`
- FriendTech's LPX Zone: `www.friendtech.com/LPX_Zone/LPX_Zone.htm`

Note that the FriendTech Web site has links to other vendors and is developing a comprehensive knowledge base of LPX-related information and possible upgrades.

LPX boards are characterized by several distinctive features (see Figure 4.6). The most noticeable is that the expansion slots are mounted on a bus riser card that plugs into the motherboard. In most designs, expansion cards plug sideways into the riser card. This sideways placement allows for the low-profile case design. Slots are located on one or both sides of the riser card depending on the system and case design. Vendors who use LPX-type motherboards in tower cases sometimes use a T-shaped riser card instead, which puts the expansion slots at the normal right angle to the motherboard but on a raised shelf above the motherboard itself.

Another distinguishing feature of the LPX design is the standard placement of connectors on the back of the board. An LPX board has a row of connectors for video (VGA 15-pin), parallel (25-pin), two serial ports (9-pin each), and mini-DIN PS/2 style mouse and keyboard connectors. All these connectors are mounted across the rear of the motherboard and protrude through a slot in the case. Some LPX motherboards might have additional connectors for other internal ports, such as network or SCSI adapters. Because LPX systems use a high degree of motherboard port integration, many vendors of LPX motherboards, cases, and systems often refer to LPX products as having an "all-in-one" design.

The standard form factor used for LPX and mini-LPX motherboards in many typical low-cost systems is shown in Figure 4.7.

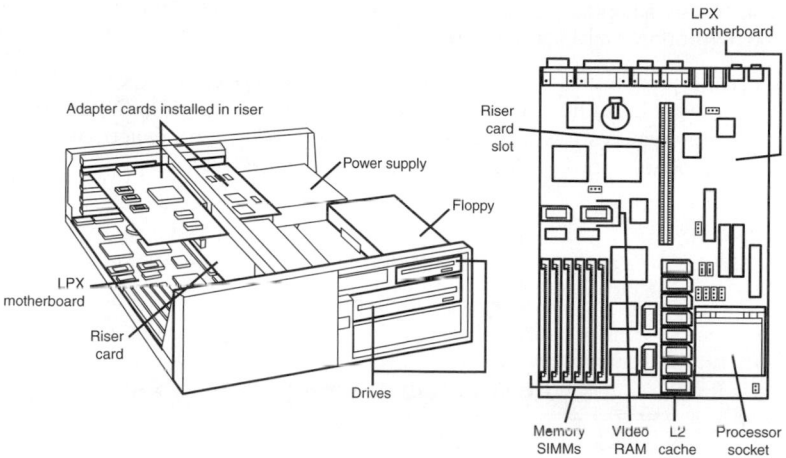

Figure 4.6 Typical LPX system chassis and motherboard.

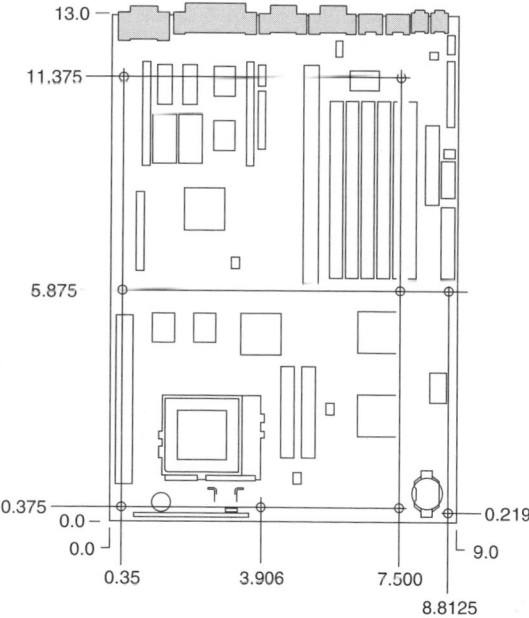

Figure 4.7 LPX motherboard dimensions.

I am often asked, "How can I tell whether a system has an LPX board without opening the cover?" Because of the many variations in riser card design, and because newer motherboards such as NLX also use riser cards, the most reliable way to distinguish an LPX motherboard from other systems is to look at the connector signature (the layout and pattern of connectors on the back of the board). As you can see in Figure 4.8, all LPX motherboards—regardless of variations in riser card shape, size, or location—place all external ports along the rear of the motherboard. By contrast, Baby-AT motherboards use case-mounted or expansion slot–mounted connectors for serial, parallel, PS/2 mouse, and USB ports, whereas ATX-family motherboards group all external ports together to the left side of the expansion slots.

On an LPX board, the riser is placed in the middle of the motherboard, whereas NLX boards have the riser to the side (the motherboard actually plugs into the riser in NLX).

Figure 4.8 shows two typical examples of the connectors on the back of LPX boards. Note that not all LPX boards have the built-in audio, so those connectors might be missing. Other ports (such as USB) might be missing from what is shown in these diagrams, depending on exactly which options are included on a specific board; however, the general layout will be the same.

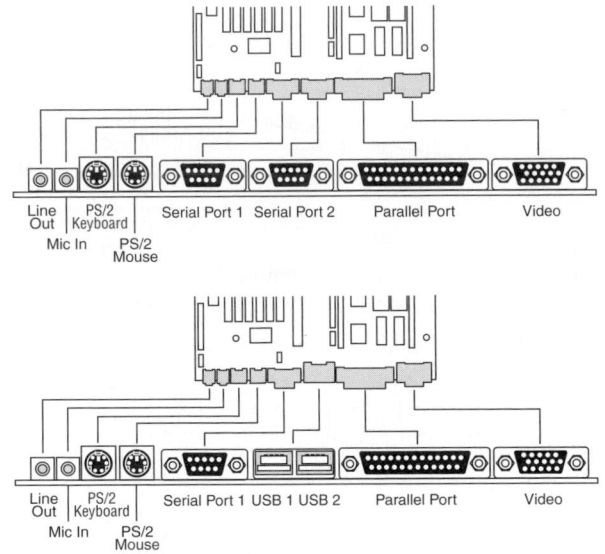

Figure 4.8 LPX motherboard back panel connectors.

The connectors along the rear of the board would interfere with locating bus slots directly on the motherboard, which accounts for why riser cards are used for adding expansion boards.

Although the built-in connectors on the LPX boards were a good idea, unfortunately the LPX design was semiproprietary (not a fully interchangeable standard) and thus, not a good choice. Newer motherboard form factors such as ATX, microATX, and NLX have both built-in connectors and use a standard board design. The riser card design of LPX allowed system designers to create a low-profile desktop system, a feature now carried by the much more standardized NLX form factor. In fact, NLX was developed as the modern replacement for LPX.

ATX

The ATX form factor was the first of a dramatic evolution in motherboard form factors. ATX is a combination of the best features of the Baby-AT and LPX motherboard designs, with many new enhancements and features thrown in. The ATX form factor is essentially a Baby-AT motherboard turned sideways in the chassis, along with a modified power supply location and connector. The most important thing to know initially about the ATX form factor is that it is physically incompatible with either the previous Baby-AT or LPX design. In other words, a different case and power supply are required to match the ATX motherboard. These case and power supply designs have become common and are found in most new systems.

Intel initially released the official ATX specification in July 1995. It was written as an open specification for the industry. ATX boards didn't hit the market in force until mid-1996, when they rapidly began replacing Baby-AT boards in new systems. The ATX specification was updated to version 2.01 in February 1997, 2.03 in May 2000, 2.1 in June 2002, and 2.2 in February 2004. Intel publishes these detailed specifications so other manufacturers can use the interchangeable ATX design in their systems. The current specifications for ATX and other current motherboard types are available online from the Desktop Form Factors site: `www.formfactors.org`. ATX is the most popular motherboard form factor for new systems through 2004. An ATX system will be upgradeable for many years to come, exactly like Baby-AT was in the past.

ATX improved on the Baby-AT and LPX motherboard designs in several major areas:

- *Built-in double high external I/O connector panel.* The rear portion of the motherboard includes a stacked I/O connector area that is 6 1/4" wide by 1 3/4" tall. This enables external connectors to be located directly on the board and negates the need for cables running from internal connectors to the back of the case as with Baby-AT designs.

- *Single main keyed internal power supply connector.* This is a boon for the average end user who always had to worry about interchanging the Baby-AT power supply connectors and subsequently blowing the motherboard. The ATX specification includes a keyed and shrouded main power connector that is easy to plug in and can't be installed incorrectly. This connector also features pins for supplying 3.3V to the motherboard, so ATX motherboards do not require built-in voltage regulators that are susceptible to failure. The ATX specification was extended to include two additional optional keyed power connectors called the Auxiliary Power connector (3.3V and 5V) and the ATX12V connector for systems that require more power than the original specification would allow.

▶▶ See "Motherboard Power Connectors," p. 1164.

- *Relocated CPU and memory.* The CPU and memory modules are relocated so they can't interfere with any bus expansion cards and can easily be accessed for upgrade without removing any of the installed bus adapters. The CPU and memory are relocated next to the power supply, which is where the primary system fan is located. The improved airflow concentrated over the processor, in the case of some older processors, eliminates the need for extra-cost CPU cooling fans (lower power configurations only). There is room for a CPU and a heatsink and fan combination of up to 2.8" in height, as well as more than adequate side clearance provided in that area.

Note

Most systems require cooling in addition to the fan in the power supply—from a secondary case-mounted fan or an active heatsink on the processor with an integral fan. Intel and AMD supply processors with attached high-quality (ball bearing) fans for CPUs sold to smaller vendors. These are so-called "boxed" processors because they are sold in single-unit box quantities instead of cases of 100 or more like the raw CPUs sold to the larger vendors. The included fan heatsink is an excellent form of thermal insurance because most smaller vendors and system self-assemblers lack the engineering knowledge necessary to perform thermal analysis, temperature measurements, and the testing required to select the properly sized passive heatsinks. The only thermal requirement spelled out for the boxed processors is that the temperature of the air entering the active heatsink (usually the same as the system interior ambient temperature) is kept to 45°C (113°F) or less in Pentium III or earlier models, or 40°C (104°F) or less in the Pentium 4 or later processors. By putting a high-quality fan on these "boxed" processors, Intel and AMD can put a warranty on the boxed processors that is independent of the system warranty. Larger vendors have the engineering talent to select the proper passive heatsink, thus reducing the cost of the system as well as increasing reliability. With an OEM non-boxed processor, the warranty is with the system vendor and not the processor manufacturer directly. Heatsink mounting instructions usually are included with a motherboard if non-boxed processors are used.

- *Relocated internal I/O connectors.* The internal I/O connectors for the floppy and hard disk drives are relocated to be near the drive bays and out from under the expansion board slot and drive bay areas. Therefore, internal cables to the drives can be much shorter, and accessing the connectors does not require card or drive removal.

- *Improved cooling.* The CPU and main memory are designed and positioned to improve overall system cooling. This can decrease—but not necessarily eliminate—the need for separate case or CPU cooling fans. Most higher-speed systems still need additional cooling fans for the CPU and chassis. Note that the ATX specification originally specified that the ATX power supply fan blows into the system chassis instead of outward. This reverse flow, or positive pressure design, pressurizes the case and minimizes dust and dirt intrusion. More recently, the ATX specification was revised to allow the more normal standard flow, which negatively pressurizes the case by having the fan blow outward. Because the specification technically allows either type of airflow, and because some overall cooling efficiency is lost with the reverse flow design, most power supply manufacturers provide ATX power supplies with fans that exhaust air from the system, otherwise called a negative pressure design. See Chapter 21 for more detailed information.

■ *Lower cost to manufacture.* The ATX specification eliminates the need for the rat's nest of cables to external port connectors found on Baby-AT motherboards, additional CPU or chassis cooling fans, or onboard 3.3V voltage regulators. Instead, ATX allows for shorter internal drive cables and no cables for standard external serial or parallel ports. These all conspire to greatly reduce the cost of the motherboard and the cost of a complete system—including the case and power supply.

Figure 4.9 shows the ATX system layout and chassis features, as you would see them looking in with the lid off on a desktop, or sideways in a tower with the side panel removed. Notice how virtually the entire motherboard is clear of the drive bays and how the devices such as CPU, memory, and internal drive connectors are easy to access and do not interfere with the bus slots. Also notice how the processor is positioned near the power supply.

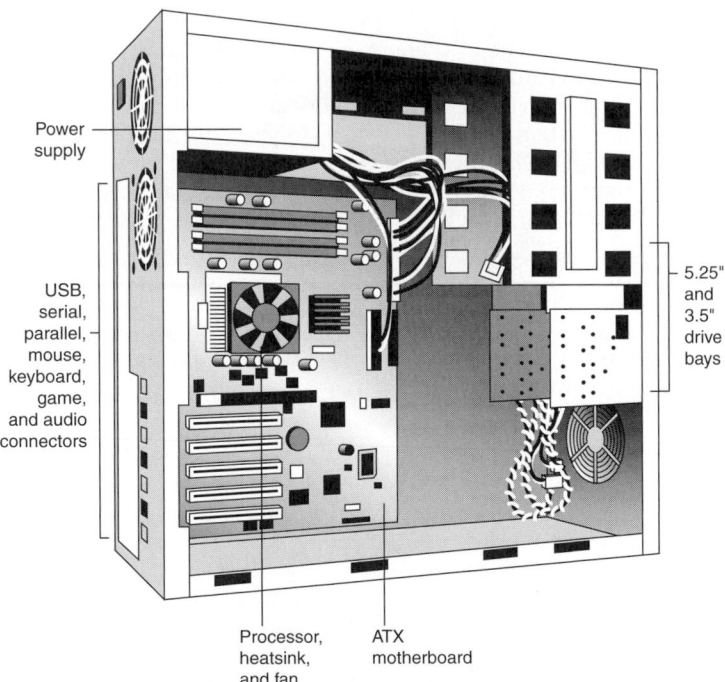

Figure 4.9 When mounted inside the case, the ATX motherboard is oriented so that the CPU socket is near the power supply fan and case fan (if your case includes one).

The ATX motherboard shape is basically a Baby-AT design rotated sideways 90°. The expansion slots are now parallel to the shorter side dimension and do not interfere with the CPU, memory, or I/O connector sockets (see Figure 4.10). There are actually two basic sizes of standard ATX boards. In addition to a full-size ATX layout, Intel also specified a MiniATX design, which is a fully compatible subset of ATX that fits into the same case:

- A full-size ATX board is 12" wide × 9.6" deep (305mm×244mm).
- The Mini-ATX board is 11.2"×8.2" (284mm×208mm).

Mini-ATX is not an official standard; instead it is simply referenced as a slightly smaller version of ATX. In fact, all references to Mini-ATX were removed from the ATX 2.1 and later specifications. Two smaller official versions of ATX exist, called microATX and FlexATX. They are discussed in the following sections.

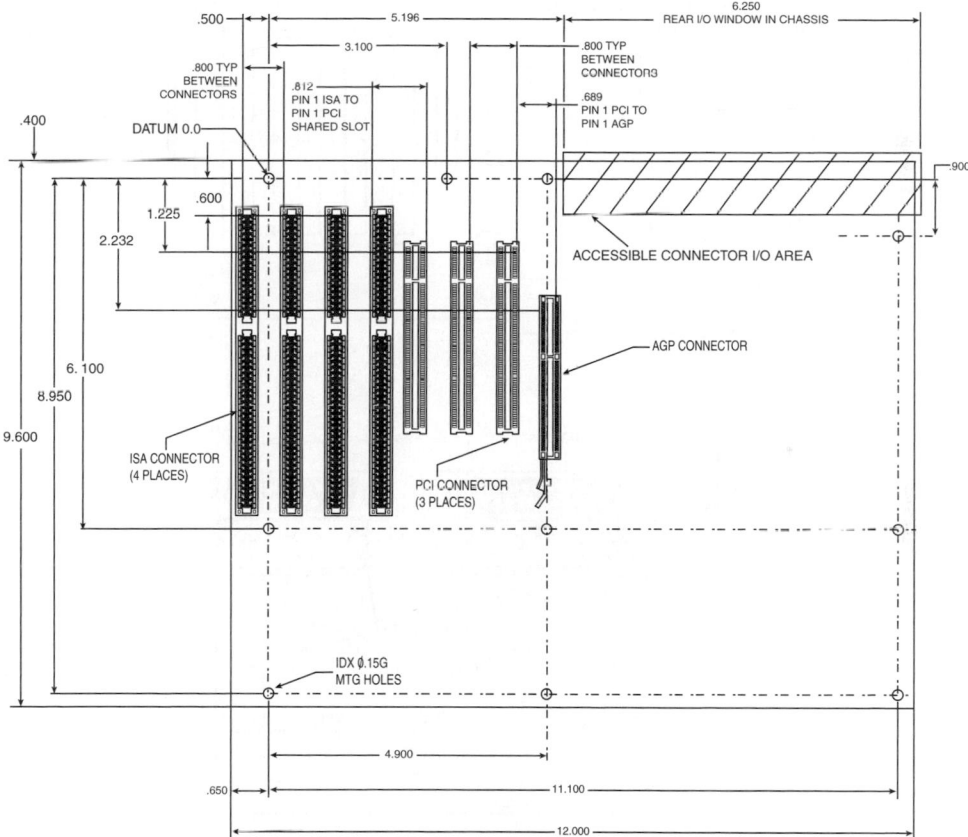

Figure 4.10   ATX specification 2.2 motherboard dimensions.

Although the case holes are similar to the Baby-AT case, cases for Baby-AT and ATX are generally incompatible. The ATX power supply design is identical in physical size to the standard Slimline power supply used with Baby-AT systems; however, they also use different connectors and supply different voltages.

The ATX form factor's design advantages have swept Baby-AT and LPX motherboards off the market. Although other form factors are now available, I have been recommending only ATX (or compatible variations such as microATX or FlexATX) systems for new system purchases since late 1996 and will probably continue to do so for the next several years.

The best way to tell whether your system has an ATX-family motherboard design without removing the lid is to look at the back of the system. Two distinguishing features identify ATX. One is that the expansion boards plug directly into the motherboard. There is usually no riser card as with LPX or NLX, so the slots are perpendicular to the plane of the motherboard. Also, ATX boards have a unique double-high connector area for all the built-in connectors on the motherboard (see Figure 4.11 and Table 4.2). This is found just to the side of the bus slot area and can be used to easily identify an ATX board.

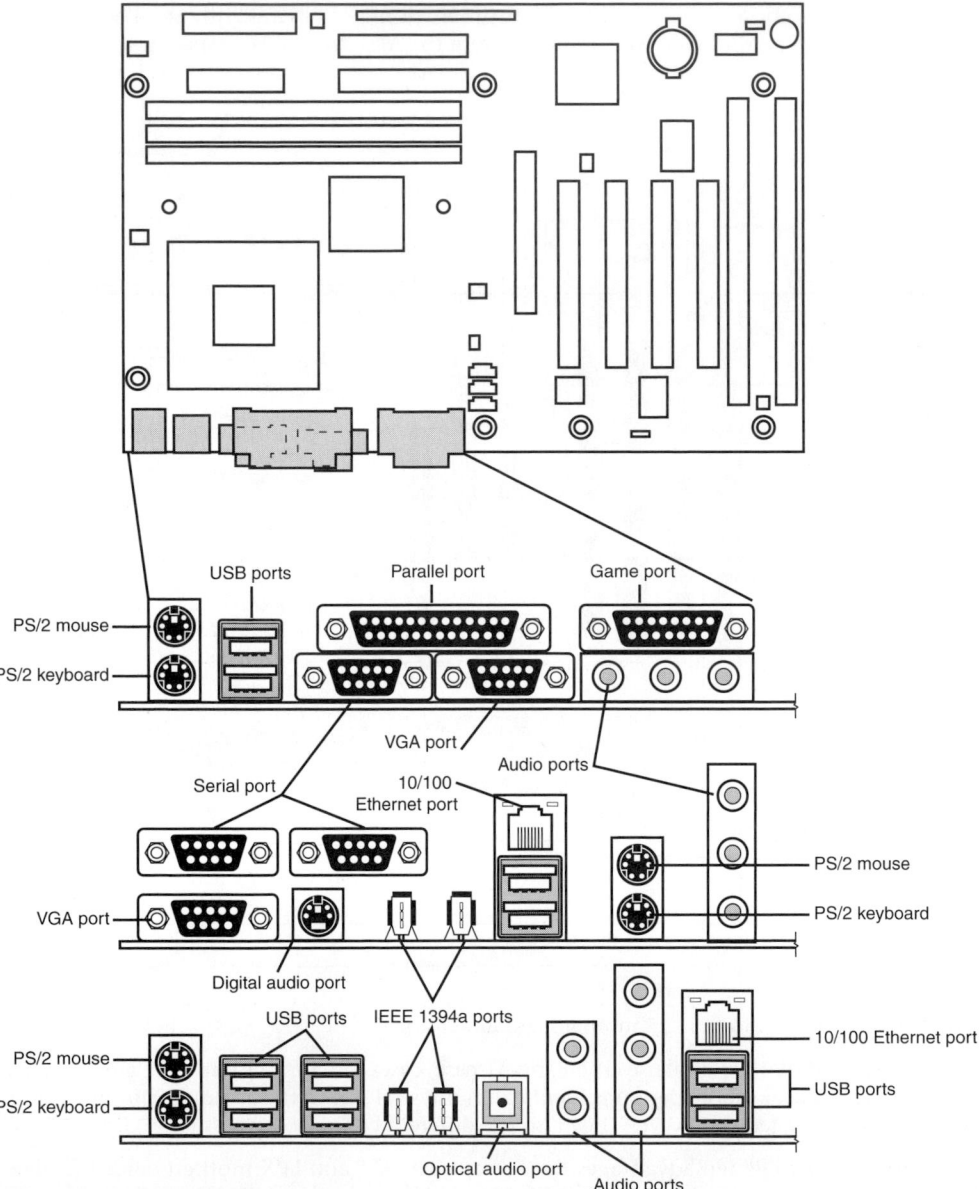

Figure 4.11   ATX motherboard and rear panel connections from systems with onboard sound and video (top and middle), networking and IEEE 1394/FireWire (middle and bottom), and a "legacy-free" system (bottom).

Table 4.2   Built-in Ports Usually Found on ATX Motherboards

Port Description	Connector Type	Connector Color
PS/2 mouse port	6-pin Mini-DIN	Green
PS/2 keyboard port	6-pin Mini-DIN	Purple
USB ports	Dual Stack USB	Black
Parallel port	25-pin D-Submini	Burgundy
Serial port	9-pin D-Submini	Teal
VGA analog video port	15-pin HD D-Submini	Dark blue
MIDI/Game port	15-pin D-Submini	Gold
Audio ports: L/R in, front L/R out, rear L/R out, center/LFE out, Microphone L/R in	1/8" (3.5mm) Mini-Phone	Light blue, lime green, black, black, pink
S-Video TV out	4-pin Mini-DIN	Black
IEEE 1394/FireWire port	6-pin IEEE 1394	Gray
10/100/1000 Ethernet LAN	8-pin RJ-45	Black
Optical S/PDIF audio out	TOSLINK	Black
DVI digital video out (not shown)	DDWG-DVI	White
Digital S/PDIF audio out (not shown)	RCA Jack	Orange
SCSI (not shown)	50/68-pin HD SCSI	Black
Modem (not shown)	4-pin RJ-11	Black
Composite Video out (not shown)	RCA Jack	Yellow

DIN = Deutsches Institut für Normung e.V.
USB = Universal serial bus
VGA = Video graphics array
HD = High density
MIDI = Musical Instrument Digital Interface
L/R = Left and right channel
LFE = Low frequency effects (subwoofer)
S-Video = Super Video
IEEE = Institute of Electrical and Electronics Engineers

LAN = Local area network
RJ = Registered jack
S/PDIF = Sony/Philips Digital Interface
TOSLINK = Toshiba optical link
DVI = Digital visual interface
DDWG = Digital Display Working Group
RCA = Radio Corporation of America
SCSI = Small computer system interface

Note

Most ATX motherboards feature connectors with industry-standardized color codes (shown in the previous table). This makes plugging in devices much easier and more foolproof: You merely match up the colors. For example, most keyboards have a cable with a purple plug, whereas most mice have a cable with a green plug. Even though the keyboard and mouse connectors on the motherboard appear the same (both are 6-pin Mini-DIN types), their color-coding matches the plugs on the respective devices. Thus, to plug them in properly, you merely insert the purple plug into the purple connector and the green plug into the green connector. This saves you from having to bend down to try to decipher small labels on the connectors to ensure you get them right.

The specification and related information about the ATX, Mini-ATX, microATX, FlexATX, or NLX form factor specifications are available from the Form Factors Web site at www.formfactors.org. The Form Factors site provides form factor specifications and design guides, as well as design considerations for new technologies, information on initiative supporters, vendor products, and a form factor discussion forum.

Note

Some motherboards, especially those used in server systems, come in nonstandard ATX variations collectively called *extended ATX*. This is a term applied to boards that are compatible with ATX but that are deeper. Standard ATX is 12"×9.6" (305mm×244mm), whereas extended ATX boards are up to 12"×13" (305mm×330mm). Because technically no official "extended ATX" standard exists, compatibility problems can exist with boards and chassis claiming to support extended ATX. When purchasing an extended ATX board, be sure it will fit in the chassis you intend to use. Dual Xeon processors fit in a standard ATX-size board, so choose a standard ATX-size board for maximum compatibility with the existing ATX chassis.

ATX Riser

In December 1999, Intel introduced a riser card design modification for ATX motherboards. The design includes the addition of a 22-pin (2×11) connector to one of the PCI slots on the motherboard, along with a two- or three-slot riser card that plugs in. The riser enables two or three PCI cards to be installed, but it does not support AGP.

ATX motherboards typically are found in vertically oriented tower-type cases, but often a horizontal desktop system is desired for a particular application. When ATX boards are installed in desktop cases, PCI cards can be as tall as 4.2", thus requiring a case that is at least 6"–7" tall. For Slimline desktop systems, most manufacturers now use the NLX format, but the more complex design and lower popularity of NLX makes that a more expensive alternative. A low-cost way to use an industry-standard ATX form factor board in a Slimline desktop case is therefore needed. The best long-term solution to this problem is the eventual adoption of a lower-profile PCI card design that is shorter than the current 4.2". The PCI Low-Profile specification was released for engineering review by the Peripheral Component Interconnect Special Interest Group (PCI SIG) on February 14, 2000, and some PCI card products have been produced in this shorter (2.5") form factor. Until Low-Profile PCI becomes widespread, Intel has suggested a riser card approach to enable standard-height PCI cards to be used in Slimline and rack-mount systems.

By adding a small 22-pin extension connector to one of the PCI slots on a motherboard, the necessary additional signals for riser card support could be implemented. The current design enables the use of a two- or three-slot riser that is either 2" or 2.8" tall, respectively. To this riser, you can attach full-length cards sideways in the system, and the motherboard can be used with or without the riser. The only caveat is that, if a riser card is installed, the remaining PCI slots on the motherboard can't be used. You can have expansion cards plugged in to only the riser or the motherboard, but not both. Also, the riser card supports only PCI cards—not AGP or ISA cards. A sample ATX board with a riser installed is shown in Figure 4.12.

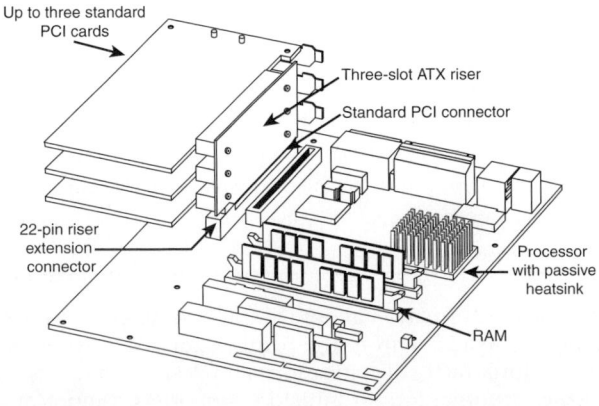

Figure 4.12   A three-slot ATX riser implementation on a microATX motherboard.

The 22-pin extension connector usually is installed in line with PCI slot 6, which is the second one from the right; the slots are usually numbered from right to left (facing the board) starting with 7 as the one closest to the processor. Some boards number the slots from right to left starting with 1; in that case, the extension connector is on PCI slot 2. The pinout of the ATX 22-pin riser extension connector is shown in Figure 4.13.

Signal	Pin	Pin	Signal
Ground	B1	A1	PCI_GNT1#
PCI_CLK1	B2	A2	Ground
Ground	B3	A3	PCI_GNT2#
PCI_REQ1#	A4	B4	Ground
Ground	A5	B5	PCI_CLK3
PCI_CLK2	A6	B6	RISER_ID1
Ground	A7	B7	Reserved
PCI_REQ2#	A8	B8	RISER_ID2
Ground	A9	B9	NOGO
PC/PCI_DREQ#	A10	B10	+12V
PC/PCI_DGNT#	A11	B11	SER_IRQ

Figure 4.13 An ATX 22-pin riser extension connector pinout.

The PCI connector that is in line with the riser extension connector is just a standard PCI slot; none of the signals are changed.

Systems that use the riser generally are low-profile designs. Therefore, they don't fit normal PCI or AGP cards in the remaining (nonriser-bound) slots. Although the ATX riser standard originally was developed for use with low-end boards—which have integrated video, sound, and network support—many rack-mounted servers are also using the ATX riser because these boards also have most of their required components already integrated. In fact, the ATX riser appears to be more popular for rack-mounted servers than for the originally intended target market of Slimline desktop systems.

ATX riser cards, compatible cases, and compatible motherboards are available from a variety of vendors, allowing you to build your own Slimline ATX system.

microATX

microATX is a motherboard form factor Intel originally introduced in December 1997, as an evolution of the ATX form factor for smaller and lower-cost systems. The reduced size as compared to standard ATX allows for a smaller chassis, motherboard, and power supply, thereby reducing the cost of the entire system. The microATX form factor is also backward-compatible with the ATX form factor and can be used in full-size ATX cases. Of course, a microATX case doesn't take a full-size ATX board. This form factor has become popular in the low-cost PC market. Currently, mini-tower chassis systems dominate the low-cost PC market, although their small sizes and cramped interiors severely limit future upgradeability.

The main differences between microATX and standard or Mini-ATX are as follows:

- Reduced width motherboard (9.6" [244mm] instead of 12" [305mm] or 11.2" [284mm])
- Fewer I/O bus expansion slots (four maximum, although most boards feature only three)
- Smaller power supply optional (SFX/TFX form factors)

The microATX motherboard maximum size is only 9.6"×9.6" (244mm×244mm) as compared to the full-size ATX size of 12"×9.6" (305mm×244mm) or the Mini-ATX size of 11.2"×8.2" (284mm×208mm). Even smaller boards can be designed as long as they conform to the location of the mounting holes, connector positions, and so on, as defined by the standard. Fewer slots aren't a problem for typical home or small-business PC users because more components such as sound and video are usually integrated on the motherboard and therefore don't require separate slots. This higher integration reduces motherboard and system costs. External buses, such as USB, 10/100 Ethernet, and optionally SCSI or 1394 (FireWire), can provide additional expansion out of the box. The specifications for microATX motherboard dimensions are shown in Figure 4.14.

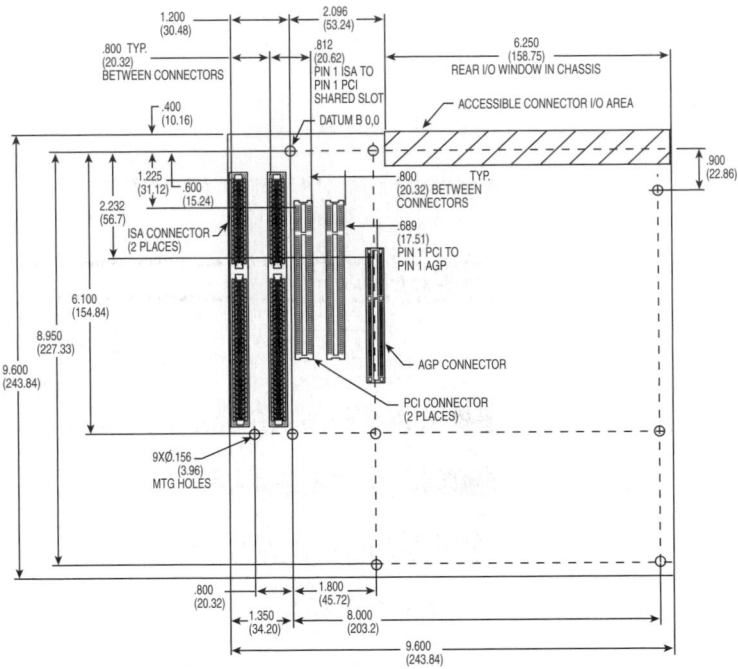

Figure 4.14 microATX specification 1.2 motherboard dimensions.

Smaller form factor (called SFX or TFX) power supplies have been defined for optional use with microATX systems, although the standard ATX supply also works fine because the connectors are the same. The smaller size SFX/TFX power supplies encourage flexibility in choosing mounting locations within the chassis and allows for smaller systems that consume less power overall. Although the smaller supplies can be used, they may lack sufficient power output for faster or more fully configured systems. Because of the high power demands of most modern systems, most third-party microATX chassis are designed to accept standard ATX power supplies, although microATX systems sold by vendors such as Compaq, HP, and eMachines typically use some type of SFX or TFX power supply to reduce costs.

▶▶ See "Power Supply Form Factors" p. 1155.

The microATX form factor is similar to ATX for compatibility. The similarities include the following:

- Standard ATX 20-pin power connector
- Standard ATX I/O panel
- Mounting holes and dimensions are a subset of ATX

These similarities ensure that a microATX motherboard can easily work in a standard ATX chassis with a standard ATX power supply, as well as the smaller microATX chassis and SFX/TFX power supply.

The overall system size for a microATX is very small. A typical case is only 12"–14" tall, about 7" wide, and 12" deep. This results in a kind of micro-tower or desktop size. A typical microATX motherboard is shown in Figure 4.15.

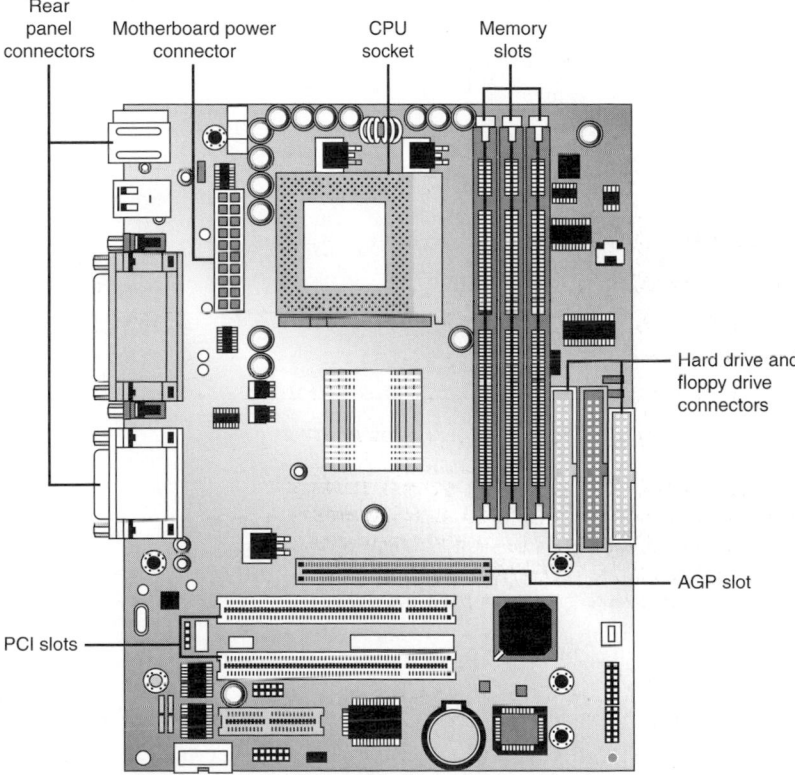

Figure 4.15 A typical microATX motherboard's dimensions are 9.6"×9.6".

As with ATX, Intel released microATX to the public domain to facilitate adoption as a de facto standard. The specification and related information on microATX are available through the Desktop Form Factors site (www.formfactors.org).

FlexATX

In March 1999, Intel released the FlexATX addendum to the microATX specification. This added a new and even smaller variation of the ATX form factor to the motherboard scene. FlexATX's smaller design is intended to allow a variety of new PC designs, especially extremely inexpensive, smaller, consumer-oriented, appliance-type systems. Some of these designs might not even have expansion slots, allowing expansion only through USB or IEEE 1394/FireWire ports.

FlexATX defines a board that is up to 9"×7.5" (229mm×191mm) in size, which is the smallest of the ATX family boards. In all other ways, FlexATX is the same as ATX and microATX, making FlexATX fully backward compatible with ATX or microATX by using a subset of the mounting holes and the same I/O and power supply connector specifications (see Figure 4.16).

Most FlexATX systems likely use SFX/TFX (small or thin form factor) type power supplies (introduced in the microATX specification), although if the chassis allows it, a standard ATX power supply can also be used.

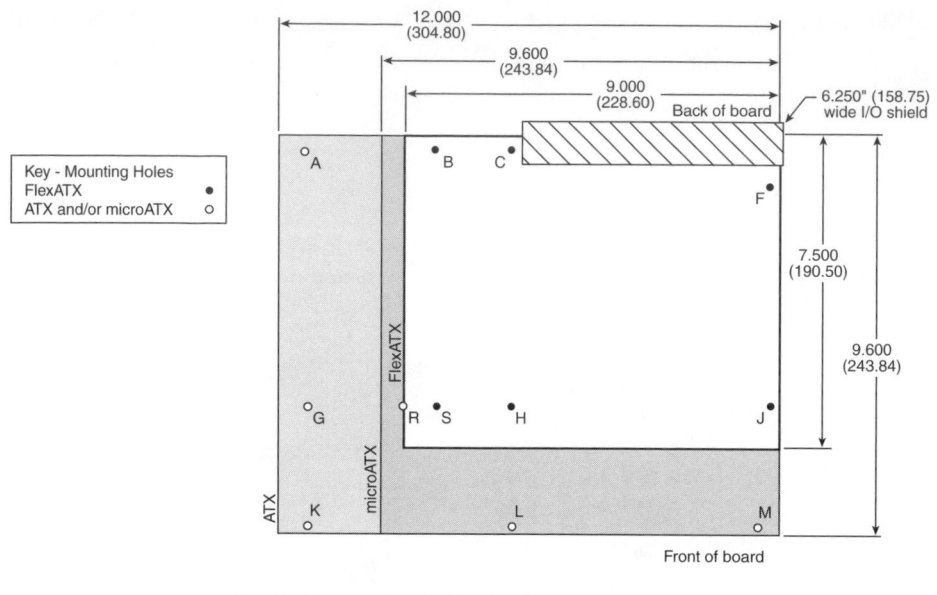

Form Factor	Mounting Hole Locations	Notes
• FlexATX	B, C, F, H, J, S	
• microATX	B, C, F, H, J, L, M, R, S	Holes R and S were added for microATX form factor. Hole B was defined in full-AT format.
• ATX	A, C, F, G, H, J, K, L, M	Hole F must be implemented in all ATX 2.03–compliant chassis assemblies. The hole was optional in the ATX 1.1 specification.

Figure 4.16 Size and mounting hole comparison between ATX, microATX, and FlexATX motherboards.

With the addition of FlexATX, the family of ATX boards has now grown to include four definitions of size (three are the official standards), as shown in Table 4.3.

Table 4.3   ATX Motherboard Form Factors

Form Factor	Max. Width	Max. Depth	Max. Area	Size Comparison
ATX	12.0" (305mm)	9.6" (244mm)	115 sq. in. (743 sq. cm)	—
Mini-ATX	11.2" (284mm)	8.2" (208mm)	92 sq. in. (593 sq. cm)	20% smaller
microATX	9.6" (244mm)	9.6" (244mm)	92 sq. in. (595 sq. cm)	20% smaller
Flex ATX	9.0" (229mm)	7.5" (191mm)	68 sq. in. (435 sq. cm)	41% smaller

Note that these dimensions are the maximums allowed. Making a board smaller in any given dimension is always possible as long as it conforms to the mounting hole and connector placement requirements detailed in the respective specifications. Each board has the same basic screw hole and connector placement requirements, so if you have a case that fits a full-size ATX board, you could also mount a microATX, or FlexATX board in that same case. Obviously, if you have a smaller case designed for microATX or FlexATX, you won't be able to put the larger Mini-ATX or full-size ATX boards in that case.

ITX and Mini-ITX

FlexATX is the smallest industry-standard form factor specification, and it defines a board that is *up to* 9"×7.5" in size. Note the *up to* part of the dimensions, which means that, even though those dimensions are the maximums, less is also allowed. Therefore, a FlexATX board can be smaller than that, but how much smaller? By analyzing the FlexATX specification—and, in particular, studying the required mounting screw locations—you can see that a FlexATX board could be made small enough to use only four mounting holes (C, F, H, and J). Refer to Figure 4.16 for the respective hole locations.

According to the FlexATX standard, the distance between holes H and J is 6.2", and the distance between hole J and the right edge of the board is 0.25". By leaving the same margin from hole H to the left edge, you could make a board with a minimum width of 6.7" (0.25" + 6.2" + 0.25") that would conform to the FlexATX specification. Similarly, the distance between holes C and H is 6.1", and the distance between hole C and the back edge of the board is 0.4". By leaving a minimum 0.2" margin from hole H to the front edge, you could make a board with a minimum depth of 6.7" (0.4" + 6.1" + 0.2") that would conform to the FlexATX specification. By combining the minimum width and depth, you can see that the minimum board size that would conform to the FlexATX specification is 6.7"×6.7" (170mm×170mm).

VIA Technologies Platform Solutions Division wanted to create a motherboard as small as possible, yet not define a completely new and incompatible form factor. To accomplish this, in March 2001 VIA created a board that was slightly narrower in width (8.5" instead of 9") but still the same depth as FlexATX, resulting in a board that was 6% smaller and yet still conformed to the FlexATX specification. VIA called this ITX but then realized that the size savings were simply too small to justify developing it further, so it was discontinued before any products were released.

In April 2002, VIA created an even smaller board that featured the absolute minimum width and depth dimensions allowed by FlexATX. It called it Mini-ITX. In essence, all Mini-ITX boards are simply FlexATX boards that are limited to the minimum allowable dimensions. All other aspects, including the I/O aperture size and location, screw hole locations, and power supply connections, are pure FlexATX. A Mini-ITX board fits in any chassis that accepts a FlexATX board; however, larger boards will not fit into a Mini-ITX chassis.

The Mini-ITX form factor was designed by VIA especially to support VIA's low-power embedded Eden and C3 E-Series processors. Only a very small number of motherboards is available in this form factor, and only from VIA and one or two other manufacturers. Because the processors used on these boards are substantially less powerful than even the Intel Celeron 4 or AMD Duron entry-level processors, the Mini-ITX form factor is intended for use mainly in nontraditional settings such as set-top boxes and computing appliances. The size of the ITX and Mini-ITX boards relate to FlexATX as shown in Table 4.4.

Table 4.4   Comparing the FlexATX, ITX, and Mini-ITX Form Factors

Form Factor	Max. Width	Max. Depth	Max. Area	Size Comparison
Flex ATX	9.0" (229mm)	7.5" (191mm)	68 sq. in. (435 sq. cm)	—
ITX	8.5" (215mm)	7.5" (191mm)	64 sq. in. (411 sq. cm)	6% smaller
Mini-ITX	6.7" (170mm)	6.7" (170mm)	45 sq. in. (290 sq. cm)	34% smaller

Again, I must point out that technically any ITX or Mini-ITX board conforms to the FlexATX specification. In particular, the Mini-ITX is the smallest board that can conform. Although the still-born ITX format was virtually the same as FlexATX in size (which is probably why it was discontinued before any were sold), Mini-ITX motherboards are 170mm×170mm (6.7"×6.7"), which is 34% smaller than the maximum allowed by FlexATX.

To take advantage of the smaller Mini-ITX format, several chassis makers are producing very small chassis to fit these boards. Most are the shape of a small cube, with one floppy and one optical drive bay visible from the front. The layout of a typical Mini-ITX motherboard, the VIA EPIA-V, is shown in Figure 4.17.

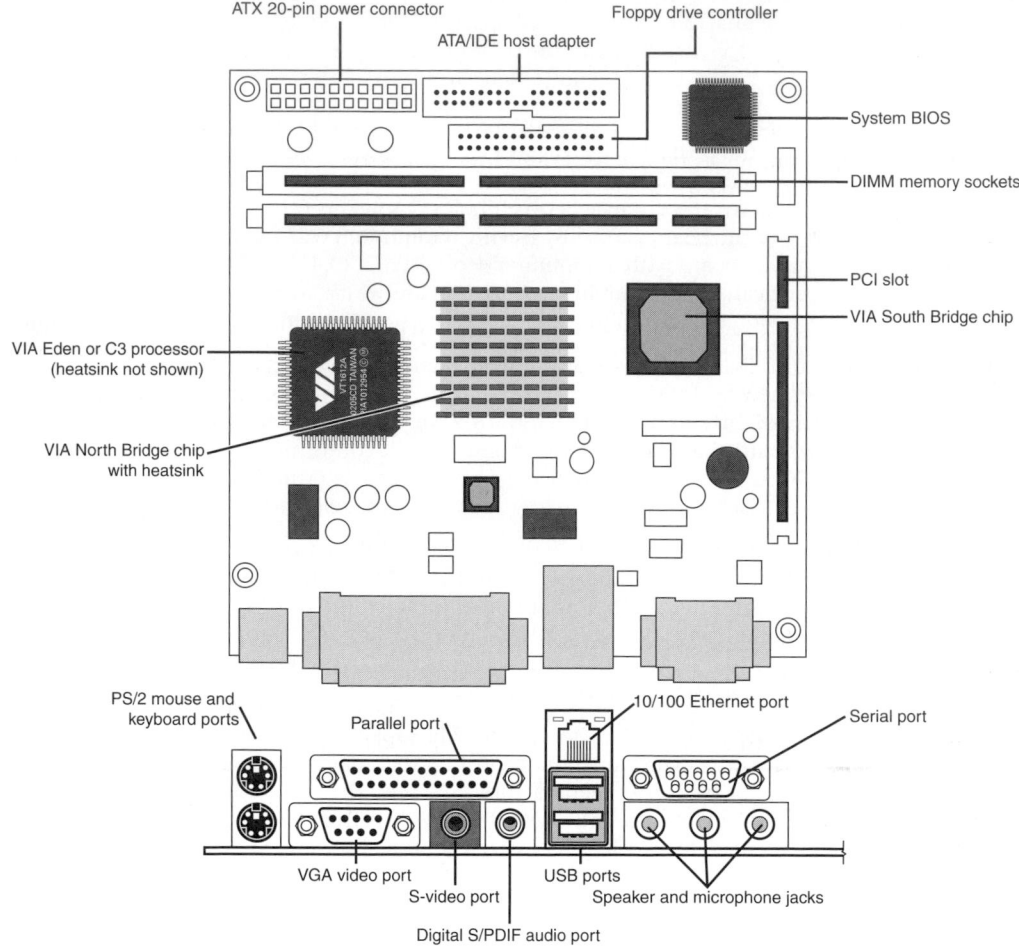

Figure 4.17 Top and rear views of the VIA EPIA-V motherboard, a typical Mini-ITX motherboard. *Photo courtesy VIA Technologies, Inc.*

As Figure 4.17 makes clear, Mini-ITX motherboards can offer a full range of input-output ports. However, several differences exist between the Mini-ITX motherboards and other ATX designs:

- The processor on a Mini-ITX motherboard is usually permanently soldered to the board, making future processor upgrades or replacements impossible.

- Most Mini-ITX chassis use TFX power supplies, for which there are currently only a few suppliers. Consequently, replacements for them are more expensive and more difficult to find.

- The available TFX power supplies are rated for less output than larger supplies, typically up to 240 watts maximum.

- There is no provision for replacing onboard video with an AGP video card.

Because Mini-ITX boards and chassis are made by only a small number of suppliers, future upgrades or parts replacements are limited. However, Mini-ITX boards are actually FlexATX boards, so they can be installed in any standard FlexATX, microATX, or full-size ATX chassis and use the corresponding power supplies. The only caveats are that the smaller Mini-ITX chassis will not accept larger FlexATX, microATX, or full-size ATX boards and most Mini-ITX chassis accept only TFX power supplies. When you select a Mini-ITX system, you must be sure to select the appropriate processor type and speed necessary for the task you need it to perform because processor replacements or upgrades almost always require changing the entire motherboard.

Both the VIA C3 E-series and the VIA Eden are x86-compatible processors, so they run the same operating systems and applications as typical AMD and Intel processors, including Windows and Linux. However, the C3 and Eden processors are significantly slower than the Celeron 4, Pentium 4, and Athlon XP processors found in typical desktop and notebook computers. Table 4.5 provides technical information about these processors.

Table 4.5 VIA C3 E-Series and Eden Processors

Processor Model	Clock Speed	FSB Speed	Voltage	L1 Cache	L2 Cache
Eden ESP 4000	400MHz	100MHz	1.05V	128KB	64KB
Eden ESP 5000	533MHz	133MHz	1.20V	128KB	64KB
Eden ESP 6000	600MHz	133MHz	1.20V	128KB	64KB
Eden ESP 8000	800MHz	133MHz	1.20V	128KB	64KB
Eden ESP 10000	1GHz	133MHz	1.20V	128KB	64KB
C3 E-series	733MHz	133MHz	1.35V	64KB	128KB
C3 E-series	800MHz	133MHz	1.35V	64KB	128KB
C3 E-series	866MHz	133MHz	1.35V	64KB	128KB
C3 E-series	933MHz	133MHz	1.35V	64KB	128KB
C3 E-series	1GHz	133MHz	1.35V	64KB	128KB
C3 E-series	1.1GHz	133MHz	1.35V	64KB	128KB

The Eden ESP series of processors uses a simplified design optimized for the most common operations. Eden ESP processors are an excellent choice for set-top boxes and Internet clients, but they are not as powerful in features or clock speed as the C3 E-series. VIA recommends Eden processors for embedded systems because the processor can be operated without a fan by using a passive heatsink for cooling. For more traditional computer tasks in a small footprint, VIA recommends the C3 E-series because it has performance similar to Intel Celeron processors running at similar speeds. C3 E-series processors can also be run with a passive heatsink, but they run hotter than Eden-series processors because they use higher voltages. VIA recommends a cooling fan for C3 E-series processors unless the case is specially designed to provide adequate cooling for the processor.

VIA uses varying combinations of the following North Bridge and South Bridge chips in its Mini-ITX motherboards. The North Bridge uses either the PLE133 or CLE266 chips, whereas the South Bridge uses either the VT8231 or VT8235 chips.

The PLE133 North Bridge chip features built-in Trident AGP 4x video and support for PC100 and PC133 SDRAM memory. The CLE266, on the other hand, features built-in S3 Savage 4 4x AGP video, a built-in MPEG2 decoder for excellent DVD playback, and support for DDR266 SDRAM memory.

The VT8231 South Bridge chip features AC'97 audio, MC'97 modem, an ATA-100 host adapter, and four USB 1.1 ports. Additional capabilities can be added through optional chips. The VT8235 South Bridge chip features six-channel audio, an ATA-133 host adapter, USB 2.0 ports, 10/100 Ethernet, PCI controller, and MC'97 modem. It also supports the new 8X V-Link interface with the North Bridge.

VIA offers a handful of Mini-ITX motherboards through its VIA Platform Solutions Division (VPSD), including the following:

- EPIA
- EPIA V (refer to Figure 4.17)
- EPIA M
- EPIA CL
- EPIA TC
- EPIA MII
- EPIA PD

Table 4.6 summarizes the differences in these motherboards.

Table 4.6   VPSD Mini-ITX Motherboards

Feature	EPIA	EPIA V	EPIA M	EPIA CL	EPIA TC	EPIA MII	EPIA PD*
North Bridge	PL133	PL133	CLE266	CLE266	CLE266	CLE266	CLE266
South Bridge	VT8231	VT8231	VT8235	VT8235	VT8235	VT8235	VT8235
RAM (#)	PC100, 133 (2)	PC133 (2)	DDR266 (1)	DDR266 (1)	DDR266 (1)	DDR266 (1)	DDR266 (1)
ATA (#)	100, 66 (1)	100, 66 (2)	133, 100, 66 (2)	133, 100, 66 (2)	133, 100, 66 (2)	133, 100, 66 (2)	133, 100, 66 (2)
USB (#)	1.1 (4)	1.1 (2)	2.0 (2)	2.0 (4)	2.0 (6)	2.0 (6)	2.0 (6)
FireWire	No	No	Yes (2)	No	No	Yes	No
Floppy controller	No	Yes	Yes	Yes	No	Yes	No
Ethernet	Yes	Yes	Yes	Yes	Yes	Yes	Yes

EPIA PD has four serial ports; other models feature one serial port.

The EPIA MII motherboard is the most sophisticated of the models listed and is the best choice for digital multimedia because of its faster memory subsystem, Hi-Speed USB (USB 2.0) and IEEE 1394a ports, and optimized DVD playback. The EPIA PD motherboard is a suitable choice for point-of-sale (POS) systems because it has four serial ports (often used for POS printers).

Obviously, with top performance only on par with sub-1GHz Celeron systems, Mini-ITX motherboards are not intended for power user applications. However, if you need a compact system for specialized uses such as home entertainment centers or for small-footprint computers for office suites and Internet access and don't mind investing in a small form factor that might make future upgrades or repairs extremely difficult, these tiny systems can be useful.

Note

The official site for ITX information is www.via.com.tw/en/VInternet/mini_itx.jsp. The site www.mini-itx.com is often mistaken for an official site, but it is actually a vendor that specializes in ITX systems and component sales.

BTX

Balanced Technology Extended (BTX) is a motherboard form factor specification Intel originally released in September 2003. A 1.0a update was released in February 2004. BTX is designed to eventually replace the venerable ATX form factor while addressing ever-increasing component power and cooling requirements, as well as enabling improved circuit routing and more flexible chassis designs.

BTX represents a completely new form factor that is not backward-compatible with ATX or other designs. A full-size BTX board is 17% larger than ATX, allowing room for more integrated components onboard.

The I/O connectors, slots, and mounting holes are in different locations than with ATX, requiring new chassis designs. However, the power supply interface connectors are the same as in the latest ATX12V specifications, and newer ATX, TFX, SFX, CFX, and LFX power supplies can be used. The latter two power supply form factors were specifically created to support compact and low-profile BTX systems.

The primary advantages to BTX include

- *Optimized inline component layout and routing.* Signals are aligned front to back, allowing connections between components and I/O connectors to run unobstructed.

- *Optimized airflow path.* Allows for a condensed system design and an optimized, unobstructed airflow path for efficient system cooling with fewer fans and lower acoustics.

- *Support and retention module (SRM).* Offers mechanical support for heavy heatsinks. It also helps to prevent board flexing or damaging board components and traces during shipping and handling.

- *Scalable board dimensions.* Flexible board sizes enable developers to use the same components for a variety of system sizes and configurations.

- *Low-profile options.* Component keep-out specifications enable lower profiles, making it easier to design slim-line or small form factor systems.

- *Flexible, compatible power supply designs.* Connectors are shared with recent ATX designs; smaller, more efficient power supply form factors can be used for small form factor systems, whereas standard ATX12V power supplies can be used for larger tower configurations.

BTX includes three definitions of motherboard size, as shown in Table 4.7.

Table 4.7   BTX Motherboard Form Factors

Form Factor	Max. Width	Depth	Max. Area	Size Versus BTX
BTX	12.8" (325mm)	10.5" (267mm)	134 sq. in. (867 sq. cm)	—
microBTX	10.4" (264mm)	10.5" (267mm)	109 sq. in. (705 sq. cm)	19% smaller
PicoATX	8.0" (203mm)	10.5" (267mm)	84 sq. in. (542 sq. cm)	37% smaller

Each board has the same basic screw hole and connector placement requirements. So, if you have a case that fits a full-size BTX board, you can also mount a microBTX or picoBTX board in that same case (see Figure 4.18). Obviously, if you have a smaller case designed for MicroBTX or picoBTX, you won't be able to put the larger microBTX or BTX boards in that case.

BTX requires up to 10 mounting holes and supports up to seven slots, depending on the size, as shown in Table 4.8.

Table 4.8   BTX Motherboard Mounting Holes

Board Size	Mounting Holes	Max. Slots
BTX	A,B,C,D,E,F,G,H,J,K	7
microBTX	A,B,C,D,E,F,G	4
picoBTX	A,B,C,D	1

BTX also clearly specifies volumetric zones around the motherboard to prevent any interference from the chassis or internal components such as drives, which allows for maximum interchangeability without physical interference or fit problems.

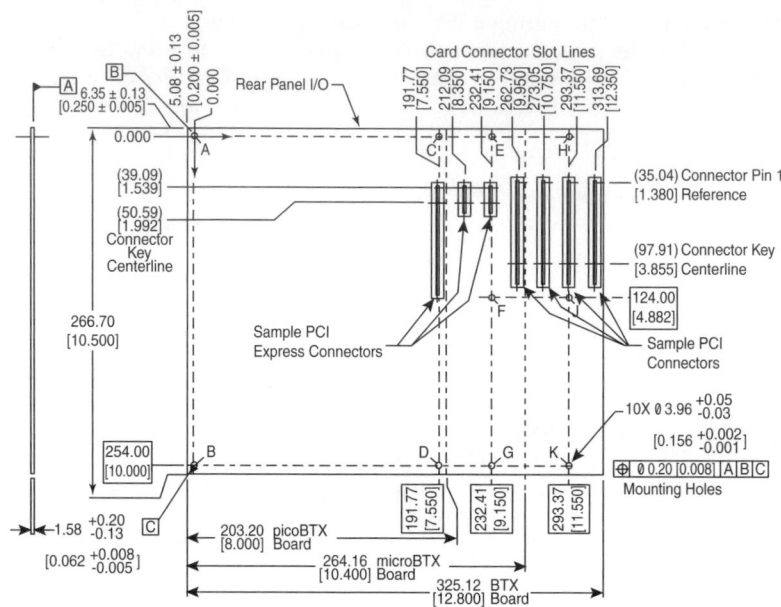

Figure 4.18 BTX specification 1.0a motherboard dimensions.

With processors exceeding 100W in thermal output, as well as voltage regulators, motherboard chipsets, and video cards adding to the thermal load in a system, BTX was designed to allow all the high-heat-producing core components to be mounted inline from front to back, so that a single high-efficiency thermal module (heatsink) can cool the system. This eliminates the need for an excessive number of fans. The thermal module includes a heatsink for the processor, a high-efficiency fan, and a duct to direct airflow through the system. Extra support for the thermal module is provided under the board via a support and retention module (SRM), which provides structural support for heatsinks that are much heavier than allowed in ATX designs (see Figure 4.19).

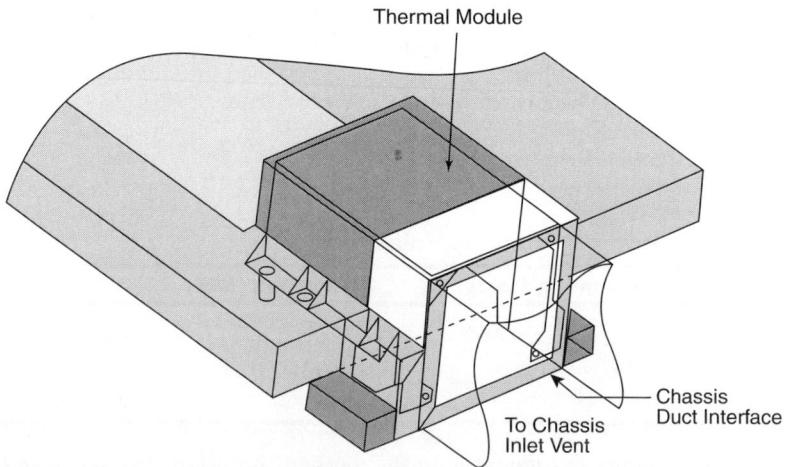

Figure 4.19 BTX thermal module containing a processor heatsink and fan.

BTX uses the same power connectors as in the latest power supply form factor specifications, including a 24-pin main connector for the board and a 4-pin ATX12V connector for the CPU voltage regulator module. The particular power supply form factor used depends mostly on the chassis selected.

A typical tower system has components arranged as shown in Figure 4.20.

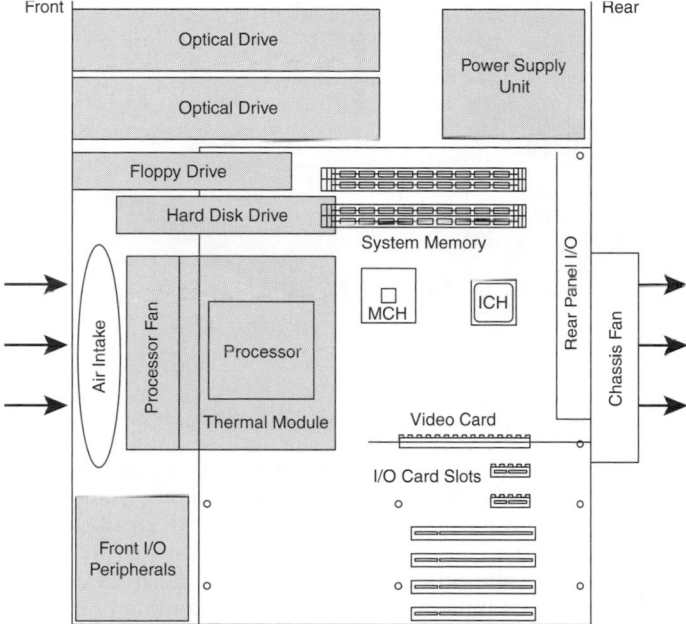

Figure 4.20   BTX tower chassis layout.

From Figure 4.20, you can see that the main heat-producing core components are centrally located inline from front to rear, allowing the most efficient thermal design. Air flows from front to rear through the center, cooling the processor, motherboard chipset, memory, and video card.

To support the heavy processor heatsink and thermal module assembly, an SRM is mounted under the board. The SRM is essentially a metal plate affixed to the chassis under the board, and the thermal module is bolted directly to the SRM instead of to the motherboard. This helps carry the weight of the module and prevents excessive loads from being applied to the processor and motherboard, especially during the shipping and handling of the system.

The BTX I/O connector area is similar to ATX, except that it is at the opposite side of the rear of the board. The size of the area is slightly shorter but wider than ATX, allowing a large number of interfaces and connectors to be built in to the motherboard.

NLX

NLX is a low-profile form factor designed to replace the nonstandard LPX design used in previous low-profile systems. First introduced in November 1996 by Intel, NLX was a popular form factor in the late 1990s for Slimline corporate desktop systems from vendors such as Compaq, HP, Toshiba, and others. Since 2000, many Slimline systems have used variations on the FlexATX motherboard instead.

NLX is similar in initial appearance to LPX, but with numerous improvements designed to enable full integration of the latest technologies. NLX is basically an improved version of the proprietary LPX design, but, unlike LPX, NLX is fully standardized, which means you should be able to replace one NLX board with another from a different manufacturer—something that was not possible with LPX.

Another limitation of LPX boards is the difficulty in handling the larger physical size of the newer processors and their larger heatsinks, as well as newer bus structures such as AGP for video. The NLX form factor has been designed specifically to address these problems (see Figure 4.21). In fact, NLX provides enough room for some vendors to support dual Slot 1 Pentium III processors in this form factor.

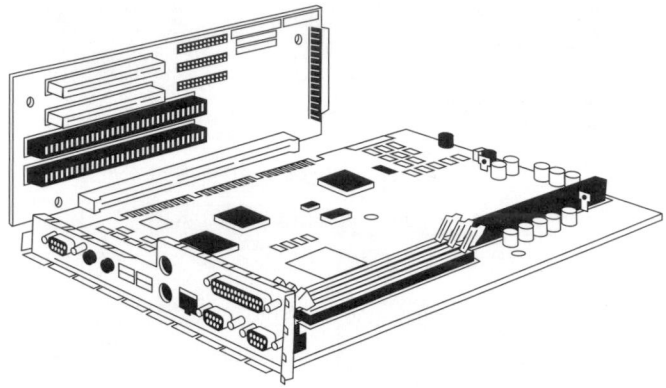

Figure 4.21   NLX motherboard and riser combination.

The main characteristic of an NLX system is that the motherboard plugs into the riser, unlike LPX where the riser plugs into the motherboard. Therefore, the motherboard can be removed from the system without disturbing the riser or any of the expansion cards plugged into it. In addition, the motherboard in a typical NLX system literally has no internal cables or connectors attached to it! All devices that normally plug into the motherboard—such as drive cables, the power supply, the front panel light, switch connectors, and so on—plug into the riser instead (see Figure 4.21). By using the riser card as a connector concentration point, you can remove the lid on an NLX system and literally slide the motherboard out the left side of the system without unplugging a single cable or connector on the inside. This allows for unbelievably quick motherboard changes; in fact, I have swapped motherboards in less than 30 seconds on NLX systems!

As Figure 4.22 shows, by using different sizes and types of riser cards, a system designer can customize the features of a given NLX system.

Such a design is a boon for the corporate market, where ease and swiftness of servicing is a major feature. Not only can components be replaced with lightning speed, but because of the industry-standard design, motherboards, power supplies, and other components can be interchanged even among different systems.

Specific advantages of the NLX form factor include

■ *Support for all desktop system processor technologies*. This is especially important because, since the NLX form factor was developed, both AMD and Intel adopted and then abandoned bulkier slot-based processors and returned to more compact socketed processors. NLX can handle both types of processors.

■ *Flexibility in the face of rapidly changing processor technologies*. Backplane-like flexibility has been built in to the form by allowing a new motherboard to be easily and quickly installed without tearing your entire system to pieces. But unlike traditional backplane systems, many industry leaders, such as Compaq, Toshiba, and HP, have sold NLX-based systems.

■ *Support for newer technologies*. This includes Accelerated Graphics Port (AGP) high-performance graphic solutions, Universal Serial Bus (USB), and memory modules in DIMM or RIMM form.

■ *Ease and speed of servicing and repair*. Compared to other industry-standard interchangeable form factors, NLX systems are by far the easiest to work on and allow component swaps or other servicing in the shortest amount of time.

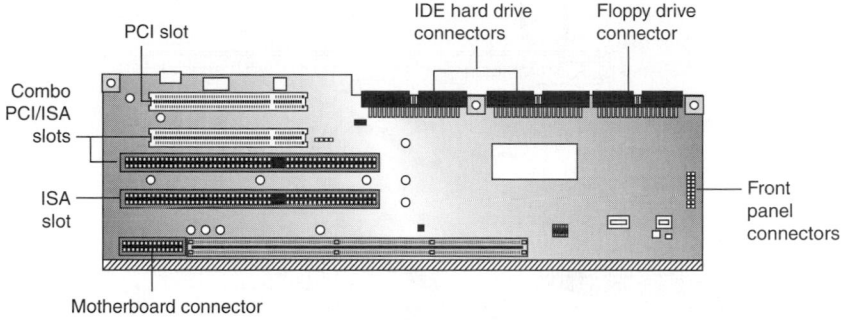

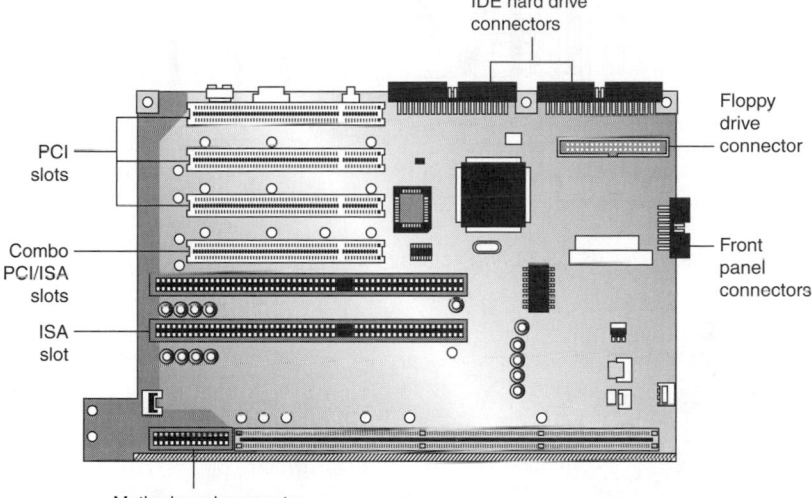

Figure 4.22 Typical NLX riser cards. Although most NLX systems use a low-profile riser card similar to the top riser card, others use a taller riser card to provide more slots for add-on cards.

Furthermore, with the importance of multimedia applications, connectivity support for such things as video playback, enhanced graphics, and extended audio has been built in to the motherboard. This should represent a good cost savings over expensive daughterboard arrangements that have been necessary for many advanced multimedia uses in the past. Although ATX also has this support, LPX and Baby-AT don't have the room for these additional connectors.

Figure 4.23 shows the basic NLX system layout. Notice that, similar to ATX, the motherboard is clear of the drive bays and other chassis-mounted components. Also, the motherboard and I/O cards (which, like the LPX form factor, are mounted parallel to the motherboard) can easily be slid in to and out of the side of the chassis, leaving the riser card and other cards in place. The processor can be easily accessed and enjoys greater cooling than in a more closed-in layout.

Note the position of the optional AGP slot shown in Figure 4.23. It is mounted on the motherboard itself, not on the riser card as with PCI or ISA slots. This location was necessary because AGP was developed well after the NLX form factor was introduced. Most NLX motherboards use chipset-integrated or motherboard-based video instead of a separate AGP card, but you must remove an AGP card installed in an NLX system before you can remove the motherboard for servicing. Also, the AGP card used in an NLX system must have a different form factor to enable it to clear the rear connector shield at the back of the NLX motherboard (see Figure 4.24).

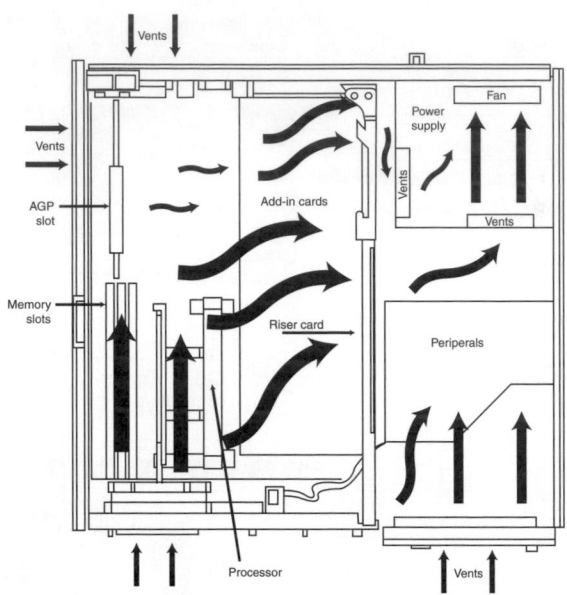

Figure 4.23 NLX system chassis layout and cooling airflow.

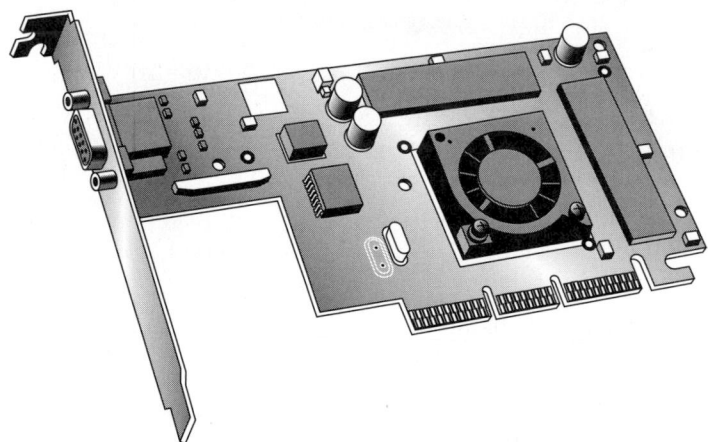

Figure 4.24 An AGP card that can be installed in either a standard ATX/Baby-AT system or an NLX system. This is because of the shape, which leaves room for the NLX motherboard's rear connector shield. *Photo courtesy Elsa AG.*

The NLX motherboard is specified in three lengths, front to back: 13.6", 11.2", or 10" total (see Figure 4.25). With proper bracketry, the shorter boards can go into a case designed for a longer board.

As with most of the form factors, you can identify NLX via the unique I/O shield or connector area at the back of the board (see Figure 4.26). You only need a quick look at the rear of any given system to determine which type of board is contained within. Figure 4.26 shows the unique stepped design of the NLX I/O connector area. This allows for a row of connectors all along the bottom and has room for double-stacked connectors on one side.

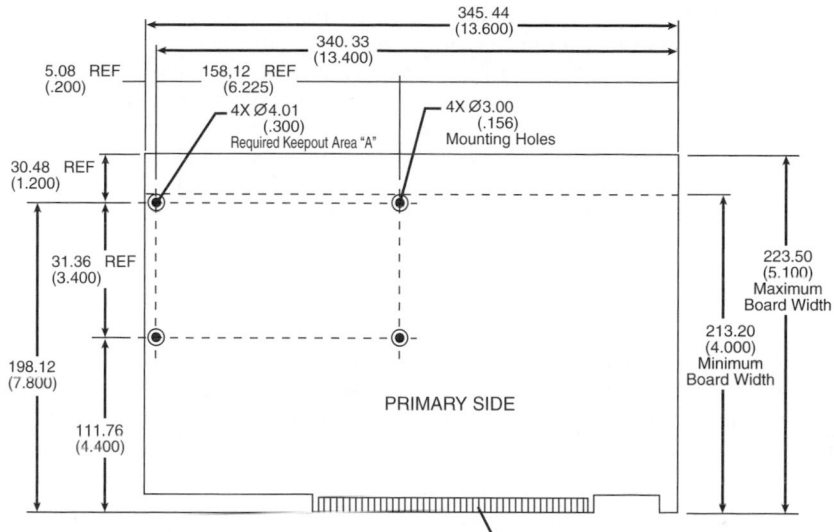

Figure 4.25 NLX form factor. This shows a 13.6" long NLX board. The NLX specification also allows shorter 11.2" and 10" versions.

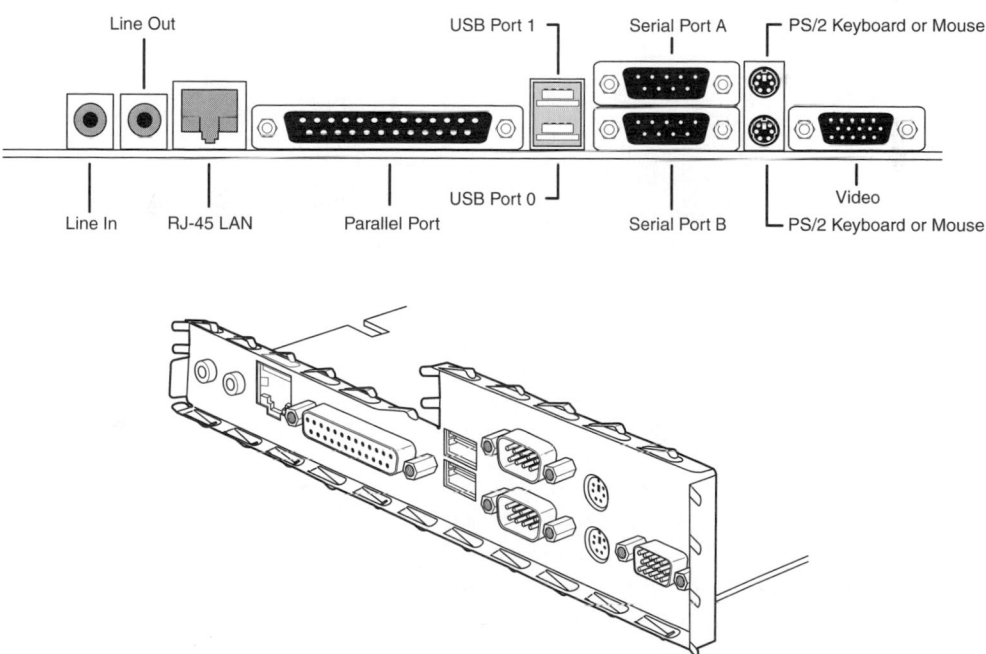

Figure 4.26 Typical NLX motherboard rear connector layout.

As you can see, the NLX form factor has been designed for maximum flexibility and space efficiency. Even extremely long I/O cards will fit easily without getting in the way of other system components—a problem with Baby-AT form factor systems.

The specification and related information about the NLX form factor are available at the Desktop Form Factor site located at www.formfactors.org (specify NLX in the search tool). Although NLX is a standard form factor—just as the ATX family is—most NLX products have been sold as part of complete systems aimed at the corporate market. Very few aftermarket motherboards have been developed in this form factor. Thus, although NLX makes swapping motherboards easy, you are more likely to encounter it in a corporate environment than in a home or small-business computer. The microATX and FlexATX form factors have largely superseded NLX in the markets formerly dominated by LPX. Overall, one of the ATX variants is still the best choice for most new systems where expandability, upgradeability, low cost, and ease of service are of prime importance. In the future, picoBTX is likely to eventually replace both the NLX and FlexATX form factors.

WTX

WTX was a board and system form factor developed for the mid-range workstation market; however, most vendors making workstations and servers have used the ATX form factor. WTX went beyond ATX and defined the size and shape of the board and the interface between the board and chassis, as well as required chassis features.

WTX was first released in September 1998 (1.0) and updated in February 1999 (1.1). The specification and other information on WTX used to be available at www.wtx.org; however, WTX has been officially discontinued and there will be no further updates.

Figure 4.27 shows a typical WTX system with the cover removed. Note that easy access is provided to internal components via pull-out drawers and swinging side panels.

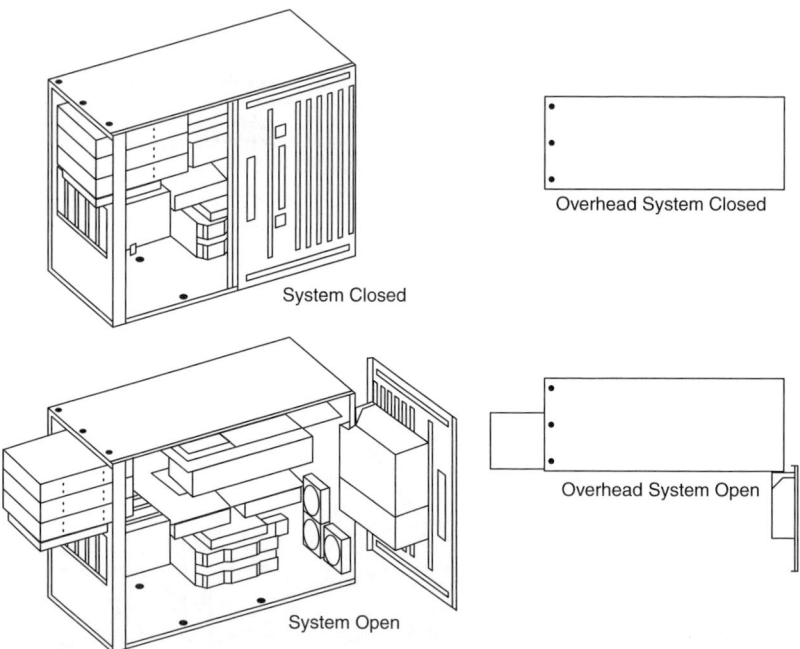

Figure 4.27   Typical WTX system chassis showing internal layout and ease of access.

WTX motherboards have a maximum width of 14" (356mm) and a maximum length of 16.75" (425 mm), which is significantly larger than ATX. There are no minimum dimensions, so board designers are free to design smaller boards as long as they meet the mounting criteria. The additional space provided by the WTX form factor provides room for two or more processors and other onboard equipment needed in a workstation or server design. Although WTX is no longer an official form factor, a number of server and workstation motherboard vendors, such as Tyan, MSI, and SuperMicro, continue to build products that use it.

The WTX specification offers flexibility by leaving motherboard mounting features and locations undefined. Instead of defining exact screw hole positions, WTX motherboards must mount to a standard mounting adapter plate, which must be supplied with the board. The WTX chassis is designed to accept the mounting plate with attached motherboard and not just a bare board alone.

WTX motherboards use different power connectors than ATX motherboards. Originally, WTX motherboards used a 24-pin power connector that supplied only 5V and 3.3V power to the motherboard and a separate 22-pin power connector that supplied 12V power. Modern WTX motherboards still use a 24-pin primary power connector, but the connector might use the EPS12V (also known as the Superset ATX or SSI) standard or the older ATX-GES standard. Both ATX-GES and EPS12V provide 3.3V, 5V, and 12V power to the motherboard, but the pinouts are completely different. EPS12V motherboards also use an 8-pin power connector to provide additional 12V power to the processor(s). Table 4.9 compares the pinouts of the ATX-GES and EPS12V 24-pin primary power connectors.

Caution

Keep in mind that motherboards using the WTX, ATX-GES, and EPS12V power supply standards all use the same connector (the 24-pin Molex 39-01-2240 connector, a longer version of the 20-pin Molex connector used by ATX power supplies). However, they use different voltages on almost every wire. If you mismatch the motherboard and power supply, you will destroy one or both of them!

Table 4.9   ATX-GES and EPS12V 24-Pin Primary Power Connector Pinouts

Pin #	ATX-GES	EPS12V	Pin #	ATX-GES	EPS12V
1	+5V red	+3.3V orange	13	+5V red	+3.3V orange and brown
2	+5V red	+3.3V orange	14	+5V red	-12V blue
3	GND black	GND black	15	GND black	GND black
4	GND black	+5V red	16	+5V SB purple	PS-On green
5	PS-On green	GND black	17	-12V blue	GND black
6	GND black	+5V red	18	GND black	GND black
7	+3.3V orange + orange	GND black	19	+3.3V orange	GND black
8	+3.3V orange	Pwr-OK gray	20	+3.3V orange	-5V white
9	GND black	+5V SB purple	21	+3.3V orange	+5V red
10	GND black	+12V yellow	22	GND black	+5V red
11	+12V yellow	+12V yellow	23	GND black	+5V red
12	+12V yellow	+3.3V orange	24	+12V yellow	GND black

Proprietary Designs

Motherboards that are *not* one of the industry standard form factors, such as AT/Baby-AT, NLX, or any of the ATX formats, are deemed *proprietary* or *semiproprietary*. LPX, ITX, and Mini-ITX systems fall into the semiproprietary category for example, while other companies have fully proprietary systems that only they manufacture. Most people purchasing PCs should avoid proprietary designs because they do not allow for a future motherboard, power supply, or case upgrade, which limits future use and serviceability of the system. To me, proprietary systems are disposable PCs because you can neither upgrade them nor easily repair them. The problem is that the proprietary parts can come only from the original system manufacturer, and they usually cost much more than nonproprietary parts. Therefore, after your proprietary system goes out of warranty, not only is it not upgradeable, but it is also essentially no longer worth repairing. If the motherboard or any component on it goes bad, you will be better off purchasing a completely new standard system than paying five times the normal price for a new proprietary motherboard. In addition, a new motherboard in a standard form factor system would be one or more generations newer and faster than the one you would be replacing. In a proprietary system, the replacement board would not only cost way too much, but it would be the same as the one that failed.

Note that you might be able to perform limited upgrades to older systems with proprietary motherboards, in the form of custom (non-OEM) processor replacements with attached voltage regulators, usually called "overdrive" or "turbo" chips. Unfortunately, these often don't perform up to the standards of a less expensive new processor and motherboard combination. Of course, I usually recommend upgrading the motherboard and processor together—but that is something that can't be done with a proprietary system.

Until the late 1990s, the LPX motherboard design was at the heart of most proprietary systems. These systems were sold primarily in the retail store channel by Compaq, IBM's Aptiva line, HP's Vectra line, and Packard Bell (no longer in business in North America). As such, virtually all their systems have problems inherent with their proprietary designs.

If the motherboard in your current ATX form factor system dies, you can find any number of replacement boards that will bolt directly in—with your choice of processors and clock speeds—at great prices. You can also find replacements for Baby-AT motherboards, but this form factor doesn't support the newest technologies and has not been used in new system designs for several years. However, if the motherboard dies in a proprietary form factor system, you'll pay for a replacement available only from the original manufacturer, and you have little or no opportunity to select a board with a faster or better processor than the one that failed. In other words, upgrading or repairing one of these systems via a motherboard replacement is difficult and usually not cost-effective.

Systems sold by the leading mail-order suppliers, such as Gateway, Micron, Dell, and others, are available in industry-standard form factors such as ATX, microATX, FlexATX, and NLX. This allows for easy upgrading and system expansion in the future. These standard factors allow you to replace your own motherboards, power supplies, and other components easily and select components from any number of suppliers other than where you originally bought the system.

Backplane Systems

One type of design that has been used in some systems over the years is the *backplane system*. These systems do not have a motherboard in the true sense of the word. In a backplane system, the components typically found on a motherboard are located instead on an expansion adapter card plugged into a slot.

In these systems, the board with the slots is called a backplane, rather than a motherboard. Systems using this type of construction are called backplane systems.

Backplane systems come in two main types—passive and active. A *passive* backplane means the main backplane board does not contain any circuitry at all except for the bus connectors and maybe some buffer and driver circuits. All the circuitry found on a conventional motherboard is contained on one or more expansion cards installed in slots on the backplane. Some backplane systems use a passive design that incorporates the entire system circuitry into a single mothercard. The mothercard is essentially a complete motherboard designed to plug into a slot in the passive backplane. The passive backplane/mothercard concept enables the entire system to be easily upgraded by changing one or more cards. Because of the expense of the high-function mothercard, this type of system design is rarely found in standard PC systems today, although it was once favored by a few early 286/386 vendors such as Zenith Data Systems. The passive backplane design does enjoy popularity in industrial systems, which are often rack-mounted. Some high-end fileservers also feature this design. Figure 4.28 shows a typical Pentium 4 single-board computer used in PICMG passive backplane systems. Figure 4.29 shows a rack-mount chassis with a passive backplane.

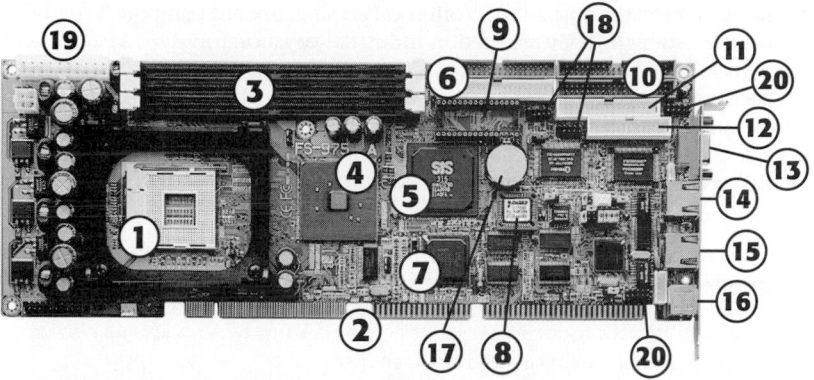

1. Pentium 4 processor socket
2. PICMG interface to backplane
3. DIMM memory sockets (3)
4. North Bridge/MCH
5. SIS 315 graphics chip
6. ATA/IDE host adapters
7. South Bridge/ICH
8. System BIOS
9. JEDEC Disk on Chip socket
10. ATA RAID host adaptors

11. Floppy controller
12. Parallel port header cable connector
    PS/2 mouse port
13. VGA port
14. 10/100 Ethernet port
15. 10/100 Ethernet port
16. PS/2 keyboard/mouse port
17. CR-2032 battery
18. USB header cable connectors (2)
19. Power connector
20. Serial port header cable connectors (2)

Figure 4.28 A typical Pentium 4 PICMG single-board computer. This single card provides PCI and ISA interfacing; integrated AGP video; two 10/100 Ethernet network interfaces; ATA RAID; and normal parallel, serial, ATA/IDE, USB, and floppy interfaces.

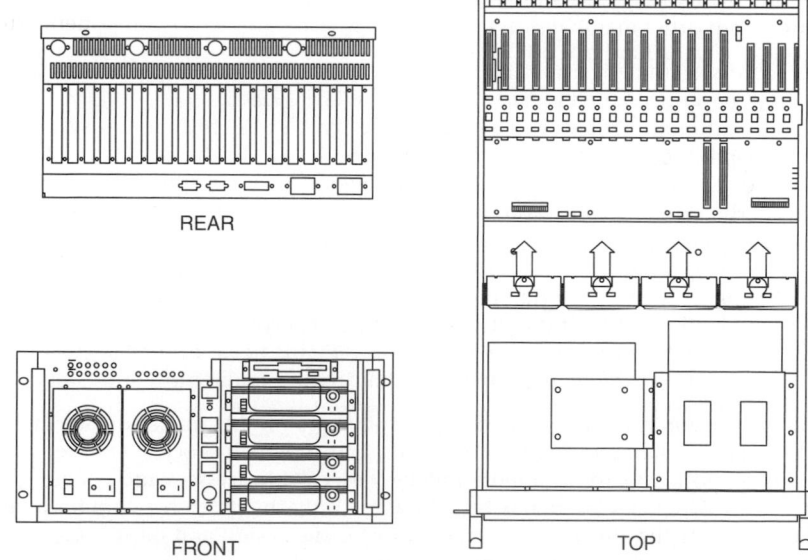

Figure 4.29 A rack-mount chassis with passive backplane.

Passive backplane systems with mothercards (often called single-board computers or SBCs) are by far the most popular backplane design. They are used in industrial or laboratory-type systems and are rack-mountable. They usually have a large number of slots and extremely heavy-duty power supplies; they also feature high-capacity, reverse flow cooling designed to pressurize the chassis with cool, filtered air. Many passive backplane systems, such as the one pictured in Figure 4.28, adhere to the PCI/ISA passive backplane and CompactPCI form factor standards set forth by the PCI Industrial Computer Manufacturers Group (PICMG). You can get more information about these standards from PICMG's Web site at www.picmg.org.

Note

Another popular standard for SBCs is the PISA standard developed by JUMPtec and Kontron. The PISA standard uses a half-length SBC that plugs in to a backplane slot similar to the old EISA slot. PISA backplanes also support PCI and ISA cards. Learn more at http://www.jumptec.de/index-en.html.

An *active* backplane means the main backplane board contains bus control and usually other circuitry as well. Most active backplane systems contain all the circuitry found on a typical motherboard except for what is then called the *processor complex*. The processor complex is the name of the circuit board that contains the main system processor and any other circuitry directly related to it, such as clock control, cache, and so forth. The processor's complex design enables the user to easily upgrade the system later to a new processor type by changing one card. In effect, it amounts to a modular motherboard with a replaceable processor section.

Many large PC manufacturers have built systems with an active backplane/processor complex. Both IBM and Compaq, for example, have used this type of design in some of their high-end (server class) systems. ALR (now owned by Gateway) once made a series of desktop and server PCs that also featured this design. This allows an easier and generally more affordable upgrade than the passive backplane/mothercard design because the processor complex board is usually much cheaper than a mothercard. Unfortunately, because no standards exist for the processor complex interface to the system, these boards are proprietary and can be purchased only from the system manufacturer. This limited market and availability causes the prices of these boards to be higher than most complete motherboards from other manufacturers.

The motherboard system design and the backplane system design have advantages and disadvantages. Most original PCs were designed as backplanes in the late 1970s. Apple and IBM shifted the market to the now traditional motherboard with a slot-type design because this kind of system generally is cheaper to mass-produce than one with the backplane design. In the late 1980s, Zenith Data manufactured a line of backplane-based 8088, 286, and 386-based systems but later abandoned this for a standard motherboard design similar to other vendors. The theoretical advantage of a backplane system, however, is that you can easily upgrade it to a new processor and level of performance by changing a single card. For example, you can upgrade a system's processor just by changing the card. In a motherboard-design system, you often must change the motherboard, a seemingly more formidable task. Unfortunately, the reality of the situation is that a backplane design is frequently much more expensive to upgrade. For example, because the bus remains fixed on the backplane, the backplane design precludes more comprehensive upgrades that involve adding local bus slots.

Another nail in the coffin of backplane designs is the upgradeable processor. Starting with the 486, Intel and AMD began standardizing the sockets or slots in which processors were to be installed, allowing a single motherboard to support a wider variety of processors and system speeds. Because board designs could be made more flexible, changing only the processor chip for a faster standard OEM type (not one of the kludgy "overdrive" chips) is the easiest and most cost-effective way to upgrade without changing the entire motherboard.

Because of the limited availability of the processor-complex boards or mothercards, they usually end up being more expensive than a complete new motherboard that uses an industry-standard form factor. The bottom line is that unless you have a requirement for a large-capacity industrial or laboratory-type system, especially one that would be rack-mounted, you are better off sticking with standard ATX form factor PCs. They will certainly be far less expensive.

Note

Some companies offer plug-in processor cards that essentially turn your existing motherboard into an active backplane, shutting down the main CPU and memory and having the card's processor and memory essentially take over. These are, unfortunately, much more expensive than a new motherboard and processor alone, use the more expensive SO DIMM memory, don't provide AGP video, and are generally not recommended.

Motherboard Components

A modern motherboard has several components built in, including various sockets, slots, connectors, chips, and so on. This section examines the components found on a typical motherboard.

Most modern motherboards have at least the following major components on them:

- Processor socket/slot
- Chipset (North/South Bridge or memory and I/O controller hubs)
- Super I/O chip
- ROM BIOS (Flash ROM/firmware hub)
- SIMM/DIMM/RIMM (RAM memory) sockets
- ISA/PCI/AGP bus slots
- CPU voltage regulator
- Battery

Some motherboards also include integrated video, audio, networking, SCSI, Audio Modem Riser (AMR), Communications and Networking Riser (CNR) connectors, or other optional interfaces, depending on the individual board.

These standard components are discussed in the following sections.

Processor Sockets/Slots

The CPU is installed in either a socket or a slot, depending on the type of chip.

Starting with the 486 processors, Intel designed the processor to be a user-installable and replaceable part and developed standards for CPU sockets and slots that would allow different models of the same basic processor to plug in. One key was to use a zero insertion force (ZIF) socket design, which meant that the processor could be easily installed or removed with no tools. ZIF sockets use a lever to engage or release the grip on the chip, and with the lever released, the chip can be easily inserted or removed. The ZIF sockets were given a designation that was usually imprinted or embossed on the socket indicating what type it was. Different socket types accepted different families of processors. If you know the type of socket or slot on your motherboard, you essentially know which types of processors are designed to plug in.

◄◄ See "Processor Socket and Slot Types," p. 88.

Sockets for processors prior to the 486 were not ZIF designs and, as such, were not designed for easy processor installation or removal. In addition, interchangeability was limited. Table 4.10 shows the designations for the various 486 and newer processor sockets/slots and lists the chips designed to plug into them.

Table 4.10   CPU Socket Specifications

	Socket	Pins	Layout	Voltage	Supported Processors
Intel/AMD 486 class	Socket 1	169	17×17 PGA	5V	486 SX/SX2, DX/DX2, DX4 OD
	Socket 2	238	19×19 PGA	5V	486 SX/SX2, DX/DX2, DX4 OD, 486 Pentium OD
	Socket 3	237	19×19 PGA	5V/3.3V	486 SX/SX2, DX/DX2, DX4, 486 Pentium OD, AMD 5x86
	Socket 6[1]	235	19×19 PGA	3.3V	486 DX4, 486 Pentium OD
Intel/AMD 586 (Pentium) class	Socket 4	273	21×21 PGA	5V	Pentium 60/66, OD
	Socket 5	320	37×37 SPGA	3.3V/ 3.5V	Pentium 75-133, OD
	Socket 7	321	37×37 SPGA	VRM	Pentium 75-233+, MMX, OD, AMD K5/K6, Cyrix M1/II
Intel 686 (Pentium II/III) class	Socket 8	387	Dual-pattern SPGA	Auto VRM	Pentium Pro, OD
	Slot 1 (SC242)	242	Slot	Auto VRM	Pentium II/III, Celeron SECC
	Socket 370	370	37×37 SPGA	Auto VRM	Celeron/Pentium III PPGA/FC-PGA
Pentium 4 class	Socket 423	423	39×39 SPGA	Auto VRM	Pentium 4 FC-PGA
	Socket 478	478	26×26 mPGA	Auto VRM	Pentium 4/Celeron FC-PGA2
	Socket T (LGA775)	775	30×33 LGA	Auto VRM	Pentium 4/Celeron LGA775
AMD K7 class	Slot A	242	Slot	Auto VRM	AMD Athlon SECC
	Socket A (462)	462	37×37 SPGA	Auto VRM	AMD Athlon/Athlon XP/ Duron PGA/FC-PGA
AMD K8 class	Socket 754	754	29×29 mPGA	Auto VRM	AMD Athlon 64
	Socket 939	939	31×31 mPGA	Auto VRM	AMD Athlon 64 v.2
	Socket 940	940	31×31 mPGA	Auto VRM	AMD Athlon 64FX, Opteron
Intel/AMD Server and Workstation class	Slot 2 (SC330)	330	Slot	Auto VRM	Pentium II/III Xeon
	Socket 603	603	31×25 mPGA	Auto VRM	Xeon (P4)
	Socket PAC418	418	38×22 split SPGA	Auto VRM	Itanium
	Socket PAC611	611	25×28 mPGA	Auto VRM	Itanium 2
	Socket 940	940	31×31 mPGA	Auto VRM	AMD Athlon 64FX, Opteron

1. Socket 6 was never actually implemented in any systems.
FC-PGA = Flip-chip pin grid array
FC-PGA2 = FC-PGA with an integrated heat spreader (IHS)
OD = OverDrive (retail upgrade processors)
PAC = Pin array cartridge
PGA = Pin grid array
PPGA = Plastic pin grid array
SC242 = Slot connector, 242 pins

SC330 = Slot connector, 330 pins
SECC = Single edge contact cartridge
SPGA = Staggered pin grid array
mPGA = Micro pin grid array
VRM = Voltage regulator module with variable voltage output determined by module type or manual jumpers
Auto VRM = Voltage regulator module with automatic voltage selection determined by processor voltage ID (VID) pins

Originally, all processors were mounted in sockets (or soldered directly to the motherboard). With the advent of the Pentium II and original Athlon processors, both Intel and AMD temporarily shifted to a slot-based approach for their processors because the processors now incorporated built-in L2 cache, purchased as separate chips from third-party Static RAM (SRAM) memory chip manufacturers. Therefore, the processor then consisted not of one but of several chips, all mounted on a daughterboard that was then plugged into a slot in the motherboard. This worked well, but there were additional expenses in the extra cache chips, the daughterboard itself, the slot, optional casings or packaging, and the support mechanisms and physical stands and latches for the processor and heatsink. All in all, slot-based processors were expensive to produce compared to the previous socketed versions.

With the advent of the second-generation Celeron, Intel integrated the L2 cache directly into the processor die, meaning within the main CPU chip circuits with no extra chips required. The second-generation (code named Coppermine) Pentium III also received on-die L2 cache, as did the K6-3, Duron (code named Spitfire), and second-generation Athlon (code named Thunderbird) processors from AMD (some early Thunderbird Athlon CPUs were also made in the Slot A configuration). With on-die L2, the processor was back to being a single chip again, which also meant that mounting it on a separate board plugged into a slot was expensive and unnecessary. Because of on-die integrated L2 cache, processor packaging shifted back to sockets and will continue that way for the foreseeable future. All modern processors now have integrated L2 cache (some also have integrated L3 cache) and use the socket form. Besides allowing a return to socketed packaging, the on-die L2 cache runs at full processor speed, instead of the one-half or one-third speed of the previous integrated (but not on-die) L2 cache.

Chipsets

We can't talk about modern motherboards without discussing chipsets. The chipset *is* the motherboard; therefore, any two boards with the same chipsets are functionally identical unless the vendor has added features to those provided by the chipset or removed support for certain chipset features.

The chipset contains the processor bus interface (called front-side bus, or FSB), memory controllers, bus controllers, I/O controllers, and more. All the circuits of the motherboard are contained within the chipset. If the processor in your PC is like the engine in your car, the chipset represents the chassis. It is the framework in which the engine rests and is its connection to the outside world. The chipset is the frame, suspension, steering, wheels and tires, transmission, drive shaft, differential, and brakes. The chassis in your car is what gets the power to the ground, allowing the vehicle to start, stop, and corner. In the PC, the chipset represents the connection between the processor and everything else. The processor can't talk to the memory, adapter boards, devices, and so on without going through the chipset. The chipset is the main hub and central nervous system of the PC. If you think of the processor as the brain, the chipset is the spine and central nervous system.

Because the chipset controls the interface or connections between the processor and everything else, the chipset ends up dictating which type of processor you have; how fast it will run; how fast the buses will run; the speed, type, and amount of memory you can use; and more. In fact, the chipset might be the single most important component in your system, possibly even more important than the processor. I've seen systems with faster processors be outperformed by systems with slower processor but a better chipset, much like how a car with less power might win a race through better cornering and braking. When deciding on a system, I start by choosing the chipset first because the chipset decision then dictates the processor, memory, I/O, and expansion capabilities.

Chipset Evolution

When IBM created the first PC motherboards, it used several discrete (separate) chips to complete the design. Besides the processor and optional math coprocessor, many other components were required to complete the system. These other components included items such as the clock generator, bus controller, system timer, interrupt and DMA controllers, CMOS RAM and clock, and keyboard controller. Additionally, many other simple logic chips were used to complete the entire motherboard circuit, plus, of course, things such as the actual processor, math coprocessor (floating-point unit), memory, and other parts. Table 4.11 lists all the primary chip components used on the original PC/XT and AT motherboards.

Table 4.11   Primary Chip Components on PC/XT and AT Motherboards

Chip Function	PC/XT Version	AT Version
Processor	8088	80286
Math Coprocessor (Floating-Point Unit)	8087	80287
Clock Generator	8284	82284
Bus Controller	8288	82288
System Timer	8253	8254
Low-order Interrupt Controller	8259	8259
High-order Interrupt Controller	—	8259
Low-order DMA Controller	8237	8237
High-order DMA Controller	—	8237
CMOS RAM/Real-Time Clock	—	MC146818
Keyboard Controller	8255	8042

In addition to the processor/coprocessor, a six-chip set was used to implement the primary motherboard circuit in the original PC and XT systems. IBM later upgraded this to a nine-chip design in the AT and later systems, mainly by adding more interrupt and DMA controller chips and the nonvolatile CMOS RAM/Real-Time Clock chip. All these motherboard chip components came from Intel or an Intel-licensed manufacturer, except the CMOS/Clock chip, which came from Motorola. To build a clone or copy of one of these IBM systems required all these chips plus many smaller discrete logic chips to glue the design together, totaling 100 or more individual chips. This kept the price of a motherboard high and left little room on the board to integrate other functions.

In 1986, a company called Chips and Technologies introduced a revolutionary component called the 82C206—the main part of the first PC motherboard chipset. This was a single chip that integrated into it all the functions of the main motherboard chips in an AT-compatible system. This chip included the functions of the 82284 Clock Generator, 82288 Bus Controller, 8254 System Timer, dual 8259 Interrupt Controllers, dual 8237 DMA Controllers, and even the MC146818 CMOS/Clock chip. Besides the processor, virtually all the major chip components on a PC motherboard could now be replaced by a single chip. Four other chips augmented the 82C206 acting as buffers and memory controllers, thus completing virtually the entire motherboard circuit with five total chips. This first chipset was called the CS8220 chipset by Chips and Technologies. Needless to say, this was a revolutionary concept in PC motherboard manufacturing. Not only did it greatly reduce the cost of building a PC motherboard, but it also made designing a motherboard much easier. The reduced component count meant the boards had more room for integrating other items formerly found on expansion cards. Later, the four chips augmenting the 82C206 were replaced by a new set of only three chips, and the entire set was called the New Enhanced AT (NEAT) CS8221 chipset. This was later followed by the 82C836 Single Chip AT (SCAT) chipset, which finally condensed all the chips in the set down to a single chip.

The chipset idea was rapidly copied by other chip manufacturers. Companies such as Acer, Erso, Opti, Suntac, Symphony, UMC, and VLSI each gained an important share of this market. Unfortunately for many of them, the chipset market has been a volatile one, and many of them have long since gone out of business. In 1993, VLSI had become the dominant force in the chipset market and had the vast majority of the market share; by the next year, VLSI (which later was merged into Philips Semiconductors), along with virtually everybody else in the chipset market, was fighting to stay alive. This is because a new chipset manufacturer had come on the scene, and within a year or so of getting serious, it was totally dominating the chipset market. That company was Intel, and after 1994, it had a virtual lock on the chipset market. If you have a motherboard built since 1994 that uses or accepts an Intel processor, chances are good that it has an Intel chipset on it as well.

Intel struggled somewhat with chipsets from 1999 through 2001 because of its reliance on RDRAM memory. Intel originally signed a contract with Rambus back in 1996 declaring it would support this memory as its primary focus for desktop PC chipsets through 2001. I suspect this has turned out to be something Intel regrets (the contract has since expired). RDRAM memory had a significantly higher price than DDR SDRAM memory. Consequently, Intel introduced the 845 chipset (code named Brookdale), which supported DDR SDRAM with the Pentium 4. After that, all of Intel's Pentium 4 chipsets have supported either DDR or DDR2 memory. Intel is not alone in the Pentium 4 chipset business: VIA Technologies, Silicon Integrated Systems (SiS), ATI, and ALi Corporation all make chipsets for the Pentium 4. In addition, almost all these chipsets also support SDRAM or DDR-SDRAM (although SiS makes a few chipsets that use RDRAM).

Although AMD has developed its own chipsets for the K6 and Athlon family of processors, it now emphasizes encouraging third-party chipset developers to support its products. Today, VIA Technologies is the leading developer of chipsets for AMD processors. The popularity of AMD processors has encouraged NVIDIA, SiS, ATI, and ALi Corporation to develop chipsets for AMD-based systems as well.

It is interesting to note that the original PC chipset maker, Chips and Technologies, survived by changing course to design and manufacture video chips and found a niche in that market specifically for laptop and notebook video chipsets. Chips and Technologies was subsequently purchased by Intel in 1998 as a part of Intel's video strategy.

Intel Chipsets

You can't talk about chipsets today without discussing Intel because it currently owns the vast majority of the chipset market. It is interesting to note that we probably have Compaq to thank for forcing Intel into the chipset business in the first place!

The thing that really started it all was the introduction of the EISA bus designed by Compaq in 1989. At that time, it had shared the bus with other manufacturers in an attempt to make it a market standard. However, Compaq refused to share its EISA bus chipset—a set of custom chips necessary to implement this bus on a motherboard.

Enter Intel, who decided to fill the chipset void for the rest of the PC manufacturers wanting to build EISA bus motherboards. As is well known today, the EISA bus failed to become a market success except for a short-term niche server business, but Intel now had a taste of the chipset business and this it apparently wouldn't forget. With the introduction of the 286 and 386 processors, Intel became impatient with how long it took the other chipset companies to create chipsets around its new processor designs; this delayed the introduction of motherboards that supported the new processors. For example, it took more than two years after the 286 processor was introduced for the first 286 motherboards to appear and just over a year for the first 386 motherboards to appear after the 386 had been introduced. Intel couldn't sell its processors in volume until other manufacturers made motherboards that would support them, so it thought that by developing motherboard chipsets for a new processor in parallel with the new processor, it could jumpstart the motherboard business by providing ready-made chipsets for the motherboard manufacturers to use.

Intel tested this by introducing the 420 series chipsets along with its 486 processor in April 1989. This enabled the motherboard companies to get busy right away, and in only a few months the first 486 motherboards appeared. Of course, the other chipset manufacturers weren't happy; now they had Intel as a competitor, and Intel would always have chipsets for new processors on the market first!

Intel then realized that it made both processors *and* chipsets, which were 90% of the components on a typical motherboard. What better way to ensure that motherboards were available for its Pentium processor when it was introduced than by making its own motherboards as well and having these boards ready on the new processor's introduction date. When the first Pentium processor debuted in

1993, Intel also debuted the 430LX chipset as well as a fully finished motherboard. Now, besides the chipset companies being upset, the motherboard companies weren't too happy, either. Intel was not only the major supplier of parts needed to build finished boards (processors and chipsets), but was now building and selling the finished boards as well. By 1994, Intel dominated the processor and chipset markets and had cornered the motherboard market as well.

Now as Intel develops new processors, it develops chipsets and motherboards simultaneously, which means they can be announced and shipped in unison. This eliminates the delay between introducing new processors and waiting for motherboards and systems capable of using them, which was common in the industry's early days. For the consumer, this means no waiting for new systems. Since the original Pentium processor in 1993, we have been able to purchase ready-made systems on the same day a new processor is released.

In my seminars, I ask how many people in the class have Intel-brand PCs. Of course, Intel does not sell or market a PC under its own name, so nobody thinks they have an "Intel-brand" PC. But, if your motherboard was made by Intel, for all intents and purposes you sure seem to have an Intel-brand PC, at least as far as the components are concerned. Does it really matter whether Dell, Gateway, or Micron PC (now MPC Computers, LLC) put that same Intel motherboard into a slightly different-looking case with their name on it? If you look under the covers, you'll find that many, if not most, of the systems from the major manufacturers are really the same because they basically use the same parts. Although more and more major manufacturers are offering AMD-based systems as alternatives to Intel's, no single manufacturer dominates AMD motherboard sales the way Intel has dominated OEM sales to major system manufacturers.

To hold down pricing, many low-cost retail systems based on microATX motherboards use non-Intel motherboards (albeit with Intel chipsets in most cases). But, even though many companies make PC-compatible motherboards for aftermarket upgrades or local computer assemblers, Intel still dominates the major vendor OEM market for midrange and high-end systems.

Intel Chipset Model Numbers

Starting with the 486 in 1989, Intel began a pattern of numbering its chipsets as shown in Table 4.12.

Table 4.12   Intel Chipset Model Numbers

Chipset Number	Processor Family	Chipset Number	Processor Family
420xx	P4 (486)	450xx	P6 server (Pentium Pro/PII/PIII Xeon)
430xx	P5 (Pentium)	E72xx	Xeon workstation with hub architecture
440xx	P6 (Pentium Pro/PII/PIII)	E75xx	Xeon server with hub architecture
8xx	P6/P7 (PII/PIII/P4) with hub architecture	460xx	Itanium processor
9xx	P7 (Pentium 4) with PCI-Express	E88xx	Itanium 2 processor with hub architecture

The chipset numbers listed here are abbreviations of the actual chipset numbers stamped on the individual chips. For example, one of the popular Pentium II/III chipsets was the Intel 440BX chipset, which consisted of two components: the 82443BX North Bridge and the 82371EB South Bridge. Likewise, the 865G chipset supports the Pentium 4 and consists of two main parts: the 82865G graphics memory controller hub (GMCH; replaces the North Bridge and includes integrated video) and an 82801EB or 82801EBR I/O controller hub (ICH5 or ICH5R; replaces the South Bridge). By reading the logo (Intel or others) as well as the part number and letter combinations on the larger chips on your motherboard, you can quickly identify the chipset your motherboard uses.

Intel has used two distinct chipset architectures: a North/South Bridge architecture and a newer hub architecture. All its more recent 800 and 900 series chipsets use the hub architecture.

Tip

In many cases, the North Bridge/GMCH/MCH chip on recent motherboards is covered up with a heatsink, and some motherboards also use a heatsink on the South Bridge or ICH chip. To determine the chipset used in these systems, watch for motherboard information displayed at system startup by some systems or use a third-party hardware reporting program such as SiSoftware Sandra (download from `http://www.sisoftware.co.uk/`).

AMD Athlon/Duron Chipsets

AMD took a gamble with its Athlon family of processors (Athlon, Athlon XP, Athlon MP, and Duron). With these processors, AMD decided for the first time to create a chip that was Intel compatible with regard to software but not directly hardware or pin compatible. Whereas the K6 series would plug into the same Socket 7 that Intel designed for the Pentium processor line, the AMD Athlon and Duron would not be pin compatible with the Pentium II/III and Celeron chips. This also meant that AMD could not take advantage of the previously existing chipsets and motherboards when the Athlon and Duron were introduced; instead, AMD would have to either create its own chipsets and motherboards or find other companies who would.

The gamble seems to have paid off. AMD bootstrapped the market by introducing its own chipset, referred to as the AMD-750 chipset (code named Irongate). The AMD 750 chipset consists of the 751 System Controller (North Bridge) and the 756 Peripheral Bus Controller (South Bridge). AMD followed with the AMD-760 chipset for the Athlon/Duron processors, which was the first major chipset on the market supporting DDR SDRAM for memory. It consists of two chips—the AMD-761 System Bus Controller (North Bridge) and the AMD-766 Peripheral Bus Controller (South Bridge). Similarly, AMD established a new standard chipset architecture for its line of 64-bit processors—the Athlon 64 and Opteron—by developing the AMD-8000 chipset. AMD's pioneering efforts have inspired other companies, such as VIA Technologies, NVIDIA, Ali, and SiS, to develop chipsets specifically designed for the Slot A and current Socket A, Socket 754, Socket 939, and Socket 940 processors from AMD. This has enabled the motherboard companies to make a variety of boards supporting these chips and the Athlon family of processors to take a fair amount of market share away from Intel in the process.

Traditional North/South Bridge Architecture

Most of Intel's earlier chipsets (and, until recently, virtually all non-Intel chipsets) are broken into a multitiered architecture incorporating what are referred to as North and South Bridge components, as well as a Super I/O chip:

- *The North Bridge.* So named because it is the connection between the high-speed processor bus (400/266/200/133/100/66MHz) and the slower AGP (533/266/133/66MHz) and PCI (33MHz) buses. The North Bridge is what the chipset is named after, meaning that, for example, what we call the 440BX chipset is derived from the fact that the actual North Bridge chip part number for that set is 82443BX.

- *The South Bridge.* So named because it is the bridge between the PCI bus (66/33MHz) and the even slower ISA bus (8MHz).

- *The Super I/O chip.* It's a separate chip attached to the ISA bus that is not really considered part of the chipset and often comes from a third party, such as National Semiconductor or Standard MicroSystems Corp. (SMSC). The Super I/O chip contains commonly used peripheral items all combined into a single chip. Note that most recent South Bridge chips now include Super I/O functions (such chips are known as Super-South Bridge chips), so that most recent motherboards no longer include a separate Super I/O chip.

▶▶   See "Super I/O Chips," p. 328.

Figure 4.30 shows a typical AMD Socket A motherboard using North/South Bridge architecture with the locations of all chips and components.

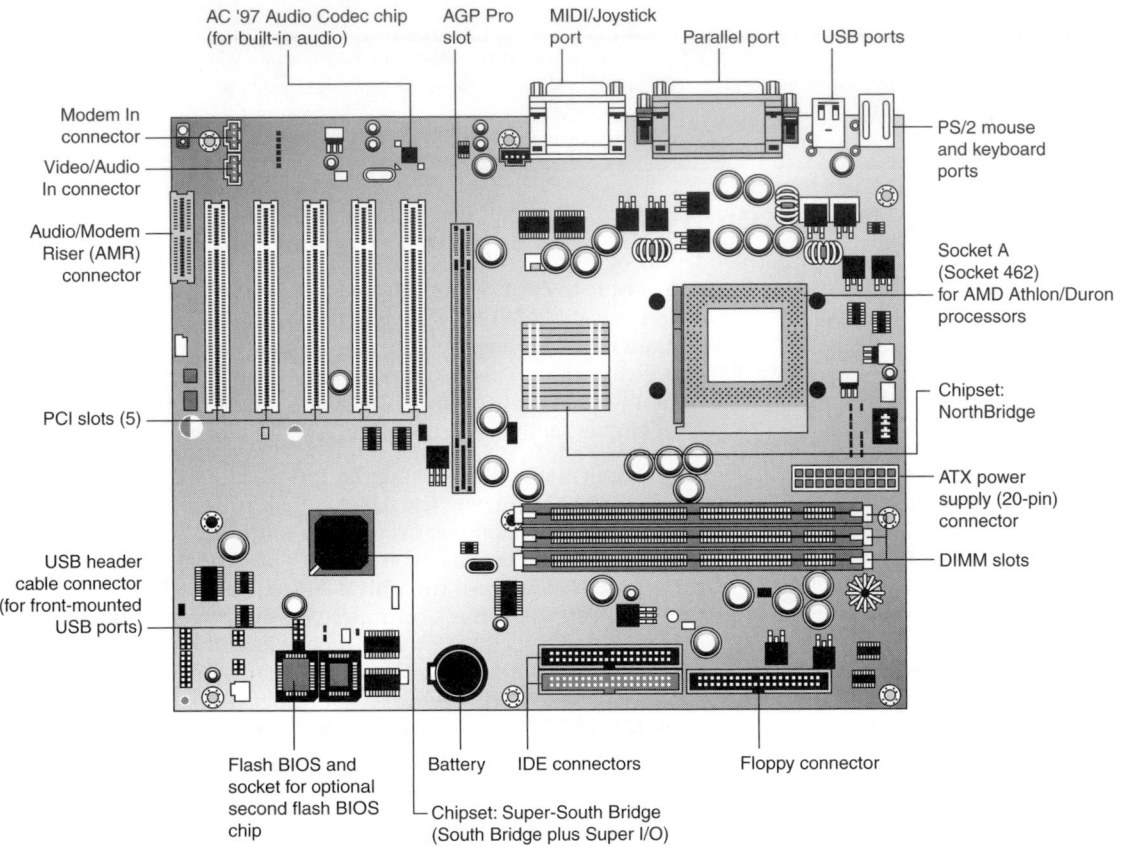

Modem In connector

Video/Audio In connector

Audio/Modem Riser (AMR) connector

PCI slots (5)

USB header cable connector (for front-mounted USB ports)

AC '97 Audio Codec chip (for built-in audio)

AGP Pro slot

MIDI/Joystick port

Parallel port

USB ports

PS/2 mouse and keyboard ports

Socket A (Socket 462) for AMD Athlon/Duron processors

Chipset: NorthBridge

ATX power supply (20-pin) connector

DIMM slots

Flash BIOS and socket for optional second flash BIOS chip

Battery

IDE connectors

Floppy connector

Chipset: Super-South Bridge (South Bridge plus Super I/O)

Figure 4.30 A typical Socket A (AMD Athlon/Duron) motherboard showing component locations.

The North Bridge is sometimes referred to as the PAC (PCI/AGP Controller). It is essentially the main component of the motherboard and is the only motherboard circuit besides the processor that normally runs at full motherboard (processor bus) speed. Most modern chipsets use a single-chip North Bridge; however, some of the older ones actually consisted of up to three individual chips to make up the complete North Bridge circuit.

The South Bridge is the lower-speed component in the chipset and has always been a single individual chip. The South Bridge is a somewhat interchangeable component in that different chipsets (North Bridge chips) often are designed to use the same South Bridge component. This modular design of the chipset allows for lower cost and greater flexibility for motherboard manufacturers. Similarly, many vendors produce several versions of pin-compatible South Bridge chips with different features to enable more flexible and lower-cost manufacturing and design. The South Bridge connects to the 33MHz PCI bus and contains the interface or bridge to the 8MHz ISA bus (if present). It also typically contains dual ATA/IDE hard disk controller interfaces, one or more USB interfaces, and in later designs even the CMOS RAM and real-time clock functions. In older designs, the South Bridge contained all the components that make up the ISA bus, including the interrupt and DMA controllers. The third motherboard component, the Super I/O chip, is connected to the 8MHz ISA bus or the low pin count (LPC) bus and contains all the standard peripherals that are built in to a motherboard. For example, most Super I/O chips contain the serial ports, parallel port, floppy controller, and keyboard/mouse interface. Optionally, they might contain the CMOS RAM/Clock, IDE controllers, and game port interface as well. Systems that integrate IEEE 1394 and SCSI ports use separate chips for these port types.

Most recent motherboards that use North/South Bridge chipset designs incorporate a Super-South Bridge, which incorporates the South Bridge and Super I/O functions into a single chip.

Hub Architecture

The newer 800 series chips from Intel use hub architectures in which the former North Bridge chip is now called a Memory Controller Hub (MCH) and the former South Bridge is called an I/O Controller Hub (ICH). Rather than connect them through the PCI bus as in a standard North/South Bridge design, they are connected via a dedicated hub interface that is twice as fast as PCI. The hub design offers several advantages over the conventional North/South Bridge design:

- *It's faster.* The hub interface used by the 8xx series is a 4X (quad-clocked) 66MHz 8-bit (4×66MHz×1 byte = 266MBps) interface, which has twice the throughput of PCI (33MHz×32 bits = 133MBps).

- *Reduced PCI loading.* The hub interface is independent of PCI and doesn't share or steal PCI bus bandwidth for chipset or Super I/O traffic. This improves performance of all other PCI bus–connected devices because the PCI bus is not involved in these transactions.

- *Reduced board wiring.* Although twice as fast as PCI, the accelerated hub interface (AHA) hub interface is only 8 bits wide and requires only 15 signals to be routed on the motherboard. By comparison, PCI requires no less than 64 signals be routed on the board, causing increased electromagnetic interference (EMI) generation, greater susceptibility to signal degradation and noise, and increased board manufacturing costs.

This hub interface design allows for a much greater throughput for PCI devices because there is no South Bridge chip (also carrying traffic from the Super I/O chip) hogging the PCI bus. Due to bypassing PCI, hub architecture also enables greater throughput for devices directly connected to the I/O Controller Hub (formerly the South Bridge), such as the higher-speed ATA-100, Serial ATA, and USB 2.0 interfaces.

The hub interface design is also very economical, being only 8 bits wide. Although this seems too narrow to be useful, there is a reason for the design. By making the interface only 8 bits wide, it uses only 15 signals, compared to the 64 signals required by the 32-bit-wide PCI bus interface used by North/South Bridge chip designs. The lower pin count means less circuit routing exists on the board, less signal noise and jitter occur, and the chips themselves have many fewer pins, making them smaller and more economical to produce.

Although it transfers only 8 bits at a time, the hub interface executes four transfers per cycle and cycles at 66MHz. This gives it an effective throughput of 4×66MHz×1 byte = 266MB per second (MBps). This is twice the bandwidth of PCI, which is 32 bits wide but runs only one transfer per 33MHz cycles for a total bandwidth of 133MBps. So, by virtue of a very narrow—but very fast—design, the hub interface achieves high performance with less cost and more signal integrity than with the previous North/South Bridge design.

The MCH interfaces between the high-speed processor bus (800/533/400/133/100/66MHz) and the hub interface (66MHz) and AGP bus (533/266/133/66MHz), whereas the ICH interfaces between the hub interface (66MHz) and the ATA (IDE) ports (66/100MHz), the SATA ports on the ICH5 (150MHz), and the PCI bus (33MHz).

The ICH also includes a new low-pin-count (LPC) bus, consisting basically of a stripped 4-bit wide version of PCI designed primarily to support the motherboard ROM BIOS and Super I/O chips. By using the same 4 signals for data, address, and command functions, only 9 other signals are necessary to implement the bus, for a total of only 13 signals. This dramatically reduces the number of traces connecting the ROM BIOS chip and Super I/O chips in a system as compared to the 98 ISA bus signals necessary for older North/South Bridge chipsets that used ISA as the interface to those devices. The LPC bus has a maximum bandwidth of 16.67MBps, which is much faster than ISA and more than enough to support devices such as ROM BIOS and Super I/O chips.

The 9xx series of chipsets uses a second-generation hub design with a new interconnect technology called direct media interface (DMI). DMI runs at 1GBps, or four times faster than the advanced hub architecture (AHA) used by most Intel 8xx-series chipsets or the updated hub interface 1.5 (HI 1.5) used by the 865/875 chipsets.

Figure 4.31 shows a typical Intel motherboard that uses bus architecture—the Intel D875PVZ, which supports the Intel Pentium 4 processor. Unlike some of Intel's less-expensive hub-based motherboards, the Intel D875PVZ's 875 chipset doesn't incorporate video.

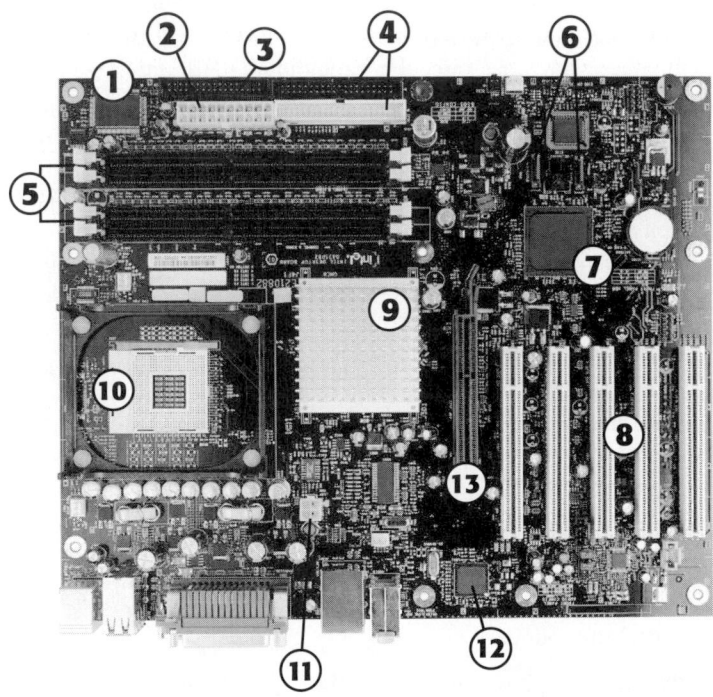

1. I/O Controller chip	8. PCI expansion slots (5)
2. ATX power supply connector	9. Chipset North Bridge
3. Floppy drive controller	10. Socket 478 for Pentium 4/Celeron
4. Primary/Secondary ATA/IDE host adapters	4 processor
5. DDR DIMM RAM banks	11. ATX12V power supply connector
6. SATA/SATA RAID host adapters (2)	12. Intel 82547 Gigabit LAN PLC chip
7. Intel ICH5-R (82801ER) I/O Controller	13. AGP 8x slot
Hub (includes SATA RAID)	

Figure 4.31 Intel's D875PVZ motherboard showing component locations and rear ports. *Illustration courtesy of Intel Corporation.*

High-Speed North-South Bridge Connections

As you learned in the previous section, Intel has developed a replacement for the traditional North Bridge/South Bridge architecture known as *hub architecture*. This 266MBps interface provides a faster connection between the memory controller hub/graphics memory controller hub (North Bridge replacements) and the I/O controller hub (South Bridge replacements) in Intel 8xx-series chipsets for the Pentium III and Pentium 4 processor families. The 9xx-series chipsets for the Pentium 4 processor have adopted a second-generation hub architecture that boosts the connection speed to 1GBps.

Intel is not alone in replacing the slow PCI bus connection between North and South Bridge–type chips with a faster architecture that bypasses the PCI bus. Other companies that have introduced high-speed chipset interconnects include

- *VIA.* VIA created the V-Link architecture to connect its North and South Bridge chips at speeds matching or exceeding Intel hub architecture. V-Link uses a dedicated 8-bit data bus and is currently implemented in three versions: 4x V-Link, 8x V-Link, and Ultra V-Link. 4x V-Link transfers data at 266MBps (4×66MHz), which is twice the speed of PCI and matches the speed of Intel's AHA and HI 1.5 hub architectures. 8x V-Link transfers data at 533MBps (4×133MHz), which is twice the speed of Intel's HI 1.5 hub architecture. Ultra V-Link transfers data at 1GBps, which is four times the speed of Intel's HI 1.5 hub architecture and equals the speed of Intel's new DMI hub architecture. All VIA South Bridge chips in the VT82xx series support V-Link. The first chipsets to use V-Link were VIA's 266-series chipsets for the Pentium III, Pentium 4, and Athlon processor families. VIA's newer chipsets also use V-Link.

- *SiS.* SiS's MuTIOL architecture provides performance comparable to VIA's 4x V-Link; the second-generation MuTIOL 1G provides performance comparable to VIA's Ultra V-Link or Intel's DMI architectures. Chipsets that support MuTIOL use separate address, DMA, input data, and output data buses for each I/O bus master. MuTIOL buffers and manages multiple upstream and downstream data transfers over a bidirectional 16-bit data bus. South Bridge chips in the SiS961 and 962 series support MuTIOL at a data transfer rate of 533MBps (4×133MHz), whereas the SiS963 and 964 series support the faster MuTIOL 1G, which supports data transfer rates exceeding 1GBps. The North Bridge chips that support MuTIOL are described in the sections listing SiS chipsets for Pentium 4 and Athlon-series processors.

- *ATI.* ATI uses a high-speed interconnect called A-Link in its 9100-series IGP integrated chipsets. A-Link runs at 266MBps, matching Intel's HI 1.5 hub architecture and first-generation V-Link and MuTIOL designs. An improved version called A-Link II is used by ATI's chipsets for the Athlon 64.

- *NVIDIA.* NVIDIA's nForce, nForce2, and nForce3 chipsets use the HyperTransport bus originally developed by AMD.

Table 4.13 compares the performance features and chipset support of major non-Intel high-speed chipset architectures.

Table 4.13   Non-Intel High-Speed Chipset Architectures

Vendor	Architecture (Performance)	Sample Chipsets	Desktop Processors Supported
ALi	HyperTransport (1.6GBps)	M1687	Athlon 64, Opteron
		M1685	
		M1683	Intel Pentium 4, Celeron
ATI	A-Link (266MBps)	9100 IGP series	Pentium 4, Celeron
	A-Link II	RS/RX480	Athlon 64
NVIDIA	HyperTransport (800MBps)	nForce, nForce2	Athlon, Athlon XP, Duron
SiS	MuTIOL 1G (1.2GBps)	SiS 656, 655, 648 series	
		SiS R659	
		SiS 661FX	Pentium 4, Celeron
		SiS 760, 756, 755 series	Athlon 64, Athlon 64 FX, Opteron
		SiS 748, 746, 741 series	Athlon XP, Duron
	MuTIOL (533MBps)	SiS 651, 650, 645 series	Pentium 4, Celeron
		SiS 740	Athlon XP, Duron

Table 4.13 Continued

Vendor	Architecture (Performance)	Sample Chipsets	Desktop Processors Supported
VIA	Ultra V-Link (1GBps)	PM880, PT880	Pentium 4, Celeron
		K8T800Pro	Athlon 64, Athlon 64 FX, Opteron
	8x V-Link (533MBps)	PT800, PM800, P4X533, P4X400, P4X333	Pentium 4, Celeron
		KT800, KT600, KM400, KT400 series	Athlon XP, Duron
		K8T800, K8M800	Athlon 64, Athlon 64 FX, Opteron
	4x V-Link (266MBps)	P4M266 series, P4X266 series	Pentium 4, Celeron
		KT333, KT266 series	Athlon, AthlonXP, Duron

1. The speed for the A-Link II was unknown at print time.

Let's examine the popular chipsets, starting with those used in 486 motherboards and working all the way through to the latest Pentium III/Celeron, Pentium 4, Athlon XP, and Athlon 64 chipsets.

Intel's Early 386/486 Chipsets

Intel's first real PC motherboard chipset was the 82350 chipset for the 386DX and 486 processors. This chipset was not very successful, mainly because the EISA bus was not very popular and many other manufacturers were making standard 386 and 486 motherboard chipsets at the time. The market changed very quickly, and Intel dropped the EISA bus support and introduced follow-up 486 chipsets that were much more successful.

Table 4.14 shows the Intel 486 chipsets.

Table 4.14 Intel 486 Motherboard Chipsets

Chipset	420TX	420EX	420ZX
Code name	Saturn	Aries	Saturn II
Date introduced	Nov. 1992	March 1994	March 1994
Processor	5V 486	5V/3.3V 486	5V/3.3V 486
Bus speed	Up to 33MHz	Up to 50MHz	Up to 33MHz
SMP (dual CPUs)	No	No	No
Memory types	FPM	FPM	FPM
Parity/ECC	Parity	Parity	Parity
Max. memory	128MB	128MB	160MB
L2 cache type	Async	Async	Async
PCI support	2.0	2.0	2.1
AGP support	No	No	No

AGP = Accelerated graphics port
FPM = Fast page mode
PCI = Peripheral component interconnect

SMP = Symmetric multiprocessing (dual processors)
Note: PCI 2.1 supports concurrent PCI operations.

The 420 series chipsets were the first to introduce the North/South Bridge design that is still used in many chipsets today.

Fifth-Generation (P5 Pentium Class) Chipsets

With the advent of the Pentium processor in March 1993, Intel also introduced its first Pentium chipset: the 430LX chipset (code named Mercury). This was the first Pentium chipset on the market and set the stage as Intel took this lead and ran with it. Other manufacturers took months to a year or more to get their Pentium chipsets out the door. Since the debut of its Pentium chipsets, Intel has dominated the chipset market. Table 4.15 shows the Intel Pentium motherboard chipsets. Note that none of these chipsets support AGP; Intel first added support for AGP in its chipsets for the Pentium II/Celeron processors.

Table 4.15   Intel Pentium Motherboard Chipsets (North Bridge)

Chipset	430LX	430NX	430FX	430MX	430HX	430VX	430TX
Code name	Mercury	Neptune	Triton	Mobile Triton	Triton II	Triton III	n/a
Date introduced	March 1993	March 1994	Jan. 1995	Oct. 1995	Feb. 1996	Feb. 1996	Feb. 1997
CPU bus speed	66MHz	66MHz	66MHz	66MHz	66MHz	66MHz	66MHz
CPUs supported	P60/66	P75+	P75+	P75+	P75+	P75+	P75+
SMP (dual CPUs)	No	Yes	No	No	Yes	No	No
Memory types	FPM	FPM	FPM/EDO	FPM/EDO	FPM/EDO	FPM/EDO/ SDRAM	FPM/EDO/ SDRAM
Parity/ECC	Parity	Parity	Neither	Neither	Both	Neither	Neither
Max. memory	192MB	512MB	128MB	128MB	512MB	128MB	256MB
Max. cacheable	192MB	512MB	64MB	64MB	512MB	64MB	64MB
L2 cache type	Async	Async	Async/ Pburst	Async/ Pburst	Async/ Pburst	Async/ Pburst	Async/ Pburst
PCI support	2.0	2.0	2.0	2.0	2.1	2.1	2.1
AGP support	No	No	No	No	No	No	No
South Bridge	SIO	SIO	PIIX	MPIIX	PIIX3	PIIX3	PIIX4

EDO = Extended data out
FPM = Fast page mode
PIIX = PCI ISA IDE Xcelerator

SDRAM = Synchronous dynamic RAM
SIO = System I/O
SMP = Symmetric multiprocessing (dual processors)

Note

PCI 2.1 supports concurrent PCI operations, enabling multiple PCI cards to perform transactions at the same time for greater speed.

Table 4.16 shows the Intel South Bridge chips used with Intel chipsets for Pentium processors. South Bridge chips are the second part of the modern Intel motherboard chipsets.

Table 4.16   Intel South Bridge Chips

Chip Name	SIO	PIIX	PIIX3	PIIX4	PIIX4E	ICH0	ICH
Part number	82378IB/ZB	82371FB	82371SB	82371AB	82371EB	82801AB	82801AA
IDE support	None	BMIDE	BMIDE	UDMA-33	UDMA-33	UDMA-33	UDMA-66
USB support	None	None	Yes	Yes	Yes	Yes	Yes
CMOS/clock	No	No	No	Yes	Yes	Yes	Yes
Power SMM/ACPI management	SMM	SMM	SMM	SMM	SMM/ACPI	SMM/ACPI	

ACPI = Advanced configuration and power interface
BMIDE = Bus master IDE (ATA)
ICH = I/O Controller Hub
IDE = Integrated Drive Electronics (AT attachment)
PIIX = PCI ISA IDE Xcelerator

SIO = System I/O
SMM = System management mode
UDMA = Ultra-DMA IDE (ATA)
USB = Universal serial bus

The Pentium chipsets listed in Tables 4.10 and 4.11 have been out of production for several years, and most computers that use these chipsets have been retired.

Intel 430LX (Mercury)

The 430LX was introduced in March 1993, concurrent with the introduction of the first Pentium processors. This chipset was used only with the original Pentiums, which came in 60MHz and 66MHz versions. These were 5V chips and were used on motherboards with Socket 4 processor sockets.

◄◄   See "Processor Socket and Slot Types," p. 88.

◄◄   See "First-Generation Pentium Processor," p. 128.

The 430LX chipset consisted of three total chips for the North Bridge portion. The main chip was the 82434LX system controller. This chip contained the processor-to-memory interface, cache controller, and PCI bus controller. There was also a pair of PCI bus interface accelerator chips, which were identical 82433LX chips.

The 430LX chipset was noted for the following:

■   Single processor

■   Support for up to 512KB of L2 cache

■   Support for up to 192MB of standard DRAM

This chipset died off along with the 5V 60/66MHz Pentium processors.

Intel 430NX (Neptune)

Introduced in March 1994, the 430NX was the first chipset designed to run the new 3.3V second-generation Pentium processor. These were noted by having Socket 5 processor sockets and an onboard 3.3V/3.5V voltage regulator for both the processor and chipset. This chipset was designed primarily for Pentiums with speeds from 75MHz to 133MHz, although it was used mostly with 75MHz–100MHz systems. Along with the lower-voltage processor, this chipset ran faster, cooler, and more reliably than the first-generation Pentium processor and the corresponding 5V chipsets.

◄◄   See "CPU Operating Voltages," p. 102.

◄◄   See "Second-Generation Pentium Processor," p. 129.

The 430NX chipset consisted of three chips for the North Bridge component. The primary chip was the 82434NX, which included the cache and main memory (DRAM) controller and the control interface to the PCI bus. The actual PCI data was managed by a pair of 82433NX chips called local bus accelerators. Together, these two chips, plus the main 82434NX chip, constituted the North Bridge.

The South Bridge used with the 430NX chipset was the 82378ZB System I/O (SIO) chip. This component connected to the PCI bus and generated the lower-speed ISA bus.

The 430NX chipset introduced the following improvements over the Mercury (430LX) chipset:

- Dual processor support
- Support for 512MB of system memory (up from 192MB for the LX Mercury chipset)

This chipset rapidly became the most popular chipset for the early 75MHz–100MHz systems, overshadowing the older 60MHz and 66MHz systems that used the 430LX chipset.

Intel 430FX (Triton)

The 430FX (Triton) chipset rapidly became popular after it was introduced in January 1995. This chipset is noted for being the first to support extended data out (EDO) memory, which subsequently became very popular. EDO was about 21% faster than the standard fast page mode (FPM) memory that had been used up until that time but cost no more than the slower FPM. Unfortunately, although it was known for faster memory support, the Triton chipset was also known as the first Pentium chipset without support for parity checking for memory. This was somewhat of a blow to PC reliability and fault tolerance, even though many did not know it at the time.

▶▶   See "Extended Data Out RAM," p. 468.

▶▶   See "Parity and ECC," p. 500.

The Triton chipset lacked parity support from the previous 430NX chipset, but it also supported only a single CPU. The 430FX was designed as a low-end chipset for home or non-mission-critical systems. As such, it did not replace the 430NX, which carried on in higher-end network fileservers and other more mission-critical systems.

The 430FX consisted of a three-chip North Bridge. The main chip was the 82437FX system controller that included the memory and cache controllers, CPU interface, and PCI bus controller, along with dual 82438FX data path chips for the PCI bus. The South Bridge was the first PIIX (PCI ISA IDE Xcelerator) chip that was a 82371FB. This chip not only acted as the bridge between the 33MHz PCI bus and the slower 8MHz ISA bus, but also incorporated for the first time a dual-channel IDE interface. By moving the IDE interface off the ISA bus and into the PIIX chip, it was now effectively connected to the PCI bus, enabling much faster Bus Master IDE transfers. This was key in supporting the ATA-2 or Enhanced IDE interface for better hard disk performance.

The major points on the 430FX are

- Support for EDO memory
- Support for higher speed—pipelined burst L2 cache
- PIIX South Bridge with high-speed Bus Master IDE

- Lack of support for parity-checked memory
- Only single CPU support
- Supported only 128MB of RAM, of which only 64MB could be cached

That last issue is one that many people are not aware of. The 430FX chipset can cache only up to 64MB of main memory. So, if you install more than 64MB of RAM in your system, performance suffers greatly. At the time, many didn't think this would be that much of a problem—after all, they didn't usually run enough software to load past the first 64MB anyway. That is another misunderstanding because Windows 9x and NT/2000 (as well as all other protected-mode operating systems including Linux and so on) load from the top down. So, for example, if you install 96MB of RAM (one 64MB and one 32MB bank), virtually all your software, including the main operating system, loads into the noncached region above 64MB. Needless to say, performance would suffer greatly. Try disabling the L2 cache via your CMOS Setup to see how slowly your system runs without it. That is the performance you can expect if you install more than 64MB of RAM in a 430FX-based system. Some thought this was a Windows limitation, but it is instead caused by the chipset design.

Intel 430HX (Triton II)

Intel created the Triton II 430HX chipset as a true replacement for the powerful 430NX chip. It added some of the high-speed memory features from the low-end 430FX, such as support for EDO memory and pipeline burst L2 cache. It also retained dual-processor support. In addition to supporting parity checking to detect memory errors, it added support for error correcting code (ECC) memory to detect and correct single bit errors on-the-fly. And the great thing was that this was implemented using plain parity memory.

The HX chipset's primary advantages over the FX are

- Symmetric multiprocessor (dual processor) support.
- Support for ECC and parity memory.
- 512MB maximum RAM support (versus 128MB).
- L2 cache functions over 512MB RAM versus 64MB (providing optional cache tag RAM is installed).
- Memory transfers in fewer cycles overall.
- PCI Level 2.1 compliance that allows concurrent PCI operations.
- PIIX3 supports different IDE/ATA transfer speed settings on a single channel.
- PIIX3 South Bridge component supports USB.

The memory problems with caching in the 430FX were corrected in the 430HX. This chipset allowed for the caching of the full 512MB of possible RAM as long as the correct amount of cache *tag* was installed. Tag is a small cache memory chip used to store the index to the data in the cache. Most 430HX systems shipped with a tag chip that could manage only 64MB of cached main memory, although you could optionally upgrade it to a larger capacity tag chip that would enable caching the full 512MB of RAM.

The 430HX chipset was a true one-chip North Bridge. It was also one of the first chips out in a ball-grid array (BGA) package, in which the chip leads are configured as balls on the bottom of the chip. This enabled a smaller chip package than the previous plastic quad flat pack (PQFP) packaging used on the older chips, and, because only one chip existed for the North Bridge, a very compact motherboard was possible. The South Bridge was the PIIX3 (82371SB) chip, which enabled independent timing of the dual IDE channels. Therefore, you could install two different speed devices on the same channel as master/slave and configure their transfer speeds independently. Previous PIIX chips allowed both devices on a single cable to work at the lowest common denominator speed supported by both. The PIIX3 also incorporated the USB for the first time on a PC motherboard. Unfortunately at the time, no devices were available to attach to USB, nor was there any operating systems or driver support for the bus. USB ports were a curiosity at the time, and nobody had a use for them.

▶▶ See "Universal Serial Bus," p. 983.

The 430HX supports the newer PCI 2.1 standard, which allowed for concurrent PCI operations and greater performance. Combined with the support for EDO and pipelined burst cache, this was perhaps the best Pentium chipset for the power user's system. It offered excellent performance, and with ECC memory it offered a truly reliable and stable system design.

The 430HX was the only modern Intel Pentium-class chipset to offer parity and error-corrected memory support. This made it the recommended Intel chipset at the time for mission-critical applications, such as fileservers, database servers, business systems, and so on.

Intel 430VX (Triton III)

The 430VX was designed to be a replacement for the low-end 430FX chipset; it was not a replacement for the higher-powered 430HX chipset. As such, the VX has only one significant technical advantage over the HX, but in almost all other respects it is more like the 430FX than the HX.

The VX has the following features:

- Support for 66MHz SDRAM
- No parity or ECC memory support
- Single processor only

- Supports only 128MB RAM
- Supports caching for only 64MB RAM

Most notable was the support for SDRAM, which was about 27% faster than the more popular EDO memory used at the time. Although the support for SDRAM was a nice bonus, the actual improvement in system speed derived from such memory was somewhat limited. This was because with a normal L1/L2 cache combination, the processor read from the caches 99% of the time. A combined miss (both L1 and L2 missing) happened only about 1% of the time while reading/writing memory. Thus with SDRAM, the system would be up to 27% faster, but only about 1% of the time. Therefore, the cache performance was actually far more important than main memory performance. See the section "How Cache Works" in Chapter 3, "Microprocessor Types and Specifications," for more information.

As with the 430FX, the VX has the limitation of being capable of caching only 64MB of main memory. Therefore, installing more than 64MB of memory actually slows down the system dramatically because none of the memory past that point can be cached. Because Windows loads from the top of memory down, installing any amount of memory greater than 64MB in a system using this chipset dramatically decreases performance.

The 430VX chipset was rapidly made obsolete in the market by the 430TX chipset that followed.

Intel 430TX

The 430TX was Intel's final Pentium chipset. It was designed not only to be used in desktop systems, but to replace the 430MX mobile Pentium chipset for laptop and notebook systems.

The 430TX had some refinements over the 430VX, but, unfortunately, it still lacked support for parity or ECC memory and retained the 64MB cacheable RAM limitation of the older FX and VX chipsets. The 430TX was not designed to replace the more powerful 430HX chipset, which still remained the chipset of choice for Pentium class mission-critical systems.

The TX chipset features include the following:

- 66MHz SDRAM support
- Cacheable memory still limited to 64MB
- Support for Ultra-ATA, or Ultra-DMA 33 (UDMA) IDE transfers

- Lower power consumption for mobile use
- No parity or ECC memory support
- Single processor only

▶▶ See "ATA/ATAPI-4," p. 539.

Third-Party (Non-Intel) P5 Pentium Class Chipsets

The development of non-Intel Pentium-class chipsets was spurred by AMD's development of its own equivalents to the Pentium processor—the K5 and K6 processor families. Although the K5 was not a successful processor, the K6 family was very successful in the low-cost (under $1,000) market and as an upgrade for Pentium systems. AMD's own chipsets aren't used as often as other third-party chipsets, but AMD's capability to support its own processors with timely chipset deliveries has helped make the K6 and its successors—the Athlon, Athlon XP, and Duron—into credible rivals for Intel's Pentium MMX and Pentium II/III/4/Celeron families and has spurred other vendors, such as VIA, Acer Laboratories, and SiS, to support AMD's processors. Major third-party chipsets for Pentium-class processors include

- AMD 640
- VIA Apollo VP1, VP2, VPX, VP3, MVP3, and MVP4

- ALi Aladdin 4, Aladdin 5, and Aladdin 7
- SiS SiS540, SiS530/5595, SiS5598, SiS5581, SiS5582, SiS5571, SiS5591, and SiS5592

Most computers that use these chipsets have been retired. For more detailed information about these chipsets, see *Upgrading and Repairing PCs, 14th Edition*, which is included on the disc packaged with this book.

Sixth-Generation (P6 Pentium Pro/II/III Class) Chipsets

Just as Intel clearly dominated the Pentium chipset world, it is also the leading vendor for chipsets supporting its P6 processor families. As discussed earlier, the biggest reason for this is that, since the Pentium first came out in 1993, Intel has been introducing new chipsets (and even complete ready-to-go motherboards) simultaneously with its new processors. This makes it hard for anybody else to catch up. Another problem for other chipset manufacturers is that they are required to license the CPU bus interface design before they can produce a matching chipset.

Note that because the Pentium Pro, Celeron, and Pentium II/III are essentially the same processor with different cache designs and minor internal revisions, the same chipset can be used for Socket 8 (Pentium Pro), Socket 370 (Celeron/Pentium III), and Slot 1 (Celeron/Pentium II/III) designs. Of course, the newer P6-class chipsets are optimized for the Socket 370 architecture and nobody is making any new designs for Socket 8 or Slot 1.

Table 4.17 shows the chipsets used on Pentium Pro motherboards.

Note

PCI 2.1 supports concurrent PCI operations.

Table 4.18   P6 Processor Chipsets Using North/South Bridge Architecture

Chipset	440FX	440LX	440EX
Code name	Natoma	None	None
Date introduced	May 1996	Aug. 1997	April 1998
Part numbers	82441FX, 82442FX	82443LX	82443EX
Bus speed	66MHz	66MHz	66MHz
Supported processors	Pentium II	Pentium II	Celeron
SMP (dual CPUs)	Yes	Yes	No
Memory types	FPM/EDO/BEDO	FPM/EDO/SDRAM	EDO/SDRAM
Parity/ECC	Both	Both	Neither
Maximum memory	1GB	1GB EDO/512MB SDRAM	256MB
Memory banks	4	4	2
PCI support	2.1	2.1	2.1
AGP support	No	AGP 2x	AGP 2x
South Bridge	82371SB (PIIX3)	82371AB (PIIX4)	82371EB (PIIX4E)

Table 4.17   Pentium Pro Motherboard Chipsets (North Bridge)

Chipset	450KX	450GX	440FX
Code name	Orion	Orion Server	Natoma
Workstation date introduced	Nov. 1995	Nov. 1995	May 1996
Bus speed	66MHz	66MHz	66MHz
SMP (dual CPUs)	Yes	Yes (up to 4)	Yes
Memory types	FPM	FPM	FPM/EDO/BEDO
Parity/ECC	Both	Both	Both
Maximum memory	1GB	1GB	1GB
L2 cache type	In CPU	In CPU	In CPU
Maximum cacheable	1GB	1GB	1GB
PCI support	2.0	2.0	2.1
AGP support	No	No	No
AGP speed	n/a	n/a	n/a
South Bridge	Various	Various	PIIX3

AGP = Accelerated graphics port
BEDO = Burst EDO
EDO = Extended data out
FPM = Fast page mode
Pburst = Pipeline burst (synchronous)

PCI = Peripheral component interconnect
PIIX = PCI ISA IDE Xcelerator
SDRAM = Synchronous dynamic RAM
SIO = System I/O
SMP = Symmetric multiprocessing (dual processors)

For the Celeron and Pentium II/III motherboards, Intel offers the chipsets in Table 4.18. 4xx series chipsets incorporate a North/South Bridge architecture, whereas 8xx series chipsets support the newer and faster hub architecture. P6/P7 (Pentium III/Celeron, Pentium 4, and Xeon) processor chipsets using hub architecture are shown in Table 4.19.

440BX	440GX	450NX	440ZX
None	None	None	None
April 1998	June 1998	June 1998	Nov. 1998
82443BX	82443GX	82451NX, 82452NX, 82453NX, 82454NX	82443ZX
66/100MHz	100MHz	100MHz	66/100MHz[1]
Pentium II/III, Celeron	Pentium II/III, Xeon	Pentium II/III, Xeon	Celeron, Pentium II/III
Yes	Yes	Yes, up to four	No
SDRAM	SDRAM	FPM/EDO	SDRAM
Both	Both	Both	Neither
1GB	2GB	8GB	256MB
4	4	4	2
2.1	2.1	2.1	2.1
AGP 2x	AGP 2x	No	AGP 2x
82371EB (PIIX4E)	82371EB (PIIX4E)	82371EB (PIIX4E)	82371EB (PIIX4E)

Table 4.19   P6 (Pentium III/Celeron) Processor Chipsets Using Hub Architecture

Chipset	810	810E	815[4]	815E[4]	815EP
Code name	Whitney	Whitney	Solano	Solano	Solano
Date introduced	April 1999	Sept. 1999	June 2000	June 2000	Nov. 2000
Part number	82810	82810E	82815	82815	82815EP
Bus speed	66/100MHz	66/100/ 133MHz	66/100/ 133MHz	66/100/ 133MHz	66/100/ 133MHz
Supported processors	Celeron, Pentium II/III	Celeron, Pentium II/III	Celeron, Pentium II/III	Celeron, Pentium II/III	Celeron, Pentium II/III
SMP (dual CPUs)	No	No	No	No	No
Memory types	EDO SDRAM	SDRAM	SDRAM	SDRAM	SDRAM
Memory speeds	PC100	PC100	PC133	PC133	PC133
Parity/ECC	Neither	Neither	Neither	Neither	Neither
Maximum memory	512MB	512MB	512MB	512MB	512MB
AGP slot	No	No	AGP 4x	AGP 4x	AGP 4x
Integrated video	AGP 2x[2]	AGP 2x[2]	AGP 2x[3]	AGP 2x[3]	No
South Bridge (ICH)	82801AA/ AB (ICH/ICH0)	82801AA (ICH)	82801AA (ICH)	82801BA (ICH2)	82801BA (ICH2)

1. *The 440ZX is available in a cheaper 440ZX-66 version that runs only at 66MHz.*
2. *These 810/815 chipsets have integral AGP 2x 3D video that is NOT upgradeable via an external AGP adapter.*
3. *The 815/815E chipsets have integral AGP 2x 3D video that IS upgradeable via an APG 4x slot.*
4. *The only difference between the 815 and 815E is in which I/O controller hub (South Bridge) is used.*
AGP = Accelerated graphics port

Note

Pentium Pro, Celeron, and Pentium II/III CPUs have their secondary caches integrated into the CPU package. Therefore, cache characteristics for these machines are not dependent on the chipset but are quite dependent on the processor instead.

Most Intel chipsets are designed as a two-part system, using a North Bridge (MCH or GMCH in hub-based designs) and a South Bridge (ICH in hub-based designs) component. Often the same South Bridge or ICH component can be used with several different North Bridge (MCH or GMCH) chipsets. Table 4.20 shows a list of all the Intel South Bridge components used with P6-class processors and their capabilities. The ICH2 is also used as part of some of the first seventh-generation (Pentium 4/Celeron 4) Intel chipsets.

The following sections examine the chipsets for P6 processors up through the Celeron and Pentium III.

820	820E	840	815P	815EG	815G
Camino	Camino	Carmel	Solano	Solano	Solano
Nov. 1999	June 2000	Oct. 1999	March 2001	Sept. 2001	Sept. 2001
82820	82820	82840	82815EP	82815G	82815G
66/100/ 133MHz	66/100/ 133MHz	66/100/ 133MHz	66/100/ 133MHz	66/100/ 133MHz	66/100/ 133MHz
Pentium II/III, Celeron	Pentium II/III, Celeron	Pentium III, Xeon	Celeron, Pentium III	Celeron, Pentium III	Celeron, Pentium III
Yes	Yes	Yes	No	No	No
RDRAM	RDRAM	RDRAM	SDRAM	SDRAM	SDRAM
PC800	PC800	PC800 dual-channel	PC100, PC133	PC66, PC100, PC133	PC66, PC100, PC133
Both	Both	Both	Neither	Neither	Neither
1GB	1GB	4GB	512MB	512MB	512MB
AGP 4x	AGP 4x	AGP 4x	AGP 4x	No	No
No	No	No	No	AGP 2x[2]	AGP 2x[2]
82801AA (ICH)	82801BA (ICH2)	82801AA (ICH)	82801AA/ AB (ICH/ICH0)	82801BA (ICH2)	82801AA/ AB (ICH/ICH0)

BEDO = Burst EDO
EDO = Extended data out
FPM = Fast page mode
ICH = I/O controller hub
Pburst = Pipeline burst (synchronous)

PCI = Peripheral component interconnect
PIIX = PCI ISA IDE Xcelerator
SDRAM = Synchronous dynamic RAM
SIO = System I/O
SMP = Symmetric multiprocessing (dual processors)

Table 4.20 Intel South Bridge—I/O Controller Hub Chips for P6

Chip Name	SIO	PIIX	PIIX3	PIIX4	PIIX4E	ICH0	ICH	ICH2
Part number	82378IB/ZB	82371FB	82371SB	82371AB	82371EB	82801AB	82801AA	82801BA
IDE support	None	BMIDE	BMIDE	UDMA-33	UDMA-33	UDMA-33	UDMA-66	UDMA-100
USB support	None	None	1C/2P	1C/2P	1C/2P	1C/2P	1C/2P	2C/4P
CMOS/clock	No	No	No	Yes	Yes	Yes	Yes	Yes
ISA support	Yes	Yes	Yes	Yes	Yes	No	No	No
LPC support	No	No	No	No	No	Yes	Yes	Yes
Power management	SMM	SMM	SMM	SMM	SMM/ACPI	SMM/ACPI	SMM/ACPI	SMM/ACPI

SIO = System I/O
PIIX = PCI ISA IDE (ATA) Xcelerator
ICH = I/O controller hub
USB = Universal serial bus
1C/2P = 1 controller, 2 ports
2C/4P = 2 controllers, 4 ports
IDE = Integrated Drive Electronics (ATA = AT attachment)

BMIDE = Bus master IDE (ATA)
UDMA = Ultra-DMA IDE (ATA)
ISA = Industry standard architecture bus
LPC = Low pin count bus
SMM = System management mode
ACPI = Advanced configuration and power interface

Intel 450KX/GX (Orion Workstation/Server)

The first chipsets to support the Pentium Pro were the 450KX and GX, both code named Orion. The 450KX was designed for networked or standalone workstations; the more powerful 450GX was designed for file-servers. The GX server chipset was particularly suited to the server role because it supports up to four Pentium Pro processors for symmetric multiprocessing (SMP) servers, up to 8GB of four-way interleaved memory with ECC or parity, and two bridged PCI buses. The 450KX is the workstation or standalone user version of Orion and as such it supports fewer processors (one or two) and less memory (1GB) than the GX. The 450GX and 450KX both have full support for ECC memory—a requirement for server and workstation use.

The 450GX and 450KX North Bridge comprises four individual chip components—an 82454KX/GX PCI bridge, an 82452KX/GX data path (DP), an 82453KX/GX data controller (DC), and an 82451KX/GX memory interface controller (MIC). Options for QFP or BGA packaging were available on the PCI Bridge and the DP. BGA uses less space on a board.

The 450's high reliability is obtained through ECC from the Pentium Pro processor data bus to memory. Reliability is also enhanced by parity protection on the processor bus, control bus, and all PCI signals. In addition, single-bit error correction is provided, thereby avoiding server downtime because of spurious memory errors caused by cosmic rays.

Until the introduction of the following 440FX chipset, these were used almost exclusively in fileservers. After the debut of the 440FX, the expensive Orion chips all but disappeared due to their complexity and high cost.

Intel 440FX (Natoma)

The first popular mainstream P6 (Pentium Pro or Pentium II) motherboard chipset was the 440FX, which was code named Natoma. Intel designed the 440FX to be a lower-cost and somewhat higher-performance replacement for the 450KX workstation chipset. It offered better memory performance through support of EDO memory, which the prior 450KX lacked.

The 440FX uses half the number of components that the previous Intel chipset used. It offers additional features, such as support for the PCI 2.1 (concurrent PCI) standard, support for USB, and reliability through ECC.

The concurrent PCI processing architecture maximizes system performance with simultaneous activity on the CPU, PCI, and ISA buses. Concurrent PCI provides increased bandwidth to better support 2D/3D graphics, video and audio, and processing for host-based applications. ECC memory support delivers improved reliability to business system users.

The main features of this chipset include

- Support for up to 1GB of EDO memory
- Full 1GB cacheability (based on the processor because the L2 cache and tag are in the CPU)
- Support for USB
- Support for Bus master IDE
- Support for full parity/ECC

The 440FX consists of a two-chip North Bridge. The main component is the 82441FX PCI Bridge and Memory controller, along with the 82442FX Data Bus accelerator for the PCI bus. This chipset uses the PIIX3 82371SB South Bridge chip that supports high-speed Bus Master DMA IDE interfaces and USB, and it acts as the bridge between the PCI and ISA buses.

Note that this was the first P6 chipset to support EDO memory, but it lacked support for the faster SDRAM. Also, the PIIX3 used with this chipset does not support the faster Ultra DMA IDE hard drives.

The 440FX was the chipset used on the first Pentium II motherboards, which have the same basic architecture as the Pentium Pro. The Pentium II was released several months before the chipset that was supposedly designed for it was ready, so early PII motherboards used the older 440FX chipset. This chipset was never designed with the Pentium II in mind, whereas the newer 440LX was optimized specifically to take advantage of the Pentium II architecture. For that reason, I normally recommended that people stay away from the original 440FX-based PII motherboards and wait for Pentium II systems that used the forthcoming 440LX chipset. When the new chipset was introduced, the 440FX was quickly superseded by the improved 440LX design.

Intel 440LX

The 440LX quickly took over in the marketplace after it debuted in August of 1997. This was the first chipset to really take full advantage of the Pentium II processor. Compared to the 440FX, the 440LX chipset offers several improvements:

- Support for the (then-new) AGP video card bus
- Support for 66MHz SDRAM memory
- Support for the Ultra DMA IDE interface
- Support for USB

The 440LX rapidly became the most popular chip for all new Pentium II systems from the end of 1997 through the beginning of 1998.

Intel 440EX

The 440EX was designed to be a low-cost, lower-performance alternative to the 440LX chipset. It was introduced in April 1998, along with the Intel Celeron processor. The 440EX lacks several features found in the more powerful 440LX, including dual processor and ECC or parity memory support. This chipset is basically designed for low-end 66MHz bus-based systems that use the Celeron processor. Note that boards with the 440EX also fully support a Pentium II but lack some of the features of the more powerful 440LX or 440BX chipsets.

The main things to note about the 440EX are listed here:

- Designed with a feature set tuned for the low-end PC market
- Primarily for the Intel Celeron processor
- Supports AGP
- Does not support ECC or parity memory
- Single processor support only

The 440EX consists of an 82443EX PCI AGP Controller (PAC) North Bridge component and the new 82371EB (PIIX4E) South Bridge chip.

Note

The original 266MHz and 300MHz Celeron processors used with the 440EX chipset provided very low performance because these processors lacked any onboard Level 2 cache memory. Starting with the 300MHz Celeron 300A, Celeron added 128KB of Level 2 cache to its SEP packaging; all Socket 370 Celerons also include Level 2 cache. You should consider upgrading to a faster Celeron CPU with Level 2 cache if your 440EX-based system uses one of the original Celeron processors.

Intel 440BX

The Intel 440BX chipset was introduced in April 1998 and was the first chipset to run the processor host bus (often called the front-side bus, or FSB) at 100MHz. The 440BX was designed specifically to support the faster Pentium II/III processors at 350MHz and higher. A mobile version of this chipset is the first Pentium II/III chipset for notebook or laptop systems.

The main change from the previous 440LX to the BX is that the 440BX chipset improves performance by increasing the bandwidth of the system bus from 66MHz to 100MHz. Because the chipset can run at either 66MHz or 100MHz, it allows one basic motherboard design to support all Pentium II/III processor speeds based on either the 66MHz or 100MHz processor bus.

Here are the Intel 440BX highlights:

- Support for 100MHz SDRAM (PC100); the now-common PC133 RAM can also be installed, but it will still run at just 100MHz
- Support for both 100MHz and 66MHz system and memory bus designs
- Support for up to 1GB of memory in up to four banks (four DIMMs)
- Support for ECC memory
- Support for ACPI
- The first chipset to support the Mobile Intel Pentium II processor

The Intel 440BX consists of a single North Bridge chip called the 82443BX Host Bridge/Controller, which is paired with a new 82371EB PCI-ISA/IDE Xcelerator (PIIX4E) South Bridge chip. The new South Bridge adds support for the ACPI specification version 1.0. Figure 4.32 shows a typical system block diagram using the 440BX.

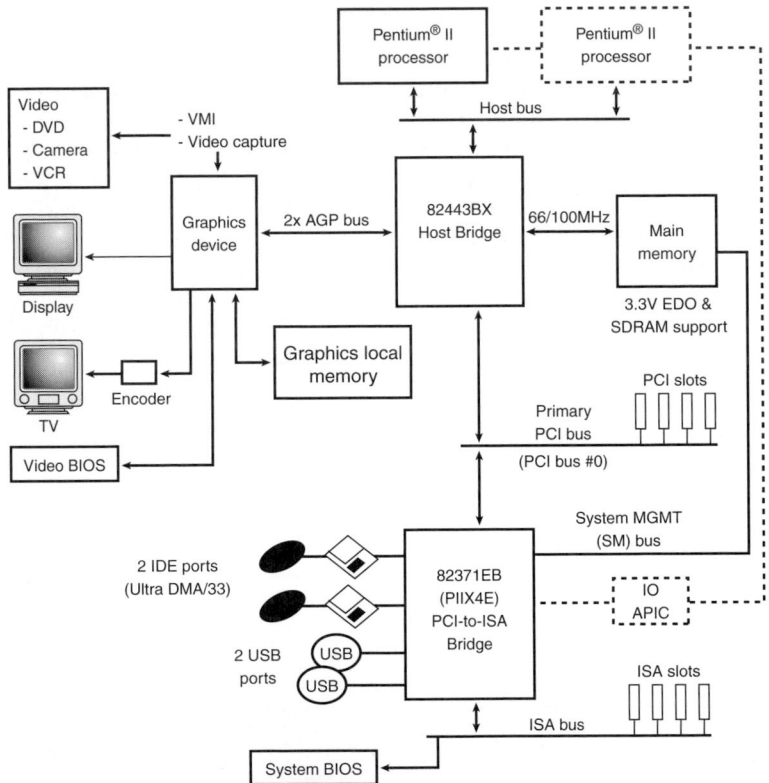

Figure 4.32 System block diagram using the Intel 440BX chipset.

The 440BX was a popular chipset during 1998 and into 1999. It offered superior performance and high reliability through the use of ECC, SDRAM, and DIMMs.

Intel 440ZX and 440ZX-66

The 440ZX was designed to be a low-cost version of the 440BX. The 440ZX brings 66MHz or 100MHz performance to entry-level Celerons (with or without Level 2 cache) and low-end Pentium II/III systems. The 440ZX is pin compatible with the more expensive 440BX, meaning existing 440BX motherboards can be easily redesigned to use this lower-cost chipset.

Note that two versions of the 440ZX are available: The standard one runs at 100MHz or 66MHz, and the 440ZX-66 runs only at the slower 66MHz.

The features of the 440ZX include the following:

- Support for Celeron and Pentium II/III processors at up to 100MHz bus speeds
- These main differences from the 440BX:
  - No parity or ECC memory support
  - Only two banks of memory (two DIMMs) supported
  - Maximum memory only 256MB

The 440ZX is not a replacement for the 440BX; instead, it was designed to be used in less expensive systems (such as those based on the microATX form factor), in which the greater memory capabilities, performance, and data integrity functions (ECC memory) of the 440BX are unnecessary.

Intel 440GX

The Intel 440GX AGP set is the first chipset optimized for high-volume midrange workstations and lower-cost servers. The 440GX is essentially a version of the 440BX that has been upgraded to support the Slot 2 (also called SC330) processor slot for the Pentium II/III Xeon processor. The 440GX can still be used in Slot 1 designs, as well. It also supports up to 2GB of memory, twice that of the 440BX. Other than these items, the 440GX is essentially the same as the 440BX. Because the 440GX is core compatible with the 440BX, motherboard manufacturers could quickly and easily modify their existing Slot 1 440BX board designs into Slot 1 or 2 440GX designs.

The main features of the 440GX include the following:

- Support for Slot 1 and Slot 2
- Support for 100MHz system bus
- Support for up to 2GB of SDRAM memory

This chipset allows for lower-cost, high-performance workstations and servers using the Slot 2–based Xeon processors.

Intel 450NX

The 450NX chipset is designed for multiprocessor systems and standard high-volume servers based on the Pentium II/III Xeon processor. The Intel 450NX chipset consists of four components: the 82454NX PCI Expander Bridge (PXB), 82451NX Memory and I/O Bridge Controller (MIOC), 82452NX RAS/CAS Generator (RCG), and 82453NX Data Path Multiplexor (MUX).

The 450NX supports up to four Pentium II/III Xeon processors at 100MHz. Two dedicated PCI Expander Bridges can be connected via the Expander Bus. Each PXB provides two independent 32-bit, 33MHz PCI buses, with an option to link the two buses into a single 64-bit, 33MHz bus.

Figure 4.33 shows a typical high-end server block diagram using the 450NX chipset.

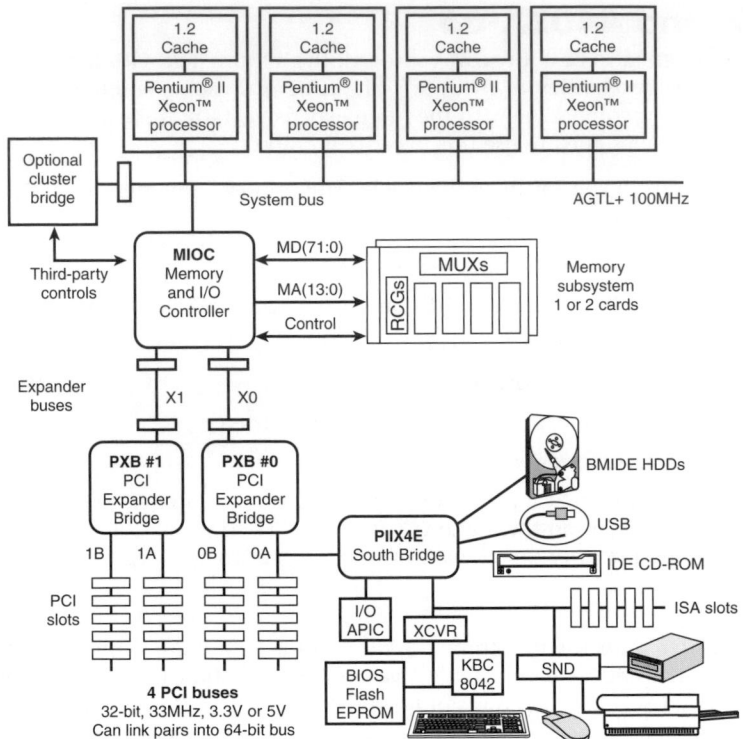

Figure 4.33 High-end server block diagram using the Intel 440NX chipset.

The 450NX supports one or two memory cards. Each card incorporates an RCG chip and two MUX chips, in addition to the memory DIMMs. Up to 8GB of memory is supported in total.

The primary features of the 450NX include the following:

- Slot 2 (SC330) processor bus interface at 100MHz
- Support for up to four-way processing
- Support for two dedicated PCI Expander Bridges
- Up to four 32-bit PCI buses or two 64-bit PCI buses

The 450NX chipset does not support AGP because high-end video is not an issue in network fileservers.

Intel 810, 810E, and 810E2

Introduced in April 1999, the Intel 810 chipset (code named Whitney) represents a major change in chipset design from the standard North and South Bridges that have been used since the 486 days. The 810 chipset allows for improvements in system performance, all for less cost and system complexity. The 810 (which supports 66MHz and 100MHz processor buses) was later revised as the 810E with support for the 133MHz processor bus.

Note

The 810E2 uses the same 82810E GMCH as the 810E but pairs it with the 82801BA I/O Controller Hub (ICH2) used by the Intel 815E. For information about the 82801BA ICH2 chip, see the section "Intel 815 Family," later in this chapter.

The major features of the 810E chipset include

- 66/100/133MHz system bus
- Integrated AGP 2x Intel 3D graphics
- Efficient use of system memory for graphics performance
- Optional 4MB of dedicated display cache video memory
- Digital Video Out port compatible with DVI specification for flat-panel displays
- Software MPEG-2 DVD playback with hardware motion compensation
- 266MBps hub interface

- Support for ATA-66
- Integrated Audio-Codec 97 (AC'97) controller
- Support for low-power sleep modes
- Random number generator (RNG)
- Integrated USB controller
- LPC bus for Super I/O and Firmware Hub (ROM BIOS) connection
- Elimination of ISA bus

The 810E chipset consists of three major components:

- *82810E Graphics Memory Controller Hub (GMCH)*. 421 BGA package (the original 810 chipset used the 82810 GMCH).
- *82801 Integrated Controller Hub (ICH)*. 241 BGA package.
- *82802 Firmware Hub (FWH)*. In either 32-pin plastic leaded chip carrier (PLCC) or 40-pin thin small outline package (TSOP) packages. Although a functional part of the chipset, this component is actually sold separately by Intel to motherboard developers.

Compared to the previous North/South Bridge designs, there are some fairly significant changes in the 810 chipset. The previous system designs had the North Bridge acting as the memory controller, talking to the South Bridge chip via the PCI bus. This new design has the GMCH taking the place of the North Bridge, which talks to the ICH via a 66MHz dedicated interface called the accelerated hub architecture (AHA) bus instead of the previously used PCI bus. In particular, implementing a direct connection between the North and South Bridges in this manner was key in implementing the new UDMA-66 high-speed IDE interface for hard disks, DVD drives, and other IDE devices.

Figure 4.34 shows a system block diagram for the 810E chipset. With the 810 chipset family, ISA is finally dead.

The 82810E GMCH uses an internal Direct AGP (integrated AGP) interface to create 2D and 3D effects and images. The video capability integrated into the 82810E chip features hardware motion compensation to improve software DVD video quality; it also features both analog and direct digital video out ports, which enable connections to either traditional TVs (via an external converter module) or a direct digital flat panel display. The GMCH chip also incorporates the System Manageability Bus, which enables networking equipment to monitor the 810 chipset platform. Using ACPI specifications, the system manageability function enables low-power sleep mode and conserves energy when the system is idle.

The 82801 I/O Controller Hub employs AHA for a direct connection from the GMCH chip. This is twice as fast (266MBps) as the previous North/South Bridge connections that used the PCI bus, and it uses far fewer pins for reduced electrical noise. Plus, the AHA bus is dedicated, meaning that no other devices will be on it. The AHA bus also incorporates optimized arbitration rules allowing more functions to run concurrently, enabling better video and audio performance.

The ICH also integrates dual IDE controllers, which run up to either 33MBps (UDMA-33 or Ultra-ATA/33) or 66MBps (UDMA-66 or Ultra-ATA/66). Note that two versions of the ICH chip exist. The 82801AA (ICH) incorporates the 66MBps-capable ATA/IDE and supports up to six PCI slots, whereas the 82801AB (ICH0) supports only 33MBps ATA/IDE maximum and supports up to four PCI slots.

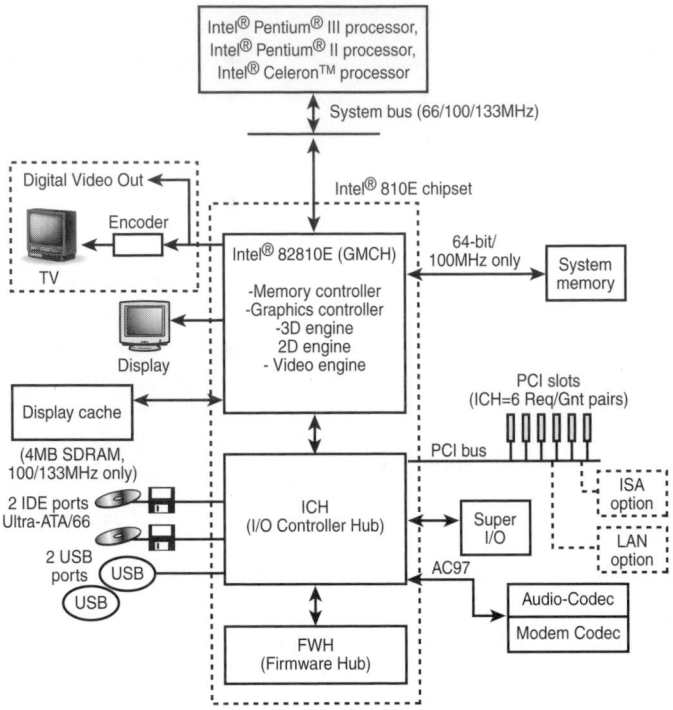

Figure 4.34 Intel 810E chipset system block diagram.

The ICH also integrates an interface to an Audio-Codec 97 (AC'97) controller, dual USB ports, and the PCI bus with up to four or six slots. The Integrated Audio-Codec 97 controller enables software audio and modem by using the processor to run sound and modem software via very simple digital-to-analog conversion circuits. Reusing existing system resources lowers the system cost by eliminating components.

The 82802 Firmware Hub (FWH) incorporates the system BIOS and video BIOS, eliminating a redundant nonvolatile memory component. The BIOS within the FWH is flash-type memory, so it can be field-updated at any time. In addition, the 82802 contains a hardware RNG. The RNG provides truly random numbers to enable fundamental security building blocks supporting stronger encryption, digital signing, and security protocols. Two versions of the FWH are available, called the 82802AB and 82802ACy. The AB version incorporates 512KB (4Mb) of Flash BIOS memory, and the AC version incorporates a full 1MB (8Mb) of BIOS ROM.

With the Intel 810 and 810E chipsets, Intel did something that many in the industry were afraid of: It integrated the video and graphics controller directly into the motherboard chipset with no means of upgrade. This means systems using the 810 chipset don't have an AGP slot and aren't capable of using conventional AGP video cards. For the low-end market for which this chipset is designed, lacking an AGP slot shouldn't be too much of a drawback. Higher-end systems, on the other hand, use the 815 or other chipsets that do support AGP slots. Intel calls the integrated interface Direct AGP, and it describes the direct connection between the memory and processor controllers with the video controller all within the same chip.

This means the video card as we know it will be reserved only for midrange and higher-end systems, as well as gaming-oriented systems. With the 810 as well as subsequent chipsets with integrated video, Intel has let it be known in a big way that it has entered the PC video business.

In fact, the theme with the 810 chipset is one of integration. The integrated video means no video cards are required; the integrated AC'97 interface means that conventional modems and sound cards are not required. Plus, there is an integrated CMOS/Clock chip (in the ICH), and even the BIOS is integrated in the FWH chip. All in all, the 810 should be taken as a sign for things to come in the PC industry, which means more integration, better overall performance for low-end and mainstream systems, and less overall cost.

Intel Random Number Generator

The 8xx chipset series features the Intel Random Number Generator (RNG). The RNG is built in to the 82802 FWH, which is the ROM BIOS component used on 8xx-based motherboards. The RNG provides software with true nondeterministic random numbers.

Most security routines, especially those providing authentication or encryption services, require random numbers for purposes such as key code generation. One method of cracking these types of codes is to predict the random numbers being used to generate the keys. Current methods that use system and user input as a seed to a conventional pseudorandom number generator have proven vulnerable to this type of attack. The Intel RNG uses thermal noise across a resistor contained in the FWH (that is, ROM BIOS in 8xx-based boards) to generate true nondeterministic, unpredictable random numbers. Therefore, "random" numbers generated by 8xx-series chipsets really are random.

Intel 815 Family

Introduced in June 2000, the 815 and 815E chipsets are mainstream PC chipsets with integral video that is also upgradeable via an AGP 4x slot. The *E* versions include the ICH2 I/O controller hub, which features two USB controllers (four ports) and ATA-100 support. The 815P and EP versions were introduced later and lacked the integrated video for lower cost. In September 2001, the last members of the family—the 815G and 815EG—were introduced. Note that the *G* indicates that these chipsets also include integrated video, which was superior to the video included with the original 815 and 815E.

The 815 chipsets are designed for Slot-1 or Socket-370 processors, such as the Celeron or Pentium III. These are the first chipsets from Intel designed to directly support PC133 SDRAM memory, allowing for a more affordable solution than other chipsets using RDRAM memory. Similar to the other 8xx series chipsets from Intel, the 815 uses hub architecture that provides a 266MBps connection between the main chipset components and does not share the PCI bus like the prior North/South Bridge designs.

Although six variations on the 815 chipset are available, only five different parts are used to create the various members of the family: one memory controller hub (82815EP MCH: North Bridge replacement without integrated graphics), two graphics memory controller hubs (82815 or 82815G GMCH: North Bridge replacement with integrated graphics), and two I/O controller hubs (ICH and ICH2). Table 4.21 shows how these parts are combined to create the various members of the family.

Table 4.21   815 Chipset Family Components

Chipset Name	82815 GMCH	82815G GMCH	82815EP MCH	82801AA ICH	82801BA ICH2
815	*			*	
815E	*				*
815EP			*		*
815P			*	*	
815G		*		*	
815EG		*			*

Figure 4.33 illustrates one member of this chipset family, the 815E.

All 815 chipsets support the following features:

- 66/100/133MHz system bus
- 266MBps hub interface
- ATA-100 (815E/EP/EG) or ATA-66 (815/P/G)
- PC100 or PC133 CL-2 SDRAM (also PC66 with 815G/EG)
- Up to 512MB RAM
- Integrated Audio-Codec 97 (AC'97) controller
- Low-power sleep modes
- RNG for stronger security products
- One (815/P/G) or two (815E/EP/EG) integrated USB controllers with either two or four ports, respectively
- LPC bus for Super I/O and Firmware Hub (ROM BIOS) connection
- Elimination of ISA Bus

The 815/E/G/EG also support the following:

- Integrated Intel AGP 2x 3D graphics
- Efficient use of system memory for graphics performance
- Optional 4MB of dedicated display cache video memory
- Digital Video Out port compatible with DVI specification for flat panel displays
- Software MPEG-2 DVD playback with hardware motion compensation

The 815E/EP/EG uses the ICH2, which is most notable for providing ATA-100 support, allowing 100MBps drive performance. Of course, few drives can really take advantage of this much throughput, but in any case, there won't be a bottleneck there. The other notable feature is having two USB 1.1 controllers and four ports on board. This allows double the USB performance by splitting up devices over the two ports and can allow up to four connections before a hub is required.

Integrated Ethernet

Another important feature of the 815 series is the integration of a fast Ethernet controller directly into the chipset. The integrated LAN controller works with one of three new physical layer components from Intel and enables three distinct solutions for computer manufacturers. These include

- Enhanced 10/100Mbps Ethernet with Alert on LAN technology
- Basic 10/100Mbps Ethernet
- 1Mbps HomePNA (phone-line) home networking

These physical layer components can be placed directly on the PC motherboard (additional chips) or installed via an adapter that plugs into the CNR slot. The CNR slot and cards enable PC assemblers to build network-ready systems for several markets.

AGP Inline Memory Module

Although the 815/815E feature is essentially the same built-in AGP 2x 3D video that comes with the 810 chipset, the difference is upgradeability. The video can easily be upgraded by adding a graphics performance accelerator (GPA) card (see Figure 4.35) or an AGP 4x card for maximum 3D graphics and video performance. The GPA card (also called the AGP Inline Memory Module, or AIMM) is essentially a high-performance video memory card that works in the AGP 4x slot and improves the performance of the integrated video by up to 30%. Unfortunately, these are not commonly sold and are somewhat expensive. For even more performance, you can install a full 4x AGP card in the AGP 4x slot, which disables the integrated video. By having the video integrated, very low-cost systems with reasonable video performance can be assembled. By later installing either the GPA or a full 4x AGP card, you can improve video performance up to 100% or more.

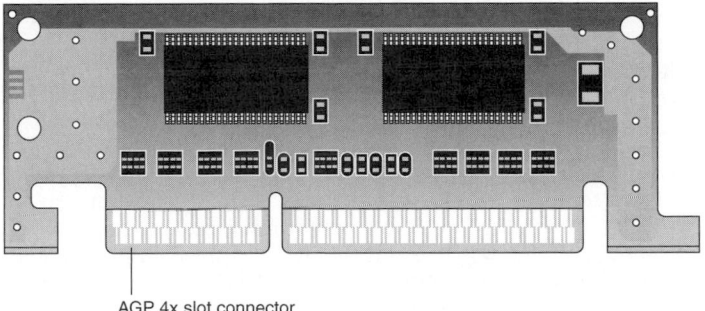

AGP 4x slot connector

Figure 4.35   A typical 4MB GPA/AIMM module, which attaches to the AGP slot of a motherboard using the 815 or 815E chipset.

PC133 Memory Support

Another important feature of the 815 chipset is the support of PC133 memory. The 815 family also uses PC100 memory. With PC133 support, Intel has also officially set a standard for PC133 memory that was higher than some of the PC133 memory on the market at the time of introduction. To meet the Intel PC133 specification, the memory must support what is called 2-2-2 timing, sometimes also known as CAS-2 (column address strobe) or CL-2 timing. The numbers refer to the number of clock cycles for the following functions to complete:

- *Precharge command to Active command.* Charges the memory's storage capacitors to prepare them for data

- *Active command to Read command.* Selects rows and columns in memory array for reading

- *Read command to Data Out.* Reads data from selected rows and columns for transmission

Some of the PC133 memory on the market takes three cycles for each of these functions and would therefore be termed PC133 3-3-3, CAS-3, or CL-3 memory. Note that the faster PC133 CL-2 can be used in place of the slower CL-3 variety, but not the other way around.

As a result of the tighter cycling timing, PC133 CL-2 offers a lead-off latency of only 30ns, instead of the 45ns required by PC133 CL-3. This results in a 34% improvement in initial access due to the decreased latency.

The 815 chipset was a popular chipset for the mainstream PC market that didn't want to pay the higher prices for RDRAM memory. The 815 was essentially designed to replace the venerable 440BX chipset.

Intel 820 and 820E

The Intel 820 chipsets use the hub-based architecture like all the 800 series chips and are designed to support slot 1 or socket 370 processors, such as the Pentium III and Celeron. The 820 chipset supports RDRAM memory technology, 133MHz system bus, and 4x AGP.

The 82820 MCH provides the processor, memory, and AGP interfaces. Two versions are available: One supports a single processor (82820), whereas the other supports two processors (82820DP). Either is designed to work with the same 82801 ICH as used with the other 800 series chipsets, such as the 810 and 840. The 820 chipset also uses the 82802 FWH for BIOS storage and for the Intel RNG.

The connection between the MCH and ICH uses what is called the Intel Hub Architecture bus instead of the PCI bus as with prior North/South Bridge chipsets. The hub architecture bus provides twice the bandwidth of PCI at 266MB per second, enabling twice as much data to flow between them. The hub architecture bus also has optimized arbitration rules, allowing more functions to run concurrently, as well as far fewer signal pins, reducing the likelihood of encountering or generating noise and signal errors.

The 820 chipset is designed to use RDRAM memory, which has a maximum throughput of up to 1.6GBps. The 820 supports PC600, PC700, and PC800 RDRAM, delivering up to 1.6GBps of theoretical memory bandwidth in the PC800 version. PC800 RDRAM is a 400MHz bus running double-clocked and transferring 16 bits (2 bytes) at a time (2×400MHz×2 bytes = 1.6GBps). Two RIMM sockets are available to support up to 1GB of total system memory.

The AGP interface in the 820 enables graphics controllers to access main memory at AGP 4x speed, which is about 1GB per second—twice that of previous AGP 2x platforms. Figure 4.36 shows the 820 chipset architecture. Because the 820 was designed for midrange to higher-end systems, it does not include integrated graphics, relying instead on the AGP 4x slot to contain a graphics card.

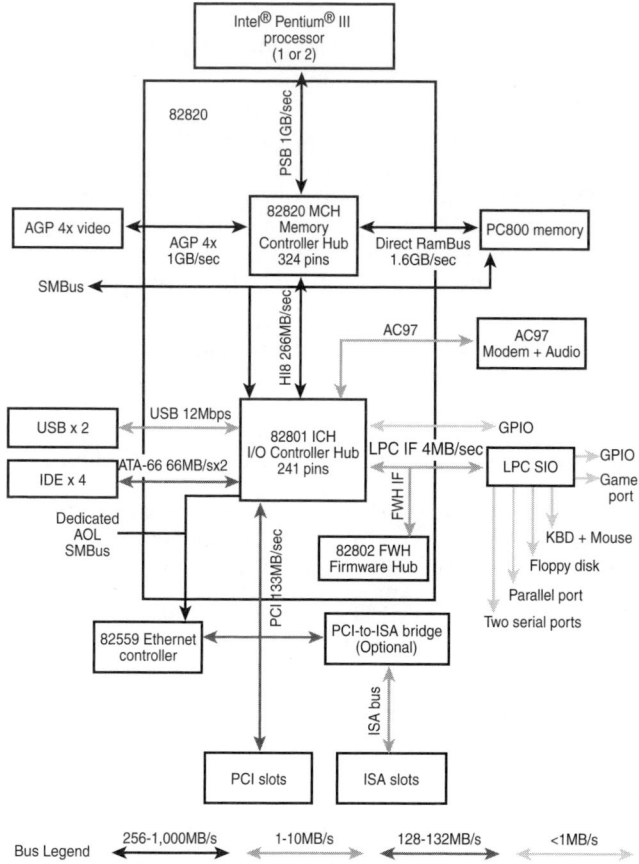

Figure 4.36 Intel 820 chipset architecture.

820 Chipset features include:

- 100/133MHz processor bus
- Intel 266MBps hub interface
- PC800 RDRAM RIMM memory support
- AGP 4x support
- ATA-100 (820E) or ATA-66 interface

- Intel RNG
- LPC interface
- AC'97 controller
- One (820) or two (820E) USB buses with either two or four ports, respectively

The 820 chipset consists of three main components with a few optional extras. The main component is the 82820 (single-processor) or 82820DP (dual-processor) MCH, which is a 324 BGA chip. That is paired with an 82801 ICH, which is a 241 BGA chip, and finally it has the 82802 FWH, which is really just a fancy Flash ROM BIOS chip. Optionally, there can be an 82380AB PCI-ISA bridge that is used only if the board is equipped with ISA slots.

The newer 820E version uses an updated 82801BA ICH2, which supports ATA-100 and incorporates dual USB controllers with two ports each, for a total of four USB ports.

820 Chipset MTH Bug

The 820 chipset is designed to support RDRAM memory directly. However, because the market still demanded lower-cost SDRAM, Intel created an RDRAM-to-SDRAM translator chip called the Memory Translator Hub (MTH). This enabled them to produce 820 chipset motherboards that supported SDRAM instead of the more expensive RDRAM.

Because the design of the MTH was proven defective, the chip (and any board using it) was simply discontinued. On May 10, 2000, Intel officially announced that it would replace any motherboards using the MTH with a new board lacking the component. The MTH translates signals from SDRAM memory to the Intel 820 chipset and is used only with motherboards utilizing SDRAM and the Intel 820 chipset; boards using RDRAM don't have an MTH and were not affected. Intel found electrical noise issues with the MTH that can cause some systems to intermittently reset, reboot, or hang. In addition, the noise issue can, under extreme conditions, potentially cause data corruption.

The MTH bug forced Intel to recall and replace more than a million motherboards in mid-2000, with new versions lacking the MTH and thus supporting only RDRAM memory. The final bill for this recall was reported at about $253 million, making it perhaps the most costly recall of computer components since the infamous Pentium math bug in 1994. I found it interesting that, due to the fact that Intel did more than $24.4 billion in sales the previous year, at least one article classified the cost of this recall as "chump change" to the chip giant!

Intel has an MTH I.D. Utility at www.intel.com/support/mth that will tell you whether you have that component and whether your board is eligible for replacement, including a 128MB RDRAM RIMM. Again, note that the 820 chipset was really designed to support RDRAM as the native type of memory, and RDRAM-based systems are not affected because they don't use the memory translator hub component.

Intel 840

The Intel 840 is a high-end chipset designed for use in high-performance multiprocessor systems using Slot 1, Slot 2 (Xeon processor), or Socket 370 processors. The 840 chipset uses the same hub architecture and modular design as the rest of the 800 family chipsets, with some additional components enabling more performance. See Figure 4.37 for a photo of the Intel 840 chipset.

As with the other 800 series chipsets, the 840 has three main components:

- *82840 Memory Controller Hub.* Provides graphics support for AGP 2x/4x, dual RDRAM memory channels, and multiple PCI bus segments for high-performance I/O.
- *82801 I/O Controller Hub.* Equivalent to the South Bridge in older chipset designs, except it connects directly to the MCH component via the high-speed Intel Hub Architecture bus. The ICH supports 32-bit PCI, IDE controllers, and dual USB ports.
- *82802 Firmware Hub.* Basically an enhanced Flash ROM chip that stores system BIOS and video BIOS, as well as an Intel RNG. The RNG provides truly random numbers to enable stronger encryption, digital signing, and security protocols.

Figure 4.37 Intel 840 chipset showing the 82840 (MCH), 82801 (ICH), 82802 (FWH), 82803 (MRH-R), 82804 (MRH-S), and 82806 (P64H) chips. *Photograph used by permission of Intel Corporation.*

In addition to the core components, parts are available for scaling up to a more powerful design. Three additional components can be added:

- *82806 64-bit PCI Controller Hub (P64H).* Supports 64-bit PCI slots at speeds of either 33MHz or 66MHz. The P64H connects directly to the MCH using Intel Hub Architecture, providing a dedicated path for high-performance I/O. This is the first implementation of the 66MHz 66-bit PCI on a PC motherboard chipset, allowing for a PCI bus four times faster than the standard 32-bit 33MHz version.

- *82803 RDRAM-based Memory Repeater Hub (MRH-R).* Converts each memory channel into two memory channels for expanded memory capacity.

- *82804 SDRAM-based Memory Repeater Hub (MRH-S).* Translates the RDRAM protocol into SDRAM-based signals for system memory flexibility. This would be used only in 840 systems that supported SDRAM.

Figure 4.38 shows the 840 chipset architecture.

840 chipset features include

- 100/133MHz processor bus

- Dual RDRAM memory channels, operating simultaneously and providing up to 3.2GBps memory bandwidth

- 16-bit wide implementation of Intel Hub Architecture (HI16), which enables high-performance concurrent PCI I/O with the optional P64H component

- AGP 4x

- Prefetch cache, unique to the 840 chipset, which enables highly efficient data flow and helps maximize system concurrency

■ Intel RNG (see the section "Intel Random Number Generator," earlier in this chapter)

■ USB support

Optionally, network interface and RAID controller interface chips can be added as well.

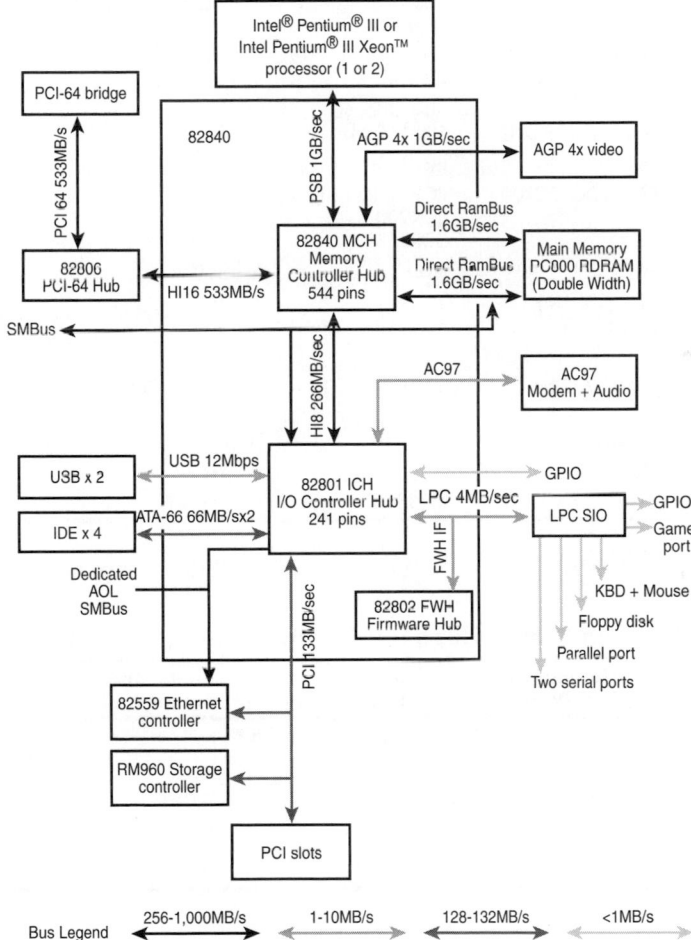

Figure 4.38   Intel 840 chipset architecture.

Third-Party (Non-Intel) P6-Class Chipsets

Several companies produce chipsets designed to support P6-class processors, including ALi Corporation (formerly known as Acer Laboratories), VIA Technologies, and SiS. The following sections discuss the offerings from these companies.

ALi Chipsets for P6-Class Processors

ALi has a variety of chipsets for the P6-class processors. Table 4.22 provides an overview of these chipsets.

Table 4.22 ALi Chipsets for Pentium Pro-II-III-Celeron

Chipset	Aladdin Pro II	Aladdin Pro 4	Aladdin TNT2	Aladdin Pro 5
Date introduced	1999	2000	1999	2000, 2001(T)
Part number	M1621	M1641/M1641B	M1631	M1651, M1651T
Bus speed	60, 66, 100MHz	100, 133, 200, 266MHZ (B)	66, 100, 133MHz	66, 100, 133, 200, 266MHz
Supported processors	Pentium II, Pentium Pro	Pentium II, III, Celeron	Pentium II, III, Celeron	Pentium II, III, Celeron (T version supports Tualatin)
Form factor	Slot 1, Socket 370	Slot 1, Socket 370	Slot 1, Socket 370	Slot 1, Socket 370
SMP (dual CPUs)	Yes	No	No	No
Memory types	FPM, EDO, PC100	PC100, PC133, DDR200, DDR266 (B)	PC66, 100, 133, EDO	PC66, PC100, PC133, DDR200, DDR266
Parity/ECC	ECC	ECC	ECC	Neither
Maximum memory	1GB (SDRAM), 2GB (EDO)	1.5GB	1.5GB	3GB
PCI support	2.2	2.2	2.2	2.2
PCI speed/ width	33MHz/32-bit	33MHz/32-bit	33MHz/32-bit	33MHz/32-bit
AGP slot	1x/2x	1x/2x/4x	No	1x/2x/4x
Integrated video	No	No	Yes—TnT2	No
South Bridge	M1533 or M1543	M1535D	M1543C	M1535D

Table 4.23 provides an overview of the features of the South Bridge chips used in these chipsets.

Table 4.23 ALi South Bridge Chips Used with P6-Class Chipsets

South Bridge Chip	Number of USB Ports	ATA Support	Integrated Sound	Integrated Super I/O
M1533	2	ATA-33	No	No
M1543	2	ATA-33	No	Yes
M1535D	4	ATA-66	Yes[1]	Yes
M1535D+	6[2]	ATA-100	Yes[3]	Yes
M1543C	3	ATA-66	No	Yes

1. *SoundBlaster 16 compatible with wavetable*

2. *Supports Legacy USB (mouse/keyboard)*

3. *3D PCI audio with Direct3D (DirectX) support, MIDI, SPDIF, SoundBlaster compatibility*

For more information about these chipsets, see *Upgrading and Repairing PCs, 14th Edition*, found in electronic form on the disc packaged with this book.

VIA Technologies Chipsets for P6-Class Processors

VIA Technologies has a variety of chipsets for the P6 processors. They are discussed in the following sections and Table 4.24.

Silicon Integrated Systems Chipsets for P6-Class Processors

Silicon Integrated Systems has a variety of chipsets for the P6-class processors. They are discussed in the following sections, and Table 4.26 provides a summary of them.

Table 4.24 VIA Technologies Chipsets for Pentium Pro-II-III-Celeron

Chipset	Apollo Pro	Apollo Pro Plus	Apollo PME133 (PM601)	ProSavage PM133	Apollo Pro133	Apollo Pro133A	Apollo Pro PL133T	Apollo Pro 266/266T
Part number	VT82C691	VT82C693	VT8601	VT8605	VT82C693A	VT82C694X	VT8605	VT8633
Bus speed	66, 100MHz	66, 100MHz	66, 100, 133MHz	66, 100, 133MHz	66, 100, 133MHz	66, 100, 133MHz	66, 100, 133MHz	66, 100, 133MHz
Supported processors	Pentium Pro, Pentium II, Celeron	Pentium II, Celeron	Pentium II, III, Celeron, VIA C3	Pentium II, III, Celeron, VIA C3	Pentium II, III, Celeron, VIA C3	Pentium II, III, Celeron, VIA C3	Pentium II, III, Celeron (Tualatin), VIA C3	Pentium III, Celeron (Tualatin), VIA C3
Form factor	Socket 8, Slot 1	Slot 1, Socket 370	Slot 1, Socket 370	Slot 1, Socket 370	Slot 1, Socket 370	Slot 1, Socket 370	Slot 1, Socket 370	Socket 370
SMP (dual CPUs)	No	No	No	No	No	Yes	No	No
Memory types	FP, EDO, PC66, 100 SDRAM	FP, EDO, PC66, 100 SDRAM	PC66, 100, 133 SDRAM	PC66, 100, 133 SDRAM	PC66, 100, 133 SDRAM	PC66, 100, 133 SDRAM, EDO	PC100, 133 SDRAM	PC100, 133 SDRAM, DDR200, 266
Parity/ECC	No	No	No	No	No	Yes	No	No
Maximum memory	1GB	1GB	1GB	1.5GB	1.5GB	4GB	1.5GB	4GB
PCI support	2.1	2.1	2.1	2.2	2.1	2.2	2.2	2.2
PCI speed/bit width	33MHz/32-bit	33MHz/32-bit	33MHz/32-bit	33MHz/32-bit	33MHz/32-bit	33MHz/32-bit	33MHz/32-bit	33MHz/32-bit
AGP slot	1x, 2x	1x, 2x	1x, 2x	2x, 4x	1x, 2x	2x, 4x	2x, 4x	2x, 4x
Integrated video	No	No	Yes[1]	Yes	No	No	Yes[2]	No
South Bridge	VT82C596 or VT82C586B	VT82C596A	VT82C686A	VT8231	VT82C596B or VT82C686A	VT82C596B or VT82C686A	VT8231	VT8233C[3]

1. *Trident Blade3D*

2. *S3 Savage 4 (3D) integrating Savage 2000 (2D)*

3. *Supports VIA 4x V-Link 266MHz high-speed interconnect between North Bridge and South Bridge*

Table 4.25 provides an overview of the features of the South Bridge chips used in these chipsets

Table 4.25 VIA South Bridge Chips Used with P6-Class Chipsets

South Bridge Chip	Number of USB Ports	ATA Support	Integrated Sound	Integrated Super I/O	Integrated 10/100 Ethernet	Supports V-Link
VT82C596	2	ATA-33	No	No	No	No
VT82C596A	2	ATA-33	No	No	No	No
VT82C686A	4	ATA-66	AC'97	Yes	No	No
VT82C586B	2	ATA-33	No	No	No	No
VT8231	4	ATA-100	AC'97	Yes	No	No
VT82C596B	4	ATA-66	AC'97	Yes	No	No
VT82C586A	No	ATA-33	No	No	No	No
VT8233(C)	6	ATA-100	AC'97	Yes	Yes*	Yes

*3Com 10/100 Ethernet on C version only

Seventh-Generation (Pentium 4) Chipsets

Because of its long-time integration of processor and chipset design, it's not surprising that Intel dominates the Pentium 4 chipset market as it has the markets for Pentium (P5) and Pentium II/III/Celeron (P6) markets in the past. Although Intel has licensed Socket 423 (used by early Pentium 4 processors) and the current Socket 478 to rival chipset vendors such as SiS, VIA, and ALi, Intel is still the leading developer of Pentium 4 chipsets. Third-party chipsets for Pentium 4 and Celeron 4 processors are discussed later in this chapter.

Because the Pentium 4 and Celeron processors using Socket 423 and those made for Socket 478 are essentially the same processors with different cache designs and minor internal revisions, the same chipset can be used for both processors.

Tables 4.27 and 4.28 show the 8xx-series chipsets made by Intel for Pentium 4 and Celeron 4 processors. These chipsets use Intel's hub architecture, providing an interconnect speed of 266MBps between the MCH/GMCH and the ICH chips.

Table 4.27 Pentium 4 8xx-Series Chipsets from Intel Introduced 2000–2002

Chipset	850	850E	845	845E
Code name	Tehama	Tehama-E	Brookdale	Brookdale-E
Date introduced	Nov. 2000	May 2002	Sept. 2001 (SDRAM); Jan. 2002 (DDR)	May 2002
Part number	82850	82850E	82845	82845E
Bus speeds	400MHz	400/533MHz	400MHz	400/533MHz
Supported processors	Pentium 4, Celeron[1]	Pentium 4, Celeron[2]	Pentium 4, Celeron[2]	Pentium 4, Celeron[2,4]
SMP (dual CPUs)	No	No	No	No
Memory types	RDRAM (PC800) dual-channel	RDRAM (PC800, 1066 dual-channel)	PC133 SDRAM, DDR 200/266 SDRAM	DDR 200/266 SDRAM
Parity/ECC	Both	Both	ECC	ECC
Maximum memory	2GB	2GB (PC800); 1.5GB (PC1066)	2GB (PC2100 DDR); 3GB (PC133 SDRAM)	2GB
Memory banks	2	2	2 (PC2100); 3 (PC133)	2
PCI support	2.2	2.2	2.2	2.2
PCI speed/width	33MHz/32-bit	33MHz/32-bit	33MHz/32-bit	33MHz/32-bit
AGP slot	AGP 4x (1.5V)	AGP 4x (1.5V)	AGP 4x (1.5V)	AGP 4x (1.5V)
Intearated video	No	No	No	No
South Bridge (hub)	ICH2	ICH2	ICH2	ICH4

1. Supports Socket 423 and Socket 478 processors.   2. Supports Socket 478 processors only.

Table 4.26   SiS 6xx-Series Chipsets for Pentium II/III/Celeron

Chipset	SiS620	SiS630	SiS630E	SiS630ET	SiS630S	SiS630ST
Bus speed	66, 100MHz	66, 100, 133MHz	66, 100, 133MHz	66, 100, 133MHz	66, 100, 133MHz	66, 100, 133MHz
Supported processors	Pentium II	Celeron, Pentium III	Celeron, Pentium III	Celeron, Pentium III, PIII Tualatin	Celeron, Pentium III	Celeron, Pentium III, PIII Tualatin
Form factor	Slot 1	Socket 370	Socket 370	Socket 370	Socket 370	Socket 370
SMP (dual CPUs)	No	No	No	No	No	No
Memory types	SDRAM PC66/100	SDRAM PC100/133	SDRAM PC100/133	SDRAM PC100/133	SDRAM PC100/133	SDRAM PC100/133
Parity/ECC	Neither	Neither	Neither	Neither	Neither	Neither
Maximum memory	1.5GB	3GB	3GB	3GB	3GB	3GB
PCI support	PCI 2.2	PCI 2.2	PCI 2.2	PCI 2.2	PCI 2.2	PCI 2.2
PCI speed/width	33MHz/ 32-bit	33MHz/ 32-bit	33MHz/ 32-bit	33MHz/ 32-bit	33MHz/ 32-bit	33MHz/ 32-bit
AGP slot	None	None	None	None	Yes	Yes
Integrated video	AGP 2.0	AGP 2.0	AGP 2.0	AGP 2.0	AGP 2.0	AGP 2.0
ATA support	ATA-33/66	ATA-33/66	ATA-33/66	ATA-33/ 66/100	ATA-33/ 66/100	ATA-33/ 66/100
USB support/ ports	USB 1.1/2 ports	USB 1.1/5 ports	USB 1.1/5 ports	USB 1.1/5 ports	USB 1.1/6 ports	USB 1.1/6 ports
10/100 Ethernet	No	Yes	Yes	Yes	Yes	Yes
Hardware audio	No	Yes	Yes	Yes	Yes	Yes
South Bridge chip	SiS 5595	No	No	No	No	No
SiS video bridge support	No	Yes	No	No	Yes	Yes

845GL	845G	845GE	845GV	845PE
Brookdale-GL	Brookdale-G	Brookdale-GE	Brookdale-GV	Brookdale-PE
July 2002	July 2002	Oct. 2002	Oct. 2002	Oct. 2002
82845GL	82845G	82845GE	82845GV	82845PE
400MHz	400/533MHz	400/533MHz	400/533MHz	400/533MHz
Pentium 4, Celeron[2]	Pentium 4, Celeron[2,3]	Pentium 4, Celeron[2,3]	Pentium 4, Celeron[2,4]	Pentium 4, Celeron[2,4]
No	No	No	No	No
PC133 SDRAM, DDR 200/ 266 SDRAM	PC133 SDRAM, DDR 200/ 266 SDRAM	DDR 333/266 SDRAM	DDR 200/266 SDRAM	DDR 333/266 SDRAM
Neither	ECC	Neither	Neither	Neither
2GB	2GB	2GB	2GB	2GB
2	2	2	2	2
2.2	2.2	2.2	2.2	2.2
33MHz/32-bit	33MHz/32-bit	33MHz/32-bit	33MHz/32-bit	33MHz/32-bit
None	AGP 4x (1.5V)	AGP 4x (1.5V)	None	AGP 4x (1.5V)
Intel Extreme Graphics 200MHz	Intel Extreme Graphics 200MHz	Intel Extreme Graphics 266MHz	Intel Extreme Graphics 200MHz	No
ICH4	ICH4	ICH4	ICH4	ICH4

3. Stepping B-1 supports HT Technology (hyper-threading).   *4. Supports HT Technology (hyper-threading).*

Table 4.28 Intel 8xx-Series Chipsets Introduced in 2003 for Pentium 4

Chipset	865P	865PE	865G	865GV	875
Codename	Springdale-P	Springdale-PE	Springdale-G	Springdale-GV	Canterwood
Date introduced	May '03	May '03	May '03	May '03	April '03
Part number	82865P	82865PE	82865G	82865GV	82875
Bus speeds	533/400MHz	800/533MHz	800/533MHz	800/533MHz	800/533MHz
Supported processors	Pentium 4, Celeron	Pentium 4, Celeron	Pentium 4, Celeron	Pentium 4, Celeron	Pentium 4, Celeron
SMP (dual CPUs)	No	No	No	No	No
Memory types	DDR266/333 dual-channel[2]	DDR333/400 dual-channel	DDR333/400 dual-channel	DDR333/400 dual-channel	DDR333/400 dual-channel
Parity/ECC	Neither	Neither	Neither	Neither	ECC
Maximum memory	4GB	4GB	4GB	4GB	4GB
Memory banks	2	2	2	2	2
PCI support	2.2	2.2	2.2	2.2	2.2
PCI speed/width	33MHz/32-bit	33MHz/32-bit	33MHz/32-bit	33MHz/32-bit	33MHz/32-bit
Video	AGP 8x	AGP 8x	AGP 8x	—	AGP 8x
Integrated video	No	No	Intel Extreme Graphics 2	Intel Extreme Graphics 2	No
Gigabit (GbE) Ethernet support*	Yes	Yes	Yes	Yes	Yes
South Bridge (hub)	ICH5/ICH5R	ICH5/ICH5R	ICH5/ICH5R	ICH5/ICH5R	ICH5/ICH5R

GbE connects directly to the MCH/GMCH chip, bypassing the PCI bus. It is implemented by the optional Intel 82547E1 Gigabit Connection chip.

Table 4.29 lists the ICH chips used by 8xx-series Pentium 4/Celeron 4 chipsets made by Intel.

Table 4.29 I/O Controller Hub Chips for Pentium 4 8xx-Series Chipsets

Chip Name	ICH0	ICH	ICH2	ICH4	ICH5	ICH5R
Part number	82801AB	82801AA	82801BA	82801DB	82801EB	82801ER
ATA support	UDMA-33	UDMA-66	UDMA-100	UDMA-100	UDMA-100	UDMA-100
SATA support	No	No	No	No	SATA-150	SATA-150
SATA RAID	No	No	No	No	No	RAID 0, RAID 1
USB support	1C/2P	1C/2P	2C/4P	3C/6P	4C/8P	4C/8P
USB 2.0	No	No	No	Yes	Yes	Yes
CMOS/clock	Yes	Yes	Yes	Yes	Yes	Yes
PCI support	2.2	2.2	2.2	2.2	2.3	2.3
ISA support	No	No	No	No	No	No
LPC support	Yes	Yes	Yes	Yes	Yes	Yes
Power management	SMM/ ACPI 1.0	SMM/ ACPI 1.0	SMM/ ACPI 1.0	SMM/ ACPI 2.0	SMM/ ACPI 2.0	SMM/ ACPI 2.0
10/100 Ethernet	No	No	No	Yes	Yes	Yes

ICH = I/O controller hub
USB = Universal serial bus
xC/xP = number of controller /number of ports
ATA = AT attachment (IDE)
UDMA = Ultra-DMA ATA

ISA = Industry-standard architecture bus
LPC = Low pin count bus
SMM = System management mode
ACPI = Advanced configuration and power interface

Starting in mid-2004, Intel introduced a new 9xx series of chipset for the Pentium 4 and Celeron 4. These chipsets, codenamed Grantsdale and Alderwood before their introduction, are optimized for the Pentium 4 Prescott design introduced in early 2004. They are the first Intel chipsets to support several new technologies, including DDR-II memory and PCI-Express for both video and other high-speed I/O uses (such as Gigabit Ethernet). They also include support for the new Socket 775—the first LGA processor socket (also known as Socket-T).

Because of the greater performance needed to support these high-speed technologies, the 9xx-series chipsets use a faster version of the HI 1.5 hub architecture used by the 8xx-series chipsets. The new interconnect design, known as Direct Media Interface (DMI), runs at 1GBps in each direction, making it comparable to the latest non-Intel interconnects listed in Table 4.13. Table 4.30 lists the 9xx-series chipsets introduced in 2004, and Table 4.31 lists the ICH6 family of I/O controller hub chips used with these chipsets.

Table 4.30   Intel 9xx-Series Chipsets for Pentium 4 Introduced in 2004

Chipset	915P	915G	915GV	915GL	925X
Code name	Grantsdale-P	Grantsdale-G	Grantsdale-GV	Grantsdale-GL	Alderwood
Part number	828915P	828915G	828915GV	828915GL	82925X
Bus speeds	800/533MHz	800/533MHz	800/533MHz	533MHz	800/533MHz
Supported processors	Pentium 4, Celeron	Pentium 4, Celeron	Pentium 4, Celeron	Pentium 4, Celeron	Pentium 4, Celeron
SMP (dual CPUs)	No	No	No	No	No
Memory types	DDR333/400 dual-channel, DDR-II	DDR333/400 dual-channel, DDR-II	DDR333/400 dual-channel, DDR-II	DDR333/400 dual-channel	DDR-II
Parity/ECC	Neither	Neither	Neither	Neither	ECC*
Maximum memory	4GB	4GB	4GB	4GB	4GB
Memory banks	2	2	2	2	2
PCI support	PCI-Express x1, x16, PCI 2.2	PCI-Express x1, x16, PCI 2.2	PCI-Express x1, PCI 2.2	PCI-Express x1, PCI 2.2	PCI-Express x1, x16, PCI 2.2
PCI speed/width	33MHz/32-bit	33MHz/32-bit	33MHz/32-bit	33MHz/32-bit	33MHz/32-bit
PCI-Express x16 video	Yes	Yes	No	No	Yes
AGP slot	No	No	No	No	No
Integrated video	No	Extreme Graphics 3	Extreme Graphics 3	Extreme Graphics 3	No
South Bridge (hub)	ICH6 family	ICH6 family	ICH6 family	ICH6 family	ICH6 family

B-2 stepping and above are required for ECC support.
915GL does not support HT Technology.

Table 4.31   I/O Controller Hub Chips for Pentium 4 9xx-Series Chipsets

Chip Name	ICH6	ICH6R	ICH6W
ATA support*	UDMA-100	UDMA-100	UDMA-100
SATA-150 support	Four drives	Four drives	Four drives
SATA RAID	No	0, 1, 0+1	No
USB support	4C/8P	4C/8P	4C/8P
USB 2.0	Yes	Yes	Yes
CMOS/clock	Yes	Yes	Yes
PCI Support	2.3, PCI-Express	2.3, PCI-Express	2.3, PCI-Express
ISA support	No	No	No
LPC support	Yes	Yes	Yes
Power management	SMM/ACPI 1.0	SMM/ACPI 1.0	SMM/ACPI 1.0
10/100 Ethernet	Yes	Yes	Yes
Integrated WAP	No	No	802.11a/b/g
High-definition audio (Dolby Pro Logic IIx-compatible 7.1-channel)	Yes	Yes	Yes

ICH = I/O controller hub
USB = Universal serial bus
xC/xP = number of USB controllers /number of ports
ATA = AT attachment (IDE)
UDMA = Ultra-DMA ATA
ISA = Industry-standard architecture bus

LPC = Low pin count bus
SMM = System management mode
ACPI = Advanced configuration and power interface
* One ATA port supporting two ATA/IDE drives
WAP = Wireless access point

Intel 850 Family

The Intel 850 family contains two members, the original 850 and an enhanced version called the 850E. The 850 is the first chipset for the Intel Pentium 4 processor and thus is also the first chipset to support the NetBurst microarchitecture. The 850 is designed for high-performance desktop computers and workstations and uses the same hub architecture and modular design as the rest of Intel's 8xx family of chipsets. See Figure 4.39 for a photo of the Intel 850 chipset.

The 850 has two main components, down from three in earlier 800-series chipsets:

- *82850 Memory Controller Hub.* Provides support for dual 400MHz RDRAM memory channels with a 3.2GBps bandwidth and a 100MHz system bus. The 82850 MCH also supports 1.5V AGP 4x video cards at a bandwidth exceeding 1GBps.

- *82801BA I/O Controller Hub 2.* The ICH2 (an enhanced version of the 82801 used by other 800-series chipsets) supports 32-bit PCI rev. 2.2, dual UDMA 33/66/100 IDE host adapters, four USB ports, an integrated LAN controller, six-channel AC'97 audio/modem codec, FWH interface support, SMBus support, and Alert on LAN and Alert on LAN 2 support.

Optionally, the Intel 82562ET/82562EM Platform LAN communication chips can be added to the 850 chipset to provide support for 10BASE-T and Fast Ethernet networking, building on the LAN features in the 82801BA ICH2 chip.

The 850 chipset, similar to most recent Intel and non-Intel chipsets, also supports the CNR card for integrated audio, modem, and network capabilities. See Figure 4.40 for a diagram of the 850's chipset architecture.

Figure 4.39 The Intel 850 chipset. *Photo used by permission of Intel Corporation.*

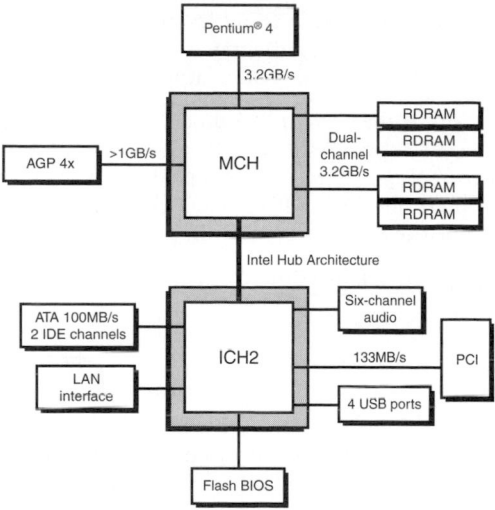

Figure 4.40 Architecture of the Intel 850 chipset.

The 850E is an enhanced version of the 850. Its 82850E MCH adds support for dual 533MHz Rambus RDRAM memory channels and support for PC1066 RIMM modules to the 850's standard features. It also uses the same ICH2 hub as the original 850.

Intel 845 Family

Unlike the 850 and 850E chipsets, the 845 family of chipsets is widely used by both Intel and third-party motherboard makers. If you purchased a Pentium 4 system from late 2001 through mid-2003, it probably uses some version of the 845 chipset. The 845, code named Brookdale during its development, was the first Pentium 4 chipset from Intel to support low-cost SDRAM instead of expensive RDRAM. Subsequent variations support DDR SDRAM at speeds up to DDR333, ATA/100, and USB 2.0.

The 845-series chipsets include the following models:

- 845
- 845GV
- 845GE
- 845PE
- 845GL
- 845G
- 845E

All members of the 845 family use the same hub-based architecture developed for the 845 family, but they also have onboard audio and support the communications and networking riser (CNR) card for integrated modem and 10/100 Ethernet networking. However, they differ in their support for different types and amounts of memory, integrated graphics, external AGP support, and which ICH chip they use.

Although the original version of the 845 supported only PC133 SDRAM memory, the so-called 845D model (a designation used by review sites but not by Intel) also supports 200/266MHz DDR SDDRAM. The Intel 845's 82845 MCH supports Socket 478–based Celeron or Pentium 4 processors and can support up to two DDR SDRAM modules or three standard SDRAM modules (depending on the motherboard). When DDR SDRAM is used, the 845 supports either 200MHz (PC2100) or 266MHz (PC2700) memory speeds, with an FSB speed of 400MHz. The 845 also supports ECC error correction when parity-checked memory modules are used and offers an AGP 4x video slot, but it has no onboard video.

The 845 uses the same ICH2 I/O controller hub chip (82801-BA) used by the Intel 850 and 850E chipsets in Rambus-based systems and the 815EP in low-cost SDRAM-based systems. The ICH2 supports ATA/100 hard disk interfacing, basic AC'97 sound, and four USB 1.1 ports.

All G-series 845 models feature Intel Extreme Graphics integrated video, which has faster core speeds and adds 3D performance to the bare-bones integrated video used by the 810 and 815 chipset families. Two chipsets—the 845G and 845GE—also offer support for AGP 4x video cards.

The 845E is an updated version of the current 845 model with ECC error correction and support for 533MHz FSB, whereas the 845PE supports the 533MHz FSB, DDR 266, and 333MHz memory, but it doesn't support ECC error correction. All models except the 845 (845D) use the enhanced ICH4 I/O Controller Hub 82801DB, which offers six USB 2.0 ports as well as integrated networking. Additionally, all models except the 845 and 845GL offer enhanced 20-bit audio.

Figure 4.41 compares the system block diagrams of the 845 and 845GE models.

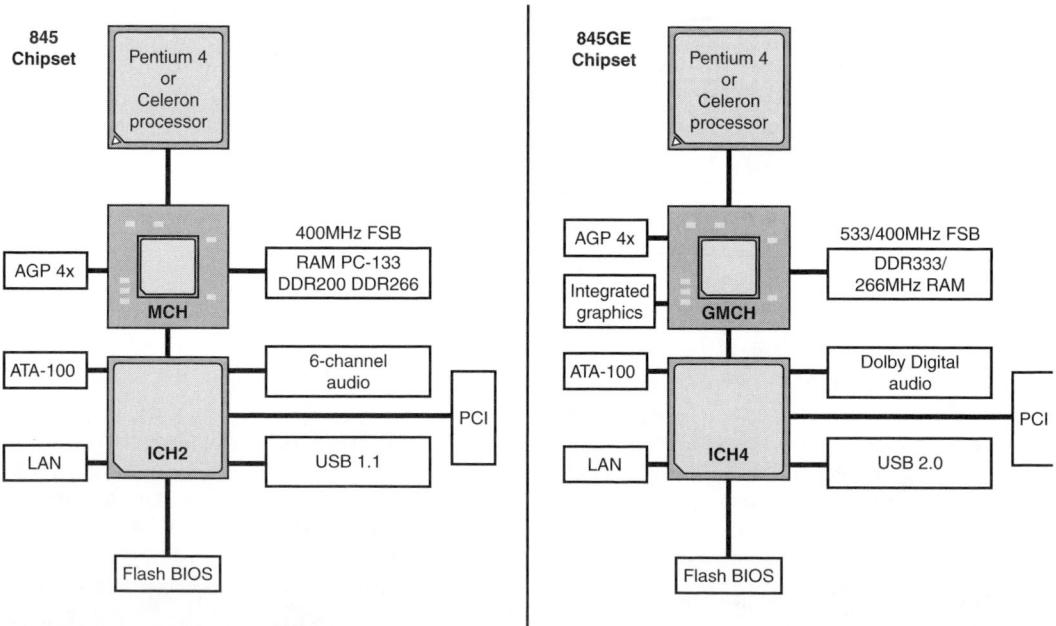

Figure 4.41   The 845GE (right) adds support for faster FSB speeds, memory, integrated graphics, and USB 2.0 to the basic 845 chipset architecture (left).

Intel Extreme Graphics Architecture

845-series chipsets with integrated video (845G-series models) support Intel's new Extreme Graphics Architecture, which supports 3D graphics and features the following four technologies to improve 3D rendering speed and quality:

- *Rapid Pixel and Texel Rendering Engine.* Uses pipelines to overlap 2D and 3D operations, provides 8x data compression to improve the use of memory bandwidth, and features a multitier cache for 3D operations

- *Zone Rendering.* Reduces memory bandwidth requirements by dividing the frame buffer into rectangular zones, sorting the triangles into memory by zone, and processing each zone to memory

- *Dynamic Video Memory Technology.* Manages memory sharing between the display, applications, and operating system depending on the memory requirements of the programs running

- *Intelligent Memory Management.* Improves memory addressing, display buffer implementation, and memory efficiency

Extreme Graphics Architecture improves 3D rendering compared to Intel's earlier integrated video chipsets (the 810 and 815-series chipsets, which have no 3D functions at all), but its performance and features still lag behind even current midrange video chipsets from NVIDIA and ATI. Extreme Graphics Architecture lacks hardware Transform and Lighting (T&L) features. T&L is a feature required by virtually all current games that support DirectX 7.0 and above. It offers frame rates which, at best, are at about the level of the now-obsolete NVIDIA GeForce 2 MX 200. Thus, even though you can play an occasional game with the G-series systems with integrated video, if you want serious game play, you'll need one of the 845 models that supports AGP 4x graphics cards and DDR333 memory, such as the 845GE or 845PE.

Intel 865 Family

The Intel 865 chipset family, code named Springdale, was released in May 2003. As the name might suggest, the 865 series is designed to replace the 845 series with chipsets that feature dual-channel memory support, the new communications streaming architecture (CSA) that provides a dedicated connection for the integrated network controller, faster performance, and support for the latest technologies (including optional Gigabit Ethernet and Serial ATA). The features of the 865 and 875 families are summarized in Table 4.28.

The 865 family includes the 865P, 865PE, 865G, and 865GV chipsets. The 865PE, 865G, and 865GV support single-channel or dual-channel DDR266, as well as dual-channel DDR333 and DDR400 SDRAM with FSB speeds up to 800MHz. Dual-channel memory provides a wider memory bandwidth for faster performance. The 865P model supports DDR266/333 and FSB speeds up to 533MHz. All models except the GV support AGP 8x, and the G and GV models include Intel Extreme Graphics 2— a faster version of the integrated graphics technology found in G-series versions of the 845 chipset family. Finally, an optional Gigabit Ethernet (GbE) port is connected to the MCH/GMCH and requires the use of an optional Intel 82547 Gigabit Ethernet controller chip on the motherboard.

All members of the 865 family use the new ICH5 or ICH5R I/O controller hub. A faster hub architecture called Hub Link 1.5 (HL 1.5) with 266MBps bandwidth connects the MCH/GMCH and ICH together.

ICH5 and ICH5R

ICH5 and ICH5R (RAID) are the latest generation of Intel's I/O controller hub for its AHA and HI 1.5 hub-based architecture, which is the equivalent of the South Bridge in Intel's hub-based architecture introduced with the 800 series of chipsets.

ICH5 and ICH5R feature four USB 2.0 controllers with eight external ports, two ATA/100 ports, and two Serial ATA/150 ports. ICH5R models add support only for RAID 0 (striping) and RAID 1 (mirroring) on the SATA ports. ICH5/ICH5R also support the PCI 2.3 bus and include an integrated 10/100 Ethernet LAN controller.

Note

RAID 1 (mirroring) support for ICH5R-equipped motherboards requires the installation of the latest version of the Intel Application Accelerator RAID Edition. In some cases, you might also need to install the latest edition of the Intel RAID Option ROM first. For more information and to download driver and option ROM updates, go to `http://support.intel.com/support/chipsets/iaa_raid/`.

Intel 875P

The Intel 875P chipset, code named Canterwood during its development, was introduced in April 2003. The 875P chipset supports Intel's HT Technology (hyper-threading), so it fully supports 3.06GHz and faster Pentium 4s, including the newer Prescott (90nm) core versions.

For faster memory access, the 875P supports four standard or ECC memory modules (up to 4GB total) using DDR333 or DDR400 memory in a dual-channel mode, and it offers a new Turbo mode that uses a faster path between DDR400 memory and the MCH to boost enhanced performance. Because multiple memory modules aren't always the same size or type, the 875P also features a new dynamic mode that optimizes system memory when different types or sizes of memory are used at the same time. The 875P also includes both Serial ATA and RAID support and uses the same ICH5/5R I/O controller hub family used by the 865 series.

Intel 915 Chipset Family

The Intel 915 chipset family, code named Grantsdale during its development, was introduced in 2004. The Grantsdale family comprises four members (915P, 915G, 915GV, and 915GL), all of which support the latest 90nm Pentium 4 Prescott core. These chipsets are the first to support the new Socket 775 processor interface outlined in Chapter 3. These chipsets are intended to replace the 865 Springdale family of chipsets.

The 915P, 915G, and 915GV models are all designed to support the HT Technology feature built in to most recent Pentium 4 processors and to support bus speeds up to 800MHz. All three chipsets support dual-channel DDR memory up to 400MHz and the new DDR-II memory standard. All three models also support PCI-Express x1 as well as PCI version 2.3 expansion slots.

The 915P uses a PCI-Express x16 slot for high-speed graphics, whereas the 915G has a PCI-Express x16 slot as well as integrated Intel Extreme Graphics 3. The 915GV uses Intel Extreme Graphics 3 but lacks a PCI-Express x16 slot. Extreme Graphics 3 is a partial implementation of DirectX 9, but it lacks the vertex shaders found on fully compatible DirectX 9 GPUs from ATI and NVIDIA.

The 915GL is the low-end member of the family, lacking support for DDR-II RAM, 800MHz bus speeds, HT Technology, and PCI-Express x16 video. The 915GL is designed to be matched with Intel Celeron processors to produce a low-cost system.

All 915-series MCH/GMCH chips use the new ICH6 family of South Bridge replacements detailed in Table 4.31.

Figure 4.42 shows which features of the 915 (Grantsdale) family are common to all versions and which vary by chipset and ICH6 version used.

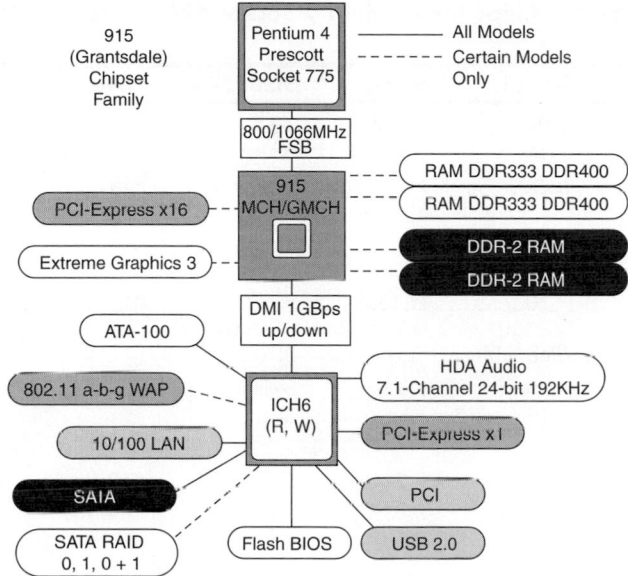

Figure 4.42   All versions of the 915 (Grantsdale) family support dual-channel memory, SATA, PCI-Express x1 slots, and 7.1-channel audio, but other features vary by model.

Intel 925X Chipset

The Intel 925X chipset, code named Alderwood before its release, was released in 2004. It is designed to replace the 875P Canterwood chipset. Unlike the 915 series of chipsets, which continue to support older DDR memory, the 925X supports only DDR-II memory. The 925X also supports ECC memory, providing a fast and accurate platform for mission-critical applications. To further improve performance, it uses an optimized memory controller design.

The 925X supports PCI-Express x1 and PCI-Express x16 (video) as well as PCI version 2.3 expansion slots. It supports the new LGA 775 processor socket and the new Intel Prescott Pentium 4 core and uses the new ICH6 family of South Bridge replacements detailed in Table 4.31.

Third-Party Pentium 4 Chipsets

SiS, the ALi Corporation, ATI, and VIA all produce chipsets for the Intel Pentium 4 and Celeron 4 processors.

Although Intel's chipsets for the Pentium 4 have dominated the market up to this point, many of these chipsets offer unique features that are worth considering. The following sections discuss these chipsets by vendor.

SiS Chipsets for Pentium 4

SiS offers several chipsets for the Pentium 4, including integrated chipsets, chipsets for use with discrete video accelerator cards, and some that support Rambus RDRAM. Details of SiS's chipsets for the Pentium 4 are available in Tables 4.32, 4.33, and 4.34. Unlike most of the chipsets SiS has created for the Pentium II/III/Celeron, the SiS chipsets for the Pentium 4 use one of several high-speed South Bridge equivalents (SiS 96x series Media I/O chips) instead of integrating North and South Bridge functions into a single chip. SiS North and South Bridge chips for the Pentium 4 use a high-speed 16-bit connection known as MuTIOL (Multi-Threaded I/O Link) instead of the slow PCI bus as with older chipsets.

Table 4.32   SiS North Bridge Chips for Pentium 4 Socket 478 (up to 533MHz Processor Bus Speed)

Chipset	SiS650	SiS651	SiS645	SiS645DX	SiS648	SiS655	SiS R658
Bus speed	400MHz	400/533MHz	400MHz	400/533MHz	400/533MHz	400/533MHz	400/533MHZ
Supports Hyper-Threading	No	Yes*	No	Yes*	Yes*	Yes*	Yes*
SMP (dual CPUs)	No	No	No	No	No	No	No
Memory types	PC133, DDR266	PC100/133, DDR200/266/333	PC133, DDR200/266	PC133, DDR266/333	DDR200/266/333	DDR266/333, dual-channel	1066/800MHz RDRAM
Parity/ECC	Neither	Neither	Neither	Neither	Neither	Neither	Neither
Maximum memory	3GB	3GB	3GB	3GB	3GB	4GB	4GB
PCI support	2.2	2.2	2.2	2.2	2.2	2.2	2.2
PCI speed/width	33MHz/32-bit	33MHz/32-bit	33MHz/32-bit	33MHz/32-bit	33MHz/32-bit	33MHz/32-bit	33MHz/32-bit
AGP slot	4x	4x	4x	4x	8x	8x	8x
Integrated video	Yes	Yes	No	No	No	No	No
South Bridge	SiS961	SiS962	SiS961	SiS961	SiS963	SiS963	SiS963
MuTIOL speed	533MBps	533MBps	533MBps	533MBps	1GBps	1GBps	1GBps

B-stepping only

Table 4.34   SiS Media I/O (South Bridge) Chips for Pentium 4

South Bridge Chip	USB Support	Number of USB Ports	ATA Support	# of SATA Ports	RAID Levels Supported
SiS961	1.1	6	33/66/100	—	—
SiS961B	1.1	6	33/66/100/133	—	—
SiS962	1.1, 2.0	6	33/66/100/133	—	—
SiS962L	1.1, 2.0	6	33/66/100/133	—	—
SiS963	1.1, 2.0	6	33/66/100/133	—	—
SiS963L	1.1, 2.0	6	33/66/100/133	—	—
SiS964	1.1, 2.0	8	33/66/100/133	2	0, 1, JBOD
SiS964L	1.1, 2.0	8	33/66/100/133	—	—
SiS965	1.1, 2.0	8	33/66/100/133	4	0, 1, 0+1, JBOD
SiS965L	1.1, 2.0	8	33/66/100/133	200	0, 1, JBOD

SiS650/651 Chipsets

The SiS650 and 651 chipsets enable Pentium 4 system builders to create low-cost systems with onboard video that can be enhanced with AGP 4x video cards at a later date. The integrated video features support for high-quality DVD playback and the optional SiS301B video bridge for TV-out and DVI LCD panels.

Both chipsets also feature SiS's own MuTIOL technology for connecting the North Bridge and South Bridge chips with a three-layer high-speed (266MHz/533MBps bandwidth) data highway.

Table 4.33   SiS North Bridge Chips for Pentium 4 Socket 478 (800MHz Processor Bus Speed)

Chipset	SiS648FX	SiS655FX	SiS655TX	SiS656	SiS R659	SiS661FX
Bus speed	800/533/ 400MHz	800/533/ 400MHz	800/533/ 400MHz	800/533/ 400MHz	800/400/ 533MHz	800/400/ 533MHz
Supports Hyper-Threading	Yes	Yes	Yes	Yes	Yes	Yes
SMP (dual CPUs)	No	No	No	No	No	No
Memory types	DDR400/333	Dual-channel DDR400/333	Dual-channel DDR400/333	Dual-channel DDR400/333, DDR-II	Quad-channel RDRAM PC1200	DDR400/ 222/266
Parity/ECC	Neither	Neither	Neither	ECC	ECC	Neither
Maximum memory	3GB	3GB	4GB	4GB	4GB	3GB
PCI support	2.3	2.3	2.3	2.3	2.3	2.3
PCI speed/ width	33MHZ, 32-bit	33MHZ, 32-bit	33MHz, 32-bit	33MHz, 32-bit	33MHz, 32-bit	33MHz, 32-bit
Video slot	AGP 8x	AGP 8x	AGP 8x	PCI-Express x16	AGP 8x	AGP 8x
Integrated video	No	No	No	No	No	SiS Mirage Graphics 32/64MB
South Bridge	SiS963L	SiS964/964L	SiS964/964L	SiS965/965L	SiS964/964L	SiS964/964L
MuTIOL speed	1GBps	1GBps	1GBps	1GBps	1GBps	1GBps

Audio	10/100 Ethernet	Gigabit Ethernet	HomePNA 1.0/2.0	IEEE 1394	MuTIOL Throughput
AC'97 2.2, 5.1 channel	Yes	No	Yes	No	533MBps
AC'97 2.2, 5.1 channel	Yes	No	Yes	No	533MBps
AC'97 2.2, 5.1 channel	Yes	No	Yes	Yes	533MBps
AC'97 2.2, 5.1 channel	Yes	No	Yes	No	533MBps
AC'97 2.2, 5.1 channel	Yes	No	Yes	Yes	533MBps
AC'97 2.2, 5.1 channel	Yes	No	Yes	No	533MBps
AC'97 2.2, 5.1 channel	Yes	No	Yes	No	1GBps
AC'97 2.2, 5.1 channel	Yes	No	Yes	No	1GBps
AC'97, 7.1 channel	Yes	Yes	Yes	No	1GBps
AC'97, 7.1 channel	Yes	No	Yes	No	1GBps

The 650 and 651 both support SDRAM and DDR SDRAM, and the 651 adds support for DDR333 memory, the 533MHz system bus of the latest Pentium 4 processors, and hyper-threading in its B-stepping version.

The 650's SiS961 South Bridge provides USB 1.1, ATA-100 (133 in its 961B version), AC'97 six-channel audio, and integrated Ethernet/HomePNA networking. The 651 also uses the newer SiS962 South Bridge, which provides ATA133 and USB 2.0 support.

SiS645/645DX

The 645 family of SiS chipsets does not include the integrated graphics of the 650/651 family, but they are otherwise similar. They support SDRAM and DDR SDRAM, AGP 4x, and the high-speed MuTIOL North Bridge/South Bridge interface. The 645DX supports DDR333 memory, the 533MHz system bus, and the HT technologies found in the most recent Pentium 4 processors.

Both the 645 and 645DX use the SiS961 South Bridge.

SiS648/648FX/655/655FX/655TX

The SiS648 chipset is a development of the 645DX chipset, with the following differences:

- Supports DDR memory only (up to DDR333)
- 8X AGP slot
- SiS963 South Bridge (USB 2.0, IEEE 1394a support)

The SiS655 chipset is essentially a dual-channel version of the 648, supporting up to 4GB of memory with DDR266/333 memory only.

The SiS648FX chipset is a development of the 648 that supports 800MHz bus speeds of the Pentium 4.

The SiS655FX is a development of the original SiS655 chipset with the following differences:

- Supports dual-channel DDR400 memory
- Supports 800MHz bus speeds of the Pentium 4
- Supports SiS's HyperStreaming Technology, SiS's marketing term for its method of reducing data latency through improved pipelining and splitting transactions
- Has SiS964 South Bridge (eight USB 2.0 ports, eight-channel audio, SATA, RAID)

The SiS655TX is based on the SiS655FX but uses second-generation Advanced HyperStreaming Technology.

SiS661FX

The SiS661FX is an integrated chipset with the following features:

- Support for Pentium 4 processors up to 800MHz processor bus with HT Technology
- Up to 2GB of DDR400 (two DIMMs) or up to 3GB of DDR333/266 (three DIMMS)
- AGP 8x video
- Integrated SiS Mirage Graphics (software compatible with DirectX9) with CRT, TV, LCD support; hardware acceleration for DVD playback; and shared memory of 32MB or 64MB
- SiS964 South Bridge

SiS656

The SiS656 is the first SiS chipset to support PCI-Express and DDR-II memory. Thus, it is roughly similar to the Intel 915 series of Pentium 4 chipsets (shown earlier). Other features include

- Support for Pentium 4 processors up to 800MHz FSB, including Prescott
- Dual-channel DDR400/333 or dual-channel DDR-II memory
- Maximum memory size of 4GB
- ECC memory support
- PCI-Express x16
- SiS965 South Bridge

SiS R658/R659

The SiS R658 is the first SiS chipset ever to support Rambus RDRAM. Other features include

- Support for Pentium 4 processors with 533MHz and HT (B-stepping only) features
- Dual-channel support for PC1066/PC800 RDRAM (requires identical pairs of memory)
- 4GB maximum memory size
- AGP 8x interface
- MuTIOL 1G (533MHz clock speed providing more than 1GBps throughput) interface to the SiS963 South Bridge

Essentially, the R658 is an RDRAM version of the 655 chipset, and, like the 655, it uses the SiS963 South Bridge.

The R659 is based on the R658 with the following differences:

- Support for 800MHz bus speeds of the Pentium 4
- SiS HyperStreaming Technology
- Quad-channel PC1200 RDRAM
- SiS964 South Bridge

ALi Corporation Chipsets for Pentium 4

ALi Corporation (formerly known as Acer Laboratories) has produced several chipsets for the Pentium 4 and Celeron 4 processors. Tables 4.35 and 4.36 provide an overview of these chipsets, which are discussed in the following sections.

Table 4.35   ALi Chipsets for Pentium 4

Chipset	ALADDiN-P4	M1681	M1683	M1685
North Bridge chip	M1671	M1681	M1563	M1563
Bus speed	400MHz	533/400MHz	800/533/400MHz	800/533/400MHz
Supports HT Technology	No	Yes	Yes	Yes
SMP (dual CPUs)	No	No	No	No
Memory types	PC100/133 DDR200/266/333	PC100/133 DDR200/266/333/400	PC133 DDR266/333/400	DDR266/333/400 DDR-II
Parity/ECC	Neither	Neither	Neither	Neither
Maximum memory	3GB	3GB	4GB	3.5GB
PCI support	2.2	2.3	2.3	2.3
PCI speed/width	33MHz, 32-bit	33MHz, 32-bit	33MHz, 32-bit	33MHz, 32-bit
Video slot	AGP 4x	AGP 8x	AGP 8x	PCI-Express x16
Integrated video	No	No	No	No
South Bridge	M1535 series	M1563	M1653	M1653
HyperTransport NB/ SB Link	N/A	400MBps	400MBps	400MBps

Also supports hyper-threaded processors

Table 4.36 provides an overview of the ALi South Bridge chips used in ALi Corporation's chipsets for the Pentium 4; ALi uses the same South Bridge chips for its chipsets for the Athlon XP.

Table 4.36   ALi South Bridge Chips for Pentium 4 and Athlon XP

South Bridge Chip	USB Support	Number of USB Ports	ATA Support	Audio	Soft Modem	10/100 Ethernet	Super I/O	HyperTransport Link Speed
M1535D	1.1	4	33/66	Stereo AC'97	Yes	No	Yes	N/A
M1535D+	1.1	6	33/66/100/133	Six-channel AC'97	Yes	No	Yes	N/A
M1563*	1.1, 2.0	6	66/100/133	Six-channel AC'97, SPDIF	Yes	Yes	Yes	400MBps

Also incorporates SD and Memory Stick flash memory interfaces and supports AMD Athlon 64/Opteron/Mobile Athlon 64 processors.

Aladdin P4 (M1671)

The ALi Aladdin P4 was ALi's first Pentium 4-compatible chipset. Because it uses the same M1535-series South Bridge chips used by its earlier Pentium and Pentium II/III chipsets, the P4 is a traditional North Bridge/South Bridge solution. Thus, it relies on the slow (133MBps) PCI interface to carry data between the bridge chips.

The P4's major features include the following:

- 400MHz system bus
- Support for PC100/133 and DDR200/266/333 memory
- ATA-133 support (when used with the M1535D+ South Bridge)
- AGP 4x interface
- USB 1.1 ports
- ACPI power management

The P4 is also available in a version for notebook computers: the ALADDiN-P4M, which uses the D1535+ South Bridge.

M1681/M1683

ALi's M1681 chipset for the Pentium 4 processor brings ALi's offerings in line with the latest from other chipset vendors. In a break with ALi tradition, it uses the HyperTransport high-speed direct connection between North and South Bridge chips instead of relying on the PCI bus, as with previous designs.

Its major features include

- Support for hyper-threading and 533MHz system bus
- Support for DDR memory up to DDR400 and PC100/133 SDRAM
- ATA-133
- USB 2.0
- AGP 8x interface
- Memory Stick and SD (Secure Digital) flash memory device interfaces
- ACPI power management
- HyperTransport high-speed link between North and South Bridge chips, running at >400MBps bandwidth in each direction (800MBps total throughput)
- M1563 South Bridge chip

The M1683 chipset is based on the M1681 but supports the 800MHz system bus.

M1685

Although the M1685 chipset is numbered in series with ALi's earlier Pentium 4 chipsets, it represents a major departure from the M1681/M1683 generation. The M1685 is ALi's first chipset for the Pentium 4 to adopt PCI-Express and DDR-II memory. Its major features include

- Support for the 800MHz system bus
- Support for HT Technology processors
- DDR266/333/400 or DDR-II memory
- PCI-Express x16 video slot
- 3.5GB maximum memory size
- M1563 South Bridge chip

Although the M1685 North Bridge supports the same DDR-II memory and PCI-Express x16 technologies used by the latest Intel and SiS chipsets, the companion M1653 South Bridge lacks significant I/O support features, such as Serial ATA and ATA RAID. Thus, a motherboard using the M1685/M1563 chipset combination will not support the latest hard disks unless a discrete SATA host adapter chip is used.

ATI Chipsets for Pentium 4

ATI's original line of chipsets for the Pentium 4 integrate Radeon VE-level 3D graphics, DVD playback, and dual-display features with high-performance North Bridge and South Bridge designs. ATI uses its high-speed A-Link bus to connect its North and South Bridge chips.

The Radeon IGP North Bridge chips for Pentium 4 include the ATI A4 family, comprised of

- Radeon IGP 330
- Radeon IGP 340

The Radeon 9x00 IGP family is ATI's second generation of chipsets for the Pentium 4. The 9x00 IGP North Bridge chips feature Radeon 9200-level graphics with DirectX 8.1 hardware support and support for multiple monitors. On the other hand, the companion IXP 300 South Bridge supports Serial ATA and USB 2.0 as well as six-channel audio. The Radeon 9x00 IGP family includes

- Radeon 9100 IGP
- Radeon 9100 Pro IGP
- Radeon 9000 Pro IGP

ATI's South Bridge chips include

- IXP 150
- IXP 200
- IXP 250
- IXP 300
- IXP 400

Table 4.37 summarizes the major features of the North Bridge chips, and Table 4.38 summarizes the major features of the South Bridge chips used in ATI's integrated chipsets for the Pentium 4. The Radeon IGP 330 and 340 chipsets were not widely used in desktop computers and have now been discontinued.

Table 4.37   Radeon IGP (North Bridge) Chips for Pentium 4

North Bridge Chip	Radeon IGP 330	Radeon IGP 340	Radeon 9100/PRO[2] IGP	Radeon 9000 PRO IGP
Bus speed	400MHz	400/533MHz	400/533/800MHz	400/533/800MHz
Hyper-Threading support	No	No	Yes	Yes
Memory types	DDR200/266	DDR200/266/333	DDR333/400 dual-channel	DDR333/400
Parity/ECC	Neither	Neither	Neither	Neither
Maximum memory	1GB	1GB	4GB	4GB
PCI support	2.2	2.2	2.3	2.3
PCI speed/width	33MHz/32-bit	33MHz/32-bit	33MHz/32-bit	33MHz/32-bit
AGP slot	4x	4x	8x	8x
Integrated video	Radeon VE[1]	Radeon VE[1]	Radeon 9200[3,4]	Radeon 9200[3,4]
NS/SB interconnect speed	266MBps	266MBps	266MBps	266MBps
NS/SB interconnect type	A-Link	A-Link	A-Link	A-Link

1. *Same core as ATI Radeon 7000 with support for dual displays.*
2. *The PRO version features improved AGP 8x performance, better memory performance, and improved DDR400 memory compatibility.*
3. *Two graphics pipelines only; discrete Radeon 9200 GPU has four.*
4. *Supports ATI SurroundView, which allows a three-monitor setup when a dual-display ATI graphics card is connected to the AGP slot. Some motherboards might not support this feature.*

Table 4.39   VIA Chipsets for Pentium 4 (up to 533MHz System Bus)

Chipset	P4X266	P4X266A	P4X266E
North Bridge chip	VT8753	VT8753A	VT8753E
Bus speed	400MHz	400MHz	400/533MHz
HT Technology support	No	No	No
SMP (dual CPUs)	No	No	No
Memory types	PC100/133, DDR200/266	PC100/133, DDR200/266	DDR200/266
Parity/ECC	Neither	Neither	Neither
Maximum memory	4GB	4GB	4GB
PCI support	2.2	2.2	2.2
PCI speed/width	33MHz/32-bit*	33MHz/32-bit*	33MHz/32-bit*
AGP slot	4x	4x	4x
Integrated video	No	No	No
South Bridge	VT8233, VT8233C, VT8233A	VT8233, VT8233C, VT8233A	VT8233, VT8233C, VT8233A, VT8235
V-Link speed	266MBps	266MBps	266MBps

*Supports 66MHz/64-bit PCI when an optional VPX-64 (VT8101) chip is used.

Table 4.38   ATI South Bridge Chips for Pentium 4

South Bridge Chip	USB Support	Number of USB Ports	ATA Support	Audio	10/100 Ethernet	High-speed Interconnect
IXP 150	2.0	6	ATA100	AC'97 2.3; 6-channel	3Com	A-Link
IXP 200/250[1]	2.0	6	ATA100	AC'97 2.3; 6-channel	3Com	A-Link
IXP 300	2.0	8	ATA133, 2 SATA	AC'97 2.3; 6-channel	3Com	A-Link
IXP 400 (SB400)	2.0	8	ATA133, 4 SATA	AC'97 2.3; 6-channel	3Com	A-Link

1. *IXP250 identical features to IXP200, plus it supports Wake On LAN (WOL), Desktop Management Interface (DMI), manage boot agent (MBA), and the Alert Standards Forum (ASF) mechanism.*

VIA Chipsets for Pentium 4

Although VIA Technologies produces a line of chipsets for the Pentium 4, it initially lacked a license from Intel for the Socket 478 interface. This slowed acceptance of VIA's chipsets by motherboard makers until VIA and Intel reached an agreement in April 2003. Before VIA received a license to the Socket 478 interface, it used its VIA Platform Solutions Division (VPSD) to produce Pentium 4–compatible motherboards for sale under a variety of brand names. With the agreement between VIA and Intel, VIA's chipsets for the Pentium 4 are now being used by most of the major third-party motherboard makers.

Tables 4.39 and 4.40 provide an overview of VIA's chipsets for the Pentium 4, including ProSavage chipsets with integrated graphics.

P4M266	P4X400 (P4X333)	P4X400A	P4X533
VT8751	VT8754	VT8754CE	P4X533
400MHz	400/533MHz	400/533MHz	400/533MHz
No	No	Yes	Yes
No	No	No	No
PC100/133, DDR200/266	DDR200/266/333	DDR266/333/400	DDR200/266/333
Neither	ECC	ECC	ECC
4GB	16GB	16GB	16GB
2.2	2.2	2.2	2.2
33MHz/32-bit	33MHz/32-bit*	33MHz/32-bit*	33MHz/32-bit*
4x	8x	8x	8x
S3 Graphics ProSavage8 3D	No	No	No
VT8233, VT8233C, VT8233A	VT8235	VT8235	VT8237
266MBps	533MBps	533MBps	533MBps

Table 4.40 VIA Chipsets for Pentium 4 (800MHz System Bus)

Chipset	PT800	PM800	PT880	PM880
North Bridge chip	PT800	PM800	PT800	PM880
Bus speed	400/533/ 800MHz	400/533/ 800MHz	400/533/ 800MHz	400/533/ 800MHz
HT Technology support	Yes	Yes	Yes	Yes
SMP (dual CPUs)	No	No	No	No
Memory types	DDR266/ 333/400	DDR266/ 333/400	Dual-channel DDR266/333/400	Dual-channel DDR266/333/400
Parity/ECC	ECC	ECC	ECC	ECC
Maximum memory	16GB	16GB	16GB	16GB
PCI support	2.2	2.2	2.2	2.2
PCI speed/width	33MHz/32-bit*	33MHz/32-bit*	33MHz/32-bit*	33MHz/32-bit*
AGP slot	8x	8x	8x	8x
Integrated video	No	S3 UniChrome Pro#	No	S3 UniChrome Pro#
South Bridge	VT8237	VT8237	VT8237	VT8237
V-Link speed	533MBps	533MBps	1066MBps	1066MBps

 # The UniChrome Pro features dual-monitor support, 350MHz RAMDAC, enhanced DVD playback, and DirectX 7/8/9 3D graphics support.

* Supports 66MHz/64-bit PCI when optional VPX-64 (VT8101) chip is used.

Table 4.41 lists the major features of the VIA South Bridge chips used in VIA's chipsets for the Pentium 4. Note that these same chips are also used by VIA chipsets for the AMD Athlon family of processors. All chipsets that use these South Bridge chips use VIA's high-speed V-Link interface between North and South Bridge chips. These chipsets connect to the VT1211 LPC (low pin count) or equivalent Super I/O chip for support of legacy devices such as serial, IR, and parallel ports and the floppy drive.

Table 4.41 VIA South Bridge Chips for Pentium 4

South Bridge Chip	USB Support	Number of USB Ports	ATA Support	Audio	10/100 Ethernet	HomePNA	V-Link Throughput
VT8233	1.1	6	33/66/100	AC'97, 6-channel[1]	Yes	Yes	266MBps
VT8233A	1.1	6	33/66/100/133	AC'97, 6-channel[1]	Yes	No	266MBps
VT8233C	1.1	6	33/66/100	AC'97, 6-channel[1]	Yes[2]	No	266MBps
VT8235	2.0	6	33/66/100/133	AC'97, 5.1 channel[1]	Yes	No	533MBps
VT8237[5]	2.0	8	33/66/100/133	AC'97, 5.1 channel[1,4]	Yes	No	1066MBps 2 (4)[3]

1. Integrated audio requires separate audio codec chip on motherboard; it also supports MC'97 soft modem.

2. 3Com 10/100 Ethernet.

3. 4 SATA ports with optional SATALite interface.

4. 8-channel (7.1) audio when optional VIA Envy 24PT PCI audio controller is used.

5. Can also be used with North Bridge chips that support 533MBps interconnect speed. It also has support for RAID 0+1 with optional SATALite.

VIA Modular Architecture Platforms (V-MAP) for Pentium 4

VIA's North and South Bridge chips for the Pentium 4 support VIA's Modular Architecture Platforms (V-MAP) designs, which enable motherboard designers to convert quickly to more advanced versions of a chipset because of a common pinout. The North Bridge chips used in all VIA Pentium 4–compatible chipsets are all pin-compatible with each other, as are the 8233/8235/8237-series South Bridge chips. Thus, motherboards using these chipsets can be built in a variety of configurations. All these chipsets also support VIA's V-Link high-speed connection between the North and South Bridge chips.

VIA Apollo P4X266 Family

The VIA Apollo P4X266 is its first chipset for the Pentium 4 and Celeron 4 processors, supporting AGP 4x, 4GB of RAM, and the 400MHz system bus used by early Pentium 4/Celeron 4 processors. The P4X266A improves the memory interface and queues more instructions (up to 12) in the processor bus interface to reduce latency and improve performance. The P4X266E adds support for the 533MHz bus used in the 2.53GHz (and faster) Pentium 4 processors. It also supports both the VT8233 and newer VT8235 series of South Bridge chips.

ProSavage P4M266

The VIA ProSavage P4M266 integrates the S3 Graphics ProSavage8 2D/3D graphics accelerators with the features of the P4X266 chipset. Unlike some other chipsets with integrated graphics, the P4M266 retains an AGP 4x slot, so users can upgrade to faster AGP 4x graphics in the future.

The ProSavage8 core uses 32MB of system RAM for its frame buffer, supports AGP 8x bandwidth internally with 128-bit data paths, and features DVD DXVA Motion Compensation to improve the quality of DVD playback. In addition, it supports all members of the 8233 family of South Bridge chips.

Apollo P4X400, P4X400A, and P4X533

The VIA Apollo P4X400 chipset is an improved version of the short-lived P4X333. It's suitable for both server and workstation/desktop computer use, thanks to its support for up to 32GB of RAM and ECC memory. It also supports 400MHz and 533MHz system bus speeds and DDR memory up to 400MHz. It uses the VT8235 South Bridge, so it also supports the latest I/O standards (USB 2.0 and ATA-133).

The P4X400A chipset features improved timings and support for DDR400 memory, supports HT Technology processors, and uses the VT8235 South Bridge.

The P4X533 chipset is similar to the P4X400A but uses the VT8237 as its South Bridge chip, providing support for SATA and RAID as well as eight USB 2.0 ports and optional 7.1 audio.

All three processors use the 8x V-Link connection (533MBps) between North and South Bridge chips.

PT800/PM800/PT880/PM880

The PT8xx-series chipsets are the first VIA Technologies chipsets to support the 800MHz processor bus versions of the Pentium 4. They use the VT8237 South Bridge chips (eight USB 2.0 ports, SATA, RAID, and optional 7.1 audio).

The major differences between these chipsets include

- PT800 uses single-channel DDR 400 memory and AGP 8x video, with 8x V-Link (533MBps).
- PM800 adds S3 UniChrome Pro integrated graphics to the PT800 feature set.
- PT880 is a dual-channel version of the PT800 and uses Ultra V-Link (1066MBps).
- PM880 adds S3 UniChrome Pro integrated graphics to the PT880 feature set.

Figure 4.43 displays the architecture of the PM880 chipset when equipped with the optional VIA Envy 24PT audio controller for eight-channel audio (left) and VIA Gigabit Ethernet controller (bottom).

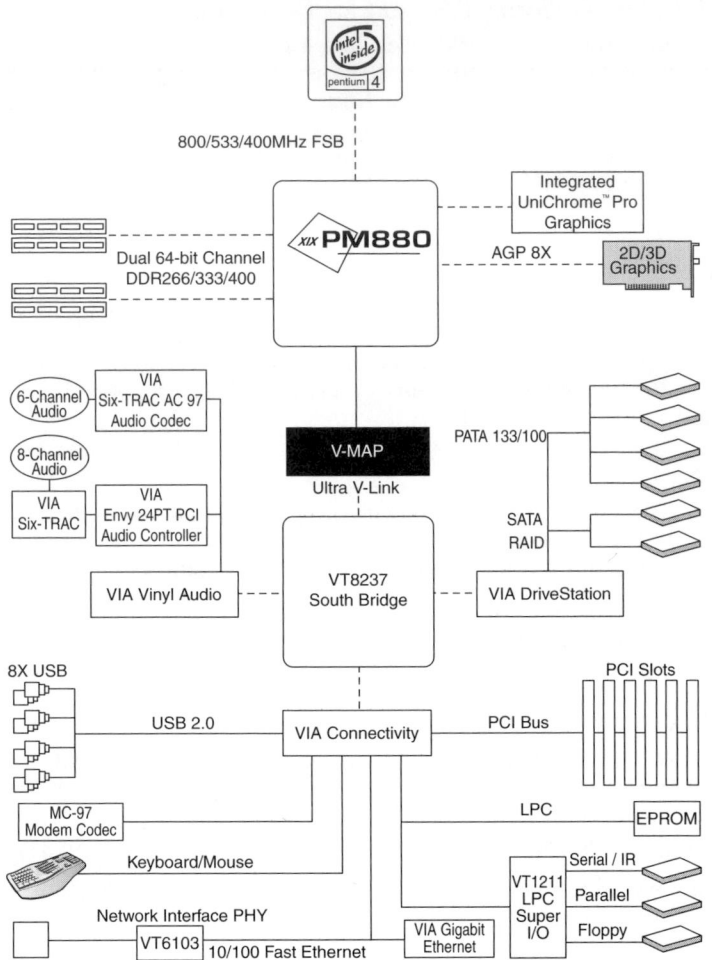

Figure 4.43 VIA's PM880 chipset for the Pentium 4 combines integrated graphics with support for AGP 8x and offers optional eight-channel audio (left) and Gigabit Ethernet (bottom). It uses a separate Super I/O chip (bottom right).

Athlon/Duron/Athlon XP Chipsets

The original AMD Athlon was a Slot A processor chip, but subsequent versions have used Socket A—as do the economical Duron and current Athlon XP. Although similar in some ways to the Pentium III and Celeron, the AMD chips use a different interface and require different chipsets. AMD was originally the only supplier for Athlon chipsets, but VIA Technology, ALi Corporation, SiS, and NVIDIA now provide a large number of chipsets with a wide range of features. These chipsets are covered in the following sections.

AMD Chipsets for Athlon/Duron Processors

AMD makes four chipsets for Athlon and Duron processors: the AMD-750 and AMD-760/MP/MPX. The major features of these chipsets are compared in Table 4.42 and described in greater detail in the following sections.

Table 4.42   AMD Athlon/Duron Processor Chipsets Using North/South Bridge Architecture

Chipset	AMD-750	AMD-760
Code name	Irongate	None
Date introduced	Aug. 1999	Oct. 2000
Part number	AMD-751	AMD-761
Bus speed	200MHz	200/266MHz
Supported processors	Athlon/Duron	Athlon/Duron
SMP (dual CPUs)	No	Yes
Memory type	SDRAM	DDR SDRAM
Memory speed	PC100	PC1600/PC2100
Parity/ECC	Both	Both
Maximum memory	768MB	2GB buffered, 4GB registered
PCI support	2.2	2.2
AGP support	AGP 2x	AGP 4x
South Bridge	AMD-756	AMD-766
ATA/IDE support	ATA-66	ATA-100
USB support	1C/4P	1C/4P
CMOS/clock	Yes	Yes
ISA support	Yes	No
LPC support	No	Yes
Power management	SMM/ACPI	SMM/ACPI

AGP = Accelerated graphics port
ATA = AT attachment (IDE) interface
DDR-SDRAM = Double data rate SDRAM
ECC = Error correcting code
ISA = Industry Standard Architecture

LPC = Low pin count bus
PCI = Peripheral component interconnect
SDRAM = Synchronous dynamic RAM
SMP = Symmetric multiprocessing (dual processors)
USB = Universal serial bus

AMD-750

AMD's first chipset for its own Slot A and Socket A processors, called the AMD-750, is a traditional North/South Bridge design specifically for the Athlon and Duron processors. The AMD-750 chipset consists of the AMD-751 North Bridge and the AMD-756 South Bridge.

The AMD-751 system controller connects between the AMD Athlon processor bus to the processor and features the memory controller, AGP 2x controller, and PCI bus controller. The AMD-756 South Bridge includes a PCI-to-ISA bridge, USB controller interface, and ATA 33/66 controller.

The AMD-750 chipset includes the following features:

- AMD Athlon 200MHz processor bus
- PCI 2.2 bus with up to six masters
- AGP 2x
- PC-100 SDRAM with ECC
- Up to 768MB of memory
- ACPI power management

- ATA-33/66 support
- USB controller
- ISA bus support
- Integrated 256-byte CMOS RAM with clock
- Integrated keyboard/mouse controller

AMD-760 Family

The AMD-760 chipset was introduced in October 2000 and is notable as the first chipset supporting DDR SDRAM memory. The AMD-760 chipset consists of the AMD-761 system controller (North Bridge) in a 569-pin plastic ball-grid array (PBGA) package and the AMD-766 peripheral bus controller (South Bridge) in a 272-pin PBGA package. See Figure 4.44 for details of the 760's block diagram.

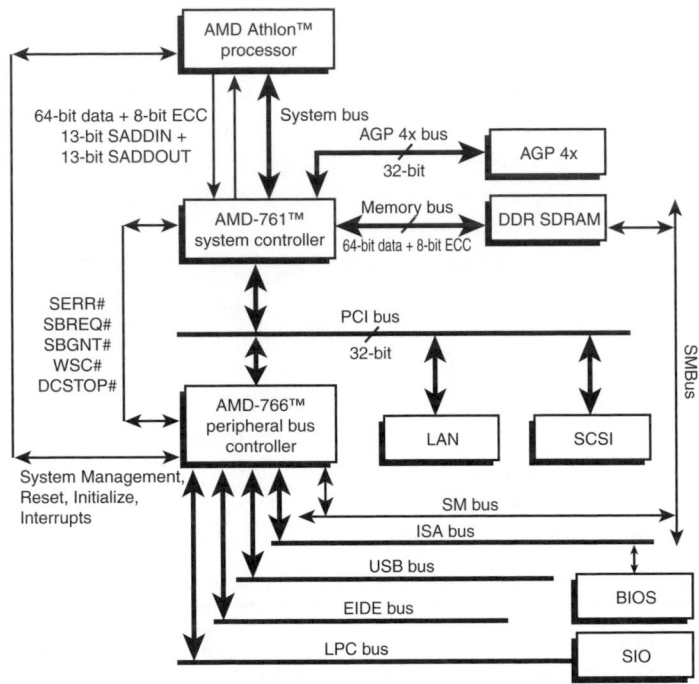

Figure 4.44   AMD-760 chipset block diagram.

The AMD-761 North Bridge features the AMD Athlon system bus, DDR-SDRAM system memory controller with support for either PC1600 or PC2100 memory, AGP 4x controller, and PCI bus controller. The 761 allows for 200MHz or 266MHz processor bus operation and supports the newer Athlon chips that use the 266MHz processor (also called front-side) bus.

The AMD-766 South Bridge includes a USB controller, dual UDMA/100 ATA/IDE interfaces, and the LPC bus for interfacing newer Super I/O and ROM BIOS components.

The AMD-760 chipset includes the following features:

- AMD Athlon 200/266MHz processor bus
- Dual processor support
- PCI 2.2 bus with up to six masters
- AGP 2.0 interface that supports 4x mode
- PC1600 or PC2100 DDR SDRAM with ECC

- Support for a maximum of 2GB buffered or 4GB registered DDR SDRAM
- ACPI power management
- ATA-100 support
- USB controller
- LPC bus for Super I/O support

The AMD-760MP chipset, which uses the AMD-762 North Bridge chip, is a development of the basic AMD-760 design that supports dual-processor Athlon MP systems. It differs from the standard 760 chipset in the following ways:

- Supports dual AMD Athlon MP processors with 200/266MHz processor bus speeds
- Up to 4GB PC2100 DDR (registered modules)
- Supports 33MHz PCI slots in 32-bit and 64-bit widths

The AMD-760MPX chipset uses the same AMD-762 North Bridge chip as the AMD-760MP to support multiple Athlon MP processors, but it uses the AMD-768 peripheral bus controller (South Bridge) chip. It differs from the 760MP chipset in the following ways:

- The AMD-762 North Bridge chip is used to support two 66MHz 32/64-bit PCI slots.
- The AMD-768 South Bridge chip is used to support 33MHz/32-bit PCI slots.

The 760MPX chipset is a better choice for a server because of its support for 66MHz and 64-bit PCI slots, whereas the 760MP is a suitable choice for a workstation.

None of these chipsets support USB 2.0, ATA-133, or DDR333 or faster memory. If you buy an Athlon, a Duron, or an Athlon XP desktop system, it's far more likely that your system will contain a third-party chipset than an AMD chipset; however, the 760MP and 760MPX chipsets continue to be popular choices for AMD-based workstations and servers. The following sections cover the third-party chipsets made for the Athlon, Duron, and Athlon XP processors.

VIA Chipsets for Athlon, Duron, and Athlon XP

VIA Technologies, Inc., is the largest chipset and processor supplier outside of Intel and AMD. Originally founded in 1987, VIA is based in Taipei, Taiwan, and is the largest integrated circuit design firm on the island. VIA is a fabless company, which means it farms out the manufacturing to other companies with chip foundry capability. Although it is best known for its chipsets, in 1999 VIA purchased the Cyrix processor division from National Semiconductor and the Centaur processor division from IDT, respectively, thereby becoming a supplier of processors in addition to chipsets. VIA has also formed a joint venture with SONICblue (formerly S3) as a means of integrating graphics capabilities into various chipset products. This joint venture is known as S3 Graphics, Inc.

VIA makes chipsets for Intel, AMD, and Cyrix (VIA) processors. Table 4.43 provides an overview of VIA's Athlon/Duron chipsets that use the traditional North/South Bridge architecture.

More recently, VIA has converted to an architecture called V-Link, which uses a fast dedicated connection between the North Bridge and South Bridge. V-Link is similar to Intel's hub architecture, as well as HyperTransport (used by ALi, NVIDIA, and ATI), MuTIOL (used by SiS), and A-Link (used by ATI). V-Link is also used by VIA's Pentium 4 chipsets. Tables 4.43, 4.44, and 4.45 provide an overview of V-Link chipsets, which also support the VIA Modular Architecture Platform (V-MAP) design. As with VIA's chipsets for the Pentium 4, V-MAP uses identical pinouts for several ranges of V-Link North and South Bridge chips so vendors can reuse a motherboard design with more advanced chipsets as they are developed.

Both types of chipsets are discussed in the following sections.

Table 4.43   VIA Athlon/Duron/Athlon XP Processor Chipsets Using North/South Bridge Architecture

Chipset	Apollo KX133	Apollo KT133	Apollo KT133A	Apollo KLE133	ProSavage KM133
Introduced	Aug. 1999	June 2000	Dec. 2000	Mar. 2001	Sep. 2000
North Bridge	VT8371	VT8363	VT8363A	VT8361	VT8365
Processor support	Athlon	Athlon/Duron	Athlon/Duron	Athlon/Duron	Athlon/Duron
CPU interface	Slot-A	Socket-A (462)	Socket-A (462)	Socket-A (462)	Socket-A (462)
CPU FSB	200MHz	200MHz	200/266MHz	200/266MHz	200/266MHz
AGP slot	4x	4x	4x	No	AGP 4x
Integrated graphics	No	No	No	Yes	S3 Savage 4
PCI	2.2	2.2	2.2	2.2	2.2
Memory type	SDRAM	SDRAM	SDRAM	SDRAM	SDRAM
Memory speed	PC133	PC133	PC100/133	PC100/133	PC100/133
Maximum memory	1.5GB	1.5GB	1.5GB	1.5GB	1.5GB
South Bridge	VT82C686A	VT82C686A	VT82C686B	VT82C686B	VT8231
ATA/IDE	ATA-66	ATA-66	ATA-100	ATA-100	ATA-100
USB ports	1C4P	1C4P	1C4P	1C4P	1C4P
Power management	SMM/ACPI	SMM/ACPI	SMM/ACPI	SMM/ACPI	SMM/ACPI
Super I/O	Yes	Yes	Yes	Yes	Yes
CMOS/Clock	Yes	Yes	Yes	Yes	Yes
NB pin count	552-pin	552-pin	552-pin	552-pin	552-pin

Table 4.44   VIA Athlon XP/Duron Processor Chipsets Using V-Link Architecture

Chipset	Apollo KT266	Apollo KT266A	Apollo KT333	ProSavage KM266
North Bridge chip	VT8366	VT8633A	VT8753E	VT8375
Bus speed	200/266MHz	200/266MHz	200/266/333MHz	200/266MHz
SMP (dual CPUs)	No	No	No	No
Memory types	PC100/133, DDR200/266	PC100/133, DDR200/266	DDR200/266/333	PC100/133, DDR200/266
Parity/ECC	Neither	Neither	Neither	Neither
Maximum memory	4GB	4GB	4GB	4GB
PCI support	2.2	2.2	2.2	2.2
PCI speed/width	33MHz/32-bit	33MHz/32-bit	33MHz/32-bit	33MHz/32-bit
AGP slot	4x	4x	4x	4x
Integrated video	No	No	No	S3 Graphics ProSavage8 3D
South Bridge	VT8233, VT8233C, VT8233A	VT8233, VT8233C, VT8233A	VT8233, VT8233C, VT8233A	VT8233, VT8233C, VT8233A
V-Link speed	266MBps	266MBps	266MBps	266MBps
NB pin count	552-pin	552-pin	552-pin	552-pin

Table 4.45 VIA South Bridge Chips for Athlon/Duron/Athlon XP

South Bridge Chip	USB Support	Number of USB Ports	ATA Support	Audio	10/100 Ethernet	HomePNA	V-Link Throughput (SATA RAID Pin Count)
VT8233	1.1	6	33/66/100	AC'97, 6-channel[1]	Yes	Yes	266MBps (376-pin)
VT8233A	1.1	6	33/66/100/133	AC'97, 6-channel[1]	Yes	No	266MBps (376-pin)
VT8233C	1.1	6	33/66/100	AC'97, 6-channel[1]	Yes[2]	No	266MBps (376-pin)
VT8235CE	2.0	6	33/66/100/133	AC'97, 5.1-channel[1]	Yes	No	533MBps (539-pin)
VT8237[6]	2.0	8	33/66/100/133	AC'97, 5.1-channel[1,5]	Yes	No	1066MBps (0, 1, JBOD[4] 539-pin)

1. *Integrated audio requires a separate audio codec chip on the motherboard; it also supports MC'97 soft modem.*
2. *3Com 10/100 Ethernet.*
3. *4 SATA ports with optional SATALite interface.*
4. *RAID 0+1 with optional SATALite.*
5. *8-channel (7.1) audio when optional VIA Envy 24PT PCI audio controller is used.*
6. *Can also be used with North Bridge chips that support 1066MBps Ultra V-Link interconnect speed.*

	Apollo KT400	UniChrome KM400	Apollo KT400A	VIA KT600	KT880
	VT8377	KM400	VT8377A	KT600	KT800
	200/266/333MHz	200/266/333MHz	200/266/333MHz	266/333/400MHz	333/400MHz
	No	No	No	No	No
	DDR200/266/333	DDR200/266/333	DDR200/266/333/400	DDR200/266/333/400	Dual-channel DDR333/400
	Neither	Neither	Neither	Neither	Neither
	4GB	4GB	4GB	4GB	8GB
	2.2		2.2	2.2	2.2
	33MHz/32-bit	33MHz/32-bit	33MHz/32-bit	33MHz/32-bit	33MHz/32-bit
	8x	8x	8x	8x	8x
	No	S3 Graphics UniChrome	No	No	No
	VT8235	VT8235CE or VT8237	VT8235CE or VT8237	VT8237	VT8237
	533MBps	533MBps	533MBps	533MBps	533MBps
	664-pin	552-pin	664-pin	664-pin	806-pin

VIA Technologies Apollo KX133

The VIA Apollo KX133 chipset brings AGP 4x, PC133, a 200MHz FSB, and ATA-66 technologies to the AMD Athlon processor platform, exceeding the performance of AMD's own 750 chipset. It was the first chipset to support AGP 4x.

Key features include the following:

- 200MHz processor bus
- AGP 4x graphics bus
- PC133 SDRAM memory
- 2GB maximum RAM
- ATA-66 support

- Four USB ports
- AC'97 link for audio and modem
- Hardware monitoring
- Power management

The VIA Apollo KX133 is a two-chip set consisting of the VT8371 North Bridge controller and the VT82C686A South Bridge controller.

VIA Technologies Apollo KT133 and KT133A

The VIA Apollo KT133/A chipsets are designed to support the AMD Athlon and Duron processors in Socket-A (462) form. Based on the prior KX133 chipset, the KT133/A differ mainly in their support for Socket-A (462) over the previous Slot-A processor interface.

The VIA Apollo KT133 and KT133A are both two-chip sets consisting of the VT8363 North Bridge and the VT82C686A South Bridge (KT133) or the VT8363A North Bridge and the VT82C686B South Bridge (KT133A).

Both the KT133 and KT133A support the following standard features:

- Athlon/Duron Socket-A (462) processors
- 200MHz CPU (front-side) bus
- AGP 4x
- 2GB RAM maximum
- PC100/PC133MHz SDRAM
- PCI 2.2

- ATA-66
- USB support
- AC-97 audio
- Integrated Super I/O
- Integrated hardware monitoring
- ACPI power management

The KT133A (VT8363A North Bridge with VT82C686B South Bridge) adds the following features:

- 266MHz CPU (front-side) bus
- ATA-100

ProSavage KM133

The VIA ProSavage KM133 integrates S3 Graphics' S3 Savage 4 and S3 Savage 2000 3D and 2D graphics engines with the Apollo Pro KT133 chipset. The major features of the chipset are the same as for the Apollo Pro KT133, with the following additions:

- 2MB–32MB shared memory architecture integrated with Savage 4 3D and Savage 2000 2D video
- Z-buffering, 32-bit true-color rendering, massive 2K-by-2K textures, single-pass multiple textures, sprite antialiasing, and other 3D features

- Support for DVD playback, DVI LCD displays, and TV-out
- PCI 2.2 compliance

An optional AGP 4x interface enables the integrated AGP 4x video to be upgraded with an add-on card if desired. This two-chip chipset consists of the VT8365 North Bridge and VT8231 South Bridge.

The VT8231 South Bridge integrates the Super I/O and supports the LPC interface.

Apollo KT266 and KT266A

The Apollo KT266 is the first VIA chipset for Athlon-based systems to support VIA's high-speed V-Link system architecture. V-Link connects the 552-pin VT8366 North Bridge to the 376-pin VT8233 series South Bridge with a 266MBps data pathway, which is twice as fast as traditional PCI-based connections.

Major features of the KT266 include system bus speeds of 200/266MHz, AGP 2x/4x interface, and up to 4GB of DDR200/266 DDR SDRAM or PC100/133 SDRAM. Other features vary with the South Bridge (VT8233, VT8233A, or VT8233C) chip used with the VT8366.

The KT266A is a pin-compatible upgrade to the original KT266's North Bridge. The KT266A's VT8366A includes VIA's Performance Driven Design, which is not a technical term but a marketing term for the A-series' chips improved memory timing and deeper command queues to improve chipset performance. Basic features of the KT266A are otherwise similar to the KT266.

ProSavage KM266

The ProSavage KM266 combines the features of the KT266 with the graphics core of the S3 Graphics ProSavage 8 2D/3D accelerator. Unlike some other chipsets with integrated graphics, the KM266 retains an AGP 4x slot, so users can upgrade to faster AGP 4x graphics in the future.

The ProSavage8 core uses 32MB of system RAM for its frame buffer, supports AGP 8x bandwidth internally with 128-bit data paths, and features DVD DXVA Motion Compensation to improve the quality of DVD playback. It supports all members of the VT8233 family of South Bridge chips and has a 266MBps 4x V-Link connection between North and South Bridge chips.

Apollo KT333

The Apollo KT333 is a pin-compatible development of the KT266A, adding support for a 333MHz system bus, 333MHz memory bus, and DDR333 memory. Unlike the KT266A, the KT333 no longer supports PC100/133 memory, but it uses the same KT8233 family of South Bridge chips.

Apollo KT400/KM400

The Apollo KT400 is the first VIA chipset for the Athlon XP processor to offer AGP 8x and a second-generation 533MB/s V-Link connection to the South Bridge. It uses the VT8235 South Bridge, which is VIA's first South Bridge chip to support USB 2.0 as well as ATA-133.

The combination of faster video, fast memory and system bus speeds, and faster V-Link connections make the KT400 among the fastest Athlon XP chipsets.

The KM400 has the same basic features as the KT400 but adds integrated UniChrome 2D/3D graphics developed by S3 Graphics. The KM400 can be matched with the VT8235CE South Bridge chip or the top-of-the-line VT8237 South Bridge chip introduced by the KT400A (see the next section).

Apollo KT400A/KT600

In previous A-series chipsets from VIA, the North Bridge component was replaced with an improved chip and the South Bridge component was retained. However, the KT400A features new designs for both its North Bridge (VT8377A) and South Bridge (VT8237) chips. The major features of the VT8377A component include

- System bus support up to 333MHz
- DDR memory support up to DDR400
- Up to 4GB of memory

- An expanded array of prefetch buffers to reduce memory latency and improve throughput (FastStream64)
- AGP 8x interface

Some motherboard vendors use the older VT8235CE South Bridge chip (refer to Table 4.45) with the VT8377A North Bridge component. However, when the VT8237 South Bridge is used, the KT400A chipset has these new features:

- Integrated six-channel Surround Sound AC'97 audio
- Optional eight-channel audio
- Eight USB 2.0 ports
- Integrated MC'97 modem
- Integrated 10/100 Ethernet
- Serial ATA

- ATA RAID 0, 1 (0+1 with optional VIA SATALite interface for two additional SATA ports)
- ATA 33/66/100/133
- ACPI/OnNow power management
- Optional VIA Velocity Gigabit Ethernet (PCI controller)

KT400A's FastStream64 enables the system to reach 3.2GBps memory transfer speeds without the need for more expensive dual-channel memory support.

Figure 4.45 shows the architecture of the KT400A (with VT8237) chipset.

The VIA KT600 is an improved version of the KT400A/VT3237 combo, adding support for the 400MHz CPU bus versions of the Athlon XP. Although a few motherboards pair the KT600's North Bridge with the older VT8235CE South Bridge, most motherboard vendors use the KT600/VT8237 combo to provide support for Serial ATA, SATA RAID, and other advanced features.

KT880

The VIA KT880 is VIA's first dual-channel chipset for the Athlon XP. Dual-channel memory support enables the system to reach very high memory transfer rates. It has the following features:

- System bus support up to 400MHz
- Dual-channel DDR memory support up to DDR400
- Up to 8GB of memory
- DualStream 64, which is VIA's marketing term for this chipset's combination of improved memory clock timings, larger on-chip branch table, and enhancements to the data prefetch protocol and memory brand predictions feature
- AGP 8x interface

- Integrated six-channel Surround Sound AC'97 audio with optional eight-channel audio
- Eight USB 2.0 ports
- Integrated MC'97 modem
- Integrated 10/100 Ethernet
- Serial ATA and SATA RAID 0, 1 (0+1 with optional VIA SATALite interface for two additional SATA ports)
- ATA 33/66/100/133
- ACPI/OnNow power management

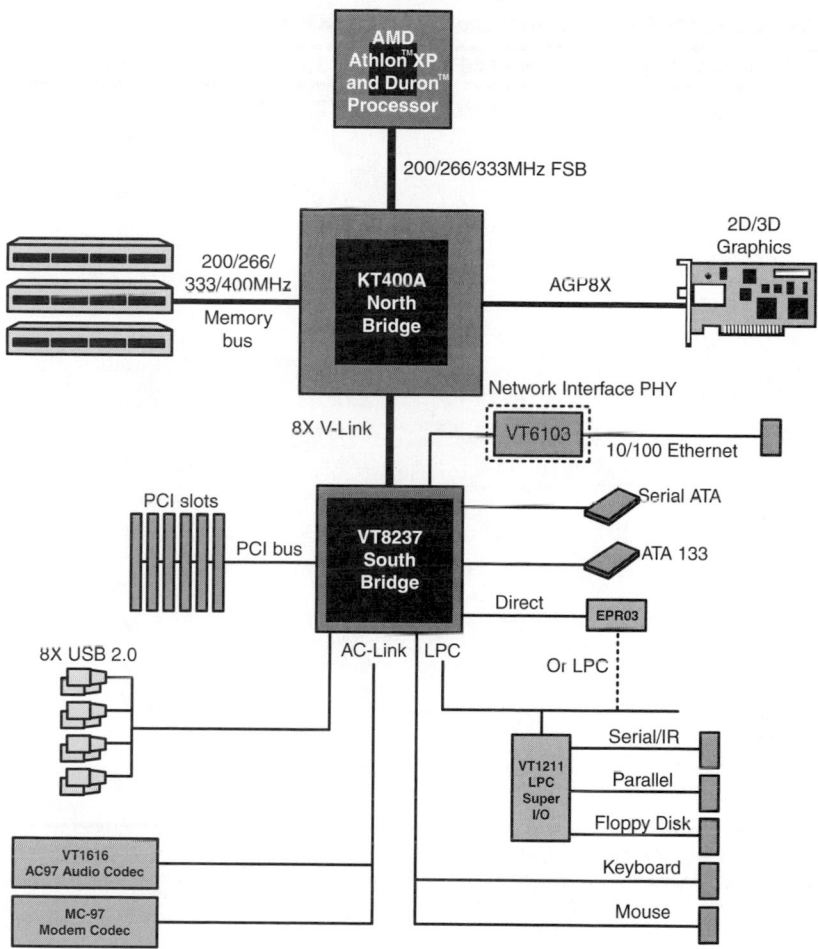

Figure 4.45   VIA KT400A block diagram.

Silicon Integrated Systems Chipsets for AMD Athlon/Duron Processors

SiS has a variety of chipsets for the Athlon, Duron, and Athlon XP processors. Tables 4.46 and 4.47 provide an overview of these chipsets, some of which use SiS's unique single-chip design and others of which use a high-speed two-chip design similar to other vendors' chipsets. These chipsets are discussed in the following sections.

Table 4.46   SiS Chipsets for Athlon/Duron/Athlon XP Processors

Chipset	SiS730S	SiS740	SiS733	SiS735	SiS745
Bus speed	200/266MHz	266MHz	200/266MHz	200/266MHz	266MHz
SMP (dual CPUs)	No	No	No	No	No
Memory type	PC133 SDRAM	DDR266 PC133	PC133	PC133/ DDDR266	DDR266/333
Parity/ECC	Neither	Neither	Neither	Neither	Neither
Maximum memory	1.5GB	1.5GB	1.5GB	1.5GB	3GB
HyperStreaming technology	No	No	No	No	No
PCI support	2.2	2.2	2.2	2.2	2.2
PCI speed/width	33MHz/ 32-bit	33MHz/ 32-bit	33MHz/ 32-bit	33MHz/ 32-bit	33MHz/ 32-bit
AGP slot	4x	None	4x	4x	4x
Integrated video	Yes[1]	Yes[2]	No	No	No
South Bridge	N/A[3]	SiS96x series	N/A[3]	N/A[3]	N/A[3]
MuTIOL speed	N/A	533MBps	N/A	N/A	N/A
ATA support	ATA-100	Varies[4]	ATA-100	ATA-100	ATA-100
USB support	1.1/6 ports	Varies[4]	1.1/6 ports	1.1/6 ports	1.1/6 ports
Audio support	AC'97	Varies[4]	AC'97	AC'97	AC'97
10/100 Ethernet	Yes	Varies[4]	No	Yes	No
IEEE 1394a	No	Varies[4]	No	No	Yes

1. 2D/3D accelerator with hardware DVD playback and optional SiS301 Video Bridge to TV and secondary monitor.
2. DirectX7-compliant 3D features, including two pixel-rendering pipelines and four texture units.
3. Single-chip (combined N/S Bridge) design.

Table 4.47   SiS MuTIOL South Bridge Chips for Athlon XP

South Bridge Chip	USB Support	Number of USB Ports	ATA Support	# of SATA Ports	RAID Levels Supported
SiS961	1.1	6	33/66/100	—	—
SiS961B	1.1	6	33/66/100/133	—	—
SiS962	1.1, 2.0	6	33/66/100/133	—	—
SiS962L	1.1, 2.0	6	33/66/100/133	—	—
SiS963	1.1, 2.0	6	33/66/100/133	—	—
SiS963L	1.1, 2.0	6	33/66/100/133	—	—
SiS964	1.1, 2.0	8	33/66/100/133	2	0, 1, JBOD
SiS964L	1.1, 2.0	8	33/66/100/133	—	—

JBOD stands for "just a bunch of disks" (spans two or more physical drives into a single logical drive).

SiS746	SiS746FX	SiS741GX	SiS748	SiS741
266MHz	266/333MHz	266/333MHz	266/333/400MHz	266/333/400MHz
No	No	No	No	No
DDR266/333	DDR266/333/400	DDR266/333	DDR266/333/400	DDR266/333/400
Neither	Neither	Neither	Neither	Neither
3GB	3GB	3GB	3GB	3GB
No	Yes	Yes	Yes	Yes
2.2	2.2	2.3	2.2	2.3
33MHz/32-bit	33MHz/32-bit	33MHz/32-bit	33MHz/32-bit	33MHz/32-bit
8x	8x	8x	8x	8x
No	No	SiS Mirage Graphics	No	SiS Mirage Graphics
SiS963 series	SiS963 series	SiS964 series	SiS963 series	SiS964 series
1GBps	1GBps[5]	1GBps[5]	1GBps[5]	1GBps[5]
Varies[4]	Varies[4]	Varies[4]	Varies[4]	Varies[4]
Varies[4]	Varies[4]	Varies[4]	Varies[4]	Varies[4]
Varies[4]	Varies[4]	Varies[4]	Varies[4]	Varies[4]
Varies[4]	Varies[4]	Varies[4]	Varies[4]	Varies[4]
Varies[4]	Varies[4]	Varies[4]	Varies[4]	Varies[4]

4. Varies with MuTIOL South Bridge chip used.
5. Chipset uses HyperStreaming technology, an improved version of MuTIOL.

Audio	10/100 Ethernet	HomePNA 1.0/2.0	IEEE 1394	MuTIOL Throughput
AC'97 2.2, 5.1 channel	Yes	Yes	No	533MBps
AC'97 2.2, 5.1 channel	Yes	Yes	No	533MBps
AC'97 2.2, 5.1 channel	Yes	Yes	Yes	533MBps
AC'97 2.2, 5.1 channel	Yes	Yes	No	533MBps
AC'97 2.2, 5.1 channel	Yes	Yes	Yes	533MBps
AC'97 2.2, 5.1 channel	Yes	Yes	No	533MBps
AC'97 2.2, 5.1 channel	Yes	Yes	No	1GBps
AC'97 2.2, 5.1 channel	Yes	Yes	No	1GBps

SiS MuTIOL High-Speed North/South Bridge Connection

The SiS96x-series South Bridge chips use a high-speed bus called MuTIOL to connect with compatible North Bridge chips. The original version of MuTIOL (supported by the SiS961- and 962-series chips) is a 16-bit wide 266MHz connection that provides 533MBps bandwidth, twice the speed of the Intel hub architecture used by Intel's 800-series chipsets.

The SiS963-, 964-, and 965-series and matching North Bridge chips use a second generation of MuTIOL called MuTIOL 1G, which supports a 16-bit-wide 533MHz connection to achieve bandwidths exceeding 1GBps.

When connected to the SiS746FX, SiS741GX, SiS748, or SiS741 North Bridge chips and newer models, the SiS963/964-series chips use a further development of MuTIOL called HyperStreaming, which integrates the following four technologies to further improve the speed of data transfer:

- *Single Stream with Low Latency Technology.* Improves performance by 5%–43% depending on the activity.

- *Multiple Stream with Pipelining and Concurrent Execution Technology.* Uses concurrent parallel data pipelines and simultaneous processing of nonsequential data. In file-copy operations, for example, performance increases as data file size increases.

- *Specific Stream with Prioritized Channel Technology.* Improves playback of Internet music, video, and applications such as IP telephony and videoconferencing.

- *Smart Stream Flow Control Technology.* Analyzes characteristics of different interfaces and improves performance.

SiS730S

The SiS730S is a high-performance, low-cost, single-chip chipset with integrated 2D/3D graphics and support for Socket A versions of the AMD Athlon and Duron.

The integrated video is based on a 128-bit graphic display interface with AGP 2x performance. In addition to providing a standard analog interface for CRT monitors, the SiS730S also provides the DFP for a digital flat panel monitor. An optional SiS301 video bridge supports NTSC/PAL TV output. The SiS730S also supports an AGP 4x slot, enabling users to upgrade to a separate AGP card in the future.

The SiS730S also includes integrated 10/100Mb Fast Ethernet as well as an AC'97-compliant interface that comprises a digital audio engine with 3D-hardware accelerator, on-chip sample rate converter, and professional wavetable along with separate modem DMA controller. SiS730S also incorporates the LPC interface for attaching newer Super I/O chips and a dual USB host controller with six USB ports. The SiS730S can also be used with ISA slots if an optional LPC/ISA bridge chip is used.

Features of the SiS730S include

- Support for AMD Athlon/Duron processors with 200/266MHz system bus
- Support for PC133 SDRAM
- Meets PC99 requirements
- PCI 2.2 compliant
- Four PCI masters
- Support for Ultra DMA100
- Integrated AGP 2x 2D/3D video/graphics accelerator
- Support for digital flat panel
- Hardware DVD decoding

- Built-in secondary CRT controller for independent secondary CRT, LCD, or TV digital output
- LPC interface
- Advanced PCI H/W audio (Sound Blaster 16 and DirectSound 3D compliant) and modem
- Meets ACPI 1.0, APM 1.2 requirements
- PCI Bus Power Management Interface Spec. 1.0
- Integrated keyboard/mouse controller
- Dual USB controller with six USB ports
- Integrated 10/100Mbps Ethernet controller

SiS733 and SiS735

The SiS733 and SiS735 are high-performance single-chip sets that support the AMD Athlon and Duron Socket A processors. Similar to other SiS single-chip sets, the SiS733 and SiS735 incorporate the features of a traditional North Bridge, South Bridge, and Super I/O chip into a single chip.

The SiS733 supports PC133 SDRAM and uses a 682-pin BGA package. The SiS735 supports either PC133 or DDR266 SDRAM and integrates 10/100 Fast Ethernet and HomePNA 1Mbps/10Mbps Home Network interfaces. The SiS735 also uses a 682-pin BGA package.

The SiS733 and SiS735 share the following features:

- Support for 4x AGP
- Up to six PCI masters
- Dual UDMA/100 IDE host adapters
- 1.5GB RAM maximum
- Six USB ports
- AC'97 audio and AMR support
- Integrated RTC
- LPC interface for support of MIDI, joystick, and legacy BIOS devices
- PC2001 compliant

SiS740

The SiS740 is a dual-chip design that provides a high-speed integrated video solution for Athlon-class processors. Its North Bridge and South Bridge chips use the high-speed MuTIOL connection to transfer data. Its major features include

- Integrated Real256 2D/3D graphics core with full DirectX 7 compatibility
- Up to 128MB of shared memory
- Hardware DVD playback
- DDR266 memory support

It is designed to use the SiS961- or 962-series South Bridge chips.

SiS745

The SiS745 is the first single-chip solution to integrate IEEE 1394a (FireWire 400) as part of its I/O. It is designed to provide a high-performance legacy-free solution. Its key features include the following:

- DDR266/333 memory support up to 3GB
- Support for Athlon XP processor as well as earlier models
- Six USB 1.1 ports
- Three IEEE 1394a ports
- Legacy keyboard, mouse, floppy, MIDI, and joystick interfaces
- ATA-100
- AC'97 audio and AMR (audio modem riser) support for a V.90 soft modem

SiS746 and SiS746FX

The SiS746 is the first Athlon/Duron/Athlon XP–compatible chipset on the market to feature an AGP 8x interface. It is a two-piece chipset designed to connect with the SiS963-series South Bridge chipsets. Major features include

- 266MHz processor bus
- DDR266/333 memory (the FX supports DDR400 memory)
- AGP 8x interface
- MuTIOL 1G second-generation connection to South Bridge (1GBps)
- SiS963 or SiS963L South Bridge

The companion SiS963L South Bridge chip adds the following features: ATA-133 support, six USB 2.0 ports, six-channel AC'97 audio, and MII interface for HomePNA or 10/100 Ethernet networking.

The SiS963 South Bridge chip adds IEEE 1394a (FireWire 400) support.

The SiS746FX North Bridge is an enhanced version of the SiS746, adding support for the 333MHz processor bus and approved DDR400 memory. It also uses the SiS963 series of South Bridge chips and uses SiS HyperStreaming technology to reduce latency in the MuTIOL interface.

SiS748

Like the SiS746FX, the SiS748 also uses the SiS963 series of South Bridge chips, as well as the SiS HyperStreaming technology for a lower-latency connection between the chips. Its other major features include

- Up to 400MHz system bus
- DDR266/333/400 memory support
- AGP 8x interface

Figure 4.46 shows the system architecture of the SiS748 chipset when using the SiS963L South Bridge chip. If the SiS963 South Bridge chip is used in place of the SiS963L pictured, three IEEE 1394a ports are also available.

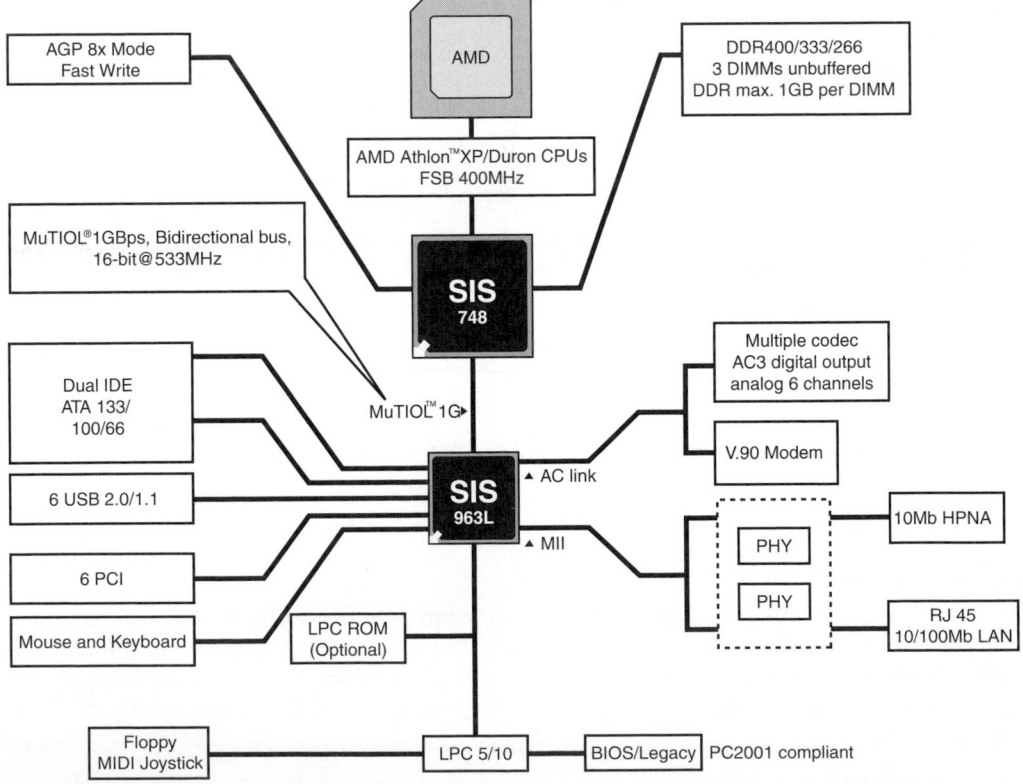

Figure 4.46 Block diagram for SiS748 chipset with SiS963L South Bridge.

SiS741/741GX

The SiS741 chipset includes integrated SiS Mirage Graphics. Its other features are similar to those of the SiS748 chipset. Major features include

- 400MHz system bus
- DDR400 memory support
- Up to 3GB of memory
- AGP 8x

- Integrated SiS Mirage Graphics with DirectX 8.1 support and 32MB or 64MB of shared memory
- Uses SiS963- or 964-series South Bridge

The SiS741GX also includes integrated SiS Mirage Graphics. Its other features are similar to those of the SiS746FX, but it is usually paired with the SiS964 South Bridge.

When paired with an SiS964-series South Bridge, the SiS741GX also supports the following:

- Serial ATA (two ports; 964 only)
- Serial ATA RAID (964 only)

- PCI version 2.3
- Up to eight USB 2.0 ports

ALiMagik1 for AMD Athlon/Duron Systems

ALi Corporation makes only one chipset for AMD Athlon/Duron processors: the ALiMagik1.

ALiMagik1 is a two-chip chipset that uses the M1647 Super North Bridge and the M1535D+ South Bridge (which is also used by its Pentium III/Celeron chipsets). The M1647 Super North Bridge is a 528-pin BGA chip.

The M1647 Super North Bridge supports SDRAM as well as DDR SDRAM at speeds of 200MHz or 266MHz. It supports up to 3GB of RAM but does not support ECC. Memory timing is x-1-1-1-1-1-1-1 in back-to-back SDRAM reads. Because the M1647 supports both conventional and DDR SDRAM, system manufacturers can use the same chipset for both memory types.

The M1647 supports AGP 4x video, PCI 2.2, up to six PCI masters beyond the North Bridge and PCI bridge, ACPI and Legacy green power management, PCI Mobile CLKRUN#, and AGP Mobile BUSY#/STOP#.

When combined with an M1535+ South Bridge chip, the chipset is called the MobileMagik1 and can be used on Athlon- or Duron-based portable systems.

Because this chipset, unlike others that use DDR memory, still uses the traditional 133MBps PCI bus connection between North and South Bridge chips, its performance is among the lowest of any Athlon chipset. This chipset is now discontinued.

NVIDIA nForce Chipsets for Athlon/Duron/Athlon XP

NVIDIA, although best known for its popular GeForce line of graphics chipsets, has also become a popular vendor of chipsets for the AMD Athlon/Duron/Athlon XP processor family with its nForce and nForce2 product families.

nForce's advanced features include

- 400MBps HyperTransport link between chipset components. nForce is the first PC chipset to use HyperTransport.
- Dual-channel crossbar memory controller to provide high-speed memory access when identical pairs of memory are used. It uses independent 64-bit memory controllers.
- nView multidisplay hardware (420 chipset with integrated video) supports dual displays with integrated video.
- AGP 4x interface.
- Dynamic adaptive speculative preprocessor (DASP) to reduce latency and improve prefetching of data.

- StreamThru architecture to improve isochronous (time-dependent) data transfers for network and broadband through the chipset's integrated 10/100 Ethernet port.
- Integrated GeForce2 MX video (420 chipset with integrated video) with support for DVI LCD flat panels.
- True hardware-based audio processing with support for Dolby Digital (AC-3) 5.1 channel audio (SoundStorm chipsets).

nForce2 improvements over nForce include the following:

- DualDDR improved dual-channel memory controller that supports up to DDR400 memory and allows dual-channel operation with two or three DIMMs
- Optional IEEE 1394a support

Table 4.48   nForce/nForce2 IGP/SPP (North Bridge) Chips

North Bridge Chip	nForce 420	nForce 415	nForce2 IGP	nForce2 SPP
Bus speed	200/266MHz	200/266MHz	200/266/ 333MHz	200/266MHz
SMP (dual CPUs)	No	No	No	No
Memory type	DDR200/266MHz PC100/133	DDR200/266MHz PC100/133	DDR200/266/ 333/400[1]	DDR200/266/ 333/400[1]
Parity/ECC	Neither	Neither	Neither	Neither
Maximum memory	4GB	4GB	3GB	3GB
Dual-channel mode	Yes[2]	Yes[2]	Yes	Yes
PCI support	2.2	2.2	2.2	2.2
PCI speed/width	33MHz/32-bit	33MHz/32-bit	33MHz/32-bit	33MHz/32-bit
AGP slot	4x	4x	8x	8x
Integrated video	GeForce2 MX	No	GeForce4 MX	No
HyperTransport speed	400MBps	400MBps	800MBps	800MBps
South Bridge chip	nForce MCP, MCP-D	nForce MCP, MCP-D	nForce2 MCP, MCP-T, Gigabit MCP	nForce2 MCP, MCP-T, Gigabit MCP

1. Requires external AGP card to support DDR400 memory.

Table 4.49   nForce/nForce2 MCP (South Bridge) Chips

South Bridge Chip	USB Support	Number of USB Ports	ATA Support	SATA Support	ATA/SATA RAID Support
nForce MCP	1.1	6	33/66/100	No	No
nForce MCP-D[1]	1.1	6	33/66/100	No	No
nForce2 MCP	1.1, 2.0	6	33/66/100/133	No	No
nForce2 MCP-T[1]	1.1, 2.0	6	33/66/100/133	No	No
nForce2 Gigabit MCP	1.1, 2.0	8	33/66/100/133	Yes	Yes
nForce2 RAID MCP	1.1, 2.0	8	33/66/100/133	Yes	Yes

1. Also known as NVIDIA SoundStorm

- Optional GeForce4 MX integrated video
- AGP 8x interface

Table 4.48 provides an overview of the North Bridge chips in the nForce and nForce2 families, and Table 4.49 provides an overview of the nForce/nForce2 South Bridge chips. Unlike most other chip makers, NVIDIA does not make Pentium 4–compatible chipsets; the nForce is a descendant of the custom chipset NVIDIA created for the Microsoft Xbox console game system.

nForce North Bridge chips with integrated graphics are known as *integrated graphics processors (IGPs)*, whereas those that require separate AGP video are known as *system platform processors (SPPs)*. All South Bridge chips are known as media and communications processors (MCP). IGP/SPP and MCP chips communicate over an 800MBps HyperTransport connection.

nForce2 400	nForce2 Ultra 400	nForce 2 Ultra 400R	nForce2 Ultra 400 Gb
200/266/ 333/400MHz	200/266/ 333/400MHz	200/266/ 333/400MHz	200/266/ 333/400MHz
No	No	No	No
DDR200/266/ 333/400[1]	DDR200/266/ 333/400[1]	DDR200/266/ 333/400[1]	DDR200/266/ 333/400[1]
Neither	Neither	Neither	Neither
3GB	3GB	3GB	3GB
No	Yes	Yes	Yes
2.2	2.2	2.2	2.2
33MHz/32-bit	33MHz/32-bit	33MHz/32-bit	33MHz/32-bit
8x	8x	8x	8x
No	No	No	No
800MBps	800MBps	800MBps	800MBps
nForce2 MCP, MCP-T, Gigabit MCP	nForce2 MCP, MCP-T 2 RAID MCP	nForce	nForce 2 Gigabit MCP

2. Use only two identical memory modules to enable this mode.

Audio	10/100 Ethernet[2]	Gigabit Ethernet	IEEE 1394	Hardware Firewall	Used with
AC'97, 5.1 channel	Yes	No	No	No	nForce IGP, SPP
AC'97, 5.1 channel	Yes	No	No	No	nForce IGP, SPP
AC'97, 6- channel, 20-bit, SPDIF out	Yes	No	No	No	nForce2 IGP, SPP, 400, Ultra 400
All features of MCP, plus Audio Processing Unit, Dolby Digital 5.1 channel, and DirectX 8 3D audio	Dual NVIDIA and 3Com	No	Yes	No	nForce2 IGP, SPP, 400, Ultra 400
AC'97, 6- channel, 20-bit, SPDIF out	Yes	Yes	No	Yes	nForce2 Ultra 400Gb
AC'97, 6- channel, 20-bit, SPDIF out	Yes	No	No	No	nForce2 Ultra 400R

2. Also supports HomePNA networking

The combination of advanced memory controllers, prefetch design, HyperTransport high-speed connection, and hardware audio processing in MCP-D and MCP-T chips makes the second-generation nForce2 chipsets among the fastest chipsets available for Athlon XP processors. The new Gigabit MCP and RAID MCP chips bring eight-port USB 2.0 and Serial ATA/ATA RAID support to nForce2-based systems. The Gigabit MCP is the first nForce2 MCP chip to offer integrated Gigabit Ethernet.

Figure 4.47 shows the architecture of the nForce2 IGP and MCP-T combination, which provides the greatest versatility. If the SPP North Bridge is used instead of the IGP, integrated video is not present. If the MCP South Bridge is used instead of the MCP-T, IEEE 1394a, hardware 5.1 Dolby Digital audio, and dual network ports are not available.

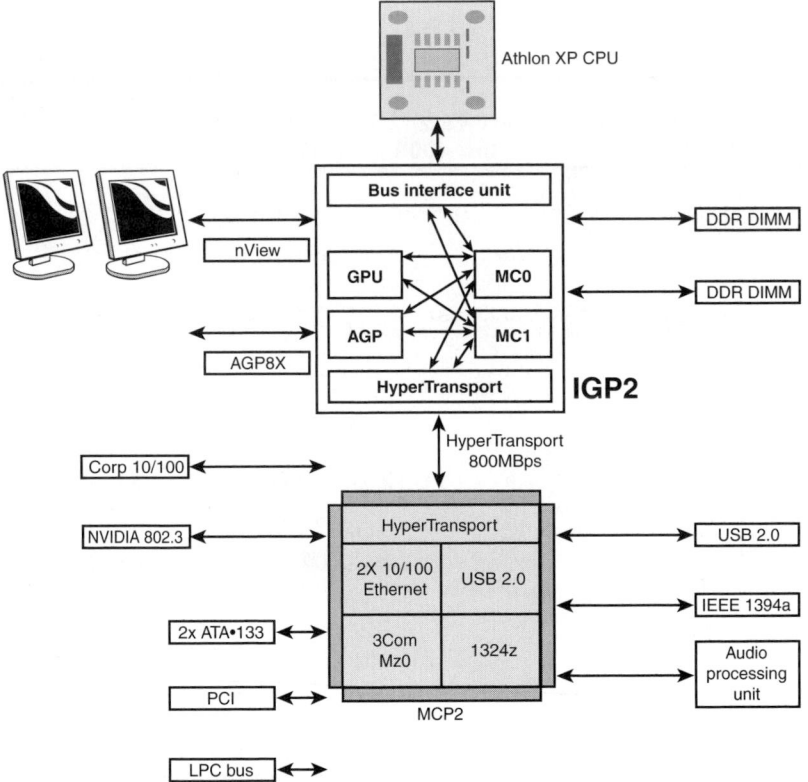

Figure 4.47   NVIDIA nForce2 IGP/MCP2 chipset architecture.

ATI Radeon IGP Chipsets for Athlon/Duron/Athlon XP

ATI made a series of chipsets for the Athlon series of processors that integrate Radeon VE-level 3D graphics, DVD playback, and dual-display features with high-performance North Bridge and South Bridge designs. These chipsets use ATI's high-speed A-Link bus to connect its North and South Bridge chips, but they also support connections to third-party South Bridge chips via the PCI bus. This has enabled system designers to create an all-ATI or a mix-and-match solution. Many of the first Radeon IGP-based systems on the market used ALi or VIA South Bridge chips. The Radeon IGP 320 North Bridge chip can be matched with either of ATI's South Bridge chips: the IXP 200 or IXP 250. Both of these chips support six USB 2.0 ports and ATA33/66/100. Although the mobile version of this chipset—the Radeon 320M IGP—is still available for use in laptop computers, the Radeon 320 IGP is now discontinued. Table 4.50 summarizes the major features of the IGP 320, and Table 4.51 summarizes the major features of the IXP 200 and 250.

Table 4.50   Radeon IGP (North Bridge) Chip for Athlon

North Bridge Chip	Radeon IGP 320	North Bridge Chip	Radeon IGP 320
Bus speed	200/266MHz	PCI support	2.2
SMP (dual CPUs)	No	PCI speed/width	33MHz/32-bit
Memory type	DDR200/266	AGP slot	4x
Parity/ECC	Neither	Integrated video	Radeon VE*
Maximum memory	1GB	A-Link speed	266MBps

Same core as ATI Radeon 7000, with support for dual displays

Table 4.51   ATI South Bridge Chips for Athlon

South Bridge Chip	IXP 200/250*	South Bridge Chip	IXP 200/250*
USB Support	6 USB 2.0 ports	Ethernet LAN	3Com 10/100
ATA Support	ATA100	Super I/O	Yes
Audio Support	AC'97, S/PDIF	High Speed Interconnect	A-Link

The IXP250 has identical features to IXP200; plus it supports Wake On LAN (WOL), Desktop Management Interface (DMI), manage boot agent (MBA), and the Alert Standards Forum (ASF) mechanism.

Intel Workstation Chipsets for Pentium 4 and Xeon

Intel has developed several chipsets for workstations based on the Pentium 4 and Xeon processors. The following sections describe these chipsets in detail; Table 4.52 provides a quick reference to their features.

Table 4.52   Workstation Chipsets

Chipset	860	E7205	E7505
Code name	Colusa	Granite Bay	Placer
Date introduced	May 2001	Dec. 2002	Dec. 2002
Part number	82860	E7205	E7505
Bus speeds	400MHz	533/400MHz	533/400MHz
Supported processors	Xeon	Pentium 4[5]	Xeon 533MHz FSB and 512KB L2 cache[5]
SMP (dual CPUs)	Yes (2)	No	Yes (2)
Memory type	4 RDRAM PC800[1]	DDR200/266 SDRAM (unbuffered)	DDR200/266 (in pairs)
Parity/ECC	Both	Both	Both
Maximum memory	4GB (with two MRHR chips)	4GB	16GB
Memory banks	Up to 4[3]	Up to 4	Up to 6 (registered memory) or 4 (unbuffered memory)
PCI support	2.2	2.2	2.2
PCI speed/width	32-bit/33MHz[2]	32-bit/33MHz	32-bit/33MHz[4]
AGP slot	AGP 4x/2x	AGP8x-1x	AGP8x-1x
Integrated video	None	None	None
South Bridge (Hub)	ICH2	ICH4	ICH4

1. Up to eight on motherboards with MRHR chips
2. 64-bit 33/66MHz on motherboards with P64H chips
3. Two banks when MRHR chip is not present
4. 64-bit 33/66MHz and PCI-X on motherboards with P64H2 chips
5. Supports HT Technology

Intel 860

The Intel 860 is a high-performance chipset designed for the Socket 602 (Pentium 4–based) Xeon processors for DP workstations. The 860 uses the same ICH2 as the Intel 850 but uses a different MCH—the 82860, which supports one or two Socket 602 ("Foster") Xeon processors. The other major features of the 82860 are similar to those of the 82850, including support for dual 400MHz RDRAM memory channels with a 3.2GBps bandwidth and a 400MHz system bus. The 82860 MCH also supports 1.5V AGP 4x video cards at a bandwidth exceeding 1GBps.

The 860 chipset uses a modular design, in which its two core chips can be supplemented by the 82860AA (P64H) 66MHz PCI Controller Hub and the 82803AA MRHR. The 82860AA supports 64-bit PCI slots at either 33MHz or 66MHz, and the 82803AA converts each RDRAM memory channel into two, which doubles memory capacity. Thus, whether a particular 860-based motherboard offers 64-bit or 66MHz PCI slots or dual-channel RDRAM memory depends on whether these supplemental chips are used in its design.

Intel E7205

The Intel E7205 chipset, known as Granite Bay during its development, is designed to support both workstation and high-performance PC applications. It supports DDR200/266 SDRAM modules with a system bus speed up to 533MHz and uses the ICH4 I/O controller hub, just as some versions of the 845 chipset do. However, the E7205 supports ECC and parity-checked memory for better system reliability and supports all standard-voltage speeds of AGP from 1x to 8x with an AGP Pro slot (nonstandard 3.5V versions of AGP once sold by some vendors such as 3dfx will not work). It supports hyper-threading for use with the 3.06GHz and faster Pentium 4 processors.

Table 4.53   Chipsets for Athlon 64

Vendor	Chipset Model	Opteron Support	Chipset Connection	South Bridge	Optional Chipset Components	Video Support
AMD	8151	Yes	HyperTransport (16b/800MHz CPU/NB)[2]	8111	8131 PCI-X tunnel[3]	AGP 8x
ALi	M1687	Yes	HyperTransport (16b/800MHz CPU/NB)	M1653[4]	—	AGP 8x
ALi	M1689	Yes	HyperTransport (16b/800MHz CPU/NB)	—[5]	—	AGP 8x
VIA	K8T800 Pro[6]	Yes	HyperTransport (16b/1GHz CPU/NB); Ultra V-Link (NB/SB)	VT8251 (also supports VT8237)	Velocity Gigabit Ethernet (PCI); VIA Vinyl Gold 8-channel audio	AGP 8x
VIA	K8T800	Yes	HyperTransport (16b/800MHz CPU/NP); 8x V-Link (NB/SB)	VT8237	Velocity Gigabit Ethernet (PCI); SATAlite SATA/SATA RAID 0+1; VIA Vinyl Gold 8-channel audio	AGP 8x
VIA	K8M800	Yes	HyperTransport (16b/800MHz CPU/NP); 8x V-Link (NB/SB)	VT8237	Velocity Gigabit Ethernet; SATAlite SATA/SATA RAID 0+1; VIA Vinyl Gold 8-channel audio	Integrated UniChrome Pro; AGP 8x

Intel E7505

The Intel E7505 chipset, known as Placer during its development, is in some ways an updated version of the 860 chipset, adding support for faster processors and more advanced hardware than the 860 offers.

The E7505 supports a system bus of up to 533MHz, matching the single or dual Xeon 533MHz FSB and 512KB L2 cache processors it supports; it also supports the HT Technology included in these processors. The E7505 supports pairs of DDR200/266 memory up to 16GB total, four times as much as the E7205 and the 860. It can use up to six registered or four unbuffered memory modules and supports ECC. Its Intel x4 single-device data correction (SDDC) can correct up to four errors per memory module for better system reliability.

Its AGP Pro slot supports all speeds of AGP from 1x to 8x (except for the nonstandard 3.5V versions of AGP once sold by some vendors), and it uses the ICH4 I/O controller hub. To achieve 66MHz/64-bit PCI and 133MHz PCI-X support, the E7505 can be used with up to three optional P64H2 (82870P2) chips, an improved version of the P64H chip that is an optional part of the 860 chipset.

Chipsets for Athlon 64

The Athlon 64 processor requires a new generation of chipsets, both to support its 64-bit processor architecture and to allow for integration of the memory controller into the processor (the memory controller has traditionally been located in the North Bridge chip or equivalent). As a consequence, some vendors do not use the term *North Bridge* to refer to the chipset component that connects the processor to AGP video.

AMD, VIA Technologies, NVIDIA, ATI, SiS, and ALi Corporation have developed chipsets for the Athlon 64. Table 4.53 lists the major features of the chipsets developed for the Athlon 64.

PCI-Express x1 Slots	ATA/Serial ATA Support	USB Support (# of Ports)	Audio	LAN
None	ATA-133	1.1/2.0 (6)	AC'97 2.2 (6-channel)	10/100 Ethernet
None	ATA-133	1.1/2.0 (6)	AC'97 2.2 (6-channel); SPDIF	10/100 Ethernet
None	ATA-133, SATA	1.1/2.0 (8)	AC'97 2.3 (6-channel; 20-bit)	10/100 Ethernet
2[7]	ATA-133, SATA, SATA RAID 0, 1, 0+1[7]	1.1/2.0 (8)	AC'97 2.2 (6-channel); Intel HDA	10/100 Ethernet
None	ATA-133, SATA, SATA RAID 0, 1	1.1/2.0 (8)	AC'97 2.2 (6-channel)	10/100 Ethernet
None	ATA-133, SATA, SATA RAID 0, 1	1.1/2.0 (8)	AC'97 2.2 (6-channel)	10/100 Ethernet

Table 4.53 Continued

Vendor	Chipset Model	Opteron Support	Chipset Connection	South Bridge	Optional Chipset Components	Video Support
VIA	K8T890	Yes	HyperTransport (16b/1GHz CPU/NB); Ultra V-Link (NB/SB)	VT8251	Velocity Gigabit Ethernet (PCI); VIA Vinyl Gold 8-channel audio	AGP 8x; PCI-Express x16
VIA	K8M890	Yes	HyperTransport (16b/1GHz CPU/NB); Ultra V-Link (NB/SB)	VT8251	Velocity Gigabit Ethernet (PCI); VIA Vinyl Gold 8-channel audio	AGP 8x; PCI- Express x16; Integrated DeltaChrome
NVIDIA	nForce3 150	No	HyperTransport (8b/600MHz up; 16b/800MHz down)[2]	—[5]	—	AGP 8x
NVIDIA	nForce3 150 Pro	Yes[10]	HyperTransport (8b/600MHz up; 16b/800MHz down)[2]	—[5]	—	AGP 8x
NVIDIA	nForce3 250	No	HyperTransport (16b/800MHz)	—[5]	—	AGP 8x
NVIDIA	nForce3 250 Gb	No	HyperTransport (16b/800MHz)	—[5]	—	AGP 8x
NVIDIA	nForce3 250 Pro	Yes[10]	HyperTransport (16b/800MHz)	—[5]	—	AGP 8x
NVIDIA	nForce3 250 Ultra	Yes[13]	HyperTransport (16b/1GHz)	—[5]	—	AGP 8x
SiS	755	Yes	HyperTransport (800MHz CPU-NB); MuTIOL 1G with HyperStreaming (NB/SB)	SiS964	—	AGP 8x
SiS	755FX	Yes[10]	HyperTransport (1GHz CPU-NB); MuTIOL 1G with HyperStreaming (NB/SB)	SiS965 (also compatible with SiS964)	—	AGP 8x
SiS	756	Yes[10]	HyperTransport (1GHz CPU-NB); MuTIOL 1G with HyperStreaming (NB/SB)	SiS965	—	PCI-Express x16
SiS	760	Yes	HyperTransport (800MHz CPU-NB); MuTIOL 1G with HyperStreaming (NB/SB)	SiS964	—	AGP 8x; integrated Mirage 2

PCI-Express x1 Slots	ATA/Serial ATA Support	USB Support (# of Ports)	Audio	LAN
4	ATA-133, SATA, SATA RAID 0, 1, 0+1[7]	1.1/2.0 (8)	AC'97 2.2 (6-channel); Intel HDA	10/100 Ethernet
4	ATA-133, SATA, SATA RAID 0, 1, 0+1[7]	1.1/2.0 (8)	AC'97 2.2 (6-channel); Intel HDA	10/100 Ethernet
None	ATA-133, RAID 0, 1, 0+1	1.1/2.0 (6)	AC'97 2.1 (6-channel; 20-bit; SPDIF)	10/100 Ethernet
None	ATA-133, RAID 0, 1, 0+1	1.1/2.0 (6)	AC'97 2.1 (6-channel; 20-bit; SPDIF)	10/100 Ethernet
None	ATA-133, SATA, ATA/SATA RAID 0, 1, 0+1	1.1/2.0 (8)	AC'97 2.1 (6-channel; 20-bit; SPDIF)	10/100 Ethernet[8]
None	ATA-133, SATA, ATA/SATA RAID 0, 1, 0+1	1.1/2.0 (6)	AC'97 2.1 (6-channel; 20-bit; SPDIF)	10/100/1000 Ethernet[8]
None	ATA-133, SATA, ATA/SATA RAID 0, 1, 0+1	1.1/2.0 (6)	AC'97 2.1 (6-channel; 20-bit; SPDIF)	10/100/1000 Ethernet[8]
None	ATA-133, SATA, ATA/SATA RAID 0, 1, 0+1	1.1/2.0 (8)	AC'97 2.1 (6-channel; 20-bit; SPDIF)	10/100/1000 Ethernet[8]
None	ATA-133, SATA, RAID 0, 1	1.1/2.0 (8)	AC'97 2.3 (6-channel)	10/100 Ethernet; HomePNA 2.0
2[9]	ATA-133, SATA, RAID 0, 1, 0+1[9]	1.1/2.0 (8)	AC'97 2.3 (8-channel)	10/100/1000 Ethernet; HomePNA 2.0
2	ATA-133, SATA, RAID 0, 1, 0+1[9]	1.1/2.0 (8)	AC'97 2.3 (8-channel)	10/100/1000 Ethernet; HomePNA 2.0
None	ATA-133, SATA, RAID 0, 1	1.1/2.0 (8)	AC'97 2.3 (6-channel)	10/100 Ethernet; HomePNA 2.0

Table 4.53   Continued

Vendor	Chipset Model	Opteron Support	Chipset Connection	South Bridge	Optional Chipset Components	Video Support
SiS	760GX	No	HyperTransport (800MHz CPU-NB); MuTIOL 1G with HyperStreaming (NB/SB)	SiS966 (also compatible with SiS965/L)	—	AGP 8x; integrated Mirage 1
SiS	761	Yes[10]	HyperTransport (1GHz CPU-NB); MuTIOL 1G with HyperStreaming (NB/SB)	SiS966 (also compatible with SiS965/L)	—	PCI-Express x16; integrated Mirage 3
SiS	761GX	No[12]	HyperTransport (1GHz CPU-NB); MuTIOL 1G with HyperStreaming (NB/SB)	SiS966 (also compatible with SiS965/L)	—	PCI-Express x16; integrated Mirage 1
ATI	RS480	Yes	HyperTransport (16b/800MHz CPU/NB); A-Link II	SB400	—	PCI-Express 16x; Integrated Radeon 9100
ATI	RX480	Yes	HyperTransport (16b/800MHz CPU/NB); A-Link II	SB400	—	PCI-Express 16x

1. This chipset is also referred to as the 8000. 8151 is the AGP 3.0 Graphics Tunnel, which performs the graphics interface functions normally performed by the North Bridge in other chipset architectures.

2. 8b = 8-bit-wide HyperTransport connection; 16b = 16-bit-wide connection.

3. This component provides two independent PCI-X bus bridges and uses HyperTransport.

4. For features of the M1653, see Table 4.36.

5. Single-chip chipset.

6. Features asynchronous bus architecture, which locks AGP and PCI buses at the correct speeds when FSB or clock multipliers are adjusted for faster performance.

7. With VT8251 South Bridge.

The following sections cover these chipsets in greater detail.

AMD 8000 (8151) Chipset

The AMD 8000 is AMD's first chipset designed for the Athlon 64 and Opteron families. Its architecture is substantially different from the North Bridge/South Bridge or hub-based architectures we are familiar with from the chipsets designed to support Pentium II/III/4/Celeron and AMD Athlon/Athlon XP/Duron processors.

The AMD-8000 chipset is often referred to as the AMD-8151 because the AMD-8151 provides the connection between the Athlon 64 or Opteron processor and the AGP video slot—the task usually performed by the North Bridge or MCH hub in other chipsets. The name of the North Bridge or MCH hub chip is usually applied to the chipset. However, AMD refers to the AMD-8151 chip as the AGP Graphics Tunnel chip because its only task is to provide a high-speed connection to the AGP slot on the motherboard. The other components of the AMD-8000 chipset include the AMD-8111 HyperTransport I/O hub (South Bridge) and the AMD-8131 PCI-X Tunnel chip.

Due to delays in the development of the AMD-8151 AGP Graphics Tunnel chip, most vendors through late 2003 used the AMD-8111 HyperTransport I/O hub alone or along with the AMD-8131

PCI-Express x1 Slots	ATA/Serial ATA Support	USB Support (# of Ports)	Audio	LAN
4[11]	ATA-133, SATA, RAID 0, 1, 0+1[13]	1.1/2.0 (10)[13]	AC'97 2.3 (6-channel); Intel HDA	10/100/1000[13] Ethernet; HomePNA 2.0
4[11]	ATA-133, SATA, RAID 0, 1, 0+1[13]	1.1/2.0 (10)[13]	AC'97 2.3 (6-channel); Intel HDA[13]	10/100/1000[13] Ethernet; HomePNA 2.0
4[11]	ATA-133, SATA, RAID 0, 1, 0+1[13]	1.1/2.0 (10)[13]	AC'97 2.3 (6-channel); Intel HDA[13]	10/100/1000[13] Ethernet; HomePNA 2.0
2	ATA-133, SATA, SATA RAID 0, 1, 0+1	1.1/2.0 (8)	AC'97 2.2 (6-channel); Intel HDA	—
2	ATA-133, SATA, SATA RAID 0, 1, 0+1	1.1/2.0 (8)	AC'97 2.2 (6-channel); Intel HDA	—

8. *Also incorporates an integrated firewall.*

9. *With SiS965 South Bridge.*

10. *Supports Athlon 64FX, Opteron processors only.*

11. *With SiS966 South Bridge.*

12. *Supports Athlon 64FX processors only.*

13. *Officially supports Athlon 64 Socket 939; some vendors also use it for motherboards with Socket 940 Opteron processors.*

HDA = High-Definition Audio (previously code named Azalia); supports CE-quality (192KHz, 32-bit multichannel) audio with support for Dolby Pro Logic IIx (7.1 surround) and multiple codecs operating independently.

PCI-X Tunnel chip to provide a mixture of PCI and PCI-X slots on motherboards optimized as servers. Some recent systems have incorporated the AMD-8151 chip to provide AGP video, but the AMD-8000 chipset continues to be used primarily as a workstation/server chipset instead of as a desktop chipset.

The AMD-8151 AGP Graphics tunnel has the following major features:

- Supports AGP 2.0/3.0 (AGP 1x–8x) graphics cards
- 16-bit up/down HyperTransport connection to the processor
- 8-bit up/down HyperTransport connection to downstream chips

The AMD-8111 HyperTransport I/O hub (South Bridge) chip's major features include

- PCI 2.2-compliant PCI bus (32-bit, 33MHz) for up to eight devices
- AC'97 2.2 audio (six-channel)
- Six USB 1.1/2.0 ports (three controllers)
- Two ATA/IDE host adapters supporting up to ATA-133 speeds
- RTC

- Low-pin-count (LPC) bus
- Integrated 10/100 Ethernet
- 8-bit up/down HyperTransport connection to upstream chips

The AMD-8131 HyperTransport PCI-X tunnel chip's major features include

- Two PCI-X bridges (A and B) supporting up to five PCI bus masters each
- PCI-X transfer rates up to 133MHz
- PCI 2.2 33MHz and 66MHz transfer rates
- Independent operational modes and transfer rates for each bridge
- 8-bit up/down HyperTransport connection to upstream and downstream chips

Figure 4.48 shows the architecture of the AMD-8151 chipset for Athlon 64.

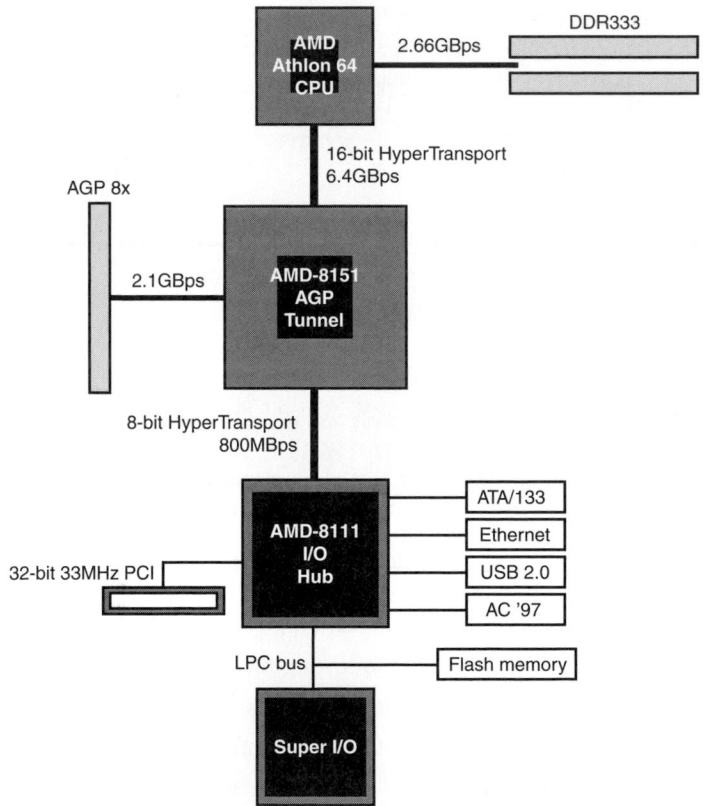

Figure 4.48   Block diagram of the AMD 8000 chipset for Athlon 64.

ALi Chipsets for Athlon 64

Although ALi has largely been absent from chipset development for the Athlon XP, it offers two chipsets for the Athlon 64 and Opteron processors: the M1687 and the M1689. The M1687 is a traditional two-chip design, whereas the M1689 is a one-chip design following in the footsteps of SiS and, more recently, NVIDIA.

ALi M1687

The M1687 uses the M1563 as its South Bridge, and the major features of this chipset are similar to the AMD-8151/AMD-8111 design:

- Support for AGP 2.0/3.0 (AGP 1x–8x) graphics cards
- 16-bit up/down HyperTransport connection between processor and M1687
- 8-bit up/down HyperTransport connection between M1687 North Bridge and M1563 South Bridge
- PCI 2.2–compliant PCI bus (32-bit, 33MHz) for up to six devices
- AC'97 2.2 audio (six-channel)
- Six USB 1.1/2.0 ports (three controllers)
- Two ATA/IDE host adapters supporting up to ATA-133 speeds
- RTC
- Low-pin-count (LPC) bus
- Integrated 10/100 Ethernet

Compared to the AMD-8151/AMD-8111, the major advantage of the ALi M1687 is the Secure Digital and Sony Memory Stick interfaces built in to the M1563.

ALi M1689

The ALi M1689 is a single-chip chipset for the Athlon 64 and Opteron processors, and it can also be used with the Mobile Athlon 64. It integrates several of the latest technologies, including Serial ATA, support for eight USB 2.0/1.1 ports, and AC'97 2.3 20-bit six-channel audio. Major features include

- AGP 1.5/3.0 (AGP 1x–8x)
- PCI 2.3 with support for up to seven bus masters
- Dual ATA-133 host adapters with support for 48-bit LBA drives
- Four USB host adapters and eight USB 1.1/2.0 ports
- 10/100 Ethernet
- AC'97 2.3 audio with 20-bit sampling
- Two Serial ATA host adapters

VIA Technologies Chipsets for Athlon 64

VIA Technologies has long been one of the leading developers of chipsets for AMD processors, and this pattern continues with the Athlon 64 and Opteron. VIA offers five chipsets for these processors:

- K8T800 Pro
- K8T800
- K8M800
- K8T890
- K8M890

The following sections cover these chipsets in more detail.

K8T800, K8T800 Pro, and K8M800

The K8T800 (originally known as the K8T400) was VIA's first chipset for the Athlon 64 and Opteron processors. It departs somewhat from the pattern established by AMD's and ALi's chipsets by using VIA's own 8x V-Link (533MBps) interconnect between the North and South Bridge chips instead of

HyperTransport (although HyperTransport is used, of course, to connect to the processor). The K8T800 uses the VT8237 South Bridge chip. Major features include

- HyperTransport 16-bit/800MHz link between the processor and North Bridge
- Support for AGP 4x/8x video cards
- PCI 2.23 with support for up to six bus masters
- Dual ATA-133 host adapters
- Eight USB 1.1/2.0 ports
- 10/100 Ethernet
- AC'97 5.1 audio
- Two Serial ATA/SATA RAID host adapters (RAID 0, 1, JBOD)

The K8T800 chipset family also includes the following optional chips, which can be used to add more features:

- SATAlite SATA (two additional ports, adding RAID 0+1)
- VPX2 expansion bridge (adds two PCI-X buses)
- VIA Vinyl Gold (7.1 surround sound via PCI bus)
- Gigabit Ethernet controller (via PCI bus)

The K8T800 Pro is based on the K8T800, but with the following improvements:

- HyperTransport 1GHz link between the processor and North Bridge
- Asynchronous operation of PCI and AGP slots
- Ultra V-Link (1GBps) connection between the North and South Bridges

The most significant of these features is the asynchronous operation of PCI and AGP slots. This feature enables the user to lock the frequency of these slots regardless of the processor bus and clock multiplier used by the processor, enabling more reliable overclocking. Many Athlon 64 chipsets lack this capability.

The K8M800 is based on the K8T800 but adds S3 UniChrome Pro integrated graphics. UniChrome Pro offers a 128-bit 2D/3D engine, dual pixel pipelines, hardware acceleration for MPEG-2 and MPEG-4 video, and support for HDTV up to 1080p and standard TV as well as LCD and CRT displays.

K8T890 and K8M890

The VIA K8T890 and K8M890 are the first Athlon 64/Opteron chipsets to support both the new PCI-Express x16 slot and the established AGP 8x slot for high-speed graphics. This support enables the user to upgrade to 64-bit computing now and upgrade to PCI-Express x16 at a later point. These chipsets use the 1GHz HyperTransport processor/NB connection and Ultra V-Link NB/SB connections.

These North Bridge chips actually have a 20-lane-wide PCI-Express interface, leaving 4 lanes available for PCI-Express x1 cards.

These chipsets are also designed to use the new VT8251 South Bridge, which includes several features that once required add-on chips:

- Four Serial ATA host adapters are included to support SATA RAID 0, 1, and 0+1.
- Support for Intel's new High-Definition Audio (HDA, formerly code named Azalia) standard. HDA provides Dolby Digital IIfx-compatible (7.1) surround sound and 24-bit/192KHz sampling rates for CE-quality sound.
- Two PCI-Express x1 slots, for a total of six possible (four connected to North Bridge and two to South Bridge).

Figure 4.49 displays the K8T890's block diagram.

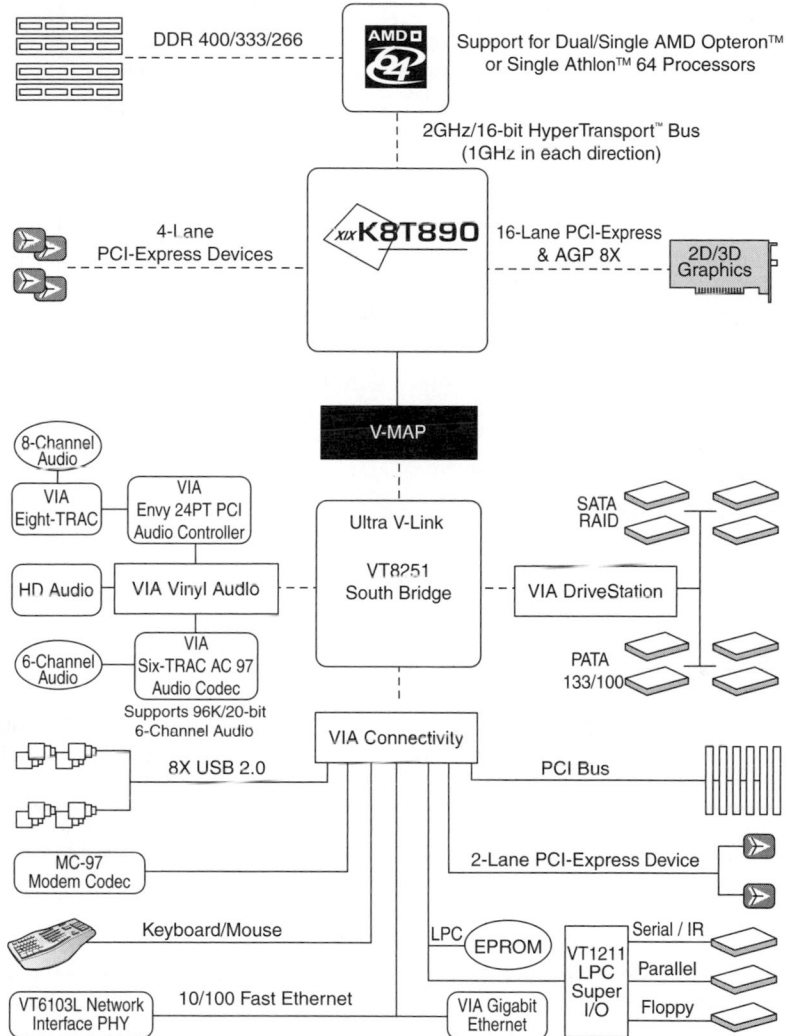

Figure 4.49 The VIA K8T890 is the first PCI-Express x16 chipset that also supports AGP 8x. It also supports two-lane and four-lane PCI-Express devices, HD Audio, and the 1GHz/each direction 16-bit HyperTransport bus.

The K8M890 adds integrated S3 Graphics DeltaChrome 2D/3D graphics with DirectX 9 graphics support to the features of the K8T890.

NVIDIA

NVIDIA offers four single-chip chipsets for the Athlon 64:

- nForce3 150
- nForce3 250
- nForce3 250Gb
- nForce3 250 Ultra

NVIDIA also offers two single-chip chipsets for the Opteron:

- nForce3 Pro 150
- nForce3 Pro 250

NVIDIA refers to these chips as *media and communications processors (MCPs)* because a single chip combines the functions of typical North and South Bridge chips. The following sections cover these chips in more detail.

nForce3 150 and nForce3 Pro 150

The NVIDIA nForce3 150 MCP was one of the first chipsets available for the Athlon 64 processor. Although it departs from the two-chip chipset standard used by most Athlon 64 chipsets by combining North Bridge and South Bridge functions, the nForce3 150 has a limited feature set. The short list of features reflects both this chipset's early development and its positioning as an entry-level chipset. The nForce3 150's major features include

- HyperTransport chipset-to-processor connection. However, it offers the standard 16-bit/800MHz speed only in the downstream (processor-to-chipset) direction. Data flowing from the chipset to the processor (upstream) runs in an 8-bit data path at only 600MHz.
- AGP 1x–8x video card support.
- Dual ATA-133 ATA/IDE hard disk host adapters.
- RAID 0, 1, and 0+1.
- AC'97 2.1 audio (six-channel) with 20-bit output and SPDIF support.
- Six USB 1.1/2.0 ports.
- 10/100 Ethernet.

The nForce3 Pro 150 has a similar feature set but is designed for use with the Opteron processor and NVIDIA's Quadro workstation graphics processor.

Note

Although some nForce3 150 and Pro 150 motherboards offer SATA and SATA RAID, this is *not* a function of the chipset; however, it can be performed with the use of an add-on SATA RAID chip.

nForce3 250, 250Gb, and 250 Ultra and nForce3 Professional 250

The nForce3 250 family of MCPs includes four members, all of which include several enhanced features over the original nForce3 150 and 150 Pro. The base model, nForce3 250, has the following major features:

- HyperTransport 16-bit/800MHz upstream/downstream connections between the processor and the MCP
- AGP 8x graphics card support
- Dual independent ATA-133 ATA/IDE host adapters with RAID 0, 1, and 0+1
- SATA and SATA RAID 0, 1, and 0+1
- Eight USB 1.1/2.0 ports
- 10/100 Ethernet with integrated hardware firewall
- AC'97 2.1 audio (six-channel) with 20-bit output and SPDIF support

The 250Gb model has the 250's features and adds support for 10/100/1000 Ethernet with integrated hardware firewall. The 250 Pro has the feature set of the 250 Gb but supports the Opteron workstation processor and the Athlon 64FX and is optimized to work with NVIDIA's Quadro workstation graphics processor.

The 250 Ultra model has the 250's features and adds support for both 10/100/1000 Ethernet with integrated hardware firewall and an Advanced 16-bit/1GHz HyperTransport upstream/downstream processor/MCP connection.

Note

The integrated firewall included in all nForce3 250-series chipsets is highly configurable and protects the computer as soon as it is turned on. Software firewalls, by contrast, cannot protect the computer until they are loaded, which is often late in the boot process.

SiS

SiS offers seven chipsets for 64-bit AMD processors. The following three chipsets require discrete graphics:

- 755
- 755FX
- 756

SiS also offers four chipsets with integrated graphics for AMD's 64-bit processors:

- 760
- 760GX
- 761
- 761GX

The following sections cover these chipsets in greater detail.

SiS755 and SiS755FX

The SiS 755 is the first SiS chipset to support the AMD Athlon 64, Opteron, and Athlon 64FX chipsets. It is a two-piece chipset that uses the SiS964 as its South Bridge component. Its major features include

- HyperTransport 16-bit/800MHz connection between the processor and North Bridge with HyperStreaming
- Support for AGP 8x graphics
- MuTIOL 1G connection between the North and South Bridge chips with HyperStreaming
- Dual ATA-133 host adapters
- Two Serial ATA ports with SATA RAID 0 and 1
- Eight USB 1.1/2.0 ports
- 10/100 Ethernet
- AC'97 version 2.3 8-channel audio

The 755FX North Bridge chip is pin-compatible with the 755; however, the preferred South Bridge chip for the 755FX—the SiS965—uses a larger 588-pin socket over the 505-pin socket used by the 964 family. The 755FX/965 chipset has the following major improvements over the 755/964 chipset:

- HyperTransport 16-bit/1GHz connection between the processor and North Bridge with HyperStreaming
- Support for two PCI-Express x1 slots
- Four Serial ATA ports with SATA RAID 0, 1, and 0+1 and JBOD (disk spanning)
- 10/100/1000 Ethernet

SiS756

The SiS756 chipset is designed specifically for use with the high-performance Athlon 64FX desktop processor. It is the first SiS chipset to support the PCI-Express x16 graphics interface. The SiS756 is usually paired with the SiS965 South Bridge. This chipset's major features include

- HyperTransport 16-bit/1GHz connection between the processor and North Bridge with HyperStreaming
- PCI-Express x16 graphics support
- Two PCI-Express x1 slots
- Eight USB 1.1/2.0 ports
- Four SATA ports with SATA RAID 0, 1, and 0+1 and JBOD
- 10/100/1000 Ethernet
- AC'97 2.3 eight-channel audio

Note

If the SiS965L is used in place of the SiS965, only two SATA ports with SATA RAID 0 and 1 are available. The other features are the same.

PCI-Express x16 replaces the AGP 8x video support found in earlier SiS chipsets.

Figure 4.50 shows the architecture of the SiS756 chipset with the SiS965 South Bridge.

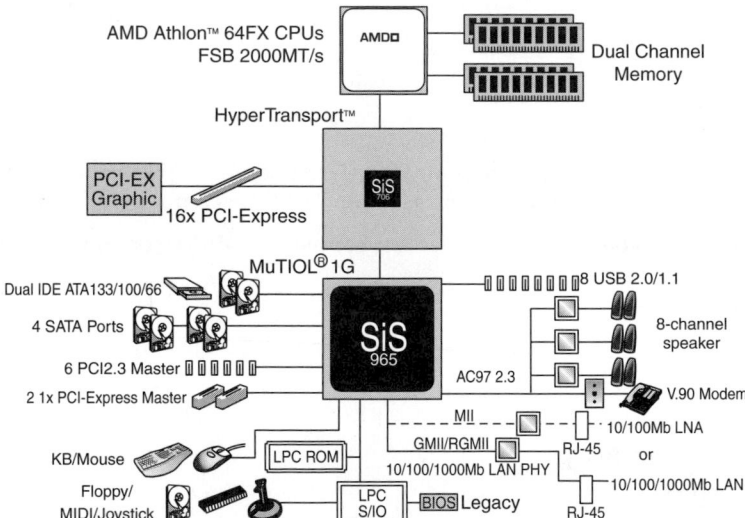

Figure 4.50   As with most Athlon 64 chipsets, the SiS756's North Bridge is used only for connection to discrete graphics (PCI-Express in this case), while a vast majority of the work is performed by the South Bridge.

SiS760 and Sis760GX

The SiS760 is the first SiS chipset with integrated graphics for the Athlon 64 and Opteron processors. Otherwise, its major features are similar to those of the SiS755. Both use the SiS964 South Bridge chip. Its features include

- HyperTransport 16-bit/800MHz connection between the processor and North Bridge with HyperStreaming

- Support for AGP 8x graphics
- MuTIOL 1G connection between the North and South Bridge chips with HyperStreaming
- Dual ATA-133 host adapters
- Two Serial ATA ports with SATA RAID 0 and 1
- Eight USB 1.1/2.0 ports
- 10/100 Ethernet
- AC'97 version 2.3 8-channel audio

The integrated SiS Mirage 2 (Ultra256) graphics features of the SiS760 include

- DirectX 8.1-compatible 3D graphics
- Dual-channel 256-bit 3D interface
- 128-bit 2D graphics
- Optional support for TV-out and a secondary CRT or LCD display
- Shared memory up to 128MB

The SiS760GX instead uses Mirage 1 single-channel (128-bit) graphics.

The SiS966 South Bridge is the preferred South Bridge for the SiS760GX, adding the following features:

- Four PCI-Express x1 slots
- SATA, SATA RAID 0, 1, and 0+1
- Ten USB 1.1/2.0 ports
- AC'97 2.3 audio with support for Intel's new High Definition Audio 7.1-channel audio
- 10/100/1000 Ethernet

SiS761 and SiS761GX

The SiS761 and SiS761GX integrated graphics chipsets support the high-performance Athlon 64FX processor family (the SiS761 can also be used with Opteron processors). Both chipsets use the SiS966 as their preferred South Bridge.

Note

The SiS966, SiS965, and SiS965L are pin compatible. Thus, some vendors might use the SiS965 or SiS965L in place of the SiS966.

Both the SiS761 and SiS761GX North Bridge chips have the following major features:

- HyperTransport 16-bit/800MHz connection between the processor and North Bridge with HyperStreaming
- Support for PCI-Express x16 graphics
- MuTIOL 1G connection between the North and South Bridge chips with HyperStreaming

When the SiS966 South Bridge chip is used, both chipsets also feature

- Four PCI-Express x1 slots
- SATA, SATA RAID 0, 1, and 0+1
- Ten USB 1.1/2.0 ports
- AC'97 2.3 six-channel audio with support for Intel's new High Definition Audio standard

Note

HDA, previously code named Azalia, provides Dolby Pro Logic IIx–compatible 7.1-channel CE-quality (192KHz, 32-bit multichannel) sound.

- 10/100/1000 Ethernet

The major difference between the SiS761GX and SiS761 is in the type of integrated graphics each North Bridge chip contains:

- The SiS761GX features conventional single-channel Mirage 1 integrated graphics.
- The SiS761 features dual-channel Mirage 3 integrated graphics.

ATI

ATI offers two two-piece chipsets for Athlon 64 processors: the RS480 (which includes Radeon 9200–equivalent DirectX 8.1 integrated graphics) and the RX480. Both chipsets use the SB400 (also known as the IXP400) South Bridge. Aside from the RS480's integrated graphics, both chipsets have the following major features:

- HyperTransport 16-bit/800MHz processor–to–North Bridge connection
- PCI-Express x16 graphics card support
- A-Link II connection between the North and South Bridge chips
- Four PCI-Express x1 slots
- Dual ATA-133 host adapters
- Four Serial ATA host adapters with SATA RAID 0, 1, and 0+1
- Eight USB 2.0 ports
- AC'97 2.3 six-channel audio with support for Intel's new HDA standard

Super I/O Chips

The third major chip seen on many PC motherboards is called the Super I/O chip. This is a chip that integrates devices formerly found on separate expansion cards in older systems.

Most Super I/O chips contain, at a minimum, the following components:

- Floppy controller
- One or two serial port controllers
- Parallel port controller

The floppy controllers on some Super I/O chips handle two drives, but some newer models can handle only one. Older systems often required a separate floppy controller card.

The serial port is another item that was formerly on one or more cards. Most of the better Super I/O chips implement a buffered serial port design known as a universal asynchronous receiver transmitter (UART), one for each port. Most mimic the standalone NS16550A high-speed UART, which was created by National Semiconductor. By putting the functions of these chips into the Super I/O chip, serial ports are essentially built in to the motherboard.

Virtually all Super I/O chips also include a high-speed multimode parallel port. Most recent models allow three modes: standard (bidirectional), Enhanced Parallel Port (EPP), and the Enhanced Capabilities Port (ECP) modes. The ECP mode is the fastest and most powerful, but selecting it also causes your port to use an ISA bus 8-bit DMA channel—usually DMA channel 3. As long as you account for this and don't set anything else to that channel (such as a sound card and so on), the EPC mode parallel port should work fine. Some of the newer printers and scanners that connect to the system via the parallel port use ECP mode, which was invented by Hewlett-Packard.

The Super I/O chip can contain other components as well. For example, the Intel VC820 ATX motherboard uses an SMC (Standard Microsystems Corp.) LPC47M102 Super I/O chip. This chip incorporates the following functions:

- Floppy drive interface
- Two high-speed serial ports
- One ECP/EPP multimode parallel port
- 8042-style keyboard and mouse controller

This chip is typical of recent Super I/O chips in that it has an integrated keyboard and mouse controller. Older Super I/O chips lacked this feature.

One thing I've noticed over the years is that the role of the Super I/O chip has decreased more and more in the newer motherboards. This is primarily due to Intel and other chipset manufacturers moving Super I/O functions, such as IDE, directly into the chipset South Bridge or ICH component, where these devices can attach to the PCI bus (North/South Bridge architecture) or to the high-speed hub interface (hub architecture) rather than the ISA bus. One of the shortcomings of the Super I/O chip is that originally it was interfaced to the system via the ISA bus and shared all the speed and performance limitations of that 8MHz bus. Moving the IDE over to the PCI bus allowed higher-speed IDE drives to be developed that could transfer at the faster 33MHz PCI bus speed.

Newer Super I/O chips interface to the system via the LPC bus, an interface designed by Intel to offer a connection running at half the speed of PCI (up to about 16.67MBps) using only 13 signals. LPC is much more efficient than ISA.

Because high-speed devices such as IDE/ATA drives are now interfaced through the South Bridge chip, PCI bus, or hub architectures, nothing interfaced through the current Super I/O chips needs any greater bandwidth anyway.

As the chipset manufacturers combine more and more functions into the main chipset, and as USB- and IEEE 1394–based peripherals replace standard serial, parallel, and floppy controller–based devices, we will probably see the Super I/O chip continue to fade away in motherboard designs. More and more chipsets are combining the South Bridge and Super I/O chips into a single component (often referred to as a Super South Bridge chip) to save space and reduce parts count on the motherboard. Several of the SiS and NVIDIA chipsets even integrate all three chips (North Bridge, South Bridge, and Super I/O) into a single chip.

Motherboard CMOS RAM Addresses

In the original AT system, a Motorola 146818 chip was used as the RTC and Complementary Metal-Oxide Semiconductor (CMOS) RAM chip. This was a special chip that had a digital clock and stored 64 bytes of data. The clock used 14 bytes of RAM and an additional 50 more bytes of leftover RAM in which you could store anything you wanted. The designers of the IBM AT used these extra 50 bytes to store the system configuration.

Modern PC systems don't use the Motorola chip; instead, they incorporate the functions of this chip into the motherboard chipset (South Bridge) or Super I/O chip, or they use a special battery and NVRAM module from companies such as Dallas or Benchmarq.

▶▶ For more details on the CMOS RAM addresses, see "Motherboard CMOS RAM Addresses," p. 425.

Motherboard Connectors

There are a variety of connectors on a modern motherboard. Figure 4.51 shows connector locations on a typical motherboard. Several of these connectors, such as power supply connectors, serial and parallel ports, and keyboard/mouse connectors, are covered in other chapters.

This section has figures and tables showing the configurations and pinouts of most of the other interface and I/O connectors you will find.

▶▶   See "AT Power Supply Connectors," p. 1164.

▶▶   See "Serial Ports," p. 997, and "Parallel Ports," p. 1007.

▶▶   See "Keyboard/Mouse Interface Connectors," p. 1031.

▶▶   See "Universal Serial Bus," p. 983.

▶▶   See "Overview of the IDE Interface," p. 532.

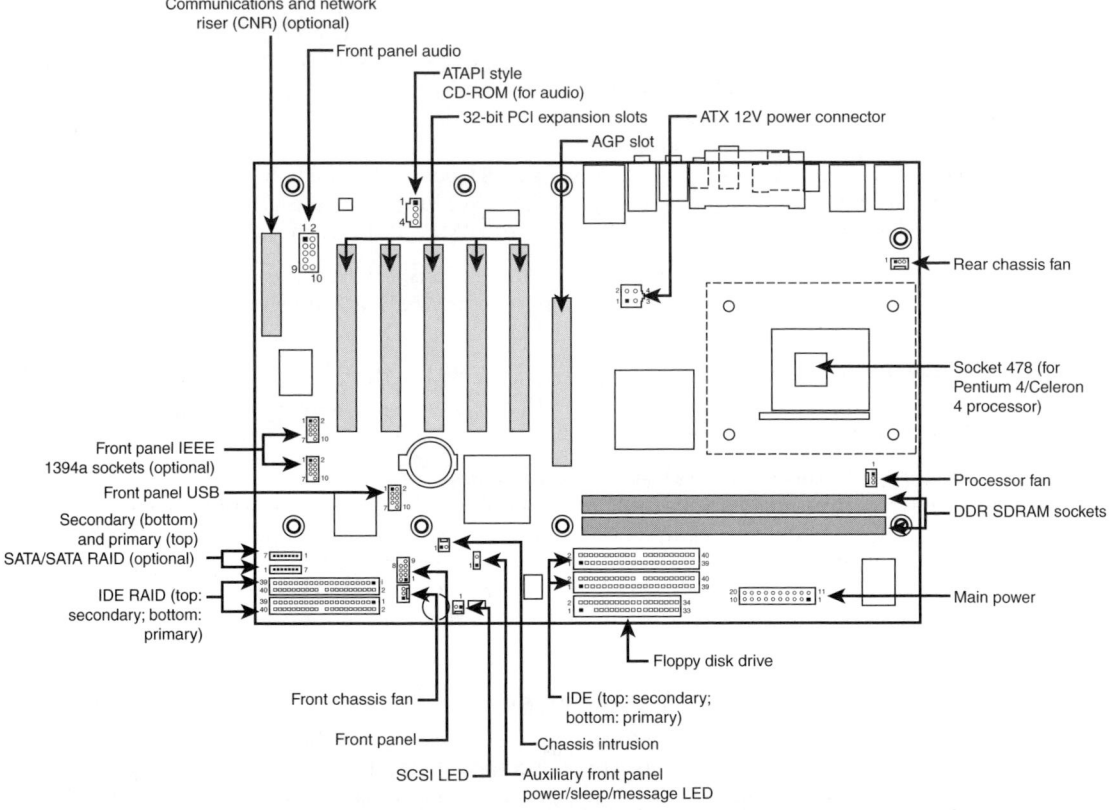

Figure 4.51   Typical motherboard connectors.

One of the biggest problems many people overlook when building and upgrading systems is the front panel connections. Connectors that don't match between the motherboard and chassis are one of the small but frustrating things that can be problematic in an otherwise smooth upgrade or system build. Having dependable standards for these connections would help, but unfortunately no official standard for the front panel connectors existed until October 2000, when Intel published the "Front

Panel I/O Connectivity Design Guide." This guide can be found, along with the motherboard form factor specifications, at www.formfactors.org.

Before this standard was published, no official standard existed (and anarchy ruled). In addition, even though most chassis gave you individual tiny connectors for each function, some of the bigger system builders (for example, Dell, Gateway, MicronPC [now MPC], and so on) began using specialized inline or dual-row header connectors so they could build systems more quickly and efficiently. Coincidentally, most of those vendors used Intel boards, hence Intel's development of a standard.

The front panel guide details a 10-pin keyed header connector for the main front panel switch/LED functions, as well as a 10-pin keyed USB header, a 10-pin keyed IEEE 1394 (FireWire/i.LINK) header, a 10-pin keyed audio header, and a 6-pin keyed IR header. The pinouts and configurations of these and other motherboard-based connectors are shown in the following figures and tables. Figure 4.52 details the front panel switch/LED header connector.

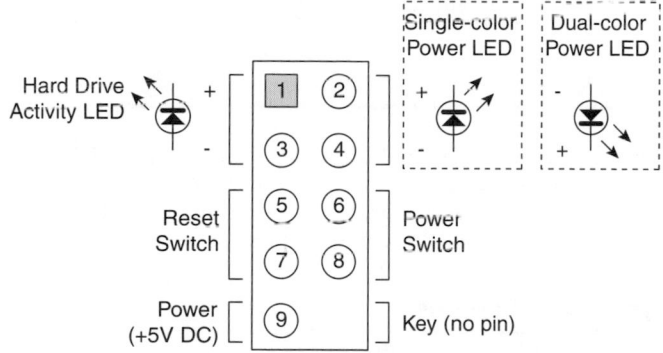

Figure 4.52   Front panel switch/LED header connector.

The pinout of the standard front panel switch/LED connector is shown in Table 4.54.

Table 4.54   Front Panel Switch/LED Connector Pinout

Signal	Description	Pin	Pin	Signal	Description
Hard Disk Activity LED			**Power/Sleep/Message LED**		
HD_LED+	Hard disk LED+	1	2	PWR_LED GRN+	Single-color LED+
HD_LED-	Hard disk LED-	3	4	PWR_LED_YEL+	Dual-color LED+
Reset Button			**Power On/Off Button**		
GND	Ground	5	6	FP_PWR	Power switch
FP_RESET	Reset switch	7	8	GND	Ground
Power			**Not Connected**		
+5V	Power	9	10	N/C	Not connected

Some chassis provide a single 10-pin header connector for the front panel switch/LED connections, but most provide individual 2-pin connectors for the various functions. If 2-pin connectors are used, they are connected as shown in Figure 4.53.

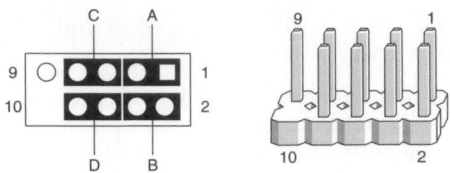

Figure 4.53 Standard front panel switch/LED connections using 2-pin connectors.

The 2-pin connections to a standard 10-pin front panel switch/LED connector are shown in Table 4.55.

Table 4.55   Front Panel Switch/LED Connections Using Multiple Connectors

Connector	Pins	Description
A	1 and 3	Hard disk activity LED
B	2 and 4	Power LED
C	5 and 7	Reset switch
D	6 and 8	Power switch

A chassis can use either a single-color or dual-color LED for the Power LED function. A dual-color LED can provide more information about the various power and message states the system might be in, including power on/off, sleep, and message-waiting indications. Table 4.56 shows the possible states and meanings for both single- and dual-color power LEDs.

Table 4.56   Power LED Indications

LED Type	LED State	Description	ACPI State
Single-color	Off	Power off or sleeping	S1, S3, S5
	Steady green	Running	S0
	Blinking green	Running, message waiting	S0
Dual-color	Off	Power off	S5
	Steady green	Running	S0
	Blinking green	Running, message waiting	S0
	Steady yellow	Sleeping	S1, S3
	Blinking yellow	Sleeping, message waiting	S1, S3

Many motherboards do not follow the industry-standard guidelines for front panel switch/LED connections, and many use alternative designs instead, one of which is shown in Figure 4.54.

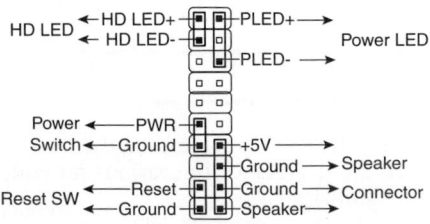

Figure 4.54   Alternative front panel switch/LED connector configuration.

Some of Intel's older motherboards, as well as those made by other motherboard manufacturers, used a single-row pin header connector for the front panel connections, as shown in Figure 4.55.

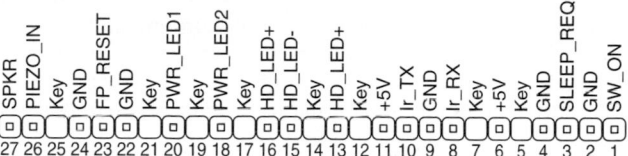

Figure 4.55 Alternative single-row front panel connector configuration.

Table 4.57 shows the designations for the front panel motherboard connectors used on some motherboards.

Table 4.57 Alternative Single-Row Front Panel Connector Pinout

Connector	Pin	Signal Name
Speaker	27	SPKR
	26	PIEZO_IN
	25	Key (no pin)
	24	GND
Reset	23	FP_RESET
	22	GND
None	21	Key (no pin)
Sleep/Power LED	20	PWR_LED1 (green)
	19	Key (no pin)
	18	PWR_LED2 (yellow)
None	17	Key (no pin)
Hard Drive LED	16	HD_LED+
	15	HD_LED-
	14	Key (no pin)
	13	HD_LED+
None	12	Key (no pin)
IrDA	11	+5V
	10	Ir_TX
	9	GND
	8	Ir_RX
	7	Key (no pin)
	6	+5V
None	5	Key (no pin)
Sleep/Resume	4	GND
	3	SLEEP_REQ
Power On	2	GND
	1	SW_ON

To adapt the connectors in your chassis to those on your motherboard, in some cases you might need to change the connector ends by removing the terminals and reinserting them into different positions. For example, I had a chassis that used a three-pin power LED connection, while the motherboard only had a two-pin connection. I had to remove one of the terminals, reinsert it into the middle position on the three-pin connector, and then plug the connector into the motherboard so that two pins were mated and the third empty position was hanging off the end of the connector. Fortunately, the terminals are easy to remove by merely lifting a latch on the side of the connector and then sliding the terminal and wire back out. When the terminal is inserted, the latch automatically grabs the terminal and locks it into position.

Most motherboards include front panel USB connectors, which are designed to be connected to front-mounted USB connectors in the chassis. The standard uses a single 10-pin keyed connector to provide two USB connections. The pinout of a standard dual USB motherboard header connector is shown in Figure 4.56 and Table 4.58.

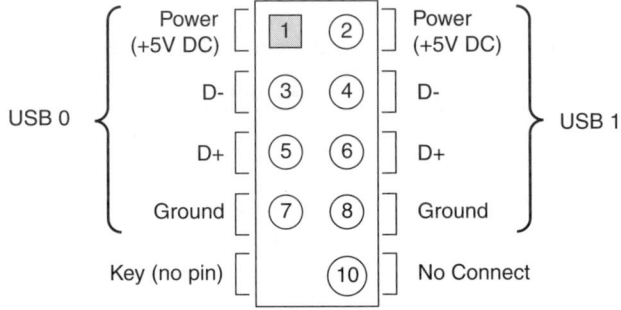

Figure 4.56   Front panel dual-USB header connector configuration.

Table 4.58   Front Panel USB Header Connector Pinout

Description	Signal Names	Pin	Pin	Signal Names	Description
Port 0 +5V	USB0_PWR	1	2	USB1_PWR	Port 1 +5V
Port 0 Data-	USB_D0-	3	4	USB_D1-	Port 1 Data-
Port 0 Data+	USB_D0+	5	6	USB_D1+	Port 1 Data+
Port 0 Ground	GND	7	8	GND	Port 1 Ground
No pin	Key	9	10	NC/Shield	No Connect/Shield

Many chassis includes multiple inline connectors for the dual-USB–to–front panel connection, instead of a single keyed connector. An example of this is shown in Figure 4.57.

Using the multiple individual connectors shown in the previous figure, you would have to plug each individual connector into the proper pin. Some internal chassis USB cables use two 5-pin inline connectors, in which case you just need to ensure that you don't put them on backward. Consult your motherboard and chassis manual for more information if you are unsure about your particular connections.

Caution

If your chassis uses multiple individual non-keyed connections, you must be sure to connect them properly to the connector on the motherboard. If you connect them improperly, you can cause a short circuit to occur that can damage the motherboard or any USB peripherals you plug into the front panel connectors. Higher-quality motherboards usually have self-healing fuses on the power signals, which can prevent damage if such a situation occurs.

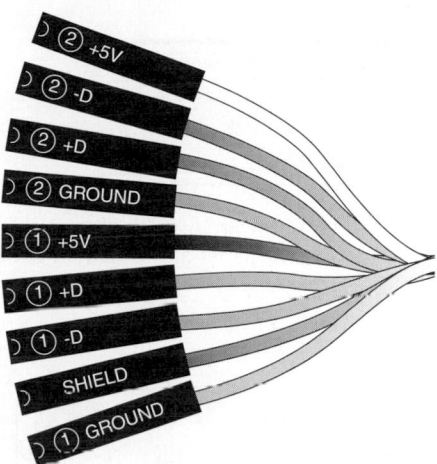

Figure 4.57 Front panel USB cable using multiple individual non-keyed connectors.

Although IEEE 1394 (FireWire/i.LINK) is not found on most motherboards, many boards do incorporate this feature or offer it as an option. FireWire can also be added via an expansion card, and many of the cards have header connectors for front panel connections similar to that found on a motherboard. Figure 4.58 and Table 4.59 show the pinout of the industry-standard FireWire header connector.

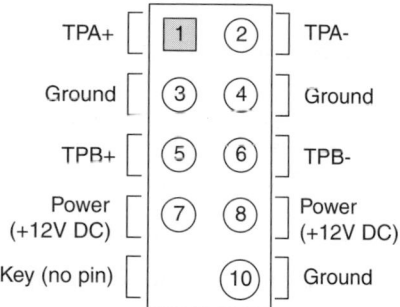

Figure 4.58 Front panel IEEE 1394 (FireWire/i.LINK) header connector configuration.

Table 4.59   Front Panel IEEE 1394 (FireWire/i.LINK) Connector Pinout

Pin	Signal Name	Pin	Signal Name
TPA+	1	2	TPA-
Ground	3	4	Ground
TPB+	5	6	TPB-
+12V (Fused)	7	8	+12V (Fused)
Key (no pin)	9	10	Ground

Note that the front panel FireWire header connector has the same physical configuration and keying as a front panel USB connector. This is unfortunate because it enables a USB front panel cable to be plugged into a FireWire connector, and vice versa. Either situation could cause a short circuit.

Caution

You must not plug a front panel USB cable into a FireWire header connector, or a front panel FireWire cable into a USB header connector. Doing so causes a short circuit that can damage the motherboard, as well as any peripherals you plug into the front panel connectors. Higher-quality motherboards usually have self-healing fuses on the power signals, which can prevent damage if such a situation occurs.

Motherboards that have integrated audio hardware usually feature a front panel audio header connector. The pinout of the industry-standard front panel audio header connector is shown in Figure 4.59 and Table 4.60.

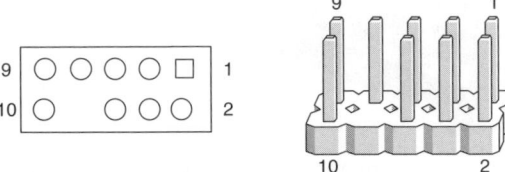

Figure 4.59 Front panel audio header connector configuration.

Table 4.60   Front Panel Audio Connector Pinout

Description	Signal Name	Pin	Pin	Signal Name	Description
Microphone input	AUD_MIC	1	2	AUD_GND	Analog audio ground
Microphone power	AUD_MIC_BIAS	3	4	AUD_VCC	Filtered +5V for analog audio
Right channel audio	AUD_FPOUT_R	5	6	AUD_RET_R	Right channel return
Ground or headphone amplifier control	GND/HP_ON	7	8	KEY	No pin
Left channel audio	AUD_FPOUT_L	9	10	AUD_RET_L	Left channel return

Some motherboards include an infrared data connector that connects to an infrared optical transceiver on the chassis front panel. This enables communicating via infrared to cell phones, PDAs, laptops, printers, or other IrDA devices. The industry-standard pinout for IrDA connections on a motherboard are shown in Figure 4.60 and Table 4.61.

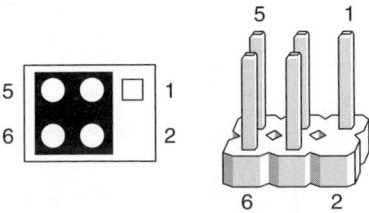

Figure 4.60 Infrared data front panel header connector configuration.

Other miscellaneous connectors might appear on motherboards as well; several are shown in Tables 4.62–4.70.

Table 4.61   Infrared Data Front Panel Connector Pinout

Description	Signal	Pin	Pin	Signal	Description
No connect	NC	1	2	Key	No pin
IR_power	+5V	3	4	GND	Ground
IrDA serial output	IR_TX	5	6	IR_RX	IrDA serial input

Table 4.62   Battery Connector

Pin	Signal	Pin	Signal
1	Gnd	3	KEY
2	Unused	4	+4 to 6V

Table 4.63   LED and Keylock Connector

Pin	Signal	Pin	Signal
1	LED Power (+5V)	4	Keyboard Inhibit
2	KEY	5	Gnd
3	Gnd		

Table 4.64   Speaker Connector

Pin	Signal	Pin	Signal
1	Ground	3	Board-Mounted Speaker
2	KEY	4	Speaker Output

Table 4.65   Chassis Intrusion (Security) Pin-Header

Pin	Signal Name
1	Ground
2	CHS_SEC

Table 4.66   Wake on LAN Pin-Header

Pin	Signal Name
1	+5 VSB
2	Ground
3	WOL

Table 4.67   Wake on Ring Pin-Header

Pin	Signal Name
1	Ground
2	RINGA

Table 4.68   CD Audio Connector

Pin	Signal Name	Pin	Signal Name
1	CD_IN-Left	3	Ground
2	Ground	4	CD_IN-Right

Table 4.69   Telephony Connector

Pin	Signal Name	Pin	Signal Name
1	Audio Out (monaural)	3	Ground
2	Ground	4	Audio In (monaural)

Table 4.70   ATAPI-Style Line In Connector

Pin	Signal Name	Pin	Signal Name
1	Left Line In	3	Ground
2	Ground	4	Right Line In (monaural)

Note

Some boards have a board-mounted piezo speaker. It is enabled by placing a jumper over pins 3 and 4, which routes the speaker output to the board-mounted speaker. Removing the jumper enables a conventional speaker to be plugged in.

Most modern motherboards have three or four fan connectors for use with the processor fan, rear chassis fan, front chassis fan, and voltage regulator (power) fan (see Table 4.71). They all generally use the same 3-pin connector, with the third pin providing a tachometer signal for optional speed monitoring. If the motherboard is capable of monitoring the fan speed, it can sound an alarm when the fans begin to slow down due to bearing failure or wear. The alarm sound can vary, but it normally comes from the internal speaker and might be an ambulance siren–type sound.

Table 4.71   Fan Power Connectors

Pin	Signal Name
1	Ground
2	+12V
3	Sense tachometer

Caution

Do not place a jumper on this connector; serious board damage will result if the 12V is shorted to ground.

System Bus Types, Functions, and Features

The heart of any motherboard is the various buses that carry signals between the components. A *bus* is a common pathway across which data can travel within a computer. This pathway is used for communication and can be established between two or more computer elements.

The PC has a hierarchy of different buses. Most modern PCs have at least three buses; some have four or more. They are hierarchical because each slower bus is connected to the faster one above it. Each device in the system is connected to one of the buses, and some devices (primarily the chipset) act as bridges between the various buses.

The main buses in a modern system are as follows:

- *Processor bus.* Also called the front-side bus (FSB), this is the highest-speed bus in the system and is at the core of the chipset and motherboard. This bus is used primarily by the processor to pass information to and from cache or main memory and the North Bridge of the chipset. The processor bus in a modern system runs at 66MHz, 100MHz, 133MHz, 200MHz, 266MHz, 400MHz, 533MHz, or 800MHz and is normally 64 bits (8 bytes) wide.

- *AGP bus.* This is a high-speed 32-bit bus specifically for a video card. It runs at 66MHz (AGP 1x), 133MHz (AGP 2x), 266MHz (AGP 4x), or 533MHz (AGP 8x), which allows for a bandwidth of up to 2133MBps. It is connected to the North Bridge or Memory Controller Hub of the chipset and is manifested as a single AGP slot in systems that support it.

- *PCI bus.* This is usually a 33MHz 32-bit bus found in virtually all newer 486 systems and Pentium and higher processor systems. Some newer systems include an optional 66MHz 64-bit version—mostly workstations or server-class systems. This bus is generated by either the chipset North Bridge in North/South Bridge chipsets or the I/O Controller Hub in chipsets using hub architecture. This bus is manifested in the system as a collection of 32-bit slots, normally white in color and numbering from four to six on most motherboards. High-speed peripherals, such as SCSI adapters, network cards, video cards, and more, can be plugged into PCI bus slots. PCI-X and PCI-Express are faster developments of the PCI bus. PCI-Express motherboards and systems began to appear in mid-2004.

- *ISA bus.* This is an 8MHz 16-bit bus that has disappeared from recent systems after first appearing in the original PC in 8-bit, 5MHz form and in the 1984 IBM AT in full 16-bit 8MHz form. It is a very slow-speed bus, but it was ideal for certain slow-speed or older peripherals. It has been used in the past for plug-in modems, sound cards, and various other low-speed peripherals. The ISA bus is created by the South Bridge part of the motherboard chipset, which acts as the ISA bus controller and the interface between the ISA bus and the faster PCI bus above it. The Super I/O chip usually was connected to the ISA bus on systems that included ISA slots.

Some newer motherboards feature a special connector called an Audio Modem Riser (AMR) or a Communications and Networking Riser (CNR). These are dedicated connectors for cards that are specific to the motherboard design to offer communications and networking options. They are *not* designed to be general-purpose bus interfaces, and few cards for these connectors are offered on the open market. Usually, they're offered only as an option with a given motherboard. They are designed such that a motherboard manufacturer can easily offer its boards in versions with and without communications options, without having to reserve space on the board for optional chips. Normal network and modem options offered publicly, for the most part, will still be PCI based because the AMR/CNR connection is somewhat motherboard specific. Figure 4.61 compares these connectors, and Figure 4.62 compares typical AMR and CNR riser cards.

Several hidden buses exist on modern motherboards—buses that don't manifest themselves in visible slots or connectors. I'm talking about buses designed to interface chipset components, such as the Hub Interface and the LPC bus. The Hub Interface is a quad-clocked (4x) 66MHz 8-bit bus that carries data between the MCH and ICH in hub architecture chipsets made by Intel. It operates at a bandwidth of 266MBps and was designed as a chipset component connection that is faster than PCI and yet uses fewer signals for a lower-cost design. Some recent workstation/server chipsets and the latest 9xx-series desktop computer chipsets from Intel use faster versions of the hub interface. The most recent chipsets from major third-party vendors also bypass the PCI bus with direct high-speed connections between chipset components.

◄◄ See "High-Speed North-South Bridge Connections," p. 246.

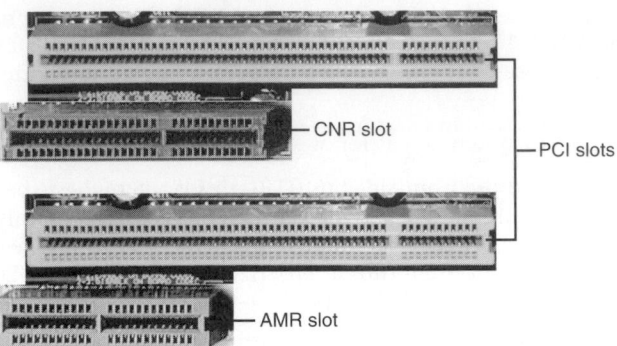

Figure 4.61 The AMR slot (top left) and CNR slot (top center) compared to PCI slots. When the AMR slot is used, the PCI slot paired with it cannot be used.

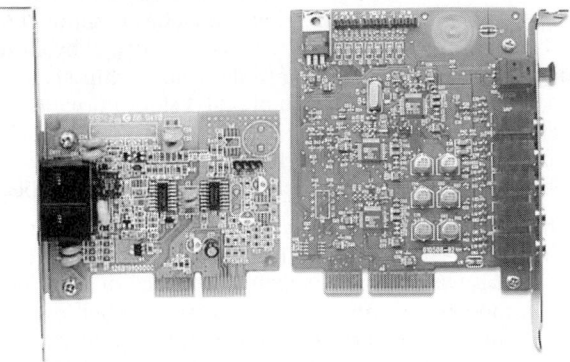

Figure 4.62 A typical AMR riser card (right) with connections for soft modem and 10/100 Ethernet ports. A typical CNR riser card (right) with analog and SPDIF digital audio ports.

In a similar fashion, the LPC bus is a 4-bit bus that has a maximum bandwidth of 16.67MBps; it was designed as an economical onboard replacement for the ISA bus. In systems that use LPC, it typically is used to connect Super I/O chip or motherboard ROM BIOS components to the main chipset. LPC is faster than ISA and yet uses far fewer pins and enables ISA to be eliminated from the board entirely.

The system chipset is the conductor that controls the orchestra of system components, enabling each to have its turn on its respective buses. Table 4.72 shows the widths, speeds, data cycles, and overall bandwidth of virtually all PC buses.

Table 4.72   Bandwidth (in MBps) and Detailed Comparison of Most PC Buses and Interfaces

Bus Type	Bus Width (Bits)	Bus Speed (MHz)	Data Cycles per Clock	Bandwidth (MBps)
8-bit ISA (PC/XT)	8	4.77	1/2	2.39
8-bit ISA (AT)	8	8.33	1/2	4.17
LPC bus	4	33	1	16.67
16-bit ISA (AT-Bus)	16	8.33	1/2	8.33

Table 4.72   Continued

Bus Type	Bus Width (Bits)	Bus Speed (MHz)	Data Cycles per Clock	Bandwidth (MBps)
DD Floppy Interface	1	0.25	1	0.03125
HD Floppy Interface	1	0.5	1	0.0625
ED Floppy Interface	1	1	1	0.125
EISA Bus	32	8.33	1	33
VL-Bus	32	33	1	133
MCA-16	16	5	1	10
MCA-32	32	5	1	20
MCA 16 Streaming	16	10	1	20
MCA-32 Streaming	32	10	1	40
MCA-64 Streaming	64	10	1	80
MCA-64 Streaming	64	20	1	160
PC-Card (PCMCIA)	16	10	1	20
CardBus	32	33	1	133
PCI	32	33	1	133
PCI 66MHz	32	66	1	266
PCI 64-bit	64	33	1	266
PCI 66MHz/64-bit	64	66	1	533
PCI-X 66	64	66	1	533
PCI-X 133	64	133	1	1066
PCI-X 266	64	266	1	2133
PCI-X 533	64	533	1	4266
PCI-Express 1.0 1-lane	1	2500	0.8	250
PCI-Express 1.0 16-lanes	16	2500	0.8	4000
PCI-Express 1.0 32-lanes	32	2500	0.8	8000
Intel Hub Interface 8-bit	8	66	4	266
Intel Hub Interface 16-bit	16	66	4	533
AMD HyperTransport 2x2	2	200	2	100
AMD HyperTransport 4x2	4	200	2	200
AMD HyperTransport 8x2	8	200	2	400
AMD HyperTransport 16x2	16	200	2	800
AMD HyperTransport 32x2	32	200	2	1600
AMD HyperTransport 2x4	2	400	2	200
AMD HyperTransport 4x4	4	400	2	400
AMD HyperTransport 8x4	8	400	2	800
AMD HyperTransport 16x4	16	400	2	1600
AMD HyperTransport 32x4	32	400	2	3200
AMD HyperTransport 2x8	2	800	2	400
AMD HyperTransport 4x8	4	800	2	800

Table 4.72   Continued

Bus Type	Bus Width (Bits)	Bus Speed (MHz)	Data Cycles per Clock	Bandwidth (MBps)
AMD HyperTransport 8x8	8	800	2	1600
AMD HyperTransport 16x8	16	800	2	3200
AMD HyperTransport 32x8	32	800	2	6400
ATI A-Link	16	66	2	266
SiS MuTIOL	16	133	2	533
SiS MuTIOL 1G	16	266	2	1066
VIA V-Link 4x	8	66	4	266
VIA V-Link 8x	8	66	8	533
AGP	32	66	1	266
AGP 2X	32	66	2	533
AGP 4X	32	66	4	1066
AGP 8X	32	66	8	2133
RS-232 Serial	1	0.1152	1/10	0.01152
RS-232 Serial HS	1	0.2304	1/10	0.02304
IEEE 1284 Parallel	8	8.33	1/6	1.38
IEEE 1284 EPP/ECP	8	8.33	1/3	2.77
USB 1.1/2.0 low-speed	1	1.5	1	0.1875
USB 1.1/2.0 full-speed	1	12	1	1.5
USB 2.0 high-speed	1	480	1	60
IEEE 1394a S100	1	100	1	12.5
IEEE 1394a S200	1	200	1	25
IEEE 1394a S400	1	400	1	50
IEEE 1394b S800	1	800	1	100
IEEE 1394b S1600	1	1600	1	200
ATA PIO-4	16	8.33	1	16.67
ATA-UDMA/33	16	8.33	2	33
ATA-UDMA/66	16	16.67	2	66
ATA-UDMA/100	16	25	2	100
ATA-UDMA/133	16	33	2	133
SATA-150	1	750	2	150
SATA-300	1	1500	2	300
SATA-600	1	3000	2	600

Table 4.72   Continued

Bus Type	Bus Width (Bits)	Bus Speed (MHz)	Data Cycles per Clock	Bandwidth (MBps)
SCSI	8	5	1	5
SCSI Wide	16	5	1	10
SCSI Fast	8	10	1	10
SCSI Fast/Wide	16	10	1	20
SCSI Ultra	8	20	1	20
SCSI Ultra/Wide	16	20	1	40
SCSI Ultra2	8	40	1	40
SCSI Ultra2/Wide	16	40	1	80
SCSI Ultra3 (Ultra160)	16	40	2	160
SCSI Ultra4 (Ultra320)	16	80	2	320
SCSI Ultra5 (Ultra640)	16	160	2	640
FPM DRAM	64	22	1	177
EDO DRAM	64	33	1	266
PC66 SDRAM DIMM	64	66	1	533
PC100 SDRAM DIMM	64	100	1	800
PC133 SDRAM DIMM	64	133	1	1066
PC1600 DDR DIMM (DDR200)	64	100	2	1600
PC2100 DDR DIMM (DDR266)	64	133	2	2133
PC2700 DDR DIMM (DDR333)	64	167	2	2666
PC3200 DDR DIMM (DDR400)	64	200	2	3200
PC3500 DDR (DDR433)	64	216	2	3466
PC3700 DDR (DDR466)	64	233	2	3733
PC2-3200 DDR2 (DDR2-400)	64	200	2	3200
PC2-4300 DDR2 (DDR2-533)	64	267	2	4266
PC2-5400 DDR2 (DDR2-667)	64	333	2	5333
PC2-6400 DDR2 (DDR2-800)	64	400	2	6400
RIMM1200 RDRAM (PC600)	16	300	2	1200
RIMM1400 RDRAM (PC700)	16	350	2	1400
RIMM1600 RDRAM (PC800)	16	400	2	1600
RIMM2100 RDRAM (PC1066)	16	533	2	2133
RIMM2400 RDRAM (PC1200)	16	600	2	2400
RIMM3200 RDRAM (PC800)	32	400	2	3200
RIMM4200 RDRAM (PC1066)	32	533	2	4266
RIMM4800 RDRAM (PC1200)	32	600	2	4800

Table 4.72   Continued

Bus Type	Bus Width (Bits)	Bus Speed (MHz)	Data Cycles per Clock	Bandwidth (MBps)
33MHz 486 FSB	32	33	1	133
66MHz Pentium I/II/III FSB	64	66	1	533
100MHz Pentium I/II/III FSB	64	100	1	800
133MHz Pentium I/II/III FSB	64	133	1	1066
200MHz Athlon FSB	64	100	2	1600
266MHz Athlon FSB	64	133	2	2133
333MHz Athlon FSB	64	167	2	2666
400MHz Athlon FSB	64	200	2	3200
533MHz Athlon FSB	64	267	2	4266
400MHz Pentium 4 FSB	64	100	4	3200
533MHz Pentium 4 FSB	64	133	4	4266
800MHz Pentium 4 FSB	64	200	4	6400
1066MHz Pentium 4 FSB	64	267	4	8533
266MHz Itanium FSB	64	133	2	2133
400MHz Itanium 2 FSB	128	100	4	6400

Note: ISA, EISA, VL-Bus, and MCA are no longer used in current motherboard designs.

MBps = Megabytes per second
ISA = Industry Standard Architecture, also known as the PC/XT (8-bit) or AT-Bus (16-bit)
LPC = Low Pin Count bus
DD Floppy = Double Density (360/720KB) Floppy
HD Floppy = High Density (1.2/1.44MB) Floppy
ED Floppy = Extra-high Density (2.88MB) Floppy
EISA = Extended Industry Standard Architecture (32-bit ISA)
VL-Bus = VESA (Video Electronics Standards Association) Local Bus (ISA extension)
MCA = MicroChannel Architecture (IBM PS/2 systems)
PC-Card = 16-bit PCMCIA (Personal Computer Memory Card International Association) interface
CardBus = 32-bit PC-Card
Hub Interface = Intel 8xx chipset bus
HyperTransport = AMD chipset bus
V-Link = VIA Technologies chipset bus
MuTIOL = Silicon Integrated System chipset bus
PCI = Peripheral Component Interconnect

AGP = Accelerated Graphics Port
RS-232 = Standard Serial port, 115.2Kbps
RS-232 HS = High Speed Serial port, 230.4Kbps
IEEE 1284 Parallel = Standard Bidirectional Parallel Port
IEEE 1284 EPP/ECP = Enhanced Parallel Port/Extended Capabilities Port
USB = Universal serial bus
IEEE 1394 = FireWire, also called i.LINK
ATA PIO = AT Attachment (also known as IDE) Programmed I/O
ATA-UDMA = AT Attachment Ultra DMA
SCSI = Small computer system interface
FPM = Fast Page Mode, based on X-3-3-3 (1/3 max) burst mode timing on a 66MHz bus
EDO = Extended Data Out, based on X-2-2-2 (1/2 max) burst mode timing on a 66MHz bus
SDRAM = Synchronous dynamic RAM
RDRAM = Rambus dynamic RAM
DDR = Double data rate SDRAM
DDR2 = Next-generation DDR
CPU FSB = Processor front-side bus

Note that many of the buses use multiple data cycles (transfers) per clock cycle to achieve greater performance. Therefore, the data transfer rate is higher than it would seem for a given clock rate, which allows for an easy way to take an existing bus and make it go faster in a backward-compatible way.

The following sections discuss the processor and other subset buses in the system and the main I/O buses mentioned in the previous table.

The Processor Bus (Front-Side Bus)

The processor bus (also called the front-side bus or FSB) is the communication pathway between the CPU and motherboard chipset, more specifically the North Bridge or Memory Controller Hub. This bus runs at the full motherboard speed—typically between 66MHz and 800MHz in modern systems, depending on the particular board and chipset design. This same bus also transfers data between the CPU and an external (L2) memory cache on Socket-7 (Pentium class) systems. Figure 4.63 shows how this bus fits into a typical Socket 7 PC system.

Figure 4.63 also shows where and how the other main buses, such as the PCI and ISA buses, fit into the system. As you can see, there is clearly a three-tier architecture with the fastest CPU bus on top, the PCI bus next, and the ISA bus at the bottom. Various components in the system are connected to one of these three main buses.

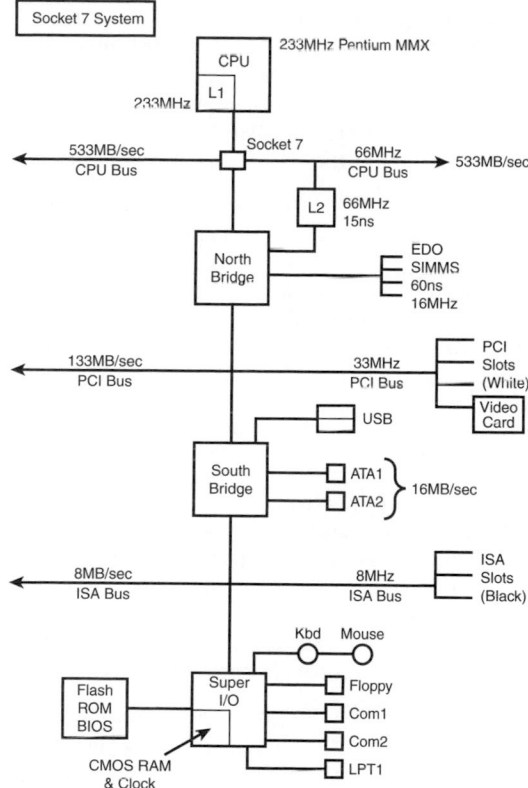

Figure 4.63   Typical Socket 7 (Pentium class) system architecture.

Socket 7 systems have an external (L2) cache for the CPU; the L2 cache is mounted on the motherboard and connected to the main processor bus that runs at the motherboard speed (usually between 66MHz and 100MHz). Thus, as the Socket 7 processors became available in faster and faster versions (through increasing the clock multiplier in the chip), the L2 cache unfortunately remained stuck on the motherboard running at the relatively slow (by comparison) motherboard speed. For example, the fastest Intel Socket 7 systems ran the CPU at 233MHz, which was 3.5x the CPU bus speed of 66MHz. Therefore, the L2 cache ran at only 66MHz. The fastest Socket 7 systems used the AMD K6-2 550 processor, which ran at 550MHz—5.5x a CPU bus speed of 100MHz. In those systems, the L2 cache ran at only 100MHz.

The problem of the slow L2 cache was first solved in the P6 class processors, such as the Pentium Pro, Pentium II, Celeron, Pentium III, and AMD Athlon and Duron. These processors used either Socket 8, Slot 1, Slot 2, Slot A, Socket A, or Socket 370. They moved the L2 cache off the motherboard and directly onto the CPU and connected it to the CPU via an on-chip back-side bus. Because the L2 cache bus was called the back-side bus, some in the industry began calling the main CPU bus the front-side bus. I still usually refer to it simply as the CPU bus.

By incorporating the L2 cache into the CPU, it can run at speeds up to the same speed as the processor itself. Most processors now incorporate the L2 cache directly on the CPU die, so the L2 cache runs at the same speed as the rest of the CPU. Others (mostly older versions) used separate die for the cache integrated into the CPU package, which ran the L2 cache at some lower multiple (one-half, two-fifth, or one-third) of the main CPU. Even if the L2 ran at half or one-third of the processor speed, it still was significantly faster than the motherboard-bound cache on the Socket 7 systems.

In a Slot-1 type system the L2 cache is built in to the CPU but running at only half the processor speed. This would also be the same for systems using Slot A. The CPU bus speed increased from 66MHz (used primarily in Socket 7 systems) to 100MHz, enabling a bandwidth of 800MBps. Note that most of these systems included AGP support. Basic AGP was 66MHz (twice the speed of PCI), but most of these systems incorporated AGP 2x, which operated at twice the speed of standard AGP and enabled a bandwidth of 533MBps. These systems also typically used PC-100 SDRAM DIMMs, which have a bandwidth of 800MBps, matching the processor bus bandwidth for the best performance.

Slot 1 was dropped in favor of Socket 370 for the Pentium III and Celeron systems. This was mainly because these newer processors incorporated the L2 cache directly into the CPU die (running at the full-core speed of the processor) and an expensive cartridge with multiple chips was no longer necessary. At the same time, processor bus speeds increased to 133MHz, which enabled a throughput of 1066MBps. Figure 4.64 shows a typical Socket 370 system design. AGP speed was also increased to AGP 4x, with a bandwidth of 1066MBps.

Note the use of what Intel calls "hub architecture" instead of the older North/South Bridge design. This moves the main connection between the chipset components to a separate 266MBps hub interface (which has twice the throughput of PCI) and enables PCI devices to use the full bandwidth of PCI without fighting for bandwidth with a South Bridge. Also note that the flash ROM BIOS chip is now referred to as a Firmware Hub and is connected to the system via the LPC bus instead of via the Super I/O chip as in older North/South Bridge designs. The ISA bus is no longer used in most of these systems, and the Super I/O is connected via the LPC bus instead of ISA. The Super I/O chip also can easily be eliminated in these designs. This is commonly referred to as a *legacy-free* system because the ports supplied by the Super I/O chip are now known as *legacy* ports. Devices that would have used legacy ports must then be connected to the system via USB instead, and such systems would feature two USB controllers, with up to four total ports (more can be added by attaching USB hubs).

AMD processor systems adopted a Socket A design, which is similar to Socket 370 except it uses faster processor and memory buses. Although early versions retained the older North/South Bridge design, more recent versions use a design similar to Intel's hub architecture. Note the high-speed CPU bus running up to 333MHz (2667MBps throughput) and the use of DDR SDRAM DIMM modules that support a matching bandwidth of 2667MBps. It is always best for performance when the bandwidth of memory matches that of the processor. Finally, note how most of the South Bridge components include functions otherwise found in Super I/O chips; when these functions are included the chip is called a Super South Bridge.

The Pentium 4 uses a Socket 423 or Socket 478 design with hub architecture (see Figure 4.65). This design is most notable for including a 400MHz, 533MHz, or 800MHz CPU bus with a bandwidth of 3200MBps, 4266MBps, or 6400MBps. The 533MHz and 800MHz models are currently faster than anything else on the market. In this example, note the use of dual-channel PC3200 (DDR400) SDRAM. A single PC-3200 DIMM has a bandwidth of 3200MBps, but when running dual-channel (identical pairs of memory) memory, it has a bandwidth of 6400MBps—which matches the bandwidth of the 800MHz CPU bus models of the Pentium 4 for best performance. Processors with the 533MHz CPU bus can use pairs of PC2100 (DDR266) or PC2700 (DDR333) memory modules in dual channel mode to match the 4266MBps throughput of this memory bus. It is always best when the throughput of the memory bus matches that of the processor bus.

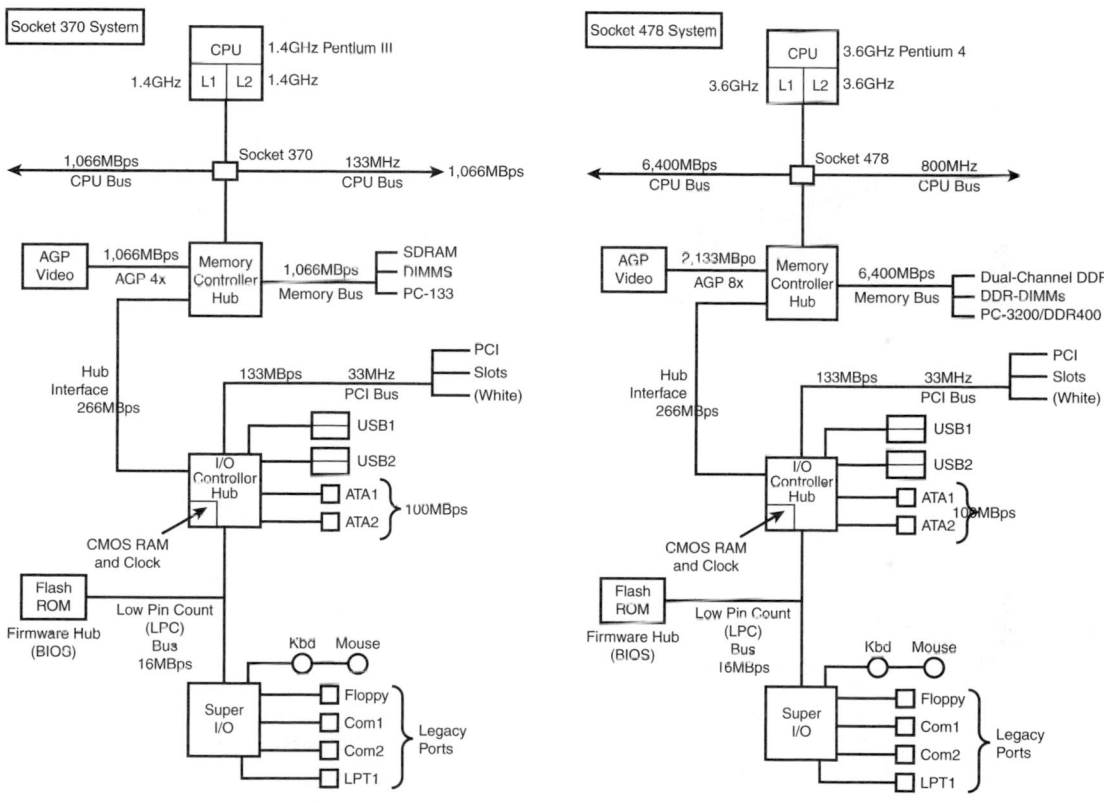

Figure 4.64 Typical Socket 370 (Pentium III/ Celeron class) system architecture.

Figure 4.65 Typical Socket 478 (Pentium 4) system architecture.

The Athlon 64 uses the high-speed HyperTransport architecture to connect the North Bridge or AGP Graphics Tunnel chip to the processor (Socket 754, 939, or 940). Most Athlon 64 chipsets use the 16-bit/800MHz version, but the latest chipsets designed for the new Socket 939 Athlon 64 FX-53 use the faster 16-bit/1GHz version to support faster DDR-2 memory.

However, the Athlon 64's most significant departure from conventional computer architecture is the location of the memory controller. Rather than being located in the North Bridge/MCH/GMCH chip, the Athlon 64/FX/Opteron architecture places the memory controller in the processor itself. This eliminates slow-downs caused by the use of an external memory controller and helps boost performance.

One drawback to the design, however, is that new memory technologies, such as DDR-2, require that the processor itself be redesigned.

Figure 4.66 illustrates an Athlon 64 FX-53–based system that uses the new PCI-Express x1 and PCI-Express x16 expansion slot designs.

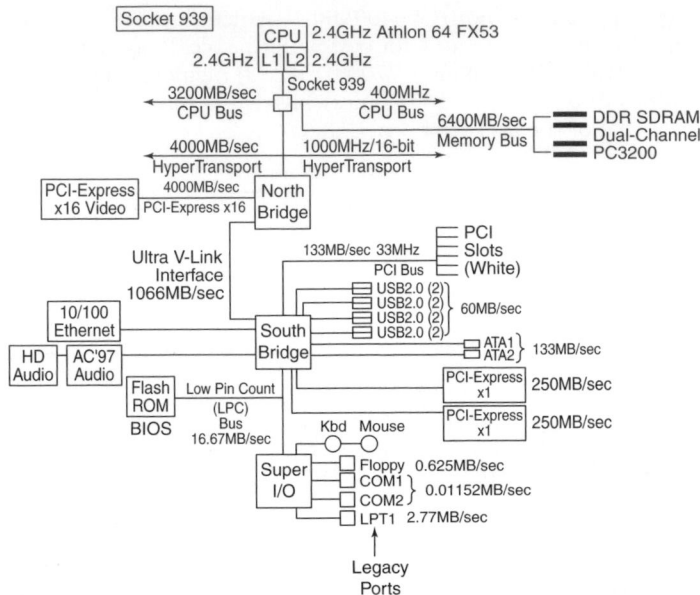

Figure 4.66 Typical Socket 939 (Athlon 64 FX-53) system architecture using PCI-Express slots.

Because the purpose of the processor bus is to get information to and from the CPU at the fastest possible speed, this bus typically operates at a rate faster than any other bus in the system. The bus consists of electrical circuits for data, addresses (the address bus, which is discussed in the following section), and control purposes. Most processors since the original Pentium have a 64-bit data bus, so they transfer 64 bits (8 bytes) at a time over the CPU bus.

The processor bus operates at the same base clock rate as the CPU does externally. This can be misleading because most CPUs these days run at a higher clock rate internally than they do externally. For example, an AMD Athlon 64 3800+ system has a processor running at 2.4GHz internally but only 400MHz externally, whereas a Pentium 4 3.4GHz runs at 3.4GHz internally but only 800MHz externally. In newer systems, the actual processor speed is some multiple (2x, 2.5x, 3x, and higher) of the processor bus.

◄◄ See "Processor Speed Ratings," p. 53.

The processor bus is tied to the external processor pin connections and can transfer 1 bit of data per data line every cycle. Most modern processors transfer 64 bits (8 bytes) of data at a time.

To determine the transfer rate for the processor bus, you multiply the data width (64 bits or 8 bytes for a Celeron/Pentium III/4 or Athlon/Duron/Athlon XP/Athlon 64) by the clock speed of the bus (the same as the base or unmultiplied clock speed of the CPU).

For example, if you are using a Pentium 4 3.6GHz processor that runs on an 800MHz processor bus, you have a maximum instantaneous transfer rate of roughly 6400MBps. You get this result by using the following formula:

$$800\text{MHz} \times 8 \text{ bytes (64 bits)} = 6400\text{MBps}$$

With slower versions of the Pentium 4, you get either

$$533.33\text{MHz} \times 8 \text{ bytes (64 bits)} = 4266\text{MBps}$$

or

$$400\text{MHz} \times 8 \text{ bytes (64 bits)} = 3200\text{MBps}$$

With Socket A (Athlon XP), you get

333.33MHz × 8 bytes (64 bits) = 2667MBps

or

266.66MHz × 8 bytes (64 bits) = 2133MBps

or

200MHz × 8 bytes (64 bits) = 1600MBps

With Socket 370 (Pentium III), you get

133.33MHz × 8 bytes (64 bits) = 1066MBps

or

100MHz × 8 bytes (64 bits) = 800MBps

This transfer rate, often called the *bandwidth* of the processor bus, represents the maximum speed at which data can move. Refer to Table 4.72 for a more complete list of various processor bus bandwidths.

The Memory Bus

The memory bus is used to transfer information between the CPU and main memory—the RAM in your system. This bus is connected to the motherboard chipset North Bridge or Memory Controller Hub chip. Depending on the type of memory your chipset (and therefore motherboard) is designed to handle, the North Bridge runs the memory bus at various speeds. The best solution is if the memory bus runs at the same speed as the processor bus. Systems that use PC133 SDRAM have a memory bandwidth of 1066MBps, which is the same as the 133MHz CPU bus. In another example, Athlon systems running a 266MHz processor bus also run PC2100 DDR-SDRAM, which has a bandwidth of 2133MBps—exactly the same as the processor bus in those systems. In addition, systems running a Pentium 4 with its 400MHz processor bus also use dual-channel RDRAM memory, which runs 1600MBps for each channel, or a combined bandwidth (both memory channels run simultaneously) of 3200MBps, which is exactly the same as the Pentium 4 CPU bus. Pentium 4 systems with the 533MHz bus run dual-channel DDR PC2100 or PC2700 modules, which match or exceed the throughput of the 4266MBps processor bus.

Running memory at the same speed as the processor bus negates the need for having cache memory on the motherboard. That is why when the L2 cache moved into the processor, nobody added an L3 cache to the motherboard. Some very high-end processors, such as the Itanium and Itanium 2 and the Intel Pentium 4 Extreme Edition, have integrated 2MB–4MB of full-core speed L3 cache into the CPU. Eventually, this should make it down to more mainstream desktop systems.

Note

Notice that the main memory bus must transfer data in the same width as the processor bus. This defines the size of what is called a *bank* of memory, at least when dealing with anything but RDRAM. Memory banks and their widths relative to processor buses are discussed in the section "Memory Banks" in Chapter 6.

The Need for Expansion Slots

The I/O bus or expansion slots enable your CPU to communicate with peripheral devices. The bus and its associated expansion slots are needed because basic systems can't possibly satisfy all the needs of all the people who buy them. The I/O bus enables you to add devices to your computer to expand its capabilities. The most basic computer components, such as sound cards and video cards, can be plugged into expansion slots; you also can plug in more specialized devices, such as network interface cards, SCSI host adapters, and others.

Note

In most modern PC systems, a variety of basic peripheral devices are built in to the motherboard. Most systems today have at least dual (primary and secondary) IDE interfaces, four USB ports, a floppy controller, two serial ports, a parallel port, keyboard, and mouse controller built directly into the motherboard. These devices are usually distributed between the motherboard chipset South Bridge and the Super I/O chip. (Super I/O chips are discussed earlier in this chapter.)

Many add even more items, such as a built-in sound card, video adapter, SCSI host adapter, network interface or IEEE 1394a port, that also are built in to the motherboard. Those items, however, might not be built in to the motherboard chipset or Super I/O chip; they are sometimes configured as additional chips installed on the board. Nevertheless, these built-in controllers and ports still use the I/O bus to communicate with the CPU. In essence, even though they are built in, they act as if they were cards plugged into the system's bus slots, including using system resources in the same manner.

Types of I/O Buses

Since the introduction of the first PC, many I/O buses have been introduced. The reason is simple: Faster I/O speeds are necessary for better system performance. This need for higher performance involves three main areas:

- Faster CPUs
- Increasing software demands
- Greater multimedia requirements

Each of these areas requires the I/O bus to be as fast as possible.

One of the primary reasons new I/O bus structures have been slow in coming is compatibility—that old catch-22 that anchors much of the PC industry to the past. One of the hallmarks of the PC's success is its standardization. This standardization spawned thousands of third-party I/O cards, each originally built for the early bus specifications of the PC. If a new high-performance bus system was introduced, it often had to be compatible with the older bus systems so the older I/O cards would not be obsolete. Therefore, bus technologies seem to evolve rather than make quantum leaps forward.

You can identify different types of I/O buses by their architectures. The main types of I/O buses are detailed earlier in this chapter.

The main differences among buses consist primarily of the amounts of data they can transfer at one time and the speeds at which they can do it. The following sections describe the various types of PC buses.

The ISA Bus

Industry Standard Architecture (ISA) is the bus architecture that was introduced as an 8-bit bus with the original IBM PC in 1981; it was later expanded to 16 bits with the IBM PC/AT in 1984. ISA is the basis of the modern personal computer and was the primary architecture used in the vast majority of PC systems until the late 1990s. It might seem amazing that such a presumably antiquated architecture was used for so long, but it provided reliability, affordability, and compatibility, plus this old bus is still faster than many of the peripherals we connect to it!

Note

The ISA bus has vanished from all recent desktop systems, and few companies make or sell ISA cards anymore. The ISA bus continues to be popular with industrial computer (PICMG) designs, but it is expected to eventually fade away from these as well.

Two versions of the ISA bus exist, based on the number of data bits that can be transferred on the bus at a time. The older version is an 8-bit bus; the newer version is a 16-bit bus. The original 8-bit version ran at 4.77MHz in the PC and XT, and the 16-bit version used in the AT ran at 6MHz and then 8MHz. Later, the industry as a whole agreed on an 8.33MHz maximum standard speed for 8/16-bit versions of the ISA bus for backward-compatibility. Some systems have the capability to run the ISA bus faster than this, but some adapter cards will not function properly at higher speeds. ISA data transfers require anywhere from two to eight cycles. Therefore, the theoretical maximum data rate of the ISA bus is about 8MBps, as the following formula shows:

$$8.33\text{MHz} \times 2 \text{ bytes (16 bits) [db] } 2 \text{ cycles per transfer} = 8.33\text{MBps}$$

The bandwidth of the 8-bit bus would be half this figure (4.17MBps). Remember, however, that these figures are theoretical maximums. Because of I/O bus protocols, the effective bandwidth is much lower—typically by almost half. Even so, at about 8MBps, the ISA bus is still faster than many of the peripherals connected to it, such as serial ports, parallel ports, floppy controllers, keyboard controllers, and so on.

The 8-Bit ISA Bus

This bus architecture is used in the original IBM PC computers and was retained for several years in later systems. Although virtually nonexistent in new systems today, this architecture still exists in hundreds of thousands of PC systems in the field, including systems with 286 and 386 processors.

Physically, the 8-bit ISA expansion slot resembles the tongue-and-groove system furniture makers once used to hold two pieces of wood together. It is specifically called a *card/edge connector*. An adapter card with 62 contacts on its bottom edge plugs into a slot on the motherboard that has 62 matching contacts. Electronically, this slot provides 8 data lines and 20 addressing lines, enabling the slot to handle 1MB of memory.

Figure 4.67 describes the pinouts for the 8-bit ISA bus; Figure 4.68 shows how these pins are oriented in the expansion slot.

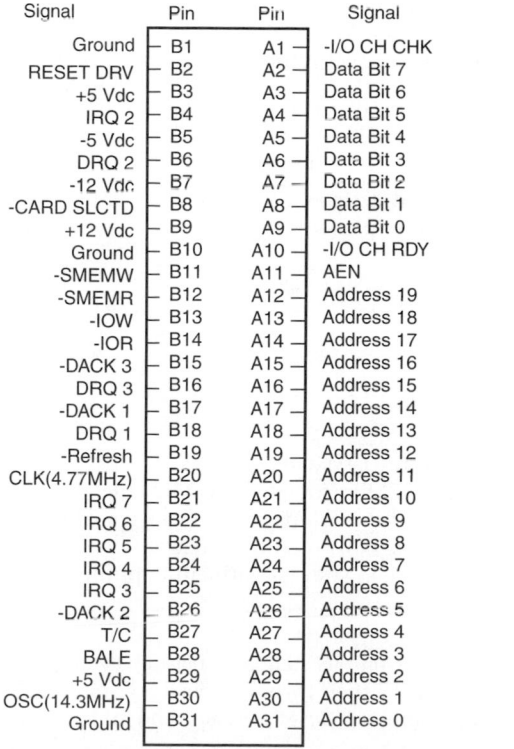

Figure 4.67 Pinouts for the 8-bit ISA bus.

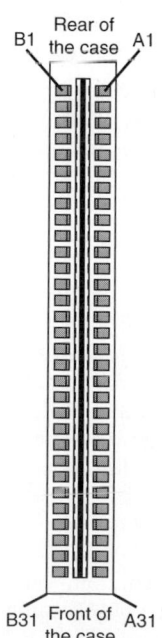

Figure 4.68 The 8-bit ISA bus connector.

Although the design of the bus is simple, IBM waited until 1987 to publish full specifications for the timings of the data and address lines, so in the early days of PC compatibles, manufacturers had to do their best to figure out how to make adapter boards. This problem was solved, however, as PC-compatible personal computers became more widely accepted as the industry standard and manufacturers had more time and incentive to build adapter boards that worked correctly with the bus.

The dimensions of 8-bit ISA adapter cards are as follows:

> 4.2" (106.68mm) high
>
> 13.13" (333.5mm) long
>
> 0.5" (12.7mm) wide

The 16-Bit ISA Bus

IBM threw a bombshell on the PC world when it introduced the AT with the 286 processor in 1984. This processor had a 16-bit data bus, which meant communications between the processor and motherboard as well as memory would now be 16 bits wide instead of only 8. Although this processor could have been installed on a motherboard with only an 8-bit I/O bus, that would have meant a huge sacrifice in the performance of any adapter cards or other devices installed on the bus.

Rather than create a new I/O bus, at that time IBM instead came up with a system that could support both 8- and 16-bit cards by retaining the same basic 8-bit connector layout but adding an optional 16-bit extension connector. This first debuted on the PC/AT in August 1984, which is why we also refer to the ISA bus as the *AT-bus*.

The extension connector in each 16-bit expansion slot adds 36 connector pins (for a total of 98 signals) to carry the extra signals necessary to implement the wider data path. In addition, two of the pins in the 8-bit portion of the connector were changed. These two minor changes did not alter the function of 8-bit cards.

Figure 4.69 describes the pinouts for the full 16-bit ISA expansion slot, and Figure 4.70 shows how the additional pins are oriented in the expansion slot.

Because of physical interference with some ancient 8-bit card designs, IBM left 16-bit extension connectors off two of the slots in the AT. This was not a problem in newer systems, so any system with ISA slots would have all of them as full 16-bit versions.

The dimensions of a typical AT expansion board are as follows:

> 4.8" (121.92mm) high
>
> 13.13" (333.5mm) long
>
> 0.5" (12.7mm) wide

Two heights actually are available for cards commonly used in AT systems: 4.8" and 4.2" (the height of older PC-XT cards). The shorter cards became an issue when IBM introduced the XT Model 286. Because this model has an AT motherboard in an XT case, it needs AT-type boards with the 4.2" maximum height. Most board makers trimmed the height of their boards; most manufacturers who still make ISA cards now make only 4.2"-tall (or less) boards so they will work in systems with either profile.

32-Bit Buses

After 32-bit CPUs became available, it was some time before 32-bit bus standards became available. Before MCA and EISA specs were released, some vendors began creating their own proprietary 32-bit buses, which were extensions of the ISA bus. Fortunately, these proprietary buses were few and far between.

The expanded portions of the bus typically are used for proprietary memory expansion or video cards. Because the systems are proprietary (meaning that they are nonstandard), pinouts and specifications are not available.

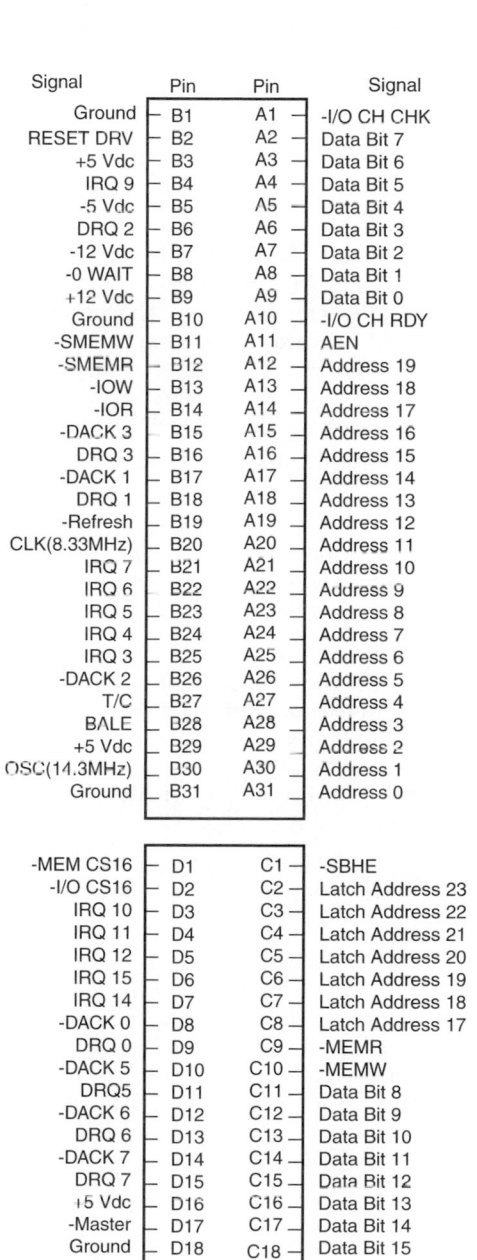

Signal	Pin	Pin	Signal
Ground	B1	A1	-I/O CH CHK
RESET DRV	B2	A2	Data Bit 7
+5 Vdc	B3	A3	Data Bit 6
IRQ 9	B4	A4	Data Bit 5
-5 Vdc	B5	A5	Data Bit 4
DRQ 2	B6	A6	Data Bit 3
-12 Vdc	B7	A7	Data Bit 2
-0 WAIT	B8	A8	Data Bit 1
+12 Vdc	B9	A9	Data Bit 0
Ground	B10	A10	-I/O CH RDY
-SMEMW	B11	A11	AEN
-SMEMR	B12	A12	Address 19
-IOW	B13	A13	Address 18
-IOR	B14	A14	Address 17
-DACK 3	B15	A15	Address 16
DRQ 3	B16	A16	Address 15
-DACK 1	B17	A17	Address 14
DRQ 1	B18	A18	Address 13
-Refresh	B19	A19	Address 12
CLK(8.33MHz)	B20	A20	Address 11
IRQ 7	B21	A21	Address 10
IRQ 6	B22	A22	Address 9
IRQ 5	B23	A23	Address 8
IRQ 4	B24	A24	Address 7
IRQ 3	B25	A25	Address 6
-DACK 2	B26	A26	Address 5
T/C	B27	A27	Address 4
BALE	B28	A28	Address 3
+5 Vdc	B29	A29	Address 2
OSC(14.3MHz)	B30	A30	Address 1
Ground	B31	A31	Address 0

Signal	Pin	Pin	Signal
-MEM CS16	D1	C1	-SBHE
-I/O CS16	D2	C2	Latch Address 23
IRQ 10	D3	C3	Latch Address 22
IRQ 11	D4	C4	Latch Address 21
IRQ 12	D5	C5	Latch Address 20
IRQ 15	D6	C6	Latch Address 19
IRQ 14	D7	C7	Latch Address 18
-DACK 0	D8	C8	Latch Address 17
DRQ 0	D9	C9	-MEMR
-DACK 5	D10	C10	-MEMW
DRQ5	D11	C11	Data Bit 8
-DACK 6	D12	C12	Data Bit 9
DRQ 6	D13	C13	Data Bit 10
-DACK 7	D14	C14	Data Bit 11
DRQ 7	D15	C15	Data Bit 12
+5 Vdc	D16	C16	Data Bit 13
-Master	D17	C17	Data Bit 14
Ground	D18	C18	Data Bit 15

Figure 4.69   Pinouts for the 16-bit ISA bus.

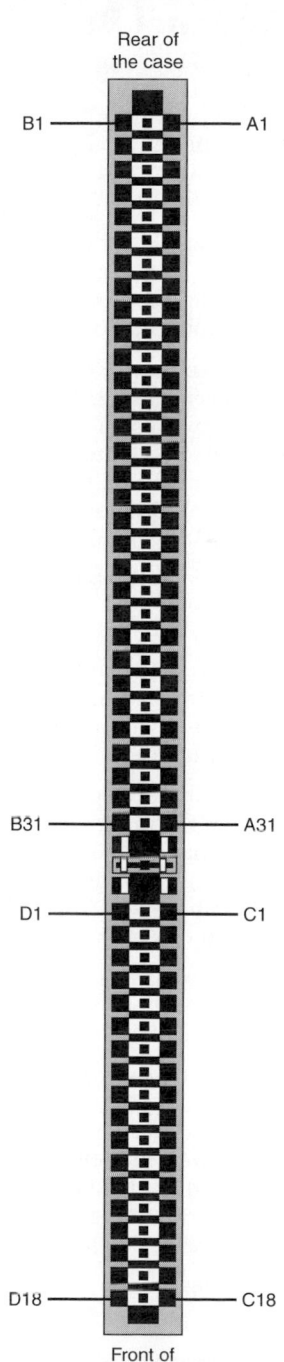

Figure 4.70   The ISA 16-bit bus connector.

The Micro Channel Bus

The introduction of 32-bit chips meant that the ISA bus could not handle the power of another new generation of CPUs. The 386DX chips could transfer 32 bits of data at a time, but the ISA bus can handle a maximum of only 16 bits. Rather than extend the ISA bus again, IBM decided to build a new bus; the result was the MCA bus. *MCA* (an abbreviation for microchannel architecture) is completely different from the ISA bus and is technically superior in every way.

IBM wanted not only to replace the old ISA standard, but also to require vendors to license certain parts of the technology. Many owed for licenses on the ISA bus technology that IBM also created, but because IBM had not been aggressive in its licensing of ISA, many got away without any license. Problems with licensing and control led to the development of the competing EISA bus (see the next section on the EISA bus) and hindered acceptance of the MCA bus.

MCA systems produced a new level of ease of use; they were plug-and-play before the official Plug and Play specification even existed. An MCA system had no jumpers and switches—neither on the motherboard nor on any expansion adapter. Instead you used a special Reference disk, which went with the particular system, and Option disks, which went with each of the cards installed in the system. After a card was installed, you loaded the Option disk files onto the Reference disk; after that, you didn't need the Option disks anymore. The Reference disk contained the special BIOS and system setup program necessary for an MCA system, and the system couldn't be configured without it.

For more information on the MCA bus, see the previous editions of this book on the included disc.

The EISA Bus

The Extended Industry Standard Architecture (EISA) standard was announced in September 1988 as a response to IBM's introduction of the MCA bus—more specifically, to the way IBM wanted to handle licensing of the MCA bus. Vendors did not feel obligated to pay retroactive royalties on the ISA bus, so they turned their backs on IBM and created their own buses.

The EISA standard was developed primarily by Compaq and was intended to be its way of taking over future development of the PC bus from IBM. Compaq knew that nobody would clone its bus if it was the only company that had it, so it essentially gave the design to other leading manufacturers. Compaq formed the EISA committee, a nonprofit organization designed specifically to control development of the EISA bus. Very few EISA adapters were ever developed. Those that were developed centered mainly around disk array controllers and server-type network cards.

The EISA bus was essentially a 32-bit version of ISA. Unlike the MCA bus from IBM, you could still use older 8-bit or 16-bit ISA cards in 32-bit EISA slots, providing for full backward-compatibility. As with MCA, EISA also allowed for automatic configuration of EISA cards via software.

The EISA bus added 90 new connections (55 new signals plus grounds) without increasing the physical connector size of the 16-bit ISA bus. At first glance, the 32-bit EISA slot looks a lot like the 16-bit ISA slot. The EISA adapter, however, has two rows of stacked contacts. The first row is the same type used in 16-bit ISA cards; the other, thinner row extends from the 16-bit connectors. Therefore, ISA cards can still be used in EISA bus slots. Although this compatibility was not enough to ensure the popularity of EISA buses, it is a feature that was carried over into the VL-Bus standard that followed. The physical specifications of an EISA card are as follows:

- 5" (127mm) high
- 13.13" (333.5mm) long
- 0.5" (12.7mm) wide

The EISA bus can handle up to 32 bits of data at an 8.33MHz cycle rate. Most data transfers require a minimum of two cycles, although faster cycle rates are possible if an adapter card provides tight timing specifications. The maximum bandwidth on the bus is 33MBps, as the following formula shows:

8.33MHz × 4 bytes (32 bits) = 33MBps

Figure 4.71 describes the pinouts for the EISA bus. Figure 4.72 shows the locations of the pins; note how some pins are offset to allow the EISA slot to accept ISA cards. Figure 4.73 shows the card connector for the EISA expansion slot.

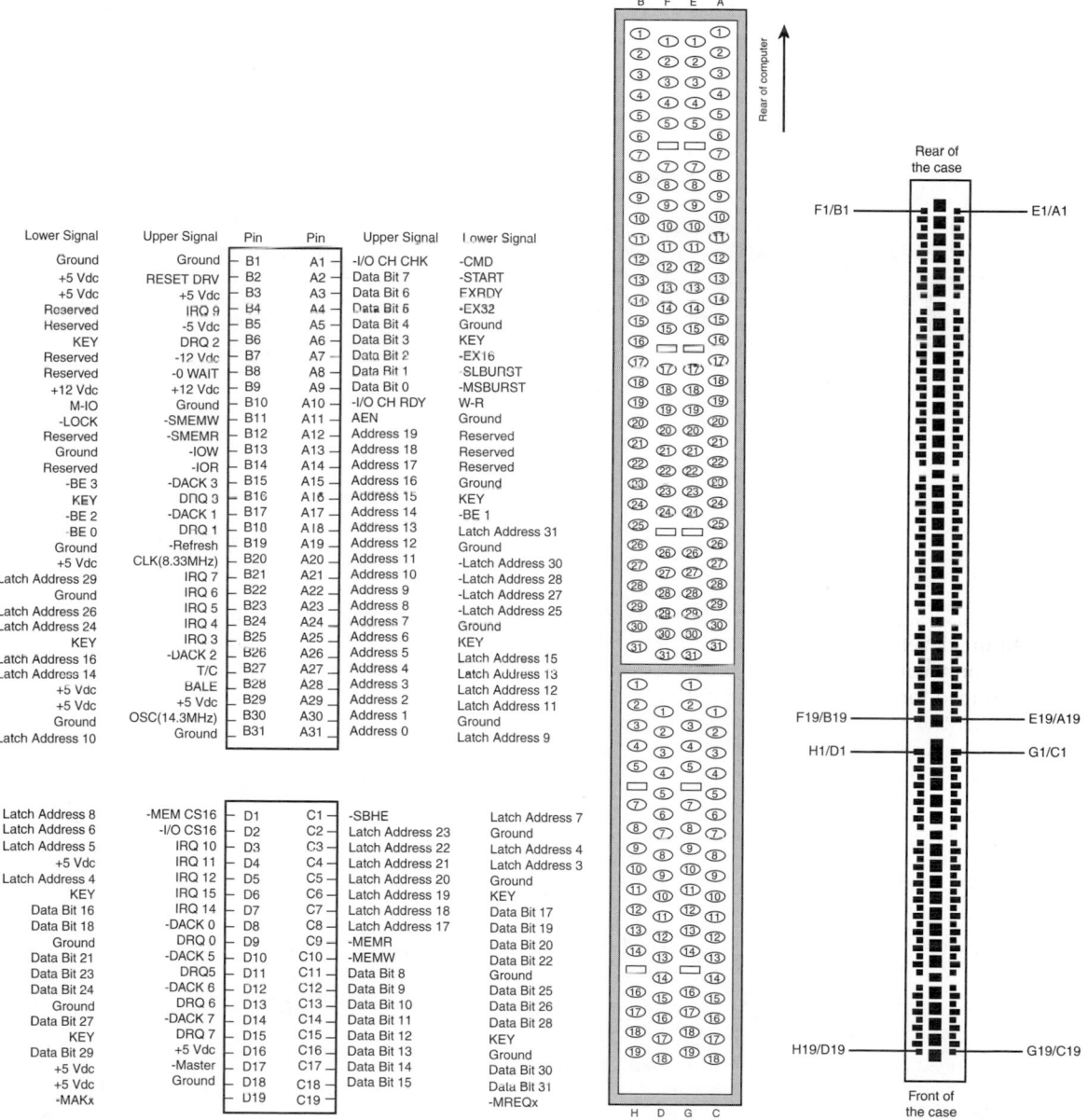

Lower Signal	Upper Signal	Pin	Pin	Upper Signal	Lower Signal
Ground	Ground	B1	A1	-I/O CH CHK	-CMD
+5 Vdc	RESET DRV	B2	A2	Data Bit 7	-START
+5 Vdc	+5 Vdc	B3	A3	Data Bit 6	EXRDY
Reserved	IRQ 9	B4	A4	Data Bit 5	-EX32
Reserved	-5 Vdc	B5	A5	Data Bit 4	Ground
KEY	DRQ 2	B6	A6	Data Bit 3	KEY
Reserved	-12 Vdc	B7	A7	Data Bit 2	-EX16
Reserved	-0 WAIT	B8	A8	Data Bit 1	-SLBURST
+12 Vdc	+12 Vdc	B9	A9	Data Bit 0	-MSBURST
M-IO	Ground	B10	A10	-I/O CH RDY	W-R
-LOCK	-SMEMW	B11	A11	AEN	Ground
Reserved	-SMEMR	B12	A12	Address 19	Reserved
Ground	-IOW	B13	A13	Address 18	Reserved
Reserved	-IOR	B14	A14	Address 17	Reserved
-BE 3	-DACK 3	B15	A15	Address 16	Ground
KEY	DRQ 3	B16	A16	Address 15	KEY
-BE 2	-DACK 1	B17	A17	Address 14	-BE 1
-BE 0	DRQ 1	B18	A18	Address 13	Latch Address 31
Ground	-Refresh	B19	A19	Address 12	Ground
+5 Vdc	CLK(8.33MHz)	B20	A20	Address 11	-Latch Address 30
Latch Address 29	IRQ 7	B21	A21	Address 10	-Latch Address 28
Ground	IRQ 6	B22	A22	Address 9	-Latch Address 27
Latch Address 26	IRQ 5	B23	A23	Address 8	-Latch Address 25
Latch Address 24	IRQ 4	B24	A24	Address 7	Ground
KEY	IRQ 3	B25	A25	Address 6	KEY
Latch Address 16	-DACK 2	B26	A26	Address 5	Latch Address 15
Latch Address 14	T/C	B27	A27	Address 4	Latch Address 13
+5 Vdc	BALE	B28	A28	Address 3	Latch Address 12
+5 Vdc	+5 Vdc	B29	A29	Address 2	Latch Address 11
Ground	OSC(14.3MHz)	B30	A30	Address 1	Ground
Latch Address 10	Ground	B31	A31	Address 0	Latch Address 9

Latch Address 8	-MEM CS16	D1	C1	-SBHE	Latch Address 7
Latch Address 6	-I/O CS16	D2	C2	Latch Address 23	Ground
Latch Address 5	IRQ 10	D3	C3	Latch Address 22	Latch Address 4
+5 Vdc	IRQ 11	D4	C4	Latch Address 21	Latch Address 3
Latch Address 4	IRQ 12	D5	C5	Latch Address 20	Ground
KEY	IRQ 15	D6	C6	Latch Address 19	KEY
Data Bit 16	IRQ 14	D7	C7	Latch Address 18	Data Bit 17
Data Bit 18	-DACK 0	D8	C8	Latch Address 17	Data Bit 19
Ground	DRQ 0	D9	C9	-MEMR	Data Bit 20
Data Bit 21	-DACK 5	D10	C10	-MEMW	Data Bit 22
Data Bit 23	DRQ5	D11	C11	Data Bit 8	Ground
Data Bit 24	-DACK 6	D12	C12	Data Bit 9	Data Bit 25
Ground	DRQ 6	D13	C13	Data Bit 10	Data Bit 26
Data Bit 27	-DACK 7	D14	C14	Data Bit 11	Data Bit 28
KEY	DRQ 7	D15	C15	Data Bit 12	KEY
Data Bit 29	+5 Vdc	D16	C16	Data Bit 13	Ground
+5 Vdc	-Master	D17	C17	Data Bit 14	Data Bit 30
+5 Vdc	Ground	D18	C18	Data Bit 15	Data Bit 31
-MAKx		D19	C19		-MREQx

Figure 4.71 Pinouts for the EISA bus.

Figure 4.72
Pin locations
inside the EISA
bus connector.

Figure 4.73
The EISA bus
connector.

Local Buses

The I/O buses discussed so far (ISA, MCA, and EISA) have one thing in common: relatively slow speed. The next three bus types that are discussed in the following few sections all use the *local bus* concept explained in this section to address the speed issue. The three main local buses found in PC systems are

- VL-Bus (VESA local bus)
- PCI
- AGP

The speed limitation of ISA, MCA, and EISA is a carryover from the days of the original PC when the I/O bus operated at the same speed as the processor bus. As the speed of the processor bus increased, the I/O bus realized only nominal speed improvements, primarily from an increase in the bandwidth of the bus. The I/O bus had to remain at a slower speed because the huge installed base of adapter cards could operate only at slower speeds.

Figure 4.74 shows a conceptual block diagram of the buses in a computer system.

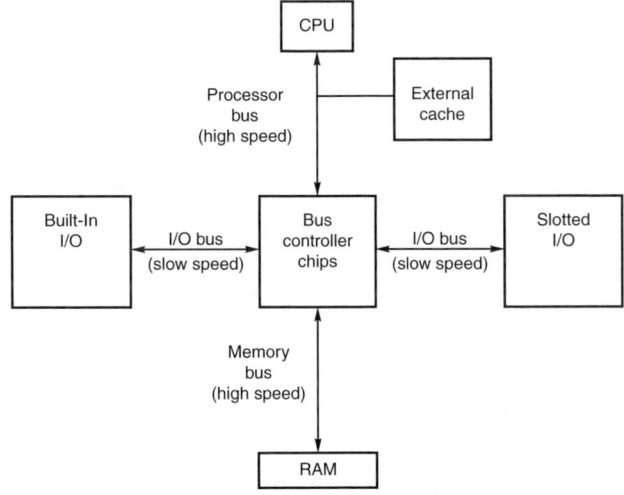

Figure 4.74   Bus layout in a traditional PC.

The thought of a computer system running more slowly than it could is very bothersome to some computer users. Even so, the slow speed of the I/O bus is nothing more than a nuisance in most cases. You don't need blazing speed to communicate with a keyboard or mouse—you gain nothing in performance. The real problem occurs in subsystems in which you need the speed, such as video and disk controllers.

The speed problem became acute when graphical user interfaces (such as Windows) became prevalent. These systems require the processing of so much video data that the I/O bus became a literal bottleneck for the entire computer system. In other words, it did little good to have a processor that was capable of 66MHz–450MHz or faster if you could put data through the I/O bus at a rate of only 8MHz.

An obvious solution to this problem is to move some of the slotted I/O to an area where it could access the faster speeds of the processor bus—much the same way as the external cache. Figure 4.75 shows this arrangement.

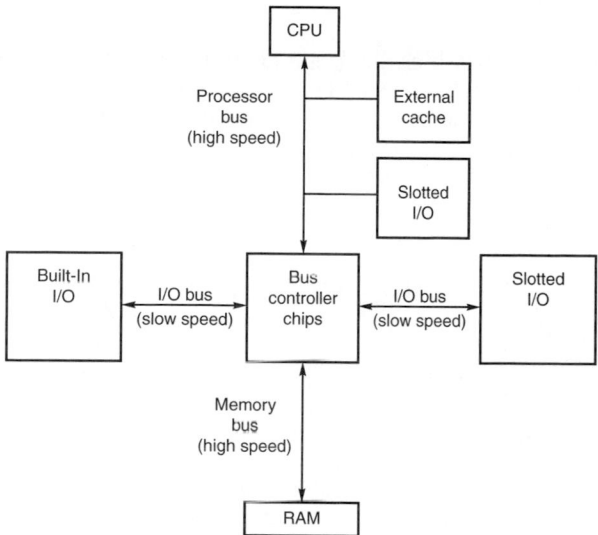

Figure 4.75   How a local bus works.

This arrangement became known as *local bus* because external devices (adapter cards) now could access the part of the bus that was local to the CPU—the processor bus. Physically, the slots provided to tap this new configuration would need to be different from existing bus slots to prevent adapter cards designed for slower buses from being plugged into the higher bus speeds, which this design made accessible.

It is interesting to note that the very first 8-bit and 16-bit ISA buses were a form of local bus architecture. These systems had the processor bus as the main bus, and everything ran at full processor speeds. When ISA systems ran faster than 8MHz, the main ISA bus had to be decoupled from the processor bus because expansion cards, memory, and so on could not keep up. In 1992, an extension to the ISA bus called the VESA local bus (VL-Bus) started showing up on PC systems, indicating a return to local bus architecture. Since then, the peripheral component interconnect (PCI) local bus has supplanted VL-Bus, and the AGP bus has been introduced to complement PCI.

Note

A system does not have to have a local bus expansion slot to incorporate local bus technology; instead, the local bus device can be built directly into the motherboard. (In such a case, the local bus–slotted I/O shown in Figure 4.75 would in fact be built-in I/O.) This built-in approach to local bus is the way the first local bus systems were designed.

Local bus solutions do not necessarily replace earlier standards, such as ISA; they are designed into the system as a bus that is closer to the processor in the system architecture. Older buses such as ISA were kept around for backward compatibility with slower types of adapters that didn't need any faster connection to the system (such as modems). Therefore, until recently a typical system might have AGP, PCI, and ISA slots. Older cards still are compatible with such a system, but high-speed adapter cards can take advantage of the AGP and PCI local bus slots as well. With the demise of ISA slots and the movement of traditionally ISA-based motherboard devices to the LPC interface, today's motherboards essentially use other buses or dedicated interfaces for most of the connections that would have previously used ISA.

The performance of graphical user interfaces such as Windows and graphical Linux interfaces such as KDE and GNOME have been tremendously improved by moving the video cards off the slow ISA bus and onto faster PCI and now AGP local buses.

VESA Local Bus

The Video Electronics Standards Association (VESA) local bus was the most popular local bus design from its debut in August 1992 through 1994. It was created by the VESA committee, a nonprofit organization originally founded by NEC to further develop video display and bus standards. In a similar fashion to how EISA evolved, NEC had done most of the work on the VL-Bus (as it would be called) and, after founding the nonprofit VESA committee, NEC turned over future development to VESA. At first, the local bus slot seemed designed to be used primarily for video cards. Improving video performance was a top priority at NEC to help sell its high-end displays as well as its own PC systems. By 1991, video performance had become a real bottleneck in most PC systems.

The VL-Bus can move data 32 bits at a time, enabling data to flow between the CPU and a compatible video subsystem or hard drive at the full 32-bit data width of the 486 chip. The maximum rated throughput of the VL-Bus is 133MBps. In other words, local bus went a long way toward removing the major bottlenecks that existed in earlier bus configurations.

Unfortunately, the VL-Bus did not seem to be a long-lived concept. The design was simple indeed—just take the pins from the 486 processor and run them out to a card connector socket. So, the VL-Bus is essentially the raw 486 processor bus. This allowed a very inexpensive design because no additional chipsets or interface chips were required. A motherboard designer could add VL-Bus slots to its 486 motherboards very easily and at a very low cost. This is why these slots appeared on virtually all 486 system designs overnight.

Problems arose with timing glitches caused by the capacitance introduced into the circuit by different cards. Because the VL-Bus ran at the same speed as the processor bus, different processor speeds meant different bus speeds, and full compatibility was difficult to achieve. Although the VL-Bus could be adapted to other processors—including the 386 or even the Pentium—it was designed for the 486 and worked best as a 486 solution only. Despite the low cost, after a new bus called PCI appeared, VL-Bus fell into disfavor very quickly. It never did catch on with Pentium systems, and there was little or no further development of the VL-Bus in the PC industry.

Physically, the VL-Bus slot was an extension of the slots used for whatever type of base system you have. If you have an ISA system, the VL-Bus is positioned as an extension of your existing 16-bit ISA slots. The VESA extension has 112 contacts and uses the same physical connector as the MCA bus.

The PCI Bus

In early 1992, Intel spearheaded the creation of another industry group. It was formed with the same goals as the VESA group in relation to the PC bus. Recognizing the need to overcome weaknesses in the ISA and EISA buses, the PCI Special Interest Group was formed.

The PCI bus specification was released in June 1992 as version 1.0 and since then has undergone several upgrades. Table 4.73 shows the various releases of PCI.

Table 4.73   PCI Specifications

PCI Specification	Released	Major Change
PCI 1.0	June 1992	Original 32/64-bit specification
PCI 2.0	April 1993	Defined connectors and expansion boards
PCI 2.1	June 1995	66MHz operation, transaction ordering, latency changes
PCI 2.2	Jan. 1999	Power management, mechanical clarifications
PCI-X 1.0	Sept. 1999	133MHz operation, addendum to 2.2
Mini-PCI	Nov. 1999	Small form factor boards, addendum to 2.2

Table 4.73   Continued

PCI Specification	Released	Major Change
PCI 2.3	March 2002	3.3V signaling, low-profile add-in cards
PCI-X 2.0	July 2002	266MHz and 533MHz operation, supports subdivision of 64-bit data bus into 32-bit or 16-bit segments for use by multiple devices, 3.3V/1.5V signaling
PCI-Express 1.0	July 2002	2.5GBps per lane per direction, using 0.8V signaling, resulting in 250MBps per lane; designed to eventually replace PCI 2.x in PC systems

PCI redesigned the traditional PC bus by inserting another bus between the CPU and the native I/O bus by means of bridges. Rather than tap directly into the processor bus, with its delicate electrical timing (as was done in the VL-Bus), a new set of controller chips was developed to extend the bus, as shown in Figure 4.76.

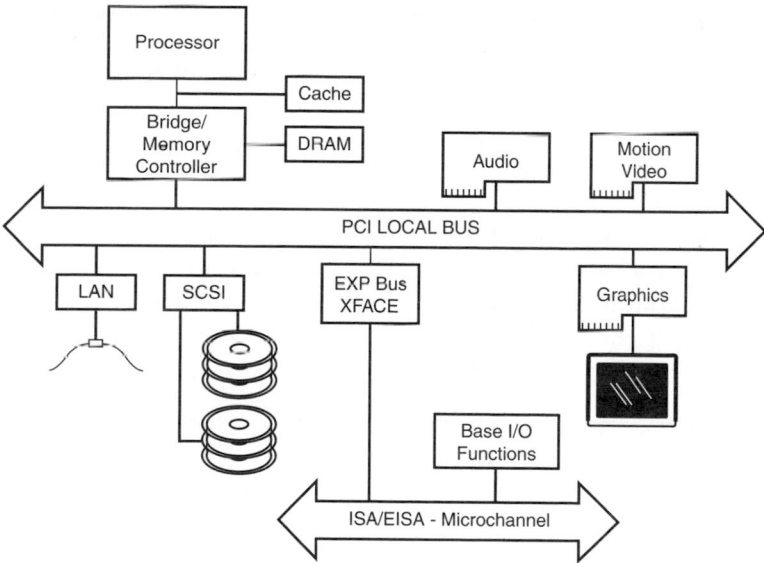

Figure 4.76   Conceptual diagram of the PCI bus.

The PCI bus often is called a *mezzanine bus* because it adds another layer to the traditional bus configuration. PCI bypasses the standard I/O bus; it uses the system bus to increase the bus clock speed and take full advantage of the CPU's data path. Systems that integrate the PCI bus became available in mid-1993 and have since become a mainstay in the PC.

Information typically is transferred across the PCI bus at 33MHz and 32 bits at a time. The bandwidth is 133MBps, as the following formula shows:

$$33.33\text{MHz} \times 4 \text{ bytes (32 bits)} = 133\text{MBps}$$

Although 32-bit 33MHz PCI is the standard found in most PCs, there are now several variations on PCI as shown in Table 4.74.

Table 4.74   PCI Bus Types

PCI Bus Type	Bus Width (Bits)	Bus Speed (MHz)	Data Cycles per Clock	Bandwidth (MBps)
PCI	32	33	1	133
PCI 66MHz	32	66	1	266
PCI 64-bit	64	33	1	266
PCI 66MHz/64-bit	64	66	1	533
PCI-X 64	64*	66	1	533
PCI-X 133	64*	133	1	1066
PCI-X 266	64*	133	2	2132
PCI-X 533	64*	133	4	4266
PCI-Express**	1	2500	0.8	250
PCI-Express**	16	2500	0.8	4000
PCI-Express**	32	2500	0.8	8000

*Bus width on PCI-X devices can be shared by multiple 32-bit or 16-bit devices.

**PCI-Express uses 8b/10b encoding, which transfers 8 bits for every 10 bits sent and can transfer 1–32 bits at a time, depending on how many lanes are in the implementation.

Currently, the 64-bit or 66MHz and 133MHz variations are used only on server- or workstation-type boards and systems. Aiding performance is the fact that the PCI bus can operate concurrently with the processor bus; it does not supplant it. The CPU can be processing data in an external cache while the PCI bus is busy transferring information between other parts of the system—a major design benefit of the PCI bus.

A PCI adapter card uses its own unique connector. This connector can be identified within a computer system because it typically is offset from the normal ISA, MCA, or EISA connectors found in older motherboards. See Figure 4.77 for an example. The size of a PCI card can be the same as that of the cards used in the system's normal I/O bus.

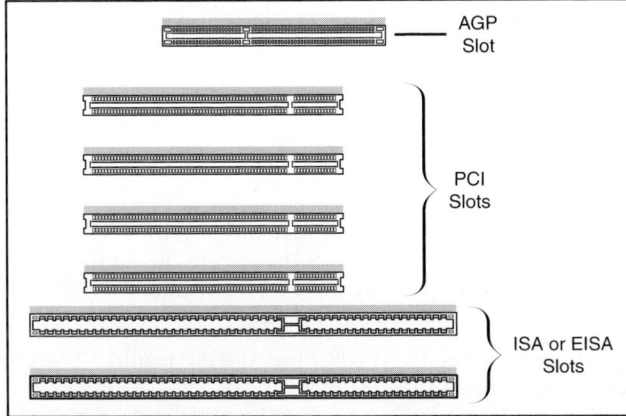

Figure 4.77   Typical configuration of 32-bit 33MHz PCI slots in relation to ISA or EISA and AGP slots.

The PCI specification identifies three board configurations, each designed for a specific type of system with specific power requirements; each specification has a 32-bit version and a longer 64-bit version. The 5V specification is for stationary computer systems (using PCI 2.2 or earlier versions), the 3.3V specification is for portable systems (also supported by PCI 2.3), and the universal specification is for motherboards and cards that work in either type of system. 64-bit versions of the 5V and universal PCI slots are found primarily on server motherboards. The PCI-X 2.0 specifications for 266 and 533 versions support 3.3V and 1.5V signaling; this corresponds to PCI version 2.3, which supports 3.3V signaling.

Note

The pinouts for the 5V, 3.3V, and universal PCI slots can be found on the disc in the Technical Reference section.

Figure 4.78 compares the 32-bit and 64-bit versions of the standard 5V PCI slot to a 64-bit universal PCI slot. Figure 4.79 shows how the connector on a 64-bit universal PCI card compares to the 64-bit universal PCI slot.

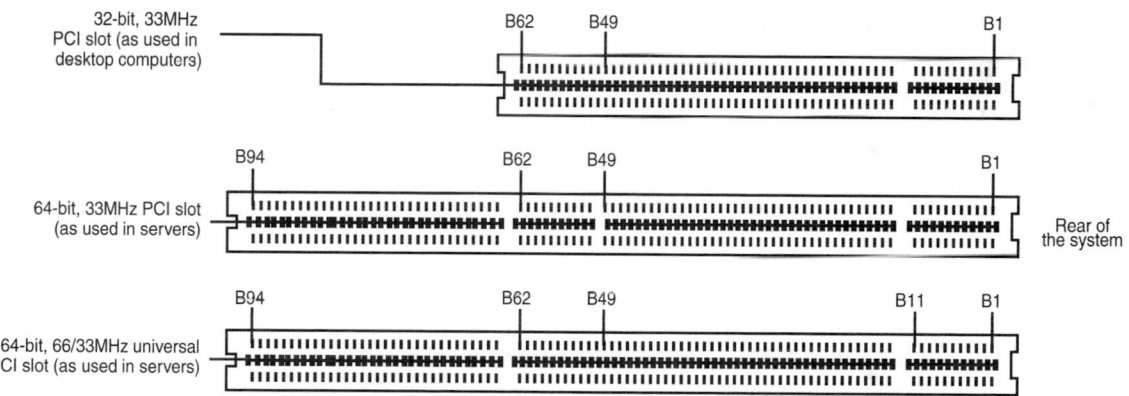

Figure 4.78 A 32-bit, 33MHz PCI slot (top) compared to a 64-bit 33MHz PCI slot (center) and a 64-bit universal PCI slot that runs at 66MHz (bottom).

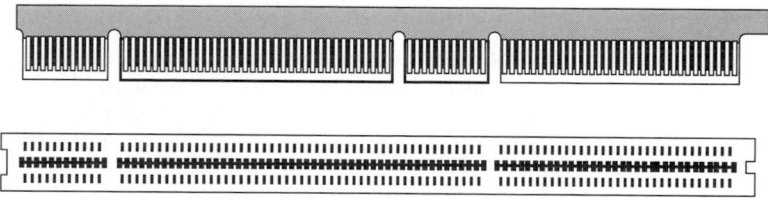

Figure 4.79 A 64-bit universal PCI card (top) compared to the 64-bit universal PCI slot (bottom).

Notice that the universal PCI board specifications effectively combine the 5V and 3.3V specifications. For pins for which the voltage is different, the universal specification labels the pin V I/O. This type of pin represents a special power pin for defining and driving the PCI signaling rail.

Another important feature of PCI is the fact that it was the model for the Intel PnP specification. Therefore, PCI cards do not have jumpers and switches and are instead configured through software. True PnP systems are capable of automatically configuring the adapters, whereas non-PnP systems with ISA slots must configure the adapters through a program that is usually a part of the system CMOS configuration. Starting in late 1995, most PC-compatible systems have included a PnP BIOS that allows the automatic PnP configuration.

PCI-Express

During 2001, a group of companies called the Arapahoe Work Group (led primarily by Intel) developed a draft of a new high-speed bus specification code named 3GIO (third-generation I/O). In August 2001, the PCI Special Interest Group (PCI-SIG) agreed to take over, manage, and promote the 3GIO architecture specification as the future generation of PCI. In April 2002, the 3GIO draft version 1.0 was completed, transferred to the PCI-SIG, and renamed PCI-Express. Finally in July 2002, the PCI-Express 1.0 specification was approved.

The original 3GIO code name was derived from the fact that this new bus specification was designed to initially augment and eventually replace the previously existing ISA/AT-Bus (first-generation) and PCI (second-generation) bus architectures in PCs. Each of the first two generations of PC bus architectures was designed to have a 10- to 15-year useful life in PCs. In being adopted and approved by the PCI-SIG, PCI-Express is now destined to be the dominant PC bus architecture designed to support the increasing bandwidth needs in PCs over the next 10–15 years.

The key features of PCI-Express are as follows:

- Compatibility with existing PCI enumeration and software device drivers.
- Physical connection over copper, optical, or other physical media to allow for future encoding schemes.
- Maximum bandwidth per pin allows small form factors, reduced cost, simpler board designs and routing, and reduced signal integrity issues.
- Embedded clocking scheme enables easy frequency (speed) changes as compared to synchronous clocking.
- Bandwidth (throughput) increases easily with frequency and width (lane) increases.
- Low latency suitable for applications requiring isochronous (time-sensitive) data delivery, such as streaming video.
- Hot plugging and hot swapping capabilities.
- Power management capabilities.

PCI-Express is another example of how the PC is moving from parallel to serial interfaces. Earlier generation bus architectures in the PC have been of a parallel design, in which multiple bits are sent simultaneously over several pins in parallel. The more bits sent at a time, the faster the bus throughput is. The timing of all the parallel signals must be the same, which becomes more and more difficult to do over faster and longer connections. Even though 32 bits can be transmitted simultaneously over a bus such as PCI or AGP, propagation delays and other problems cause them to arrive slightly skewed at the other end, resulting in a time difference between when the first and last of all the bits arrive.

A serial bus design is much simpler, sending 1 bit at a time over a single wire, at much higher rates of speed than a parallel bus would allow. By sending the bits serially, the timing of individual bits or the length of the bus becomes much less of a factor. By combining multiple serial data paths, even faster throughputs can be realized that dramatically exceed the capabilities of traditional parallel buses.

PCI-Express is a very fast serial bus design that is backward-compatible with current PCI parallel bus software drivers and controls. In PCI-Express, data is sent full duplex (simultaneously operating one-way paths) over two pairs of differentially signaled wires called a *lane*. Each lane allows for about 250MBps throughput in each direction initially, and the design allows for scaling from 1 to 2, 4, 8, 16, or 32 lanes. For example, a high-bandwidth configuration with 8 lanes allowing 8 bits to be sent in each direction simultaneously would allow up to 2000MBps bandwidth (each way) and use a total of only 40 pins (32 for the differential data pairs and 8 for control). Future increases in signaling speed could increase that to 8000MBps each way over the same 40 pins. This compares to PCI, which has only 133MBps bandwidth (one way at a time) and requires more than 100 pins to carry the signals.

For expansion cards, PCI-Express will take on the physical format of a smaller connector that appears adjacent to any existing PCI slots on the motherboard. Figure 4.80 compares the PCI-Express x1–x16 connectors, and Figure 4.81 shows how PCI-Express x1 and x16 slots compare to PCI slots on a typical motherboard implementation. Note that the PCI-Express x4 and x8 connectors shown in Figure 4.80 are intended primarily for use in servers.

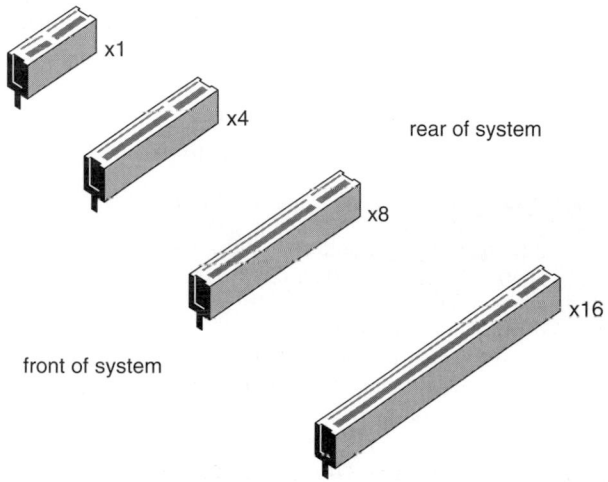

Figure 4.80   PCI-Express x1, x4, x8, and x16 slots.

PCI-Express uses an IBM-designed 8-bit–to–10-bit encoding scheme, which allows for self-clocked signals that will easily allow future increases in frequency. The starting frequency is 2.5GHz, and the specification will allow increasing up to 10GHz in the future, which is about the limit of copper connections. By combining frequency increases with the capability to use up to 32 lanes, PCI-Express will be capable of supporting future bandwidths up to 32GBps.

PCI-Express is designed to augment and eventually replace many of the buses currently used in PCs. It will not only be a supplement to (and the eventual replacement for) PCI slots, but can also be used to replace the existing Intel hub architecture, HyperTransport, and similar high-speed interfaces between motherboard chipset components. Additionally, it will replace video interfaces such as AGP and act as a mezzanine bus to attach other interfaces, such as Serial ATA, USB 2.0, 1394b (FireWire or i.LINK), Gigabit Ethernet, and more.

Because PCI-Express can be implemented over cables as well as onboard, it can be used to create systems constructed with remote "bricks" containing the bulk of the computing power. Imagine the motherboard, processor, and RAM in one small box hidden under a table, with the video, disk drives, and I/O ports in another box sitting out on a table within easy reach. This will enable a variety of flexible PC form factors to be developed in the future without compromising performance.

PCI-Express will not replace PCI or other interfaces overnight. System developers will continue to integrate PCI, AGP, and other bus architectures into system designs for several more years. Just as with PCI and the ISA/AT-Bus before, there will likely be a long period of time during which both buses will be found on motherboards. Gradually, though, fewer PCI and more PCI-Express connections will appear. Over time, PCI-Express will eventually become the preferred general-purpose I/O interconnect over PCI. I expect the move to PCI-Express will be similar to the transition from ISA/AT-Bus to PCI during the 1990s.

Although it will take some time for PCI-Express to replace PCI, many high-performance systems sold in the second half of 2004 and beyond will no longer feature AGP 8x video card slots. Instead,

PCI-Express x16 (a 16-lane-wide PCI-Express slot) will be used to provide video. Although a few systems will offer both PCI-Express x16 and AGP 8x slots, AGP is likely to be the first bus design replaced by PCI-Express.

The first desktop PCs using PCI-Express began to emerge in mid- to late 2004. These feature a mix of PCI and PCI-Express slots. After that, PCI-Express is expected to appear in portable devices and low-end servers and workstations by late 2004, and in high-end servers and workstations by late 2005. These are just estimates, of course, and might change according to the dynamics of the industry. The PCI-Express Bridge 1.0 and Mini PCI-Express Card specifications are designed to help bring PCI-Express products into being by using existing PCI technology. These specifications might help shorten the time-to-market for PCI-Express products.

For more information on PCI-Express, I recommend consulting the PCI-SIG Web site (`www.pcisig.org`).

Accelerated Graphics Port

Intel created AGP as a new bus specifically designed for high-performance graphics and video support. AGP is based on PCI, but it contains several additions and enhancements and is physically, electrically, and logically independent of PCI. For example, the AGP connector is similar to PCI, although it has additional signals and is positioned differently in the system. Unlike PCI, which is a true bus with multiple connectors (slots), AGP is more of a point-to-point high-performance connection designed specifically for a video card in a system because only one AGP slot is allowed for a single video card. Intel originally released the AGP specification 1.0 in July 1996 and defined a 66MHz clock rate with 1x or 2x signaling using 3.3V. AGP version 2.0 was released in May 1998 and added 4x signaling as well as a lower 1.5V operating capability.

The latest revision for the AGP specification for PCs is AGP 8x, also called AGP 3.0. AGP 8x defines a transfer speed of 2133MBps, which is twice that of AGP 4x. The AGP 8x specification was first publicly announced in November 2000. AGP 8x support is now widely available in motherboard chipsets and graphics chipsets from major vendors. Although AGP 8x has a maximum speed twice that of AGP 4x, the real-world differences between AGP 4x- and 8x-compatible devices with otherwise identical specifications are minimal. However, many 3D chipsets that support AGP 8x are also upgrading memory and 3D graphics core speeds and designs to better support the faster interface.

Most recent AGP video cards are designed to conform to the AGP 4X or AGP 8X specification, each of which runs on only 1.5 volts. Most older motherboards with AGP 2X slots are designed to accept only 3.3V cards. If you plug a 1.5V card into a 3.3V slot, both the card and motherboard could be damaged, so special keys have been incorporated into the AGP specification to prevent such disasters. Normally, the slots and cards are keyed such that 1.5V cards fit only in 1.5V sockets and 3.3V cards fit only in 3.3V sockets. However, universal sockets do exist that accept either 1.5V or 3.3V cards. The keying for the AGP cards and connectors is dictated by the AGP standard, as shown in Figure 4.81.

As you can see from Figure 4.81, AGP 4X or 8X (1.5V) cards fit only in 1.5V or universal (3.3V or 1.5V) slots. Due to the design of the connector and card keys, a 1.5V card cannot be inserted into a 3.3V slot. So, if your new AGP card won't fit in the AGP slot in your existing motherboard, consider that a good thing because if you were able to plug it in, you would fry both the card and possibly the board as well! In that case, you'd either have to return the 4X/8X card or get a new motherboard that supports the 4X/8X (1.5V) cards.

Caution

Some AGP 4x/8x-compatible motherboards require you to use 1.5V AGP 4x/8x cards only; be sure to check compatibility between the motherboard and the AGP card you want to buy to avoid problems. Some AGP 4x/8x-compatible slots use the card retention mechanism shown in Figure 4.81. Note that AGP 1x/2x slots have a visible divider not present on the newer AGP 4x slot. AGP 4x slots can also accept AGP 8x cards, and vice versa.

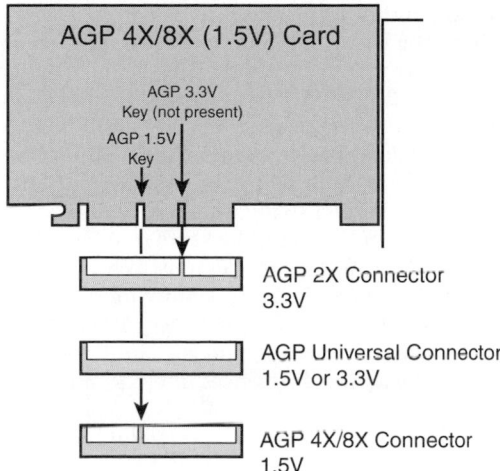

Figure 4.81   AGP 4X/8X (1.5V) card and AGP 3.3V, universal, and 1.5V slots.

Additionally, a newer specification was introduced as AGP Pro 1.0 in August 1998 and was revised in April 1999 as AGP Pro 1.1a. It defines a slightly longer slot with additional power pins at each end to drive bigger and faster AGP cards that consume more than 25 watts of power, up to a maximum of 110 watts. AGP Pro cards are likely to be used for high-end graphics workstations and are not likely to be found in any normal PCs. However, AGP Pro slots are backward-compatible, meaning a standard AGP card will plug in, and a number of motherboard vendors are using AGP Pro slots rather than AGP 4x slots in recent products. Because AGP Pro slots are longer, an AGP 1x/2x card can be incorrectly inserted into the slot, which could damage it, so some vendors supply a cover or an insert for the AGP Pro extension at the rear of the slot. This protective cover or insert should be removed only if you want to install an AGP Pro card.

The standard AGP 1x/2x, AGP 4x, and AGP Pro slots are compared to each other in Figure 4.82.

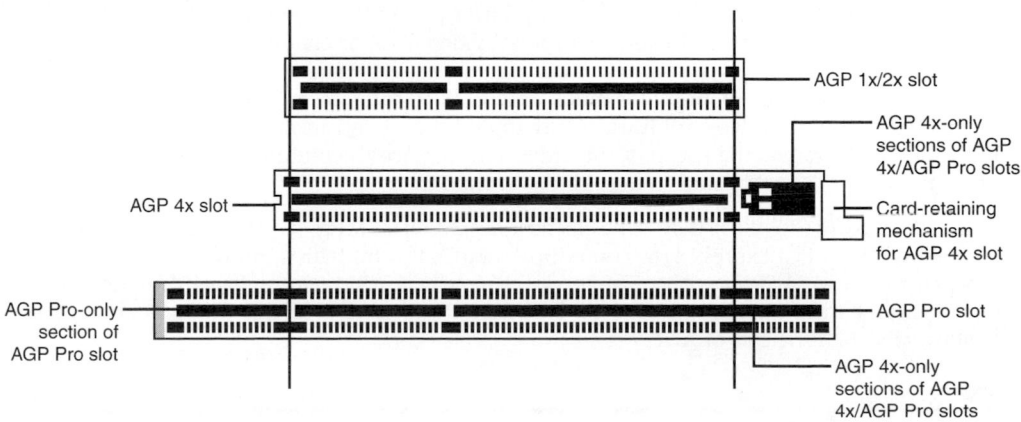

Figure 4.82   AGP standard (1x/2x), AGP 4x, and AGP Pro slots compared to each other. AGP 4x and AGP Pro can accept AGP 1x, 2x, and 4x cards. AGP 4x and AGP Pro slots can also accept AGP 8x cards.

AGP is a high-speed connection and runs at a base frequency of 66MHz (actually 66.66MHz), which is double that of standard PCI. In the basic AGP mode, called 1x, a single transfer is done every cycle. Because the AGP bus is 32 bits (4 bytes) wide, at 66 million times per second it would be capable of transferring data at a rate of about 266MBps! The original AGP specification also defines a 2x mode, in which two transfers are performed every cycle, resulting in 533MBps. Using an analogy in which every cycle is equivalent to the back-and-forth swing of a pendulum, the 1x mode is thought of as transferring information at the start of each swing. In 2x mode, an additional transfer would occur every time the pendulum completed half a swing, thereby doubling performance while technically maintaining the same clock rate, or in this case, the same number of swings per second. Although the earliest AGP cards supported only the AGP 1x mode, most vendors quickly shifted to the AGP 2x mode. The newer AGP 2.0 specification adds the capability for 4x transfers, in which data is transferred four times per cycle and equals a data transfer rate of 1066MBps. Most newer AGP cards now have support for the 4x standard as a minimum, and the latest graphics chipsets from NVIDIA and ATI support AGP 8x. Table 4.75 shows the differences in clock rates and data transfer speeds (bandwidth) for the various AGP modes.

Table 4.75   AGP Modes Showing Clock Speeds and Bandwidth

AGP Bus Type	Bus Width (Bits)	Bus Speed (MHz)	Data Cycles per Clock	Bandwidth (MBps)
AGP	32	66	1	266
AGP 2x	32	66	2	533
AGP 4x	32	66	4	1066
AGP 8x	32	66	8	2133

Because AGP is independent of PCI, using an AGP video card frees up the PCI bus for more traditional input and output, such as for IDE/ATA or SCSI controllers, USB controllers, sound cards, and so on.

Besides faster video performance, one of the main reasons Intel designed AGP was to allow the video card to have a high-speed connection directly to the system RAM, which would enable a reasonably fast and powerful video solution to be integrated at a lower cost. AGP allows a video card to have direct access to the system RAM, either enabling lower-cost video solutions to be directly built in to a motherboard without having to include additional video RAM or enabling an AGP card to share the main system memory. However, few AGP cards in recent years share main memory. Instead, they have their own high-speed memory (as much as 256MB in some recent models). Using dedicated memory directly on the video card is especially important when running high-performance 3D video applications. AGP enables the speed of the video card to pace the requirements for high-speed 3D graphics rendering as well as full-motion video on the PC.

Although AGP 8x (2133MBps) is 16 times faster than 32-bit 33MHz PCI (133MBps), AGP 8x is only about half as fast as PCI-Express x16 (4000MBps). Starting in mid-2004, motherboard and system vendors began to replace AGP 8x with PCI-Express x16 expansion slots in high-performance systems using Pentium 4 and Athlon 64 processors. This trend is likely to accelerate in 2005 and beyond and will eventually spell the end of AGP.

Note

If you want to purchase a motherboard that uses PCI-Express x16 but don't want to replace your AGP video card at the same time, look for motherboards that offer both AGP 8x and PCI-Express x16 slots. These are available for both Pentium 4 and AMD Athlon 64 processors.

System Resources

System resources are the communications channels, addresses, and other signals hardware devices use to communicate on the bus. At their lowest level, these resources typically include the following:

- Memory addresses
- IRQ (interrupt request) channels
- DMA (direct memory access) channels
- I/O port addresses

I have listed these roughly in the order you would experience problems with them. Memory conflicts are perhaps the most troublesome of these and certainly the most difficult to fully explain and overcome. These are discussed in Chapter 6. This chapter focuses on the others listed here in the order you will likely have problems with them.

IRQs cause more problems than DMAs because they are in much higher demand; virtually all cards use IRQ channels. Fewer problems exist with DMA channels because fewer cards use them, DMA channels are used only by the obsolete ISA standard, and there are usually more than enough channels to go around. I/O ports are used by all hardware devices on the bus, but there are technically 64KB of them, which means there are plenty to go around. With all these resources, you must ensure that a unique card or hardware function uses each resource; in most cases they cannot or should not be shared.

These resources are required and used by many components of your system. Adapter cards need these resources to communicate with your system and accomplish their purposes. Not all adapter cards have the same resource requirements. A serial communications port, for example, needs an IRQ channel and I/O port address, whereas a sound card needs these resources and at least one DMA channel. Most network cards use an IRQ channel and an I/O port address, and some also use a 16KB block of memory addresses.

As your system increases in complexity, the chance for resource conflicts increases. Modern systems with several additional devices can really push the envelope and become a configuration nightmare for the uninitiated. Sometimes under these situations the automatic configuration capability of Plug and Play can get confused or fail to optimally configure resources so that everything will work. Most adapter cards enable you to modify resource assignments by using the Plug and Play software that comes with the card or the Device Manager in Windows 9x and later, thus you can sometimes improve on a default configuration by making some changes. Even if the automatic configuration gets confused (which happens more often than it should), fortunately, in almost all cases a logical way to configure the system exists—once you know the rules.

Interrupts

Interrupt request channels, or hardware interrupts, are used by various hardware devices to signal the motherboard that a request must be fulfilled. This procedure is the same as a student raising his hand to indicate that he needs attention.

These interrupt channels are represented by wires on the motherboard and in the slot connectors. When a particular interrupt is invoked, a special routine takes over the system, which first saves all the CPU register contents in a stack and then directs the system to the interrupt vector table. This vector table contains a list of memory addresses that correspond to the interrupt channels. Depending on which interrupt was invoked, the program corresponding to that channel is run.

The pointers in the vector table point to the address of whatever software driver is used to service the card that generated the interrupt. For a network card, for example, the vector might point to the address of the network drivers that have been loaded to operate the card; for a hard disk controller, the vector might point to the BIOS code that operates the controller.

After the particular software routine finishes performing whatever function the card needed, the interrupt-control software returns the stack contents to the CPU registers, and the system then resumes whatever it was doing before the interrupt occurred.

Through the use of interrupts, your system can respond to external events in a timely fashion. Each time a serial port presents a byte to your system, an interrupt is generated to ensure that the system reads that byte before another comes in. Keep in mind that in some cases a port device—in particular, a modem with a 16550 or higher UART chip—might incorporate a byte buffer that allows multiple characters to be stored before an interrupt is generated.

Hardware interrupts are generally prioritized by their numbers; with some exceptions, the highest-priority interrupts have the lowest numbers. Higher-priority interrupts take precedence over lower-priority interrupts by interrupting them. As a result, several interrupts can occur in your system concurrently, with each interrupt nesting within another.

If you overload the system—in this case, by running out of stack resources (too many interrupts were generated too quickly)—an internal stack overflow error occurs and your system halts. The message usually appears as `Internal stack overflow - system halted` at a DOS prompt. If you experience this type of system error and run DOS, you can compensate for it by using the `STACKS` parameter in your `CONFIG.SYS` file to increase the available stack resources. Most people will not see this error in Windows 9x/Me or Windows NT/2000/XP.

The ISA bus uses *edge-triggered* interrupt sensing, in which an interrupt is sensed by a changing signal sent on a particular wire located in the slot connector. A different wire corresponds to each possible hardware interrupt. Because the motherboard can't recognize which slot contains the card that used an interrupt line and therefore generated the interrupt, confusion results if more than one card is set to use a particular interrupt. Each interrupt, therefore, is usually designated for a single hardware device. Most of the time, interrupts can't be shared.

Originally, IBM developed ways to share interrupts on the ISA bus, but few devices followed the necessary rules to make this a reality. The PCI bus inherently allows interrupt sharing; in fact, virtually all PCI cards are set to PCI interrupt A and share that interrupt on the PCI bus. The real problem is that there are technically two sets of hardware interrupts in the system: PCI interrupts and ISA interrupts. For PCI cards to work in a PC, the PCI interrupts are first mapped to ISA interrupts, which are then configured as non-shareable. Therefore, in many cases you must assign a nonconflicting interrupt for each card, even PCI cards. The conflict between assigning ISA IRQs for PCI interrupts caused many configuration problems for early users of PCI motherboards and continued to cause problems even after the development of Windows 95 and its Plug and Play technology.

The solution to the interrupt sharing problem for PCI cards was something called *PCI IRQ Steering*, which is supported in the more recent operating systems (starting with Windows 95 OSR 2.x) and BIOS. PCI IRQ Steering allows a plug-and-play operating system such as Windows to dynamically map or "steer" PCI cards (which almost all use PCI INTA#) to standard PC interrupts and allows several PCI cards to be mapped to the same interrupt. More information on PCI IRQ Steering is found in the section "PCI Interrupts," later in this chapter.

Hardware interrupts are sometimes referred to as *maskable interrupts*, which means the interrupts can be masked or turned off for a short time while the CPU is used for other critical operations. It is up to the system BIOS and programs to manage interrupts properly and efficiently for the best system performance.

Because interrupts usually can't be shared in an ISA bus system, you often run into conflicts and can even run out of interrupts when you are adding boards to a system. If two boards or onboard devices use the same IRQ to signal the system, the resulting conflict prevents either board from operating properly. The following sections discuss the IRQs that any standard devices use, as well as what might be free in your system.

8-Bit ISA Bus Interrupts

The PC and XT (the systems based on the 8-bit 8086 CPU) provide for eight different external hardware interrupts. Table 4.76 shows the typical uses for these interrupts, which are numbered 0–7.

Table 4.76   8-Bit ISA Bus Default Interrupt Assignments

IRQ	Function	Bus Slot
0	System Timer	No
1	Keyboard Controller	No
2	Available	Yes (8-bit)
3	Serial Port 2 (COM2:)	Yes (8-bit)
4	Serial Port 1 (COM1:)	Yes (8-bit)
5	Hard Disk Controller	Yes (8-bit)
6	Floppy Disk Controller	Yes (8-bit)
7	Parallel Port 1 (LPT1:)	Yes (8-bit)

If you have a system that has one of the original 8-bit ISA buses, you will find that the IRQ resources provided by the system present a severe limitation. Installing several devices that need the services of system IRQs in a PC/XT-type system can be a study in frustration because the only way to resolve the interrupt-shortage problem is to remove the adapter board that you need the least.

16-Bit ISA, EISA, and MCA Bus Interrupts

The introduction of the AT, based on the 286 processor, was accompanied by an increase in the number of external hardware interrupts the bus would support. The number of interrupts was doubled to 16 by using two Intel 8259 interrupt controllers, piping the interrupts generated by the second one through the unused IRQ2 in the first controller. This arrangement effectively makes only 15 IRQ assignments available, and IRQ2 effectively became inaccessible.

By routing all the interrupts from the second IRQ controller through IRQ2 on the first, all these new interrupts are assigned a nested priority level between IRQ1 and IRQ3. Thus, IRQ15 ends up having a higher priority than IRQ3. Figure 4.83 shows how the two 8259 chips were wired to create the cascade through IRQ2 on the first chip.

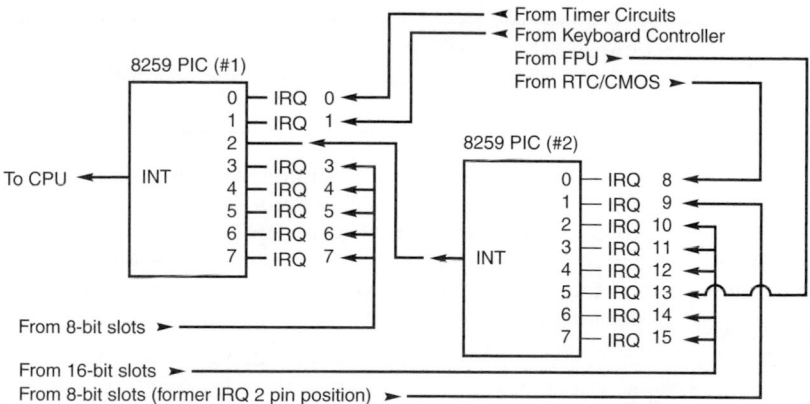

Figure 4.83   Interrupt controller cascade wiring.

To prevent problems with boards set to use IRQ2, the AT system designers routed one of the new interrupts (IRQ9) to fill the slot position left open after removing IRQ2. This means that any card you install in a modern system that claims to use IRQ2 is really using IRQ9 instead.

Table 4.77 shows the typical uses for interrupts in the 16-bit ISA and 32-bit PCI/AGP buses and lists them in priority order from highest to lowest. The obsolete EISA and MCA buses used a similar IRQ map.

Table 4.77   16/32-Bit ISA/PCI/AGP Default Interrupt Assignments

IRQ	Standard Function	Bus Slot	Card Type	Recommended Use
0	System Timer	No	—	—
1	Keyboard Controller	No	—	—
2	2nd IRQ Controller Cascade	No	—	—
8	Real-Time Clock	No	—	—
9	Avail. (as IRQ2 or IRQ9)	Yes	8/16-bit	Network Card
10	Available	Yes	16-bit	USB
11	Available	Yes	16-bit	SCSI Host Adapter
12	Mouse Port/Available	Yes	16-bit	Mouse Port
13	Math Coprocessor	No	—	—
14	Primary IDE	Yes	16-bit	Primary IDE (hard disks)
15	Secondary IDE	Yes	16-bit	2nd IDE (CD-ROM/Tape)
3	Serial 2 (COM2:)	Yes	8/16-bit	COM2:/Internal Modem
4	Serial 1 (COM1:)	Yes	8/16-bit	COM1:
5	Sound/Parallel 2 (LPT2:)	Yes	8/16-bit	Sound Card
6	Floppy Controller	Yes	8/16-bit	Floppy Controller
7	Parallel 1 (LPT1:)	Yes	8/16-bit	LPT1:

Notice that interrupts 0, 1, 2, 8, and 13 are not on the bus connectors and are not accessible to adapter cards. Interrupts 8, 10, 11, 12, 13, 14, and 15 are from the second interrupt controller and are accessible only by boards that use the 16-bit extension connector because this is where these wires are located. IRQ9 is rewired to the 8-bit slot connector in place of IRQ2, so IRQ9 replaces IRQ2 and, therefore, is available to 8-bit cards, which treat it as though it were IRQ2.

Note

Although the 16-bit ISA bus has twice as many interrupts as systems that have the 8-bit ISA bus, you still might run out of available interrupts because only 16-bit adapters can use most of the newly available interrupts. Any 32-bit PCI adapter can be mapped to any ISA IRQs.

The extra IRQ lines in a 16-bit ISA system are of little help unless the adapter boards you plan to use enable you to configure them for one of the unused IRQs. Some devices are hard-wired so they can use only a particular IRQ, and some of the early 16-bit ISA adapters weren't designed to use 16-bit IRQs (9–15). If you have a device that already uses that IRQ, you must resolve the conflict before installing the second adapter. If neither adapter enables you to reconfigure its IRQ use, chances are that you can't use the two devices in the same system.

PCI Interrupts

The PCI bus supports hardware interrupts (IRQs) that can be used by PCI devices to signal to the bus that they need attention. The four PCI interrupts are called INTA#, INTB#, INTC#, and INTD#. These INTx# interrupts are *level-sensitive*, which means that the electrical signaling enables them to be shared among PCI cards. In fact, all single device or single function PCI chips or cards that use only one interrupt must use INTA#. This is one of the rules in the PCI specification. If additional devices are within a chip or onboard a card, the additional devices can use INTB# through INTD#. Because there are very few multifunction PCI chips or boards, practically all the devices on a given PCI bus share INTA#.

For the PCI bus to function in a PC, the PCI interrupts must be mapped to ISA interrupts. Because ISA interrupts can't be shared, in most cases each PCI card using INTA# on the PCI bus must be mapped to a different non-shareable ISA interrupt. For example, you could have a system with four PCI slots and four PCI cards installed, each using PCI interrupt INTA#. These cards would each be mapped to a different available ISA interrupt request, such as IRQ9, IRQ10, IRQ11, or IRQ5 in most cases.

Finding unique IRQs for each device on both the ISA and PCI buses has always been a problem; there simply aren't enough free ones to go around. Setting two ISA devices to the same IRQ has never been possible (the so-called *IRQ sharing* of IRQ4 by COM1/3 and IRQ3 by COM2/4 didn't allow both COM ports to work at the same time), but on most newer systems sharing IRQs between multiple PCI devices might be possible. Newer system BIOSs as well as plug-and-play operating systems, such as Windows 95B (OSR 2) or later, Windows 98, and Windows 2000/XP, all support a function known as PCI IRQ Steering. For this to work, both your system BIOS and operating system must support IRQ Steering. Older system BIOSs and Windows 95 or 95A do not have support for PCI IRQ Steering.

Generally, the BIOS assigns unique IRQs to PCI devices. If your system supports PCI IRQ Steering and it is enabled, Windows assigns IRQs to PCI devices. Even when IRQ Steering is enabled, the BIOS still initially assigns IRQs to PCI devices. Although Windows has the capability to change these settings, it typically does not do so automatically, except where necessary to eliminate conflicts. If there are insufficient free IRQs to go around, IRQ Steering allows Windows to assign multiple PCI devices to a single IRQ, thus enabling all the devices in the system to function properly. Without IRQ Steering, Windows begins to disable devices after it runs out of free IRQs to assign.

To determine whether your Windows 9x/Me system is using IRQ Steering, you can follow these steps:

1. Open the Device Manager.
2. Double-click the System Devices branch.
3. Double-click the PCI Bus, and then click the IRQ Steering tab. There will be a check that displays IRQ Steering as either Enabled or Disabled. If enabled, it also specifies where the IRQ table has been read from.

Note that with Windows 2000 and XP, you can't disable IRQ steering and no IRQ Steering tab appears in the Device Manager.

IRQ Steering is controlled by one of four routing tables Windows attempts to read. Windows searches for the tables in order and uses the first one it finds. You can't control the order in which Windows searches for these tables, but by selecting or deselecting the Get IRQ Table Using check boxes, you can control which table Windows finds first by disabling the search for specific tables. Windows searches for the following tables:

- ACPI BIOS table
- MS Specification table
- Protected Mode PCIBIOS 2.1 table
- Real Mode PCIBIOS 2.1 table

Windows first tries to use the ACPI BIOS table to program IRQ Steering, followed by the MS Specification table, the Protected Mode PCIBIOS 2.1 table, and the Real Mode PCIBIOS 2.1 table. Windows 95 OSR2 and later versions offer only a choice for selecting the PCIBIOS 2.1 tables via a single check box, which is disabled by default. Under Windows 98, all IRQ table choices are selected by default, except the third one, which is the Protected Mode PCIBIOS 2.1 table.

If you are having a problem with a PCI device related to IRQ settings under Windows 95, try selecting the PCIBIOS 2.1 table and restarting. Under Windows 98, try clearing the ACPI BIOS table selection and restarting. If the problem persists, try selecting the Protected Mode PCIBIOS 2.1 table and restarting.

You should select Get IRQ Table from Protected Mode PCIBIOS 2.1 Call only if a PCI device is not working properly. To access these settings in the Windows 98 Device Manager, do the following:

1. Open the Device Manager.

2. Scroll down to the System Devices category, and double-click to open it.

3. Select PCI Bus and click Properties.

4. Click the IRQ Steering tab to see or change the current settings.

If IRQ Steering is shown as disabled in Device Manager, be sure the Use IRQ Steering check box is selected. After selecting this and restarting, if IRQ Steering is still showing as disabled, the IRQ routing table that must be provided by the BIOS to the operating system might be missing or contain errors. Check your BIOS Setup to ensure PCI IRQ Steering is enabled. If there is still no success, you might have to select the Get IRQ Table from Protected Mode PCIBIOS 2.1 Call check box, or your BIOS might not support PCI bus IRQ Steering. Contact the manufacturer of your motherboard or BIOS to see whether your board or BIOS supports IRQ Steering.

On systems that have support for IRQ Steering, an IRQ Holder for PCI Steering might be displayed when you view the System Devices branch of Device Manager. This indicates that an IRQ has been mapped to PCI and is unavailable for ISA devices, even if no PCI devices are currently using the IRQ. To view IRQs programmed for PCI-mode, follow these steps:

1. Select Start, Settings, Control Panel, and then double-click System.

2. Click the Device Manager tab.

3. Double-click the System Devices branch.

4. Double-click the IRQ Holder for PCI Steering you want to view, and then click the Resources tab.

I have found this interrupt steering or mapping to be the source of a great deal of confusion. Even though PCI interrupts (INTx#) can be (and are by default) shared, each card or device that might be sharing a PCI interrupt must be mapped or steered to a unique ISA IRQ, which in turn can't normally be shared. You can have several PCI devices mapped to the same ISA IRQ only if

■ No ISA devices are using the IRQ.

■ The BIOS and operating system support PCI IRQ Steering.

■ PCI IRQ Steering is enabled.

Without PCI IRQ Steering support, the sharing capabilities of the PCI interrupts are of little benefit because all PCI-to-ISA IRQ assignments must then be unique. Without PCI IRQ Steering, you can easily run out of available ISA interrupts. If IRQ Steering is supported and enabled, multiple PCI devices will be capable of sharing a single IRQ, allowing for more system expansion without running out of available IRQs. Better support for IRQ Steering is one of the best reasons for upgrading to Windows 98 or newer versions, especially if you are using the original OSR1 release of 95.

Another source of confusion is that the interrupt listing shown in the Windows 9x Device Manager might show the PCI to ISA interrupt mapping as multiple entries for a given ISA interrupt. One entry would be for the device actually mapped to the interrupt—for example, a built-in USB controller—whereas the other entry for the same IRQ would say IRQ Holder for PCI Steering. This latter entry, despite claiming to use the same IRQ, does not indicate a resource conflict; instead it represents the chipset circuitry putting a reservation on that interrupt for mapping purposes. This is part of the plug-and-play capabilities of PCI and the modern motherboard chipsets. Windows 2000 and XP can also map multiple devices to the same IRQ, but they don't use the term *IRQ Holder* to avoid confusion.

Note that you can have internal devices on the PCI bus even though all the PCI slots are free. For example, most systems today have two IDE controllers and at least one USB controller as devices on the PCI bus. Normally, the PCI IDE controllers are mapped to ISA interrupts 14 (primary IDE) and 15 (secondary IDE), whereas the USB controller can be mapped to the available ISA interrupts 9, 10, 11, and 5. Many recent systems have two or more USB controllers (typically one per every two USB ports), so each USB controller needs to be mapped to an ISA interrupt.

▶▶   See "Universal Serial Bus," p. 983.

The PCI bus enables two types of devices to exist, called *bus masters* (initiators) and *slaves* (targets). A bus master is a device that can take control of the bus and initiate a transfer. The target device is the intended destination of the transfer. Most PCI devices can act as both masters and targets, and to be compliant with the PC'97 and newer system design guides, all PCI slots must support bus master cards.

The PCI bus is an arbitrated bus: A central arbiter (part of the PCI bus controller in the motherboard chipset) governs all bus transfers, giving fair and controlled access to all the devices on the bus. Before a master can use the bus, it must first request control from the central arbiter, and then it is granted control for only a specified maximum number of cycles. This arbitration allows equal and fair access to all the bus master devices, prevents a single device from hogging the bus, and also prevents deadlocks because of simultaneous multiple device access. In this manner, the PCI bus acts much like a local area network (LAN), albeit one that is contained entirely within the system and runs at a much higher speed than conventional external networks between PCs.

IRQ Conflicts

One of the more common IRQ conflicts is the potential one between the integrated COM2: port found in most modern motherboards and an internal (card-based) ISA modem. The problem stems from the fact that true PC card–based modems (not the so-called WinModems, which are software based) incorporate a serial port as part of the card's circuitry. This serial port is set as COM2: by default. Your PC sees this as having two COM2: ports, each using the same IRQ and I/O port address resources.

The solution to this problem is easy: Enter the system BIOS Setup and disable the built-in COM2: port in the system. While you are there, you might think about disabling the COM1: port too because you are unlikely to use it. Disabling unused COMx: ports is one of the best ways to free up a couple of IRQs for other devices to use.

Another common IRQ conflict also involves serial (COM) ports. You might have noticed in the preceding two sections that two IRQs are set aside for two COM ports. IRQ3 is used for COM2:, and IRQ4 is used for COM1:. The problem occurs when you have more than two serial ports in a system. When people add COM3: and COM4: ports, they often don't set them to nonconflicting interrupts, which results in a conflict and the ports not working.

Contributing to the problem are poorly designed COM port boards that do not allow IRQ settings other than 3 or 4. What happens is that they end up setting COM3: to IRQ4 (sharing it with COM1:), and COM4: to IRQ3 (sharing it with COM2:). This is not acceptable because it prevents you from using the two COM ports on any one of the interrupt channels simultaneously. This was somewhat acceptable under plain DOS because single-tasking (running only one program at a time) was the order of the day, but it is totally unacceptable with Windows and OS/2. If you must share IRQs, you can usually get away with sharing devices on the same IRQ as long as they use different COM ports. For instance, a scanner and an internal modem could share an IRQ, but if the two devices are used simultaneously, a conflict results. Fortunately, most devices that formerly used serial ports (such as mice and other pointing devices, label printers, external modems, and PDA cradles) have been redesigned to use USB ports. Thus, many users no longer have any devices that must be plugged into a serial port.

If you need to use serial ports, the best solution is to purchase a multiport serial I/O card that allows nonconflicting interrupt settings or an intelligent card with its own processor that can handle the multiple ports onboard and use only one interrupt in the system. Some older multiport serial cards used the ISA slot, but PCI-slot cards have replaced these in recent systems and have the additional advantages of faster speed and a sharable interrupt.

▶▶ See "Serial Ports," p. 997.

If a device listed in the table is not present, such as the motherboard mouse port (IRQ12) or parallel port 2 (IRQ5), you can consider those interrupts as available. For example, a second parallel port is a rarity, and most systems have a sound card installed and set for IRQ5 (if it is used to emulate a SoundBlaster Pro or 16). Also, on most systems IRQ15 is assigned to a secondary IDE controller. If you do not have an IDE hard or optical drive connected to the secondary controller, you could disable the secondary IDE controller to free up that IRQ for another device.

Note that an easy way to check your interrupt settings is to use the Device Manager in Windows 95/98, Windows NT, or Windows 2000/XP. By double-clicking the Computer Properties icon in the Device Manager, you can get concise lists of all used system resources. Microsoft has also included a program called HWDIAG on Windows 95B; Windows 98 and above feature the System Information program. HWDIAG and System Information do an excellent job of reporting system resource usage, as well as details about device drivers and Windows Registry entries for each hardware component. If you are running Windows XP, a program called MSinfo32 will also give you a report of detailed system information.

To provide the maximum number of shareable interrupts in a recent system without ISA slots, I recommend performing the following steps in the system BIOS:

1. Disable any unused legacy ports in the system BIOS. For example, if you use USB ports instead of serial and parallel ports, disable the serial and parallel ports. This can free up as many as three IRQs.

2. Select the IRQs freed up in step 1 as available for PCI/PnP use. Depending on the BIOS, the screen to use might be known as the PnP/PCI Resource Exclusion screen or the PnP/PCI Configuration screen.

3. Enable the Reset Configuration Data option so the IRQ routing tables in the CMOS are cleared.

4. Save your changes and exit the BIOS setup program.

DMA Channels

Direct Memory Access (DMA) channels are used by communications devices that must send and receive information at high speeds. A serial or parallel port does not use a DMA channel, but an ISA-based sound card or SCSI adapter often does. DMA channels sometimes can be shared if the devices are not the type that would need them simultaneously. For example, you can have a network adapter and a tape backup adapter sharing DMA channel 1, but you can't back up while the network is running. To back up during network operation, you must ensure that each adapter uses a unique DMA channel.

Note

There are several types of DMA in a modern PC. The DMA channels referred to in this section involve the ISA bus. Other buses, such as the ATA/IDE bus used by hard drives, have different DMA uses. The DMA channels explained here don't involve your ATA/IDE drives, even if they are set to use DMA or Ultra DMA transfers.

8-Bit ISA Bus DMA Channels

In the 8-bit ISA bus, four DMA channels support high-speed data transfers between I/O devices and memory. Three of the channels are available to the expansion slots. Table 4.78 shows the typical uses of these DMA channels.

Table 4.78   8-Bit ISA Default DMA-Channel Assignments

DMA	Standard Function	Bus Slot
0	Dynamic RAM Refresh	No
1	Available	Yes (8-bit)
2	Floppy disk controller	Yes (8-bit)
3	Hard disk controller	Yes (8-bit)

Because most systems typically have both a floppy and hard disk drive, only one DMA channel is available in 8-bit ISA systems.

16-Bit ISA DMA Channels

Since the introduction of the 286 CPU, the ISA bus has supported eight DMA channels, with seven channels available to the expansion slots. Similar to the expanded IRQ lines described earlier in this chapter, the added DMA channels were created by cascading a second DMA controller to the first one. DMA channel 4 is used to cascade channels 0–3 to the microprocessor. Channels 0–3 are available for 8-bit transfers, and channels 5–7 are for 16-bit transfers only. Table 4.79 shows the typical uses for the DMA channels.

Table 4.79   16-Bit ISA Default DMA-Channel Assignments

DMA	Standard Function	Bus Slot	Card Type	Transfer	Recommended Use
0	Available	Yes	16-bit	8-bit	Sound
1	Available	Yes	8/16-bit	8-bit	Sound
2	Floppy Disk Controller	Yes	8/16-bit	8-bit	Floppy Controller
3	Available	Yes	8/16-bit	8-bit	LPT1: in ECP Mode
4	1st DMA Controller Cascade	No	—	16-bit	—
5	Available	Yes	16-bit	16-bit	Sound
6	Available	Yes	16-bit	16-bit	Available
7	Available	Yes	16-bit	16-bit	Available

Note that PCI adapters don't use these ISA DMA channels; these are only for ISA cards. However, some PCI cards emulate the use of these DMA channels (such as sound cards) to work with older software.

The only standard DMA channel used in all systems is DMA 2, which is universally used by the floppy controller. DMA 4 is not usable and does not appear in the bus slots. DMA channels 1 and 5 are most commonly used by ISA sound cards, such as the Sound Blaster 16, or by newer PCI sound cards that emulate an older one for backward compatibility. These cards use both an 8-bit and a 16-bit DMA channel for high-speed transfers. DMA 3 is used when a parallel port is configured to work in ECP mode or EPP/ECP mode. Some nonstandard systems, such as older Packard Bell computers, use DMA 1 instead of DMA 3 for the parallel port by default. However, a jumper block on the motherboard on many of these systems can be set to use DMA 3 for the parallel port and avoid conflicts with sound cards that use DMA 1.

Note

Although DMA channel 0 appears in a 16-bit slot connector extension and therefore can be used only by a 16-bit card, it performs only 8-bit transfers! Because of this, you generally don't see DMA 0 as a choice on 16-bit cards. Most 16-bit cards (such as SCSI host adapters) that use DMA channels have their choices limited to DMA 5–7.

I/O Port Addresses

Your computer's I/O ports enable communications between devices and software in your system. They are equivalent to two-way radio channels. If you want to talk to your serial port, you need to know on which I/O port (radio channel) it is listening. Similarly, if you want to receive data from the serial port, you need to listen on the same channel on which it is transmitting.

Unlike IRQs and DMA channels, our systems have an abundance of I/O ports. There are 65,535 ports to be exact—numbered from 0000h to FFFFh—which is an artifact of the Intel processor design more than anything else. Even though most devices use up to 8 ports for themselves, with that many to spare, you won't run out anytime soon. The biggest problem you have to worry about is setting two devices to use the same port.

Most modern plug-and-play systems resolve any port conflicts and select alternative ports for one of the conflicting devices.

One confusing issue is that I/O ports are designated by hexadecimal addresses similar to memory addresses. They are not memory; they are ports. The difference is that when you send data to memory address 1000h, it gets stored in your SIMM or DIMM memory. If you send data to I/O port address 1000h, it gets sent out on the bus on that "channel," and anybody listening in could then "hear" it. If nobody is listening to that port address, the data reaches the end of the bus and is absorbed by the bus terminating resistors.

Driver programs are primarily what interact with devices at the various port addresses. The driver must know which ports the device is using to work with it, and vice versa. That is not usually a problem because the driver and device come from the same company.

Motherboard and chipset devices usually are set to use I/O port addresses 0h–FFh, and all other devices use 100h–FFFFh. Table 4.80 shows the commonly used motherboard and chipset-based I/O port usage.

Table 4.80   Motherboard and Chipset-Based Device Port Addresses

Address (hex)	Size	Description
0000–000F	16 bytes	Chipset - 8237 DMA 1
0020–0021	2 bytes	Chipset - 8259 interrupt controller 1
002E–002F	2 bytes	Super I/O controller configuration registers
0040–0043	4 bytes	Chipset - Counter/Timer 1
0048–004B	4 bytes	Chipset - Counter/Timer 2
0060	1 byte	Keyboard/Mouse controller byte - reset IRQ
0061	1 byte	Chipset - NMI, speaker control
0064	1 byte	Keyboard/Mouse controller, CMD/STAT byte
0070, bit 7	1 bit	Chipset - Enable NMI
0070, bits 6:0	7 bits	MC146818 - Real-time clock, address
0071	1 byte	MC146818 - Real-time clock, data
0078	1 byte	Reserved - Board configuration

Table 4.80   Continued

Address (hex)	Size	Description
0079	1 byte	Reserved - Board configuration
0080–008F	16 bytes	Chipset - DMA page registers
00A0–00A1	2 bytes	Chipset - 8259 interrupt controller 2
00B2	1 byte	APM control port
00B3	1 byte	APM status port
00C0–00DE	31 bytes	Chipset - 8237 DMA 2
00F0	1 byte	Math Coprocessor Reset Numeric Error

To find out exactly which port addresses are being used on your motherboard, consult the board documentation or look up these settings in the Windows Device Manager.

Bus-based devices typically use the addresses from 100h on up. Table 4.81 lists the commonly used bus-based device addresses and some common adapter cards and their settings.

Table 4.81   Bus-Based Device Port Addresses

Address (hex)	Size	Description
0130–0133	4 bytes	Adaptec SCSI adapter (alternate)
0134–0137	4 bytes	Adaptec SCSI adapter (alternate)
0168–016F	8 bytes	Fourth IDE interface
0170–0177	8 bytes	Secondary IDE interface
01E8–01EF	8 bytes	Third IDE interface
01F0–01F7	8 bytes	Primary IDE/AT (16-bit) hard disk controller
0200–0207	8 bytes	Gameport or joystick adapter
0210–0217	8 bytes	IBM XT expansion chassis
0220–0233	20 bytes	Creative Labs Sound Blaster 16 audio (default)
0230–0233	4 bytes	Adaptec SCSI adapter (alternate)
0234–0237	4 bytes	Adaptec SCSI adapter (alternate)
0238–023B	4 bytes	MS bus mouse (alternate)
023C–023F	4 bytes	MS bus mouse (default)
0240–024F	16 bytes	SMC Ethernet adapter (default)
0240–0253	20 bytes	Creative Labs Sound Blaster 16 audio (alternate)
0258–025F	8 bytes	Intel above board
0260–026F	16 bytes	SMC Ethernet adapter (alternate)
0260–0273	20 bytes	Creative Labs Sound Blaster 16 audio (alternate)
0270–0273	4 bytes	Plug and Play I/O read ports
0278–027F	8 bytes	Parallel port 2 (LPT2)
0280–028F	16 bytes	SMC Ethernet adapter (alternate)
0280–0293	20 bytes	Creative Labs Sound Blaster 16 audio (alternate)
02A0–02AF	16 bytes	SMC Ethernet adapter (alternate)
02C0–02CF	16 bytes	SMC Ethernet adapter (alternate)

Table 4.81   Continued

Address (hex)	Size	Description
02E0–02EF	16 bytes	SMC Ethernet adapter (alternate)
02E8–02EF	8 bytes	Serial port 4 (COM4)
02EC–02EF	4 bytes	Video, 8514, or ATI standard ports
02F8–02FF	8 bytes	Serial port 2 (COM2)
0300–0301	2 bytes	MPU-401 MIDI port (secondary)
0300–030F	16 bytes	SMC Ethernet adapter (alternate)
0320–0323	4 bytes	XT (8-bit) hard disk controller
0320–032F	16 bytes	SMC Ethernet adapter (alternate)
0330–0331	2 bytes	MPU-401 MIDI port (default)
0330–0333	4 bytes	Adaptec SCSI adapter (default)
0334–0337	4 bytes	Adaptec SCSI adapter (alternate)
0340–034F	16 bytes	SMC Ethernet adapter (alternate)
0360–036F	16 bytes	SMC Ethernet adapter (alternate)
0366	1 byte	Fourth IDE command port
0367, bits 6:0	7 bits	Fourth IDE status port
0370–0375	6 bytes	Secondary floppy controller
0376	1 byte	Secondary IDE command port
0377, bit 7	1 bit	Secondary floppy controller disk change
0377, bits 6:0	7 bits	Secondary IDE status port
0378–037F	8 bytes	Parallel Port 1 (LPT1)
0380–038F	16 bytes	SMC Ethernet adapter (alternate)
0388–038B	4 bytes	Audio - FM synthesizer
03B0–03BB	12 bytes	Video, Mono/EGA/VGA standard ports
03BC–03BF	4 bytes	Parallel port 1 (LPT1) in some systems
03BC–03BF	4 bytes	Parallel port 3 (LPT3)
03C0–03CF	16 bytes	Video, EGA/VGA standard ports
03D0–03DF	16 bytes	Video, CGA/EGA/VGA standard ports
03E6	1 byte	Third IDE command port
03E7, bits 6:0	7 bits	Third IDE status port
03E8–03EF	8 bytes	Serial port 3 (COM3)
03F0–03F5	6 bytes	Primary floppy controller
03F6	1 byte	Primary IDE command port
03F7, bit 7	1 bit	Primary floppy controller disk change
03F7, bits 6:0	7 bits	Primary IDE status port
03F8–03FF	8 bytes	Serial port 1 (COM1)
04D0–04D1	2 bytes	Edge/level triggered PCI interrupt controller
0530–0537	8 bytes	Windows sound system (default)
0604–060B	8 bytes	Windows sound system (alternate)
0678–067F	8 bytes	LPT2 in ECP mode
0778–077F	8 bytes	LPT1 in ECP mode

Table 4.81   Continued

Address (hex)	Size	Description
0A20–0A23	4 bytes	IBM Token-Ring adapter (default)
0A24–0A27	4 bytes	IBM Token-Ring adapter (alternate)
0CF8–0CFB	4 bytes	PCI configuration address registers
0CF9	1 byte	Turbo and reset control register
0CFC–0CFF	4 bytes	PCI configuration data registers
FF00–FF07	8 bytes	IDE bus master registers
FF80–FF9F	32 bytes	Universal serial bus
FFA0–FFA7	8 bytes	Primary bus master IDE registers
FFA8–FFAF	8 bytes	Secondary bus master IDE registers

To find out exactly what your devices are using, again I recommend consulting the documentation for the device or looking up the device in the Windows Device Manager. Note that the documentation for some devices might list only the starting address instead of the full range of I/O port addresses used.

Virtually all devices on the system buses use I/O port addresses. Most of these are fairly standardized, meaning conflicts or problems won't often occur with these settings. In the next section, you learn more about working with I/O addresses.

Resolving Resource Conflicts

The resources in a system are limited. Unfortunately, the demands on those resources seem to be unlimited. As you add more and more adapter cards to your system, you will find that the potential for resource conflicts increases. If your system is fully PnP-compatible, potential conflicts should be resolved automatically, but often are not.

How do you know whether you have a resource conflict? Typically, one of the devices in your system stops working. Resource conflicts can exhibit themselves in other ways, though. Any of the following events could be diagnosed as a resource conflict:

- A device transfers data inaccurately.
- Your system frequently locks up.
- Your sound card doesn't sound quite right.
- Your mouse doesn't work.
- Garbage appears on your video screen for no apparent reason.
- Your printer prints gibberish.
- You can't format a floppy disk.
- The PC starts in Safe mode (Windows 9x/Me) or can start only in Last Known Good Configuration (Windows 2000/XP).

Windows 9x/Me and Windows 2000/XP also show conflicts by highlighting a device in yellow or red in the Device Manager representation. By using the Windows Device Manager, you can usually spot the conflicts quickly.

In the following sections, you learn some of the steps you can take to head off resource conflicts or track them down when they occur.

Caution

Be careful when diagnosing resource conflicts; a problem might not be a resource conflict at all, but a computer virus. Many computer viruses are designed to exhibit themselves as glitches or periodic problems. If you suspect a resource conflict, it might be worthwhile to run a virus check first to ensure that the system is clean. This procedure could save you hours of work and frustration.

One way to resolve conflicts is to help prevent them in the first place. Especially if you are building up a new system, you can take several steps to avoid problems. One is to avoid using older ISA devices. By definition, they cannot share IRQs, and that is the resource most in demand. PCI (and AGP) cards can share IRQs with IRQ Steering and as such are a much better choice.

Tip

The serial, PS/2 mouse, and parallel ports still found in most recent systems are all ISA devices that cannot share IRQs. If you no longer use these ports, you can use these devices' IRQs for other devices if you

- Disable the unused port in the system BIOS.
- Configure the system BIOS to use the IRQ formerly used by the device(s) for PnP configuration; this might be automatic in some systems.

Another way you can help is to install cards in a particular sequence, and not all at once. Modifying the installation sequence often helps because many cards can use only one or two out of a predefined selection of IRQs that is specific to each brand or model of card. By installing the cards in a controlled sequence, the plug-and-play software can more easily work around IRQ conflicts caused by the default configurations of different cards.

The first time you start up a new system you have assembled or done major upgrades on, the first thing you should check is the BIOS Setup. If you have a setting for PnP Operating System in your BIOS, be sure it is enabled if you are running an operating system with plug-and-play support, such as Windows 9x/Me/2000/XP. Otherwise, make sure it's disabled if you are running an OS that is not plug-and-play, such as Windows NT.

On initial startup I recommend a minimum configuration with only the graphics card, memory, and storage drives (floppy, hard disk, CD-ROM, and DVD). This allows for the least possibility of system conflicts in the initial configuration. If your motherboard came with a CD including drivers specific to the chipset or other built-in features of the board, now is the time to load or install them. Complete the configuration of all built-in devices before installing any other cards or external devices.

After the basic system has been configured (and after you have successfully loaded your operating system and any updates or patches), you can then begin adding one device at a time in a specific order. So, you will power down, install the new device, power up, and proceed to install any necessary drivers and configure the device. You'll probably have to restart your system after you are done to fully complete the configuration.

Tip

I sometimes recommend that between installing devices you enter the Device Manager in Windows and print out the resource settings as they are configured at the time. This way you have a record of how the configuration changes during the entire device installation and configuration process.

Here's the loading sequence for additional cards:

1. Sound card
2. Internal or external modem

3. Network card

4. Auxiliary video devices, such as MPEG decoders, 3D accelerators, and so on

5. SCSI adapter

6. Anything else

Normally, using this controlled sequence of configuring or building up your system results in easier integration with less conflicts and configuration hassles.

Resolving Conflicts Manually

In the past, the only way to resolve conflicts manually was to take the cover off your system and start changing switches or jumper settings on the adapter cards. Fortunately, this is a bit easier with plug-and-play because all the configuration is done via the Device Manager software included in the operating system. Although some early plug-and-play cards also had jumper switches or setup options to enable them to be configured manually, this feature was found primarily on ISA PnP-compatible cards.

Be sure you write down or print out your current system settings before you start making changes. That way, you will know where you began and can go back to the original configuration (if necessary).

Finally, dig out the manuals for all your adapter boards; you might need them, particularly if they can be configured manually or be switched to PnP mode. Additionally, you could look for more current information online at the manufacturers' Web sites.

Now you are ready to begin your detective work. As you try various resource settings, keep the following questions in mind, the answers will help you narrow down the conflict areas:

- *When did the conflict first become apparent?* If the conflict occurred after you installed a new adapter card, that new card probably is causing the conflict. If the conflict occurred after you started using new software, the software probably uses a device that is taxing your system's resources in a new way.

- *Are there two similar devices in your system that do not work?* For example, if your modem, integrated serial ports, or mouse— devices that use a COM port—do not work, chances are good that these devices are conflicting with each other.

- *Have other people had the same problem, and if so, how did they resolve it?* Public forums, such as those on CompuServe, Internet newsgroups, and America Online, are great places to find other users who might be able to help you solve the conflict.

Whenever you make changes in your system, reboot and see whether the problem persists. When you believe that you have solved the problem, be sure to test all your software. Fixing one problem often seems to cause another to crop up. The only way to ensure that all problems are resolved is to test everything in your system.

One of the best pieces of advice I can give you is to try changing one thing at a time, and then retest. That is the most methodical and the simplest way to isolate a problem quickly and efficiently.

As you attempt to resolve your resource conflicts, you should work with and update a system-configuration template, as discussed in the following section.

Using a System-Configuration Template

A *system-configuration template* is helpful because remembering something that is written down is easier than keeping it in your head. To create a configuration template, you need to start writing down which resources are used by which parts of your system. Then, when you need to make a change or add an adapter, you can quickly determine where conflicts might arise. You can also use the Windows 9x/Me/2000/XP Device Manager to list and print this information.

I like to use a worksheet split into three main areas—one for interrupts, another for DMA channels, and a middle area for devices that do not use interrupts. Each section lists the IRQ or DMA channel on the left and the I/O port device range on the right. This way, I get the clearest picture of which resources are used and which ones are available in a given system.

The next page shows the system-configuration template I have developed over the years and still use almost daily.

This type of configuration sheet is resource based instead of component based. Each row in the template represents a different resource and lists the component using the resource as well as the resources used. The chart has pre-entered all the fixed items in a modern PC for which the configuration cannot be changed.

To fill out this type of chart, you would perform the following steps:

1. Enter the default resources used by standard components, such as serial and parallel ports, disk controllers, and video. You can use the filled-out example I have provided to see how most standard devices are configured.

2. Enter the default resources used by additional add-on components, such as sound cards, SCSI cards, network cards, proprietary cards, and so on.

3. Change any configuration items that are in conflict. Try to leave built-in devices at their default settings, as well as sound cards. Other installed adapters might have their settings changed, but be sure to document the changes.

Of course, a template such as this is best used when first installing components, not after. After you have it completely filled out to match your system, you can label it and keep it with the system. Whenever you add more devices, the template will be your guide as to how any new devices should be configured if you need to configure devices manually.

Note

Thanks to plug-and-play configuration, the days of fixed IRQ and other hardware resources are receding into the past. Don't be surprised if your system has assigned different IRQ, I/O port address, or DMA settings after you install a new card. That's why I recommend recording information both before and after you add a new device to your system.

You also might want to track which PCI slot is used by a particular card because some systems convert PCI IRQs to different ISA IRQs depending on which slot is used for a card. Also, some systems pair PCI slots or might pair the AGP slot and a PCI slot, assigning cards installed in both paired slots to the same ISA IRQ.

Page 384 shows the same template filled out for a typical PC system with a mixture of PCI and ISA devices.

System Resource Map

PC Make and Model: _____

Serial Number: _____

Date: _____

Interrupts (IRQs):

0	-	Timer Circuits _____
1	-	Keyboard/Mouse Controller _____
2	-	2nd 8259 IRQ Controller _____
8	-	Real-time Clock/CMOS RAM_____
9	-	_____
10	-	_____
11	-	_____
12	-	_____
13	-	Math Coprocessor_____
14	-	_____
15	-	_____
3	-	_____
4	-	_____
5	-	_____
6	-	_____
7	-	_____

I/O Port Addresses:

040–04B_____

060 & 064 _____

0A0–0A1 _____

070–071_____

_____

_____

_____

_____

0F0 _____

Devices Not Using Interrupts:

Mono/EGA/VGA Standard Ports_____

EGA/VGA Standard Ports_____

CGA/EGA/VGA Standard Ports _____

_____

_____

_____

_____

_____

I/O Port Addresses:

3B0–3BB _____

3C0–3CF _____

3D0–3DF _____

_____

_____

_____

_____

_____

DMA Channels:

0	-	_____
1	-	_____
2	-	_____
3	-	_____
4	-	DMA Channel 0–3 Cascade _____
5	-	_____
6	-	_____
7	-	_____

System Resource Map

PC Make and Model: Intel SE440BX-2 _____

Serial Number: 100000 _____

Date: 06/09/99 _____

Interrupts (IRQs):   I/O Port Addresses:

0 - Timer Circuits _____   040–04B _____

1 - Keyboard/Mouse Controller _____   060 & 064 _____

2 - 2nd 8259 IRQ Controller _____   0A0–0A1 _____

8 - Real-time Clock/CMOS RAM_____   070–071_____

9 - SMC EtherEZ Ethernet Card _____   340–35F _____

10 - _____   _____

11 - Adaptec 1542CF SCSI Adapter (scanner) _   334–337[1] _____

12 - Motherboard Mouse Port _____   060 and 064 _____

13 - Math Coprocessor _____   0F0 _____

14 - Primary IDE (hard disk 1 and 2) _____   1F0–1F7, 3F6_____

15 - Secondary IDE (CD-ROM/tape) _____   170–177, 376 _____

3 - Serial Port 2 (Modem)_____   3F8–3FF _____

4 - Serial Port 1 (COM1) _____   2F8–2FF _____

5 - Sound Blaster 16 Audio _____   220–233_____

6 - Floppy Controller_____   3F0–3F5 _____

7 - Parallel Port 1 (Printer) _____   378–37F _____

Devices Not Using Interrupts: I/O Port Addresses:

Mono/EGA/VGA Standard Ports _____   3B0–3BB _____

EGA/VGA Standard Ports _____   3C0–3CF _____

CGA/EGA/VGA Standard Ports _____   3D0–3DF _____

ATI Mach 64 Video Card Additional Ports_   102,1CE–1CF, 2EC–2EF _____

Sound Blaster 16 MIDI Port _____   330–331_____

Sound Blaster 16 Game Port (joystick) ____   200–207_____

Sound Blaster 16 FM Synthesizer (music)__   388–38B_____

_____   _____

DMA Channels:

0 - _____

1 - Sound Blaster 16 (8-bit DMA) _____

2 - Floppy Controller_____

3 - Parallel Port 1 (in ECP mode)_____

4 - DMA Channel 0–3 Cascade _____

5 - Sound Blaster 16 (16-bit DMA) _____

6 - Adaptec 1542CF SCSI Adapter[1] _____

7 - _____

1. Represents a resource setting that had to be changed to resolve a conflict.

As you can see from this template, only one IRQ and two DMA channels remain available, and that would be *no* IRQs if I enabled the USB on the motherboard! As you can see, interrupt shortages are a big problem in modern systems, particularly when ISA and PCI devices are in use. In that case, I would probably find a way to recover one of the other interrupts; for example, I am not really using COM1, so I could disable that port and gain back IRQ4. In this sample configuration, the primary and secondary IDE connectors were built in to the motherboard:

- Floppy controller
- Two serial ports
- One parallel port

Whether these devices are built in to the motherboard or on a separate card makes no difference because the resource allocations are the same in either case. All default settings are typically used for these devices and are indicated in the completed configuration. Next, the accessory cards were configured. In this example, the following cards were installed:

- SVGA video card (ATI Mach 64)
- Sound card (Creative Labs Sound Blaster 16)
- SCSI host adapter (Adaptec AHA-1542CF)
- Network interface card (SMC EtherEZ)

It helps to install the cards in this order. Start with the video card; next, add the sound card. Because of problems with software that must be configured to the sound card, it is best to install it early and ensure that only default settings are used. It is better to change settings on cards other than the sound card.

After the sound card, the SCSI adapter was installed; however, the default I/O port addresses (330–331) and DMA channel (DMA 5) used were in conflict with other cards (mainly the sound card). These settings were changed to their next logical settings that did not cause a conflict.

Finally, the network card was installed, which also had default settings that conflicted with other cards. In this case, the Ethernet card came preconfigured to IRQ3, which was already in use by COM2:. The solution was to change the setting, and IRQ9 was the next logical choice in the card's configuration settings.

Even though this is a fully loaded configuration, only three individual items among all the cards had to be changed to achieve an optimum system configuration. As you can see, using a configuration template such as the one shown can make what would otherwise be a jumble of settings lay out in an easy-to-follow manner. The only real problems you will run into after you work with these templates are cards that do not allow for enough adjustment in their settings or cards that are lacking in documentation. As you can imagine, you will need the documentation for each adapter card, as well as the motherboard, to accurately complete a configuration table such as the one shown.

Tip

Do not rely too much on third-party DOS-based software diagnostics, such as MSD.EXE, which claim to be capable of showing hardware settings such as IRQ and I/O port settings. Even though they can be helpful in certain situations, they are often wrong with respect to at least some of the information they display about your system. One or two items shown incorrectly can be very troublesome if you believe the incorrect information and configure your system based on it!

Some third-party products such as AMIDiag and CheckIt do a better job, but a much better utility to view these settings is the Device Manager built in to Windows 9x/Me/2000/XP. With plug-and-play hardware, it not only reports settings, but it allows you to change them in some cases (sometimes this requires moving the card to another PCI slot). On older legacy hardware, you can view the settings but not change them. To change the settings of legacy (non–plug-and-play) hardware, you must manually move jumpers or switches and run the special configuration software that came with the card. Consult the card manufacturer or documentation for more information.

Heading Off Problems: Special Boards

A number of devices that you might want to install in a computer system require IRQ lines or DMA channels, which means that a world of conflict could be waiting in the box the device comes in. As mentioned in the preceding section, you can save yourself problems if you use a system-configuration template to keep track of the way your system is configured.

You also can save yourself trouble by carefully reading the documentation for a new adapter board before you attempt to install it, particularly if you are still using ISA boards. The documentation details the IRQ lines the board can use as well as its DMA-channel requirements. In addition, the documentation details the adapter's upper-memory needs for ROM and adapter.

Note

Although PCI cards also use all the resources discussed earlier except DMA channels, most are designed to use any available resource. Thus, the resources used by a particular PCI card are controlled less by the card's design than by the configuration of the particular system in use. For example, if IRQ3 or IRQ4 (normally set aside for use by COM2 and COM1) are not used by COM ports and are made available for PCI/PnP use on a given system, a PCI card might use one of these IRQs. However, on a system that has only IRQ9, IRQ10, and IRQ11 available for PCI/PnP configuration, the identical card might use one of these IRQs instead. In addition, some systems assign different IRQs to different PCI expansion slots.

The following sections describe some of the conflicts you might encounter when you install some popular adapter boards. Although the list of adapter boards covered in these sections is far from comprehensive, the sections serve as a guide to installing complex hardware with minimum hassle. Included are tips on soundboards, SCSI host adapters, and network adapters.

Sound Cards

Sound cards are probably the biggest single resource hog in your system. They typically use at least one IRQ, two DMA channels (in DOS emulation mode), and multiple I/O port address ranges. This is because a sound card is actually several different pieces of hardware all on one board. Most sound cards, including PCI-based models, emulate the Sound Blaster 16 from Creative Labs.

Table 4.82 shows the default resources used by a typical PCI sound card, the Creative Labs SB512. Because sound cards are multifunction devices, each function is listed separately as it appears in the Windows Device Manager.

Table 4.82   Default Resources Used by Creative Labs SB512

Device	IRQ	I/O Port Address	16-Bit DMA Channel	8-Bit DMA Channel
Sound Blaster 16 emulation	5	0220–022F 0330–0331[1] 0388–038B[2]	5	1
Creative Multimedia Interface	N/A	D400–D407	n/a	n/a
Creative Gameport Joystick	N/A	0200–0207	n/a	n/a
Creative SB512	9[3]	C860–C87F	n/a	n/a

1. Used for MIDI interface

2. Used for FM Synthesis

3. Varies with system and PCI expansion slot used

Although other brands of sound cards might use a slightly different configuration, the pattern is the same; Sound Blaster emulation requires a large number of resources. Even if SB emulation isn't used (you might be able to disable it if you no longer play DOS games), the card still uses a single IRQ and several I/O port address ranges. If you take the time to read your soundboard's documentation and determine its communications-channel needs, compare those needs to the IRQ lines and DMA channels that already are in use in your system, and then change the settings of the other adapters to avoid conflicts with the sound card, your installation will go quickly and smoothly. Unfortunately, many vendors no longer provide detailed information on their plug-and-play–compatible cards. That's why you need to install the sound card first and use the system resource map to record which settings the card uses before you install other cards.

Tip

The best advice I can give you for installing a sound card is to put the sound card in before all other cards—except for video. In other words, let the sound card retain all its default settings if you can. Try to change the settings of other adapters when a conflict with the sound card arises. The problem here is that many older programs that use sound are very poorly written with respect to supporting alternative resource settings on sound cards. Save yourself some grief, and let the sound card have its way!

Even the latest sound cards can have problems if they're installed after other cards. I know a user who had to remove all his plug-and-play cards before his system would recognize his plug-and-play sound card.

If your system has integrated sound but you prefer to use a sound card, don't forget to use the BIOS configuration program to disable onboard sound before you install the sound card.

One example of a potential soundboard conflict is the combination of a Sound Blaster 16 and an Adaptec SCSI adapter, as I noted earlier in this chapter. The Sound and SCSI adapters conflict on DMA 5 as well as on I/O ports 330–331. Rather than changing the settings of the sound card, it is best to alter the SCSI adapter to the next available settings that will not conflict with the sound card or anything else. The reason to use the defaults for the sound card is that some older (mostly DOS-based) software often assumes default settings for sound hardware and won't work when alternative settings are used. However, devices that use SCSI ports can use any available setting. The final settings are shown in the previous configuration template.

The cards in question (Sound Blaster 16 and AHA-1542CF) are not singled out here because there is something wrong with them, but instead because they happen to be very popular cards of their respective types and, as such, often are paired together in older systems.

Most people would be using PCI versions of these cards today, but they still require the same types of resource settings with the only exception being DMA channels. Unfortunately, it wasn't DMA channels that we were really running out of! The interrupt shortage often continues even with PCI cards because for older real-mode applications or Windows 95 and earlier, they must be mapped to discrete ISA IRQs. The real solutions to the ISA IRQ problem are to use only PCI cards, use Windows 98 or newer (which support IRQ Steering), and have that support in your ROM BIOS. Then, full sharing is possible. Every desktop system sold today is equipped with a motherboard that lacks ISA slots and breaks ties with that bus forever. These motherboards free us of the interrupt restrictions we have been under for so many years.

Tip

The newer PCI sound cards are largely incompatible with older DOS-based software because they don't use DMA channels like their ISA counterparts. If you don't update your software to 32-bit Windows versions, you won't be able to use these newer PCI bus sound cards. Most of the newer PCI cards do include an emulation program that allows the card to work with older DMA-dependent software, but the results are often problematic. If you use integrated sound, the drivers for your motherboard might include a Sound Blaster emulation driver.

For the best results, use the PC/PCI connector found on some motherboards to connect a patch cable to a PC/PCI-compatible sound card. The PC/PCI connector enables the sound card to use ISA-style DMA channels without clumsy emulation software.

SCSI Adapter Boards

SCSI adapter boards use more resources than just about any other type of add-in device except perhaps a sound card. They often use resources that are in conflict with sound cards or network cards, especially if the card has an onboard BIOS for handling bootable drives. A typical ISA SCSI host adapter with onboard BIOS requires an IRQ line, a DMA channel, a range of I/O port addresses, plus a 16KB range of unused upper memory for its ROM and possible scratch-pad RAM use. Even a simple SCSI host adapter designed for use with scanners still requires an IRQ and a range of I/O port addresses. Fortunately, the typical SCSI adapter is also easy to reconfigure, and changing any of these settings should not affect performance or software operation. PCI-based SCSI host adapters require all of the preceding, except for the DMA channel.

Before installing a SCSI adapter, be sure to read the documentation for the card, and ensure that any IRQ lines, DMA channels, I/O ports, and upper memory the card needs are available. If the system resources the card needs are already in use, use your system-configuration template to determine how you can alter the settings on the SCSI card or other cards to prevent any resource conflicts before you attempt to plug in the adapter card.

Note

Some ISA-based SCSI and network cards can be configured to work in PnP mode or use manual configuration settings. With these cards, you can use the configuration method you prefer. If PnP doesn't work, set the card manually (through jumpers, DIP switches, or software).

Network Interface Cards

Networks are becoming more and more popular all the time, thanks to the rise of easy-to-configure small office/home office networks and the use of network cards to connect to broadband Internet devices such as cable and DSL modems. A typical network adapter does not require as many resources as some of the other cards discussed here, but it requires at least a range of I/O port addresses and an interrupt. Some network interface cards (NICs) also require a 16KB range of free upper memory to be used for the RAM transfer buffer on the network card. As with any other cards, be sure that all these resources are unique to the card and are not shared with any other devices. If your network adapter is built in to the motherboard, it still uses IRQ and I/O port address resources.

Multiple-COM-Port Adapters

A serial port adapter usually has two or more ports onboard. These COM ports require an interrupt and a range of I/O ports each. There aren't too many problems with the I/O port addresses because the ranges used by up to four COM ports in a system are fairly well defined. The real problem is with the interrupts. Most older installations of more than two serial ports have any additional ones sharing the same interrupts as the first two. This is incorrect and causes nothing but problems with software that runs under Windows or OS/2. With these older boards, ensure that each serial port in your system has a unique I/O port address range and, more importantly, a unique interrupt setting.

Many newer multiport adapter cards—such as those offered by Byte Runner Technologies—allow "intelligent" interrupt sharing among ports. In some cases, you can have up to 12 COM port settings without conflict problems. Check with your adapter card's manufacturer to determine whether it allows for automatic or "intelligent" interrupt sharing.

Although most people have problems incorrectly trying to share interrupts when installing more than two serial ports in a system, a fairly common problem exists with the I/O port addressing that should be mentioned. Many of the high-performance video chipsets, such as those from S3, Inc., and ATI, use some additional I/O port addresses that conflict with the standard I/O port addresses used by COM4:.

In the sample system configuration just covered, you can see that the ATI video card uses some additional I/O port addresses, specifically 2EC–2EF. This is a problem because COM4: usually is configured as 2E8–2EF, which overlaps with the video card. The video cards that use these addresses are not normally adjustable for this setting, so you either must change the address of COM4: to a nonstandard setting or disable COM4: and restrict yourself to using only three serial ports in the system. If you do have a serial adapter that supports nonstandard I/O address settings for the serial ports, you must ensure that those settings are not used by other cards, and you must inform any software or drivers, such as those in Windows, of your nonstandard settings.

In many cases, USB or 10/100 Ethernet connections can be used to perform the tasks formerly handled by serial ports. If you no longer need serial ports for any devices in your system, I recommend that you disable the onboard serial ports, remove multiport serial cards, and assign the IRQs used by the serial ports in the BIOS to be available for PCI/AGP Plug and Play assignment. This helps eliminate any IRQ conflicts that could occur.

Universal Serial Bus

USB ports corresponding to USB 1.1 or USB 2.0 are now found on most motherboards, and Windows 98, Windows Me, Windows 2000, and Windows XP provide you with a wide range of operating systems that support them properly. One potential problem is that USB takes another interrupt from your system (in some cases, more than one), and many computers either don't have any free or are down to their last one. If your system supports PCI IRQ Steering, this shouldn't be much of a problem because the IRQ used by your USB controller should be sharable with other PCI devices. If you are out of interrupts, you should look at what other devices you can disable (such as COM or LPT ports) to gain back a necessary interrupt for other devices.

The big advantage of either type of USB from an IRQ or a resource perspective is that the USB bus uses only one IRQ no matter how many devices (up to 127) are attached or how many USB ports are installed on systems with a single USB controller. Some systems with multiple USB controllers use additional IRQs, but USB controllers can share IRQs with each other or with other PCI devices. Therefore, you can freely add or remove devices from the USB without worrying about running out of resources or having resource conflicts.

If you aren't using any USB devices, you should turn off the port using your motherboard CMOS Setup so that the IRQ it was using will be freed. As we continue to move to USB-based keyboards, mice, modems, printers, and so on, the IRQ shortage will be less of a problem. As we have already seen, the elimination of the ISA bus in our systems will also go a long way toward solving this problem.

For the best performance—especially with high-capacity removable media, CD/DVD rewriteable drives, scanners, and printers—look for motherboards that have USB 2.0 (High-speed USB) ports. These ports are also completely backward compatible with USB 1.1 devices and provide better performance when several USB devices are in use simultaneously. You can also add a USB 2.0 card to an existing motherboard to provide the same benefits to an existing system.

Miscellaneous Boards

Some video cards ship with advanced software that allows special video features, such as oversized desktops, custom monitors, switch modes on-the-fly, and so on. Unfortunately, this software requires that the card be configured to use an IRQ. If your video card doesn't require an IRQ, I suggest you dispense with this unnecessary software and configure the card to free up the interrupt for other devices. However, keep in mind that many of the latest 3D accelerators must use an IRQ to enable their bus-mastering feature to work correctly. See your video card's manual for details.

Also related to video is the use of an MPEG decoder add-on card that works in addition to your normal graphics adapter. These are used more in specialized video production and editing and in playing DVD movies; however, they do use additional system resources that must be available. If your CPU runs at speeds above 300MHz and you have an AGP video card, you can probably use your video card for DVD playback and remove the MPEG decoder card. You will need a DVD player program, which might be supplied with your video card. See your video card's manual for details.

Plug-and-Play Systems

Plug and Play (PnP) represents a major revolution in interface technology. PnP first came on the market in 1995, and most motherboards and adapter cards since 1996 take advantage of it. Prior to that, PC users were forced to muddle through a nightmare of DIP switches and jumpers every time they wanted to add new devices to their systems. The results, all too often, were system resource conflicts and nonfunctioning cards.

PnP was not an entirely new concept. It was a key design feature of MCA and EISA interfaces that preceded it by almost 10 years, but the limited appeal of MCA and EISA meant that they never became true de facto industry standards. Therefore, mainstream PC users still had to worry about I/O addresses, DMA channels, and IRQ settings. Early PCI-based systems also used a form of PnP configuration, but because there was no provision for managing conflicts between PCI and ISA cards, many users still had configuration problems. But now that PnP has become prevalent, worry-free hardware setup is available to all computer buyers.

For PnP to work, the following components are desired:

- PnP hardware
- PnP BIOS
- PnP operating system

Each of these components needs to be PnP-compatible, meaning that it complies with the PnP specifications.

The Hardware Component

The *hardware component* refers to both computer systems and adapter cards. The term does not mean, however, that you can't use your older ISA adapter cards (referred to as *legacy cards*) in a PnP system. You can use these cards; in fact, your PnP BIOS automatically reassigns PnP-compatible cards around existing legacy components. Also, many late-model ISA cards can be switched into PnP-compatible mode.

PnP adapter cards communicate with the system BIOS and the operating system to convey information about which system resources are necessary. The BIOS and operating system, in turn, resolve conflicts (wherever possible) and inform the adapter card which specific resources it should use. The adapter card then can modify its configuration to use the specified resources.

The BIOS Component

The BIOS component means that most users of pre-1996 PCs need to update their BIOSs or purchase new machines that have PnP BIOSs. For a BIOS to be compatible, it must support 13 additional system function calls, which can be used by the OS component of a PnP system. The PnP BIOS specification was developed jointly by Compaq, Intel, and Phoenix Technologies.

The PnP features of the BIOS are implemented through an expanded POST. The BIOS is responsible for identification, isolation, and possible configuration of PnP adapter cards. The BIOS accomplishes these tasks by performing the following steps:

1. Disables any configurable devices on the motherboard or on adapter cards
2. Identifies any PnP PCI or ISA devices
3. Compiles an initial resource-allocation map for ports, IRQs, DMAs, and memory
4. Enables I/O devices

5. Scans the ROMs of ISA devices

6. Configures initial program-load (IPL) devices, which are used later to boot the system

7. Enables configurable devices by informing them which resources have been assigned to them

8. Starts the bootstrap loader

9. Transfers control to the operating system

The Operating System Component

The operating system component is found in most modern operating systems, such as Windows 9x/Me/2000/XP. In some cases system manufacturers have provided extensions to the operating system for their specific hardware. Such is especially true for notebook systems, for example. Be sure you load these extensions if they are required by your system.

It is the responsibility of the operating system to inform users of conflicts that can't be resolved by the BIOS. Depending on the sophistication of the operating system, the user then could configure the offending cards manually (onscreen) or turn off the system and set switches on the physical cards. When the system is restarted, the system is checked for remaining (or new) conflicts, any of which are brought to the user's attention. Through this repetitive process, all system conflicts are resolved.

Note

Because of revisions in some of the Plug and Play specifications, especially the ACPI specification, it can help to ensure you are running the latest BIOS and drivers for your system. With the Flash ROM used in most PnP systems, you can download the new BIOS image from the system vendor or manufacturer and run the supplied BIOS update program.

Motherboard Selection Criteria (Knowing What to Look For)

I am often asked to make a recommendation for purchases. Without guidance, many individuals don't have any rhyme or reason to their selections and instead base their choices solely on magazine reviews or, even worse, on some personal bias. To help eliminate this haphazard selection process, I have developed a simple checklist that will help you select a system. This list takes into consideration several important system aspects overlooked by most checklists. The goal is to ensure that the selected system truly is compatible and has a long life of service and upgrades ahead.

It helps to think like an engineer when you make your selection. Consider every aspect and detail of the motherboards in question. For instance, you should consider any future uses and upgrades. Technical support at a professional (as opposed to a user) level is extremely important. What support will be provided? Is there documentation, and does it cover everything else?

In short, a checklist is a good idea. Here is one for you to use in evaluating any PC-compatible system. A system might not have to meet every one of these criteria for you to consider purchasing it, but if it misses more than a few, consider staying away from that system. The items at the top of the list are the most important, and the items at the bottom are perhaps of lesser importance (although I think each item is important). The rest of this chapter discusses in detail the criteria in this checklist:

- ■ *Motherboard chipset.* Motherboards should use a high-performance chipset that supports DDR or DDR-2 SDRAM DIMMs or RDRAM RIMMs—preferably one that allows ECC memory as well if you are concerned about catching possible memory errors before they corrupt your data. Also look for AGP 4x or faster video support and ATA-100 or faster hard drive support. The motherboard chipset is the backbone of a system and is perhaps the single most important part you'll consider. I spend the most time deciding on my next chipset because it affects and influences virtually every other component in the system.

- *Processor.* A modern system should use a socket-based processor with on-die L2 cache. Evaluate the processor choices you have, and try to get the one with the highest-speed CPU bus (front-side bus). Don't get too hung up on L2 cache size; a little cache goes a long way. It is more important that the cache run at full core speed (which it will if it is on-die). Current processors such as the Athlon XP, Pentium 4, Celeron 4, and Athlon 64 all meet this criteria. I usually recommend only "boxed" processors as sold by Intel and AMD, which include a high-quality active heatsink as well as installation instructions and a 3-year warranty direct with the manufacturer.

- *Processor sockets.* For maximum upgradeability and performance, you should stick with a system that uses a socket for the CPU. The main sockets in use today on new systems include Socket A (Socket 462) for the Duron/Athlon/Athlon XP, Socket 478 (which has replaced the original Socket 423) for the Pentium 4 and Celeron 4, and Socket 754 for the Athlon 64 or Socket 939 (which is replacing Socket 940) for the Athlon 64FX. As long as your motherboard has one of these sockets, you should be in good shape.

- *Motherboard speed.* The motherboard typically offers a choice of speeds, including anywhere from 200MHZ to 400MHz for the Duron/Athlon/Athlon XP-based boards, or from 400MHz to 800MHz for the Pentium 4–based boards. Check to ensure the board you are buying runs at the speeds necessary to support the processors you want to install.

- *Cache memory.* All modern systems use processors with integral cache, most of them now having the cache directly on the processor die for maximum speed. As such, there won't be any cache memory on the motherboard in a modern system. The tip is to make sure you are using a processor with full core speed on-die L2 cache because this offers the maximum in performance. All the modern processors now incorporate full-speed on-die L2 cache.

- *SIMM/DIMM/RIMM memory.* SIMMs are obsolete by today's standards, so stay away from any boards that use them. Your board should support either standard or DDR DIMMs or RIMMs that contain SDRAM, DDR SDRAM, or RDRAM, respectively. What you use depends mainly on your motherboard chipset, so choose the chipset and board that accepts the memory type you want to use. Currently, DDR and DDR-2 SDRAM and RDRAM are the fastest types of memory available, with RDRAM being by far the most costly. SDRAM is now much more expensive than DDR SDRAM because current systems no longer use SDRAM.

  Mission-critical systems should use ECC memory and ensure that the motherboard fully supports ECC operation. Note that many of the low-end chipsets from Intel and others do not support ECC and should not be used for mission-critical applications. This is something you should know before purchasing the system.

  Finally, note that most motherboards support either three or four DIMM sockets, or two or three RIMM sockets. Be sure that you populate them wisely so you don't have to resort to removing memory later to add more, which is not very cost-effective.

- *Bus type.* No recent desktop motherboards incorporate ISA bus slots, so if you have any ISA cards, you'll have to discard them or use them in older systems. Instead you should find anywhere from one to five or more PCI local bus slots. Be sure the PCI slots conform to the PCI 2.1 or later revision (primarily based on the chipset). Take a look at the layout of the slots to ensure that cards inserted in them will not block access to memory sockets or be blocked by other components in the case. Systems without onboard video should also feature one AGP 4x or 8x slot for a high-performance AGP video card. Some very high-performance systems use the new PCI-Express x16 slot instead of (or sometimes along with) an AGP 4x/8x slot. Some boards also feature AMR (audio modem riser) or CNR (communications networking riser) slots for special cards that are included with the board to provide sound, modem, or other similar features. If a motherboard has an AMR or a CNR slot but doesn't include the riser card, you should check with the vendor to determine whether riser cards are available with the features you want.

- *BIOS.* The motherboard should use an industry-standard BIOS, such as those from AMI, Phoenix, or Award. The BIOS should be of a Flash ROM or EEPROM design for easy updating. Look for a BIOS Recover jumper or mode setting, as well as possibly a Flash ROM write-protect jumper on some systems.

- *Form factor.* For maximum flexibility, performance, reliability, and ease-of-use, the ATX form factor (including microATX and FlexATX) cannot be beat. ATX has several distinct performance and functional advantages over Baby-AT and is vastly superior to any proprietary designs, such as LPX. Additionally, the NLX form factor might be a consideration for low-profile or low-cost desktop systems, although FlexATX is also becoming popular for these designs. The newest form factor, BTX, offers superior cooling but is more expensive than ATX and requires a new power supply and case design.

- *Built-in interfaces.* Ideally, a motherboard should contain as many built-in standard controllers and interfaces as possible (except perhaps video). There is a trend toward legacy-free PCs that lack the conventional Super I/O component and therefore have only USB and sometimes IEEE 1394 for external expansion. Legacy-free PCs lack the conventional keyboard and mouse ports, serial and parallel ports, and possibly even the internal floppy controller. Systems that use an integrated Super I/O component have these interfaces.

  Built-in 10/100 or 10/100/1000 Ethernet network adapters are also handy, especially if you are using a cable modem or DSL connection to the Internet. A built-in sound card is a great feature, usually offering full Sound Blaster compatibility and functions, and possibly offering additional features such as 5.1 (six-channel) or 7.1 (eight-channel) surround sound and SPDIF connections to a home theater system. If your sound needs are more demanding, you might find the built-in solutions less desirable, and you might want to have a separate sound card in your system. Built-in video adapters are also a bonus in some situations, but because there are many video chipset and adapter designs from which to choose, generally you'll find better choices in external local bus video adapters. This is especially true if you need the highest performance video available.

  Built-in devices usually can be disabled to allow future add-ons, but problems can result.

- *Onboard IDE interfaces.* All motherboards on the market have included onboard IDE interfaces for some time now, but not all IDE interfaces are equal. Your motherboard should support at least UDMA/66 (ATA-66) speeds, which matches the best real-world performance currently available from IDE drives. UDMA/66, UDMA/100, and UDMA/133 actually exceed the real-world performance of current drives using these standards and thus provide you with headroom for future drives. For even greater speed, consider motherboards with onboard IDE RAID controllers. These motherboards can be configured to perform data striping for extra speed or data mirroring for extra reliability when two or more identical IDE drives are used. These motherboards are based on a variety of standard chipsets with RAID functions added by RAID chipsets from AMI, HighPoint, or Promise. Many recent systems now include Serial ATA drive interfaces, some of which include RAID functions. SATA is even faster than ATA-133 and exceeds the real-world performance of current (first-generation) SATA drives by a wide margin.

Tip

With a never-ending stream of motherboards coming onto the market, finding motherboards with the features you want can be difficult. Motherboard Homeworld's Mobot search engine helps you find motherboards based on your choice of form factor, platform, chipset, CPU type, processor, manufacturer, memory type, slot types, built-on ports, and more. Check it out at `iceberg.pchomeworld.com/cgi-win/mobotGen/mobot.asp`.

- *Power management.* The motherboard should fully support the latest standard for power management, which is ACPI. An Energy Star–compliant system is also a bonus because it uses less than 30 watts of electrical energy when in sleep mode, saving energy as well as your electric bill.

- *Documentation.* Good technical documentation is a requirement. Documents should include information on any and all jumpers and switches found on the board, connector pinouts for all connectors, specifications for other plug-in components, and any other applicable technical information. Most vendors provide this information in electronic form (using the Adobe Reader PDF format) on their Web sites, so you can preview the information available for a given motherboard before you buy.

- *Technical support.* Good online technical support goes beyond documentation. It includes driver and BIOS updates, FAQs, updated tables of processor and memory compatibility, and utility programs to help you monitor the condition of your system. In addition to these online support features, make sure the vendor can be contacted through email and by phone.

You might notice that these selection criteria seem fairly strict and might disqualify many motherboards on the market, including what you already have in your system! These criteria will, however, guarantee you the highest-quality motherboard offering the latest in PC technology that will be upgradeable, be expandable, and provide good service for many years.

Most of the time I recommend purchasing boards from better-known motherboard manufacturers such as Intel, Acer, ABIT, AsusTek, SuperMicro, Tyan, FIC, and others. These boards might cost a little more, but there is some safety in the more well-known brands. That is, the more boards they sell, the more likely that any problems will have been discovered by others and solved long before you get yours. Also, if service or support is necessary, the larger vendors are more likely to be around in the long run.

Documentation

As mentioned, documentation is an important factor to consider when you're planning to purchase a motherboard. Most motherboard manufacturers design their boards around a particular chipset, which actually counts as the bulk of the motherboard circuitry. Many manufacturers, such as Intel, VIA, ALi, SiS, and others, offer chipsets. I recommend obtaining the data book or other technical documentation on the chipset directly from the chipset manufacturer.

For example, one of the more common questions I hear about a system relates to the BIOS Setup program. People want to know what the "Advanced Chipset Setup" features mean and what the effects of changing them will be. Often they go to the BIOS manufacturer thinking that the BIOS documentation will offer help. Usually, however, people find that there is no real coverage of what the chipset setup features are in the BIOS documentation. You will find this information in the data book provided by the chipset manufacturer. Although these books are meant to be read by the engineers who design the boards, they contain all the detailed information about the chipset's features, especially those that might be adjustable. With the chipset data book, you will have an explanation of all the controls in the Advanced Chipset Setup section of the BIOS Setup program.

Besides the main chipset data books, I also recommend collecting any data books on the other major chips in the system. This includes any floppy or IDE controller chips, Super I/O chips, and of course the main processor. You will find an incredible amount of information on these components in the data books.

Caution

Most chipset manufacturers make a particular chip for only a short time, rapidly superseding it with an improved or changed version. The data books are available only during the time the chip is being manufactured, so if you wait too long, you will find that such documents might no longer be available. The time to collect documentation on your motherboard is *now*!

Using Correct Speed-Rated Parts

Some vendors use substandard parts in their systems to save money. Because the CPU is one of the most expensive components on the motherboard and motherboards are sold to system assemblers without the CPU installed, it is tempting for the assembler to install a CPU rated for less than the actual operating speed. A system could be sold as a 2.4GHz system, for example, but when you look under the hood, you might find it's rated for only 2GHz. This is called *overclocking*, and many vendors have practiced this over the last few years. Some even go so far as to re-mark the CPUs, so that even if you look, the part appears to have the correct rating. The best way to stop this is to purchase systems from known, reliable vendors and purchase processors from distributors that are closely connected with the manufacturer. Overclocking is fine if you want to do it yourself and understand the risks, but when I purchase a new system, I expect that all the parts included will be rated to run at the speed to which they are set.

◀◀   See "Processor Speed Ratings," p. 53.

When a chip is run at a speed higher than it is rated for, it runs hotter than it would normally. This can cause the chip to occasionally overheat, which would appear as random lockups, glitches, and frustration. I highly recommend that you check to ensure you are getting the right speed-rated parts you are paying for.

Also be sure to use the recommended heatsink compound (thermal grease). This can improve the efficiency of your heatsink by up to 30%.

This practice is easy to fall into because the faster-rated chips cost more money. Intel and other chip manufacturers usually rate their chips very conservatively. Over the years, I have overclocked many processors, running them sometimes well beyond their rated speeds. Although I might purchase a Pentium 4 2.4GHz and run it at 2.6GHz, if I were to experience lockups or glitches in operation, I would immediately return it to the original speed and retest. If I purchase a 2.6GHz system from a vendor, I fully expect it to have a 2.6GHz part, not slower parts running past their rated speeds!

Overclocking has been made more difficult by Intel and AMD, who have both started locking the bus multipliers in their chips to prevent easy overclocking by changing the multiplier setting on the motherboard. This is done mainly to combat re-marking CPUs and deceiving customers, although it unfortunately can also prevent those who want to from hotrodding their chips. Still, you can overclock most chips by increasing the CPU bus (front-side bus) speed within certain tolerances. Many of the motherboards on the market have tweakable CPU bus speeds specifically designed to allow overclocking. Check with your motherboard manual, or download the documentation from the manufacturer's Web site. You might find that your board is capable of things you didn't realize.

If you purchase a processor or system, verify that the markings are the original Intel or AMD markings and that the speed rating on the chip is what you really paid for.

The bottom line: If the price is too good to be true, ask before you buy. Are the parts really manufacturer-rated for the system speed?

To determine the rated speed of a CPU chip, look at the writing on the chip. See Chapter 3 for details on how to interpret the marks to see what the rating on the chip actually is.

Caution

Be careful when running software to detect processor speed. Most programs can only estimate at what speed the chip is currently running, not what the true original rating is. The current speed of the processor might not be its actual rated speed, either because of overclocking or because some recent systems reduce processor speed when the system is not heavily tasked. One exception to this is the Intel Processor Frequency ID Utility, which can determine whether an Intel processor is operating at the correct and rated frequency intended. Although it gives only basic information about any Intel processor, it can uniquely identify the original speed ratings of the Pentium III, third-generation Celeron (Coppermine-based), and any newer processors, accurately determining whether they have been overclocked. You can download the Intel Processor Frequency ID Utility from `developer.intel.com/support/processors/tools/frequencyid/download.htm`.

Older system chassis with speed markings or even indicator lights are usually no indication of the actual or rated speed of the processor inside. Those displays can literally be set via jumpers to read any speed you desire! They have no true relation to actual system speed.

Most of the better diagnostics on the market, such as Norton Utilities from Symantec or SiSoftware Sandra, read the processor ID and stepping information, as well as show current operating (but not rated) speed. You can consult the processor manufacturer or Chapter 3 for tables listing the various processor steppings to see exactly how yours stacks up.

CHAPTER 5

BIOS

BIOS Basics

It is often difficult for people to understand the difference between hardware and software in a PC system. The differences can be difficult because they are both very much intertwined in the system design, construction, and operation. Understanding these differences is essential to understanding the role of the BIOS in the system.

BIOS is a term that stands for *basic input/output system*, which consists of low-level software that controls the system hardware and acts as an interface between the operating system and the hardware. Most people know the term BIOS by another name—*device drivers*, or just *drivers*. In other words, the BIOS is drivers, meaning all of them. BIOS is essentially the link between hardware and software in a system.

When the PC was first introduced, the BIOS software containing all the device drivers for the entire system was collectively burned into one or more nonvolatile (meaning they retain their data even when the power is turned off) read-only memory (ROM) chips and placed on the motherboard. In essence, the drivers were self-contained, preloaded into memory, and accessible anytime the PC was powered on.

This ROM chip also contained a power on self test (POST) program and a bootstrap loader. The bootstrap program was designed to initiate the loading of an OS by checking for and loading the boot sector from a floppy disk and, if one was not present, a hard disk. After the OS was loaded, it could call on the low-level routines (device drivers) in the BIOS to interact with the system hardware. In the early days, all the necessary device drivers were in the BIOS stored in the motherboard ROM. This included drivers for the keyboard, MDA/CGA video adapters, serial/parallel ports, floppy controller, hard disk controller, joystick, and clock.

When the OS loaded, you didn't have to load a driver to interact with those pieces of hardware because the drivers were already preloaded in the ROM. That worked great as long as you didn't add any new hardware for which there wasn't a driver in ROM. If you did, you then had two choices: If the hardware you were adding was an adapter card, that card could have a ROM onboard containing the necessary device drivers. The motherboard ROM was preprogrammed to scan a predetermined area of memory looking for any adapter card ROMs and, if any were found, their code was tested and subsequently executed, essentially linking them into and adding their functionality to the existing BIOS. In essence, the motherboard ROM "assimilated" any adapter card ROMs, adding to the "collective" functionality.

This method of adding drivers was required for certain items, such as video cards, that needed to be functional immediately when the PC was powered on. The BIOS code in the motherboard ROM had drivers only for the IBM monochrome display adapter (MDA) and color graphics adapter (CGA) video cards. If you added any card that was different from that, the drivers in the motherboard ROM would not work. That wouldn't be a problem if the new video card had its own onboard drivers in a ROM that would be linked into the BIOS immediately upon throwing the power switch.

If the device did not use an adapter card, there had to be another way to add the necessary driver to the BIOS collective. A scheme was devised whereby during the early stages of loading, the OS startup file (IO.SYS) checked for a configuration file (called CONFIG.SYS) that specified any additional drivers to load to support new hardware. The CONFIG.SYS file, along with any drivers named within, would be placed on the boot drive. Then, when the IO.SYS program read them, it loaded the specified drivers into memory and linked them into the rest of the BIOS, again adding their functionality to the collective whole. In essence, these drivers were loaded from disk into RAM and linked into the BIOS so they could be called on when necessary.

At this point, the BIOS had grown from being entirely contained in the motherboard ROM, to having additional drivers linked in from adapter card ROMs, to having even more drivers linked in after being loaded into RAM during the early stages of the boot process. The BIOS was now constructed of programs located in three different physical locations in the system, and yet it functioned as a single entity because all the programs were linked together via the BIOS subroutine calling system-of-software interrupts. The OS or an application program needing to talk to a specific piece of hardware (for example, to read from the CD-ROM drive) would make a call to a specific software interrupt, and the interrupt vector table would then route the call to the specific part of the BIOS (meaning the specific driver) for the device being called. It did not matter whether that driver was in the motherboard ROM, adapter ROM, or RAM. As far as the system was concerned, memory is memory, and as long as the routine existed at a memory address, it could be called.

The combination of the motherboard BIOS, adapter card BIOS, and device drivers loaded from disk contributed to the BIOS as a whole. The portion of the BIOS contained in ROM chips, both on the motherboard and in some adapter cards, is sometimes called *firmware*, which is a name given to software stored in chips rather than on disk. Of course, after you turned off the system, the drivers in nonvolatile ROM would remain intact but those in volatile RAM would instantly vanish. That was not a problem, however, because the next time the system was turned back on, it went through the boot process and again loaded the necessary supplemental drivers from disk all over again.

As the PC has evolved, more and more accessories and new hardware have been devised to add to the system. This means that more and more drivers have needed to be loaded to support this hardware. Adding new drivers to the motherboard ROM has been extremely difficult because ROM chips were relatively fixed (difficult to change) and limited space was available. The PC architecture allotted only 128KB for the motherboard ROM, and most of it was already used by the existing drivers, POST, BIOS Setup program, and of course the bootstrap loader. Putting the driver on an adapter card ROM is also difficult and expensive, and only 128KB is allocated for all adapter card ROMs to exist, not to mention the fact that the video cards have already stolen 32KB of that. So, most companies developing new hardware for the PC simply wrote a driver that was designed to be loaded into RAM during boot.

As time went on, more and more drivers were being loaded from disk—in some cases, even drivers that were replacing those in the motherboard. For example, Windows 95 introduced a new hard disk driver that used 32-bit code, which shut down the existing 16-bit driver that existed in the motherboard ROM. At that point, the hard disk driver in the motherboard ROM was used for only a few seconds after the system was turned on, and after the 32-bit driver was loaded into RAM during the boot process, the vector table was changed to point to that one instead of the one in the ROM. Windows 95, 98, and Me allowed the use of both 16-bit and 32-bit drivers, easing the transition to full 32-bit operation.

This has progressed to today, when 32-bit drivers have been designed to be loaded from disk to replace *all* the drivers in the motherboard ROM. This is the case for any system today running Windows NT, 2000, or XP. Those operating systems cannot use any of the 16-bit drivers found in either the motherboard ROMs or any adapter card ROMs and must use only 32-bit drivers. The 16-bit code in the motherboard ROM is used only to get the system functioning long enough to get the initial 32-bit drivers and OS loaded, at which point they take over and the 16-bit code is shut down.

The same issue is true for 64-bit versions of Windows, which require all 64-bit drivers and cannot use any 32-bit or 16-bit drivers. In fact, the all-or-nothing approach requiring all 64-bit drivers will delay the acceptance of systems running 64-bit Windows for some time.

When running 32-bit Windows XP, for example, after XP is loaded, no more calls are made to any of the 16-bit routines in the motherboard or adapter ROMs. Instead, only 32-bit device drivers loaded into RAM are called. So, the instant the PC is powered on, the BIOS might be mostly in ROM, but after XP is loaded, the BIOS resides entirely in RAM.

That is most likely the way things will continue for the future. The motherboard ROM exists only to get the system started, to initialize specific hardware, to offer security in the way of power-on passwords and such, and to perform some basic initial configuration. However, after the OS is loaded, a whole new set of drivers takes over.

A PC system can be described as a series of layers—some hardware and some software—that interface with each other. In the most basic sense, you can break a PC down into four primary layers, each of which can be broken down further into subsets. Figure 5.1 shows the four layers in a typical PC.

The purpose of the layered design is to enable a given operating system and applications to run on different hardware. Figure 5.1 shows how two different machines with different hardware can each use different sets of drivers (BIOS) to interface the unique hardware to a common operating system and applications. Thus, two machines with different processors, storage media, video display units, and so on can run the same OS and applications.

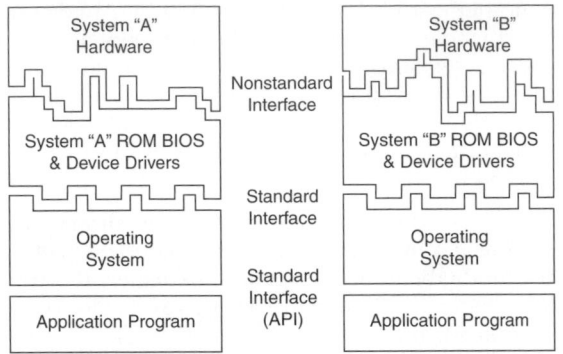

Figure 5.1 PC system layers.

In this layered architecture, the application software programs talk to the operating system via what is called an Application Program Interface (API). The API varies according to the operating system you are using and consists of the various commands and functions the operating system can perform for an application. For example, an application can call on the operating system to load or save a file. This prevents the application itself from having to know how to read the disk, send data to a printer, or perform any other of the many functions the operating system can provide. Because the application is completely insulated from the hardware, you can essentially run the same applications on different machines; the application is designed to talk to the operating system rather than the hardware.

The operating system then interfaces with or talks to the BIOS or driver layer. The BIOS consists of all the individual driver programs that operate between the operating system and the actual hardware. As such, the operating system never talks to the hardware directly; instead, it must always go through the appropriate drivers. This provides a consistent way to talk to the hardware. It is usually the responsibility of the hardware manufacturer to provide drivers for its hardware. Because the drivers must act between both the hardware and the operating system, the drivers typically are operating system specific. Thus, the hardware manufacturer must offer different drivers so that its hardware works under DOS, Windows 9x, Windows 2000, Windows XP, OS/2, Linux, and so on. Because many operating systems use the same internal interfaces, some drivers can work under multiple operating systems. For example, a driver that works under Windows Me will usually also work under Windows 98 and 95, and a driver that works under Windows XP will also often work under Windows 2000 and NT (and vice versa). This is because Windows 95, 98, and Me are essentially variations on the same OS, as are Windows NT, 2000, and XP.

Because the BIOS layer looks the same to the operating system no matter what hardware is above it (or underneath, depending on your point of view), the same operating system can run on a variety of systems. For example, you can run Windows XP on two systems with different processors, hard disks, video adapters, and so on, yet Windows XP will look and feel pretty much the same on both of them. This is because the drivers provide the same basic functions no matter which specific hardware is used.

As you can see from Figure 5.1, the application and operating systems layers can be identical from system to system, but the hardware can differ radically. Because the BIOS consists of software drivers that act to interface the hardware to the software, the BIOS layer adapts to the unique hardware on one end but looks consistently the same to the operating system at the other end.

The hardware layer is where most differences lie between various systems. It is up to the BIOS to mask the differences between unique hardware so that the given operating system (and subsequently the application) can be run. This chapter focuses on the BIOS layer of the PC.

BIOS Hardware/Software

The BIOS itself is software running in memory that consists of all the various drivers that interface the hardware to the operating system. The BIOS is unique compared to normal software in that it doesn't all load from disk; some of it is preloaded into memory chips (read-only memory, or ROM) installed in the system or on adapter cards.

The BIOS in a PC comes from three possible sources:

- Motherboard ROM
- Adapter card ROM (such as that found on a video card)
- Loaded into RAM from disk (device drivers)

The motherboard ROM BIOS is most often associated with hardware rather than software. This is because the BIOS on the motherboard is contained in a ROM chip on the board, which contains the initial software drivers needed to get the system running. Years ago, when only DOS was running on basic PCs, this was enough, so no other drivers were needed—the motherboard BIOS had everything that was necessary. The motherboard BIOS usually includes drivers for all the basic system components, including the keyboard, floppy drive, hard drive, serial and parallel ports, and more. As systems became more complex, new hardware was added for which no motherboard BIOS drivers existed. These included devices such as newer video adapters, CD-ROM drives, SCSI hard disks, USB ports, and so on.

Rather than requiring a new motherboard BIOS that would specifically support the new devices, it was far simpler and more practical to copy any new drivers that were necessary onto the system hard disk and configure the operating system to load them at boot time. This is how most CD-ROM drives, sound cards, scanners, printers, PC Card (PCMCIA) devices, and so on are supported. Because these devices don't need to be active during boot time, the system can boot up from the hard disk and wait to load the drivers during the initial operating system load.

Some drivers, however, must be active during boot time. For example, how could you boot from a hard disk if the drivers necessary to make the disk interface work must be loaded from that disk? Obviously, the hard disk drivers must be preloaded into ROM either on the motherboard or on an adapter card.

How will you be able to see anything onscreen if your video card doesn't have a set of drivers in a ROM? The solution to this could be to provide a motherboard ROM with the appropriate video drivers built in; however, this is impractical because of the variety of video cards, each needing its own drivers. You would end up with hundreds of different motherboard ROMs, depending on which video card you had. Instead, when IBM designed the original PC, it created a better solution. It designed the PC's motherboard ROM to scan the slots looking for adapter cards with ROMs on them. If a card was found with a ROM on it, the ROM was executed during the initial system startup phase, before the system began loading the operating system from the hard disk.

By putting the ROM-based drivers right on the card, you didn't have to change your motherboard ROM to have built-in support for new devices, especially those that needed to be active during boot time. A few cards (adapter boards) almost always have a ROM onboard, including the following:

- *Video cards.* All have an onboard BIOS.
- *SCSI adapters.* Those that support booting from SCSI hard drives or CD-ROMs have an onboard BIOS. Note that, in most cases, the SCSI BIOS does not support any SCSI devices other than a hard disk; if you use a SCSI CD-ROM, scanner, Zip drive, and so on, you still need to load the appropriate drivers for those devices from your hard disk. Most newer SCSI adapters support booting from a SCSI CD-ROM, but CD-ROM drivers are still necessary to access the CD-ROM when booting from another drive or device.

- *Network cards.* Those that support booting directly from a file server have what is usually called a boot ROM or IPL (initial program load) ROM onboard. This enables PCs to be configured on a LAN as diskless workstations—also called Net PCs, NCs (network computers), thin clients, or even smart terminals.

- *ATA or floppy upgrade boards.* Boards that enable you to attach more or different types of drives than what is typically supported by the motherboard alone. These cards require an onboard BIOS to enable these drives to be bootable.

- *Y2K boards.* Boards that incorporate BIOS fixes to update the century byte in the CMOS RAM. These boards have a small driver contained in a BIOS, which monitors the year byte for a change from 99 to 00. When this is detected, the driver updates the century byte from 19 to 20, correcting a flaw in some older motherboard ROM BIOS. Although it might seem strange to list Y2K boards because the century changed a few years ago, if installed these boards often remain in use until the systems using them are retired.

BIOS and CMOS RAM

Some people confuse BIOS with the CMOS RAM in a system. This confusion is aided by the fact that the Setup program in the BIOS is used to set and store the configuration settings in the CMOS RAM. They are, in fact, two totally separate components.

The BIOS on the motherboard is stored in a fixed ROM chip. Also on the motherboard is a chip called the RTC/NVRAM chip, which stands for real-time clock/nonvolatile memory. This is where the BIOS Setup information is stored, and it is actually a digital clock chip with a few extra bytes of memory thrown in. It is usually called the CMOS chip because it is made using CMOS (complementary metal-oxide semiconductor) technology.

The first example of this ever used in a PC was the Motorola MC146818 chip, which had 64 bytes of storage, of which 14 bytes were dedicated to the clock function, leaving 50 bytes to store BIOS Setup settings. Although it is called non-volatile, it is actually volatile, meaning that without power, the time/date settings and the data in the RAM portion will in fact be erased. It is considered *nonvolatile* by many because it is designed using CMOS technology, which results in a chip that still requires power but very little compared to other chips. A battery in the system, rather than the AC wall current, provides that power. This is also why most people call this chip the CMOS RAM chip; although not technically accurate (almost all modern chips use a form of CMOS technology), the term has stuck. Most RTC/NVRAM chips run on as little as 1 micro amp (millionth of an amp), so they use very little battery power to run. Most lithium coin cell batteries can last up to 5 years or more before the battery runs out and the information stored (as well as the date and time) is lost. Some systems use special versions of these chips made by Dallas Semiconductor, Benchmarq, or Odin (such as the DS12885 and DS12887) that include both the RTC/NVRAM chip and the battery in a single component.

When you enter your BIOS Setup, configure your hard disk parameters or other BIOS Setup settings, and save them, these settings are written to the storage area in the RTC/NVRAM (otherwise called CMOS RAM) chip. Every time your system boots up, it reads the parameters stored in the CMOS RAM chip to determine how the system should be configured. A relationship exists between the BIOS and CMOS RAM, but they are two distinctly different parts of the system.

Motherboard BIOS

All motherboards must have a special chip containing software called the ROM BIOS. This ROM chip contains the startup programs and drivers used to get the system running and act as the interface to the basic hardware in the system. When you turn on a system, the power on self test (POST) in the BIOS also tests the major components in the system. Additionally, you can run a setup program to store system configuration data in the CMOS memory, which is powered by a battery on the mother-board. This CMOS RAM is often called NVRAM (nonvolatile RAM) because it runs on about 1 millionth of an amp of electrical current and can store data for years when powered by a tiny lithium battery.

The BIOS is a collection of programs embedded in one or more chips, depending on the design of your computer. That collection of programs is the first thing loaded when you start your computer, even before the operating system. Simply put, the BIOS in most PCs has four main functions:

- *POST (power on self test).* The POST tests your computer's processor, memory, chipset, video adapter, disk controllers, disk drives, keyboard, and other crucial components.

- *Setup.* The system configuration and setup program is usually a menu-driven program activated by pressing a special key during the POST, and it enables you to configure the motherboard and chipset settings along with the date and time, passwords, disk drives, and other basic system settings. You also can control the power-management settings and boot-drive sequence from the BIOS Setup, and on some systems, you can also configure CPU timing and clock-multiplier settings. Some older 286 and 386 systems did not have the Setup program in ROM and required that you boot from a special setup disk, and some newer systems use a Windows-based application to access BIOS Setup settings.

- *Bootstrap louder.* A routine that reads the first physical sector of various disk drives looking for a valid master boot record (MBR). If one meeting certain minimum criteria (ending in the signature bytes 55AAh) is found, the code within is executed. The MBR program code then continues the boot process by reading the first physical sector of the bootable volume, which is the start of the volume boot record (VBR). The VBR then loads the first operating system startup file, which is usually IO.SYS (DOS/Windows 9x/Me) or NTLDR (Windows NT/2000/XP), upon which the operating system is then in control and continues the boot process.

- *BIOS (basic input/output system).* This refers to the collection of actual drivers used to act as a basic interface between the operating system and your hardware when the system is booted and running. When running DOS or Windows in safe mode, you are running almost solely on ROM-based BIOS drivers because none are loaded from disk.

ROM Hardware

Read-only memory (ROM) is a type of memory that can permanently or semipermanently hold data. It is called read-only because it is either impossible or difficult to write to. ROM is also often called nonvolatile memory because any data stored in ROM remains even if the power is turned off. As such, ROM is an ideal place to put the PC's startup instructions—that is, the software that boots the system (the BIOS).

Note that ROM and RAM are not opposites, as some people seem to believe. In fact, ROM is technically a subset of the system's RAM. In other words, a portion of the system's random access memory address space is mapped into one or more ROM chips. This is necessary to contain the software that enables the PC to boot up; otherwise, the processor would have no program in memory to execute when it is powered on.

For example, when a PC is turned on, the processor automatically jumps to address FFFF0h, expecting to find instructions to tell the processor what to do. This location is exactly 16 bytes from the end of the first megabyte of RAM space, as well as the end of the ROM itself. If this location were mapped into regular RAM chips, any data stored there would have disappeared when the power was previously turned off, and the processor would subsequently find no instructions to run the next time the power was turned on. By placing a ROM chip at this address, a system startup program can be permanently loaded into the ROM and will be available every time the system is turned on.

▶▶ For more information about Dynamic RAM, see "DRAM," p. 460.

Normally, the system ROM starts at address E0000h or F0000h, which is 128KB or 64KB prior to the end of the first megabyte. Because the ROM chip usually is up to 128KB in size, the ROM programs are allowed to occupy the entire last 128KB of the first megabyte, including the critical FFFF0h startup instruction address, which is located 16 bytes from the end of the BIOS space. Some motherboard ROM chips are larger, up to 256KB or 512KB in size. The additional code in these is configured to act as a video card ROM (addresses C0000h–C7FFFh) on motherboards with built-in video and might even contain additional ROM drivers configured anywhere from C8000h to DFFFFh to support additional onboard devices, such as SCSI or network adapters.

Figure 5.2 shows a map of the first megabyte of memory in a PC; notice the upper memory areas reserved for adapter card and motherboard ROM BIOS at the end of the first megabyte.

```
    . = RAM
    G = Graphics Mode Video RAM
    M = Monochrome Text Mode Video RAM
    C = Color Text Mode Video RAM
    V = Video adapter ROM BIOS
    a = Reserved for other adapter board ROM
    r = Additional Motherboard ROM BIOS in some systems
    R = Motherboard ROM BIOS

    Conventional (Base) Memory

          : 0---1---2---3---4---5---6---7---8---9---A---B---C---D---E---F---
    000000: ................................................................
    010000: ................................................................
    020000: ................................................................
    030000: ................................................................
    040000: ................................................................
    050000: ................................................................
    060000: ................................................................
    070000: ................................................................
    080000: ................................................................
    090000: ................................................................

    Upper Memory Area (UMA)

          : 0---1---2---3---4---5---6---7---8---9---A---B---C---D---E---F---
    0A0000: GGGGGGGGGGGGGGGGGGGGGGGGGGGGGGGGGGGGGGGGGGGGGGGGGGGGGGGGGGGGGGGGG
    0B0000: MMMMMMMMMMMMMMMMMMMMMMMMMMMMMMMMMCCCCCCCCCCCCCCCCCCCCCCCCCCCCCCCCC
          : 0---1---2---3---4---5---6---7---8---9---A---B---C---D---E---F---
    0C0000: VVVVVVVVVVVVVVVVVVVVVVVVVVVVVVVVVaaaaaaaaaaaaaaaaaaaaaaaaaaaaaaaaa
    0D0000: aaaaaaaaaaaaaaaaaaaaaaaaaaaaaaaaaaaaaaaaaaaaaaaaaaaaaaaaaaaaaaaaa
          : 0---1---2---3---4---5---6---7---8---9---A---B---C---D---E---F---
    0E0000: rrrrrrrrrrrrrrrrrrrrrrrrrrrrrrrrrrrrrrrrrrrrrrrrrrrrrrrrrrrrrrrrr
    0F0000: RRRRRRRRRRRRRRRRRRRRRRRRRRRRRRRRRRRRRRRRRRRRRRRRRRRRRRRRRRRRRRRRR
```

Figure 5.2   PC memory map showing ROM BIOS.

Some think it is strange that the PC would start executing BIOS instructions 16 bytes from the end of the ROM, but this design was intentional. All the ROM programmer has to do is place a JMP (jump) instruction at that address that instructs the processor to jump to the actual beginning of the ROM—in most cases, close to F0000h—which is about 64KB earlier in the memory map. It's like deciding to read every book starting 16 pages from the end and then having all book publishers agree to place an instruction there to jump back the necessary number of pages to get to page 1. By setting the startup location in this way, Intel enabled the ROM to grow to be any size, all the while keeping it at the upper end of addresses in the first megabyte of the memory address space.

The main ROM BIOS is contained in a ROM chip on the motherboard, but adapter cards with ROMs contain auxiliary BIOS routines and drivers needed by the particular card, especially for those cards that must be active early in the boot process, such as video cards. Cards that don't need drivers active during boot (such as sound cards) typically don't have a ROM because those drivers can be loaded from the hard disk later in the boot process.

Because the BIOS is the main portion of the code stored in ROM, we often call the ROM the ROM BIOS. In older PCs, the motherboard ROM BIOS could consist of up to five or six total chips, but most PCs have required only a single chip for many years now.

Adapter card ROMs, such as those used for video, SCSI, add-on ATA cards, and network cards for disk-less workstations, are automatically scanned and read by the motherboard ROM during the early part of the boot process—during the POST. The motherboard ROM scans a special area of RAM reserved for adapter ROMs (addresses C0000–DFFFFh) looking for 55AAh signature bytes that indicates the start of a ROM.

All adapter ROMs must start with 55AAh; otherwise, the motherboard won't recognize them. The third byte indicates the size of the ROM in 512-byte units called *paragraphs*, and the fourth byte is the actual start of the driver programs. The size byte is used by the motherboard ROM for testing purposes. The motherboard ROM adds all the bytes in the ROM and divides the sum by the number of bytes. The result should produce a remainder of 100h. Thus, when creating a ROM for an adapter, the programmer typically uses a "fill" byte at the end to get the checksum to come out right. Using this checksum, the motherboard tests each adapter ROM during the POST and flags any that appear to have been corrupted.

The motherboard BIOS automatically runs the programs in any adapter ROMs it finds during the scan. You see this in most systems when you turn on your system, and during the POST you see the video card BIOS initialize and announce its presence.

ROM Shadowing

ROM chips by their natures are very slow, with access times of 150ns (nanoseconds, or billionths of a second), compared to DRAM access times of less than 10ns on the newest systems. Because of this, in virtually all systems the ROMs are *shadowed*, which means they are copied into DRAM chips at startup to allow faster access during normal operation. The shadowing procedure copies the ROM into RAM and then assigns that RAM the same address as the ROM originally used, disabling the actual ROM in the process. This makes the system seem as though it has ROM running at the same speed as RAM.

The performance gain from shadowing is often very slight, and it can cause problems if not set up properly. Therefore, in most cases, it is wise to shadow only the motherboard (and maybe the video card BIOS) and leave the others alone.

Typically, shadowing is useful only if you are running 16-bit operating systems, such as DOS or Windows 3.x. If you are running a 32-bit operating system, such as Windows 9x, Windows Me, Windows 2000, Windows NT, or Windows XP, shadowing is virtually useless because those operating systems do not use the 16-bit ROM code while running. Instead, those operating systems load 32-bit drivers into RAM, which replace the 16-bit BIOS code used only during system startup.

Shadowing controls are found in the CMOS Setup program in the motherboard ROM, which is covered in more detail later in this chapter.

ROM Chip Types

The four main types of ROM chips that have been used in PCs are as follows:

- *ROM.* Read-only memory
- *PROM.* Programmable ROM
- *EPROM.* Erasable PROM
- *EEPROM.* Electrically erasable PROM, also sometimes called a flash ROM

No matter which type of ROM your system uses, the data stored in a ROM chip is nonvolatile and remains indefinitely unless intentionally erased or overwritten (in those cases where that is possible).

Table 5.1 lists the identifying part numbers typically used for each type of ROM chip, along with any other identifying information.

Table 5.1 ROM Chip Part Numbers

ROM Type	Part Number
ROM	No longer in use
PROM	27xxxx
EPROM*	27xxxx
EEPROM/Flash	28xxxx or 29xxxx

xxxx = numbers normally indicating capacity in K-bits or M-bits
*Has a clear quartz window over the internal chip die allowing UV (ultraviolet) exposure to erase the chip

ROM (True or Mask ROM)

Originally, most ROMs were manufactured with the binary data (0s and 1s) already "cast in" or integrated into the die. The die represents the actual silicon chip itself. These are called Mask ROMs because the data is formed into the mask from which the ROM die is photolithographically produced. This type of manufacturing method is economical if you are making hundreds of thousands of ROMs with the same information. If you must change a single bit, however, you must remake the mask, which is an expensive proposition. Because of costs and inflexibility, nobody uses Mask ROMs anymore.

Mask ROMs are exactly analogous to prerecorded CD-ROMs. Some people think a CD-ROM is first manufactured as a blank and then the data is written to it by a laser, but that is not true. A CD-ROM is literally a piece of plastic that is stamped in a press, and the data is directly molded in, not written. The only actual recording is done with the master disc from which the molds or stamps are made.

PROM

PROMs are a type of ROM that is blank when new and that must be programmed with whatever data you want. The PROM was invented in the late 1970s by Texas Instruments and has been available in sizes from 1KB (8Kb) to 2MB (16Mb) or more. They can be identified by their part numbers, which usually are 27nnnn—where the 27 indicates the TI type PROM and the nnnn indicates the size of the chip in kilobits (not bytes). For example, most PCs that used PROMs came with 27512 or 271000 chips, which indicate 512Kb (64KB) or 1Mb (128KB).

Note

Since 1981, all cars sold in the United States have used onboard computers with some form of ROM containing the control software. For example, my 1989 Pontiac Turbo Trans Am came with an onboard computer containing a 2732 PROM, which was a 32Kb (4KB) chip in the ECM (electronic control module or vehicle computer) under the dash. This chip contained the vehicle operating software as well as all the data tables describing spark advance, fuel delivery, and other engine and vehicle operating parameters. Many devices with integrated computers use PROMs to store their operating programs.

Although we say these chips are blank when new, they are technically preloaded with binary 1s. In other words, a 1Mb ROM chip used in a PC would come with 1 million (actually 1,048,576) bit locations, each containing a binary 1. A blank PROM can then be programmed, which is the act of writing to it. This usually requires a special machine called a device programmer, ROM programmer, or ROM burner (see Figure 5.3).

Programming the ROM is sometimes referred to as *burning* it because that is technically an apt description of the process. Each binary 1 bit can be thought of as a fuse, which is intact. Most chips run on 5 volts, but when a PROM is programmed, a higher voltage (normally 12 volts) is placed at the various addresses within the chip. This higher voltage actually blows or burns the fuses at the desired locations, thus turning any given 1 into a 0. Although you can turn a 1 into a 0, you should note that the process is irreversible; that is, you can't turn a 0 back into a 1.

The device programmer examines the program you want to write into the chip and then selectively changes only the 1s to 0s where necessary in the chip.

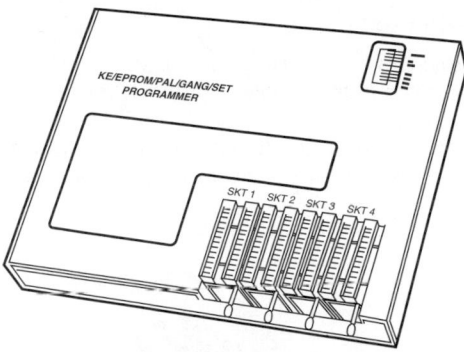

Figure 5.3 Typical gang (multisocket) device programmer (PROM burner).

PROM chips are often referred to as OTP (one-time programmable) chips for this reason. They can be programmed once and never erased. Most PROMs are very inexpensive—about $3 for a typical PC motherboard PROM—so if you want to change the program in a PROM, you discard it and program a fresh one with the new data.

The act of programming a PROM takes anywhere from a few seconds to a few minutes, depending on the size of the chip and the algorithm used by the programming device. Figure 5.3 shows an illustration of a typical PROM programmer that has multiple sockets. This is called a *gang programmer* and can program several chips at once, saving time if you have several chips to write with the same data. Less expensive programmers are available with only one socket, which is fine for most individual use.

I use and recommend a very inexpensive programmer from a company called Andromeda Research Labs (www.arlabs.com). Besides being economical, its unit has the advantage of connecting to a PC via the parallel port for fast and easy data transfer of files between the PC and programming unit. The unit is also portable and comes built into a convenient carrying case. It is operated by a menu-driven program you install on the connected PC. The program contains several features, including a function that enables you to read the data from a chip and save it in a file on your system, as well as write a chip from a data file, verify that a chip matches a file, and verify that a chip is blank before programming begins. A low-cost BIOS backup option makes backing up the flash BIOS chip in your system easy (if it is removable) as a safeguard against disaster.

Custom Programming of PROM Chips

I even used my PROM programmer to reprogram the chip in my 1989 Turbo Trans Am, changing the factory preset speed and rpm limiters, turbocharger boost, torque converter lockup points, spark advance, fuel delivery, idle speed, and much more! I also incorporated a switch box under the dash that enables me to switch among four different chips, even while the vehicle is running. One chip I created I call the "valet chip," which, when engaged, cuts off the fuel injectors at 36 miles per hour and restarts them when the vehicle coasts down to 35mph. By rewriting the chip, I could set the cutoff/restore speeds anywhere from 0mph to 255mph. I imagine this type of modification would be useful for those with teenage drivers because you could set the mph or engine rpm limit to whatever you want! Another chip I created cuts off fuel to the engine altogether, which I engage for security purposes when the vehicle is parked. No matter how clever, a thief will not be able to steal this car unless he tows it away. If you are interested in such a chip-switching device or custom chips for your Turbo Trans Am or Buick Grand National, contact Casper's Electronics at **www.casperselectronics.com**. For other vehicles with replaceable PROMs, companies such as Fastchip (**www.fastchip.com**), Superchips (**www.superchips.com**), Hypertech (**www.hypertech.com**), and Mopar Performance (**www.mopar.com/perf.html**) offer custom PROMs or vehicle powertrain control modules (PCMs) for improved performance (see the Vendor List on the DVD packaged with this book). I installed a Mopar Performance PCM in my 5.9L Jeep Grand Cherokee, and it made a noticeable improvement in engine operation and vehicle performance.

EPROM

One variation of the PROM that has been very popular is the EPROM. An *EPROM* is a PROM that is erasable. An EPROM chip can be easily recognized by the clear quartz crystal window set in the chip package directly over the die (see Figure 5.4). You can actually see the die through the window! EPROMs have the same 27xxxx part-numbering scheme as the standard PROM, and they are functionally and physically identical except for the clear quartz window above the die.

Figure 5.4   An EPROM showing the quartz window for ultraviolet erasing.

The purpose of the window is to allow ultraviolet light to reach the chip die because the EPROM is erased by exposure to intense UV light. The window is quartz crystal because regular glass blocks UV light. You can't get a suntan through a glass window!

Note

The quartz window makes the EPROMs more expensive than the OTP PROMs. This extra expense is needless if erasability is not important.

The UV light erases the chip by causing a chemical reaction, which essentially melts the fuses back together. Thus, any binary 0s in the chip become 1s, and the chip is restored to a new condition with binary 1s in all locations. To work, the UV exposure must be at a specific wavelength (2,537 angstroms), at a fairly high intensity (12,000 uw/cm²), in close proximity (2cm–3cm, or about 1"), and last for between 5 and 15 minutes duration. An EPROM eraser is a device that contains a UV light source (usually a sunlamp-type bulb) above a sealed compartment drawer in which you place the chip or chips (see Figure 5.5).

Figure 5.5 shows a professional-type EPROM eraser that can handle up to 50 chips at a time. I use a much smaller and less expensive one called the DataRase by Walling Co. This device erases up to four chips at a time and is both economical and portable. The current version is called DataRase II; the DataRase II and similar products are sold by DigiKey (www.digikey.com) and other sources of EPROM programming equipment.

The quartz crystal window on an EPROM typically is covered by tape, which prevents accidental exposure to UV light. UV light is present in sunlight, of course, and even in standard room lighting, so that over time a chip exposed to the light can begin to degrade. For this reason, after a chip is programmed, you should put a sticker over the window to protect it.

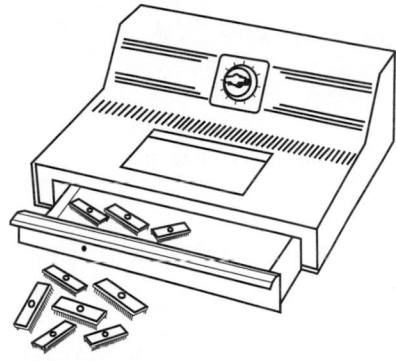

Figure 5.5 A professional EPROM eraser.

EEPROM/Flash ROM

A newer type of ROM is the *EEPROM*, which stands for electrically erasable PROM. These chips are also called flash ROMs and are characterized by their capability to be erased and reprogrammed directly in the circuit board they are installed in, with no special equipment required. By using an EEPROM, or flash ROM, you can erase and reprogram the motherboard ROM in a PC without removing the chip from the system or even opening up the system chassis.

With a flash ROM or EEPROM, you don't need a UV eraser or device programmer to program or erase chips. Not only do virtually all PC motherboards built since 1994 use flash ROMs or EEPROMs, but most automobiles built since then use them as well. For example, my 1994 Chevy Impala SS had a PCM with an integral flash ROM, as do virtually all 1993 and newer vehicles.

The EEPROM or flash ROM can be identified by a 28xxxx or 29xxxx part number, as well as by the absence of a window on the chip. Having an EEPROM or a flash ROM in your PC motherboard means you now can easily upgrade the motherboard ROM without having to swap chips. In most cases, you download the updated ROM from the motherboard manufacturer's Web site and then run a special program it provides to update the ROM. This procedure is described in more detail later in this chapter.

I recommend that you periodically check with your motherboard manufacturer to see whether an updated BIOS is available for your system. An updated BIOS might contain bug fixes or enable new features not originally found in your system. You might find fixes for ATA hard drive support over 8.4GB or new drivers to support booting from LS-120 (120MB floppy) drives or USB drives.

Non-PC ROM Upgrades

For the auto enthusiasts out there, you might want to do the same for your car; that is, check to see whether ROM upgrades are available for your vehicle's computer. Now that updates are so easy and inexpensive, vehicle manufacturers are releasing bug-fix ROM upgrades that correct operational problems or improve vehicle performance. In most cases, you must check with your dealer to see whether any new vehicle ROMs are available. If you have a GM car, GM has a Web site where you can get information about the BIOS revisions available for your car, which it calls Vehicle Calibrations. The GM Vehicle Calibration Information site address is `http://calid.gm.com`.

When you enter your VIN (vehicle identification number), this page displays the calibration history for the vehicle, which is a list of all the different flash ROM upgrades (calibrations) developed since the vehicle was new. For example, when I entered the VIN on the 1994 Impala SS I had, I found that five flash ROM calibrations had been released over the years, and my car had only the second revision installed originally, meaning there had been three newer ROMs than the one I had! The fixes in the various calibration updates are also listed. A trip to the dealer with this information enabled them to use their diagnostic computer to connect to my car and reflash the PCM with the latest software, which, in my case, fixed several problems, including the engine surging under specific conditions, shift clunks, erroneous "check engine" light warnings, and several other minor problems.

With the flash ROM capability, I began experimenting with running calibrations originally intended for other vehicles. For example, I ran a modified Camaro '94 calibration in the '94 Impala SS. The spark-advance curve and fuel delivery parameters were much more aggressive in the Camaro calibration, as were the transmission shift points and other features. If you are interested in having a custom program installed in your flash ROM–equipped vehicle, I recommend you contact Fastchip at www.fastchip.com or Superchips at www.superchips.com. If you want to write and program your own vehicle calibrations, see www.diy-efi.org for more information.

These days, many objects with embedded computers controlling them are using flash ROMs. Pretty soon you'll be downloading flash ROM upgrades into your toaster as well!

▶▶ See the section "Upgrading the BIOS," p. 415, for more information on updating your PC motherboard flash ROMs.

Many other devices have flash ROMs; for example, I have updated the flash ROM code (often called *firmware*) in my network routers, wireless access points, and even some digital cameras. Installing flash ROM or firmware upgrades is as easy as downloading a file from the device manufacturer Web site and running the update program included in the file.

Flash ROM updates can also be used to add new capabilities to existing peripherals, such as modems or rewriteable DVD or CD drives, to the latest standards; for example, updating a modem from X2 or K56Flex to V.90 or V.92 or adding support for the latest types of media to a rewriteable drive.

ROM BIOS Manufacturers

Several popular BIOS manufacturers in the market today supply the majority of motherboard and system manufacturers with the code for their ROMs. This section discusses the various available versions.

Several companies have specialized in the development of a compatible ROM BIOS product. The three major companies that come to mind in discussing ROM BIOS software are American Megatrends, Inc. (AMI); Phoenix Technologies; and Award Software (now owned by Phoenix Technologies). Each company licenses its ROM BIOS to motherboard manufacturers so those manufacturers can worry about the hardware rather than the software. To obtain one of these ROMs for a motherboard, the original equipment manufacturer (OEM) must answer many questions about the design of the system so that the proper BIOS can be either developed or selected from those already designed. Combining a ROM BIOS and a motherboard is not a haphazard task. No single, generic, compatible ROM exists, either. AMI, Award, Microid Research (MR BIOS), and Phoenix ship many variations of their BIOS code to different board manufacturers, each one custom tailored to that specific motherboard.

Over the years, some major changes have occurred in the BIOS industry. Intel, the largest BIOS customer, has gone from using mostly Phoenix to using AMI, back to Phoenix, and now back to AMI for most of its motherboards. Intel originally used the Phoenix BIOS core in its motherboards up through 1995, when it changed to an AMI core. It then used AMI until 1997, when it switched back to Phoenix. More recently in 1999 Intel switched again, this time back to AMI. In all these cases, Intel takes the core BIOS from Phoenix or AMI and highly customizes it for its particular motherboards. It is always a big deal which BIOS Intel uses because Intel manufactures more motherboards than any other company. What that basically means is that if you purchase a PC today, you have a good chance of receiving an Intel-made motherboard with AMI BIOS.

Another major development in BIOS occurred in late 1998, when Phoenix bought Award. For several years, Phoenix continued to sell the Award BIOS as a separate product line. However, in March 2002, Phoenix introduced two new product lines based on the previous BIOS. The Phoenix FirstBIOS is based on Award 6.x code, and the Phoenix FirstBIOS Pro is based on Phoenix 4.x code.

Currently, the BIOS market is divided between AMI and Phoenix; however, Phoenix not only develops the BIOS for many systems, but is also the primary BIOS developer responsible for new BIOS development and new BIOS standards.

Another development in recent years has been the creation of separate BIOS products for 32-bit and 64-bit desktop systems, mobile systems, 32-bit and 64-bit servers, and embedded devices. Although all BIOS chips must perform some of the same tasks, a BIOS product optimized for a mobile computer often needs additional support for features such as docking modules, advanced battery power management, as well as bootable USB and removable Flash memory devices, whereas a BIOS optimized for a server needs support for features such as advanced hardware monitoring and 64-bit PCI slots. By creating customized BIOS versions for different platforms, BIOS vendors provide support for the features needed by a particular computing platform and provide better performance and stability.

OEMs

Although most use either the AMI or Phoenix offerings, some OEMs have developed their own compatible BIOS ROMs independently. Companies such as Compaq, AT&T, and Acer have developed their own BIOS products that are comparable to those offered by AMI and Phoenix. These companies also offer upgrades to newer versions that often can provide more features and improvements or fix problems with the older versions. If you use a system with a proprietary ROM, ensure that it is from a larger company with a track record and one that will provide updates and fixes as necessary. Ideally, upgrades should be available for download from the Internet.

Most OEMs have their BIOS written for them by a third-party company. For example, IBM and Hewlett-Packard contract with Phoenix to develop the motherboard BIOS for some HP PCs. Note that even though Phoenix might have done the development, you still must get upgrades or fixes from the OEM. This is really true for all systems because all motherboard manufacturers customize the BIOS for their boards.

AMI

Although AMI customizes the ROM code for a particular system, it does not sell the ROM source code to the OEM. An OEM must obtain each new release as it becomes available. Because many OEMs don't need or want every new version developed, they might skip several version changes before licensing a new one. The AMI BIOS is currently the most popular BIOS in PC systems. Some versions of the AMI BIOS are called Hi-Flex because of the high flexibility found in the BIOS configuration program. The AMI Hi-Flex BIOS products are used in Intel, AMI, and many other manufacturers' motherboards. One special AMI feature is that it is the only third-party BIOS manufacturer to make its own motherboards and other hardware devices.

During power up, the BIOS ID string is displayed on the lower-left part of the screen. This string tells you valuable information about which BIOS version you have and about certain settings that are determined by the built-in setup program.

Tip

A good trick to help you view the BIOS ID string is to shut down and either unplug your keyboard or hold down a key as you power back on. This causes a keyboard error, and the string remains displayed.

You also can download the AMI Motherboard ID Utility program (AMIMBID) from AMI's Web site (**www.ami.com/support/mbid.cfm**) and run it to determine the contents of ID String 1.

The primary BIOS Identification string (ID String 1) is displayed by any AMI BIOS during the POST in the bottom-left corner of the screen, below the copyright message. Two additional BIOS ID strings (ID Strings 2 and 3) can be displayed by the AMI Hi-Flex BIOS by pressing the Insert key during the POST. These additional ID strings display the options installed in the BIOS.

The general BIOS ID String 1 format for older AMI BIOS versions is shown in Table 5.2. In addition, the BIOS ID String 1 format for AMI Hi-Flex BIOS versions is shown in Table 5.3, the AMI Hi-Flex BIOS ID String 2 in Table 5.4, and the AMI Hi-Flex BIOS ID String 3 in Table 5.5.

Table 5.2   The ABBB-NNNN-mmddyy-KK String 1 Format for Older AMI BIOS Versions

Position	Description

A	BIOS Options:
	    D = Diagnostics built in
	    S = Setup built in
	    E = Extended Setup built in

BBB	Chipset or Motherboard Identifier:
	    C&T = Chips & Technologies chipset
	    NET = C&T NEAT 286 chipset
	    286 = Standard 286 motherboard
	    SUN = Suntac chipset
	    PAQ = Compaq motherboard
	    INT = Intel motherboard
	    AMI = AMI motherboard
	    G23 = G2 chipset 386 motherboard

NNNN	The manufacturer license code reference number
mmddyy	The BIOS release date, mm/dd/yy
KK	The AMI keyboard BIOS version number

Table 5.3   The AB-CCcc-DDDDDD-EFGHIJKL-mmddyy-MMMMMMMM-N String 1 Format for the AMI Hi-Flex BIOS

Position	Description

A	Processor Type:
	    0 = 8086 or 8088
	    2 = 286
	    3 = 386
	    4 = 486
	    5 = Pentium
	    6 = Pentium Pro/II/III/Celeron/Athlon/Duron

B	Size of BIOS:
	    0 = 64KB BIOS
	    1 = 128KB BIOS
	    2 = 256KB BIOS

CCcc	Major and minor BIOS version number

DDDDDD	Manufacturer license code reference number
	    0036xx = AMI 386 motherboard, xx = Series #
	    0046xx = AMI 486 motherboard, xx = Series #
	    0056xx = AMI Pentium motherboard, xx = Series #
	    0066xx = AMI Pentium Pro motherboard, xx = Series #

E	1 = Halt on POST Error
F	1 = Initialize CMOS every boot
G	1 = Block pins 22 and 23 of the keyboard controller
H	1 = Mouse support in BIOS/keyboard controller
I	1 = Wait for <F1> key on POST errors
J	1 = Display floppy error during POST

Table 5.3   Continued

Position	Description
K	1 = Display video error during POST
L	1 = Display keyboard error during POST
mmddyy	BIOS Date, mm/dd/yy
MMMMMMMM	Chipset identifier or BIOS name
N	Keyboard controller version number

Table 5.4   The AAB-C-DDDD-EE-FF-GGGG-HH-II-JJJ Format for the AMI Hi-Flex BIOS String 2

Position	Description
AA	Keyboard controller pin number for clock switching
B	Keyboard controller clock switching pin function: H = High signal switches clock to high speed L = High signal switches clock to low speed
C	Clock switching through chipset registers 0 = Disable 1 = Enable
DDDD	Port address to switch clock high
EE	Data value to switch clock high
FF	Mask value to switch clock high
GGGG	Port address to switch clock low
HH	Data value to switch clock low
II	Mask value to switch clock low
JJJ	Pin number for Turbo Switch Input

Table 5.5   The AAB-C-DDD-EE-FF-GGGG-HH-II-JJ-K-L Format for the AMI Hi-Flex BIOS ID String 3

Position	Description
AA	Keyboard controller pin number for cache control.
B	Keyboard controller cache control pin function: H = High signal enables the cache. L = High signal disables the cache.
C	1 = High signal is used on the keyboard controller pin.
DDD	Cache control through chipset registers: 0 = Cache control off. 1 = Cache control on.
EE	Port address to enable cache.
FF	Data value to enable cache.
GGGG	Mask value to enable cache.
HH	Port address to disable cache.

Table 5.5   Continued

Position	Description
II	Data value to disable cache.
JJ	Mask value to disable cache.
K	Pin number for resetting the 82335 memory controller.
L	BIOS Modification Flag: 0 = The BIOS has not been modified. 1–9, A–Z = Number of times the BIOS has been modified.

The AMI BIOS has many features, including a built-in setup program activated by pressing the Delete or Esc key in the first few seconds of booting up your computer. The BIOS prompts you briefly as to which key to press and when to press it. The AMI BIOS offers user-definable hard disk types, essential for optimal use of many ATA or ESDI drives. The 1995 and newer BIOS versions also support enhanced ATA drives and autoconfigure the drive parameters.

A unique feature of some of the AMI BIOS versions was that in addition to the setup, they had a built-in, menu-driven diagnostics package—essentially a very limited version of the standalone AMIDIAG product. The internal diagnostics are not a replacement for more comprehensive disk-based programs, but they can help in a pinch. The menu-driven diagnostics do not do extensive memory testing, for example, and the hard disk low-level formatter works only at the BIOS level rather than at the controller register level. These limitations often have prevented it from being capable of formatting severely damaged disks. Most newer AMI BIOS versions no longer include the full diagnostics.

AMI doesn't produce BIOS documentation; it leaves that up to the motherboard manufacturers who include their BIOS on the motherboard. However, AMI has published a detailed version of its documentation called the *Programmer's Guide to the AMIBIOS: Includes Descriptions of PCI, APM, and Socket Services BIOS Functions*, published by Windcrest/McGraw-Hill, ISBN 0-07-001561-9. This book, written by AMI engineers, describes all the BIOS functions, features, error codes, and more. Unfortunately, this book is out of print. If you can locate it (try searching with Google or at Amazon.com), I recommend this book for users with an AMI BIOS in their systems because this provides a complete version of the documentation for which they might have been looking.

The AMI BIOS is sold through distributors, a list of which is available at its Web site. However, keep in mind that you can't buy upgrades and replacements directly from AMI, and AMI produces upgrades only for its own motherboards. If you have a non-AMI motherboard with a customized AMI BIOS, you must contact the motherboard manufacturer for an upgrade or use a third-party BIOS upgrade vendor such as those discussed later in this chapter.

Award

Phoenix now refers to the Award BIOS as FirstBIOS. The FirstBIOS has all the features you expect, including a built-in setup program activated by pressing Ctrl+Alt+Esc or a particular key on startup (usually prompted on the screen). This setup offers user-definable drive types, required to fully use ATA or ESDI hard disks. The POST is good, although the few beep codes supported means that a POST card is necessary if you want to diagnose most power-on problems. Phoenix provides technical support on its Web site at www.phoenix.com. eSupport.com (formerly Unicore Software) provides limited Award BIOS upgrades for end users.

Phoenix

The Phoenix BIOS (now sold by Phoenix as FirstBIOS Pro) for many years has been a standard of compatibility by which others are judged. It was one of the first third-party companies to legally reverse-engineer the IBM BIOS using a *clean-room* approach. In this approach, a group of engineers studied the IBM BIOS and wrote a specification for how that BIOS should work and what features should be incorporated.

This information then was passed to a second group of engineers who had never seen the IBM BIOS. They could then legally write a new BIOS to the specifications set forth by the first group. This work was then unique and not a copy of IBM's BIOS; however, it functioned the same way.

The Phoenix (FirstBIOS Pro) BIOS excels in two areas that put it high on my list of recommendations. One is that the POST is excellent. The BIOS outputs an extensive set of beep codes that can be used to diagnose severe motherboard problems that would prevent normal operation of the system. In fact, with beep codes alone, this POST can isolate memory failures in Bank 0 right down to the individual SIMM or DIMM module. The Phoenix BIOS also has an excellent setup program free from unnecessary frills, but one that offers all the features the user would expect, such as user-definable drive types and so on. The built-in setup is activated by pressing Ctrl+Alt+S; Ctrl+Alt+Esc; or a particular key on startup, such as F1 or F2 on most newer systems, depending on the version of BIOS you have.

The second area in which Phoenix excels is the documentation. Not only are the manuals you get with the system detailed, but Phoenix has also written a set of BIOS technical reference manuals that are a standard in the industry. The original set consists of three books, titled *System BIOS for IBM PC/XT/AT Computers and Compatibles, CBIOS for IBM PS/2 Computers and Compatibles,* and *ABIOS for IBM PS/2 Computers and Compatibles;* an updated version is called *System BIOS for IBM PCs, Compatibles, and EISA Computers: The Complete Guide to ROM-Based System Software.* In addition to being excellent references for the Phoenix BIOS, these books serve as an outstanding overall reference to the BIOS in general. These are out of print but might be available through bookfinder services such as Amazon.com.

Phoenix has extensive technical support and documentation on its Web site at www.phoenix.com, and you can also find documentation on the Micro Firmware site (www.firmware.com) as well as the eSupport site (www.esupport.com). You also can check the phone numbers listed in the Vendor List on the disc packaged with this book. Micro Firmware and eSupport offer upgrades to some older systems with an AMI or a Phoenix/Award BIOS, including many Packard Bell, Gateway (with Micronics motherboards), Micron Technologies, and other systems. For most systems, especially newer ones, you need to get any BIOS updates from the system or motherboard manufacturer.

These companies' products are established as ROM BIOS standards in the industry, and frequent updates and improvements ensure that a system containing these ROMs will have a long life of upgrades and service.

Microid Research BIOS

Microid Research (MR) is an interesting BIOS supplier. It primarily markets upgrade BIOS for older Pentium and 486 motherboards that were abandoned by their original manufacturers. As such, it is an excellent upgrade for adding new features and performance to an older system. Microid Research BIOS upgrades are sold through eSupport.com.

Tip

If you support several BIOS types, consider adding Phil Croucher's *The BIOS Companion* to your bookshelf or PDF file collection. This book provides detailed BIOS options and configuration information for today's leading BIOS. You can purchase various editions from Amazon.com and other bookstores, but for the most up-to-date (and least expensive) edition, I suggest ordering the PDF (Adobe Acrobat) version of *The BIOS Companion* from Electrocution.com.

Upgrading the BIOS

In this section, you learn how ROM BIOS upgrades can improve a system in many ways. You also learn why upgrades can be difficult and can require much more than plugging in a generic set of ROM chips.

The ROM BIOS provides the crude brains that get your computer's components working together. A simple BIOS upgrade can often give your computer better performance and more features.

The BIOS is the reason various operating systems can operate on virtually any PC-compatible system despite hardware differences. Because the drivers in the BIOS communicate with the hardware, the BIOS must be specific to the hardware and match it completely. As discussed earlier, instead of creating their own BIOS, many computer makers buy a BIOS from specialists such as American Megatrends, Inc. (AMI) or Phoenix Technologies Ltd. A motherboard manufacturer that wants to license a BIOS must tailor the BIOS code to the hardware. This is what makes upgrading a BIOS somewhat problematic; the BIOS usually resides on ROM chips on the motherboard and is specific to that motherboard model or revision. In other words, you must get your BIOS upgrades from your motherboard manufacturer or from a BIOS upgrade company that supports the motherboard you have, rather than directly from the BIOS developer.

Often, in older systems, you must upgrade the BIOS to take advantage of some other upgrade. To install some of the larger and faster Integrated Drive Electronics (IDE) hard drives and LS-120 (120MB) floppy drives in older machines, for example, you might need a BIOS upgrade. Some of the machines you have might be equipped with older BIOSs that do not support hard drives larger than 8GB, for example.

The following list shows some of the primary functions of a ROM BIOS upgrade; the exact features and benefits of a particular BIOS upgrade depend on your system:

- Added support for newer-type and faster-speed processors
- Support for bootable ATAPI CD-ROM drives (called the El Torito specification)
- Support for bootable LS-120 (120MB) SuperDisk floppy or Iomega Zip drive support
- Support for bootable USB drives
- Fast POST for decreasing boot times
- Support for Ultra-DMA/100 or Ultra-DMA/133 ATA drives
- Support for ATA hard drives greater than 8.4GB or 137GB (48-bit LBA)
- Support for Serial ATA (SATA) drives
- Support for a preboot environment and recovery software in the host protected area (HPA)
- Plug and Play (PnP) support and compatibility
- Correction of calendar-related and leap-year bugs
- Correction of known bugs or compatibility problems with certain hardware and application or operating system software
- Support for ACPI power management
- Support for temperature monitoring and fan speed monitoring and control
- Support for legacy USB devices (keyboards and mice)
- Support for chassis intrusion detection

Part of the PC 2001 standard published by Intel and Microsoft requires something called Fast POST to be supported. Fast POST means that the time it takes from turning on the power until the system starts booting from disk must be 12 seconds or less (for systems not using SCSI as the primary storage connection). This time limit includes the initialization of the keyboard, video card, and ATA bus. For systems containing adapters with onboard ROMs, an additional 4 seconds are allowed per ROM. Intel calls the Fast POST feature Rapid BIOS Boot (RBB), and it is supported in all its motherboards from 2001 and beyond—some of which can begin booting from power-on in as little as 6 seconds or less.

If you install newer hardware or software and follow all the instructions properly, but you can't get it to work, specific problems might exist with the BIOS that an upgrade can fix. This is especially true for newer operating systems. Many systems need to have a BIOS update to properly work with the

Plug and Play features of Windows 9x, Me, XP, and 2000. Because these problems are random and vary from board to board, it pays to periodically check the board manufacturer's Web site to see whether any updates are posted and what problems they fix. Because new hardware and software that are not compatible with your system could cause it to fail, I recommend you check the BIOS upgrades available for your system before you install new hardware or software, particularly processors.

You can use the BIOS Wizard utility available from eSupport.com (formerly Unicore) to test your BIOS for compatibility with popular BIOS features, such as Zip/LS-120 booting, ACPI power management, PCI IRQ routing, and more. Download it from www.esupport.com/techsupport/award/awardutils.htm.

Where to Get Your BIOS Update

For most BIOS upgrades, you must contact the motherboard manufacturer by phone or download the upgrade from its Web site. The BIOS manufacturers do not offer BIOS upgrades because the BIOS in your motherboard did not actually come from them. In other words, although you think you have a Phoenix, AMI, or Award BIOS, you really don't! Instead, you have a custom version of one of these BIOS, which was licensed by your motherboard manufacturer and uniquely customized for its board. As such, you must get any BIOSs upgrades from the motherboard or system manufacturer because they must be customized for your board or system as well.

In the case of Phoenix or Award, another option might exist. A company called eSupport (formerly Unicore) specializes in providing Award BIOS upgrades. eSupport might be able to help you if you can't find your motherboard manufacturer or if it is out of business. Phoenix has a similar deal with Micro Firmware, a company it has licensed to provide various BIOS upgrades. If you have a Phoenix or an Award BIOS and your motherboard manufacturer can't help you, contact one of these companies for a possible solution. Microid Research (sold through eSupport, formerly Unicore) is another source of BIOS upgrades for a variety of older and otherwise obsolete boards. These upgrades are available for boards that originally came with AMI, Award, or Phoenix BIOS, and they add new features to older boards that have been abandoned by their original manufacturers. Contact eSupport for more information.

Determining Your BIOS Version

When seeking a BIOS upgrade for a particular motherboard (or system), you need to know the following information:

- The make and model of the motherboard (or system)
- The version of the existing BIOS
- The type of CPU (for example, Pentium MMX, AMD K6, Cyrix/IBM 6x86MX, MII, Pentium II, Pentium III and later, AMD Athlon, Athlon XP, and so on)

You usually can identify the BIOS you have by watching the screen when the system is first powered up. It helps to turn on the monitor first because some take a few seconds to warm up and the BIOS information is often displayed for only a few seconds.

Note

Many newer PCs now do not display the typical POST screen. Instead, many show a logo for the motherboard or PC manufacturer, which is usually referred to as a *splash screen*. To enter BIOS Setup, you must press a key or keys (specific to the BIOS manufacturer). See the section "Running or Accessing the CMOS Setup Program," later in this chapter, for more information. You might hear some in the industry refer to displaying a manufacturer's logo instead of the default POST screen as a *quiet boot*. Often you can change these BIOS splash screens to your own liking, even including your own company logo or graphic of choice. Intel has free software at `developer.intel.com/design/motherbd/gen_indx.htm` that enables you to change or restore the splash screen on Intel motherboards.

> **Tip**
>
> Look for any copyright notices or part number information. Sometimes you can press the Pause key on the keyboard to freeze the POST, allowing you to take your time to write down the information. Pressing any other key then causes the POST to resume.

In addition, you often can find the BIOS ID information in the BIOS Setup screens. eSupport also offers a downloadable BIOS Agent that can be used to determine this information, as well as the motherboard chipset and Super I/O chip used by your motherboard. After you have this information, you should be able to contact the motherboard manufacturer to see whether a new BIOS is available for your system. If you go to the Web site, check to see whether a version exists that is newer than the one you have. If so, you can download it and install it in your system.

Most BIOS display version information onscreen when the system is first powered up. In some cases, the monitor takes too long to warm up, and you might miss this information because it is displayed for only a few seconds. Try turning on your monitor first, and then your system, which makes this information easier to see. You usually can press the Pause key on the keyboard when the BIOS ID information is being displayed, which freezes it so you can record the information. Pressing any other key allows the system startup to resume.

Checking the BIOS Date

One method of determining the relative age and capabilities of your motherboard ROM is to check the date. The BIOS date is stored in virtually all PCs as an 8-byte text string at memory address FFFF5h. The date generally indicates when the BIOS code was last updated or compiled by the motherboard manufacturer. Knowing the date of a particular BIOS might give you some clue as to which features might or might not be present. You can use the DEBUG command-line utility supplied with Windows and DOS to view these addresses. DEBUG is a command-line program that presents a - prompt of its own, to which you can enter various commands. For example, the ? command displays help information. To find the BIOS date, open a command-prompt window (or boot to a DOS floppy) and execute the DEBUG command. Then at the DEBUG - prompt, enter **D FFFF:5 L 8**, which instructs DEBUG to display memory at FFFF5 for a length of 8 bytes. DEBUG then displays both the hexadecimal and ASCII codes found at those addresses. When the - prompt returns, you can enter **Q** to quit DEBUG and return to the command prompt. Figure 5.6 shows how this looked when I ran it on my system.

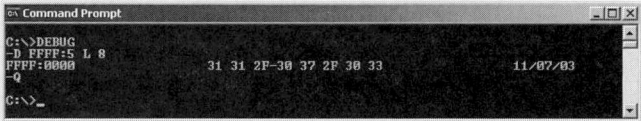

Figure 5.6 Using DEBUG to display the motherboard ROM BIOS date.

In this example, the system shows a motherboard ROM BIOS date of 11/07/03.

Backing Up Your BIOS

One often-overlooked benefit of an EPROM programmer is that you can use it to essentially back up your ROMs in case they are later damaged. Many hardware vendors do not sell preprogrammed ROM chips for their systems, and the only way to repair an older motherboard or card with a damaged ROM is to burn a new copy from a backup. The backup can be in the form of another EPROM or flash ROM chip with the original program burned in or even in the form of a disk file. I keep files containing images of the ROMs in each of my motherboards and expansion cards in case I have to burn a new copy to repair one of my systems. A file-based backup of your ROMs can also prove interesting for snooping around because you can look for the copyright and other strings, disassemble the code to see how it works, and otherwise check it out.

To create a disk-file copy of your motherboard ROM BIOS, you can place the ROM in an EPROM programmer and use the function provided by the device to read the EPROM into a disk file, or you can use the DOS DEBUG program to read your ROM BIOS from memory and transfer it to disk as a file. Because most ROMs are soldered in, removal is difficult at best, so the DEBUG routine is much easier.

The ROM code in a PC normally consumes 128KB of RAM in two 64KB segments, E0000–EFFFF and F0000–FFFFF. Video and other auxiliary BIOS routines normally reside in C0000–CFFFF and D0000–DFFFF. Because of the nature of DEBUG, each 64KB segment must be saved separately.

To use DEBUG to save segments E000 and F000 in this manner, follow these instructions:

```
C:\>DEBUG                  ;Run DEBUG
-R BX                      ;Change BX register (high-order file size)
BX 0000                    ;  from 0
:1                         ;  to 1 (indicates 64K file)
-N SEG-E.ROM               ;Name the file
-M E000:0 FFFF CS:0        ;Move 64K of BIOS data to current code segment
-W 0                       ;Write file from offset 0 in code segment
Writing 10000 bytes        ;  10000h = 64K
-N SEG-F.ROM               ;Name the file
-M F000:0 FFFF CS:0        ;Move 64K of BIOS data to current code segment
-W 0                       ;Write file from offset 0 in code segment
Writing 10000 bytes        ;  10000h = 64K
-Q                         ;Quit DEBUG
```

Figure 5.7 shows how this will look when entered in a Windows XP command-prompt window.

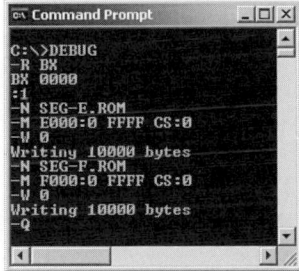

Figure 5.7   Using DEBUG to save E0000–EFFFF and F0000–FFFFF as files.

These instructions effectively save the 64K segment ranges E0000–EFFFF and F0000–FFFFF as files by first setting up the size of the file to be saved, then setting up the name of the file, and then moving (essentially, copying) the ROM BIOS code to the current code segment when DEBUG was loaded. The data then can be written to the disk.

If you want to save the segments including the video BIOS and other possible adapter card ROMs in your system, repeat the previous procedure but use C000:0 and D000:0 as the starting addresses in the DEBUG commands. Be sure to use different file names as well. Note that the video BIOS might not use all of the C0000 segment; also, you might not have any other adapters using ROM in the remainder of the C0000 and D0000 segments, in which case Windows can sometimes use this area for other code.

One important quirk of this procedure is that the commands should be entered in the relative order indicated here. In particular, the Name command must precede the Move command; otherwise, some of the data at the beginning of the current code-segment area will be trashed.

Backing Up Your BIOS's CMOS Settings

A motherboard BIOS upgrade usually wipes out the BIOS Setup settings in the CMOS RAM. Therefore, you should record these settings, especially the important ones such as hard disk parameters. Some software programs, such as the Norton Utilities, can save and restore CMOS settings, but unfortunately, these types of programs are often useless in a BIOS upgrade situation. This is because sometimes the new BIOS offers new settings or changes the positions of the stored data in the CMOS RAM, which means you don't want to do an exact restore. Also, with the variety of BIOS available, I have yet to find a CMOS RAM backup and restore program that works on more than just a few specific systems.

You are better off manually recording your BIOS Setup parameters, or possibly connecting a printer to your system and using the Shift+Prtsc (Print Screen) function to print each of the setup screens. Turn on your printer, start your computer normally, and restart it without turning off the system to initialize the printer to try this option. Some shareware programs could print or even save and restore the BIOS Setup settings stored in the CMOS RAM, but these were BIOS version specific and would not work on any other system. Most of these programs were useful during the 286/386 era, but most systems released since— especially those with Plug and Play capabilities—have rendered most of these older programs useless.

Tip

If you are unable to print your screens, use a digital camera to take a picture of each BIOS setup screen. Be sure to set the camera to its close-up mode, and use the LCD display rather than the optical viewfinder to ensure you get the entire screen in the photo.

Keyboard Controller Chips

In addition to the main system ROM, older AT-class (286 and later) computers also have a keyboard controller or keyboard ROM, which is a keyboard-controller microprocessor with its own built-in ROM. This often is found in the Super I/O or South Bridge chips on most newer boards. The keyboard controller was originally an Intel 8042 microcontroller, which incorporates a microprocessor, RAM, ROM, and I/O ports. This was a 40-pin chip that often had a copyright notice identifying the BIOS code programmed into the chip. Modern motherboards have this function integrated into the chipset, specifically the Super I/O or South Bridge chips, so you won't see the old 8042 chip anymore.

The keyboard controller controls the reset and A20 lines and also deciphers the keyboard scan codes. The A20 line is used in extended memory and other protected-mode operations. In many systems, one of the unused ports is used to select the CPU clock speed. Because of the tie-in with the keyboard controller and protected-mode operation, many problems with keyboard controllers became evident on these older systems when upgrading from DOS to Windows 95/98, NT, or 2000.

Problems with the keyboard controller were solved in most systems in the early 1990s, so you shouldn't have to deal with this issue in systems newer than that. With older systems, when you upgraded the BIOS in the system, the BIOS vendor often included a new keyboard controller.

Using a Flash BIOS

Virtually all PCs built since 1996 include a flash ROM to store the BIOS. A flash ROM is a type of EEPROM chip you can erase and reprogram directly in the system without special equipment. Older EPROMs required a special ultraviolet light source and an EPROM programmer device to erase and reprogram them, whereas flash ROMs can be erased and rewritten without even removing them from the system. On many recent systems, the flash ROM is not a separate chip but might be incorporated into the South Bridge chip.

Using flash ROM enables you to download ROM upgrades from a Web site or receive them on disk; you then can load the upgrade into the flash ROM chip on the motherboard without removing and replacing the chip. Normally, these upgrades are downloaded from the manufacturer's Web site, and then an included utility is used to create a bootable floppy with the new BIOS image and update program. It is important to run this procedure from a boot floppy so that no other software or drivers are in the way that might interfere with the update. This method saves time and money for both the system manufacturer and end user.

Sometimes the flash ROM in a system is write-protected, and you must disable the protection before performing an update—usually by means of a jumper or switch that controls the lock on the ROM update. Without the lock, any program that knows the correct instructions can rewrite the ROM in your system—not a comforting thought. Without the write-protection, virus programs could be written that copy themselves directly into the ROM BIOS code in your system. Even without a physical write-protect lock, modern flash ROM BIOSs have a security algorithm that helps prevent unauthorized updates. This is the technique Intel uses on its motherboards.

Note that motherboard manufacturers will not notify you when they upgrade the BIOS for a particular board. You must periodically log on to their Web sites to check for updates. Usually, any flash updates are free.

Before proceeding with a BIOS upgrade, you first must locate and download the updated BIOS from your motherboard manufacturer. Consult the Vendor List on the accompanying DVD to find the Web site address or other contact information for your motherboard manufacturer. Log on to its Web site, and follow the menus to the BIOS updates page; then select and download the new BIOS for your motherboard.

Note

If a flash BIOS upgrade is identified as being for only certain board revisions of a particular model, be sure you determine that it will work with your motherboard before you install it. You might need to open your system and look for a revision number on the motherboard or for a particular component. Check the vendor's Web site for details.

The BIOS upgrade utility is contained in a self-extracting archive file that can initially be downloaded to your hard drive, but it must be extracted and copied to a floppy before the upgrade can proceed. Different motherboard manufacturers have slightly different procedures and programs to accomplish a flash ROM upgrade, so you should read the directions included with the update. I include instructions here for Intel motherboards because they are by far the most common.

Intel and other typical flash BIOS upgrades fit on a bootable floppy disk; some recent BIOS upgrades from Intel and other vendors can also be run from within the Windows GUI. Older Intel and some other flash BIOS upgrades also provide the capability to save and verify the current BIOS version before replacing it with the new version and also provide the capability to install alternative languages for BIOS messages and the BIOS setup utility.

Tip

Before you start the flash BIOS upgrade process, you should disconnect all USB devices except for your keyboard and mouse. On some systems, leaving USB drives connected prevents a BIOS upgrade from working properly.

If you have Byte Merge enabled in an Award BIOS or a FirstBIOS-based system, disable this feature before you perform the BIOS upgrade. On some systems, leaving byte merge enabled during a BIOS upgrade can destroy your BIOS. You can re-enable this feature after you complete the upgrade.

If the BIOS setup is performed with a bootable floppy disk, the first step in the upgrade after downloading the new BIOS file is to enter the CMOS Setup and write down or record your existing CMOS settings because they will be erased during the upgrade. Then, you create a DOS boot floppy and uncompress or extract the BIOS upgrade files to the floppy from the file you downloaded. Next, you reboot on the newly created upgrade disk and follow the menus for the actual reflash procedure.

The iFlash procedure covered in this section is similar to the BIOS update process used by most non-Intel motherboards and must be used for systems running Windows 95, MS-DOS, or non-Windows operating systems such as Linux. Intel's Express BIOS update (for Windows 98, Windows NT 4, and current Windows versions) uses the InstallShield loader program familiar to Windows users to install BIOS upgrades within the Windows GUI. Here is a step-by-step procedure for the process using Intel's iFlash (DOS-based) BIOS update:

1. Save your CMOS RAM setup configuration. You can do so by pressing the appropriate key during boot to start the BIOS setup program (usually F1 with an AMI BIOS and F2 with a Phoenix BIOS) and writing down all your current CMOS settings. You also might be able to print the screens if you have a printer connected, using the PrtScr key on the keyboard. You must reset these settings after you have upgraded to the latest BIOS. Write down all the settings that are unique to the system. These settings will be needed later to reconfigure the system. Pay special attention to any hard drive settings for geometry (Cylinder/Head/Sectors per track) and translation (LBA, Large, CHS); these are very important. If you fail to restore these properly, you might not be able to boot from the drive or access the data on it.

2. Exit the BIOS Setup and restart the system. Allow the system to fully start Windows and bring up a DOS prompt window or boot directly to a DOS prompt via the Windows Start menu (for example, press F8 when you see Starting Windows, and select Command Prompt).

3. Place a formatted blank floppy disk in the A: floppy drive. If the disk contains data, format the floppy using the normal format command:

    `C:\>FORMAT A:`

    You also can use Windows Explorer to format the floppy disk.

4. The file you originally downloaded from the Intel Web site is a self-extracting compressed archive that includes other files that need to be extracted. Put the file in a temporary directory, and then from within this directory, double-click the BIOS file you downloaded or type the filename of the file and press Enter. This causes the file to self-extract. For example, if the file you downloaded is called `CB-P06.EXE` (for the Intel D810E2CB motherboard), you would enter the following command:

    `C:\TEMP>CB-P06 <enter>`

5. The extracted files are stored in the same temporary folder as the downloaded BIOS. Recent Intel flash BIOS upgrades contain the following files: `Desc.txt`, `License.txt`, `Readme.txt`, `Run.bat` (which is run to create the bootable floppy), and `SW.EXE` (which contains the BIOS code).

6. To create the bootable floppy disk, open `Run.bat`—which extracts files from `SW.EXE`—and transfer the necessary files to the blank disk in Drive A:.

7. Now you can restart the system with the bootable floppy in drive A: containing the new BIOS files you just extracted. Upon booting from this disk, the iFlash program automatically starts and updates the BIOS boot block and the main BIOS area.

8. When you're told that the BIOS has been successfully loaded, remove the bootable floppy from the drive and press Enter to reboot the system.

9. Press F1 or F2 to enter Setup. On the first screen within Setup, check the BIOS version to ensure that it is the new version.

10. In Setup, load the default values. If you have an AMI BIOS, press the F5 key. With a Phoenix BIOS, go to the Exit submenu and highlight Load Setup Defaults, and then press Enter.

Caution

If you do not set the values back to default, the system might function erratically.

11. If the system had unique settings, reenter those settings now. Press F10 to save the values, exit Setup, and restart the system. Your system should now be fully functional with the new BIOS.

Note

If you encounter a CMOS checksum error or other problems after rebooting, try rebooting the system again. CMOS checksum errors require that you enter Setup, check and save your settings, and exit Setup a second time.

Note

The procedure for older Intel BIOS upgrades differs from that described previously. If your BIOS upgrade contains the `BIOS.EXE` program, see the BIOS upgrade description contained in *Upgrading and Repairing PCs, 12th Edition*, included in electronic form on the DVD packaged with this book.

Flash BIOS Recovery

When you performed the flash reprogramming, you should have seen a warning message onscreen similar to the following:

```
The BIOS is currently being updated. DO NOT REBOOT OR POWER DOWN until the update
is completed (typically within three minutes)...
```

If you fail to heed this warning or something interrupts the update procedure, you will be left with a system that has a corrupted BIOS. This means you will not be able to restart the system and redo the procedure, at least not easily. Depending on the motherboard, you might have to replace the flash ROM chip with one that was preprogrammed by the motherboard manufacturer or from a vendor such as BIOSWorld (www.biosworld.com), which provides replacement BIOS chips containing the same BIOS code as that provided by your motherboard vendor. This is an unfortunate necessity because your board will be nonfunctional until a valid ROM is present. This is why I still keep my trusty ROM burner around; it is very useful for those motherboards with socketed flash ROM chips. In minutes, I can use the ROM burner to reprogram the chip and reinstall it in the board. If you need a ROM programmer, I recommend Andromeda Research Labs (see the Vendor List on the accompanying DVD).

In many of the latest systems, the flash ROM is soldered into the motherboard so it can't be replaced, rendering the reprogramming idea moot. However, this doesn't mean the only way out is a complete motherboard replacement. Most motherboards with soldered-in flash ROMs have a special BIOS Recovery procedure that can be performed. This hinges on a special nonerasable part of the flash ROM that is reserved for this purpose.

In the unlikely event that a flash upgrade is interrupted catastrophically, the BIOS might be left in an unusable state. Recovering from this condition requires the following steps. A minimum of a power supply, a speaker, and a floppy drive configured as drive A: should be attached to the motherboard for this procedure to work:

1. Change the Flash Recovery jumper to the recovery mode position. Virtually all Intel motherboards and many third-party motherboards have a jumper or switch for BIOS recovery, which in most cases is labeled "Recover/Normal." Figure 5.8 shows this jumper on a typical motherboard.

2. Install the bootable BIOS upgrade disk you previously created to do the flash upgrade into drive A: and reboot the system.

   Because of the small amount of code available in the nonerasable flash boot block area, no video prompts are available to direct the procedure. So, you will see nothing onscreen. In fact, it is not even necessary for a video card to be connected for this procedure to work. The procedure can be monitored by listening to the speaker and looking at the floppy drive LED. When the system beeps and the floppy drive LED is lit, the system is copying the BIOS recovery code into the flash device.

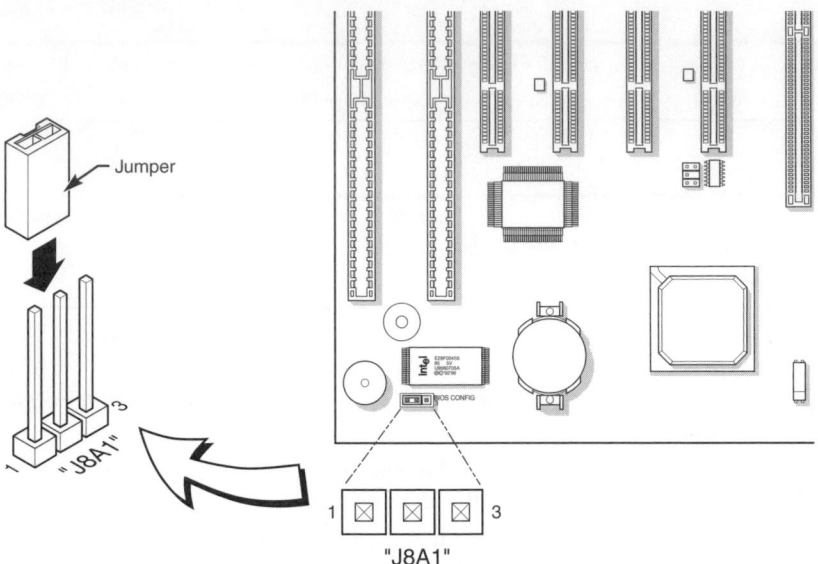

Figure 5.8 Motherboard BIOS recovery jumper.

3. As soon as the drive LED goes off and the system beeps (normally twice), the recovery should be complete. Sometimes there might be pauses where the drive stops reading during the recovery process; however, the process might not be complete. Be sure to wait for a minute or so to ensure a complete recovery before turning off the system. When you are sure the recovery is complete and there is no further activity, power off the system.

4. Change the flash recovery jumper back to the default position for normal operation.

When you power the system back on, the new BIOS should be installed and functional. However, you might want to leave the BIOS upgrade floppy in drive A: and check to see that the proper BIOS version was installed.

Note

Note that this BIOS recovery procedure is often the fastest way to update a large number of machines, especially if you are performing other upgrades at the same time. This is how it is typically done in a system assembly or production environment.

Using IML System Partition BIOS

IBM and Compaq used a scheme similar to a flash ROM, called Initial Microcode Load (IML), in some of their older Pentium and 486 systems. IML is a technique in which the BIOS code is installed on the hard disk in a special hidden-system partition and is loaded every time the system is powered up. Of course, the system still has a core BIOS on the motherboard, but all that BIOS does is locate and load updated BIOS code from the system partition. This technique enabled Compaq and IBM to distribute ROM updates on disk for installation in the system partition. The IML BIOS is loaded every time the system is reset or powered on.

Along with the system BIOS code, the system partition contains a complete copy of the Setup and Diagnostics or Reference Disk, which provides the option of running the setup and system-configuration software at any time during a reboot operation. This option eliminates the need to boot from this disk to reconfigure the system and gives the impression that the entire Setup and Diagnostics or Reference Disk is contained in ROM.

One drawback to this technique is that the BIOS code is installed on the hard disk; the system can't function properly without the correctly set-up hard disk connected. You can always boot from the Reference Disk floppy should the hard disk fail or become disconnected, but you can't boot from a standard floppy disk.

Although this might seem similar to newer systems using the host protected area (reserved space past the "end" of the hard disk), it is not quite the same thing. Systems using the HPA use it only for recovery, diagnostic, and backup applications. The BIOS itself, as well as the BIOS Setup, is still contained in the actual ROM (flash ROM) chip.

Motherboard CMOS RAM Addresses

In the original IBM AT system, a Motorola 146818 chip was used as the real-time clock (RTC) and CMOS RAM chip. This special chip had a simple digital clock that used 14 bytes of RAM and an additional 50 more bytes of leftover RAM in which you could store anything you wanted. The designers of the IBM AT used these extra 50 bytes to store the system configuration.

Modern PC systems don't use the Motorola chip; instead, they incorporate the functions of this chip into the motherboard chipset (South Bridge) or Super I/O chip, or they use a special battery and NVRAM module from companies such as Dallas or Benchmarq.

Table 5.6 shows the standard format of the information stored in the 64-byte standard CMOS RAM module. This information controls the configuration of the system and is read and written by the system setup program.

Table 5.6   CMOS RAM Addresses

Offset (hex)	Offset (dec)	Field Size	Function
00h	0	1 byte	Current second in BCD (00–59)
01h	1	1 byte	Alarm second in BCD
02h	2	1 byte	Current minute in BCD (00–59)
03h	3	1 byte	Alarm minute in BCD
04h	4	1 byte	Current hour in BCD (00–23)
05h	5	1 byte	Alarm hour in BCD
06h	6	1 byte	Current day of week in BCD (00–06)
07h	7	1 byte	Current day of month in BCD (00–31)
08h	8	1 byte	Current month in BCD (00–12)
09h	9	1 byte	Current year in BCD (00–99)
0Ah	10	1 byte	Status register A
0Bh	11	1 byte	Status register B
0Ch	12	1 byte	Status register C
0Dh	13	1 byte	Status register D
0Eh	14	1 byte	Diagnostic status
0Fh	15	1 byte	Shutdown code
10h	16	1 byte	Floppy drive types
11h	17	1 byte	Advanced BIOS Setup options
12h	18	1 byte	Hard disk 0/1 types (0–15)
13h	19	1 byte	Keyboard typematic rate and delay
14h	20	1 byte	Installed equipment
15h	21	1 byte	Base memory in 1K multiples, LSB

Table 5.6   Continued

Offset (hex)	Offset (dec)	Field Size	Function
16h	22	1 byte	Base memory in 1K multiples, MSB
17h	23	1 byte	Extended memory in 1K multiples, LSB
18h	24	1 byte	Extended memory in 1K multiples, MSB
19h	25	1 byte	Hard Disk 0 Extended Type (0–255)
1Ah	26	1 byte	Hard Disk 1 Extended Type (0–255)
1Bh	27	9 bytes	Hard Disk 0 user-defined type information
24h	36	9 bytes	Hard Disk 1 user-defined type information
2Dh	45	1 byte	Advanced BIOS Setup options
2Eh	46	1 byte	CMOS checksum MSB
2Fh	47	1 byte	CMOS checksum LSB
30h	48	1 byte	POST reported extended memory LSB
31h	49	1 byte	POST reported extended memory MSB
32h	50	1 byte	Date century in BCD (00–99)
33h	51	1 byte	POST information flag
34h	52	2 bytes	Advanced BIOS Setup options
36h	54	1 byte	Chipset-specific BIOS Setup options
37h	55	7 bytes	Power-On Password (usually encrypted)
3Eh	62	1 byte	Extended CMOS checksum MSB
3Fh	63	1 byte	Extended CMOS checksum LSB

BCD = Binary-coded decimal   *MSB = Most significant byte*
LSB = Least significant byte   *POST = Power on self test*

Note that many newer systems have extended CMOS RAM with 2KB, 4KB, or more. The extra room is used to store the Plug and Play information detailing the configuration of adapter cards and other options in the system. As such, no 100% compatible standard exists for how CMOS information is stored in all systems. You should consult the BIOS manufacturer for more information if you want the full details of how CMOS is stored because the CMOS configuration and Setup program typically are part of the BIOS. This is another example of how close the relationship is between the BIOS and the motherboard hardware.

Backup programs and utilities are available in the public domain for CMOS RAM information, which can be useful for saving and later restoring a configuration. Unfortunately, these programs are BIOS specific and function only on a BIOS for which they are designed. As such, I don't usually rely on these programs because they are too motherboard and BIOS specific and will not work on all my systems seamlessly.

Table 5.7 shows the values that might be stored by your system BIOS in a special CMOS byte called the diagnostic status byte. By examining this location with a diagnostics program, you can determine whether your system has set trouble codes, which indicate that a problem previously has occurred.

Table 5.7   CMOS RAM Diagnostic Status Byte Codes

| Bit Number | | | | | | | | Hex | Function |
7	6	5	4	3	2	1	0		
1	•	•	•	•	•	•	•	80	Real-time clock (RTC) chip lost power.
•	1	•	•	•	•	•	•	40	CMOS RAM checksum is bad.
•	•	1	•	•	•	•	•	20	Invalid configuration information found at POST.
•	•	•	1	•	•	•	•	10	Memory size compare error at POST.
•	•	•	•	1	•	•	•	08	Fixed disk or adapter failed initialization.
•	•	•	•	•	1	•	•	04	Real-time clock (RTC) time found invalid.
•	•	•	•	•	•	1	•	02	Adapters do not match configuration.
•	•	•	•	•	•	•	1	01	Time-out reading an adapter ID.
•	•	•	•	•	•	•	•	00	No errors found (Normal).

If the diagnostic status byte is any value other than 0, you typically get a CMOS configuration error on bootup. These types of errors can be cleared by rerunning the setup program.

Replacing a BIOS ROM

Systems dating from 1995 or earlier usually don't have a flash ROM and instead use an EPROM. To upgrade the BIOS in one of these systems, you replace the EPROM chip with a new one preloaded with the new BIOS. As with a flash ROM upgrade, you must get this from your motherboard manufacturer. There is usually a fee for this because the manufacturer must custom-burn a chip just for you and mail it out. Most boards older than 1995 are probably not worth upgrading the BIOS, so this option might no longer be available. Even if it is available, it most likely doesn't make sense to spend up to $50 on a new BIOS for an ancient board when a more modern board can be had for nearly the same cost—especially since that new board will include a flash BIOS and many other new features.

Tip

You can get a replacement BIOS chip identical to the motherboard manufacturer's product for many systems for around $30 from BIOSWorld (**www.biosworld.com**). See its Web site for details.

The procedure for replacing the BIOS chip is also useful if you have made a backup copy of your socketed system BIOS chip and need to replace a damaged original with the backup copy. This can also be useful if you have a socketed flash ROM, which was common on motherboards without a BIOS recovery jumper.

To replace the BIOS chip, follow these steps:

1. Back up the CMOS RAM settings.
2. Power down the system and unplug the power cord.
3. Remove the cover and any other components in the way of the BIOS EPROM chip. Remember to use caution with respect to static discharges; you should wear an antistatic wrist strap for this procedure or ground yourself to the chassis before touching any internal components.
4. Using a chip puller or a thin flat-blade screwdriver, gently pry the chip out of its socket.
5. Remove the new EPROM from the antistatic packing material in which it came.
6. Install the new EPROM chip into the socket. A standard rectangular BIOS chip has a dimple at one end that corresponds to a cutout on the socket. You can install the chip in the socket backward, but if you do, you will destroy the chip.

7. Reinstall anything you removed to gain access to the chip.

8. Put the cover back on, plug in the system, and power on.

9. Enter the BIOS setup information you saved earlier.

10. Reboot and enjoy the new BIOS!

As you can see, things are much easier with a modern motherboard with a flash ROM because you usually don't even have to remove the lid (unless the flash BIOS is write-protected as discussed earlier in this chapter).

Year 2000 BIOS Issues

All systems now in use should be compliant with twenty-first century dates, either through BIOS updates or through software or hardware patches. However, if you are returning stored systems built before 1999 to service, you might want to test them for year-2000 compliance. For details, see *Upgrading and Repairing PCs, 12th Edition*, available in electronic form on the DVD packaged with this book.

Preboot Environment

Both the standard and Pro versions of the Phoenix FirstBIOS have a common preboot environment with a graphical user interface that allows a user to access the BIOS Setup, extended diagnostics, a backup/restore application, or a full recovery of the original system contents (product restoration to factory-delivered contents). All these applications (except the BIOS Setup) are stored in the HPA, a hidden area of the hard drive literally situated past the reported end of the drive. The number and type of applications accessible via the preboot environment depend on which options the OEM selected when designing the system. Figure 5.9 shows IBM's implementation of the Phoenix FirstBIOS Pro preboot environment. This environment is activated by pressing the Enter key on the keyboard during the POST.

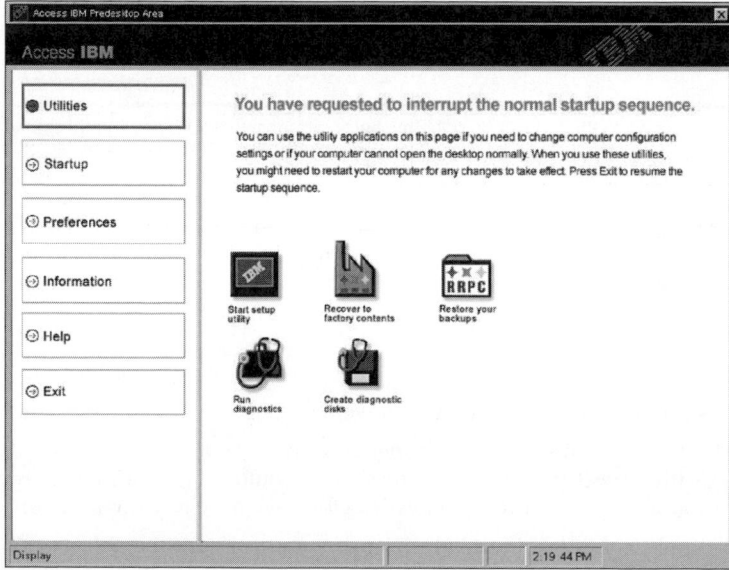

Figure 5.9   Phoenix FirstBIOS Pro preboot environment: IBM implementation shown.

A graphical preboot environment is especially useful for product recovery. For example, most of the larger system OEMs do a lot more than just install Windows on a system before they deliver it. After installing Windows, they install all the service packs and updates available at the time, as well as all the updated drivers unique to their systems. Then they add customizations, such as special wallpapers or interface customizations, support contact information, online system documentation, and custom utilities designed to make their systems easier to use. Finally, they install applications such as DVD players, Office applications or other productivity software, and more.

This OEM customization represents a lot of work if a user were to have to duplicate this from scratch, so most manufacturers like to include the ability to easily recover the system to the factory-delivered contents, including the OS, drivers, application, and custom configuration. This is normally provided via several CDs, which could be lost or damaged by the user, are sometimes problematic to use, and which cost money to produce and deliver with the system. By using a BIOS such as the Phoenix FirstBIOS, an OEM can instead deliver the contents of the recovery CDs directly on the hard disk and make it accessible via the preboot menu in the BIOS.

Originally, this was done using a hidden partition, which unfortunately could easily be damaged or overwritten by partitioning software or other utilities. In many newer systems, the contents of the recovery CDs is instead preinstalled in the HPA, which is accessible via Protected Area Run Time Interface Extension Services (PARTIES), a standard supported on all ATA-4 or newer drives. HPA/ PARTIES works by using the ATA SET MAX ADDRESS command to essentially make the drive appear to the system as a slightly smaller drive. Most manufacturers use the last 3GB of the drive for the HPA. Anything from the new max address (the newly reported end of the drive) to the true end of the drive is considered the HPA and is accessible only using PARTIES commands. Figure 5.10 shows the contents of the HPA and the relationship between the HPA and the rest of the drive.

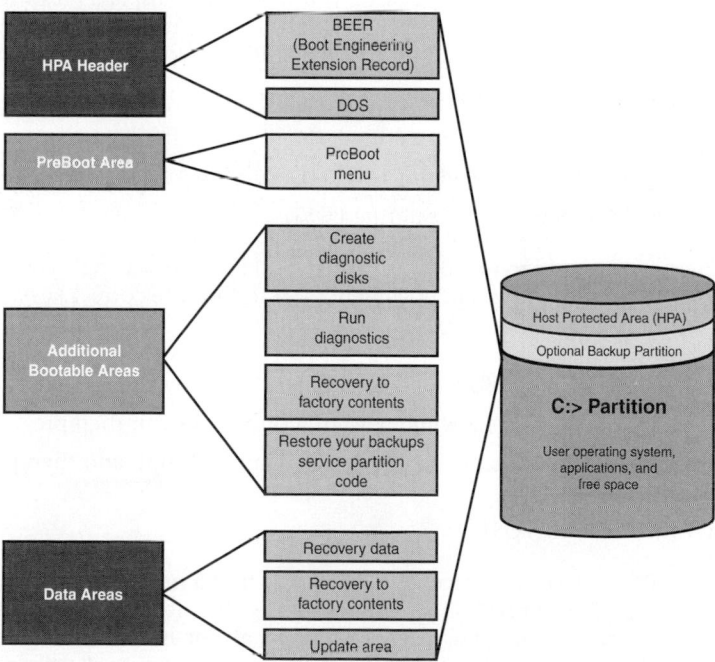

Figure 5.10 The HPA.

The HPA is more secure than a hidden partition because any data past the end of the drive simply cannot be seen by any normal application, or even a partitioning utility such as Partition Magic or Partition Commander. This makes it far more secure and immune to damage. Still, if you wanted to remove the HPA, there is a way to reset the max address, thus exposing the HPA. Then you could run something like Partition Magic or Partition Commander to resize the main partition to include the extra space that was formerly hidden and unavailable. The only consequence is that you would lose access to the product recovery, diagnostics, and backup applications preloaded by the OEM. For some people, this might be desirable because future product recoveries could still be done via the recovery CDs (not usually shipped with the system anymore, but still available separately either free or for a minimal charge), and true hardware diagnostics can still be run via bootable floppies or CDs. Also, if you are replacing the hard disk, you can temporarily unhide the HPA on the original drive, allowing it to be copied to a new drive. Alternatively, you can use the OEM-supplied recovery CDs to install the HPA on the new drive.

Most new systems using Phoenix FirstBIOS come with their recovery software and diagnostics in the HPA because this is part of the new Phoenix FirstBIOS core managed environment (cME), which is used by a large number of OEMs (including IBM) on most desktop and laptop systems starting in 2003.

CMOS Setup Specifications

The CMOS RAM must be configured with information about your system's drives and user-selected options before you can use your computer. The Setup program provided with your system is used to select the options you want to use to start your computer.

Running or Accessing the CMOS Setup Program

If you want to run the BIOS Setup program, you usually have to reboot and press a particular key or key combination during the POST. Normally, the correct key to press is displayed onscreen momentarily during the POST. If it flashes past too quickly to read, try pressing the Pause key on the keyboard when it appears. This freezes the system, allowing you to read the display. Pressing any other key (such as the spacebar) un-pauses the system and allows the POST to continue. The major vendors have standardized the following keystrokes to enter the BIOS Setup in recent systems:

- *AMI BIOS.* Press Delete during POST.
- *Phoenix BIOS (FirstBIOS Pro).* Press F2 during POST.
- *Award BIOS (FirstBIOS).* Press Delete or Ctrl+Alt+Esc during POST.
- *Microid Research (MR) BIOS.* Press Esc during POST.

If your system does not respond to one of these common keystroke settings, you might have to contact the manufacturer or read the system documentation to find the correct keystrokes.

Some unique ones are as follows:

- *IBM Aptiva/Valuepoint or ThinkPad.* Press F1 during POST or while powering on the system.
- *Toshiba notebook/laptop.* Press Esc while powering on the system; then press F1 when prompted.
- *Older Phoenix BIOS.* Boot to a safe mode DOS command prompt, and then press Ctrl+Alt+Esc or Ctrl+Alt+S.
- *Compaq.* Press F10 during POST.

After you are at the BIOS Setup main screen, you'll usually find a main menu allowing access to other menus and submenus of different sections or screens. Using the Intel D875PBZ motherboard as an example (one of Intel's recent motherboards), let's go through the menus and submenus of this typical (and popular) motherboard. Although other motherboards might feature slightly different settings, most are very similar.

BIOS Setup Menus

Most modern BIOSs offer a menu bar at the top of the screen when you're in the BIOS Setup that controls navigation through the various primary menus. A typical menu bar offers the choices shown in Table 5.8.

Note

Because most common BIOSs use similar settings, I've chosen the Setup used by modern Intel motherboards as an example in the following tables. Because the BIOS is customized by the motherboard manufacturer, even the same BIOS can offer different options for different boards. The settings covered here will help you get a general idea of the type of settings to expect and how the BIOS Setup settings affect your computer.

Table 5.8   Typical BIOS Setup Menus

Setup Menu Screen	Description
Maintenance	Specifies the processor speed and clears the setup passwords. This menu is available only in Configure mode, set by a jumper on the board.
Main	Allocates resources for hardware components.
Advanced	Specifies advanced features available through the chipset.
Security	Specifies passwords and security features.
Power	Specifies power management features.
Boot	Specifies boot options and power supply controls.
Exit	Saves or discards changes to the setup program options.

Settings based on the BIOS used in the Intel D875PBZ motherboard. Used by permission of Intel Corporation.

Choosing each of these selections takes you to another menu with more choices. The following sections examine all the choices available in a typical motherboard, such as the Intel D875PBZ.

Maintenance Menu

The Maintenance menu is a special menu for setting the processor speed and clearing the setup passwords. Older motherboards used jumpers to configure the processor bus speed (motherboard speed) and processor multiplier. Most newer boards from Intel and others now offer this control via the BIOS Setup rather than moving jumpers. In the case of Intel, one jumper still remains on the board called the configuration jumper, and it must be set to Configure mode for the Maintenance menu to be available.

Setup displays this menu only if the system is set in Configure mode. To set Configure mode, power off the system and move the configuration jumper on the motherboard from *Normal* to *Configure* (see Figure 5.6, earlier in this chapter). Because this is the only jumper on a modern Intel board, it is pretty easy to find. When the system is powered back on, the BIOS Setup automatically runs, and you will be able to select the Maintenance menu shown in Table 5.9. After making changes and saving, power off the system and reset the jumper to Normal mode for normal operation.

Table 5.9   Typical Maintenance Menu Settings

Feature	Options	Description
Clear All Passwords	OK (default) Cancel	Clears the user and supervisor passwords
Clear BIOS	OK (default) Cancel	Clears the Wired for Management Boot Integrity Service (BIS) credentials
CPU Stepping Signature	No options	Displays CPU's stepping revision
CPU Microcode Update Revision	No options	Displays CPU's microcode update revision

Settings based on the BIOS used in the Intel D875PBZ motherboard. Used by permission of Intel Corporation.

Note that most newer Intel processors are designed to allow operation only at or below their rated speeds (a feature called *speed locking*), whereas others allow higher-than-rated speeds to be selected.

If a user forgets his password, all he has to do is set the configuration jumper, enter the Maintenance menu in BIOS Setup, and use the option provided to clear the password. This function doesn't tell the user what the password was; it simply clears it, allowing a new one to be set if desired. This means the security is only as good as the lock on the system case because anybody who can get to the configuration jumper can clear the password and access the system. This is why most better cases come equipped with locks.

Extended Configuration Submenu

The Extended Configuration submenu on some Intel motherboards has memory setup options similar to those found in the section "Additional Advanced Features," later in this chapter. See this section for details.

Main Menu

The standard CMOS Setup menu dates back to the 286 days, when the complete BIOS Setup consisted of only one menu. In the standard menu, you can set the system clock and record hard disk and floppy drive parameters and the basic video type. Newer BIOSs have more complicated setups with more menus and submenus, so the main menu often is fairly sparse compared to older systems.

The main menu in a modern system reports system information such as the BIOS version, the processor type and speed, the amount of memory, and whether the memory or cache is configured for ECC functionality. The main menu also can be used to set the system date and time.

Table 5.10 shows a typical main menu.

Table 5.10 Typical Main Menu Settings

Feature	Options	Description
BIOS Version	—	Displays the version of the BIOS.
Processor Type	—	Displays the processor type.
Hyper-Threading Technology	Enabled (default); Disabled	Enables/disables. Hyper-Threading Technology. This option is present only when a processor that supports Hyper-Threading Technology is installed.
Processor Speed	—	Displays the processor speed.
System Bus Speed	—	Displays the system bus speed.
System Memory Speed	—	Displays the system memory speed.
Cache RAM	—	Displays the size of the L2 cache.
Total Memory	—	Displays the total amount of RAM.
Memory Mode	—	Displays the memory mode (dual channel or single channel).
Memory Channel A Slot 0; Memory Channel A Slot 1; Memory Channel B Slot 0; Memory Channel B Slot 1	—	Displays the amount and type of RAM in the DIMM sockets.

Table 5.10 Continued

Feature	Options	Description
Memory Configuration	Non-ECC (default); ECC	ECC turns on error reporting if the system and all the memory installed supports ECC. This setting is available only when ECC memory is installed.
Language	English (default); others might be listed	Selects the current default language used by the BIOS.
System Time	Hour:minute:second	Specifies the current time.
System Date	Month/day/year	Specifies the current date.

Settings based on the BIOS used in the Intel D875PBZ motherboard. Used by permission of Intel Corporation.

ECC stands for error correcting code, which is the use of extra bits on the memory modules to detect and even correct memory errors on-the-fly. For ECC to be enabled, more expensive ECC DIMMs would have to be installed in the system. Note that all DIMMs would need to be ECC versions for this to work; if even one is non-ECC, ECC can't be enabled. For mission-critical systems (such as servers), I recommend purchasing ECC memory and enabling this function because it makes the system more fault tolerant and prevents corrupted data due to soft errors in memory. Random memory errors can occur at the rate of up to 1 bit error per month for every 64–256 megabytes installed. ECC ensures that these errors don't creep into your data files, corrupt the system, or cause it to crash.

▶▶ See "Error Correcting Code," p. 506.

Be sure to check whether your motherboard supports ECC before purchasing ECC memory. You can install ECC memory in a non-ECC-capable board, but the ECC functionality will not be available. Also, make sure you are aware of the memory requirements for your board. Don't try to install more memory than the board supports, and be sure the modules you use meet the specifications required by the board. See the documentation for the motherboard for more information on the type and amount of memory that can be installed.

Most older BIOSs report memory as base and extended memory instead of as a single value. Base memory is typically 640KB and sometimes is called *conventional* memory. Extended memory is that which is beyond the first megabyte in the system.

You can't change any values in the memory fields; they are only for your information because they are automatically counted up by the system. If the memory count doesn't match what you have installed, a problem has likely occurred with some of the memory: It is defective, is not fully seated or properly installed, or is a type that is incompatible with your system.

Advanced Menu

The Advanced menu is a doorway to submenus for setting advanced features that are available through the motherboard chipset. This part of your BIOS setup is specific to the particular chipset the motherboard uses. Many chipsets are available on the market today, and each has unique features. The chipset setup is designed to enable the user to customize these features and control some of the chipset settings. Table 5.11 shows the typical Advanced submenus available.

Table 5.11   Typical Advanced BIOS Submenus

Submenu	Description
PCI Configuration	Configures the IRQ priority of individual PCI slots
Boot Configuration	Configures Plug and Play, resets PnP configuration data, and configures the NumLock key
Peripheral Configuration	Configures peripheral ports and devices
Drive Configuration	Configures ATA devices
Floppy Configuration	Configures the floppy drive
Event Log Configuration	Configures event logging
Video Configuration	Configures video features
USB Configuration	Configures USB support
Chipset Configuration	Configures advanced chipset features
Fan Control Configuration	Configures fan operation
Hardware Monitoring	Monitors system temperatures, voltages, and fan speeds

Settings based on the BIOS used in the Intel D875PBZ motherboard. Used by permission of Intel Corporation.

PCI Configuration Submenu

The PCI Configuration submenu is used to select the IRQ priority of add-on cards plugged into the PCI slots. Auto (the default) should be used to allow the BIOS and operating system to assign IRQs to each slot unless specific PCI cards require unique IRQs. See Table 5.12 for a typical example.

Table 5.12   Typical PCI Configuration Submenu Settings

Feature	Options	Description
PCI Slot 1 IRQ Priority	Auto (default), 3, 5, 9, 10, 11	Allows selection of the IRQ priority for PCI bus connector 1
PCI Slot 2 IRQ Priority	Auto (default), 3, 5, 9, 10, 11	Allows selection of the IRQ priority for PCI bus connector 2
PCI Slot 3 IRQ Priority	Auto (default), 3, 5, 9, 10, 11	Allows selection of the IRQ priority for PCI bus connector 3
PCI Slot 4 IRQ Priority	Auto (default), 3, 5, 9, 10, 11	Allows selection of the IRQ priority for PCI bus connector 4
PCI Slot 5 IRQ Priority	Auto (default), 3, 5, 9, 10, 11	Allows selection of the IRQ priority for PCI bus connector 5

Settings based on the BIOS used in the Intel D875PBZ motherboard. Used by permission of Intel Corporation.

Additional IRQs might be available if onboard devices such as the serial and parallel ports are disabled.

Boot Configuration Submenu

The options in Table 5.13 configure the system's PnP and keyboard configuration during initial boot.

Table 5.13   Typical Boot Configuration Submenu Settings

Feature	Options	Description
Plug and Play O/S	No (default) Yes	Specifies whether a PnP operating system is being used. No lets the BIOS configure all devices. Yes lets the operating system configure plug-and-play devices. Either setting works with a PnP operating system; however, No must be selected if using a non-PnP OS.
NumLock	On (default) Off	Specifies the power-on state of the NumLock feature on the numeric keypad of the keyboard.

Settings based on the BIOS used in the Intel D875PBZ motherboard. Used by permission of Intel Corporation.

Additional Advanced Features

Many boards differ in the advanced chipset menus. In most cases, unless you know exactly which chipset and what type of memory and other items are found in your system, it is best to leave these settings on Auto. In that case, the modern boards use the configuration ROM found on the DIMM or RIMM memory modules to properly configure the memory settings. In fact, many newer boards no longer allow these settings to be manually adjusted because, in most cases, all that does is lead to trouble in the form of an unstable or a failing system. If you do want to play with these settings, I recommend first finding out exactly which memory modules and chipset you have and contacting the manufacturers of them to get their databooks. The databooks have all the technical information related to those devices.

Table 5.14 lists settings used by a typical motherboard's Chipset Configuration submenu.

Table 5.14   Typical Chipset Configuration Menu

Feature	Options	Description
ISA Enable Bit	Enabled (default) Disabled	When enabled, a PCI-to-PCI bridge recognizes only 16-bit I/O addresses that are not aliases of 10-bit ISA addresses (within the bridge's assigned I/O range). This helps prevent resource conflicts with ISA devices that might be present in the system (such as serial or parallel ports) and allows VGA-compatible address range mapping for ISA devices.
PCI Latency Timer	32 (default) 64 96 128 160 192 224 248	Allows you to control the time (in PCI bus clock cycles) that an agent on the PC bus can hold the bus when another agent has requested the bus.
Burn-In Mode	—	Selects a submenu used to set Burn-In mode configuration options.
Extended Configuration	Default (default) User-defined	Allows the setting of extended configuration options.
SDRAM Frequency[1]	Auto (default) 266MHz 333MHz[2] 400MHz[3]	Allows an override of the detected memory frequency[4].
SDRAM Timing Control[1]	Auto (default) Manual-Aggressive Manual-User-defined	When Auto is selected, timings are programmed according to the memory detected. Manual-Aggressive selects the most aggressive user-defined timings. Manual-User-defined allows manual override of detected SDRAM settings.
CPC Override	Auto (default) Enabled Disabled	Controls the CPC/1n rule mode. Enabled allows the DRAM controller to attempt chip select assertions in two consecutive common clocks.
SDRAM RAS Active to Precharge[5]	8 7 6 (default) 5	Corresponds to tRAS, or the minimum page open time.
SDRAM CAS# Latency[5]	2.0 2.5 (default) 3.0	Selects the number of clock cycles required to address a column in memory.

Table 5.14   Continued

Feature	Options	Description
SDRAM RAS# to CAS# Delay[5]	4 3 2 (default)	Selects the number of clock cycles between addressing a row and addressing a column.
SDRAM RAS# Precharge[5]	4 3 2 (default)	Selects the length of time required before accessing a new row.

1. *This feature is displayed only if Extended Configuration is set to User-defined.*

2. *This option is displayed only if the installed processor has a 533MHz system bus.*

3. *This option is displayed only if the installed processor has an 800MHz system bus.*

4. *If SDRAM Frequency is changed, you must reboot for the change to take effect. After changing this setting and rebooting, the System Memory Speed parameter in the Main menu reflects the new value.*

5. *This feature is normally controlled by the serial presence detect (SPD) ROM in the DIMM and is displayed only if SDRAM Timing Control is set to Manual-User-defined.*

Settings based on the BIOS used in the Intel D875PBZ motherboard. Used by permission of Intel Corporation.

Some motherboards might also have advanced chipset options similar to those described in Table 5.15.

Table 5.15   Additional Advanced Chipset Options

Setting	Description
System BIOS Cacheable	Allows caching of the system BIOS ROM at F0000h–FFFFFh, resulting in better system performance when 16-bit applications are run. If any program writes to this memory area, a system error can result.
Video BIOS Cacheable	Allows caching of the video BIOS ROM at C0000h–C7FFFh, resulting in better video performance when 16-bit applications are run. If any program writes to this memory area, a system error can result.
Video RAM Cacheable (Video Memory Cache Mode)	Selecting Enabled allows caching of the video memory (RAM) at A0000h–AFFFFh, resulting in better video performance when 16-bit applications are run. If any program writes to this memory area, a memory access error can result. Uncacheable Speculative Write-Combining (USWC) mode is the same as Enabled on some systems.
8/16 Bit I/O Recovery Time	The I/O recovery mechanism adds bus clock cycles between PCI-originated I/O cycles to the ISA bus. This delay takes place because the PCI bus is so much faster than the ISA bus.
Memory Hole at 15M–16M	Places a 1MB empty RAM area between 15MB and 16MB. Older software sometimes would not run with 16MB or more memory in the system; enabling this provides a workaround. This is not normally used.
Passive Release	When Enabled, CPU-to-PCI bus accesses are allowed during passive release. Otherwise, the arbiter accepts only another PCI master access to local DRAM.
Delayed Transaction	The chipset has an embedded 32-bit posted write buffer to support delay transaction cycles. Select Enabled to support compliance with PCI specification version 2.1.

Overclocking/Burn-in Test Features

Many motherboards include features designed to overclock the system, which enables you to set the system to run the CPU bus (and therefore the CPU itself) and possibly other buses at higher-than-normal rated speeds. These settings are especially useful for stress testing a system after initial assembly, which is often called a *burn-in* test. Table 5.16 shows typical overclock/burn-in test features found in the BIOS Setup.

Table 5.16   Overclocking/Burn-in Test Settings

Feature	Options	Description
Do you wish to continue?	No (default) Continue	Enables or disables setting of burn-in (overclocking) mode options. Burn-in Mode is an unsupported overclocking capability for use by system engineers, technicians, or experienced users for validation and test purposes.
Host and I/O Burn-In Mode	Default (default) -2.0% -1.0% +1.0% +2.0% +3.0% +4.0%	Alters the host clock (system bus) and I/O clocks (AGP and PCI) by the percentage selected. If this option is set to anything other than Default, the AGP/PCI Burn-In Mode (shown below) is automatically set to Default.
AGP/PCI Burn In Mode	Default (default) 63.88/31.94MHz 68.05/34.02MHz 69.44/34.72MHz 70.83/35.41MHz 72.22/36.11MHz 73.60/36.80MHz	The Default settings are 66.66/33.33MHz. Using other settings enables the selection of specific AGP/PCI clock frequencies, but only if the host clock (system bus speed) is not changed. If this option is set to anything other than Default, the Host and I/O Burn-In Mode (shown above) is automatically set to Default.

Settings based on the BIOS used in the Intel D875PBZ motherboard. Used by permission of Intel Corporation.

These settings can be used to speed up the processor and interconnected buses such as PCI and AGP by a specified percentage. For specifically testing AGP video or PCI adapter cards, some motherboards allow the AGP/PCI bus speed to be set independently of the CPU bus. If you intend to use these settings to speed up a system, beware that—depending on the specific hardware and software you have—running faster than default clock speeds can reduce system stability and shorten the useful life of the processor, and it might not be covered under warranty. If any problems occur, return the settings to the default values.

Peripheral Configuration

The Peripheral Configuration menu is used to configure the devices built into the motherboard, such as serial ports, parallel ports, and built-in audio and USB ports.

Table 5.17 shows a typical Peripheral Configuration menu and choices.

Table 5.17   Typical Peripheral Configuration Menu

Feature	Options	Description
Serial Port A	Auto (default) Disabled Enabled	Configures serial port A. Auto assigns the first free COM port (normally COM 1) I/O address 3F8h and IRQ4.
Base I/O address	3F8h (default) 2F8h 3E8h 2E8h	Specifies the base I/O address for serial port A.
Interrupt	IRQ 4 (default) IRQ 3	Specifies the interrupt for serial port A.
Parallel port	Auto (default) Enabled Disabled	Configures the parallel port. Auto assigns I/O addresses 378h and IRQ7.

Table 5.17 Continued

Feature	Options	Description
Mode	Output Only Bi-directional (default) EPP ECP	Selects the mode for the parallel port. EPP is Extended Parallel Port mode, a high-speed, bidirectional mode. ECP is Enhanced Capabilities Port mode, another high-speed, bidirectional mode.
Base I/O address	378 (default) 278	Specifies the base I/O address for the parallel port.
Interrupt	IRQ 7 (default) IRQ 5	Specifies the interrupt for the parallel port.
DMA	DMA 3 (default) DMA 1	Specifies the DMA channel for the parallel port.
Audio	Enabled (default) Disabled	Enables or disables the onboard audio subsystem.
Onboard LAN	Enabled (default) Disabled	Enables or disables the onboard LAN (network card) device.

An asterisk (*) displayed next to an address indicates a conflict with another device.

(EPP and ECP are IEEE-1284-compliant modes and require the use of an IEEE-1284-compliant printer cable.)

Settings based on the BIOS used in the Intel D875PBZ motherboard. Used by permission of Intel Corporation.

I recommend disabling the serial and parallel ports if they are not being used because this frees up those resources for other devices.

ATA Configuration Submenu

The ATA Configuration submenu is for configuring ATA devices, such as hard drives, CD-ROM drives, LS-120 (SuperDisk) drives, tape drives, and so on. Table 5.18 shows the ATA Configuration menu and options for a typical modern motherboard.

Table 5.18 Typical ATA Configuration Menu Settings

Feature	Options	Description
ATA Configuration	Enhanced (default) Disabled Legacy	Enhanced causes all Serial ATA (SATA) and Parallel ATA (PATA) resources to be enabled. Disabled causes all ATA resources to be disabled. Legacy causes up to two ATA channels to be enabled for operating systems that require legacy ATA operation.
Legacy ATA Channels	PATA Pri Only PATA Sec Only PATA Pri and Sec SATA P0/P1 Only SATA P0/P1, PATA Sec SATA P0/P1, PATA Pri	Configures PATA and SATA resources for operating systems that require legacy ATA operation. This feature is present only when the ATA configuration option is set to Legacy.
PCI ATA Bus Master	Enabled (default) Disabled	Enables/disables the use of DMA for hard drive BIOS INT13 reads and writes.

Table 5.18   Continued

Feature	Options	Description
Hard Disk Pre-Delay	Disabled (default) 3 Seconds 6 Seconds 9 Seconds 12 Seconds 15 Seconds 21 Seconds 30 Seconds	Specifies the hard disk drive predelay.
SoftRAID Support	Disabled (default) Enabled	Configures SoftRAID support.
SATA Port-0	—	Select this to display a submenu (if a device is attached).
SATA Port-1	—	Select this to display a submenu (if a device is attached).
PATA Primary Master	—	Select this to display a submenu (if a device is attached).
PATA Primary Slave	—	Select this to display a submenu (if a device is attached).
PATA Secondary Master	—	Select this to display a submenu (if a device is attached).
PATA Secondary Slave	—	Select this to display a submenu (if a device is attached).

PATA = Parallel ATA   *P0 = Serial ATA connector 0*
SATA = Serial ATA   *P1 = Serial ATA connector 1*
Pri = Primary   *Settings based on the BIOS used in the Intel D875PBZ*
Sec = Secondary   *motherboard. Used by permission of Intel Corporation.*

The hard disk predelay function is to delay accessing drives that are slow to spin up. Some drives aren't ready when the system begins to look for them during boot, causing the system to display Fixed Disk Failure messages and fail to boot. Setting this delay allows time for the drive to become ready before continuing the boot. Of course, this slows down the boot process, so if your drives don't need this delay, it should be disabled.

ATA Configuration Submenus

These submenus are for configuring each ATA device. Of all the BIOS Setup menus, the hard disk settings are by far the most important. In fact, they are the most important of all the BIOS settings. Most modern motherboards incorporate two ATA controllers that support up to four drives. Most modern BIOSs have an autodetect feature that enables automatic configuration of the drives. If this is available, in most cases you should use it because it will prevent confusion in the future. With the Auto setting, the BIOS sends a special Identify Drive command to the drive, which responds with information about the correct settings. From this, the BIOS can automatically detect the specifications and optimal operating mode of almost all ATA hard drives. When you select Auto for a hard drive, the BIOS redetects the drive specifications during POST, every time the system boots. You could swap drives with the power off, and the system would automatically detect the new drive the next time it was turned on.

In addition to the Auto setting, most older BIOSs offered a standard table of up to 47 drive types with specifically prerecorded parameters. Each defined drive type has a specified number of cylinders, number of heads, write precompensation factor, landing zone, and number of sectors. This often was used many years ago, but it is rarely used today because virtually no drives conform to the parameters on these drive type lists.

Another option is to select a setting called User or User Defined, which is where you can enter the specific drive CHS (Cylinder, Head, and Sector) parameters into the proper fields. These parameters are saved in the CMOS RAM and reloaded every time the system is powered up.

Most BIOSs today offer control over the drive translation settings if the type is set to User and not Auto. Usually, two translation settings are available, called Standard and LBA. Standard or LBA-disabled is used only for drives of 528MB or less, where the maximum number of cylinders, heads, and sectors are 1,024, 16, and 63, respectively. Because most drives today are larger, this setting is rarely used.

LBA (logical block addressing) is used for virtually all ATA drives that are larger than 528MB. Note that systems dating from 1997 and earlier usually are limited to a maximum drive size of 8.4GB unless they have a BIOS upgrade. Systems from 1998 and later usually support drives up to 136.9GB; systems dating from 2002 and beyond usually support drives beyond 137GB (48-bit LBA support), although a BIOS upgrade might be necessary. During drive access, the ATA controller transforms the data address described by sector, head, and cylinder number into a physical block address, significantly improving data transfer rates.

Table 5.19 shows the ATA drive settings found in a typical modern motherboard BIOS.

Table 5.19   Typical ATA Drive Settings

Feature	Options	Description
Drive Installed	—	Displays the type of drive installed.
Type	Auto (default) User	Specifies the ATA configuration mode for ATA devices. Auto reads settings from the ATA/ATAPI device. User allows settings to be changed.
Maximum Capacity	—	Displays the drive capacity.
LBA/Large Mode	Auto (default) Disabled	Displays whether automatic translation mode is enabled for the hard disk.
Block Mode	Auto (default) Disabled	Displays whether automatic multiple sector data transfers are enabled.
PIO Mode	Auto (default) 0 1 2 3 4	Sets the Programmed I/O mode.
DMA Mode	Auto (default) SWDMAx MWDMAx UDMAx	Specifies the DMA mode for the drive. SWDMA = SingleWord DMA; MWDMA = MultiWord DMA; UDMA = Ultra DMA.
SMART	Auto (default) Disabled Enabled	Enables/disables Self-Monitoring, Analysis, and Reporting Technology (SMART). Auto enables SMART if it's supported by the drive.
Cable Detected	—	Displays the type of cable connected to the Parallel ATA interface: 40-conductor or 80-conductor.
ARMD (ATAPI Removable Media Device) Emulation Type	Floppy	This is displayed only when an LS-120 SuperDisk drive is connected.

Settings based on the BIOS used in the Intel D875PBZ motherboard. Used by permission of Intel Corporation.

Setting the drive type to Auto causes the other values to be automatically configured correctly. I recommend this for virtually all standard system configurations. When set to Auto, the BIOS sends an Identify command to the drive, causing it to report back all the options and features found on that drive. Using this information, the BIOS then automatically configures all the settings on this menu for maximum performance with that drive, including selecting the fastest possible transfer modes and other features.

For hard drives, the only option available other than Auto is User. When set to User, the other choices are made available and are not automatically set. This can be useful for somebody who wants to "play" with these settings, but in most cases, all you will get by doing so is lower performance and possibly even trouble in the form of corrupted data or a nonfunctional drive. User should be used only if a drive was originally prepared with a set of values different from those recognized automatically with the default Auto configuration setting.

Floppy Configuration Submenu

The Floppy Configuration submenu is for configuring the floppy drive and interface. Table 5.20 shows the options in a typical BIOS Setup.

Table 5.20   Typical Diskette Configuration Settings

Feature	Options	Description
Diskette Controller	Enabled (default) Disabled	Disables or enables the integrated diskette controller
Diskette A:	Disabled 360KB, 5 1/4" 1.2MB, 5 1/4" 1.44MB, 3 1/2" (default) 720KB, 3 1/2" 2.88MB, 3 1/2"	Specifies the capacity and physical size of floppy disk drive A:
Diskette Write Protect	Disabled (default) Enabled	Disables or enables write protect for floppy disk drive A:

Settings based on the BIOS used by the Intel D845PEBT2 motherboard. Used by permission of Intel Corporation.

By enabling the write-protect feature, you can disallow writing to floppy disks. This can help prevent the theft of data as well as help to prevent infecting disks with viruses should they be on the system.

Event Logging

The Event Logging menu is for configuring the System Management (SMBIOS) event logging features. SMBIOS is a DMI-compliant method for managing computers on a managed network. DMI stands for Desktop Management Interface, a special protocol that software can use to communicate with the motherboard.

Using SMBIOS, a system administrator can remotely obtain information about a system. Applications such as the LANDesk Client Manager (originally developed by Intel but now sold by LANDesk Software) can use SMBIOS to report the following DMI information:

- BIOS data, such as the BIOS revision level
- System data, such as installed peripherals, serial numbers, and asset tags
- Resource data, such as memory size, cache size, and processor speed
- Dynamic data such as event detection, including event detection and error logging

Table 5.21 shows a typical Event Logging menu in BIOS Setup.

Table 5.21   Typical Event Logging Menu

Feature	Options	Description
Event Log	—	Indicates whether space is available in the event log
View Event Log	[Enter]	Displays the event log
Clear Event Log	OK (default) Cancel	Clears the event log after rebooting
Event Logging	Enabled (default) Disabled	Enables/disables logging of Desktop Management Interface events
ECC Event Logging	Enabled (default) Disabled	Enables/disables logging of ECC events
Mark Events As Read	OK (default) Cancel	Marks all events as read

Settings based on the BIOS used in the Intel D875PBZ motherboard. Used by permission of Intel Corporation.

Some motherboards with ECC memory also support log ECC events. I find event logging particularly useful for tracking errors such as ECC errors. Using the View Log feature, you can see whether any errors have been detected (and corrected) by the system.

Video Configuration

The Video Configuration menu is for configuring video features. Table 5.22 shows the functions of this menu in a typical modern motherboard BIOS.

Table 5.22   Typical Video Configuration Menu

Feature	Options	Description
AGP Aperture Size	4MB 8MB 16MB 32MB 64MB (default) 128MB 256MB	Specifies the aperture size for the AGP video controller
Primary Video Adapter	AGP (default) PCI	Selects the type of video card used for the boot display device

Settings based on the BIOS used by the Intel D875PBZ motherboard. Used by permission of Intel Corporation.

Other motherboards might also include features such as those shown in Table 5.23.

Table 5.23   Additional Video Configuration Menu Options

Feature	Options	Description
Palette Snooping	Disabled (default) Enabled	Controls the capability of a primary PCI graphics controller to share a common palette with an ISA add-in video card
AGP Hardware Detected	No options	Indicates whether a 1x, 2x, or 4x AGP card is installed; disables onboard graphics subsystem

The most common use of this menu is to change the primary video device. This is useful under Windows 98 and later versions, which support dual-monitor configurations. Using this feature, you can set either the AGP or PCI video card to be the primary boot device.

USB Configuration Submenu

The USB Configuration submenu is used for configuring the USB ports on the system. Table 5.24 shows the functions of this menu in a typical modern motherboard BIOS.

Table 5.24   Typical USB Configuration Menu

Feature	Options	Description
High-Speed USB	Enabled (default) Disabled	Set to Disabled when a USB 2.0 driver is not available
Legacy USB Support	Enabled (default) Disabled	Enables/disables legacy USB support
USB 2.0 Legacy Support	FullSpeed (default) HiSpeed	Configures the USB 2.0 Legacy support: HiSpeed = 480Mbps; FullSpeed = 12Mbps

Settings based on the BIOS used in the Intel D875PBZ motherboard. Used by permission of Intel Corporation.

Some motherboards that have separate USB 1.1 and USB 2.0 ports might offer additional configuration options.

Legacy USB support means support for USB keyboards and mice. If you are using USB keyboards and mice, you will find that the keyboard is not functional until a USB-aware operating system is loaded. This can be a problem when running DOS; diagnostics software; or other applications that run outside of USB-aware operating systems, such as Windows 98, Windows Me, Windows XP, and Windows 2000. In that case, you should enable the USB legacy support via this menu.

Even with legacy support disabled, the system still recognizes a USB keyboard and enables it to work during the POST and BIOS Setup. If USB legacy support is disabled (the default on some systems), the system operates as follows:

1. When you power up the computer, USB legacy support is disabled.
2. POST begins.
3. USB legacy support is temporarily enabled by the BIOS. This enables you to use a USB keyboard to enter the setup program or Maintenance mode.
4. POST completes and disables USB legacy support (unless it was set to *Enabled* while in Setup).
5. The operating system loads. While the operating system is loading, USB keyboards and mice are not recognized. After the operating system loads the USB drivers, the USB devices are recognized.

To install an operating system that supports USB, enable USB legacy support in BIOS Setup and follow the operating system's installation instructions. After the operating system is installed and the USB drivers are configured, USB legacy support is no longer used and the operating system USB drivers take over. However, I recommend that you leave legacy support enabled so the USB keyboard functions in DOS while running self-booting or DOS-based diagnostics or when running other non-USB-aware operating systems.

If USB legacy support is enabled, you shouldn't mix USB and PS/2 port keyboards and mice. For example, don't use a PS/2 keyboard with a USB mouse or a USB keyboard and a PS/2 mouse. Also remember that this legacy support is for keyboards and mice only; it won't work for USB hubs or other USB devices. For devices other than keyboards or mice to work, you need a USB-aware operating system with the appropriate USB drivers.

Fan Control Configuration Submenu

Most systems have one or more chassis fans to help cool the system. Table 5.25 shows the function of the Fan Control Configuration submenu on a typical high-performance PC.

Table 5.25   Fan Control Configuration Submenu

Feature	Options	Description
Fan Control	Enabled (default) Disabled	Enables or disables fan control.
Lowest Fan Speed	Slow (default) Off	Defines the lower limit of chassis fan speed operation. When set to *Slow*, at low system temperatures the fans will continue o run at slow speed. When set to *Off*, at low system temperatures the fans will turn off.

These options do not take effect until AC power has been completely removed from the system. After saving the BIOS settings and turning off the system, unplug the power cord from the system and wait at least 30 seconds before reapplying power and turning the system back on.

Settings based on the BIOS used in the Intel D875PBZ motherboard. Used by permission of Intel Corporation.

Many newer boards have built-in monitor chips that can read temperature, voltage, and fan speeds. Those that do often include a screen in the BIOS Setup that allows you to view the readings from the monitor chip. Usually such boards also include a hardware monitor program that runs under Windows for more convenient monitoring while the system is in use (see Table 5.26).

Table 5.26   Hardware Monitoring Display

Feature	Description
Processor Zone Temperature	Displays temperature near the CPU in Celsius and Fahrenheit
System Zone 1 Temperature	Displays temperature of Zone 1 in Celsius and Fahrenheit
System Zone 2 Temperature	Displays temperature of Zone 2 in Celsius and Fahrenheit
Processor Fan Speed	Displays CPU fan speed in RPM
Rear Fan Speed	Displays chassis rear fan speed in RPM
Front Fan Speed	Displays chassis front fan speed in RPM
Voltage Regulator Fan Speed	Displays VR fan speed in RPM
+1.5V in	Displays voltage level of +1.5V supply
Vccp	Displays voltage level of CPU core supply
+3.3V in	Displays voltage level of +3.3V supply
+5V in	Displays voltage level of +5V supply
+12V in	Displays voltage level of +12V supply

Settings based on the BIOS used in the Intel D875PBZ motherboard. Used by permission of Intel Corporation.

Resource Configuration/PnP Configuration Menu

If you have a motherboard with one or more ISA slots, you need to use the Resource Configuration or PnP Configuration menu to determine which IRQs and memory addresses are available for ISA devices. This is not necessary on motherboards that have only PCI or PCI and AGP slots. For more information about this menu, see *Upgrading and Repairing PCs, 12th Edition*, included in electronic form on the DVD packaged with this book.

Security Menu

Most BIOSs include two passwords for security, called the supervisor and user passwords. These passwords help control who is allowed to access the BIOS Setup program and who is allowed to boot the computer. The supervisor password is also called a setup password because it controls access to the setup program. The user password is also called a system password because it controls access to the entire system.

If a supervisor password is set, a password prompt is displayed when an attempt is made to enter the BIOS Setup menus. When entered correctly, the supervisor password gives unrestricted access to view and change all the Setup options in the Setup program. If the supervisor password is not entered or is entered incorrectly, access to view and change Setup options in the Setup program is restricted.

If the user password is set, the password prompt is displayed before the computer boots up. The password must be entered correctly before the system is allowed to boot. Note that if only the supervisor password is set, the computer boots without asking for a password because the supervisor password controls access only to the BIOS Setup menus. If both passwords are set, the password prompt is displayed at boot time, and either the user or the supervisor password can be entered to boot the computer. In most systems, the password can be up to seven or eight characters long.

If you forget the password, most systems have a jumper on the board that allows all passwords to be cleared. This means that for most systems, the password security also requires that the system case be locked to prevent users from opening the cover and accessing the password-clear jumper. This jumper is often not labeled on the board for security reasons, but it can be found in the motherboard or system documentation.

Provided you know the password and can get into the BIOS Setup, a password can also be cleared by entering the BIOS Setup and selecting the Clear Password function. If no Clear function is available, you can still clear the password by selecting the Set Password function and pressing Enter (for no password) at the prompts.

Table 5.27 shows the security functions in a typical BIOS Setup.

Table 5.27   Typical Security Settings

Feature	Options	Description
Supervisor Password	—	Reports if a supervisor password is set.
User Password	—	Reports if a user password is set.
Set Supervisor Password[1]	—	Specifies the supervisor password.
User Access Level[2]	Full (default) No Access View Only Limited	Sets the user access rights to the BIOS Setup Utility. Full allows the user to change all fields except the supervisor password. No Access prevents user access to the BIOS Setup Utility. View Only allows the user to view but not change the BIOS Setup Utility fields. Limited allows the user to change some fields.
Set User Password[1]	—	Specifies the user password.
Clear User Password[3]	OK (default) Cancel	Clears the user password.
Chassis Intrusion	Disabled (default) Log Log, notify once Log, notify until cleared	Disabled disables chassis intrusion; Log logs the intrusion in the event log. Log, notify once halts the system during POST, the user must press F4 to continue, the intrusion flag is cleared, and the event log is updated. Log, notify until cleared halts the system during POST and the user must enter the BIOS Setup Security menu and select Clear Chassis Intrusion Status to clear the chassis intrusion flag.

1. *Passwords can be up to seven alphanumeric characters, including A–Z, a–z, and 1–9.*
2. *This feature is displayed only if a supervisor password has been set.*
3. *This feature is displayed only if a user password has been set.*
Settings based on the BIOS used in the Intel D875PBZ motherboard. Used by permission of Intel Corporation.

To clear passwords if the password is forgotten, most motherboards have a password-clear jumper or switch. Intel motherboards require that you set the configuration jumper, enter the Maintenance menu in BIOS Setup, and select the Clear Password feature. If you can't find the documentation for your board and aren't sure how to clear the passwords, you can try removing the battery for 15 minutes or so—it clears the CMOS RAM. It can take that long for the CMOS RAM to clear on some systems because they have capacitors in the circuit that retain a charge. Note that this also erases all other BIOS settings, including the hard disk settings, so they should be recorded beforehand.

Power Menu

Power management is defined as the capability of the system to automatically enter power-conserving modes during periods of inactivity. Two main classes of power management exist; the original standard was called Advanced Power Management (APM) and was supported by most systems since the 386 and 486 processors. More recently, a new type of power management called Advanced Configuration and Power Interface (ACPI) has been developed and began appearing in systems during 1998. Most systems sold in 1998 or later support the more advanced ACPI type of power management. In APM, the hardware does the actual power management, and the operating system or other software had little control. With ACPI, the power management is now done by the operating system and BIOS, and not the hardware. This makes the control more centralized and easier to access and enables applications to work with the power management. Instead of using the BIOS Setup options, you merely ensure that ACPI is enabled in the BIOS Setup and then manage all the power settings through Windows 98/Me, 2000/XP, or later.

Tables 5.28 and 5.29 show the typical power settings found in a managed system.

Table 5.28   Typical Power Settings for a Managed System

Feature	Options	Description
ACPI	—	Selects a submenu that sets the ACPI power management options.
After Power Failure	Last State (default) Stay Off Power On	Specifies the mode of operation if an AC power loss occurs. Last State restores the computer to the power state it was in before the power loss. Stay Off keeps the computer powered off until the power button is pressed. Power On boots the computer when power is restored.
Wake on PCI PME	Stay Off (default) Power On	Specifies how the computer responds when system power is off and a PCI power management event occurs.

Settings based on the BIOS used in the Intel D875PBZ motherboard. Used by permission of Intel Corporation.

Table 5.29   ACPI Submenu

Feature	Options	Description
ACPI Suspend State	S3 State (default) S1 State	S3 consumes less power, but some drivers might not support this state. S1 is the safest mode but consumes more power.
Wake on LAN from S5	Stay Off (default) Power On	In ACPI stay-off mode only, it determines how the system responds to a LAN wake-up event.

Settings based on the BIOS used in the Intel D875PBZ motherboard. Used by permission of Intel Corporation.

When in Standby mode, the BIOS reduces power consumption by spinning down hard drives and reducing power to or turning off monitors that comply with Video Electronics Standards Organization (VESA) and Display Power Management Signaling (DPMS). While in Standby mode, the system can still respond to external interrupts, such as those from keyboards, mice, fax/modems, or network adapters. For example, any keyboard or mouse activity brings the system out of Standby mode and immediately restores power to the monitor.

In most systems, the operating system takes over most of the power management settings, and in some cases, it can even override the BIOS settings. This is definitely true if the operating system and motherboard both support ACPI.

Some systems feature additional power management settings in their BIOS. These options are listed in "Additional Power Management Settings" in the Technical Reference section of the DVD packaged with this book.

Boot Menu (Boot Sequence, Order)

The Boot menu is used for setting the boot features and the boot sequence (through submenus). If your operating system includes a bootable CD—Windows XP, for example—use this menu to change the boot drive order to check your CD before your hard drive. Table 5.30 shows the functions and settings available on a typical motherboard.

Table 5.30   Typical Boot Menu Settings

Feature	Options	Description
Silent Boot	Enabled (default) Disabled	Enabled displays the OEM graphic instead of POST messages. Disabled displays normal POST messages.
Add-On ROM Display Mode	Enabled (default) Disabled	Enables/disables the splash screen for add-in cards.
Intel Rapid BIOS Boot	Enabled (default) Disabled	Enables the computer to boot with or without running certain POST tests.
PXE Boot to LAN	Disabled (default) Enabled	Disables/enables PXE boot from LAN. When set to Enabled, you must reboot for the Intel Boot Agent device to be available in the boot Device menu.
USB Boot	Enabled (default) Disabled	Enables/disables booting from USB devices.
Boot Device Priority	—	Selects a submenu that specifies the boot sequence from the available types of boot devices.
Hard Disk Drives*	—	Selects a submenu that specifies the boot sequence from the available hard disk drives.
Removable Devices*	—	Selects a submenu that specifies the boot sequence from the available removable devices.
ATAPI CD-ROM Drives*	—	Selects a submenu that specifies the boot sequence from the available ATAPI CD-ROM drives.

This feature is displayed only if this type of device is present.

Settings based on the BIOS used in the Intel D875PBZ motherboard. Used by permission of Intel Corporation.

Using this menu, you can configure which devices your system boots from and in which order the devices are sequenced. From this menu, you also can access Hard Drive and Removable Devices submenus, which enable you to configure the ordering of these devices in the boot sequence. For example, you can set hard drives to be the first boot choice, and then in the hard drive submenu, decide to boot from the secondary drive first and the primary drive second. Normally, the default with two drives would be the other way around.

Some recent systems also enable you to boot from external USB drives, such as Zip or LS-120 SuperDisk drives.

Boot Device Priority Submenu

This submenu is used to select the order in which boot devices will be read to start the system. Table 5.31 shows the options found on a typical motherboard.

Table 5.31 Boot Device Priority Submenu

Feature	Options	Description
1st Boot Device 2nd Boot Device 3rd Boot Device 4th Boot Device	Removable (Floppy) Hard Drive device ATAPI CD-ROM device Disabled	Specifies the boot sequence according to the device type. The default settings for the first through fourth boot devices are: 1. Removable, 2. Hard Drive, 3. ATAPI CD-ROM, 4. Disabled

Settings based on the BIOS used in the Intel D875PBZ motherboard. Used by permission of Intel Corporation.

If more than four boot devices are available, they are also displayed in this submenu.

The Hard Disk Drives submenu (not shown) for the D875PBZ motherboard lists up to 12 hard disks, enabling you to choose the preferred boot device; older systems usually list only primary and secondary master and slave (four) drives. This BIOS option enables you to install more than 1 bootable hard disk in your computer and select which one you want to boot from at a BIOS level, rather than by using a boot manager program. If you need to work with multiple operating systems, this menu can be very useful.

The Removable Devices and ATAPI CD-ROM Drives submenus (not shown) list up to four devices of each type, enabling you to select from which removable device or ATAPI drive to boot. On older systems, these options might be included in the boot sequence menu. Some motherboards also list Zip and SCSI drives as bootable drives.

Exit Menu

The Exit menu is for exiting the Setup program, saving changes, and loading and saving defaults. Table 5.32 shows the typical selections found in most motherboard BIOSs.

Table 5.32 Typical Exit Menu Settings

Feature	Description
Exit Saving Changes	Exits and saves the changes in CMOS RAM.
Exit Discarding Changes	Exits without saving any changes made in the BIOS Setup.
Load Optimal Defaults	Loads the factory (optimal) default values for all the Setup options.
Load Custom Defaults	Loads the custom defaults for Setup options.
Save Custom Defaults	Saves the current values as custom defaults in CMOS RAM. Normally, the BIOS reads the saved Setup values from CMOS RAM. If this memory is corrupted, the BIOS reads the custom defaults. If no custom defaults are set, the BIOS reads the factory defaults from the flash ROM.
Discard Changes	Discards changes without exiting Setup. The option values present when the computer was turned on are used.

Settings based on the BIOS used in the Intel D875PBZ motherboard. Used by permission of Intel Corporation.

After you have selected an optimum set of BIOS Setup settings, you can save them using the Save Custom Defaults option. This enables you to quickly restore your settings if they are corrupted or lost. All BIOS settings are stored in the CMOS RAM memory, which is powered by a battery attached to the motherboard.

Additional BIOS Setup Features

Some systems have additional features in their BIOS Setup screens, which might not be found in all BIOSs. Some of the more common features you might see are listed in Table 5.33.

Table 5.33   Additional BIOS Setup Features

Feature	Description
CPU Hyper-threading	Displayed on motherboards designed for use with the Intel Pentium 4 3.06GHz and faster processors with HT Technology when such processors are installed. When enabled, this feature enables hyper-threading for faster performance when multiple applications are running.
PC Health (menu)	This menu can display information such as CPU Vcore; 3.3V, 5V, and 12V actual voltage values; chassis and processor temperature; and fan speeds. The information can be used by system management programs to warn you of problems or shut down the computer automatically.
Serial ATA Controller	When enabled, Serial ATA (SATA) drives can be used.
IEEE-1394a Port	When enabled, you can use IEEE-1394a ports for DV camcorders, external hard drives, and other IEEE-1394a devices.
ATA RAID Controller	When enabled, additional ATA ports provided for RAID or individual ATA drives can be used.
Virus Warning	When enabled, you receive a warning message if a program attempts to write to the boot sector or the partition table of the hard disk drive. If you get this warning during normal operation, you should run an antivirus program to see whether an infection has occurred. This feature protects only the master boot sector, not the entire hard drive. Note that programs that usually write to the master boot sector, such as FDISK, can trigger the virus warning message.
CPU Internal Cache/ External Cache	This allows you to disable the L1 (internal) and L2 (external) CPU caches. This is often used when testing memory, in which case you don't want the cache functioning. For normal operation, both caches should be enabled.
Quick Power On Self Test	When enabled, this reduces the amount of time required to run the POST. A quick POST skips certain steps, such as the memory test. If you trust your system, you can enable the quick POST, but in most cases I recommend leaving it disabled so you get the full-length POST version.
Swap Floppy Drive	This field is functional only in systems with two floppy drives. Selecting Enabled assigns physical drive B: to logical drive A: and physical drive A: to logical drive B:.
Boot Up Floppy Seek	When enabled, the BIOS tests (seeks) floppy drives to determine whether they have 40 or 80 tracks. Only 360KB floppy drives have 40 tracks; drives with 720KB, 1.2MB, and 1.44MB capacity all have 80 tracks. Because very few modern PCs have 40-track floppy drives, you can disable this function to save time.
Boot Up System Speed	Select High to boot at the default CPU speed; select Low to boot at a simulated 8MHz speed. The 8MHz option often was used in the past with certain copy-protected programs, which would fail the protection scheme if booted at full speed. This option is not used today.
Gate A20 Option	Gate A20 refers to the way the system addresses memory above 1MB (extended memory). When set to Fast, the system chipset controls Gate A20. When set to Normal, a pin in the keyboard controller controls Gate A20. Setting Gate A20 to Fast improves system speed, particularly with protected-mode operating systems such as Windows 9x and Windows 2000/XP.

Table 5.33   Continued

Feature	Description
Typematic Rate Setting	When disabled, the following two items (Typematic Rate and Typematic Delay) are irrelevant. Keystrokes repeat at a rate determined by the keyboard controller in your system. When enabled, you can select a typematic rate and typematic delay.
Typematic Rate (Chars/Sec)	When the typematic rate setting is enabled, you can select a typematic rate (the rate at which characters repeat when you hold down a key) of 6, 8, 10, 12, 15, 20, 24, or 30 characters per second.
Typematic Delay (Msec)	When the typematic rate setting is enabled, you can select a typematic delay (the delay before key strokes begin to repeat) of 250, 500, 750, or 1,000 milliseconds.
Security Option	If you have set a password, select whether the password is required every time the system boots or only when you enter Setup.
PS/2 Mouse Function Control	If your system has a PS/2 (motherboard) mouse port and you install a serial or USB pointing device, select Disabled.
HDD SMART Capability	SMART is an acronym for Self-Monitoring Analysis and Reporting Technology system. SMART is a hard drive self-diagnostic feature available on some ATA hard drives. Enabling this option is recommended if you use diagnostic software that can monitor SMART-compatible drives to warn you of impending failures.
Report No FDD for WIN 95	Select Yes to release IRQ6 when the system contains no floppy drive, for compatibility with Windows 95 logo certification. In the Integrated Peripherals screen, select Disabled for the Onboard FDC Controller field.
ROM Shadowing	ROM chips typically are very slow, around 150ns (nanoseconds), and operate only 8 bits at a time, whereas RAM runs 60ns or even 10ns or less and is either 32 bits or 64 bits wide in most systems. Shadowing is the copying of BIOS code from ROM into RAM, where the CPU can read the BIOS drivers at the higher speed of RAM.
Operating Frequency	Some motherboards enable you to select the FSB (front-side bus) and CPU clock multiplier speeds within the BIOS rather than through the normal motherboard-based DIP switches or jumper blocks. Select this option to enable customized settings for the CPU Clock Multiplier and CPU Frequency options.
CPU Frequency	This option enables you to vary the CPU FSB frequency from the default 66MHz, 100MHz, or 133MHz to higher values, enabling you to overclock your system.
CPU Clock Multiplier	This option enables you to vary the CPU clock multiplier from its default values to higher values *if* the CPU is not multiplier-locked. Recent and current Intel CPUs ignore nonstandard CPU clock multiplier settings, but AMD Athlon and Duron CPUs can be overclocked with this option.
CPU Vcore Setting	This option enables you to vary the core voltage of the CPU to improve the stability of your system during overclocking or to install CPUs not specifically supported by the default Automatic voltage settings.

Plug and Play BIOS

Traditionally, installing and configuring devices in PCs has been a difficult process. During installation, the user is faced with the task of configuring the new card by selecting the IRQ, I/O ports, and DMA channel. In the past, users were required to move jumpers or set switches on the add-in cards to control these settings. They needed to know exactly which resources were already in use so they could find a set of resources that did not conflict with the devices already in the system. If a conflict existed, the system might not boot and the device might fail or cause the conflicting hardware to fail.

PnP is technology designed to prevent configuration problems and provide users with the capability to easily expand a PC. With PnP, the user simply plugs in the new card and the system configures it automatically for proper operation.

PnP is composed of three principal components:

- Plug and Play BIOS
- Extended System Configuration Data (ESCD)
- Plug and Play operating system

The PnP BIOS initiates the configuration of the PnP cards during the bootup process. If the cards previously were installed, the BIOS reads the information from ESCD, initializes the cards, and boots the system. During the installation of new PnP cards, the BIOS consults the ESCD to determine which system resources are available and needed for the add-in card. If the BIOS is capable of finding sufficient available resources, it configures the card. However, if the BIOS is incapable of locating sufficient available resources, the Plug and Play routines in the operating system complete the configuration process. During the configuration process, the configuration registers (in flash BIOS) on the card and the ESCD are updated with the new configuration data.

PnP Device IDs

All Plug and Play devices must contain a Plug and Play device ID to enable the operating system to uniquely recognize the device so it can load the appropriate driver software. Each device manufacturer is responsible for assigning the Plug and Play ID for each product and storing it in the hardware.

Each manufacturer of Plug and Play devices must be assigned an industry-unique, three-character vendor ID. Then, the device manufacturer is responsible for assigning a unique product ID to each individual product model. After an ID is assigned to a product model, it must not be assigned to any other product model manufactured by the same company (that is, one that uses the same vendor ID).

Note

For a comprehensive, printable list of PnP device IDs, see "PnP Device IDs" on pages 401–408 in *Upgrading and Repairing PCs, 11th Edition*, included in the Previous Editions section of the disc accompanying this book.

ACPI

ACPI stands for Advanced Configuration and Power Interface, which defines a standard method for integrating power management as well as system configuration features throughout a PC, including the hardware, operating system, and application software. ACPI goes far beyond the previous standard, called Advanced Power Management (APM), which consists mainly of processor, hard disk, and display control. ACPI controls not only power, but also all the Plug and Play hardware configuration throughout the system. With ACPI, system configuration (Plug and Play) as well as power management configuration is no longer controlled via the BIOS Setup; it is controlled entirely within the operating system instead.

ACPI enables the system to automatically turn peripherals on and off (such as CD-ROMs, network cards, hard disk drives, and printers), as well as external devices connected to the PC (such as VCRs, televisions, telephones, and stereos). ACPI technology also enables peripherals to turn on or activate the PC. For example, inserting a tape into a VCR can turn on the PC, which could then activate a large-screen television and high-fidelity sound system.

ACPI enables system designers to implement a range of power management features with various hardware designs while using the same operating system driver. ACPI also uses the Plug and Play BIOS data structures and takes control over the Plug and Play Interface, providing an operating-system-independent interface for configuration and control. ACPI is supported in Windows 98/Me, Windows 2000, XP, and later versions.

During the system setup and boot process, Windows versions supporting ACPI perform a series of checks and tests to see whether the system hardware and BIOS supports ACPI. If support for ACPI is either not detected or found to be faulty, the system typically reverts to standard Advanced Power Management control, but problems can also cause a lockup with either a red or blue screen with an ACPI error code.

Red screens indicate that the problem is probably related to hardware or the BIOS. Blue screens, on the other hand, indicate that the problem is probably related to software or is an obscure problem. The ACPI error codes are described in Table 5.34.

Table 5.34 ACPI Error Codes

Error Code	Description
1xxx -	Indicates an error during the initialization phase of the ACPI driver and usually means the driver can't read one or more of the ACPI tables
2xxx -	Indicates an ACPI machine language (AML) interpreter error
3xxx -	Indicates an error within the ACPI driver event handler
4xxx -	Indicates thermal management errors
5xxx -	Indicates device power management errors

Virtually all these errors are the result of partial or incomplete ACPI implementations or incompatibilities in either the BIOS or device drivers. If you encounter any of these errors, contact your motherboard manufacturer for an updated BIOS or the device manufacturers for updated drivers.

Initializing a PnP Device

One responsibility of a Plug and Play BIOS during POST is to isolate and initialize all Plug and Play cards and assign them a valid Card Select Number (CSN). After a CSN is assigned, the system BIOS can then designate resources to the cards. The BIOS is responsible only for the configuration of boot devices; all the remaining Plug and Play devices can be configured dynamically by the operating system software.

The following steps outline a typical flow of a Plug and Play BIOS during the POST:

1. Disable all configurable devices.
2. Identify all Plug and Play devices.
3. Construct a resource map of resources that are statically allocated to devices in the system.
4. Enable input and output devices.
5. Perform ISA ROM scan.
6. Configure the boot device.
7. Enable Plug and Play ISA and other configurable devices.
8. Start the bootstrap loader.

If the loaded operating system is Plug and Play compliant, it takes over management of the system resources. Any unconfigured Plug and Play devices are configured by the appropriate system software or the Plug and Play operating system.

At this point, the operating system is loaded and takes control over Plug and Play system resources. Using the Device Manager in the operating system (such as Windows), the user can now control any Plug and Play devices.

BIOS Error Messages

When a PC system is first powered on, the system runs a POST. If errors are encountered during the POST, you usually see a text error message displayed onscreen. Errors that occur very early in the POST might happen before the video card is initialized. These types of errors can't be displayed, so the system uses two other alternatives for communicating the error message. One is beeping—the system beeps the speaker in a specific pattern that indicates which error has occurred.

▶▶ For detailed lists of the BIOS POST beep codes, see Chapter 24, "PC Diagnostics, Testing, and Maintenance," p. 1285.

The other alternative is to send a hexadecimal error code to I/O port address 80h, which can be read by a special card in one of the bus slots. When the ROM BIOS is performing the POST, in most systems the results of these tests are continuously sent to I/O Port 80h so they can be monitored by special diagnostics cards called POST cards (see Figure 5.11). These tests sometimes are called *manufacturing tests* because they were designed into the system for testing systems on the assembly line without a video display attached.

Figure 5.11 A typical POST card with two-digit hexadecimal code display (left) and a POST card in operation (right).

The POST cards have a two-digit hexadecimal display used to report the number of the currently executing test routine. Before executing each test, a hexadecimal numeric code is sent to the port and then the test is run. If the test fails and locks up the machine, the hexadecimal code of the last test being executed remains on the card's display.

Note

The DVD accompanying this book contains an exhaustive listing of additional error codes, error messages, and BIOS POST codes for BIOSs from Phoenix, AMI, Award, Microid Research, and IBM.

Many tests are executed in a system before the video display card is enabled, especially if the display is EGA or VGA. Therefore, many errors can occur that would lock up the system before the system could possibly display an error code through the video system. Because not all these errors generate beep codes, to most normal troubleshooting procedures, a system with this type of problem (such as a memory failure in Bank 0) would appear completely "dead." By using one of the commercially available POST cards, however, you can often diagnose the problem.

These codes are completely BIOS dependent because the card does nothing but display the codes sent to it. Some BIOSs have more detailed POST procedures and therefore send more informative codes. POST cards can be purchased from JDR Microdevices or other sources and are available in both ISA and PCI bus versions.

For simple but otherwise fatal errors that can't be displayed onscreen, most of the BIOS versions also send audio codes that can be used to help diagnose such problems. The audio codes are similar to POST codes, but they are read by listening to the speaker beep rather than by using a special card.

The following section details the text error codes for all the popular BIOS versions. For detailed lists of the BIOS POST beep codes, see Chapter 24, "PC Diagnostics, Testing, and Maintenance."

General BIOS Boot Text Error Messages

During the boot process, the bootstrap loader routine in the motherboard ROM BIOS reads the first physical sector of each of the bootable drives or devices, which is cylinder 0, head 0, sector 1 in CHS mode or logical block address 0 in LBA mode. The code from the first sector is loaded into RAM, and the last two bytes are checked to see whether they match a signature value of 55AAh. If the signature bytes match, that tells the ROM that the first sector contains a valid MBR and that the ROM can continue by transferring control to the MBR code.

If the last two bytes of the first physical sector do not match 55AAh, the ROM continues by checking the first physical sector of the next bootable device in the boot sequence until it either finds one with a valid MBR or runs out of devices to check. If after checking all the drives or devices in the boot sequence, none are found to have the proper signature bytes indicating a valid MBR, the ROM invokes an interrupt 18h that calls a subroutine that displays an error message. The specific text or wording of the message varies according to the ROM manufacturer and version. The messages are detailed in the following section.

ROM BIOS Messages Indicating Boot Failure (No Valid MBR Found)

With no valid MBR or bootable device found, systems with a very old IBM BIOS display the infamous ROM BASIC interpreter, which looks like this:

```
The IBM Personal Computer Basic
Version C1.10 Copyright IBM Corp 1981
62940 Bytes free
Ok
```

IBM ROM BASIC

The ROMs of most PCs are similar to the original IBM systems with which they are compatible—with the exception of the ROM BASIC interpreter (also called Cassette BASIC). It might come as a surprise to some PC users, but the original IBM PC actually had a jack on the rear of the system for connecting a cassette tape recorder. This was to be used for loading programs and data to or from a cassette tape. IBM included the cassette port because cassette tapes were used by several early personal computers (including the Apple) because floppy drives were very expensive and hard disks were not even an option yet. However, floppy drives came down in price quickly right at the time the PC was first released, and the cassette port never appeared on any subsequent IBM systems. The cassette port also never appeared on any PC-compatible systems because floppy drives were cheap by the time they came out.

The reason for having BASIC in ROM was so the original PC could come standard with only 16KB of memory and no floppy drives in the base configuration. Many computer users at the time either wrote their own programs in the BASIC language or ran BASIC programs written by others. The BASIC language interpreter built in to the ROM BIOS of these early IBM systems was designed to access the cassette port on the back of the system, and by having the interpreter in ROM, all the 16KB of RAM could be used to store a program.

Even after the cassette port was eliminated, IBM left the BASIC code in the motherboard ROM until the early 1990s! I liken this to our having an appendix. The ROM BASIC in those IBM systems is sort of like a vestigial organ—a leftover that had some use in prehistoric evolutionary ancestors but has no function today.

You can catch a glimpse of this ROM BASIC on older IBM systems that have it by disabling all the disk drives in the system. In that case, with nothing to boot from, those systems unceremoniously dump you into the strange (vintage 1981) ROM BASIC screen.

People used to dread seeing this because it usually meant that the floppy disk or hard disk they were trying to boot from had become corrupted or had failed. Because no compatible systems ever had the BASIC interpreter in ROM, they came up with different messages to display for the same situations in which an IBM system would invoke this BASIC. The most confusing of these was the message from AMI BIOS, which simply said **NO ROM BASIC - SYSTEM HALTED**, which really meant that the system was incapable of booting.

With no valid MBR or bootable device found, systems with a more recent IBM BIOS display a screen using text graphic characters that look similar to Figure 5.12.

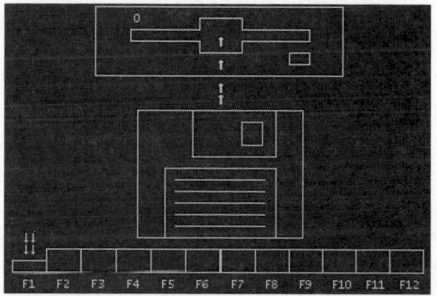

Figure 5.12   When the PC can't find the master boot record on a modern IBM BIOS, you are confronted with this graphic.

The meaning here is, "Insert a bootable floppy disk into the A: drive and press the F1 key."

With no valid MBR or bootable device found, systems with an AMI BIOS display the following message:

```
NO ROM BASIC - SYSTEM HALTED
```

This message is confusing to some because it seems to point to a problem with ROM BASIC, which of course is not what it really means! The AMI ROM does not include a BASIC interpreter in the ROM (neither do any other ROMs except those found in very old IBM machines), so instead of jumping into BASIC or displaying a useful message indicating there are no bootable devices, it displays this confusing message. The real meaning is the same as for all these messages, which is to say that none of the bootable devices in the boot sequence were found to contain signature bytes indicating a valid MBR in their first physical sectors.

With no valid MBR or bootable device found, systems with a Compaq BIOS display the following message:

```
Non-System disk or disk error
replace and strike any key when ready
```

This is another confusing message because this very same (or similar) error message is contained in the DOS/Windows 9X/Me VBR and normally is displayed if the system files are missing or corrupted. So, if you see this message on a Compaq system, you can't be sure whether the problem is in the MBR, VBR, or the system files, which makes tracking down and solving the problem more difficult.

With no valid MBR or bootable device found, systems with an Award BIOS display the following message:

```
DISK BOOT FAILURE, INSERT SYSTEM DISK AND PRESS ENTER
```

So far, that appears to be the least confusing of these messages. You don't need a secret decoder ring to figure out what it is really trying to say.

With no valid MBR or bootable device found, systems with a Phoenix BIOS display either this message:

```
No boot device available -
strike F1 to retry boot, F2 for setup utility
```

or this one:

```
No boot sector on fixed disk -
strike F1 to retry boot, F2 for setup utility
```

Which of these two messages you see depends on whether no boot devices were found or readable, or a boot sector could be read but was found not to have the proper signature bytes.

Although the message displayed varies from BIOS to BIOS, the causes are the same for all of them. Several things can cause these messages to be displayed, and many of them relate to the MBR.

The primary causes are disks that are new (have never been partitioned) or that have had the MBR corrupted.

The MBR, including the signature bytes, is written to the hard disk by the FDISK, DISKPART, or Disk Management program. When a drive is new or freshly low-level formatted, all the sectors are initialized with a default pattern of bytes. At that point, the first sector contains a test pattern or all 0s and the last two bytes of the sector do not contain the 55AAh signature. In other words, these ROM error messages are exactly what you see if you attempt to boot from a new hard disk or one that has been low-level formatted but not yet partitioned.

Now consider another situation that can cause these messages. If the signature bytes are correct, the BIOS executes the MBR code, which performs a test of the Boot Indicator bytes in each of the four partition table entries. These bytes are at offset 446 (1BEh), 462 (1CEh), 478 (1DEh), and 494 (1EEh), respectively. They are used to indicate which of the four possible primary partition table entries contains an active (bootable) partition. A value of 80h at any of these byte offsets indicates that the particular table contains the active partition, whereas all other values must be 00h. If more than one of these bytes is 80h (indicating multiple active partitions), or any of the byte values is anything other than 80h or 00h, you see the following error message:

```
Invalid partition table
```

If all these four boot indicator bytes are 00h—which indicates that no active (bootable) partitions exist—then the MBR returns control to the motherboard ROM. Also, if no other bootable devices exist, interrupt 18h is called and displays the same error messages as listed earlier.

▶▶ See "Master Boot Record," p. 1355.

This is exactly what occurs if you were to remove the existing partitions from a drive but had not created new partitions on the drive, or if you had failed to make one of the partitions Active (bootable) during partitioning before rebooting your system.

▶▶ For more information on repairing or restoring the master boot sector (MBR), see Chapter 25, "File Systems and Data Recovery," p. 1353.

Another cause for these errors can occur with hard disks that are 8.4GB in size or less, which run in CHS mode. The problem is caused by tampering with the translation mode in the system BIOS for drives less than 8.4GB in size. Translation is used by drives between 528MB and 8.4GB, which alters the reported CHS geometry of the drive into a format that enables the entire disk (up to 8.4GB) to be used by DOS and Windows. Typically, three settings exist for translation: It can be disabled (often indicated by a setting of normal) or enabled using either CHS or LBA values. Translation using CHS values is often indicated by a setting of large, and translation using LBA values is indicated by a setting of LBA. If a drive is partitioned and formatted with LBA translation and the setting is later changed to CHS (often indicated as large), the bootstrap loader in the BIOS translates drive sector locations differently and might not properly load the MBR or make the proper jump from the MBR to the VBR of the bootable volume. This can cause one of the previously discussed error messages to appear, or it can cause the MBR to display the following message:

```
Missing operating system
```

Thus, if you see such errors on a system with a hard drive between 528MB (504MiB) and 8.4GB (7.9GiB), be sure to check the translation settings for the drive. On some of the older AMI BIOS Hi-Flex and WinBIOS (graphical) versions, the translation mode setting is not on the same screen as the hard disk setup but is buried in the Advanced or Built-in Peripherals setup screens where it can be turned off by autoconfiguring BIOS setup options.

CHAPTER 6

Memory

Memory Basics

This chapter discusses memory from both a physical and logical point of view. First, we'll examine what memory is, where it fits into the PC architecture, and how it works. Then we'll look at the various types of memory, speeds, and packaging of the chips and memory modules you can buy and install.

This chapter also covers the logical layout of memory, defining the various areas and their uses from the system's point of view. Because the logical layout and uses are within the "mind" of the processor, memory mapping and logical layout remain perhaps the most difficult subjects to grasp in the PC universe. This chapter contains useful information that removes the mysteries associated with memory and enables you to get the most out of your system.

Memory is the workspace for the computer's processor. It is a temporary storage area where the programs and data being operated on by the processor must reside. Memory storage is considered temporary because the data and programs remain there only as long as the computer has electrical power or is not reset. Before being shut down or reset, any data that has been changed should be saved to a more permanent storage device (usually a hard disk) so it can be reloaded into memory in the future.

Memory often is called *RAM*, for *random access memory*. Main memory is called RAM because you can randomly (as opposed to sequentially) access any location in memory. This designation is somewhat misleading and often misinterpreted. Read-only memory (ROM), for example, is also randomly accessible, yet is usually differentiated from the system RAM because it maintains data without power and can't normally be written to. Disk memory is also randomly accessible, but we don't consider that RAM either.

Over the years, the definition of RAM has changed from a simple acronym to become something that means the primary memory workspace the processor uses to run programs, which usually is constructed of a type of chip called dynamic RAM (DRAM). One of the characteristics of DRAM chips (and therefore RAM in general) is that they store data dynamically, which really has two meanings. One meaning is that the information can be written to RAM repeatedly at any time. The other has to do with the fact that DRAM requires the data to be refreshed (essentially rewritten) every 15ms (milliseconds) or so. A type of RAM called static RAM (SRAM) does not require the periodic refreshing. An important characteristic of RAM in general is that data is stored only as long as the memory has electrical power.

When we talk about a computer's memory, we usually mean the RAM or physical memory in the system, which is mainly the memory chips or modules the processor uses to store primary active programs and data. This often is confused with the term *storage*, which should be used when referring to things such as disk and tape drives (although they can be used as a form of RAM called virtual memory).

RAM can refer to both the physical chips that make up the memory in the system and the logical mapping and layout of that memory. *Logical mapping* and *layout* refer to how the memory addresses are mapped to actual chips and what address locations contain which types of system information.

People new to computers often confuse main memory (RAM) with disk storage because both have capacities that are expressed in similar megabyte or gigabyte terms. The best analogy to explain the relationship between memory and disk storage I've found is to think of an office with a desk and a file cabinet.

In this popular analogy, the file cabinet represents the system's hard disk, where both programs and data are stored for long-term safekeeping. The desk represents the system's main memory, which allows the person working at the desk (acting as the processor) direct access to any files placed on it. Files represent the programs and documents you can "load" into the memory. To work on a particular file, it must first be retrieved from the cabinet and placed on the desk. If the desk is large enough, you might be able to have several files open on it at one time; likewise, if your system has more memory, you can run more or larger programs and work on more or larger documents.

Adding hard disk space to a system is similar to putting a bigger file cabinet in the office—more files can be permanently stored. And adding more memory to a system is like getting a bigger desk—you can work on more programs and data at the same time.

One difference between this analogy and the way things really work in a computer is that when a file is loaded into memory, it is a copy of the file that is actually loaded; the original still resides on the hard disk. Because of the temporary nature of memory, any files that have been changed after being loaded into memory must then be saved back to the hard disk before the system is powered off (which erases the memory). If the changed file in memory is not saved, the original copy of the file on the hard disk remains unaltered. This is like saying that any changes made to files left on the desktop are discarded when the office is closed, although the original files are still preserved in the cabinet.

Memory temporarily stores programs when they are running, along with the data being used by those programs. RAM chips are sometimes termed *volatile storage* because when you turn off your computer or an electrical outage occurs, whatever is stored in RAM is lost unless you saved it to your hard drive. Because of the volatile nature of RAM, many computer users make it a habit to save their work frequently. (Some software applications can do timed backups automatically.)

Launching a computer program brings files into RAM, and as long as they are running, computer programs reside in RAM. The CPU executes programmed instructions in RAM and also stores results in RAM. RAM stores your keystrokes when you use a word processor and also stores numbers used in calculations. Telling a program to save your data instructs the program to store RAM contents on your hard drive as a file.

Physically, the *main memory* in a system is a collection of chips or modules containing chips that are usually plugged into the motherboard. These chips or modules vary in their electrical and physical designs and must be compatible with the system into which they are being installed to function properly. This chapter discusses the various types of chips and modules that can be installed in different systems.

Next to the processor and motherboard, memory can be one of the more expensive components in a modern PC, although the total amount spent on memory for a typical system has declined over the past few years. Before the big memory price crash in mid-1996, memory had maintained a fairly consistent price for many years of about $40 per megabyte. A typical configuration back then of 16MB cost more than $600. In fact, memory was so expensive at that time that it was worth more than its weight in gold. These high prices caught the attention of criminals and memory module manufacturers were robbed at gunpoint in several large heists. These robberies were partially induced by the fact that memory was so valuable, the demand was high, and stolen chips or modules were virtually impossible to trace. After the rash of armed robberies and other thefts, memory module manufacturers began posting armed guards and implementing beefed-up security procedures.

By the end of 1996, memory prices had cooled considerably to about $4 per megabyte—a tenfold price drop in less than a year. Prices continued to fall after the major crash until they were at or below 50 cents per megabyte in 1997. All seemed well, until events in 1998 conspired to create a spike in memory prices, increasing them by four times their previous levels. The main culprit was Intel, who had driven the industry to support a then-new type of memory called Rambus DRAM (RDRAM) and then failed to deliver the supporting chipsets on time. The industry was caught in a bind by shifting production to a type of memory for which there were no chipsets or motherboards to plug into, which then created a shortage of the existing (and popular) SDRAM memory. An earthquake in Taiwan during that year served as the icing on the cake, disrupting production and furthering the spike in prices.

Since then, things have cooled considerably, and memory prices have dropped to all-time lows, with actual prices of under 20 cents per megabyte. In particular, 2001 was a disastrous year in the semiconductor industry, prompted by the dot-com crash as well as worldwide events, and sales dropped well below that of previous years. This conspired to bring memory prices down further than they had ever been and even forced some companies to merge or go out of business.

Memory is less expensive now than ever, but its useful life has become much shorter. New types of memory are being adopted more quickly than before, and any new systems you purchase now most likely will not accept the same memory as your existing ones. In an upgrade or a repair situation, that means you often have to change the memory if you change the motherboard. The chance that you can reuse the memory in an existing motherboard when upgrading to a new one is slim.

Because of this, you should understand all the various types of memory on the market today, so you can best determine which types are required by which systems, and thus more easily plan for future upgrades and repairs.

To better understand physical memory in a system, you should see where and how it fits into the system. Three main types of physical memory are used in modern PCs:

- *ROM.* Read-only memory
- *DRAM.* Dynamic random access memory
- *SRAM.* Static RAM

ROM

Read-only memory, or ROM, is a type of memory that can permanently or semipermanently store data. It is called read-only because it is either impossible or difficult to write to. ROM also is often referred to as *nonvolatile memory* because any data stored in ROM remains there, even if the power is turned off. As such, ROM is an ideal place to put the PC's startup instructions—that is, the software that boots the system.

Note that ROM and RAM are not opposites, as some people seem to believe. Both are simply types of memory. In fact, ROM could be classified as technically a subset of the system's RAM. In other words, a portion of the system's random access memory address space is mapped into one or more ROM chips. This is necessary to contain the software that enables the PC to boot up; otherwise, the processor would have no program in memory to execute when it was powered on.

◀◀   For more information on ROM, see "Motherboard BIOS," p. 402.

The main ROM BIOS is contained in a ROM chip on the motherboard, but there are also adapter cards with ROMs on them as well. ROMs on adapter cards contain auxiliary BIOS routines and drivers needed by the particular card, especially for those cards that must be active early in the boot process, such as video cards. Cards that don't need drivers active at boot time typically don't have a ROM because those drivers can be loaded from the hard disk later in the boot process.

Most systems today use a type of ROM called electrically erasable programmable ROM (EEPROM), which is a form of Flash memory. Flash is a truly nonvolatile memory that is rewritable, enabling users to easily update the ROM or firmware in their motherboards or any other components (video cards, SCSI cards, peripherals, and so on).

DRAM

Dynamic RAM (DRAM) is the type of memory chip used for most of the main memory in a modern PC. The main advantages of DRAM are that it is very dense, meaning you can pack a lot of bits into a very small chip, and it is inexpensive, which makes purchasing large amounts of memory affordable.

The memory cells in a DRAM chip are tiny capacitors that retain a charge to indicate a bit. The problem with DRAM is that it is dynamic. Also, because of the design, it must be constantly refreshed; otherwise, the electrical charges in the individual memory capacitors will drain and the data will be lost. Refresh occurs when the system memory controller takes a tiny break and accesses all the rows of data in the memory chips. Most systems have a memory controller (normally built into the North Bridge portion of the motherboard chipset), which is set for an industry-standard refresh rate of 15ms (milliseconds). This means that every 15ms, all the rows in the memory are automatically read to refresh the data.

◀◀   See "Chipsets," p. 239.

Refreshing the memory unfortunately takes processor time away from other tasks because each refresh cycle takes several CPU cycles to complete. In older systems, the refresh cycling could take up to 10% or more of the total CPU time, but with modern systems running in the multi-gigahertz range, refresh overhead is now on the order of a fraction of a percent or less of the total CPU time. Some systems allow you to alter the refresh timing parameters via the CMOS Setup, but be aware that increasing the time between refresh cycles to speed up your system can allow some of the memory cells to begin draining, which can cause random soft memory errors to appear. A *soft error* is a data error that is not caused by a defective chip. It is usually safer to stick with the recommended or default refresh timing. Because refresh consumes less than 1% of modern system overall bandwidth, altering the refresh rate has little effect on performance. It is almost always best to use default or automatic settings for any memory timings in the BIOS Setup. Many modern systems don't allow changes to memory timings and are permanently set to automatic settings. On an automatic setting, the motherboard reads the timing parameters out of the serial presence detect (SPD) ROM found on the memory module and sets the cycling speeds to match.

DRAMs use only one transistor and capacitor pair per bit, which makes them very dense, offering more memory capacity per chip than other types of memory. Currently, DRAM chips are available with densities of up to 1Gb or more. This means that DRAM chips are available with one billion or more transistors! Compare this to a Pentium 4, which has 55 million transistors, and it makes the processor look wimpy by comparison. The difference is that in a memory chip, the transistors and capacitors are all consistently arranged in a (normally square) grid of simple repetitive structures, unlike the processor, which is a much more complex circuit of different structures and elements interconnected in a highly irregular fashion.

The transistor for each DRAM bit cell reads the charge state of the adjacent capacitor. If the capacitor is charged, the cell is read to contain a 1; no charge indicates a 0. The charge in the tiny capacitors is constantly draining, which is why the memory must be refreshed constantly. Even a momentary power interruption, or anything that interferes with the refresh cycles, can cause a DRAM memory cell to lose the charge and therefore the data. If this happens in a running system, it can lead to blue screens, global protection faults, corrupted files, and any number of system crashes.

DRAM is used in PC systems because it is inexpensive and the chips can be densely packed, so a lot of memory capacity can fit in a small space. Unfortunately, DRAM is also slow, typically much slower than the processor. For this reason, many types of DRAM architectures have been developed to improve performance. These architectures are covered later in the chapter.

Cache Memory: SRAM

Another distinctly different type of memory exists that is significantly faster than most types of DRAM. SRAM stands for static RAM, which is so named because it does not need the periodic refresh rates like DRAM. Because of how SRAMs are designed, not only are refresh rates unnecessary, but SRAM is much faster than DRAM and much more capable of keeping pace with modern processors.

SRAM memory is available in access times of 2ns or less, so it can keep pace with processors running 500MHz or faster. This is because of the SRAM design, which calls for a cluster of six transistors for each bit of storage. The use of transistors but no capacitors means that refresh rates are not necessary because there are no capacitors to lose their charges over time. As long as there is power, SRAM remembers what is stored. With these attributes, why don't we use SRAM for all system memory? The answers are simple.

Compared to DRAM, SRAM is much faster but also much lower in density and much more expensive (see Table 6.1). The lower density means that SRAM chips are physically larger and store fewer bits overall. The high number of transistors and the clustered design mean that SRAM chips are both physically larger and much more expensive to produce than DRAM chips. For example, a DRAM module might contain 64MB of RAM or more, whereas SRAM modules of the same approximate physical size would have room for only 2MB or so of data and would cost the same as the 64MB DRAM module. Basically, SRAM is up to 30 times larger physically and up to 30 times more expensive than DRAM. The high cost and physical constraints have prevented SRAM from being used as the main memory for PC systems.

Table 6.1   Comparing DRAM and SRAM

Type	Speed	Density	Cost
DRAM	Slow	High	Low
SRAM	Fast	Low	High

Even though SRAM is too expensive for PC use as main memory, PC designers have found a way to use SRAM to dramatically improve PC performance. Rather than spend the money for all RAM to be SRAM memory, which can run fast enough to match the CPU, designing in a small amount of high-speed SRAM memory, called cache memory, is much more cost-effective. The cache runs at speeds close to or even equal to the processor and is the memory from which the processor usually directly reads from and writes to. During read operations, the data in the high-speed cache memory is resupplied from the lower-speed main memory or DRAM in advance. Up until recently, DRAM was limited to about 60ns (16MHz) in speed. To convert access time in nanoseconds to MHz, use the following formula:

1 / nanoseconds × 1000 = MHz

Likewise, to convert from MHz to nanoseconds, use the following inverse formula:

1 / MHz × 1000 = nanoseconds

When PC systems were running 16MHz and less, the DRAM could fully keep pace with the motherboard and system processor and there was no need for cache. However, as soon as processors crossed the 16MHz barrier, DRAM could no longer keep pace, and that is exactly when SRAM began to enter PC system designs. This occurred back in 1986 and 1987 with the debut of systems with the 386 processor running at speeds of 16MHz and 20MHz or faster. These were among the first PC systems to employ what's called *cache memory*, a high-speed buffer made up of SRAM that directly feeds the processor. Because the cache can run at the speed of the processor, the system is designed so that the cache controller anticipates the processor's memory needs and preloads the high-speed cache memory with that data. Then, as the processor calls for a memory address, the data can be retrieved from the high-speed cache rather than the much lower-speed main memory.

Cache effectiveness is expressed as a hit ratio. This is the ratio of cache hits to total memory accesses. A *hit* occurs when the data the processor needs has been preloaded into the cache from the main memory, meaning the processor can read it from the cache. A cache *miss* is when the cache controller did not anticipate the need for a specific address and the desired data was not preloaded into the cache. In that case the processor must retrieve the data from the slower main memory, instead of the faster cache. Anytime the processor reads data from main memory, the processor must wait longer because the main memory cycles at a much slower rate than the processor. If the processor with integral on-die cache is running at 3400MHz (3.4GHz), both the processor and the integral cache would be cycling at 0.29ns, while the main memory would most likely be cycling 8.5 times more slowly at 2.5ns (200MHz DDR). Therefore, the memory would be running at only a 400MHz equivalent rate. So, every time the 3.4GHz processor reads from main memory, it would effectively slow down 8.5-fold to only 400MHz! The slowdown is accomplished by having the processor execute what are called *wait states*, which are cycles in which nothing is done; the processor essentially cools its heels while waiting for the slower main memory to return the desired data. Obviously, you don't want your processors slowing down, so cache function and design become more important as system speeds increase.

To minimize the processor being forced to read data from the slow main memory, two or three stages of cache usually exist in a modern system, called Level 1 (L1), Level 2 (L2), and Level 3 (L3). The L1 cache is also called *integral* or *internal cache* because it has always been built directly into the processor as part of the processor die (the raw chip). Because of this, L1 cache always runs at the full speed of the processor core and is the fastest cache in any system. All 486 and higher processors incorporate integral L1 cache, making them significantly faster than their predecessors. L2 cache was originally called *external cache* because it was external to the processor chip when it first appeared. Originally, this meant it was installed on the motherboard, as was the case with all 386, 486, and Pentium systems. In those systems, the L2 cache runs at motherboard and CPU bus speed because it is installed on the motherboard and is connected to the CPU bus. You typically find the L2 cache directly next to the processor socket in Pentium and earlier systems.

◀◀   See "How Cache Works," p. 68.

In the interest of improved performance, later processor designs from Intel and AMD included the L2 cache as a part of the processor. In all processors since late 1999 (and some earlier models), the L2 cache is directly incorporated as a part of the processor die just like the L1 cache. In chips with on-die L2, the cache runs at the full core speed of the processor and is much more efficient. By contrast, most processors from 1999 and earlier with integrated L2 had the L2 cache in separate chips that were external to the main processor core. The L2 cache in many of these older processors ran at only half or one-third the processor core speed. Cache speed is very important, so systems having L2 cache on the motherboard were the slowest. Including L2 inside the processor made it faster, and including it directly on the processor die (rather than as chips external to the die) is the fastest yet. Any chip that has on-die full core speed L2 cache has a distinct performance advantage over any chip that doesn't.

Processors with built-in L2 cache, whether it's on-die or not, still run the cache more quickly than any found on the motherboard. Thus, most motherboards designed for processors with built-in cache don't have any cache on the board; all the cache is contained in the processor module instead.

L3 cache has been present in high-end workstation and server processors such as the Xeon and Itanium families since 2001. The first desktop PC processor with L3 cache was the Pentium 4 Extreme Edition, a high-end chip introduced in late 2003 with 2MB of on-die L3 cache. In the future you can expect L3 cache to become more commonplace in mainstream processors because more levels of cache help mitigate the speed differential between the fast processor core and the relatively slow motherboard and main memory.

The key to understanding both cache and main memory is to see where they fit in the overall system architecture.

See Chapter 4, "Motherboards and Buses," for diagrams showing recent systems with different types of cache memory. Table 6.2 illustrates the need for and function of cache memory in modern systems.

Cache designs originally were *asynchronous*, meaning they ran at a clock speed that was not identical or in sync with the processor bus. Starting with the 430FX chipset released in early 1995, a new type of synchronous cache design was supported. It required that the chips now run in sync or at the same identical clock timing as the processor bus, further improving speed and performance. Also added at that time was a feature called *pipeline burst mode*, which reduces overall cache latency (wait states) by allowing single-cycle accesses for multiple transfers after the first one. Because both synchronous and pipeline burst capability came at the same time in new modules, specifying one usually implies the other. Synchronous pipeline burst cache allowed for about a 20% improvement in overall system performance, which was a significant jump.

The cache controller for a modern system is contained in either the North Bridge of the chipset, as with Pentium and lesser systems, or within the processor, as with the Pentium Pro/II and newer systems. The capabilities of the cache controller dictate the cache's performance and capabilities. One important thing to note is that most external cache controllers have a limitation on the amount of memory that can be cached. Often, this limit can be quite low, as with the 430TX chipset-based Pentium systems. Most original Pentium class chipsets such as the 430FX/VX/TX can cache data only within the first 64MB of system RAM. If you add more memory than that, you will see a noticeable slowdown in system performance because all data outside the first 64MB is never cached and is always accessed with all the wait states required by the slower DRAM. Depending on what software you use and where data is stored in memory, this can be significant. For example, 32-bit operating systems such as Windows load from the top down, so if you had 96MB of RAM, the operating system and applications would load directly into the upper 32MB (past 64MB), which is not cached. This results in a dramatic slowdown in overall system use. Removing the additional memory to bring the system total down to the cacheable limit of 64MB is the solution. In short, it is unwise to install more main RAM memory than your system (CPU or chipset) can cache.

Table 6.2   The Relationship Between L1 (Internal) Cache, L2 (External) Cache, and Main Memory in Modern Systems

CPU Type	Pentium	Pentium Pro	Pentium II	AMD K6-2	AMD K6-3	Duron
CPU speed	233MHz	200MHz	450MHz	550MHz	450MHz	1.3GHz
L1 cache speed	4.3ns (233MHz)	5.0ns (200MHz)	2.2ns (450MHz)	1.8ns (550MHz)	2.2ns (450MHz)	0.77ns (1.3GHz)
L1 cache size	16K	32K	32K	64K	64K	128K
L2 cache type	onboard	on-chip	on-chip	onboard	on-die	on-die
CPU/L2 speed ratio	—	1/1	1/2	—	1/1	1/1
L2 cache speed	15ns (66MHz)	5ns (200MHz)	4.4ns (225MHz)	10ns (100MHz)	2.2ns (450MHz)	0.77ns (1.3GHz)
L2 cache size	varies[1]	256K[2]	512K	varies[1]	256K	64K
CPU bus speed	66MHz	66MHz	100MHz	100MHz	100MHz	200MHz
Memory bus speed	60ns (16MHz)	60ns (16MHz)	10ns (100MHz)	10ns (100MHz)	10ns (100MHz)	5ns (200MHz)

1. *The L2 cache is on the motherboard, and the amount depends on which board is chosen and how much is installed.*

2. *The Pentium Pro also was available with 512KB and 1024KB L2 cache.*

Chipsets made for the Pentium Pro/II and later processors did not control the L2 cache because it was moved into the processor instead. So, with the Pentium Pro/II and beyond, the processor sets the cacheability limits. The Pentium Pro and some of the earlier Pentium IIs can address up to 64GB but only cache up to 512MB. The later Pentium IIs and all Pentium III and Pentium 4 processors can cache up to 4GB. Most desktop chipsets for those processors allow only up to 1GB, 2GB, or 4GB of RAM anyway, making cacheability limits moot. All the server-oriented Xeon processors can cache up to 64GB. This is beyond the maximum RAM support of any of the chipsets.

In any case, it is important not to install more memory than the cache controller can support. If you want to know the cacheability limit for your system, consult the chipset documentation if you have a Pentium class or older system (or any system with cache on the motherboard), or check the processor documentation if you have a Pentium II class or newer system (or any system with all the cache integrated into the CPU).

RAM Types

The speed and performance issue with memory is confusing to some because memory speed is usually expressed in ns (nanoseconds) and processor speed has always been expressed in MHz (megahertz). Recently, however, some newer and faster types of memory have speeds expressed in MHz, adding to the confusion. Fortunately, you can translate one to the other.

A *nanosecond* is defined as one billionth of a second—a very short time indeed. To put some perspective on that, the speed of light is 186,282 miles (299,792 kilometers) per second in a vacuum. In one billionth of a second, a beam of light travels a mere 11.80 inches or 29.98 centimeters—less than the length of a typical ruler!

Chip and system speed has been expressed in megahertz (MHz), which is millions of cycles per second, or gigahertz (GHz), which is billions of cycles per second. During 2005, systems will exceed 5GHz or 5 billion cycles per second.

Because it is confusing to speak in these different terms for speeds, I thought it would be interesting to see how they compare. Earlier in this chapter I listed formulas you could use to mathematically convert these values. Table 6.3 shows the relationship between common nanosecond (ns) and megahertz (MHz) speeds associated with PCs from yesterday to today and tomorrow.

Athlon	Athlon XP	Pentium III	Celeron/370	Celeron/478	Pentium 4
1.4GHz	2.2GHz	1.4GHz	1.4GHz	2.4GHz	3.6GHz
0.71ns (1.4GHz)	0.45ns (2.2GHz)	0.71ns (1.4GHz)	0.71ns (1.4GHz)	0.42ns (2.4GHz)	0.28ns (3.6GHz)
128K	128K	32K	32K	20K	20K
on-die	on-die	on-die	on-die	on-die	on-die
1/1	1/1	1/1	1/1	1/1	1/1
0.71ns (1.4GHz)	0.45ns (2.2GHz)	0.71ns (1.4GHz)	0.71ns (1.4GHz)	0.42ns (2.4GHz)	0.28ns (3.6GHz)
256K	512K	512K	256K	128K	1M
266MHz	400MHz	133MHz	100MHz	400MHz	800MHz
3.8ns (266MHz)	2.5ns (400MHz)	7.5ns (133MHz)	10ns (100MHz)	2.5ns (400MHz)	1.25ns (800MHz)

Table 6.3 The Relationship Between Megahertz (MHz) and Cycle Times in Nanoseconds (ns)

Clock Speed	Cycle Time	Clock Speed	Cycle Time	Clock Speed	Cycle Time	Clock Speed	Cycle Time
4.77MHz	210ns	250MHz	4.0ns	850MHz	1.18ns	2,700MHz	0.37ns
6MHz	167ns	266MHz	3.8ns	866MHz	1.15ns	2,800MHz	0.36ns
8MHz	125ns	300MHz	3.3ns	900MHz	1.11ns	2,900MHz	0.34ns
10MHz	100ns	333MHz	3.0ns	933MHz	1.07ns	3,000MHz	0.333ns
12MHz	83ns	350MHz	2.9ns	950MHz	1.05ns	3,100MHz	0.323ns
16MHz	63ns	366MHz	2.7ns	966MHz	1.04ns	3,200MHz	0.313ns
20MHz	50ns	400MHz	2.5ns	1,000MHz	1.00ns	3,300MHz	0.303ns
25MHz	40ns	433MHz	2.3ns	1,100MHz	0.91ns	3,400MHz	0.294ns
33MHz	30ns	450MHz	2.2ns	1,133MHz	0.88ns	3,500MHz	0.286ns
40MHz	25ns	466MHz	2.1ns	1,200MHz	0.83ns	3,600MHz	0.278ns
50MHz	20ns	500MHz	2.0ns	1,300MHz	0.77ns	3,700MHz	0.270ns
60MHz	17ns	533MHz	1.88ns	1,400MHz	0.71ns	3,800MHz	0.263ns
66MHz	15ns	550MHz	1.82ns	1,500MHz	0.67ns	3,900MHz	0.256ns
75MHz	13ns	566MHz	1.77ns	1,600MHz	0.63ns	4,000MHz	0.250ns
80MHz	13ns	600MHz	1.67ns	1,700MHz	0.59ns	4,100MHz	0.244ns
100MHz	10ns	633MHz	1.58ns	1,800MHz	0.56ns	4,200MHz	0.238ns
120MHz	8.3ns	650MHz	1.54ns	1,900MHz	0.53ns	4,300MHz	0.233ns
133MHz	7.5ns	666MHz	1.50ns	2,000MHz	0.50ns	4,400MHz	0.227ns
150MHz	6.7ns	700MHz	1.43ns	2,100MHz	0.48ns	4,500MHz	0.222ns
166MHz	6.0ns	733MHz	1.36ns	2,200MHz	0.45ns	4,600MHz	0.217ns
180MHz	5.6ns	750MHz	1.33ns	2,300MHz	0.43ns	4,700MHz	0.213ns
200MHz	5.0ns	766MHz	1.31ns	2,400MHz	0.42ns	4,800MHz	0.208ns
225MHz	4.4ns	800MHz	1.25ns	2,500MHz	0.40ns	4,900MHz	0.204ns
233MHz	4.3ns	833MHz	1.20ns	2,600MHz	0.38ns	5,000MHz	0.200ns

As you can see from Table 6.3, as clock speeds increase, cycle time decreases proportionately.

If you examine Table 6.3, you can clearly see that the 60ns DRAM memory used in the original Pentium and Pentium II PCs up until 1998 works out to be 16.7MHz! This super-slow 16MHz memory had been installed in systems running up to 300MHz or faster, and you can see that a large mismatch existed between processor and main memory performance. The dominant standard in 2000 was to have 100MHz and even 133MHz memory, called PC100 and PC133, respectively. Starting in early 2001, double data rate (DDR) memory of 200MHz and 266MHz become popular, along with 800MHz RDRAM. In 2002 standard 333MHz DDR memory arrived, and in 2003, the speeds increased to 400MHz. During 2004, we saw the introduction of DDR2 first at 400MHz and then at 533MHz.

System memory timing is a little more involved than simply converting nanoseconds to megahertz. The transistors for each bit in a memory chip are most efficiently arranged in a grid, using a row and column scheme to access each transistor. All memory accesses involve selecting a row address and then a column address and then transferring the data. The initial setup for a memory transfer where the row and column addresses are selected is a necessary overhead referred to as *latency*. The access time for memory is the cycle time plus latency for selecting the row and column addresses. For example, SDRAM memory rated at 133MHz (7.5ns) typically takes five cycles to set up and complete the first transfer (5×7.5ns = 37.5ns) and then perform three additional transfers with no additional setup. Thus, four transfers take a total of eight cycles, or an average of about two cycles per transfer.

Over the development life of the PC, memory has had a difficult time keeping up with the processor, requiring several levels of high-speed cache memory to intercept processor requests for the slower main memory. Table 6.4 shows the progress and relationship between system board (motherboard) speeds in PCs and the various types and speeds of main memory or RAM used and how these changes have affected total bandwidth. Many of the faster specifications listed in this table are only proposed future standards and not yet officially released.

Table 6.4   DRAM Memory Module and Bus Standards/Bandwidth (Past, Current, and Future)

Module Standard	Module Format	Chip Type	Clock Speed (MHz)	Cycles per Clock	Bus Speed (MT/s)	Bus Width (Bytes)	Transfer Rate (MBps)
FPM	SIMM	60ns	22	1	22	8	177
EDO	SIMM	60ns	33	1	33	8	266
PC66	SDR DIMM	10ns	66	1	66	8	533
PC100	SDR DIMM	8ns	100	1	100	8	800
PC133	SDR DIMM	7/7.5ns	133	1	133	8	1,066
PC1600	DDR DIMM	DDR200	100	2	200	8	1,600
PC2100	DDR DIMM	DDR266	133	2	266	8	2,133
PC2400	DDR DIMM	DDR300	150	2	300	8	2,400
PC2700	DDR DIMM	DDR333	166	2	333	8	2,667
PC3000	DDR DIMM	DDR366	183	2	366	8	2,933
PC3200	DDR DIMM	DDR400	200	2	400	8	3,200
PC3500	DDR DIMM	DDR433	216	2	433	8	3,466
PC3700	DDR DIMM	DDR466	233	2	466	8	3,733
PC4000	DDR DIMM	DDR500	250	2	500	8	4,000
PC4300	DDR DIMM	DDR533	266	2	533	8	4,266
PC2-3200	DDR2 DIMM	DDR2-400	200	2	400	8	3,200
PC2-4300	DDR2 DIMM	DDR2-533	266	2	533	8	4,266

Table 6.4 Continued

Module Standard	Module Format	Chip Type	Clock Speed (MHz)	Cycles per Clock	Bus Speed (MT/s)	Bus Width (Bytes)	Transfer Rate (MBps)
PC2-5400	DDR2 DIMM	DDR2-667	333	2	667	8	5,333
PC2-6400	DDR2 DIMM	DDR2-800	400	2	800	8	6,400
RIMM1200	RIMM-16	PC600	300	2	600	2	1,200
RIMM1400	RIMM-16	PC700	350	2	700	2	1,400
RIMM1600	RIMM-16	PC800	400	2	800	2	1,600
RIMM2100	RIMM-16	PC1066	533	2	1,066	2	2,133
RIMM2400	RIMM-16	PC1200	600	2	1,200	2	2,400
RIMM3200	RIMM-32	PC800	400	2	800	4	3,200
RIMM4200	RIMM-32	PC1066	533	2	1,066	4	4,266
RIMM4800	RIMM-32	PC1200	600	2	1,200	4	4,800

MT/s = Megatransfers per second
MBps = Megabytes per second
ns = Nanoseconds (billionths of a second)
FPM = Fast Page Mode
EDO = Extended data out

SIMM = Single inline memory module
DIMM = Dual inline memory module
RIMM = Rambus inline memory module
SDR = Single data rate
DDR = Double data rate

Generally, things work best when the throughput of the memory bus matches the throughput of the processor bus. Compare the memory bus transfer speeds (bandwidth) to the speeds of the processor bus as shown in Table 6.5, and you'll see that some of the memory bus rates match that of some of the processor bus rates. In most cases the type of memory that matches the CPU bus transfer rate is the best type of memory for systems with that type of processor.

Table 6.5 Processor Bus Bandwidth

CPU Bus Type	Clock Speed (MHz)	Cycles per Clock	Bus Speed (MT/s)	Bus Width (Bytes)	Bandwidth (MBps)
33MHz 486 FSB	33	1	33	4	133
66MHz Pentium I/II/III FSB	66	1	66	8	533
100MHz Pentium I/II/III FSB	100	1	100	8	800
133MHz Pentium I/II/III FSB	133	1	133	8	1,066
200MHz Athlon FSB	100	2	200	8	1,600
266MHz Athlon FSB	133	2	266	8	2,133
333MHz Athlon FSB	166	2	333	8	2,667
400MHz Athlon FSB	200	2	400	8	3,200
400MHz Pentium 4 FSB	100	4	400	8	3,200
533MHz Pentium 4 FSB	133	4	533	8	4,266
800MHz Pentium 4 FSB	200	4	800	8	6,400

FSB = Front side bus
MBps = Megabytes per second
MT/s = Megatransfers per second

Because the processor is fairly well insulated from directly dealing with main memory by the L1 and L2 cache, memory performance has often lagged behind the performance of the processor bus. More recently, however, systems using SDRAM, DDR SDRAM, and RDRAM have memory bus performance equaling that of the processor bus. When the speed of the memory bus equals the speed of the processor bus, memory performance is optimum for that system.

Fast Page Mode DRAM

Standard DRAM is accessed through a technique called *paging*. Normal memory access requires that a row and column address be selected, which takes time. Paging enables faster access to all the data within a given row of memory by keeping the row address the same and changing only the column. Memory that uses this technique is called *Page Mode* or *Fast Page Mode* memory. Other variations on Page Mode were called *Static Column* or *Nibble Mode* memory.

Paged memory is a simple scheme for improving memory performance that divides memory into pages ranging from 512 bytes to a few kilobytes long. The paging circuitry then enables memory locations in a page to be accessed with fewer wait states. If the desired memory location is outside the current page, one or more wait states are added while the system selects the new page.

To improve further on memory access speeds, systems have evolved to enable faster access to DRAM. One important change was the implementation of burst mode access in the 486 and later processors. Burst mode cycling takes advantage of the consecutive nature of most memory accesses. After setting up the row and column addresses for a given access, using burst mode, you can then access the next three adjacent addresses with no additional latency or wait states. A burst access usually is limited to four total accesses. To describe this, we often refer to the timing in the number of cycles for each access. A typical burst mode access of standard DRAM is expressed as x-y-y-y; *x* is the time for the first access (latency plus cycle time), and *y* represents the number of cycles required for each consecutive access.

Standard 60ns DRAM normally runs 5-3-3-3 burst mode timing. This means the first access takes a total of five cycles (on a 66MHz system bus, this is about 75ns total or 5×15ns cycles), and the consecutive cycles take three cycles each (3×15ns = 45ns). As you can see, the actual system timing is somewhat less than the memory is technically rated for. Without the bursting technique, memory access would be 5-5-5-5 because the full latency is necessary for each memory transfer.

DRAM memory that supports paging and this bursting technique is called Fast Page Mode (FPM) memory. The term comes from the capability of memory accesses to data on the same page to be done with less latency. Most 486 and Pentium systems from 1995 and earlier use FPM memory.

Another technique for speeding up FPM memory was called *interleaving*. In this design, two separate banks of memory are used together, alternating access from one to the other as even and odd bytes. While one is being accessed, the other is being precharged, when the row and column addresses are being selected. Then, by the time the first bank in the pair is finished returning data, the second bank in the pair is finished with the latency part of the cycle and is now ready to return data. While the second bank is returning data, the first bank is being precharged, selecting the row and column address of the next access. This overlapping of accesses in two banks reduces the effect of the latency or precharge cycles and allows for faster overall data retrieval. The only problem is that to use interleaving, you must install identical pairs of banks together, doubling the amount of SIMMs or DIMMs required. This method was popular on 32-bit wide memory systems on 486 processors but fell out of favor on Pentiums because of their 64-bit wide memory widths. To perform interleaving on a Pentium machine, you would need to install memory 128 bits at a time, meaning four 72-pin SIMMs or two DIMMs at a time.

Extended Data Out RAM

In 1995, a newer type of memory called extended data out (EDO) RAM became available for Pentium systems. EDO, a modified form of FPM memory, is sometimes referred to as *Hyper Page mode*. EDO was invented and patented by Micron Technology, although Micron licensed production to many other memory manufacturers.

EDO memory consists of specially manufactured chips that allow a timing overlap between successive accesses. The name *extended data out* refers specifically to the fact that unlike FPM, the data output drivers on the chip are not turned off when the memory controller removes the column address to begin the next cycle. This enables the next cycle to overlap the previous one, saving approximately 10ns per cycle.

The effect of EDO is that cycle times are improved by enabling the memory controller to begin a new column address instruction while it is reading data at the current address. This is almost identical to what was achieved in older systems by interleaving banks of memory, but unlike interleaving, with EDO you didn't need to install two identical banks of memory in the system at a time.

EDO RAM allows for burst mode cycling of 5-2-2-2, compared to the 5-3-3-3 of standard fast page mode memory. To do four memory transfers, then, EDO would require 11 total system cycles, compared to 14 total cycles for FPM. This is a 22% improvement in overall cycling time, but in actual testing, EDO typically increases overall system benchmark speed by about 5%. Even though the overall system improvement might seem small, the important thing about EDO was that it used the same basic DRAM chip design as FPM, meaning that there was practically no additional cost over FPM. In fact, in its heyday, EDO cost less than FPM and yet offered higher performance.

EDO RAM generally comes in 72-pin SIMM form. Figure 6.3 (later in this chapter) shows the physical characteristics of these SIMMs.

To actually use EDO memory, your motherboard chipset must support it. Most motherboard chipsets on the market from 1995 (Intel 430FX) through 1997 (Intel 430TX) offered support for EDO. Because EDO memory chips cost the same to manufacture as standard chips, combined with Intel's support of EDO in all its chipsets, the PC market jumped on the EDO bandwagon full force.

◄◄ See "Fifth-Generation (P5 Pentium Class) Chipsets," p. 249, and "Sixth-Generation (P6 Pentium Pro/Pentium II/III Class) Chipsets," p. 254.

EDO RAM was ideal for systems with bus speeds of up to 66MHz, which fit perfectly with the PC market up through 1997. However, since 1998 with the advent of faster system bus speeds (100MHz and above), the market for EDO has rapidly declined as the newer and faster SDRAM architecture has become the standard for new PC system memory.

A variation of EDO is burst EDO (BEDO). *BEDO* is basically EDO memory with special burst features for even speedier data transfers than standard EDO. Unfortunately, the technology was owned by Micron and not a free industry standard, so only one chipset (Intel 440FX Natoma) ever supported it. BEDO was therefore quickly overshadowed by industry-standard SDRAM, which was favored among PC system chipset and system designers over proprietary designs. As such, BEDO never really saw the light of production, and to my knowledge no systems ever really used it.

SDRAM

SDRAM is short for *synchronous DRAM*, a type of DRAM that runs in synchronization with the memory bus. SDRAM delivers information in very high-speed bursts using a high-speed, clocked interface. SDRAM removes most of the latency involved in asynchronous DRAM because the signals are already in synchronization with the motherboard clock.

Like EDO RAM, your chipset must support this type of memory for it to be usable in your system. Starting in 1996 with the 430VX and 430TX, most of Intel's chipsets began to support industry-standard SDRAM, making it the most popular type of memory for new systems through 2000 and even into 2001.

SDRAM performance is dramatically improved over that of FPM or EDO RAM. Because SDRAM is still a type of DRAM, the initial latency is the same, but overall cycle times are much faster than with FPM or EDO. SDRAM timing for a burst access would be 5-1-1-1, meaning that four memory reads would complete in only eight system bus cycles, compared to eleven cycles for EDO and fourteen cycles for FPM. This makes SDRAM almost 20% faster than EDO.

Besides being capable of working in fewer cycles, SDRAM is also capable of supporting up to 133MHz (7.5ns) system bus cycling. As such, most new PC systems sold from 1998 to 2000 have included SDRAM memory.

SDRAM is sold in DIMM form and is often rated by megahertz speed rather than nanosecond cycling time, which was confusing during the change from FPM and EDO DRAM. Figure 6.4 (later in this chapter) shows the physical characteristics of DIMMs.

To meet the stringent timing demands of its chipsets, Intel created specifications for SDRAM called PC66, PC100, and PC133. To meet the PC100 specification, 8ns chips usually are required. Normally, you would think 10ns would be considered the proper rating for 100MHz operation, but the PC100 specification calls for faster memory to ensure all timing parameters are met.

In May 1999, the Joint Electron Device Engineering Council (JEDEC) created a specification called PC133. They achieved this 33MHz speed increase by taking the PC100 specification and tightening up the timing and capacitance parameters. The faster PC133 quickly caught on as the most popular version of SDRAM for any systems running a 133MHz processor bus. The original chips used in PC133 modules were rated for exactly 7.5ns or 133MHz; later ones were rated at 7.0ns or 143MHz. These faster chips were still used on PC133 modules, but they allowed for improvements in column address strobe latency (abbreviated as CAS or CL), which somewhat improves overall memory cycling time.

Note

JEDEC is the semiconductor engineering standardization body of the Electronic Industries Alliance (EIA), a trade association that represents all areas of the electronics industry. JEDEC was originally created in 1960 and governs the standardization of all types of semiconductor devices, integrated circuits, and modules. JEDEC has about 300 member companies, including memory, chipset, and processor manufacturers as well as practically any company involved in manufacturing computer equipment using industry-standard components.

The idea behind JEDEC is simple: For example, if one company were to create a proprietary memory technology, other companies who wanted to manufacture components compliant with that memory would have to pay license fees, assuming the company that owned it was interested in licensing at all! Parts would be more proprietary in nature, causing problems with interchangeability or sourcing reasonably priced replacements. In addition, those companies licensing the technology would have no control over future changes or evolution made by the owner company.

The idea behind JEDEC is to prevent this type of scenario for things such as memory by getting all the memory manufacturers to work together to create shared industry standards covering memory chips and modules. JEDEC-approved standards for memory can then be freely shared by all the member companies, and no one single company has control over a given standard, or any of the companies producing compliant components. FPM, SDRAM, DDR SDRAM, and DDR2 SDRAM are examples of JEDEC memory standards used in PCs, whereas EDO and RDRAM are proprietary examples. You can find out more about JEDEC standards for memory and other semiconductor technology at www.jedec.org.

Table 6.6 shows the timing, rated chip speeds, and standard module speeds for various SDRAM DIMMs.

Table 6.6   SDRAM Timing, Actual Speed, and Rated Speed

Timing	Rated Chip Speed	Standard Module Speed
15ns	66MHz	PC66
10ns	100MHz	PC66
8ns	125MHz	PC100
7.5ns	133MHz	PC133
7.0ns	143MHz	PC133

Note that several module manufacturers sell modules they claim are "PC150" or "PC166" even though those speeds do not exist as official JEDEC or Intel standards and no chipsets or processors officially support these speeds. Normally, these modules actually use hand-picked 7.5ns (133MHz) or 7.0ns (143MHz) rated chips that can run overclocked at 150MHz or 166MHz speeds. In essence, PC150 or PC166 memory would more accurately be called PC133 memory that has been tested to run at overclocked speeds not supported by the original chip manufacturer. This specially selected overclockable memory is sold at a premium to enthusiasts who want to overclock their motherboard chipsets, thereby increasing the speed of the processor and memory bus. Table 6.7 shows the standard SDRAM module types and resulting bandwidths.

Table 6.7   SDRAM Module Types and Bandwidths

Module Standard	Module Format	Chip Type	Clock Speed (MHz)	Cycles per Clock	Bus Speed (MT/s)	Bus Width (Bytes)	Transfer Rate (MBps)
PC66	SDR DIMM	10ns	66	1	66	8	533
PC100	SDR DIMM	8ns	100	1	100	8	800
PC133	SDR DIMM	7/7.5ns	133	1	133	8	1,066

MT/s = Megatransfers per second

MBps = Megabytes per second

ns = Nanoseconds (billionths of a second)

DIMM = Dual inline memory module

SDR = Single data rate

▶▶   See "SIMMs, DIMMs, and RIMMS," p. 477.

DDR SDRAM

Double data rate (DDR) SDRAM memory is a JEDEC-created standard that is an evolutionary upgrade of standard SDRAM in which data is transferred twice as quickly. Instead of doubling the actual clock rate, DDR memory achieves the doubling in performance by transferring twice per transfer cycle: once at the leading (falling) edge and once at the trailing (rising) edge of the cycle (see Figure 6.1). This effectively doubles the transfer rate, even though the same overall clock and timing signals are used.

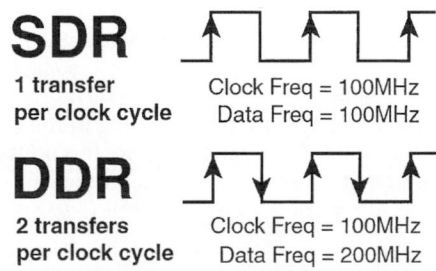

Figure 6.1   SDR (single data rate) versus DDR (double data rate) cycling.

DDR found initial support in the graphics card market and since then has become the mainstream PC memory standard. As such, DDR SDRAM is supported by all the major processor, chipset, and memory manufacturers.

DDR SDRAM first came to market during 2000, but it didn't really catch on until 2001 with the advent of mainstream motherboards and chipsets supporting it. DDR SDRAM uses a new DIMM module design with 184 pins. Figure 6.5 (later in this chapter) shows the DDR SDRAM DIMM.

DDR DIMMs come in a variety of speed or throughput ratings and normally run on 2.5 volts. They are basically an extension of the standard SDRAM DIMMs redesigned to support double clocking, where data is sent on each clock transition (twice per cycle) rather than once per cycle as with standard SDRAM. To eliminate confusion with DDR, regular SDRAM is often called single data rate (SDR). Table 6.8 compares the various types of standard DDR SDRAM modules. As you can see, the raw chips are designated by their speed in megatransfers per second, whereas the modules are designated by their approximate throughput in megabytes per second.

Table 6.8   DDR SDRAM Module Types and Bandwidths

Module Standard	Module Format	Chip Type	Clock Speed (MHz)	Cycles per Clock	Bus Speed (MT/s)	Bus Width (Bytes)	Transfer Rate (MBps)
PC1600	DDR DIMM	DDR200	100	2	200	8	1,600
PC2100	DDR DIMM	DDR266	133	2	266	8	2,133
PC2400	DDR DIMM	DDR300	150	2	300	8	2,400
PC2700	DDR DIMM	DDR333	166	2	333	8	2,667
PC3000	DDR DIMM	DDR366	183	2	366	8	2,933
PC3200	DDR DIMM	DDR400	200	2	400	8	3,200
PC3500	DDR DIMM	DDR433	216	2	433	8	3,466
PC3700	DDR DIMM	DDR466	233	2	466	8	3,733
PC4000	DDR DIMM	DDR500	250	2	500	8	4,000
PC4300	DDR DIMM	DDR533	266	2	533	8	4,266

MT/s = Megatransfers per second

MBps = Megabytes per second

DIMM = Dual inline memory module

DDR = Double data rate

The bandwidths listed in these tables are per module. Many recent chipsets support dual-channel DDR memory—a technique in which two DDR DIMMs are installed at one time and function as a single bank with double the bandwidth of a single module. For example, the Intel 865 and 875 family chipsets use dual-channel DDR memory. They support the 800MHz Pentium 4 processor front-side bus (FSB), which transfers 8 bytes (64 bits) at a time for a bandwidth of 6,400MBps (800×8 = 6400). With an 800MHz FSB processor installed, these boards use standard PC3200 modules, installed two at a time (dual-channel), for a total bandwidth of 6,400MBps (3,200MBps × 2 = 6,400MBps). This design allows the memory bus throughput to match the CPU bus throughput exactly, resulting in the best possible performance. You can optimize PC design by ensuring that the CPU bus and memory bus both run at exactly the same speeds (meaning bandwidth, not MHz), so that data can move synchronously between the buses without delays.

DDR2 SDRAM

JEDEC and its members began working on the DDR2 specification in April 1998, and published the standard in September 2003. DDR2 chip and module production actually began in mid-2003 (mainly samples and prototypes), and the first chipsets, motherboards, and systems supporting DDR2 appeared in mid-2004.

DDR2 SDRAM is simply a faster version of conventional DDR-SDRAM memory: It achieves higher throughput by using differential pairs of signal wires to allow faster signaling without noise and interference problems. DDR2 is still double data rate just as with DDR, but the modified signaling method enables higher speeds to be achieved with more immunity to noise and cross-talk between the signals. The additional signals required for differential pairs add to the pin count—DDR2 DIMMs have

240 pins, which is more than the 184 pins of DDR. The original DDR specification tops out at 400MHz, whereas DDR2 starts at 400MHz and goes up to 533MHz, 800MHz, and beyond. Table 6.9 shows the various DDR2 module types and bandwidth specifications.

Table 6.9   DDR2 SDRAM Module Types and Bandwidths

Module Standard	Module Format	Chip Type	Clock Speed (MHz)	Cycles per Clock	Bus Speed (MT/s)	Bus Width (Bytes)	Transfer Rate (MBps)
PC2-3200	DDR2 DIMM	DDR2-400	200	2	400	8	3,200
PC2-4300	DDR2 DIMM	DDR2-533	266	2	533	8	4,266
PC2-5400	DDR2 DIMM	DDR2-667	333	2	667	8	5,333
PC2-6400	DDR2 DIMM	DDR2-800	400	2	800	8	6,400

MT/s = Megatransfers per second

MBps = Megabytes per second

DIMM = Dual inline memory module

DDR = Double data rate

In addition to providing greater speeds and bandwidth, DDR2 has other advantages. It uses lower voltage than conventional DDR (1.8V versus 2.5V), so power consumption and heat generation are reduced. Because of the greater number of pins required on DDR2 chips, the chips typically use fine-pitch ball grid array (FBGA) packaging rather than the thin small outline package (TSOP) chip packaging used by most DDR and conventional SDRAM chips. FPGA chips are connected to the substrate (meaning the memory module in most cases) via tightly spaced solder balls on the base of the chip.

Volume production of DDR2 chips and modules started in the latter part of 2003, with supporting chipsets and motherboards arriving in mid-2004. Variations of DDR2 such as G-DDR2 (Graphics DDR2) are being used in some of the higher-end graphics cards as well. Because all the major memory and chipset manufacturers are supporting DDR2, there is little doubt that DDR2 will quickly become the most popular form of memory after conventional DDR.

DDR2 DIMMs resemble conventional DDR DIMMs but have more pins and slightly different notches to prevent confusion or improper application. For example, the different physical notches prevent you from plugging a DDR2 module in to a conventional DDR (or SDR) socket. DDR2 memory module designs incorporate 240 pins, significantly more than conventional DDR or standard SDRAM DIMMs.

RDRAM

Rambus DRAM (RDRAM) is a fairly radical memory design found in high-end PC systems from late 1999 through 2002. Intel signed a contract with Rambus in 1996 ensuring it would support RDRAM into 2001. After 2001, Intel continued to support RDRAM in existing systems, but new chipsets and motherboards primarily shifted to DDR SDRAM, and all future Intel chipsets and motherboards are being designed for either conventional DDR or the new DDR2 standard. RDRAM standards had been proposed that will support faster processors through 2006; however, without Intel's commitment to future chipset development and support, very few RDRAM-based systems were sold in 2003, and almost none after that. Due to the lack of industry support from chipset and motherboard manufacturers, RDRAM will most likely not play a big part in future PCs.

With RDRAM, Rambus developed what is essentially a chip-to-chip memory bus, with specialized devices that communicate at very high rates of speed. What might be interesting to some is that this technology was first developed for game systems and first made popular by the Nintendo 64 game system, and it subsequently was used in the Sony Playstation 2.

Conventional memory systems that use FPM/EDO or SDRAM are known as *wide-channel systems*. They have memory channels as wide as the processor's data bus, which for the Pentium and up is 64 bits. The dual inline memory module (DIMM) is a 64-bit wide device, meaning data can be transferred to it 64 bits (or 8 bytes) at a time.

RDRAMs, on the other hand, are narrow-channel devices. They transfer data only 16 bits (2 bytes) at a time (plus 2 optional parity bits), but at much faster speeds. This is a shift away from a more parallel to a more serial design and is similar to what is happening with other evolving buses in the PC.

16-bit single channel RIMMs originally ran at 800MHz, so the overall throughput is 800×2, or 1.6GB per second for a single channel—the same as PC1600 DDR SDRAM. Pentium 4 systems typically used two banks simultaneously, creating a dual-channel design capable of 3.2GBps, which matches the bus speed of the original Pentium 4 processors. The RDRAM design features less latency between transfers because they all run synchronously in a looped system and in only one direction.

Newer RIMM versions run at 1,066MHz or 1,200MHz in addition to the original 800MHz rate and are available in single-channel, 16-bit versions as well as multiple-channel, 32-bit versions for throughputs up to 4.8GBps per module.

A single Rambus memory channel can support up to 32 individual RDRAM devices (the RDRAM chips), and more if buffers are used. Each individual chip is serially connected to the next on a package called a Rambus inline memory module (RIMM), but all memory transfers are done between the memory controller and a single device, not between devices. The individual RDRAM chips are contained on RIMMs, and a single channel typically has three RIMM sockets. The RDRAM memory bus is a continuous path through each device and module on the bus, with each module having input and output pins on opposite ends. Therefore, any RIMM sockets not containing a RIMM must then be filled with a continuity module to ensure that the path is completed. The signals that reach the end of the bus are terminated on the motherboard.

Each RDRAM chip on a RIMM1600 essentially operates as a standalone module sitting on the 16-bit data channel. Internally, each RDRAM chip has a core that operates on a 128-bit wide bus split into eight 16-bit banks running at 100MHz. In other words, every 10ns (100MHz), each RDRAM chip can transfer 16 bytes to and from the core. This internally wide yet externally narrow high-speed interface is the key to RDRAM.

Other improvements to the design include separating control and data signals on the bus. Independent control and address buses are split into two groups of pins for row and column commands, while data is transferred across the 2-byte wide data bus. The actual memory bus clock runs at 400MHz; however, data is transferred on both the falling and rising edges of the clock signal, or twice per clock pulse. The falling edge is called an *even cycle*, and the rising edge is called an *odd cycle*. Complete memory bus synchronization is achieved by sending packets of data beginning on an even cycle interval. The overall wait before a memory transfer can begin (latency) is only one cycle, or 2.5ns maximum.

Figure 6.1 (shown earlier) depicts the relationship between clock and data cycles; you can see the DDR clock and data cycles used by RDRAM and DDR SDRAM. An RDRAM data packet always begins on an even (falling) transition for synchronization purposes.

The architecture also supports multiple, simultaneous interleaved transactions in multiple separate time domains. Therefore, before a transfer has even completed, another can begin.

Another important feature of RDRAM is that it is a low-power memory system. The RIMMs themselves as well as the RDRAM devices run on only 2.5 volts and use low-voltage signal swings from 1.0V to 1.8V, a swing of only 0.8V total. RDRAMs also have four power-down modes and can automatically transition into standby mode at the end of a transaction, which offers further power savings.

As discussed, RDRAM chips are installed in modules called RIMMs. A RIMM is similar in size and physical form to current DIMMs, but they are not interchangeable. RIMMs are available in module sizes up to 1GB or more and can be added to a system one at a time because each individual RIMM technically represents multiple banks to a system. They have to be added in pairs if your motherboard implements dual-channel RDRAM and you are using 16-bit wide RIMMs.

An RDRAM memory controller with a single Rambus channel supports up to three RIMM modules according to the design. However, most motherboards implement only two modules per channel to avoid problems with signal noise.

RIMMs are available in three primary speed grades, with three different width versions in each grade. The 16-bit versions are usually run in a dual-channel environment, so they have to be installed in pairs, with each one of the pairs in a different set of sockets. Each set of RIMM sockets on such boards is a channel. The 32-bit version incorporates multiple channels within a single device and, as such, is designed to be installed individually, eliminating the requirement for matched pairs. Table 6.10 compares the various types of RDRAM modules. Note that the once-common names for RIMM modules, such as PC800, have been replaced by names that reflect the actual bandwidth of the module to avoid confusion with DDR memory.

Table 6.10   RDRAM Module Types and Bandwidth

Module Standard	Module Format	Chip Type	Clock Speed (MHz)	Cycles per Clock	Bus Speed (MT/s)	Bus Width (Bytes)	Transfer Rate (MBps)
RIMM1200	RIMM-16	PC600	300	2	600	2	1,200
RIMM1400	RIMM-16	PC700	350	2	700	2	1,400
RIMM1600	RIMM-16	PC800	400	2	800	2	1,600
RIMM2100	RIMM-16	PC1066	533	2	1,066	2	2,133
RIMM2400	RIMM-16	PC1200	600	2	1,200	2	2,400
RIMM3200	RIMM-32	PC800	400	2	800	4	3,200
RIMM4200	RIMM-32	PC1066	533	2	1,066	4	4,266
RIMM4800	RIMM-32	PC1200	600	2	1,200	4	4,800

MT/s = Megatransfers per second

MBps = Megabytes per second

RIMM = Rambus inline memory module

When Intel initially threw its weight behind the Rambus memory, it seemed destined to be a sure thing for success. Unfortunately, technical delays in the chipsets caused the supporting motherboards to be significantly delayed, and with few systems to support the RIMMs, most memory manufacturers went back to making SDRAM or shifted to DDR SDRAM instead. This caused the remaining available RIMMs being manufactured to be originally priced three or more times that of a comparatively sized DIMM. More recently the cost for RDRAM RIMMs has come down to approximately that of DDR SDRAM, but by the time that happened, Intel had shifted all future chipset development to support only DDR and DDR2 memory.

As I've stated many times, one of the main considerations for memory is that the throughput of the memory bus should match the throughput of the processor bus, and in that area RDRAM RIMMs were originally more suited to the initial Pentium 4 processor systems. However, with the increases in speed of the Pentium 4 processor bus from 400MHz to 533MHz and then 800MHz and the advent of chipsets supporting dual-channel DDR memory, DDR and DDR2 are currently the best match for the CPU bus speeds of both Intel and AMD processors. In short, the advent of newer chipsets supporting dual-channel DDR in 2002 and DDR2 in 2004 has rendered DDR and DDR2 as the best choices for modern systems, offering the maximum memory performance possible.

Note

Unfortunately for the memory chip manufacturers, Rambus has claimed patents that cover both standard and DDR SDRAM designs. So, regardless of whether these companies manufacture SDRAM, DDR, or RDRAM, it is the contention of Rambus that these memory manufacturers must pay the company royalties. Several court cases are ongoing with companies challenging these patents, and a lot is riding on the outcome. Most of the cases that have gone to trial have so far ruled against Rambus, essentially invalidating its patents and claims on DDR and SDRAM. Many appeals are pending, and it will likely be a long time before the patent issues are resolved.

Memory Modules

The CPU and motherboard architecture (chipset) dictates a particular computer's physical memory capacity and the types and forms of memory that can be installed. Over the years, two main changes have occurred in computer memory—it has gradually become faster and wider. The CPU and the memory controller circuitry indicate the speed and width requirements. The memory controller in a modern PC resides in the motherboard chipset. Even though a system might physically support a given amount of memory, the type of software you run could dictate whether all the memory can be used.

The 8088 and 8086 CPUs, with 20 address lines, can use as much as 1MB (1,024KB) of RAM. The 286 and 386SX CPUs have 24 address lines and can keep track of as much as 16MB of memory. The 386DX, 486, Pentium, and Pentium-MMX CPUs have a full set of 32 address lines, so they can keep track of 4GB of memory; the Pentium Pro, Pentium II/III, and 4, as well as the AMD Athlon and Duron, have 36 address lines and can manage an impressive 64GB. The Itanium processor, on the other hand, has 44-bit addressing, which allows for up to 16TB (terabytes) of physical RAM!

◀◀   See "Processor Specifications," p. 41.

When the 286 and higher chips emulate the 8088 chip (as they do when running 16-bit software, such as DOS or Windows 3.x), they implement a hardware operating mode called *real mode*. Real mode is the only mode available on the 8086 and 8088 chips used in PC and XT systems. In real mode, all Intel processors—even the mighty Pentium family—are restricted to using only 1MB of memory, just as their 8086 and 8088 ancestors were, and the system design reserves 384KB of that amount. Only in protected mode can the 286 or better chips use their maximum potentials for memory addressing.

◀◀   See "Processor Modes," p. 49.

P5 class systems can address as much as 4GB of memory, and P6/P7 class systems can address up to 64GB. To put these memory-addressing capabilities into perspective, 64GB (65,536MB) of memory would cost nearly $20,000! Even if you could afford all this memory, some of the largest memory modules available today are 1GB DIMMs. Installing 64GB of RAM would require 64 of the largest 1GB DIMMs available, and most systems today support up to only four DIMM sockets.

Most motherboards have a maximum of only three to six DIMM sockets, which allows a maximum of 1.5GB–3GB if all the sockets are filled. These limitations are from the chipset, not the processor. Although some processors can address 64GB, there isn't a chipset on the market that will allow that! Most of the chipsets today are limited to 2GB of memory, although some handle up to 4GB or more.

Some systems have even more limitations. P5 class systems have been available since 1993, but only those built in 1997 or later use a motherboard chipset that supports SDRAM DIMMs. Even those using the most recent P5 class chipset from Intel, such as the 430TX, do not support more than 256MB of total memory and should not have more than 64MB actually installed because of memory-caching limitations. Don't install more than 64MB of RAM in one of these older systems unless you are sure the motherboard and chipset will allow the L2 cache to function with the additional memory.

Note

See the "Chipsets" section in Chapter 4 for the maximum cacheable limits on all the Intel and other motherboard chipsets.

SIMMs, DIMMs, and RIMMs

Originally, systems had memory installed via individual chips. They are often referred to as *dual inline package (DIP)* chips because of their designs. The original IBM XT and AT had 36 sockets on the motherboard for these individual chips; then more of them were installed on the memory cards plugged into the bus slots. I remember spending hours populating boards with these chips, which was a tedious job.

Besides being a time-consuming and labor-intensive way to deal with memory, DIP chips had one notorious problem—they crept out of their sockets over time as the system went through thermal cycles. Every day, when you powered the system on and off, the system heated and cooled, and the chips gradually walked their way out of the sockets. Eventually, good contact was lost and memory errors resulted. Fortunately, reseating all the chips back in their sockets usually rectified the problem, but that method was labor intensive if you had a lot of systems to support.

The alternative to this at the time was to have the memory soldered into either the motherboard or an expansion card. This prevented the chips from creeping and made the connections more permanent, but it caused another problem. If a chip did go bad, you had to attempt desoldering the old one and resoldering a new one or resort to scrapping the motherboard or memory card on which the chip was installed. This was expensive and made memory troubleshooting difficult.

A chip was needed that was both soldered and removable, and that is exactly what was found in the module called a *SIMM*. For memory storage, most modern systems have adopted the single inline memory module (SIMM), DIMM, or RIMM as an alternative to individual memory chips. These small boards plug into special connectors on a motherboard or memory card. The individual memory chips are soldered to the module, so removing and replacing them is impossible. Instead, you must replace the entire module if any part of it fails. The module is treated as though it were one large memory chip.

Two main types of SIMMs, three main types of DIMMs, and so far one type of RIMM are used in desktop systems. The various types are often described by their pin count, memory row width, or memory type.

SIMMs, for example, are available in two main physical types—30-pin (8 bits plus an option for 1 additional parity bit) and 72-pin (32 bits plus an option for 4 additional parity bits)—with various capacities and other specifications. The 30-pin SIMMs are physically smaller than the 72-pin versions, and either version can have chips on one or both sides. SIMMs were widely used from the late 1980s to the late 1990s but have become obsolete.

DIMMs are also available in three main types. DIMMs usually hold standard SDRAM or DDR SDRAM chips and are distinguished by different physical characteristics. Standard DIMMs have 168 pins, one notch on either side, and two notches along the contact area. DDR DIMMs, on the other hand, have 184 pins, two notches on each side, and only one offset notch along the contact area. DDR2 DIMMs have 240 pins, two notches on each side, and one in the center of the contact area. All DIMMs are either 64-bits (non-ECC/parity) or 72-bits (parity or error correcting code [ECC]) wide (data paths). The main physical difference between SIMMs and DIMMs is that DIMMs have different signal pins on each side of the module. That is why they are called *dual* inline memory modules, and why with only 1" of additional length, they have many more pins than a SIMM.

Note

There is confusion among users and even in the industry over regarding the terms single-sided or double-sided with respect to memory modules. In truth, the single- or double-sided designation actually has *nothing* to do with whether chips are physically located on one or both sides of the module, and it has *nothing* to do with whether the module is a SIMM or DIMM (meaning whether the connection pins are single- or double-inline). Instead the terms *single-sided* and *double-sided* are used to indicate whether the module has one or two banks of memory chips installed. A double-banked DIMM module has two complete 64-bit-wide banks of chips logically stacked so that the module is twice as deep (has twice as many 64-bit rows). In most (but not all) cases, this requires chips to be on both sides of the module; therefore, the term *double-sided* has often been used to indicate that a module has two banks, even though the term is technically incorrect. Single-banked modules (incorrectly referred to as *single-sided*) can have chips physically mounted on both sides of the module, and double-banked modules (incorrectly referred to as *double-sided*) can have chips physically mounted on only one side. I recommend using the terms *single-banked* and *double-banked* instead because they are much more accurate and easily understood.

RIMMs also have different signal pins on each side. Three different physical types of RIMMs are available: a 16/18-bit version with 184 pins, a 32/36-bit version with 232 pins, and a 64/72-bit version with 326 pins. Each of these plugs into the same sized connector, but the notches in the connectors and RIMMs are different to prevent a mismatch. A given board will accept only one type. By far the most common type is the 16/18-bit version. The 32-bit version was introduced in late 2002, and the 64-bit version was introduced in 2004.

The standard 16/18-bit RIMM has 184 pins, one notch on either side, and two notches centrally located in the contact area. 16-bit versions are used for non-ECC applications, whereas the 18-bit versions incorporate the additional bits necessary for ECC.

Figures 6.2–6.7 show a typical 30-pin (8-bit) SIMM, 72-pin (32-bit) SIMM, 168-pin SDRAM DIMM, 184-pin DDR SDRAM (64-bit) DIMM, 240-pin DDR2 DIMM, and 184-pin RIMM, respectively. The pins are numbered from left to right and are connected through to both sides of the module on the SIMMs. The pins on the DIMM are different on each side, but on a SIMM, each side is the same as the other and the connections carry through. Note that all dimensions are in both inches and millimeters (in parentheses), and modules are generally available in error correcting code (ECC) versions with 1 extra ECC (or parity) bit for every 8 data bits (multiples of 9 in data width) or versions that do not include ECC support (multiples of 8 in data width).

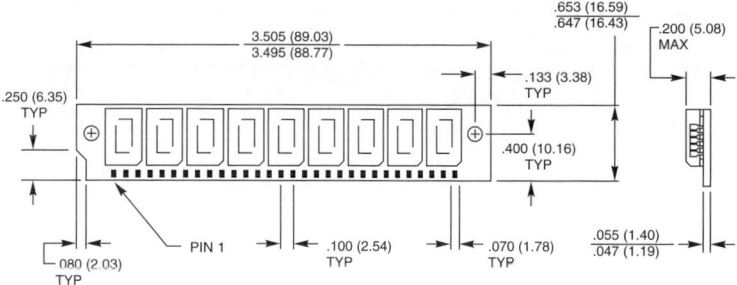

Figure 6.2   A typical 30-pin SIMM.

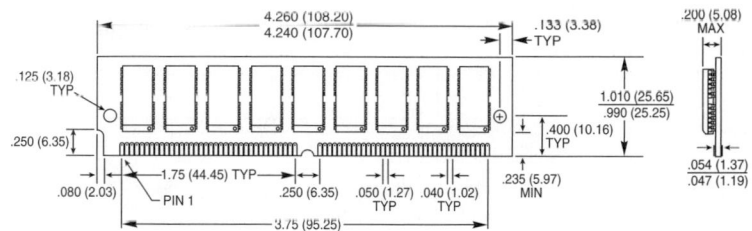

Figure 6.3   A typical 72-pin SIMM.

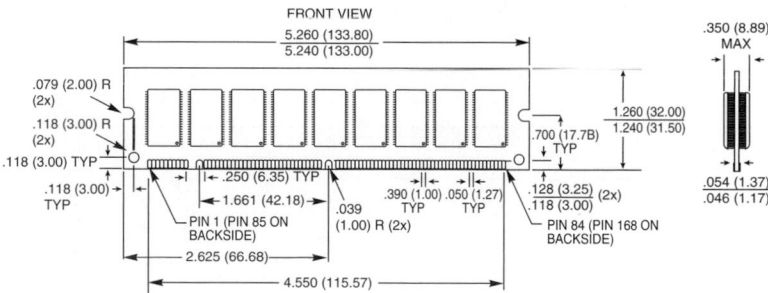

Figure 6.4   A typical 168-pin SDRAM DIMM.

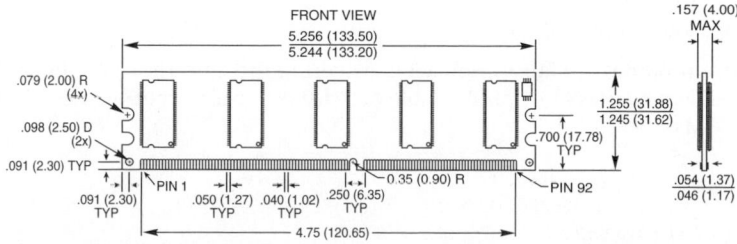

Figure 6.5   A typical 184-pin DDR DIMM.

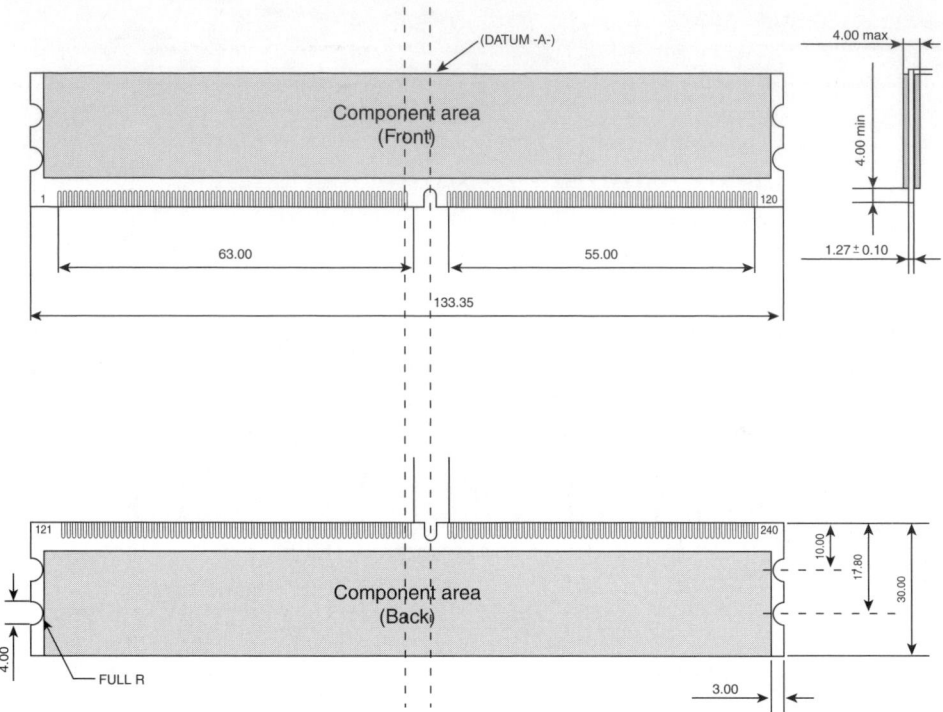

Figure 6.6 A typical 240-pin DDR2 DIMM.

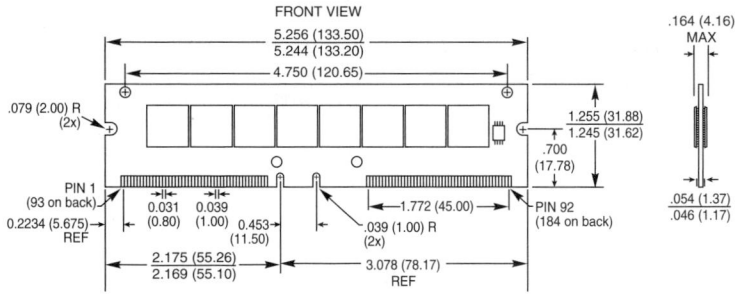

Figure 6.7 A typical 184-pin RIMM.

All these memory modules are fairly compact considering the amount of memory they hold and are available in several capacities and speeds. Table 6.11 lists the various capacities available for SIMMs, DIMMs, and RIMMs.

Table 6.11   SIMM, DIMM, and RIMM Capacities

Capacity	Standard	Parity/ECC
30-Pin SIMM		
256KB	256KB×8	256KB×9
1MB	1MB×8	1MB×9
4MB	4MB×8	4MB×9
16MB	16MB×8	16MB×9
72-Pin SIMM		
1MB	256KB×32	256KB×36
2MB	512KB×32	512KB×36
4MB	1MB×32	1MB×36
8MB	2MB×32	2MB×36
16MB	4MB×32	4MB×36
32MB	8MB×32	8MB×36
64MB	16MB×32	16MB×36
128MB	32MB×32	32MB×36
168/184-Pin DIMM/DDR DIMM		
8MB	1MB×64	1MB×72
16MB	2MB×64	2MB×72
32MB	4MB×64	4MB×72
64MB	8MB×64	8MB×72
128MB	16MB×64	16MB×72
256MB	32MB×64	32MB×72
512MB	64MB×64	64MB×72
1,024MB	128MB×64	128MB×72
2,048MB	256MB×64	256MB×72
4,096MB	512MB×64	512MB×72
240-Pin DDR2 DIMM		
256MB	32MB×64	32MB×72
512MB	64MB×64	64MB×72
1,024MB	128MB×64	128MB×72
2,048MB	256MB×64	256MB×72
4,096MB	512MB×64	512MB×72
184-Pin RIMM		
64MB	32MB×16	32MB×18
128MB	64MB×16	64MB×18
256MB	128MB×16	128MB×18
512MB	256MB×16	256MB×18
1,024MB	512MB×16	512MB×18

SIMMs, DIMMs, DDR/DDR2 DIMMs, and RIMMs of each type and capacity are available in various speed ratings. Consult your motherboard documentation for the correct memory speed and type for your system. It is usually best for the memory speed (also called throughput or bandwidth) to match the speed of the processor data bus (also called the front side bus or FSB).

If a system requires a specific speed, you can almost always substitute faster speeds if the one specified is not available. Generally, no problems occur in mixing module speeds, as long as you use modules equal to or faster than what the system requires. Because there's little price difference between the various speed versions, I often buy faster modules than are necessary for a particular application. This might make them more usable in a future system that could require the faster speed.

Because DIMMs and RIMMs have an onboard serial presence detect (SPD) ROM that reports their speed and timing parameters to the system, most systems run the memory controller and memory bus at the speed matching the slowest DIMM/RIMM installed. Most DIMMs are SDRAM memory, which means they deliver data in very high-speed bursts using a clocked interface. DDR DIMMs are also SDRAM, but they transfer data two times per clock cycle and thus are twice as fast.

Note

A *bank* is the smallest amount of memory needed to form a single row of memory addressable by the processor. It is the minimum amount of physical memory that is read or written by the processor at one time and usually corresponds to the data bus width of the processor. If a processor has a 64-bit data bus, a bank of memory also is 64 bits wide. If the memory is interleaved or runs dual-channel, a virtual bank is formed that is twice the absolute data bus width of the processor.

You can't always replace a module with a higher-capacity unit and expect it to work. Systems might have specific design limitations for the maximum capacity of module they can take. A larger-capacity module works only if the motherboard is designed to accept it in the first place. Consult your system documentation to determine the correct capacity and speed to use.

Registered Modules

SDRAM and DDR DIMMs are available in buffered, unbuffered, and registered versions. A *buffered* module has additional buffer circuits between the memory chips and the connector to condition or buffer the signals. Virtually all PC motherboards designed to use SDRAM or DDR require unbuffered or registered modules instead. In fact, no PCs that I am aware of use plain buffered modules. Some of the early PowerPC Macs might have used buffered SDRAM, but no PCs do. Because so few systems ever used them, you will not find buffered modules available for sale.

Most PC motherboards are designed to use *unbuffered* modules, which allow the memory controller signals to pass directly to the memory chips on the module with no interference. This is not only the cheapest design, but also the fastest and most efficient. The only drawback is that the motherboard designer must place limits on how many modules (meaning module sockets) can be installed on the board, and possibly also limit how many chips can be on a module. So-called double-sided modules that really have two banks of chips (twice as many as normal) onboard might be restricted on some systems in certain combinations.

Systems designed to accept extremely large amounts of RAM often require registered modules. A registered module uses an architecture which has register chips on the module that act as an interface between the actual RAM chips and the chipset. The registers temporarily hold data passing to and from the memory chips and enable many more RAM chips to be driven or otherwise placed on the module than the chipset could normally support. This allows for motherboard designs that can support many modules and enables each module to have a larger number of chips. In general, registered modules are required by server or workstation motherboards designed to support more than 1GB or 2GB of RAM. The important thing to note is that you can use only the type of module your motherboard (or chipset) is designed to support. For most, that is standard unbuffered modules or, in some cases, registered modules.

SIMM Pinouts

Table 6.12 shows the interface connector pinouts for standard 72-pin SIMMs. They also include a special presence detect table that shows the configuration of the presence detect pins on various 72-pin SIMMs. The motherboard uses the presence detect pins to detect exactly what size and speed SIMM is installed. Industry-standard 30-pin SIMMs do not have a presence detect feature, but IBM did add this capability to its modified 30-pin configuration. Note that all SIMMs have the same pins on both sides of the module. SIMM pins are usually tin plated. The plating on the module pins must match the socket pins because corrosion will result otherwise.

Table 6.12   Standard 72-Pin SIMM Pinout

Pin	SIMM Signal Name	Pin	SIMM Signal Name	Pin	SIMM Signal Name
1	Ground	25	Data Bit 22	49	Data Bit 8
2	Data Bit 0	26	Data Bit 7	50	Data Bit 24
3	Data Bit 16	27	Data Bit 23	51	Data Bit 9
4	Data Bit 1	28	Address Bit 7	52	Data Bit 25
5	Data Bit 17	29	Address Bit 11	53	Data Bit 10
6	Data Bit 2	30	+5 Vdc	54	Data Bit 26
7	Data Bit 18	31	Address Bit 8	55	Data Bit 11
8	Data Bit 3	32	Address Bit 9	56	Data Bit 27
9	Data Bit 19	33	Address Bit 12	57	Data Bit 12
10	+5 Vdc	34	Address Bit 13	58	Data Bit 28
11	Presence Detect 5	35	Parity Data Bit 2	59	+5 Vdc
12	Address Bit 0	36	Parity Data Bit 0	60	Data Bit 29
13	Address Bit 1	37	Parity Data Bit 1	61	Data Bit 13
14	Address Bit 2	38	Parity Data Bit 3	62	Data Bit 30
15	Address Bit 3	39	Ground	63	Data Bit 14
16	Address Bit 4	40	Column Address Strobe 0	64	Data Bit 31
17	Address Bit 5	41	Column Address Strobe 2	65	Data Bit 15
18	Address Bit 6	42	Column Address Strobe 3	66	EDO
19	Address Bit 10	43	Column Address Strobe 1	67	Presence Detect 1
20	Data Bit 4	44	Row Address Strobe 0	68	Presence Detect 2
21	Data Bit 20	45	Row Address Strobe 1	69	Presence Detect 3
22	Data Bit 5	46	Reserved	70	Presence Detect 4
23	Data Bit 21	47	Write Enable	71	Reserved
24	Data Bit 6	48	ECC Optimized	72	Ground

Notice that the 72-pin SIMMs use a set of four or five pins to indicate the type of SIMM to the motherboard. These presence detect pins are either grounded or not connected to indicate the type of SIMM to the motherboard. Presence detect outputs must be tied to the ground through a 0-ohm resistor or jumper on the SIMM—to generate a high logic level when the pin is open or a low logic level when the motherboard grounds the pin. This produces signals the memory interface logic can decode. If the motherboard uses presence detect signals, a power on self test (POST) procedure can determine the size and speed of the installed SIMMs and adjust control and addressing signals automatically. This enables autodetection of the memory size and speed.

Note

In many ways, the presence detect pin function is similar to the industry-standard DX coding used on modern 35mm film rolls to indicate the ASA (speed) rating of the film to the camera. When you drop the film into the camera, electrical contacts can read the film's speed rating via an industry-standard configuration.

Table 6.13 shows the Joint Electronic Devices Engineering Council (JEDEC) industry-standard presence detect configuration listing for the 72-pin SIMM family. JEDEC is an organization of U.S. semiconductor manufacturers and users that sets semiconductor standards.

Table 6.13   Presence Detect Pin Configurations for 72-Pin SIMMs

Size	Speed	Pin 67	Pin 68	Pin 69	Pin 70	Pin 11
1MB	100ns	Gnd	—	Gnd	Gnd	—
1MB	80ns	Gnd	—	—	Gnd	—
1MB	70ns	Gnd	—	Gnd	—	—
1MB	60ns	Gnd	—	—	—	—
2MB	100ns	—	Gnd	Gnd	Gnd	—
2MB	80ns	—	Gnd	—	Gnd	—
2MB	70ns	—	Gnd	Gnd	—	—
2MB	60ns	—	Gnd	—	—	—
4MB	100ns	Gnd	Gnd	Gnd	Gnd	—
4MB	80ns	Gnd	Gnd	—	Gnd	—
4MB	70ns	Gnd	Gnd	Gnd	—	—
4MB	60ns	Gnd	Gnd	—	—	—
8MB	100ns	—	—	Gnd	Gnd	—
8MB	80ns	—	—	—	Gnd	—
8MB	70ns	—	—	Gnd	—	—
8MB	60ns	—	—	—	—	—
16MB	80ns	Gnd	—	—	Gnd	Gnd
16MB	70ns	Gnd	—	Gnd	—	Gnd
16MB	60ns	Gnd	—	—	—	Gnd
16MB	50ns	Gnd	—	Gnd	Gnd	Gnd
32MB	80ns	—	Gnd	—	Gnd	Gnd
32MB	70ns	—	Gnd	Gnd	—	Gnd
32MB	60ns	—	Gnd	—	—	Gnd
32MB	50ns	—	Gnd	Gnd	Gnd	Gnd

— = No connection (open)   Pin 68 = Presence detect 2   Pin 70 = Presence detect 4

Gnd = Ground   Pin 69 = Presence detect 3   Pin 11 = Presence detect 5

Pin 67 = Presence detect 1

Unfortunately, unlike the film industry, not everybody in the computer industry follows established standards. As such, presence detect signaling is not a standard throughout the PC industry. Different system manufacturers sometimes use different configurations for what is expected on these four pins. Compaq, IBM (mainly PS/2 systems), and Hewlett-Packard are notorious for this type of behavior. Many of the systems from these vendors require special SIMMs that are basically the same as standard 72-pin SIMMs, except for special presence detect requirements. Table 6.14 shows how IBM defines these pins.

Table 6.14 Presence Detect Pins for IBM 72-Pin SIMMs

67	68	69	70	SIMM Type	IBM Part Number
—	—	—	—	Not a valid SIMM	n/a
Gnd	—	—	—	1MB 120ns	n/a
—	Gnd	—	—	2MB 120ns	n/a
Gnd	Gnd	—	—	2MB 70ns	92F0102
—	—	Gnd	—	8MB 70ns	64F3606
Gnd	—	Gnd	—	Reserved	n/a
—	Gnd	Gnd	—	2MB 80ns	92F0103
Gnd	Gnd	Gnd	—	8MB 80ns	64F3607
—	—	—	Gnd	Reserved	n/a
Gnd	—	—	Gnd	1MB 85ns	90X8624
—	Gnd	—	Gnd	2MB 85ns	92F0104
Gnd	Gnd	—	Gnd	4MB 70ns	92F0105
—	—	Gnd	Gnd	4MB 85ns	79F1003 (square notch) L40-SX
Gnd	—	Gnd	Gnd	1MB 100ns	n/a
Gnd	—	Gnd	Gnd	8MB 80ns	79F1004 (square notch) L40-SX
—	Gnd	Gnd	Gnd	2MB 100ns	n/a
Gnd	Gnd	Gnd	Gnd	4MB 80ns	87F9980
Gnd	Gnd	Gnd	Gnd	2MB 85ns	79F1003 (square notch) L40SX

— = No connection (open) *Pin 67 = Presence detect 1* *Pin 69 = Presence detect 3*
Gnd = Ground *Pin 68 = Presence detect 2* *Pin 70 = Presence detect 4*

Because these pins can have custom variations, you often must specify IBM, Compaq, HP, or generic SIMMs when you order memory.

DIMM Pinouts

Table 6.15 shows the pinout configuration of a 168-pin standard unbuffered SDRAM DIMM. Note again that the pins on each side of the DIMM are different. All pins should be gold plated.

Table 6.15 168-Pin SDRAM DIMM Pinouts

Pin	Signal	Pin	Signal	Pin	Signal	Pin	Signal
1	GND	43	GND	85	GND	127	GND
2	Data Bit 0	44	Do Not Use	86	Data Bit 32	128	Clock Enable 0
3	Data Bit 1	45	Chip Select 2#	87	Data Bit 33	129	Chip Select 3#
4	Data Bit 2	46	I/O Mask 2	88	Data Bit 34	130	I/O Mask 6
5	Data Bit 3	47	I/O Mask 3	89	Data Bit 35	131	I/O Mask 7
6	+3.3V	48	Do Not Use	90	+3.3V	132	Reserved
7	Data Bit 4	49	+3.3V	91	Data Bit 36	133	+3.3V
8	Data Bit 5	50	NC	92	Data Bit 37	134	NC
9	Data Bit 6	51	NC	93	Data Bit 38	135	NC
10	Data Bit 7	52	Parity Bit 2	94	Data Bit 39	136	Parity Bit 6

Table 6.15   Continued

Pin	Signal	Pin	Signal	Pin	Signal	Pin	Signal
11	Data Bit 8	53	Parity Bit 3	95	Data Bit 40	137	Parity Bit 7
12	GND	54	GND	96	GND	138	GND
13	Data Bit 9	55	Data Bit 16	97	Data Bit 41	139	Data Bit 48
14	Data Bit 10	56	Data Bit 17	98	Data Bit 42	140	Data Bit 49
15	Data Bit 11	57	Data Bit 18	99	Data Bit 43	141	Data Bit 50
16	Data Bit 12	58	Data Bit 19	100	Data Bit 44	142	Data Bit 51
17	Data Bit 13	59	+3.3V	101	Data Bit 45	143	+3.3V
18	+3.3V	60	Data Bit 20	102	+3.3V	144	Data Bit 52
19	Data Bit 14	61	NC	103	Data Bit 46	145	NC
20	Data Bit 15	62	NC	104	Data Bit 47	146	NC
21	Parity Bit 0	63	Clock Enable 1	105	Parity Bit 4	147	NC
22	Parity Bit 1	64	GND	106	Parity Bit 5	148	GND
23	GND	65	Data Bit 21	107	GND	149	Data Bit 53
24	NC	66	Data Bit 22	108	NC	150	Data Bit 54
25	NC	67	Data Bit 23	109	NC	151	Data Bit 55
26	+3.3V	68	GND	110	+3.3V	152	GND
27	WE#	69	Data Bit 24	111	CAS#	153	Data Bit 56
28	I/O Mask 0	70	Data Bit 25	112	I/O Mask 4	154	Data Bit 57
29	I/O Mask 1	71	Data Bit 26	113	I/O Mask 5	155	Data Bit 58
30	Chip Select 0#	72	Data Bit 27	114	Chip Select 1#	156	Data Bit 59
31	Do Not Use	73	+3.3V	115	RAS#	157	+3.3V
32	GND	74	Data Bit 28	116	GND	158	Data Bit 60
33	Address Bit 0	75	Data Bit 29	117	Address Bit 1	159	Data Bit 61
34	Address Bit 2	76	Data Bit 30	118	Address Bit 3	160	Data Bit 62
35	Address Bit 4	77	Data Bit 31	119	Address Bit 5	161	Data Bit 63
36	Address Bit 6	78	GND	120	Address Bit 7	162	GND
37	Address Bit 8	79	Clock 2	121	Address Bit 9	163	Clock 3
38	Address Bit 10	80	NC	122	Bank Address 0	164	NC
39	Bank Address 1	81	SPD Write Protect	123	Address Bit 11	165	SPD Address 0
40	+3.3V	82	SPD Data	124	+3.3V	166	SPD Address 1
41	+3.3V	83	SPD Clock	125	Clock 1	167	SPD Address 2
42	Clock 0	84	+3.3V	126	Reserved	168	+3.3V

Gnd = Ground   *SPD = Serial presence detect*   *NC = No connection*

The DIMM uses a completely different type of presence detect than a SIMM, called *serial presence detect (SPD)*. It consists of a small EEPROM or Flash memory chip on the DIMM that contains specially formatted data indicating the DIMM's features. This serial data can be read via the serial data pins on the DIMM, and it enables the motherboard to autoconfigure to the exact type of DIMM installed.

DIMMs can come in several varieties, including unbuffered or buffered and 3.3V or 5V. Buffered DIMMs have additional buffer chips on them to interface to the motherboard. Unfortunately, these buffer chips slow down the DIMM and are not effective at higher speeds. For this reason, all PC systems use unbuffered DIMMs. The voltage is simple—DIMM designs for PCs are almost universally

3.3V. If you install a 5V DIMM in a 3.3V socket, it would be damaged, but fortunately, keying in the socket and on the DIMM prevents that.

Modern PC systems use only unbuffered 3.3V DIMMs. Apple and other non-PC systems can use the buffered 5V versions. Fortunately, the key notches along the connector edge of a DIMM are spaced differently for buffered/unbuffered or 3.3V/5V DIMMs, as shown in Figure 6.8. This prevents inserting a DIMM of the wrong type into a given socket.

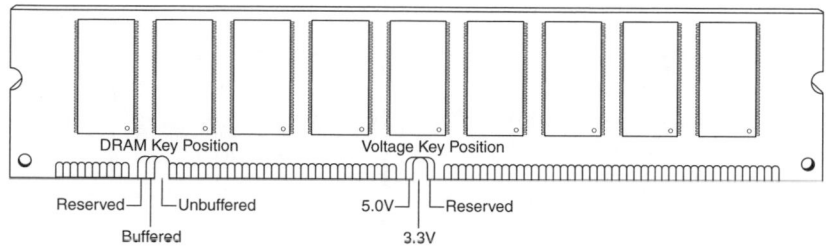

Figure 6.8   168-pin DRAM DIMM notch key definitions.

DDR DIMM Pinouts

Table 6.16 shows the pinout configuration of a 184-pin DDR SDRAM DIMM. Note again that the pins on each side of the DIMM are different. All pins should be gold plated.

Table 6.16   184-Pin DDR DIMM Pinouts

Pin	Signal	Pin	Signal	Pin	Signal	Pin	Signal
1	Reference +1.25V	47	Data Strobe 8	93	GND	139	GND
2	Data Bit 0	48	Address Bit 0	94	Data Bit 4	140	Data Strobe 17
3	GND	49	Parity Bit 2	95	Data Bit 5	141	Address Bit 10
4	Data Bit 1	50	GND	96	I/O +2.5V	142	Parity Bit 6
5	Data Strobe 0	51	Parity Bit 3	97	Data Strobe 9	143	I/O +2.5V
6	Data Bit 2	52	Bank Address 1	98	Data Bit 6	144	Parity Bit 7
7	+2.5 V	53	Data Bit 32	99	Data Bit 7	145	GND
8	Data Bit 3	54	I/O +2.5 V	100	GND	146	Data Bit 36
9	NC	55	Data Bit 33	101	NC	147	Data Bit 37
10	NC	56	Data Strobe 4	102	NC	148	+2.5V
11	GND	57	Data Bit 34	103	Address Bit 13	149	Data Strobe 13
12	Data Bit 8	58	GND	104	I/O +2.5V	150	Data Bit 38
13	Data Bit 9	59	Bank Address 0	105	Data Bit 12	151	Data Bit 39
14	Data Strobe 1	60	Data Bit 35	106	Data Bit 13	152	GND
15	I/O +2.5V	61	Data Bit 40	107	Data Strobe 10	153	Data Bit 44
16	Clock 1	62	I/O +2.5V	108	+2.5V	154	RAS#
17	Clock 1#	63	WE#	109	Data Bit 14	155	Data Bit 45
18	GND	64	Data Bit 41	110	Data Bit 15	156	I/O +2.5V
19	Data Bit 10	65	CAS#	111	Clock Enable 1	157	S0#
20	Data Bit 11	66	GND	112	I/O +2.5V	158	S1#

Table 6.16   Continued

Pin	Signal	Pin	Signal	Pin	Signal	Pin	Signal
21	Clock Enable 0	67	Data Strobe 5	113	Bank Address 2	159	Data Strobe 14
22	I/O +2.5V	68	Data Bit 42	114	Data Bit 20	160	GND
23	Data Bit 16	69	Data Bit 43	115	Address Bit 12	161	Data Bit 46
24	Data Bit 17	70	+2.5V	116	GND	162	Data Bit 47
25	Data Strobe 2	71	S2#	117	Data Bit 21	163	S3#
26	GND	72	Data Bit 48	118	Address Bit 11	164	I/O +2.5V
27	Address Bit 9	73	Data Bit 49	119	Data Strobe 11	165	Data Bit 52
28	Data Bit 18	74	GND	120	+2.5V	166	Data Bit 53
29	Address Bit 7	75	Clock 2#	121	Data Bit 22	167	FETEN
30	I/O +2.5V	76	Clock 2	122	Address Bit 8	168	+2.5V
31	Data Bit 19	77	I/O +2.5V	123	Data Bit 23	169	Data Strobe 15
32	Address Bit 5	78	Data Strobe 6	124	GND	170	Data Bit 54
33	Data Bit 24	79	Data Bit 50	125	Address Bit 6	171	Data Bit 55
34	GND	80	Data Bit 51	126	Data Bit 28	172	I/O +2.5V
35	Data Bit 25	81	GND	127	Data Bit 29	173	NC
36	Data Strobe 3	82	+2.5VID	128	I/O +2.5V	174	Data Bit 60
37	Address Bit 4	83	Data Bit 56	129	Data Strobe 12	175	Data Bit 61
38	+2.5V	84	Data Bit 57	130	Address Bit 3	176	GND
39	Data Bit 26	85	+2.5V	131	Data Bit 30	177	Data Strobe 16
40	Data Bit 27	86	Data Strobe 7	132	GND	178	Data Bit 62
41	Address Bit 2	87	Data Bit 58	133	Data Bit 31	179	Data Bit 63
42	GND	88	Data Bit 59	134	Parity Bit 4	180	I/O +2.5V
43	Address Bit 1	89	GND	135	Parity Bit 5	181	SPD Address 0
44	Parity Bit 0	90	SPD Write Protect	136	I/O +2.5V	182	SPD Address 1
45	Parity Bit 1	91	SPD Data	137	Clock 0	183	SPD Address 2
46	+2.5V	92	SPD Clock	138	Clock 0#	184	SPD +2.5V

Gnd = Ground   *SPD = Serial presence detect*   *NC = No connection*

DDR DIMMs use a single key notch to indicate voltage, as shown in Figure 6.9.

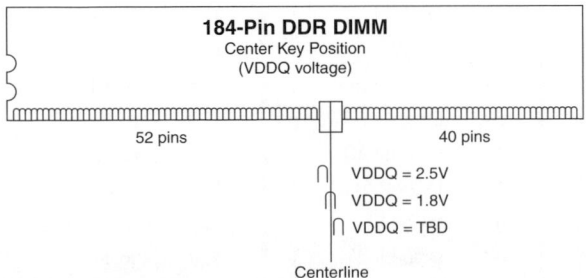

Figure 6.9   184-pin DDR SDRAM DIMM keying.

184-pin DDR DIMMs use two notches on each side to enable compatibility with both low- and high-profile latched sockets. Note that the key position is offset with respect to the center of the DIMM to prevent inserting it backward in the socket. The key notch is positioned to the left, centered, or to the right of the area between pins 52 and 53. This is used to indicate the I/O voltage for the DDR DIMM and to prevent installing the wrong type into a socket that might damage the DIMM.

DDR2 DIMM Pinouts

Table 6.17 shows the pinout configuration of a 240-pin DDR2 SDRAM DIMM. Pins 1–120 are on the front side, and pins 121–240 are on the back. All pins should be gold plated.

Table 6.17   240-Pin DDR2 DIMM Pinouts

Pin	Signal	Pin	Signal	Pin	Signal	Pin	Signal
1	VREF	61	A4	121	VSS	181	VDDQ
2	VSS	62	VDDQ	122	DQ4	182	A3
3	DQ0	63	A2	123	DQ5	183	A1
4	DQ1	64	VDD	124	VSS	184	VDD
5	VSS	65	VSS	125	DM0	185	CK0
6	-DQS0	66	VSS	126	NC	186	-CK0
7	DQS0	67	VDD	127	VSS	187	VDD
8	VSS	68	NC	128	DQ6	188	A0
9	DQ2	69	VDD	129	DQ7	189	VDD
10	DQ3	70	A10/-AP	130	VSS	190	BA1
11	VSS	71	BA0	131	DQ12	191	VDDQ
12	DQ8	72	VDDQ	132	DQ13	192	-RAS
13	DQ9	73	-WE	133	VSS	193	-CS0
14	VSS	74	-CAS	134	DM1	194	VDDQ
15	-DQS1	75	VDDQ	135	NC	195	ODT0
16	DQS1	76	-CS1	136	VSS	196	A13
17	VSS	77	ODT1	137	CK1	197	VDD
18	NC	78	VDDQ	138	-CK1	198	VSS
19	NC	79	SS	139	VSS	199	DQ36
20	VSS	80	DQ32	140	DQ14	200	DQ37
21	DQ10	81	DQ33	141	DQ15	201	VSS
22	DQ11	82	VSS	142	VSS	202	DM4
23	VSS	83	-DQS4	143	DQ20	203	NC
24	DQ16	84	DQS4	144	DQ21	204	VSS
25	DQ17	85	VSS	145	VSS	205	DQ38
26	VSS	86	DQ34	146	DM2	206	DQ39
27	-DQS2	87	DQ35	147	NC	207	VSS
28	DQS2	88	VSS	148	VSS	208	DQ44
29	VSS	89	DQ40	149	DQ22	209	DQ45
30	DQ18	90	DQ41	150	DQ23	210	VSS
31	DQ19	91	VSS	151	VSS	211	DM5
32	VSS	92	-DQS5	152	DQ28	212	NC

Table 6.17   Continued

Pin	Signal	Pin	Signal	Pin	Signal	Pin	Signal
33	DQ24	93	DQS5	153	DQ29	213	VSS
34	DQ25	94	VSS	154	VSS	214	DQ46
35	VSS	95	DQ42	155	DM3	215	DQ47
36	-DQS3	96	DQ43	156	NC	216	VSS
37	DQS3	97	VSS	157	VSS	217	DQ52
38	VSS	98	DQ48	158	DQ30	218	DQ53
39	DQ26	99	DQ49	159	DQ31	219	VSS
40	DQ27	100	VSS	160	VSS	220	CK2
41	VSS	101	SA2	161	NC	221	-CK2
42	NC	102	NC	162	NC	222	VSS
43	NC	103	VSS	163	VSS	223	DM6
44	VSS	104	-DQS6	164	NC	224	NC
45	NC	105	DQS6	165	NC	225	VSS
46	NC	106	VSS	166	VSS	226	DQ54
47	VSS	107	DQ50	167	NC	227	DQ55
48	NC	108	DQ51	168	NC	228	VSS
49	NC	109	VSS	169	VSS	229	DQ60
50	VSS	110	DQ56	170	VDDQ	230	DQ61
51	VDDQ	111	DQ57	171	CKE1	231	VSS
52	CKE0	112	VSS	172	VDD	232	DM7
53	VDD	113	-DQS7	173	NC	233	NC
54	NC	114	DQS7	174	NC	234	VSS
55	NC	115	VSS	175	VDDQ	235	DQ62
56	VDDQ	116	DQ58	176	A12	236	DQ63
57	A11	117	DQ59	177	A9	237	VSS
58	A7	118	VSS	178	VDD	238	VDDSPD
59	VDD	119	SDA	179	A8	239	SA0
60	A5	120	SCL	180	A6	240	SA1

240-pin DDR2 DIMMs use two notches on each side to enable compatibility with both low- and high-profile latched sockets. The connector key is offset with respect to the center of the DIMM to prevent inserting it backward in the socket. The key notch is positioned in the center of the area between pins 64 and 65 on the front (184/185 on the back), and there is no voltage keying because all DDR2 DIMMs run on 1.8V.

RIMM Pinouts

RIMM modules and sockets are gold-plated and designed for 25 insertion/removal cycles. Each RIMM has 184 pins, split into two groups of 92 pins on opposite ends and sides of the module. The pinout of the RIMM is shown in Table 6.18.

Table 6.18 RIMM Pinout

Pin	Signal	Pin	Signal	Pin	Signal	Pin	Signal
A1	GND	B1	GND	A47	NC	B47	NC
A2	LData Bit A8	B2	LData Bit A7	A48	NC	B48	NC
A3	GND	B3	GND	A49	NC	B49	NC
A4	LData Bit A6	B4	LData Bit A5	A50	NC	B50	NC
A5	GND	B5	GND	A51	VREF	B51	VREF
A6	LData Bit A4	B6	LData Bit A3	A52	GND	B52	GND
A7	GND	B7	GND	A53	SPD Clock	B53	SPD Address 0
A8	LData Bit A2	B8	LData Bit A1	A54	+2.5V	B54	+2.5V
A9	GND	B9	GND	A55	SDA	B55	SPD Address 1
A10	LData Bit A0	B10	Interface Clock+	A56	SVDD	B56	SVDD
A11	GND	B11	GND	A57	SPD Write Protect	B57	SPD Address 2
A12	LCTMN	B12	Interface Clock-	A58	+2.5V	B58	+2.5V
A13	GND	B13	GND	A59	RSCK	B59	RCMD
A14	LCTM	B14	NC	A60	GND	B60	GND
A15	GND	B15	GND	A61	Rdata Bit B7	B61	RData Bit B8
A16	NC	B16	LROW2	A62	GND	B62	GND
A17	GND	B17	GND	A63	Rdata Bit B5	B63	RData Bit B6
A18	LROW1	B18	LROW0	A64	GND	B64	GND
A19	GND	B19	GND	A65	Rdata Bit B3	B65	RData Bit B4
A20	LCOL4	B20	LCOL3	A66	GND	B66	GND
A21	GND	B21	GND	A67	Rdata Bit B1	B67	RData Bit B2
A22	LCOL2	B22	LCOL1	A68	GND	B68	GND
A23	GND	B23	GND	A69	RCOL0	B69	RData Bit B0
A24	LCOL0	B24	LData Bit B0	A70	GND	B70	GND
A25	GND	B25	GND	A71	RCOL2	B71	RCOL1
A26	LData Bit B1	B26	LData Bit B2	A72	GND	B72	GND
A27	GND	B27	GND	A73	RCOL4	B73	RCOL3
A28	LData Bit B3	B28	LData Bit B4	A74	GND	B74	GND
A29	GND	B29	GND	A75	RROW1	B75	RROW0
A30	LData Bit B5	B30	LData Bit B6	A76	GND	B76	GND
A31	GND	B31	GND	A77	NC	B77	RROW2
A32	LData Bit B7	B32	LData Bit B8	A78	GND	B78	GND
A33	GND	B33	GND	A79	RCTM	B79	NC
A34	LSCK	B34	LCMD	A80	GND	B80	GND
A35	VCMOS	B35	VCMOS	A81	RCTMN	B81	RCFMN
A36	SOUT	B36	SIN	A82	GND	B82	GND
A37	VCMOS	B37	VCMOS	A83	Rdata Bit A0	B83	RCFM
A38	NC	B38	NC	A84	GND	B84	GND
A39	GND	B39	GND	A85	Rdata Bit A2	B85	RData Bit A1
A40	NC	B40	NC	A86	GND	B86	GND
A41	+2.5V	B41	+2.5V	A87	Rdata Bit A4	B87	RData Bit A3
A42	+2.5V	B42	+2.5V	A88	GND	B88	GND
A43	NC	B43	NC	A89	Rdata Bit A6	B89	RData Bit A5
A44	NC	B44	NC	A90	GND	B90	GND
A45	NC	B45	NC	A91	Rdata Bit A8	B91	RData Bit A7
A46	NC	B46	NC	A92	GND	B92	GND

16/18-bit RIMMs are keyed with two notches in the center. This prevents a backward insertion and prevents the wrong type (voltage) RIMM from being used in a system. Currently, all RIMMs run on 2.5V, but future 64-bit versions will run on only 1.8V. To allow for changes in the RIMMs, three keying options are possible in the design (see Figure 6.10). The left key (indicated as "DATUM A" in Figure 6.10) is fixed in position, but the center key can be in three different positions spaced 1mm or 2mm to the right, indicating different types of RIMMs. The current default is option A, as shown in Figure 6.10 and Table 6.19, which corresponds to 2.5V operation.

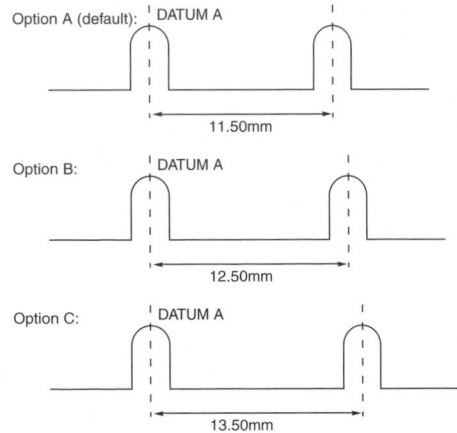

Figure 6.10   RIMM keying options.

Table 6.19   Possible Keying Options for RIMMs

Option	Notch Separation	Description
A	11.5mm	2.5V RIMM
B	12.5mm	Reserved
C	13.5mm	Reserved

RIMMs incorporate an SPD device, which is essentially a Flash ROM onboard. This ROM contains information about the RIMM's size and type, including detailed timing information for the memory controller. The memory controller automatically reads the data from the SPD ROM to configure the system to match the RIMMs installed.

Figure 6.11 shows a typical PC RIMM installation. The RDRAM controller and clock generator are typically in the motherboard chipset North Bridge component. As you can see, the Rambus memory channel flows from the memory controller through each of up to three RIMM modules in series. Each module contains 4, 8, 16, or more RDRAM devices (chips), also wired in series, with an onboard SPD ROM for system configuration. Any RIMM sockets without a RIMM installed must have a continuity module, shown in the last socket in Figure 6.11. This enables the memory bus to remain continuous from the controller through each module (and, therefore, each RDRAM device on the module) until the bus finally terminates on the motherboard. Note how the bus loops from one module to another. For timing purposes, the first RIMM socket must be 6" or less from the memory controller, and the entire length of the bus must not be more than it would take for a signal to go from one end to another in four data clocks, or about 5ns.

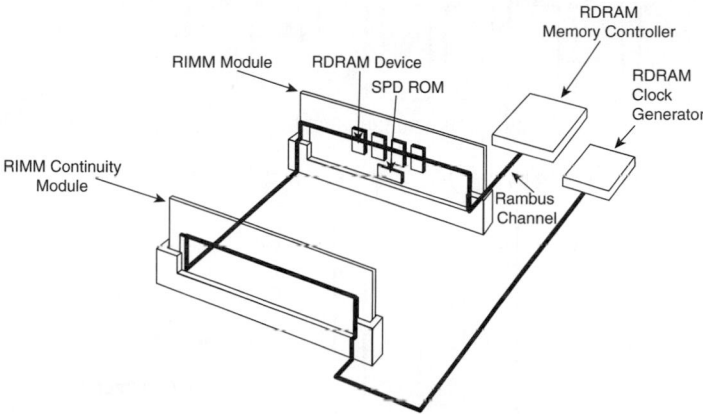

Figure 6.11 Typical RDRAM bus layout showing a RIMM and one continuity module.

Interestingly, Rambus does not manufacture the RDRAM devices (the chips) or the RIMMs; that is left to other companies. Rambus is merely a design company, and it has no chip fabs or manufacturing facilities of its own. It licenses its technology to other companies who then manufacture the devices and modules.

Physical RAM Capacity and Organization

Several types of memory chips have been used in PC system motherboards. Most of these chips are single-bit-wide chips and are available in several capacities.

Note that chip capacity typically goes up by factors of four because the dies that make up the chips are square. When they increase capacity, this results in four times more transistors and four times more capacity. Most modern SIMMs and DIMMs use 16Mb–256Mb chips onboard.

Figure 6.12 shows the markings on a typical memory chip from Micron Technologies, one of the most popular chip and module manufacturers. Many memory manufacturers use similar schemes for numbering their chips; however, if you are really trying to identify a particular chip, you should consult the manufacturer catalog for more information.

The -75 marking corresponds to the chip speed in nanoseconds—in this case, a 7.5-nanosecond or 133MHz designation.

The part number usually contains a clue about the chip's type and capacity. The chip here is MT48LC8M8A2TG-75L. This decodes as

MT = Micron Technologies

48 = SDRAM

LC = 3.3V CMOS

8M8 = 8 million rows deep × 8 bits wide

A2 = Device version

TG = TSOP (thin small outline package)

-75 = 7.5ns (133MHz) rating

L = Low power

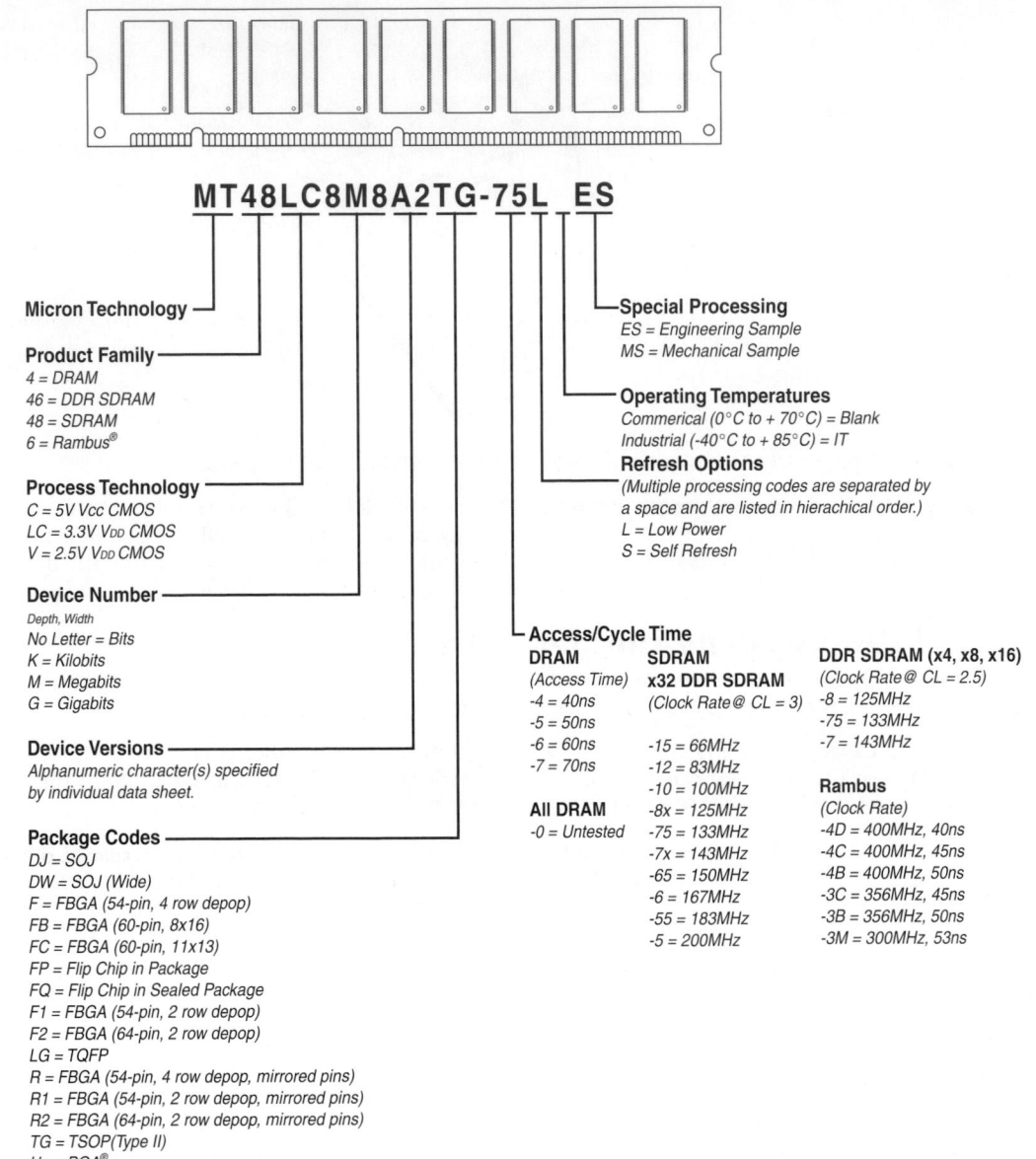

Figure 6.12 The markings on a typical memory chip (Micron shown).

Note

Markings vary from manufacturer to manufacturer. The example shown here is for illustrative purposes only.

Because this chip is 8 bits wide, I'd expect to see either 8 or 16 of them on a DIMM to make up the 64 bits of width for the complete DIMM. If 16 chips were used, this would be known as a *double-sided DIMM* and the chips would be arranged in a logically stacked form in which the two banks of 8MB×8 chips work together as if they were a single bank of 16MB×8 chips. If 8 of these chips were on a

DIMM, it would be 8MB×64 bits, which is the same as saying 8MB×8 bytes, which is the same as calling it a 64MB DIMM. If there were 16 of these chips, it would be a 128MB double-sided DIMM, and if there were either 9 or 18 of these chips, it would be a 72-bit wide DIMM with parity/ECC support.

Most chips also feature a four-digit number separate from the part number that indicates the date of manufacture by week and day. For example, 0021 indicates the chip was made in the 21st week of 2000. To further decode the chip, contact the manufacturer or chip vendor for its catalog information.

SIMMs and DIMMs also have part numbers that can be difficult to decode. Unfortunately, no industry standard exists for numbering these modules, so you must contact the manufacturer if you want to decode the numbers.

Sometimes you can't find any writing on the module that tells you the capacity or other information. In that case, just look up the chip part numbers on the chip manufacturer's Web site, and from there you should be able to figure out what it is (see Figure 6.13).

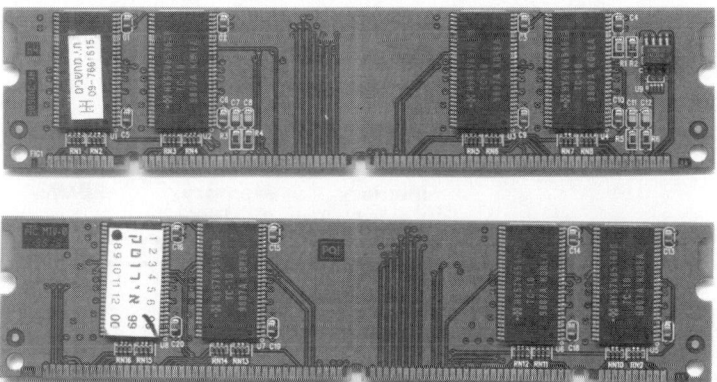

Figure 6.13   DIMM front/rear view with indecipherable markings indicating part number, capacity, or speed.

The fact that I can't decipher the information on the stickers about the DIMM is not a problem, as long as I can read the chip part numbers.

The chips carry the Hyundai (HY) logo, with a part number of HY57V651620-TC10. I found the data sheet for these chips at the Hyundai Memory Web site. I can't tell who made the actual DIMM; at first I suspected Hyundai might have made it because of the HY-3U1606 number on the left side, but I can't find any corresponding information in the Hyundai catalog that matches this designation. No matter; I can still deduce all the information I need about this module by looking at the chip information.

According to the data sheet for the chips on this DIMM, these are 10ns chips, which, although technically rated 100MHz, would classify this as a 66MHz SDRAM DIMM (PC66). If they were 8ns (125MHz) chips, this would be a PC100 DIMM, and if they were 7.5ns, this would be a PC133 DIMM. These are 64Mb chips, organized as 4MB×16 (rows by columns). Four chips are on one side, resulting in a full 64-bit wide bank of 4MB×64 bits (4MB×8 bytes or 32MB total). The other side contains the same number of chips, which would be electronically or logically "stacked" to double the depth (number of rows). This is because DIMMs can be only 64 bits wide, resulting in a total of 8MB×64 bits, which is 8MB×8 bytes, which is 64MB total. The additional tiny Atmel brand chip on the right side is the serial EEPROM, which contains the data about this DIMM that can be read by the motherboard to configure the chipset memory controllers. Because there are no additional memory chips, this DIMM lacks the additional 8 bits of width to make it a 72 bit wide ECC DIMM.

So, by deciphering the chip part numbers and adding things up, I have figured out that this is a 64MB, double-sided, non-ECC, PC66 SDRAM DIMM.

Tip

If you are unable to decipher the chip part number, you can use the HWinfo or SiSoftware Sandra program to identify your memory module as well as many other facts about your computer, including chipset, processor, empty memory sockets, and much more. You can download shareware versions of HWinfo from `www.hwinfo.com` or SiSoft Sandra from `www.sisoftware.net`.

Memory Banks

Memory chips (DIPs, SIMMs, SIPPs, and DIMMs) are organized in banks on motherboards and memory cards. You should know the memory bank layout and position on the motherboard and memory cards.

You need to know the bank layout when adding memory to the system. In addition, memory diagnostics report error locations by byte and bit addresses, and you must use these numbers to locate which bank in your system contains the problem.

The banks usually correspond to the data bus capacity of the system's microprocessor. Table 6.20 shows the widths of individual banks based on the type of PC.

Table 6.20   Memory Bank Widths on Various Systems

Processor	Data Bus	Memory Bank Size (No Parity)	Memory Bank Size (Parity/ECC)	30-Pin SIMMs per Bank	72-Pin SIMMs per Bank	168-Pin DIMMs per Bank
8088	8-bit	8 bits	9 bits	1	n/a	n/a
8086	16-bit	16 bits	18 bits	2	n/a	n/a
286	16-bit	16 bits	18 bits	2	n/a	n/a
386SX, SL, SLC	16-bit	16 bits	18 bits	2	n/a	n/a
486SLC, SLC2	16-bit	16 bits	18 bits	2	n/a	n/a
386DX	32-bit	32 bits	36 bits	4	1	n/a
486SX, DX, DX2, DX4, 5x86	32-bit	32 bits	36 bits	4	1	n/a
Pentium, K6 series	64-bit	64 bits	72 bits	8*	2	1
PPro, PII, Celeron, PIII, P4, Athlon/Duron, Athlon XP	64-bit	64 bits	72 bits	8*	2	1

Very few if any motherboards using this type of memory were made for these processors.

The number of bits for each bank can be made up of single chips, SIMMs, or DIMMs. Modern systems don't use individual chips; instead, they use only SIMMs or DIMMs. If the system has a 16-bit processor, such as a 386SX, it probably uses 30-pin SIMMs and has two SIMMs per bank. All the SIMMs in a single bank must be the same size and type.

A 486 system requires four 30-pin SIMMs or one 72-pin SIMM to make up a bank. A single 72-pin SIMM is 32 bits wide, or 36 bits wide if it supports parity. You can often tell whether a SIMM supports parity by counting its chips. To make a 32-bit SIMM, you could use 32 individual 1-bit-wide chips, or you could use eight individual 4-bit-wide chips to make up the data bits. If the system uses parity, four extra bits are required (36 bits total), so you would see one more 4-bit-wide or four individual 1-bit-wide chips added to the bank for the parity bits.

As you might imagine, 30-pin SIMMs are less than ideal for 32-bit or 64-bit systems (that is, 486 or Pentium) because you must use them in increments of four or eight per bank. Because these SIMMs are currently available in 1MB, 4MB, and 16MB capacities, a single bank of 30-pin SIMMs in a 486 system would be 4MB, 16MB, or 64MB; for a Pentium system, this would be 8MB, 32MB, or 128MB of memory, with no in-between amounts. Using 30-pin SIMMs in 32- and 64-bit systems artificially constrains memory configurations, and such systems are not recommended. If a 32-bit system (such as any PC with a 486 processor) uses 72-pin SIMMs, each SIMM represents a separate bank and the SIMMs can be added or removed on an individual basis rather than in groups of four, as would be required with 30-pin SIMMs. This makes memory configuration much easier and more flexible. In 64-bit systems that use SIMMs, two 72-pin SIMMs are required per bank.

DIMMs are ideal for Pentium and higher systems because the 64-bit width of the DIMM exactly matches the 64-bit width of the Pentium processor data bus. Therefore, each DIMM represents an individual bank, and they can be added or removed one at a time.

The physical orientation and numbering of the SIMMs or DIMMs used on a motherboard is arbitrary and determined by the board's designers, so documentation covering your system or card comes in handy. You can determine the layout of a motherboard or an adapter card through testing, but that takes time and might be difficult, particularly after you have a problem with a system.

Memory Module Speed

When you replace a failed memory module or install a new module as an upgrade, you typically must install a module of the same type and speed as the others in the system. You can substitute a module with a different (faster) speed but only if the replacement module's speed is equal to or faster than that of the other modules in the system.

Some people have had problems when "mixing" modules of different speeds. With the wide variety of motherboards, chipsets, and memory types, few ironclad rules exist. When in doubt as to which speed module to install in your system, consult the motherboard documentation for more information.

Substituting faster memory of the same type doesn't result in improved performance if the system still operates the memory at the same speed. Systems that use DIMMs or RIMMs can read the speed and timing features of the module from a special SPD ROM installed on the module and then set chipset (memory controller) timing accordingly. In these systems, you might see an increase in performance by installing faster modules, to the limit of what the chipset will support.

To place more emphasis on timing and reliability, there are Intel and JEDEC standards governing memory types that require certain levels of performance. Intel, for example, has created the PC66, PC100, and PC133 standards supported by many newer chipsets. These standards certify that memory modules perform within Intel's timing and performance guidelines. At 100MHz or higher, there is not much "forgiveness" or slop allowed in memory timing.

The same common symptoms result when the system memory has failed or is simply not fast enough for the system's timing. The usual symptoms are frequent parity check errors or a system that does not operate at all. The POST might report errors, too. If you're unsure of which chips to buy for your system, contact the system manufacturer or a reputable chip supplier.

▶▶ See "Parity Checking," p. 502.

Gold Versus Tin

Many people don't understand the importance of the memory module electrical contacts in a computer system. Modules (SIMMs, DIMMs, and RIMMs) are available in gold- or tin-plated contact form. I initially thought that gold contact modules were the best way to go for reliability in all situations, but that is not true. To have the most reliable system, you must install modules with gold-plated contacts into gold-plated sockets and modules with tin-plated contacts into tin-plated sockets only.

If you don't heed this warning and install memory with gold-plated contacts into tin sockets or vice versa, you will have problems with memory errors and reliability in the long run. In my experiences, they occur six months to one year after installation. I have encountered this problem several times in my own systems and in several systems I have serviced. I have even been asked to assist one customer in a lawsuit as an expert witness. The customer had bought several hundred machines from a vendor, and severe memory failures began appearing in most of the machines approximately a year after delivery. The cause was traced to dissimilar metals between the memory modules and sockets (gold-plated contact SIMMs in tin-plated contact sockets, in this case). The vendor refused to replace the SIMMs with tin-plated versions, hence the lawsuit.

Most systems using 72-pin SIMMs have tin-plated sockets, so they must have tin-plated SIMM memory installed. Studies done by the connector manufacturers, such as AMP, show that a type of corrosion called *fretting* occurs when tin comes in pressure contact with gold or any other metal. With fretting corrosion, tin oxide transfers to the harder gold surface, eventually causing a high-resistance connection. This happens whenever gold comes into contact with tin, no matter how thick or thin the gold coating is. Over time, depending on the environment, fretting corrosion can and will cause high resistance at the contact point and thus cause memory errors.

You might think tin makes a poor connector material because it readily oxidizes. Even so, electrical contact is easily made between two tin surfaces under pressure because the oxides on the softer tin surfaces bend and break, ensuring contact. In most memory modules, the contacts are under fairly high pressure when the modules are installed.

When tin and gold come into contact, because one surface is hard, the oxidation builds up and does not break easily under pressure. Increased contact resistance ultimately results in memory failures.

The connector manufacturer AMP has published several documents from the AMP Contact Physics Research Department that discuss this issue, but two are the most applicable. One is titled "Golden Rules: Guidelines for the Use of Gold on Connector Contacts," and the other is called "The Tin Commandments: Guidelines for the Use of Tin on Connector Contacts." Both can be downloaded in PDF form from the AMP Web site. Commandment Number Seven from the Tin Commandments specifically states "7. Mating of tin-coated contacts to gold-coated contacts is not recommended." For further technical details, you can contact Intel or AMP.

Certainly, the best type of arrangement is having gold-plated modules installed in gold-plated sockets. Most systems using DIMMs or RIMMs are designed this way.

If you have mixed metals in your memory now, the correct solution is to replace the memory modules with the appropriate contact type to match the socket. Another much less desirable solution is to wait until problems appear (about six months to a year, in my experience) and then remove the modules, clean the contacts, reinstall, and repeat the cycle. This is probably fine if you are an individual with one or two systems, but it is not fine if you are maintaining hundreds of systems. If your system does not feature parity or ECC memory (most systems sold today do not), when the problems do occur, you might not be able to immediately identify them as memory related (General Protection Faults, crashes, file and data corruption, and so on).

One problem with cleaning is that the hard tin oxide deposits that form on the gold surface are difficult to remove and often require abrasive cleaning (by using an eraser or a crocus cloth, for example). This should never be done dry because it generates static discharges that can damage the chips. Instead, use a contact cleaner to lubricate the contacts; wet contacts minimize the potential for static discharge damage when rubbing the eraser or other abrasive on the surface.

To further prevent this problem from occurring, I highly recommend using a liquid contact enhancer and lubricant called Stabilant 22 from D.W. Electrochemicals when installing SIMMs or DIMMs. Its Web site has a detailed application note on this subject if you are interested in more technical details; see the Vendor List on the disc accompanying this book.

Some people have accused me of being too picky by insisting that the memory match the socket. On several occasions, I have returned either memory or motherboards because the vendor putting them together did not have a clue that this is a problem. When I tell some people about it, they tell me they have a lot of PCs with mixed metal contacts that run fine and have been doing so for many years.

Of course, that is certainly a poor argument against sound engineering practices. Many people are running SCSI buses that are way too long, with improper termination, and they say they run "fine." Parallel port cables are by the spec limited to 10 feet, yet I see many that have longer cables, which people claim work "fine." The IDE cable limit is 18"; that spec is violated and people get away with it, saying their drives run just "fine." I see cheap, crummy power supplies that put out noise, ripple, and loosely regulated voltages, and I have even measured up to 69 volts AC of ground leakage, and yet the systems appeared to be running "fine." I have encountered numerous systems without proper CPU heatsinks, or in which the active heatsink (fan) was seized, and the system ran "fine." This reminds me of when Johnny Carson would interview 100-year-old people and often got them to admit that they drank heavily and smoked cigarettes every day, as if those are good practices that ensure longevity!

The truth is I am often amazed at how poorly designed or implemented some systems are, and yet they do seem to work...for the most part. The occasional lockup or crash is just written off by the user as "that's the way they all are." All, except *my* systems, of course. In my systems, I adhere to proper design and engineering practices. In fact, I am often guilty of engineering or specifying overkill into things. Although it adds to the cost, they do seem to run better because of it.

In other words, what one individual can "get away" with does not change the laws of physics. It does not change the fact that for those supporting many systems or selling systems where the maximum in reliability and service life is desired, the gold/tin issue does matter.

Another issue that was brought to my attention was the thickness of the gold on the contacts; people are afraid that it is so thin that it will wear off after one or two insertions. Certainly, the choice of gold coating thickness depends on the durability required by the application; because of gold's high cost, it is prudent to keep the gold coating thickness as low as is appropriate for the durability requirements.

To improve durability, a small amount of cobalt or nickel added to the gold usually hardens the gold coatings. Such coatings are defined as "hard gold" and produce coatings with a low coefficient of friction and excellent durability characteristics. Hard gold-coated contacts can generally withstand hundreds to thousands of durability cycles without failing. Using an underlayer with a hardness value greater than that of gold alone that provides additional mechanical support can enhance the durability of hard gold coatings. Nickel is generally recommended as an underlayer for this purpose. Special electronic contact lubricants or enhancers, such as Stabilant 22 from D.W. Electrochemicals, are also effective at increasing the durability of gold coatings. Generally, lubrication can increase the durability of a gold contact by an order of magnitude. These and other chemicals are discussed in more detail in Chapter 24, "PC Diagnostics, Testing, and Maintenance."

Increasing the thickness of a hard gold coating increases durability. AMP obtained the laboratory results in Table 6.21 for the wear-through of a hard gold coating to the 1.3 micron (50 micro-inch) thick nickel underplate. The following data is for a 0.635cm (0.250") diameter ball wiped a distance of 1.27cm (0.500") under a normal force of 100 grams for each cycle.

Table 6.21 Plating Thickness for Gold-Plated Contacts

Thickness Microns	Thickness Micro-inch	Cycles to Failure
0.4	15	200
0.8	30	1000
1.3	50	2000

As you can see from this table, an 0.8 micron (30 micro-inches) coating of hard gold results in durability that is more than adequate for most connector applications because it allows 1,000 insertion and removal cycles before wearing through. I studied the specification sheets for DIMM and SIMM sockets produced by AMP and found that its gold-plated sockets come mostly as .000030 (30 micro-inches) thick gold over .000050 (50 micro-inches) thick nickel in the contact area. As far as I can determine, the coating on virtually all memory module contacts would be similar in thickness, allowing for the same durability.

AMP also has a few gold-plated sockets with specifications of .001020-thick (1,020 micro-inches) gold over .001270-thick (1,270 micro-inches) nickel. I'd guess that the latter sockets were for devices such as SIMM testers, in which many insertions were expected over the life of the equipment. They could also be used in high-vibration or high-humidity environments.

For reference, all its tin-contact SIMM and DIMM sockets have the following connector plating specifications: .000030 (30 micro-inches) minimum thick tin on mating edge over .000050 (50 micro-inches) minimum thick nickel on entire contact.

The bottom line is that the thickness of the coating in current module sockets and modules is not an issue for the expected use of these devices. The thickness of the plating used is also not relevant to the tin versus gold compatibility issue. The only drawback to a thinner gold plating is that it will wear after fewer insertion/removal cycles, exposing the nickel underneath and allowing the onset of fretting corrosion.

In my opinion, this tin/gold issue is even more important for those using DIMMs and RIMMs, for two reasons. With SIMMs, you really have two connections for each pin (one on each side of the module), so if one of them goes high resistance, it will not matter; there is a built-in redundancy. With DIMMs and RIMMs, you have many, many more connections (168 or 184 versus 72) and no redundant connections. The chance for failure is much greater. Also, DIMMs and RIMMs run much faster, at speeds of up to 800MHz or faster, where the timing is down in the single-digit nanosecond range. At these speeds, the slightest additional resistance in the connection causes problems.

Bottom line: Definitely don't mix metal types, but for the utmost in reliability for systems using DIMMs or RIMMs, be sure both the motherboard sockets as well as the modules themselves have gold-plated contacts. You usually can tell easily because tin is silver-colored, whereas gold is, well, gold-colored.

Parity and ECC

Part of the nature of memory is that it inevitably fails. These failures are usually classified as two basic types: hard fails and soft errors.

The best understood are *hard fails*, in which the chip is working and then, because of some flaw, physical damage, or other event, becomes damaged and experiences a permanent failure. Fixing this type of failure normally requires replacing some part of the memory hardware, such as the chip, SIMM, or DIMM. Hard error rates are known as *HERs*.

The other more insidious type of failure is the *soft error*, which is a nonpermanent failure that might never recur or could occur only at infrequent intervals. (Soft fails are effectively "fixed" by powering the system off and back on.) Soft error rates are known as *SERs*.

About 20 years ago, Intel made a discovery about soft errors that shook the memory industry. It found that alpha particles were causing an unacceptably high rate of soft errors or single event upsets (SEUs, as they are sometimes called) in the 16KB DRAMs that were available at the time. Because alpha particles are low-energy particles that can be stopped by something as thin and light as a sheet of paper, it became clear that for alpha particles to cause a DRAM soft error, they would have to be coming from within the semiconductor material. Testing showed trace elements of thorium and uranium in the plastic and ceramic chip packaging materials used at the time. This discovery forced all the memory manufacturers to evaluate their manufacturing processes to produce materials free from contamination.

Today, memory manufacturers have all but totally eliminated the alpha-particle source of soft errors. Many people believed that was justification for the industry trend to drop parity checking. The argument is that, for example, a 16MB memory subsystem built with 4MB technology would experience a soft error caused by alpha particles only about once every 16 years! The real problem with this thinking is that it is seriously flawed, and many system manufacturers and vendors were coddled into removing parity and other memory fault-tolerant techniques from their systems even though soft errors continue to be an ongoing problem. More recent discoveries prove that alpha particles are now only a small fraction of the cause of DRAM soft errors.

As it turns out, the biggest cause of soft errors today are cosmic rays. IBM researchers began investigating the potential of terrestrial cosmic rays in causing soft errors similar to alpha particles. The difference is that cosmic rays are very high-energy particles and can't be stopped by sheets of paper or other more powerful types of shielding. The leader in this line of investigation was Dr. J.F. Ziegler of the IBM Watson Research Center in Yorktown Heights, New York. He has produced landmark research into understanding cosmic rays and their influence on soft errors in memory.

One example of the magnitude of the cosmic ray soft-error phenomenon demonstrated that with a certain sample of non-IBM DRAMs, the SER at sea level was measured at 5950 FIT (failures in time, which is measured at 1 billion hours) per chip. This was measured under real-life conditions with the benefit of millions of device hours of testing. In an average system, this would result in a soft error occurring every six months or less. In power-user or server systems with a larger amount of memory, it could mean one or more errors per month! When the exact same test setup and DRAMs were moved to an underground vault shielded by more than 50 feet of rock, thus eliminating all cosmic rays, absolutely no soft errors were recorded. This not only demonstrates how troublesome cosmic rays can be, but it also proves that the packaging contamination and alpha-particle problem has indeed been solved.

Cosmic-ray-induced errors are even more of a problem in SRAMs than DRAMS because the amount of charge required to flip a bit in an SRAM cell is less than is required to flip a DRAM cell capacitor. Cosmic rays are also more of a problem for higher-density memory. As chip density increases, it becomes easier for a stray particle to flip a bit. It has been predicted by some that the soft error rate of a 64MB DRAM will be double that of a 16MB chip, and a 256MB DRAM will have a rate four times higher.

Unfortunately, the PC industry has largely failed to recognize this cause of memory errors. Electrostatic discharge, power surges, or unstable software can much more easily explain away the random and intermittent nature of a soft error, especially right after a new release of an operating system or major application.

Studies have shown that the soft error rate for ECC systems is on the order of 30 times greater than the hard error rate. This is not surprising to those familiar with the full effects of cosmic-ray-generated soft errors. The number of errors experienced varies with the density and amount of memory present. Studies show that soft errors can occur from once a month or less to several times a week or more!

Although cosmic rays and other radiation events are the biggest cause of soft errors, soft errors can also be caused by the following:

- *Power glitches or noise on the line.* This can be caused by a defective power supply in the system or by defective power at the outlet.
- *Incorrect type or speed rating.* The memory must be the correct type for the chipset and match the system access speed.
- *RF (radio frequency) interference.* Caused by radio transmitters in close proximity to the system, which can generate electrical signals in system wiring and circuits. Keep in mind that the increased use of wireless networks, keyboards, and mice can lead to a greater risk of RF interference.
- *Static discharges.* Causes momentary power spikes, which alter data.
- *Timing glitches.* Data doesn't arrive at the proper place at the proper time, causing errors. Often caused by improper settings in the BIOS Setup, by memory that is rated slower than the system requires, or by overclocked processors and other system components.

Most of these problems don't cause chips to permanently fail (although bad power or static can damage chips permanently), but they can cause momentary problems with data.

How can you deal with these errors? Just ignoring them is certainly not the best way to deal with them, but unfortunately that is what many system manufacturers and vendors are doing today. The best way to deal with this problem is to increase the system's fault tolerance. This means implementing ways of detecting and possibly correcting errors in PC systems. Three basic levels and techniques are used for fault tolerance in modern PCs:

- Nonparity
- Parity
- ECC

Nonparity systems have no fault tolerance at all. The only reason they are used is because they have the lowest inherent cost. No additional memory is necessary, as is the case with parity or ECC techniques. Because a parity-type data byte has 9 bits versus 8 for nonparity, memory cost is approximately 12.5% higher. Also, the nonparity memory controller is simplified because it does not need the logic gates to calculate parity or ECC check bits. Portable systems that place a premium on minimizing power might benefit from the reduction in memory power resulting from fewer DRAM chips. Finally, the memory system data bus is narrower, which reduces the amount of data buffers. The statistical probability of memory failures in a modern office desktop computer is now estimated at about one error every few months. Errors will be more or less frequent depending on how much memory you have.

This error rate might be tolerable for low-end systems that are not used for mission-critical applications. In this case, the extreme market sensitivity to price probably can't justify the extra cost of parity or ECC memory, and such errors then must be tolerated.

At any rate, having no fault tolerance in a system is simply gambling that memory errors are unlikely. You further gamble that if they do occur, memory errors will result in an inherent cost less than the additional hardware necessary for error detection. However, the risk is that these memory errors can lead to serious problems. A memory error in a calculation could cause the wrong value to go into a bank check. In a server, a memory error could force a system to hang and bring down all LAN-resident client systems with subsequent loss of productivity. Finally, with a nonparity or non-ECC memory system, tracing the problem is difficult, which is not the case with parity or ECC. These techniques at least isolate a memory source as the culprit, thus reducing both the time and cost of resolving the problem.

Parity Checking

One standard IBM set for the industry is that the memory chips in a bank of nine each handle 1 bit of data: 8 bits per character plus 1 extra bit called the *parity bit*. The parity bit enables memory-control circuitry to keep tabs on the other 8 bits—a built-in cross-check for the integrity of each byte in the system. If the circuitry detects an error, the computer stops and displays a message informing you of the malfunction. If you are running a GUI operating system, such as Windows or OS/2, a parity error generally manifests itself as a locked system. When you reboot, the BIOS should detect the error and display the appropriate error message.

SIMMs and DIMMs are available both with and without parity bits. Originally, all PC systems used parity-checked memory to ensure accuracy. Starting in 1994, a disturbing trend developed in the PC-compatible marketplace. Most vendors began shipping systems without parity checking or any other means of detecting or correcting errors! These systems can use cheaper nonparity SIMMs, which saves about 10%–15% on memory costs for a system. Parity memory results in increased initial system cost, primarily because of the additional memory bits involved. Parity can't correct system errors, but because parity can detect errors, it can make the user aware of memory errors when they happen. This has two basic benefits:

- Parity guards against the consequences of faulty calculations based on incorrect data.
- Parity pinpoints the source of errors, which helps with problem resolution, thus improving system serviceability.

PC systems can easily be designed to function using either parity or nonparity memory. The cost of implementing parity as an option on a motherboard is virtually nothing; the only cost is in actually purchasing the parity SIMMs or DIMMs. This enables a system manufacturer to offer its system purchasers the choice of parity if the purchasers feel the additional cost is justified for their particular applications.

Unfortunately, several of the big names began selling systems without parity to reduce their prices, and they did not make it well known that the lower cost meant parity memory was no longer included as standard. This began happening mostly in 1994 and 1995, and it has continued until recently, with few people understanding the full implications. After one or two major vendors did this, most of the others were forced to follow to remain price-competitive.

Because nobody wanted to announce this information, it remained sort of a dirty little secret within the industry. Originally, when this happened you could still specify parity memory when you ordered a system, even though the default configurations no longer included it. There was a 10%–15% surcharge on the memory, but those who wanted reliable, trustworthy systems could at least get them, provided they knew to ask, of course. Then a major bomb hit the industry, in the form of the Intel Triton 430FX Pentium chipset, which was the first major chipset on the market that did not support parity checking at all! It also became the most popular chipset of its time and was found in practically all Pentium motherboards sold in the 1995 timeframe. This set a disturbing trend for the next few years. All but one of Intel's Pentium processor chipsets after the 430FX did not support parity-checked memory; the only one that did was the 430HX Triton II.

Since then, Intel and other chipset manufacturers have put support for parity and ECC memory in most of their chipsets (especially so in their higher-end models). The low-end chipsets, however, typically do lack support for either parity or ECC. If more reliability is important to you, make sure the systems you purchase have this support. In Chapter 4, you can learn which recent chipsets support parity and ECC memory and which ones do not.

Let's look at how parity checking works, and then examine in more detail the successor to parity checking, called ECC, which can not only detect but correct memory errors on-the-fly.

How Parity Checking Works

IBM originally established the odd parity standard for error checking. The following explanation might help you understand what is meant by odd parity. As the 8 individual bits in a byte are stored in memory, a parity generator/checker, which is either part of the CPU or located in a special chip on the motherboard, evaluates the data bits by adding up the number of 1s in the byte. If an even number of 1s is found, the parity generator/checker creates a 1 and stores it as the ninth bit (parity bit) in the parity memory chip. That makes the sum for all 9 bits (including the parity bit) an odd number. If the original sum of the 8 data bits is an odd number, the parity bit created would be a 0, keeping the sum for all 9 bits an odd number. The basic rule is that the value of the parity bit is always chosen so that the sum of all 9 bits (8 data bits plus 1 parity bit) is stored as an odd number. If the system used even parity, the example would be the same except the parity bit would be created to ensure an even sum. It doesn't matter whether even or odd parity is used; the system uses one or the other, and it is completely transparent to the memory chips involved. Remember that the 8 data bits in a byte are numbered 0 1 2 3 4 5 6 7. The following examples might make it easier to understand:

```
Data bit number:    0 1 2 3 4 5 6 7     Parity bit
Data bit value:     1 0 1 1 0 0 1 1     0
```

In this example, because the total number of data bits with a value of 1 is an odd number (5), the parity bit must have a value of 0 to ensure an odd sum for all 9 bits.

Here is another example:

```
Data bit number:    0 1 2 3 4 5 6 7     Parity bit
Data bit value:     1 1 1 1 0 0 1 1     1
```

In this example, because the total number of data bits with a value of 1 is an even number (6), the parity bit must have a value of 1 to create an odd sum for all 9 bits.

When the system reads memory back from storage, it checks the parity information. If a (9-bit) byte has an even number of bits, that byte must have an error. The system can't tell which bit has changed or whether only a single bit has changed. If 3 bits changed, for example, the byte still flags a parity-check error; if 2 bits changed, however, the bad byte could pass unnoticed. Because multiple bit errors (in a single byte) are rare, this scheme gives you a reasonable and inexpensive ongoing indication that memory is good or bad.

The following examples show parity-check messages for three types of older systems:

```
For the IBM PC:                    PARITY CHECK x
For the IBM XT:                    PARITY CHECK x    yyyyy (z)
For the IBM AT and late model XT:  PARITY CHECK x    yyyyy
```

where x is 1 or 2:

> 1 = Error occurred on the motherboard

> 2 = Error occurred in an expansion slot

In this example, *yyyyy* represents a number from 00000 through FFFFF that indicates, in hexadecimal notation, the byte in which the error has occurred.

Where (z) is (S) or (E):

> (S) = Parity error occurred in the system unit

> (E) = Parity error occurred in an optional expansion chassis

Note

An expansion chassis was an option IBM sold for the original PC and XT systems to add more expansion slots.

When a parity-check error is detected, the motherboard parity-checking circuits generate a nonmaskable interrupt (NMI), which halts processing and diverts the system's attention to the error. The NMI causes a routine in the ROM to be executed. On some older IBM systems, the ROM parity-check routine halts the CPU. In such a case, the system locks up, and you must perform a hardware reset or a power-off/power-on cycle to restart the system. Unfortunately, all unsaved work is lost in the process.

Most systems do not halt the CPU when a parity error is detected; instead, they offer you the choice of rebooting the system or continuing as though nothing happened. Additionally, these systems might display the parity error message in a different format from IBM, although the information presented is basically the same. For example, most systems with a Phoenix BIOS display one of these messages:

```
Memory parity interrupt at xxxx:xxxx
Type (S)hut off NMI, Type (R)eboot, other keys to continue
```

or

```
I/O card parity interrupt at xxxx:xxxx
Type (S)hut off NMI, Type (R)eboot, other keys to continue
```

The first of these two messages indicates a motherboard parity error (Parity Check 1), and the second indicates an expansion-slot parity error (Parity Check 2). Notice that the address given in the form *xxxx:xxxx* for the memory error is in a segment:offset form rather than a straight linear address, such as with IBM's error messages. The segment:offset address form still gives you the location of the error to a resolution of a single byte.

You have three ways to proceed after viewing this error message:

■ You can press S, which shuts off parity checking and resumes system operation at the point where the parity check first occurred.

■ You can press R to force the system to reboot, losing any unsaved work.

■ You can press any other key to cause the system to resume operation with parity checking still enabled.

If the problem occurs, it is likely to cause another parity-check interruption. It's usually prudent to press S, which disables the parity checking so you can then save your work. In this case, it's best to save your work to a floppy disk to prevent the possible corruption of the hard disk. You should also avoid overwriting any previous (still good) versions of whatever file you are saving because you could be saving a bad file caused by the memory corruption. Because parity checking is now disabled, your save operations will not be interrupted. Then, you should power the system off, restart it, and run whatever memory diagnostics software you have to try to track down the error. In some cases, the POST finds the error on the next restart, but you usually need to run a more sophisticated diagnostics program—perhaps in a continuous mode—to locate the error.

Systems with an AMI BIOS display the parity error messages in the following forms:

```
ON BOARD PARITY ERROR ADDR (HEX) = (xxxxx)
```

or

```
OFF BOARD PARITY ERROR ADDR (HEX) - (xxxxx)
```

These messages indicate that an error in memory has occurred during the POST, and the failure is located at the address indicated. The first one indicates that the error occurred on the motherboard, and the second message indicates an error in an expansion slot adapter card. The AMI BIOS can also display memory errors in the following manners:

```
Memory Parity Error at xxxxx
```

or

```
I/O Card Parity Error at xxxxx
```

These messages indicate that an error in memory has occurred at the indicated address during normal operation. The first one indicates a motherboard memory error, and the second indicates an expansion slot adapter memory error.

Although many systems enable you to continue processing after a parity error and even allow disabling further parity checking, continuing to use your system after a parity error is detected can be dangerous. The idea behind letting you continue using either method is to give you time to save any unsaved work before you diagnose and service the computer, but be careful how you do this.

Note that these messages can vary depending not only on the ROM BIOS but also on your operating system. Protected mode operating systems, such as most versions of Windows, trap these errors and run their own handler program that displays a message different from what the ROM would have displayed. The message might be associated with a blue screen or might be a trap error, but it usually indicates that it is memory or parity related. For example, Windows 98 displays a message indicating `Memory parity error detected. System halted.` when such an error has occurred.

Caution

When you are notified of a memory parity error, remember the parity check is telling you that memory has been corrupted. Do you want to save potentially corrupted data over the good file from the last time you saved? Definitely not! Be sure you save your work with a different filename. In addition, after a parity error, save only to a floppy disk if possible and avoid writing to the hard disk; there is a slight chance that the hard drive could become corrupt if you save the contents of corrupted memory.

After saving your work, determine the cause of the parity error and repair the system. You might be tempted to use an option to shut off further parity checking and simply continue using the system as though nothing were wrong. Doing so is like unscrewing the oil pressure warning indicator bulb on a car with an oil leak so the oil pressure light won't bother you anymore!

A few years ago, when memory was more expensive, a few companies marketed SIMMs with bogus parity chips. Instead of actually having the extra memory chips needed to store the parity bits, these "logic parity" or parity "emulation" SIMMs used an onboard parity generator chip. This chip ignored any parity the system was trying to store on the SIMM, but when data was retrieved, it always ensured that the correct parity was returned, thus making the system believe all was well even though there might have been a problem.

These bogus parity modules were used because memory was much more expensive and a company could offer a "parity" SIMM for only a few dollars more with the fake chip. Unfortunately, identifying them can be difficult. The bogus parity generator doesn't look like a memory chip and has different markings from the other memory chips on the SIMM. Most of them had a "GSM" logo, which indicated the original manufacturer of the parity logic device, not necessarily the SIMM itself.

One way to positively identify these bogus fake parity SIMMs is by using a hardware SIMM test machine, such as those by Tanisys (www.tanisys.com), CST (www.simmtester.com), or Innoventions (www.memorytest.com). I haven't seen DIMMs or RIMMs with fake parity/ECC bits, and memory prices have come down far enough that it probably isn't worth the trouble anymore.

Error Correcting Code

ECC goes a big step beyond simple parity-error detection. Instead of just detecting an error, ECC allows a single bit error to be corrected, which means the system can continue without interruption and without corrupting data. ECC, as implemented in most PCs, can only detect, not correct, double-bit errors. Because studies have indicated that approximately 98% of memory errors are the single-bit variety, the most commonly used type of ECC is one in which the attendant memory controller detects and corrects single-bit errors in an accessed data word (double-bit errors can be detected but not corrected). This type of ECC is known as *single-bit error-correction double-bit error detection (SEC-DED)* and requires an additional 7 check bits over 32 bits in a 4-byte system and an additional 8 check bits over 64 bits in an 8-byte system. ECC in a 4-byte (32-bit, such as a 486) system obviously costs more than nonparity or parity, but in an 8-byte-wide bus (64-bit, such as Pentium/Athlon) system, ECC and parity costs are equal because the same number of extra bits (8) is required for either parity or ECC. Because of this, you can purchase parity SIMMs (36-bit), DIMMs (72-bit), or RIMMs (18-bit) for 32-bit systems and use them in an ECC mode if the chipset supports ECC functionality. If the system uses SIMMs, two 36-bit (parity) SIMMs are added for each bank (for a total of 72 bits), and ECC is done at the bank level. If the system uses DIMMs, a single parity/ECC 72-bit DIMM is used as a bank and provides the additional bits. RIMMs are installed in singles or pairs, depending on the chipset and motherboard. They must be 18-bit versions if parity/ECC is desired.

ECC entails the memory controller calculating the check bits on a memory-write operation, performing a compare between the read and calculated check bits on a read operation, and, if necessary, correcting bad bits. The additional ECC logic in the memory controller is not very significant in this age of inexpensive, high-performance VLSI logic, but ECC actually affects memory performance on writes. This is because the operation must be timed to wait for the calculation of check bits and, when the system waits for corrected data, reads. On a partial-word write, the entire word must first be read, the affected byte(s) rewritten, and then new check bits calculated. This turns partial-word write operations into slower read-modify writes. Fortunately, this performance hit is very small, on the order of a few percent at maximum, so the tradeoff for increased reliability is a good one.

Most memory errors are of a single-bit nature, which ECC can correct. Incorporating this fault-tolerant technique provides high system reliability and attendant availability. An ECC-based system is a good choice for servers, workstations, or mission-critical applications in which the cost of a potential memory error outweighs the additional memory and system cost to correct it, along with ensuring that it does not detract from system reliability. If you value your data and use your system for important (to you) tasks, you'll want ECC memory. No self-respecting manager would build or run a network server, even a lower-end one, without ECC memory.

By designing a system that allows the user to make the choice of ECC, parity, or nonparity, users can choose the level of fault tolerance desired, as well as how much they want to gamble with their data.

Installing RAM Upgrades

Adding memory to a system is one of the most useful upgrades you can perform and also one of the least expensive—especially when you consider the increased capabilities of Windows 9x/Me, Windows NT/2000/XP, and OS/2 when you give them access to more memory. In some cases, doubling the memory can practically double the speed of a computer.

The following sections discuss adding memory, including selecting memory chips, installing memory chips, and testing the installation.

Upgrade Options and Strategies

Adding memory can be an inexpensive solution; at this writing, the cost of memory has fallen to about 12 cents per megabyte or less. A small dose can give your computer's performance a big boost.

How do you add memory to your PC? You have two options, listed in order of convenience and cost:

- Adding memory in vacant slots on your motherboard
- Replacing your current motherboard's memory with higher-capacity memory

If you decide to upgrade to a more powerful computer system or motherboard, you usually can't salvage the memory from your previous system. Most of the time it is best to plan on equipping a new board with the optimum type of memory that it supports.

Be sure to carefully weigh your future needs for computing speed and a multitasking operating system (OS/2, Windows 9x, Windows NT, Windows 2000, or Linux, for example) against the amount of money you spend to upgrade current equipment.

Before you add RAM to a system (or replace defective RAM chips), you must determine the memory chips required for your system. Your system documentation has this information.

If you need to replace a defective memory module and do not have the system documentation, you can determine the correct module for your system by inspecting the ones that are already installed. Each module has markings that indicate the module's capacity and speed. RAM capacity and speed are discussed in detail earlier in this chapter.

If you do not have the documentation for your system and the manufacturer does not offer technical support, open your system case and carefully write down the markings that appear on your memory chips. Then contact a local computer store or module vendor, such as Kingston, Micron (Crucial), PNY, or others, for help in determining the proper RAM chips for your system. Adding the wrong modules to a system can make it as unreliable as leaving a defective module installed and trying to use the system in that condition.

Note

Before upgrading an older Pentium (P5 class) system beyond 64MB of RAM, be sure your chipset supports caching more than 64MB. Adding RAM beyond the amount supported by your L2 cache slows performance rather than increases it. See the section "Cache Memory: SRAM," earlier in this chapter, and the discussion of chipsets in Chapter 4 for a more complete explanation of this common system limitation. This limitation was mostly with Pentium (P5) class chipsets. Pentium II and later processors, including the AMD Athlon and Duron, have the L2 cache controller integrated in the processor (not the chipset), which supports caching up to 1GB, or 4GB on most newer models. With the higher price of older SIMM-type memory modules per megabyte compared to SDRAM and DDR-SDRAM, you might find it more cost-effective to replace your motherboard, processor, and memory with new components than to add memory to an older system that uses SIMMs.

Selecting and Installing Memory

If you are upgrading a motherboard by adding memory, follow the manufacturer's guidelines on which memory chips or modules to buy. As you learned earlier, memory comes in various form factors, including SIMMs, DIMMs, and RIMMs.

No matter which type of memory modules you have, the chips are installed in memory banks. A *memory bank* is a collection of memory chips that make up a complete row of memory. Your processor reads each row of memory in one pass. A memory bank does not work unless the entire row is filled with memory chips. (Banks are discussed in more detail earlier in this chapter in the section "Memory Banks.")

Installing extra memory on your motherboard is an easy way to add memory to your computer. Most systems have at least one vacant memory bank where you can install extra memory at a later time and speed up your computer.

If your system requires dual-channel memory, as some high-performance systems do, you must use two identical memory modules (same size, speed, and type).

Purchasing Memory

When purchasing memory, there are some issues you need to consider. Some are related to the manufacturing and distribution of memory, whereas others depend on the type of memory you are purchasing. This section covers some of the issues you should consider when purchasing memory.

Suppliers

Many companies sell memory, but only a few companies actually *make* memory. Additionally, only a few companies make memory chips, but many more companies make memory modules such as SIMMs, DIMMs, and RIMMs. Most of the companies that make the actual RAM chips also make modules containing their own chips. Other companies, however, strictly make modules; these companies purchase memory chips from several chip makers and then produce modules with these chips. Finally, some companies don't make either the chips or modules. Instead, they purchase modules made by other companies and relabel them.

I refer to memory modules made by the chip manufacturers as first-party modules, whereas those made by module (but not chip) manufacturers I call second-party modules. Finally, those that are simply relabeled first- or second-party modules under a different name are called third-party modules. I always prefer to purchase first- or second-party modules if I can because they are better documented. In essence they have a better pedigree and their quality is generally more assured. Not to mention that purchasing from the first or second party eliminates one or more middlemen in the distribution process as well.

First-party manufacturers (where the same company makes the chips and the modules) include Micron (http://www.crucial.com), Infineon (formerly Siemens), Samsung, Mitsubishi, Toshiba, NEC, and others. Second-party companies that make the modules (but not the chips) include Kingston, Viking, PNY, Simple Tech, Smart, Mushkin, and OCZ Technologies.

At the third-party level you are not purchasing from a manufacturer but from a reseller or remarketer instead. Although I call this third-party memory, some people call these modules *major on third*, which is British slang used to indicate that the memory modules are sourced from a third-party manufacturer (which might be unspecified) even though they are using name brand chips. It is derived from saying that a given memory module is made from memory chips supplied by a "major" memory chip manufacturer "on third"-party manufactured SIMM/DIMM boards. That particular slang term is not often used in the United States.

Most of the large manufacturers don't sell small quantities of memory to individuals, but some have set up factory outlet stores where individuals can purchase as little as a single module. Two of the largest memory manufacturers in the world, Samsung and Micron, both have factory outlet stores you can use. Because you are buying direct, the pricing is often highly competitive with the second- and third-party suppliers. Micron's factory outlet store is http://www.crucial.com.

SIMMs

When purchasing SIMMs, the main things to consider are as follows:

- Do you need FPM (Fast Page Mode) or EDO (extended data out) versions?
- Do you need ECC or non-ECC?
- What speed grade do you need?

Most Pentium systems after 1995 used EDO SIMMs that were non-ECC and rated for 60ns access time. If your system is older than that, you might need regular FPM versions. The FPM and EDO types are interchangeable in many systems, but some older systems do not accept the EDO type. If your system is designed for high-reliability using ECC, you might need (or want) ECC versions; otherwise, standard non-ECC types are typically used. You can mix the two, but in that case the system defaults to non-ECC mode.

Unfortunately, FPM and EDO SIMMs are obsolete by today's standards, so they are much more expensive than newer, better, and faster types of memory. This can make adding memory to older systems cost prohibitive.

Tip

Instead of buying new SIMM memory for older systems, check with computer repair shops or other users who might have a collection of old parts.

DIMMs

When purchasing DIMMs, the main things to consider are as follows:

- Do you need SDR or DDR versions?
- Do you need ECC or non-ECC?
- Do you need registered or unbuffered versions?
- What speed grade do you need?
- Do you need a specific column address strobe (CAS) latency?

Currently, DIMMs come in single data rate (SDR) and double data rate (DDR) versions, with most newer systems using the DDR type; look for the first DDR2 modules and systems in late 2003. They are not interchangeable because they use completely different signaling and have different notches to prevent a mismatch. High-reliability systems such as servers can use ECC versions, although most systems use the less-expensive non-ECC types. Most systems use standard unbuffered DIMMs, but file server or workstation motherboards designed to support very large amounts of memory might require registered DIMMs. Registered DIMMs contain their own memory registers, enabling the module to hold more memory than a standard DIMM. DIMMs come in a variety of speeds, with the rule that you can always substitute a faster one for a slower one, but not vice versa. As an example, if your system requires PC2100 DDR DIMMs, you can install faster PC2700 DDR DIMMs but not slower PC1600 versions.

Another speed-related issue is the column address strobe (CAS) latency. Sometimes this specification is abbreviated CAS or CL and is expressed in a number of cycles, with lower numbers indicating higher speeds (fewer cycles). The lower CAS latency shaves a cycle off a burst mode read, which marginally improves memory performance. Single data rate DIMMs are available in CL3 or CL2 versions, with the CL2 being faster. DDR DIMMs are available in CL2.5 or CL2 versions, with CL2 being the faster and better version in that case. You can mix DIMMs with different CAS latency ratings, but the system usually defaults to cycling at the slower speeds of the lowest common denominator.

RIMMs

When purchasing RIMMs, the main things to consider are as follows:

- Do you need 184-pin (16/18-bit) or 232-pin (32/36-bit) versions?
- Do you need ECC or non-ECC?
- What speed grade do you need?

RIMMs are available in 184-pin and 232-pin versions, and although they appear to be the same size, they are not interchangeable. Differences exist in the notches that prevent a mismatch. High-reliability systems might want or need ECC versions, which have extra ECC bits. As with other memory types, you can mix ECC and non-ECC types, but systems can't use the ECC capability.

Replacing Modules with Higher-Capacity Versions

If all the memory module slots on your motherboard are occupied, your best option is to remove an existing bank of memory and replace it with higher-capacity modules. For example, if you have a motherboard that supports two DIMM modules (each representing one bank on a processor with a 64-bit data bus), you could remove one of them and replace it with a higher-capacity version. For example, if you have two 64MB modules giving a total of 128MB, you could remove one of the 64MB modules and replace it with a 128MB unit, in which case you'd then have a total of 192MB of RAM.

However, just because higher-capacity modules are available that are the correct pin count to plug into your motherboard, don't automatically assume the higher-capacity memory will work. Your system's chipset and BIOS set limits on the capacity of the memory you can use. Check your system or motherboard documentation to see which size modules work with it before purchasing the new RAM. You should make sure you have the latest BIOS for your motherboard when installing new memory.

Installing Memory

This section discusses installing memory—specifically, new SIMM or DIMM modules. It also covers the problems you are most likely to encounter and how to avoid them. You also get information on configuring your system to use new memory.

When you install or remove memory, you are most likely to encounter the following problems:

- Electrostatic discharge
- Improperly seated modules
- Incorrect memory configuration settings in the BIOS Setup

To prevent electrostatic discharge (ESD) when you install sensitive memory chips or boards, you shouldn't wear synthetic-fiber clothing or leather-soled shoes because these promote the generation of static charges. Remove any static charge you are carrying by touching the system chassis before you begin, or better yet, wear a good commercial grounding strap on your wrist. You can order one from any electronics parts store. A grounding strap consists of a conductive wristband grounded at the other end through a 1-meg ohm resistor by a wire clipped to the system chassis. Be sure the system you are working on is unplugged.

Caution

Be sure to use a properly designed commercial grounding strap; do not make one yourself. Commercial units have a 1-meg ohm resistor that serves as protection if you accidentally touch live power. The resistor ensures that you do not become the path of least resistance to the ground and therefore become electrocuted. An improperly designed strap can cause the power to conduct through you to the ground, possibly killing you.

Each memory chip or module must be installed in a specific orientation. Interference fit notches and tangs are designed to prevent improper installation of the module into the socket. As long as you are observant and don't try to force anything, the proper orientation should be fairly easy to figure out. As you insert the module, be sure the notches align with the appropriate tangs on the socket.

I would hope it goes without saying, but before installing memory, be sure the system power is off! You should make sure the system is unplugged from any power outlets just to be sure. If you were to install memory while the power was on (even if the system was in a sleep mode), you would probably fry not only the memory but possibly the entire motherboard as well. Most newer systems incorporate standby power connections, so they are partially powered on even when the system is powered off. The only way to ensure such systems are really powered off completely is to unplug them from the wall socket.

You remove SIMMs, DIMMs, or RIMMs by releasing the locking tabs and either pulling or rolling them out of their sockets. The installation is exactly the opposite.

After adding the memory and putting the system back together, you might have to run the BIOS Setup and resave with the new amount of memory being reported. Most newer systems automatically detect the new amount of memory and reconfigure the BIOS Setup settings for you. Most newer systems also don't require setting any jumpers or switches on the motherboard to configure them for your new memory.

After configuring your system to work properly with the additional memory, you might want to run a memory-diagnostics program to ensure that the new memory works properly. Some are run automatically for you. At least two and sometimes three memory-diagnostic programs are available for all systems. In order of accuracy, these programs are as follows:

- POST (power on self test)
- Disk-based advanced diagnostics software

The POST is used every time you power up the system.

Many additional diagnostics programs are available from aftermarket utility software companies. More information on aftermarket testing facilities can be found in Chapter 24.

Installing SIMMs

SIMM memory is oriented by a notch on one side of the module that is not present on the other side, as shown in Figure 6.14. The socket has a protrusion that must fit into this notched area on one side of the module. This protrusion makes installing a SIMM backward impossible unless you break the connector or the module. Figure 6.15 details the notch and locking clip.

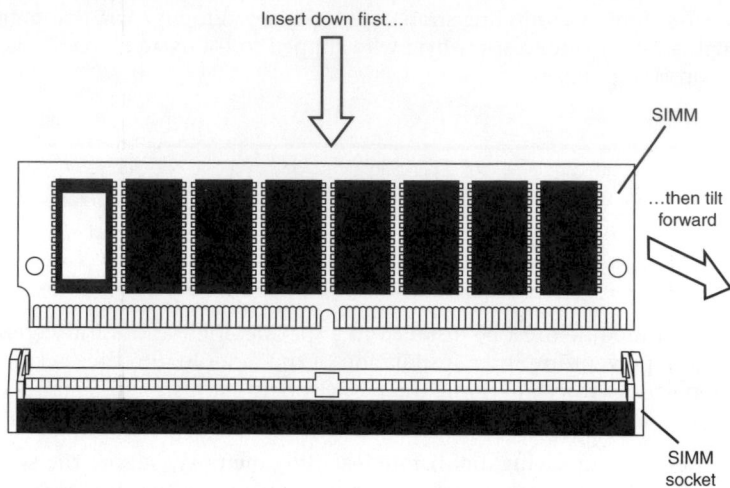

Figure 6.14 The notch on this SIMM is shown on the left side. Insert the SIMM at a 45° angle and then tilt it forward until the locking clips snap into place.

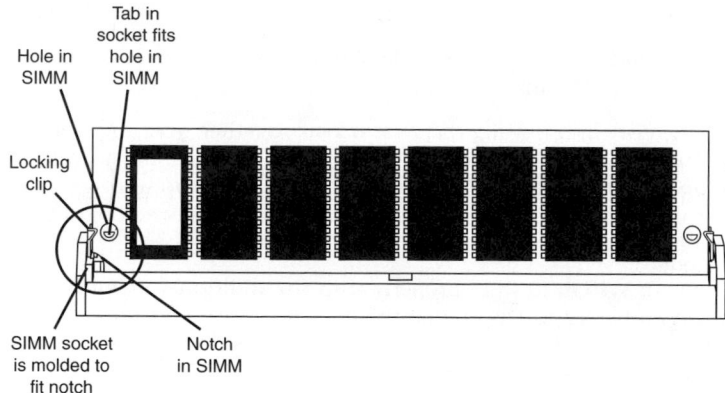

Figure 6.15 This figure shows the SIMM inserted in the socket with the notch aligned, the locking clip locked, and the hole in the SIMM aligned with the tab in the socket.

Installing DIMMs and RIMMs

Similarly, DIMMs and RIMMs are keyed by notches along the bottom connector edge that are offset from the center so they can be inserted in only one direction, as shown in Figure 6.16.

The DIMM/RIMM ejector tab locks into place in the notch on the side of the DIMM when it is fully inserted. Some DIMM sockets have ejector tabs on both ends. Take care not to force the module into the socket. If the module does not slip easily into the slot and then snap into place, the module is probably not oriented or aligned correctly. Forcing the module could break the module or the socket. If the retaining clips on the socket break, the memory isn't held firmly in place, and you likely will get random memory errors because the module can't make consistent electrical contact if it is loose.

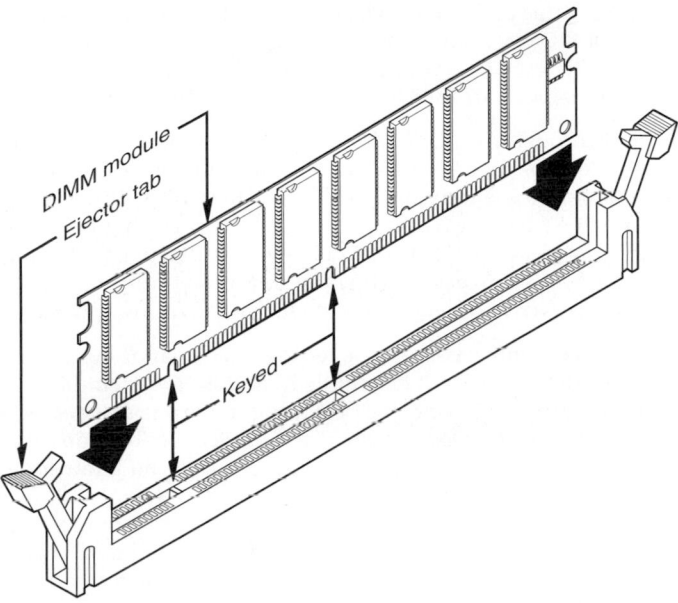

Figure 6.16 DIMM keys match the protrusions in the DIMM sockets. DDR DIMM and RIMM keys are similar but not exactly the same.

Installing RIMMs

RIMMs install in exactly the same manner as DIMMs, although in different sockets. The ejector tabs on the sides are similar, and they go in at a straight 90° angle just like DIMMs. The key notches on the RIMM prevent backward installation and aid alignment when inserting them.

You'll also need to fill any empty RIMM sockets with a continuity module. Refer to Figure 6.11 for details on this module.

Troubleshooting Memory

Memory problems can be difficult to troubleshoot. For one thing, computer memory is still mysterious to people because it is a kind of "virtual" thing that can be hard to grasp. The other difficulty is that memory problems can be intermittent and often look like problems with other areas of the system, even software. This section shows simple troubleshooting steps you can perform if you suspect you are having a memory problem.

To troubleshoot memory, you first need some memory-diagnostics testing programs. You already have several, and might not know it. Every motherboard BIOS has a memory diagnostic in the POST that runs when you first turn on the system. In most cases, you also receive a memory diagnostic on a utility disk that came with your system. Many commercial diagnostics programs are on the market, and almost all of them include memory tests.

When the POST runs, it not only tests memory, but also counts it. The count is compared to the amount counted the last time BIOS Setup was run; if it is different, an error message is issued. As the POST runs, it writes a pattern of data to all the memory locations in the system and reads that pattern back to verify that the memory works. If any failure is detected, you see or hear a message. Audio messages (beeping) are used for critical or "fatal" errors that occur in areas important for the system's operation. If the system can access enough memory to at least allow video to function, you see error messages instead of hearing beep codes.

See the disc accompanying this book for detailed listings of the BIOS beep and other error codes, which are specific to the type of BIOS you have. These BIOS codes are found in the Technical Reference section of the disc in printable PDF format for your convenience. For example, most Intel motherboards use the Phoenix BIOS. Several beep codes are used in that BIOS to indicate fatal memory errors.

If your system makes it through the POST with no memory error indications, there might not be a hardware memory problem, or the POST might not be able to detect the problem. Intermittent memory errors are often not detected during the POST, and other subtle hardware defects can be hard for the POST to catch. The POST is designed to run quickly, so the testing is not nearly as thorough as it could be. That is why you often have to boot from a DOS or diagnostic disk and run a true hardware diagnostic to do more extensive memory testing. These types of tests can be run continuously and be left running for days if necessary to hunt down an elusive intermittent defect.

Still, even these programs do only pass/fail type testing; that is, all they can do is write patterns to memory and read them back. They can't determine how close the memory is to failing—only whether it worked. For the highest level of testing, the best thing to have is a dedicated memory test machine, usually called a *SIMM/DIMM/RIMM module tester*. These devices enable you to insert a module and test it thoroughly at a variety of speeds, voltages, and timings to let you know for certain whether the memory is good or bad. Versions of these testers are available to handle all types of memory from older SIMMs to the latest DDR DIMMs or RIMMs. I have defective modules, for example, that work in some systems (slower ones) but not others. What I mean is that the *same* memory test program fails the module in one machine but passes it in another. In the module tester, it is always identified as bad right down to the individual bit, and it even tells me the actual speed of the device, not just its rating. Companies that offer memory module testers include Tanisys (www.tanisys.com), CST (www.simmtester.com), and Innoventions (www.memorytest.com). They can be expensive, but for a professional in the PC repair business, using one of these SIMM/DIMM testers is the only way to go.

After your operating system is running, memory errors can still occur, typically identified by error messages you might receive. These are the most common:

- *Parity errors*. Indicates that the parity-checking circuitry on the motherboard has detected a change in memory since the data was originally stored. (See the "How Parity Checking Works" section earlier in this chapter.)

- *General or global protection faults*. A general-purpose error indicating that a program has been corrupted in memory, usually resulting in immediate termination of the application. This can also be caused by buggy or faulty programs.

- *Fatal exception errors*. Error codes returned by a program when an illegal instruction has been encountered, invalid data or code has been accessed, or the privilege level of an operation is invalid.

- *Divide error*. A general-purpose error indicating that a division by 0 was attempted or the result of an operation does not fit in the destination register.

If you are encountering these errors, they could be caused by defective or improperly configured memory, but they can also be caused by software bugs (especially drivers), bad power supplies, static discharges, close proximity radio transmitters, timing problems, and more.

If you suspect the problems are caused by memory, there are ways to test the memory to determine whether that is the problem. Most of this testing involves running one or more memory test programs.

I am amazed that most people make a critical mistake when they run memory test software. The biggest problem I see is that people run memory tests with the system caches enabled. This effectively invalidates memory testing because most systems have what is called a *write-back cache*. This means that data written to main memory is first written to the cache. Because a memory test program first writes data and then immediately reads it back, the data is read back from the cache, not the main memory. It makes the memory test program run very quickly, but all you tested was the cache. The bottom line is that if you test memory with the cache enabled, you aren't really writing to the

SIMM/DIMMs, but only to the cache. Before you run any memory test programs, be sure your cache is disabled. The system will run very slowly when you do this, and the memory test will take much longer to complete, but you will be testing your actual RAM, not the cache.

The following steps enable you to effectively test and troubleshoot your system RAM. Figure 6.17 provides a boiled-down procedure to help you step through the process quickly.

First, let's cover the memory testing and troubleshooting procedures.

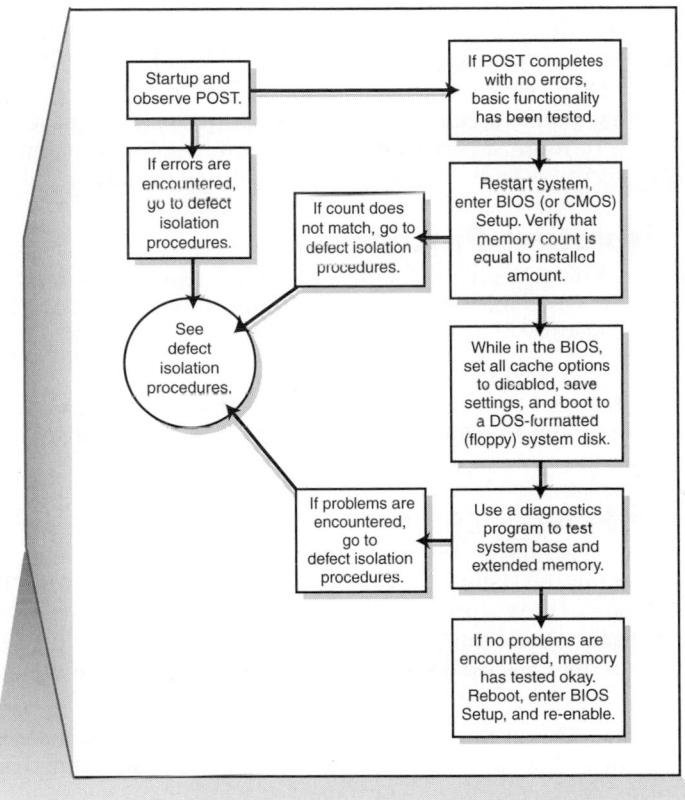

Figure 6.17   Testing and troubleshooting memory.

1. Power up the system and observe the POST. If the POST completes with no errors, basic memory functionality has been tested. If errors are encountered, go to the defect isolation procedures.

2. Restart the system, and enter your BIOS (or CMOS) Setup. In most systems, this is done by pressing the F2 key during the POST but before the boot process begins. Once in BIOS Setup, verify that the memory count is equal to the amount that has been installed. If the count does not match what has been installed, go to the defect isolation procedures.

3. Find the BIOS Setup options for cache, and set all cache options to disabled. Save the settings and reboot to a DOS-formatted system disk (floppy) containing the diagnostics program of your choice. If your system came with a diagnostics disk, you can use that, or you can use one of the many commercial PC diagnostics programs on the market, such as PC-Technician by Windsor Technologies (which comes in self-booting form), the Norton Utilities by Symantec, or others.

4. Follow the instructions that came with your diagnostic program to have it test the system base and extended memory. Most programs have a mode that enables them to loop the test—that is, to run it continuously, which is great for finding intermittent problems. If the program encounters a memory error, proceed to the defect isolation procedures.

5. If no errors are encountered in the POST or in the more comprehensive memory diagnostic, your memory has tested okay in hardware. Be sure at this point to reboot the system, enter the BIOS Setup, and re-enable the cache. The system will run very slowly until the cache is turned back on.

6. If you are having memory problems yet the memory still tests okay, you might have a problem undetectable by simple pass/fail testing, or your problems could be caused by software or one of many other defects or problems in your system. You might want to bring the memory to a SIMM/DIMM tester for a more accurate analysis. Most PC repair shops have such a tester. I would also check the software (especially drivers, which might need updating), power supply, and system environment for problems such as static, radio transmitters, and so forth.

Memory Defect Isolation Procedures

To use these steps, I am assuming you have identified an actual memory problem that is being reported by the POST or disk-based memory diagnostics. If this is the case, see the following steps and Figure 6.18 for the steps to identify or isolate which SIMM or DIMM in the system is causing the problem.

1. Restart the system and enter the BIOS Setup. Under a menu usually called Advanced or Chipset Setup might be memory timing parameters. Select BIOS or Setup defaults, which are usually the slowest settings. Save the settings, reboot, and retest using the testing and troubleshooting procedures listed earlier. If the problem has been solved, improper BIOS settings were the problem. If the problem remains, you likely do have defective memory, so continue to the next step.

2. Open the system for physical access to the SIMM/DIMM/RIMMs on the motherboard. Identify the bank arrangement in the system. For example, Pentium systems use 64-bit banks, which means two SIMMs or one DIMM per bank. Pentium 4 systems require two 184-pin RIMMs at a time (in separate channels) or a single 232-pin RIMM if the system uses that type. Using the manual or the legend silk-screened on the motherboard, identify which modules correspond to which banks.

3. Remove all the memory except the first bank, and retest using the troubleshooting and testing procedures listed earlier. If the problem remains with all but the first bank removed, the problem has been isolated to the first bank, which must be replaced.

4. Replace the memory in the first bank, preferably with known good spare modules, but you can also swap in others that you have removed and retest. If the problem *still* remains after testing all the memory banks (and finding them all to be working properly), it is likely the motherboard itself is bad (probably one of the memory sockets). Replace the motherboard and retest.

5. At this point, the first (or previous) bank has tested good, so the problem must be in the remaining modules that have been temporarily removed. Install the next bank of memory and retest. If the problem resurfaces now, the memory in that bank is defective. Continue testing each bank until you find the defective module.

6. Repeat the preceding step until all remaining banks of memory are installed and have been tested. If the problem has not resurfaced after removing and reinstalling all the memory, the problem was likely intermittent or caused by poor conduction on the memory contacts. Often simply removing and replacing memory can resolve problems because of the self-cleaning action between the module and the socket during removal and reinstallation.

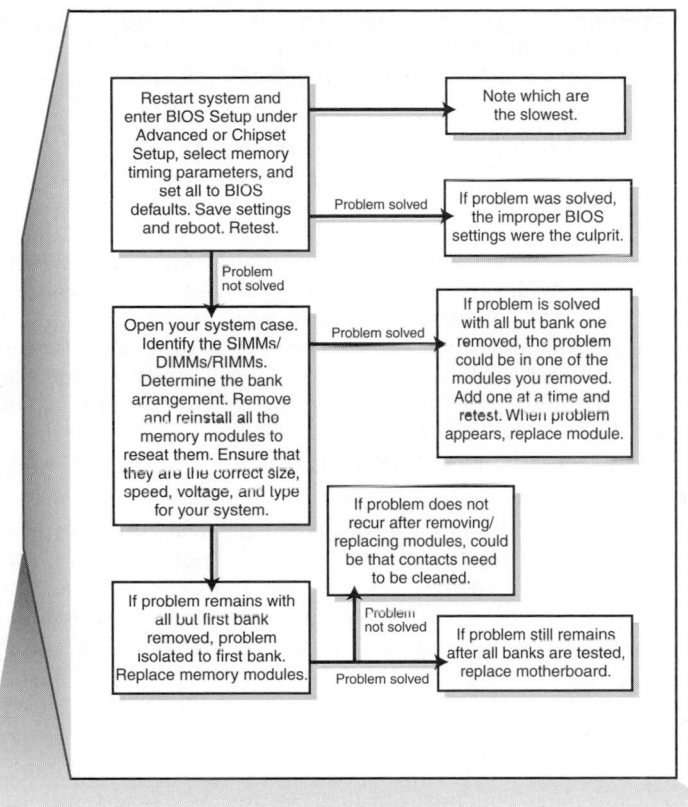

Figure 6.18   Follow these steps if you are still encountering memory errors after completing the steps in Figure 6.17.

The System Logical Memory Layout

The original PC had a total of 1MB of addressable memory, and the top 384KB of that was reserved for use by the system. Placing this reserved space at the top (between 640KB and 1024KB instead of at the bottom, between 0KB and 640KB) led to what is often called the *conventional memory barrier*. The constant pressures on system and peripheral manufacturers to maintain compatibility by never breaking from the original memory scheme of the first PC has resulted in a system memory structure that is (to put it kindly) a mess. Almost two decades after the first PC was introduced, even the newest Pentium 4–based systems are limited in many important ways by the memory map of the first PCs.

What we end up with is a PC with a split personality. There are two primary modes of operation that are very different from each other. The original PC used an Intel 8088 processor that could run only 16-bit instructions or code, which ran in what was called the real mode of the processor. These early processors had only enough address lines to access up to 1MB of memory, and the last 384KB of that was reserved for use by the video card as video RAM, other adapters (for on-card ROM BIOS), and finally the motherboard ROM BIOS.

The 286 processor brought more address lines, enough to allow up to 16MB of RAM to be used, and a new mode called *protected mode* that you had to be in to use it. Unfortunately, all the operating systems software at the time was designed to run only within the first 1MB, so extender programs were added and other tricks performed to eventually allow DOS and Windows 3.x access up to the first 16MB. One area of confusion was that RAM was now noncontiguous; that is, the operating system could use the first 640KB and the last 15MB, but not the 384KB of system reserved area that sat in between.

When Intel released the first 32-bit processor in 1985 (the 386DX), the memory architecture of the system changed dramatically. There were now enough address lines for the processor to use 4GB of memory, but this was accessible only in a new 32-bit *protected mode* in which only 32-bit instructions or code could run. This mode was designed for newer, more advanced operating systems, such as Windows 9x, NT, 2000, XP, OS/2, Linux, Unix, and so forth. With the 386 came a whole new memory architecture in which this new 32-bit software could run. Unfortunately, it took 10 years for the mainstream user to upgrade to 32-bit operating systems and applications, which shows how stubborn we are! From a software instruction perspective, all the 32-bit processors since the 386 are really just faster versions of the same. Other than the more recent additions of MMX and SSE (or AMD's 3DNow) instructions to the processor, for all intents and purposes, a Pentium 4 or Athlon is just a "turbo" 386. Even more advanced server-oriented, 64-bit instruction set processors such as the Intel Itanium and AMD Opteron processors fit into this category because they can also run 32-bit software.

The real problem now is that the 32-bit processors have two distinctly different modes, with different memory architectures in each. For backward compatibility, you could still run the 32-bit processors in real mode, but only 16-bit software could run in that mode, and such software could access only the first 1MB or 16MB, depending on how it was written. For example, 16-bit drivers could load into and access only the first 1MB. Also, it is worth noting that the system ROM BIOS, including the POST, BIOS configuration, boot code, and all the internal drivers, is virtually all 16-bit software. This is because all Intel-compatible PC processors begin operation in 16-bit real mode when they are powered on. When a 32-bit operating system loads, it is that operating system code that instructs the processor to switch into 32-bit protected mode.

When an operating system such as Windows is loaded, the processor is switched into 32-bit protected mode early in the loading sequence. Then, 32-bit drivers for all the hardware can be loaded, and then the rest of the operating system can load. In 32-bit protected mode, the operating systems and applications can access all the memory in the system, up to the maximum limit of the processor (64GB for most of the Pentium II and later chips).

Unfortunately, one problem with protected mode is just that: It is protected. The name comes from the fact that only driver programs are allowed to talk directly to the hardware in this mode; programs loaded by the operating system, such as by clicking an icon in Windows, are not allowed to access memory or other hardware directly. This protection is provided so that a single program can't crash the machine by doing something illegal. You might have seen the error message in Windows indicating this, and that the program will be shut down.

Diagnostics software by nature must talk to the hardware directly. This means that little intensive diagnostics testing can be done while a protected mode operating system such as Windows 9x, NT, 2000, XP, Linux, and so forth is running. For system testing, you usually have to boot from a DOS floppy or interrupt the loading of Windows (press the F8 key when Starting Windows appears during the boot process) and select Command Prompt Only, which boots you into DOS. In Windows 9x (but not Me), you can execute a shutdown and select Restart the Computer in MS-DOS mode. Many of the higher-end hardware diagnostics programs include their own special limited 16-bit operating systems so they can more easily access memory areas even DOS would use. With Windows 2000 and XP, you can format a floppy disk with MS-DOS startup files by selecting that option from the Format menu in My Computer.

For example, when you boot from a Windows 9x startup disk, you are running 16-bit DOS, and if you want to access your CD-ROM drive to install Windows, you must load a 16-bit CD-ROM driver program from that disk as well. In this mode, you can do things such as partition and format your hard disk, install Windows, or test the system completely. OEM versions of Windows 98 and all versions of Windows Me and newer come on bootable CDs, so if your system supports booting from a CD-ROM drive, be sure to set that option in the BIOS Setup to eliminate the need for a formatted floppy disk.

The point of all this is that although you might not be running DOS very much these days, at least for system configuration and installation, as well as for high-level hardware diagnostics testing, data recovery, and so forth, you might still have to boot to a 16-bit OS occasionally. When you are in that mode, the system's architecture changes, less memory is accessible, and some of the software you are running (16-bit drivers and most application code) must fight over the first 1MB or even 640KB for space.

The system memory areas discussed in this chapter, including the 384KB at the top of the first megabyte, which is used for video, adapter BIOS, and motherboard BIOS, as well as the remaining extended memory, are all part of the PC hardware design. They exist whether you are running 16-bit or 32-bit software; however, the limitations on their use in 16-bit (real) mode are much more severe. Because most people run 32-bit operating systems, such as Windows 9x, 2000, XP, Linux, and so on, these operating systems automatically manage the use of RAM, meaning you don't have to interact with and manage this memory yourself as you often did with the 16-bit operating systems.

The following sections are intended to give you an understanding of the PC hardware memory layout, which is consistent no matter which operating system you use. The only things that change are how your operating system uses these areas and how they are managed by the OS.

The following sections detail the various types of memory installed on a modern PC. The kinds of memory covered in the following sections include

- Conventional (base) memory
- Upper memory area (UMA)
- High memory area (HMA)
- Extended memory (XMS)
- Expanded memory (obsolete)
- Video RAM memory (part of UMA)
- Adapter ROM and special-purpose RAM (part of UMA)
- Motherboard ROM BIOS (part of UMA)

Figure 6.19 shows the logical address locations for a 16-bit or higher system. If the processor is running in real mode, only the first megabyte is accessible. If the processor is in protected mode, the full 16MB, 4096MB, or 65536MB are accessible. Each symbol is equal to 1KB of memory, and each line or segment is 64KB. This map shows the first two megabytes of system memory.

◄◄   See "Processor Modes," p. 49.

Note

To save space, this map stops after the end of the second megabyte. In reality, this map continues to the maximum of addressable memory.

```
    . = Program-accessible memory (standard RAM)
    G = Graphics Mode Video RAM
    M = Monochrome Text Mode Video RAM
    C = Color Text Mode Video RAM
    V = Video ROM BIOS (would be "a" in PS/2)
    a = Adapter board ROM and special-purpose RAM (free UMA space)
    r = Additional PS/2 Motherboard ROM BIOS (free UMA in non-PS/2 systems)
    R = Motherboard ROM BIOS
    b = IBM Cassette BASIC ROM (would be "R" in IBM compatibles)
    h = High Memory Area (HMA), if HIMEM.SYS is loaded.

Conventional (Base) Memory:

        : 0---1---2---3---4---5---6---7---8---9---A---B---C---D---E---F---
000000: ................................................................
010000: ................................................................
020000: ................................................................
030000: ................................................................
040000: ................................................................
050000: ................................................................
060000: ................................................................
070000: ................................................................
080000: ................................................................
090000: ................................................................

Upper Memory Area (UMA):

        : 0---1---2---3---4---5---6---7---8---9---A---B---C---D---E---F---
0A0000: GGGGGGGGGGGGGGGGGGGGGGGGGGGGGGGGGGGGGGGGGGGGGGGGGGGGGGGGGGGGGGGGG
0B0000: MMMMMMMMMMMMMMMMMMMMMMMMMMMMMMMMCCCCCCCCCCCCCCCCCCCCCCCCCCCCCCCCCC
        : 0---1---2---3---4---5---6---7---8---9---A---B---C---D---E---F---
0C0000: VVVVVVVVVVVVVVVVVVVVVVVVVVVVVVVVVaaaaaaaaaaaaaaaaaaaaaaaaaaaaaaaaa
0D0000: aaaaaaaaaaaaaaaaaaaaaaaaaaaaaaaaaaaaaaaaaaaaaaaaaaaaaaaaaaaaaaaaa
        : 0---1---2---3---4---5---6---7---8---9---A---B---C---D---E---F---
0E0000: rrrrrrrrrrrrrrrrrrrrrrrrrrrrrrrrrrrrrrrrrrrrrrrrrrrrrrrrrrrrrrrrr
0F0000: RRRRRRRRRRRRRRRRRRRRRRRRRRRRRRRRbbbbbbbbbbbbbbbbbbbbbbbbbbbbbbbbbbRRRRRRRR

Extended Memory:

        : 0---1---2---3---4---5---6---7---8---9---A---B---C---D---E---F---
100000: hhhhhhhhhhhhhhhhhhhhhhhhhhhhhhhhhhhhhhhhhhhhhhhhhhhhhhhhhhhhhhhhhh

Extended Memory Specification (XMS) Memory:

110000: ................................................................
120000: ................................................................
130000: ................................................................
140000: ................................................................
150000: ................................................................
160000: ................................................................
170000: ................................................................
180000: ................................................................
190000: ................................................................
1A0000: ................................................................
1B0000: ................................................................
1C0000: ................................................................
1D0000: ................................................................
1E0000: ................................................................
1F0000: ................................................................
```

Figure 6.19   The logical memory map of the first 2MB.

Conventional (Base) Memory

The original PC/XT-type system was designed to use 1MB of RAM. This 1MB of RAM is divided into several sections, some of which have special uses. DOS can read and write to the entire megabyte but can manage the loading of programs only in the portion of RAM space called *conventional memory*, which was 512KB at the time the first PC was introduced. The other 512KB was reserved for use by the system, including the motherboard and adapter boards plugged into the system slots.

After introducing the system, IBM decided that only 384KB was needed for these reserved uses, and the company began marketing PCs with 640KB of user memory. Therefore, 640KB became the standard for memory that can be used by DOS for running programs and often is termed the 640KB memory barrier. The remaining memory after 640KB was reserved for use by the graphics boards, other adapters, and the motherboard ROM BIOS.

This barrier largely affects 16-bit software, such as DOS and Windows 3.1, and is much less of a factor with 32-bit software and operating systems, such as Windows 9x, NT/2000/XP, and so on.

Upper Memory Area

The term *Upper Memory Area (UMA)* describes the reserved 384KB at the top of the first megabyte of system memory on a PC/XT and the first megabyte on an AT-type system. This memory has the addresses from A0000 through FFFFF. The way the 384KB of upper memory is used breaks down as follows:

- *The first 128KB after conventional memory is called video RAM.* It is reserved for use by video adapters. When text and graphics are displayed onscreen, the data bits that make up those images reside in this space. Video RAM is allotted the address range A0000–BFFFF.

- *The next 128KB is reserved for the adapter BIOS that resides in read-only memory chips on some adapter boards plugged into the bus slots.* Most VGA-compatible video adapters use the first 32KB of this area for their onboard BIOS. Any other adapters installed can use the rest. Many network adapters also use this area for special-purpose RAM called *shared memory*. Adapter ROM and special-purpose RAM is allotted the address range C0000–DFFFF.

- *The last 128KB of memory is reserved for motherboard BIOS (the basic input/output system, which is stored in read-only RAM chips or ROM).* The POST and bootstrap loader, which handles your system at boot-up until the operating system takes over, also reside in this space. Most systems use only the last 64KB (or less) of this space, leaving the first 64KB or more free for remapping with memory managers. Some systems also include the CMOS Setup program in this area. The motherboard BIOS is allotted the address range E0000–FFFFF.

Not all the 384KB of reserved memory is fully used on most 16-bit and higher systems. For example, according to the PC standard, reserved video RAM begins at address A0000, which is right at the 640KB boundary. Normally, it is used for VGA graphics modes, whereas the monochrome and color text modes use B0000–B7FFF and B8000–BFFFF, respectively. Older non-VGA adapters used memory only in the B0000 segment. Different video adapters use varying amounts of RAM for their operations, depending mainly on the mode they are in. To the processor, however, it always appears as the same 128KB area, no matter how much RAM is really on the video card. This is managed by bank switching areas of memory on the card in and out of the A0000–BFFFF segments.

Although the top 384KB of the first megabyte was originally termed *reserved memory*, it is possible to use previously unused regions of this memory to load 16-bit device drivers (such as the ANSI.SYS screen driver that comes with DOS) and memory-resident programs (such as MOUSE.COM, the DOS mouse driver), which frees up the conventional memory they would otherwise require. Note that this does not affect 32-bit device drivers such as those used with Windows 9x, NT/2000/XP, and so forth because they load into extended memory with no restrictions. The amount of free UMA space varies from system to system, depending mostly on the adapter cards installed on the system. For example, most video adapters, SCSI adapters, and some network adapters require some of this area for built-in ROMs or special-purpose RAM use.

Segment Addresses and Linear Addresses

See the "General Troubleshooting and Diagnostics," section in the Technical Reference section of the disc accompanying this book for a discussion of segment and linear addressing.

Video RAM Memory

A video adapter installed in your system uses a portion of your system's first megabyte of memory to hold graphics or character information for display, but this typically is used or active only when in basic VGA mode.

Note that even though a modern video card can have 64MB or more of onboard memory, only 128KB of this memory appears available to the system in the video RAM area. The rest of the memory is accessible only by the video processor (on the video card) directly, or by your system processor via a memory aperture positioned near the 4GB top of the system address space. Because this aperture can be configured differently by various cards, you should consult the technical documentation for your card or video chipset for more information. Some motherboard ROM have BIOS Setup options for controlling the video card memory aperture, but unless you are experiencing some type of problem related to the video card, it is best to leave those options to their default settings.

When in basic VGA mode, such as when at a DOS prompt or when running in Windows safe mode, your processor can directly access up to 128KB of the video RAM from address A0000–BFFFFh. All modern video cards also have onboard BIOS normally addressed at C0000–C7FFFh, which is part of the memory space reserved for adapter card BIOS. Generally, the higher the resolution and color capabilities of the video adapter, the more system memory the video adapter uses, but again, that additional memory (past 128KB) is not usually accessible by the processor. Instead, the system tells the video chip what should be displayed, and the video chip generates the picture by putting data directly into the video RAM on the card.

In the standard system-memory map, a total of 128KB is reserved for use by the video card to store currently displayed information when in basic VGA modes. The reserved video memory is located in segments A000 and B000. The video adapter ROM uses additional upper memory space in segment C000. Even with the new multiple monitor feature in Windows 98 and later, only one video card (the primary video card) is in the memory map; all others use no low system memory.

Note

The location of video adapter RAM is responsible for the infamous 640KB DOS conventional memory barrier. DOS can use all available contiguous memory in the first megabyte of memory up to the point where the video adapter RAM is encountered. The use of ancient video adapters, such as the MDA and CGA, can enable DOS access to more than 640KB of system memory. For more information, see Chapter 5 of *Upgrading and Repairing PCs, 10th Anniversary Edition*, included on the disc.

To learn how the older video adapters use the system's memory, see "Obsolete Video Adapter Types," also in Chapter 5 of the *10th Edition*.

Video Graphics Array Memory

All VGA-compatible cards, including those running in PCI or AGP slots, use all 128KB of the system allocated video RAM from A0000–BFFFF, but not all at once. This video RAM area is used depending on the mode the card is in. Figure 6.20 shows the VGA adapter memory map.

You can see that the typical VGA card uses a full 32KB of space for the onboard ROM containing driver code. Some VGA cards might use slightly less, but this is rare. The video RAM areas are active only when the adapter is in the particular mode designated. In other words, when a VGA adapter is in graphics mode, only segment A000 is used; when it is in color text mode, only the last half of segment B000 is used. Because the VGA adapter is almost never run in monochrome text mode, the first half of segment B000 remains unused (B0000–B7FFF). Figure 6.20 shows the standard motherboard ROM BIOS so that you can get an idea of how the entire UMA is laid out with this adapter.

```
   . = Empty Addresses
   G = Video Graphics Array (VGA) Adapter Graphics Mode Video RAM
   M = VGA Monochrome Text Mode Video RAM
   C = VGA Color Text Mode Video RAM
   V = Standard VGA Video ROM BIOS
   R = Standard Motherboard ROM BIOS


        : 0---1---2---3---4---5---6---7---8---9---A---B---C---D---E---F---
 0A0000: GGGGGGGGGGGGGGGGGGGGGGGGGGGGGGGGGGGGGGGGGGGGGGGGGGGGGGGGGGGGGGGGG
 0B0000: MMMMMMMMMMMMMMMMMMMMMMMMMMMMMMMMCCCCCCCCCCCCCCCCCCCCCCCCCCCCCCCCC
        : 0---1---2---3---4---5---6---7---8---9---A---B---C---D---E---F---
 0C0000: VVVVVVVVVVVVVVVVVVVVVVVVVVVVVVVVVV..............................
 0D0000: ...............................................................
        : 0---1---2---3---4---5---6---7---8---9---A---B---C---D---E---F---
 0E0000: ...............................................................
 0F0000: RRRRRRRRRRRRRRRRRRRRRRRRRRRRRRRRRRRRRRRRRRRRRRRRRRRRRRRRRRRRRRRRR
```

Figure 6.20 The VGA adapter memory map.

Some systems incorporate the video adapter into the motherboard or even directly in the motherboard chipset. In these systems, even though the video BIOS and motherboard BIOS might be from the same manufacturer, they are always set up to emulate a standard VGA-type adapter card. In other words, the video BIOS appears in the first 32KB of segment C000 just as though a standalone VGA-type card were plugged into a slot. The built-in video circuit in these systems can in many cases be disabled with a switch or jumper or sometimes by simply plugging in a video card. By having the built-in VGA act exactly as though it were a separate card, disabling it allows a new adapter to be installed with no compatibility problems that might arise if the video drivers had been incorporated into the motherboard BIOS.

Adapter ROM and Special-Purpose RAM Memory

The second 128KB of upper memory beginning at segment C000 is reserved for the software programs, or BIOS, on the adapter boards plugged into the system slots. These BIOS programs are stored on special chips known as ROM. Most adapters today use EEPROM or Flash ROM, which can be erased and reprogrammed right in the system without removing the chip or card. Updating the Flash ROM is as simple as running the update program you get from the manufacturer and following the directions onscreen. It pays to check periodically with your card manufacturers to see whether they have Flash ROM updates for their cards.

ROM is useful for semipermanent programs that must always be present while the system is running, and especially for booting. Graphics boards, hard disk controllers, communications boards, and expanded memory boards, for example, are adapter boards that might have adapter ROM. These adapter ROMs are in an area of memory separate from the VGA video RAM and motherboard ROM areas.

On systems based on the 386 CPU chip or higher, memory managers that are included with DOS 6 or third-party programs can load device drivers and memory-resident programs into unused regions in the UMA.

To actually move the RAM usage on any given adapter requires that you consult the documentation for the card. Most older cards require that specific switches or jumpers be changed, and the settings will probably not be obvious without the manual. Plug and Play cards allow these settings to be changed by software that comes with the card or the Device Manager program included in Windows.

Video Adapter BIOS

The video adapter ROM BIOS controls the video card during the boot sequence and anytime the system is in basic VGA modes (such as when running DOS). You also are using the video ROM BIOS code whenever you are running Windows in safe mode. All modern video adapters (even AGP cards) use 32KB for their onboard BIOS, from addresses C0000–C7FFF.

Depending on the basic VGA mode selected (color text, monochrome text, or VGA graphics), the video card uses some or all of the 128KB of upper memory beginning at segment C000. In addition, graphics cards can contain up to 64MB or more of onboard memory for use in their native high-resolution modes in which to store currently displayed data and more quickly fetch new screen data for display.

Hard Disk Controller and SCSI Host Adapter BIOS

The upper memory addresses C0000–DFFFF are also used for the built-in BIOS contained on many hard drive and SCSI controllers. Table 6.22 lists the amount of memory and the addresses commonly used by the BIOS contained on hard drive adapter cards.

Table 6.22   Memory Addresses Used by Various Hard Drive Adapter Cards

Disk Adapter Type	Onboard BIOS Size	BIOS Address Range
Most XT-compatible controllers	8KB	C8000–C9FFF
Most AT controllers	None	Drivers in motherboard BIOS
Most standard IDE adapters	None	Drivers in motherboard BIOS
Most enhanced IDE adapters	16KB	C8000–CBFFF
Some SCSI host adapters	16KB	C8000–CBFFF
Some SCSI host adapters	16KB	DC000–DFFFF

The hard drive or SCSI adapter card used on a particular system might use a different amount of memory, but it is most likely to use the memory segment beginning at C800 because this address is considered part of the IBM standard for personal computers. Virtually all the disk controller or SCSI adapters today that have an onboard BIOS allow the BIOS starting address to be easily moved in the C000 and D000 segments. The locations listed in Table 6.22 are only the default addresses that most of these cards use. If the default address is already in use by another card, you have to consult the documentation for the new card to see how to change the BIOS starting address to avoid any conflicts.

Figure 6.21 shows a sample memory map for an Adaptec AHA-2940 SCSI adapter.

```
        .  = Empty Addresses
        G  = Video Graphics Array (VGA) Adapter Graphics Mode Video RAM
        M  = VGA Monochrome Text Mode Video RAM
        C  = VGA Color Text Mode Video RAM
        V  = Standard VGA Video ROM BIOS
        S  = SCSI Host Adapter ROM BIOS
        R  = Standard Motherboard ROM BIOS


        : 0---1---2---3---4---5---6---7---8---9---A---B---C---D---E---F---
0A0000: GGGGGGGGGGGGGGGGGGGGGGGGGGGGGGGGGGGGGGGGGGGGGGGGGGGGGGGGGGGGGGGGG
0B0000: MMMMMMMMMMMMMMMMMMMMMMMMMMMMMMMMMCCCCCCCCCCCCCCCCCCCCCCCCCCCCCCCCC
        : 0---1---2---3---4---5---6---7---8---9---A---B---C---D---E---F---
0C0000: VVVVVVVVVVVVVVVVVVVVVVVVVVVVVVVVV...............................
0D0000: ..............................................SSSSSSSSSSSSSSSSSS
        : 0---1---2---3---4---5---6---7---8---9---A---B---C---D---E---F---
0E0000: ...............................................................
0F0000: RRRRRRRRRRRRRRRRRRRRRRRRRRRRRRRRRRRRRRRRRRRRRRRRRRRRRRRRRRRRRRRRR
```

Figure 6.21   Adaptec AHA-2940U SCSI adapter default memory use.

Network Adapters

Network adapter cards can also use upper memory in segments C000 and D000. The exact amount of memory used and the starting address for each network card vary with the card's type and manufacturer. Some network cards do not use any memory at all. A network card might have two primary uses for memory. They are as follows:

- IPL (Initial Program Load or Boot) ROM
- Shared memory (RAM)

An IPL ROM is usually an 8KB ROM that contains a bootstrap loader program that enables the system to boot directly from a file server on the network. This enables the removal of all disk drives from the PC, creating a diskless workstation. Because no floppy or hard disk is in the system to boot from, the IPL ROM gives the system the instructions necessary to locate an image of the operating system on the file server and load it as though it were on an internal drive.

Shared memory refers to a small portion of RAM contained on the network card that is mapped into the PC's upper memory area. This region is used as a memory window onto the network and offers rapid data transfer from the network card to the system. IBM pioneered the use of shared memory for its first Token-Ring network adapters, and now shared memory is commonly used in other companies' network adapters. Shared memory first was devised by IBM because it found that transfers using the DMA channels were not fast enough in most systems. This mainly had to do with some quirks in the DMA controller and bus design, which especially affected 16-bit ISA bus systems. Network adapters that do not use shared memory use DMA or Programmed I/O (PIO) transfers to move data to and from the network adapter.

Although shared memory is faster than either DMA or PIO for ISA systems, it does require 16KB of UMA space to work. Most standard performance network adapters use PIO because it makes them easier to configure, and they require no free UMA space. However, most high-performance adapters use shared memory. The shared memory region on most network adapters that use one is usually 16KB in size and can be located at any user-selected 4KB increment of memory in segments C000 or D000.

Figure 6.22 shows the default memory addresses for the IPL ROM and shared memory of an IBM Token-Ring network adapter, although many other network adapters, such as Ethernet adapters, are similar. One thing to note is that most Ethernet adapters use either a DMA channel or standard PIO commands to send data to and from the network and don't use shared memory, as many Token-Ring cards do.

```
         . = Empty Addresses
         G = Video Graphics Array (VGA) Adapter Graphics Mode Video RAM
         M = VGA Monochrome Text Mode Video RAM
         C = VGA Color Text Mode Video RAM
         V = Standard VGA Video ROM BIOS
         I = Token Ring Network Adapter IPL ROM
         N = Token Ring Network Adapter Shared RAM
         R = Standard Motherboard ROM BIOS


           : 0---1---2---3---4---5---6---7---8---9---A---B---C---D---E---F---
   0A0000: GGGGGGGGGGGGGGGGGGGGGGGGGGGGGGGGGGGGGGGGGGGGGGGGGGGGGGGGGGGGGGGGG
   0B0000: MMMMMMMMMMMMMMMMMMMMMMMMMMMMMMMMMMMCCCCCCCCCCCCCCCCCCCCCCCCCCCCCCC
           : 0---1---2---3---4---5---6---7---8---9---A---B---C---D---E---F---
   0C0000: VVVVVVVVVVVVVVVVVVVVVVVVVVVVVVVVV................IIIIIIII........
   0D0000: ..........................NNNNNNNNNNNNNNNN.................
           : 0---1---2---3---4---5---6---7---8---9---A---B---C---D---E---F---
   0E0000: ................................................................
   0F0000: RRRRRRRRRRRRRRRRRRRRRRRRRRRRRRRRRRRRRRRRRRRRRRRRRRRRRRRRRRRRRRRRRR
```

Figure 6.22   Network adapter default memory map.

I have also included the standard VGA video BIOS in Figure 6.22 because nearly every system would have a VGA-type video adapter as well. Note that these default addresses for the IPL ROM and the shared memory can easily be changed by reconfiguring the adapter. Most other network adapters are similar in that they also have an IPL ROM and a shared memory address, although the sizes of these areas and the default addresses might be different. Most network adapters that incorporate an IPL ROM option can disable the ROM and socket so that those addresses are not needed at all. This helps conserve UMA space and prevent possible future conflicts if you are never going to use the function.

Note that the Plug and Play feature in Win 9x, Me, 2000, and XP does not attempt to optimize memory use, only to resolve conflicts. Of course, with 32-bit drivers, the locations and sizes of free upper memory blocks don't really matter because 32-bit drivers are loaded into extended memory. If you are still occasionally running DOS-based programs, such as games, you could manually optimize the upper memory area configuration for maximum memory and performance, but for the most part it isn't worth the effort.

Motherboard BIOS Memory

The last 128KB of reserved memory is used by the motherboard BIOS. The BIOS programs in ROM control the system during the boot-up procedure and remain as drivers for various hardware in the system during normal operation. Because these programs must be available immediately, they can't be loaded from a device such as a disk drive.

◀◀ See Chapter 5, "BIOS," p. 397.

Both segments E000 and F000 in the memory map are considered reserved for the motherboard BIOS, but only some systems actually use this entire area. Older 8-bit systems require only segment F000 and enable adapter card ROM or RAM to use segment E000. Most 16-bit or greater systems use all F000 for the BIOS and might decode but not use any of segment E000. By decoding an area, the motherboard essentially grabs control of the addresses, which precludes installing any other hardware in this region. In other words, configuring adapter cards to use this area isn't possible. That is why you will find that most adapters that use memory simply do not allow any choices for memory use in segment E000. Although this might seem like a waste of 64KB of memory space, any 386 or higher system can use the powerful MMU in the processor to map RAM from extended memory into segment E000 as an upper memory block. The system can subsequently load 16-bit driver software in this UMB if necessary. This is a nice solution to what otherwise would be wasted memory, although it is not important if you use 32-bit drivers.

Figure 6.23 shows the motherboard ROM BIOS memory use of most 16-bit or greater systems.

```
        . = Empty Addresses
        R = Standard Motherboard ROM BIOS

               : 0---1---2---3---4---5---6---7---8---9---A---B---C---D---E---F---
        0E0000: ................................................................
        0F0000: RRRRRRRRRRRRRRRRRRRRRRRRRRRRRRRRRRRRRRRRRRRRRRRRRRRRRRRRRRRRRRRRRR
```

Figure 6.23 Motherboard ROM BIOS memory use of most systems.

Note that the standard system BIOS uses only segment F000 (64KB). In almost every case, the remainder of the BIOS area (segment E000) is completely free and can be used as UMA block space.

Extended Memory

As mentioned previously in this chapter, the memory map on a system based on the 286 or higher processor can extend beyond the 1MB boundary that exists when the processor is in real mode. On a 286 or 386SX system, the extended memory limit is 16MB (24-bit addressing); on a 386DX, 486, Pentium, or Pentium MMX system, the extended memory limit is 4GB (4,096MB using 32-bit addressing). Systems based on the Pentium Pro, Pentium II, and newer processors have a limit of 64GB (65,536MB using 36-bit addressing).

Note

36-bit memory addressing is enabled through a method called physical address extension (PAE). PAE is an Intel-provided memory address extension that enables support of up to 64GB of physical memory for applications running on most 32-bit Intel Pentium Pro and later processors. PAE enables the processor to expand the number of bits that can be used to address physical memory from 32 bits to 36 bits, but it requires operating system support as well. Support for PAE is provided only in server-oriented operating systems such as Windows 2000 and later versions of the Advanced Server and Datacenter Server operating systems. Without PAE support, memory addressing is limited to 32 bits or 4GB of physical RAM.

For a system to address memory beyond the first megabyte, the processor must be in protected mode—the native mode of 286 and higher processors. On a 286, only programs designed to run in protected mode can take advantage of extended memory; 386 and higher processors offer another mode, called virtual real mode, which enables extended memory to be, in effect, chopped into 1MB pieces (each its own real-mode session). Virtual real mode also enables several of these sessions to be running simultaneously in protected areas of memory. They can be seen as DOS prompt sessions or windows within Windows 9x/Me, NT, 2000, XP, or OS/2. Although several DOS programs can be running at once, each is still limited to a maximum of 640KB of memory because each session simulates a real-mode environment, right down to the BIOS and Upper Memory Area. Running several programs at once in virtual real mode, called *multitasking*, requires software that can manage each program and keep them from crashing into one another. OS/2; Windows 9x/Me; and Windows NT, 2000, and XP all do this.

The 286 and higher CPU chips also run in what is termed *real mode*, which enables full compatibility with the 8088 CPU chip installed on the PC/XT-type computer. Real mode enables you to run DOS programs one at a time on an AT-type system just as you would on a PC/XT. However, an AT-type system running in real mode, particularly a system based on the 386 through Pentium 4 or Athlon, is really functioning as little more than a turbo PC. In real mode, these processors can emulate the 8086 or 8088, but they can't operate in protected mode at the same time. For that reason, the 386 and above also provide a virtual real mode that operates under protected mode. This enables real-mode programs to execute under the control of a protected-mode operating system, such as Win9x/Me or NT/2000/XP.

Note

Extended memory is basically all memory past the first megabyte, which can be accessed only while the processor is in protected mode.

XMS Memory

Microsoft, Intel, AST Corp., and Lotus Development developed the extended memory specification (XMS) in 1987 to specify how programs would use extended memory. The XMS specification functions on systems based on the 286 or higher and enables real-mode programs (those designed to run in DOS) to use extended memory and another block of memory usually out of the reach of DOS.

Before XMS, there was no way to ensure cooperation between programs that switched the processor into protected mode and used extended memory. There was also no way for one program to know what another had been doing with the extended memory because none of them could see that memory while in real mode. HIMEM.SYS becomes an arbitrator of sorts that first grabs all the extended memory for itself and then doles it out to programs that know the XMS protocols. In this manner, several programs that use XMS memory can operate together under DOS on the same system, switching the processor into and out of protected mode to access the memory. XMS rules prevent one program from accessing memory that another has in use. Because Windows 3.x is a program manager that switches the system to and from protected mode in running several programs at once, it has been set up to require XMS memory to function. Windows 9x/Me operates mostly in protected mode, but still calls on real mode for access to many system components. Windows NT, 2000, and XP are true protected-mode operating systems, as is OS/2.

Extended memory can be made to conform to the XMS specification by installing a device driver in the CONFIG.SYS file. The most common XMS driver is HIMEM.SYS, which is included with Windows 3.x and later versions of DOS, starting with 4.0 and up. Windows 9x/Me and NT/2000/XP automatically allow XMS functions in DOS prompt sessions, and you can configure full-blown DOS-mode sessions to allow XMS functions as well.

Note

To learn more about the high memory area and expanded memory, see Chapter 5 of *Upgrading and Repairing PCs, 10th Anniversary Edition*, on the disc.

Preventing ROM BIOS Memory Conflicts and Overlap

As explained previously, C000 and D000 are reserved for use by adapter-board ROM and RAM. If two adapters have overlapping ROM or RAM addresses, usually neither board operates properly. Each board functions if you remove or disable the other one, but they do not work together.

With many adapter boards, you can change the actual memory locations to be used with jumpers, switches, or driver software, which might be necessary to allow two boards to coexist in one system. This type of conflict can cause problems for troubleshooters. You must read the documentation for each adapter to find out which memory addresses the adapter uses and how to change the addresses to allow coexistence with another adapter. Most of the time, you can work around these problems by reconfiguring the board or by changing jumpers, switch settings, or software-driver parameters. This change enables the two boards to coexist and stay out of each other's way.

Additionally, you must ensure that adapter boards do not use the same IRQ, DMA channel, or I/O port address. You can easily avoid adapter board memory, IRQ, DMA channel, and I/O port conflicts by creating a chart or template to mock up the system configuration by penciling on the template the resources already used by each installed adapter. You end up with a picture of the system resources and the relationship of each adapter to the others.

If you are running a Plug and Play operating system, such as Windows 9x/Me or 2000/XP, you can use the Device Manager to view and optionally print all the device settings. I highly recommend you use this to print out all the settings in your system before and after you make modifications to see what has been changed. This will help you anticipate conflicts and ensures that you configure each adapter board correctly the first time. The template also becomes important documentation when you consider new adapter purchases. New adapters must be configurable to use the available resources in your system.

◄◄   See "System Resources," p. 367.

If your system has Plug and Play capabilities, and you use PnP adapters, it can resolve conflicts between the adapters by moving the memory usage on any conflict. Unfortunately, this routine is not intelligent and still requires human intervention—that is, manual specification of addresses to achieve the most optimum location for the adapter memory.

ROM Shadowing

Virtually all 386 and higher systems enable you to use what is termed *shadow memory* for the motherboard and possibly some adapter ROMs as well. Shadowing essentially moves the programming code from slow ROM chips into fast 32-bit system memory. Shadowing slower ROMs by copying their contents into RAM can greatly speed up these BIOS routines—sometimes making them four to five times faster.

Note that shadowing ROMs is not very important when running a 32-bit operating system, such as Win9x/Me or NT/2000/XP. This is because those operating systems use the 16-bit BIOS driver code only during booting; then they load 32-bit replacement drivers into faster extended memory and use them. Therefore, shadowing normally affects only DOS or other 16-bit software and operating systems. Because of this, some people are tempted to turn off the Video BIOS shadowing feature in the BIOS setup. Unfortunately, it won't gain you any memory back (you've lost it anyway) and will make the system slightly slower to boot up and somewhat slower when in Windows safe mode. The 16-bit BIOS video driver code is used at those times.

Note

To learn more about ROM shadowing, see Chapter 5 of *Upgrading and Repairing PCs, 10th Anniversary Edition*, on the disc accompanying this book.

Total Installed Memory Versus Total Usable Memory

Most people don't realize that not all the RAM you purchase and install in a system is available. Because of some quirks in system design, the system usually has to "throw away" up to 384KB of RAM to make way for the Upper Memory Area.

For example, most systems with 16MB of RAM (which is 16,384KB) installed show a total of only 16,000KB installed during the POST or when running Setup. This indicates that 16,384KB–16,000KB = 384KB of missing memory! Some systems might show 16,256KB with the same 16MB installed, which works out to 16,384KB–16,256KB = 128KB missing.

If you run your Setup program and check out your base and extended memory values, you will find more information than just the single figure for the total shown during the POST. In most systems with 4,096KB (4MB), you have 640KB base and 3,072KB extended. In some systems, Setup reports 640KB base and 3,328KB extended memory, which is a bonus. In other words, most systems come up 384KB short, but some come up only 128KB short.

This shortfall is not easy to explain, but it is consistent from system to system. Say that you have a 486 system with two installed 72-pin (32-bit) 16MB SIMMs. This results in a total installed memory of 32MB in two separate banks because the processor has a 32-bit data bus. Each SIMM is a single bank in this system. The first bank (or SIMM, in this case) starts at address 0000000h (the start of the first megabyte), and the second starts at 1000000 (the start of the seventeenth megabyte).

One of the cardinal rules of memory is that you absolutely cannot have two hardware devices wired to the same address. This means that 384KB of the first memory bank in this system would be in direct conflict with the video RAM (segments A000 and B000), any adapter card ROMs (segments C000 and D000), and of course the motherboard ROM (segments E000 and F000). This means all SIMM RAM that occupies these addresses must be shut off; otherwise, the system will not function! Actually, a motherboard designer can do three things with the SIMM memory that would overlap from A0000–FFFFF:

- Use the faster RAM to hold a copy of any slow ROMs (shadowing), disabling the ROM in the process
- Turn off any RAM not used for shadowing, eliminating any UMA conflicts
- Remap any RAM not used for shadowing, adding to the stack of currently installed extended memory

Most systems shadow the motherboard ROM (usually 64KB) and the video ROM (32KB) and simply turn off the rest. Some motherboard ROMs allow additional shadowing to be selected between C8000 and DFFFF, usually in 16KB increments.

Note

You can shadow only ROM, never RAM, so if any card (such as a network card) has a RAM buffer in the C8000–DFFFF area, you must not shadow the RAM buffer addresses; otherwise, the card will not function. For the same reason, you can't shadow the A0000–BFFFF area because it is the video adapter RAM buffer.

Most motherboards do not do any remapping, which means that any of the 384KB not shadowed is simply turned off. That is why enabling shadowing does not seem to use any memory. The memory used for shadowing would otherwise be discarded in most systems. These systems would appear to be short by 384KB compared to what is physically installed in the system. For example, in a system with 32MB, no remapping would result in 640KB of base memory and 31,744KB of extended memory, for a total of 32,384KB of usable RAM—384KB short of the total (32,768KB–384KB).

Systems that show 384KB of "missing" memory do not do remapping. If you want to determine whether your system has any missing memory, all you need to know are three things. One is the total physical memory actually installed. Running your Setup program can discover the other two items. You want to know the total base and extended memory numbers recognized by the system. Then simply subtract the base and extended memory from the total installed to determine the missing memory. You usually will find that your system is missing 384KB, but you could be lucky and have a system that remaps 256KB of what is missing and thus shows only 128KB of memory missing.

Virtually all systems use some of the missing memory for shadowing ROMs, especially the motherboard and video BIOS, so what is missing is not completely wasted. Systems missing 128KB will find that it is being used to shadow your motherboard BIOS (64KB from F0000 to FFFFF) and video BIOS (32KB from C0000 to C8000). The remainder of segment C0000 (32KB from C8000 to CFFFF) is simply being turned off. All other segments (128KB from A0000 to BFFFF and 128KB from D0000 to EFFFF) are being remapped to the start of the fifth megabyte (400000–43FFFF). Most systems simply disable these remaining segments rather than take the trouble to remap them.

Note that with the relatively large amount of memory in modern PCs, losing a paltry 384KB hardly has an impact on performance. Also, because shadowing has a performance benefit only when running under a 16-bit OS such as DOS, systems running Windows aren't affected by any changes to the shadowing settings. If these settings are present in your BIOS Setup, I usually recommend they be left at default settings.

Adapter Memory Configuration and Optimization

Adapter boards use upper memory for their BIOS and as working RAM. If two boards attempt to use the same BIOS area or RAM area of upper memory, a conflict occurs that can keep your system from booting. In most cases, the plug-and-play software in the operating system ensures that such cards are automatically reconfigured so that they are not in conflict; however, sometimes problems can occur and you must step in and manually resolve a conflict. The following sections cover ways to avoid these potential unresolved conflicts and how to troubleshoot if they do occur. In addition, these sections discuss moving adapter memory to resolve conflicts and provide some ideas on optimizing adapter memory use.

How to Determine What Adapters Occupy the UMA

You can determine which adapters are using space in upper memory in the following two ways:

- Study the documentation for each adapter on your system to determine the memory addresses they use.
- Use a software utility or the Device Manager in your operating system to determine which upper memory areas your adapters are using.

The simplest way (although by no means always the most foolproof) is to use a software utility to determine the upper memory areas used by the adapters installed on your system. One such utility, Microsoft Diagnostics (MSD), comes with Windows 3.x and DOS 6 or higher versions. The Device Manager in the Windows 9x/Me and 2000/XP Control Panel also supplies this information in much more detail than MSD, as does the new System Information utility that comes with Windows 98 and later. These utilities examine your system configuration and determine not only the upper memory used by your adapters, but also the IRQs used by each of these adapters.

True plug-and-play systems also shut down one of the cards involved in a conflict to prevent a total system lockup. This could cause Windows to boot in safe mode.

After you run MSD, Device Manager, or another utility to determine your system's upper memory configuration, make a printout of the memory addresses used. Thereafter, you can quickly refer to the printout when you are adding a new adapter to ensure that the new board does not conflict with any devices already installed on your system.

Moving Adapter Memory to Resolve Conflicts

After you identify a conflict or potential conflict using one of the two methods discussed in the previous section, you might have to reconfigure one or more of your adapters to move the upper memory space used by a problem adapter.

Most adapter boards make moving adapter memory a somewhat simple process, enabling you to change a few jumpers or switches to reconfigure the board. With plug-and-play cards, use the configuration program that comes with the board or the Windows Device Manager to make the changes. The following steps help you resolve most problems that arise because adapter boards conflict with one another:

1. Determine the upper memory addresses currently used by your adapter boards and write them down.
2. Determine whether any of these addresses are overlapping, which results in a conflict.
3. Consult the documentation for your adapter boards to determine which boards can be reconfigured so that all adapters have access to unique memory addresses.
4. Configure the affected adapter boards so that no conflict in memory addresses occurs.

For example, if one adapter uses the upper memory range C8000–CBFFF and another adapter uses the range CA000–CCFFF, you have a potential address conflict. One of them must be changed. Note that plug-and-play cards allow these changes to be made directly from the Windows Device Manager.

CHAPTER 7

The ATA/IDE Interface

An Overview of the IDE Interface

The interface used to connect hard disk and optical drives to a modern PC is typically called IDE (Integrated Drive Electronics); however, I always like to point out that the true name of this interface is ATA (AT Attachment). The ATA designation refers to the fact that this interface was originally designed to connect a combined drive and controller directly to the 16-bit bus found in the 1984 vintage IBM AT (Advanced Technology) and compatible computers. The AT bus is otherwise known as the ISA (Industry Standard Architecture) bus. Although ATA is the official name of the interface, *IDE* is a marketing term originated by some of the drive manufacturers to describe the drive/controller combination used in drives with the ATA interface. *Integrated Drive Electronics* refers to the fact that the interface electronics or controller is built in to the drive and is not a separate board, as with earlier drive interfaces. Although the correct name for the particular IDE interface we most commonly use is technically ATA, many persist in using the IDE designation today. If you are being picky, you could say that *IDE* refers generically to any drive interface in which the controller is built in to the drive, whereas *ATA* refers to the specific implementation of IDE that is used in most PCs.

ATA is used to connect not only hard disks, but also optical (CD and DVD) drives, high-capacity SuperDisk or Zip floppy drives, and tape drives. Even so, ATA is still thought of primarily as a hard disk interface, and it evolved directly from the separate controller and hard drive interfaces that were used prior to ATA. This chapter covers the standard parallel version of ATA as well as the newer Serial ATA interfaces in detail; it also briefly mentions the original interfaces from which ATA evolved. Because the ATA interface is directly integrated into virtually all motherboard chipsets, ATA is the primary storage device interface used by most PCs.

Note

Even Apple recognized the value of ATA and began incorporating it into virtually all modern Macintosh systems released from 1995 to the present (before that, Apple used a semiproprietary version of SCSI). In fact, Apple has quietly adopted many other industry standards taken directly from the PC, including PCI, AGP, USB, and both SDR and DDR SDRAM, to name a few.

▶▶ See "SuperDisk LS-120 and LS-240," p. 710.

Precursors to IDE

A variety of hard disk interfaces has been used for PC hard disks over the years. As time has passed, the number of choices has increased; however, many of the older interface standards are obsolete and no longer viable in newer systems.

The primary job of the hard disk controller or interface is to transmit and receive data to and from the drive. The various interface types limit how fast data can be moved from the drive to the system and offer different features as well as levels of performance. If you are putting together a system in which performance is a primary concern, you need to know how these various interfaces affect performance and what you can expect from them. Many statistics that appear in technical literature are not indicative of the real performance figures you will see in practice. I will separate the myths presented by some of these overly optimistic figures from the reality of what you will actually see.

Several types of hard disk interfaces have been used in PCs over the years, as shown in Table 7.1.

Table 7.1 PC Drive Interfaces

Interface	When Used	Interface	When Used
ST-506/412	1978–1989 (obsolete)	SCSI	1986–present
ESDI	1983–1991 (obsolete)	ATA (IDE)	1986–present
Non-ATA IDE	1987–1993 (obsolete)	Serial ATA	2003–present

Of these interfaces, only ST-506/412 and ESDI are what you could call true disk-controller–to–drive interfaces, and they are obsolete. Non-ATA versions of IDE were used primarily in the IBM PS/2 systems and are also obsolete. Current SCSI, ATA, and Serial ATA are system-level interfaces that usually internally incorporate a chipset-based controller interface. For example, many SCSI, parallel ATA, and Serial ATA drives incorporate the same basic controller circuitry inside the actual drive. The SCSI interface then adds another layer that connects between the drive controller and the PCI (or ISA) bus, whereas PATA and Serial ATA have a more direct connection from the controller to the AT bus attachment interface. Despite their differences, we call a SCSI, ATA, or Serial ATA card a *host interface adapter* instead of a controller card because the actual controllers are inside the drives. Virtually all modern disk drives use parallel ATA, Serial ATA, or SCSI interfaces to connect to a system.

IDE Origins

Any drive with an integrated controller could be called an IDE drive, although normally when we say *IDE*, we really mean the specific version of IDE called ATA. No matter what you call it, combining the drive and controller greatly simplifies installation because there are no separate power or signal cables that run from the controller to the drive. Also, when the controller and drive are assembled as a unit, the number of total components is reduced, signal paths are shorter, and the electrical connections are more noise-resistant. This results in a more reliable and less expensive design than is possible when a separate controller, connected to the drive by cables, is used.

Placing the controller, including the digital-to-analog encoder/decoder (endec), on the drive offers an inherent reliability advantage over interfaces with separate controllers such as ST506 and ESDI. Reliability is increased because the data encoding, from digital to analog, is performed directly on the drive in a tight noise-free environment. The timing-sensitive analog information does not have to travel along crude ribbon cables that are likely to pick up noise and insert propagation delays into the signals. The integrated configuration enables increases in the clock rate of the encoder and the storage density of the drive.

Integrating the controller and drive also frees the controller and drive engineers from having to adhere to the strict guidelines imposed by the earlier interface standards. Engineers can design what essentially are custom drive and controller implementations because no other controller will ever have to be connected to the drive. The resulting drive and controller combinations can offer higher performance than earlier standalone controller and drive setups. IDE drives sometimes are called drives with embedded controllers.

The earliest IDE drives were called hardcards and were nothing more than hard disks and controllers bolted directly together and plugged into a slot as a single unit. Companies such as the Plus Development Division of Quantum took small 3 1/2" drives (either ST-506/412 or ESDI) and attached them directly to a standard controller. The drive/controller assembly then was plugged into an ISA bus slot as though it were a normal disk controller card. Unfortunately, the mounting of a heavy, vibrating hard disk in an expansion slot with nothing but a single screw to hold it in place left a lot to be desired—not to mention the physical interference with adjacent cards because many of these units were much thicker than a controller card alone.

Several companies got the idea to redesign the controller to replace the logic board assembly on a standard hard disk and then mount it in a standard drive bay just like any other drive. Because the built-in controller in these drives still needed to plug directly into the expansion bus just like any other controller, a cable was run between the drive and one of the slots. This is the origin of IDE.

IDE Variations

There have been four main types of IDE interfaces based on three bus standards:

- Serial AT Attachment (SATA)
- Parallel AT Attachment (ATA, based on the 16-bit AT-bus, also called ISA)
- XT IDE (based on 8-bit ISA, obsolete)
- MCA IDE (based on 16-bit Micro Channel, obsolete)

Of these, only the parallel and Serial ATA versions are used today. ATA and Serial ATA have evolved with newer, faster, and more powerful versions. The newer versions of parallel ATA are referred to as ATA-2 and higher. They are also sometimes called EIDE (Enhanced IDE), Fast-ATA, Ultra-ATA, or Ultra-DMA. Even though parallel ATA has hit the end of the evolutionary road with ATA-7, Serial ATA picks up where parallel ATA leaves off and offers greater performance, higher reliability, easier installation, lower cost, and an established roadmap for future upgrades.

In 1987, IBM developed its own Micro Channel Architecture (MCA) IDE drives for systems such as the PS/2 Model 70, and connected them to the bus through a bus adapter device called an *interposer card*. These bus adapters (sometimes called *paddle boards* or *angle boards*) needed only a few buffer chips and did not require any real circuitry because the drive-based controller was designed to plug directly into the bus. The *paddle board* nickname came from the fact that they resemble game paddle or joystick adapters, which do not have much circuitry on them. MCA IDE uses a non-standard 72-pin connector, and was designed for MCA bus systems only.

An 8-bit variation of IDE appeared in 8-bit ISA systems such as the PS/2 Model 30. The XT IDE interface used a 40-pin connector similar to, but not compatible with, the 16-bit version. Neither MCA nor XT versions of IDE became very popular, and they have been off the market for several years.

Note

It is important to note that only the ATA IDE interface has been standardized by the industry. The XT and MCA IDE interfaces never were adopted as industry-wide standards and never became very popular. These interfaces were only used from 1987 to 1993 and only in IBM PS/2 (and some early ThinkPad) systems.

In most modern systems you will find at least two ATA connectors on the motherboard, and systems that offer ATA RAID have two additional ATA connectors which can be used for an ATA RAID array or for additional ATA drives running as independent devices. If your motherboard does not have one of these connectors and you want to attach an ATA drive to your system, you can purchase an adapter card that adds an ATA interface (or two) to a system via the ISA or PCI bus slots. Some of the cards offer additional features, such as an onboard ROM BIOS or cache memory.

Because only the parallel and serial ATA versions of IDE are in use today, they are what this chapter focuses on.

Origins of ATA

Control Data Corporation (CDC; its disk drive division was later called Imprimis), Western Digital, and Compaq actually created what could be called the first ATA IDE interface drive and were the first to establish the 40-pin ATA connector pinout. The first ATA IDE drive was a 5 1/4" half-height CDC Wren II 40MB drive with an integrated WD controller and was initially used in the first Compaq 386 systems in 1986. I remember seeing this drive for the first time in 1986 at the fall Comdex show, and besides the (at the time) unique 40-pin ribbon cable, I remember being surprised by the green activity LED on the front bezel (most drives up until then used red LEDs).

Compaq was the first to incorporate a special bus adapter in its system to adapt the 98-pin AT-bus (also known as ISA) edge connector on the motherboard to a smaller 40-pin, header-style connector into which the drive would plug. The 40-pin connectors were all that was necessary because it was known that a disk controller never would need more than 40 of the ISA bus lines. Smaller 2 1/2" ATA drives found in notebook computers use a superset 44-pin or 50-pin connection, which includes additional pins for power and configuration. The pins from the original ISA bus used in ATA are the only signal pins required by a standard-type AT hard disk controller. For example, because a primary AT-style disk controller uses only interrupt request (IRQ) line 14, the primary motherboard ATA connector supplies only that IRQ line; no other IRQ lines are necessary. Even if your ATA interface is integrated within the motherboard chipset South Bridge or I/O Controller Hub chip (as it would be in newer systems) and runs at higher bus speeds, the pinout and functions of the pins are still the same as the original design taken right off the ISA bus.

◀◀ See "Motherboard Connectors," p. 330.

◀◀ See "The ISA Bus," p. 350.

Note

Many people who use systems with ATA connectors on the motherboard believe that a hard disk controller is built in to their motherboards, but in a technical sense the controller is actually in the drive. Although the integrated ATA ports on a motherboard often are referred to as *controllers*, they are more accurately called *host adapters* (although you'll rarely hear this term). A host adapter can be thought of as a device that connects a controller to a bus.

Eventually, the 40-pin ATA connector and drive interface design was placed before one of the ANSI standards committees that, in conjunction with drive manufacturers, ironed out some deficiencies, tied up some loose ends, and then published what was known as the CAM ATA (Common Access Method AT Attachment) interface. The CAM ATA Committee was formed in October 1988, and the first working document of the AT Attachment interface was introduced in March 1989. Before the CAM ATA standard, many companies, such as Conner Peripherals (which later merged with Seagate Technology), made proprietary changes to the original interface as designed by CDC. As a result, many older ATA drives from the late 1980s are very difficult to integrate into a dual-drive setup because minor differences in the interfaces can cause compatibility problems among the drives. By the early 1990s, most drive manufacturers brought their drives into full compliance with the official standard, which eliminated many of these compatibility problems.

Some areas of the ATA standard have been left open for vendor-specific commands and functions. These vendor-specific commands and functions are the main reason it is so difficult to low-level format ATA drives. To work to full capability, the format program you are using typically must know the specific vendor-unique commands for remapping defects. Unfortunately, these and other specific drive commands differ from OEM to OEM, clouding the "standard" somewhat. Most ATA drive manufacturers publish their drive formatting/initialization software on their Web sites.

Note

Many people are confused about 16- versus 32-bit bus connections and 16- versus 32-bit hard drive connections. A PCI bus connection allows for a 32-bit (and possibly 64-bit in some versions) connection between the bus and the ATA host interface, which is typically in the motherboard chipset South Bridge or I/O Controller Hub (ICH) chip. However, the actual parallel ATA interface between the host connector on the motherboard and the drive (or drives) itself is only a 16-bit interface. Thus, in a parallel ATA drive configuration, you are still getting only 16-bit transfers between the drive and the motherboard-based host interface. Even so, the clock speeds of the ATA interface are high enough that one or two hard drives normally can't supply the controller enough data to saturate even a 16-bit channel. The same is true with Serial ATA, which—although it transmits only 1 bit at a time—does so at extremely high speeds.

Parallel ATA is a 16-bit parallel interface, meaning that 16 bits are transmitted simultaneously down the interface cable. A serial interface called Serial ATA was officially introduced in late 2000 and began appearing in systems starting in 2003. Serial ATA (SATA) sends 1 bit down the cable at a time, enabling thinner and smaller cables to be used and providing higher performance due to the higher cycling speeds allowed. SATA is a completely new and updated physical interface design, while remaining compatible on the software level with parallel ATA. Throughout this book, *ATA* refers to both the parallel and serial versions, whereas parallel ATA (PATA) and Serial ATA (SATA) refer to the specific version as indicated. Figure 7.1 shows how the power and data cables used by SATA compare in size to those used by parallel ATA.

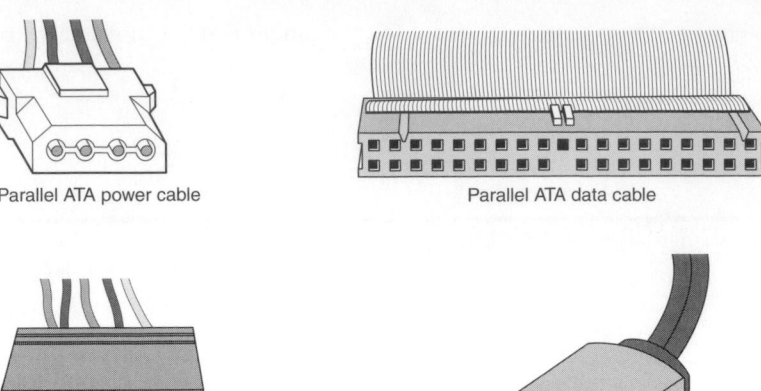

Parallel ATA power cable   Parallel ATA data cable

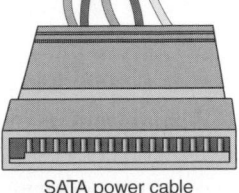   

SATA power cable   SATA data cable

Figure 7.1 Serial ATA data cables (lower right) are much smaller than those used by parallel ATA (upper right), whereas the power cables (left) are similar in size.

The primary advantage of ATA drives over the older, separate controller-based interfaces and newer host bus interface alternatives, such as USB, SCSI, and IEEE 1394 (i.LINK or FireWire), is cost. Because the separate controller or host adapter is eliminated and the cable connections are simplified, ATA drives cost much less than a standard controller and drive combination.

▶▶ See "Small Computer System Interface," p. 584.

▶▶ See "USB and IEEE1394 (i.LINK or FireWire)," p. 982.

In terms of performance, ATA drives are often some of the highest performance drives available—but they can also be among the lowest performance drives. This apparent contradiction is a result of the fact that all ATA drives are different. You can't make a blanket statement about the performance of ATA drives because each drive is unique. The high-end models, however, offer performance equal or superior to that of any other type of drive on the market for a single-user, single-tasking operating system.

ATA Standards

Today, the ATA interface is controlled by an independent group of representatives from major PC, drive, and component manufacturers. This group is called Technical Committee T13 (http://www.t13.org) and is responsible for all standards relating to the parallel and Serial AT Attachment storage interfaces. T13 is a part of the International Committee on Information Technology Standards (INCITS), which operates under rules approved by the American National Standards Institute (ANSI), a governing body that sets rules that control nonproprietary standards in the computer industry as well as many other industries. A second group called the Serial ATA Working Group (http://www.serialata.org) was formed to initially create the Serial ATA standards, which are then passed on to the T13 Committee for refinement and official publication under ANSI. The ATA-7 standard incorporates both parallel and serial standards and represents the end of the road for parallel ATA because ATA-8 and beyond will contain only serial versions.

The rules these committees operate under are designed to ensure that voluntary industry standards are developed by the consensus of people and organizations in the affected industry. INCITS specifically develops Information Processing System standards, whereas ANSI approves the process under which they are developed and then publishes them. Because T13 is essentially a public organization, all the working drafts, discussions, and meetings of T13 are open for all to see.

Copies of any of the published standards can be purchased from ANSI or Global Engineering Documents (see the Vendor List on the disc that accompanies this book). Draft versions of the standards can be downloaded from the T13 Committee or Serial ATA Working Group Web site.

The parallel ATA interface has evolved into several successive standard versions, introduced as follows:

- ATA-1
- ATA-2 (also called Fast-ATA, Fast-ATA-2, or EIDE)
- ATA-3
- ATA-4 (Ultra-ATA/33)
- ATA-5 (Ultra-ATA/66)
- ATA-6 (Ultra-ATA/100)
- ATA-7 (Ultra-ATA/133 or Serial ATA)
- SATA-8 (Serial ATA II)

Since ATA-1, newer versions of the ATA interface and complementary BIOS support larger and faster drives, as well as different types of devices other than hard disks. ATA-2 and later have improved the original ATA interface in five main areas:

- Secondary two-device channel
- Increased maximum drive capacity
- Faster data transfer
- ATAPI (ATA Program Interface)
- SATA (Serial ATA)

Each newer version of ATA is backward-compatible with the previous versions. In other words, older ATA-1 or ATA-2 devices work fine on ATA-6 and ATA-7 interfaces. ATA-7 includes both parallel and Serial ATA, but SATA-8 is serial only. Newer versions of ATA are normally built on older versions and with few exceptions can be thought of as extensions of the previous versions. This means that ATA-7, for example, is generally considered equal to ATA-6 with the addition of some features.

Table 7.2 breaks down the various ATA standards. The following sections describe all the ATA versions in more detail.

Table 7.2 ATA Standards

Standard	Proposed	Published	Withdrawn	PIO Modes	DMA Modes	UDMA Modes	Parallel Speed (MBps)[1]	Serial Speed (MBps)	Features
ATA-1	1988	1994	1999	0–2	0	—	8.33	—	Drives support up to 136.9GB; BIOS issues not addressed
ATA-2	1993	1996	2001	0–4	0–2	—	16.67	—	Faster PIO modes; CHS/LBA BIOS translation defined up to 8.4GB; PC-Card
ATA-3	1995	1997	2002	0–4	0–2	—	16.67	—	SMART; improved signal integrity; LBA support mandatory; eliminated single-word DMA modes
ATA-4	1996	1998	—	0–4	0–2	0–2	33.33	—	Ultra-DMA modes; ATAPI Packet Interface; BIOS support up to 136.9GB
ATA-5	1998	2000	—	0–4	0–2	0–4	66.67	—	Faster UDMA modes; 80-pin cable with autodetection
ATA-6	2000	2002	—	0–4	0–2	0–5	100	—	100MBps UDMA mode; extended drive and BIOS support up to 144PB

Table 7.2   Continued

Standard	Proposed	Published	Withdrawn	PIO Modes	DMA Modes	UDMA Modes	Parallel Speed (MBps)[1]	Serial Speed (MBps)	Features
ATA-7	2001	2004	—	0–4	0–2	0–6	133	150	133MBps UDMA mode; Serial ATA
SATA-8	2004	—	—	—	—	—	—	300	Serial ATA II

SMART = Self-Monitoring, Analysis, and Reporting Technology
ATAPI = AT Attachment Packet Interface
MB = Megabyte; million bytes
GB = Gigabyte; billion bytes
PB = Petabyte; quadrillion bytes

CHS = Cylinder, Head, Sector
LBA = Logical block address
PIO = Programmed I/O
DMA = direct memory access
UDMA = Ultra DMA (direct memory access)

ATA-1 (AT Attachment Interface for Disk Drives)

ATA-1 defined the original AT Attachment interface, which was an integrated bus interface between disk drives and host systems based on the ISA (AT) bus. These major features were introduced and documented in the ATA-1 specification:

- 40/44-pin connectors and cabling
- Master/slave or cable select drive configuration options
- Signal timing for basic Programmed I/O (PIO) and direct memory access (DMA) modes
- Cylinder, head, sector (CHS) and logical block address (LBA) drive parameter translations supporting drive capacities up to 2^{28}–2^{20} (267,386,880) sectors, or 136.9GB

Although ATA-1 had been in use since 1986, work on turning it into an official standard began in 1988 under the Common Access Method (CAM) committee. The ATA-1 standard was finished and officially published in 1994 as ANSI X3.221-1994, AT Attachment Interface for Disk Drives. ATA-1 was officially withdrawn as a standard on August 6, 1999.

Although ATA-1 supported theoretical drive capacities up to 136.9GB (2^{28}–2^{20} = 267,386,880 sectors), it did not address BIOS limitations that stopped at 528MB ($1024 \times 16 \times 63$ = 1,032,192 sectors). The BIOS limitations would be addressed in subsequent ATA versions because, at the time, no drives larger than 528MB had existed.

ATA-2 (AT Attachment Interface with Extensions-2)

ATA-2 first appeared in 1993 and was a major upgrade to the original ATA standard. Perhaps the biggest change was almost a philosophical one. ATA-2 was updated to define an interface between host systems and storage devices in general and not only disk drives. The major features added to ATA-2 as compared to the original ATA standard include

- Faster PIO and DMA transfer modes
- Support for power management
- Support for removable devices
- PCMCIA (PC Card) device support
- Identify Drive command that reports more information
- Defined standard CHS/LBA translation methods for drives up to 8.4GB in capacity

The most important additions in ATA-2 were the support for faster PIO and DMA modes, as well as methods to enable BIOS support up to 8.4GB. The BIOS support was necessary because, although ATA-1 was designed to support drives of up to 136.9GB in capacity, the PC BIOS could originally handle drives of up to 528MB. Adding parameter-translation capability now allowed the BIOS to handle drives up to 8.4GB. This is discussed in more detail later in this chapter.

ATA-2 also featured improvements in the Identify Drive command that enabled a drive to tell the software exactly what its characteristics are; this is essential for both Plug and Play (PnP) and compatibility with future revisions of the standard.

ATA-2 was also known by unofficial marketing terms such as fast-ATA or fast-ATA-2 (Seagate/Quantum) and EIDE (Enhanced IDE, Western Digital).

Although work on ATA-2 began in 1993, the standard was not officially published until 1996 as ANSI X3.279-1996 AT Attachment Interface with Extensions. ATA-2 was officially withdrawn in 2001.

ATA-3 (AT Attachment Interface-3)

First appearing in 1995, ATA-3 was a comparatively minor revision to the ATA-2 standard that preceded it. It consisted of a general cleanup of the specification and had mostly minor clarifications and revisions. The most major changes included the following:

- Eliminated single-word (8-bit) DMA transfer protocols.
- Added SMART (Self-Monitoring, Analysis, and Reporting Technology) support for prediction of device performance degradation.
- LBA mode support was made mandatory (previously it had been optional).
- Added ATA Security mode, allowing password protection for device access.
- Recommendations for source and receiver bus termination to solve noise issues at higher transfer speeds.

ATA-3 built on ATA-2, adding improved reliability, especially of the faster PIO mode 4 transfers; however, ATA-3 did not define any faster modes. ATA-3 did add a simple password-based security scheme, more sophisticated power management, and SMART. This enables a drive to keep track of problems that might result in a failure and therefore avoid data loss. SMART is a reliability prediction technology that was initially developed by IBM.

Work on ATA-3 began in 1995, and the standard was finished and officially published in 1997 as ANSI X3.298-1997, AT Attachment 3 Interface. ATA-3 was officially withdrawn in 2002.

ATA/ATAPI-4 (AT Attachment with Packet Interface Extension-4)

First appearing in 1996, ATA-4 included several important additions to the standard. It included the Packet Command feature known as the AT Attachment Packet Interface (ATAPI), which allowed devices such as CD-ROM and CD-RW drives, LS-120 SuperDisk floppy drives, Zip drives, tape drives, and other types of storage devices to be attached through a common interface. Until ATA-4 came out, ATAPI was a separately published standard. ATA-4 also added the 33MB per second (MBps) transfer mode known as Ultra-DMA or Ultra-ATA. ATA-4 is backward-compatible with ATA-3 and earlier definitions of the ATAPI.

Work on ATA-4 began in 1996, and the standard was finished and officially published in 1998 as ANSI NCITS 317-1998, AT Attachment - 4 with Packet Interface Extension.

The major revisions added in ATA-4 were as follows:

- Ultra-DMA (UDMA) transfer modes up to Mode 2, which is 33MBps (called UDMA/33 or Ultra-ATA/33)
- Integral ATAPI support

- Advanced power management support
- Defined an optional 80-conductor, 40-pin cable for improved noise resistance
- Host protected area (HPA) support
- Compact Flash Adapter (CFA) support
- Introduced enhanced BIOS support for drives over 9.4ZB (zettabytes or trillion gigabytes) in size (even though ATA was still limited to 136.9GB)

The speed and level of ATA support in your system is mainly dictated by your motherboard chipset. Most motherboard chipsets come with a component called either a South Bridge or an I/O Controller Hub that provides the ATA interface (as well as other functions) in the system. Check the specifications for your motherboard or chipset to see whether yours supports the faster ATA/33, ATA/66, ATA/100, or ATA/133 mode. One indication is to enter the BIOS Setup, put the hard disk on manual parameter settings (user defined), and see which (if any) Ultra-DMA modes are listed. Most boards built during 1998 support ATA/33; in 2000 they began to support ATA/66; and by late 2000 most started supporting ATA/100. ATA/133 support became widespread in mid-2002.

◀◀ See "Chipsets," p. 254.

ATA-4 made ATAPI support a full part of the ATA standard, and thus ATAPI was no longer an auxiliary interface to ATA but merged completely within it. Thus, ATA-4 promoted ATA for use as an interface for many other types of devices. ATA-4 also added support for new Ultra-DMA modes (also called Ultra-ATA) for even faster data transfer. The highest-performance mode, called UDMA/33, had 33MBps bandwidth—twice that of the fastest programmed I/O mode or DMA mode previously supported. In addition to the higher transfer rate, because UDMA modes relieve the load on the processor, further performance gains were realized.

An optional 80-conductor cable (with cable select) is defined for UDMA/33 transfers. Although this cable was originally defined as optional, it would later be required for the faster ATA/66, ATA/100, and ATA/133 modes in ATA-5 and later. Many hard drives purchased in retail kits include the 80-conductor cable, although other types of devices, such as optical drives, include only a 40-conductor cable.

Support for a reserved area on the drive called the host protected area (HPA) was added via an optional SET MAX ADDRESS command. This enables an area of the drive to be reserved for recovery software.

Also included was support for queuing commands, which is similar to that provided in SCSI-2. This enabled better multitasking as multiple programs make requests for ATA transfers.

▶▶ See "SCSI Versus ATA," p. 585.

Another standard approved by the T13 committee in 1998 is "ANSI NCITS 316-1998 1394 to AT Attachment - Tailgate," which is a bridge protocol between the IEEE 1394 (i.LINK/FireWire) bus and ATA that enables ATA drives to be adapted to FireWire. A *tailgate* is an adapter device (basically a small circuit board) that converts IEEE 1394 (i.LINK or FireWire) to ATA, essentially allowing ATA drives to be plugged into a FireWire bus. This has enabled vendors such as Maxtor, Western Digital, and others to quickly develop IEEE 1394 (FireWire) external drives for backup and high-capacity removable data storage. Inside almost any external FireWire drive enclosure you will find the tailgate device and a standard ATA drive.

▶▶ See "IEEE 1394," p. 992.

ATA/ATAPI-5 (AT Attachment with Packet Interface-5)

ATA-5 first appeared in 1998 and built on the previous ATA-4 interface. ATA-5 includes Ultra-ATA/66 (also called Ultra-DMA or UDMA/66), which doubles the Ultra-ATA burst transfer rate by reducing setup times and increasing the clock rate. The faster clock rate increases interference, which causes problems with the standard 40-pin cable used by ATA and Ultra-ATA. To eliminate noise and interference, the newer 40-pin, 80-conductor cable has now been made mandatory for drives running in

UDMA/66 or faster modes. This cable was first announced in ATA-4 but is now mandatory in ATA-5 to support the Ultra-ATA/66 mode. This cable adds 40 additional ground lines between each of the original 40 ground and signal lines, which helps shield the signals from interference. Note that this cable works with older, non–Ultra-ATA devices as well because it still has the same 40-pin connectors.

Work on ATA-5 began in 1998, and the standard was finished and officially published in 2000 as ANSI NCITS 340-2000, AT Attachment - 5 with Packet Interface.

The major additions in the ATA-5 standard include the following:

- Ultra-DMA (UDMA) transfer modes up to Mode 4, which is 66MBps (called UDMA/66 or Ultra-ATA/66).

- 80-conductor cable now mandatory for UDMA/66 operation.

- Added automatic detection of 40- or 80-conductor cables.

- UDMA modes faster than UDMA/33 are enabled only if an 80-conductor cable is detected.

The 40-pin, 80-conductor cables will support the cable select feature and have color-coded connectors. The blue (end) connector should be connected to the ATA host interface (usually the motherboard). The black (opposite end) connector is known as the *master position*, which is where the primary drive plugs in. The gray (middle) connector is for slave devices.

To use either the UDMA/33 or UDMA/66 mode, your ATA interface, drive, BIOS, and cable must be capable of supporting the mode you want to use. The operating system also must be capable of handling direct memory access. Windows 95 OSR2 or later, Windows 98/Me, and Windows 2000/XP are ready out of the box, but older versions of Windows 95 and NT (prior to Service Pack 3) require additional or updated drivers to fully exploit these faster modes. Contact the motherboard or system vendor for the latest drivers.

For reliability, Ultra-DMA modes incorporate an error-detection mechanism known as *cyclical redundancy checking (CRC)*. CRC is an algorithm that calculates a checksum used to detect errors in a stream of data. Both the host (controller) and the drive calculate a CRC value for each Ultra-DMA transfer. After the data is sent, the drive calculates a CRC value, and this is compared to the original host CRC value. If a difference is reported, the host might be required to select a slower transfer mode and retry the original request for data.

ATA/ATAPI-6 (AT Attachment with Packet Interface-6)

ATA-6 began development during 2000 and includes Ultra-ATA/100 (also called Ultra-DMA or UDMA/100), which increases the Ultra-ATA burst transfer rate by reducing setup times and increasing the clock rate. As with ATA-5, the faster modes require the improved 80-conductor cable. Using the ATA/100 mode requires both a drive and motherboard interface that supports that mode.

Work on ATA-6 began in 2000, and the standard was finished and officially published in 2002 as ANSI NCITS 361-2002, AT Attachment - 6 with Packet Interface.

The major changes or additions in the standard include the following:

- Ultra-DMA (UDMA) Mode 5 added, which allows 100MBps (called UDMA/100, Ultra-ATA/100, or just ATA/100) transfers.

- Sector count per command increased from 8-bits (256 sectors or 131KB) to 16-bits (65,536 sectors or 33.5MB), allowing larger files to be transferred more efficiently.

- LBA addressing extended from 2^{28} to 2^{48} (281,474,976,710,656) sectors supporting drives up to 144.12PB (petabytes = quadrillion bytes). This feature is often referred to as *48-bit LBA* or *greater than 137GB* support by vendors; Maxtor refers to this feature as *Big Drive*.

- CHS addressing made obsolete; drives must use 28-bit or 48-bit LBA addressing only.

Besides adding the 100MBps UDMA Mode 5 transfer rate, ATA-6 also extended drive capacity greatly, and just in time. ATA-5 and earlier standards supported drives of up to only 137GB in capacity, which became a limitation as larger drives were becoming available. Commercially available 3 1/2" drives exceeding 137GB were introduced during 2001, but they were originally available only in SCSI versions because SCSI doesn't share the same limitations as ATA. With ATA-6, the sector addressing limit has been extended from (2^{28}) sectors to (2^{48}) sectors. What this means is that LBA addressing previously could use only 28-bit numbers, but with ATA-6, LBA addressing can use larger 48-bit numbers if necessary. With 512 bytes per sector, this raises maximum supported drive capacity to 144.12PB. That is equal to more than 144.12 quadrillion bytes! Note that the 48-bit addressing is optional and necessary only for drives larger than 137GB. Drives 137GB or smaller can use either 28-bit or 48-bit addressing.

ATA/ATAPI-7 (AT Attachment with Packet Interface-7)

Work on ATA-7 began late in 2001 and, as with the earlier ATA standards, ATA-7 was built on the previous standard (ATA-6)—with some additions.

The primary addition in ATA-7 is another transfer mode for parallel ATA, called UDMA Mode 6, that allows for data transfers up to 133MBps. As with the UDMA Mode 5 (100MBps) and UDMA Mode 4 (66MBps), the use of an 80-conductor cable is required. Slower speeds don't require the 80-conductor cable, although they will work and are always preferred over the 40-conductor type.

Another major change in the specification was the inclusion of the Serial ATA 1.0 specification into ATA-7. This makes SATA an official part of the ATA standard. Work on ATA-7 began in 2001, and the standard was finished and officially published in 2004.

Note that although the throughput has been increased from the drive controller (on the drive) to the motherboard via the UDMA modes, most ATA drives—even those capable of UDMA Mode 6 (133MBps) from the drive to the motherboard—still have an average maximum sustained transfer rate while reading data of under 60MBps. This means that although newer ATA drives can transfer at speeds up to 133MBps from the circuit board on the drive to the motherboard, data from the drive media (platters) through the heads to the circuit board on the drive moves at less than half that rate. For that reason, running a drive capable of UDMA Mode 6 (133MBps) on a motherboard capable of only UDMA Mode 5 (100MBps) really doesn't slow things down much, if at all. Likewise, upgrading your ATA host adapter from one that does 100MBps to one that can do 133MBps won't help much if your drive reads data off the disk platters at only half that speed. Always remember that the media transfer rate is far more important than the interface transfer rate when selecting a drive because the media transfer rate is the limiting factor.

As a historical note, ATA-7 is the last revision of the venerable parallel ATA standard. ATA is evolving into Serial ATA, which was incorporated into the ATA-7 specification and is covered in detail later in this chapter.

SATA/ATAPI-8

In 2004, work began on SATA-8, which is a new ATA standard based on ATA-7 that will carry forward the development of Serial ATA while removing parallel ATA from the standard entirely. The main features of SATA-8 include

- The removal of parallel ATA from the standard
- The replacement of read long/write long functions
- Improved HPA management

The most dramatic change is the removal of parallel ATA from the SATA-8 standard. This is not intended to make parallel ATA obsolete, but instead is designed to allow new features and functions to be made available in SATA-8-compliant Serial ATA drives, while also allowing parallel ATA drives to continue to be manufactured in compliance with ATA-7. In other words, parallel drives will continue to be compliant with ATA-7 and earlier, and Serial ATA drives will be compliant with ATA-7 and later. Simplifying the ATA standard in this manner allows obsolete parallel ATA features to be removed, resulting in a clearer and more concise description of the Serial ATA interface for future standards. It is expected that SATA-8 will be finalized and officially published in 2006.

Parallel ATA

Parallel ATA has unique specifications and requirements regarding the physical interface, cabling, and connectors as compared to Serial ATA. The following sections detail the unique features of parallel ATA.

Parallel ATA I/O Connector

The parallel ATA interface connector is normally a 40-pin header-type connector with pins spaced 0.1" (2.54mm) apart, and generally it is keyed to prevent the possibility of installing it upside down (see Figures 7.2 and 7.3). To create a keyed connector, the manufacturer usually removes pin 20 from the male connector and blocks pin 20 on the female cable connector, which prevents the user from installing the cable backward. Some cables also incorporate a protrusion on the top of the female cable connector that fits into a notch in the shroud surrounding the mating male connector on the device. The use of keyed connectors and cables is highly recommended. Plugging an ATA cable in backward normally doesn't cause any permanent damage; however, it can lock up the system and prevent it from running.

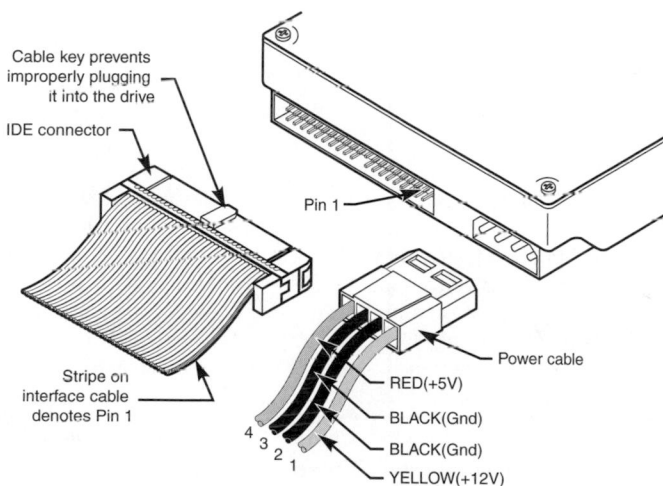

Figure 7.2 Typical parallel ATA (IDE) hard drive connectors.

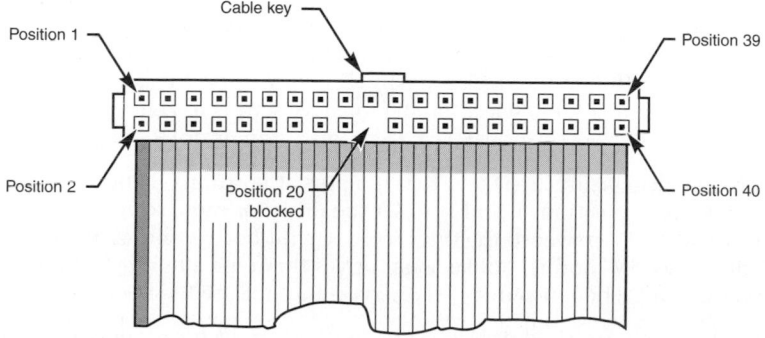

Figure 7.3 Parallel ATA (IDE) 40-pin interface connector detail.

Table 7.3 shows the standard 40-pin parallel ATA (IDE) interface connector pinout.

Table 7.3   40-Pin Parallel ATA Connector

Signal Name	Pin	Pin	Signal Name
-RESET	1	2	GROUND
Data Bit 7	3	4	Data Bit 8
Data Bit 6	5	6	Data Bit 9
Data Bit 5	7	8	Data Bit 10
Data Bit 4	9	10	Data Bit 11
Data Bit 3	11	12	Data Bit 12
Data Bit 2	13	14	Data Bit 13
Data Bit 1	15	16	Data Bit 14
Data Bit 0	17	18	Data Bit 15
GROUND	19	20	KEY (pin missing)
DRQ 3	21	22	GROUND
-IOW	23	24	GROUND
-IOR	25	26	GROUND
I/O CH RDY	27	28	CSEL:SPSYNC[1]
-DACK 3	29	30	GROUND
IRQ 14	31	32	Reserved[2]
Address Bit 1	33	34	-PDIAG
Address Bit 0	35	36	Address Bit 2
-CS1FX	37	38	-CS3FX
-DA/SP	39	40	GROUND
+5V (Logic)	41	42	+5V (Motor)
GROUND	43	44	Reserved

1. Pin 28 is usually cable select, but some older drives could use it for spindle synchronization between multiple drives.

2. Pin 32 was defined as -IOCS16 in ATA-2 but is no longer used.

Note that "-" preceding a signal name (such as with -RESET) indicates the signal is "active low."

The 2 1/2" drives found in notebook/laptop-size computers typically use a smaller unitized 50-pin header connector with pins spaced only 2.0mm (0.079") apart. The main 40-pin part of the connector is the same as the standard parallel ATA connector (except for the physical pin spacing), but there are added pins for power and jumpering. The cable that plugs into this connector typically has 44 pins, carrying power as well as the standard ATA signals. The jumper pins usually have a jumper on them (the jumper position controls cable select, master, or slave settings). Figure 7.4 shows the unitized 50-pin connector used on the 2 1/2" parallel ATA drives in laptop or notebook computers.

Note the jumper pins at positions A–D and that the pins at positions E and F are removed. A jumper usually is placed between positions B and D to set the drive for cable select operation. On this connector, pin 41 provides +5V power to the drive logic (circuit board), pin 42 provides +5V power to the motor (2 1/2" drives use 5V motors, unlike larger drives that typically use 12V motors), and pin 43 provides a power ground. The last pin (44) is reserved and not used.

Table 7.4 shows the 50-pin unitized parallel ATA interface connector pinout as used on most 2 1/2" (laptop or notebook computer) drives.

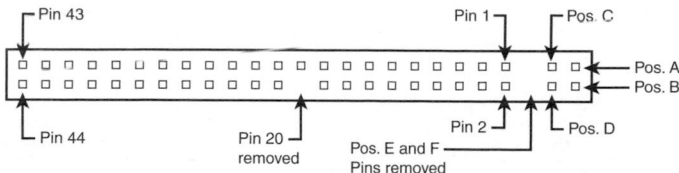

Figure 7.4 50-pin unitized parallel ATA connector detail (used on 2 1/2" notebook/laptop parallel ATA drives with a 44-pin cable).

Table 7.4   50-Pin Unitized Parallel ATA 2 1/2" (Notebook/Laptop Drive) Connector Pinout

Signal Name	Pin	Pin	Signal Name
Jumper pin	A	B	Jumper pin
Jumper pin	C	D	Jumper pin
KEY (pin missing)	E	F	KEY (pin missing)
-RESET	1	2	GROUND
Data Bit 7	3	4	Data Bit 8
Data Bit 6	5	6	Data Bit 9
Data Bit 5	7	8	Data Bit 10
Data Bit 4	9	10	Data Bit 11
Data Bit 3	11	12	Data Bit 12
Data Bit 2	13	14	Data Bit 13
Data Bit 1	15	16	Data Bit 14
Data Bit 0	17	18	Data Bit 15
GROUND	19	20	KEY (pin missing)
DRQ 3	21	22	GROUND
-IOW	23	24	GROUND
-IOR	25	26	GROUND
I/O CH RDY	27	28	CSEL
-DACK 3	29	30	GROUND
IRQ 14	31	32	Reserved
Address Bit 1	33	34	-PDIAG
Address Bit 0	35	36	Address Bit 2
-CS1FX	37	38	-CS3FX
-DA/SP	39	40	GROUND
+5V (Logic)	41	42	+5V (Motor)
GROUND	43	44	Reserved

Not All Cables and Connectors Are Keyed

Many lower-cost board and cable manufacturers leave out the keying. Cheaper motherboards often don't have pin 20 removed on their ATA connectors; consequently they don't supply a cable with pin 20 blocked. If they don't use a shrouded connector with a notch and a corresponding protrusion on the cable connector, no keying exists and the cables can be inserted backward. Fortunately, the only consequence of this in most cases is that the device won't work until the cable is attached with the correct orientation.

Note that some systems do not display any video until the ATA drives respond to a spin-up command, which they can't receive if the cable is connected backward. So, if you connect an unkeyed ATA drive to your computer, turn on the computer, and it seems as if the system is locked up (you don't see anything on the screen), check the ATA cable. (See Figure 7.6 for examples of unkeyed and keyed ATA cables.)

In rare situations in which you are mixing and matching items, you might encounter a cable with pin 20 blocked (as it should be) and a board with pin 20 still present. In that case, you can break off pin 20 from the board—or for the more squeamish, remove the block from the cable or replace the cable with one without the blocked pin. Some cables have the block permanently installed as a part of the connector housing, in which case you must break off pin 20 on the board or device end or use a different cable.

The simple rule of thumb is that pin 1 should be oriented toward the power connector on the device, which normally corresponds to the stripe on the cable.

Parallel ATA I/O Cable

A 40-conductor ribbon cable is specified to carry signals between the bus adapter circuits and the drive (controller). To maximize signal integrity and eliminate potential timing and noise problems, the cable should not be longer than 18" (0.46 meters), although testing shows that 80-conductor cables can be used reliably up to 27" (0.69 meters) in length.

Note that ATA drives supporting the higher-speed transfer modes, such as PIO Mode 4 or any of the Ultra-DMA (UDMA) modes, are especially susceptible to cable integrity problems and cables that are too long. If the cable is too long, you can experience data corruption and other errors that can be maddening. This is manifested in problems reading from or writing to the drive. In addition, any drive using UDMA Mode 5 (66MBps transfer rate), Mode 6 (100MBps transfer rate), or Mode 7 (133MBps transfer rate) must use a special, higher-quality 80-conductor cable (the extra conductors are grounds to reduce noise). I also recommend this type of cable if your drive is running at UDMA Mode 2 (33MBps) or slower because it can't hurt and can only help. I always keep a high-quality 80-conductor ATA cable in my toolbox for testing drives where I suspect cable integrity or cable length problems. Figure 7.5 shows the typical ATA cable layout and dimensions.

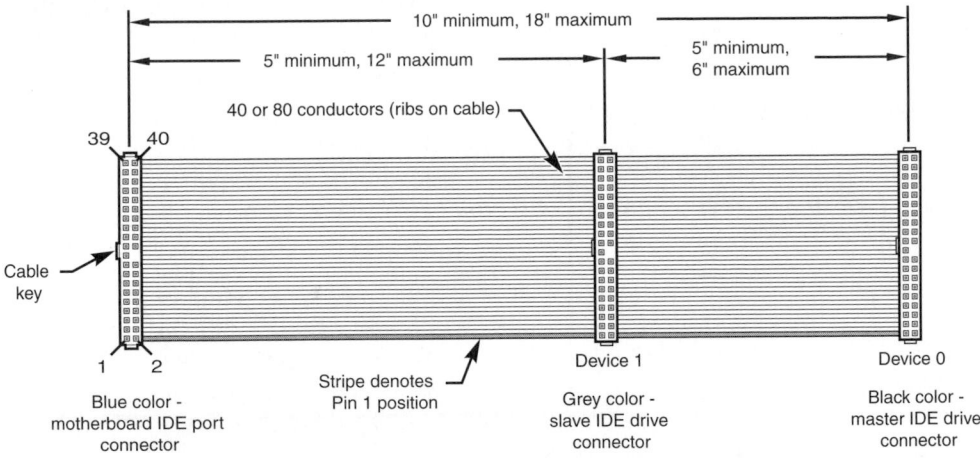

Figure 7.5   Parallel ATA (IDE) cable, with 40-pin connectors and either 40- or 80-conductor cables (additional wires are grounded in 80-conductor versions).

Note

Most 40-conductor cables do not color-code the connectors, whereas all 80-conductor cables do color-code the connectors.

Two primary variations of parallel ATA cables are used today: one with 40 conductors and the other with 80 conductors (see Figure 7.6). Both use 40-pin connectors, and the additional wires in the 80-conductor version are simply wired to ground. The additional conductors are designed to reduce noise and interference and are required when setting the interface to run at 66MBps (ATA/66) or faster. The drive and host adapter are designed to disable the higher-speed ATA/66, ATA/100, or ATA/133 modes if an 80-conductor cable is not detected. In such cases, you might see a warning message when you start your computer if an ATA/66 or faster drive is connected to a 40-conductor cable. The 80-conductor cable can also be used at lower speeds; although this is unnecessary, it improves the signal integrity. Therefore, it is the recommended version no matter which drive you use.

I once had a student ask me how to tell an 80-conductor cable from a 40-conductor cable. I thought to myself, "Is this a trick question?" Perhaps they didn't know that each conductor in a ribbon cable can be seen as a rib or ridge in the cable. The simple answer is to count the ridges (conductors) in the cable. If you count only 40, it must be a 40-conductor cable, and if you count to 80, well...you get the idea! If you observe them side by side, the difference is clear: The 80-conductor cable has an obviously smoother, less ridged appearance than the 40-conductor cable.

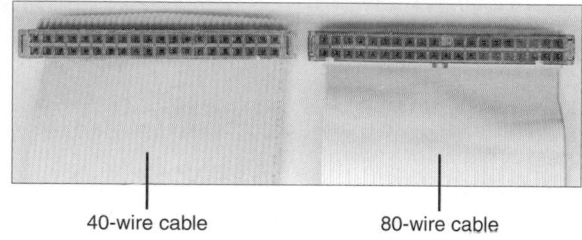

40-wire cable   80-wire cable

Figure 7.6   40-conductor (left) and 80-conductor (right) parallel ATA cables.

Note the keying on the 80-conductor cable that is designed to prevent backward installation, but note also that the poorly constructed 40-conductor cable shown in this example lacks keying. Most good 40-conductor cables include the keying; however, because it is optional, many cheaply constructed versions do not include it. Keying was made mandatory for all 80-conductor cables as part of the standard.

Longer or Rounded Cables

The official parallel ATA standard limits cable length to 18" (0.46 meters); however, many of these cables that are sold are longer, up to even 36" (0.91 meters) or more in length. I've had many readers write me questioning the length, asking, "Why would people sell cables longer than 18" if the standard doesn't allow it?" Well, just because something is for sale doesn't mean it conforms to the standards and will work properly! I see improperly designed, poorly manufactured, and nonconforming items for sale all the time. Still, many people have used the longer cables and yet their systems seem to work fine, but I've also documented numerous cases where using longer cables has caused problems, so I decided to investigate this issue more thoroughly.

What I've discovered is that you can use longer 80-conductor cables reliably up to 27" (0.69 meters) in length, but 40-conductor cables should remain limited to 18" just as the standard indicates.

In fact, an attempt was made to change the parallel ATA standard to allow 27" cables. If you read www.t13.org/technical/e00151r0.pdf, you'll see data from a proposal that shows "negligible differences in Ultra DMA Mode 5 signal integrity between a 27", 80-conductor cable and an 18", 80-conductor cable." This extended cable design was actually proposed back in October 2000, but it was never incorporated into the standard. Even though it was never officially approved, I take the information presented in this proposal as empirical evidence for allowing the use of 80-conductor cables up to 27" in length without problems.

To that, I would add another recommendation, which is that in general I do not recommend "rounded" ATA cables. A rounded design has not been approved in the ATA standard, and there is some evidence that they can cause problems with crosstalk and noise. The design of 80-conductor cables is such that a ground wire is interspersed between each data wire in the ribbon, and *rounding* the cable causes some of the data lines to run parallel or adjacent to each other at random, thereby causing crosstalk and noise and resulting in signal errors.

In support of this, I read an interview with Rahul Sood in the March 2004 issue of *CPU* (www.computerpoweruser.com). Sood is the chief technology officer of a popular builder of high-end systems, called Voodoo PC (www.voodoopc.com). In the *CPU* interview, he said, "I don't agree with rounded cables, I never have. SATA cables are great, of course, but rounded [parallel ATA] cables are a different story because there is potential for noise. Any benchmarks that I've run on any of the rounded cables that we've tested show either errors generating over time or they're slower than good quality flat IDE cables."

Of course, many people are using rounded cables with success, but my knowledge of electrical engineering as well as the ATA standard has always made me somewhat uncomfortable with their use. Although I cannot offer any specific test data to corroborate the findings of Sood, I do prefer to stick with 80-conductor ribbon cables of 27" or less in length in my own systems.

Parallel ATA Signals

This section describes some of the most important parallel ATA signals having to do with drive configuration and installation in more detail. This information can help you understand how the cable select feature works, for example.

Pin 20 is used as a key pin for cable orientation and is not connected to the interface. This pin should be missing from any ATA connectors, and the cable should have the pin-20 hole in the connector plugged off to prevent the cable from being plugged in backward.

Pin 39 carries the drive active/slave present (DASP) signal, which is a dual-purpose, time-multiplexed signal. During power-on initialization, this signal indicates whether a slave drive is present on the interface. After that, each drive asserts the signal to indicate that it is active. Early drives could not multiplex these functions and required special jumper settings to work with other drives. Standardizing this function to allow for compatible dual-drive installations is one of the features of the ATA standard. This is why some drives require a slave present (SP) jumper whereas others do not.

Pin 28 carries the cable select signal (CSEL). In some older drives, it could also carry a spindle synchronization signal (SPSYNC), but that is not commonly found on newer drives. The CSEL function is the most widely used and is designed to control the designation of a drive as master (drive 0) or slave (drive 1) without requiring jumper settings on the drives. If a drive sees the CSEL as being grounded, the drive is a master; if CSEL is open, the drive is a slave.

You can install special cabling to ground CSEL selectively. This installation usually is accomplished through a Y-cable arrangement, with the ATA bus connector in the middle and each drive at opposite ends of the cable. One leg of the Y has the CSEL line connected through, indicating a master drive; the other leg has the CSEL line open (conductor interrupted or removed), making the drive at that end the slave.

Parallel ATA Dual-Drive Configurations

Dual-drive parallel ATA installations can be problematic because each drive has its own controller and both controllers must function while being connected to the same bus. There has to be a way to ensure that only one of the two controllers will respond to a command at a time.

The ATA standard provides the option of operating on the AT bus with two drives in a daisy-chained configuration. The primary drive (drive 0) is called the *master*, and the secondary drive (drive 1) is called the *slave*. You designate a drive as being master or slave by setting a jumper or switch on the drive or by using a special line in the interface called the *cable select (CS) pin* and setting the CS jumper on the drive.

When only one drive is installed, the controller responds to all commands from the system. When two drives (and, therefore, two controllers) are installed, both controllers receive all commands from the system. Each controller then must be set up to respond only to commands for itself. In this situation, one controller must be designated as the master and the other as the slave. When the system sends a command for a specific drive, the controller on the other drive must remain silent while the selected controller and drive are functioning. Setting the jumper to master or slave enables discrimination between the two controllers by setting a special bit (the DRV bit) in the drive/head register of a command block.

Configuring ATA drives can be simple, as is the case with most single-drive installations. Or it can be troublesome, especially when it comes to mixing two older drives from different manufacturers on a single cable.

Most ATA drives can be configured with four possible settings:

- Master (single-drive)
- Master (dual-drive)
- Slave (dual-drive)
- Cable select

Many drives simplify this to three settings: master, slave, and cable select. Because each ATA drive has its own controller, you must specifically tell one drive to be the master and the other to be the slave. No functional difference exists between the two, except that the drive that's specified as the slave will assert a signal called DASP after a system reset informs the master that a slave drive is present in the system. The master drive then pays attention to the drive select line, which it otherwise ignores. Telling a drive that it's the slave also usually causes it to delay its spinup for several seconds to allow the master to get going and thus to lessen the load on the system's power supply.

Until the ATA specification, no common implementation for drive configuration was in use. Some drive companies even used different master/slave methods for different models of drives. Because of these incompatibilities, some drives work together only in a specific master/slave or slave/master order. This situation mostly affects older IDE drives introduced before the ATA specification.

Most drives that fully follow the ATA specification now need only one jumper (master/slave) for configuration. A few also need a slave present jumper, as well. Table 7.5 shows the jumper settings required by most ATA drives.

Table 7.5   Jumper Settings for Most ATA-Compatible Drives on Standard (Non–Cable Select) Cables

Jumper Name	Single-Drive	Dual-Drive Master	Dual-Drive Slave
Master (M/S)	On	On	Off
Slave Present (SP)	Off	On	Off
Cable Select (CS)	Off	Off	Off

Note

If a cable select cable is used, the CS jumper should be set On and all others should be Off. The cable connector then determines which drive will be master or slave.

Figure 7.7 shows the jumpers on a typical ATA drive.

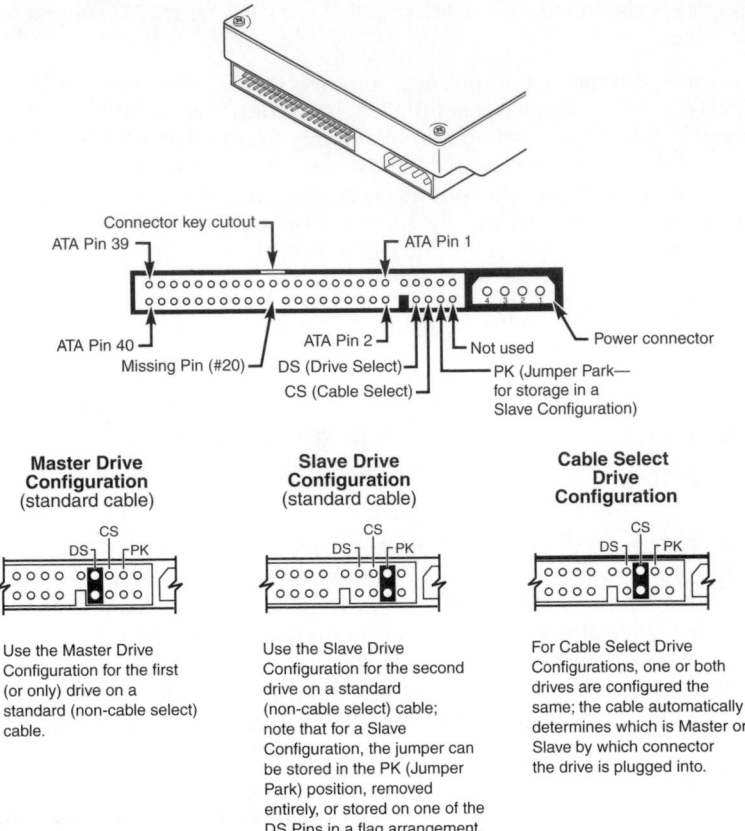

Figure 7.7   Parallel ATA (IDE) drive jumpers for most drives.

The master jumper indicates that the drive is a master or a slave. Some drives also require a slave present jumper, which is used only in a dual-drive setup and then installed only on the master drive—which is somewhat confusing. This jumper tells the master that a slave drive is attached. With many parallel ATA drives, the master jumper is optional and can be left off. Installing this jumper doesn't hurt in these cases and can eliminate confusion; I recommend that you install the jumpers listed here.

Note

Note that some drives have these jumpers on the drive circuit board on the bottom of the drive, and as such they might not be visible on the rear.

To eliminate confusion over master/slave settings, most newer systems now use the cable select option. This involves two things. The first is having a special parallel ATA cable that has all the wires except pin 28 running from the motherboard connector to both drive connectors. Pin 28 is used for cable select and is connected to one of the drive connectors (labeled master) and not to the other (labeled slave). Both drives are then configured in cable select mode via the CS jumper on each drive.

With cable select, the drive that receives signals on pin 28 automatically becomes the master, and the other becomes the slave. Most cables implement this by removing the metal insulation displacement bit from the pin-28 hole, which can be difficult to see at a glance. Other cables have a section of pin 28 visibly cut from the cable somewhere along the ribbon. Because this is such a minor modification to the cable and can be difficult to see, cable select cables typically have the connectors labeled master, slave, and system, indicating that the cable controls these options rather than the drive. All 80-conductor UltraATA cables are designed to use cable select.

With cable select, you simply set the CS jumper on all drives and then plug the drive you want to be the master into the connector labeled master on the cable and the drive you want to be the slave into the connector labeled slave.

The only downside I see to using cable select is that it can restrict how the cable is routed or where you mount the drive that is to be master versus slave because they must be plugged in to specific cable connector positions.

Parallel ATA PIO Transfer Modes

ATA-2 and ATA-3 defined the first of several higher-performance modes for transferring data over the parallel ATA interface, to and from the drive. These faster modes were the main part of the newer specifications and were the main reason they were initially developed. The following section discusses these modes.

The PIO (programmed I/O) mode determines how fast data is transferred to and from the drive using PIO transfers. In the slowest possible mode—PIO Mode 0—the data cycle time can't exceed 600 nanoseconds (ns). In a single cycle, 16 bits are transferred into or out of the drive, making the theoretical transfer rate of PIO Mode 0 (600ns cycle time) 3.3MBps, whereas PIO Mode 4 (120ns cycle time) achieves a 16.6MBps transfer rate.

Table 7.6 shows the PIO modes, with their respective transfer rates.

Table 7.6   PIO Modes and Transfer Rates

PIO Mode	Bus Width (Bits)	Cycle Speed (ns)	Bus Speed (MHz)	Cycles per Clock	Transfer Rate (MBps)	ATA Specification
0	16	600	1.67	1	3.33	ATA-1
1	16	383	2.61	1	5.22	ATA-1
2	16	240	4.17	1	8.33	ATA-1
3	16	180	5.56	1	11.11	ATA-2
4	16	120	8.33	1	16.67	ATA-2

ATA-2 was also referred to as EIDE (Enhanced IDE) or Fast-ATA.

ns = nanoseconds (billionths of a second)

MB = million bytes

Most motherboards with ATA-2 or greater support have dual ATA connectors on the motherboard. Most of the motherboard chipsets include the ATA interface in their South Bridge components, which in most systems is tied into the PCI bus.

Older 486 and some early Pentium boards have only the primary connector running through the system's PCI local bus. The secondary connector on those boards usually runs through the ISA bus and therefore supports up to Mode 2 operation only.

When interrogated with an Identify Drive command, a hard disk returns, among other things, information about the PIO and DMA modes it is capable of using. Most enhanced BIOSs automatically set the correct mode to match the capabilities of the drive. If you set a mode faster than the drive can handle, data corruption results.

ATA-2 and newer drives also perform Block Mode PIO, which means they use the Read/Write Multiple commands that greatly reduce the number of interrupts sent to the host processor. This lowers the overhead, and the resulting transfers are even faster.

Parallel ATA DMA Transfer Modes

ATA drives also support *direct memory access (DMA)* transfers. DMA means that the data is transferred directly between drive and memory without using the CPU as an intermediary, as opposed to PIO. This has the effect of offloading much of the work of transferring data from the processor, in effect allowing the processor to do other things while the transfer is taking place.

There are two distinct types of direct memory access: singleword (8-bit) and multiword (16-bit) DMA. Singleword DMA modes were removed from the ATA-3 and later specifications and are obsolete. DMA modes are also sometimes called *busmaster* ATA modes because they use a host adapter that supports busmastering. Ordinary DMA relies on the legacy DMA controller on the motherboard to perform the complex task of arbitration, grabbing the system bus and transferring the data. In the case of busmastering DMA, all this is done by a higher-speed logic chip in the host adapter interface (which is also on the motherboard).

Systems using the Intel PIIX (PCI IDE ISA eXcelerator) and later South Bridge chips (or equivalent) have the capability of supporting busmaster ATA. The singleword and doubleword busmaster ATA modes and transfer rates are shown in Tables 7.7 and 7.8.

Table 7.7   Singleword (8-bit) DMA Modes and Transfer Rates

8-bit DMA Mode	Bus Width (Bits)	Cycle Speed (ns)	Bus Speed (MHz)	Cycles per Clock	Transfer Rate (MBps)	ATA Specification
0	16	960	1.04	1	2.08	ATA-1*
1	16	480	2.08	1	4.17	ATA-1*
2	16	240	4.17	1	8.33	ATA-1*

Singleword (8-bit) DMA modes were removed from the ATA-3 and later specifications.

Table 7.8   Multiword (16-bit) DMA Modes and Transfer Rates

16-bit DMA Mode	Bus Width (Bits)	Cycle Speed (ns)	Bus Speed (MHz)	Cycles per Clock	Transfer Rate (MBps)	ATA Specification
0	16	480	2.08	1	4.17	ATA-1
1	16	150	6.67	1	13.33	ATA-2*
2	16	120	8.33	1	16.67	ATA-2*

ATA-2 was also referred to as EIDE (Enhanced IDE) or Fast-ATA.

Note that doubleword DMA modes are also called busmaster DMA modes by some manufacturers. Unfortunately, even the fastest doubleword DMA Mode 2 results in the same 16.67MBps transfer speed as PIO Mode 4. However, even though the transfer speed is the same as PIO, because DMA offloads much of the work from the processor, overall system performance is higher. Even so, multiword DMA modes were never very popular and have been superseded by the newer Ultra-DMA modes supported in devices that are compatible with ATA-4 through ATA-7.

Table 7.9 shows the Ultra-DMA modes now supported in the ATA-4 through ATA-7 specifications. Note that you need to install the correct drivers for your host adapter and version of Windows to use this feature.

Table 7.9 Ultra-DMA Support in ATA-4 Through ATA-7

Ultra DMA Mode	Bus Width	Cycle Speed (Bits)	Bus Speed (ns)	Cycles per (MHz)	Transfer Rate Clock	ATA Specification (MBps)
0	16	240	4.17	2	16.67	ATA-4
1	16	160	6.25	2	25.00	ATA-4
2	16	120	8.33	2	33.33	ATA-4
3	16	90	11.11	2	44.44	ATA-5
4	16	60	16.67	2	66.67	ATA-5
5	16	40	25.00	2	100.00	ATA-6
6	16	30	33.00	2	133.00	ATA-7

ATA-4 UDMA Mode 2 is sometimes called Ultra-ATA/33 or ATA-33.
ATA-5 UDMA Mode 4 is sometimes called Ultra-ATA/66 or ATA-66.
ATA-6 UDMA Mode 5 is sometimes called Ultra-ATA/100 or ATA-100.
ATA-7 UDMA Mode 6 is sometimes called Ultra-ATA/133 or ATA-133.

Serial ATA

With the release of ATA-7, it seems that the parallel ATA standard that has been in use for more than 10 years has finally reached the end of the line. Sending data at rates faster than 133MBps down a parallel ribbon cable is fraught with all kinds of problems because of signal timing, electromagnetic interference (EMI), and other integrity problems. The solution is called Serial ATA, which is an evolutionary replacement for the venerable parallel ATA physical storage interface. Serial ATA is software-compatible with parallel ATA, which means it fully emulates all the commands, registers, and controls so existing software will run on the new architecture without any changes. In other words, the existing BIOSs, operating systems, and utilities that work on parallel ATA also work on Serial ATA.

Of course, they do differ physically—that is, you can't plug parallel ATA drives into Serial ATA host adapters and vice versa, although signal converters make that possible. The physical changes are all for the better because Serial ATA uses much smaller and thinner cables with only seven conductors that are easier to route inside the PC and easier to plug in with smaller, redesigned cable connectors. The interface chip designs also are improved with far fewer pins and lower voltages. These improvements are all designed to eliminate the design problems inherent in parallel ATA.

Figure 7.8 shows the official Serial ATA working group logo used to identify most Serial ATA devices.

Figure 7.8 Serial ATA official logo, which is used to identify SATA devices.

Although Serial ATA won't immediately replace parallel ATA, most new systems include Serial ATA interfaces alongside parallel ATA interfaces. Eventually, SATA will replace parallel ATA as the de facto standard internal storage device interface found in PCs. As current motherboard designs indicate, the transition from ATA to SATA is a gradual one, and during this transition parallel ATA capabilities will continue to be available. I also expect that, with more than a 10-year history, parallel ATA devices will continue to be available even after most PCs have gone to SATA.

Development for Serial ATA started when the Serial ATA Working Group effort was announced at the Intel Developer Forum in February 2000. The initial members of the Serial ATA Working Group included APT Technologies, Dell, IBM, Intel, Maxtor, Quantum, and Seagate. The first Serial ATA 1.0 draft specification was released in November 2000 and was officially published as a final specification in August 2001. The Serial ATA II extensions to this specification, which make Serial ATA suitable for network storage, were released in October 2002. Both can be downloaded from the Serial ATA Working Group Web site at http://www.serialata.org. Since forming, the group has added more than 150 Contributor and Adopter companies to the membership from all areas of industry. Systems using Serial ATA were first released in late 2002 using discrete PCI interface boards and chips. SATA was finally integrated directly into the motherboard chipset in April 2003 with the introduction of the Intel ICH5 (I/O controller hub) chipset component. Since then, most new motherboard chipsets have included Serial ATA.

The performance of SATA is impressive, although current hard drive designs can't fully take advantage of its bandwidth. Three variations of the standard have been proposed that all use the same cables and connectors; they differ only in transfer rate performance. Currently, only the first two speeds are available, with higher speeds coming in the future. Table 7.10 shows the specifications for the current and future proposed SATA versions; the next-generation 300MBps version is not expected until 2005, whereas the 600MBps version is expected in 2007.

Table 7.10   Serial ATA Transfer Modes

Serial ATA Type	Signal Rate (Gbps)	Bus Width (Bits)	Bus Speed (MHz)	Data Cycles per Clock	Bandwidth (MBps)
SATA-150	1.5	1	1500	1	150
SATA-300	3.0	1	3000	1	300
SATA-600	6.0	1	6000	1	600

From Table 7.10, you can see that Serial ATA sends data only a single bit at a time. The cable used has only seven wires (four signal and three ground) and is a very thin design, with keyed connectors only 14mm (0.55") wide on each end. This eliminates problems with airflow compared to the wider parallel ATA ribbon cables. Each cable has connectors only at each end, and each cable connects the device directly to the host adapter (typically on the motherboard). There are no master/slave settings because each cable supports only a single device. The cable ends are interchangeable—the connector on the motherboard is the same as on the device, and both cable ends are identical. Maximum SATA cable length is 1 meter (39.37"), which is considerably longer than the 18" maximum for parallel ATA. Even with this thinner, longer, and less-expensive cable, you initially get transfer rates of 150MBps (nearly 13% greater than parallel ATA/133). Serial ATA-II supports 300MBps, and even 600MBps is possible.

Serial ATA uses a special encoding scheme called 8B/10B to encode and decode data sent along the cable. The 8B/10B transmission code originally was developed (and patented) by IBM in the early 1980s for use in high-speed data communications. This encoding scheme is now used by many high-speed data transmission standards, including Gigabit Ethernet, Fibre Channel, FireWire, and others. The main purpose of the 8B/10B encoding scheme is to guarantee that there are never more than four 0s (or 1s) transmitted consecutively. This is a form of run length limited (RLL) encoding called RLL 0,4, in which the 0 represents the minimum and the 4 represents the maximum number of consecutive 0s in each encoded character.

8B/10B encoding also ensures that there are never more than six or fewer than four 0s (or 1s) in a single encoded 10-bit character. Because 1s and 0s are sent as voltage changes on a wire, this ensures that the spacing between the voltage transitions sent by the transmitter is fairly balanced, with a more regular and steady stream of pulses. This presents a steadier load on the circuits, increasing reliability. The conversion from 8-bit data to 10-bit encoded characters for transmission leaves several 10-bit patterns unused. Many of these additional patterns are used to provide flow control, delimit packets of data, perform error checking, or perform other special functions.

Serial ATA Cables and Connectors

The physical transmission scheme for SATA uses *differential NRZ (nonreturn to zero)*. This uses a balanced pair of wires, each carrying +0.25V (one-quarter volt). The signals are sent differentially: If one wire in the pair carries +0.25V, the other wire carries –0.25V, where the differential voltage between the two wires is always 0.5V (one-half volt). So, for a given voltage waveform, the opposite voltage waveform is sent along the adjacent wire. Differential transmission minimizes electromagnetic radiation and makes the signals easier to read on the receiving end.

A 15-pin power cable and power connector is optional with SATA, providing 3.3V power in addition to the 5V and 12V provided via the industry-standard 4-pin device power connectors. Although it has 15 pins, this new power connector design is only 24mm (0.945"). With 3 pins designated for each of the 3.3V, 5V, and 12V power levels, enough capacity exists for up to 4.5 amps of current at each voltage, which is plenty for even the most power-hungry drives. For compatibility with existing power supplies, SATA drives can be made with the original, standard 4-pin device power connector or the new 15-pin SATA power connector—or both. If the drive doesn't have the type of connector you need, adapters are available to convert from one type to the other.

Figure 7.9 shows what the new SATA signal and power connectors look like.

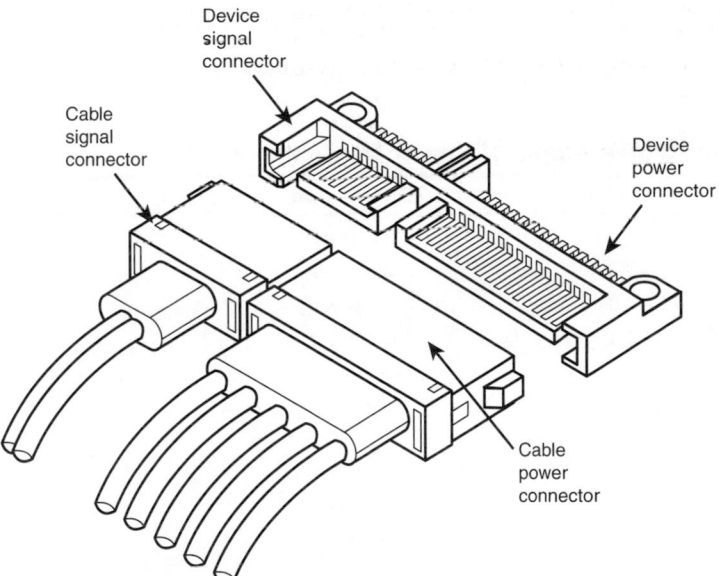

Figure 7.9   SATA (Serial ATA) signal and power connectors on a typical SATA hard drive.

Figure 7.10 shows SATA and parallel ATA host adapters on a typical motherboard.

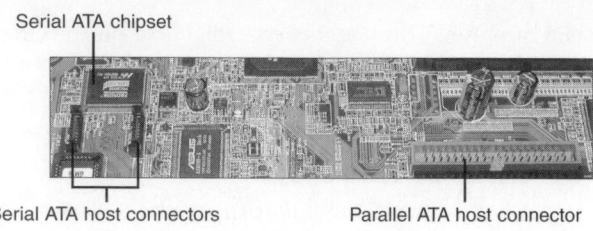

Serial ATA chipset

Serial ATA host connectors   Parallel ATA host connector

Figure 7.10   A motherboard with Serial and parallel ATA host adapters.

The pinouts for the Serial ATA data and optional power connectors are shown in Tables 7.11 and 7.12, respectively.

Table 7.11   Serial ATA Data Connector Pinout

Signal Pin	Signal	Description
S1	Gnd	First mate
S2	A+	Host Transmit +
S3	A-	Host Transmit -
S4	Gnd	First mate
S5	B-	Host Receive -
S6	B+	Host Receive +
S7	Gnd	First mate

All pins are in a single row spaced 1.27mm (.050'') apart.
All ground pins are longer so they will make contact before the signal/power pins to allow hot plugging.

Table 7.12   Serial ATA Optional Power Connector Pinout

Power Pin	Signal	Description
P1	+3.3V	3.3V power
P2	+3.3V	3.3V power
P3	+3.3V	3.3V power
P4	Gnd	First mate
P5	Gnd	First mate
P6	Gnd	First mate
P7	+5V	5V power
P8	+5V	5V power
P9	+5V	5V power
P10	Gnd	First mate
P11	Gnd	First mate
P12	Gnd	First mate
P13	+12V	12V power
P14	+12V	12V power
P15	+12V	12V power

All pins are in a single row spaced 1.27mm (.050'') apart.
All ground pins are longer so they will make contact before the signal/power pins to allow hot plugging.
Three power pins are used to carry 4.5 amps, a maximum current for each voltage.

Serial ATA Configuration

Configuration of Serial ATA devices is also much simpler because the master/slave or cable select jumper settings used with parallel ATA are no longer necessary.

BIOS setup for Serial ATA drives is also quite simple. Because Serial ATA is based on ATA, autodetection of drive settings on systems with Serial ATA connectors is performed in the same way as on parallel ATA systems. Depending on the system, Serial ATA interfaces might be enabled by default or might need to be enabled in the BIOS setup program (see Chapter 5, "BIOS," for details).

Because Serial ATA is based on parallel ATA, you can adapt ATA-100 and ATA-133 hard disks to a Serial ATA host adapter with a converter such as the HighPoint RocketHead 100 device shown in Figure 7.11. This converter is included with HighPoint Serial ATA RAID host adapters, and similar devices can be purchased from aftermarket vendors.

Parallel ATA connector (plugs into hard disk)

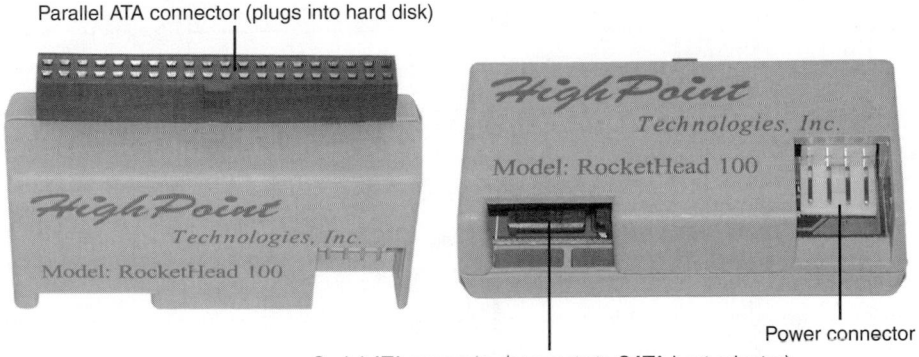

Serial ATA connector (connects to SATA host adapter)

Power connector

Figure 7.11 Two views of the HighPoint RocketHead 100 converter.

If you want to use Serial ATA drives but don't want to install a new motherboard with Serial ATA host adapters already included, you can install a separate Serial ATA host adapter into a PCI expansion slot (see Figure 7.12). Most of these adapters include ATA RAID functions.

Some of the first Serial ATA host adapters, such as models from HighPoint and 3Ware, use a parallel-to-Serial ATA bridge technology that consumes as much as half of the available bandwidth. Other adapters, such as those made by Promise Technology, use native Serial ATA controller chips, which is a better solution in theory because it preserves all the bandwidth for use by the drive. However, current Serial ATA drives, like their parallel ATA siblings, cannot transfer data at anything close to the 150MBps rate of the host adapter; 40MBps–50MBps is the typical range for average transfer speeds of 7200rpm Serial ATA drives.

Serial ATA II

As with parallel ATA, Serial ATA was designed to be the primary storage interface used inside a PC and was not initially designed to be used as an external interface. However, with Serial ATA II (SATA-8, under development), Serial ATA will evolve to include external connections, storage enclosures with multiple drives, and port multipliers that allow up to 15 SATA drives to be connected to a single SATA port. The external connection is designed to support four lanes, with 300MBps per lane, for a total of 1200MBps. This competes with external SCSI for RAID enclosures but most likely won't compete with general-purpose high-speed external device interfaces such as USB 2.0 and IEEE 1394 (i.LINK/FireWire). Because of the lower cost and smaller size of the internal cabling, there is little doubt that Serial ATA will replace parallel ATA inside both desktop and laptop systems over the next few years.

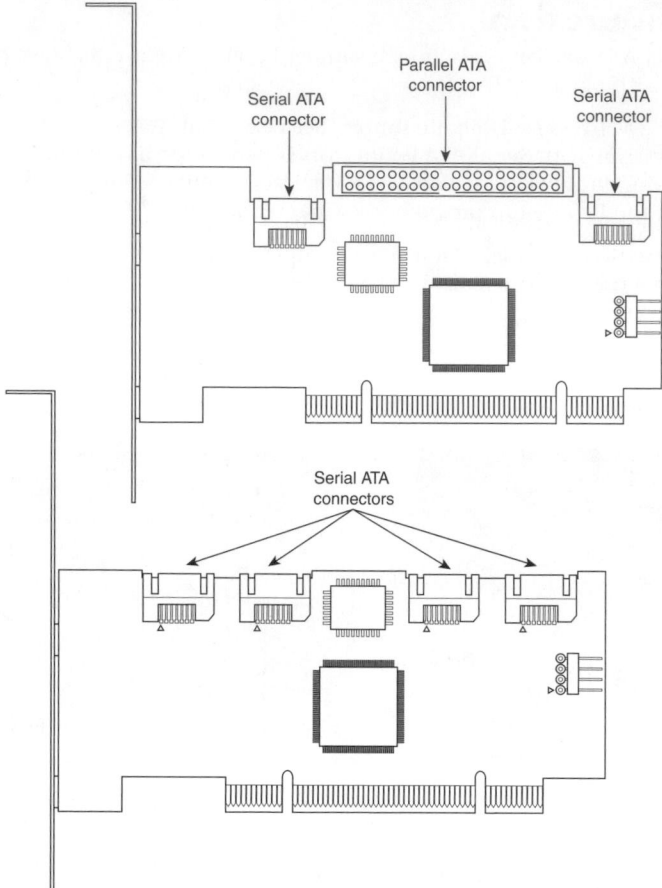

Figure 7.12   Typical two-channel (top) and four-channel (bottom) Serial ATA RAID host adapters. The two-channel adapter also includes a parallel ATA host adapter.

Advanced Host Controller Interface

Serial ATA was designed not only as a replacement for parallel ATA, but also as an interface that would evolve into something with many more capabilities and features than its predecessor. Initially, compatibility with parallel ATA was one of the most important features of Serial ATA because it enabled a smooth and easy transition from one to the other. This compatibility extends to the driver level, allowing Serial ATA devices to use the same BIOS-level drivers and software as legacy parallel ATA devices.

Although the intent of Serial ATA was to allow an easy transition from parallel ATA, it was also designed to allow future growth and expansion of capabilities. To accomplish this, an enhanced software interface called the Advanced Host Controller Interface (AHCI) was initially developed by the AHCI Contributor Group, a group chaired by Intel and originally consisting of AMD, Dell, Marvell, Maxtor, Microsoft, Red Hat, Seagate, and StorageGear. The AHCI Contributor Group released a preliminary version of AHCI v0.95 in May 2003 and released the final specification in 2004.

AHCI provides a standard, high-performance interface to system driver/OS software for discovering and implementing such advanced SATA features as command queuing, hot plugging, and power management. AHCI was integrated into Serial ATA–supporting chipsets in 2004 and is supported by AHCI drivers for Windows.

Serial ATA Transfer Modes

Serial ATA transfers data in a completely different manner from parallel ATA. As indicated previously, the transfer rates are 150MBps, 300MBps, and 600MBps, with most drives today using the 150MBps rate. However, because SATA is designed to be backward-compatible with parallel ATA, some confusion can result because SATA drives can report and emulate parallel ATA mode settings for backward compatibility. This means that the drive is merely lying for backward compatibility with existing software.

For example, many motherboards detect and report a Serial ATA drive as supporting Ultra DMA Mode 5 (ATA/100), which is a parallel ATA mode operating at 100MBps. This is obviously incorrect because even the slowest Serial ATA mode (SATA-150) is 150MBps and Ultra DMA modes simply do not apply to Serial ATA drives.

Parallel and Serial ATA are completely different electrical and physical specifications, but Serial ATA does *emulate* parallel ATA in a way that makes it completely software transparent. In fact, the parallel ATA emulation in Serial ATA specifically conforms to the ATA-5 specification.

This is especially apparent in the IDENTIFY DEVICE command used by the autodetect routines in the BIOS to read the drive parameters. The Serial ATA specification indicates that many of the items returned by IDENTIFY DEVICE are to be "set as indicated in ATA/ATAPI-5," including available UDMA modes and settings.

The SATA 1 specification also says, "Emulation of parallel ATA device behavior as perceived by the host BIOS or software driver, is a cooperative effort between the device and the Serial ATA host adapter hardware. The behavior of Command and Control Block registers, PIO and DMA data transfers, resets, and interrupts are all emulated. The host adapter contains a set of registers that shadow the contents of the traditional device registers, referred to as the Shadow Register Block. All Serial ATA devices behave like Device 0 devices. Devices shall ignore the DEV bit in the Device/Head field of received Register FISs, and it is the responsibility of the host adapter to gate transmission of Register FISs to devices, as appropriate, based on the value of the DEV bit."

This means the shadow register blocks are "fake" parallel ATA registers, allowing all ATA commands, modes, and so on to be emulated. Serial ATA was designed to be fully software compatible with ATA/ATAPI-5, which is why a Serial ATA drive can report in some ways as if it were parallel ATA or running in parallel ATA modes, even though it isn't.

ATA Features

The ATA standards have gone a long way toward eliminating incompatibilities and problems with interfacing IDE drives to ISA/PCI bus systems. The ATA specifications define the signals on the 40-pin connector, the functions and timings of these signals, cable specifications, and so on. The following section lists some of the elements and functions defined by the ATA specifications.

ATA Commands

One of the best features of the ATA interface is the enhanced command set. The ATA interface was modeled after the WD1003 controller IBM used in the original AT system. All ATA drives must support the original WD command set (eight commands) with no exceptions, which is why ATA drives are so easy to install in systems today. All IBM-compatible systems have built-in ROM BIOS support for the WD1003, so they essentially support ATA as well.

In addition to supporting all the WD1003 commands, the ATA specification added numerous other commands to enhance performance and capabilities. These commands are an optional part of the ATA interface, but several of them are used in most drives available today and are very important to the performance and use of ATA drives in general.

Perhaps the most important is the IDENTIFY DRIVE command. This command causes the drive to transmit a 512-byte block of data that provides all details about the drive. Through this command, any program (including the system BIOS) can find out exactly which type of drive is connected, including the drive manufacturer, model number, operating parameters, and even the serial number of the drive. Many modern BIOSs use this information to automatically receive and enter the drive's parameters into CMOS memory, eliminating the need for the user to enter these parameters manually during system configuration. This arrangement helps prevent mistakes that can later lead to data loss when the user no longer remembers what parameters he used during setup.

The Identify Drive data can tell you many things about your drive, including the following:

- Number of logical block addresses available using LBA mode
- Number of physical cylinders, heads, and sectors available in P-CHS mode
- Number of logical cylinders, heads, and sectors in the current translation L-CHS mode
- Transfer modes (and speeds) supported
- Manufacturer and model number
- Internal firmware revision
- Serial number
- Buffer type/size, indicating sector buffering or caching capabilities

Several public-domain programs can execute this command to the drive and report the information onscreen. In the past, I've used the IDEINFO program available at http://www.tech-pro.co.uk/ideinfo.html. However, because this program was created almost a decade ago, it doesn't provide the best information about recent drives. For more up-to-date information, use IDEDIAG, which is available from http://www.penguin.cz/~mhi/idediag, or HWINFO, which is available from http://www.hwinfo.com. (I find these programs especially useful when I am trying to install ATA drives on a system that has a user-defined drive type but doesn't support autodetection and I need to know the correct parameters for a user-definable BIOS type. These programs get the information directly from the drive.)

Two other important commands are the Read Multiple and Write Multiple commands. These commands permit multiple-sector data transfers and, when combined with block-mode PIO capabilities in the system, can result in incredible data-transfer rates many times faster than single-sector PIO transfers. Some older systems require you to select the correct number of sectors supported by the drive, but most recent systems automatically determine this information for you.

Many other enhanced commands are available, including room for a given drive manufacturer to implement what are called *vendor-unique* commands. Certain vendors often use these commands for features unique to that vendor. Often, vendor-unique commands control features such as low-level formatting and defect management. This is why low-level format programs can be so specific to a particular manufacturer's ATA drives and why many manufacturers make their own LLF programs available.

ATA Security Mode

Support for hard disk passwords (called ATA Security Mode) was added to the ATA-3 specification during 1995. The proposal adopted in the ATA specification was originally from IBM, which had developed this capability and which had already begun incorporating it into ThinkPad systems and IBM 2.5" drives. Because it was then incorporated into the official ATA-3 standard (finally published in 1997), most other drive and system manufacturers have also adopted this, especially for laptop systems and 2.5" drives. Note that these passwords are *very* secure. Also, if you lose or forget them, they usually cannot be recovered and you will never be able to access the drive. More on that later....

Hard disk security passwords are set via the BIOS Setup, and not all systems support this feature. Most laptops support hard disk security, but most desktops do not. If supported, two types of hard disk passwords can be set, called user and master. The user password locks and unlocks the disk, whereas the master password is used to only unlock. You can set only a user password, or you can set user+master, but you cannot set a master password alone.

When a user password is set (with no master), or when both user+master passwords are set, access to the drive is prevented (even if the drive is moved to a different system) unless the user (or master) password is entered upon system startup.

The master password is designed to be an alternative or backup password for system administrators as a master unlock. With both master and user passwords set, the user is told the user password but not the master password. Subsequently, the user can change the user password as desired; however, a system administrator can still gain access by using the master password.

If a user or user+master password is set, the disk must be unlocked at boot time via a BIOS-generated password prompt. The appearance of the prompt varies from system to system, but in IBM systems the prompt is graphical. An icon consisting of a cylinder with a number above it (indicating the drive number) next to a padlock appears onscreen. If the hard disk password prompt appears, you must enter it; otherwise, you will be denied access to the drive and the system will not boot.

As I said earlier, if you forget the user password (with no master) or both the user and master passwords (if both are set), you will not be able to gain access to the drive, even if you move it to another system and even if the other system does not support ATA Security Mode. The drive will have essentially become a paper weight.

As with many security features, a workaround might be possible if you forget your password. In this case, at least one company can either restore the drive to operation (with all the data lost) or restore the drive and the data. That company is Nortek (see http://www.nortek.on.ca for more information). The password removal procedure costs $85–$295, and you must provide proof of ownership when you send in the drive. As you can see, the cost is generally more than the cost of a new drive, so it is worthwhile only if you absolutely need the data back.

Hard disk passwords are not preset on a brand-new drive, but they might be preset if you are buying a used drive or if the people or company you purchased the drive or system from entered them. This is a common ploy when selling drives or systems on eBay—for example, the seller might set supervisor or hard disk passwords and hold them until payment is received. Or he might be selling used product "as-is" for which he doesn't have the passwords, which renders them useless to the purchaser. Because of this, I *never* recommend purchasing a laptop or hard drive used unless you are certain that no supervisor or hard disk passwords are set.

Most systems also support other power-on or supervisor passwords in the BIOS Setup. In most systems, when you set a supervisor password, it automatically sets the hard disk password to the same value as well. In most cases, if a supervisor password is set and it matches the hard disk user or master password, when you enter the supervisor password, the BIOS automatically enters the hard disk password at the same time. This means that even though a hard disk password is set, you might not even know it because the hard disk password is entered automatically at the same time as you enter the supervisor password; therefore, you won't see a separate prompt for the hard disk password. However, if the drive is later separated from the system, it will not work on another system until the correct hard disk password is entered. Without the services of a company such as Nortek, you can remove a hard disk password only if you know the password to begin with.

Host Protected Area

Most PCs sold on the market today include some form of automated product recovery or restoration feature that allows a user to easily restore the operating system and other software on the system to the state it was in when the system was new. Originally, this was accomplished via one or more product recovery CDs containing automated scripts that reinstalled all the software that came preinstalled on the system when it was new.

Unfortunately, the CDs could be lost or damaged, they were often problematic to use, and including them by default cost manufacturers a lot of money. This prompted PC manufacturers to move the recovery software to a hidden partition of the boot hard drive. Although this wastes some space on the drive, the recovery software normally fits on from one to four CDs, which occupies 1GB–3GB of drive space. With 60GB or larger drives, this amounts to 5% or less of the total space. Still, even the hidden partition was less than satisfactory because the partition could easily be damaged or overwritten by partitioning software or other utilities, so there was no way to make it secure.

In 1996, Gateway proposed a change to the ATA-4 standard under development that would allow a space called the host protected area to be reserved on a drive. This change was ratified, and the HPA feature set was incorporated into the ATA-4 specification that was finally published in 1998. A separate BIOS firmware interface specification called Protected Area Run Time Interface Extension Services (PARTIES) was initiated in 1999 that defined services an operating system could use to access the HPA. The PARTIES standard was completed and published in 2001 as NCITS 346-2001, Protected Area Run Time Interface Extension Services.

The HPA works by using the optional ATA SET MAX ADDRESS command to make the drive appear to the system as a slightly smaller drive. Anything from the new max address (the newly reported end of the drive) to the true end of the drive is considered the HPA and is accessible only using PARTIES commands. This is more secure than a hidden partition because any data past the end of the drive simply cannot be seen by any normal application, or even a partitioning utility such as PartitionMagic or Partition Commander. Still, if you want to remove the HPA, you can use some options in the BIOS Setup or separate commands to reset the max address, thus exposing the HPA. At that point, you can run something such as PartitionMagic or Partition Commander to resize the adjacent partition to include the extra space that was formerly hidden and unavailable.

Most new systems using Phoenix FirstBIOS come with their recovery software and diagnostics in the HPA because this is part of the new Phoenix FirstBIOS core managed environment (cME), which is used by a large number of OEMs (including IBM) on most desktop and laptop systems starting in 2003.

◀◀   For more information on the HPA and what might be stored there, see "Preboot Environment," p. 428.

ATA Packet Interface

ATA Packet Interface (ATAPI) is a standard designed to provide the commands necessary for devices such as CD-ROMs, removable media drives such as SuperDisk and Zip, and tape drives that plug in to an ordinary ATA (IDE) connector. The principal advantage of ATAPI hardware is that it's cheap and works on your current adapter. For CD-ROMs, it has a somewhat lower CPU usage compared to proprietary adapters, but there's no performance gain otherwise. For tape drives, ATAPI has the potential for superior performance and reliability compared to the popular floppy controller attached tape devices. Although ATAPI CD-ROMs use the hard disk interface, this does not mean they look like ordinary hard disks. To the contrary, from a software point of view, they are a completely different kind of animal. They most closely resemble a SCSI device. All modern ATA CD-ROMs support the ATAPI protocols, and generally the terms are synonymous. In other words, an ATAPI CD-ROM is an ATA CD-ROM, and vice versa.

Caution

Most systems starting in 1998 began supporting the Phoenix El Torito specification, which enables booting from ATAPI CD or DVD drives. Systems without El Torito support in the BIOS can't boot from an ATAPI CD or DVD drive. Even with ATAPI support in the BIOS, you still must load a driver to use ATAPI under DOS or Windows. Windows 95 and later (including 98 and Me) and Windows NT (including Windows 2000 and XP) have native ATAPI support. Some versions of the Windows 98 and Me CD-ROMs are bootable, whereas all NT, 2000, and XP CD-ROMs are directly bootable on those systems, greatly easing installation.

I normally recommend keeping ATA devices you will be accessing simultaneously on separate channels. Because ATA does not typically support overlapping access, when one drive is being accessed on
a given channel, the other drive on the same channel can't be accessed. By keeping the CD-ROM and
hard disk on separate channels, you can more effectively overlap accessing between them. One other
caveat is that a parallel ATA device such as a hard drive might be incapable of functioning if another
parallel ATAPI device (CD or DVD drive) is master. Therefore, in most cases you should try to set parallel ATA hard drives as master (device 0) and parallel ATAPI drives as slave (device 1) on a given
cable.

ATA Drive Capacity Limitations

ATA interface versions up through ATA-5 suffered from a drive capacity limitation of about 137GB
(billion bytes). Depending on the BIOS used, this limitation can be further reduced to 8.4GB, or even
as low as 528MB (million bytes). This is due to limitations in both the BIOS and the ATA interface,
which when combined create even further limitations. To understand these limits, you have to look
at the BIOS (software) and ATA (hardware) interfaces together.

Note

In addition to the BIOS/ATA limitations discussed in this section, various operating system limitations also exist. These are
described later in this chapter.

The limitations when dealing with ATA drives are those of the ATA interface itself as well as the BIOS
interface used to talk to the drive. A summary of the limitations is shown in Table 7.13.

This section details the differences between the various sector addressing methods and the limitations
incurred by using them.

Prefixes for Decimal and Binary Multiples

Many readers are unfamiliar with the MiB (mebibyte), GiB (gibibyte), and so on designations I am
using in this section and throughout the book. These are part of a standard designed to eliminate
confusion between decimal- and binary-based multiples, especially in computer systems. Standard SI
(system international or metric system) units are based on multiples of 10. This worked well for most
things, but not for computers, which operate in a binary world where most numbers are based on
powers of 2. This has resulted in different meanings being assigned to the same prefix—for example
1KB (kilobyte) could mean either 1,000 (10^3) bytes or 1,024 (2^{10}) bytes. To eliminate confusion, in
December 1998 the International Electrotechnical Commission (IEC) approved as an international
standard the prefix names and symbols for binary multiples used in data processing and transmission.
Some of these prefixes are shown in Table 7.14.

Under this standard terminology, an MB (megabyte) would be 1,000,000 bytes, whereas an MiB
(mebibyte) would be 1,048,576 bytes.

Note

For more information on these industry-standard decimal and binary prefixes, check out the National Institute for Standards
and Technology (NIST) Web site at **physics.nist.gov/cuu/Units/prefixes.html**.

Table 7.13   ATA/IDE Capacity Limitations for Various Sector Addressing Methods

Sector Addressing Method	Total Sectors Calculation	Max. Total Sectors
CHS: BIOS w/o TL	1024×16×63	1,032,192
CHS: BIOS w/bit-shift TL	1024×240×63	15,482,880
CHS: BIOS w/LBA-assist TL	1024×255×63	16,450,560
CHS: BIOS INT13h	1024×256×63	16,515,072
CHS: ATA-1/ATA-5	65536×16×255	267,386,880
LBA: ATA-1/ATA-5	2^{28}	268,435,456
LBA: ATA-6+	2^{48}	281,474,976,710,655
LBA: EDD BIOS	2^{64}	18,446,744,073,709,551,616

BIOS = Basic input output system   w/ = with
ATA = AT Attachment (IDE)   w/o = without
CHS = Cylinder head sector   TL = Translation
LBA = Logical block (sector) address   INT13h = Interrupt 13 hex

Table 7.14   Standard Prefix Names and Symbols for Binary Multiples

Decimal Prefixes:

Factor	Symbol	Name	Value
10^3	k	Kilo	1,000
10^6	M	Mega	1,000,000
10^9	G	Giga	1,000,000,000
10^{12}	T	Tera	1,000,000,000,000
10^{15}	P	Peta	1,000,000,000,000,000
10^{18}	E	Exa	1,000,000,000,000,000,000
10^{21}	Z	Zetta	1,000,000,000,000,000,000,000

Note that the symbol for kilo (k) is in lowercase (which is technically correct according to the SI standard), whereas all other decimal prefixes are uppercase.

BIOS Limitations

Motherboard ROM BIOSs have been updated throughout the years to support larger and larger drives. Table 7.15 shows the most important relative dates when drive capacity limits were changed.

Table 7.15   Dates of Changes to Drive Capacity Limitations in the ROM BIOS

BIOS Date	Capacity Limit
August 1994	528MB
January 1998	8.4GB
September 2002	137GB

These are when the limits were broken, such that BIOSs older than August 1994 are generally limited to drives of up to 528MB, whereas BIOSs older than January 1998 are generally limited to 8.4GB. Most BIOSs dated 1998 or newer support drives up to 137GB, and those dated September 2002 or

Maximum Capacity (Bytes)	Capacity (Decimal)	Capacity (Binary)
528,482,304	528.48MB	504.00MiB
7,927,234,560	7.93GB	7.38GiB
8,422,686,720	8.42GB	7.84GiB
8,455,716,864	8.46GB	7.88GiB
136,902,082,560	136.90GB	127.50GiB
137,438,953,472	137.44GB	128.00GiB
144,115,188,075,855,872	144.12PB	128.00PiB
9,444,732,965,739,290,427,392	9.44ZB	8.00ZiB

EDD = Enhanced Disk Drive specification
  (Phoenix/ATA)

MB = megabyte (million bytes)

MiB = mebibyte

GB = gigabyte (billion bytes)

GiB = gibibyte

PB = petabyte (quadrillion bytes)

PiB = pebibyte

ZB = zettabyte (sextillion bytes)

ZiB = zebibyte

Binary Prefixes:

Factor	Symbol	Name	Derivation	Value
2^{10}	Ki	Kibi	Kilobinary	1,024
2^{20}	Mi	Mebi	Megabinary	1,048,576
2^{30}	Gi	Gibi	Gigabinary	1,073,741,824
2^{40}	Ti	Tebi	Terabinary	1,099,511,627,776
2^{50}	Pi	Pebi	Petabinary	1,125,899,906,842,624
2^{60}	Ei	Exbi	Exabinary	1,152,921,504,606,846,976
2^{70}	Zi	Zebi	Zettabinary	1,180,591,620,717,411,303,424

newer should support drives larger than 137GB. These are only general guidelines, though; to accurately determine this for a specific system, you should check with your motherboard manufacturer. You can also use the BIOS Wizard utility from http://www.unicore.com/bioswiz/index2.html, which will tell you the BIOS date from your system and specifically whether your system supports the Enhanced Hard Disk Drive specification (which means drives over 8.4GB).

If your BIOS does not support EDD (drives over 8.4GB), the three possible solutions are

- Upgrade your motherboard BIOS to a 1998 or newer version that supports >8.4GB.
- Install a BIOS upgrade card, such as the Ultra ATA 133 PCI card from www.maxtordirect.com.
- Install a software patch to add >8.4GB support.

Of these, the first one is the most desirable because it is usually free. Visit your motherboard manufacturer's Web site to see whether it has any newer BIOSs available for your motherboard that will support large drives. If it doesn't, the next best thing is to use a card such as the ATA Pro Flash from Micro Firmware or the Ultra ATA 133 PCI card from Maxtor. I almost never recommend the last solution because it merely installs a software patch in the boot sector area of the hard drive, which can result in numerous problems when booting from different drives, installing new drives, or recovering data.

CHS Versus LBA

There are two primary methods to address (or number) sectors on an ATA drive. The first method is called CHS (cylinder head sector) after the three respective coordinate numbers used to address each sector of the drive. The second method is called LBA (logical block address) and uses a single number to address each sector on a drive. CHS was derived from the physical way drives were constructed (and is how they work internally), whereas LBA evolved as a simpler and more logical way to number the sectors regardless of the internal physical construction.

▶▶   For more information on cylinders, heads, and sectors as they are used internally within the drive, see "Hard Disk Drive Operation," p. 645.

When reading a drive sequentially in CHS mode, the process starts with cylinder 0, head 0, and sector 1 (which is the first sector on the disk). Next, all the remaining sectors on that first track are read; then the next head is selected; and then all the sectors on that track are read—and so on until all the heads on the first cylinder are read. Then the next cylinder is selected, and the sequence starts again. Think of CHS as an odometer of sorts: The sector numbers must roll over before the head number can change, and the head numbers must roll over before the cylinder can change.

When reading a drive sequentially in LBA mode, the process starts with sector 0, then read 1, then 2, and so on. The first sector on the drive in CHS mode would be 0,0,1, and the same sector in LBA mode would be 0.

As an example, imagine a drive with one platter, two heads (both sides of the platter are used), two tracks on each platter (cylinders), and two sectors on each track. We would say the drive has two cylinders (tracks per side), two heads (sides), and two sectors per track. This would result in a total capacity of eight (2×2×2) sectors. Noting that cylinders and heads begin numbering from 0—whereas physical sectors on a track number from 1—using CHS addressing, we would say the first sector on the drive is cylinder 0, head 0, sector 1 (0,0,1); the second sector is 0,0,2; the third sector is 0,1,1; the fourth sector is 0,1,2; and so on until we get to the last sector, which would be 1,1,2.

Now imagine that we could take the eight sectors and, rather than refer directly to the physical cylinder, head, and sector, number the sectors in order from 0 to 7. Thus, if we wanted to address the fourth sector on the drive, we could reference it as sector 0,1,2 in CHS mode or as sector 3 in LBA mode. Table 7.16 shows the correspondence between CHS and LBA sector numbers for this eight-sector imaginary drive.

Table 7.16   CHS and LBA Sector Numbers for an Imaginary Drive with Two Cylinders, Two Heads, and Two Sectors per Track (Eight Sectors Total)

Mode	Equivalent Sector Numbers							
CHS:	0,0,1	0,0,2	0,1,1	0,1,2	1,0,1	1,0,2	1,1,1	1,1,2
LBA:	0	1	2	3	4	5	6	7

As you can see from this example, using LBA numbers is simpler and generally easier to handle; however, when the PC was first developed, all BIOS and ATA drive-level addressing was done using CHS addressing.

CHS/LBA and LBA/CHS Conversions

You can address the same sectors in either CHS or LBA mode. The conversion from CHS to LBA is always consistent in that for a given drive, a particular CHS address always converts to a given LBA address, and vice versa. The ATA-1 document specifies a simple formula that can be used to convert CHS parameters to LBA:

$$LBA = (((C \times HPC) + H) \times SPT) + S - 1$$

By reversing this formula, you can convert the other way— that is, from LBA back to CHS:

C = int (LBA / SPT / HPC)
H = int ((LBA / SPT) mod HPC)
S = (LBA mod SPT) + 1

For these formulae, the acronyms are defined as follows:

LBA = Logical block address
C = Cylinder
H = Head
S = Sector
HPC = Heads per cylinder (total number of heads)
SPT = Sectors per track
int X = Integer portion of X
X mod Y = Modulus (remainder) of X/Y

Using these formulas you can calculate the LBA for any given CHS address, and vice versa. Given a drive of 16,383 cylinders, 16 heads, and 63 sectors per track, Table 7.17 shows the equivalent CHS and LBA addresses.

Table 7.17   Equivalent CHS and LBA Sector Numbers for a Drive with 16,383 Cylinders, 16 Heads, and 63 Sectors per Track (16,514,064 Sectors Total)

Cylinder	Head	Sector	LBA
0	0	1	0
0	0	63	62
0	1	0	63
999	15	63	1,007,999
1,000	0	1	1,008,000
9,999	15	63	10,079,999
10,000	0	1	10,080,000
16,382	15	63	16,514,063

BIOS Commands Versus ATA Commands

In addition to the two methods of sector addressing (CHS or LBA), there are two levels of interface where sector addressing occurs. One interface is where the operating system talks to the BIOS (using BIOS commands); the other is where the BIOS talks to the drive (using ATA commands). The specific commands at these levels are different, but both support CHS and LBA modes. Figure 7.13 illustrates the two interface levels.

When the operating system talks to the BIOS to read or write sectors, it issues commands via software interrupt (not the same as an IRQ) INT13h, which is how the BIOS subroutines for disk access are called. Various INT13h subfunctions allow sectors to be read or written using either CHS or LBA addressing. The BIOS routines then convert the BIOS commands into ATA hardware-level commands, which are sent over the bus I/O ports to the drive controller. Commands at the ATA hardware level can also use either CHS or LBA addressing, although the limitations are different. Whether your BIOS and drive use CHS or LBA addressing depends on the drive capacity, age of the BIOS and drive, BIOS Setup settings used, and operating system used.

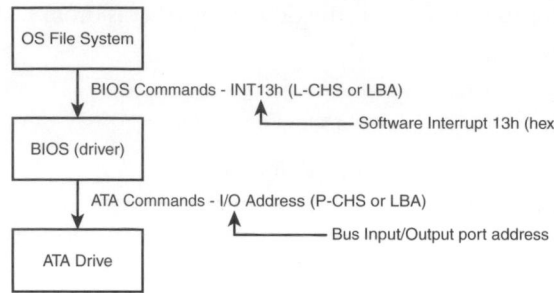

Figure 7.13 The relationship between BIOS and physical sector addressing. (In this figure, L-CHS stands for Logical CHS and P-CHS stands for Physical CHS.)

CHS Limitations (the 528MB Barrier)

The original BIOS-based driver for hard disks is accessed via software interrupt 13h (13 hex) and offers functions for reading and writing drives at the sector level. Standard INT13h functions require that a particular sector be addressed by its cylinder, head, and sector location—otherwise known as *CHS addressing*. This interface is used by the operating system and low-level disk utilities to access the drive. IBM originally wrote the INT13h interface for the BIOS on the PC XT hard disk controller in 1983, and in 1984, incorporated it into the AT motherboard BIOS. This interface used numbers to define the particular cylinder, head, and sector being addressed. Table 7.18, which shows the standard INT13h BIOS CHS parameter limits, includes the maximum values for these numbers.

Table 7.18   INT13h BIOS CHS Parameter Limits

Field	Field Size	Maximum Value	Range	Total Usable
Cylinder	10 bits	1024	0–1023	1024
Head	8 bits	256	0–255	256
Sector	6 bits	64	1–63	63

The concept of a maximum value given a number of digits is simple: If you had, for example, a hotel with two-digit decimal room numbers, you could have only 100 (10^2) rooms, numbered 0–99. The CHS numbers used by the standard BIOS INT13h interface are binary, and with a 10-bit number being used to count cylinders, you can have only 1,024 (2^{10}) maximum, numbered 0–1023. Because the head is identified by an 8-bit number, the maximum number of heads is 256 (2^8), numbered 0–255. Finally, with sectors per track there is a minor difference. Sectors on a track are identified by a 6-bit number, which would normally allow a maximum of 64 (2^6) sectors; however, because sectors are numbered starting with 1 (instead of 0), the range is limited to 1–63, which means a total of 63 sectors per track is the maximum the BIOS can handle.

These BIOS limitations are true for all BIOS versions or programs that rely on CHS addressing. Using the maximum numbers possible for CHS at the BIOS level, you can address a drive with 1,024 cylinders, 256 heads, and 63 sectors per track. Because each sector is 512 bytes, the math works out as follows:

```
              Max. Values
      ---------------------------
      Cylinders         1,024
          Heads           256
  Sectors/Track            63
      ===========================
```

```
Total Sectors     16,515,072
- - - - - - - - - - - - - - - - - - - - - - - - - -
Total Bytes     8,455,716,864
Megabytes (MB)         8,456
Mebibytes (MiB)        8,064
Gigabytes (GB)           8.4
Gibibytes (GiB)          7.8
```

From these calculations, you can see that the maximum capacity drive addressable via the standard BIOS INT13h interface is about 8.4GB (where GB equals roughly 1 billion bytes), or 7.8GiB (where GiB means *gigabinarybytes*).

Unfortunately, the BIOS INT13h limits are not the only limitations that apply. Limits also exist in the ATA interface itself. The ATA CHS limits are shown in Table 7.19.

Table 7.19   Standard ATA CHS Parameter Limitations

Field	Field Size	Maximum Value	Range	Total Usable
Cylinder	16 bits	65536	0–65535	65536
Head	4 bits	16	0–15	16
Sector	8 bits	256	1–255	255

As you can see, the ATA interface uses different sized fields to store CHS values. Note that the ATA limits are higher than the BIOS limits for cylinders and sectors but lower than the BIOS limit for heads. The CHS limits for capacity according to the ATA-1 through ATA-5 specification are as follows:

```
                Max. Values
- - - - - - - - - - - - - - - - - - - - - - - - - -
    Cylinders         65,536
        Heads             16
Sectors/Track            255
==============================
Total Sectors    267,386,880
- - - - - - - - - - - - - - - - - - - - - - - - - -
Total Bytes    136,902,082,560
Megabytes (MB)       136,902
Mebibytes (MiB)      130,560
Gigabytes (GB)         136.9
Gibibytes (GiB)        127.5
```

When you combine the limitations of the BIOS and ATA CHS parameters, you end up with the situation shown in Table 7.20.

Table 7.20   Combined BIOS and ATA CHS Parameter Limits

Field	BIOS CHS Parameter Limits	ATA CHS Parameter Limits	Combined CHS Parameter Limits
Cylinder	1,024	65,536	1,024
Head	256	16	16
Sector	63	255	63
Total Sectors	16,515,072	267,386,880	1,032,192
Maximum Capacity	8.4GB	136.9GB	528MB

As you can see, the lowest common denominator of the combined CHS limits results in maximum usable parameters of 1,024 cylinders, 16 heads, and 63 sectors, which results in a maximum drive capacity of 528MB. This became known as the 528MB barrier (also called the 504MiB barrier), and it affects virtually all PCs built in 1993 or earlier.

CHS Translation (Breaking the 528MB Barrier)

Having a barrier limiting drive capacity to 528MB or less wasn't a problem when the largest drives available were smaller than that. But by 1994, drive technology had developed such that making drives larger than what the combined BIOS and ATA limitations could address was possible. Clearly a fix for the problem was needed.

Starting in 1993, the BIOS developer Phoenix Technologies began working on BIOS extensions to work around the combined CHS limits. In January 1994, it released the BIOS Enhanced Disk Drive (EDD) Specification, which was later republished by the T13 committee (also responsible for ATA) as "BIOS Enhanced Disk Drive Services (EDD)." The EDD documents detail several methods for circumventing the limitations of previous BIOSs without causing compatibility problems with existing software. These include

- BIOS INT13h extensions supporting 64-bit LBA
- Bit-shift geometric CHS translation
- LBA-assist geometric CHS translation

The method for dealing with the CHS problem was called *translation* because it enabled additional subroutines in the BIOS to translate CHS parameters from ATA maximums to BIOS maximums (and vice versa). In an effort to make its methods standard among the entire PC industry, Phoenix released the EDD document publicly and allowed the technology to be used free of charge, even among its competitors such as AMI and Award. The T13 committee in charge of ATA subsequently adopted the EDD standard and incorporated it into official ATA documents.

Starting in 1994, most BIOSs began implementing the Phoenix-designed CHS translation methods, which enabled drives up to the BIOS limit of 8.4GB to be supported. The fix involved what is termed *parameter translation* at the BIOS level, which adapted or translated the cylinder, head, and sector numbers to fit within the allowable BIOS parameters. There are two types of translation: One works via a technique called CHS bit-shift (usually called "Large" or "Extended CHS" in the BIOS Setup), and the other uses a technique called LBA-assist (usually called "LBA" in the BIOS Setup). These refer to the different mathematical methods of doing essentially the same thing: converting one set of CHS numbers to another.

CHS bit-shift translation manipulates the cylinder and head numbers but does not change the sector number. It begins with the physical (drive reported) cylinders and heads and, using some simple division and multiplication, comes up with altered numbers for the cylinders and heads. The sectors per track value is not translated and is passed unaltered. The term *bit-shift* is used because the division and multiplication math is actually done in the BIOS software by shifting bits in the CHS address.

With CHS bit-shift translation, the drive reported (physical) parameters are referred to as P-CHS and the BIOS altered logical parameters are referred to as L-CHS. After the settings are made in the BIOS Setup, L-CHS addresses are automatically translated to P-CHS at the BIOS level. This enables the operating system to send commands to the BIOS using L-CHS parameters, which the BIOS automatically converts to P-CHS when it talks to the drive using ATA commands. Table 7.21 shows the rules for calculating CHS bit-shift translation.

CHS bit-shift translation is based on dividing the physical cylinder count by a power of 2 to bring it under the 1,024 cylinder BIOS INT13h limit and then multiplying the heads by the same power of 2, leaving the sector count unchanged. The power of 2 used depends on the cylinder count, as indicated in Table 7.21.

Table 7.21   CHS Bit-Shift Translation Rules

Physical (Drive Reported) Cylinders	Physical Heads	Logical Cylinders	Logical Heads	Max. Capacity
1 < C <= 1,024	1 < H <= 16	C = C	H = H	528MB
1,024 < C <= 2,048	1 < H <= 16	C = C/2	H = H×2	1GB
2,048 < C <= 4,096	1 < H <= 16	C = C/4	H = H×4	2.1GB
4,096 < C <= 8,192	1 < H <= 16	C = C/8	H = H×8	4.2GB
8,192 < C <= 16,384	1 < H <= 16	C = C/16	H = H×16	8.4GB

The drive reported sector count is not translated.

The logical heads value can't exceed 255 with some operating systems, such as DOS/Win9x/Me.

Here is an example of CHS bit-shift translation:

```
                                      Bit-shift
                         P-CHS        L-CHS
                      Parameters     Parameters
------------------------------------------------
       Cylinders         8,000          1,000
           Heads            16            128
    Sectors/Track           63             63
================================================
    Total Sectors     8,064,000      8,064,000
------------------------------------------------
    Total Bytes   4,128,768,000  4,128,768,000
  Megabytes (MB)          4,129          4,129
  Mebibytes (MiB)         3,938          3,938
  Gigabytes (GB)           4.13           4.13
  Gibibytes (GiB)          3.85           3.85
```

This example shows a drive with 8,000 cylinders and 16 heads. The physical cylinder count is way above the BIOS limit of 1,024, so if CHS bit-shift translation is selected in the BIOS Setup, the BIOS then divides the cylinder count by 2, 4, 8, or 16 to bring it below 1,024. In this case it would divide by 8, which results in a new logical cylinder count of 1,000—which is below the 1,024 maximum. Because the cylinder count is divided by 8, the head count is then multiplied by the same number, resulting in 128 logical heads, which is also below the limit the BIOS can handle.

So, although the drive reports having 8,000 cylinders and 16 heads, the BIOS and all software (including the operating system) instead see the drive as having 1,000 cylinders and 128 heads. Note that the 63 sectors/track figure is simply carried over without change. The result is that by using the logical parameters, the BIOS can see the entire 4.13GB drive and won't be limited to just the first 528MB.

When you install a drive, you don't have to perform the translation math to convert the cylinders and heads; the BIOS does that for you automatically. All you have to do is allow the BIOS to autodetect the P-CHS parameters and then enable the translation in the BIOS Setup. Selecting Large or ECHS translation in the BIOS Setup enables the CHS bit-shift. The BIOS does the rest of the work for you.

CHS bit-shift is a simple and fast (code-wise) scheme that can work with all drives, but unfortunately it can't properly translate all theoretically possible drive geometries for drives under 8.4GB. To solve this, an addendum was added to the ATA-2 specification to specifically require drives to report certain ranges of geometries to allow bit-shift translation to work. Thus, all drives that conform to the ATA-2 specification (or higher) can be translated using this method.

The 2.1GB Barrier

Some BIOSs incorrectly allocated only 12 bits for the P-CHS cylinder field, thereby allowing a maximum of 4,096 cylinders. Combined with the standard 16-head and 63-sector limits, this resulted in the inability to support any drives over 2.1GB in capacity. Fortunately, this BIOS defect affected only a limited number of systems with BIOS dates prior to about mid-1996.

The 4.2GB Barrier

Even so, some problems still existed with bit-shift translation. Because of the way DOS and Windows 9x/Me were written, they could not properly handle a drive with 256 heads. This was a problem for drives larger than 4.2GB because the CHS bit-shift translation rules typically resulted in 256 heads as a logical value, as seen in the following example:

	P-CHS Parameters	Bit-shift L-CHS Parameters
Cylinders	12,000	750
Heads	16	256
Sectors/Track	63	63
Total Sectors	12,096,000	12,096,000
Total Bytes	6,193,152,000	6,193,152,000
Megabytes (MB)	6,193	6,193
Mebibytes (MiB)	5,906	5,906
Gigabytes (GB)	6.19	6.19
Gibibytes (GiB)	5.77	5.77

This scheme failed when you tried to install Windows 9x/Me (or DOS) on a drive larger than 4.2GB because the L-CHS parameters included 256 heads. Any BIOS that implemented this scheme essentially had a 4.2GB barrier, so installing a drive larger than that and selecting CHS bit-shift translation caused the drive to fail. Note that this was not a problem for Windows NT/2000/XP.

Note

It is interesting to note that the BIOS is not actually at fault here; the problem instead lies with the DOS/Win9x/Me file system code, which stores the sector per track number as an 8-bit value. The number 256 causes a problem because 256 = 100000000b, which takes 9 bits to store. The value 255 = 11111111b is the largest value that can fit in an 8-bit binary register and is therefore the maximum number of heads those operating systems can support.

To solve this problem, CHS bit-shift translation was revised by adding a rule such that if the drive reported 16 heads and more than 8,192 cylinders (which would result in a 256-head translation), the P-CHS head value would be assumed to be 15 (instead of 16) and the P-CHS cylinder value would be multiplied by 16/15 to compensate. These adjusted cylinder and head values would then be translated. The following example shows the results:

	P-CHS Parameters	Bit-shift L-CHS Parameters	Revised Bit-shift L-CHS Parameters
Cylinders	12,000	750	800
Heads	16	256	240
Sectors/Track	63	63	63

Total Sectors	12,096,000	12,096,000	12,096,000

Total Bytes	6,193,152,000	6,193,152,000	6,193,152,000
Megabytes (MB)	6,193	6,193	6,193
Mebibytes (MiB)	5,906	5,906	5,906
Gigabytes (GB)	6.19	6.19	6.19
Gibibytes (GiB)	5.77	5.77	5.77

As you can see from this example, a drive with 12,000 cylinders and 16 heads translates to 750 cylinders and 256 heads using the standard CHS bit-shift scheme. The revised CHS bit-shift scheme rule does a double translation in this case, first changing the 16 heads to 15 and then multiplying the 12,000 cylinders by 16/15, resulting in 12,800 cylinders. Then, the new cylinder value is CHS bit-shift translated by dividing it by 16, resulting in 800 logical cylinders. Likewise, the 15 heads are multiplied by 16, resulting in 240 logical heads. If the logical cylinder count calculates to over 1,024 then it is truncated to 1,024. In this case, what started out as 12,000 cylinders and 16 heads P-CHS becomes 800 cylinders and 240 heads (instead of 750 cylinders and 256 heads) L-CHS, which works around the bug in the DOS/Win9x/Me operating systems.

So far, all my examples have been very clean—that is, the L-CHS parameters have calculated to the same capacity as the P-CHS parameters. Unfortunately, it doesn't always work out that way. The following example shows a more typical example in the real world. Several 8.4GB drives from Maxtor, Quantum, Seagate, and others report 16,383 cylinders and 16 heads P-CHS. For those drives, the translations would work out as follows:

	P-CHS Parameters	Bit-shift L-CHS Parameters	Revised Bit-shift L-CHS Parameters
Cylinders	16,383	1,023	1,024
Heads	16	256	240
Sectors/Track	63	63	63
Total Sectors	16,514,064	16,498,944	15,482,880
Total Bytes	8,455,200,768	8,447,459,328	7,927,234,560
Megabytes (MB)	8,455	8,447	7,927
Mebibytes (MiB)	8,064	8,056	7,560
Gigabytes (GB)	8.46	8.45	7.93
Gibibytes (GiB)	7.87	7.87	7.38

Note that the revised CHS bit-shift translation rules result in supporting only 7.93GB of the 8.46GB total on the drive. In fact, the parameters shown (with 240 heads) are the absolute maximum that revised CHS bit-shift supports. Fortunately, another translation mode is available that improves this situation.

LBA-Assist Translation

The LBA-assist translation method places no artificial limits on the reported drive geometries, but it works only on drives that support LBA addressing at the ATA interface level. Fortunately, though, virtually all ATA drives larger than 2GB support LBA. LBA-assist translation takes the CHS parameters the drive reports, multiplies them together to get a calculated LBA maximum value (total number of sectors), and then uses this calculated LBA number to derive the translated CHS parameters. Table 7.22 shows the rules for LBA-assist translation.

Table 7.22   LBA-Assist Translation Rules

Total Sectors	Logical Cylinders	Logical Heads	Logical Sectors
1 < T <= 1,032,192	T/1,008	16	63
1,032,192 < T <= 2,064,384	T/2,016	32	63
2,064,384 < T <= 4,128,768	T/4,032	64	63
4,128,768 < T <= 8,257,536	T/8,064	128	63
8,257,536 < T <= 16,450,560	T/16,065	255	63

T = Total sectors, calculated by multiplying the drive-reported P-CHS parameters (C×H×S)

LBA-assist translation fixes the sectors at 63 no matter what and divides and multiplies the cylinders and heads by predetermined values depending on the total number of sectors. This results in a set of L-CHS parameters the operating system uses to communicate with the BIOS. The L-CHS numbers are then translated to LBA numbers at the ATA interface level. Because LBA mode is more flexible at translating, it should be used in most cases instead of CHS bit-shift.

Normally, both the CHS bit-shift and LBA-assist translations generate the same L-CHS geometry for a given drive. This should always be true if the drive reports 63 sectors per track and 4, 8, or 16 heads. In the following example both translation schemes result in identical L-CHS values:

```
                                  Revised bit-   LBA-assist
                         P-CHS    shift L-CHS       L-CHS
                    Parameters     Parameters    Parameters
           ---------------------------------------------------
        Cylinders        8,192          1,024         1,024
            Heads           16            128           128
     Sectors/Track           63             63            63
           ===================================================
     Total Sectors    8,257,536      8,257,536     8,257,536
           ---------------------------------------------------
       Total Bytes  4,227,858,432  4,227,858,432  4,227,858,432
   Megabytes (MB)        4,228          4,228         4,228
   Mebibytes (MiB)       4,032          4,032         4,032
   Gigabytes (GB)         4.23           4.23          4.23
   Gibibytes (GiB)        3.94           3.94          3.94
```

However, if the drive reports a value other than 63 sectors per track or has other than 4, 8, or 16 heads, LBA-assist translation does not result in the same parameters as CHS bit-shift translation. In the following example, different translations result:

```
                                  Revised bit-   LBA-assist
                         P-CHS    shift L-CHS       L-CHS
                    Parameters     Parameters    Parameters
           ---------------------------------------------------
        Cylinders       16,383          1,024         1,024
            Heads           16            240           255
     Sectors/Track           63             63            63
           ===================================================
     Total Sectors   16,514,064     15,482,880    16,450,560
           ---------------------------------------------------
       Total Bytes  8,455,200,768  7,927,234,560  8,422,686,720
   Megabytes (MB)        8,455          7,927         8,423
   Mebibytes (MiB)       8,064          7,560         8,033
   Gigabytes (GB)         8.46           7.93          8.42
   Gibibytes (GiB)        7.87           7.38          7.84
```

The LBA-assist translation supports 8.42GB, which is nearly 500MB more than the revised CHS bit-shift translation. More importantly, these translations are different, which can result in problems if you change translation modes with data on the drive. If you were to set up and format a drive using CHS bit-shift translation and then change to LBA-assist translation, the interpreted geometry could change and the drive could then become unreadable until it is repartitioned and reformatted (which would destroy all the data). Bottom line: After you select a translation method, don't plan on changing it unless you have your data securely backed up.

Virtually all PC BIOSs since 1994 have translation capability in the BIOS Setup, and virtually all offer both translation modes as well as an option to disable translation entirely. If both CHS bit-shift and LBA-assist translation modes are offered, you should probably choose the LBA method of translation because it is the more efficient and flexible of the two. LBA-assist translation also gets around the 4.2GB operating system bug because it is designed to allow a maximum of 255 logical heads no matter what.

You usually can tell whether your BIOS supports translation by the capability to specify more than 1,024 cylinders in the BIOS Setup, although this can be misleading. The best clue is to look for the translation setting parameters in the ATA/IDE drive setup page in the BIOS Setup. See Chapter 5, "BIOS," for more information on how to enter the BIOS Setup on your system. If you see drive-related settings, such as LBA or ECHS (sometimes called Large or Extended), these are telltale signs of a BIOS with translation support. Most BIOSs with a date of 1994 or later include this capability, although some AMI BIOS versions from the mid-1990s locate the LBA setting on a screen different from the hard drive configuration screen. If your system currently does not support parameter translation, you might be able to get an upgrade from your motherboard manufacturer or install a BIOS upgrade card with this capability, such as the ATA Pro Flash by Micro Firmware (see the Vendor List on the disc that accompanies this book). Another option for drives larger than 137GB is the Ultra ATA/133 PCI Adapter Card from Maxtor. This card also supports the ATA/133 transfer rate of the fastest ATA drives.

Table 7.23 summarizes the four ways today's BIOSs can handle addressing sectors on the drive: Standard CHS (no translation), Extended CHS translation, LBA translation, and pure LBA addressing.

Table 7.23   Drive Sector Addressing Methods

BIOS Mode	OS to BIOS	BIOS to Drive
Standard (Normal) - No Translation	P-CHS	P-CHS
CHS Bit-Shift (ECHS) Translation	L-CHS	P-CHS
LBA-Assist (LBA) Translation	L-CHS	LBA
Pure LBA (EDD BIOS)	LBA	LBA

In Standard CHS, there is only one possible translation step internal to the drive. The drive's actual physical geometry is completely invisible from the outside with all zoned recorded ATA drives today. The cylinders, heads, and sectors printed on the label for use in the BIOS Setup are purely logical geometry and do not represent the actual physical parameters. Standard CHS addressing is limited to 16 heads and 1,024 cylinders, which provides a limit of 504MiB (528MB).

This is often called "Normal" in the BIOS Setup and causes the BIOS to behave like an old-fashioned one without translation. Use this setting if your drive has fewer than 1,024 cylinders or if you want to use the drive with a non-DOS operating system that doesn't understand translation.

ECHS or Large in the BIOS Setup is CHS bit-shift, and most BIOSs from 1997 and later use the revised method (240 logical heads maximum).

LBA, as selected in the BIOS Setup, indicates LBA-assist translation, not pure LBA mode. This enables software to operate using L-CHS parameters while the BIOS talks to the drive in LBA mode.

The only way to select a pure LBA mode, from the OS to the BIOS as well as from the BIOS to the drive, is with a drive that is over 8.4GB. All drives over 137GB must be addressed via LBA at both the BIOS and drive levels, and most PC BIOSs automatically address any drive over 8.4GB in that manner, as well. In that case no special BIOS Setup settings are necessary, other than setting the type to auto or autodetect.

Caution

A word of warning with these BIOS translation settings: If you have a drive 8.4GB or less in capacity and switch between Standard CHS, ECHS, or LBA, the BIOS can change the (translated) geometry. The same thing can happen if you transfer a disk that has been formatted on an old, non-LBA computer to a new one that uses LBA. This causes the logical CHS geometry seen by the operating system to change and the data to appear in the wrong location from where it actually is! This can cause you to lose access to your data if you are not careful. I always recommend recording the CMOS Setup screens associated with the hard disk configuration so you can properly match the setup of a drive to the settings to which it was originally set. This does not affect drives over 8.4GB because in those cases pure LBA is automatically selected.

The 8.4GB Barrier

Although CHS translation breaks the 528MB barrier, it runs into another barrier at 8.4GB. Supporting drives larger than 8.4GB requires leaving CHS behind and changing from CHS to LBA addressing at the BIOS level. The ATA interface had always supported LBA addressing, even in the original ATA-1 specification. One problem was that LBA support at the ATA level originally was optional, but the main problem was that there was no LBA support at the BIOS interface level. You could set LBA-assist translation in the BIOS Setup, but all that did was convert the drive LBA numbers to CHS numbers at the BIOS interface level.

Phoenix Technologies recognized that the BIOS interface needed to move from CHS to LBA early on and, beginning in 1994, published the "BIOS Enhanced Disk Drive Specification (EDD)," which addressed this problem with new extended INT13h BIOS services that worked with LBA rather than CHS addresses.

To ensure industry-wide support and compatibility for these new BIOS functions, in 1996 Phoenix turned this document over to the InterNational Committee on Information Technology Standards (INCITS) T13 technical committee for further enhancement and certification as a standard called the "BIOS Enhanced Disk Drive Specification (EDD)." Starting in 1998, most of the other BIOS manufacturers began installing EDD support in their BIOSs, enabling BIOS-level LBA mode support for ATA drives larger than 8.4GB. Coincidentally (or not), this support arrived just in time because ATA drives of that size and larger became available that same year.

The EDD document describes new extended INT13h BIOS commands that allow LBA addressing up to 2^{64} sectors, which results in a theoretical maximum capacity of more than 9.44ZB (zettabytes, or quadrillion bytes). That is the same as saying 9.44 trillion GB: 9.44×10^{21} bytes or, to be more precise, 9,444,732,965,739,290,427,392 bytes! I say theoretical capacity because even though by 1998 the BIOS could handle up to 2^{64} sectors, ATA drives were still using only 28-bit addressing (2^{28} sectors) at the ATA interface level. This limited an ATA drive to 268,435,456 sectors, which was a capacity of 137,438,953,472 bytes, or 137.44GB. Thus, the 8.4GB barrier had been broken, but another barrier remained at 137GB because of the 28-bit LBA addressing used in the ATA interface. The numbers work out as follows:

```
                    Max. Values
----------------------------------
Total Sectors       268,435,456
----------------------------------
Total Bytes     137,438,953,472
Megabytes (MB)          137,439
Mebibytes (MiB)         131,072
Gigabytes (GB)           137.44
Gibibytes (GiB)          128.00
```

By using the new extended INT13h 64-bit LBA mode commands at the BIOS level, as well as the existing 28-bit LBA mode commands at the ATA level, no translation would be required and the LBA numbers would be passed unchanged. The combination of LBA at the BIOS as well as the ATA interface levels meant that the clumsy CHS addressing could finally die. This also means that when you install an ATA drive larger than 8.4GB in a PC that has an EDD-capable BIOS (1998 or newer), both the BIOS and the drive are automatically set to use LBA mode.

An interesting quirk is that to allow backward-compatibility when you boot an older operating system that doesn't support LBA mode addressing (DOS or the original release of Win95, for example), most drives larger than 8.4GB report 16,383 cylinders, 16 heads, and 63 sectors per track, which is 8.4GB. For example, this enables a 120GB drive to be seen as an 8.4GB drive by older BIOSs or operating systems. That sounds strange, but I guess having a 120GB drive being recognized as an 8.4GB is better than not having it work at all. If you did want to install a drive larger than 8.4GB into a system dated before 1998, the recommended solution is either a motherboard BIOS upgrade or an add-on BIOS card with EDD support (available from Micro Firmware and others).

The 137GB Barrier and Beyond

By 2001, the 137GB barrier had become a problem because 3 1/2" hard drives were poised to breach that capacity level. The solution came in the form of ATA-6, which was being developed during that year. To enable the addressing of drives of greater capacity, ATA-6 upgraded the LBA functions from using 28-bit numbers to using larger 48-bit numbers.

The ATA-6 specification extends the LBA interface such that it can use 48-bit sector addressing. This means that the maximum capacity is increased to 2^{48} (281,474,976,710,656) total sectors. Because each sector stores 512 bytes, this results in a maximum drive capacity of

```
                       Max. Values
--------------------------------------------
Total Sectors      281,474,976,710,656
--------------------------------------------
Total Bytes    144,115,188,075,855,872
Megabytes  (MB)    144,115,188,076
Mebibytes  (MiB)   137,438,953,472
Gigabytes  (GB)        144,115,188
Gibibytes  (GiB)       134,217,728
Terabytes  (TB)            144,115
Tebibytes  (TiB)           131,072
Petabytes  (PB)             144.12
Pebibytes  (PiB)            128.00
```

As you can see, the 48-bit LBA in ATA-6 allows a capacity of just over 144PB (petabytes = quadrillion bytes)!

Because the EDD BIOS functions use a 64-bit LBA number, they have a much larger limit:

```
                          Max. Values
-----------------------------------------------------
Total Sectors      18,446,744,073,709,551,616
-----------------------------------------------------
Total Bytes    9,444,732,965,739,290,427,392
Megabytes  (MB)    9,444,732,965,739,290
Mebibytes  (MiB)   9,007,199,254,740,992
Gigabytes  (GB)        9,444,732,965,739
Gibibytes  (GiB)       8,796,093,022,208
Terabytes  (TB)            9,444,732,966
Tebibytes  (TiB)           8,589,934,592
Petabytes  (PB)                9,444,733
Pebibytes  (PiB)               8,388,608
Exabytes   (EB)                    9,445
Exbibytes  (EiB)                   8,192
Zettabytes (ZB)                     9.44
Zebibytes  (ZiB)                    8.00
```

Although the BIOS services use 64-bit LBA (allowing up to 2^{64} sectors) for even greater capacity, the 144 peta-byte ATA-6 limitation is the lower of the two that applies. Still, that should hold us for some time to come.

Because hard disk drives have been doubling in capacity every 1.5–2 years (Moore's Law), and considering that 200GB+ ATA drives were available in late 2003, I estimate that it will take us until between the years 2031 and 2041 before we reach the 144PB barrier (assuming hard disk technology hasn't been completely replaced by then). Similarly, I estimate that the 9.44ZB EDD BIOS barrier won't be reached until between the years 2055 and 2073! Phoenix originally claimed that the EDD specification would hold us until 2020, but it seems they were being quite conservative.

The 137GB barrier has proven a bit more complicated than previous barriers because, in addition to BIOS issues, operating system issues must also be considered.

Internal ATA drives larger than 137GB require 48-bit LBA (logical block address) support. This support absolutely needs to be provided in the OS, but it can also be provided in the BIOS. It is best if both OS and BIOS support it, but it can be made to work if only the OS has the support.

To have 48-bit LBA support in the OS requires one of the following:

- Windows XP with Service Pack 1 (SP1) or later.
- Windows 2000 with Service Pack 4 (SP4) or later.
- Windows 98/98SE/Me or NT 4.0 with the Intel Application Accelerator (IAA) loaded. This solution works only if your motherboard has an IAA-supported chipset. See `www.intel.com/support/chipsets/IAA/instruct.htm` for more information.

To have 48-bit LBA support in the BIOS requires either

- A motherboard BIOS with 48-bit LBA support (most of those dated September 2002 or later)
- An ATA host adapter card with onboard BIOS that includes 48-bit LBA support

If your motherboard BIOS does not have the support and an update is not available from your motherboard manufacturer, you can use a card. Cards that offer 48-bit LBA support include the LBA Pro ISA card from eSupport (`www.esupport.com`) and the Maxtor Ultra ATA/133 PCI card (`www.maxtor.com`). The Maxtor card has two additional ATA-133 ports you can use to connect up to four additional drives, whereas the eSupport card has only a BIOS with no ports. In both cases, you could continue to use your existing motherboard ports; the BIOS on the cards would allow 48-bit LBA support for both motherboard-based and card-based ports.

Note that if you have both BIOS and OS support as well, you can simply install and use the drive like any other. If you have no BIOS support, but you do have OS support, portions of the drive past 137GB are not recognized or accessible until the OS is loaded. If you are installing the OS to a blank hard drive and booting from an original XP (pre-SP1) CD or earlier, you need to partition and install up to the first 137GB of the drive at installation time. After installing the OS and then the SP1 update, you can either partition the remainder of the drive using standard partitioning software or use a third-party partitioning program such as PartitionMagic or Partition Commander to resize the first partition to use the full drive. If you are booting from an XP SP1 or later CD, you can recognize and access the entire drive during the OS installation and partition the entire drive as a single partition greater than 137GB, if you want.

Finally, keep in mind that the original version of Windows XP, as well as Windows 2000/NT or Windows 95/98/Me, does not currently provide native support for ATA hard drives that are larger than 137GB. You will therefore need to use XP and ensure you have Service Pack 1 or later installed.

Operating System and Other Software Limitations

Note that if you use older software including utilities, applications, or even operating systems that rely exclusively on CHS parameters, they will see all drives over 8.4GB as 8.4GB only. You will need not only a newer BIOS, but also newer software designed to handle the direct LBA addressing to work with drives over 8.4GB.

Operating system limitations with respect to drives over 8.4GB are shown in Table 7.24.

Table 7.24   Operating System Limitations

Operating System	Limitations for Hard Drive Size
DOS/Windows 3x	DOS 6.22 or lower can't support drives greater than 8.4GB. DOS 7.0 or higher (included with Windows 95 or later) is required to recognize a drive over 8.4GB.
Windows 9x/Me	Windows 95a (original version) does support the INT13h extensions, which means it does support drives over 8.4GB; however, due to limitations of the FAT16 file system, the maximum individual partition size is limited to 2GB. Windows 95B/OSR2 or later (including Windows 98/Me) supports the INT13h extensions, which allows drives over 8.4GB, and also supports FAT32, which allows partition sizes up to the maximum capacity of the drive. However, Windows 95 doesn't support hard drives larger than 32GB because of limitations in its design. Windows 98 requires an update to FDISK to partition drives larger than 64GB.
Windows NT	Windows NT 3.5x does not support drives greater than 8.4GB. Windows NT 4.0 does support drivers greater than 8.4GB; however, when a drive larger than 8.4GB is being used as the primary bootable device, Windows NT will not recognize more than 8.4GB. Microsoft has released Service Pack 4, which corrects this problem.
Windows 2000/XP	Windows 2000/XP supports drives greater than 8.4GB.
OS/2 Warp	Some versions of OS/2 are limited to a boot partition size of 3.1GB or 4.3GB. IBM has a Device Driver Pack upgrade that enables the boot partition to be as large as 8.4GB. The HPFS file system in OS/2 will support drives up to 64GB.
Novell	NetWare 5.0 or later supports drives greater than 8.4GB.

In the case of operating systems that support drives over 8.4GB, the maximum drive size limitations are dependent on the BIOS and hard drive interface standard, not the OS. Instead, other limitations come into play for the volumes (partitions) and files that can be created and managed by the various operating systems. These limitations are dependent on not only the operating system involved, but also the file system that is used for the volume. Table 7.25 shows the minimum and maximum volume (partition) size and file size limitations of the various Windows operating systems. As noted in the previous section, the original version of XP, as well as Windows 2000/NT or Windows 95/98/Me, does not currently provide native support for ATA hard drives that are larger than 137GB. You will need to use XP and ensure you have Service Pack 1 or later installed to use an ATA drive over 137GB. This does not affect drives interfaced via USB, FireWire, SCSI, or other interfaces.

Table 7.25   Operating System Volume/File Size Limitations by File System

OS Limitations by File System	FAT16	FAT32	NTFS
Min. Volume Size (9x/Me)	2.092MB	33.554MB	—
Max. Volume Size (95)	2.147GB	33.554MB	—
Max. Volume Size (98)	2.147GB	136.902GB	—
Max. Volume Size (Me)	2.147GB	8.796TB	—
Min. Volume Size (NT/2000/XP)	2.092MB	33.554MB	1.000MB
Max. Volume Size (NT/2000/XP)	4.294GB	8.796GB	281.475TB
Max. File Size (all)	4.294GB	4.294GB	16.384TB

— = not applicable   GB = gigabyte = 1,000,000,000 bytes
MB = megabyte = 1,000,000 bytes   TB = terabyte = 1,000,000,000,000 bytes

ATA RAID

RAID is an acronym for redundant array of independent (or inexpensive) disks and was designed to improve the fault tolerance and performance of computer storage systems. RAID was first developed at the University of California at Berkeley in 1987, and was designed so that a group of smaller, less expensive drives could be interconnected with special hardware and software to make them appear as a single larger drive to the system. By using multiple drives to act as one drive, increases in fault tolerance and performance could be realized.

Initially, RAID was conceived to simply enable all the individual drives in the array to work together as a single, larger drive with the combined storage space of all the individual drives added up. However, this actually reduced reliability and didn't do much for performance, either. For example, if you had four drives connected in an array acting as one drive, you would be four times as likely to experience a drive failure than if you used just a single larger drive. To improve the reliability and performance, the Berkeley scientists proposed six levels (corresponding to different methods) of RAID. These levels provide varying emphasis on either fault tolerance (reliability), storage capacity, performance, or a combination of the three.

An organization called the RAID Advisory Board (RAB) was formed in July 1992 to standardize, classify, and educate on the subject of RAID. The RAB has developed specifications for RAID, a conformance program for the various RAID levels, and a classification program for RAID hardware.

Currently, seven standard RAID levels are defined by the RAID Advisory Board, called RAID 0–6. RAID typically is implemented by a RAID controller board, although software-only implementations are possible (but not recommended). The levels are as follows:

- *RAID Level 0—Striping.* File data is written simultaneously to multiple drives in the array, which act as a single larger drive. Offers high read/write performance but very low reliability. Requires a minimum of two drives to implement.

- *RAID Level 1—Mirroring.* Data written to one drive is duplicated on another, providing excellent fault tolerance (if one drive fails, the other is used and no data lost), but no real increase in performance as compared to a single drive. Requires a minimum of two drives to implement (same capacity as one drive).

- *RAID Level 2—Bit-level ECC.* Data is split one bit at a time across multiple drives, and error correction codes (ECCs) are written to other drives. Intended for storage devices that do not incorporate ECC internally (all SCSI and ATA drives have internal ECC). Provides high data rates with good fault tolerance, but large numbers of drives are required, and no commercial RAID 2 controllers or drives without ECC, that I am aware of, are available on the market.

- *RAID Level 3—Striped with parity.* Combines RAID Level 0 striping with an additional drive used for parity information. This RAID level is really an adaptation of RAID Level 0 that sacrifices some capacity, for the same number of drives. However, it also achieves a high level of data integrity or fault tolerance because data usually can be rebuilt if one drive fails. Requires a minimum of three drives to implement (two or more for data and one for parity).

- *RAID Level 4—Blocked data with parity.* Similar to RAID 3 except data is written in larger blocks to the independent drives, offering faster read performance with larger files. Requires a minimum of three drives to implement (two or more for data and one for parity).

- *RAID Level 5—Blocked data with distributed parity.* Similar to RAID 4 but offers improved performance by distributing the parity stripes over a series of hard drives. Requires a minimum of three drives to implement (two or more for data and one for parity).

- *RAID Level 6—Blocked data with double distributed parity.* Similar to RAID 5 except parity information is written twice using two different parity schemes to provide even better fault tolerance in case of multiple drive failures. Requires a minimum of four drives to implement (two or more for data and two for parity).

Additional RAID levels exist that are not supported by the RAID Advisory Board but which are instead custom implementations by specific companies. Note that a higher number doesn't necessarily mean increased performance or fault tolerance; the numbered order of the RAID levels was entirely arbitrary.

At one time virtually all RAID controllers were SCSI based, meaning they used SCSI drives. For a professional setup, SCSI RAID is definitely the best choice because it combines the advantages of RAID with the advantages of SCSI—an interface that already was designed to support multiple drives. Now, however, ATA RAID controllers are available that allow for even less expensive RAID implementations. These ATA RAID controllers typically are used in single-user systems for performance rather than reliability increases.

Most ATA RAID implementations are much simpler than the professional SCSI RAID adapters used on network file servers. ATA RAID is designed more for the individual who is seeking performance or simple drive mirroring for redundancy. When set up for performance, ATA RAID adapters run RAID Level 0, which incorporates data striping. Unfortunately, RAID 0 also sacrifices reliability such that if one drive fails, all data is lost. With RAID 0, performance scales up with the number of drives you add in the array. If you use four drives, you won't necessarily have four times the performance of a single drive, but it can be close to that for sustained transfers. Some overhead is still involved in the controller performing the striping and issues still exist with latency—that is, how long it takes to find the data—but performance will be higher than any single drive can normally achieve.

When set up for reliability, ATA RAID adapters generally run RAID Level 1, which is simple drive mirroring. All data written to one drive is written to the other. If one drive fails, the system can continue to work on the other drive. Unfortunately, this does not increase performance at all, and it also means you get to use only half of the available drive capacity. In other words, you must install two drives, but you get to use only one (the other is the mirror). However, in an era of high capacities and low drive prices, this is not a significant issue. If you want to eliminate a lot of bulky cabling, consider Serial ATA RAID, which uses the narrow Serial ATA cables shown earlier in this chapter.

Combining performance with fault tolerance requires using one of the other RAID levels, such as 3 or 5. For example, virtually all professional RAID controllers used in network file servers are designed to use RAID Level 5. Controllers that implement RAID Level 5 are more expensive, and at least three drives must be connected. To improve reliability, but at a lower cost, many of the ATA RAID controllers enable combinations of the RAID levels—such as 0 and 1 combined. This usually requires four drives, two of which are striped together in a RAID Level 0 arrangement, which is then redundantly written to a second set of two drives in a RAID Level 1 arrangement. This enables you to have approximately double the performance of a single drive, and you have a backup set should one of the primary sets fail.

Today, you can get parallel or Serial ATA RAID controllers from companies such as Arco Computer Products, Iwill, Promise Technology, HighPoint, and more. A typical low-cost ATA RAID controller enables up to four drives to be attached, and you can run them in RAID Level 0, 1, or 0+1 mode. Remember that performance suffers somewhat when running two drives (master/slave) on a single parallel ATA channel because only one drive can transfer on the cable at a time, which cuts performance in half. Four-channel parallel ATA RAID cards are available, but most new RAID cards are moving to Serial ATA, which doesn't have the master/slave channel sharing problems of parallel ATA. Serial ATA RAID cards use a separate Serial ATA data channel (cable) for each drive, allowing maximum performance. I recommend Serial ATA RAID cards for best performance.

If you are looking for an ATA RAID controller (or a motherboard with an integrated ATA RAID controller), things to look for include

- RAID levels supported (most support 0, 1, and 0+1 combined, although some ATA RAID 5 card products are now available)
- Two or four channels (I recommend four channels for best performance with four devices using parallel ATA)

- Support for ATA/100 or ATA/133 speeds for parallel ATA
- Support for 33MHz or 66MHz PCI slots (some servers have 66MHz slots)
- Serial ATA RAID implementations for maximum performance, ease of installation, and reliability

If you want to experiment with RAID inexpensively, you can implement RAID without a custom controller when using certain higher-end (often server-based) operating systems. For example, Windows NT/2000 and XP or Server 2003 operating systems provide a software implementation for RAID using both striping and mirroring. In these operating systems, the Disk Administrator tool is used to set up and control the RAID functions, as well as to reconstruct the volume when a failure has occurred. Normally, though, if you are building a server in which the ultimate in performance and reliability is desired, you should look for Serial ATA or SCSI RAID controllers that support RAID Level 3 or 5.

CHAPTER 8

The SCSI Interface

Small Computer System Interface

SCSI (pronounced "scuzzy") stands for Small Computer System Interface and is a general-purpose interface used for connecting many types of devices to a PC. This interface has its roots in SASI, the Shugart Associates System Interface. SCSI is a popular interface for attaching high-speed disk drives to higher-performance PCs, such as workstations or especially to high-end network servers. SCSI is also very flexible; it is not just a disk interface, but is a systems-level interface allowing many types of devices to be connected, including scanners and printers. SCSI is a bus that supports as many as 7 or 15 total devices. Multichannel adapters exist that can support up to 7 or 15 devices per channel.

The SCSI card, called the *host adapter*, functions as the gateway between the SCSI bus and the PC system bus. Each device on the bus has a SCSI controller chip built in. The SCSI host adapter does not talk directly with actual devices such as hard disks; instead, it talks to the SCSI interface controller that is built into the drive.

A single SCSI bus can support as many as 8 or 16 physical units, usually called SCSI *IDs*. One of these units is the SCSI host adapter card in your PC; the other 7 or 15 can be other peripherals. You could have hard disks, tape drives, CD-ROM drives, a graphics scanner, or other devices attached to a single SCSI host adapter. Most systems can support up to four host adapters, each with up to 15 devices, for a total of 60 devices! There are even dual-channel adapters that could double that figure.

SCSI is a fast interface, generally suited to high-performance workstations, servers, or anywhere the ultimate in performance for a storage system interface is needed. The latest Ultra5 (Ultra640) SCSI version supports transfer speeds of up to 640MB per second (MBps)! By comparison, parallel ATA (also known as IDE) transfers at speeds up to 133MBps, and Serial ATA transfers at 150MBps. Note that these figures are raw interface transfer speeds; the speeds of individual devices are normally much lower. The higher speeds of the SCSI bus are utilized when multiple devices share the bus, in which case they can overlap reads and writes and more fully utilize the higher bandwidth available. The slower ATA buses allow only one or two devices, making higher throughputs unnecessary because they would be unusable.

When you purchase a SCSI device such as a SCSI hard disk, you usually are purchasing the device, device controller, and SCSI interface controller in one circuit; as such the device is ready to connect directly to the SCSI bus. This type of drive usually is called an *embedded* SCSI device—the SCSI interface is built in. For example, most SCSI hard drives are technically the same or similar as compared to their ATA counterparts except for the addition of the SCSI interface controller circuits (normally a single chip) added to the logic board. Your system cannot talk directly to the device controller as though it were plugged into the system bus, like on a standard ATA drive. Instead, communications go through the SCSI host adapter installed in the system bus, then to the SCSI interface controller on the drive logic board, and finally to the device controller (also on the logic board) and disk drive. You can access the drive only through the SCSI protocols.

Apple originally rallied around SCSI as being an inexpensive way out of the bind in which it put itself with the Macintosh. When the engineers at Apple realized their mistake in making the Macintosh a closed system (no expansion slots!), they decided that the easiest way to gain expandability was to build a SCSI port into the system, which is how external peripherals were originally added to the slotless Macs. Of course, in keeping with Apple tradition of proprietary designs, they used a nonstandard SCSI connector. Now that Apple is designing systems with expansion slots, Universal Serial Bus (USB), and FireWire (also known as iLink or IEEE 1394), the nonstandard Apple SCSI interface has been dropped from most Macs as a built-in option. Because PC systems have always been expandable, the push toward SCSI was not as urgent. With up to eight or more bus slots supporting various devices in PC-compatible systems, it seemed as though SCSI was not as necessary for system expansion. In fact, with modern PCs sporting inexpensive built-in USB and FireWire ports for external expansion, in most cases SCSI devices are necessary only when top performance or reliability (using hot-swappable drive arrays) is a critical issue. However, USB 2.0 as well as IEEE 1394a/b (FireWire) offer performance comparable to many of the lower-speed versions of SCSI and should be considered as an alternative for devices such as external hard drives and scanners. In fact, for most anything except server-oriented drive arrays, you should probably choose one of the other interfaces over SCSI.

SCSI originally became popular in the PC-based workstation and server market because of the performance and expandability it offers. One block that stalled acceptance of SCSI in the early PC marketplace was the lack of a complete standard; the SCSI standard originally was designed by one company and then turned into a committee-controlled public standard where it eventually became comprehensive and complete. Since then, no single manufacturer has controlled it.

Note

Most SCSI host adapters bundled with hardware, such as graphics scanners or SCSI CD-RW drives, do not include all the features necessary to support multiple SCSI devices or bootable SCSI hard drives. This has nothing to do with any limitations in the SCSI specification. The situation is simply that the manufacturer has included the most stripped-down version of a SCSI host adapter available to save money. It has all the functionality necessary to support the device it came with, but usually lacks the onboard ROM BIOS chip with drivers necessary for booting SCSI drives. Fortunately, with the right adapter and drivers, one SCSI card could support all the SCSI devices in a system from hard drives to optical drives, scanners, tape drives, and more.

In the beginning, SCSI adapters lacked the capability to boot from hard disks on the SCSI bus. Booting from these drives and using a variety of operating systems was a problem that resulted from the lack of a software interface standard. The standard BIOS software in PC systems is designed to talk to ST-506/412, ESDI, or ATA hard disks and devices. SCSI is so different from ATA that a new set of ROM BIOS routines is necessary to support the system so it can self-boot. Also, this BIOS support is unique to the SCSI host adapter you are using; so, unless the host adapter is built in to your motherboard, this support won't be found in your motherboard BIOS. Instead, SCSI host adapters are available with BIOS support for SCSI hard disk drives right on the SCSI host adapter itself.

Note

For more information about the ancient ST-506/412 and ESDI Interfaces, see "ST-506/412 Interface" and "ESDI Interface," respectively, in the Technical Reference section of the disc accompanying this book. Although PCs have not used these interfaces since the early '90s, several current interfaces evolved from them, so I include the information for historical reasons.

Because of the lead taken by Apple in developing systems software (operating systems and ROM) support for SCSI, peripherals connect to Apple systems in fairly standard ways. Until recently, this type of standard-setting leadership was lacking for SCSI in the PC world. This situation changed dramatically with Windows 95 and later versions, which include drivers for most popular SCSI adapters and peripherals on the market. These days, Windows 98/Me, Windows NT/2000/XP includes even more drivers and support for SCSI adapters and devices built in.

Many system manufacturers have standardized SCSI for high-end workstation or server systems. In these systems, a SCSI host adapter card is placed in one of the slots, or the system has a SCSI host adapter built in to the motherboard. This arrangement is similar in appearance to the ATA interface because a single cable runs from the motherboard to the SCSI drive. SCSI supports as many as 7 or 15 additional devices per bus (some of which might not be hard disks), whereas ATA supports only 4 devices (2 per host adapter). Additionally, SCSI supports more types of devices other than hard disks than ATA supports. ATA devices must be a hard disk, an ATA-type CD-ROM drive, a tape drive, an LS-120 or LS-240 SuperDisk drive, a Zip drive, and so on. Systems with SCSI drives are easy to upgrade because virtually any third-party SCSI drive will plug in and function.

SCSI Versus ATA

When you compare the performance and capabilities of ATA (AT attachment, sometimes also known as IDE for integrated drive electronics) interface and SCSI interface drives, you must consider several factors. These two types of drives are the most popular drives used in PC systems today, and a single manufacturer might make seemingly identical drives in both interfaces. Deciding which drive type is best for your system is a difficult decision that depends on many factors.

In most cases, you will find that an ATA drive using the same head-disk assembly as a SCSI drive from the same manufacturer performs about the same or outperforms the equivalent SCSI drive at a given task or benchmark. This is particularly true when using a single disk drive with a single-user operating system, such as Windows 9x/Me. More powerful operating systems, such as Windows NT, Windows 2000, or Windows XP, can more effectively use the command queuing and other features of SCSI, thus improving performance over ATA—especially when supporting multiple drives.

It is interesting to see that SCSI really evolved from ATA, or you could say that both evolved from the ST-506/412 and ESDI interfaces that were once used.

◀◀ See "Precursors to IDE," p. 532.

SCSI Hard Disk Evolution and Construction

SCSI is not a disk interface, but a bus that supports SCSI bus interface controllers connected to disk and other device controllers. The first SCSI drives for PCs were standard ST-506/412 or ESDI drives with a separate SCSI bus interface controller card (sometimes called a *bridge controller*) that converted the ST-506/412 or ESDI interfaces to SCSI. This interface originally was in the form of a secondary logic board, and the entire assembly often was mounted in an external case.

The next step was to build the SCSI bus interface controller directly into the drive's own logic board. Today, we call these drives *embedded* SCSI drives because the SCSI interface is built in.

At that point, there was no need to conform to the absolute specifications of ST-506/412 or ESDI on the internal disk interface because the only other device the interface ever would have to talk to was built in as well. Thus, the disk controller chipset manufacturers began to develop more customized chipsets that were based on the ST-506/412 or ESDI chipsets already available but offered more features and higher performance.

Today, if you look at a typical SCSI drive logic board, you often can identify the chip that serves as the disk controller on the board as being the same kind that would be used on an ATA drive.

Consider some examples. An ATA drive must fully emulate the system-level disk-controller interface introduced with the Western Digital WD1003 controller series IBM used in the original 1984 AT system. Most of these built-in controllers have more capabilities than the original WD1003 series (usually in the form of additional commands), but they must at least respond to all the original commands that were used with the WD1003.

In some cases a manufacturer makes ATA and SCSI drives with the same capacity and specifications, which use the same head disk assembly (HDA). If you study these virtually identical drives, the only major difference you will find is an additional chip on the logic board of the SCSI version, called a SCSI Bus Adapter Chip (SBAC) or SCSI controller chip.

Figures 8.1 and 8.2 show the logic-block diagrams of an ATA and a SCSI drive from the same manufacturer. These drives use the same HDA; they differ only in their logic boards, and even the logic boards are the same except for the addition of an SBIC on the SCSI drive's logic board.

Notice that even the circuit designs of these two drives are almost identical. Both drives use an LSI (large scale integrated circuit) chip called the WD42C22 Disk Controller and Buffer Manager chip. In the ATA drive, this chip is connected through a DMA control chip directly to the AT bus. In the SCSI version, a WD33C93 SCSI bus interface controller chip is added to interface the disk-controller logic to the SCSI bus. In fact, the logic diagrams of these two drives differ only in the fact that the SCSI version has a complete subset of the ATA drive, with the SCSI bus interface controller logic added. This essentially is a very condensed version of the separate drive and bridge controller setups that were used in the early days of PC SCSI.

◀◀ See "Parallel ATA DMA Transfer Modes," p. 552.

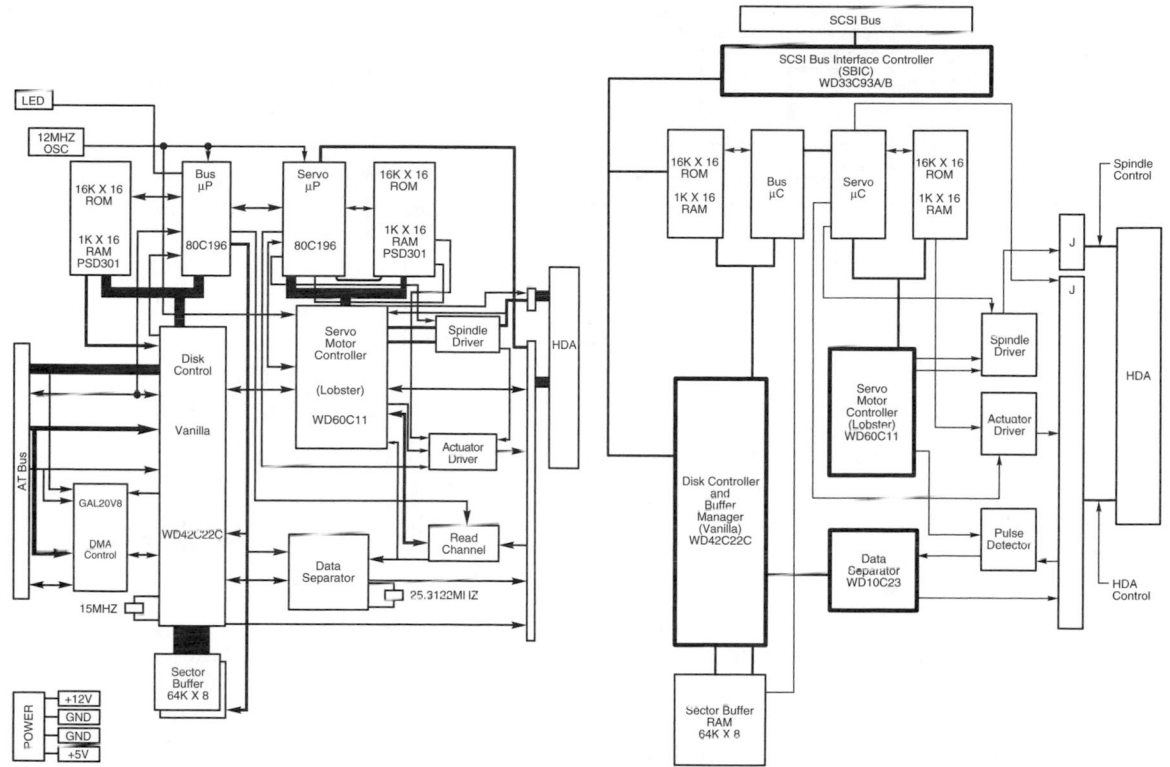

Figure 8.1 Typical ATA (also called IDE) drive logic board block diagram.

Figure 8.2 Typical SCSI drive logic board block diagram.

To top off this example, study the logic diagram in Figure 8.3 for the WD 1006V-MM1, which is an old ST-506/412 controller used in early AT-compatible computers.

You can clearly see that the main LSI chip onboard is the same WD42C22 disk controller chip used in the ATA and SCSI drives. Here is what the technical reference literature says about that chip:

> *The WD42C22 integrates a high-performance, low-cost Winchester controller's architecture. The WD42C22 integrates the central elements of a Winchester controller subsystem such as the host interface, buffer manager, disk formatter/controller, encoder/decoder, CRC/ECC (Cyclic Redundancy Check/Error Correction Code) generator/checker, and drive interface into a single 84-pin PQFP (Plastic Quad Flat Pack) device.*

You can now see that many SCSI drives are "regular" ATA drives with a SCSI bus interface controller chip added to the logic board. This fact will come up again later in this chapter in the section "SCSI Versus ATA Performance: Advantages and Limitations," which discusses performance and other issues differentiating these interfaces.

For another example, I have several old IBM 320MB and 400MB embedded SCSI-2 hard disks; each of these drives has onboard a WD-10C00 Programmable Disk Controller in the form of a 68-pin Plastic Leaded Chip Carrier (PLCC) chip. The technical literature states

> *This chip supports ST412, ESDI, SMD, and Optical interfaces. It has 27Mbps maximum transfer rate and an internal, fully programmable 48- or 32-bit ECC, 16-bit CRC-CCITT or external user-defined ECC polynomial, fully programmable sector sizes, and 1.25 micron low power CMOS design.*

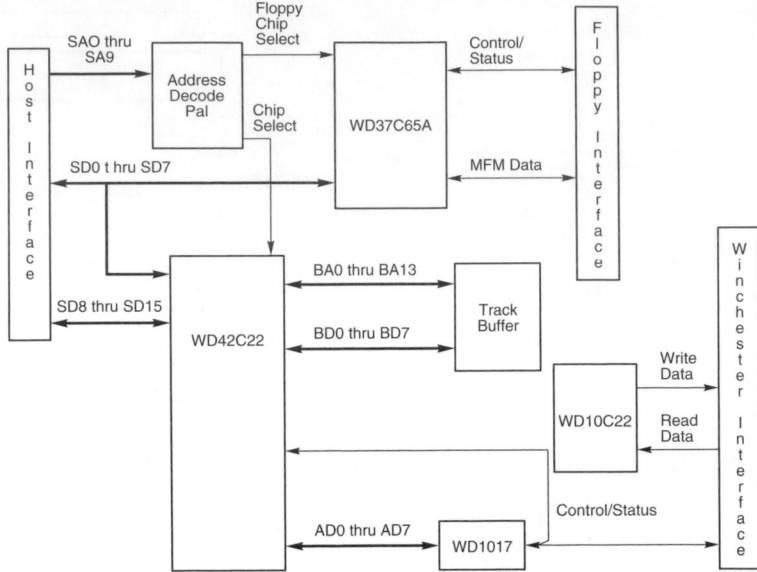

Figure 8.3   Western Digital WD1006V-MM1 ST-506/412 Disk Controller block diagram.

In addition, these particular embedded SCSI drives include the 33C93 SCSI Bus Interface Controller chip, which also is used in the other SCSI drive that I mentioned. Again, there is a distinctly separate disk controller, and the SCSI interface controller is added on top of that.

So again, most embedded SCSI drives have a built-in disk controller (usually based on previous ST-506/412 or ESDI designs) and additional logic to interface that controller to the SCSI bus (a built-in bridge controller, if you like). Now think about this from a performance standpoint. If SCSI drives really are ATA drives with a SCSI Bus Interface Controller chip added, what conclusions can you draw?

First, no drive can perform sustained data transfers faster than the data can actually be read from the disk platters. In other words, the HDA limits performance to whatever it is capable of achieving. Drives can transmit data in short bursts at very high speeds because they often have built-in cache or read-ahead buffers that store data. Many of the newer high-performance SCSI and ATA drives have 8MB or more of cache memory onboard. No matter how big or intelligent the cache is, however, sustained data transfer is still limited by the HDA.

◄◄   See "ATA Standards," p. 536.

Data from the HDA must pass through the disk controller circuits, which, as you have seen, are virtually identical between similar SCSI and ATA drives. In the ATA drive, this data then is presented directly to the system bus. In the SCSI drive, however, the data must pass through a SCSI bus interface controller chip on the drive, travel through the SCSI bus, and then pass through another SCSI bus interface controller chip in the SCSI host adapter card in your system. The longer route a SCSI transfer must take makes this type of transfer slower than the much more direct ATA transfer, when communicating with a single device.

The conventional wisdom has been that SCSI always is much faster than ATA; unfortunately, this wisdom is usually wrong. One cannot compare ATA and SCSI by merely looking at the raw ATA and SCSI bus performance capabilities. An Ultra4 SCSI drive can transfer data at an interface transfer rate of 320MBps, whereas an UltraATA/133 drive can transfer data at an interface transfer rate of 133MBps. Based on these raw transfer rates, SCSI seems to be much faster, but the raw transfer rate of the interface is not the limiting factor. As discussed previously, the actual HDA and disk-controller circuitry place limits on this performance of each drive. The key figure to check is what is reported as the internal or media transfer rate for the drive itself. For example, here are the specs on two similar drives (one ATA and one SCSI):

ATA Drive

Drive	Maxtor DiamondMax+ 60 ATA
Interface	UltraATA/100
Platters	3
Data heads	6
Capacity	60GB
Areal density (max)	15.4Gb/sq. in.
Rotational speed	7,200rpm
Internal cache buffer	2MB
Interface transfer rate	Up to 100MBps
Media transfer rate	Up to 57MBps
Sustained data transfer rate	28.5MBps–57MBps
Average sustained transfer rate	42.75MBps

SCSI Drive

Drive	IBM Ultrastar 73LZX SCSI
Interface	Ultra4 (Ultra320) SCSI
Platters	6
Data heads	12
Capacity	73.4GB
Areal density (max)	13.2Gb/sq. in.
Rotational speed	10,000rpm
Internal cache buffer	4MB
Interface transfer rate	Up to 320MBps
Media transfer rate	Up to 58MBps
Sustained data transfer rate	29.8MBps–58MBps
Average sustained transfer rate	43.9MBps

Note that although the SCSI drive can claim a much higher external transfer rate of 320MBps as compared to the ATA drive's 100MBps, in actuality these drives are almost identical performers. The real specs to look at are in the last two lines of the tables, which detail how fast data can actually be read from the drive. In particular, the sustained transfer rates are the true transfer rates for reading data from these drives; as you can see, they are very close indeed. The rotational speed, track density, and things such as internal buffers or caches mainly influence the true transfer rate of a drive.

Then you have to factor in that the SCSI drive would cost 50%–100% more than the ATA counterpart. Not to mention the cost of springing for an Ultra4 SCSI host adapter to plug the drive into. Decent SCSI adapters, especially Ultra-SCSI versions, can easily cost $300 or more, which is 2 or 3 times the cost of most desktop PC motherboards. When you consider that UltraATA and/or Serial ATA interfaces are built in to modern motherboards for free, you can see that, depending on your needs, spending a ton of extra cash for SCSI can be a significant waste of money.

Now to present the counterpoint: Although these two drives are basically equivalent, the ATA version was one of the top ATA drives offered at the time, whereas the SCSI drive listed was only a middle-of-the-pack performer. Hitachi and others make SCSI drives that have rotational speeds of 15,000rpm; increased track density; and larger buffers. Of course, these drives cost even more. So, the bottom line is that if you must have the absolute best-performing drives, by all means get the top-of-the-line SCSI drives and Ultra SCSI Wide adapters. However, if you want something that is literally one third or one fourth the cost and three-fourths or more the performance, stick with ATA.

ANSI SCSI Standards

The SCSI standard defines the physical and electrical parameters of a parallel I/O bus used to connect computers and peripheral devices in daisy-chain fashion. The standard supports devices such as disk drives, tape drives, and CD-ROM drives. The original SCSI standard (ANSI X3.131-1986) was approved in 1986, SCSI-2 was approved in January 1994, and the first portions of SCSI-3 were approved in 1995. Note that SCSI-3 has evolved into an enormous standard with numerous sections and is an evolving, growing standard still very much under development. Because it has been broken down into multiple standards, there really is no single SCSI-3 standard.

The SCSI interface is defined as a standard by ANSI (the American National Standards Institute), specifically by a committee currently known as T10. T10 is a technical committee of the InterNational Committee on Information Technology Standards (INCITS, pronounced "insights"). INCITS is accredited by ANSI and operates under rules approved by ANSI. These rules are designed to ensure that voluntary standards are developed by the consensus of industry groups. INCITS develops information-processing system standards, whereas ANSI approves the processes under which they are developed and publishes them. Working draft copies of all SCSI-related standards can be downloaded from the T10 Technical Committee site (www.t10.org).

One problem with the original SCSI-1 document was that many of the commands and features were optional, and there was little or no guarantee that a particular peripheral would support the expected commands. This problem caused the industry as a whole to define a set of 18 basic SCSI commands called the Common Command Set (CCS) to become the minimum set of commands supported by all peripherals. SCSI-1 plus the CCS became the basis for the SCSI-2 specification.

Along with formal support for CCS, SCSI-2 provided additional definitions for commands to access CD-ROM drives (and their sound capabilities), tape drives, removable drives, optical drives, and several other peripherals. In addition, an optional higher-speed version called Fast SCSI-2 and a 16-bit version called Wide SCSI-2 were defined. Another feature of SCSI-2 is *command queuing*, which enables a device to accept multiple commands and execute them in the order that the device deems to be most efficient. This feature is most beneficial when you are using a multitasking operating system that could be sending several requests on the SCSI bus at the same time.

The X3T9 group approved the SCSI-2 standard as X3.131-1990 in August 1990, but the document was recalled in December 1990 for changes before final ANSI publication. Final approval for the SCSI-2 document was made in January 1994, although it changed little from the original 1990 release. The SCSI-2 document is now called ANSI X3.131-1994. The official document is available from Global Engineering Documents and the ANSI committee—both are listed in the Vendor List on the disc packaged with this book. You can also download the final working drafts of these documents from the T10 Technical Committee home page, as listed previously.

Most companies indicate that their host adapters follow both the ANSI X3.131-1986 (SCSI-1) and the X3.131-1994 (SCSI-2) standards. Note that because virtually all parts of SCSI-1 are supported in SCSI-2, most SCSI-1 devices are also considered SCSI-2 by default. Many manufacturers advertise that their devices are SCSI-2, but this does not mean they support any of the additional optional features that were incorporated in the SCSI-2 revision.

For example, an optional part of the SCSI-2 specification includes a fast synchronous mode that doubles the standard synchronous transfer rate from 5MBps to 10MBps. This Fast SCSI transfer mode can be combined with 16-bit Wide SCSI for transfer rates of up to 20MBps. An optional 32-bit version was defined in SCSI-2, but component manufacturers have shunned this as too expensive. In essence, 32-bit SCSI was a stillborn specification, as it was withdrawn from the SCSI-3 standard. Most SCSI implementations are 8-bit standard SCSI or 16-bit Fast/Wide SCSI. Even devices that support none of the Fast or Wide modes can still be considered SCSI-2.

SCSI-3 is broken down into a number of standards. The SCSI Parallel Interface (SPI) standard controls the parallel interconnection between SCSI devices, which is mostly what we are talking about here. So far, five versions of SPI have been created, including SPI, SPI-2, SPI-3, SPI-4, and SPI-5.

What can be confusing is that several terms can be used to describe the newer SPI standards, as shown in Table 8.1.

Table 8.1   SPI (SCSI Parallel Interface) Standards

SCSI-3 Standard	Also Known As	Speed	Throughput
SPI	Ultra SCSI	Fast-20	20/40MBps
SPI-2	Ultra2 SCSI	Fast-40	40/80MBps
SPI-3	Ultra3 SCSI or Ultra160(+)	Fast-80DT	160MBps
SPI-4	Ultra4 SCSI or Ultra320	Fast-160DT	320MBps
SPI-5	Ultra5 SCSI or Ultra640	Fast-320DT	640MBps

To add to the confusion, SPI-3 or Ultra3 SCSI is also called Ultra160 or Ultra160+, SPI-4 or Ultra4 SCSI is also called Ultra320, and SPI-5 or Ultra5 SCSI is also called Ultra640. The Ultra160 designation refers to any device that includes the first three of the five main features from the Ultra3 SCSI specification. Ultra160+ refers to any device that supports all five main features of Ultra3 SCSI. Ultra320 and Ultra640 includes all the features of Ultra160+, as well as several additional features.

Table 8.2 shows the maximum transfer rates for the SCSI bus at various speeds and widths and the cable type required for the specific transfer widths.

Note

The A cable listed in Table 8.2 is the standard 50-pin SCSI cable, whereas the P cable is a 68-pin cable designed for 16-bit transfers. High Voltage Differential (HVD) signaling was never popular and is now considered obsolete. Low Voltage Differential (LVD) signaling is used in the Ultra2 and Ultra3 modes to increase performance and cabling lengths. Pinouts for the cable connections are listed in this chapter in Tables 8.3–8.6, and you can see the connectors in Figures 8.8–8.10.

SCSI is both forward and backward compatible, meaning one can run faster devices on buses with slower host adapters or vice versa. In each case, the entire bus runs at the lowest common-denominator speed. Thus, although you can mix and match different speeds of devices on the same bus, you should place fast devices on a separate SCSI adapter (or connector, if you use dual-bus adapters) from slower devices. In fact, as was stated earlier, virtually any SCSI-1 device can also legitimately be called SCSI-2 (or even SCSI-3) because most of the improvements in the later versions are optional. Of course, you can't take advantage of the faster modes on an older, slower host adapter. By the same token, you can purchase an Ultra3-capable SCSI host adapter and still run older standard SCSI devices. You can even mix standard 8-bit and wide 16-bit devices on the same bus using cable adapters.

SCSI-1

SCSI-1 was the first implementation of SCSI and was officially known as ANSI X3.131-1986. The major features of SCSI-1 were as follows:

- 8-bit parallel bus
- 5MHz asynchronous or synchronous operation
- 4MBps (asynchronous) or 5MBps (synchronous) throughput
- 50-pin cables with low-density pin-header internal and Centronics-style external connectors

- Single-ended (SE) unbalanced transmission
- Passive termination
- Optional bus parity

SCSI-1 is now considered obsolete; in fact, the standard has been withdrawn by ANSI and replaced by SCSI-2.

SCSI-2

SCSI-2 is officially known as ANSI X3.131-1994. The SCSI-2 specification is essentially an improved version of SCSI-1 with some parts of the specification tightened and several new features and options added. Normally, SCSI-1 and SCSI-2 devices are compatible, but SCSI-1 devices ignore the additional features in SCSI-2.

Some of the changes in SCSI-2 are very minor. For example, SCSI-1 allowed SCSI bus parity to be optional, whereas parity must be implemented in SCSI-2. Parity is an extra bit that is sent as a verification bit to ensure that the data is not corrupted. Another requirement is that initiator devices, such as host adapters, provide terminator power to the interface; most devices already did so, though.

Table 8.2   SCSI Types, Data-Transfer Rates, and Cables

SCSI Standard	SCSI Technology	Marketing Term	Clock Speed (MHz)	Transfer Width	ST/DT
SCSI-1	Async	Asynchronous	5	8-bit	ST
SCSI-1	Fast-5	Synchronous	5	8-bit	ST
SCSI-2	Fast-5/Wide	Wide	5	16-bit	ST
SCSI-2	Fast-10	Fast	10	8-bit	ST
SCSI-2	Fast-10/Wide	Fast/Wide	10	16-bit	ST
SCSI-3/SPI	Fast-20	Ultra	20	8-bit	ST
SCSI-3/SPI	Fast-20/Wide	Ultra/Wide	20	16-bit	ST
SCSI-3/SPI-2	Fast-40	Ultra2	40	8-bit	ST
SCSI-3/SPI-2	Fast-40/Wide	Ultra2/Wide	40	16-bit	ST
SCSI-3/SPI-3	Fast-80DT	Ultra3 (Ultra160)	40^5	16-bit	DT
SCSI-3/SPI-4	Fast-160DT	Ultra4 (Ultra320)	80^5	16-bit	DT
SCSI-3/SPI-5	Fast-320DT	Ultra5 (Ultra640)	160^5	16-bit	DT

Cable lengths are in meters: 25M = 80ft., 12M = 40ft., 6M = 20ft., 3M = 10ft., 1.5M = 5ft.
SE = Single-ended signaling.
HVD = High Voltage Differential signaling; obsolete.
LVD = Low Voltage Differential signaling.
SPI = SCSI Parallel Interface; part of SCSI-3.
ST = Single transition, or one transfer per clock cycle.
DT = Double transition, or two transfers per clock cycle; 16-bit only.

SCSI-2 also added several optional features:

- Fast SCSI (10MHz)
- Wide SCSI (16-bit transfers)
- Command queuing
- New commands
- High-density, 50-pin cable connectors

- Active (Alternative 2) termination for improved single-ended (SE) transmission
- High Voltage Differential transmission (incompatible with SE on the same bus) for longer bus lengths

Wide SCSI enables parallel data transfers at a bus width of 16 bits. The wider connection requires a new cable design. The standard 50-conductor, 8-bit cable is called the A cable. SCSI-2 originally defined a special 68-conductor B cable that was supposed to be used in conjunction with the A cable for 32-bit wide transfers. However, because of a lack of industry support and the added expenses involved, 32-bit SCSI was never actually implemented and was finally removed as part of the SCSI-3 specifications. Therefore, two different types of SCSI cables are now available, called the A cable and the P cable. A cables are any SCSI cables with 50-pin connectors, whereas P cables are any SCSI cables with 68-pin connectors. You need a P cable if you are connecting a Wide SCSI device and want it to work in 16-bit mode. The P cable was not officially included in the standard until SCSI-3.

Fast SCSI refers to high-speed synchronous transfer capability. Fast SCSI achieves a 10MBps transfer rate on the standard 8-bit SCSI cabling. When combined with a 16-bit Wide SCSI interface, this configuration results in data-transfer rates of 20MBps (called Fast/Wide).

The high-density connectors enable smaller, more efficient connector and cable designs.

Transfer Speed (MB/s)	Max. No. of Devices[1]	Cable Type	Max. Length (SE)	Max. Length (HVD)	Max. Length (LVD)
4	7	A (50-pin)	6M	25M	-
5	7	A (50-pin)	6M	25M	-
10	15	P (68-pin)	6M	25M	-
10	7	A (50-pin)	3M	25M	-
20	15	P (68-pin)	3M	25M	-
20	7	A (50-pin)	3/1.5M[2]	25M	-
40	7	P (68-pin)	3/1.5M[2]	25M	-
40	7	A (50-pin)	-	-	12M[3]
80	15	P (68-pin)	-	-	12M[3]
160	15	P (68-pin)	-	-	12M[3]
320	15	P (68-pin)	-	-	12M[3]
640	15	P (68-pin)	-	-	10M[4]

1 = Not including the host adapter.

2 = Ultra SCSI cable total length is restricted to 1.5M if more than three devices exist on the bus (not including the host adapter). A maximum of seven devices is allowed.

3 = A 25M cable can be used if only one device exists (point-to-point interconnect).

4 = For Ultra5 (Ultra640) only, cable length is restricted to 2M using ribbon cable, and a 20M cable can be used if only one device exists (point-to-point interconnect).

5 = Ultra3 (Ultra160), Ultra4 (Ultra320), and Ultra5 (Ultra640) SCSI transfer twice per clock cycle and are 16-bit only.

In SCSI-1, an initiator device, such as a host adapter, was limited to sending one command per device. In SCSI-2, the host adapter can send as many as 256 commands to a single device, which will store and process those commands internally before responding on the SCSI bus. The target device can even resequence the commands to enable the most efficient execution or performance possible. This is especially useful in multitasking environments, such as OS/2 and Windows NT, which can take advantage of this feature.

SCSI-2 took the Common Command Set that was being used throughout the industry and made it an official part of the standard. The CCS was designed mainly for disk drives and did not include specific commands designed for other types of devices. In SCSI-2, many of the old commands are reworked, and several new commands have been added. New command sets have been added for CD-ROMs, optical drives, scanners, communications devices, and media changers (jukeboxes).

The single-ended SCSI bus depends on very tight termination tolerances to function reliably. Unfortunately, the original 132-ohm passive termination defined in the SCSI-1 document was not designed for use at the higher synchronous speeds now possible. These passive terminators, which are sometimes built in to SCSI devices, can cause signal reflections to generate errors when transfer rates increase or when more devices are added to the bus. SCSI-2 defines an active (voltage-regulated) terminator that lowers termination impedance to 110 ohms and improves system integrity. Note that LVD SCSI requires special LVD terminators. If you use SE terminators on a bus with LVD devices, they either won't work or, if they are multimode devices, will default to SE operation.

These features are not required; they are optional under the SCSI-2 specification. If you connect a standard SCSI host adapter to a Fast SCSI drive, for example, the interface will work, but only at standard SCSI speeds.

SCSI-3

SCSI-3 is a term used to describe a set of standards currently being developed. Simply put, it is the next generation of documents a product conforms to. Unlike SCSI-1 and SCSI-2, SCSI-3 is not one document that covers all the layers and interfaces of SCSI, but is instead a collection of documents that covers the primary commands, specific command sets, and electrical interfaces and protocols. The command sets include hard disk interface commands, commands for tape drives, commands for redundant array of inexpensive drives (RAID), and other commands. Additionally, an overall SCSI Architectural Model (SAM) exists for the physical and electrical interfaces, as does a SCSI Parallel Interface (SPI) standard that controls the form of SCSI most commonly used. Each document within the standard is now a separate publication with its own revision level—for example, within SCSI-3, five versions of the SCSI Parallel Interface have been published. Usually, we don't refer to SCSI-3 anymore as a specific interface and instead refer to the specific subsets of SCSI-3, such as SPI-3 (Ultra3 SCSI).

The main additions to SCSI-3 include

- Ultra2 (Fast-40) SCSI
- Ultra3 (Fast-80DT) SCSI
- Ultra4 (Fast-160DT) SCSI

- Ultra5 (Fast-320DT) SCSI
- New Low Voltage Differential signaling
- Elimination of High Voltage Differential signaling

Breaking SCSI-3 into many smaller individual standards has enabled the standard as a whole to develop more quickly. The individual standards can now be published more quickly rather than waiting for an entire large standard to be approved.

Figure 8.4 shows the main parts of SCSI today.

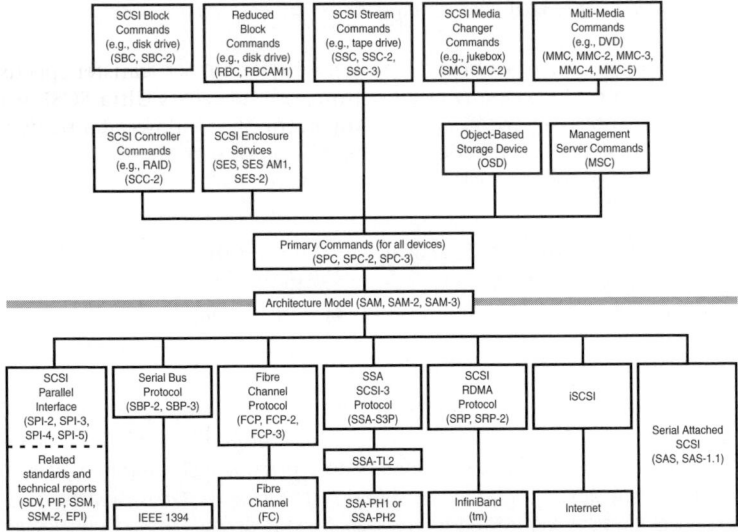

Figure 8.4   SCSI architecture.

The most recent changes or additions to SCSI include the Ultra320 (Ultra4) and Ultra640 (Ultra5) SCSI standards, which have taken the performance of SCSI up to 320MBps or 640MBps. Ultra2 SCSI and beyond also include the LVD (low-voltage differential) electrical interface standard, which enables greater cable lengths. The older high-voltage differential signaling has also been removed from the standard.

A number of people are confused over the speed variations in SCSI. Part of the problem is that speeds are quoted as either clock speeds (MHz) or transfer speeds. With 8-bit transfers, you get 1 byte per transfer, so if the clock is 40MHz (Fast-40 or Ultra2 SCSI), the transfer speed is 40MBps. On the other hand, if you are using a Wide (16-bit) interface, the transfer speed doubles to 80MBps, even though the clock speed remains at 40MHz. With Fast-80DT, the bus speed technically remains at 40MHz; however, two transfers are made per cycle, resulting in a throughput speed of 160MBps. The same is true for Ultra4 SCSI, which runs at 80MHz, transfers 2 bytes at a time, and has two transfers per cycle, for a throughput of 320MBps. Ultra5 doubles the clock speed again, running at 160MHz, transferring 2 bytes at a time, two times per cycle, for a throughput of 640MBps.

Finally, confusion exists because SCSI speeds or modes are often discussed using either the official terms—such as Fast-10, Fast-20, Fast-40, Fast-80DT, Fast-160DT—or the equivalent marketing terms, such as Fast, Ultra, Ultra2, Ultra3 (also called Ultra160) and Ultra4 (Ultra320). Refer to Table 8.2 for a complete breakdown of SCSI official terms, marketing terms, and speeds.

The further evolution of the most commonly used form of SCSI is defined under the SPI standards within SCSI-3. The SPI standards are detailed in the following sections.

SPI or Ultra SCSI

The SCSI Parallel Interface standard was published on January 1, 1995, and is the first SCSI standard that fell under the SCSI-3 designation. The SPI standard is officially known as ANSI/INCITS 253-1995 (formerly ANSI X3.253-1995). SPI is also called Ultra SCSI by most marketing departments and defines the parallel bus electrical connections and signals. A separate document called the SCSI Interlock Protocol (SIP) defines the parallel command set. SIP was included in the later SPI-2 and SPI-3 revisions and is no longer carried as a separate document. The main features added in SPI or Ultra SCSI are

- Fast-20 (Ultra) speeds (20MBps or 40MBps)
- 68-pin P-cable and connectors defined for Wide SCSI

SPI initially included speeds up to Fast SCSI (10MHz), which enabled transfer speeds up to 20MBps using a 16-bit wide bus. Later, Fast-20 (20MHz), commonly known as Ultra SCSI, was added through an addendum document (ANSI/INCITS 253-1995 Amendment 1), allowing a throughput of 40MBps on a 16-bit wide bus (commonly called Ultra/Wide).

SPI-2 or Ultra2 SCSI

SPI-2 is also called Ultra2 SCSI and was officially published on April 14, 1998 as ANSI/INCITS 302-1998 (formerly ANSI X3.302-1998). SPI-2 or Ultra2 SCSI adds several features to the prior versions:

- Fast-40 (Ultra2) speeds (40MBps or 80MBps)
- Low-voltage differential (LVD) signaling
- Single Connector Attachment (SCA-2) connectors
- 68-pin Very High Density Connector (VHDC)

The most notable of these is a higher speed called Fast-40, which is commonly called Ultra2 SCSI and runs at 40MHz. On a narrow (8-bit) bus, this results in 40MBps throughput, whereas on a wide bus (16-bit), this results in 80MBps throughput and is commonly referred to as Ultra2/Wide.

To achieve these speeds, a new electrical interface called LVD must be used. The slower single-ended electrical interface is only good for speeds up to Fast-20; Fast-40 mode requires LVD operation. The LVD signaling also enables longer cable lengths up to 12 meters with multiple devices or 25 meters with only one device. LVD and SE devices can share the same cable, but in that case, the bus runs in SE mode and is restricted in length to as little as 1.5 meters in Fast-20 mode. LVD operation requires special LVD-only or LVD/SE multimode terminators. If multimode terminators are used, the same terminators work on either SE or LVD buses.

The SPI-2 standard also includes SCSI Interlink Protocol (SIP) and defines the Single Connector Attachment (SCA-2) 80-pin connector for hot-swappable drive arrays. There is also a new 68-pin Very High Density Connector (VHDC), which is smaller than the previous types.

SCSI Signaling

"Normal," or standard, SCSI uses a signaling technique called *single-ended (SE)* signaling. SE signaling is a low-cost technique, but it also has performance and noise problems.

Single-ended signaling is also called *unbalanced* signaling. Each signal is carried on a pair of wires, usually twisted to help reduce noise. With SE, one of the pair is grounded—often to a common ground for all signals—and the other carries the actual voltage transitions. It is up to a receiver at the other end of the cable to detect the voltage transitions, which are really just changes in voltage.

Unfortunately, this type of unbalanced signaling is very prone to problems with noise, electromagnetic interference, and ground leakage; these problems get worse the longer the cable is. This is why Ultra SCSI was limited to such short maximum bus lengths—as little as 1.5 meters, or 5 feet.

When SCSI was first developed, a signaling technique called High Voltage Differential signaling was also introduced into the standard. Differential signaling, also known as *balanced signaling*, is still done with a pair of wires. In fact, the first in the pair carries the same type of signal that single-ended SCSI carries. The second in the pair, however, carries the logical inversion of that signal. The receiving device detects the difference between the pair (hence the name differential). By using the wires in a balanced pair, the receiver no longer needs to detect voltage magnitude, only the differential between voltages in two wires. This is much easier for circuits to do reliably, which makes them less susceptible to noise and enables greater cable length. Because of this, differential SCSI can be used with cable lengths of up to 25 meters, whereas single-ended SCSI is good only for 6 meters maximum, or as little as 1.5 meters in the faster modes.

Figure 8.5 shows the circuit differences between balanced (differential) and unbalanced (single-ended) transmission lines.

Figure 8.5   Balanced (differential) versus unbalanced (single-ended) signaling.

Unfortunately, the original standard for HVD signaling called for high-voltage differentials between the two wires. This meant that small, low-power, single-chip interfaces using HVD signaling could not be developed. Instead, circuits using several chips were required. This worked at both ends, meaning both the host adapter and device circuitry had to be larger and more expensive.

Another problem with HVD SCSI is that although the cables and connectors look (and are) exactly the same as for SE SCSI, both types of devices can't be mixed on the same bus. If they are, the high voltage from the HVD device burns out the receiver circuits on all SE devices attached to the bus. In other words, the result is smoked hardware—not a pretty sight.

Because SE SCSI worked well enough for the speeds that were necessary up until recently, HVD SCSI signaling never really caught on. It was used only in minicomputers and very rarely, if at all, in PCs. Because of this fact, the extra cost of this interface, and the fact that it is electrically incompatible with standard SE SCSI devices, HVD signaling was removed from the SCSI specification in the latest SCSI-3 documents. So, as far as we are concerned, it is obsolete.

Still, a need existed for a more reliable signaling technique that would allow for longer cable lengths. The answer came in the form of LVD signaling. By designing a new version of the differential interface, it can be made to work with inexpensive and low-power SCSI chips. Another advantage of LVD is that because it uses low voltage, if you plug an LVD device into an SE SCSI bus, nothing will be damaged. In fact, as an optional part of the LVD standard, the LVD device can be designed as a multimode device, which means it works on both SE and LVD buses. In the case of installing a multimode LVD device into an SE bus, the device detects that it is installed in an SE bus and defaults to SE mode.

Therefore, all multimode LVD/SE SCSI devices can be used on either LVD or SE SCSI buses. However, when on a bus with even one other SE device, all the LVD devices on the bus run only in SE mode. Because SE mode supports only SCSI speeds of up to 20MHz (Fast-20 or UltraSCSI) and cable lengths of up to 1.5 or 3 meters, the devices also work only at that speed or lower; you also might have problems with longer cables. Although you can purchase an Ultra3 SCSI multimode LVD/SE drive and install it on a SCSI bus along with single-ended devices, you will certainly be wasting the capabilities of the faster device.

Note that all Ultra2 and Ultra3 devices support LVD signaling because that is the only way they can be run at the Ultra2 (40MHz) or Ultra3 (80MHz) speeds. Ultra SCSI (20MHz) or slower devices can support LVD signaling, but in most cases, LVD is synonymous with Ultra2 or Ultra3 only.

Table 8.2, shown earlier, lists all the SCSI speeds and maximum lengths for each speed using the supported signaling techniques for that speed.

Because the connectors are the same for SE, HVD, LVD, or multimode SE/LVD devices, and because putting an HVD device on any bus with SE or LVD devices causes damage, it would be nice to be able to tell them apart. One way is to look for a special symbol on the unit; the industry has adopted different universal symbols for single-ended and differential SCSI. Figure 8.6 shows these symbols.

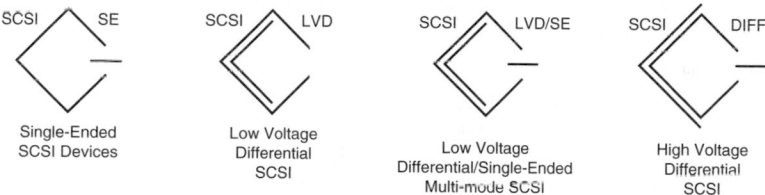

Figure 8.6   Universal symbol icons identifying SE, LVD, multimode LVD/SE, and HVD devices.

If you do not see such symbols, you can tell whether you have a High Voltage Differential device by using an ohmmeter to check the resistance between pins 21 and 22 on the device connector:

- On a single-ended or Low Voltage Differential device, the pins should be tied together and also tied to the ground.

- On a High Voltage Differential device, the pins should be open or have significant resistance between them.

Although you will blow up stuff if you plug HVD devices into LVD or SE buses, this generally should not be a problem because virtually all devices used in the PC environment are SE, LVD, or LVD/SE. HVD has essentially been rendered obsolete because it has been removed from the SCSI standard with Ultra3 SCSI (SPI-3).

SPI-3 or Ultra3 SCSI (Ultra160)

SPI-3—also known as Ultra3 or Ultra160 SCSI—was published on November 1, 2000, and built on the previous standard primarily by doubling the speed to Fast-80DT (double transition). This results in a maximum throughput of 160MBps. The main features added to SPI-3 (Ultra3) are

- DT (double transition) clocking
- Cyclic redundancy checking (CRC)
- Domain validation
- Packetization
- Quick Arbitrate and Select (QAS)

Double transition clocking sends data on both the rising and falling edges of the REQ/ACK clock. This enables Ultra3 SCSI to transfer data at 160MBps, while still running at a bus clock rate of 40MHz. This mode is defined for 16-bit wide bus use only.

Cyclic redundancy checking (CRC) is a form of error checking incorporated into Ultra3 SCSI. Previous versions of SCSI used simple parity checking to detect transmission errors. CRC is a much more robust form of error-detection capability that is far superior for operation at higher speeds.

Domain validation allows better negotiation of SCSI transfer speeds and modes. With prior SCSI versions, when the bus is initialized, the host adapter sends an INQUIRY command at the lowest 5MHz speed to each device to determine which data-transfer rate the device can use. The problem is that, even though both the host adapter and device might support a given speed, there is no guarantee that the interconnection between the devices will reliably work at that speed. If a problem occurs, the device becomes inaccessible. With domain validation, after a maximum transfer speed is negotiated between the host and device, it is then tested at that rate. If errors are detected, the rate is stepped down until the connection tests error-free. This is similar to how modems negotiate transmission speeds before communicating and really improves the flexibility and perceived reliability of SCSI.

Packetization is a protocol that enables information to be transferred between SCSI devices in a much more efficient manner. Traditional parallel SCSI uses multiple bus phases to communicate different types of information between SCSI devices: one for command information, two for messages, one for status, and two for data. In contrast, packetized SCSI communicates all this information by using only two phases: one for each direction. This dramatically reduces the command and protocol overhead, especially as higher and higher speeds are used.

Packetized SCSI is fully compatible with traditional parallel SCSI, which means packetized SCSI devices can reside on the same bus as traditional SCSI devices. As long as the host adapter supports the packetization, it can communicate with one device using packets and another using traditional protocol. Not all Ultra3 or Ultra160 SCSI devices include packetization support, however. Ultra3 devices that support packetization typically are referred to as Ultra160+ SCSI.

Quick Arbitrate and Select (QAS) is a feature in Ultra3 SCSI that reduces arbitration time by eliminating bus free time. QAS enables a device to transfer control of the bus to another device without an intervening BUS FREE phase. SCSI devices that support QAS report that capability in the INQUIRY command.

Ultra160 and Ultra160+

Because the five main new features of Ultra3 SCSI are optional, drives could claim Ultra3 capability and not have a consistent level of functionality. To ensure truth in advertising and a minimum level of performance, a group of manufacturers got together and created a substandard within Ultra3 SCSI that requires a minimum set of features. These are called Ultra160 and Ultra160+ because both indicate 160MBps throughput. These are technically not an official part of the SPI-3 standard. Even so, they do guarantee that certain specifications will be met and certain performance levels will be attained.

Ultra160 is a specific implementation of Ultra3 (SPI-3) SCSI that includes the first three additional features of Ultra3 SCSI:

- Fast-80DT clocking for 160MBps operation
- CRC
- Domain validation

Ultra160 SCSI runs in LVD mode and is backward compatible with all Ultra2 SCSI (LVD) devices. The only caveat is that no SE devices must be on the bus. When Ultra2 and Ultra160 (Ultra3) devices are mixed, each device can operate at its full-rated speed independent of the other. The bus will dynamically switch from single- to double-transition mode to support the differences in speeds.

Ultra160+ adds the other two features, ensuring a full implementation of Ultra3:

- Packetization
- Quick Arbitrate and Select

With Ultra160 and Ultra160+, a known level of functionality ensures that a minimum level of performance will be met. Ultra160+ SCSI is the highest-performance PC-level storage interface and is best suited for high-traffic environments, such as high-end network servers or workstations. The adaptability and scalability of the interface enables high performance with high reliability.

SPI-4 or Ultra4 SCSI (Ultra320)

SPI-4, also known as Ultra4 or Ultra320 SCSI was published on December 1, 2002, as ANSI/INCITS 362-2002, and has all the same features as the previous Ultra3 (Ultra160) SCSI plus several new features to ensure reliable data transmission at twice the speed.

Ultra320 SCSI integrates both the Packetization and Quick Arbitrate and Select features from Ultra160+ SCSI as mandatory features.

Ultra320 SCSI then adds the following new features:

- *Transfer speed.* Ultra320 transfers data 2 bytes (16 bits) at a time at 80MHz using double-transition (DT) cycling, meaning it transfers twice per cycle (hertz). This results in a burst transfer rate of 320MBps.

- *Read/write data streaming.* This minimizes the overhead for queued data transfers by enabling a device to send one data stream queue-tag packet followed by multiple data packets. Previously, only one data packet could be sent with each queue-tag packet. Write performance is also increased because there are fewer bus turnarounds from data in to data out.

- *Flow control.* This allows a target device to indicate when the last packet of a data stream will be transferred, which enables the initiator to terminate the data prefetch or begin flushing data buffers sooner than previously possible.

At the high 80MHz DT (dual transition) signaling speeds used with Ultra320, problems were discovered with high-frequency roll-off (signal degradation) and skew (timing variations) in the cables and logic boards. To compensate for this, Ultra320 can use one of two methods: write precompensation (WPC) in the transmitters or adjustable active filters (AAF) in the receivers. Write precompensation alters the transmitted signals by driving the first bit after a clock transition harder than the subsequent bits. Write precompensation can be turned off if receivers with AAF are used instead, which are capable of compensating for roll-off and skew problems in the transmission line at the receiving end. When using AAF, a special training pattern with low- and high-frequency signals is sent before each data transfer to allow the receiver to dynamically adjust for the high-frequency roll-off and skew problems. AAF is considered the best method because it is dynamic and automatically adjusts to compensate for the particular conditions in the bus at the time of each data transfer. Because of this, the faster Ultra640 standard requires AAF and WPC is not an option.

SPI-5 or Ultra5 SCSI (Ultra640)

SPI-5 (also known as Ultra5 or Ultra640 SCSI) was published on July 10, 2003, as ANSI/INCITS 367-2003 and is twice as fast as the previous Ultra4 (Ultra320) standard. Most importantly, SPI-5 or Ultra640 is being promoted as the last of the parallel SCSI standards according to Technical Committee T10. With the announcement of Ultra640, the new Serial Attached SCSI (SAS) standard was mentioned for the future as picking up where parallel SCSI leaves off.

Ultra640 includes all the same features of Ultra320 SCSI, with the following additional features or requirements:

- Signal and clock speeds double (160MHz, 2 bytes per transfer, and two transfers per cycle).
- Write precompensation (WPC) is no longer allowed.
- Adjustable active filters (AAF) are required.
- The AAF receiver adjusts the clocking for both the rising and falling edges of the signal.

- The AAF training pattern is changed to compensate for crosstalk effects.

- Cable length is restricted to 2M using a multidrop ribbon cable, or up to 20M for a shielded cable if only one device exists (point-to-point interconnect).

With Ultra640 SCSI, ribbon cables are restricted to 2M in total length. This is because ribbon cable has high crosstalk, or signal noise transfer, between adjacent wires. The maximum length for a shielded cable bus is 10M, or 20M if a single device is connected.

SPI-5 (Ultra640) SCSI will almost certainly be the last generation of the parallel SCSI physical interface. In fact, currently there are no Ultra640 products on the market. Additionally, because SAS has been released and is being touted as the future of SCSI, there might never be any Ultra640 products. Because SAS uses the same basic physical layer and connections as Serial ATA, SAS is expected to be the next step in both SCSI and high-end SATA solutions.

Serial Attached SCSI

With parallel SCSI reaching the end of the road with the development of Ultra320 and Ultra640, and future upgrades in speed to the parallel bus both extremely difficult and expensive to engineer, it was deemed that serial architectures should be investigated by the T10 committee as possible solutions for future SCSI implementations. Starting in April 2002, the committee began work on a future serial SCSI standard. Rather than reinvent the wheel, it was decided to adopt the same signaling, cable, and connector designs as used in SATA and combine the SCSI command protocol with a somewhat modified SATA physical layer design. The result was called Serial Attached SCSI and was officially published on October 30, 2003, as ANSI/INCITS 376-2003. An extension featuring incremental enhancements and fixes is called Serial Attached SCSI 1.1 and is currently under development.

SAS was designed to leverage the cost economies of the SATA physical interface, cable, and connector designs while preserving the robust software and reliability of SCSI. SAS was designed as an extendable standard with future increases in speed and performance in mind. As with SATA, the serial interface is self-clocking, which allows data rates to be more easily pushed higher and higher. The main features of Serial Attached SCSI include

- 300MBps point-to-point connections with up to 1200MBps with future backward-compatible enhancements.

- Wide-port devices will allow multiple serial connections, multiplying the bandwidth available by the number of connections.

- SAS utilizes the robust and refined (20 years in development) SCSI protocol.

- SAS supports both 300MBps SAS and 150MBps SATA drives, enabling a motherboard or host adapter with SAS connectors to support both SAS and SATA drives.

The most important feature of SAS is that it will actually support two types of drives. SATA drives can be attached for low-cost storage, and true SAS drives can be attached for higher-performance systems. The SAS connector design enables both SAS and SATA drives to be plugged in; however, it is impossible to plug an SAS drive into a SATA interface. Because the SATA connector signals are a subset of SAS signals, SATA drives will operate on SAS host adapters. SAS drives, on the other hand, will not operate on SATA adapters. The SAS connectors are specially keyed to prevent plugging them into SATA host adapters.

SAS uses three protocols, each for transferring different types of data depending on which type of device is being accessed:

- *Serial SCSI Protocol (SSP).* Sends SCSI commands to SAS devices

- *SCSI Management Protocol (SMP).* Sends management information to expanders

- *SATA Tunneled Protocol (STP).* Sends SATA commands to SATA devices

By including these protocols, SAS provides full compatibility with existing SCSI devices and applications software as well as SATA devices and software. Combined with the backward compatibility of SAS and SATA physical connections, this enables SAS to operate as a universal interconnection for both SAS and SATA devices. If SAS is onboard, a user could upgrade her system from SATA to SAS by either replacing the SATA drive with an SAS drive or by keeping the SATA drive and adding the SAS drive to the system and using both simultaneously. To further ensure compatibility, in January 2003, the SCSI Trade Association (STA) and the Serial ATA (SATA) II Working Group announced a partnership to enable system-level compatibility with SAS and SATA hard drives.

Serial Attached SCSI is designed for extremely high bandwidth. Data transfer rates start at 3GBps (300MBps) with a roadmap enabling increases up to 12GBps (1200MBps), which is nearly four times that of Ultra320 SCSI. Additionally, Serial Attached SCSI is a point-to-point connection that allows full bandwidth to each drive, rather than sharing it among multiple drives as with parallel SCSI. Devices can also use Wide-Port connections, meaning they can have multiple connections to a single device. The total bandwidth available in that case is multiplied by the total number of connections to the device.

Internal connections use cables up to 1 meter long; these are similar to SATA cables except for a modified connector key. External connections, on the other hand, use Infiniband-type cables supporting four physical connections, along with an adapter allowing four internal connections to be mated to the external cable via an open expansion slot. The device connector looks a lot like the connector on a SATA drive; however, it also features a key and optional secondary signals for Wide-Port device connections. The design of the host connector enables both SATA and SAS cables to be attached. The pinout of each connection uses seven pins, and the pinout is identical to SATA.

Figure 8.7 shows the icon used to identify SAS devices and connections compliant with the SAS standard.

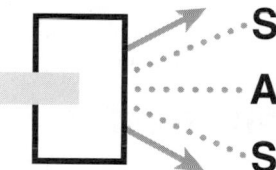

Figure 8.7   Serial Attached SCSI (SAS) icon.

A key feature of SAS is expandability. Devices called *expanders* enable SAS to be scaled up to connect large numbers of drives. Expanders are essentially low-cost switches that enable up to 128 individual point-to-point connections to be made—a total of up to 16,384 SAS devices can be connected via multiple expanders to a single host. By contrast, parallel SCSI imposes a limit of 15 devices per SCSI chain and severely limits total cable length.

Although the SAS specification was released in October 2003, prototype SAS adapters and drives were first demonstrated by Seagate and HP in March 2003. Retail SAS products (including host adapters and drives) are expected to be available to the public in the second half of 2004. All the major disk drive manufacturers have announced plans to develop SAS disk drives, and SAS allows existing SATA drives to be used as well.

RAID Arrays

Most servers, especially at levels above the workgroup, use SCSI drives rather than ATA drives because of their superior performance. You can enhance performance and data reliability further by creating a drive array. RAID (redundant array of inexpensive/independent disks) technologies are used by both SCSI and ATA drives. Current SCSI-based RAID products primarily support Ultra320 and Ultra160 drives and are used in traditional servers and rack-mounted computers. For a complete description of RAID levels and terminologies, see Chapter 7, "The ATA/IDE Interface."

Fibre Channel SCSI

Fibre Channel (FC) SCSI is a specification for a serial interface using a fibre channel physical and protocol characteristic, with a SCSI command set. It can achieve 200MBps or 400MBps over either fiber or coaxial cable of several kilometers in length. Fibre Channel is designed for long-distance connectivity (such as several kilometers) and connecting multiple systems, and it has become a popular choice for storage area networks (SANs) and server clusters. Fibre Channel SCSI complements, rather than replaces, Ultra160 and Ultra320 SCSI, which are designed for direct connection to servers.

200MBps versions of Fibre Channel SCSI use the gigabit interface connector (GBIC), whereas 400MBps versions use either the small form factor pluggable (SFP) connector for optical connections or the high-speed serial data connector (HSSDC) for copper cable (these connectors are shown later in this chapter, in Figures 8.13–8.15).

Because SAS and iSCSI will offer much the same performance and benefits of FC at a much lower cost, it is expected that SAS and iSCSI will replace FC in many high-end server applications.

iSCSI

Another variation on SCSI, iSCSI, combines the performance of SCSI drives with Ethernet networking up to gigabit speeds. Because iSCSI uses Ethernet to transport data between systems, iSCSI storage can be located anywhere an Ethernet network can reach, including Internet access. In addition, iSCSI storage enables secure remote storage for computers that could be hundreds of kilometers away. Because iSCSI data can be routed the same way any other type of Ethernet data can be routed, it enables data to be transported even when some connections between the server and the storage devices are unavailable.

Eventually, iSCSI is expected to replace Fibre Channel in uses such as network attached storage (NAS), SANs, and storage clusters. Similar to Fibre Channel, iSCSI cards can be purchased in both copper-wire and fiber-optic versions to match the Ethernet network already in use. The first iSCSI devices were produced by Adaptec and Cisco Systems in mid-2002.

SCSI Cables and Connectors

The SCSI standards are very specific when it comes to cables and connectors. The most common connectors specified in this standard are the 50-position unshielded pin header connector for internal SCSI connections and the 50-position shielded Centronics latch-style connectors for external connections. The shielded Centronics-style connector also is called Alternative 2 in the official specification. Passive or Active termination (Active is preferred) is specified for both single-ended and differential buses. The 50-conductor bus configuration is defined in the SCSI-2 standard as the A cable.

Older narrow (8-bit) SCSI adapters and external devices use a full-size Centronics-type connector. Figure 8.8 shows what the low-density, 50-pin SCSI connector looks like.

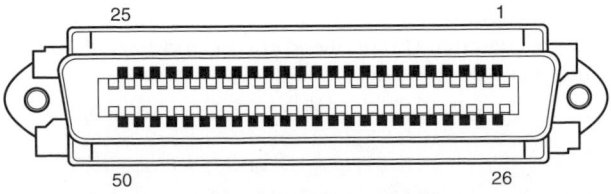

Figure 8.8   Low-density, 50-pin SCSI device connector.

The SCSI-2 revision added a high-density, 50-position, D-shell connector option for the A-cable connectors. This connector now is called Alternative 1. Figure 8.9 shows the 50-pin, high-density SCSI connector.

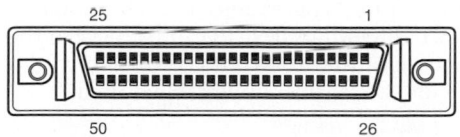

Figure 8.9 High-density, 50-pin SCSI device connector.

The Alternative 2 Centronics latch-style connector remains unchanged from SCSI-1. A 68-conductor B-cable specification was added to the SCSI-2 standard to provide for 16- and 32-bit data transfers; the connector, however, had to be used in parallel with an A cable. The industry did not widely accept the B-cable option, which has been dropped from the SCSI-3 standard.

To replace the ill-fated B cable, a new 68-conductor P cable was developed as part of the SCSI-3 specification. Shielded and unshielded high-density D-shell connectors are specified for both the A and P cables. The shielded high-density connectors use a squeeze-to-release latch rather than the wire latch used on the Centronics-style connectors. Active termination for single-ended buses is specified, providing a high level of signal integrity. Figure 8.10 shows the 68-pin, high-density SCSI connector.

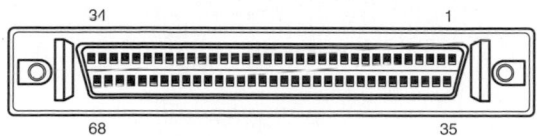

Figure 8.10 High-density, 68-pin SCSI device connector.

Drive arrays normally use special SCSI drives with what is called an 80-pin Alternative-4 connector, which is capable of Wide SCSI and also includes power signals. Drives with the 80-pin connector are usually *hot-swappable*—they can be removed and installed with the power on—in drive arrays. The 80-pin Alt-4 connector is shown in Figure 8.11.

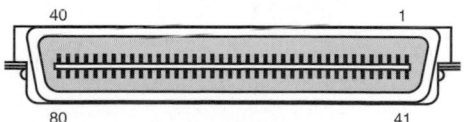

Figure 8.11 80-pin Alt-4 SCSI device connector.

Apple and some other nonstandard implementations from other vendors used a 25-pin cable and connector for SCSI devices. They did this by eliminating most of the grounds from the cable, which unfortunately results in a noisy, error-prone connection. These 25-pin connectors and cables are not compliant with any SCSI standard; you should avoid them if possible. The connector used in these cases was a standard female DB-25 connector, which looks exactly like a PC parallel port (printer) connector.

Unfortunately, you can damage equipment by plugging printers into DB-25 SCSI connectors or by plugging SCSI devices into DB-25 printer connectors. So, if you use this type of SCSI connection, be sure it is well marked because there is no way to tell DB-25 SCSI from DB-25 parallel printer connectors by looking at them. The nonstandard DB-25 SCSI connector is shown in Figure 8.12.

Again, I recommend avoiding making SCSI connections using this type of nonstandard cable or connector.

Fibre Channel SCSI devices running at 200MBps can connect to various types of devices, depending on the gigabit interface connector (GBIC) module installed in the host adapter. The module could use a subscriber connector (SC) for fiber-optic cable, a high-speed serial data connector (HSSDC) for copper cable, or a DB-9 connector for copper cable. The GBIC module can be removed from the host adapter, as shown in Figure 8.13. 400MBps devices can connect to the HSSDC connector shown in Figure 8.14 if copper wire is used, or they can connect to the modular small form factor pluggable (SFP) connector shown in Figure 8.15 if fiber-optic cable is used.

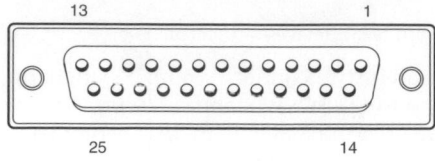

Figure 8.12   Nonstandard DB-25 SCSI device connector.

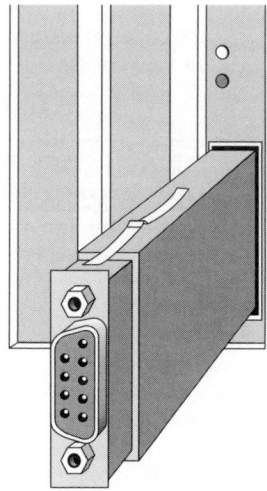

Figure 8.13   The GBIC module used for 200MBps versions of Fibre Channel can accept DB-9 (shown), SC, or HSSDC modules.

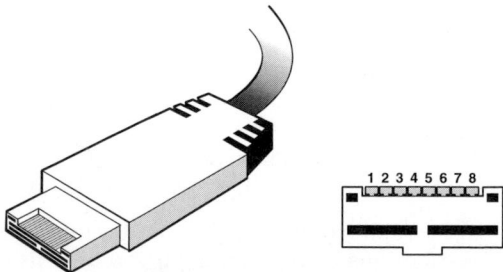

Figure 8.14   The HSSDC used for 400MBps versions of Fibre Channel over copper wire.

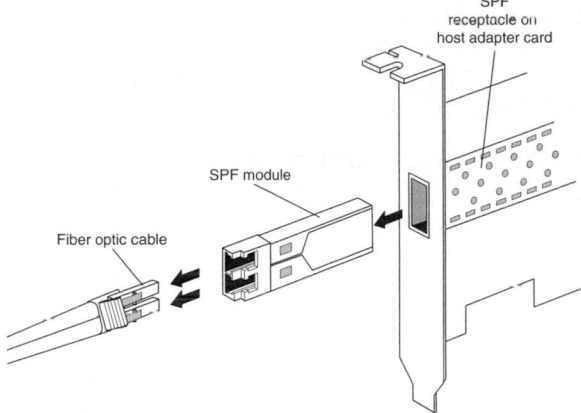

Figure 8.15 The SFP module used for 400MBps versions of Fibre Channel over fiber-optic cable.

Parallel SCSI Cable and Connector Pinouts

The following section details the pinouts of the various SCSI cables and connectors. Two electrically different versions of SCSI exist: single-ended and differential. These two versions are electrically incompatible and must not be interconnected; otherwise, damage will result. Fortunately, very few differential SCSI applications are available in the PC industry, so you will rarely (if ever) encounter one. Within each electrical type (single-ended or differential), there are basically two SCSI cable types:

■ A cable (Standard 8-bit SCSI)

■ P cable (16-bit Wide SCSI)

The 50-pin A-cable is used in most SCSI-1 and SCSI-2 installations and is the most common cable you will encounter. SCSI-2 Wide (16-bit) applications use a P cable instead, which has 68 pins. You can intermix standard and Wide SCSI devices on a single SCSI bus by interconnecting A and P cables with special adapters. SCSI-3 applications that are 32-bit wide would have used an additional Q cable, but this was finally dropped from the SCSI-3 standard after it was never implemented in actual products.

SCSI cables are specially shielded with the most important high-speed signals carried in the center of the cable and less important, slower ones in two additional layers around the perimeter. A typical SCSI cable is constructed as shown in Figure 8.16.

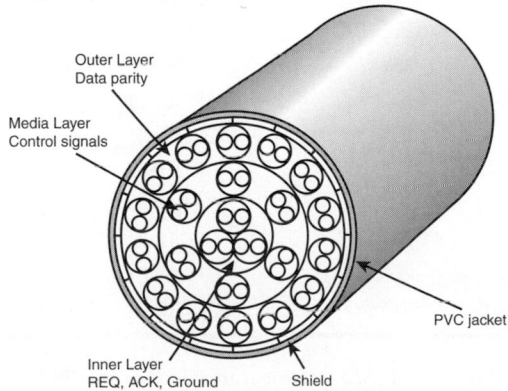

Figure 8.16 Cross section of a typical SCSI cable.

This specialized construction is what makes SCSI cables so expensive, as well as thicker than other types of cables. Note this specialized construction is necessary only for external SCSI cables. Cables used to connect devices inside a shielded enclosure (such as inside a PC) can use much less expensive ribbon cables.

The A cables can have pin-header–type (internal) connectors or external shielded connectors, each with a different pinout. The P cables feature the same connector pinout on either internal or external cable connections.

Single-Ended SCSI Cables and Connectors

The single-ended electrical interface is the most popular type for PC systems. Tables 8.3 and 8.4 show all the possible single-ended cable and connector pinouts. The A cable is available in both internal unshielded and external shielded configurations. A hyphen preceding a signal name indicates the signal is Active Low. The RESERVED lines have continuity from one end of the SCSI bus to the other. In an A cable bus, the RESERVED lines should be left open in SCSI devices (but may be connected to ground) and are connected to ground in the bus terminator assemblies. In the P and Q cables, the RESERVED lines are left open in SCSI devices and the bus terminator assemblies.

Table 8.3   A-Cable (Single-Ended) Internal Unshielded Header Connector

Signal	Pin	Pin	Signal
GROUND	1	2	-DB(0)
GROUND	3	4	-DB(1)
GROUND	5	6	-DB(2)
GROUND	7	8	-DB(3)
GROUND	9	10	-DB(4)
GROUND	11	12	-DB(5)
GROUND	13	14	-DB(6)
GROUND	15	16	-DB(7)
GROUND	17	18	-DB(Parity)
GROUND	19	20	GROUND
GROUND	21	22	GROUND
RESERVED	23	24	RESERVED
Open	25	26	TERMPWR
RESERVED	27	28	RESERVED
GROUND	29	30	GROUND
GROUND	31	32	-ATN
GROUND	33	34	GROUND
GROUND	35	36	-BSY
GROUND	37	38	-ACK
GROUND	39	40	-RST
GROUND	41	42	-MSG
GROUND	43	44	-SEL
GROUND	45	46	-C/D
GROUND	47	48	-REQ
GROUND	49	50	-I/O

Table 8.4   A-Cable (Single-Ended) External Shielded Connector

Signal	Pin	Pin	Signal
GROUND	1	26	-DB(0)
GROUND	2	27	-DB(1)
GROUND	3	28	-DB(2)
GROUND	4	29	-DB(3)
GROUND	5	30	-DB(4)
GROUND	6	31	-DB(5)
GROUND	7	32	-DB(6)
GROUND	8	33	-DB(7)
GROUND	9	34	-DB(Parity)
GROUND	10	35	GROUND
GROUND	11	36	GROUND
RESERVED	12	37	RESERVED
Open	13	38	TERMPWR
RESERVED	14	39	RESERVED
GROUND	15	40	GROUND
GROUND	16	41	-ATN
GROUND	17	42	GROUND
GROUND	18	43	-BSY
GROUND	19	44	-ACK
GROUND	20	45	-RST
GROUND	21	46	-MSG
GROUND	22	47	-SEL
GROUND	23	48	-C/D
GROUND	24	49	-REQ
GROUND	25	50	-I/O

IBM used the SCSI interface in virtually all PS/2 systems introduced after 1990. These systems use a Micro-Channel SCSI adapter or have the SCSI Host Adapter built in to the motherboard. In either case, IBM's SCSI interface uses a special 60-pin, mini-Centronics–type external shielded connector that is unique in the industry.

A special IBM cable is required to adapt this connector to the standard 50-pin Centronics-style connector used on most external SCSI devices. The pinout of the IBM 60-pin, mini-Centronics–style external shielded connector is shown in Table 8.5. Notice that although the pin arrangement is unique, the pin-number-to–signal designations correspond with the standard unshielded internal pin header type of SCSI connector. IBM has discontinued this design in all its systems because after the PS/2 series, all have used conventional SCSI connectors.

The P cable (single-ended) and connectors are used in 16-bit Wide SCSI-2 applications (see Table 8.6 for the pinout).

Table 8.5   IBM PS/2 SCSI External

Signal Name	Pin	Pin	Signal Name
GROUND	1	60	Not Connected
-DB(0)	2	59	Not Connected
GROUND	3	58	Not Connected
-DB(1)	4	57	Not Connected
GROUND	5	56	Not Connected
-DB(2)	6	55	Not Connected
GROUND	7	54	Not Connected
-DB(3)	8	53	Not Connected
GROUND	9	52	Not Connected
-DB(4)	10	51	GROUND
GROUND	11	50	-I/O
-DB(5)	12	49	GROUND
GROUND	13	48	-REQ
-DB(6)	14	47	GROUND
GROUND	15	46	-C/D
-DB(7)	16	45	GROUND
GROUND	17	44	-SEL
-DB(Parity)	18	43	GROUND
GROUND	19	42	-MSG
GROUND	20	41	GROUND
GROUND	21	40	-RST
GROUND	22	39	GROUND
RESERVED	23	38	-ACK
RESERVED	24	37	GROUND
Open	25	36	-BSY
TERMPWR	26	35	GROUND
RESERVED	27	34	GROUND
RESERVED	28	33	GROUND
GROUND	29	32	-ATN
GROUND	30	31	GROUND

Table 8.6   P-Cable (Single-Ended) Internal or External Shielded Connector

Signal Name	Pin	Pin	Signal Name
GROUND	1	35	-DB(12)
GROUND	2	36	-DB(13)
GROUND	3	37	-DB(14)
GROUND	4	38	-DB(15)
GROUND	5	39	-DB(Parity 1)
GROUND	6	40	-DB(0)
GROUND	7	41	-DB(1)
GROUND	8	42	-DB(2)
GROUND	9	43	-DB(3)
GROUND	10	44	-DB(4)
GROUND	11	45	-DB(5)
GROUND	12	46	-DB(6)
GROUND	13	47	-DB(7)
GROUND	14	48	-DB(Parity 0)
GROUND	15	49	GROUND
GROUND	16	50	GROUND
TERMPWR	17	51	TERMPWR
TERMPWR	18	52	TERMPWR
RESERVED	19	53	RESERVED
GROUND	20	54	GROUND
GROUND	21	55	-ATN
GROUND	22	56	GROUND
GROUND	23	57	-BSY
GROUND	24	58	-ACK
GROUND	25	59	-RST
GROUND	26	60	-MSG
GROUND	27	61	-SEL
GROUND	28	62	-C/D
GROUND	29	63	-REQ
GROUND	30	64	-I/O
GROUND	31	65	-DB(8)
GROUND	32	66	-DB(9)
GROUND	33	67	-DB(10)
GROUND	34	68	-DB(11)

High-Voltage Differential SCSI Signals

High Voltage Differential SCSI is not normally used in a PC environment but is very popular with minicomputer installations because of the very long bus lengths that are allowed. This has changed with the introduction of Low Voltage Differential signaling for SCSI, bringing the benefits of differential signaling to lower-end and more mainstream SCSI products.

Differential signaling uses drivers on both the initiator and target ends of the bus and makes each signal work in a push/pull arrangement, rather than a signal/ground arrangement as with standard single-ended SCSI. This enables much greater cable lengths and eliminates some of the problems with termination.

Almost all PC peripherals produced since the beginning of SCSI have been SE types. These are incompatible with HVD devices, although HVD devices can be used on an SE bus with appropriate (and expensive) adapters. The LVD devices, on the other hand, can be used on an SE bus if they are multimode devices, in which case they switch into SE mode. If all devices—including the host adapter—support LVD mode, all the devices switch into that mode and much longer cable lengths and higher speeds can be used. The normal limit for an SE SCSI bus is 1.53 meters maximum (about 5–10 feet) and up to 20MHz. If run in LVD mode, the maximum bus length goes up to 12 meters (about 40 feet) and speeds can go up to 80MHz. HVD SCSI supports bus lengths of up to 25 meters (about 80 feet).

Note that almost all modern SCSI hard disks are Ultra2 or Ultra3 devices, which means by default they are also LVD or multimode LVD/SE devices.

Expanders

SCSI expanders separate a SCSI bus into more than one physical segment, each of which can have the full SCSI cable length for that type of signaling. They provide a complete regeneration of the SCSI bus signals, allowing greater cable lengths and incompatible devices to essentially share the same bus. An expander also can be used to separate incompatible parts of a SCSI bus—for example, to keep SE and HVD SCSI devices in separate domains.

Expanders are transparent to the software and firmware on the bus, and they don't take up a device ID. They are usually capable of providing termination if located at the end of a bus segment, or they can have termination disabled if they are in the middle of a bus segment.

Because of their expense, expanders are not normally used except in extreme situations in which no other alternative remains. In most cases, it is better to stick within the recommended cable and bus length requirements and keep incompatible devices, such as HVD devices, off a standard SE or LVD bus.

Termination

Because a SCSI bus carries high-speed electrical signals, it can be affected by electrical reflections that might occur within any transmission line system. A terminator is designed to minimize the potential for reflections or noise on the bus, as well as to create the proper load for the bus transmitter circuits. Terminators are placed at each end of the bus to minimize these problems.

Despite the simple rules that only two terminators must be on the bus and they must be at each end, I still see improper termination as the most common cause of problems in SCSI installations.

Several types of SCSI terminators are available, dependent on the bus signaling and speed requirements:

- Passive
- Active (also called Alternative 2)
- Forced Perfect Termination (FPT): FPT-3, FPT-18, and FPT-27
- HVD termination
- LVD termination

The first three are used on single-ended SCSI buses only. Passive terminators use a passive network of 220-ohm and 330-ohm resistors to control bus termination. They should be used only in narrow

(8-bit) SCSI buses running at 5MHz. Passive terminators allow signal fluctuations in relation to the terminator power signal on the bus. Usually, passive terminating resistors suffice over short distances, such as 2 or 3 feet, but for longer distances or higher speeds, active termination is a real advantage. Active termination is required with Fast SCSI.

Passive terminators can be plugged in to the unused SCSI port or be built in to many low-speed SCSI devices such as scanners, optical drives, and removable-media drives. On such devices, you can activate or deactivate built-in passive termination with jumper blocks, a toggle switch, or some other form of selector switch—depending on the device.

Active terminators use built-in voltage regulator ICs combined with 110-ohm resistors. An active terminator actually has one or more voltage regulators to produce the termination voltage, rather than resistor voltage dividers alone. This arrangement helps ensure that the SCSI signals always are terminated to the correct voltage level. Active terminators often have some type of LED indicating the termination activity. The SCSI-2 specification recommends active termination on both ends of the bus and requires active termination whenever Fast or Wide SCSI devices are used. Most high-performance host adapters have an "auto-termination" feature, so if it is the end of a chain, it terminates itself.

A variation on active termination is available for single-ended buses: *forced perfect termination (FPT)*. Forced perfect termination is an even better form of active termination in which diode clamps are added to eliminate signal overshoot and undershoot. The trick is that instead of clamping to +5 and ground, these terminators clamp to the output of two regulated voltages. This arrangement enables the clamping diodes to eliminate signal overshoot and undershoot, especially at higher signaling speeds and over longer distances. Forced perfect termination is technically not found in the SCSI specifications but is the superior type of termination for single-ended applications that experience high levels of electrical noise.

FPT terminators are available in several versions. FPT-3 and FPT-18 versions are available for 8-bit standard SCSI, whereas the FPT-27 is available for 16-bit (Wide) SCSI. The FPT-3 version forces perfect the three most highly active SCSI signals on the 8-bit SCSI bus, whereas the FPT-18 forces perfect all the SCSI signals on the 8-bit bus except grounds. FPT-27 also forces perfect all the 16-bit Wide SCSI signals except grounds.

HVD buses require HVD terminators, constructed using a passive network of 330-ohm/150-ohm/330-ohm resistors. The only choice is that the terminator matches your cable or device connection.

The same is true for Low Voltage Differential buses. They require LVD terminators for the bus to function properly. One twist is that special LVD/SE (active) multimode terminators are available. These function as LVD types on an LVD bus and as active types on an SE bus. Note that if any SE devices are on the bus, it functions in SE mode and never uses LVD mode, severely limiting bus length and performance. If any SE-only terminators or SE devices are on the bus, the bus defaults into SE mode.

Schematic diagrams of passive, active, and FPT terminators can be found in *Upgrading and Repairing PCs, 15th Edition*, which is included on the disc packaged with this book.

▶▶ See "SCSI Drive Configuration," p. 610.

Note

Several companies make high-quality terminators for the SCSI bus, including East/West Manufacturing Enterprises, Inc. (formerly Aeronics) and the Data Mate division of Methode. Both companies make a variety of terminators. EWE is well noted for some unique FPT versions that are especially suited to problem configurations that require longer cable runs or higher signal integrity. One of the best investments you can make in any SCSI installation is in high-quality cables and terminators. Contact information for both of these companies is in the Vendor List on the accompanying disc.

Special terminators also are required for LVD and HVD SCSI, so if you are using those interfaces, be sure your terminators are compatible.

With LVD or HVD buses, you don't have much choice in terminator types, but for single-ended buses, you have at least three choices.

Tip

The best rule for terminators, as well as for cables, is to get the best you can. My recommendation is to *never* use passive terminators; instead, use active or, if you want the best in reliability and integrity, use only FPT.

SCSI Drive Configuration

SCSI drives are not too difficult to configure, but they are more complicated than ATA drives. The SCSI standard controls the way the drives must be set up. You need to set up two or three items when you configure a SCSI drive:

- SCSI ID setting (0–7 or 0–15)
- Terminating resistors

The SCSI ID setting is very simple. Up to 7 SCSI devices can be used on a single narrow SCSI bus or up to 15 devices on a Wide SCSI bus, and each device must have a unique SCSI ID address. There are 8 or 16 addresses respectively, and the host adapter takes 1 address, so the rest are free for up to 7 or 15 SCSI peripherals. Most SCSI host adapters are factory-set to ID 7 or 15, which is the highest-priority ID. All other devices must have unique IDs that do not conflict with one another. Some host adapters boot only from a hard disk set to a specific ID. Older Adaptec host adapters required the boot hard disk to be ID 0; newer ones can boot from any ID.

Setting the ID usually involves changing jumpers on the drive. If the drive is installed in an external chassis, the chassis might have an ID selector switch that is accessible at the rear. This selector makes ID selection a simple matter of pressing a button or rotating a wheel until the desired ID number appears. If no external selector is present, you must open the external device chassis and set the ID via the jumpers on the drive.

Three jumpers are required to set the SCSI ID; the particular ID selected actually is derived from the binary representation of the jumpers themselves. One example is setting all three ID jumpers to off, resulting in a binary number of 000b, which translates to an ID of 0. A binary setting of 001b equals ID 1, 010b equals 2, 011b equals 3, and so on. (Notice that as I list these values, I append a lowercase b to indicate binary numbers.)

Unfortunately, the jumpers can appear either forward or backward on the drive, depending on how the manufacturer set them up. To keep things simple, I have recorded all the various ID jumper settings in the following tables. Table 8.7 shows the settings for drives that order the jumpers with the most significant bit (MSB) to the left; Table 8.8 shows the settings for drives that have the jumpers ordered so that the MSB is to the right.

Table 8.7 SCSI ID Jumper Settings with the Most Significant Bit to the Left

SCSI	ID	Jumper	Settings
0	0	0	0
1	0	0	1
2	0	1	0
3	0	1	1
4	1	0	0
5	1	0	1
6	1	1	0
7	1	1	1

1 = Jumper On; 0 = Jumper Off

Table 8.8 SCSI ID Jumper Settings with the Most Significant Bit to the Right

SCSI	ID	Jumper	Settings
0	0	0	0
1	1	0	0
2	0	1	0
3	1	1	0
4	0	0	1
5	1	0	1
6	0	1	1
7	1	1	1

1 = Jumper On; 0 = Jumper Off

SCSI termination is very simple. Termination is required at both ends of the bus; there are no exceptions. If the host adapter is at one end of the bus, it must have termination enabled. If the host adapter is in the middle of the bus, and if both internal and external bus links are present, the host adapter must have its termination disabled and the devices at each end of the bus must have terminators installed. Unfortunately, the majority of problems I see with SCSI installations are the result of improper termination.

Figure 8.17 shows a representation of a SCSI bus with several devices attached. In this case, the host adapter is at one end of the bus and a CD-ROM drive is at the other. For the bus to work properly, those devices must be terminated, whereas the others do not have to be.

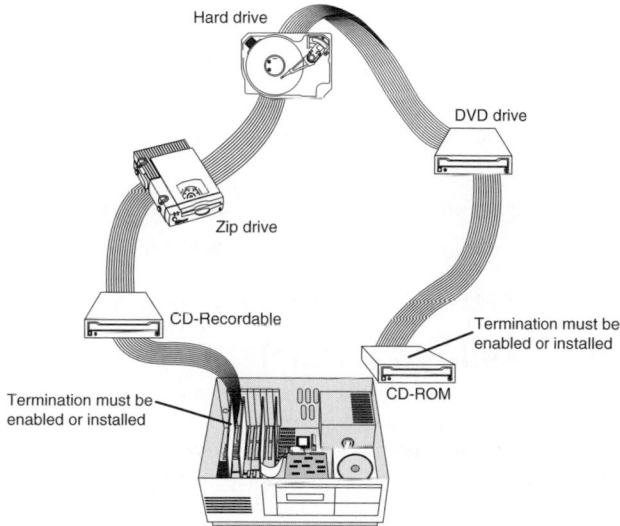

Figure 8.17   SCSI bus daisy-chain connections; the first and last devices must be terminated.

When installing an external SCSI device, you usually find the device in a storage enclosure with both input and output SCSI connectors, so you can use the device in a daisy-chain. If the enclosure is at the end of the SCSI bus, an external terminator module most likely will have to be plugged into the second (outgoing) SCSI port to provide proper termination at that end of the bus (see Figure 8.18).

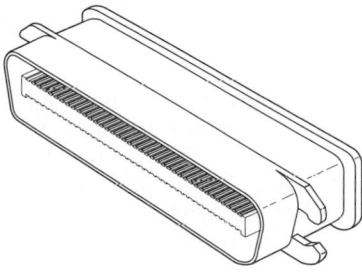

Figure 8.18   External SCSI device terminator.

External terminator modules are available in a variety of connector configurations, including pass-through designs, which are necessary if only one port is available. Pass-through terminators also are commonly used in internal installations in which the device does not have built-in terminating resistors. Many hard drives use pass-through terminators for internal installations to save space on the logic-board assembly (see Figure 8.19).

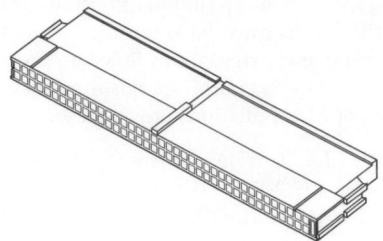

Figure 8.19   Internal pin-header connector pass-through SCSI terminator.

The pass-through models are required when a device is at the end of the bus and only one SCSI connector is available.

Other configuration items on a SCSI drive can be set via jumpers. Following are several of the most common additional settings:

- Start on Command (delayed start)
- SCSI Parity
- Terminator Power
- Synchronous Negotiation

These configuration items are described in the following sections.

Start on Command (Delayed Start)

If you have multiple drives installed in a system, it is wise to set them up so that not all the drives start to spin immediately when the system is powered on. A hard disk drive can consume three or four times more power during the first few seconds after power-on than during normal operation. The motor requires this additional power to get the platters spinning quickly. If several drives are drawing all this power at the same time, the power supply can be overloaded, which can cause the system to hang or have intermittent startup problems.

Nearly all SCSI drives provide a way to delay drive spinning so this problem does not occur. When most SCSI host adapters initialize the SCSI bus, they send out a command called Start Unit to each of the ID addresses in succession. By setting a jumper on the hard disk, you can prevent the disk from spinning until it receives the Start Unit command from the host adapter. Because the host adapter sends this command to all the ID addresses in succession, from the highest-priority address (ID 7) to the lowest (ID 0), the higher-priority drives can be made to start first, with each lower-priority drive spinning up sequentially. Because some host adapters do not send the Start Unit command, some drives might simply delay spin-up for a fixed number of seconds rather than wait for a command that never will arrive.

If drives are installed in external chassis with separate power supplies, you need not implement the delayed-start function. This function is best applied to internal drives that must be run from the same power supply that runs the system. For internal installations, I recommend setting Start on Command (delayed start) even if you have only one SCSI drive; this setting eases the load on the power supply by spinning the drive up after the rest of the system has full power. This method is especially good for portable systems and other systems in which the power supply is limited.

SCSI Parity

SCSI Parity is a limited form of error checking that helps ensure that all data transfers are reliable. Virtually all host adapters support SCSI parity checking, so this option should be enabled on every device. The only reason it exists as an option is that some older host adapters do not work with SCSI parity, so the parity must be turned off.

Terminator Power

The terminators at each end of the SCSI bus require power from at least one device on the bus. In most cases, the host adapter supplies this terminator power; in some cases, however, it does not. For example, parallel port SCSI host adapters typically do not supply terminator power. It is not a problem if more than one device supplies terminator power because each source is diode-protected. For simplicity's sake, many people often configure all devices to supply terminator power. If no device supplies terminator power, the bus is not terminated correctly and will not function properly.

SCSI Synchronous Negotiation

The SCSI bus can run in two modes: asynchronous (the default) and synchronous. The bus actually switches modes during transfers through a protocol called *synchronous negotiation*. Before data is transferred across the SCSI bus, the sending device (called the *initiator*) and the receiving device (called the *target*) negotiate how the transfer will take place. If both devices support synchronous transfers, they will discover this fact through the negotiation and the transfer will take place at the faster synchronous rate.

Unfortunately, some older devices do not respond to a request for synchronous transfer and can actually be disabled when such a request is made. For this reason, both host adapters and devices that support synchronous negotiation often have a jumper that can be used to disable this negotiation so it can work with older devices. By default, all devices today should support synchronous negotiation, and this function should be enabled.

Plug and Play SCSI

Plug and Play (PnP) SCSI originally was released in April 1994. This specification enables SCSI device manufacturers to build PnP peripherals that are automatically configured when used with a PnP operating system. This enables you to easily connect or reconfigure external peripherals, such as hard disk drives, backup tapes, and CD-ROMs.

To connect SCSI peripherals to the host PC, the specification requires a PnP SCSI host adapter. PnP add-in cards enable a PnP operating system to automatically configure software device drivers and system resources for the host bus interface.

The PnP SCSI specification includes these technical highlights:

- A single cable connector configuration
- Automatic termination of the SCSI bus
- SCAM (SCSI Configured AutoMagically*) automatic ID assignment
- Full backward compatibility of PnP SCSI devices with the installed base of SCSI systems

Note

"AutoMagically" is not a misspelling. The word is actually used in the official name for the original specification, which the X3T9.2 committee designated X3T9.2/93-109r5.

This helps make SCSI easier to use for the average user.

Each SCSI peripheral you add to your SCSI bus (other than hard disk drives) requires an external driver to make the device work. Hard disks are the exception; driver support for them typically is provided as part of the SCSI host adapter BIOS. These external drivers are specific not only to a particular device, but also to the host adapter.

Recently, two types of standard host adapter interface drivers have become popular, greatly reducing this problem. By having a standard host adapter driver to write to, peripheral makers can more quickly create new drivers that support their devices and then talk to the universal host adapter driver. This arrangement eliminates dependence on one particular type of host adapter. These primary or universal drivers link the host adapter and operating system.

The Advanced SCSI Programming Interface (ASPI) currently is the most popular universal driver, with most peripheral makers writing their drivers to talk to ASPI. The *A* in ASPI used to stand for Adaptec, the company that introduced it, but other SCSI device vendors have licensed the right to use ASPI with their products. DOS does not support ASPI directly, but it does when the ASPI driver is loaded. Windows 9x/Me, Windows NT/2000/XP, and OS/2 2.1 and later versions provide automatic ASPI support for several SCSI host adapters.

Future Domain (now merged into Adaptec) and NCR created another interface driver called the Common Access Method (CAM). CAM is an ANSI-approved protocol that enables a single driver to control several host adapters. CAM is widely used by Linux and Unix operating systems for SCSI device interfacing using open-source drivers.

SCSI Configuration Troubleshooting

When you are installing a chain of devices on a single SCSI bus, the installation can get complicated very quickly. If you have a problem during installation, check these items first:

- Make sure you are using the latest BIOS from your motherboard manufacturer. Some have had problems with their PCI bus slots not working properly.

- Make sure that all SCSI devices attached to the bus are powered on.

- Make sure all SCSI cables and power cables are properly connected. Try removing and reseating all the connectors to be sure.

- Check that the host adapter and each device on each SCSI bus channel have a unique SCSI ID setting.

- Make sure the SCSI bus is terminated properly. Remember there should be only two terminators on the bus, one at each end. All other terminations should be removed or disabled.

- If your system BIOS setup has settings for controlling PCI bus configuration, make sure the PCI slot containing the SCSI adapter is configured for an available interrupt. If your system is Plug and Play, use the Windows Device Manager to check and possibly change the resource configuration.

- Make sure the host adapter is installed in a PCI slot that supports bus mastering. Some older motherboards (mainly old 486 processor boards) did not allow bus mastering to work in all PCI slots. Check your motherboard documentation and try moving the SCSI host adapter to a different PCI slot. This should not be an issue on any Pentium or newer boards.

- If you have a SCSI hard disk installed and your system will not boot from the SCSI drive, there can be several causes for this problem. Note that if both SCSI and non-SCSI disk drives are installed in your computer, in almost all cases the non-SCSI drive is the boot device. If you want to boot from a SCSI drive, check the boot sequence configuration in your BIOS. If your system allows it, change the boot sequence to allow SCSI devices to boot first. If not, try removing the non-SCSI drives from your system.

If the system has only SCSI disk drives and still won't boot, check the following items:

- Be sure your computer's BIOS Setup drive configuration is set to No Drives Installed. The PC BIOS supports only ATA (also called IDE) drives; by setting this to no drives, the system will then try to boot from another device, such as SCSI.

- Make sure the drive is partitioned and that a primary partition exists. Use FDISK from DOS or Windows 9x/Me or the Windows Disk Management tool in Windows 2000/XP to check.

- Make sure the boot partition of the boot hard disk is set to active. This can be checked or changed with the FDISK or Disk Management program.

- Finally as a last resort, you can try backing up all data on the SCSI hard disk and then perform a low-level format with the Format utility built in to or included with the host adapter.

Here are some tips for getting your setup to function quickly and efficiently:

- *Start by adding one device at a time.* Rather than plugging numerous peripherals into a single SCSI card and then trying to configure them at the same time, start by installing the host adapter and a single hard disk. Then, you can continue installing devices one at a time, checking to ensure that everything works before moving on.

- *Keep good documentation.* When you add a SCSI peripheral, write down the SCSI ID address and any other switch and jumper settings, such as SCSI Parity, Terminator Power, and Delayed or Remote Start. For the host adapter, record the BIOS addresses, Interrupt, DMA channel, and I/O Port addresses used by the adapter, and any other jumper or configuration settings (such as termination) that might be important to know later. If you use the System Configuration Template provided in Chapter 4, "Motherboards and Buses," to record information about your system, attach the SCSI information sheet to the System Configuration Template to provide more complete information about your system.

- *Use proper termination.* Each end of the bus must be terminated, preferably with active or forced perfect terminators. If you are using any Fast SCSI-2 device, you must use active terminators rather than the cheaper passive types. Even with standard (slow) SCSI devices, active termination is highly recommended. If you have only internal or external devices on the bus, the host adapter and last device on the chain should be terminated. If you have external and internal devices on the chain, you generally will terminate the first and last of these devices, but not the SCSI host adapter (which is in the middle of the bus).

- *Use high-quality shielded SCSI cables.* Be sure your cable connectors match your devices. Use high-quality shielded cables, and observe the SCSI bus-length limitations. Use cables designed for SCSI use, and, if possible, stick to the same brand of cable throughout a single SCSI bus. Different brands of cables have different impedance values; this situation sometimes causes problems, especially in long or high-speed SCSI implementations.

Following these simple tips will help minimize problems and leave you with a trouble-free SCSI installation.

SCSI Versus ATA Performance: Advantages and Limitations

Modern operating systems are multitasking, and SCSI devices (with all their additional controller circuitry) function independently of one another, unlike ATA. Therefore, data can be read and written to any of the SCSI devices simultaneously. This enables smoother multitasking and increased overall data throughput. The most advanced operating systems, such as Windows NT/2000/XP, even allow drive striping. A *striped drive set* is two or more drives that appear to the user as one drive. Data is split between the drives equally, again increasing overall throughput. Increased fault tolerance and performance are readily implemented and supported in SCSI drive arrays.

Ultra4 (Ultra320) SCSI drives offer advantages when compared with ATA. Ultra320 SCSI is 140% faster than UltraATA/133, which has a maximum data rate of 133MBps. Ultra320 SCSI also fully supports multitasking and can significantly improve system performance in workstations and servers running Windows NT, 2000, or XP. ATA limits cable lengths to 18 inches, effectively eliminating the ability to connect remote or external devices, whereas Ultra4 (Ultra320) SCSI allows external connections of up to 12 meters or more in length. Also note that ATA allows only 2 devices per cable, whereas Ultra320 SCSI can connect up to 15 devices. Finally, the domain validation feature of Ultra320 SCSI enables noise and other problems on the bus to be handled properly, whereas with ATA, if a problem occurs with the connection (and that is more common at the UltraATA/100 and 133 speeds), the ATA drives simply fail.

ATA drives have much less command overhead for a given sector transfer than do SCSI drives. In addition to the drive-to-controller command overhead that both ATA and SCSI must perform, a SCSI transfer involves negotiating for the SCSI bus; selecting the target drive; requesting data; terminating the transfer over the bus; and finally converting the logical data addresses to the required cylinder, head, and sector addresses. This arrangement gives ATA an advantage in sequential transfers handled by a single-tasking operating system. In a multitasking system that can take advantage of the extra intelligence of the SCSI bus, SCSI can have the performance advantage.

SCSI drives offer significant architectural advantages over ATA and other drives. Because each SCSI drive has its own embedded disk controller that can function independently from the system CPU, the computer can issue simultaneous commands to every drive in the system. Each drive can store these commands in a queue and then perform the commands simultaneously with other drives in the system. The data could be fully buffered on the drive and transferred at high speed over the shared SCSI bus when a time slot was available.

Although ATA drives also have their own controllers, they do not normally operate simultaneously, and command queuing is not supported. In effect, the dual controllers in a dual-drive ATA installation work one at a time so as not to step on each other.

ATA does not fully support overlapped, multitasked I/O, which enables a device to take on multiple commands and work on them independently and in an order different from which they were received, releasing the bus for other devices to use. The ATA bus instead waits for each command to be completed before the next one can be sent.

As you can see, SCSI has some advantages over ATA, especially where expansion is concerned, and also with regard to support for multitasking operating systems. Unfortunately, it also costs more to implement.

One final advantage of SCSI is in the portability of external devices. It is easy to take an external SCSI CD-ROM, tape drive, scanner, or even a hard disk and quickly move it to another system. This allows moving peripherals more freely between systems and can be a bonus if you have several systems with which you might want to share a number of peripherals. Installing a new external SCSI device on a system is easier because you normally will not need to open it up.

Of course, moving an external SCSI device from one system to another is not nearly as easy as it would be with a USB or FireWire (IEEE-1394) device, which is one reason the latter two (especially USB) are catching on in the mainstream market. USB and FireWire devices are Plug and Play and hot-swappable, allowing you to attach or remove the device with the power on. Plus, no device ID or other configuration is necessary. Narrow and Wide SCSI devices must normally be attached with the device and system power turned off; they also must be configured to use a unique device ID and have proper termination set for existing and new devices.

Recommended SCSI Host Adapters, Cables, and Terminators

For SCSI host adapters, I usually recommend Adaptec. Its adapters work well and come with the necessary formatting and operating software. Windows 9x/Me, Windows NT/2000/XP, and even OS/2 have built-in support for Adaptec SCSI adapters. This support is a consideration in many cases because it frees you from having to deal with additional drivers.

Standard or Fast SCSI is adequately supported by the now-obsolete ISA bus, but if you are going to install a Wide SCSI bus—or especially an Ultra, Ultra2, or Ultra160/320 bus—you should consider a PCI host adapter. This is because ISA supports a maximum transfer speed of only about 8MBps, whereas a Fast-Wide SCSI bus runs up to 20MBps. Even faster versions such as Ultra3 (Ultra160) or

Ultra4 (Ultra320) SCSI run up to a blazing 320MBps! In virtually every case, a local bus SCSI adapter would be a PCI bus version, which is supported in all current PC systems. For maximum performance, you should use a 64-bit-wide, 66MHz version of the PCI slot if your host adapter supports this version of the PCI standard.

◄◄   See "The ISA Bus," p. 350.

◄◄   See "The PCI Bus," p. 358.

Like all modern PCI adapters, plug and play is supported, meaning virtually all functions on the card can be configured and set through software. No more digging through manuals or looking for inter-rupt, DMA, I/O port, and other jumper settings—everything is controlled by software and saved in a flash memory module on the card. Following are some features found on recent SCSI cards:

- Complete configuration utility built in to the adapter's ROM
- Software-configurable IRQ, ROM addresses, DMA, I/O port addresses, SCSI parity, SCSI ID, and other settings
- Software-selectable automatic termination (no resistors to pull out!)
- Enhanced BIOS support for up to 15 drives
- No drivers required for more than two hard disks
- Drive spin-up on a per-drive basis available
- Boots from any SCSI ID

Adaptec has full PnP support on all its SCSI adapters. These adapters either are automatically config-ured in any PC that supports the PnP specification or can be configured manually through supplied software in non-PnP systems. The PnP SCSI adapters are highly recommended because they can be configured without opening up the PC! All functions are set by software, and there are no jumpers or switches to attend to. Most peripheral manufacturers write drivers for Adaptec's cards first, so you will not have many compatibility or driver-support problems with any Adaptec card.

For SCSI cables, I recommend CS Electronics (http://www.scsi-cables.com), which can supply or cus-tom manufacture virtually any SCSI cable or adapter. It can also supply a wide range of terminators, as can a company called East/West Manufacturing Enterprises, Inc. (formerly Aeronics), which is also worth a look. Visit its Web site at http://www.ewme.com.

CHAPTER 9

Magnetic Storage Principles

Magnetic Storage

Permanent or semipermanent computer data storage works by either optical or magnetic principles—or, in some cases, a combination of the two. In the case of magnetic storage, a stream of binary computer data bits (0s and 1s) is stored by magnetizing tiny pieces of metal embedded on the surface of a disk or tape in a pattern that represents the data. Later, this magnetic pattern can be read and converted back into the exact same stream of bits you started with. This is the principle of magnetic storage and the subject of this chapter.

Magnetic storage is often difficult for people to understand because magnetic fields can't be seen by the human eye. This chapter explains the principles, concepts, and techniques behind modern computer magnetic storage, enabling you to understand what happens behind the scenes. This information is designed for those who have an insatiable curiosity about how these things work; it is not absolutely necessary to know this to use a PC or perform routine troubleshooting, maintenance, or upgrades. Because the data I store on my hard drives, tape drives, floppy drives, and other magnetic storage devices happens to be far more important to me than the devices themselves, knowing how my data is handled makes me feel much more comfortable with the system in general. Having an understanding of the underlying technology does help when it comes to dealing with problems that might arise.

This chapter covers magnetic storage principles and technology and can be considered an introduction to several other chapters in the book, including the following:

- Chapter 10, "Hard Disk Storage"
- Chapter 11, "Floppy Disk Storage"
- Chapter 12, "High-Capacity Removable Storage"
- Chapter 13, "Optical Storage"
- Chapter 14, "Physical Drive Installation and Configuration"

Consult these chapters for more specific information on various types of magnetic and optical storage, as well as drive installation and configuration.

History of Magnetic Storage

Before there was magnetic storage for computers, the primary storage medium was punch cards (paper cards with holes punched in to indicate character or binary data), originally invented by Herman Hollerith for use in the 1890 Census. What amazes me is that I missed contact with punch cards by about a year; the college I went to discontinued using them during my freshman year, before I was able to take any computer-related courses. I have to believe that this was more a reflection on their budget and lack of focus on current technology at the time (in 1979, there really weren't many punch-card readers being used in the field) than it is on my age! Although long obsolete in computer use, punch cards in various forms are still used in older voting equipment.

The history of magnetic storage dates back to June 1949, when a group of IBM engineers and scientists began working on a new storage device. What they were working on was the first magnetic storage device for computers, and it revolutionized the industry. On May 21, 1952, IBM announced the IBM 726 Tape Unit with the IBM701 Defense Calculator, marking the transition from punched-card calculators to electronic computers.

Four years later, on September 13, 1956, a small team of IBM engineers in San Jose, California, introduced the first computer disk storage system as part of the 305 RAMAC (Random Access Method of Accounting and Control) computer.

The 305 RAMAC drive could store 5 million characters (that's right, only 5MB!) of data on 50 disks, each a whopping 24" in diameter. Unlike tape drives, RAMAC's recording heads could go directly to any location on a disk surface without reading all the information in between. This random accessibility had a profound effect on computer performance at the time, enabling data to be stored and retrieved significantly faster than if it were on tape.

From these beginnings, the magnetic storage industry has progressed such that today you can store 75GB or more on tiny 3 1/2" drives that fit into a single computer drive bay.

IBM's contributions to the history and development of magnetic storage are incredible; in fact, most have either come directly from IBM or as a result of IBM research. Not only did IBM invent computer magnetic tape storage as well as the hard disk drive, but it also invented the floppy drive. The same San Jose facility where the hard drive was created introduced the first floppy drive, then using 8" diameter floppy disks, in 1971. The team that developed the drive was led by Alan Shugart, a now legendary figure in computer storage.

Since then, IBM has pioneered advanced magnetic data encoding schemes, such as Modified Frequency Modulation (MFM) and Run Length Limited (RLL); drive head designs, such as Thin Film, magneto-resistive (MR), and giant magneto-resistive (GMR) heads; and drive technologies, such as Partial Response Maximum Likelihood (PRML), No-ID recording, and Self-Monitoring Analysis and Reporting Technology (S.M.A.R.T.). Today, the combined hard disk drive operations of IBM and Hitachi (called Hitachi Global Storage Technology) is arguably the leader in developing and implementing new drive technology and is second in sales only to Seagate Technology in PC hard drives.

How Magnetic Fields Are Used to Store Data

All magnetic storage devices read and write data by using electromagnetism. This basic principle of physics states that as an electric current flows through a conductor (wire), a magnetic field is generated around the conductor (see Figure 9.1). Note that electrons actually flow from negative to positive as shown in the figure, although we normally think of current flowing in the other direction.

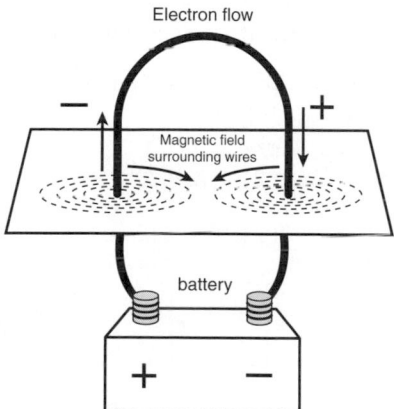

Figure 9.1   A magnetic field is generated around a wire when current is passed through it.

Electromagnetism was discovered in 1819 by Danish physicist Hans Christian Oersted, when he found that a compass needle would deflect away from pointing north when brought near a wire conducting an electric current. When the current was shut off, the compass needle resumed its alignment with the Earth's magnetic field and again pointed north.

The magnetic field generated by a wire conductor can exert an influence on magnetic material in the field. When the direction of the flow of electric current or polarity is reversed, the magnetic field's polarity also is reversed. For example, an electric motor uses electromagnetism to exert pushing and pulling forces on magnets attached to a rotating shaft.

Another effect of electromagnetism was discovered by Michael Faraday in 1831. He found that if a conductor is passed through a moving magnetic field, an electrical current is generated. As the polarity of the magnetic field changes, so does the direction of the electric current's flow (see Figure 9.2).

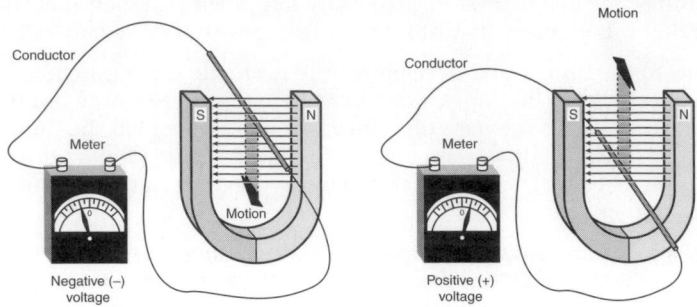

Figure 9.2 Current is induced in a wire when passed through a magnetic field.

For example, an alternator, which is a type of electrical generator used in automobiles, operates by rotating electromagnets on a shaft past coils of stationary wire conductors, which consequently generates large amounts of electrical current in those conductors. Because electromagnetism works two ways, a motor can become a generator and vice versa. When applied to magnetic storage devices, this two-way operation of electromagnetism makes recording data on a disk and reading that data back later possible. When recording, the head changes electrical impulses to magnetic fields, and when reading, the head changes magnetic fields back into electrical impulses.

The read/write heads in a magnetic storage device are U-shaped pieces of conductive material, with the ends of the U situated directly above (or next to) the surface of the actual data storage medium. The U-shaped head is wrapped with coils or windings of conductive wire, through which an electric current can flow (see Figure 9.3). When the drive logic passes a current through these coils, it generates a magnetic field in the drive head. Reversing the polarity of the electric current causes the polarity of the generated field to change also. In essence, the heads are electromagnets whose voltage can be switched in polarity very quickly.

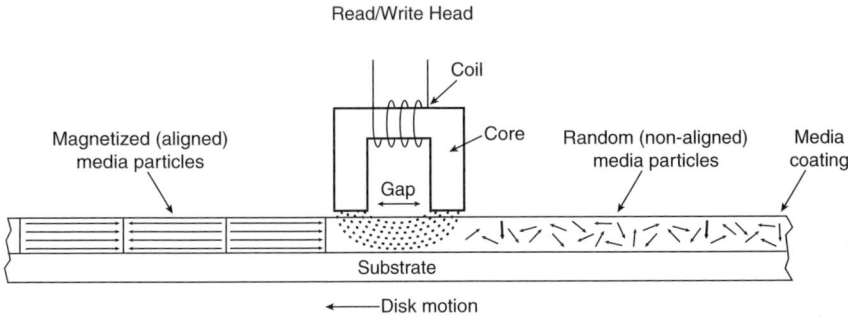

Figure 9.3 A magnetic read/write head.

The disk or tape that constitutes the actual storage medium consists of some form of substrate material (such as Mylar for floppy disks or aluminum or glass for hard disks) on which a layer of magnetizable material has been deposited. This material usually is a form of iron oxide with various other elements added. Each of the individual magnetic particles on the storage medium has its own magnetic field. When the medium is blank, the polarities of those magnetic fields are normally in a state of random disarray. Because the fields of the individual particles point in random directions, each tiny magnetic field is canceled out by one that points in the opposite direction; the cumulative effect of this is a surface with no observable field polarity. With many randomly oriented fields, the net effect is no observable unified field or polarity.

When a drive's read/write head generates a magnetic field, the field jumps the gap between the ends of the U shape. Because a magnetic field passes through a conductor much more easily than through the air, the field bends outward from the gap in the head and actually uses the adjacent storage medium as the path of least resistance to the other side of the gap. As the field passes through the medium directly under the gap, it polarizes the magnetic particles it passes through so they are aligned with the field. The field's polarity or direction—and, therefore, the polarity or direction of the field induced in the magnetic medium—is based on the direction of the flow of electric current through the coils. A change in the direction of the current flow produces a change in the direction of the magnetic field. During the development of magnetic storage, the distance between the read/write head and the media has decreased dramatically. This enables the gap to be smaller and also makes the size of the recorded magnetic domain smaller. The smaller the recorded magnetic domain, the higher the density of data that can be stored on the drive.

When the magnetic field passes through the medium, the particles in the area below the head gap are aligned in the same direction as the field emanating from the gap. When the individual magnetic domains of the particles are in alignment, they no longer cancel one another out, and an observable magnetic field exists in that region of the medium. This local field is generated by the many magnetic particles that now are operating as a team to produce a detectable cumulative field with a unified direction.

The term *flux* describes a magnetic field that has a specific direction or polarity. As the surface of the medium moves under the drive head, the head can generate what is called a *magnetic flux* of a given polarity over a specific region of the medium. When the flow of electric current through the coils in the head is reversed, so is the magnetic field polarity or flux in the head gap. This flux reversal in the head causes the polarity of the magnetized particles on the disk medium to reverse.

The flux reversal or flux transition is a change in the polarity of the aligned magnetic particles on the surface of the storage medium. A drive head creates flux reversals on the medium to record data. For each data bit (or bits) that a drive writes, it creates a pattern of positive-to-negative and negative-to-positive flux reversals on the medium in specific areas known as *bit cells* or *transition cells*. A bit cell or transition cell is a specific area of the medium—controlled by the time and speed at which the medium travels—in which the drive head creates flux reversals. The particular pattern of flux reversals within the transition cells used to store a given data bit (or bits) is called the *encoding method*. The drive logic or controller takes the data to be stored and encodes it as a series of flux reversals over a period of time, according to the pattern dictated by the encoding method it uses.

Note

The two most popular encoding methods for magnetic media are Modified Frequency Modulation and Run Length Limited. All floppy disk drives and some older hard disk drives use the MFM scheme. Today's hard disk drives use one of several variations on the RLL encoding method. These encoding methods are described in more detail later in this chapter in the section "Data Encoding Schemes."

During the write process, voltage is applied to the head. As the polarity of this voltage changes, the polarity of the magnetic field being recorded also changes. The flux transitions are written precisely at the points where the recording polarity changes. Strange as it might seem, during the read process, a head does not generate exactly the same signal that was written. Instead, the head generates a voltage pulse or spike only when it crosses a flux transition. When the transition changes from positive to negative, the pulse that the head detects is a negative voltage. When the transition changes from negative to positive, the pulse is a positive voltage spike. This effect occurs because current is generated in a conductor only when passing through lines of magnetic force at an angle. Because the head moves parallel to the magnetic fields it created on the media, the only time the head generates voltage when reading is when passing through a polarity or flux transition (flux reversal).

In essence, while reading from the medium, the head becomes a flux transition detector, emitting voltage pulses whenever it crosses a transition. Areas of no transition generate no pulse. Figure 9.4 shows the relationship between the read and write waveforms and the flux transitions recorded on a storage medium.

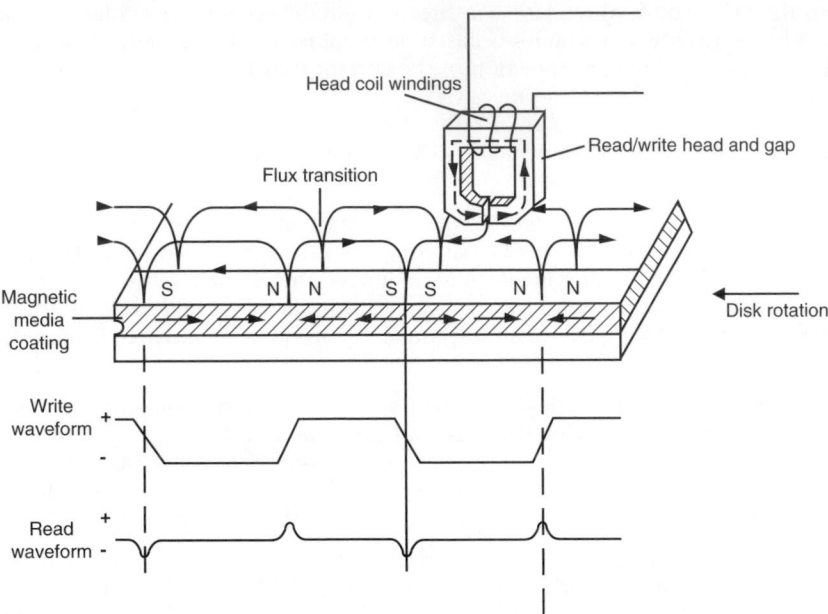

Figure 9.4   Magnetic write and read processes.

You can think of the write pattern as being a square waveform that is at a positive or negative voltage level. When the voltage is positive, a field is generated in the head, which polarizes the magnetic media in one direction. When the voltage changes to negative, the magnetic field induced in the media also changes direction. Where the waveform actually transitions from positive to negative voltage, or vice versa, the magnetic flux on the disk also changes polarity. During a read, the head senses these flux transitions and generates a pulsed positive or negative waveform, rather than the continuously positive or negative waveform used during the original recording. In other words, the signal when reading is 0 volts unless the head detects a magnetic flux transition, in which case it generates a positive or negative pulse accordingly. Pulses appear only when the head is passing over flux transitions on the medium. By knowing the clock timing the drive uses, the controller circuitry can determine whether a pulse (and therefore a flux transition) falls within a given transition cell time period.

The electrical pulse currents generated in the head while it is passing over the storage medium in read mode are very weak and can contain significant noise. Sensitive electronics in the drive and controller assembly amplify the signal above the noise level and decode the train of weak pulse currents back into binary data that is (theoretically) identical to the data originally recorded.

As you can see, hard disk drives and other storage devices read and write data by means of basic electromagnetic principles. A drive writes data by passing electrical currents through an electromagnet (the drive head), generating a magnetic field that is stored on the medium. The drive reads data by passing the head back over the surface of the medium. As the head encounters changes in the stored magnetic field, it generates a weak electrical current that indicates the presence or absence of flux transitions in the signal as it was originally written.

Read/Write Head Designs

As disk drive technology has evolved, so has the design of the read/write head. The earliest heads were simple iron cores with coil windings (electromagnets). By today's standards, the original head designs were enormous in physical size and operated at very low recording densities. Over the years, head designs have evolved from the first simple ferrite core designs into the several types and technologies available today. This section discusses the various types of heads found in PC hard disk drives, including the applications and relative strengths and weaknesses of each.

Five main types of heads have been used in hard disk drives over the years:

- Ferrite
- Thin-Film (TF)
- Metal-In-Gap (MIG)

- Magneto-resistive (MR)
- Giant magneto-resistive (GMR)

A sixth type, perpendicular, is in the experimental stage and is expected to be introduced in 2004 or later. It is discussed at the end of this section.

Ferrite

Ferrite heads, the traditional type of magnetic-head design, evolved from the original IBM 30-30 Winchester drive. These heads have an iron-oxide core wrapped with electromagnetic coils. The drive produces a magnetic field by energizing the coils or passing a magnetic field near them. This gives the heads full read/write capability. Ferrite heads are larger and heavier than thin-film heads and therefore require a larger floating height to prevent contact with the disk while it is spinning.

Manufacturers have made many refinements to the original (monolithic) ferrite head design. One type of ferrite head, called a composite ferrite head, has a smaller ferrite core bonded with glass in a ceramic housing. This design permits a smaller head gap, which enables higher track densities. These heads are less susceptible to stray magnetic fields than the older monolithic design heads.

During the 1980s, composite ferrite heads were popular in many low-end drives, such as the Seagate ST-225. As density demands grew, the competing MIG and thin-film head designs came to be used in place of ferrite heads, which are virtually obsolete today. Ferrite heads can't write to the higher coercivity media necessary for high-density disk designs and have poor frequency response with higher noise levels. The main advantage of ferrite heads is that they are the cheapest type available.

Metal-In-Gap

Metal-In-Gap heads are a specially enhanced version of the composite ferrite design. In MIG heads, a metal substance is applied to the head's recording gap. Two versions of MIG heads are available: single-sided and double-sided. Single-sided MIG heads are designed with a layer of magnetic alloy placed along the trailing edge of the gap. Double-sided MIG designs apply the layer to both sides of the gap. The metal alloy is applied through a vacuum-deposition process called sputtering.

This magnetic alloy has twice the magnetization capability of raw ferrite and enables the head to write to the higher coercivity thin-film media needed at the higher densities. MIG heads also produce a sharper gradient in the magnetic field for a better-defined magnetic pulse. Double-sided MIG heads offer even higher coercivity capability than the single-sided designs.

Because of these increases in capabilities through improved designs, MIG heads were for a time the most popular head design and were used in many hard disk drives in the late '80s and early '90s. They are still used today in LS-120 (SuperDisk) drives.

Thin Film

Thin-film heads are manufactured much the same way as a semiconductor chip—through a photolithographic process. This process creates many thousands of heads on a single circular wafer and produces a very small, high-quality product.

TF heads have an extremely narrow and controlled head gap that is created by sputtering a hard aluminum material. Because this material completely encloses the gap, the area is very well protected, minimizing the chance of damage from contact with the spinning disk. The core is a combination of iron and nickel alloy that has two to four times more magnetic power than a ferrite head core.

TF heads produce a sharply defined magnetic pulse that enables them to write at extremely high densities. Because they do not have a conventional coil, TF heads are more immune to variations in coil impedance. These small, lightweight heads can float at a much lower height than the ferrite and MIG heads; in some designs, the floating height is 2 micro-inches or less. Because the reduced height enables the heads to pick up and transmit a much stronger signal from the platters, the signal-to-noise ratio increases and improves accuracy. At the high track and linear densities of some drives, a standard ferrite head would not be capable of picking out the data signal from the background noise. Another advantage of TF heads is that their small size enables the platters to be stacked closer together, enabling more platters to fit into the same space.

When first introduced, TF heads were relatively expensive compared with older technologies, such as ferrite and MIG. Better manufacturing techniques and the need for higher densities, however, have driven the market to TF heads. The widespread use of these heads has also made them cost-competitive with, if not cheaper than, MIG heads.

Many of the drives in the 100MB–2GB range used TF heads, especially in the smaller form factors. TF heads displaced MIG heads as the most popular head design, but they have now themselves been displaced by newer magneto-resistive heads.

Magneto-Resistive Heads

A more recent development in magnetic recording—or more specifically, the read phase of magnetic recording—is the magneto-resistive head, sometimes also referred to as the anisotropic magneto-resistant (AMR) head. In the last few years, virtually all modern hard disk designs have shifted to using MR heads. MR heads are capable of increasing density four times or greater as compared to the previous inductive-only heads. IBM introduced the first commercially available drive with MR heads in 1991, in a 1GB 3 1/2" model.

All heads are detectors; that is, they are designed to detect the flux transitions in the media and convert them back to electrical signals that can be interpreted as data. One problem with magnetic recording is the ever-increasing desire for more and more density, which is putting more information (flux transitions) in a smaller and smaller space. As the magnetic domains on the disk get smaller, the signal from the heads during reading operations becomes weaker; distinguishing the true signal from the random noise or stray fields present becomes difficult. A more efficient read head, which is a more efficient way to detect these transitions on the disk, is therefore necessary.

Another magnetic effect that is well known today is being used in modern drives. When a wire is passed through a magnetic field, not only does the wire generate a small current, but the resistance of the wire also changes. Standard read heads use the head as a tiny generator, relying on the fact that the heads will generate a pulsed current when passed over magnetic flux transitions. A newer type of head design pioneered by IBM instead relies on the fact that the resistance in the head wires will also change.

Rather than use the head to generate tiny currents, which must then be filtered, amplified, and decoded, a magneto-resistive head uses the head as a resistor. A circuit passes a voltage through the head and watches for the voltage to change, which will occur when the resistance of the head changes as it passes through the flux reversals on the media. This mechanism for using the head results in a much stronger and clearer signal of what was on the media and enables the density to be increased.

MR heads rely on the fact that the resistance of a conductor changes slightly when an external magnetic field is present. Rather than put out a voltage by passing through a magnetic-field flux reversal—as a normal head would—the MR head senses the flux reversal and changes resistance. A small current flows through the heads, and this sense current measures the change in resistance. This design provides an output that is three or more times more powerful than a TF head during a read. In effect, MR heads are power-read heads, acting more like sensors than generators.

MR heads are more costly and complex to manufacture than other types of heads because several special features or steps must be added:

- Additional wires must be run to and from the head to carry the sense current.
- Four to six more masking steps are required.
- Because MR heads are so sensitive, they are very susceptible to stray magnetic fields and must be shielded.

Because the MR principle can only read data and is not used for writing, MR heads are really two heads in one. The assembly includes a standard inductive TF head for writing data and an MR head for reading. Because two separate heads are built into one assembly, each head can be optimized for its task. Ferrite, MIG, and TF heads are known as single-gap heads because the same gap is used for both reading and writing, whereas the MR head uses a separate gap for each operation.

The problem with single-gap heads is that the gap length is always a compromise between what is best for reading and what is best for writing. The read function needs a thinner gap for higher resolution; the write function needs a thicker gap for deeper flux penetration to switch the medium. In a dual-gap MR head, the read and write gaps can be optimized for both functions independently. The write (TF) gap writes a wider track than the read (MR) gap reads. Thus, the read head is less likely to pick up stray magnetic information from adjacent tracks.

A typical IBM-designed MR head is shown in Figure 9.5. This figure first shows the complete MR head-and-slider assembly on the end of an actuator arm. This is the part you would see if you opened up a drive. The slider is the block device on the end of the triangular-shaped arm that carries the head. The actual head is the tiny piece shown magnified at the end of the slider, and then the MR read sensor in the head is shown further magnified.

The read element, which is the actual magneto-resistive sensor, consists of a nickel-ferrite (NiFe) film separated by a spacer from a magnetically soft layer. The NiFe film layer changes resistance in the presence of a magnetic field. Layers of shielding protect the MR sensor read element from being corrupted by adjacent or stray magnetic fields. In many designs, the second shield also functions as one pole of the write element, resulting in what is called a *merged* MR head. The write element is not of MR design but is instead a traditional thin film inductive head.

IBM's MR head design employs a Soft Adjacent Layer (SAL) structure, consisting of the MR NiFe film, as well as a magnetically soft alloy layer separated by a film with high electrical resistance. In this design, a resistance change occurs in the NiFe layer as the MR sensor passes through a magnetic field.

As areal densities have increased, heads have been designed with narrower and thinner MR elements. The newest heads have reduced the film width between the side contacts to as little as half a micron or less.

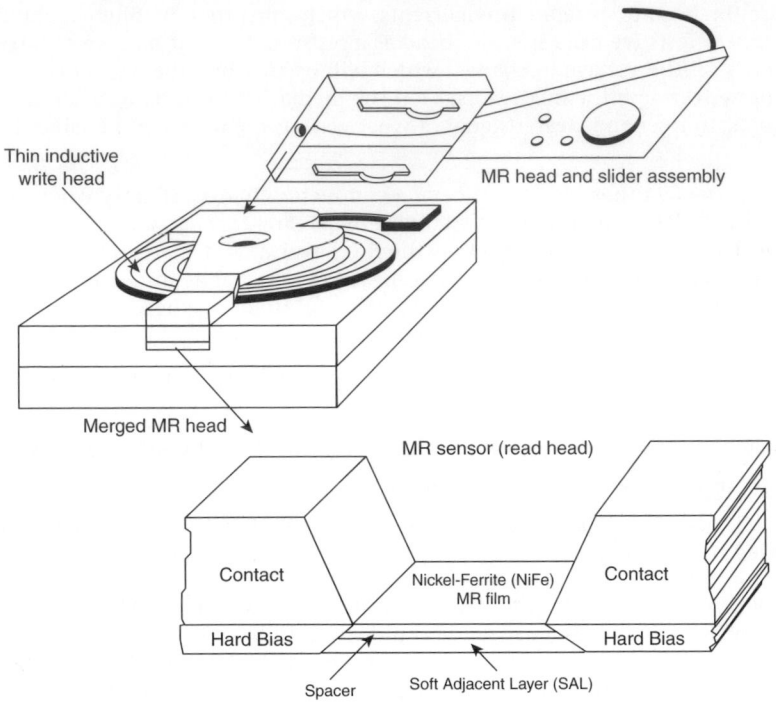

Figure 9.5 Cross section of a magneto-resistive head.

Giant Magneto-Resistive Heads

In the quest for even more density, IBM introduced a new type of MR head in 1997. Called giant magneto-resistive heads, they are physically smaller than standard MR heads but are so named for the GMR effect on which they are based. The design is very similar; however, additional layers replace the single NiFe layer in a conventional MR design. In MR heads, a single NiFe film changes resistance in response to a flux reversal on the disk. In GMR heads, two films (separated by a very thin copper conducting layer) perform this function.

The GMR effect was first discovered in 1988 in crystal samples exposed to high-powered magnetic fields (1,000 times the fields used in HDDs). Scientists Peter Gruenberg of Julich, Germany, and Albert Fert of Paris discovered that large resistance changes were occurring in materials comprised of alternating very thin layers of various metallic elements. The key structure in GMR materials is a spacer layer of a nonmagnetic metal between two layers of magnetic metals. One of the magnetic layers is *pinned*, which means it has a forced magnetic orientation. The other magnetic layer is *free*, which means it is free to change orientation or alignment. Magnetic materials tend to align themselves in the same direction. So if the spacer layer is thin enough, the free layer takes on the same orientation as the pinned layer. What was discovered was that the magnetic alignment of the free magnetic layer would periodically swing back and forth from being aligned in the same magnetic direction as the pinned layer to being aligned in opposite magnetic directions. The overall resistance is relatively low when the layers are in the same alignment and relatively high when in opposite magnetic alignment.

Figure 9.6 shows a GMR read element.

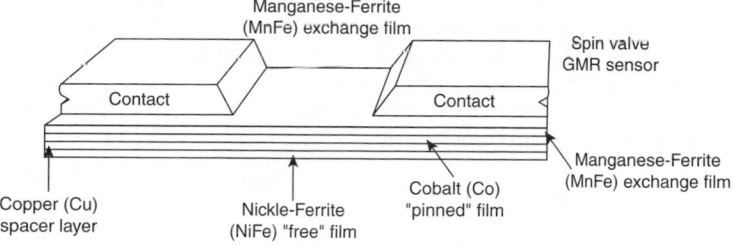

Figure 9.6 Cross section of a giant magneto-resistive head.

When a weak magnetic field, such as that from a bit on a hard disk, passes beneath a GMR head, the magnetic orientation of the free magnetic layer rotates relative to that of the other and generates a significant change in electrical resistance due to the GMR effect. Because the physical nature of the resistance change was determined to be caused by the relative spin of the electrons in the different layers, GMR heads are often referred to as *spin-valve heads*.

IBM announced the first commercially available drive using GMR heads (a 16.8GB 3 1/2" drive) in December 1997. Since then, GMR heads have become the standard in most drives of 20GB and beyond. GMR enables drives to store up to 20Gb of data per square inch of disk surface, enabling drives with capacities exceeding 100GB to be produced in the standard 3 1/2" wide, 1" high form factor.

Perpendicular

Virtually all hard drives and other types of magnetic media record data using longitudinal recording, which stores magnetic bits horizontally across the surface of the media. However, perpendicular recording, which aligns magnetic signals vertically on the media surface, has the potential to achieve higher data densities because vertically oriented magnetic bits use less space than longitudinally stored bits (see Figure 9.7). Professor Shun-ich Iwasaki was the first to propose this method of magnetic storage in 1976. However, until recently, the only major product to use this recording method was the short-lived 2.88MB floppy drive introduced in 1989 by Toshiba and first used in IBM PS/2 systems starting in 1991. Currently, major drive vendors such as Seagate and Maxtor are experimenting with perpendicular recording as a way to achieve signal density surpassing that achievable even with AFC pixie dust media (see the section "Increasing Areal Density with Pixie Dust," later in this chapter).

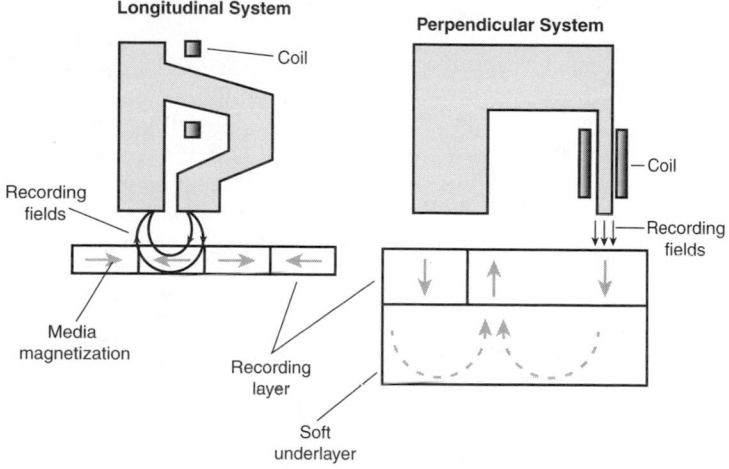

Figure 9.7 Longitudinal recording (left) compared to perpendicular recording (right).

In April 2002, Read-Rite Corporation, a major maker of read/write heads, reached areal densities of 130Gb per square inch in a prototype drive using media provided by Maxtor subsidiary MMC Technology. In November 2002, Seagate Technology announced it had achieved areal densities of more than 100Gb per square inch in a prototype drive using this technology as well. According to two independent studies published in 2000, perpendicular recording could enable densities of 500Gb–1000Gb (1 terabit) per square inch in the future.

Unlike GMR heads and AFC media (discussed later in this chapter), which can be added relatively easily to existing drive technologies, perpendicular recording requires entirely new read/write head designs. Because of the cost of such a changeover, and because GMR and AFC technologies are sufficient for the present, drives using perpendicular recording are not expected to reach the market until 2004 or later.

Head Sliders

The term *slider* is used to describe the body of material that supports the actual drive head itself. The slider is what actually floats or slides over the surface of the disk, carrying the head at the correct distance from the medium for reading and writing. Older sliders resemble a trimaran, with two outboard pods that float along the surface of the disk media and a central "hull" portion that actually carries the head and read/write gap. Figure 9.8 shows a typical mini slider. Note that the actual head, with the read/write gap, is on the trailing end of the slider.

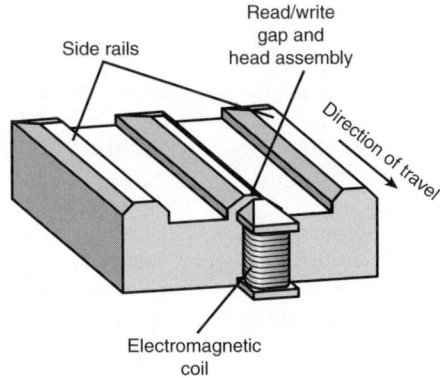

Figure 9.8   The underside of a typical head mini slider.

The trend toward smaller and smaller form factor drives has forced sliders to become smaller as well. The typical Mini-Winchester slider design was about 4mm × 3.2mm × 0.86mm in size. Most head manufacturers have since shifted to smaller Micro, Nano, Pico, or Femto sliders. The Femto sliders in use today are extremely small—about the size of the ball in the tip of a ballpoint pen. Pico and Femto sliders are assembled by using flex interconnect cable (FIC) and chip on ceramic (COC) technology that enables the process to be completely automated.

Table 9.1 shows the characteristics of the various types of sliders used in hard disk drives.

Table 9.1   Hard Disk Drive Slider Types

Slider Type	Year Introduced	Relative Size	Dimensions L (mm)	W (mm)	H (mm)	Mass (mg)
Mini	1980	100%	4.00	3.20	0.86	55.0
Micro	1986	70%	2.80	2.24	0.60	16.2
Nano (+ Pressure)	1991	62%	2.50	1.70	0.43	7.8
Nano (- Pressure)	1994	50%	2.00	1.60	0.43	5.9
Pico	1997	30%	1.25	1.00	0.30	1.6
Femto	2003	20%	0.85	0.70	0.23	0.6

Smaller sliders reduce the mass carried at the end of the head actuator arms, which provides increased acceleration and deceleration leading to faster seek times. The smaller sliders also require less surface area, allowing the head to track closer to the outer and inner diameters, thus increasing the usable area of the disk platters. Further, the smaller slider contact area reduces the slight wear on the platter surface that occurs during normal startup and spindown of the drive platters. Figure 9.9 shows a magnified photo of a Femto slider mounted on the head gimbal assembly, which is on the end of the head actuator arm.

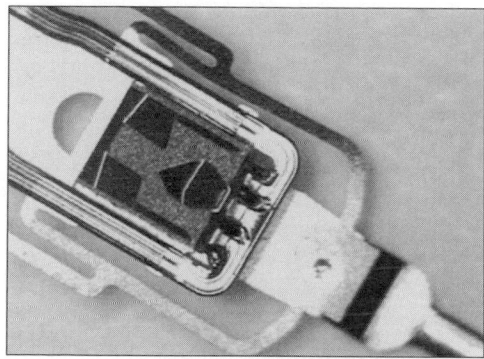

Figure 9.9   Magnified head gimbal assembly featuring a Femto slider (photo courtesy Hitachi Global Storage Technologies).

The newer slider designs also have specially modified surface patterns that are designed to maintain the same floating height above the disk surface, whether the slider is positioned above the inner or outer cylinders. Conventional sliders would increase or decrease their floating heights considerably according to the velocity of the disk surface traveling beneath them. Above the outer cylinders, the velocity and floating height would be higher. This arrangement is undesirable in newer drives that use zoned bit recording, in which the bit density is the same on all the cylinders. When the bit density is uniform throughout the drive, the head floating height should also be relatively constant for maximum performance. Special textured surface patterns and manufacturing techniques enable the sliders to float at a much more consistent height, making them ideal for zoned bit recording drives. For more information on zoned recording, see the section "Disk Formatting" in Chapter 10.

A typical Femto air-bearing slider surface design is shown in Figure 9.10.

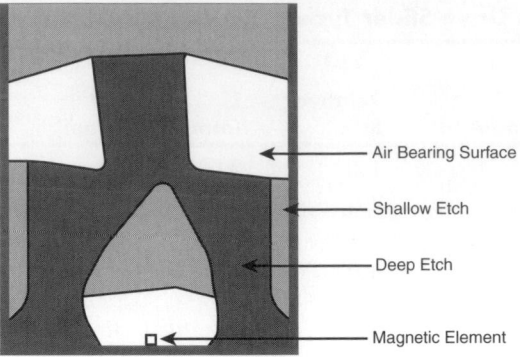

Figure 9.10 Femto air-bearing slider surface design.

A Femto slider has three distinct areas with complex shapes designed to achieve a consistent head-to-disk floating height across the disk as well as minimal height loss under high-altitude (low-pressure) conditions. The shallow etch area creates a stepped air inlet allowing airflow to create a positive pressure under the air-bearing surface that lifts the slider away from the disk. The deep etch area creates an opposite negative pressure pocket that simultaneously pulls the slider closer to the disk surface. The combination of positive and negative pressures is designed to balance the force of the suspension arm pushing the slider toward the disk, while keeping the slider at the desired floating height away from the disk surface. The balance of positive and negative pressures stabilizes and reduces the floating height variations commonly found in older slider designs. The first drive using the Femto slider design was the Hitachi 7K60 2 1/2" drive released in May 2003.

Data Encoding Schemes

Magnetic storage is essentially an analog medium. The data a PC stores on it, however, is digital information—that is, 1s and 0s. When the drive sends digital information to a magnetic recording head, the head creates magnetic domains on the storage medium with specific polarities corresponding to the positive and negative voltages the drive applies to the head. The flux reversals form the boundaries between the areas of positive and negative polarity that the drive controller uses to encode the digital data onto the analog medium. During a read operation, each flux reversal the drive detects generates a positive or negative pulse that the device uses to reconstruct the original binary data.

To optimize the placement of flux transitions during magnetic storage, the drive passes the raw digital input data through a device called an encoder/decoder (endec), which converts the raw binary information to a waveform designed to optimally place the flux transitions (pulses) on the media. During a read operation, the endec reverses the process and decodes the pulse train back into the original binary data. Over the years, several schemes for encoding data in this manner have been developed; some are better or more efficient than others, which you see later in this section.

Other descriptions of the data encoding process might be much simpler, but they omit the facts that make some of the issues related to hard drive reliability so critical—namely, timing. Engineers and designers are constantly pushing the envelope to stuff more and more bits of information into the limited quantity of magnetic flux reversals per inch. What they've come up with, essentially, is a design in which the bits of information are decoded not only from the presence or absence of flux reversals, but from the timing between them. The more accurately they can time the reversals, the more information that can be encoded (and subsequently decoded) from that timing information.

In any form of binary signaling, the use of timing is significant. When interpreting a read or write waveform, the timing of each voltage transition event is critical. Timing is what defines a particular bit or transition cell—that is, the time window within which the drive is either writing or reading a transition. If the timing is off, a given voltage transition might be recognized at the wrong time as being in a different cell, which would throw the conversion or encoding off, resulting in bits being missed, added, or misinterpreted. To ensure that the timing is precise, the transmitting and receiving devices must be in perfect synchronization. For example, if recording a 0 is done by placing no transition on the disk for a given time period or cell, imagine recording ten 0 bits in a row—you would have a long period of ten time periods or cells with no transitions.

Imagine now that the clock on the encoder was slightly off time while reading data as compared to when it was originally written. If it were fast, the encoder might think that during this long stretch of 10 cells with no transitions, only 9 cells had actually elapsed. Or if it were slow, it might think that 11 cells had elapsed instead. In either case, this would result in a read error, meaning the bits that were originally written would not be read as being the same. To prevent timing errors in drive encoding/decoding, perfect synchronization is necessary between the reading and writing processes. This synchronization often is accomplished by adding a separate timing signal, called a *clock signal*, to the transmission between the two devices. The clock and data signals also can be combined and transmitted as a single signal. Most magnetic data encoding schemes use this type of combination of clock and data signals.

Adding a clock signal to the data ensures that the communicating devices can accurately interpret the individual bit cells. Each bit cell is bounded by two other cells containing the clock transitions. By sending clock information along with the data, the clocks remain in sync, even if the medium contains a long string of identical 0 bits. Unfortunately, the transition cells used solely for timing take up space on the medium that could otherwise be used for data.

Because the number of flux transitions a drive can record in a given space on a particular medium is limited by the physical nature or density of the medium and the head technology, drive engineers have developed various ways of encoding the data by using a minimum number of flux reversals (taking into consideration the fact that some flux reversals used solely for clocking are required). Signal encoding enables the system to make the maximum use of a given drive hardware technology.

Although various encoding schemes have been tried, only a few are popular today. Over the years, these three basic types have been the most popular:

- Frequency Modulation
- Modified Frequency Modulation
- Run Length Limited

The following sections examine these codes, how they work, where they are used, and any advantages or disadvantages that apply to them. It will help to refer to Figure 9.9 (later in the chapter) as you read the descriptions of each of these encoding schemes because this figure depicts how each of these schemes would store an "X" on the same media.

FM Encoding

One of the earliest techniques for encoding data for magnetic storage is called Frequency Modulation encoding. This encoding scheme—sometimes called Single-Density encoding—was used in the earliest floppy disk drives installed in PC systems. The original Osborne portable computer, for example, used these Single-Density floppy disk drives, which stored about 80KB of data on a single disk. Although it was popular until the late 1970s, FM encoding is no longer used.

MFM Encoding

Modified Frequency Modulation encoding was devised to reduce the number of flux reversals used in the original FM encoding scheme and, therefore, to pack more data onto the disk. MFM encoding minimizes the use of clock transitions, leaving more room for the data. It records clock transitions only when a stored 0 bit is preceded by another 0 bit; in all other cases, a clock transition is not required. Because MFM minimizes the use of clock transitions, it can double the clock frequency used by FM encoding, enabling it to store twice as many data bits in the same number of flux transitions.

Because MFM encoding writes twice as many data bits by using the same number of flux reversals as FM, the clock speed of the data is doubled and the drive actually sees the same number of total flux reversals as with FM. This means a drive using MFM encoding reads and writes data at twice the speed of FM, even though the drive sees the flux reversals arriving at the same frequency as in FM.

Because it is twice as efficient as FM encoding, MFM encoding also has been called Double-Density recording. MFM is used in virtually all PC floppy disk drives today and was used in nearly all PC hard disks for a number of years. Today, virtually all hard disks use variations of RLL encoding, which provides even greater efficiency than MFM.

Table 9.2 shows the data bit-to-flux reversal translation in MFM encoding.

Table 9.2   MFM Data-to-Flux Transition Encoding

Data Bit Value	Flux Encoding
1	NT
0 preceded by 0	TN
0 preceded by 1	NN

T = Flux transition
N = No flux transition

RLL Encoding

Today's most popular encoding scheme for hard disks, called Run Length Limited, packs up to twice the information on a given disk than MFM does and three times as much information as FM. In RLL encoding, the drive combines groups of bits into a unit to generate specific patterns of flux reversals. By combining the clock and data signals in these patterns, the clock rate can be further increased while maintaining the same basic distance between the flux transitions on the storage medium.

IBM invented RLL encoding and first used the method in many of its mainframe disk drives. During the late 1980s, the PC hard disk industry began using RLL encoding schemes to increase the storage capabilities of PC hard disks. Today, virtually every drive on the market uses some form of RLL encoding.

Instead of encoding a single bit, RLL typically encodes a group of data bits at a time. The term *Run Length Limited* is derived from the two primary specifications of these codes, which are the minimum number (the run length) and maximum number (the run limit) of transition cells allowed between two actual flux transitions. Several variations of the scheme are achieved by changing the length and limit parameters, but only two have achieved any real popularity: RLL 2,7 and RLL 1,7.

You can even express FM and MFM encoding as a form of RLL. FM can be called RLL 0,1 because as few as zero and as many as one transition cells separate two flux transitions. MFM can be called RLL 1,3 because as few as one and as many as three transition cells separate two flux transitions. (Although these codes can be expressed as variations of RLL form, it is not common to do so.)

RLL 2,7 was initially the most popular RLL variation because it offers a high-density ratio with a transition detection window that is the same relative size as that in MFM. This method provides high storage density and fairly good reliability. In very high-capacity drives, however, RLL 2,7 did not prove to be reliable enough. Most of today's highest capacity drives use RLL 1,7 encoding, which offers a density ratio 1.27 times that of MFM and a larger transition detection window relative to MFM. Because of the larger relative timing window or cell size within which a transition can be detected, RLL 1,7 is a more forgiving and more reliable code, which is important when media and head technology are being pushed to their limits.

Another little-used RLL variation called RLL 3,9—sometimes also called Advanced RLL (ARLL)—allows an even higher density ratio than RLL 2,7. Unfortunately, reliability suffered too greatly under the RLL 3,9 scheme; the method was used by only a few now-obsolete controllers and has all but disappeared.

Understanding how RLL codes work is difficult without looking at an example. Within a given RLL variation, such as RLL 2,7 or 1,7, you can construct many flux transition encoding tables to demonstrate how particular groups of bits are encoded into flux transitions.

In the conversion table shown in Table 9.3, specific groups of data that are 2, 3, and 4 bits long are translated into strings of flux transitions 4, 6, and 8 transition cells long, respectively. The selected transitions for a particular bit sequence are designed to ensure that flux transitions do not occur too closely together or too far apart.

Limiting how close two flux transitions can be is necessary because of the fixed resolution capabilities of the head and storage medium. Limiting how far apart two flux transitions can be ensures that the clocks in the devices remain in sync.

Table 9.3   RLL 2,7 Data-to-Flux Transition Encoding

Data Bit Values	Flux Encoding
10	NTNN
11	TNNN
000	NNNTNN
010	TNNTNN
011	NNTNNN
0010	NNTNNTNN
0011	NNNNTNNN

T = Flux transition

N = No flux transition

In studying Table 9.3, you might think that encoding a byte value such as 00000001b would be impossible because no combinations of data bit groups fit this byte. Encoding this type of byte is not a problem, however, because the controller does not transmit individual bytes; instead, the controller sends whole sectors, making encoding such a byte possible by including some of the bits in the following byte. The only real problem occurs in the last byte of a sector if additional bits are necessary to complete the final group sequence. In these cases, the endec in the controller adds excess bits to the end of the last byte. These excess bits are then truncated during any reads so the controller always decodes the last byte correctly.

Encoding Scheme Comparisons

Figure 9.11 shows an example of the waveform written to store the ASCII character X on a hard disk drive by using three different encoding schemes.

In each of these encoding scheme examples, the top line shows the individual data bits (01011000b, for example) in their bit cells separated in time by the clock signal, which is shown as a period (.). Below that line is the actual write waveform, showing the positive and negative voltages as well as head voltage transitions that result in the recording of flux transitions. The bottom line shows the transition cells, with T representing a transition cell that contains a flux transition and N representing a transition cell that is empty.

The FM encoding example shown in Figure 9.11 is easy to explain. Each bit cell has two transition cells: one for the clock information and one for the data itself. All the clock transition cells contain flux transitions, and the data transition cells contain a flux transition only if the data is a 1 bit. No transition is present when the data is a 0 bit. Starting from the left, the first data bit is 0, which decodes as a flux transition pattern of TN. The next bit is a 1, which decodes as TT. The next bit is 0, which decodes as TN, and so on.

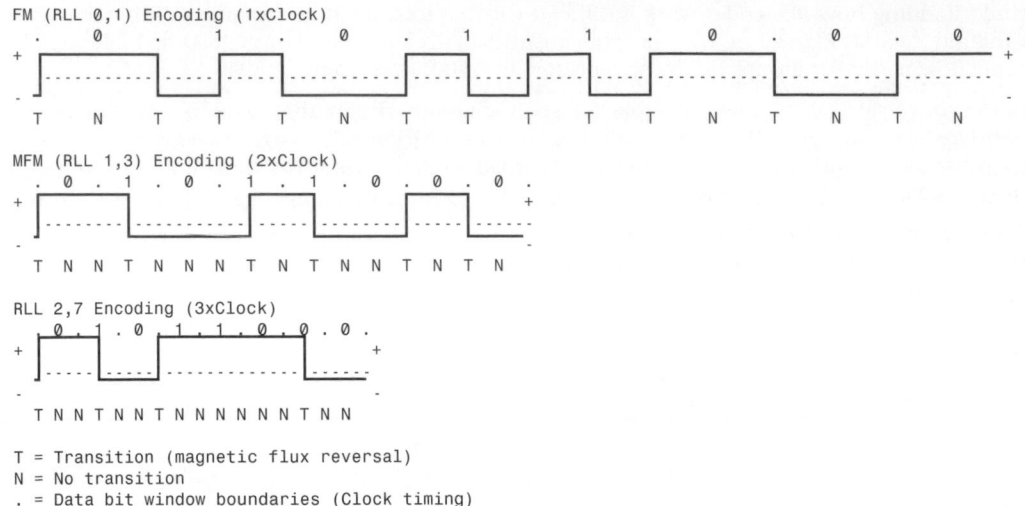

T = Transition (magnetic flux reversal)
N = No transition
. = Data bit window boundaries (Clock timing)

Figure 9.11 ASCII character X write waveforms using FM; MFM; and RLL 2,7 encoding.

The MFM encoding scheme also has clock and data transition cells for each data bit to be recorded. As you can see, however, the clock transition cells carry a flux transition only when a 0 bit is stored after another 0 bit. Starting from the left, the first bit is a 0, and the preceding bit is unknown (assume 0), so the flux transition pattern is TN for that bit. The next bit is a 1, which always decodes to a transition-cell pattern of NT. The next bit is 0, which was preceded by 1, so the pattern stored is NN. By using Table 9.2 (shown earlier), you easily can trace the MFM encoding pattern to the end of the byte. You can see that the minimum and maximum numbers of transition cells between any two flux transitions are one and three, respectively, which explains why MFM encoding can also be called RLL 1,3.

The RLL 2,7 pattern is more difficult to see because it encodes groups of bits rather than individual bits. Starting from the left, the first group that matches the groups listed in Table 9.3 is the first three bits, 010. These bits are translated into a flux transition pattern of TNNTNN. The next two bits, 11, are translated as a group to TNNN; and the final group, 000 bits, is translated to NNNTNN to complete the byte. As you can see in this example, no additional bits are needed to finish the last group.

Notice that the minimum and maximum numbers of empty transition cells between any two flux transitions in this example are 2 and 6, although a different example could show a maximum of seven empty transition cells. This is where the RLL 2,7 designation comes from. Because even fewer transitions are recorded than in MFM, the clock rate can be increased to three times that of FM or 1.5 times that of MFM, thus storing more data in the same space. Notice, however, that the resulting write waveform itself looks exactly like a typical FM or MFM waveform in terms of the number and separation of the flux transitions for a given physical portion of the disk. In other words, the physical minimum and maximum distances between any two flux transitions remain the same in all three of these encoding scheme examples.

Partial-Response, Maximum-Likelihood Decoders

Another feature often used in modern hard disk drives involves the disk read circuitry. Read channel circuits using Partial-Response, Maximum-Likelihood (PRML) technology enable disk drive manufacturers to increase the amount of data stored on a disk platter by up to 40%. PRML replaces the standard "detect one peak at a time" approach of traditional analog peak-detect, read/write channels with digital signal processing.

As the data density of hard drives increases, the drive must necessarily record the flux reversals closer together on the medium. This makes reading the data on the disk more difficult because the adjacent magnetic peaks can begin to interfere with each other. PRML modifies the way the drive reads the data from the disk. The controller analyzes the analog data stream it receives from the heads by using digital signal sampling, processing, and detection algorithms (this is the partial response element) and predicts the sequence of bits the data stream is most likely to represent (the maximum likelihood element). PRML technology can take an analog waveform, which might be filled with noise and stray signals, and produce an accurate reading from it.

This might not sound like a very precise method of reading data that must be bit-perfect to be usable, but the aggregate effect of the digital signal processing filters out the noise efficiently enough to enable the drive to place the flux change pulses much more closely together on the platter, thus achieving greater densities. Most drives with capacities of 2GB or above use PRML technology in their endec circuits.

Capacity Measurements

In December 1998, the International Electrotechnical Commission (IEC)—the leading international organization for worldwide standardization in electrotechnology—approved as an IEC International Standard names and symbols for prefixes for binary multiples for use in the fields of data processing and data transmission. Prior to this, a lot of confusion had existed as to whether a megabyte stood for 1 million bytes (10^6) or 1,048,576 bytes (2^{20}). Even so, these new prefixes have yet to be widely adopted and confusion still reigns. The industry-standard abbreviations for the units used to measure the capacity of magnetic (and other) drives are shown in Table 9.4.

Table 9.4   Standard Abbreviations and Meanings

Abbreviation	Description	Power	Value
K	Kilo	10^3	1,000
Ki	Kibi	2^{10}	1,024
M	Mega	10^6	1,000,000
Mi	Mebi	2^{20}	1,048,576
G	Giga	10^9	1,000,000,000
Gi	Gibi	2^{30}	1,073,741,824
T	Tera	10^{12}	1,000,000,000,000
Ti	Tebi	2^{40}	1,099,511,627,776
P	Peta	10^{15}	1,000,000,000,000,000
Pi	Pebi	2^{50}	1,125,899,906,842,624

According to the new prefix standard, 1 mebibyte (1 MiB = 2^{20} B = 1,048,576 B) and 1 megabyte (1MB = 10^6 B = 1,000,000 B) are not equal. Because the new prefixes are not in widespread use (and they might never be), M in most cases can indicate both decimal *millions of bytes* and binary *megabytes*. Similarly, G is often used to refer to decimal *billions of bytes* and binary *gigabytes*. In general, memory values are expressed by using the binary values, although disk capacities can go either way. This often leads to confusion in reporting disk capacities because many manufacturers tend to use whichever value makes their products look better. For example, drive capacities are often rated in decimal billions (G - Giga), whereas most BIOS chips and operating system utilities, such as the Windows FDISK, rate the same drive in binary gigabytes (Gi - Gibi). Note also that when bits and bytes are used as part of some other measurement, the difference between bits and bytes is often distinguished by the use of a lower- or uppercase *B*. For example, megabits are typically abbreviated with a lowercase *b*, resulting in the abbreviation *Mbps* for *megabits per second*, whereas *MBps* indicates *megabytes per second*.

Areal Density

Areal density is often used as a technology growth-rate indicator for the hard disk drive industry. *Areal density* is defined as the product of the linear bits per inch (BPI), measured along the length of the tracks around the disk, multiplied by the number of tracks per inch (TPI), measured radially on the disk (see Figure 9.12). The results are expressed in units of megabits or gigabits per square inch (Mbit/sq. inch or Gbit/sq. inch) and are used as a measure of efficiency in drive recording technology. Current high-end 3 1/2" drives record at areal densities exceeding 60Gbit/sq. inch (such as the 400GB Hitachi 7K400, which records at 61.7Gbit/sq. inch), whereas 2 1/2" drives such as the 80GB Hitachi 5K80 record at areal densities of 70Gbit/sq. inch or more. Prototype drives with densities of 130Gbit/sq. inch or more now exist, which will enable 3 1/2" drives with capacities of 1 terabyte (TB) or more in the next few years.

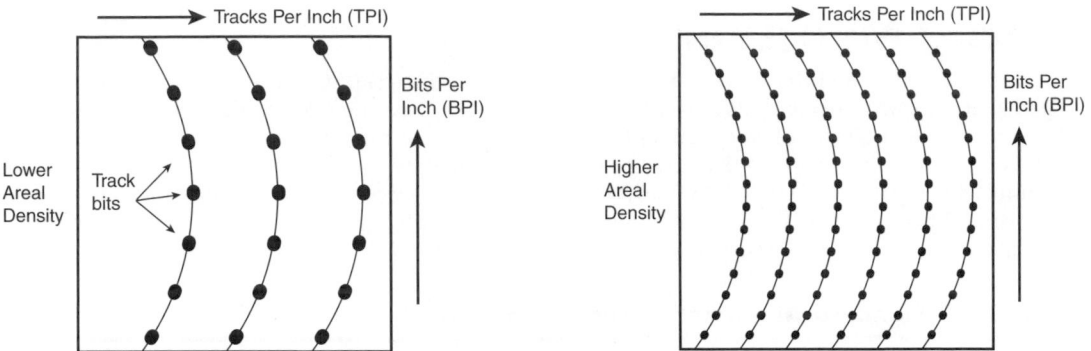

Figure 9.12   Areal density, combining tracks per inch and bits per inch.

Drives record data in tracks, which are circular bands of data on the disk. Each track is divided into sectors. Figure 9.13 shows an actual floppy disk sprayed with magnetic developer (powdered iron) such that an image of the actual tracks and sectors can be clearly seen. The disk shown is a 5 1/4" 360KB floppy, which has 40 tracks per side, with each track divided into 9 sectors. Note that each sector is delineated by gaps in the recording, which precede and postcede the track and sector headers (where ID and address information resides). You can clearly see the triple gap preceding the first sector, which includes the track and sector headers. Then following in a counterclockwise direction, you see each subsequent sector, preceded by gaps delineating the header for that sector. The area between the headers is where the sector data is written.

Notice that sector 9 is longer than the others; this is to enable rotational speed differences between drives, so that all the data can be written before running into the start of the track. Also notice that a good portion of the disk surface isn't used because it is simply impractical to have the heads travel in and out that far, and the difference in length between the sectors on the inner and outer tracks becomes more of a problem.

Areal density has been rising steadily since the first magnetic storage drive (IBM RAMAC) was introduced in 1956, initially at a growth rate of about 25% per year (doubling every four years), and since the early 1990s at a growth rate of about 60% per year (doubling every year and a half). The development and introduction of magneto-resistive heads in 1991, giant magneto-resistive heads in 1997, and AFC pixie dust media in 2001 have propelled the increase in the areal density growth rate. In the 47+ years since the RAMAC drive was introduced, the areal density of magnetic storage has increased more than 17 million fold.

At the current growth rate, within the next three years or so, drive manufacturers will achieve areal densities of approximately 100Gbit/sq. inch, which is considered near the point at which the superparamagnetic effect takes place. This is an effect in which the magnetic domains become so small that they are intrinsically unstable at room temperature. Techniques such as extremely high coercivity media and vertical polarity recording are projected to enable magnetic storage densities of

400Gbit/sq. inch or more, but beyond that, scientists and engineers will have to look toward other technologies. One such technology being considered for the future is holographic storage, in which a laser writes data three-dimensionally in a crystal plate or cube.

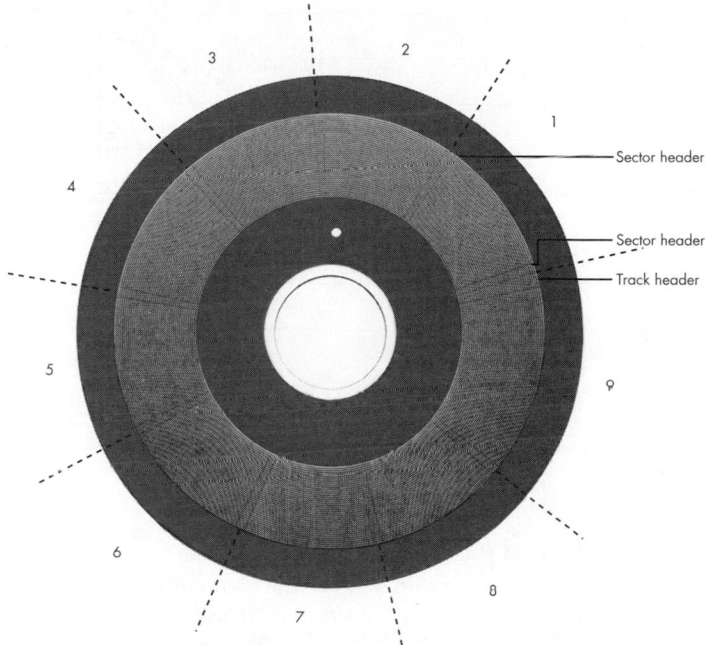

Figure 9.13 360KB floppy disk media sprayed with magnetic developer (powdered iron) showing the actual track and sector images.

Figure 9.14 shows how areal density has increased from when magnetic storage was first developed (1956 RAMAC) through the present time.

To increase areal density while maintaining the same external drive form factors, drive manufacturers have developed media and head technologies to support these higher areal densities, such as ceramic/glass platters, GMR heads, pseudo-contact recording, and PRML electronics, as discussed earlier in this chapter. The primary challenge in achieving higher densities is manufacturing drive heads and disks to operate at closer tolerances. Improvements in tolerances and the use of more platters in a given form factor continue to fuel improvements in drive capacity, but drive makers continue to seek even greater capacity increases, both by improving current technologies and by developing new ones.

To fit more data on a platter of a given size, the tracks must be placed more closely together and the heads must be capable of achieving greater precision in their placements over the tracks. This also means that as hard disk capacities increase, heads must float ever closer to the disk surface during operation. The gap between the head and disk is as close as 10 nanometers (0.01 microns) in some drives, which is approximately the thickness of a cell membrane. By comparison, a human hair is typically 80 microns in diameter, which is 8,000 times thicker than the gap between the head and disk in some drives. The prospect of actual contact or near contact recording is being considered for future drives to further increase density.

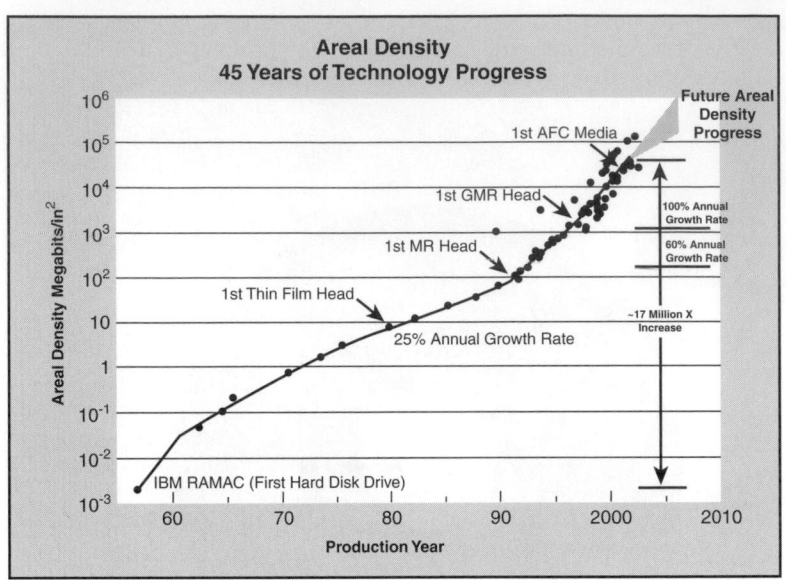

Figure 9.14   Evolution of areal density in magnetic disk storage.

Increasing Areal Density with Pixie Dust

In 1990, IBM scientists discovered that a thin layer of the element ruthenium was the most effective nonmagnetic element that could be used for spacers in devices such as GMR heads. However, more than a decade passed before the first commercially available application of this principle was used to increase disk drive storage densities by improving the storage density of the drives' platters.

In May 2001, IBM began to produce drives using "pixie dust" technology in its Travelstar 2 1/2" hard drive series for notebook computers. In November 2001, Deskstar GXP drives using the same technology were introduced, and these drives had capacities of 80GB and 120GB.

These drives achieved data densities exceeding 25Gb per square inch through the use of a thin (three-atom-thick) layer of ruthenium used to separate two magnetic surfaces on each side of the drive's platters. Traditional drives use platters with a single magnetic surface per side. Media using the ruthenium coating, commonly referred to as pixie dust, is technically known as antiferromagnetically coupled (AFC) media. IBM continues to use AFC media in its latest drives for notebook, desktop, and server computers and has licensed AFC media to other drive and media vendors.

AFC media was developed because achieving greater and greater densities of magnetic storage requires individual magnetic areas on the media to become smaller and smaller. However, when magnetic areas become too small, a problem called the superparamagnetic effect (which causes magnetic areas to lose their magnetism over time) can occur.

When a thin layer of ruthenium is placed between two magnetic layers, the layers are forced to orient themselves magnetically in opposite directions to each other. Although the three-layer structure is physically thicker than a conventional magnetic surface, the opposing magnetic orientations make the layers appear to be thinner than a conventional surface. As a result, disk drive read/write heads can record smaller, high-density signals, increasing the storage capacity of a given platter size without the risk of the signal degrading. Figure 9.15 compares a normal single-layer disk platter to a disk platter using pixie dust AFC media technology.

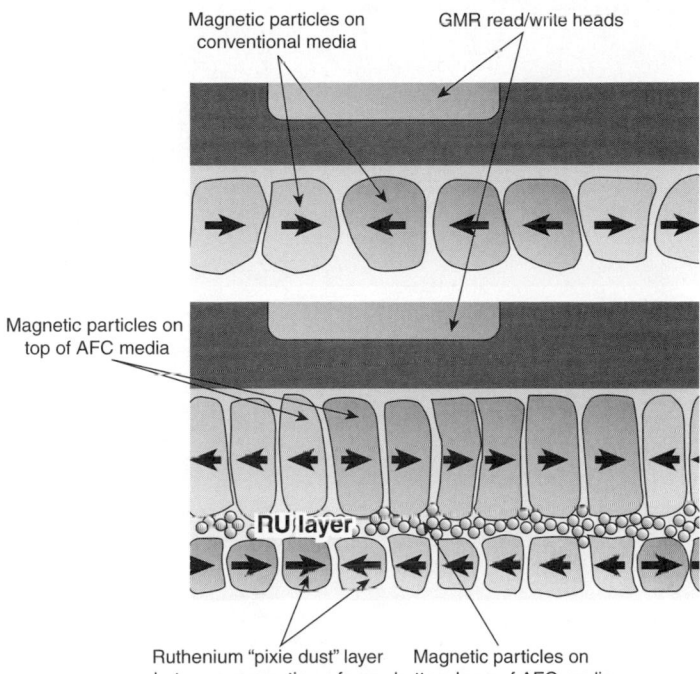

Figure 9.15 Conventional media uses a single magnetic surface, whereas AFC media uses two magnetic surfaces separated by a thin layer of ruthenium, a process IBM refers to as *pixie dust*.

Just as GMR heads use two layers separated by a thin conductive layer to increase data storage density, AFC media uses a similar principle. In essence, AFC media represents an extension of GMR principles from the read/write heads to the media's data recording surfaces. Over time, AFC media is expected to quadruple the storage capacity of magnetic media, enabling drives to reach capacities of 100Gb per square inch or more. In practical terms, such capacity could result in desktop 3 1/2" hard drives of up to 1TB, 2 1/2" notebook hard drives of up to 300GB, and IBM Microdrives (which have a 1" wide platter) of 8GB or more.

CHAPTER 10

Hard Disk Storage

Definition of a Hard Disk

To many users, the hard disk drive is the most important and yet the most mysterious part of a computer system. A *hard disk drive* is a sealed unit that a PC uses for nonvolatile data storage. *Nonvolatile*, or semipermanent, storage means that the storage device retains the data even when no power is supplied to the computer. Because the hard disk drive is expected to retain data until deliberately erased or overwritten, the hard drive is used to store crucial programming and data. As a result, when the hard disk fails, the consequences are usually very serious. To maintain, service, and upgrade a PC system properly, you must understand how the hard disk functions.

A hard disk drive contains rigid, disk-shaped platters, usually constructed of aluminum or glass (see Figure 10.1). Unlike floppy disks, the platters can't bend or flex—hence the term *hard disk*. In most hard disk drives, you can't remove the platters, which is why they are sometimes called *fixed* disk drives. Removable hard disk drives are also available. Usually, this term refers to a device in which the entire drive unit (that is, the disk unit containing the platters as well as the rest of the drive) is removable, but it can also refer to cartridge drives, where the platters are contained in a removable cartridge.

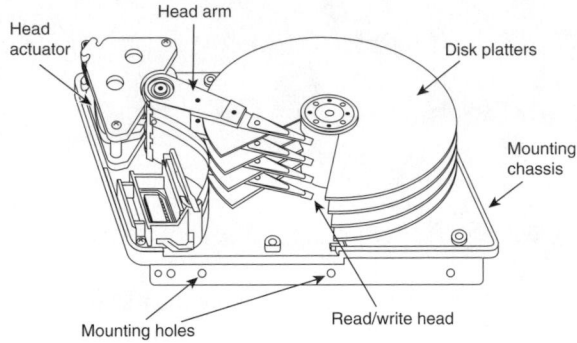

Figure 10.1   Hard disk heads and platters.

Note

Hard disk drives are sometimes referred to as *Winchester drives*. This term dates back to 1973, when IBM introduced the model 3340 drive, which had 30MB of fixed platter and 30MB of removable platter storage on separate spindles. The drive was codenamed Winchester by project leader Ken Haughton because the original capacity designation (30-30) sounded like the popular .30-30 (caliber-grains of charge) cartridge used by the Winchester 94 rifle introduced in 1895. The original 3340 "Winchester" drive was the first to use a sealed head/disk assembly, and the name has since been applied to all subsequent drives with similar technology.

Hard Drive Advancements

In 1957, Cyril Northcote Parkinson published his famous compilation of essays titled *Parkinson's Law*, which begins with the statement, "Work expands so as to fill the time available for its completion." A corollary of Parkinson's most famous "law" can be applied to hard drives: "Data expands so as to fill the space available for its storage." This, of course, means that no matter how big a drive you get, you *will* find a way to fill it. I know that I have lived by that dictum since purchasing my first hard disk drive 20 years ago.

Even though I am well aware of the exponential growth of everything associated with computers, I am still amazed at how large and fast modern drives have become. The first hard drive I purchased in

1983 was a 10MB (that's 10 megabyte, *not* gigabyte) Miniscribe model 2012, which was a 5 1/4" (platter) drive that was 203.2mm×146mm×82.6mm or 8"×5.75"×3.25" (L×W×H) in overall size and weighed 2.5kg (5.5 lb., which is more than some laptop computers)! By comparison, the 400GB Hitachi Deskstar 7K400 drive (currently the highest-capacity 3 1/2" hard drive) uses smaller 3 1/2" platters, is about 147mm×101.6mm×26.1mm or 5.8"×4"×1" in overall size and weighs only 0.7kg (1.54 lb.). It stores a whopping 400GB, which is 40,000 times more storage in a package that is less than one-sixth the size and about one-fourth the weight. That's a pretty large step in just over 20 years' time!

Note

The book *Parkinson's Law* (ISBN: 1-5684-9015-1) is still in print and is in fact considered one of the essential tomes of business and management study even today.

To give you an idea of how far hard drives have come in the 20+ years they have been used in PCs, I've outlined some of the more profound changes in PC hard disk storage:

- Maximum storage capacities have increased from the 5MB and 10MB 5 1/4" full-height drives available in 1982 to 300GB or more for even smaller 3 1/2" half-height drives (Maxtor MaXLine II) and 80GB or more for notebook system 2 1/2" drives (Hitachi Travelstar 5K80) that are 9.5mm (or less) in height. Hard drives smaller than 30GB are rare in today's desktop personal computers.

- Data transfer rates to and from the media (sustained transfer rates) have increased from between 85KBps and 102KBps for the original IBM XT in 1983 to an average of 62MBps or more for some of the fastest drives today (Seagate Cheetah X15.3).

- Average seek times (how long it takes to move the heads to a particular cylinder) have decreased from more than 85ms (milliseconds) for the 10MB drives used by IBM in the 1983 vintage PC-XT to 3.6ms or less for some of the fastest drives today. The Maxtor Atlas 15K features an average seek time of just 3.2ms.

- In 1982–1983, a 10MB drive and controller cost more than $2,000 ($200 per megabyte), which would be more than double that in today's dollars. Today, the cost of hard drives (with integrated controllers) has dropped to one-eighth of a cent per megabyte or less, or about 80GB for $100!

Note

In a rather stunning move, IBM sold its Hard Disk Drive operations division to Hitachi on January 6, 2003. The resulting new company is called Hitachi Global Storage Technologies (www.hitachigst.com); comprises the hard disk drive operations of Hitachi and IBM; and is headquartered in San Jose, California. Hitachi Global Storage Technologies now manufactures, sells, and supports the former IBM Travelstar, Microdrive, Ultrastar, and Deskstar product lines. The new company is 70% owned by Hitachi, with the remaining shares held by IBM. Hitachi will assume full ownership at the end of 2005, and IBM has no involvement in the management of the new company. What is stunning about this is that IBM invented the hard drive, so it is sad to see it exit the business.

Hard Disk Drive Operation

The basic physical construction of a hard disk drive consists of spinning disks with heads that move over the disks and store data in tracks and sectors. The heads read and write data in concentric rings called *tracks*, which are divided into segments called *sectors*, which typically store 512 bytes each (see Figure 10.2).

Hard disk drives usually have multiple disks, called *platters*, that are stacked on top of each other and spin in unison, each with two sides on which the drive stores data. Most drives have two or three platters, resulting in four or six sides, but some PC hard disks have up to 12 platters and 24 sides with 24 heads to read them (Seagate Barracuda 180). The identically aligned tracks on each side of every platter together make up a cylinder (see Figure 10.3). A hard disk drive usually has one head per platter side, with all the heads mounted on a common carrier device or rack. The heads move radially across the disk in unison; they can't move independently because they are mounted on the same carrier or rack, called an *actuator*.

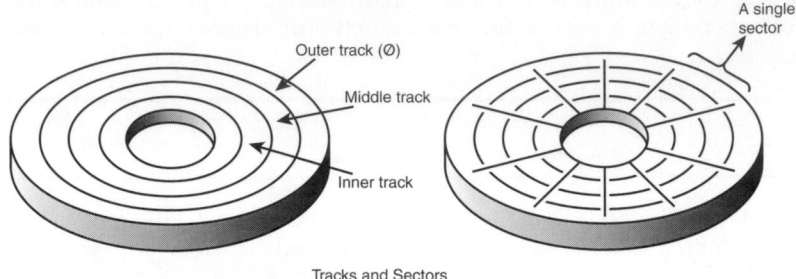

Tracks and Sectors

Figure 10.2   The tracks and sectors on a disk.

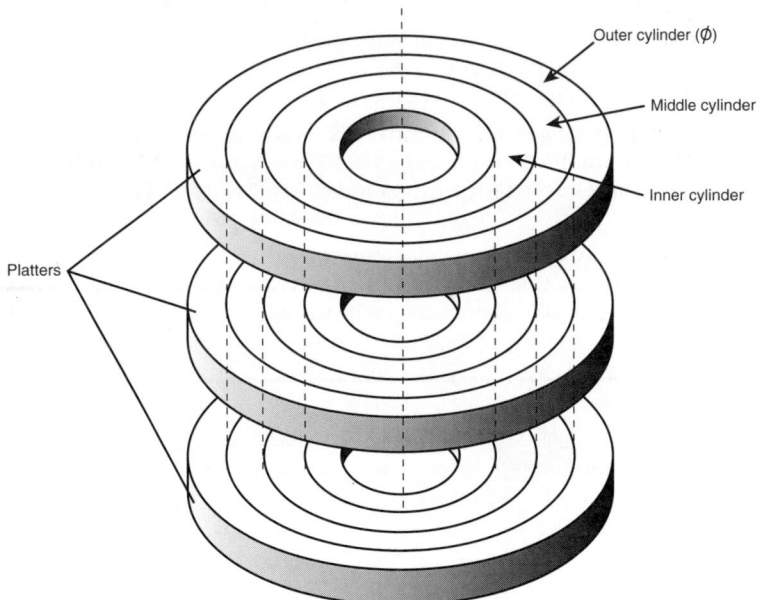

Figure 10.3   Hard disk cylinders.

Originally, most hard disks spun at 3,600rpm—approximately 10 times faster than a floppy disk drive. For many years, 3,600rpm was pretty much a constant among hard drives. Now, however, most drives spin even faster. Although speeds can vary, modern drives typically spin the platters at either 4,200rpm; 5,400rpm; 7,200rpm; 10,000rpm; or 15,000rpm. Most standard-issue drives found in PCs today spin at 5,400rpm, with high-performance models spinning at 7,200rpm. Some of the small 2 1/2" notebook drives run at only 4,200rpm to conserve power, and the 10,000rpm or 15,000rpm drives are usually found only in very high-performance workstations or servers, where their higher prices, heat generation, and noise can be more easily dealt with. High rotational speeds combined with a fast head-positioning mechanism and more sectors per track are what make one hard disk faster overall than another.

The heads in most hard disk drives do not (and should not!) touch the platters during normal operation. However, on most drives, the heads do rest on the platters when the drive is powered off. In most drives, when the drive is powered off, the heads move to the innermost cylinder, where they land on the platter surface. This is referred to as *contact start stop (CSS)* design. When the drive is powered on, the heads slide on the platter surface as they spin up, until a very thin cushion of air builds up between the heads and platter surface, causing the heads to lift off and remain suspended a short distance above or below the platter. If the air cushion is disturbed by a particle of dust or a shock, the head can come into contact with the platter while it is spinning at full speed. When contact with the spinning platters is forceful enough to do damage, the event is called a *head crash*. The result of a head crash can be anything from a few lost bytes of data to a completely ruined drive. Most drives have special lubricants on the platters and hardened surfaces that can withstand the daily "takeoffs and landings" as well as more severe abuse.

Some newer drives do not use CSS design and instead use a load/unload mechanism that does not allow the heads to contact the platters, even when the drive is powered off. First used in the 2 1/2" form factor notebook or laptop drives where resistance to mechanical shock is more important, traditional load/unload mechanisms use a ramp positioned just off the outer part of the platter surface, whereas some newer designs position the ramp near the spindle. When the drive is powered off or in a power-saving mode, the heads ride up on the ramp. When powered on, the platters are allowed to come up to full speed before the heads are released down the ramp, allowing the airflow (air bearing) to prevent any head/platter contact.

Because the platter assemblies are sealed and nonremovable, the track densities on the disk can be very high. Hard drives today have up to 96,000 or more tracks per inch (TPI) recorded on the media (Hitachi Travelstar 5K80). Head disk assemblies (HDAs), which contain the platters, are assembled and sealed in clean rooms under absolutely sanitary conditions. Because few companies repair HDAs, repair or replacement of the parts inside a sealed HDA can be expensive. Every hard disk ever made eventually fails. The only questions are when the failure will occur and whether your data is backed up.

Caution

It is strongly recommended that you do not even attempt to open a hard disk drive's HDA unless you have the equipment and expertise to make repairs inside. Most manufacturers deliberately make the HDA difficult to open to discourage the intrepid do-it-yourselfer. Opening the HDA voids the drive's warranty.

Many PC users know that hard disks are fragile, and comparatively speaking, they are certainly one of the more fragile components in your PC. That being the case, it comes as somewhat of a surprise to the students in some of my PC Hardware and Troubleshooting or Data Recovery seminars when I run various hard disks with the covers removed—and in some cases I've even removed and installed the covers while the drives were operating! Those drives continue to store data perfectly to this day with their lids either on or off. Of course, I do not recommend that you try this with your own drives.

The Ultimate Hard Disk Drive Analogy

There is an old analogy that compares the interaction of the heads and the medium in a typical hard disk drive as being similar in scale to a 747 Jumbo Jet flying a few feet off the ground at cruising speed (500+ mph). I have heard this analogy used repeatedly for years, and in the past I even used it myself without checking to see whether the analogy is technically accurate with respect to modern hard drives. It isn't.

Perhaps the most inaccurate aspect of the 747 analogy is the use of an airplane of any type to describe the head-and-platter interaction. This analogy implies that the heads fly very low over the surface of the disk, but technically, this is not true. The heads do not fly at all in the traditional aerodynamic sense; instead, they float or ski on a cushion of air that is being dragged around by the platters.

A much better analogy would use a hovercraft instead of an airplane; the action of a hovercraft much more closely emulates the action of the heads in a hard disk drive. Like a hovercraft, the drive heads rely somewhat on the shape of the bottom of the head to capture and control the cushion of air that keeps them floating over the disk. By nature, the cushion of air on which the heads float forms only in very close proximity to the platter and is often called an *air bearing* by those in the disk drive industry.

I thought it was time to come up with a new analogy that more correctly describes the dimensions and speeds at which a hard disk drive operates today. I looked up the specifications on a specific modern hard disk drive and then magnified and rescaled all the dimensions involved by a factor of more than 300,000. For my example, I use an IBM Deskstar 75GXP drive, which is a 75GB (formatted capacity), 3 1/2" ATA (AT Attachment interface) drive. The head sliders (called *pico* sliders) in this drive are about 0.049" long, 0.039" wide, and 0.012" high. They float on a cushion of air about 15 nanometers (nm or billionths of a meter) over the surface of the disk while traveling at an average true speed of 53.55 miles per hour (figuring an average track diameter of about 2 1/2"). These heads read and write individual bits spaced only 2.56 micro-inches (millionths of an inch) apart, along tracks separated by only 35.27 micro-inches. The heads can move from one track to another in 8.5 milliseconds during an average seek.

To create my analogy, I magnified the scale to make the head floating height equal to 5 millimeters (about 0.2"). Because 5 millimeters is about 333,333 times greater than 15 nanometers (nm), I scaled up everything else by the same amount.

Magnified to such a scale, the heads in this typical hard disk would be about 1,361 feet long, 1,083 feet wide, and 333 feet high (the length and height would be about equal to the Sears Tower if it were tipped over sideways). These skyscraper-sized heads would float on a cushion of air that to scale would be only 5mm thick (about 0.2") while traveling at a speed of 17.8 million miles per hour (4,958 miles per second), all while reading data bits spaced a mere 0.85" apart on tracks separated by only 0.98 feet!

The proportionate forward speed of this imaginary head is difficult to comprehend, so I'll elaborate. The diameter of the Earth at the equator is 7,926 miles, which means a circumference of about 24,900 miles. At 4,958 miles per second, this imaginary skyscraper-sized head would circle the earth once every 5 seconds (at only two-tenths of an inch over the surface)! It would also read 231.33MB in one lap around this equatorial track.

There is also sideways velocity to consider. Because the average seek time of 8.5 milliseconds is defined as the time it takes to move the heads over one-third of the total tracks (about 9,241 tracks in this example), the heads could move sideways within a scale distance of 1.71 miles in that short time. This results in a scale seek velocity of more than 726,321mph, or 202 miles per second!

This analogy should give you a new appreciation of the technological marvel that the modern hard disk drive actually represents. It makes the old Jumbo Jet analogy look rather pathetic (not to mention grossly inaccurate), doesn't it?

Tracks and Sectors

A *track* is a single ring of data on one side of a disk. A disk track is too large to manage data effectively as a single storage unit. Many disk tracks can store 100,000 or more bytes of data, which would be very inefficient for storing small files. For that reason, tracks are divided into several numbered divisions known as sectors. These sectors represent arc-shaped pieces of the track.

Various types of disk drives split their disk tracks into different numbers of sectors, depending on the density of the tracks. For example, floppy disk formats use 8–36 sectors per track, although hard disks usually store data at a higher density and today can have 900 or more sectors per track physically. The sectors created by the standard formatting procedure on a PC system have a capacity of 512 bytes, which has been one constant throughout the history of the PC. One interesting phenomenon of the

PC standard is that to be compatible with most older BIOSs and drivers, drives usually perform an internal translation so that they pretend to have 63 sectors per track when addressed in CHS (cylinder, head, sector) mode.

The sectors on a track are numbered starting with 1, unlike the heads or cylinders that are numbered starting with 0. For example, a 1.44MB floppy disk contains 80 cylinders numbered 0–79 and two heads numbered 0 and 1, whereas each track on each cylinder has 18 sectors numbered 1–18.

When a disk is formatted, the formatting program creates ID areas before and after each sector's data that the disk controller uses for sector numbering and identifying the start and end of each sector. These areas precede and follow each sector's data area and consume some of the disk's total storage capacity. This accounts for the difference between a disk's unformatted and formatted capacities. Note that most modern hard drives are sold preformatted and advertise only the formatted capacity. The unformatted capacity is usually not mentioned anymore. Another interesting development is that many new drives use what is called No-ID sector formatting, which means the sectors are recorded without ID marks before and after each sector. Therefore, more of the disk can be used for actual data.

Each sector on a disk usually has a prefix portion, or header, that identifies the start of the sector and contains the sector number, as well as a suffix portion, or trailer, that contains a checksum (which helps ensure the integrity of the data contents). Many newer drives omit this header and have what is called a No-ID recording, allowing more space for actual data. With a No-ID recording, the start and end of each sector are located via predetermined clock timing.

Each sector contains 512 bytes of data. The low-level formatting process typically fills the data bytes with some specific value, such as F6h (hex), or some other repeating test pattern used by the drive manufacturer. Some patterns are more difficult for the electronics on the drive to encode/decode, so these patterns are used when the manufacturer is testing the drive during initial formatting. A special test pattern might cause errors to surface that a normal data pattern would not show. This way, the manufacturer can more accurately identify marginal sectors during testing.

Note

The type of disk formatting discussed here is a physical or low-level format, not the high-level format you perform when you use a Windows DOS-based FORMAT program. See the section "Disk Formatting," later in this chapter, to learn about the difference between these two types of formatting.

The sector headers and trailers are independent of the operating system, file system, and files stored on the drive. In addition to the headers and trailers, gaps exist within the sectors, between the sectors on each track, and between tracks, but none of these gaps contain usable data space. The gaps are created during the low-level format process when the recording is turned off momentarily. They serve the same function as having gaps of no sound between the songs recorded on a cassette tape. The prefix, suffix, and gaps account for the lost space between the unformatted capacity of a disk and the formatted capacity. For example, a 4MB (unformatted) floppy disk (3 1/2") has a capacity of 2.88MB when it is formatted, a 2MB (unformatted) floppy has a formatted capacity of 1.44MB, and an older 38MB unformatted capacity (for instance, Seagate ST-4038) hard disk has a capacity of only 32MB when it is formatted. Because the ATA/IDE and SCSI hard drives you purchase today are low-level formatted at the factory, the manufacturers now advertise only the formatted capacity. Even so, nearly all drives use some reserved space for managing the data that will be stored on the drive. Thus, although I stated earlier that each disk sector is 512 bytes in size, this statement is technically untrue. Each sector does allow for the storage of 512 bytes of data, but the data area is only a portion of the sector. Each sector on a disk typically occupies up to 571 bytes of the disk, of which only 512 bytes are available for the storage of user data. The actual number of additional bytes required for the sector header and trailer can vary from drive to drive. As mentioned earlier, though, many modern drives now use a No-ID recording scheme that virtually eliminates the storage overhead of the sector header information.

You might find it helpful to think of each disk sector as being a page in a book. In a book, each page contains text, but the entire page is not filled with text; rather, each page has top, bottom, left, and right margins. Information such as chapter titles (track and cylinder numbers) and page numbers (sector numbers) is placed in the margins. The "margin" areas of a sector are created during the low-level formatting process. Formatting also fills the data area of each sector with dummy values. After you perform a high-level format on the disk, the PC's file system can write to the data area of each sector, but the sector header and trailer information can't be altered during normal write operations unless the disk is low-level formatted again.

Table 10.1 shows the format for each track and sector on a typical hard disk drive with 17 sectors per track.

Table 10.1 Typical Disk Track/Sector Format Using ID Marks

Bytes	Name	Description
16	POST INDEX GAP	All 4Eh, at the track beginning after the Index mark.
The following sector data (shown between the lines in this table) is repeated as many times as there are sectors on the track.		
13	ID VFO LOCK	All 00h; synchronizes the VFO for the sector ID.
1	SYNC BYTE	A1h; notifies the controller that data follows.
1	ADDRESS MARK	FEh; defines that ID field data follows.
2	CYLINDER NUMBER	A value that defines the head actuator position.
1	HEAD NUMBER	A value that defines the particular head selected.
1	SECTOR NUMBER	A value that defines the sector.
2	CRC	Cyclic Redundancy Check to verify ID data.
3	WRITE TURN-ON GAP	00h written by format to isolate the ID from DATA.
13	DATA SYNC VFO LOCK	All 00h; synchronizes the VFO for the DATA.
1	SYNC BYTE	A1h; notifies the controller that data follows.
1	ADDRESS MARK	F8h; defines that user DATA field follows.
512	DATA	The area for user DATA.
2	CRC	Cyclic Redundancy Check to verify DATA.
3	WRITE TURN-OFF GAP	00h; written by DATA update to isolate DATA.
15	INTER-RECORD GAP	All 00h; a buffer for spindle speed variation.
693	PRE-INDEX GAP	All 4Eh, at track end before Index mark.

571 = Total bytes per sector; 512 = Data (usable) bytes per sector
Note: "All XXh" indicates that field will be filled with XXh bytes.

As you can see, the usable space for data on each track is about 15% less than its total unformatted capacity. This is true for most disks, although the percentage can vary slightly, depending on how many sectors exist per track. The following paragraphs detail each piece of the sector data listed in Table 10.1.

The POST INDEX GAP provides a head-switching recovery period, so when switching from one track to another, the heads can read sequential sectors without waiting for an additional revolution of the disk. Because the disk is continuously spinning and the heads take some small amount of time to move radially from track to track, reading consecutive sectors on two different tracks, one right after the other, is not possible. By the time the head moves to the new track, the beginning of the second sector has already spun past it. Leaving a gap between sectors provides the heads with time to move to another track.

In some drives, this gap does not provide sufficient time for the heads to move. When this is the case, a drive can gain additional time by skewing the sectors on different tracks so the arrival of the first sector is delayed. In other words, the low-level formatting process offsets the sector numbering, so instead of the same numbered sectors on each track being adjacent to each other, Sector 9 on one track might be next to Sector 8 of the next track, which is next to Sector 7 on the next, and so forth. The optimum skew value is based on the rotational speed of the disk as compared to the lateral speed of the heads.

Note

At one time, the head skew was a parameter you could set yourself while low-level formatting a drive. Today's ATA/IDE and SCSI drives are low-level formatted at the factory with the optimum skew values.

The Sector ID data consists of the Cylinder, Head, and Sector Number fields, as well as a CRC field used to verify the ID data. Most controllers use bit 7 of the Head Number field to mark a sector as bad during a low-level format or surface analysis. This convention is not absolute, however. Some controllers use other methods to mark a bad sector, but the mark usually involves one of the ID fields.

The WRITE TURN-ON GAP follows the ID field's CRC bytes and provides a pad to ensure a proper recording of the user data area that follows, as well as to enable full recovery of the ID CRC.

The user DATA field consists of all 512 bytes of data stored in the sector. This field is followed by a CRC field to verify the data. Although many controllers use two bytes of CRC here, the controller might implement a longer error correction code (ECC) that requires more than two CRC bytes to store. The ECC data stored here provides the possibility of correcting errors in the DATA field as well as detecting them. The correction/detection capabilities depend on the ECC code the drive uses and its implementation by the controller. The WRITE TURN-OFF GAP is a pad that enables the ECC (CRC) bytes to be fully recovered.

The INTER-RECORD GAP provides a means to accommodate variances in drive spindle speeds. A track might have been formatted while the disk was running slightly more slowly than normal and then written to while the disk was running slightly more quickly than normal. In such cases, this gap prevents the accidental overwriting of any information in the next sector. The actual size of this padding varies, depending on the speed of the DATA disk's rotation when the track was formatted and each time the DATA field is updated.

The PRE-INDEX GAP enables speed tolerance over the entire track. This gap varies in size, depending on the variances in disk rotation speed and write-frequency tolerance at the time of formatting.

This sector prefix information is extremely important because it contains the numbering information that defines the cylinder, head, and sector. So this information, except the DATA field, DATA CRC bytes, and WRITE TURN-OFF GAP, is written only during a low-level format.

Disk Formatting

Two formatting procedures are required before you can write user data to a disk:

- Physical, or low-level formatting
- Logical, or high-level formatting

When you format a blank floppy disk, the Windows Explorer or DOS FORMAT command performs both types of formats simultaneously. If the floppy was already formatted, DOS and Windows will default to doing only a high-level format.

A hard disk, however, requires two separate formatting operations. Moreover, a hard disk requires a third step, between the two formatting procedures, to write the partitioning information to the disk. Partitioning is required because a hard disk is designed to be used with more than one operating system. Using multiple operating systems on one hard drive is possible by separating the physical formatting in a procedure that is always the same, regardless of the operating system used and the high-level format (which is different for each operating system). Partitioning enables a single hard disk drive to run more than one type of operating system, or it can enable a single operating system to use the disk as several volumes or logical drives. A *volume* or *logical drive* is any section of the disk to which the operating system assigns a drive letter or name.

Consequently, preparing a hard disk drive for data storage involves three steps:

1. Low-level formatting (LLF)
2. Partitioning
3. High-level formatting (HLF)

Low-Level Formatting

During a low-level format, the formatting program divides the disk's tracks into a specific number of sectors, creating the intersector and intertrack gaps and recording the sector header and trailer information. The program also fills each sector's data area with a dummy byte value or a pattern of test values. For floppy disks, the number of sectors recorded on each track depends on the type of disk and drive. For hard disks, the number of sectors per track depends on the drive and the controller interface.

Originally, PC hard disk drives used a separate controller that took the form of an expansion card or was integrated into the motherboard. Because the controller could be used with various disk drives and might even have been made by a different manufacturer, some uniformity had to exist in the communications between the controller and the drive. For this reason, the number of sectors written to a track tended to be relatively consistent.

The original ST-506/412 MFM controllers always placed 17 sectors per track on a disk, although ST-506/412 controllers with RLL encoding increased the number of sectors to 25 or 26 per track; ESDI drives had 32 or more sectors per track. The ATA/IDE and SCSI drives found in PCs today can have anywhere from 17 to 900 or more sectors per track.

Virtually all ATA and SCSI drives use a technique called *zoned-bit recording (ZBR)*, sometimes shortened to *zoned recording*, which writes a variable number of sectors per track. Without zoned recording, the number of sectors, and therefore bits, on each track is a constant. This means the actual number of bits per inch will vary. More bits per inch will exist on the inner tracks, and fewer will exist on the outer. The data rate and rotational speed will remain constant, as will the number of bits per track. Figure 10.4 shows a drive recorded with the same number of sectors per track.

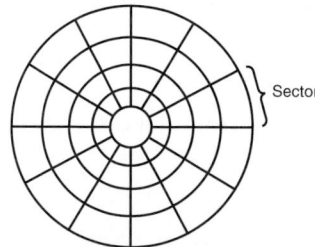

Figure 10.4 Standard recording, where the same number of sectors comprise every track.

A standard recording wastes capacity on the outer tracks because it is longer and yet holds the same amount of data (more loosely spaced) as the inner tracks. One way to increase the capacity of a hard drive during the low-level format is to create more sectors on the disks' outer cylinders than on the inner ones. Because they have a larger circumference, the outer cylinders can hold more data. Drives without zoned recording store the same amount of data on every cylinder, even though the tracks of the outer cylinders might be twice as long as those of the inner cylinders. The result is wasted storage capacity because the disk medium must be capable of storing data reliably at the same density as on the inner cylinders. When the number of sectors per track is fixed, as in older controllers, the drive capacity is limited by the density of the innermost (shortest) track.

Drives that use zoned recording split the cylinders into groups called *zones*, with each successive zone having more sectors per track as you move outward from the center of the disk. All the cylinders in a particular zone have the same number of sectors per track. The number of zones varies with specific drives, but most drives have 10 or more zones.

Figure 10.5 shows a drive with zoned-bit recording.

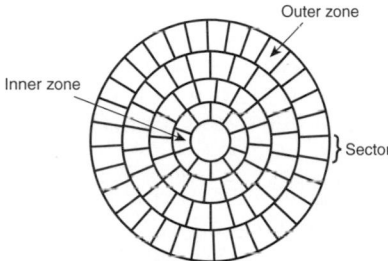

Figure 10.5   Zoned recording, where the number of sectors per track increases within each zone, moving out from the center.

Another effect of zoned recording is that transfer speeds vary depending on which zone the heads are in. A drive with zoned recording still spins at a constant speed. Because more sectors exist per track in the outer zones, however, data transfer is fastest there. Consequently, data transfer is slowest when reading or writing to the inner zones. That is why virtually all drives today report minimum and maximum sustained transfer rates, which depend on where on the drive you are reading from or writing to.

As an example, see Table 10.2, which shows the zones defined for a Hitachi Travelstar 7K60 2 1/2" notebook drive, the sectors per track for each zone, and the resulting data transfer rate. This is one of the fastest laptop hard drives on the market.

Table 10.2   Zoned Recording Information for the Hitachi Travelstar 7K60 2 1/2" Hard Disk Drive

Zone	Sectors per Track	Bytes per Track	Transfer Rate (MBps)
0	720	368640	44.24
1	704	360448	43.25
2	696	356352	42.76
3	672	344064	41.29
4	640	327680	39.32
5	614	314368	37.72
6	592	303104	36.37
7	556	284672	34.16
8	528	270336	32.44
9	480	245760	29.49

Table 10.2   Continued

Zone	Sectors per Track	Bytes per Track	Transfer Rate (MBps)
10	480	245760	29.49
11	456	233472	28.02
12	432	221184	26.54
13	416	212992	25.56
14	384	196608	23.59
15	360	184320	22.12

This drive has a total of 54,288 cylinders, which are divided into 16 zones averaging 3,393 cylinders each. Zone 0 consists of the outermost cylinders, which are the longest and contain the most sectors: 720 for each track. Because each sector is 512 bytes, each track in the outer zone contains 368,640 bytes of data. The inner zone has only 360 sectors per track, which means each track in the inner zone holds 184,320 bytes.

With zoned recording, this drive averages 545.63 sectors per track. Without zoned recording, the number of sectors per track would be limited to 360 for all tracks. The use of zoned recording therefore provides nearly a 52% increase in the storage capacity of this particular drive.

Also notice the difference in the data transfer rates for each of the zones. Because the drive spins at 7,200 rpm, it completes a single revolution every 1/120 of a second, or every 8.33 milliseconds. Therefore, the data transfer speed varies depending on which zone you are reading and writing. In the outer zone, the data transfer rate is 44.24MBps, whereas in the inner zone it is only 22.12MBps. The average transfer rate for this drive is 33.52MBps. This is one reason you might notice huge discrepancies in the results produced by disk drive benchmark programs. A test that reads or writes files on the outer tracks of the disk naturally yields far better results than one conducted on the inner tracks. It might appear as though your drive is running more slowly when the problem is actually that the test results you are comparing stem from disk activity on different zones.

Another thing to note is that this drive conforms to the ATA-6 specification and is capable of running in Ultra-ATA/100 mode (also called UDMA-100), which implies a transfer speed of 100MBps. As you can see, that is entirely theoretical because the true media transfer speed of this drive varies between about 22MBps and 44MBps, averaging about 33MBps overall. The interface transfer rate is just that: what the interface is capable of. It has little bearing on the actual capabilities of the drive.

Drives with separate controllers used in the past could not handle zoned recording because no standard way existed to communicate information about the zones from the drive to the controller.

With SCSI and ATA disks, however, formatting individual tracks with different numbers of sectors became possible because these drives have the disk controller built in. The built-in controllers on these drives are fully aware of the zoning algorithm and can translate the physical cylinder, head, and sector numbers to logical cylinder, head, and sector numbers so the drive appears to have the same number of sectors on each track. Because the PC BIOS is designed to handle only a single number of sectors per track throughout the entire drive, a zoned drive must run by using a sector translation scheme.

The use of zoned recording enables drive manufacturers to increase the capacity of their hard drives by 20%–50% or more when compared with a fixed–sector-per-track arrangement. All modern drives use zoned recording.

Partitioning

Creating a partition on a hard disk drive enables it to support separate file systems, each in its own partition.

Each file system can then use its own method to allocate file space in logical units called *clusters* or *allocation units*. Every hard disk drive must have at least one partition on it and can have up to four partitions, each of which can support the same or different type file systems. Three common file systems are used by PC operating systems today:

- *FAT (file allocation table).* The standard file system supported by DOS and Windows 9x/Me. FAT partitions support filenames of 11 characters maximum (8 characters + a 3-character extension) under DOS, and 255 characters under Windows 9x (or later). The standard FAT file system uses 12- or 16-bit numbers to identify clusters, resulting in a maximum volume size of 2GB.

   Using FDISK, you can create only two physical FAT partitions on a hard disk drive—primary and extended—but you can subdivide the extended partition into as many as 25 logical volumes. Alternative partitioning programs, such as Partition Magic, can create up to four primary partitions or three primary and one extended.

- *FAT32 (file allocation table, 32-bit).* An optional file system supported by Windows 95 OSR2 (OEM Service Release 2), Windows 98, Windows Me, and Windows 2000/XP.

   FAT32 uses 32-bit numbers to identify clusters, resulting in a maximum single volume size of 2TB or 2,048GB.

- *NTFS (Windows NT File System).* The native file system for Windows NT/2000/XP that supports filenames up to 256 characters long and partitions up to (a theoretical) 16 exabytes. NTFS also provides extended attributes and file system security features that do not exist in the FAT file system.

Up until the release of XP, FAT32 was by far the most popular file system. Because NTFS is native to XP, NTFS is now becoming more popular in newer systems. Still, the FAT file system is accessible by nearly every operating system, which makes it the most compatible in a mixed OS environment. FAT32 and NTFS provide additional features but are not universally accessible by other operating systems.

▶▶ See "FAT32," p. 1373.

Partitioning normally is accomplished by running the disk partitioning program that comes with your operating system. The name and exact operation of the disk partitioning program varies with the operating system. For example, FDISK is used by DOS and Windows 9x/Me for this task, whereas the DISKPART command or the Disk Management snap-in component of the Computer Management service are used with Windows XP. FDISK, DISKPART, and other disk partitioning tools enable you to select the amount of space on the drive to use for a partition, from a single megabyte (or 1%) of the drive up to the entire capacity of the drive or as much as the particular file system will allow. You usually should have as few partitions as possible, and many people (myself included) try to stick with only one or two at the most. This was more difficult before FAT32 because the maximum partition size for a FAT16 partition was only 2GB. With FAT32, though, the maximum partition size can be up to 2048GB.

Caution

FDISK, DISKPART, and other disk partitioning tools included in operating systems can't be used to change the size of a partition; all they can do is remove or create partitions. The act of removing or creating a partition destroys and loses access to data that was contained in the partition or that was on that part of the disk. To manipulate partitions without destroying data, you can use third-party utility programs, such as Partition Magic from PowerQuest or Partition Commander from V-Communications.

After a drive is partitioned, each partition must then be high-level formatted by the operating system that will use it.

High-Level Formatting

During the high-level format, the operating system writes the structures necessary for managing files and data on the disk. For example, FAT partitions have a Volume Boot Sector (VBS), two copies of a file allocation table (FAT), and a root directory on each formatted logical drive. These data structures enable the operating system to manage the space on the disk, keep track of files, and even manage defective areas so they do not cause problems.

High-level formatting is not really a physical formatting of the drive, but rather the creation of a table of contents for the disk. In low-level formatting, which is the real physical formatting process, tracks and sectors are written on the disk. As mentioned, the DOS and Windows 9x/Me FORMAT command can perform both low-level and high-level format operations on a floppy disk, but it performs only the high-level format for a hard disk. Low-level formats of ATA and SCSI hard disk drives are performed by the manufacturer and should almost never be performed by the end user. The only time I low-level format ATA or SCSI drives is when I am attempting to repair a format that has become damaged (parts of the disk become unreadable) or in some cases when I want to wipe away all data on the drive.

Basic Hard Disk Drive Components

Many types of hard disk drives are on the market, but nearly all share the same basic physical components. Some differences might exist in the implementation of these components (and in the quality of the materials used to make them), but the operational characteristics of most drives are similar. The basic components of a typical hard disk drive are as follows (see Figure 10.6):

- Disk platters
- Read/write heads
- Head actuator mechanism
- Spindle motor (inside platter hub)
- Logic board (controller or Printed Circuit Board)
- Cables and connectors
- Configuration items (such as jumpers or switches)

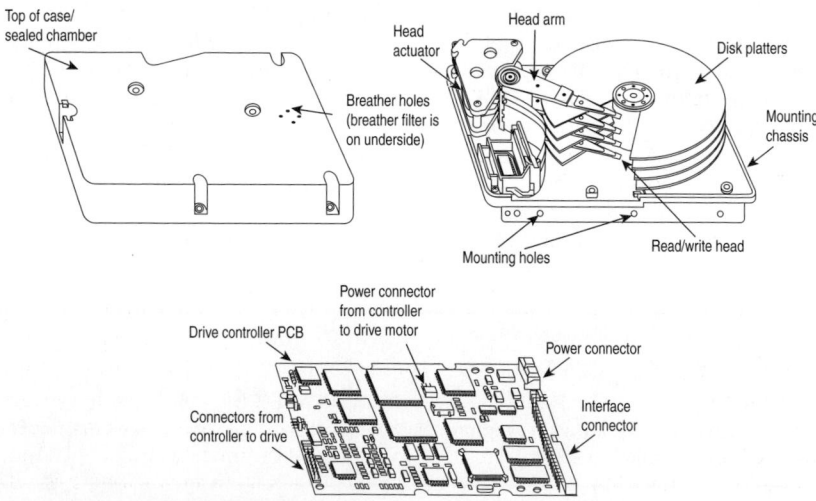

Figure 10.6   Typical hard disk drive components.

The platters, spindle motor, heads, and head actuator mechanisms usually are contained in a sealed chamber called the head disk assembly (HDA). The HDA is usually treated as a single component; it is rarely opened. Other parts external to the drive's HDA, such as the logic boards, bezel, and other configuration or mounting hardware, can be disassembled from the drive.

Hard Disk Platters (Disks)

A hard disk drive has one or more platters, or disks. Hard disks for PC systems have been available in several form factors over the years. Normally, the physical size of a drive is expressed as the size of the platters. Following are the platter sizes that have been associated with PC hard disk drives:

- 5 1/4" (actually 130mm, or 5.12")
- 3 1/2" (actually 95mm, or 3.74")
- 2 1/2" (actually 65mm, or 2.56")
- 1.8" (actually 48mm, or 1.89")
- 1" (actually 34mm, or 1.33")
- 0.85" (actually 21.5mm)

Larger hard disk drives that have 8", 14", or even larger platters are available, but these drives are not used with PC systems. Currently, the 3 1/2" drives are the most popular for desktop and some portable systems, whereas the 2 1/2" and smaller drives are very popular in portable or notebook systems.

During 1998, IBM introduced a drive called the MicroDrive (now manufactured by Hitachi Global Storage Technologies), which currently can store up to 4GB or more on a single platter about the size of a quarter. These drives are in the physical and electrical format of a Type II Compact Flash (CF) card, which means they can be used in any device that takes CF cards, including digital cameras, personal digital assistants (PDAs), MP3 players, and anywhere else Compact Flash memory cards can be used.

In 2004, Toshiba followed with an even smaller drive, the 0.85" drive, which is about the size of a postage stamp and stores up to 4GB. This drive is not really designed for PCs but will be used in cell phones, digital audio players, PDAs, digital still cameras, camcorders, and more.

Several companies have introduced 1.8" drives over the years, most notably HP, Calluna, Toshiba, and Hitachi. Of those, only Toshiba and Hitachi continue to manufacture drives in that format. In 2000, Toshiba introduced its 1.8" drives, which are available in the physical format of a Type II PC Card, or in a format designed to be mounted internally in a device. Hitachi introduced its 1.8" drives in 2003. These drives are available in capacities of up to 40GB or more and can be used in extremely thin and light laptop computers as well as PDAs, MP3 players, or other small digital devices.

Most hard disk drives have two or more platters, although some of the smaller drives used in portable systems and some entry-level drives for desktop computers have only one. The number of platters a drive can have is limited by the drive's vertical physical size. The maximum number of platters I have seen in any 3 1/2" drive is 12; however, most drives have 6 or fewer.

Platters have traditionally been made from an aluminum/magnesium alloy, which provides both strength and light weight. However, manufacturers' desire for higher and higher densities and smaller drives has led to the use of platters made of glass (or, more technically, a glass-ceramic composite). One such material, produced by the Dow Corning Corporation, is called MemCor. MemCor is composed of glass with ceramic implants, enabling it to resist cracking better than pure glass. Glass platters offer greater rigidity than metal (because metal can be bent and glass can't) and can therefore be machined to one-half the thickness of conventional aluminum disks—sometimes less. Glass platters are also much more thermally stable than aluminum platters, which means they do not expand or contract very much with changes in temperature. Several hard disk drives made by companies such as Hitachi, Seagate, Toshiba, Areal Technology, and Maxtor currently use glass or glass-ceramic platters; in fact, Hitachi Global Storage Technologies (Hitachi and IBM's joint hard disk venture) is designing all its new drives with only glass platters. For most other manufacturers as well, glass disks will probably replace the standard aluminum/magnesium substrate over the next few years.

Recording Media

No matter which substrate is used, the platters are covered with a thin layer of a magnetically retentive substance, called the *medium*, on which magnetic information is stored. Three popular types of magnetic media are used on hard disk platters:

- Oxide media
- Thin-film media
- AFC (antiferromagnetically coupled) media

Oxide Media

The oxide medium is made of various compounds, containing iron oxide as the active ingredient. The magnetic layer is created on the disk by coating the aluminum platter with a syrup containing iron-oxide particles. This syrup is spread across the disk by spinning the platters at high speed; centrifugal force causes the material to flow from the center of the platter to the outside, creating an even coating of the material on the platter. The surface is then cured and polished. Finally, a layer of material that protects and lubricates the surface is added and burnished smooth. The oxide coating is usually about 30 millionths of an inch thick. If you could peer into a drive with oxide-coated platters, you would see that the platters are brownish or amber.

As drive density increases, the magnetic medium needs to be thinner and more perfectly formed. The capabilities of oxide coatings have been exceeded by most higher-capacity drives. Because the oxide medium is very soft, disks that use it are subject to head-crash damage if the drive is jolted during operation. Most older drives, especially those sold as low-end models, use oxide media on the drive platters. Oxide media, which have been used since 1955, remained popular because of their relatively low cost and ease of application. Today, however, very few drives use oxide media.

Thin-Film Media

The thin-film medium is thinner, harder, and more perfectly formed than oxide medium. Thin film was developed as a high-performance medium that enabled a new generation of drives to have lower head-floating heights, which in turn made increases in drive density possible. Originally, thin-film media were used only in higher-capacity or higher-quality drive systems, but today, virtually all drives use thin-film media.

The thin-film medium is aptly named. The coating is much thinner than can be achieved by the oxide-coating method. Thin-film media are also known as plated, or sputtered, media because of the various processes used to deposit the thin film on the platters.

Thin-film plated media are manufactured by depositing the magnetic medium on the disk with an electroplating mechanism, in much the same way that chrome plating is deposited on the bumper of a car. The aluminum/magnesium or glass platter is immersed in a series of chemical baths that coat the platter with several layers of metallic film. The magnetic medium layer itself is a cobalt alloy about 1 µ-inch thick.

Thin-film sputtered media are created by first coating the aluminum platters with a layer of nickel phosphorus and then applying the cobalt-alloy magnetic material in a continuous vacuum-deposition process called *sputtering*. This process deposits magnetic layers as thin as 1 µ-inch or less on the disk, in a fashion similar to the way that silicon wafers are coated with metallic films in the semiconductor industry. The same sputtering technique is again used to lay down an extremely hard, 1 µ-inch protective carbon coating. The need for a near-perfect vacuum makes sputtering the most expensive of the processes described here.

The surface of a sputtered platter contains magnetic layers as thin as 1 µ-inch. Because this surface also is very smooth, the head can float more closely to the disk surface than was previously possible. Floating heights as small as 10nm (nanometers, or about 0.4 μ-inch) above the surface are possible. When the head is closer to the platter, the density of the magnetic flux transitions can be increased to provide greater storage capacity. Additionally, the increased intensity of the magnetic field during a closer-proximity read provides the higher signal amplitudes necessary for good signal-to-noise performance.

Both the sputtering and plating processes result in a very thin, hard film of magnetic medium on the platters. Because the thin-film medium is so hard, it has a better chance of surviving contact with the heads at high speed. In fact, modern thin-film media are virtually uncrashable. If you could open a drive to peek at the platters, you would see that platters coated with the thin-film medium look like mirrors.

AFC Media

The latest advancement in drive media is called antiferromagnetically coupled (AFC) media and is designed to allow densities to be pushed beyond previous limits. Anytime density is increased, the magnetic layer on the platters must be made thinner and thinner. Areal density (tracks per inch times bits per inch) has increased in hard drives to the point where the grains in the magnetic layer used to store data are becoming so small that they become unstable over time, causing data storage to become unreliable. This is referred to as the *superparamagnetic limit*, and it has been determined to be between 30Gb/sq. in. and 50Gb/sq. in. Drives today have already reached 35Gb/sq. in., which means the superparamagnetic limit is now becoming a factor in drive designs.

AFC media consists of two magnetic layers separated by a very thin 3-atom (6 angstrom) film layer of the element ruthenium. IBM has coined the term "pixie dust" to refer to this ultra-thin ruthenium layer. This sandwich produces an antiferromagnetic coupling of the top and bottom magnetic layers, which causes the apparent magnetic thickness of the entire structure to be the difference between the top and bottom magnetic layers. This allows the use of physically thicker magnetic layers with more stable larger grains, so they can function as if they were really a single layer that was much thinner overall.

IBM has introduced AFC media into several drives, starting with the 2 1/2" Travelstar 30GN series of notebook drives introduced in 2001; they were the first drives on the market to use AFC media. In addition, IBM has introduced AFC media in desktop 3 1/2" drives starting with the Deskstar 120 GXP. AFC media is also used by Hitachi Global Storage Technologies, which owns the former IBM hard drive lines. I expect other manufacturers to introduce AFC media into their drives as well. The use of AFC media is expected to allow areal densities to be extended to 100Gb/sq. in. and beyond.

▶▶ For more information about AFC media and other advanced storage technologies, see Chapter 9, "Magnetic Storage Principles," p. 619.

Read/Write Heads

A hard disk drive usually has one read/write head for each platter surface (meaning that each platter has two sets of read/write heads—one for the top side and one for the bottom side). These heads are connected, or ganged, on a single movement mechanism. The heads, therefore, move across the platters in unison.

Mechanically, read/write heads are simple. Each head is on an actuator arm that is spring-loaded to force the head into contact with a platter. Few people realize that each platter actually is "squeezed" by the heads above and below it. If you could open a drive safely and lift the top head with your finger, the head would snap back down into the platter when you released it. If you could pull down on one of the heads below a platter, the spring tension would cause it to snap back up into the platter when you released it.

Figure 10.7 shows a typical hard disk head-actuator assembly from a voice coil drive.

When the drive is at rest, the heads are forced into direct contact with the platters by spring tension, but when the drive is spinning at full speed, air pressure develops below the heads and lifts them off the surface of the platter. On a drive spinning at full speed, the distance between the heads and the platter can be anywhere from 0.5 μ-inches to 5 μ-inches or more in a modern drive.

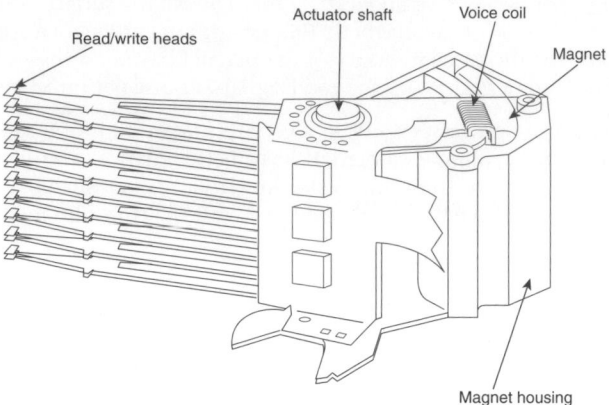

Actuator shaft   Voice coil

Read/write heads   Magnet

Magnet housing

Figure 10.7   Read/write heads and rotary voice coil actuator assembly.

In the early 1960s, hard disk drive recording heads operated at floating heights as large as 200 µ-inches–300 µ-inches; today's drive heads are designed to float as low as 10nm (nanometers) or 0.4 µ-inches above the surface of the disk. To support higher densities in future drives, the physical separation between the head and disk is expected to drop even further, such that on some drives there will even be contact with the platter surface. New media and head designs will be required to make full or partial contact recording possible.

Caution

The small size of the gap between the platters and the heads is why you should never open the disk drive's HDA except in a clean-room environment. Any particle of dust or dirt that gets into this mechanism could cause the heads to read improperly or possibly even to strike the platters while the drive is running at full speed. The latter event could scratch the platter or the head, causing permanent damage.

To ensure the cleanliness of the interior of the drive, the HDA is assembled in a class-100 or better clean room. This specification means that a cubic foot of air can't contain more than 100 particles that measure up to 0.5 microns (19.7 µ-inches). A single person breathing while standing motionless spews out 500 such particles in a single minute! These rooms contain special air-filtration systems that continuously evacuate and refresh the air. A drive's HDA should not be opened unless it is inside such a room.

Although maintaining a clean-room environment might seem to be expensive, many companies manufacture tabletop or bench-size clean rooms that sell for only a few thousand dollars. Some of these devices operate like a glove box; the operator first inserts the drive and any tools required, closes the box, and then turns on the filtration system. Inside the box, a clean-room environment is maintained, and a technician can use the built-in gloves to work on the drive.

In other clean-room variations, the operator stands at a bench where a forced-air curtain maintains a clean environment on the bench top. The technician can walk in and out of the clean-room field by walking through the air curtain. This air curtain is very similar to the curtain of air used in some stores and warehouses to prevent heat from escaping in the winter while leaving a passage wide open.

Because the clean environment is expensive to produce, few companies except those that manufacture the drives are properly equipped to service hard disk drives.

Read/Write Head Designs

As disk drive technology has evolved, so has the design of the read/write head. The earliest heads were simple iron cores with coil windings (electromagnets). By today's standards, the original head designs were enormous in physical size and operated at very low recording densities. Over the years, head designs have evolved from the first simple ferrite core designs into the magneto-resistive and giant magneto-resistive types available today.

For more information on the various head designs, see Chapter 9.

Head Actuator Mechanisms

Possibly more important than the heads themselves is the mechanical system that moves them: the head actuator. This mechanism moves the heads across the disk and positions them accurately above the desired cylinder. Many variations on head actuator mechanisms are in use, but all fall into one of two basic categories:

- Stepper motor actuators
- Voice coil actuators

The use of one or the other type of actuator has profound effects on a drive's performance and reliability. The effects are not limited to speed; they also include accuracy, sensitivity to temperature, position, vibration, and overall reliability. The head actuator is the single most important specification in the drive, and the type of head actuator mechanism in a drive tells you a great deal about the drive's performance and reliability characteristics. Table 10.3 shows the two types of hard disk drive head actuators and the affected performance characteristics.

Table 10.3 Characteristics of Stepper Motor Versus Voice Coil Drives

Characteristic	Stepper Motor	Voice Coil
Relative access speed	Slow	Fast
Temperature sensitive	Yes (very)	No
Positionally sensitive	Yes	No
Automatic head parking	Not usually	Yes
Preventive maintenance	Periodic reformat	None required
Relative reliability	Poor	Excellent

Stepper motor actuators were commonly used on hard drives made during the 1980s and early 1990s with capacities of 100MB or less. All the drives I've seen with greater storage capacity use a voice coil actuator.

Floppy disk drives position their heads by using a stepper motor actuator. The accuracy of the stepper mechanism is suited to a floppy disk drive because the track densities usually are nowhere near those of a hard disk. The track density of a 1.44MB floppy disk is 135 tracks per inch, whereas hard disk drives have densities of more than 5,000 tracks per inch. All hard disk drives being manufactured today use voice coil actuators because stepper motors can't achieve the degree of accuracy necessary.

Stepper Motor Actuators

A stepper motor is an electrical motor that can "step," or move from position to position, with mechanical detents or click-stop positions. If you were to grip the spindle of one of these motors and spin it manually, you would hear a clicking or buzzing sound as the motor passed each detent position with a soft click.

Stepper motors can't position themselves between step positions; they can stop only at the predetermined detent positions. The motors are small (between 1" and 3") and can be square, cylindrical, or flat. Stepper motors are outside the sealed HDA, although the spindle of the motor penetrates the HDA through a sealed hole.

Stepper motor mechanisms are affected by a variety of problems, but the greatest problem is temperature. As the drive platters heat and cool, they expand and contract, and the tracks on the platters move in relation to a predetermined track position. The stepper mechanism can't move in increments of less than a single track to correct for these temperature-induced errors. The drive positions the heads to a particular cylinder according to a predetermined number of steps from the stepper motor, with no room for nuance.

Figure 10.8 shows a common stepper motor design, in which a split metal band is used to transfer the movement from the rotating motor shaft to the head actuator itself.

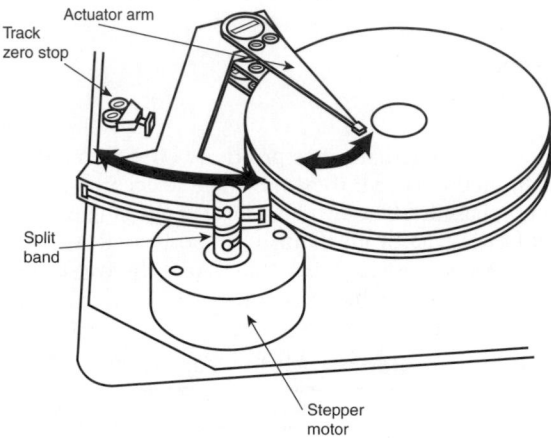

Figure 10.8   A stepper motor actuator.

Voice Coil Actuators

The voice coil actuators used in virtually all hard disk drives made today—unlike stepper motor actuators—use a feedback signal from the drive to accurately determine the head positions and adjust them, if necessary. This arrangement provides significantly greater performance, accuracy, and reliability than traditional stepper motor actuator designs.

A voice coil actuator works by pure electromagnetic force. The construction of the mechanism is similar to that of a typical audio speaker, from which the term *voice coil* is derived. An audio speaker uses a stationary magnet surrounded by a voice coil, which is connected to the speaker's paper cone. Energizing the coil causes it to move relative to the stationary magnet, which produces sound from the cone. In a typical hard disk drive's voice coil system, the electromagnetic coil is attached to the end of the head rack and placed near a stationary magnet. No physical contact occurs between the coil and the magnet; instead, the coil moves by pure magnetic force. As the electromagnetic coils are energized, they attract or repulse the stationary magnet and move the head rack. Systems like these are extremely quick, efficient, and usually much quieter than systems driven by stepper motors.

Unlike a stepper motor, a voice coil actuator has no click-stops or detent positions; rather, a special guidance system stops the head rack above a particular cylinder. Because it has no detents, the voice coil actuator can slide the heads in and out smoothly to any position desired. Voice coil actuators use a guidance mechanism called a *servo* to tell the actuator where the heads are in relation to the cylinders and to place the heads accurately at the desired positions. This positioning system often is called a *closed loop feedback mechanism*. It works by sending the index (or servo) signal to the positioning electronics, which return a feedback signal that is used to position the heads accurately. The system also is called *servo-controlled*, which refers to the index or servo information that is used to dictate or control head-positioning accuracy.

A voice coil actuator with servo control is not affected by temperature changes, as a stepper motor is. When temperature changes cause the disk platters to expand or contract, the voice coil system compensates automatically because it never positions the heads in predetermined track positions. Rather, the voice coil system searches for the specific track, guided by the prewritten servo information, and then positions the head rack precisely above the desired track, wherever it happens to be. Because of the continuous feedback of servo information, the heads adjust to the current position of the track at all times. For example, as a drive warms up and the platters expand, the servo information enables the heads to "follow" the track. As a result, a voice coil actuator is sometimes called a *track following system*.

The two main types of voice-coil positioner mechanisms are

- Linear voice-coil actuators
- Rotary voice-coil actuators

The two types differ only in the physical arrangement of the magnets and coils.

Linear Actuators

A linear actuator moves the heads in and out over the platters in a straight line (see Figure 10.9). The coil moves in and out on a track surrounded by the stationary magnets. The primary advantage of the linear design is that it eliminates the head azimuth variations that occur with rotary positioning systems. (*Azimuth* refers to the angular measurement of the head position relative to the tangent of a given cylinder.) A linear actuator does not rotate the head as it moves from one cylinder to another, thus eliminating this problem.

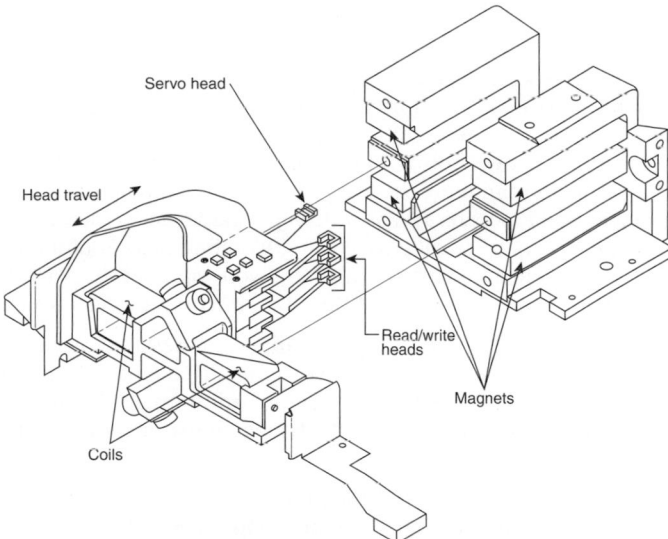

Figure 10.9   A linear voice coil actuator.

Although the linear actuator seems to be a good design, it has one fatal flaw: The devices are much too heavy. As drive performance has increased, the desire for lightweight actuator mechanisms has become very important. The lighter the mechanism, the faster it can accelerate and decelerate from one cylinder to another. Because they are much heavier than rotary actuators, linear actuators were popular only for a short time; they are virtually nonexistent in drives manufactured today.

Rotary actuators also use stationary magnets and a movable coil, but the coil is attached to the end of an actuator arm. As the coil moves relative to the stationary magnet, it swings the head arms in and out over the surface of the disk. The primary advantage of this mechanism is its light weight, which means the heads can accelerate and decelerate very quickly, resulting in very fast average seek times. Because of the lever effect on the head arm, the heads move faster than the actuator, which also helps to improve access times. (Refer to Figure 10.7, which shows a rotary voice coil actuator.)

The disadvantage of a rotary system is that as the heads move from the outer to the inner cylinders, they rotate slightly with respect to the tangent of the cylinders. This rotation results in an azimuth error and is one reason the area of the platter in which the cylinders are located is somewhat limited. By limiting the total motion of the actuator, the azimuth error is contained to within reasonable specifications. Virtually all voice coil drives today use rotary actuator systems.

Servo Mechanisms

Three servo mechanism designs have been used to control voice coil positioners over the years:

- Wedge servo
- Embedded servo
- Dedicated servo

The three designs are slightly different, but they accomplish the same basic task: They enable the head positioner to adjust continuously so it is precisely positioned above a given cylinder on the disk. The main difference between these servo designs is where the gray code information is actually written on the drive.

All servo mechanisms rely on special information that is written to the disk when it is manufactured. This information is usually in the form of a special code called a *gray code*. A gray code is a special binary notational system in which any two adjacent numbers are represented by a code that differs in only one bit place or column position. This system enables the head to easily read the information and quickly determine its precise position.

At the time of manufacture, a special machine called a servowriter writes the servo gray code on the disk. The servowriter is basically a jig that mechanically moves the heads to a given reference position and then writes the servo information at that position. Many servowriters are themselves guided by a laser-beam reference that calculates its own position by calculating distances in wavelengths of light. Because the servowriter must be capable of moving the heads mechanically, the process requires either that the lid of the drive be removed or that access be available through special access ports in the HDA. After the servowriting is complete, these ports are usually covered with sealing tape. You often see these tape-covered holes on the HDA, usually accompanied by warnings that you will void the warranty if you remove the tape. Because servowriting exposes the interior of the HDA, it requires a clean-room environment.

A servowriter is an expensive piece of machinery, costing up to $50,000 or more, and often must be custom-made for a particular make or model of drive. Some drive-repair companies have servowriting capability, which means they can rewrite the servo information on a drive if it becomes damaged. If a servowriter is not available, a drive with servo-code damage must be sent back to the drive manufacturer for the servo information to be rewritten.

Fortunately, damaging the servo information through disk read and write processes is impossible. Drives are designed so the heads can't overwrite the servo information, even during a low-level format. One myth that has been circulating (especially with respect to ATA drives) is that you can damage the servo information by improper low-level formatting. This is not true. An improper low-level format can compromise the performance of the drive, but the servo information is totally protected and can't be overwritten. Even so, the servo information on some drives can be damaged by a strong adjacent magnetic field or by jarring the drive while it is writing, which causes the heads to move off track.

The track-following capabilities of a servo-controlled voice coil actuator eliminate the positioning errors that occur over time with stepper motor drives. Voice coil drives are not affected by conditions such as thermal expansion and contraction of the platters. In fact, many voice coil drives today perform a special thermal-recalibration procedure at predetermined intervals while they run. This procedure usually involves seeking the heads from cylinder 0 to some other cylinder one time for every head on the drive. As this sequence occurs, the control circuitry in the drive monitors how much the track positions have moved since the last time the sequence was performed, and a thermal-recalibration adjustment is calculated and stored in the drive's memory. This information is then used every time the drive positions the heads to ensure the most accurate positioning possible.

Most drives perform the thermal-recalibration sequence every 5 minutes for the first 30 minutes that the drive is powered on and then once every 25 minutes after that. With some drives, this thermal-recalibration sequence is very noticeable; the drive essentially stops what it is doing, and you hear rapid ticking for a second or so. Some people think this is an indication that their drive is having a problem reading something and perhaps is conducting a read retry, but this is not true. Most drives today (ATA and SCSI) employ this thermal-recalibration procedure to maintain positioning accuracy.

As multimedia applications grew in popularity, thermal recalibration became a problem with some manufacturers' drives. The thermal-recalibration sequence sometimes interrupted the transfer of a large data file, such as an audio or a video file, which resulted in audio or video playback jitter. Some companies released special A/V (audio visual) drives that hide the thermal-recalibration sequences so they never interrupt a file transfer. Most of the newer ATA and SCSI drives are A/V capable, which means the thermal-recalibration sequences will not interrupt a transfer such as a video playback. A/V-capable ATA drives are also used in set-top boxes that are utilized for digital recording, such as the popular TiVo and ReplayTV devices.

While we are on the subject of automatic drive functions, most of the drives that perform thermal-recalibration sequences also automatically perform a function called a *disk sweep*. Also called *wear leveling* by some manufacturers, this procedure is an automatic head seek that occurs after the drive has been idle for a period of time. The disk-sweep function moves the heads to a cylinder in the outer portion of the platters, which is where the head float-height is highest (because the head-to-platter velocity is highest). Then, if the drive continues to remain idle for another period, the heads move to another cylinder in this area, and the process continues indefinitely as long as the drive is powered on.

The disk-sweep function is designed to prevent the head from remaining stationary above one cylinder in the drive for too long, where friction between the head and platter eventually would dig a trench in the medium. Although the heads are not in direct contact with the medium, they are so close that the constant air pressure from the head floating above a single cylinder could cause friction and excessive wear. Figure 10.10 shows both a wedge and an embedded servo.

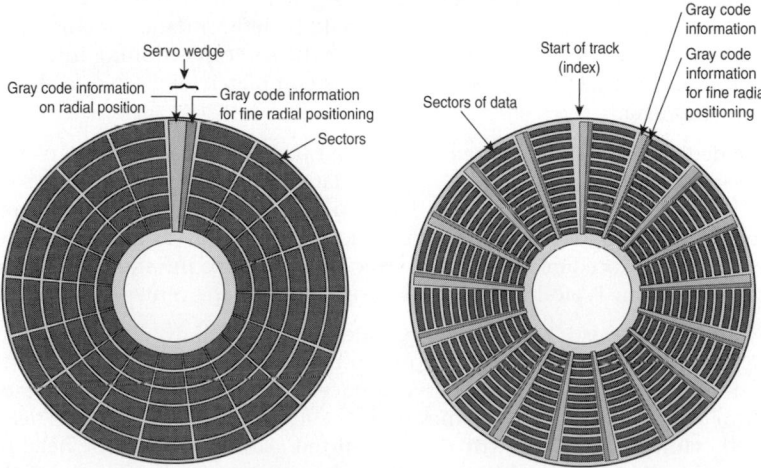

Figure 10.10   A wedge and an embedded servo.

Wedge Servo

Early servo-controlled drives used a technique called a *wedge servo*. In these drives, the gray-code guidance information is contained in a "wedge" slice of the drive in each cylinder immediately preceding the index mark. The index mark indicates the beginning of each track, so the wedge-servo information was written in the PRE-INDEX GAP, which is at the end of each track. This area is provided for speed tolerance and normally is not used by the controller.

Some controllers had to be notified that the drive was using a wedge servo so they could shorten the sector timing to allow for the wedge-servo area. If they were not correctly configured, these controllers would not work properly with the drive.

Another problem was that the servo information appears only one time every revolution, which means that the drive often needed several revolutions before it could accurately determine and adjust the head position. Because of these problems, the wedge servo never was a popular design; it no longer is used in drives.

Embedded Servo

An embedded servo is an enhancement of the wedge servo. Instead of placing the servo code before the beginning of each cylinder, an embedded servo design writes the servo information before the start of each sector. This arrangement enables the positioner circuits to receive feedback many times in a single revolution, making the head positioning much faster and more precise. Another advantage is that every track on the drive has its own positioning information, so each head can quickly and efficiently adjust position to compensate for any changes in the platter or head dimensions, especially for changes due to thermal expansion or physical stress.

Most drives today use an embedded servo to control the positioning system. As in the wedge servo design, the embedded servo information is protected by the drive circuits and any write operations are blocked whenever the heads are above the servo information. Thus, it is impossible to overwrite the servo information with a low-level format, as some people incorrectly believe.

Although the embedded servo works much better than the wedge servo because the servo feedback information is made available several times in a single disk revolution, a system that offered continuous servo feedback information would be better.

Dedicated Servo

A dedicated servo is a design in which the servo information is written continuously throughout the entire track, rather than just once per track or at the beginning of each sector. Unfortunately, if this procedure were used on the entire drive, no room would be left for data. For this reason, a *dedicated servo* uses one side of one of the platters exclusively for the servo-positioning information. The term "dedicated" comes from the fact that this platter side is completely dedicated to the servo information and can't contain any data.

When building a dedicated servo drive, the manufacturer deducts one side of one platter from normal read/write usage and records a special set of gray-code data there that indicates the proper track positions. Because the head that rests above this surface can't be used for normal reading and writing, the gray code can never be erased and the servo information is protected—as in the other servo designs. No low-level format or other procedure can possibly overwrite the servo information. Figure 10.11 shows a dedicated servo mechanism. Typically, the head on top or one in the center is dedicated for servo use.

When the drive moves the heads to a specific cylinder, the internal drive electronics use the signals received by the servo head to determine the position of the read/write heads. As the heads move, the track counters are read from the dedicated servo surface. When the servo head detects the requested track, the actuator stops. The servo electronics then fine-tune the position so the heads are precisely above the desired cylinder before any writing is permitted. Although only one head is used for servo tracking, the other heads are attached to the same rack so that if one head is above the desired cylinder, all the others are as well.

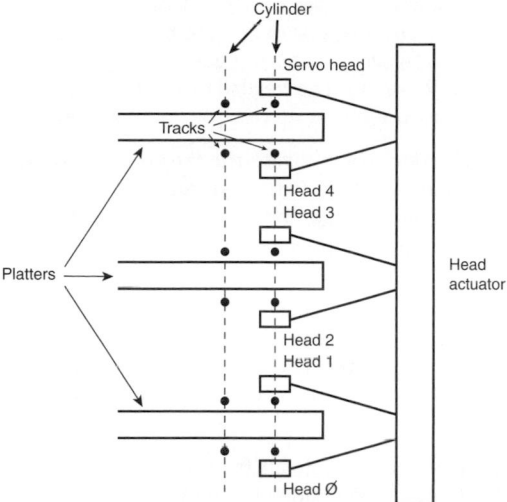

Figure 10.11   A dedicated servo, showing one entire head/side used for servo reading.

One way of telling whether a drive uses a dedicated servo platter is if it has an odd number of heads. For example, the Toshiba MK-538FB 1.2GB drive that I used to have in one of my systems had eight platters, but only 15 read/write heads. That drive uses a dedicated servo positioning system, and the 16th head is the servo head. The advantage of the dedicated servo concept is that the servo information is continuously available to the drive, making the head positioning process faster and more precise.

The drawback to a dedicated servo is that dedicating an entire platter surface for servo information is wasteful. Virtually all drives today use a variation on the embedded servo technique instead. Some drives combined a dedicated servo with an embedded servo, but this type of hybrid design is rare. Regardless of whether the servo mechanism is dedicated or embedded, it is far more accurate than the stepper motor mechanisms of the past.

Of course, as mentioned earlier, today's ATA and SCSI drives have head, track, and sector-per-track parameters that are translated from the actual physical numbers. Therefore, you usually can't tell from the published numbers exactly how many heads or platters are contained within a drive.

Automatic Head Parking

When you power off a hard disk drive using CSS (contact start stop) design, the spring tension in each head arm pulls the heads into contact with the platters. The drive is designed to sustain thousands of takeoffs and landings, but it is wise to ensure that the landing occurs at a spot on the platter that contains no data. Older drives required manual head parking; you had to run a program that positioned the drive heads to a landing zone—usually the innermost cylinder—before turning off the system. Modern drives automatically park the heads, so park programs are no longer necessary.

Some amount of abrasion occurs during the landing and takeoff process, removing just a "micro puff" from the magnetic medium, but if the drive is jarred during the landing or takeoff process, real damage can occur. Newer drives that use load/unload designs incorporate a ramp positioned outside the outer surface of the platters to prevent any contact between the heads and platters, even if the drive is powered off. Load/unload drives automatically park the heads on the ramp when the drive is powered off.

One benefit of using a voice coil actuator is automatic head parking. In a drive that has a voice coil actuator, the heads are positioned and held by magnetic force. When the power to the drive is removed, the magnetic field that holds the heads stationary over a particular cylinder dissipates, enabling the head rack to skitter across the drive surface and potentially cause damage. In the voice coil design, the head rack is attached to a weak spring at one end and a head stop at the other end. When the system is powered on, the spring is overcome by the magnetic force of the positioner. When the drive is powered off, however, the spring gently drags the head rack to a park-and-lock position before the drive slows down and the heads land. On some drives, you could actually hear the "ting...ting...ting...ting" sound as the heads literally bounce-parked themselves, driven by this spring.

On a drive with a voice coil actuator, you activate the parking mechanism by turning off the computer; you do not need to run a program to park or retract the heads, as was necessary with early hard disk designs. In the event of a power outage, the heads park themselves automatically. (The drives unpark automatically when the system is powered on.)

Air Filters

Nearly all hard disk drives have two air filters. One is called the recirculating filter, and the other is called either a barometric or breather filter. These filters are permanently sealed inside the drive and are designed never to be changed for the life of the drive, unlike many older mainframe hard disks that had changeable filters.

A hard disk on a PC system does not circulate air from inside to outside the HDA or vice versa. The recirculating filter permanently installed inside the HDA is designed to filter only the small particles scraped off the platters during head takeoffs and landings (and possibly any other small particles dislodged inside the drive). Because PC hard disk drives are permanently sealed and do not circulate outside air, they can run in extremely dirty environments (see Figure 10.12).

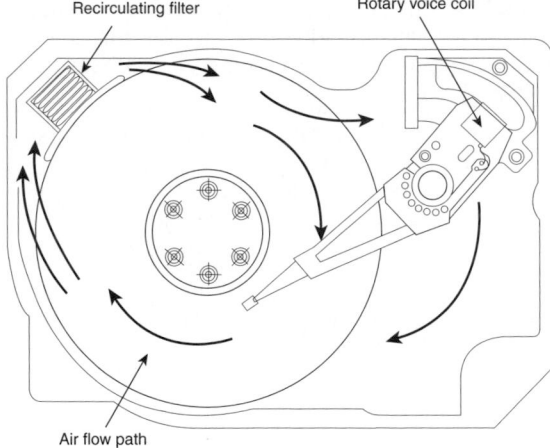

Figure 10.12 Air circulation in a hard disk.

The HDA in a hard disk drive is sealed but not airtight. The HDA is vented through a barometric or breather filter element that enables pressure equalization (breathing) between the inside and outside of the drive. For this reason, most hard drives are rated by the drive's manufacturer to run in a specific range of altitudes, usually from 1,000 feet below to 10,000 feet above sea level. In fact, some hard drives are not rated to exceed 7,000 feet while operating because the air pressure would be too low inside the drive to float the heads properly. As the environmental air pressure changes, air bleeds into or out of the drive so internal and external pressures are identical. Although air does bleed through a vent, contamination usually is not a concern because the barometric filter on this vent is designed to filter out all particles larger than 0.3 microns (about 12 µ-inches) to meet the specifications for cleanliness inside the drive. You can see the vent holes on most drives, which are covered internally by this breather filter. Some drives use even finer grade filter elements to keep out even smaller particles.

I conducted a seminar in Hawaii several years ago, and several of the students were from one of the astronomical observatories atop Mauna Kea. They indicated that virtually all the hard disk drives they had tried to use at the observatory site had failed very quickly, if they worked at all. This was no surprise because the observatories are at the 13,796-foot peak of the mountain, and at that altitude, even people don't function very well! At the time, they had to resort to solid-state (RAM) disks, tape drives, or even floppy disk drives as their primary storage medium. IBM's Adstar division, which made all IBM hard drives before the creation of the Hitachi Global Storage Technologies joint venture, developed a line of rugged 3 1/2" drives that are hermetically sealed (airtight), although they do have air inside the HDA. Because they carry their own internal air under pressure, these drives can operate at any altitude and can withstand extremes of shock and temperature. The drives are designed for military and industrial applications, such as systems used aboard aircraft and in extremely harsh environments. They are, of course, more expensive than typical hard drives that operate under ambient pressures. Other vendors, such as MBM Rugged Systems Ltd. (www.lago.co.uk), have also introduced hermetically sealed drives.

Hard Disk Temperature Acclimation

Because most hard drives have a filtered port to bleed air into or out of the HDA, moisture can enter the drive, and after some period of time, it must be assumed that the humidity inside any hard disk is similar to that outside the drive. Humidity can become a serious problem if it is allowed to condense—and especially if you power up the drive while this condensation is present. Most hard disk manufacturers have specified procedures for acclimating a hard drive to a new environment with different temperature and humidity ranges, and especially for bringing a drive into a warmer environment in which condensation can form. This situation should be of special concern to users of laptop or portable systems. If you leave a portable system in an automobile trunk during the winter, for example, it could be catastrophic to bring the machine inside and power it up without allowing it to acclimate to the temperature indoors.

The following text and Table 10.4 are taken from the factory packaging that Control Data Corporation (later Imprimis and eventually Seagate) used to ship with its hard drives:

> If you have just received or removed this unit from a climate with temperatures at or below 50°F (10°C) do not open this container until the following conditions are met, otherwise condensation could occur and damage to the device and/or media may result. Place this package in the operating environment for the time duration according to the temperature chart.

Table 10.4   Hard Disk Drive Environmental Acclimation Table

Previous Climate Temperature	Acclimation Time	Previous Climate Temperature	Acclimation Time
+40°F (+4°C)	13 hours	−10°F (−23°C)	20 hours
+30°F (−1°C)	15 hours	−20°F (−29°C)	22 hours
+20°F (−7°C)	16 hours	−30°F (−34°C) or less	27 hours
+10°F (−12°C)	17 hours		
0°F (−18°C)	18 hours		

As you can see from this table, you must place a hard disk drive that has been stored in a colder-than-normal environment into its normal operating environment for a specified amount of time to allow it to acclimate before you power it on.

Spindle Motors

The motor that spins the platters is called the spindle motor because it is connected to the spindle around which the platters revolve. Spindle motors in hard disk drives are always connected directly; no belts or gears are involved. The motor must be free of noise and vibration; otherwise, it can transmit a rumble to the platters, which can disrupt reading and writing operations.

The spindle motor also must be precisely controlled for speed. The platters in hard disk drives revolve at speeds ranging from 3,600rpm to 15,000rpm (60–250 revolutions per second) or more, and the motor has a control circuit with a feedback loop to monitor and control this speed precisely. Because the speed control must be automatic, hard drives do not have a motor-speed adjustment. Some diagnostics programs claim to measure hard drive rotation speed, but all these programs do is estimate the rotational speed by the timing at which sectors pass under the heads.

There is actually no way for a program to measure the hard disk drive's rotational speed; this measurement can be made only with sophisticated test equipment. Don't be alarmed if some diagnostics program tells you that your drive is spinning at an incorrect speed; most likely, the program is wrong, not the drive. Platter rotation and timing information is not provided through the hard disk controller interface. In the past, software could give approximate rotational speed estimates by performing multiple sector read requests and timing them, but this was valid only when all drives had the same number of sectors per track and spun at the same speed. Zoned-bit recording—combined with the many various rotational speeds used by modern drives, not to mention built-in buffers and caches—means that these calculation estimates can't be performed accurately by software.

On most drives, the spindle motor is on the bottom of the drive, just below the sealed HDA. Many drives today, however, have the spindle motor built directly into the platter hub inside the HDA. By using an internal hub spindle motor, the manufacturer can stack more platters in the drive because the spindle motor takes up no vertical space.

Note

Spindle motors, particularly on the larger form-factor drives, can consume a great deal of 12-volt power. Most drives require two to three times the normal operating power when the motor first spins the platters. This heavy draw lasts only a few seconds or until the drive platters reach operating speed. If you have more than one drive, you should try to sequence the start of the spindle motors so the power supply does not have to provide such a large load to all the drives at the same time. Most SCSI and some ATA drives have a delayed spindle-motor start feature.

Fluid Dynamic Bearings

Traditionally, spindle motors have used ball bearings in their design, but limitations in their performance have now caused drive manufacturers to look for alternatives. The main problem with ball bearings is that they have approximately 0.1 micro-inch (millionths of an inch) of runout, which is lateral side-to-side play in the bearings. Even though that might seem small, with the ever increasing density of modern drives, it has become a problem. This runout allows the platters to move randomly that distance from side to side, which causes the tracks to wobble under the heads. Additionally, the runout plus the metal-to-metal contact nature of ball bearings allows an excessive amount of mechanical noise and vibration to be generated, and that is becoming a problem for drives that spin at higher speeds.

The solution is a new type of bearing called a fluid dynamic bearing, which uses a highly viscous lubricating fluid between the spindle and sleeve in the motor. This fluid serves to dampen vibrations and movement, allowing runout to be reduced to 0.01 micro-inches or less. Fluid dynamic bearings also allow for better shock resistance, improved speed control, and reduced noise generation. Several of the more advanced drives on the market today already incorporate fluid dynamic bearings, especially those designed for very high spindle speeds, high areal densities, or low noise. Over the next few years, I expect to see fluid dynamic bearings become standard issue in most hard drives.

Logic Boards

All hard disk drives have one or more logic boards mounted on them. The logic boards contain the electronics that control the drive's spindle and head actuator systems and present data to the controller in some agreed-upon form. On ATA drives, the boards include the controller itself, whereas SCSI drives include the controller and the SCSI bus adapter circuit.

Many disk drive failures occur in the logic board, not in the mechanical assembly. (This statement does not seem logical, but it is true.) Therefore, you sometimes can repair a failed drive by replacing the logic board rather than the entire drive. Replacing the logic board, moreover, enables you to regain access to the data on the drive—something that replacing the entire drive does not provide. Unfortunately, none of the drive manufacturers sell logic boards separately. The only way to obtain a replacement logic board for a given drive is to purchase a functioning identical drive and then cannibalize it for parts. Of course, it doesn't make sense to purchase an entire new drive just to repair an existing one except in cases in which data recovery from the old drive is necessary.

If you have an existing drive that contains important data, and the logic board fails, you will be unable to retrieve the data from the drive unless the board is replaced. Because the value of the data in most cases far exceeds the cost of the drive, a new drive that is identical to the failed drive can be purchased and cannibalized for parts such as the logic board, which can be swapped onto the failed drive. This method is common among companies that offer data recovery services. They stock a large number of popular drives they can use for parts to allow data recovery from defective customer drives they receive.

Most of the time the boards are fairly easy to change with nothing more than a screwdriver. Merely removing and reinstalling a few screws as well as unplugging and reconnecting a cable or two are all that is required to remove and replace a typical logic board.

Cables and Connectors

Hard disk drives typically have several connectors for interfacing to the computer, receiving power, and sometimes grounding to the system chassis. Most drives have at least these three types of connectors:

- Interface connector(s)
- Power connector
- Optional ground connector (tab)

Of these, the interface connectors are the most important because they carry the data and command signals between the system and the drive. In most cases, the drive interface cables can be connected in a daisy-chain or bus-type configuration. Most interfaces support at least two devices, and SCSI (Small Computer System Interface) can support up to seven (Wide SCSI can support up to fifteen) devices in the chain, in addition to the host adapter. Older interfaces, such as ST-506/412 or ESDI (Enhanced Small Device Interface), used separate cables for data and control signals, but today's SCSI, ATA (AT Attachment), and Serial ATA drives have a single data connector on each drive.

◄◄   See "Parallel ATA I/O Connector," p. 543, and "SCSI Cables and Connectors," p. 602.

The power is supplied via the larger four-pin peripheral power connector found on all PC power supplies. Most hard disk drives use both 5- and 12-volt power, although some of the smaller drives designed for portable applications use only 5-volt power. In most cases, the 12-volt power runs the spindle motor and head actuator, and the 5-volt power runs the circuitry. Make sure your power supply can supply adequate power for the hard disk drives installed in your system.

The 12-volt power consumption of a drive usually varies with the physical size of the unit. The larger the drive is, the faster it spins. In addition, the more platters there are to spin, the more power it requires. For example, most of the 3 1/2" drives on the market today use roughly one-half to one-fourth the power (in watts) of the older 5 1/4" drives. Some of the very small (2 1/2" or 1.8") hard disks barely sip electrical power and actually use 1 watt or less!

A grounding tab provides an optional ground connection between the drive and the system's chassis. In most computers, the hard disk drive is mounted directly to the chassis using screws, or the drive is grounded via the ground wires in the power connector, so an extra ground wire is unnecessary.

Configuration Items

To configure a hard disk drive for installation in a system, you usually must set several jumpers (and, possibly, terminating resistors) properly. These items typically vary according to the type of interface the drive supports but can vary somewhat from drive to drive as well.

▶▶ See Chapter 14, "Physical Drive Installation and Configuration," p. 831.

The Faceplate or Bezel

At one time, hard disk drive vendors offered a front faceplate, or *bezel*, as an option (see Figure 10.13). In most systems today, the bezel is a part of the case and not the drive itself.

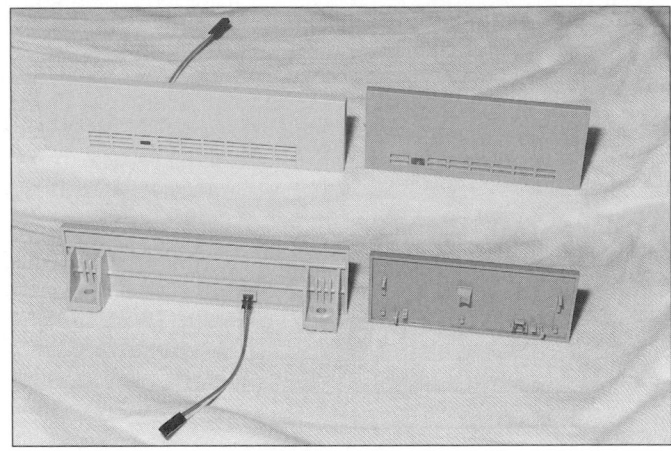

Figure 10.13   Typical 5 1/4" and 3 1/2" hard drive bezel shown from the front (as seen on the outside of the PC case) (top) and from the back (bottom—the inside mounting and LED wiring).

Older systems had the drive installed so it was visible outside the system case. To cover the hole in the case, you would use an optional bezel or faceplate. Because today's drives are almost always mounted in an internal bay or an external bay behind a blank faceplate, you seldom need to buy a drive bezel. If you need to use one, you typically use one included with your system or case. However, drive bezels are still available from several vendors in several sizes and colors to match various PC systems. Many faceplate configurations for 3 1/2" drives are available, including bezels that fit 3 1/2" drive bays as well as 5 1/4" drive bays. You even have a choice of colors (usually black, cream, or white).

Some bezels feature a light-emitting diode (LED) that flickers when your hard disk is in use. The LED is mounted in the bezel; the wire hanging off the back of the LED plugs into the drive. In some drives, the LED is permanently mounted on the drive, and the bezel has a clear or colored window so you can see the LED flicker while the drive is being accessed. Most systems today have an LED indicating drive access on the case's front panel, which is connected to a hard drive LED connector on the motherboard.

In systems in which the hard disk is hidden by the unit's cover, a bezel is unnecessary. In fact, using a bezel can prevent the cover from resting on the chassis properly, in which case the bezel must be removed. If you are installing a drive that does not have a proper bezel, frame, or rails to attach to the system, check the Vendor List on the disc accompanying this book; several listed vendors offer these accessories for a variety of drives. If you are using a 7200rpm or faster hard disk, you should consider placing the drive into a drive bay with a removable cover and using a drive bay cooler, which fits on the front of an external drive bay just as a normal bezel would. It has a power connector to provide power for one or more fans used to cool the drive for greater reliability.

Hard Disk Features

To make the best decision in purchasing a hard disk for your system or to understand what distinguishes one brand of hard disk from another, you must consider many features. This section examines some of the issues you should consider when you evaluate drives:

- Capacity
- Performance
- Reliability
- Cost

Capacity

As stated earlier, a corollary of Parkinson's famous "law" can be applied to hard drives: "Data expands so as to fill the space available for its storage." This of course means that no matter how big a drive you get, you *will* find a way to fill it.

If you've exhausted the space on your current hard disk, you might be wondering, "How much storage space is enough?" Because you are more likely to run out of space than have too much, you should aim high and get the largest drive that will fit within your budget. Modern systems are used to store many space-hungry file types, including digital photos, music, video, newer operating systems, applications, and games. As an example, according to hard drive manufacturer Western Digital, storing 600 high-res photos (500KB each), 12 hours of digital music, 5 games, 20 applications, and just 90 minutes of digital video requires an estimated 43GB of space, exceeding the capacity of the typical hard drive installed in many low-end systems sold at retail.

Running out of space causes numerous problems in a modern system, mainly because Windows, as well as many newer applications, uses a large amount of drive space for temporary files and virtual memory. When Windows runs out of room, system instability, crashes, and data loss are inevitable.

Capacity Limitations

How big a hard drive you can use depends somewhat on the interface you choose. Although the ATA interface is by far the most popular interface for hard drives, SCSI interface drives are also available. Each has different limitations, but those of ATA have always been lower than those of SCSI.

When ATA was first created in 1986, it had a maximum capacity limitation of 137GB (65,536×16×255 sectors). BIOS issues further limited capacity to 8.4GB in systems earlier than 1998, and 528MB in systems earlier than 1994. Even after the BIOS problems were resolved, however, the 137GB limit of ATA remained. Fortunately, this was broken in the ATA-6 specification drafted in 2001. ATA-6 augments the addressing scheme used by ATA to allow drive capacity to grow to 144PB (petabytes, or quadrillion bytes), which is 2^{48} sectors. This has opened the door allowing ATA drives over 137GB to be released. Obviously any drives larger than 137GB would by nature conform to ATA-6. However, if you are installing a drive larger than that, you should also ensure that your motherboard BIOS has ATA-6 support.

BIOS Limitations

If your current hard drive is 8GB or smaller, your system might not be capable of handling a larger drive without a BIOS upgrade because many older (pre-1998) BIOSs can't handle drives above the 8.4GB limit, and others (pre-2002) have other limits such as 137GB. Most ATA hard drives ship with a setup disk containing a software BIOS substitute such as Ontrack's Disk Manager or Phoenix Technologies' EZ-Drive (Phoenix purchased EZ-Drive creator StorageSoft in January 2002), but I don't recommend using a software BIOS replacement. Ez-Drive, Disk Manager, and their OEM offshoots (Drive Guide, MAXBlast, Data Lifeguard, and others) can cause problems if you need to boot from floppy or CD media or if you need to repair the nonstandard master boot record these products use.

If your motherboard ROM BIOS dates before 1998 and is limited to 8.4GB or dates before 2002 and is limited to 137GB, and you want to install a larger drive, I recommend you first contact your motherboard (or system) manufacturer to see whether an update is available. Virtually all motherboards incorporate a flash ROM, which allows for easy updates via a utility program.

Internal ATA drives larger than 137GB require 48-bit logical block address (LBA) support. This support *must* be provided in the operating system; it can also be provided in the BIOS, or both. It is best if both the OS and the BIOS support it, but it can be made to work if only the OS has the support.

48-bit LBA support in the OS requires

- Windows XP with Service Pack 1 (SP1) or later.
- Windows 2000 with Service Pack 4 (SP4) or later.
- Windows 98/98SE/Me or NT 4.0 with the Intel Application Accelerator (IAA) loaded. This solution works only if your motherboard has an IAA-supported chipset. See `www.intel.com/support/chipsets/IAA/instruct.htm` for more information.

48-bit LBA support in the BIOS requires either of the following:

- A motherboard BIOS with 48-bit LBA support (usually dated September 2002 or later)
- An adapter card with onboard BIOS that includes 48-bit LBA support, such as the LBA Pro card from eSupport (`www.esupport.com`)

These cards use an ISA slot and contain a flash ROM that adds 48-bit LBA support for your existing ATA host adapters. These cards are ROM only. They don't have onboard ATA interfaces, and your drives remain connected to your previously existing ATA host adapters (normally built in to the motherboard).

If you have both OS and BIOS support for 48-bit LBA, you can simply install and use the drive like any other internal drive. On the other hand, if you do not have 48-bit LBA support in the BIOS, but you do have it in the OS, portions of the drive past 137GB are not recognized or accessible until the OS is loaded. This means that if you are installing the OS to a blank hard drive and booting from an original XP (pre-SP1) CD or earlier, you need to partition up to the first 137GB of the drive at installation time. After the OS is fully installed and the service packs added, the remainder of the drive beyond 137GB is recognized. At that point, you can then either partition the remainder of the drive beyond 137GB using the XP Disk Management tools or use a third-party partitioning program such as PartitionMagic or Partition Commander to resize the first partition to use the full drive.

If you are booting from an XP SP1 or later CD (meaning a CD with Service Pack 1 already applied), you can recognize and access the entire drive during the OS installation and partition the entire drive as a single partition greater than 137GB if you like.

If you need more or faster ATA interface connections, or if you don't have ISA slots on your motherboard, you can use PCI-based add-on cards (such as the Ultra133 TX2 and Ultra100 TX2) from companies like Maxtor and Promise Technologies. These cards support drives up to and beyond the 137GB limit imposed by the ATA-5 and older standards. These cards also have two ATA host adapter interfaces onboard that support two drives each (four drives per card). These cards do support ATA-133 and ATA-100 interface speeds and are backward-compatible with older, slower ATA drives.

Maxtor and Western Digital sell drives in kits bundled with an ATA-133 PCI host adapter card that also provides BIOS support for drives beyond 137GB.

USB, FireWire, and SCSI drives don't have these capacity issues because they don't rely on the ROM BIOS for support and use OS managed drivers instead.

SCSI was designed from the beginning with fewer limitations than ATA, which is why SCSI is more commonly used in high-performance file servers, workstations, and other high-performance computer systems. Even though SCSI originated prior to ATA, the architects had the foresight to allow SCSI to address devices up to 2.2TB (terabytes, or trillion bytes) in capacity (2^{32} sectors). In 2001, the SCSI command set was further upgraded to support drives up to 9.44ZB (zettabytes, or sextillion bytes) in capacity (2^{64} sectors). Because SCSI was initially designed with fewer limitations and greater performance in mind, manufacturers have always released their largest capacity drives in SCSI versions first. If you absolutely must have the biggest drive, it will almost always be a SCSI drive you are looking for.

Because of the changes in 2001 to both ATA and SCSI, it will be many years before the capacity limitations of either interface become a problem.

Operating System Limitations

More recent operating systems such as Windows Me, as well as Windows 2000 and XP, fortunately don't have any problems with larger drives. However, older operating systems might have limitations when it comes to using large drives.

DOS generally does not recognize drives larger than 8.4GB because those drives are accessed using LBA and DOS versions 6.x and lower use only CHS addressing.

Windows 95 has a 32GB hard disk capacity limit, and there is no way around it other than upgrading to Windows 98 or newer. Additionally, the retail or upgrade versions of Windows 95 (also called Windows 95 OSR 1 or Windows 95a) are further limited to using only the FAT16 (16-bit file allocation table) file system, which carries a maximum partition size limitation of 2GB. Therefore, if you had a 30GB drive, you would be forced to divide it into 15 2GB partitions, with each appearing as a separate drive letter (drives C:–Q: in this example). Windows 95B and 95C can use the FAT32 file system, which allows partition sizes up to 2TB. Note that because of internal limitations, no version of FDISK can create partitions larger than 512MB.

Windows 98 supports large drives, but a bug in the FDISK program included with Windows 98 reduces the reported drive capacity by 64GB for drives over that capacity. The solution is an updated version of FDISK that can be downloaded from Microsoft. Another bug appears in the FORMAT command with Windows 98: If you run FORMAT from a command prompt on a partition over 64GB, the size isn't reported correctly, although the entire partition is formatted.

Performance

When you select a hard disk drive, one of the important features you should consider is the performance (speed) of the drive. Hard drives can have a wide range of performance capabilities. As is true of many things, one of the best indicators of a drive's relative performance is its price. An old saying from the automobile-racing industry is appropriate here: "Speed costs money. How fast do you want to go?"

The speed of a disk drive is typically measured in two ways:

- Transfer rate
- Average access time

Transfer Rate

The transfer rate is probably more important to overall system performance than any other statistic, but it is also one of the most misunderstood specifications. The problem stems from the fact that several transfer rates can be specified for a given drive; however, the most important of these is usually overlooked.

Don't be fooled by interface transfer rate hype, especially around ATA-133 or SATA-150. A far more important gauge of a drive's performance is the average media transfer rate, which is significantly lower than the interface rate of 133MBps or 150MBps. The media transfer rate represents the average speed at which the drive can actually read or write data. By comparison, the interface transfer rate merely indicates how quickly data can move between the motherboard and the buffer on the drive. The rotational speed of the drive has the biggest effect on the drive's true transfer speed; in general, drives that spin at 10,000rpm transfer data faster than 7,200rpm drives, and 7,200rpm drives transfer data faster than those that spin at 5,400rpm. If you are looking for performance, be sure to check the true *media* transfer rates of any drives you are comparing.

The confusion results from the fact that drive manufacturers can report up to seven different transfer rates for a given drive. Perhaps the least important (but one that people seem to focus on the most) is the raw interface transfer rate, which for most modern ATA drives is either 100MBps or 133MBps, or 150MBps for Serial ATA drives. Unfortunately, few people seem to realize that the drives actually read and write data much more slowly than that. The more important transfer rate specifications are the media transfer rates, which express how fast a drive can actually read or write data. Media transfer rates can be expressed as a raw maximum, a raw minimum, a formatted maximum, formatted minimum, or averages of either. Few report the averages, but they can be easily calculated.

The media transfer rate is far more important than the interface transfer rate because the media transfer rate is the true rate at which data can be read from (or written to) the disk. In other words, it tells how fast data can be moved to and from the drive platters (media). It is the rate that any sustained transfer can hope to achieve. This rate is usually reported as a minimum and maximum figure, although many drive manufacturers report the maximum only.

Media transfer rates have minimum and maximum figures because drives today use zoned recording with fewer sectors per track on the inner cylinders than the outer cylinders. Typically, a drive is divided into 16 or more zones, with the inner zone having about half the sectors per track (and therefore about half the transfer rate) of the outer zone. Because the drive spins at a constant rate, data can be read twice as fast from the outer cylinders than from the inner cylinders.

Another issue is the raw transfer rate versus the formatted transfer rate. The *raw* rate refers to how fast bits can be read off the media. Because not all bits represent data (some are intersector, servo, ECC, or ID bits), and because some time is lost when the heads have to move from track to track (latency), the *formatted* transfer rate represents the true rate at which user data can be read from or written to the drive.

Note that some manufacturers report only raw internal media transfer rates, but you usually can calculate that the formatted transfer rates are about three-fourths of the raw rates. This is because the user data on each track is only about three-fourths of the actual bits stored due to servo, ECC, ID, and other overhead that is stored. Likewise, some manufacturers report only maximum transfer rates (either raw, formatted, or both); in that case, you generally can assume the minimum transfer rate is one-half of the maximum and that the average transfer rate is three-fourths of the maximum.

Let's look at a specific drive as an example. The Hitachi (formerly IBM) Deskstar 120GXP is considered a fast ATA drive. It spins at 7,200rpm and supports the ATA/100 interface transfer rate (Ultra DMA Mode 5, which is 100MBps from the drive controller to the motherboard host adapter). As with all drives I know of, the actual (media) transfer rate is much less.

Table 10.5 shows the specifications for the 7,200rpm Ultra-ATA/100 Hitachi (IBM) Deskstar 120GXP drive.

Table 10.5   Media Transfer Rate Specifications for the Hitachi (IBM) Deskstar 120GXP Drive

Media Zone	Sectors/Track	Rotational Speed	Transfer Rate
Outer Zone	928	7,200rpm	57.02MBps
Inner Zone	448	7,200rpm	27.53MBps
Average	688	7,200rpm	42.27MBps

As you can see, the *true* transfer rate for this drive is between 57.02MBps and 27.53MBps, or an average of about 42.27MBps—less than half of the ATA/100 interface transfer rate. Of course, if this were your drive, you wouldn't be disappointed because 42.27MBps is excellent performance. In fact, this is one of the fastest ATA drives on the market. Many other ATA drives would have equal or slower performance.

A common question I get is about upgrading the ATA interface in a system. Many people are using older motherboards that support only ATA/33 (Ultra DMA Mode 2) or ATA/66 (Ultra DMA Mode 4) modes and not the faster ATA/100 (Ultra DMA Mode 5) or ATA/133 (Ultra DMA Mode 6) specifications. After studying the true formatted media transfer rates of most drives, you can see why I generally do not recommend installing a separate ATA/100 or ATA/133 host adapter for those systems, unless you need the additional host adapters to attach more drives. From a pure performance perspective, those who perform such an upgrade will most likely see little, if any, increase in performance. This is because in almost all cases, the drives they are using are on average slower than even ATA/33— and often significantly slower than the ATA/66, ATA/100, or ATA/133 interface speeds.

Two primary factors contribute to transfer rate performance: rotational speed and the linear recording density or sector-per-track figures. When comparing two drives with the same number of sectors per track, the drive that spins more quickly transfers data more quickly. Likewise, when comparing two drives with identical rotational speeds, the drive with the higher recording density (more sectors per track) is faster. A higher-density drive can be faster than one that spins faster—both factors have to be taken into account.

Let's look at another example. Similar to the IBM 120GXP, the Maxtor DiamondMax D540X-4G120J6 is also a 120GB ATA drive. It spins at 5,400rpm and supports the ATA/133 interface transfer rate (Ultra DMA Mode 6, which is 133MBps from the drive controller to the motherboard host adapter). Table 10.6 shows the specifications for the 5,400rpm Ultra-ATA/133 Maxtor DiamondMax D540X-4G120J6 120GB ATA drive.

Table 10.6   Media Transfer Rate Specifications for the Maxtor DiamondMax D540X-4G120J6 120GB ATA Drive

Media Zone	Sectors/Track	Rotational Speed	Transfer Rate
Outer Zone	896	5,400rpm	41.29MBps
Inner Zone	448	5,400rpm	20.64MBps
Average	672	5,400rpm	30.97MBps

As you can see, the *true* transfer rate for this drive is between 41.29MBps and 20.64MBps, or an average of about 30.97MBps—less than one-fourth of the interface transfer rate.

Note the comparison between the two 120GB drives:

Drive	Rotational Speed	Interface Transfer Rate	Average Media Transfer Rate
Hitachi (IBM) 120GXP	7,200rpm	100MBps	42.27MBps
Maxtor D540X	5,400rpm	133MBps	30.97MBps

It is interesting to note that the drive with the *faster* interface transfer rate (133MBps versus 100MBps) is actually *slower* overall by a fairly large margin (about 37%). Because the drives have about the same average number of sectors per track, the differential in the transfer speed performance is mainly due to the 33% greater rotational speed in one drive over the other.

If you were choosing among 120GB drives and looking for the highest performance, you should almost always choose the drive with the fastest *media* transfer rate. Even though it operates at a slower 100MBps (ATA-100) interface transfer speed, it actually reads and writes data 37% faster overall than the other drive, even though the other drive supports 133MBps interface transfers (ATA-133).

As you can see from this example, the interface transfer speed is almost meaningless. In fact, because neither drive can actually transfer data faster than 66MBps (even from the outer cylinders), using an interface transfer rate higher than that does not help performance much. So, if you were thinking about getting a new motherboard or maybe a separate host adapter card for the sole purpose of increasing drive performance, save your money. To be fair, there will be a slight benefit to higher interface transfer speeds in that data from the buffer on the drive controller can be transferred to the motherboard at interface speed, rather than media speed. These buffers are usually 2MB or less and help only with repetitive transfers of small amounts of data. However, if you perform repetitive transfers frequently, drives with larger 8MB buffers can improve performance with applications that perform repetitive transfers. Refer to Table 10.5 for information on current drives with 8MB buffers.

All other things being equal, a drive that spins faster transfers data faster, regardless of the interface transfer rate. Unfortunately, it is rare that all other things are exactly equal, so you should consult the drive specifications listed in the data sheet or manual for the drive to be sure.

One of the fastest rotating drives today is the Seagate Cheetah X15, which spins at 15,000rpm. Table 10.7 shows the specifications for the 15,000rpm Ultra4-SCSI/320 Seagate Cheetah X15-36LP (ST-336732LW) drive.

Table 10.7   Transfer Rate Specifications for the Seagate Cheetah X15-36LP (ST-336732LW) 15,000rpm Drive

Transfer Rate	Megabits/Sec	Megabytes/Sec
Interface Transfer Rate	2560Mbps	320.0MBps
Raw Media Transfer Rate (Max)	709Mbps	88.6MBps
Raw Media Transfer Rate (Min)	522Mbps	65.3MBps
Formatted Media Transfer Rate (Max)	552Mbps	69.0MBps
Formatted Media Transfer Rate (Min)	408Mbps	51.0MBps
Formatted Media Transfer Rate (Avg)	480Mbps	60.0MBps

As a comparison, Table 10.8 contains the specifications for the 10,000rpm Ultra4-SCSI/320 Seagate Cheetah 36ES (ST-336746LW) drive.

Table 10.8   Transfer Rates for the Seagate Cheetah 36ES (ST-336746LW) 10,000rpm Drive

Transfer Rate	Megabits/Sec	Megabytes/Sec
Interface Transfer Rate	2560Mbps	320.0MBps
Raw Media Transfer Rate (Max)	682Mbps	85.3MBps
Raw Media Transfer Rate (Min)	520Mbps	65.0MBps
Formatted Media Transfer Rate (Max)	506Mbps	63.2MBps
Formatted Media Transfer Rate (Min)	393Mbps	49.1MBps
Formatted Media Transfer Rate (Avg)	449Mbps	56.2MBps

As you can see, although the 15,000rpm drive spins 50% faster, it actually transfers data only about 7% faster. It also costs about 38% more for the same capacity. Note that neither of these drives comes close to the Ultra4 SCSI (320MBps) bandwidth the interface would allow. One difference between ATA and SCSI, though, is that all the SCSI drives on a given channel can more effectively share the bandwidth.

With a comparison such as this, you can see that you need to be careful. Don't just compare one specification, such as interface speed or rotational speed, because these can be misleading. The interface speed is relatively meaningless, and although the rotational speed is much more important, some drives have a slower media transfer rate than others even though they spin faster. Be careful with simplistic comparisons. With hard drives, the bottom line is that the media transfer rate is probably the most important specification you can know about a drive—and faster is better.

To find the transfer specifications for a given drive, look in the data sheet or preferably the documentation or manual for the drive. These can usually be downloaded from the drive manufacturer's Web site. This documentation often reports the maximum and minimum sector per track specifications, which—combined with the rotational speed—can be used to calculate true formatted media performance. You should be looking for the true number of physical sectors per track for the outer and inner zones. Therefore, you should be aware that many drives (especially zoned-bit recording drives) are configured with sector translation, which means the number of sectors per track reported by the BIOS has little to do with the actual physical characteristics of the drive. You must know the drive's true physical parameters, rather than the values the BIOS uses.

When you know the sector per track (SPT) and rotational speed figures, you can use the following formula to determine the true media data transfer rate in millions of bytes per second (MBps):

Media Transfer Rate (MBps) = SPT×512 bytes×rpm/60 seconds/1,000,000 bytes

For example, the Hitachi Deskstar 120GXP drive spins at 7,200rpm and has an average of 688 sectors per track. The average media transfer rate for this drive is figured as follows:

688×512×(7,200/60)/1,000,000 = 42.27MBps

Using this formula, you can calculate the media transfer rate of any drive if you know the rotational speed and average sectors per track.

Average Seek Time

Average seek time, usually measured in milliseconds (ms), is the average amount of time it takes to move the heads from one cylinder to another a random distance away. One way to measure this specification is to run many random track-seek operations and then divide the timed results by the number of seeks performed. This method provides an average time for a single seek.

The standard method used by many drive manufacturers when reporting average seek times is to measure the time it takes the heads to move across one-third of the total cylinders. Average seek time depends only on the drive itself; the type of interface or controller has little effect on this specification. The average seek rating is primarily a gauge of the capabilities of the head actuator mechanism.

Note

Be wary of benchmarks that claim to measure drive seek performance. Most ATA/IDE and SCSI drives use a scheme called sector translation, so any commands the drive receives to move the heads to a specific cylinder might not actually result in the intended physical movement. This situation renders some benchmarks meaningless for those types of drives. SCSI drives also require an additional step because the commands first must be sent to the drive over the SCSI bus. These drives might seem to have the fastest access times because the command overhead is not factored in by most benchmarks. However, when this overhead is factored in by benchmark programs, these drives receive poor performance figures.

Latency

Latency is the average time (in milliseconds) it takes for a sector to be available after the heads have reached a track. On average, this figure is half the time it takes for the disk to rotate once. A drive that spins twice as fast would have half the latency.

Latency is a factor in disk read and write performance. Decreasing the latency increases the speed of access to data or files and is accomplished only by spinning the drive platters more quickly. Latency figures for most popular drive rotational speeds are shown in Table 10.9.

Table 10.9   Hard Disk Rotation Speeds and Their Latencies

Revs/Minute	Revs/Second	Latency
3,600	60	8.33
4,200	70	7.14
5,400	90	5.56
7,200	120	4.17
10,000	167	3.00
15,000	250	2.00

Many drives today spin at 7,200rpm, resulting in a latency time of only 4.17ms, whereas others spin at 10,000rpm or even 15,000rpm, resulting in incredible 3.00ms or 2.00ms latency figures. In addition to increasing performance where real-world access to data is concerned, spinning the platters more quickly also increases the data-transfer rate after the heads arrive at the desired sectors.

Average Access Time

A measurement of a drive's average access time is the sum of its average seek time plus latency. The average access time is usually expressed in milliseconds.

A measurement of a drive's average access time (average seek time plus latency) provides the average total amount of time required for the drive to access a randomly requested sector.

Cache Programs and Caching Controllers

At the software level, disk cache programs such as SMARTDRV (DOS) and VCACHE (Windows) can have a major effect on disk drive performance. These cache programs hook into the BIOS hard drive interrupt and intercept the read and write calls to the disk BIOS from application programs and device drivers.

When an application program wants to read data from a hard drive, the cache program intercepts the read request, passes the read request to the hard drive controller in the usual way, saves the data read from the disk in its cache memory buffer, and then passes the data back to the application program. Depending on the size of the cache buffer, data from numerous sectors can be read into and saved in the buffer.

When the application wants to read more data, the cache program again intercepts the request and examines its buffers to see whether the requested data is still in the cache. If so, the program passes the data back from the cache to the application immediately, without another hard drive operation. Because the cached data is stored in memory, this method speeds access tremendously and can greatly affect disk drive performance measurements.

Most controllers now have some form of built-in hardware buffer or cache that doesn't intercept or use any BIOS interrupts. Instead, the drive caches data at the hardware level, which is invisible to normal performance-measurement software. Manufacturers originally included track read-ahead buffers in controllers to permit 1:1 interleave performance. Some manufacturers now increase the size of these read-ahead buffers in the controller, whereas others add intelligence by using a cache instead of a simple buffer.

Many ATA and SCSI drives have cache memory built directly into the drive's onboard controller. Most newer ATA drives have 2MB of built-in cache; many high-performance ATA drives have 8MB of cache. Most SCSI drives have 8MB while some have up to 16MB. I remember the days when 1MB or 2MB of RAM was a lot of memory for an entire system. Nowadays, some 3 1/2" hard disk drives can have up to 16MB of cache memory built right in!

Although software and hardware caches can make a drive faster for routine or repetitive data transfer operations, a cache will not affect the true maximum transfer rate the drive can sustain.

Interleave Selection

In a discussion of disk performance, the issue of interleave often comes up. Although traditionally this was more a controller performance issue than a drive issue, modern ATA/IDE and SCSI hard disk drives with built-in controllers are fully capable of processing the data as fast as the drive can send it. In other words, all modern ATA and SCSI drives are formatted with no interleave (sometimes expressed as a 1:1 interleave ratio). On older hard drive types, such as MFM and ESDI, you could modify the interleave during a low-level format to optimize the drive's performance. Today, drives are low-level formatted at the factory and interleave adjustments are a moot topic.

Note

For more information on interleaving and cylinder skewing as used on older drives, see the sections "Interleave Selection" and "Head and Cylinder Skewing" in Chapter 10 of *Upgrading and Repairing PCs, 12th Edition,* included in its entirety on the disc accompanying this book.

Reliability

When you shop for a drive, you might notice a statistic called the mean time between failures (MTBF) described in the drive specifications. MTBF figures usually range from 300,000 to 1,000,000 hours or more. I usually ignore these figures because they are derived theoretically.

In understanding the MTBF claims, you must understand how the manufacturers arrive at them and what they mean. Most manufacturers have a long history of building drives, and their drives have seen millions of hours of cumulative use. They can look at the failure rate for previous drive models with the same components and calculate a failure rate for a new drive based on the components used to build the drive assembly. For the electronic circuit board, they also can use industry-standard techniques for predicting the failure of the integrated electronics. This enables them to calculate the predicted failure rate for the entire drive unit.

To understand what these numbers mean, you must know that the MTBF claims apply to a population of drives, not an individual drive. This means that if a drive claims to have an MTBF of 500,000 hours, you can expect a failure in that population of drives in 500,000 hours of total running time. If 1,000,000 drives of this model are in service and all 1,000,000 are running simultaneously, you can expect one failure out of this entire population every half-hour. MTBF statistics are not useful for predicting the failure of any individual drive or a small sample of drives.

You also need to understand the meaning of the word *failure*. In this sense, a failure is a fault that requires the drive to be returned to the manufacturer for repair, not an occasional failure to read or write a file correctly.

Finally, as some drive manufacturers point out, this measure of MTBF should really be called mean time to first failure. "Between failures" implies that the drive fails, is returned for repair, and then at some point fails again. The interval between repair and the second failure here would be the MTBF. Because in most cases, a failed hard drive that would need manufacturer repair is replaced rather than repaired, the whole MTBF concept is misnamed.

The bottom line is that I do not really place much emphasis on MTBF figures. For an individual drive, they are not accurate predictors of reliability. However, if you are an information systems manager considering the purchase of thousands of PCs or drives per year or a system vendor building and supporting thousands of systems, it might be worth your while to examine these numbers and study the methods used to calculate them by each vendor. Most hard drive manufacturers designate their premium drives as Enterprise class drives, meaning they are designed for use in environments requiring full-time usage and high reliability and carry the highest MTBF ratings. If you can understand the vendor's calculations and compare the actual reliability of a large sample of drives, you can purchase more reliable drives and save time and money in service and support.

SMART

Self-Monitoring, Analysis, and Reporting Technology (SMART) is an industry standard providing failure prediction for disk drives. When SMART is enabled for a given drive, the drive monitors predetermined attributes that are susceptible to or indicative of drive degradation. Based on changes in the monitored attributes, a failure prediction can be made. If a failure is deemed likely to occur, SMART makes a status report available so the system BIOS or driver software can notify the user of the impending problems, perhaps enabling the user to back up the data on the drive before any real problems occur.

Predictable failures are the types of failures SMART attempts to detect. These failures result from the gradual degradation of the drive's performance. According to Seagate, 60% of drive failures are mechanical, which is exactly the type of failures SMART is designed to predict.

Of course, not all failures are predictable, and SMART can't help with unpredictable failures that occur without any advance warning. These can be caused by static electricity; improper handling or sudden shock; or circuit failure, such as thermal-related solder problems or component failure.

SMART was originally created by IBM in 1992. That year IBM began shipping 3 1/2" hard disk drives equipped with Predictive Failure Analysis (PFA), an IBM-developed technology that periodically measures selected drive attributes and sends a warning message when a predefined threshold is exceeded. IBM turned this technology over to the ANSI organization, and it subsequently became the ANSI-standard SMART protocol for SCSI drives, as defined in the ANSI-SCSI Informational Exception Control (IEC) document X3T10/94-190.

Interest in extending this technology to ATA drives led to the creation of the SMART Working Group in 1995. Besides IBM, other companies represented in the original group were Seagate Technology, Conner Peripherals (now a part of Seagate), Fujitsu, Hewlett-Packard, Maxtor, Quantum, and Western Digital. The SMART specification produced by this group and placed in the public domain covers both ATA and SCSI hard disk drives and can be found in most of the more recently produced drives on the market.

The SMART design of attributes and thresholds is similar in ATA and SCSI environments, but the reporting of information differs.

In an ATA environment, driver software on the system interprets the alarm signal from the drive generated by the SMART "report status" command. The driver polls the drive on a regular basis to check the status of this command and, if it signals imminent failure, sends an alarm to the operating system where it is passed on via an error message to the end user. This structure also enables future enhancements, which might allow reporting of information other than drive failure conditions. The system can read and evaluate the attributes and alarms reported in addition to the basic "report status" command.

SCSI drives with SMART communicate a reliability condition only as either good or failing. In a SCSI environment, the failure decision occurs at the disk drive and the host notifies the user for action. The SCSI specification provides for a sense bit to be flagged if the drive determines that a reliability issue exists. The system then alerts the end user via a message.

Note that traditional disk diagnostics such as Scandisk work only on the data sectors of the disk surface and do not monitor all the drive functions that are monitored by SMART. Most modern disk drives keep spare sectors available to use as substitutes for sectors that have errors. When one of these spares is reallocated, the drive reports the activity to the SMART counter but still looks completely defect-free to a surface analysis utility, such as Scandisk.

Drives with SMART monitor a variety of attributes that vary from one manufacturer to another. Attributes are selected by the device manufacturer based on their capability to contribute to the prediction of degrading or fault conditions for that particular drive. Most drive manufacturers consider the specific set of attributes being used and the identity of those attributes as vendor specific and proprietary.

Some drives monitor the floating height of the head above the magnetic media. If this height changes from a nominal figure, the drive could fail. Other drives can monitor different attributes, such as ECC circuitry that indicates whether soft errors are occurring when reading or writing data. Some of the attributes monitored on various drives include the following:

- Head floating height
- Data throughput performance
- Spin-up time
- Reallocated (spared) sector count

- Seek error rate
- Seek time performance
- Drive spin-up retry count
- Drive calibration retry count

Each attribute has a threshold limit that is used to determine the existence of a degrading or fault condition. These thresholds are set by the drive manufacturer, can vary among manufacturers and models, and can't be changed.

The basic requirements for SMART to function in a system are simple: You just need a SMART-capable hard disk drive and a SMART-aware BIOS or hard disk driver for your particular operating system. If your BIOS does not support SMART, utility programs are available that can support SMART on a given system. These include Norton Utilities from Symantec, EZ Drive from StorageSoft, and Data Advisor from Ontrack.

When sufficient changes occur in the monitored attributes to trigger a SMART alert, the drive sends an alert message via an IDE/ATA or a SCSI command (depending on the type of hard disk drive you have) to the hard disk driver in the system BIOS, which usually reports the problem during the POST the next time the system boots.

If you want more immediate reporting, you can run a utility that queries the SMART status of the drive, such as SMART Explorer by Adenix (www.adenix.net) or HDD Health by Panterasoft (www.panterasoft.com).

The first thing to do if you receive a SMART warning is to back up all the data on the drive. I recommend you back up to new media and do not overwrite any previous backups you might have, just in case the drive fails before the new backup is complete.

After backing up your data, what should you do? SMART warnings can be caused by an external source and might not actually indicate that the drive itself is going to fail. For example, environmental changes such as high or low ambient temperatures can trigger a SMART alert, as can excessive vibration in the drive caused by an external source. Additionally, electrical interference from motors or other devices on the same circuit as your PC can induce these alerts.

If the alert was not caused by an external source, a drive replacement might be indicated. If the drive is under warranty, contact the vendor and ask whether they will replace it. If no further alerts occur, the problem might have been an anomaly, and you might not need to replace the drive. If you receive further alerts, replacing the drive is recommended. If you can connect both the new and existing (failing) drive to the same system, you might be able to copy the entire contents of the existing drive to the new one, saving you from having to install or reload all the applications and data from your backup.

Cost

The cost of hard disk storage is continually falling. You can now purchase a 200GB ATA drive for around $100, which is about 1/20 of a cent per megabyte.

A drive I bought in 1983 had a maximum capacity of 10MB and cost $1,800. At current pricing (0.05 cents per megabyte), that drive is worth about half a penny!

Of course, the cost of drives continues to fall, and we can expect even greater capacities and lower prices in the future.

CHAPTER 11

Floppy Disk Storage

Floppy Storage Basics

This chapter examines the standard types of floppy disk drives and disks that have been used in PCs since the beginning. It explores the various types of drives and disks, how they function, and how to properly install and service them. The high-capacity floppy drives such as the SuperDisk (LS-120 and LS-240) and flash memory devices such as USB keychain are covered separately in Chapter 12, "High-Capacity Removable Storage." Magnetic storage in general—that is, how data is actually stored on the disk media—is covered in Chapter 9, "Magnetic Storage Principles."

Although no longer used for primary storage, the floppy is still sometimes used as a system installation and configuration device, especially when troubleshooting. In older systems that don't support the El Torito CD-ROM boot specification, the floppy drive is the only way to load an operating system from scratch or to run bootable diagnostics. Newer systems that support El Torito (bootable CDs) don't require floppy drives because they can boot operating systems and diagnostics directly from a CD.

Starting in 2002, many companies started selling systems without floppy drives. This started with note-book computers, where internal floppy drives were first eliminated and replaced with external (normally USB) drives. Most newer notebooks no longer include a floppy drive with the system, offering only external USB models as an option. In 2003, many desktop system manufacturers likewise stopped including floppy drives in their standard system configurations. In March 2003, Dell dropped the floppy drive as a standard feature from most of its desktop models and instead offers it as an optional extra.

Many alternatives to floppy storage are available. Both Zip and LS-120/LS-240 (SuperDisk) drives have failed in the marketplace as floppy drive replacements in new PCs. The Mt. Rainier standard, which was introduced in 2002, allows CD-RW and DVD+-RW drives to serve as replacements for the floppy. Prior to Mt. Rainier, the CD/DVD drives lacked defect management, as well as native OS support.

▶▶   See "Mount Rainier," p. 779.

Many people are also now using USB flash memory devices, often called *thumb drives* or *keychain drives*, to transport small to medium amounts of data (up to 2GB or more) between systems. Floppy drives remain useful for data recovery or computer forensics, where data retrieval from older media is often necessary. Even though I don't use floppy drives much for storing new information, I maintain systems with both 5 1/4" and 3 1/2" drives so that I can read data from older media in a forensics or data recovery situation.

History of the Floppy

Alan Shugart is generally credited with inventing the floppy disk drive in 1967 while working for IBM. One of Shugart's senior engineers, David Noble, actually proposed the flexible medium (then 8" in diameter) and the protective jacket with the fabric lining. Shugart left IBM in 1969, and in 1976 his company, Shugart Associates, introduced the minifloppy (5 1/4") disk drive. It, of course, became the standard eventually used by personal computers, rapidly replacing the 8" drives. He also helped create the Shugart Associates System Interface (SASI), which was later renamed small computer system interface (SCSI) when approved as an ANSI standard.

Sony introduced the first 3 1/2" microfloppy drives and disks in 1981. The first significant company to adopt the 3 1/2" floppy for general use was Hewlett-Packard in 1984 with its partially PC-compatible HP-150 system. The adoption of the 3 1/2" drive in the PC was solidified when IBM started using the drive in 1986 in some systems and finally switched its entire PC product line to 3 1/2" drives in 1987.

Note that all PC floppy disk drives are still based on (and mostly compatible with) the original Shugart designs, including the electrical and command interfaces. Compared to other parts of the PC, the floppy disk drive has undergone relatively few changes over the years.

Floppy Drive Interfaces

Floppy drives are interfaced to the PC in several ways. Most use the traditional floppy controller interface, which is covered in this chapter, but some now use the USB interface. Because the traditional floppy controller only works internally, all external drives are interfaced via USB or some other alternative interface.

USB drives often have a standard floppy drive inside an external box with a USB-to-floppy controller interface converter inside. Newer systems that are "legacy free" don't include a traditional floppy controller and typically use USB as the floppy interface. In the past, some drives have been available in FireWire (IEEE-1394) or even parallel interfaces as well. For more information on USB or the parallel port, see Chapter 17, "I/O Interfaces from Serial and Parallel to IEEE 1394 and USB."

Drive Components

All floppy disk drives, regardless of type, consist of several basic common components. To properly install and service a disk drive, you must be able to identify these components and understand their functions (see Figure 11.1).

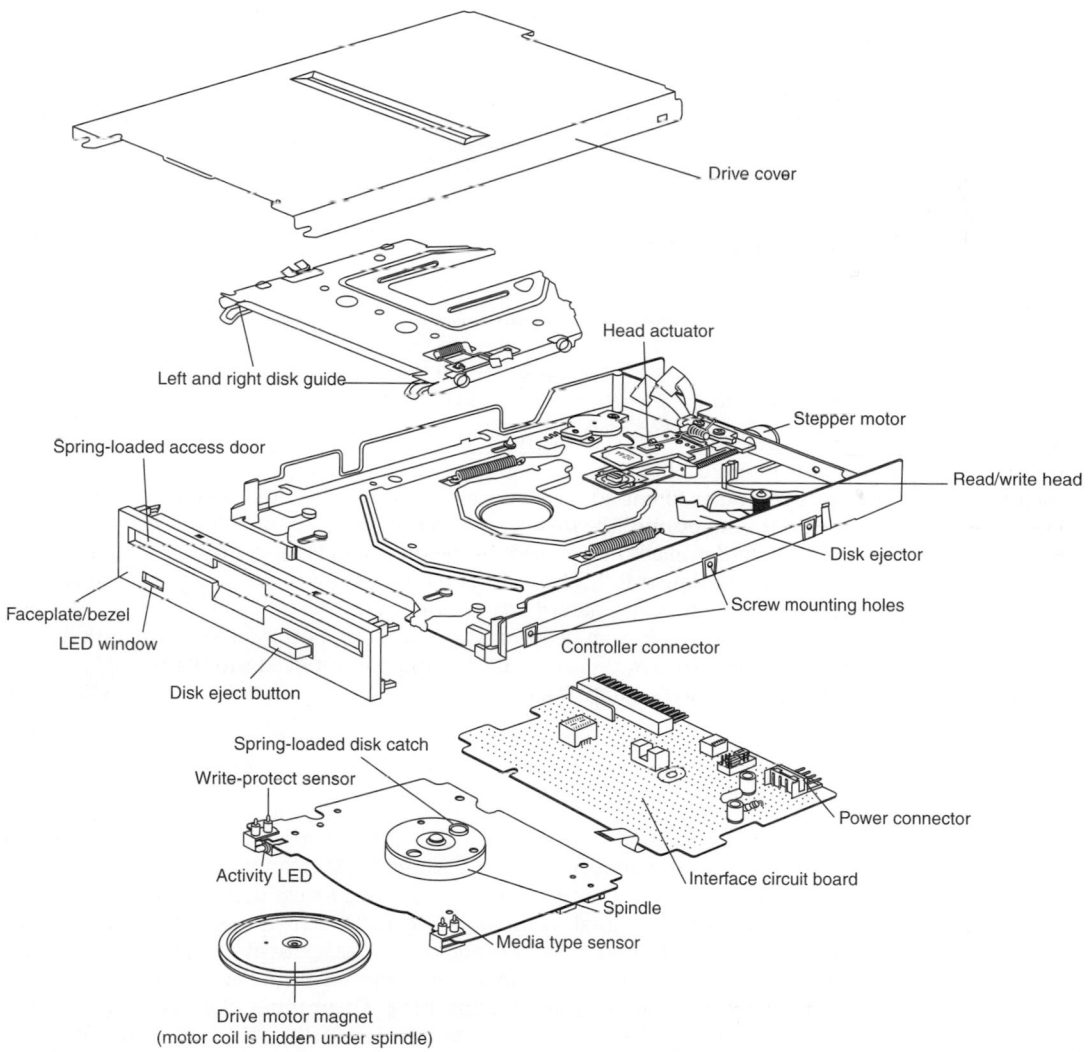

Figure 11.1 A typical floppy disk drive.

Read/Write Heads

A floppy disk drive usually has two read/write heads—one for each side of the disk, with both heads being used for reading and writing on their respective disk sides (see Figure 11.2). At one time, single-sided drives were available for PC systems (the original PC had such drives), but today single-sided drives are a faded memory.

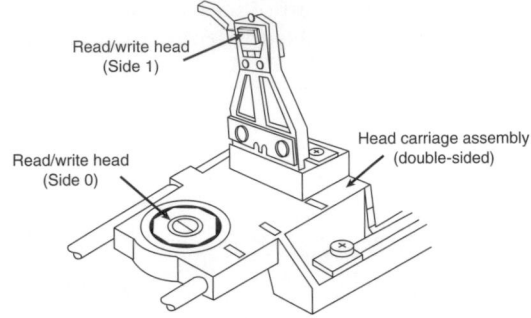

Figure 11.2   A double-sided drive head assembly.

Note

Many people do not realize that Head 0, or the first head on a floppy disk drive, is the bottom one. Single-sided drives, in fact, used only the bottom head; the top head has been replaced by a felt pressure pad. Another bit of disk trivia is that the top head (Head 1) is not positioned directly over the bottom head (Head 0). The top head is instead offset by either four or eight tracks inward from the bottom head, depending on the drive type.

A motor called a *head actuator* moves the head mechanism. The heads can move in and out over the surface of the disk in a straight line to position themselves over various tracks. On a floppy drive, the heads move in and out tangentially to the tracks they record on the disk. This is different from hard disks, where the heads move on a rotating arm similar to the tone-arm of a record player. Because the top and bottom heads are mounted on the same rack, or mechanism, they move in unison and can't move independently of each other. The upper and lower heads each define tracks on their respective sides of the disk medium, whereas at any given head position, the tracks under the top and bottom head simultaneously are called a *cylinder*. Most floppy disks are recorded with 80 tracks on each side (160 tracks total), which is 80 cylinders.

The heads themselves are made of soft ferrous (iron) compounds with electromagnetic coils. Each head is a composite design, with a read/write head centered within two tunnel-erase heads in the same physical assembly (see Figure 11.3).

Floppy disk drives use a recording method called *tunnel erasure*. As the drive writes to a track, the trailing tunnel-erase heads erase the outer bands of the track, trimming it cleanly on the disk. The heads force the data into a specified narrow "tunnel" on each track. This process prevents the signal from one track from being confused with the signals from adjacent tracks, which would happen if the signal were allowed to naturally "taper off" to each side. *Alignment* is the placement of the heads with respect to the tracks they must read and write. Head alignment can be checked only against some sort of reference-standard disk recorded by a perfectly aligned machine. These types of disks are available, and you can use one to check your drive's alignment. However, this is usually not practical for the end user because one calibrated analog alignment disk can cost more than a new drive.

The floppy disk drive's two heads are spring-loaded and physically grip the disk with a small amount of pressure, which means they are in direct contact with the disk surface while reading from and writing to the disk. Because floppy disk drives spin at only 300rpm or 360rpm, this pressure does not present an excessive friction problem. Some newer disks are specially coated with Teflon or other compounds to further reduce friction and enable the disk to slide more easily under the heads. Because of the contact between the heads and disk, a buildup of the magnetic material from the disk eventually forms on the heads. The buildup should periodically be cleaned off the heads as part of a preventive maintenance or normal service program. Most manufacturers recommend cleaning the heads after every 40 hours of drive operation, which—considering how often people use these drives today—could be a lifetime.

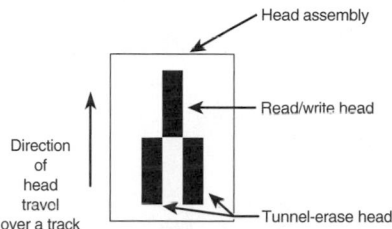

Figure 11.3 Composite construction of a typical floppy disk drive head.

To read and write to the disk properly, the heads must be in direct contact with the magnetic medium. Very small particles of loose oxide, dust, dirt, smoke, fingerprints, or hair can cause problems with reading and writing the disk. Disk and drive manufacturers' tests have found that a spacing as little as .000032" (32 millionths of an inch) between the heads and medium can cause read/write errors. You now can understand why it is important to handle disks carefully and avoid touching or contaminating the surface of the disk medium in any way. The rigid jacket and protective shutter for the head access aperture on 3 1/2" disks is excellent for preventing problems caused by contamination. Disks that are 5 1/4" do not have the same protective elements, which is perhaps one reason they initially began to fall into disuse. If you still use 5 1/4" floppy disks, you should exercise extra care in their handling. I recommend copying any archival data over to recordable CD or DVD media if your situation doesn't require keeping the data on the original media.

The Head Actuator

The *head actuator* for a floppy disk drive is what moves the heads across the disk and is driven by a special kind of motor, called a *stepper motor* (see Figure 11.4). This type of motor does not spin around continuously; rather, the motor turns a precise specified distance and stops. Stepper motors are not infinitely variable in their positioning; they move in fixed increments—or *detents*—and must stop at a particular detent position. This is ideal for disk drives because the location of each track on the disk can then be defined by moving one or more increments of the motor's motion. The disk controller can instruct the motor to position itself any number of steps within the range of its travel. To position the heads at cylinder 25, for example, the controller instructs the motor to go to the 25th detent position or step from Cylinder 0.

The stepper motor can be linked to the head rack in one of two ways. In the first, the link is a coiled, split-steel band. The band winds and unwinds around the spindle of the stepper motor, translating the rotary motion into linear motion. Some drives, however, use a worm-gear arrangement rather than a band. In this type of drive, the head assembly rests on a worm gear driven directly off the stepper motor shaft. Because this arrangement is more compact, you usually find worm-gear actuators on the smaller 3 1/2" drives.

Most stepper motors used in floppy disk drives can step in specific increments that relate to the track spacing on the disk. Older 48-track-per-inch (TPI) drives have a motor that steps in increments of 3.6°. This means that each 3.6° of stepper motor rotation moves the heads from one track to the next. Most 96 or 135 TPI drives have stepper motors that move in 1.8° increments, which is exactly half of what the 48 TPI drives use. Sometimes you see this information actually printed or stamped on the stepper motor itself, which is useful if you are trying to figure out which type of drive you have. The 5 1/4" 360KB drives are the only 48 TPI drives that use the 3.6° increment" stepper motor; all other drive types typically use the 1.8° stepper motor. On most drives, the stepper motor is a small, cylindrical object near one corner of the drive.

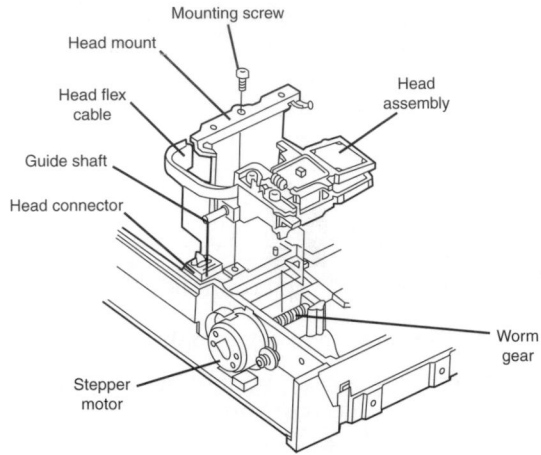

Figure 11.4   An expanded view of a stepper motor and head actuator.

A stepper motor usually has a full travel time of about one fifth of a second—about 200ms. On average, a one-half stroke is 100ms, and a one-third stroke is 66ms. The timing of a one-half or one-third stroke of the head-actuator mechanism is often used to determine the reported average access time for a disk drive. Average access time is the normal amount of time the heads spend moving at random from one track to another.

The Spindle Motor

The *spindle motor* is what spins the disk. The normal speed of rotation is either 300rpm or 360rpm, depending on the type of drive. The 5 1/4" high-density (HD) drive is the only drive that spins at 360rpm. All others, including the 5 1/4" double-density (DD), 3 1/2" DD, 3 1/2" HD, and 3 1/2" extra-high density (ED) drives, spin at 300rpm. This is a slow speed when compared to a hard disk drive, which helps explain why floppy disk drives have much lower data transfer rates. However, this slow speed also enables the drive heads to be in physical contact with the disk while it is spinning, without causing friction damage.

Many earlier drives used a mechanism by which the spindle motor physically turned the disk spindle with a belt, but all modern drives use a direct-drive system with no belts. The direct-drive systems are more reliable and less expensive to manufacture, as well as smaller in size. The earlier belt-driven systems did have more rotational torque available to turn a sticky disk because of the torque multiplication factor of the belt system. Most newer direct-drive systems, on the other hand, use an automatic torque-compensation capability that sets the disk-rotation speed to a fixed 300rpm or 360rpm and compensates with additional torque for high-friction disks or less torque for more slippery ones. Besides compensating for varying amounts of friction, this arrangement eliminates the need to adjust the rotational speed of the drive—something that was frequently required on older drives.

Circuit Boards

A disk drive always incorporates one or more *logic boards*, which are circuit boards that contain the circuitry used to control the head actuator, read/write heads, spindle motor, disk sensors, and other components on the drive. The logic board implements the drive's interface to the controller board in the system unit.

The standard interface that all PC floppy disk drives use is termed the Shugart Associates SA400 interface, was invented in the 1970s, and is based on the NEC 765 controller chip. All modern floppy controllers contain circuits that are compatible with the original NEC 765 chip. This industry-standard interface is why you can purchase drives from almost any manufacturer and they will all be compatible.

The Controller

At one time, the controller for a computer's floppy disk drives took the form of a dedicated expansion card installed in an Industry Standard Architecture (ISA) bus slot. Later implementations used a multi-function card that provided the IDE/ATA, parallel, and serial port interfaces in addition to the floppy disk drive controller. Today's PCs have the floppy controller integrated into the motherboard, usually in the form of a Super I/O chip that also includes the serial and parallel interfaces, among other things. Even though the floppy controller can be found in the Super I/O chip on the motherboard, it is still interfaced to the system via the ISA or LPC (low pin count) bus and functions exactly as if it were a card installed in an ISA slot. These built-in controllers are typically configured via the system BIOS Setup routines and can be disabled if an actual floppy controller card is going to be installed.

Whether it is built in or not, each primary floppy controller uses a standard set of system resources:

- IRQ 6 (interrupt request)
- DMA 2 (direct memory address)
- I/O ports 3F0–3F5, 3F7 (input/output)

These system resources are standardized and generally not changeable. This usually does not present a problem because no other devices will try to use these resources (which would result in a conflict). Systems advertised as "legacy free" don't include a Super I/O chip and therefore don't have a built-in floppy controller. Such systems can still use a floppy drive, but only in the form of an external USB drive.

Unlike the ATA interface used primarily by hard disks and optical drives, the floppy disk controller has not changed much over the years. Virtually the only thing that has changed is the controller's maximum speed. As the data density of floppy disks (and their capacity) has increased over the years, the controller speed has had to increase, as well. Nearly all floppy disk controllers in computers today support speeds of up to 1 megabit per second (Mbps), which supports all the standard floppy disk drives. 500 kilobits per second (Kbps) controllers can support all floppy disk drives except the 2.88MB extra high-density models. Older computers used 250Kbps controllers that could support only 360KB 5 1/4" and 720KB 3 1/2" drives. To install a standard 1.44MB 3 1/2" drive in an older machine, you might have to replace the floppy controller with a faster model.

Tip

The best way to determine the speed of the floppy disk drive controller in your computer is to examine the floppy disk drive options provided by the system BIOS.

▶▶ See Chapter 5, "BIOS," p. 397.

Even if you do not intend to use a 2.88MB floppy disk drive, you still might want to ensure that your computer has the fastest possible controller. Some of the older tape drives on the market use the floppy disk interface to connect to the system, and in this case, the controller has a profound effect on the overall throughput of the tape drive. Although traditional floppy controller cards and multi I/O cards have provisions for two floppy drives—A: and B:—many recent systems that integrate Super I/O features into the South Bridge chip on the motherboard support only a single floppy drive.

The Faceplate

The *faceplate*, or *bezel*, is the plastic piece that comprises the front of the drive. This piece, usually removable, comes in various colors and configurations.

Most floppy drive manufacturers offer drives with matching faceplates in gray, beige, or black and with a choice of red, green, or yellow activity LEDs as well. This enables a system builder to better match the drive to the aesthetics of the case for a seamless, integrated, and more professional look.

Connectors

Nearly all floppy disk drives have two connectors—one for power to run the drive and the other to carry the control and data signals to and from the drive. These connectors are fairly standardized in the computer industry. A 4-pin inline connector (called Mate-N-Lock by AMP) in both large and small styles is used for power (see Figure 11.5), and a 34-pin connector in both edge and pin header designs is used for the data and control signals. Typically, 5 1/4" drives use the large-style power connector and the 34-pin edge-type connector, whereas most 3 1/2" drives use the smaller version of the power connector and the 34-pin header-type logic connector. The drive controller and logic connectors and pinouts are detailed later in this chapter, as well as on the Vendor List on this book's disc.

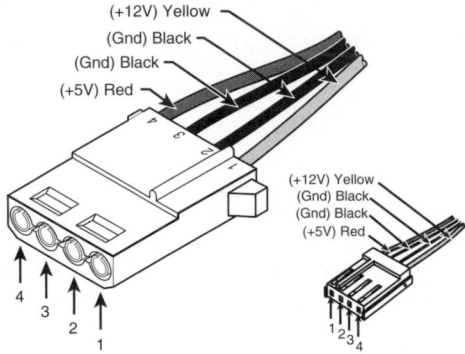

Figure 11.5   Large (5 1/4" drive) and small (3 1/2" drive) disk drive female power supply cable connectors.

Both the large and small power connectors from the power supply are female plugs. They plug into the male portion, which is attached to the drive itself. Note that the pin-to-signal designations on the small connector are the opposite of those on the large connector.

One common problem with installing 3 1/2" drives in older systems, or in some cases adding a second drive to newer systems, is that the power supply has only one or none of the small-style power connectors used by the smaller drives. An adapter cable that converts the large-style peripheral power connector to the proper small-style connector used on most 3 1/2" drives is available from Dalco (www.dalco.com) under p/n 47425 and from other sources.

Most standard PCs use 3 1/2" drives with a 34-pin signal connector and a separate small-style power connector. For older systems, many drive manufacturers also sell 3 1/2" drives installed in a 5 1/4" frame assembly with a special adapter built in that enables you to use the larger power connector and older edge-type signal connectors. External floppy drives are available in USB or parallel interfaces. For more information on these interfaces, see Chapter 17.

The Floppy Disk Controller Cable

The 34-pin connector on a floppy disk drive takes the form of either an edge connector (on 5 1/4" drives) or a pin connector (on 3 1/2" drives). The pinouts for the floppy controller connector are shown in Table 11.1.

Table 11.1   Floppy Disk Drive Controller Connector Pinout

Pin	Signal	Pin	Signal
1	Ground	2	DD/HD Density Select
3	Key[1]	4	Reserved (unused)
5	Key[1]	6	ED Density Select[2]
7	Ground	8	Index
9	Ground	10	Motor-On 0 (A:)
11	Ground	12	Drive Select 1 (B:)
13	Ground	14	Drive Select 0 (A:)
15	Ground	16	Motor-On 1 (B:)
17	Ground	18	Direction (stepper motor)
19	Ground	20	Step Pulse
21	Ground	22	Write Data
23	Ground	24	Write Enable
25	Ground	26	Track 0
27	Ground	28	Write Protect
29	Ground	30	Read Data
31	Ground	32	Head Select
33	Ground	34	Disk Change

1. *Controllers and drives can use one, both, or no key (missing) pins.*
2. *For controllers supporting ED (Extra-high Density 2.88M) drives only; otherwise unused.*

The cable used to connect the floppy disk drive(s) to the controller on the motherboard is quite strange. To support various drive configurations, the cable might have up to five connectors on it—two edge connectors and two pin connectors to attach to the drives and one pin connector to connect to the controller. The cable has redundant connectors for each of the two drives (A and B) supported by the standard floppy disk drive controller, so you can install any combination of 5 1/4" and 3 1/2" drives (see Figure 11.6).

In addition to the connectors, the cable has a special twist that inverts the signals of wires 10–16. These are the wires carrying the Drive Select (DS) and Motor Enable signals for each of the two drives. Older floppy disk drives have DS jumpers designed to enable you to select whether a given drive should be recognized as A or B (really old ones allow a third and fourth setting as well).

You might not even know that these jumpers exist because the twist in the cable prevents you from having to adjust them, and as such they have been eliminated from most newer drives. When installing two floppy disk drives in one system (admittedly a rarity nowadays), the cable electrically changes the DS configuration of the drive that is plugged in after the twist. Thus, the twist causes a drive physically set to the second DS position (B) to appear to the controller to be set to the first DS position (A). The adoption of this cable has enabled the use of a standard jumper configuration for all floppy disk drives, regardless of whether you install one or two drives in a computer.

If you install only a single floppy disk drive, you use the connector after the twist, which causes the drive to be recognized as drive A. Although it's seldom necessary today, many computer BIOS setup programs have an option enabling you to swap drives A: and B: without adjusting drive cables. If you have a computer with the old 5 1/4" floppy as B: for use with old software and need to use it as A:, you can use this BIOS option, if present, to change the drive setup without opening your system.

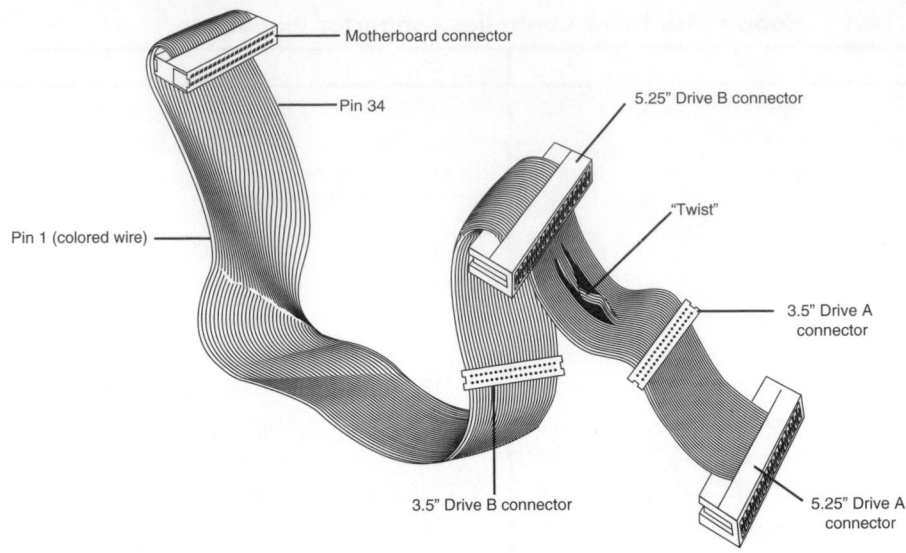

Figure 11.6   Standard five-connector floppy interface cable.

Secrets of the Cable Twist

The original Shugart SA400 floppy interface was designed to support up to four drives on a single cable. However, IBM modified the controller pinout so it could make a less-expensive controller that would work with only two drives and at the same time eliminate the need to change drive select jumpers on the drives.

If you check the documentation for older floppy drives and controllers using the industry-standard Shugart SA400 interface, you will see that they incorporate four separate drive select signals (DS0/DS1/DS2/DS3 on pins 10/12/14/6, respectively) and that pin 16 is the Motor-On (also called Motor Enable) signal shared by all drives (see Table 11.2).

Table 11.2   Industry-Standard Shugart Floppy Drive Interface

Pin	Signal
10	Drive Select 0 (A:)
12	Drive Select 1 (B:)
14	Drive Select 2 (C:)
16	Motor-On (all drives)

Drive Select 3 (D:) would be pin 6, but I am showing only the pins that will be involved in the cable twist because PCs support only up to two drives anyway and the twist is where the confusion lies.

When the floppy controller wants to talk to a drive, it raises the drive select line (DS0 for A: and DS1 for B:) as well as the Motor-On line. Only the selected drive responds and turns on its spindle motor. The controller then uses the other signals to seek, read, write, and so on; only the selected drive responds.

IBM, however, did not use the industry-standard Shugart floppy interface exactly as it was. Instead, the IBM floppy controller provides only two Drive Select signals and puts DS0 (A:) where DS2 (C:) was originally supposed to be. IBM also provided *separate* Motor-On signals for drives 0 and 1 (A: and B:) on pins 10 and 16, respectively (see Table 11.3). Note that pin 10 was originally supposed to be used for DS0, and not a Motor-On signal for drive 0 (A:). Also, pin 16 was supposed to be used as a common Motor-On line for all drives, not a private Motor-On line for drive 1 (B:).

Table 11.3   IBM's Modified Shugart Floppy Controller Interface

Pin	Signal
10	Motor-On 0 (A:)
12	Drive Select 1 (B:)
14	Drive Select 0 (A:)
16	Motor-On 1 (B:)

As you can see, the pinout of the IBM floppy disk controller does not match the pinout of the standard floppy drives! Then, how does it work?

Drive B: works fine as is: The DS1 (Drive Select B:) signal comes from the controller on pin 12 and is expected at the drive on pin 12. The Motor-On 1 (Motor B:) signal comes from the controller on pin 16 and is expected at the drive on pin 16. This is why Drive B: works with a straight-through cable. The only concern is that the drive must be jumpered as DS1, which is how all PC floppy drives are set up by default.

What about Drive A:? This is where the twist comes into play, along with the fact that Drive A: is also supposed to be jumpered as DS1 (same as Drive B:).

Here's how it works: The twist in the cable swaps pins 10 and 16, as well as pins 12 and 14. When accessing Drive A:, the DS0 (Drive Select A:) signal comes from the controller on pin 14 and is swapped by the twist to pin 12 at the drive, which is DS1 (Drive Select B:). This works because the A: drive is also jumpered to respond to DS1, the same as the B: drive. The Motor-On 0 (Motor A:) signal comes from the controller on pin 10 and is swapped by the twist to pin 16 at the drive, which is the Motor-On signal for all drives. As you can see, Drive A: would then work fine.

The interface between the original IBM floppy controller and the standard floppy drive does not quite match. The twisted cable combined with setting both drives to DS1 allows things to work properly. This controller and cable twist design is standard in all PCs since the IBM original.

Disk Physical Specifications and Operation

Most PCs sold today are equipped with a 3 1/2" 1.44MB floppy disk drive. In rare cases, you might run into a very old system that has a 5 1/4" 1.2MB drive instead of, or in addition to, the 3 1/2" drive. Plus, a few older PC systems have a 2.88MB 3 1/2" drive that can also read and write 1.44MB disks. The older drive types—5 1/4" 360KB and 3 1/2" 720KB—are obsolete and rarely found anymore.

The physical operation of a disk drive is fairly simple to describe. The disk rotates in the drive at either 300rpm or 360rpm. Most drives spin at 300rpm; only the 5 1/4" 1.2MB drives spin at 360rpm. With the disk spinning, the heads can move in and out approximately one inch and write 80 tracks. The tracks are written on both sides of the disk and are therefore sometimes called *cylinders*. A single cylinder comprises the tracks on the top and bottom of the disk. The heads record by using a tunnel-erase procedure that writes a track to a specified width and then erases the edges of the track to prevent interference with any adjacent tracks.

Different drives record tracks at different widths. Table 11.4 shows the track widths in both millimeters and inches for the various types of floppy disk drives found in modern PC systems.

Table 11.4   Floppy Disk Drive Track-Width Specifications

Drive Type	No. of Tracks	Track Width	
5 1/4" 360KB	40 per side	0.300mm	0.0118"
5 1/4" 1.2MB	80 per side	0.155mm	0.0061"
3 1/2" 720KB	80 per side	0.115mm	0.0045"
3 1/2" 1.44MB	80 per side	0.115mm	0.0045"
3 1/2" 2.88MB	80 per side	0.115mm	0.0045"

How the Operating System Uses a Disk

To the operating system, data on your PC disks is organized in tracks and sectors, just as on a hard disk drive. *Tracks* are narrow, concentric circles on a disk; *sectors* are pie-shaped slices of the individual tracks.

Table 11.5 summarizes the standard disk formats for PC floppy disk drives.

Table 11.5   5 1/4" and 3 1/2" Floppy Disk Drive Formats

	5 1/4" Floppy Disks	
	Double-Density 360KB (DD)	High-Density 1.2MB (HD)
Bytes per sector	512	512
Sectors per track	9	15
Tracks per side	40	80
Sides	2	2
Capacity (KiB)	360	1,200
Capacity (MiB)	0.352	1.172
Capacity (MB)	0.369	1.229

	3 1/2" Floppy Disks		
	Double-Density 720KB (DD)	High-Density 1.44MB (HD)	Extra High-Density 2.88MB (ED)
Bytes per sector	512	512	512
Sectors per track	9	18	36
Tracks per side	80	80	80
Sides	2	2	2
Capacity (KiB)	720	1,440	2,880
Capacity (MiB)	0.703	1.406	2.813
Capacity (MB)	0.737	1.475	2.949

You can calculate the capacity differences between various formats by multiplying the sectors per track by the number of tracks per side together with the constants of two sides and 512 bytes per sector. Note that the floppy disk's capacity can actually be expressed in various ways. For example, what we call a 1.44MB disk really stores 1.475MB if you go by the correct decimal prefix definition for a megabyte. The discrepancy comes from the fact that in the past floppies were designated by their kilobinary (1024-byte) capacities, which were originally (and improperly) abbreviated as KB. To prevent ambiguities in binary versus decimal number interpretations, the International Electrotechnical Commission (IEC) has designated KiB as the correct abbreviation for kilobinary.

Despite the IEC standards, the traditional method when discussing floppy drives or disks is to refer to the capacity of a floppy by the number of kilobinary bytes (1,024 bytes equals 1KiB) but to use the otherwise improper abbreviation KB instead. This has also been improperly extended to the abbreviation MB. Therefore, a floppy disk with an actual capacity of 1,440KiB is instead denoted as a 1.44MB disk, even though it would really be 1.406MiB (megabinary bytes) or 1.475MB (million bytes) if we went by the correct definitions for MiB (mebibyte) and MB (megabyte).

For the remainder of this chapter, I will refer to the capacity of the various floppy disks according to the previously used conventions rather than the more technically accurate IEC-designated binary and decimal prefixes.

Note

As with hard disk drives, using the same prefixes for both decimal and binary multiples has resulted in a great deal of confusion. The IEC prefixes for binary multiples was designed to eliminate this confusion. For more information on prefixes for binary multiples, see `http://physics.nist.gov/cuu/Units/binary.html`. Also, see the section "Capacity Measurements" in Chapter 9.

Like blank sheets of paper, new, unformatted disks contain no information. Formatting a disk is similar to adding lines to the paper so you can write straight across. Formatting the disk writes the information the operating system needs to maintain a directory and file table of contents. On a floppy disk, no distinction exists between a high-level and low-level format, nor do you have to create any partitions. When you format a floppy disk with Windows Explorer or the command prompt `FORMAT.COM`, both the high- and low-level formats are performed simultaneously.

When you format a floppy disk, the operating system reserves the track nearest to the outside edge of a disk (track 0) almost entirely for its purposes. Track 0, Side 0, Sector 1 contains the Volume Boot Record (VBR), or Boot Sector, that the system needs to begin operation. The next few sectors contain the file allocation tables (FATs), which keep records of which clusters or allocation units on the disk contain file information and which are empty. Finally, the next few sectors contain the root directory, in which the operating system stores information about the names and starting locations of the files on the disk.

Note that most floppies today are sold preformatted. This saves time because the formatting can take a minute or more per disk. Even if disks come preformatted, they can always be reformatted later.

Cylinders

The cylinder number is normally used in place of the track number because all floppy drives today are double-sided. A cylinder on a floppy disk includes two tracks: the one on the bottom of the disk above Head 0 and the one on the top of the disk below Head 1. Because a disk can't have more than two sides and the drive has two heads, there are always two tracks per cylinder for floppy disks. Hard disk drives, on the other hand, can have multiple disk platters—each with two heads—resulting in many tracks per single cylinder. The simple rule is that there are as many tracks per cylinder as there are heads on the drive.

Cylinders are discussed in more detail in Chapter 10, "Hard Disk Storage," and Chapter 25, "File Systems and Data Recovery."

Clusters or Allocation Units

A *cluster* also is called an *allocation unit*. The term is appropriate because a single cluster is the smallest unit of the disk that the operating system can allocate when it writes a file. A cluster or an allocation unit consists of one or more sectors—usually a power of two (1, 2, 4, 8, and so on). Having more than one sector per cluster reduces the FAT size and enables the OS to run more quickly because it has fewer individual clusters to manage. The tradeoff is in some wasted disk space. Because the OS can manage space only in the cluster size unit, every file consumes space on the disk in increments of one cluster.

▶▶ For more information on allocation units, see "File Allocation Table Types," p. 1367.

Table 11.6 lists the default cluster sizes used for various floppy disk formats.

Table 11.6   Default Cluster and Allocation Unit Sizes

Floppy Disk Capacity	Cluster/Allocation Unit Size	FAT Type	
5 1/4" 360KB	2 sectors	1,024 bytes	12-bit
5 1/4" 1.2MB	1 sector	512 bytes	12-bit
3 1/2" 720KB	2 sectors	1,024 bytes	12-bit
3 1/2" 1.44MB	1 sector	512 bytes	12-bit
3 1/2" 2.88MB	2 sectors	1,024 bytes	12-bit

KB = 1,024 bytes (by convention)

MB = 1,000 KB bytes (by convention)

Disk Change

The standard PC floppy controller and drive use a special signal on pin 34 called *Disk Change* to determine whether the disk has been changed—or more accurately, to determine whether the same disk loaded during the previous disk access is still in the drive. Disk Change is a pulsed signal that changes a status register in the controller to let the system know that a disk has been either inserted or ejected. This register is set to indicate that a disk has been inserted or removed (changed) by default.

The register is cleared when the controller sends a step pulse to the drive and the drive responds, acknowledging that the heads have moved. At this point, the system knows that a specific disk is in the drive. If the Disk Change signal is not received before the next access, the system can assume that the same disk is still in the drive. Any information read into memory during the previous access can therefore be reused without rereading the disk.

Because of this process, systems can buffer or cache the contents of the FAT or directory structure of a disk in the system's memory. By eliminating unnecessary rereads of these areas of the disk, the apparent speed of the drive is increased. If you move the door lever or eject button on a drive that supports the Disk Change signal, the DC pulse is sent to the controller, thus resetting the register and indicating that the disk has been changed. This procedure causes the system to purge buffered or cached data that had been read from the disk because the system then can't be sure that the same disk is still in the drive.

One interesting problem can occur when certain drives are installed in a 16-bit or greater system. As mentioned, some drives use pin 34 for a "Ready" (RDY) signal. The RDY signal is sent whenever a disk is installed and rotating in the drive. If you install a drive that has pin 34 set to send RDY, the system thinks it is continuously receiving a Disk Change signal, which causes problems. Usually, the drive fails with a Drive Not Ready error and is inoperable. The only reason the RDY signal exists on some drives is that it happens to be a part of the standard Shugart SA400 disk interface; however, it has never been used in PC systems.

The biggest problem occurs if the drive should be sending the DC signal on pin 34 but isn't. If a system is told (through CMOS setup) that the drive is any type other than a 360KB (which can't ever send the DC signal), the system expects the drive to send DC whenever a disk has been ejected. If the drive is not configured properly to send the signal, the system never recognizes that a disk has been changed. Therefore, even if you do change the disk, the system still acts as though the first disk is in the drive and holds the first disk's directory and FAT information in RAM. This can be dangerous because the FAT and directory information from the first disk can be partially written to any subsequent disks written to in the drive.

If the drive you are installing is a 5 1/4" 1.2MB or 3 1/2" 720KB, 1.44MB, or 2.88MB drive, be sure to set pin 34 to send the Disk Change (DC) signal. Most drives come permanently preset this way, but some have used a jumper (usually labeled DC) to set this option.

Caution

If you have ever seen a system with a floppy disk drive that shows "phantom directories" of the previously installed disk, even after you have changed or removed it, you have experienced this problem firsthand. The negative side effect is that all disks after the first one you place in this system are in extreme danger. You likely will overwrite the directories and FATs of many disks with information from the first disk.

If it's even possible at all, data recovery from such a catastrophe can require quite a bit of work with utility programs, such as Norton Utilities (part of the Norton SystemWorks suite). These problems with Disk Change most often are traced to an incorrectly configured drive.

Note that Windows Explorer doesn't always display the new contents of a drive. Press the F5 key to refresh the display after you change floppy disks to force the computer to read the new disk.

Types of Floppy Disk Drives

The characteristics of the floppy disk drives you might encounter in PC-compatible systems are summarized in Table 11.7. As you can see, the different disk capacities are determined by several parameters, some of which seem to remain constant on all drives, although others change from drive to drive. For example, all drives use 512-byte physical sectors, which is true for hard disks as well.

Table 11.7   Floppy Disk Logical Formatted Parameters

	Current Formats					Obsolete Formats		
Disk Size (Inches)	3 1/2	3 1/2	3 1/2	5 1/4	5 1/4	5 1/4	5 1/4	5 1/4
Disk Capacity (KB)	2,880	1,440	720	1,200	360	320	180	160
Media descriptor byte	F0h	F0h	F9h	F9h	FDh	FFh	FCh	FEh
Sides (heads)	2	2	2	2	2	2	1	1
Tracks per side	80	80	80	80	40	40	40	40
Sectors per track	36	18	9	15	9	8	9	8
Bytes per sector	512	512	512	512	512	512	512	512
Sectors per cluster	2	1	2	1	2	2	1	1
FAT length (sectors)	9	9	3	7	2	1	2	1
Number of FATs	2	2	2	2	2	2	2	2
Root dir. length (sectors)	15	14	7	14	7	7	4	4
Maximum root entries	240	224	112	224	112	112	64	64
Total sectors per disk	5,760	2,880	1,440	2,400	720	640	360	320
Total available sectors	5,726	2,847	1,426	2,371	708	630	351	313
Total available clusters	2,863	2,847	713	2,371	354	315	351	313

1.44MB 3 1/2" Drives

The 3 1/2", 1.44MB, high-density (HD) drives first appeared from IBM in the PS/2 product line introduced in 1987. Most other computer vendors started offering the drives as an option in their systems immediately afterward. For systems that include floppy drives, the 1.44MB type is still by far the most popular.

The drive records 80 cylinders consisting of 2 tracks each with 18 sectors per track, resulting in a formatted capacity of 1.44MB. Some disk manufacturers label these disks as 2.0MB, and the difference between this unformatted capacity and the formatted usable result is lost during the format. Note that the 1440KB of total formatted capacity does not account for the areas the FAT file system reserves for file management, leaving only 1423.5KB of actual file-storage area.

The drive spins at 300rpm and in fact must spin at that speed to operate properly with existing high- and low-density controllers. To use the 500KHz data rate (the maximum from most standard high- and low-density floppy controllers), these drives must spin at a maximum of 300rpm. If the drives were to spin at the faster 360rpm rate of the 5 1/4" drives, they would have to reduce the total number of sectors per track to 15; otherwise, the controller could not keep up. In short, the 1.44MB 3 1/2" drives store 1.2 times the data of the 5 1/4" 1.2MB drives, and the 1.2MB drives spin exactly 1.2 times faster than the 1.44MB drives. The data rates used by both of these HD drives are identical and compatible with the same controllers. In fact, because these 3 1/2" HD drives can run at the 500KHz data rate, a controller that can support a 1.2MB 5 1/4" drive can also support the 1.44MB drives.

Other Floppy Drive Types

Other types of floppy drives that have been used in the past include the following:

- *2.88MB 3 1/2"*. This size was used on some IBM PS/2 and ThinkPad models in the early 1990s.
- *720KB 3 1/2"*. This size was used by IBM and others starting in 1986 before the 1.44MB 3 1/2" was introduced.
- *1.2MB 5 1/4"*. It was introduced by IBM for the IBM AT in 1984 and widely used throughout the rest of the decade.
- *360KB 5 1/4"*. An improved version of the floppy disk drive originally used by the IBM PC, it was used throughout the 1980s on XT-class machines and some AT-class machines.

If you need more information about these drives, see the Technical Reference section of the disc included with this book.

Analyzing 3 1/2" Floppy Disk Construction

3 1/2" disks differ from the older 5 1/4" disks in both construction and physical properties. The flexible (or floppy) disk is contained within a plastic jacket. The 3 1/2" disks are covered by a more rigid jacket than are the 5 1/4" disks. The disks within the jackets, however, are virtually identical except, of course, for size.

For more information about the construction of a 5 1/4" floppy disk, see the Technical Reference section on the disc packaged with this book.

The 3 1/2" disks use a much more rigid plastic case than 5 1/4" disks, which helps stabilize the magnetic medium inside. Therefore, the disks can store data at track and data densities greater than the 5 1/4" disks (see Figure 11.7). A metal shutter protects the media-access hole. The drive manipulates the shutter, leaving it closed whenever the disk is not in a drive. The medium is then completely insulated from the environment and from your fingers. The shutter also obviates the need for a disk jacket.

Because the shutter is not necessary for the disk to work, you can remove it from the plastic case if it becomes bent or damaged. Pry it off the disk case; it will pop off with a snap. You also should remove the spring that pushes it closed. Additionally, after removing the damaged shutter, you should copy the data from the damaged disk to a new one.

Rather than an index hole in the disk, the 3 1/2" disks use a metal center hub with an alignment hole. The drive "grasps" the metal hub, and the hole in the hub enables the drive to position the disk properly.

On the lower-left part of the disk is a hole with a plastic slider—the write-protect/enable hole. When the slider is positioned so the hole is visible, the disk is *write-protected*, meaning the drive is prevented from recording on the disk. When the slider is positioned to cover the hole, writing is enabled, and you can save data to the disk. For more permanent write-protection, some commercial software programs are supplied on disks with the slider removed so you can't easily enable recording on the disk. This is exactly opposite of a 5 1/4" floppy, in which covered means write-protected, not write-enabled.

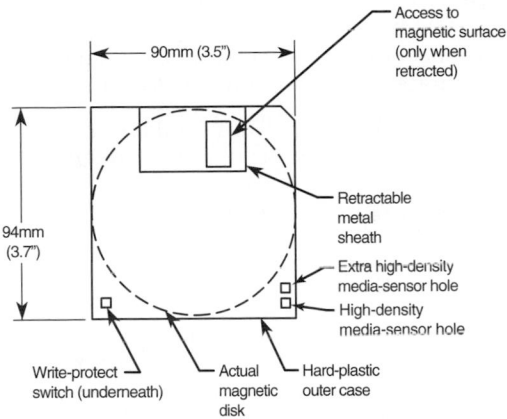

Figure 11.7   Construction of a 3 1/2" floppy disk.

On the other (right) side of the disk from the write-protect hole is usually another hole called the media-density-selector hole. If this hole is present, the disk is constructed of a special medium and is therefore an HD or ED disk. If the media-sensor hole is exactly opposite the write-protect hole, it indicates a 1.44MB HD disk. If the media-sensor hole is located more toward the top of the disk (the metal shutter is at the top of the disk), it indicates an ED disk. No hole on the right side means that the disk is a low-density disk. Most 3 1/2" drives have a media sensor that controls recording capability based on the absence or presence of these holes.

The actual magnetic medium in both the 3 1/2" and 5 1/4" disks is constructed of the same basic materials. They use a plastic base (usually Mylar) coated with a magnetic compound. High-density disks use a cobalt-ferric compound; extended-density disks use a barium-ferric media compound. The rigid jacket material on the 3 1/2" disks has occasionally caused people to believe incorrectly that these disks are some sort of "hard disk" and not really a floppy disk. The disk cookie inside the 3 1/2" case is just as floppy as the 5 1/4" variety.

Floppy Disk Media Types and Specifications

This section examines the types of disks that have been available to PC owners over the years. Especially interesting are the technical specifications that can separate one type of disk from another, as Table 11.8 shows. The following sections define all the specifications used to describe a typical disk.

Table 11.8   Floppy Disk Media Specifications

	5 1/4"			3 1/2"		
Media Parameters	**Double-Density (DD)**	**Quad-Density (QD)**	**High-Density (HD)**	**Double-Density (DD)**	**High-Density (HD)**	**Extra High-Density (ED)**
Tracks per inch (TPI)	48	96	96	135	135	135
Bits per inch (BPI)	5,876	5,876	9,646	8,717	17,434	34,868
Media formulation	Ferrite	Ferrite	Cobalt	Cobalt	Cobalt	Barium
Coercivity (oersteds)	300	300	600	600	720	750
Thickness (micro-in.)	100	100	50	70	40	100
Recording polarity	Horiz.	Horiz.	Horiz.	Horiz.	Horiz.	Vert.

Density

Density, in simplest terms, is a measure of the amount of information that can be reliably packed into a specific area of a recording surface. The keyword here is *reliably*.

Disks have two types of densities: longitudinal density and linear density. *Longitudinal density* is indicated by how many tracks can be recorded on the disk and is often expressed as a number of tracks per inch (TPI). *Linear density* is the capability of an individual track to store data and is often indicated as a number of bits per inch (BPI). Unfortunately, these types of densities are often confused when discussing different disks and drives.

Media Coercivity and Thickness

The *coercivity* specification of a disk refers to the magnetic-field strength required to make a proper recording. Coercivity, measured in oersteds, is a value indicating magnetic strength. A disk with a higher coercivity rating requires a stronger magnetic field to make a recording on that disk. With lower ratings, the disk can be recorded with a weaker magnetic field. In other words, the lower the coercivity rating, the more sensitive the disk.

HD media demands higher coercivity ratings so the adjacent magnetic domains don't interfere with each other. For this reason, HD media is actually less sensitive and requires a stronger recording signal strength.

Another factor is the thickness of the disk. The thinner the disk, the less influence a region of the disk has on another adjacent region. The thinner disks, therefore, can accept many more bits per inch without eventually degrading the recording.

Caring for and Handling Floppy Disks and Drives

Most computer users know the basics of disk care. Disks can be damaged or destroyed easily by the following:

- Touching the recording surface with your fingers or anything else
- Writing on a disk label (which has been affixed to a disk) with a ball-point pen or pencil
- Bending the disk
- Spilling coffee or other substances on the disk
- Overheating a disk (leaving it in the hot sun or near a radiator, for example)
- Exposing a disk to stray magnetic fields

Despite all these cautions, disks are rather hardy storage devices; I can't say that I have ever destroyed one by just writing on it with a pen because I do so all the time. I am careful, however, not to press too hard, so I don't put a crease in the disk. Also, touching a disk does not necessarily ruin a disk, but rather makes the disk and your drive head dirty with oil and dust. The real danger to your disks comes from magnetic fields that, because they are unseen, can sometimes be found in places you never imagined.

For example, all color monitors (and color TV sets) that use cathode-ray tube (CRT) technology have a degaussing coil around the face of the tube that demagnetizes the shadow mask when you turn on the monitor. If you keep your disks anywhere near (within 1[pr] of) the front of a color monitor, you expose them to a strong magnetic field every time you turn on the monitor. Keeping disks in this area is not a good idea because the field is designed to demagnetize objects, and it indeed works well for demagnetizing disks. The effect is cumulative and irreversible. Note that LCD or plasma displays don't have degaussing coils and therefore do not affect magnetic media.

Another source of powerful magnetic fields is an electric motor found in vacuum cleaners, heaters, air conditioners, fans, electric pencil sharpeners, and so on. Do not place these devices near areas where you store disks. Audio speakers also contain magnets, but most of the speakers sold for use with PCs are shielded to minimize disk corruption.

Store 3 1/2" disks between 40° and 127° Fahrenheit (4°–53° Celsius), and store 5 1/4" disks between 40° and 140° Fahrenheit (4°–60° Celsius). In both cases, humidity should not exceed 90%.

Airport X-Ray Machines and Metal Detectors

One of my favorite myths to dispel is that the airport X-ray machine somehow damages disks. I have a great deal of experience in this area from having traveled around the country for the past 20 years or so with disks and portable computers in hand. I fly about 150,000 miles per year, and my portable computer equipment and disks have been through X-ray machines hundreds of times.

X-rays are essentially just a form of light, and disks and computers are not affected by X-rays at anywhere near the levels found in these machines.

What could potentially damage your magnetic media is the metal detector. Metal detectors work by monitoring disruptions in a weak magnetic field. A metal object inserted in the field area causes the field's shape to change, which the detector observes. This principle, which is the reason the detectors are sensitive to metal objects, can be dangerous to your disks; the X-ray machine, however, is the safest area through which to pass either your disk or your computer.

The X-ray machine is not dangerous to magnetic media because it merely exposes the media to electromagnetic radiation at a particular (very high) frequency. Blue light is an example of electromagnetic radiation of a different frequency. The only difference between X-rays and blue light is in the frequency, or wavelength, of the emission.

Some people worry about the effect of X-ray radiation on their system's EPROM (erasable programmable read-only memory) chips. This concern might actually be more valid than worrying about disk damage because EPROMs are erased by certain forms of electromagnetic radiation. In reality, however, you do not need to worry about this effect either. EPROMs are erased by direct exposure to very intense ultraviolet light. Specifically, to be erased, an EPROM must be exposed to a 12,000uw/cm^2 UV light source with a wavelength of 2,537 angstroms for 15–20 minutes, and at a distance of 1". Increasing the power of the light source or decreasing the distance from the source can shorten the erasure time to a few minutes.

The airport X-ray machine is different by a factor of 10,000 in wavelength. The field strength, duration, and distance from the emitter source are nowhere near what is necessary for EPROM erasure. Many circuit-board manufacturers even use X-ray inspection on circuit boards (with components including EPROMs installed) to test and check quality control during manufacture.

Now, you might not want to take my word for it, but scientific research has been published that corroborates what I have stated. A study was published by two scientists—one of whom actually designs X-ray tubes for a major manufacturer. Their study was titled "Airport X-rays and Floppy Disks: No Cause for Concern" and was published in 1993 in the journal *Computer Methods and Programs in Biomedicine*. According to the abstract,

> A controlled study was done to test the possible effects of X-rays on the integrity of data stored on common sizes of floppy disks. Disks were exposed to doses of X-rays up to seven times that to be expected during airport examination of baggage. The readability of nearly 14 megabytes of data was unaltered by X-irradiation, indicating that floppy disks need not be given special handling during X-ray inspection of baggage.

In fact, the disks were retested after two years of storage, and there still has been no measurable degradation since the exposure.

Drive Installation Procedures

In most cases, installing a floppy disk drive is a matter of physically attaching the drive to the computer chassis or case and then plugging the power and signal cables into the drive. Some types of brackets and screws are usually required to attach the drive to the chassis, and these are normally included with the chassis or case itself. Several companies listed in the Vendor List on the disc specialize in cases, cables, brackets, screw hardware, and other items useful in assembling systems or installing drives.

Note

Because floppy disk drives are generally installed into the same half-height bays as hard disk drives, the physical mounting of the drive in the computer case is the same for both units. See the section "Hard Disk Installation Procedures" in Chapter 14, "Physical Drive Installation and Configuration," for more information on the process.

Troubleshooting Floppy Drives

For information on troubleshooting floppy drives, see "Troubleshooting Floppy Drives" in the Technical Reference section on the disc packaged with this book.

CHAPTER 12

High-Capacity Removable Storage

The Role of Removable Media Drives

Since the mid-1980s, the primary storage device used by computers has been the hard disk drive. However, for data backup, data transport between computers, and temporary storage, secondary storage devices such as high-capacity removable media drives, floptical drives, magneto-optical drives, flash memory devices, and tape drives are useful supplements to primary storage. Pure optical storage—such as CD-R, CD-RW, DVD-RAM, DVD+RW, DVD-RW, and others—is covered in Chapter 13, "Optical Storage." These types of drives can also be used as a supplement to hard disk storage as well as for primary storage.

The options for purchasing removable devices vary. Some removable-media drives use media as small as a quarter or your index finger, whereas others use larger media up to 5 1/4". Most popular removable-storage drives today have capacities that range from as little as 16MB to as much as 100GB or more. These drives offer fairly speedy performance and the capability to store anything from a few data files or less frequently used programs to complete hard disk images on a removable disk or tape.

The next two sections examine the primary roles of these devices.

Extra Storage

As operating systems and applications continue to grow in size and features, more and more storage space is needed for these programs as well as for the data they create.

Operating systems aren't the only program types that are growing. Applications whose MS-DOS versions once fit on a few floppy disks have now mutated into "everything but the kitchen sink" do-it-all behemoths that can take 500MB or more of disk space. The multimedia revolution—fueled by powerful, low-cost digital cameras, scanners, and video recorders—enables you to capture and store images that easily can consume hundreds of megabytes of space, and the MP3 craze is filling countless gigabytes of storage on individual users' systems with digitized musical hits and classics.

High-capacity removable storage devices provide the capability to easily transport huge data files— computer-aided drawing (CAD) files and graphics files, for example—from one computer to another. Or, you can use removable storage to take sensitive data away from your office so you can lock it safely away from prying eyes. Some types of removable-media storage feature archival durability, whereas others are designed for the "shoot it today, delete it tomorrow" world of digital photography.

Backing Up Your Data

Any computer book worth reading warns repeatedly that you should back up your system regularly. Backups are necessary because at any time a major problem, or even some minor ones, can corrupt the important information and programs stored on your computer's hard disk drive and render this information useless. A wide range of problems can damage the data on your hard drive. Here is a list of some of these data-damaging problems:

- *Sudden fluctuations in the electricity that powers your computer (power spikes), resulting in data damage or corruption.*

- *Overwriting a file by mistake.*

- *Mistakenly formatting your hard disk when you meant to format a floppy.*

- *Hard drive failure resulting in loss of data that has not been backed up.* Not only do you have to install a new drive, but, because you have no backup, you also must reinstall all your software.

- *Catastrophic damage to your computer (storm, flood, lightning strike, fire, theft, and so on).* A single lightning strike near your office or home can destroy the circuitry of your computer, including your hard drive. Theft of your computer (increasingly common for laptop users), of course, is equally devastating. A recent, complete backup greatly simplifies the process of setting up a replacement computer.

■ *Loss of valuable data due to a computer-related virus.* One single download or floppy disk can contain a virus that can damage valuable files and even your entire hard disk. With several hundred new viruses appearing each month, no antivirus software program can keep you entirely safe. A recent backup of uninfected, critical files can help repair even the worst damage.

Backups are also the cure for such common headaches as a full hard drive and the need to transfer data between computers. By backing up data you rarely use and deleting the original data from your hard drive, you free up space once occupied by that data. If you later need a particular data file, you can retrieve that file from your backup. You also can more easily share large amounts of data between computers—when you send data from one city to another, for example—by backing up the data to a tape or other media and sending the media.

Regardless of how important regular backups are, many people avoid making them. A major reason for this lapse is that for many people, backing up their systems is tedious work when they have to use floppy disks or other low-capacity media. When you use these media, you might have to insert and remove many disks to back up all the important programs and data.

Optical storage, high-capacity magnetic media, and tape backups are all useful devices for making backups. Historically, tape backups have been regarded as the most powerful of these technologies because tape backups are among the few backup devices capable of recording the contents of today's multi-gigabyte drives to a single cartridge for restoration.

Comparing Disk, Tape, and Flash Memory Technologies

Several types of removable-media disk drives are commonly used. Traditionally, the most common varieties have used magnetic media, but some use one of two combinations of magnetic and optical storage: floptical or magneto-optical. Magnetic media drives use technology similar to that of a floppy or hard disk drive to encode data for storage. Floptical and magneto-optical media drives encode information on disk by using different combinations of laser and magnetic technologies.

Flash memory devices, which are becoming increasingly popular, emulate disk drives and are also discussed in this chapter. Some tape drives are also capable of emulating disk drives by providing drive letter access to a portion of the media but are used primarily to perform streaming backups of large disk drives and network drive arrays.

Magnetic Disk Media

Whether you are looking at "pure" magnetic media, floptical media, or magneto-optical drives, all types of magnetic disk media share similar characteristics. Disk media is more expensive per megabyte or gigabyte than tape, usually has a lower capacity, and is more easily used on a file-by-file basis as compared to tape. Disk media uses random access, which enables you to find, use, modify, or delete any file or group of files on a disk without disturbing the rest of the disk's contents. Disk media is faster for copying a few files but is typically slower for copying large numbers of files or entire drives.

Magnetic Tape Media

Tape media has much less expensive costs overall per megabyte or gigabyte than disk media, has a higher total capacity, and is more easily used on an image or multiple-file basis. Tape drives use sequential access, meaning that the contents of a tape must be read from the beginning and that individual files must be retrieved in the order found on the tape. Also, individual files usually can't be modified on the tape or removed from the tape; the contents of the entire cartridge must be deleted and rewritten. Thus, tape drives are more suited for complete backups of entire hard disks including all applications and data. Because it is suited for mass backup, tape can be difficult to use for copying single files.

Note

Removable-media disk drives can be used as system backup devices similar to tape. However, the higher price of the medium itself (disks or cartridges) and the generally slower speed at which they perform can make this use somewhat prohibitive on a large scale. For file-by-file backups, disk media is ideal; if, however, you're completely backing up entire drives or systems, tape is faster and more economical.

Flash Memory Media

The newest type of removable storage is not magnetically based but uses flash memory—a special type of solid-state memory chip that requires no power to maintain its contents. Flash memory cards can easily be moved from digital cameras to notebook or desktop computers and can even be connected directly to photo printers or self-contained display units. Flash memory can be used to store any type of computer data, but its original primary application was digital photography. However, more and more digital music players have removable flash memory cards, and so-called *thumb* or *keychain* flash memory devices that plug directly into a USB port are helping to make flash memory a mainstream storage medium and an increasingly popular replacement for some types of magnetic removable-media storage.

Tip

Literally dozens of removable storage devices are currently on the market. Be sure to compare your chosen solution against the competition before making a final purchase. Be especially wary of missing statistics in press releases and product packaging—manufacturers are apt to omit a specification if their drives don't measure up to the competition.

Interfaces for Removable Media Drives

In addition to choosing a type of device, you must choose which type of interface is ideally suited for connecting it to your PC. Several connection options are available for the leading removable drives. The most common interface (and one of the fastest) for internally mounted drives is the same AT Attachment (ATA) interface used for most hard drives. SCSI interfacing is as fast or even faster for use with either internal or external drives but requires adding an interface card to most systems. Most high-end tape backups require a SCSI interface.

The most common external interface is now the USB port, which has largely replaced the venerable parallel port for printing as well as for interfacing low-cost external drives and other types of I/O devices. The USB port is available on virtually all recent PCs (both desktop and notebook models); can be hot-swapped; and is supported by Windows 98 and later, including Windows Me, Windows 2000, and Windows XP. For small-capacity (under 300MB) removable-media devices, the performance of USB 1.1 (12Mbps) is adequate, but larger removable-media devices should be connected to the faster USB 2.0 port (480Mbps) or the 400Mbps IEEE 1394a (FireWire/i.Link) port if possible. Most flash memory devices must be connected to a card reader, which usually plugs into a USB port; some can be plugged into a CardBus adapter on laptop computers, and some recent laptop computers have integrated slots for some types of flash memory cards (primarily SD or MMC).

Many of the latest flash memory card readers and keychain USB drives now support Hi-Speed USB (USB 2.0), so if you're not satisfied with the speed of data transfer from USB 1.1 devices, use Hi-Speed USB storage devices if your system has Hi-Speed USB ports.

Older interfaces such as the parallel port and PC Card (for notebook computers) are still used on some devices but have limited performance. These are recommended only for systems that don't support USB (such as those still running Windows 95 or Windows NT). Some external removable-media drives allow you to interchange interfaces to enable a single drive to work with a variety of systems.

Note

Although late versions of Windows 95 ("Win95C" or OSR2.1 and above) also have USB drivers, many developers of USB devices do not support their use with Windows 95. For reliable results and manufacturer support, use Windows 98, Windows Me, Windows 2000, or Windows XP.

Hi-Speed USB ports can be added to desktop systems that have an available PCI slot and to notebook computers that have an available CardBus (32-bit PC Card) slot.

As you will see in the following sections, most removable-media drives are available in two or more of these interface types, allowing you to choose the best interface option for your needs.

Note

Connecting or installing removable-media drives is similar to connecting and installing other internal and external peripherals. The external USB, IEEE 1394, or parallel port drives are the simplest of the available interfaces, requiring only a special cable that comes with the drive and installation of special software drivers. See the instructions that come with each drive for the specifics of its installation.

See Chapter 7, "The ATA/IDE Interface"; Chapter 8, "The SCSI Interface"; and Chapter 17, "I/O Interfaces from Serial and Parallel to IEEE 1394 and USB," for details on how these interfaces operate.

Overview of Removable Magnetic Storage Devices

A small group of companies dominates the changing market for magnetic removable-media drives. Currently, Iomega and Castlewood are the leading names in removable magnetic media drives and media. Until recently, 3M's spin-off company Imation was also among the leaders, but it has now discontinued production of SuperDisk media as well as SuperDisk drives.

Removable magnetic media drives are usually floppy or hard disk based. For example, the popular Zip drive is a 3 1/2" version of the original Bernoulli flexible disk drive made by Iomega. The now-discontinued Imation SuperDisk LS-120 drive is a floppy-based drive that stores 120MB on a disk that looks almost exactly like a 1.44MB floppy; the second-generation LS-240 SuperDisk drives store up to 240MB and can format standard 1.44MB floppy disks to hold 32MB of data. Both LS-120 and LS-240 drives are read/write-compatible with 1.44MB and 720KB floppy media at normal capacities. The former SyQuest SparQ, the discontinued Iomega Jaz and Peerless, and the Castlewood Orb drives are all based on hard disk technology. The latest removable-media drive from Iomega (the Iomega REV) uses a newly designed, sealed, hard disk mechanism and features a native capacity of 35GB per cartridge with a compressed capacity of up to 90GB per cartridge.

Until recently, both the Imation LS-120 SuperDisk and Iomega Zip drives could be considered de facto industry standards for high-capacity flexible disk storage. However, with Imation's decision in 2003 to discontinue production of SuperDisk media, both the LS-120 and second-generation LS-240 drives are on the way to becoming orphan products. Although Iomega Zip drives are no longer as popular as they were in the late 1990s, their widespread industry adoption and easy media and drive availability make them the leading bigger-than-floppy magnetic removable-media storage de facto standard. Various models can be purchased as upgrades for existing computers, and media is available from both Iomega and Fujifilm.

Note

Although Imation no longer produces SuperDisk drives or media, internal SuperDisk LS-120 and LS-240 drives are still available for certain models of IBM and HP laptop computers and for desktop computers that use the ATA/IDE interface. Some vendors might still offer USB-based versions of the LS-240 drive, and Maxell still produces LS-120 and LS-240 media.

The following sections provide information about all types of magnetic media, including floptical and magneto-optical drive types.

Iomega Zip

Unlike the LS-120 and LS-240 SuperDisk drives, the Iomega Zip drive can't use standard 3 1/2" floppy disks. It is a descendent of a long line of removable-media drives from Iomega that go back to the first Bernoulli cartridge drives released in the early 1980s.

Note

For more information about Iomega Bernoulli drives, see *Upgrading and Repairing PCs, 14th Edition*, available in electronic form on the disc packaged with this book.

The current form of Bernoulli-technology drive from Iomega is the popular Zip drive. These devices are available in 100MB, 250MB, and 750MB versions with either ATA (internal), USB (external), or FireWire (external) interfaces. They also sell specific external models with either SCSI or parallel port interfaces. In addition, low-power PC Card or internal drive bay versions are available from various aftermarket vendors designed for use in notebook computers.

Zip 100 drives can store up to 100MB of data on a small removable magnetic cartridge that resembles a 3 1/2" floppy disk. The newer Zip 250 drives store up to 250MB of data on the same size cartridge and can read and write to the Zip 100 cartridges. The latest Zip 250 cartridges have a U-shaped case and use media containing titanium particles for greater durability. The most recent Zip drive holds 750MB of data. It's available in separate ATAPI internal versions for PC and Mac and in USB 2.0 and FireWire (IEEE 1394a) versions for use with both platforms. It has read/write compatibility with Zip 250 media, but it has read-only compatibility with Zip 100 media. For best performance, you should use the native media size with Zip 250 and Zip 750 drives; these drives read and write much more slowly when smaller Zip media is used than when their native media size is used.

For more information about Zip drives, see the Technical Reference section of the disc packaged with this book.

SuperDisk LS-120 and LS-240

Imation developed the LS-120 SuperDisk in the late 1990s as a rival to the Iomega Zip disk. The SuperDisk uses floptical technology, which uses optical tracking to precisely position read-write heads on floppy-type media. Although the SuperDisk is capable of reading and writing to standard 1.44MB and 720KB floppy media as well as to its own 120MB media, it was unable to overcome the huge lead Iomega had gained by being first-to-market with the Zip drives and media in the mid-1990s.

The second-generation LS-240 SuperDisk uses both LS-120 and its own 240MB LS-240 media. It can also write to standard 1.44MB and 720KB floppy disks and format a 1.44MB floppy disk to hold 32MB of data. However, similar to its predecessor, it has been incapable of making a significant impact in the marketplace.

Imation no longer sells any type of SuperDisk drives or media. Maxell continues to sell LS-120 and LS-240 SuperDisk media, and a few vendors still offer LS-120 and LS-240 drives in proprietary notebook form factors and for ATA/IDE and USB interfaces, using Matsushita/Panasonic's 1" high form factor versions of the LS-120 and LS-240 drive mechanisms. Because of the spotty availability of drives and media, SuperDisk products should be considered obsolescent at best, and I recommend that you move to other types of removable storage for your long-term needs.

For more information about SuperDisk technology, see the Technical Reference section of the disc packaged with this book.

Hard-Disk-Size Removable-Media Drives

The following drives have capacities of 1GB or larger and are fast enough to be considered removable-media hard drives:

- *Iomega Jaz*. Features 1GB and 2GB capacities
- *Castlewood Orb*. Features 2.2GB and 5.7GB capacities

- *Iomega Peerless.* Features 10GB and 20GB capacities
- *Iomega REV.* Features 35GB (native) and 90GB (compressed) capacities

The now-discontinued Jaz and Peerless drives and the currently available Orb and new REV drives can be used as bootable drives: You can install an entire operating system and a major application on the cartridge and use it to customize your system's operation. Unfortunately, these drives use proprietary designs, so the drives and media are available only from the manufacturer and are not interchangeable with other companies' products. I usually do not recommend proprietary products, preferring instead devices that conform to industry standards.

Various factors—including the high prices of traditional removable-media drives and cartridges, the rise of high-speed external hard disks using USB or IEEE 1394a ports, and the low cost of rewritable DVD drives—have led to a decline in the popularity of this category of removable storage in recent years.

Iomega discontinued its Jaz removable-media drives in 2001, but it still offers 1GB and 2GB cartridges and support. Its Peerless drive was discontinued in 2002, and additional cartridges are no longer available from Iomega. Castlewood Orb drives are still sold by Castlewood, although most retail stores don't carry them.

For more information about Orb, Jaz, and Peerless drives and media, see the Technical Reference section of the disc packaged with this book.

The newest hard disk–sized removable-media drive, the Iomega REV, was introduced in early 2004. It uses a specially designed compact cartridge (10mm × 77mm × 75mm) that contains a 2.5" motor and hard disk platters, with the read/write heads and electronics being built in to the body of the drive. By moving the drive motor into the cartridge, instead of keeping it in the drive itself as with earlier types of removable-media drives, the cartridge can be sealed against contamination. Gaskets in the drive and airflow around the read/write heads are designed to further minimize the chances of head or media contamination, and ECC is used during data writing. The native capacity of the cartridge is 35GB. However, up to 90GB of compressed storage per cartridge is possible when using the included Iomega Automatic Backup Pro software. In practice, expect your average compressed capacity to fall somewhere between 35GB and 90GB per cartridge, depending on the data you're transferring.

The internal data transfer rate of the REV drive is 25MBps, which makes it somewhat slower than most recent ATA/IDE hard disks. By the end of 2004, the drive will be available in Hi-Speed USB, ATA/IDE, SCSI, FireWire, and Serial ATA interfaces; Hi-Speed USB and ATA/IDE interfaces are used for the initial models.

"Orphan" Removable-Media Drives

Several removable-media drives have become "orphans" because of the closing of their manufacturers. Orphan drives include

- SyQuest (all models)
- Avatar Shark

Because orphan drives have very small capacities, limited performance, and limited or no support for current and forthcoming operating systems, I recommend that you transfer all data on orphan drive media to a current removable-media or optical-technology drive. Continuing to depend on an orphan can leave you stranded in the case of a drive or media failure. If you need support for these drives, see the Technical Reference section of the disc packaged with this book.

Magneto-Optical Drives

One of the most neglected types of removable-drive technologies is the magneto-optical (MO) drive. Introduced commercially in 1985, magneto-optical drives are now available in capacities exceeding 9GB.

Two sizes of magneto-optical media and drives are available for desktop computers: 3 1/2" and 5 1/4". The 3 1/2" drives have capacities up to 2.3GB, and the 5 1/4" drives have capacities up to 9.1GB. 12" MO drives are also available for enterprise systems. Originally, magneto-optical drives were strictly WORM (write once, read many) drives that produced media that could be added to, but not erased. WORM drives are still available on the market, but for desktop computer users, read/write MO drives are preferable.

Magneto-Optical Technology

At normal temperatures, the magnetic surface of an MO disk is very stable, with archival ratings of up to 30 years.

One surface of an MO disk faces a variable-power laser, whereas the other surface of the disk faces a magnet. Both the laser beam and the magnet are used to change the data on an MO disk. Figure 12.1 illustrates the magneto-optical writing and reading process.

The "optical" portion of an MO drive is the laser beam, which is used at high power during the erasing process to heat the destination area of the MO drive to a temperature of about 200° Celsius (the Curie point, at which a normally magnetic surface ceases to be magnetic). This enables any existing information in that area to be erased by a uniform magnetic field, which doesn't affect the other portions of the disk that are at normal temperature.

Next, the laser beam and magnetic field are used together to write information to the location by applying high power to the laser and applying a controlled magnetic signal to the media to change it to either a binary 0 or 1.

During the read process, the laser is used at low power to send neutrally polarized light to the surface of the MO disk. The areas of the MO disk that store binary 0s reflect light at a polarization angle different from those that store binary 1s. This difference of one degree is called the *Kerr effect*.

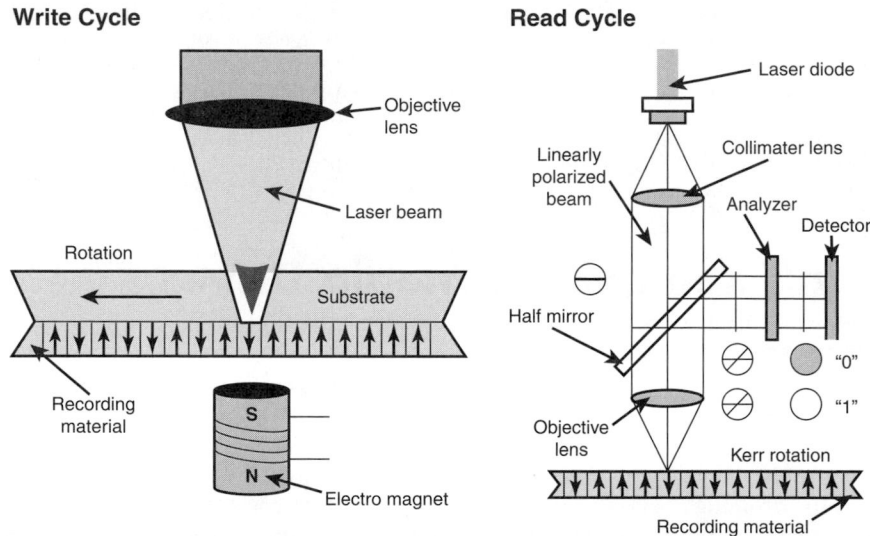

Figure 12.1   Magneto-optical drives use the laser at high power to heat the magnetic surface to enable its contents to be magnetically changed during the write cycle (left) and use the laser at low power to determine the angle of polarization (the Kerr effect) during the read cycle (right).

In older MO drives, the erase and write process involved two separate operations, but most recent MO drives starting with the Plasmon DW260 of 1997 use the LIMDOW method (light intensity modulated direct overwrite) for a single-pass operation with some media types. LIMDOW drives use magnets built into the disk itself, rather than separate magnets as in older MO drives. LIMDOW drives are fast enough to store MPEG-2 streaming video and make achieving higher capacities easier.

MO drives are available from many manufacturers at a variety of price points.

Most internal MO drives connect to SCSI interfaces. ATAPI/IDE models are sold by some vendors but aren't as easy to find, and external MO drives are available in SCSI, USB 2.0, and IEEE 1394a interfaces.

Comparing MO to "Pure" Magnetic Media

Compared to most high-capacity removable-media drives, MO drive hardware is more expensive (especially in the 5 1/4" media size), but media costs are far less per MB, durability is far better, and performance is as good or better than the 200MB-or-under class magnetic removable-media drives. The use of SCSI interfaces for most models was a drawback when MS-DOS/Windows 3.1 were the leading operating systems, but Windows 9x/Me/NT/2000/XP have much easier SCSI installation processes, and SCSI interfaces have dropped in price (and are included with some internal drives). IEEE 1394a and Hi-Speed USB (USB 2.0) interfaces available on some models allow the easiest installation process of all for external drives. If you can afford the high initial cost of the 5 1/4" media MO drives, you'll have a fairly fast, durable, long-term storage solution that's also a good storage area for works in progress.

Key Factors in Selecting a Removable Drive

When shopping for a removable drive, keep the following in mind:

- *Price per megabyte of storage.* Take the cost of the drive's cartridge or disk and divide it by the storage capacity to see how much you are paying per megabyte of storage. This difference in price becomes quite apparent as you buy more cartridges or disks for the drive. (Don't forget to factor in the cost of the drive itself if you are trying to decide which removable-media drive to buy!) If you plan to use removable storage for temporary data storage only, as with flash memory devices, the cost per megabyte is a less important factor than if you plan to leave data on a cartridge or disk for long periods of time.

- *Access time versus need of access.* The access and data transfer speeds are important only if you need to access the data frequently or quickly. If your primary use is archiving data, a slower drive might be fine. However, if you plan to run programs off the drive, choose a faster drive instead.

- *Compatibility and portability.* Opt for an external SCSI, IEEE 1394a, USB, or parallel port solution if you need to move the drive between various computers. Hi-Speed USB is the lowest-cost and friendliest solution because it's built in to recent systems, supports hot-swapping, and can be used on machines with USB 1.1 ports (albeit with much slower data transfer and access speeds). Also verify that drivers are available for each type of machine and operating system you want to use with the drive, and consider whether you need to exchange disks with other users. The Iomega Zip drive has become the standard for magnetic removable-cartridge media. However, if you don't want the expense of buying a separate drive for each machine, USB keychain storage devices using flash memory can perform the same tasks and don't need a separate drive for each computer. For some users, this might be the most important factor in choosing a drive.

- *Storage capacity.* For maximum safety and ease of use, the capacity of your storage device should be the largest available that meets your other requirements. Digital camera users, for example, will want the largest possible flash or disk storage supported by their cameras to allow more photos or higher-quality photos to be stored. Desktop and notebook computer users will want the largest drives possible for data backup or program storage.

Note

For many uses, the rewritable DVD drive is the best choice for two reasons: low media cost (well under $1 each in quantity for CD-RW media; less than $3 each for rewritable DVD) and near-universal compatibility (virtually all systems sold since the mid-1990s can read CD-RW media in ordinary CD-ROM drives, and many systems with DVD-ROM drives can read rewritable DVD media). For permanent storage, use CD-R or recordable DVD media.

USB keychain drives are now available in capacities above 1GB for situations demanding high storage density in a very small space.

- *Internal versus external.* Most users find external USB drives the easiest to install; additionally, they give you the option of using the drive on several systems. Internal drives are usually faster because of their ATA, Serial ATA, or SCSI interfaces and are more cleanly integrated into the system from a physical perspective.

- *Bootable or not.* Most systems dating from 1995 or later have a BIOS that supports the Phoenix El Torito standard, which enables them to boot from CD or DVD drives or drives that emulate them, such as the Iomega REV. Most also support the ATAPI/IDE version of the Imation LS-120 or LS-240 SuperDisk as a bootable device; however, those drives are obsolete and difficult to find. Some systems support ATA Zip drives as a bootable drive, but Zip drives are a proprietary format and incompatible with standard 3 1/2" floppy disks.

Flash Memory Devices

Flash memory has been around for several years as a main or an auxiliary storage medium for notebook computers. However, the rise of devices such as digital cameras and MP3 players and the presence of USB ports on practically all recent systems have transformed this technology from a niche product into a mainstream must-have accessory.

How Flash Memory Works

Flash memory is a type of nonvolatile memory that is divided into blocks, rather than bytes as with normal RAM memory modules. Flash memory, which also is used in most recent computers for BIOS chips, is changed by a process known as Fowler-Nordheim tunneling. This process removes the charge from the floating gate associated with each memory cell. Flash memory then must be erased before it can be charged with new data.

The speed, low reprogramming current requirements, and compact size of recent flash memory devices have made flash memory a perfect counterpart for portable devices such as notebook computers and digital cameras, which often refer to flash memory devices as so-called "digital film." Unlike real film, digital film can be erased and reshot. Ultra-compact, USB-based keychain drives that use flash memory are replacing both traditional floppy drives and Zip/SuperDisk drives for transporting data between systems.

Types of Flash Memory Devices

Several types of flash memory devices are in common use today, and it's important to know which ones your digital camera is designed to use. The major types include

- ATA Flash
- CompactFlash (CF)
- SmartMedia (SM)
- MultiMediaCards (MMC)
- Reduced Size MMC (RS-MMC)

- SecureDigital (SD)
- Memory Stick
- xD-Picture Card
- Thumb or keychain USB devices

Some of these are available in different sizes (Type I/Type II). Table 12.1 shows the various types of solid-state storage used in digital cameras and other devices, listed in order of physical size.

Table 12.1   Different Flash Memory Devices and Physical Sizes

Type	L (mm)	W (mm)	H (mm)	Volume (cc)	Date Introduced
ATA Flash Type II	54.00	85.60	5.00	23.11	Nov. 1992
ATA Flash Type I	54.00	85.60	3.30	15.25	Nov. 1992
CompactFlash (CF) Type II	42.80	36.40	5.00	7.79	Mar. 1998
CompactFlash (CF) Type I	42.80	36.40	3.30	5.14	Oct. 1995

Table 12.1   Continued

Type	L (mm)	W (mm)	H (mm)	Volume (cc)	Date Introduced
Memory Stick	21.45	50.00	2.80	3.00	Jul. 1998
Secure Digital (SD)	24.00	32.00	2.10	1.61	Aug. 1999
SmartMedia (SM)	37.00	45.00	0.76	1.27	Apr. 1996
MultiMediaCard (MMC)	24.00	32.00	1.40	1.08	Nov. 1997
xD-Picture Card (xD)	20.00	25.00	1.70	0.85	Jul. 2002
Reduced Size MMC (RS-MMC)	24.00	18.00	1.40	0.60	Nov. 2002

Note: USB flash drives are not listed because they do not have a standardized form factor.

CompactFlash

CompactFlash was developed by SanDisk Corporation in 1994 and uses ATA architecture to emulate a disk drive; a CompactFlash device attached to a computer has a disk drive letter just like your other drives.

The original size was Type I (3.3mm thick); a newer Type II size (5mm thick) accommodates higher-capacity devices. Both CompactFlash cards are 1.433" wide by 1.685" long, and adapters allow them to be inserted into notebook computer PC Card slots. The CompactFlash Association (http://www.compactflash.org) oversees development of the standard.

SmartMedia

Ironically, SmartMedia (originally known as SSFDC for solid state floppy disk card) is the simplest of any flash memory device; SmartMedia cards contain only flash memory on a card without any control circuits. This simplicity means that compatibility with different generations of SmartMedia cards can require manufacturer upgrades of SmartMedia-using devices. The Solid State Floppy Disk Forum (http://www.ssfdc.or.jp/english) oversees development of the SmartMedia standard. If you use a SmartMedia-based Olympus digital camera that has the panorama feature, be sure to use Olympus-brand SmartMedia because other brands lack support for the panorama feature.

MultiMediaCard

The MultiMediaCard (MMC) was codeveloped by SanDisk and Infineon Technologies AG (formerly Siemens AG) in November 1997 for use with smart phones, MP3 players, digital cameras, and camcorders. The MMC uses a simple 7-pin serial interface to devices and contains low-voltage flash memory. The MultiMediaCard Association (www.mmca.org) was founded in 1998 to promote the MMC standard and aid development of new products. In November 2002, MMCA announced the development of the Reduced Size MultiMedia Card (RS-MMC), which reduces the size of the standard MMC by about 40% and can be adapted for use with standard MMC devices. The first flash memory cards in this form factor were introduced in early 2004 to support compact smart phones.

SecureDigital

A SecureDigital (SD) storage device is about the same size as MMC (many devices can use both types of flash memory), but it's a more sophisticated product. SD, which was codeveloped by Toshiba, Matsushita Electric (Panasonic), and SanDisk in 1999, gets its name from two special features. The first is encrypted storage of data for additional security, meeting current and future Secure Digital Music Initiative (SDMI) standards for portable devices. The second is a mechanical write-protection switch. The SD slot can also be used for adding memory to Palm PDAs. The SDIO standard was created in January 2002 to enable SD slots to be used for small digital cameras and other types of expansion with various brands of PDAs and other devices. The SD Card Association (http://www.sdcard.org) was established in 2000 to promote the SD standard and aid the development of new products. Note that some new laptop computers have built-in SD slots.

Sony Memory Stick and Memory Stick Pro

Sony, which is heavily involved in both notebook computers and a wide variety of digital cameras and camcorder products, has its own proprietary version of flash memory known as the Sony Memory Stick. These devices feature an erase-protection switch, which prevents accidental erasure of your photographs. Sony has also licensed Memory Stick technology to other companies, such as Lexar Media.

Lexar introduced the enhanced Memory Stick PRO in 2003, with capacities ranging from 256MB up to 1GB. Memory Stick Pro includes MagicGate encryption technology, which enables digital rights management, and Lexar's proprietary high-speed memory controller. Memory Stick Pro is sometimes referred to as MagicGate Memory Stick.

ATA Flash PC Card

Although the PC Card (PCMCIA) form factor is now used for everything from game adapters to modems, from SCSI interfacing to network cards, its original use was computer memory, as the old PCMCIA (Personal Computer Memory Card International Association) acronym indicated.

Unlike normal RAM modules, PC Card memory acts like a disk drive, using the PCMCIA ATA (AT Attachment) standard. PC Cards come in three thicknesses (Type I is 3.3mm, Type II is 5mm, and Type III is 10.5mm), but all are 3.3" long by 2.13" wide. Type I and Type II cards are used for ATA-compliant flash memory and the newest ATA-compliant hard disks. Type III cards are used for older ATA-compliant hard disks; a Type III slot also can be used as two Type II slots.

xD-Picture Card

In July 2002, Olympus and Fujifilm, the major supporters of the SmartMedia flash memory standard for digital cameras, announced the xD-Picture Card as a much smaller, more durable replacement for SmartMedia. In addition to being about one-third the size of SmartMedia—making it the smallest flash memory format yet—xD-Picture Card media has a faster controller to enable faster image capture. Currently, xD-Picture Cards are available in capacities of 16MB–1GB.

16MB and 32MB cards (commonly packaged with cameras) record data at speeds of 1.3MBps, whereas 64MB and larger cards record data at 3MBps. The read speed for all sizes is 5MBps. The media is manufactured for Olympus and Fujifilm by Toshiba, and because xD-Picture media is optimized for the differences in the cameras (Olympus's media supports the panorama mode found in some Olympus xD-Picture cameras, for example), you should buy media that's the same brand as your digital camera.

USB Keychain Drives

As an alternative to floppy and Zip/SuperDisk-class removable-media drives, USB-based flash memory devices are rapidly becoming the preferred way to move data between systems. The first successful drive of this type—Trek's ThumbDrive—was introduced in 2000 and has spawned many imitators, including many that incorporate a keychain or pocket clip to emphasize their portability.

Unlike other types of flash memory, USB keychain drives don't require a separate card reader; they can be plugged into any USB port or hub. Although a driver is usually required for Windows 98 and Windows 98SE, most USB keychain drives can be read immediately by newer versions of Windows, particularly Windows XP. As with other types of flash memory, USB keychain drives are assigned a drive letter when connected to the computer. Most have capacities ranging from 32MB to 256MB, with some capacities as high as 2GB. However, typical read/write performance of USB 1.1-compatible drives is about 1MBps. Hi-Speed USB keychain drives are much faster, providing read speeds ranging from 5MBps to 15MBps and write speeds ranging from 5MBps to 13MBps. Because Hi-Speed USB keychain drives vary in performance, be sure to check the specific read/write speeds for the drives you are considering before you purchase one.

Tip

If you have a card reader plugged into a USB hub or port on your computer, you might need to disconnect it before you can attach a USB keychain drive. This is sometimes necessary because of conflicts between the drivers used by some devices. Use the Windows Safely Remove Hardware icon in the system tray to stop the card reader before you insert the USB keychain drive. After the USB keychain drive has been recognized by the system, you should be able to reattach the card reader.

For additional protection of your data, some USB keychain drives have a mechanical write-protect switch; others include or support password-protected data encryption as an option, and some are capable of being a bootable device (if supported in the BIOS). The Kanguru MicroDrive+ can be upgraded with SD or MMC flash cards for additional capacity.

Figure 12.2 shows the features of a typical USB keychain drive, the NexDisk USB storage device from Jungsoft.

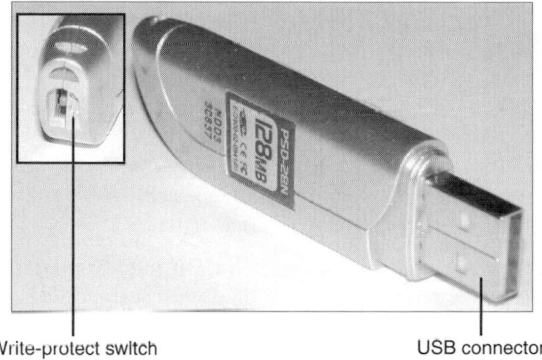

Write-protect switch   USB connector

Figure 12.2   The Jungsoft NexDisk USB storage device holds 128MB of data, which can be write-protected to help prevent accidental erasure.

If you use MMC, SD, or Memory Stick flash memory cards in digital cameras or other devices, you can use them as interchangeable storage in the Lexar Media JumpDrive Trio. This device is essentially a USB 1.1/ Hi-Speed USB keychain drive without flash memory storage onboard, enabling you to add your own. The JumpDrive Trio also doubles as a card reader. SimpleTech's Bonzai flash drive provides similar functionality for SD and MMC cards only and is available with or without preinstalled SD memory.

Comparing Flash Memory Devices

As with any storage issue, you must compare each product's features to your needs. You should check the following issues before purchasing flash memory devices:

- *Which flash memory products does your camera or other device support?* Although adapters allow some interchange of the various types of flash memory devices, for best results, you should stick with the flash memory type your device was designed to use.

- *Which capacities does your device support?* Flash memory devices are available in ever-increasing capacities, but not every device can handle the higher-capacity devices. Check the device and flash memory card's Web sites for compatibility information.

- *Are some flash memory devices better than others?* Some manufacturers have added improvements to the basic requirements for the flash memory device. For example, Lexar makes four series of faster-than-normal Compact Flash+ cards (4x, 12x, 16x, and 24x), a series of Write Acceleration Technology (WA) cards for even faster performance with professional digital SLR cameras, and USB-enabled models that can be attached to USB ports for fast data transfer using a simple USB cable rather than an expensive and bulky card reader.

Only the ATA Flash cards can be attached directly to a notebook computer's PC Card slots. All other devices need their own socket or some type of adapter to transfer data. Figure 12.3 shows how the most common types of flash memory cards compare in size to each other and to a penny.

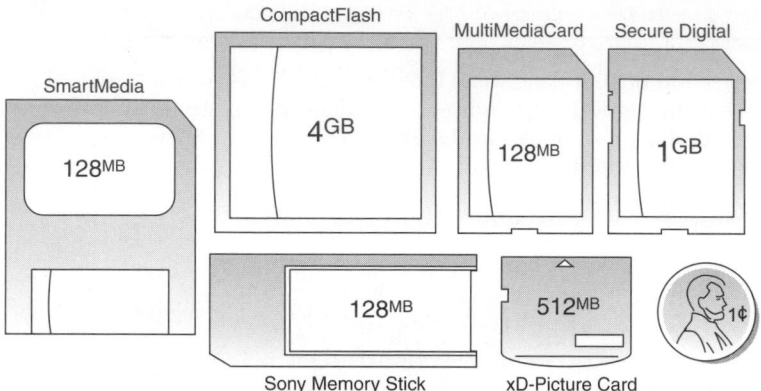

Figure 12.3 SmartMedia, CompactFlash, MultiMediaCard, SecureDigital, xD-Picture Card, and Sony Memory Stick flash memory devices. Shown in maximum capacity versions and in relative scale to a U.S. penny (lower right).

Table 12.2 provides an overview of the major types of flash memory devices and their current capacities. Note that smaller-capacity cards might be bundled with some digital cameras.

Table 12.2 Flash Memory Card Capacities

Device	Maximum Available Capacity	Notes
CompactFlash+	4GB	Highest capacity, most flexible format, supported by the best cameras. Lexar Media and SanDisk also make faster versions of CF+ media; Lexar Media also makes USB-enabled CF+ media.
Secure Digital (SD)	1GB	Next-best format to CompactFlash, SD cards do not work in MMC sockets.
MultiMediaCard (MMC)	128MB	Obsolete format; MMC cards can work in most SD sockets.
Memory Stick	128MB	Proprietary format developed by Sony and licensed to Lexar Media.
Memory Stick Pro	1GB	Enhanced high-speed version of Memory Stick with digital rights management support; also called Memory Stick Magic Gate.
ATA Flash	2GB	Plugs directly into a PC-Card (PCMCIA) slot without an adapter.
xD-Picture Card	512MB	Use the same brand as your digital camera for the best results.
SmartMedia	128MB	Becoming obsolete, very thin.
USB keychain drive	2GB	Some include password-protection and write-protect features.

I normally recommend devices (cameras, PDAs, and so on) that use CompactFlash (CF), Secure Digital (SD), or xD-Picture flash memory cards. Any of the others I generally do not recommend due to limitations in capacity, performance, proprietary designs, and higher costs.

CompactFlash is the most widely used format in professional and consumer devices and offers the highest capacity, at the lowest prices, in a reasonably small size. CF cards plug directly into PC Card slots on all laptops by using a simple passive adapter that is extremely inexpensive. Therefore, when you're not using one of those cards in your camera, you can use it as a solid-state hard disk in a laptop. For a long time I would not even consider a camera or other device that did not use CF storage. I have relaxed on that stance a little bit, but it is still by far the best overall format and is available in capacities of up to 8GB or higher. It is also significantly faster than the other formats.

Secure Digital is becoming more popular, is reasonably fast, and is available in capacities up to 1GB. SD sockets also take MultiMediaCard (MMC) cards, which are basically thinner versions of SD. Note that the opposite is not true—MMC sockets do not accept SD cards. MMC is also available in versions up to 128MB. Finally, xD-Picture is a very compact format that has grown in popularity and offers capacities up to 1GB.

In general I would not consider any device that uses other formats, especially Memory Stick, which is a Sony proprietary format (didn't Sony learn anything from the Betamax versus VHS war?). The RS-MMC format is too new to consider and as such is found in a limited number of devices with very limited capacity. ATA Flash is great, but the cards are physically big, mostly obsolete, and can easily be replaced by a CompactFlash card in a PC Card adapter. SmartMedia was once a popular format, but it's relatively fragile now, limited to 128MB in capacity, and camera vendors who once used it have now switched to the higher-capacity xD-Picture card format.

Moving Data in Flash Memory Devices to Your Computer

Several types of devices can be purchased to enable the data on flash memory cards to be moved from digital cameras and other devices to a computer. Although some digital cameras come with an RS-232 serial cable for data downloading, this is a painfully slow method, even for low-end cameras with less than a megapixel (1,000 pixel horizontal width) resolution.

Card Readers

The major companies who produce flash card products sell card readers that can be used to transfer data from proprietary flash memory cards to PCs. These card readers typically plug into the computer's USB ports (some older versions might use the parallel port) for fast access to the data on the card.

In addition to providing fast data transfer, card readers enable the reuse of expensive digital film after the photos are copied from the camera and save camera battery power because the camera is not needed to transfer information. External card readers can be used with any computer with the correct port type and a supported operating system. USB readers, for example, should be used with Windows 98 or above. Some readers don't support write functions (such as erasing pictures after they're transferred from the media to your computer); I recommend devices with read/write functionality.

Because many computer and electronics device users might have devices that use two or more types of flash memory, many vendors now offer multiformat flash memory card readers, such as the SanDisk 8-in-1 Card Reader/Writer shown in Figure 12.4.

Type II PC Card Adapters

For use in the field, you might prefer to adapt flash memory cards to the Type II PC Card slot. You insert the flash memory into the adapter; then, you slide the adapter into the notebook computer's Type II PC Card slot. Figure 12.5 shows how a CompactFlash card Type II PC Card adapter works. As with card readers, check with the major companies who produce your type of flash memory device for the models available.

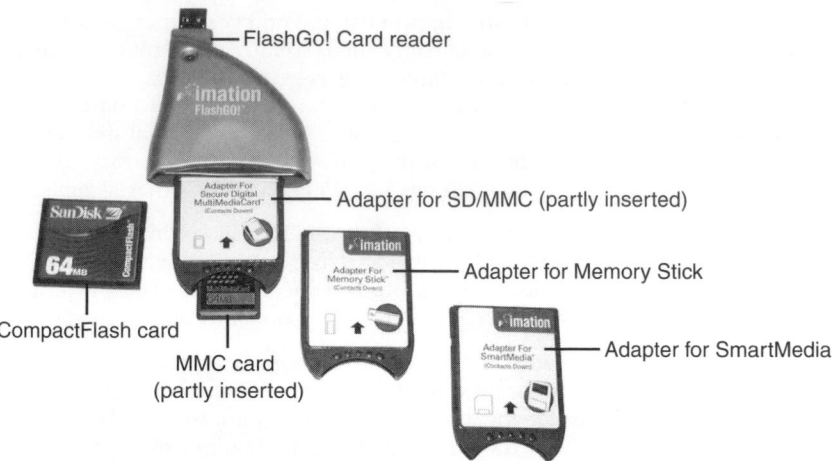

Figure 12.4 The SanDisk 8-in-1 Card Reader/Writer plugs into a Hi-Speed USB port.

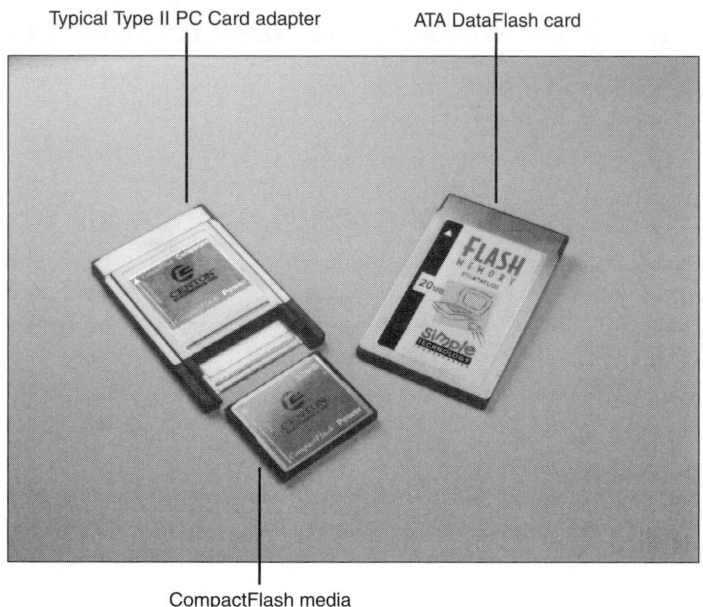

Figure 12.5 A typical Type II PC Card adapter for CompactFlash media (left) compared to an ATA DataFlash card (right).

Floppy Adapters

If you have a standard 3 1/2" floppy drive connected to a standard floppy controller, you have a third alternative for reading the contents of flash memory cards: SmartDisk (http://www.smartdisk.com) makes the FlashPath line of flash memory card adapters that fit in place of a 3 1/2" floppy disk. Separate models are available for SmartMedia, Sony Memory Stick, and CompactFlash cards. As shown in Figure 12.6, the flash memory devices are inserted into the FlashPath adapter. Then, the FlashPath adapter is inserted into a 3 1/2" floppy drive.

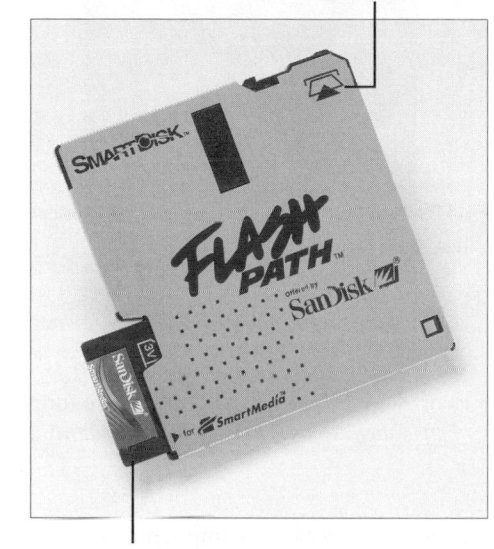

Assembly is inserted into a
standard 3.5-inch floppy disk drive

Compact Flash module is
inserted into the FlashPath adapter

Figure 12.6 A CompactFlash module is inserted into the FlashPath adapter; the assembly is then inserted into a standard 3 1/2" floppy drive. *Photo courtesy of SanDisk.*

Note that this adapter does not work with the SuperDisk LS-120/LS-240 drives found in some computers; it works only with 1.44MB floppy drives.

Microdrive Technology

If you prefer magnetic storage for digital camera data storage, consider the Hitachi Microdrive, originally developed by IBM and now manufactured and sold by Hitachi Global Storage Technologies. The Hitachi Microdrive is also sold by various other companies under OEM agreements.

When first introduced by IBM, the Microdrive was released in a 170MB capacity. Current models, though, have capacities of 512MB, 1GB, 2GB, and 4GB. The 4GB model uses a new five-layer version of the Pixie Dust AFC media technology originally developed by IBM. Microdrives can be used with several digital cameras, many notebook computers, and other devices. The Microdrive is a true hard drive with a rotational speed of 3,600rpm and a 128KB cache buffer. At 1" wide, it works in CompactFlash+ Type II slots, enabling it to be a direct replacement for standard CompactFlash memory cards on compatible equipment. The Microdrive is also available as part of a Travel Kit containing a PC Card adapter, and the drive is compatible with many standard CompactFlash card readers. See the www.hitachigst.com Web site for more information about Microdrive products, a compatibility matrix, and other information. Figure 12.7 shows how Microdrive's mechanism compares in size to a standard U.S. quarter.

Note

Depending on the version of Windows you use and the type of removable-media storage you select, you might see changes in existing drive letters when you install a new removable-media drive or flash memory device into a system.

Figure 12.7 A U.S. quarter is just slightly smaller than the Hitachi (originally IBM) Microdrive. *Courtesy of International Business Machines Corporation. Unauthorized use not permitted.*

Tape Drives

The data backup and archive needs of a personal computer can be overwhelming. People with large hard drives and numerous applications installed and those who generate a large amount of data might need to back up their computers on a weekly or even a daily basis.

In addition, a critical need on today's PCs is data storage space. Sometimes it seems as though the storage requirements of a PC can never be satisfied. On nearly any PC used for business, study, or even fun, the amount of software installed can quickly overwhelm even a large hard drive. To save space on the primary storage devices, you can archive infrequently used data to another storage medium. Depending on the method you use for archiving data to secondary storage, you might be able to read the data directly from the device, or you might need to restore the data to the drive before you can access it. If you copy data to the drive with drag-and-drop, the data can be read from the media directly. However, if you use a backup program to create the backup, you will need to use that same program to access the data and restore it to a drive before it can be reused.

Historically, a popular method for backing up full hard disks or modified files has been a tape backup drive. This section focuses on current tape backup drive technologies to help you determine whether this type of storage technology is right for you.

Tape backup drives are the most simple and efficient device for creating a full backup of your hard disk if the tape is large enough. With a tape backup drive installed in your computer, you insert a tape into the drive, start your backup software, and select the drive and files you want to back up. The backup software copies your selected files onto the tape while you attend to other business. Later, when you need to retrieve some or all of the files on the backup tape, you insert the tape in the drive, start your backup program, and select the files you want to restore. The tape backup drive takes care of the rest of the job.

This section examines the various types of tape backup drives on the market, describing the capacities of different drives as well as the system requirements for installation and use of a tape drive. The following topics are covered in this section:

- Hard-disk-based alternatives to tape backup
- Advantages and disadvantages to tape backup
- Common standards for tape backup drives
- Common backup tape capacities
- Newer higher-capacity tape drives
- Common tape drive interfaces
- Portable tape drives
- Tape backup software

Hard-Disk-Based Alternatives to Tape Backup

Before you decide to adopt a tape backup as your backup strategy, keep the following alternatives in mind:

- *External hard drives.* Maxtor, Western Digital, SimpleTech, and others have developed external hard drives with capacities ranging from 20GB up to 400GB. These drives attach through USB 1.1, USB 2.0, or IEEE 1394a ports and can be used for data backup with backup software or drag-and-drop file copying. Many external drives include backup software, and some offer additional features. For example, the Maxtor One Touch and Personal Storage 5000 family feature an exclusive OneTouch feature that starts the file-copying process automatically and can be used to launch Dantz Retrospect Express backup software. Western Digital's Media Center combines Hi-Speed USB/IEEE 1394a external drives with capacities up to 250GB with a two-port Hi-Speed USB hub and an 8-in-1 flash memory card reader.

- *Removable-media drives based on hard disk technology.* The Iomega REV drive's native capacity of 35GB per cartridge and compressed capacity of up to 90GB per cartridges makes it a promising alternative for tape backup drives.

◄◄ To learn more about the Iomega REV, see "Hard-Disk-Size Removable-Media Drives," p. 710.

- *RAID arrays.* By connecting identical hard disks to a RAID array using RAID 1 data mirroring or RAID 5 data striping with parity, your data is automatically backed up as soon as it is created. RAID arrays were once used strictly for SCSI drives on networks because of their high cost. However, recent developments in high-performance, low-cost, RAID 1-compatible ATA or Serial ATA host adapters on motherboards and PCI add-on cards make this another useful backup strategy to consider. RAID 5 arrays generally require a separate host adapter.

◄◄ To learn more about RAID, see "ATA RAID," p. 580.

Disadvantages of Tape Backup Drives

Many computer users who once used tape backups for data backup purposes have turned to other technologies for the following reasons:

- *Creating a tape backup copy of files or of a drive requires the use of a special backup program in almost all cases.* A few tape drives allow drive letter access to at least part of the tape capacity, but this feature is far from universal.

- *Retrieving data from most tape backup drives requires that the data files be restored to the hard disk.* Other types of backup storage can be treated as a drive letter for direct use from the media.

- *Tape backups store and retrieve data sequentially.* The last file backed up can't be accessed until the rest of the tape is read; other types of backup storage use random access, which enables any file on the device to be located and used in mere seconds.

- *Low-cost tape backups using QIC (Quarter Inch Committee), QIC-Wide, or Travan technology once had little problem keeping up with increases in hard disk capacity and once sold for prices comparable to or less than the hard disks they protected.* Today's hard disks have capacities of 20GB–400GB or larger and are far less expensive than most comparably sized tape backups. As a result, more expensive, higher-capacity tape drives are needed to achieve single-cartridge backups.

- *Newer backup and restore techniques, such as drive imaging/ghosting, rival the ease of use of tape backups and permit data restoration with lower-cost optical storage devices such as CD-RW or rewritable DVD drives.* These alternatives are particularly useful if only a few GB of data needs to be backed up on a continuing basis.

For these reasons, the once-unassailable position of a tape backup drive as being the must-have data protection accessory is no longer a secure one; plenty of rivals to tape backups are on the market. However, if you can afford a high-quality DDS or AIT tape drive, you can get a high-performance and high-reliability solution because these same drives are used in the demanding roles of network backup.

Advantages to Tape Backup Drives

Although tape backup drives are no longer the one-size-fits-all panacea for all types of bigger-than-floppy storage problems, they have their place in keeping your data safe. Following are several good reasons for using tape backup drives:

- *Tape backups are a true one-cartridge backup process for individual client PCs, standalone computers, or network servers when high-capacity tape drives and cartridges are used.* Anytime multiple tapes or disks must be used to make a backup, the chances of backup failure increase.

- *If you or your company has made previous backup tapes, you must keep a tape drive to access that data or perform a restore from it.* Tape backup drives are necessary if you need to restore from previously made backup tapes.

- *If you want an easy media rotation method for preserving multiple full-system backups, tape backup drives are a good choice.*

In general, tape drives are used where high capacity and high reliability are paramount. They can be expensive initially but are extremely inexpensive when you factor in the low cost of the media over time.

Common Tape Backup Standards

Tape drives come in a variety of industry-standard as well as some proprietary formats. The following list details several of the available formats:

- *QIC, QIC-Wide, and Travan.* Travan is a development of the QIC and QIC-Wide family of low-cost, entry-level tape backup drives. Travan drives can handle data up to 40GB at 2:1 compression.

- *DAT (Digital Audio Tape).* This is a newer technology than QIC and its offshoots, and it uses Digital Data Storage (DDS) technology to store data up to 40GB at 2:1 compression (DDS-4) and up to 72GB in the new DDS fifth-generation drives. DAT drives are often referred to as DDS drives for this reason.

- *AIT (Advanced Intelligent Tape).* This is becoming the successor to DAT/DDS because it can handle higher capacities than DAT.

- *Exabyte (formerly Ecrix)'s VXA-1 and VXA-2 drives.* VXA-1 offers a capacity of 66GB at 2:1 compression and a variety of high-speed SCSI and IEEE 1394 interface options. The VXA-1 format has been approved by the ECMA, an important international organization that establishes standards for information and communication systems. The improved VXA-2 drives have capacities up to 160GB (2:1 compression).

Other tape backup standards, such as DLT (Digital Linear Tape) and 8mm, are used primarily with larger network file servers and are beyond the scope of this book.

QIC and Its Variants (QIC-Wide and Travan)

The first 1/4" tape drive was introduced in 1972 by 3M, and it used a cartridge size of 6"×4"×5/8". This pioneering cartridge established the so-called "DC" data cartridge standard that was used with the first true QIC-standard drive—the 60MB QIC-02, introduced in 1983–1984. The QIC-02-compatible drives were sold for several years and, like many early tape backup drives, used a dedicated host adapter board. QIC-02's small capacity began to be a problem in the mid-1980s, and many other QIC standards were created for larger drives.

The QIC (http://www.qic.org) has introduced more than 120 standards over the years in both the older DC and newer minicartridge (MC) forms. This huge number of standards has actually led to a fragmented marketplace that makes it increasingly difficult to determine the backward-compatibility and cross-compatibility factors that QIC, ironically, was established to provide. QIC-Wide technology, developed by Sony, is not an official QIC standard, but QIC-Wide drives can read and write some types of QIC minicartridge media.

This section focuses on the recent and current minicartridge versions of Travan, the latest development of the QIC and QIC-Wide standards.

Note

For more information on QIC and QIC-Wide standards, see Chapter 12 of *Upgrading and Repairing PCs, 11th Edition*, and Chapter 12 of *Upgrading and Repairing PCs, 12th Edition*, found in their entirety on the disc accompanying this book.

Travan Cartridge Tape

The successor to both QIC-MC and QIC-Wide drives was created in 1994 by 3M (now Imation). Travan drives maintain backward compatibility with various QIC standards and provide backup capabilities up to 20GB uncompressed and 40GB at 2:1 compression.

The Travan platform features a unique drive/minicartridge interface patented by Imation. The Travan platform fits in a 3 1/2" form factor, enabling easy installation in a variety of systems and enclosures. Travan drives can accept current QIC, QIC-Wide, and Travan minicartridges—a critical need for users, given the installed base of more than 200 million QIC-compatible minicartridges worldwide.

Currently, several levels of Travan cartridges and drives are available, each based on a particular QIC standard. Table 12.3 lists the standard Travan cartridges and capacities. All Travan cartridges use .315" (8mm) wide tape.

Table 12.3   Travan Family Cartridges and Capacities

Travan Cartridge (Previous Name)	Capacity/2:1 Compression	Read/Write Compatible with	Read Compatible with
Travan-1 (TR-1)	400MB/800MB	QIC-80, QW5122	QIC-40
Travan-3 (TR-3)	1.6GB/3.2GB	TR-2, QIC-3020, QIC-3010, QW-3020XLW, QW-3010XLW	QIC-80, QW-5122, TR-1
Travan 8GB (Travan 4/TR-4)	4GB/8GB	Travan 8, QIC-3080, QIC-Wide (3080)	QIC-80, QIC-3010, QIC-Wide (3010), QIC-3020, QIC-Wide (3020), TR-1, TR-3
Travan NS-8[1]	4GB/8GB	TR-4, QIC-3080	QIC-Wide (3080)
Travan NS-20 (Travan TR-5)	10GB/20GB		Travan 8GB, QIC-3095
Travan 40GB (Travan TR-7)	20GB/40GB		Travan NS-20

1. *This cartridge can be used in place of the Travan 8GB (TR-4); the same cartridge can be used on either NS8 or TR-4 drives.*

Note

Backward compatibility can vary with drive; consult the manufacturer before purchasing any drive to verify backward-compatibility issues.

Most Travan drives on the market today use the Network Series (NS) technology described in the following section.

The Travan NS

Drives that support Travan NS technology are designed to solve two problems that have plagued tape backup users for many years: data compression and data verification.

On QIC-40 and above, QIC-Wide, and standard Travan drives, data compression is performed by the backup software used by the drive. This could cause the following problems:

■ Drives might have difficulty reading data if different backup software was used to make the backup and perform the restoration.

■ The speed of the computer had a major impact on how fast backups could be performed; a typical backup program (such as Iomega's Ditto Tools) would offer three settings—no compression, compress to save time, and compress to save space—forcing the user to choose between maximum data storage and maximum speed.

On the same drives, backup software supports a verification step that compares the data written to the tape with the data on the drive. Unfortunately, this requires that the tape be rewound to the beginning of the current backup and be read to the end while the hard disk is also read. The result? A backup that took 45 minutes without verification would take more than 90 minutes with verification enabled. This inefficient write-rewind-reread process has discouraged many users from relying on this safer backup method. Also, errors caused by changes in the state of a Windows 9x computer (such as screensavers being enabled or swapfiles changing in size) during the time passage between backup and verify tended to create the erroneous notion that the backup wasn't accurate.

Travan NS–compatible drives (including the Travan 40) use a dual-head design, shown in Figure 12.8, that enables data to be verified as soon as it is written (read-while-write). They also feature hardware data compression, which allows a higher data capacity (up to 40GB at 2:1 compression). The result is faster and more reliable backups. The Travan NS20 and Travan 40 cartridges also use a different metal media formula for greater data density than older Travan drives do.

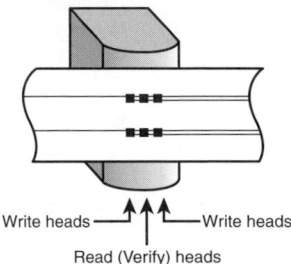

Write heads ——— Write heads

Read (Verify) heads

Figure 12.8 Travan NS and Travan 40 tape drives use separate read and write heads to enable data to be verified as soon as it is written, saving the time-consuming rewind and verify operation used with QIC, QIC-Wide, and earlier Travan drives.

Currently, Travan NS20 and Travan 40–based drives are sold primarily by Certance (formerly Seagate Removable Storage Solutions LLC).

Proprietary Versions of Travan Technology

Ironically, because Travan technology was designed to bring an end to the QIC MC—QIC-Wide tape "wars," some drives use proprietary versions of the Travan standard. Nonstandard sizes include

■ 5GB Tecmar/Iomega DittoMax[1]

■ 5GB HP/Colorado

■ 6.6GB AIWA Bolt[2]

■ 7GB Tecmar/Iomega DittoMax[1]

■ 10GB Tecmar DittoMax[1]

■ 14GB HP/Colorado

1. *Iomega sold the Ditto and DittoMax backup product line to Tecmar, which went out of business in 2002. Although media is still available for these drives from Imation, they are orphans without technical support and should be replaced.*

2. *AIWA Computer Systems Division was shut down in October 1999. These are orphan drives that should be replaced.*

The drive manufacturer is the principal supplier of media for some of these drives, whereas others are also supported with third-party media. Consult the drive manufacturers' Web sites for details.

OnStream ADR Drives

OnStream Data B.V.—the successor to the original OnStream, Inc., spinoff from Philips Electronics— declared bankruptcy in April 2003, making the OnStream ADR (introduced in 1999) and newer ADR[2] tape backup product lines orphans. The remaining stock of OnStream drives, as well as some sizes of tape cartridges, drivers, manuals, and technical information, is available from Hastec B.V. (http://www.hastec.nl). Verbatim continues to sell cartridges for some sizes of ADR drives. For more information about OnStream ADR drives and tape cartridges, see *Upgrading and Repairing PCs, 15th Anniversary Edition*, contained in electronic form on the disc packaged with this book.

DAT/DDS, AIT, and Other High-Capacity Tape Drive Standards

Although Travan capacities have now reached 40GB compressed, users of today's high-capacity hard drives must turn to larger tape backup standards. The same tape backup standards long supported by workstation and large network servers can also be used with today's versions of Windows for both individual desktop computers and small network servers. Additionally, new high-capacity technologies are available to support today's larger drives.

4mm digital audio tape (DAT/DSS), 8mm videotape, 8mm AIT, digital linear tape, scalable linear recording (SLR), and Exabyte (originally Ecrix) VXA are the major choices available for users who need higher-capacity backups. An emerging choice for very high-capacity (100GB and up) drives is the Ultrium version of the LTO Technology standard. All these technologies are available in autoloading tape libraries suitable for large networks, as well as single-cartridge drives intended for small network servers or desktop use.

Proprietary Versus Open Standards

If you want a wider variety of choices in drives, media, and pricing, you might prefer to purchase a high-performance drive type that is made by several companies. However, some of the most advanced technologies are controlled by a single vendor.

Drive technologies available from multiple vendors include

- *DAT/DDS.* Introduced and licensed by Sony to numerous manufacturers. Fifth-generation DDS drives are sold by HP and Certance (formerly Seagate RSS).
- *AIT.* Introduced and licensed by Sony to numerous manufacturers.
- *DLT.* Originally developed by Digital Equipment Corporation, but was purchased by Quantum in 1994.
- *LTO (Linear Tape-Open).* Developed by HP, IBM, and Seagate RSS (now Certance).

The following drive technologies are sold by a single vendor:

- *SLR.* Tandberg Data
- *VXA.* Exabyte (originally developed by Ecrix)

However, third-party vendors might sell tape cartridges compatible with even so-called "proprietary" standards.

DAT/DDS Tape Drives

Of the many high-performance tape drives on the market, this author's longtime favorite has been the DAT/DDS tape drive family because of its combination of performance, capacity, reliability, and reasonable price. Five levels of DAT/DDS drive capacity are available:

- *DDS-1.* This entry-level member of the family (2GB native/4GB at 2:1 compression) is now obsolete.
- *DDS-2.* Has the same capacity as drives based on Travan NS8 (4GB native/8GB at 2:1 compression).

- *DDS-3.* Has a slightly larger capacity (12GB native/24GB at 2:1 compression) than Travan NS20.

- *DDS-4.* Has a 20GB native/40GB at 2:1 compression capacity, which is double the capacity of Travan NS20 and equal to Travan 40GB. It also works with DDS-3 media.

- *DAT72 (DDS Fifth Generation).* The newest member of the DAT/DDS family, it has a 36GB native/72GB at 2:1 compression capacity. It works with DDS-4 and DDS-3 media.

Even though DAT/DDS drives are more expensive than Travan drives with similar capacities, the media cost is much lower because of the drive's design. For example, you will pay about three times as much for a Travan NS20 cartridge as for a slightly higher-capacity DDS-3 cartridge. A DDS-4 cartridge, which offers double the capacity of Travan NS20, still sells for about 30% less. DDS drives are more reliable than Travan or earlier QIC-based drives, which is a vital consideration because the most important reason to use a tape backup is to perform a restore. The enhanced reliability of DDS drives is aided by the inclusion of automatic head-cleaning features built into most DDS drives and media.

After Sony announced in April 2001 that DDS-4 tape drives would be the end of the DAT/DDS lineup of drives, the future of DAT/DDS tapes was uncertain. However, in January 2003, HP and Certance announced the development of a fifth generation of DDS drives (DAT72), which features a higher capacity than DDS-4 and backward read/write compatibility with DDS-4 and DDS-3 tapes. The first DAT72 drives were introduced in July 2003. DAT72 nearly doubles the capacity of DDS-4.

Certance's DAT72 drives feature a combination of technologies called TapeShield that are designed to protect drives and data. TapeShield, previously available on Certance's DDS-4 drives, features

- A sealed chamber for the head-to-tape interface

- A continuous-contact capstan cleaner

- A sapphire media-cleaning blade that removes debris from the tape before it contaminates the drive

These improvements enable DAT72 drives to run 10 times longer in dusty conditions than similar drives lacking these features. DAT72 drives from Certance also feature SmartShield, which uses multiple reads to improve data recovery when reading from out-of-spec or weak recorded tapes.

HP's DAT72 drives include One Button Disaster Recovery, an easy-to-use disaster-recovery feature designed to restore a system to its most recent backed-up condition.

Helical Scan Recording on DAT, 8mm, and AIT Drives

Exabyte 8mm, Sony DAT/DDS, and Sony AIT use helical scan recording. The read/write heads used in helical scan recording are mounted on a drum and write data at a slight angle to the tape, using a mechanism highly reminiscent of that in a VCR (refer to Figure 12.9). The entire surface of the tape is used to store data, enabling more data to be placed in a given length of tape than with the linear recording techniques used by the QIC family of drives.

AIT Unique Features

Sony's AIT has several unique features designed to make backup and restoration faster and more reliable. An optional Memory In Cassette (MIC) chip allows the cartridge to remember which of the 256 on-tape partitions were used for the data you want to restore, so the correct starting point can be located in seconds. AIT drives also have a servo tracking system called Auto Tracking Following (ATF), which is used for accurate data-track writing, and Advanced Lossless Data Compression (ALDC), a mainframe-style compression method that can compress data to a greater extent than other methods. The drives have several other features, including built-in head cleaning that is activated when soft (correctable) errors reach a preset limit, metal-evaporated tape media that avoids head contamination, and a 3 1/2" form factor.

DLT Unique Features

DLT segments the tape into parallel horizontal tracks and records data by streaming the tape across a single stationary head at 100"–150" per second during read/write operations. This is a dramatic contrast to traditional helical-scan technology, in which the data is recorded in diagonal stripes with a rotating drumhead while a much slower tape motor draws the media past the recording head.

The result is a very durable drive and a robust medium. DLT drive heads have a minimum life expectancy of 15,000 hours under worst-case temperature and humidity conditions, and the tapes have a life expectancy of 500,000 passes.

SLR Unique Features

Tandberg's SLR drives use a linear recording method; the tape used by the SLR 40, SLR 60, SLR 75, SLR 100, and SLR 140 is divided into 192 tracks. Twenty-four prewritten servo tracks are used to adjust the position of the read/write head as necessary. This feature is designed to ensure compatibility of SLR tapes between drives, enabling a tape written by one drive unit to be readable by another unit. Four tracks are written at the same time in parallel. The entry-level SLR 7 uses a simplified recording method that uses 72 tracks, writing 2 tracks at a time in parallel. Both tape types have fault-tolerance features that enable the drive to switch to another track for data recording if the original track fails. SLR media is available from most major tape vendors.

Exabyte VXA Unique Features

The Exabyte VXA drives (originally developed by Ecrix, which merged with Exabyte in November 2001) combine special recording and playback methods. The recording method used somewhat resembles a normal helical scan, but the tape is guided past the magnetic drum with a completely different type of mechanism and the data is recorded at variable speeds that change according to how fast the host can transmit data. This eliminates the need to wind tape backward because of data underruns (back-hitching). Data is recorded in 64-byte groups of 387 data packets rather than in linear blocks. VXA drives use a special read feature called overscan operation (OSO). OSO performs redundant reads of each group of data packets, enabling data to be retrievable even from damaged tapes. The packetizing of data works the same way as on the Internet: Data can be read in any order and reassembled into its original form when all packets are received. In tests, Exabyte and Ecrix have boiled, frozen, and even poured hot coffee over VXA tapes and been able to retrieve 100% of the stored data.

LTO Technology Unique Features

Linear Tape-Open, better known as LTO, is a very high-performance tape backup technology that offers two distinct types of mechanisms:

- *Ultrium.* This implementation of LTO is optimized for very high capacities. For example, Ultrium drives have an uncompressed capacity of 100GB (200GB at 2:1 compression) and transfer rates of 20MBps–40MBps. Ultrium Generation 2 drives have an uncompressed capacity of 200GB (400GB at 2:1 compression) and transfer rates of 40MBps–80MBps. Both types of drives also have special features such as dynamic power-down (protects tapes from damage during a power interruption), intelligent data compression, intelligent media analysis to avoid suspect tape areas, and variable tape speed to minimize back-hitching (moving the tape backward because of a data underrun). Ultrium drives are popular in both single-drive and tape-library formats, although they are quite expensive: Basic single-cartridge Ultrium Generation 1 units start at around $3,500, with 100GB (uncompressed) cartridges selling for about $40 each. Ultrium Generation 2 cartridges sell for about $80 each.

- *Accelis.* This proposed implementation of LTO is optimized for very high speeds, using a dual-reel cartridge that enables tape to be loaded from the mid-point instead of the beginning. It has a native capacity of 25GB (50GB at 2:1 compression) and features cartridge memory (used to retrieve data about the cartridge's previous use to make locating data faster) and throughput of 20MB–40MB per second. Because Ultrium drives achieve the same speeds at much higher capacities, it's no surprise that Accelis appears to be an on-paper variation at this point, with no drives on the market using this variation on LTO.

Comparing Tape Backup Technologies

As the preceding sections indicate, you have many choices in large, high-performance tape backup. All the drive technologies discussed in this section use various SCSI interface versions and can be purchased as internal or external drives; some are also available with USB 2.0 or IEEE 1394a interfaces. Even though they are more expensive than Travan drives, they offer the capacities needed by today's larger hard drives.

Unlike the confusing backward-compatibility picture for QIC-family drives, the more advanced drives in each family are backward compatible with smaller drives.

Table 12.4 summarizes the performance and other characteristics of these tape technologies and compares them to Travan NS20 and 40GB drives. The prices of the tape drives vary tremendously depending on which version of SCSI is selected, whether the drive is internal or external, and whether a single-tape or tape-library drive is selected. The standards shown in Table 12.4 are listed in order by native capacity. All drive interfaces are SCSI, except as noted. Maximum prices listed are for the most expensive single-drive SCSI interface model except as noted; most models of a given drive will be cheaper, depending on the SCSI version supported, whether the drive is sold bare or as a kit, and whether it is internal (less expensive) or external.

Table 12.4   High-Performance Tape Backup Standards Compared

Drive Type	Capacity/2:1 Compressed	Backup Speed (Native/Compressed)	Drive Price Range	Media Cost
Travan NS20	10GB/20GB	1–2MBps	under $250	around $40
DAT DDS-3	12GB/24GB	1.1–2.2MBps	around $600	around $7
Travan 40GB	20GB/40GB	2–4MBps ATA 1–2MBps USB 2	under $350 around $430	around $45 around $45
DAT DDS-4	20GB/40GB	2–4.8MBps	around $700	around $14
SLR 7	20GB/40GB	3–6MBps	under $800	around $50
DLT 4000	20GB/40GB	1.5–3MBps	around $1,500	around $40
SLR 50	25GB/50GB	2–4MBps	around $1,300	around $80
SLR 60	30GB/60GB		around $960	around $70
VXA-1	33GB/66GB	3–6MBps	under $750	around $67 (33/66GB); around $40 (20/40GB); around $30 (12/24GB)
AIT-1	35GB/70GB	3–6MBps	under $900	around $50
DAT72	36GB/72GB	3.5–7MBps	around $1,200	around $30
DLT 8000	40GB/80GB	3–6MBps	around $1,700	around $50
SLR 100	50GB/100GB	5–10MBps	around $1,400	around $80
AIT-2	50GB/100GB	6–12MBps	under $1,400	around $55
VXA-2	80GB/160GB	6–12MBps	around $1,000	around $90

From Table 12.4, you can see that the Travan NS20 drives are among the least expensive SCSI-based drives to purchase, but the cost per MB for media is much lower with DAT/DDS drives. The performance is higher with all 20GB and up drives of other types. For an individual computer or small network server, the DDS-3, DDS-4, DAT72, SLR 7, VXA-1, and VXA-2 drive families represent the best balance of initial cost, performance, and media cost per MB. DLT and AIT drives are better choices for larger network server backup, especially if purchased in their more expensive tape-library forms (not listed).

Note

To learn more about DAT, DLT, and Exabyte 8mm tape drives, see *Upgrading and Repairing PCs, 11th Edition*, which is included in printable PDF format on the disc accompanying this book.

Choosing a Tape Backup Drive

Choosing a tape backup drive can be a simple job if you need to back up a single standalone system with a relatively small hard drive. The decision becomes more complex if the system has a larger hard drive or if you must back up a desktop system as well as a laptop. Choosing a tape backup drive type can be an even more complex program if you must back up a network server's hard drives and perhaps even back up the workstations from the server. As you ponder which backup tape drive you should select, consider the following factors:

- The amount of data you must back up
- The interfaces your equipment supports
- The data throughput you need
- The tape standard that is best for your needs

- The cost of the drive and tapes
- The capabilities and compatibility of the included driver and backup software
- Support for disaster recovery

By balancing the considerations of price, capacity, throughput, compatibility, and tape standard, you can find a tape drive that best meets your needs.

Note

When purchasing a tape backup drive, take the time to look through magazines in which dealers or distributors advertise. Several publications specialize in PCs and carry advertising from many hardware and software distributors. I recommend publications such as *Computer Reseller News* and *Computer Shopper*. CNet's online shopping service (`http://shopper.cnet.com`) can help you locate multiple sources for both popular and rare items quickly.

These publications cater to people or companies willing to go around the middlemen and buy direct. By reading such publications, you can get an excellent idea of the drives available and the price you can expect to pay.

While reading about drive capabilities and prices, don't neglect to read reviews of the software included with each drive. Verify that the software capabilities match your expectations and needs. This is especially important if you intend to use the drive on a non–Windows system because most backup software today is tailored for Windows. If you are not satisfied with the backup software included with a backup drive, check with the vendor to see whether a bare drive (no software) is available; then check with your preferred backup software vendor to verify that the drive you prefer is supported.

Capacity

The first rule for selecting a tape backup drive is to buy a drive with a capacity large enough for your needs, both now and for the foreseeable future. The ideal is to buy a drive with enough capacity so you can start your backup software, insert a blank tape in the drive, walk away from the system, and find the backup completed when you return. Because tape backups are generally rated by their maximum (2:1 compression) capacities—which is seldom reached in practice—you should calculate the "true" size of a tape backup drive by multiplying the native (noncompressed) capacity of a drive by 1.5 (equal to rating the drive as 1.5:1 compression). Thus, a so-called "20GB" tape backup might be better described as having a "15GB" capacity (10GB uncompressed times 1.5). Of course, the compressed capacity of a drive depends on the backup software you use, the settings you use, and the type of data you back up. Already compressed data, such as Zip archives, JPEG and GIF, and some types of TIFF graphics files, can't be compressed further, whereas text and database files can be compressed significantly. If you find that you have higher or lower compression ratios during backup, use the compression ratio you normally achieve to help estimate your true backup capacity.

You should always ensure that your tape backup medium supports a capacity larger than your largest single drive or partition. This makes automated backups possible because you won't have to change a tape in the middle of a backup. And, even if you don't mind replacing tapes in the middle of a backup, a single-tape backup is safer. If the first tape of a multiple-tape backup is damaged or lost, the entire backup is unusable with most backup systems!

Tape Standards and Compatibility

The next most important consideration, after adequate capacity, is choosing a drive whose tapes meet a standard that is useful to you. If you have existing tapes you want to restore, or you receive tapes from other users that you must read, you need a drive that can work with those tapes. Use the backward-compatibility information listed earlier to help you decide on a drive to purchase if this feature is important to you.

If your ability to work with older tape media is only an occasional issue, you might prefer to buy a high-performance drive for current backups and maintain an older drive that matches the older standard. Most Travan-type and QIC-Wide drives can read QIC-80 tape cartridges, for example.

Tip

It is important that you make a choice you can live with. If you manage a large installation of computers, mixing QIC, Travan, DAT, and 8mm drives among systems is seldom a good idea.

Software Compatibility

Equally important to your consideration is the software required to operate each drive. Currently, most parallel port and ATA drives come with software that runs under Windows operating system versions from 98 to XP. SCSI tape drives usually also support Windows NT, Windows 2000/XP, or Unix. USB-based drives are primarily designed for Windows 98/Me/2000/XP, although Windows 2000/XP might not support as many devices as Windows 9x/Me does. Check the manufacturers' Web sites for operating system compliance if your office's computers use more than one operating system.

Most operating systems have their own software for backing up data to a tape drive. If you intend to use this software, you should verify that the drive you purchase is supported by each piece of software on each system you intend to use with the drive. Third-party programs usually offer more features, but you might need to buy separate programs for the various operating systems your office uses.

Data Throughput

Any of the ATA, IEEE 1394a, Hi-Speed USB, or SCSI interface drives covered earlier should provide adequate performance (1MBps or above when backing up compressed data), but performance suffers if you opt for the convenience of USB 1.1 or parallel port drives. Floppy-interface QIC, QIC-Wide, and Travan drives should be considered obsolete for large-drive backups because of the limitations of the floppy interface and their small capacities.

Cost

You can figure the cost per MB for a drive in two ways: media cost only (which is valid for users with an existing drive) or drive plus media costs (which is a better method for new purchasers). Regardless of your favorite choice(s) in removable storage, be sure to look at the total picture, taking into account the savings from multipack data and the benefits of the extra speed of SCSI and ATA.

Tip

One point worth remembering when you evaluate whether to buy a tape drive is that the cost of the tapes and drive, taken as a whole, is nowhere near as high as the costs (in terms of frustration and lost productivity) of a single data-damaging hard drive problem. Considering that most people are more likely to back up a system if they have a tape drive installed than if they must use another medium for the backup, the cost of a drive and tapes is quite small, even on a standalone PC used mostly for fun.

Support for Disaster Recovery

Disaster recovery, which enables you to create a tape backup and floppy disk set that can be used to reinstall an entire operating system and data file set without installing Windows first, is a function of both the backup software and the drive interface. Disaster recovery is supported with most backup programs, but drives that connect to the USB or IEEE 1394a interfaces cannot support disaster recovery because they use Windows drivers. Because a disaster recovery data restore process starts in the MS-DOS mode, these drives can't be accessed because DOS lacks drivers for these ports.

Tape Drive Installation

Because most tape drives today use the same ATA, SCSI, USB, or parallel-port connection options that are used by other types of storage devices, you should see the appropriate sections of this book for more details about these devices:

- Chapter 14, "Physical Drive Installation and Configuration," provides detailed instructions for installing hard drives, floppy drives, and CD drives.
- Chapter 7 provides exhaustive coverage of the ATA interface.
- Chapter 8 provides detailed coverage of the SCSI interface.
- Chapter 17 provides information on USB and serial interfaces.

Note

For more details about installing the older floppy-interface tape backup drives, see *Upgrading and Repairing PCs, 11th Edition*, available in printable PDF format on the disc included with this book.

Tape Drive Backup Software

The most important decision you can make after you choose the tape standard and capacity of your backup tape drive is the backup software you will use with it.

The three sources for tape backup software are

- Software bundled with the drive
- Software bundled with the operating system
- Software obtainable from third parties

Use the following checklist to evaluate the software you plan to use with your tape backup drive:

- *Device support.* You might prefer to use tape for most backups, but can you change your mind and use high-capacity removable magnetic or optical storage if you need to? Some backup software bundled with a particular drive will work only with that drive; check whether a full version with more options is available.
- *Compatibility with existing backups.* If you have replaced an older tape drive with a new one, can the backup software as well as the tape drive read your old data?
- *Adjustable compression options.* If you are using a drive without hardware data compression, you should be able to adjust the compression methods used, or even turn them off to make sending the tape to the user of another drive easier.
- *Data safety options.* In addition to verification, good tape software should also include some form of ECC error correction to make recovering the data in case of media damage easier.
- *Disaster recovery.* Many bundled or operating-system-standard backup programs require you to reinstall the operating system before you can restore the contents of a crashed drive. Insist on a disaster recovery feature that will allow you to restore a drive from bootable disks and the tape

backup without taking the time to reinstall the operating system first. Keep in mind that you need to verify that the tape drive and interface support disaster recovery. If you want to use a USB or an IEEE 1394a drive for disaster recovery, you usually need to make a boot disk or CD with disaster-recovery software that supports these interfaces. Some backup programs support only SCSI or ATAPI drives for disaster recovery.

Other useful features to look for include

- *Unattended backup scheduling.* Enables you to schedule a backup for a time when you won't need to use your computer. You might be able to use the scheduling features in Windows if the software itself lacks this option.

- *Macro capability.* Use when selecting options and the files to back up.

- A *quick tape-erase capability.* Use when erasing the entire contents of a tape.

- *Partial tape-erase capability.* Use when erasing only part of a tape.

- *Tape unerase capability.* Use when recovering erased data.

- *Password-protect capability.* Enables you to protect backup data from access by unauthorized persons.

Read reviews, check compatibility, look for trial versions, and be sure to test the backup and restore features as you look for the best tape backup program for your needs.

Tip

Backup software vendor Novastor (`www.novastor.com`) has a unique solution for a major problem caused by moving from an older backup system to a new one: What to do with the data on the older tapes? Its TapeCopy 2.1 software enables you to move data archives from your outmoded SCSI, ATA/IDE, USB, or FireWire tape backup to a new SCSI- or ATA-based backup system. You can also use it to make hard disk copies of your tapes and to duplicate a backup tape on a similar drive. If you have extensive backup data and don't want to retain your old tape backup drive, TapeCopy 2.1 might be the answer. See the Web site for specific model compatibility and to download a trial version.

Tape Drive Troubleshooting

Tape drives can be troublesome to install and operate. Any type of removable media is more susceptible to problems or damage, and tape is no exception. This section lists some common problems and resolutions. After each problem or symptom is a list of troubleshooting steps.

Can't detect the drive:

- For parallel port drives, use the tape backup as the only device on the drive and check the IEEE 1284 (EPP or ECP) mode required by the drive against the parallel port configuration.

- For USB drives, be sure you're using Windows 98 or higher and that the USB port is enabled in the BIOS; many systems originally shipped with Windows 95 have this port disabled. Check the USB port by connecting another device (such as a flash memory card reader or a Webcam) to the port.

- For ATA drives, ensure that the master/slave jumpers on both drives are set properly.

- For SCSI drives, check termination and Device ID numbers.

- For external drives of any type, ensure that the drive is turned on a few seconds before starting the system. If not, you might be able to use the Windows Device Manager to refresh the list of devices, but if this doesn't work, you must restart the computer.

Backup or restore operation failure:

If your tape drive suffers a backup or restore operation failure, follow these steps:

1. Make sure you are using the correct type of tape cartridge.
2. Remove and replace the cartridge.
3. Restart the system.
4. Retension the tape.
5. Try a new tape.
6. Clean the tape heads.
7. Make sure all cables are securely connected.
8. Rerun the confidence test that checks data-transfer speed with a blank tape (this test overwrites any data already on the tape).

Bad block or other tape media errors:

To troubleshoot bad block or other types of media errors, follow these steps:

1. Retension the tape.
2. Clean the heads.
3. Try a new tape.
4. Restart the system.
5. Try initializing the tape.
6. Perform a secure erase on the tape (previous data will no longer be retrievable from the tape).

Caution

Note that most minicartridge tapes are preformatted and can't be reformatted by your drive. Do not attempt to bulk-erase preformatted tape because this renders the tapes unusable.

System lockup or system freezing when running a tape backup:

If your system locks up or freezes while running a tape backup, follow these steps:

1. Ensure that your system meets at least the minimum requirements for both the tape drive and the backup software.
2. Check for driver or resource (IRQ, DMA, or I/O port address) conflicts with your tape drive controller card or interface; using the floppy drive while making a floppy or parallel port tape backup is a major cause of DMA conflicts.
3. Set the CD-ROM to master and the tape drive to slave if both are using the same ATA port.
4. Check the BIOS boot sequence; ensure that it is not set to ATAPI (tape/CD-ROM) devices if the tape drive is configured as a master device or as a slave with no master.
5. Make sure the hard drive has sufficient free space; most backup programs temporarily use hard drive space as a buffer for data transfer.
6. Hard drive problems can cause the backup software to lock up. Check your hard disk for errors with SCANDISK or a comparable utility.
7. Check for viruses.

8. Check for previous tape drive installations; ensure that any drivers from previous installations are removed.

9. Temporarily disable the current VGA driver and test with the standard 640×480×16 VGA driver supplied by Microsoft; in Windows 2000/XP, start the computer in VGA mode. If the problem does not recur, contact your graphics board manufacturer for an updated video driver.

10. Empty the Recycle Bin before attempting a backup. Files in some third-party Recycle Bins can cause backup software to lock up.

11. Disable antivirus programs and Advanced Power Management.

12. Try the tape drive on another computer system and different operating system, or try swapping the drive, card, and cable with known-good, working equipment.

Other tape drive problems:

Other issues that might cause problems in general with tape backups include

- Corrupted data or ID information on the tape.
- Incorrect BIOS (CMOS) settings.
- Networking problems (outdated network drivers and so on).
- A tape that was recorded by another tape drive. If the other drive can still read the tape, this might indicate a head-alignment problem or incompatible environment.

Tape Retensioning

Retensioning a tape is the process of fast-forwarding and then rewinding the tape to ensure that there is even tension on the tape and rollers throughout the entire tape travel. Retensioning is recommended as a preventive maintenance operation when using a new tape or after an existing tape has been exposed to temperature changes or shock (for example, dropping the tape). Retensioning restores the proper tension to the media and removes unwanted tight spots that can develop.

Some general rules for retensioning include the following:

- Retension any tapes that have not been used for more than a month or two.
- Retension tapes if you have errors reading them.
- Retension any tapes that have been dropped.
- In some cases, you might need to perform the retension operation several times to achieve the proper effect. Most tape drive or backup software includes a Retension feature as a menu selection.

CHAPTER 13

Optical Storage

Optical Technology

There are basically two types of disk storage for computers: magnetic and optical. *Magnetic* storage is represented by the standard floppy and hard disks installed in most PC systems, where the data is recorded magnetically on rotating disks. *Optical* disc storage is similar to magnetic disk storage in basic operation, but it reads and records using light (optically) instead of magnetism. Although most magnetic disk storage is fully read- and write-capable many times over, many optical storage media are either read-only or write-once. Note the convention in which we refer to magnetic as *disk* and optical as *disc*. This is not a law or rule but seems to be followed by most in the industry.

Some media combine magnetic and optical techniques, using either an optical guidance system (called a laser servo) to position a magnetic read/write head (as in the LS-120/LS-240 SuperDisk floppy drive) or a laser to heat the disk so it can be written magnetically, thus polarizing areas of the track, which can then be read by a lower-powered laser, as in magneto-optical (MO) drives. These technologies are covered in Chapter 12, "High-Capacity Removable Storage."

At one time, it was thought that optical storage would replace magnetic as the primary online storage medium. However, optical storage has proven to be much slower and far less dense than magnetic storage and is much more adaptable to removable-media designs. As such, optical storage is more often used for backup or archival storage purposes and as a mechanism by which programs or data can be loaded onto magnetic drives. Magnetic storage, being significantly faster and capable of holding much more information than optical media in the same amount of space, is more suited for direct online storage and most likely won't be replaced in that role by optical storage anytime soon.

The most promising development in the optical area is that CD-RW (compact disc-rewritable) or DVD+RW (DVD+rewritable) drives with EasyWrite (Mount Rainier) support are starting to replace the venerable floppy disk as the de facto standard, interchangeable, transportable drive and media of choice for PCs. In fact, some would say that has already happened. Most new systems today include a CD-RW drive, and some also include some type of rewritable DVD drive. Even though a floppy drive is also included with most systems, it is rarely used except for running tests; running diagnostics; or doing basic system maintenance, disk formatting, preparation for OS installation, or configuration.

Optical technology standards for computers can be divided into two major types:

- CD (CD-ROM, CD-R, CD-RW)
- DVD (DVD-ROM, DVD-RAM, DVD-RW, DVD-R, DVD+RW, DVD+R)

Both CD and DVD storage devices are descended from popular entertainment standards; CD-based devices can also play music CDs, and DVD-based devices can play the same DVD videos you can purchase or rent. However, computer drives that can use these types of media also offer many additional features.

In the following sections, you will learn how CD and DVD drives and media are similar, how they differ from each other, and how they can be used to enhance your storage and playback options.

CD-Based Optical Technology

The first type of optical storage that became a widespread computing standard is the CD-ROM. CD-ROM, or *compact disc read-only memory*, is an optical read-only storage medium based on the original CD-DA (digital audio) format first developed for audio CDs. Other formats, such as CD-R (CD-recordable) and CD-RW (CD-rewritable), are expanding the compact disc's capabilities by making it writable. As you will see later in this chapter, technologies such as DVD (digital versatile disc) enable you to store more data than ever on the same size disc.

CD-ROM drives have been considered standard equipment on most PCs for many years. The primary exceptions to this rule are *thin clients*—PCs intended for use only on networks and which normally lack drives of any type.

CD-ROM discs are capable of holding up to 74 or 80 minutes of high-fidelity audio (depending on the disc used). If used for data, the traditional 74-minute disc can hold up to 650MiB (or 682MB), whereas the newer 80-minute disc can hold up to 700MiB (or 737MB). A combination of music and data can be stored on one side (only the bottom is used) of a 120mm (4.72") diameter, 1.2mm (0.047") thick plastic disc.

CD-ROM has exactly the same form factor (physical shape and layout) of the familiar CD-DA audio compact disc and can, in fact, be inserted in a normal audio player. It usually isn't playable, though, because the player reads the subcode information for the track, which indicates that it is data and not audio. If it could be played, the result would be noise—unless audio tracks precede the data on the CD-ROM (see the section "Blue Book—CD EXTRA," later in this chapter). Accessing data from a CD-ROM using a computer is much faster than from a floppy disk but slower than a modern hard drive. The term *CD-ROM* refers to both the discs themselves and the drive that reads them.

Although only a few dozen CD-ROM discs, or titles, were published by 1988, currently hundreds of thousands of individual titles exist that contain data and programs ranging from worldwide agricultural statistics to preschool learning games. Individual businesses, local and federal government offices, and large corporations also publish thousands of their own limited-use titles. As one example, the storage space and expense that so many business offices once dedicated to the maintenance of a telephone book library can now be replaced by two discs containing the telephone listings for the entire United States.

CDs: A Brief History

In 1979, the Philips and Sony corporations joined forces to coproduce the CD-DA (Compact Disc-Digital Audio) standard. Philips had already developed commercial laserdisc players, and Sony had a decade of digital recording research under its belt. The two companies were poised for a battle—the introduction of potentially incompatible audio laser disc formats—when instead they came to terms on an agreement to formulate a single industry-standard digital audio technology.

Philips contributed most of the physical design, which was similar to the laserdisc format it had previously created with regards to using pits and lands on the disk that are read by a laser. Sony contributed the digital-to-analog circuitry, and especially the digital encoding and error-correction code designs.

In 1980, the companies announced the CD-DA standard, which has since been referred to as the Red Book format (so named because the cover of the published document was red). The Red Book included the specifications for recording, sampling, and—above all—the 120mm (4.72") diameter physical format you live with today. This size was chosen, legend has it, because it could contain all of Beethoven's approximately 70-minute Ninth Symphony without interruption.

After the specification was set, both manufacturers were in a race to introduce the first commercially available CD audio drive. Because of its greater experience with digital electronics, Sony won that race and beat Philips to market by one month, when on October 1, 1982 Sony introduced the CDP-101 player and the world's first commercial CD recording—Billy Joel's *52nd Street* album. The player was first introduced in Japan and then Europe; it wasn't available in the United States until early 1983. In 1984, Sony also introduced the first automobile and portable CD players.

Sony and Philips continued to collaborate on CD standards throughout the decade, and in 1983 they jointly released the Yellow Book CD-ROM standard. It turned the CD from a digital audio storage medium to one that could now store read-only data for use with a computer. The Yellow Book used the same physical format as audio CDs but modified the decoding electronics to allow data to be stored reliably. In fact, all subsequent CD standards (usually referred to by their colored book binders) have referred back to the original Red Book standard for the physical parameters of the disc. With the advent of the Yellow Book standard (CD-ROM), what originally was designed to hold a symphony could now be used to hold practically any type of information or software.

For more information on the other CD book formats, see the section "Compact Disc and Drive Formats" later in this chapter.

CD-ROM Construction and Technology

Although identical in appearance to CD-DAs, CD-ROMs store data instead of (or in addition to) audio. The CD-ROM drives in PCs that read the data discs are almost identical to audio CD players, with the main changes in the circuitry to provide additional error detection and correction. This is to ensure data is read without errors because what would be a minor—if not unnoticeable—glitch in a song would be unacceptable as missing data in a file.

A CD is made of a polycarbonate wafer, 120mm in diameter and 1.2mm thick, with a 15mm hole in the center. This wafer base is stamped or molded with a single physical track in a spiral configuration starting from the inside of the disc and spiraling outward. The track has a pitch, or spiral separation, of 1.6 microns (millionths of a meter, or thousandths of a millimeter). By comparison, an LP record has a physical track pitch of about 125 microns. When viewed from the reading side (the bottom), the disc rotates counterclockwise. If you examined the spiral track under a microscope, you would see that along the track are raised bumps, called *pits*, and flat areas between the pits, called *lands*. It seems strange to call a raised bump a *pit*, but that is because when the discs are pressed, the stamper works from the top side. So, from that perspective, the pits are actually depressions made in the plastic.

The laser used to read the disc would pass right through the clear plastic, so the stamped surface is coated with a reflective layer of metal (usually aluminum) to make it reflective. Then, the aluminum is coated with a thin protective layer of acrylic lacquer, and finally a label or printing is added.

Caution

CD-ROM media should be handled with the same care as a photographic negative. The CD-ROM is an optical device and degrades as its optical surface becomes dirty or scratched. Also it is important to note that, although discs are read from the bottom, the layer containing the track is actually much closer to the top of the disc because the protective lacquer overcoat is only 6–7 microns thick. Writing on the top surface of a disc with a ballpoint pen, for example, will easily damage the recording underneath. You need to be careful even when using a marker to write on the disc. The inks and solvents used in some markers can damage the print and lacquer overcoat on the top of the disc, and subsequently the information layer right below. The important thing is to treat both sides of the disc carefully, especially the top (label) side.

Mass-Producing CD-ROMs

Commercial mass-produced CDs are stamped or pressed and not burned by a laser as many people believe (see Figure 13.1). Although a laser is used to etch data onto a glass master disc that has been coated with a photosensitive material, using a laser to directly burn discs would be impractical for the reproduction of hundreds or thousands of copies.

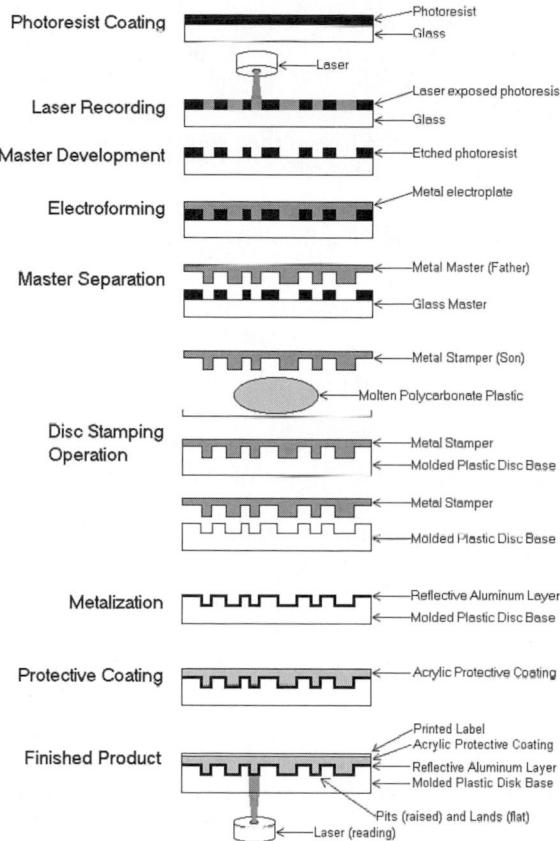

Photoresist Coating — Photoresist, Glass

Laser Recording — Laser, Laser exposed photoresist, Glass

Master Development — Etched photoresist

Electroforming — Metal electroplate

Master Separation — Metal Master (Father), Glass Master

Disc Stamping Operation — Metal Stamper (Son), Molten Polycarbonate Plastic, Metal Stamper, Molded Plastic Disc Base, Metal Stamper, Molded Plastic Disc Base

Metalization — Reflective Aluminum Layer, Molded Plastic Disc Base

Protective Coating — Acrylic Protective Coating

Finished Product — Printed Label, Acrylic Protective Coating, Reflective Aluminum Layer, Molded Plastic Disk Base, Pits (raised) and Lands (flat), Laser (reading)

Figure 13.1 CD manufacturing process.

The steps in manufacturing CDs are as follows (use Figure 13.1 as a visual):

1. *Photoresist Coating.* A circular 240mm diameter piece of polished glass 6mm thick is spin-coated with a photoresist layer about 150 microns thick and then hardened by baking at 80°C (176°F) for 30 minutes.

2. *Laser Recording.* A Laser Beam Recorder (LBR) fires pulses of blue/violet laser light to expose and soften portions of the photoresist layer on the glass master.

3. *Master Development.* A sodium hydroxide solution is spun over the exposed glass master, which then dissolves the areas exposed to the laser, thus etching pits in the photoresist.

4. *Electroforming.* The developed master is then coated with a layer of nickel alloy through a process called *electroforming*. This creates a metal master called a *father*.

5. *Master Separation.* The metal master father is then separated from the glass master. The father is a metal master that can be used to stamp discs, and for short runs, it may in fact be used that way. However, because the glass master is damaged when the father is separated, and because a stamper can produce only a limited number of discs before it wears out, the father often is electroformed to create several reverse image *mothers*. These mothers are then subsequently electroformed to create the actual stampers. This enables many more discs to be stamped without ever having to go through the glass mastering process again.

6. *Disc Stamping Operation.* A metal stamper is used in an injection molding machine to press the data image (pits and lands) into approximately 18 grams of molten (350°C or 662°F) polycarbonate plastic with a force of about 20,000psi. Normally, one disc can be pressed every 2–3 seconds in a modern stamping machine.

7. *Metalization.* The clear stamped disc base is then sputter-coated with a thin (0.05–0.1 micron) layer of aluminum to make the surface reflective.

8. *Protective Coating.* The metalized disc is then spin-coated with a thin (6–7 micron) layer of acrylic lacquer, which is then cured with UV (ultraviolet) light. This protects the aluminum from oxidation.

9. *Finished Product.* Finally, a label is affixed or printing is screen-printed on the disc and cured with UV light.

This manufacturing process is identical for both data CD-ROMs and audio CDs.

Pits and Lands

Reading the information back from a disc is a matter of bouncing a low-powered laser beam off the reflective layer in the disc. The laser shines a focused beam on the underside of the disc, and a photosensitive receptor detects when the light is reflected back. When the light hits a land (flat spot) on the track, the light is reflected back; however, when the light hits a pit (raised bump), no light is reflected back.

As the disc rotates over the laser and receptor, the laser shines continuously while the receptor sees what is essentially a pattern of flashing light as the laser passes over pits and lands. Each time the laser passes over the edge of a pit, the light seen by the receptor changes in state from being reflected to not reflected or vice versa. Each change in state of reflection caused by crossing the edge of a pit is translated into a 1 bit digitally. Microprocessors in the drive translate the light/dark and dark/light (pit edge) transitions into 1 bits, translate areas with no transitions into 0 bits, and then translate the bit patterns into actual data or sound.

The individual pits on a CD are 0.125 microns deep and 0.6 microns wide. Both the pits and lands vary in length from about 0.9 microns at their shortest to about 3.3 microns at their longest. The track is a spiral with 1.6 microns between adjacent turns (see Figure 13.2).

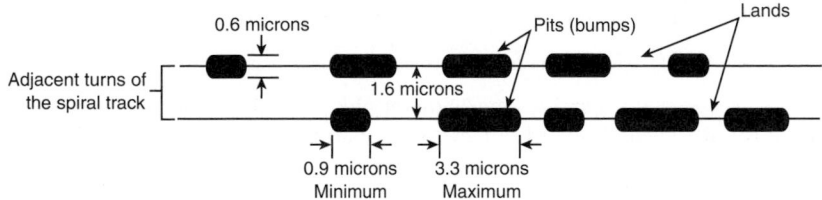

Figure 13.2   Pit, land, and track geometry on a CD.

The height of the pits above the land is especially critical as it relates to the wavelength of the laser light used when reading the disc. The pit (bump) height is exactly 1/4 of the wavelength of the laser light used to read the disc. Therefore, the light striking a land travels 1/2 of a wavelength of light farther than light striking the top of a pit (1/4 + 1/4 = 1/2). This means the light reflected from a pit is 1/2 wavelength out of phase with the rest of the light being reflected from the disc. The out-of-phase waves cancel each other out, dramatically reducing the light that is reflected back and making the pit appear dark even though it is coated with the same reflective aluminum as the lands.

The read laser in a CD drive is a 780nm (nanometer) wavelength laser of about 1 milliwatt in power. The polycarbonate plastic used in the disc has a refractive index of 1.55, so light travels through the plastic 1.55 times more slowly than through the air around it. Because the frequency of the light passing through the plastic remains the same, this has the effect of shortening the wavelength inside the plastic by the same factor. Therefore, the 780nm light waves are now compressed to 780/1.55 = 500nm. One quarter of 500nm is 125nm, which is 0.125 microns—the specified height of the pit.

Drive Mechanical Operation

A CD-ROM drive operates by using a laser to reflect light off the bottom of the disc. The reflected light is then read by a photo detector. The overall operation of a CD-ROM drive is as follows (see Figure 13.3):

1. The laser diode emits a low-energy infrared beam toward a reflecting mirror.

2. The servo motor, on command from the microprocessor, positions the beam onto the correct track on the CD-ROM by moving the reflecting mirror.

3. When the beam hits the disc, its refracted light is gathered and focused through the first lens beneath the platter, bounced off the mirror, and sent toward the beam splitter.

4. The beam splitter directs the returning laser light toward another focusing lens.

5. The last lens directs the light beam to a photo detector that converts the light into electric impulses.

6. These incoming impulses are decoded by the microprocessor and sent along to the host computer as data.

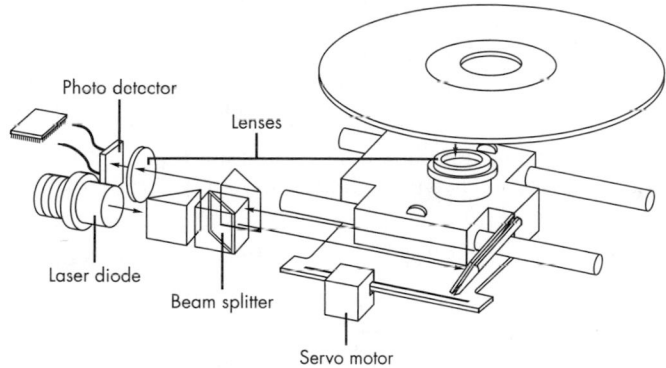

Figure 13.3   Typical components inside a CD-ROM drive.

When first introduced, CD-ROM drives were too expensive for widespread adoption. In addition, drive manufacturers were slow in adopting standards, causing a lag time for the production of CD-ROM titles. Without a wide base of software to drive the industry, acceptance was slow.

After the production costs of both drives and discs began to drop, however, CD-ROMs were rapidly assimilated into the PC world. This was particularly due to the ever-expanding size of PC applications. Virtually all software is now supplied on CD-ROM, even if the disc doesn't contain data representing a tenth of its potential capacity. As the industry stands now, if a software product requires more than one or two floppy disks, it is more economical to put it on a CD-ROM.

For large programs, the advantage is obvious. The Windows 98SE operating system would require more than 75 floppy disks, certainly an amount nobody would want to deal with.

Tracks and Sectors

The pits are stamped into a single spiral track with a spacing of 1.6 microns between turns, corresponding to a track density of 625 turns per millimeter, or 15,875 turns per inch. This equates to a total of 22,188 turns for a typical 74-minute (650MiB) disc. The disc is divided into six main areas (discussed here and shown in Figure 13.4):

■ *Hub clamping area.* The hub clamp area is just that: a part of the disc where the hub mechanism in the drive can grip the disc. No data or information is stored in that area.

■ *Power calibration area (PCA).* This is found only on writable (CD-R/RW) discs and is used only by recordable drives to determine the laser power necessary to perform an optimum burn. A single CD-R or CD-RW disc can be tested this way up to 99 times.

■ *Program memory area (PMA).* This is found only on writable (CD-R/RW) discs and is the area where the TOC (table of contents) is temporarily written until a recording session is closed. After the session is closed, the TOC information is written to the lead-in area.

■ *Lead-in.* The lead-in area contains the disc (or session) TOC in the Q subcode channel. The TOC contains the start addresses and lengths of all tracks (songs or data), the total length of the program (data) area, and information about the individual recorded sessions. A single lead-in area exists on a disc recorded all at once (Disc At Once or DAO mode), or a lead-in area starts each session on a multisession disc. The lead-in takes up 4,500 sectors on the disc (1 minute if measured in time, or about 9.2MB worth of data). The lead-in also indicates whether the disc is multisession and what the next writable address on the disc is (if the disc isn't closed).

■ *Program (data) area.* This area of the disc starts at a radius of 25mm from the center.

■ *Lead-out.* The lead-out marks the end of the program (data) area or the end of the recording session on a multisession disc. No actual data is written in the lead-out; it is simply a marker. The first lead-out on a disc (or the only one if it is a single session or Disk At Once recording) is 6,750 sectors long (1.5 minutes if measured in time, or about 13.8MB worth of data). If the disc is a multisession disc, any subsequent lead-outs are 2,250 sectors long (0.5 minutes in time, or about 4.6MB worth of data).

The hub clamp, lead-in, program, and lead-out areas are found on all CDs, whereas only recordable CDs (such as CD-Rs and CD-RWs) have the additional power calibration area and program memory area at the start of the disc.

Figure 13.4 shows these areas in actual relative scale as they appear on a disc.

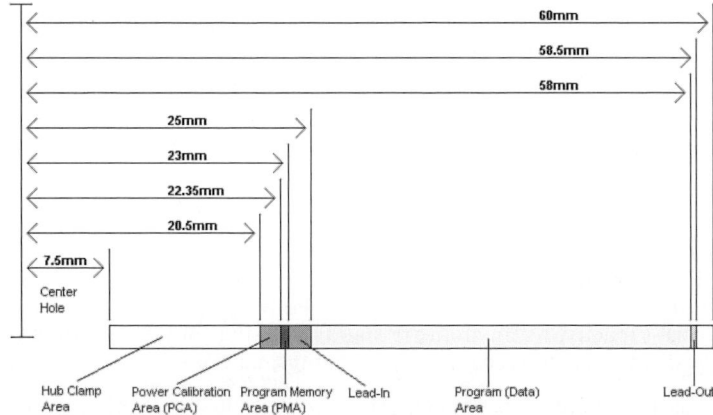

Figure 13.4 Areas on a CD (side view).

Officially, the spiral track of a standard CD-DA or CD-ROM disc starts with the lead-in area and ends at the finish of the lead-out area, which is 58.5mm from the center of the disc, or 1.5mm from the outer edge. This single spiral track is about 5.77 kilometers, or 3.59 miles, long. An interesting fact is that in a 56x CAV (constant angular velocity) drive, when reading the outer part of the track, the data moves at an actual speed of 162.8 miles per hour (262km/h) past the laser. What is more amazing is that even when the data is traveling at that speed, the laser pickup can accurately read bits (pit/land transitions) spaced as little as only 0.9 microns (or 35.4 millionths of an inch) apart!

Table 13.1 shows some of the basic information about the two main CD capacities, which are 74- and 80-minute. The CD standard originally was created around the 74-minute disc; the 80-minute versions were added later and basically stretch the standard by tightening up the track spacing within the limitations of the original specification. A poorly performing or worn out drive can have trouble reading the 80-minute discs.

Table 13.1 CD-ROM Technical Parameters

Advertised CD length (minutes)	74	80
Advertised CD capacity (MiB)	650	700
1x read speed (m/sec)	1.3	1.3
Laser wavelength (nm)	780	780
Numerical aperture (lens)	0.45	0.45
Media refractive index	1.55	1.55
Track (turn) spacing (um)	1.6	1.48
Turns per mm	625	676
Turns per inch	15,875	17,162
Total track length (m)	5,772	6,240
Total track length (feet)	18,937	20,472
Total track length (miles)	3.59	3.88
Pit width (urn)	0.6	0.6
Pit depth (um)	0.125	0.125
Min. nominal pit length (um)	0.90	0.90
Max. nominal pit length (um)	3.31	3.31
Lead-in inner radius (mm)	23	23
Data zone inner radius (mm)	25	25
Data zone outer radius (mm)	58	58
Lead-out outer radius (mm)	58.5	58.5
Data zone width (mm)	33	33
Total track area width (mm)	35.5	35.5
Max. rotating speed 1x CLV (rpm)	540	540
Min. rotating speed 1x CLV (rpm)	212	212
Track revolutions (data zone)	20,625	22,297
Track revolutions (total)	22,188	23,986

B = Byte (8 bits)
KB = Kilobyte (1,000 bytes)
KiB = Kibibyte (1,024 bytes)
MB = Megabyte (1,000,000 bytes)
MiB = Mebibyte (1,048,576 bytes)

m = Meters
mm = Millimeters (thousandths of a meter)
um = Micrometers = microns (millionths of a meter)
CLV = Constant linear velocity
rpm = Revolutions per minute

The spiral track is divided into sectors that are stored at the rate of 75 sectors per second. On a disc that can hold a total of 74 minutes of information, that results in a maximum of 333,000 sectors. Each sector is then divided into 98 individual frames of information. Each frame contains 33 bytes: 24 bytes are audio data, 1 byte contains subcode information, and 8 bytes are used for parity/ECC (error correction code) information. Table 13.2 shows the sector, frame, and audio data calculations.

Table 13.2   CD-ROM Sector, Frame, and Audio Data Information

Advertised CD length (minutes)	74	80
Sectors/second	75	75
Frames/sector	98	98
Number of sectors	333,000	360,000
Sector length (mm)	17.33	17.33
Byte length (um)	5.36	5.36
Bit length (um)	0.67	0.67
Each Frame:		
Subcode bytes	1	1
Data bytes	24	24
Q+P parity bytes	8	8
Total bytes/frame	33	33
Audio Data:		
Audio sampling rate (Hz)	44,100	44,100
Samples per Hz (stereo)	2	2
Sample size (bytes)	2	2
Audio bytes per second	176,400	176,400
Sectors per second	75	75
Audio bytes per sector	2,352	2,352
Each Audio Sector (98 Frames):		
Q+P parity bytes	784	784
Subcode bytes	98	98
Audio data bytes	2,352	2,352
Bytes/sector RAW (unencoded)	3,234	3,234

Hz = Hertz (cycles per second)
mm = Millimeters (thousandths of a meter)
um = Micrometers = microns (millionths of a meter)

Sampling

When music is recorded on a CD, it is sampled at a rate of 44,100 times per second (Hz). Each music sample has a separate left and right channel (stereo) component, and each channel component is digitally converted into a 16-bit number. This allows for a resolution of 65,536 possible values, which represents the amplitude of the sound wave for that channel at that moment.

The sampling rate determines the range of audio frequencies that can be represented in the digital recording. The more samples of a wave that are taken per second, the closer the sampled result will be to the original. The Nyquist theorem (originally published by American physicist Harry Nyquist in 1928) states that the sampling rate must be at least twice the highest frequency present in the sample to reconstruct the original signal accurately. That explains why Philips and Sony intentionally chose the 44,100Hz sampling rate when developing the CD—that rate could be used to accurately reproduce sounds of up to 20,000Hz, which is the upper limit of human hearing.

So, you can see that audio sectors combine 98 frames of 33 bytes each, which results in a total of 3,234 bytes per sector, of which only 2,352 bytes are actual audio data. Besides the 98 subcode bytes per frame, the other 784 bytes are used for parity and error correction.

Subcodes

Subcode bytes enable the drive to find songs (which are confusingly also called *tracks*) along the spiral track and also contain or convey additional information about the disc in general. The subcode bytes are stored as 1 byte per frame, which results in 98 subcode bytes for each sector. Two of these bytes are used as start block and end block markers, leaving 96 bytes of subcode information. These are then divided into eight 12-byte subcode blocks, each of which is assigned a letter designation P–W. Each subcode channel can hold about 31.97MB of data across the disc, which is about 4% of the capacity of an audio disc. The interesting thing about the subcodes is that the data is woven continuously throughout the disc; in other words, subcode data is contained piecemeal in every sector on the disc.

The P and Q subcode blocks are used on all discs, and the R–W subcodes are used only on CD+G (graphics) or CD TEXT–type discs.

The P subcode is used to identify the start of the tracks on the CD. The Q subcode contains a multitude of information, including

- *Whether the sector data is audio (CD-DA) or data (CD-ROM).* This prevents most players from trying to "play" CD-ROM data discs, which might damage speakers due to the resulting noise that would occur.
- *Whether the audio data is two or four channel.* Four channel is rarely if ever used.
- *Whether digital copying is permitted.* PC-based CD-R and RW drives ignore this; it was instituted to prevent copying to DAT (digital audio tape) or home audio CD-R/RW drives.
- *Whether the music is recorded with pre-emphasis.* This is a hiss or noise reduction technique.
- *The track (song) layout on the disc.*
- *The track (song) number.*
- *The minutes, seconds, and frame number from the start of the track (song).*
- *A countdown during an intertrack (intersong) pause.*
- *The minutes, seconds, and frames from the start of the first track (song).*
- *The barcode of the CD.*
- *The ISRC (International Standard Recording Code).* This is unique to each track (song) on the disc.

The R-W subcodes are used on CD+G (graphics) discs to contain graphics and text. This enables a limited amount of graphics and text to be displayed while the music is being played. These same subcodes are used on CD TEXT discs to store disc- and track-related information that is added to standard audio CDs for playback on compatible CD audio players. The CD TEXT information is stored as ASCII characters in the R-W channels in the lead-in and program areas of a CD. On a CD TEXT disc, the lead-in area subcodes contain text information about the entire disc, such as the album, track (song) titles, and artist names. The program area subcodes, on the other hand, contain text information for the current track (song), including track title, composer, performers, and so on. The CD TEXT data is repeated throughout each track to reduce the delay in retrieving the data.

CD TEXT–compatible players typically have a text display to show this information, ranging from a simple one- or two-line, 20-character display such as on many newer RBDS (radio broadcast data system) automobile radio/CD players to up to 21 lines of 40-color, alphanumeric or graphics characters on home- or computer-based players. The specification also allows for future additional data, such as Joint Photographics Expert Group (JPEG) images. Interactive menus also can be used for the selection of text for display.

Handling Read Errors

Handling errors when reading a disc was a big part of the original Red Book CD standard. CDs use parity and interleaving techniques called *cross-interleave Reed-Solomon code (CIRC)* to minimize the effects of errors on the disk. This works at the frame level. When being stored, the 24 data bytes in each frame are first run through a Reed-Solomon encoder to produce a 4-byte parity code called "Q" parity, which then is added to the 24 data bytes. The resulting 28 bytes are then run though another encoder that uses a different scheme to produce an additional 4-byte parity value called "P" parity. These are added to the 28 bytes from the previous encoding, resulting in 32 bytes (24 of the original data plus the Q and P parity bytes). An additional byte of subcode (tracking) information is then added, resulting in 33 bytes total for each frame. Note that the P and Q parity bytes are not related to the P and Q subcodes mentioned earlier.

To minimize the effects of a scratch or physical defect that would damage adjacent frames, several interleaves are added before the frames are actually written. Parts of 109 frames are cross-interleaved (stored in different frames and sectors) using delay lines. This scrambling decreases the likelihood of a scratch or defect affecting adjacent data because the data is actually written out of sequence.

With audio CDs and CD-ROMs, the CIRC scheme can correct errors up to 3,874 bits long (which would be 2.6mm in track length). In addition, for audio CDs, only the CIRC can also conceal (through interpolation) errors up to 13,282 bits long (8.9mm in track length). Interpolation is the process in which the data is estimated or averaged to restore what is missing. That would of course be unacceptable on a CD-ROM data disc, so this applies only to audio discs. The Red Book CD standard defines the *block error rate (BLER)* as the number of frames (98 per sector) per second that have any bad bits (averaged over 10 seconds) and requires that this be less than 220. This allows a maximum of up to about 3% of the frames to have errors, and yet the disc will still be functional.

An additional layer of error detection and correction circuitry is the key difference between audio CD players and CD-ROM drives. Audio CDs convert the digital information stored on the disc into analog signals for a stereo amplifier to process. In this scheme, some imprecision is acceptable because it would be virtually impossible to hear in the music. CD-ROMs, however, can't tolerate any imprecision. Each bit of data must be read accurately. For this reason, CD-ROM discs have a great deal of additional ECC information written to the disc along with the actual stored information. The ECC can detect and correct most minor errors, improving the reliability and precision to levels that are acceptable for data storage.

In the case of an audio CD, missing data can be interpolated—that is, the information follows a predictable pattern that enables the drive to guess the missing values. For example, if three values are stored on an audio disc, say 10, 13, and 20 appearing in a series, and the middle value is missing—because of damage or dirt on the CD's surface—you could interpolate a middle value of 15, which is midway between 10 and 20. Although this might not be exactly correct, in the case of audio recording, it probably won't be noticeable to the listener. If those same three values appear on a CD-ROM in an executable program, there is no way to guess at the correct value for the middle sample. Interpolation can't work because executable program instructions or data must be exact; otherwise, the program will crash or improperly read data needed for a calculation. Using the previous example with a CD-ROM running an executable program, guessing 15 is not merely slightly off—it is completely wrong.

In a CD-ROM on which data is stored instead of audio information, additional information is added to each sector to detect and correct errors as well as to identify the location of data sectors more accurately. To accomplish this, 304 bytes are taken from the 2,352 that originally were used for audio data and are instead used for sync (synchronizing bits), ID (identification bits), ECC, and EDC information. This leaves

2,048 bytes for actual user data in each sector. Just as when reading an audio CD, on a 1x (standard speed) CD-ROM, sectors are read at a constant speed of 75 per second. This results in a standard CD-ROM transfer rate of 2,048 × 75 = 153,600 bytes per second, which is expressed as either 153.6KBps or 150KiBps.

Note

Some of the copy protection schemes used on audio CDs intentionally interfere with the audio data and CIRC information in such a way as to make the disc appear to play correctly, but copies of the audio files or of the entire disc will be filled with noise. Copy protection for both audio and data CDs is discussed in more detail later in this chapter.

CD Capacity

Because a typical disc can hold a maximum of 74 minutes of data, and each second contains 75 blocks of 2,048 bytes each, you can calculate the absolute maximum storage capacity of a CD-ROM at 681,984,000 bytes—rounded as 682MB (megabytes) or 650MiB (mebibytes). Table 13.3 shows the structure and layout of each sector on a CD-ROM on which data is stored.

Table 13.3   CD-ROM Sector Information and Capacity

Each Data Sector (Mode 1):	74-Minute	80-Minute
Q+P parity bytes	784	784
Subcode bytes	98	98
Sync bytes	12	12
Header bytes	8	8
ECC/EDC bytes	284	284
Data bytes	2,048	2,048
Bytes/sector RAW (unencoded)	3,234	3,234
Actual CD-ROM Data Capacity:		
B	681,984,000	737,280,000
KiB	666,000	720,000
KB	681,984	737,280
MiB	650.39	703.13
MB	681.98	737.28

B = Byte (8 bits)
KB = Kilobyte (1,000 bytes)
KiB = Kibibyte (1,024 bytes)
MB = Megabyte (1,000,000 bytes)

MiB = Mebibyte (1,048,576 bytes)
ECC = Error correction code
EDC = Error detection code

This information assumes the data is stored in Mode 1 format, which is used on virtually all data discs. You can learn more about the Mode 1/Mode 2 formats in the section on the Yellow Book and XA standards later in this chapter.

With data sectors, you can see that out of 3,234 actual bytes per sector, only 2,048 are actual CD-ROM user data. Most of the 1,186 other bytes are used for the intensive error detection and correction schemes to ensure error-free performance.

Data Encoding on the Disc

The final part of how data is actually written to the CD is very interesting. After all 98 frames are composed for a sector (whether audio or data), the information is then run through a final encoding process called EFM (eight to fourteen modulation). This scheme takes each byte (8 bits) and converts it into a 14-bit value for storage. The 14-bit conversion codes are designed so that there are never fewer than 2 or more than 10 adjacent 0 bits. This is a form of Run Length Limited (RLL) encoding called RLL 2,10 (RLL x,y where x = the minimum and y = the maximum run of 0s). This is designed to prevent long strings of 0s, which could more easily be misread, as well as to limit the minimum and maximum frequency of transitions actually placed on the recording media. With as few as 2 or as many as 10 0 bits separating 1 bits in the recording, the minimum distance between 1s is 3 bit time intervals (usually referred to as 3T) and the maximum spacing between 1s is 11 time intervals (11T).

Because some of the EFM codes start and end with a 1 or more than five 0s, three additional bits called *merge bits* are added between each 14-bit EFM value written to the disc. The merge bits usually are 0s but might contain a 1 if necessary to break a long string of adjacent 0s formed by the adjacent 14-bit EFM values. In addition to the now 17-bits created for each byte (EFM plus merge bits), a 24-bit sync word (plus 3 more merge bits) is added to the beginning of each frame. This results in a total of 588 bits (73.5 bytes) actually being stored on the disc for each frame. Multiply this for 98 frames per sector and you have 7,203 bytes actually being stored on the disc to represent each sector. A 74-minute disc, therefore, really has something like 2.4GB of actual data being written, which after being fully decoded and stripped of error correcting codes and other information, results in about 682MB (650MiB) of actual user data.

The calculations for EFM-encoded frames and sectors are shown in Table 13.4.

Table 13.4 EFM-Encoded Data Calculations

EFM-Encoded Frames:	74-Minute	80-Minute
Sync word bits	24	24
Subcode bits	14	14
Data bits	336	336
Q+P parity bits	112	112
Merge bits	102	102
EFM bits per frame	588	588
EFM-Encoded Sectors:		
EFM bits per sector	57,624	57,624
EFM bytes per sector	7,203	7,203
Total EFM data on disc (MB)	2,399	2,593

B = Byte (8 bits)
KB = Kilobyte (1,000 bytes)
KiB = Kibibyte (1,024 bytes)
MB = Megabyte (1,000,000 bytes)
MiB = Mebibyte (1,048,576 bytes)
EFM = Eight to fourteen modulation

To put this into perspective, see Table 13.5 for an example of how familiar data would actually be encoded when written to a CD. As an example, I'll use the letters "N" and "O" as they would be written on the disk. Table 13.5 shows the digitally encoded representations of these letters.

Table 13.5   EFM Data Encoding on a CD

Character	"N"	"O"
ASCII decimal code	78	79
ASCII hexadecimal code	4E	4F
ASCII binary code	01001110	01001111
EFM code	00010001000100	00100001000100

ASCII = American Standard Code for Information Interchange
EFM = Eight to fourteen modulation

Figure 13.5 shows how the encoded data would actually appear as pits and lands stamped into a CD.

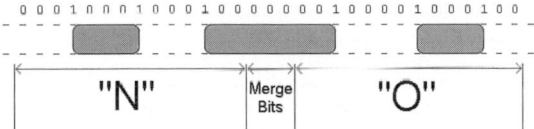

Figure 13.5   EFM data physically represented as pits and lands on a CD.

The edges of the pits are translated into the binary 1 bits. As you can see, each 14-bit grouping is used to represent a byte of actual EFM encoded data on the disc, and each 14-bit EFM code is separated by three merge bits (all 0s in this example). The three pits produced by this example are 4T (4 transitions), 8T, and 4T long. The string of 1s and 0s on the top of the figure represent how the actual data would be read; note that a 1 is read wherever a pit-to-land transition occurs. It is interesting to note that this drawing is actually to scale, meaning the pits (raised bumps) would be about that long and wide relative to each other. If you could use a microscope to view the disc, this is what the word "NO" would look like as actually recorded.

Caring for Optical Media

Some people believe that optical discs and drives are indestructible when compared to their magnetic counterparts. Actually, modern optical drives are far less reliable than modern hard disk drives. Reliability is the bane of any removable media, and CD-ROMs and DVD-ROMs are no exceptions.

By far the most common causes of problems with optical discs and drives are scratches, dirt, and other contamination. Small scratches or fingerprints on the bottom of the disc should not affect performance because the laser focuses on a point inside the actual disc, but dirt or deep scratches can interfere with reading a disc.

To remedy this type of problem, you can clean the bottom surface of the CD with a soft cloth, but be careful not to scratch the surface in the process. The best technique is to wipe the disc in a radial fashion, using strokes that start from the center of the disc and emanate toward the outer edge. This way, any scratches will be perpendicular to the tracks rather than parallel to them, minimizing the interference they might cause. You can use any type of solution on the cloth to clean the disc, so long as it will not damage plastic. Most window cleaners are excellent at removing fingerprints and other dirt from the disc and don't damage the plastic surface.

If your disc has deep scratches, they can often be buffed or polished out. A commercial plastic cleaner such as that sold in auto parts stores for cleaning plastic instrument cluster and tail-lamp lenses is very good for removing these types of scratches. This type of plastic polish or cleaner has a very mild abrasive that polishes scratches out of a plastic surface. Products labeled as cleaners usually are designed for more serious scratches, whereas those labeled as polishes are usually milder and work well as a final buff after using the cleaner. Polishes can be used alone if the surface is not scratched very deeply. The Skip Doctor device made by Digital Innovations (www.skipdoctor.com) can be used to make the polishing job easier.

Most people are careful about the bottom of the disc because that is where the laser reads, but the top is actually more fragile! This is because the lacquer coating on top of the disc is very thin, normally only 6–7 microns (0.24–0.28 thousandths of an inch). If you write on a disc with a ball point pen, for example, you will press through the lacquer layer and damage the reflective layer underneath, ruining the disc. Also, certain types of markers have solvents that can eat through the lacquer and damage the disc as well. You should write on discs only with felt tip pens that have compatible inks, such as the Sharpie or Staedtler Lumocolor brand, or other markers specifically sold for writing on CDs. In any case, remember that scratches or dents on the top of the disc are more fatal than those on the bottom.

Read errors can also occur when dust accumulates on the read lens of your CD-ROM drive. You can try to clean out the drive and lens with a blast of "canned air" or by using a drive cleaner (which can be purchased at most stores that sell audio CDs).

If your discs and your drive are clean, but you still can't read a particular disc, your trouble might be due to disc capacity. Many older CD-ROM drives are unreliable when they try to read the outermost tracks of newer discs where the last bits of data are stored. You're more likely to run into this problem with a CD that has a lot of data—including some multimedia titles. If you have this problem, you might be able to solve it with a firmware or driver upgrade for your CD-ROM drive, but the only solution might be to replace the drive.

Sometimes too little data on the disc can be problematic as well. Some older CD-ROM drives use an arbitrary point on the disc's surface to calibrate their read mechanism, and if there happens to be no data at that point on the disc, the drive will have problems calibrating successfully. Fortunately, this problem usually can be corrected by a firmware or driver upgrade for your drive.

Many older drives have had problems working under Windows 9x. If you are having problems, contact your drive manufacturer to see whether a firmware or software-driver upgrade is available that might take care of your problem. With new high-speed drives available for well under $100, it might not make sense to spend any time messing with an older drive that is having problems. It might be more cost-effective to upgrade to a new drive (which won't have these problems and will likely be much faster) instead.

If you have problems reading a particular brand or type of disk in some drives but not others, you might have a poor drive/media match. Use the media types and brands recommended by the drive vendor.

If you are having problems with only one particular disc and not the drive in general, you might find that your difficulties are in fact caused by a defective disc. See whether you can exchange the disc for another to determine whether that is indeed the cause.

DVD

DVD stands for digital versatile disc and in simplest terms is a high-capacity CD. In fact, every DVD-ROM drive *is* a CD-ROM drive; that is, they can read CDs as well as DVDs (many standalone DVD players can't read CD-R or CD-RW discs, however). DVD uses the same optical technology as CD, with the main difference being higher density. The DVD standard dramatically increases the storage capacity of, and therefore the useful applications for, CD-ROM-sized discs. A CD-ROM can hold a maximum of about 737MB (80-minute disc) of data, which might sound like a lot but is simply not enough for many up-and-coming applications, especially where the use of video is concerned. DVDs, on the other hand, can hold up to 4.7GB (single layer) or 8.5GB (dual layer) on a single side of the disc, which is more than 11 1/2 times greater than a CD. Double-sided DVDs can hold up to twice that amount, although you currently must manually flip the disc over to read the other side.

Up to two layers of information can be recorded to DVDs, with an initial storage capacity of 4.7GB of digital information on a single-sided, single-layer disc—a disk that is the same overall diameter and thickness of a current CD-ROM. With Moving Picture Experts Group–standard 2 (MPEG-2) compression, that's enough to contain approximately 133 minutes of video, which is enough for a full-length, full-screen, full-motion feature film—including three channels of CD-quality audio and four channels of subtitles. Using both layers, a single-sided disc could easily hold 240 minutes of video or more. This initial capacity is no coincidence; the creation of DVD was driven by the film industry, which has long sought a storage medium cheaper and more durable than videotape.

Note

It is important to know the difference between the DVD-Video and DVD-ROM standards. DVD-Video discs contain only video programs and are intended to be played in a DVD player connected to a television and possibly an audio system. DVD-ROM is a data storage medium intended for use by PCs and other types of computers. The distinction is similar to that between an audio CD and a CD-ROM. Computers might be capable of playing audio CDs as well as CD-ROMs, but dedicated audio CD players can't use a CD-ROM's data tracks. Likewise, computer DVD drives can play DVD-video discs (with MPEG-2 decoding in either hardware or software), but DVD video players can't access data on a DVD-ROM. This is the reason you must select the type of DVD you are trying to create when you make a writable or rewritable DVD.

The initial application for DVDs was as an upgrade for CDs as well as a replacement for prerecorded videotapes. DVDs can be rented or purchased like prerecorded VCR tapes, but they offer much higher resolution and quality with greater content. As with CDs, which initially were designed only for music, DVDs have since developed into a wider range of uses, including computer data storage and high-quality audio.

DVD History

DVD had a somewhat rocky start. During 1995, two competing standards for high-capacity CD-ROM drives were being developed to compete with each other for future market share. One standard, called Multimedia CD, was introduced and backed by Philips and Sony, whereas a competing standard, called the Super Density (SD) disc, was introduced and backed by Toshiba, Time Warner, and several other companies. If both standards had hit the market as is, consumers as well as entertainment and software producers would have been in a quandary over which one to choose.

Fearing a repeat of the Beta/VHS situation that occurred in the videotape market, several organizations, including the Hollywood Video Disc Advisory Group and the Computer Industry Technical Working Group, banded together to form a consortium to develop and control the DVD standard. The consortium insisted on a single format for the industry and refused to endorse either competing proposal. With this incentive, both groups worked out an agreement on a single, new, high-capacity CD-type disc in September 1995. The new standard combined elements of both previously proposed standards and was called DVD, which originally stood for digital video disc, but has since been changed to digital versatile disc. The single DVD standard has avoided a confusing replay of the VHS versus Beta tape fiasco for movie fans and has given the software, hardware, and movie industries a single, unified standard to support.

After agreeing on copy protection and other items, the DVD-ROM and DVD-Video standards were officially announced in late 1996. Players, drives, and discs were announced in January 1997 at the Consumer Electronics Show (CES) in Las Vegas, and the players and discs became available in March 1997. The initial players were about $1,000 each. Only 36 movies were released in the first wave, and they were available only in seven cities nationwide (Chicago, Dallas, Los Angeles, New York,

San Francisco, Seattle, and Washington, D.C.) until August 1997 when the full release began. After a somewhat rocky start (much had to do with agreements on copy protection to get the movie companies to go along, and there was a lack of titles available in the beginning), DVD has become an incredible success. It will continue to grow as DVD moves from a read-only to a fully rewritable consumer as well as computer device.

The organization that controls the DVD video standard is called the DVD Forum and was founded by 10 companies, including Hitachi, Matsushita, Mitsubishi, Victor, Pioneer, Sony, Toshiba, Philips, Thomson, and Time Warner. Since its founding in April 1997, more than 230 companies have joined the forum. Because it is a public forum, anybody can join and attend the meetings; the site for the DVD forum is www.dvdforum.org. Because the DVD Forum was unable to agree on a universal recordable format, its members who are primarily responsible for CD and DVD technology (Philips, Sony, and others) split off to form the DVD+RW Alliance in June 2000; their site is www.dvdrw.com. They have since introduced the DVD+RW format, which is the fastest, most flexible and backward-compatible recordable DVD format. DVD+RW might someday replace the VCR at home, and it's already well on its way to replacing the CD-RW and floppy drives in your PC.

DVD Construction and Technology

DVD technology is similar to CD technology. Both use the same size (120mm diameter, 1.2mm thick, with a 15mm hole in the center) discs with pits and lands stamped in a polycarbonate base. Unlike a CD, though, DVDs can have two layers of recordings on a side and be double-sided as well. Each layer is separately stamped, and they are all bonded together to make the final 1.2mm-thick disc. The manufacturing process is largely the same, with the exception that each layer on each side is stamped from a separate piece of polycarbonate plastic and are then bonded together to form the completed disc. The main difference between CD and DVD is that DVD is a higher-density recording read by a laser with a shorter wavelength, focused more closely to the disc, which enables more information to be stored. Also, whereas CDs are single-sided and have only one layer of stamped pits and lands, DVDs can have up to two layers per side and can have information on both sides.

As with CDs, each layer is stamped or molded with a single physical track in a spiral configuration starting from the inside of the disc and spiraling outward. The disc rotates counterclockwise (as viewed from the bottom), and each spiral track contains pits (bumps) and lands (flat portions) just as on a CD. Each recorded layer is coated with a thin film of metal to reflect the laser light. The outer layer has a thinner coating to allow the light to pass through to read the inner layer. If the disc is single-sided, a label can be placed on top; if it's double-sided, only a small ring near the center provides room for labeling.

Just as with a CD, reading the information back on a DVD is a matter of bouncing a low-powered laser beam off one of the reflective layers in the disc. The laser shines a focused beam on the underside of the disc, and a photosensitive receptor detects when the light is reflected back. When the light hits a land (flat spot) on the track, the light is reflected back; when the light hits a pit (raised bump), the phase differential between the projected and reflected light causes the waves to cancel and no light is reflected back.

The individual pits on a DVD are 0.105 microns deep and 0.4 microns wide. Both the pits and lands vary in length from about 0.4 microns at their shortest to about 1.9 microns at their longest (on single-layer discs).

Refer to the section "CD-ROM Construction and Technology," earlier in this chapter, for more information on how the pits and lands are read and converted into actual data, as well as how the drives physically and mechanically work.

DVD uses the same optical laser read pit and land storage that CDs do. The greater capacity is made possible by several factors, including the following:

- A 2.25 times smaller pit length (0.9–0.4 microns)
- A 2.16 times reduced track pitch (1.6–0.74 microns)
- A slightly larger data area on the disc (8,605–8,759 square millimeters)
- About 1.06 times more efficient channel bit modulation
- About 1.32 times more efficient error correction code
- About 1.06 times less sector overhead (2,048/2,352–2,048/2,064 bytes)

The DVD disc's pits and lands are much smaller and closer together than those on a CD, allowing the same physical-sized platter to hold much more information. Figure 13.6 shows how the grooved tracks with pits and lands are just over four times as dense on a DVD as compared to a CD.

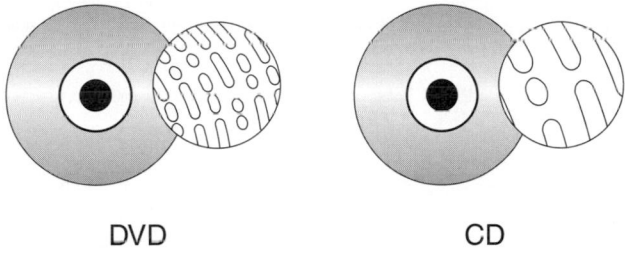

DVD   CD

Figure 13.6   DVD data markings (pits and lands) versus those of a standard CD.

DVD drives use a shorter wavelength laser to read these smaller pits and lands. A DVD can have nearly double the initial capacity by using two separate layers on one side of a disc and double it again by using both sides of the disc. The second data layer is written to a separate substrate below the first layer, which is then made semireflective to enable the laser to penetrate to the substrate beneath it. By focusing the laser on one of the two layers, the drive can read roughly twice the amount of data from the same surface area.

DVD Tracks and Sectors

The pits are stamped into a single spiral track (per layer) with a spacing of 0.74 microns between turns, corresponding to a track density of 1,351 turns per millimeter or 34,324 turns per inch. This equates to a total of 49,324 turns and a total track length of 11.8km or 7.35 miles in length. The track is comprised of sectors, with each sector containing 2,048 bytes of data. The disc is divided into four main areas:

- *Hub clamping area.* The hub clamp area is just that, a part of the disc where the hub mechanism in the drive can grip the disc. No data or information is stored in that area.

- *Lead-in zone.* The lead-in zone contains buffer zones, reference code, and mainly a control data zone with information about the disc. The control data zone consists of 16 sectors of information repeated 192 times for a total of 3,072 sectors. Contained in the 16 (repeated) sectors is information about the disc, including disc category and version number, disc size and maximum transfer rate, disc structure, recording density, and data zone allocation. The entire lead-in zone takes up to 196,607 (2FFFFh) sectors on the disc. Unlike CDs, the basic structure of all sectors on a DVD are the same. The buffer zone sectors in the lead-in zone have all 00h (zero hex) recorded for data.

- *Data zone.* The data zone contains the video, audio, or other data on the disc and starts at sector number 196,608 (30000h). The total number of sectors in the data zone can be up to 2,292,897 per layer for single layer discs.

- *Lead-out (or middle) zone.* The lead-out zone marks the end of the data zone. The sectors in the lead-out zone all contain zero (00h) for data. This is called the middle zone if the disc is dual layer and is recorded in opposite track path (OPT) mode, in which the second layer starts from the outside of the disc and is read in the opposite direction from the first layer.

The center hole in a DVD is 15mm in diameter, so it has a radius of 7.5mm from the center of the disc. From the edge of the center hole to a point at a radius of 16.5mm is the hub clamp area. The lead-in zone starts at a radius of 22mm from the center of the disc. The data zone starts at a radius of 24mm from the center and is followed by the lead-out (or middle) zone at 58mm. The disc track officially ends at 58.5mm, which is followed by a 1.5mm blank area to the edge of the disc. Figure 13.7 shows these zones in actual relative scale as they appear on a DVD.

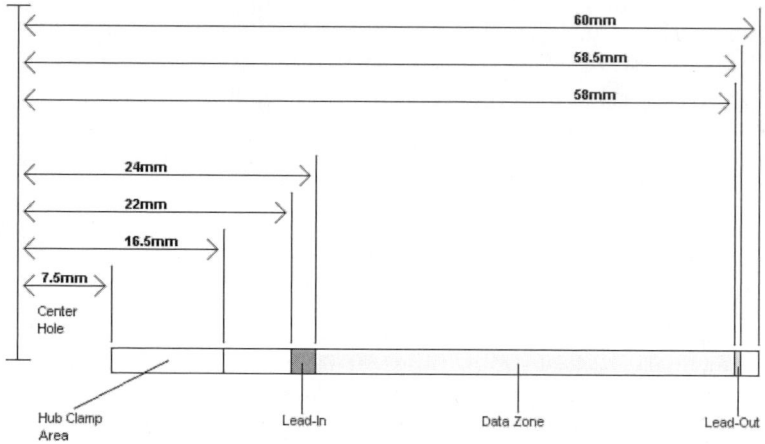

Figure 13.7   Areas on a DVD (side view).

Officially, the spiral track of a standard DVD starts with the lead-in zone and ends at the finish of the lead-out zone. This single spiral track is about 11.84 kilometers or 7.35 miles long. An interesting fact is that in a 20x CAV drive, when reading the outer part of the track, the data moves at an actual speed of 156 miles per hour (251km/h) past the laser. What is more amazing is that even when the data is traveling at that speed, the laser pickup can accurately read bits (pit/land transitions) spaced as little as only 0.4 microns or 15.75 millionths of an inch apart!

DVDs come in both single- and dual-layer as well as single- and double-sided versions. The double-sided discs are essentially the same as two single-sided discs glued together back to back, but subtle differences do exist between the single- and dual-layer discs. Table 13.6 shows some of the basic information about DVD technology, including single- and dual-layer DVDs. The dual-layer versions are recorded with slightly longer pits, resulting in slightly less information being stored in each layer.

Table 13.6   DVD Technical Parameters

DVD Type:	Single-Layer	Dual-Layer
1x read speed (m/sec)	3.49	3.84
Laser wavelength (nm)	650	650
Numerical aperture (lens)	0.60	0.60
Media refractive index	1.55	1.55
Track (turn) spacing (um)	0.74	0.74
Turns per mm	1,351	1,351
Turns per inch	34,324	34,324
Total track length (m)	11,836	11,836
Total track length (feet)	38,832	38,832
Total track length (miles)	7.35	7.35
Media bit cell length (nm)	133.3	146.7
Media byte length (um)	1.07	1.17
Media sector length (mm)	5.16	5.68
Pit width (um)	0.40	0.40
Pit depth (um)	0.105	0.105
Min. nominal pit length (um)	0.40	0.44
Max. nominal pit length (um)	1.87	2.05
Lead-in inner radius (mm)	22	22
Data zone inner radius (mm)	24	24
Data zone outer radius (mm)	58	58
Lead-out outer radius (mm)	58.5	58.5
Data zone width (mm)	34	34
Data zone area (mm2)	8,759	8,759
Total track area width (mm)	36.5	36.5
Max. rotating speed 1x CLV (rpm)	1,515	1,667
Min. rotating speed 1x CLV (rpm)	570	627
Track revolutions (data zone)	45,946	45,946
Track revolutions (total)	49,324	49,324
Data zone sectors per layer per side	2,292,897	2,083,909
Sectors per second	676	676
Media data rate (mbits/sec)	26.15625	26.15625
Media bits per sector	38,688	38,688
Media bytes per sector	4,836	4,836
Interface data rate (mbits/sec)	11.08	11.08
Interface data bits per sector	16,384	16,384
Interface data bytes per sector	2,048	2,048
Track time per layer (minutes)	56.52	51.37
Track time per side (minutes)	56.52	102.74
MPEG-2 video per layer (minutes)	133	121
MPEG-2 video per side (minutes)	133	242

B = Byte (8 bits)
KB = Kilobyte (1,000 bytes)
KiB = Kibibyte (1,024 bytes)
MB = Megabyte (1,000,000 bytes)
MiB = Mebibyte (1,048,576 bytes)
GB = Gigabyte (1,000,000,000 bytes)

GiB = Gibibyte (1,073,741,824 bytes)
m = Meters
mm = Millimeters (thousandths of a meter)
mm2 = Square millimeters
um = Micrometers = microns (millionths of a meter)
nm = Nanometers (billionths of a meter)

rpm = Revolutions per minute
ECC = Error correction code
EDC = Error detection code
CLV = Constant linear velocity
CAV = Constant angular velocity

As you can see from the information in Table 13.6, the spiral track is divided into sectors that are stored at the rate of 676 sectors per second. Each sector contains 2,048 bytes of data.

When being written, the sectors are first formatted into data frames of 2,064 bytes: 2,048 are data, 4 bytes contain ID information, 2 bytes contain ID error detection (IED) codes, 6 bytes contain copyright information, and 4 bytes contain EDC for the frame.

The data frames then have ECC information added to convert them into ECC frames. Each ECC frame contains the 2,064-byte data frame plus 182 parity outer (PO) bytes and 120 parity inner (PI) bytes, for a total of 2,366 bytes for each ECC frame.

Finally, the ECC frames are converted into physical sectors on the disc. This is done by taking 91 bytes at a time from the ECC frame and converting them into recorded bits via 8 to 16 modulation. This is where each byte (8 bits) is converted into a special 16-bit value, which is selected from a table. These values are designed using an RLL 2,10 scheme, which is designed so that the encoded information never has a run of fewer than 2 or more than 10 0 bits in a row. After each group of 91 bytes is converted via the 8 to 16 modulation, 32 bits (4 bytes) of synchronization information is added. After the entire ECC frame is converted into a physical sector, 4,836 total bytes are stored.

Table 13.7 shows the sector, frame, and audio data calculations.

Table 13.7   DVD Data Frame, ECC Frame, and Physical Sector Layout and Information

DVD Data Frame:	
Identification data (ID) bytes	4
ID error detection code (IED) bytes	2
Copyright info (CI) bytes	6
Data bytes	2,048
Error detection code (EDC)	4
Data frame total bytes	2,064
DVD ECC Frame:	
Data frame total bytes	2,064
Parity outer (PO) bytes	182
Parity inner (PI) bytes	120
ECC frame total bytes	2,366
DVD Media Physical Sectors:	
ECC frame bytes	2,366
8 to 16 modulation bits	37,856
Synchronization bits	832
Total encoded media bits/sector	38,688
Total encoded media bytes/sector	4,836
Original data bits/sector	16,384
Original data bytes/sector	2,048
Ratio of original to media data	2.36

Unlike CDs, DVDs do not use subcodes and instead use the ID bytes in each data frame to store the sector number and information about the sectors.

Handling Errors

DVDs use more powerful error correcting codes than were first devised for CDs. Unlike CDs, which have different levels of error correction depending on whether audio/video or data is being stored, DVDs treat all information equally and apply the full error correction to all sectors.

The main error correcting in DVDs takes place in the ECC frame. Parity outer (column) and parity inner (row) bits are added to detect and correct errors. The scheme is simple and yet very effective. The information from the data frames is first broken up into 192 rows of 172 bytes each. Then, a polynomial equation is used to calculate and add 10 PI bytes to each row, making the rows now 182 bytes each. Finally, another polynomial equation is used to calculate 16 PO (Parity Outer) bytes for each column, resulting in 16 bytes (rows) being added to each column. What started out as 192 rows of 172 bytes becomes 208 rows of 182 bytes with the PI and PO information added.

The function of the PI and PO bytes can be explained with a simple example using simple parity. In this example, 2 bytes are stored (01001110 = N, 01001111 = O). To add the error correcting information, they are organized in rows, as shown in the following:

```
            Data bits
            1 2 3 4 5 6 7 8
------------------------------------
Byte 1      0 1 0 0 1 1 1 0
Byte 2      0 1 0 0 1 1 1 1
------------------------------------
```

Then, 1 PI bit is added for each row, using odd parity. This means you count up the 1 bits: In the first row there are 4, so the parity bit is created as a 1, making the sum an odd number. In the second row, the parity bit is a 0 because the sum of the 1s was already an odd number. The result is as follows:

```
            Data bits        |
            1 2 3 4 5 6 7 8   |    PI
-------------------------------|---------
Byte 1      0 1 0 0 1 1 1 0   |    1
Byte 2      0 1 0 0 1 1 1 1   |    0
-------------------------------|---------
```

Next, the parity bits for each column are added and calculated the same as before. In other words, the parity bit will be such that the sum of the 1s in each column is an odd number. The result is as follows:

```
            Data bits        |
            1 2 3 4 5 6 7 8   |    PI
-------------------------------|---------
Byte 1      0 1 0 0 1 1 1 0   |    1
Byte 2      0 1 0 0 1 1 1 1   |    0
-------------------------------|---------
    PO      1 1 1 1 1 1 1 0   |    1
```

Now the code is complete, and the extra bits are stored along with the data. So, instead of just the 2 bytes being stored, 11 additional bits are stored for error correction. When the data is read back, the error correction bit calculations are repeated and they're checked to see whether they are the same as before. To see how it works, let's change one of the data bits (due to a read error) and recalculate the error correcting bits as follows:

```
                 Data bits       |
                 1 2 3 4 5 6 7 8  |  PI
       -----------------------------------|---------
       Byte 1    0 1 0 0 1 0 1 0  |   0
       Byte 2    0 1 0 0 1 1 1 1  |   0
       -----------------------------------|---------
          PO     1 1 1 1 1 0 1 0  |   1
```

Now, when you compare the PI and PO bits you calculated after reading the data to what was originally stored, you see a change in the PI bit for byte (row) 1 and in the PO bit for bit (column) 6. This identifies the precise row and column where the error was, which is at byte 1 (row 1), bit 6 (column 6). That bit was read as a 0, and you now know it is wrong, so it must have been a 1. The error correction circuitry then simply changes it back to a 1 before passing it back to the system. As you can see, with some extra information added to each row and column, error correction codes can indeed detect and correct errors on-the-fly.

Besides the ECC frames, DVDs also scramble the data in the frames using a bit-shift technique and also interleave parts of the ECC frames when they are actually recorded on the disc. These schemes serve to store the data somewhat out of sequence, preventing a scratch from corrupting consecutive pieces of data.

DVD Capacity (Sides and Layers)

Four main types of DVDs are available, categorized by whether they are single- or double-sided, and single- or dual-layered. They are designated as follows:

- *DVD-5 - 4.7GB Single-Side, Single-Layer.* A DVD-5 is constructed from two substrates bonded together with adhesive. One is stamped with a recorded layer (called Layer 0), and the other is blank. An aluminum coating typically is applied to the single recorded layer.

- *DVD-9 - 8.5GB Single-Side, Dual-Layer.* A DVD-9 is constructed of two stamped substrates bonded together to form two recorded layers for one side of the disc, along with a blank substrate for the other side. The outer stamped layer (0) is coated with a semitransparent gold coating to both reflect light if the laser is focused on it and pass light if the laser is focused on the layer below. A single laser is used to read both layers; only the focus of the laser is changed.

- *DVD-10 - 9.4GB Double-Side, Single-Layer.* A DVD-10 is constructed of two stamped substrates bonded together back to back. The recorded layer (Layer 0 on each side) usually is coated with aluminum. Note that these discs are double-sided; however, drives have a read laser only on the bottom, which means the disc must be removed and flipped to read the other side.

- *DVD-18 - 17.1GB Double-Side, Dual-Layer.* A DVD-18 combines both double layers and double sides. Two stamped layers form each side, and the substrate pairs are bonded back to back. The outer layers (Layer 0 on each side) are coated with semitransparent gold, whereas the inner layers (Layer 1 on each side) are coated with aluminum. The reflectivity of a single-layer disc is 45%–85%, and for a dual-layer disc the reflectivity is 18%–30%. The automatic gain control (AGC) circuitry in the drive compensates for the different reflective properties.

Figure 13.8 shows the construction of each of the DVD disc types.

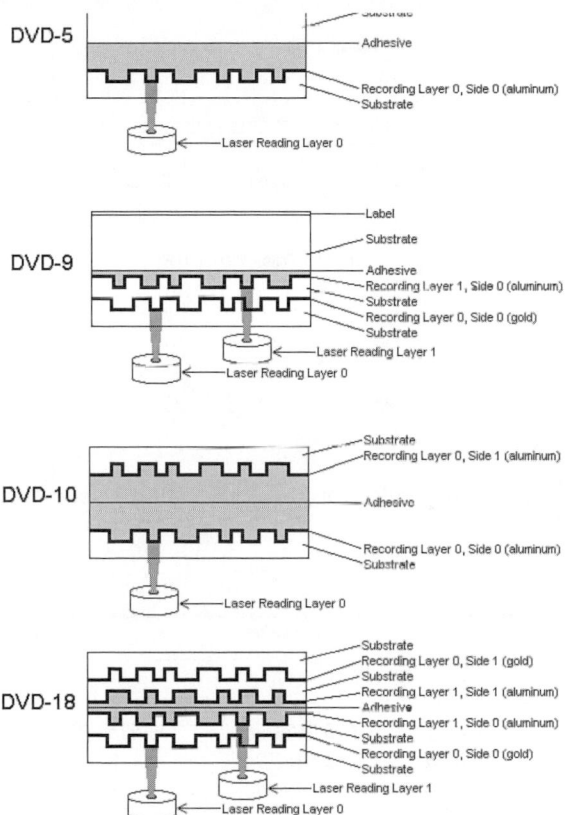

Figure 13.8 DVD disk types and construction.

Note that although Figure 13.8 shows two lasers reading the bottom of the dual-layer discs, in actual practice only one laser is used. Only the focus is changed to read the different layers.

Dual-layer discs can have the layers recorded in two ways: either OTP or parallel track path (PTP). OTP minimizes the time needed to switch from one layer to the other when reading the disc. When reaching the inside of the disc (end of Layer 0), the laser pickup remains in the same location—it merely moves toward the disc slightly to focus on Layer 1. When written in OTP mode, the lead-out zone toward the outer part of the disc is called a middle zone instead.

Discs written in PTP have both spiral layers written (and read) from the inside out. When changing from Layer 0 to Layer 1, PTP discs require the laser pickup to move from the outside (end of the first layer) back to the inside (start of the second layer), as well as for the focus of the laser to change. Virtually all discs are written in OTP mode to make the layer change quicker.

To allow the layers to be read more easily even though they are on top of one another, discs written in PTP mode have the spiral direction changed from one layer to the other. Layer 0 has a spiral winding clockwise (which is read counterclockwise), whereas Layer 1 has a spiral winding counterclockwise. This typically requires that the drive spin the disc in the opposite direction to read that layer, but with OTP the spiral is read from the outside in on the second layer. So Layer 0 spirals from the inside out, and Layer 1 spirals from the outside in.

Figure 13.9 shows the differences between PTP and OTP on a DVD.

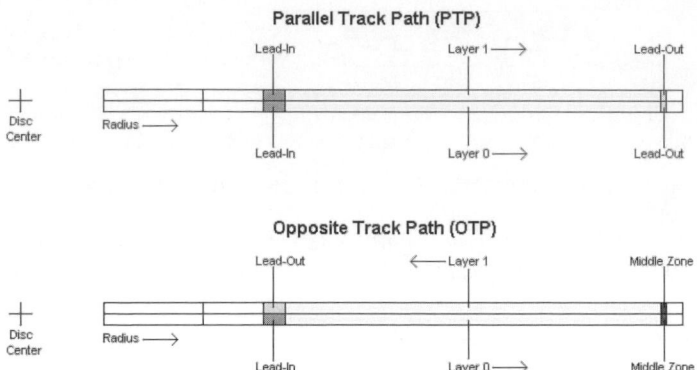

Figure 13.9   PTP versus OTP.

DVDs store up to 4.7GB–17.1 GB, depending on the type. Table 13.8 shows the precise capacities of the various types of DVDs.

Table 13.8   DVD Capacity

	Single-Layer	Dual-Layer
DVD Designation	DVD-5	DVD-9
B	4,695,853,056	8,535,691,264
KiB	4,585,794	8,335,636
KB	4,695,853	8,535,691
MiB	4,478	8,140
MB	4,696	8,536
GiB	4.4	7.9
GB	4.7	8.5
MPEG-2 video (approx. minutes)	133	242
MPEG-2 video (hours:minutes)	2:13	4:02
	Single-Layer Double-Sided	Dual-Layer Double-Sided
DVD Designation	DVD-10	DVD-18
B	9,391,706,112	17,071,382,528
KiB	9,171,588	16,671,272
KB	9,391,706	17,071,383
MiB	8,957	16,281
MB	9,392	17,071
GiB	8.7	15.9
GB	9.4	17.1
MPEG-2 video (approx. minutes)	266	484
MPEG-2 video (hours:minutes)	4:26	8:04

B = Byte (8 bits)
KB = Kilobyte (1,000 bytes)
KiB = Kibibyte (1,024 bytes)
MB = Megabyte (1,000,000 bytes)

MiB = Mebibyte (1,048,576 bytes)
GB = Gigabyte (1,000,000,000 bytes)
GiB = Gibibyte (1,073,741,824 bytes)

As you might notice, the capacity of dual-layer discs is slightly less than twice of single-layer discs, even though the layers take up the same space on the discs (the spiral tracks are the same length). This was done intentionally to improve the readability of both layers in a dual-layer configuration. To do this, the bit cell spacing was slightly increased, which increases the length of each pit and land. When reading a dual-layer disc, the drive spins slightly faster to compensate, resulting in the same data rate. However, because the distance on the track is covered more quickly, less overall data can be stored.

Besides the standard four capacities listed here, a double-sided disc with one layer on one side and two layers on the other can also be produced. This would be called a DVD-14 and have a capacity of 13.2GB, or about 6 hours and 15 minutes of MPEG-2 video. Additionally, 80mm discs, which store less data in each configuration than the standard 120mm discs, can be produced.

Because of the manufacturing difficulties and the extra expense of double-sided discs—and the fact that they must be ejected and flipped to play both sides—most DVDs are configured as either a DVD-5 (single-sided, single-layer) or a DVD-9 (single-sided, dual-layer), which allows up to 8.5GB of data or 242 minutes of uninterrupted MPEG-2 video to be played. The 133-minute capacity of DVD-5 video discs accommodates 95% or more of the movies ever made.

Note

When you view a dual-layer DVD movie, you will see a momentary pause onscreen when the player starts to play the second layer. This is normal, and it takes so little time that if you blink, you might miss it.

Data Encoding on the Disc

As with CDs, the pits and lands themselves do not determine the bits; instead, the transitions (changes in reflectivity) from pit to land and land to pit determine the actual bits on the disc. The disc track is divided into bit cells or time intervals (T), and a pit or land used to represent data is required to be a minimum of 3T or a maximum of 11T intervals (cells) long. A 3T long pit or land represents a 1001, and a 11T long pit or land represents a 100000000001.

Data is stored using 8 to 16 modulation, which is a modified version of the eight to fourteen modulation (EFM) used on CDs. Because of this, 8 to 16 modulation is sometimes called EFM+. This modulation takes each byte (8 bits) and converts it into a 16-bit value for storage. The 16-bit conversion codes are designed so that there are never fewer than 2 or more than 10 adjacent 0 bits (resulting in no fewer than 3 or no more than 11 time intervals between 1s). EFM+ is a form of RLL encoding called RLL 2,10 (RLL x,y where x = the minimum and y = the maximum run of 0s). This is designed to prevent long strings of 0s, which could more easily be misread due to clocks becoming out of sync, as well as to limit the minimum and maximum frequency of transitions actually placed on the recording media. Unlike CDs, no merge bits exist between codes. The 16-bit modulation codes are designed so that they will not violate the RLL 2,10 form without needing merge bits. Because the EFM used on CDs really requires more than 17 bits for each byte (because of the added merge and sync bits), EFM+ is slightly more efficient since only slightly more than 16 bits are generated for each byte encoded.

Note that although no more than 10 0s are allowed in the modulation generated by EFM+, the sync bits added when physical sectors are written can have up to 13 0s, meaning a time period of up to 14T between 1s written on the disc and pits or lands up to 14T intervals or bit cells in length.

Blu-ray Disc

In February 2002, the leading optical storage companies formed the Blu-ray Disc Founders (BDF) and announced the initial specifications for Blu-ray Disc, a high-capacity CD/DVD-type optical disc format. By May 2002, the Blu-ray Disc (BD) specification 1.0 was released, and in April 2003, Sony released the BDZ-S77 for the Japanese market, the first commercially available BD recorder. Blu-ray is a fully rewritable format that enables recording up to 27GB of data or up to 2 hours of high-definition video on a single-sided, single-layer 12cm diameter disc (which is the same as existing CDs and DVDs) using a 405nm blue-violet laser. Dual-layer BD recorders are also being developed and will record up to 54GB. Current Blu-ray discs are contained in a cartridge that protects them from dust and fingerprints; however, versions with hard-coated discs that do not require a cartridge are being developed. Although backward compatibility with DVD and CD is not a requirement of the Blu-ray specification, it is a feature drive manufacturers can easily include. In fact, all the Blu-ray drives announced so far have full backward compatibility with DVD and CD formats.

One of the main applications for higher-capacity optical storage is recording high-definition TV, which takes an incredible amount of storage. Current DVD recorders can't store enough data to handle high-definition video. Blu-ray, on the other hand, is designed to store up to 2 hours of high-definition video (or more than 13 hours of standard broadcast-quality TV) on a single-layer disc, or double that when dual-layer versions become available. As with DVD, Blu-ray uses the industry-standard MPEG-2 compression technology.

The Blu-ray Disc 1.0 specification includes the following formats:

- *BD-ROM.* Read-only for prerecorded content
- *BD-R.* Recordable for PC data storage
- *BD-RW.* Rewritable for PC data storage
- *BD-RE.* Rewritable for HDTV recording

Standard CDs use a 780nm (infrared) laser combined with a 0.45 numerical aperture lens, whereas DVDs use a 650nm (red) laser combined with a 0.60 numerical aperture lens. Blu-ray uses a much shorter 405nm (blue-violet) laser with a 0.85 numerical aperture lens. *Numerical aperture* is a measurement of the light-gathering capability of a lens, as well as the focal length and relative magnification. The numerical aperture of a lens is derived by taking the sine of the maximum angle of light entering the lens. For example, the lens in a CD-ROM drive gathers light at up to a 26.7° angle, which results in a numerical aperture of SIN(26.7) = 0.45. By comparison, the lens in a DVD drive gathers light at up to a 36.9° angle, resulting in a numerical aperture of SIN(36.9) = 0.60. Blu-ray drives gather light at up to a 58.2° angle, resulting in a numerical aperture of SIN(58.2) = 0.85. Higher numerical apertures allow increasingly oblique (angled) rays of light to enter the lens and therefore produce a more highly resolved image.

The higher the aperture, the shorter the focal length and the greater the magnification. The lens in a CD-ROM drive magnifies roughly 20 times, whereas the lens in a DVD drive magnifies about 40 times. The Blu-ray lens magnifies about 60 times. This greater magnification is necessary because the distance between tracks on a Blu-ray disc is reduced to 0.32um, which is almost half of that of a regular DVD. Because of the very high densities involved, a simple cartridge is normally used to hold the disc, which prevents it from being impaired by dust, fingerprints, or scratches.

The most important features of a Blu-ray disc are summarized in Table 13.9.

Table 13.9   Blu-ray Disc Specifications

Specification	Value	Specification	Value
Capacity (single-layer)	23.3GB/25GB/27GB	Tracking pitch	0.32um
Capacity (dual-layer)	46.6GB/50GB/54GB	Shortest pit length	0.160/0.149/0.138um
Laser wavelength	405nm (blue-violet)	Recording density	16.8/18.0/19.5Gb/sq. in.
Lens numerical aperture	0.85	Data transfer rate	36Mbps
Cartridge dimensions	Approximately 129×131×7mm	Recording format	Phase change recording
Disc diameter	120mm	Tracking format	Groove recording
Disc thickness	1.2mm	Video format	MPEG2
Optical protection layer	0.1mm		

Blu-ray, or perhaps some other blue-laser disc drive, will eventually become the replacement for today's DVD drives. For more information about Blu-ray, see the official BDF Web site at www.blu-raydisc-official.org, as well as the unofficial Blue-ray site at www.blu-ray.com.

HD-DVD

HD-DVD, also known as Advanced Optical Disc (AOD), is another next-generation blue laser optical disc format developed by Toshiba and NEC. HD-DVD is similar to Blu-ray (but not compatible) and also uses blue-laser technology to achieve a higher storage capacity. HD-DVD-R (recordable) versions store 15GB on a single-layer disc and 30GB on a dual-layer disc. HD-DVD-RW (rewritable) versions store 20GB on a single-layer disc and 32GB on a dual-layer disc. The DVD Forum has approved the HD-DVD format for further study as the successor to the current DVD technology. Unfortunately, the development of HD-DVD and the endorsement by the DVD Forum means that there will be another format war over the next-generation blue laser DVD drives. Blu-ray has the lead, with drives and discs already on the market, and most of the major manufacturers have already committed to producing drives. Still, another format war is only going to cause additional confusion in the market place, just as it has with DVD recordables.

Optical Disc Formats

CD and DVD drives can use many types of disc formats and standards. The following sections discuss the formats and file systems used by CD and DVD drives, so you can make sure you can use media recorded in a particular format with your drive.

Compact Disc and Drive Formats

After Philips and Sony created the Red Book CD-DA format discussed earlier in the chapter, they began work on other format standards that would allow CDs to store computer files, data, and even video and photos. These standards control how the data is formatted so that the drive can read it, and additional file format standards can then control how the software and drivers on your PC can be designed to understand and interpret the data properly. Note that the physical format and storage of data on the disc as defined in the Red Book was adopted by all subsequent CD standards. This refers to the encoding and basic levels of error correction provided by CD-DA discs. The other "books" specify primarily how the 2,352 bytes in each sector are to be handled, what type of data can be stored, how it should be formatted, and more.

All the official CD standard books and related documents can be purchased from Philips for $100–$150 each. See the Philips licensing site at www.licensing.philips.com for more information.

Table 13.10 describes the various standard CD formats, which are discussed in more detail in the following sections.

Table 13.10   Compact Disc Formats

Format	Name	Introduced	Notes
Red Book	CD-DA (compact disc digital audio)	1980 - by Philips and Sony	• The original CD audio standard on which all subsequent CD standards are based.
Yellow Book	CD-ROM (compact disc read-only memory)	1983 - by Philips and Sony	• Specifies additional ECC and EDC for data in several sector formats, including Mode 1 and Mode 2.
Green Book	CD-i (compact disc-interactive)	1986 - by Philips and Sony	• Specifies an interactive audio/video standard for nonPC-dedicated player hardware (now mostly obsolete) and discs used for interactive presentations. • Defines Mode 2, Form 1 and Mode 2, Form 2 sector formats along with interleaved MPEG-1 video and ADPCM audio.
CD-ROM XA	CD-ROM XA (extended architecture)	1989 - by Philips, Sony, and Microsoft	• Combines Yellow Book and CD-i to bring CD-i audio and video capabilities to PCs.

Table 13.10   Continued

Format	Name	Introduced	Notes
Orange Book	CD-R (recordable) and CD-RW (rewritable)	1989 - by Philips and Sony (Part I/II); 1996 - by Philips and Sony (Part III)	• Defines single session, multisession, and packet writing on recordable discs. • Part I—CD-MO (magneto-optical, withdrawn). • Part II—CD-R (recordable). • Part III—CD-RW (rewritable).
Photo-CD	CD-P	1990 - by Philips and Kodak	• Combines CD-ROM XA with CD-R multisession capability in a standard for photo storage on CD-R discs.
White Book	Video CD	1993 - by Philips, JVC, Matsushita, and Sony	• Based on CD-i and CD-ROM XA. It stores up to 74 minutes of MPEG-1 video and ADPCM digital audio data.
Blue Book	CD EXTRA (formerly CD-Plus or enhanced music)	1995 - by Philips and Sony	• Multisession format for stamped discs; used by musical artists to incorporate videos, liner notes, and other information on audio CDs.
Purple Book	CD Double-Density	2000 – by Philips and Sony	• Double-density (1.3GB) versions of CD-ROM, CD-R, and CD-RW (DD-ROM, DD-R, DD-RW).

Red Book—CD-DA

The Red Book introduced by Philips and Sony in 1980 is the father of all compact-disc specifications because all other "books" or formats are based on the original CD-DA Red Book format. The Red Book specification includes the main parameters, audio specification, disc specification, optical stylus, modulation system, error correction system, and control and display system. The latest revision of the Red Book is dated May 1999.

For more information on the original Red Book format, see the section "CDs: A Brief History" earlier in this chapter.

Yellow Book—CD-ROM

The Yellow Book was first published by Philips, Sony, and Microsoft in 1983 and has been revised and amended several times since. The Yellow Book standard took the physical format of the original CD-DA, or Red Book, standard and added another layer of error detection and correction to enable data to be stored reliably. It also added additional synchronization and header information to enable sectors to be more accurately located. Yellow Book specifies two types of sectoring—called Mode 1 (with error correction) and Mode 2—which offer different levels of error detection and correction schemes. Some data (computer files, for example) can't tolerate errors. However, other data, such as a video image or sound, can tolerate minor errors. By using a mode with less error correction information, more data can be stored, but with the possibility of uncorrected errors.

In 1989, the Yellow Book was issued as an international standard by the ISO as *ISO/IEC 10149, Data Interchange on Read-Only 120mm Optical Discs (CD-ROM)*. The latest version of the Yellow Book is dated May 1999.

Green Book—CD-i

The Green Book was published by Philips and Sony in 1986. CD-i is much more than just a disc format; instead it is a complete specification for an entire interactive system consisting of custom hardware (players) designed to be connected to a television, software designed to deliver video and audio together with user interactivity in real time, and the media and format. A CD-i player is actually a dedicated computer usually running a variant on the Motorola 68000 processor line, as well as a customized version of the Microware OS/9 Real Time Operating System.

CD-i enables both audio and video to share a disc and enables the information to be interleaved so as to maintain synchronization between the pictures and sounds. To fit both audio and video in the same space originally designed for just audio, compression was performed. The video was compressed using the Moving Picture Experts Group-1 (MPEG-1) compression standard, whereas the audio was compressed with adaptive differential pulse code modulation (ADPCM). ADPCM is an audio encoding algorithm that takes about half the space for the same quality of standard PCM, and even less if quality is reduced by lowering the sampling rate or bits per sample. Using ADPCM, up to 8 hours of stereo or 16 hours of mono sound can fit on one CD. The "differential" part of ADPCM refers to the fact that it records the differences between one signal and the next (using only 4-bit numbers), which reduces the total amount of data involved. ADPCM audio can be interleaved with video in CD-i (and CD-ROM XA) applications.

The Yellow Book defines two CD-ROM sector structures, called Mode 1 and Mode 2. The Green Book (CD-i) refines the Mode 2 sector definition by adding two forms, called Mode 2, Form 1 and Mode 2, Form 2. The Mode 2, Form 1 sector definition uses ECC and allows for 2,048 bytes of data storage like the Yellow Book Mode 1 sectors, but it rearranged things slightly to use the 8 formerly unused (blank or 0) bytes as a subheader containing additional information about the sector. The Mode 2, Form 2 definition drops the ECC and allows 2,324 bytes for data. Without the ECC, only video or audio information should be stored in Form 2 sectors because that type of information can tolerate minor errors.

All types of media were produced for CD-i, but because the files use the OS/9 file format, they can't be viewed by a PC without special drivers. One of the best resources for CD-i technical information, utility software, drivers, and emulators is The New International CD-I Association Web site at www.icdia.org.

Today, the CD-i format is largely obsolete. The last revision of the standard was produced in May 1994. Philips sold off its entire consumer CD-i catalog to Infogrames Multimedia in 1998, which now owns the rights for virtually all consumer CD-i titles ever produced. Philips made a final run of CD-i players in 1999, and it is doubtful any new ones will ever be produced. The legacy of CD-i lives on in the other formats that use specifications originally devised for CD-i, such as the Mode 2, Form 1 and Form 2 sector structures found in CD-XA and the MPEG-1 video format later used in the White Book (CD-Video).

CD-ROM XA

CD-ROM XA originally was defined in 1989 by Philips, Sony, and Microsoft as a supplement to the Yellow Book. CD-ROM XA brings some of the features originally defined in the Green Book (CD-i) to the Yellow Book (CD-ROM) standard, especially for multimedia use. CD-ROM XA adds three main features to the Yellow Book standard. The first consists of the CD-i-enhanced sector definitions (called forms) for the Mode 2 sectors; the second is a capability called interleaving (mixing audio and video information); and the third is ADPCM for compressed audio. The latest version of the CD-ROM XA standard was released in May 1991.

Interleaving

CD-ROM XA drives can employ a technique known as *interleaving*. The specification calls for the capability to encode on disc whether the data directly following an identification mark is graphics, sound, or text. Graphics can include standard graphics pictures, animation, or full-motion video. In addition, these blocks can be interleaved, or interspersed, with each other. For example, a frame of video can start a track followed by a segment of audio, which would accompany the video, followed by yet another frame of video. The drive picks up the audio and video sequentially, buffering the information in memory and then sending it along to the PC for synchronization.

In short, the data is read off the disc in alternating pieces and then synchronized at playback so that the result is a simultaneous presentation of the data. Without interleaving, the drive would have to read and buffer the entire video track before it could read the audio track and synchronize the two for playback.

Sector Modes and Forms

Mode 1 is the standard Yellow Book CD sector format with ECC and EDC to enable error-free operation. Each Mode 1 sector is broken down as shown in Tables 13.11 and 13.12.

Table 13.11   Yellow Book Mode 1 Sector Format Breakdown

Yellow Book (CD-ROM) Sectors (Mode 1):	
Q+P parity bytes	784
Subcode bytes	98
Sync bytes	12
Header bytes	4
Data bytes	2,048
EDC bytes	4
Blank (0) bytes	8
ECC bytes	276
Bytes/sector RAW (unencoded)	3,234

Table 13.12   Yellow Book (CD-ROM) Mode 1 Sector Format

Sync	Header	User Data	EDC	Blank	ECC
12	4	2,048	4	8	276

In the original Yellow Book, Mode 2 was defined as a sector without any ECC or EDC. Unfortunately, Mode 1 (which had ECC and EDC) couldn't be mixed with Mode 2 sectors on the same track (program or song). To enable data with and without error detection and correction in a single track, new sector format subsets for Mode 2 sectors were added in the Green Book (CD-i) and subsequently adopted in the CD-ROM XA extensions. This enabled information that would not tolerate errors (such as programs or computer data) to be interleaved or mixed within the same track with information that would tolerate errors (such as audio or video data). These variations on Mode 2 include Form 1 and Form 2 sectors. Each Mode 2, Form 1 sector is broken down as shown in Tables 13.13, 13.14, 13.15, and 13.16.

Table 13.13   Green Book Mode 2 Sector Format Breakdown

Green Book/CD-ROM XA Sectors (Mode 2, Form 1):	
Q+P parity bytes	784
Subcode bytes	98
Sync bytes	12
Header bytes	4
Subheader bytes	8
Data bytes	2,048
EDC bytes	4
ECC bytes	276
Bytes/sector RAW (unencoded)	3,234

Table 13.14   Green Book/CD-ROM XA (Yellow Book Extensions) Mode 2, Form 1 Sector Format

Sync	Header	Subheader	User Data	EDC	ECC
12	4	8	2,048 bytes	4	276

Table 13.15   Green Book Mode 2 Sector Format Breakdown

Green Book/CD-ROM XA Sectors (Mode 2, Form 2):	
Q+P parity bytes	784
Subcode bytes	98
Sync bytes	12
Header bytes	4
Subheader bytes	8
Data bytes	2,324
EDC bytes	4
Bytes/sector RAW (unencoded)	3,234

Table 13.16   Green Book/CD-ROM XA (Yellow Book Extensions) Mode 2, Form 2 Sector Format

Sync	Header	Subheader	User Data	EDC
12	4	8	2,324 bytes	4

Both Mode 2 sector formats add a subheader field that identifies the type of information (such as audio or video) carried in the user data field. The Form 2 sector lacks the ECC of the Form 1 sector and increases the size of the user data field instead. This type of sector is for storing audio or video data that can tolerate errors.

Because they don't use any third-level error correction, CD-ROMs that use the Mode 2, Form 2 sector format (such as MPEG video CDs) can hold more user information than other CD-ROM types in the same number of sectors and as a result also have a higher data transfer rate of 174.3KBps instead of the standard 153.6KBps. Note that Form 2 sectors are never used to store data or program files because errors can't be tolerated in that type of information. In that case, the Mode 2, Form 1 sector format would be used.

For a drive to be truly XA compatible, the audio data written in Form 2 sectors on the disc as audio must be ADPCM audio—specially compressed and encoded audio. This requires that the drive or the SCSI controller have a signal processor chip that can decompress the audio during the synchronization process.

Some earlier drives were called XA-ready, which meant they were capable of Mode 2, Form 1 and Form 2 reading but did not incorporate the ADPCM chip. This is not a significant shortcoming, however, because only certain multimedia titles use the ADPM encoding (with interleaved audio and video). The main benefit XA brought to the table was the additional sector modes and forms taken from the Green Book.

Orange Book

The Orange Book defines the standards for recordable CDs and originally was announced in 1989 by Philips and Sony. The Orange Book comes in three parts: Part I describes a format called CD-MO (magneto-optical), which was to be a rewritable format but was withdrawn before any products really came to market; Part II (1989) describes CD-R; and Part III (1996) describes CD-RW. Note that originally CD-R was referred to as CD-WO (write-once), and CD-RW originally was called CD-E (erasable).

The Orange Book Part II CD-R design is known as a WORM (write once read mostly) format. After a portion of a CD-R disc is recorded, it can't be overwritten or reused. Recorded CD-R discs are Red Book and Yellow Book compatible, which means they are readable on conventional CD-DA or CD-ROM drives. The CD-R definition in the Orange Book Part II is divided into two volumes. Volume 1 defines recording speeds of 1x, 2x, and 4x the standard CD speed; the last revision, dated December 1998, is 3.1. Volume 2 defines recording speeds up to 48x the standard CD speed. The latest version released, 1.2, is dated April 2002.

The Orange Book Part III describes CD-RW. As the name implies, CD-RW enables you to erase and overwrite information in addition to reading and writing. The Orange Book Part III CD-RW definition is broken into three volumes. Volume 1 defines recording speeds of 1x, 2x, and 4x times the standard CD speed; the latest version, 2.0, is dated August 1998. Volume 2 (high-speed) defines recording speeds from 4x to 10x standard CD speed; the latest version, 1.1, is dated June 2001. Volume 3 (ultra-speed) defines recording speeds from 8x to 32x; the latest version, 1.0, is dated September 2002.

Besides the capability to record on CDs, the most important feature instituted in the Orange Book specification is the capability to perform multisession recording.

Multisession Recording Overview

Before the Orange Book specification, CDs had to be written as a single session. A *session* is defined as a lead-in, followed by one or more tracks of data (or audio), followed by a lead-out. The lead-in takes up 4,500 sectors on the disc (1 minute if measured in time or about 9.2MB worth of data). The lead-in also indicates whether the disc is multisession and what the next writable address on the disc is (if the disc isn't closed). The first lead-out on a disc (or the only one if it is a single session or Disk At Once recording) is 6,750 sectors long (1.5 minutes if measured in time or about 13.8MB worth of data). If the disc is a multisession disc, any subsequent lead-outs are 2,250 sectors long (0.5 minutes in time or about 4.6MB worth of data).

A multisession CD has multiple sessions, with each individual session complete from lead-in to lead-out. The mandatory lead-in and lead-out for each session do waste space on the disc. In fact, 48 sessions would literally use up all of a 74-minute disc even with no data recorded in each session! Therefore, the practical limit for the number of sessions you can record on a disc would be much less than that.

CD-DA and older CD-ROM drives couldn't read more than one session on a disc, so that is the way most pressed CDs are recorded. The Orange Book allows multiple sessions on a single disc. To allow this, the Orange Book defines three main methods or modes of recording:

- Disk-at-Once (DAO)
- Track-at-Once (TAO)
- Packet Writing

Disc-at-Once

Disc-at-Once means pretty much what it says: It is a single- session method of writing CDs in which the lead-in, data tracks, and lead-out are written in a single operation without ever turning off the writing laser; then the disc is closed. A disc is considered closed when the last (or only) lead-in is fully written and the next usable address on the disc is not recorded in that lead-in. In that case, the CD recorder is incapable of writing any further data on the disc. Note that it is not necessary to close a disc to read it in a normal CD-ROM drive, although if you were submitting a disc to a CD duplicating company for replication, most require that it be closed.

Track-at-Once

Multisession discs can be recorded in either Track-at-Once (TAO) or Packet Writing mode. In Track-at-Once recording, each track can be individually written (laser turned on and off) within a session, until the session is closed. Closing a session is the act of writing the lead-out for that session, which means no more tracks can be added to that session. If the disc is closed at the same time, no further sessions can be added either.

The tracks recorded in TAO mode are typically divided by gaps of 2 seconds. Each track written has 150 sectors of overhead for run-in, run-out, pre-gap, and linking. A CD-R/RW drive can read the tracks even if the session is not closed, but to read them in a CD-DA or CD-ROM drive, the session must be closed. If you intend to write more sessions to the disc, you can close the session and not close the disc. At that point, you could start another session of recording to add more tracks to the disc. The main thing to remember is that each session must be closed (lead-out written) before another session can be written or before a normal CD-DA or CD-ROM drive can read the tracks in the session.

Packet Writing

Packet writing is a method whereby multiple writes are allowed within a track, thus reducing the overhead and wasted space on a disc. Each packet uses four sectors for run-in, two for run-out, and one for linking. Packets can be of fixed or variable length, but most drives and packet-writing software use a fixed length because dealing with file systems that way is much easier and more efficient.

With packet writing, you use the Universal Disk Format (UDF) version 1.5 or later file system, which enables the CD to be treated essentially like a big floppy drive. That is, you can literally drag and drop files to it, use the copy command to copy files onto the disc, and so on. The packet-writing software and UDF file system manage everything. If the disc you are using for packet writing is a CD-R, every time a file is overwritten or deleted, the file seems to disappear, but you don't get the space back on the disc. Instead, the file system simply forgets about the file. If the disc is a CD-RW, the space is indeed reclaimed and the disc won't be full until you literally have more than the limit of active files stored there.

Unfortunately, Windows versions up through Windows XP don't support packet writing or the UDF file system directly, so drivers must be loaded to read packet-written discs and a packet-writing application must be used to write them. Fortunately, though, these typically are included with CD-RW drives. One of the most popular packet-writing programs is DirectCD from Roxio. You can even download a universal UDF reader application from Roxio for free that enables you to read UDF 1.5 (packet-written) discs on any CD-ROM or CD-RW drive.

Note

Windows XP also has limited CD-RW support in the form of something called IMAPI (image mastering application program interface), which enables data to be temporarily stored on the hard drive (staged) before being written to the CD in one session. Additional sessions can be written to the same disc, but a 50MB overhead exists for each session. This gives some of the appearance of packet writing, but it is not really the same thing. To read packet-written discs in the UDF 1.5 or later format, you must install a UDF reader just as with previous versions of Windows. Instead of using IMAPI, I recommend installing a third-party CD-mastering program that also includes packet-writing UDF support, such as Roxio's Easy DVD-CD Creator with DirectCD or Ahead Nero Burning ROM with InCD.

When you remove a packet-written disc from the drive, the packet-writing software first asks whether you want the files to be visible to normal CD-ROM drives. If you do then the session must be closed. Even if the session is closed, you can still write more to the disc later, but there is an overhead of wasted space every time you close a session. If you are going to read the disc in a CD-RW drive, you don't have to close the session because it will be capable of reading the files even if the session isn't closed.

A newer standard called Mount Rainier adds even more capability to packet writing and is one of the most important developments in CD and DVD drives. With Mount Rainier, packet writing can become an official part of the operating system and the drives can support the defect management necessary to make them usable as removable storage in the real world. For more information, see the section "Mount Rainier" later in this chapter.

Note

Microsoft has released updates for Windows XP that add native support for the Mount Rainier standard, which supports full drag-and-drop packet writing through CD-MRW drives as well as DVD+MRW drives.

Photo CD

First announced back in 1990 but not available until 1992, Photo CD is a standard for CD-R discs and drives to store photos. The current version 1.0 of the Photo CD standard was published in December 1994. You simply drop off a roll of film at a participating Kodak developer, and they digitize and store the photos on a specially formatted CD-R disc called a Photo CD, which you can then read on virtually any CD-ROM drive connected to a PC running the appropriate software. Originally, Kodak sold Photo CD "players" designed to display the photos to a connected TV, but these have since been dropped in favor of simply using a PC with software to decode and display the photos.

Perhaps the main benefit Photo CD has brought to the table is that it was the first CD format to use the Orange Book Part II (CD-R) specification with multisession recordings. Additionally, the data is recorded in CD-ROM XA Mode 2, Form 2 sectors so more photo information could be stored on the disc.

Using the Photo CD software, you can view your photographs at any one of several resolutions and manipulate them using standard graphics software packages.

When you drop off your roll of film, the Kodak developers produce prints as they normally do. After prints are made, they scan the prints with ultra-high-resolution scanners. To give you an idea of the amount of information each scan carries, one color photograph can take 15MB–20MB of storage. The compressed, stored images are then encoded onto special writable CDs, and the finished product is packaged and shipped back to your local developer for pickup. Some developers can do the scanning onsite.

Photo CD Disc Types

The images on the disc are compressed and stored using Kodak's own PhotoYCC encoding format, which includes up to six resolutions for each image, as shown in Table 13.17. Kodak has defined several types of Photo CDs to accommodate the needs of various types of users. The Photo CD Master disc is the standard consumer format and contains up to 100 photos in all the resolutions shown in the table except for base x64.

Table 13.17 Photo CD Resolutions

Base	Resolution (Pixels)	Description
/16	128×192	Thumbnail
/4	256×384	Thumbnail
x1	512×768	TV resolution
x4	1,024×1,536	HDTV resolution
x16	2,048×3,072	Print size
x64	4,096×6,144	Pro Photo CD master only

The various resolutions supply you with images appropriate for various applications. If, for example, you wanted to include a Photo CD image on a Web page, you would choose a low-resolution image. A professional photographer shooting photos for a print ad would want to use the highest resolution possible.

The Pro Photo CD Master disc is intended for professional photographers using larger film formats, such as 70mm, 120mm, or 4"×5". This type of disc adds an even higher-resolution image (4,096×6,144 pixels) to those already furnished on the Photo CD Master disc. Because of this added high-resolution image, this type of disc can hold anywhere from 25 to 100 images, depending on the film format.

The Photo CD Portfolio disc is designed for interactive presentations that include sound and other multimedia content. The high-resolution images that take up the most space are not necessary here, so this type of disc can contain up to 700 images, depending on how much other content is included.

Multisession Photo CDs

One breakthrough of the Photo CD concept is that each of the disc types is capable of containing multiple sessions. Because the average consumer wouldn't usually have enough film processed to fill an entire disc, you can bring back your partially filled CDs each time you have more film to develop. A new session can then be added to your existing CD until the entire disc is filled. You pay less for the processing because a new CD is not necessary, and all your images are stored on a smaller number of discs.

Any XA-compliant or XA-ready CD-ROM drive can read the multiple sessions on a Photo CD disc, and even if your drive is not multisession capable, it can still read the first session on the disc. If this is the case, you must purchase a new disc for each batch of film you process, but you can still take advantage of Photo CD technology.

Kodak provides software that enables you to view the Photo CD images on your PC and licenses a Photo CD import filter to the manufacturers of many desktop publishing, image-editing, and paint programs. Therefore, you can modify your Photo CD images using a program such as Adobe Photoshop and integrate them into documents for printing or electronic publication with a page layout program such as Adobe PageMaker.

Picture CD

Although Kodak still offers Photo CD services, the high cost has led to limited popularity. Kodak now offers the simpler Picture CD service. Unlike Photo CD, Picture CD uses the industry-standard JPEG file format. It uses a CD-R, with up to 40 images stored at a single medium-resolution scan of 1,024×1,536 pixels. This resolution is adequate for 4"×6" and 5"×7" prints. The images can also be made available via Kodak PhotoNet, where the same images are posted online and can be downloaded. In addition, Kodak has a service called Picture Disk that stores up to 28 images on a 1.44MB floppy disk at a resolution of 400×600, suitable for screensavers and slide shows.

The software provided with Picture CD enables the user to manipulate images with various automatic or semiautomatic operations, but unlike Photo CD, the standard JPEG (JPG) file format used for storage enables any popular image-editing program to work with the images without conversion. Although the image quality of Picture CD isn't as high as with Photo CD, the much lower price of the service should make it far more popular with amateur photographers. Services similar to Picture CD are also offered by Fujifilm and Agfa, and some stores allow you to order Kodak Picture CD with your choice of store-brand or Kodak film processing.

White Book—Video CD

The White Book was introduced in 1993 by Philips, JVC, Matsushita, and Sony. It is based on the Green Book (CD-i) and CD-ROM XA standards and allows for storing up to 74 minutes of MPEG-1 video and ADPCM digital audio data on a single disc. The latest version (2.0) was released in April 1995. Video CD 2.0 supports MPEG-1 compression with a 1.15Mbps bit rate. The screen resolution is 352×240 for NTSC format and 352×288 for European PAL format. In addition, it supports Dolby Pro Logic–compatible stereo sound.

You can think of video CDs as a sort of poor man's DVD format, although the picture and sound quality can actually be quite good—certainly better than VHS or most other videotape formats. You can play video CDs on virtually any PC with a CD-ROM drive using the free Windows Media Player (other media player applications can be used as well). They also can be played on most DVD players and even some game consoles, such as the Playstation (with the correct options). Video CDs are an especially big hit with people who travel with laptop computers, and the prerecorded discs are much cheaper than DVD—many cost as little as $5.

Super Video CD

The Super Video CD specification 1.0, published in May 1999, is an enhanced version of the the White Book Video CD specification. It uses MPEG-2 compression, an NTSC screen resolution of 480×480, and a PAL screen resolution of 480×576; it also supports MPEG-2 5.1 surround sound and multiple languages.

Most home DVD-creation programs can create Video CDs or Super Video CDs.

Blue Book—CD EXTRA

Manufacturers of CD-DA media were looking for a standard method to combine both music and data on a single CD. The intention was for a user to be able to play only the audio tracks in a standard audio CD player while remaining unaware of the data track. However, a user with a PC or dedicated combination audio/data player could access both the audio and data tracks on the same disc.

The fundamental problem with nonstandard mixed-mode CDs is that if or when an audio player tries to play the data track, the result is static that could conceivably damage speakers and possibly hearing if the volume level has been turned up. Various manufacturers originally addressed this problem in different ways, resulting in a number of confusing methods for creating these types of discs, some of which still allowed the data tracks to be accidentally "played" on an audio player. In 1995, Philips and Sony developed the CD EXTRA specification, as defined in the Blue Book standard. CDs conforming to this specification usually are referred to as CD EXTRA (formerly called CD Plus or CD Enhanced Music) discs and use the multisession technology defined in the CD-ROM XA standard to separate the audio and data tracks. These are a form of stamped multisession disc. The audio portion of the disc can consist of up to 98 standard Red Book audio tracks, whereas the data track typically is composed of XA Mode 2 sectors and can contain video, song lyrics, still images, or other multimedia content. Such discs can be identified by the CD EXTRA logo, which is the standard CD-DA logo with a plus sign to the right. Often the logo or markings on the disc package are overlooked or somewhat obscure, and you might not know that an audio CD contains this extra data until you play it in a CD-ROM drive.

A CD EXTRA disc normally contains two sessions. Because audio CD players are only single-session capable, they play only the audio session and ignore the additional session containing the data. A CD-ROM drive in a PC, however, can see both sessions on the disc and access both the audio and data tracks.

Note

Many artists have released audio CDs in the CD EXTRA format that include things such as lyrics, video, artist bio, photos, and so on in data files on the disc. *Tidal* by Fiona Apple (released in 1996) was one of the first CD EXTRA discs from Sony Music. There have been many CD EXTRA releases since then. For examples of other CD EXTRA (Enhanced CD) discs, including current releases, see `www.musicfan.com`.

Purple Book

The Purple Book defines the standards for double-density CD-ROM (DDCD), CD-R (DDCD-R), and CD-RW (DDCD-RW) media and drives. It was announced by Sony and Philips in July 2000, and the current 1.0 standard was released in July 2001.

Purple Book–compliant rewritable drives can read and write standard CD, CD-R, and CD-RW media and achieve their higher 1.3GB (versus 650MB for standard drives) by modifying the following features of existing CD-ROM, CD-R, and CD-RW standards:

- The track pitch has been reduced from 1.6 micrometers to 1.1 micrometers, and the minimum pit length has been reduced from 0.833 micrometers to 0.623 micrometers to enable double-density recording.
- CIRC7, instead of regular CIRC, error correction is used.
- An expanded ATIP address format is used.

DD drives support digital rights management. They are designed to prevent the creation of DD music CDs. Tables 13.18 and 13.19 provide the details of the sector format used by DD drives.

Table 13.18   Purple Book Mode 2 Sector Format Breakdown

Purple Book/DD CD-ROM Sectors (Mode 2, Form 2):	
Q+P parity bytes	276
Subcode bytes	98
Sync bytes	12
Header bytes	4
Subheader bytes	8
Data bytes	2,048
EDC bytes	4
Bytes/sector RAW (unencoded)	2,352

Table 13.19   Purple Book/DD CD-ROM Mode 2, Form 2 Sector Format

Sync	Header	Subheader	User Data	EDC
12	4	8	2,048 bytes	4

Although DDCD drives have twice the capacity of traditional drives, very few of them were sold. Sony offered several models in 2001 but has since discontinued them, although DDCD media is still available.

CD-ROM File Systems

Manufacturers of early CD-ROM discs required their own custom software to read the discs. This is because the Yellow Book specification for CD-ROM details only how data sectors—rather than audio sectors—can be stored on a disc and did not cover the file systems or deal with how data should be stored in files and how these should be formatted for use by PCs with different operating systems. Obviously, noninterchangeable file formats presented an obstacle to the industry-wide compatibility for CD-ROM applications.

In 1985–1986, several companies got together and published the High Sierra file format specification, which finally enabled CD-ROMs for PCs to be universally readable. That was the first industry-standard CD-ROM file system that made CD-ROMs universally usable in PCs. Today several file systems are used on CDs, including

- High Sierra
- ISO 9660 (based on High Sierra)
- Joliet
- UDF (Universal Disk Format)
- Mac HFS (Hierarchical File Format)
- Rock Ridge
- Mount Rainier

Not all CD file system formats can be read by all operating systems. Table 13.20 shows the primary file systems used and which operating systems support them.

Table 13.20   CD File System Formats

CD File System	DOS/Win 3.x	Win 9x/Me	Win NT/2000/XP	Mac OS
High Sierra	Yes	Yes	Yes	Yes
ISO 9660	Yes	Yes	Yes	Yes
Joliet	Yes[1]	Yes	Yes	Yes[1]
UDF	No	Yes[2]	Yes[2]	Yes[2]
Mac HFS	No	No	No	Yes
Rock Ridge	Yes[1]	Yes[1]	Yes[1]	Yes[1]
Mount Rainier	No	Yes[3]	Yes[3]	Yes[3]

1. A short name, such as (SHORTN~1.TXT), will be shown in place of long filenames.

2. Only if a third-party UDF reader is installed.

3. Requires Mount Rainier (also called EasyWrite) hardware and driver software (Win98 or above) or a third-party reader program.

Note

The Mac HFS and Unix Rock Ridge file systems are not supported by PC operating systems such as DOS or Windows and therefore are not covered in depth here.

High Sierra

To make CD-ROM discs readable on all systems without having to develop custom file systems and drivers, it was in the best interests of all PC hardware and software manufacturers to resolve the CD-ROM file format standardization issue. In 1985, representatives from TMS, DEC, Microsoft, Hitachi, LaserData, Sony, Apple, Philips, 3M, Video Tools, Reference Technology, and Xebec met at what was then called the High Sierra Hotel and Casino in Lake Tahoe, Nevada, to create a common logical format and file structure for CD-ROMs. In 1986, they jointly published this standard as the "Working Paper for Information Processing: Volume and File Structure of CD-ROM Optical Discs for Information Exchange (1986)." This standard was subsequently referred to as the High Sierra format.

This agreement enabled all drives using the appropriate driver (such as MSCDEX.EXE supplied by Microsoft with DOS) to read all High Sierra format discs, opening the way for the mass production and acceptance of CD-ROM software publishing. Adoption of this standard also enabled disc publishers to provide cross-platform support for their software and easily manufacture discs for DOS, Unix, and other operating system formats. Without this agreement, the maturation of the CD-ROM marketplace would have taken years longer and the production of CD-ROM-based information would have been stifled.

The High Sierra format was submitted to the International Organization for Standardization (ISO). Two years later (in 1988), with several enhancements and changes, it was republished as the ISO 9660 standard. ISO 9660 was not exactly the same as High Sierra, but all drivers that would read High Sierra–formatted discs were quickly updated to handle both ISO 9660 and the original High Sierra format on which it was based.

For example, Microsoft wrote the MSCDEX.EXE (Microsoft CD-ROM extensions) driver in 1988 and licensed it to CD-ROM hardware and software vendors to include with their products. It wasn't until 1993 when MS-DOS 6.0 was released that MSCDEX was included with DOS as a standard feature. MSCDEX enables DOS to read ISO 9660–formatted (and High Sierra–formatted) discs. This driver works with the AT Attachment Packet Interface (ATAPI) or Advanced SCSI Programming Interface (ASPI) hardware-level device driver that comes with the drive. Microsoft built ISO 9660 and Joliet file system support directly into Windows 95 and later, with no additional drivers necessary.

ISO 9660

The ISO 9660 standard enabled full cross compatibility among different computer and operating systems. ISO 9660 was released in 1988 and was based on the work done by the High Sierra group. Although based on High Sierra, ISO 9660 does have some differences and refinements. It has three levels of interchange that dictate the features that can be used to ensure compatibility with different systems.

ISO 9660 Level 1 is the lowest common denominator of all CD file systems and is capable of being read by almost every computer platform, including Unix and Macintosh. The downside of this file system is that it is very limited with respect to filenames and directories. Level 1 interchange restrictions include

- Only uppercase characters A–Z, numbers 0–9, and the underscore (_) are allowed in filenames.
- 8.3 characters maximum for the name.extension (based on DOS limits).
- Directory names are eight characters maximum (no extension allowed).
- Directories are limited to eight levels deep.
- Files must be contiguous.

Level 2 interchange rules have the same limitations as Level 1, except that the filename and extension can be up to 30 characters long (both added together, not including the . separator). Finally, Level 3 interchange rules are the same as Level 2 except that files don't have to be contiguous.

Note that Windows 95 and later versions enable you to use file and folder names up to 255 characters long, which can include spaces as well as lowercase and many other characters not allowed in ISO 9660. To maintain backward compatibility with DOS, Windows 95 and later associate a short 8.3 format filename as an alias for each file that has a longer name. These alias short names are created automatically by Windows and can be viewed in the Properties for each file or by using the `DIR` command at a command prompt. To create these alias names, Windows truncates the name to six (or fewer) characters followed by a tilde (~) and a number starting with 1 and truncates the extension to three characters. Other numbers are used in the first part if other files that would have the same alias when truncated already exist. For example, the filename `This is a.test` gets `THISIS~1.TES` as an alias.

This filename alias creation is independent of your CD drive, but it is important to know that if you create or write to a CD using the ISO 9660 format using Level 1 restrictions, the alias short names are used when recording files to the disc, meaning any long filenames will be lost in the process. In fact, even the alias short name will be modified because ISO 9660 Level 1 restrictions don't allow a tilde—that character is converted to an underscore in the names written to the CD.

The ISO 9660 data starts at 2 seconds and 16 sectors into the disc, which is also known as *logical sector 16 of track one*. For a multisession disc, the ISO 9660 data is present in the first data track of each session containing CD-ROM tracks. This data identifies the location of the volume area—where the actual data is stored. The system area also lists the directories in this volume as the volume table of contents (VTOC), with pointers or addresses to various named areas, as illustrated in Figure 13.10. A significant difference between the CD directory structure and that of a normal hard disk is that the CD's system area also contains direct addresses of the files within the subdirectories, allowing the CD to seek specific sector locations on the spiral data track. Because the CD data is all on one long spiral track, when speaking of tracks in the context of a CD, we're actually talking about sectors or segments of data along that spiral.

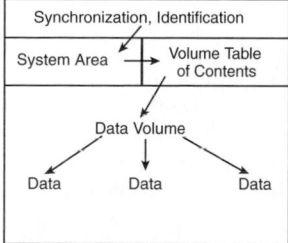

Figure 13.10 A diagam of basic ISO 9660 file organizational format.

To put the ISO 9660 format in perspective, the disc layout is roughly analogous to that of a floppy disk. A floppy disk has a system track that not only identifies itself as a floppy disk and reveals its density and operating system, but also tells the computer how it's organized (into directories, which are made up of files).

Joliet

Joliet is an extension of the ISO 9660 standard that Microsoft developed for use with Windows 95 and later. Joliet enables CDs to be recorded using filenames up to 64 characters long, including spaces and other characters from the Unicode international character set. Joliet also preserves an 8.3 alias for those programs that can't use the longer filenames.

In general, Joliet features the following specifications:

- File or directory names can be up to 64 Unicode characters (128 bytes) in length.
- Directory names can have extensions.

- Directories can be deeper than eight levels.
- Multisession recording is inherently supported.

Tip

Because Joliet supports a shorter path than Windows 9x and newer versions, you might have difficulties mastering a Joliet-format CD that contains extremely long pathnames. I recommend you shorten folder names in the file structure you create with the CD mastering software to avoid problems. Unfortunately, many CD mastering programs don't warn you about a pathname that is too long until after the burning process starts.

Due to backward-compatibility provisions, systems that don't support the Joliet extensions (such as older DOS systems) should still be capable of reading the disc. However, it will be interpreted as an ISO 9660 format using the short names instead.

Note

A bit of trivia: "Chicago" was the code name used by Microsoft for Windows 95. Joliet is the town outside of Chicago where Jake was locked up in the movie *The Blues Brothers*.

Universal Disk Format

UDF is a relatively new file system created by the Optical Storage Technology Association (OSTA) as an industry-standard format for use on optical media such as CD-ROM and DVD. UDF has several advantages over the ISO 9660 file system used by standard CD-ROMs but is most noted because it is designed to work with packet writing, a technique for writing small amounts of data to a CD-R/RW disc, treating it much like a standard magnetic drive.

The UDF file system allows long filenames up to 255 characters per name. There have been several versions of UDF, with most packet-writing software using UDF 1.5 or later. Packet-writing software such as DirectCD from Roxio writes in the UDF file system. However, standard CD-ROM drives, drivers, or operating systems such as DOS can't read UDF-formatted discs. Recordable drives can read them, but regular CD-ROM drives must conform to the MultiRead specification (see the section "MultiRead Specifications," later in this chapter) to be capable of reading UDF discs.

After you are sure that your drive can read UDF, you must check the OS. Most operating systems can't read UDF natively—the support has to be added via a driver. DOS can't read UDF at all; however, with Windows 95 and later, UDF-formatted discs can be read by installing a UDF driver. Typically, such a driver is included with the software that comes with most CD-RW drives. If you don't have a UDF driver, you can download one for free from Roxio at www.roxio.com. The Roxio UDF Reader is included with DirectCD 3.0 and later. After the UDF driver is installed, you do not need to take any special steps to read a UDF-formatted disc. The driver will be in the background waiting for you to insert a UDF-formatted disc.

You can close a DirectCD for Windows disc to make it readable in a normal CD-ROM drive, which converts the filenames to Joliet format and causes them to be truncated to 64 characters.

You can download the latest (revision 2.01) version of the Universal Disk Format from the OSTA Web site at www.osta.org/specs/index.htm.

Macintosh HFS

HFS is the file system used by the Macintosh OS. HFS can also be used on CD-ROMs; however, if that is done, they will not be readable on a PC. A hybrid disc can be produced with both Joliet and HFS or ISO 9660 and HFS file systems, and the disc would then be readable on both PCs and Macs. In that case, the system will see only the disc that is compatible, which is ISO 9660 or Joliet in the case of PCs.

Rock Ridge

The Rock Ridge Interchange Protocol (RRIP) was developed by an industry consortium called the Rock Ridge group. It was officially released in 1994 by the IEEE CD-ROM File System Format Working Group and specifies an extension to the ISO 9660 standard for CD-ROM that enables the recording of additional information to support Unix/POSIX file system features. Neither DOS nor Windows include support for the Rock Ridge extensions. However, because it is based on ISO 9660, the files are still readable on a PC and the RRIP extensions are simply ignored.

Note

An interesting bit of trivia is that the Rock Ridge name was taken from the fictional Western town in the movie *Blazing Saddles.*

Mount Rainier

Mount Rainier is a recent standard being promoted by Philips, Sony, Microsoft, and HP (Compaq). Also called EasyWrite (see Figure 13.11), Mount Rainier enables native operating system support for data storage on CD-RW and DVD+RW. This makes the technology much easier to use (no special drivers or packet-writing software is necessary) and enables CD-RW and DVD+RW drives to become fully integrated storage solutions.

Figure 13.11   The EasyWrite logo is used on CD-RW and DVD+R/RW drives manufactured in 2003 and beyond that support the Mount Rainier standard.

The main features of Mount Rainier are as follows:

- *Integral defect management.* Standard drives rely on driver software to manage defects.

- *Direct addressing at the 2KB sector level to minimize wasted space.* Standard CD-RW media uses a block size of 64KB.

- *Background formatting so that new media can be used in seconds after first insertion.* Standard CD-RW formatting can take up to 45 minutes depending on drive speed.

- *Standardized command set.* Standard software cannot work with new drives until revised command files are available.

- *Standardized physical layout.* Differences in standard UDF software can make reading media written by another program difficult.

To use Mount Rainier, you must have a drive that supports the standard. These are sometimes called CD-MRW or DVD+MRW drives and might instead bear either the Mount Rainier or EasyWrite logo. Some existing CD-RW drives can be updated to MRW status by reflashing the firmware in the drive; however, most older drives will need to be replaced instead.

Also required is software support directly in the operating system (such as with Windows XP or later), or software support can be added via a third-party add-on application for older operating systems.

Software Architects (www.softarch.com) produces WriteCD-RW Pro! Software, which enables interchange between Mount Rainier and conventional UDF media, as well as between UDF media written with different programs and to different standards.

The first Mount Rainier drive (Philips RWDV1610B) was released in April 2002, and since then many more have followed. Because only minor changes are required in the drive circuitry and firmware to enable Mount Rainier support, many newer drives include Mount Rainier capability; check the drive vendor's Web site or manual to determine compatibility. In addition, the DVD+RW standard was designed with Mount Rainier compatibility in mind—defect management was included inherently from the beginning. (DVD-RW drives don't support defect management, so they are not compatible with Mount Rainier.) The first DVD+RW drives with Mount Rainier/EasyWrite compatibility began shipping in early 2003.

Because Mount Rainier essentially makes CD-MRW and DVD+MRW drives function as high-capacity replacements for floppy, Zip, and SuperDisk drives, it won't be long before those are but a distant memory.

The latest version of the Mount Rainier specification, version 1.1., includes DVD+RW as well as CD-RW drives. It can be ordered from the Philips Intellectual Property and Standards Web site (www.licensing. philips.com). For more information, go to the Mount Rainier Web site at www.mt-rainier.org.

DVD Formats and Standards

As with the CD standards, the DVD standards are published in reference books produced mainly by the DVD Forum, but also by other companies.

The DVD-Video and DVD-ROM standards are pretty well established, but recordable DVD technology is still evolving. The standards situation for recordable DVD is more confusing than usual, especially because there are at least four different (and somewhat incompatible) recording formats! It remains to be seen which will have the best support and become the most popular, but so far the DVD-RW and DVD+RW formats are both very popular. However, DVD+RW looks to be by far the most promising for the future with higher speed, features that make it ideal for both video and data recording, higher compatibility with existing DVD players and drives, and finally Microsoft's endorsement via including support in upcoming versions of Windows. At this point, the only type of recordable DVD I recommend for both home DVD recorders and PC-based DVD recordable drives are units that conform to the DVD+RW format. That also includes DVD±R/RW drives (which support both formats in a single unit), making them essentially compatible with everything. I recommend avoiding drives that do not support the DVD+R/RW format.

The current standard DVD formats are shown in Table 13.21.

Table 13.21   Standard DVD Formats and Capacities

Format	Disc Size	Sides	Layers	Data Capacity	MPEG-2 Video Capacity
DVD-ROM Formats and Capacities					
DVD-5	120mm	Single	Single	4.7GB	2.2 hours
DVD-9	120mm	Single	Double	8.5GB	4.0 hours
DVD-10	120mm	Double	Single	9.4GB	4.4 hours
DVD-14	120mm	Double	Both	13.2GB	6.3 hours
DVD-18	120mm	Double	Double	17.1GB	8.1 hours
DVD-1	80mm	Single	Single	1.5GB	0.7 hours
DVD-2	80mm	Single	Double	2.7GB	1.3 hours
DVD-3	80mm	Double	Single	2.9GB	1.4 hours
DVD-4	80mm	Double	Double	5.3GB	2.5 hours

Table 13.21   Continued

Format	Disc Size	Sides	Layers	Data Capacity	MPEG-2 Video Capacity
Recordable DVD Formats and Capacities					
DVD-R 1.0	120mm	Single	Single	3.95GB	1.9 hours
DVD-R 2.0	120mm	Single	Single	4.7GB	2.2 hours
DVD-RAM 1.0	120mm	Single	Single	2.58GB	N/A
DVD-RAM 1.0	120mm	Double	Single	5.16GB	N/A
DVD-RAM 2.0	120mm	Single	Single	4.7GB	N/A
DVD-RAM 2.0	120mm	Double	Single	9.4GB	N/A
DVD-RAM 2.0	80mm	Single	Single	1.46GB	N/A
DVD-RAM 2.0	80mm	Double	Single	2.65GB	N/A
DVD-RW 2.0	120mm	Single	Single	4.7GB	N/A
DVD+RW 2.0	120mm	Single	Single	4.7GB	2.2hours
DVD+RW 2.0	120mm	Double	Single	9.4GB	4.4 hours
DVD+R 1.0	120mm	Single	Single	4.7GB	2.2 hours
CD-ROM Formats and Capacities (for comparison)					
CD-ROM/R/RW	120mm	Single	Single	0.737GB	N/A
CD-ROM/R/RW	80mm	Single	Single	0.194GB	N/A

With advancements coming in blue-light lasers, this capacity will be increased several-fold in the future with an HD-DVD format that can store up to 20GB per layer. Prototype players have already been shown by major manufacturers, although you shouldn't expect to see HD-DVD on the market just yet.

DVD drives are fully backward-compatible and as such are capable of playing today's CD-ROMs as well as audio CDs. When playing existing CDs, the performance of current models is equivalent to a 40x or faster CD-ROM drive. Therefore, users who currently own slower CD-ROM drives might want to consider a DVD drive instead of upgrading to a faster CD-ROM drive. Several manufacturers have announced plans to phase out their CD-ROM drive products in favor of DVD. DVD is rapidly making CD-ROMs obsolete in the same way that audio CDs displaced vinyl records in the 1980s. The only thing keeping the CD-ROM format alive is the battle between competing DVD recordable standards and the fact that CD-R and CD-RW are rapidly becoming the de facto replacements for the floppy drive.

The current crop of DVD drives features several improvements over the first-generation models of 1997. Those units were expensive, slow, and incompatible with either CD-R or CD-RW media. Many early units asked your overworked video card to try to double as an MPEG decoder to display DVD movies, with mediocre results in speed and image quality. As is often the case with "leading-edge" devices, their deficiencies make them eminently avoidable.

Many PC vendors have integrated DVD-ROM drives into their new high-end computers, usually as an option. Originally, most of these installations included an MPEG-2 decoder board for processing the compressed video on DVDs. This offloads the intensive MPEG calculations from the system processor and enables the display of full-screen, full-motion video on a PC. After processors crossed 400MHz in speed, performing MPEG-2 decoding reliably in software became possible, so any systems faster than that usually don't include a hardware decoder card.

Some manufacturers of video display adapters have begun to include MPEG decoder hardware on their products. These adapters are known as "DVD MPEG-2 accelerated" and call for some of the MPEG decoding tasks to be performed by software. Any software decoding involved in an MPEG solution places a greater burden on the main system processor and can therefore yield less satisfactory results on slower systems.

DIVX (Discontinued Standard)

DIVX (Digital Video Express) was a short-lived proprietary DVD format developed by Digital Video Express (a Hollywood law firm) and Circuit City. It was discontinued on June 16, 1999, less than a year after it was released.

The name now lives on as an open encoding standard for DVD video. However, this encoding standard actually has no relation to the original DIVX format other than the name.

Note

More detailed coverage of DIVX is included in Chapter 13 of the 11th and 12th editions of this book, both of which are included in their entirety on the disc accompanying this book.

DVD Drive Compatibility

When DVD drives first appeared on the market, they were touted to be fully backward-compatible with CD-ROM drives. Although that might be the case when reading commercially pressed CD-ROM discs, that was not necessarily true when reading CD-R or CD-RW media. Fortunately, the industry has responded with standards that let you know in advance how compatible your DVD drive will be. These standards are called *MultiRead* for computer-based drives and *MultiPlay* for consumer standalone devices, such as DVD-Video or CD-DA players. See the section "MultiRead Specifications," later in this chapter.

DVD Movie Playback on a PC

Almost all DVD-ROM and rewritable DVD drives (except for some DVD-RAM drives) include a DVD playback program such as MyDVD or SoftDVD. These programs enable you to interact with a DVD movie the same way you would if it were being played through a DVD player.

However, if your video card doesn't have built-in MPEG-2 decoding, you might want to consider upgrading to a better video card that has this feature (all recent ATI and NVIDIA chipsets support MPEG-2 decoding in hardware) or install a separate MPEG-2 decoder. Hardware decoding is very important for best quality, particularly if your processor has a clock speed below 1GHz (it's possible with a 400MHz machine, but at least 1GHz is ideal).

If you are using a hardware decoder, it requires an open PCI expansion slot, as well as an interrupt request (IRQ) resource from your system. Also, to view the movies on your PC's display, you must somehow connect the decoder card to your existing video card. This can be accomplished via an internal connection to the card, or it can use a loop-through connection to the monitor port on the back of the card. Some video cards include MPEG-2 decoders (players) built in. Table 13.22 compares MPEG decoder hardware (built in to a separate card or integrated into a video card's 3D accelerator chip) with MPEG player.

Table 13.22   MPEG Decoder Hardware Versus MPEG Player Software

Consideration	MPEG Decoder	MPEG Player Software
PCI/AGP slot usage	One for decoder; one for VGA* or integrated into video chipset	Video card (or integrated video)
Movie image quality	High	Varies
Playback speed	High	Varies
MPEG game compatibility	Yes	No

*If integrated into graphics card, uses one slot (AGP or PCI) only

DVD Copy Protection

DVD video discs employ several levels of protection that are mainly controlled by the DVD Copy Control Association (DVD CCA) and a third-party company called Macrovision. This protection typically applies only to DVD-Video discs, not DVD-ROM software. So, for example, copy protection might affect your ability to make backup copies of *The Matrix*, but it won't affect a DVD encyclopedia or other software application distributed on DVD-ROM discs.

Note that every one of these protection systems has been broken, so with a little extra expense or the correct software, you can defeat the protection and make copies of your DVDs either to other digital media (hard drive, DVD+RW, CD-R/RW, and so on) or analog media (such as a VHS or other tape format).

A lot of time and money are wasted on these protection schemes, which can't really foil the professional bootleggers willing to spend the time and money to work around them. But they can make it difficult for the average person to legitimately back up his expensive media.

The three main protection systems used with DVD-Video discs are:

- Regional Playback Control (RPC)
- Content Scrambling System (CSS)
- Analog Protection System (APS)

Caution

The Digital Millennium Copyright Act (DMCA) signed into law in 1998 prohibits the breaking of copy-protection schemes or the distribution of information (such as tools, Web site links, and so forth) on how to break these schemes.

Regional Playback Control

Regional playback was designed to allow discs sold in specific geographical regions of the world to play only on players sold in those same regions. The idea was to allow a movie to be released at different times in different parts of the world and to prevent people from ordering discs from regions in which the movie had not been released yet.

Eight regions are defined in the RPC standard. Discs (and players) usually are identified by a small logo or label showing the region number superimposed on a world globe. Multiregion discs are possible, as are discs that are not region locked. If a disc plays in more than one region, it has more than one number on the globe. The regions are

- *Region Code 1*. United States, Canada, U.S. Territories
- *Region Code 2*. Japan, Europe, South Africa, and the Middle East
- *Region Code 3*. Southeast Asia and East Asia
- *Region Code 4*. Australia, New Zealand, Pacific Islands, Central America, Mexico, South America, and the Caribbean
- *Region Code 5*. Eastern Europe (east of Poland and the Balkans), Indian subcontinent, Africa, North Korea, and Mongolia
- *Region Code 6*. China and Tibet
- *Region Code All*. Special international or mobile venues, such as airplanes, cruise ships, and so on

The region code is embedded in the hardware of DVD video players. Most players are preset for a specific region and can't be changed. Some companies who sell the players modify them to play discs from all regions; these are called *region-free* or *code-free* players. Some newer discs have an added region code enhancement (RCE) function that checks to see whether the player is configured for multiple or all regions and then, if it is, refuses to play. Most newer region-free modified players know how to query the disc first to circumvent this check as well.

DVD-ROM drives used in PCs originally did not have RPC in the hardware, placing that responsibility instead on the software used to play DVD video discs on the PC. The player software would usually lock the region code to the first disc that was played and then from that point on, play only discs from that region. Reinstalling the software enabled the region code to be reset, and numerous patches were posted on Web sites to enable resetting the region code even without reinstalling the software. Because of the relative ease of defeating the region-coding restrictions with DVD-ROM drives, starting on January 1, 2000, all DVD-ROM drives were required to have RPC-II, which embeds the region coding directly into the drive.

RPC-II (or RPC-2) places the region lock in the drive, and not in the playing or MPEG-2 decoding software. You can set the region code in RPC-II drives up to five times total, which basically means you can change it up to four times after the initial setting. Usually, the change can be made using the player software you are using, or you can download region change software from the drive manufacturer. Upon making the fourth change (which is the fifth setting), the drive is locked on the last region set.

Content Scramble System

The Content Scramble System (CSS) provides the main protection for DVD-Video discs. It wasn't until this protection was implemented that the Motion Picture Association of America (MPAA) agreed to release movies in the DVD format, which is the main reason the rollout of DVD had been significantly delayed.

CSS originally was developed by Matsushita (Panasonic) and is used to digitally scramble and encrypt the audio and video data on a DVD-Video disc. Descrambling requires a pair of 40-bit (5-byte) keys (numeric codes). One of the keys is unique to the disc, whereas the other is unique to the video title set (VTS file) being descrambled. The disc and title keys are stored in the lead-in area of the disc in an encrypted form. The CSS scrambling and key writing are carried out during the glass mastering procedure, which is part of the disc manufacturing process.

You can see this encryption in action if you put a DVD disc into a DVD-ROM drive on a PC, copy the files to your hard drive, and then try to view the files. The files are usually called VTS_*xx_yy*.VOB (video object), where *xx* represents the title number and *yy* represents the section number. Typically, all the files for a given movie have the same title number and the movie is spread out among several 1GB or smaller files with different section numbers. These .VOB files contain both the encrypted video and audio streams for the movie interleaved together. Other files with a .IFO extension contain information used by the DVD player to decode the video and audio streams in the .VOB files. If you copy the .VOB and .IFO files onto your hard drive and try to click or play the .VOB files directly, you either see and hear scrambled video and audio or receive an error message about playing copy-protected files.

This encryption is not a problem if you use a CSS-licensed player (either hardware or software) and play the files directly from the DVD disc. All DVD players, whether they are consumer standalone units or software players on your PC, have their own unique CSS unlock key assigned to them. Every DVD video disc has 400 of these 5-byte keys stamped onto the disc in the lead-in area (which is not usually accessible by programs) on the DVD in encrypted form. The decryption routine in the player uses its unique code to retrieve and unencrypt the disc key, which is then used to retrieve and unencrypt the title keys. CSS is essentially a three-level encryption that originally was thought to be very secure but has proven otherwise.

In October 1999, a 16-year-old Norwegian programmer was able to extract the first key from one of the commercial PC-based players, which allowed him to very easily decrypt disc and title keys. A now famous program called DeCSS was then written that can break the CSS protection on any DVD video title and save unencrypted .VOB files to a hard disk that can be played by any MPEG-2 decoder program. Needless to say, this utility (and others based on it) has been the cause of much concern in the movie industry and has caused many legal battles over the distribution and even links to this code on the Web. Do a search on DeCSS for some interesting legal reading.

As if that weren't enough, in March 2001, two MIT students published an incredibly short (only seven lines long!) and simple program that can unscramble CSS so quickly that a movie can essentially be unscrambled in real-time while it is playing. They wrote and demonstrated the code as part of a two-day seminar they conducted on the controversial Digital Millennium Copyright Act, illustrating how trivial the CSS protection really is.

Because of the failure of CSS, the DVD forum is now actively looking into other means of protection, especially including digital watermarks, which consists essentially of digital noise buried into the data stream, which is supposed to be invisible to normal viewing. Unfortunately, when similar technology was applied to DIVX (the discontinued proprietary DVD standard), these watermarks caused a slight impairment of the image—a raindrop or bullet-hole effect could be seen by some in the picture. Watermarks also might require new equipment to play the discs.

Analog Protection System

APS (also called CopyGuard by Macrovision) is an analog protection system developed by Macrovision and is designed to prevent making VCR tapes of DVD-Video discs. APS requires codes to be added to the disc, as well as special modifications in the player. APS starts with the creation or mastering of a DVD, where APS is enabled by setting predefined control codes in the recording. During playback in an APS-enabled (Macrovision-enabled) player, the digital-to-analog converter (DAC) chip inside the player adds the APS signals to the analog output signal being sent to the screen. These additions to the signal are designed so that they are invisible when viewed on a television or monitor but cause copies made on most VCRs to appear distorted. Unfortunately, some TVs or other displays can react to the distortions added to create a less-than-optimum picture.

APS uses two signal modifications called automatic gain control and colorstripe. The automatic gain control process consists of pulses placed in the vertical scan interval of the video signal, which TVs can't detect but which cause dim and noisy pictures, loss of color, loss of video, tearing, and so forth on a VCR. This process has been used since 1985 on many prerecorded video tapes to prevent copying. The colorstripe process modifies colorburst information that is also transparent on television displays but produces lines across the picture when recorded on a VCR.

Note that many older players don't have the licensed Macrovision circuits and simply ignore the code to turn on the APS signal modifications. Also, various image stabilizer, enhancer, or copyguard decoder units are available that can plug in between the player and VCR to remove the APS copyguard signal and allow a perfect recording to be made.

CD/DVD Read-Only Drives and Specifications

When evaluating a CD-ROM or DVD-ROM drive for your PC, you should consider three distinct sets of criteria, as follows:

- The drive's performance specifications
- The interface the drive requires for connection to your PC
- The physical disc-handling system the drive uses

These criteria will affect how fast the drive operates, how it is connected to your system, and how convenient (or inconvenient) it is to use. These same criteria, plus media and speed issues, are also important considerations when selecting a rewritable drive.

Performance Specifications

Many factors in a drive can affect performance, and several specifications are involved. Typical performance figures published by manufacturers are the data transfer rate, the access time, the internal cache or buffers (if any), and the interface the drive uses. The following sections examine these specifications.

CD Data Transfer Rate

The data transfer rate for a CD-ROM or CD-RW drive tells you how quickly the drive can read from the disc and transfer to the host computer. Normally, transfer rates indicate the drive's capability for reading large, sequential streams of data.

Transfer speed is measured two ways. The one most commonly quoted with CD/DVD drives is the "x" speed, which is defined as a multiple of the particular standard base rate. For example, CD-ROM drives transfer at 153.6KBps according to the original standard. Drives that transfer twice that are 2x, 40 times that are 40x, and so on. DVD drives transfer at 1,385KBps at the base rate, whereas drives that are 20 times faster than that are listed as 20x. Note that because almost all faster drives feature CAV, the "x" speed usually indicated is a maximum that is seen only when reading data near the outside (end) of a disc. The speed near the beginning of the disc might be as little as half that, and of course, average speeds are somewhere in the middle.

With recordable CD drives, the speed is reported for various modes. CD-R drives have two speeds listed (one for writing, the other for reading), CD-RW drives have three, and CD-RW/DVD-ROM drives have four. On a CD-RW drive, the speeds are in the form A/B/C, where A is the speed when writing CD-Rs, B is the speed when writing CD-RWs, and C is the speed when reading. The first CD-RW drive on the market was 2/2/6, with versions up to 54/24/52 available today. CD-RW/DVD-ROM drives use the format A/B/C-D, where the fourth number represents the DVD-ROM reading speed. Some of the fastest CD-RW/DVD-ROM drives today report 20/10/40-12.

CD Drive Speed

When a drive seeks out a specific data sector or musical track on the disc, it looks up the address of the data from a table of contents contained in the lead-in area and positions itself near the beginning of this data across the spiral, waiting for the right string of bits to flow past the laser beam.

Because CDs originally were designed to record audio, the speed at which the drive reads the data had to be constant. To maintain this constant flow, CD-ROM data is recorded using a technique called *constant linear velocity (CLV)*. This means that the track (and thus the data) is always moving past the read laser at the same speed, which originally was defined as 1.3 meters per second. Because the track is a spiral that is wound more tightly near the center of the disc, the disc must spin at various rates to maintain the same track linear speed. In other words, to maintain a CLV, the disk must spin more quickly when reading the inner track area than when reading the outer track area. The speed of rotation in a 1x drive (1.3 meters per second is considered 1x speed) varies from 540rpm when reading the start (inner part) of the track down to 212rpm when reading the end (outer part) of the track.

In the quest for greater performance, drive manufacturers began increasing the speeds of their drives by making them spin more quickly. A drive that spins twice as fast was called a 2x drive, one that spins four times faster was called 4x, and so on. This was fine until about the 12x point, where drives were spinning discs at rates from 2,568rpm to 5,959rpm to maintain a constant data rate. At higher speeds than this, it became difficult to build motors that could change speeds (spin up or down) as quickly as necessary when data was read from different parts of the disc. Because of this, most drives rated faster than 12x spin the disc at a fixed rotational, rather than linear speed. This is termed *constant angular velocity (CAV)* because the angular velocity (or rotational speed) remains a constant.

CAV drives are also generally quieter than CLV drives because the motors don't have to try to accelerate or decelerate as quickly. A drive (such as most rewritables) that combines CLV and CAV technologies is referred to as *Partial-CAV* or *P-CAV*. Most writable drives, for example, function in CLV mode when burning the disc and in CAV mode when reading. Table 13.23 compares CLV and CAV.

Table 13.23   CLV Versus CAV Technology Quick Reference

	CLV (Constant Linear Velocity)	**CAV (Constant Angular Velocity)**
Speed of CD rotation	Varies with data position on CD—faster on inner tracks than on outer tracks	Constant
Data transfer rate	Constant	Varies with data position on CD—faster on outer tracks than on inner tracks
Average noise level	Higher	Lower

CD-ROM drives have been available in speeds from 1x up to 52x and beyond. Most nonrewritable drives up to 12x were CLV; most drives from 16x and up are CAV. With CAV drives, the disc spins at a constant speed, so track data moves past the read laser at various speeds, depending on where the data is physically located on the CD (near the inner or outer part of the track). This also means that CAV drives read the data at the outer edge (end) of the disk more quickly than data near the center (beginning). This allows for some misleading advertising. For example, a 12x CLV drive reads data at 1.84MBps no matter where that data is on the disc. On the other hand, a 16x CAV drive reads data at speeds up to 16x (2.46MBps) on the outer part of the disc, but it also reads at a much lower speed of only 6.9x (1.06MBps) when reading the inner part of the disc (that is the part they don't tell you). On average, this would be only 11.5x, or about 1.76MBps. In fact, the average is actually overly optimistic because discs are read from the inside (slower part) out, and an average would relate only to reading completely full discs. The real-world average could be much less than that.

What this all means is that on average the 12x CLV drive would be noticeably faster than the 16x drive, and faster than even a 20x drive! Remember that all advertised speeds on CAV drives are only the maximum transfer speed the drive can achieve, and it can achieve that only when reading the very outer (end) part of the disc.

Table 13.24 contains data showing CD-ROM drive speeds along with transfer rates and other interesting data.

Vibration problems can cause high-speed drives to drop to lower speeds to enable reliable reading of CD-ROMs. Your CD-ROM can become unbalanced, for example, if you apply a small paper label to its surface to identify the CD or affix its serial number or code for easy reinstallation. For this reason, many of the faster CD and DVD drives come with autobalancing or vibration-control mechanisms to overcome these problems. The only drawback is that if they detect a vibration, they slow down the disc, thereby reducing the transfer rate performance.

A company called Zen Research developed a technology called TrueX in the late 1990s, which used multiple laser beams to achieve constant high transfer rates with lower spin rates. Unfortunately, TrueX drives made by vendors such as Kenwood didn't live up to the promised performance of TrueX technology and suffered from many reliability problems. Zen Research closed in mid-2002, and TrueX drives are no longer sold. Instead of TrueX, most are now moving to Z-CLV (zoned CLV) or P-CAV (partial CAV) designs, which help increase average performance while keeping rotational speeds under control.

Table 13.24   CD-ROM Drive Speeds and Transfer Rates

Column 1	Column 2	Column 3	Column 4	Column 5	Column 6
Advertised CD-ROM Speed (Max. if CAV)	Time to Read 74-Minute CD if CLV	Time to Read 80-Minute CD if CLV	Transfer Rate (Bps) (Max. if CAV)	Actual CD-ROM Speed Minimum if CAV	Minimum Transfer Rate if CAV (Bps)
1x	74.0	80.0	153,600	0.4x	61,440
2x	37.0	40.0	307,200	0.9x	138,240
4x	18.5	20.0	614,400	1.7x	261,120
6x	12.3	13.3	921,600	2.6x	399,360
8x	9.3	10.0	1,228,800	3.4x	522,240
10x	7.4	8.0	1,536,000	4.3x	660,480
12x	6.2	6.7	1,843,200	5.2x	798,720
16x	4.6	5.0	2,457,600	6.9x	1,059,840
20x	3.7	4.0	3,072,000	8.6x	1,320,960
24x	3.1	3.3	3,686,400	10.3x	1,582,080
32x	2.3	2.5	4,915,200	13.8x	2,119,680
40x	1.9	2.0	6,144,000	17.2x	2,641,920
48x	1.5	1.7	7,372,800	20.7x	3,179,520
50x	1.5	1.6	7,680,000	21.6x	3,317,760
52x	1.4	1.5	7,987,200	22.4x	3,440,640
56x	1.3	1.4	8,601,600	24.1x	3,701,760

Each of the columns in Table 13.24 is explained here:

Column 1 indicates the advertised drive speed. This is a constant speed if the drive is CLV (most 12x and lower) or a maximum speed only if CAV.

Columns 2 and 3 indicate how long it would take to read a full disc if the drive was CLV. For CAV drives, those figures would be longer because the average read speed is less than the advertised speed. The fourth column indicates the data transfer rate, which for CAV drives would be a maximum figure only when reading the end of a disc.

Columns 3–6 indicate the actual minimum "x" speed for CAV drives, along with the minimum transfer speed (when reading the start of any disc) and an optimistic average speed (true only when reading a full disc; otherwise, it would be even lower) in both "x" and byte-per-second formats.

DVD Drive Speed

As with CDs, DVDs rotate counterclockwise (as viewed from the reading laser) and typically are recorded at a constant data rate called CLV. Therefore, the track (and thus the data) is always moving past the read laser at the same speed, which originally was defined as 3.49 meters per second (or 3.84mps on dual-layer discs). Because the track is a spiral that is wound more tightly near the center of the disc, the disc must spin at varying rates to maintain the same track linear speed. In other words, to maintain a CLV, the disk must spin more quickly when reading the inner track area and more slowly when reading the outer track area. The speed of rotation in a 1x drive (3.49 meters per second is considered 1x speed) varies from 1,515rpm when reading the start (inner part) of the track down to 570rpm when reading the end (outer part) of the track.

Single-speed (1x) DVD-ROM drives provide a data transfer rate of 1.385MBps, which means the data transfer rate from a DVD-ROM at 1x speed is roughly equivalent to a 9x CD-ROM (1x CD-ROM data transfer rate is 153.6KBps, or 0.1536MBps). This does not mean, however, that a 1x DVD drive can read CDs at 9x rates: DVD drives actually spin at a rate that is just under three times faster than a CD-ROM drive of the same speed. So, a 1x DVD drive spins at about the same rotational speed as a 2.7x CD drive. Many DVD

Column 7	Column 8	Column 9	Column 10	Column 11	Column 12
Average CD-ROM Speed if CAV	Average Transfer Rate if CAV (Bps)	Maximum Linear Speed (mps)	Maximum Linear Speed (mph)	Rotational Speed Min. if CLV Max. if CAV (rpm)	Rotational Speed Max. if CLV (rpm)
0.7x	107,520	1.3	2.9	214	497
1.5x	222,720	2.6	5.8	428	993
2.9x	437,760	5.2	11.6	856	1,986
4.3x	660,480	7.8	17.4	1,284	2,979
5.7x	875,520	10.4	23.3	1,712	3,973
7.2x	1,098,240	13.0	29.1	2,140	4,966
8.6x	1,320,960	15.6	34.9	2,568	5,959
11.5x	1,758,720	20.8	46.5	3,425	7,945
14.3x	2,196,480	26.0	58.2	4,281	9,931
17.2x	2,634,240	31.2	69.8	5,137	11,918
22.9x	3,517,440	41.6	93.1	6,849	15,890
28.6x	4,392,960	52.0	116.3	8,561	19,863
34.4x	5,276,160	62.4	139.6	10,274	23,835
35.8x	5,498,880	65.0	145.4	10,702	24,828
37.2x	5,713,920	67.6	151.2	11,130	25,821
40.1x	6,151,680	72.8	162.8	11,986	27,808

Columns 7–8 indicate the maximum linear speeds the drive will attain, in both meters per second and miles per hour. CLV drives maintain those speeds everywhere on the disc, whereas CAV drives reach those speeds only on the outer part of a disc.

Columns 9–12 indicate the rotational speeds of a drive. The first of those shows how fast the disc spins when reading the start of a disc; this would apply to either CAV or CLV drives. For CAV drives, that figure is constant no matter where on the disc it is reading. The last column shows the maximum rotational speed if the drive were a CLV type. Because most drives over 12x are CAV, those figures are mostly theoretical for the 16x and faster drives.

drives list two speeds, one for reading DVDs and another for reading CDs. For example, a DVD-ROM drive listed as a 16x/40x would indicate the performance when reading DVDs/CDs, respectively.

As with CDs, drive manufacturers began increasing the speeds of their drives by making them spin more quickly. A drive that spins twice as fast was called a 2x drive, a drive that spins four times as fast was 4x, and so on. At higher speeds, it became difficult to build motors that could change speeds (spin up or down) as quickly as needed when data was read from different parts of the disc. Because of this, faster DVD drives spin the disc at a fixed rotational, rather than linear speed. This is termed *constant angular velocity (CAV)* because the angular velocity (or rotational speed) remains a constant.

The faster drives are useful primarily for data, not video. Having a faster drive can reduce or eliminate the pause during layer changes when playing a DVD video disc, but having a faster drive has no effect on video quality.

DVD-ROM drives have been available in speeds up to 20x or more, but because virtually all are CAV, they actually achieve the rated transfer speed only when reading the outer part of a disc. Table 13.25 shows the data rates for DVD drives reading DVDs and how that rate compares to a CD-ROM drive.

Table 13.25 DVD Speeds and Transfer Rates

Column 1	Column 2	Column 3	Column 4	Column 5	Column 6
Advertised DVD-ROM Speed (Max. if CAV)	Time to Read Single Layer DVD if CLV	Time to Read Dual Layer DVD if CLV	Transfer Rate (Bytes/sec) (Max. if CAV)	Actual DVD Speed Minimum if CAV	Minimum Transfer Rate if CAV (Bytes/sec)
1x	56.5	51.4	1,384,615	0.4x	553,846
2x	28.3	25.7	2,769,231	0.8x	1,107,692
4x	14.1	12.8	5,538,462	1.7x	2,353,846
6x	9.4	8.6	8,307,692	2.5x	3,461,538
8x	7.1	6.4	11,076,923	3.3x	4,569,231
10x	5.7	5.1	13,846,154	4.1x	5,676,923
12x	4.7	4.3	16,615,385	5.0x	6,923,077
16x	3.5	3.2	22,153,846	6.6x	9,138,462
20x	2.8	2.6	27,692,308	8.3x	11,492,308
24x	2.4	2.1	33,230,769	9.9x	13,707,692
32x	1.8	1.6	44,307,692	13.2x	18,276,923
40x	1.4	1.3	55,384,615	16.6x	22,984,615
48x	1.2	1.1	66,461,538	19.9x	27,553,846
50x	1.1	1.0	69,230,769	20.7x	28,661,538

Column 1 indicates the advertised drive speed. This is a constant speed if the drive is CLV or a maximum speed only if CAV (most DVD-ROM drives are CAV).

Columns 2 and 3 indicate how long it would take to read a full disc (single- or dual-layer) if the drive were CLV. For CAV drives, those figures are longer because the average read speed is less than the advertised speed. The fourth column indicates the data transfer rate, which for CAV drives is a maximum figure seen only when reading the end of a disc.

Columns 4–8 indicate the actual minimum "x" speed for CAV drives, along with the minimum transfer speed (when reading the start of any disc) and an optimistic average speed (true only when reading a full disc; otherwise, it's even lower) in both "x" and byte-per-second formats.

Columns 9 and 10 indicate the maximum linear speeds the drive attains, in both meters per second and miles per hour. CLV drives maintain those speeds everywhere on the disc, whereas CAV drives reach those speeds only on the outer part of a disc.

Access Time

The access time for a CD or DVD drive is measured the same way as for PC hard disk drives. In other words, the access time is the delay between the drive receiving the command to read and its actual first reading of a bit of data. The time is recorded in milliseconds; a typical manufacturer's rating would be listed as 95ms. This is an average access rate; the true access rate depends entirely on where the data is located on the disc. When the read mechanism is positioned to a portion of the disc nearer to the narrower center, the access rate is faster than when it is positioned at the wider outer perimeter. Access rates quoted by many manufacturers are an average taken by calculating a series of random reads from a disc.

Obviously, a faster (that is, a lower) average access rate is desirable, especially when you rely on the drive to locate and pull up data quickly. Access times for CD and DVD drives have been steadily improving, and the advancements are discussed later in this chapter. Note that these average times are significantly slower than PC hard drives, ranging from 200ms to below 100ms, compared to the 8ms

Column 7	Column 8	Column 9	Column 10	Column 11	Column 12	Column 13
Average DVD Speed if CAV	Average Transfer Rate if CAV (Bytes/sec)	Maximum Linear Speed (m/sec)	Maximum Linear Speed (mph)	Single Layer Rot. Speed Min. if CLV Max. if CAV (rpm)	Single Layer Rot. Speed Max. if CLV (rpm)	Usual Transfer Rate When Reading CD-ROMs
0.7x	969,231	3.5	7.8	570	1,515	2.7x
1.4x	1,938,462	7.0	15.6	1,139	3,030	5.4x
2.9x	3,946,154	14.0	31.2	2,279	6,059	11x
4.3x	5,884,615	20.9	46.8	3,418	9,089	16x
5.7x	7,823,077	27.9	62.5	4,558	12,119	21x
7.1x	9,761,538	34.9	78.1	5,697	15,149	27x
8.5x	11,769,231	41.9	93.7	6,836	18,178	32x
11.3	15,646,154	55.8	124.9	9,115	24,238	43x
14.2	19,592,308	69.8	156.1	11,394	30,297	54x
17.0	23,469,231	83.8	187.4	13,673	36,357	64x
22.6	31,292,308	111.7	249.8	18,230	48,476	86x
28.3	39,184,615	139.6	312.3	22,788	60,595	107x
34.0	47,007,692	167.5	374.7	27,345	72,714	129x
35.4	48,946,154	174.5	390.3	28,485	75,743	134x

Columns 11 and 12 indicate the rotational speeds of a drive. The first of those shows how quickly the disc spins when reading the start of a disc. This applies to either CAV or CLV drives. For CAV drives, that figure is constant no matter where on the disc it is being read. The second of those two columns shows the maximum rotational speed if the drive were a CLV type. Because most faster drives are CAV, those figures are mostly theoretical for the faster drives.

Column 13 shows the speed the drive would be rated if it were a CD-ROM drive. This is based on the rotational speed, not the transfer rate. In other words, a 12x DVD drive would perform as a 32x CD-ROM drive when reading CDs. Most DVD drives list their speeds when reading CDs in the specifications. Due to the use of PCAV (Partial CAV) designs, some might have higher CD performances than the table indicates.

access time of a typical hard disk drive. Most of the speed difference lies in the construction of the drive itself. Hard drives have multiple-read heads that range over a smaller surface area of the medium; CD/DVD drives have only one laser pickup, and it must be capable of accessing the entire range of the disc. In addition, the data on a CD is organized in a single long spiral. When the drive positions its head to read a track, it must estimate the distance into the disc and skip forward or backward to the appropriate point in the spiral. Reading off the outer edge requires a longer access time than the inner segments, unless you have a CAV drive, which spins at a constant rate so the access time to the outer tracks is equal to that of the inner tracks.

Access times have fallen a great deal since the original single-speed drives came out. However, recently a plateau seems to have been reached with most CD/DVD drives hovering right around the 100ms area, with some as low as 80ms. With each increase in data transfer speed, you usually see an improvement in access time as well. But as you can see in Table 13.26, these improvements are much less significant because of the physical limitation of the drive's single-read mechanism design.

Table 13.26 Typical CD-ROM Drive Access Times

Drive Speed	Access Time (ms)
1x	400
2x	300
3x	200
4x	150
6x	150
8x–12x	100
16x–24x	90
32x–52x or greater	85 or less

The times listed here are typical examples for good drives; within each speed category some drives are faster and some are slower. Because of the additional positioning accuracy required and the overall longer track, DVD drives usually report two access speeds—one when reading DVDs and the other when reading CDs. The DVD access times typically run 10ms–20ms slower than when reading CDs.

Buffer/Cache

Most CD/DVD drives include internal buffers or caches of memory installed onboard. These buffers are actual memory chips installed on the drive's circuit board that enable it to stage or store data in larger segments before sending it to the PC. A typical buffer for a CD/DVD drive is 128KB, although drives are available that have either more or less (more is usually better). Recordable CD or DVD drives typically have much larger buffers of 2MB–8MB or more to prevent buffer underrun problems and to smooth writing operations. Generally, faster drives come with more buffer memory to handle the higher transfer rates.

Having buffer or cache memory for the CD/DVD drive offers a number of advantages. Buffers can ensure that the PC receives data at a constant rate; when an application requests data from the drive, the data can be found in files scattered across different segments of the disc. Because the drive has a relatively slow access time, the pauses between data reads can cause a drive to send data to the PC sporadically. You might not notice this in typical text applications, but on a drive with a slower access rate coupled with no data buffering, it is very noticeable—and even irritating—during the display of video or some audio segments. In addition, a drive's buffer, when under the control of sophisticated software, can read and have ready the disc's table of contents, speeding up the first request for data. A minimum size of 128KB for a built-in buffer or cache is recommended and is standard on many 24x and faster drives. For greater performance, look for drives with 256KB or larger buffers.

CPU Utilization

A once-neglected but very real issue in calculating computer performance is the impact that any piece of hardware or software has on the central processing unit (CPU). This "CPU utilization" factor refers to how much attention the CPU (such as Pentium 4, Athlon 64, and so on) must provide to the hardware or software to help it work. A low CPU utilization percentage score is desirable because the less time a CPU spends on any given hardware or software process, the more time it has for other tasks and thus the greater the performance for your system. On CD-ROM drives, three factors influence CPU utilization: drive speed, drive buffer size, and interface type.

Drive buffer size can influence CPU utilization. For CD-ROM drives with similar performance ratings, the drive with a larger buffer is likely to require less CPU time (lower CPU utilization percentage) than the one with a smaller buffer.

Because drive speed and buffer size are more of a given, the most important factor influencing CPU utilization is the interface type. Traditionally, SCSI-interface CD-ROM drives have had far lower CPU utilization rates than ATAPI drives of similar ratings. One review of 12x drives done several years ago rated CPU utilization for ATAPI CD-ROM drives at 65%–80%, whereas SCSI CD-ROM drives checked in at less than 11%. By using DMA or Ultra-DMA modes with an ATA interface drive, near-SCSI levels of low CPU utilization can be realized. Using DMA or Ultra-DMA modes can cut CPU utilization down to the 10% or lower range, leaving the CPU free to run applications and other functions.

Direct Memory Access and Ultra-DMA

Busmastering ATA controllers use Direct Memory Access (DMA) or Ultra-DMA transfers to improve performance and reduce CPU utilization. Virtually all modern ATA drives support Ultra-DMA. With busmastering, CPU utilization for ATA/ATAPI and SCSI CD-ROM drives is about equal at around 11%. Thus, it's to your benefit to enable DMA access for your CD-ROM drives (and your ATA hard drives, too) if your system permits it.

Most recent ATA/ATAPI CD-ROM drives (12x and above) support DMA or Ultra-DMA transfers, as does Windows 95B and above and most recent Pentium-class or newer motherboards. To determine whether your Win9x, Me, or XP system has this feature enabled, check the System Properties' Device Manager tab and click the + mark next to Hard Disk Controllers. A drive interface capable of handling DMA transfers lists "Bus Master" in the name. Next, check the hard drive and CD-ROM information for your system. You can use the properties sheet for your system's CD-ROM drives under Windows 9x/Me and Windows 2000/XP to find this information; you might need to open the system to determine your hard drive brand and model. Hard disk drives and CD-ROM drives that support MultiWord DMA Mode 2 (16.6MBps), UltraDMA Mode 2 (33MBps), UltraDMA Mode 4 (66MBps), or faster can use DMA transfers. Check your product literature or the manufacturer's Web site for information.

To enable DMA transfers if your motherboard and drives support it, open the Device Manager and then open the properties sheet for the controller or drive. Click the Settings or Advanced Settings tab, and make sure DMA is enabled if available. Depending on which version of Windows you are using, some have the DMA setting in the controller properties and others have it with the individual drives.

Repeat the same steps to enable DMA transfers for any additional hard drives and ATAPI CD-ROM drives in your computer. Restart your computer after making these changes.

Note

If your system hangs after you enable this feature, you must restart the system in Safe mode and uncheck the DMA box. Because DMA transfers bypass the CPU to achieve greater speed, DMA problems could result in data loss. Make backups first, instead of wishing you had later.

Also, if your drive is a parallel ATA model that supports any of the Ultra-DMA (also called Ultra-ATA) modes, you should be sure to use the 80-conductor-style ATA cables. Also be wary of using cables longer than the 18" limit according to the ATA standard. Using these cables prevents noise and signal distortion that will occur if you try to use a standard 40-conductor cable with the Ultra-DMA modes. Most drives and motherboards refuse to enable Ultra-DMA modes faster than 33MBps if an 80-conductor cable is not detected. Note that these cabling issues affect only parallel ATA drives. If your drives are newer Serial ATA (SATA) models, these cabling issues do not apply.

Drive interfaces that don't mention busmastering either can't perform this speedup or need to have the correct driver installed. In some cases, depending on your Windows version and when your motherboard chipset was made, you must install chipset drivers to enable Windows to properly recognize the chipset and enable DMA modes. A good Web site for both Intel and non-Intel chipset support of this important feature is the Bus Mastering – Drivers and Links page at www.hardwaresite.net/drvbmide.html. Follow the links at this site to the motherboard chipset vendors, their technical notes (to determine whether your chipset supports busmastering), and the drivers you need to download. Virtually all motherboard chipsets produced since 1995 provide busmaster ATA support. Most of those produced since 1997 also provide UltraDMA support for up to 33MHz (Ultra-ATA/33) or 66MHz (Ultra-ATA/66) speed operation. Still, you should make sure that DMA is enabled to ensure you are benefiting from the performance it offers. Enabling DMA can dramatically improve DVD performance, for example.

Interface

The drive's interface is the physical connection of the drive to the PC's expansion bus. The interface is the data pipeline from the drive to the computer, and its importance shouldn't be minimized. Five types of interfaces are available for attaching a CD-ROM, CD-R, or CD-RW drive to your system:

- SCSI/ASPI (Small Computer System Interface/Advanced SCSI Programming Interface)
- ATA/ATAPI (AT Attachment/AT Attachment Packet Interface)
- Parallel port
- USB port
- FireWire (IEEE 1394)

The following sections examine these interface choices.

SCSI/ASPI

SCSI (pronounced *scuzzy*), or the Small Computer System Interface, is a name given to a special interface bus that allows many types of peripherals to communicate.

A standard software interface called ASPI (Advanced SCSI Programming Interface) enables CD-ROM drives (and other SCSI peripherals) to communicate with the SCSI host adapter installed in the computer. SCSI offers the greatest flexibility and performance of the interfaces available for CD-ROM drives and can be used to connect many other types of peripherals to your system as well.

The SCSI bus enables computer users to string a group of devices along a chain from one SCSI host adapter, avoiding the complication of installing a separate adapter card into the PC bus slots for each new hardware device, such as a tape unit or additional CD-ROM drive added to the system. These traits make the SCSI interface preferable for connecting a peripheral such as a CD-ROM to your PC.

Not all SCSI adapters are created equal, however. Although they might share a common command set, they can implement these commands differently, depending on how the adapter's manufacturer designed the hardware. ASPI was created to eliminate these incompatibilities. ASPI was originally developed by Adaptec, Inc., a leader in the development of SCSI controller cards and adapters who originally named it the Adaptec SCSI Programming Interface before it became a de facto standard. ASPI consists of two main parts. The primary part is an ASPI-Manager program, which is a driver that functions between the operating system and the specific SCSI host adapter. The ASPI-Manager sets up the ASPI interface to the SCSI bus.

The second part of an ASPI system is the individual ASPI device drivers. For example, you would get an ASPI driver for your SCSI CD-ROM drive. You can also get ASPI drivers for your other SCSI peripherals, such as tape drives and scanners. The ASPI driver for the peripheral talks to the ASPI-Manager for the host adapter. This is what enables the devices to communicate together on the SCSI bus.

The bottom line is that if you are getting a SCSI interface CD-ROM, be sure it includes an ASPI driver that runs under your particular operating system. Also, be sure that your SCSI host adapter has the corresponding ASPI-Manager driver as well. Substantial differences exist between SCSI adapters because SCSI can be used for a wide variety of peripherals. Low-cost, SCSI-3-compliant ISA or PCI adapters can be used for CD-ROM interfacing. In contrast, higher-performance PCI adapters that support more advanced SCSI standards, such as Wide, Ultra, UltraWide, Ultra2Wide, and so on, can be used with both CD-ROM drives and other devices, such as CD-R/CD-RW drives, hard drives, scanners, and tape backups. To help you choose the appropriate SCSI adapter for both your CD-ROM drive and any other SCSI-based peripheral you're considering, visit Adaptec's Web site.

The SCSI interface offers the most powerful and flexible connection for CD-ROMs and other devices. It provides better performance, and seven or more drives can be connected to a single host adapter. The drawback is cost. If you do not need SCSI for other peripherals and intend to connect only one CD-ROM drive to the system, you will be spending a lot of money on unused potential. In that case, an ATAPI interface CD-ROM drive is a more cost-effective choice.

◄◄   See "Small Computer System Interface," p. 584.

ATA/ATAPI

The ATA/ATAPI (AT Attachment/AT Attachment Packet Interface) is an extension of the same ATA (AT Attachment) interface most computers use to connect to their hard disk drives. ATA is sometimes also referred to as IDE (Integrated Drive Electronics). ATAPI is an industry-standard ATA interface used for CD/DVD and other drives. ATAPI is a software interface that adapts the SCSI/ASPI commands to the ATA interface. This enables drive manufacturers to take their high-end CD/DVD drive products and quickly adapt them to the ATA interface. This also enables the ATA drives to remain compatible with the extensions that provide the CD/DVD drive with a software interface with DOS. With Windows 9x and later, the CD-ROM extensions are contained in the CD file system (CDFS) VxD (virtual device) driver.

ATA/ATAPI drives are sometimes also called enhanced IDE (EIDE) drives because this is an extension of the original IDE (technically the ATA) interface. In most cases, an ATA drive connects to the system via a second ATA interface connector and channel, leaving the primary one for hard disk drives only. This is preferable because ATA does not share the single channel well and would cause a hard disk drive to wait for CD/DVD commands to complete and vice versa. SCSI does not have this problem because a SCSI host adapter can send commands to different devices without having to wait for each previous command to complete.

The ATA interface represents the most cost-effective and high-performance interface for CD-ROM drives. Most new systems that include a CD and/or DVD drive have it connected through ATA. You can connect up to two drives to the secondary ATA connector; for more than that, SCSI is your only choice and provides better performance as well.

Many systems on the market today can use the ATA/ATAPI CD/DVD drive as a bootable device, which allows the vendor to supply a recovery CD that can restore the computer's software to its factory-shipped condition. Later, you'll see how bootable CDs differ from ordinary CDs and how you can use low-cost CD-R/CD-RW drives, along with mastering and imaging software to make your own bootable CDs with your own preferred configuration.

◄◄   See "An Overview of the IDE Interface," p. 532.

▶▶   See "Bootable CDs and DVDs—El Torito," p. 824.

Parallel Port

In the past, some external CD-ROM or CD-RW drives were available in versions that connected to a PC's parallel port. USB has for the most part replaced the parallel port for this type of use.

If you use a parallel port drive, for best performance you should set your printer port to use IEEE 1284 standards, such as ECP/EPP or ECP, before connecting your parallel-port CD-ROM. These are bidirectional, high-speed extensions to the normal Centronics parallel port standard and provide better performance for virtually any recent parallel device. If your operating system supports Plug and Play (PnP) (such as Windows 9x/Me or 2000/XP does), simply plugging a PnP drive into the parallel port enables the OS to detect the new hardware and load the appropriate driver automatically.

▶▶   See "IEEE 1284 Parallel Port Standard," p. 1007.

Note

Parallel port CD-ROM drives nearly always include a cable with a pass-through connector. This connector plugs into the parallel port and, if necessary, a printer cable can plug into the connector. This enables you to continue using the port to connect to your printer while sharing the interface with the CD-ROM drive. Note there might be performance problems when trying to print and read from the drive at the same time.

With the popularity, performance, and ease of use of USB, I recommend a USB external drive over a parallel port version. USB drives are much faster, more compatible, and easier to install and use. If you need parallel port support for some systems, look for drives that feature parallel and USB interfaces, such as the Backpack product line from Micro Solutions, Inc. See the Vendor List on the disc for Web site and contact information.

USB Interface

Universal Serial Bus (USB) has proven to be extremely flexible and has been used for everything from keyboards and joysticks to CD/DVD drives from several vendors.

USB 1.1 and earlier drives provide read and write transfer rates that match the fastest rates possible with IEEE 1284 parallel ports, with read rates on typical 6x models ranging from 1,145KBps to 1,200KBps. USB 2.0 and later provide a transfer rate up to 60MBps, which is 40 times faster than USB 1.1 and yet is fully backward-compatible.

USB also provides benefits that no parallel port drive can match: for example, hot-swappability, which is the capability to be plugged in or unplugged without removing the power or rebooting the system. Additionally, USB devices are fully Plug and Play, allowing the device to be automatically recognized by the system and the drivers automatically installed.

For Windows 98/Me or Windows 2000/XP systems with USB ports, USB-based CD-RW drives are an excellent solution for backup and archiving of data onto low-cost, durable optical media.

FireWire

In addition, external CD/DVD drives are now available on the market with a FireWire (also called IEEE 1394 or iLink) interface. FireWire is a high-performance external interface designed mainly for video use. It evolved as an Apple standard and is used primarily on Macintosh systems. Because few PCs include FireWire ports as a standard item—whereas all PCs include USB—I usually recommend the more universally supported USB for external CD/DVD drives. Make sure any external drives you purchase use the faster USB 2.0 (also known as Hi-Speed USB), which is faster and far more readily available than FireWire versions. FireWire drives can be useful if you work in a two-platform environment (both PCs and Macs). However, because most Macs also support USB (and you can easily add a USB interface to those that don't), if your primary platform is the PC, I'd still recommend USB over FireWire.

If you do want to use a FireWire drive and your system does not include FireWire integrated into the motherboard, you can easily add a FireWire interface card to your PC. Additionally, some video and sound cards are available with FireWire ports as an option.

▶▶   See "Universal Serial Bus," p. 983, and "IEEE 1394," p. 992.

Loading Mechanism

Three distinctly different mechanisms exist for loading a disc into a CD/DVD drive: the tray, caddy, and slot. Each one offers some benefits and features. Which type you select has a major impact on your use of the drive because you interact with this mechanism every time you load a disc.

Some drives on the market allow you to insert more than one disc at a time. Some of these use a special cartridge that you fill with discs, much like multidisc CD changers used in automobiles. Newer models are slot-loading, allowing you to push a button to select which internal cartridge slot you want to load with a CD/DVD. The drive's door opens and you slide in the CD, which the drive mechanism grabs and pulls into place. Typical capacities range from three to six discs or more, and these are available in both SCSI and ATA interfaces.

Tray

Most current SCSI and ATAPI CD/DVD drives use a tray-loading mechanism. This is similar to the mechanism used with a stereo system. Because you don't need to put each disc into a separate caddy, this mechanism is much less expensive overall. However, it also means that you must handle each disc every time you insert or remove it.

Tray loading is less expensive than a caddy system (see the section, "Caddy," later in this chapter) because you don't need a caddy. It is also more convenient, unless you have caddies for all your discs. However, this can make it much more difficult for young children or those who work in harsh environments to use the discs without smudging or damaging them due to excess handling.

The tray loader itself is also subject to damage. The trays can easily break if bumped or if something is dropped on them while they are extended. Also, any contamination you place on the tray or disc is brought right into the drive when the tray is retracted. Tray-loaded drives should not be used in a harsh environment, such as a commercial or an industrial application. Make sure both the tray and the data surface of the disc are clean whenever you use a tray-loading drive.

The tray mechanism also does not hold the disc as securely as the caddy. If you don't have the disc placed in the tray properly when it retracts, the disc or tray can be damaged. Even a slight misalignment can prevent the drive from reading the disc properly, forcing you to open the tray and reset the disc.

Some tray drives can't operate in a vertical (sideways) position because gravity prevents proper loading and operation. Check to see whether the drive tray has retaining clips that grab the hub of the disc or tabs that fold in or flip over from the outside of the tray to retain the disc. If so, you can run the drive in either a horizontal or vertical position.

The main advantage of the tray mechanism over the others is in cost, and that is a big factor. Most drives today use the tray mechanism for handling discs.

Caddy

At one time, the caddy system was used on most high-end CD-ROM drives as well as the early CD-R and DVD-RAM drives. The caddy system requires that you place the disc itself into a special caddy, which is a sealed container with a metal shutter. The caddy has a hinged lid you open to insert the disc, but after that the lid remains shut. When you insert the caddy containing the disc into the drive, the drive opens a metal shutter on the bottom of the caddy, allowing access to the disc by the laser.

When caddy-loaded drives were popular, they were extremely convenient to use if you had a caddy for each drive and extremely inconvenient if you shared a single caddy among all your media. The caddy was inserted into the drive, much the way you would insert a 3 1/2" floppy disk. The caddy protected the CD from scratches, contamination, and careless handling.

The drawbacks to the caddy system included the expense and the inconvenience of having to put the discs into the caddies.

When DVD-RAM was first introduced, the disc had to remain in a caddy because the recordable surface is delicate. Since then, DVD-RAM drives have been made caddy-less, but especially with double-sided discs the information is at risk every time you handle the disc. Because of this fragility, as well as the general incompatibility of DVD-RAM with DVD-ROM, I recommend DVD+RW as the best solution for recordable DVD. No caddy is required with DVD+RW, and the format is fully two-way compatible with most recent DVD-Video players and DVD-ROM drives.

The caddy-loading system has declined in popularity because of the convenience of the tray. Today only a few drives on the market use caddies, and they are generally not for mainstream use (most have a SCSI interface, for example).

Slot

Some drives now use a slot-loading mechanism, identical to that used in most automotive CD players. This is very convenient because you just slip the disc into the slot, where the mechanism grabs it and draws it inside. Some drives can load several CDs at a time this way, holding them internally inside the drive and switching discs as access is required.

The primary drawback to this type of mechanism is that if a jam occurs, it can be much more difficult to repair because you might have to remove the drive to free the disc. Another drawback is that slot-loading drives usually can't handle the smaller 80mm discs, card-shaped discs, or other modified disc physical formats or shapes.

Other Drive Features

Although drive specifications are of the utmost importance, you should also consider other factors and features when evaluating CD-ROM drives. Besides quality of construction, the following criteria bear scrutiny when making a purchasing decision:

- Drive sealing
- Self-cleaning lenses
- Internal versus external drive

Drive Sealing

Dirt is your CD/DVD drive's biggest enemy. Dust or dirt, when it collects on the lens portion of the mechanism, can cause read errors or severe performance loss. Many manufacturers seal off the lens and internal components from the drive bay in airtight enclosures. Other drives, although not sealed, have double dust doors—one external and one internal—to keep dust from the inside of the drive. All these features help prolong the life of your drive.

Some drives are sealed, which means no air flows through the chamber in which the laser and lens reside. Always look for sealed drives in harsh industrial or commercial environments. In a standard office or home environment, it is probably not worth the extra expense.

Self-Cleaning Lenses

If the laser lens gets dirty, so does your data. The drive will spend a great deal of time seeking and reseeking or will finally give up. Lens-cleaning discs are available, but built-in cleaning mechanisms are now included on virtually all good-quality drives. This might be a feature you'll want to consider, particularly if you work in a less-than-pristine work environment or have trouble keeping your desk clean, let alone your drive laser lens. You can clean the lens manually, but it is generally a delicate operation requiring that you partially disassemble the drive. Also, damaging the lens mechanism by using too much force is pretty easy to do. Because of the risks involved, in most cases I do not recommend the average person disassemble and try to manually clean the laser lens.

Internal Versus External Drives

When deciding whether you want an internal or external drive, think about where and how you're going to use your drive. What about the future expansion of your system? Both types of drives have advantages and disadvantages, such as the following:

- *External enclosure.* These tend to be rugged, portable, and large—in comparison to their internal versions. External drives are ideal for sharing a drive with multiple systems or especially with laptops or notebook portable systems. Parallel port drives are very portable and supported on a broad range of machines, but USB drives are a better choice for Windows 98 or later systems that have USB ports. Connect recent drives to the faster USB 2.0 port for best performance.

SCSI drives are also ideal for external configurations because performance is even better than with internal ATA drives. If each PC has its own SCSI adapter with an external connection, all you need to do is unplug the drive from one adapter and plug it in to the other. I use SCSI drives extensively, and with SCSI I can get the same level of performance when the drive is connected to my laptop as when it is connected to a desktop system.

If you have an IEEE 1394 (FireWire, i.LINK) port and don't have a USB 2.0 port, this port type provides speed comparable to SCSI and USB 2.0 and the hot-swappability of USB. Some optical drives are now equipped with both USB 2.0 and IEEE 1394 ports.

■ *Internal enclosure.* Internal drives won't take up any space on your desk. Buy an internal drive if you have a free drive bay and a sufficient power supply and you plan to keep the drive exclusively on one machine. The internal drives are also nice because you can connect the audio connector to your sound card and leave the external audio connectors free for other inputs. Internal drives can be ATA or SCSI.

Writable CDs

Although the CD originally was conceived as a read-only device, these days you easily can create your own data and audio CDs. By purchasing CD-R or CD-RW discs and drives, you can record (or burn) your own CDs. This enables you to store large amounts of data at a cost that is lower than most other removable, random-access mediums.

It might surprise newcomers to the world of PCs to see just how far recordable CD technology, performance, and pricing has come. Today you can buy recorders that operate at up to 52x speeds and cost under $100. You can even purchase Slimline CD drives for laptops. Compare this to the first CD-R recording system on the market in 1988, which cost more than $50,000 (back then, they used a $35,000 Yamaha audio recording drive along with thousands of dollars of additional error correction and other circuitry for CD-ROM use), operated at 1x speed only, and was part of a subsystem that was the size of a washing machine! The blank discs also cost about $100 each—a far cry from the 25 cents or less they cost today (if you purchase in bulk and are willing to supply your own jewel cases). With prices that high, the main purpose for CD recording was to produce prototype CDs that could then be replicated via the standard stamping process.

In 1991, Philips introduced the first 2x recorder (the CDD 521), which was about the size of a stereo receiver and cost about $12,000. Sony in 1992 and then JVC in 1993 followed with their 2x recorders, and the JVC was the first drive that had the half-height 5 1/4" form factor that most desktop system drives still use today. In 1995, Yamaha released the first 4x recorder (the CDR100), which sold for $5,000. A breakthrough in pricing came in late 1995 when Hewlett-Packard released a 2x recorder (the 4020i, which was actually made for them by Philips) for under $1,000. This proved to be exactly what the market was waiting for. With a surge in popularity after that, prices rapidly fell to below $500, and then down to $200 or less. In 1996, Ricoh introduced the first CD-RW drive.

Compared with either tape or other removable media, using a CD burner is a very cost-effective and easy method for transporting large files or making archival copies. Another benefit of the CD for archiving data is that CDs have a much longer shelf life than tapes or other removable media.

Two main types of recordable CD drives and discs are available, called CD-R (recordable) and CD-RW (rewritable). Because all CD-RW drives can also function as CD-R drives, and the prices of CD-R and RW drives are similar, virtually all drives sold today are CD-RW. Those drives can work with either CD-R or CD-RW discs. In addition, because the CD-RW discs are 1.5–4 times more expensive than CD-R discs, only half as fast (or less) as CD-R discs, and won't work in all CD audio or CD-ROM drives, people usually write to CD-R media in their CD-RW drives.

Note

Because of differences in reflectivity of the media, older CD and DVD drives can't read CD-RW media. Most newer CD or DVD-ROM drives conform to the MultiRead specification and as such can read CD-RWs. But many older drives are still out there that do not conform. As such, if you are recording something that many people or systems will need to read, CD-R is your best choice for overall compatibility.

CD-R media is a WORM (write once, read many) media, meaning that after you fill a CD-R with data, it is permanently stored and can't be erased. The write-once limitation makes this type of disc less than ideal for system backups or other purposes in which it would be preferable to reuse the same media over and over. However, because of the low cost of CD-R media, you might find that making permanent back-ups to essentially disposable CD-R discs is as economically feasible as tape or other media.

CD-RW discs can be reused up to 1,000 times, making them suitable for almost any type of data storage task. When first introduced, there were many CD-R-only drives; however, today most recordable CD drives are both CD-R and CD-RW in one. The following sections examine these two standards and how you can use them for your own data storage needs.

CD-R

Once recorded, CD-R discs can be played back or read in any standard CD-ROM drive. CD-R discs are useful for archival storage and creating master CDs, which can be duplicated for distribution within a company.

CD-Rs function using the same principle as standard CD-ROMs, by bouncing laser light off the disc and tracking the changes in reflectivity when pit/land and land/pit boundaries are encountered. The main difference is that instead of being stamped or embossed into plastic as on regular CDs, CD-Rs have images of pits burned onto a raised groove instead. Therefore, the pits are not really raised bumps like on a standard CD, but instead are rendered as dark (burned) areas on the groove that reflect less light. Because the overall reflectivity of pit and land areas remains the same as on a stamped disc, normal CD-ROM or CD audio drives can read CD-Rs exactly as if they were stamped discs.

Part of the recording process with CD-Rs starts before you even insert the disc into the drive. CD-R media is manufactured much like a standard CD—a stamper is used to mold a base of polycarbonate plastic. However, instead of stamping pits and lands, the stamper imprints a spiral groove (called a *pre-groove*), into the disc. From the perspective of the reading (and writing) laser underneath the disc, this groove is seen as a raised spiral ridge and not a depression.

The pre-groove (or ridge) is not perfectly straight; instead it has a slight wobble. The amplitude of the wobble is generally very small compared to the track pitch (spacing). The groove separation is 1.6 microns, but it wobbles only 0.030 microns from side to side. The wobble of a CD-R groove is modulated to carry supplemental information read by the drive. The signal contained in the wobble is called absolute time in pre-groove (ATIP) because it is modulated with time code and other data. The time code is the same minutes:seconds:frame format that will eventually be found in the Q-subcode of the frames after they are written to the disc. The ATIP enables the drive to locate positions on the disc before the frames are actually written. Technically, the wobble signal is frequency shift keyed with a carrier frequency of 22.05KHz and a deviation of 1KHz. The wobble uses changes in frequency to carry information.

To complete the CD-R disc, an organic dye is evenly applied across the disc by a spin-coating process. Next, a gold reflective layer is applied, followed by a protective coat of UV-cured lacquer to protect the gold and dye layers. Gold is used in CD-R discs to get the reflectivity as high as possible, and it was found that the organic dye tends to oxidize aluminum. Then, silk-screen printing is applied on top of the lacquer for identification and further protection. When seen from the underside, the laser used to read (or write) the disc first passes through the clear polycarbonate and the dye layer, hits the gold layer where it is reflected back through the dye layer and the plastic, and finally is picked up by the optical pickup sensor in the drive.

The dye and reflective layer together have the same reflective properties as a *virgin* CD. In other words, a CD reader would read the groove of an unrecorded CD-R disc as one long land. To record on a CD-R disc, a laser beam of the same wavelength (780nm) as is normally used to read the disc, but with 10 times the power, is used to heat up the dye. The laser is fired in a pulsed fashion at the top of the ridge (groove), heating the layer of organic dye to between 482°F and 572°F (250°–300°C). This temperature literally burns the organic dye, causing it to become opaque. When read, this prevents the light from passing through the dye layer to the gold and reflecting back, having the same effect of canceling the laser reflection that an actual raised pit would on a normal stamped CD.

Figure 13.12 shows the CD-R media layers, along with the pre-groove (raised ridge from the laser perspective) with burned pits.

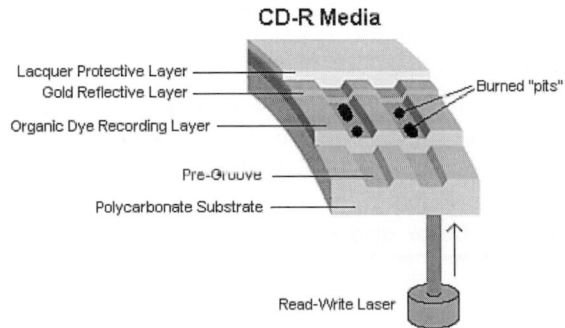

Figure 13.12 CD-R media layers.

The drive reading the disc is fooled into thinking a pit exists, but no actual pit exists—there's simply a spot of less-reflective material on the ridge. This use of heat to create the pits in the disc is why the recording process is often referred to as *burning* a CD. When burned, the dye changes from a reflective to a nonreflective state. This change of state is permanent and can't be undone, which is why CD-R is considered a write-once medium.

CD-R Capacity

All CD-R drives can work with the standard 650MiB (682MB) CD-R media (equal to 74 minutes of recorded music), as well as the higher-capacity 700MiB (737MB) CD-R blanks (equal to 80 minutes of recorded music). The 80-minute discs cost only about 2 cents more than the 74-minute discs, so most would figure why not purchase only the higher-capacity media? Although the extra 55MB of storage can be useful and the cost difference is negligible, the 80-minute discs can actually be harder to read on older CD-ROM and CD-DA drives, especially car audio units. This is because to get the extra 55MB/6 minutes of capacity, the spiral track is wound a little more tightly, making them a bit more difficult to read. If you'll be using the discs for audio or interchange purposes and might be dealing with older equipment, you might want to stick with the 74-minute discs instead. If not, the 80-minute media will be just fine.

Some drives and burning software are capable of overburning, whereby they write data partially into the lead-out area and essentially extend the data track. This is definitely risky as far as compatibility is concerned. Many drives, especially older ones, fail when reading near the end of an overburned disc. It's best to consider this form of overclocking CDs somewhat experimental. It might be useful for your own purposes if it works with your drives and software, but interchangeability will be problematic.

Some vendors now sell 90-minute (790MiB) and 99-minute (870MiB) media to make overburning easier. Although experiments performed by the Tom's Hardware Web site (www.tomshardware.com) indicate that most standard CD-RW drives can reliably burn up to 89:59 of music onto the 90-minute media and the CD-R can be played on a wide variety of auto and home electronics players, very few drives can burn a full 90 minutes or more of music (or the equivalent amount of computer data) to this media.

Tip

Wondering whether your drive can handle 90-minute or 99-minute media? Your drive vendor will probably say it can't, but the media compatibility list put together by Jan Distribudora (a major electronics distributor in the Dominican Republic; `www.jan.com.do/Archivos/90minCompatibilityBurnersFinal.pdf`) can provide a field-tested answer. Check drive compatibility before you buy the longer media.

Note that Roxio (makers of Easy CD Creator and other CD mastering/writing programs) states that trying to write 90-minute or longer media could result in damage to the drive that is writing or reading the media.

CD-R Media Color

There has been some controversy over the years about which colors of CD-R media provide the best performance. Table 13.27 shows the most common color combinations, along with which brands use them and some technical information.

Some brands are listed with more than one color combination, due to production changes or different product lines. You should check color combinations whenever you purchase a new batch of CD-R media if you've found that particular color combinations work better for you in your applications.

Table 13.27   CD-R Media Color and Its Effect on Recording

Media Color (first color is reflective layer; second is die layer)	Brands	Technical Notes
Gold-gold	Mitsui, Kodak, Maxell, Ricoh	Phthalocyanine dye. Less tolerance for power variations. Has a rate life span of up to 100 years. Might be less likely to work in a wide variety of drives. Invented by Mitsui Toatsu Chemicals. Works best in drives that use a Long Write Strategy (longer laser pulse) to mark media.
Gold-green	Imation (nee 3M), Memorex, Kodak, BASF, TDK	Cyanine dye. More forgiving of disc-write and disc-read variations. Has a rated lifespan of 10 years (older media). Recent media has a rated lifespan of 20–50 years (silver/green). Color combination developed by Taiyo Yuden. Used in the development of the original CD-R standards. De facto standard for CD-R industry and was the original color combination used during the development of CD-R technology. Works best in drives that use a Short Write Strategy (shorter laser pulse) to mark media.
Silver-blue	Verbatim, DataLifePlus, HiVal, Maxell, TDK	Process developed by Verbatim. Azo dye. Similar performance to green media plus rated to last up to 100 years. A good choice for long-term archiving.

Note

Playstation games originally came on discs that were tinted black for appearance. Soon blank CD-R recordable discs were also available with this same black tint in the polycarbonate. The black tint is purely cosmetic—it is invisible to the infrared laser that reads/writes the disc. In other words, "black" CD-R discs are functionally identical to clear discs and can be made using any of the industry-standard dyes in the recording layer. The black tint hides the recording layer visually, so although the laser passes right through it, the black tint prevents you from observing the color of the dye in the recording layer directly.

Ultimately, although the various color combinations have their advantages, the best way to choose a media type is to try a major brand of media in your CD-R/CD-RW drive with both full-disc and small-disc recording jobs and then try the completed CD-R in as wide a range of CD-ROM drive brands and speeds as you can.

The perfect media for you will be the ones that offer you the following:

- High reliability in writing (check your drive model's list of recommended media)
- No dye or reflective surface dropouts (areas where the media won't record properly)
- Durability through normal handling (scratch-resistant coating on media surface)
- Compatibility across the widest range of CD-ROM drives
- Lowest unit cost

If you have problems recording reliably with certain types of media, or if you find that some brands with the same speed rating are much slower than others, contact your drive vendor for a firmware upgrade. Firmware upgrades can also help your drive recognize new types of faster media from different vendors.

▶▶ See "Updating the Firmware in a CD-RW or Rewritable DVD Drive," p. 828.

Choosing the Best Media

After you determine which media works best for you and your target drives, you might still be faced with a wide variety of choices, including conventional surface, printable surface, unbranded, jewel case, and bulk on spindle. The following list discusses these options:

- *Conventional surface.* Choose this type of media if you want to use a marker to label the CD rather than adding a paper label. This type of CD often has elaborate labeling, including areas to indicate CD title, date created, and other information as well as prominent brand identification. Because of the surface marking, it's not suitable for relabeling unless you use very opaque labels. It's a good choice for internal backups and data storage, though, where labeling is less important.

- *Printable surface.* Choose this type of media if you have a CD printer (a special type of inkjet printer that can print directly onto the face of the CD). Because the brand markings are usually low-contrast or even nonexistent (to allow overprinting), this type also works well with labeling kits such as NEATO and others.

- *Unbranded.* Usually sold in bulk on spindle, these are good choices for economy or use with labeling kits.

- *Jewel case.* Any of the preceding versions can be sold with jewel cases (the same type of case used for CD-ROM software and music CDs). This is a good choice if you plan to distribute the media in a jewel case, but it raises your costs if you plan to distribute or store the media in paper, Tyvek, or plastic sleeves. Hint: Use extra jewel cases to replace your broken jewel cases in your CD software or music collection!

■ *Bulk on spindle.* This media generally comes with no sleeves and no cases. It is usually the lowest-priced packaging within any brand of media. This is an excellent choice for mass duplication, or for those who don't use jewel cases for distribution.

CD-R Media Recording Speed Ratings

With CD-R mastering speeds ranging from 1x (now-discontinued first-generation units) up through the latest state-of-the-art 48x–52x rates, it's important to check the speed rating (x-rating) of your CD-R media.

Most branded media on the market today is rated to work successfully at up to 32x recording speeds. Some brands indicate this specifically on their packaging, whereas you must check the Web sites for others to get this information. If your drive is faster than 32x (new drives are now reaching 48x–52x speeds), look for media that supports the maximum speed of your drive and comes from a manufacturer supported by your drive. If necessary, install the latest firmware updates to reach maximum recording speed.

▶▶ See "Updating the Firmware in a CD-RW or Rewritable DVD Drive," p. 828.

Note

The current 52x CD-R recording speed might be the fastest speed ever achieved by CD-RW drives. Many vendors believe that the risk of damage to media and drives at faster spin rates and the technical difficulties in reliably recording data at higher speeds, plus the rising popularity of rewritable DVD, might make the 52x generation the last generation of CD-RW drives. However, even if you prefer a DVD rewritable drive for making DVDs, you might want a fast CD-RW drive as well. 40x or faster CD-RW drives create CD-Rs much more quickly than many current rewritable DVD drives do.

If speed ratings are unavailable for your media, you might want to restrict your burning to 32x or lower for data. If you are burning audio CDs, you might find that some devices work better with media burned at 8x or lower speeds than with media burned at higher speeds.

Tip

Some drives and mastering software support a setting that automatically determines the best speed to use for burning a CD-R. For example, Plextor calls this feature PowerRec (Plextor Optimized Writing Error Reduction Control). PowerRec and similar features used by other vendors analyze the media and adjust writing methods and write speed during the write process to ensure the best results. Using this feature with media with an unknown speed rating helps you get a reliable burn no matter what the speed rating of the media is.

CD-RW

Beginning in early 1996, an industry consortium that included Ricoh, Philips, Sony, Yamaha, Hewlett-Packard, and Mitsubishi Chemical Corporation announced the CD-RW format. The design was largely led by Ricoh, and it was the first manufacturer to introduce a CD-RW drive in May 1996. This drive was the MP6200S, which was a 2/2/6 (2x record, 2x rewrite, 6x read) rated unit. At the same time, the Orange Book Part III was published, which officially defined the CD-RW standard.

Since that time, CD-RW drives have pretty much replaced CD-R-only drives in the market today, mainly because CD-RW drives are fully backward-compatible with CD-R drives and can read and write the same CD-R media with the same capabilities. So, a CD-RW drive can also function as a CD-R drive. CD-RW discs can be burned or written to just like CD-Rs; the main difference is that they can be erased and reburned again and again. They are very useful for prototyping a disc that will then be duplicated in less expensive CD-R or even stamped CDs for distribution. They can be rewritten at least 1,000 times or more. Additionally, with packet-writing software, they can even be treated like giant floppy disks, where you can simply drag and drop or copy and delete files at will. Although CD-RW discs are about twice as expensive as CD-R media, CD-RWs are still far cheaper than optical cartridges and other removable formats. This makes CD-RW a viable technology for system backups, file archiving, and virtually any other data storage task.

Note

The CD-RW format originally was referred to as CD-Erasable, or CD-E.

Four main differences exist between CD-RW and CD-R media. In a nutshell, CD-RW discs are

- Rewritable
- More expensive
- Slower when writing
- Less reflective

Besides the CD-RW media being rewritable and costing a bit more, they also are writable at about half (or less) the speed of CD-R discs. This is because the laser needs more time to operate on a particular spot on the disk when writing. They also have a lower reflectivity, which limits readability in older drives. Many older standard CD-ROM and CD-R drives can't read CD-RWs. However, MultiRead capability is now found in virtually all CD-ROM drives of 24x speed or above, enabling them to read CD-RWs without problems. In general, CD-DA drives—especially the car audio players—seem to have the most difficulty reading CD-RWs. So, for music recording or compatibility with older drives, you should probably stick to CD-R media. Look for the MultiRead logo on a CD-ROM drive, which indicates the capability to read CD-RW. When you shop for a new standalone CD player, look for those that specify the capability to read CD-R/CD-RW media.

CD-RW drives and media use a phase change process to create the illusion of pits on the disc. As with CD-R media, the disc starts out with the same polycarbonate base with a wobbled pre-groove molded in, which contains ATIP information. Then, on top of the base a special dielectric (insulating) layer is spin-coated, followed by the phase change recording layer, another dielectric layer, an aluminum reflective layer, and finally a UV-cured lacquer protective layer (and optional screen printing). The dielectric layers above and below the recording layer are designed to insulate the polycarbonate and reflective layers from the intense heat used during the phase-change process.

Figure 13.13 shows the CD-RW media layers, along with the pre-groove (raised ridge from the laser perspective) with burned pits in the phase change layer.

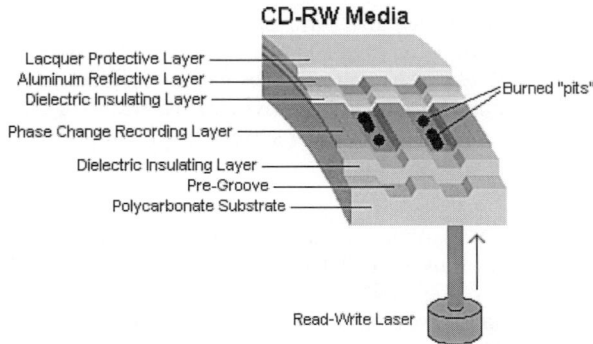

CD-RW Media

Lacquer Protective Layer
Aluminum Reflective Layer
Dielectric Insulating Layer
Burned "pits"
Phase Change Recording Layer
Dielectric Insulating Layer
Pre-Groove
Polycarbonate Substrate
Read-Write Laser

Figure 13.13 CD-RW media layers.

Instead of burning an organic dye as with CD-R, the recording layer in a CD-RW disc is made up of a phase-change alloy consisting of silver, indium, antimony, and tellurium (Ag-In-Sb-Te). The reflective part of the recording layer is an aluminum alloy, the same as used in normal stamped discs. As a result, the recording side of CD-RW media looks like a mirror with a slight blue tint. The read/write laser works from the underside of the disk, where the groove again appears like a ridge, and the recording is made in the phase-change layer on top of this ridge. The recording layer of Ag-In-Sb-Te alloy normally has a polycrystalline structure that is about 20% reflective. When data is written to a

CD-RW disc, the laser in the drive alternates between two power settings, called P-write and P-erase. The higher power setting (P-write) is used to heat the material in the recording layer to a temperature between 500°C and 700°C (932°–1,292°F), causing it to melt. In a liquid state the molecules of the material flow freely, losing their polycrystalline structure and taking what is called an *amorphous* (random) state. When the material then solidifies in this amorphous state, it is only about 5% reflective. When being read, these areas lower in reflectivity simulate the pits on a stamped CD-ROM disc.

That would be all to the story if CD-RW discs were read-only, but because they can be rewritten, there must be a way to bring the material back to a polycrystalline state. This is done by setting the laser to the lower-power P-erase mode. This heats the active material to approximately 200°C (392°F), which is well below the liquid melting point but high enough to soften the material. When the material is softened and allowed to cool more slowly, the molecules realign from a 5% reflective amorphous state back to a 20% reflective polycrystalline state. These higher reflective areas simulate the lands on a stamped CD-ROM disc.

Note that despite the name of the P-erase laser power setting, the disc is not ever explicitly "erased." Instead, CD-RW uses a recording technique called *direct overwrite*, in which a spot doesn't have to be erased to be rewritten; it is simply rewritten. In other words, when data is recorded the laser remains on and pulses between the P-write and P-erase power levels to create amorphous and polycrystalline areas of low and high reflectivity, regardless of which state the areas were in prior. It is similar in many ways to writing data on a magnetic disk that also uses direct overwrite. Every sector already has data patterns, so when you write data, all you are really doing is writing new patterns. Sectors are never really erased; they are merely overwritten. The media in CD-RW discs is designed to be written and rewritten up to 1,000 times.

CD-RW Speeds

The original Orange Book Part III Volume 1 (CD-RW specification) allowed for CD-RW writing at up to 4x speeds. New developments in the media and drives were required to support speeds higher than that. So in May 2000, Part III Volume 2 was published, defining CD-RW recording at speeds from 4x to 10x. This revision of the CD-RW standard is called High-Speed Rewritable, and both the discs and drives capable of CD-RW speeds higher than 4x will indicate this via the logos printed on them. Part III Volume 3 was published in September 2002 and definines Ultra-Speed drives, which are CD-RW drives capable of recording speeds 8x–24x.

Because of the differences in High-Speed and UltraSpeed media, High-Speed media can be used only in High-Speed and Ultra-Speed drives; Ultra-Speed Media can be used only in Ultra-Speed drives. Both High-Speed and Ultra-Speed drives can use standard 2x–4x media, enabling them to interchange data with computers that have standard-speed CD-RW drives. Thus, choosing the wrong media to interchange with another system can prevent the other system from reading the media. If you don't know which speed of CD-RW media the target computer supports, I recommend you either use standard 2x–4x media or create a CD-R.

Because of differences in the UDF standards used by the packet-writing software that drags and drops files to CD-RW drives, the need to install a UDF reader on systems with CD-ROM drives, and the incapability of older CD-ROM and first-generation DVD-ROM drives to read CD-RW media, I recommend using CD-RW media for personal backups and data transfer between your own computers. However, when you send CD data to another user, CD-R is universally readable, making it a better choice.

MultiRead Specifications

The original Red and Yellow Book CD standards specified that on a CD the lands should have a minimum reflectance value of about 70% and the pits should have a maximum reflectance of about 28%. Therefore, the area of a disc that represents a land should reflect back no less than 70% of the laser light directed at it, whereas the pits should reflect no more than 28%. In the early 1980s when these standards were developed, the photodetector diodes used in the drives were relatively insensitive, and these minimum and maximum reflectance requirements were deliberately designed to create enough brightness and contrast between pits and lands to accommodate them.

On a CD-RW disc, the reflectance of a land is approximately 20% (plus or minus 5%) and the reflectivity of a pit is only 5%—obviously well below the original requirements. Fortunately, it was found that by the addition of a relatively simple AGC circuit, the ratio of amplification in the detector circuitry can be changed dynamically to allow for reading the lower-reflective CD-RW discs. Thus, although CD-ROM drives were not initially capable of reading CD-RW discs, modifying the existing designs to enable them to do so wasn't difficult. Where you might encounter problems reading CD-RW discs is with CD audio drives, especially older ones. Because CD-RW first came out in 1996 (and took a year or more to become popular), most CD-ROM drives manufactured in 1997 or earlier have problems reading CD-RW discs. Reflectivity is also a problem on DVD-Video and DVD-ROM drives—because they use a different frequency laser, they actually have more trouble reading CD-R discs than CD-RWs.

DVDs also have some compatibility problems. With DVD, the problem isn't just simple reflectivity as it is an inherent incompatibility with the laser wavelength used for DVD versus CD-R and RW. The problem in this case stems from the dyes used in the recording layer of CD-R and RW discs, which are very sensitive to the wavelength of light used to read them. At the proper CD laser wavelength of 780nm, they are very reflective, but at other wavelengths, the reflectivity falls off markedly. Normally, CD-ROM drives use a 780nm (infrared) laser to read the data, whereas DVD drives use a shorter wavelength 650nm (red) laser. Although the shorter wavelength laser works well for reading commercial CD-ROM discs because the aluminum reflective layer they use is equally reflective at the shorter DVD laser wavelength, it doesn't work well at all for reading CD-R or RW discs.

Fortunately, a solution was first introduced by Sony and then similarly by all the other DVD drive manufacturers. This solution consists of a dual-laser pickup that incorporates both a 650nm (DVD) and 780nm (CD) laser. Some of these used two discrete pickup units with separate optics mounted to the same assembly, but they eventually changed to dual-laser units that use the same optics for both, making the pickup smaller and less expensive. Because most manufacturers wanted to make a variety of drives—including cheaper ones without the dual-laser pickup—a standard needed to be created so that someone purchasing a drive would know the drive's capabilities.

So, how can you tell whether your drive is compatible with CD-R and RW discs? To demonstrate the compatibility of a particular drive, OSTA created industry standard tests and logos that would guarantee specific levels of compatibility. These are called the MultiRead specifications. Currently there are two levels, as follows:

- *MultiRead*. For CD-ROM drives
- *MultiRead2*. For DVD-ROM drives

In addition, a similar MultiPlay standard exists that is for consumer DVD-Video and CD-DA devices.

Table 13.28 shows the two levels of MultiRead capability that can be assigned to drives and the types of media guaranteed to be readable in such drives.

Table 13.28   MultiRead and MultiRead2 Compatibility Standards for CD/DVD Drives

Media	MultiRead	MultiRead2	Media	MultiRead	MultiRead2
CD-DA	X	X	DVD-ROM	—	X
CD-ROM	X	X	DVD-Video	—	X
CD-R	X	X	DVD-Audio	—	X
CD-RW	X	X	DVD-RAM	—	X

X = Compatible; drive will read this media
— = Incompatible; drive won't read

Note that MultiRead also indicates that the drive is capable of reading discs written in Packet Writing mode because this mode is now being used more commonly with both CD-R and RW media.

To determine whether your drive meets either of these standards, merely look for the MultiRead or MultiRead2 logo on the drive, as shown in Figure 13.14.

Figure 13.14 MultiRead and MultiRead2 logos.

The presence of these logos guarantees that particular level of compatibility. If you are purchasing a CD-ROM or DVD-ROM drive and want to be able to read recordable or rewritable discs, be sure to look for the MultiRead or MultiRead2 logo on your drive. Especially in the case of DVD drives, MultiRead2 versions are generally more expensive because of the extra cost of the dual-mode laser pickup required. Virtually all DVD-ROM drives for computers have the dual pickup mechanism, enabling them to properly read CD-R or CD-RW discs. However, most DVD video players used in entertainment systems do not have the dual pickups.

You can obtain the latest versions of the MultiRead specification (revision 1.11, October 23, 1997) and MultiRead 2 specification (revision 1.0, December 6, 1999) from the OSTA Web site.

How to Reliably Record CDs

With typical burn times for full CD-Rs ranging from under 3 minutes (40x or faster speeds) to as long as 80 minutes (1x), it is frustrating when a buffer underrun or some other problem forces you to rewrite your CD-RW disc, or worse yet, turn your CD-R media to a coaster—an unusable disc that must be discarded.

Five major factors influence your ability to create a working CD-R: interface type, drive buffer size, the location and condition of the data you want to record to CD-R, the recording speed, and whether the computer is performing other tasks while trying to create the CD-R.

To improve the odds of getting reliable CD-R/RW creation, look for drives with the following:

- *A large data buffer (2MB or larger), or better yet some form of buffer underrun protection.* The data buffer in the drive holds information read from the original data source, so that if a pause in data reading occurs, there's less of a possibility of a buffer underrun until the on-drive buffer runs empty. A larger buffer minimizes the chance of "running out of data." Newer drives with buffer underrun protection virtually eliminate this problem, no matter what size buffer is in the drive.

- *Support for UDMA operating modes.* As you've already seen, UDMA modes transfer data more quickly and with less CPU intervention than earlier versions of ATA. To use this feature, you'll also need a motherboard with a busmastering UDMA interface with the appropriate drivers installed.

Tip

Also, if you have problems with reliable CD-R creation at the drive's maximum speed, try using a lower speed (24x instead of 48x, for example). Your mastering job will take twice as long, but it's better to create a working CD-R slowly than ruin a blank quickly.

An alternative approach is to use packet-writing software to create your CD-R. All late-model CD-R/CD-RW drives support packet writing, which allows drag-and-drop copying of individual files to the CD-R/RW rather than transferring all the files at once as with normal mastering software. This "a little at a time" approach means that less data must be handled in each write and can make the difference between success and failure. If your drive supports this feature, it probably includes packet-writing software in the package. Note that although packet-written CDs can be read with Windows 9x/Me and NT/2000/XP, they can't be read with Windows 3.1 and MS-DOS because these operating systems don't have drivers available that support packet-written CDs. Note that some CD-mastering software supports packet-writing to CD-Rs, but others don't. For example, the DirectCD program included with Roxio Easy CD Creator can packet-write to both CD-R and CD-RW media and close CD-R media for reading on any drive, but Nero Burning ROM's InCD packet-writing software doesn't support CD-R.

Note

Imaging software such as PowerQuest DriveImage works from a DOS prompt but uses packet-writing to copy data to CD-R media. Because a backup created with DriveImage must be restored from a DOS prompt in some versions of the program, DriveImage includes a special DOS-compatible packet-writing driver that is loaded during its startup process.

If your CD-R/RW drive is SCSI based, be sure you have the correct type of SCSI interface card and cables. Although many drive vendors take the uncertainty out of this issue by supplying an appropriate card and cables, others don't.

If you must buy your own SCSI card for your recorder, follow these tips:

- *Forget about ISA cards.* Many new motherboards no longer include ISA slots, and even if they do, the performance of the ISA bus presents a bottleneck that will seriously inhibit drive performance.

- *PCI or Cardbus SCSI works well.* As discussed in Chapter 17, "I/O Interfaces from Serial and Parallel to IEEE 1394 and USB," PCI's 32-bit data bus and 33MHz typical performance is far faster than ISA's 16-bit data bus and 8.33MHz typical performance. Cardbus is PCI for notebooks, so the same benefits apply there as well.

- *Make sure the SCSI card is rated for CD-RW/CD-R use.* The SCSI host adapters that are designed for use with and are sometimes bundled with low-performance devices such as scanners and Zip drives are not adequate for use with a CD-R or CD-RW drive.

Tip

Several manufacturers, including Adaptec, Promise Tech, SIIG, Tekram, and Advansys, offer high-performance PCI SCSI cards.

Buffer Underruns

Whenever a drive writes data to a CD-R/RW disc in either Disk at Once or Track at Once mode, it writes to the spiral track on the CD, alternating on and off to etch the pattern into the raw media. Because the drive can't easily realign where it starts and stops writing like a hard drive can, after it starts writing it must typically continue until it's finished with the track or disc. Otherwise, the recording (and disc if it is a CD-R) will be ruined. This means that the CD recording software, in combination with your system hardware, must be capable of delivering a consistent stream of data to the drive while it's writing. To aid in this effort, the software uses a buffer that it creates on your hard disk to temporarily store the data as it is being sent to the drive.

If the system is incapable of delivering data at a rate sufficient to keep the drive happy, you receive a buffer underrun message and the recording attempt fails. The buffer underrun message indicates that the drive had to abort recording because it ran out of data in its buffer to write to the CD. For many years, this was the biggest problem people had when recording to CD-R/RW media. And for many years, the best way to prevent buffer underruns was to either slow down the writing speeds or have a large buffer in the recording drive, as well as to use the fastest interface and reading drive as possible. Nobody wants to write at lower speeds (otherwise, why buy a fast drive?), so buffer sizes grew as did the interface speeds. Still, it was possible to get a buffer underrun if, for example, you tried browsing Web pages or doing other work while burning a disc.

Buffer Underrun Protection

Sanyo was the first to develop a technology that eliminates buffer underruns once and for all. It calls the technology BURN-Proof ("BURN" stands for "buffer underrun"), which sounds a little confusing (some people thought it prevented any writing on discs), but in practice it has proven to be excellent.

After Sanyo, several other companies have developed similar and compatible technology with various names. Including Sanyo's, the most common you'll see are

- BURN-Proof, from Sanyo
- JustLink, from Ricoh
- Waste-Proof, from Yamaha
- Safeburn, from Yamaha
- Superlink, from Mediatek

You will see these technologies on many vendors' drives because most developers of this technology license it to various drive makers.

Buffer underrun protection technology involves having a special chipset in the drive that monitors the drive buffer. When it anticipates that a buffer underrun might occur (the buffer is running low on data), it temporarily suspends the recording until more data fills the buffer. When the buffer is sufficiently restocked, the drive then locates exactly where the recording left off earlier and restarts recording again immediately after that position.

According to the Orange Book specification, gaps between data in a CD recording must not be more than 100 milliseconds in length. The buffer underrun technology can restart the recording with a gap of 40–45 milliseconds or less from where it left off, which is well within the specification. These small gaps are easily compensated for by the error correction built into the recording, so no data is lost.

Note that it is important that the drive incorporate buffer underrun technology, but the recording software must support it as well for everything to work properly. Fortunately, all the popular CD recording programs on the market now support this technology.

If your drive incorporates buffer underrun protection, you can multitask—do other things while burning CDs—without fear of producing a bad recording.

Producing Error-Free Recordings

If you have an older drive that doesn't feature buffer underrun protection, follow these recommendations to help ensure error-free recordings and prevent buffer underruns:

- *Whenever possible, move all the data you want to put onto a CD-R to a fast local hard drive.* If you can't do this, avoid using the following sources for data: floppy drives, parallel port–connected storage drives, and slower CD-ROM drives (especially 8x or slower). These locations for data usually can't feed data quickly enough to maintain data flow to the recording drive.

- *Before you master the CD-R, check your hard disk or data source for errors (the Windows 9x/Me Scandisk or Windows 2000/XP error-checking program can often be used for this).* Also try defragmenting the drive. This ensures that disk errors or file fragmentation, both of which slow down disk access, won't be a factor in program or data search and retrieval.

- *Avoid trying to burn from active files or zero-byte files (often used for temporary storage).* If you must burn these files to make an archival copy of your current system configuration, use a program such as Norton Ghost or PowerQuest Drive Image. These programs create a single compressed file from your drive's contents. Then, burn the disc using the resulting compressed file.

- *Turn off power management for your hard disk and other peripherals.* In Windows you normally do this through the Power icon in the Control Panel.

■ *Make sure your temporary drive has at least twice the empty space of your finished CD.* Your CD's estimated space requirements are shown during the mastering process with programs such as Roxio Easy CD-Creator or NERO Burning ROM. Thus, if you're creating a CD with 500MB of data, your temporary drive should have at least 1GB of empty space.

■ *With Windows 9x/Me, you'll improve disk caching by adjusting the typical role of the computer from workstation to server in the Performance tab of the System Properties dialog box.* Note that this change works correctly with Windows 95B and 95C (OSR 2.x) and Windows 98/Me, but the Registry keys are incorrect in Windows 95 original retail and OSR1 (95A) versions. Check Microsoft's Web site for the correct Registry key settings for Windows 95/95A, back up and edit the Registry, and restart the computer before making this change with those versions.

■ *If your original data is coming from a variety of sources, consider using the Create Disk Image option found in most CD mastering software.* This feature creates an image file on your hard drive that contains all the files you want to put onto a CD. Then, use Create CD from Disk Image to actually master the CD from that information.

■ *If you're uncertain of success, why waste a CD-R blank?* Use a CD-RW instead, which usually is written at a slower speed, or use the "test-then-create" option found in most recording software that does a simulated burn of the CD before the actual creation. After the simulation, you're warned of any problems before the actual process begins. This is not always foolproof, but it can help.

■ *Small files are harder to use in mastering a CD than large ones because of the excessive drive tracking necessary to find them and load them.* You might want to use the Packet Writing mode instead if your drive and software support it.

■ *Keep your drives clean and free from dust.* Use a cleaning CD if necessary. Dirty drives cause data-read errors or data-write errors if your recording drive is the dirty one.

■ *Don't multitask.* If you run another program during the mastering process, the computer is forced to perform time-slicing, which causes it to start a process, switch away from it to start the next process, switch back to the first process, and so forth. This switching process could cause the recording drive to run out of data because it isn't receiving data in a steady stream. Forget about surfing the Internet, playing Solitaire, or creating a label for your new CD during the burning process if you want reliable mastering on a drive that doesn't feature buffer underrun protection.

If you're still having buffer underrun problems despite taking all the precautions listed here, try dropping down a speed. Go to the next lower speed and see how you do. Using a lower speed than the drive is rated for can be frustrating, but it's preferable to wasting time creating unusable discs.

As a final note, I have also seen problems with burning CDs caused by inadequate power supplies. An inadequate or overtaxed power supply can cause myriad recording problems (including buffer underruns). I've seen cases in which the system seemed to be normal in most respects, but there were tremendous problems recording CDs, from buffer underruns to power calibration errors. After upgrading the power supply with a high-quality, high-output unit, the problems all but disappeared. I've said it many times, but the power supply is the foundation of a PC, and in general it is the most failure-prone or problematic piece of hardware in the system. See Chapter 21, "Power Supply and Chassis/Case," for more information on power supplies, including recommended suppliers for upgraded units.

Recording Software

Another difficulty with CD-R/RW devices is that they usually require special software to write them. Although most cartridge drives and other removable media mount as standard devices in the system and can be accessed exactly like a hard drive, the CD-R/RW drives and most types of rewritable DVD drives use special CD-ROM/DVD burning software to write to the disc (DVD-RAM drives don't require special software to write to DVD-RAM media). This software handles the differences between how data is stored on a CD and how it is stored on a hard drive. As you learned earlier, there are several

CD-ROM standards for storing information. The CD-ROM-burning software arranges the data into one of these formats so a CD-ROM reader can read the CD later. Windows XP and later include CD writing software built in; operating systems prior to that required that you purchase and install third-party CD writing software. Still, most have found that the popular third-party CD writing applications such as CD-Creator (Roxio) or Nero Burning ROM (Ahead Software) are far more powerful and easier to use than what Windows includes or what is packaged with some drives.

At one time, CD recording technology required that you have what amounted to a replica of the CD on a local hard drive. In fact, some software packages even required a separate, dedicated disk partition for this purpose. You would copy all the files to the appropriate place on the hard drive, creating the directory structure for the CD, and then the software would create an exact replica of every sector for the proposed CD-ROM—including every file, all the directory information, and the volume information—and copy it to the CD-R drive. The result was that you had to have about 1.5GB of storage to burn a single CD (650MB/CD×2 = 1.3GB + overhead = 1.5GB). This is no longer a requirement because most software supports virtual images. You select the files and directories you want to write to the CD from your hard drive and create a virtual directory structure for the CD-ROM in the software. This means you can select files from different directories on different hard drives, or even files from network or other CD-ROM drives, and combine them any way you want on the CD-R. This works well provided the drives have adequate speed and your drive has a large buffer or features buffer underrun protection. If you have problems, follow the advice given earlier to overcome slow data sources.

The software assembles the directory information, burns it onto the CD, opens each file on the CD, and copies the data directly from the original source. This generally works well, but you must be aware of the access times for the media you select as data sources. If, for example, you select directories from a slow hard drive or from a busy network, the software might not be capable of reading the data quickly enough to maintain a consistent stream to the recorder. In drives lacking buffer underrun protection, this causes the write to fail, resulting in a wasted disc.

Don't Forget the Software!

If you have persistent problems with making CDs, your recording software or drive might be to blame. Check the vendor's Web site for tips and software updates. Some drives offer software-upgradable firmware similar to the motherboard's flash BIOS; if so, be sure your drive has the latest firmware available. Also make sure that your recording software is up-to-date and compatible with your drive and your drive's firmware revision.

Each of the major CD-R/CD-RW drive vendors provides extensive technical notes to help you achieve reliable recordings. You can also find helpful information on SCSI adapter vendors' Web sites and the Web sites of the media vendors.

▶▶   See "Updating the Firmware in a CD-RW or Rewritable DVD Drive," p. 828.

Digital Audio Extraction

All CD-ROM drives can *play* Red Book–formatted CD-DA discs, but not all CD-ROM drives can *read* CD-DA discs. The difference sounds subtle, but it is actually quite dramatic. If you enjoy music and want to use your PC to manage your music collection, the ability to read the audio data digitally is an important function for your CD (and DVD) drives because it enables you to much more easily and accurately store, manipulate, and eventually write back out audio tracks.

CD-ROM drives installed in PCs can play audio discs. The playing function is simple: Using a CD or Media player application (such as the one included with Windows), you can insert a CD-DA disc into a CD-ROM drive and play it just as you could with a standard audio CD player. While playing, the analog sound waveform is sent over a thin stereo cable (usually referred to as the CD audio cable) connected between your CD-ROM drive and the sound card in your PC. The same analog waveform usually is also sent to the headphone jack on the front of the drive (or sound card). Your sound card then amplifies the analog signal so you can hear it through the speakers plugged into your sound card or via headphones plugged into the front of the drive (or the sound card).

That is just fine if all you want to do is play discs, but if you ever want to record one of the songs on your hard disk, you will run into some problems. To transfer the song to your hard drive, you would have to play the song as you did normally and simultaneously use a sound recorder application, such as the Sound Recorder supplied with Windows 95 and later (similar recording software is also typically supplied with your sound card), to redigitize the audio waveform for storage as a .WAV file on the PC. This means the sound goes from digital as originally stored on the disc to analog in the CD-ROM drive and back to digital in your sound card, with the resulting digital file being only an approximation of the original digital data. Another drawback is that this procedure runs only at 1x speed—hardly an ideal situation!

It would be much better if you could read the original digital data directly off the disc. That was not possible with older CD-ROM drives, but newer drives can do what is called *digital audio extraction (DAE)*. In this process they read the digital audio sectors directly and, rather than decode them into analog signals, pass each 2,352-byte sector of raw (error-corrected) digital audio data directly to the PC's processor via the drive interface cable (ATA, SCSI, USB, or FireWire). Therefore, no digital-to-analog conversion (and back) occurs, and you essentially get the audio data exactly as it was originally recorded on the CD (within the limits of the CD-DA error-correction standards). You would have essentially extracted the exact digital audio data from the disc onto your PC.

Another term for digital audio extraction is *ripping*, so named because you can "rip" the raw audio data from the drive at full drive read speed, rather than the normal 1x speed at which you listen to audio discs. Actually, most drives can't perform DAE at their full rated speeds. Although some are faster (or slower) than others, most perform DAE at speeds from about one-quarter to about one-half of their rated read speed. So, you might be able to extract audio data at speeds only up to 20x on a 40x rated drive. However, that is still quite a bit better than at 1x as it would be on drives that can't do DAE (not to mention skipping the conversion to analog and back to digital with the resultant loss of information).

Virtually all newer CD/DVD drives can perform digital audio extraction on music discs. How fast or accurately they do this varies from model to model. One might think any extraction (digital copy) of a given track (song) should be the same because it is a digital copy of the original; however, that is not always the case. The CD-DA format was designed to play music, not to transfer data with 100% accuracy. Errors beyond the capability of the CIRC in the CD-DA format cause the firmware in the drive to interpolate or approximate the data. In addition, time-based problems due to clock inaccuracies can occur in the drive, causing it to get slightly out of step when reading the frames in the sector (this is referred to as *jitter*). Differences in the internal software (firmware) in the drive and differences in the drivers used are other problems that can occur.

Positioning can also be a problem because the CD-DA format was designed to stream (play continuously) and not to read individual sectors. CD-ROM sectors are 2,352 bytes long, and these bytes are further divided into 2,048 bytes of data plus 304 bytes of synchronization, header, and additional ECC information to control positioning and allow for error-free reads. No such synchronization, header, or extra ECC information exists for audio sectors; instead, all 2,352 bytes are used for pure audio data. To address an audio sector, the Q subcode information is used instead (see the section "Subcodes," earlier in this chapter). Most audio players position to within only 75 sectors (1 second) using the Q subcode information. CD-ROM drives that can perform digital audio extraction are usually much more accurate than that, but because of how the subcode works (as well as the cross-interleaved way audio data is stored), designing a drive that can position every time to the precise audio sector that starts the track can be difficult.

All of this conspires to cause inaccuracies or slight differences in multiple extractions of the same track (song). Perfect extractions are possible, but making perfect extractions is difficult to achieve for many reasons. For example, even a slight amount of dirt or scratches on the disc has a great effect on the quality of your extractions, so be sure the discs are clean. As a test of your drive's capability to perform DAE, try extracting the same track (song) multiple times from a new, clean, scratch-free disc, using a different filename for each extraction. Then, bring up a command prompt and use the FC (file compare) command to compare the different files to each other. If they compare exactly, you have a combination of hardware and software that can do perfect or near-perfect extractions.

If you intend to do a lot of extracting, you should ask around to see what hardware and software others are using for this purpose. As a general rule, SCSI drives work better than ATA, but some ATA drives are just as good as the better SCSI drives. Plextor is well known for drives that are excellent when it comes to digital audio extraction, and I've always had good luck with Toshiba drives.

The bottom line is that DAE enables you to extract audio data tracks directly to your PC as .WAV files. Once on the PC, you can play the WAV files as is or convert them to other (usually more compressed) formats, such as MP3 (MPEG-1/2 Layer III) for use with the MP3 audio players on the market.

Note

Because the WAV files extracted match the high 44.1KHz sampling rate used on the CD, you have 176,400 bytes per second of sound information, which means 1 minute of music consumes nearly 10.6MB worth of space on your hard drive! MP3 compression can reduce that by a factor of 6 or more, with little to no perceptible loss in quality.

You can also use a CD-R/RW drive that can perform DAE to make copies of audio CDs (for backup purposes only) or to compile several songs into your own greatest hits collections that you can use to burn your own custom audio CDs.

"For Music Use Only" CD-R/RW discs

According to the Audio Home Recording Act of 1992, consumer CD recordable drives *and media* sold specifically for recording music are required to have specific safeguards against copying discs, mainly SCMS. That means these recorders can make digital copies only from original prerecorded discs. You can copy a copy, but in that case, the data being recorded goes from digital to analog and back to digital on the second copy, resulting in a generational loss of quality.

The media for these recorders must be special as well. They work only with special discs labeled "For Music Use," "For Audio," or "For Consumer." These carry the standard Compact Disk Digital Audio Recordable logo that most are familiar with, but below that, as part of the logo, is an added line that says "For Consumer." These discs feature a special track prerecorded onto the disc, which the consumer music recorders look for. Built into the price of the AHRA-compliant media is a royalty for the music industry that this track protects. The media costs about 20%–30% more than what regular CD-R/RW media costs. If you try to use standard non-AHRA-compliant CD-R/RW discs in these drives, the drive refuses to recognize the disc. These music devices also refuse to copy CD-ROM or data discs.

Note that this does not apply to the CD-R/RW drive you have installed or attached to your PC. It does not have to be AHRA compliant, nor does it need to use AHRA-compliant "For Music Use" media, even if you are copying or recording music discs. Additionally, you can make digital copies of copies—the SCMS does not apply, either. The bottom line is that you do not have to purchase AHRA-compliant discs for the CD-R/RW drives in your PC. If you do purchase such discs, despite the "For Music Use Only" designation, AHRA-compliant discs can be used in your CD-R/RW drives just as regular CD-R/RW discs can be used for storing data. The extra information indicating AHRA compliance is simply ignored.

CD Copy Protection

Worries about the public copying of software and music CDs has prompted the development of copy protection techniques that attempt to make these discs uncopyable. There are different methods of protecting software CDs versus music CDs, but the end result is the same: You are prevented from making normal copies, or the copies don't work properly. In the case of music CDs, the copy protection can be quite obtrusive, adding noise to the recording, and in extreme cases preventing the disc from even playing in a PC drive.

Several copy protection schemes are available for CD-DA (digital audio) discs, ranging from the simple to sophisticated. The most popular protection scheme for digital audio discs is called SafeAudio by Macrovision. Macrovision won't explain exactly how SafeAudio works, but it purchased the technology from a company called TTR Technologies and patents filed by TTR describe the scheme in detail. According to the patents, the disc is deliberately recorded with grossly erroneous values (bursts of noise) in both the audio data and the codes, which would typically be used to correct these errors. When reading the disc, the normal error correction scheme fails, leaving small gaps in the music.

When this happens on a standard audio CD player, the gaps are automatically bridged by circuitry or code in the player, which looks at the audio data on either side of the gap and interpolates (guesses) the missing values. The CD drive in a PC can do the same thing, so the interpolation occurs only when playing CDs in an audio player mode. However, the drive in a PC does not perform this same interpolation when "ripping" the data—that is, copying it directly to a hard drive, another CD, or some other medium. In that case the unbridged gaps are heard as extremely loud clicks, pops, and noise. Both TTR and Macrovision claim that the interpolation that occurs when playing a SafeAudio disc is not discernable to the human ear, but many audio experts disagree. To an audiophile, the addition of any distortion or noise to the audio signal is unconscionable.

Even more rigorous protection can be added that can render the audio disc unplayable on a PC and even cause problems on audio players. Of course, the final problem is that you can't make legal backups of your music—something that is allowed by law.

For software (rather than audio), several protection schemes are used, although most are similar to one another. Again the most popular is by Macrovision, but for CD-ROMs it is called SafeDisc. As with SafeAudio, Macrovision purchased the technology from another company; in this case it was a company called C-Dilla.

SafeDisc works by first encrypting all the software code on the disc and then adding a routine to the code that looks for a unique authentication signature (called a *watermark*) which would have been added to the disc during the mastering process. When executed, the authentication code attempts to read the watermark on the disc. If the watermark is present, the main program code is unencrypted and executed. But if the watermark is not present, the program does not run. Because the watermark does not conform to the normal structures written to a CD, most CD burners can't duplicate it.

The authentication process basically requires that the original CD be present in the drive whenever the program is run. This, however, can be set up so that the original disc is required only during program installation, or it can be checked anytime the program is run, even if run from a hard disk. The latter is quite inconvenient because it requires you to have the original CD with you at all times to run the program.

To circumvent this type of protection, people have developed software that can fool the authentication code into believing the watermark is present. Some software even strips the authentication code from the software completely. Others have found ways to copy the watermark such that it would appear on any copies of the original CD. As with other forms of copy protection, it has been easily defeated and represents more of a nuisance to the legitimate user rather than to the thief.

Recordable DVD Standards

The history of recordable DVD drives is a troubled one. It dates back to April 1997, when the DVD Forum announced specifications for rewritable DVD, DVD-RAM, and DVD-R. Later, it added DVD-RW to the mix. Dissatisfied with these standards, the industry leaders in optical recording and drives formed their own group called the DVD+RW Alliance and created another standard—DVD+R and DVD+RW.

In a war that brings back unhappy memories of the VHS/Beta struggle of the 1980s, as well as the problems in bringing DVD video to light, the computer and movie industries are locked in a struggle to see which enhancements to the basic DVD standard will win out. Table 13.29 compares the competing recordable DVD standards, and Table 13.30 breaks down the compatibilities between the drives and media.

Table 13.29   Recordable DVD Standards

Format	Introduced	Capacity	Compatibility
DVD-RAM	July '97	Up to 4.7GB per side	Incompatible with existing DVD drives unless they support the MultiRead2 standard
DVD-R/RW	July '97/ Nov. '99	4.7GB per side	Readable by many existing DVD recorders/drives
DVD+R/RW	Mar. '01/ May '01	4.7GB per side	Readable by most existing DVD recorders/drives, with enhancements for video and data recording

Table 13.30   DVD Drive and Media Compatibility

	Media (Discs)									
Drives	**CD-ROM**	**CD-R**	**CD-RW**	**DVD-Drive**	**DVD-ROM**	**DVD-R**	**DVD-RAM**	**DVD-RW**	**DVD+RW**	**DVD+R**
DVD-Video Player	R	?	?	R	—	R	?	R	R	R
DVD-ROM Drive	R	R	R	R	R	R	?	R	R[1]	R
DVD-R Drive	R	R/W	R/W	R	R	R/W	—	R	R	R
DVD-RAM Drive	R	R	R	R	R	R[6]	R/W	R	R[1]	R
DVD-RW Drive	R	R/W	R/W	R	R	R/W	—	R/W	R	R
DVD+R/RW Drive	R	R/W	R/W	R	R	R	R[3]	R	R/W	R/W[2]
DVD-Multi Drive[4]	R	R/W	R/W	R	R	R	R/W	R/W	R[1]	R
DVD±R/RW Drive	R	R/W	R/W	R	R	R/W	R[5]	R/W	R/W	R/W

R = Read.

W = Write.

— = Will not read or write.

? = MultiRead/MultiPlay drives will read.

1 = Might require media's compatibility bit be changed to alternate (Type 2).

2 = Some first-generation DVD+RW drives will not write DVD+R discs; see your drive manufacturer for an update or trade-in.

3 = Read compatibility with DVD-RAM varies by drive; check documentation for details.

4 = DVD Forum specification for drives that are compatible with all DVD Forum standards (DVD+R/RW is not a DVD Forum standard).

5 = Some of these drives can also write to DVD-RAM media.

6 = Some of these drives can also write to DVD-R media.

As you can see from looking at both the horizontal rows and vertical columns of Table 13.30, the following factors are worth noting:

■ Of the single-format drives, DVD+R/RW drives are the most compatible with other media from a read standpoint.

■ Increasing numbers of vendors are shipping multiformat drives to solve the persistent issues of drive/media compatibility.

DVD+R/RW offers low drive and media prices, provides the highest compatibility with existing formats, and has features that make it the most ideal for both video recording and data storage in PCs.

DVD-RAM

DVD-RAM is the rewritable DVD standard endorsed by Panasonic, Hitachi, and Toshiba; it is part of the DVD Forum's list of supported standards. DVD-RAM uses a phase-change technology similar to that of CD-RW. Unfortunately, DVD-RAM discs can't be read by most standard DVD-ROM drives because of differences in both reflectivity of the media and the data format. (DVD-R, by comparison, is backward compatible with DVD-ROM.) DVD-ROM drives that can read DVD-RAM discs began to come on the market in early 1999 and follow the MultiRead2 specification. DVD-ROM drives and DVD-Video players labeled as MultiRead2 compliant are capable of reading DVD-RAM discs. See the section "MultiRead Specifications," earlier in this chapter, for more information.

The first DVD-RAM drives were introduced in spring 1998 and had a capacity of 2.6GB (single-sided) or 5.2GB (double-sided). DVD-RAM Version 2 discs with 4.7GB arrived in late 1999, and double-sided 9.4GB discs arrived in 2000. DVD-RAM drives typically read DVD-Video, DVD-ROM, and CD media. The current installed base of DVD-ROM drives and DVD-Video players can't read DVD-RAM media; most DVD+R/RW and DVD-R/RW drives can't read DVD-RAM media. To improve compatibility with other formats, many recent DVD-RAM drives can also write to DVD-R media, and the DVD Forum has developed a DVD Multi specification for drives that can read/write DVD-RAM, DVD-R, and DVD-RW media.

DVD-RAM uses what is called the wobbled land and groove recording method, which records signals on both the lands (the areas between grooves) and inside the grooves that are preformed on the disc. The tracks wobble, which provides clock data for the drive. Special sector header pits are prepressed into the disc during the manufacturing process as well. See Figure 13.15, which shows the wobbled tracks (lands and grooves) with data recorded both on the lands and in the grooves. This is unlike CD-R or CD-RW, in which data is recorded on the groove only.

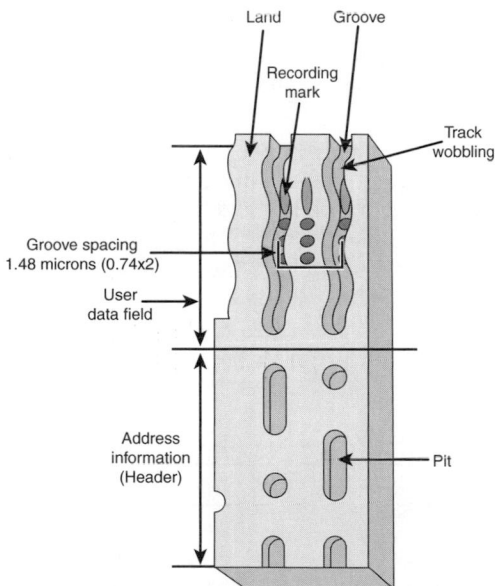

Figure 13.15   DVD-RAM wobbled land and groove recording.

The disc is recorded using phase-change recording, in which data is written by selectively heating spots in the grooves or on the lands with a high-powered laser. The DVD-RAM drive write laser transforms the film from a crystalline to an amorphous state by heating a spot, which is then rendered less reflective than the remaining crystalline portions. The signal is read as the difference of the laser reflection rate between the crystalline and amorphous states. The modulation and error correction codes are the same as for DVD-Video and DVD-ROM, ensuring compatibility with other DVD formats. For rewriting, a lower-powered laser reheats the spot to a lower temperature, where it recrystallizes.

Disc cartridges or caddies originally were required for both single- and double-sided discs but have now been made optional for single-sided discs. Double-sided discs must remain inside the caddy at all times for protection; however, single-sided discs can be taken out of the cartridge if necessary.

DVD-RAM specifications are shown in Table 13.31.

Table 13.31   DVD-RAM Specifications

Storage capacity	2.6GB single-sided; 5.2GB double sided
Disc diameter	80mm–120mm
Disc thickness	1.2mm (0.6mm×2: bonded structure)
Recording method	Phase change
Laser wavelength	650nm
Data bit length	0.41–0.43 microns
Recording track pitch	0.74 microns
Track format	Wobbled land and groove

DVD-R

DVD-R is a write-once medium very similar to CD-R, which was originally created by Pioneer and released by the DVD Forum in July 1997. DVD-R discs can be played on standard DVD-ROM drives. Some recent DVD-RAM drives can also write to DVD-R media.

DVD-R has a single-sided storage capacity of 4.7GB—about seven times that of a CD-R—and double that for a double-sided disc. These discs use an organic dye recording layer that allows for a low material cost, similar to CD-R.

To enable positioning accuracy, DVD-R uses a wobbled groove recording, in which special grooved tracks are pre-engraved on the disc during the manufacturing process. Data is recorded within the grooves only. The grooved tracks wobble slightly right and left, and the frequency of the wobble contains clock data for the drive to read, as well as clock data for the drive. The grooves are spaced more closely together than with DVD-RAM, but data is recorded only in the grooves and not on the lands (see Figure 13.16).

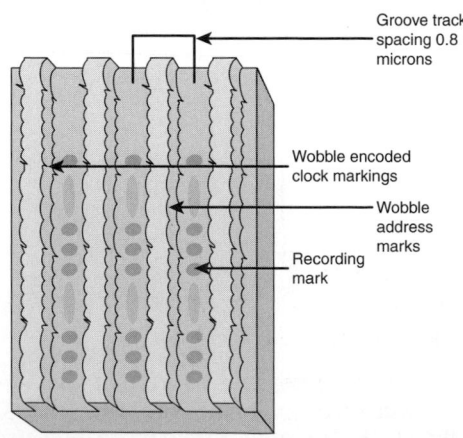

Figure 13.16   DVD-R wobbled groove recording.

Table 13.32 has the basic specifications for DVD-R drives.

Table 13.32   DVD-R Specifications

Storage capacity	4.7GB single-sided; 9.4GB double-sided
Disc diameter	80mm–120mm
Disc thickness	1.2mm (0.6mm×2: bonded structure)
Recording method	Organic dye layer recording method
Laser wavelength	635nm (recording); 635/650nm (playback)
Data bit length	0.293 microns
Recording track pitch	0.80 microns
Track format	Wobbled groove

DVD-RW

The DVD Forum introduced DVD-RW in November 1999. Created and endorsed originally by Pioneer, DVD-RW is basically an extension to DVD-R just as CD-RW is an extension to CD-R. DVD-RW uses a phase-change technology and is somewhat more compatible with standard DVD-ROM drives than DVD-RAM. Drives based on this technology began shipping in late 1999, but early models achieved only moderate popularity because Pioneer was the only source for the drives and because of limitations in their performance.

Currently, DVD-RW drives are available in 1x DVD-RW/2x DVD-R and the newer 2x DVD-RW/4x DVD-R models. 2x/4x drives have several advantages over older drives, including these:

- *Quick formatting.* 1x/2x drives require that the entire DVD-RW disc be formatted before the media can be used, a process that can take about an hour. 2x/4x drives can use DVD-RW media in a few seconds after inserting, formatting the media in the background as necessary. This is similar to the way in which DVD+RW drives work.

- *Quick grow.* Instead of erasing the media to add files, as with 1x/2x DVD-RW drives, 2x/4x DVD-RW drives can unfinalize the media and add more files without deleting existing files.

- *Quick finalizing.* 2x/4x DVD-RW drives close media containing small amounts of data (under 1GB) more quickly than 1x/2x drives.

However, DVD-RW drives still don't support lossless linking, Mount Rainier, or selective deletion of files—all of which are major features of DVD+RW.

DVD-RW is currently supported by most major makers of CD/DVD-burning software (including Ahead Nero Burning ROM, Roxio Easy CD-DVD Creator, and others) and by several drive manufacturers (including Panasonic, Toshiba, and Teac).

DVD+RW

DVD+RW, also called DVD Phase Change Rewritable, is rapidly becoming the premier DVD recordable standard because it is the least expensive, easiest to use, and most compatible with existing formats. It was developed and is supported by Philips, Sony, Hewlett-Packard, Mitsubishi Chemical (MCC/Verbatim), Ricoh, Yamaha, and Thomson, who are all part of an industry standard group called the DVD+RW Alliance (www.dvdrw.com). Microsoft joined the alliance in February 2003. DVD+RW is also supported by major DVD/CD creation software vendors and many drive vendors, including HP, Philips, Ricoh, and many remarketers of OEM drive mechanisms. Although DVD-RW has increased in popularity with the advent of faster and easier burning times, DVD+RW is still the most popular rewritable DVD format.

Table 13.33 lists the basic specifications for DVD+RW drives.

Table 13.33   DVD+RW Specifications

Storage capacity	4.7GB single-sided; 9.4GB double-sided (future product)
Disc diameter	120mm
Disc thickness	1.2mm (0.6mm×2: bonded structure)
Recording method	Phase change
Laser wavelength	650nm (recording/playback)
Data bit length	0.4 microns
Recording track pitch	0.74 microns
Track format	Wobbled groove

Note that DVD+R, the recordable version of DVD+RW, was actually introduced *after* DVD+RW. This is the opposite of DVD-RW, which grew out of DVD-R. One of the major reasons for the development of DVD+R was to provide a lower-cost method for permanent data archiving with DVD+RW drives, and another was because of compatibility issues with DVD-ROM and DVD video players being incapable of reading media created with DVD+RW drives. However, writing DVD+RW media is relatively simple with most drives that can be read by a DVD-ROM or DVD player. See the section "DVD+RW Compatibility Mode," later in this chapter, for details.

The basic structure of a DVD+RW or DVD+R disc resembles that of a DVD-R disc with data written in the grooves only (refer to Figure 13.16), but the groove is wobbled at a frequency different from that used by DVD-R/RW or DVD-RAM. The DVD+R/RW groove also contains positioning information. These differences mean that DVD+R/RW media offers more accurate postioning for lossless linking, but DVD+R/RW drives can't write to other types of DVD rewritable media.

Although some first-generation DVD+RW drives worked only with rewritable media, all current and future DVD+RW drives are designed to work with both DVD+R (writable) and DVD+RW (rewritable) media. The +R discs can be written only once and are less expensive than the +RW discs.

Some of the features of DVD+RW includes are as follows:

- Single-sided discs (4.7GB).
- Double-sided discs (9.4GB).
- Up to 4 hours video recording (single-sided discs).
- Up to 8 hours video recording (double-sided discs).
- Bare discs—no caddy required.
- 650nm laser (same as DVD-Video).
- Constant linear data density.
- CLV and CAV recording.
- Write speeds 1x–4x and higher (depending on the drive).
- DVD-Video data rates.
- UDF (Universal Disc Format) file system.
- Defect management integral to the drive.
- Quick formatting.
- Uses same eight to sixteen modulation and error correcting codes as DVD-ROM.
- Sequential and random recording.
- Lossless linking (multiple recording sessions don't waste space).
- Spiral groove with radial wobble.
- After recording, all physical parameters comply with the DVD-ROM specification.

DVD+RW technology is very similar to CD-RW, and DVD+RW drives can read DVD-ROMs and all CD formats, including CD-R and CD-RW.

With DVD+RW, the writing process can be suspended and continued without a loss of space linking the recording sessions together. This increases efficiency in random writing and video applications. This "lossless linking" also enables the selective replacement of any individual 32KB block of data (the minimum recording unit) with a new block, accurately positioning with a space of 1 micron. To enable this high accuracy for placement of data on the track, the pre-groove is wobbled at a higher frequency. The timing and addressing information read from the groove is very accurate.

The quick formatting feature means you can pop a DVD+R or DVD+RW blank into the drive and almost instantly begin writing to it. The actual formatting is carried out in the background ahead of where any writing will occur.

DVD+RW is also designed to work with existing DVD video players, DVD+RW-compatible video recorders such as those made by Philips and Yamaha, and DVD-ROM drives. However, because of the wide variance in equipment, DVD+RW tends to work better in newer equipment rather than in older equipment, particularly set-top players. As with DVD-RW, you might prefer to use writable (DVD+R) media to improve the odds of compatibility with older drives and players whose compatibility with DVD+RW is unknown.

DVD+RW is the format I prefer and recommend, and I expect that in the long run it will be the one preferred by most users. However, if you need to work with both DVD+R/RW and DVD-R/RW media because of device compatibility, I recommend one of the DVD±R/RW multiformat drives from Sony, NEC, and other vendors. I do not recommend DVD-RAM because it is not supported by set-top players or by most other types of DVD drives.

DVD+RW Compatibility Mode

When DVD+RW drives were introduced in 2001, some users of DVD-ROM and standalone DVD players were unable to read DVD+RW media, even though others were able to do so. The first drives to support DVD+R (writable) media (which works with a wider range of older drives) was not introduced until mid-2002, so this was a significant problem.

The most common reason for this problem turned out to be the contents of the Book Type Field located in the lead-in section of every DVD disc. Some drives require that this field indicate that the media is a DVD-ROM before they can read it. However, by default, DVD+RW drives write DVD+RW as the type into this field when DVD+RW media is used.

The following are two possible solutions:

■ Upgrade the firmware in the DVD+RW recorder so it writes compatible information into the Book Type Field automatically

■ Use a compatibility utility to change the contents of the Book Type Field for a particular DVD+RW disc as necessary

▶▶   See "Updating the Firmware in a CD-RW or Rewritable DVD Drive," p. 828.

In some cases, the manufacturer of the DVD+RW or DVD+R/RW drive provides a utility as well as a firmware download to perform this task for you. For example, HP includes a compatibility utility with the software provided for the HP DVD200 series and offers it as a download along with updated firmware for the DVD100i drive. Mode 1 (DVD+RW compatibility bits) is the default with these drives, whereas Mode 2 writes DVD-ROM compatibility bits to DVD+RW media (HP drives mark all DVD+R media as DVD-ROM).

Multiformat Rewritable Drives

Because of the fragmented nature of the rewritable DVD marketplace, there are two new categories of drives that provide for wider read/write media compatibility:

■ DVD Multi

■ DVD±R/RW

DVD Multi is a specification developed by the DVD Forum for drives and players that are compatible with all DVD Forum standards, including DVD-R/RW, DVD-RAM, DVD-ROM, DVD-Video, and eventually DVD Audio (DVD+R/RW are not DVD Forum specifications and are not supported). The original version of DVD Multi was published in February 2001; the current version, version 1.01, was approved by the DVD Forum and published in December 2001. The first DVD Multi products for computers reached the market in early 2003. Figure 13.17 compares the DVD Multi logos to the DVD+RW and other DVD forum logos.

Figure 13.17 The DVD-R/RAM, DVD-RW, and DVD+RW logos (top left to right), compared to new DVD Multi logos in vertical (lower left) and horizontal variations (lower right).

DVD±R/RW, unlike DVD Multi, is not a specification. Instead, it is used to indicate drives that work with both DVD+R/RW and DVD-R/RW media (DVD-RAM is not typically supported by these drives). Such drives usually carry both the DVD-RW and DVD+RW logos shown in Figure 13.17. Thus, DVD±R/RW drives are designed to handle the most common formats supported by the DVD Forum and the DVD+RW Alliance.

DVD Multi drives are a good choice for users who have been using DVD-RAM drives but want to enjoy a wider degree of compatibility with the rest of the DVD Forum world. However, if you need to work with the most common types of DVD rewritable media, DVD±R/RW is a better choice. Because of the need to support different read/write technologies, DVD±R/RW drives are more expensive than DVD-R/RW or DVD+R/RW drives.

CD/DVD Drive and Software Installation and Support

CD and DVD drives are installed and configured in the same way as any other drive with the same interface. For details, see the appropriate section:

- For ATA/IDE drives, see Chapter 7, "The ATA/IDE Interface," and Chapter 14, "Physical Drive Installation and Configuration."

- For IEEE 1394a and USB drives, see Chapter 17, "I/O Interfaces from Serial and Parallel to IEEE 1394 and USB."

- For SCSI drives, see Chapter 8, "The SCSI Interface," and Chapter 14.

After you've physically installed the drive, you're ready for the last step—installing the drivers and other CD-ROM/DVD-ROM software. As usual, this process can be simple with a PnP operating system such as Windows 9x or later. In that case the drivers for Windows will automatically be installed. Things are different, however, if you need to access the drive after booting from a floppy, such as when installing an operating system, running diagnostics, or running DOS.

Booting from a Floppy Disk with CD/DVD Drive Support

You might need to boot from a floppy drive on a modern PC for many reasons. One reason is to install an operating system on a newly built system or one with a new or unformatted hard drive. In that case, because the system cannot boot from the hard drive, it must boot from a CD or floppy instead.

For a CD or DVD drive to function in a floppy (or CD) boot environment, several drivers might be necessary:

- *An ATAPI host adapter driver (not needed for SCSI drives).* This driver is included with your motherboard, or you can use the generic ATAPI drivers found on Windows 98 and later startup disks.

- *SCSI adapter drivers (not needed for ATAPI drives).* Most SCSI cards include these drivers, or you can use the generic versions included on Windows 98 and later startup disks.

- *MSCDEX.* Microsoft CD Extensions, which is included with DOS 6.0 and later. It is also built into Windows 95 and later as the CDFS VxD.

If you need to start a PC from a bootable floppy, the floppy must contain not only a bootable OS, but also the previously mentioned drivers; otherwise, the CD-ROM will be inaccessible.

Generic ATAPI and SCSI drivers can be found on the Windows 98 and newer startup disks. Rather than create custom CONFIG.SYS and AUTOEXEC.BAT files, the best advice I can give is to merely boot from a Windows 98 or Me startup floppy because each time you boot from these, the proper drivers load and autodetect the CD/DVD drives, after which the drives are accessible. You can generate a Windows 98/Me startup disk on any system running Windows 98 or Me. If you don't have access to a Windows 98 or Me system, you can download an equivelant bootable floppy from www.bootdisk.com.

After you boot from a Win98/Me floppy, you see a menu that asks whether you want to boot with or without CD-ROM (and DVD) support. If you select yes, after the floppy finishes loading, you should be able to read any discs in the CD or DVD drives.

One possible, and useful, task with this capability is to install any version of Windows in a situation where the installation CD is not bootable (such as with most versions of Windows 9x/Me) or where the system is older than 1998 and cannot boot from a CD. In such a case, all you need to install any version of Windows is the Windows CD and your bootable Windows 98/Me startup floppy. In addition, the fact that the startup floppy is from Windows 98 or Me does not matter—you can install *any* Windows OS using that floppy.

For example, to install Windows 9x/Me onto a system, you could do the following:

1. Boot from the Windows 98/Me startup floppy, and then select Start Computer with CD-ROM support from the menu. Wait for the A: prompt to appear.

2. Insert the operating system CD you want to install (Windows 95, 98, or Me) into the CD/DVD drive.

3. Type **D:SETUP** at the A: prompt and press Enter. Make sure you substitute the drive letter of your CD/DVD drive for the *D:*.

4. The SETUP program will run from the CD and begin the operating system installation. Merely follow the prompts as necessary to complete the install.

To install Windows NT, 2000, or XP onto a system, do the following:

1. Boot from the Windows 98/Me startup floppy and select Start Computer with CD-ROM Support from the menu. Wait for the A: prompt to appear.

2. Insert the operating system CD you want to install (Windows NT, 2000, or XP) into the CD/DVD drive.

3. Type **D:\i386\WINNT** at the A: prompt and press Enter. Make sure you substitute the drive letter of your CD/DVD drive for the *D:*.

4. The WINNT program will run from the CD and begin the operating system installation. Merely follow the prompts as necessary to complete the install.

Another useful function you can perform with a Windows 98/Me startup floppy is to format a hard drive larger than 32GiB with FAT32 for use with Windows 2000 or XP. The Format program in Windows 2000 and XP is intentionally restricted by Microsoft from formatting volumes larger than 32GiB even though Windows 2000 and XP support FAT32 volumes up to 2TiB in size. In most cases it is recommended to use NTFS on Windows 2000 or XP systems, but if you are creating a dual-boot environment in which you want to run other operating systems that do not support NTFS, FAT32 is the best choice. The restriction on the Windows 2000/XP format command is a nuisance in such a situation, but the only way around it is to use the format from 98/Me.

Although I've often used a Windows 98/Me startup floppy to install Windows XP, Microsoft does have official XP startup floppies available for downloading from its Web site. The file is an executable file that creates the startup floppies. To locate this file, visit the Microsoft Knowledge Base at support.microsoft.com and search for article number 310994.

Using a CD-ROM or DVD-ROM drive that conforms to the ATAPI specification under Windows does not require you to do anything. All the driver support for these drives is built into Windows 9x and later versions, including the ATAPI driver and the CDFS VxD driver.

If you are running a SCSI CD-ROM drive under Windows, you may still need the ASPI driver that goes with your drive. The ASPI driver for your drive usually comes from the drive manufacturer and is included with the drive in most cases. However, by arrangement with hardware manufacturers, Windows typically includes the ASPI driver for most SCSI host adapters and also automatically runs the CDFS VxD virtual device driver. In some rare cases, you might have to install an updated driver that you have obtained from the manufacturer.

When you install a PnP SCSI host adapter in a Windows system, simply booting the computer should cause the operating system to detect, identify, and install drivers for the new device. When the driver for the host adapter is active, the system should detect the SCSI devices connected to the adapter and again load the appropriate drivers automatically.

For DOS users, merely use the Windows 98 or Me startup disk, which includes the necessary DOS SCSI and CD-ROM drivers that support most SCSI cards and CD/DVD drives on the market.

To learn more about the process of preparing to use a CD/DVD drive from a DOS prompt, see "DOS ATAPI CD-ROM Device Driver" in the Technical Reference portion of the disc packaged with this book.

Bootable CDs and DVDs—El Torito

If your system BIOS is a version dated from 1998 or later, most likely it has "El Torito" support, which means it supports booting from a bootable CD or DVD. The El Torito name comes from the Phoenix/IBM Bootable CD-ROM Format Specification, which was actually named after the El Torito restaurant located near the Phoenix Software offices where the two engineers who developed the standard ate lunch. What El Torito means for the PC is the capability to boot from CDs or DVDs, which opens up several new possibilities, including creating bootable CD/DVD rescue discs, booting from newer OS discs when installing to new systems, creating bootable diagnostics and test CDs, and more.

To create a bootable CD, ideally you need a CD/DVD burning application that allows the creation of bootable discs. Additionally, in some cases you need a bootable floppy that contains the drivers to support your CD drive in DOS mode (sometimes called real-mode drivers). The best source for these drivers (if needed) is a Windows 98 or Me startup floppy, which can be generated by any Windows 98 or Me system. Windows 98/Me startup disks can be used because these have the DOS-level CD-ROM support already configured and installed. If you don't have access to such a system to generate the disk, you can download one from www.bootdisk.com.

Before creating the bootable CD/DVD, test your boot floppy (with CD-ROM drivers) by first booting to the floppy. Then, with a CD or DVD containing files in the CD/DVD drive, see whether you can change to the CD/DVD drive and read a directory of the files (try the DIR command). The CD/DVD usually is the next drive letter after your last hard drive letter. For example, if your last hard drive letter is C:, the CD/DVD will be D:.

If you can display a directory listing of the CD/DVD after booting from the floppy, your drivers are properly loaded.

To create a bootable CD or DVD, simply follow the directions included with your CD/DVD burning application. Programs such as CD/DVD Creator by Roxio and Nero Burning ROM by Ahead Software make the creation of bootable discs a relatively easy procedure.

Creating a Rescue CD

Several programs on the market today allow you to make a compressed image file of the contents of any drive. These programs, such as the Ghost program sold by Symantec or PowerQuest's Drive Image, enable you to lock in the condition of any drive as of a particular time.

This enables you to create an image file of your system when it's working and use the image-restore feature to reset your system when it fails.

The perfect place to store a compressed image file is on a CD-R. At a minimum, your rescue disk should contain the compressed image file (a 737MB, 80-minute CD-R/RW could contain the equivalent of a nearly 1.5GB drive's normal contents if the maximum compression option is used). It's also desirable to place a copy of the image-restore program on the CD. Mastering this type of rescue CD is done exactly the same as a conventional CD mastering process. To use the rescue CD, you must boot your system with drivers that allow the CD-ROM drive to work, run the restore program to read the data from the CD, and overwrite the drive's existing contents.

If you're looking for a single-CD solution to rescuing your system, one that won't require you to lug around a bootable floppy disk, you can burn a rescue CD that is bootable all by itself.

Making a Bootable CD/DVD for Emergencies

A little-known capability to PC users is that they can create their own versions of what is standard with more and more new computers: a bootable CD/DVD that can be used to start up a system and restore it to a previously saved state.

The minimum requirements for a bootable CD/DVD include

- *A system supporting the El Torito standard in which the CD/DVD can be designated as a boot drive.* Check your BIOS under Advanced Setup or similar options. Recent and current BIOS code supplied by AMI, Award Software, and Phoenix Technologies typically support El Torito, meaning the CD/DVD can be assigned as a bootable device.

- *A CD/DVD burner and media.*

- *Recording software that allows creation of a bootable CD.* Most modern CD recording software, such as NERO Burning ROM or Roxio CD/DVD Creator, support creating bootable CD/DVDs. If your current CD/DVD-recording software lacks this option, you must upgrade to something that does.

- *A floppy disk containing your operating system boot files.*

ATAPI Drives Are Bootable

Most ATAPI drives connected to a motherboard ATA interface can be used as bootable devices if the BIOS permits it. If your CD-ROM is connected to a sound card, this procedure won't work. If your CD/DVD is connected to a SCSI interface, you'll need a SCSI interface with a BIOS chip that permits booting as well as a bootable disc.

Check your BIOS Setup for a page on which boot devices are listed to see whether yours supports a CD/DVD drive as a bootable device.

Because the procedures can vary for different burning software, you should follow the directions that come with your software for the exact procedure for creating a bootable CD or DVD.

Troubleshooting Optical Drives

Failure Reading a CD/DVD

If your drive fails to read a CD or DVD, try the following solutions:

- Check for scratches on the disc data surface.
- Check the drive for dust and dirt; use a cleaning disc.
- Make sure the drive shows up as a working device in System Properties.
- Try a disc that you know works.
- Restart the computer (the magic cure-all).
- Remove the drive from Device Manager in Windows 9x or later versions, allow the system to redetect the drive, and then reinstall the drivers (if PnP-based system).

Failure to Read CD-R, CD-RW Discs in CD-ROM or DVD Drive

If your CD-ROM or DVD drive fails to read CD-R and CD-RW discs, try the following solutions:

- Check compatibility; some very old 1x CD-ROM drives can't read CD-R media. Replace the drive with a newer, faster, cheaper model.
- Many early-model DVD drives can't read CD-R, CD-RW media; check compatibility.
- The CD-ROM drive must be MultiRead compatible to read CD-RW because of the lower reflectivity of the media; replace the drive.
- If some CD-Rs but not others can be read, check the media color combination to see whether some color combinations work better than others; change the brand of media.
- Packet-written CD-Rs (from Adaptec DirectCD and backup programs) can't be read on MS-DOS/Windows 3.1 CD-ROM drives because of the limitations of the operating system.
- Record the media at a slower speed. The pits/lands created at faster speeds sometimes can't be read by older drives.
- If you are trying to read a packet-written CD-R created with Adaptec/Roxio DirectCD on a CD-ROM drive, reinsert the media into the original drive, eject the media, and select the option Close to Read on Any Drive.
- Download and install a UDF reader compatible with the packet-writing software used to create the CD-RW on the target computer. If you are not sure how the media was created, Software Architects offers a universal UDF reader/media repair program called FixUDF! (also included as part of WriteCD-RW! Pro). WriteDVD! Pro includes the similar FixDVD! UDF reader/media repair program for DVD drives.

Failure to Read a Rewritable DVD in DVD-ROM Drive or Player

If your DVD-ROM or DVD player fails to read a rewritable DVD, try the following solutions:

- *Reinsert DVD-RW media into the original drive and finalize the media.* Make sure you don't need to add any more data to the media if you use a first-generation (DVD-R 2x/DVD-RW 1x) drive because you must erase the entire disc to do so. You can unfinalize media written by second-generation DVD-R 4x/DVD-RW 2x drives. See your DVD-RW disc-writing software instructions or help file for details.
- *Reinsert DVD+RW media into the original drive and change the compatibility setting to emulate DVD-ROM.* See the section "DVD+RW Compatibility Mode," earlier in this chapter, for details.
- *Make sure the media contains more than 521MB of data.* Some drives can't read media that contains a small amount of data.

Failure to Create a Writable DVD

If you can't create a writable DVD but the drive can be used with CD-R, CD-RW, or rewritable DVD media, try the following solutions:

- *Make sure you are using the correct media.* +R and –R media can't be interchanged unless the drive is a DVD±R/RW dual-mode drive.
- *Be sure you select the option to create a DVD project in your mastering software.* Some CD/DVD-mastering software defaults to the CD-R setting.
- *Select the correct drive as the target.* If you have both rewritable DVD and rewritable CD drives on the same system, be sure to specify the rewritable DVD drive.
- *Try a different disc.*
- *Contact the mastering software vendor for a software update.*

Failure Writing to CD-RW or DVD-RW 1x Media

If you can't write to CD-RW or DVD-RW 1x media, try the following solutions:

- *Make sure the media is formatted.* Use the format tool provided with the UDF software to prepare the media for use.
- *If the media was formatted, verify it was formatted with the same or compatible UDF program.* Different packet-writing programs support different versions of the UDF standard. I recommend you use the same UDF packet-writing software on the computers you use or use drives that support the Mount Rainier standard.
- *Make sure the system has identified the media as CD-RW or DVD-RW.* Eject and reinsert the media to force the drive to redetect it.
- *Contact the packet-writing software vendor for a software update.*
- *Disc might have been formatted with Windows XP's own limited CD writing software instead of a true UDF packet-writing program.* Erase the disc with Windows XP after transferring any needed files from the media; then format it with your preferred UDF program.
- *Contact the drive vendor for a firmware update.* See "Updating the Firmware in a CD-RW or Rewritable DVD Drive," later in this chapter.

ATAPI CD-ROM or DVD Drive Runs Slowly

If your ATAPI CD-ROM or DVD drive performs poorly, check the following items:

- Check the cache size in the Performance tab of the System Properties control panel. Select the quad-speed setting (largest cache size).
- Check to see whether the drive is set as the slave to your hard disk; move the drive to the secondary controller if possible.
- Your PIO (Programmed I/O) or UDMA mode might not be set correctly for your drive in the BIOS; check the drive specs and use autodetect in BIOS for the best results (see Chapter 5, "BIOS").
- Check that you are using busmastering drivers on compatible systems; install the appropriate drivers for the motherboard's chipset and the operating system in use. See the section "Direct Memory Access and Ultra-DMA," earlier in this chapter.
- Check to see whether you are using the CD-ROM interface on your sound card instead of the ATA connection on the motherboard. Move the drive connection to the ATA interface on the motherboard and disable the sound card ATA if possible to free up IRQ and I/O port address ranges.

- Open the System Properties control panel and select the Performance tab to see whether the system is using MS-DOS Compatibility Mode for CD-ROM drive. If all ATA drives are running in this mode, see www.microsoft.com and query on "MS-DOS Compatibility Mode" for a troubleshooter. If only the CD-ROM drive is in this mode, see whether you're using CD-ROM drivers in CONFIG.SYS and AUTOEXEC.BAT. Remove the lines containing references to the CD-ROM drivers (don't actually delete the lines—REM them), reboot the system, and verify that your CD-ROM drive still works and that it's running in 32-bit mode. Some older drives require at least the CONFIG.SYS driver to operate.

Poor Results or Slow Performance When Writing to CD-R Media

If you are having problems successfully writing data to a CD, see "How to Reliably Record CDs," earlier in this chapter. See the section "Updating the Firmware in a CD-RW or Rewritable DVD Drive."

Trouble Reading CD-RW Discs on CD-ROM

If you can't read CD-RW discs in your CD-ROM, try the following solutions:

- Check the vendor specifications to see whether your drive is MultiRead compliant. Some are not.
- If your drive is MultiRead compliant, try the CD-RW disc on a known-compliant CD-ROM drive (a drive with the MultiRead feature).
- Insert CD-RW media back into the original drive and check it for problems with the packet-writing software program's utilities.
- Insert CD-RW media back into the original drive and eject the media. Use the right-click Eject command in My Computer or Windows Explorer to properly close the media.
- Create a writable CD or DVD to transfer data to a computer that continues to have problems reading rewritable media.

Trouble Reading CD-R Discs on DVD Drive

If your DVD drive can't read a CD-R disc, check to see that the drive is MultiRead2 compliant because non-compliant DVDs can't read CD-R media. Newer DVD drives generally support reading CD-R media.

Trouble Making Bootable CDs

If you are having problems creating a bootable CD, try these possible solutions:

- Check the contents of the bootable floppy disk from which you copied the boot image. To access the entire contents of a CD, a bootable disk must contain CD-ROM drivers, AUTOEXEC.BAT, and CONFIG.SYS.
- Use the ISO 9660 format. Don't use the Joliet format because it is for long-filename CDs and can't boot.
- Check your system's BIOS for boot compliance and boot order; the CD-ROM should be listed first.
- SCSI CD-ROMs need a SCSI card with BIOS and bootable capability as well as special motherboard BIOS settings.

Updating the Firmware in a CD-RW or Rewritable DVD Drive

Just as updating the motherboard BIOS can solve compatibility problems with CPU and memory, support, USB ports, and system stability, upgrading the firmware in a rewritable CD or DVD drive can also solve problems with media compatibility, writing speed, and digital audio extraction from scratched discs and even prevent potentially fatal mismatches between media and drives.

For example, I noticed that a Plextor CD-RW drive with a maximum CD-R writing speed of 40x was working near its maximum speed when writing to green-gold media brands such as Philips and Imation. However, when using azo blue/silver Verbatim media, performance sank to an average of 10x or less. A check of the Plextor Web site (www.plextor.com) revealed that the latest firmware upgrade improved results when Verbatim media was used. After I installed the update, the drive wrote at top speed to azo blue/silver, green-gold, and other types of CD-R media.

To determine exactly which problems a firmware update can solve for you, be sure to check your drive vendor's Web site. This is especially important if you have a Pioneer DVD-RW drive; it can be a matter of life and death to your drive!

Several Pioneer DVD-RW drive models—including the DVR-A03, 103, A04, and 104 models, as well as the DVR-7000 and PRV-9000 standalone recorders—can be damaged or destroyed if they attempt to write to high-speed DVD-RW/R media (4x DVD-R, 2x DVD-RW speeds) before the firmware update is installed. Now that high-speed media is also available for DVD+RW drives, firmware updates are available for these drives to prevent problems with 2.4x drives writing to 4x media.

Determining Whether You Might Need a Firmware Update

If you encounter any of the following issues, a firmware update might be necessary:

- Your drive can't use a particular type of media, or it performs much more slowly with one type of media than other types/brands of media.
- Your writing software stops recognizing the drive as a rewritable drive.
- You want to use faster media than what the drive was originally designed to use (particularly true with Pioneer drives).

Because any firmware update runs a risk of failure and a failed firmware update can render your drive useless (I've seen it happen), you shouldn't install firmware updates casually. However, as the preceding examples make clear, sooner or later you'll probably need one.

Note that firmware updates don't fix the following problems:

- Drive not recognized by a newly installed CD or DVD mastering program
- Drive not recognized by Windows XP's built-in CD writing program

Because each rewritable CD or DVD drive has special characteristics at present (in the future, Mount Rainier support will standardize drive characteristics), CD or DVD writing programs you buy at retail must have model-specific updates to work. Get the update from the software vendor, or use the software provided with the drive. If you are trying to use an OEM version of a program with a different drive model from the original, you will also need an update from the software vendor (in some cases, an OEM version works only with the original drive with which it was packaged).

Windows XP's built-in CD writing feature is a pale imitation of even the worst third-party CD mastering program, but if you insist on using it, be sure your drive is listed in the Windows Catalog of supported drives and devices (www.microsoft.com/windows/catalog). To install the latest updates for Windows XP, including updates to the CD writing feature, use Windows Update. Microsoft Knowledge Base article 320174 discusses an update to the CD writing feature. Search the Microsoft Web site for other solutions.

Determining Which Drive Model and Firmware Are Installed

Before you can determine whether you need a firmware update for your rewritable drive, you need to know your drive model and which firmware version it's using. This is especially important if you use a drive that is an OEM product produced by a vendor other than the one that packaged the drive for resale. You can use the following methods to determine this information:

- Windows Device Manager (Windows 9x/Me)
- CD/DVD Mastering Software Drive Information

With the Windows 9x/Me Device Manager, follow this procedure:

1. Right-click My Computer and select Properties.
2. Click the Device Manager tab.
3. Click the plus (+) sign next to CDROM in the list of device types.
4. Double-click the rewritable drive icon to display its properties sheet.
5. Click the Settings tab; the firmware version and drive name will be displayed.

With Roxio Easy CD Creator 5, follow this procedure:

1. Click Tools.
2. Click CD-Drive Properties.
3. Click the drive letter.
4. The firmware revision and drive brand/model are listed along with other information.

With Nero Burning ROM 5.5, follow this procedure:

1. Click Recorder from the top-level menu.
2. Click the drive desired.
3. The drive model and firmware version are displayed along with other information.

After you have this information, you can go to your rewritable drive vendor's Web site and see whether a firmware update is available and what the benefits of installing the latest version would be.

Installing New Drive Firmware

Generally speaking, the firmware update procedure works like this, but you should be sure to follow the particular instructions given for your drive:

1. If the firmware update is stored as a Zip file, you need to use an unzipping program or the integrated unzipping utility found in some versions of Windows to uncompress the update to a folder.
2. If the drive maker provides a readme file, be sure to read it for help and troubleshooting. If the update file is an EXE file, it might display a readme file as part of step 3.
3. Double-click the EXE file to start the update process. Be sure to leave the system powered on during the process (which can take 2–3 minutes).
4. Follow the vendor's instructions for restarting your system.
5. After you restart your system, the computer might redetect the drive and assign it the next available drive letter. If you previously assigned the drive a customized drive letter (for example, on one computer in my organization, Q: is used for a CD-RW drive and R: for a DVD+RW drive), use the Device Manager in Windows 9x/Me or the Computer Management service in Windows 2000/XP to reassign the correct drive letter to the drive.

Troubleshooting Firmware Updates

If you have problems performing a rewritable drive firmware update, check the vendor's readme file or Web site for help. In addition, here are some tips we've found useful.

If the firmware update fails to complete, there might be interference from programs that control the drive, such as packet-writing programs (InCD, DirectCD) or the built-in Windows XP CD writing feature. To disable resident software, restart the computer in Safe Mode (Windows 2000/XP) and retry the update. Restart the system normally after the update is complete.

With Windows 9x/Me, you can use MSConfig (System Configuration Utility), select the Selective Startup option, and uncheck Load Startup Group Items and Process Win.INI File Before Restarting. After completing the firmware update, be sure to rerun MSConfig and select Normal Startup before restarting the computer.

To disable Windows XP's own CD writing feature for a particular drive, right-click the drive icon in My Computer, select Properties, click the Recording tab, and clear the check mark in the box next to Enable CD Recording on This Drive.

If the firmware update doesn't improve drive performance on a system running Windows 9x/Me, DMA might not be enabled on the rewritable drive. See the section "Direct Memory Access and Ultra-DMA," earlier in this chapter, for details.

CHAPTER 14

Physical Drive Installation and Configuration

Installing All Types of Drives

This chapter covers the actual installation of hard drives, optical drives (CD/DVD), floppy drives, and tape drives. This includes everything from preparing the components to setting jumpers to installing the actual cabling and physical installation. I also dig into some initial system software configuration issues, right up to the point of installing the operating system. From that point on, the steps you take depend on which operating system you are installing.

For more information on drive interfaces, magnetic storage, drive operation, and operating system issues, see the following chapters:

- Chapter 7, "The ATA/IDE Interface"
- Chapter 8, "The SCSI Interface"
- Chapter 9, "Magnetic Storage Principles"
- Chapter 10, "Hard Disk Storage"
- Chapter 11, "Floppy Disk Storage"
- Chapter 12, "High-Capacity Removable Storage"
- Chapter 13, "Optical Storage"
- Chapter 17, "I/O Interfaces from Serial and Parallel to IEEE 1394 and USB"

Although most of the drives you would install in a PC are covered here, the primary emphasis is on hard disks and other devices using Parallel ATA (also called IDE), Serial ATA (SATA), or SCSI interfaces. For USB or FireWire (IEEE 1394) devices, see Chapter 17.

Hard Disk Installation Procedures

This section describes the hard disk drive installation process, particularly the configuration, physical installation, and formatting of a hard disk drive.

To install a hard drive in a PC, you must perform some or all of the following procedures:

- Configure the drive.
- Configure the host adapter (if used).
- Physically install the drive.
- Configure the system to recognize the drive.
- Partition the drive (FDISK, DISKPART, or SETUP).
- High-level format the partitions (FORMAT or SETUP).

As you perform the procedure, you might need to know various details about the hard disk drive, host adapter (if used), and system ROM BIOS, as well as many of the other devices in the system. This information usually appears in the various manuals or reference sheets that come with these devices. When you purchase these items, be sure the vendor includes any documentation that came with the original components. (Many do not include the manuals unless you ask for them.) For most equipment sold today, you will get enough documentation from the vendor to enable you to proceed.

If you are like me, however, and want all the technical documentation on the device, you should contact the original manufacturer of the device and order the technical specification manual. For example, if you purchase a system that comes with a particular ATA drive, the seller probably will give you some limited information on the drive, but not nearly the amount that the technical manual for the drive provides. To get this documentation, you normally download it from the drive manufacturer's Web site. The same rule applies for any of the other components in most of the systems sold today. I find the OEM technical manuals essential in providing the highest level of technical support possible.

For reference, you can look up the hard disk manufacturer names in the Vendor List on the disc packaged with this book; you will find numbers to call for technical support, as well as URLs for their Web sites.

Note

You also will find a drive specification database on the disc. This database contains an exhaustive list of drive specs for thousands of drives. If you don't have ready access to your drive specs, check out this searchable database.

Drive Configuration

Before you physically install a hard disk drive in the computer, you must ensure that it is properly configured. For an ATA drive, this generally means designating the drive as a master/slave or using the Cable Select (CS) feature and a special cable to determine the relationship. For SCSI drives, you must set the device's SCSI ID and possibly its SCSI bus termination state.

◀◀ These procedures are covered in "ATA Standards," p. 536, and "Small Computer System Interface," p. 584.

Serial ATA drives do not require configuration with jumper blocks. Although some SATA drives might have jumper blocks, they are intended for factory use only. Each SATA drive connects to the SATA host adapter in a point-to-point configuration using its own cable; there is no master or slave as there is with Parallel ATA drives. For compatibility, some SATA host adapters emulate master and slave configurations.

Host Adapter Configuration

Older hard disk drive types used separate disk controller cards you had to install in a bus slot. The ATA, SCSI, and SATA hard disk drives used in today's PCs, however, have the disk controller integrated into the drive assembly. For ATA drives, the I/O interface is nearly always integrated into the system's motherboard, and you configure the interface through the BIOS Setup. No separate host adapter exists; therefore, if you have an ATA drive, you can proceed to the section "Physical Installation" later in this chapter. Some systems might use ATA/IDE adapters in lieu of the built-in interface. This is because some of the motherboard-integrated ATA interfaces might not support the faster modes (such as Ultra-ATA/33 through Ultra-ATA/133) that most newer drives can use. In most cases, I would recommend upgrading the motherboard rather than getting an ATA host adapter because a new motherboard has other benefits and the cost isn't much higher. SATA drives can be connected to a system with a standard ATA interface by installing an SATA adapter card (see Figure 14.1). If the system has an SATA host adapter built in to the motherboard, no additional card is necessary.

SCSI drives, however, usually require a host adapter card you must install in a bus slot like any other card. A few motherboards have integrated SCSI adapters, but these are rare. Configuring a SCSI host adapter card involves setting the various system resources the adapter requires. As with most expansion cards, a SCSI host adapter requires some combination of the following system resources:

- Boot ROM address (optional)
- Interrupt request (IRQ)
- Direct Memory Access (DMA) channel
- I/O port address

Not all adapters use every one of these resources, but some might use them all. In most cases with modern plug-and-play adapters and systems, the BIOS and your operating system automatically configure these resources. The computer sets the required hardware resource settings to values that do not conflict with other devices in the computer.

◀◀ See "Plug and Play BIOS," p. 450.

Note

A detailed list of PnP device IDs is included in the Technical Reference section of the disc included with this book.

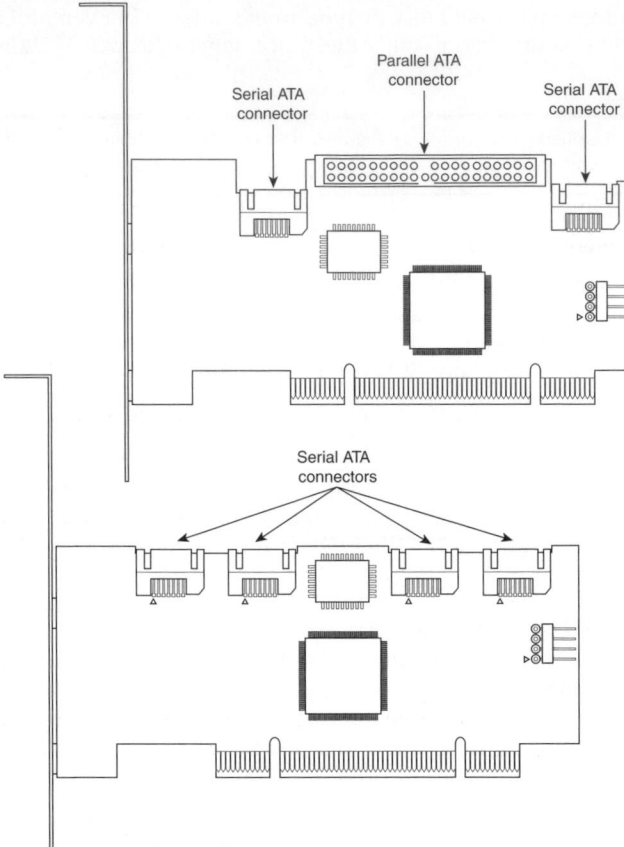

Figure 14.1 You can install a combo SATA/ATA host adapter (top) or a pure SATA host adapter (bottom) to enable you to install SATA drives into a computer that has standard ATA host adapters.

If your hardware or operating system does not support Plug and Play, you must manually configure the adapter to use the appropriate resources. Some adapters provide software that enables you to reconfigure or change the hardware resources, whereas others might use jumpers or DIP switches on the adapter card.

◄◄ See "System Resources," p. 367.

The ATA interface driver is part of the standard PC BIOS, which enables booting from an ATA drive. Systems that include SATA interfaces on the motherboard also incorporate support for SATA into the BIOS. The BIOS provides the device driver functionality the system needs to access the drive before any files can be loaded from disk. However, a SCSI interface driver is not part of the standard PC BIOS, so most SCSI host adapters have their own onboard ROM BIOS that enables SCSI drives to function as bootable devices.

Note

Although standard ATA drivers are provided with Windows, this interface is typically built in to the motherboard chipset South Bridge or I/O Controller Hub (ICH) component, and it usually requires that specific chipset drivers be loaded. If you are using a motherboard that is newer than your operating system version (for example, a new board purchased in late 2002 with Windows XP), be sure you install the chipset drivers that came with your motherboard immediately after installing Windows. If the board is older than the OS, the chipset drivers will most likely be present on the OS installation CD; however, it is still a good idea to update to the latest chipset drivers immediately after the OS installation.

Use of the SCSI BIOS is usually optional. If you are not booting from a SCSI drive, you can leave the BIOS on the card disabled and merely install the appropriate device driver to access the SCSI devices. Most host adapters have switches, jumpers, or configuration software you can use to enable or disable SCSI BIOS support.

In addition to providing boot functionality, the SCSI BIOS can provide many other functions, including any or all of the following:

- Low-level formatting
- Drive-type (parameter) control
- Host adapter configuration
- SCSI diagnostics
- Support for nonstandard I/O port addresses and interrupts

If the adapter's onboard BIOS is enabled, it uses specific memory address space in the upper memory area (UMA). The UMA is the top 384KB in the first megabyte of system memory. It is divided into three areas of two 64KB segments each, with the first and last areas being used by the video adapter circuits and the motherboard BIOS, respectively. Segments C000h and D000h are reserved for use by adapter ROMs, such as those found on disk controllers or SCSI host adapters.

Note

You must ensure that any adapters using space in these segments of the UMA (upper memory area) do not overlap with another adapter that uses this space. No two adapters can share this memory space. Most adapters have software, jumpers, or switches that can adjust the configuration of the board and change the addresses it uses to prevent conflict.

Physical Installation

The procedure for the physical installation of a hard disk drive is much the same as that for installing any other type of drive. You must have the correct screws, brackets, and faceplates for the specific drive and system before you can install the drive.

Some computer cases require plastic or metal rails that are secured to the sides of a hard disk drive so it can slide into the proper place in the system (see Figure 14.2). Other case designs have drive bays that directly accept the drive via screws through the side supports and no other hardware is necessary, whereas others use a cage arrangement where you first install the drives into a cage and then slide the cage into the case (see Figure 14.3). If your case uses rails or a cage, these are usually included with the case. With the proper mounting mechanism supplied via the case, all you need is the bare drive to install.

Because ATA, SCSI, and SATA drives use different cables, be sure you have the proper cable for both your drive and controller/host adapter. For example, to run ATA-66 or faster modes (through ATA-133), you need a special 80-conductor cable that supports the CS feature. This cable is also recommended if you are running Ultra-ATA/33, and it works for all slower modes as well. To determine whether your cable has 40 or 80 conductors, simply count the ridges on the ribbon cable—each ridge contains a conductor (wire). Another indication is that the 80-conductor cable typically has the motherboard connector end color-coded blue, and the master and slave drive connectors color-coded black and gray, respectively.

If you need additional drive-mounting hardware not included with either your case or the drive, several companies that specialize in drive-mounting brackets, cables, and other hardware accessories are listed in the Vendor List (on the accompanying disc). If you intend to install a 3 1/2" hard drive in a 5 1/4" drive bay, you need yet another type of mounting bracket (as shown in Figure 14.4). Many 3 1/2" hard drives come with these brackets, or one might be supplied with your case or chassis.

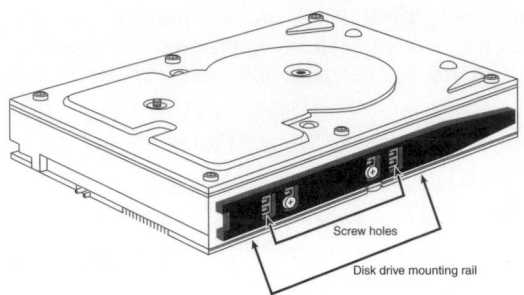

Figure 14.2 A typical 3 1/2" hard disk with mounting rails for a 3 1/2" drive bay.

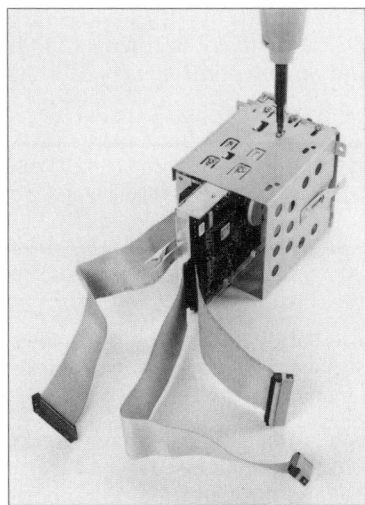

Figure 14.3 A typical hard disk mounted in a removable drive cage.

Note

You should also note the length of the drive cable itself when you plan to add a hard disk drive. It can be very annoying to assemble everything you think you'll need to install a drive and then find that the drive cable is not long enough to reach the new drive location. You can either try to reposition the drive to a location closer to the interface connector on the host adapter or motherboard or just get a longer cable. ATA cables are limited to 18" in overall length according to the standard; shorter is fine, but longer ones can cause signal integrity problems. This is most important if your drive is going to use the faster ATA-33 through ATA-133 modes. Using a cable that is too long causes timing errors and signal degradation, possibly corrupting the data on your drive. I see many 24"–36" cable assemblies being sold or used in systems; you are asking for trouble if you violate the 18" maximum-length specification.

Different faceplate, or bezel, options are also available. Make sure you have the correct bezel for your application. Some systems, for example, do not need a bezel; if a bezel exists on the drive, you must remove it.

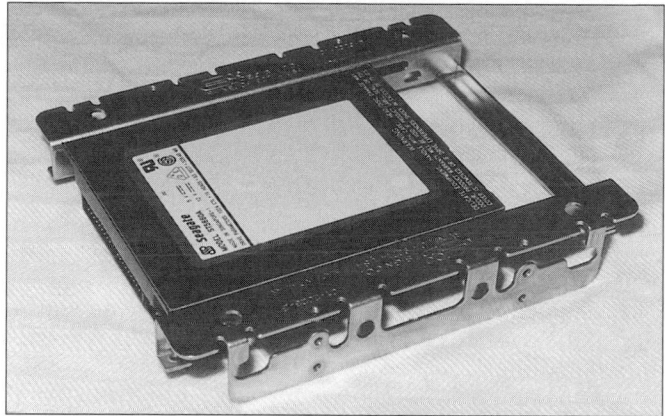

Figure 14.4 A typical bracket used to mount a 3 1/2" drive in a 5 1/4" drive bay. The bracket is screwed to the drive and then mounted in the bay by using screws or rails, as determined by the case.

Caution

Be sure you use only the screws that come with your new drive. Many drives come with special short-length screws that may have the same size thread as other screws you might use in your system, but that should not be interchanged. If you use screws that are too long, they might protrude too far into the drive casing and cause problems.

The step-by-step procedures for installing an ATA hard drive are as follows:

1. Check your computer for an unused ATA/IDE connector. Typical Pentium-class and newer PCs have two ATA/IDE connectors, allowing for up to four ATA/IDE devices.

You might need an additional cable if both master and slave connectors are used on the primary cable and you are adding a third device.

Tip

Usually it is best for performance to keep devices that will be simultaneously active, such as hard drives and optical drives, on separate cables.

2. Double-check the pin configuration and cable type. The colored (normally red or red-flecked) stripe on one edge of the cable goes to pin 1 of the hard drive's data connector. Most cables and drive connectors are keyed to prevent improper (backward) installation, but many are not. Keying can be done via missing and plugged pins, a ridge on one side of the connector, or both. One tip to note is that pin 1 on the drive connector is almost always oriented nearest to the power connector.

Tip

Newer ATA drives that operate in the faster Ultra-DMA modes (ATA-66 through ATA-133) require a special 80-conductor cable, whereas lesser drives can use a 40-conductor cable. Note that you can always use the superior 80-conductor cable for slower drives, so normally that is all I recommend purchasing. SCSI drives use either 50-pin or 68-pin (wide) cables.

3. Configure the drive jumpers. If the drive is ATA/IDE and you are using a cable that supports CS, you must set the CS jumper on any drives connected to that cable. Otherwise, you must set the drives on the cable as either master or slave. Note that some older drives also required a slave-present jumper be set if the drive was configured as a master with a slave drive on the same cable. You'll find more detail on the drive configuration procedures later in this chapter.

4. Slide the drive carefully into a drive bay of the correct size. Most hard drives—except for a few very high-capacity SCSI drives meant for servers and the now-discontinued Quantum Bigfoot series—are 3 1/2" wide and 1" high. If you have no 3 1/2" drive bays left for your hard disk, attach a drive-adapter kit to the sides of the drive to make it wide enough to fit into a 5 1/4" wide drive bay (refer to Figure 14.4). Some case designs require you to attach rails to the side of the hard drive. If so, attach them to the drive using the screws supplied with either the case or the drive. Be sure the screws aren't too long; if you bottom the screws in the drive, you can damage it. Then, slide the drive into the bay in the case until the rails latch into place.

Note

You can find more visual step-by-step instructions for installing a hard drive in Chapter 22, "Building or Upgrading Systems."

5. Attach the data cable connector to the back of the drive, unless you are adding the drive and cable at the same time. In that case, attach the cable to the drive before you slide it into the drive bay and fasten it into place (step 2).

6. Attach the appropriate power connector to the drive. Most hard drives use the larger, or "Molex," four-wire power connector. If necessary, purchase a Y-splitter cable (see Figure 14.5) to create two power connectors from one (many computers have fewer power connectors than drive bays).

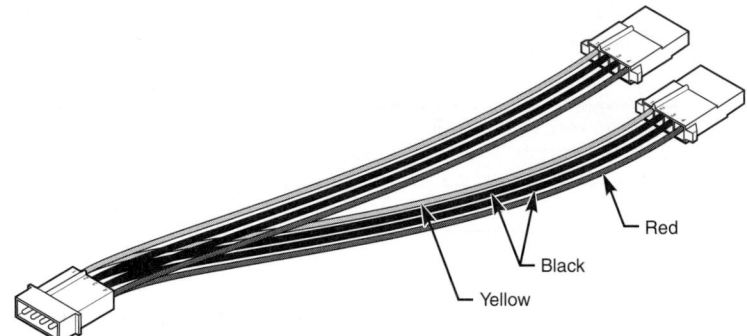

Red

Black

Yellow

Figure 14.5 Power cord splitter and connector.

7. Turn on the computer and listen for the new hard disk to spin up. Even though today's drives are very quiet compared to early hard disks, you should still hear a faint rattling or clicking as the new hard disk starts to run. If you don't hear anything from the drive, double-check the data and power cables.

8. Restart the computer and access the BIOS setup screens to configure the new hard disk. If your BIOS has an autodetect or auto type setting, I recommend you use it because it will configure the parameters automatically using optimal settings. For ATA hard drives above 528MB (504MiB), you also must set logical block address (LBA) translation to access the drive's full capacity. If autodetect was selected, LBA translation should already be set correctly. Many systems have a Peripherals Configuration screen, which also enables you to set transfer speeds for maximum drive performance, but again these should be configured automatically if you enabled autodetect. If your BIOS can't autodetect your drive, see the documentation that came with the drive for the correct settings. Most drives have the CHS parameters as well as jumper setting information displayed on a sticker attached to the drive, and all modern BIOSs support autodetect, as well. Save the BIOS configuration and exit the BIOS Setup screen to continue. See the section "System Configuration," later in this chapter, for more information on this step because it can be complicated.

9. With your operating system boot CD or floppy in the appropriate drive, restart the computer. If you intend to install the operating system, Windows 98 or later will automatically guide you through the partitioning and formatting process during the operating system installation. If you want, you can partition and format the drive before installing the OS, by using the operating system's disk partitioning software.

   If you use Windows 9x or Me, FDISK can be found on the operating system start disk, such as the Windows startup disk. Simply insert the startup disk in the floppy drive, boot from it, and type the **FDISK** command at the A: prompt. Windows 2000 and XP use the DISKPART command or the Disk Management utility.

◄◄ See "ATA Standards," p. 536, and "Small Computer System Interface," p. 584.

Physical Installation Issues for SATA Drives

The step-by-step procedure for installing an SATA hard drive differs from the ATA drive installation as follows:

1. Check your computer for an unused SATA connector. Even though some new computers and motherboards have one or two SATA connectors, you might need to install a separate SATA host adapter card on most systems. If you need to install a separate SATA host adapter, consult its manual for physical and driver installation instructions.

2. Connect the SATA data cable to the SATA host adapter. SATA data cables can be combined with the SATA power cable or be separate. If the SATA data cable is separate from the SATA power cable, either end of the cable can be used for the drive or host adapter (see Figure 14.6).

3. Slide the drive carefully into a drive bay of the correct size, as in step 4 of the ATA host adapter installation in the previous section.

4. Attach the SATA data cable connector to the back of the drive, unless you are adding the drive and cable at the same time. In that case, attach the cable to the drive before you slide it into the drive bay and fasten it into place.

5. Attach the appropriate power connector to the drive. Because most power supplies don't have an SATA power connector, you might need to purchase a Molex 12V-to-SATA power converter cable if one was not provided with your drive. This converter connects to a standard 4-pin Molex power connector into an SATA power connector.

From this point, the remainder of the installation is the same as with a standard ATA drive.

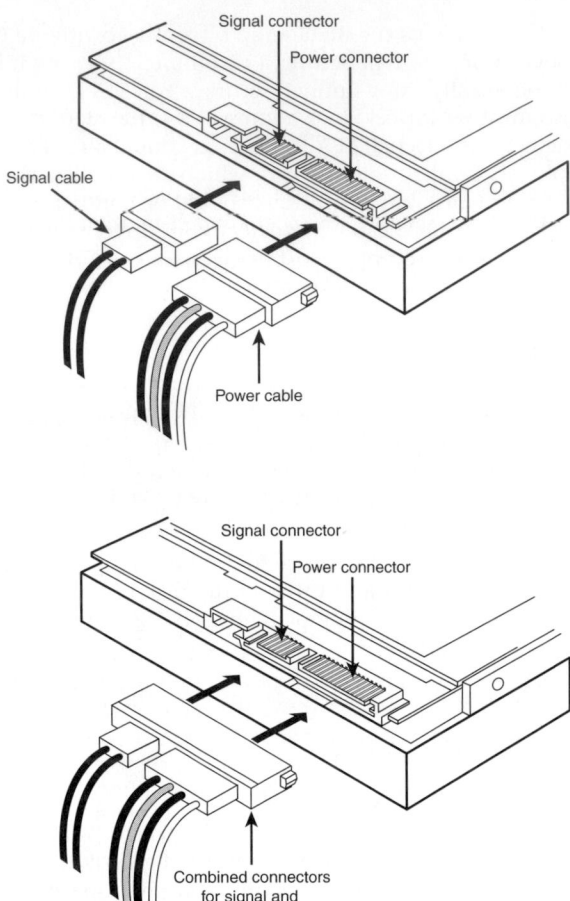

Figure 14.6 SATA data and power cables can be separate (top) or be combined into a single molded assembly (bottom).

Physical Installation Issues for SCSI Drives

The step-by-step procedure for installing a SCSI hard drive differs from the ATA drive installation as follows:

1. Check your computer for a SCSI host adapter card unless your computer has a SCSI host adapter on the motherboard. If the SCSI host adapter already has a ribbon cable connected to it, verify that an empty connector is available. If the SCSI host adapter doesn't have a ribbon cable connected to it, you must attach a ribbon cable with the correct pinout to the host adapter.

2. Verify that the SCSI drive has been configured to use a unique SCSI device ID number. Generally, this is done by adjusting jumpers on the rear of the drive.

3. Configure the terminator jumpers correctly, according to whether the drive is the only internal drive (termination on) or is being added to a cable after an existing drive (termination on for the new drive and termination off for the existing drive).

4. Slide the drive carefully into a drive bay of the correct size, as in step 4 of the ATA host adapter installation.

5. Attach the SCSI data cable connector to the back of the drive, unless you are adding the drive and cable at the same time. In that case, attach the cable to the drive before you slide it into the drive bay and fasten it into place.

6. Attach the appropriate power connector to the drive, as in step 6 of the ATA host adapter installation.

7. Turn on the computer and listen to the drive, as in step 7 of the ATA host adapter installation.

8. After the computer starts, start the SCSI host adapter drive configuration utility and configure your host adapter and drive. See the SCSI host adapter manual for details.

9. Run your operating system's disk preparation program, as described in step 9 of the ATA host adapter installation.

System Configuration

After your drive is physically installed, you must provide the computer with basic information about the drive so the system can access and boot from it. How you set and store this information depends on the type of drive and system you have. Standard ATA setup procedures apply for most hard disks (including SATA drives) except SCSI drives. SCSI drives usually follow a custom setup procedure that varies depending on the host adapter you are using. If you have a SCSI drive, follow the instructions included with the host adapter to configure the drive.

Automatic Drive Detection

For ATA drives, virtually all new BIOS versions in today's PCs have automatic parameter detection (autodetect). The BIOS sends a special Identify Drive command to all the devices connected to the ATA interface during the system startup sequence; the drives are intelligent enough to respond with the correct parameters. The BIOS then automatically enters the parameter information returned by the drive. This procedure eliminates errors or confusion in parameter selection.

Manual Drive Parameters

If you are dealing with a motherboard that does not support autodetect, you must enter the appropriate drive information in the system BIOS manually. The BIOS has a selection of preconfigured drive types, but these are woefully outdated in most cases, providing support only for drives holding a few hundred megabytes or less. In nearly every case, you must select the user-defined drive type and provide values for the following settings:

- Cylinders
- Heads
- Sectors per track

The values you use for these settings should be provided in the documentation for the hard disk drive, but they also might be printed on the drive itself. It's a good idea to check for these settings and write them down because they might not be visible after you've installed the drive. You also should maintain a copy of these settings in case your system BIOS loses its data due to a battery failure. One of the best places to store this information is inside the computer itself. Taping a note with vital settings such as these to the inside of the case can be a lifesaver.

In the event that you are unable to determine the correct settings for your hard drive from either the drive case or the Technical Reference, utility programs are available on the Internet that can query the drive for this information.

Note

The setup parameters for more than 1,000 popular drive models are included in the Technical Reference on the accompanying disc.

Depending on the maker and version of your system BIOS, you might have to configure other settings as well, such as which transfer mode to use and whether the BIOS should use logical block addressing.

◄◄   See "ATA Drive Capacity Limitations," p. 563.

Formatting

Proper setup and formatting are critical to a drive's performance and reliability. This section describes the procedures used to format a hard disk drive correctly. Use these procedures when you install a new drive in a system or immediately after you recover data from a hard disk that has been exhibiting problems.

The three major steps in the formatting process for a hard disk drive subsystem are as follows:

1. Low-level formatting
2. Partitioning
3. High-level formatting

Low-Level Formatting

All new hard disk drives are low-level formatted by the manufacturer, and you do not have to perform another LLF before you install the drive. In fact, under normal circumstances, you should not ever have to perform a low-level format on an ATA or SCSI drive. Most manufacturers no longer recommend that you low-level format any ATA type drive.

This recommendation has been the source of some myths about ATA. Many people say, for example, that you can't perform a low-level format on an ATA drive, and that if you do, you will destroy the drive. This statement is untrue! What can happen with some of the earliest ATA drives is that you might lose the optimal head and cylinder skew factors that were set by the manufacturer for the drive, as well as the map of drive defects. This can have a negative effect on the drive's performance, but you can still reliably use the drive. Note that all drives that internally use a zoned recording (where there is a variable number of sectors per track internally) are immune to any problems due to low-level formatting because the actual sector marks can't be rewritten. This includes pretty much all modern ATA drives made in the last 10 years.

However, sometimes you must perform a low-level format on an ATA or a SCSI drive. The following sections discuss the software you can use to do this.

SCSI Low-Level Format Software

SCSI drives also come preformatted, and unless there is a problem with the drive, you will not have to perform this operation yourself. If you do want to low-level format a SCSI drive, you must use the LLF program provided by the manufacturer of the SCSI host adapter. The designs of these devices vary enough that a register-level program can work only if it is tailored to the individual controller. Fortunately, all SCSI host adapters include low-level format software, either in the host adapter's BIOS or in a separate disk-based program.

The interface to the SCSI drive is through the host adapter. SCSI is a standard, but no true standards exist for what a host adapter is supposed to look like. This means that any formatting or configuration software is specific to a particular host adapter.

Note

Notice that SCSI format and configuration software is keyed to the host adapter and is not specific in any way to the particular SCSI hard disk drive you are using. Because of differences in how various SCSI host adapters view the contents of a SCSI hard disk, if you move a SCSI hard disk containing data to a different SCSI host adapter, the data on the hard disk might not be recognized.

ATA Low-Level Format Software

ATA drive manufacturers have defined and standardized extensions to the original WD1002/1003 hard disk controller card to AT-bus (ISA) interface, which is known as the ATA (AT Attachment) interface. The ATA specification provides for vendor-unique commands, which are manufacturer proprietary extensions to the standard. To prevent improper low-level formatting, many of these ATA drives have special codes that must be sent to the drive to unlock the format routines. These codes vary among manufacturers. If possible, you should obtain LLF and defect management software from the drive manufacturer; this software usually is specific to that manufacturer's products and often is model specific. Check the brand and model number of your hard disk to determine the utility program you need.

Most ATA drives are protected from any alteration to the skew factors or defect map erasure because they are always in a translated mode internally. Zoned bit recording drives are always under translation and are fully protected. Most ATA drives have a custom command set that must be used in the format process; the standard format commands defined by the ATA specification usually do not work, especially with intelligent or zoned bit recording ATA drives. Without the proper manufacturer-specific format commands, you can't perform the defect management by the manufacturer-specified method, in which bad sectors often can be spared.

Most manufacturers supply low-level format programs for their drives. Here are a few examples:

- *Seagate/Conner Peripherals.* `ftp.seagate.com/techsuppt/seagate_utils/sgatfmt4.zip` or `www.seagate.com/support/seatools`

- *Hitachi/IBM.* `http://www.hitachigst.com/hdd/support/download.htm`

- *Maxtor/Quantum.* `www.maxtor.com/en/support/downloads/index.htm`

- *Samsung.* `www.samsung.com/Products/HardDiskDrive/utilities/hutil.htm` or `www.samsung.com/Products/HardDiskDrive/utilities/sutil.htm` or `www.samsung.com/Products/HardDiskDrive/utilities/shdiag.htm`

- *Western Digital.* `http://support.wdc.com/download/`

You should try the manufacturer-specific format programs first. They are free, can often work at a lower level, and can handle defects in ways that the more generic ones can't. If formatting software is not available from your drive's manufacturer, I recommend Disk Manager by Ontrack and the Micro-Scope program by Micro 2000. Another excellent, inexpensive, general-purpose PC hardware diagnostic that includes low-level format capability is the Hitachi (formerly IBM) Drive Fitness Test (DFT) program. The Drive Fitness Test program works on non-Hitachi and non-IBM drives as well and performs a detailed and thorough test of your hard drive. I recommend this as one of the best general-purpose drive test programs on the market because it can do a fairly thorough test in nondestructive mode. It performs an LLF (destructive) only on IBM- and Hitachi-brand drives. You can download DFT from the Hitachi site listed previously.

Note

Although Ontrack Disk Manager can be purchased in a "generic" version that works with any manufacturer's hard drives, brand-specific OEM versions are often available free of charge on the utility disks or CD-ROMs shipped with new retail-packaged hard disk drives. You should also check your drive maker's Web site for updated versions of Disk Manager. These OEM versions are designed to check for a particular brand's drive firmware and do not work on any brand other than the one for which they are modified.

Nondestructive Formatters

General-purpose, BIOS-level, nondestructive formatters, such as Calibrate (older Symantec Norton Utilities) and SpinRite (Gibson Research), are not recommended in most situations in which a real LLF is required. These programs have several limitations and problems that decrease their effectiveness; in some cases, they can even cause problems with the way defects are handled on a drive. These programs attempt to perform a track-by-track LLF by using BIOS functions, while backing up and restoring the track data as they go. These programs do not actually perform a complete LLF because they do not even try to low-level format the first track (Cylinder 0, Head 0) due to problems with some controller types that store hidden information on the first track.

These programs also do not perform defect mapping in the way standard LLF programs do, and they even can remove the carefully applied sector header defect marks during a proper LLF. This situation potentially enables data to be stored in sectors that originally were marked defective and might actually void the manufacturer's warranty on some drives. Another problem is that these programs work only on drives that have already been formatted and can format only drives that are formattable through BIOS functions.

Note

SpinRite is useful for recovering data found on drives with read errors because of its thorough method of repeatedly rereading the errors and analyzing the results to reconstruct the missing data.

A true LLF program bypasses the system BIOS and sends commands directly to the disk controller hardware. For this reason, many LLF programs are specific to the disk controller hardware for which they are designed. Having a single format program that will run on all types of controllers is virtually impossible. Many hard drives have been incorrectly diagnosed as being defective because the wrong format program was used and the program did not operate properly.

Drive Partitioning

Partitioning a hard disk is the act of defining areas of the disk for an operating system to use as a volume.

When you partition a disk, the partitioning software writes a master partition boot sector at Cylinder 0, Head 0, Sector 1—the first sector on the hard disk. This sector contains data that describes the partitions by their starting and ending cylinder, head, and sector locations. The partition table also indicates to the ROM BIOS which of the partitions is bootable and, therefore, where to look for an operating system to load.

▶▶ See "File Systems and Data Recovery," p. 1353.

The FDISK program is the accepted standard for partitioning hard disk drives for use with all operating systems up through Windows Me. Windows 2000 and XP use a similar command-line program called DISKPART, or you can partition and format hard disks with the Disk Management tool. All versions of Windows starting with Windows 95 can also partition and format the drive using the SETUP program for installing the OS. These programs are included with your operating system, and although they might have the same name and basic functions with any OS, you should typically use the tools that specifically came with your OS. Partitioning prepares the boot sector of the disk in such a way that the FORMAT program or the Windows SETUP format utility can operate correctly. Partitioning also enables various operating systems to coexist on a single hard disk. No matter which operating system you use, it should come with an FDISK, DISKPART, or SETUP program that can be used to partition the drive.

Note

Because FDISK, DISKPART, and SETUP depend on BIOS information about the hard disk to determine the size and drive geometry of the hard disk, having correct BIOS settings saved in the BIOS Setup is vital to the correct operation of these programs. If a 100GB hard drive is defined in the BIOS as a 100MB hard drive, for example, all these programs will see is 100MB.

With any version of Windows—as with MS-DOS—FDISK or other disk preparation tools enable you to create two types of disk partitions: primary and extended. A primary partition can be bootable but an extended partition can't. If you have only a single hard disk in your system, at least part of the drive must be prepared as a primary partition if you want to start your computer from the hard disk (and who doesn't?). A primary partition is seen as a single volume or drive letter (C: on one-drive systems), whereas an extended partition acts as a sort of logical container for additional volumes (drive letters D: and beyond). A single extended partition can contain a single volume (also referred to by FDISK as a *logical DOS drive*) or several volumes (logical DOS drives) of various sizes.

Don't get hung up on the fact that FDISK calls partitions "DOS" partitions or "DOS" drives. This is true even though the operating system you are installing is Windows 95, 98, Me, NT, 2000, XP, Linux, and so on.

Depending on the version of Windows in use (and with any version of MS-DOS), you might need to subdivide a hard drive through the use of FDISK. The original release of Windows 95 and all MS-DOS versions support a file system known as FAT16, which allows no more than 65,536 files per drive and a single drive letter or volume size of no more than 2.1GB. Thus, a 10GB hard disk prepared with MS-DOS or the original Windows 95 (or 95A) must have a minimum of five drive letters and could have more (see Figure 14.7).

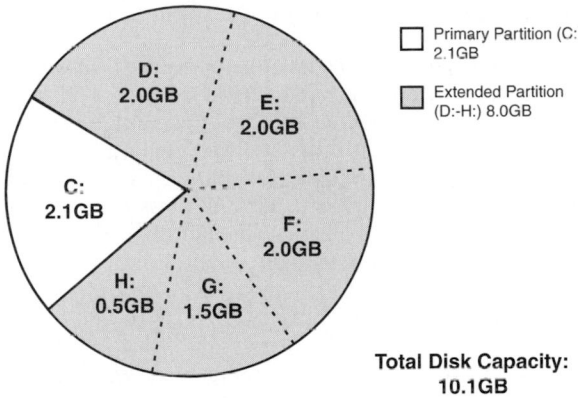

Figure 14.7 Adding a hard drive above 2.1GB in size to an MS-DOS or original Windows 95A computer forces the user to create multiple drive letters to use the entire drive capacity. The logical DOS drives are referenced like any other drive, although they are portions of a single physical hard disk.

▶▶ See "File Allocation Table Types," p. 1367.

Another reason for subdividing a single drive into multiple volumes is increased data security. For example, PowerQuest (the creator of PartitionMagic) suggests a three-volume partitioning scheme that looks like this:

> C: for the operating system and utilities
>
> D: for applications
>
> E: and above for data

In this example, primary and extended partitions would be assigned as shown here:

> C: the primary partition
>
> D: and E: in the extended partition as logical DOS drives (volumes)

If a catastrophic failure to the disk structure wipes out C: or D:, drive E:—which contains the data—is usually still intact. This method also makes backing up the data easier; just set the backup program to back up all of E:, or all the changed files on E:.

Note

Although external USB and IEEE 1394a drives are normally preformatted and partitioned to allow immediate use, you can normally use FDISK/FORMAT or Disk Management to change the partitions and file system used on the drive. See the external drive's instruction manual or the drive vendor's Web site for details.

Large Hard Disk Support

If you use the Windows 95B or above (Win95 OSR 2.x), Windows 98, Windows Me, or Windows 2000 versions of FDISK with a hard drive greater than 512MB, FDISK offers to enable large disk support.

Choosing to enable large disk support provides several benefits:

- *You can use a large hard disk (greater than 2.1GB) as a single drive letter.* In fact, your drive can be as large as 2TB and still be identified by a single drive letter. This is because of the FAT32 file system, which allows for many more files per drive than FAT16.

▶▶ See "FAT32," p. 1373.

- *Because of the more efficient storage methods of FAT-32, your files will use less hard disk space overall.*

However, keep in mind that all disk operations must be performed through an operating system with FAT32 support (Windows 95B or later, Windows 98, Windows Me, or Windows 2000). If you have old MS-DOS games or applications that are bootable, you won't be able to access a FAT32 volume unless you replace the DOS version on the disk with the DOS included on Win95B or Windows 98. This normally can be done by using the SYS A: command from the \Windows\Command folder. Another option is to use the Windows Startup menu in Win95B or Win98 (press F8 as Windows starts to load) and select Command Prompt to get to a FAT32-capable DOS. On the other hand, you can select Start, Shutdown, Restart the Computer in MS-DOS Mode from the Windows desktop.

A drive prepared with the large hard disk support (FAT32) option enabled can still be partitioned into primary and secondary partitions with FDISK, as with FAT16 for the data-security reasons listed earlier.

Another type of file system is NTFS, which is supported by only Windows NT, Windows 2000, and Windows XP. This is a high-performance file system with additional security and networking features. NTFS was revised to NTFS5 in Windows NT 4.0 with Service Pack 4 and later, as well as Windows 2000 and Windows XP. It is discussed in more detail in Chapter 25, "File Systems and Data Recovery." Note that Windows 9x can't read NTFS partitions, and Windows NT can't read FAT32 partitions. Windows 2000 and Windows XP, however, can handle both FAT32 and NTFS.

Assigning Drive Letters with FDISK

FDISK can be used in many ways, depending on the number of hard drives you have in your system and the number of drive letters you want to create.

With a single drive, creating a primary partition (C:) and an extended partition with two logical DOS drives within it results in the following drive letters:

Partition Type	Drive Letter(s)
Primary	C:
Extended	D: and E:

Most people think that a second physical drive added to this system should have drive letters that follow the E: drive.

However, you must understand how drive letters are allocated by the system to know how to use FDISK correctly in this situation. Table 14.1 shows how FDISK assigns drive letters by drive and partition type.

Table 14.1   Drive Letter Allocations by Drive and Partition Type

Drive	Partition	Order	Drive Letter
1st	Primary	1st	C:
1st	Extended	3rd	E:
2nd	Primary	2nd	D:
2nd	Extended	4th	F:

How does this affect you when you add another hard drive? If you prepare the second hard drive with a primary partition and your first hard drive has an extended partition on it, the second hard drive takes the primary partition's D: drive letter. This moves all the drive letters in the first hard drive's extended partition up one drive letter.

In the first example, a drive is listed with C: (primary partition), D:, and E: (extended partition volumes) as the drive letters (D: and E: were in the extended partition). Table 14.2 indicates what happens if a second drive is added with a primary partition and an extended partition with two volumes (same setup as the first drive).

Table 14.2   Drive Letter Changes Caused by Addition of Second Drive with Primary Partition

Drive	Partition Type	Order	Original Drive Letters (First Drive Only)	New Drive Letters After Adding Second Drive
1st	Primary	1st	C:	C:
1st	Extended	3rd	D:, E:	E:, F:
2nd	Primary	2nd		D:
2nd	Extended	4th		G:, H:

After adding the second drive, the original drive letters D: and E: have now become E: and F:. The primary partition on the new drive has become D:, and the extended partition volumes on the second drive are G: and H:. Confused? Well, you better not be or you'll find yourself deleting or copying data to or from the wrong drive.

This principle extends to third and fourth physical drives as well: The primary partitions on each drive get their drive letters first, followed by logical DOS drives in the extended partitions.

One way to effect this is to partition additional drives with only extended partitions—in other words, do not create primary partitions on them. That enables the new drive's partitions to be seen only as additional letters, and the letters used by the first drive's partitions to remain unchanged.

If you're *adding* a drive to your system, you should now understand why preparing that second, third, or fourth drive with a primary partition is a bad idea. If you're installing an additional hard drive (not a replacement), remember that it can't be a bootable drive. And if it can't be bootable, there's no reason to make it a primary partition. FDISK allows you to create an extended partition using 100% of the space on any drive. Table 14.3 shows the same example used in Table 14.2 with the second drive installed as an extended partition.

Table 14.3   Drive Letter Allocations After Addition of Second Drive with Extended Partition Only

Drive	Partition Type	Order	Original Drive Letters (First Drive Only)	New Drive Letters (After Adding Second Drive)
1st	Primary	1st	C:	C:
1st	Extended	3rd	D:, E:	D:, E:
2nd	Primary	2nd	—	—
2nd	Extended	4th		F:

When a new drive is added with only extended partition volumes, you can see that the original drive letters remain undisturbed. This arrangement is much easier to understand, and it prevents accidents with data because of drive letters changing. This operating system behavior also explains why some of the first computers with ATA-based (ATAPI) Iomega Zip drives had the Zip drive as D:, with a single hard disk identified as C: and E:. The Zip drive was treated as the second hard drive with a primary partition. Subsequently, Iomega changed the Zip drive format and driver so that the Zip disk is recognized as an extended partition at the end of the drive letter chain.

Running FDISK

When you run newer versions of FDISK, the first thing that happens is you are prompted with the following:

```
Do you wish to enable large disk support (Y/N)..........? [Y]
```

If you answer Yes to this question, FDISK creates FAT32 volumes for all volumes created that are larger than 512MB. Answering No to this question forces FDISK to create only FAT16 volumes, which are limited to a 2GB maximum size and waste more space on the disk due to larger cluster sizes.

Normally, in a modern system you would answer Yes, allowing the use of FAT32. After answering the question, FDISK shows a menu similar to the following:

```
Current fixed disk drive: 1

    Choose one of the following:

    1. Create DOS partition or Logical DOS Drive
    2. Set active partition
    3. Delete partition or Logical DOS Drive
    4. Display partition information
    5. Change current fixed disk drive

    Enter choice: [1]
```

Option 5 is shown only if FDISK detects more than one drive on your system (if more than one is entered via your BIOS Setup). In that case, FDISK defaults to the first drive, and via option 5 you can cause FDISK to work with any of the other hard disks on the system.

To create partitions, you select option 1. If the drive is already partitioned, however, you can use option 4 to display the current layout of the drive.

After selecting option 1, the menu changes to enable you to create primary or extended partitions on a drive as follows:

```
Create DOS Partition or Logical DOS Drive

    Current fixed disk drive: 1

    Choose one of the following:

    1. Create Primary DOS Partition
    2. Create Extended DOS Partition
    3. Create Logical DOS Drive(s) in the Extended DOS Partition

    Enter choice: [1]
```

The rules require you to create a primary partition first on the boot drive, but on a secondary or non-boot drive, you can create just an extended partition if you choose. So, if you are partitioning the first drive in a system and it will be bootable, you would choose option 1.

At this point, you are prompted to decide whether you want to use the maximum available size for a Primary DOS Partition. If you say Yes and you're using FAT32, the primary partition uses the entire drive. Conversely, if you say Yes and you did not enable large drive support (meaning you are using FAT16), the partition uses the entire drive or 2GB, whichever is smaller.

If you decide to create a primary partition that is not the full drive, you should go back through the menus and create an extended partition using the rest of the drive, and then further divide it into logical drives. Normally, I recommend making the primary partition the full size of the drive, keeping all of the drive as one letter. But there are various reasons you might want to split the drive into multiple partitions, such as for different operating systems, different file systems, applications, and so on.

After all the partitions are created, the final operation is to make one of them active (bootable), which is option 2 from the main FDISK menu. Typically, the only one that can be active is the primary partition. After that is done, all FDISK operations are complete, and you can exit the program.

When exiting FDISK after making partition changes, the system must be rebooted before these changes will be recognized. After rebooting, you must then high-level format each of the volumes with the operating system FORMAT command, which then allows the operating system to store files on them.

The C: volume usually must be formatted with the system files, although when you install Windows via the Windows Setup command, it detects whether the system files are present and offers to install them for you.

Drive Partitioning and Formatting with Disk Management

Even though Windows 2000 and Windows XP have a very powerful command-line tool called DISKPART that provides FDISK-like capabilities, along with additional options useful for working with advanced disk structures such as RAID arrays and dynamic disks, most Windows 2000 and Windows XP users utilize the GUI-based Disk Management component of the Microsoft Management Console to perform hard disk partitioning and formatting when installing a new hard disk on an existing system.

As with FDISK, you can select the type of file system you want to use, but the following differences exist between FDISK and Disk Management:

■ *Disk Management is a true GUI-based utility.* Color-coded indicators for partition type and drive condition let you easily see which tasks you've performed with a drive. Wizards enable you to partition and format a drive under the guidance of Windows.

■ *Disk Management supports more file systems than FDISK.* Whereas FDISK is limited to FAT-16 (and FAT-32 on Windows 95B and above, Windows 98, and Windows Me), Disk Management also supports NTFS.

■ *Disk Management partitions and formats hard disks with a simple process.* Unlike FDISK, which requires you to restart the system before a new hard disk can be formatted and uses a separate FORMAT program to finish the job, Disk Management can perform both tasks without the need to restart the computer.

■ *Disk Management uses drive letters not already in use for hard disk or optical drives, regardless of the partition type.* Unlike FDISK, which can scramble existing drive letter assignments if you prepare a new hard disk with a primary partition, Disk Management assigns a drive letter(s) to the new hard drive that follows those already in use. And, if installing a new drive causes conflicts with removable-media drives such as USB keychain or flash memory card readers you use occasionally, you can use Disk Management to select a different drive letter for the new hard disk or for existing hard disks or optical drives.

To use Disk Management to partition a new hard disk in Windows XP, do the following:

1. Open the Start menu, right-click My Computer, and select Manage from the context menu.

2. From the Computer Management screen, click Disk Management in the left window. The current hard disk drive letter is displayed in the upper-right window, and physical hard disks are displayed in the bottom-right window (see Figure 14.8). A newly installed drive is shown as unallocated space.

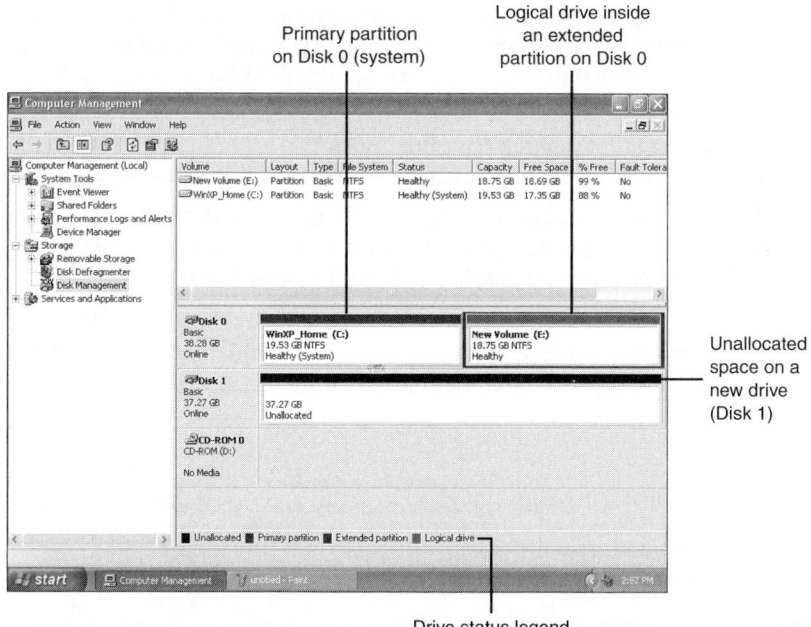

Figure 14.8 The Computer Management view of a system with a newly installed hard disk (Disk 1). Because New Volume (E:) was prepared after the CD-ROM drive (D:) was installed, it has a higher drive letter.

3. Select the new hard disk, right-click it, and select New Partition from the right-click menu to start the partitioning process.

4. Click Next at the opening screen of the New Partition Wizard.

5. Select Primary or Extended partition. Generally, you should choose an extended partition unless you want to create a primary partition that you can use to start the computer. Click Next to continue.

6. If you want to leave part of the hard disk unallocated, change the partition size. Otherwise, click Next to continue.

7. The New Partition Wizard displays the changes it's about to make to the new drive (see Figure 14.9). Click Finish to complete the partitioning process.

Figure 14.9   The New Partition Wizard prepares to create an extended partition from Disk 1.

8. After the wizard finishes, the Computer Management view displays the newly partitioned hard disk as free space. Right-click the partition, and select New Logical Drive to continue.

9. Click Next to continue with the wizard. Click Next again to select a logical drive.

10. To create more than one logical drive, change the maximum size of the partition size. To create a single logical drive, click Next.

11. Select the drive letter to assign. By default, the next available drive letter is displayed, but you can choose any unused drive letter. If you prefer, you can mount the new logical drive into an empty NTFS folder, or even not assign a drive letter or path. Click Next to continue.

12. Select the format options. By default, the new logical drive is formatted with NTFS, but you can choose FAT32 if the logical drive is 34.36GB (32GiB) or less. If the logical drive is larger than 32GiB, XP can only format the drive using NTFS. You can also specify the volume label, select a particular allocation unit (cluster) size, enable file/folder compression, and perform a quick format. If you want to format the drive later, select Do Not Format This Partition. Click Next to continue.

13. Again, the New Partition Wizard displays a list of changes to be made. Click Back to return to a particular menu if you need to make any changes, or click Finish to format the logical drive with the options selected (see Figure 14.10).

14. Repeat steps 10–14 if you didn't use all the free space as a logical drive and want to prepare additional logical drives.

Figure 14.10 The New Partition Wizard prepares to format a logical drive on Disk 1 with the options shown.

No rebooting is necessary, and the color-coded legend at the bottom of the Disk Management display helps you track the status of the disk preparation process.

Drive Partitioning with Aftermarket Utilities

Alternative partitioning programs such as PartitionMagic by PowerQuest and Partition Commander by V-Communications enable you to take an existing hard drive and perform the following changes to it without loss of data:

- Create, resize, split, move, and merge partitions on the fly without losing data.

- Convert between file systems without losing data—conversions include FAT to FAT32 and NTFS; FAT32 to FAT; NTFS to FAT and FAT32; primary to logical and vice versa; and FAT32 to NTFS under Windows 2000 and XP. It also includes support for ext2 and Linux SWAP file systems.

- Move applications between partitions and automatically update the drive-letter references after partitioning with their DriveMapper utility.

- Undelete FAT, FAT32, Linux ext2, and NTFS partitions that have been deleted. You can restore partitions that have been deleted on disk as long as the space has not been reallocated or written over.

- Copy or move a partition to another partition or drive.

Note

I still recommend FDISK, DISKPART, Disk Management, or SETUP be used for initial partitioning and setup of any drive (these utilities destroy existing data), but these aftermarket utilities can be very useful for reconfiguring a system that is already partitioned.

Although the program recommends a full backup before starting, I've used these utilities many times to turn a single "big drive" into two or more drive letters in less than 10 minutes. Performing the same task with backup software and FDISK/FORMAT can take several hours because you must back up your existing drive, remove existing partitions with FDISK, create new partitions with FDISK, restart your computer, format the new drives, and reload your operating system and your backup.

High-Level (Operating System) Formatting

The final step in the installation of a hard disk drive is the high-level format. Similar to the partitioning process, the high-level format is specific to the file system you've chosen to use on the drive. On Windows 9x and DOS systems, the primary function of the high-level format is to create a FAT and a directory system on the disk so the operating system can manage files. You must run FDISK before formatting a drive. Each drive letter created by FDISK must be formatted before it can be used for data storage. As you learned in the section "Drive Partitioning and Formatting with Disk Management," Windows 2000 and Windows XP perform the high-level format with the New Partition Wizard.

Usually, you perform the high-level format with the FORMAT.COM program or the formatting utility in Windows 9x/Me Explorer. FORMAT.COM uses the following syntax:

```
FORMAT C: /S /V
```

This command high-level formats drive C:, writes the hidden operating system files in the first part of the partition, and prompts for the entry of a volume label to be stored on the disk at the completion of the process.

The FAT high-level format program performs the following functions and procedures:

1. Scans the disk (read-only) for tracks and sectors marked as bad during the LLF, and notes these tracks as being unreadable.

2. Returns the drive heads to the first cylinder of the partition, and at that cylinder (Head 1, Sector 1) writes a DOS volume boot sector.

3. Writes a FAT at Head 1, Sector 2. Immediately after this FAT, it writes a second copy of the FAT. These FATs are essentially blank except for bad-cluster marks noting areas of the disk that were found to be unreadable during the marked-defect scan.

4. Writes a blank root directory.

5. If the /S parameter is specified, copies the system files, IO.SYS and MSDOS.SYS (or IBMBIO.COM and IBMDOS.COM, depending on which DOS you run), and COMMAND.COM to the disk (in that order).

6. If the /V parameter is specified, prompts the user for a volume label, which is written as the fourth file entry in the root directory.

Now, the operating system can use the disk for storing and retrieving files, and the disk is a bootable disk.

During the first phase of the high-level format, the program performs a marked defect scan. Defects marked by the LLF operation show up during this scan as being unreadable tracks or sectors. When the high-level format encounters one of these areas, it automatically performs up to five retries to read these tracks or sectors. If the unreadable area was marked by the LLF, the read fails on all attempts.

After five retries, the DOS FORMAT program gives up on this track or sector and moves to the next one. If an area remains unreadable after the initial read and five retries, it is marked in the FAT as a bad cluster.

Note

Because the high-level format doesn't overwrite data areas beyond the root directory of the hard disk, using programs such as Norton Utilities to unformat the hard disk that contains data from previous operations is possible, provided no programs or data has been copied to the drive after high-level formatting. Unformatting can be performed because the data from the drive's previous use is still present.

If you create an extended partition, the logical DOS drive letters found there need a simpler FORMAT command because system files aren't necessary—for example, FORMAT D:/V for drive D:, FORMAT E:/V for drive E:, and so on.

FDISK and FORMAT Limitations

The biggest problem with FDISK is that it is destructive. If you change your mind about disk structure, you must back up your system and start over again. That alone is cause for using FDISK with care, but here are other limitations you should keep in mind:

- FDISK doesn't provide any help with issues of drive letter changes.

- FDISK requires FORMAT before the drive is ready for use.

- FORMAT must check the entire drive before making it ready for use. Its error management is rudimentary and can waste a lot of disk space with older drives that have disk errors.

- FDISK and FORMAT are designed for a single operating system environment, with no provision for multiboot options (Windows 9x and NT or Windows 9x and Linux, for example).

- FDISK and FORMAT offer no procedure for migrating data to a new drive, and the XCOPY command is tricky to use.

- FDISK and FORMAT might cause conflicts with existing CD-ROM drives, which often use the next available drive letter after the existing hard drive.

Although Disk Management in Windows 2000 and Windows XP does a better job than FDISK/FORMAT of avoiding drive letter conflicts with existing drives, it's still a destructive process if you need to change your disk partitions, and it has no provision for migrating data.

For these reasons, many drive vendors offer some type of automatic disk installation software with their hard drives. These routines can make the task of disk migration a fast, easy, and reliable operation.

Typical features of automatic disk installation programs include the following:

- *Replacement for FDISK and FORMAT.* A single program performs both functions more quickly than FDISK and FORMAT separately.

- *Database of drive jumpers for major brands and models.*

- *Drive copy function.* Copies contents of old MS-DOS or Windows 9x drive to the new drive, retaining long filenames, file attributes, and so on.

- *CD-ROM drive letter relocation utility.* Moves CD-ROM to new drive letter (to make room for new hard drive letters) and resets Windows Registry and INI file references to new drive letter so CD-ROM software works without reinstallation.

- *Menu-driven or wizard-driven process for installing new hard drive.*

- *Optional override of BIOS limitations for installation of large hard drives (>504MB, 2.1GB, 8.4GB, and so on).*

The two major vendors in the automated disk-utility business are Ontrack Data Recovery, Inc., and StorageSoft. These companies sell their disk-installation products to OEM hard drive vendors for use with particular brands of drives. They also sell to the public "generic" versions that can be purchased for use with any brand or model of hard disk. Table 14.4 provides a basic overview of the most popular disk-installation programs.

Disk Manager and EZ-Drive are DOS-based utility programs, whereas DiscWizard, MaxBlast, and Disk Manager version 4.x offer a Windows-like interface. Seagate's DiscWizard and MaxBlast actually analyze the system, ask the user questions about the intended installation, and prepare a customized procedure based on the user's responses.

OEM versions of disk-installation programs are available from the drive makers' Web sites; retail versions of Disk Manager v4.x usable with any combination of drives can be purchased from retail stores or at the vendor's online store.

Table 14.4   Overview of Automatic Disk-Installation Programs

Vendor	Software	OEM	Retail
Ontrack	Disk Manager[1]	Yes	Yes
StorageSoft[2]	DriveGuide	Yes	No
Western Digital[3]	Data Lifeguard	Yes	No
Seagate[4]	DiscWizard	Yes	No
Maxtor[5]	MaxBlast	Yes	No

1. Disk Manager v4.xx has replaced Disk Manager DiskGo!
2. Phoenix Technologies acquired StorageSoft in 2002.
3. Data Lifeguard includes a customized version of StorageSoft's EZ-Drive and DriveGuide tools.
4. Seagate's DiscWizard was codeveloped with Ontrack and contains Ontrack Disk Manager. It is designed for installation of an additional drive. To install the first drive in a new system, download DiscWizard Starter Edition. DiscWizard Online is an online version of DiscWizard 2002.
5. Maxtor's MaxBlast Plus II is a customized version of DriveGuide. MaxBlast! Software v9.x is a customized version of EZ-Drive. Versions 7.x and 8.x of MaxBlast! are customized versions of Ontrack Disk Manager.

Replacing an Existing Drive

Previous sections discussed installing a single hard drive or adding a new hard drive to a system. Although formatting and partitioning a new hard disk can be challenging, replacing an existing drive and moving your programs and files to it can be a lot more challenging.

Drive Migration for MS-DOS Users

When MS-DOS 6.x was dominant, many users used this straightforward method to transfer the contents of their old hard drive to their new hard drive:

1. The user creates a bootable disk containing FDISK, FORMAT, and XCOPY.

2. The new hard drive is prepared with a primary partition (and possibly an extended partition, depending on the user's desires).

3. The new hard drive is formatted with system files, although the operating system identifies it as D:.

4. The XCOPY command is used to transfer all nonhidden files from C:\ (the old hard drive) to D:\, thus:

```
XCOPY C:\ D:\/S/E
```

The XCOPY command also is used as necessary to transfer files from any remaining drive letters on the old hard drive to the corresponding drive letters on the new drive.

Because the only hidden files such a system would have were probably the operating system boot files (already installed) and the Windows 3.1 permanent swap file (which could be re-created after restarting Windows), this "free" data transfer routine worked well for many people.

After the original drive was removed from the system, the new drive would be jumpered as master and assigned C:. The user then would need to run FDISK from a floppy and set the primary partition on the new C: drive as Active. Then, the user would exit FDISK and the drive would boot.

Drive Migration for Windows 9x/Me Users

Windows 9x/Me have complicated the once-simple act of data transfer to a new system by their frequent use of hidden files and folders (such as \Windows\Inf, where Windows 9x hardware drivers are stored). The extensive use of hidden files was a major reason for a greatly enhanced version of XCOPY being included in Windows 9x/Me.

Note

XCOPY32 is automatically used in place of XCOPY when XCOPY is started within a command prompt session under Windows.

XCOPY32 for Windows 9x Data Transfer

Compared to "classic" XCOPY, XCOPY32 can copy hidden files; can preserve file attributes such as system, hidden, read-only, and archive; can automatically create folders; and is compatible with long filenames. Thus, using it to duplicate an existing drive is possible, but with these cautions:

- The XCOPY32 command is much more complex.
- Errors might occur during the copy process because of Windows's use of temporary files during normal operation, but XCOPY32 can be forced to continue.

This command line calls XCOPY32 and transfers all files and folders with their original attributes intact from the original drive (C:) to the new drive (D:). This command, however, must be run from an MS-DOS prompt window (and not MS-DOS Mode) under Windows 9x/Me, as follows:

```
xcopy32 c:\. d:\ /e/c/h/r/k
```

The command switches are explained here:

- /e. Copies folders, even if empty; also copies all folders beneath the starting folder.
- /c. Continues to copy after errors. The Windows swap file can't be copied due to being in use.
- /h. Copies hidden and system files.
- /r. Overwrites read-only files.
- /k. Preserves file attributes.

Repeat the command with appropriate drive-letter changes for any additional drive letters on your old drive.

After the original drive is removed from the system, the new drive must be jumpered as master (or single), and the operating system assigns it C:. You next need to run FDISK from a floppy and set the primary partition on the new C: drive as Active. Then, exit FDISK, and the drive will boot.

Note that although the XCOPY method has worked for me, some people have problems with it. A much more automated and easy approach to cloning drives is to use commercial software designed for that purpose, such as Drive Copy by PowerQuest or Norton Ghost by Symantec. Drive copying programs included with older versions of hard disk installation programs provided by drive vendors have not always worked well, but the latest versions of these programs can be very useful for drive copying and other preparation tasks. In recent installations, I've found that the Maxtor MaxBlast disk copying program worked perfectly in transferring a Windows XP installation to a much larger target drive. So, I recommend you try the drive vendor's copying program first. If you have problems, you can use a third-party product instead.

Even though many users have prepared new hard drives for use with nothing but FDISK and FORMAT, today's more complex systems are presenting increasingly good reasons for looking at alternatives.

Hard Disk Drive Troubleshooting and Repair

If a hard drive has a mechanical problem inside the sealed head disk assembly (HDA), repairing the drive is usually unfeasible. It might be doable, but purchasing a new drive will be far less expensive. If the failure is in the logic board, that board can be replaced with one from a donor drive. Typically, this is done only for the purposes of reading the information on the failed drive because you must purchase a complete second drive to cannibalize for the logic board. The drive manufacturers usually don't sell spare parts for their drives anymore.

Most hard disk drive problems are not mechanical hardware problems; instead, they are "soft" problems that can be solved by a new LLF and defect-mapping session. Soft problems are characterized by a drive that sounds normal but produces various read and write errors.

Hard problems are mechanical, such as when the drive sounds as though it contains loose marbles. Constant scraping and grinding noises from the drive, with no reading or writing capability, also qualify as hard errors. In these cases, an LLF is unlikely to put the drive back into service. If a hardware problem is indicated, first replace the logic-board assembly. You can make this repair yourself and, if successful, you can recover the data from the drive.

If replacing the logic assembly does not solve the problem, contact the manufacturer or a specialized repair shop that has clean-room facilities for hard disk repair. (See the Vendor's List on the accompanying disc for a list of drive manufacturers and companies that specialize in hard disk drive repair.) However, because of the costs, simply purchasing a new drive is probably more economical.

Testing a Drive

When accessing a drive, determining whether the drive has been partitioned and formatted properly is easy. A simple test can tell you whether a stored drive is in its "raw" condition or has been partitioned and formatted properly. These tests work best if you have a boot disk available and if the spare hard drive is the only hard drive attached.

First, attach the drive to your system. If you can attach power and data cables to it, you need not install it into a drive bay unless you are planning to use it immediately. If the drive will be run loose, I recommend placing it on a nonconductive foam pad or other soft surface. This insulates the drive from potential shocks and other hazards. After detecting the drive in the BIOS and saving the changes, start your operating system from the boot disk.

Then, from the A: prompt, enter the following command:

```
DIR C:
```

This produces one of the following responses:

- *Invalid drive specification.* This indicates the drive does not have a valid partition (created by FDISK) or that the existing Master Boot Sector or partition tables have been damaged. No matter what, the drive must be partitioned and formatted before use. You also get this warning on a FAT32 or NTFS partitioned drive if you use a Windows 95 (original version) or MS-DOS boot disk when checking. Use a Windows 95B, Windows 98/Me, or Windows 2000 boot disk to avoid this false message from FAT32 partitions. Or, use a Windows NT, Windows 2000, or Windows XP boot disk to detect NTFS partitions.

- *Invalid media type.* This drive has been partitioned but not FORMATted, or the format has been corrupted. You should use FDISK's #4 option to examine the drive's existing partitions and either delete them and create new ones or keep the existing partitions and run FORMAT on each drive letter.

- *Directory of C:.* The contents of the C: drive are listed, indicating the drive was stored with a valid FDISK and FORMAT structure and data.

Tip

If you know to which computer the drive was previously connected, you should connect the drive to that computer to perform the test. If you move the drive to another computer, differences in BIOS and ATA host adapter translation could cause a working drive with data to appear to be empty. This is particularly the case with systems that have onboard Promise ATA RAID controllers—even if the ATA RAID feature is not used or you move the drive from a system using an Award or AMI BIOS to a system with a Phoenix BIOS.

Installing an Optical Drive

Installation of a CD-ROM, CD-R, CD-RW, DVD-ROM, or rewriteable DVD drive can be as difficult or as easy as you make it. If you plan ahead, the installation should go smoothly.

This section walks you through the installation of a typical internal (SCSI or ATA) and external (SCSI only) optical drive, with tips that often aren't included in the manufacturers' installation manuals. After you install the hardware, your job might be finished if you are running Windows and using a Plug and Play drive, or you might have to manually load the software necessary to access the drive.

Note

CD-ROM and DVD-ROM drives use the same ATA, SATA, and SCSI system interfaces and can be installed using the same basic procedures. Some DVD-ROM drives come with an MPEG-2 decoder board or MPEG decoder software that enables you to view DVD movies and video on your PC. If a board is included, it usually installs in a PCI bus slot like any other expansion card and performs the video decoding process that would otherwise fall to the system processor. Software decoding does not require a board and instead uses your processor to do the decoding work. Software decoding normally requires a fast processor (see the software manufacturer's recommendations for how fast); otherwise, the video appears jumpy, jerky, or unsynchronized with the sound. Although many premium DVD setups have included hardware decoding for this reason in the past, today's computers typically have 1GHz and faster processors to make software playback smooth. Also, many video cards now feature onboard DVD hardware decoding, eliminating the need for a separate DVD decoder.

Note that a separate analog or digital audio connection typically exists between the drive and the sound card as well, used primarily for playing audio CDs.

Avoiding Conflict: Get Your Cards in Order

Regardless of the type of installation—internal or external drive—you must have a functioning ATA or SCSI host adapter before the drive can function. In most cases, you will be connecting the optical drive to an existing ATA or SCSI adapter. If so, the adapter should already be configured not to conflict with other devices in your system. All you have to do is connect the drive with the appropriate cable and proceed from there.

Most computers today have an ATA adapter integrated into the motherboard. However, if you are adding SCSI to your system for the first time, you must install a SCSI host adapter into an expansion slot and ensure it is configured to use the appropriate hardware resources, such as the following:

- IRQ
- DMA channel
- I/O port address

As always, Windows 9x/Me/2000/XP and PnP hardware can completely automate this process; however, if you're using another operating system, you might have to configure the adapter manually.

Drive Configuration

Configuration of your new optical drive is paramount to its proper functioning. Examine your new drive and locate any jumpers (see Figure 14.11). For an ATA drive, here are the typical ways to jumper the drive:

- As the primary (master) drive on the secondary ATA connection
- As the secondary (slave) drive to a current hard disk drive
- Using Cable Select (CS), where the cable connector determines which drive is master or slave automatically

If the drive is to be the only device on your secondary ATA interface, the factory settings are usually correct. Consult the manual to make sure this is so.

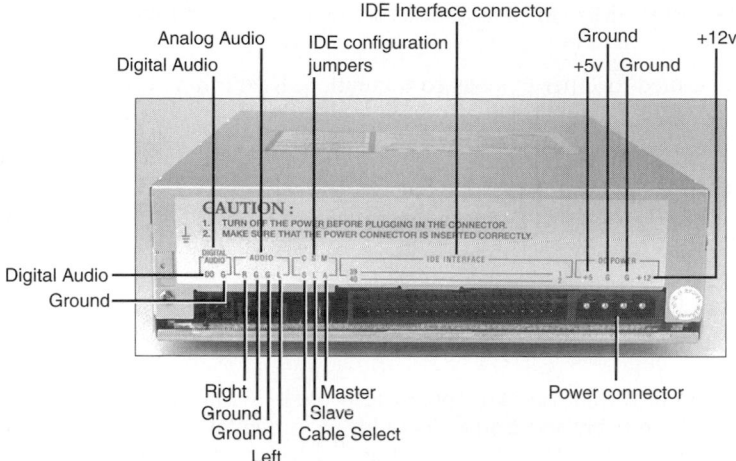

Figure 14.11 The rear connection interfaces of a typical ATA internal CD-ROM drive.

When you use the CD-ROM or DVD-ROM as a secondary drive—that is, the second drive on the same ribbon cable with another device—be sure it is jumpered as the slave drive, and configure the other device so it is the master drive (see Figure 14.12). In most cases, the drive shows up as the next logical drive, or the D: drive.

Caution

Whenever possible, you should not connect a CD-ROM or DVD-ROM drive to the same channel as a hard disk drive because devices on the same channel can't simultaneously read or write data. If your computer has the two ATA channels standard in systems today, you should connect the optical drive to the secondary channel, even if you have only one hard disk drive on the primary.

Figure 14.12 An embedded ATA interface with primary and secondary ATA connections (the pen is pointing to the primary ATA connector).

◄◄ These procedures are covered in "Parallel ATA," p. 543, and "Small Computer System Interface," p. 584.

Depending on how you look at it, SCSI drives can be a bit easier to configure because you need only to select the proper SCSI ID for the drive. By convention, the boot disk (the C: drive) in a SCSI system is set as ID0, and the host adapter has an ID of 7. You are free to choose any ID in between that is not being used by another device. Most SCSI devices use some type of rotating or pushbutton selector to cycle between the SCSI IDs, but some might use jumpers.

SCSI devices are cabled together in a bus configuration. If your new SCSI drive falls at the end of the SCSI bus, you also must terminate the drive. Note that the SCSI bus refers to the physical arrangement of the devices, and not the SCSI IDs selected for each one.

External (SCSI) Drive Hookup

Unpack the drive carefully. With the purchase of an external drive, you should receive the following items:

- CD-ROM or DVD-ROM drive
- SCSI adapter cable

With the exception of the SCSI host adapter, this is the bare minimum you need to get the drive up and running. You'll probably also find a CD caddy, documentation for the drive, driver software, a SCSI terminator plug, and possibly a sampling of CDs to get you started. SCSI drives almost never come with the SCSI host adapter necessary to connect them to the system. Because SCSI is designed to support up to seven devices on the same system (or up to fifteen devices for Ultra2 SCSI), including a host adapter with every peripheral is impractical. Although a few computers have SCSI interfaces integrated into the motherboard, in most cases you have to purchase a SCSI adapter as a separate expansion card.

To begin the installation, take a look at your work area and the SCSI cable that came with the drive. Where will the drive find a new home? You're limited by the length of the cable. Find a spot for the drive, and insert the power cable into the back of the unit. Be sure you have an outlet or, preferably, a free socket in a surge-suppressing power strip to plug in the new drive.

SCSI devices generally use one of two cable types. Some older drives use a 50-pin Centronics cable, referred to as an A-cable. Most drives today, though, use a 68-pin cable called a P-cable. Plug one end of the supplied cable into the connector socket of the drive and one into the SCSI connector on the adapter card. Most external drives have two connectors on the back—either connector can be hooked to the PC (see Figure 14.13). You use the other connector to attach another SCSI device or, if the drive is at the end of the bus, to connect a terminator plug. Secure the cable with the guide hooks on both the drive and adapter connectors, if provided.

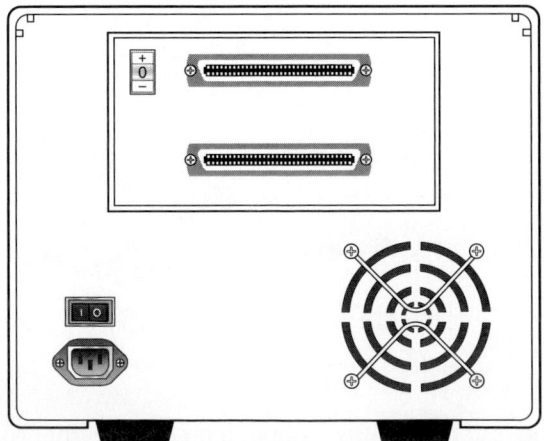

Figure 14.13 External drive with dual SCSI connectors.

Note

A SCSI device should include some means of terminating the bus, when necessary. The terminator might take the form of a cableless plug you connect to the second SCSI connector on the drive, or the drive might be self-terminating, in which case there should be a jumper or a switch you can set to activate termination.

Finally, your external drive should have a SCSI ID select switch on the back. This switch sets the identification number the host adapter uses to distinguish the drive from the other devices on the bus. The host adapter, by most manufacturers' defaults, should be set for SCSI ID 7, and some (but not all) manufacturers reserve the IDs 0 and 1 for use by hard disk drives. Be sure you set the SCSI ID for the CD-ROM or DVD-ROM drive to any other number—6, 5, or 4, for example. The only rule to follow is to be sure you do not set the drive for an ID that is already occupied—by either the adapter or any other SCSI peripheral on the bus.

Internal Drive Installation

Unpack your internal drive kit. You should have the following pieces:

- The drive
- The internal CD-audio cable
- Floppy disks/CD-ROM with device driver software and manual
- Drive rails and mounting screws

Your manufacturer also might have provided a power cable splitter—a bundle of wires with plastic connectors on each of three ends. A disc caddy and owner's manual might also be included. If you do not already have one in the computer, you also will need a SCSI host adapter to connect SCSI peripherals.

Make sure the PC is turned off, and remove the cover from the case. Before installing a SCSI adapter into the PC's expansion bus, connect the SCSI ribbon cable to the adapter card (see Figure 14.14).

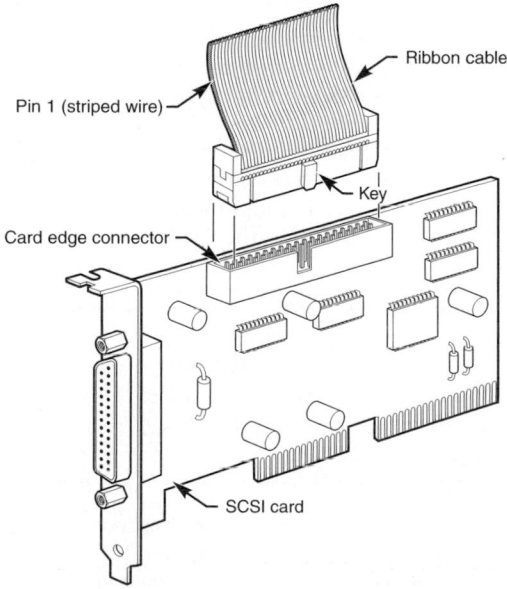

Figure 14.14 Connecting a ribbon cable to a SCSI adapter.

Ribbon Cable and Card Edge Connector

The ribbon cable should be identical on both ends. You'll find a red stripe or dotted line down one side of the outermost edge of the cable. This stripe indicates a pin-1 designation and ensures that the SCSI cable is connected properly to the card and drive. If you're lucky, the manufacturer has supplied a cable with notches or keys along one edge of the connector. With such a key, you can insert the cable into the card and drive in only one way. Unkeyed cables must be hooked up according to the pin-1 designation.

Along one edge of your SCSI adapter is a double row of 50 brass-colored pins. This is the card edge connector. In small print along the base of this row of pins you should find at least two numbers next to the pins—1 and 50. Aligning the ribbon cable's marked edge over pin 1, carefully and evenly insert the ribbon cable connector.

Next, insert the adapter card into a free bus slot in the computer, leaving the drive end of the cable loose for the time being.

Choose a bay in the front of your computer's case for your internal drive. Make sure it's easily accessible from the outside and not blocked by other items on your desk. You'll be inserting the CDs or DVDs here, and you'll need the elbow room.

Remove the drive bay cover from the computer case. You might have to loosen some screws to do this, or the cover might just pop off. Inside the drive bay, you should find a metal enclosure with screw holes for mounting the drive. If the drive has mounting holes along its side and fits snugly into the enclosure, you won't need mounting rails. If it's a loose fit, however, mount the rails along the sides of the drive with the rail screws, and then slide the drive into the bay. Secure the drive into the bay with four screws—two on each side. If the rails or drive don't line up evenly with four mounting holes, be sure you use at least two screws—one mounting screw on each side. Because you'll be inserting and ejecting many discs over the years, mounting the drive securely is a must.

Once again, find the striped side of the ribbon cable and align it with pin 1 on the drive's edge connector. Either a diagram in your owner's manual or a designation on the connector itself tells you which is pin 1.

The back of the drive has a four-pin power connector outlet. Inside the case of your PC, at the back of your floppy or hard disk, are power cords—bundled red and yellow wires with plastic connectors on them. You might already have a power connector lying open in the case. Take the open connector and plug it into the back of the power socket on the CD-ROM or DVD-ROM drive. These connectors can go in only one way. If you do not have an open connector, use a drive power splitter (refer to Figure 14.5). Disconnect an existing drive power cord from the device that uses the least power. Next, attach the splitter to the detached power cord. Plug one of the free ends back into the drive you removed the power from and plug the other into the CD-ROM or DVD-ROM drive.

Note

It's preferable to "borrow" power from the drive that consumes the least power so you don't overload the connection. Check the specification sheets for your drives to determine their power consumption. In general, devices that are physically smaller or that spin more slowly draw less power. If you have no choice—if the splitter and ribbon cable won't reach, for example—you can split off any power cord that hasn't already been split. Check the power cable to ensure that you have a line not already overloaded with another splitter.

Do not replace the PC cover yet—you need to make sure that everything is running perfectly before you seal the case. You're now ready to turn on the computer. If everything runs normally, it's time to put that cover back on.

SCSI Chains: Internal, External, or Both

Remember, one of the primary reasons for using the SCSI interface for your CD-ROM or DVD-ROM drive is the capability to connect a string of peripherals from one adapter, thus saving card slots inside the PC and limiting the nightmare of tracking IRQs, DMAs, and I/O memory addresses.

You can add hard drives, scanners, tape backup units, and other SCSI peripherals to this chain (see Figure 14.15). You must keep a few things in mind, however, and chief among them is SCSI termination.

◄◄   See "Termination," p. 608.

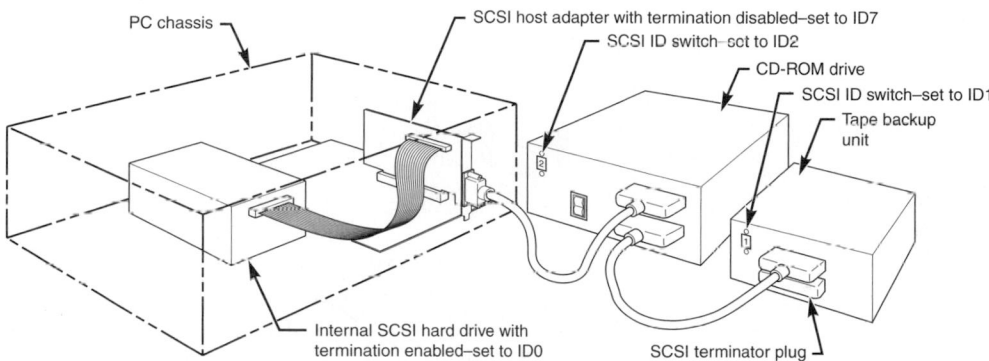

Figure 14.15   A SCSI chain of devices on one adapter card.

Example One: All External SCSI Devices. Say that you installed your CD-ROM or DVD-ROM drive and added a tape device to the SCSI bus with the extra connector on the back of the optical drive. The first device in this SCSI bus is the adapter card itself. Most modern host adapters are *autoterminating*, meaning they will terminate themselves without your intervention if they are at the end of the bus.

From the card, you ran an external cable to the optical drive, and from the optical drive, you added another cable to the back of the tape unit. You must now terminate the tape unit as well. Most external units are terminated with a SCSI cap—a small connector that plugs into the unused external SCSI connector. These external drive connectors come in two varieties: a SCSI cap and a pass-through terminator. The cap is just that; it plugs over the open connector and covers it. The pass-through terminator, however, plugs into the connector and has an open end into which you can plug the SCSI cable. This type of connector is essential if your external drive has only one SCSI connector; you can plug the drive in and make sure it's terminated—all with one connector.

Example Two: Internal Chain and Termination. On an internal SCSI bus, the same rules apply: All the internal devices must have unique SCSI ID numbers, and the first and last devices must be terminated. In the case of internal devices, however, you must check for termination. Internal devices typically have DIP switches or terminator packs similar to those on your adapter card. If you install a tape unit as the last device on the chain, it must have some means of terminating the bus. If you place your optical drive in the middle of the bus, you must deactivate its termination. The host adapter at the end of the chain must still be terminated.

Note

Most internal SCSI devices ship with terminating resistors or DIP switches onboard, usually the latter. Check your user manuals for their locations. Any given device can have one, two, or even three such resistors.

Example Three: Internal and External SCSI Devices. If you mix and match external as well as internal devices, follow the same rules. The bottom example shown in Figure 14.16 has an internal CD-ROM drive, terminated and set for SCSI ID 6; the external hard drive also is terminated and is using SCSI ID 5. The SCSI adapter itself is set for ID 7 and, most importantly, its termination has been disabled because it is no longer at the end of the bus.

Note

As with any adapter card, be careful when handling the card itself. Be sure to ground yourself first.

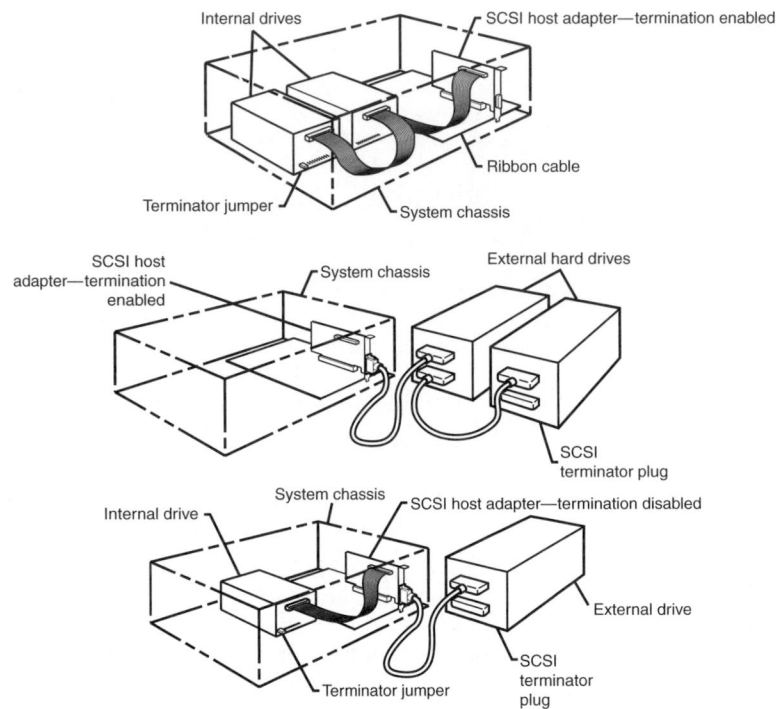

Figure 14.16 Examples of various SCSI termination scenarios.

To help you determine whether your SCSI interface card and devices are functioning properly, Adaptec supplies a utility program called SCSI Interrogator. Use it to determine which logical unit numbers (LUNs) are available for new devices.

If you don't see any devices listed, you might have a termination problem. Shut down your system and your devices. Then, check terminator plugs, switches, or resistor packs. If they appear correct, turn on the external devices about 5 seconds before you start the system. A multiswitch power director with high-quality surge protection works well for this because it allows you to turn on individual devices. If the devices fail to show up after you restart the system, you might have a problem with the SCSI BIOS or device driver software. Check the documentation for your particular card and device to ensure you have installed the proper drivers.

One peculiarity of the Adaptec SCSI Interrogator is that it lists a "host adapter #1" that's actually your ATA interface! If your SCSI card isn't working, both "host adapter #0" and "host adapter #1" are actually ATA. You can tell whether this is happening with Windows 9x because it will list "ESDI_506" as the driver version.

Floppy Drive Installation Procedures

A floppy drive is one of the simplest types of drives to install. In most cases, installing a floppy disk drive is a matter of attaching the drive to the computer chassis or case and then plugging the power and signal cables into the drive. Some type of brackets and screws are usually required to attach the drive to the chassis; however, some chassis are designed to accept the drive with no brackets at all. Any brackets, if necessary, are normally included with the chassis or case itself. Several companies listed in the Vendor List on the accompanying disc specialize in cases, cables, brackets, screw hardware, and other items useful in assembling systems or installing drives.

Note

Because floppy disk drives are generally installed into the same half-height bays as hard disk drives, the physical mounting of the drive in the computer case is the same for both units. See the section "Hard Disk Installation Procedures," earlier in this chapter, for more information on the process.

When you connect the drive, make sure the power cable is installed properly. The cable is usually keyed so you can't plug it in backward, but the keying can be defeated by somebody forcing the connection. If that is done, the drive will be fried the instant the power is turned on.

Next, install the interface cable. A floppy interface cable is a 34-pin cable that typically has a twist in it. What I mean is that pins 10–16 are twisted around before they reach the last (A:) drive connector. Normally, the A: drive must be plugged in after this twist; any drive plugged into a connector before the twist is seen by the system as drive B:. The twist reverses the drive select and motor enable signals, letting A: and B: drives coexist without rejumpering. This is similar to the way Cable Select works for ATA/IDE drives. Because of this, all floppy drives are jumpered the same way, in the second Drive Select (DS) position.

Older drives used to require various jumpers to be set to enable the drive to work properly. The two most common jumpers were the Drive Select jumper and the Disk Change (DC) jumper. If you encounter an older drive with these jumpers, you should follow a few simple rules. The DS jumper typically has two positions, labeled 0 and 1—or in some cases, 1 and 2. In all PC installations, the DS jumper should be set on the second position, no matter what it is numbered. This enables the drive on the cable before the twist to function as drive B: and the drive at the end of the cable after the twist to function as drive A:. The DC jumper setting is normally an on or off setting. For PC use, if the drive has a DC jumper, it must be set on or enabled. This enables the PC to detect when you have changed disks in the drive. For more information on floppy drives and interfacing, see Chapter 11.

The interface cable is usually keyed to prevent backward installation. If no key exists in this cable, use the colored wire in the cable as a guide to the position of pin 1. Normally, pin 1 is oriented closest to the power connector, which is the same as other drives. If the drive LED stays on continuously when you power up the system or when the system is running, that is a sure sign you have the floppy cable on backward either at the drive end or at the controller (motherboard) end.

CHAPTER 15

Video Hardware

Video Display Technologies

Along with the mouse and keyboard, the video display is a vital part of the user interface of any computer. Actually, it is a latecomer to computing; before CRT monitors came into general use, the teletypewriter was the standard computer interface—a large, loud device that printed the input and output characters on a roll of paper. The first CRT displays used on computers were primitive by today's standards; they displayed only text in a single color (usually green), but to users at the time they were a great improvement, allowing real-time display of input and output data. Over time, color displays were introduced, screen sizes increased, and LCD technologies moved from the portable computer to the desktop. The latest trends, large-screen plasma displays and LCD/DLP projectors, reflect the increasing convergence of entertainment and computer technologies exemplified by developments such as Windows XP Media Center PCs.

Today, PC video displays are much more sophisticated, but you must be careful when selecting video hardware for your computer. A slow video adapter or monitor can slow down even the fastest and most powerful PC. Incorrect monitor and video adapter combinations can also cause eyestrain or be unsuitable for the tasks you want to accomplish.

The video subsystem of a PC consists of two main components:

- *Monitor (or video display).* The monitor can be a CRT or an LCD panel for desktop use, or a wide-screen LCD TV, plasma display, or projector using LCD or DLP technology.

- *Video adapter (also called the video card or graphics adapter).* On many recent low-cost desktop systems and virtually all portable systems, video might be built into the motherboard or included as part of this motherboard's chipset.

This chapter explores the range of PC video adapters on the market today and the displays that work with them. The remainder of this section covers the various types of display technologies.

Note

The term *video*, as it is used in this context, does not necessarily imply the existence of a moving image, such as on a television screen. All adapters that feed signals to a monitor or other display are video adapters, regardless of whether they are used with applications that display moving images, such as multimedia or videoconferencing software.

How CRT Display Technology Works

A monitor can use one of several display technologies. The original display technology, and still the most popular, is cathode ray tube (CRT) technology—the same technology used in television sets. CRTs consist of a vacuum tube enclosed in glass. One end of the tube contains an electron gun assembly that projects three electron beams, one each for the red, green, and blue phosphors used to create the colors you see onscreen; the other end contains a screen with a phosphorous coating.

When heated, the electron gun emits a stream of high-speed electrons that are attracted to the other end of the tube. Along the way, a focus control and deflection coil steer the beam to a specific point on the phosphorous screen. When struck by the beam, the phosphor glows. This light is what you see when you watch TV or look at your computer screen. Three layers of phosphors are used: red, green, and blue. A metal plate called a *shadow mask* is used to align the electron beams; it has slots or holes that divide the red, green, and blue phosphors into groups of three (one of each color). Various types of shadow masks affect picture quality, and the distance between each group of three (the *dot pitch*) affects picture sharpness.

▶▶ See "Dot Pitch (CRTs)," p. 884.

Figure 15.1 illustrates the interior of a typical CRT.

The phosphor chemical has a quality called *persistence*, which indicates how long this glow remains onscreen. Persistence is what causes a faint image to remain on your TV screen for a few seconds after you turn off the set. The scanning frequency of the display specifies how often the image is refreshed. You should have a good match between persistence and scanning frequency so the image has less flicker (which occurs when the persistence is too low) and no ghost images (which occurs when the persistence is too high).

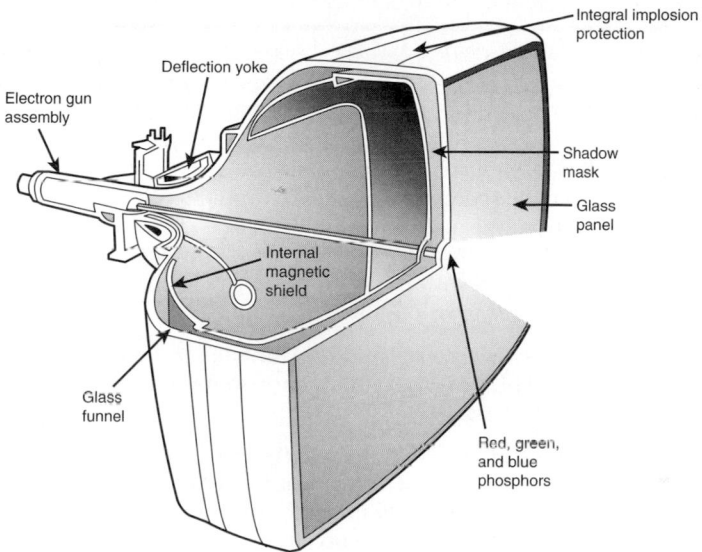

Electron gun assembly

Deflection yoke

Integral implosion protection

Shadow mask

Glass panel

Internal magnetic shield

Glass funnel

Red, green, and blue phosphors

Figure 15.1 A typical CRT monitor is a large vacuum tube. It contains three electron guns (red, green, and blue) that project the picture toward the front glass of the monitor. High voltage is used to produce the magnetism that controls the electron beams that create the picture displayed on the front of the CRT.

The electron beam moves very quickly, sweeping the screen from left to right in lines from top to bottom, in a pattern called a *raster*. The horizontal scan rate refers to the speed at which the electron beam moves laterally across the screen.

During its sweep, the beam strikes the phosphor wherever an image should appear onscreen. The beam also varies in intensity to produce different levels of brightness. Because the glow begins to fade almost immediately, the electron beam must continue to sweep the screen to maintain an image—a practice called *redrawing* or *refreshing* the screen.

Most current CRT displays have an ideal refresh rate (also called the vertical scan frequency) of about 85 hertz (Hz), which means the screen is refreshed 85 times per second. Refresh rates that are too low cause the screen to flicker, contributing to eyestrain. The higher the refresh rate, the better for your eyes. Low-cost monitors often have flicker-free refresh rates available only at 640×480 and 800×600 resolutions; you should insist on high refresh rates at resolutions such as 1024×768 or higher.

It is important that the refresh rates expected by your monitor match those produced by your video card. If you have mismatched rates, you will not see an image and can actually damage your monitor. Generally speaking, video card refresh rates cover a higher range than most monitors. For this reason, the default refresh rate used by most video cards is relatively low (usually 60Hz) to avoid monitor damage. The refresh rate can be adjusted through the Windows display properties sheets.

Multiple Frequency Monitors

Although a few very old monitors had fixed refresh rates, most monitors support a range of frequencies. This support provides built-in compatibility with a wide range of current and future video standards (described in the "Video Display Adapters" section later in this chapter). A monitor that supports many video standards is called a *multiple-frequency monitor*. Virtually all monitors sold today are multiple frequency, which means they support operation with a variety of popular video signal standards. Different vendors have used a variety of trade names to identify their multiple-frequency monitors, including multisync, multifrequency, multiscan, autosynchronous, and autotracking among others.

Note

Even though a monitor is capable of displaying a wide range of video standards, you usually need to fine-tune the display through its onscreen display (OSD) controls and Windows display properties sheets to achieve the best possible pictures.

Curved Versus Flat Picture Tubes

Phosphor-based screens come in two styles: curved and flat. Until recently, the typical display screen has been curved; it bulges outward from the middle of the screen. This design is consistent with the vast majority of CRT designs (the same as the tube in most television sets). Although this type of CRT is inexpensive to produce, the curved surface can cause distortion and glare, especially when used in a brightly lit room. Some vendors use antiglare treatments to reduce the reflectivity of the typical curved CRT surface.

The traditional screen is curved both vertically and horizontally. Some monitor models use the Sony Trinitron CRT, some versions of which are curved only horizontally and flat vertically; these are referred to as *flat square tube (FST)* designs.

Most manufacturers are now selling monitors featuring CRTs that are flat both horizontally and vertically. Sony's FD Trinitron, NEC-Mitsubishi's DiamondTron NF, and ViewSonic's PerfectFlat are some of the more popular flat CRT designs, the first such screens for PCs since the short-lived Zenith FTM monitors of the late 1980s. Many people prefer this type of flatter screen because these picture tubes show less glare and provide a higher-quality, more accurate image. Although flat-screen CRTs are slightly more expensive than conventional curved CRTs, they are only one-third to one-half the price of comparably sized flat-panel LCDs.

Figure 15.2 compares the cross-section of typical curved and flat CRT picture tubes.

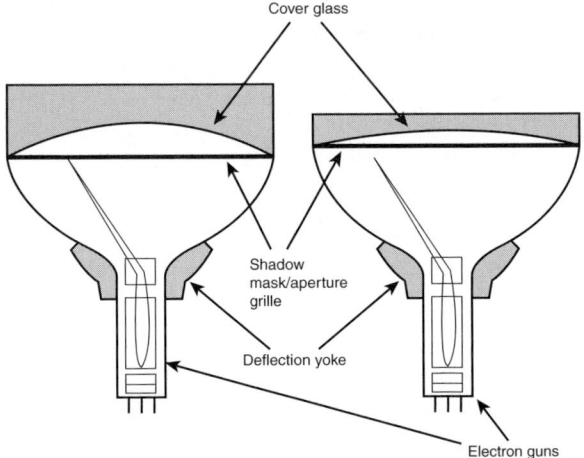

Figure 15.2 A typical curved-tube CRT (left) compared to a Sony Trinitron FD flat tube (right).

DVI—Digital Signals for CRT Monitors

The latest trend in CRT monitor design is the use of digital input signals using the same Digital Video Interface (DVI) standard used for LCD flat-panel displays. Although several major monitor vendors announced support for DVI-I interfaces for their CRT monitors in 1999, most CRT monitors (except for a few 19" or larger high-end monitors) continue to use the conventional 15-pin analog VGA connector. CRT monitors that use the DVI-I connector—unlike the TTL digital displays of the 1980s that supported only a few colors—support the same unlimited color spectrum as analog CRTs. Users benefit from digital displays because these displays can feature better picture quality, better signal reception, and precise auto setup.

Because most low-end and mid-range video cards still feature only analog (DB-15) VGA connectors, many of these monitors feature both analog and 20-pin DVI interfaces. However, as all-digital LCD panels that also use the DVI interface increase in popularity and DVI interfaces on video cards continue to increase in popularity, analog VGA eventually might be replaced by DVI-based CRT and LCD panels.

▶▶ See "LCD Panels," p. 871.

▶▶ See "Flat-Panel LCD Monitors," p. 874.

LCD Panels

Borrowing technology from laptop manufacturers, most major monitor makers sell monitors with liquid crystal displays (LCDs). LCDs have low-glare, completely flat screens and low power requirements (5 watts versus nearly 100 watts for an ordinary monitor). The color quality of an active-matrix LCD panel actually exceeds that of most CRT displays.

At this point, however, LCD screens usually are more limited in resolution than typical CRTs. Table 15.1 compares the typical resolutions of LCD monitors from 15" to 22" to mainstream CRT monitors ranging from 17" to 22" with comparable viewable areas.

Table 15.1 LCD and CRT Resolutions Compared

LCD Size	LCD Resolution	CRT Size	CRT Viewable Area	CRT Maximum Resolution
15"	1024×768	17"	16"	1024×768 1280×1024 1600×1200*
17"	1280×1024	—	—	—
18.1"	1280×1024	19"	18"	1600×1200 1920×1440*
19"	1280×1024	—	—	—
20.1"	1600×1200	21"	20"	1600×1200 1920×1440*

Available on high-end monitors only

As you can see from Table 15.1, you need a 20.1" or larger LCD panel to achieve resolutions above 1280×1024, although most 18" CRT displays can achieve 1600×1200.

Despite recent price drops, LCD panels continue to be more expensive than comparably sized CRTs. A typical 15" LCD panel sells for around $250–$400, compared to flat-screen 17" CRTs, which sell for around $150–$250. However, as Table 15.1 shows, it is important to consider that an LCD screen provides a larger viewable image than a CRT monitor of the same size. See Figure 15.3 for an example of a typical desktop LCD panel.

Figure 15.3 Note the small footprint of this 15" LCD, which makes these panels ideal for use in cramped quarters.

Two basic LCD choices are available today on notebook computers: active-matrix analog color and active-matrix digital—the latest development. Monochrome LCDs are obsolete for PCs, although they remain popular for Palm and similar organizer devices and are sometimes used for industrial display panels. Passive-matrix displays using dual-scan technology were popular for low-cost notebook models until a few years ago, but they have been completely replaced by analog or digital active-matrix displays. Passive-matrix displays are still used with handheld organizers or for industrial-use desktop display panels because of their relatively low cost and enhanced durability compared to active-matrix models.

Note

The most common type of passive-matrix display uses a supertwist numatic design, so these panels are often referred to as STNs. Active-matrix panels usually use a thin-film transistor design and are thus referred to as TFTs.

Desktop LCD panels are analog or digital active-matrix units. Typically, lower-cost 15" LCD panels use the traditional analog VGA connector and must convert analog signals back into digital, whereas more expensive 15" and most larger LCD panels provide both the analog VGA and the DVI digital connector found on most high-end and mid-range video cards. Note that some LCD vendors of VGA/DVI-compatible panels might provide only the cheaper analog VGA cable, leaving it to you to buy your own DVI cable. If you plan to connect your new LCD to your video card's DVI port, be sure that the panel supports DVI and that the cable is included. And, while you're shopping for an LCD panel, be sure to note which models include the DVI cable; the presence of a DVI cable in the box of a nominally more expensive display can more than make up the difference in price between it and an apparently less expensive panel that doesn't include the cable.

The latest trend in LCD displays is the so-called TV monitor. These LCD displays integrate TV tuners and AV video inputs to enable a single device to be used for business, gaming, and video entertainment. Many of these displays, particularly those with a 17" or larger LCD panel, also incorporate a wide-screen (16×9 aspect ratio) design for better display of wide-screen video and TV content.

How LCDs Work

In an LCD, a polarizing filter creates two separate light waves. The polarizing filter allows light waves that are aligned only with the filter to pass through. After passing through the polarizing filter, the remaining light waves are all aligned in the same direction. By aligning a second polarizing filter at a right angle to the first, all those waves are blocked. By changing the angle of the second polarizing filter, the amount of light allowed to pass can be changed. It is the role of the liquid crystal cell to change the angle of polarization and control the amount of light that passes. The liquid crystals are rod-shaped molecules that flow like a liquid. They enable light to pass straight through, but an electrical charge alters their orientations and the orientation of light passing through them. Although monochrome LCDs do not have color filters, they can have multiple cells per pixel for controlling shades of gray.

In a color LCD, an additional filter has three cells for each pixel—one each for displaying red, green, and blue—with a corresponding transistor for each cell. The red, green, and blue cells, which make up a pixel, are sometimes referred to as *subpixels*. The ability to control each cell individually has enabled Microsoft to develop a new method of improving LCD text quality. Beginning with Windows XP, you can enable a feature called ClearType through the Display properties sheet. However, individual cells can also fail.

Dead Pixels

A so-called *dead pixel* is one in which the red, green, or blue cell is stuck on or off. Failures in the on state are more common. In particular, those that fail when on are very noticeable on a dark background, such as bright red, green, or blue dots. Although even a few of these can be distracting, manufacturers vary in their warranty policies regarding how many dead pixels are required before you can get a replacement display. Some vendors look at both the total number of dead pixels and their locations. Fortunately, improvements in manufacturing quality make it less and less likely that you will see a screen with dead pixels either on your desktop or in your notebook computer display.

Although there is no normal way to repair bad pixels, there might be a simple fix that can help. I have actually repaired bad pixels by gently tapping on the screen at the pixel location. This seems to work in many cases, especially in cases in which the pixel is always illuminated instead of dead (dark). Because I find a constantly lit pixel to be more irritating than one that is constantly dark, this fix has saved me a lot of aggravation.

Active-Matrix Displays

Most active-matrix displays use a thin film transistor (TFT) array. TFT is a method for packaging from one (monochrome) to three (RGB color) transistors per pixel within a flexible material that is the same size and shape as the display. Therefore, the transistors for each pixel lie directly behind the liquid crystal cells they control.

Two TFT manufacturing processes account for most of the active-matrix displays on the market today: hydrogenated amorphous silicon (a-Si) and low-temperature polysilicon (p-Si). These processes differ primarily in their costs. At first, most TFT displays were manufactured using the a-Si process because it required lower temperatures (less than 400°C) than the p-Si process of the time. Now, lower-temperature p-Si manufacturing processes are making this method an economically viable alternative to a-Si.

To improve horizontal viewing angles in the latest LCDs, some vendors have modified the classic TFT design. For example, Hitachi's in-plane switching (IPS) design—also known as STFT—aligns the individual cells of the LCD parallel to the glass, running the electric current through the sides of the cells and spinning the pixels to provide more even distribution of the image to the entire panel area.

Hitachi's Super-IPS technology also rearranges the liquid crystal molecules into a zig-zag pattern, rather than the typical row-column arrangement, to reduce color shift and improve color uniformity. The similar multidomain vertical alignment (MVA) technology developed by Fujitsu divides the screen into different regions and changes the angle of the regions.

Both Super-IPS and MVA provide a wider viewing angle than traditional TFT displays. Other companies have different names for the same technology—for example, Sharp calls it Ultra High Aperture (UHA). Manufacturers often like to think up their own buzzwords for the same technology because it makes their products seem different. Because larger LCDs (17" and wider) are large enough to cause shifts in viewing angle even for an individual user, these advanced technologies are being used primarily on larger and more expensive panels and have been licensed to other display vendors.

Flat-Panel LCD Monitors

LCD desktop monitors, once seen mainly on the office sets of futuristic TV shows, are now becoming a common choice for use in today's office computing environment. Many users with dual-display-capable video cards have added an LCD panel as a second monitor or use one as their only monitor.

LCD monitors offer a number of benefits when compared to conventional CRT "glass tube" monitors. LCD panels feature a larger effective viewable area than CRTs; a 17" LCD is essentially equal in usability to a 19" CRT. Because LCDs use direct addressing of the display (each pixel in the picture corresponds with a transistor), they produce a high-precision image. LCDs can't have the common CRT display problems of pin-cushion, barrel distortion, or convergence errors (halos around the edges of onscreen objects).

LCD panels are less expensive to operate because they feature lower power consumption and much less heat buildup than CRTs. Because LCD units lack a CRT, no concerns exist about electromagnetic VLF or ELF emissions. Although LCDs offer a comparable mean time between failures (MTBF) to CRT displays, the major reason for LCD failures is the backlight, which is relatively inexpensive to replace. CRT failures usually involve the picture tube, which is the most expensive portion of the display and is often—especially on displays 17" and smaller—not cost-effective to replace.

LCD panels offer a smaller footprint (front-to-back dimensions), and some offer optional wall or stand mounting. Several LCD panels offer a pivoting feature, enabling the unit to swivel 90° and providing a choice between the traditional landscape horizontal mode for Web surfing and the portrait vertical mode for word processing and page-layout programs. LCD panels weigh substantially less than comparably sized CRTs. For example, the ViewSonic VE175, a 17" LCD, weighs only 13.6 lbs., compared to the 50 lbs. weight of typical 19" CRTs.

There have been two major digital LCD panel standards and specifications:

- *The Digital Flat Panel (DFP) standard approved by the Video Electronic Standards Association (VESA) in February 1999.* DFP was previously known as PanelLink; DFP has now been replaced by DVI.

- *The Digital Visual Interface (DVI) standard proposed by the Digital Display Working Group (DDWG) in April 1999.* DVI has become a de facto standard supported by most recent mid-range and high-end VGA display cards, including models with dual-display capabilities.

Figure 15.4 shows how DFP and DVI connectors found on some video cards and digital LCDs compare to the standard VGA connector used on conventional video cards, CRTs, and analog-compatible LCDs.

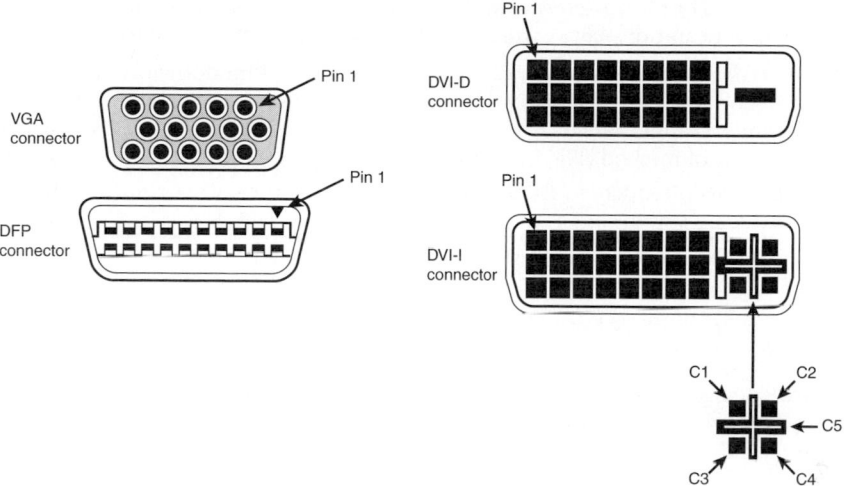

Figure 15.4 Conventional VGA cards, CRTs, and analog-compatible LCDs use the standard VGA connector. Early digital LCDs and their matching video cards often used the DFP connector. Most recent digital LCD panels use the DVI-D connector, whereas video cards used with both analog and digital displays use the DVI-I connector.

Before you rush to the store to purchase an LCD desktop monitor, you should consider several potential drawbacks:

- *If you routinely switch display resolutions (as Web developers do to preview their work), LCD monitors must take one of two approaches to change resolutions.* Some older units might reduce the onscreen image to occupy only the pixels of the new resolution, thus using only a portion of a typical 1024×768 LCD panel to display a 640×480 image, whereas newer units might scale the image to occupy the entire screen. Scaling is becoming common because the Digital Display Work Group standard for LCD desktop displays specifies that the scaling must take place in the display panel, the graphics controller, or both places. Look at the quality of a scaled image if using different resolutions is important to you.

- *If you choose an analog LCD panel, you'll usually save money and be able to use your existing video card or onboard video port.* However, image quality for both text and graphics can suffer because of the conversion of the computer's digital signal to analog (at the video card) and back to digital again (inside the LCD panel). The conversion can lead to pixel jitter or pixel swim, in which adjacent LCD cells are turned on and off by the display's incapability to determine which cells should stay on and stay off. Most panels come with adjustment software to reduce this display-quality problem, but you might not be able to eliminate it entirely.

- *Digital LCD panels avoid conversion problems when attached to a digital-compatible display card.* However, most low-cost, off-the-shelf display cards don't support digital signals yet, and the onboard video circuits built into some motherboards don't support DVI yet.

Note

Video card and chipset makers, such as NVIDIA, Matrox, and ATI, have added support for digital and analog display panels to most of their recent 3D chipsets and video cards. Check the specifications for a particular video card to verify support.

- *High-quality LCD panels of either digital or analog type are great for displaying sharp text and graphics.* But they often can't display as wide a range of very light and very dark colors as CRTs can.

- *Many LCDs don't react as quickly as CRTs.* This can cause full-motion video, full-screen 3D games, and animation to look smeared onscreen. To avoid this problem, look for LCDs that offer a response time of 16ms or faster. Some LCDs now have response times as low as 12ms. These displays use an improved control method called feed forward driving (FFD) technology developed by Mitsubishi.

Note

Instead of applying the same voltage level to LCD cells when the image changes, FFD uses the optimum voltage level for each cell when it changes. Because cells require different voltage levels depending on the shade needed, FFD displays reduce blur by improving display performance. FFD displays first became available at retail late in 2002.

Thanks to price decreases, larger panel sizes, improved performance, and widespread support for DVI digital connectors on current video cards, this is the best time ever to consider buying an LCD panel for your desktop PC.

Be sure that you use the following criteria when you consider purchasing an LCD monitor:

- *Evaluate the panel both at its native resolution and at any other resolutions you plan to use.*

- *If you're considering a digital LCD panel, determine whether your existing video card supports the features you need.* Features you might find necessary include OpenGL and high-speed 3D support (for gaming), VGA-to-TV support (for video producers), and DVD playback software (for watching DVD movies). Because most mid-range and high-end video cards based on the latest NVIDIA and ATI chipsets do offer a DVI port for connection with current and forthcoming digital LCD panels, you can upgrade to a high-performance video card that will support your display. Even though some notebook computers now support DVI displays, most still feature only analog VGA connectors.

- *Look for displays that support both analog and DVI inputs if you want to use the same display on different systems.* Because LCD panels are much lighter and smaller than normal CRT displays, they're a natural choice for connecting to both desktop and notebook computers. If you use multiple computers in a small work area, you might also want to look for displays that support multiple inputs, which enables you to connect two computers to one screen.

- *Make sure your system has a suitable expansion slot for the recommended video card type.* Many low-cost systems today feature onboard AGP video but no AGP slot, which can't be upgraded unless the user opts for the obsolescent (for video) PCI slot. As the move to LCD panels continues, more of these systems should feature built-in support for LCDs, but this could be a problem for some time to come.

Note

Although many recent chipsets with integrated video—such as NVIDIA's nForce2; ATI's Radeon IGP; and Intel's 865G, 845G, and 845GE—feature DVI support, most motherboards using these chipsets do not provide a built-in DVI port. Instead, an optional add-on card that plugs in to the AGP slot is used to enable DVI support. Otherwise, the onboard video can be disabled and replaced with a dual-display video card with VGA and DVI ports.

- *Evaluate the panel and card combo's performance on video clips and animation if you work with full-motion video, animated presentation programs, or games.*

- *Although active-matrix (analog) and digital LCD monitors have much wider viewing areas than do passive-matrix and dual-scan LCD panels used in older notebook computers, their viewing angles are still usually much less than CRTs.* This is an important consideration if you're planning to use your LCD monitor for group presentations. To improve the horizontal viewing area, several vendors have developed patented improvements to the basic TFT display, such as Hitachi's in-plane switching (IPS), Fujitsu's multidomain vertical adjustment (MVA), and Mitsubishi's FFD—all of which have been licensed to other leading LCD makers.

■ *A high-contrast ratio (luminance difference between white and black) makes for sharper text and vivid colors.* A typical CRT has a contrast ratio of about 245:1. Although LCD panels in the May 23, 2000 *PC Magazine* test had contrast ratios ranging from a low of 186:1 to a high of 370:1, newer LCD panels have even higher contrast ratios (up to 400:1). Panels could be viewed at an average horizontal angle of as much as 129° without loss of contrast.

■ *Features such as integrated speakers and Universal Serial Bus (USB) hubs are pleasant additions, but your eyes should make the final decision about which panel is best for you.* Because reviews of LCD panels often don't provide detailed analysis of horizontal and vertical viewing angles and contrast ratios, check display units in stores yourself. Be sure to view the displays from several angles. If you're adding the panel as a second display, be sure to check its off-axis image quality.

■ *Look for pivoting displays that enable you to rotate the display to match an upright page layout if you use your computer for text-editing or page layout.* This feature is supported by many LCD panels—particularly those that are 17" or larger—but the display performance in portrait mode is usually lower than in normal landscape mode, especially for rapid motion. If possible, test the display in portrait mode if you plan to use this mode frequently.

LCD and DLP Projectors

Originally, data projectors were intended for use in boardrooms and training facilities. However, with the rise of home theater systems, the increasing popularity of working from home, and major price reductions and improvements in projector technology, portable projectors are an increasingly popular alternative to large-screen TVs and plasma displays. They can be used with Windows XP Media Center PCs and video players as well as their traditional partners, conventional laptop and desktop computers.

Two technologies are used in the construction of data projectors:

■ Liquid crystal display (LCD)

■ Digital light processing (DLP)

Instead of using triads of subpixels as in a flat-panel or portable LCD, an LCD projector works by separating white light into red, green, and blue wavelengths and directing each wavelength through a corresponding LCD panel. Each LCD panel's pixels are opened or closed according to the signals received from the signal source (computer, DVD, or video player) and are combined into a single RGB image that is projected onto the screen.

LCD projectors are relatively low in cost (some 800×600 SVGA models are available for under $1,000) but require some cool-down time before they can be stored.

The other major technology for presentation and home theater projectors uses Texas Instruments' own digital light processing (DLP) technology. DLP projectors use a combination of a rapidly spinning color wheel and a microprocessor-controlled array of tiny mirrors known as a *digital micromirror device (DMD)*. Each mirror in a DMD corresponds to a pixel, and the mirrors reflect light toward or away from the projector optics. Depending on how frequently the mirrors are switched on, the image varies from white (always on) to black (never on) through as many as 1,024 gray shades. The color wheel provides color data to complete the projected image. Compared to LCD projectors, DLP projectors are more compact, are lighter, and cool down more quickly after use; however, they are more expensive.

Figure 15.5 illustrates how a DLP-based processor produces the image.

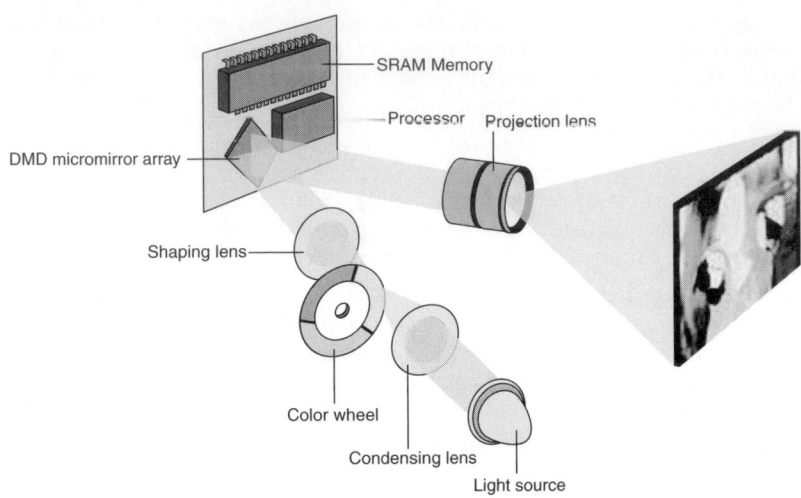

SRAM Memory

Processor Projection lens

DMD micromirror array

Shaping lens

Color wheel

Condensing lens

Light source

Figure 15.5 How a typical DLP projector works.

The earliest DLP projectors used a simple three-color (RGB) wheel, as shown in Figure 15.5. However, more recent models have used a four-segment (RGB and clear) or a six-segment (RGBRGB) wheel to improve picture quality.

Note

For more information about digital light processing, see the official Texas Instruments Web site about DLP technology at http://www.dlp.com.

Plasma Displays

Plasma, the latest technology for large wide-screen displays, actually has a long history. In the late 1980s, IBM developed a monochrome plasma screen that displayed orange text and graphics on a black background. Toshiba used this display in its T3100 and T3200 laptop computers, which featured double-scan CGA/AT&T 6300-compatible 640×400 graphics.

Unlike the early IBM monochrome plasma screen, today's plasma displays are RGB devices capable of displaying 24-bit or 32-bit color, TV, or DVD signals. Plasma screens produce an image by using electrically charged gas (plasma) to illuminate triads of red, green, and blue phosphors, as shown in Figure 15.6.

The display and address electrodes create a grid that enables each subpixel to be individually addressed. By adjusting the differences in charge between the display and address electrodes for each triad's subpixels, the signal source controls the picture.

Typical plasma screens range in size from 42" to 50" or larger. Because they are primarily designed for use with DVD, TV, or HDTV video sources, their resolution is typically 852×480 with a 16:9 aspect ratio (some 50" units have 1366×768 resolution WXGA resolution). Although 852×480 is too low for mainstream computer applications, many displays can accept VGA and DVI inputs as well as S-video or composite inputs, so they can be used with a PC for DVD or similar entertainment applications.

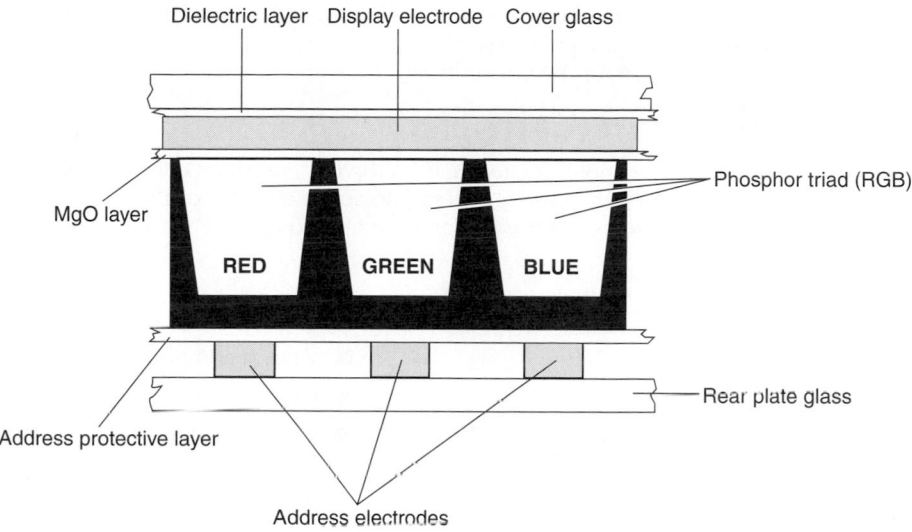

Figure 15.6 A cross-section of a typical plasma display.

Video Adapter Types

A monitor requires a source of input. The signals that run to your monitor come from a video adapter inside or plugged into your computer.

The three ways computer systems connect to either CRT or LCD panels are as follows:

- *Add-on video cards.* This method requires the use of an AGP or a PCI expansion slot but provides the highest possible level of performance, the greatest amount of memory, and the largest choice of features.

- *Video-only chipset on motherboard.* Performance is generally less than with add-on video cards because older chipset designs are often used. Although many systems with the LPX design used this type of video, it has fallen out of fashion on recent systems. Mid-range and high-end note-book computers typically use a discrete video chip instead of integrated video.

- *Motherboard chipset with integrated video.* This has the lowest cost of any video solution, but performance can also be very low, especially for 3D gaming or other graphics-intensive applications. Resolution and color-depth options are also more limited than those available with add-on video cards. However, new motherboard chipset designs from video-chipset makers such as NVIDIA (nForce, nForce2, and nForce3 series) and ATI (RADEON IGP) perform significantly better than other motherboard chipsets but still achieve results comparable to low-end add-on video cards. Most low-end and some mid-range notebooks use this type of video instead of a discrete video chip on the motherboard.

Most systems that use Baby-AT or ATX motherboards typically use add-on video cards, whereas the obsolete LPX, the new Mini-ITX, and most current NLX and Micro-ATX motherboards typically use some type of motherboard-based video. Many of the most recent low-cost computers built on the Micro-ATX, Flex-ATX, NLX, or Mini-ITX form factor use motherboard chipsets that integrate video from Intel, NVIDIA, VIA, or other vendors. Systems with integrated video (either with video chipsets or motherboard chipsets that include video) usually can be upgraded with an add-on video card, but some do not include an AGP slot, which is best suited for high-speed video today.

▶▶ See "Integrated Video/Motherboard Chipsets," p. 898.

▶▶ See "3D Chipsets," p. 922.

The term *video adapter* applies to either integrated or separate video circuitry. The term *graphics adapter* is essentially interchangeable with *video adapter* because all video options developed since the original IBM monochrome display adapter (MDA) can display graphics as well as text.

Monitor Selection Criteria

Stores offer a dizzying variety of monitor choices, from the low-cost units bundled with computers to large-screen tubes that cost more than many systems. Because a monitor can account for a large part of the price of your computer system, you need to know what to look for when you shop for a monitor.

Important factors to consider include:

- Viewable image size
- Resolution
- Dot pitch (CRTs)
- Image brightness and contrast (LCDs)

- Power management and safety certifications
- Vertical and horizontal frequencies
- Picture controls
- Environmental issues (lighting, size, weight)

This section helps you understand these issues so you can make a wise choice for your next display, regardless of the display technology you prefer.

The Right Size

CRT-based monitors come in various sizes ranging from 15" to 42" diagonal measure. The larger the monitor, the higher the price tag—after you get beyond 19" displays, the prices skyrocket. The most common CRT monitor sizes are 17", 19", and 21". These diagonal measurements, unfortunately, often represent not the size of the actual image the screen displays, but the size of the tube. Refer to Table 15.1 to see how CRT monitors' viewing areas compare to LCDs' actual sizes.

As a result, comparing one company's 17" CRT monitor to that of another might be unfair unless you actually measure the active screen area. The active screen area refers to the diagonal measure of the lighted area on the screen. In other words, if you are running Windows, the viewing area is the actual diagonal measure of the desktop.

This area can vary widely from monitor to monitor, so one company's 17" monitor can display a 16" image, and another company's 17" monitor can present a 15 1/2" image. Typically, you can expect to lose 1"–1 1/2" from the diagonal screen size to the actual active viewing area. Consult the monitor's packaging, advertising, or manufacturer's Web site for precise information for a given model. For example, ViewSonic lists the size of its G73f CRT monitor as the following: 17" (16.0" VIS [viewable image size]). I recommend that you concern yourself with the VIS, not the tube size, when you select a CRT monitor.

Note

Most CRTs currently on the market are 17" in size or larger; 17" has become the current standard, with 19" CRTs becoming much more common since the prices have dropped below $400.

You can adjust many better-quality CRT monitors to display a high-quality image that completely fills the tube from edge to edge. Less-expensive monitors can fill the screen also, but some of them do so only by pushing the monitor beyond its comfortable limits. The result is a distorted image that is worse than the monitor's smaller, properly adjusted picture.

In most cases today, the 17" CRT monitor is the best bargain in the industry. A 17" monitor is recommended for new systems, especially when running Windows, and is not much more expensive than a 15" display. I recommend a 17" monitor as the minimum you should consider for most normal applications. Displays of 19"–21" or larger are recommended for high-end systems, especially in situations where graphics applications are the major focus.

Note

One of the many reasons I don't recommend low-cost computers sold by major retail stores is because they often are bundled with low-quality CRT or LCD monitors. Although 15" CRT monitors are now less common than 17" CRT monitors, many bundled monitors in either size have lower refresh rates, are bulkier, or have other deficiencies compared to high-quality third-party monitors. If you buy the computer and monitor separately, you have a wider choice of displays and can get one of higher quality. You can also opt for an LCD if space, rather than cost, is a major factor. Note that some vendors who make or sell both computers and LCDs, such as Sony and HP, now bundle some of their computer models with LCDs.

Larger monitors are particularly handy for applications such as CAD and desktop publishing, in which the smallest details must be clearly visible. With a 17" or larger display, you can see nearly an entire 8 1/2"×11" print page in 100% view; in other words, what you see onscreen virtually matches the page that will be printed. Being able to see the entire page at its actual size can save you the trouble of printing several drafts of a document or project to get it right.

With the popularity of the Internet, monitor size and resolution become even more of an issue. Many Web pages are designed for 800×600 or higher resolutions. Whereas a 15" monitor can handle 800×600 fairly well, a 17" monitor set to 1024×768 resolution enables you to comfortably view any Web site without eyestrain (if the monitor supports 75Hz or higher refresh rates) or excessive scrolling.

Note

Although many monitors smaller than 17" are physically capable of running at 1024×768 and even higher resolutions, most people have trouble reading print at that size. A partial solution is to enable large icons in the Windows Display properties (right-click your desktop and select Properties). In Windows 98/Me/2000/XP, select Effects, Use Large Icons. Windows 95 doesn't have an option to enlarge only the icons; you can use the Settings tab to select Large Fonts, but some programs will not work properly with font sizes larger than the default Small Fonts setting.

Wide-Screen Monitors for Media Center PCs

A number of manufacturers are now shipping wide-screen (16×9 aspect ratio) LCD TV displays that include TV tuners, AV inputs, built-in speakers, and VGA/DVI ports at sizes up to 30". Compared to conventional LCD displays (refer to Table 15.1), these units have relatively low resolution for the panel size: 1280×768 (WXGA) is typical. However, these displays are intended primarily for home-entertainment applications such as Windows XP Media Center PCs or DVD and VCR playback. At the longer viewing distances used for TV and video viewing, the resolution is adequate.

Wide-screen plasma TVs that include VGA/DVI ports can also be used with Media Center PCs as well as other video sources. These units range in size up to 50" and feature HD-ready resolutions of 852×480 (up to 46") or 1366×768 (50").

Resolution

Resolution is the amount of detail a monitor can render. This quantity is expressed in the number of horizontal and vertical picture elements, or *pixels*, contained in the screen. The greater the number of pixels, the more detailed the images. The resolution required depends on the application. Character-based applications (such as DOS command-line programs) require little resolution, whereas graphics-intensive applications (such as desktop publishing and Windows software) require a great deal.

It's important to realize that CRTs are designed to handle a range of resolutions natively, but LCD panels (both desktop and notebook) are built to run a single native resolution and must scale to other choices. Older LCD panels handled scaling poorly, but even though current LCD panels perform scaling better, the best results with various resolutions are still found with CRTs.

As PC video technology developed, the screen resolutions video adapters support grew at a steady pace. Table 15.2 shows standard resolutions used in PC graphics adapters and displays and the terms commonly used to describe them.

Table 15.2   Graphics Display Resolution Standards

Display Standard	Linear Pixels (H×V)	Total Pixels	Aspect Ratio
CGA	320×200	64,000	1.60
EGA	640×350	224,000	1.83
VGA	640×480	307,200	1.33
WVGA	854×480	409,920	1.78
SVGA	800×600	480,000	1.33
XGA	1024×768	786,432	1.33
XGA+	1152×864	995,328	1.33
WXGA	1280×800	1,024,000	1.60
WXGA+	1440×900	1,296,000	1.60
SXGA	1280×1024	1,310,720	1.25
SXGA+	1400×1050	1,470,000	1.33
WSXGA	1600×1024	1,638,400	1.56
WSXGA+	1680×1050	1,764,000	1.60
UXGA	1600×1200	1,920,000	1.33
HDTV	1920×1080	2,073,600	1.78
WUXGA	1920×1200	2,304,000	1.60
QXGA	2048×1536	3,145,728	1.33
QSXGA	2560×2048	5,242,880	1.25
QUXGA-W	3840×2400	9,216,000	1.60

Aspect ratios:
1.25 = 5:4
1.33 = 4:3
1.56 = 25:16

1.60 = 16:10
1.78 = 16:9
1.83 = 11:6
W = Wide-screen (aspect ratios wider than 1.33)

The Color Graphics Adapter (CGA) and Enhanced Graphics Adapter (EGA) cards and monitors were the first PC graphics standards in the early to mid-1980s. The Video Graphics Array (VGA) standard was released by IBM in April 1987, and all the subsequent resolutions and modes introduced since then have been based on it in one way or another. VGA mode is still in common use as a reference to the standard 640×480 16-color display that most versions of the Windows operating systems use as their default; Windows XP, however, defaults to SVGA mode, which is 800×600. The 15-pin connector through which you connect the analog display to most video adapters is also often called a *VGA port*. A newer 20-pin connector is used for DFP-compatible LCD panels. A larger 24-pin connector is used on DVI-D displays, whereas DVI-I displays use a 29-pin version of the DVI-D connector (refer to Figure 15.4).

Nearly all video adapters sold today support SXGA (1280×1024) resolutions at several color depths, and many support UXGA (1600×1200) and higher as well. Typically, in addition to the highest setting your card and display will support, any lower settings are automatically supported as well.

Because all CRT and most new and upcoming LCDs can handle various resolutions, you have a choice. As you'll see later in this chapter, the combinations of resolution and color depth (number of colors onscreen) you can choose might be limited by how much RAM your graphics adapter has onboard or, if you have motherboard chipset-based video, how much system memory is allocated to your video function. If you switch to a larger display and you can't set the color depth you want to use, a new video card with more RAM is a desirable upgrade. Video cards once featured upgradeable memory, but this is no longer an option with current models.

Which resolution do you want for your display? Generally, the higher the resolution, the larger the display you will want. Why? Because Windows icons and text use a constant number of pixels, higher display resolutions make these screen elements a smaller part of the desktop onscreen. By using a larger display (17" or larger), you can use higher resolution settings and still have text and icons that are readable.

To understand this issue, you might want to try various resolutions on your system. As you change from 800×600 to 1024×768 and beyond, you'll notice several changes to the appearance of your screen.

At 800×600 or less, text and onscreen icons are very large. Because the screen elements used for the Windows desktop and software menus are at a fixed pixel width and height, you'll notice that they shrink in size onscreen as you change to the higher resolutions. You'll be able to see more of your document or Web page onscreen at the higher resolutions because each object requires less of the screen.

If you are operating at 800×600 resolution, for example, you should find a 15" monitor to be comfortable. At 1024×768, you probably will find that the display of a 15" monitor is too small; therefore, you will probably prefer to use a larger one, such as a 17" monitor. Table 15.3 shows the smallest monitors I recommend to properly display the resolutions users typically select.

Table 15.3   Recommended Resolutions for CRT and LCD Displays

Resolution	Minimum Recommended CRT Monitor	Minimum Recommended LCD Panel
800×600	15"	15"
1024×768	17"	15"
1280×1024	19"	17"
1600×1200	21"	18"

If you compare the recommended resolutions in Table 15.3 with those listed in Table 15.1, you'll notice that the recommended resolutions are not necessarily the limits of a given monitor's capabilities. However, I recommend these resolutions to help ensure a comfortable computing experience. On small monitors set to high resolutions, characters, icons, and other information are too small for most users and can cause eyestrain. Low-cost CRT monitors and those bundled with many systems often produce blurry results when set to their maximum resolution and often have low refresh rates at their highest resolution. Low refresh rates cause screen flicker, leading to increased eyestrain.

Whereas CRTs can produce poor-quality results at very high resolutions, LCDs are always crisp and perfectly focused by nature. Also, the dimensions advertised for the LCD screens represent the exact size of the viewable image, unlike most conventional CRT-based monitors. In addition, the LCD is so crisp that screens of a given size can easily handle resolutions that are higher than what would otherwise be acceptable on a CRT.

For example, many of the high-end notebook systems now use 14" or 15" LCD panels that feature SXGA+ (1400×1050) or even UXGA (1600×1200) resolution. Although these resolutions would be unacceptable on a CRT display of the same size, they work well on the LCD panel built in to the laptop because of the crystal-clear image and because you generally sit closer to a laptop display. In fact, it is for this reason that such high resolutions might not work on desktop LCD panels unless they are larger 17" or 18" models.

Dot Pitch (CRTs)

Another important specification that denotes the quality of a given CRT monitor is its dot pitch, which is controlled by the design of the shadow mask or aperture grille inside the CRT. A *shadow mask* is a metal plate built into the front area of the CRT, next to the phosphor layers. It has thousands of holes that are used to help focus the beam from each electron gun so that it illuminates only one correctly colored phosphor dot at a time. Because of the immense speed of screen rewriting (60–85 times per second), all dots appear to be illuminated at the same time. The mask prevents the electron gun from illuminating the wrong dots.

In a monochrome monitor, the picture element is a screen phosphor, but in a color monitor, the picture element is a phosphor triad—which is a group of three phosphor dots (red, green, and blue). Dot pitch, which applies only to color monitors, is the distance (in millimeters) between phosphor triads, measured from the center of a phosphor dot in a given triad to the same color phosphor dot in the next triad. Screens with a small dot pitch have a smaller space between the phosphor triads. As a result, the picture elements are closer together, producing a sharper picture onscreen. Conversely, screens with a large dot pitch tend to produce images that are less clear. Figure 15.7 illustrates dot pitch.

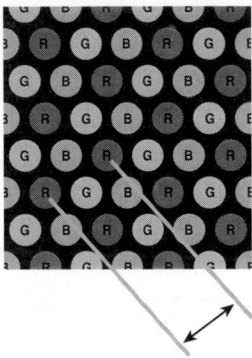

Figure 15.7 Dot pitch is the distance between each group (triad) of red, green, and blue (RGB) phosphors. A smaller dot pitch helps produce sharper, clearer images.

Note

Dot pitch is not an issue with LCD portable or desktop display panels because of their designs, which use transistors rather than phosphor triads.

The original IBM PC color monitor had a dot pitch of .43mm, which is considered to be poor by almost any standard. Smaller pitch values indicate sharper images. Most recent monitors have a dot pitch between .25mm and .30mm, with state-of-the-art monitors down to .24mm or less. To avoid grainy images, look for a dot pitch of .26mm or smaller. Be wary of monitors with anything larger than a .28mm dot pitch; they lack clarity for fine text and graphics. Although you can save money by buying monitors with smaller tubes or a higher dot pitch, the trade-off isn't worth it.

Monitors based on Sony's Trinitron picture tubes and Mitsubishi's DiamondTron picture tubes use an aperture grille, which uses vertical stripes (rather than a shadow mask) to separate red, green, and blue phosphors. This produces a brighter picture, although the stabilizing wires shown in Figure 15.8 are visible on close examination. Monitors using an aperture grille–type picture tube use a stripe pitch measurement instead of dot pitch. An aperture grille monitor stripe pitch of .25mm is comparable to a .27mm dot pitch on a conventional monitor.

Some of NEC's monitors use a variation on the aperture grille called the slotted mask, which is brighter than standard shadow-mask monitors and more mechanically stable than aperture grille–based monitors (see Figure 15.8).

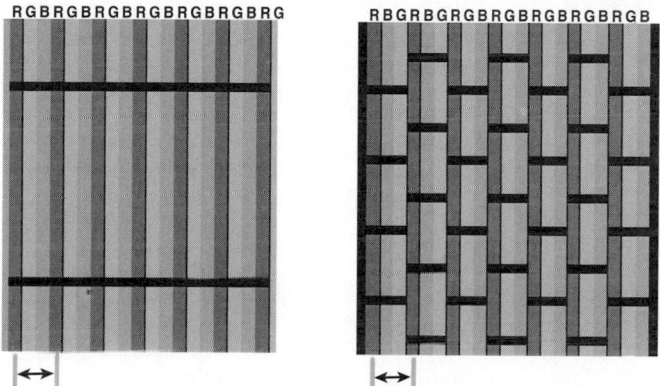

Figure 15.8 Aperture-grille picture tubes (left) have their phosphors arranged in vertical stripes with one or two reinforcing wires, depending on CRT size. NEC's CromaClear slotted mask picture tube design (right) provides many of the benefits of both the shadow-mask and aperture-grille designs.

The dot pitch or stripe pitch measurement is one of the most important specifications of any monitor, but it is not the only specification. You might find the image on a monitor with a slightly higher dot pitch superior to that of a monitor with a lower dot pitch. There is no substitute for actually looking at images and text on the monitors you're considering purchasing.

Image Brightness and Contrast (LCD Panels)

As previously mentioned, dot pitch is not a factor in deciding which LCD panel to purchase. Although it's a consideration that applies to both LCDs and CRTs, the brightness of a display is especially important in judging the quality of an LCD panel.

Although a dim CRT display is almost certainly a sign of either improper brightness control or a dying monitor, brightness in LCD panels can vary a great deal from one model to another. Brightness for LCD panels is measured in candelas per square meter, which is abbreviated "nt" and pronounced as a *nit*. Typical ratings for good display panels are between 200 and 400 nits, but the brighter the better. A good combination is a rating of 250 nits or higher and a contrast rating of 300:1 or higher.

Note

When you evaluate an LCD TV monitor, be sure to note the brightness settings available in computer mode and TV mode. Many of these displays provide a brighter picture in TV mode than in computer mode.

Interlaced Versus Noninterlaced

Monitors and video adapters can support interlaced or noninterlaced resolution. In *noninterlaced* (conventional) mode, the electron beam sweeps the screen in lines from top to bottom, one line after the other, completing the screen in one pass. In *interlaced* mode, the electron beam also sweeps the screen from top to bottom, but it does so in two passes—sweeping the odd lines first and the even lines second. Each pass takes half the time of a full pass in noninterlaced mode. Early high-resolution monitors, such as the IBM 8514/A, used interlacing to reach their maximum resolutions, but all recent and current high-resolution (1,024×768 and higher) monitors are noninterlaced, avoiding the slow screen response and flicker caused by interlacing.

For more information about interlaced displays, see "Interlaced Versus Noninterlaced" in Chapter 15 of *Upgrading and Repairing PCs, 12th Edition,* included in electronic form on the disc accompanying this book.

Energy and Safety

Monitors, like virtually all power-consuming computer devices, have been designed to save energy for a number of years. Virtually all monitors sold in recent years have earned the Environmental Protection Agency's Energy Star logo by reducing their current draw to 30 watts or less when idle. Power-management features in the monitor, as well as controls provided in the system BIOS and in the latest versions of Windows, help monitors and other types of computing devices use less power.

▶▶ For more information about power management, see Chapter 21, "Power Supply and Chassis/Case," p. 1151.

Power Management

One of the first energy-saving standards for monitors was VESA's Display Power-Management Signaling (DPMS) spec, which defined the signals a computer sends to a monitor to indicate idle times. The computer or video card decides when to send these signals.

In Windows 9x/Me/2000/XP, you must enable this feature if you want to use it because it's turned off by default. To enable it in Windows 9x/Me, open the Display properties in the Control Panel, switch to the Screen Saver tab, and make sure the Energy Star Low-Power settings and Monitor Shutdown settings are checked. You can adjust how long the system remains idle before the monitor picture is blanked or the monitor shuts down completely. Use the Power icon in Windows 2000/XP to set power management for the monitor and other peripherals. You can also access power management by selecting the Screen Saver tab on the Display properties sheet and clicking the Power button.

Intel and Microsoft jointly developed the Advanced Power Management (APM) specification, which defines a BIOS-based interface between hardware that is capable of power-management functions and an operating system that implements power-management policies. In short, this means you can configure an OS such as Windows 9x to switch your monitor into a low-power mode after an interval of nonuse and even to shut it off entirely. For these actions to occur, however, the monitor, system BIOS, and operating system must all support the APM standard.

With Windows 98, Windows Me, Windows 2000, and Windows XP, Microsoft introduced a more comprehensive power-management method called Advanced Configuration and Power Interface (ACPI). ACPI also works with displays, hard drives, and other devices supported by APM and allows the computer to automatically turn peripherals, such as CD-ROMs, network cards, hard disk drives, and printers, on and off. It also enables the computer to turn consumer devices connected to the PC, such as VCRs, televisions, telephones, and stereos, on and off.

Although APM compatibility has been standard in common BIOSs for several years, a number of computers from major manufacturers required BIOS upgrades to add ACPI support when Windows 98 was introduced.

Note

ACPI support is installed on Windows 98, Windows Me, Windows 2000, and Windows XP computers *only* if an ACPI-compliant BIOS is present when either version of Windows is first installed. If an ACPI-compliant BIOS is installed after the initial Windows installation, it is ignored. Fortunately, both versions of Windows still support APM as well. See Microsoft's FAQ for ACPI on the Microsoft Web site.

Use Table 15.4 to select the most appropriate DPMS power-management setting(s) for your needs. Most recent systems enable you to select separate values for standby (which saves minimal amounts of power) and for monitor power-down (which saves more power but requires the user to wait several seconds for the monitor to power back up).

Table 15.4   Display Power Management Signaling

State	Horizontal	Vertical	Video	Power Savings	Recovery Time
On	Pulses	Pulses	Active	None	n/a
Stand-By	No Pulses	Pulses	Blanked	Minimal	Short
Suspend	Pulses	No Pulses	Blanked	Substantial	Longer
Off	No Pulses	No Pulses	Blanked	Maximum	System Dependent

Virtually all monitors with power management features meet the requirements of the United States EPA's Energy Star labeling program, which requires that monitor power usage be reduced to 15 watts or less in standby mode. However, some current monitors also comply with the far more stringent Energy 2000 (E2000) standard developed in Switzerland. E2000 requires that monitors use less than 5 watts when in standby mode.

Emissions

Another trend in green monitor design is to minimize the user's exposure to potentially harmful electromagnetic fields. Several medical studies indicate that these electromagnetic emissions can cause health problems, such as miscarriages, birth defects, and cancer. The risk might be low, but if you spend a third of your day (or more) in front of a computer monitor, that risk is increased.

The concern is that VLF (very low frequency) and ELF (extremely low frequency) emissions might affect the body. These two emissions come in two forms: electric and magnetic. Some research indicates that ELF magnetic emissions are more threatening than VLF emissions because they interact with the natural electric activity of body cells. Monitors are not the only culprits; significant ELF emissions also come from electric blankets and power lines.

Note

ELF and VLF are a form of electromagnetic radiation; they consist of radio frequencies below those used for normal radio broadcasting.

The standards shown in Table 15.5 have been established to regulate emissions and other aspects of monitor operations. Even though these standards originated with Swedish organizations, they are recognized and supported throughout the world.

Table 15.5   Monitor Emissions Standards

Standard Name	Established by	Date Established	Regulates	Notes
MPR I	SWEDAC[1]	1987	Monitor emissions	Replaced by MPR II
MPR II	SWEDAC[1]	1990	Monitor emissions	Added maximums for ELF and VLF; minimum standard in recent monitors
TCO[2]	TCO[2]	1992, 1995, 1999, 2003		Tighter monitor emissions limits than MPR- II; power management TCO '95, '99, and '03 add other classes of devices to the TCO standard

1. The Swedish Board for Accreditation and Conformity Assessment
2. Swedish abbreviation for the Swedish Confederation of Professional Employees

Today, virtually all monitors on the market support TCO standards.

If you aren't using a low-emission monitor yet, you can take other steps to protect yourself. The most important is to stay at arm's length (about 28 inches) from the front of your monitor. When you move a couple of feet away, ELF magnetic emission levels usually drop to those of a typical office with fluorescent lights. Likewise, monitor emissions are weakest at the front of a monitor, so stay at least 3 feet from the sides and backs of nearby monitors and 5 feet from any photocopiers, which are also strong sources of ELF.

Electromagnetic emissions should not be your only concern; you also should be concerned about screen glare. In fact, some of the antiglare panels that fit in front of a monitor screen not only reduce eyestrain, but also cut ELF and VLF emissions.

Note that because plasma and LCD panels don't use electron guns or magnets, they don't produce ELF emissions.

Frequencies

One essential buying decision is to choose a monitor that works with your selected video adapter. Today, virtually all monitors are multiple-frequency (also called multiscanning and multifrequency) units that accommodate a range of standards, including those that are not yet standardized. However, big differences exist in how well various monitors cope with various video adapters.

Tip

High-quality monitors retain their value longer than most other computer components. Although it's common for a newer, faster processor to come out right after you have purchased your computer or to find the same model with a bigger hard disk for the same money, a good quality monitor should outlast your computer. If you purchase a unit with the expectation that your own personal requirements will grow over the years, you might be able to save money on your next system by reusing your old monitor.

Some useful features include the following:

- Front-mounted digital controls that can memorize screen settings
- Onscreen programmability to enable you to precisely set desired values for screen size and position
- Self-test mode, which displays a picture even when your monitor is not receiving a signal from the computer

With multiple-frequency CRT monitors, you must match the range of horizontal and vertical frequencies the monitor accepts with those generated by your video adapter. The wider the range of signals, the more expensive—and more versatile—the monitor. Your video adapter's vertical and horizontal frequencies must fall within the ranges your monitor supports. The vertical frequency (or refresh/frame rate) determines the stability of your image (the higher the vertical frequency, the better). Typical vertical frequencies range from 50Hz to 160Hz, but multiple-frequency monitors support different vertical frequencies at different resolutions. You might find that a bargain monitor has a respectable 120Hz vertical frequency at 640×480 but drops to a less desirable 66Hz at 1280×1024. The horizontal frequency (or line rate) typically ranges from 31.5KHz to 90KHz or more. By default, most video adapters use a 60Hz default vertical scan frequency to avoid monitor damage.

Although LCD monitors use lower vertical frequencies than CRTs, they avoid problems with screen flicker because of their design. Because they use transistors to activate all the pixels in the image at once, as opposed to a scanning electron beam that must work its way from the top to the bottom of the screen to create an image, LCD panels never flicker.

Refresh Rates (Vertical Scan Frequency)

The *refresh rate* (also called the vertical scan frequency) is the rate at which the screen display is rewritten. This is measured in hertz. A refresh rate of 72Hz means that the screen is refreshed 72 times per second. A refresh rate that is too low causes CRT screens to flicker, contributing to eyestrain. The higher the refresh rate you use with a CRT display, the better for your eyes and your comfort during long sessions at the computer.

A *flicker-free refresh rate* is a refresh rate high enough to prevent you from seeing any flicker. The flicker-free refresh rate varies with the resolution of your monitor setting (higher resolutions require higher refresh rates) and must be matched by both your monitor and display card. Because a refresh rate that is too high can slow down your video display, use the lowest refresh rate that is comfortable for you.

One important factor to consider when purchasing a CRT monitor is the refresh rate, especially if you are planning to use the monitor at 1024×768 or higher resolutions. Low-cost monitors sometimes have refresh rates that are too low to achieve flicker-free performance for most users and thus can lead to eyestrain.

Table 15.6 compares two typical 17" CRT monitors and a typical mid-range graphics card.

Note the differences in the refresh rates supported by the ATI RADEON 9000 Pro and two 17" CRT monitors from ViewSonic: the E70 and P75f.

The E70 sells for around $130, and the P75f+ sells for about $185. The P75f+ offers flicker-free refresh rates at higher resolutions than the cheaper E70.

Although the ATI RADEON 9000 Pro video card supports higher refresh rates than either monitor, these rates can't be used safely. Use of video adapter refresh rates in excess of the monitor's maximum refresh rate can damage the monitor!

Table 15.6   Refresh Rates Comparison

| | Refresh Rates | | |
Resolution	ATI Radeon 9000 Pro	Viewsonic E70	Viewsonic P75f+
1024×768	60Hz–200Hz*	87Hz*	85Hz*
1280×1024	60Hz–160Hz*	66Hz	89Hz*
1600×1200	60Hz–120Hz*	Not supported	77Hz*

Rates above 72Hz will be flicker-free for many users; the VESA standard for flicker-free refresh is 85Hz or above.

To determine a monitor's refresh rates for the resolutions you're planning to use, check out the monitor manufacturer's Web site.

Note

Many manufacturers use the term *optimal resolution* to refer to the highest CRT monitor resolution that supports the VESA standard for flicker-free viewing (85Hz or higher). I recommend that you consider the monitor's optimal resolution as its highest practical resolution because higher resolutions, which don't support flicker-free viewing, are likely to provide poor visual quality.

During installation, Windows 2000, Windows 98, Windows 95B (OSR 2.x), Windows Me, and Windows XP support Plug and Play (PnP) monitor configuration if both the monitor and video adapter support the Data Display Channel (DDC) feature. When DDC communication is available, the monitor can send signals to the operating system that indicate which refresh rates it supports, as well as other display information; this data is reflected by the Display Properties sheet for that monitor.

Monitors that don't support PnP configuration via DDC can be configured with an .INF (information) file, just as with other Windows-compatible devices. This might be supplied with a setup disk or CD or can be downloaded from the monitor vendor's Web site.

Note

Because CRT monitors are redrawing the screen many times per second, the change in a noninterlaced CRT screen display is virtually invisible to the naked eye, but it is very obvious when computer screens are photographed, filmed, or videotaped. Because these cameras aren't synchronized to the monitor's refresh cycle, it's inevitable that the photo, film, or videotape will show the refresh in progress as a line across the picture.

If you need to capture moving images from a monitor to videotape, use a video card with a TV-out option to send your picture to a VCR. If you need to take still photos of a monitor (for example, to record BIOS/CMOS setup information), use an LCD display instead of a CRT monitor.

In my experience, a 60Hz vertical scan frequency (frame rate) is the minimum anybody should use with a CRT, and even at this frequency, most people notice a flicker. Especially on a larger display, onscreen flicker can cause eyestrain and fatigue. If you can select a frame rate (vertical scan frequency) of 72Hz or higher, most people are not able to discern any flicker; 72Hz is the minimum refresh rate I recommend. Most modern mid-range or better CRT displays easily handle vertical frequencies up to 85Hz or more at resolutions up to 1024×768. This greatly reduces the flicker a user sees. However, note that increasing the frame rate, although it improves the quality of the image, can also slow down the video hardware because it now needs to display each image more times per second. If you're a gamer, slower frame rates can reduce your score. In general, I recommend that you set the lowest frame rate you find comfortable. To adjust the video card's refresh rate with Windows 9x/Me/2000/XP, use the Display icon in Control Panel.

Depending on your flavor of Windows, the refresh rates supported by the video card will appear on one of the Display tabs. Optimal is the default setting, but this really is a "safe" setting for any monitor. Select a refresh rate of at least 72Hz or higher to reduce or eliminate flicker. Click Apply for the new setting to take effect. If you choose a refresh rate other than Optimal, you might see a warning about possible monitor damage. This is a warning you should take seriously, especially if you don't have detailed information about your monitor available. You can literally smoke a monitor if you try to use a refresh rate higher than the monitor is designed to accept. Before you try using a custom refresh rate, do the following:

- Make sure Windows has correctly identified your monitor as either a Plug and Play monitor or by brand and model.
- Check the manual supplied with the monitor (or download the statistics) to determine which refresh rates are supported at a given resolution. As in the example listed earlier in Table 15.6, low-cost monitors often don't support high refresh rates at higher resolutions.

Click OK to try the new setting. The screen changes to show the new refresh rate. If the screen display looks scrambled, wait a few moments and the screen will be restored to the previous value; you'll see a dialog box asking whether you want to keep the new setting. If the display was acceptable, click Yes; otherwise, click No to restore your display. If the screen is scrambled and you can't see your mouse pointer, just press the Enter key on your keyboard because No is the default answer. With some older video drivers, this refresh rate dialog box is not available. Get an updated video driver, or check with the video card vendor for a separate utility program that sets the refresh rate for you.

If you have a scrambled display with a high refresh rate, but you think the monitor should be capable of handling the refresh rate you chose, you might not have the correct monitor selected. To check your Windows 9x/Me/2000/XP monitor selection, check the Display Properties dialog box. If your monitor is listed as Standard VGA, Super VGA, or Default Monitor, Windows is using a generic driver that will work with a wide variety of monitors. However, this generic driver doesn't support refresh rates above 75Hz because some monitors could be damaged by excessive refresh rates.

In some cases, you might need to manually select the correct monitor brand and model in the Windows Display Properties dialog box. If you don't find your brand and model of monitor listed, check with your monitor vendor for a driver specific for your model. After you install it, see whether your monitor will safely support a higher refresh rate.

Horizontal Frequency

Different video resolutions use different horizontal frequencies. For example, the standard VGA resolution of 640×480 requires a horizontal resolution of 31.5KHz, whereas the 800×600 resolution requires a vertical frequency of at least 72Hz and a horizontal frequency of at least 48KHz. The 1024×768 image requires a vertical frequency of 60Hz and a horizontal frequency of 58KHz, and the 1280×1024 resolution requires a vertical frequency of 60Hz and a horizontal frequency of 64KHz. If the vertical frequency increases to 75Hz at 1280×1024, the horizontal frequency must be 80KHz. For a super-crisp display, look for available vertical frequencies of 75Hz or higher and horizontal frequencies of up to 90KHz or more. My favorite 17" NEC monitor supports vertical resolutions of up to 75Hz at 1600×1200 pixels, 117Hz at 1024×768, and 160Hz at 640×480!

Virtually all the analog monitors on the market today are, to one extent or another, multiple-frequency. Because literally hundreds of manufacturers produce thousands of monitor models, it is impractical to discuss the technical aspects of each monitor model in detail. Suffice it to say that before investing in a monitor, you should check the technical specifications to ensure that the monitor meets your needs. If you are looking for a place to start, check out some of the magazines that periodically feature reviews of monitors. If you can't wait for a magazine review, investigate monitors at the Web sites run by any of the following vendors: IBM, Sony, NEC-Mitsubishi, and ViewSonic. Each of these manufacturers creates monitors that set the standards by which other monitors can be judged. Although you typically pay a bit more for these manufacturers' monitors, they offer a known, high level of quality and compatibility, as well as service and support. Note that most monitor companies sell several lines of monitors, varying by refresh rates, CRT type, antiglare coatings, energy efficiency, and warranties. For best results at resolutions of 1024×768 and above, avoid the lowest-cost 17" monitors because these models tend to produce fuzzy onscreen displays with low refresh rates.

Controls

Most of the newer CRT monitors and LCD panels use digital controls instead of analog controls. This has nothing to do with the signals the monitor receives from the computer, but only the controls (or lack of them) on the front panel that enable you to adjust the display. Monitors with digital controls have a built-in menu system that enables you to set parameters such as brightness (which adjusts the black level of the display), contrast (which adjusts the luminance of the display), screen size, vertical and horizontal shifts, color, phase, and focus. A button brings the menu up onscreen, and you use controls to make menu selections and vary the settings. When you complete your adjustments, the monitor saves the settings in nonvolatile RAM (NVRAM) located inside the monitor. This type of memory provides permanent storage for the settings with no battery or other power source. You can unplug the monitor without losing your settings, and you can alter them at any time in the future. Digital controls provide a much higher level of control over the monitor and are highly recommended.

Tip

Digital video engineer Charles Poynton's notes on adjusting brightness and contrast controls provide an excellent tutorial on the use of these often misunderstood monitor adjustments. Find them online at `http://www.vision.ee.ethz.ch/~buc/brechbuehler/mirror/color/Poynton-color.html`.

Digital controls make adjusting CRT monitors suffering from any of the geometry errors shown in Figure 15.9 easy. Before making these adjustments, be sure the vertical and horizontal size and position are correct.

Tip

Get a monitor with positioning and image controls that are easy to reach, preferably on the front of the case. Look for more than just basic contrast and brightness controls; a good monitor should enable you to adjust the width and height of your screen images and the placement of the image on the screen. The monitor should also be equipped with a tilt-swivel stand so you can adjust the monitor to the best angle for your use.

Figure 15.9 Typical geometry errors in CRT monitors; these can be corrected on most models that have digital picture controls.

Although LCD panels aren't affected by geometry errors as CRT monitors can be, they can have their own set of image-quality problems, especially if they use the typical 15-pin analog VGA video connector. Pixel jitter and pixel swim (in which adjacent pixels turn on and off) are relatively common problems that occur when using an LCD monitor connected to your PC with an analog VGA connector.

Testing a Display

Unlike most of the other peripherals you can connect to your computer, you can't really tell whether a monitor suits you by examining its technical specifications. Price might not be a reliable indicator either. Testing monitors is a highly subjective process, and it is best to "kick the tires" of a few at a dealer showroom or in the privacy of your home or office (if the dealer has a liberal return policy).

Testing should also not be simply a matter of looking at whatever happens to be displayed on the monitor at the time. Many computer stores display movies, scenic photos, or other flashy graphics that are all but useless for a serious evaluation and comparison. If possible, you should look at the same images on each monitor you try and compare the manner in which they perform a specific series of tasks.

Before running the tests listed here, set your display to the highest resolution and refresh rate allowed by your combination of display and graphics card.

One good series of tasks is as follows:

■ *Draw a perfect circle with a graphics program.* If the displayed result is an oval, not a circle, this monitor will not serve you well with graphics or design software.

■ *Using a word processor, type some words in 8- or 10-point type (1 point equals 1/72").* If the words are fuzzy or the black characters are fringed with color, select another monitor.

■ *Display a screen with as much white space as possible and look for areas of color variance.* This can indicate a problem with only that individual unit or its location, but if you see it on more than one monitor of the same make, it might indicate a manufacturing problem; it could also indicate problems with the signal coming from the graphics card. Move the monitor to another system equipped with a different graphics card model and retry this test to see for certain whether it's the monitor or the video card.

■ *Display the Microsoft Windows desktop to check for uniform focus and brightness.* Are the corner icons as sharp as the rest of the screen? Are the lines in the title bar curved or wavy? Monitors usually are sharply focused at the center, but seriously blurred corners indicate a poor design. Bowed lines can be the result of a poor video adapter or incorrect configuration of the monitor's digital picture controls. Before you decide to replace the monitor, you should first adjust the digital picture controls to improve the display. Next, try attaching the monitor to another display adapter. If the display quality does not improve, replace the monitor.

Adjust the brightness up and down to see whether the image blooms or swells, which indicates the monitor is likely to lose focus at high brightness levels. You can also use diagnostics that come with the graphics card or third-party system diagnostics programs to perform these tests.

■ *With LCD panels in particular, change to a lower resolution from the panel's native resolution using the Microsoft Windows Display properties settings.* Because LCD panels have only one native resolution, the display must use scaling to handle other resolutions full-screen. If you are a Web designer, are a gamer, or must capture screens at a particular resolution, this test will show you whether the LCD panel produces acceptable display quality at resolutions other than normal. You can also use this test on a CRT, but CRTs, unlike LCD panels, are designed to handle a wide variety of resolutions.

■ *A good CRT monitor is calibrated so that rays of red, green, and blue light hit their targets (individual phosphor dots) precisely.* If they don't, you have bad convergence. This is apparent when edges of lines appear to illuminate with a specific color. If you have good convergence, the colors are crisp, clear, and true, provided there isn't a predominant tint in the phosphor.

■ *If the monitor has built-in diagnostics (a recommended feature), try them as well to test the display independently of the graphics card and system to which it's attached.*

Maintaining Your Monitor

Because a good 17" or larger CRT or 15" or larger LCD monitor can be used for several years on more than one computer, proper care is essential to extend its life to the fullest extent.

Use the following guidelines for proper care of your monitors:

■ *Although phosphor burn (in which an image left onscreen eventually leaves a permanent shadow onscreen) is next-to-impossible with VGA-type displays—unlike the old TTL displays—screensavers are still useful for casual security.* You can password-protect your system with both the standard Windows screensaver and third-party programs (although a determined snoop can easily thwart screensaver password protection). Windows includes several screensavers that can be enabled via the Display Control Panel. A bevy of free and inexpensive screensavers is available for download from the Internet. Keep in mind, though, that add-on screensavers can cause crashes and lockups if they're poorly written or out-of-date and that many "free" versions available online might install spyware (software that reports your Web-surfing habits to advertisers). Use screensavers written for your particular operating system version to minimize problems.

Note

Phosphor burn *is* possible with plasma displays, so if you decide to connect a plasma display to your PC, be sure to use a screensaver to protect your display.

■ *To prevent premature failure of the monitor's power supply, use the power-management feature of the Display Properties or Power (Management) sheet to put the monitor into a low-power standby mode after a reasonable period of inactivity (10–15 minutes) and to turn it off after about 60 minutes.* Using the power management feature is far better than using the on/off switch when you are away from the computer for brief periods. Turn off the monitor only at the end of your computing "day."

How can you tell whether the monitor is really off or in standby mode? Look at the power LCD on the front of the monitor. A monitor that's in standby mode usually has a blinking green or solid amber LCD in place of the solid green LCD displayed when it's running in normal mode. Because monitors in standby mode still consume some power, they should be shut off at the end of the computing day.

If the monitor will not go into standby when the PC isn't sending signals to it, make sure the monitor is properly defined in Windows's Display Properties sheet. In addition, the Energy Star check box should be selected for any monitor that supports power management, unless the monitor should be left on at all times (such as when used in a retail kiosk or self-standing display).

■ *Make sure the monitor has adequate ventilation along the sides, rear, and top.* Because monitors use passive cooling, a lack of adequate airflow caused by piling keyboards, folders, books, or other office debris on top of the monitor will cause it to overheat and considerably shorten its life. If you're looking at a monitor with a partly melted grille on the top of the case, you're looking at a victim of poor cooling. If you need to use a monitor in an area with poor airflow, use an LCD panel instead of a CRT because LCDs run much cooler than CRTs.

■ *The monitor screen and case should be kept clean.* Turn off the power, spray a cleaner such as Endust for Electronics onto a soft cloth (never directly onto the monitor!), and wipe the screen and the case gently.

■ *If your CRT monitor has a degaussing button or feature, use it periodically to remove stray magnetic signals.* Keep in mind that CRTs have powerful magnets around the picture tube, so keep magnetic media away from them.

Video Display Adapters

A video adapter provides the interface between your computer and your monitor and transmits the signals that appear as images on the display. Throughout the history of the PC, there have been a succession of standards for video display characteristics that represent a steady increase in screen resolution and color depth. The following list of standards can serve as an abbreviated history of PC video-display technology:

MDA (Monochrome Display Adapter)

HGC (Hercules Graphics Card)

CGA (Color Graphics Adapter)

EGA (Enhanced Graphics Adapter)

VGA (Video Graphics Array)

SVGA (Super VGA)

XGA (Extended Graphics Array)

IBM pioneered most of these standards, but other manufacturers of compatible PCs adopted them as well. Today, IBM is no longer the industry leader it once was (and hasn't been for some time), and many of these standards are obsolete. Those that aren't obsolete seldom are referred to by these names anymore. The sole exception to this is *VGA*, which is a term that is still used to refer to a baseline graphics display capability supported by virtually every video adapter on the market today.

When you shop for a video adapter today, you are more likely to see specific references to the screen resolutions and color depths that the device supports than a list of standards such as VGA, SVGA, XGA, and UVGA. However, reading about these standards gives you a good idea of how video-display technology developed over the years and prepares you for any close encounters you might have with legacy equipment from the dark ages.

Today's VGA and later video adapters can also display most older color graphics software written for CGA, EGA, and most other obsolete graphics standards. This enables you to use older graphics software (such as games and educational programs) on your current system. Although not a concern for most users, some older programs wrote directly to hardware registers that are no longer found on current video cards.

Obsolete Display Adapters

Although many types of display systems were at one time considered to be industry standards, few of these are viable standards for today's hardware and software.

Note

If you are interested in reading more about MDA, HGC, CGA, EGA, or MCGA display adapters, see Chapter 8 of *Upgrading and Repairing PCs, 10th Anniversary Edition,* included on the disc with this book.

Current Display Adapters

When IBM introduced the PS/2 systems on April 2, 1987, it also introduced the VGA display. On that day, in fact, IBM also introduced the lower-resolution MCGA and higher-resolution 8514 adapters. The MCGA and 8514 adapters did not become popular standards like the VGA did, and both were discontinued.

All current display adapters that connect to the 15-pin VGA analog connector or the DVI analog/digital connector are based on the VGA standard.

Digital Versus Analog Signals

Unlike earlier video standards, which are digital, VGA is an analog system. Why have displays gone from digital to analog when most other electronic systems have gone digital? Compact disc players (digital) have replaced most turntables (analog), mini DV camcorders are replacing 8MM and VHS-based analog camcorders, and TiVo and UltimateTV digital video recorders are performing time-shifting in place of analog VCRs for many users. With a digital television set, you can watch several channels on a single screen by splitting the screen or placing a picture within another picture.

Most personal computer displays introduced before the PS/2 are digital. This type of display generates different colors by firing the RGB electron beams in on-or-off mode, which allows for the display of up to eight colors (2^3). In the IBM displays and adapters, another signal doubles the number of color combinations from 8 to 16 by displaying each color at one of two intensity levels. This digital display is easy to manufacture and offers simplicity with consistent color combinations from system to system. The real drawback of the older digital displays such as CGA and EGA is the limited number of possible colors.

In the PS/2 systems, IBM went to an analog display circuit. Analog displays work like the digital displays that use RGB electron beams to construct various colors, but each color in the analog display system can be displayed at varying levels of intensity—64 levels, in the case of the VGA. This versatility provides 262,144 possible colors (64^3), of which 256 could be simultaneously displayed. For realistic computer graphics, color depth is often more important than high resolution because the human eye perceives a picture that has more colors as being more realistic. IBM moved to analog graphics to enhance the color capabilities of its systems.

Video Graphics Array

PS/2 systems incorporated the primary display adapter circuitry onto the motherboard, and both IBM and third-party companies introduced separate VGA cards to enable other types of systems to enjoy the advantages of VGA.

Although the IBM MicroChannel (MCA) computers, such as the PS/2 Model 50 and above, introduced VGA, it's impossible today to find a brand-new replacement for VGA that fits into the obsolete MCA-bus systems. However, a few surplus and used third-party cards might be available if you look hard enough.

The VGA BIOS is the control software residing in the system ROM for controlling VGA circuits. With the BIOS, software can initiate commands and functions without having to manipulate the VGA directly. Programs become somewhat hardware independent and can call a consistent set of commands and functions built into the system's ROM-control software.

◄◄ See "Video Adapter BIOS," p. 523.

Other implementations of the VGA differ in their hardware but respond to the same BIOS calls and functions. New features are added as a superset of the existing functions, and VGA remains compatible with the graphics and text BIOS functions built into the PC systems from the beginning. The VGA can run almost any software that originally was written for the CGA or EGA, unless it was written to directly access the hardware registers of these cards.

A standard VGA card displays up to 256 colors onscreen, from a palette of 262,144 (256KB) colors; when used in the 640×480 graphics or 720×400 text mode, 16 colors at a time can be displayed. Because the VGA outputs an analog signal, you must have a monitor that accepts an analog input.

VGA displays originally came not only in color, but also in monochrome VGA models, which use color summing. With color summing, 64 gray shades are displayed instead of colors. The summing routine is initiated if the BIOS detects a monochrome display when the system boots. This routine uses an algorithm that takes the desired color and rewrites the formula to involve all three color guns, producing varying intensities of gray. Users who preferred a monochrome display, therefore, could execute color-based applications.

Note

For a listing of the VGA display modes supported by the original IBM VGA card (and thus all subsequent VGA-type cards), see "VGA Display Modes" in Chapter 15 of *Upgrading and Repairing PCs, 12th Edition*, available in electronic form on the disc supplied with this book.

Even the least-expensive video adapters on the market today can work with modes well beyond the VGA standard. VGA, at its 16-color, 640×480 graphics resolution, has come to be the baseline for PC graphical display configurations. VGA is accepted as the least common denominator for all Windows systems and must be supported by the video adapters in all systems running Windows. The installation programs of all Windows versions use these VGA settings as their default video configuration. In addition to VGA, virtually all adapters support a range of higher screen resolutions and color depths, depending on the capabilities of the hardware. If a Windows 9x/Me or Windows XP/2000 system must be started in Safe Mode because of a startup problem, the system defaults to VGA in the 640×480, 16-color mode. Windows 2000 and Windows XP also offer a VGA Mode startup that also uses this mode (Windows XP uses 800×600 resolution) but doesn't slow down the rest of the computer the way Safe Mode (which replaces 32-bit drivers with BIOS services) does.

IBM introduced higher-resolution versions of VGA called XGA and XGA-2 in the early 1990s, but most of the development of VGA standards has come from the third-party video card industry and its trade group, the Video Electronic Standards Association (VESA).

Note

If you are interested in reading more about the XGA and XGA-2 display adapters, see "XGA and XGA-2" in Chapter 8 of *Upgrading and Repairing PCs, 10th Anniversary Edition*, included on the disc with this book.

Super VGA

When IBM's XGA and 8514/A video cards were introduced, competing manufacturers chose not to attempt to clone these incremental improvements on their VGA products. Instead, they began producing lower-cost adapters that offered even higher resolutions. These video cards fall into a category loosely known as Super VGA (SVGA).

SVGA provides capabilities that surpass those offered by the VGA adapter. Unlike the display adapters discussed so far, SVGA refers not to an adapter that meets a particular specification, but to a group of adapters that have different capabilities.

For example, one card might offer several resolutions (such as 800×600 and 1024×768) that are greater than those achieved with a regular VGA, whereas another card might offer the same or even greater resolutions but also provide more color choices at each resolution. These cards have different capabilities; nonetheless, both are classified as SVGA.

The SVGA cards look much like their VGA counterparts. They have the same connectors, but because the technical specifications from different SVGA vendors vary tremendously, it is impossible to provide a definitive technical overview in this book. The connector is shown in Figure 15.10; the pinouts are shown in Table 15.7.

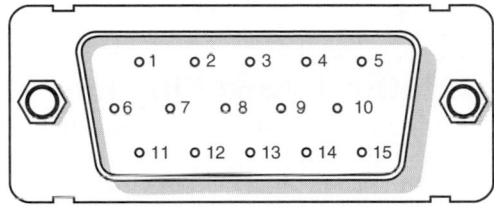

Figure 15.10   VGA connector used for SVGA and other VGA-based standards.

Table 15.7   Standard 15-Pin VGA Connector Pinout

Pin #	Function	Direction	Pin #	Function	Direction
1	Red video	Out	9	Key (plugged hole)	–
2	Green video	Out	10	Synch Ground	–
3	Blue video	Out	11	Monitor ID 0	In
4	Monitor ID 2	In	12	Monitor ID 1	In
5	TTL Ground (monitor self-test)	–	13	Horizontal Synch	Out
6	Red analog ground	–	14	Vertical Synch	Out
7	Green analog ground	–	15	Monitor ID 3	In
8	Blue analog ground	–			

On the VGA cable connector that plugs into your video adapter, pin 9 is often pinless. Pin 5 is used only for testing purposes, and pin 15 is rarely used; these are often pinless as well. To identify the type of monitor connected to the system, some manufacturers use the presence or absence of the monitor ID pins in various combinations.

VESA SVGA Standards

The Video Electronics Standards Association includes members from various companies associated with PC and computer video products. In October 1989, VESA recognized that programming applications to support the many SVGA cards on the market was virtually impossible and proposed a standard for a uniform programmer's interface for SVGA cards; it is known as the VESA BIOS extension (VBE). VBE support might be provided through a memory-resident driver (used by older cards) or through additional code added to the VGA BIOS chip itself (the more common solution). The benefit of the VESA BIOS extension is that a programmer needs to worry about only one routine or driver to support SVGA. Various cards from various manufacturers are accessible through the common VESA interface. Today, VBE support is a concern primarily for real-mode DOS applications, usually older games, and for non-Microsoft operating systems that need to access higher resolutions and color depths. VBE supports resolutions up to 1280×1024 and color depths up to 24-bit (16.8 million colors), depending on the mode selected and the memory on the video card. VESA compliance is of virtually no consequence to Windows versions 95 and up. These operating systems use custom video drivers for their graphics cards.

Note

For a listing of VESA BIOS modes by resolution, color depth, and scan frequency, see "VESA SVGA Standards" in the Technical Reference portion of the disc accompanying this book.

Integrated Video/Motherboard Chipsets

Although built-in video has been a staple of low-cost computing for a number of years, until the late 1990s most motherboard-based video simply moved the standard video components discussed earlier in this chapter to the motherboard. Many low-cost systems—especially those using the semi-proprietary LPX motherboard form factor—have incorporated standard VGA-type video circuits on the motherboard. The performance and features of the built-in video differed only slightly from add-on cards using the same or similar chipsets, and in most cases the built-in video could be replaced by adding a video card. Some motherboard-based video also had provisions for memory upgrades.

◄◄   See "LPX," p. 207.

However, in recent years the move toward increasing integration on the motherboard has led to the development of chipsets that include 3D accelerated video and audio support as part of the chipset design. In effect, the motherboard chipset takes the place of most of the video card components listed earlier and uses a portion of main system memory as video memory. The use of main system memory for video memory is often referred to as *unified memory architecture (UMA)*, and although this memory-sharing method was also used by some built-in video that used its own chipset, it has become much more common with the rise of integrated motherboard chipsets.

The pioneer of integrated chipsets containing video (and audio) features was Cyrix (now owned by VIA Technologies). While Cyrix was owned by National Semiconductor, it developed a two-chip product called MediaGX. MediaGX incorporated the functions of a CPU, memory controller, sound, and video and made very low-cost computers possible (although with performance significantly slower than that of Pentium-class systems with similar clock speeds). National Semiconductor retained the MediaGX after it sold Cyrix to VIA Technologies. National Semiconductor went on to develop improved versions of the MediaGX, called the Geode GX1 and Geode GX2, for use in thin clients (a terminal that runs Windows and has a high-res display), interactive set-top boxes, and other embedded devices. National Semiconductor sold its information appliance business, including the Geode family, to Advanced Micro Devices (AMD) in August 2003. AMD currently offers a variety of Geode-based solutions.

Intel became the next major player to develop integrated chipsets, with its 810 chipset for the Pentium III and Celeron processors. The 810 (codenamed Whitney before its official release) heralded the beginning of widespread industry support for this design. Intel later followed the release of the 810 series (810 and 810E) with the 815 series for the Pentium III and Celeron, most of which also feature integrated video. Currently, Intel offers integrated video for the Pentium 4 and Celeron 4 processors in the 845 and 865 families. Table 15.8 compares the major video features of Intel's 8xx-series chipsets, which include integrated video. Note that chipsets listed together share the same video features but differ in other ways such as memory support, I/O features, and so forth.

Table 15.8   Integrated Video Features of Intel 8xx Chipsets

Chipset	Supported Processors	Integrated Graphics Type	External AGP Graphics Support	Video Memory Size
810, 810E, 810E[2]	Pentium III, Celeron III	Intel 3D with Direct AGP	—	6MB[1], 10MB[2], 12MB[3]
815, 815E	Pentium III, Celeron III	Intel 3D with Direct AGP	AGP 4x	6MB[1], 10MB[2], 12MB[3]
815G, 815EG	Pentium III, Celeron III	Intel 3D with Direct AGP	—	6MB[1], 10MB[2], 12MB[3]
845GL	Pentium 4, Celeron 4	Intel Extreme Graphics	—	32MB[4], 64MB[5]
845G, 845GE	Pentium 4, Celeron 4	Intel Extreme Graphics	AGP 4x	32MB[6], 64MB[7]
845GV	Pentium 4, Celeron 4	Intel Extreme Graphics	—	32MB[6], 64MB[7]
865GV	Pentium 4, Celeron 4	Intel Extreme Graphics 2	—	32MB[4], 64MB[5]
865G	Pentium 4, Celeron 4	Intel Extreme Graphics 2	AGP 8x	32MB[4], 64MB[5]
915G[8]	Pentium 4, Celeron 4	Intel Extreme Graphics 3	PCI Express x16	32MB[4], 64MB[5]
915GV, 915GL[8]	Pentium 4, Celeron 4	Intel Extreme Graphics 3	—	32MB[4], 64MB[5]

1. *Systems with 32MB of RAM, PV 5.x, or greater graphics drivers.*
2. *Systems with 64MB of RAM, PV 5.x, or greater graphics drivers.*
3. *Systems with 128MB or more of RAM, PV 5.x, or greater graphics drivers.*
4. *Systems with up to 128MB of RAM.*
5. *Systems with more than 128MB of RAM.*
6. *Systems with up to 255MB of RAM.*
7. *Systems with 256MB or more of RAM.*
8. *This family of chipsets was code-named Grantsdale before its release.*
Intel 3D with Direct AGP—Basic 2D and 3D acceleration.
Intel Extreme Graphics—Supports alpha blending, fog, anisotropic filtering, hardware motion compensation, and advanced textures.
Intel Extreme Graphics 2—Enhanced version of original Extreme Graphics, adding better memory management, zone rendering, and faster pixel and texturing rendering.
Intel Extreme Graphics 3—Enhanced version of Extreme Graphics 2, adding support for most DirectX 9 features (does not support vertex shaders) and optional dual-display support.

Besides Intel, other major vendors of integrated chipsets include NVIDIA, VIA, ATI, and Acer Labs. Table 15.9 compares the video features of major integrated chipsets from these vendors.

Table 15.9   Video Features of Current Non-Intel Integrated Chipsets

Vendor	Chipset	External AGP Supported Processors	Integrated Graphics Type	Graphics Support	Video Memory Size
ATI	RADEON IGP 9100	Intel Pentium 4, Celeron 4	ATI RADEON 9000	AGP 8x	Up to 128MB
ATI	RADEON IGP 9100PRO	Intel Pentium 4, Celeron 4	ATI RADEON 9000	AGP 8x	Up to 128MB
NVIDIA	nForce2	AMD Athlon/Duron/ Athlon XP	NVIDIA GeForce4 MX420	AGP 8x	Up to 64MB
SiS	SiS661FX	Intel Pentium 4, Celeron 4	SiS Ultra-AGPII Mirage	AGP 8x	Up to 64MB
SiS	SiS760	AMD Athlon 64, Opteron	SiS Ultra-AGPII Mirage 2	AGP 8x	Up to 128MB
SiS	SiS741	AMD Athlon XP/ Athlon/Duron	SiS Ultra-AGPII Mirage	AGP 8x	Up to 64MB
VIA	PM880, PM800	Intel Pentium 4, Celeron 4	S3 Graphics Unichrome Pro	AGP 8x	Up to 64MB
VIA	K8M800	AMD Athlon 64, Opteron	S3 Graphics Unichrome Pro	AGP 8x	Up to 64MB
VIA	KM400	AMD Athlon XP/ Athlon/Duron	S3 Graphics Unichrome	AGP 8x	Up to 64MB

Although a serious 3D gamer will not be satisfied with the performance of most integrated chipsets (NVIDIA's nForce2 and ATI's RADEON 9100 IGPs being notable exceptions), business, home/office, and casual gamers will find that integrated chipset-based video on Pentium 4, Athlon XP, or Athlon 64 platforms are satisfactory in performance and provide cost savings compared with separate video cards. If you decide to buy a motherboard with an integrated chipset, I recommend that you select one that also supports an AGP 8x or PCI Express x16 video expansion slot. This enables you to add a faster video card in the future if you decide you need it.

Video Adapter Components

All video display adapters contain certain basic components, such as the following:

- Video BIOS.
- Video processor/video accelerator.
- Video memory.
- Digital-to-analog converter (DAC). Formerly a separate chip, the DAC is usually incorporated into the video processor/accelerator chip on recent chipsets. The DAC is not necessary on a purely digital subsystem (digital video card and display), but because most display subsystems have an analog VGA video card, an analog display, or both, video cards will continue to have DAC features for some time to come.
- Bus connector.
- Video driver.

Figure 15.11 indicates the locations of many of these components on a typical AGP 8x video card. Note that the acronym GPU refers to the graphics processing unit.

Heatsinks over GDDR-3 memory chips

Connectors to system power supply

Cooling fan over 6800 Ultra GPU

GDDR-3 memory chips

TV-out (S-video)

AGP 4x/8x slot connector

DVI-out (can be
converted to VGA-out)

Power connector for fan

Figure 15.11 A typical example of a high-end video card based on the NVIDIA GeForce FX 6800 Ultra GPU, a GPU optimized for gaming and dual-display support.

Virtually all video adapters on the market today use chipsets that include 3D acceleration features. The following sections examine these components and features in greater detail.

The Video BIOS

Video adapters include a BIOS that is similar in construction but completely separate from the main system BIOS. (Other devices in your system, such as SCSI adapters, might also include their own BIOS.) If you turn on your monitor first and look quickly, you might see an identification banner for your adapter's video BIOS at the very beginning of the system startup process.

Similar to the system BIOS, the video adapter's BIOS takes the form of a ROM (read-only memory) chip containing basic instructions that provide an interface between the video adapter hardware and the software running on your system. The software that makes calls to the video BIOS can be a stand-alone application, an operating system, or the main system BIOS. The programming in the BIOS chip enables your system to display information on the monitor during the system POST and boot sequences, before any other software drivers have been loaded from disk.

◄◄ See "BIOS Basics," p. 398.

The video BIOS also can be upgraded, just like a system BIOS, in one of two ways. The BIOS uses a rewritable chip called an EEPROM (electrically erasable programmable read-only memory) that you can upgrade with a utility the adapter manufacturer provides. On older cards, you might be able to completely replace the chip with a new one—again, if supplied by the manufacturer and if the manufacturer did not hard solder the BIOS to the printed circuit board. Most recent video cards use a surface-mounted BIOS chip rather than a socketed chip. A BIOS you can upgrade using software is referred to as a *flash* BIOS, and most current-model video cards that offer BIOS upgrades use this method.

Video BIOS upgrades (sometimes referred to as *firmware* upgrades) are sometimes necessary in order to use an existing adapter with a new operating system, or when the manufacturer encounters a significant bug in the original programming. Occasionally, a BIOS upgrade is necessary because of a major revision to the video card chipset's video drivers. As a general rule, the video BIOS is a component that falls into the "if it ain't broke, don't fix it" category. Try not to let yourself be tempted to upgrade just because you've discovered that a new BIOS revision is available. Check the documentation for the upgrade, and unless you are experiencing a problem the upgrade addresses, leave it alone.

◄◄ See "Video Adapter BIOS," p. 523.

The Video Processor

The video processor, or chipset, is the heart of any video adapter and essentially defines the card's functions and performance levels. Two video adapters built using the same chipset often have many of the same capabilities and deliver comparable performance. Also, the software drivers that operating systems and applications use to address the video adapter hardware are written primarily with the chipset in mind. You often can use a driver intended for an adapter with a particular chipset on any other adapter using the same chipset. Of course, cards built using the same chipset can differ in the amount and type of memory installed, so performance can vary.

Since the first VGA cards were developed, several main types of processors have been used in video adapters; these technologies are compared in Table 15.10.

Table 15.10   Video Processor Technologies

Processor Type	Where Video Processing Takes Place	Relative Speed	Relative Cost	How Used Today
Frame-buffer	Computer's CPU.	Very slow	Very low	Obsolete; mostly ISA video cards
Graphics coprocessor	Video card's own processor.	Very fast	Very high	CAD and engineering workstations
Graphics accelerator	Video chip draws lines, circles, shapes; CPU sends commands to draw them.	Fast	Low to moderate	All mainstream video cards; is combined with 3D GPU on current cards
3D graphics processor (GPU)	Video card's 3D GPU (in accelerator chipset) renders polygons and adds lighting and shading effects as needed.	Fast 2D and 3D display	Most price ranges depending on chipset, memory, and RAMDAC speed	All gaming-optimized video cards and almost all mainstream video cards

Identifying the Video and System Chipsets

Before you purchase a system or a video card, you should find out which chipset the video card or video circuit uses or, for systems with integrated chipset video, which integrated chipset the system uses. This allows you to have the following:

- Better comparisons of card or system to others
- Access to technical specifications
- Access to reviews and opinions
- Better buying decisions
- Choice of card manufacturer or chipset manufacturer support and drivers

Because video card performance and features are critical to enjoyment and productivity, find out as much as you can before you buy the system or video card by using the chipset or video card manufacturer's Web site and third-party reviews. Poorly written or buggy drivers can cause several types of problems, so be sure to check periodically for video driver updates and install any that become available. With video cards, support after the sale can be important. So, you should check the manufacturer's Web site to see whether it offers updated drivers and whether the product seems to be well supported.

The Vendor List on the disc has information on most of the popular video chipset manufacturers, including how to contact them. You should note that NVIDIA (the leading video chipset vendor) makes only chipsets, whereas ATI (the #2 video vendor) makes branded video cards and supplies chipsets to vendors. This means a wide variety of video cards use the same chipset; it also means that you are likely to find variations in card performance, software bundles, warranties, and other features between cards using the same chipset.

Video RAM

Most video adapters rely on their own onboard memory that they use to store video images while processing them; although the AGP specification supports the use of system memory for 3D textures, this feature is seldom supported now that video cards routinely ship with 32MB, 64MB, or more of onboard memory. Many low-cost systems with onboard video use the universal memory architecture (UMA) feature to share the main system memory. In any case, the memory on the video card or borrowed from the system performs the same tasks.

The amount of memory on the adapter or used by integrated video determines the maximum screen resolution and color depth the device can support. You often can select how much memory you want on a particular video adapter; for example, 32MB, 64MB, and 128MB are common choices today. Although adding more memory is not guaranteed to speed up your video adapter, it can increase the speed if it enables a wider bus (from 64 bits wide to 128 bits wide) or provides nondisplay memory as a cache for commonly displayed objects. It also enables the card to generate more colors and higher resolutions and, for AGP cards (see the following), allows 3D textures to be stored and processed on the card, rather than in slower main memory.

Many types of memory have been used with video adapters. These memory types are summarized in Table 15.11.

Table 15.11   Memory Types Used in Video Display Adapters

Memory Type	Definition	Relative Speed	Usage
FPM DRAM	Fast Page-Mode RAM	Slow	Low-end ISA cards; obsolete
VRAM[1]	Video RAM	Fast	Expensive; obsolete
WRAM[1]	Window RAM	Fast	Expensive; obsolete
EDO DRAM	Extended Data Out DRAM	Moderate	Low-end PCI-bus
SDRAM	Synchronous DRAM	Fast	Low-end PCI/AGP
MDRAM	Multibank DRAM	Fast	Little used; obsolete
SGRAM	Synchronous Graphics DRAM	Very fast	High-end PCI/AGP; replaced by DDR SDRAM
DDR SDRAM	Double-Data Rate SDRAM	Very fast	High-end AGP
DDR-II SDRAM	DDR SDRAM, 4-bit per-cycle memory fetch	Extremely fast	High-end AGP, PCI Express
GDDR-3 SDRAM	Modified DDR SDRAM	Extremely fast	High-end AGP, PCI Express

1. *VRAM and WRAM are dual-ported memory types that can read from one port and write data through the other port. This improves performance by reducing wait times for accessing the video RAM compared to FPM DRAM and EDO DRAM.*

Note

To learn more about memory types used on older video cards (FPD DRAM, VRAM, WRAM, EDO DRAM, and MDRAM), see Chapter 15 of *Upgrading and Repairing PCs, 12th Edition*, available in electronic form on the disc packaged with this book.

SGRAM, SDRAM, DDR, and DDR-II SDRAM—which are derived from popular motherboard memory technologies—have replaced VRAM, WRAM, and MDRAM as high-speed video RAM solutions. Their high speeds and low production costs have enabled even inexpensive video cards to have 16MB or more of high-speed RAM onboard.

SDRAM

Synchronous DRAM (SDRAM) is the same type of RAM used on many current systems based on processors such as the Pentium III, Pentium 4, Athlon, and Duron. The SDRAMs found on video cards are usually surface-mounted individual chips; on a few early models, a small module containing SDRAMs might be plugged into a proprietary connector. This memory is designed to work with bus speeds up to 200MHz and provides performance just slightly slower than SGRAM. SDRAM is used primarily in current low-end video cards and chipsets such as NVIDIA's GeForce2 MX and ATI's RADEON VE.

SGRAM

Synchronous Graphics RAM (SGRAM) was designed to be a high-end solution for very fast video adapter designs. SGRAM is similar to SDRAM in its capability to be synchronized to high-speed buses up to 200MHz, but it differs from SDRAM by including circuitry to perform block writes to increase the speed of graphics fill or 3D Z-buffer operations. Although SGRAM is faster than SDRAM, most video card makers have dropped SGRAM in favor of even faster DDR SDRAM in their newest products.

DDR SDRAM

Double Data Rate SDRAM (also called DDR SDRAM) is the most common video RAM technology on recent video cards. It is designed to transfer data at speeds twice that of conventional SDRAM by transferring data on both the rising and falling parts of the processing clock cycle. Today's mid-range and low-end video cards based on chipsets such as NVIDIA's GeForce FX and ATI's RADEON 9xxx series use DDR SDRAM for video memory.

DDR-II SDRAM

The second generation of DDR SDRAM fetches 4 bits of data per cycle, instead of 2 as with DDR SDRAM. This doubles performance at the same clock speed. The first video chipset to support DDR-II was NVIDIA's GeForce FX, which became the top of NVIDIA's line of GPUs in late 2002. DDR-II (also spelled DDR-2) is also used by ATI's high-end graphics cards.

GDDR-3 SDRAM

GDDR-3 SDRAM, which began appearing on NVIDIA's high-end graphics cards in early 2004, is based on DDR-II memory, but with two major differences:

- GDDR-3 separates reads and writes with a single-ended unidirectional strobe, whereas DDR-II uses differential bidirectional strobes. This method enables much higher data transfer rates.

- GDDR-3 uses an interface technique known as *pseudo-open drain*, which uses voltage instead of current. This method makes GDDR-3 memory compatible with GPUs designed to use DDR or DDR-II memory.

◀◀ For more information about DDR, DDR-II, and GDDR-3, see Chapter 6, "Memory."

Video RAM Speed

Video cards with the same type of 3D graphics processor chip (GPU) onboard might use different speeds of memory. For example, two cards that use the NVIDIA GeForce FX 5200—the Prolink PixelView and the Chaintech A-FX20—use different memory speeds. The Prolink card uses 4ns memory, whereas the Chaintech card uses 5ns memory.

Sometimes, video card makers also match different memory speeds with different versions of the same basic GPU, as with ATI's Radeon 9800 XT and 9800 Pro. The 9800XT has a core clock speed of

412MHz, versus the 9800 Pro's 380MHz clock speed. Thus, the 9800 XT supports memory running at 730MHz, whereas the 9800 Pro supports memory running at 680MHz. By using the slower Pro part, vendors can use slower memory to create a less expensive graphics card.

Unless you dig deeply into the technical details of a particular 3D graphics card, determining whether a particular card uses SDRAM, DDR SDRAM, DDR-II, SGRAM, or GDDR-3 can be difficult. Because none of today's 3D accelerators feature upgradeable memory, I recommend that you look at the performance of a given card and choose the card with the performance, features, and price that's right for you.

RAM Calculations

The amount of memory a video adapter needs to display a particular resolution and color depth is based on a mathematical equation. A location must be present in the adapter's memory array to display every pixel on the screen, and the resolution determines the number of total pixels. For example, a screen resolution of 1024×768 requires a total of 786,432 pixels.

If you were to display that resolution with only two colors, you would need only 1 bit of memory space to represent each pixel. If the bit has a value of 0, the dot is black, and if its value is 1, the dot is white. If you use 24 bits of memory space to control each pixel, you can display more than 16.7 million colors because 16,777,216 combinations are possible with a 4-digit binary number (2^{24}=16,777,216). If you multiply the number of pixels necessary for the screen resolution by the number of bits required to represent each pixel, you have the amount of memory the adapter needs to display that resolution. Here is how the calculation works:

$$1024 \times 768 = 786432 \text{ pixels} \times 24 \text{ bits per pixel}$$
$$= 18,874,368 \text{ bits}$$
$$= 2,359,296 \text{ bytes}$$
$$= 2.25\text{MB}$$

As you can see, displaying 24-bit color (16,777,216 colors) at 1024×768 resolution requires exactly 2.25MB of RAM on the video adapter. Because most adapters support memory amounts of only 256KB, 512KB, 1MB, 2MB, or 4MB, you would need to use a video adapter with at least 4MB of RAM onboard to run your system using that resolution and color depth.

To use the higher-resolution modes and greater numbers of colors common today, you would need much more memory on your video adapter than the 256KB found on the original IBM VGA. Table 15.12 shows the memory requirements for some of the most common screen resolutions and color depths used for 2D graphics operations, such as photo editing, presentation graphics, desktop publishing, and Web page design.

Table 15.12   Video Display Adapter Minimum Memory Requirements for 2D Operations

Resolution	Color Depth	Max. Colors	Memory Required	Memory Used
640×480	16-bit	65,536	1MB	614,400 bytes
640×480	24-bit	16,777,216	1MB	921,600 bytes
640×480	32-bit	4,294,967,296	2MB	1,228,800 bytes
800×600	16-bit	65,536	1MB	960,000 bytes
800×600	24-bit	16,777,216	2MB	1,440,000 bytes
800×600	32-bit	4,294,967,296	2MB	1,920,000 bytes

Table 15.12   Continued

Resolution	Color Depth	Max. Colors	Memory Required	Memory Used
1024×768	16-bit	65,536	2MB	1,572,864 bytes
1024×768	24-bit	16,777,216	4MB	2,359,296 bytes
1024×768	32-bit	4,294,967,296	4MB	3,145,728 bytes
1280×1024	16-bit	65,536	4MB	2,621,440 bytes
1280×1024	24-bit	16,777,216	4MB	3,932,160 bytes
1280×1024	32-bit	4,294,967,296	8MB	5,242,880 bytes
1400×1050	16-bit	65,536	4MB	2,940,000 bytes
1400×1050	24-bit	16,777,216	8MB	4,410,000 bytes
1400×1050	32-bit	4,294,967,296	8MB	5,880,000 bytes
1600×1200	16-bit	65,536	4MB	3,840,000 bytes
1600×1200	24-bit	16,777,216	8MB	5,760,000 bytes
1600×1200	32-bit	4,294,967,296	8MB	7,680,000 bytes

From this table, you can see that a video adapter with 4MB can display 65,536 colors in 1600×1200 resolution mode, but for a true color (16.8 million colors) display, you would need to upgrade to 8MB. In most cases you can't add memory to your video card—you would need to replace your current video card with a new one with more memory.

3D video cards require more memory for a given resolution and color depth because the video memory must be used for three buffers: the front buffer, back buffer, and Z-buffer. The amount of video memory required for a particular operation varies according to the settings used for the color depth and Z-buffer. Triple buffering allocates more memory for 3D textures than double-buffering but can slow down performance of some games. The buffering mode used by a given 3D video card usually can be adjusted through its properties sheet.

Table 15.13 lists the memory requirements for 3D cards in selected modes. For memory sizes used by other combinations of color depth and Z-buffer depth, see the eTesting Labs' Memory Requirements for 3D Applications Web site at the following address:

www.etestinglabs.com/benchmarks/3dwinbench/d5memfor3d.asp

Table 15.13   Video Display Adapter Memory Requirements for 3D Operations

Resolution	Color Depth	Z-Buffer Depth	Buffer Mode	Actual Memory Used	Onboard Video Memory Size Required
640×480	16-bit	16-bit	Double	1.76MB	2MB
			Triple	2.34MB	4MB
	24-bit	24-bit	Double	2.64MB	4MB
			Triple	3.52MB	4MB
	32-bit	32-bit	Double	3.52MB	4MB
			Triple	4.69MB	8MB
800×600	16-bit	16-bit	Double	2.75MB	4MB
			Triple	3.66MB	4MB
	24-bit	24-bit	Double	4.12MB	8MB
			Triple	5.49MB	8MB
	32-bit	32-bit	Double	5.49MB	8MB
			Triple	7.32MB	8MB

Table 15.13   Continued

Resolution	Color Depth	Z-Buffer Depth	Buffer Mode	Actual Memory Used	Onboard Video Memory Size Required
1024×768	16-bit	16-bit	Double	4.50MB	8MB
			Triple	6.00MB	8MB
	24-bit	24-bit	Double	6.75MB	8MB
			Triple	9.00MB	16MB
	32-bit[1]	32-bit	Double	9.00MB	16MB
			Triple	12.00MB	16MB
1280×1024	16-bit	16-bit	Double	7.50MB	8MB
			Triple	10.00MB	16MB
	24-bit	24-bit	Double	11.25MB	16MB
			Triple	15.00MB	16MB
	32-bit	32-bit	Double	15.00MB	16MB
			Triple	20.00MB	32MB
1600×1200	16-bit	16-bit	Double	10.99MB	16MB
			Triple	14.65MB	16MB
	24-bit	24-bit	Double	16.48MB	32MB
			Triple	21.97MB	32MB
	32-bit	32-bit	Double	21.97MB	32MB
			Triple	29.30MB	32MB

Note

Although 3D adapters typically operate in a 32-bit mode (refer to Table 15.12), this does not necessarily mean they can produce more than the 16,277,216 colors of a 24-bit true-color display. Many video processors and video memory buses are optimized to move data in 32-bit words, and they actually display 24-bit color while operating in a 32-bit mode, instead of the 4,294,967,296 colors you would expect from a true 32-bit color depth.

If you spend a lot of time working with graphics and want to enjoy 3D games, you might want to invest in a 32-bit 3D video card with at least 64MB or more of RAM. Although 2D operations can be performed with as little as 4MB of RAM, 32-bit color depths for realistic 3D operation with large Z-buffers use most of the RAM available on a 16MB card at 1024×768 resolution; higher resolutions use more than 16MB of RAM at higher color depths. Today's video cards provide more RAM and more 2D/3D performance for less money than ever before. Note that recent and current-model video cards don't use socketed memory anymore, so you must be sure to buy a video card with all the memory you might need now and in the future. Otherwise, you must replace a card with inadequate memory.

Note

If your system uses integrated graphics and you have less than 256MB of RAM, you might be able to increase your available graphics memory by upgrading system memory (system memory is used by the integrated chipset). Most recent Intel chipsets with integrated graphics automatically detect additional system memory and adjust the size of graphics memory automatically. Refer to Table 15.8 for details.

Windows Can't Display More Than 256 Colors

If you have a video card with 1MB or more of video memory, but the Windows Display Settings properties sheet won't allow you to select a color depth greater than 256 colors, Windows might have misidentified the video card during installation or the video driver installation might be corrupted. To see which video card Windows recognizes, click the Advanced Properties button, and then click the Adapter tab if necessary. Your adapter type might be listed either by the video card's brand name and model or by the video card's chipset maker and chipset model.

If the card model or chipset appears to be incorrect or not specific enough, click Change and see what other drivers your system lists that appear to be compatible, or use a utility program provided by your video card/chipset maker to identify your card and memory size. Then, manually select the correct driver if necessary. If the video card model or chipset appears to be correct, open the System properties sheet, locate the Device Manager, and remove the display adapter listing. Restart the computer and Windows will redetect the video card/chipset and install the correct driver.

Video Bus Width

Another issue with respect to the memory on the video adapter is the width of the bus connecting the graphics chipset and memory on the adapter. The chipset is usually a single large chip on the card that contains virtually all the adapter's functions. It is wired directly to the memory on the adapter through a local bus on the card. Most of the high-end adapters use an internal memory bus that is 256 bits wide. This jargon can be confusing because video adapters that take the form of separate expansion cards also plug into the main system bus, which has its own speed rating. When you read about a 128-bit or 256-bit video adapter, you must understand that this refers to the local video bus and that the bus connecting the adapter to the system is actually the PCI, AGP, or PCI-Express bus on the system's motherboard.

◀◀   See "System Bus Types, Functions, and Features," p. 338.

The Digital-to-Analog Converter

The digital-to-analog converter on a video adapter (commonly called a RAMDAC) does exactly what its name describes. The RAMDAC is responsible for converting the digital images your computer generates into analog signals the monitor can display. The speed of the RAMDAC is measured in MHz; the faster the conversion process, the higher the adapter's vertical refresh rate. The speeds of the RAMDACs used in today's high-performance video adapters range from 300MHz to 500MHz. Most of today's video card chipsets include the RAMDAC function inside the 3D accelerator chip, but some dual-display-capable video cards use a separate RAMDAC chip to allow the second display to work at different refresh rates than the primary display. Systems that use integrated graphics include the RAMDAC function in the North Bridge or GMCH chip portion of the motherboard chipset.

The benefits of increasing the RAMDAC speed include higher vertical refresh rates, which allows higher resolutions with flicker-free refresh rates (72Hz–85Hz or above). Typically, cards with RAMDAC speeds of 300MHz or above display flicker-free (75Hz or above) at all resolutions up to 1920×1200. Of course, as discussed earlier in this chapter, you must ensure that any resolution you want to use is supported by both your monitor and video card.

The Bus

You've learned in this chapter that certain video adapters were designed for use with certain system buses. Earlier bus standards, such as the IBM MCA, ISA, EISA, and VL-Bus, have all been used for VGA and other video standards. Because of their slow performances, all are now obsolete; current video cards use the PCI, AGP, or PCI-Express bus standard.

Although a few PCI-based video cards are still sold, primarily as upgrades for systems with integrated video that lack AGP ports, the most common high-speed video standard is AGP. The eventual successor to AGP—PCI Express—was introduced in mid-2004.

◄◄ See "Accelerated Graphics Port," p. 364.

◄◄ See "The PCI Bus," p. 358.

◄◄ See "PCI–Express," p. 362.

The Accelerated Graphics Port (AGP), an Intel-designed dedicated video bus introduced in 1997, delivers a maximum bandwidth up to 16 times larger than that of a comparable PCI bus. AGP has been the mainstream high-speed video standard for several years. The AGP slot is essentially an enhancement to the existing PCI bus; it's intended for use with only video adapters and provides them with high-speed access to the main system memory array. This enables the adapter to process certain 3D video elements, such as texture maps, directly from system memory rather than having to copy the data to the adapter memory before the processing can begin. This saves time and eliminates the need to upgrade the video adapter memory to better support 3D functions. Although AGP version 3.0 provides for two AGP slots, this feature has never been implemented in practice. Systems with AGP have only one AGP slot.

Note

Although the earliest AGP cards had relatively small amounts of onboard RAM, most recent and all current implementations of card-based AGP use large amounts of on-card memory and use a memory aperture (a dedicated memory address space above the area used for physical memory) to transfer data more quickly to and from the video card's own memory. Integrated chipsets featuring built-in AGP do use system memory for all operations, including texture maps.

Ironically, the memory aperture used by AGP cards can actually cause out-of-memory errors with Windows 9x and Windows Me on systems with more than 512MB of RAM. See Microsoft Knowledge Base document #253912 for details.

All recent nonintegrated motherboard chipsets from major vendors (Intel, Acer Labs, VIA Technologies, and SiS) for Pentium II and newer Intel processors and AMD Athlon and Duron processors support some level of AGP. However, some of the early integrated chipsets don't support an AGP slot.

Even with the proper chipset, however, you can't take full advantage of AGP's capabilities without the proper operating system support. AGP's Direct Memory Execute (DIME) feature uses main memory instead of the video adapter's memory for certain tasks to lessen the traffic to and from the adapter. Windows 98/Me and Windows 2000/XP support this feature, but Windows 95 and Windows NT 4 do not. However, with the large amounts of memory found on current AGP video cards, this feature is seldom implemented.

Four speeds of AGP are available: 1X, 2X, 4X, and 8X (see Table 15.14 for details).

Table 15.14   AGP Speeds and Technical Specifications

AGP Speed	AGP Specification	Clock Speed	Transfer Rate	Slot Voltages
1x	1.0	66MHz	266MBps	3.3V
2x	1.0	133MHz	533MBps	3.3V, 1.5V[1]
4x	2.0	266MHz	1,066MBps	1.5V
8x	3.0	533MHz	2,132GBps	1.5V[2]

1. Varies with card implementation.
2. Uses 0.8V internal signaling.

Because of the bandwidth AGP 3.0 requires, systems featuring this version of AGP also support DDR333 or faster memory, which is significantly faster than DDR266 (also known as PC2100 memory). AGP 3.0 was announced in 2000, but support for the standard required the development of motherboard chipsets that were not introduced until mid-2002. Virtually all current motherboard chipsets and AGP video cards support AGP 8x; however, differences in GPU design, memory bus design, and core and memory clock speed mean (as always) that AGP 8x cards with faster and wider memory and faster GPU speeds provide faster performance than AGP 8x cards with slower and narrower components.

Although some systems with AGP 4x or 8x slots use a universal slot design that can handle 3.3V or 1.5V AGP cards, others do not. If a card designed for 3.3V (2x mode) is plugged in to a motherboard that supports only 1.5V (4x mode) signaling, the motherboard will be damaged.

◄◄ See "Accelerated Graphics Port," p. 364.

Caution

Be sure to check AGP compatibility before you insert an older (AGP 1x/2x) card into a recent or current system. Even if you can physically insert the card, a mismatch between the card's required voltage and the AGP slot's voltage output can damage the motherboard. Check the motherboard manual for the card types and voltage levels supported by the AGP slot.

Some AGP cards can use either 3.3V or 1.5V voltage levels by adjusting an onboard jumper. These cards typically use an AGP connector that is notched for use with either AGP 2x or AGP 4x slots, as pictured in Chapter 4, "Motherboards and Buses." Be sure to set these cards to use 1.5V before using them in motherboards that support only 1.5V signaling, such as motherboards based on the Intel 845 or 850 chipsets.

PCI Express, which will eventually succeed both AGP and PCI, began to show up in high-performance systems in mid-2004. Despite the name, PCI Express uses a high-speed bidirectional serial data transfer method, and PCI Express channels (also known as *lanes*) can be combined to create wider and faster expansion slots (each lane provides 250MBps data rate in each direction). Unlike PCI, PCI Express slots do not compete with each other for bandwidth. PCI Express graphics cards use 16 lanes (x16) to enable speeds of 4GBps in each direction; when PCI Express is used for other types of cards, fewer lanes are used.

PCI, AGP, and x16 PCI Express have some important differences, as Table 15.15 shows.

Table 15.15   High-Speed Video Card Bus Specifications

Feature	PCI	AGP	PCI Express
Theoretical maximum	133MBps[1]	533MBps throughput (2X) 1066GBps throughput (4X)[2] 2133GBps throughput (8X)[2]	250MBps/lane[3] 4GBps (x16)[3]
Slots[2]	4/5 (typical)	1	1/more[4]

1. At 33MHz bus speed and 32 bits.
2. Most current systems support AGP 4X/8X only.
3. In each direction; multiply by 2 for bidirectional throughput.
4. Only one PCI Express slot (x16 – video) per system in early implementations; motherboards with multiple PCI Express slots with fewer lanes for use by other card types will be available by 2005.

The Video Driver

The software driver is an essential, and often problematic, element of a video display subsystem. The driver enables your software to communicate with the video adapter. You can have a video adapter with the fastest processor and the most efficient memory on the market but still have poor video performance because of a badly written driver.

Video drivers generally are designed to support the processor on the video adapter. All video adapters come equipped with drivers the card manufacturer supplies, but often you can use a driver the chipset maker created as well. Sometimes you might find that one of the two provides better performance than the other or resolves a particular problem you are experiencing.

Most manufacturers of video adapters and chipsets maintain Web sites from which you can obtain the latest drivers; drivers for chipset-integrated video are supplied by the system board or system vendor. A driver from the chipset manufacturer can be a useful alternative, but you should always try the adapter manufacturer's driver first. Before purchasing a video adapter, you should check out the manufacturer's site and see whether you can determine how up-to-date the available drivers are. At one time, frequent driver revisions were thought to indicate problems with the hardware, but the greater complexity of today's systems means that driver revisions are a necessity. Even if you are installing a brand-new model of a video adapter, be sure to check for updated drivers on the manufacturer's Web site for best results.

Note

Although most devices work best with the newest drivers, video cards can be a notable exception. Both NVIDIA and ATI now use unified driver designs, creating a single driver installation that can be used across a wide range of graphics chips. However, in some cases, older versions of drivers sometimes work better with older chipsets than the newest drivers do. If you find that system performance or stability, especially in 3D gaming, drops when you upgrade to the newest driver for your 3D graphics card, revert to the older driver.

The video driver also provides the interface you can use to configure the display your adapter produces. On a Windows 9x/Me/2000/XP system, the Display Control Panel identifies the monitor and video adapter installed on your system and enables you to select the color depth and screen resolution you prefer. The driver controls the options that are available for these settings, so you can't choose parameters the hardware doesn't support. For example, the controls would not allow you to select a 1024×768 resolution with 24-bit color if the adapter had only 1MB of memory.

When you click the Advanced button on the Settings page, you see the Properties dialog box for your particular video display adapter. The contents of this dialog box can vary, depending on the driver and the capabilities of the hardware. Typically, on the General page of this dialog box, you can select the size of the fonts (large or small) to use with the resolution you've chosen. Windows 98/Me/2000 (but not Windows XP) also add a control to activate a convenient feature. The Show Settings Icon on Task Bar check box activates a tray icon that enables you to quickly and easily change resolutions and color depths without having to open the Control Panel. This feature is often called QuickRes. The Adapter page displays detailed information about your adapter and the drivers installed on the system, and it enables you to set the Refresh Rate for your display; with Windows XP, you can use the List All Modes button to view and choose the resolution, color depth, and refresh rate with a single click. The Monitor page lets you display and change the monitor's properties and switch monitor drivers if necessary. In Windows XP, you can also select the refresh rate on this screen.

If your adapter includes a graphics accelerator, the Performance page contains a Hardware Acceleration slider you can use to control the degree of graphic display assistance provided by your adapter hardware. In Windows XP, the Performance page is referred to as the Troubleshoot page.

Setting the Hardware Acceleration slider to the Full position activates all the adapter's hardware acceleration features. The necessary adjustments for various problems can be seen in Table 15.16 for Windows XP and in Table 15.17 for other versions of Windows.

Table 15.16 Using Graphics Acceleration Settings to Troubleshoot Windows XP

Acceleration Setting	When to Use	Effect of Setting	Long-Term Solution
Left*	The display works in Safe or VGA mode but is corrupted in other modes.	There's no acceleration.	Update display, DirectX, and mouse drivers.
One click from left*	2D and 3D graphics driver problems; mouse driver problems.	It disables all but basic acceleration.	Update display, DirectX, and mouse drivers.
Two clicks from left*	3D acceleration problems.	It disables DirectX, DirectDraw, and Direct 3D acceleration (mainly used by 3D games).	Update DirectX drivers.
Two clicks from right*	Display driver problems.	It disables cursor and drawing accelerations.	Update display drivers.
One click from right*	Mouse pointer corruption.	It disables mouse and pointer acceleration.	Update mouse drivers.
Right	Normal operation.	It enables full acceleration.	N/A

Disable write combining, which is a method for speeding up screen display, whenever you select any setting other than full acceleration to improve stability. Reenable write combining after you install updated drivers and retry.

Table 15.17 Using Graphics Acceleration Settings to Troubleshoot Other Windows Versions

Mouse Pointer Location	When to Use	Effects of Setting	Long-Term Solution
Left	Display works in Safe or VGA mode, but it is corrupted in other modes.	It disables all acceleration.	Update display and mouse drivers.
One click from left	2D and 3D graphics driver problems, mouse driver problems.	Basic acceleration only.	Update display and mouse drivers.
One click from right	Mouse pointer corruption.	It disables mouse pointer acceleration.	Update mouse drivers.
Right	Normal operation.	Full acceleration.	N/A

If you're not certain of which setting is the best for your situation, use this procedure: Move the slider one notch to the left to address mouse display problems by disabling the hardware's cursor support in the display driver. This is the equivalent of adding the SWCursor=1 directive to the [Display] section of the System.ini file in Windows 9x/Me.

If you are having problems with 2D graphics in Windows XP only, but 3D applications work correctly, move the slider to the second notch from the right to disable cursor drawing and acceleration.

Moving the slider another notch (to the third notch from the right in Windows XP or the second notch from the right in earlier versions) prevents the adapter from performing certain bit-block transfers; it disables 3D functions of DirectX in Windows XP. With some drivers, this setting also disables memory-mapped I/O. This is the equivalent of adding the Mmio=0 directive to the [Display] section of System.ini and the SafeMode=1 directive to the [Windows] section of Win.ini (and the SWCursor directive mentioned previously) in Windows 9x/Me.

Moving the slider to the None setting (the far left) adds the `SafeMode=2` directive to the `[Windows]` section of the `Win.ini` file in Windows 9x/Me. This disables all hardware acceleration support on all versions of Windows and forces the operating system to use only the device-independent bitmap (DIB) engine to display images, rather than bit-block transfers. Use this setting when you experience frequent screen lockups or receive invalid page fault error messages.

Note

If you need to disable any of the video hardware features listed earlier, this often indicates a buggy video or mouse driver. If you download and install updated video and mouse drivers, you should be able to revert to full acceleration. You should also download an updated version of DirectX for your version of Windows.

In most cases, another tab called Color Management is also available. You can select a color profile for your monitor to enable more accurate color matching for use with graphics programs and printers.

Video cards with advanced 3D acceleration features often have additional properties; these are discussed later in this chapter.

Multiple Monitors

Macintosh systems pioneered multiple-monitor support long before Windows, but starting with Windows 98, all current Windows versions also offer the ability to use multiple monitors on a single system. Windows 98/Me support up to nine monitors (and video adapters), each of which can provide a different view of the desktop. Windows 2000 and Windows XP support up to ten monitors and video adapters. When you configure a Windows 98/Me or Windows 2000/XP system to use multiple monitors, the operating system creates a virtual desktop—that is, a display that exists in video memory that can be larger than the image actually displayed on a single monitor. You use the multiple monitors to display various portions of the virtual desktop, enabling you to place the windows for different applications on separate monitors and move them around at will.

Unless you use multiple-head video cards, each monitor you connect to the system requires its own video adapter. So, unless you have nine bus slots free, the prospects of seeing a nine-screen Windows display are slim, for now. However, even two monitors can be a boon to computing productivity. For example, you can leave an email client or Web browser maximized on one monitor and use the other monitor for additional programs.

On a multimonitor Windows system, one display is always considered to be the primary display. The primary display can use any PCI or AGP VGA video adapter that uses a Windows minidriver with a linear frame buffer and a packed (nonplanar) format, meaning that most of the brand-name adapters sold today are eligible. Additional monitors are called secondaries and are much more limited in their hardware support. To install support for multiple monitors, be sure you have only one adapter installed first; then reboot the system, and install each additional adapter one at a time. For more information about multiple-monitor support for Windows 98/Me, including a list of supported adapters, see the Microsoft Knowledge Base article #182708.

It's important that the computer correctly identifies which one of the video adapters is the primary one. This is a function of the system BIOS, and if the BIOS on your computer does not let you select which device should be the primary VGA display, it decides based on the order of the PCI slots in the machine. You should, therefore, install the primary adapter in the highest-priority PCI slot. In some cases, an AGP adapter might be considered secondary to a PCI adapter. Depending on the BIOS used by your system, you might need to check in various places for the option to select the primary VGA display. For example, the AMI BIOS used by the MSI KT4 Ultra motherboard for Socket A processors lists this option, which it calls Primary Graphics Adapter, in the PCI/PnP menu. In contrast, the Intel/AMI BIOS used by the Intel D865PERL motherboard lists this option, which it calls Primary Video Adapter, in the Video Configuration menu.

◄◄   See "The PCI Bus," p. 358.

After the hardware is in place, you can configure the display for each monitor from the Display control panel's Settings page. The primary display is always fixed in the upper-left corner of the virtual desktop, but you can move the secondary displays to view any area of the desktop you like. You can also set the screen resolution and color depth for each display individually. For more information about configuring multiple-monitor support in Windows 98/Me, see Microsoft Knowledge Base article #179602. The multiple-monitor support included with Windows 2000 and Windows XP is somewhat different from that of Windows 98/Me. These versions of Windows support ten monitors, rather than nine as with Windows 98/Me. In addition, because Windows 2000 and XP use different display drivers than Windows 98/Me, some configurations that work with 98/Me might not work with Windows 2000/XP. For more information about configuring multiple-monitor support in Windows 2000, see Microsoft Knowledge Base article #238886. For details of the display cards compatible with Windows XP in multiple-display modes, see Microsoft Knowledge Base article #307397.

Windows XP also supports DualView, an enhancement to Windows 2000's multiple-monitor support. DualView supports the increasing number of dual-head video cards as well as notebook computers connected to external displays. With systems supporting DualView, the first video port is automatically assigned to the primary monitor. On a notebook computer, the primary display is the built-in LCD panel.

Note

Many recent notebook computers that have integrated graphics do not support DualView; however, most recent notebook computers that use a discrete graphics chip do support DualView. To determine whether your notebook computer supports DualView, open its Display properties sheet and click the Settings tab. If two monitor icons are visible, your computer supports DualView. You can activate secondary monitor support after you attach a monitor to the external VGA port.

Even if your BIOS enables you to specify the primary video card and you use video cards that are listed as compatible, determining exactly which display cards will work successfully in a multimonitor configuration can be difficult. Microsoft provides a list of compatible display cards in the Hcl.txt file located on the Windows 2000 CD-ROM, but this list does not contain the latest video cards and chipsets from NVIDIA, ATI, or other companies, nor does it take into account changes in supported chipsets caused by improved drivers. Unfortunately, the online version of the Microsoft Windows Catalog (www.Microsoft.com/windows/catalog/) doesn't list information about multiple-monitor support for any version of Windows.

Consequently, you should check with your video card or chipset maker for the latest information on Windows 2000 or Windows XP and multiple-monitor support issues.

Because new chipsets, updated drivers, and combinations of display adapters are a continuous issue for multiple-monitor support when separate video cards are used, I recommend the following online resources:

- http://www.realtimesoft.com/ultramon. Home of the UltraMon multiple-monitor support enhancement program ($39.95); an extensive database of user-supplied multiple-monitor configurations for Windows 98/Me, Windows 2000/XP, and Linux; product reviews; and tips

- http://www.digitalroom.net (click Tech Articles and then Multiple Monitor Guide); excellent tips on multiple-monitor setups and links to other resources

Multiple-monitor support can be enabled through either of the following:

- Installation of a separate AGP or PCI graphics card for each monitor you want to use
- Installation of a single AGP or PCI graphics card that can support two or more monitors

A card that supports multiple monitors (also called a multiple-head or dual-head card) saves slots inside your system and eliminates the headaches of driver and BIOS updates or system reconfiguration sometimes necessary when using two or more video cards for multiple-monitor capability.

Most recent video cards with multiple-monitor support feature a 15-pin analog VGA connector for CRTs, a DVI-I digital/analog connector for digital LCD panels, and a TV-out connector for S-video or composite output to TVs and VCRs. Thus, you can connect any of the following to these cards:

- One analog LCD or CRT display *and* one digital LCD
- Two analog LCD or CRT displays (when the DVI-I–to–VGA adapter is used)
- One analog LCD or CRT display *and* one TV
- One digital LCD *and* one TV

The major video chipsets that support multiple CRT and LCD displays are listed in Table 15.18.

Table 15.18   Major Multiple-Head Video Chipsets and Cards

Brand	Chipset	Bus Type(s) Supported	Number of Monitors Supported
ATI[1]	RADEON VE	AGP 4x	2
	RADEON 7500[7]	AGP 4x, PCI	2
	RADEON 8500	AGP 4x	2
	RADEON 8500LE	AGP 4x	2
	RADEON 9000 PRO	AGP 4x	2
	RADEON 9500 PRO	AGP 8x	2
	RADEON 9600 PRO	AGP 8x	2
	AIW 9600 PRO	AGP 8x	2
	RADEON 9700 PRO	AGP 8x	2
	RADEON 9800, PRO, XT	AGP 8x	2
Matrox[2]	M200MMS	PCI	2,4[3]
	Millennium G450	AGP 4x, PCI	2[3]
	G450MMS	PCI	2,4[4]
	G550	AGP 4x	2[3]
	Millennium P650	AGP 8x	2[6]
	Millennium P750	AGP 8x	3[3]
	Parhelia	AGP 8x	3[3]
NVIDIA[5]	GeForce 2 MX series[7]	AGP 4x, PCI	2
	GeForce 4 MX 440[7]	AGP 4x	2
	GeForce 4 Ti series[7]	AGP 4x, 8x	2
	GeForce FX series	AGP 8x	2
	GeForce 6800 series	AGP 8x	2
	GeForce MX 4000 series	AGP 8x	2

1. *ATI sells video cards using these chipsets under the ATI brand and also supplies chipsets to third-party vendors.*
2. *Matrox is the only vendor using its chipsets; this table lists Matrox card models.*
3. *Features a separate accelerator chip for each display, enabling the independent selection of the refresh rate and the resolution under Windows 2000.*
4. *Features a separate RAMDAC chip for each display, enabling the independent selection of the refresh rate and the resolution under Windows 2000.*
5. *NVIDIA does not manufacture video cards; it sells chipsets only.*
6. *Upgradeable to three-monitor support.*
7. *Some video cards based on this chipset might not support multiple monitors.*
AIW—All-in-Wonder; includes TV tuner and other AV features.

As Table 15.18 notes, some video cards that use a chipset capable of multiple-monitor support might not provide the additional DVI or VGA connector necessary to enable that support. Table 15.18 does not include video chipsets that support TV-out or video in-video out (VIVO) but do not support a second CRT or LCD display.

Caution

Some vendors whose cards provide a single VGA or DVI port (DVI-I ports can be converted to VGA with an adapter) and a TV-out port refer to such cards as "supporting multiple monitors." Table 15.18 lists only chipsets or cards that support two or more CRT or LCD displays.

3D Graphics Accelerators

Since the late 1990s, 3D acceleration—once limited to exotic add-on cards designed for hardcore game players—has become commonplace in the PC world. Although mainstream business users are not likely to encounter 3D imaging until the next major release of Windows (code-named Longhorn) is released in 2006, full-motion 3D graphics are used in sports, first-person shooters, team combat, driving, and many other types of PC gaming. Because even low-cost integrated chipsets offer some 3D support and 3D video cards are now in their sixth generation of development, virtually any user of a recent-model computer has the ability to enjoy 3D lighting, perspective, texture, and shading effects in her favorite games. The latest 3D sports games provide lighting and camera angles so realistic that a casual observer could almost mistake the computer-generated game for an actual broadcast, and the latest 3D accelerator chips enable fast PCs to compete with high-performance dedicated game machines, such as Sony's PlayStation 2, Nintendo's GameCube, and Microsoft's Xbox, for the mind and wallet of the hard-core game player.

Note

At a minimum, Longhorn requires graphics hardware that supports DirectX 7 3D graphics; however, for maximum functionality of the 3D GUI, graphics hardware that supports DirectX 9 or greater is required.

How 3D Accelerators Work

To construct an animated 3D sequence, a computer can mathematically animate the sequences between keyframes. A keyframe identifies specific points. A bouncing ball, for example, can have three keyframes: up, down, and up. Using these frames as a reference point, the computer can create all the interim images between the top and bottom. This creates the effect of a smoothly bouncing ball.

After it has created the basic sequence, the system can then refine the appearance of the images by filling them in with color. The most primitive and least effective fill method is called *flat shading*, in which a shape is simply filled with a solid color. *Gouraud shading*, a slightly more effective technique, involves the assignment of colors to specific points on a shape. The points are then joined using a smooth gradient between the colors.

A more processor-intensive, and much more effective, type of fill is called *texture mapping*. The 3D application includes patterns—or textures—in the form of small bitmaps that it tiles onto the shapes in the image, just as you can tile a small bitmap to form the wallpaper for your Windows desktop. The primary difference is that the 3D application can modify the appearance of each tile by applying perspective and shading to achieve 3D effects. When lighting effects that simulate fog, glare, directional shadows, and others are added, the 3D animation comes very close indeed to matching reality.

Until the late 1990s, 3D applications had to rely on support from software routines to convert these abstractions into live images. This placed a heavy burden on the system processor in the PC, which has a significant impact on the performance not only of the visual display, but also of any other applications the computer might be running. Starting in the period from 1996 to 1997, chipsets on most video adapters began to take on many of the tasks involved in rendering 3D images, greatly lessening the load on the system processor and boosting overall system performance.

There have been roughly eight generations of 3D graphics hardware on PCs, as detailed in Table 15.19.

Table 15.19   Brief 3D Acceleration History

Generation	Dates	Technologies	Example Product/Chipset
1st	1996–1997	3D PCI card with passthrough to 2D graphics card; OpenGL and GLIDE APIs	3dfx Voodoo
2nd	1997–1998	2D/3D PCI card	ATI Rage, NVIDIA RIVA 128
3rd	1999	2D/3D AGP 1x/2x card	3dfx Voodoo 3, ATI Rage Pro, NVIDIA TnT2
4th	1999–2000	DirectX 7 API, AGP 4x	NVIDIA GeForce 256, ATI Radeon
5th	2001	DirectX 8 API, programmable vertex and pixel shaders	NVIDIA GeForce 3, NVIDIA GeForce 4 Ti
6th	2001–2002	DirectX 8.1 API	ATI Radeon 8500, ATI Radeon 9000
7th	2002–2003	DirectX 9 API, AGP 8x	ATI Radeon 9700, NVIDIA GeForce FX 5900
8th	2004–2005	PCI Express	ATI X800, NVIDIA GeForce 6800

With virtually every recent graphics card on the market featuring DirectX 8.x or greater capabilities, you don't need to spend a fortune to achieve a reasonable level of 3D graphics. Many cards in the $75–$200 range use lower-performance variants of current high-end GPUs, or they might use the previous year's leading GPU. These cards typically provide more-than-adequate performance for 2D business applications. Most current 3D accelerators also support dual-display and TV-out capabilities, enabling you to work and play at the same time.

However, keep in mind that the more you spend on a 3D accelerator card, the greater the onboard memory and faster the accelerator chip you can enjoy. Current high-end video cards featuring NVIDIA or ATI's top graphics chips, 128MB–256MB of video memory, and AGP 8x or the new PCI Express x16 interfaces sell for $300–$500 each. These cards are aimed squarely at hardcore gamers for whom money is no object. Mid-range cards costing $200–$300 are often based on GPUs that use designs similar to the high-end products but might have slower memory and core clock speeds or a smaller number of rendering pipelines. These cards provide a good middle ground for users who play games fairly often but can't cost-justify high-end cards.

Before purchasing a 3D accelerator adapter, you should familiarize yourself with some of the terms and concepts involved in the 3D image generation process.

The basic function of 3D software is to convert image abstractions into the fully realized images that are then displayed on the monitor. The image abstractions typically consist of the following elements:

- *Vertices.* Locations of objects in three-dimensional space, described in terms of their x, y, and z coordinates on three axes representing height, width, and depth.

- *Primitives.* The simple geometric objects the application uses to create more complex constructions, described in terms of the relative locations of their vertices. This serves not only to specify the location of the object in the 2D image, but also to provide perspective because the three axes can define any location in three-dimensional space.

- *Textures.* Two-dimensional bitmap images or surfaces designed to be mapped onto primitives. The software enhances the 3D effect by modifying the appearance of the textures, depending on the location and attitude of the primitive. This process is called *perspective correction.* Some applications use another process, called *MIP mapping*, which uses different versions of the same texture that contain varying amounts of detail, depending on how close the object is to the viewer in the three-dimensional space. Another technique, called *depth cueing*, reduces the color and intensity of an object's fill as the object moves farther away from the viewer.

Using these elements, the abstract image descriptions must then be rendered, meaning they are converted to visible form. Rendering depends on two standardized functions that convert the abstractions into the completed image that is displayed onscreen. The standard functions performed in rendering are

- *Geometry*. The sizing, orienting, and moving of primitives in space and the calculation of the effects produced by the virtual light sources that illuminate the image
- *Rasterization*. The converting of primitives into pixels on the video display by filling the shapes with properly illuminated shading, textures, or a combination of the two

A modern video adapter that includes a chipset capable of 3D video acceleration has special built-in hardware that can perform the rasterization process much more quickly than if it were done by software (using the system processor) alone. Most chipsets with 3D acceleration perform the following rasterization functions right on the adapter:

- *Scan conversion*. The determination of which onscreen pixels fall into the space delineated by each primitive
- *Shading*. The process of filling pixels with smoothly flowing color using the flat or Gouraud shading technique
- *Texture mapping*. The process of filling pixels with images derived from a 2D sample picture or surface image
- *Visible surface determination*. The identification of which pixels in a scene are obscured by other objects closer to the viewer in three-dimensional space
- *Animation*. The process of switching rapidly and cleanly to successive frames of motion sequences
- *Antialiasing*. The process of adjusting color boundaries to smooth edges on rendered objects

Common 3D Techniques

Virtually all 3D cards use the following techniques:

- *Fogging*. Fogging simulates haze or fog in the background of a game screen and helps conceal the sudden appearance of newly rendered objects (buildings, enemies, and so on).
- *Gouraud shading*. Interpolates colors to make circles and spheres look more rounded and smooth.
- *Alpha blending*. One of the first 3D techniques, alpha blending creates translucent objects onscreen, making it a perfect choice for rendering explosions, smoke, water, and glass. Alpha blending also can be used to simulate textures, but it is less realistic than environment-based bump mapping (see the section "Environment-Based Bump Mapping and Displacement Mapping," later in this chapter). Because they are so common, data sheets for advanced cards frequently don't mention them, although these features are present.

Advanced 3D Techniques

The following are some of the latest techniques that leading 3D accelerator cards use. Not every card uses every technique.

Stencil Buffering

Stencil buffering is a technique useful for games such as flight simulators, in which a static graphic element—such as a cockpit windshield frame, which is known as a HUD (heads up display) and used by real-life fighter pilots—is placed in front of dynamically changing graphics (such as scenery, other aircraft, sky detail, and so on). In this example, the area of the screen occupied by the cockpit windshield frame is not re-rendered. Only the area seen through the "glass" is re-rendered, saving time and improving frame rates for animation.

Z-Buffering

A closely related technique is *Z-buffering*, which originally was devised for computer-aided drafting (CAD) applications. The Z-buffer portion of video memory holds depth information about the pixels in a scene. As the scene is rendered, the Z-values (depth information) for new pixels are compared to the values stored in the Z-buffer to determine which pixels are in "front" of others and should be rendered. Pixels that are "behind" other pixels are not rendered. This method increases speed and can be used along with stencil buffering to create volumetric shadows and other complex 3D objects.

Environment-Based Bump Mapping and Displacement Mapping

Environment-based bump mapping (standard starting in DirectX 6) introduces special lighting and texturing effects to simulate the rough texture of rippling water, bricks, and other complex surfaces. It combines three separate texture maps (for colors, for height and depth, and for environment—including lighting, fog, and cloud effects). This creates enhanced realism for scenery in games and could also be used to enhance terrain and planetary mapping, architecture, and landscape-design applications. This represents a significant step beyond alpha blending. However, a feature called displacement mapping produces even more accurate results.

Special grayscale maps called displacement maps have long been used for producing accurate maps of the globe. Microsoft DirectX 9 supports the use of grayscale hardware displacement maps as a source for accurate 3D rendering. GPUs that fully support DirectX 9 in hardware all support displacement mapping. The Matrox Parhelia series, which supports some DirectX 9 features, also supports displacement mapping.

Texture Mapping Filtering Enhancements

To improve the quality of texture maps, several filtering techniques have been developed, including MIP mapping, bilinear filtering, trilinear filtering, and anisotropic filtering. These techniques and several others are explained here:

- *Bilinear filtering*. Improves the image quality of small textures placed on large polygons. The stretching of the texture that takes place can create blockiness, but bilinear filtering applies a blur to conceal this visual defect.

- *MIP mapping*. Improves the image quality of polygons that appear to recede into the distance by mixing low-res and high-res versions of the same texture; a form of antialiasing.

- *Trilinear filtering*. Combines bilinear filtering and MIP mapping, calculating the most realistic colors necessary for the pixels in each polygon by comparing the values in two MIP maps. This method is superior to either MIP mapping or bilinear filtering alone.

Note

Bilinear and trilinear filtering work well for surfaces viewed straight-on but might not work so well for oblique angles (such as a wall receding into the distance).

- *Anisotropic filtering*. Some video card makers use another method, called anisotropic filtering, for more realistically rendering oblique-angle surfaces containing text. This technique is used when a texture is mapped to a surface that changes in two of three spatial domains, such as text found on a wall down a roadway (for example, advertising banners at a raceway). The extra calculations used take time, and for that reason, it can be disabled. To balance display quality and performance, you can also adjust the sampling size: Increase the sampling size to improve display quality, or reduce it to improve performance.

■ *T-buffer.* This technology eliminates aliasing (errors in onscreen images due to an undersampled original) in computer graphics, such as the "jaggies" seen in onscreen diagonal lines; motion stuttering; and inaccurate rendition of shadows, reflections, and object blur. The T-buffer replaces the normal frame buffer with a buffer that accumulates multiple renderings before displaying the image. Unlike some other 3D techniques, T-buffer technology doesn't require rewriting or optimization of 3D software to use this enhancement. The goal of T-buffer technology is to provide a movie-like realism to 3D-rendered animations. The downside of enabling antialiasing using a card with T-buffer support is that it can dramatically impact the performance of an application. This technique originally was developed by now-defunct 3dfx. However, this technology is incorporated into Microsoft DirectX 8.0 and above.

■ *Integrated transform and lighting (T&L).* The 3D display process includes transforming an object from one frame to the next and handling the lighting changes that result from those transformations. T&L is a standard feature of DirectX starting with version 7. The NVIDIA GeForce 256 and original ATI RADEON were the first GPUs to integrate the T&L engines into the accelerator chip, a now-standard feature.

■ *Full-screen antialiasing.* This technology reduces the jaggies visible at any resolution by adjusting color boundaries to provide gradual, rather than abrupt, color changes. Whereas early 3D products used antialiasing for certain objects only, accelerators from NVIDIA (GeForce 4 Ti, GeForce FX, and the 6800 series) and ATI (RADEON 9xxx and the X800 series) use various types of highly optimized FSAA methods that allow high visual quality at high frame rates.

■ *Vertex skinning.* Also referred to as vertex blending, this technique blends the connection between two angles, such as the joints in an animated character's arms or legs. NVIDIA's GeForce2, 3, and 4 series cards use a software technique to perform blending at two matrices, whereas the ATI RADEON series chips use a more realistic hardware-based technique called 4-matrix skinning.

■ *Keyframe interpolation.* Also referred to as vertex morphing, this technique animates the transitions between two facial expressions, allowing realistic expressions when skeletal animation can't be used or isn't practical. See the ATI Web site for details.

■ *Programmable vertex and pixel shading.* Programmable vertex and pixel shading became a standard part of DirectX starting with version 8.0. However, NVIDIA introduced this technique with the GeForce3's nfiniteFX technology, enabling software developers to customize effects such as vertex morphing and pixel shading (an enhanced form of bump mapping for irregular surfaces that enables per-pixel lighting effects), rather than applying a narrow range of predefined effects. The NVIDIA GeForce4 Ti's nfiniteFXII pixel shader is DirectX 8 compatible and supports up to four textures, whereas its dual vertex shaders provide high-speed rendering up to 50% faster than the GeForce3. The ATI RADEON 8500 and 9000's version, SmartShader, is supported by DirectX 8.1. DirectX 8.1 supports more complex programs than nfiniteFX and provides comparable quality to nfiniteFXII. ATI 9700, 9800, and 9500 support DirectX 9's floating-point pixel shaders and more complex vertex shader. NVIDIA GeForce FX cards also support DirectX 9 pixel and vertex shaders, but they add more features. NVIDIA's 6800 series supports the new DirectX 9 Shader Model 3.0.

■ *Floating-point calculations.* Microsoft DirectX 9 supports floating-point data for more vivid and accurate color and polygon rendition. ATI Radeon 9500, 9600, 9700, and 9800-series GPUs support standard DirectX 9 floating-point data, whereas the NVIDIA GeForce FX series supports DirectX 9 and has additional precision. The NVIDIA 6800 series further increases precision beyond the basic DirectX 9 requirements. The Matrox Parhelia supports this, but doesn't support other DirectX 9 features.

Single- Versus Multiple-Pass Rendering

Various video card makers handle application of these advanced rendering techniques differently. The current trend is toward applying the filters and basic rendering in a single pass rather than multiple passes. Video cards with single-pass rendering and filtering typically provide higher frame-rate performance in 3D-animated applications and avoid the problems of visible artifacts caused by errors in multiple floating-point calculations during the rendering process.

Hardware Acceleration Versus Software Acceleration

Compared to software-only rendering, hardware-accelerated rendering provides faster animation. Although most software rendering would create more accurate and better-looking images, software rendering is too slow. Using special drivers, these 3D adapters can take over the intensive calculations needed to render a 3D image that software running on the system processor formerly performed. This is particularly useful if you are creating your own 3D images and animation, but it is also a great enhancement to the many modern games that rely extensively on 3D effects. Note that motherboard-integrated video solutions, such as those listed in Tables 15.8 and 15.9, typically have significantly lower 3D performance than even low-end GPUs because they use the CPU for more of the 3D rendering than 3D video adapter chipsets do.

To achieve greater performance, many of the latest 3D accelerators run their accelerator chips at very high speeds, and some even allow overclocking of the default RAMDAC frequencies. Just as CPUs at high speeds produce a lot of heat, so do high-speed video accelerators. Both the chipset and the memory are heat sources, so most mid-range and high-end 3D accelerator cards feature a fan to cool the chipset. Also, most current high-end 3D accelerators use finned passive heatsinks to cool the memory chips and make overclocking the video card easier (refer to Figure 15.11).

Software Optimization

It's important to realize that the presence of an advanced 3D-rendering feature on any given video card is meaningless unless game and application software designers optimize their software to take advantage of the feature. Although various 3D standards exist (OpenGL and DirectX), video card makers provide drivers that make their games play with the leading standards. Because some cards do play better with certain games, you should read the reviews in publications such as *Maximum PC* to see how your favorite graphics card performs with them. It's important to note that, even though the latest video cards based on recent ATI and NVIDIA chips support DirectX 9.x, many games still support only DirectX 8.x. As with previous 3D features, it takes time for the latest hardware features to be supported by game vendors.

Some video cards allow you to perform additional optimization by adjusting settings for OpenGL, Direct 3D, RAMDAC, and bus clock speeds, as well as other options. Note that the bare-bones 3D graphics card drivers provided as part of Microsoft Windows usually don't provide these dialog boxes. Be sure to use the drivers provided with the graphics card or download updated versions from the graphics card vendor's Web site. Although you can sometimes use generic drivers provided by the GPU vendor, you should use drivers that have been specifically developed for your card to ensure that your card's particular features are fully supported.

Note

If you want to enjoy the features of your newest 3D card immediately, be sure to purchase the individual retail-packaged version of the card from a hardware vendor. These packages typically come with a sampling of games (full and demo versions) designed or compiled to take advantage of the card with which they're sold. The lower-cost OEM or "white box" versions of video cards are sold without bundled software, come only with driver software, and might differ in other ways from the retail advertised product. Some even use modified drivers, use slower memory or RAMDAC components, or lack special TV-out or other features. Some 3D card makers use different names for their OEM versions to minimize confusion, but others don't. Also, some card makers sell their cards in bulk packs, which are intended for upgrading a large organization with its own support staff. These cards might lack individual documentation or driver CDs and also might lack some of the advanced hardware features found on individual retail-pack video cards.

Application Programming Interfaces

Application programming interfaces (APIs) provide hardware and software vendors a means to create drivers and programs that can work quickly and reliably across a wide variety of platforms. When APIs exist, drivers can be written to interface with the API rather than directly with the operating system and its underlying hardware.

Currently, the leading game APIs include SGI's OpenGL and Microsoft's Direct3D (part of DirectX). OpenGL and Direct3D are available for virtually all leading graphics cards. A third popular game API was Glide, an enhanced version of OpenGL that is restricted to graphics cards that use 3Dfx chipsets, which are no longer on the market.

The latest version of OpenGL is version 1.5, released on July 29, 2003. It adds programmable shading support through the OpenGL Shading Language specification and other enhancements. To learn more about OpenGL, see the OpenGL Web site at `www.opengl.org`. Although the video card maker must provide OpenGL support through driver updates, Microsoft provides support for Direct3D as part of a much larger API called DirectX.

The latest version of DirectX is DirectX 9.x, which enhances 3D video support, enhances DirectPlay (used for Internet gaming), and provides other advanced gaming features. For more information about DirectX or to download the latest version, see Microsoft's DirectX Web site at `www.microsoft.com/windows/directx`.

Note

DirectX 9.x is for Windows 98 and later versions (98SE, Me, 2000, and XP) only. However, Microsoft still provides DirectX 8.0a for Windows 95 users.

Although DirectX 8.0, 8.1, and 9.0 all provide support for higher-order surfaces (converting 3D surfaces into curves), vertex shaders, and pixel shaders, significant differences exist between DirectX 8.0/8.1 and 9.0 in how these operations are performed.

The difference between DirectX 8.0 (used by NVIDIA) and DirectX 8.1 (used by ATI and Matrox) involves the pixel shader portion of the 3D rendering engine. DirectX 8.1's pixel shader can handle more texture maps (6 versus 4) and more texture instructions (8 versus 4) than DirectX 8.0. DirectX 8.1 also handles integer data with 48-bit precision, versus DirectX 9.0's 32-bit precision. However, both pale in comparison to DirectX 9.0's pixel shader, which handles up to 16 texture maps, up to 32 texture instructions, and up to 64 color instructions and uses floating-point data at 128-bit precision.

To create higher-order surfaces, DirectX 9 supports continuous *tessellation* (the process of converting a surface into small triangles using floating-point math for greater precision) and displacement mapping in addition to the n-patches method used by DirectX 8.0 and 8.1.

DirectX 9.0's vertex shader is capable of handling much more complex commands than the DirectX 8.x shader: 1,024 instructions versus 128 and up to 256 constants versus 96. DirectX 9.0 also supports flow control.

DirectX 9.0c (supported by the NVIDIA GeForce FX 6800 series) includes Vertex Shader and Pixel Shader 3.0. Both support up to 65,535 instructions and 32-bit floating-point precision.

DirectX 9.x support is becoming commonplace in major new game releases, including leading titles such as Half-Life 2, Doom 3, Far Cry, Painkiller, and others. As noted previously, the next major revision of Microsoft Windows (code-named Longhorn) will offer a DirectX 9.0–compliant 3D GUI as an option.

3D Chipsets

Virtually every mainstream video adapter in current production features a 3D acceleration–compatible chipset. With several generations of 3D adapters on the market from the major vendors, keeping track of the latest products can be difficult. Table 15.20 lists the major 3D chipset manufacturers, the various chipsets they make, and the major features of each chipset.

The following manufacturers' products are not included in Table 15.20 for the reasons listed:

- *3Dfx Interactive*. Out of business; obtain last-available official and third-party drivers from www.voodoofiles.com.

- *3Dlabs*. Now manufacturers Open GL–compatible workstation cards only.

- *Intel*. No longer manufactures graphics boards.

- *Micron*. No longer manufactures chipsets.

- *VideoLogic*. No longer manufactures graphics boards.

- *PowerVR/ST Microelectronics*. Now makes graphics cores for mobile and embedded applications.

Note

See Chapter 15 in both *Upgrading and Repairing PCs, 12th Edition* and *13th Edition* on this book's disc for more information about these companies' products and other older chipsets.

Note

Table 15.20 is designed to be a reference to recent and current GPUs (and graphics cards) from current vendors. In most cases, only GPUs that meet fourth-generation (DirectX 7) or newer standards are included; a few third-generation GPUs still in wide use are listed. Refer to Table 15.19 for the criteria I use to describe each 3D generation. Because most graphics card vendors now use the GPU name as part of the product name, Table 15.20 does not include product examples. See *Upgrading and Repairing PCs, 15th Anniversary Edition*, available in electronic form on the disc packaged with this book, for a table matching older graphics card GPUs and product names.

Be sure to use this information in conjunction with application-specific and game-specific tests to help you choose the best card/chipset solution for your needs. Consult the chipset vendors' Web sites for the latest information about third-party video card sources using a specific chipset.

Table 15.20   3D Video Chipset Manufacturers and Products

				Manufacturer: ATI			
GPU (Codename)	**DirectX Version**	**Hard-ware T&L**	**Rendering Pipelines**	**Program-mable Vertex Shader Pipelines**	**Memory Bus**	**Mfr. Process**	**Notes**
RADEON (R100/ Rage 6C)	7	Yes	2	N/A	128-bit	.18 micron	—
RADEON VE, 7000 (RV100)	6	No	1	N/A	64-bit	.18 micron	VE features dual-display; AGP 4x
RADEON 7500, 7200 (RV200)	7	Yes	2	N/A	128-bit	.15 micron	AIW (7500); AGP 4x
RADEON 8500 (R200)	8.1	Yes	4	2	128-bit	.15 micron	Dual-display; AIW; AGP 4x
RADEON 9700 PRO, 9700 (R300)	9	Yes	8	4	256-bit	.15 micron	Dual-display; AIW; AGP 8x
RADEON 9500 PRO	9	Yes	8	4	128-bit	.15 micron	Based on 9700 Pro; AGP 8x

Table 15.20   Continued

Manufacturer: ATI

GPU (Codename)	DirectX Version	Hard-ware T&L	Rendering Pipelines	Program-mable Vertex Shader Pipelines	Memory Bus	Mfr. Process	Notes
RADEON 9500	9	Yes	4	4	128-bit	.15 micron	AGP 8x
RADEON 9000 PRO, 9000 (RV250)	8.1	Yes	4	2	128-bit	.15 micron	Updated 8500 core; dual-display (PRO); AIW; AGP 8x
RADEON 9800 PRO (R350)	9	Yes	8	4	256-bit	.15 micron	Update of 9700 Pro; dual-display; AGP 8x
RADEON 9600 PRO, XT (RV350)	9	Yes	4	4	128-bit	.13 micron	Dual-display; AGP 8x; AIW version has dual VGA
RADEON 9200, SE, Pro (RV280)	8.1	Yes	4	2	64-bit (SE); 128-bit	.15 micron	Dual-display (PRO); AGP 8x
RADEON 9800XT (R360)	9	Yes	8	4	256-bit	.15 micron	Dual-display; AGP 8x
RADEON 9600XT (RV360)	9	Yes	4	4	128-bit	.13 micron	Dual-display; AGP 8x
RADEON X800 PRO (R420)	9	Yes	12	6	256-bit	.13 micron	Dual-display; GDDR-3 memory; AGP 8x or PCI-Express x16
RADEON X800 XT Platinum (R420)	9	Yes	16	6	256-bit	.13 micron	GDDR-3 memory; AGP 8x or PCI-Express x16

Manufacturer: Matrox

GPU (Codename)	DirectX Version	Hard-ware T&L	Rendering Pipelines	Program-mable Vertex Shader Pipelines	Memory Bus	Mfr. Process	Notes
Millennium G450	6	No	2	N/A	64-bit	.18 micron	Triple-head display option; AGP 4x
Millennium G550	6	No	2	N/A	64-bit	.18 micron	Triple-head display option; AGP 4x

Table 15.20   Continued

Manufacturer: Matrox

GPU (Codename)	DirectX Version	Hard-ware T&L	Rendering Pipelines	Program-mable Vertex Shader Pipelines	Memory Bus	Mfr. Process	Notes
Millennium P650, P750 (Parhelia-LX)	8.1	Yes	2	2	128-bit	.15 micron	Based on Parhelia-512; triple-head display; AGP 8x
Parhelia (Parhelia-512)	8.1	Yes	4	4	256-bit	.15 micron	Has some DirectX 9 features; triple-head display; AGP 8x

Manufacturer: NVIDIA

GPU/Card (Codename)	DirectX Version	Hard-ware T&L	Rendering Pipelines	Program-mable Vertex Shader Pipelines	Memory Bus	Mfr. Process	Notes
GeForce2 GTS, Ultra	7	Yes	4	N/A	128-bit	.18 micron	AGP 4x
GeForce2 Ti	7	Yes	4	N/A	128-bit	.15 micron	AGP 4x
GeForce2 MX, MX400	7	Yes	2	N/A	64-bit, 128-bit	.18 micron	Some available with dual-display option; AGP 4x
GeForce3, GeForce Ti 200, 500 (NV20)	8	Yes	4	1	128-bit	.15 micron	Various core/memory speeds; AGP 4x
GeForce2 MX200	7	Yes	2	N/A	64-bit	.18 micron	AGP 4x
GeForce4 Ti 4600, 4400, 4200 (NV25)	8	Yes	4	2	128-bit	.15 micron	Dual-display; most 4200 uses standard memory; others use faster BGA; AGP 4x
GeForce4 MX 400, 420, 440, 460 (NV17)	7	Yes	2	N/A	128-bit	.15 micron	Updated GeForce2 MX core; AGP 4x; PCinema
GeForce4 MX 440-8x (NV18)	7	Yes	2	N/A	128-bit	.15 micron	AGP 8x version of GeForce 4 MX 440

Table 15.20   Continued

<table>
<tr><th colspan="8" style="text-align:center;">*Manufacturer: NVIDIA*</th></tr>
<tr>
<th>GPU/Card
(Codename)</th>
<th>DirectX
Version</th>
<th>Hard-
ware
T&L</th>
<th>Rendering
Pipelines</th>
<th>Program-
mable
Vertex
Shader
Pipelines</th>
<th>Memory
Bus</th>
<th>Mfr.
Process</th>
<th>Notes</th>
</tr>
<tr>
<td>GeForce4 Ti
4600-8x, 4200-
8x (NV28)</td>
<td>8</td>
<td>Yes</td>
<td>4</td>
<td>2</td>
<td>128-bit</td>
<td>.15 micron</td>
<td>AGP 8x version
of GeForce 4 Ti
4600 and 4200;
dual-display</td>
</tr>
<tr>
<td>GeForce FX
5800 (NV30)</td>
<td>9</td>
<td>Yes</td>
<td>8</td>
<td>1</td>
<td>128-bit</td>
<td>.13 micron</td>
<td>Dual-display;
AGP 8x</td>
</tr>
<tr>
<td>GeForce FX
5600 (NV31)</td>
<td>9</td>
<td>Yes</td>
<td>4</td>
<td>1</td>
<td>128-bit</td>
<td>.13 micron</td>
<td>Dual-display;
AGP 8x;
PCinema</td>
</tr>
<tr>
<td>GeForce FX
5200 (NV34)</td>
<td>9</td>
<td>Yes</td>
<td>4</td>
<td>1</td>
<td>128-bit</td>
<td>.13 micron</td>
<td>Dual-display;
AGP 8x;
PCinema</td>
</tr>
<tr>
<td>GeForce FX
5900 (NV35)</td>
<td>9</td>
<td>Yes</td>
<td>8</td>
<td>1</td>
<td>256-bit</td>
<td>.13 micron</td>
<td>Dual-display;
AGP 8x;
requires two slots
for fan; PCinema</td>
</tr>
<tr>
<td>GeForce FX
5700 (NV36)</td>
<td>9</td>
<td>Yes</td>
<td>4</td>
<td>1</td>
<td>128-bit</td>
<td>.13 micron</td>
<td>Dual-display;
based on FX
5900; AGP 8x</td>
</tr>
<tr>
<td>GeForce FX 5950
Ultra (NV38)</td>
<td>9</td>
<td>Yes</td>
<td>8</td>
<td>1</td>
<td>256-bit</td>
<td>.13 micron</td>
<td>Dual-display;
faster version of
FX 5900; AGP
8x; requires two
slots for fan</td>
</tr>
<tr>
<td>GeForce 6800
Ultra (NV40)</td>
<td>9.0c</td>
<td>Yes</td>
<td>16</td>
<td>6</td>
<td>256-bit</td>
<td>.13 micron</td>
<td>Dual-display;
GDDR-3
memory; AGP
8x or PCI-
Express x16;
requires 480-
watt power
supply and two
separate Molex
power connectors</td>
</tr>
<tr>
<td>GeForce 6800
(NV40)</td>
<td>9.0c</td>
<td>Yes</td>
<td>12</td>
<td>6</td>
<td>256-bit</td>
<td>.13 micron</td>
<td>Dual-display;
GDDR-3 mem-
ory; AGP 8x or
PCI-Express x16</td>
</tr>
</table>

Table 15.20   Continued

Manufacturer: SiS

GPU/Card (Codename)	DirectX Version	Hardware T&L	Rendering Pipelines	Programmable Vertex Shader Pipelines	Memory Bus	Mfr. Process	Notes
SiS315	7	Yes	2	N/A	64-bit, 128-bit	.15 micron	AGP 4x
Xabre 80	8.1	Yes	4	2	64-bit, 128-bit	.15 micron	AGP 4x
Xabre 200, 400	8.1	Yes	4	2	128-bit	.15 micron	Dual-display (400); AGP 8x
Xabre 600	8.1	Yes	4	2	128-bit	.13 micron	Dual-display; AGP 8x; faster version of Xabre 400

Manufacturer: XGI

GPU/Card (Codename)	DirectX Version	Hardware T&L	Rendering Pipelines	Programmable Vertex Shader Pipelines	Memory Bus	Mfr. Process	Notes
Volari V8, V8 Ultra (V8 Duo: 2-chip version)	9.0	Yes	8 (16)	2 (4)	128-bit (256-bit)	.13 micron	Dual-display; AGP 8x
Volari V5, V5 Ultra (V5 Duo: 2-chip version)	9.0	Yes	4 (8)	2 (4)	128-bit (256-bit)	.13 micron	Dual-display; AGP 8x
Volari V3	8.1	Yes	2	1	64-bit; 128-bit	.13 micron	Up to four displays; based on Trident XP4; AGP 8x

AIW: Indicates ATI GPUs also used in the ATI All-in-Wonder series of TV-tuner/capture graphics cards.
PCinema: Indicates NVIDIA GPUs also used in Personal Cinema TV-tuner/capture graphics cards.
XGI: Spinoff of SiS's graphics chip division; later acquired Trident's graphics subsidiary.

Upgrading or Replacing Your Video Card

With today's video cards offering sophisticated 3D graphics supporting DirectX 8.x and 9.x, multiple-monitor support at most price points, and massive amounts of display memory (up to 256MB!), it makes little sense to add most upgrades to an existing video card. The component-level upgrades that can be added generally include:

- TV tuners, permitting you to watch cable or broadcast TV on your monitor
- Video capture devices, allowing you to capture still or moving video to a file

In many cases, a single device provides both features. However, if you need better 3D performance or features, more memory, or support for DVI digital displays, you need to replace your video card.

TV Tuner and Video Capture Upgrades

With a few notable exceptions, such as ATI's Radeon All-in-Wonder and NVIDIA's Personal Cinema series, most video cards don't have TV tuner and video capture upgrade features built in. New cards with these features tend to be either in the middle to high range of their manufacturers' price structures or less expensive but of poor quality.

These features are exciting if you are already into video editing, want to add video to your Web site, or are trying to create CD- or DVD-based archives of your home video. If you have an up-to-date video card with acceptable 2D and 3D performance and at least 64MB of video RAM, compare the price of the add-ons to the price of a new card with these features. You'll probably find the add-ons to be less expensive. If your card has less than 64MB of video RAM and you play 3D games, I recommend replacing it with a new card with these features. Look at sample video captures before making your decision because all video capture solutions require image compression with at least some loss of quality. If you have a digital camcorder with IEEE 1394 (also called FireWire or i.LINK) ports, you should purchase an IEEE 1394 interface board to use high-quality pure digital video that needs no conversion.

Note

Although ATI's All-in-Wonder RADEON 8500 DV includes an IEEE 1394a (FireWire 400) port, more recent All-in-Wonder boards don't include this port. However, a wide variety of multifunction PCI cards include IEEE 1394a ports, including high-end sound cards from Hercules and Creative Labs and combination Hi-Speed USB (USB 2.0)/IEEE 1394a cards from many vendors.

The USB port can be used to connect TV tuner and video-capture options compatible with any manufacturer's video card from vendors such as Dazzle, Hauppauge, and others. Because the wide variety of TV and computer hardware on the market can cause compatibility problems with USB TV/capture devices, be sure to check review sites such as http://reviews.cnet.com and http://www.epinions.com. For best image capture quality, look for products designed for Hi-Speed USB (USB 2.0) and connect them to a Hi-Speed USB port.

If HDTV is in your future, look for products compatible with HDTV, such as an HDTV tuner (some plug in to an empty PCI slot, and others plug in to a USB port). HDTV tuners enable you to watch HDTV broadcasts on any monitor connected to your PC, including large-screen monitors and projectors. Some of the major vendors of HDTV cards include ATI Technologies, Hauppauge Computer Works, and Sasem Co, Ltd.

Warranty and Support

Because a video card can go through several driver changes during its effective lifetime (about three years or two operating-system revisions), buying a video card from a major manufacturer usually assures you of better support during the card's lifetime. If you buy a card that uses widely available chipsets (such as NVIDIA's or ATI's), you might be able to try a different vendor's version of drivers or use the chipset vendor's "generic" drivers if you don't get satisfactory support from your card vendor.

Keep in mind that using generic drivers (chipset level) or a different brand of drivers can cause problems if your original card's design was tweaked from the chipset maker's reference design. Look at the vendor's technical support forums or third-party discussions on newsgroups, computer information Web sites such as ZDNet, or magazine Web sites to get a feel for the stability, reliability, and usefulness of a vendor's support and driver services. These sources generally also provide alternatives in case of difficulties with a specific brand or chipset. If you use Windows Me, Windows 2000, or Windows XP, make sure you use WHQL-certified drivers for best results. These drivers have been passed by Microsoft's Windows Hardware Quality Labs and might be available through Windows Update or from the vendor's own Web site.

Note

With the rise in popularity of Linux, many graphics card and GPU vendors now provide downloadable Linux drivers. Be sure to check compatibility carefully because some vendors customize drivers for different Linux distributions or might provide drivers that work with only certain Linux kernels or XFree86 drivers.

Comparing Video Cards with the Same Chipset

Many manufacturers create a line of video cards with the same chipset to sell at different pricing points. Why not save some dollars and get the cheapest model? Why not say "price is no object" and get the most expensive one? When you're faced with various cards in the "chipsetX" family, look for differences such as those shown in Table 15.21.

Table 15.21   Comparing Video Cards with the Same Features

Feature	Effect on You
RAMDAC speed	Most current high-end 3D GPUs integrate 400MHz RAMDACs to provide flicker-free resolutions beyond 1280×1024. However, less-expensive cards and older designs often incorporate a slower RAMDAC, which reduces maximum and flicker-free resolutions. If you use a 17" or larger monitor, this could be an eye-straining problem.
Amount of RAM	Although AGP video cards can use AGP memory (a section of main memory borrowed for texturing), performing as much work as possible on the card's own memory is still faster. PCI cards must perform all functions within their own memory. Less expensive cards in a chipset family often have lower amounts of memory onboard, and graphics cards haven't featured expandable memory for several years. Buy a card with enough memory for your games or applications—today and tomorrow; at least 64MB or more for business and 128MB or more for gaming, 3D graphics, and video-related work.
Memory type	Virtually all video cards on the market today use SDRAM or its faster variants (SGRAM, DDR SDRAM, DDR-II, or GDDR-3 SDRAM). Any of these provides you with high performance in business applications, although DDR, DDR-II, or GDDR-3 SDRAM is preferable when running high-resolution, high-quality 3D games faster.
Core clock speed	Many suppliers adjust the recommended speed of graphics controllers in an effort to provide users with maximum performance. Sometimes the supplier can choose to exceed the rated specification of the graphics chip. Be cautious: Current controller chips are large and can overheat. An overclocked device in an open system with great airflow might work, or it might fail in a period of months from overstress of the circuitry. If you have questions about the rated speed of a controller, check the chip supplier's Web site. Many reputable companies do use overclocked parts, but the best vendors supply large heatsinks or powered fans to avoid overheating. Some vendors even provide on-card temperature monitoring.
RAM Speed (ns rating)	Just as faster system RAM improves overall computer performance, faster video card RAM improves video card performance. Some high-performance 3D video cards now use DDR SDRAM memory chips with a 2.8ns access time.
TV-out	Once a rare feature, most mid-range and most high-end video cards now feature TV-out, enabling you to display DVD movies or video games on a big-screen TV. Some of the latest models have hardware-based MPEG-2 compression for higher video quality in less disk space. Some of the latest video cards are now using a VIVOport to support either RCA or S-video inputs on VCRs and TVs.

The speed of the RAMDAC is not the same as the core clock speed of a given graphics card. Even though most current GPUs incorporate the RAMDAC in the GPU, the RAMDAC and the GPU core run at different speeds.

Video Cards for Multimedia

Multimedia—including live full-motion video feeds, videoconferencing, and animations—has become an important element of the personal computing industry and is helping to blur the once-solid lines between computer and broadcast media. As the demand for multimedia content increases, so do the capabilities of the hardware and software used to produce the content. Video is just one, albeit important, element of the multimedia experience, and the graphics adapters on the market today reflect the demand for these increased capabilities. Producing state-of-the-art multimedia content today often requires that the PC be capable of interfacing with other devices, such as cameras, VCRs, and television sets, and many video adapters are now equipped with these capabilities.

Other multimedia technologies, such as 3D animation, place an enormous burden on a system's processing and data-handling capabilities, and many manufacturers of video adapters are redesigning their products to shoulder this burden more efficiently.

The following sections examine some of the video adapter components that make these technologies possible and practical, including VFC, VAFC, VMC, and VESA VIP.

Because none of these specifications for internal video feature connectors has become a true industry standard, some manufacturers of auxiliary video products—such as dedicated 3D accelerator boards and MPEG decoders—have taken an alternative route through the standard VGA connector.

Video Feature Connectors

To extend the capabilities of the VGA standard beyond direct connections to a monitor, several auxiliary connector standards have been devised, first by individual card makers and later by VESA.

Four early attempts to create a common connector were the Video Feature Connector (VFC) that IBM devised in 1987, the VESA Advanced Feature Connector (VAFC), the VESA Media Channel (VMC), and the VESA Video Interface Port (VESA VIP). These connector designs were not widely used, though.

Note

If you are interested in reading more about VFC, VAFC, VMC, and VESA VIP, see "Video Feature Connectors," in the Technical Reference section of the disc with this book.

Replacements for the VESA VIP and Other Video Connectors

Currently, most systems interface with video devices through their USB or IEEE 1394 ports. Add-on TV tuner cards and USB devices such as the ATI TV Wonder VE can be used with most DirectX-compatible video chipsets from ATI and NVIDIA for video capture. The ATI All-in-Wonder series provides TV-in, TV-out, and full-power graphics support in a single slot. The latest version, the ATI All-in-Wonder 9800 Pro, has S-video and composite input and output ports and a 125-channel stereo TV tuner. An adapter for component video is available from ATI for interfacing with big-screen televisions. If you prefer NVIDIA graphics, look for GeForce FX–based cards that include the Personal Cinema breakout box and software bundle.

Video Output Devices

When video technology first was introduced, it was based on television. However, a difference exists between the signals used by a television and those used by a computer. In the United States, the National Television System Committee (NTSC) established color TV standards in 1953. Some other countries, such as Japan, followed this standard. Many countries in Europe, though, developed more sophisticated standards, including Phase Alternate Line (PAL) and Sequential Couleur Avec Mémoire (SECAM). Table 15.22 shows the differences among these standards.

Table 15.22   Television Versus Computer Monitors

Standard	Year Est.	Country	Lines	Rate
		Television		
NTSC	1953 (color) 1941 (b&w)	U.S., Japan	525	60 fields/sec
PAL	1941	Europe[1]	625	50 fields/sec
SECAM	1962	France	625	25 fields/sec
		Computer		
VGA	1987	U.S.	640×480[2]	72Hz

Field = 1/2 (.5 frame)
1. England, Holland, and West Germany.
2. VGA is based on more lines and uses pixels (480) versus lines; genlocking is used to lock pixels into lines and synchronize computers with TV standards.

A video-output (or VGA-to-NTSC) adapter enables you to display computer screens on a TV set or record them onto videotape for easy distribution. These products fall into two categories: those with genlocking (which enables the board to synchronize signals from multiple video sources or video with PC graphics) and those without. Genlocking provides the signal stability necessary to obtain adequate results when recording to tape, but it isn't necessary for using a television as a video display.

VGA-to-NTSC converters are available as internal expansion boards, external boxes that are portable enough to use with a laptop for presentations on the road, and TV-out ports on the rear of most video cards using chipsets from NVIDIA, ATI, and others. Indeed, many laptop and notebook systems these days come equipped with a built-in VGA-to-NTSC converter.

The converter does not replace your existing video adapter but instead connects to the adapter using an external cable. In addition to VGA input and output ports, a video output board has a video output interface for S-video and composite video.

Most VGA-to-TV converters support the standard NTSC television format and might also support the European PAL format. The resolution these devices display on a TV set or record on videotape often is limited to straight VGA at 640×480 pixels, although some TV-out ports on recent video cards can also display 800×600 resolution. The converter also might contain an antiflicker circuit to help stabilize the picture because VGA-to-TV products, as well as TV-to-VGA solutions, often suffer from a case of the jitters.

Video Capture Devices

You can capture individual screen images or full-motion video for reuse in several ways, including:

- 3D accelerator cards with TV-in ports
- TV tuner cards
- USB- or parallel port–based devices such as TV tuner/capture devices discussed earlier or a dedicated device such as the SnapMAGIC (available from www.snapnsend.com)
- Webcams with video input ports

These units capture still or moving images from NTSC video sources, such as camcorders and VCRs. Although image quality is limited by the input signal, the results are still good enough for presentations and desktop publishing applications. These devices work with 8-, 16-, and 24-bit VGA cards and usually accept video input from VHS, Super VHS, and Hi-8 devices. As you might expect, however,

Super VHS and Hi-8 video sources give better results, as do configurations using more than 256 colors. For the best results, use DV camcorders equipped with IEEE 1394 (i.LINK/FireWire) connectors; these can output high-quality digital video direct to your computer without the need to perform an analog-to-digital conversion. If your computer doesn't include an IEEE 1394a or 1394b port, you must install an IEEE 1394 add-in card if you want to capture output from a DV camcorder.

Desktop Video Boards

You can also capture NTSC (television) signals to your computer system for display or editing. In other words, you can literally watch TV in a window on your computer. When capturing video, you should think in terms of digital versus analog. The biggest convenience of an analog TV signal is efficiency; it is a compact way to transmit video information through a low-bandwidth pipeline. The disadvantage is that although you can control how the video is displayed, you can't edit it.

Actually capturing and recording video from external sources and saving the files onto your PC requires special technology. To do this, you need a device called a *video capture board* (also called a TV tuner, video digitizer, or video grabber).

Note

In this context, the technical nomenclature again becomes confusing because the term *video* here has its usual connotation; that is, it refers to the display of full-motion photography on the PC monitor. When evaluating video hardware, be sure to distinguish between devices that capture still images from a video source and those that capture full-motion video streams.

Today, video sources come in two forms:

- Analog
- Digital

Analog video can be captured from traditional sources such as broadcast or cable TV, VCRs, and camcorders using VHS or similar tape standards. This process is much more demanding of storage space and system performance than still images are. Here's why:

The typical computer screen was designed to display mainly static images. The storing and retrieving of these images requires managing huge files. Consider this: A single, full-screen color image in an uncompressed format can require as much as 2MB of disk space; a 1-second video would therefore require 45MB. Likewise, any video transmission you want to capture for use on your PC must be converted from an analog NTSC signal to a digital signal your computer can use. On top of that, the video signal must be moved inside your computer at 10 times the speed of the conventional ISA bus structure. You need not only a superior video card and monitor, but also an excellent expansion bus, such as PCI or AGP.

Considering that full-motion video can consume massive quantities of disk space, it becomes apparent that data compression is all but essential. Compression and decompression apply to both video and audio. Not only does a compressed file take up less space, it also performs better simply because less data must be processed. When you are ready to replay the video/audio, the application decompresses the file during playback. In any case, if you are going to work with video, be sure that your hard drive is large enough and fast enough to handle the huge files that can result.

Compression/decompression programs and devices are called *codecs*. Two types of codecs exist: hardware-dependent codecs and software (or hardware-independent) codecs. Hardware codecs typically perform better; however, they require additional hardware—either an add-on card or a high-end video card with hardware codecs built in. Software codes do not require hardware for compression or playback, but they typically do not deliver the same quality or compression ratio. Following are two of the major codec algorithms:

■ *JPEG (Joint Photographic Experts Group).* Originally developed for still images, JPEG can compress and decompress at rates acceptable for nearly full-motion video (30fps). JPEG still uses a series of still images, which makes editing easier. JPEG is typically lossy (meaning that a small amount of the data is lost during the compression process, slightly diminishing the quality of the image), but it can also be lossless. JPEG compression functions by eliminating redundant data for each individual image (intraframe). Compression efficiency is approximately 30:1 (20:1–40:1).

■ *MPEG (Motion Picture Experts Group).* MPEG by itself compresses video at approximately a 30:1 ratio, but with precompression through oversampling, the ratio can climb to 100:1 and higher, while retaining high quality. Thus, MPEG compression results in better, faster videos that require less storage space. MPEG is an interframe compressor. Because MPEG stores only incremental changes, it is not used during editing phases.

If you will be capturing or compressing video on your computer, you'll need software based on standards such as Microsoft's DirectShow (the successor to Video for Windows and ActiveMovie), Real Network's Real Producer series, or Apple's QuickTime Pro. Players for files produced with these technologies can be downloaded free from the vendors' Web sites.

To play or record video on your multimedia PC (MPC), you need some extra hardware and software:

■ Video system software, such as Apple's QuickTime for Windows or Microsoft's Windows Media Player.

■ A compression/digitization video adapter that enables you to digitize and play large video files.

■ An NTSC-to-VGA adapter that combines TV signals with computer video signals for output to a VCR. Video can come from a variety of sources: TV, VCR, video camera, laserdisc player, or DVD player. When you record an animation file, you can save it in a variety of file formats: AVI (Audio Video Interleave), MOV (Apple QuickTime format), or MPG (MPEG format).

Depending on the video-capture product you use, you have several choices for capturing analog video. The best option is to use component video. Component video uses three RCA-type jacks to carry the luminance (Y) and two chrominance (PR and PB) signals; this type of connector commonly is found on DVD players and high-end conventional and HDTV television sets. However, home-market video capture devices usually don't support component video. A typical professional capture device designed for component video, such as Pinnacle Systems' DC2000DV, retails for about $2,000.

The next best choice, and one that is supported by many home-market video-capture devices, is the S-video (S-VHS) connector. This cable transmits separate signals for color (chroma) and brightness (luma). Otherwise, you must use composite video, which mixes luma and chroma. This results in a lower-quality signal, and the better your signal, the better your video quality will be.

You also can purchase devices that display only NTSC (TV) signals on your computer. The built-in digital movie editing features found in Windows Me and Windows XP, the increasing popularity of computer/TV solutions, and broadband Internet connections make onscreen full-motion video an increasingly common part of the computing experience. Because of the growing importance of onscreen full-motion video, more and more recent CPUs have added features to enhance playback—including MMX and SSE instructions found in the Pentium II, Pentium III, Celeron, and AMD Athlon and Duron and the instruction set found in the Intel Pentium 4's NetBurst microarchitecture and SSE2. Computers that use Windows XP Media Center Edition are ready out of the box to capture and digitally record video from TV for playback later, functioning as a personal video recorder (PVR).

In addition, many graphics cards with TV-in, such as ATI's Radeon-based All-in-Wonder series and NVIDIA's Personal Cinema FX also include PVR software. A remote control and onscreen program guide is often included to make TV viewing and recording even easier.

Table 15.23 provides a breakdown of some common video cards and capture devices supporting key features. This table is not inclusive and is meant to serve only as a reference example.

Table 15.23 Video Capture Devices

Device Type	Example
Video card with TV tuner and PVR	ATI All-in-Wonder 9800 Pro, XT
Video card with TV tuner and PVR	ATI All-in-Wonder 9800 XT, XT, NVIDIA Personal Cinema FX
PCI TV-tuner and PVR	ATI-TV Wonder VE, HDTV Wonder
USB TV-tuner and PVR	Hauppauge WinTV-PVR-USB2
USB port video capture	Dazzle Digital Video Creator series
Parallel port still image capture	Invisco SnapMagic
PCI video capture card	Broadway Pro DVD
IEEE 1394 (FireWire)	AVerMedia DVD EzMaker

Figure 15.12 shows a typical video adapter incorporating TV tuner and video-in and video-out features: the ATI All-in-Wonder 9600 XT.

Figure 15.12 ATI's All-in-Wonder 9600 XT is a mid-range video accelerator with integrated TV and FM tuners, dual-display capabilities, and video-capture/PVR features. A multihead AV output cable, AV input breakout box, and remote control are also included. *Photo courtesy of ATI Technologies.*

Each type of device has advantages and potential disadvantages. Table 15.24 provides a summary that will help you decide which solution is best for you.

Table 15.24   Multimedia Device Comparison

Device Type	Pros	Cons
Graphics card with built-in TV tuner and capture	Convenience; single-slot solution	Upgrading requires card replacement.
TV-tuner card	Allows upgrade to existing graphics cards; might be movable to newer models	Might not work with all current chipsets.
Parallel port attachment	Universal usage on desktop or notebook computer; inexpensive	Frame rate limited by speed of port; best for still-image capture.
USB port attachment	Easy installation on late-model USB-equipped computers with Windows 98/Me and Windows 2000/XP	Might not work on Windows 95B OSR 2.x with USB; requires active USB port; not all devices may be compatible with Windows 2000/XP; low bandwidth with USB 1.1–compatible devices; not suitable for high res or full-motion applications unless Hi-Speed USB (USB) is specifically supported.
Dedicated PCI interface card	Fast frame rate for realistic video; works with any graphics card	High resource requirements (IRQ and so on) on some models; requires internal installation.
IEEE 1394 (FireWire) connection to digital video	No conversion from analog to digital needed; all-digital image is very high quality without compression artifacts (blocky areas) in video; fast throughput	Requires IEEE 1394 port, IEEE 1394 digital video source; card requires internal installation; some cards don't include capture/editing software; verify that editing software purchased separately works with card.

Troubleshooting Video Capture Devices

Table 15.25 provides some advice for troubleshooting problems with video capture devices. Note that IRQ conflicts can be an issue with both parallel port and add-on card devices and that low-bandwidth devices such as parallel port or USB devices might not be capable of supporting full-motion video capture except in a small window.

Table 15.25   Troubleshooting Video Capture Devices

Device Type	Problem	Solutions
Parallel port attachment	Can't detect device, but printers work okay.	Check port settings; device might require IEEE 1284 settings (EPP and ECP); change in BIOS; ensure device is connected directly to port; avoid daisy-chaining devices unless device specifically allows it; check Windows Device Manager for IRQ conflicts.
TV tuners (built-in graphics card or add-on)	No picture.	Check cabling; set signal source correctly in software; update software.

Table 15.25   Continued

Device Type	Problem	Solutions
All devices	Video capture is jerky.	Frame rate is too low. Increasing it might require capturing video in a smaller window; use fastest parallel port setting you can; use faster CPU and increase RAM to improve results.
All devices	Video playback has pauses, dropped frames.	Hard disk might be pausing for thermal recalibration; use AV-rated SCSI hard drives or UDMA EIDE drives; install correct busmastering EIDE drivers for motherboard chipset to improve speed. Reinstall video playback software.
USB devices	Device can't be detected or doesn't work properly.	Use Windows 98/Me/2000/XP; late versions of Windows 95 have USB drivers, but they often don't work. If you use a USB hub, be sure it's self-powered.
Interface cards (all types)	Card can't be detected or doesn't work.	Check for IRQ conflicts in Windows Device Manager; move card to different slot if possible.
IEEE 1394 cards	Card can't be detected or doesn't work.	Make sure power connector is attached to card if card has 4-pin power jack. Make sure correct drivers are installed.
All devices	Capture or installation problems	Use the newest drivers available; check manufacturers' Web site for updates, FAQs, and so on.

Adapter and Display Troubleshooting

Solving most graphics adapter and monitor problems is fairly simple, although costly, because replacing the adapter or display is the normal procedure. However, before you take this step, be sure that you have exhausted all your other options. One embarrassingly obvious fix to monitor display problems that is often overlooked by many users is to adjust the controls on the monitor, such as contrast and brightness. Although most monitors today have a control panel on the front of the unit, other adjustments might be possible as well.

Some NEC monitors, for example, have a focus adjustment screw on the left side of the unit. Because the screw is deep inside the case, the only evidence of its existence is a hole in the plastic grillwork on top of it. To adjust the monitor's focus, you must stick a long-shanked screwdriver about 2" into the hole and feel around for the screw head. This type of adjustment can save you both an expensive repair bill and the humiliation of being ridiculed by the repair technician. Always examine the monitor case, documentation, and manufacturer's Web site or other online services for the locations of adjustment controls. Most recent CRT and LCD monitors use front-mounted controls with onscreen display (OSD).

A defective or dysfunctional adapter or display usually is replaced as a single unit rather than being repaired. Except for specialized CAD or graphics workstation–oriented adapters, virtually all of today's adapters cost more to service than to replace, and the documentation required to service the hardware properly is not always available. You usually can't get schematic diagrams, parts lists, wiring diagrams, and other documents for most adapters or monitors. Also, virtually all adapters now are constructed with surface-mount technology that requires a substantial investment in a rework station before you can remove and replace these components by hand. You can't use a $25 pencil-type soldering iron on these boards!

Servicing monitors is a slightly different proposition. Although a display often is replaced as a whole unit, some displays—particularly 20" or larger CRTs or most LCD panels—might be cheaper to repair than to replace. If you decide to repair the monitor, your best bet is to either contact the company from which you purchased the display or contact one of the companies that specializes in monitor depot repair. If your CRT monitor has a 15" diagonal measurement or less, consider replacing it with a unit that is 17" or larger because repair costs on small monitors come close to replacement costs and large monitors aren't much more expensive these days.

Depot repair means you send in your display to repair specialists who either fix your particular unit or return an identical unit they have already repaired. This usually is accomplished for a flat-rate fee; in other words, the price is the same no matter what they have done to repair your actual unit.

Because you usually get a different (but identical) unit in return, they can ship out your repaired display immediately on receiving the one you sent in, or even in advance in some cases. This way, you have the least amount of downtime and can receive the repaired display as quickly as possible. In some cases, if your particular monitor is unique or one they don't have in stock, you must wait while they repair your specific unit.

Troubleshooting a failed monitor is relatively simple. If your display goes out, for example, a swap with another monitor can confirm that the display is the problem. If the problem disappears when you change the display, the problem is almost certainly in the original display or the cable; if the problem remains, it is likely in the video adapter or PC itself.

Many of the better quality, late-model monitors have built-in self-diagnostic circuitry. Check your monitor's manual for details. Using this feature, if available, can help you determine whether the problem is really in the monitor, in a cable, or somewhere else in the system. If self diagnostics produce an image onscreen, look to other parts of the video subsystem for your problem.

The monitor cable can sometimes be the source of display problems. A bent pin in the DB-15 connector that plugs into the video adapter can prevent the monitor from displaying images, or it can cause color shifts. Most of the time, you can repair the connector by carefully straightening the bent pin with sharp-nosed pliers. A loose cable or DVI/VGA adapter can also cause color shifts; tighten the cable and adapter securely.

If the pin breaks off or the connector is otherwise damaged, you can sometimes replace the monitor cable. Some monitor manufacturers use cables that disconnect from the monitor and video adapter, whereas others are permanently connected. Depending on the type of connector the device uses at the monitor end, you might have to contact the manufacturer for a replacement.

If you narrow down the problem to the display, consult the documentation that came with the monitor or call the manufacturer for the location of the nearest factory repair depot. Third-party depot repair service companies are also available that can repair most displays (if they are no longer covered by a warranty); their prices often are much lower than factory service. Check the Vendor List on the disc for several companies that do depot repair of computer monitors and displays.

Caution

You should *never* attempt to repair a CRT monitor yourself. Touching the wrong component can be fatal. The display circuits can hold extremely high voltages for hours, days, or even weeks after the power is shut off. A qualified service person should discharge the cathode ray tube and power capacitors before proceeding.

For most displays, you are limited to making simple adjustments. For color displays, the adjustments can be quite formidable if you lack experience. Use the OSD controls to adjust color, brightness, picture size, and other settings. To quickly adjust an LCD, try the auto-tune feature available on many models. Even factory service technicians often lack proper documentation and service information for newer models; they usually exchange your unit for another and repair the defective one later. Never buy a display for which no local factory repair depot is available.

If you have a problem with a display or an adapter, it pays to call the manufacturer, who might know about the problem and make repairs available. Sometimes, when manufacturers encounter numerous problems with a product, they might offer free repair, replacements, or another generous offer that you would never know about if you did not call.

Remember, also, that many of the problems you might encounter with modern video adapters and displays are related to the drivers that control these devices rather than to the hardware. Be sure you have the latest and proper drivers before you attempt to have the hardware repaired; a solution might already be available.

Troubleshooting Monitors

Problem

No picture.

Solution

If the LED on the front of the monitor is yellow or flashing green, the monitor is in power-saving mode. Move the mouse or press Alt+Tab on the keyboard and wait up to 1 minute to wake up the system if the system is turned on.

If the LED on the front of the monitor is green, the monitor is in normal mode (receiving a signal), but the brightness and contrast are set incorrectly; adjust them.

If no lights are lit on the monitor, check the power and power switch. Check the surge protector or power director to ensure that power is going to the monitor. Replace the power cord with a known-working spare if necessary. Retest. Replace the monitor with a known-working spare to ensure that the monitor is the problem.

Check data cables at the monitor and video card end.

Problem

Jittery picture quality.

Solution

LCD monitors. Use display-adjustment software or onscreen menus to reduce or eliminate pixel jitter and pixel swim.

All monitors. Check cables for tightness at the video card and the monitor (if removable):

- Remove the extender cable and retest with the monitor plugged directly into the video card. If the extended cable is bad, replace it.
- Check the cables for damage; replace as needed.
- If problems are intermittent, check for interference. (Microwave ovens near monitors can cause severe picture distortion when turned on.)

CRT monitors. Check refresh-rate settings; reduce them until acceptable picture quality is achieved:

- Use onscreen picture adjustments until an acceptable picture quality is achieved.
- If problems are intermittent and can be "fixed" by waiting or gently tapping the side of the monitor, the monitor power supply is probably bad or has loose connections internally. Service or replace the monitor.

Troubleshooting Video Cards and Drivers

Problem

Display works in DOS but not in Windows.

Solution

If you have an acceptable picture quality in MS-DOS mode (system boot) but no picture in Windows, most likely you have an incorrect or corrupted video driver installed in Windows. Boot Windows 9x/Me in Safe Mode (which uses a VGA driver), boot Windows 2000/XP in Enable VGA mode, or install the VGA driver and restart Windows. If Safe Mode or VGA Mode works, get the correct driver for the video card and reinstall.

If you have overclocked your card with a manufacturer-supplied or third-party utility, you might have set the speed too high. Restart the system in Safe Mode, and reset the card to run at its default speed. If you have adjusted the speed of AGP/PCI slots in the BIOS setup program, restart the system, start the BIOS setup program, and reset the AGP and PCI slots to run at the normal speed.

Problem

Can't replace built-in video card with add-on PCI or AGP video card.

Solution

Check with the video card and system vendor for a list of acceptable replacement video cards. Try another video card with a different chipset. Check the BIOS or motherboard for jumper or configuration settings to disable built-in video. Place the add-on card in a different PCI slot. Be sure the card is fully inserted into the PCI or AGP slot.

Problem

Can't select desired color depth and resolution combination.

Solution

Verify that the card is properly identified in Windows and that the card's memory is working properly. Use diagnostic software provided by the video card or chipset maker to test the card's memory. If the hardware is working properly, check for new drivers. Use the vendor's drivers rather than the ones provided with Windows.

Problem

Can't select desired refresh rate.

Solution

Verify that the card and monitor are properly identified in Windows. Obtain updated drivers for the card and monitor.

Problem

Can't adjust OpenGL or Direct3D (DirectX) settings.

Solution

Install the graphic card or chipset vendor's latest drivers instead of using the drivers included with Microsoft Windows. Standard Microsoft drivers often don't include 3D or other advanced dialog boxes.

DisplayMate

DisplayMate is a unique diagnostic and testing program designed to thoroughly test your video adapter and display. It is somewhat unique in that most conventional PC hardware diagnostics programs do not emphasize video testing the way this program does.

I find it useful not only in testing whether a video adapter is functioning properly, but also in examining video displays. You easily can test the image quality of a display, which allows you to make focus, centering, brightness and contrast, color level, and other adjustments much more accurately than before. If you are purchasing a new monitor, you can use the program to evaluate the sharpness and linearity of the display and to provide a consistent way of checking each monitor you are considering. If you use projection systems for presentations—as I do in my PC hardware seminars—you will find it invaluable for setting up and adjusting the projector.

DisplayMate also can test a video adapter thoroughly. It sets the video circuits into each possible video mode so you can test all its capabilities. It even helps you determine the performance level of your card, both with respect to resolution and colors as well as speed. You can then use the program to benchmark the performance of the display, which enables you to compare one type of video adapter system to another. The Video Edition also supports various types of multimedia projectors and TVs used in home theater and presentation environments.

See the Vendor List on the CD for more information on DisplayMate (formerly Sonera) Technologies, or visit **www. displaymate.com**.

Some video-card vendors supply a special version of DisplayMate for use in diagnostics testing.

CHAPTER 16

Audio Hardware

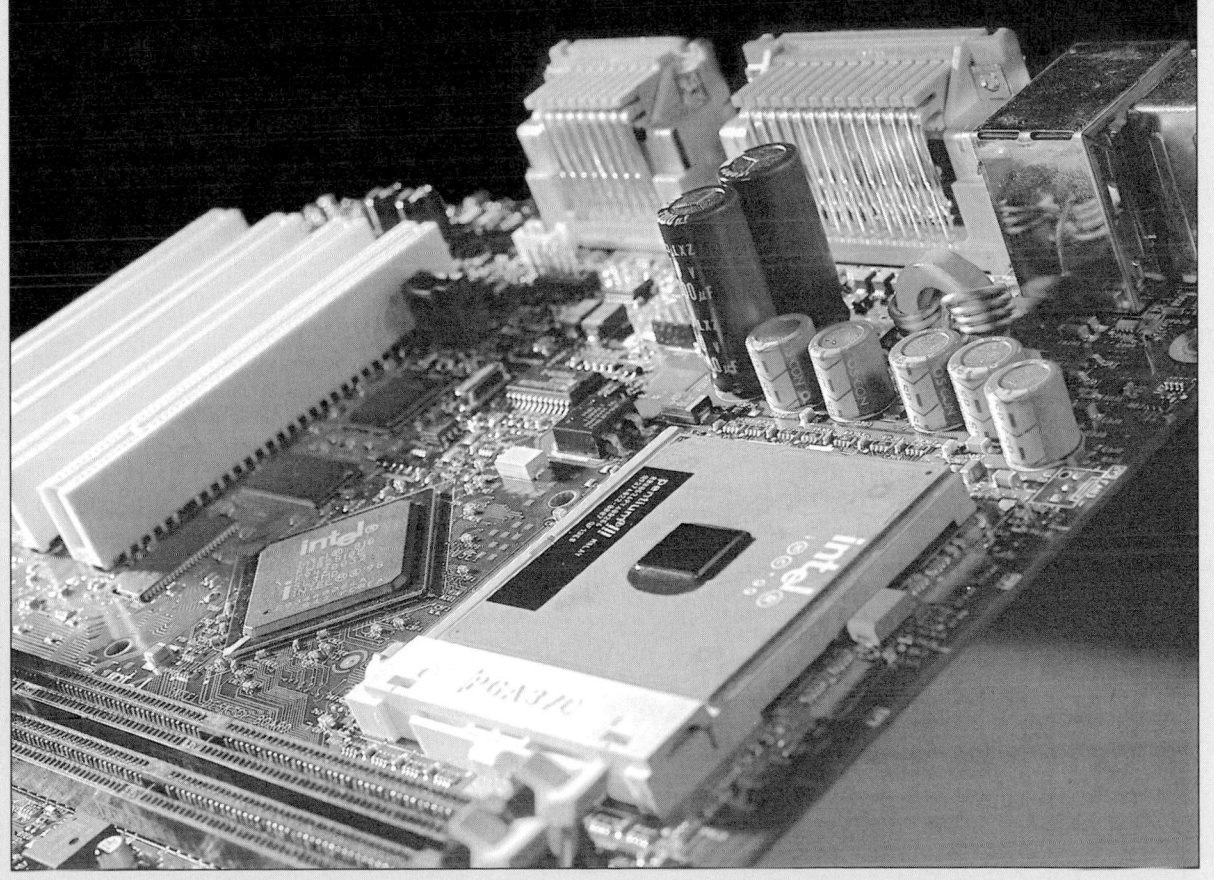

Since the first edition of this book was published in 1988, a lot has happened to audio hardware. Although rudimentary audio capabilities were part of the original IBM PC of 1981 and its many successors, audio was used on early computers for troubleshooting rather than for creative tasks. Computers used beeps for little other than to signal problems such as a full keyboard buffer or errors during the power on self test (POST) sequence. The Macintosh, first introduced in 1984, included high-quality audio capabilities in its built-in hardware, but PCs did not gain comparable audio capabilities until the first add-on sound cards from companies such as Ad Lib and Creative Labs were developed in the late 1980s.

Thanks to competition among many companies, we now enjoy widely supported d e facto hardware and software standards for audio. Audio hardware has gone from being an expensive, exotic add-on to being an assumed part of virtually any system configuration.

Today's PC audio hardware might take one of the following forms:

- An audio adapter on a PCI expansion card that you install into a bus slot in the computer.
- An AC'97 sound codec chip located on the motherboard, using sound chips from companies such as Crystal, Analog Devices, Sigmatel, ESS, or others.
- Hardware that's integrated into the motherboard's main chipset, as with some of the most recent chipsets for computers developed by Intel, SiS, NVIDIA, and VIA Technologies. A unique series of motherboards from Aopen combines this with a vacuum tube in the amplifier circuit catering to the audio purist.

Regardless of their location, the audio features use jacks for speakers and a microphone. In addition, many of them provide dedicated jacks for MIDI hardware (older cards usually provided an analog game port for joysticks). As you will see later in this chapter, many mid-range and high-end audio adapters also support sophisticated digital audio input and output. On the software side, the audio adapter requires the support of a driver that you install either directly from an application or in your computer's operating system. This chapter focuses on the audio products found in today's PCs, their uses, and how you install and operate them.

Early PC Audio Adapters

When the first audio adapters were introduced in the late 1980s by companies such as AdLib, Roland, and Creative Labs, they were aimed squarely at a gaming audience, were not compatible with each other, and often cost more than $100.

Note

About the same time as the release of the Creative Labs Game Blaster, hardware supporting the Musical Instrument Digital Interface (MIDI) became available for the PC. At this time, however, such hardware was used only in very specialized recording applications. As MIDI support became a more common feature in musical instruments, though, it also became a more affordable PC add-on.

The Game Blaster, which was compatible with only a handful of games, was soon replaced by the Sound Blaster, which was compatible with the AdLib sound card and the Creative Labs Game Blaster card, enabling it to support games that specified one sound card or the other. The Sound Blaster included a built-in microphone jack, stereo output, and a MIDI port for connecting the PC to a synthesizer or other electronic musical instrument. This established a baseline of features that would be supported by virtually all other sound cards and onboard sound features up to the present. Finally, the audio adapter had the potential for uses other than games. The follow-up Sound Blaster Pro featured improved sound when compared to the original Sound Blaster. The Sound Blaster Pro and its successors eventually triumphed over earlier rivals to become de facto standards for PC sound reproduction.

Note

Unlike de jure standards such as the IEEE-1394 port, which is an official standard of the IEEE organization, de facto standards are those that develop informally due to the widespread acceptance of the market leader's products in a particular segment of the marketplace. The Sound Blaster Pro is just one of many examples of a de facto standard: IBM's VGA card became a de facto baseline standard for video, and HP and Apple's different printer languages (HP PCL and Adobe PostScript) became de facto standards for printers.

Limitations of Sound Blaster Pro Compatibility

Through the mid-1990s, while MS-DOS was the standard gaming platform, many users of non–Creative Labs sound cards struggled with the limitations of their hardware's imperfect emulation of the Sound Blaster Pro. Unfortunately, some cards required two separate sets of hardware resources, using one set of IRQ, DMA, and I/O port addresses for native mode and a second set for Sound Blaster Pro compatibility. Others worked well within Windows or within an MS-DOS session running with Windows in the background but required the user to install a DOS-based Terminate and Stay Resident (TSR) driver program to work in MS-DOS itself.

However, the rise of 32-bit Windows games has made audio support very simple by comparison. Windows applications use the operating system's drivers to interface with hardware, relieving the software developer from needing to write different code for different sound cards, 3D graphics cards, and so on. For 3D sound and gaming graphics, Microsoft Windows uses a technology called DirectX, which was first introduced in December 1995; the current version is DirectX 9.0b.

DirectX and Audio Adapters

Microsoft's DirectX is a series of application program interfaces (APIs) that sit between multimedia applications and hardware. Unlike MS-DOS applications that required developers to develop direct hardware support for numerous models and brands of audio cards, video cards, and game controllers, Windows uses DirectX to "talk" to hardware in a more direct manner than normal Windows drivers do. This improves program performance and frees the software developer from the need to change the program to work with different devices. Instead, a game developer must work with only the DirectX sound engine, DirectX 3D renderer, and DirectX modem or network interface routines.

▶▶ For more information about DirectX and sound hardware, see "3D Audio," p. 966.

Thanks to DirectX, sound card and chipset developers are assured that their products will work with recent and current versions of Windows. However, if you still enjoy playing MS-DOS–based games, current audio adapters, chipsets, and integrated audio solutions still might present a compatibility challenge to you because of fundamental hardware differences between the ISA expansion slots used by classic Creative Labs and other sound cards and PCI slots, chipsets, and integrated audio.

▶▶ For more information about using PCI sound hardware with MS-DOS games, see "Legacy (MS-DOS and Gameport) Game Support Issues," p. 955.

PC Multimedia History

Virtually every computer on the market today is equipped with some type of audio adapter and a 0CD-ROM or CD-ROM–compatible drive such as a CD-RW or DVD drive. Computers equipped with an audio adapter and a CD-ROM–compatible drive are often referred to as *multimedia* PCs after the old MPC-1, MPC-2, and MPC-3 standards that were used to rate early multimedia computers. Since 1996, all computers with onboard sound and a CD-ROM or compatible optical drive have exceeded MPC-3 standards by increasingly huge margins.

Note

For more information about the MPC series of multimedia standards, see the section "Multimedia" in Chapter 20 of *Upgrading and Repairing PCs, 11th Edition*, available in electronic form on the disc accompanying this book.

Because the MPC specifications reflect multimedia's past, users who want to know what comes next need to turn somewhere else for guidance. Microsoft and Intel have jointly produced a series of PC System Design Guides. Although the PC System Design Guide's last version is known as PC 2001 and no further updates are planned, it and its predecessor (PC 99) are still useful references for multimedia hardware and software design and are still widely followed by the industry. For example, most I/O ports on recent systems use the PC 99 color-coding standard.

Note

You can download the PC 2001 and earlier PC System Design Guides from Microsoft's Web site at `http://www.microsoft.com/whdc/hwdev/platform/pcdesign/desguide/pcguides.mspx`.

Updated Microsoft-specific system design information is available at `http://www.microsoft.com/whdev/platform/pcdesign/desguide/default.mspx`.

Although virtually every computer is a "multimedia PC" today, the features of the audio adapter or onboard audio solution in your system will help determine how satisfied you will be with the wide range of specialized uses for multimedia-equipped systems.

Later in this chapter, you learn more about the features you need to specify to ensure your audio adapter—regardless of type—is ready to work for you.

Audio Adapter Features

To make an intelligent purchasing decision, you should be aware of some audio adapter basic components and the features they provide, as well as the advanced features you can get on better audio adapters. The following sections discuss the features you should consider while evaluating audio adapters for your PC.

Basic Connectors

Most audio adapters have the same basic external connectors. These 1/8" minijack connectors provide the means of passing sound signals from the adapter to speakers, headphones, and stereo systems, and of receiving sound from a microphone, CD player, tape player, or stereo. The four types of connectors your audio adapter should have at a minimum are shown in Figure 16.1. Note that computers with onboard audio also feature some or all of these jacks.

The jacks shown in Figure 16.1 are usually labeled, but when setting up a computer on or under a desk, the labels on the back of the PC can be difficult to see. One of the most common reasons a PC fails to produce any sound is that the speakers are plugged into the wrong socket. To avoid this problem, many consumer-oriented audio cards color-code the jacks according to specifications found in the PC 99 Design Guide available from the Microsoft Web site. The color-coding can vary on some audio adapters (or not be present at all). Regardless, the basic set of connections included on most audio cards is as follows:

- *Stereo line, or audio, out connector (lime green).* The line-out connector is used to send sound signals from the audio adapter to a device outside the computer. You can hook up the cables from the line-out connector to stereo speakers, a headphone set, or your stereo system. If you hook up the PC to your stereo system, you can have amplified sound.

- *Stereo line, or audio, in connector (light blue).* With the line-in connector, you can record or mix sound signals from an external source, such as a stereo system or VCR, to the computer's hard disk.

- *Rear out or speaker/headphone connector (no standard color).* Older sound cards often provided an amplified jack supplying up to 4 watts of power for use with unpowered speakers or head-phones along with the line-out connector. Today, you are more likely to find this jack used for rear speakers in four-speaker setups. The rear out jack often is disabled by default; check your audio adapter properties or setup program to see whether you need to enable this port when you connect rear speakers.

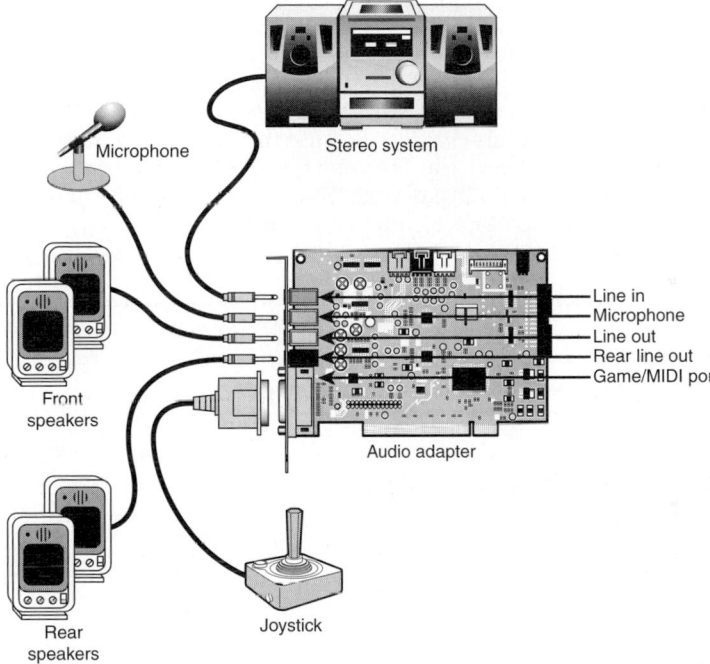

Figure 16.1 The basic input and output connectors that most audio adapters have in common.

Note

If you have only a single speaker/line-out connector, you must carefully adjust your mixer volume control and the volume control on your amplified speakers to find the best quality sound. Don't use powered speakers with an already-amplified sound if you can avoid it.

- *Microphone, or mono, in connector (pink).* The mono-in connector is used to connect a micro-phone for recording your voice or other sounds to disk. This microphone jack records in mono—not in stereo—and is therefore not suitable for high-quality music recordings. Many audio adapter cards use Automatic Gain Control (AGC) to improve recordings. This feature adjusts the recording levels on-the-fly. A 600ohm–10,000ohm dynamic or condenser micro-phone works best with this jack. Some inexpensive audio adapters use the line-in connector instead of a separate microphone jack.

- *Game port (gold).* The game port (also called the joystick connector) is a 15-pin, D-shaped connector that can connect to any standard joystick or game controller. Sometimes the joystick port can accommodate two joysticks if you purchase an optional Y-adapter. Many computers already contain a joystick port as part of a multifunction I/O circuit on the motherboard or an expansion card. If this is the case, you must note which port your operating system or application is configured to use when connecting the game controller. Some of the latest sound cards and systems with onboard sound omit this connector or put this connector on an optional bracket because most recent game controllers support USB connectors.

- *MIDI connector (gold).* Audio adapters typically use the same joystick port as their MIDI connector. Two of the pins in the connector are designed to carry signals to and from a MIDI device, such as an electronic keyboard. In most cases, you must purchase a separate MIDI connector from the audio adapter manufacturer that plugs into the joystick port and contains the two round, 5-pin DIN connectors used by MIDI devices, plus a connector for a joystick. However, high-end sound cards might use 5-pin MIDI ports connected to a daughtercard or a breakout box (see Figure 16.3, later in this chapter). Because their signals use separate pins, you can connect the joystick and a MIDI device at the same time. You need this connector only if you plan to connect your PC to external MIDI devices. You can still play the MIDI files found on many Web sites by using the audio adapter's internal synthesizer.

Note

Some recent systems with onboard audio lack the joystick/MIDI connector, but you can use digital game controllers that feature a USB connector to attach your game controllers to the USB port. And, as mentioned earlier, you can attach MIDI devices through the same USB connector with a suitable interface box.

In addition to the external connections, most sound cards feature at least one (and possibly multiple) internal CD-audio connectors. Most audio adapters have an internal 4-pin connector you can use to plug an internal CD-ROM drive directly into the audio adapter, using a small round cable. This connection enables the drive to send analog audio signals from the CD-ROM directly to the audio adapter, so you can play the sound through the computer's speakers. Some sound cards use a different connector than the CD-ROM, whereas others use the same type of connector as the CD-ROM (see Figure 16.2).

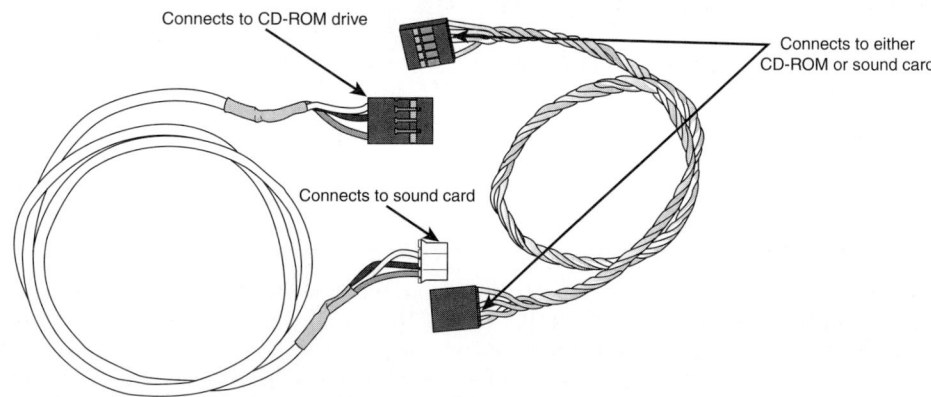

Figure 16.2 Typical CD-ROM analog audio cables.

Note

See Figure 16.10, later in this chapter, for an example of a typical sound card with analog and digital audio cables attached.

To play audio CDs, you have two choices: The playback can be either analog or digital. Analog playback is supported via an analog audio cable connected between the drive and sound card. This cable does not carry data from the CD-ROM to the system bus; it connects the analog audio output of the CD-ROM drive directly to the audio amplifier in the sound card. With many drives and sound cards—especially on older systems—if you don't connect an analog audio cable between the drive and card, you might be unable to play music CDs or hear some game audio.

Most newer drives and cards support digital playback as well as the standard direct analog connection. If your drive and card support digital playback, open the Control Panel in Windows, click the Multimedia icon, and then select the CD Music tab. You should see settings for changing the default drive for playing CD music and a box you can check to enable digital CD audio for that drive. If the box is grayed out (meaning you can't check it), digital audio is not supported for that drive or card.

Using digital audio enables multiple drives to play audio CDs. Typically, a sound card has only a single analog audio connector, so if you have multiple optical drives, only one can have an analog audio connection to the sound card for playing audio CDs. If you want to play audio CDs on multiple drives, you must either enable digital CD audio for those drives or purchase a CD audio Y-cable. By either enabling digital audio or installing an analog audio cable, you should be able to play audio CDs with any given CD/DVD drive.

Note

Many recent versions of audio player programs, such as Windows Media Player, can perform digital audio playback without using the two-wire digital audio cable between the CD-ROM drive and sound card. Instead, these programs read the CD music tracks and convert them on-the-fly into digital form.

Connectors for Advanced Features

Many of the newest sound cards and motherboards with onboard sound are designed for advanced gaming, DVD audio playback, and sound production uses and have additional connectors to support these uses, such as the following:

- *MIDI in and MIDI out.* Some advanced sound cards don't require you to convert the game port (joystick port) to MIDI interfacing by offering these ports on a separate external connector. This permits you to use a joystick and have an external MIDI device connected at the same time. Typical location: external device.

- *SPDIF (also called SP/DIF) in and SPDIF out.* The Sony/Philips Digital Interface receives digital audio signals directly from compatible devices without converting them to analog format first. Typical location: external device. (SPDIF interfaces are also referred to by some vendors as "Dolby Digital" interfaces.)

Note

SPDIF connectors use cables with the standard RCA jack connector but are designed to work specifically at an impedance of 75ohms—the same as composite video cables. Thus, you can use RCA-jack composite video cables with your SPDIF connectors. Although audio cables are also equipped with RCA jacks, their impedance is different, making them a less desirable choice.

- *CD SPDIF.* Connects compatible CD-ROM drives with SPDIF interfacing to the digital input of the sound card. Typical location: side of audio card. The cable used resembles the cable shown in Figure 16.2, but it uses only two wires. See Figure 16.10, later in this chapter, for an example of a typical sound card using a CD SPDIF cable.

- *TAD in.* Connects internal modems with Telephone Answering Device support to the sound card for sound processing of voice messages. Typical location: side of audio card.

- *Digital DIN out.* This supports multispeaker digital speaker systems, such as those produced by Cambridge for use with the SoundBlaster Live! series. Typical location: external device.

- *Optical SPDIF in/out.* This supports home theater and digital speaker systems with optical inputs. Typical locations: rear of card or external device.

- *Aux in.* Provides input for other sound sources, such as a TV tuner card. Typical location: side of audio card.

- *I2S in.* This enables the sound card to accept digital audio input from an external source, such as two-channel decoded AC-3 from DVD decoders and MPEG-2 Zoom Video. Typical location: side of audio card.

- *USB port.* This enables the sound card to connect to USB speakers, game controllers, and other types of USB devices. The Hercules Game Theater XP series, the first sound card with built-in USB ports, supports USB 1.1 only. Typical location: external breakout box.

- *IEEE 1394.* This enables the sound card to connect to IEEE 1394–compatible DV camcorders, scanners, hard drives, and other devices. The Creative Labs Sound Blaster Audigy, Audigy 2 series, and Hercules Digifire 7.1 all feature one or more IEEE 1394 ports. Typical location: card bracket or external cable or breakout box.

Sometimes, these additional connectors are found on the card itself, or sometimes they are attached to an internal or external breakout box, daughtercard, or external rack. Currently, the Sound Blaster Audigy 2 ZS Platinum and Platinum Pro sound cards from Creative Labs are two-piece units. Other recent models that feature a similar design include the Audigy 2 Platinum EX, Audigy 2 Platinum, Audigy Platinum, and the Hercules Game Theater XP 6.1 and 7.1. Although details vary, each of these models features a PCI-based sound card with basic I/O ports and a separate component with additional and more advanced I/O ports. The Audigy 2 ZS Platinum routes its additional connections to an internal breakout box that fits into an unused 5 1/4" drive bay (see Figure 16.3). The top-of-the-line Platinum Pro uses an external breakout box with the same connection options. Both models feature a remote control (not shown) and external volume controls (visible in Figure 16.3). The Hercules Game Theater XP series also featured an external breakout box, which Hercules refers to as an audio rack.

Figure 16.4 shows Chaintech's AV-710 audio adapter card with the internal connectors common on today's 3D sound cards.

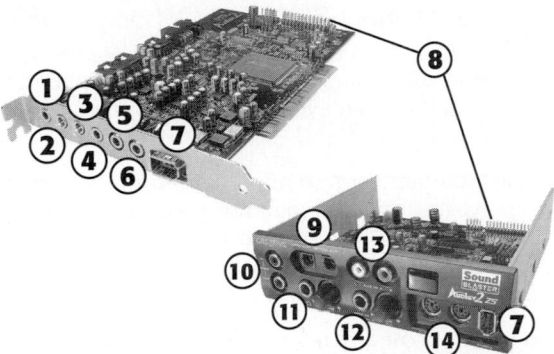

1. 6-channel digital out
2. Line in
3. Microphone in
4. Line out 1 (front/headphones; used with all analog speakers)
5. Line out 2 (rear; used with 4.1, 5.1, 6.1, 7.1 analog speakers)
6. Line out 3 (center/subwoofer; used with 5.1, 6.1, 7.1 analog speakers)

7. SB1394 ports (one each on the card bracket and on the Audigy drive)
8. Connection between Audigy 2 card and Audigy 2 Drive breakout box
9. Optical in/out
10. Coaxial SPDIF in/out
11. Headphone out
12. Line in/Mic IN
13. Left/right Aux in
14. MIDI in/out

Figure 16.3 The Sound Blaster Audigy 2 ZS Platinum (left) includes the Audigy 2 ZS Drive internal, front-panel breakout box (right) to support the Audigy 2 ZS's many features.

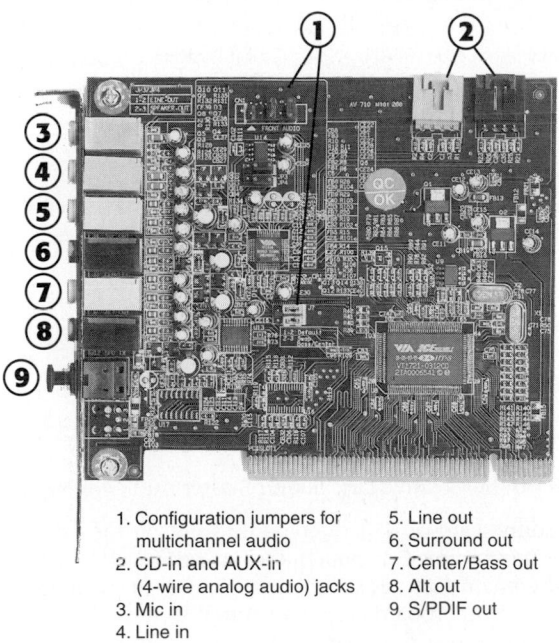

1. Configuration jumpers for multichannel audio
2. CD-in and AUX-in (4-wire analog audio) jacks
3. Mic in
4. Line in

5. Line out
6. Surround out
7. Center/Bass out
8. Alt out
9. S/PDIF out

Figure 16.4 Chaintech's AV-710 is a typical example of a mid-range 3D sound card with 7.1 audio support.

Adding Advanced Sound Features Without Replacing Onboard Audio

Traditionally, audio card upgrades have been designed specifically for users of desktop computers, leaving the growing number of notebook computer users out in the cold if they decided that the bare-bones features of their integrated audio weren't sufficient. However, several companies have recently developed USB-based audio processors that can be used by both notebook and desktop computers.

When you consider a USB-based solution, keep in mind that, unlike a normal sound card upgrade, you don't need to disable your existing onboard sound or remove a sound card. USB-based audio can coexist with existing sound cards. Typically, as with most hardware, the most recently installed hardware in a category becomes the default, but you can switch back to the original audio hardware through the Windows Control Panel Sound properties sheet.

Beyond the ability to add audio to almost any recent system, USB-based audio is particularly appealing if your current sound card or onboard audio doesn't support 5.1 or 7.1 audio, can't digitize sound at 24-bit/96KHz rates, or lacks digital outputs. Table 16.1 lists the major features of current and recent USB-based audio products.

Table 16.1 USB-Based Audio Processors

Manufacturer	Product	Output Quality	Recording Quality	Speaker Support	Notes
Audiotrak	MAYA EX	16-bit/48KHz	16-bit/48KHz	Up to 5.1	Dolby Digital AC-3
Audiotrak	MAYA EX7	16-bit/48KHz	16-bit/48KHz	Up to 7.1	Dolby Digital AC-3
Creative Labs	Sound Blaster Extigy	24-bit/96KHz	16-bit/48KHz	Up to 5.1	Dolby Digital AC-3
Creative Labs	Sound Blaster MP3+	16-bit/48KHz	16-bit/48KHz	2.1	Optical SPDIF input/output
Creative Labs	Audigy 2 NX	24-bit/96KHz	24-bit/96KHz	Up to 7.1	Dolby Digital AC-3, EX; supports Hi-Speed USB
Hercules	Gamesurround MUSE Pocket	16-bit/48KHz	16-bit/48KHz	Up to 5.1	No SPDIF connector
M-Audio	Sonica	24-bit/96KHz	N/A	Up to 5.1	Dolby Digital AC-3 with optical output only
M-Audio	Sonica Theater	24-bit/96KHz	24-bit/96KHz	Up to 7.1	Dolby Digital AC-3
Philips	PSC805 Aurilium	24-bit/96KHz	N/A	Up to 5.1	Dolby Digital AC-3; supports Hi-Speed USB
TerraTec	Aureon 5.1 USB	16-bit/48KHz	16-bit/48KHz	Up to 5.1	Dolby Digital AC-3

The connectors and controls on the Creative Labs Sound Blaster Audigy 2 NX are shown in Figure 16.5.

Before you purchase a new sound card or USB-based audio solution for a desktop computer, you should check your system or motherboard documentation to see whether you already have six-channel audio onboard. If your motherboard features six-channel (5.1) or better audio output but the only ports built in to the rear of the motherboard are for a normal stereo (2.0/2.1) configuration, you need to add a header cable to the motherboard similar to the one shown in Figure 16.6. If the motherboard did not ship with the header cable, contact the vendor.

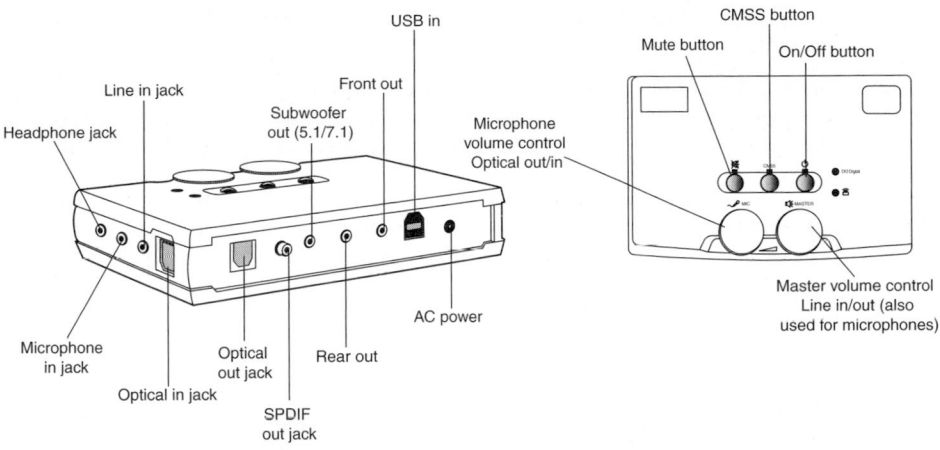

Figure 16.5 The Sound Blaster Audigy 2 NX expands bare-bones onboard audio by adding advanced I/O and sampling features similar to those found on the Sound Blaster Audigy 2 series.

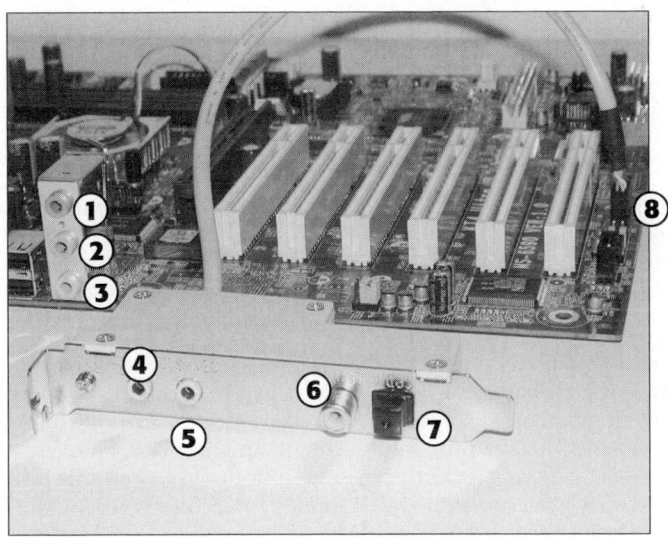

1. Microphone in	5. Speaker out (center/subwoofer)
2. Line in	6. Coaxial SPDIF digital audio out
3. Speaker out (front)	7. Optical SPDIF digital audio out
4. Speaker out (rear)	8. Header cable connection to motherboard

Figure 16.6 The built-in ports on the ATX port cluster (left) support stereo output, but the header cable (center) adds support for four-channel and six-channel audio and digital sound.

Volume Control

With virtually all recent sound cards, the volume is controlled through a Windows Control Panel speaker icon that can also be found in the system tray (near the onscreen clock). If you're switching from a bare-bones stereo sound card to a more sophisticated one featuring Dolby Digital 5.1, 6.1, or 7.1 output or input, you will need to use the mixing options in the volume control to select the proper sources and appropriate volume levels for incoming and outgoing audio connected to the card or a breakout box. Keep in mind that if you are sending sound to an external audio receiver, you will need to adjust the volume on that device as well.

If the PC speakers are amplified but you aren't hearing any sound, remember to check that the power is on, the volume control on the speakers is turned up, and the correct speakers are selected and properly connected. If the sound card has a thumbwheel volume control (as some older ones do), make sure it is turned up as well.

MIDI Support Features

At one time, when evaluating audio adapters, you had to decide whether to buy a monophonic or stereophonic card. Today, all audio adapters are stereophonic and can play music using the MIDI standard, which plays scores using either synthesized instruments or digital samples stored on the audio adapter or in RAM.

Stereophonic cards produce many voices concurrently and from two sources. A voice is a single sound produced by the adapter. A string quartet uses four voices, one for each instrument. On the other hand, a polyphonic instrument, such as a piano, requires one voice for each note of a chord. Thus, fully reproducing the capabilities of a pianist requires 10 voices—one for each finger. The more voices an audio adapter is capable of producing, the better the sound fidelity. The best audio adapters on the market today can produce up to 1,024 simultaneous voices.

Early audio adapters used FM synthesis for MIDI support; the Yamaha OPL2 (YM3812) featured 11 voices, whereas the OPL3 (YMF262) featured 20 voices and stereophonic sound. However, virtually all audio adapters today use recorded samples for MIDI support; audio adapters using this feature are referred to as *wavetable* adapters.

Wavetable audio adapters use digital recordings of real instruments and sound effects instead of imitations generated by an FM chip. When you hear a trumpet in a MIDI score played on a wavetable sound card, you hear the sound of an actual trumpet, not a synthetic imitation of a trumpet. The first cards featuring wavetable support stored 1MB of sound clips embedded in ROM chips on the card or on an optional daughtercard. However, with the widespread use of the high-speed PCI bus for sound cards and large amounts of RAM in computers, most soundcards now use a so-called "soft wavetable" approach, loading 2MB–8MB of sampled musical instruments into the computer's RAM.

While early games supported only digitized audio samples (because most early sound cards had very poor MIDI support), late DOS games such as DOOM began to exploit the widespread wavetable-based MIDI support found on most mid-1990s and more recent sound cards. With all current sound hardware supporting wavetable MIDI and the improvements in DirectX 8.x and above for MIDI support, MIDI sound has become far more prevalent for game soundtracks. Many Web sites also offer instructions for patching existing games to allow MIDI support. Whether you play the latest games or like music, good MIDI performance is likely to be important to you.

The most important factor for high-performance MIDI is the number of hardware voices. Even the best sound cards, such as Creative Labs' Sound Blaster Audigy 2 series, support only 64 voices in hardware; the remainder of the voices required by a MIDI soundtrack must come from software. If your sound card supports only 32 MIDI voices in hardware or uses software synthesis only, consider replacing it with a newer model. Many of the models currently on the market support more than 500 simultaneous voices and 64 hardware voices for under $100.

Data Compression

Virtually all audio adapters on the market today can easily produce CD-quality audio, which is sampled at 44.1KHz. At this rate, recorded files (even of your own voice) can consume more than 10MB for every minute of recording. To counter this demand for disk space, many audio adapters include their own data-compression capability. For example, the Sound Blaster series includes on-the-fly compression of sound files in ratios of 2:1, 3:1, and 4:1.

Most manufacturers of audio adapters use an algorithm called Adaptive Differential Pulse Code Modulation (ADPCM) compression (it's also called IMA-ADPCM), which was developed by the Interactive Multimedia Association (IMA) to reduce file size by more than 50%. IMA-ADPCM compresses 16-bit linear samples down to 4 bits per sample. However, a simple fact of audio technology is that when you use such compression, you lose sound quality. Unfortunately, no standard exists for the use of ADPCM. For example, although both Apple and Microsoft support IMA-ADPCM compression, they implement it in different ways. Apple's standard AIFF and Microsoft's standard WAV file formats are incompatible with each other unless you use a media player that can play both.

When you install an audio adapter, several codecs (programs that perform compression and decompression) are installed. Typically, some form of ADPCM is installed along with many others. To see which codecs are available on your system, open the Windows Control Panel and open the Multimedia icon (Windows 9x), the Sounds and Multimedia icon (Windows 2000), or the Sounds and Audio Devices icon (Windows XP). In Windows 9x, click the Devices tab followed by the plus sign next to Audio Compression to see the installed codecs. In Windows 2000 and Windows XP, click the Hardware tab, followed by Audio Codecs and Properties. The codecs are listed in order of priority, highest to lowest. You can also change the priority if you prefer a different order of priority. If you create your own recorded audio for use on another computer, both computers must use the same codec. You can select which codec you want to use for recording sounds with most programs, including the Windows Sound Recorder.

The most popular compression standard is the Motion Pictures Experts Group (MPEG) standard, which works with both audio and video compression and is gaining support in the non-PC world from products such as DVD players. MPEG by itself provides a potential compression ratio of 30:1, and largely because of this, full-motion-video MPEG DVD and CD-ROM titles are now available. The popular MP3 sound compression scheme is an MPEG format, and it can be played back on most versions of the Windows Media Player, as well as by various other audio player programs and devices.

Multipurpose Digital Signal Processors

Many audio adapters use digital signal processors (DSPs) to add intelligence to the adapter, freeing the system processor from work-intensive tasks, such as filtering noise from recordings or compressing audio on-the-fly.

The Sound Blaster Audigy 2 ZS's CA0102-ICT programmable DSP, for example, supports hardware sound acceleration needed by the latest version of Microsoft DirectX/DirectSound 3D, which enables multiple sounds to be played at the same time to synchronize with the onscreen action in a video game. The DSP can be upgraded with software downloads to accommodate more simultaneous audio streams. The widespread use of DSPs in better-quality audio adapters enables you to upgrade them through software instead of the time-consuming, expensive process of physical replacement.

For additional examples of DSPs, see the section "Who's Who in Audio," later in this chapter.

Sound Drivers

As with many PC components, a software driver provides a vital link between an audio adapter and the application or operating system that uses it. Operating systems such as Windows 9x/Me and Windows 2000/XP include a large library of drivers for most of the audio adapters on the market (Windows NT 4.0 also supports some sound hardware but not as much as other versions of Windows). In most cases, these drivers are written by the manufacturer of the audio adapter and distributed only by Microsoft. You might find that the drivers that ship with the adapter are more recent than those included with the operating system. Although traditionally the best place to find the most recent drivers for a piece of hardware has been the manufacturer's own Web site or other online service, Windows Me, 2000, and XP prefer digitally signed drivers that have been certified by the Microsoft Hardware Quality Labs. You might find these drivers available at the vendor's own Web site, but you can also download and install them automatically through Windows Update.

Any DOS applications you might still use do not typically include as wide a range of driver support as an operating system, but you should find that most games and other programs support the Sound Blaster adapters. If you are careful to buy an adapter that is compatible with Sound Blaster, you should have no trouble finding driver support for all your applications. Older ISA Sound Blaster cards provided hardware support for DOS games, but recent models (including the Sound Blaster Audigy/Audigy 2/Audigy 2 ZS series), as well as most comparable sound cards, require you to run software drivers to obtain Sound Blaster compatibility for DOS games. This software must be run before the game starts.

If your game program locks up when you try to detect the sound card during configuration, set the card type and settings manually. This is often a symptom of inadequate emulation for Sound Blaster by a third-party card. If you have problems, check the game developer's or audio adapter's Web site for patches or workarounds.

Choosing the Best Audio Adapter for Your Needs

Although sound features in computers have become commonplace, the demand for sophisticated uses for sound hardware have grown and demanded more and more powerful hardware. If your idea of a perfect multimedia PC includes any of the following, the plain-vanilla multimedia hardware found in many of today's PCs won't be sufficient:

- Realistic 3D and 360° sound for games
- Theater-quality audio for DVD movies
- Voice dictation and voice command
- Creating and recording MIDI, MP3, CD-Audio, and WAV audio files

Table 16.2 summarizes the additional hardware features and software you'll need to achieve the results you want with your high-performance audio adapter. The following sections examine in detail these advanced uses and the features you'll need for each.

Table 16.2   Audio Adapter Intended Uses and Features Comparison

Intended Use	Features You Need	Additional Hardware	Additional Software
Gaming	Game or USB port; 3D sound; audio accelerator	4.1 or greater speaker configuration; game controller	Games
DVD movie playback	5.1 or greater analog or Dolby Digital AC-3 support	5.1 or greater speaker configuration	DVD player program with 5.1 or greater audio support
Voice dictation and voice command	Audio adapter equivalent or better than Sound Blaster 16 and supported by software	Microphone optimized for voice-recognition	Voice-dictation or voice-command software
Creating MIDI files	MIDI-in connector	MIDI keyboard	MIDI composing software
Creating digital music (MP3, WMA) files	Digital connection to CD or DVD drive	CD or DVD drive with digital audio extraction (DAE) support	MP3 or WMA ripping software
Creating WAV (uncompressed audio) files	Line-in/microphone jack	Microphone or other sound source	Sound recording program
Creating CD audio files	Line-in jack	External sound source (microphone, CD audio, or others)	Digital (WAV, MP3, or WMA) to CD audio track conversion program

The following sections discuss many of these special uses in detail.

Gaming

Thanks to the widespread availability of audio adapters, game playing has taken on a new dimension. Support for 3D and surround digitized sound and realistic MIDI music in current games has added a level of realism that would otherwise be impossible even with today's sophisticated graphics hardware. Gaming enthusiasts should choose audio solutions with support for four or more speakers and some form of directional sound, such as the Creative Labs EAX technology used in Sound Blaster Live! and the Audigy/Audigy 2 series or Sensaura 3D Positional Audio (3DPA) used by ESS, VideoLogic, Cirrus Crystal Logic, Analog Devices, C-Media, and NVIDIA. Most recent sound cards feature support for one or more of these standards, either through direct hardware support or through software emulation and conversion. As with 3D video cards (see Chapter 15, "Video Hardware"), most cards today merely need to work with the 3D audio APIs included in the current revision of Microsoft's DirectX technology.

Any audio adapter built in the last few years will still work with today's games, thanks in large part to the Hardware Emulation Layer (HEL) built into DirectX. HEL emulates the features of newer hardware, such as 3D sound, on older hardware. However, as you can imagine, the task of emulating advanced performance on older hardware can slow down gameplay and doesn't produce sounds as realistic as those available with today's best audio adapters.

Sound Card Minimums for Gameplay

The replacement of the old ISA Sound Blaster Pro standard by PCI sound card standards has helped improve audio performance a great deal, but for the best gameplay with current and forthcoming titles, you need to consider sound cards with the following features:

- *3D audio support in the chipset.* 3D audio means you'll be able to hear sounds appear to move toward you, away from you, and at various angles corresponding to what's happening onscreen. Microsoft's DirectX, version 9.0b, includes support for 3D audio, but you'll have faster 3D audio performance if you use an audio adapter with 3D support built in. DirectX 9.0b works along with proprietary 3D audio APIs, such as Creative's EAX and EAX 2.0, Sensaura's 3D Positional Audio, and the A3D technology from now-defunct Aureal.

- *3D sound acceleration.* Sound cards using chipsets with this feature require very little CPU utilization, which speeds up overall gameplay. For best results, use a chipset that can accelerate a large number of 3D streams; otherwise, the CPU will be bogged down with managing 3D audio. This can slow down gameplay, particularly on systems with processors running under 1GHz or that are running at a high-resolution, high-color depth setting (1,024×768/32-bit).

Features such as these don't necessarily cost a ton of money; many of the mid-range audio adapters on the market ($50–$100 at retail) support these features. With new 3D audio chipsets available from a number of vendors, it might be time for you to consider an upgrade if you're heavily into 3D gaming.

Legacy (MS-DOS and Gameport) Game Support Issues

Support for the classic Sound Blaster Pro standard and 15-pin game port were once the primary requirements for a good gaming audio adapter. However, with the rise of great Windows-based games, the development of DirectX, and the replacement of game ports by USB ports, these are no longer issues for many users.

If you need to play MS-DOS games or work with game ports, see Chapter 16 of *Upgrading and Repairing PCs, 15th Anniversary Edition* on the disc packaged with this book to learn about compatibility considerations.

DVD Movies on Your Desktop

You don't need a dedicated DVD player to enjoy the clarity, control, extra features, and excitement of DVD movies. DVD-ROM drives help bring the DVD movie experience to your PC, but having a DVD-ROM and a DVD movie player program is only part of what you need to bring the big screen to your desktop.

To get the most out of your desktop DVD experience, you need the following:

- *DVD playback software that supports Dolby Digital 5.1 or better output.* One of the best choices is Cyberlink's PowerDVD 5.x, available from www.gocyberlink.com.

- *An audio adapter that supports Dolby Digital input from the DVD drive and will output to Dolby Digital 5.1–compatible audio hardware.* Some will remix Dolby 5.1 to work on four-speaker setups if you don't have Dolby 5.1 hardware or will accept S/PDIF AC3 (Dolby Surround) input designed for a four-speaker system; some can also pass through Dolby Digital audio to speakers that can perform the Dolby Digital 5.1 decoding. Some high-end audio adapters now support 6.1 and 7.1 speaker configurations; these also work with Dolby Digital 5.1 sound.

- *Dolby Digital 5.1–compatible stereo receiver and speakers.* Most high-end sound cards with Dolby Digital 5.1 support connection to analog-input Dolby Digital 5.1 receivers, but some, such as the Creative Labs Sound Blaster Live!, Audigy, and Audigy 2 Platinum series and the Hercules Digifire 7.1, Game Theater XP 7.1, and Fortissimo III 7.1 support digital-input speaker systems. Depending on which types of speakers you are using and how they are attached, you might need to switch your mixer settings in Windows from analog to digital to hear sounds from your applications (movies, games, and so on).

To learn more about speaker terminology and how to ensure your speaker configuration is correct, see the section "Speakers," later in this chapter.

Voice Dictation and Control

Voice dictation and voice control are a long-time dream of computer users, but unlike science-fiction movies in which the computer always understands the speaker, real-life applications for voice interfacing to computers haven't always been satisfying in practice.

Current vendors of voice-dictation software available in English include

- *ScanSoft.* Dragon NaturallySpeaking; IBM ViaVoice (www.scansoft.com)
- *Microsoft.* Microsoft Office XP and 2003 (www.microsoft.com)

Although the number of vendors of voice-dictation and control software is smaller than it was a few years ago, results are getting better, particularly if you

- Take time to train the software adequately.
- Use a computer with a 1GHz or faster processor and 256MB of RAM or greater.

Note

You can find an excellent summary of the current state of voice recognition, links to products and articles, as well as historical information at Itamar Even-Zohar's Page on Speech Recognition (http://www.tau.ac.il/~itamarez/Voice/).

For more information about voice recognition, see "Voice Dictation Software" in Chapter 20 of *Upgrading and Repairing PCs, 12th Edition*, included on the disc accompanying this book.

Sound Producers

Sound producers are people who intend to create their own sound files. These can range from casual business users recording low-fidelity voice annotations to professional musicians and MIDI maniacs. These users need an adapter that can perform as much of the audio processing as possible itself, so as not to place an additional burden on the system processor. Adapters that use DSPs to perform compression and other tasks are highly recommended in this case. Musicians will certainly want an adapter with as many voices as possible and a wavetable synthesizer. Adapters with expandable memory arrays and the capability to create and modify custom wavetables are also preferable.

Many of the best sound cards for hardcore gamers also are suitable for sound producers by adding the appropriate sound-editing programs, such as Sound Forge, and by equipping the card with the appropriate connectors for SPDIF digital audio and MIDI interfaces. The latest Sound Blaster Audigy 2 ZS Platinum and Platinum Pro include internal (Platinum) and external (Platinum Pro) breakout boxes with these features. The Creative Labs Audigy 2 NX and other USB devices with 24-bit/96KHz sampling provide features similar to those found on the Audigy 2 ZS Platinum series, but can be added to any system with a USB port. Most other audio cards designed for sound production features add jacks to the traditional trio of connectors on the rear card bracket.

Playing and Creating Digitized Sound Files

You can use two basic types of files to store audio on your PC. One type is generically called a sound file and uses formats such as WAV, VOC, AU, and AIFF. Sound files contain waveform data, which means they are analog audio recordings that have been digitized for storage on a computer. Just as you can store graphic images at different resolutions, you can have sound files that use various resolutions, trading off sound quality for file size. The default sound resolution levels used by the Windows Sound Recorder are shown in Table 16.3.

Table 16.3   Windows Default Sound File Resolutions

Format	Resolution	Frequency	Bandwidth	File Size
PCM	Telephone quality	11025Hz	8-bit mono	11KBps
	Radio quality	22050Hz	8-bit mono	22KBps
	CD quality	44100Hz	16-bit stereo	172KBps

If you have a sound card that supports DVD-quality (48000Hz, 16-bit stereo, 187KBps), you can also save sounds at that frequency with the Windows Sound Recorder, but you must select that setting manually. Note that the Windows Sound Recorder applet uses the Pulse Code Modulation (PCM) method for storing sounds as its default. PCM produces the highest quality of sound, but because it doesn't use any type of data compression, file sizes can be enormous.

Note

When you use the Windows Sound Recorder, you can reduce the size of the audio files you create by choosing a different format and sampling frequency and selecting stereo or mono recording. If you want to experiment with the results of various formats, save the audio at the highest quality setting using PCM, retrieve the original audio file, change one or more settings, and save the changes under a different name.

As you can see from Table 16.3, the difference in file sizes between the highest and lowest audio resolution levels is substantial. CD-quality sound files can occupy enormous amounts of disk space. At this rate, just 60 seconds of audio would require more than 10MB of storage. For applications that don't require or benefit from such high resolution, such as voice annotation, telephone-quality audio is sufficient and generates much smaller files. To achieve a balance between high quality and smaller file sizes, you can convert conventional WAV files into compressed formats, such as MP3 or WMA audio files.

The other type of file is a MIDI file, which consists of a musical score that is played back by synthesized or sampled musical instruments incorporated into the sound card's MIDI support.

Note

To learn more about the differences between MP3, WMA, and MIDI files, see "Audio Compression and MIDI Files" in the Technical Reference located on the disc packaged with this book.

On a multimedia PC, it is often possible for two or more sound sources to require the services of the audio adapter at the same time. Any time you have multiple sound sources you want to play through a single set of speakers, a mixer is necessary.

Most audio adapters include a mixer that enables all the different audio sources, MIDI, WAV, line in, and CD to use the single line-out jack. Starting with Windows 95 through the latest Windows versions (XP Pro/XP Home), Windows uses a single mixer for both recording and playback features, instead of using separate mixers as with Windows 3.x. Normally, the adapter ships with software that displays visual sliders like you would see on an actual audio mixer in a recording studio. With these controls, you can set the relative volume of each of the sound sources.

Tip

Whenever you change from analog to digital speakers or add speakers to a two-speaker configuration, you must adjust the mixer controls to match your current speaker configuration. If you don't, you will be unable to hear anything through your speakers.

Audio Adapter Concepts and Terms

To fully understand audio adapters and their functions, you need to understand various concepts and terms. Terms such as 16-bit, CD quality, and MIDI port are just a few. Concepts such as sampling and digital-to-audio conversion (DAC) are often sprinkled throughout stories about new sound products. You've already learned about some of these terms and concepts; the following sections describe many others.

The Nature of Sound

To understand an audio adapter, you must understand the nature of sound. Every sound is produced by vibrations that compress air or other substances. These sound waves travel in all directions, expanding in balloon-like fashion from the source of the sound. When these waves reach your ear, they cause vibrations that you perceive as sound.

Two of the basic properties of any sound are its pitch and intensity.

Pitch is the rate at which vibrations are produced. It is measured in the number of hertz (Hz), or cycles per second. One cycle is a complete vibration back and forth. The number of Hz is the frequency of the tone; the higher the frequency, the higher the pitch.

Humans can't hear all possible frequencies. Very few people can hear sounds with frequencies less than 16Hz or greater than about 20KHz (kilohertz; 1KHz equals 1000Hz). In fact, the lowest note on a piano has a frequency of 27Hz, and the highest note has a frequency a little higher than 4KHz. Frequency-modulation (FM) radio stations can broadcast notes with frequencies as high as 15KHz.

The amazing compression ratios possible with MP3 files, compared to regular CD-quality WAV files, is due in part to the discarding of sound frequencies that are higher or lower than normal hearing range during the ripping process.

The intensity of a sound is called its *amplitude*. This intensity determines the sound's volume and depends on the strength of the vibrations producing the sound. A piano string, for example, vibrates gently when the key is struck softly. The string swings back and forth in a narrow arc, and the tone it sends out is soft. If the key is struck more forcefully, however, the string swings back and forth in a wider arc, producing a greater amplitude and a greater volume. The loudness of sounds is measured in decibels (db). The rustle of leaves is rated at 20db, average street noise at 70db, and nearby thunder at 120db.

Evaluating the Quality of Your Audio Adapter

The quality of an audio adapter is often measured by three criteria: frequency response (or range), total harmonic distortion, and signal-to-noise ratio.

The *frequency response* of an audio adapter is the range in which an audio system can record or play at a constant and audible amplitude level. Many cards support 30Hz–20KHz. The wider the spread, the better the adapter.

The *total harmonic distortion* measures an audio adapter's linearity and the straightness of a frequency response curve. In layman's terms, the harmonic distortion is a measure of accurate sound reproduction.

Any nonlinear elements cause distortion in the form of harmonics. The smaller the percentage of distortion, the better. This harmonic distortion factor might make the difference between cards that use the same audio chipset. Cards with cheaper components might have greater distortion, making them produce poorer-quality sound.

The *signal-to-noise ratio (S/N or SNR)* measures the strength of the sound signal relative to background noise (hiss). The higher the number (measured in decibels), the better the sound quality. For example, the top-of-the-line Sound Blaster Audigy 2 sound card features an SNR of 106db, whereas the older Sound Blaster Audigy is rated at 100db and the AWE64 series has an SNR of 90db.

These factors affect all types of audio adapter use, from WAV file playback to speech recognition. Keep in mind that low-quality microphones and speakers can degrade the performance of a high-quality sound card.

Sampling

With an audio adapter, a PC can record waveform audio. Waveform audio (also known as sampled or digitized sound) uses the PC as a recording device (like a tape recorder). Small computer chips built into the adapter, called analog-to-digital converters (ADCs), convert analog sound waves into digital bits that the computer can understand. Likewise, digital-to-analog converters (DACs) convert the recorded sounds to an audible analog format.

Sampling is the process of turning the original analog sound waves into digital (binary) signals that the computer can save and later replay (see Figure 16.7). The system samples the sound by taking snapshots of its frequency and amplitude at regular intervals. For example, at time X the sound might be measured with an amplitude of Y. The higher (or more frequent) the sample rate, the more accurately the digital sound replicates its real-life source and the larger the amount of disk space needed to store it.

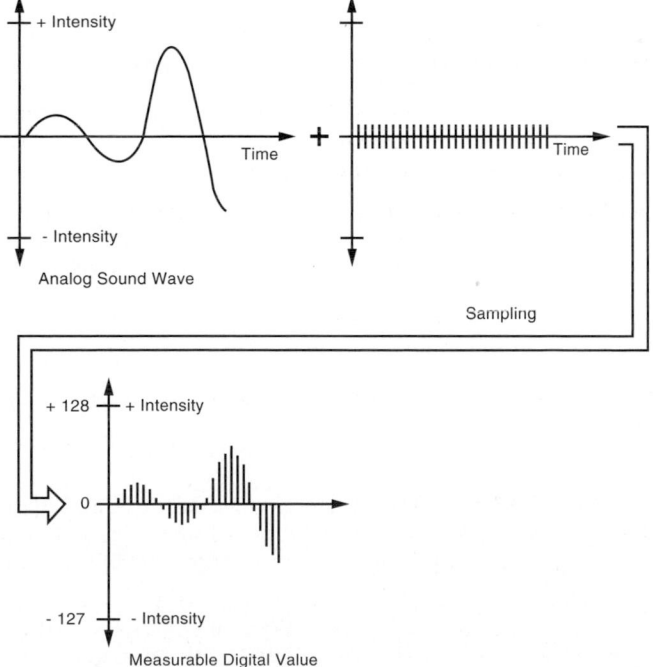

Figure 16.7 Sampling turns a changing sound wave into measurable digital values.

Originally, sound cards used 8-bit digital sampling that provided for only 256 values (2^8), which could be used to convert a sound. More recently, sound cards have increased the quality of digitized sound by using 16-bit (2^{16}) sampling to produce 65,536 distinct values. Today's highest-quality sound cards feature 24-bit sampling (2^{24}), which translates into more than 16.8 million possible digital values that can be matched to a given sound.

Note

For more information on the differences between 8-bit and 16-bit audio sampling, see "8-Bit Versus 16-Bit," in Chapter 16 of *Upgrading and Repairing PCs, 13th Edition*, included on the disc accompanying this book.

You can experiment with the effects of various sampling rates (and compression technologies) by recording sound with the Windows Sound Recorder or a third-party application set to CD-quality sound. Save the sound and play it back at that highest-quality setting. Then convert the file to a lower-quality setting, and save the sound file again with a different name. Play back the various versions, and determine the lowest quality (and smallest file size) you can use without serious degradation to sound quality.

Who's Who in Audio

Because audio adapters have become common features in systems, many vendors have produced audio adapters, audio chips, integrated motherboard chipsets with audio features, and even specialized vacuum tube audio. This section examines some of these companies and their products.

As you've learned in other chapters, I believe it is very important to get all the technical information you can about your computer and its components. By knowing who makes the audio chip your computer depends on, you can find out what the hardware can do and be better able to find upgrades to the software drivers you need to get the most out of your audio hardware.

Chipset Makers Who Make Their Own Audio Adapters

Just as graphics card vendors are divided into two camps, chipset makers are divided into these two categories:

- Card and device makers who produce their own chipsets
- Card and device makers who use chipsets from other vendors

Audio adapter vendors fall into the same categories. One of the pioneers of the audio adapter business, Creative Labs, has also been among the leaders in developing audio chips. Creative Labs develops audio chips primarily for its own Sound Blaster–branded products, but it has sold some of its older Sound Blaster 16 products into OEM markets.

Creative's major audio chips have included the following:

- *Vibra-16.* This was used in the later Sound Blaster 16 cards; it doesn't support wavetable or 3D effects.

- *Ensoniq ES137x series (ES1370/71/73).* These were used in the Sound Blaster PCI64 and PCI 128 series as well as the Ensoniq Audio PCI and Vibra PCI series. They support soft wavetable features, four speakers on some models and Microsoft Direct 3D but don't support 3D acceleration or EAX positional audio.

- *EMU-8000.* This audio chip was used by the AWE32/64 series and features 32-voice wavetable synthesis but no 3D acceleration. The AWE64 used software to generate 32 additional voices for a total of 64 voices.

- **EMU10K1.** This audio chip was at the heart of the Live! and Live 5.1 series sound cards as well as the PCI 512; it features 3D acceleration, EAX positional audio for one audio stream, a reprogrammable DSP, and soft wavetable support.

- **EMU10K2 (also known as Audigy).** This is the audio chip at the heart of Creative Labs' Sound Blaster Audigy series sound cards; it features 3D acceleration, EAX HD positional audio for up to four audio streams, a reprogrammable DSP, and soft wavetable support. This chip supports professional-level 24-bit sampling at 96KHz and real-time sampling at Dolby Digital–quality 24-bit samples at 48KHz.

- **CA0102 (also known as Audigy 2).** This audio chip is the one used by the Creative Labs Audigy 2 series. It's a development of the EMU10K2 chip, adding support for 24-bit 96KHz output, Dolby Digital EX 6.1 decoding and 6.1 sound in DirectX games, and 64 hardware polyphonic voices.

- **CA0185.** This audio chip is used by the Sound Blaster MP3+. It features 2.1 audio support for analog and digital speakers, 48KHz/16-bit playback and recording, and 3D acceleration.

- **CA0186.** This audio chip is used by the Audigy 2 NX. It features Dolby Digital EX 7.1 decoding, 7.1 sound in DirectX games, 96KHz/24-bit stereo output, and 3D audio acceleration.

- **CA0102-ICT (also known as Audigy 2 ZS).** This audio chip is used by the Creative Labs Audigy 2 ZS series. It's a development of the CA0102 chip, adding support for Dolby Digital EX 7.1 decoding, Dolby ETS decoding, 7.1 sound in DirectX games, and 192KHz/24-bit stereo output.

Various other companies have produced their own sound chips in the past but no longer do so. The primary makers that fit in this category are

- **Aureal.** Its A3D technology was regarded by many as superior to Creative Labs' original EAX 3D positional audio, but the company was absorbed by Creative Labs in mid-2000. Because Creative's new EAX HD is superior to A3D, there will be no further development of this technology.

- **Yamaha.** Its OPL2 and OPL3 chips were among the best FM-synthesis chips used on older sound cards, and its MIDI performance in later models was outstanding. However, its emphasis is now on MIDI daughtercards and professional sound-recording cards such as the SW1000XG. Some of its retail and OEM products might still be available, though. Yamaha maintains drivers and support links for its branded and some OEM cards at www.yamaha.co.jp/english/lsi/us.

- **Philips.** ItsIts ThunderBird Q3D (SAA7780) and ThunderBird Avenger (SAA7785) chips, jointly developed with QSound Labs, provided high-quality 3D acceleration for Philips's now-discontinued line of PCI-based sound cards. Some third-party sound cards also used the SAA7780 chip, but the six-channel SAA7785 was used only by Philips. See Table 16.4 for details.

Table 16.4   Philips ThunderBird Audio Chips

Audio Chip	Sound Cards	3D Audio	Speaker Support	Other Features
ThunderBird Q3D (SAA7780)	Philips PSC702, PSC704; Aztech PCI-368DSP; I/O Magic MagicQuad 8; Labway Thunder	64 3D hardware streams; EAX and QSound	4.1	DOS Sound 3D Blaster emulation; wavetable MIDI
ThunderBird Avenger (SAA7785)	Philips PSC604, PSC605, PSC703, PSC705, PSC706	96 3D hardware streams; EAX and QSound	Dolby Digital 5.1	DOS Sound Blaster emulation; wavetable MIDI

Should you panic if your favorite audio adapter is an "orphan?" Not necessarily. If the audio adapter vendor provides good technical support and up-to-date drivers, you're okay for now. But, the next time an operating system update or new audio API shows up, you probably won't be able to take advantage of it unless you replace your audio adapter.

Major Sound Chip Makers

Most companies other than Creative Labs depend on third parties to make their audio chips. Some of the major vendors include:

- *Atech.* The Sonix SN11116 USB audio controller is designed especially for the USB interface. It supports up to 48KHz sampling for digital and analog recording and playback. It supports six-channel analog output and SPDIF digital stereo output and can transmit AC-3 5.1 data via SPDIF to an external Dolby Digital decoder for 5.1 digital audio.

- *Cirrus Logic/Crystal Semiconductors.* The top-of-the-line Sound Fusion CS4630, an enhanced version of the CS4624, features 3D acceleration, support for both EAX and Sensaura positional audio, unlimited-voice wavetable synthesis, and S/PDIF support for AC3 and Dolby 5.1 input and output at rates up to 48KHz. The CS4630 is used in the Hercules Game Theater XP, Voyetra Turtle Beach Santa Cruz, TerraTec SiXPack 5.1, Video Logic Sonic Fury, and SonicXplosion audio adapters. The CS4624 is used by the Hercules Gamesurround Fortissimo II/III 7.1, Hercules DigiFire 7.1, TerraTec DMX Xfire, and Hoontech SoundTrack I-Phone Digital CS audio adapters.

- *ESS Technology.* The Canyon3D-2 (ESS1990/1992) is ESS Technology's flagship audio chip, featuring four-channel analog output, support for Dolby and THX digital sound, SPDIF input and output, and Sensaura 3D positional audio, and it is optimized for use with DirectX 8.0. It is used by the I/O Magic Hurricane Extreme, Diamond Monster Sound 3D, Hercules MaxiSound Fortissimo, and TerraTec DMX audio adapters.

  The Maestro-2 series features wavetable, positional 3D from Sensaura, and 3D audio acceleration; the Maestro 2E and 2EM also support S/PDIF output for DVD movie support. The Maestro series chips are optimized for notebook computers, and Maestro chips are used in recent models of Dell, Toshiba, Gateway, Compaq, and HP portables.

  The Allegro series (ESS-1989 for desktops and ESS-1988 for notebook computers) features DirectSound, Direct3D, S/PDIF output, and Sensaura 3D positional sound. The ESS-1989 is used by the Philips Harmonic Edge (PSC602) sound card as well as models sold by Pine Technologies and others.

  ESS's earlier AudioDrive series was popular with many notebook computers and second-tier sound card makers in the mid-1990s.

- *C-Media Electronics.* The CMI 8738 series features 4.1 and 5.1 speaker support for quadraphonic and Dolby Digital output, Direct Sound 3D and A3D positional audio, and wavetable and is available for desktop or notebook computers; some versions also integrate a software modem and SDPIF port. It is used by sound cards such as Guillemot's MUSE, Leadtek's WinFast 4x Sound, and various generic sound cards; and motherboards made by Asus, Soyo, Shuttle, Chaintech, and others.

- *ForteMedia, Inc.* The FM-801 is the first audio chip to feature Dolby Digital 5.1 output to analog speakers for both DVD movies and games. The FM-801 also features QSound's Q3D 2.0 3D API and optional support for SPDIF input/output. It uses host signal processing (HSP), which shifts some of the signal processing load onto the CPU, so it's a less desirable choice for slower systems than some other audio chips. The FM-801 is used by many smaller sound card makers and some motherboard makers, such as Shuttle. For a review of the sound chip and a feature comparison of some sound cards using this chip, see www.3dsoundsurge.com/reviews/FM801/FM801.html.

- *VIA Technologies.* VIA Technologies produces a wide range of audio controller chips sold under the Envy24 brand, all of which feature 24-bit resolution and DirectX 3D acceleration. The original Envy24 is designed for professional sound recording. The Envy24HT and Envy24HT-S are designed for use in high-performance (up to 192KHz sampling) sound cards for gamers and audiophiles; the Envy24PT features up to 96KHz sampling rate for use on low-cost motherboards with integrated audio. These chips are paired with the VIA Six-TRAC AC'97 codec for 5.1 audio. To achieve 7.1 audio, the Six-TRAC codec and an additional DAC are required, or the VIA Eight-TRAC AC'97 codec can be used instead of the Six-TRAC codec. The Envy24HT is used in the Audiotrak Prodigy 7.1, Aureon 7.1 Space, Aureon 5.1 Sky, and M-Audio Revolution 7.1 PCI sound cards. Envy24PT is used in motherboards from Albatron and Chaintech.

Discontinued and Orphan Sound Chips and Sound Card Producers

The following sound chips are no longer being sold, and ongoing support is limited or no longer available. If you use an audio adapter based on one of these products, you might need to upgrade if you can't get drivers for new and forthcoming operating systems.

Discontinued products include

- *Oak Technology OTI-601 series.* Oak left the audio chipset business in early 1998.
- *Trident 4DWave-NX series.* This 3D audio chipset was used on some cards from smaller audio adapter vendors, such as Aztech, Jaton, and Hoontech.

Note

The former Diamond Multimedia division of S3 (later Sonic Blue, now out of business) sold sound cards using chips from various vendors, including ESS Technology, Aureala, and others. The current Diamond Multimedia product line of graphics cards and modems is sold and supported by Best Data Products; the new Diamond Multimedia offers limited support for old Diamond Multimedia modem and graphics card products, but not sound cards. You can search the Web to locate drivers for S3-built Diamond sound cards.

Motherboard Chipsets with Integrated Audio

The Intel 810 chipset was the first mainstream chipset for a major CPU to integrate audio; it works with Celeron CPUs. Its inspiration might have been the Cyrix/National Semiconductor Media GX series, which used a trio of chips to substitute for the CPU, VGA video, onboard audio, memory, and I/O tasks.

Thanks to improvements in chipset design and faster CPU performance, today's best integrated chipsets can provide solid mid-range performance. Almost all recent chipsets from Intel, VIA, ALi, and SiS have integrated audio (see Chapter 4, "Motherboards and Buses," for details). In almost every case, integrated audio supports the AC'97 audio standard.

AC'97 Integrated Audio

The phrase *AC'97 integrated audio* can be found in the descriptions of most recent systems. Because AC'97 can replace the need for a separate audio card but might not be a satisfactory replacement, you need to understand what it is and how it works.

AC'97 (often referred to as *AC97*) is an Intel specification that connects an audio codec (compression/decompression) architecture to a section of a South Bridge, an I/O Communications Hub chip called the AC-Link control, or an audio controller such as the VIA Envy24 series. The AC-Link control works with the CPU and an AC'97 digital signal processor (DSP) to create audio.

The AC'97 audio codec could be a physical chip on the motherboard, a chip on a small daughterboard called a *communications and networking riser (CNR)*, or a software program. Thus, a motherboard with AC'97 integrated sound support doesn't require the use of a separate audio card for sound playback. Sometimes *AC'97* is also used to refer to audio chips on a sound card, but in this discussion we will use it to refer only to integrated audio. Sometimes motherboards also integrate an analog modem through an MC '97 codec chip, or they might have an AMC '97 (audio/modem) codec chip to combine both functions.

Note

Some low-cost sound cards and some USB-based audio products use AC'97 codec chips along with additional components instead of traditional single-chip audio solutions.

It's important to realize that, although most recent chipsets support AC'97 audio, this does not mean that every motherboard built on a particular chipset uses the same AC'97 codec, or even the same method of creating sound. In most cases, AC'97 is implemented through a small AC'97 codec chip on the motherboard (see Figure 16.8). It can be surface-mounted as shown in Figure 16.8, but many vendors use a small socket instead.

Figure 16.8 The VIA VT1612A is a typical AC'97 2.2–compliant codec chip. *Photo courtesy of VIA Technologies, Inc.*

A few motherboards use an AMR or a CNR riser card to implement AC'97 audio along with audio ports.

For various reasons, including audio codec features and price, different motherboard vendors might use different AC'97 codec chips on motherboards that use the same chipset.

For example, compare the following motherboards based on the Intel 865PE chipsets as listed in Table 16.5.

Table 16.5   Sample AC'97 Codecs Used with Intel 865–Based Motherboards

Vendor	Motherboard Model	AC'97 Codec Chip
FIC	P4-865PE Max II	Analog Devices AD1980
Soyo	Sy-P4I865PE Plus Dragon 2	C-Media 9739A
Giga-Byte	GA-8IPE1000-G	Realtek ALC850

Major vendors of AC'97 codecs include Analog Devices (SoundMAX), C-Media, Cirrus Logic (Crystal Audio), National Semiconductor, Realtek (includes former Avance Logic products), SigmaTel (STAC C-Major), VIA Technologies, and Wolfson Microelectronics plc.

Note

The drivers for a particular AC'97 codec chip are supplied by your motherboard vendor because they must be customized to the combination of codec and South Bridge/ICH chip your motherboard uses.

Although the AC'97 specification recommends a standard pinout, differences do exist between AC'97 codec chips. Some vendors of AC'97 chips provide technical information to help motherboard builders design sockets that can be used with different models of the AC'97 codec chip. However, in other cases, AC'97 codecs are surface-mounted to the motherboard.

The four versions of the AC'97 codec are as follows:

- *AC'97 1.0.* Has fixed 48KHz sampling rate and stereo output
- *AC'97 2.1.* Has options for variable sampling rate and multichannel output
- *AC'97 2.2.* Has AC'97 2.1 features plus optional S/PDIF digital audio and enhanced riser card support; released in September 2000
- *AC'97 2.3.* Has AC'97 2.1/2.2 features plus support for true Plug and Play detection of audio devices; released in July 2002

Note

Audio solutions that use AC'97 2.3–compliant codecs can detect whether you have connected a speaker to the microphone jack or a microphone to the speaker jack and warn you that the wrong jack is being used for the device. This helps eliminate one of the most common causes of audio failures.

Most recent motherboards with integrated audio support AC'97 2.2 or 2.3. To learn more about the AC'97 specifications, see the Intel – Research and Development, Audio Codec site at `www.intel.com/labs/media/audio/index.htm`.

To determine whether a particular motherboard's implementation of AC'97 audio will be satisfactory, follow these steps:

1. Determine which codec chip the motherboard uses. Read the motherboard manual or see which driver the motherboard uses for audio.
2. Look up the chip's features and specifications. If you are not sure of the chip manufacturer, look up the part number with a search engine such as Google.
3. Use a search engine to find reviews of the chip's sound quality and performance (typically found as part of a motherboard review).
4. Look at the motherboard's features to determine whether it uses the full capabilities of the codec chip. Chips that support AC'97 2.1 can offer up to six-channel analog audio; those that support AC'97 2.2 can also offer S/PDIF digital audio. However, motherboard makers don't always provide the proper outputs.
5. Analyze how you use audio. If you play a lot of 3D games, you're not likely to be satisfied with the performance of any integrated audio solution, no matter what its features might be. You can disable onboard audio with a BIOS setting if you prefer to install your own audio card.

◄◄ For details on how to enable and disable onboard audio, see "Peripheral Configuration," p. 437.

AOpen TubeSound

The Taiwan-based motherboard maker AOpen, part of the Acer Group, came up with a very interesting gimmick in June 2002 when it introduced the world's first PC motherboard with a vacuum tube–based audio amplifier—the AOpen AX4B-533 Tube. The motherboard was based on the Intel 845E chipset, and uses a Realtek ALC650 AC'97 audio codec chip. At first, many PC users wondered whether this was an April Fool's joke that showed up late. Why a vacuum tube? AOpen engineers pointed out that serious audiophiles have continued to use vacuum-tube amplifiers because of their rich sound. They felt that audiophiles would pay a premium price for similar technology in the sound circuitry of a PC. AOpen used the following design features to bring the vacuum tube into the twenty-first century:

- *A switching mode power supply to provide adequate tube power.* Tubes fell out of favor in the late 1950s because they require more power than transistors and integrated circuits.

- *A dual-triode.* This design has one tube with two front stereo channels and is modeled after the design used by classic pre-amp circuits, which can also accept input from standard sound cards.

- *Frequency isolation wall (FIW) noise reduction.* This shields the tube circuitry from the normal EFI/RFI interference inside the computer.

- *High mean time between failure (MTBF) design for motherboard and tube circuitry.*

The additional circuitry used by the AX4B-533 Tube made it one of the most expensive motherboards using the 845E chipset (see Figure 16.9). However, it has received rave reviews from many computer publications and users for audio quality, performance, and (not least) the snob appeal of having the first motherboard on the block like it.

Figure 16.9   A close look at the A4XB-533's vacuum tube sound system.

The AX4B-533 Tube's audio quality is optimized for classical and jazz music listening. AOpen has now released additional vacuum-tube-based motherboards: the AX4GE Tube and AX4PE Tube for Pentium 4 processors and the AK79G Tube for Athlon XP processors. These motherboards are optimized for rock and pop music thanks to a slightly revised tube and amplifier design.

Tip

To compare these motherboards in more detail, see the AOpen TubeSound technology Web site at `http://english.aopen.com.tw/tech/techinside/Tube.htm`.

3D Audio

One of the biggest issues for serious game players when audio adapters are considered is how well they perform 3D audio tasks. This has been complicated by several factors, including the following:

- Differing standards for positional audio
- Hardware versus software processing of 3D audio
- DirectX support issues

Positional Audio

The underlying issue common to all 3D sound cards is that of positional audio, which refers to adjusting features such as reverberation; balance; and apparent sound "location" to produce the illusion of sound coming from in front of, beside, or even behind the user. One very important element in positional audio is HRTF (Head Related Transfer Function), which refers to how the shape of the ear and the angle of the listener's head changes the perception of sound. Because HRTF factors mean that a "realistic" sound at one listener's head angle might sound artificial when the listener turns to one side or the other, the addition of multiple speakers that "surround" the user, as well as sophisticated sound algorithms that add controlled reverberation to the mix, are making computer-based sound more and more realistic.

Creative Labs' Environmental Audio Extensions (EAX) has become the de facto standard for 3D audio since the demise of Aureal's A3D in mid-2000. There are four versions of EAX:

- EAX 1.0
- EAX 2.0
- EAX Advanced HD (also known as EAX 3.0)
- EAX 4.0 Advanced HD

EAX 1.0 introduced 26 presets designed to simulate the audio effects caused by typical building and natural environments along with the capability to adjust volume, reverberation, decay time, and damping. EAX 2.0 adds occlusions (how sound originating in one room is heard in another room) and obstructions (how sound is heard when an object blocks direct sound waves and only reflections can be heard).

EAX 1.0 and EAX 2.0 are supported both by Creative's Sound Blaster and Audigy series of sound cards but also by most recent third-party sound cards and integrated audio solutions, thanks to Creative's release of these standards to the industry.

EAX Advanced HD, introduced by the Sound Blaster Audigy, adds support for multienvironment— each sound (up to four) can have its own environmental effects. It also adds environment morphing, environment panning, and environment reflection, three methods used to change environment sounds as the player moves through the game. Environmental filtering fine-tunes how sounds change from environment to environment. Audigy 2's version of EAX Advanced HD adds the capability to convert DirectX 3D audio (Direct3D) into 6.1 audio on systems with 6.1 speaker systems. EAX Advanced HD supports up to 32 channels of Direct 3D hardware voice acceleration.

EAX 4.0 Advanced HD, introduced by the Sound Blaster Audigy 2 ZS, adds sound effects such as pitch and frequency shifting, automatic gain control compression, a wah-wah pedal, chorus, distortion, a whooshing effect (flanger), and a ring modulator. EAX 4.0 Advanced HD also adds a comb filter to remove audio artifacts, HRTF filters, cross-talk cancellation algorithms that support speaker types from headphones (2.0) up through 7.1, and 64 channels of Direct 3D hardware voice acceleration.

Note

Audigy 2 cards (but not the low-end Audigy LS) can also use EAX 4.0 Advanced HD through a driver update.

The major alternative to EAX is Sensaura's 3D positional audio technology (3DPA). Most third-party sound cards support Sensaura 3DPA along with EAX 1.0/2.0. The full range of Sensaura 3DPA features include

- *Digital Ear.* HRTF filters
- *Virtual Ear.* Customizes Digital Ear for the listener's ear size and positioning
- *MacroFX.* Improves realism of close sound sources, such as a buzzing insect
- *ZoomFX.* Improves realism of sounds from different sizes of objects, such as trains versus motorcycles
- *EnvironmentFX.* Preset environments with adjustable properties
- *XTC and MultiDrive.* Crosstalk cancellation for speaker systems up to 7.1
- *Headphone Theater.* Simulates 5.1 audio for headset users

Note

Some audio cards that use Sensaura 3DPDA technology might not support all the features, or they might require a software upgrade. Contact your audio card or motherboard vendor for details.

3D Audio Processing

A second important issue for game players is how the sound cards produce 3D audio. As with 3D video, there are two major methods:

- Host-based processing (which uses the CPU to process 3D, which can slow down overall system operation)
- Processing on the audio adapter (referred to as 3D acceleration)

Some 3D audio cards perform some or all of the processing necessary for 3D using the host's CPU, whereas others use a powerful DSP that performs the processing on the audio adapter itself. Cards that use host-based processing for 3D audio as well as systems that use AC'97 audio codecs for integrated 3D audio can cause major drops in frame rate (frames per second of animation displayed onscreen by a 3D game) when 3D sound is enabled on systems with processors running at speeds under 1GHz. However, cards with their own 3D audio processors onboard have little change in frame rate whether 3D sound is enabled or disabled. Many of the latest chips from major audio adapter and chipset vendors support 3D acceleration, but the number of 3D audio streams supported varies greatly by chip—and it can sometimes be limited by problems with software drivers.

A good rule of thumb for realistic gaming is to have an overall average frame rate of at least 30fps (frames per second). With CPUs running at 1GHz or above, this is easy to achieve with any recent 3D audio card or recent onboard integrated audio solutions. However, gamers using older CPUs, such as those running slower than 1GHz, will find that cards using the host CPU for some of the 3D processing will have frame rates that fall below the desired average of 30fps, making for clumsy gameplay. To see the effect of enabling 3D sound on the speed of popular games, you can use the built-in frame-rate tracking feature found in many games or check online game-oriented hardware review sources, such as www.anandtech.com. Frame rates are closely related to CPU utilization; the more CPU attention your 3D audio card or integrated audio solution requires, the slower the frame rate will be.

As with 3D video, the main users of 3D sound are game developers, but business uses for ultra-realistic sound will no doubt follow.

DirectX Support Issues

The latest version of DirectX, DirectX 9.0b, is designed to give all sound cards with 3D support a major boost in performance compared to DirectX 8.x and earlier versions. Previous versions of DirectX supported 3D with DirectSound3D, but the performance of DirectSound3D was limited. Game programmers needed to test the audio adapter to see whether it supported DirectSound3D acceleration and then would either enable or disable 3D sounds based on the host hardware. Starting with DirectX 5.0, DirectSound3D works with third-party 3D acceleration features. Compared to DirectX 8.x, DirectX 9.0b improves 3D audio quality and performance. You can download it from the Microsoft DirectX Web site at www.microsoft.com/windows/directx.

Installing the Sound Card

Before you can install a sound card, you must open your computer. In almost all cases today, you will install a PCI audio adapter that supports Plug and Play configuration. Compared to the previous generation of ISA audio adapters, PCI audio adapters use fewer hardware resources, feature a lower CPU utilization rate, and provide better support for advanced 3D gaming APIs.

If you need to install an ISA audio adapter, see "Installing the Sound Card (Detailed Procedure)" in Chapter 20 of *Upgrading and Repairing PCs, 11th Edition*, supplied in electronic form on the disc packaged with this book.

If your computer has integrated audio, in most cases you should disable it. You could have audio conflicts with AC'97 codec-based solutions and resource conflicts with solutions that emulate the Creative Labs Sound Blaster. See Chapter 5, "BIOS," for details.

If you have several empty bus slots from which to choose, install the audio adapter in the slot that is as far away as possible from the other cards in the computer. This reduces any possible electromagnetic interference; that is, it reduces stray radio signals from one card that might affect the sound card. The analog components on audio adapters are highly susceptible to interference, and even though they are shielded, they should be protected as well as is possible. Next, you must remove the screw that holds the metal cover over the empty expansion slot you've chosen. Remove your audio adapter from its protective packaging. When you open the bag, carefully grab the card by its metal bracket and edges. Do not touch any of the components on the card because any static electricity you might transmit can damage the card. Also, do not touch the gold-edge connectors. You might want to invest in a grounding wrist strap, which continually drains you of static build-up as you work on your computer.

Before you make your final decision about which slot to use for your audio adapter, take a careful look at the external cables you must attach to the card. Front and rear speakers, microphone, game controller, line in, S/PDIF, and other cables that attach to your system can interfere with (or be interfered by) existing cables already attached to your system. It's usually best to choose a slot that allows you to route the audio cables away from other cables. If you're installing a sound card that uses an internal 5 1/4" breakout box, be sure the ribbon cable from the drive bay used for the breakout box can comfortably reach the connector on the sound card. You might have to move a CD-ROM, CD-RW, or DVD drive to a different drive bay to free up a drive bay needed by the breakout box.

Figure 16.10 shows a Creative Labs Audigy sound card after installation in a computer. The four-wire analog and two-wire digital cables to the CD-ROM drive are connected to the card, as is the ribbon cable to the Audigy Drive internal breakout box. However, the cable to the Audigy Drive's SB1394 (IEEE-1394a-compatible) port has not yet been connected to the card.

1. Mounting screw
2. TAD (telephone answering device) analog audio connector
3. CD audio analog cable
4. Aux in analog audio connector
5. SB1394 (IEEE-1394a) I/0 connector
6. CD SPDIF digital audio cable
7. Audigy Drive I/O cable
8. Game port (joystick) header pins

Figure 16.10   A Creative Labs Audigy sound card installed in a typical PC.

If your system has an internal CD-ROM drive with an analog audio cable, connect the audio cable to the adapter's CD Audio In connector, as shown in Figure 16.10. This connector is a four-pin connector and is keyed so that you can't insert it improperly. Note that no true standard exists for this audio cable, so be sure you get the correct one that matches your drive and adapter. If you need to purchase one, you can find cables with multiple connectors designed for various brands of CD-ROM drives. This will allow you to play music CDs through the sound card's speakers and to use analog ripping if you want to create MP3 files from your CDs.

Many recent CD-ROM and DVD drives also have a digital audio connector that supports a two-wire connector. Attach one end of the digital audio cable to the rear of the drive and the other end to the CD SPDIF or CD Digital Audio connector on the sound card (refer to Figure 16.10). This enables you to perform digital ripping if you want to create MP3 files from your CDs. Note that some ripping programs can also use digital signals received through the drive's data cable.

Next, insert the adapter's edge connector in the bus slot, but first touch a metal object, such as the inside of the computer's cover, to drain yourself of static electricity. When the card is firmly in place, attach the screw (refer to Figure 16.10) to hold the expansion card and then reassemble your computer.

Connecting PC Speakers and Completing the Installation

After the adapter card is installed, you can connect small speakers to the external speaker jack(s). Typically, sound cards provide 4 watts of power per channel to drive unpowered bookshelf speakers. If you are using speakers rated for less than 4 watts, do not turn up the volume on your sound card to the maximum; your speakers might burn out from the overload. You'll get better results if you plug your sound card into powered speakers—that is, speakers with built-in amplifiers. If your sound card supports a four-speaker system, check the documentation to see which jack is used for the front speakers and which for the rear speakers. To use the rear speakers for 3D audio, adjust the properties with the mixer control software supplied with your sound card.

Tip

If you have powered speakers but don't have batteries in them or have them connected to an AC adapter, don't turn on the speakers! Turning on the speakers without power will prevent you from hearing anything at all. Leave the speakers turned off and use the volume control built into your sound card's mixer software instead. Powered speakers sound better, but most small models can run without power in an emergency.

Some computer power supplies feature small jacks to provide power for computer speakers.

When the sound card installation is finished, you should have a speaker icon in the Windows System Tray. If the speaker icon (indicating the Volume Control) isn't visible, you can install it through the Control Panel's Add/Remove Programs icon. With Windows 9x/Me, select the Windows Setup tab and open the Multimedia section. Then, check the box labeled Volume Control. With Windows XP, open the Sounds and Audio Devices icon in Control Panel, click the Volume tab, and click the Place Volume icon in the taskbar box. In some cases you might be asked to insert the Windows CD-ROM if additional drivers are required to complete the installation.

If you use digital sound sources or output such as Dolby 5.1, CD digital, or S/PDIF, open the properties sheet for your mixer device and enable display of these volume controls.

Use the Volume Control to ensure your speakers are receiving a sound signal. The mixer sometimes defaults to Mute. You can usually adjust volume separately for wave (WAV) files, MIDI, microphone, and other components.

Using Your Stereo Instead of Speakers

Another alternative is to patch your sound card into your stereo system for greatly amplified sound and for support of advanced Dolby Digital sound for DVD playback. Check the plugs and jacks at both ends of the connection. Most stereos use pin plugs, also called RCA or phono plugs, for input. Although pin plugs are standard on some sound cards or breakout boxes, most use miniature 1/8" phono plugs, which require an adapter when connecting to your stereo system. For example, from Radio Shack you can purchase an audio cable that provides a stereo 1/8" miniplug on one end and phono plugs on the other (Cat. No. 42-2481A). If you want to attach your sound card to Dolby 5.1 speakers, be sure you use cabling designed for the S/PDIF connectors on your sound card. Some might use RCA-type plugs, whereas others use an optical cable with a square end (also known as a Toslink connector).

Make sure that you get stereo—not mono—plugs, unless your sound card supports only mono. To ensure that you have enough cable to reach from the back of your PC to your stereo system, get a 6-ft. long cable.

Hooking up your stereo to an audio adapter is a matter of connecting the plugs into the proper jacks. If your audio adapter gives you a choice of outputs—speaker/headphone and stereo line-out—choose the stereo line-out jack for the connection. This will give you the best sound quality because the signals from the stereo line-out jack are not amplified. The amplification is best left to your stereo system. In some cases, you'll attach a special DIN plug to your audio adapter that has multiple connections to your stereo system.

Connect this cable output from your audio adapter to the auxiliary input of your stereo receiver, pre-amp, or integrated amplifier. If your stereo doesn't have an auxiliary input, other input options include—in order of preference—tuner, CD, or Tape 2. (Do not use phono inputs, however, because the level of the signals will be uneven.) You can connect the cable's single stereo miniplug to the sound card's stereo line-out jack, for example, and then connect the two RCA phono plugs to the stereo's Tape/VCR 2 Playback jacks.

The first time you use your audio adapter with a stereo system, turn down the volume on your receiver to prevent blown speakers. Barely turn up the volume control and then select the proper input (such as Tape/VCR 2) on your stereo receiver. Finally, start your PC. Never increase the volume to more than three-fourths of the way up. Any higher and the sound might become distorted.

Note

If your stereo speakers are not magnetically shielded, you might hear a lot of crackling if they are placed close to your computer. Try moving them away from the computer, or use magnetically shielded speakers.

Tricks for Using the Tape Monitor Circuit of Your Stereo

Your receiver might be equipped with something called a tape monitor. This outputs the sound coming from the tuner, tape, or CD to the tape-out port on the back; it then expects the sound to come back in on the tape-in port. These ports, in conjunction with the line-in and line-out ports on your audio adapter, enable you to play computer sound and the radio through the same set of speakers.

Here's how you do it:

1. Turn off the tape monitor circuit on your receiver.
2. Turn down all the controls on the sound card's mixer application.
3. Connect the receiver's tape-out ports to the audio adapter's line-in port.
4. Connect the audio adapter's line-out port to the receiver's tape-in ports.
5. Turn on the receiver, select some music, and set the volume to a medium level.
6. Turn on the tape monitor circuit.
7. Slowly adjust the line-in and main-out sliders in the audio adapter's mixer application until the sound level is about the same as before.
8. Disengage and re-engage the tape monitor circuit while adjusting the output of the audio adapter so that the sound level is the same regardless of whether the tape monitor circuit is engaged.
9. Start playing a WAV file.
10. Slowly adjust up the volume slider for the WAV file in the audio adapter's mixer application until it plays at a level (slightly above or below the receiver) that is comfortable.

Now you can get sounds from your computer and the radio through the receiver's speakers.

Different connectors might be needed if you have digital surround speakers and newer PCI-based sound cards. Check your speakers and sound card before you start this project.

Troubleshooting Sound Card Problems

To operate, an audio adapter needs hardware resources, such as IRQ numbers, a base I/O address, and DMA channels that don't conflict with other devices. Most adapters come preconfigured to use the standard Sound Blaster resources that have come to be associated with audio adapters. However, problems occasionally arise even with Plug and Play adapters. Troubleshooting might mean that you have to change the settings used by your system BIOS for PnP devices, move the sound card to another slot, or even reconfigure the other devices in your computer. No one said life was fair.

Hardware (Resource) Conflicts

The most common problem for audio adapters (particularly if you still use ISA cards) is that they might conflict with other devices installed in your PC. You might notice that your audio adapter simply doesn't work (no sound effects or music), repeats the same sounds over and over, or causes your PC to freeze. This situation is called a device, or hardware, conflict. What are they fighting over? Mainly the same bus signal lines or channels (called resources) used for talking to your PC. The sources of conflict in audio adapter installations are generally threefold:

- *Interrupt Requests (IRQs).* Hardware devices use IRQs to "interrupt" your PC's CPU and get its attention. PCI cards can share IRQs, but ISA cards and onboard legacy ports such as serial, parallel, and PS/2 mouse ports can't.

- *Direct Memory Access (DMA) channels.* DMA channels move information directly to your PC's memory, bypassing the system processor. DMA channels enable sound to play while your PC is doing other work. ISA sound cards and PCI sound cards emulating the Sound Blaster standard require DMA settings; PCI sound cards running in native mode don't use DMA channels.

- *Input/output (I/O) port addresses.* Your PC uses I/O port addresses to channel information between the hardware devices on your audio adapter and PC. The addresses usually mentioned in a sound card manual are the starting or base addresses. An audio adapter has several devices on it, and each one uses a range of addresses starting with a particular base address.

PCI-based sound cards and PCI-based onboard audio can share IRQs, don't use DMA channels (except when emulating a Sound Blaster card), and can use a wide variety of I/O port addresses. Consequently, resource conflicts involving PCI-based audio are extremely rare today, in part because systems no longer use ISA slots or ISA cards (ISA devices cannot share IRQs). However, if you still work with ISA sound cards or ISA or PCI cards that use game ports, you might encounter resource conflicts.

▶▶   See Chapter 20 of *Upgrading and Repairing PCs, 12th Edition* on the disc accompanying this book for details on resolving conflicts involving ISA sound cards and game ports.

Other Sound Card and Onboard Audio Problems

Like the common cold, audio adapter problems have common symptoms. Use the following sections to diagnose your problem.

No Sound

If you don't hear anything from your audio adapter, consider these solutions:

- Make sure the audio adapter is set to use all default resources and that all other devices using these resources have been either reconfigured or removed if they cause a conflict. Use the Device Manager to determine this information.

- Are the speakers connected? Check that the speakers are plugged into the sound card's stereo line-out or speaker jack (not the line-in or microphone jack).

- Are the speakers receiving power? Check that the power "brick" or power cord is plugged in securely and that the speakers are turned on.

- Are the speakers stereo? Check that the plug inserted into the jack is a stereo plug, not mono.

- Are the mixer settings correct? Many audio adapters include a sound mixer application. The mixer controls the volume settings for various sound devices, such as the microphone or the CD player. There might be separate controls for both recording and playback. Increase the master volume or speaker volume when you are in the play mode.

  If the Mute option is selected in your sound mixer software, you won't hear anything. Depending on the speaker type and sound source type, you might need to switch from analog to digital sound for some types of sound output. Make sure that the correct digital audio volume controls are enabled in your audio device's mixer control.

- Use your audio adapter's setup or diagnostic software to test and adjust the volume of the adapter. Such software usually includes sample sounds used to test the adapter.

- Turn off your computer for 1 minute and then turn it back on. A hard reset (as opposed to pressing the Reset button or pressing Ctrl+Alt+Delete) might clear the problem.

- If your computer game lacks sound, check that it is designed to work with your audio adapter. For example, some legacy (DOS-based) and early Windows games might require the exact settings of IRQ 7 (or IRQ 5), DMA 1, and I/O address 220 to be Sound Blaster compatible. You also might need to load DOS drivers to enable some recent sound cards to work with DOS games.

- If you're using motherboard-integrated audio, make sure the onboard audio is enabled (check the BIOS setup program) and that the proper drivers and player program have been installed (check the Windows Control Panel). With some motherboards, you might need to run a setup program on the motherboard driver CD to enable onboard sound.

- If you're using motherboard-integrated audio that uses a removable header cable (such as with many SDPIF optical or 4/6-channel analog speaker configurations), make sure the header cable is properly connected to the motherboard.

One-Sided Sound

If you hear sound coming from only one speaker, check out these possible causes:

- *Are you using a mono plug in the stereo jack?* A common mistake is to use a mono plug in the sound card's speaker or stereo-out jacks. Seen from the side, a stereo connector has two darker stripes. A mono connector has only one stripe.

- *If you're using amplified speakers, are they powered on?* Check the strength of the batteries or the AC adapter's connection to the electrical outlet. If each speaker is powered separately, be sure that both have working batteries.

- *Are the speakers wired correctly?* When possible, use keyed and color-coded connectors to avoid mistakes.

- *Is the audio adapter driver loaded?* Some sound cards provide only left-channel sound if the driver is not loaded correctly. Rerun your adapter's setup software or reinstall it in the operating system.

- *Are both speakers set to the same volume?* Some speakers use separate volume controls on each speaker. Balance them for best results. Separate speaker volume controls can be an advantage if one speaker must be farther away from the user than the other.

- *Is the speaker jack loose?* If you find that plugging your speaker into the jack properly doesn't produce sound but pulling the plug half-way out or "jimmying" it around in its hole can temporarily correct the problem, you're on the road to a speaker jack failure. There's no easy solution; buy a new adapter or whip out your soldering iron and spend a lot more time on the test bench than most audio adapters are worth. To avoid damage to the speaker jack, be sure you insert the plug straight in, not at an angle.

Volume Is Low

If you can barely hear your sound card, try these solutions:

■ *Are the speakers plugged into the proper jack?* Speakers require a higher level of drive signal than headphones. Again, adjust the volume level in your mixer application.

■ *Are the mixer settings too low?* Again, adjust the volume level in your mixer application. If your mixer lets you choose between speakers and headphones, be sure to select the correct speaker configuration.

■ *Is the initial volume too low?* If your audio adapter has an external thumbwheel volume control located on the card bracket, check to ensure that it is not turned down too low. Check the speakers' own volume controls as well.

■ *Are the speakers too weak?* Some speakers might need more power than your audio adapter can produce. Try other speakers or put a stereo amplifier between your sound card and speakers.

Some Speakers Don't Play

If you can hear sound coming from some speakers, but not others, check the following:

■ *Incorrect sound mixer settings.* Most systems assume that you are using two-channel (stereophonic) sound, even if you have plugged in four or more speakers. Select the correct speaker type with the Windows Speaker icon or a third-party sound mixer.

■ *Additional speakers are connected to the wrong jacks.* Make sure you connect the additional speakers needed for four-channel or six-channel audio to the correct jacks. If you connect them to line-in or microphone jacks, they won't work.

■ *Incorrect balance settings.* The volume control also adjusts the balance between the left and right speakers. If you hear audio from the left speakers only or the right speakers only, the balance control needs to be centered with the Windows Speaker icon or a third-party sound mixer.

Note

On some systems with integrated audio, audio jacks have multiple uses. For example, in six-channel mode on some systems, the normal line-in and microphone jacks might be reconfigured to work with rear and center/subwoofer speakers. In such cases, the mixer controls need to be reset.

Some Types of Sounds Play, But Others Don't

If you can hear CDs but not WAV or MP3 digital music, or can play WAV and MP3 but not CD or MIDI files, check the following:

■ *Low volume or mute settings for some audio types.* Some audio mixers have separate volume controls for WAV/MP3, MIDI, CD digital, CD audio, and other sound types and sources. Unmute any audio types you play back and adjust the volume as desired.

■ *I/O port or DMA conflicts when playing DOS games.* On most ISA-based sound cards or PCI-based sound cards or integrated audio solutions, separate I/O port address ranges and DMA channels are used for MIDI, FM synthesis, and normal audio. A conflict can cause some types of sounds not to play.

▶▶ See Chapter 20 of *Upgrading and Repairing PCs, 12th Edition* on the disc packaged with this book for details on resolving conflicts involving ISA sound cards and game ports.

Scratchy Sound

Scratchy or static-filled sound can be caused by several problems. Improving the sound can be as simple as rearranging your hardware components. The following list suggests possible solutions to the problem of scratchy sound:

- *Is your audio adapter near other expansion cards?* The adapter might be picking up electrical interference from other expansion cards inside the PC. Move the audio card to an expansion slot as far away as possible from other cards.

- *An ISA-based audio adapter requires a lot of CPU attention.* Frequent hard disk access can cause dropouts due to the CPUs switching between managing the sound card and the hard drive.

- *Are your speakers too close to your monitor?* The speakers can pick up electrical noise from your monitor. Move them farther away. Subwoofers should *never* be placed near the monitor because their powerful magnets can interfere with the picture. They should be on the floor to maximize low-frequency transmission.

- *Are you experiencing compatibility problems between particular games and your sound card?* If you notice sound problems such as stuttering voices and static on some games but not others, check with the game vendor for a software patch or with the sound card vendor for updated drivers. If the game uses DirectX, run the DXDIAG diagnostics program (select Start, Run; type **DXDIAG**; and click OK) and click the Sound tab. Adjust the slider for Hardware Sound Acceleration Level down one notch from Full (the default) to Standard, click Save All Information, and exit. Retry the game. If the problem persists, adjust the Hardware Sound Acceleration Level to Basic. If other games have performance problems after you adjust the Hardware Sound Acceleration Level, be sure to reset it to Full before playing those games.

Your Computer Won't Start

If your computer won't start at all, you might not have inserted the audio adapter completely into its slot. Turn off the PC and then press firmly on the card until it is seated correctly.

If you can't start your computer after installing a new sound card and its drivers, you can use the Windows "bootlog" feature to record every event during startup; this file records which hardware drivers are loaded during startup and indicates whether the file loaded successfully, didn't load successfully, or froze the computer. See the documentation for your version of Windows for details on how to create a bootlog when necessary.

Parity Errors or Other Lockups

Your computer might display a memory parity error message or simply crash. This is usually caused by resource conflicts in one of the following areas:

- IRQ
- DMA
- I/O ports

If other devices in your system are using the same resources as your audio adapter, crashes, lockups, or parity errors can result. You must ensure that multiple devices in your system do not share these resources.

▶▶ See Chapter 20 of *Upgrading and Repairing PCs, 12th Edition* on the disc packaged with this book for details on resolving conflicts involving ISA sound cards and game ports.

Advanced Features

If you are having problems playing DVD audio, playing MP3 files, or using SPDIF connections, make sure that

- You have enabled the hardware resources on the sound card.
- You are using the correct playback program.
- Your mixer has the correct volume control setting for the device.
- Your cabling is correct for the device.

Other Problems

Sometimes sound problems can be difficult to solve. Due to quirks and problems with the way DMA is implemented in some motherboard chipsets, problems interacting with certain cards or drivers can occur. Sometimes altering the Chipset Setup options in your CMOS settings can resolve problems. These types of problems can take a lot of trial and error to solve.

The PC standard is based loosely on the cooperation among a handful of companies. Something as simple as one vendor's BIOS or motherboard design can make the standard nonstandard.

A good way to solve problems of all types with Plug and Play cards, a PnP BIOS, and a PnP operating system (Windows 9x/Me/2000/XP) is to use the Device Manager to remove the sound card, restart the system, and allow the card's components to be redetected. This installs a "fresh" copy of the software and reinserts Registry entries.

If you are using a motherboard with a VIA chipset, be sure to download and install the latest versions of VIA drivers.

Speakers

Successful business presentations, multimedia applications, and MIDI work demand external high-fidelity stereo speakers. Although you can use standard stereo speakers, they are often too big to fit on or near your desk. Smaller bookshelf speakers are better.

Sound cards offer little or none of the amplification needed to drive external speakers. Although some sound cards have small 4-watt amplifiers, they are not powerful enough to drive quality speakers. Also, conventional speakers sitting near your display can create magnetic interference, which can distort colors and objects onscreen or jumble the data recorded on nearby floppy disks or other magnetic media.

To solve these problems, computer speakers need to be small, efficient, and self-powered. Also, they should be provided with magnetic shielding, either in the form of added layers of insulation in the speaker cabinet or electronic cancellation of the magnetic distortion.

Caution

Although most computer speakers are magnetically shielded, do not leave recorded tapes, watches, credit cards, or floppy disks in front of the speakers for long periods of time.

Quality sound depends on quality speakers. A 16-bit audio adapter might provide better sound to computer speakers, but even an 8-bit adapter sounds good from a good speaker. Conversely, an inexpensive speaker makes both 8-bit and 16-bit adapter cards sound tinny.

Now dozens of models of PC speakers are on the market, ranging from inexpensive minispeakers from Sony, Creative, and LabTech to larger self-powered models from prestigious audio companies such as Bose, Cambridge Sound Works, Klipsch, Monsoon, and Altec Lansing. Many of the medium- to higher-end speaker systems even include subwoofers to provide additional bass response. To evaluate speakers, it helps to know the jargon. Speakers are measured by three criteria:

- *Frequency response.* A measurement of the range of high and low sounds a speaker can reproduce. The ideal range is 20Hz–20KHz, the range of human hearing. No speaker system reproduces this range perfectly. In fact, few people hear sounds above 18KHz. An exceptional speaker might cover a range of 30Hz–23000Hz, and lesser models might cover only 100Hz–20000Hz. Frequency response is the most deceptive specification because identically rated speakers can sound completely different.

- *Total Harmonic Distortion (THD).* An expression of the amount of distortion or noise created by amplifying the signal. Simply put, distortion is the difference between the sound sent to the speaker and the sound you hear. The amount of distortion is measured in percentages. An acceptable level of distortion is less than .1% (one-tenth of 1%). For some CD-quality recording equipment, a common standard is .05%, but some speakers have a distortion of 10% or more. Headphones often have a distortion of about 2% or less.

- *Watts.* Usually stated as watts per channel, this is the amount of amplification available to drive the speakers. Check that the company means "per channel" (or RMS) and not total power. Many audio adapters have built-in amplifiers, providing up to 8 watts per channel (most provide 4 watts). This wattage is not enough to provide rich sound, however, which is why many speakers have built-in amplifiers. With the flick of a switch or the press of a button, these speakers amplify the signals they receive from the audio adapter. If you do not want to amplify the sound, you typically leave the speaker switch set to "direct." In most cases, you'll want to amplify the signal.

Inexpensive PC speakers sometimes use batteries to power the amplifiers. Because these speakers require so much power, you might want to invest in an AC adapter or purchase speakers that use AC power. With an AC adapter, you won't have to buy new batteries every few weeks. If your speakers didn't come with an AC adapter, you can pick one up from your local Radio Shack or hardware store. Be sure that the adapter you purchase matches your speakers in voltage and polarity; most third-party adapters are multiple voltage, featuring interchangeable tips and reversible polarity.

You can control the volume and other sound attributes of your speakers in various ways, depending on their complexity and cost. Typically, each speaker has a volume knob, although some share a single volume control. If one speaker is farther away than the other, you might want to adjust the volume accordingly. Many computer speakers include a dynamic bass boost (DBB) switch. This button provides a more powerful bass and clearer treble, regardless of the volume setting. Other speakers have separate bass and treble boost switches or a three-band equalizer to control low, middle, and high frequencies. When you rely on your audio adapter's power rather than your speakers' built-in amplifier, the volume and dynamic bass boost controls have no effect. Your speakers are at the mercy of the adapter's power.

For best audio quality, adjust the master volume on the sound card near the high end and use the volume control on powered speakers to adjust the volume. Otherwise, your speakers will try to amplify any distortions coming from the low-power input from the PC's audio adapter.

A 1/8" stereo minijack connects from the audio adapter's output jack to one of the speakers. The speaker then splits the signal and feeds through a separate cable from the first speaker to the second one (often referred to as the "satellite speaker").

Before purchasing a set of speakers, check that the cables between the speakers are long enough for your computer setup. For example, a tower case sitting alongside your desk might require longer speaker wires than a desktop computer.

Beware of speakers that have a tardy built-in sleep feature. Such speakers, which save electricity by turning themselves off when they are not in use, might have the annoying habit of clipping the first part of a sound after a period of inactivity.

Speakers that are USB based will not be capable of playing CD music unless the CD-ROM drive can perform digital audio extraction. Check your drive's specifications for information.

Headphones are an option when you can't afford a premium set of speakers. Headphones also provide privacy and enable you to play your PC audio as loud as you like.

For best results with newer sound cards that support four speakers or more, check the properties sheet for the audio adapter and set whether you're using headphones, stereo speakers, or a larger number of speakers.

Make sure that speakers are placed properly. If you use a subwoofer, put it on the floor for better bass sound and to reduce EMI interference with other devices.

How can you tell whether wireless satellite speakers are causing interference? Watch your monitor; frequencies as high as 2KHz can interfere with your video display. Move the speakers away from the monitor and check the display again.

Theater and Surround Sound Considerations

If you're a serious gamer or DVD movie lover, you won't be content with ordinary stereophonic sound. Most audio adapters now support front and rear speakers, and many of the best audio adapters also support Dolby-compatible 4.1 and 5.1 speaker setups.

To ensure you get the sound you expect from four or more speakers, check the following:

- *Use the properties sheet for your audio adapter to properly describe your speaker setup.* This includes selecting the number of speakers you are using, setting options for 3D environmental audio and positional sound such as reverb, and setting up your subwoofer if present.

- *Make sure you use the correct cabling between your speakers and audio adapter.* If you are planning to use AC3/Dolby speaker setups, such as 4.1, 5.1, 6.1, or 7.1, be sure you use the correct S/PDIF connection and configuration. This varies from audio adapter to audio adapter; check the vendor's Web site for details.

- *Make sure you have placed your speakers correctly.* In some cases you can adjust the audio adapter's properties to improve sound quality, but sometimes you might need to move the speakers themselves.

- *Make sure you have connected your speakers to the proper jacks.* Mixing up left and right or front and rear causes poor sound quality.

Typical Speaker Setups

The simplest audio configuration available today is stereo, which uses two speakers placed to overlap sound. Most audio adapters now support at least four speakers, but depending on the audio adapter, settings, and sound output options in the program, the rear speakers might simply mirror the front speakers' output, or you might have four distinct sound streams.

4-point surround sound uses four speakers plus a subwoofer to surround you with music and gaming sound effects; the four speakers are placed around the listener, and the subwoofer is usually placed near a wall or in the corner to amplify its low-frequency sound. The subwoofer in stereo or four-point surround sound setups is not on a separate circuit but is controlled by the same signals sent to the other speakers. A stereo speaker system with a subwoofer is often referred to as a *2.1 speaker configuration*, and a four-point surround sound configuration with a subwoofer is often referred to as a *4.1 speaker configuration*.

5.1 Surround sound, also referred to as Dolby Digital or DTS Surround sound, uses five speakers plus a subwoofer. The fifth speaker is placed between the front two speakers to fill in any missing sound caused by incorrect speaker placement. The subwoofer is independently controlled. This is the preferred sound system for use with DVD movies. Most lower-cost audio adapters lack support for 5.1 Surround sound.

Some of the latest sound cards support 6.1 and 7.1 Surround sound. The 6.1 configuration resembles the 5.1 Surround setup but adds a middle speaker along with a subwoofer. 7.1 Surround sound uses left-middle and right-middle speakers to flank the listener, along with a subwoofer. Depending on the sound card, some cards play back 5.1 or greater Surround sound configurations with analog speakers only, whereas others can also transmit Dolby Digital (AC-3), DTS Surround, or Dolby EX digital audio through the SPDIF digital audio port to a home theater system.

Microphones

Some audio adapters come complete with a microphone, but most do not. You'll need one to record your voice to a WAV file. Selecting a microphone is quite simple. You need one that has a 1/8" mini-jack to plug into your audio adapter's microphone, or audio in, jack. Most handheld microphones have an on/off switch. However, you can also use the Mute control in the audio mixer to shut off the microphone.

Like speakers, microphones are measured by their frequency ranges. This is not an important buying factor, however, because the human voice has a limited range. If you are recording only voices, consider an inexpensive microphone that covers a limited range of frequencies. An expensive microphone's recording capabilities extend to frequencies outside the voice's range. Why pay for something you won't be needing?

If you are recording music, invest in an expensive microphone, but be sure that your audio adapter can do justice to the signal produced by the microphone. A high-quality microphone can produce mediocre results when paired with a cheap 8-bit audio adapter.

Your biggest decision is to select a microphone that suits your recording style. If you work in a noisy office, you might want a unidirectional microphone that will prevent extraneous noises from being recorded. An omnidirectional microphone is best for recording a group conversation.

Some audio adapters include a microphone. This can be a small lapel microphone, a handheld microphone, or one with a desktop stand. If you want to keep your hands free, you might want to shun the traditional handheld microphone for a lapel or desktop model. If your audio adapter does not come with a microphone, see your local stereo or electronics parts store. Be sure that any microphone you purchase has the correct impedance to match the audio adapter's input.

If you're using software such as Dragon Naturally Speaking, IBM Via Voice, Philips FreeSpeech, or other voice-recognition software, use the microphone supplied with the software or choose from alternative models the software vendor recommends. Run the microphone setup program again if your software has trouble recognizing your voice. Some models feature a battery pack to boost sound quality; be sure to check the batteries and replace them to keep recognition quality high.

If you're talking but your voice-recognition or recording software isn't responding, check the following:

- *Incorrect jack.* It's easy to plug the microphone into the wrong jack. Try using a magic marker to color-code the microphone wire and jack to make matching up easier if your microphone or audio jack isn't color-coded or uses competing standards.

- *Check the recording volume in the mixer control.* This usually defaults to Mute to avoid spurious noise.

- *Make sure the microphone is turned on in the voice-recognition or recording software.* You must click the Record button in recording software, and many voice-recognition programs let you "pick up" the microphone for use or "put it down" when you need to answer the phone. Look for an onscreen microphone icon in the Windows System Tray for fast toggling between modes.

I/O Interfaces from Serial and Parallel to IEEE 1394 and USB

Introduction to Input/Output Ports

This chapter covers the primary peripheral input/output ports on a modern PC system. This includes a discussion of both the so-called "legacy" serial and parallel ports that have been standard on PCs since the beginning, as well as a discussion of the more current Universal Serial Bus (USB), which is replacing both serial and parallel ports, and IEEE 1394 (i.LINK or FireWire) interfaces. (IEEE stands for the Institute of Electrical and Electronic Engineers.) Although SCSI and IDE are also I/O interfaces, they are mainly used as internal interfaces and are important or complicated enough to warrant their own chapters for more specific and detailed coverage.

USB and IEEE 1394 (i.LINK or FireWire)

The two most popular high-speed serial-bus architecture families for desktop and portable PCs are Universal Serial Bus (USB) and IEEE 1394, which is also called i.LINK or FireWire. Each interface type is available in two versions: USB 1.1 and USB 2.0; IEEE 1394a and IEEE 1394b (also called FireWire 800). The USB and IEEE 1394 port families are high-speed communications ports that far outstrip the capabilities of older standard serial and parallel ports. They can also be used as an alternative to SCSI for high-speed external peripheral connections. In addition to performance, these newer ports offer I/O device consolidation, which means that all types of external peripherals can connect to these ports.

Why Serial?

The recent trend in high-performance peripheral bus design is to use a serial architecture, in which 1 bit at a time is sent down a wire. Because parallel architecture (used by SCSI, ATA, and LPT ports) uses 8, 16, or more wires to send bits simultaneously, the parallel bus is actually much faster at the same clock speed. However, increasing the clock speed of a serial connection is much easier than increasing that of a parallel connection.

Parallel connections in general suffer from several problems, the biggest being signal skew and jitter. Skew and jitter are the reasons high-speed parallel buses such as SCSI (small computer systems interface) are limited to short distances of 3 meters or less. The problem is that, although the 8 or 16 bits of data are fired from the transmitter at the same time, by the time they reach the receiver, propagation delays have conspired to allow some bits to arrive before the others. The longer the cable, the longer the time between the arrival of the first and last bits at the other end! This *signal skew*, as it is called, prevents you from running a high-speed transfer rate or a longer cable—or both. *Jitter* is the tendency for the signal to reach its target voltage and float above and below for a short period of time.

With a serial bus, the data is sent 1 bit at a time. Because there is no worry about when each bit will arrive, the clocking rate can be increased dramatically. For example, the top transfer rate possible with EPP/ECP parallel ports is 2.77MBps, whereas IEEE 1394a ports (which use high-speed serial technology) support transfer rates as high as 400Mbps (about 50MBps)—25 times faster than parallel ports. USB 2.0 supports transfer rates of 480Mbps (about 60MBps), which is about 30 times faster than parallel ports, and the new IEEE 1394b (FireWire 800) ports reach transfer rates as high as 800Mbps (or about 100MBps), which is about 50 times faster than parallel ports!

At high clock rates, parallel signals tend to interfere with each other. Serial again has an advantage because, with only one or two signal wires, crosstalk and interference between the wires in the cable are negligible.

In general, parallel cabling is more expensive than serial cabling. Besides the many additional wires needed to carry the multiple bits in parallel, the cable also must be specially constructed to prevent crosstalk and interference between adjacent data lines. This is one reason external SCSI cables are so expensive. Serial cabling, by comparison, is very inexpensive. For one thing, it has significantly fewer wires. Furthermore, the shielding requirements are far simpler, even at very high speeds. Because of this, transmitting serial data reliably over longer distances is also easier, which is why parallel interfaces have shorter recommended cable lengths than do serial interfaces.

For these reasons—in addition to the need for new Plug and Play external peripheral interfaces and the elimination of the physical port crowding on portable computers—these high-performance serial buses were developed. USB is a standard feature on virtually all PCs today; is used for most general-purpose, high-speed external interfacing; and is the most compatible, widely available, and fastest general-purpose external interface. In addition, IEEE 1394 (more commonly known as FireWire), although mainly used in certain niche markets—such as connecting DV (digital video) camcorders—is also spreading into other high-bandwidth uses, such as high-resolution scanners, external hard drives, and networking.

Universal Serial Bus

Universal Serial Bus (USB) is an external peripheral bus standard designed to bring Plug and Play capability for attaching peripherals externally to the PC. USB eliminates the need for special-purpose ports, reduces the need to use special-purpose I/O cards (thus reducing the need to reconfigure the system with each new device added), and saves important system resources such as interrupts (IRQs); regardless of the number of devices attached to a system's USB ports, only one IRQ is required. PCs equipped with USB enable peripherals to be automatically recognized and configured as soon as they are physically attached, without the need to reboot or run setup. USB allows up to 127 devices to run simultaneously on a single bus, with peripherals such as monitors and keyboards acting as additional plug-in sites, or hubs. USB cables, connectors, hubs, and peripherals can be identified by icons, as shown in Figure 17.1. Note the "plus" symbol added to the upper icon, which indicates that port supports USB 2.0 (Hi-Speed USB) in addition to the standard 1.x support.

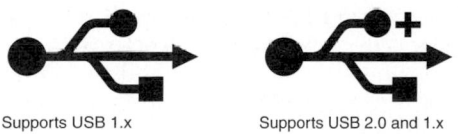

Supports USB 1.x   Supports USB 2.0 and 1.x

Figure 17.1   These icons identify USB cables, connectors, hubs, and peripherals.

Intel has been the primary proponent of USB, and all its PC chipsets starting with the PIIX3 South Bridge chipset component (introduced in February 1996) have included USB support as standard. Other chipset vendors have followed suit, making USB as standard a feature of today's desktop and notebook PCs as the serial and parallel ports once were.

Six other companies initially worked with Intel in codeveloping the USB, including Compaq, Digital, IBM, Microsoft, NEC, and Northern Telecom. Together, these companies have established the USB Implementers Forum (USB-IF) to develop, support, and promote USB architecture.

◄◄   See "Chipsets," p. 239.

The USB-IF formally released USB 1.0 in January 1996, USB 1.1 in September 1998, and USB 2.0 in April 2000. The 1.1 revision was mostly a clarification of some issues related to hubs and other areas of the specification. Most devices and hubs should be 1.1 compliant, even if they were manufactured before the release of the 1.1 specification. The biggest change was USB 2.0, which is 40 times faster than the original USB and yet fully backward compatible. USB ports can be retrofitted to older computers that lack built-in USB connectors through the use of either an add-on PCI card (for desktop computers) or a PC Card on Cardbus-compatible notebook computers. You can also use USB add-on cards to update an older system that has only USB 1.1 on the motherboard. As of mid-2002, virtually all motherboards include four or more USB 2.0 ports as standard. Notebook computers were slower to catch on—it wasn't until early 2003 that most notebook or laptop computers included USB 2.0 ports as standard.

USB Technical Details

USB 1.1 runs at 12Mbps (1.5MBps) over a simple four-wire connection. The bus supports up to 127 devices connected to a single root hub and uses a tiered-star topology, built on expansion hubs that can reside in the PC, any USB peripheral, or even standalone hub boxes.

Note that although the standard allows up to 127 devices to be attached, they all must share the 1.5MBps bandwidth, meaning that for every active device you add, the bus will slow down some. In practical reality, few people will have more than 8 devices attached at any one time.

For low-speed peripherals, such as pointing devices and keyboards, the USB also has a slower 1.5Mbps subchannel. The subchannel connection is used for slower interface devices, such as keyboards and mice.

USB employs what is called Non Return to Zero Invert (NRZI) data encoding. NRZI is a method of encoding serial data in which 1s and 0s are represented by opposite and alternating high and low voltages where there is no return to a zero (or reference) voltage between the encoded bits. In NRZI encoding, a 1 is represented by no change in signal level, and a 0 is represented by a change in level. A string of 0s causes the NRZI data to toggle each bit time; a string of 1s causes long periods with no transitions in the data. This is an efficient transfer encoding scheme because it eliminates the need for additional clock pulses that would otherwise waste time and bandwidth.

USB devices are considered either *hubs* or *functions*, or both. Functions are the individual devices that attach to the USB, such as a keyboard, mouse, camera, printer, telephone, and so on. Hubs provide additional attachment points to the USB, enabling the attachment of more hubs or functions. The initial ports in the PC system unit are called the *root hub*, and they are the starting point for the USB. Most motherboards have two, three, or four USB ports, any of which can be connected to functions or additional hubs. Some systems place one or two of the USB ports in the front of the computer, which is very convenient for devices you use only occasionally, such as digital cameras or flash memory card readers. External hubs (also called *generic hubs*) are essentially wiring concentrators, and through a star-type topology they allow the attachment of multiple devices. Each attachment point is referred to as a *port*. Most hubs have either four or eight ports, but more are possible. For more expandability, you can connect additional hubs to the ports on an existing hub. The hub controls both the connection and distribution of power to each of the connected functions. A typical hub is shown in Figure 17.2.

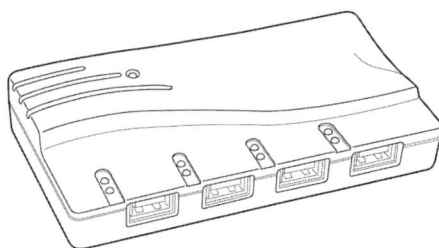

Figure 17.2   A typical USB hub with four ports.

Besides providing additional sockets for connecting USB peripherals, a hub provides power to any attached peripherals. A hub recognizes the dynamic attachment of a peripheral and provides at least 0.5W of power per peripheral during initialization. Under control of the host PC driver software, the hub can provide more device power, up to a maximum of 2.5W, for peripheral operation.

Tip

For the most reliable operation, I recommend that you use self-powered hubs, which plug into an AC adapter. Bus-powered hubs pull power from the PC's USB root hub connector and aren't always capable of providing adequate power for high-power requirement devices, such as optical mice.

A newly attached hub is assigned a unique address, and hubs can be cascaded up to five levels deep (see Figure 17.3). A hub operates as a bidirectional repeater and repeats USB signals as required both upstream (toward the PC) and downstream (toward the device). A hub also monitors these signals and handles transactions addressed to itself. All other transactions are repeated to attached devices. A USB 1.1 hub supports both 12Mbps (full-speed) and 1.5Mbps (low-speed) peripherals.

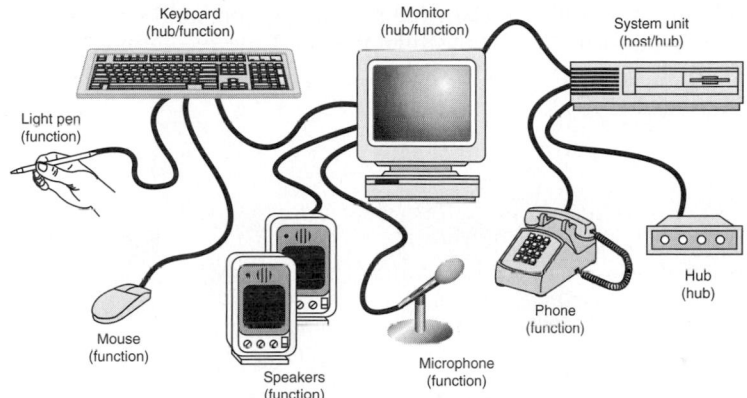

Figure 17.3 A typical PC with USB devices can use multiple USB hubs to support a variety of peripherals, connected to whichever hub is most convenient.

Maximum cable length between two full-speed (12Mbps) devices or a device and a hub is 5 meters using twisted-pair shielded cable with 20-gauge wire. Maximum cable length for low-speed (1.5Mbps) devices using non-twisted-pair wire is 3 meters. These distance limits are shorter if smaller-gauge wire is used (see Table 17.1).

Table 17.1   Maximum Cable Lengths Versus Wire Gauge

Gauge	Resistance (in Ohms/Meter Ω/m)	Length (Max.)
28	0.232 Ω/m	0.81m
26	0.145 Ω/m	1.31m
24	0.091 Ω/m	2.08m
22	0.057 Ω/m	3.33m
20	0.036 Ω/m	5.00m

Although USB 1.1 is not as fast at data transfer as FireWire or SCSI, it is still more than adequate for the types of peripherals for which it is designed. USB 2.0 operates a surprising 40 times faster than USB 1.1 and allows transfer speeds of 480Mbps or 60MBps. Because it is fully backward-compatible and supports older 1.1 devices, I recommend purchasing only motherboards and add-in USB cards that conform to the faster USB 2.0 (Hi-Speed USB) standard. One of the additional benefits of USB 2.0 is the capability to handle concurrent transfers, which enables your USB 1.1 devices to transfer data at the same time without tying up the USB bus.

USB 2.0 drivers were not provided with the initial launch of Windows XP but are available through system update downloads or service packs. Use the Windows Update feature to connect to the Microsoft site and download any updates as necessary. Add-on USB 2.0 cards might include their own drivers, which should be installed.

Four main styles of connectors are specified for USB, called Series A, Series B, Mini-A, and Mini-B connectors. The A connectors are used for upstream connections between a device and the host or a hub. The USB ports on motherboards and hubs are usually Series A connectors. Series B connectors are designed for the downstream connection to a device that has detachable cables. In all cases, the mini connectors are simply smaller versions of the larger ones, in a physically smaller form factor for smaller devices.

The physical USB plugs are small (especially the mini plugs) and, unlike a typical serial or parallel cable, the plug is not attached by screws or thumbscrews. There are no pins to bend or break, making USB devices very user friendly to install and remove. The USB plug shown in Figure 17.4 snaps into place on the USB connector.

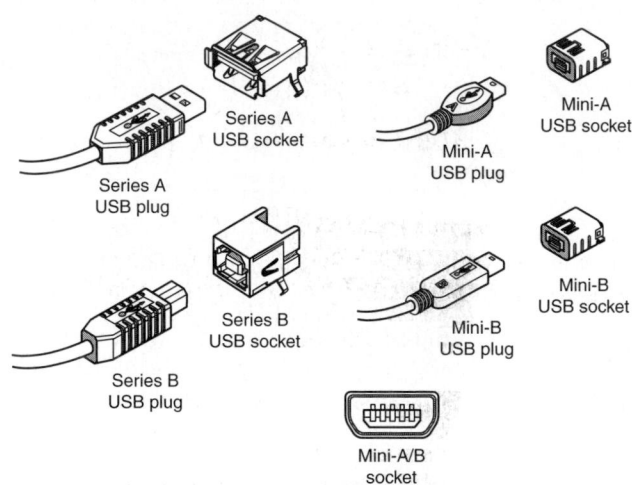

Figure 17.4 USB Series A and Series B plugs and receptacles.

Note that a Mini-A/B socket is a dual-purpose socket that can accept either Mini-A or Mini-B plugs. The newer mini plugs and sockets have plastic portions inside the connectors that are required to be color-coded as shown in Table 17.2.

Table 17.2 Color-Coding for USB Mini-Plugs and Sockets

Connector	Color
Mini-A socket	White
Mini-A plug	White
Mini-B socket	Black
Mini-B plug	Black
Mini-A/B socket	Gray

Tables 17.3 and 17.4 show the pinouts for the USB connectors and cables. Most systems with USB connectors feature one or two pairs of Series A plugs on the rear of the system. Some also feature one or two pairs on the front of the system for ease of use with items that are not permanently connected.

Table 17.3   USB Connector Pinouts for Series A/B Connectors

Pin	Signal Name	Wire Color	Comment
1	Vbus	Red	Bus power
2	- Data	White	Data transfer
3	+ Data	Green	Data transfer
4	Ground	Black	Cable ground
Shell	Shield	—	Drain wire

Table 17.4   USB Connector Pinouts for Mini-A/B Connectors

Pin	Signal Name	Wire Color	Comment
1	Vbus	Red	Bus power
2	- Data	White	Data transfer
3	+ Data	Green	Data transfer
4	ID	—	A/B identification*
4	Ground	Black	Cable ground
Shell	Shield	—	Drain wire

*Used to identify a Mini-A from a Mini-B connector to the device. ID is connected to Ground in a Mini-A plug and not connected (open) in a Mini-B plug.

USB conforms to Intel's Plug and Play (PnP) specification, including hot plugging, which means that devices can be plugged in dynamically without powering down or rebooting the system. Simply plug in the device, and the USB controller in the PC detects the device and automatically determines and allocates the required resources and drivers. Microsoft has developed USB drivers and included them automatically in Windows 98 and later.

Windows 95B and 95C have very limited support for USB 1.1; the necessary drivers are not present in the original Windows 95 or 95A. With Windows 95B, the USB drivers are not automatically included; they are provided separately, although a late release of Windows 95—Windows 95C—includes USB support. Many USB devices will not work with *any* Windows 95 release, including those that have the USB support files included.

Windows 98 and later have USB 1.1 support built in; however, additional drivers are required for USB 2.0 or later. In most cases, these drivers can be downloaded from Microsoft using the Windows Update feature.

USB support is also required in the BIOS for devices such as keyboards and mice. This is included in all newer systems with USB ports built in. Aftermarket PCI and PC Card boards also are available for adding USB to systems that don't include it as standard on the motherboard. USB peripherals include printers, CD-ROMs, modems, scanners, telephones, joysticks, keyboards, and pointing devices such as mice and trackballs.

A free utility called USBready is available from http://www.usb.org; it examines your PC's hardware and software and informs you of your PC's USB capabilities. Most PCs built in 1995 or earlier don't support USB. During 1996 most PC motherboards began supporting USB, and if your system dates from 1997 to 1998 or later, USB support is almost a certainty.

One interesting feature of USB is that, with certain limitations, attached devices can be powered by the USB bus. The PnP aspects of USB enable the system to query the attached peripherals as to their power requirements and issue a warning if available power levels are being exceeded. This is important for USB when it is used in portable systems because the battery power that is allocated to run the external peripherals might be limited. You can determine the amount of power available to each port in a USB root or generic hub and the amount of power required by a USB peripheral with the Windows Device Manager (see Figure 17.5).

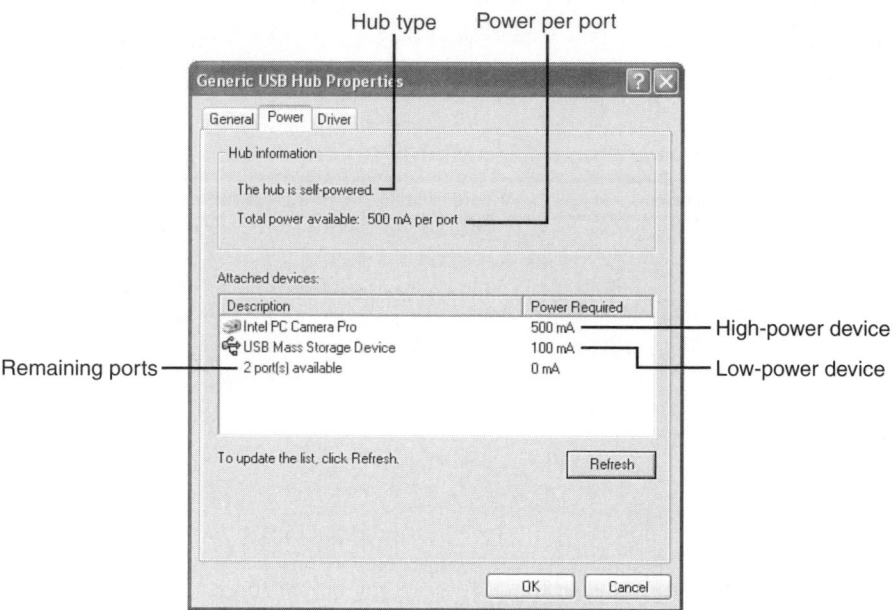

Figure 17.5   The Power tab of the properties sheet for a USB generic hub lists available power and power usage by device.

Devices that use more than 100mA, such as the Webcam shown in Figure 17.5, must be connected to a root hub or a self-powered generic hub. Devices that use 100mA or less can be connected to bus-powered hubs, such as those built in to some keyboards and monitors.

Tip

If a device plugged in to a self-powered hub stops working, check the power source for the self-powered hub—it might have failed or been disconnected. In such cases, a self-powered hub becomes a bus-powered hub, providing only 100mA per port instead of the 500mA per port available in self-powered mode.

To avoid running out of power when connecting USB devices, use a self-powered hub.

Another of the benefits of the USB specification is the self-identifying peripheral, a feature that greatly eases installation because you don't have to set unique IDs or identifiers for each peripheral—the USB handles that automatically. Also, USB devices can be "hot" plugged or unplugged, meaning that you do not have to turn off your computer or reboot every time you want to connect or disconnect a peripheral. However, to prevent data loss with USB drives and storage devices, you need to use the Eject Hardware or Safely Remove Hardware feature in the Windows system tray. Click the device, select Stop, click OK, and wait for the system to indicate that the device has been stopped before you remove it.

Enabling USB Support

Many systems shipped before Windows 98 was introduced in mid-1998 have onboard USB ports that were disabled at the factory. In some cases, especially with Baby-AT motherboards, there is no way to tell from the outside which systems have USB support built in. This is because many of these same systems were not shipped with the USB header cables necessary to bring the USB root hub connectors from the motherboard to the rear of the system.

If USB support is disabled in the system BIOS, restart your system and locate the BIOS setup screen that refers to the USB ports. Enable the USB feature. If you see a separate entry for USB IRQ, enable this as well. After you restart the computer with a USB-aware operating system, your "new" USB root hub will be detected and the drivers will be installed if you are using Windows 98 or newer; you might need to manually install drivers with late releases of Windows 95.

If your system has USB connectors present, you also will be able to use the "new" USB ports as soon as the system is rebooted after the USB drivers are installed. However, if your motherboard vendor didn't provide USB connectors, you must buy USB header cables. Before you order them, check the configuration of your motherboard's USB header pins. The standard is two rows of five pins each. Companies such as Belkin, CyberGuys, and Cables To Go sell header cables that are compatible with standard USB header pins if your motherboard supplier doesn't have the header cable in stock. Figure 17.6 shows a typical USB header cable set.

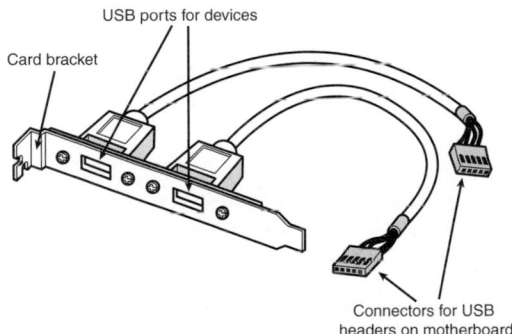

Figure 17.6 A typical USB header cable set; plug it into your motherboard to connect devices to the additional onboard USB ports (if present).

One of the biggest advantages of an interface such as USB is that it requires only a single interrupt (IRQ) from the PC. Therefore, you can connect up to 127 devices and they will not use separate interrupts, as they might if each were connected over a separate interface. This is a major benefit of the USB interface.

The USB interface can also be adapted to older peripherals. See the section "USB Adapters," later in this chapter, for details.

USB 2.0/Hi-Speed USB

USB 2.0 (also called Hi-Speed USB) is a backward-compatible extension of the USB 1.1 specification that uses the same cables, connectors, and software interfaces, but it runs 40 times faster than the original 1.0 and 1.1 versions. The higher speed enables higher-performance peripherals, such as higher-resolution Web/videoconferencing cameras, scanners, and faster printers, to be connected externally with the same easy plug-and-play installation of current USB peripherals. From the end user's point of view, USB 2.0 works exactly the same as 1.1—only faster and with more interesting, higher-performance devices available. All existing USB 1.1 devices work in a USB 2.0 bus because USB 2.0 supports all the slower-speed connections. USB data rates are shown in Table 17.5.

Table 17.5   USB Data Rates

Interface	Megabits per Second	Megabytes per Second
USB 1.1 low speed	1.5Mbps	0.1875MBps
USB 1.1 full speed	12Mbps	1.5MBps
USB 2.0 high speed	480Mbps	60MBps

If your motherboard or system features USB 2.0–compatible (Hi-Speed USB) ports, you might need to enable USB 2.0/Hi-Speed USB support in the system BIOS and install an appropriate driver. Otherwise, USB 2.0/Hi-Speed USB ports will be used as USB 1.1 ports.

◀◀   See "USB Configuration Submenu," p. 443, for details.

The support of higher-speed USB 2.0 peripherals requires using a USB 2.0 hub. You can still use older USB 1.1 hubs on a 2.0 bus, but any peripherals or additional hubs connected downstream from a 1.1 hub will operate at the slower 1.5MBps USB 1.1 maximum speed. Devices connected to USB 2.0 hubs will operate at the maximum speed of the device, up to the full USB 2.0 speed of 60MBps. The higher transmission speeds through a 2.0 hub are negotiated on a device-by-device basis, and if the higher speed is not supported by a peripheral, the link operates at a lower USB 1.1 speed.

As such, a USB 2.0 hub accepts high-speed transactions at the faster USB 2.0 frame rate and must deliver them to high-speed USB 2.0 peripherals as well as USB 1.1 peripherals. This data rate matching responsibility requires increased complexity and buffering of the incoming high-speed data. When communicating with an attached USB 2.0 peripheral, the 2.0 hub simply repeats the high-speed signals; however, when communicating with USB 1.1 peripherals, a USB 2.0 hub buffers and manages the transition from the high speed of the USB 2.0 host controller (in the PC) to the lower speed of a USB 1.1 device. This feature of USB 2.0 hubs means that USB 1.1 devices can operate along with USB 2.0 devices and not consume any additional bandwidth. Some manufacturers of add-on USB 2.0 cards are equipping the cards with both external and internal USB 2.0 ports.

How can you tell which devices are designed to support USB 1.1 and which support the emerging USB 2.0 standard? The USB Implementer's Forum (USB-IF), which owns and controls the USB standard, introduced new logos in late 2000 for products that have passed its certification tests. The logos are shown in Figure 17.7.

Figure 17.7   The USB-IF USB 1.1–compliant logo (left) compared to the USB-IF USB 2.0–compliant logo (right).

As you can see from Figure 17.7, USB 1.1 is also known simply as USB, and USB 2.0 is also known as Hi-Speed USB. Also note the icons shown earlier, where the addition of the plus symbol to the standard USB trident is used to identify ports that support USB 2.0.

USB On-The-Go

In December 2001, the USB-IF released a supplement to the USB 2.0 standard called USB On-The-Go. It was designed to address the one major shortcoming of USB: the fact that a PC was required to transfer data between two devices. In other words, you couldn't connect two cameras together and transfer pictures between them without a PC orchestrating the transfer. With USB On-The-Go, however, devices that conform to the specification still work normally when they are connected to a PC, but they also have additional capabilities when connected to other devices supporting the standard.

Although this capability can also work with PC peripherals, it was mainly added to address issues using USB devices in the consumer electronics area, where a PC might not be available. Using this standard, devices such as digital video recorders can connect to other recorders to transfer recorded movies or shows, items such as personal organizers can transfer data to other organizers, and so on. The addition of the On-The-Go supplement to USB 2.0 greatly enhances the use and capabilities of USB both in the PC and consumer electronics markets.

USB Adapters

If you still have a variety of older peripherals and yet you want to take advantage of the USB connector on your motherboard, several signal converters or adapters are available. Companies such as Belkin and others currently have adapters in the following types:

- USB-to-parallel (printer)
- USB-to-serial
- USB-to-SCSI
- USB-to-Ethernet
- USB-to-keyboard/mouse
- USB-to-TV/video

These adapters usually look just like a cable, with a USB connector at one end (which you plug into your USB port) and various other interface connectors at the other end. In some cases, you attach standard USB and device cables to a standalone adapter, such as with the USB-to-Ethernet adapter shown in Figure 17.8.

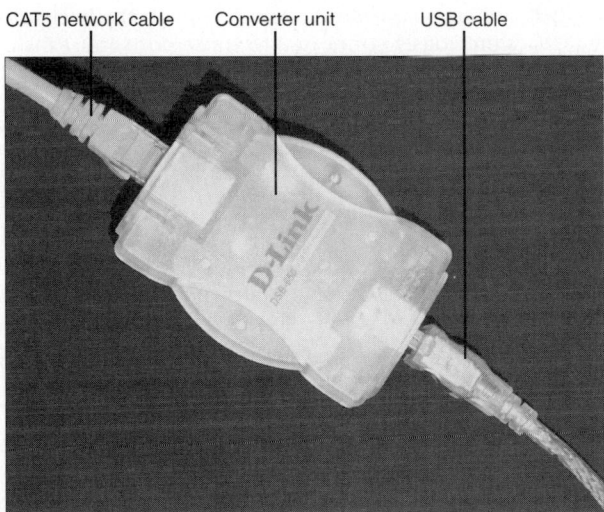

CAT5 network cable   Converter unit   USB cable

Figure 17.8 A typical USB-to-Ethernet adapter from D-Link.

There is more to these devices than just a cable: If the unit is a one-piece device, active electronics are hidden in a module along the cable or are sometimes packed into one of the cable ends. The electronics are powered by the USB bus and convert the signals to the appropriate other interface. If you cannot install a native adapter card for your device, converting it to use the USB port through an adapter is much better than not using the device at all. For example, a USB-to-Ethernet adapter such as the one shown in Figure 17.8 can enable a computer without expansion slots to connect to a broadband Internet device such as a cable or DSL modem.

However, some drawbacks do exist to these adapters. One is cost: They typically cost $30–$60 or more. It can be tough to spend up to $40 on a USB-to-parallel adapter to drive a printer that barely cost twice that amount. In addition, other limitations might apply. For example, USB-to-parallel converters work only with printers and not other parallel-connected devices, such as scanners, cameras, external drives, and so on. Before purchasing one of these adapters, ensure that it will work with the device or devices you have in mind. If you need to use more than one non-USB device with your system, consider special USB hubs that also contain various combinations of other port types; these are sometimes referred to as *multifunction USB hubs*, *USB port replicators*, or *USB docking stations*. These special hubs are more expensive than USB-only hubs but are less expensive than the combined cost of a comparable USB hub and two or more USB adapters.

Another type of adapter available is a direct-connect cable, which enables you to connect two USB-equipped PCs directly together using USB as a network. These are popular for people playing two-player games, with each player on his own system. Another use is for transferring files because this connection usually works as well or better than the direct parallel connection that otherwise might be used. Also available are USB switchboxes that enable one peripheral to be shared among two or more USB buses. Note that both the direct connect cables and USB switchboxes are technically not allowed as a part of the USB specification, although they do exist.

Legacy-Free PCs

USB adapters might find more use in the future as more and more legacy-free PCs are shipped. A *legacy-free PC* is one that lacks any components that were connected to or a part of the traditional ISA bus. This especially includes the otherwise standard Super I/O chip, which integrated serial, parallel, keyboard, mouse, floppy, and other connections. A legacy-free motherboard therefore does not have the standard serial, parallel, and keyboard/mouse connectors on the back and lacks an integrated floppy controller. The devices previously connected to those ports must instead be connected via USB, ATA/IDE, PCI, and other interfaces.

Legacy-free systems are primarily found on the low-end, consumer-oriented systems. For those systems, USB will likely be one of the only external connections provided. To compensate for the loss of the other external interfaces, most legacy-free motherboards feature four or more integrated USB connectors on one or two buses.

IEEE 1394

The *Institute of Electrical and Electronic Engineers* Standards Board introduced IEEE 1394 (or just 1394 for short) in late 1995. The number comes from the fact that this happened to be the 1,394th standard they published. It is the result of the large data-moving demands of today's audio and video multimedia devices. The key advantage of 1394 is that it's extremely fast; the popular 1394a standard supports data transfer rates up to an incredible 400Mbps.

1394 Standards

The most common version of the 1394 standard is actually referred to as 1394a, or sometimes as 1394a-2000 for the year it was adopted. The 1394a standard was introduced to solve interoperability and compatibility issues in the original 1394 standard; it uses the same connectors and supports the same speeds as the original 1394 standard.

The first products to use the 1394b standard were introduced in early 2003. Initially, 1394b supports 800Mbps transfer rates, but future versions of the standard might reach speeds of up to 3,200Mbps. 1394b will be capable of reaching much higher speeds than the current 1394/1394a standard because it will also support network technologies such as glass and plastic fiber-optic cable and Category 5 UTP cable, increased distances when Category 5 cabling is used between devices, and improvements in signaling. 1394b will also be fully backward-compatible with 1394a devices. 1394 is also known by two other common names: i.LINK and FireWire. *i.LINK* is an IEEE 1394 designation initiated by Sony in an effort to put a more user-friendly name on IEEE 1394 technology. Most companies that produce 1394 products for PCs have endorsed this new name initiative. Originally, the term *FireWire* was an Apple-specific trademark that Apple licensed to vendors on a fee basis. However, in May 2002, Apple and the 1394 Trade Association announced an agreement to allow the trade association to provide no-fee licenses for the FireWire trademark on 1394-compliant products that pass the trade association's tests. Apple continues to use *FireWire* as its marketing term for IEEE 1394 devices. FireWire 400 refers to Apple's IEEE 1394a–compliant products, whereas FireWire 800 refers to Apple's IEEE 1394b–compliant products.

1394a Technical Details

The IEEE 1394a standard currently exists with three signaling rates—100Mbps, 200Mbps, and 400Mbps (12.5MBps, 25MBps, and 50MBps). Most PC adapter cards support the 400Mbps (50MBps) rate, although device speeds can vary. A maximum of 63 devices can be connected to a single IEEE 1394 adapter card by way of daisy-chaining or branching. 1394 devices, unlike USB devices, can be used in a daisy-chain without using a hub, although hubs are recommended for devices that will be hot-swapped. Cables for IEEE 1394/1394a devices use Nintendo GameBoy–derived connectors and consist of six conductors: Four wires transmit data, and two wires conduct power. Connection with the motherboard is made either by a dedicated IEEE 1394 interface or by a PCI adapter card. Figure 17.9 shows the 1394/1394a cable, socket, and connector.

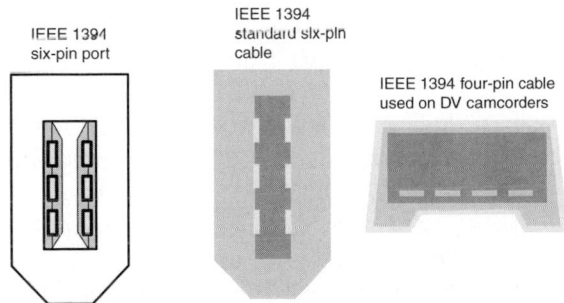

IEEE 1394
six-pin port

IEEE 1394
standard six-pin
cable

IEEE 1394 four-pin cable
used on DV camcorders

Figure 17.9   IEEE 1394 port, 6-pin cable, and 4-pin cable.

The 1394 bus was derived from the FireWire bus originally developed by Apple and Texas Instruments, and it is also a part of a new Serial SCSI standard.

1394a uses a simple six-wire cable with two differential pairs of clock and data lines, plus two power lines; the four-wire cable end shown in Figure 17.9 is used with self-powered devices, such as DV camcorders. Just as with USB, 1394 is fully PnP, including the capability for hot-plugging (insertion and removal of components without powering down). Unlike the much more complicated parallel SCSI bus, 1394 does not require complicated termination, and devices connected to the bus can draw up to 1.5 amps of electrical power. 1394 offers equal or greater performance compared to ultra-wide SCSI, with a much less expensive and less complicated connection.

1394 is built on a daisy-chained and branched topology, and it allows up to 63 nodes, with a chain of up to 16 devices on each node. If this is not enough, the standard also calls for up to 1,023 bridged buses, which can interconnect more than 64,000 nodes! Additionally, as with SCSI, 1394 can support devices with various data rates on the same bus. Most 1394 adapters have three nodes, each of which can support 16 devices in a daisy-chain arrangement. Some 1394 adapters also support internal 1394 devices.

The types of devices that can be connected to the PC via 1394 mainly include video cameras; editing equipment; and all forms of disk drives, including hard disk, optical, floppy, CD-ROM, and DVD-ROM drives. Also, digital cameras, tape drives, high-resolution scanners, and many other high-speed peripherals that feature 1394 have interfaces built in. The 1394 bus appears in some desktop and portable computers as a replacement or supplement for other external high-speed buses, such as USB or SCSI.

Chipsets and PCI adapters for the 1394 bus are available from a number of manufacturers, including some models that support both 1394 and other port types in a single slot. Microsoft has developed drivers to support 1394 in Windows 9x and later, including Windows XP. The most popular devices that conform to the IEEE 1394 standard are camcorders and VCRs with digital video capability. Sony was among the first to release such devices (under the i.LINK name). In typical Sony fashion, however, its products have a unique four-wire connector that requires an adapter cord to be used with IEEE 1394 PC Cards, and Sony doesn't even call it IEEE 1394 or FireWire—it created its own designation (i.LINK) instead. DV products using 1394 also are available from Panasonic, Sharp, Matsushita, and others. Noncomputer IEEE 1394 applications include DV conferencing devices, satellite audio and video data streams, audio synthesizers, DVD, and other high-speed disc drives.

Because of the current DV emphasis for IEEE 1394 peripherals, many FireWire cards currently offered are bundled with DV capturing and editing software. With a DV camera or recording equipment, these items provide substantial video editing and dubbing capabilities on your PC. Of course, you need IEEE 1394 I/O connectivity, which is a growing, but still somewhat rare, feature on current motherboards.

IEEE 1394b Technical Details

IEEE 1394b is the second generation of the 1394 standard, with the first products (high-performance external hard drives) introduced in January 2003. IEEE 1394b uses one of two new nine-pin cables and connectors to support speeds of 800Mbps–3200Mbps with copper or fiber-optic cabling. In addition to supporting faster transfer rates, 1394b has other new features, including

- *Self-healing loops.* If you improperly connect 1394b devices together to create a logical loop, the interface corrects the problem instead of failing as with 1394a.

- *Continuous dual simplex.* Of the two wire pairs used, each pair transmits data to the other device, so that speed remains constant.

- *Support for fiber-optic and CAT5 network cable as well as standard 1394a and 1394b copper cable.*

- *Improved arbitration of signals to support faster performance and longer cable distances.*

- *Support for CAT5 cable, even though it uses pairs on pins 1 and 2 and 7 and 8 only for greater reliability.* It also doesn't require crossover cables.

The initial implementations of IEEE 1394b use a new nine-wire interface with two pairs of signaling wires. However, to enable a 1394b port to connect to 1394a-compatible devices, there are two different versions of the 1394b port:

- Beta

- Bilingual

Beta connectors support only 1394b devices, whereas bilingual connectors can support both 1394b and 1394a devices. As Figure 17.10 shows, the connectors and cables have the same pinout but are keyed differently.

Note that bilingual sockets and cables have a narrower notch than beta sockets and cables. This prevents cables designed for 1394a devices from being connected to the beta socket. Figure 17.11 compares a beta-to-beta 1394b cable to bilingual-to-1394a cables.

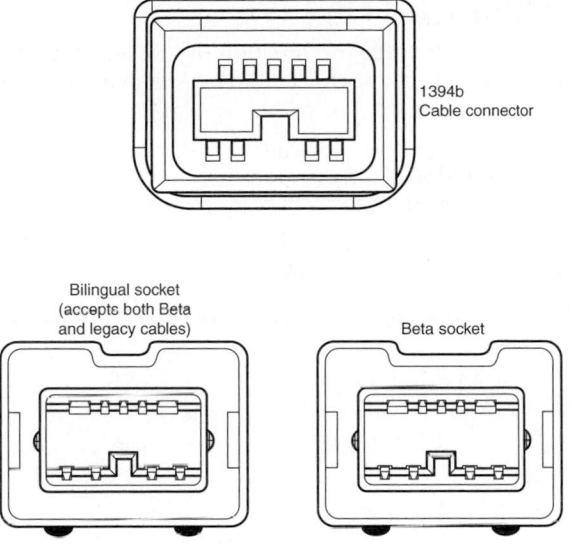

Figure 17.10   Bilingual and beta 1394b connectors and cables. Many 1394b implementations use both types of connectors.

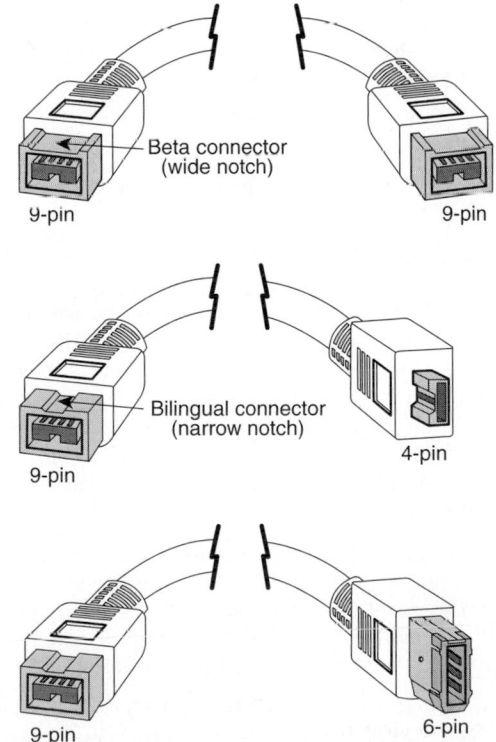

Figure 17.11   A beta-to-beta cable (top) compared to bilingual–to–4-pin (middle) and bilingual–to 6-pin 1394a devices (bottom).

Comparing IEEE 1394 and USB

Because of the similarity in both the form and function of USB and 1394 ports, there has been some confusion about the differences between them. Table 17.6 summarizes the differences between these technologies.

Table 17.6   IEEE 1394 and USB Comparison

	IEEE 1394a (also called I.LINK or FireWire 400)	IEEE 1394b (also called FireWire 800)	USB 1.1	USB 2.0
PC-host required	No	No	Yes	Yes/No[1]
Maximum number of devices	63	63	127	127
Hot-swappable	Yes	Yes	Yes	Yes
Maximum cable length between devices	4.5 meters	4.5 meters (9-pin copper); 100 meters (glass optical fiber)[2]	5 meters	5 meters
Transfer rate	400Mbps (50MBps)	800Mbps (100MBps)	12Mbps (1.5MBps)	480Mbps (60MBps)
Proposed future transfer rates	None	1,600Mbps (400MBps); 3,200Mbps (800MBps)	None	None
Typical devices	DV camcorders; high-res digital cameras; HDTV; set-top boxes; high-speed drives; high-res scanners; electronic musical instruments	All 1394a devices	Keyboards; mice; joysticks; low-res digital cameras; low-speed drives; modems; printers; low-res scanners	All USB 1.1 devices; DV camcorders; high-res digital cameras; HDTV; set-top boxes; high-speed drives; high-res scanners

1. *No with USB On-The-Go.*

2. *CAT-5 UTP supported for 100Mbps speeds (100 meters max.); step-index plastic optical fiber supported for 100Mbps and 200Mbps speeds (50 meters max.).*

Because the overall performance and physical specifications are similar, the main difference between USB and 1394 is popularity. The bottom line is that USB is by far the most popular external interface for PCs, eclipsing all others by comparison. This is primarily because Intel developed most of USB and has placed built-in USB support in all its motherboard chipsets and motherboards since 1996. Virtually no motherboard chipsets integrate 1394a or 1394b; in most cases, it has to be added as an extra-cost chip to the motherboard. The cost of the additional 1394 circuitry (and a $0.25 royalty paid to Apple Computer per system) and the fact that all motherboards already have USB, have limited the popularity of 1394 (FireWire) in the PC marketplace.

Even with the overwhelming popularity of USB, a market for 1394 still exists. Perhaps the main reason 1394 will survive in conjunction with the USB 2.0 interface is that USB is normally PC-centric, whereas 1394 is not. In other words, USB and Hi-Speed USB require a PC as the host, whereas 1394 can connect two devices directly without a PC between them. As such, 1394 can be used to directly connect a DV camcorder to a DV-VCR for dubbing tapes or editing.

Even this has changed, however, as a supplement called USB On-The-Go was added to the USB 2.0 specification in December 2001. USB On-The-Go enables the same device-to-device connections as was capable in 1394 (FireWire) and essentially nullifies the one advantage 1394 had over USB. Because of the popularity and capabilities of USB, I recommend seeking out only USB peripherals over their 1394 (FireWire) counterparts where possible.

Many people like to bring any comparison of USB and 1394 down to speed, but that is a constantly changing parameter. 1394a offers a data transfer rate more than 33 times faster than that of USB 1.1, but is only about 83% as fast as USB 2.0. However, 1394b is about 66% faster than USB 2.0.

Because both USB 2.0 and 1394a (FireWire) offer relatively close to the same overall capabilities and performance, you make your choice based on which devices you intend to connect. If the digital video camera you want to connect has only a 1394 (FireWire/i.LINK) connection, you will need to add a 1394 FireWire card to your system, if such a connection isn't already present on your motherboard. Most general-purpose PC storage, I/O, and other devices are USB, whereas only video devices usually have 1394 connections. However, many devices now offer both USB 2.0 and 1394 interfaces to enable use with the widest range of computers.

Standard Serial and Parallel Ports

Traditionally, the most basic communications ports in any PC system have been the serial and parallel ports, and these ports continue to be important.

Serial ports (also known as *communication* or *COM* ports) originally were used for devices that had to communicate bidirectionally with the system. Such devices include modems, mice, scanners, digitizers, and any other devices that "talk to" and receive information from the PC. Newer parallel port standards now allow the parallel port to perform high-speed bidirectional communications.

Several companies manufacture communications programs that perform high-speed transfers between PC systems using serial or parallel ports. Versions of these file transfer programs have been included with DOS 6.0 and higher (Interlink) and with Windows 95 and newer versions (Direct Cable Connection [DCC]). Although USB continues to replace the parallel port in new computers, you can still purchase products that make nontraditional use of the parallel port. For example, external drive vendors continue to make CD-ROM, CD-RW, and DVD drives; floppy drives; print servers; and tape backups that connect to the parallel port, although many of these devices also include USB connections as well.

Serial Ports

The asynchronous serial interface was designed as a system-to-system communications port. *Asynchronous* means that no synchronization or clocking signal is present, so characters can be sent with any arbitrary time spacing.

Each character that is sent over a serial connection is framed by a standard start-and-stop signal. A single 0 bit, called the *start bit*, precedes each character to tell the receiving system that the next eight bits constitute a byte of data. One or two stop bits follow the character to signal that the character has been sent. At the receiving end of the communication, characters are recognized by the start-and-stop signals instead of by the timing of their arrival. The asynchronous interface is character oriented and has an approximate 20% overhead for the extra information that is needed to identify each character.

Serial refers to data that is sent over a single wire, with each bit lining up in a series as the bits are sent. This type of communication is used over the phone system because it provides one wire for data in each direction.

Typical Locations for Serial Ports

Typical systems include one or two serial ports, with connectors typically located at the rear of the system. Some recent consumer-oriented computers label a front-mounted serial port the "digital camera port." This name comes from the use of serial ports for data transfer from low-end digital cameras. On recent systems, these built-in serial ports are controlled by a highly integrated South Bridge chip in the latest motherboard designs.

If you need more serial ports than your system has as standard, you can purchase single- or multi-port serial port cards or so-called *multi-I/O* cards that feature one or two serial ports and one or two parallel ports. Older systems based on the ISA or VL-Bus standard often have the serial ports attached to a multifunction card that also has IDE hard disk and floppy disk interfaces.

Note that card-based modems also incorporate a built-in serial port on the card as part of the modem circuitry. Figure 17.12 shows the standard 9-pin connector used with most modern external serial ports. Figure 17.13 shows the original standard 25-pin version.

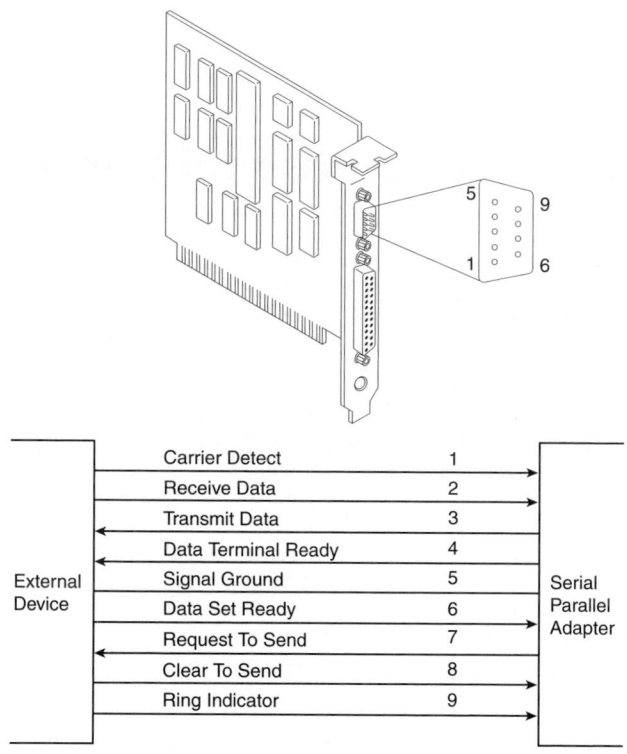

Figure 17.12 AT-style 9-pin serial-port connector specifications.

Serial ports can connect to a variety of devices, such as modems, plotters, printers, PDA docking devices, other computers, bar code readers, scales, and device control circuits.

The official specification recommends a maximum cable length of 50 feet. The limiting factor is the total load capacitance of cable and input circuits of the interface. The maximum capacitance is specified as 2500pF (picofarads). Special low-capacitance cables can effectively increase the maximum cable length greatly, to as much as 500 feet or more. Also available are line drivers (amplifier/repeaters) that can extend cable length even further. Tables 17.7, 17.8, and 17.9 show the pinouts of the 9-pin (AT-style), 25-pin, and 9-pin–to–25-pin serial connectors, respectively.

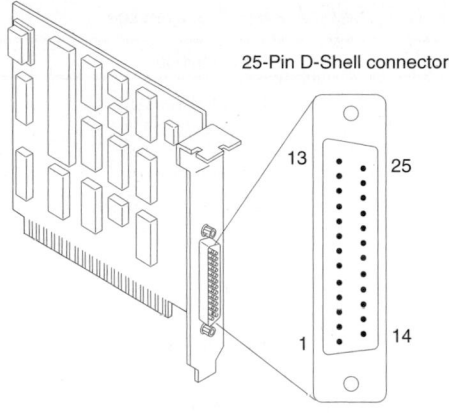

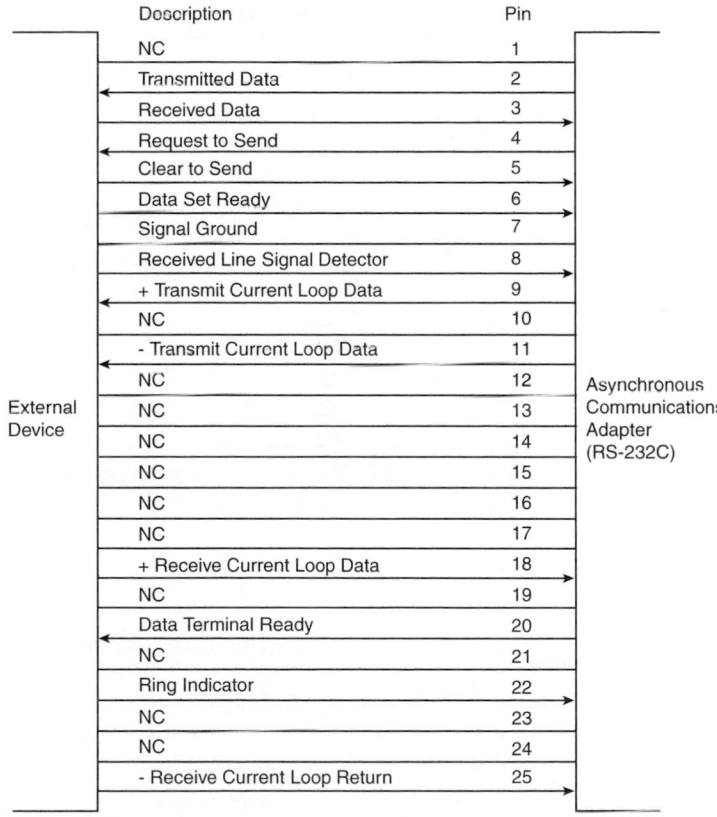

Figure 17.13 Standard 25-pin serial-port connector specifications. NC stands for no connect, which indicates a dead pin.

Table 17.7   9-Pin (AT) Serial Port Connector

Pin	Signal	Description	I/O
1	CD	Carrier detect	In
2	RD	Receive data	In
3	TD	Transmit data	Out
4	DTR	Data terminal ready	Out
5	SG	Signal ground	—
6	DSR	Data set ready	In
7	RTS	Request to send	Out
8	CTS	Clear to send	In
9	RI	Ring indicator	In

Table 17.8   25-Pin (PC, XT, and PS/2) Serial Port Connector

Pin	Signal	Description	I/O
1	—	Chassis ground	—
2	TD	Transmit data	Out
3	RD	Receive data	In
4	RTS	Request to send	Out
5	CTS	Clear to send	In
6	DSR	Data set ready	In
7	SG	Signal ground	—
8	CD	Carrier detect	In
9	—	+Transmit current loop return	Out
11	—	-Transmit current loop data	Out
18	—	+Receive current loop data	In
20	DTR	Data terminal ready	Out
22	RI	Ring indicator	In
25	—	-Receive current loop return	In

Table 17.9   9-Pin–to–25-Pin Serial Cable Adapter Connections

9-Pin	25-Pin	Signal	Description
1	8	CD	Carrier detect
2	3	RD	Receive data
3	2	TD	Transmit data
4	20	DTR	Data terminal ready
5	7	SG	Signal ground
6	6	DSR	Data set ready
7	4	RTS	Request to send
8	5	CTS	Clear to send
9	22	RI	Ring indicator

Note

Macintosh systems use a similar serial interface, defined as RS-422. Most external modems in use today can interface with either RS-232 or RS-422, but it is safest to make sure that the external modem you get for your PC is designed for a PC, not a Macintosh.

UARTs

The heart of any serial port is the Universal Asynchronous Receiver/Transmitter (UART) chip. This chip completely controls the process of breaking the native parallel data within the PC into serial format and later converting serial data back into the parallel format.

Several types of UART chips have been available on the market. The original PC and XT used the 8250 UART, which was used for many years in low-priced serial cards. Starting with the first 16-bit systems, the 16450 UART typically was used. The only difference between these chips is their suitability for high-speed communications. The 16450 is better suited for high-speed communications than is the 8250; otherwise, both chips appear identical to most software. The 16550 UART was the first serial chip used in the IBM PS/2 line. Other 386 and higher systems rapidly adopted it. The 16550 functioned as the earlier 16450 and 8250 chips, but it also included a 16-byte buffer that aided in faster communications. This is sometimes referred to as a *FIFO (first in first out)* buffer. Unfortunately, the early 16550 chips had a few bugs, particularly in the buffer area. These bugs were corrected with the release of the 16550A. The most current version of the chip is the 16550D, which was released in 1995 and is produced by National Semiconductor.

Tip

The high-speed buffered 16550A (or newer) UART chip is pin for pin compatible with the 16450 UART. If your 16450 UART is socketed, a cheap and easy way to improve serial performance is to install a 16550 UART chip in the socket.

Because the 16550 is a faster, more reliable chip than its predecessors, it is best to ensure that your serial ports have either that chip or an equivalent. If you are in doubt about which type of UART you have in your system, you can use the Microsoft MSD program (provided with MS-DOS 6.x and Windows 9x/Me/2000) to determine the type of UART you have. Note that MSD often reports a 16450 UART as an 8250.

Note

Another way to tell whether you have a 16650 UART in Windows is to click the Start menu and then select Settings, Control Panel. Next, double-click Modems, and then click the Diagnostics tab. The Diagnostics tab shows a list of all COM ports in the system, even if they don't have a modem attached to them. Select the port you want to check in the list and click More Info. Windows communicates with the port to determine the UART type, and that information is listed in the Port Information portion of the More Info box. If a modem is attached, additional information about the modem is displayed.

The original designer of these UARTs is National Semiconductor (NS). So many other manufacturers are producing clones of these UARTs that you probably don't have an actual NS brand part in your system. Even so, the part you have is compatible with one of the NS parts, hopefully the 16550. In other words, check to see that whatever UART chip you have does indeed feature the 16-byte FIFO buffer, as found in the NS 16550 part.

◀◀ See "Super I/O Chips," p. 328.

8250

IBM used this original chip in the PC serial port card. This chip had no transmit/receive buffer, so it was very slow. The chip also had several bugs, none of which were serious. The PC and XT ROM BIOSs were written to anticipate at least one of the bugs. The 8250B replaced this chip.

8250A

Do not use the second version of the 8250 in any system. This upgraded chip fixes several bugs in the 8250, including one in the interrupt enable register, but because the PC and XT ROM BIOSs expect the bug, this chip does not work properly with those systems. The 8250A works in an AT system that does not expect the bug, but it does not work adequately at 9600bps.

8250B

The last version of the 8250 fixes bugs from the previous two versions. The interrupt enable bug in the original 8250, which is expected by the PC and XT ROM BIOS software, has been put back into this chip, making the 8250B the most desirable chip for any non-AT serial port application. The 8250B chip might work in an AT under DOS, but it does not run properly at 9600bps because, like all 8250s, it has no transmit/receive buffer.

16450

IBM selected the higher-speed version of the 8250 for the AT. The higher performance comes mainly from a 1-byte transmit/receive buffer contained within the chip. Because this chip has fixed the afore-mentioned interrupt enable bug, the 16450 does not operate properly in many PC or XT systems because they expect this bug to be present. OS/2 requires this chip as a minimum; otherwise, the serial ports do not function properly. It also adds a scratch-pad register as the highest register. The 16450 is used primarily in AT systems because of its increase in throughput over the 8250B.

16550 Series

This chip is pin compatible with the 16450 but is much faster due to a built-in 16-character transmit/receive FIFO buffer. It also allows multiple DMA channel access. The original version of this chip did not allow the buffer to work, but all 16550A or later revisions have the bug fixed. The last version produced by National Semiconductor was called the 16550D. Use a version of this UART in your serial port if you do any communications at 9600bps or higher. If your communications program uses the FIFO—and all of them do today—it can greatly increase communications speed and eliminate lost characters and data at the higher speeds. Virtually all Super I/O chips contain the equivalent of dual 16550A or later chips. Most 16550 UARTs have a maximum communications speed of 115Kbps.

16650, 16750, and 16850

Several companies have produced versions of the 16550 with larger buffers:

- The 16550 has a 32-byte buffer.
- The 16750 has a 64-byte buffer.
- The 16850 has a 128-byte buffer.
- The 16950 has a 128-byte buffer and the option to run at normal or 4x normal baud rates.

These chips are not from National Semiconductor, and the designations only imply that they are compatible with the 16550 but have a larger buffer. These larger-buffered versions allow speeds of 230Kbps (16650), 460Kbps (16750), and 920Kbps (16850 and 16950) and are recommended when running a high-speed external communications link, such as an ISDN terminal adapter or external 56Kbps modem. These are discussed more in the following section.

High-Speed Serial Port Cards

If you are using external RS-232 devices designed to run at speeds higher than 115Kbps (the maximum speed of the 16550 series UARTs and equivalents), you can't achieve maximum performance unless you replace your existing serial ports with add-on cards using one of the 16650, 16750, 16850, or 16950 UARTs discussed earlier. Most cards allow raw port speed settings of 230Kbps, 460Kbps, or even higher, which is valuable when connecting a PC to a high-speed external component that is connected to a serial port, such as an ISDN terminal adapter. You can't really get the full-speed benefit of an external ISDN modem (terminal adapter) unless your serial port can go at least 230Kbps. Lava Computer Mfg. and SIIG are two of the companies that offer a complete line of high-speed serial and parallel port cards (see the Vendor List on the accompanying disc).

Onboard Serial Ports

Starting with late-model 486-based systems in the mid-1990s, a component on the motherboard called a *Super I/O* chip began to replace separate UART chips. This usually has two serial port UARTs as well as a multimode parallel port, floppy controller, keyboard controller, and sometimes the CMOS memory—all built into a single tiny chip. Still, this chip acts as if all these separate devices were installed: That is, from a software point of view, both the operating system and applications still act as if separate UART chips were installed on serial port adapter cards. The most recent systems integrate the functions of a Super I/O chip into the South Bridge chip. As with the Super I/O chip, South Bridge chips with integrated I/O are transparent to software. Super I/O and South Bridge chips are discussed throughout this chapter and in Chapter 4, "Motherboards and Buses."

Serial Port Configuration

Each time a character is received by a serial port, it has to get the attention of the computer by raising an interrupt request line (IRQ). Eight-bit ISA bus systems have eight of these lines, and systems with a 16-bit ISA bus have 16 lines. The 8259 interrupt controller chip or equivalent typically handles these requests for attention. In a standard configuration, COM1 uses IRQ4, and COM2 uses IRQ3. Even on the latest systems, the default COM port assignments remain the same for compatibility with older software and hardware.

When a serial port is installed in a system, it must be configured to use specific I/O addresses (called ports) and interrupts (called IRQs). The best plan is to follow the existing standards for how these devices are to be set up. For configuring serial ports, use the addresses and interrupts indicated in Table 17.10.

Table 17.10   Standard Serial I/O Port Addresses and Interrupts

COMx	I/O Ports	IRQ
COM1	3F8–3FFh	IRQ4
COM2	2F8–2FFh	IRQ3
COM3	3E8–3EFh	IRQ4[1]
COM4	2E8–2EFh[2]	IRQ3[1]

1. *Note that although many serial ports can be set up to share IRQ3 and IRQ4 with COM1 and COM2, it is not recommended. The best recommendation is setting COM3 to IRQ10 and COM4 to IRQ11 (if available). If ports above COM3 are required, it is recommended that you purchase a special multiport serial board, preferably a PCI-based board that supports IRQ sharing without conflicts.*

2. *This I/O address can conflict with registers in some video cards. In such cases, you cannot use COM4 unless COM4 or the video card can be configured to use a different I/O port address range.*

Be sure that, if you are adding more than the standard COM1 and COM2 serial ports, they use unique and nonconflicting interrupts. If you purchase a serial port adapter card and intend to use it to supply ports beyond the standard COM1 and COM2, be sure it can use interrupts other than IRQ3 and IRQ4; PCI-based serial port boards take advantage of IRQ sharing features to allow COM3 and above to use a single IRQ without conflicts.

Note that BIOS manufacturers never built support for COM3 and COM4 into the BIOS. Therefore, DOS can't work with serial ports above COM2 because DOS gets its I/O information from the BIOS. The BIOS finds out what is installed in your system, and where it is installed, during the power-on self test (POST). The POST checks only for the first two installed ports. This is not a problem under Windows because Windows 95 and later have built-in support for up to 128 ports.

With support for up to 128 serial ports in Windows, using multiport boards in the system is much easier. Multiport boards give your system the capability to collect or share data with multiple devices while using only one slot and one interrupt.

Caution

Sharing interrupts between COM ports—or any devices—can function properly sometimes and not others. It is recommended that you never share interrupts between multiple ISA-based serial ports, such as the COM ports built into your motherboard or found on an ISA modem. Trying to track down drivers, patches, and updates to allow this to work successfully—if it's even possible in your system—can cause you hours of frustration.

◀◀ See "Resolving Resource Conflicts," p. 379.

Testing Serial Ports

You can perform several tests on serial and parallel ports. The two most common types of tests are those that involve software only and those that involve both hardware and software. The software-only tests are done with diagnostic programs, such as Microsoft's MSD or the Modem diagnostics built into Windows, whereas the hardware and software tests involve using a wrap plug to perform loopback testing.

▶▶ See "Testing Parallel Ports," p. 1014.

▶▶ See "Advanced Diagnostics Using Loopback Testing," p. 1005.

Microsoft Diagnostics

Microsoft Diagnostics (MSD) is a diagnostic program supplied with MS-DOS 6.x, Windows 3.x, and Windows 9x/Me/2000. In Windows 95 this program can be found on the CD-ROM in the \other\msd directory, and in Windows 98/Me/2000, you can find it on the CD-ROM in the \tools\oldmsdos directory. MSD is not automatically installed when you install the operating system. To use it, you must run it from the CD-ROM directly or copy the program from the CD-ROM to your hard disk.

For the most accurate results, many diagnostics programs, such as MSD, are best run in a DOS-only environment. Because of this, you need to restart the machine in DOS mode before using them. If you use Windows 2000 or XP, you can format a floppy disk with MS-DOS startup files and use it to start your computer. Then, to use MSD, switch to the directory in which it is located. This is not necessary, of course, if the directory that contains the program is in your search path—which is often the case with the DOS 6.x or Windows-provided versions of MSD. Then, simply type **MSD** at the DOS prompt and press Enter. Soon you see the MSD screen.

Select the Serial Ports option. Notice that you are given information about which type of serial chip you have in your system, as well as information about which ports are available. If any of the ports are in use (with a mouse, for example), that information is provided as well.

MSD is helpful in at least determining whether your serial ports are responding. If MSD can't determine the existence of a port, it does not provide the report that indicates that the port exists. This sort of "look-and-see" test is the first action I usually take to determine why a port is not responding.

Troubleshooting Ports in Windows

Windows 9x/Me can tell you whether your ports are functioning. First, you must verify that the required communications files are present to support the serial ports in your system:

1. Verify the file sizes and dates of both COMM.DRV (16-bit serial driver) and SERIAL.VXD (32-bit serial driver) in the SYSTEM directory, compared to the original versions of these files from the Windows 9x/Me CD-ROM.

2. Confirm that the following lines are present in SYSTEM.INI:

```
[boot]
comm.drv=comm.drv
[386enh]
device=*vcd
```

The SERIAL.VXD driver is not loaded in SYSTEM.INI; instead, it is loaded through the Registry.

Windows 2000 and XP use the SERIAL.SYS and SERENUM.SYS drivers for handling RS-232 devices. You can compare the file sizes and dates for these files to those on the Windows 2000 CD-ROM.

If both drivers are present and accounted for, you can determine whether a particular serial port's I/O address and IRQ settings are properly defined by following these steps for Windows 9x/Me/2000:

1. Right-click the My Computer icon on the desktop and select Properties, or double-click the System icon in the Control Panel. Click the Device Manager tab, click Ports, and then select a specific port (such as COM1).

2. Click the Properties button, and then click the Resources tab to display the current resource settings (IRQ, I/O) for that port.

3. Check the Conflicting Devices List to see whether the port is using resources that conflict with other devices. If the port is in conflict with other devices, click the Change Setting button, and then select a configuration that does not cause resource conflicts. You might need to experiment with these settings until you find the correct one.

4. If the resource settings can't be changed, most likely they must be changed via the BIOS Setup. Shut down and restart the system, enter the BIOS Setup, and change the port configurations there.

◄◄ See "Resolving Resource Conflicts," p. 379.

A common problem with non–Plug and Play modems can occur when people try to use a modem on COM3 with a serial mouse or other device on COM1. Typically, COM1 and COM3 ports use the same IRQ, meaning that they can't be used simultaneously. The COM2 and COM4 ports have the same problem sharing IRQs. If possible, change the COM3 or COM4 port to an IRQ setting that is not in conflict with COM1 or COM2. Note also that some video adapters have an automatic address conflict with COM4.

Advanced Diagnostics Using Loopback Testing

One of the most useful types of diagnostic test is the loopback test, which can be used to ensure the correct function of the serial port and any attached cables. Loopback tests are basically internal (digital) or external (analog). You can run internal tests by simply unplugging any cables from the port and executing the test via a diagnostics program.

The external loopback test is more effective. This test requires that a special loopback connector or wrap plug be attached to the port in question. When the test is run, the port is used to send data out to the loopback plug, which simply routes the data back into the port's receive pins so the port is transmitting and receiving at the same time. A loopback or wrap plug is nothing more than a cable that is doubled back on itself. Most diagnostics programs that run this type of test include the loopback plug, and if not, these types of plugs easily can be purchased or even built.

Following is a list of the wiring necessary to construct your own serial port loopback or wrap plugs:

- *Standard IBM-type 25-pin serial (female DB25S) loopback connector (wrap plug).* Connect the following pins:

  1 to 7

  2 to 3

  4 to 5 to 8

  6 to 11 to 20 to 22

  15 to 17 to 23

  18 to 25

- *Norton Utilities (Symantec) 25-pin serial (female DB25S) loopback connector (wrap plug).* Connect the following pins:

  2 to 3

  4 to 5

  6 to 8 to 20 to 22

- *Standard IBM-type 9-pin serial (female DB9S) loopback connector (wrap plug).* Connect the following pins:

  1 to 7 to 8

  2 to 3

  4 to 6 to 9

- *Norton Utilities (Symantec) 9-pin serial (female DB9S) loopback connector (wrap plug).* Connect the following pins:

  2 to 3

  7 to 8

  1 to 4 to 6 to 9

◄◄ See "Serial Ports," p. 997.

To make these loopback plugs, you need a connector shell with the required pins installed. Then, wire wrap or solder the wires, interconnecting the appropriate pins inside the connector shell as specified in the preceding list.

In most cases, purchasing a set of loopback connectors that are premade is less expensive than making them yourself. Most companies that sell diagnostics software can also sell you a set of loopback plugs. Some hardware diagnostic programs include loopback plugs with the software.

One advantage of using loopback connectors is that you can plug them into the ends of a cable that is included in the test. This can verify that both the cable and the port are working properly.

If you need to test serial ports further, see Chapter 24, "PC Diagnostics, Testing, and Maintenance," which describes third-party testing software.

Parallel Ports

Parallel ports are normally used for connecting printers to a PC. Even though that was their sole original intention, parallel ports have become much more useful over the years as a more general-purpose, relatively high-speed interface between devices (when compared to serial ports). Today, USB 1.1–compliant ports are almost as fast as parallel ports, and USB 2.0, IEEE 1394a, and IEEE 1394b ports are significantly faster. Originally, parallel ports were one way only; however, modern parallel ports can send and receive data when properly configured.

Parallel ports are so named because they have eight lines for sending all the bits that comprise 1 byte of data simultaneously across eight wires. This interface is fast and traditionally has been used for printers. However, programs that transfer data between systems always have used the parallel port as an option for transmitting data because it can do so 4 bits at a time, rather than 1 bit at a time as with a serial interface.

The following section looks at how these programs transfer data between parallel ports. The only problem with parallel ports is that their cables can't be extended for any great length without amplifying the signal; otherwise, errors occur in the data. Table 17.11 shows the pinout for a standard PC parallel port.

Table 17.11   25-Pin PC-Compatible Parallel Port Connector

Pin	Description	I/O		Pin	Description	I/O
1	-Strobe	Out		14	-Auto Feed	Out
2	+Data Bit 0	Out		15	-Error	In
3	+Data Bit 1	Out		16	-Initialize Printer	Out
4	+Data Bit 2	Out		17	-Select Input	Out
5	+Data Bit 3	Out		18	-Data Bit 0 Return (GND)	In
6	+Data Bit 4	Out		19	-Data Bit 1 Return (GND)	In
7	+Data Bit 5	Out		20	-Data Bit 2 Return (GND)	In
8	+Data Bit 6	Out		21	-Data Bit 3 Return (GND)	In
9	+Data Bit 7	Out		22	-Data Bit 4 Return (GND)	In
10	-Acknowledge	In		23	-Data Bit 5 Return (GND)	In
11	+Busy	In		24	-Data Bit 6 Return (GND)	In
12	+Paper End	In		25	-Data Bit 7 Return (GND)	In
13	+Select	In				

IEEE 1284 Parallel Port Standard

The IEEE 1284 standard, called Standard Signaling Method for a Bidirectional Parallel Peripheral Interface for Personal Computers, was approved for final release in March 1994. This standard defines the physical characteristics of the parallel port, including data-transfer modes and physical and electrical specifications. IEEE 1284 defines the electrical signaling behavior external to the PC for a multi-modal parallel port that can support 4-bit modes of operation. Not all modes are required by the 1284 specification, and the standard makes some provision for additional modes.

The IEEE 1284 specification is targeted at standardizing the behavior between a PC and an attached device, specifically attached printers. However, the specification is also of interest to vendors of parallel port peripherals (removable-media drives, scanners, and so on).

IEEE 1284 pertains only to hardware and line control and does not define how software is to talk to the port. An offshoot of the original 1284 standard has been created to define the software interface. The IEEE 1284.3 committee was formed to develop a standard for software that is used with IEEE 1284–compliant hardware. This standard, designed to address the disparity among providers of parallel port chips, contains a specification for supporting EPP (the Enhanced Parallel Port) mode via the PC's system BIOS.

IEEE 1284 enables much higher throughput in a connection between a computer and a printer or two computers. The result is that the printer cable is no longer the standard printer cable. The IEEE 1284 printer cable uses twisted-pair technology, which results in a much more reliable and error-free connection.

The IEEE 1284 standard also defines the parallel port connectors, including the two preexisting types (called Type A and Type B), as well as an additional high-density Type C connector. Type A refers to the standard DB25 connector used on most PC systems for parallel port connections, whereas Type B refers to the standard 36-pin Centronics-style connector found on most printers. Type C is a high-density 36-pin connector that can be found on some of the newer printers on the market, such as those from HP. The three connectors are shown in Figure 17.14.

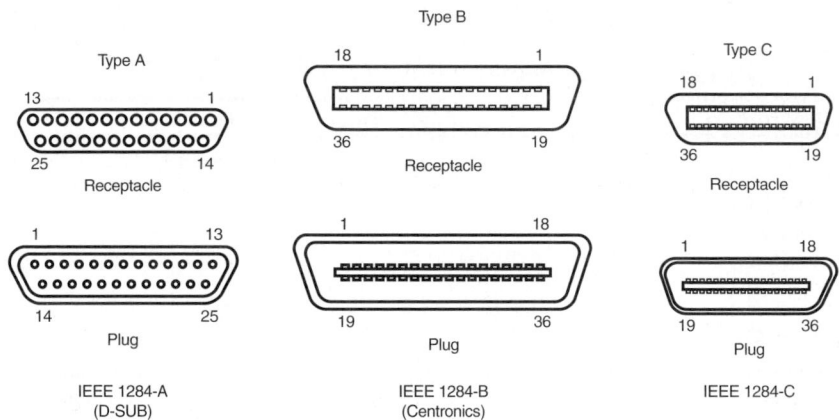

Figure 17.14   The three different types of IEEE 1284 parallel port connectors.

The IEEE 1284 parallel port standard defines five port-operating modes, emphasizing the higher-speed EPP and ECP modes. Some of the modes are input only, whereas others are output only. These five modes combine to create four types of ports, as shown in Table 17.12.

Table 17.12   Types of IEEE 1284 Ports

Parallel Port Type	Input Mode	Output Mode	Comments
SPP (Standard Parallel Port)	Nibble	Compatible	4-bit input, 8-bit output
Bidirectional	Byte	Compatible	8-bit I/O
EPP (Enhanced Parallel Port)	EPP	EPP	8-bit I/O
ECP (Enhanced Capabilities Port)	ECP	ECP	8-bit I/O, uses DMA

The 1284-defined parallel port modes are shown in Table 17.13, which also shows the approximate transfer speeds.

Table 17.13   IEEE 1284 Parallel Port Modes

Parallel Port Mode	Direction	Transfer Rate
Nibble (4-bit)	Input only	50KBps
Byte (8-bit)	Input only	150KBps
Compatible	Output only	150KBps
EPP (Enhanced Parallel Port)	Input/Output	500KBps–2.77MBps
ECP (Enhanced Capabilities Port)	Input/Output	500KBps–2.77MBps

Each of the port types and modes is discussed in the following sections.

Standard Parallel Ports

Older PCs did not have different types of parallel ports available. The only available port was the parallel port that was used to send information from the computer to a device such as a printer. The unidirectional nature of the original PC parallel port is consistent with its primary use—that is, sending data to a printer. There were times, however, when it was desirable to have a bidirectional port—for example, when it was necessary to receive feedback from a printer, which was common with PostScript printers. This could not be done easily with the original unidirectional ports.

Although it was never intended to be used for input, a clever scheme was devised in which four of the signal lines can be used as a 4-bit input connection. Thus, these ports can do 8-bit (byte) output (called compatible mode) and 4-bit input (called nibble mode). This is still very common on low-end desktop systems. Systems built after 1993 are likely to have more capable parallel ports, such as bidirectional, EPP, or ECP.

Standard parallel ports are capable of effective transfer rates of about 150KBps output and about 50KBps input.

Bidirectional (8-bit) Parallel Ports

With the introduction of the PS/2 series of machines in 1987, IBM introduced the bidirectional parallel port. These are commonly found in PC-compatible systems today and can be designated "bidirectional," "PS/2 type," or "extended" parallel ports. This port design opened the way for true communication between the computer and the peripheral across the parallel port. This was done by defining a few of the previously unused pins in the parallel connector, and by defining a status bit to indicate in which direction information was traveling across the channel. This allowed for a true 8-bit (called byte mode) input.

These ports can do both 8-bit input and output using the standard eight data lines and are considerably faster than the 4-bit ports when used with external devices. Bidirectional ports are capable of approximately 150KBps transfer rates on both output and input.

Enhanced Parallel Port

EPP is a newer specification, sometimes referred to as the Fast Mode parallel port. Intel, Xircom, and Zenith Data Systems developed and announced the EPP in October 1991. The first products to offer EPP were Zenith Data Systems laptops, Xircom Pocket LAN adapters, and the Intel 82360 SL I/O chip. Currently, almost all systems include a multimode parallel port that supports EPP mode; it's usually built into the Super I/O chip or South Bridge chip on the motherboard.

EPP operates at almost ISA bus speed and offers a tenfold increase in the raw throughput capability over a conventional parallel port. EPP is especially designed for parallel port peripherals, such as LAN adapters, disk drives, and tape backups. EPP has been included in the IEEE 1284 Parallel Port standard. Transfer rates of up to 2.77MBps are possible with EPP.

Since the original Intel 82360 SL I/O chip in 1992, other major chip vendors (such as National Semiconductor, SMC, Western Digital, and VLSI) have also produced I/O chipsets that offer some form of EPP capability. One problem is that the procedure for enabling EPP across the various chips differs widely from vendor to vendor, and many vendors offer more than one I/O chip.

EPP version 1.7 (March 1992) identifies the first popular version of the hardware specification. With minor changes, this has since been abandoned and folded into the IEEE 1284 standard. Some technical reference materials have erroneously made reference to "EPP specification version 1.9," causing confusion about the EPP standard. Note that "EPP version 1.9" technically does not exist, and any EPP specification after the original version 1.7 is more accurately referred to as a part of the IEEE 1284 specification.

Unfortunately, this has resulted in two somewhat incompatible standards for EPP parallel ports: the original EPP Standards Committee version 1.7 standard and the IEEE 1284 Committee standard, usually called EPP version 1.9. The two standards are similar enough that new peripherals can be designed to support both, but older EPP 1.7 peripherals might not operate with EPP 1284 (EPP 1.9) ports. For this reason, many multimode ports allow configuration in either EPP 1.7 or 1.9 mode, normally selected via the BIOS Setup.

EPP ports are now supported in virtually all Super I/O chips that are used on modern motherboards and in South Bridge chips that integrate I/O functions. Because the EPP port is defined in the IEEE 1284 standard, it also has gained software and driver support, including support in Windows NT.

Enhanced Capabilities Port

In 1992, Microsoft and Hewlett-Packard announced the Enhanced Capabilities Port (ECP), another type of high-speed parallel port. Similar to EPP, ECP offers improved performance for the parallel port and requires special hardware logic.

Since the original announcement, ECP is included in IEEE 1284—just like EPP. Unlike EPP, however, ECP is not tailored to support portable PCs' parallel port peripherals; its purpose is to support an inexpensive attachment to a very high-performance printer or scanner. Furthermore, ECP mode requires the use of a DMA channel, which EPP did not define and which can cause troublesome conflicts with other devices that use DMA, such as ISA sound cards or high-performance ISA SCSI host adapters. Most PCs with newer Super I/O chips or integrated South Bridge I/O support can support either EPP or ECP mode.

Most new systems are being delivered with ECP ports that support high-throughput communications. In most cases, the ECP ports can be turned into EPP or standard parallel ports via BIOS. However, it's recommended that the port be placed in ECP mode for the best throughput.

Depending on the motherboard, the DMA channel assignment used for ECP mode on a built-in parallel might be performed through the BIOS setup program or through moving a jumper block on the motherboard itself.

Upgrading to EPP/ECP Parallel Ports

If you want to test the parallel ports in a system, especially to determine which type they are, I highly recommend a utility called Parallel (PARA14.ZIP). This is a handy parallel port information utility that examines your system's parallel ports and reports the port type, I/O address, IRQ level, BIOS name, and an assortment of informative notes and warnings in a compact and easy-to-read display. The output can be redirected to a file for tech support purposes. Parallel uses very sophisticated techniques for port and IRQ detection, and it is aware of a broad range of quirky port features. You can get it from Parallel Technologies (www.1pt.com).

If you have an older system that does not include an EPP/ECP port and you want to upgrade, several companies now offer boards with the correct Super I/O chips to implement these features. I recommend that you check with Parallel Technologies, Byterunner Technologies, Lava Computer Mfg., or SIIG; they are listed in the Vendor List on the disc accompanying this book.

Although USB ports are replacing most nontraditional parallel port uses, high-speed parallel ports such as EPP and ECP are still used for supporting external peripherals, such as Zip drives, CD-ROM drives, scanners, tape drives, and even hard disks. Most of these devices attach to the parallel port using a pass-through connection. This means your local printer can still work through the port, along with the device. The device will have its own drivers that mediate both the communications with the device and the printer pass-through. Using EPP or ECP mode, communications speeds that are as high as 2.77MBps can be achieved. This can enable a relatively high-speed device to function almost as if it were connected to the system bus internally.

Parallel Port Configuration

The configuration of parallel ports is not as complicated as it is for serial ports. Even the original IBM PC had BIOS support for three LPT ports. Table 17.14 shows the standard I/O address and interrupt settings for parallel port use.

Table 17.14   Parallel Interface I/O Port Addresses and Interrupts

Standard LPTx	Alternate LPTx	I/O Ports	IRQ
LPT1	—	3BC–3BFh	IRQ7
LPT1	LPT2	378–37Ah	IRQ5
LPT2	LPT3	278h–27Ah	IRQ5

Because the BIOS and DOS have always provided three definitions for parallel ports, problems with older systems are infrequent. Problems can arise, however, from the lack of available interrupt-driven ports for ISA/PCI bus systems. Usually, an interrupt-driven port is not absolutely required for printing operations; in fact, many programs do not use the interrupt-driven capability. However, some programs do use the interrupt, such as network print programs and other types of background or spooler-type printer programs.

Also, high-speed laser-printer utility programs often use the interrupt capabilities to enable printing. If you use these types of applications on a port that is not interrupt driven, you see the printing slow to a crawl—if it works at all. The only solution is to use an interrupt-driven port. MS-DOS and Windows 9x/Me/2000/XP now support up to 128 parallel ports.

To configure parallel ports in ISA/PCI bus systems, you normally use the BIOS Setup program for ports that are built into the motherboard, or you might need to set jumpers and switches or use a setup program for adapter-card-based ports. Because each board on the market is different, you always should consult the OEM manual for that particular card if you need to know how the card should be configured.

◀◀   See "BIOS Hardware/Software," p. 401.

Linking Systems with Serial or Parallel Ports

You can connect two systems locally using their serial or parallel ports along with specially wired cables. This form of connection has been used over the years to enable a quick and easy mini-LAN to be set up that allows for the transfer of data between two systems. This can be especially useful when you are migrating your data to a new system you have built or purchased.

Even though using serial or parallel ports to connect two systems to migrate data can be useful, a much better way to connect two systems is to use Ethernet cards and what is commonly called a *crossover* cable. Using this type of connection, you can establish a LAN connection between the two systems and transfer data at the full speed of the Ethernet network, which is 10Mbps, 100Mbps, or 1,000Mbps (1.25MBps, 12.5MBps, or 125MBps). Using serial or parallel ports to transfer data between two systems was more prevalent when most systems did not include some form of network interface card (NIC).

Several free and commercial programs can support serial or parallel-port file transfers. MS-DOS 6.0 and later include a program Interlink, whereas Windows 95 and later include software called either Direct Cable Connection or Direct Parallel Connection. Other commercially available software includes Laplink.com's LapLink series, Smith Micro's CheckIt FastMove, and Symantec's PC Anywhere, among others.

Serial Port Transfers

Serial ports have always been used for communications between systems, but the ports were usually connected to modems that convert the data to be transmitted over telephone lines, enabling long-distance connections. If the systems were in the same room, you could connect the serial ports directly without using modems by instead using what is commonly referred to as a *null modem cable*. The name comes from the fact that there really aren't any modems present—the cable effectively replaces the modems that would be used at either end. The only drawback is that, because serial ports evolved to support relatively low-speed modem communications, even when using a null modem cable, the connection would be slow because most ports can transmit at 115.2Kbps (14.4KBps).

By using a null modem cable, serial ports can be used to transfer data between systems, although the performance is much lower than when using parallel ports. A serial null modem cable has either a 9-pin or a 25-pin female connector on both ends. The cable should be wired as shown in Table 17.15.

Table 17.15   Serial Null Modem Cable Wiring (9-pin or 25-pin Connectors)

9-Pin	25-Pin	Signal	<-to->	Signal	25-Pin	9-Pin
Pin 5	Pin 7	Ground	<->	Ground	Pin 7	Pin 5
Pin 3	Pin 2	Transmit	<->	Receive	Pin 3	Pin 2
Pin 7	Pin 4	RTS	<->	CTS	Pin 5	Pin 8
Pin 6	Pin 6	DSR	<->	DTR	Pin 20	Pin 4
Pin 2	Pin 3	Receive	<->	Transmit	Pin 2	Pin 3
Pin 8	Pin 5	CTS	<->	RTS	Pin 4	Pin 7
Pin 4	Pin 20	DTR	<->	DSR	Pin 6	Pin 6

If both systems feature infrared serial ports, you can connect the two systems via an infrared connection that uses no cable at all. This type of connection is subject to the limitations of the infrared ports, which allow only very short (a few feet at most) distances with fairly slow data rates.

Because they work so slowly, I usually recommend using serial ports to transfer data between two systems only as a last resort. If possible, you should try to use Ethernet cards and a crossover cable, a USB direct connect cable, or parallel ports with an interlink cable for faster connections.

Parallel Port Transfers

Although the original intention for the parallel port was for it to be used to connect a printer, later implementations allowed for bidirectional data transfer. Bidirectional parallel ports can be used to quickly and easily transfer data between one system and another. If both systems use an EPP/ECP port, you can actually communicate at rates of up to 2.77MBps, which is far faster than the speeds achievable with serial port or infrared (IR) data transfers.

Connecting computers with parallel ports requires a special cable known as a *Direct Cable Connection (DCC)*, *Interlink*, *LapLink*, *parallel crossover*, or *parallel null modem* cable. Many of the commercial file transfer programs provide these cables with their software, or you can purchase them separately from most computer stores or companies that sell cables. However, if you need to make one for yourself, Table 17.16 provides the wiring diagram you need.

Table 17.16   Direct Cable Connection, Interlink, Laplink, or Parallel Null Modem Cable Wiring (25-pin Connectors)

25-Pin	Signal Description	<-to->	Signal Description	25-Pin
Pin 2	Data Bit 0	<->	-Error	Pin 15
Pin 3	Data Bit 1	<->	Select	Pin 13
Pin 4	Data Bit 2	<->	Paper End	Pin 12
Pin 5	Data Bit 3	<->	-Acknowledge	Pin 10
Pin 6	Data Bit 4	<->	Busy	Pin 11
Pin 15	-Error	<->	Data Bit 0	Pin 2
Pin 13	Select	<->	Data Bit 1	Pin 3
Pin 12	Paper End	<->	Data Bit 2	Pin 4
Pin 10	-Acknowledge	<->	Data Bit 3	Pin 5
Pin 11	Busy	<->	Data Bit 4	Pin 6
Pin 25	Ground	<->	Ground	Pin 25

Tip

Even though cables usually are provided for data-transfer programs, notebook users might want to look for an adapter that makes the appropriate changes to a standard parallel printer cable. This can make traveling lighter by preventing the need for additional cables. A DB25 null modem adapter, such as Belkin's F4A602, can be used for this purpose.

Although the prebuilt parallel cables referred to in the previous tip work for connecting two machines with ECP/EPP ports, they can't take advantage of the advanced transfer rates of these ports. Special cables are needed to communicate between ECP/EPP ports. Parallel Technologies is a company that sells ECP/EPP cables for connecting to other ECP/EPP computers, as well as a universal cable for connecting any two parallel ports to use the highest speed.

Windows 9x/Me include a special program called Direct Cable Connection or Direct Parallel Connection, which enables two systems to be networked together via a parallel transfer cable. With Windows 2000 and XP, use the Network Connections dialog box to set up a direct connection. Consult the Windows documentation for information on how to establish a DCC/Direct Parallel connection. Parallel Technologies has been contracted by Microsoft to supply the special DCC cables used to connect the systems, including a special type of cable that uses active electronics to ensure a reliable high-speed interconnection.

Parallel-to-SCSI Converters

Parallel ports can also be used to connect SCSI peripherals to a PC. With a parallel-to-SCSI converter, you can connect any type of SCSI device—such as hard disks, CD-ROM drives, tape drives, Zip drives, or scanners—to your PC, all via the parallel port. To connect to a SCSI device and also continue to be able to print, most parallel-to-SCSI converters include a pass-through connection for a printer.

Therefore, at one end of the converter is a connection to your parallel port, and at the other end is both SCSI and parallel-port connections. Thus, you can plug in a single SCSI device and still connect your printer as well. The drivers for the parallel-to-SCSI converter automatically pass through any information to the printer, so the printer works normally. Some of these converters handle only one SCSI device, but others can handle up to seven SCSI devices, just as normal SCSI host adapters do. SCSI devices are much slower when connected to a parallel port than when they are connected to a native SCSI host adapter.

Testing Parallel Ports

Testing parallel ports is, in most cases, simpler than testing serial ports. The procedures are effectively the same as those used for serial ports, except that when you use the diagnostics software, you (obviously) select choices for parallel ports rather than serial ports.

Even though the software tests are similar, the hardware tests require the proper plugs for the loopback tests on the parallel port. Several loopback plugs are required, depending on what software you are using. Most use the IBM-style loopback, but some use the style that originated in the Norton Utilities diagnostics.

You can purchase loopback plugs or build them yourself. The following wiring is needed to construct your own parallel loopback or wrap plugs to test a parallel port:

■ *IBM 25-pin parallel (male DB25P) loopback connector (wrap plug).* Connect the following pins:

1 to 13

2 to 15

10 to 16

11 to 17

12 to 14

■ *Norton Utilities 25-pin parallel (male DB25P) loopback connector (wrap plug).* Connect the following pins:

2 to 15

3 to 13

4 to 12

5 to 10

6 to 11

CHAPTER 18

Input Devices

Keyboards

One of the most basic system components is the keyboard, which is the primary input device. It is used for entering commands and data into the system. This section looks at the keyboards available for PC-compatible systems, examining the various types of keyboards, how the keyboard functions, the keyboard-to-system interface, and keyboard troubleshooting and repair.

In the years since the introduction of the original IBM PC, IBM has created three keyboard designs for PC systems, and Microsoft has augmented one of them. These designs have become de facto standards in the industry and are shared by virtually all PC manufacturers.

The primary keyboard types are as follows:

- 101-key Enhanced keyboard
- 104-key Windows keyboard
- 83-key PC and XT keyboard (obsolete)
- 84-key AT keyboard (obsolete)

This section discusses the 101-key Enhanced keyboard and the 104-key Windows keyboard, showing the layout and physical appearance of both. Although you can still find old systems that use the 83-key and 84-key designs, these are rare today. Because all new systems today use the 101- or 104-key keyboard design, these versions are covered here.

Note

If you need to learn more about the 83-key PC and XT keyboard or the 84-key AT keyboard, see Chapter 7 of *Upgrading and Repairing PCs, 10th Anniversary Edition*, on the disc included with this book.

Enhanced 101-Key (or 102-Key) Keyboard

In 1986, IBM introduced the "corporate" Enhanced 101-key keyboard for the newer XT and AT models. I use the word *corporate* because this unit first appeared in IBM's RT PC, which was a RISC (reduced instruction set computer) system designed for scientific and engineering applications. Keyboards with this design were soon supplied with virtually every type of system and terminal IBM sold. Other companies quickly copied this design, which became the standard on Intel-based PC systems until the introduction of the 104-key Windows keyboard in 1995 (discussed later in this chapter).

The layout of this universal keyboard was improved over that of the 84-key unit, with perhaps the exception of the Enter key, which reverted to a smaller size. The 101-key Enhanced keyboard was designed to conform to international regulations and specifications for keyboards. In fact, other companies such as Digital Equipment Corporation (DEC) and Texas Instruments (TI) had already been using designs similar to the IBM 101-key unit. The IBM 101-key units originally came in versions with and without the status-indicator LEDs, depending on whether the unit was sold with an XT or AT system. Now many other variations are available from which to choose, including some with integrated pointing devices, such as the IBM TrackPoint II pointing stick, trackballs and touch pads, and programmable keys useful for automating routine tasks.

The Enhanced keyboard is available in several variations, but all are basically the same electrically and all can be interchanged. IBM—with its Lexmark keyboard and printer spinoff—and Unicomp (which now produces these keyboards) have produced a number of keyboard models, including versions with built-in pointing devices and new ergonomic layouts. With the replacement of the Baby-AT motherboard and its five-pin DIN (an acronym for Deutsches Institut für Normung e.V.) keyboard connector by ATX motherboards, which use the six-pin mini-DIN keyboard connector, virtually all keyboards on the market today come with cables for the six-pin mini-DIN connector introduced on the IBM PS/2s.

Although the connectors might be physically different, the keyboards are not, and you can either interchange the cables or use a cable adapter to plug one type into the other; some keyboards you can buy at retail include the adapter in the package. See the section "Keyboard/Mouse Interface Connectors" and Figure 18.8 later in this chapter for the physical and electronic details of these connectors. Many keyboards now include both the standard mini-DIN as well as USB connectors for maximum flexibility when attaching to newer systems. See the section "USB Keyboards" later in this chapter for details on connecting keyboards via USB.

The 101-key keyboard layout can be divided into the following four sections:

- Typing area
- Numeric keypad
- Cursor and screen controls
- Function keys

The 101-key arrangement is similar to the Selectric keyboard layout, with the exception of the Enter key. The Tab, Caps Lock, Shift, and Backspace keys have a larger striking area and are located in the familiar Selectric locations. Ctrl and Alt keys are on each side of the spacebar, and the typing area and numeric keypad have home-row identifiers for touch typing.

The cursor- and screen-control keys have been separated from the numeric keypad, which is reserved for numeric input. (As with other PC keyboards, you can use the numeric keypad for cursor and screen control when the keyboard is not in Num Lock mode.) A division-sign key (/) and an additional Enter key have been added to the numeric keypad.

The cursor-control keys are arranged in the inverted T format that is now expected on all computer keyboards. The Insert, Delete, Home, End, Page Up, and Page Down keys, located above the dedicated cursor-control keys, are separate from the numeric keypad. The function keys, spaced in groups of four, are located across the top of the keyboard. The keyboard also has two additional function keys: F11 and F12. The Esc key is isolated in the upper-left corner of the keyboard. In addition, dedicated Print Screen/Sys Req, Scroll Lock, and Pause/Break keys are provided for commonly used functions.

Foreign-language versions of the Enhanced keyboard include 102 keys and a slightly different layout from the 101-key U.S. versions.

One of the many useful features of the IBM/Lexmark enhanced keyboard (now manufactured by Unicomp) is removable keycaps. This permits the replacement of broken keys and provides access for easier cleaning. Also, with clear keycaps and paper inserts, you can customize the keyboard. Keyboard templates are also available to provide specific operator instructions.

104-Key (Windows 9x/Me/2000/XP) Keyboard

With the introduction of Windows 95, a modified version of the standard 101-key design (created by Microsoft) appeared, called the 104-key Windows keyboard.

If you are a touch typist as I am, you probably really hate to take your hands off the keyboard to use a mouse. Windows 9x and newer versions make this even more of a problem because they use both the right and left mouse buttons (the right button is used to open shortcut menus). Many new keyboards, especially those in portable computers, include a variation of the IBM TrackPoint or the Cirque GlidePoint pointing devices (discussed later in this chapter), which enable touch typists to keep their hands on the keyboard even while moving the pointer. However, another alternative is available that can help. When Microsoft released Windows 95, it also introduced the Microsoft Natural Keyboard, which implemented a revised keyboard specification that added three new Windows-specific keys to the keyboard.

The Microsoft Windows keyboard specification, which has since become a de facto industry standard for keyboard layouts, outlines a set of additional keys and key combinations. The 104-key layout includes left and right Windows keys and an Application key (see Figure 18.1). These keys are used for operating system and application-level keyboard combinations, similar to the existing Ctrl and Alt combinations. You don't need the new keys to use Windows, but software vendors are adding specific functions to their Windows products that use the new Application key (which provides the same functionality as clicking the right mouse button). The recommended Windows keyboard layout calls for the Left and Right Windows keys (called WIN keys) to flank the Alt keys on each side of the space-bar, as well as an Application key on the right of the Right Windows key. Note that the exact placement of these keys is up to the keyboard designer, so variations exist from keyboard to keyboard.

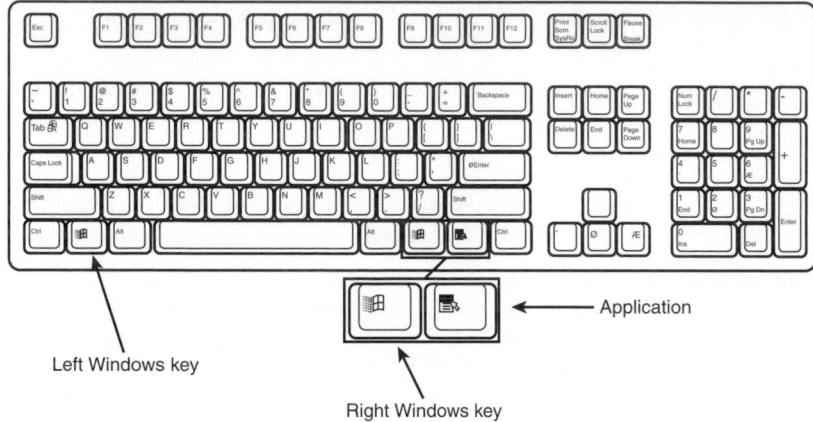

Left Windows key

Right Windows key

Application

Figure 18.1   The 104-key Windows keyboard layout.

The WIN keys open the Windows Start menu, which you can then navigate with the cursor keys. The Application key simulates the right mouse button; in most applications, it brings up a context-sensitive pop-up menu. Several WIN key combinations offer preset macro commands as well. For example, you can press WIN+E to launch the Windows Explorer application. Table 18.1 shows a list of all the Windows key combinations used with the 104-key keyboard.

Table 18.1   Windows 9x/Me/2000/XP Key Combinations

Key Combination	Resulting Action
WIN+R	Runs dialog box
WIN+M	Minimize All
Shift+WIN+M	Undo Minimize All
WIN+D	Minimize All or Undo Minimize All
WIN+F1	Help
WIN+E	Starts Windows Explorer
WIN+F	Find Files or Folders
Ctrl+WIN+F	Find Computer
WIN+Tab	Cycles through taskbar buttons
WIN+Break	Displays System Properties dialog box
Application key	Displays a context menu for the selected item

The preceding keystroke combinations work with any manufacturer's 104-key keyboard, but users of certain Microsoft 104-key keyboards can enhance their keyboard use further by installing the IntelliType Pro software supplied by Microsoft with the keyboard.

The Windows keys are not mandatory when running Windows. In fact, preexisting standard key combinations perform the same functions as these newer keys. I also have noticed that only power users wanting to work as efficiently as possible by keeping their hands on the keyboard (and off the mouse) primarily use these combinations.

The Windows keyboard specification requires that keyboard makers increase the number of trilograms in their keyboard designs. A *trilogram* is a combination of three rapidly pressed keys that perform a special function, such as Ctrl+Alt+Delete. Designing a keyboard so that the switch matrix correctly registers the additional trilograms plus the additional Windows keys adds somewhat to the cost of these keyboards compared to the previous 101-key standard models.

Virtually all keyboard manufacturers have standardized on 104-key keyboards that include these Windows-specific keys. Some manufacturers have added browser control or other keys that, although not standard, can make them easier to use for navigating Web pages and launching various applications.

For additional keyboard combinations you can use, see "Running Windows Without a Mouse" in the Technical Reference section of the disc included with this book.

USB Keyboards

Most keyboards now on the market can connect to the PC via a USB port instead of the standard PS/2 keyboard port. Because USB is a universal bus that uses a hub to enable multiple devices to connect to a single port, a single USB port in a system can replace the standard serial and parallel ports as well as the keyboard and mouse ports. Most current systems and motherboards still include the standard ports (now called *legacy* ports) as well as USB, but most so-called *legacy-free* systems and replacement motherboards have only USB ports for interfacing external devices.

Most keyboard manufacturers now market USB keyboards, but if you want to use your keyboard with both legacy (PS/2) and legacy-free (USB) systems, the most economic way to do so is to specify a keyboard that includes both a USB connector and an adapter to permit the keyboard to work with PS/2 ports. Although Microsoft's Natural Keyboard Elite was the first widely available model to offer USB and PS/2 compatibility, other wired and wireless models from Microsoft, Logitech, Belkin, and others now offer this feature. You can also purchase third-party USB-to-PS/2 adapters, but these can be expensive and might not work with all keyboards.

Not all systems accept USB keyboards, even those with USB ports, because the standard PC BIOS has a keyboard driver that expects a standard keyboard port interface to be present. When a USB keyboard is installed on a system that lacks USB keyboard support, the system can't use it because no driver exists in the BIOS to make it work. In fact, some systems see the lack of a standard keyboard as an error and halt the boot process until one is installed.

To use a keyboard connected via the USB port, you must meet three requirements:

- Have a USB port in the system
- Run Microsoft Windows 98, Windows Me, Windows 2000, or Windows XP (all of which include USB keyboard drivers)
- Have a system chipset and BIOS that feature USB Legacy support

USB Legacy support means your motherboard has a chipset and ROM BIOS drivers that enable a USB keyboard to be used outside the Windows GUI environment. When a system has USB Legacy support enabled, a USB keyboard can be used with MS-DOS (for configuring the system BIOS) when using a command prompt within Windows or when installing Windows on the system for the first time. If USB Legacy support is not enabled on the system, a USB keyboard will function only when Windows is running.

Most recent systems include USB Legacy support, although it might be disabled by default in the system BIOS.

Also, if the Windows installation fails and requires manipulation outside of Windows, the USB keyboard will not function unless it is supported by the chipset and the BIOS. Almost all 1998 and newer systems with USB ports include a chipset and BIOS with USB Legacy (meaning USB Keyboard) support.

Even though USB Legacy support enables you to use a USB keyboard in almost all situations, don't scrap your standard-port keyboards just yet. Some Windows-related bugs and glitches reported by users include the following:

■ *Can't log on to Windows the first time after installing a USB keyboard.* The solution in some cases is to click Cancel when you are asked to log on and then allow the system to detect the keyboard and install drivers. The logon should work normally thereafter. In other cases, you might have to leave the keyboard unplugged when first booting and then plug it in after the OS desktop is up and running. This allows the keyboard to be detected and drivers loaded.

■ *Some USB keyboards won't work when the Windows Emergency Boot Disk (EBD) is used to start the system.* The solution is to turn off the system, connect a standard keyboard, and restart the system.

■ *Some users of Windows 98 and Windows 98 SE have reported conflicts between Windows and the BIOS when USB Legacy support is enabled on some systems.* This conflict can result in an incapability to detect the USB keyboard if you use the Windows 9x shutdown menu and choose to restart the computer in MS-DOS mode. Check with the system or BIOS vendor for an updated BIOS or a patch to solve this conflict.

If you have problems with Legacy USB support, look at these possible solutions:

■ Microsoft's Knowledge Base might address your specific combination of hardware.

■ Your keyboard vendor might offer new drivers.

■ Your system or motherboard vendor might have a BIOS upgrade you can install.

■ Connect the keyboard to the PS/2 port with its adapter (or use a PS/2 keyboard) until you resolve the problem.

◄◄ See "Universal Serial Bus," p. 983.

Notebook Computer Keyboards

One of the biggest influences on keyboard design in recent years has been the proliferation of laptop and notebook systems. Because of size limitations, it is obviously impossible to use the standard keyboard layout for a portable computer. Manufacturers have come up with many solutions. Unfortunately, none of these solutions has become an industry standard, as the 101-key layout is. Because of the variations in design, and because a portable system keyboard is not as easily replaceable as that of a desktop system, the keyboard arrangement should be an important part of your purchasing decision.

Early laptop systems often used smaller-than-normal keys to minimize the size of the keyboard, which resulted in many complaints from users. Today, the keytops on portable systems are usually comparable in size to that of a desktop keyboard, although some systems include half-sized keytops for the function keys and other less frequently used keyboard elements. In addition, consumer demand has caused most manufacturers to retain the inverted-T design for the cursor keys after a few abortive attempts at changing their arrangement.

Of course, the most obvious difference in a portable system keyboard is the sacrifice of the numeric keypad. Most systems now embed the keypad into the standard alphabetical part of the keyboard, as shown in Figure 18.2. To switch the keys from their standard values to their keypad values, you typically must press a key combination involving a proprietary function key, often labeled Fn.

This is an extremely inconvenient solution, and many users abandon their use of the keypad entirely on portable systems. Unfortunately, some activities—such as the entry of ASCII codes using the Alt key—require the use of the keypad numbers, which can be quite frustrating on systems using this arrangement.

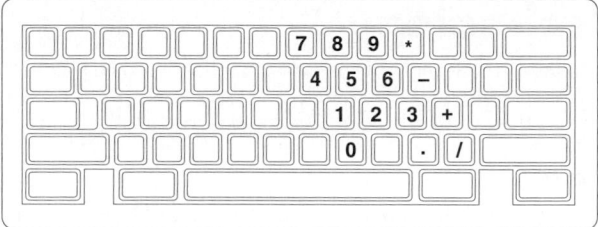

Figure 18.2 Most portable systems today embed the numeric keypad into an oddly shaped block of keys on the alphabetical part of the keyboard.

To alleviate this problem, many portable system manufacturers sell external numeric keypads that plug into the external keyboard port, a serial port, or a USB port. This is a great feature for somebody performing a lot of numeric data entry.

In addition to keypad control, the Fn key often is used to trigger other proprietary features in portable systems, such as toggling between an internal and external display and controlling screen brightness and sound volume.

Some portable system manufacturers have gone to great lengths to provide users with adequate keyboards. For a short time, IBM marketed systems with a keyboard that used a "butterfly" design. The keyboard was split into two halves that rested on top of one another when the system was closed. When you opened the lid, the two halves separated to rest side by side, forming a keyboard that was actually larger than the computer case.

Ironically, the trend toward larger-sized displays in portable systems has made this sort of arrangement unnecessary. Many manufacturers have increased the footprint of their notebook computers to accommodate 14.1" and even 15" display panels, leaving more than adequate room for a keyboard with full-size keys. However, even on the newest systems, there still isn't enough room for a separate numeric keypad.

Num Lock

On IBM systems that support the Enhanced keyboard, when the system detects the keyboard on powerup, it enables the Num Lock feature and the light goes on. If the system detects an older 84-key AT-type keyboard, it does not enable the Num Lock function because these keyboards do not have cursor keys separate from the numeric keypad. When the Enhanced keyboards first appeared in 1986, many users (including me) were irritated to find that the numeric keypad was automatically enabled every time the system booted. Most system manufacturers subsequently began integrating a function into the BIOS setup that enabled you to specify the Num Lock status imposed during the boot process.

Some users thought that the automatic enabling of Num Lock was a function of the Enhanced keyboard because none of the earlier keyboards seemed to operate in this way. Remember that this function is not really a keyboard function but instead a function of the motherboard ROM BIOS, which identifies an Enhanced 101-key unit and turns on the Num Lock as a "favor." In systems with a BIOS that can't control the status of the numeric keypad, you can use the DOS 6.0 or higher version NUMLOCK= parameter in CONFIG.SYS to turn Num Lock on or off, as desired. Some versions of Windows, particularly Windows NT and Windows 2000 (but not Windows XP), disable Num Lock by default.

Keyboard Technology

The technology that makes up a typical PC keyboard is very interesting. This section focuses on all the aspects of keyboard technology and design, including the keyswitches, the interface between the keyboard and the system, the scan codes, and the keyboard connectors.

Keyswitch Design

Today's keyboards use any one of several switch types to create the action for each key. Most keyboards use a variation of the mechanical keyswitch. A mechanical keyswitch relies on a mechanical momentary contact-type switch to make the electrical contact that forms a circuit. Some high-end keyboards use a more sophisticated design that relies on capacitive switches. This section discusses these switches and the highlights of each design.

The most common type of keyswitch is the mechanical type, available in the following variations:

- Pure mechanical
- Foam element
- Rubber dome
- Membrane

Pure Mechanical Switches

The pure mechanical type is just that—a simple mechanical switch that features metal contacts in a momentary contact arrangement. The switch often includes a tactile feedback mechanism, consisting of a clip and spring arrangement designed to give a "clicky" feel to the keyboard and offer some resistance to the keypress (see Figure 18.3).

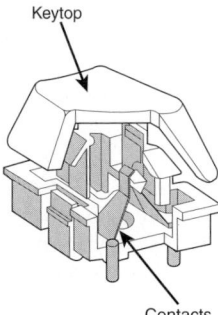

Keytop

Contacts

Figure 18.3   A typical mechanical switch used in older NMB keyboards. As the key is pressed, the switch pushes down on the contacts to make the connection.

Mechanical switches are very durable, usually have self-cleaning contacts, and are normally rated for 20 million keystrokes (which is second only to the capacitive switch in longevity). They also offer excellent tactile feedback.

Despite the tactile feedback and durability provided by mechanical keyswitch keyboards, they have become much less popular than membrane keyboards (discussed later in this chapter). In addition, many companies that produce keyboards that use mechanical keyswitches either use them for only a few of their high-priced models or have phased out their mechanical keyswitch models entirely. With the price of keyboards nose-diving along with other traditional devices, such as mice and drives, the pressure on keyboard makers to cut costs has led many of them to abandon or de-emphasize mechanical-keyswitch designs in favor of the less expensive membrane keyswitch.

The Alps Electric mechanical keyswitch is used by many of the vendors who produce mechanical-switch keyboards, including Alps Electric itself. Other vendors who use mechanical keyswitches for some of their keyboard models include Adesso, Inc. (www.adesso.com), Avant Prime and Stellar (revivals of the classic Northgate keyboards and available from Ergonomic Resources; www.ergo-2000.com), Kinesis (www.kinesis-ergo.com), SIIG (www.siig.com), and Focus (www.focustaipei.com). Many of these vendors sell through the OEM market, so you must look carefully at the detailed specifications for the keyboard to see whether it is a mechanical keyswitch model.

Foam Element Switches

Foam element mechanical switches were a very popular design in some older keyboards. Most of the older PC keyboards, including models made by Key Tronic and many others, used this technology. These switches are characterized by a foam element with an electrical contact on the bottom. This foam element is mounted on the bottom of a plunger that is attached to the key (see Figure 18.4).

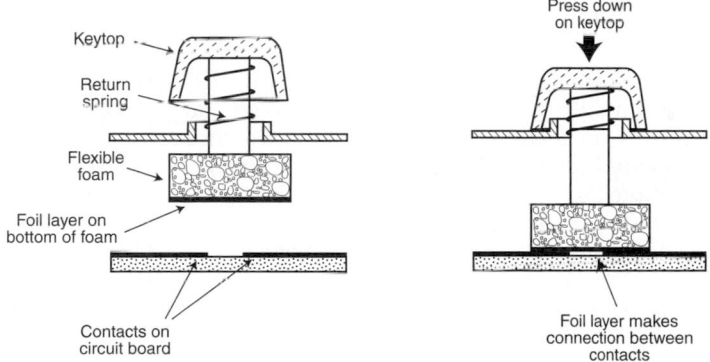

Figure 18.4   Typical foam element mechanical keyswitch.

When the switch is pressed, a foil conductor on the bottom of the foam element closes a circuit on the printed circuit board below. A return spring pushes the key back up when the pressure is released. The foam dampens the contact, helping to prevent bounce, but unfortunately it gives these keyboards a "mushy" feel. The big problem with this type of keyswitch design is that little tactile feedback often exists. These types of keyboards send a clicking sound to the system speaker to signify that contact has been made. Preferences in keyboard feel are somewhat subjective; I personally do not favor the foam element switch design.

Another problem with this type of design is that it is more subject to corrosion on the foil conductor and the circuit board traces below. When this happens, the key strikes can become intermittent, which can be frustrating. Fortunately, these keyboards are among the easiest to clean. By disassembling the keyboard completely, you usually can remove the circuit board portion—without removing each foam pad separately—and expose the bottoms of all the pads. Then, you easily can wipe the corrosion and dirt off the bottoms of the foam pads and the circuit board, thus restoring the keyboard to a "like-new" condition. Unfortunately, over time, the corrosion problem will occur again. I recommend using some Stabilant 22a from D.W. Electrochemicals (www.stabilant.com) to improve the switch contact action and prevent future corrosion. Because of such problems, the foam element design is not used much anymore and has been superseded in popularity by the rubber dome design.

KeyTronicEMS, the most well-known user of this technology, now uses a center-bearing membrane switch technology in its keyboards, so you are likely to encounter foam-switch keyboards only on very old systems.

Rubber Dome Switches

Rubber dome switches are mechanical switches similar to the foam element type but are improved in many ways. Instead of a spring, these switches use a rubber dome that has a carbon button contact on the underside. As you press a key, the key plunger presses on the rubber dome, causing it to resist and then collapse all at once, much like the top of an oil can. As the rubber dome collapses, the user feels the tactile feedback, and the carbon button makes contact between the circuit board traces below. When the key is released, the rubber dome re-forms and pushes the key back up.

The rubber eliminates the need for a spring and provides a reasonable amount of tactile feedback without any special clips or other parts. Rubber dome switches use a carbon button because it resists corrosion and has a self-cleaning action on the metal contacts below. The rubber domes themselves are formed into a sheet that completely protects the contacts below from dirt, dust, and even minor spills. This type of switch design is the simplest, and it uses the fewest parts. This made the rubber dome keyswitch very reliable for several years. However, its relatively poor tactile feedback has led most keyboard manufacturers to switch to the membrane switch design covered in the next section.

Membrane Switches

The membrane keyswitch is a variation on the rubber dome type, using a flat, flexible circuit board to receive input and transmit it to the keyboard microcontroller. Industrial versions of membrane boards use a single sheet for keys that sits on the rubber dome sheet for protection against harsh environments. This arrangement severely limits key travel. For this reason, flat-surface membrane keyboards are not considered usable for normal touch typing. However, they are ideal for use in extremely harsh environments. Because the sheets can be bonded together and sealed from the elements, membrane keyboards can be used in situations in which no other type could survive. Many industrial applications use membrane keyboards for terminals that do not require extensive data entry but are used instead to operate equipment, such as cash registers and point-of-sale terminals in restaurants.

Membrane keyswitches are no longer relegated to fast food or industrial uses, though. Over the last few years, the membrane keyswitch used with conventional keyboard keytops has replaced the rubber dome keyswitch to become the most popular keyswitch used in low-cost to mid-range keyboards. Inexpensive to make, membrane switches have become the overwhelming favorite of low-cost Pacific Rim OEM suppliers and are found in most of the keyboards you'll see at your local computer store or find inside the box of your next complete PC. Although low-end membrane keyswitches have a limited life of only 5–10 million keystrokes, some of the better models are rated to handle up to 20 million keystrokes, putting them in the range of pure mechanical switches for durability (see Figure 18.5). A few membrane switches are even more durable: Cherry Corporation's G8x-series keyboards use Cherry's own 50-million-keystroke membrane switch design (www.cherrycorp.com).

Membrane keyboards provide a firmer touch than rubber dome keyboards or the old foam-element keyboards, but they are still no match for mechanical or capacitive keyswitch models in their feel. One interesting exception is the line of keyboards made by KeyTronicEMS using its center-bearing version of membrane keyswitches. Most of its keyboards feature Ergo Technology, which has five levels of force from 35 grams to 80 grams, depending on the relative strength of the fingers used to type various keys. As little as 35 grams of force is required for keys that are used by the little finger, such as Q, Z, and A, and greater levels of force are required for keys used by the other fingers. The spacebar requires the most force: 80 grams. This compares to the standard force level of 55 grams for all keys on normal keyboards (see Figure 18.6). For more information about keyboards with Ergo Technology, visit the KeyTronicEMS Web site (www.keytronic.com).

To find the best membrane keyboards from the vast numbers on the market, look at the lifespan rating of the keyswitches. Longer-lasting keyswitches make the keyboard cost more but will lead to a better experience over the life of the keyboard.

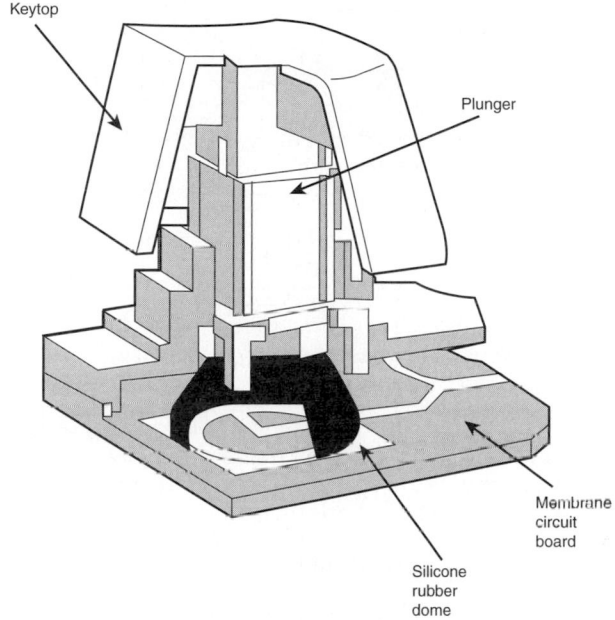

Figure 18.5 A typical membrane keyswitch used in NMB keyboards.

Figure 18.6 Force levels used on KeyTronicEMS keyboards with Ergo Technology.

Capacitive Switches

Capacitive switches are the only nonmechanical keyswitch in use today (see Figure 18.7). The capacitive switch is the Cadillac of keyswitches. It is much more expensive than the more common mechanical membrane switch, but it is more resistant to dirt and corrosion and offers the highest-quality tactile feedback of any type of switch. This type of keyboard is sometimes referred to as a *buckling spring* keyboard because of the coiled spring used to provide feedback.

A capacitive switch does not work by making contact between conductors. Instead, two plates usually made of plastic are connected in a switch matrix designed to detect changes in the capacitance of the circuit.

When the key is pressed, the plunger moves the top plate in relation to the fixed bottom plate. Typically, a buckling spring mechanism provides for a distinct over-center tactile feedback with a resounding "click." As the top plate moves, the capacitance between the two plates changes. The comparator circuitry in the keyboard detects this change.

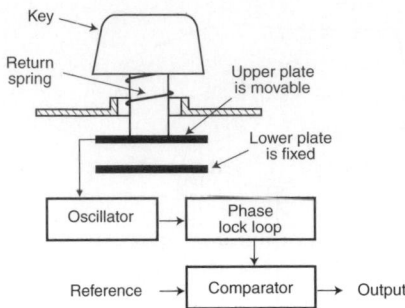

Figure 18.7 A capacitive buckling spring keyswitch.

Because this type of switch does not rely on metal contacts, it is nearly immune to corrosion and dirt. These switches are also very resistant to the key bounce problems that result in multiple characters appearing from a single strike. In addition, they are the most durable in the industry—rated for 25 million or more keystrokes, as opposed to 10–20 million for other designs. The tactile feedback is unsurpassed because the switch provides a relatively loud click and a strong over-center feel. The only drawback to the design is the cost. Capacitive switch keyboards are among the most expensive designs. The quality of the feel and their durability make them worth the price, however.

Originally, the only vendor of capacitive keyswitch keyboards was IBM. Although some of IBM's older keyboards still feature capacitive keyswitches, most current IBM keyboards use rubber-dome or other lower-cost keyswitches. In 1991, IBM spun off its keyboard/printer division as Lexmark, which then spun off the keyboard division as Unicomp in 1996. Today, Unicomp still manufactures and sells "IBM" keyboards with the classic buckling spring capacitive switch ("clickety" as some would say) technology. As a bonus, it also has models with the IBM trackpoint built in. You can purchase new Unicomp (IBM) keyboards direct by calling its toll-free number (800-777-4886) or by visiting its online store (http://www.pckeyboard.com).

My personal recommendations are for either the EnduraPro/104 (http://www.pckeyboard.com/ep104.html) or the Customizer 101 or 104 (http://www.pckeyboard.com/customizer.html). These are brand-new, not reconditioned or rebuilt, keyboards.

The EnduraPro/104 is notable for including a built-in TrackPoint pointing device and a pass-through mini-DIN mouse port, being programmable and reconfigurable, requiring no special drivers, and of course having the famous buckling spring keyswitches.

Because of the buckling spring capacitive keyswitches (and the resulting clickety feel), I've always been a huge fan of the IBM, Lexmark, and now Unicomp keyboards. In my opinion, they are the absolute best keyboards in the world and the only ones I willingly use on desktop systems. I especially like the fact that they include the IBM TrackPoint because I use a laptop system as my main machine and therefore use only laptops that include the TrackPoint device (mainly IBM, Toshiba, and some Dell/HP/others). The feel and durability of the buckling spring capacitive keyswitches is outstanding, and with the integrated TrackPoint, I never have to move my hands off the keyboard, resulting in much greater efficiency when working with my systems.

The Keyboard Interface

A keyboard consists of a set of switches mounted in a grid or an array called the *key matrix*. When a switch is pressed, a processor in the keyboard identifies which key is pressed by determining which grid location in the matrix shows continuity. The keyboard processor, which also interprets how long the key is pressed, can even handle multiple keypresses at the same time. A 16-byte hardware buffer in the keyboard can handle rapid or multiple keypresses, passing each one to the system in succession.

When you press a key, the contact bounces slightly in most cases, meaning that several rapid on/off cycles occur just as the switch makes contact. This is called *bounce*. The processor in the keyboard is designed to filter this, or *debounce* the keystroke. The keyboard processor must distinguish bounce from a double key strike the keyboard operator intends to make. This is fairly easy, though, because the bouncing is much more rapid than a person could simulate by striking a key quickly several times.

The keyboard in a PC is actually a computer itself. It communicates with the main system in one of two ways:

- Through a special serial data link if a standard keyboard connector is used
- Through the USB port

The serial data link used by conventional keyboards transmits and receives data in 11-bit packets of information, consisting of 8 data bits, plus framing and control bits. Although it is indeed a serial link (in that the data flows on one wire), the keyboard interface is incompatible with the standard RS-232 serial port commonly used to connect modems.

The processor in the original PC keyboard was an Intel 8048 microcontroller chip. Newer keyboards often use an 8049 version that has built-in ROM or other microcontroller chips compatible with the 8048 or 8049. For example, in its Enhanced keyboards, IBM has always used a custom version of the Motorola 6805 processor, which is compatible with the Intel chips. The keyboard's built-in processor reads the key matrix, debounces the keypress signals, converts the keypress to the appropriate scan code, and transmits the code to the motherboard. The processors built into the keyboard contain their own RAM, possibly some ROM, and a built-in serial interface.

In the original PC/XT design, the keyboard serial interface is connected to an 8255 Programmable Peripheral Interface (PPI) chip on the motherboard of the PC/XT. This chip is connected to the interrupt controller IRQ1 line, which is used to signal to the system that keyboard data is available. The data is then sent from the 8255 to the processor via I/O port address 60h. The IRQ1 signal causes the main system processor to run a subroutine (INT 9h) that interprets the keyboard scan code data and decides what to do.

In an AT-type keyboard design, the keyboard serial interface is connected to a special keyboard controller on the motherboard. This controller was an Intel 8042 Universal Peripheral Interface (UPI) slave micro-controller chip in the original AT design. This microcontroller is essentially another processor that has its own 2KB of ROM and 128 bytes of RAM. An 8742 version that uses erasable programmable read-only memory (EPROM) can be erased and reprogrammed. In the past, when you purchased a motherboard ROM upgrade for an older system from a motherboard manufacturer, the upgrade included a new key-board controller chip as well because it had somewhat dependent and updated ROM code in it. Some older systems might use the 8041 or 8741 chips, which differ only in the amount of built-in ROM or RAM. However, recent systems incorporate the keyboard controller into the main system chipset.

In an AT system, the (8048-type) microcontroller in the keyboard sends data to the (8042-type) key-board controller on the motherboard. The motherboard-based controller also can send data back to the keyboard. When the keyboard controller on the motherboard receives data from the keyboard, it sig-nals the motherboard with an IRQ1 and sends the data to the main motherboard processor via I/O port address 60h, just as in the PC/XT. Acting as an agent between the keyboard and the main system processor, the 8042-type keyboard controller can translate scan codes and perform several other func-tions as well. The system also can send data to the 8042 keyboard controller via port 60h, which then passes it on to the keyboard. Additionally, when the system needs to send commands to or read the status of the keyboard controller on the motherboard, it reads or writes through I/O port 64h. These commands usually are followed by data sent back and forth via port 60h.

In older systems, the 8042 keyboard controller is also used by the system to control the A20 memory address line, which provides access to system memory greater than 1MB. More modern motherboards typically incorporate this functionality directly into the motherboard chipset. The AT keyboard con-nector was renamed the "PS/2" port after the IBM PS/2 family of systems debuted in 1987. That was the time when the connector changed in size from the DIN to the min-DIN, and even though the signals were the same, the mini-DIN version became known from that time forward as the PS/2 port.

Keyboards connected to a USB port work in a surprisingly similar fashion to those connected to conventional DIN or mini-DIN (PS/2) ports after the data reaches the system. Inside the keyboard a variety of custom controller chips is used by various keyboard manufacturers to receive and interpret keyboard data before sending it to the system via the USB port. Some of these chips contain USB hub logic to enable the keyboard to act as a USB hub. After the keyboard data reaches the USB port on the system, the USB port routes the data to the 8042-compatible keyboard controller, where the data is treated as any other keyboard information.

This process works very well after a system has booted into Windows. But what about users who need to use the keyboard at a command prompt or within the BIOS configuration routine? As discussed earlier in this chapter, USB Legacy support must be enabled in the BIOS. A BIOS with USB Legacy support is capable of performing the following tasks:

- Configure the host controller
- Enable a USB keyboard and mouse
- Set up the host controller scheduler
- Route USB keyboard and mouse input to the 8042 Keyboard Controller

Systems with USB Legacy support enabled use the BIOS to control the USB keyboard until a supported operating system is loaded. At that point, the USB host controller driver in the operating system takes control of the keyboard by sending a command called StopBIOS to the BIOS routine that was managing the keyboard. When Windows shuts down to MS-DOS, the USB host controller sends a command called StartBIOS to restart the BIOS routine that manages the keyboard.

When the BIOS controls the keyboard, after the signals reach the 8042 Keyboard Controller, the USB keyboard is treated just like a conventional keyboard if the BIOS is correctly designed to work with USB keyboards. As discussed previously in this chapter, a BIOS upgrade might be necessary in some cases to provide proper support of USB keyboards on some systems. The system chipset also must support USB Legacy features.

Typematic Functions

If a key on the keyboard is held down, it becomes *typematic*, which means the keyboard repeatedly sends the keypress code to the motherboard. In the AT-style keyboards, the typematic rate is adjusted by sending the appropriate commands to the keyboard processor. This is impossible for the earlier PC/XT keyboard types because the keyboard interface for these types is not bidirectional.

AT-style keyboards have programmable typematic repeat rate and delay parameters. You can adjust the typematic repeat rate and delay parameters with settings in your system BIOS (although not all BIOS chips can control all functions) or in your operating system. In Windows you use the Keyboard icon in the Control Panel; in DOS you use the MODE command. The next section describes how to adjust the keyboard parameters in Windows because this is more convenient than the other methods and enables the user to make further adjustments at any time without restarting the system.

Adjusting Keyboard Parameters in Windows

You can modify the default values for the typematic repeat rate and delay parameters in any version of Windows using the Keyboard icon in the Control Panel. The Repeat Delay slider controls the number of times a key must be pressed before the character begins to repeat, and the Repeat Rate slider controls how fast the character repeats after the delay has elapsed.

Note

The increments on the Repeat Delay and Repeat Rate sliders in Keyboard Properties in the Control Panel correspond to the timings given for the **MODE** command's **RATE** and **DELAY** values. Each mark in the Repeat Delay slider adds about 0.25 seconds to the delay, and the marks in the Repeat Rate slider are worth about one character per second each.

The dialog box also contains a text box you can use to test the settings you have chosen before committing them to your system. When you click in the box and press a key, the keyboard reacts using the settings currently specified by the sliders, even if you have not yet applied the changes to the Windows environment.

To learn how to adjust keyboard parameters in DOS, see "Adjusting Keyboard Parameters in DOS" in Chapter 17 of *Upgrading and Repairing PCs, 11th Edition*, which is available in electronic form on the disc included with this book.

Keyboard Key Numbers and Scan Codes

When you press a key on the keyboard, the processor built into the keyboard (8048- or 6805-type) reads the keyswitch location in the keyboard matrix. The processor then sends to the motherboard a serial packet of data containing the scan code for the key that was pressed.

This is called the *Make code*. When the key is released, a corresponding *Break code* is sent, indicating to the motherboard that the key has been released. The Break code is equivalent to the Make scan code plus 80h. For example, if the Make scan code for the "A" key is 1Eh, the Break code would be 9Eh. By using both Make and Break scan codes, the system can determine whether a particular key has been held down and determine whether multiple keys are being pressed.

In AT-type motherboards that use an 8042-type keyboard controller, the 8042 chip translates the actual keyboard scan codes into one of up to three sets of system scan codes, which are sent to the main processor. It can be useful in some cases to know what these scan codes are, especially when troubleshooting keyboard problems or when reading the keyboard or system scan codes directly in software.

When a keyswitch on the keyboard sticks or otherwise fails, the Make scan code of the failed keyswitch usually is reported by diagnostics software, including the power on self test (POST), as well as conventional disk-based diagnostics. This means you must identify the malfunctioning key by its scan code. See the Technical Reference section of the disc included with this book for a comprehensive listing of keyboard key numbers and scan codes for both the 101/102-key (Enhanced) keyboard and 104-key Windows keyboard. By looking up the reported scan code on these charts, you can determine which keyswitch is defective or needs to be cleaned.

Note

The 101-key Enhanced keyboards are capable of three scan code sets. Set 1 is the default. Some systems, including some of the IBM PS/2 machines, use one of the other scan code sets during the POST. For example, my IBM P75 uses Scan Code Set 2 during the POST but switches to Set 1 during normal operation. This is rare, and it really threw me off in diagnosing a stuck key problem one time. It is useful to know whether you are having difficulty interpreting the scan code number, however.

IBM also assigns each key a unique key number to distinguish it from the others. This is important when you are trying to identify keys on foreign keyboards that might use symbols or characters different from what the U.S. models do. In the Enhanced keyboard, most foreign models are missing one of the keys (key 29) found on the U.S. version and have two additional keys (keys 42 and 45). This accounts for the 102-key total instead of the 101 keys found on the U.S. version.

Note

See the Technical Reference section of the disc included with this book for a comprehensive listing of keyboard key numbers and scan codes for both the 101/102-key (Enhanced) keyboard and 104-key Windows keyboard, including HID and hotkey scan codes used on the latest USB and hotkey keyboards.

Knowing these key number figures and scan codes can be useful when you are troubleshooting stuck or failed keys on a keyboard. Diagnostics can report the defective keyswitch by the scan code, which varies from keyboard to keyboard on the character it represents and its location.

Many enhanced and USB keyboards now feature hotkeys that either have fixed uses—such as opening the default Web browser, sending the system into standby mode, and adjusting the speaker volume— or are programmable for user-defined functions. Each of these keys also has scan codes. USB keyboards use a special series of codes called Human Interface Device (HID), which are translated into PS/2 scan codes.

International Keyboard Layouts

After the keyboard controller in the system receives the scan codes generated by the keyboard and passes them to the main processor, the operating system converts the codes into the appropriate alphanumeric characters. In the United States, these characters are the letters, numbers, and symbols found on the standard American keyboard.

However, no matter which characters you see on the keytops, adjusting the scan code conversion process to map different characters to the keys is relatively simple. Windows (post 3.x) takes advantage of this capability by enabling you to install multiple keyboard layouts to support various languages.

In Windows 9x/Me, open the Keyboard icon in the Control Panel and select the Language page. The Language box should display the keyboard layout you selected when you installed the operating system. In Windows XP, click the Details button found on the Languages tab in the Regional and Language Options applet (in the Windows Control Panel). By clicking the Add button, you can select any one of several additional keyboard layouts supporting other languages.

These keyboard layouts map various characters to certain keys on the standard keyboard. The standard French layout provides easy access to the accented characters commonly used in that language. For example, pressing the 2 key produces the é character. To type the numeral 2, you press the Shift+2 key combination. Other French-speaking countries have different keyboard conventions for the same characters, so Windows includes support for several keyboard layout variations for some languages, based on nationality.

Note

It is important to understand that this feature is not the same as installing the operating system in a different language. These keyboard layouts do not modify the text already displayed onscreen; they only alter the characters generated when you press certain keys.

The alternative keyboard layouts also do not provide support for non-Roman alphabets, such as Russian and Chinese. The accented characters and other symbols used in languages such as French and German are part of the standard ASCII character set. They are always accessible to English-language users through the Windows Character Map utility or through the use of Alt+keypad combinations. An alternative keyboard layout simply gives you an easier way to access the characters used in certain languages.

If you work on documents using more than one language, you can install as many keyboard layouts as necessary and switch between them at will. When you click the Enable Indicator on Taskbar check box on the Language page of the Keyboard control panel, a selector appears in the taskbar's tray area that enables you to switch languages easily. On the same page, you can enable a key combination that switches between the installed keyboard layouts.

Keyboard/Mouse Interface Connectors

Keyboards have a cable with one of two primary types of connectors at the system end. On most aftermarket keyboards, the cable is connected inside the keyboard case on the keyboard end, requiring you to open the keyboard case to disconnect or test it; different vendors use different connections, making cable interchange between brands of keyboards unlikely. When IBM manufactured its own enhanced keyboards, it used a unique cable assembly that plugged into both the keyboard and the system unit to make cable replacement or interchange easy. Current IBM keyboards, unfortunately, no longer use either the shielded data link (SDL) connector inside the keyboard or the telephone cable-style removable plug-in external keyboard connector used on some more recent models.

Although the method of connecting the keyboard cable to the keyboard can vary, all PC keyboards (except those using the USB port) use either of the following two connectors to attach to the computer:

- *5-pin DIN connector.* Used on most PC systems with Baby-AT form factor motherboards
- *6-pin mini-DIN connector.* Used on PS/2 systems and most PCs with LPX, ATX, and NLX motherboards

Figure 18.8 and Table 18.2 show the physical layout and pinouts of all the respective keyboard connector plugs and sockets; although the 6-pin SDL connector is not used in this form by most keyboard vendors, most non-IBM keyboards use a somewhat similar connector to attach the keyboard cable to the inside of the keyboard. You can use the pinouts listed in Table 18.2 to test the continuity of each wire in the keyboard connector.

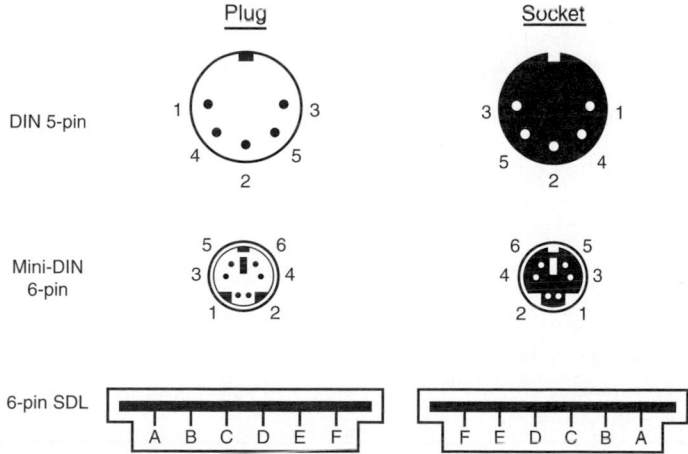

Figure 18.8 Keyboard and mouse connectors.

Table 18.2   Keyboard Connector Signals and Specifications

Signal Name	5-Pin DIN	6-Pin Mini-DIN	6-Pin SDL	Test Voltage
Keyboard Data	2	1	B	+4.8V to +5.5V
Ground	4	3	C	—
+5V Power	5	4	E	+2.0V to +5.5V
Keyboard Clock	1	5	D	+2.0V to +5.5V
Not Connected	—	2	A	—
Not Connected	—	6	F	—
Not Connected	3	—	—	

DIN = Deutsches Institut für Normung e.V., a committee that sets German dimensional standards

SDL = Shielded data link, a type of shielded connector created by AMP and used by IBM and others for keyboard cables

Motherboard non-USB mouse connectors also use the 6-pin mini-DIN connector and have the same pinout and signal descriptions as the keyboard connector; however, the data packets are incompatible. Therefore, you can easily plug a motherboard mouse (PS/2-style) into a mini-DIN keyboard connector or plug the mini-DIN keyboard connector into a motherboard mouse port. Neither one will work properly in this situation, though.

Caution

I have also seen PCs with external power supplies that used the same standard DIN connectors to attach the keyboard and power supply. Although cross-connecting the mini-DIN connectors of a mouse and keyboard is a harmless annoyance, connecting a power supply to a keyboard socket can be disastrous.

USB keyboards use the Series A USB connector to attach to the USB port built into modern computers. For more information on USB, see Chapter 17, "I/O Interfaces from Serial and Parallel to IEEE 1394 and USB."

Keyboards with Special Features

Several keyboards on the market have special features not found in standard designs. These additional features range from simple things, such as built-in calculators, clocks, and volume control, to more complicated features, such as integrated pointing devices, special character layouts, shapes, and even programmable keys.

Note

In 1936, August Dvorak patented a simplified character layout called the Dvorak Simplified Keyboard (DSK). The Dvorak keyboard was designed to replace the common QWERTY layout used on nearly all keyboards available today. The Dvorak keyboard was approved as an ANSI standard in 1982 but has seen limited use. For a comparison between the Dvorak keyboard and the common QWERTY keyboard you most likely use, see "The Dvorak Keyboard" in the Technical Reference section of the disc accompanying this book.

Ergonomic Keyboards

A trend that began in the late 1990s is to change the shape of the keyboard instead of altering the character layout. This trend has resulted in several so-called ergonomic designs. The goal is to shape the keyboard to better fit the human hand. The most common of these designs splits the keyboard in the center, bending the sides outward. Some designs allow the angle between the sides to be adjusted, such as the now-discontinued Lexmark Select-Ease, the Goldtouch keyboard designed by Mark Goldstein (who also designed the Select-Ease), and the Kinesis Maxim split keyboards. Others, such as the Microsoft Natural keyboard series, PC Concepts Wave, and Cirque Smooth Cat, are fixed. These split or bent designs more easily conform to the hands' natural angles while typing than the standard keyboard. They can improve productivity and typing speed and help prevent repetitive strain injuries (RSI), such as carpal tunnel syndrome (tendon inflammation). Even more radical keyboard designs are available from some vendors, including models such as the 3-part Comfort and ErgoMagic keyboards, the Kinesis concave contoured keyboard, and others. A good source for highly ergonomic keyboards, pointing devices, and furniture is Ergonomic Resources (www.ergo-2000.com).

Because of their novelty and trendy appeal, some ergonomic keyboards can be considerably more expensive than traditional designs, but for users with medical problems caused or exacerbated by improper positioning of the wrists at the keyboard, they can be an important remedy to a serious problem. General users, however, are highly resistant to change, and these designs have yet to significantly displace the standard keyboard layout. If you don't want to spend big bucks on the more radical ergonomic keyboards but want to give yourself at least limited protection from RSI, consider keyboards with a built-in wrist rest or add a gel-based wrist rest to your current keyboard. These provide hand support without making you learn a modified or brand-new keyboard layout.

USB Keyboards with Hubs

Some of the latest USB keyboards feature a built-in USB hub designed to add two or more USB ports to your system. Even though this sounds like a good idea, keep in mind that a keyboard-based hub won't provide additional power to the USB connectors. Powered hubs work better with a wider variety of devices than unpowered hubs do. I wouldn't choose a particular model based solely on this feature, although if your keyboard has it and your devices work well when plugged into it, that's great. I'd recommend that you use this type of keyboard with your USB mouse or other devices that don't require much power. Bus-powered devices such as scanners and Webcams should be connected to a self-powered hub or directly to the USB ports built in to the computer. USB keyboards and mice correspond to the USB 1.1 standard but can also be connected to the faster USB 2.0 ports on the latest systems.

Multimedia and Web-Enabled Keyboards

As I discussed earlier in this chapter, many keyboards sold at retail and bundled with systems today feature fixed-purpose or programmable hotkeys that can launch Web browsers, run the Microsoft Media Player, adjust the volume on the speakers, change tracks on the CD player, and so forth. You need Windows 98 or later to use these hotkeys; Windows Me, Windows 2000, and Windows XP add additional support for these keyboards.

For the best results, you should download the latest drivers for your keyboard and version of Windows from the keyboard vendor's Web site.

Keyboard Troubleshooting and Repair

Keyboard errors are usually caused by two simple problems. Other more difficult, intermittent problems can arise, but they are much less common. The most frequent problems are as follows:

- Defective cables
- Stuck keys

Defective cables are easy to spot if the failure is not intermittent. If the keyboard stops working altogether or every keystroke results in an error or incorrect character, the cable is likely the culprit. Troubleshooting is simple, especially if you have a spare cable on hand. Simply replace the suspected cable with one from a known, working keyboard to verify whether the problem still exists. If it does, the problem must be elsewhere.

If you remove the cable from the keyboard, you can test it for continuity with a digital multimeter (DMM). DMMs that have an audible continuity tester built in make this procedure much easier to perform. To test each wire of the cable, insert the DMM's red pin into the keyboard connector and touch the DMM's black pin to the corresponding wire that attaches to the keyboard's circuit board. Wiggle the ends of the cable as you check each wire to ensure no intermittent connections exist. If you discover a problem with the continuity in one of the wires, replace the cable or the entire keyboard, whichever is cheaper. Because replacement keyboards are so inexpensive, it's almost always cheaper to replace the entire unit than to get a new cable, unless the keyboard is a deluxe model.

For more information about using digital multimeters for testing hardware, see Chapter 24, "PC Diagnostics, Testing, and Maintenance."

Many times you first discover a problem with a keyboard because the system has an error during the POST. Many systems use error codes in a 3xx numeric format to distinguish the keyboard. If you encounter any such errors during the POST, write them down. Some BIOS versions do not use cryptic numeric error codes; they simply state something such as the following:

```
Keyboard stuck key failure
```

This message is usually displayed by a system with a Phoenix BIOS if a key is stuck. Unfortunately, the message does not identify which key it is!

If your system displays a 3xx (keyboard) error preceded by a two-digit hexadecimal number, the number is the scan code of a failing or stuck keyswitch. Look up the scan code in the tables provided in the Technical Reference section on the disc to determine which keyswitch is the culprit. By removing the keycap of the offending key and cleaning the switch, you often can solve the problem.

For a simple test of the motherboard keyboard connector, you can check voltages on some of the pins. Using Figure 18.8, which was shown earlier in the chapter, as a guide, measure the voltages on various pins of the keyboard connector. To prevent possible damage to the system or keyboard, turn off the power before disconnecting the keyboard. Then, unplug the keyboard and turn the power back on. Make measurements between the ground pin and the other pins according to Table 18.2, shown earlier in the chapter. If the voltages are within these specifications, the motherboard keyboard circuitry is probably okay.

If your measurements do not match these voltages, the motherboard might be defective. Otherwise, the keyboard cable or keyboard might be defective. If you suspect that the cable is the problem, the easiest thing to do is replace the keyboard cable with a known good one. If the system still does not work normally, you might have to replace the entire keyboard or the motherboard.

In many newer systems, the motherboard's keyboard and mouse connectors are protected by a fuse that can be replaced. Look for any type of fuse on the motherboard in the vicinity of the keyboard or mouse connectors. Other systems might have a socketed keyboard controller chip (8042-type). In that case, you might be able to repair the motherboard keyboard circuit by replacing this chip. Because these chips have ROM code in them, you should get the replacement from the motherboard or BIOS manufacturer. If the motherboard uses a soldered keyboard controller chip or a chipset that integrates the keyboard controller with other I/O chips, you'll need to replace the motherboard.

See the disc included with this book for a listing of the standard POST and diagnostic keyboard error codes used by some systems.

Keyboard Disassembly

Although disassembling a keyboard is possible, most likely you won't need or want to do that given the reasonable prices of keyboards. If you do want to disassemble your keyboard, see "Keyboard Disassembly" in the Technical Reference section of the disc accompanying this book.

Cleaning a Keyboard

One of the best ways to keep a keyboard in top condition is periodic cleaning. As preventive maintenance, you should vacuum the keyboard weekly, or at least monthly. When vacuuming, you should use a soft brush attachment; this will help dislodge the dust. Also note that many keyboards have keycaps that can come off easily. Be careful when vacuuming; otherwise, you'll have to dig them out of the vacuum cleaner. I recommend using a small, handheld vacuum cleaner made for cleaning computers and sewing machines; these have enough suction to get the job done with little risk of removing your keytops.

You also can use canned compressed air to blow the dust and dirt out instead of using a vacuum. Before you dust a keyboard with the compressed air, turn the keyboard upside down so that the particles of dirt and dust collected inside can fall out.

On all keyboards, each keycap is removable, which can be handy if a key sticks or acts erratically. For example, a common problem is a key that does not work every time you press it. This problem usually results from dirt collecting under the key. An excellent tool for removing keycaps on almost any keyboard is the U-shaped chip puller included in many computer tool kits. Simply slip the hooked ends of the tool under the keycap, squeeze the ends together to grip the underside of the keycap, and lift up. IBM sells a tool designed specifically for removing keycaps from its keyboards, but the chip puller works even better. After removing the cap, spray some compressed air into the space under the cap to dislodge the dirt. Then replace the cap and check the action of the key.

Caution

When you remove the keycaps, be careful not to remove the spacebar on the original 83-key PC and the 84-key AT-type keyboards. This bar is difficult to reinstall. The newer 101-key units use a different wire support that can be removed and replaced much more easily.

When you remove the keycap on some keyboards, you are actually detaching the entire key from the keyswitch. Be careful during the removal or reassembly of the keyboard; otherwise, you'll break the switch. The classic IBM/Lexmark-type keyboards (now made by Unicomp) use a removable keycap that leaves the actual key in place, enabling you to clean under the keycap without the risk of breaking the switches. If your keyboard doesn't have removable keycaps, consider using cleaning wands with soft foam tips to clean beneath the keytops.

Spills can be a problem, too. If you spill a soft drink or cup of coffee into a keyboard, you do not necessarily have a disaster. Many keyboards that use membrane switches are spill resistant. However, you should immediately (or as soon as possible) disconnect the keyboard and flush it out with distilled water. Partially disassemble the keyboard and use the water to wash the components. (See "Keyboard Disassembly" in the Technical Reference section of the disc accompanying this book for disassembly instructions.) If the spilled liquid has dried, soak the keyboard in some of the water for a while. When you are sure the keyboard is clean, pour another gallon or so of distilled water over it and through the keyswitches to wash away any residual dirt. After the unit dries completely, it should be perfectly functional. You might be surprised to know that drenching your keyboard with water does not harm the components. Just make sure you use distilled water, which is free from residue or mineral content (bottled water is *not* distilled; the distinct taste of many bottled waters comes from the trace minerals they contain!). Also, make sure the keyboard is fully dry before you try to use it; otherwise, some of the components might short out.

Tip

If spills or excessive dust or dirt are expected because of the environment or conditions in which the PC is used, several companies make thin membrane skins that mold over the top of the keyboard, protecting it from liquids, dust, and other contaminants. These skins are generally thin enough so that they don't interfere too much with the typing or action of the keys.

Keyboard Recommendations

In most cases, replacing a keyboard is cheaper or more cost effective than repairing it. This is especially true if the keyboard has an internal malfunction or if one of the keyswitches is defective. Replacement parts for keyboards are almost impossible to procure, and installing any repair part is usually difficult. In addition, many of the keyboards supplied with lower-cost PCs leave much to be desired. They often have a mushy feel, with little or no tactile feedback. A poor keyboard can make using a system a frustrating experience, especially if you are a touch typist. For all these reasons, it is often a good idea to replace an existing keyboard with something better.

Perhaps the highest-quality keyboards in the entire computer industry are those made by IBM, or, more accurately today, Unicomp. Unicomp maintains an extensive selection of more than 1,400 Lexmark and IBM keyboard models and continues to develop and sell a wide variety of traditional and customized models, including keyboards that match the school colors of several universities. Unicomp sells keyboards directly via its Web site at www.pckeyboard.com. My personal favorite is the black EnduraPro 104.

Note

See the section "Replacement Keyboards" in Chapter 17 of *Upgrading and Repairing PCs, 11th Edition* on this book's disc for a listing of IBM keyboard and cable part numbers.

Some of the classic-design IBM keyboards are available in the retail market under either the IBM or IBM Options brand name. Items under the IBM Options program are sold direct by IBM's Web site (www.pc.ibm.com) or through normal retail channels, such as CompUSA and Computer Discount Warehouse (CDW). These items are also priced much more cheaply than items purchased as spare parts. They include a full warranty and are sold as complete packages, including cables. Table 18.3 lists some of the IBM Options keyboards and part numbers; even though the IBM Web site no longer offers these models, they can be purchased from various online retailers. Models marked with an * are also available from Unicomp.

Table 18.3   IBM Options Keyboards (Sold Retail)

Description	Part Number
IBM Enhanced keyboard (cable w/DIN plug)	92G7454*
IBM Enhanced keyboard (cable w/mini-DIN plug)	92G7453*
IBM Enhanced keyboard, built-in Trackball (cable w/DIN plug)	92G7456*
IBM Enhanced keyboard, built-in Trackball (cable w/mini-DIN plug)	92G7455*
IBM Enhanced keyboard, integrated TrackPoint II (cables w/mini-DIN plugs)	92G7461*
IBM TrackPoint IV keyboard, Black	01K1260
IBM TrackPoint IV keyboard, White	01K1259
IBM TrackPoint USB Space Saver keyboard (black)	22P5150
IBM USB Keyboard with two-port hub (black)	10K3849
IBM Rapid Access III (black)	22P5185

Keep in mind, though, that because IBM spun off its keyboard business some years ago, many recent and current IBM-labeled keyboards no longer have the distinct feel, quality, or durability found in the older models. Ironically, one of the best ways to get an "IBM" keyboard is to buy the model with the features you want from Unicomp, most of whose keyboards still use the capacitive buckling spring technology IBM originally made famous.

The extremely positive tactile feedback of the IBM/Lexmark/Unicomp design is also a benchmark for the rest of the industry. Although keyboard feel is an issue of personal preference, I have never used a keyboard that feels better than the IBM/Lexmark/Unicomp designs. I now equip every system I use with a Unicomp keyboard, including the many non-IBM systems I use. You can purchase these keyboards directly from Unicomp at very reasonable prices.

Many models are available, including some with a built-in trackball or even the revolutionary TrackPoint pointing device. (TrackPoint refers to a small stick mounted between the G, H, and B keys.) This device was first featured on the IBM ThinkPad laptop systems, although the keyboards are now sold for use on other manufacturers' PCs. The technology is being licensed to many other manufacturers, including Toshiba. Other manufacturers of high-quality keyboards that are similar in feel to the IBM/Lexmark/Unicomp units are Alps, Lite-On, NMB Technologies, and the revived Northgate designs sold under the Avant Prime and Avant Stellar names by Creative Vision Technologies. These keyboards have excellent tactile feedback, with a positive click sound. They are my second choice, after a Unicomp unit.

Pointing Devices

The mouse was invented in 1964 by Douglas Englebart, who at the time was working at the Stanford Research Institute (SRI), a think tank sponsored by Stanford University. The mouse was officially called an X-Y Position Indicator for a Display System. Xerox later applied the mouse to its revolutionary Alto computer system in 1973. At the time, unfortunately, these systems were experimental and used purely for research.

In 1979, several people from Apple—including Steve Jobs—were invited to see the Alto and the software that ran the system. Steve Jobs was blown away by what he saw as the future of computing, which included the use of the mouse as a pointing device and the graphical user interface (GUI) it operated. Apple promptly incorporated these features into what was to become the Lisa computer and lured away 15–20 Xerox scientists to work on the Apple system.

Although Xerox released the Star 8010 computer that used this technology in 1981, it was expensive, poorly marketed, and perhaps way ahead of its time. Apple released the Lisa computer, its first system that used the mouse, in 1983. It was not a runaway success, largely because of its $10,000 list price, but by then Jobs already had Apple working on the low-cost successor to the Lisa: the Macintosh. The Apple Macintosh was introduced in 1984. Although it was not an immediate hit, the Macintosh has grown in popularity since that time.

Many credit the Macintosh with inventing the mouse and GUI, but as you can see, this technology was actually borrowed from others, including SRI and Xerox. Certainly the Macintosh, and now Microsoft Windows and OS/2, have gone on to popularize this interface and bring it to the legion of Intel-based PC systems.

Although the mouse did not catch on quickly in the PC marketplace, today the GUIs for PC systems, such as Windows, practically demand the use of a mouse. Therefore, virtually every new system sold at retail comes with a mouse. And, because the mice packaged with retail systems are seldom high-quality or up-to-date designs, sooner or later most users are in the market for a better mouse or compatible pointing device.

Mice come in many shapes and sizes from many manufacturers. Some have taken the standard mouse design and turned it upside down, creating the trackball. In the trackball devices, you move the ball with your hand directly rather than moving the unit itself. Trackballs were originally found on arcade video games, such as Missile Command, but have become popular with users who have limited desk space. In most cases, the dedicated trackballs have a much larger ball than would be found on a standard mouse. Other than the orientation and perhaps the size of the ball, a trackball is identical to a mouse in design, basic function, and electrical interface. Like many recent mice, trackballs often come in ergonomic designs, and the more recent models even use the same optical tracking mechanisms used by the latest Microsoft and Logitech mice.

The largest manufacturers of mice are Microsoft and Logitech; these two companies provide designs that inspire the rest of the industry and each other and are popular OEM choices as well as retail brands. Even though mice can come in different varieties, their actual use and care differ very little. The standard mouse consists of several components:

- A housing that you hold in your hand and move around on your desktop
- A method of transmitting movement to the system: either ball/roller or optical sensors
- Buttons (two or more, and often a wheel or toggle switch) for making selections
- An interface for connecting the mouse to the system; conventional mice use a wire and connector, whereas wireless mice use a radio-frequency or infrared transceiver in both the mouse and a separate unit connected to the computer to interface the mouse to the computer

The housing, which is made of plastic, consists of very few moving parts. On top of the housing, where your fingers normally rest, are buttons. There might be any number of buttons, but in the PC world, two is the standard. If your mouse has additional buttons or a wheel, specialized driver software provided by the mouse vendor is required for them to operate to their full potential. Although the latest versions of Windows support scrolling mice, other features supported by the vendor still require installing the vendor's own mouse driver software.

Ball-Type Mice

The bottom of the mouse housing is where the detection mechanisms or electronics are located. On traditional mice, the bottom of the housing contains a small, rubber ball that rolls as you move the mouse across the tabletop. The movements of this rubber ball are translated into electrical signals transmitted to the computer across the cable.

Internally, a ball-driven mouse is very simple, too. The ball usually rests against two rollers: one for translating the x-axis movement and the other for translating the y-axis movement. These rollers are typically connected to small disks with shutters that alternately block and allow the passage of light. Small optical sensors detect movement of the wheels by watching an internal infrared light blink on and off as the shutter wheel rotates and "chops" the light. These blinks are translated into movement along the axes. This type of setup, called an *opto-mechanical mechanism*, is still the most popular type of mouse mechanism (see Figure 18.9), although optical mice are gaining in popularity. Figure 18.10 shows a PS/2 mouse connector.

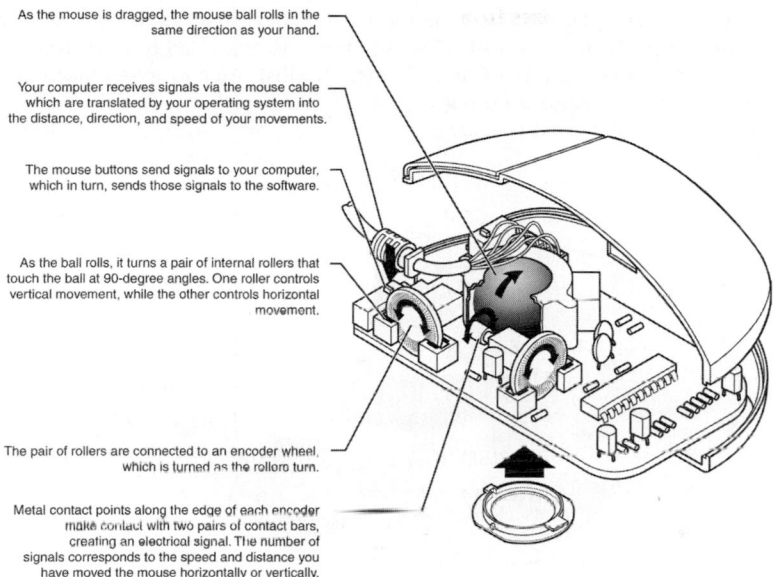

As the mouse is dragged, the mouse ball rolls in the same direction as your hand.

Your computer receives signals via the mouse cable which are translated by your operating system into the distance, direction, and speed of your movements.

The mouse buttons send signals to your computer, which in turn, sends those signals to the software.

As the ball rolls, it turns a pair of internal rollers that touch the ball at 90-degree angles. One roller controls vertical movement, while the other controls horizontal movement.

The pair of rollers are connected to an encoder wheel, which is turned as the rollers turn.

Metal contact points along the edge of each encoder make contact with two pairs of contact bars, creating an electrical signal. The number of signals corresponds to the speed and distance you have moved the mouse horizontally or vertically.

Figure 18.9   Typical opto-mechanical mouse mechanism.

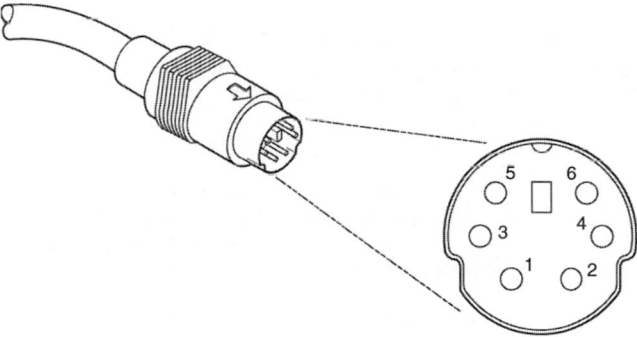

Figure 18.10   Typical PS/2-type mouse connector.

Optical Mice

The other major method of motion detection is optical. Some of the early mice made by Mouse Systems and a few other vendors used a sensor that required a special grid-marked pad. Although these mice were very accurate, the need to use them with a pad caused them to fall out of favor.

Microsoft's IntelliMouse Explorer pioneered the return of optical mice. The IntelliMouse Explorer and the other new-style optical mice from Logitech and other vendors use optical technology to detect movement, and they have no moving parts of their own (except for the scroll wheel and buttons on top). Today's optical mice need no pad; they can work on virtually any surface. This is done by upgrading the optical sensor from the simple type used in older optical mice to a more advanced CCD (charge coupled device). This essentially is a crude version of a video camera sensor that detects movement by seeing the surface move under the mouse. An LED is used to provide light for the sensor.

The IntelliMouse Explorer revolutionized the mouse industry; first Logitech, then virtually all other mouse makers, including both retail and OEM suppliers, have moved to optical mice for most of their product lines, offering a wide variety of optical mice in most price ranges. Figure 18.11 shows the essential features of a typical optical mouse.

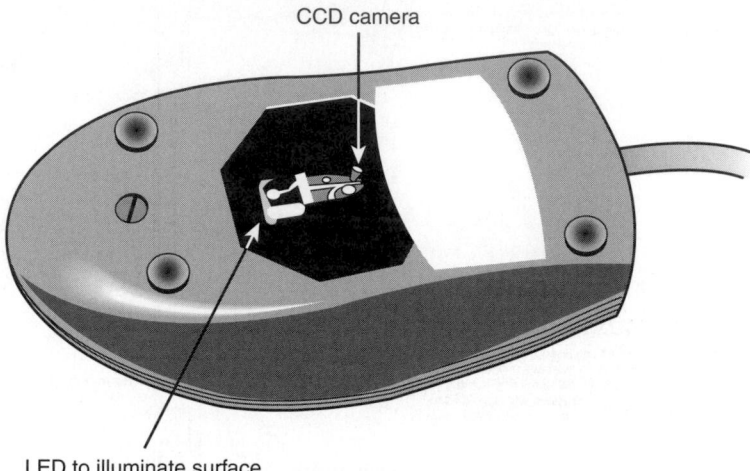

Figure 18.11   The bottom of the Logitech iFeel optical mouse.

Their versatility and low maintenance (not to mention that neat red or blue glow out the sides!) make optical mice an attractive choice, and the variety of models available from both vendors means you can have the latest optical technology for about the price of a good ball-type mouse. Figure 18.12 shows the interior of a typical optical mouse.

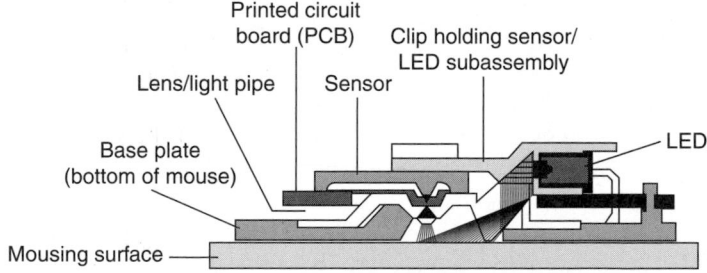

Figure 18.12   The LED inside an optical mouse illuminates the surface by blinking many times per second. The light is reflected from the mousing surface back to the sensor, which converts the information into digital form and sends it to the computer.

All optical mice have a resolution of at least 400dpi and at least one sensor. However, for better performance, some optical mice have improved on these basic features, as listed in Table 18.4.

Table 18.4   Enhanced Optical Mouse Features

Feature	Benefit	Sample Product
800dpi optical resolution	Improves accuracy for mouse positioning	Logitech MX series, Microsoft IntelliMouse Explorer and Optical series
Larger sensor size	Improves tracking on surfaces with repetitive patterns, such as wood desktops	Logitech MX series
Faster tracking speed	Able to keep up with fast hand movements, such as when playing games	Microsoft IntelliMouse Explorer and Optical series
Dual sensors	Faster speed and accuracy, especially for gaming	Logitech MouseMan Dual Optical

Optical mice, similar to traditional ball-type mice, are available as corded or cordless models. Cordless ball-type mice are usually much larger than ordinary mice because of the need to find room for both the bulky ball mechanism and batteries, but cordless optical mice are about the same size as high-end corded mice.

The cable can be any length, but it is typically between 4 and 6 feet long. Mice are also available in a cordless design, which uses either infrared or RF transceivers to replace the cable. A receiver is plugged into the mouse port, while the battery-powered mouse contains a compatible transmitter.

Tip

If you have a choice on the length of cable to buy, get a longer one. This allows easier placement of the mouse in relation to your computer. Extension cables can be used if necessary.

After the mouse is connected to your computer, it communicates with your system through the use of a device driver, which can be loaded explicitly or built into the operating system software. For example, no separate drivers are necessary to use a mouse with Windows or OS/2, but using the mouse with most DOS-based programs requires a separate driver to be loaded from the CONFIG.SYS or AUTOEXEC.BAT file. Regardless of whether it is built in, the driver translates the electrical signals sent from the mouse into positional information and indicates the status of the buttons.

The standard mouse drivers in Windows are designed for the traditional two-button mouse or scroll mouse (in Windows Me/2000/XP or later), but increasing numbers of mice feature additional buttons, toggles, or wheels to make them more useful. These additional features require special mouse driver software supplied by the manufacturer.

Pointing Device Interface Types

The connector used to attach your mouse to the system depends on the type of interface you are using. Three main interfaces are used for mouse connections, with a fourth option you also occasionally might encounter. Mice are most commonly connected to your computer through the following three interfaces:

- Serial interface
- Dedicated motherboard (PS/2) mouse port
- USB port

Serial

A popular method of connecting a mouse to older PCs is through the standard serial interface. As with other serial devices, the connector on the end of the mouse cable is typically a 9-pin female connector; some very old mice used a 25-pin female connector. Only a couple of pins in the DB-9 or DB-25 connector are used for communications between the mouse and the device driver, but the mouse connector typically has all 9 or 25 pins present.

Because most older PCs come with two serial ports, a serial mouse can be plugged into either COM1 or COM2. The device driver, when initializing, searches the ports to determine to which one the mouse is connected. Some mouse drivers can't function if the serial port is set to COM3 or COM4, but most newer drivers can work with any COM port 1–4.

Because a serial mouse does not connect to the system directly, it does not use system resources by itself. Instead, the resources are those used by the serial port to which it is connected. For example, if you have a mouse connected to COM2, and if COM2 is using the default IRQ and I/O port address range, both the serial port and the mouse connected to it use IRQ3 and I/O port addresses 2F8h–2FFh.

◄◄   See "Serial Ports," p. 997.

Motherboard Mouse Port (PS/2)

Most computers include a dedicated mouse port built into the motherboard. This practice was introduced by IBM with the PS/2 systems in 1987, so this interface is often referred to as a *PS/2 mouse interface*. This term does not imply that such a mouse can work only with a PS/2; instead, it means the mouse can connect to any system that has a dedicated mouse port on the motherboard.

From a hardware perspective, a motherboard mouse connector is usually exactly the same as the mini-DIN connector used for newer keyboards. In fact, the motherboard mouse port is connected to the 8042-type keyboard controller found on the motherboard. All the PS/2 computers include mini-DIN keyboard and mouse port connectors on the back. Most computers based on the semiproprietary LPX motherboards and all ATX-series motherboards use these same connectors for space reasons. Most Baby-AT motherboards have a pin-header type connector for the mouse port because most standard cases do not have a provision for the mini-DIN mouse connector. If that is the case, an adapter cable is usually supplied with the system. This cable adapts the pin-header connector on the motherboard to the standard mini-DIN type connector used for the motherboard mouse.

Caution

As mentioned in the "Keyboard/Mouse Interface Connectors" section earlier in this chapter, the mini-DIN sockets used for both keyboard and mouse connections on many systems are physically and electrically interchangeable, but the data packets they carry are not. Be sure to plug each device into the correct socket; otherwise, neither will function correctly. Don't panic if you mix them up, though. They are electrically identical to each other, so you can't damage the ports or the devices.

Connecting a mouse to the built-in mouse port is the best method of connection on systems that don't have USB ports because you do not sacrifice any of the system's interface slots or any serial ports, and the performance is not limited by the serial port circuitry. The standard resource usage for a motherboard (or PS/2) mouse port is IRQ12, as well as I/O port addresses 60h and 64h. Because the motherboard mouse port uses the 8042-type keyboard controller chip, the port addresses are those of this chip. IRQ12 is an interrupt that is usually free on most systems, but if you use a USB mouse, you can probably disable the mouse port to make IRQ12 available for use by another device.

Hybrid Mice

Hybrid mice are those designed to plug into two types of ports. Although a few low-cost mice sold at retail are designed to plug into either the serial port or the PS/2 port, most mice on the retail market today are designed to plug into either the PS/2 port or the USB port. These combination mice are more flexible than the mice typically bundled with systems, which are designed to work only with the PS/2 or USB port to which they attach.

Circuitry in a hybrid mouse automatically detects the type of port to which it is connected and configures the mouse automatically. Serial-PS/2 hybrid mice usually come with a mini-DIN connector on the end of their cable and an adapter that converts the mini-DIN to a 9- or 25-pin serial port connector, although the reverse is sometimes true on early examples of these mice. PS/2-USB mice usually come with the USB connector on the end of their cable and include a mini-DIN (PS/2) adapter, as shown in Figure 18.13.

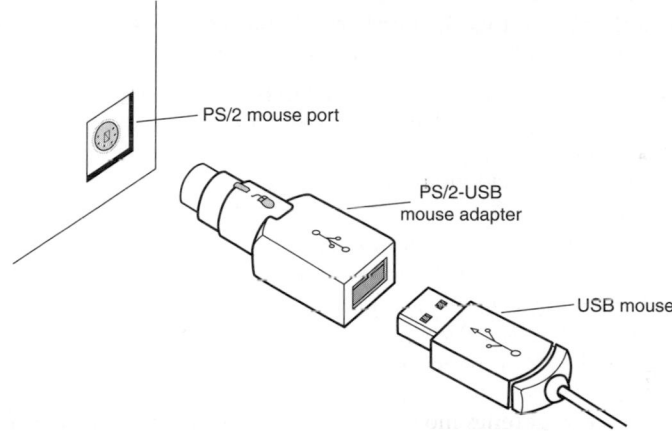

Figure 18.13 A typical USB mouse with a PS/2 adapter.

Sometimes people use adapters to try to connect a serial mouse to a motherboard mouse port or a motherboard mouse to a serial port. If this does not work, it is not the fault of the adapter. If the mouse does not explicitly state that it is both a serial and a PS/2-type mouse, it works only on the single interface for which it was designed. Most of the time, you find the designation for which type of mouse you have printed on its underside. A safe rule of thumb to follow is if the mouse didn't come with an adapter or come bundled with a system, it probably won't work with an adapter.

USB

The extremely flexible USB port has become the most popular port to use for mice as well as keyboards and other I/O devices. Compared to the other interfaces, USB mice (and other USB pointing devices such as trackballs) have the following advantages:

- *USB mice move much more smoothly than the traditional PS/2-type.* This is because the frequency with which the mouse reports its position is much higher. A typical PS/2 mouse has a reporting rate of about 40Hz, whereas an average USB-wired mouse has a reporting rate of 125Hz (most USB wireless mice have a reporting rate of 40Hz–50Hz). Several utilities are available to test and adjust the mouse frequency.

- *Mice with the most advanced features are usually made especially for the USB port.* One example is the Logitech iFeel mouse, the first mouse with an optical sensor plus force feedback. It vibrates gently as you move the mouse over clickable buttons on Web pages, software menus, and the Windows desktop, and it's made especially for USB.

- *USB mice and pointing devices, similar to all other USB devices, are hot-swappable.* If you like to use a trackball and your computing partners prefer mice, you can just lean over and unplug the other users' pointing device and plug in your own, or move it from PC to PC. You can't do that with the other port types.

- *USB mice can be attached to a USB hub, such as the hubs contained in some USB keyboards, as well as standalone hubs.* Using a hub makes attaching and removing your mouse easy without crawling around on the floor to reach the back of the computer. Many computers now have front-mounted USB ports, letting you easily attach and remove a USB mouse without the use of an external hub.

Although the early USB mice were decidedly on the premium end of the price scale, low-cost USB mice are now available for less than $20.

If you want to use a USB mouse at an MS-DOS prompt, in Windows safe mode, or in some other environment outside of normal Windows 98 or later, make sure that USB Legacy mode is enabled in your PC's BIOS, as discussed earlier in this chapter. Legacy mode enables non-USB-aware systems to recognize a USB keyboard and mouse.

A fourth type of connection, the bus mouse (referred to by Microsoft as the Inport mouse), used a dedicated adapter card and is now obsolete. For more information about the bus mouse, see Chapter 17 of *Upgrading and Repairing PCs, 11th Edition*, which is included on the disc supplied with this book.

Mouse Troubleshooting

If you are experiencing problems with your mouse, you need to look in only two general places—hardware or software. Because mice are basically simple devices, looking at the hardware takes very little time. Detecting and correcting software problems can take a bit longer, however. To troubleshoot wireless mice, see "Troubleshooting Wireless Input Devices," later in this chapter.

Cleaning Your Mouse

If you notice that the mouse pointer moves across the screen in a jerky fashion, it might be time to clean your mouse. For a mouse with a roller-ball, this jerkiness is caused when dirt and dust become trapped around the mouse's ball-and-roller assembly, thereby restricting its free movement.

From a hardware perspective, the mouse is a simple device, so cleaning it is easy. The first step is to turn the mouse housing over so that you can see the ball on the bottom. Notice that surrounding the ball is an access panel you can open. Sometimes instructions indicate how the panel is to be opened. (Some off-brand mice might require you to remove some screws to get at the roller ball.) Remove the panel to see more of the roller ball and the socket in which it rests.

If you turn the mouse back over, the rubber roller ball should fall into your hand. Take a look at the ball. It might be gray or black, but it should have no visible dirt or other contamination. If it does, wash it in soapy water or a mild solvent, such as contact lens cleaner solution or alcohol, and dry it off.

Now take a look at the socket in which the roller ball normally rests. You will see two or three small wheels or bars against which the ball usually rolls. If you see dust or dirt on or around these wheels or bars, you need to clean them. The best way is to use a compressed air duster, which can blow out any dust or dirt. You also can use some electrical contact cleaner to clean the rollers. Remember, any remaining dirt or dust impedes the movement of the roller ball and results in the mouse not working as it should.

Put the mouse back together by inserting the roller ball into the socket and then securely attaching the cover panel. The mouse should look just as it did before you removed the panel, except that it will be noticeably cleaner.

One of the major advantages of the new breed of optical mice is the lack of moving parts. Just wipe away dust from the optical sensor, and that's all the cleaning an optical mouse needs.

Interrupt Conflicts

Interrupts are internal signals used by your computer to indicate when something needs to happen. With a mouse, an interrupt is used whenever the mouse has information to send to the mouse driver. If a conflict occurs and the same interrupt used by the mouse is used by a different device, the mouse will not work properly—if at all.

Interrupt conflicts caused by mice can occur when a serial or PS/2 mouse is used, but not when a USB mouse is used. Mouse ports built in to modern motherboards are almost always set to IRQ12. If your system has a motherboard mouse port, be sure you don't set any other adapter cards to IRQ12; otherwise, a conflict will result.

If you are using a serial mouse, interrupt conflicts typically occur if you add third and fourth serial ports, using either an expansion card or internal serial device, such as a modem. This happens because in ISA bus systems, the odd-numbered serial ports (1 and 3) usually are configured to use the same interrupts as the even-numbered ports (2 and 4) are; IRQ4 is shared by default between COM1 and COM3, and IRQ 2 is shared by default between COM2 and COM4. Therefore, if your mouse is connected to COM2 and an internal modem uses COM4, they both might use the same interrupt, and you can't use them at the same time.

Because the mouse generates interrupts only when it is moved, you might find that the modem functions properly until you touch the mouse, at which point the modem is disconnected. Another example is when your system will run properly until you try to go online with your modem; then the conflict usually locks up the system. You might be able to use the mouse and modem at the same time by moving one of them to a different serial port. For instance, if your mouse uses COM1 and the modem still uses COM4, you can use them both simultaneously because odd and even ports use different interrupts.

The best way around these interrupt conflicts is to make sure no two devices use the same interrupt. Serial port adapters are available for adding COM3 and COM4 serial ports that do not share the interrupts used by COM1 and COM2. These boards enable the new COM ports to use other normally available interrupts, such as IRQs 10, 11, 12, 15, and 5. I never recommend configuring a system with shared ISA interrupts; it is a sure way to run into problems later. However, interrupts used by PCI boards can be shared if you use Windows 95 OSR 2.x, Windows 98, Windows Me, Windows 2000, or Windows XP with recent chipsets that support a feature called IRQ steering.

◀◀ See "PCI Interrupts," p. 370.

If you suspect an interrupt problem with a bus-type mouse, you can use the Device Manager built into Windows (which is accessible from the System control panel).

▶▶ See "Operating System Diagnostics," p. 1299.

The Device Manager in Windows 9x/Me/2000/XP is part of the Plug-and-Play (PnP) software for the system, and it is usually 100% accurate on PnP hardware. Although some of these interrupt-reporting programs can have problems, most can easily identify the mouse IRQ if the mouse driver has been loaded. After the IRQ is identified, you might need to change the IRQ setting of the bus mouse adapter or one or more other devices in your system so that everything works together properly.

If your driver refuses to recognize the mouse at all, regardless of its type, try using a different mouse that you know works. Replacing a defective mouse with a known good one might be the only way to know whether the problem is indeed caused by a bad mouse.

I have had problems in which a bad mouse caused the system to lock right as the driver loaded or when third-party diagnostics were being run on the system. If you use a DOS-based diagnostic, such as Microsoft MSD or AMIDIAG, and the system locks up during the mouse test, you have found a problem with either the mouse or the mouse port. Try replacing the mouse to see whether that helps. If it does not, you might need to replace the serial port or bus mouse adapter. If a motherboard-based mouse port goes bad, you can replace the entire motherboard—which is usually expensive—or you can just disable the motherboard mouse port via jumpers or the system BIOS setup program and install a serial mouse instead. This method enables you to continue using the system without having to replace the motherboard. On systems with Windows 98/Me/2000/XP, you also can switch to a USB mouse, using USB ports on your motherboard or by installing a PCI-based USB card—provided your system has a USB port.

Note

To learn more about using the Microsoft MSD diagnostic program to test for mouse or mouse-port problems, see Chapters 17 and 25 of *Upgrading and Repairing PCs, 11th Edition*, which is included on the disc packaged with this book.

Driver Software

Most mice and other pointing devices in use today emulate a Microsoft mouse, enabling you to have basic two-button plus scrolling functions with current versions of Windows without loading any special drivers. However, if your mouse has additional buttons or other special features, you will need to install device-specific drivers available from the mouse vendor.

If you plan to use the mouse from a Windows 9x/Me command prompt or with DOS, you must load the driver manually. To learn more about this process, see "Mouse Driver Software" in the Technical Reference section of the disc packaged with this book.

Scroll Wheels

Late in 1996, Microsoft introduced the IntelliMouse, which differed from standard Microsoft mice by adding a small gray wheel between the mouse buttons. This was the first scrolling mouse, and since then, Logitech, IBM, and virtually all other mouse vendors have made scroll wheels or similar devices standard across almost all models, including OEM mice bundled with computer systems.

The wheel has two main functions. The primary function is to act as a scrolling device, enabling you to scroll through documents or Web pages by manipulating the wheel with your index finger. The wheel also functions as a third mouse button when you press it.

Although three-button mice have been available for years from vendors such as Logitech, the scrolling function provided a real breakthrough. No longer do you have to move the mouse pointer to click the scrollbar on the right side of your screen or take your hand off the mouse to use the arrow keys on the keyboard. You just push or pull on the wheel. This is a major convenience, especially when browsing Web pages or working with word processing documents or spreadsheets. Also, unlike three-button mice from other vendors, the IntelliMouse's wheel-button doesn't seem to get in the way and you are less likely to click it by mistake. Although it took a while for software vendors to support the wheel, improvements in application software and Windows support allow today's wheel mice to be fully useful with almost any recent or current Windows program.

Each vendor's mouse driver software offers unique features to enhance the basic operation of the mouse. For example, Logitech's MouseWare 9.7 driver enables you to select many uses for all three mouse buttons (the scroll wheel is treated as a third mouse button), as well as provides various options for how to scroll with each wheel click (three lines, six lines, or one screen). Microsoft's IntelliMouse driver offers a feature called ClickLock, which allows you to drag items without holding down the primary mouse button. In addition, it offers a Universal Scroll feature that adds scrolling mouse support to applications that lack such support. To get the most from whatever scrolling or other advanced-feature mouse you have, be sure you periodically download and install new mouse drivers.

Instead of the wheel used by Microsoft and Logitech, IBM and other mouse vendors frequently use various types of buttons for scrolling. Some inexpensive mice use a rocker switch, but the most elegant of the non-wheel alternatives is IBM's ScrollPoint Pro, which uses a pressure-sensitive scroll stick similar to the TrackPoint pointing device used on IBM's notebook computer and some PC keyboards made by IBM and Unicomp. The scrollpointer in the center of the mouse enables you to smoothly scroll through documents without having to lift your finger to roll the wheel, as you do on the Microsoft version, which makes it much easier and more convenient to use. Because no moving parts exist, the ScrollPoint is also more reliable.

TrackPoint II/III/IV

On October 20, 1992, IBM introduced a revolutionary new pointing device called TrackPoint II as an integrated feature of its new ThinkPad 700 and 700C computers. Often referred to as a *pointing stick device*, TrackPoint II and its successors consist primarily of a small rubber cap that appears on the keyboard right above the B key, between the G and H keys. This was the first significant new pointing device since the mouse had been invented nearly 30 years earlier!

This device occupies no space on a desk, does not have to be adjusted for left-handed or right-handed use, has no moving parts to fail or become dirty, and (most importantly) does not require you to move your hands from the home row to use it. This is an absolute boon for touch typists.

I was fortunate enough to meet the actual creator and designer of this device in early 1992 at the spring Comdex/Windows World in Chicago. He was in a small corner of the IBM booth showing off his custom-made keyboards with a small silicone rubber nub in the middle. In fact, the devices he had were hand-built prototypes installed in standard desktop keyboards, and he was there trying to get public reaction and feedback on his invention. I was invited to play with one of the keyboards, which was connected to a demonstration system. By pressing on the stick with my index finger, I could move the mouse pointer on the screen. The stick itself did not move, so it was not a joystick. Instead, it had a silicone rubber cap that was connected to pressure transducers that measured the amount of force my finger was applying and the direction of the force and moved the mouse pointer accordingly. The harder I pressed, the faster the pointer moved. After playing around with it for just a few minutes, the movements became automatic—almost as though I could just think about where I wanted the pointer to go.

The gentleman at the booth turned out to be Ted Selker, the primary inventor of the device. He and Joseph Rutledge created this integrated pointing device at the IBM T.J. Watson Research Center. When I asked him when such keyboards would become available, he could not answer. At the time, there were apparently no plans for production, and he was only trying to test user reaction to the device.

Just over six months later, IBM announced the ThinkPad 700, which included this revolutionary device—then called the TrackPoint II Integrated Pointing Device. Since the original version came out, enhanced versions with greater control and sensitivity, called the TrackPoint III and IV, have become available.

Note

The reason the device was called TrackPoint II is that IBM had previously been selling a convertible mouse/trackball device called the TrackPoint. No relationship exists between the original TrackPoint mouse/trackball, which has since been discontinued, and the TrackPoint II integrated device. Since the original TrackPoint II came out, improved versions known as TrackPoint III and TrackPoint IV have become available. In the interest of simplicity, I will refer to all the TrackPoint II, III, and successive devices as just *TrackPoint*.

In its final production form, the TrackPoint consists of a small, red, silicone rubber knob nestled between the G, H, and B keys on the keyboard. The primary and secondary mouse buttons are placed below the spacebar where you can easily reach them with your thumbs without taking your hands off the keyboard.

IBM studies conducted by Selker found that the act of removing your hand from the keyboard to reach for a mouse and replacing the hand on the keyboard takes approximately 1.75 seconds. If you type 60wpm, that can equal nearly two lost words per minute, not including the time lost while you regain your train of thought. Almost all this time can be saved each time you use TrackPoint to move the pointer or make a selection (click or double-click). The combination of the buttons and the positioning knob also enable you to perform drag-and-drop functions easily.

IBM's research also found that people can get up to 20% more work accomplished using the TrackPoint instead of a mouse, especially when the application involves a mix of typing and pointing activities, such as with word processing, spreadsheets, and other typical office applications. In usability tests with the TrackPoint III, IBM gave a group of desktop computer users a TrackPoint and a traditional mouse. After two weeks, 80% of the users had unplugged their mice and switched solely to the TrackPoint device. Selker is convinced (as am I) that the TrackPoint is the best pointing solution for both laptop and desktop systems.

Another feature of the TrackPoint is that a standard mouse can be connected to the system at the same time to enable dual-pointer use. This setup not only enables a single person to use both devices, but also enables two people to use the TrackPoint and the mouse simultaneously to move the pointer on the screen. The first pointing device that moves (thus issuing a system interrupt) takes precedence and retains control over the mouse pointer on the screen until it completes its movement action. The second pointing device is automatically locked out until the primary device is stationary. This enables the use of both devices and prevents each one from interfering with the other.

IBM has added various versions of the TrackPoint to its notebook computers, as well as to high-end keyboards sold under the IBM, Lexmark, and Unicomp names. Notebook computer makers, such as HP and Toshiba, also have licensed the TrackPoint device (Toshiba calls it Accupoint).

I have compared the TrackPoint device to other pointing devices for notebooks, such as the trackballs and even the capacitive touch pads, but nothing compares in terms of accuracy and control—and, of course, you don't have to take your hands off the keyboard!

Some notebook computer makers copied the TrackPoint instead of licensing it, but with poor results that include sluggish response to input and poor accuracy. One way of telling whether the TrackPoint device is licensed from IBM and uses the IBM technology is if it accepts IBM TrackPoint II/III/IV rubber caps. They have a square hole in them and will properly lock on to any of the licensed versions, such as those found in Toshiba systems.

IBM has upgraded its pointing stick to the TrackPoint III and the current TrackPoint IV. Two main differences exist in the III/IV system, but the most obvious one is in the rubber cap. The IBM TrackPoint II and Toshiba Accupoint caps are made from silicone rubber, which is grippy and works well in most situations. However, if the user has greasy fingers, the textured surface of the rubber can absorb some of the grease and become slippery. Cleaning the cap (and the user's hands) solves the problem, but it can be annoying at times. The TrackPoint III/IV caps are made from a different type of rubber, which Selker calls "plastic sandpaper." This type of cap is much more grippy and does not require cleaning except for cosmetic purposes. I have used both types of caps and can say for certain that the TrackPoint III/IV cap is superior.

Note

Because the Accupoint device used in the Toshiba notebooks is licensed from IBM, it uses the same hardware (a pressure transducer called a *strain gauge*) and takes the same physical caps. I ordered a set of the TrackPoint III caps and installed them on my Toshiba portable systems, which dramatically improved the grip. You can get these caps by ordering them from IBM Parts directly or from others who sell IBM parts, such as Compu-Lock (`www.compu-lock.com`). The cost is under $15 for a set of four "plastic sandpaper" red caps.

Replacing the cap is easy—grab the existing cap with your fingers and pull straight up; it pops right off. Then, push on the new red IBM TrackPoint III/IV cap in its place. You will thank me when you feel how you can grip the new IBM cap much more easily than you can grip the designs used by others.

The other difference between the TrackPoint II and III/IV from IBM is in the control software. IBM added routines that implement a subtle technique Selker calls "negative inertia," which is marketed under the label *QuickStop response*. This software not only takes into account how far you push the pointer in any direction, but also how quickly you push or release it. Selker found that this improved software (and the sandpaper cap) enables people to make selections up to 8% faster.

TrackPoint IV includes an extra scroll button, as well as the ability to press the TrackPoint nub to select as if using the left mouse button. These new features make the TrackPoint even better to use.

The bottom line is that anyone who touch types should strongly consider only portable systems that include an IBM-licensed TrackPoint device (such as Toshiba). TrackPoints are far superior to other pointing devices, such as the touch pads, because the TrackPoint is faster to use (you don't have to take your hands off the keyboard's home row), easier to adapt to (especially for speedy touch typists), and far more precise. It takes some getting accustomed to, but the benefits are worth it.

The benefits of the TrackPoint are not limited to portable systems, however. If you use a notebook computer with TrackPoint like I do, you can have the same features on your desktop keyboard. For desktop systems, I use a Lexmark keyboard with the IBM-licensed TrackPoint device built in. This makes for a more consistent interface between desktop and notebook use because I can use the same pointing device in both environments. You also can buy these keyboards directly from Unicomp (Unicomp keyboards are TrackPoint III compatible); IBM also offers TrackPoint IV in some of its high-end keyboards available at retail.

Mouse and Pointing Stick Alternatives

Because of Windows, many users spend at least as much time moving pointers around the screen as they do in typing, making pointing device choices very important. In addition to the mouse and the pointing stick choices discussed earlier in this chapter, several other popular pointing devices are available, including

- Track pads, such as the Cirque GlidePoint
- Trackballs from many vendors
- Upright mice, such as the 3M Renaissance Mouse

All these devices are treated as mice by the operating system but offer radically different options for the user in terms of comfort. If you're not satisfied with a regular mouse and don't want to use an integrated pointing stick such as the TrackPoint II/III/IV, look into these options.

GlidePoint/Touch Pad

Cirque originated the touch pad (also called a *track pad*) pointing device in 1994. Cirque refers to its technology as the GlidePoint and has licensed the technology to other vendors such as Alps Electric, which also uses the term GlidePoint for its touch pads. The GlidePoint uses a flat, square pad that senses finger position through body capacitance. This is similar to the capacitance-sensitive elevator button controls you sometimes encounter in office buildings or hotels.

When it is used on a portable computer's keyboard, the touch pad is mounted below the spacebar, and it detects pressure applied by your thumbs or fingers. Transducers under the pad convert finger movement into pointer movement. Several laptop and notebook manufacturers have licensed this technology from Cirque and have incorporated it into their portable systems. Touch pads are also integrated into a number of mid-range to high-end keyboards from many vendors. When used on a desktop keyboard, touch pads are often offset to the right side of the keyboard's typing area.

Touch pads feature mouse buttons, although the user also can tap or double-tap on the touch pad's surface to activate an onscreen button located under the touch pad's cursor. Dragging and dropping is accomplished without touching the touch pad's buttons; just move the cursor to the object to be dragged, press down on the pad, hold while moving the cursor to the drop point, and raise the finger to drop the object. Some recent models also feature additional hot buttons with functions similar to those on hot-button keyboards.

The primary use for touch pads has been for notebook computer– and desktop keyboard–integrated pointing devices, although Cirque and Alps have both sold standalone versions of the touch pad for use as a mouse alternative on desktop systems. Cirque's touch pads are now available at retail under the Fellowes brand name, as well as direct from the Cirque Web site. The Internet Touchpad (also sold by Fellowes) has enhanced software to support touch gestures, has programmable hot buttons, and includes other features to make Web surfing easier.

Although it has gained wide acceptance, especially on portable computers, touch pad technology can have many drawbacks for some users. Operation of the device can be erratic, depending on skin resistance and moisture content. The biggest drawback is that to operate the touch pad, users must remove their hands from the home row on the keyboard, which dramatically slows their progress. In addition, the operation of the touch pad can be imprecise, depending on how pointy your finger or thumb is! On the other hand, if you're not a touch typist, removing your hands from the keyboard to operate the touch pad might be easier than using a TrackPoint. Even with their drawbacks, touch pad pointing devices are still vastly preferable to using a trackball or a cumbersome external mouse with portable systems.

Unless you want to use a "real" mouse with a portable system, I recommend you sit down with portable computers that have both touch pad and TrackPoint pointing devices. Try them yourself for typing, file management, and simple graphics and see which type of integrated pointing device you prefer. I know what I like, but you might have different tastes.

Trackballs

The first trackball I ever saw outside of an arcade was the Wico trackball, a perfect match for mid-1980s video games and computer games, such as Missile Command and others. It emulated the eight-position Atari 2600 analog joystick but was capable of much more flexibility.

Unlike the mid-80s trackballs, today's trackballs are used primarily for business instead of gaming. Most trackballs use a mouse-style positioning mechanism—the differences being that the trackball is on the top or side of the case and is much larger than a mouse ball. The user moves the trackball rather than the input device case, but rollers or wheels inside most models translate the trackball's motion and move a cursor onscreen the same way that mouse rollers or wheels convert the mouse ball's motion into cursor movement.

Trackballs come in a variety of forms, including ergonomic models shaped to fit the (right) hand, ambidextrous models suitable for both lefties and right-handers, optical models that use the same optical sensors found in the latest mice in place of wheels and rollers, and multibutton monsters that look as if they're the result of an encounter with a remote control.

Because they are larger than mice, trackballs lend themselves well to the extra electronics and battery power needed for wireless use. Logitech offers several wireless trackball models that use radio-frequency transceivers; for details of how this technology works, see the section "Wireless Input Devices," later in this chapter.

Trackballs use the same drivers and connectors as conventional mice. For basic operations, the operating-system-supplied drivers will work, but you should use the latest version of the vendor-supplied drivers to achieve maximum performance with recent models.

Cleaning and Troubleshooting Trackballs

Trackball troubleshooting is similar to mouse troubleshooting. For issues other than cleaning the trackball, see the section "Mouse Troubleshooting," earlier in this chapter.

Because trackballs are moved by the user's hand rather than by rolling against a tabletop or desktop, they don't need to be cleaned as often as mouse mechanisms do. However, occasional cleaning is recommended, especially with trackballs that use roller movement-detection mechanisms. If the trackball pointer won't move, skips, or drags when you move the trackball, try cleaning the trackball mechanism.

Trackballs can be held into place by a retaining ring, an ejection tab, or simply by gravity. Check the vendor's Web site for detailed cleaning instructions if your trackball didn't come with such instructions. Swabs and isopropyl alcohol are typically used to clean the trackball and rollers or bearings; see the trackball's instructions for details.

3M's Ergonomic Mouse

Many PC users who grew up using joysticks on the older video games experienced some "interface shock" when they turned in their joysticks for mice. And even long-time mouse users nursing sore arms and elbows have wondered whether the mouse was really as "ergonomic" as it is sometimes claims to be.

3M's solution, developed late in 2000, is to keep the traditional ball-type mouse positioning mechanism but change the user interface away from the hockey puck/soap bar design used for many years to a slanted handle that resembles a joystick (see Figure 18.14). 3M's Ergonomic Mouse (originally called the Renaissance Mouse) is available in two hand sizes and attaches to either the PS/2 port or USB port (serial ports are not supported). The single button on the top of the handle is a rocker switch; push on the left side to left-click and on the right side to right-click. The front handgrip provides scrolling support when the special Ergonomic Mouse driver software is installed.

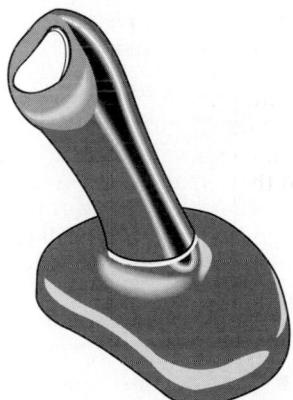

Figure 18.14 The 3M Ergonomic Mouse combines an ergonomic shape with a standard mouse-movement mechanism.

The Ergonomic Mouse enables the user to hold the pointing device with a "handshake"-style hand and arm position. 3M's Web site provides detailed ergonomic information to encourage the proper use of the Ergonomic Mouse, which comes with software to support scrolling and other advanced functions. It's available in various colors and separate models for Windows-based PCs and Macs.

Input Devices for Gaming

Originally, game players on the PC used the arrow keys or letter keys on the keyboard to play all types of games. As you can imagine, this limited the number and type of games that could be played on the PC.

Analog Joysticks and the Game Port

As video standards improved, making games more realistic, input devices made especially for game play also became more and more popular. The first joysticks made for the IBM PC were similar to joysticks made for its early rival, the Apple II series. Both the IBM and Apple II joysticks were analog devices that lacked much of the positive feedback game players were accustomed to from the Atari 2600, Commodore 64, or arcade joysticks. These joysticks also required frequent recalibration to work properly and were far from satisfactory to hardcore game players. Also, these devices required their own connector—the 15-pin game port. The game port found its way onto many sound cards as well as onto multi-I/O cards made for ISA and VL-Bus systems.

Even though joysticks began to add better features, including spring action, video game-style gamepads, and flight control options, the analog nature and slow speed of the gameport began to restrict performance as CPU speeds climbed above 200MHz and high-speed AGP and PCI video cards made ultra-realistic flying, driving, and fighting simulators possible. USB controllers offer the additional speed necessary for more sophisticated gamers.

USB Ports for Gaming

The USB port has become the preferred connector for all types of gaming controllers, including joysticks, gamepads, and steering wheels. Instead of making a single inadequate joystick work for all types of games, users can now interchange controllers using the hot-swap benefits of USB and use the best controller for each type of game.

Although a few low-end game controllers still on the market can connect to either the venerable game port or the serial port, serious gamers want USB because of its higher speed, better support for force feedback (which shakes the game controller realistically to match the action onscreen), and tilting (tilt the gamepad and the onscreen action responds).

As with USB mice, your USB-connected gaming controllers are only as good as their software drivers. Be sure to install the latest software available to keep up with the latest games.

Compatibility Concerns

If you play a lot of older games designed in the heyday of the 15-pin gameport, consider keeping a gameport-type controller. Even though the vendors of USB game controllers strive to make the USB port emulate a game port for use with older games, some older games can't be fooled. If you have problems using a USB game controller with a specific game, check the game's Web site for patches, as well as your game controller's Web site for tips and workarounds.

Wireless Input Devices

For several years, many manufacturers have offered cordless versions of mice and keyboards. In most cases, these devices have used either infrared or short-range radio transceivers to attach to standard serial or PS/2 ports, with matching transceivers located in the mouse or keyboard. Wireless input devices are designed to be easier to use in cramped home-office environments and where a large-screen TV/monitor device is used for home entertainment and computing.

Many manufacturers, including Microsoft, Logitech, and second-tier vendors, offer bundled kits that include a wireless keyboard and mouse which share a transceiver. Because many of these keyboards and mice have the latest features, including programmable keys, multimedia and Internet-access keys, and optical sensors, these wireless combos are often the top-of-the-line products from a given vendor and are often less expensive than buying the keyboard and mouse separately.

How Wireless Input Devices Work

The three major technologies used by wireless input devices are as follows:

- Infrared (IR)
- Proprietary radio frequency
- Bluetooth

All three technologies use a transceiver connected to the PS/2 or USB ports on the computer. Because many wireless transceivers are designed for use with a mouse and keyboard, PS/2-compatible versions have two cables—one for the mouse port and one for the keyboard port. A USB-compatible transceiver needs only one USB port to handle both devices if the system supports USB Legacy (keyboard) functions. The transceiver attached to the computer draws its power from the port.

The transceiver receives signals from the transceiver built in to the mouse or keyboard. These devices require batteries to function; therefore, a common cause of wireless device failure is battery run-down. Early generations of wireless devices used unusual battery types, but most recent products use off-the-shelf alkaline AA or AAA batteries. Rechargeable batteries are usually not supported, although Logitech's MX 700 has built-in rechargeable batteries and a transceiver that doubles as a charger.

Although all three technologies rely on battery power, the similarities end there. IR devices have a relatively short range (12 ft. maximum) and must have a clear line-of-sight between the input device and transceiver. Anything from a Mountain Dew can to a sheet of paper can block the IR signal from reaching the transceiver, assuming you're aiming the transmitter built in to your input device correctly in the first place. Some late-model IR devices have transceivers that can receive signals through a relatively wide 120° range, but this technology is much more temperamental than the others and has been abandoned by most vendors. Figure 18.15 shows how range and line-of-sight issues can prevent IR input devices from working correctly.

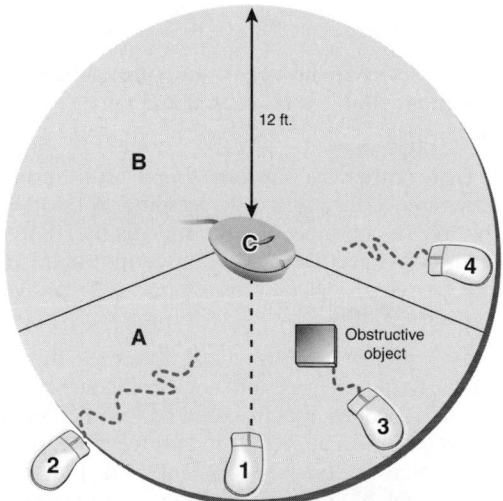

A. Acceptable angle for receiving transmissions
B. Not acceptable
C. IR transceiver

1. Mouse with IR-connection to transceiver
2. Mouse can't connect (out of range)
3. Mouse can't connect (line-of-sight blocked)
4. Mouse can't connect (wrong angle to transceiver)

Figure 18.15   A wireless mouse using IR technology must be within range of the transceiver, at the correct angle to the transceiver, and not blocked by any objects. Otherwise, it cannot work.

Because of the problems with IR devices shown in Figure 18.15, almost all vendors of wireless input devices now use radio waves (RF) for transmission between the device and transceiver. RF-based wireless devices have no line-of-sight problems, but most have a limited range of about 6 ft. from the transmitter (see Figure 18.16).

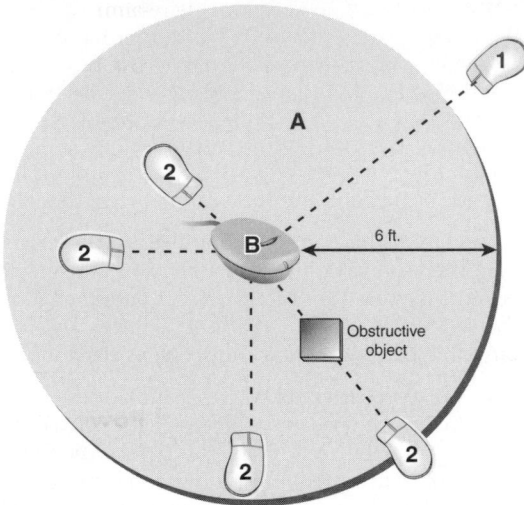

A. Acceptable angle for receiving transmissions (360)
B. RF transceiver

1. Mouse can't connect (out of range)
2. Mouse with connection to RF transceiver

Figure 18.16   A wireless mouse using RF must be within range of the transceiver, but unlike IR-based wireless mice, the angle of the mouse to the transceiver doesn't matter and radio signals can't be blocked by books, paper, or other obstacles.

Although RF overcomes line-of-sight issues that can cripple an IR mouse, early versions of RF products had a high potential for interference from other devices and from other devices in use in the same room because of a limited range of channels. For example, early Logitech wireless MouseMan products required the user to manually select the channel used by the transceiver and mouse. If more than six users in a small room had wireless devices, interference was practically inevitable and user error could lead to a user's mouse movements showing up on the wrong computer screen.

Fortunately, improvements in frequency bands used and automatic tuning have enabled all users of a particular type of device to avoid interference with other electronic devices or with each other. For example, Logitech's current line of wireless products uses its patented Palomar technology. Although the 27MHz frequency used by Palomar has become a de facto standard for most recent wireless input devices (it's also used by Microsoft and IBM for their wireless products), Logitech allows users to enable a digital security feature that uses one of more than 4,000 unique codes to prevent accidentally activating another computer with a wireless device or signal snooping by another user. Most vendors use similar technology but might use a much smaller number of codes. The range of 27MHz RF devices is short—about 6 ft.—but the transmitter can be located behind the computer or under the desk without loss of signal.

Although most wireless products use proprietary radio transceivers, the Bluetooth wireless standard can now be used by some keyboards and mice, such as Microsoft's pioneering Wireless Optical Desktop mouse and keyboard bundle or the Wireless IntelliMouse Explorer for Bluetooth. Logitech also offers a Bluetooth-enabled input device: its Cordless Presenter handheld pointing device. Bluetooth-enabled devices have an effective range of up to 30 ft. and might be compatible with other brands of devices that are also Bluetooth enabled.

▶▶ For more information about Bluetooth, see Chapter 20, "Local Area Networking," p. 1101.

Having used both IR and RF types of wireless devices, I can tell you that a radio-frequency input device beats an infrared input device hands down for use at home or in a small one- or two-person office. Because infrared requires an unobstructed direct line between the transceivers, when I used an infrared keyboard/ pointing stick combination at a client site, I was constantly re-aiming the keyboard at the transceiver to avoid losing my signal. When I used a radio mouse, on the other hand, there were no line-of-sight issues to worry about. Historically, the only advantage to infrared was cost, but the problems of reliability in my mind outweigh any cost savings. Additionally, a wide range of prices for RF wireless products, including attractive keyboard and mouse combinations, make RF input devices affordable for almost everyone. If you're planning to use a computer to drive a big-screen TV or as a presentation unit, consider Bluetooth-enabled devices available from Microsoft, Logitech, and others because of their longer range (up to 10 meters, or 33 ft.).

Power Management Features of Wireless Input Devices

A wireless mouse is useless if its batteries fail, so several vendors of wireless products have developed sophisticated power-management features to help preserve battery life—especially with optical mice, which use power-eating LEDs to illuminate the mousing surface. For example, the Logitech Cordless MouseMan Optical's LED sensor has four operating modes, as shown in Table 18.5.

Table 18.5   Logitech Cordless MouseMan Optical Power Management

Mode	LED Flashing Rate	Notes
Normal	1,500 per second	Used only when mouse is being moved across a surface
Glow	1,000 per second	Used when mouse stops moving
Strobe	10 per second	Mouse not moved for more than 2 minutes
Flash	2 per second	Mouse not moved for more than 10 minutes

Wireless keyboards are activated only when you press a key or use the scroll wheel available on some models, so they tend to have longer battery lives than mice. Conventional ball-type mice also have longer battery lives than optical mice, but the convenience and accuracy of optical mice outweigh battery-life issues for most users.

Wireless Pointing Device Issues

Before you invest in wireless pointing devices for multiple computers, you should be aware of the following issues:

- *Line-of-site issues.* Infrared devices won't work if the IR beam between the pointing device and the transceiver attached to the system is blocked. These units are not as suitable for casual in-the-lap use as radio-frequency units are.

- *Radio-frequency interference.* Although early wireless mice used analog tuners that were hard to synchronize, today's wireless input devices typically use digital selectors. However, if several similar devices are used in close quarters, a transceiver might actually receive data from the wrong mouse or keyboard. Also, metal desks and furniture can reduce range and cause erratic cursor movement. Most wireless devices operate around 27MHz, minimizing interference from devices such as cordless phones. If you plan to install several different computers using wireless input devices in the same room, set up one at a time and allow about half an hour between installations if possible to let each unit synchronize with its transceiver. Check with the vendor for other tips on overcoming interference issues.

- *Battery life and availability.* Early wireless devices sometimes used unusual, expensive batteries. Today's units run on common battery types, such as AAA or AA. Battery life is usually rated at about 6 months for keyboards or ball-type mice and about 2–3 months for optical mice. Be sure you have spare batteries for the input device to avoid failures due to running out of battery power. Some vendors provide software that gives users an onscreen warning when batteries run low. Furthermore, when using an optical wireless mouse, you should try working on brighter or whiter surfaces. Many optical mice adjust their sensors based on the illumination of the surface, which is why you might see the light in the mouse change intensity. The less intense the internal LED operates, the less battery power being used.

■ *Location.* The range of wireless devices can vary from 6 ft. with conventional RF devices to as much as 30 ft. with Bluetooth-based devices. Consider where the device will be used before making your purchase. For instance, in an office where multiple devices might be used at the same time, a close-range device might be more desirable to avoid crosstalk among devices. On the other hand, the home user who wants to sit away from the screen while maintaining control might want an extended range, making Bluetooth-enabled devices a better choice.

■ *User experience.* Different users will have different expectations of wireless input devices, but in general, the more a wireless input device acts like its wired siblings, the better. The fact that a device is wireless should not compromise its functionality. If things such as reliability, connection, or driver problems hinder proper usage, the device isn't worth using. Hardcore gamers who need the fastest response time possible generally favor the responsiveness of a wired optical mouse over any wireless mouse. Although minimal, some lag time does exist. Some mice can require up to 0.25 centimeter of movement before responding. This lag time can also affect users doing graphical work requiring the superior consistency and accuracy of a wired optical mouse, although the latest dual-sensor wireless optical mice have accuracy on par with wired optical mice.

■ *Pointer speed.* Conventional wired optical mice transmit their positions about 120 times per second, whereas wireless mice that use a USB receiver transmit their positions about 40–50 times per second. If you use a mouse to play fast-action games, you might find a corded mouse a better choice because of the more frequent position updates it provides.

Troubleshooting Wireless Input Devices

If your wireless input device does not work, check the following:

■ *Battery failure.* The transceivers attached to the computer are powered by the computer, but the input devices themselves are battery-powered. Check the battery life suggestions published by the vendor; if your unit isn't running as long as it should, try using a better brand of battery or turning off the device if possible.

■ *Lost synchronization between device and transceiver.* Both the device and the transceiver must be using the same frequency to communicate. Depending on the device, you might be able to resynchronize the device and transceiver by pressing a button, or you might need to remove the battery, reinsert the battery, and wait for several minutes to reestablish contact.

■ *Interference between units.* Check the transmission range of the transceivers in your wireless units and visit the manufacturer's Web site for details on how to reduce interference. Typically, you should use different frequencies for wireless devices on adjacent computers.

■ *Blocked line of sight.* If you are using infrared wireless devices, check the line of sight carefully at the computer, the space between your device and the computer, and the device itself. You might be dangling a finger or two over the infrared eye and cutting off the signal—the equivalent of putting your finger over the lens on a camera.

■ *Serial port IRQ conflicts.* If the wireless mouse is connected to a serial port and it stops working after you install another add-on card, check for conflicts using the Windows Device Manager.

■ *Disconnected transceiver.* If you have moved the computer around, you might have disconnected the transceiver from its keyboard, PS/2 mouse, serial, or USB port. You can plug a USB device in without shutting down the system, but the other types require you to shut down, reattach the cable, and restart to work correctly.

■ *USB Legacy support not enabled.* If your wireless keyboard uses a transceiver connected to the USB port and the device works in Windows, but not at a command prompt, make sure you have enabled USB Legacy support in the BIOS or use the PS/2 connector from the transceiver to connect to the PS/2 keyboard port.

CHAPTER 19

Internet Connectivity

Relating Internet and LAN Connectivity

Communication between computers is a major part of the PC computing industry. Thanks to the World Wide Web (WWW), no computer user is an island. Whether using a dialup modem or broadband technology, virtually all PCs can be connected to other computers, enabling them to share files, send and receive email, and access the Internet. This chapter explores the various technologies you can use to expand the reach of your PC around the block and around the world.

It might surprise you to see discussions of protocols and networking setup in both this chapter and the LAN chapter of this book, but a modem connection is really just another form of networking. In fact, 32-bit versions of Windows from Windows NT and Windows 9x all the way through Windows XP have all but blended the two services into a single entity.

The reason for this combination is that the typical target for a modem connection has changed over the years. Computer users a decade ago dialed in to *bulletin board systems (BBSs)*, which are proprietary services that provide terminal access to other computers. However, BBSs are practically extinct today. Similarly, proprietary online services such as America Online and CompuServe (now owned by AOL but maintained as a separate service), which have also been around for many years, have almost entirely dropped their proprietary client software and protocols and have been reborn as gateways to the Internet.

With the explosive growth of the Internet, modem and network technologies were joined because both could use the same client software and protocols. Today, the most popular suite of networking protocols—TCP/IP—is used on both LANs and the Internet. When you dial in to an Internet service provider (ISP), you are actually connecting to a network using a modem instead of a network interface card, and when you use most broadband services, your path to the Internet typically starts with a network interface card, built-in network port, network-to-USB adapter, or even a wireless connection.

Although most new PCs still include a dialup modem, an increasing number of PC users are abandoning dialup Internet access for the faster world of broadband access. In fact, according to the Broadband Update report by eMarketer.com, in 2005 more than one-half (53%) of online households in the United States will have high-speed connections, up from 45.1% in 2004, 36.3% in 2003, 8.9% in 2000, and 0% in 1995. In other words, although dialup has been the dominant Internet access technology from 1995 to 2005, in 2005 a major transition will occur: For the first time, there will be more broadband users than dialup both in the United States and worldwide.

A milestone was reached in 2004 when the worldwide total of broadband connections reached and exceeded 100 million. By the end of 2004, the Asia-Pacific region had the most broadband subscribers with 56.6 million households, topping 37.7 million in North America, 28.7 million in Western Europe, and 2.3 million in Latin America. Nearly 250 million broadband subscribers are forecast by 2007.

By the end of 2003, there were 37.7 million broadband subscribers in the United States. In February 2004, about 54% of these used cable modems and about 42% used digital subscriber line (DSL) connections. The remainder generally used a form of satellite or wireless connection.

Although broadband is growing at a rapid rate and is replacing dialup for the majority of users, dialup connections still have their uses and a large user base. Those without broadband options, those on a budget, or those who travel still need a dialup connection. Also, dialup connections are sometimes required for certain types of broadband services and serve as a backup Internet access source. Even though I use broadband when I can, I still configure new PCs with dialup modems for emergency use when the broadband connection is down. You'll find dialup modem coverage in the second portion of the chapter.

Comparing Broadband and Dialup Modem Internet Access

Even though most new PCs purchased at retail include some type of dialup modem you can use for Internet and email access, you are likely to find that Internet and email access with a dialup modem aren't sufficient for your needs if you use these services for more than a few minutes each day. Here are some reasons you should consider switching to a broadband service:

- *Speed*. The fastest dialup modems can download data at a maximum rate of 56Kbps (limited in the United States to just 53Kbps by the FCC), whereas broadband services start at 128Kbps for ISDN. Newer forms of broadband, such as DSL and cable modems, start at 384Kbps and typically exceed 500Kbps. Similarly, broadband services can upload data at several times the speed of a dialup modem.

- *Convenience*. Cable modems and some types of DSL and satellite broadband Internet service are always on, providing you with an immediate connection as soon as you open your Web browser or email client. Dialup modems require you to dial up the server and wait up to a minute before you can check your email or surf the Web. Similarly, always-on broadband services can provide you with immediate notification of incoming email, whereas dialup systems can check for incoming email only if you stay online and tie up your phone line.

- *Telephone line usage*. In the wake of the September 11th terrorist attacks on the United States, keeping telephone communications lines open for emergencies has been a major consideration for many people. Most dialup modems do not support call waiting, making it difficult for callers to reach you with important messages while you're online unless you use call-forwarding or call-notification software. Although some dialup ISPs provide software that can alert you to incoming calls, in most cases you must find and install such software yourself. By contrast, most broadband services keep your telephone line free so you can check email or surf the Web and use the telephone at the same time.

- *Price*. One disadvantage of broadband communications is apparent when you see your bill: It costs two to three times as much per month as dialup access with a dialup modem. However, millions of U.S. users believe the additional speed and convenience of broadband make the extra cost of the service per month a worthwhile investment. If you use the Internet enough to justify installing a second phone line just for Internet use, the price gap narrows considerably because you can use most broadband services without tying up your single existing phone line. If you have cable TV, most cable TV providers now also offer cable broadband service and provide a discount off the normal price for customers who have both cable TV and cable Internet service.

- *Ease of reconnection after an operating system upgrade*. Because broadband Internet is usually based on automatically configured TCP/IP network settings, you should be able to keep your broadband connection running during a Windows upgrade with little difficulty. Just verify that you have the correct drivers for your Ethernet adapter (used for most broadband connections) before you perform the upgrade, note your computer and workgroup name, and you should be able to go online as soon as the upgrade is completed. A dialup connection is often much tougher to keep working, especially because of the different methods used by various Windows versions for handling dialup networking.

Broadband Internet Access Types

Thanks to the combination of huge multimegabyte downloads needed to update software and support hardware, dynamic Web sites with music and full-motion video, and increased demand for online services, even the fastest dialup modem (which can download at just 53Kbps) isn't sufficient for heavy Internet use. More and more users are taking advantage of various types of broadband Internet access solutions, including:

- Cable modem
- DSL
- Fixed-base wireless
- Satellite-based services
- ISDN
- Leased lines

At least one of these services might be available to you, and if you live in a large- to medium-size city, you might be able to choose from two or more of these broadband solutions. The first portion of this chapter focuses on these solutions.

High Speed = Less Freedom

Although high-speed services such as cable modems, DSL, and others all represent major improvements in speed over existing dialup 56Kbps connections, one big drawback you should consider is the loss of freedom in choosing an ISP.

With a 56Kbps dialup modem, you can choose from a wide variety of services, including

- Local ISPs (personalized service)
- National ISPs with dialup access across the country (great for travelers)
- Online services with customized content plus Web access (AOL and CompuServe)
- Family-friendly filtered Internet access (Mayberry USA and Lightdog)
- Business-oriented Web hosting plus Internet access plans from many vendors

At present, if you want faster speed, you must use the ISP provided with your high-speed service. Whether it's your local telephone company, a third-party vendor, or your friendly cable TV operator, their ISP is your ISP. When you evaluate a high-speed service, remember to look at the special features and services provided by the ISP and its track record for reliability and keeping customers happy. After all, the quality of the work your ISP does is reflected in the quality of your broadband connection.

Tip

If you want the extra speed and convenience of broadband Internet but want to shield your family from some types of Internet content, several filtering services are available that work with your preferred broadband service, including these:

- Cleanweb's Filter Your Internet (FYI) at `www.cleanweb.net`
- S4F FamilyConnect FilterPak at `www.familyconnect.com`
- Bsafe Online at `http://www.bsafehome.com`

Cable Modems and CATV Networks

For many users, cable modem service—which piggybacks on the same cable TV (CATV) service lines that bring your TV many channels—represents both a big boost in speed from that available with ISDN and a major savings in initial costs and monthly charges. Unlike ISDN, cable modem service normally is sold as an "all you can eat" unlimited-access plan with a modest installation charge (often waived) and a small monthly fee for the rental of the cable modem. Because more and more cable networks support a single standard, you can also choose to buy your cable modem from any of several vendors in some cases, saving even more money over the long term.

Connecting to the Internet with a "Cable Modem"

As with ISDN, the device used to connect a PC to a CATV network is somewhat inaccurately called a modem. In fact, the so-called "cable modem" (a name I will continue to use, for the sake of convenience) is actually a great deal more. The device does indeed modulate and demodulate, but it also functions as a tuner, a network bridge, an encryptor, and an SNMP agent. To connect your PC to a CATV network, you do not use a serial port as with dialup modem technologies or ISDN terminal adapters. Instead, the most typical connection today uses 10/100 Ethernet or USB (10/100 Ethernet is faster). If your computer doesn't include an Ethernet adapter or 10/100 Ethernet card, you can install a 10/100 Ethernet adapter into a PCI slot or connect most recent cable modem models to a USB port on your computer. Some older cable modem services utilize an internal adapter for one-way service and use the conventional modem for uploads; this type of service is called *telco return*. Even though you get fast downloading, telco return systems tie up your phone line and are not recommended.

Tip

For maximum speed and ease of sharing, I recommend that you connect your cable modem to a 10/100 Ethernet card or port or use a USB 2.0 port (built into many new machines or available as an add-on card for older systems). USB 1.1 ports limit the throughput of your cable modem.

The Cable Modem and the CATV Network

The cable modem connects to the CATV network using the same coaxial cable connection as your cable TV service (see Figure 19.1). Thus, the cable modem functions as a bridge between the tiny twisted-pair network in your home and the hybrid fiber/coax (HFC) network that connects all the cable customers in your neighborhood.

A few cable modem CATV systems have been built using the older one-way (download-only) coax cable, but this type of cable is much slower for cable modem use and is obsolete for both CATV and data communications. The industry has largely replaced coax with HFC. Before you sign up for CATV Internet service, find out which type of service is being offered. Only the two-way, HFC-based systems allow you to use the Internet independently of the telephone system; one-way cable modem service requires a dialup modem for uploading page requests, files, and email. The modem can be built into your one-way cable modem (these are called *bundled* cable modems) or be a separate external dialup modem. In either case, going online with a one-way cable modem ties up your phone line.

Digital CATV service, which brings your TV many more channels and a clearer picture, requires the cable TV provider to upgrade to an HFC physical plant. Thus, digital CATV service is a precursor to two-way cable modem service; pure-coax CATV systems can't be used to transmit digital service or handle two-way cable modem traffic. CATV systems that have been upgraded to digital service are capable of providing two-way cable modem service, after suitable head-end equipment is installed at the CATV central office. A good rule of thumb, therefore, is that CATV systems that don't offer digital cable TV might offer only one-way cable modem service or no cable modem service at all. A typical two-way cable modem connection is shown in Figure 19.1.

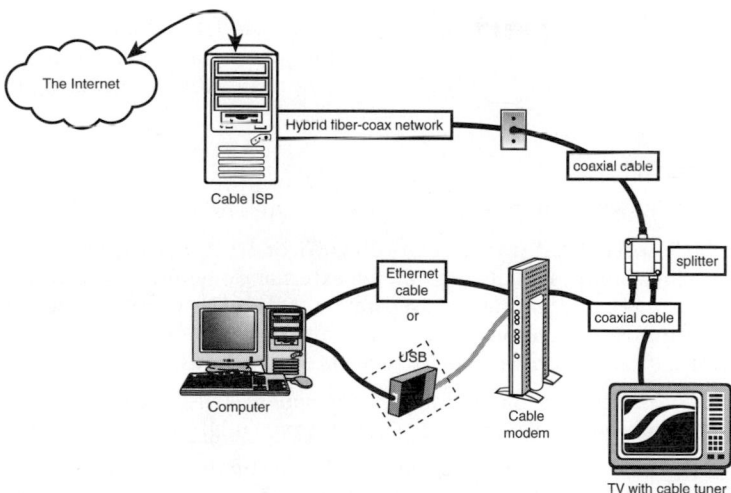

Figure 19.1   A typical hybrid fiber-coax cable TV network that also includes two-way cable modem service.

Originally, cable modems were not sold to users of CATV Internet access but were leased by the CATV companies offering Internet access to their cable modem customers. This is because each cable modem on a particular CATV network had to match the proprietary technology used by the network. In late 1998, DOCSIS-compliant cable modems began to be used by some CATV companies. DOCSIS refers to devices that meet the Data Over Cable Service Interface Specification standards established by Cable Television Laboratories, Inc. (CableLabs). Modems that meet DOCSIS standards are now referred to as CableLabs Certified cable modems. Visit the CableLabs Web site at www.cablelabs.org for a complete list of cable modems that are CableLabs Certified.

Many vendors of traditional modems and other types of communications products, such as Zoom Telephonics, 3Com, GVC, General Instruments, Philips, Motorola, Cabletron, Toshiba, Cisco, D-Link, and many others, now make CableLabs Certified Cable Modem–compliant hardware. The models supported by your CATV Internet provider might vary according to the DOCSIS standard it supports. Table 19.1 provides a brief overview of the differences in these standards.

Table 19.1   DOCSIS Standards Overview

DOCSIS Standard	Benefits	Notes
1.0	Basic broadband CATV (cable modem) service	Original DOCSIS version
1.1	Supports tiered service (different speeds at different costs), faster uploading, home networking, and packet telephony while reducing costs	Backward-compatible with DOCSIS 1.0
2.0	Faster performance for downloading and uploading compared to DOCSIS 1.0 and 1.1; supports high-speed two-way business services	Backward-compatible with DOCSIS 1.1, 1.0

Although most cable modems are now available for about $100, compared to $30–$70 for typical dialup modems, you should check with your CATV Internet provider before purchasing one to determine which models are supported by your provider and whether your CATV Internet provider still requires you to lease the cable modem.

If you plan to keep cable modem service for more than a year, I recommend purchasing a CableLabs Certified cable modem, but if you're unsure of your long-term plans, leasing isn't all that expensive. Typical lease costs for the device add only about $10/month to the monthly rate of $30–$40 for cable modem service.

Types of Cable Modems

Cable modems come in several forms:

- *External cable modem "box."* It requires a 10BASE-T or 10/100 Ethernet NIC or a USB port. Some vendors provide "bundles" that combine the external cable modem with the NIC at a lower price than leasing or purchasing both separately. This type of cable modem is designed for fast uploads as well as fast downloads and works only on newer "two-way" CATV Internet connections. Almost all cable modems sold by retailers fall into this category.

- *Internal cable modem with a 56Kbps dialup modem built in.* This type of cable modem provides fast downloads but uploads at dialup speeds only; this type might use either an ISA or a PCI slot.

- *Internal cable modem for use with a separate 56Kbps dialup modem.* This type might use either an ISA or a PCI slot. As with the previous model, uploads are at dialup speeds only.

- *Internal cable modem for use with two-way service.* This type of cable modem is rare, but because some internal cable modems are now CableLabs Certified, you might see some cable ISPs offer these. Some also might be designed for one-way service, enabling the cable ISP to install a single modem for use with both types of service.

- *External cable modem with a 56Kbps dialup modem built in.* This type of cable modem is sometimes designed to work with both one-way and two-way services.

Cable modem models that must be used with (or include) a dialup modem are designed for older "one-way" CATV Internet connections; these will tie up your phone line when transmitting page requests as well as when sending uploads.

Note

For more comprehensive coverage of cable modem service types, installation, sharing, security, and use, see the *Absolute Beginner's Guide to Cable Internet Connections* by Mark Edward Soper (published by Que, 2002).

CATV Bandwidth

Cable TV uses what is known as a *broadband network*, meaning the bandwidth of the connection is split to simultaneously carry many signals at different frequencies. These signals correspond to the channels you see on your TV. A typical HFC network provides approximately 750MHz of bandwidth, and each channel requires 6MHz. Therefore, because the television channels start at about 50MHz, you would find channel 2 in the 50MHz–56MHz range, channel 3 at 57MHz–63MHz, and so on up the frequency spectrum. At this rate, an HFC network can support about 110 channels.

For data networking purposes, cable systems typically allocate one channel's worth of bandwidth in the 50MHz–750MHz range for downstream traffic—that is, traffic coming into the cable modem from the CATV network. In this way, the cable modem functions as a tuner, just like your cable TV box, ensuring that your PC receives signals from the correct frequency.

Upstream traffic (data sent from your PC to the network) uses a different channel. Cable TV systems commonly reserve the bandwidth from 5MHz to 42MHz for upstream signals of various types (such as those generated by cable TV boxes that enable you to order pay-per-view programming). Depending on the bandwidth available, you might find that your CATV provider does not furnish the same high speed upstream as it does downstream. This is called an *asymmetrical network*.

Note

Because the upstream speed often does not match the downstream speed (and to minimize noise, which tends to accumulate because of the tree-and-branch nature of the network), cable TV connections usually are not practical for hosting Web servers and other Internet services. This is largely deliberate because most CATV providers are currently targeting their traditional home user market. As the technology matures, however, this type of Internet connection is likely to spread to the business world as well. There are now specialized domain name services that can be used to "point" Web surfers to your cable modem or DSL connection.

Some cable ISPs require you to switch to a more expensive business plan if you want to host a server (including a P2P server such as Gnutella) on your cable modem connection. In fact, hosting a server on a residential cable modem service could be a violation of your contract and could lead to cancellation of your service.

The amount of data throughput that the single 6MHz downstream channel can support depends on the type of modulation used at the head end (that is, the system to which your PC connects over the network). Using a technology called 64 QAM (quadrature amplitude modulation), the channel might be capable of carrying up to 27Mbps of downstream data. A variant called 256 QAM can boost this to 36Mbps.

You must realize, however, that you will not achieve anything even approaching this throughput on your PC. First of all, if you are using a 10BASE-T Ethernet adapter to connect to the cable modem, you are limited to 10Mbps. A USB 1.1 port is limited to 12Mbps, but even this is well beyond the real-life results you will achieve. As with any LAN, you are sharing the available bandwidth with other users in your neighborhood. All your neighbors who also subscribe to the service use the same 6MHz channel. As more users are added, more systems are contending for the same bandwidth, and throughput goes down.

In November 1999, ZDTV (now TechTV) tested five brands of cable modems in typical operations and found that the overhead of CATV proved to be a major slowdown factor. The cable modems were first connected directly to the server to provide a baseline for comparisons. Some of these tests showed speeds as high as 4Mbps. However, when the CATV cable was connected and the same tests were run, the best performer dropped to just 1.1Mbps, with others running even slower.

Tip

You can improve the performance of your cable modem or other broadband Internet access device by making changes to your system Registry that affect the size of the TCP receive window and other settings. I recommend the system tweaks available at the SpeedGuide.net Web site (**www.speedguide.net**). You can find tweaks for all Windows versions from Windows 95 through Windows XP, along with instructions on how to make the changes manually and easy methods for setting your system's Registry back to its default values.

Widespread reports from cable modem users across the country indicate that rush hour–type conditions occur at certain times of the day on some systems, with big slowdowns. This rush hour is due to increasing use of cable modem systems in the late afternoon and early evening, as daytime workers get home and pull up the day's news, weather, stocks, and sports on their Internet connections. Because cable modems are shared access, this type of slowdown is inevitable and becomes exceptionally severe if the CATV Internet provider doesn't use a fast enough connection to the rest of the Internet. To minimize this problem, many CATV Internet providers use caching servers at their point-of-presence connections to the Internet. These servers store frequently accessed Web pages to enable users to view pages without the delays in retrieving them from the original Web sites. By adding multiple T1 or T3 connections to the Internet backbones and using caching servers, ISPs can minimize delays during peak usage hours.

CATV Performance

The fact that you are sharing the CATV network with other users doesn't mean the performance of a cable modem isn't usually spectacular. Although the CATV network takes a big cut out of the maximum speeds, you'll still realize a throughput that hovers around 512Kbps, almost 10 times that of the fastest modem connection and 4 times that of ISDN. You will find the Web to be an entirely new experience at this speed. Those huge audio and video clips you avoided in the past now download in seconds, and you will soon fill your hard drives with all the free software available.

Add to this the fact that the service is typically quite reasonably priced. Remember that the CATV provider is replacing both the telephone company (if you have two-way service) and your ISP in your Internet access solution. The price can be about $40–$50 per month (including cable modem rental), which is twice that of a normal dialup ISP account, but it is far less than ISDN, does not require a telephone line (if your provider has two-way service), and provides 24-hour access to the Internet. The only drawback is that the service might not be available yet in your area. In my opinion, this technology exceeds all the other Internet access solutions available today in speed, economy, convenience, and widespread availability. Its nearest rival is DSL, which is still not as widely available geographically and is plagued with poor coordination between ISPs and telephone companies. Because cable modem Internet service providers provide the physical plant, provide ISP services, and can provide equipment, you can get service installed in just days and avoid the finger-pointing common with other types of broadband Internet service.

CATV Internet Connection Security

Because your PC is sharing a network with other users in your neighborhood and because the traffic is bidirectional on systems using two-way cable modems, the security of your PC and the network becomes an issue. In most cases, some form of encryption is involved to prevent unauthorized access to the network. CableLabs Certified (DOCSIS) cable modems have built-in encryption, but older one-way modems might not have this feature.

If you use an operating system such as 32-bit Windows that has built-in peer networking capabilities and your provider doesn't use CableLabs Certified cable modems or some other form of encryption, you might be able to see your neighbors' computers on the network. The operating system has settings that enable you to specify whether other network users can access your drives. If these settings are configured improperly, your neighbors might be able to view, access, and even delete the files on your hard drives. Be sure the technician from the cable company installing the service addresses this problem if your cable modem hardware doesn't provide encryption. If you want to use a cable modem along with sharing access on your computer (for printing, file storage, and so on), I'd recommend that you use passwords for any shared drives, but you're even safer if you disable file and printer sharing on the system you connect to the cable modem.

▶▶   For more information on securing any type of Internet access, see "Securing Your Internet Connection," p. 1079.

Digital Subscriber Line

The biggest rival to the cable modem in the broadband Internet business is the digital subscriber line (DSL). DSL, like its predecessor ISDN, appeals to the telephone companies who might be able to use the existing POTS wiring to provide high-speed Internet access. Not every type of DSL is suitable for existing wiring; however, all but the fastest, most expensive types can sometimes be used with the existing POTS plant. DSL is also appealing to businesses that don't have access to cable modems but are looking for a high-performance, lower-cost alternative to the expensive ISDN services that top out at 128Kbps.

Note

Some technical discussions of DSL refer to xDSL. The x stands for the various versions of DSL being proposed and offered by local telephone companies and ISPs. DSL generally is used to refer to any type of digital subscriber line service.

One advantage of DSL compared to its most popular rival—cable modems—is that cable modems share common bandwidth, which means that a lot of simultaneous use by your neighbors can slow down your connection. If you use DSL you don't have this concern; whatever bandwidth speed you pay for is yours—period.

How DSL Works

DSL takes advantage of the broadband nature of the telephone system, using the system's capability to carry signals at multiple frequencies to allow both high-speed Internet traffic and phone calls at the same time. Two methods for sending and receiving signals are used by the most common type of DSL, Asymmetric DSL (ADSL):

- Carrierless Amplitude/Phase (CAP)
- Discrete Multitone (DMT)

Most early DSL installations used CAP, which splits the telephone line into three frequency bands. Exact frequency usage varies by system, but most typically, the divisions resemble the following:

- Voice calls use frequencies from 30Hz to 4KHz. This frequency is also used by answering machines, fax machines, and alarm systems.
- Upstream data such as Web page requests and sent email uses frequencies between 25Hz and 160Hz.
- Downstream data such as received Web pages and email uses frequencies between 240KHz and 1.5MHz.

Some systems use the 300Hz–700Hz range for downstream data and frequencies of 1MHz and above for upstream data.

Because voice, downstream, and upstream data use different frequencies, you can talk, surf, and send email at the same time.

DMT, the system used by most recent ADSL installations, divides the telephone line into 247 channels that are 4KHz wide. If a particular channel has problems, a different channel with better signal quality is used automatically. Unlike CAP, DMT uses some channels starting at around 8KHz to send and receive information.

Both types of signaling can have problems with interference from telephones and similar devices, so devices called *low-pass filters* are used to prevent telephone signals from interfering with signals above the 4KHz range, where DSL signals begin. The location of these filters depends on the type of DSL you use and whether you are installing DSL service yourself.

At the central switch, DSL data is transferred to a device called a *DSL access multiplexer (DSLAM)*, which transfers outgoing signals to the Internet and sends incoming signals to the correct DSL *transceiver* (the correct name for the so-called "DSL modem" that connects to your computer).

Who Can Use DSL—and Who Can't

DSL services are slowly rolling out across the country, first to major cities and then to smaller cities and towns. As with 56Kbps modems, rural and small-town users are probably out of luck and should consider satellite-based or fixed wireless Internet services where available for a faster-than-56Kbps experience.

Just as distance to a telephone company's central switch (CS) is an important consideration for people purchasing an ISDN connection, distance also affects who can use DSL in the markets offering it. For example, most DSL service types require that you be within about 18,000 feet (about 3 miles) wire distance to a telco offering DSL; some won't offer it if you're beyond 15,000 feet wire distance because the speed drops significantly at longer distances. Repeaters or a local loop that has been extended by the telco with fiber-optic line might provide longer distances. The speed of your DSL connection varies with distance: The closer you are to the telco, the faster your DSL access is. Many telcos that offer some type of DSL service provide Web sites that help you determine whether, and what type of, DSL is available to you.

If you want to locate DSL service providers in your area, compare rates, and see reviews from users of the hundreds of ISPs now providing DSL service, set your browser to http://www.dslreports.com. The site provides a verdict on many of the ISPs reviewed, summarizing users' experiences and ranking each ISP in five categories.

Note

If you want to connect DSL to your SOHO or office LAN, check first to see what the provider's attitude is. Some users report good cooperation, whereas others indicate they were told "we can't help you" or were told that DSL "couldn't be connected to a LAN." Again, check around for the best policies. Low-cost switch/router combinations from companies such as Linksys and D-Link and Microsoft's Internet Connection Sharing provide relatively easy ways to share both DSL and other types of high-speed connections.

Even if your telco's central switch is well within wire distance range of your location, that's no guarantee that you qualify for DSL service. The design and condition of the wiring plant connecting your location with the central switch can prevent you from qualifying for DSL service. Because DSL service depends on successful sending and receiving of high-frequency data, a telephone wiring plant that blocks high-frequency signals can't be used for DSL service. Some of the typical issues with telephone lines that aren't DSL-friendly include

- *Loading coils*. These amplifiers boost voice signals and are sometimes called voice coils. Unfortunately, these block the high-frequency signals needed by DSL service.

- *Bridge taps*. Used to extend service to new customers without running separate lines all the way back to the central switch. Bridge taps can create a circuit that's too long for DSL service.

- *Fiber-optic cables*. Used to carry a lot of signals in a small physical space, fiber-optic cables use analog-to-digital (A/D) and digital-to-analog (D/A) converters where they connect to copper telephone lines. A/D and D/A converters can't pass DSL signals through to their destinations.

Major Types of DSL

Although the term *DSL* is used in advertising and popular discussions to refer to any form of DSL, many, many variations of DSL are used in different markets and for different situations. This section discusses the most common forms of DSL and provides a table that compares the various types of DSL service. Although many types of DSL service exist, you can choose only from the service types offered by your DSL provider:

- *ADSL (Asymmetrical DSL).* The type of DSL used most often, especially in residential installations. Asymmetrical means that downstream (download) speeds are much faster than upstream (upload) speeds. For most users, this is no problem because downloads of Web pages, graphics, and files are the major use of Internet connections. Maximum downstream speeds are up to 9Mbps, with up to 640Kbps upstream. Most vendors who offer ADSL provide varying levels of service at lower speeds and prices, as well. Voice calls are routed over the same wire using a small amount of bandwidth, making a single-line service that carries voice and data possible. ADSL is more expensive to set up than some other forms of DSL because a splitter must be installed at the customer site, meaning that you must pay for a service call (also called a truck roll) as part of the initial setup charge.

- *CDSL (Consumer DSL).* A slower (1Mbps downstream) form of DSL that was developed by modem chipset maker Rockwell. It doesn't require a service call because no splitter is required at the customer site.

- *G.Lite (Universal DSL, and also called DSL Lite or Splitterless DSL).* Another version that splits the line at the telco end rather than at the consumer end. Downstream speeds range from 1.544Mbps to 6.0Mbps, and upstream speeds can be from 128Kbps to 384Kbps. This is becoming one of the most popular forms of DSL because it enables consumers to use self-install kits. Note that the DSL vendor might cap the service at rates lower than those listed earlier in the chapter; check with the vendor for details.

- *SDSL (Symmetrical DSL).* This type of DSL service provides the same speed for upstream as for downstream service. Generally, SDSL is offered to business rather than residential customers because it requires new cabling (rather than reusing existing phone lines). A long-term contract frequently is required.

Table 19.2 summarizes the various types of DSL.

Table 19.2   DSL Type Comparison

DSL Type	Description	Data Rate Downstream; Upstream	Distance Limit	Application
IDSL	ISDN Digital Subscriber Line	128Kbps	18,000 feet on 24-gauge wire	Similar to the ISDN BRI service but data only (no voice on the same line)
CDSL	Consumer DSL from Rockwell	1Mbps downstream; less upstream	18,000 feet on 24-gauge wire	Splitterless home and small business service; similar to DSL Lite
DSL Lite (same as G.Lite)	Splitterless DSL	From 1.544Mbps to 6Mbps downstream, depending on the subscribed service	18,000 feet on 24-gauge wire	Sacrifices speed for not having to install splitters
HDSL	High bit-rate Digital Subscriber Line	1.544Mbps duplex on two twisted-pair lines; 2.048Mbps duplex on three twisted-pair lines	12,000 feet on 24-gauge wire	T-1/E1 service between server and phone company or within a company

Table 19.2   Continued

DSL Type	Description	Data Rate Downstream; Upstream	Distance Limit	Application
SDSL	Symmetric DSL	1.544Mbps duplex (U.S. and Canada); 2.048Mbps (Europe) on a single-duplex line downstream and upstream	12,000 feet on 24-gauge wire	Same as for HDSL but requiring only one line of twisted pair
ADSL	Asymmetric Digital Subscriber Line	1.544Mbps to 8.448Mbps downstream; 16Kbps to 640Kbps upstream	1.544Mbps at 18,000 feet; 2.048Mbps at 16,000 feet; 6.312Mbps at 12,000 feet; 8.448Mbps at 9,000 feet	The most common DSL used for Internet access
VDSL	Very High Digital Subscriber Line	12.9Mbps to 52.8Mbps downstream; 1.6Mbps to 2.3Mbps upstream	4,500 feet at 12.96Mbps; 3,000 feet at 25.82Mbps; 1,000 feet at 51.84Mbps	ATM networks; Fiber to the Neighborhood

With any type of DSL, an external device called a DSL *modem* is attached to the computer through either of the following:

■ A crossover cable running to a 10BASE-T or 10/100 Ethernet card or port in the computer

■ A USB cable running to a USB port in the computer

An RJ-11 (standard telephone) cable is attached between the DSL modem and the RJ-11 port that has been set up for DSL service.

To prevent telephone signals from interfering with DSL frequencies, splitters or microfilters must be installed on a DSL line. If you choose a technician-installed form of DSL, a device called a *splitter* is used at your location to prevent interference. Splitter-based DSL allows faster speeds than splitterless DSL installations, but the wait for a technician to show up and add the splitter can add days or weeks to your installation process.

If you self-install DSL, you will install small devices called *microfilters* to block interference from telephones, answering machines, and similar devices. These devices might fit behind the faceplate of the wall outlet used for DSL service or inline between the phone, answering machine, or fax machine and the wall outlet (see Figure 19.2).

Tip

If you have a security system attached to your telephone line, watch out for problems if you select DSL as your preferred broadband access method. Security systems are often designed to seize the line, interrupting a phone call in progress to send an alarm to the security company. This feature won't work with normal microfilters, so you should purchase a special DSL Alarm filter to allow your alarm system to coexist with your DSL installation. Get more information about the alarm microfilter and alternative DSL installation options from `www.hometech.com/learn/dsl.html`.

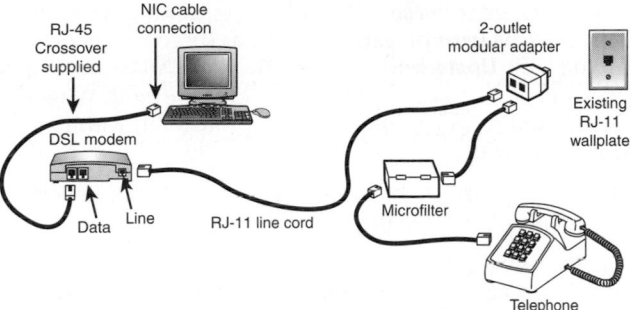

DSL Installation with In-line Microfilter

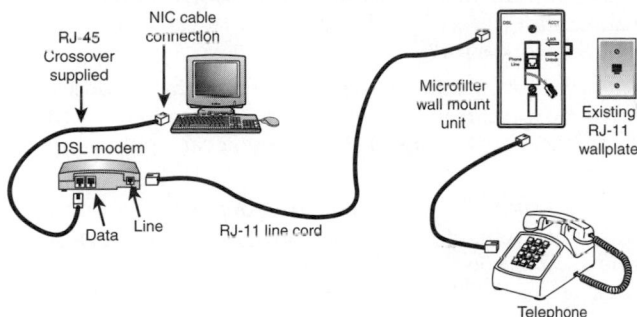

DSL Installation with Wall Outlet Microfilter

Figure 19.2 Two types of DSL self-installations; if a splitter is used to set up a separate DSL line, the microfilters shown here are not necessary.

DSL Pricing

DSL pricing varies widely, with different telephone companies offering different speeds of DSL and different rates. One thing that's true about the most commonly used flavors of DSL is that they are usually an asymmetrical service—with download speeds faster than upload speeds. ADSL installations can typically be run over existing copper wires, whereas SDSL installations usually require that new high-quality copper wires be installed between the CO and the subscriber's location.

For unlimited use, typical residential DSL pricing ranges anywhere from $30 to $80 a month depending on whether you want a static or dynamic IP address and the download speed, which ranges from 256Kbps to 1.5Mbps. Business DSL pricing ranges from $50 to as high as $500 per month.

The wide variance is partly due to the upload speeds permitted. The lower-cost plans typically use a lower upload speed (some variation on ADSL or G.Lite); in contrast, the more expensive plans often use SDSL. Check carefully with your vendor because your traditional telephone company might not be the only DSL game in town. Some major cities might have as many as half a dozen vendors selling various flavors of DSL.

DSL Security Issues

Unlike other types of broadband access, DSL is a direct one-to-one connection that isn't shared; you have no digital "neighbors" who could casually snoop on your activities. However, as with any broadband "always-on" connection, intrusion from the Internet to your computer is a very real possibility.

▶▶ For more information on securing any type of Internet access, see "Securing Your Internet Connection," p. 1079.

Technical Problems with DSL

Telecommunications has always had its share of difficulties, starting with the incredibly slow and trouble-plagued 300bps modems used on early PCs, but as speed increases, so do problems. DSL connections are often very difficult to get working correctly because DSL, as you've seen, combines the problems of adding high-speed data access to the telephone line with network configuration using TCP/IP (the most powerful and most complex network protocol in widespread use; see Chapter 20, "Local Area Networking," for details).

A review of comments from DSL users in various forums, such as DSLReports.com and others, shows that the most common problems include the following:

- *Poor coordination between the DSL sales department of the telco or third-party provider and the installers.* This can lead to broken or very late appointments for installation; if possible, contact the installer company to verify the appointment. If possible, opt for a self-install version of DSL to avoid problems with late or missing appointments.

- *Installers who install the hardware and software and then leave without verifying it works properly.* Ask whether the installer carries a notebook computer that can test the line; don't let the installer leave until the line is working.

- *Poor technical support before and after installation.* Record the IP address and other information used during the installation; read reviews and tips from sources listed earlier in the chapter to help you find better DSL providers and solutions you can apply yourself or ask your telco or provider to perform.

- *Lower speeds than anticipated.* This can be due to a poor-quality connection to the telco from your home or business or problems at the central switch; ask the installer to test the line for you during initial installation and tell you the top DSL speed the line can reach. On a healthy line, the problem is often traceable to a very low value for the Windows Registry key called RWIN (receive window), which should be adjusted from its default of 8192 (8KB) to a value as high as 32768 (32KB) or even 65535 (64KB). If your system previously was used with a dialup modem, the value for RWIN can be as low as 2144; low values force your DSL connection to receive data at rates hardly faster than those for a dialup modem connection. For interactive tests that will help you find the best value to use for RWIN or other Registry options, find line problems, and adjust your configuration, go to http://www.dslreports.com and follow the DSLR Tools link from the home page.

Because of the problems with trying to retrofit an aging voice-oriented telephone network with high-speed Internet service, many pure DSL companies are having financial problems. Some once-prominent DSL ISPs went out of business in 2000–2001, leading to service cancellations in some cases. Before you sign a long-term contract for DSL service, you should determine what your options are if your telco, DSL line provider, or ISP drops DSL service.

Fixed-Base Wireless Broadband

If cable modem or DSL service isn't available at your location, you still might be able to get broadband Internet service through a fixed wireless broadband Internet provider. These services use various frequencies of microwave signals to connect to the Internet. Most of these are based on the same 2.4GHz frequencies 802.11 Wi-Fi connections use. These services typically require a small directional panel antenna to be mounted at the highest point on your roof and must have a clear line-of-sight view of the transmitter, which is usually mounted on a tower only a few miles away. Such services are therefore local, so you generally need to check your area to see whether they are available. Normally, I recommend fixed-base wireless only if cable modem or DSL service is unavailable, but I'd place it as a better overall choice than satellite service. In general, the initial equipment fees are less than satellite and the signals are more immune to weather problems.

To learn more about fixed-base wireless broadband, see the Technical Reference section on the disc packaged with this book.

Internet Connectivity via Satellite with DirecWAY or StarBand

If you're in an area where cable modem, DSL, or fixed wireless services don't exist, you might be able to use a satellite connection as a last resort. To see whether this is possible, take a look at the southern sky from your home, condo, or apartment building. If you have a good, clear 45° window view to the sky toward the equator and you want fast downloads of big files, a satellite-based service such as DirecWAY or StarBand might be the best (or only viable) high-speed choice for you.

Note

Geosynchronous satellites used for satellite Internet/TV service are visible in the southern sky for users in the Northern Hemisphere (North America, Europe, and Asia); if you're in the Southern Hemisphere (South America, Australia, Africa), these satellites are located in the northern sky.

Depending on the product you choose for satellite Internet, you might be able to use a single dish for both satellite Internet and satellite TV.

Tip

If you want both high-speed Internet access and satellite TV with a single dish, you can add DirecTV to the DirecWAY dish at any time. The StarBand dish can work with both Dish Network (TV) and StarBand (Internet) services in the continental United States and Canada. However, if you decide to add DirecWAY to an existing DirecTV setup, you will need to replace your existing DirecTV dish unless you installed the larger DirecDUO dish (which works with DirecTV and DirecPC or DirecWAY).

DirecWAY

DirecWAY was originally called DirecPC, but Hughes Network Systems renamed it in mid-2001, shortly after rolling out a two-way version of the DirecPC service; this section discusses the two-way service. The original version of DirecPC/DirecWAY was a one-way service that used satellite for downloading and a conventional dialup modem for uploads. Starting in 2002, this was replaced with a two-way satellite connection.

Currently, DirecWAY is advertised at 500Kbps for downloads, although most people experience much higher speeds of 1000Kbps–2000Kbps. Uploads are more limited in speed to about 60Mbps. This might be slower than cable modems or DSL, but satellite connections are often the only available broadband connection for people living away from urban areas.

DirecWAY Requirements

The DirecWAY service requires you to purchase and install a small satellite dish as part of the necessary hardware. It's similar to and slightly larger than the dishes used for satellite TV services, such as DirecTV and DishNetwork. In fact, you can combine DirecTV and DirecWAY service on the same dish in many cases, although generally you are better off keeping them separate. DirecWAY uses a 35" wide DirecWAY satellite dish to send and receive data. The dish is connected to a DW6000 satellite modem, which provides a shareable Ethernet connection to which you can plug an individual PC or a router to share the access on your network for Windows PC, Mac, and other systems. The DW6000 is functionally identical to a cable modem as far as setup and operation is concerned. This means that no custom software is required on the PC end. Older modems connected via USB and required a PC for connection, but those have since been phased out.

Purchasing DirecWAY Service

DirecWAY can be purchased from DirecWAY (www.direcway.com) as well as from partners such as EarthLink (www.earthlink.com).

You can either purchase the equipment up front (installation is included) and then pay a lower monthly fee or pay a higher monthly fee and avoid the greater upfront costs. Either way, you have to accept a minimum 15-month contract with penalties for early termination.

DirecWAY's FAP—Brakes on High-speed Downloading?

A big concern for those wanting to exploit the high-speed download feature continues to be DirecWAY's Fair Access Policy (FAP). FAP uses unpublished algorithms to determine who is "abusing" the service with large downloads. This has proven to be a controversial feature. For example, the current guidelines for residential customers state that you might experience the FAP if the cumulative requested downloads in a 1-hour to 4-hour time period exceeds 169MB. The restrictions are lifted within 8–12 hours of the original application of the FAP if the usage in that period stays below the FAP threshold. The limits are higher for business customers. For a more detailed discussion of the real-world impact of FAP on both residential and business users and software you can use to track downloading, see the Fair Access Policy page at http://www.copperhead.cc/fap.html.

Note

Because different satellites are used by the different DirecWAY partners, it pays to research which DirecWAY versions perform best. In addition to the DirecPC/DirecWAY newsgroup, check out the DirecPC Uncensored! Web site at **www. copperhead.cc** as well as the forums on **www.dslreports.com** for speed tests and tweaks you can make to your system.

You can also use the freeware FAPBuster software available from **http://home.mindspring.com/~testftptest/** to help track usage and determine when you are close to exceeding FAP.

StarBand

In April 2000, StarBand—the first consumer-oriented two-way satellite network—was introduced after being tested as Gilat-At-Home. After some initial teething pains, StarBand has achieved success but is not as popular as DirecWAY. Even so, the feature set of StarBand in its current two-way form is almost identical to DirecWAY.

StarBand provides download speeds ranging from 500Kbps to 1000Kbps and upload speeds ranging from 50Kbps to 100Kbps, depending on the satellite modem used. StarBand's satellite modems include the new StarBand Model 480Pro, released in early 2003. The 480Pro contains a four-port router and can be used with non-Windows operating systems. StarBand has partnered with several other companies, including SIA (satellite-internet-access.net) and US Online (www.usonline.com). StarBand equipment pricing and monthly service fees are generally similar to DirecWAY's two-way price structure, although some vendors might offer special promotional packages and bundles.

Tip

You can find excellent tips, tricks, utility software, and user-provided help at the StarBand Users Web site (**www. starbandusers.com**) as well as **www.dslreports.com**.

DirecWAY and StarBand services work as shown in Figure 19.3.

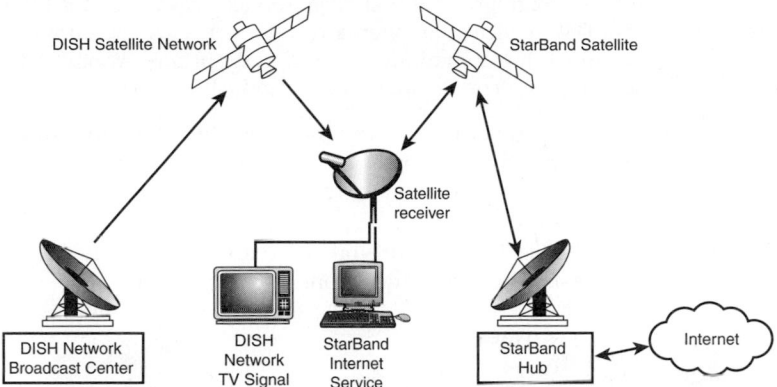

Figure 19.3 The DirecWay and StarBand services can receive both TV programs (left) and Internet traffic (right) with a single 24"×36" satellite dish.

Real-world Satellite Performance

Benchmark addicts will find that satellite Internet access performs poorly on ping tests because the complex pathway your data must travel (ground to space and back again) results in pings taking at least 400ms–600ms. Interactive benchmarks are also disappointing. The delays caused by communicating with a geosynchronous satellite over 22,500 miles in space make satellite a poor choice for these applications, although download speeds are significantly faster than dialup modems. Speeds vary widely, but speeds of 1000Kbps are common, and some can reach download speeds of more than 2000Kbps. To achieve results like this, use the tips available on the various forums and sites covering satellite connections to adjust your system's configuration.

Weather can be a problem for satellite connections, but not in the way you might think. Clouds and storms don't generally affect the signal, unless the storm is so severe you should probably be taking shelter anyway. What can be a problem, however, is snow and ice accumulation on the dish. If you live in an area where it snows, you can have signal problems even though the sky is clear; those problems are invariably caused by snow and ice accumulation on the dish. With that in mind, try to have the dish mounted in a location where you can periodically get to it to brush off any snow and ice accumulation.

Because of the higher latency, slower overall speeds, greater equipment costs, and sensitivity to snow and ice, few would recommend satellite service when alternatives are available. But when the only alternatives are dialup or having an expensive T1 line, satellite is certainly more attractive than the alternatives. Although the costs are higher than cable modem or DSL access, satellite might be the only even remotely cost-effective option for people outside urban areas. Many people have creatively adapted the dishes for use on a recreational vehicle (RV) when stationary or in various tripods and platforms for use while camping.

Integrated Services Digital Network

The connection speed of dialup modems is limited by Shannon's Law (see the section "56Kbps Modems," later in this chapter). To surpass the speed limitations of dialup modems, you need to use digital signals. Integrated Services Digital Network (ISDN) was the first step in the move to digital telecommunications. With ISDN, you can connect to the Internet at speeds of up to 128Kbps. Because ISDN was developed by the telephone companies, you can purchase a variety of service plans. Depending on the ISDN service you choose, you can use it strictly for Internet service or use it to service multiple telephony applications such as voice, fax, and teleconferencing.

Depending on where you live, you might find that ISDN service is available for Internet uses, or your local telco might offer faster DSL service as an alternative. Because ISDN was not originally designed for Internet use, its speed is much lower than other broadband options. Also, ISDN costs about twice what a typical ADSL or cable modem connection costs per month.

ISDN doesn't require as high a line quality as DSL, so it can be offered in areas where DSL can't work without a major upgrade of the telephone system.

How Standard ISDN Works

Because ISDN carries three channels, it allows integrated services that can include combinations such as voice+data, data+data, voice+fax, fax+data, and so on (see Figure 19.4).

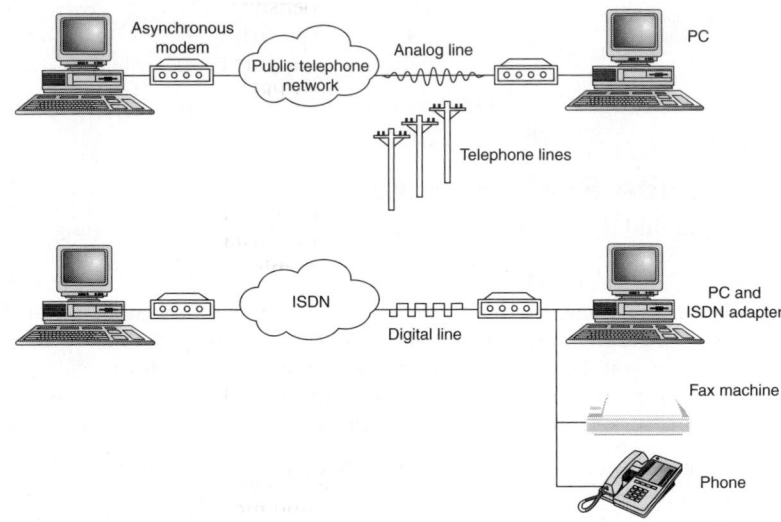

Figure 19.4 A dialup modem connection (top) connects only your PC to the Internet or other online services, whereas ISDN (bottom) can connect your computer, fax, and many other devices via a single ISDN terminal adapter.

On a standard ISDN connection, bandwidth is divided into bearer channels (B channels) that run at 64Kbps and a delta channel (D channel) that runs at either 16Kbps or 64Kbps, depending on the type of service. The B channels carry voice transmissions or user data, and the D channel carries control traffic. In other words, you talk, surf, or fax through the B-channel lines.

Two types of ISDN service exist: basic rate interface (BRI) and primary rate interface (PRI). The BRI service is intended for private and home users and consists of two B channels and one 16Kbps D channel, for a total of 144Kbps. The typical BRI service enables you to use one B channel to talk at 64Kbps and one B channel to run your computer for Web surfing at 64Kbps. Hang up the phone, and both B channels become available. If your ISDN service is configured appropriately, your Web browsing becomes supercharged because you're now running at 128Kbps.

The PRI service is oriented more toward business use, such as for PBX connections to the telephone company's central office. In North America and Japan, the PRI service consists of 23 B channels and 1 64Kbps D channel for a total of 1536Kbps, running over a standard T-1 interface. In Europe, the PRI service is 30 B channels and 1 64Kbps D channel, totaling 1984Kbps, which corresponds to the E1 telecommunications standard. For businesses that require more bandwidth than one PRI connection provides, 1 D channel can be used to support multiple PRI channels using non-facility associated signaling (NFAS).

The BRI limit of two B channels might seem limiting to anyone other than a small office or home office user, but this is misleading. The BRI line can actually accommodate up to eight ISDN devices, each with a unique ISDN number. The D channel provides call routing and "on-hold" services, also called *multiple call signaling*, allowing all the devices to share the two B channels.

Note

When speaking of ISDN connections, 1 kilobyte equals 1,000 bytes, not 1,024 bytes as in standard computer applications.

As you saw earlier, this is also true of speed calculations for modems. Calculations that use 1,000 as a base are often referred to as *decimal* kilobytes, whereas the ones based on 1,024 are now called *kibibytes* or *binary* kilobytes.

If you need a more powerful, more flexible (and more expensive) version of ISDN, use the PRI version along with a switching device, such as a PBX or server. Although PRI allows only one device per B channel, it can dynamically allocate unused channels to support high-bandwidth uses, such as video-conferencing, when a switching device is in use along with PRI.

Acquiring ISDN Service

To have an ISDN connection installed, you must be within 18,000 wire feet (about 3.4 miles or 5.5km) of the CO (telco central office or central switch) for the BRI service; *wire feet* refers to the distance traveled by the telephone wires serving your location, not straight-line distance. For greater distances, expensive repeater devices are needed, and some telephone companies might not offer the service at all.

Prices for ISDN service vary widely depending on your location. In the United States, the initial installation fee can range from $35 to $150, depending on whether you are converting an existing line or installing a new one. The monthly charges typically range from $30 to $50, and sometimes you must pay a connect-time charge as well, ranging from 1 to 6 cents per minute or more, depending on the state. Keep in mind that you also must purchase an ISDN terminal adapter for your PC and possibly other hardware as well, and these charges are only for the telephone company's ISDN service. In addition, you must pay your ISP for access to the Internet at ISDN speeds. Typically, when all charges are included, you can pay up to $100 or more per month for ISDN service in a residential setting, and more for a small business connection. Residential plans are often dialup, requiring you to make a connection to the ISP's server every time you want to go online, whereas business plans are usually always-on, with immediate connection.

Note

Although ISDN Internet access provided by your local telephone company usually has a single price for the ISDN line and ISDN Internet access, most third-party ISDN ISPs provide pricing for only Internet access. These costs might appear to be much less expensive at startup and per month than what the telco's ISDN package costs, but this is misleading because the telco's charges for ISDN service aren't included. Add up the costs from both the ISP and the telephone company for a true picture of third-party ISDN Internet service pricing.

Because ISDN pricing plans offer many options depending on the channels you want and how you want to use them, be sure you carefully plan how you want to use ISDN. Check the telco's Web site for pricing and package information to get a jump on the decision-making process. Although ISDN is unique among broadband Internet services for its capability to handle both voice and data traffic, its relatively high cost and low speed make it a poor choice for most small-office and home-office users.

ISDN Hardware

To connect a PC to an ISDN connection, you must have a hardware component called a *terminal adapter (TA)*. The terminal adapter takes the form of an expansion board or an external device connected to a serial port, much like a modem. In fact, terminal adapters often are mistakenly referred to as ISDN modems. Actually, they are not modems at all because they do not perform analog/digital conversions.

Because an ISDN connection originally was designed to service telephony devices, most ISDN terminal adapters have connections for telephones, fax machines, and similar devices, as well as for your computer. Some terminal adapters can also be used as routers to enable multiple PCs to be networked to the ISDN connection.

Caution

To achieve the best possible performance, you should either purchase an external ISDN terminal adapter that connects to your computer's USB port or use an internal version. A terminal adapter with compression enabled easily can exceed a serial port's capability to reliably send and receive data. Consider that even a moderate 2:1 compression ratio exceeds the maximum rated speed of 232Kbps, which most high-speed COM ports support. USB 1.1 ports, on the other hand, can handle signals up to 12Mbps, easily supporting even the fastest ISDN connection. USB 2.0 ports available on the latest computers support speeds up to 480Mbps.

Note

For more information about ISDN hardware and configuration, see *Upgrading and Repairing PCs, 11th Edition*, available in electronic form on the disc packaged with this book.

Comparing High-speed Internet Access

One way of making sense out of the confusing morass of plans available from cable modem, DSL, fixed wireless Internet, and satellite vendors is to calculate the average cost per Kbps of data downloaded ($/Kbps). You can calculate this figure yourself by dividing the service cost ($SC) per month by the rated or average speed of the service ($SPD):

$SC / $SPD = $/Kbps

For example, a typical cable modem service costs $50 per month, including cable modem lease, and has an average (not peak) speed of 500Kbps. Divide $50 by 500Kbps, and the cost per Kbps equals 10 cents.

Use this formula with any broadband or dialup service to find the best values. Don't forget to calculate the cost of required equipment (as in the example). If you must pay for equipment or installation upfront—as you will need to do with satellite, fixed wireless, and ISDN Internet plans—divide the upfront cost by the number of months you plan to keep the service and add the result to the monthly service charge to get an accurate figure.

How does a typical 56Kbps modem compare, assuming 50Kbps download speeds? Using Juno Web ($14.95 per month) and assuming no charge for a dialup modem, the cost per Kbps is 29.9 cents per Kbps—almost three times as much for service that is at least 10 times slower than a typical cable modem.

Generally, the services stack up as shown in Table 19.3, from slowest to fastest when download speeds are compared.

Table 19.3   Comparing Typical Speeds for Various Types of Internet Connections

Connection Type	Speed (Kbps)	Connection Type	Speed (Kbps)
V.34 dialup	33.6/33.6	Basic DSL	384/128
V.90/92 dialup	53/33.6	Satellite (two-way)	500/60
ISDN (1BRI)	64/64	Premium DSL	3000/128
ISDN (2BRI)	128/128	Premium wireless	3000/256
Basic wireless	256/256	Cable modem	3000/384

The values in this table indicate various vendor maximum ratings; maximum values available in your area will depend on specific vendors and offerings. These figures do not indicate actual average speeds and do not take into account turn-around (ping) speeds or other issues such as network traffic.

Another way to compare Internet connection types is by feature, as in Table 19.4.

Table 19.4 Comparing High-speed Internet Access by Feature

Service	Always On?	Reliability Affected By?	Connection to Network
Cable modem	Yes	Cable outages	Ethernet
DSL	Yes	Phone line outages	Ethernet
Fixed wireless	Yes	Transmitter outages; obstructions	Ethernet
Satellite (two-way)	Yes	Weather; satellite outages	Ethernet

Having a Backup Plan in Case of Service Interruptions

Because no high-speed connection is immune to service interruptions, you should consider having some type of backup plan in place in case of a significant service outage.

If your high-speed Internet access uses an ISP that can also accept dialup connections, you can use your regular modem for emergencies. However, this might require an extra charge in some cases. You could also consider using a free trial subscription to an ISP that uses a conventional modem. If you temporarily switch to a different ISP—especially one that uses its own client, such as AOL—be sure to back up your current Internet configuration information before you install the client software. Your best bet is to use an Internet-only ISP whose dialup connection can be configured manually with the Dialup Networking Connection Wizard or Network Setup Wizard in XP. Then, you can construct a new connection without destroying your existing configuration.

If you don't want to spend $15–$25/month for an additional dialup service, or if you travel occasionally and want a low-cost way to work online when you're away from broadband, consider using a broadband vendor who also offers dialup connections such as EarthLink (www.earthlink.com) or SpeakEasy (www.speakeasy.net). Having both broadband and dialup access is essential for those who travel because broadband connections are not always available when on the road. Also, if your broadband connection goes down for some reason, you can usually check the broadband carrier or network status online using a dialup connection to access the company's Web pages.

Note

Each type of Internet connection uses a particular combination of TCP/IP settings. TCP/IP is the protocol (software rules) used by all computers on the Internet. TCP/IP is covered in Chapter 20, but for now keep in mind that different TCP/IP settings are required for modem access and access through a NIC or USB port device (cable modem, DSL, and DirecWAY or StarBand). Modems usually have an IP address provided dynamically by the ISP when the modem connects with the ISP. The other types of Internet access devices might have static IP addresses that don't change or have dynamically assigned IP addresses. IP addresses are just one of the network settings that, if changed, prevent you from connecting to the Internet.

Leased Lines

For users with high bandwidth requirements (and deep pockets), dedicated leased lines provide digital service between two locations at speeds that can far exceed ISDN and are as fast or faster than DSL or cable modem. A *leased line* is a permanent 24-hour connection to a particular location that can be changed only by the telephone company. Businesses use leased lines to connect LANs in remote locations or to connect to the Internet through a service provider. Leased lines are available at various speeds, as described in the following sections.

T-1 and T-3 Connections

To connect networks in distant locations, networks that must support a large number of Internet users, or especially organizations that will be hosting their own Internet services, a T-1 connection might be a wise investment. A *T-1* is a digital connection running at about 1.5Mbps. This is more than 10 times faster than an ISDN link and is more than double the speed of most fast DSL connections. A T-1 can be split (or fractioned), depending on how it is to be used. It can be split into 24 individual 64Kbps lines or left as a single high-capacity pipeline. Some ISPs allow you to lease any portion of a T-1 connection that you want (in 64Kbps increments). SBC (formerly Ameritech), for example, offers a flexible T-1 service it calls DS1; it's available at full bandwidth or in various fractional sizes. Figure 19.5 shows how a T-1 line is fractioned.

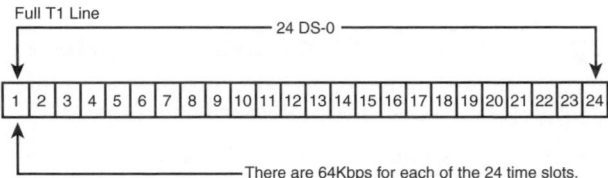

Figure 19.5 Full T-1 service uses all 24 lines (each one is 64Kbps) as a single pipeline; a fractional T-1 service of 256Kbps could use slots 1–4 only, for example.

An individual user of the Internet interacts with a T-1 line only indirectly. No matter how you're accessing the Internet (dialup modem, ISDN, DSL, cable modem, DirecWAY, StarBand, or fixed-base wireless), your ISP typically will have a connection to one or more T-1 or T-3 lines, which connect to the backbone of the Internet. This connection to the backbone is sometimes referred to as a *point of presence (PoP)*. When you make your connection to the Internet, your ISP shares a small chunk of that T-1 pipe with you. Depending on how many other users are accessing the Internet at your ISP or elsewhere, you might experience very fast to slow throughput, even if your modem connection speed remains constant. It's a bit like splitting up a pizza into smaller and smaller slices to accommodate more people at a party: The more users of a high-speed connection, the slower each individual part of it will be. To keep user connections fast while growing, ISPs add full or fractional T-1 lines to their points of presence. Or, they might switch from a T-1 connection to the even faster T-3 if available.

Note

Equivalent in throughput to approximately 28 T-1 lines, a T-3 connection runs at 45Mbps and is suitable for use by very large networks and university campuses. Pricing information falls into the "if-you-have-to-ask-you-can't-afford-it" category.

If your Internet connection is on a corporate LAN or your office is located in a downtown building, your relationship to a T-1 line might be much closer. If your building or office is connected directly to a T-1, you're sharing the capacity of that line with just a relatively few other users rather than with the hundreds or thousands of dialup users a normal ISP is hosting at one time. Full or fractional T-1 lines are being added to more and more apartments and office buildings in major cities to allow residents and workers faster Internet access. In these cases, a LAN connection to the T-1 is usually provided, so your Internet access device is a network card, rather than a modem or ISDN terminal adapter.

With the rise of the Internet and the demand for high-speed data access for networks, the price of T-1 links in the United States has fallen drastically since the late 1990s, although you will still pay in the hundreds of dollars for typical service offerings. T-1 service can be acquired from either your local telco or third-party firms. Fractional T-1 or burstable T-1 (which allows you to have differing levels of bandwidth up to the entire T-1 1.5Mbps depending on demand) costs less than full T-1 service. For a large organization that requires a lot of bandwidth, the lower cost of T-1 services today make installing a higher-capacity service and growing into it—rather than constantly upgrading the link—more economical than ever. Although the speed of T-1 links resembles the maximum rates available with DSL or cable modem service, most types of T-1 service provide constant bandwidth (unlike cable modems) and bypass the potentially severe problems of trying to retrofit old phone lines with digital service (unlike DSL).

Comparing Conventional High-speed Services

Some telcos who formerly posted pricing for ISDN, T-1, or other high-end telecommunications services now have a "call us" button on their Web sites because pricing is complicated by many factors, including

- Location (state and locality because telephone companies are regulated public utilities)
- Fixed and variable costs
- Usage
- Installation costs
- Your needs

Be sure to consider hardware and usage costs when you price services, and (for items such as ISDN terminal adapters and network cards) compare the official offerings with products available elsewhere. If you decide to provide some of the equipment yourself, find out whose responsibility repairs become. Some companies provide lower-cost "value" pricing for services in which you agree to configure the hardware yourself and maintain it. If you have knowledgeable staffers who can handle routers and other network configuration, you can save money every month, but if not, go with the full-service option.

Securing Your Internet Connection

Because any Internet connection must use TCP/IP, which uses built-in logical ports numbered 0–65,535 to service different types of activity, any user of the Internet can be vulnerable to various types of Internet attacks, even if precautions such as turning off drive and folder sharing have been followed. Such vulnerabilities increase drastically with always-on broadband services such as DSL and cable modems.

Steve Gibson of Gibson Research Corporation (makers of the classic SpinRite disk maintenance program) has established a free Web-based service called Shields Up that you should try with *any* Internet-connected PC to see how safe or vulnerable you are.

The Shields Up portion of the Gibson Research Corporation Web site (http://www.grc.com) probes your system's Internet connection security and Internet service ports.

After testing your system, Shields Up provides reviews and recommendations for proxy server and firewall software (such as ZoneAlarm, Norton Internet Security, and Sygate Personal Firewall) that you can use to help secure your system.

With the increasing importance of the Internet and the multiple vulnerabilities we've seen since 2000 to Internet-borne viruses, Trojan horses, and denial-of-service attacks, Shields Up provides a valuable service for *any* Internet user.

Chapter 20 discusses how using a router to share your Internet connection can also help protect your system against intruders.

Note

Proxy servers and firewalls are subjects that go far beyond the scope of this book. If you want to learn more, I suggest you pick up a copy of *Upgrading and Repairing Networks* also published by Que.

Que's *Absolute Beginner's Guide to Personal Firewalls* by Jerry Lee Ford is another excellent resource for users who want to install a personal firewall, such as ZoneAlarm or BlackICE PC Protection, instead of a hardware firewall.

Asynchronous (Dialup) Modems

If you want to connect to the Internet without spending a lot of money, a dialup modem can serve as your on-ramp to the rest of the computing world. Modems are standard equipment with most recent systems and continue to be popular upgrades for systems that do not have access to broadband solutions, such as two-way cable modem or DSL lines. Even with some types of broadband access (such as one-way DirecWAY and one-way cable modem), modems are still needed to send page requests and email.

The word *modem* (from modulator/demodulator) basically describes a device that converts the digital data used by computers into analog signals suitable for transmission over a telephone line and converts the analog signals back to digital data at the destination. To distinguish modems that convert analog and digital signals from other types of access devices, modems are frequently referred to as *analog modems*; because you must dial a telephone number to reach a remote computer, they are also referred to as *dialup modems*. The typical PC modem is an asynchronous device, meaning it transmits data in an intermittent stream of small packets. The receiving system takes the data in the packets and reassembles it into a form the computer can use.

Note

Because it has become such a familiar term, even to inexperienced computer users, the word *modem* is sometimes used to describe devices that are, strictly speaking, not modems at all. For example, earlier in this chapter you read about broadband solutions such as ISDN, cable modems, DirecWAY, DSL, and StarBand. Although all these services use devices commonly called "modems" to connect your PC to fast online services, not all of them convert digital information to analog signals. However, because these devices look similar to a standard modem and are used to connect PCs to the Internet or to other networks, they are called modems.

Asynchronous modems transmit each byte of data individually as a separate packet. One byte equals 8 bits, which, using the standard ASCII codes, is enough data to transmit a single alphanumeric character. For a modem to transmit asynchronously, it must identify the beginning and end of each byte to the receiving modem. It does this by adding a start bit before and a stop bit after every byte of data, thus using 10 bits to transmit each byte (see Figure 19.6). For this reason, asynchronous communications have sometimes been referred to as *start-stop* communications. This is in contrast to synchronous communications, in which a continuous stream of data is transmitted at a steady rate.

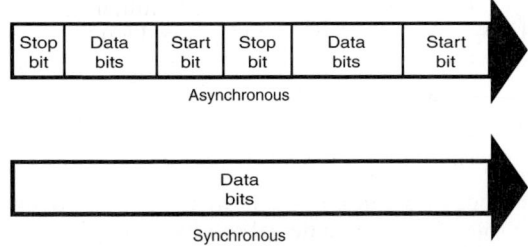

Figure 19.6   Asynchronous modems frame each byte of data with a start bit and a stop bit, whereas synchronous communications use an uninterrupted stream of data.

Synchronous modems generally are used in leased-line environments and in conjunction with multiplexers to communicate between terminals to Unix- or Linux-based servers and mainframe computers. Thus, this type of modem is outside the scope of this book.

Whenever modems are referred to in this book, I will be discussing the asynchronous, analog variety. (Synchronous modems are not found in typical computer stores and aren't included in normal computer configurations, so you might not ever see one unless you go into the data center of a corporation that uses them.)

Note

During high-speed modem communications, the start and stop bits are usually not transmitted over the telephone line. Instead, the modem's data compression algorithm eliminates them. However, these bits are part of the data packets generated by the communications software in the computer, and they exist until they reach the modem hardware. If both ends of a dialup modem connection don't use the same value for start and stop bits, the connection transmits gibberish instead of usable data.

The use of a single start bit is required in all forms of asynchronous communication, but some protocols use more than one stop bit. To accommodate systems with different protocols, communications software products usually enable you to modify the format of the frame used to transmit each byte. The standard format used to describe an asynchronous communications format is parity/data bits/stop bits. Almost all asynchronous connections today are therefore abbreviated as N-8-1 (No parity/8 data bits/ 1 stop bit). The meanings for each of these parameters and their possible variations are as follows:

- *Parity.* Before error-correction protocols became standard modem features, a simple parity mechanism was used to provide basic error checking at the software level. Today, this is almost never used, and the value for this parameter is nearly always set to none. Other possible parity values you might see in a communications software package are odd, even, mark, and space.

- *Data Bits.* This parameter indicates how many bits are actually carried in the data portion of the packet (exclusive of the start and stop bits). PCs typically use 8 data bits, but some types of computers use a 7-bit byte, and others might call for other data lengths. Communications programs provide this option to prevent a system from confusing a stop bit with a data bit.

- *Stop Bits.* This parameter specifies how many stop bits are appended to each byte. PCs typically use 1 stop bit, but other types of protocols might call for the use of 1.5 or 2 stop bits.

In most situations, you will never have to modify these parameters manually, but the controls are almost always provided. In Windows 9x/Me/2000/XP, for example, if you open the Modems control panel and look at the Connection page of your modem's Properties dialog box, you will see Data Bits, Parity, and Stop Bits selectors.

Unless you use the Windows HyperTerminal program to establish a direct connection to another computer via phone lines, you might never need to modify these parameters. However, if you need to call a mainframe computer to perform terminal emulation for e-banking, checking a library's catalog, or working from home, you might need to adjust these parameters. (*Terminal emulation* means using software to make your PC keyboard and screen act like a terminal, such as a DEC VT-100 and so on.) Many mainframe computers use even parity and a 7-bit word length. If your PC is set incorrectly, you'll see garbage text on your monitor instead of the other system's login or welcome screen.

Modem Standards

For two modems to communicate, they must share the same *protocol*. A protocol is a specification that determines how two entities will communicate. Just as humans must share a common language and vocabulary to speak with each other, two computers or two modems must share a common protocol. In the case of modems, the protocol determines the nature of the analog signal the device creates from the computer's digital data.

Bell Labs (which set standards for early 300bps modems) and the CCITT are two of the bodies that have set standards for modem protocols. CCITT is an acronym for Comité Consultatif International Téléphonique et Télégraphique, a French term that translates into English as the Consultative Committee on International Telephone and Telegraph. The organization was renamed the International Telecommunication Union (ITU) in the early 1990s, but the protocols developed under the old name are often referred to as such. Newly developed protocols are called ITU-T standards, which refers to the Telecommunication Standardization Sector of the ITU. Most modems built in recent years conform to the standards developed by the CCITT/ITU.

The ITU, headquartered in Geneva, Switzerland, is an international body of technical experts responsible for developing data communications standards for the world. The group falls under the organizational umbrella of the United Nations, and its members include representatives from major modem manufacturers, common carriers (such as AT&T), and governmental bodies. The ITU establishes communications standards and protocols in many areas, so one modem often adheres to many different standards, depending on its various features and capabilities.

All modems sold today support the following ITU protocols:

- ITU V.90 (modulation)
- ITU V.42 (error correction)
- ITU V.42bis (data compression)

However, earlier modems supported many industry-standard and proprietary protocols for modulation, error correction, and data compression.

Most modems today also support the proprietary Microcom Network Protocol (MNP) MNP10 and MNP10EC error-correction standards to provide better connection during conventional wired and wireless (cellular) communication sessions. The latest modems also support the newest ITU standards: V.92 (modulation) and V.44 (data compression). All current protocols are discussed later in this chapter.

Note

To learn more about earlier industry-standard and proprietary protocols, see Chapter 18 of *Upgrading and Repairing PCs, 11th Edition*, available in electronic form on the disc packaged with this book.

Note

The term *protocol* is also used to describe software standards that must be established between different computers to allow them to communicate, such as TCP/IP.

Modems are controlled through AT commands, which are text strings sent to the modem by software to activate the modem's features. For example, the ATDT command followed by a telephone number causes the modem to dial that number using tone dialing mode. Applications that use modems typically generate AT commands for you, but you can control a modem directly using a communications program with a terminal mode or even the DOS ECHO command.

Because almost every modem uses the AT command set (originally developed by modem-maker Hayes), this compatibility is a given and should not really affect your purchasing decisions about modems. The basic modem commands might vary slightly from manufacturer to manufacturer, depending on a modem's special features, but the basic AT command set is all but universal.

Note

A list of the basic AT commands can be found in the Technical Reference on the disc included with this book. However, the best source for the commands used by your modem is the manual that came with the device.

Although most modem users will never need to review these commands, if you use MS-DOS–based communication programs or some specialized Windows programs, you might be required to enter or edit an *initialization string*, which is a series of AT commands sent to the modem before dialing. If these commands are not correct, the modem will not work with these programs.

Bits and Baud Rates

When discussing modem transmission speeds, the terms *baud rate* and *bit rate* are often confused. Baud rate (named after a Frenchman named Emile Baudot, the inventor of the asynchronous telegraph printer) is the rate at which a signal between two devices changes in 1 second. If a signal between two modems can change frequency or phase at a rate of 300 times per second, for example, that device is said to communicate at 300 baud.

Thus, baud is a signaling rate, not a data-transmission rate. The number of bits transmitted by each baud is used to determine the actual data-transmission rate (properly expressed as bps or Kbps). Modern dialup modems transmit and receive more bits per baud than the original 300bps modems (which also ran at 300 baud).

Note

To learn more about bits versus baud, see Chapter 18 of *Upgrading and Repairing PCs, 11th Edition*, available in electronic form on the disc packaged with this book.

Modulation Standards

Modems start with modulation, which is the electronic signaling method used by the modem. Modulation is a variance in some aspect of the transmitted signal. By modulating the signal using a predetermined pattern, the modem encodes the computer data and sends it to another modem that demodulates (or decodes) the signal. Modems must use the same modulation method to understand each other. Each data rate uses a different modulation method, and sometimes more than one method exists for a particular rate.

Regardless of the modulation method, all modems must perform the same task: Change the digital data used inside the computer (ON-OFF, 1-0) into the analog (variable tone and volume) data used by the telephone company's circuits, which were built over a period of years and were never intended for computer use. That's the "mo(dulate)" in modem. When the analog signal is received by the other computer, the signal is changed back from the analog waveform into digital data (see Figure 19.7). That's the "dem(odulate)" in modem.

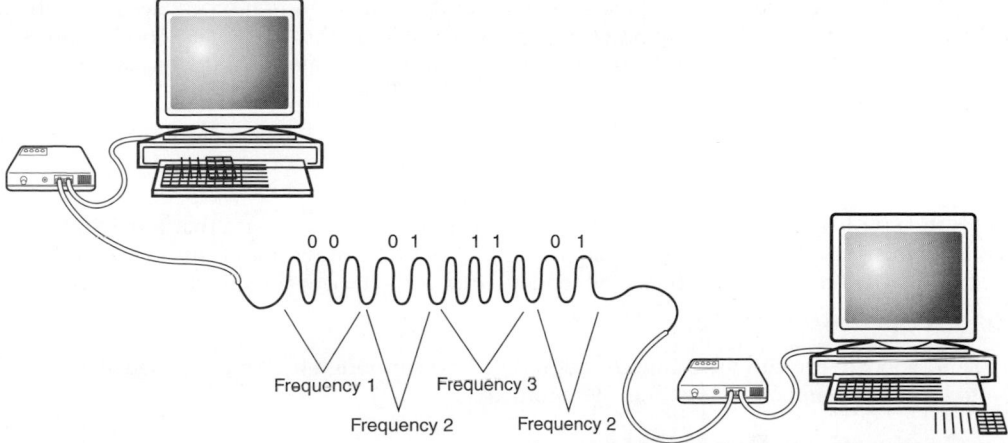

Figure 19.7 The modem at each computer changes digital (computer) signals to analog (telephone) signals when transmitting data or analog back to digital when receiving data.

The three most popular modulation methods are as follows:

- *Frequency-shift keying (FSK).* A form of frequency modulation, otherwise known as FM. By causing and monitoring frequency changes in a signal sent over the phone line, two modems can send information.

- *Phase-shift keying (PSK).* A form of phase modulation in which the timing of the carrier signal wave is altered and the frequency stays the same.

- *Quadrature amplitude modulation (QAM).* A modulation technique that combines phase changes with signal-amplitude variations, resulting in a signal that can carry more information than the other methods.

All modem protocols since ITU V.34 (33.6Kbps maximum speed) up through the current ITU V.90 and ITU V.92 standards (56Kbps maximum speed) are full-duplex protocols. A *full-duplex* protocol is one in which communications can travel in both directions at the same time and at the same speed. A telephone call, for example, is full duplex because both parties can speak at the same time. In *half-duplex* mode, communications can travel in both directions, but only one side can transmit at a time. A radio call in which only one party can speak at a time is an example of half-duplex communications.

These protocols are automatically negotiated between your modem and the modem at the other end of the connection. Basically, the modems start with the fastest protocol common to both and work their way down to a speed/protocol combination that will work under the line conditions existing at the time of the call.

The ITU V.90 and V.92 protocols are the industry-standard protocols most commonly used today; V.92 modems also support V.90.

Note

The 56Kbps standards that represent the highest current increment in modem communication speed require a digital connection at one end and are therefore not purely analog. Other high-speed communication technologies such as ISDN and cable network connections don't perform digital-to-analog conversions, so they should not be called modems, strictly speaking.

V.90

V.90 is the ITU-T designation for a 56Kbps communication standard that reconciles the conflict between the proprietary U.S. Robotics (3Com) x2 and Rockwell K56flex modem specifications developed in 1996 and 1997. The last ISA modems manufactured by major vendors typically support V.90, as do many PC Card and PCI modems built from 1998 to 2001.

▶▶ See "56Kbps Modems," p. 1086.

V.92

V.92 is the ITU-T designation for an improved version of the V.90 standard that provides faster negotiation of the connection, call-waiting support, and faster uploading than is possible with V.90. Most PCI and PC Card modems sold by major vendors since mid-2001 to the present are V.92 compatible.

▶▶ See "56Kbps Modems," p. 1086.

V.90 and V.92 are the current communication protocols supported by ISPs; any modem you want to use today should support at least the V.90 protocol.

Error-Correction Protocols

Error correction refers to the capability of some modems to identify errors during a transmission and to automatically resend data that appears to have been damaged in transit. Although you can implement error correction using software, this places an additional burden on the computer's expansion bus and processor. By performing error correction using dedicated hardware in the modem, errors are detected and corrected before any data is passed to the computer's CPU.

As with modulation, both modems must adhere to the same standard for error correction to work. Fortunately, most modem manufacturers use the same error-correction protocols.

V.42, MNP10, and MNP10EC Error-Correction Protocols

The current error-correction protocols supported by modems include Microcom's proprietary MNP10 (developed to provide a better way to cope with changing line conditions) and MNP10EC (an enhanced version developed to enable modems to use constantly changing cellular telephone connections).

V.90 and V.92 modems (as well as some older models) also support the ITU V.42 error-correction protocol, with fallback to the MNP 4 protocol (which also includes data-compression). Because the V.42 standard includes MNP compatibility through Class 4, all MNP 4–compatible modems can establish error-controlled connections with V.42 modems.

This standard uses a protocol called Link Access Procedure for Modems (LAPM). LAPM, similar to MNP, copes with phone-line impairments by automatically retransmitting data corrupted during transmission, ensuring that only error-free data passes between the modems. V.42 is considered to be better than MNP 4 because it offers approximately a 20% higher transfer rate due to its more intelligent algorithms.

Note

For information about the MNP 1–4 protocols, see Chapter 18 of *Upgrading and Repairing PCs, 11th Edition*, included in electronic form on the disc packaged with this book.

Data-Compression Standards

Data compression refers to a built-in capability in some modems to compress the data they're sending, thus saving time and money for modem users. Depending on the type of files the modem is sending, data can be compressed to nearly one-fourth its original size, effectively quadrupling the speed of the modem—at least in theory. This assumes that the modem has V.42bis data compression built in (true since about 1990) *and* that the data hasn't already been compressed by software. Thus, in reality, the higher throughput caused by data compression applies only to HTML and plain-text files on the Web. Graphics and Zip or EXE archives have already been compressed, as have most PDF (Adobe Acrobat Reader) files. Another factor that influences the throughput of a modem is the type of UART chip used by the serial port included in an internal modem or connected to an external modem, or the use of a USB port instead of a serial port.

Note

To learn more, see "Can Non-56Kbps Modems Achieve Throughput Speeds Above 115,200bps?" in the Technical Reference section of the disc packaged with this book.

As with error correction, data compression can also be performed with software. Data can be compressed only once, so if you are transmitting files that are already in a compressed form, such as Zip archives, GIF or JPEG images, or Adobe Acrobat PDF files, there will be no palpable increase in speed from the modem's hardware compression. The transmission of plain-text files (such as HTML pages) and uncompressed bitmaps, however, is accelerated greatly by modem compression.

MNP5 and V.42bis

Current data-compression standards in modems include Microcom's MNP 5 and the ITU V.42bis protocols. V.42bis is a CCITT data-compression standard similar to MNP Class 5, but it provides about 35% better compression. V.42bis is not actually compatible with MNP Class 5, but nearly all V.42bis modems include the MNP 5 data-compression capability as well.

V.42bis is superior to MNP 5 because it analyzes the data first and then determines whether compression would be useful. V.42bis compresses only data that needs compression. MNP 5, on the other hand, always attempts to compress the data, which slows down throughput on previously compressed files.

To negotiate a standard connection using V.42bis, V.42 also must be present. Therefore, a modem with V.42bis data compression is assumed to include V.42 error correction. When combined, these two protocols result in an error-free connection that has the maximum data compression possible.

V.44

At the same time that the V.92 protocol was introduced by the ITU in mid-2000, a companion data-compression protocol called V.44 was also introduced by the ITU. V.44 uses a new lossless LZJH compression protocol designed by Hughes Network Systems (developers of the DirecWAY satellite broadband Internet service) to achieve performance more than 25% better than that of V.42. Data throughput with V.44 can reach rates of as much as 300Kbps, compared to 150Kbps–200Kbps with V.42bis. V.42bis was developed in the late 1980s, long before the advent of the World Wide Web, so it is not optimized for Web surfing the way V.44 is. V.44 is especially designed to optimize compression of HTML text pages.

Note

V.44 is the latest compression algorithm to be based in part on the work of mathematicians Abraham Lempel and Jakob Ziv in the late 1970s. Lempel and Ziv's work also has been used in the development of LZW (Lempel-Ziv-Welch) compression for TIFF image files, GIF compressed image files, PKZIP-compatible compression, and other data compression methods.

Proprietary Standards

In addition to the industry-standard protocols for modulation, error correction, and data compression that are generally defined and approved by the ITU-T, several protocols in these areas were invented by various companies and included in their products without any official endorsement by any standards body. Some of these protocols have been quite popular at times and became pseudo-standards of their own. The only proprietary standards that continue to enjoy widespread support are the Microcom MNP standards for error correction and data compression. Others, such as 3Com's HST, CompuCom's DIS, and Hayes' V-series, are no longer popular. For details about the MNP classes, see "MNP Classes" in the Technical Reference section of the disc packaged with this book.

Note

For more information about older proprietary protocols, see Chapter 18 of *Upgrading and Repairing PCs, 11th Edition*, included in electronic form on this book's disc.

56Kbps Modems

At one time, the V.34 annex speed of 33,600bps (33.6Kbps) was regarded as the absolute speed limit for asynchronous modem usage. However, starting in 1996, modem manufacturers began to produce modems that supported speeds of up to 56,000bps. These so-called "56K" or "56Kbps" modems are now universal, although the methods for breaking the 33.6Kbps barrier have changed several times. To understand how this additional speed was achieved, you must consider the basic principle of modem technology—that is, the digital-to-analog conversion.

As you've learned, a traditional modem converts data from digital to analog form so it can travel over the Public Switched Telephone Network (PSTN). At the destination system, another modem converts the analog data back to its digital form. This conversion from digital to analog and back causes some speed loss. Even though the phone line is physically capable of carrying data at 56Kbps or more, the effective maximum speed because of the conversions is about 33.6Kbps. An AT&T engineer named Claude Shannon came up with a law (Shannon's Law) stating that the maximum possible error-free data communications rate over an all-analog PSTN is approximately 35Kbps, depending on the noise present.

However, because many parts of the United States's urban telephone system is digital—being converted to analog only when signals reach the telephone company's central office (or central switch)—it's possible to "break" Shannon's Law and achieve faster download rates. You can, in some cases, omit the initial digital-to-analog conversion and send a purely digital signal over the PSTN to the recipient's CO (see Figure 19.8). Thus, only one digital-to-analog conversion is necessary, instead of two or more. The result is that you theoretically can increase the speed of the data transmission, in one direction only, beyond the 35Kbps specified by Shannon's Law—to nearly the 56Kbps speed supported by the telephone network. Prior to the new ITU V.92 standard, the transmission in the other direction was still limited to the V.34 annex maximum of 33.6Kbps. However, both the modem and the ISP must have support for the ITU V.92 standard to overcome this limitation for uploading speeds.

▶▶ See "ITU V.92 and V.44—Breaking the Upload Barrier," p. 1089, for more information on how the V.92 standard enables faster uploading.

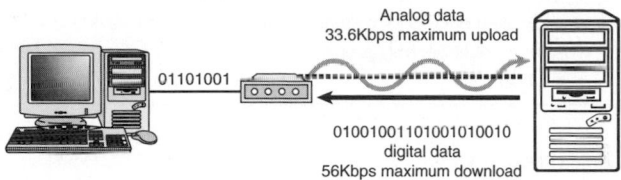

Figure 19.8 V.90-based 56Kbps connections enable you to send data at standard analog modem rates (33.6Kbps maximum) but enable you to receive data nearly twice as fast, depending on line conditions.

56Kbps Limitations

Thus, 56Kbps modems can increase data transfer speeds beyond the limits of V.34 modems, but they are subject to certain limitations. Unlike standard modem technologies, you can't buy two 56Kbps modems, install them on two computers, and achieve 56Kbps speeds. One side of the connection must use a special digital modem that connects directly to the PSTN without a digital-to-analog conversion.

Therefore, 56Kbps modems can be used at maximum speeds only to connect to ISPs or other hosting services that have invested in the necessary infrastructure to support the connection. Because the ISP has the digital connection to the PSTN, its downstream transmissions to your computer are accelerated. If both sides of the connection support standards predating V.92, your communications back to the ISP are not accelerated.

On a practical level, this means you can surf the Web and download files more quickly, but if you host a Web server on your PC, your users will realize no speed gain because the upstream traffic is not accelerated unless you and your ISP both use V.92-compliant modems. If you connect to another regular modem, your connection is made at standard V.34 annex rates (33.6Kbps or less).

Also, only one digital-to-analog conversion can be in the downstream connection from the ISP to your computer. This is dictated by the nature of the physical connection to your local telephone carrier. If additional conversions are involved in your connection, 56Kbps technology will not work for you; 33.6Kbps will be your maximum possible speed.

Note

Although most advertising for 56Kbps modems refers to them as simply "56K" modems, this is inaccurate. "K" is most often used in the computer business to refer to kilobytes. If that were true, a "real" 56K modem would be downloading at 56,000 bytes per second (or 448,000 bits per second)!

With the way the telephone system has had to grow to accommodate new exchanges and devices, even neighbors down the street from each other might have different results when using a 56Kbps modem.

Caution

56Kbps modem communications are highly susceptible to slowdowns caused by line noise. Your telephone line might be perfectly adequate for voice communications and even lower-speed modem communications, but inaudible noise easily can degrade a 56Kbps connection to the point at which there is only a marginal increase over a 33.6Kbps modem, or even no increase at all. If you do have a problem with line noise, getting a surge suppressor with noise filtration might help.

Hotel connections through telephones with data jacks typically provide very slow connections with any type of modem. Even if you have a V.90- or V.92-compliant 56Kbps modem, you will be lucky to achieve even a 24Kbps transmission rate. The analog-to-digital conversions that occur between your room's telephone and the hotel's digital PBX system eliminate the possibility of using any of the 56Kbps standards the modem supports because they depend on a direct digital connection to the central switch (CS).

As an alternative, more and more hotels and motels provide Ethernet-based access to broadband Internet service; a growing number even provide wireless Ethernet access with Wi-Fi/IEEE-802.11b hardware. Depending on the location, you might be able to use your normal Ethernet card or connect to a USB adapter provided by the hotel. If you want high-speed Internet access as part of the package with your next hotel or motel stay, contact the specific lodging location or chain Web site for details and pricing.

Early 56Kbps Standards

To achieve a high-speed connection, both modems and your ISP (or other hosting service to which you connect) must support the same 56Kbps technology. The first 56Kbps chipsets were introduced in late 1996:

- U.S. Robotics's x2 used Texas Instruments (TI) chipsets.
- Rockwell's K56flex was supported by Zoom and other modem makers.

These rival methods for achieving performance up to 56Kbps were incompatible with each other and were replaced in 1998 by the ITU's V.90 standard.

Note

For more information about K56flex and x2, see *Upgrading and Repairing PCs, 11th Edition*, available in electronic format on the disc supplied with this book.

Unfortunately, the 56Kbps name is rather misleading, in regards to actual transmission speeds. Although all 56Kbps modems theoretically are capable of this performance on top-quality telephone lines, the power requirements for telephone lines specified in the FCC's Part 68 regulation limit the top speed of these modems to 53Kbps. The FCC has been considering lifting this speed limitation since the fall of 1998, but it still applies to modems as of early 2003.

V.90

V.90 was introduced on February 5, 1998, and was ratified by the ITU-T on September 15, 1998. Its ratification ended the K56flex/x2 standards "war": Shortly thereafter, most modem manufacturers announced upgrade options for users of x2 and K56flex modems to enable these products to become V.90 compliant.

Some modem vendors offer upgrades for K56flex and x2 modems to the V.90 standard. If you purchased your modem before the V.90 standard became official, see your modem vendor's Web site for information about upgrading to V.90.

ITU V.92 and V.44—Breaking the Upload Barrier

56Kbps protocols, such as the early proprietary x2 and K56flex and the ITU V.90 standard, increased the download speed from its previous maximum of 33.6Kbps to 56Kbps. However, upload speeds, which affect how quickly you can send email, page requests, and file transfers, were not affected by the development of 56Kbps technologies. Upload speeds with any of these 56Kbps technologies are limited to a maximum of 33.6Kbps. This causes severe speed lags for both pure dialup users and those who depend on dialup modems for upstream traffic, such as users of one-way broadband solutions—for example, one-way (Telco Return) cable modems, one-way DirecWAY, and one-way (Telco Return) fixed-base wireless Internet services. Other shortcomings of existing 56Kbps technology include the amount of time it takes the user's modem to negotiate its connection with the remote modem and the lack of uniform support for call-waiting features.

In mid-2000, the ITU unveiled a multifaceted solution to the problem of slow connections and uploads: the V.92 and V.44 protocols (V.92 was previously referred to as V.90 Plus).

V.92, as the name implies, is a successor to the V.90 protocol, and any modem that supports V.92 also supports V.90. V.92 doesn't increase the download speed beyond the 56Kbps barrier, but offers these major features:

- *QuickConnect.* QuickConnect cuts the amount of time needed to make a connection by storing telephone line characteristics and using the stored information whenever the same phone line is used again. For users who connect to the Internet more than once from the same location, the amount of time the modem beeps and buzzes to make the connection will drop from as much as 27 seconds to about half that time. Bear in mind, though, that this reduction in connection time does not come about until after the initial connection at that location is made and its characteristics are stored for future use.

- *Modem-on-Hold.* The Modem-on-Hold feature allows the user to pick up incoming calls and talk for a longer amount of time than the few seconds allowed by current proprietary call-waiting modems. Modem-on-Hold enables the ISP to control how long you can take a voice call while online without interrupting the modem connection; the minimum amount of time supported is 10 seconds, but longer amounts of time (up to unlimited!) are also supported by this feature. Modem-on-Hold also allows you to make an outgoing call without hanging up the modem connection. Modem-on-Hold, similar to previous proprietary solutions, requires that you have the call-waiting feature enabled on your telephone line and also requires that your ISP support this feature of V.92.

Note

Although Modem-on-Hold is good for the Internet user with only one phone line (because it allows a single line to handle incoming as well as outgoing calls), it's not as good for ISPs because when you place your Internet connection on hold, the ISP's modem is not capable of taking other calls. ISPs that support Modem-on-Hold might need to add more modems to maintain their quality of service if this feature is enabled. More modems are necessary because the ISP won't be able to count on users dropping their Internet connections to make or receive voice calls when Modem-on-Hold is available.

- *PCM Upstream.* PCM Upstream breaks the 33.6Kbps upload barrier, boosting upload speed to a maximum of 48Kbps. Unfortunately, because of power issues, enabling PCM Upstream can reduce your downstream (download) speed by 1.3Kbps–2.7Kbps or more. PCM Upstream is an optional feature of V.92, and ISPs who support V.92 connections might not support this feature.

Modems that support V.92 typically also support the V.44 data-compression standard. V.44, which replaces V.42bis, provides for compression of data at rates up to 6:1—that's more than 25% better than V.42bis. This enables V.92/V.44 modems to download pages significantly faster than V.90/V.42bis modems can at the same connection speed.

When will you be able to enjoy the benefits of V.92/V.44? Although most major modem vendors have been offering V.92/V.44-compliant modems since late 2000, ISP interest in this standard has been tepid. Only one national ISP, Navipath (which provided support for many local and regional ISPs), offered V.92 access in 2001, and Navipath went out of business in September 2001. Prodigy began to offer V.92 service early in 2002.

According to the V.92 News & Updates page at Richard Gamberg's Modemsite (`www.modemsite.com/56K/v92s.htm`), many vendors of ISP equipment continue to drag their feet on V.92/V.44 support, in part because it often requires expensive upgrades to terminal equipment. Even after upgrading to support V.92/V.44, some existing terminal hardware is incapable of working with the desirable PCM Upstream feature. Additionally, many major modem vendors have produced so-called "V.92" modems that don't support major V.92 features. Check user reviews available at the Modemsite Web site and others before you buy a particular V.92 modem model.

Tip

Wondering whether it's time to get a V.92/V.44 modem? Before you update your current model or buy a new modem, do the following:

- Contact your ISP to see whether (or when) it plans to support V.92/V.44 and to determine which features will be supported.

- Check the V.92 ISPs listing at (`www.v92.com`) and contact ISPs in your area for more details.

Although the change from x2/K56flex to V.90 was a no-cost one for many modem owners, the upgrade from V.90 to V.92/V.44 isn't as painless. In many cases, only the most recent V.90 modems will be eligible for a free upgrade to V.92/V.44 firmware. Contact your modem vendor for details.

Can your existing V.90-compatible modem be upgraded to V.92/V.44? As with earlier 56Kbps modem standards, the answer will likely be, "It depends." Some Lucent LT Winmodem (Agere Systems) modem drivers for V.90 also might include V.92 commands; see Modemsite's Lucent modem section for the latest information (`http://www.modemsite.com/56k/ltwin.asp`). For modems based on other chipsets, check with your modem vendor.

As with earlier 56Kbps standards, you shouldn't worry about V.92/V.44 support until your ISP announces that it is supporting these standards. Because the V.92 standard has several components, find out which features of V.92 your ISP is planning to support before you look into a modem firmware update or modem replacement.

Fax Modem Standards

Even though the first experimental facsimile equipment was developed at the end of World War II, it took many years for faxing to become commonplace. Similarly, the first fax boards for computers were not introduced until the late 1980s as separate devices. Later, fax capabilities were incorporated into modems. Today, virtually all modems also meet the ITU-T Class 3 fax standards, enabling them to send data to and receive data from other ITU-T Class 3 fax machines and multifunction devices.

Many recent multifunction devices also support the newer ITU-T.30E recommendation for color faxing. Fax modems don't meet this standard as shipped from the manufacturer, but you can download free color fax software developed by HP (Impact ColorFax) that works with most fax modems. Find Impact ColorFax at the BlackICE Software Web site (`www.blackice.com`).

For more information about ITU-T fax protocols, see "ITU-T Fax Protocols" in the Technical Reference on the disc packaged with this book.

Dialup Modem Recommendations

A dialup modem for a PC can take the form either of an external device with its own power supply that plugs into a PC's serial port or USB port or of an internal expansion card you insert into a PCI or PC Card bus slot inside the computer. Very few ISA-slot dialup modems are still on the market because the majority of recent systems no longer have ISA slots. Most manufacturers of modems have both internal and external versions.

External versions are slightly more expensive because they include a separate case and power supply and sometimes require you to buy a serial modem cable or USB cable. The decision as to which type to use should typically depend on whether you have a free bus slot or serial port, whether you have USB ports and Windows 98/Me/2000/XP, how much room you have on your desk, the capabilities of your system's internal power supply, and how comfortable you are with opening up your computer.

I often prefer external modems because of the visual feedback they provide through their LED indicator lights. These lights let you easily see whether the modem is still connected and transmitting or receiving data. However, Windows and many communication programs today include onscreen indicators that provide some of the same information.

In many situations, however, an internal modem is preferable. If you are using an older computer whose serial ports do not have buffered UART chips, such as the 16550, some more advanced controller-based internal modems include an onboard 16550 UART-equivalent controller chip. This onboard UART with the modem saves you the trouble of upgrading the UART serial port. However, controller-less (or "Windows") modems do not include such chips and rely on the processor for their power and speed, which can degrade the performance of other applications while online. External 56Kbps modems can be hampered from achieving their full speeds by the limitations of the computer's serial port. An external USB model or an internal model using the PCI slot might be preferable instead. Use Table 19.5 to see how internal and external units compare.

Table 19.5   External Versus Internal Modems

Features	External	Internal
Price	Higher	Lower
Extras required	Serial or USB cable	Nothing
Migration between systems	Easy	Difficult (must open case)
Power supply	External AC adapter brick	None—powered by host bus
Status monitoring	External signal LEDs	Tray icon or none
Interface	Serial or USB	PCI or ISA

Although late versions of Windows 95 OSR 2.x have USB support, many USB devices actually require Windows 98 or better. Use Windows 98/Me/2000/XP to achieve more reliable support for USB devices.

◄◄   See "UARTs," p. 1001.

Not all modems that function at the same speed have the same functionality. Many modem manufacturers produce modems running at the same speed but with different feature sets at different price points. The more expensive modems usually support advanced features, such as distinctive ring support, caller ID, voice and data, video teleconferencing, and call-waiting support. When purchasing a modem, be sure it supports all the features you need. You also should make sure the software you plan to use, including the operating system, has been certified for use with the modem you select.

If you live in a rural area, or in an older city neighborhood, your telephone line quality might influence your decision. Look at comparison test results carefully and pay particular attention to how well various modems perform with noisy lines. If your phone line sounds crackly during a rainstorm, that poor-quality line makes reliable modem communications difficult, too, and it can limit your ability to connect at speeds above 33.6Kbps.

Another feature to consider is the modem's resistance to electrical damage. Some brands feature built-in power protection to shield against damage from digital telephone lines (higher powered and not compatible with modems) or power surges. However, every modem should be used with a surge protector that allows you to route the RJ-11 telephone cable through the unit for protection against high-voltage surges.

All modems on the market today support V.90 or V.92, and even if your particular location can't support those speeds, your modem might still offer advanced features, such as voicemail or simultaneous voice and data. Keep in mind that V.90/V.92 connections seem to work better for many users if their modems also support x2. If you prefer a modem made by a vendor that also supports K56flex, try to buy a modem that contains both types of standards in its firmware (referred to by some vendors as "Dualmode" modems).

Choosing to Upgrade

If you bought your modem in 1997 or later, or if it was included in your computer, chances are good that it came with 56Kbps support or that you've upgraded it to some form of 56Kbps support. However, even though today's V.90/V.92 modems still have the same maximum speed, other changes in modem design have occurred that might make a modem upgrade desirable for you. And if you are still using a 33.6Kbps modem or even slower model, you should get a 56Kbps modem if your line quality can support it.

Dialup modems introduced from 2001 to the present still run at the 53Kbps FCC maximum with the potential to run at up to 56Kbps if the FCC regulations change, but they might offer one or more of the following advanced features:

- *MNP10EC support.* Improves performance on poor-quality phone lines by quickly adjusting line speed up and down with changing conditions. MNP10EC includes MNP10 and is superior.

- *PCI bus.* Newer systems don't have ISA slots. It can share IRQs. Unfortunately, most PCI modems are WinModems; see "Modems Without a UART (WinModems)," later in this chapter.

- *USB connection.* Most new systems include USB, but some no longer include serial ports. Requires Win98 or better.

- *Game-optimized.* Provides faster ping response for gaming but is not as useful for ordinary Web surfing. These modems are more expensive than others.

- *Modem-on-hold.* Allows you to answer the phone and not lose the modem connection. Maximum hold time might be limited.

- *V.92/V.44 support.* Includes faster negotiation, modem-on-hold, and 56Kbps support. Not all ISPs have full V.92/V.44 support.

- *Voice support.* Allows the digitizing of received calls for answering machine functionality.

Modems Without a UART (WinModems)

Modems without a UART chip, sometimes referred to as *WinModems* after the pioneering U.S. Robotics version, can save you money at purchase time but can cause problems with speed and operating-system compatibility later.

For users wanting an inexpensive internal modem, a modem that doesn't use a traditional UART instead of a UART-equipped internal or external modem looks like a great deal, often costing less than $40, compared to $80 or more for a UART-equipped "hardware" modem. But, there is no free lunch for modem users. What can you lose with a modem that lacks a UART?

First, you need to realize that there are actually two types of UART-less modems: those that rely on Windows and the CPU for all operations (these modems are also called *controllerless* modems) and those that use a programmable digital signal processor (DSP) chip to replace the UART. Both types of modems use less power than traditional UART-based modems, making them better for use with notebook computers. Although both are "software modems," there's an enormous difference in what you're getting.

A Windows-based modem must run under Windows because Windows provides the brains of the modem, a cost-cutting move similar to that used by some low-cost host-based printers. You should avoid this if you're planning to try Linux, move the modem to a Macintosh, or use an old MS-DOS–based communications program. If you have no drivers for your modem/operating system combination, you'll have no luck using the software modem.

Software modems that lack a DSP have a second major strike against them: They make your CPU do all the work. Although today's computers have much faster CPUs than those required for typical software modems (Pentium 133 minimum), your modem can still slow down your computer if you multitask while downloading or surfing the Web.

Most of the modems bundled with computer systems are software modems, and the major chipsets used include Lucent LT (now Agere Systems), Conexant (formerly Rockwell) HCF, U.S. Robotics WinModem, ESS Technology's HSP-compliant chipsets, Intel's Modem Silicon Operation (formerly Ambient), and PCTel.

Except for U.S. Robotics, the other companies produce chipsets that can be found in the modems made by many manufacturers.

For best results, do the following:

- *Make sure your modem uses a DSP.* Typically, these modems don't require a particular CPU or a particular speed of CPU.

- *Consider modems built around the Lucent/Agere LT chipset.* These modems have a DSP, and Lucent/Agere's firmware is frequently revised to achieve the best results in a rapidly changing telephony environment.

- *Use the modem manufacturer's own drivers first.* But software modems can often use any manufacturer's drivers for the same chipset with excellent results; in particular, Lucent/Agere LT chipset modems typically can use any Lucent/Agere LT driver from any modem manufacturer.

- *Don't delete the old software driver when you download and install new modem software.* As with UART-equipped modems, the latest firmware isn't always the best.

- *Look carefully at the CPU, RAM, and operating system requirements before you buy your modem.*

Tip

Many manufacturers sell both traditional and UART-free modems. If you have an older system or want the option to use MS-DOS– or Linux-based communications programs, the hardware modem with a traditional UART might cost more but be a better choice.

Finding Support for "Brand-X" Modems

Many computer users today didn't install their modems, or even purchase them as a separate unit. Their modems came bundled inside the computer and often have a bare-bones manual that makes no mention of the modem's origin or where to get help. Getting V.90 firmware updates, drivers, or even jumper settings for OEM modems such as this can be difficult.

One of the best Web sites for getting help when you don't know where to start is the "Who Made My Modem?" page (www.56K.com), which features

- Links to the FCC's equipment authorization database (enter the FCC ID to locate the vendor)
- Using ATI commands to query the modem chipset
- Lookup by chipset manufacturer
- Search engine tips
- Links to major modem and chipset manufacturers

Squeezing Performance from Your 56Kbps Modem

Although many users of 56Kbps modems have seen significant improvements in their connect speeds and throughputs over their previous V.34-type modems, many have not or have seen only sporadic improvements. According to the research of Richard Gamberg, available online at his Modemsite Web site (http://www.modemsite.com), a combination of five factors comes into play to affect your ability to get reliable connections in the range of 45Kbps–53Kbps (the current FCC maximum):

- The modem
- The modem firmware/driver
- Your line conditions
- The ISP's modems
- The ISP's modem firmware

It's up to you to ensure that you match your modem's 56Kbps type to the 56Kbps standards your ISP supports, and that you use the best (not always the latest!) modem firmware and drivers, as discussed in the previous section.

Other modem adjustments recommended by Modemsite include

- Modifying existing modem .INF files used by Windows 9x to accurately reflect connection speed
- Disabling 56Kbps connections (!) when playing games to minimize lag times

Note

This last suggestion might seem odd, but "fast" modems are designed to push a large amount of data through for downloads, and gameplay over modems actually deals with small amounts of data instead. The lag time caused by 56Kbps data handling can make a regular "fast" modem seem slow. If you want a fast modem for both downloading and game playing, see "Choosing to Upgrade," earlier in this chapter.

The site also hosts a forum area for discussing modem configuration, reliability, and performance issues.

Telco "Upgrades" and Your Modem

In addition to the well-known analog-to-digital conversion issue that prevents some phone lines from handling 56Kbps modems at anything beyond 33.6Kbps, other local telephone company (telco) practices and services can either prevent 56Kbps from ever working or take it away from you after you've enjoyed it for a while.

If you were getting 45Kbps or faster connections with your 56Kbps modem but can no longer get past 33.6Kbps, what happened? Some local telephone companies have been performing network "upgrades" that improve capacity for voice calls but prevent 56Kbps modems from running faster than 28Kbps. The cause seems to be the telephone companies' change from a signaling type called RBS (Robbed Bit Signaling) to SS7 (Signaling System 7), which changes how data used by the modem for high-speed access is detected. Caller ID devices connected to your phone line use RBS or SS7 signals to obtain information from incoming phone calls. If you use a caller ID box on the same phone circuit as your modem (even if it's connected in another room), you might not be able to get fast connections, or you might experience frequent disconnects. If you notice a drop in connection speed or reliability after you install caller ID, disconnect the caller ID box from the wall jack while you're online and see whether the speed and reliability of your modem connections improve.

What else can you do? You can install the latest firmware available for your modem model or chipset. You can also check with your local telephone company to see whether it can update its firmware to solve the problem. Even if your modem has different firmware, checking on an upgrade might still be useful because this problem is likely to become widespread as telephone numbers, exchanges, and area codes continue to multiply like weeds and telephone network upgrades must keep pace.

Sharing Your Internet Connection

Whether you have a 56Kbps dialup modem or a broadband connection, one connection is often not enough for a home or small-office setting. You can share your connection with other computer users with one of the following methods:

- *Computer-based sharing solutions.* These work by connecting the computer with Internet access to a network with the other computers with which you want to share the connection. The computer with the connection acts as a gateway to the Internet.

- *Router-based sharing solutions.* These work by connecting all the computers on a network with a router or gateway connected to the Internet. Most routers are designed to work with broadband devices that use a USB or 10BASE-T connection, but a few work with dialup modems.

Typical computer-based sharing solutions include

- *Microsoft Internet Connection Sharing (ICS).* Introduced in Windows 98 Second Edition (Win98SE) and also a part of Windows Me, Windows 2000, and Windows XP

- *Third-party gateway or proxy-server programs such as Wingate, Winproxy, and others*

Both ICS and third-party programs can also work with non-Windows computers because the TCP/IP network protocol, the standard protocol of the Internet, is used for networking.

▶▶ See "Network Protocols," p. 1136, for details of the TCP/IP protocol.

Router-based solutions are available for popular types of home and small-office networks, including:

- 10BASE-T and 10/100 Ethernet
- IEEE 802.11a and 802.11b wireless Ethernet
- HomePNA (phone-line) networks

Comparing Gateways, Proxy Servers, and Routers

To the typical user, it doesn't matter whether a gateway, proxy server, or router is used to provide shared Internet access. Traditional gateway programs such as Microsoft ICS, Sygate Home Network, and WinGate use a method of shared access called Network Address Translation (NAT), which enables sharing by converting network addresses into Internet-compatible addresses during the file request and download process. This process requires little client PC configuration but doesn't permit page caching, content filtration, firewalls, or other useful services that can be provided by a proxy server. Proxy servers traditionally have required tricky configuration—sometimes at an individual application level. However, products such as WinProxy combine the ease of configuration of a gateway with the extra features of a proxy server.

Popular third-party sharing programs include WinProxy (www.winproxy.com), WinGate (www.wingate.com), and Sybergen SyGate (smb.sygate.com). Many home-oriented networks and modems are bundled with these or similar products, so if you're in the market for a new modem or are building a small network, ask whether a proxy server or gateway program for Internet sharing is included. If not, you can download free trial versions from the previously listed Web sites.

If you don't like leaving a computer on at all times to provide Internet access to the network, a router is the only way to go. Routers also provide better firewall protection for all computers on the network, and some, such as certain Linksys models, can be configured to require networked PCs to be running specified firewall or antivirus software before Internet access is granted. The most common routers for broadband Internet access also contain a switch, so you won't need a separate connection device for your home network.

Routers for Internet Sharing

Just as an ICS gateway has two IP addresses—one for the network and one for the Internet—so does a router. Most routers are sold for use with two-way broadband Internet access devices such as two-way cable modems and fixed wireless broadband services or DSL lines. Most of these devices connect to the computer via a 10BASE-T Ethernet port, as seen in Figure 19.9.

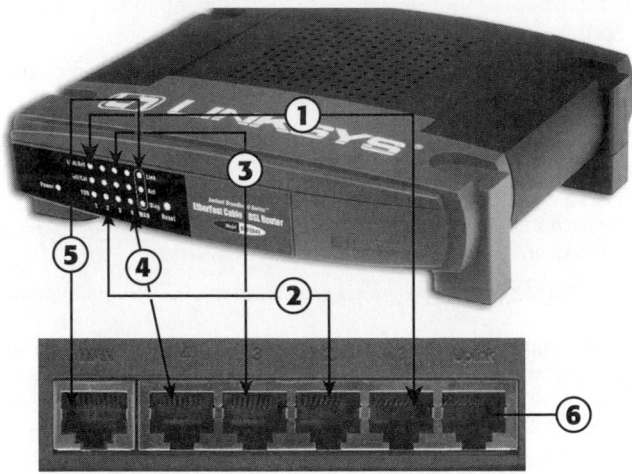

1. LAN port #1
2. LAN port #2
3. LAN port #3
4. LAN port #4
5. WAN port (connects to cable or DSL modem)
6. Uplink port (connects to a hub or switch to allow additional users to connect to the Internet)

Figure 19.9   Front (top) and rear (bottom) views of a typical broadband router with a built-in four-port switch, the Linksys EtherFast Cable/DSL Router, BEFSR41. *Top photo courtesy Linksys.*

When you use a router to share your Internet connection, the WAN port on the router replaces the network card connection originally used to connect your computer with the cable modem or DSL modem. All computers on the network connect to LAN ports and can share files and printers with each other as well as share Internet access.

The router can be configured to provide either dynamically assigned or fixed IP addresses to each computer connected to it through the LAN ports and can be configured to use the same MAC address (a unique hardware address assigned to each network component) originally used by the network card first connected to the cable modem or DSL modem. This prevents the ISP from determining that you're sharing the connection. The WAN port on the router can be configured to obtain an IP address from the cable modem or DSL modem or to have a fixed IP address, depending on the configuration required by the ISP.

As long as the router is running and properly connected to the cable modem or DSL modem, any computer connected to it can go online just by opening its email client or Web browser.

Figure 19.10 shows a typical 10/100 Ethernet home network configuration that uses a router with a built-in switch to share a cable modem.

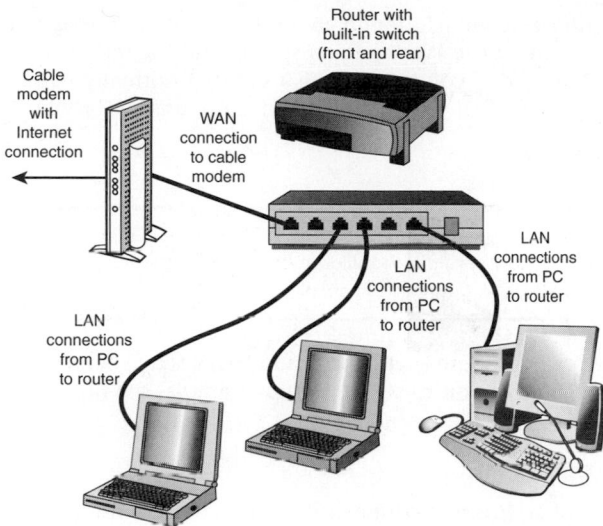

Figure 19.10 When you use a router to share a cable modem or DSL modem, you need only one network card in each computer. This router incorporates a switch that can connect up to four computers to the cable modem.

If you have a wireless network, connect the wireless access point or gateway device designed for your network to the cable modem or other broadband Internet device (some also work with dialup modems). The wireless access point or gateway device will transfer data to and from computers on the wireless network and the Internet.

For more information about choosing and installing wired and wireless networks, see Chapter 20.

Internet Troubleshooting

This section deals with hardware problems that can cause Internet problems. Software problems usually are caused by incorrect configuration of the TCP/IP protocol required by all types of Internet connections. For more information about TCP/IP or other software problems, see Chapter 20.

Diagnosing Problems with a Shared Internet Connection

Although each Internet sharing product has individual configuration issues, the following tips provide general guidelines useful for solving problems with all of them.

Check Your Host Configuration

If your host isn't set up correctly, it can't share its connection with clients. Check the bindings for TCP/IP or other protocols used to create the shared connection. If you are using Microsoft's ICS and two Ethernet cards, you will see entries in the Network configuration on the host computer for each Ethernet card and for the ICS software itself.

Check Your Client Configuration

Make sure your clients have correct TCP/IP, DHCP, and other protocol settings for the host. The ping command can be used at a command prompt to check the Internet connection; try pinging a Web site by opening a Windows command prompt and typing a command such as ping www.dslreports.com. Note that many sites are designed to reject ping requests, in which case you receive timeout errors.

If you have a working Internet connection and are pinging a site not designed to reject ping requests, you should see the IP address for the Web site you specify and the round-trip time (or ping rate) for four signals sent to the Web site. If you are pinging a site that normally responds and yet you still get no response or see an error message, you might have a configuration problem with your TCP/IP configuration.

Note

Because pinging can also be used for denial-of-service (DoS) attacks by hackers on Web sites, some Web sites don't respond to pings. Use **ping** when your system is working properly to find a Web site that will respond to **ping** and use that site for troubleshooting as described previously.

Verify that the host has a working Internet connection that's active before you try to share it. Check the sharing program's documentation to see how guests can dial the host's modem to start a connection if necessary.

Speed Will Drop with Multiple Users

It's normal for the speed of an Internet connection to drop with multiple users, but if you're concerned about the degree of decline, check with the sharing software provider for Registry tweaks and other options to improve performance.

Diagnosing Connection Problems with Signal Lights

Signal lights are found on most external broadband devices, such as cable modems, wireless broadband routers, and DSL modems. The signal lights indicate whether the unit is receiving signals from the computer, sending data to the network, or receiving data from the network and whether the unit can "see" the network—even if no data is currently flowing through the unit.

On many units, the power light also is used to indicate problems. If the light is normally green, for example, a red light might indicate the unit has failed. Other lights flash when data is being sent or received. On cable modem or wireless broadband routers, look for a signal lock light; this light flashes if the unit is trying to lock onto a signal from the cable network or wireless transmitter.

Learn the meaning of the lights on your broadband device to help you diagnose problems; the user manual or vendor's Web site will provide the troubleshooting information you need for the particular broadband device you use.

Modem Fails to Dial

1. Check line and phone jacks on the modem. Use the line jack to attach the modem to the telephone line. The phone jack takes the same RJ-11 silver cord cable, but it's designed to let you daisy-chain a telephone to your modem, so you need only a single line for modem and telephone use. If you have reversed these cables, you will not get a dial tone.

2. If the cables are attached properly, check the cable for cuts or breaks. The outer jacket used on RJ-11 telephone cables is minimal. If the cable looks bad, replace it.

3. If the modem is external, make sure the RS-232 modem cable is running from the modem to a working serial port on your computer and that it is switched on. Signal lights on the front of the modem can be used to determine whether the modem is on and whether it is responding to dialing commands.

4. If the modem is a PC Card (PCMCIA card), make sure it is fully plugged into the PCMCIA/PC slot. With Windows 9x/Me/2000/XP, you should see a small PCMCIA/PC Card icon on the toolbar. Double-click it to view the cards that are currently connected. If your modem is properly attached, it should be visible. Otherwise, remove it, reinsert it into the PCMCIA/PC Card slot, and see whether the computer detects it.

Connecting a PC Card Modem via a Dongle

Some PC Card modems do not use a standard RJ-11 cable because the card is too thin. Instead, they use a connection called a *dongle*, which runs from the PC Card to the telephone. If this proprietary cable is damaged, your modem is useless. You should purchase a spare from the modem vendor and carry it with you. And if you find the dongle is too short to reach the data jacks in a hotel room, buy a coupler from your local RadioShack or telephone-parts department and attach a standard RJ-11 cable to your dongle via the coupler. Dongles are also used with some PC Card network cards for the same reason; the RJ-45 twisted-pair cable connector is too wide to attach to a standard PC Card. To avoid using dongles, look for a network or modem card that has a standard RJ-11 or RJ-45 connection built in to it.

5. Make sure your modem has been properly configured by your OS. With Windows 9x/Me/2000, use the Modems control panel to view and test your modem configuration (with Windows XP, you can use the Modem Troubleshooter). Select your modem and click the Diagnostics tab. This displays the COM (serial) ports in your computer. Select the COM port used by the modem, and click the More Info tab. This sends test signals to your modem. A properly working modem responds with information about the port and modem.

6. If you get a `Couldn't Open Port` error message, your modem isn't connected properly. It might be in use already by a program running in the background, or there might be an IRQ or I/O port address conflict with another card in your computer. Whether you have a modem installed, every COM port that is working will display its IRQ, I/O port address, and UART chip type when you run Diagnostics. The UART type should be 16550 or above for use with any modern modem.

Note

You can also test your modem response by setting up a HyperTerminal session (discussed earlier) to send the modem commands. If the modem fails to respond, this is another indication of a problem with the modem-PC connection.

Computer Locks Up After Installing or Using Internal Modem, Terminal Adapter, or Network Card

The usual cause of lockups after you install an internal card is an IRQ conflict. Internal dialup modems that use ISA slots typically cause the "curse of the shared IRQ," especially if a serial mouse is also used. PC Card and PCI modems can share IRQs safely, and USB mice use the same IRQ as the USB port itself. For more information about shared IRQs with ISA modems and serial mice, see the Technical Reference section on the disc packaged with this book.

Computer Can't Detect External Modem

1. Make sure the modem has been connected to the computer with the correct type of cable.

For external modems that use an RS-232 serial port, you might need a separate RS-232 modem cable, which has a 9-pin connector on one end (to connect to the computer) and a 25-pin connector on the other end (to connect to the modem). Some external modems have an integrated modem cable. Because RS-232 is a very flexible standard encompassing many pinouts, be sure the cable is constructed according to the diagram on the following page.

If you purchase an RS-232 modem cable prebuilt at a store, you'll have a cable that works with your PC and your modem. However, you can use the preceding chart to build your own cable or, by using a cable tester, determine whether an existing RS-232 cable in your office is actually made for modems or some other device.

PC (with 9-pin COM port—male)		Modem (25-pin port—female)
3	TX data	2
2	RX data	3
7	RTS	4
8	CTS	5
6	DSR	6
5	SIG GND	7
1	CXR	8
4	DTR	20
9	RI	22

2. Make sure the COM (serial) port or USB port to which the modem is connected to is working.

The Windows 9x/Me/2000/XP diagnostics test listed earlier can be useful in testing the serial port, but third-party testing programs such as AMIDIAG have more thorough methods for testing the system's COM ports. These programs can use loopback plugs to test the serial ports. The loopback plug loops signals that would be sent to the modem or other serial device back to the serial port. These programs normally work best when run from the MS-DOS prompt.

Some diagnostics include a loopback plug to test serial ports. Loopback plugs may vary in design depending on the vendor.

To ensure that the USB port is working, check the Device Manager in Windows; a working USB port is listed as a USB Root hub and a PCI to USB Universal Host Controller in the Universal Serial Bus device category. Any external USB hubs also are listed in the same category. If this category is not listed and the ports are physically present on the computer, make sure you are using Windows 98/Me/2000/XP (only a few late versions of Windows 95 have USB support). If you are, be sure the USB ports are enabled in the system BIOS.

3. Check the power cord and power switch.

Using Your Modem Sound to Diagnose Your Modem

If you listen to your modem when it makes a connection, you might have realized that different types of modems make distinctive connection sounds and that different connection speeds also make distinctive sounds.

The various types of 56Kbps modems have distinctly different handshakes of tones, buzzes, and warbles as they negotiate speeds with the ISP's modem. Learning what your modem sounds like when it makes a 56Kbps connection and when it settles for a V.34-speed connection can help you determine when you should hang up and try to connect at a faster speed.

The Modemsite's troubleshooting section has a number of sound samples of various modems during the handshaking process. Use RealPlayer to play the samples, available at www.modemsite.com/56k/trouble.asp (click the Handshakes link).

Compare these sound samples to your own modem; be sure you adjust the speaker volume for your modem so you can hear it during the call.

CHAPTER 20

Local Area Networking

Focus of This Chapter

This chapter concentrates on how to build and use a peer-to-peer network, the lowest-cost network that is still highly useful to small business and home-office users. This type of network can be created by adding network hardware to any recent version of Windows, from Windows 9x and NT through Windows Me, 2000, and XP. As you'll see, most peer-to-peer networks can be "grown" into client/server networks at a later point by adding a dedicated server and the appropriate software to the server and client PCs.

Thus, this chapter provides the hands-on and practical information you need to create a small-office, workgroup, or home-office network. If you are managing a corporate network using Linux, Unix, Windows NT Server, Windows 2000 Server, Windows Server 2003, or Novell NetWare, you will also be concerned with matters such as security, user profiles, SIDs, and other factors beyond the scope of this book.

Note

Networking is an enormous topic. For more information about client/server networking, wide area networking, the Internet, and corporate networking, I recommend *Upgrading and Repairing Networks, Fourth Edition*, from Que.

Defining a Network

A *network* is a group of two or more computers that *intelligently* share hardware or software devices with each other. A network can be as small and simple as two computers that share the printer and CD-ROM drive attached to one of them or as large as the world's largest network: the Internet.

Intelligently sharing means that each computer that shares resources with another computer or computers maintains control of that resource. Thus, a switchbox for sharing a single printer between two computers doesn't qualify as a network device; because the switchbox—not the computers—handles the print jobs, neither computer knows when the other one needs to print, and print jobs can interfere with each other.

A shared printer, on the other hand, can be controlled remotely and can store print jobs from different computers on the print server's hard disk. Users can change the sequence of print jobs, hold them, or cancel them. And, sharing of the device can be controlled through passwords, further differentiating it from a switchbox.

Virtually any storage or output device can be shared over a network, but the most common devices include:

- Printers
- Disk drives
- CD-ROM and optical drives
- Modems

- Fax machines
- Tape backup units
- Scanners

Entire drives, selected folders, or individual files can be shared with other users via the network.

In addition to reducing hardware costs by sharing expensive printers and other peripherals among multiple users, networks provide additional benefits to users:

- Multiple users can share access to software and data files.
- Electronic mail (email) can be sent and received.
- Multiple users can contribute to a single document using collaboration features.
- Remote-control programs can be used to troubleshoot problems or show new users how to perform a task.
- A single Internet connection can be shared among multiple computers.

Types of Networks

Several types of networks exist, from small, two-station arrangements to networks that interconnect offices in many cities:

- *Local area networks.* The smallest office network is referred to as a local area network (LAN). A LAN is formed from computers and components in a single office or building. A LAN can also be built at home from the same components used in office networking, but, as you'll see later, special home-networking components now exist to allow the creation of what can be called a home area network (HAN).

- *Home area networks.* A home area network (HAN) often uses the same hardware components as a LAN, but it is mainly used to share Internet access. Powerline, low-speed wireless, and phoneline networks are used primarily in HAN rather than LAN environments. HANs are often referred to as small-office/home-office (SOHO) LANs.

- *Wide area networks.* LANs in different locations can be connected together by high-speed fiber-optic, satellite, or leased phone lines to form a wide area network (WAN).

- *The Internet.* The World Wide Web is the most visible part of the world's largest network, the Internet. Although many users of the Internet still use modems over a dialup connection rather than a LAN or WAN connection, any user of the Internet is a network user. The Internet is really a network of networks, all of which are connected to each other through the TCP/IP protocol. Programs such as Web browsers, File Transfer Protocol (FTP) clients, and newsreaders are some of the most common ways users work with the Internet.

- *Intranets.* Intranets use the same Web browsers and other software and the same TCP/IP protocol as the public Internet, but intranets exist as a portion of a company's private network. Typically, intranets comprise one or more LANs that are connected to other company networks, but, unlike the Internet, the content is restricted to authorized company users only. Essentially, an intranet is a private Internet.

- *Extranets.* Intranets that share a portion of their content with customers, suppliers, or other businesses, but not with the general public, are called extranets. As with intranets, the same Web browsers and other software are used to access the content.

Note

Both intranets and extranets rely on firewalls and other security tools and procedures to keep their private contents private.

Requirements for a Network

Unless the computers that are connected know they are connected and agree on a common means of communication and what resources are to be shared, they can't work together. Networking software is just as important as networking hardware because it establishes the logical connections that make the physical connections work.

At a minimum, each network requires the following:

- Physical (cable) or wireless (infrared [IRDA] or radio-frequency) connections between computers
- A common set of communications rules, known as a *network protocol*
- Software that enables resources to be shared with other PCs and controls access to shared resources, known as a *network operating system*
- Resources that can be shared, such as printers, disk drives, and CD-ROMs
- Software that enables computers to access other computers with shared resources, known as a *network client*

These rules apply to the simplest and most powerful networks, and all the ones in between, regardless of their nature. The details of the hardware and software you need are discussed more fully later in this chapter.

Client/Server Versus Peer Networks

Although every computer on a LAN is connected to every other computer, they do not necessarily all communicate with each other. There are two basic types of LANs, based on the communication patterns between the machines—client/server networks and peer-to-peer networks.

Client/Server Networks

On a *client/server* network, every computer has a distinct role, that of either a client or a server. A *server* is designed to share its resources among the client computers on the network. Typically, servers are located in secured areas, such as locked closets or data centers, because they hold an organization's most valuable data and do not have to be accessed by operators on a continuous basis. The rest of the computers on the network function as *clients* (see Figure 20.1).

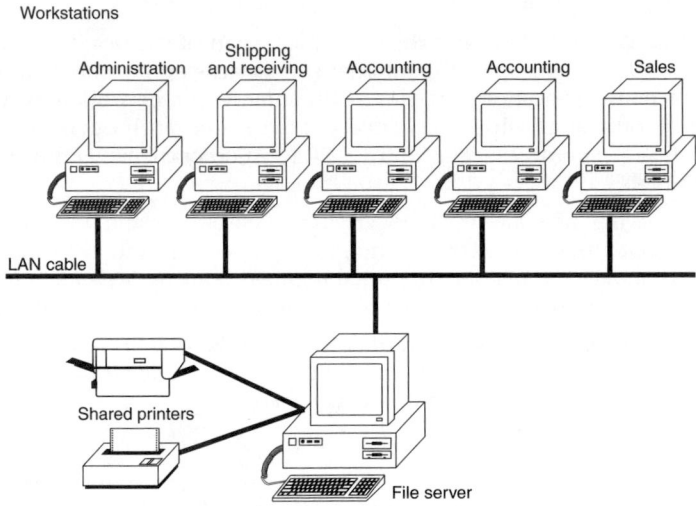

Figure 20.1 The components of a client/server LAN.

Servers

A dedicated server computer typically has a faster processor, more memory, and more storage space than a client because it might have to service dozens or even hundreds of users at the same time. High-performance servers also might use two or more processors, use the 64-bit version of the PCI expansion slot for server-optimized network interface cards, and have redundant power supplies. The server runs a special network operating system—such as Windows NT Server, Windows 2000 Server, Windows Server 2003, Linux, Unix, or Novell NetWare—that is designed solely to facilitate the sharing of its resources. These resources can reside on a single server or on a group of servers. When more than one server is used, each server can "specialize" in a particular task (file server, print server, fax server, email server, and so on) or provide redundancy (duplicate servers) in case of server failure. For very demanding computing tasks, several servers can act as a single unit through the use of parallel processing.

Clients

A client computer communicates only with servers, not with other clients. A client system is a standard PC that is running an operating system such as Windows 9x, Windows Me, Windows 2000 Professional, or Windows XP. These versions of Windows contain the client software that enables the client computers to access the resources that servers share. Older operating systems, such as Windows 3.x and DOS, require add-on network client software.

Peer-to-Peer Network

By contrast, on a peer-to-peer network, every computer is equal and can communicate with any other computer on the network to which it has been granted access rights (see Figure 20.2). Essentially, every computer on a peer-to-peer network can function as both a server and a client; any computer on a peer-to-peer network is considered a server if it shares a printer, a folder, a drive, or some other resource with the rest of the network. This is why you might hear about client and server activities, even when the discussion is about a peer-to-peer network. Peer-to-peer networks can be as small as two computers or as large as hundreds of systems. Although there is no theoretical limit to the size of a peer-to-peer network, performance drops significantly and security becomes a major headache on peer-based networks with more than 10 computers. Also, Microsoft imposes a 10-station limit on computers running Windows 2000 Professional or XP Professional that are sharing resources with other systems. For these reasons, I recommend that you switch to a client/server network when your network climbs above about 10 stations.

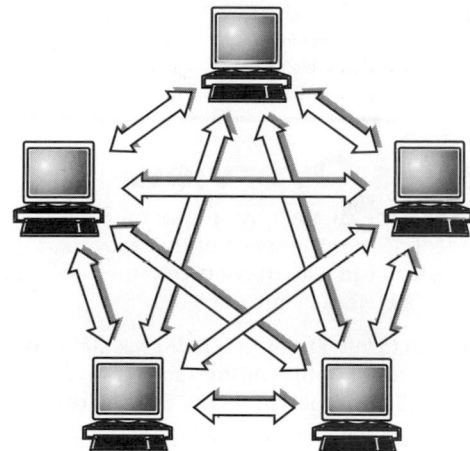

Figure 20.2   The logical architecture of a typical peer-to-peer network.

Peer-to-peer networks are more common in small offices or within a single department of a larger organization. The advantage of a peer-to-peer network is that you don't have to dedicate a computer to function as a file server. Instead, every computer can share its resources with any other. The potential disadvantages to a peer-to-peer network are that typically less security and less control exist because users normally administer their own systems, whereas client/server networks have the advantage of centralized administration.

Comparing Client/Server and Peer-to-Peer Networks

Client/server LANs offer enhanced security for shared resources, greater performance, increased backup efficiency for network-based data, and the potential for the use of redundant power supplies and RAID drive arrays. Client/server LANs also have a much greater cost to purchase and maintain. Table 20.1 compares client/server and peer-to-peer server networking.

Table 20.1   Comparing Client/Server and Peer-to-Peer Networking

Item	Client/Server	Peer-to-Peer
Access control	Via user/group lists of permissions; a user has access to only the resources granted, different users can be given different levels of access	Via password lists by resource; each resource requires a separate password, all-or-nothing access, no centralized user list
Security	High; access is controlled by user or by group identity	Low; knowing the password gives anybody access to a shared resource
Performance	High; the server is dedicated and doesn't handle other tasks	Low; servers often act as workstations
Hardware cost	High; specialized high-performance server hardware with redundancy features	Low; any workstation can become a server by sharing resources
Software cost	Higher; license fees per user are part of the cost of the server OS	Lower; client software is included with OS
Backup	Centralized on the server; managed network administrator, backup by device and media only required at server	Decentralized; managed by users, backup devices and media required at each workstation
Redundancy	Yes; duplicate power supplies, hot-swappable drive arrays, and even redundant servers are common; network OS normally is capable of using redundant devices automatically	No true redundancy among peer "servers" or clients; failures require manual intervention to correct, with a high possibility of data loss

Network Protocols Overview

The protocol you choose to run is the single most important decision you make when setting up a local area network. This protocol defines the speed of the network, the medium access control mechanism it uses, the types of cables you can use, the network interface adapters you must buy, and the adapter drivers you install in the network client software.

The Institute of Electrical and Electronic Engineers (IEEE) has defined and documented a set of standards for the physical characteristics of both collision-detection and token-passing networks. These standards are known as IEEE 802.3 (Ethernet) and IEEE 802.5 (Token-Ring). IEEE 802.11 defines wireless versions of Ethernet.

Note

Be aware, however, that the colloquial names Ethernet and Token-Ring actually refer to earlier versions of these protocols, on which the IEEE standards were based. Minor differences exist between the frame definitions for true Ethernet and true IEEE 802.3. In terms of the standards, IBM's 16Mbps Token-Ring products are an extension of the IEEE 802.5 standard. There is also an older data-link protocol called ARCnet that is now rarely used.

The two major choices today for wired networks are Ethernet and Token-Ring, although Ethernet and its variations are by far the most popular. Other network data-link protocols you might also encounter are summarized in Table 20.2. The abbreviations used for the cable types are explained in the following sections.

Table 20.2   Wired LAN Protocol Summary

Network Type	Speed	Maximum Number of Stations	Cable Types	Notes
ARCnet	2.5Mbps	255	RG-62 coax UTP/Type1 STP	Obsolete for new installations; used same cable as IBM 3270 terminals
Ethernet	10Mbps	Per network: 1024; per segment: 10BASE-T=2 10BASE-2=30 10BASE-5=100 10BASE-FL=2	UTP Cat 3 (10BASE-T), Thicknet (coax; 10BASE-5), Thinnet (RG-58 coax; 10BASE-2), fiber-optic (10BASE-F)	Largely replaced by Fast Ethernet; backward compatible with Fast or Gigabit Ethernet
Fast Ethernet	100Mbps	Per network: 1024; per segment: 2	Cat 5 UTP	The most popular networking standard
Gigabit Ethernet	1,000Mbps	Per network: 1024; per segment: 2	Cat 5/5e/6 UTP	Uses all four signal pairs in the cable
Token-Ring	4Mbps; 16Mbps; 100Mbps	72 on UTP; 250-260 on type 1 STP	UTP, Type 1 STP, and fiber optic	Largely replaced by Fast Ethernet

▶▶ Wireless protocols, such as Wireless Ethernet IEEE 802.11 variants, are discussed later in this chapter. See "Wireless Network Standards," p. 1128.

A few years ago, the choice between Token-Ring or Ethernet wasn't easy. The original versions of standard Ethernet (10BASE-5 "Thick Ethernet" and 10BASE-2 "Thin Ethernet") used hard-to-install coaxial cable and were expensive to build beyond a certain point because of the technical limitations expressed by the "5-4-3" rule (see the following note).

Note

The 5-4-3 rule gets its name from the fact that Ethernet signals can travel through no more than five segments, four repeaters or hubs, and three populated segments (cable segments with two or more stations) before they become unreliable. Because 10BASE-T hubs act as repeaters and a 10BASE-T segment has only one station per cable, creating large networks is easier with 10BASE-T Ethernet than with older forms of Ethernet.

Initially, Token-Ring's 16Mbps version was substantially faster than 10BASE versions of Ethernet and had larger limits on the numbers of workstations permitted per segment. Currently, however, the popularity and low cost of Fast Ethernet; the use of easy-to-install twisted-pair cabling for standard, 100Mbps Fast, and even 1,000Mbps Gigabit Ethernet; and the use of hubs and switches to overcome classic Ethernet station limitations have made Fast Ethernet the preferred choice for workgroup-size networks and a competitor to Token-Ring for larger networks. A properly designed Fast Ethernet network can be upgraded to Gigabit Ethernet in the future.

Ethernet

With tens of millions of computers connected by Ethernet cards and cables, Ethernet is the most widely used data link layer protocol in the world. Ethernet-based LANs enable you to interconnect a wide variety of equipment, including Unix and Linux workstations, Apple computers, printers, and PCs. You can buy Ethernet adapters from dozens of competing manufacturers. Older adapters supported one, two, or all three of the cable types defined in the standard: Thinnet, Thicknet, and Unshielded Twisted Pair (UTP). Current adapters, on the other hand, almost always support UTP only.

Traditional Ethernet operates at a speed of 10Mbps, but the more recent (and most popular of the Ethernet flavors) Fast Ethernet standards push this speed to 100Mbps. The latest version of Ethernet, Gigabit Ethernet, reaches speeds of 1,000Mbps, or 100 times the speed of original Ethernet.

Fast Ethernet

Fast Ethernet requires adapters, hubs, and UTP or fiber-optic cables designed to support the higher speed. Some early Fast Ethernet products supported only 100Mbps, but almost all current Fast Ethernet products are combination devices that run at both 10Mbps and 100Mbps, enabling you to gradually upgrade an older 10Mbps Ethernet network by installing new NICs and hubs over an extended period of time.

Both the most popular form of Fast Ethernet (100BASE-TX) and 10BASE-T standard Ethernet use two of the four wire pairs found in UTP Category 5 cable. An alternative Fast Ethernet standard called 100BASE-T4 uses all four wire pairs in UTP Category 5 cable, but this Fast Ethernet standard was never popular and is seldom seen today.

Gigabit Ethernet

Gigabit Ethernet also requires special adapters, hubs, and cables. Most users of Gigabit Ethernet use fiber-optic cables, but you can run Gigabit Ethernet over the same Category 5 UTP (although better Cat 5e or Cat 6 is recommended) cabling that Fast Ethernet and newer installations of standard Ethernet use. Gigabit Ethernet for UTP is also referred to as 1000BASE-T.

Unlike Fast Ethernet and standard Ethernet over UTP, Gigabit Ethernet uses all four wire pairs. Thus, Gigabit Ethernet requires dedicated Ethernet cabling; you can't "borrow" two wire pairs for telephone or other data signaling with Gigabit Ethernet as you can with the slower versions. Most Gigabit Ethernet adapters can also handle 10BASE-T and 100BASE-TX Fast Ethernet traffic, enabling you to interconnect all three UTP-based forms of Ethernet on a single network.

Neither Fast Ethernet nor Gigabit Ethernet support the use of thin or thick coaxial cable originally used with traditional Ethernet, although you can interconnect coaxial-cable-based and UTP-based Ethernet networks by using media converters or specially designed hubs and switches.

Note

For more information about Ethernet, Fast Ethernet, Token-Ring, and other network data-link standards, see the "Data Link Layer Protocols" and "High-Speed Networking Technologies" sections found in Chapter 19 of *Upgrading and Repairing PCs, 11th Edition*, available in electronic form on the disc provided with this book.

Hardware Elements of Your Network

The choice of a data-link protocol affects the network hardware you choose. Because Ethernet, Fast Ethernet, Token-Ring, and other data-link protocols use different hardware, you must select the protocol before you can select appropriate hardware, including network interface cards, cables, and hubs or switches.

Network Interface Cards

On most computers, the network interface adapter takes the form of a network interface card (NIC) that fits into a PCI slot on a desktop computer or a PC Card (PCMCIA) slot on a notebook computer. Although network cards for older systems might use the ISA or EISA slot standards, these don't support high-speed network standards and are obsolete. Many recent systems incorporate the network interface adapter onto the motherboard, but this practice is more commonly found in workstations and portable computers and rarely in servers because most network administrators prefer to select their own NICs.

Ethernet and Token-Ring adapters have unique hardware addresses coded into their firmware. The data link layer protocol uses these addresses to identify the other systems on the network. A packet gets to the correct destination because its data link layer protocol header contains the hardware addresses of both the sending and receiving systems.

Note

You can also adapt the USB port for Ethernet use with a USB-to-Ethernet adapter, but because USB 1.1 ports run at only 12Mbps (compared to Fast Ethernet running at 100Mbps), a performance bottleneck results. USB 2.0–to–Fast Ethernet adapters are now available from several vendors and are a suitable choice if your system has USB 2.0 ports but lacks a free PCI or PC Card slot.

10/100 Ethernet network adapters range in price from under $10 for client adapters to as much as $300 or more for server-optimized adapters. Token-Ring adapters are much more expensive, ranging in price from around $100 for client adapters to more than $500 for server-optimized adapters. Network adapters are built in all the popular interface-card types and are also optimized for either workstation or server use. For first-time network users, so-called network-in-a-box kits are available that contain two 10/100 Fast Ethernet NICs, a small hub or switch, and prebuilt UTP cables for less than $90. When combined with the built-in networking software in Windows, these kits make networking very inexpensive. A number of 10/100/1000-BASE-TX Gigabit Ethernet adapters for use with UTP cable can be purchased for under $60, and some 10/100 switches now also feature Gigabit Ethernet ports.

For client workstations (including peer servers on peer-to-peer networks), the following sections contain my recommendations on the features you need.

Speed

Your NIC should run at the maximum speed you want your network to support. For a Fast Ethernet network, for example, you should purchase Ethernet cards that support 100BASE-TX's 100Mbps speed. Most Fast Ethernet cards also support standard Ethernet's 10Mbps speed, allowing the same card to be used on both older and newer portions of the network. To verify dual-speed operation, look for network cards identified as 10/100 Ethernet.

Your NIC should support both half-duplex and full-duplex operation:

- *Half-duplex* means that the network card can only send or only receive data in a single operation.
- *Full-duplex* means that the network card can both receive and send simultaneously. Full-duplex options boost network speed if switches are used in place of hubs. For example, 100Mbps Fast Ethernet cards running in full-duplex mode have a maximum true throughput of 200Mbps, with half going in each direction.

Unlike hubs, which broadcast data packets to all computers connected to it, switches create a direct connection between the sending and receiving computers. Thus, switches provide faster performance than hubs; most switches also support full-duplex operation, doubling the rated speed of the network when full-duplex network cards are used.

Although, at one time, switches were hard to justify on a workgroup peer-to-peer LAN because of their extra cost, switches are now available for little more than the price of hubs with a similar number of ports and are recommended for LANs of any size. If you plan to use your Ethernet-based home or office network to share an Internet connection, consider purchasing a router with an integrated switch. This combination makes networking simple and requires less space than separate routers and switches. Many router/switch combinations cost little more than a switch or router would separately. You can also purchase a wireless access point and router with an integrated switch so both wired and wireless workstations can share a single Internet connection. For other types of networks, you can use a gateway to connect your network with the Internet.

Bus Type

If you are networking desktop computers built from 1995 to the present, you should consider only PCI-based NICs (these computers typically have three or more PCI slots). Although many older computers still have at least one ISA or combo ISA/PCI expansion slot, the superior data bus width and data transfer rate of PCI make it the only logical choice for networks of all types. The integrated NIC found on some recent PC motherboards is also a PCI device. Alternative interfaces include USB or PC Card/Cardbus adapters that are often used for portable systems.

Table 20.3 summarizes the differences between all the types of interfaces used by network cards.

Table 20.3   Bus Choices for Client PC NICs

Bus Type	Bus Width (Bits)	Bus Speed (MHz)	Data Cycles per Clock	Bandwidth (MBps)
8-bit ISA (AT)	8	8.33	1/2	4.17
16-bit ISA (AT-Bus)	16	8.33	1/2	8.33
EISA Bus	32	8.33	1	33
MCA-16 Streaming	16	10	1	20
MCA-32 Streaming	32	10	1	40
MCA-64 Streaming	64	10	1	80
PC-Card (PCMCIA)	16	10	1	20
CardBus	32	33	1	133
PCI	32	33	1	133
PCI 66MHz	32	66	1	266
PCI 64-bit	64	33	1	266
PCI 66MHz/64-bit	64	66	1	533
USB 1.1	1	12	1	1.5
USB 2.0	1	480	1	60

Note: ISA, EISA, and MCA are no longer used in current motherboard designs.

MBps = Megabytes per second

ISA = Industry Standard Architecture, also known as the PC/XT (8-bit) or AT-Bus (16-bit)

EISA = Extended Industry Standard Architecture (32-bit ISA)

MCA = Microchannel Architecture (IBM PS/2 systems)

PC-Card = 16-bit PCMCIA (Personal Computer Memory Card International Association) interface

CardBus = 32-bit PC-Card

PCI = Peripheral Component Interconnect

USB = universal serial bus

Although a few ISA-based NICs are still on the market, their slow speeds and narrow bus widths severely restrict their performance. Most ISA-based Ethernet cards can't support speeds above 10Mbps and thus don't support Fast Ethernet or Gigabit Ethernet. A few vendors make 10/100 Ethernet cards for the ISA slot, but their performance is substantially lower than PCI cards. If you are shopping for a network card for a laptop or notebook system, look for Cardbus types, which are significantly faster than PC Cards and those using USB.

Network Adapter Connectors

Ethernet adapters typically have a connector that looks like a large telephone jack called an RJ-45 (for 10BASE-T and Fast Ethernet twisted-pair cables), a single BNC connector (for Thinnet coaxial cables), or a D-shaped 15-pin connector called a DB15 (for Thicknet coaxial cables). A few older 10Mbps adapters have a combination of two or all three of these connector types; adapters with two or more connectors are referred to as *combo* adapters. Token-Ring adapters can have a 9-pin connector called a DB9 (for Type 1 STP cable) or sometimes an RJ-45 jack (for Type 3 UTP cable). Figure 20.3 shows all three of the Ethernet connectors.

The following figures provide profile views of the most common types of NIC connections. Figure 20.4 shows a 10BASE-2 NIC configured to be at the end of a network; the T-adapter connected to the BNC connector has a Thinnet (RG-58) cable attached to one side and a 50-ohm terminator at the other end.

Figure 20.5 shows a 10BASE-T NIC with its UTP cable attached.

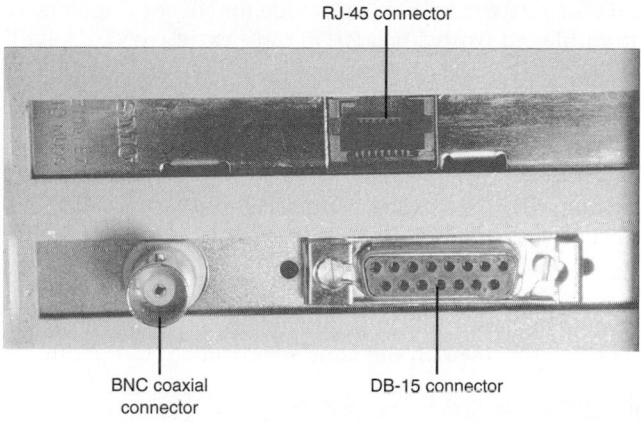

RJ-45 connector

BNC coaxial connector

DB-15 connector

Figure 20.3   Three Ethernet connectors on two NICs: RJ-45 connector (top center), DB-15 connector (bottom right), and BNC connector (bottom left).

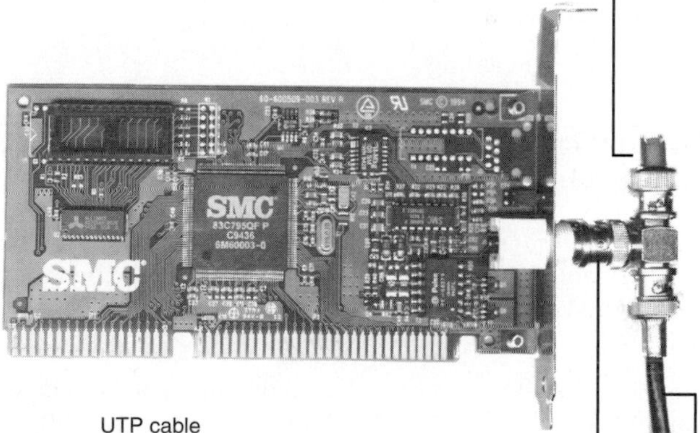

50-ohm terminator

UTP cable

T-connector

Thinnet (RG-58) cable

Figure 20.4   An Ethernet 10BASE-2 NIC configured as the last station in a Thin Ethernet network.

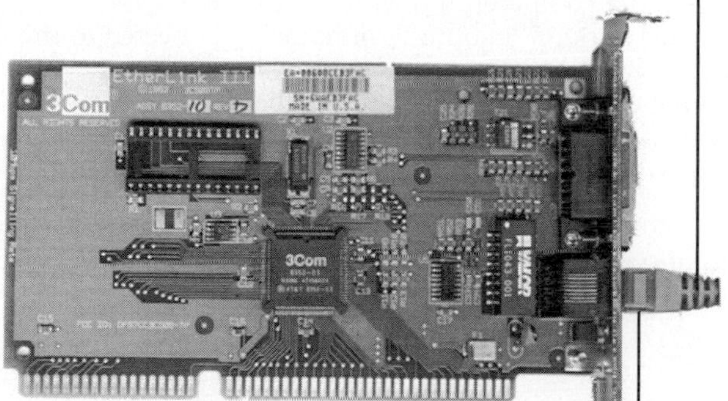

RJ-45 connector

Figure 20.5   An Ethernet 10BASE-T NIC with a UTP cable attached.

Virtually all standard and 10/100 Ethernet NICs made for client-PC use on the market today are designed to support unshielded twisted-pair (UTP) cable exclusively; Gigabit Ethernet cards made for wired (not fiber-optic) networks also use only UTP cable. If you are adding a client PC to an existing network that uses some form of coaxial cable, you have three options:

- Purchase a combo NIC that supports coaxial cable as well as RJ-45 twisted-pair cabling.

- Purchase a media converter that can be attached to the coaxial cable to allow the newer UTP-based NICs to connect to the existing network.

- Use a switch or hub that has both coaxial cable and RJ-45 ports. A dual-speed (10/100) device is needed if you are adding one or more Fast Ethernet clients.

For maximum economy, NICs and network cables must match, although media converters can be used to interconnect networks based on the same standard, but using different cable.

Network Cables

Originally, all networks used some type of cable to connect the computers on the network to each other. Although various types of wireless networks are now on the market, most office and home networks are still based on one of the following media types:

- Coaxial cable
- Twisted-pair cabling

Thick and Thin Ethernet Coaxial Cable

The first versions of Ethernet were based on coaxial cable. The original form of Ethernet, 10BASE-5, used a thick coaxial cable (called Thicknet) that was not directly attached to the NIC. A device called an attachment unit interface (AUI) ran from a DB15 connector on the rear of the NIC to the cable. The cable had a hole drilled into it to allow the "vampire tap" to be connected to the cable. NICs designed for use with thick Ethernet cable are almost impossible to find as new hardware today.

10BASE-2 Ethernet cards use a BNC (Bayonet-Neill-Concilman) connector on the rear of the NIC. Although the thin coaxial cable (called Thinnet or RG-58) used with 10BASE-2 Ethernet has a bayonet connector that can physically attach to the BNC connector on the card, this configuration is incorrect and won't work. Instead, a BNC T-connector attaches to the rear of the card, allowing a thin Ethernet cable to be connected to either both ends of the T (for a computer in the middle of the networ]k) or to one end only (for a computer at the end of the network). A 50-ohm terminator is connected to the other arm of the T to indicate the end of the network and prevent erroneous signals from being sent to other clients on the network. Some early Ethernet cards were designed to handle thick (AUI/DB15), thin (RG-58), and UTP (RJ-45) cables. Combo cards with both BNC and RJ-45 connectors are still available but can run at only standard Ethernet speeds.

Figure 20.6 compares Ethernet DB-15 to AUI, BNC coaxial T-connector, and RJ-45 UTP connectors to each other, and Figure 20.7 illustrates the design of coaxial cable.

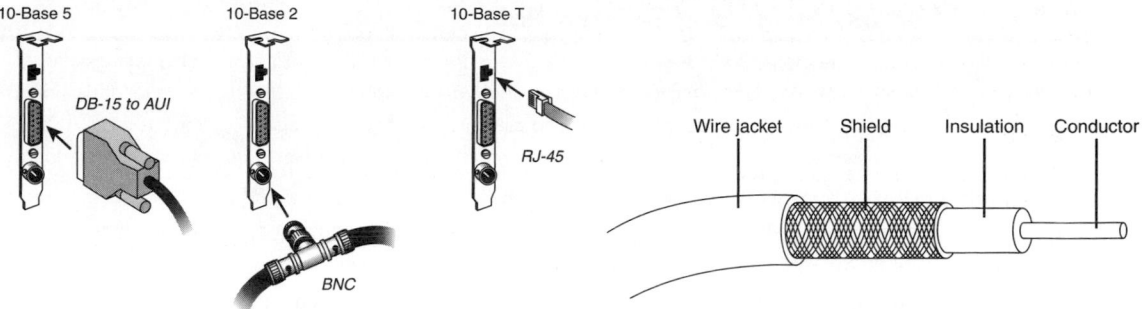

Figure 20.6 An Ethernet network card with thick Ethernet (DB-15), thin Ethernet (RG-58 with T-connector), and UTP (RJ-45) connectors.

Figure 20.7 Coaxial cable.

Twisted-Pair Cable

Twisted-pair cable is just what its name implies: insulated wires within a protective casing with a specified number of twists per foot. Twisting the wires reduces the effect of electromagnetic interference (that can be generated by nearby cables, electric motors, and fluorescent lighting) on the signals being transmitted. Shielded twisted pair (STP) refers to the amount of insulation around the cluster of wires and therefore its immunity to noise. You are probably familiar with unshielded twisted-pair (UTP) cable; it is often used for telephone wiring. Figure 20.8 shows unshielded twisted-pair cable; Figure 20.9 illustrates shielded twisted-pair cable.

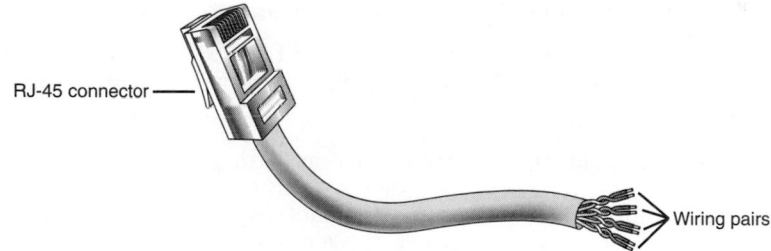

Figure 20.8 An unshielded twisted-pair (UTP) cable.

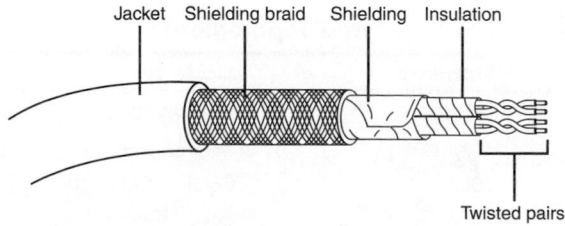

Figure 20.9 A shielded twisted-pair (STP) cable.

Shielded Versus Unshielded Twisted Pair

When cabling was being developed for use with computers, it was first thought that shielding the cable from external interference was the best way to reduce interference and provide for greater transmission speeds. However, it was discovered that twisting the pairs of wires is a more effective way to prevent interference from disrupting transmissions. As a result, earlier cabling scenarios relied on shielded cables rather than the unshielded cables more commonly in use today.

Shielded cables also have some special grounding concerns because one, and only one, end of a shielded cable should be connected to an earth ground; issues arose when people inadvertently caused grounding loops to occur by connecting both ends or caused the shield to act as an antenna because it wasn't grounded.

Grounding loops are situations in which two different grounds are tied together. This is a bad situation because each ground can have a slightly different potential, resulting in a circuit that has very low voltage but infinite amperage. This causes undue stress on electrical components and can be a fire hazard.

Most Ethernet and Fast Ethernet installations that use twisted-pair cabling use UTP because the physical flexibility and small size of the cable and connectors makes routing it very easy. However, its lack of electrical insulation can make interference from fluorescent lighting, elevators, and alarm systems (among other devices) a major problem. If you use UTP in installations where interference can be a problem, you need to route the cable away from the interference, use an external shield, or substitute STP for UTP near interference sources.

Network Topologies

Each computer on the network is connected to the other computers with cable (or some other medium). The physical arrangement of the cables connecting computers on a network is called the network *topology*.

The three types of basic topologies used in computer networks are as follows:

- *Bus.* Connects each computer on a network directly to the next computer in a linear fashion. The network connection starts at the server and ends at the last computer in the network.
- *Star.* Connects each computer on the network to a central access point.
- *Ring.* Connects each computer to the others in a loop or ring.

These different topologies are often mixed, forming what is called a *hybrid network*. For example, you can link the hubs of several star networks together with a bus, forming a star-bus network. Rings can be connected in the same way.

Table 20.4 summarizes the relationships between network types and topologies.

Table 20.4   Network Cable Types and Topologies

Network Type	Standard	Cable Type	Topology
Ethernet	10BASE-2	Thin (RG-58) coaxial	Bus
Ethernet	10BASE-5	Thick coaxial	Bus
Ethernet	10BASE-T	Cat 3 or Cat 5 UTP	Star
Fast Ethernet	100BASE-TX	Cat 5 UTP	Star
Gigabit Ethernet	1000BASE-TX	Cat 5, 5e, or 6 UTP	Star
Token-Ring	(all)	UTP or STP	Logical ring

Bus Topology

The earliest type of network topology was the *bus topology*, which uses a single cable to connect all the computers in the network to each other, as shown in Figure 20.10. This network topology was adopted initially because running a single cable past all the computers in the network is easier and less wiring is used than with other topologies. Because early bus topology networks used bulky coaxial cables, these factors were important advantages. Both 10BASE-5 (thick) and 10BASE-2 (thin) Ethernet networks are based on the bus topology.

However, the advent of cheaper and more compact unshielded twisted-pair cabling, which also supports faster networks, has made the disadvantages of a bus topology apparent. If one computer or cable connection malfunctions, it can cause all the stations beyond it on the bus to lose their network connections. Thick Ethernet (10BASE-5) networks often fail because the vampire tap connecting the AUI device to the coaxial cable comes loose. In addition, the T-adapters and terminating resistors on a 10BASE-2 Thin Ethernet network can also come loose or be removed by the user, causing all or part of the network to fail. Another drawback of Thin Ethernet (10BASE-2) networks is that adding a new computer to the network between existing computers might require replacement of the existing network cable between the computers with shorter segments to connect to the new computer's network card and T-adapter.

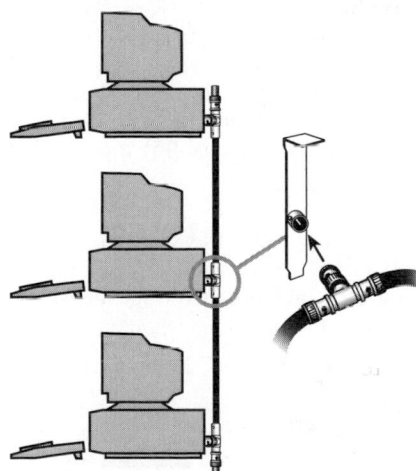

Figure 20.10   A 10BASE-2 network is an example of a linear bus topology, attaching all network devices to a common cable.

Ring Topology

Another topology often listed in discussions of this type is a *ring*, in which each workstation is connected to the next and the last workstation is connected to the first again (essentially a bus topology with the two ends connected). Two major network types use the ring topology:

- *Fiber Distributed Data Interface (FDDI)*. A network topology used for large, high-speed networks using fiber-optic cables in a physical ring topology
- *Token-Ring*. Uses a logical ring topology

A Token-Ring network resembles a 10BASE-T or 10/100 Ethernet network at first glance because both networks use a central connecting device and a physical star topology. Where is the "Ring" in Token-Ring?

The ring exists only within the device that connects the computers, which is called a *multistation access unit (MSAU)* on a Token-Ring network (see Figure 20.11).

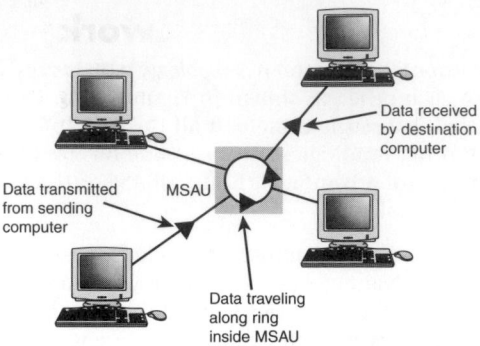

Figure 20.11   A Token-Ring network during the sending of data from one computer to another.

Signals generated from one computer travel to the MSAU, are sent out to the next computer, and then go back to the MSAU again. The data is then passed to each system in turn until it arrives back at the computer that originated it, where it is removed from the network. Therefore, although the physical wiring topology is a star, the data path is theoretically a ring. This is called a *logical ring*.

A logical ring that Token-Ring networks use is preferable to a physical ring network topology because it affords a greater degree of fault tolerance. As on a bus network, a cable break anywhere in a physical ring network topology, such as FDDI, affects the entire network. FDDI networks use two physical rings to provide a backup in case one ring fails. By contrast, on a Token-Ring network, the MSAU can effectively remove a malfunctioning computer from the logical ring, enabling the rest of the network to function normally.

Star Topology

The most popular type of topology in use today has separate cables to connect each computer to a central wiring nexus, often called a *hub* or *concentrator*; a switch can also be used in place of a hub. Figure 20.12 shows this arrangement, which is called a *star topology*.

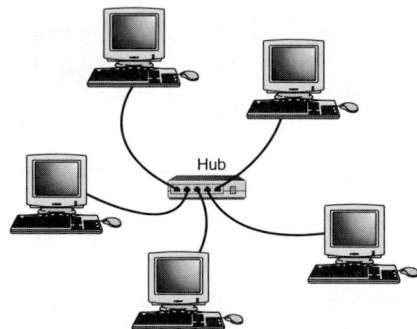

Figure 20.12   The star topology, linking the LAN's computers and devices to one or more central hubs, or access units.

Because each computer uses a separate cable, the failure of a network connection affects only the single machine involved. The other computers can continue to function normally. Bus cabling schemes use less cable than the star but are harder to diagnose or bypass when problems occur. At this time, Fast Ethernet in a star topology is the most commonly implemented type of LAN; this is the type of network you build with most preconfigured network kits. 10BASE-T Ethernet and 1000BASE-TX Gigabit Ethernet also use the star topology. 10BASE-T can use either Category 3 or Category 5 UTP, whereas Fast Ethernet and Gigabit Ethernet require Category 5 UTP or greater.

Hubs and Switches for Ethernet Networks

As you have seen, modern Ethernet workgroup networks are based on UTP cable with workstations arranged in a star topology. The center of the star uses a multiport connecting device that can be either a hub or a switch. Although hubs and switches can be used to connect the network—and can have several features in common—the differences between them are also significant and are covered in the following sections.

All Ethernet hubs and switches have the following features:

- Multiple RJ-45 UTP connectors
- Diagnostic and activity lights
- A power supply

Ethernet hubs and switches are made in two forms: managed and unmanaged. *Managed* hubs and switches can be configured, enabled or disabled, or monitored by a network operator and are commonly used on corporate networks. Workgroup and home-office networks use less expensive *unmanaged* hubs, which simply connect computers on the network.

Note

The now-obsolete ARCnet network used its own types of hubs: passive hubs, which were unpowered, and active hubs, which used a power supply. Neither type of hub is compatible with Ethernet.

The connection between each workstation and the hub or switch is the UTP cable running from the RJ-45 jack on the rear of the NIC to the RJ-45 jack on the rear of the hub or switch.

Signal lights on the front of the hub or switch indicate which connections are in use by computers; switches also indicate whether a full-duplex connection is in use. Multispeed hubs and switches also indicate which connection speed is in use on each port. Your hub or switch must have at least one RJ-45 UTP connector for each computer you want to connect to it. Figure 20.13 shows a typical five-port, 10/100 Ethernet hub suitable for small networks at home or in a small business.

Link/activity lights
Power light
100Mbps connection lights

Figure 20.13   A typical 10/100, five-port workgroup hub. *Photo courtesy Linksys.*

How Hubs Work

A computer on an Ethernet network broadcasts (sends) a request for network information or programs from a specific computer through the cable to the hub, which broadcasts the request to all computers connected to it. When the destination computer receives the message, it sends the requested information back to the hub, which broadcasts it again to all computers, although only the requesting computer acts on the information. Thus, a hub acts similarly to a radio transmitter and receiver that sends a signal to all radios, but only the radios set for the correct station can send or receive the information.

How Switches Differ from Hubs

Switches are similar to hubs in that they connect computers on a UTP-based Ethernet network to each other and physically resemble hubs (see Figure 20.14). However, instead of broadcasting data to all computers on the network as hubs do, switches use a feature called *address storing*, which checks the destination for each data packet and sends it directly to the computer it's intended for. Thus, a switch can be compared to a telephone exchange, making direct connections between the originator of a call and the receiver.

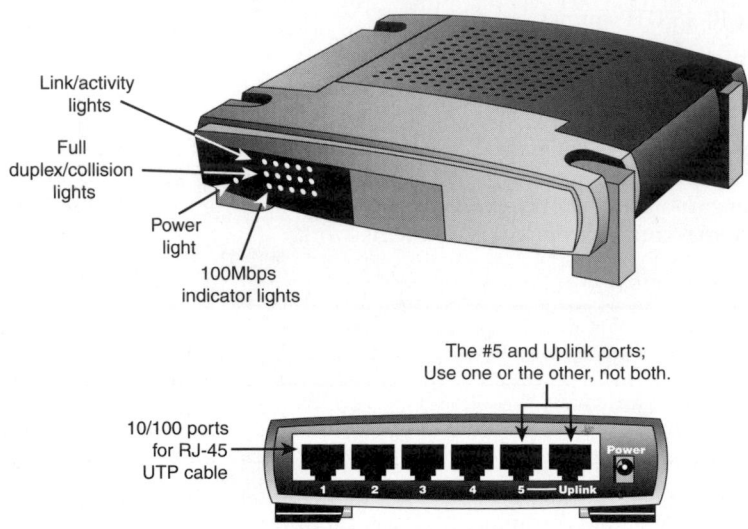

Figure 20.14   Front (top) and rear (bottom) of a typical five-port, 10/100 Ethernet switch.

Because switches establish a direct connection between the originating and receiving PC, they also provide the full bandwidth of the network to each port. Hubs, by contrast, must subdivide the network's bandwidth by the number of active connections on the network, meaning that bandwidth rises and falls depending on network activity.

For example, assume you have a four-station network workgroup using 10/100 NICs and a Fast Ethernet hub. The total bandwidth of the network is 100Mbps. However, if two stations are active, the effective bandwidth available to each station drops to 50Mbps (100Mbps divided by 2). If all four stations are active, the effective bandwidth drops to just 25Mbps (100Mbps divided by 4)! Add more active users, and the effective bandwidth continues to drop.

By replacing the hub with a switch, the effective bandwidth for each station remains 100Mbps because the switch doesn't broadcast data to all stations.

Most 10/100 NICs and Fast Ethernet or 10/100 switches also support full-duplex (simultaneous transmit and receive), enabling actual bandwidth to be double the nominal 100Mbps rating: 200Mbps. Table 20.5 summarizes the differences between the two devices.

Table 20.5   Ethernet Hub and Switch Comparison

Feature	Hub	Switch
Bandwidth	Divided by total number of ports in use	Dedicated to each port in use
Data transmission	Broadcast to all connected computers	Broadcast only to the receiving computer
Duplex support	Half-duplex	Full-duplex when used with full-duplex NICs

As you can see, using a switch instead of a hub greatly increases the effective speed of a network, even if all other components remain the same.

Because of the improved performance of switches, I recommend them instead of hubs for networks of any size.

Additional Hub and Switch Features You Might Need

Although older hubs and switches run at only a single speed and have only a few RJ-45 connectors, it makes sense to upgrade to newer, more flexible equipment. Most recent hubs and switches have the following useful features, which are worth asking for:

- *Dual-speed hubs/switches.* If you are adding Fast Ethernet (100BASE-TX) clients to an existing 10BASE-T network, you need a dual-speed hub or switch to connect the various types of Ethernet together.

  Even if you are building a brand-new Fast Ethernet network, a dual-speed hub or switch is useful for occasionally hosting a "guest" PC that has only a standard 10BASE-T Ethernet NIC onboard. Even though most Fast Ethernet switches and hubs on the market today are actually 10/100 dual-speed models, you might still encounter a Fast Ethernet–only unit. These should be used only on networks that will never have a 10BASE-T connection.

- *Stackable hub or switch with an uplink port.* A *stackable* hub or switch is one that can be connected to another hub, enabling you to add computers to your network without replacing the hub or switch every time it runs out of connections. Most hubs and switches on the market today are stackable (but very small) hubs, and some older models might lack this feature. You can use this feature to add 10/100 features to an older 10BASE-T-only network and connect a dual-speed hub or switch to the uplink port on your 10BASE-T hub.

- *"Extra" ports beyond your current requirements.* If you are connecting four computers together into a small network, you need a four-port hub or switch (the smallest available). But, if you buy a hub or switch with only four ports and want to add another client PC to the network, you must add a second hub or switch or replace the hub or switch with a larger one with more ports.

  Instead, plan for the future by buying a hub or switch that can handle your projected network growth over the next year. If you plan to add two workstations, buy at least a six-port hub or switch (the cost per connection drops as you buy hubs with more connections). Even though most hubs and switches are stackable to support the growth of your network, the more ports a hub or switch has, the less expensive per port it will be.

To determine whether a hub or switch is stackable, look for an uplink port, as shown in Figure 20.15. This port looks like an ordinary RJ-45 UTP port, but it is wired differently, enabling you to use a standard-pinout RJ-45 UTP cable to connect it to another hub. Without the uplink port, you'd have to use a specially wired crossover cable.

Typically, hubs and switches with an uplink port allow you to use the port along with all but one of the normal ports on the hub (see Figure 20.15). For example, one of my associates uses a five-port switch from Linksys that also contains a router (for Internet access) and an uplink port. If his office network expands beyond five computers, he can use the uplink port to add another switch to expand the network and provide the new stations, as well as the original network, with Internet access.

The uplink port connects
this hub to another hub.

Up to five devices (computers and
printers) can be connected to this hub.

Figure 20.15 The connectors on a typical five-port workgroup hub with an uplink port (at left) for connecting this hub to another hub (stacking the hubs). Either port #5 or the uplink port can be used, but not both.

Hub and Switch Placement

Although large networks have a wiring closet near the server, the workgroup-size LANs you'll be building don't need a wiring closet. However, the location of the hub or switch is important.

Ethernet hubs and switches require electrical power, whether they are small units that use a power "brick" or larger units that have an internal power supply and a standard three-prong AC cord.

In addition to electrical power, consider placing the hub or switch where its signal lights will be easy to view for diagnostic purposes and where its RJ-45 connectors can be reached easily when it's time to add another user or two. In many offices, the hub or switch sits on the corner of the desk, enabling the user to see network problems just by looking at the hub or switch.

If the hub or switch also integrates a router for use with a broadband Internet device, such as a DSL or cable modem, you can place it near the cable or DSL modem or at a distance if the layout of your home or office requires it. Because the cable or DSL modem usually connects to your computer by the same Category 5 cable used for UTP Ethernet networking, you can run the cable from the cable or DSL modem to the router/switch's WAN port and connect all the computers to the LAN ports on the router/switch.

Except for the 328-ft. (100-meter) limit for all forms of UTP Ethernet (10BASE-T, 100BASE-TX, and 1000BASE-TX), distances between each computer on the network and the hub or switch aren't critical, so put the hub or switch wherever you can supply power and gain easy access.

Tip

Decide where you plan to put your hub or switch before you buy prebuilt UTP wiring or make your own; if you move the hub or switch, some of your wiring will no longer be the correct length. Although excess lengths of UTP cable can be coiled and secured with cable ties, cables that are too short should be replaced. You can buy RJ-45 connectors to create one long cable from two short cables, but you must ensure the connectors are Category 5 if you are running Fast Ethernet; some vendors still sell Category 3 connectors that support only 10Mbps. You're really better off replacing the too-short cable with the correct length.

Network Cable Installations

If you have to run cables (of any type) through existing walls and ceilings, the cable installation can be the most expensive part of setting up a LAN. At every branching point, special fittings connect the intersecting wires. Sometimes, you also need various additional components along the way, such as hubs, repeaters, or MSAUs.

Note

As an alternative to wired networks, more and more companies and home users are exploring wireless networks using radio waves and other technologies. Although these networks are not yet as fast as wired solutions such as Fast Ethernet, they are useful for solutions in which wiring isn't feasible or when speed is not important. See the section "Wireless Network Standards," later in this chapter, for details.

With the development of easy-to-build (or prebuilt) Category 5 twisted-pair cabling, high-speed and low-cost NICs and hubs, and built-in basic networking in current versions of Windows, installing and setting up a network today is far easier than ever before. For small cubicle/office networking in which no wire must be routed through walls and in which Windows peer networking software will be used, you should be able to set up the network yourself.

If your wiring must go through walls, be run through dropped ceilings, be piggybacked on air ducts, or be run between floors, you might want to have professional network-cable specialists install the cable. A good company knows the following:

- When UTP (unshielded twisted-pair) cabling is adequate
- Where STP (shielded twisted-pair) cabling might be necessary to avoid excessive cable runs and interference
- How to route cable between rooms, floors, and nonadjacent offices
- How to use wall panels to make cable attachments look better and more professional
- When you must use fireproof Plenum cable
- How to deal with sources of electrical interference, such as elevator motors, transmitters, alarm systems, and even florescent office lighting, by using fiber-optic or shielded cable

If you decide you need professional cable installation, be sure to get a firm price quote first because the cost of a complex cable installation might make a wireless network a more appealing choice.

Selecting the Proper Cable

A network is only as fast as its slowest component; to achieve the maximum speeds of the network, all its components, including cables, must meet the standards. Two standard types of twisted-pair cabling exist:

- *Category 3 cable.* The original type of UTP cable used for Ethernet networks was also the same as that used for business telephone wiring. This is known as Category 3, or voice-grade UTP cable, and is measured according to a scale that quantifies the cable's data-transmission capabilities. The cable itself is 24 AWG (American Wire Gauge, a standard for measuring the diameter of a wire), copper-tinned with solid conductors, 100–105 ohm characteristic impedance, and a minimum of two twists per foot. Category 3 cable is adequate for networks running at up to 16Mbps. This cable usually looks like "silver" telephone cable, but with the larger RJ-45 connector. Category 3 cabling is obsolete because it doesn't support Fast Ethernet or greater network speeds.

- *Category 5 cable.* The newer, faster network types require greater performance levels. Fast Ethernet (100BASE-TX) uses the same two-wire pairs as 10BASE-T, but Fast Ethernet needs a greater resistance to signal crosstalk and attenuation. Therefore, the use of Category 5 UTP cabling is essential with 100BASE-TX Fast Ethernet. Although the 100BASE-T4 version of Fast Ethernet can use all four-wire pairs of Category 3 cable, this flavor of Fast Ethernet is not widely supported and has practically vanished from the marketplace. Thus, for practical purposes, if you mix Category 3 and Category 5 cables, you should use only 10BASE-T (10Mbps) Ethernet hubs; if you try to run Fast Ethernet 100BASE-TX over Category 3 cable, you will have a slow and unreliable network. Category 5 cable is commonly called CAT5 and is also referred to as Class D cable.

Many cable vendors also sell an enhanced form of Category 5 cable called Category 5e (specified by Addendum 5 of the ANSI/TIA/EIA-568-A cabling standard). Category 5e cable can be used in place of Category 5 cable and is especially well suited for use in Fast Ethernet networks that might be upgraded to Gigabit Ethernet in the future. Category 5e cabling must pass several tests not required for Category 5 cabling. Even though you can use both Category 5 and Category 5e cabling on a Gigabit Ethernet network, Category 5e cabling provides better transmission rates and a greater margin of safety for reliable data transmission.

Category 6 cabling (also called CAT 6 or Class E) can be used in place of CAT 5 or 5e cabling and uses the same RJ-45 connectors as CAT 5 and 5e. CAT 6 cable handles a frequency range of 1MHz–250MHz, compared to CAT5 and CAT5e's 1MHz–100MHz frequency range.

You should use existing Category 3 cable for your LAN only if you are content with the 10Mbps speeds of 10BASE-T and if the cable is in good condition. The silver exterior on Category 3 cabling can become brittle and deteriorate, leading to frequent network failures. If you are installing new wiring for a new network or replacing deteriorated Category 3 cable, you should use Category 5, Category 5e, or Category 6 cabling. All three types are widely available either in prebuilt assemblies or in bulk.

The newest standard—Category 7 cabling (also called CAT 7 or Class F)—handles a frequency range of 1MHz–600MHz and reduces propagation delay and delay skew, which enables longer network cables and larger numbers of workstations on a network. CAT 7 uses the GG45 connector developed by Nexans. The GG45 connector resembles the RJ-45 connector but has four additional contacts (see Figure 20.16). The GG45 connector contains a switch that activates a maximum of 8 out of 12 contacts. The upper 8 RJ45 contacts are used for up to 250MHz (CAT 6) operation, whereas the 8 contacts in the outer edges are used for 600MHz (CAT 7) operation. Only 8 contacts are used at a given time. In other words, this connector is designed to be backward-compatible with cables using RJ-45 connectors, while supporting the newer standard.

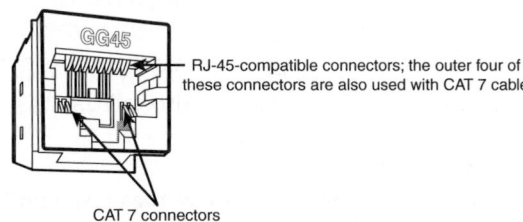

Figure 20.16   The GG45 connector from Nexans can accept CAT 5 and other standard network cabling using the RJ-45 connector or the new CAT 7 cabling.

Caution

If you choose to install Category 5/5e UTP cable, be sure that all the connectors, wall plates, and other hardware components involved are also Category 5-rated.

If you are trying to connect prebuilt Category 5 cabling together on a Fast Ethernet network, use Category 5–grade or better connectors; otherwise, you'll create a substandard section that might fail in your network.

Choosing the correct type of Category 5/5e cable is also important. Use solid PVC cable for network cables that represent a permanent installation. However, the slightly more expensive stranded cables are a better choice for a notebook computer or temporary wiring of no more than 10 ft. lengths (from a computer to a wall socket, for example) because it is more flexible and is therefore capable of withstanding frequent movement.

If you plan to use air ducts or suspended ceilings for cable runs, you should use Plenum cable, which doesn't emit harmful fumes in a fire. It is much more expensive, but the safety issue is a worthwhile reason to use it (and it is required by some localities).

Building Your Own Twisted-Pair Cables

When it's time to wire your network, you have two choices. You can opt to purchase prebuilt cables, or you can build your own cables from bulk wire and connectors.

You should build your own twisted-pair cables if you

■ Plan to perform a lot of networking

■ Need cable lengths longer than the lengths you can buy preassembled at typical computer departments

■ Want to create both standard and crossover cables

■ Want to choose your own cable color

■ Want maximum control over cable length

■ Want to save money

■ Have the time necessary to build cables

TP Wiring Standards

If you want to create twisted-pair (TP) cables yourself, be sure your cable pairs match the color-coding of any existing cable or the color-coding of any prebuilt cabling you want to add to your new network. Because there are eight wires in TP cables, many incorrect combinations are possible. Several standards exist for UTP cabling.

Tip

The key is to be consistent and use the same scheme for all your cables and to ensure that anyone else working on your network understands the scheme used in it.

One common standard is the AT&T 258A configuration (also called EIA/TIA 568B). Table 20.6 lists the wire pairing and placement within the standard RJ-45 connector.

Table 20.6 RJ-45 Connector Wire Pairing and Placement for AT&T 258A/EIA 568B Standard

Wire Pairing	Wire Connected to Pin #	Pair Used for
White/blue and blue	White/blue - #5 Blue - #4	Not used[1]
White/orange and orange	White/orange - #1 Orange - #2	Transmit
White/green and green	White/green - #3 Green - #6	Receive
White/brown and brown	White/brown - #7 Brown - #8	Not used[1]

1. This pair is not used with 10BASE-T or Fast Ethernet 100BASE-TX, but all four pairs are used with Fast Ethernet 100BASE-T4 and Gigabit Ethernet 1000BASE-TX standards.

In Figure 20.17 you can see an RJ-45 cable connector wired to the EIA 568B/AT&T 258A standard.

Note

You also might encounter the similar EIA 568A standard. It reverses the position of the orange and green pairs listed previously.

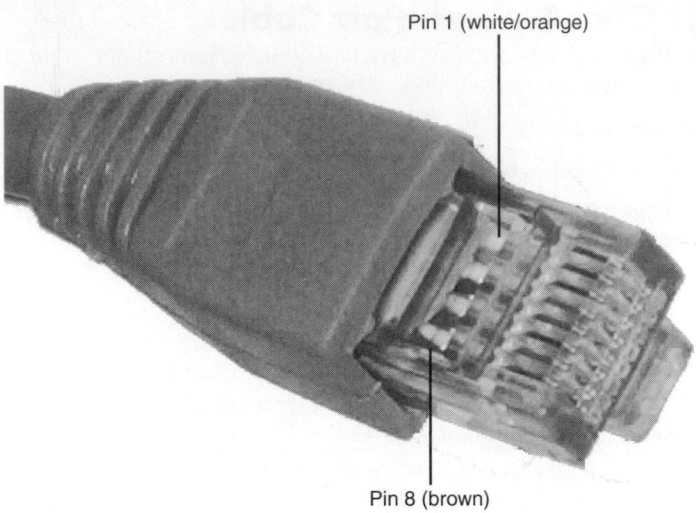

Pin 1 (white/orange)

Pin 8 (brown)

Figure 20.17 An AT&T 258A/EIA 568B standard compliant RJ-45 connector.

Crossover UTP Cables

Crossover cables, which change the wiring at one end of the cable, are used to connect two (and only two) computers together when no hub or switch is available or to connect a hub or switch without an uplink (stacking) port to another hub or switch. The pinout for a crossover cable is shown in Table 20.7. This pinout is for one end of the cable only; the other end of the cable should correspond to the standard TIA 568B pinout, as shown previously in Figure 20.17.

Table 20.7 RJ-45 Connector Wire Pairing and Placement for Crossover Variation on EIA 568B Standard

Wire	Pin #	Wire	Pin #
White/blue	5	White/orange	3
Blue	4	Orange	6
White/green	1	White/brown	7
Green	2	Brown	8

Note

It should be noted that other wiring schemes exist, such as IEEE and USOC. All told, at least eight agreed-on standards exist for connecting UTP cables and RJ-45 connectors. The ones listed in this chapter are the most common.

Making Your Own UTP Cables

Making your own UTP cables requires a few tools that aren't commonly found in a typical toolbox. Those items that you might not already have you can typically purchase for a single price from many network-products vendors. You will need the following tools and supplies to build your own Ethernet cables (see Figure 20.18):

- UTP cable (Category 5 or better)
- RJ-45 connectors
- Wire stripper
- RJ-45 crimping tool

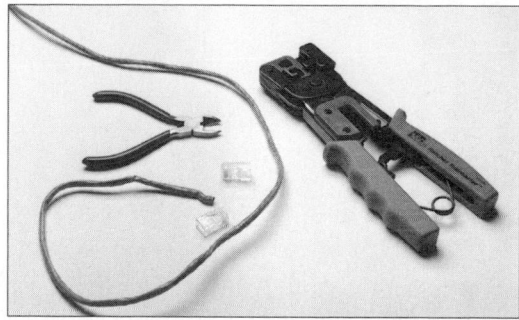

Figure 20.18   You'll need wire strippers, a crimping tool, bulk UTP cable, and RJ-45 connectors to make your own 10BASE-T (100BASE-T) cables.

Before you make a "real" cable of any length, you should practice on a short length of cable. RJ-45 connectors and bulk cable are cheap; network failures are not. Follow these steps for creating your own twisted-pair cables:

1. Determine how long your UTP cable should be. You should allow adequate slack for moving the computer and for avoiding strong interference sources. Keep the maximum distances for UTP cables listed later in this chapter in mind.

2. Roll out the appropriate length of cable.

3. Cut the cable cleanly from the box of wire.

4. Use the wire stripper to strip only the insulation jacket off the cable to expose the TP wires (see Figure 20.19); you'll need to rotate the wire about 1 1/4 turns to strip away all the jacket. If you turn it too far, you'll damage the wires inside the cable.

5. Check the outer jacket and inner TP wires for nicks; adjust the stripper tool and repeat steps 3 and 4 if you see damage.

6. As shown in Figure 20.20, arrange the wires according to the EIA 568B standard. This arrangement is listed earlier in the chapter, in the section "TP Wiring Standards."

7. Trim the wire edges so the eight wires are even with one another and are slightly less than 1/2" past the end of the jacket. If the wires are too long, crosstalk (wire-to-wire interference) can result; if the wires are too short, they can't make a good connection with the RJ-45 plug.

8. With the clip side of the RJ-45 plug facing away from you, push the cable into place (see Figure 20.21). Verify that the wires are arranged according to the EIA/TIA 568B standard *before* you crimp the plug onto the wires (refer to Table 20.6 and Figure 20.17 earlier in this chapter). Adjust the connection as necessary.

9. Use the crimping tool to squeeze the RJ-45 plug onto the cable (see Figure 20.22). The end of the cable should be tight enough to resist being removed by hand.

10. Repeat steps 4–9 for the other end of the cable. Recut the end of the cable if necessary before stripping it.

11. Label each cable with the following information:
    - Wiring standard
    - Length
    - End with crossover (if any)
    - _____ (blank) for computer ID

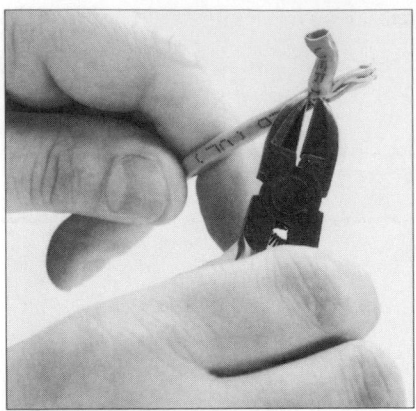

Figure 20.19 Carefully strip the cable jacket away to expose the four wire pairs.

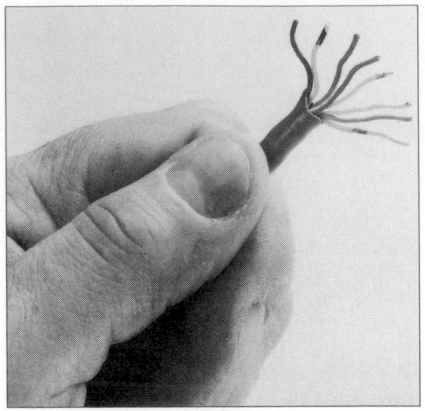

Figure 20.20 Arrange the wire pairs for insertion into the RJ-45 connector according to your chosen scheme (EIA 568B for instance).

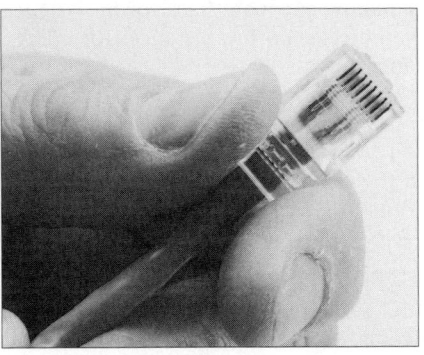

Figure 20.21 Push the RJ-45 connector into place, ensuring the cable pairs are ordered properly.

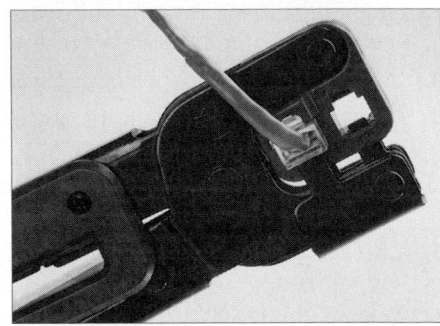

Figure 20.22 Firmly squeeze the crimping tool to attach the connector to the cable.

The cables should be labeled at both ends to make matching the cable with the correct computer easy and to facilitate troubleshooting at the hub. Check with your cable supplier for suitable labeling stock or tags you can attach to each cable.

An excellent online source for this process is `http://www.duxcw.com/digest/Howto/network/cable/`.

Cable Distance Limitations

The people who design computer systems love to find ways to circumvent limitations. Manufacturers of Ethernet products have made possible the building of networks in star, branch, and tree designs that overcome the basic limitations already mentioned. You can have thousands of computers on a complex Ethernet network.

LANs are local because the network adapters and other hardware components typically can't send LAN messages more than a few hundred feet. Table 20.8 lists the distance limitations of various types of LAN cable. In addition to the limitations shown in the table, keep the following points in mind:

■ You can't connect more than 30 computers on a single Thinnet Ethernet segment.

■ You can't connect more than 100 computers on a Thicknet Ethernet segment.

- You can't connect more than 72 computers on a UTP Token-Ring cable.
- You can't connect more than 260 computers on an STP Token-Ring cable.

Table 20.8   Network Distance Limitations

Network Adapter	Cable Type	Maximum	Minimum
Ethernet	10BASE-2	185m (607 ft.)	0.5m (1.6 ft.)
	10BASE-5 (drop)	50m (164 ft.)	2.5m (8.2 ft.)
	10BASE-5 (backbone)	500m (1,640 ft.)	2.5m (8.2 ft.)
	10BASE-T	100m (328 ft.)	2.5m (8.2 ft.)
	100BASE-TX	100m (328 ft.)	2.5m (8.2 ft.)
	1000BASE-TX	100m (328 ft.)	2.5m (8.2 ft.)
Token-Ring	STP	100m (328 ft.)	2.5m (8.2 ft.)
	UTP	45m (147 ft.)	2.5m (8.2 ft.)
ARCnet	Passive hub drop	30m (98 ft.)	Varies by cable type
	Active hub	600m (1,968 ft.)	Varies by cable type

If you have a station wired with Category 5 cable that is more than 328 feet (100 meters) from a hub, you must use a repeater. If you have two or more stations beyond the 328 ft. limit of UTP Ethernet, connect them to a hub or switch that is less than 328 feet away from the primary hub or switch and connect the new hub or switch to the primary hub or switch via its uplink port. Because hubs and switches can act as repeaters, this feature enables you to extend the effective length of your network (see Figure 20.23).

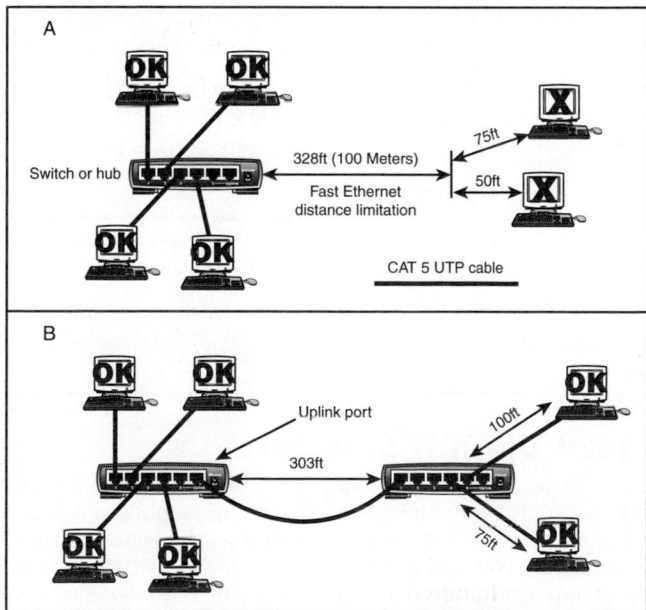

Figure 20.23   In case A (top), the workstations on the right are too far away from the hub to connect to a Fast Ethernet network. In case B (bottom), an additional hub or switch is used to allow the workstations to be added to the network.

Wireless Network Standards

Various forms of wireless networks using either radio or IR (infrared) have been developed over the years, but until recently, the benefits of a wireless network (no wires to pull or holes to drill) were outweighed by the lack of standards and relatively slow speed. In conventional Ethernet networks, you can use various brands of NICs, hubs, and switches without any problems, as long as each device corresponds to the same Ethernet standard.

Even though early forms of wireless networking were much slower than wired networks and often were single-vendor proprietary solutions, today's newest wireless networks offer speeds comparable to or faster than 10BASE-T wired networks and offer multivendor mix-and-match equipment sources. Prices have also dropped dramatically, making wireless networking an increasingly appealing alternative to traditional wired network solutions.

The most common forms of wireless networking in the United States and Canada are built around various versions of the IEEE 802.11 wireless Ethernet standards, including IEEE 802.11b, IEEE 802.11a, and the newer IEEE 802.11g standard.

Wi-Fi (Wireless Fidelity) is a logo and term given to any IEEE 802.11 wireless network product that is certified to conform to specific interoperability standards. Wi-Fi Certification comes from the Wi-Fi Alliance, a nonprofit international trade organization that tests 802.11-based wireless equipment to ensure it meets the Wi-Fi standard. To wear the Wi-Fi logo, an 802.11 networking product must pass specific compatibility and performance tests, which ensure that the product will work with all other manufacturers' Wi-Fi equipment on the market. This certification arose from the fact that certain ambiguities in the 802.11 standards allowed for potential problems with interoperability between devices. By purchasing only devices bearing the Wi-Fi logo, you ensure that they will work together and not fall into loopholes in the standards.

The Bluetooth standard for short-range wireless networking is designed to complement, rather than rival, IEEE 802.11–based wireless networks. In Europe, HiperLAN, which has performance and frequency usage similar to that of 802.11a, is the wireless networking standard.

The widespread popularity of IEEE 802.11–based wireless networks has led to the abandonment of other types of wireless networking, including RadioLAN and HomeRF. RadioLAN now markets long-range antennas that work with 802.11a-based wireless networks.

Note

The HomeRF Working Group, an industry group that supported the development of HomeRF 1.0 (1Mbps) and HomeRF 2.0 (10Mbps) wireless networks, disbanded at the start of 2003 and closed down its Web site (www.homerf.org). Although some vendors might still have HomeRF-compatible products available for sale, it is essentially an orphan technology. For more information about HomeRF, see Chapter 20 of *Upgrading and Repairing PCs, 14th Edition*, available in electronic form on the disc packaged with this book.

Wi-Fi—A Standard Upon a Standard

When the first 802.11b networking products appeared, compatibility problems existed due to certain aspects of the 802.11 standards being ambiguous or leaving loopholes. A group of companies formed an alliance designed to ensure that their products would work together, eliminating any ambiguities or loopholes in the standards. This was originally known as the Wireless Ethernet Compatibility Alliance (WECA) but is now known simply as the Wi-Fi Alliance (www.wi-fi.org). The term *Wi-Fi* is now used to refer to any IEEE 802.11 wireless network products that have passed the Wi-Fi Alliance certification tests. Currently, the alliance has certified 802.11b, 802.11a, and dual-band (a/b) products. It is also working on certification standards for the newer 802.11g products.

Caution

Dual-band hardware can access either of the 802.11b and 802.11a flavors of Wi-Fi. The new 802.11g wireless standard has the speed of 802.11a, but connects to 802.11b networks without special hardware. As 802.11g hardware passes Wi-Fi Alliance tests, it will also be known as Wi-Fi-compliant hardware. Be sure you find out which flavor of Wi-Fi is in use in a particular location to determine whether you can connect to it.

Table 20.9 provides an overview of 802.11-compliant networks.

Table 20.9   IEEE 802.11–based Wireless Networks

IEEE Standard	Maximum Speed	Typical Range	Wi-Fi Alliance Term	Number of Nonoverlapping Channels	Also Known As	Notes
802.11a	54Mbps	75 ft.	5GHz band	12	Wireless-A	Dual-band hardware needed to connect with 802.11b or 802.11g
802.11b	11Mbps	150 ft.	2.4GHz band	3	Wireless-B	Interoperable with 802.11g; dual-band hardware needed to connect with 802.11a
802.11g	54Mbps	150 ft.	2.4GHz band	3	Wireless-G	Interoperable with 802.11b; dual-band hardware needed to connect with 802.11a

Although you are likely to see retail products identified by their Wi-Fi band designations as in Table 20.9, in this book I will normally use the IEEE designations.

Caution

In the past, *Wi-Fi* has been used as a synonym for IEEE 802.11b hardware. Because the Wi-Fi Alliance now certifies other types of 802.11 wireless networks, the term *Wi-Fi* should always be accompanied by the frequency band (as in Wi-Fi 2.4GHz band) to make it clear which products will work with the device.

Figure 20.24 shows the labels used by the Wi-Fi Alliance on 11Mbps, 54Mbps, and dual-band equipment along with the name of the official IEEE standard for each type of product.

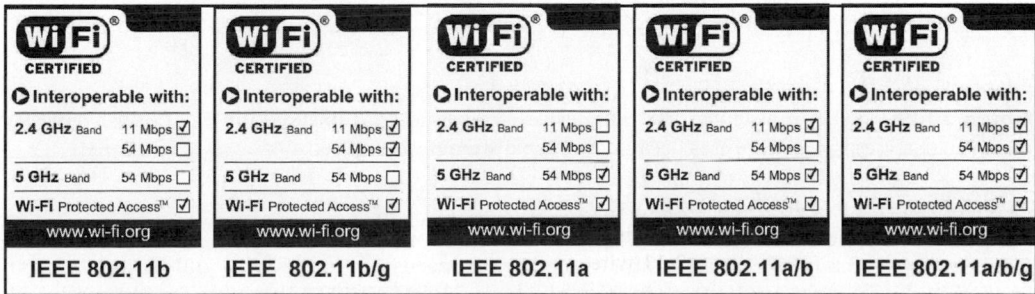

Figure 20.24   The Wi-Fi Alliance's certification labels for Wi-Fi-compliant 802.11 hardware.

IEEE 802.11b—11Mbps Wi-Fi

IEEE 802.11b (Wi-Fi 2.4GHz band–compliant) wireless networks run at a maximum speed of 11Mbps, about the same as 10BASE-T Ethernet (the original version of IEEE 802.11 supported data rates up to 2Mbps only). Other data rates supported by 802.11b include 1Mbps, 2Mbps, and 5.5Mbps. 802.11b networks can connect to conventional Ethernet networks or be used as independent networks, similar to other wireless networks. Wireless networks running 802.11b hardware use the same 2.4GHz spectrum that many portable phones, wireless speakers, security devices, microwave ovens, and the Bluetooth short-range networking products use. Although the increasing use of these products is a potential source of interference, the short range of wireless networks (indoor ranges up to 300 feet and outdoor ranges up to 1,500 feet, varying by product) minimizes the practical risks. Many devices use a spread-spectrum method of connecting with other products to minimize potential interference.

Although 802.11b supports a maximum speed of 11Mbps, that top speed is seldom reached in practice, and speed varies by distance. Most 802.11b hardware is designed to run at four speeds, using three different data-encoding methods depending on the speed range:

- *11Mbps.* Uses quatenery phase-shift keying/complimentary code keying (QPSK/CCK)
- *5.5Mbps.* Also uses quatenery phase-shift keying/complimentary code keying (QPSK/CCK)
- *2Mbps.* Uses differential quaternary phase-shift keying (DQPSK)
- *1Mbps.* Uses differential binary phase-shift keying (DBPSK)

As distances change and signal strength increases or decreases, 802.11b hardware switches to the most suitable data-encoding method. The overhead required to track and change signaling methods, along with the additional overhead required when security features are enabled, helps explain why wireless hardware throughput is lower than the rated speed. Figure 20.25 is a simplified diagram showing how speed is reduced with distance. Figures given are for best-case situations—building design and antenna positioning can also reduce speed and signal strength, even at relatively short distances.

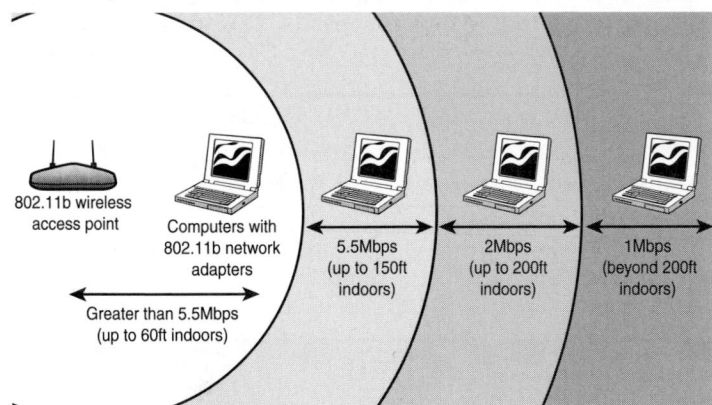

Figure 20.25   At short distances, 802.11b devices can connect at top speed (up to 11Mbps). However, as distance increases, speed decreases because the signal strength is reduced.

IEEE 802.11a—Wi-Fi in the 5GHz Band

The second flavor of Wi-Fi is the wireless network known officially as IEEE 802.11a. 802.11a uses the 5GHz frequency band, which allows for much higher speeds (up to 54Mbps) and helps avoid interference from devices that cause interference with lower-frequency 802.11b networks. Although real-world 802.11a hardware seldom, if ever, reaches that speed (almost five times that of 802.11b), 802.11a maintains relatively high speeds at both short and relatively long distances.

For example, in a typical office floor layout, the real-world throughput (always slower than rated speed due to security and signaling overhead) of a typical 802.11b device at 100 feet might drop to about 5Mbps, whereas a typical 802.11a device at the same distance could have a throughput of around 15Mbps. At a distance of about 50 feet, 802.11a real-world throughput can be four times faster than 802.11b. 802.11a has a shorter maximum distance than 802.11b, but you get your data much faster.

Given the difference in throughput, especially at long distances, why not skip 802.11b altogether? In a single word, frequency. By using the 5GHz frequency instead of the 2.4GHz frequency used by 802.11b, standard 802.11a hardware cuts itself off from the already vast 802.11b universe, including the growing number of public and semipublic 802.11b wireless Internet connections (called *hot spots*) showing up in cafes, airports, hotels, and business campuses.

The current solution for maximum flexibility is to use dual-band hardware. As Figure 20.24 demonstrated earlier in this chapter, the Wi-Fi Alliance is encouraging the manufacture of dual-band hardware through its certification program. Dual-band hardware can work with either 802.11a or 802.11b networks, enabling you to move from an 802.11b wireless network at home or at Starbucks to a faster 802.11a office network.

802.11g—A Compatible 54Mbps Standard

IEEE 802.11g, also known to some as *Wireless-G*, is a promising newcomer that combines compatibility with 802.11b with the speed of 802.11a at longer distances at a price only slightly higher than 802.11b hardware. The final 802.11g standard was ratified in mid-2003, although many network vendors were already rushing products based on the draft 802.11g standard to market before the final standard was approved.

Although 802.11g promises to connect seamlessly with existing 802.11b hardware, early 802.11g hardware was slower and less compatible than the specification promises. In some cases, problems with early-release 802.11g hardware can be solved through firmware upgrades.

As with previous types of 802.11 wireless Ethernet network hardware, I recommend that you wait for 802.11g hardware that meets Wi-Fi Alliance or comparable certifications before you purchase it. You want the same mix-and-match assurance that different brands of network hardware work together in the wireless world that we've long enjoyed with wired Ethernet.

Figure 20.26 demonstrates how the different 802.11-based wireless networks can interact with each other.

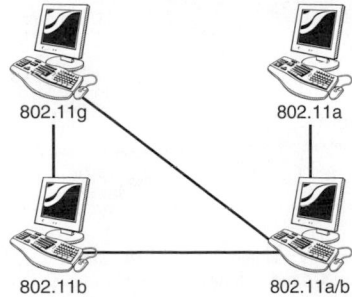

Figure 20.26 Computers running 802.11b and 802.11g wireless Ethernet can connect with each other, and with computers with dual-band 802.11a/b hardware. 802.11a hardware can connect only with other 802.11a or with dual-band 802.11a/b hardware.

802.11 Network Hardware

All types of 802.11 wireless networks have two basic components:

- Access points
- NICs equipped with radio transceivers

An *access point* is a bookend-size device that uses an RJ-45 port to attach to a 10BASE-T or 10/100 Ethernet network (if desired) and contains a radio transceiver, encryption, and communications software. It translates conventional Ethernet signals into wireless Ethernet signals it broadcasts to wireless NICs on the network and performs the same role in reverse to transfer signals from wireless NICs to the conventional Ethernet network.

For coverage of a large area, purchase two or more access points and connect them to an Ethernet switch or hub. This enables users to "roam" inside a building without losing contact with the network. Some access points can communicate directly with each other via radio waves, enabling you to create a wireless backbone that can cover a wide area, such as a warehouse, without the need to run any network cabling.

Access points are not necessary for direct peer-to-peer networking (also called *ad hoc mode*), but they are required for a shared Internet connection or a connection with another network. When access points are used, the network is operating in the *infrastructure mode*.

NICs equipped for wireless Ethernet communications have a fixed or detachable radio antenna in place of the usual coaxial or RJ-45 port or dongle. Because a major market for wireless Ethernet use is notebook computer users, a few vendors sell only PC Cards in their wireless Ethernet product lines, but most vendors support PCI cards for desktop computers. Most vendors also offer wireless USB adapters for use in both desktop and notebook computers. Because you can mix and match Wi-Fi-certified products that use the same frequency band, you can incorporate any mix of desktop and notebook computers into your wireless network. Figure 20.27 illustrates typical wireless network hardware.

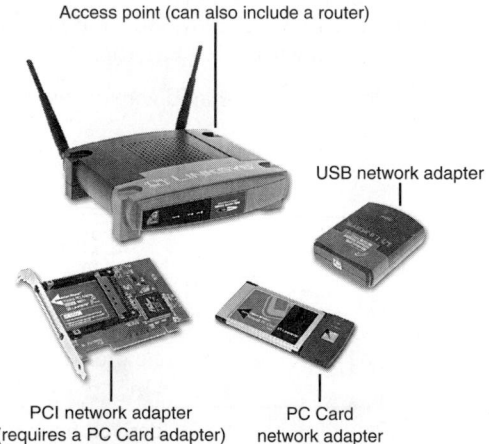

Access point (can also include a router)

USB network adapter

PCI network adapter
(requires a PC Card adapter)

PC Card
network adapter

Figure 20.27   A typical family of Wi-Fi 2.4GHz band (802.11b) wireless products, including a wireless access point, USB, PC Card, and PCI wireless network adapters. The PC Card is used in notebook computers that lack Wi-Fi support and also acts as the transceiver for the PCI card used in desktop computers. *Photos courtesy of Linksys.*

Client systems lock onto the strongest signal from access points and automatically roam (switch) to another access point when the signal strength is stronger and the error level is lower than the current connection.

Additional hardware you might want to add to your network include

- *Wireless bridges*. These devices enable you to connect a wired Ethernet device, including non-computer items such as video games or set-top boxes, to a wireless network.

- *Wireless repeaters*. A repeater can be used to stretch the range of an existing wireless network. Some can also be used as access points or wireless bridges.

- *Wireless router*. Use this in place of a standard access point to enable a wireless network to connect to the Internet through a cable modem or other broadband device (see Chapter 19, "Internet Connectivity," for details). For additional flexibility, many wireless routers also include a multiport switch for use with wired Ethernet networks, and some also include a print server.

- *Specialized*. The "rabbit ears" antennas used by most access points and routers are adequate for short distances, but longer distances or problems with line-of-sight reception can be solved by attaching specialized ceiling, wall, omnidirectional, or directional antennas in place of the standard antenna.

- *Signal boosters*. In addition to or as an alternative to replacement antennas, some vendors also sell signal boosters that piggyback onto an existing access point or router.

Security and Other Features

When I was writing the original edition of *Upgrading and Repairing PCs*, the hackers' favorite way of trying to get into a network without authorization was discovering the telephone number of a modem on the network, dialing in with a computer, and guessing the password, as in the movie *War Games*. Today, *war driving* has largely replaced this pasttime as a popular hacker sport. War driving is the popular name for driving around neighborhoods with a notebook computer equipped with a wireless network card on the lookout for unsecured networks. They're all too easy to find, and after someone gets onto your network, all the secrets in your computer can be hers for the taking.

Because wireless networks can be accessed by anyone with a compatible NIC, most models of NICs and access points provide for encryption options. Some devices with this feature enable you to set a security code known as an SSID on the wireless devices on your network. This seven-digit code prevents unauthorized users from sneaking onto your network and acts as an additional layer of security along with your normal network authentication methods, such as user passwords. Others use a list of authorized MAC numbers (each NIC has a unique MAC) to limit access to authorized devices only.

All Wi-Fi products support at least 40-bit encryption through the wired equivalent privacy (WEP) specification, but the minimum standard on recent products is 64-bit WEP encryption. Many vendors offer 128-bit or 256-bit encryption on some of their products. However, the 128-bit and stronger encryption feature is more common among enterprise products than small-office/home-office–oriented products. Unfortunately, the WEP specification has been shown to be notoriously insecure against determined hacking. Enabling WEP will keep a casual snooper at bay, but someone who wants to get into your wireless network won't have much trouble breaking WEP.

For that reason, many network products introduced in 2003 and beyond now incorporate a new security standard known as Wi-Fi Protected Access (WPA). WPA is derived from the developing IEEE 802.11i security standard, which will not be completed until mid-decade. WPA-enabled hardware works with existing WEP-compliant devices, and software upgrades might be available for existing devices.

You should match the encryption level and encryption type used on both the access points and the NICs for best security. Remember: If some of your network supports WPA but other parts support only WEP, your network must use the lesser of the two security standards (WEP). If you want to use the more robust WPA security, you must ensure that all the devices on your wireless network support WPA. Because WEP is easily broken and the specific WEP implementations vary between manufacturers, I recommend using only devices that support WPA.

Some products' access points can be managed via a Web browser and provide diagnostic and monitoring tools to help you optimize the positioning of access points.

Many products feature support for Dynamic Host Configuration Protocol (DHCP), allowing a user to move from one subnet to another without difficulties.

Figure 20.28 illustrates how a typical IEEE 802.11b wireless network uses multiple access points.

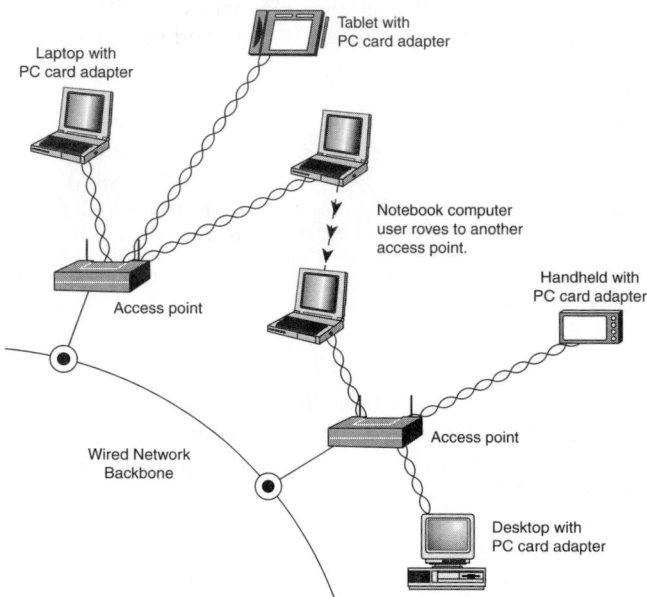

Figure 20.28   A typical wireless network with multiple access points. As users with wireless NICs move from one office to another, the roaming feature of the NIC automatically switches from one access point to another, permitting seamless network connectivity without wires or logging off the network and reconnecting.

Users per Access Point

The number of users per access point varies with the product; Wi-Fi access points are available in capacities supporting anywhere from 15 to as many as 254 users. You should contact the vendor of your preferred Wi-Fi access point device for details.

Although wired Ethernet networks are still the least expensive network to build if you can do your own wiring, Wi-Fi networking is now cost-competitive with wired Ethernet networks when the cost of a professional wiring job is figured into the overall expense.

Because Wi-Fi is a true standard, you can mix and match access point and wireless NIC hardware to meet your desired price, performance, and feature requirements for your wireless network, just as you can for conventional Ethernet networks provided you match up frequency bands or use dual-band hardware.

Notebook Computers with Integrated Wi-Fi Adapters

Major notebook computer makers, including Dell, IBM, and Toshiba, are now integrating built-in 802.11b or dual-band 802.11a/b wireless adapters and antennas into some of their notebook computers. Although computers with built-in Wi-Fi hardware are a little more expensive than comparable models lacking Wireless Ethernet support, building the adapter and antenna into notebook computers provides for a more durable and less cumbersome way to equip portable systems than the normal PC Card and external antenna arrangement that must be fitted to ordinary notebook computers.

Most notebook computers with Wi-Fi hardware onboard use the mini-PCI interface for the wireless adapter and place the antenna inside the screen housing. This enables computers with built-in Wi-Fi hardware to have one more open PC Card slot than computers that must use an external PC Card adapter and antenna.

Bluetooth

Bluetooth is a low-speed (up to 700Kbps), low-power standard originally designed to interconnect notebook computers, PDAs, cell phones, and pagers for data synchronization and user authentication in public areas, such as airports, hotels, rental car pickups, and sporting events. Bluetooth is also used for a wide variety of wireless devices on PCs, including printer adapters, keyboards and mice (Microsoft's Bluetooth keyboard and mouse are available at many stores selling computer hardware), DV camcorders, data projectors, and many others. Bluetooth-compliant devices are becoming widely available, after first reaching the market in the second half of 2000. A list of Bluetooth products and announcements is available at the official Bluetooth wireless information Web site: www.bluetooth.com. Bluetooth devices also use the same 2.4GHz frequency range Wi-Fi/IEEE 802.11b devices use. However, in an attempt to avoid interference with Wi-Fi, Bluetooth uses a signaling method called *frequency hopping spread spectrum*, which switches the exact frequency used during a Bluetooth session 1,600 times per second over the 79 channels Bluetooth uses. Unlike Wi-Fi, which is designed to allow a device to be part of a network at all times, Bluetooth is designed for ad hoc temporary networks in which two devices connect only long enough to transfer data and then break the connection.

Interference Issues Between Bluetooth and IEEE 802.11b/g

Despite the frequency-hopping nature of Bluetooth, studies have shown that Bluetooth (up through version 1.1) and IEEE 802.11b devices can interfere with each other, particularly at close range (under 2 meters) or when users attempt to use both types of wireless networking at the same time (as with an 802.11b wireless Internet connection on a computer with Bluetooth wireless keyboard and mouse). Although 802.11g has not been specifically studied, it uses the same frequencies as 802.11b, and interference between 802.11g and Bluetooth can also take place under similar circumstances. Interference reduces throughput and in some circumstances can cause data loss.

An improved version of the Bluetooth specification, version 1.2, adds adaptive frequency hopping to solve interference problems when devices are more than 1 meter (3.3 feet) away from each other. However, close-range (under 1 meter) interference can still take place.

IEEE has developed 802.15.2, a specification for enabling coexistence between 802.11b/g and Bluetooth. It can use various time-sharing or time-division methods to enable coexistence. However, these specifications are not yet part of typical 802.11b/g implementations.

Chipset makers Silicon Wave (www.siliconwave.com) and Intersil (www.intersil.com) have developed Blue802 Technology, a combination of chipsets that enable coexistence between Bluetooth and 802.11b wireless networks at any distance.

Wireless Network Logical Topologies

Wireless networks have different topologies, just as wired networks do. However, wireless networks use only two logical topologies:

- *Star.* The star topology, used by Wi-Fi/IEEE 802.11–based products in the infrastructure mode, resembles the topology used by 10BASE-T and faster versions of Ethernet that use a hub. The access point takes the place of the hub because stations connect via the access point, rather than directly with each other. This method is much more expensive per unit but permits performance near 10BASE-T Ethernet speeds and easier management.

- *Point-to-Point.* Bluetooth products (as well as Wi-Fi products in the *ad hoc* mode) use the point-to-point topology. These devices connect directly with each other and require no access point or other hub-like device to communicate with each other, although shared Internet access with HomeRF does require that all computers connect to a common wireless gateway. The point-to-point topology is much less expensive per unit than a star topology. It is, however, best suited for temporary data sharing with another device (Bluetooth) and is currently much slower than 100BASE-TX networks.

Figure 20.29 shows a comparison of wireless networks using these two topologies.

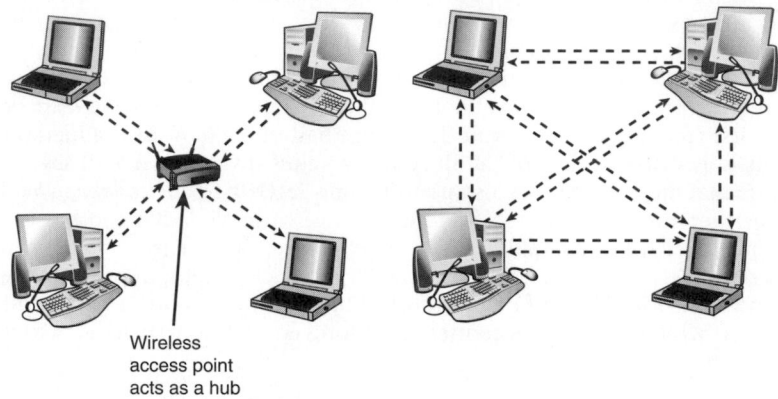

Wireless
access point
acts as a hub

Figure 20.29   A logical star topology (left) as used by IEEE 802.11–based wireless Ethernet in infrastructure mode compared to a point-to-point topology as used by Bluetooth and 802.11 in ad hoc mode (right).

Network Protocols

The second-most important choice you must make when you create your network is which network protocol to use. The network protocol affects which types of computers your network can connect.

The three major network protocols are TCP/IP, IPX/SPX, and NetBEUI. Unlike data-link protocols, though, network protocols are not tied to particular hardware (NIC or cable) choices. Network protocols are software and can be installed to or removed from any computer on the network at any time as necessary. Table 20.10 summarizes the differences between these protocols.

Table 20.10   Overview of Network Protocols and Suites

Protocol	Best Used for	Notes
TCP/IP	Most Windows-based networks	Native protocol suite for Windows 2000/XP and Novell NetWare 5.x/6.x; also used for dial-up Internet access
IPX/SPX	Novell 4.x and earlier networks	Used by NetWare 5.x for certain special features only
NetBIOS	Older Windows for Workgroups or DOS-based peer networks	Simplest protocol; can't be routed between networks; also used with Direct Cable Connection "networking"

All the computers on any given network must use the same network protocol or protocol suite to communicate with each other.

IP and TCP/IP

IP stands for Internet Protocol; it is the network layer of the collection of protocols (or protocol suite) developed for use on the Internet and commonly known as TCP/IP (Transmission Control Protocol/Internet Protocol).

Later, the TCP/IP protocols were adopted by the Unix operating systems, and they have now become the most commonly used protocol suite on PC LANs. Virtually every operating system with networking capabilities supports TCP/IP, and it is well on its way to displacing all the other competing protocols. Novell NetWare 6 and Windows XP both use TCP/IP as their native protocol for most services.

TCP/IP—LAN and Dialup Networks

TCP/IP, unlike the other network protocols listed in the previous section, is also a protocol used by people who have never seen a NIC. People who access the Internet via modems (with what Windows 9x calls Dial-Up Networking) use TCP/IP just as those whose Web access is done with their existing LANs. Although the same protocol is used in both cases, the settings vary a great deal.

Table 20.11 summarizes the differences you're likely to encounter. If you access the Internet with both modems and a LAN, you must ensure that the TCP/IP properties for modems and LANs are set correctly. You also might need to adjust your browser settings to indicate which connection type you are using. Table 20.11 provides general guidelines; your ISP or network administrator can give you the specific details.

Table 20.11   TCP/IP Properties by Connection Type—Overview

TCP/IP Property Tab	Setting	Modem Access (Dialup Adapter)	LAN Access (Network Card)
IP Address	IP Address	Automatically assigned by ISP	Specified (get value from network administrator) or automatically assigned by a DHCP server on the network (DHCP servers are often built in to gateways and routers)
WINS Configuration	Enable/Disable WINS Resolution	Disabled	Indicate server or enable DHCP to allow NetBIOS over TCP/IP
Gateway	Add Gateway/ List of Gateways	None (PPP is used to connect modem to Internet)	IP address of gateway used to connect LAN to Internet
DNS Configuration	Enable/Disable Host Domain	Usually disabled, unless proxy server used by ISP	Enabled, with host and domain specified (get value from network administrator)

As you can see from Table 20.11, correct settings for LAN access to the Internet and dialup networking (modem) settings are almost always completely different. In general, the best way to get your dialup networking connection working correctly is to use your ISP's automatic setup software. This is usually supplied as part of your ISP's signup software kit. After the setup is working, view the properties and record them for future troubleshooting use.

Note

In Windows 98 and Me, Microsoft recommends that TCP/IP properties be viewed through the Dial-Up Networking icon for the connection, rather than through the Network icon in the Control Panel. This is because different dialup connections could use different TCP/IP properties, which would override the default properties for the Dial-Up Adapter listing in the Network properties.

In Windows 2000 and XP, all types of networking are viewed and configured through a single interface.

IPX

The IPX protocol suite (often referred to as IPX/SPX) is the collective term for the proprietary protocols Novell created for its NetWare operating system. Although based loosely on some of the TCP/IP protocols, Novell privately holds the IPX protocol standards. However, this has not prevented Microsoft from creating its own IPX-compatible protocol for the Windows operating systems.

IPX (Internetwork Packet Exchange) itself is a network layer protocol that is equivalent in function to IP. The suite's equivalent to TCP is the Sequenced Packet Exchange (SPX) protocol, which provides connection-oriented, reliable service at the transport layer.

The IPX protocols typically are used today only on networks with NetWare servers running older versions of NetWare and often are installed along with another protocol suite, such as TCP/IP. Novell has phased out its use of IPX for NetWare support and switched to TCP/IP—along with the rest of the networking industry—starting with NetWare 5. NetWare 5 uses IPX/SPX only for specialized operations. Most of the product uses TCP/IP. NetWare 6, the latest version of NetWare, uses TCP/IP exclusively.

NetBEUI

NetBIOS Extended User Interface (NetBEUI) is a protocol used primarily on small Windows NT networks, as well as on peer networks based on Windows for Workgroups and Windows 9x. It was the default protocol in Windows NT 3.1, the first version of that operating system. Later versions, however, use the TCP/IP protocols as their default.

NetBEUI is a simple protocol that lacks many of the features that enable protocol suites such as TCP/IP to support networks of almost any size. NetBEUI is not routable, so it can't be used on large internetworks. It is suitable for small peer-to-peer networks, but any serious Windows NT/2000/XP network installation should use TCP/IP.

NetBEUI is still useful for creating "instant networks" with the Direct Cable Connection (see the following), and it is the minimum protocol required for use in a Windows 9x peer-to-peer network.

Other Home Networking Solutions

If you are working at home or in a small office, you have an alternative to hole-drilling; pulling specialized network cabling; and learning how to configure TCP/IP, IPX, or NetBEUI protocols.

So-called "home" networking is designed to minimize the complexities of cabling and protocol configuration by providing users with a sort of instant network that requires no additional wiring and configures with little technical understanding.

HomePNA

Other than using Ethernet, the most popular form of home networking involves adapting existing telephone wiring to networking by running network signals at frequencies above those used by the telephone system. Other, less popular forms of home networking piggyback on household or office electrical wiring or are wireless, taking advantage of previously unused parts of the electromagnetic spectrum.

Because it is the most developed and most broadly supported type of home networking, this discussion focuses on the HomePNA standards the Home Phoneline Networking Alliance (http://www.homepna.org) has created. This alliance has most of the major computer hardware and telecommunications vendors among its founding and active membership.

A companion Web site focusing on products that use HomePNA standards is http://www.homepna.com.

The Home Phoneline Networking Alliance has developed two versions of its HomePNA standard. Both versions are designed to work over existing telephone lines, but they have big differences in speed and hardware usage.

HomePNA 1.0

The original HomePNA standard, introduced in 1998, was designed to make home networking as much of a no-brainer as possible. HomePNA 1.0 has a speed of just 1Mbps, which is just 1/10 the speed of 10BASE-T or other forms of standard Ethernet. HomePNA 1.0 was designed for ease of use—rather than performance—and utilized parallel ports, USB ports, and PCI cards for use with desktop computers, and PC Card (PCMCIA) devices for use with notebook computers. HomePNA 1.0 is now obsolete, having been replaced by HomePNA 2.0; HomePNA 1.0 products can be used on the same network as HomePNA 2.0 products.

HomePNA 2.0

HomePNA 2.0–compatible products began to appear in late 1999. HomePNA 2.0 runs up to 10Mbps, making it comparable to standard Ethernet speeds, and is implemented through 32-bit PCI network cards for desktop computers and PC Card devices for use with notebook computers (see Figure 20.30). The newest HomePNA 2.0–compatible devices include broadband modems, Internet appliances, and broadband gateways. Some home-office computers include HomePNA 2.0 interface cards.

HomePNA 2.0–compatible products are fast enough to make Internet connection sharing a workable reality and are backward-compatible with HomePNA 1.0 products.

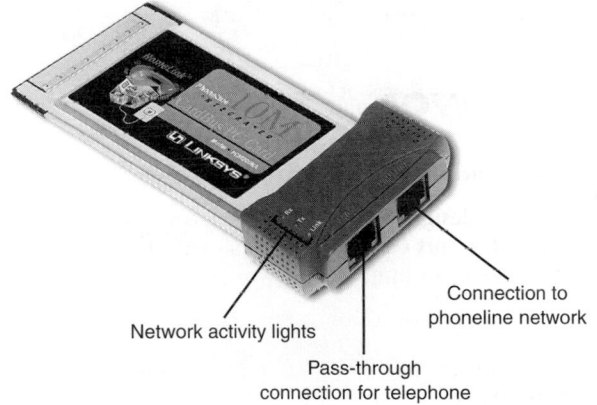

Network activity lights

Pass-through
connection for telephone

Connection to
phoneline network

Figure 20.30   A typical HomePNA 2.0 PC Card network adapter from Linksys. *Photo courtesy Linksys.*

After HomePNA network adapters are installed, they use the same network protocols as do other adapters. A default installation might install only the nonrouteable NetBEUI protocol, but if you use your HomePNA network to share an Internet connection (see Figure 20.31 in the following section), you will also need to install the TCP/IP protocol on each computer if it is not already installed. See the documentation for your HomePNA router for details on installation and client configuration.

HomePNA Topology

HomePNA uses a simplified form of the bus topology described earlier in this chapter. The telephone wiring is the backbone of a HomePNA network, and each HomePNA network adapter has two connectors: one that connects to the telephone wiring in the wall and another that enables you to plug a telephone into the adapter and use the phone at the same time as the network is active. This pass-through feature is similar to that found on most telephone modems. Figure 20.31 illustrates a typical HomePNA network being used to share a broadband Internet connection.

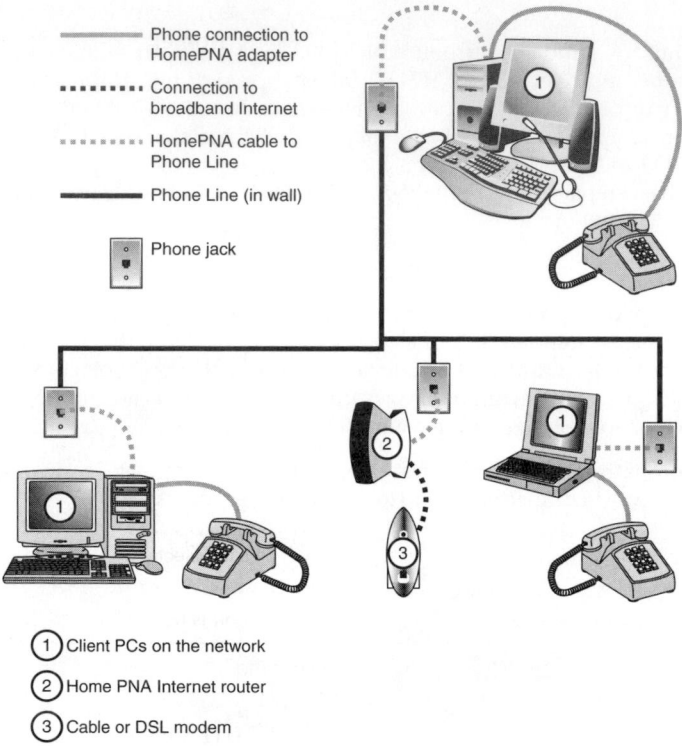

Phone connection to
HomePNA adapter

Connection to
broadband Internet

HomePNA cable to
Phone Line

Phone Line (in wall)

Phone jack

(1) Client PCs on the network

(2) Home PNA Internet router

(3) Cable or DSL modem

Figure 20.31 A typical HomePNA network with three stations; this network enables data and peripheral sharing and shared access to a broadband Internet cable or DSL modem.

◄◄ For more information about sharing Internet access and broadband Internet devices, see Chapter 19, "Internet Connectivity," p. 1057.

Powerline Networking

Home networking via power lines has been under development for several years, but electrical interference, inconsistent voltage, and security issues made the creation of a workable standard difficult until mid-2001. In June 2001, the HomePlug Powerline Alliance, a multivendor industry trade group, introduced its HomePlug 1.0 specification for 14Mbps home networking using power lines. The HomePlug Powerline Alliance (www.homeplug.org) conducted field tests in about 500 households early in 2001 to develop the HomePlug 1.0 specification.

HomePlug 1.0 is based on the PowerPacket technology developed by Intellon. PowerPacket uses a signaling method called orthogonal frequency division multiplexing (OFDM), which combines multiple signals at different frequencies to form a single signal for transmission. Because OFDM uses multiple frequencies, it can adjust to the constantly changing characteristics of AC power. To provide security, PowerPacket also supports 56-bit DES encryption and an individual key for each home network. By using PowerPacket technology, HomePlug 1.0 is designed to solve the power quality and security issues of concern to a home or small-office network user. Although HomePlug 1.0 is rated at 14Mbps, typical real-world performance is usually around 4Mbps for LAN applications and around 2Mbps when connected to a broadband Internet device such as a cable modem.

HomePlug 1.0 products include USB and Ethernet adapters, bridges, and routers, enabling most recent PCs with USB or Ethernet ports to use powerline networking for LAN and Internet sharing. Linksys was the first to introduce HomePlug 1.0 products in late 2001; other leading vendors producing HomePlug hardware include Phonex, NetGear, and Asoka. HomePlug 1.0–certified products bear the HomePlug certification label seen in Figure 20.32.

Figure 20.32   The HomePlug Powerline Alliance 1.0 (14Mbps) certification mark.

An improved HomePlug AV specification with support for faster speeds (up to 100Mbps), multimedia hardware, and guaranteed bandwidth for multimedia applications was announced in the fall of 2002; the final HomePlug AV specification and first products are expected in 2004.

Note

The rival powerline network adapter technology known as the Consumer Electronics Association R7.3 specification has been discontinued. Based on Inari's Passport parallel-port network adapter technology, very few products were ever produced for this technology, which is not compatible with HomePlug. Inari is now owned by Thompson Multimedia.

Home Networking Compared to Ethernet UTP Solutions

The pricing of home networks is comparable to Ethernet UTP solutions, but which one is best for you? Use Table 20.12 to determine which way to go in networking your small office or home office. Networks are listed in order of speed, from slowest to fastest.

Table 20.12   Comparing Wired and Wireless Home Networking Adapters to Ethernet UTP Networking—Adapters

Network Type	Media	Speed
10BASE-T	UTP	10Mbps
HomePNA 2.0	Phone	10Mbps
802.11b	Wireless	11Mbps
HomePlug 1.0	Power	14Mbps
802.11a	Wireless	54Mbps
802.11g	Wireless	54Mbps
100BASE-TX	UTP	100Mbps
1000BASE-TX	UTP	1,000Mbps

In addition to speed and cable types, consider the issue of interconnecting a HomePNA network to a standard Ethernet network. You'll need a special PC Card or a HomePNA/Ethernet hub to interconnect the two networks, and some products of this type support only HomePNA 1.0 1Mbps speeds. You can't simply install HomePNA networking software onto a system that already has standard networking software installed; they aren't designed to coexist unless you use these types of dual-purpose hardware. HomePlug 1.0 has multiple-vendor support, but its real-world performance is the lowest of any nonwireless technology and fewer products are available than for other types of home networks.

I recommend HomePNA 2.0–compatible networking for use only in a home-office environment in which technical expertise is scant and installing UTP wiring is out of the question. With the current rock-bottom pricing of Fast Ethernet 100BASE-TX NICs and hubs, Fast Ethernet is very close to the pricing of HomePNA 2.0 products, offers 10 times the speed, and has compatibility with a broad range of network protocols. As you learned earlier in this chapter, 802.11-based wireless networks are now cost-competitive with home network standards and allow you to cut the cord and work anywhere.

Putting Your Network Together

You've bought or built your cables, bought your NICs and hub, and located your Windows CD-ROM. Now it's time to make your network a reality!

In this section is a detailed checklist of the hardware and software you need to build your network.

First, start with the number of computers you plan to network together. You need the items discussed in the following sections to set up your network.

Network Adapter

You need a network adapter for every computer on the network that doesn't have a network port or wireless network adapter already included; if the computer has a built-in network port or wireless network adapter, be sure it will work with your network.

Traditionally, network adapters are also called network interface cards (NICs), but the widespread use of USB devices and built-in ports makes this term less accurate. To simplify technical support, buy the same model of NIC for each computer in your network (if possible). If you are creating a Windows NT/2000/Windows Server or Novell NetWare network with a dedicated server, you should buy server-optimized NICs for the server and less-expensive client NICs for the client PCs. However, you should still purchase the same brand to simplify support issues. Some vendors use the same driver for both their server and client NICs, further simplifying your support issue.

For the best performance, I recommend that you use PCI-based NICs for desktop computers or PC Card CardBus NICs for notebook computers with CardBus slots (CardBus and PCI slots have a 32-bit wide data bus, whereas typical PC Card slots have a 16-bit data bus). USB devices are more convenient, but USB 1.1 devices are much slower than 10/100 Ethernet. USB 2.0 devices are a satisfactory substitute for 10/100 Ethernet but require that both the computer and the device be USB 2.0–compliant to achieve the 480Mbps speed of USB 2.0. If either the device or the computer is only USB 1.1–compliant, the connection is limited to 12Mbps.

You should record the brand name and model number of the network adapters you are using, as well as the driver version or source. Use Table 20.13 in the "Recording Information About Your Network" section, later in this chapter, as a template for storing this information.

Installing the Network Adapter

Before you can connect computers to the network, you must install network adapters. If the network adapter is an internal card, follow this procedure:

1. Open the case and locate an open expansion slot that matches the type of NIC you purchased (preferably PCI).
2. Using a screwdriver, remove the screw securing the slot cover at the rear of the case.
3. Insert the card gently, ensuring that the edge connector is seated solidly in the slot.
4. Fasten down the card with the same screw that held the slot cover.

▶▶ See Figures 22.27 and 22.28 in Chapter 22, "Building or Upgrading Systems," p. 1245, for an example of installing an add-on card.

Tip

If you are a realist like me, you might not want to close the case until you are certain the NIC is working (see the next section, "Testing Your Network Adapters and Connections").

A NIC uses the same hardware configuration settings most other expansion cards use:

- An IRQ
- An I/O port address range

Note

Some older network cards might require an upper memory block range for RAM buffers. Cards used on diskless work-stations use a boot ROM, which also requires an upper memory block range. See your network card's documentation to find out whether this issue applies to you.

If you are using Windows 9x, Me, 2000, or XP with a PnP (Plug and Play) BIOS and a PnP NIC, the computer and Windows configure your card for you in most cases. In a few cases, you might need to adjust PnP settings in the BIOS, and in a rare case you might even need to remove your other PnP cards and put the NIC in first if your system doesn't recognize it after you restart the system.

◄◄ For general BIOS information, see Chapter 5, "BIOS," p. 397, or see your system manual for details about your computer's BIOS.

If you install the card in a non-PnP system or under Windows NT, be sure the card comes with configuration software or manual switch settings for hardware configuration. A pure PnP card can't be installed on a system that lacks PnP support.

USB and PC Card/CardBus network adapters are automatically detected and installed when connected because USB ports and PC Card/CardBus slots are hot-swap connections.

And, if you are using an older network adapter with the newest version of Windows—Windows XP— you might need to download drivers from the adapter vendors' Web sites. Even if you have drivers for your current version of Windows, getting the latest driver release will help you avoid setup and installation problems.

Testing Your Network Adapters and Connections

The configuration software disk or CD-ROM included with the network adapter usually features diagnostic software. Some diagnostics should be performed before the card is connected to the network and should be run from a command prompt.

After the network adapter passes these tests, connect the network adapter to the network. With an Ethernet network using UTP cable, run the cable from the card to the hub or switch, turn on the computer and hub, and watch for signal lights to light up on the NIC's back bracket (if so equipped) and on the hub or switch. Hubs and switches use green LEDs to indicate the presence of a computer on a particular RJ-45 port. Connect a second computer with NIC installed to the hub or switch. Then, run the diagnostics program on both computers to send and receive data. For other types of networks, see the diagnostics provided with the network hardware for testing details.

Cables and Connections Between Computers

Depending on the network you choose, you might need to run cables. If you are installing a 100BASE-TX, or 1000BASE-TX Ethernet network (both of which use UTP cables), you need cables that are long enough to reach comfortably between each computer's network port and the network's hub or switch. Use

Table 20.13 in the "Recording Information About Your Network" section, later in this chapter, as a template for storing this information.

Because HomePNA networks are based on your existing telephone line, the patch cord included with the NIC is usually long enough to connect with your existing RJ-11 telephone jack. The HomePNA NIC has two jacks: one for the connection to the telephone line and the other to enable you to connect your telephone to the NIC. Be sure you use the correct jack for each cable; otherwise, your network won't work. HomePNA enables you to use your telephone system for voice and networking at the same time.

Wireless network NICs use an external antenna to make the connection between computers. In some cases, the antenna is built in to the NIC, whereas in other cases the antenna is attached to the NIC or needs to be extended from a storage position inside the NIC.

Hub/Switch/Access Point

UTP Ethernet networks require a hub or switch if more than two computers will be networked (you can use a crossover cable between two computers only). Wireless Ethernet networks also require an access point if more than two computers will be networked, or if the network will be used to share an Internet connection.

For a UTP-based Ethernet network, buy a hub or switch (preferred) of the correct speed with at least enough RJ-45 ports for each computer on the network. For a wireless Ethernet network, you will need at least one access point, depending on the range of your wireless network. Most IEEE 802.11b/Wi-Fi network access points have a range of 300 feet indoors (and up to 1,500 feet outdoors), which should be adequate for most homes and many small businesses. You can add more access points if you need a wider area of coverage.

If you are going to use the network to share Internet access, you can save money if you buy a router that contains a switch for a wired Ethernet network or a wireless access point that contains a router for a wireless Ethernet network.

Use Table 20.13 in the "Recording Information About Your Network" section, later in this chapter, as a template for storing this information. Table 20.13 also provides a space for recording whether you plan to use the network for Internet sharing.

Gateways for Non-Ethernet Networks

If you plan to share Internet access through a non-Ethernet network such as HomePNA or HomePlug and you don't want to use a software-sharing solution such as Microsoft Internet Connection Sharing, you must install a gateway or router between the broadband device (such as a cable or DSL modem) and your network. Some gateway/router devices can also act as print servers; in addition, some, such as those from 2Wire, support HomePNA, Ethernet, or Wi-Fi networks.

Recording Information About Your Network

Networks are terrific when they work, but they're a potential nightmare when they fail. By keeping careful notes about network configuration, you can reinstall network drivers, set up new computers on the network, and handle other network crises without breaking a sweat.

Use the worksheet shown in Table 20.13 as a guide for recording information about your network hardware.

Table 20.13   Network Hardware Worksheet

Network Type:	Number of Stations:	Internet Sharing:	
Computer Location/ID:	Brand Name/Model:	NIC Brand/Model:	Speed:
Driver:	Cable Type/ Wiring Standard:	Cable Length:	
Hub/Switch Location/ID:	Hub/Switch Brand/ Model:	Hub/Switch Speed:	
No. Ports:	Hub or Switch:		
Router Location/ID:	Router Brand/Model:	Router Speed:	
No. Ports:	Router IP Address:	Router Password:	

Installing Networking Software

To access network resources with a PC—whether it is connected to a client/server or peer-to-peer network—you must install network client software on the computer. The network client can be part of the operating system or a separate product, but it is this software that enables the system to use the network interface adapter to communicate with other machines.

On a properly configured network workstation, accessing network resources is no different from accessing local ones (except that they might be slightly slower). You can open a file on a network drive just as you would open the same file on your local hard disk. This is because the network client software is completely integrated into every level of the computer's operating system.

In most cases, the network client software is part of the operating system. Windows 9x, NT, 2000, and XP, for example, include all the software you need to participate in a peer-to-peer Windows network or to connect to Windows NT, Windows 2000, Windows Server 2003, and Novell NetWare servers. To connect to a network using DOS or Windows 3.1, however, you must install a separate client software package.

When you install a NIC under Windows 95 or Windows 98, the following network protocols are installed by default:

- NetBEUI
- TCP/IP
- IPX/SPX

Windows Me, Windows 2000, and Windows XP use TCP/IP by default. If you need to install particular protocols or other network components, use the Networks icon in the Windows Control Panel or right-click the Network Neighborhood (Windows 9x) or My Network Places (Windows Me/2000) icon on the Windows desktop and select Properties. If you need to use NetBEUI with Windows XP, it must be manually installed from the Windows XP CD-ROM.

Configuring Your Network Software

You might have a few problems installing your NICs. They might pass their diagnostics flawlessly, but until each station on your network can speak the same language, has correct client or server software setups, and uses the same protocols, your network will not function properly.

Table 20.14 shows the minimum network software configuration you must install for Windows 9x/Me, Windows NT, Windows 2000, and Windows XP peer-to-peer networking.

Table 20.14   Minimum Network Software for Peer-to-Peer Networking

Item	Workstation	Server
Windows Network client	Yes	No
NetBEUI or TCP/IP* protocol	Yes	Yes
File and print sharing for Microsoft Networks	No	Yes
NIC installed and bound to protocols and services above	Yes	Yes
Workgroup identification (same for all PCs in workgroup)	Yes	Yes
Computer name (each PC needs a unique name)	Yes	Yes

If TCP/IP is used as the standard protocol, each workstation must have a different IP address—either manually assigned or received from a DHCP server built in to a server, router, or gateway computer or device.

Although the networking settings in Table 20.14 enable a Windows peer-to-peer network to function, you might need to add more networking components. If the computer can access a Novell NetWare client/server network running NetWare 4.x, the IPX/SPX protocol must also be installed. It also might be required for certain operations with NetWare 5. If the computer is used to access the Internet or any other TCP/IP-based network, the TCP/IP protocol must also be installed. In most cases, you can now use TCP/IP as the only network protocol because it can be used for both Internet and LAN access.

Use the Network icon in the Windows Control Panel to select your network settings. To set up your network, you'll need the operating system CDs, disks, or hard-disk image files and the network adapter drivers. (Workgroup hubs and switches require no software.)

To install a network component, follow this procedure:

1. Open the Network icon in the Control Panel.

2. The Configuration tab is displayed; select Add.

3. Select from the following:

   - *Client.* Select if you want to install the Microsoft or other network clients for your network. Every PC on a peer-to-peer network needs the Client for Microsoft Networks.

   - *Adapter.* This should already be installed, but you can use this to install a new adapter.

   - *Protocol.* For a simple, non-Internet network with versions of Windows before XP, install NetBEUI. If you want to use Internet Connection Sharing along with networking, install both TCP/IP and NetBEUI. With Windows XP, use the Network Setup Wizard to configure TCP/IP easily.

   - *Service.* Install File and Printer Sharing for Microsoft Networks on any computer that will be used as a server.

4. Click the Identification tab. Enter a unique name for each computer on the network; use the same workgroup name for all computers on the network.

5. Click OK. Supply the Windows CD-ROM or other media as necessary to install the network components you requested.

6. You are prompted to insert a CD or disk or browse to the appropriate files during the installation procedure, if they're not available on the Windows 9x CD-ROM or on your hard disk in the default location.

You might need to reboot your PC to complete the process, particularly if you're using Windows 9x or Me. After this is completed, you'll be ready to share resources.

After the network hardware and software installation is complete, your network is ready to use. However, if you are using Windows NT, Windows 2000, or Windows XP Professional, you must set up users and groups for security. Windows 9x, Me, and Windows XP Home use peer-to-peer access control, which can be protected with passwords if you desire.

For more information about these processes, see "Configuring Users, Groups, and Resources" in the Technical Reference section of the disc packaged with this book.

Tips and Tricks

Network configuration can take a long time unless you have a few tricks up your sleeve. Use this section to help you find faster, easier, and better ways to set up and use your network.

Installation

- If you are setting up several systems with identical hardware, NICs, and software, consider making an image file of the first system after you complete its installation with a program such as Drive Image Professional and then connecting the other computers and "cloning" the first computer's hard disk to each additional system. Check with the imaging software vendor for details.

- Don't click OK in the Windows Networks properties sheet until you have made all the changes you want to make (see the previous list) on a Windows 9x or Me system. Whenever you click OK, you are prompted to reboot the system to apply the changes.

- If you're salvaging old 10BASE-T Ethernet cards for a network, use Category 5 UTP and dual-speed hubs to make switching to Fast Ethernet in the future easier. I recommend this only if your systems use ISA cards; new 10/100 Ethernet cards cost less than $20 each.

Sharing Resources

- If you want to have network drives or folders show up as part of My Computer so you can search them and see them easily in Windows Explorer, map a drive letter to each one. This step is desirable with any combination of operating systems and is a virtual necessity on networks in which Windows 2000 or Windows XP computers are accessing shared resources on a Windows 9x computer. Browsing the network is very slow without mapped drives, but access to shares through a mapped drive letter is very fast.

- To more easily keep drive mappings straight, I use the drive letter I plan to use for mapping on other workstations as the name of the shared resource on my peer server. In other words, if I want to map the D: drive on my peer server as "P:", I name it "P" when I set its sharing properties. Then, as I view the folder from another computer, I know from its name that I should map it as "P:". This enables multiple PCs to easily map the same resource as the same drive letter on different systems, which makes it easier if people in your office play musical computers.

Setting Up Security

- If you're building a peer-to-peer network, keep in mind that passwords are the only way to keep unwanted users out of your system.

- Create a group of several users and assign rights on a group basis when you have several users who need the same access rights.

Sharing Internet Connections

- If you are planning to share an Internet connection using Microsoft Internet Connection Sharing or other computer-based sharing programs, *don't* set up File and Printer Sharing on the computer that does the sharing (the proxy server or gateway computer); share drives on other computers instead, or install a self-contained network storage device. See Chapter 19 for software you can add to your computer to keep it safe on the Internet.

- Routers and gateway devices are an economical way to share broadband access in a home or small office, and they are easier to manage and more reliable than using ICS or other sharing programs. Routers and gateways can also act as firewalls to protect your computer from unauthorized access from the Internet.

Direct Cable Connections

Direct Cable Connection is a technology that enables you to connect two PCs together via their serial, parallel, or IR ports to make an instant network. Windows 9x, Me, 2000, and XP all include Direct Connect client and server software, but special parallel (preferred) or serial cables are required; IR (infrared) ports on notebook computers can also be used for direct connections. See the section "Direct Cable Connections" in Chapter 19, "Local Area Networking," of *Upgrading and Repairing PCs, 12th Edition*, included on this book's disc, for details.

Troubleshooting a Network

The following sections list a series of common networking problems along with solutions that can usually set things right again.

Network Software Setup

Problem

Duplicate computer IDs.

Solution

Make sure that every computer on the network has a unique ID (use Control Panel, Network, Identification to view this information). Otherwise, you'll get an error message when you reboot the workstations with networking cables attached.

Problem

Different workgroup names.

Solution

Make sure every computer that's supposed to be working together has the same workgroup name. The Windows 9x/NT Network Neighborhood and Windows Me/2000/XP My Network Places icons display computers by workgroup name. Different workgroup names actually create different workgroups, and you'd need to access them by browsing via Entire Network. This wastes time.

Problem

Shared resources are not available.

Solution

Make sure that shared resources have been set for any servers on your network (including peer servers on Windows 9x). If you can't share a resource through Windows Explorer on the peer server, ensure that File and Printer Sharing has been installed.

Problem

Network doesn't work after making changes.

Solution

Did you reboot? Any change in the Network icon in Windows 9x/Me Control Panel requires a system reboot!

Did you log in? Any network resources can't be accessed unless you log in when prompted. You can use Start, Shutdown, and Close All Programs and Logon As a New User with Windows 9x/Me to recover quickly from a failure to log on.

Networks in Use

Problem

A user can't access any shared resources (but others can).

Solution

First, have the user log off and log back on. Pressing Cancel or Esc instead of logging in would keep a user off the network.

Next, check cable connections at the server and workstation. Loose terminators or BNC T-connectors can cause trouble for all workstations on a Thinnet cable segment. A loose or disconnected RJ-45 cable affects only the computer (or hub) using it. If a Category 5 UTP cable seems to be connected tightly but the user still can't get on the network, check the cable with a cable tester or replace the cable.

Problem

Wrong access level.

Solution

If you save your passwords in a password cache, entering the read-only password instead of the full-access password limits your access with peer servers. Try unsharing the resource and try to reshare it, or have the user of that peer server set up new full-access and read-only passwords. Alternatively, don't use password caching by unchecking the Save Password box when you log on to a shared resource. With a client/server network with user lists and rights, check with your network administrator because she will need to change the rights for you.

TCP/IP

Problem

Incorrect settings in Network Properties.

Solution

Get the correct TCP/IP settings from the administrator and enter them; restart the PC.

Problem

Can't keep connection running in Dial-Up Networking.

Solution

You might have the wrong version of PPP running; change the server type in Properties under Dial-Up Networking, not Networks.

Problem

Message about duplicate IP addresses—can't connect to anything.

Solution

Duplicate IP addresses disable both TCP/IP and NetBEUI networking. Internet sharing products such as ICS, third-party sharing programs, and routers are usually configured to assign IP addresses automatically to avoid duplication. If some computers on a network have fixed IP addresses and others have dynamically assigned IP addresses, conflicts could occur. The entire network should use dynamic IP addressing (DHCP) or each computer should be assigned a unique IP address.

Problem

No error message—can't connect to Internet or other computers.

Solution

Check the router, switch, or hub used to connect the computers to each other and the Internet. It needs to be powered, and the data cables must be properly connected between it and each PC (and between the Internet connection and the switch or hub, if applicable).

If your network uses DHCP to dynamically assign IP addresses and the router has lost power or connection, users won't have valid IP addresses. Restart the router, and have all users log off and shut down. When they restart their systems, they should be able to obtain valid IP addresses and connect with each other.

CHAPTER 21

Power Supply and Chassis/Case

Considering the Importance of the Power Supply

The power supply is not only one of the most important parts in a PC, but it is unfortunately also the most overlooked. In the words of a famous comedian, the power supply gets no respect! People spend hours discussing their processor speeds, memory capacity, disk storage capacity and speed, video adapter performance, monitor size, and so forth but rarely even mention or consider their power supply. When a system is put together to meet the lowest possible price point, what component do you think the manufacturer skimps on? Yes, the power supply. To most people, the power supply is a rather nondescript, unglamorous metal box that sits inside their systems, something to which they pay virtually no attention at all. The few who do pay any mind seem concerned only with how many watts of power it is rated to put out (even though no practical way exists to verify those ratings), without regard as to whether the power being produced is clean and stable or whether it is full of noise, spikes, and surges.

I have always placed great emphasis on selecting a power supply for my systems. I consider the power supply the core of the system and am willing to spend more to get a better unit. The power supply function is critical because it supplies electrical power to every other component in the system. In my experience, the power supply is also one of the most failure-prone components in any computer system. I have replaced more power supplies in PCs than any other part. This is especially due to the fact that so many system builders use the cheapest power supplies they can find. A malfunctioning power supply can not only cause other components in the system to malfunction, but also can damage the other components in your computer by delivering an improper or erratic voltage. Because of its importance to proper and reliable system operation, you should understand both the function and limitations of a power supply, as well as its potential problems and their solutions.

This chapter covers the power supply in detail. I focus on the electrical functions of the supply and the mechanical form factors and physical designs that have been used in PC systems in the past, as well as today. Because the physical shape (*form factor*) of the power supply relates to the case, some of this information also relates to the type of chassis or case you have.

Primary Function and Operation

The basic function of the power supply is to convert the type of electrical power available at the wall socket to the type the computer circuitry can use. The power supply in a conventional desktop system is designed to convert either 120-volt (nominal) 60Hz AC (alternating current) or 240V (nominal) 50Hz AC power into +3.3V, +5V, and +12V DC (direct current) power. Some power supplies require you to switch between the two input ranges, whereas others auto-switch.

Positive DC Voltages

Usually, the digital electronic components and circuits in the system (motherboard, adapter cards, and disk drive logic boards) use the +3.3V or +5V power, and the motors (disk drive motors and any fans) use the +12V power. Table 21.1 lists these devices and their power consumptions.

Table 21.1   Power Consumption Ratings for PC Devices

Voltage	Devices Powered
+3.3V	Chipsets, DIMMs, PCI/AGP cards, miscellaneous chips
+5V	Disk drive logic, SIMMs, PCI/AGP cards, ISA cards, voltage regulators, miscellaneous chips
+12V	Motors, voltage regulators (high output)

The power supply must deliver a good, steady supply of DC power so the system can operate properly. Devices that run on voltages other than these must be powered by onboard voltage regulators. For example, RIMMs and DDR dual inline memory modules (DIMMs) require 2.5V, whereas AGP 4x and faster cards require 1.5V—both of which are supplied by simple onboard regulators. Processors also require a wide variety of voltages (as low as 1.3V or less) that are supplied by a sophisticated voltage regulator module (VRM) that is either built in or plugged in to the motherboard as well. You'll commonly find three or more different voltage regulator circuits on a modern motherboard.

Note

When Intel began releasing processors that required a +3.3V power source, power supplies that supplied the additional output voltage were not yet available. As a result, motherboard manufacturers began adding voltage regulators to their boards, which converted +5V current to +3.3V for the processor. When other chips began using 3.3V as well, Intel created the ATX power supply specification, which supplied 3.3V to the motherboard. DIMMs also run on +3.3V as supplied by the power supply. You would think that having 3.3V direct from the power supply would have eliminated the need for onboard voltage regulators, but by that time, processors began running on a wide variety of voltages lower than 3.3V. Motherboard manufacturers then included adaptable regulator circuits called voltage regulator modules to accommodate the widely varying processor voltage requirements. Other regulators are also used to power any other devices on the motherboard that don't use +3.3V, +5V, or +12V.

◀◀ See "CPU Operating Voltages," p. 102.

Negative DC Voltages

If you look at a specification sheet for a typical PC power supply, you can see that the supply generates not only +3.3V, +5V, and +12V, but also –5V and –12V. The positive voltages seemingly power everything in the system (logic and motors), so what are the negative voltages used for? The answer is not much! Some of the power supply designs, such as the small form factor (SFX) design, no longer include the –5V output for that reason. The only reason it has remained in most power supply designs is that –5V is required on the Industry Standard Architecture (ISA) bus for full backward-compatibility.

Although –5V and –12V are supplied to the motherboard via the power supply connectors, the motherboard normally uses only the +3.3V, +5V, and +12V. The –5V is simply routed to the ISA bus on pin B5 so any ISA cards can use it, even though not many do today. However, as an example, the analog data separator circuits found in older floppy controllers do use –5V.

The motherboard logic typically doesn't use –12V either; however, it might be used in some board designs for serial port or LAN circuits.

Note

The load placed on the –12V output by an integrated LAN adapter is very small. For example, the integrated 10/100 Ethernet adapter in the Intel D815EEAL motherboard uses only 10mA of +12V and 10mA of –12V (0.01 amps each) to operate.

Although older serial port circuits used +/–12V outputs, today most run only on +3.3V or +5V.

The main function of the +12V power is to run disk drive motors as well as the higher-output processor voltage regulators in some of the newer boards. Usually, a large amount of +12V current is available from the power supply, especially in those designed for systems with a large number of drive bays (such as in a tower configuration). Besides disk drive motors and newer CPU voltage regulators, the +12V supply is used by any cooling fans in the system—which, of course, should always be running. A single cooling fan can draw between 100mA and 250mA (0.1–0.25 amps); however, most newer fans use the lower 100mA figure. Note that although most fans in desktop systems run on +12V, portable systems can use fans that run on +5V or even +3.3V.

Most systems with newer motherboard form factors, such as the ATX, micro-ATX, or NLX, include another special signal. This feature, called PS_ON, can be used to turn the power supply (and thus the system) on or off via software. It is sometimes known as the *soft-power feature*. PS_ON is most evident when you use it with an operating system such as Windows that supports the Advanced Power Management (APM) or Advanced Configuration and Power Interface (ACPI) specification. When you select the Shut Down the Computer option from the Start menu, Windows automatically turns off the computer after it completes the OS shutdown sequence. A system without this feature only displays a message that it's safe to shut down the computer.

The Power_Good Signal

In addition to supplying electrical power to run the system, the power supply also ensures that the system does not run unless the voltages supplied are sufficient to operate the system properly. In other words, the power supply actually prevents the computer from starting up or operating until all the power supply voltages are within the proper ranges.

The power supply completes internal checks and tests before allowing the system to start. If the tests are successful, the power supply sends a special signal to the motherboard, called Power_Good. This signal must be continuously present for the system to run. Therefore, when the AC voltage dips and the power supply can't maintain outputs within regulation tolerance, the Power_Good signal is withdrawn (goes low) and forces the system to reset. The system will not restart until the Power_Good signal returns.

The Power_Good signal (sometimes called Power_OK or PWR_OK) is a +5V (nominal) active high signal (with a variation from +2.4V through +6.0V generally being considered acceptable) that is supplied to the motherboard when the power supply has passed its internal self tests and the output voltages have stabilized. This typically takes place anywhere from 100ms to 500ms (0.1–0.5 seconds) after you turn on the power supply switch. The power supply then sends the Power_Good signal to the motherboard, where the processor timer chip that controls the reset line to the processor receives it.

In the absence of Power_Good, the timer chip holds the reset line on the processor, which prevents the system from running under bad or unstable power conditions. When the timer chip receives the Power_Good signal, it releases the reset and the processor begins executing whatever code is at address FFFF:0000 (usually the ROM BIOS).

If the power supply can't maintain proper outputs (such as when a brownout occurs), the Power_Good signal is withdrawn and the processor is automatically reset. When the power output returns to its proper levels, the power supply regenerates the Power_Good signal and the system again begins operation (as if you had just powered on). By withdrawing Power_Good before the output voltages fall out of regulation, the system never sees the bad power because it is stopped quickly (reset) rather than being allowed to operate using unstable or improper power levels, which can cause memory parity errors and other problems.

Note

You can use the Power_Good feature as a method of implementing a reset switch for the PC. The Power_Good line is wired to the clock generator circuit, which controls the clock and reset lines to the microprocessor. When you ground the Power_Good line with a switch, the timer chip and related circuitry reset the processor. The result is a full hardware reset of the system. Instructions for making and installing a reset switch can be found in the section "Making and Installing a Reset Switch" in the Technical Reference portion of the disc included with this book.

◄◄   See "Parity and ECC," p. 500.

On pre-ATX systems, the Power_Good connection is made via connector P8-1 (P8 pin 1) from the power supply to the motherboard. ATX and later systems use pin 8 of the 20-pin connector, which is usually a gray wire.

A well-designed power supply delays the arrival of the Power_Good signal until all the voltages stabilize after you turn on the system. Badly designed power supplies, which are found in many low-cost systems, often do not delay the Power_Good signal properly and enable the processor to start too soon. (The normal Power_Good delay is 0.1–0.5 seconds.) Improper Power_Good timing also causes CMOS memory corruption in some systems.

Note

If you find that a system consistently fails to boot up properly the first time you turn on the switch, but that it subsequently boots up if you press the reset or Ctrl+Alt+Delete warm boot command, you likely have a problem with the Power_Good timing. You should install a new, higher-quality power supply and see whether that solves the problem.

Some cheaper power supplies do not have proper Power_Good circuitry and might just tie any +5V line to that signal. Some motherboards are more sensitive to an improperly designed or improperly functioning Power_Good signal than others. Intermittent startup problems are often the result of improper Power_Good signal timing. A common example is when you replace a motherboard in a system and then find that the system intermittently fails to start properly when you turn on the power. This can be very difficult to diagnose, especially for the inexperienced technician, because the problem appears to be caused by the new motherboard. Although it seems as though the new motherboard is defective, it usually turns out that the power supply is poorly designed. It either can't produce stable enough power to properly operate the new board or has an improperly wired or timed Power_Good signal (which is more likely). In these situations, replacing the supply with a higher-quality unit, in addition to the new motherboard, is the proper solution.

Power Supply Form Factors

The shape and general physical layout of a component is called the *form factor*. Items that share a form factor are generally interchangeable, at least as far as their sizes and fits are concerned. When designing a PC, the engineers can choose to use one of the popular standard power supply unit (PSU) form factors, or they can elect to build their own. Choosing the former means that a virtually inexhaustible supply of inexpensive replacement parts will be available in a variety of quality and power output levels. Going the custom route means additional time and expense for development. In addition, the power supply is unique to the system and available only from the original manufacturer.

If you can't tell already, I am a fan of the industry-standard form factors! Having standards and then following them allows us to upgrade and repair our systems by easily replacing physically (and electrically) interchangeable components. Having interchangeable parts means that we have a better range of choices for replacement items, and the competition makes for better pricing, too.

In the PC market, IBM originally defined the standards and everybody else copied them. This included power supplies. All the popular PC power supply form factors up through 1995 were based on one of three IBM models, including the PC/XT, AT, and PS/2 Model 30. The interesting thing is that these three power supply definitions all had the same motherboard connectors and pinouts; where they differed was mainly in shape, maximum power output, the number of peripheral power connectors, and switch mounting. PC systems using knock-offs of one of those three designs were popular through 1996 and beyond, and some systems still use them today.

Intel gave the power supply a new definition in 1995 with the introduction of the ATX form factor. ATX became popular in 1996 and started a shift away from the previous IBM-based standards. ATX and the related standards that followed have different connectors with additional voltages and signals that allow systems with greater power consumption and additional features that would otherwise not be possible with the AT-style supplies.

Technically, the power supply in most PCs is described as a *constant voltage switching power supply*, which is defined as follows:

- *Constant voltage* means that the power supply puts out the same voltage to the computer's internal components, no matter what the voltage of AC current running it or the capacity (wattage) of the power supply.

- *Switching* refers to the design and power regulation technique that most suppliers use. Compared to other types of power supplies, this design provides an efficient and inexpensive power source and generates a minimum amount of heat. It also maintains a small size and low price.

Note

Although two power supplies can share the same basic design and form factor, they can differ greatly in quality and efficiency. Later in this chapter, you'll learn about some of the features and specifications to look for when evaluating PC power supplies.

Seven power supply physical form factors have existed that can be called industry standard. Five of these are based on IBM designs, whereas two are based on Intel designs. Of these, only the two Intel-based designs are used in most modern systems; the others are pretty much obsolete.

Note that although the names of the power supply form factors seem to be the same as those of motherboard form factors, the power supply form factor is more closely related to the system chassis (case) than the motherboard. That is because all the form factors use one of only two types of connector designs: either AT or ATX.

For example, all PC/XT, AT, and LPX form factor supplies use the same pair of six-pin connectors to plug into the motherboard and will therefore power any board having the same type of power connections. Plugging into the motherboard is one thing, but for the power supply to physically work in the system, it must fit the case. The bottom line is that it is up to you to ensure that the power supply you purchase not only plugs into your motherboard, but also fits into the chassis or case you plan to use.

Table 21.2 shows these power supply form factors, their connection types, and associated motherboards.

Table 21.2   Power Supply Connector Types and Form Factors

Obsolete PS Form Factors	Originated From	Connector Type	Associated MB Form Factors
PC/XT style	IBM PC, PC-XT (1981/1983)	AT	PC/XT, Baby-AT
AT/Desk style	IBM PC-AT (1984)	AT	Full-size AT, Baby-AT
AT/Tower style	IBM PC-AT (1984)	AT	Full-size AT, Baby-AT
Baby-AT style	IBM PC-AT (1984)	AT	Full-size AT, Baby-AT
LPX style*	IBM PS/2 Model 30 (1987)	AT	Baby-AT, Mini-AT, LPX
Modern PS Form Factors	**Originated From**	**Connector Type**	**Associated MB Form Factors**
ATX style	Intel ATX, ATX12V (1995/2000)	ATX	ATX, NLX, Micro-ATX, Mini-ITX
SFX style	Intel SFX (1997)	ATX	Flex-ATX, Micro-ATX, Mini-ITX

Note: LPX is also sometimes called Slimline or PS/2.

Each of these power supply form factors is available in numerous configurations and power output levels. The LPX form factor supply was the standard used on most systems from the late 1980s to mid-1996, when the ATX form factor started to gain in popularity. Since then, ATX has become by far the dominant form factor for power supplies, with the new SFX style being added as an ATX derivative for use in very compact systems that mainly use Flex-ATX-sized boards. The earlier IBM-derived form factors have been largely obsolete for some time now. Any power supply that does not conform to one of these standards is considered *proprietary*. Any systems that use proprietary designs should generally be avoided because replacements are difficult to obtain and upgrades are generally not available.

◄◄ See "Motherboard Form Factors," p. 202.

PC/XT Style

IBM's PC and XT systems (circa 1981 and 1983, respectively) used the same power supply form factor; the only difference was that the XT supply had more than double the power output capability. Because they were identical in external appearance and the type of connectors they used, you easily could install the higher-output XT supply as an upgrade for a PC system; thus, the idea of upgrading the power supply was born. The tremendous popularity of the original PC and XT systems led several manufacturers to begin building systems that mimicked their shapes and layouts. These clones or compatibles, as they have been called, could interchange virtually all components with the IBM systems, including the power supply. Numerous manufacturers then began producing components that followed the form factor of these systems. The PC/XT power supply and connectors are shown in Figure 21.1. This form factor, however, is not used in modern systems today.

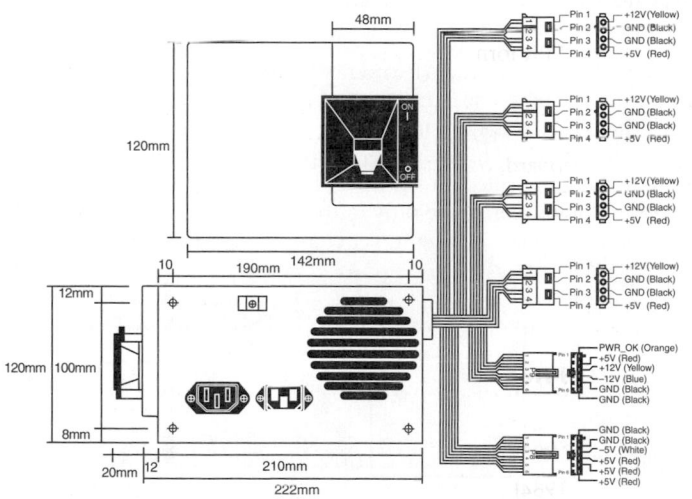

Figure 21.1   PC/XT form factor power supply.

AT/Desk Style

The AT desktop system that IBM introduced in August 1984 had a larger power supply and a form factor different from the original PC/XT. Other manufacturers rapidly cloned this system, which represented the basis for many subsequent IBM-compatible designs. The power supply used in these systems was called the AT/Desktop-style power supply (see Figure 21.2). Hundreds of manufacturers began making motherboards, power supplies, cases, and other components that were physically interchangeable with the original IBM AT. This form factor is no longer used today.

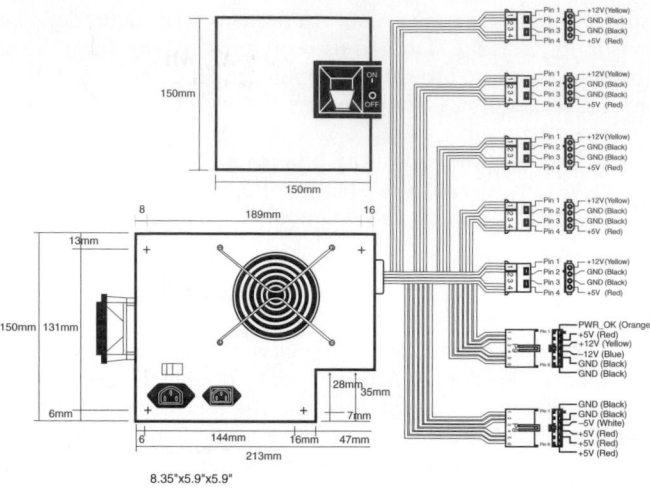

Figure 21.2   AT/Desktop form factor power supply.

AT/Tower Style

The AT/Tower configuration was basically a full-sized, AT-style desktop system running on its side. The tower configuration was not new; in fact, even IBM's original AT had a specially mounted logo that could be rotated when you ran the system on its side in the tower configuration.

The type of power supply used in most of the AT tower systems was identical to that used in a desktop system, except for the location of the power switch. On the original AT/Desktop systems, the power switch was built in to the side of the power supply (usually in the form of a large toggle switch). AT/Tower systems instead used an external switch attached to the power supply through a four-wire cable. A full-sized AT power supply with a remote switch is called an AT/Tower form factor power supply and is identical to the AT/Desktop supply in size and dimensions. The only difference is the use of an external switch (see Figure 21.3). This form factor is still used today in large server chassis that run AT form factor motherboards.

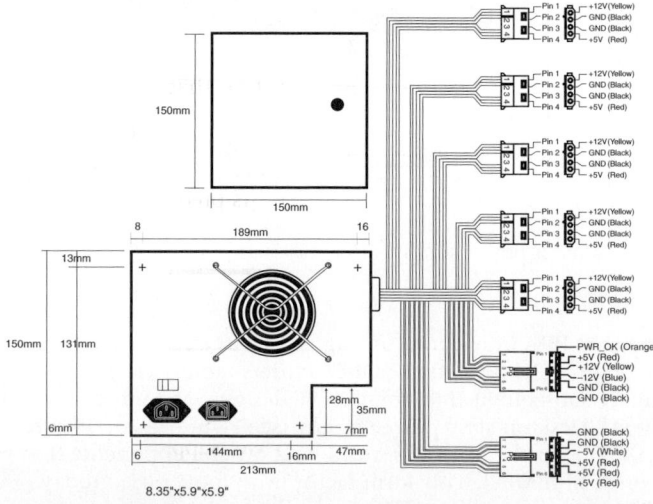

Figure 21.3   AT/Tower form factor power supply.

Baby-AT Style

Another type of AT-based form factor is the so-called Baby-AT, which is a shortened version of the full-size AT form factor. The power supply in these systems is shortened in one dimension but matches the AT design in all other respects. Baby-AT-style power supplies could fit in place of the larger AT/Desktop-style supply; however, the full-size AT/Tower supply would not fit in the Baby-AT chassis (see Figure 21.4). Because the Baby-AT PSU performed the same functions as the AT-style power supply but was in a smaller package, it became a common form factor until it was overtaken by later designs. This form factor is rarely used today.

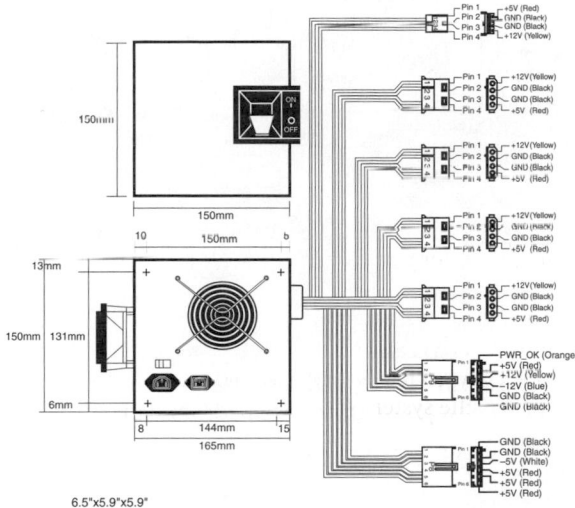

Figure 21.4 Baby-AT form factor power supply.

LPX Style

The next power supply form factor to gain popularity was the LPX style, also called the PS/2 type, Slimline, or slim style (see Figure 21.5). The LPX-style power supply has the exact same motherboard and disk drive connectors as the previous standard power supply form factors; it differs mainly in the shape. LPX systems were designed to have a smaller footprint and a lower height than AT-size systems. These computers used a different motherboard configuration that mounts the expansion bus slots on a "riser" card that plugs into the motherboard. The expansion cards plug into this riser and are mounted sideways in the system, parallel to the motherboard. Because of its smaller case, an LPX system needs a smaller power supply. The power supply designed for LPX systems is smaller than the Baby-AT style in every dimension and takes up less than half the space of its predecessor.

Note

IBM used the LPX power supply in some of its PS/2 systems in the late 1980s; hence it is sometimes called a PS/2-type supply.

As with the Baby-AT design in its time, the LPX power supply does the same job as its predecessor but comes in a smaller package. The LPX power supply quickly found its way into many manufacturers' systems and soon became a de facto standard. This style of power supply became the staple of the industry for many years, coming in everything from low-profile systems using actual LPX motherboards to full-size towers using Baby-AT or even full-size AT motherboards. It still is used in some PCs produced today; however, since 1996 the popularity of LPX has been overshadowed by the increasing popularity of the ATX design.

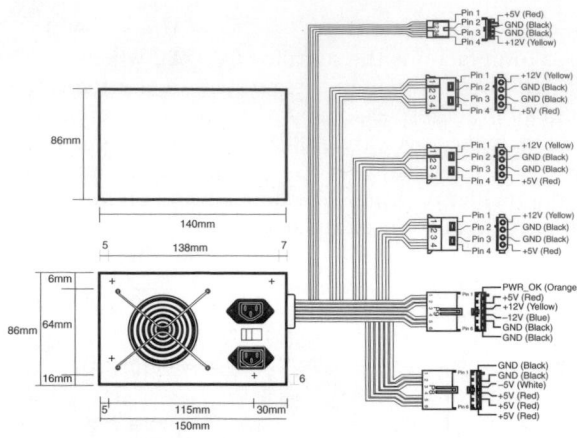

Figure 21.5   LPX form factor power supply.

ATX Style

The current standard in the industry is the ATX form factor (see Figure 21.6). The ATX specification, now in version 2.03, defines a new motherboard shape from its predecessors, as well as a new case and power supply form factor.

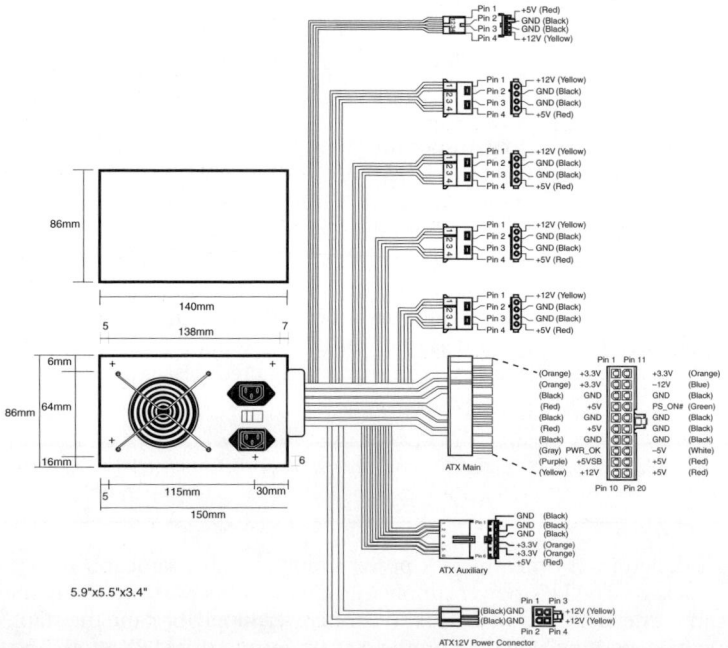

Figure 21.6   ATX form factor power supply with optional Auxiliary and ATX12V connectors.

The shape of the ATX power supply is based on the LPX design, but some important differences are worth noting.

One difference is that the ATX specification originally called for the fan to be mounted along the inner side of the supply, where it could draw air in from the rear of the chassis and blow it inside across the motherboard. This kind of airflow runs in the opposite direction as most standard supplies, which exhaust air out the back of the supply through a hole in the case where the fan protrudes. The idea was that the reverse-flow design could cool the system more efficiently with only a single fan, eliminating the need for a fan (active) heatsink on the CPU.

Another benefit of the reverse-flow cooling is that the system would run cleaner, freer from dust and dirt. The case would be pressurized, so air would be continuously forced out of the cracks in the case—the opposite of what happens with a negative pressure design. For this reason, the reverse-flow cooling design is often referred to as a positive-pressure-ventilation design. On an ATX system with reverse-flow cooling, the air is blown out away from the drive because the only air intake is the single fan vent on the power supply at the rear. For systems that operate in extremely harsh environments, you can add a filter to the fan intake vent to further ensure that all the air entering the system is clean and free of dust.

Although this sounds like a good way to ventilate a system, the positive-pressure design needs to use a more powerful fan to pull the required amount of air through a filter and pressurize the case. Also, if a filter is used, it must be serviced on a periodic basis—depending on operating conditions, it could need changing or cleaning as often as every week. In addition, the heat load from the power supply on a fully loaded system heats the air being ingested, blowing warm air over the CPU and reducing the overall cooling capability.

As CPUs evolved to generate more and more heat, the cooling capability of the system became more critical and the positive-pressure design was simply not up to the task. Therefore, subsequent versions of the ATX specification were rewritten to allow both positive- and negative-pressure designs, but they emphasized the standard negative-pressure system with an exhaust fan on the power supply and an additional high-quality cooling fan blowing cool air right on the CPU as the best solution.

Because a standard negative-pressure system offers the greatest cooling capacity for a given fan's air-speed and flow, virtually all the newer ATX-style power supplies use a negative-pressure design, in which air flows out the back of the power supply.

Intel first released the ATX specification in 1995. In 1996, it became increasingly popular in Pentium and Pentium Pro–based PCs, capturing 18% of the motherboard market within the first year. Since 1996, ATX has become the dominant motherboard form factor, displacing the previously popular Baby-AT. ATX and its derivatives are likely to remain the most popular form factor for several years to come.

The ATX form factor addressed several problems with the previous AT-type and LPX-type supplies. One is that the power supplies used with Baby-AT boards have two connectors that plug into the motherboard. If you insert these connectors backward or out of their normal sequence, you will fry the motherboard! Most responsible system manufacturers "key" the motherboard and power supply connectors so that you can't install them backward or out of sequence. However, most vendors of cheaper systems did not feature this keying on the boards or supplies they used. The ATX form factor includes intelligently designed power plugs for the motherboard to prevent users from plugging in their power supplies incorrectly. The ATX design features up to three motherboard power connectors that are definitively keyed, making plugging them in backward virtually impossible. The new ATX connectors also supply +3.3V, reducing the need for voltage regulators on the motherboard to power the chipset, DIMMs, and other +3.3V circuits.

Besides the new +3.3V outputs, ATX power supplies furnish another set of outputs that is not typically seen on standard power supplies. The set consists of the Power_On (PS_ON) and 5V_Standby (5VSB) outputs mentioned earlier, known collectively as *Soft Power*. This enables features to be implemented, such as Wake on Ring or Wake on LAN, in which a signal from a modem or network adapter can actually cause a PC to wake up and power on. Many such systems also have the option of setting a wake-up time, at which the PC can automatically turn itself on to perform scheduled tasks. These signals also can enable the optional use of the keyboard to power the system on—just like Apple systems. Users can enable these features because the +5V Standby power is always active, giving the motherboard a limited source of power even when off. Check your BIOS Setup for control over these features.

NLX Style

The NLX specification—one that Intel also developed—defines a low-profile case and motherboard design with many of the same attributes as the ATX. In fact, for interchangeability, NLX systems were designed to use ATX power supplies, even though the case and motherboard dimensions are different.

As in previous LPX systems, the NLX motherboard uses a riser board for the expansion bus slots. Where NLX differs is that it is a true (and not proprietary) standard. See Chapter 4, "Motherboards and Buses," for more information on the NLX form factor.

For the purposes of this discussion, NLX systems use ATX power supplies. The only real difference is that the supply plugs into the riser card and not the motherboard, enabling NLX motherboards to be more quickly and easily removed from their chassis for service.

SFX Style

Intel released the smaller Micro-ATX motherboard form factor in December 1997, and at the same time also released a new smaller SFX power supply design to go with it (see Figure 21.7). Even so, most Micro-ATX chassis used the standard ATX power supply instead. Then in March 1999, Intel released the Flex-ATX addendum to the Micro-ATX specification, which was a very small board designed for low-end PCs or PC-based appliances. Now, the SFX supply has found use in many new compact system designs.

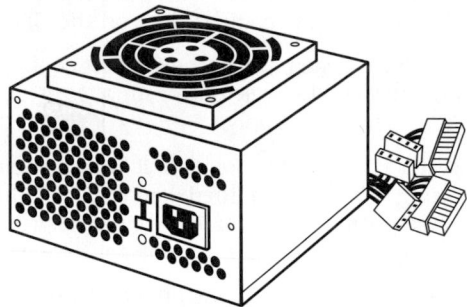

Figure 21.7   SFX-style power supply (with 80mm top-mounted cooling fan).

The SFX power supply is specifically designed for use in small systems containing a limited amount of hardware and limited upgradability. Most SFX supplies can provide 90 watts of continuous power (135 watts at its peak) in four voltages (+5V, +12V, –12V, and +3.3V). This amount of power has proven to be sufficient for a small system with a processor, an AGP interface, up to four expansion slots, and three peripheral devices—such as hard drives and CD-ROMs.

Although Intel designed the SFX power supply specification with the Micro-ATX and Flex-ATX motherboard form factors in mind, SFX is a wholly separate standard that is compliant with other motherboards as well. SFX power supplies use the same 20-pin connector defined in the ATX standard and include both the Power_On and 5V_Standby outputs. Whether you will use an ATX or SFX power supply in a given system depends more on the case or chassis than the motherboard. Each has the same basic electrical connectors; the main difference is which type of power supply the case is physically designed to accept.

One limiting factor of the SFX design is that it lacks the –5V and so shouldn't be used with motherboards that have ISA slots (most Micro-ATX and Flex-ATX boards do *not* have ISA slots; the Mini-ITX boards don't have ISA slots either). SFX power supplies also don't have the Auxiliary (3.3V and 5V) or ATX12V power connectors and therefore shouldn't be used with full-size ATX boards that require those connections.

On a standard model SFX power supply, a 60mm diameter cooling fan is located on the surface of the housing, facing the inside of the computer's case (see Figure 21.8). The fan draws the air into the power supply housing from the system cavity and expels it through a port at the rear of the system. Internalizing the fan in this way reduces system noise and results in a standard negative-pressure design. In many cases, additional fans might be needed in the system to cool the processor.

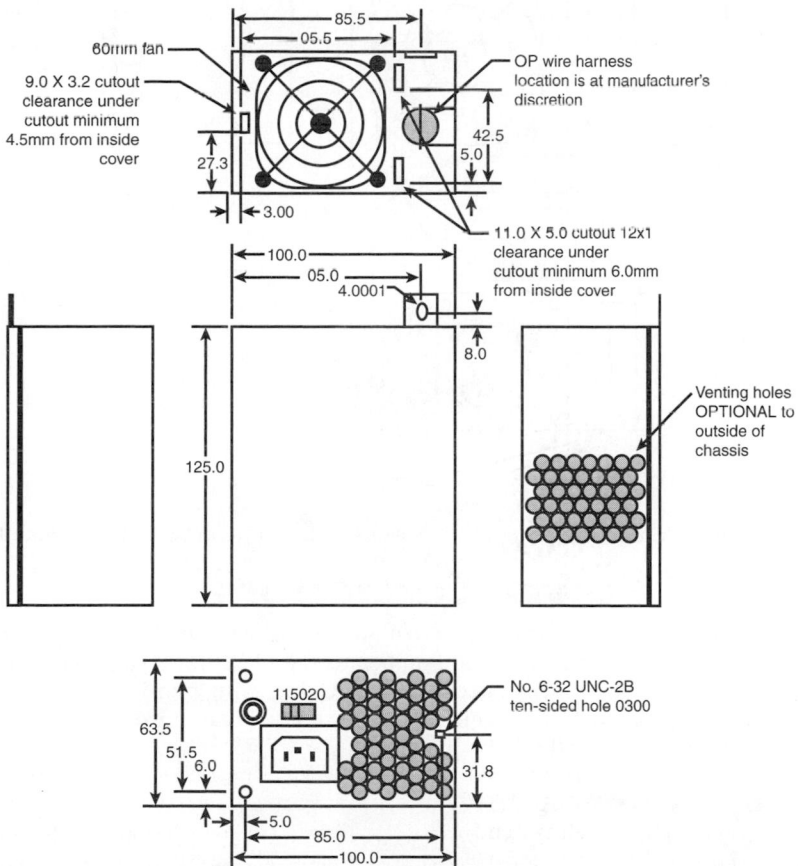

Figure 21.8　SFX form factor power supply dimensions with a standard internal 60mm fan.

For systems that require more cooling capability, a version that allows for a larger, 80mm top-mounted cooling fan also is available. The larger fan provides more cooling capability and airflow for systems that need it (see Figure 21.9).

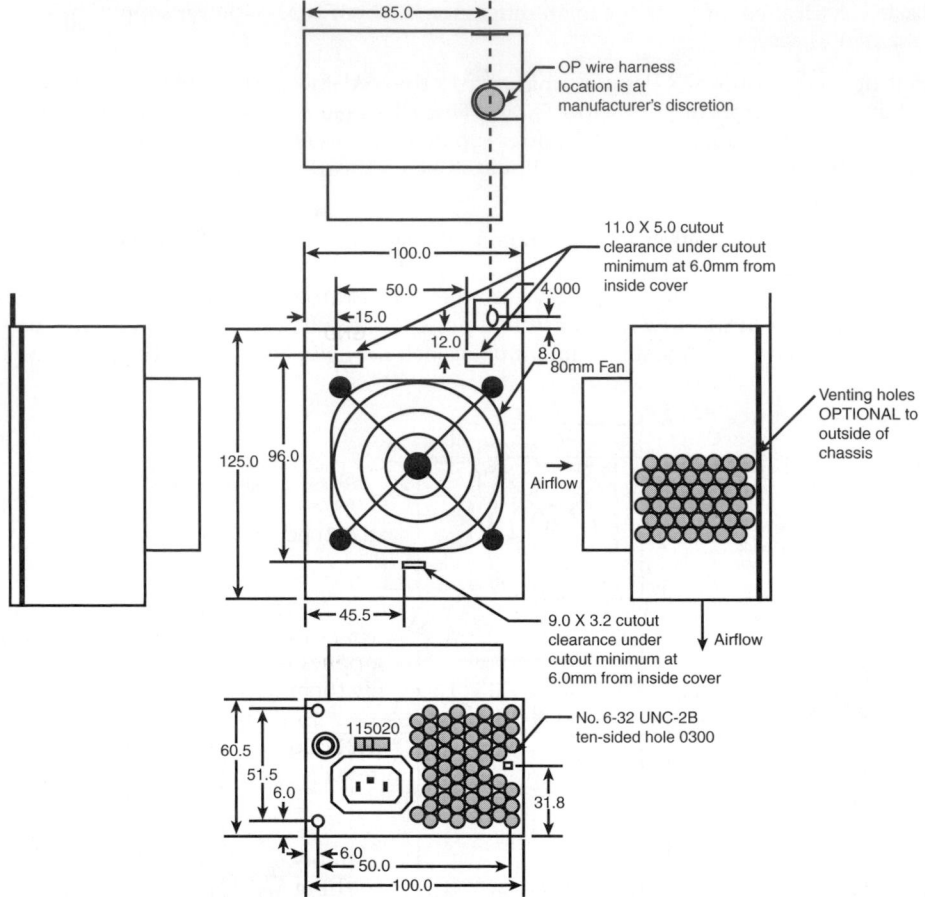

Figure 21.9   SFX form factor power supply dimensions with an internal 80mm top-mounted fan.

Motherboard Power Connectors

Every PC power supply has special connectors that attach to the motherboard, giving power to the system processor, memory, and all slotted add-on boards (ISA, PCI, and AGP). Attaching these connectors improperly can have a devastating effect on your PC, including burning up both your power supply and motherboard. The following sections detail the motherboard power connectors used by various power supplies.

AT Power Supply Connectors

AT power supplies feature two main power connectors (P8 and P9), each with six pins that attach the power supply to the motherboard. These are rated at 5 amps per pin, at up to 250V. These two connectors are shown in Figure 21.10.

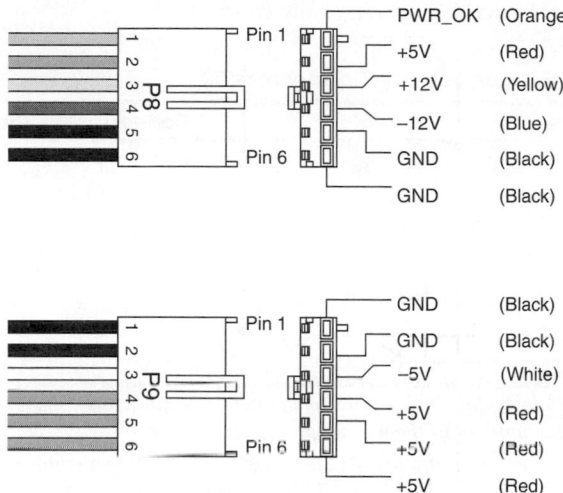

Figure 21.10   AT/LPX main P8/P9 (sometimes also called P1/P2) power connectors.

All standard PC power supplies that use the P8 and P9 connectors have them installed end to end so that the two black wires (ground connections) on both power cables are next to each other. Note the designations "P8" and "P9" are not fully standardized, although most use those designations because that is what IBM stamped on the originals. Some power supplies have them labeled as P1/P2 instead. Because these connectors usually have a clasp that prevents them from being inserted backward on the motherboard's pins, the major concern is getting the two connectors in the correct orientation side by side and also not missing a pin offset on either side. Following the black-to-black rule keeps you safe. You must take care, however, to ensure that no remaining unconnected motherboard pins exist between or on either side of the two connectors after you install them. A properly installed connector connects to and covers every motherboard power pin. If any power pins are showing on either side of or between the connectors, the entire connector assembly is installed incorrectly, which can result in catastrophic failure for the motherboard and everything plugged into it at the time of power-up. Figure 21.11 shows the P8 and P9 connectors (sometimes also called P1/P2) in their proper orientation when connecting.

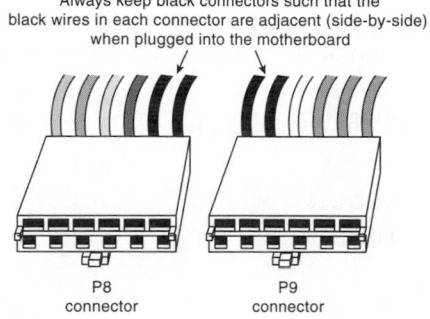

Figure 21.11   The P8/P9 power connectors (sometimes also called P1/P2) that connect an AT/LPX power supply to the motherboard.

Table 21.3 shows typical AT and LPX power supply connections.

Table 21.3   AT/LPX Power Supply Connectors

Connector	Pin	Signal	Color[2]	Connector	Pin	Signal	Color[2]
P8 (or P1)	1	Power_Good (+5V)	Orange	P9 (or P2)	1	Ground	Black
	2	+5V[1]	Red		2	Ground	Black
	3	+12V	Yellow		3	−5V	White
	4	−12V	Blue		4	+5V	Red
	5	Ground	Black		5	+5V	Red
	6	Ground	Black		6	+5V	Red

1. First-generation PC/XT motherboards and power supplies did not require this voltage, so the pin might be missing from the motherboard and terminal and the wire might be missing from the connector (P8 pin 2).

2. I have seen some supplies where the manufacturer did not follow industry-standard wire color-codes even though the signals were correct.

Tip

Although older PC/XT power supplies do not have any connection at connector P8 pin 2, you still can use them on AT-type motherboards, or vice versa. The presence or absence of the +5V on that pin has little or no effect on system operation because the remaining +5V wires usually can carry the load.

Note that all the AT- and LPX-type power supplies use the same connectors and pin configurations.

ATX Main Power Connector

The industry-standard ATX power supply–to–motherboard main connector is the Molex Mini-Fit, Jr. connector number 39-29-9202 (or equivalent), which is more commonly known as the 20-pin ATX-style connector (see Figure 21.12). Molex rates each pin to handle 6 amps of current (at up to 600V). First used in the ATX form factor power supply, it also is used in the SFX form factor or any other ATX-based variations. This is a 20-pin keyed connector with pins configured as shown in Table 21.4. The colors for the wires listed are those the ATX standard recommends; however, to enable them to vary from manufacturer to manufacturer, they are not required for compliance to the specification. I like to show these connector pinouts in a wire side view, which shows how the pins are arranged looking at the back of the connector (from the wire and not terminal side). This is because it shows how they would be oriented if you were back-probing the connector with the connector plugged in.

Figure 21.13 shows a view of the connector as if you were looking at it facing the terminal side.

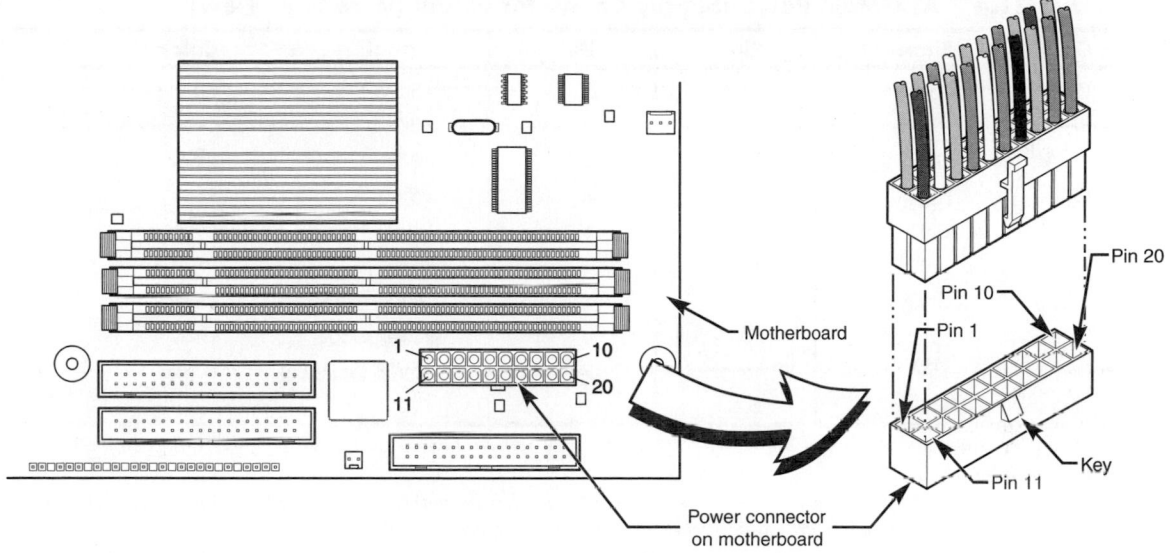

Figure 21.12   ATX-style 20-pin motherboard main power connector, perspective view.

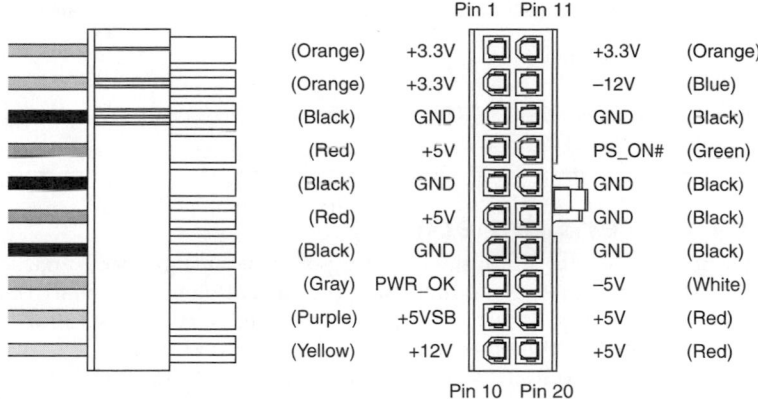

Pin 1   Pin 11

(Orange)	+3.3V			+3.3V	(Orange)
(Orange)	+3.3V			−12V	(Blue)
(Black)	GND			GND	(Black)
(Red)	+5V			PS_ON#	(Green)
(Black)	GND			GND	(Black)
(Red)	+5V			GND	(Black)
(Black)	GND			GND	(Black)
(Gray)	PWR_OK			−5V	(White)
(Purple)	+5VSB			+5V	(Red)
(Yellow)	+12V			+5V	(Red)

Pin 10   Pin 20

Figure 21.13   ATX/NLX 20-pin main power connector, terminal side view.

Table 21.4   ATX Main Power Supply Connector Pinout (Wire Side View)

Color	Signal	Pin	Pin	Signal	Color
Orange[1]	+3.3V	11	1	+3.3V	Orange
Blue	−12V	12	2	+3.3V	Orange
Black	GND	13	3	GND	Black
Green	PS_On	14	4	+5V	Red
Black	GND	15	5	GND	Black
Black	GND	16	6	+5V	Red
Black	GND	17	7	GND	Black
White	−5V[2]	18	8	Power_Good	Gray
Red	+5V	19	9	+5VSB (Standby)	Purple
Red	+5V	20	10	+12V	Yellow

1. *Might have a second orange or brown wire, used for +3.3V sense feedback—used by the power supply to monitor 3.3V regulation.*

2. *Also might be N/C (no connection) on some later model supplies or motherboards. Supplies with no connection at pin 18 should be used only with motherboards that do not incorporate ISA Bus slots.*

Note

The ATX supply features several voltages and signals not seen before, such as the +3.3V, PS_On, and +5V_Standby. Therefore, adapting a standard LPX form factor supply to make it work properly in an ATX system is impossible—even though the shapes of the power supplies themselves are virtually identical.

However, because ATX is a superset of the older LPX power supply standard, you can use a connector adapter to allow an ATX power supply to connect to an older Baby-AT-style motherboard. PC Power and Cooling (see the Vendor List on the disc) sells this type of adapter.

ATX Auxiliary Power Connector

As motherboards and processors evolved, the need for power became greater. In particular, chipsets and DIMMs were designed to run on 3.3V, increasing the current demand at that voltage. In addition, most boards included CPU voltage regulators that were designed to convert +5V power into the unique voltage levels required by the processors the board supported. Eventually, the high current demands on the +3.3V and +5V outputs were proving too much for the design of the connectors and terminals. Each of the terminals in the main power connector are rated for 6 amps (A), which allows for a maximum draw of 18A of +3.3V power and 24A of +5V power. These maximums match the ratings of an approximately 250-watt-rated power supply. Because motherboards with high-speed processors and multiple cards installed could draw more power than that and power supply manufacturers were building supplies with 300-watt and higher ratings, melted connectors were becoming more and more common. The terminals in the main connector would overheat under such a load.

To allow for additional power from the supply to the motherboard, Intel modified the ATX specification to add a second auxiliary power connector for high power draw ATX motherboards and 250-watt or higher rated supplies. The criteria was such that if the motherboard could draw more than 18A of +3.3V power, and/or more than 24A of +5V power, then the auxiliary connector would be required to carry the additional load. These higher levels of power are needed in systems using 250- to 300-watt or greater supplies.

The ATX Auxiliary Connector is a 6-pin Molex-type connector, similar to one of the motherboard power connectors used on AT/LPX supplies (see Figure 21.14). The terminals in this type of connector are rated for 5 amps per pin at up to 250 volts. The connector is normally keyed to prevent a mis-aligned connection. The additional +5V wire allows a total of 29A of +5V to be available to the motherboard, and the additional two +3.3V wires allow a total of 28A of +3.3V power to be available to the motherboard.

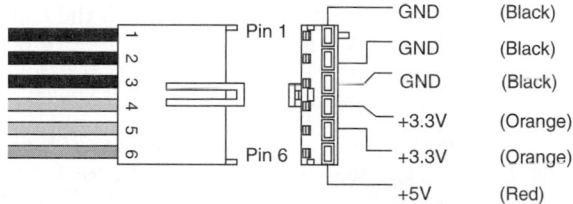

Figure 21.14   ATX auxiliary power connector.

The pinouts of the auxiliary connector are shown in Table 21.5.

Table 21.5   ATX Auxiliary Power Connector Pinout

Pin	Signal	Color	Pin	Signal	Color
1	Gnd	Black	4	+3.3V	Orange
2	Gnd	Black	5	+3.3V	Orange
3	Gnd	Black	6	+5V	Red

If your motherboard does not feature a mate for the auxiliary connector then it probably wasn't designed to consume a large amount of power. In that case, the auxiliary connector from the power supply (if present) can be left unconnected. If your power supply is rated at 250 watts or higher, you should ensure that it has the Auxiliary Connector. Consequently, if your motherboard is capable of drawing more than 18A of +3.3V power or more than 24A of +5V power, you should also ensure that your motherboard has the mating auxiliary power connector. Using the auxiliary connector eases the load on the main power connector and prevents melted contacts.

ATX12V Connector

Power for the processor comes from a device called the voltage regulator module (VRM), which is built in to most modern motherboards. This device senses the CPU voltage requirements (usually via sense pins on the processor) and calibrates itself to provide the proper voltage to run the CPU. The design of a VRM enables it to run on either 5V or 12V for input power. Most have used 5V over the years, but many are now converting to 12V because of the lower current requirements at that voltage. In addition, other devices might have already loaded the 5V, whereas, typically, only drive motors use the 12V. Whether the VRM on your board uses 5V or 12V depends on the particular motherboard or regulator design. Many modern voltage regulator ICs are designed to run on anything from a 4V to a 36V input, so it is up to the motherboard designer as to how they will be configured.

For example, I studied a system using an FIC (First International Computer) SD-11 motherboard, which used a Semtech SC1144ABCSW voltage regulator. This board design uses the +5V to convert to the lower voltage the CPU needs. Most motherboards use voltage regulator circuits controlled by chips from Semtech (http://www.semtech.com) or Linear Technology (http://www.linear.com). You can visit their sites for more data on these chips.

That motherboard accepts an Athlon 1GHz Cartridge version (Model 2), which according to AMD has a maximum power draw of 65W and a nominal voltage requirement of 1.8V. 65W at 1.8V would equate to 36.1A of current at that voltage (volts × amps = watts). If the voltage regulator used +5V as a feed, 65W would equate to only 13A at +5V. That would assume 100% efficiency in the regulator, which is impossible. Therefore, assuming 80% efficiency (which is typical), there would be about 16.25A actual draw on the +5V due to the regulator and processor combined.

When you consider that other circuits on the motherboard also use +5V power—plus ISA or PCI cards are drawing that power as well—you can see how easy it is to overload the +5V lines from the supply to the motherboard.

Although most motherboard VRM designs up through the Pentium III and Athlon/Duron use 5V-based regulators, a transition is underway to use 12V-powered regulators. This is because the higher voltage will significantly reduce the current draw. As an example, using the same 65W AMD Athlon 1GHz CPU, you end up with the levels of draw at the various voltages shown in Table 21.6.

Table 21.6   Levels of Draw at Various Voltages

Watts	Volts	Amps	Amps at 80% Regulator Efficiency
65	1.8	36.1	—
65	3.3	19.7	24.6
65	5.0	13.0	16.3
65	12.0	5.4	6.8

As you can see, using 12V to power the chip results in only 5.4A of draw, or 6.8A assuming 80% efficiency on the part of the regulator.

So, modifying the motherboard VRM circuit to use the +12V power feed would seem simple. Unfortunately, the standard ATX 2.03 power supply design has only a single +12V lead in the main power connector. The auxiliary connector has no +12V leads at all, so that is no help. Pulling up to 8A more through a single 18-gauge wire supplying +12V power to the motherboard is a recipe for a melted connector because the contacts in the main ATX connector are rated for only 6A.

To augment the supply of +12V power to the motherboard, Intel created a new ATX12V power supply specification. This adds a third power connector, called the ATX12V connector, specifically to supply additional +12V power to the board. This connector has two +12V power pins, each rated for 8A total, allowing for up to 16A of additional 12V current to the motherboard, for a total of 22A of +12V. This connector is shown in Figure 21.15.

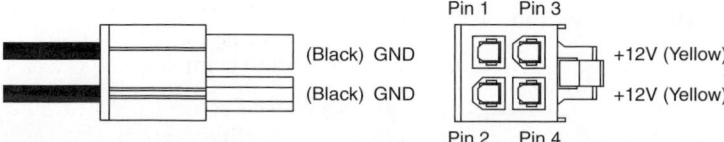

Figure 21.15   An ATX12V power connector.

The pinout of the +12V power connector is shown in Table 21.7.

Table 21.7   ATX +12V Power Connector Pinout (Wire Side View)

Color	Signal	Pin	Pin	Signal	Color
Yellow	+12V	3	1	Gnd	Black
Yellow	+12V	4	2	Gnd	Black

If you are replacing your motherboard with a new one that requires the ATX12V connection for the CPU voltage regulator, and yet your existing power supply doesn't have that connector, an easy solution is available. Merely convert one of the peripheral power connectors to an ATX12V type. PC Power and Cooling has released just such an adapter that can instantly make any standard ATX power supply into one with an ATX12V connector. This connector works because the issue is not whether the power supply can generate the necessary 12V—that has always been available via the peripheral connectors. The ATX12V adapter shown in Figure 21.16 solves the connector problem quite nicely.

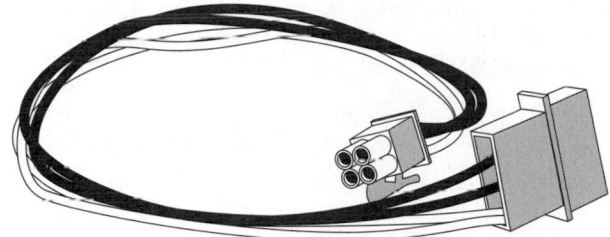

Figure 21.16   ATX12V adapter from PC Power and Cooling.

Dell Proprietary (Nonstandard) ATX Design

If you currently own a desktop system made between 1996 and 2000 from Dell, you will definitely want to pay attention to this section. A potential booby trap is waiting to nail the unsuspecting Dell system owner who decides to upgrade either the motherboard or power supply in his system. This hidden trap can cause the destruction of the motherboard, power supply, or both! Okay, now that I have your attention, read on....

As those of you who have attended my seminars or read previous editions of this book will know, I have long been a promoter of industry-standard PCs and components and wouldn't think of purchasing a desktop PC that didn't have what I consider an industry-standard form factor motherboard, power supply, and chassis (ATX, for example). I've been down the proprietary road before with systems from Packard Bell, Compaq, IBM, and other companies that used custom, unique, or proprietary components. For example, during a momentary lapse of reason in the early '90s, I purchased a Packard Bell system. I quickly outgrew the capabilities of the system, so I thought I'd upgrade it with a new motherboard and a faster processor. It was then that I discovered, to my horror, that LPX systems were not an interchangeable standard. Because of riser card differences, virtually no interchangeability of motherboards, riser cards, chassis, and power supplies existed. I had what I now refer to as a "disposable PC"—the kind you can't upgrade and have to throw away instead. Suddenly, the money I thought I had saved when initially purchasing the system paled in comparison to what I'd now have to spend to completely replace it. Lesson learned.

After several upgrade and repair experiences like that, I decided never again would I be trapped by systems using proprietary or nonstandard components. By purchasing only systems built with industry-standard parts, I could easily and inexpensively upgrade, maintain, or repair the systems for many years into the future. I have been preaching the gospel of industry-standard components in my seminars and in this book ever since.

Of course, building your own system from scratch is one way to avoid proprietary components, but often that route is more costly in both time and money than purchasing a prebuilt system. And what systems should I recommend for people who want an inexpensive prebuilt system but one that uses industry-standard parts so it can be inexpensively upgraded and repaired later? Although many system vendors and assemblers exist, I've settled on companies such as Gateway, MPC (formerly MicronPC), and Dell. In fact, those are really the three largest system vendors that deal direct, and they mostly sell systems that use industry-standard ATX form factor components in all their main desktop system product lines. Or so I thought.

It seems that when Dell converted to the ATX motherboard form factor in mid-1996, it unfortunately defected from the newly released standard and began using specially modified Intel-supplied ATX motherboards with custom-wired power connectors. Inevitably, it also had custom power supplies made that duplicated the nonstandard pinout of the motherboard power connectors.

An even bigger crime than simply using nonstandard power connectors is that only the pinout is nonstandard; the connectors look like and are keyed the same as is dictated by true ATX. Therefore, nothing prevents you from plugging the Dell nonstandard power supply into a new industry-standard ATX motherboard you installed in your Dell case as an upgrade, or even plugging a new upgraded industry-standard ATX power supply into your existing Dell motherboard. But mixing either a new ATX board with the Dell supply or a new ATX supply with the existing Dell board is a recipe for silicon toast. How do you like your fried chips: medium or well-done?

Frankly, I'm amazed I haven't heard more about this because Dell has climbed to the lead in worldwide PC sales. In any case, I figure by getting this information out I can save thousands of innocent motherboards and power supplies from instant death upon installation.

If you've already fallen victim to this nasty circumstance, believe me, I feel your pain. I discovered this the hard way as well—by frying parts. At first, I thought the upgraded power supply I installed in one of my Dell systems was bad, especially considering the dramatic way it smoked when I turned on the system: I actually saw fire through the vents! Good thing I decided to check the color codes on the connectors and verify the pinout on another Dell system by using a voltmeter before I installed and fried a second supply. I was lucky in that the smoked supply didn't take the motherboard with it; I can only surmise that the supply fried so quickly it sacrificed itself and saved the motherboard. You might not be so lucky, and in most cases I'd expect you'd fry the board and supply together.

Call me a fool, but I didn't think I'd have to check the color-coding or get out my voltmeter to verify the Dell "pseudo-ATX" power connector pinouts before I installed a new ATX supply or motherboard. You'll also find that motherboard and power supply manufacturers don't like to replace these items under warranty when they are fried in this manner due to nonstandard connector wiring.

Dell's official explanation for its lack of conformance to the ATX standard was, "In the mid-90s the industry moved to a higher use of 3.3V motherboard components. Dell engineers designed a connector that supported the increased use of 3.3V current which differed from the industry proposed designs that we deemed less than robust." Unfortunately, this explanation doesn't hold much water because the standard ATX connector incorporated three 3.3V pins, allowing for up to 18A of current and the addition of the Auxiliary Connector added two more pins with 10A of additional current. Dell's pseudo-ATX design had only three 3.3V pins in the Auxiliary Connector, which could supply only up to 15A to the board. You can see that even the main ATX Connector alone had more 3.3V current than Dell's design using two connectors!

Because its technical explanation fails to address the issue, the only other reason I can imagine it did this is to lock people into purchasing replacement motherboards or power supplies from Dell. What makes this worse is that Dell uses virtually all Intel-manufactured boards in its systems. One system I have uses an Intel D815EEA motherboard, which is the same board used by many of the other major system builders, including Gateway and Micron. It's the same, except for the power connectors, that is. The difference is that Dell has Intel custom make the boards for Dell with the nonstandard connectors. Everybody else gets virtually the same Intel boards, but with industry-standard connectors.

Tables 21.8 and 21.9 show the nonstandard Dell main and auxiliary power supply connections. This nonstandard wiring is used on Dell's pseudo-ATX systems.

Table 21.8 Dell Proprietary (Nonstandard) ATX Main Power Connector Pinout (Wire Side View)

Color	Signal	Pin	Pin	Signal	Color
Gray	PS_On	11	1	+5V	Red
Black	Gnd	12	2	Gnd	Black
Black	Gnd	13	3	+5V	Red
Black	Gnd	14	4	Gnd	Black
White	−5V	15	5	Power_Good	Orange
Red	+5V	16	6	+5VSB (Standby)	Purple
Red	+5V	17	7	+12V	Yellow
Red	+5V	18	8	−12V	Blue
KEY (blank)	—	19	9	Gnd	Black
Red	+5V	20	10	Gnd	Black

Table 21.9 Dell Proprietary (Nonstandard) ATX Auxiliary Power Connector Pinout

Pin	Signal	Color	Pin	Signal	Color
1	Gnd	Black	4	+3.3	Blue/White
2	Gnd	Black	5	+3.3	Blue/White
3	Gnd	Black	6	+3.3	Blue/White

At first I thought that if all Dell did was switch some of the terminals around, I could use a terminal pick to remove the terminals from the connectors (with the wires attached) and merely reinsert them into the proper connector positions, enabling me to use the Dell power supply with an upgraded ATX motherboard in the future. Unfortunately, if you study the Dell main and auxiliary connector pinouts I've listed here and compare them to the industry-standard ATX pinouts listed earlier, you'll see that not only are the voltage and signal positions changed, but the number of terminals carrying specific voltages and grounds has changed as well. You could modify a Dell supply to work with a standard ATX board or modify a standard ATX supply to work with a Dell board, but you'd have to do some cutting and splicing in addition to swapping some terminals around. Usually, it isn't worth the time and effort.

If you do decide to upgrade the motherboard in any Dell system purchased between 1996 and 2000, a simple solution is available—just be sure you replace both the motherboard *and* power supply with industry-standard ATX components at the same time. That way nothing gets fried, and you'll be back to having a true industry-standard ATX system. If you want to replace just the Dell motherboard, you're out of luck unless you get your replacement board from Dell. On the other hand, if you want to replace just the power supply, you do have one alternative. PC Power and Cooling now makes a version of its high-performance 300W ATX power supply with the modified Dell wiring for about $90. The internals are identical to its industry-standard, high-performance 300W ATX supply (which it sells for about 30% less)—only the number and arrangement of wires has changed.

Fortunately, starting in 2000, Dell switched to using industry-standard ATX power connections in its Dimension 4300, 4400, 8200, and newer systems. That means barring any other unforeseen glitches, these systems should be more easily upgradeable by just replacing either the power supply or the motherboard alone. I, for one, am glad to see Dell moving back toward industry standardization because its systems are now more appealing to purchase as a starting point for a system that will be user upgradeable and repairable in the future.

Power Switch Connectors

Three main types of power switches are used on PCs. They can be described as follows:

- Integral Power Supply AC switch
- Front Panel Power Supply AC switch
- Front Panel Motherboard Controlled switch

The earliest systems had power switches integrated or built directly into the power supply, which turned the main AC power to the system on and off. This was a simple design, but because the power supply was mounted to the rear or side of the system, it required reaching around to the back to actuate the switch. Also, switching the AC power directly meant the system couldn't be remotely started without special hardware.

Starting in the late '80s, systems began using remote front panel switches. These were essentially the same power supply design as the first type. The only difference was that the AC switch was now mounted remotely (usually on the front panel of the chassis), rather than integrated in the power supply unit. The switch was connected to the power supply via a four-wire cable, and the ends of the cable were fitted with spade connector lugs, which plugged onto the spade connectors on the power switch. The cable from the power supply to the switch in the case contained four color-coded wires. In addition, a fifth wire supplying a ground connection to the case was sometimes included. The switch was usually included with the power supply and heavily shrink-wrapped or insulated where the connector lugs attached to prevent electric shock.

This solved the ergonomic problem of reaching the switch, but it still didn't enable remote or auto-mated system power-up without special hardware. Plus, you now had a 120V AC switch mounted in the chassis, with wires carrying dangerous voltage through the system. Some of these wires are hot anytime the system is plugged in (all are hot with the system turned on), creating a dangerous environment for the average person when messing around inside the system.

Caution

At least two of the remote power switch leads to a remote-mounted AC power switch in an AT/LPX supply are energized with 120V AC at all times. You could be electrocuted if you touch the ends of these wires with the power supply plugged in, even if the unit is turned off! For this reason, always make sure the power supply is unplugged before connecting or discon-necting the remote power switch or touching any of the wires connected to it.

The four or five wires are usually color-coded as follows:

- *Brown and blue.* These wires are the live and neutral feed wires from the 120V power cord to the power supply. These are always hot when the power supply is plugged in.
- *Black and white.* These wires carry the AC feed from the switch back to the power supply. These leads should be hot only when the power supply is plugged in and the switch is turned on.
- *Green or green with a yellow stripe.* This is the ground lead. It should be connected to the PC case and should help ground the power supply to the case.

On the switch, the tabs for the leads are usually color-coded; if not, you'll find that most switches have two parallel tabs and two angled tabs. If no color-coding is on the switch, plug the blue and brown wires onto the tabs that are parallel to each other and the black and white wires to the tabs that are angled away from each other. If none of the tabs are angled, simply make sure the blue and brown wires are plugged into the most closely spaced tabs on one side of the switch and the black and white wires on the most closely spaced tabs on the other side (see Figure 21.17).

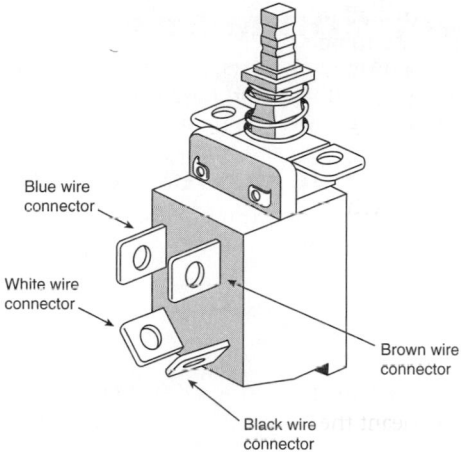

Blue wire
connector

White wire
connector

Brown wire
connector

Black wire
connector

Figure 21.17 Power supply remote push button switch connections.

Caution

Although these wire color-codings and parallel/angled tabs are used on most power supplies, they are not necessarily 100% universal. I have encountered power supplies that do not use the same coloring or tab placement scheme described here. One thing is sure: Two of the wires will be hot with potentially fatal AC voltage anytime the power supply is plugged in. No matter what, always disconnect the power supply from the wall socket before handling any of these wires. Be sure to insulate the connections with electrical tape or heat-shrink tubing so you won't be able to touch the wires when working inside the case in the future.

As long as the blue and brown wires are on the one set of tabs and the black and white leads are on the other, the switch and supply will work properly. If you incorrectly mix the leads, you will likely blow the circuit breaker for the wall socket because mixing them can create a direct short circuit.

All ATX and subsequent power supplies that employ the 20-pin motherboard connector use the PS_ON signal to power up the system. As a result, the remote switch does not physically control the power supply's access to the 120V AC power, as in the older-style power supplies. Instead, the power supply's on or off status is toggled by a PS_ON signal received on pin 14 of the ATX connector.

The PS_ON signal can be generated physically by the computer's power switch or electronically by the operating system. PS_ON is an active low signal, meaning that the power supply voltage outputs are disabled (the system is off) when the PS_ON is high (greater than or equal to 2.0V). This excludes the +5VSB (Standby) on pin 9, which is active whenever the power supply is connected to an AC power source. The power supply maintains the PS_ON signal at either 3.3V or 5V. This signal is then routed through the motherboard to the remote switch on the front of the case. When the switch is pressed, the PS_ON signal is grounded. When the power supply sees the PS_ON signal drop to 0.8V or less, the power supply (and system) is turned on. Thus, the remote switch in an ATX-style system (which includes NLX and SFX systems as well) carries up to only +5V of DC power, rather than the full 120V–240V AC current like that of the older AT/LPX form factors.

Caution

The continuous presence of the +5VSB power on pin 9 of the ATX connector means that the motherboard is always receiving standby power from the power supply when connected to an AC source, even when the computer is turned off. As a result, it is even more crucial to unplug an ATX system from the power source before working inside the case than it is on an earlier model system.

Peripheral Power Connectors

In addition to the motherboard power connectors, power supplies include a variety of peripheral power connectors for everything from floppy and hard drives to internal case fans. The following sections discuss the various types of connectors you're likely to find in your PC.

Peripheral and Floppy Drive Power Connectors

The disk drive connectors on power supplies are fairly universal with regard to pin configuration and even wire color. Figure 21.18 shows the peripheral and floppy power connectors.

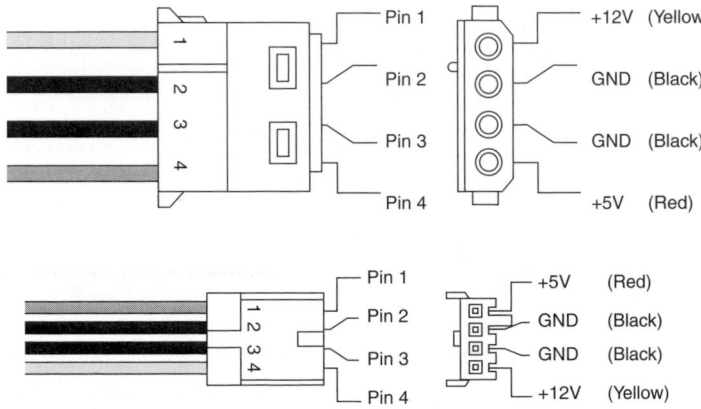

Figure 21.18   Peripheral and floppy power connectors.

Table 21.10 shows the standard disk drive power connector pinout and wire colors, whereas Table 21.11 shows the pinouts for the smaller floppy drive power connector.

Table 21.10   Peripheral Power Connector Pinout (Large Drive Power Connector)

Pin	Signal	Color	Pin	Signal	Color
1	+12V	Yellow	3	Gnd	Black
2	Gnd	Black	4	+5V	Red

Table 21.11   3 1/2" Floppy Power Connector Pinout (Small Drive Power Connector)

Pin	Signal	Color	Pin	Signal	Color
1	+5V	Red	3	Gnd	Black
2	Gnd	Black	4	+12V	Yellow

Note that the pin numbering and voltage designations are reversed on the two connectors. Be careful if you are making or using an adapter cable from one type of connector to another. Reversing the red and yellow wires will fry the drive or device you plug into.

To determine the location of pin 1, look at the connector carefully. It is usually embossed in the plastic connector body; however, it is often tiny and difficult to read. Fortunately, these connectors are keyed and therefore difficult to insert incorrectly. Figure 21.19 shows the keying with respect to pin numbers on the larger drive power connector.

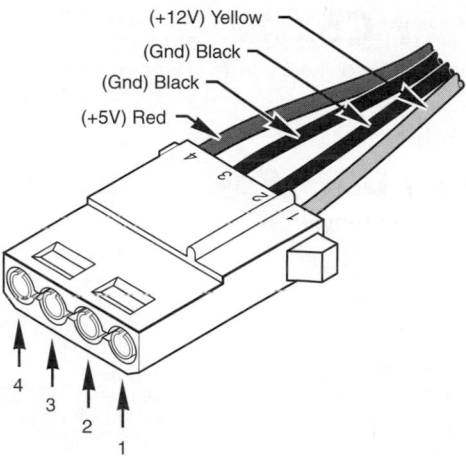

Figure 21.19 A peripheral female power supply connector.

Note

Some drive connectors might supply only two wires—usually the +5V and a single ground (pins 3 and 4)—because the floppy drives in most newer systems run only on +5V and do not use the +12V at all.

Early power supplies featured only two large style drive connectors, usually called peripheral connectors today. Later power supplies featured four or more of the larger peripheral (drive) connectors, and one or two of the smaller 3 1/2" floppy drive connectors. Depending on their power ratings and intended uses, some supplies have as many as eight peripheral/drive connectors.

If you are adding drives and need additional disk drive power connectors, Y splitter cables (see Figure 21.20) as well as large to small drive power connector adapters (see Figure 21.21) are available from many electronics supply houses (including RadioShack). These cables can adapt a single power connector to service two drives or enable you to convert the large peripheral power connector to a smaller floppy drive power connector. If you are using several Y-adapters, be sure that your total power supply output is capable of supplying the additional power.

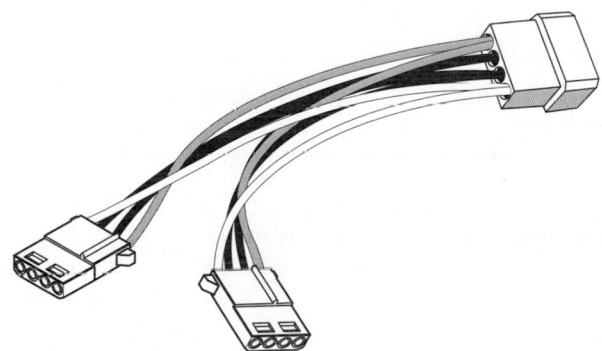

Figure 21.20 A common Y-adapter power cable.

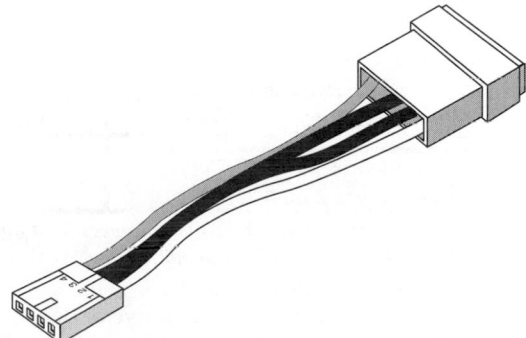

Figure 21.21 A peripheral-to-floppy drive power adapter cable.

If you want to add Serial ATA drives to an existing system, you will also need a Serial ATA–to–4-pin adapter, such as the one shown in Figure 21.22. This adapter converts a standard 4-pin power connector used by conventional hard drives to the 15-pin connector used by Serial ATA.

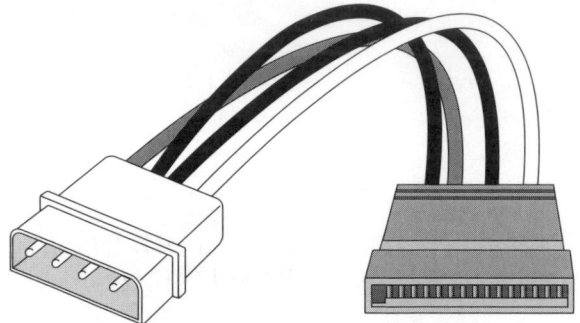

Figure 21.22   A 4-pin–to–Serial ATA drive power adapter cable.

Physical Connector Part Numbers

The physical connectors used in industry-standard PC power supplies were originally specified by IBM for the supplies used in the original PC/XT/AT systems. They used a specific type of connector between the power supply and the motherboard (the P8 and P9 connectors) and specific connectors for the disk drives. The motherboard connectors used in all the industry-standard power supplies were unchanged from 1981 (when the IBM PC appeared) until 1995 (when Intel released the ATX standard). The original PC's four-pin disk drive connector was augmented by a smaller (also four-pin) power connector when 3 1/2" floppy drives appeared in 1986. Table 21.12 lists the standard connectors used for motherboard and disk drive power.

Table 21.12   Physical Power Connectors

Connector Description	Female (on Power Cable)	Male (on Component)
ATX/NLX/SFX (20-pin)	Molex 39-01-2200	Molex 39-29-9202
ATX Optional (6-pin)	Molex 8993[1]	Molex 8619[2]
ATX12V Optional (4-pin)	Molex 39-01-2040	Molex 39-29-9042
PC/XT/AT/LPX P8/P9	Molex 8993[1]	Molex 8619[2]
Peripheral (large style)	AMP 1-480424-0	AMP 1-480426-0
Floppy drive (small style)	AMP 171822-4	AMP 171826-4
Serial ATA	Molex 88751[3]	Molex 87679-0001[4]

1. *Can also use Burndy GTC6P-1.*

2. *Can also use Burndy GTC6RI.*

3. *Add -1310 or -1311 to this part number for a dual-end version, including a 4-pin connector (refer to Figure 21.22). Add -1410 or -1411 for a pigtail version.*

4. *Includes SATA data connector.*

You can get these raw connectors through the electronics supply houses (Allied, Newark, and Digi-Key, for example) found in the Vendor List on the disc. You also can get complete cable assemblies, including drive adapters that convert the large connectors into small connectors, disk drive Y splitter cables, and motherboard power extension cables, from several of the cable and miscellaneous supply houses, such as Ci Design and Key Power, as well as PC Power and Cooling.

Caution

Before you install additional connectors to your power supply using Y splitters or any other type of connector, be sure your power supply is capable of delivering sufficient power for all your internal peripherals. Overloading the power supply can cause damage to electrical components and stored data.

▶▶ See "Power Supply Ratings," p. 1180.

Power Supply Specifications

Power supplies have several specifications that define their input and output capabilities as well as their operational characteristics. The following sections define and examine most of the common specifications related to power supplies.

Power Supply Loading

PC power supplies are of a *switching* rather than a *linear* design. The switching type of design uses a high-speed oscillator circuit to convert the higher wall-socket AC voltage to the much lower DC voltage used to power the PC and PC components. Switching-type power supplies are noted for being very efficient in size, weight, and energy in comparison to the linear design, which uses a large internal transformer to generate various outputs. This type of transformer-based design is inefficient in at least three ways. First, the output voltage of the transformer linearly follows the input voltage (hence the name *linear*), so any fluctuations in the AC power going into the system can cause problems with the output. Second, the high current-level (power) requirements of a PC system require the use of heavy wiring in the transformer. Third, the 60Hz frequency of the AC power supplied from your building is difficult to filter out inside the power supply, requiring large and expensive filter capacitors and rectifiers.

The switching supply, on the other hand, uses a switching circuit that chops up the incoming power at a relatively high frequency. This enables the use of high-frequency transformers that are much smaller and lighter. Also, the higher frequency is much easier and cheaper to filter out at the output, and the input voltage can vary widely. Input ranging from 90V to 135V still produces the proper output levels, and many switching supplies can automatically adjust to 240V input.

One characteristic of all switching-type power supplies is that they do not run without a *load*. Therefore, you must have something such as a motherboard and hard drive plugged in and drawing power for the supply to work. If you simply have the power supply on a bench with nothing plugged into it, either the supply burns up or its protection circuitry shuts it down. Most power supplies are protected from no-load operation and shut down automatically. Some of the cheapest supplies, however, lack the protection circuit and relay and can be destroyed after a few seconds of no-load operation. A few power supplies have their own built-in load resistors, so they can run even though there isn't a normal load (such as a motherboard or hard disk) plugged in.

Some power supplies have minimum load requirements for both the +5V and +12V sides. According to IBM specifications for the 192-watt power supply used in the original AT, a minimum load of 7.0 amps was required at +5V and a minimum of 2.5 amps was required at +12V for the supply to work properly. As long as a motherboard was plugged into the power supply, the motherboard would draw sufficient +5V at all times to keep those circuits in the supply happy. However, +12V is typically used only by motors (and not motherboards), and the floppy or CD/DVD drive motors are off most of the time. Because floppy or optical (CD/DVD) drives don't present any +12V load unless they are spinning, systems without a hard disk drive could have problems because there wouldn't be enough load on the +12V circuit in the supply.

To alleviate problems, when IBM used to ship the original AT systems without a hard disk, it plugged the hard disk drive power cable into a large 5-ohm, 50-watt sandbar resistor that was mounted in a small, metal cage assembly where the drive would have been. The AT case had screw holes on top of where the hard disk would go, specifically designed to mount this resistor cage.

Note

Several computer stores I knew of in the mid-1980s ordered the diskless AT and installed their own 20MB or 30MB drives, which they could get more cheaply from sources other than IBM. They were throwing away the load resistors by the hundreds! I managed to grab a couple at the time, which is how I know the type of resistor they used.

This resistor would be connected between pin 1 (+12V) and pin 2 (Ground) on the hard disk power connector. This placed a 2.4-amp load on the supply's +12V output, drawing 28.8 watts of power (it would get hot!) and thus enabling the supply to operate normally. Note that the cooling fan in most power supplies draws approximately 0.1–0.25 amps, bringing the total load to 2.5 amps or more. If the load resistor were missing, the system would intermittently fail to start up.

Most of the power supplies in use today do not require as much of a load as the original IBM AT power supply. In most cases, a minimum load of 0–0.3 amps at +3.3V, 2.0–4.0 amps at +5V, and 0.5–1.0 amps at +12V is considered acceptable. Most motherboards easily draw the minimum +5V current by themselves. The standard power supply cooling fan draws only 0.1–0.25 amps, so the +12V minimum load might still be a problem for a diskless workstation. Generally, the higher the rating on the supply, the more minimum load required. However, exceptions do exist, so this is a specification you should check when evaluating power supplies.

Some switching power supplies have built-in load resistors and can run in a no-load situation. Most power supplies don't have internal load resistors but might require only a small load on the +5V line to operate properly. Some supplies, however, might require +3.3V, +5V, and +12V loads to work—the only way to know is by checking the documentation for the particular supply in question.

No matter what, if you want to properly and accurately bench test a power supply, be sure you place a load on at least one (or preferably all) of the positive voltage outputs. This is one reason it is best to test a supply while it is installed in the system, instead of testing it separately on the bench. For impromptu bench testing, you can use a spare motherboard and one or more hard disk drives to load the outputs.

Power Supply Ratings

A system manufacturer should be able to provide you the technical specifications of the power supplies it uses in its systems. This type of information can be found in the system's technical reference manual, as well as on stickers attached directly to the power supply. Power supply manufacturers can also supply this data, which is preferable if you can identify the manufacturer and contact them directly or via the Web.

The input specifications are listed as voltages, and the output specifications are listed as amps at several voltage levels. IBM reports output wattage level as "specified output wattage." If your manufacturer does not list the total wattage, you can convert amperage to wattage by using the following simple formula:

watts = volts × amps

For example, if a motherboard is listed as drawing 6 amps of +5V current, that equals 30 watts of power according to the formula.

By multiplying the voltage by the amperage available at each main output and then adding the results, you can calculate the total capable output wattage of the supply. Note that only positive voltage outputs are normally used in calculating outputs; the negative outputs, Standby, Power_Good, or other signals that are not used to power components are exempt.

Table 21.13 shows the standard power supply output levels available in industry-standard form factors. Most manufacturers offer supplies with ratings from 100 watts to 450 watts or more. Table 21.14 shows the rated outputs at each of the voltage levels for supplies with different manufacturer-specified output ratings. To compile the table, I referred to the specification sheets for supplies from Astec Power (note that they no longer make PC power supplies) and PC Power and Cooling. Although most of the ratings are fairly accurate, there appears to be overly optimistic rounding going on in some of the ratings.

Table 21.13   Typical Non-ATX Power Supply Output Ratings

Rated Output (Watts)	100W	150W	200W	250W	300W	375W	450W
Output current (amps):							
+5V	10.0	15.0	20.0	25.0	32.0	35.0	45.0
+12V	3.5	5.5	8.0	10.0	10.0	13.0	15.0
−5V	0.3	0.3	0.3	0.5	0.5	0.5	1.0
−12V	0.3	0.3	0.3	0.5	0.5	0.5	1.0
Calc. output (watts)	92	141	196	245	280	331	405

Adding a +3.3V output to the power supply modifies the equation significantly. Table 21.14 contains data for various ATX/ATX12V power supplies from PC Power and Cooling.

Table 21.14   PC Power and Cooling ATX/ATX12V Power Supply Output Ratings

Model (Rated Output)	235W	250W	275W	300W	350W	400W	425W	510W
+3.3V	13	13	14	14	28	40	40	30
+5V	22	25	30	30	32	40	40	40
+12V	8	10	10	12	15	15	15	34
−5V	0.3	0.3	0.3	0.3	0.3	0.3	0.3	0.3
−12V	0.5	0.5	1.0	1.0	0.8	1.0	1.0	2.0
+5VSB	2.0	2.0	2.0	2.0	2.0	2.0	2.0	3.0
Total watts (3.3+5+12)*	249	288	316	340	432	512	512	707
+3.3V and +5V Max.	125	150	150	150	215	300	300	300

Note the calculated maximum output is theoretical, assuming the maximum draw from the +3.3V, +5V, and +12V simultaneously. Virtually all power supplies place limits on the maximum combined draw for the +3.3V and +5V combined. This would make the true maximum rating somewhat less than the calculated maximum shown here.

The 400W and 425W supplies listed here seem to have the same specs; however, the 400W version uses a special low-speed quiet fan which has slightly less cooling ability, hence the lower maximum rating figure.

If you compute the total output using the formula described earlier, these power supplies seem to produce an output that is much higher than their ratings. The 300W model, for example, comes out at 340 watts. However, notice that the supply also has a maximum combined output for the +3.3V and +5V of 150 watts. This means you can't draw the maximum rating on both the +5V and +3.3V circuits simultaneously but must keep the total combined draw between them at 150W or less. This brings the total output to a more logical 294 watts.

Most PC power supplies have ratings between 150 and 300 watts. Although lesser ratings are not usually desirable, you can purchase heavy-duty power supplies for most systems that have outputs as high as 600 watts or more.

The 300-watt and larger units are recommended for fully optioned desktops or tower systems. These supplies run any combination of motherboard and expansion card, as well as a large number of disk drives and other peripherals. In most cases, you can't exceed the ratings on these power supplies—the system will run out of room for additional items first!

Most power supplies are considered to be universal, or worldwide. That is, they also can run on the 240V, 50-cycle current used in Europe and many other parts of the world. Many power supplies that can switch from 120V to 240V input do so automatically, but a few require you to set a switch on the back of the power supply to indicate which type of power you will access.

Note

In North America, power companies are required to supply split-phase 240V (plus or minus 5%) AC, which equals two 120V legs. Resistive voltage drops in the building wiring can cause the 240V to drop to 220V or the 120V to drop to 110V by the time the power reaches an outlet at the end of a long circuit run. For this reason, the input voltage for an AC-powered device might be listed as anything between 220V and 240V, or 110V and 120V. I use the 240/120V numbers throughout this chapter because that is the intended standard figure.

Caution

If your supply does not switch input voltages automatically, make sure the voltage setting is correct. If you plug the power supply into a 120V outlet while it's set in the 240V setting, no damage will result, but the supply won't operate properly until you correct the setting. On the other hand, if you plug into a 240V outlet and have the switch set for 120V, you can cause damage.

Other Power Supply Specifications

In addition to power output, many other specifications and features go into making a high-quality power supply. I have had many systems over the years. My experience has been that if a brownout occurs in a room with several systems running, the systems with higher-quality power supplies and higher output ratings are far more likely to make it through the power disturbances unscathed, whereas others choke.

High-quality power supplies also help protect your systems. A high-quality power supply from a vendor such as PC Power and Cooling will not be damaged if any of the following conditions occur:

- A 100% power outage of any duration
- A brownout of any kind
- A spike of up to 2,500V applied directly to the AC input (for example, a lightning strike or a lightning simulation test)

Decent power supplies have an extremely low current leakage to ground of less than 500 microamps. This safety feature is important if your outlet has a missing or an improperly wired ground line.

As you can see, these specifications are fairly tough and are certainly representative of a high-quality power supply. Make sure that your supply can meet these specifications.

You can also use many other criteria to evaluate a power supply. The power supply is a component many users ignore when shopping for a PC, and it is therefore one that some system vendors choose to skimp on. After all, a dealer is far more likely to be able to increase the price of a computer by spending money on additional memory or a larger hard drive than by installing a better power supply.

When buying a computer (or a replacement power supply), you always should learn as much as possible about the power supply. However, many consumers are intimidated by the vocabulary and statistics found in a typical power supply specification. Here are some of the most common parameters found on power supply specification sheets, along with their meanings:

- *Mean Time Between Failures (MTBF) or Mean Time To Failure (MTTF).* The (calculated) average interval, in hours, that the power supply is expected to operate before failing. Power supplies typically have MTBF ratings (such as 100,000 hours or more) that are clearly not the result of real-time empirical testing. In fact, manufacturers use published standards to calculate the results based on the failure rates of the power supply's individual components. MTBF figures for power supplies often include the load to which the power supply was subjected (in the form of a percentage) and the temperature of the environment in which the tests were performed.

- *Input Range (or Operating Range).* The range of voltages that the power supply is prepared to accept from the AC power source. For 120V AC power, an input range of 90V–135V is common; for 240V power, a 180V–270V range is typical.

- *Peak Inrush Current.* The greatest amount of current drawn by the power supply at a given moment immediately after it is turned on, expressed in terms of amps at a particular voltage. The lower the current, the less thermal shock the system experiences.

- *Hold-up Time.* The amount of time (in milliseconds) that a power supply can maintain output within the specified voltage ranges after a loss of input power. This enables your PC to continue running without resetting or rebooting if a brief interruption in AC power occurs. Values of 15–30 milliseconds are common for today's power supplies, and the higher (longer), the better. The ATX12V specification calls for a minimum of 17ms hold-up time.

- *Transient Response.* The amount of time (in microseconds) a power supply takes to bring its output back to the specified voltage ranges after a steep change in the output current. In other words, the amount of time it takes for the output power levels to stabilize after a device in the system starts or stops drawing power. Power supplies sample the current being used by the computer at regular intervals. When a device stops drawing power during one of these intervals (such as when a floppy drive stops spinning), the power supply might supply too high a voltage to the output for a brief time. This excess voltage is called *overshoot*, and the transient response is the time that it takes for the voltage to return to the specified level. This is seen as a spike in voltage by the system and can cause glitches and lockups. Once a major problem that came with switching power supplies, overshoot has been greatly reduced in recent years. Transient response values are sometimes expressed in time intervals, and at other times they are expressed in terms of a particular output change, such as "power output levels stay within regulation during output changes of up to 20%."

- *Overvoltage Protection.* Defines the trip points for each output at which the power supply shuts down or squelches that output. Values can be expressed as a percentage (for example, 120% for +3.3 and +5V) or as raw voltages (for example, +4.6V for the +3.3V output and +7.0V for the +5V output).

- *Maximum Load Current.* The largest amount of current (in amps) that safely can be delivered through a particular output. Values are expressed as individual amperages for each output voltage. With these figures, you can calculate not only the total amount of power the power supply can supply, but also how many devices using those various voltages it can support.

- *Minimum Load Current.* The smallest amount of current (in amps) that must be drawn from a particular output for that output to function. If the current drawn from an output falls below the minimum, the power supply could be damaged or automatically shut down.

- *Load Regulation (or Voltage Load Regulation).* When the current drawn from a particular output increases or decreases, the voltage changes slightly as well—usually increasing as the current rises. Load regulation is the change in the voltage for a particular output as it transitions from its minimum load to its maximum load (or vice versa). Values, expressed in terms of a +/– percentage, typically range from +/–1% to +/–5% for the +3.3V, +5V, and +12V outputs.

- *Line Regulation.* The change in output voltage as the AC input voltage transitions from the lowest to the highest value of the input range. A power supply should be capable of handling any AC voltage in its input range with a change in its output of 1% or less.

- *Efficiency.* The ratio of power input to power output, expressed in terms of a percentage. Values of 65%–85% are common for power supplies today. The remaining 15%–35% of the power input is converted to heat during the AC/DC conversion process. Although greater efficiency means less heat inside the computer (always a good thing) and lower electric bills, it should not be emphasized at the expense of precision, stability, and durability, as evidenced in the supply's load regulation and other parameters.

■ *Ripple (or Ripple and Noise, or AC Ripple, or PARD [Periodic and Random Deviation]).* The average voltage of all AC effects on the power supply outputs, usually measured in millivolts peak-to-peak or as a percentage of the nominal output voltage. The lower this figure, the better. Higher-quality units are typically rated at 1% ripple (or less), which if expressed in volts would be 1% of the output. Consequently, for +5V that would be 0.05V or 50mV (millivolts). Ripple can be caused by internal switching transients, feed through of the rectified line frequency, and other random noise.

Power Factor Correction

Recently, the power line efficiency and harmonic distortion generation of PC power supplies has come under examination. This generally falls under the topic of the power factor of the supply. Interest in power factor is not only due to an improvement in power efficiency, but also because of a reduction in the generation of harmonics back on the power line. In particular, new standards are now mandatory in many European Union (EU) countries that require harmonics be reduced below a specific amount. The circuitry required to do this is called power factor correction (PFC).

The *power factor* measures how effectively electrical power is being used and is expressed as a number between 0 and 1. A high power factor means that electrical power is being used effectively, whereas a low power factor indicates poor utilization of electrical power. To understand the power factor, you must understand how power is used.

Generally, two types of loads are placed on AC power lines:

■ *Resistive.* Power converted into heat, light, motion, or work

■ *Inductive.* Sustains an electromagnetic field, such as in a transformer or motor

A resistive load is often called *working power* and is measured in kilowatts (KW). An inductive load, on the other hand, is often called *reactive power* and is measured in kilovolt-amperes-reactive (KVAR). Working power and reactive power together make up *apparent power*, which is measured in kilovolt-amperes (KVA). The power factor is measured as the ratio of working power to apparent power, or working power/apparent power (KW/KVA). The ideal power factor is 1, where the working power and apparent power are the same.

The concept of a resistive load or working power is fairly easy to understand. For example, a light bulb that consumes 100W of power generates 100W worth of heat and light. This is a pure resistive load. An inductive load, on the other hand, is a little harder to understand. Think about a transformer, which has coil windings to generate an electromagnetic field and then induce current in another set of windings. A certain amount of power is required to saturate the windings and generate the magnetic field, even though no work is being done. A power transformer that is not connected to anything is a perfect example of a pure inductive load. An apparent power draw exists to generate the fields, but no working power exists because no actual work is being done.

When the transformer is connected to a load, it uses both working power and reactive power. In other words, power is consumed to do work (for example, if the transformer is powering a light bulb), and apparent power is used to maintain the electromagnetic field in the transformer windings. In an AC circuit, these loads can become out of sync or phase, meaning they don't peak at the same time, which can generate harmonic distortions back down the power line. I've seen examples where electric motors have caused distortions in television sets plugged into the same power circuit.

PFC usually involves adding capacitance to the circuit to maintain the inductive load without drawing additional power from the line. This makes the working power and apparent power the same, which results in a power factor of 1. It usually isn't just as simple as adding some capacitors to a circuit, although that can be done and is called *passive* power factor correction. *Active* power factor correction involves a more intelligent circuit designed to match the resistive and inductive loads so they are seen as the same by the electrical outlet.

A power supply with active power factor correction draws low distortion current from the AC source and has a power factor rating of 0.9 or greater. A nonpower factor corrected supply draws highly distorted current and is sometimes referred to as a *nonlinear* load. The power factor of a noncorrected supply is typically 0.6–0.8. Therefore, only 60% of the apparent power consumed is actually doing real work!

Having a power supply with active PFC might or might not lower your electric bill (it depends on how your power is measured), but it will definitely reduce the load on the building wiring. With PFC, all the power going into the supply is converted into actual work and the wiring is less overworked. For example, if you ran a number of computers on a single breaker-controlled circuit and found that you were blowing the breaker periodically, you could switch to systems with active PFC power supplies and reduce the load on the wiring by up to 40%, meaning you would be less likely to blow the breaker.

The International Electrical Committee (IEC) has released standards dealing with the low-frequency public supply system. The initial standards were 555.2 (Harmonics) and 555.3 (Flicker), but they have since been refined and are now available as IEC 1000-3-2 and IEC 1000-3-3, respectively. As governed by the EMC directive, most electrical devices sold within the member countries of the EU must meet the IEC standards. The IEC1000-3-2/3 standards became mandatory in 1997 and 1998.

Even if you don't live in a country where PFC is required, I highly recommend specifying PC power supplies with active PFC. The main benefits of PFC supplies is that they do not overheat building wiring or distort the AC source waveform, which causes less interference on the line for other devices.

Power Supply Safety Certifications

Many agencies around the world certify electric and electronic components for safety and quality. The most commonly known agency in the United States is Underwriters Laboratories, Inc. (UL). UL standard #60950—*Safety of Information Technology Equipment, Third Edition*—covers power supplies and other PC components. You should always purchase power supplies and other devices that are UL-certified. It has often been said that, although not every good product is UL-certified, no bad products are.

In Canada, electric and electronic products are certified by the Canadian Standards Agency (CSA). The German equivalents are TÜV Rheinland and VDE, and NEMKO operates in Norway. These agencies are responsible for certification of products throughout Europe. Power supply manufacturers that sell to an international market should have products that are certified at least by UL, the CSA, and TÜV—if not by all the agencies listed, and more.

Apart from UL-type certifications, many power supply manufacturers, even the most reputable ones, claim that their products have a Class B certification from the Federal Communications Commission, meaning that they meet FCC standards for electromagnetic and radio frequency interference (EMI/RFI). This is a contentious point, however, because the FCC does not certify power supplies as individual components. Title 47 of the Code of Federal Regulations, Part 15, Section 15.101(c) states as follows:

> The FCC does NOT currently authorize motherboards, cases, and internal power supplies. Vendor claims that they are selling 'FCC-certified cases,' 'FCC-certified motherboards,' or 'FCC-certified internal power supplies' are false.

In fact, an FCC certification can be issued collectively only to a base unit consisting of a computer case, motherboard, and power supply. Thus, a power supply purported to be FCC-certified was actually certified along with a particular case and motherboard—not necessarily the same case and motherboard you are using in your system. This does not mean, however, that the manufacturer is being deceitful or that the power supply is inferior. If anything, this means that when evaluating power supplies, you should place less weight on the FCC certification than on other factors, such as UL certification.

Power-Use Calculations

When expanding or upgrading your PC, you should ensure that your power supply is capable of providing sufficient current to power all the system's internal devices. One way to see whether your system is capable of expansion is to calculate the levels of power drain in the various system components and deduct the total from the maximum power supplied by the power supply. This calculation can help you decide whether you must upgrade the power supply to a more capable unit. Unfortunately, these calculations can be difficult to make because many manufacturers do not publish power consumption data for their products.

In addition, getting power-consumption data for many +5V devices, including motherboards and adapter cards, can be difficult. Motherboards can consume different power levels, depending on numerous factors. Most motherboards consume about 5 amps or so, but try to get information on the one you are using. For adapter cards, if you can find the actual specifications for the card, use those figures. To be on the conservative side, however, I usually go by the maximum available power levels set forth in the respective bus standards.

For example, consider the power-consumption figures for components in a modern PC, such as a desktop or Slimline system with a 200-watt power supply rated for 20 amps at +5V and 8 amps at +12V. The ISA specification calls for a maximum of 2.0 amps of +5V power and 0.175 amps of +12V power for each slot in the system. Most systems have eight slots, and you can assume that four are filled for the purposes of calculating power draw. The calculation shown in Table 21.15 shows what happens when you subtract the amount of power necessary to run the various system components.

Table 21.15   Power Consumption Calculation

	Available 5V Power (Amps):	20.0A		Available 12V Power (Amps):	8.0A
Less:	Motherboard	−5.0A	Less:	4 slots filled at 0.175 each	−0.7A
	4 slots filled at 2.0 each	−8.0A		3 1/2" hard disk drive motor	−1.0A
	3 1/2" floppy drive logic	−0.5A		3 1/2" floppy drive motor	−1.0A
	3 1/2" hard disk drive logic	−0.5A		Cooling fan motor	−0.1A
	CD-ROM/DVD drive logic	−1.0A		CD-ROM/DVD drive motor	−1.0A
	Remaining Power (Amps):	**5.0A**		**Remaining Power (Amps):**	**4.2A**

In the preceding example, everything seems okay for now. With half the slots filled, a floppy drive, and one hard disk, the system still has room for more. Problems with the power supply could come up, however, if this system were expanded to the extreme. With every slot filled and two or more hard disks, problems with the +5V current definitely would occur. However, the +12V does seem to have room to spare. You could add a CD-ROM drive or a second hard disk without worrying too much about the +12V power, but the +5V power would be strained.

If you anticipate loading up a system to the extreme—as in a high-end multimedia system, for example—you might want to invest in the insurance of a higher-output power supply. For example, a 250-watt supply usually has 25 amps of +5V current and 10 amps of +12V current, whereas a 300-watt unit usually has 32 amps of +5V current available. These supplies enable you to fully load the system and are likely to be found in full-sized desktop or tower case configurations in which this type of expansion is expected.

Motherboards can draw anywhere from 4 to 15 amps or more of +5V power to run. Depending on which processor is installed, the figure can go higher. As an example, the AMD Athlon XP 3000+ (2.167GHz) processor draws up to 74.3 watts of 1.65V power, which is supplied by motherboard-based voltage regulators. These regulators are powered by +5V in most Socket A motherboards, so assuming an 80% (typical) efficiency in the regulator power conversion, this would equate to consuming 18.57

amps of +5V power. This, plus the power draw from the rest of the motherboard, would put the +5V power draw near the 24A–30A maximum allowed by the power supply connectors.

By comparison, the 3.06GHz version of the Pentium 4 draws up to 81.8 watts of 1.55V power. Intel wisely decided that Pentium 4 systems were power hungry enough that the motherboard-based voltage regulators should run on +12V instead of +5V. Again, assuming an 80% efficiency, the regulators would require 20.45 amps if running on +5V but only 8.52 amps if running on +12V. By moving the regulators to the 12V power, the load on the 5V is greatly eased. I assume Socket A motherboards will also make the move to 12V regulators due to the better balanced design. If your motherboard has the ATX12V connector, you can be assured that the CPU voltage regulator module is running off 12V and not 5V.

Considering that systems with two or more processors are now becoming common, you could have up to 40 amps of 5V (using 5V-powered CPU voltage regulators) or up to 16 amps of 12V power being drawn by the processors alone. A dual processor system using 5V-based regulators would almost certainly exceed the 30A maximum allowable power draw through the ATX main and auxiliary connectors! Add in the power draw for the motherboard, video card, memory, and disk drives, and you'll see that very few "no-name" power supplies can supply this kind of current. For these applications, you should consider only high-quality, high-capacity power supplies from a reputable manufacturer, such as PC Power and Cooling.

In these calculations, bus slots are allotted maximum power in amps, as shown in Table 21.16.

Table 21.16   Maximum Power Consumption in Amps per Bus Slot

Bus Type	+5V Power	+12V Power	+3.3V Power
ISA	2.0	0.175	n/a
EISA	4.5	1.5	n/a
VL-bus	2.0	n/a	n/a
16-bit MCA	1.6	0.175	n/a
32-bit MCA	2.0	0.175	n/a
PCI	5	0.5	7.6

As you can see from the table, ISA slots are allotted 2.0 amps of +5V and 0.175 amps of +12V power. Note that these are maximum figures; not all cards draw this much power. If the slot has a VL-bus extension connector, an additional 2.0 amps of +5V power are allowed for the VL-bus.

Floppy drives can vary in power consumption, but most of the newer 3 1/2" drives have motors that run on +5V current in addition to the logic circuits. These drives usually draw 1.0 amp of +5V power and use no +12V at all. 5 1/4" drives use standard +12V motors that draw about 1.0 amp. These drives also require about 0.5 amps of +5V for the logic circuits. Most cooling fans draw about 0.1 amps of +12V power, which is negligible.

Typical 3 1/2" hard disks today draw about 1 amp of +12V power to run the motors and only about 0.5 amps of +5V power for the logic. 5 1/4" hard disks, especially those that are full-height, draw much more power. A typical full-height hard drive draws 2.0 amps of +12V power and 1.0 amp of +5V power.

Another problem with hard disks is that they require much more power during the spin-up phase of operation than during normal operation. In most cases, the drive draws double the +12V power during spin-up, which can be 4.0 amps or more for the full-height drives. This tapers off to a normal level after the drive is spinning.

The figures that most manufacturers report for maximum power supply output are full duty-cycle figures. The power supply can supply these levels of power continuously. You usually can expect a unit that continuously supplies a given level of power to be capable of exceeding this level for some noncontinuous amount of time. A supply normally can offer 50% greater output than the continuous figure indicates for as long as 1 minute. Systems often use this cushion to supply the necessary power to spin up a hard disk drive. After the drive has spun to full speed, the power draw drops to a value within the system's continuous supply capabilities. Drawing anything over the rated continuous figure for any extended length of time causes the power supply to run hot and fail early, and it can create nasty symptoms in the system.

Tip

If you are using internal SCSI hard drives, you can ease the startup load on your power supply. The key is to enable the SCSI drive's Remote Start option, which causes the drive to start spinning only when it receives a startup command over the SCSI bus. The effect is that the drive remains stationary (drawing very little power) until the very end of the POST and spins up right when the SCSI portion of the POST begins.

If you have multiple SCSI drives, they all spin up sequentially based on their SCSI ID settings. This is designed so that only one drive is spinning up at any one time and so that no drives start spinning until the rest of the system has had time to start. This greatly eases the load on the power supply when you first power the system on.

In most cases, you enable Remote Start through your SCSI host adapter's setup program. This program might be supplied with the adapter on separate media, or it might be integrated into the adapter's BIOS and activated with a specific key combination at boot time.

The biggest cause of power supply overload problems has historically been filling up the expansion slots and adding more drives. Multiple hard drives, CD-ROM drives, and floppy drives can create quite a drain on the system power supply. Be sure you have enough +12V power to run all the drives you plan to install. Tower systems can be especially problematic because they have so many drive bays. Just because the case has room for the devices doesn't mean the power supply can support them. Be sure you have enough +5V power to run all your expansion cards, especially PCI cards. It pays to be conservative, but remember that most cards draw less than the maximum allowed. Today's newest processors can have very high current requirements for the +5V or +3.3V supplies. When selecting a power supply for your system, be sure to take into account any future processor upgrades.

Many people wait until an existing component fails to replace it with an upgraded version. If you are on a tight budget, this "if it ain't broke, don't fix it" attitude might be necessary. Power supplies, however, often do not fail completely all at once; they can fail in an intermittent fashion or allow fluctuating power levels to reach the system, which results in unstable operation. You might be blaming system lockups on software bugs when the culprit is an overloaded power supply. In addition, an inadequate or failing supply causing lockups can result in file system corruption, which causes even further system instabilities (that could remain present even after replacing the power supply). If you use bus-powered USB devices, a failing power supply can also cause these devices to fail or malfunction. If you have been running your original power supply for a long time and have upgraded your system in other ways, you should expect some problems, and you might want to consider reloading the operating system and applications from scratch.

Although there is certainly an appropriate place for the exacting power-consumption calculations you've read about in this section, a great many experienced PC users prefer the "don't worry about it" power calculation method. This technique consists of buying or building a system with a good-quality 300-watt or higher power supply (or upgrading to such a supply in an existing system) and then upgrading the system freely, without concern for power consumption.

Tip

My preference is the 425W supply from PC Power and Cooling, which is probably overkill for most people, but for those who keep a system for a long time and put it through several upgrades, it is an excellent choice.

Unless you plan to build a system with arrays of SCSI drives and a dozen other peripherals, you will probably not exceed the capabilities of the power supply, and this method certainly requires far less effort.

Power Cycling

Should you turn off a system when it is not in use? To answer this frequent question, you should understand some facts about electrical components and what makes them fail. Combine this knowledge with information on power consumption, cost, and safety to come to your own conclusion. Because circumstances can vary, the best answer for your own situation might be different from the answer for others, depending on your particular needs and applications.

Frequently powering a system on and off does cause deterioration and damage to the components. This seems logical, but the simple reason is not obvious to most people. Many believe that flipping system power on and off frequently is harmful because it electrically "shocks" the system. The real problem, however, is temperature or thermal shock. As the system warms up, the components expand; as it cools off, the components contract. In addition, various materials in the system have different thermal expansion coefficients, so they expand and contract at different rates. Over time, thermal shock causes deterioration in many areas of a system.

From a pure system-reliability viewpoint, you should insulate the system from thermal shock as much as possible. When a system is turned on, the components go from ambient (room) temperature to as high as 185°F (85°C) within 30 minutes or less. When you turn off the system, the same thing happens in reverse, and the components cool back to ambient temperature in a short period of time.

Thermal expansion and contraction remains the single largest cause of component failure. Chip cases can split, allowing moisture to enter and contaminate them. Delicate internal wires and contacts can break, and circuit boards can develop stress cracks. Surface-mounted components expand and contract at rates different from the circuit boards on which they are mounted, causing enormous stress at the solder joints. Solder joints can fail due to the metal hardening from the repeated stress, resulting in cracks in the joint. Components that use heatsinks, such as processors, transistors, or voltage regulators, can overheat and fail because the thermal cycling causes heatsink adhesives to deteriorate and break the thermally conductive bond between the device and the heatsink. Thermal cycling also causes socketed devices and connections to loosen, or *creep*, which can cause a variety of intermittent contact failures.

◀◀ See "SIMMs, DIMMs, and RIMMs," p. 477.

Thermal expansion and contraction affect not only chips and circuit boards, but also things such as hard disk drives. Most hard drives today have sophisticated thermal compensation routines that make adjustments in head position relative to the expanding and contracting platters. Most drives perform this thermal compensation routine once every 5 minutes for the first 30 minutes the drive is running and then every 30 minutes thereafter. In many drives, this procedure can be heard as a rapid "tick-tick-tick-tick" sound.

In essence, anything you can do to keep the system at a constant temperature prolongs the life of the system, and the best way to accomplish this is to leave the system either permanently on or permanently off. Of course, if the system is never turned on in the first place, it should last a long time indeed!

Now, I am not saying that you should leave all systems on 24 hours a day. A system powered on and left unattended can be a fire hazard (I have witnessed at least two monitors spontaneously catch fire—luckily, I was there at the time), is a data security risk (from cleaning crews and other nocturnal visitors), can be easily damaged if moved while running, and wastes electrical energy.

I currently pay 8 cents for a kilowatt-hour of electricity. A typical desktop-style PC with display consumes at least 300 watts (0.3 kilowatt) of electricity (and that is a conservative estimate). This means it would cost 2.4 cents to run my typical PC for an hour. Multiplying by 168 hours in a week means that it would cost $4.03 per week to run this PC continuously. If the PC were turned on at 9 a.m. and off at 5 p.m., it would be on only 40 hours per week and would cost only $0.96—a savings of $3.07 per week! Multiply this savings by 100 systems, and you are saving $307 per week. Multiply this by 1,000 systems, and you are saving $3,070 per week! Using systems certified under the EPA Energy Star program (so-called green PCs) would account for an additional savings of around $1 per system per week—or $1,000 per week for

1,000 systems. The great thing about Energy Star systems is that the savings are even greater if the systems are left on for long periods of time because the power management routines are automatic.

Based on these facts, my recommendations are that you power on the systems at the beginning of the workday and off at the end of the workday. Do not power the systems off for lunch, breaks, or any other short periods of time. If you are a home user, leave your computer on if you are going to be using it later in the day or if instant access is important. I'd normally recommend home users turn off the system when leaving the house or when sleeping. Servers, of course, should be left on continuously. This seems to be the best compromise of system longevity with pure economics. No matter what, these are just guidelines; if it works better for you to leave your system on 24 hours a day, seven days a week, make it so.

Power Management

As the standard PC configuration has grown to include capabilities formerly considered options, the power requirements of the system have increased steadily. Larger displays, CD-ROM drives, and audio adapters all need more power to run, and the cost of operating a PC rises steadily. To address these concerns, several programs and standards are now being developed that are intended to reduce the power needed to run a PC as much as possible.

For standard desktop systems, power management is a matter of economy and convenience. By turning off specific components of the PC when they are not in use, you can reduce the electric bill and avoid having to power the computer up and down manually.

For portable systems, power management is far more important. Adding CD-ROMs, speakers, and other components to a laptop or notebook computer reduces even further what is in many cases a short battery life. By adding new power management technology, a portable system can supply power only to the components it actually needs to run, thus extending the life of the battery charge.

Energy Star Systems

The EPA has started a certification program for energy-efficient PCs and peripherals. To be a member of this program, the PC or display must drop to a power draw at the outlet of 30 watts or less during periods of inactivity. Systems that conform to this specification get to wear the Energy Star logo. This is a voluntary program; however, many PC manufacturers are finding that it helps them sell their systems if they can advertise these systems as energy efficient.

One problem with this type of system is that the motherboard and disk drives can go to sleep, which means they can enter a standby mode in which they draw very little power. This causes havoc with some of the older power supplies because the low power draw does not provide enough of a load for them to function properly. Most of the newer supplies on the market, which are designed to work with these systems, have a very low minimum-load specification. I suggest you ensure that the minimum load will be provided by the equipment in your system if you buy a power supply upgrade. Otherwise, when the PC goes to sleep, it might take a power switch cycle to wake it up again. This problem would be most noticeable if you invested in a very high-output supply and used it in a system that draws very little power to begin with.

Advanced Power Management

Advanced Power Management (APM) is a specification jointly developed by Intel and Microsoft that defines a series of interfaces between power management–capable hardware and a computer's operating system. When it is fully activated, APM can automatically switch a computer between five states, depending on the system's current activity. Each state represents a further reduction in power use, accomplished by placing unused components into a low-power mode. The five system states are as follows:

- *Full On.* The system is completely operational, with no power management occurring.
- *APM Enabled.* The system is operational, with some devices being power managed. Unused devices can be powered down and the CPU clock slowed or stopped.

- *APM Standby.* The system is not operational, with most devices in a low-power state. The CPU clock can be slowed or stopped, but operational parameters are retained in memory. When triggered by a specific user or system activity, the system can return to the APM Enabled state almost instantaneously.

- *APM Suspend.* The system is not operational, with most devices unpowered. The CPU clock is stopped, and operational parameters are saved to disk for later restoration. When triggered by a wake-up event, the system returns to the APM Enabled state relatively slowly.

- *Off.* The system is not operational. The power supply is off.

APM requires support from both hardware and software to function. In this chapter, you've already seen how ATX-style power supplies can be controlled by software commands using the Power_On signal and the six-pin optional power connector. Manufacturers are also integrating the same type of control features into other system components, such as motherboards, monitors, and disk drives.

Operating systems that support APM, such as Windows, trigger power management events by monitoring the activities performed by the computer user and the applications running on the system. However, the OS does not directly address the power management capabilities of the hardware.

A system can have many hardware devices and many software functions participating in APM functions, which makes communication difficult. To address this problem, both the operating system and the hardware have an abstraction layer that facilitates communication between the various elements of the APM architecture.

The operating system runs an APM driver that communicates with the various applications and software functions that trigger power management activities, while the system's APM-capable hardware devices all communicate with the system BIOS. The APM driver and the BIOS communicate directly, completing the link between the OS and the hardware.

Thus, for APM to function, support for the standard must be built in to the system's individual hardware devices, the system BIOS, and the operating system (which includes the APM driver). Without all these components, APM activities can't occur.

Advanced Configuration and Power Interface

Advanced Configuration and Power Interface (ACPI) is a newer power management and system configuration standard supported by newer system BIOS software running Windows 98 and later operating systems. If your BIOS and operating system support ACPI, full power management control is now done by the operating system, rather than by the BIOS. ACPI is intended to offer a single place for power management and system configuration control; in the past, with APM you often could make power management settings in the BIOS setup as well as the operating system that overlapped or could have conflicting settings. ACPI is supported in newer systems in lieu of APM.

Tip

If, for any reason, you find that power management activities cause problems on your system, such as operating system freeze-ups or hardware malfunctions, the easiest way to disable APM is through the system BIOS. Most BIOSs that support APM include an option to disable it. This breaks the chain of communication between the operating system and the hardware, causing all power management activities to cease. Although you also can achieve the same end by removing the APM driver from the operating system, Windows 9x's Plug and Play (PnP) feature detects the system's APM capabilities whenever you restart the computer and attempts to reinstall the APM driver.

If you have a newer system with ACPI, you can disable the power management settings via the Power Management icon in the Windows Control Panel.

Power Supply Troubleshooting

Troubleshooting the power supply basically means isolating the supply as the cause of problems within a system and, if necessary, replacing it.

Caution

It is rarely recommended that an inexperienced user open a power supply to make repairs because of the dangerous high voltages present. Even when unplugged, power supplies can retain dangerous voltage and must be discharged (like a monitor) before service. Such internal repairs are beyond the scope of this book and are specifically not recommended unless the technician knows what she is doing.

Many symptoms lead me to suspect that the power supply in a system is failing. This can sometimes be difficult for an inexperienced technician to see because at times little connection seems to exist between the symptom and the cause—the power supply.

For example, in many cases a parity check error message can indicate a problem with the power supply. This might seem strange because the parity check message specifically refers to memory that has failed. The connection is that the power supply powers the memory, and memory with inadequate power fails.

It takes some experience to know when this type of failure is power related and not caused by the memory. One clue is the repeatability of the problem. If the parity check message (or other problem) appears frequently and identifies the same memory location each time, I would suspect that defective memory is the problem. However, if the problem seems random, or if the memory location the error message cites as having failed seems random, I would suspect improper power as the culprit. The following is a list of PC problems that often are related to the power supply:

- Any power-on or system startup failures or lockups
- Spontaneous rebooting or intermittent lockups during normal operation
- Intermittent parity check or other memory-type errors
- Hard disk and fan simultaneously failing to spin (no +12V)
- Overheating due to fan failure
- Small brownouts that cause the system to reset
- Electric shocks felt on the system case or connectors
- Slight static discharges that disrupt system operation
- Erratic recognition of bus-powered USB peripherals

In fact, just about any intermittent system problem can be caused by the power supply. I always suspect the supply when flaky system operation is a symptom. Of course, the following fairly obvious symptoms point right to the power supply as a possible cause:

- System that is completely dead (no fan, no cursor)
- Smoke
- Blown circuit breakers

If you suspect a power supply problem, some of the simple measurements and the more sophisticated tests outlined in this section can help you determine whether the power supply is at fault. Because these measurements might not detect some intermittent failures, you might have to use a spare power supply for a long-term evaluation. If the symptoms and problems disappear when a known good spare unit is installed, you have found the source of your problem.

Following is a simple flowchart to help you zero in on common power supply–related problems:

1. Check the AC power input. Make sure the cord is firmly seated in the wall socket and in the power supply socket. Try a different cord.

2. Check the DC power connections. Make sure the motherboard and disk drive power connectors are firmly seated and making good contact. Check for loose screws.

3. Check the DC power output. Use a digital multimeter to check for proper voltages. If it's below spec, replace the power supply.

4. Check the installed peripherals. Remove all boards and drives and retest the system. If it works, add items back in one at a time until the system fails again. The last item added before the failure returns is likely defective.

Many types of symptoms can indicate problems with the power supply. Because the power supply literally powers everything else in the system, everything from disk drive problems to memory problems to motherboard problems can often be traced back to the power supply as the root cause.

Overloaded Power Supplies

A weak or inadequate power supply can put a damper on your ideas for system expansion. Some systems are designed with beefy power supplies, as if to anticipate a great deal of system add-ons and expansion components. Most desktop or tower systems are built in this manner. Some systems have inadequate power supplies from the start, however, and can't adequately service the power-hungry options you might want to add.

The wattage rating can sometimes be very misleading. Not all 300-watt supplies are created the same. People familiar with high-end audio systems know that some watts are better than others. This is true for power supplies, too. Cheap power supplies might in fact put out the rated power, but what about noise and distortion? Some of the supplies are under-engineered to just barely meet their specifications, whereas others might greatly exceed their specifications. Many of the cheaper supplies provide noisy or unstable power, which can cause numerous problems with the system. Another problem with under-engineered power supplies is that they can run hot and force the system to do so as well. The repeated heating and cooling of solid-state components eventually causes a computer system to fail, and engineering principles dictate that the hotter a PC's temperature, the shorter its life. Many people recommend replacing the original supply in a system with a heavier-duty model, which solves the problem. Because power supplies come in common form factors, finding a heavy-duty replacement for most systems is easy, as is the installation process.

Inadequate Cooling

Some of the available replacement power supplies have higher-capacity cooling fans than the originals, which can greatly prolong system life and minimize overheating problems—especially for the newer, hotter-running processors. If system noise is a problem, models with special fans can run more quietly than the standard models. These power supplies often use larger-diameter fans that spin more slowly, so they run more quietly but move the same amount of air as the smaller fans. PC Power and Cooling specializes in heavy-duty and quiet supplies.

Ventilation in a system is also important. You must ensure adequate airflow to cool the hotter items in the system. Many systems today (especially those from larger vendors such as Dell, Gateway, MPC, and so on) still use passive heatsinks that require a steady stream of air to cool the chip. If the processor heatsink has its own fan, this is not much of a concern. If you have free expansion slots, you should space out the boards in your system to permit airflow between them. Place the hottest running boards nearest the fan or the ventilation holes in the system. Make sure that adequate airflow exists around the hard disk drive, especially for those that spin at high rates of speed. Some hard disks can generate quite a bit of heat during operation. If the hard disks overheat, data can be lost.

Always be sure you run your computer with the case cover on, especially if you have a loaded system using passive heatsinks. Removing the cover in that situation can actually cause the system to overheat. With the cover off, the power supply and chassis fans no longer draw air through the system. Instead, the fans end up cooling only the supply, and the rest of the system must be cooled by simple convection. Systems that use an active heatsink on the processor aren't as prone to this type of problem; in fact, the cooler air from outside the normally closed chassis can help them to run cooler.

In addition, be sure that any empty slot positions have the filler brackets installed. If you leave these brackets off after removing a card, the resultant hole in the case disrupts the internal airflow and can cause higher internal temperatures.

If you experience intermittent problems that you suspect are related to overheating, a higher-capacity replacement power supply is usually the best cure. Specially designed supplies with additional cooling fan capacity also can help. At least one company sells a device called a fan card, but I am not convinced these are a good idea. Unless the fan is positioned to draw air to or from outside the case, all it does is blow hot air around inside the system and provide a spot cooling effect for anything it is blowing on. In fact, adding fans in this manner contributes to the overall heat inside the system because the fan consumes power and generates heat.

CPU-mounted fans are an exception because they are designed only for spot cooling of the CPU. Most newer processors run so much hotter than the other components in the system that a conventional, passive heatsink can't do the job. In this case, a small fan placed directly over the processor provides a spot cooling effect that keeps the processor temperatures down. One drawback to these active processor cooling fans is that the processor overheats instantly and can be damaged if they fail. Newer Intel processors have built-in safeguards that prevent damage. The Pentium III, for example, automatically shuts down if overheated, and the Pentium 4 automatically throttles the speed down, which allows it to continue to run even if the heatsink is completely removed! Still, it is best not to depend on these safeguards because not all processors have them. Until recently, systems based on AMD Athlon processors didn't have thermal protection for the processor. Whenever possible, try to use a high-quality heatsink that is designed to properly cool your processor.

Using Digital Multimeters

One simple test you can perform on a power supply is to check the output voltages. This shows whether a power supply is operating correctly and whether the output voltages are within the correct tolerance range. Note that you must measure all voltages with the power supply connected to a proper load, which usually means testing while the power supply is still installed in the system and connected to the motherboard and peripheral devices.

Selecting a Meter

You need a simple digital multimeter (DMM) or digital volt-ohm meter (DVOM) to perform voltage and resistance checks on electronic circuits (see Figure 21.23). You should use only a DMM instead of the older needle-type multimeters because the older meters work by injecting 9V into the circuit when measuring resistance, which damages most computer circuits.

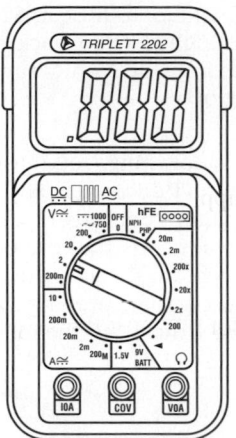

Figure 21.23 A typical DMM.

A DMM uses a much smaller voltage (usually 1.5V) when making resistance measurements, which is safe for electronic equipment. You can get a good DMM with many features from several sources. I prefer the small, pocket-size meters for computer work because they are easy to carry around.

Some features to look for in a good DMM are as follows:

- *Pocket size.* This is self-explanatory, but small meters are available that have many, if not all, of the features of larger ones. The elaborate features found on some of the larger meters are not really necessary for computer work.

- *Overload protection.* If you plug the meter into a voltage or current beyond the meter's capability to measure, the meter protects itself from damage. Cheaper meters lack this protection and can be easily damaged by reading current or voltage values that are too high.

- *Autoranging.* The meter automatically selects the proper voltage or resistance range when making measurements. This is preferable to the manual range selection; however, really good meters offer both autoranging capability and a manual range override.

- *Detachable probe leads.* The leads easily can be damaged, and sometimes a variety of differently shaped probes are required for different tests. Cheaper meters have the leads permanently attached, which means you can't easily replace them. Look for a meter with detachable leads that plug into the meter.

- *Audible continuity test.* Although you can use the ohm scale for testing continuity (0 ohms indicates continuity), a continuity test function causes the meter to produce a beep noise when continuity exists between the meter test leads. By using the sound, you quickly can test cable assemblies and other items for continuity. After you use this feature, you will never want to use the ohms display for this purpose again.

- *Automatic power off.* These meters run on batteries, and the batteries can easily be worn down if the meter is accidentally left on. Good meters have an automatic shutoff that turns off the unit when it senses no readings for a predetermined period of time.

- *Automatic display hold.* This feature enables you to hold the last stable reading on the display even after the reading is taken. This is especially useful if you are trying to work in a difficult-to-reach area single-handedly.

- *Minimum and maximum trap.* This feature enables the meter to trap the lowest and highest readings in memory and hold them for later display, which is especially useful if you have readings that are fluctuating too quickly to see on the display.

Although you can get a basic pocket DMM for as little as $20, one with all these features is priced closer to $100, and some can be much higher. RadioShack carries some nice inexpensive units, and you can purchase the high-end models from electronics supply houses, such as Newark or Digi-Key.

Measuring Voltage

To measure voltages on a system that is operating, you must use a technique called *back probing* on the connectors (see Figure 21.24). You can't disconnect any of the connectors while the system is running, so you must measure with everything connected. Nearly all the connectors you need to probe have openings in the back where the wires enter the connector. The meter probes are narrow enough to fit into the connector alongside the wire and make contact with the metal terminal inside. The technique is called back probing because you are probing the connector from the back. You must use this back-probing technique to perform virtually all the following measurements.

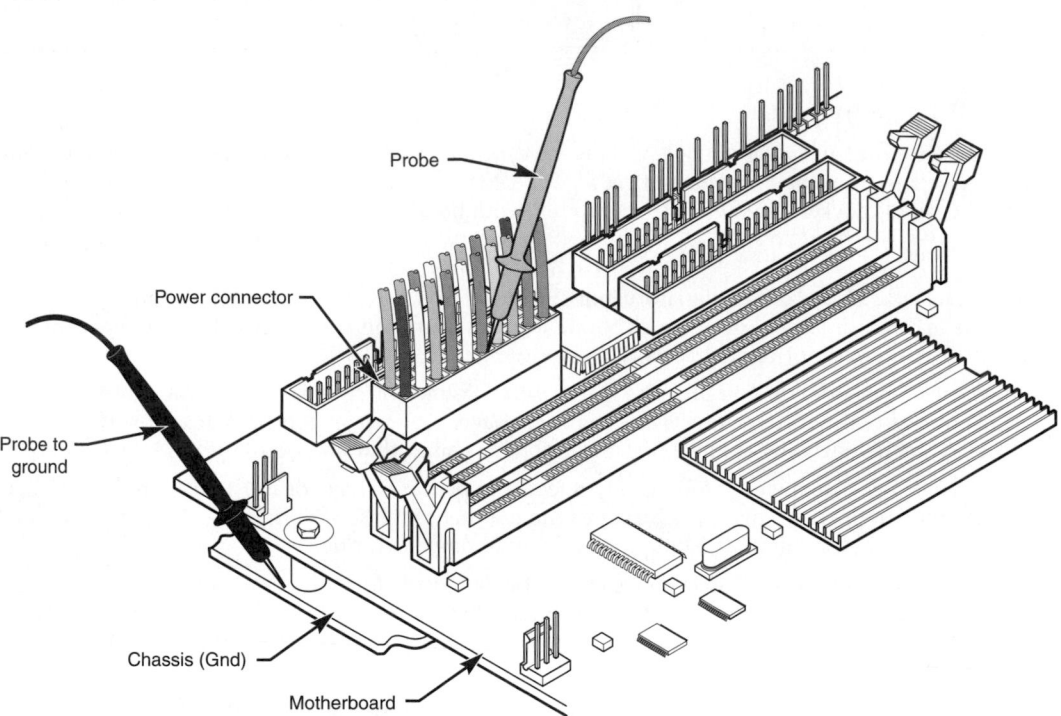

Figure 21.24   Back probing the power supply connectors.

To test a power supply for proper output, check the voltage at the Power_Good pin (P8-1 on AT, Baby-AT, and LPX supplies; pin 8 on the ATX-type connector) for +3V to +6V of power. If the measurement is not within this range, the system never sees the Power_Good signal and therefore does not start or run properly. In most cases, the power supply is bad and must be replaced.

Continue by measuring the voltage ranges of the pins on the motherboard and drive power connectors. If you are measuring voltages for testing purposes, any reading within 10% of the specified voltage is considered acceptable, although most manufacturers of high-quality power supplies specify a tighter 5% tolerance. For ATX power supplies, the specification requires that voltages must be within 5% of the rating, except for the 3.3V current, which must be within 4%. The following table shows the voltage ranges within these tolerances.

	Loose Tolerance		Tight Tolerance	
Desired Voltage	Min. (−10%)	Max. (+8%)	Min. (−5%)	Max. (+5%)
+3.3V	2.97V	3.63V	3.135V	3.465V
+/−5.0V	4.5V	5.4V	4.75V	5.25V
+/−12.0V	10.8V	12.9V	11.4V	12.6V

The Power_Good signal has tolerances that are different from the other voltages, although it is nominally +5V in most systems. The trigger point for Power_Good is about +2.4V, but most systems require the signal voltage to be within the tolerances listed here:

Signal	Minimum	Maximum
Power_Good (+5V)	3.0V	6.0V

Replace the power supply if the voltages you measure are out of these ranges. Again, it is worth noting that any and all power supply tests and measurements must be made with the power supply properly loaded, which usually means it must be installed in a system and the system must be running.

Specialized Test Equipment

You can use several types of specialized test gear to test power supplies more effectively. Because the power supply is one of the most failure-prone items in PCs today, you should have these specialized items if you service many PC systems.

Digital Infrared Thermometer

One of the greatest additions to my toolbox is a digital infrared thermometer (illustrated in Chapter 24, "PC Diagnostics, Testing, and Maintenance"). They also are called noncontact thermometers because they measure by sensing infrared energy without having to touch the item they are reading. This enables me to make instant spot checks of the temperature of a chip, a board, or the system chassis. They are available from companies such as Raytek (http://www.raytek.com) for under $100. To use these handheld items, you point at an object and then pull the trigger. Within seconds, the display shows a temperature readout accurate to +/−3°F (2°C). These devices are invaluable in checking to ensure the components in your system are adequately cooled.

Variable Voltage Transformer

When testing power supplies, it is sometimes desirable to simulate different AC voltage conditions at the wall socket to observe how the supply reacts. A variable voltage transformer is a useful test device for checking power supplies because it enables you to exercise control over the AC line voltage used as input for the power supply (see Figure 21.25). This device consists of a large transformer mounted in a housing with a dial indicator that controls the output voltage. You plug the line cord from the transformer into the wall socket and plug the PC power cord into the socket provided on the transformer. The knob on the transformer can be used to adjust the AC line voltage the PC receives.

Most variable transformers can adjust their AC outputs from 0V to 140V no matter what the AC input (wall socket) voltage is. Some can cover a range from 0V to 280V, as well. You can use the transformer to simulate brownout conditions, enabling you to observe the PC's response. Thus, you can check a power supply for proper Power_Good signal operation, among other things.

By running the PC and dropping the voltage until the PC shuts down, you can see how much reserve is in the power supply for handling a brownout or other voltage fluctuations. If your transformer can output voltages in the 200V range, you can test the capability of the power supply to run on foreign voltage levels. A properly functioning supply should operate between 90V and 135V but should shut down cleanly if the voltage is outside that range.

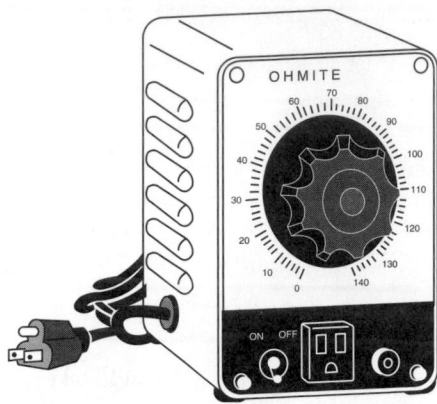

Figure 21.25 A variable voltage transformer.

One indication of a problem is seeing parity check-type error messages when you drop the voltage to 80V. This indicates that the Power_Good signal is not being withdrawn before the power supply output to the PC fails. The PC should simply stop operating as the Power_Good signal is withdrawn, causing the system to enter a continuous reset loop.

Variable voltage transformers are sold by a number of electronic parts supply houses, such as Newark and Digi-Key. You should expect to pay anywhere from $100 to $300 for this device.

Repairing the Power Supply

Hardly anyone actually repairs power supplies anymore, primarily because simply replacing the supply with a new one is usually cheaper. Even high-quality power supplies are not that expensive when compared to the labor required to repair them.

A defective power supply is typically discarded unless it happens to be one of the higher-quality or more expensive units. In that case, it is usually wise to send the supply to a company that specializes in repairing power supplies and other components. These companies normally provide what is called depot repair, which means you send the supply to them and they repair it and return it to you. If time is of the essence, most of the depot repair companies immediately send you a functional equivalent to your defective supply and take yours in as a core charge. Depot repair is the recommended way to service many PC components, such as power supplies, monitors, and printers. If you take your PC to a conventional service outlet, they often determine which component has the problem and send it to be depot repaired. You can do that yourself and save the markup the repair shop usually charges in such cases.

For those with experience around high voltages, you might be able to repair a failing supply with two relatively simple operations (replacing the internal fuse or the fan); however, these require opening the supply—something I do not normally recommend. I mention it only as an alternative to replacement in some cases. Besides, in all cases where I've seen the internal fuse blown, there were more serious problems and just replacing the fuse only caused it to immediately blow again. On the other hand, if the only problem with the supply is that the fan has failed (motor or bearing failure), you might be able to save the supply from the trash by simply replacing the internal fan.

Most manufacturers try to prevent you from entering the supply by sealing it with special tamperproof Torx screws. These screws use the familiar Torx star driver but also have a tamper-prevention pin in the center that prevents a standard driver from working. Most tool companies, such as Jensen or Specialized, sell sets of TT (tamperproof Torx) bits that remove the tamper-resistant screws. Other manufacturers rivet the power supply case shut, which means you must drill out the rivets to gain access.

Caution

The manufacturers place these obstacles there for a reason—to prevent entry by those who are inexperienced with high voltage. Consider yourself warned!

Obtaining Replacement Units

Most of the time, it is simply easier, safer, or less expensive (considering the time and materials involved) to replace the power supply than to repair it. As mentioned earlier, replacement power supplies are available from many manufacturers. Before you can shop for a supplier, however, you should consider other purchasing factors.

Deciding on a Power Supply

When you are shopping for a new power supply, you should take several factors into account. First, consider the power supply's shape, or form factor. ATX supplies are consistent in size, so any ATX supply should fit any ATX chassis. Some systems use the smaller SFX supplies, and those are available from third-party suppliers as well.

Apart from electrical considerations, power supply form factors can differ physically in their sizes, shapes, screw-hole positions, connector types, number of connectors, fan locations, and switch positions. However, systems that use the same form factor can easily interchange power supplies. When ordering a replacement supply, you need to know which form factor your system requires.

Some systems use proprietary power supply designs, which makes replacement more difficult. If a system uses one of the common form factor power supplies, replacement units are available from hundreds of vendors. An unfortunate user of a system with a nonstandard form factor supply does not have this kind of choice and must get a replacement from the original manufacturer of the system—and usually must pay through the nose for the unit. Although you can find standard form factor supplies for under $100, the proprietary units from some manufacturers cost as much as $400 or more. PC buyers often overlook this and discover too late the consequences of having nonstandard components in a system.

◄◄   See "Power Supply Form Factors," p. 1155.

Cheaper retail-store systems are notorious for using proprietary form factor power supplies. Even Dell has been using proprietary supplies in many of its systems. Be sure you consider this if you intend to own these types of systems out of warranty. Personally, I always insist on systems that use industry-standard power supplies, such as the ATX form factor supply found in many systems today.

Sources for Replacement Power Supplies

Because one of the most failure-prone items in PC systems is the power supply, I am often asked to recommend a replacement. Literally hundreds of companies manufacture PC power supplies, and I certainly have not tested them all. I can, however, recommend some companies whose products I have come to know and trust.

Although other high-quality manufacturers exist, at this time I recommend power supplies from PC Power and Cooling or Antec.

PC Power and Cooling has a complete line of power supplies for PC systems. It makes supplies in all the standard PC form factors used today. Versions are available in a variety of quality and output levels, from inexpensive replacements to very high-quality, high-output models with ratings of up to 600 watts. It even makes versions with built-in battery backup and redundant power systems, as well as a series of special models with high-volume, low-speed (quiet) fan assemblies. Its quiet models are especially welcome to people who work in quiet homes or offices and are annoyed by the fan noise some power supplies emanate. My favorite models are PC Power and Cooling's top-of-the-line 400W Silencer and the 475W Turbo-Cool ATX supplies, which have specs that put most others to shame.

PC Power and Cooling also has units available that fit some of Dell's proprietary designs. This can be a real boon if you have to service or repair Dell systems purchased between 1996 and 2000 because the PC Power and Cooling units are available in higher output ratings than Dell's. These units cost much less than Dell's and bolt in as direct replacements.

Tip

PC Power and Cooling also has SFX-style supplies that can be used to upgrade systems with Flex-ATX boards and chassis, including E-machines, HP's 67xx series, and other low-cost systems. If you have one of these systems and need a high-quality replacement supply to support your upgrades, PC Power and Cooling can help.

The support offered by PC Power and Cooling is excellent as well, and the company has been in business a long time—which is rare in this industry. Besides power supplies, it also offers an excellent line of cases.

Antec, Inc., also offers high-quality power supplies, particularly its TruePower series. It also offers power supplies in both its TruePower and lower-cost Solution series, which feature the popular blue neon effect when plugged in, making them a popular choice for case modding.

A high-quality power supply from either of these vendors can be one of the best cures for intermittent system problems and can go a long way toward ensuring trouble-free operation in the future.

Chassis/Case

The components of a PC system are mounted within a chassis or case. The main feature you must first decide on is which form factor the case needs to be. Several somewhat standardized form factors are available for PC chassis, including

- Slimline Desktop
- Desktop
- Mini-Tower
- Mid-Tower
- Full Tower (Server)
- Large Server
- Rackmount

The Slimline chassis are typically used with NLX form factor boards that are a riser card design. Recently, an addendum to the ATX form factor was created that enables riser cards to be used, allowing ATX boards to be used even in Slimline systems.

In addition to the case form factor, the following are several other things you should consider before purchasing your case:

- *Motherboard form factor supported.* A given chassis usually accepts one or more standard motherboard form factors. Most of the chassis accept ATX (or Micro-ATX or Flex-ATX) form factor motherboards, whereas some accept Baby-AT form factor motherboards as well.
- *Motherboard mounting mechanism.* Some chassis include removable plates or trays that allow the board to be mounted outside the chassis. This enables the board to be more easily installed and facilitates easier servicing later.
- *Power supply form factor supported.* Most modern chassis support ATX or SFX form factor power supplies.
- *Power supply included or separate.* Many include the power supply as standard, but others do not. Usually, I prefer cases in which the supply is separate because that enables me to choose the specific power supply myself.

- *Number of 3 1/2" drive bays (internal and external).* Hard drives are typically installed in the internal 3 1/2" drive bays, whereas floppy, LS-120, Zip, and some tape drives are installed in external 3 1/2" bays.

- *Number of 5 1/4" drive bays (external).* CD and DVD drives as well as some tape drives install in 5 1/4" drive bays, which are almost always external.

- *Number and size of cooling fans supported.* Most modern cases have mounting provisions for several additional cooling fans of different sizes. Be sure the case you choose has sufficient fan mounting provisions to provide the cooling your system will require.

- *Ease of disassembly (tool-free or not).* Some cases are easily disassembled without the use of tools, whereas others require simple hand tools.

- *Front panel USB supported.* Many newer cases feature front-mounted USB connectors, which are a major convenience.

These are just some of the criteria you should use when selecting the case for your next system.

Custom Cases

Sometimes the standard cases don't fit the bill; in those situations you might want to investigate using a more specialized or custom case. Several companies make specialized cases for unique systems. These cases offer features such as multiple drive bays, unique appearances, and specialized cooling.

Perhaps the most unique cases on the market are those by Koolance (www.koolance.com) or Chip-Con (www.chip-con.com). These companies market cases with built-in refrigeration units in the base, which are connected directly to a thermal plate that mounts on the CPU. The plate runs at temperatures as low as –40°F (–40°C) and can maintain a CPU temperature in the –18°F (–28°C) range with processors generating up to 150W. These cases also feature an LCD temperature display on the front for monitoring the temperature, and a safety system shutdown is designed to trip if the processor overheats. They have models available for Socket A through Socket 478 processors.

The only drawback to these cases is the expense; they cost about $500–$600 each. They also do not include a power supply, which would cost another $100–$200 for something 300W or greater to go with it.

Another company offering special cases is PC Power and Cooling. It offers a line of heavy-duty, solid steel cases with multiple drive bays for serious expansion and server use. For those who want something that's different and sure to evoke stares from all who see it, PC Power and Cooling also offers a tower case with a chrome-plated front bezel and black cover.

Power-Protection Systems

Power-protection systems do just what the name implies: They protect your equipment from the effects of power surges and power failures. In particular, power surges and spikes can damage computer equipment, and a loss of power can result in lost data. In this section, you learn about the four primary types of power-protection devices available and when you should use them.

Before considering any further levels of power protection, you should know that a quality power supply already affords you a substantial amount of protection. High-end power supplies from the vendors I recommend are designed to provide protection from higher-than-normal voltages and currents, and they provide a limited amount of power-line noise filtering. Some of the inexpensive aftermarket power supplies probably do not have this sort of protection. If you have an inexpensive computer, further protecting your system might be wise.

Caution

All the power-protection features in this chapter and the protection features in the power supply inside your computer require that the computer's AC power cable be connected to a ground.

Many older homes do not have three-prong (grounded) outlets to accommodate grounded devices.

Do not use a three-pronged adapter (that bypasses the three-prong requirement and enables you to connect to a two-prong socket) to plug a surge suppressor, computer, or UPS into a two-pronged outlet. They often don't provide a good ground and can inhibit the capabilities of your power-protection devices.

You also should test your power sockets to ensure they are grounded. Sometimes outlets, despite having three-prong sockets, are not connected to a ground wire; an inexpensive socket tester (available at most hardware stores) can detect this condition.

Of course, the easiest form of protection is to turn off and unplug your computer equipment (including your modem) when a thunderstorm is imminent. However, when this is not possible, other alternatives are available.

Power supplies should stay within operating specifications and continue to run a system even if any of these power line disturbances occur:

- Voltage drop to 80V for up to 2 seconds
- Voltage drop to 70V for up to .5 seconds
- Voltage surge of up to 143V for up to 1 second

Most high-quality power supplies (or the attached systems) will not be damaged by the following occurrences:

- Full power outage
- Any voltage drop (brownout)
- A spike of up to 2,500V

Because of their internal protection, many computer manufacturers that use high-quality power supplies state in their documentation that external surge suppressors are not necessary with their systems.

To verify the levels of protection built in to the existing power supply in a computer system, an independent laboratory subjected several unprotected PC systems to various spikes and surges of up to 6,000V—considered the maximum level of surge that can be transmitted to a system through an electrical outlet. Any higher voltage would cause the power to arc to the ground within the outlet. None of the systems sustained permanent damage in these tests. The worst thing that happened was that some of the systems rebooted or shut down when the surge was more than 2,000V. Each system restarted when the power switch was toggled after a shutdown.

I do not use any real form of power protection on my systems, and they have survived near-direct lightning strikes and powerful surges. The most recent incident, only 50 feet from my office, was a direct lightning strike to a brick chimney that blew the top of the chimney apart. None of my systems (which were running at the time) were damaged in any way from this incident; they just shut themselves down. I was able to restart each system by toggling the power switches. An alarm system located in the same office, however, was destroyed by this strike. I am not saying that lightning strikes or even much milder spikes and surges can't damage computer systems—another nearby lightning strike did destroy a modem and serial adapter installed in one of my systems. I was just lucky that the destruction did not include the motherboard.

This discussion points out an important oversight in some power-protection strategies: Do not forget to provide protection from spikes and surges on the phone line.

The automatic shutdown of a computer during power disturbances is a built-in function of most high-quality power supplies. You can reset the power supply by flipping the power switch from on to off and back on again. Some power supplies even have an auto-restart function. This type of power supply acts the same as others in a massive surge or spike situation: It shuts down the system. The difference is that after normal power resumes, the power supply waits for a specified delay of 3–6 seconds and then resets itself and powers the system back up. Because no manual switch resetting is required, this feature might be desirable in systems functioning as network servers or in those found in other unattended locations.

The first time I witnessed a large surge cause an immediate shutdown of all my systems, I was extremely surprised. All the systems were silent, but the monitor and modem lights were still on. My first thought was that everything was blown, but a simple toggle of each system-unit power switch caused the power supplies to reset, and the units powered up with no problem. Since that first time, this type of shutdown has happened to me several times, always without further problems.

The following types of power-protection devices are explained in the sections that follow:

- Surge suppressors
- Phone-line surge protectors
- Line conditioners

- Standby power supplies (SPS)
- Uninterruptible power supplies (UPS)

Surge Suppressors (Protectors)

The simplest form of power protection is any one of the commercially available surge protectors—that is, devices inserted between the system and the power line. These devices, which cost between $20 and $200, can absorb the high-voltage transients produced by nearby lightning strikes and power equipment. Some surge protectors can be effective for certain types of power problems, but they offer only very limited protection.

Surge protectors use several devices, usually metal-oxide varistors (MOVs), that can clamp and shunt away all voltages above a certain level. MOVs are designed to accept voltages as high as 6,000V and divert any power above 200V to ground. MOVs can handle normal surges, but powerful surges such as direct lightning strikes can blow right through them. MOVs are not designed to handle a very high level of power and self-destruct while shunting a large surge. These devices therefore cease to function after either a single large surge or a series of smaller ones. The real problem is that you can't easily tell when they no longer are functional. The only way to test them is to subject the MOVs to a surge, which destroys them. Therefore, you never really know whether your so-called surge protector is protecting your system.

Some surge protectors have status lights that let you know when a surge large enough to blow the MOVs has occurred. A surge suppressor without this status indicator light is useless because you never know when it has stopped protecting.

Underwriters Laboratories has produced an excellent standard that governs surge suppressors, called UL 1449. Any surge suppressor that meets this standard is a very good one and definitely offers a line of protection beyond what the power supply in your PC already offers. The only types of surge suppressors worth buying, therefore, should have two features:

- Conformance to the UL 1449 standard
- A status light indicating when the MOVs are blown

Units that meet the UL 1449 specification say so on the packaging or directly on the unit. If this standard is not mentioned, it does not conform. Therefore, you should avoid it.

Another good feature to have in a surge suppressor is a built-in circuit breaker that can be manually reset rather than a fuse. The breaker protects your system if it or a peripheral develops a short. These better surge suppressors usually cost about $40.

Phone Line Surge Protectors

In addition to protecting the power lines, it is critical to provide protection to your systems from any connected phone lines. If you are using a modem or fax board that is plugged into the phone system, any surges or spikes that travel through the phone line can damage your system. In many areas, the phone lines are especially susceptible to lightning strikes, which are the leading cause of fried modems and damage to the computer equipment attached to them.

Several companies manufacture or sell simple surge protectors that plug in between your modem and the phone line. These inexpensive devices can be purchased from most electronics supply houses. Most of the cable and communication product vendors listed in the Vendor List (on the disc that accompanies this book) sell these phone line surge protectors. Some of the standard power line surge protectors include connectors for phone line protection as well.

Line Conditioners

In addition to high-voltage and current conditions, other problems can occur with incoming power. The voltage might dip below the level needed to run the system, resulting in a brownout. Forms of electrical noise other than simple voltage surges or spikes might travel through the power line, such as radio-frequency interference or electrical noise caused by motors or other inductive loads.

Remember two things when you wire together digital devices (such as computers and their peripherals):

- Any wire can act as an antenna and have voltage induced in it by nearby electromagnetic fields, which can come from other wires, telephones, CRTs, motors, fluorescent fixtures, static discharge, and, of course, radio transmitters.

- Digital circuitry responds with surprising efficiency to noise of even a volt or two, making those induced voltages particularly troublesome. The electrical wiring in your building can act as an antenna, picking up all kinds of noise and disturbances.

A line conditioner can handle many of these types of problems. A line conditioner is designed to remedy a variety of problems. It filters the power, bridges brownouts, suppresses high-voltage and current conditions, and generally acts as a buffer between the power line and the system. A line conditioner does the job of a surge suppressor, and much more. It is more of an active device, functioning continuously, rather than a passive device that activates only when a surge is present. A line conditioner provides true power conditioning and can handle myriad problems. It contains transformers, capacitors, and other circuitry that can temporarily bridge a brownout or low-voltage situation. These units usually cost $100–$300, depending on the power-handling capacity of the unit.

Backup Power

The next level of power protection includes backup power-protection devices. These units can provide power in case of a complete blackout, thereby providing the time necessary for an orderly system shutdown. Two types are available: the standby power supply (SPS) and the uninterruptible power supply (UPS). The UPS is a special device because it does much more than just provide backup power—it is also the best kind of line conditioner you can buy.

Standby Power Supplies

A standby power supply is known as an offline device: It functions only when normal power is disrupted. An SPS system uses a special circuit that can sense the AC line current. If the sensor detects a loss of power on the line, the system quickly switches over to a standby battery and power inverter. The power inverter converts the battery power to 120V AC power, which is then supplied to the system.

SPS systems do work, but sometimes a problem occurs during the switch to battery power. If the switch is not fast enough, the computer system shuts down or reboots anyway, which defeats the purpose of having the backup power supply. A truly outstanding SPS adds to the circuit a ferroresonant transformer, which is a large transformer with the capability to store a small amount of power and deliver it during the switch time. This device functions as a buffer on the power line, giving the SPS almost uninterruptible capability.

Tip

Look for SPS systems with a switchover time of less than 10 milliseconds (ms). This is shorter than the hold-over time of typical power supplies.

SPS units also might have internal line conditioning of their own. Under normal circumstances, most cheaper units place your system directly on the regular power line and offer no conditioning. The addition of a ferroresonant transformer to an SPS gives it extra regulation and protection capabilities because of the buffer effect of the transformer. SPS devices without the ferroresonant transformer still require the use of a line conditioner for full protection. SPS systems usually cost between a hundred and several thousand dollars, depending on the quality and power-output capacity.

Uninterruptible Power Supplies

Perhaps the best overall solution to any power problem is to provide a power source that is conditioned and that can't be interrupted—which is the definition of an uninterruptible power supply. UPSs are known as online systems because they continuously function and supply power to your computer systems. Because some companies advertise ferroresonant SPS devices as though they were UPS devices, many now use the term *true UPS* to describe a truly online system. A true UPS system is constructed in much the same way as an SPS system; however, because the computer is always operating from the battery, there is no switching circuit.

In a true UPS, your system always operates from the battery. A voltage inverter converts from 12V DC to 120V AC. You essentially have your own private power system that generates power independently of the AC line. A battery charger connected to the line or wall current keeps the battery charged at a rate equal to or greater than the rate at which power is consumed.

When the AC current supplying the battery charger fails, a true UPS continues functioning undisturbed because the battery-charging function is all that is lost. Because the computer was already running off the battery, no switch takes place and no power disruption is possible. The battery begins discharging at a rate dictated by the amount of load your system places on the unit, which (based on the size of the battery) gives you plenty of time to execute an orderly system shutdown. Based on an appropriately scaled storage battery, the UPS functions continuously, generating power and preventing unpleasant surprises. When the line power returns, the battery charger begins recharging the battery, again with no interruption.

Note

Occasionally, a UPS can accumulate too much storage and not enough discharge. When this occurs, the UPS emits a loud alarm, alerting you that it's full. Simply unplugging the unit from the AC power source for a while can discharge the excess storage (as it powers your computer) and drain the UPS of the excess.

Many SPS systems are advertised as though they are true UPS systems. The giveaway is the unit's switch time. If a specification for switch time exists, the unit can't be a true UPS because UPS units never switch. However, a good SPS with a ferroresonant transformer can virtually equal the performance of a true UPS at a lower cost.

Note

Many UPSs and SPSs today come equipped with a cable and software that enables the protected computer to shut down in an orderly manner on receipt of a signal from the UPS. This way, the system can shut down properly even if the computer is unattended. Some operating systems designed for server environments, such as Windows NT/2000/XP, contain their own UPS software components.

UPS cost is a direct function of both the length of time it can continue to provide power after a line current failure and how much power it can provide. You therefore should purchase a UPS that provides enough power to run your system and peripherals and enough time to close files and provide an orderly shutdown. Remember, however, to manually perform a system shutdown procedure during a power outage. You will probably need your monitor plugged into the UPS and the computer. Be sure the UPS you purchase can provide sufficient power for all the devices you must connect to it.

Because of a true UPS's almost total isolation from the line current, it is unmatched as a line conditioner and surge suppressor. The best UPS systems add a ferroresonant transformer for even greater power conditioning and protection capability. This type of UPS is the best form of power protection available. The price, however, can be high. To find out just how much power your computer system requires, look at the UL sticker on the back of the unit. This sticker lists the maximum power draw in watts, or sometimes in just volts and amperes. If only voltage and amperage are listed, multiply the two figures to calculate the wattage.

As an example, if the documentation for a system indicates that the computer can require as much as 120V at a maximum current draw of 5 amps, the maximum power the system can draw is about 550 watts. This wattage is for a system with every slot full, two hard disks, and one floppy—in other words, a system at the maximum possible level of expansion. The system should never draw any more power than that; if it does, a 5-amp fuse in the power supply will blow. This type of system usually draws an average of 300 watts. However, to be safe when you make calculations for UPS capacity, be conservative; use the 550-watt figure. Adding a monitor that draws 100 watts brings the total to 650 watts or more. Therefore, to run two fully loaded systems, you'd need a 1,100-watt UPS. And don't forget two monitors, each drawing 100 watts. Therefore, the total is 1,300 watts. A UPS of that capacity or greater costs approximately $500–$700. Unfortunately, that is what the best level of protection costs. Most companies can justify this type of expense only for critical-use PCs, such as network servers.

Note

The highest-capacity UPS sold for use with a conventional 15-amp outlet is about 1,400 watts. If it's any higher, you risk tripping a 15-amp circuit when the battery is charging heavily and the inverter is drawing maximum current.

In addition to the total available output power (wattage), several other factors can distinguish one UPS from another. The addition of a ferroresonant transformer improves a unit's power conditioning and buffering capabilities. Good units also have an inverter that produces a true sine wave output; the cheaper ones might generate a square wave. A square wave is an approximation of a sine wave with abrupt up-and-down voltage transitions. The abrupt transitions of a square wave are not compatible with some computer equipment power supplies. Be sure that the UPS you purchase produces power that is compatible with your computer equipment. Every unit has a specification for how long it can sustain output at the rated level. If your systems draw less than the rated level, you have some additional time.

Caution

Be careful! Most UPS systems are not designed for you to sit and compute for hours through an electrical blackout. They are designed to provide power only to essential components and to remain operating long enough to allow for an orderly shutdown. You pay a large amount for units that provide power for more than 15 minutes or so. At some point, it becomes more cost-effective to buy a generator than to keep investing in extended life for a UPS.

Some of the many sources of power protection equipment include American Power Conversion (APC), Tripp Lite, and Best Power. These companies sell a variety of UPS, SPS, line, and surge protector products.

Caution

Don't connect a laser printer to a backed-up socket in any SPS or UPS unit. Such printers are electrically noisy and have widely varying current draws. This can be hard on the inverter in an SPS or a UPS and frequently cause the inverter to fail or detect an overload and shut down. Either case means that your system will lose power, too.

Printers are normally noncritical because whatever is being printed can be reprinted. Don't connect them to a UPS unless there's a good business need to do so.

Some UPSs and SPSs have sockets that are conditioned but not backed up—that is, they do not draw power from the battery. In cases such as this, you can safely plug printers and other peripherals into these sockets.

RTC/NVRAM (CMOS RAM) Batteries

All 16-bit and higher systems have a special type of chip in them that combines a real-time clock (RTC) with at least 64 bytes (including the clock data) of nonvolatile RAM (NVRAM) memory. This chip is officially called the RTC/NVRAM chip, but it is often referred to as the CMOS or CMOS RAM chip because the type of chip used is produced using a CMOS (complementary metal-oxide semiconductor) process. CMOS design chips are known for very low power consumption. This special RTC/NVRAM chip is designed to run off a battery for several years.

The original chip of this type used in the IBM AT was the Motorola MC146818 chip. Although the chips used today have different manufacturers and part numbers, they all are designed to be compatible with this original Motorola part. Most modern motherboards have the RTC/NVRAM built in to the motherboard chipset South Bridge or I/O Controller Hub (ICH) component.

The function of the real-time clock should be obvious: The clock enables software to read the date and time and preserves the date and time data even when the system is powered off or unplugged.

The NVRAM portion of the chip has another function. It is designed to store basic system configuration, including the amount of memory installed, types of floppy and hard disk drives, and other information. Some of the more modern motherboards use extended NVRAM chips with as much as 4KB or more of space to hold this configuration information. This is especially true for plug-and-play systems, which store the motherboard configuration as well as the configuration of adapter cards. The system can then read this information every time you power it on.

These chips typically are powered by some type of battery while the system is off. This battery preserves the information in the NVRAM and powers the clock. Most systems use a lithium-type battery because they have a very long life, especially at the low power draw from the typical RTC/NVRAM chip.

Some systems have a chip that has the battery embedded within it. These are made by several companies—including Dallas Semiconductor and Benchmarq. These chips are notable for their long lives. Under normal conditions, the integral battery lasts for 10 years—which is, of course, longer than the useful life of the system. If your system uses one of the Dallas or Benchmarq modules, the battery and chip must be replaced as a unit because they are integrated. Most of the time, these chip/battery combinations are installed in a socket on the motherboard just in case a problem requires an early replacement. You can get new modules direct from the manufacturers for $18 or less, which is often less than the cost of the older separate battery alone.

Some systems do not use a battery at all. Hewlett-Packard, for example, includes a special capacitor in some of its systems that is automatically recharged anytime the system is plugged in. Note that the system does not have to be running for the capacitor to charge; it only has to be plugged in. If the system is unplugged, the capacitor powers the RTC/NVRAM chip for up to a week or more. If the system remains unplugged for a duration longer than that, the NVRAM information is lost. In that case, these systems can reload the NVRAM from a backup kept in a special flash ROM chip contained on the motherboard. The only pieces of information that will actually be missing when you repower the system are the date and time, which will have to be reentered. By using the capacitor combined with an NVRAM backup in flash ROM, these systems have a very reliable solution that lasts indefinitely.

Many systems use a separate battery, which can be either directly soldered into the motherboard (mostly older obsolete systems) or plugged in via a battery connector. For those older systems with the battery soldered in, a spare battery connector exists on the motherboard where you can insert a conventional plug-in battery, should the original ever fail.

Motherboard NVRAM (CMOS RAM) batteries come in many forms. The best are of a lithium design because they last 2–5 years or more. I have seen systems with conventional alkaline batteries mounted in a holder; these are much less desirable because they fail more frequently and do not last as long. Also, they are prone to leak, and if a battery leaks on the motherboard, the motherboard can be severely damaged. By far, the most commonly used battery for motherboards today is the type 2032 lithium coin cell battery, which is about the size of a quarter and is readily available at electronics supply stores, camera shops, and even drugstores.

Besides the various battery types, the chip can require any one of several voltages. The batteries in PCs are usually 3.0V, but some systems have used 3.6V, 4.5V, or 6V types as well. If you are replacing the battery, be sure your replacement is the same voltage as the one you removed from the system. Some motherboards can use batteries of several voltages, and you use a jumper or switch to select the various settings. If you suspect your motherboard has this capability, consult the documentation for instructions on changing the settings. Of course, the easiest thing to do is to replace the existing battery with another of the same type.

Symptoms that indicate that the battery is about to fail include having to reset the clock on your PC every time you shut down the system (especially after moving it) and problems during the system's POST, such as drive-detection difficulties. If you experience problems such as these, you should make note of your system's CMOS settings and replace the battery as soon as possible.

Caution

When you replace a PC battery, be sure you get the polarity correct; otherwise, you will damage the RTC/NVRAM (CMOS) chip. Because the chip is soldered onto most motherboards, this can be an expensive mistake! The battery connector on the motherboard and the battery are usually keyed to prevent a backward connection. The pinout of this connector is on the disc, but it should also be listed in your system documentation.

When you replace a battery, in most cases the existing data stored in the NVRAM is lost. Sometimes, however, the data remains intact for several minutes (I have observed NVRAM retain information with no power for an hour or more), so if you make the battery swap quickly, the information in the NVRAM might be retained. Just to be sure, I recommend that you record all the system configuration settings stored in the NVRAM by your system Setup program. In most cases, you should run the BIOS Setup program and copy or print out all the screens showing the various settings. Some Setup programs offer the capability to save the NVRAM data to a file for later restoration if necessary.

Tip

If your system BIOS is password-protected and you forget the password, one possible way to bypass the block is to remove the battery for a few minutes and then replace it. This resets the BIOS to its default settings, removing the password protection.

After replacing a battery, power up the system and use the Setup program to check the date and time setting and any other data that was stored in the NVRAM.

CHAPTER 22

Building or Upgrading Systems

System Components

In these days of commodity parts and component pricing, building your own system from scratch is no longer the daunting process it once was. Every component necessary to build a PC system is available off the shelf at competitive pricing. In many cases, the system you build can use the same or even better components than the top name-brand systems.

There are, however, some cautions to heed. The main thing to note is that you rarely save money when building your own system; purchasing a complete system from a mail-order vendor or mass merchandiser is almost always less expensive. The reason for this is simple: Most system vendors who build systems to order use many, if not all, of the same components you can use when building your own system. The difference is that they buy these components in quantity and receive a much larger discount than you can by purchasing only one of a particular item.

In addition, you pay only one shipping and handling charge when you purchase a complete system instead of the multiple shipping charges you pay when you purchase separate components. In fact, the shipping and handling charges from ordering all the separate parts needed to build a PC through the mail often add up to $100 or more, and this doesn't count the additional time spent as well as additional telephone or Internet access charges accrued in the process. The cost rises if you encounter problems with any of the components and have to make additional calls or pay for shipping charges to send improper or malfunctioning parts back for replacement. Also, many companies charge restocking fees if you purchase something and then determine you don't need it or can't use it.

Finally, if you purchase parts locally, you typically must pay the additional state sales tax, as well as the higher prices usually associated with retail store sales.

Then there is the included software. Although I can sometimes come close in price to a commercial system when building my own from scratch, the bundled software really adds value to the commercial system. A copy of Windows XP costs $100 or more, and many commercial systems also include Microsoft Office or other applications as well.

It is clear that the reasons for building a system from scratch often have less to do with saving money and more to do with the experience you gain and the results you achieve. In the end, you have a custom system that contains the exact components and features you have selected. Most of the time when you buy a preconfigured system, you have to compromise in some way. For example, you might get the video adapter you want, but you would prefer a different make or model of motherboard. By building your own system, you can select the exact components you want and build the ultimate system for your needs. The experience is also very rewarding. You know exactly how your system is constructed and configured because you have done it yourself. This makes future support and installation of additional accessories much easier.

Another benefit of building your own system is that you are guaranteed an industry-standard system that will be easily upgradeable in the future. Many of the larger system vendors use proprietary components that can make future upgrades difficult or impossible. Of course, if you have been reading the book up to this point, you already know everything you need to ensure any preassembled systems you purchase would use industry-standard components, and therefore be upgradeable and repairable in the future.

You might be able to save some money using components from your current system when building your new system. You might have recently upgraded your hard drive and optical drive in an attempt to extend the life of your current computer. In most cases, you can take those components with you to the new system. For example, if you bought a 120GB hard drive and a DVD+/-RW drive for your old system, you can move them to a newer system.

Your monitor, keyboard, mouse, storage devices, most PCI adapter cards, and some AGP video cards from your old system will likely work in your new system. The bad news is that most newer systems require different memory from an older system and most older AGP 1X or 2X cards might not work in newer motherboards with 4X or 8X slots.

So, if you are interested in a rewarding experience, want a customized and fully upgradeable system that is not exactly the same as that offered by any vendor, are able to take on all system repair and troubleshooting tasks, want to save some money by reusing some of the components from your current system, and are not in a hurry, building your own PC might be the way to go.

On the other hand, if you are interested in getting a PC with the most value for the best price, want one-stop support for in-warranty repairs and technical problems, and need an operational system quickly, building your own system should be avoided. In that case, you should consider purchasing a system from a name-brand vendor. Also, if you are unable to provide self-support or will not be upgrading the system, you might consider an extended warranty. An extended warranty essentially prevents you from doing any upgrades to the system because an upgrade is not covered and, in some cases, can even invalidate the warranty on the rest of the system. If you do plan to upgrade your system after a year or so of use, you should avoid purchasing any extended warranties.

This chapter details the components necessary to assemble your own system, explains the assembly procedures, and lists some recommendations for components and their sources.

The components used in building a typical PC are as follows:

- Case and power supply
- Motherboard
- Processor with heatsink and fan
- Memory
- Floppy drive (optional)
- Hard disk drive
- Optical drive(s) (CD and/or DVD)
- Keyboard and pointing device (mouse)
- Video card and display
- Sound card (optional) and speakers
- Modem (optional) or LAN card (optional)
- Cables
- Hardware (nuts, bolts, screws, and brackets)
- Operating system software

Each of these components is discussed in the following sections.

Case and Power Supply

The case and power supply are typically sold as a unit, although some vendors do sell them separately. There are a multitude of designs from which to choose, usually dependent on the motherboard form factor you want to use, the number of drive bays available, and whether the system is desktop or floor mounted. There are cases with extra fans for cooling (recommended), air filters on the air inlets to keep out the dust, removable side panels, or motherboard trays; cases that require no tools for assembly, rack-mounted versions, and more. For most custom-built systems, a mid-tower case supporting either ATX or BTX form factor motherboards and ATX12V or CFX form factor power supplies is the recommended choice. The size and shape of a component is called the *form factor*. The most popular case form factors are as follows:

- Full-tower
- Mid- or mini-tower
- Desktop
- Low-profile (also called Slimline)

Each specific case is designed to accept a specific motherboard and power supply form factor as well. You have to ensure that the particular case you choose will accept the type of motherboard and power supply you want to use.

When deciding which type of case to purchase, you should consider where you will place your computer. Will it be on a desk? Or is it more feasible to put the system on the floor and just have the monitor, keyboard, and mouse on the desk? The amount of space you have available for the computer can affect other purchasing decisions, such as the length of the monitor, keyboard, and mouse cables.

After you have settled on a case form factor, you need to choose one that supports the motherboard and power supply form factors you want to use. The smaller mini-tower or slimline cases often accept only MicroATX, FlexATX, MicroBTX, or PicoBTX motherboards, which somewhat limit your choices. If the case you choose fits a full-size ATX board, you can be sure it also accepts the smaller MicroATX and FlexATX boards. The same is true for BTX: A chassis that can handle BTX also accepts MicroBTX and PicoBTX. FlexATX (and variations such as MiniITX) and PicoBTX motherboards are used in some of the latest small form factor systems.

◄◄ See "Motherboard Form Factors," p. 202.

Most mid-tower and larger cases accept full-size ATX or BTX boards, which have become the standard for most full-function systems. If you are interested in the most flexible type of case and power supply that will support the widest variety of future upgrades, I recommend getting a chassis that supports full-size ATX or BTX boards and ATX12V power supplies.

Note

Generally, any ATX case, motherboard, and power supply of sufficient wattage for your equipment can be put together to form the basis of a new system. However, there are two major exceptions you need to know about:

■ *Many Dell systems built from 1996 through 2000 use nonstandard motherboards and power supplies with what appears to be a standard ATX power supply physical connector; however, the pinout and voltage levels have changed.* If you mix a nonstandard Dell motherboard and a standard ATX power supply, or a standard ATX motherboard and a nonstandard Dell power supply, you will destroy the power supply and possibly your motherboard as well! If you want to upgrade newer Dell systems, you must either buy Dell-compatible power supplies for use with the Dell motherboard or replace both Dell components with standard ATX components. See Chapter 21, "Power Supply and Chassis/Case," for more details. Many of Dell's newer systems also use nonstandard power supplies and motherboards, but these are more obvious in that they do not use standard connectors either, which means a standard ATX motherboard or power supply will not physically plug in. This makes an upgrade difficult or impossible, but at least you won't blow up any hardware in the process.

■ *Intel Pentium 4 and AMD Athlon CPUs require heavy heatsinks and fans for cooling.* Be sure to use a heatsink designed for your particular processor, and make sure it is properly installed. These high-powered systems also require an ATX12V power supply, which has an additional 12V connector for the motherboard-based CPU voltage regulators. ATX12V adapters are available to convert standard ATX power supplies, but in general you should upgrade to an ATX12V supply that has upgraded internal circuitry and wiring to handle the additional 12V power required.

Whether you choose a desktop or one of the tower cases is really a matter of personal preference and system location. Most people feel that the tower systems are roomier and easier to work on, and the full-sized tower cases have a lot of bays for various storage devices. Tower cases typically have enough bays to hold floppy drives, multiple hard disk drives, CD-ROM drives, tape drives, and anything else you might want to install. However, some of the desktop cases can have as much room as the towers, particularly the mini- or mid-tower models. In fact, a tower case is sometimes considered a desktop case turned sideways or vice versa. Some cases are convertible—that is, they can be used in either a desktop or tower orientation.

Tip

Mini-tower systems are an exception to the roomy tower case rule. These systems normally use the MicroATX, FlexATX, MicroBTX, or PicoBTX motherboards and might have only two or three drive bays. These systems are compact and somewhat difficult to work on.

When it comes to the power supply, the most important consideration is how many devices you plan to install in the system and how much power they require. Chapter 21 describes the process for calculating the power your system hardware requires and selecting an appropriate power supply for your needs.

◄◄ See "Power-Use Calculations," p. 1186.

When you build your own system, you should always keep upgradeability and repairability in mind. A properly designed custom PC should last you far longer than an off-the-shelf model because you can more easily add or replace components. When choosing a case and power supply, leave yourself some room for expansion, on the assumption that you will eventually want to install an additional hard drive or some other new device that appears on the market that you can't live without. To be specific, be sure you have at least two empty internal drive bays and choose a higher output power supply than you need for your current equipment, so it won't be overtaxed when additional components are added later.

Processor

Both Intel and AMD sell processors through two primary channels or methods. They are referred to as *boxed* (or retail) and *OEM*.

A boxed processor and an OEM processor might have the same specifications, but they are packaged differently, include different supplemental components, and have different warranties. Even though the boxed processors are sometimes also called *retail* processors, they are technically not intended to be sold in the normal retail channel. Both boxed and OEM processors are technically wholesale items and, as such, can be purchased from Intel or AMD only by signing up as a dealer with them and meeting their requirements to achieve and maintain dealer status. After you are registered as an Intel or AMD dealer, you can purchase boxed processors directly from them.

OEM processors are sold only to major accounts that purchase hundreds of chips at a time. Although neither the boxed nor OEM processors are intended to be sold in the retail channel, after Intel or AMD sells them to one of their dealers, that dealer is free to resell the chips as he chooses. Therefore, an individual can purchase either boxed or OEM processors from many sources.

The most obvious difference between the boxed and OEM processors is the physical packaging. It could be argued that both technically come in boxes, but the Intel or AMD *boxed* processors come individually packaged in a colorful shrink-wrapped box that includes the processor, the heatsink and fan, installation instructions, a certificate of authenticity, warranty paperwork, as well as an "Intel inside" or "AMD instead" sticker that is supposed to be affixed to the front of the system chassis (see Figure 22.1).

Figure 22.1 Boxed Intel Pentium 4. *Photo used by permission of Intel Corporation.*

On the other hand, OEM processors come in a much larger box with multiple trays containing up to 10 processors each, or up to 100 total. No heatsinks, fans, installation instructions, warranties, or other paperwork are included. These are purchased in large quantities by the major system manufacturers.

A boxed processor generally includes a 3-year warranty direct with the processor manufacturer. So, if the chip fails within 3 years of purchase, the end user can contact Intel or AMD directly and they will replace the chip. OEM processors have *no* warranty with the manufacturer (Intel or AMD); however, the company from which you purchased it will likely offer a 30- or 90-day warranty. The warranty length and the way in which it is administered are entirely up to the dealer from which you purchased the chip, which could be a problem if, for example, that dealer has gone out of business.

Boxed processors also include a high-quality, manufacturer-supplied heatsink and cooling fan. Typically, the cooling system provided with a boxed processor is designed to work under worst-case thermal environments and is a very high-quality and heavy-duty unit. When you think about it, it wouldn't serve Intel or AMD to provide cheap heatsinks and fans on a processor they are warranting for 3 years!

OEM processors, on the other hand, include no heatsink or fan, but the dealer from which you purchase the processor will likely provide one. Unfortunately, these are often of very uneven quality and performance, up to the whims of the particular dealer you are using. With only a 30- or 90-day warranty, it doesn't matter as much if the manufacturer skimps on the heatsink because, if the chip fails beyond the short warranty period, the company isn't obligated to replace it. If you purchase an OEM processor with a motherboard, most dealers install the processor into the motherboard and provide a single warranty covering both items.

The motherboards you consider should have one of the following processor sockets or slots:

- *Socket 775.* Supports the third-generation Intel Pentium 4 processors
- *Socket 478.* Supports the second- and third-generation Intel Pentium 4 and compatible Celeron processors
- *Socket 939.* Supports the second-generation Athlon 64 FX processors
- *Socket 940.* Supports the original Athlon 64 FX processors
- *Socket 754.* Supports the Athlon 64 processors
- *Socket A (462).* Supports the AMD Athlon, Athlon XP, and Duron processors

The following slot and socket types also can be purchased but are not compatible with the latest CPU models and will limit your future processor upgrade options:

- *Socket 370 (also called PGA370).* Supports the PGA versions of the Intel Pentium III and compatible Celeron processors
- *Socket 423.* Supports the original version of the Intel Pentium 4 processor
- *Slot 1 (also called SC-242).* Supports the SECC versions of the Intel Pentium III, Celeron, and Pentium II processors
- *Slot A.* Supports the original SECC version of the AMD Athlon processors
- *Socket 7 (also called Super7 if faster than 66MHz).* Supports the Intel Pentium; Pentium MMX; AMD K5, K6, K6-2, and K6-3; Cyrix 6x86 and 6x86MX; and MII processors

Because the motherboard you choose dictates or limits your choice in processor, you should choose your processor first, which will then dictate the type of CPU socket (or slot) that must be present. For more information on processors, see Chapter 3, "Microprocessor Types and Specifications."

◄◄ See "Processor Socket and Slot Types," p. 88.

Depending on the type of motherboard you select, there might be jumpers on the motherboard to set for processor type and speed. It also might have jumpers to control the voltage supplied to the processor. Typically, older Socket 7 or Super7 boards have jumpers for motherboard bus speed, CPU multiplier, and CPU voltage settings. If you purchase this type of board, be sure you get these settings correct; otherwise, the system won't run properly. In a worst-case situation, you can damage the processor with too high a voltage setting, for example.

All modern processor sockets handle these settings automatically, so there is little danger of incorrect settings. Even so, several boards have overrides for the automatic settings, which can be useful for those intending to hotrod or overclock their processors. Most of these boards use the BIOS Setup to control these overrides, so no jumpers or switches need to be set.

Motherboard

Several compatible form factors are used for motherboards. The form factor refers to the physical dimensions and size of the board and dictates into which type of case the board will fit. The types of compatible industry-standard motherboard form factors generally available for system builders are as follows:

Modern form factors

- BTX
- ATX
- MicroATX
- FlexATX
- NLX
- MiniITX (semiproprietary)

All others

- Proprietary designs (some Compaq, Dell Optiplex, Hewlett-Packard, notebook/portable systems, and so on); many Dell Dimension systems from 1996 through 2000 use ATX form factors, but with different electrical pinouts; newer Dell Dimension XPS systems use proprietary motherboards and power supplies as well.

BTX is the latest form factor, designed as an improved replacement for ATX; however, BTX is not physically compatible with and requires a different chassis from ATX. Because BTX is new, it hasn't become as popular as ATX yet, but it will likely become the most popular design in future systems.

Currently, the ATX motherboard form factor is far and away the most popular.

Note

For more information on all the motherboard form factors, see Chapter 4, "Motherboards and Buses." You can also find the reference standard documents detailing the modern form factors at the Desktop Form Factors Web site: `http://www.formfactors.org`.

In addition to processor support and form factor, you should consider several other features when selecting a motherboard. The following sections examine each feature.

Chipsets

Aside from the processor, the main component on a motherboard is called the *chipset*. This usually is a set of one to five chips that contains the main motherboard circuits. These chipsets replace the 150 or more distinct components that were used in the original IBM AT systems and enable a motherboard designer to easily create a functional system from just a few parts. The chipset contains all the motherboard circuitry except the processor and memory in most systems.

Because the chipset really *is* the motherboard, the chipset used in a given motherboard has a profound effect on the performance of the board. It dictates all the performance parameters and limitations of the board, such as memory size and speed, processor types and speeds, supported buses and their speeds, and more. If you plan to incorporate technologies such as the Accelerated Graphics Port (AGP) or the Universal Serial Bus (USB) into your system, you must ensure that your motherboard has a chipset that supports these features.

Because chipsets are constantly being introduced and improved over time, I can't list all of them and their functions here; however, you will find a detailed description of many of them in Chapter 4. Several popular high-performance chipsets are on the market today.

◄◄ See "Chipsets," p. 239.

◄◄ See "Motherboard Selection Criteria," p. 391.

Clearly, the selection of a chipset must be based largely on the processor you choose and the additional components you intend to install in the computer.

However, no matter which chipset you look for, I recommend checking the following supported features to ensure they match your needs and desires:

- CPU bus speed support
- The type of main memory supported
- AGP4X/8X or PCI Express video support
- Parallel or Serial ATA interfaces
- USB 2.0 (high-speed USB) or FireWire support
- Support for the fastest available processor in the processor family you choose, even if you are installing a slower model

If you are intent on building the ultimate PC (at least by this week's standards), you also should consider the faster processors available. Be sure not to waste your investment on the most capable processor by using a chipset that doesn't fully exploit its capabilities.

When you are designing your system, carefully consider the number and type of expansion cards you intend to install. Then, ensure that the motherboard you select has the correct number of slots and that they are of the correct bus type for your peripherals (ISA, PCI, AGP, and PCI Express). Because most newer boards don't have ISA slots, it might be time to get rid of any ISA boards you have and replace them with more capable PCI or PCI Express versions.

When you buy a motherboard, I highly recommend you contact the chipset manufacturer and obtain the documentation (usually called the *data book*) for your particular chipset. This explains how the memory and cache controllers, as well as many other devices in the system, operate. This documentation should also describe the Advanced Chipset Setup functions in your system's Setup program. With this information, you might be able to fine-tune the motherboard configuration by altering the chipset features. Because chipsets are frequently discontinued and replaced with newer models, don't wait too long to get the chipset documentation because most manufacturers make it available only for chips currently in production.

Note

One interesting fact about chipsets is that in the volume that the motherboard manufacturers purchase them, the chipsets usually cost about $40 each. If you have an older motherboard that needs repair, you usually can't purchase the chipsets because they aren't stocked by the manufacturer after they are discontinued. Not to mention that most chipsets feature surface mounting with ball grid array (BGA) packages that are extremely difficult to manually remove and replace. The low-cost chipset is one of the reasons motherboards have become disposable items that are rarely, if ever, repaired.

BIOS

Another important feature on the motherboard is the basic input/output system (BIOS). This is also called the ROM BIOS because the code is stored in a read-only memory (ROM) chip. There are several things to look for here. One is that the BIOS is supplied by one of the major BIOS manufacturers, such as AMI (American Megatrends International), Phoenix, or Award (owned by Phoenix). Also, be sure that the BIOS is contained in a special type of reprogrammable chip called a Flash ROM or EEPROM (electrically erasable programmable read-only memory). This enables you to download BIOS updates from the manufacturer and, using a program it supplies, easily update the code in your BIOS. If you do not have the Flash ROM or EEPROM type, you must physically replace the chip if an update is required.

◀◀ See "Upgrading the BIOS," p. 415.

Virtually all motherboards built in the last few years include a BIOS with support for the Plug and Play (PnP) specification. This makes installing new cards, especially PnP cards, much easier. PnP automates the installation and uses special software built into the BIOS and the operating system (such as Windows 9x/Me and Windows 2000/XP) to automatically configure adapter cards and resolve adapter resource conflicts.

You also need to verify that the BIOS supports both the processor you plan to install initially and the processor you might upgrade to in the future. If the motherboard and chipset can handle a new processor but the BIOS cannot, a BIOS upgrade can be used to provide proper support.

Note

For more information on PnP, see "Plug and Play BIOS" in Chapter 5, "BIOS." Also, an exhaustive listing of PnP device IDs can be found in the Technical Reference section of the disc included with this book.

Memory

Older systems had L2 cache memory on the motherboard, but for almost all systems starting with the Pentium II, this cache is a part of the processor. The few remaining Socket 7 or Super7 motherboards do still include cache onboard, and it is normally soldered in and not removable or upgradeable.

◀◀ See "Cache Memory: SRAM," p. 461.

Main memory typically is installed in the form of dual inline memory modules (DIMMs). Five physical types of main memory modules are used in PC systems today, with several variations of each. The four main types are as follows:

- 168-pin SDRAM DIMMs
- 184-pin DDR DIMMs
- 240-pin DDR2 DIMMs
- 184-pin RDRAM RIMMs

The 168-pin SDRAM DIMMs are found only in older or lower-end systems today. DIMMs have become popular because they are 64 bits wide and can be used as a single bank on a Pentium or higher-class processor that has a 64-bit external data bus.

Double data rate (DDR) SDRAM memory is a newer variation on SDRAM in which data is transferred twice as quickly, and it is the most common type of memory used in recent systems. DDR2 DIMMs came out in new systems during 2004. Note that although both DDR DIMMs and RDRAM RIMMs use 184-pin connectors, their pin configurations are completely different and the modules are *not* interchangeable.

RDRAM RIMMs were used in a limited number of systems from 1999 through 2002 but have since been phased out.

◄◄   See "DDR SDRAM," p. 471.

Systems using a 64-bit CPU bus require two 72-pin SIMMs (32 bits wide each) or a single DIMM (64 bits wide) to make a single bank. Systems using DDR or DDR2 DIMMs can also use dual-channel memory, in which pairs of matching DIMMs enable double the memory throughput.

Memory modules can include an extra bit for each 8 for parity checking or ECC use. If ECC is important to you, be sure your chipset (and motherboard) supports ECC before purchasing the more expensive ECC modules.

◄◄   See "Parity and ECC," p. 500.

Another thing to watch out for is the type of metal on the memory module contacts, especially on motherboards using SIMMs. SIMMs were widely available with either tin- or gold-plated contacts. Although it might seem that gold-plated contacts are better (they are), you should not use them in all systems. You should instead always match the type of plating on the module contacts to what is also used on the socket contacts. In other words, if the motherboard sockets have tin-plated contacts, you must use modules with tin-plated contacts and likewise must match gold to gold. Most motherboards using SIMMs had sockets with tin-plated contacts, requiring tin-plated SIMMs, whereas virtually all DIMM and RIMM sockets are gold-plated, requiring gold-plated DIMMs and RIMMs.

If you mix dissimilar metals (tin with gold), corrosion on the tin side is rapidly accelerated and tiny electrical currents are generated. The combination of the corrosion and tiny currents causes havoc, and several types of memory problems and errors can occur.

◄◄   See "Gold Versus Tin," p. 497.

For more information on PC memory of all types, see Chapter 6, "Memory."

I/O Ports

Most motherboards today have built-in I/O ports. If these ports are not built in, they must be supplied via a plug-in expansion board that, unfortunately, wastes an expansion slot. The following ports might be included in any new system you assemble:

- PS/2 Keyboard connector (mini-DIN type)
- PS/2 Mouse port (mini-DIN type)
- One or two serial ports
- Parallel port
- Four or more USB ports
- Two or more FireWire ports
- Analog VGA or DVI video connector (integrated video)
- RJ-45 port for 10/100 or 10/100/1000 Ethernet
- Audio/game connectors (speaker, microphone, and MIDI/joystick)
- Two or more parallel ATA ports
- Two or more serial ATA ports
- Floppy controller connector

Some motherboards lack the serial, parallel, keyboard, and mouse ports (referred to as legacy ports), instead relying on USB for those connections. You might want to avoid "legacy-free" motherboards if you still use peripherals with those types of connections. Most motherboards feature integrated sound, and many have optional integrated video as well.

All the integrated ports are supported either directly by the motherboard chipset or by an additional Super I/O chip and additional interface components. Adding the optional video and sound interfaces directly to the motherboard saves both money and the use of an expansion slot, especially important in the less expensive systems sold today.

If these devices are not present on the motherboard, various Super I/O or multi-I/O boards that implement all these ports are available. Again, most of the newer versions of these boards use a single-chip implementation because it is cheaper and more reliable.

◄◄ See "Super I/O Chips," p. 328.

It has become an increasingly popular practice in recent years (especially in Slimline-style systems) to integrate other standard computer functions into the motherboard design, such as video, sound, and even network adapters. The advantages of this practice include freeing up expansion slots that would normally be occupied by separate adapter cards and saving money. The price difference between a motherboard with integrated video and sound and one without would be far less than the cost of good-quality sound and video cards.

The drawback, of course, is that you have little or no choice about the features or quality of the integrated adapters. Integrated components such as these are nearly always of serviceable quality, but they certainly do not push the performance envelope of higher-end expansion cards. Most people who decide to build a system themselves do so because they want optimum performance from every component, which you do not get from integrated video and sound.

Buying a motherboard with integrated adapters, however, does not preclude you from adding expansion devices of the same type. You usually can install a video or sound card into a system with an integrated sound or video adapter without major problems, except that the additional cost of the integrated component is wasted. You also might encounter difficulties with the automated hardware detection routines in operating systems such as Windows 9x/Me/2000/XP detecting the wrong adapter in your system, but you can remedy this by manually identifying the expansion card to the OS. If you want the convenience of integrated video but want to maintain the option of installing a faster AGP (4x or 8x) video card later, look for systems that provide both integrated video and an AGP slot.

◄◄ See "Integrated Video/Motherboard Chipsets," p. 898, "Intel 845 Family," p. 279, and "Intel 865 Family," p. 281.

If four or more USB ports exist, they often are split among two or more buses, with one set of connections on the back of the board and another set as a pin-header connector on the motherboard. A cable then plugs into this connector, enabling you to route the second USB bus port to the front of the PC case. Most newer cases have provisions for front-mounted USB ports in this manner, which makes temporarily connecting devices such as digital cameras or MP3 players for transferring files easier. Even though USB 2.0 support is increasingly common, some systems use a separate USB 2.0 support chip; therefore, some USB ports on such systems support only the older USB 1.1 standard. Also, you might need to enable USB 2.0 support in the system BIOS and load USB 2.0 drivers before USB 2.0 ports will support USB 2.0 devices at top speed.

Note that if your motherboard has integrated devices such as video and sound, you must go into the BIOS Setup to disable these devices if you want to add a card-based replacement device. Check your BIOS Setup menus for an Enable/Disable setting for any integrated devices.

A trend with some newer low-cost systems is the complete elimination of the integrated ports supported by the Super I/O chip or the Super I/O features of recent South Bridge chips. These are called legacy-free PCs and lack any serial ports, parallel ports, and standard keyboard and mouse connections. All external expansion must be done via the USB ports. This means your keyboard, mouse, printer, external modem, and so on must be of the USB type. Some so-called "legacy-free" systems still have PS/2 mouse and keyboard ports but have eliminated serial and parallel ports.

Floppy Disk and Removable Drives

Since the advent of the CD-RW, the floppy disk drive has largely been relegated to a minor role as an alternative system boot device. Usually, today's systems are equipped with a 1.44MB 3 1/2" drive. All systems today are capable of booting from CD, making CD-R (or especially CD-RW discs) a useful high-capacity replacement for floppy or Zip drives.

For additional removable storage, I recommend a CD-RW (CD-rewriteable) or DVD+/-RW drive over the Zip or even LS-120 formats, particularly if you have a limited amount of money. These are now relatively inexpensive, and the media is low priced as well. A CD-RW drive can also write on even more inexpensive CD-R media, and DVD+/-RW drives can use less expensive DVD+/-R media. This provides an easy way to back up or archive up to 700MB (using CD-R/RW) or 4.7GB (using DVD+/-R or RW) of data.

Combo CD-RW/DVD-ROM drives also support DVD movie playback. You can also get a rewriteable DVD+/-RW drive, which can read and write CD-R/RW discs as well as play and record DVDs. The versatility of a DVD+/-RW drive is tremendous because it enables you to work with virtually any type of optical media and lets you store up to 4.7GB on a single rewriteable or recordable DVD. The newest dual-layer recordable drives can store double that amount on dual-layer discs.

Hard Disk Drives

Your system also needs at least one hard disk drive. In most cases, a drive with a minimum capacity of 80GB is recommended, although in some cases you can get away with less for a low-end configuration. High-end systems should have drives of 120GB or higher. One of the cardinal rules of computer shopping is that you can never have too much storage. Buy as much as you can afford, and you'll almost certainly end up filling it anyway.

Tip

If you are an Internet user, one informal method of estimating how much disk space you will need is to go by the speed of your Internet connection. If you have a high-speed link, such as that provided by a DSL connection, a cable modem, or a LAN, you will find that the ease of downloading large amounts of data fills disk drives amazingly quickly. I would recommend at least a 120GB hard drive in these cases. In addition, a removable storage system with a large capacity, such as a CD-RW drive, is also a good idea.

Note that Windows 95 does not support any drives larger than 32GB. You should upgrade to at least Windows 98 or 2000, although at this point I recommend taking the leap to Windows XP.

The most popular hard drive interface for desktop systems is parallel ATA, although serial ATA is becoming more popular.

Some of the newest motherboards now feature RAID-compatible ATA or SATA interfaces. These enable you to install two identical IDE drives (a pair of 80GB drives, for example) and treat them as a single very large and very fast 160GB hard drive.

Most new motherboards now feature Serial ATA (SATA) interfaces, many of which are also RAID compatible. Although the SATA drive interface is technically faster than the fastest ATA interface on the market (ATA-133), real-world SATA drive performance is currently on par with ATA drive performance because both are limited by the throughput of the drive mechanism and media. However, if your motherboard supports SATA, the smaller cable size used for data and the promise of higher performance in the future can still make using SATA drives a better choice.

Most all systems have USB 2.0, and more and more systems have IEEE 1394 (FireWire) built in to the motherboard or added as PCI expansion cards. Although FireWire and USB 2.0–based drives have performance similar to ATA drives and can be moved from system to system, they are not recommended as primary drives. However, they can be used for additional portable storage or system backup.

◀◀ See "ATA RAID," p. 580 and "Serial ATA," p. 553.

Several brands of high-quality hard disk drives are available from which to choose, and most offer similar performance within their price and capacity categories. In fact, you might notice that the capacities and specifications of the various ATA and SATA drives certain manufacturers offer are remarkably similar. This is because a single drive assembly is manufactured for use with both interfaces.

Optical Drives

An optical drive is considered a mandatory item in any PC you construct these days. This is because virtually all software is now distributed on CD-ROM, and some newer titles are on DVD. DVD drives can read CD-ROMs as well as DVD-ROMs, so they are more flexible. Systems can now even boot from CD-ROM drives as long as the system BIOS provides the proper support.

DVD-ROM is a high-density data storage format that uses a CD-size disc to store a great deal more data than a CD-ROM—from 4.7GB to 17GB, depending on the format. These drives can read standard CD-ROMs and audio CDs, as well as the higher-capacity DVD data and video discs.

◀◀ See "DVD," p. 752.

At one time, rewriteable CD and DVD drives were extremely expensive, but today, I recommend that you start with a rewriteable drive. I recommend a minimum of a CD-RW drive with 40x read, 40x write, and 12x rewrite connected to the ATA interface on the motherboard. This results in the best possible performance with the minimum amount of hassle. Combo CD-RW/DVD-ROM drives are available that add DVD read capabilities as fast as 12x to the CD-RW features. For the ultimate combination of features, I recommend DVD+R/RW drives as the best overall optical drives on the market. The DVD+R/RW format is the fastest and most compatible, has the most features, and is designed to support the integrated EasyWrite capability (also called Mt. Rainier) coming in the next Windows release in 2005. This will finally allow the replacement of the floppy drive because CDs and DVDs will be usable for burning right out of the box, with no format time (formatting is done in the background) and no extra packet writing software needed.

If you need compatibility with DVD-R/RW media, most DVD recorders are dual-format and support both the +R/RW as well as the –R/RW format.

Burning your own CDs or DVDs can be a convenient and relatively inexpensive data storage method. Drives advertised as RW handle both RW (rewriteable) and R (record once) media. Note, however, that many older CD-ROM drives can't read CD-RW media (drives labeled as MultiRead can read CD-RW media), whereas virtually all drives can read CD-R discs.

Tip

For the highest reliability when using CD-RW drives, be sure your drive incorporates one of the forms of buffer underrun protection, such as BURN-proof, JustLink, or Waste-Proof. This prevents you from making coasters (unusable discs) when burning CDs.

Input Devices

Obviously, your system needs a keyboard and some type of pointing device, such as a mouse. Different people prefer different types of keyboards, and the "feel" of one type can vary considerably from other types. If possible, I suggest you try a variety of keyboards until you find the type that suits you best. I prefer a stiff action with tactile feedback myself, but others prefer a lighter, quieter touch.

Keyboards and mice are typically available in either PS/2 or USB versions. The PS/2 versions plug in to a 6-pin mini-DIN (PS/2) connector and have traditionally been the most popular. The newest keyboard and mouse interface is USB, driven by the widespread availability of the USB connector and the rise of legacy-free PCs that have only USB ports.

As with any USB device, you must have support in the operating system for USB, and in the case of USB keyboards and mice, your system BIOS must support a function called Legacy USB or USB Keyboard and Mouse if you want to use the USB keyboard or mouse outside the Windows graphical user interface. Most recent BIOSs have this feature. However, to enable you to use your USB keyboard or mouse on both new and older systems, I recommend you look for models that also support the traditional PS/2 ports. This type usually ships with a USB-to-PS/2 adapter. These adapters can also be purchased separately if necessary.

If you prefer a wireless keyboard or mouse, be sure to choose one that uses RF (radio) instead of IR (infrared) signaling, and get one that can use a single transceiver for both the keyboard and mouse. RF signaling might use either short-range proprietary frequencies or the industry-standard Bluetooth wireless network. Bluetooth devices are preferable if you want to use the keyboard or mouse with a wide variety of devices or at distances greater than 6 feet or so from the system.

◄◄   See "Keyboards," p. 1016.

◄◄   See "Keyboard Technology," p. 1022.

Tip

You might be tempted to skimp on your keyboard and mouse to save a few dollars. Don't! You do all your interacting with your new PC through these devices, and cheap ones make their presence known every time you use your system. I insist on high-quality mechanical switch–type keyboards on all my systems.

The Universal Serial Bus (USB) is rendering the standard I/O ports on the PC obsolete. Essentially, USB brings PnP support to external peripherals by enabling you to plug up to 127 devices into a single port supporting data transfer rates up to 12Mbps with USB 1.1 or 480Mbps (60MBps) with USB 2.0. Typically, you plug a USB hub into a port integrated into the motherboard and then plug other devices into that. Virtually all current motherboards support USB, and you can update a USB 1.1–only system to USB 2.0 with an add-on card.

◄◄   See "USB and IEEE 1394 (i.LINK) FireWire," p. 982.

There are virtually no limits to the types of devices available for USB. Modems, keyboards, mice, CD-ROM drives, speakers, joysticks, hard drives, tape drives, floppy drives, scanners, cameras, MP3 players, and printers are just some of the devices available. However, before you start buying all USB peripherals for your new system, be aware that performance problems can occur with some devices if used on a single bus, and sometimes compatibility problems can occur as well. USB 2.0 (also called High-Speed USB) solves these problems, so you should be sure that any new systems you buy or build include USB 2.0 ports.

Video Card and Display

You need a video adapter and a monitor or display to complete your system. Numerous choices are available in this area, but the most important piece of advice I have to give is to choose a good monitor. The display is your main interface to the system and can be the cause of many hours of either pain or pleasure, depending on which monitor you choose.

I usually recommend a minimum of a 17" CRT display these days (equivalent to a 15" LCD display). Anything smaller can't acceptably display a 1,024×768 pixel resolution. If you opt for a 15" or smaller CRT display, you might find that the maximum tolerable resolution is 800×600. This might be confusing because many 15" monitors are capable of displaying 1,024×768 resolution or even higher, but the characters and features are so small onscreen at that resolution that excessive eyestrain and headaches are often the result; the display often is blurry when a monitor is run at its maximum resolution. If you spend a lot of time in front of your system and want to work in the higher screen resolutions, a 17" CRT display should be considered mandatory. If you can afford it, I recommend a 19" CRT display; they work even better at the higher resolutions and have come down in price considerably from previous years. Look for CRT displays with lower dot-pitch (0.28dpi or less), which indicates the size and spacing of dots in the CRT mask. Lower means higher resolution and a clearer picture.

If your desk space is limited and you can afford it, consider the wide variety of flat-screen LCD panels now available (a 15" LCD panel is about equal in viewable area to a 17" CRT). In most cases, they attach to the normal VGA analog port, but the most current models work with the DVI connector available on some of the newest video cards. LCD panels are an excellent choice if you always use the native resolution (typically 1024×768 on 15" displays or 1280×1024 on 17" displays), but if you need to change resolutions (for previewing Web page designs or game playing), CRTs are better.

Your video card and monitor should be compatible in terms of refresh rate. The minimum refresh rate for a solid, nonflickering CRT display is 70Hz–72Hz (the higher, the better). If your new video card can display 16 million colors at a resolution of 1,024×768 and a refresh rate of 76Hz, but your monitor's maximum refresh rate at 1,024×768 is 56Hz, you can't use the video card to its maximum potential. Configuring a video adapter to deliver signals the monitor can't support is one of the few software configuration processes that can physically damage the system hardware. Pushing a monitor beyond its capabilities can cause it irreparable harm. Note that LCD displays don't flicker, regardless of the refresh rate.

Video adapters in recent years have become standardized on the accelerated graphics port (AGP) interface, although many older systems used PCI-based video cards. You might need to use a PCI video card if you are adding a secondary video adapter to your system to run a second monitor and prefer not to replace your primary video card. Windows 98, Me, 2000, and XP support this feature, and it can be very useful for some applications. Newer cards are available in PCI Express versions to support the high-speed PCI Express bus found in the latest systems.

If you are into gaming, you need one of the high-performance 3D video cards currently available. Modern games are very video-intensive, so be sure to check the Web sites, manuals, and even game boxes for the games you play to see which cards they recommend. Although early 3D cards connected to the standard 2D graphics card, this design is now obsolete. High-performance 3D cards based on chipsets from NVIDIA and ATI provide both fast 2D graphics and excellent 3D performance.

◀◀ See "Accelerated Graphics Port," p. 364.

◀◀ See "3D Graphics Accelerators," p. 916.

If you are adding a video card to a newly constructed system, the video card should be inserted into the AGP slot. Most current motherboards support AGP4X, AGP Pro, or AGP8X. I recommend video cards with at least 32MB of memory if you don't play 3D games or are a casual gamer; 128MB or more is a necessity if you play a lot of 3D games. Look for a TV-out connector if you want to attach your system to a big-screen TV for presentations or watching DVD movies. If you want to add TV viewing and recording features to your system, consider a video card with video capture and editing features such as the All-in-Wonder series from ATI or NVIDIA-based systems featuring the Personal Cinema TV tuner.

If you are installing a newer AGP video card as an upgrade to your current system, you can remove the current video card and replace it with any video card that supports the motherboard's AGP standard. You can also replace an existing PCI video card with another PCI video card if there is no AGP slot, but you should consider a motherboard upgrade instead to provide an AGP slot for faster video.

Many motherboards with onboard video also have an AGP slot; if your motherboard has one, you can insert an AGP card into this slot. The onboard video should be automatically disabled in most cases. If the motherboard has only PCI slots, you might want to consider upgrading to a motherboard that has an AGP slot instead.

If you are replacing an existing video card, be sure to check the chipset on the video card against the list of video card chipsets provided in the section "3D Chipsets" in Chapter 15, "Video Hardware." You should avoid chipsets marked as OLD if you are looking for acceptable performance and support for the latest versions of Windows.

Audio Hardware

You need a motherboard with integrated audio or a sound card and a set of external speakers for any system that you want to be multimedia capable. Most systems today, even those without integrated video, now feature integrated audio, but you might prefer to add a high-quality sound card if you want the best possible sound quality for DVD playback or audio capture and editing. Almost any motherboard-integrated audio system and sound card on the market today are compatible with both the Creative Labs Sound Blaster series and Windows DirectX and other sound APIs. Although a few stores still stock ISA sound cards, for best performance, I recommend you get a PCI-based sound card. There can be some problems with support for older DOS-based games with some of the new cards, but most of these issues have been addressed by special drivers for the newer cards.

Speakers designed for use with PCs range from tiny, underpowered devices to large audiophile systems. Many of the top manufacturers of stereo speakers now produce speaker systems for PCs. Some include subwoofers or even a full Dolby 5.1, 6.1, or 7.1 surround sound implementation.

Accessories

Apart from the major components, you need several other accessories to complete your system. These are the small parts that can make the assembly process a pleasure or a chore. If you are purchasing your system components from mail-order sources, you should make a complete list of all the parts you need, right down to the last cable and screw, and be sure you have everything before you begin the assembly process. It is excruciating to have to wait several days with a half-assembled system for the delivery of a forgotten part.

Heatsinks/Cooling Fans

Most of today's faster processors produce a lot of heat, and this heat has to be dissipated so your system doesn't operate intermittently or even fail completely. Heatsinks are available in two main types: passive and active.

Passive heatsinks are simply finned chunks of metal (usually aluminum or copper) that are clipped or glued to the top of the processor. They act as a radiator and, in effect, give the processor more surface area to dissipate the heat. *Active* heatsinks are required by many processors today because of their higher capacity and smaller space requirements. Often you have no control over which heatsink you use because it comes already attached to the processor. If you have to attach it yourself, you should use a thermal transfer grease or sticky tape to fill any air gaps between the heatsink and the processor. This allows for maximum heat transfer and the best efficiency.

An active heatsink includes a built-in fan. These can offer greater cooling capacity than the passive types, and some processors—especially "boxed" processors from Intel and AMD—are sold with the heatsink and fan included. OEM processors don't include a heatsink from the processor manufacturer, but most vendors who sell them add an aftermarket heatsink and fan to the package; often, aftermarket heatsinks and fans provide significantly better cooling than those shipped with boxed processors. Thus, an OEM processor is a better candidate for overclocking. Note that all modern heatsinks require a thermal interface material (usually grease or paste) be applied to the base of the heatsink before installation.

Another consideration for cooling is with the case. The fan in the power supply and the one on the CPU heatsink often are not enough for a modern high-performance system. I recommend you get a case that includes at least one additional cooling fan. This is typically mounted in the rear of the chassis, directing additional air out the back. Some cases include an extra fan in the front or side cover as well.

If you are upgrading an existing system, several companies make fan assemblies that insert into a drive bay for additional cooling. They take the place of a 5 1/4" drive and take air in through the front bezel, directing it back into the case. Bay-mounted fans are an especially good idea if you are using the 10,000rpm or faster SCSI drives on the market because they run extremely hot. There are even fan assemblies mounted on cards that blow air out the rear of the case. Keep in mind that it is best to keep the interior of the PC below 100°F; anything over 110° dramatically reduces component life and leads to stability problems.

Cables

PC systems need many different cables to hook up everything. These can include power cables or adapters, disk drive cables, internal or external CD-ROM cables, and many others. Frequently, the motherboard includes the cables for any of the internal ports, such as floppy or hard drives. Other external devices you purchase come with included cables, but in some cases, they aren't supplied. The Vendor List on the disc included with the book contains contact information for several cable and small parts suppliers that can get you the cables or other parts you need to complete your system.

If you build your system using all OEM (what the industry calls *white box*) components, be aware that these sometimes don't include the accessories, such as cables, software, and additional documentation, that you would get with a boxed-retail version of the same component.

Hardware

You might need screws, standoffs, mounting rails (if your case requires them), and other miscellaneous hardware to assemble your system. Most of these parts are included with the case or your other system components. This is especially true of any card or disk drive brackets or screws. When you purchase a component such as a hard drive, some vendors offer you the option of purchasing the bare drive or a kit containing the required cables and mounting hardware for the device. Most of the time bare drives don't include any additional hardware, but you might not need it anyway if the mounting hardware comes with your case. Even so, spending the few additional dollars for the complete drive kit is rarely a waste of money. Even if you're left with some extra bits and pieces after assembling your system, they will probably come in handy someday.

In situations in which you need other hardware not included with your system components, you can consult the Vendor List for suppliers of small parts and hardware necessary to get your system operational.

Hardware and Software Resources

When you are planning to build a system, it is important to consider how all your selected components will work together and how the software you run must support them. It is not enough to be sure that you have sufficient slots on the motherboard for all your expansion cards and enough bays in the case for all your drives. You must also consider the resources required for all the components.

For example, if you are planning to use USB 2.0 devices, you need to know whether your new motherboard has USB 2.0 ports built in or whether you will need to add a card to achieve USB 2.0 compatibility. With the many changes in processor speed and voltage, you need to verify that the processor and motherboard combination you prefer will work correctly.

Essentially, you should completely configure the system before you begin ordering any parts. Planning a system to this level of detail can be a lot of work, which is one reason the vast majority of PCs are prebuilt.

Tip

In most cases, you can download or view online the manuals for the motherboard, processor, and other major components before you purchase them. Check the component vendors' Web sites for these manuals and technical notes and read them carefully. You will need Adobe Acrobat Reader, available free from **www.adobe.com**, to view most online manuals.

Another consideration is the operating system and other software you will need. Prebuilt systems nearly always arrive with the operating system installed, but when you build your own, you must be prepared with a copy of your selected operating system—including a system disk so you can boot the system the first time. Because nearly any operating system in use today is distributed on CD-ROM, you must get your computer to recognize the CD-ROM drive before you can install an operating system. To make this process simpler, you should create a bootable CD. Note that the OEM versions of Windows 98 and later are bootable, but the retail upgrade versions of Windows 98 and Windows Me aren't. You can boot from both OEM and upgrade versions of Windows 2000 and Windows XP.

◄◄   See "Making a Bootable CD/DVD for Emergencies," p. 825.

The operating system you select for your new computer is another important decision. You must be certain that the OS supports all the hardware you've selected, which can occasionally be a difficult task. For example, you will need Windows 98 or later to properly support USB devices in your system.

Note

Although Windows 98 has been a long-time favorite of system builders, Microsoft no longer sells licenses for it to system builders. Microsoft plans to provide online operating system and driver updates through Windows Update for Windows 98 until mid-2005 and online support until mid-2006. You might prefer to use a newer version of Windows or a non-Windows operating system such as Linux if you want support for a longer period of time.

Windows 98 and later come on bootable CD-ROMs if you get what is called the OEM version of the operating system. The so-called retail or upgrade editions often are restricted, aren't bootable in their Windows 9x/Me versions, and might also search for preexisting files or operating systems before they will load. For this reason, you should keep the CD-ROM of your previous operating system so you can use it for verification during installation of a new version. Because Microsoft doesn't allow OEM versions of its operating systems to be sold separately, be sure you get an OEM edition of whatever operating system you will be running when you buy your hardware. The terms of the Microsoft dealer (or system builder) agreement allow dealers to sell the OS only with hardware. At one time you needed to buy a complete PC, a motherboard, or a hard disk to get an OEM version of the operating system, but you can now buy any hardware—even a device as inexpensive as a case fan or mouse—and qualify to buy the OEM version. No matter what, be sure you get the original OEM version on CD-ROM.

Tip

If you don't have the OEM version of your OS, or the system you are assembling does not support booting from CD (called El Torito support after the Phoenix-created standard), you must create a boot floppy with CD-ROM drivers. Windows 98 and later include a disk with a set of universal CD-ROM drivers that work for most systems; for Windows 95 and older operating systems, you must either borrow a Windows 98 or later startup disk or create your own bootable floppy with the correct drivers.

Drivers for specific hardware components, such as your motherboard chipset, might also be a problem. It is a good idea to gather all the latest driver revisions for your hardware, as well as BIOS flashes, firmware updates, and other software components, and have them available when you begin the assembly process.

System Assembly and Disassembly

Actually assembling the system is easy after you have lined up all the components. In fact, you will find the parts procurement phase the most lengthy and trying of the entire experience. Completing the system is basically a matter of screwing everything together, plugging in all the cables and connectors, and configuring everything to operate properly together.

In short order, you will find out whether your system operates as you had planned or whether some incompatibilities exist between some of the components. Be careful and pay attention to how you install all your components. It is rare that a newly assembled system operates perfectly the first time, even for people who are somewhat experienced. It is very easy to forget a jumper, switch, or cable connection that later causes problems in system operation. Most people's first reaction when problems occur is to blame defective hardware, but that is usually not the source. The problem can typically be traced to some missed step or error made in the assembly process.

Above all, the most crucial rule of assembling your own system is to save every piece of documentation and software that comes with every component in your system. This material can be indispensable in troubleshooting problems you encounter during the assembly process or later. You should also retain all the packing materials used to ship mail-order components to you until you are certain they will not have to be returned.

Assembly Preparation

The process of physically assembling a PC requires only a few basic tools: a 1/4" nut driver or Phillips-head screwdriver for the external screws that hold the cover in place and a 3/16" nut driver or Phillips-head screwdriver for all the other screws. Needle-nose pliers can also help in removing motherboard standoffs, jumpers, and stubborn cable connectors. Because of marketplace standardization, only a couple types and sizes of screws (with a few exceptions) are used to hold a system together. Also, the physical arrangement of the major components is similar even among different manufacturers. Figure 22.2 shows the components that go into a typical system, and Figure 22.3 shows the system with those components assembled. Note that the components shown here are for a standard PC. Your final component list might vary.

You'll find more information on tools used to work on PCs in Chapter 24, "PC Diagnostics, Testing, and Maintenance."

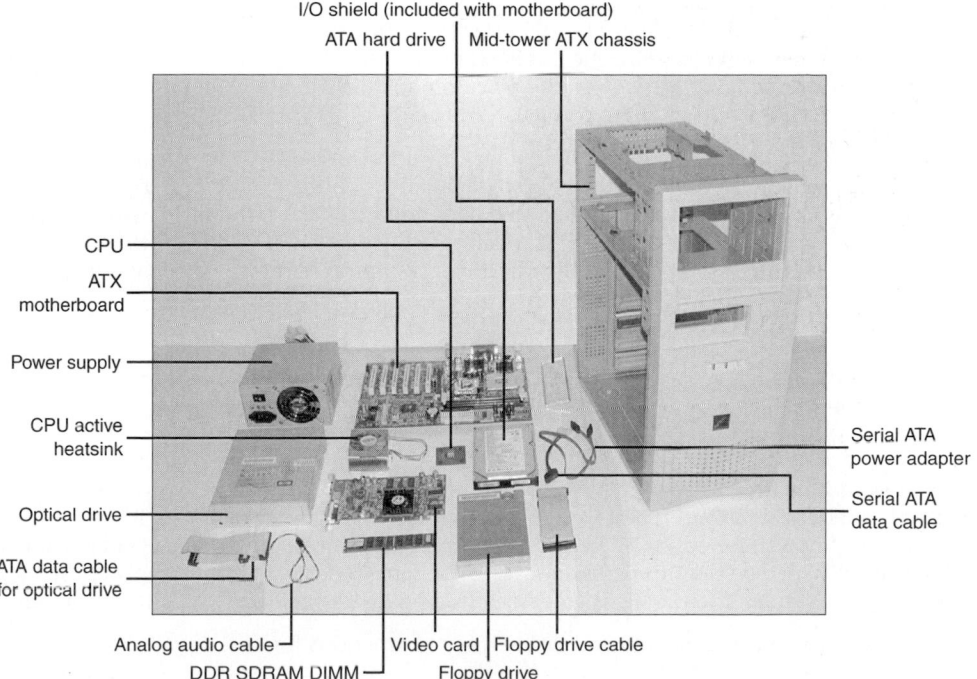

Figure 22.2 Components used in building a typical PC. The case and drive screws and the standoffs are not shown but are usually provided with the case and drives.

Figure 22.3 A completed system using components similar to those shown in Figure 22.2.

Other tools you'll need are software related. You'll need the master operating system CD-ROM, and if your particular CD-ROM version isn't bootable or your system is older and doesn't support booting from CD, you'll also need an operating system startup floppy disk with CD-ROM drivers installed. This way, your system will recognize the CD-ROM drive and enable you to install the operating system from it. Newer operating systems often come on bootable CDs, but sometimes only the OEM (and not retail) versions of the OS are configured that way.

The Windows 98 and later versions' startup floppies include generic ATAPI and SCSI CD-ROM drivers on them, enabling virtually all CD-ROMs to be recognized after booting from them. If you are installing Windows 95 or some other operating system that does not include a startup disk with CD-ROM drivers already installed, you can either use a Win98 or later startup disk or take your existing startup disk and install the CD-ROM drivers that came with your drive. That procedure is covered later in this chapter.

The following sections cover the assembly and disassembly procedure:

- Case or cover assembly
- Power supply
- Adapter boards
- Motherboard
- Disk drives

Later, you learn how to install and remove these components for several types of systems. With regard to assembly and disassembly, it is best to consider each system by the type of case it uses. All systems that have AT-type cases, for example, are assembled and disassembled in much the same manner. Tower cases are basically AT-type cases turned sideways, so the same basic instructions apply. Most Slimline and XT-style cases are similar; these systems are assembled and disassembled in much the same way.

The following section lists assembly and disassembly instructions for several case types.

ESD Protection

One issue you must be aware of is electrostatic discharge (ESD) protection. Another is recording the configuration of the system with regard to the physical aspects of the system (such as jumper or switch settings and cable orientations) and the logical configuration of the system (especially in terms of elements such as CMOS settings).

When you are working on the internal components of a computer, you must take the necessary precautions to prevent accidental static discharges to the components. At any time, your body can hold a large static voltage charge that can easily damage components of your system. Before I ever put my hands into an open system, I first touch a grounded portion of the chassis, such as the power supply case. This action serves to equalize the electrical charges the device and my body might be carrying. Be sure the power supply is unplugged during all phases of the assembly process. Some will claim that you should leave the system plugged in to provide an earth ground through the power cord and outlet, but that is unnecessary. If you leave the system plugged in, you open yourself up to other problems, such as accidentally turning it on or leaving it on when installing a board or device, which can damage the motherboard or other devices.

Caution

Also note that power supplies used in many systems today deliver a +5V current to the motherboard continuously—that is, whenever they are plugged in. Bottom line: Be sure any system you are working on is completely unplugged from the wall outlet.

High-end workbenches at repair facilities have the entire bench grounded, so it's not as big of a problem; however, you need something to be a good ground source to prevent a current from building up in you.

A more sophisticated way to equalize the charges between you and any of the system components is to use an ESD protection kit. These kits consist of a wrist strap and mat, with ground wires for attachment to the system chassis. When you are going to work on a system, you place the mat next to or partially below the system unit. Next, you clip the ground wire to both the mat and the system's chassis, tying the grounds together. You then put on the wrist strap and attach that wire to a ground. Because the mat and system chassis are already wired together, you can attach the wrist-strap wire to the system chassis or to the mat. If you are using a wrist strap without a mat, clip the wrist-strap wire to the system chassis. When clipping these wires to the chassis, be sure to use an area that is free of paint so a good ground contact can be achieved. This setup ensures that any electrical charges are carried equally by you and any of the components in the system, preventing the sudden flow of static electricity that can damage the circuits.

As you install or remove disk drives; adapter cards; and especially delicate items such as the entire motherboard, SIMMs, or processors, you should place these components on the static mat. Sometimes people put the system unit on top of the mat, but the unit should be alongside the mat so you have room to lay out all the components as you work with them. If you are going to remove the motherboard from a system, be sure you leave enough room for it on the mat.

If you do not have such a mat, place the removed circuits and devices on a clean desk or table. Always pick up a loose adapter card by the metal bracket used to secure the card to the system. This bracket is tied into the ground circuitry of the card, so by touching the bracket first, you prevent a discharge from damaging the components of the card. If the circuit board has no metal bracket (a motherboard, for example), handle the board carefully by the edges, and try not to touch any of the connectors or components. If you don't have proper ESD equipment such as a wrist strap or mat, be sure to periodically touch the chassis while working inside the system to equalize any charge you might have built up.

Caution

Some people recommend placing loose circuit boards and chips on sheets of aluminum foil. I absolutely *do not recommend* this procedure because it can actually result in an explosion! Many motherboards, adapter cards, and other circuit boards today have built-in lithium or NiCad batteries. These batteries react violently when they are shorted out, which is exactly what you would be doing by placing such a board on a piece of aluminum foil. The batteries will quickly overheat and possibly explode like a large firecracker (with dangerous shrapnel). Because you will not always be able to tell whether a board has a battery built into it somewhere, the safest practice is to never place any board on any conductive metal surface. Instead, use cardboard or newspapers if you don't have an antistatic work mat or sufficient antistatic bags.

Recording Physical Configuration

While you are assembling a system, you should record all the physical settings and configurations of each component, including jumper and switch settings, cable orientations and placement, ground wire locations, and even adapter board placement. Keep a notebook handy for recording these items, and write down all the settings. See Chapter 4 for more information on motherboard connector, jumper, and other component locations. Figure 22.4 shows a typical motherboard jumper.

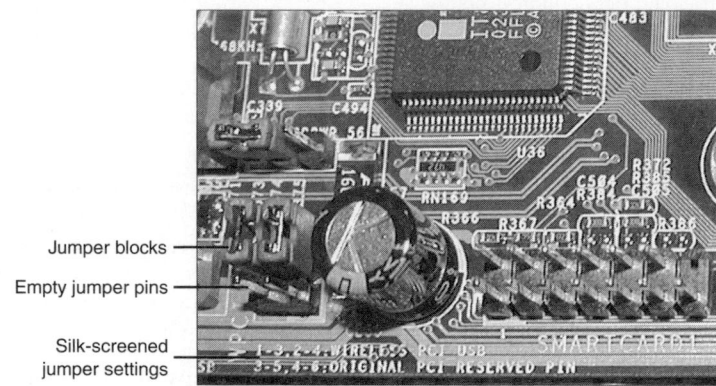

Jumper blocks

Empty jumper pins

Silk-screened
jumper settings

Figure 22.4 Motherboard jumpers often are silk-screened on the motherboard, as shown here; the jumper position shown here is used to configure the motherboard's PCI and USB interface.

It is especially important to record all the jumper and switch settings on the motherboard, as well as those on any card you install in the system (cards seldom use jumpers or switches today, but some motherboards still do). If you accidentally disturb these jumpers or switches, you will know how they were originally set. This knowledge is very important if you do not have all the documentation for the system handy. Even if you do, undocumented jumpers and switches often do not appear in the manuals but must be set a certain way for the item to function. Also, record all cable orientations. Most name-brand systems use cables and connectors that are keyed so that they can't be plugged in backward, but some generic PCs do not have this added feature. You should mark or record what each cable was plugged into and its proper orientation. Ribbon cables usually have an odd-colored (red, green, blue, or black) wire at one end that indicates pin 1. There might also be a mark on the connector, such as a triangle or even the number 1. The devices the cables are plugged into are also marked in some way to indicate the orientation of pin 1. Often, a dot appears next to the pin 1 side of the connector, or a 1 or other mark might appear.

Although cable orientation and placement seem to be very simple, we rarely get through the entire course of my PC troubleshooting seminars without at least one group of people having cable-connection problems. Fortunately, in most cases (except power cables), plugging any of the ribbon cables inside the system backward doesn't cause any permanent damage.

Power and battery connections on pre-ATX systems are exceptions; plugging them in backward in most cases causes damage. In fact, plugging the motherboard power connectors in backward or in the wrong plug location on these older systems puts 12V where only 5V should be—a situation that can cause components of the board to violently explode. I know of several people who have facial scars caused by shrapnel from components that exploded because of improper power supply connections! As a precaution, I always turn my face away from the system when I power it on for the first time. If you are using an ATX board and power supply, there is little chance of this happening because of the superior type of power connector used *unless* you mix a September 1998 or newer Dell power supply or motherboard with a standard motherboard or power supply.

Plugging in the CMOS battery backward can damage the CMOS chip, which usually is soldered into the motherboard; in such a case, the motherboard must be replaced.

Finally, you should record miscellaneous items such as the placement of any ground wires, adapter cards, and anything else that you might have difficulty remembering later. Some configurations and setups might be particular about the slots in which the adapter cards are located, so you should put everything back exactly the way it was originally.

Motherboard Installation

When you are installing your system's motherboard, unpack the motherboard and check to ensure you have everything that should be included. If you purchase a new board, you typically get at least the motherboard, some I/O cables, and a manual. If you order the motherboard with a processor or memory, it is usually installed on the board for you but might also be included separately. Some board kits include an antistatic wrist strap to help prevent damage due to static electricity when installing the board.

Installing the CPU and Heatsink

Before your new motherboard is installed, you should install the processor and memory. This usually is much easier to do before the board is installed in the chassis. Some motherboards have jumpers that control both the CPU speed and the voltage supplied to it. If these are set incorrectly, the system might not operate at all, might operate erratically, or might possibly even damage the CPU. If you have any questions about the proper settings, contact the vendor who sold you the board before making any jumper changes.

◀◀ See "CPU Operating Voltages," p. 102.

Most processors today run hot enough to require some form of heatsink to dissipate heat from the processor. To install the processor and heatsink, use the following procedure:

1. Take the new motherboard out of the antistatic bag it was supplied in and set it on the bag or the antistatic mat, if you have one.

2. Install the processor. There are two procedures—one for socketed processors and the other for slot-based processors. Slot-based processors are outdated, but you might need to install one in an older system.

   Follow the appropriate instructions for the type you are installing:

   - *For socketed processors, the procedure is as follows:* Find pin 1 on the processor; it usually is denoted by a corner of the chip that is marked by a dot or bevel. Next, find the corresponding pin 1 of the ZIF socket for the CPU on the motherboard; it also is usually marked on the board or with a bevel in one corner of the socket. Be sure the pins on the processor are straight and not bent; if they are bent, the chip won't insert properly into the socket. If necessary, use small needle-nose pliers or a hemostat to carefully straighten any pins. Don't bend them too much—they might break off, ruining the chip. Insert the CPU into the ZIF socket by lifting the release lever until it is vertical. Then, align the pins on the processor with the holes in the socket and drop it down into place. If the processor does not seem to want to drop in all the way, remove it to check for proper alignment and any possibly bent pins. When the processor is fully seated in the socket, push the locking lever on the socket down until it latches to secure the processor (see Figure 22.5).

   - *For slot-based processors, the procedure is different.* You need the processor, the universal retention mechanism brackets with included fasteners, and the heatsink supports. Most slot-based processors come with either an active or a passive heatsink already installed. Start by positioning the two universal retention mechanism brackets on either side of the processor slot so that the holes in the brackets line up with the holes in the motherboard (see Figure 22.6). Push the included fasteners through the mounting holes in the retention bracket and the motherboard until you feel them snap into place. Insert the fastener retainer pins through the holes in the fastener to lock them into place. Then, slide the processor/heatsink down between the brackets until it is firmly seated in the slot. The latches on the top sides of the processor lock into place when the processor is fully seated. Install the heatsink supports into the holes provided in the motherboard and processor.

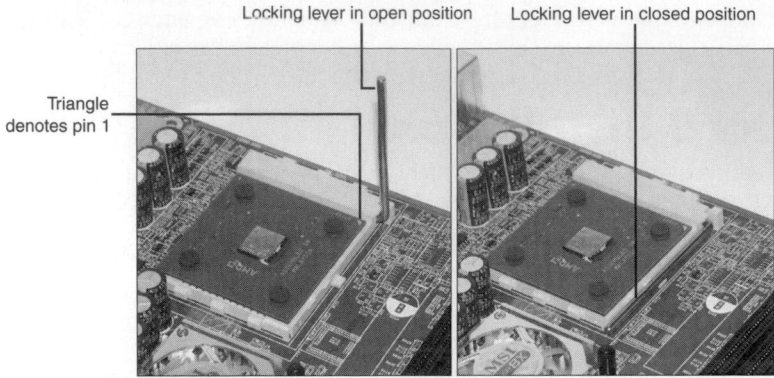

Figure 22.5 The lever on a ZIF socket locks the processor into the socket when lowered. Note the triangle on the corner of the processor, denoting pin 1.

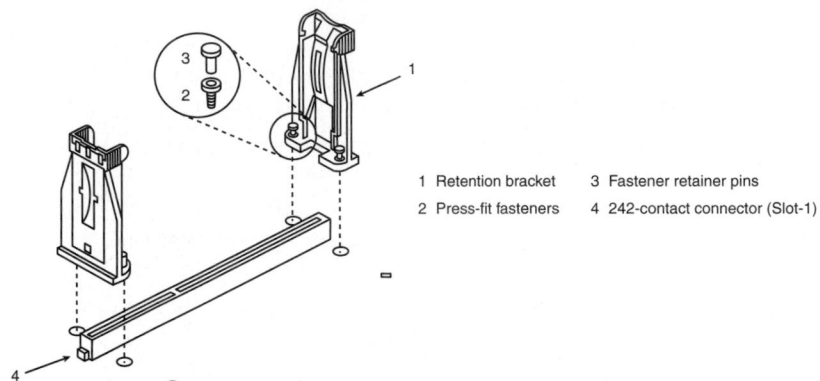

1 Retention bracket   3 Fastener retainer pins
2 Press-fit fasteners   4 242-contact connector (Slot-1)

Figure 22.6 Universal retention mechanism for slot-based processors. *Illustration used by permission of Intel Corporation.*

Most heatsinks clip to the socket with one or more retainer clips (see Figure 22.7). Be careful when attaching the clip to the socket; you don't want it to scrape against the motherboard, which can damage circuit traces or components. You also need to keep the heatsink steady on the chip while attaching the clips, so do not move, tilt, or slide the heatsink while you attach it. Most heatsinks have a preapplied thermal pad; otherwise, you will need to put a dab of heatsink thermal transfer compound (normally a white- or silver-colored grease) on the CPU before installing the heatsink. This prevents any air gaps and enables the heatsink to work more effi- ciently. If the CPU has an active heatsink (with a fan), plug the fan power connector into one of the fan connectors supplied on the motherboard (see Figure 22.8). Optionally, some heatsinks use a disk drive power connector for fan power.

3. Refer to the motherboard manufacturer's manual to set the jumpers, if any, to match the CPU you are going to install. Look for the diagram of the motherboard to find the jumper location, and look for the tables for the correct settings for your CPU. If the CPU supplied was already installed on the motherboard, the jumpers should already be correctly set for you, but it is still a good idea to check them.

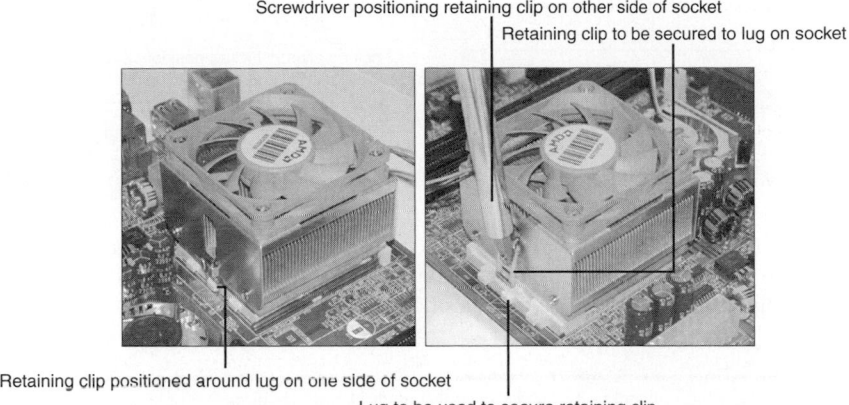

Screwdriver positioning retaining clip on other side of socket

Retaining clip to be secured to lug on socket

Retaining clip positioned around lug on one side of socket

Lug to be used to secure retaining clip

Figure 22.7 Attaching the heatsink to a socketed processor. The retaining clip is spring-loaded, so it must be positioned with a screwdriver or similar tool that can push the clip down and swing it into place.

Heatsink fan power connector

Figure 22.8 Attaching the heatsink fan power connector to the motherboard.

Installing Memory Modules

To function, the motherboard must have memory installed on it. Modern motherboards use either DIMMs or RIMMs. Depending on the module type, it will have a specific method of sliding into and clipping to the sockets. Usually, you install modules in the lowest-numbered sockets or banks first. Note that some boards require modules to be installed in pairs; this is most common with boards that use dual-channel RDRAM and systems using the Intel 865 and 875 dual-channel DDR SDRAM chipsets. Consult the motherboard documentation for more information on which sockets to use first and in what order and how to install the specific modules the board uses.

◀◀   See "Memory Banks," p. 496.

Memory modules frequently are keyed to the sockets by a notch on the side or bottom, so they can go in only one way. Figure 22.9 shows how to install a DIMM or RIMM; more detailed instructions for installing memory modules can be found in Chapter 6.

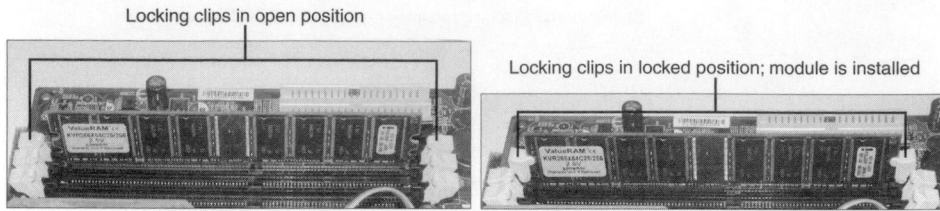

Figure 22.9   Installing the memory modules. Make sure the locking clips are open on both sides of the module before the module is inserted into the memory socket (top). Press down on the module until the module locking clips swing up into the locked position (bottom).

Caution

Be careful not to damage the connector. If you damage the motherboard memory connector, you could be facing an expensive repair. Never force the module; it should come out easily. If it doesn't, you are doing something wrong.

Mounting the New Motherboard in the Case

The motherboard attaches to the case with one or more screws and often several plastic standoffs. If you are using a new case, you might have to attach one or more metal spacers or plastic standoffs in the proper holes before you can install the motherboard. Use the following procedure to install the new motherboard in the case:

1. Find the holes in the new motherboard for the metal spacers and plastic standoffs. You should use metal spacers wherever there is a ring of solder around the hole. Use plastic standoffs where there is no ring of solder (see Figure 22.10).

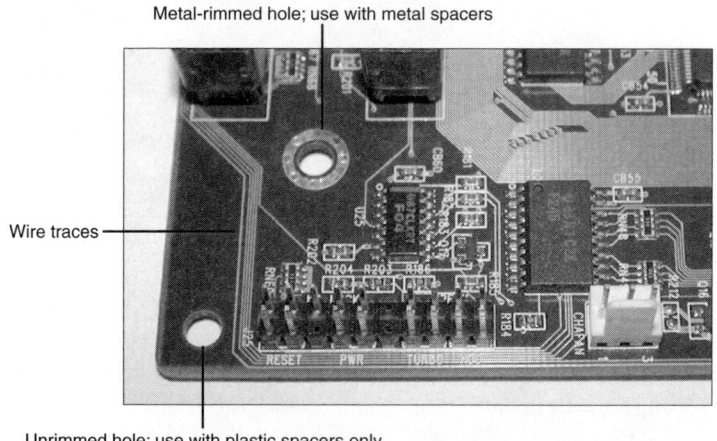

Figure 22.10   The corner of a typical motherboard. Be sure not to damage the wire traces when attaching the motherboard to the case.

2. Screw any metal spacers into the new case in the proper positions to align with the screw holes in the motherboard (see Figure 22.11).

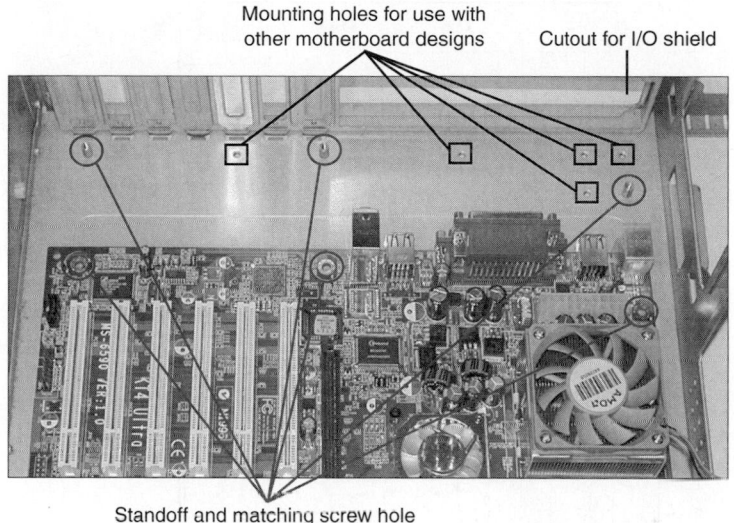

Figure 22.11   Make sure the standoffs align with the holes in the motherboard. Note that this chassis has a variety of mounting holes so you can adjust the position of the standoffs to match various motherboard designs.

3. Most motherboards today attach directly to the chassis or to a removable motherboard tray with screws that thread into brass standoffs attached to the chassis or tray. Figure 22.12 shows three types of standoffs, including two brass types and one plastic. One screws directly to the chassis or tray, whereas the others attach to the motherboard and then slide into notches in the case or tray.

Figure 22.12   Various types of motherboard standoffs, used to support the board when installed in the chassis or motherboard tray.

If the board uses the type of standoff that fits into slots in the chassis or tray, rather than screwing directly in, insert the standoffs directly into the new motherboard from underneath until they snap into place (see Figure 22.13). Or attach them to the board with a screw if necessary. Figure 22.14 shows a typical ATX-style motherboard with arrows indicating the typical location of the screw holes for mounting the motherboard to the case (see your motherboard manual for the exact location of these screw holes).

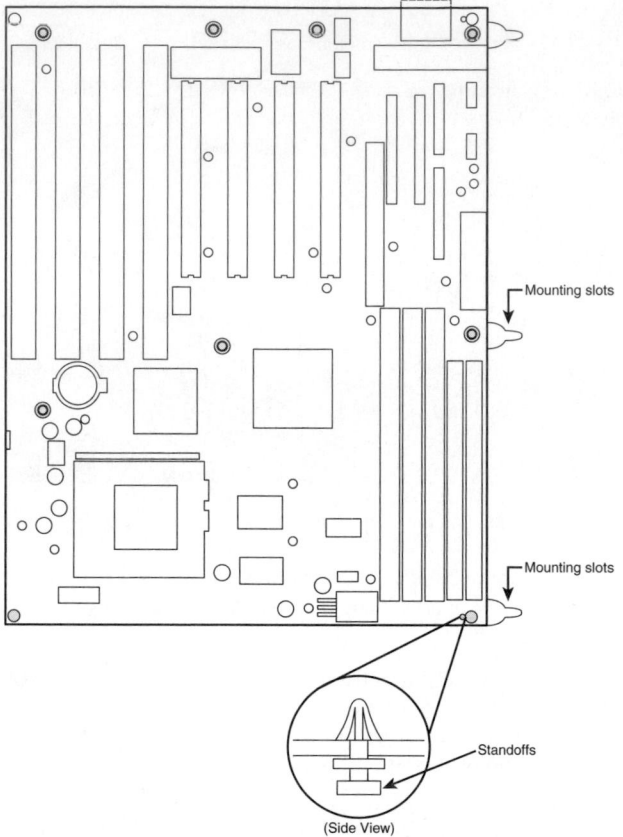

Figure 22.13 Insert standoffs into their mounting slots by sliding a Baby-AT motherboard into place after attaching standoffs.

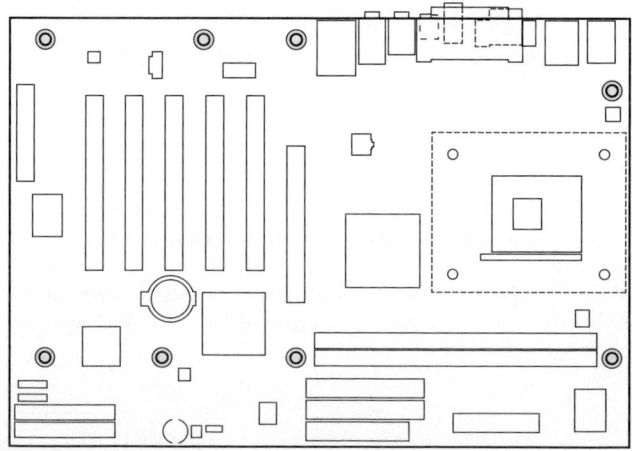

Figure 22.14 Mounting screw holes in a typical ATX motherboard. The highlighted circles mark the screw holes for mounting the motherboard to the case.

After you have inserted the standoffs and lined them up with the screw holes on the mother-board, carefully attach the screws to secure the motherboard to the motherboard tray or case, depending on your chassis design. Figure 22.15 shows a motherboard attached to a tray. Note the use of the thumb and forefinger to stabilize the screwdriver tip. This prevents accidental slippage of the screwdriver tip off of the screw, which is one of the biggest causes of new board failures.

Figure 22.15   Attaching a motherboard to the motherboard tray. *Motherboard courtesy of Intel Corporation.*

4. Install the I/O shield (if used) into the chassis by snapping it into place (see Figure 22.16).

Figure 22.16   The I/O shield after being snapped into place in the chassis.

5. Install the new motherboard into the case or motherboard tray. Either screw it directly to the standoffs or slide the standoffs already attached to the board by sliding the entire board into position. Be sure you align the I/O shield with the case or the ports on the back of the board with the I/O shield already in the case. Often, you will have to set the board into the case and slide it side-ways to engage the standoffs into the slots in the case. When the board is in the proper position, the screw holes in the board should be aligned with all the metal spacers or screw holes in the case. Figure 22.17 shows a motherboard attached to a motherboard tray being installed in the chassis.

Some cases and boards, particularly ATX types, don't use any plastic spacers. Instead they use up to seven screws into metal standoffs that are installed in the case (refer to Figure 22.11). These are somewhat easier to install because the board drops into place and doesn't require that it be moved to the side to engage any standoffs.

Figure 22.17   Installing a motherboard and tray into the chassis. *Case courtesy of PC Power & Cooling, Inc. Motherboard courtesy of Intel Corporation.*

  6. Take the screws and any plastic washers that were supplied with the new motherboard and screw the board into the case (see Figure 22.18).

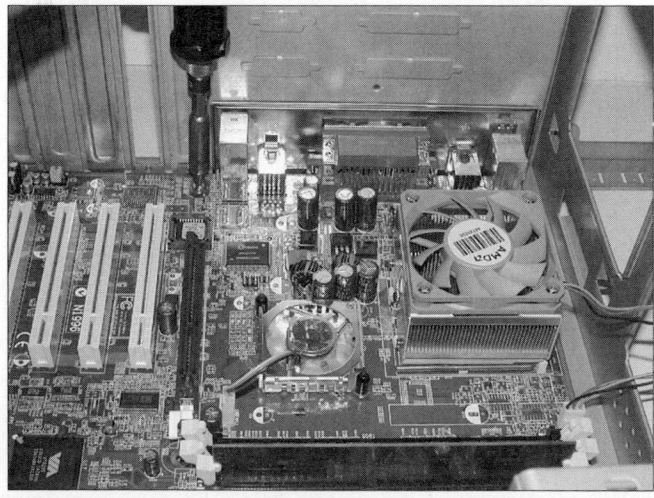

Figure 22.18   Installing the screws that hold the motherboard to the chassis.

Connecting the Power Supply

The power supply is very easy to install, and it usually attaches to the chassis with four screws. Figures 22.19 and 22.20 show installing the power supply into the chassis and tightening the screws.

Figure 22.19 Installing the power supply into the chassis.

Figure 22.20 Installing the screws to retain the power supply.

ATX-style motherboards have a single power connector that can go on only one way and an optional secondary connector that is also keyed (see Figure 22.21). Although BTX power supplies were not standardized at the time of writing, ATX supplies can be used in a standard BTX case (but not Pico/Micro). Baby-AT and other old-style board designs such as LPX usually have two separate six-wire power connectors from the power supply to the board, which might not be keyed and therefore might be interchangeable. If you still work with Baby-AT or LPX systems, see Chapter 21 for important information on proper installation of Baby-AT power supplies. Even though you might be able to insert them several ways, only one way is correct! These power leads usually are labeled P8 and P9 in most systems. The order in which you connect them to the board is crucial; if you install them backward, you can damage the motherboard when you power it up. Many systems use a CPU cooling fan, which should also be connected. To attach the power connectors from the power supply to the motherboard, do the following:

1. If the system uses a single ATX-style power connector, plug it in; it can go on only one way. Some ATX systems also use a 6-pin auxiliary connector as well as a 4-pin ATX12V connector. These are also keyed and plug in only one way. If the system is not ATX and two separate six-wire connectors are used instead, the two black ground wires on the ends of the connectors must meet in the middle. Align the power connectors such that the black ground wires are adjacent to each other and plug in the connectors. Consult the documentation with your board to ensure that the power supply connection is correct. Incorrectly connecting the power connectors can destroy the motherboard.

2. Plug in the power lead for the CPU fan if one is used. The fan will either connect to the power supply via a disk drive power connector or connect directly to a fan power connector on the motherboard.

Figure 22.21 Attaching an ATX motherboard power connector.

◄◄ See "Motherboard Power Connectors," p. 1164.

Note

See Chapter 21 of this book for detailed coverage of the various types of power supply connectors, including new connectors used with the Intel Pentium 4.

Connecting I/O and Other Cables to the Motherboard

Several connections must be made between a motherboard and the case. These include LEDs for the hard disk and power, an internal speaker connection, a reset button, and a power button. Most modern motherboards also have several built-in I/O ports that have to be connected. This includes dual IDE host adapters, a floppy controller, and front-mounted USB or IEEE 1394 ports. Some boards also include additional items such as built-in video, sound, or SCSI adapters.

If the board is an ATX type, the connectors for all the external I/O ports are already built into the rear of the board. If you are using a legacy Baby AT–type board, you might have to install cables and brackets to run the serial, parallel, and other external I/O ports to the rear of the case.

If your motherboard has onboard I/O (nearly all PCs today use onboard I/O), use the following procedure to connect the cables:

1. Connect the floppy cable between the floppy drives and the 34-pin floppy controller connector on the motherboard.

2. Connect the IDE cables between the hard disk, IDE CD-ROM, and 40-pin primary and secondary IDE connectors on the motherboard (see Figure 22.22). Typically, you will use the primary IDE channel connector for hard disks only and the secondary IDE channel connector to attach an IDE CD-ROM or other device, such as a tape drive. If you have a Serial ATA hard disk and a Serial ATA host adapter on the motherboard, connect the Serial ATA cable from the hard disk to the host adapter connection on the motherboard.

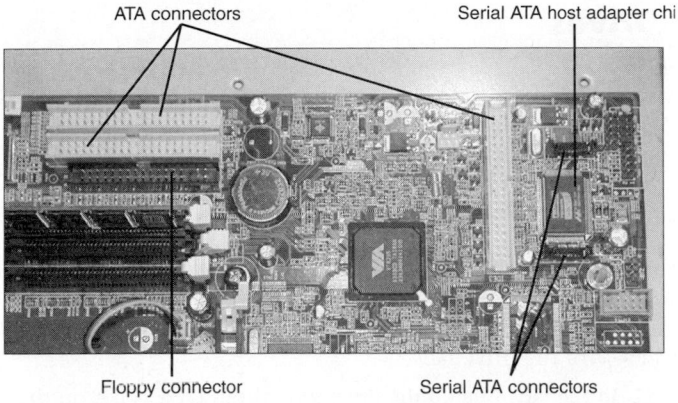

Figure 22.22 Floppy, ATA, and Serial ATA hard drive connectors.

3. On non-ATX boards, a 25-pin female cable port bracket is used for the parallel port. Usually two serial ports exist: a 9-pin and either another 9-pin or a 25-pin male connector port. Align pin 1 on the serial and parallel port cables with pin 1 on the motherboard connector, and then plug them in.

4. If the ports don't have card slot-type brackets or if you need all your expansion slots, the back of the case might have port knockouts you can use instead. Find ones that fit the ports, and push them out, removing the metal piece covering the hole. Unscrew the hex nuts on each side of the port connector, and position the connector in the hole. Install the hex nuts back in through the case to hold the port connector in place.

5. Most newer motherboards also include a built-in mouse port. If the connector for this port is not built into the back of the motherboard (typically next to the keyboard connector), you probably have a card bracket-type connector to install. In that case, plug the cable into the motherboard mouse connector and then attach the external mouse connector bracket to the case.

6. Attach the front-panel switch, LED, internal speaker wires, and front-mounted ports such as USB and IEEE 1394 from the case front panel to the motherboard. If they are not marked on the board, check where each one is on the diagram in the motherboard manual. Figure 22.23 shows the front-panel connectors.

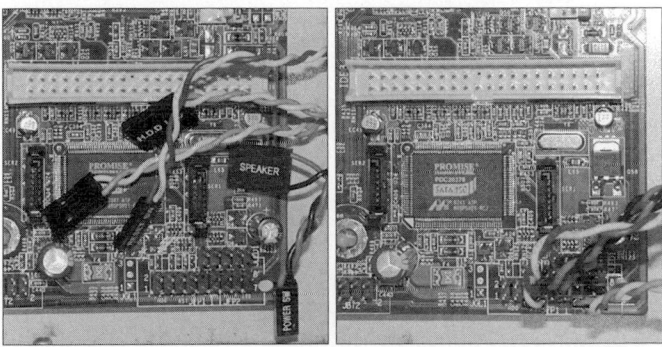

Figure 22.23 The motherboard front-panel connectors (speaker, power switch, LEDs, and so on) must be connected to the appropriate pins on the motherboard (bottom center).

Installing the Drives

At this point you should install your hard drive, floppy drive, CD-ROM or DVD drive, and optionally your CD-RW drive. This is covered in detail in Chapter 14, "Physical Drive Installation and Configuration."

The basic process for mounting CD drives, hard drives, and floppy drives is as follows:

1. Remove the drive bay plates (if needed). Simply bend or knock the plate out of the way.

2. To install a CD drive, simply slide the drive into the chassis. Note that it is easier to connect the IDE cable to the rear of the drive and make jumper selections before mounting the drive. See Chapters 7 and 14 for more about IDE jumpers and drive installation. Note that some cases come with rails that must be added to 5 1/4" wide drives, such as the CD. In such cases, use the screws from step 3 for the drive rails.

3. After the drive is in the bay, line up the drive-mounting screw holes on the drive with the holes in the case chassis. Secure the drive with four screws, using the ones that came with your case or the drive you are installing (see Figure 22.24). If the drive uses rails, the rails hold the drive in place.

Figure 22.24   Secure the drive to the chassis using four screws.

4. Connect the other end of the IDE cable to your motherboard's IDE connector or to the back of another IDE device if you are chaining drives.

5. If your system has a removable drive cage, for floppy and hard disk drives, you should remove the cage.

6. To install floppy and hard drives, slide your drives into the drive cage and secure them with the screws that came with your case or with the drive you are installing (see Figure 22.25). As with the CD drive, it's easier to connect the floppy and IDE cables to the rear of the drives and make any jumper selections prior to placing the drives or the drive cage into the chassis.

Note

If your chassis does not include a removable drive cage, as shown in Figure 22.25, you'll simply have to mount the drives in the chassis. This is a little more difficult because there's not much working room inside a PC.

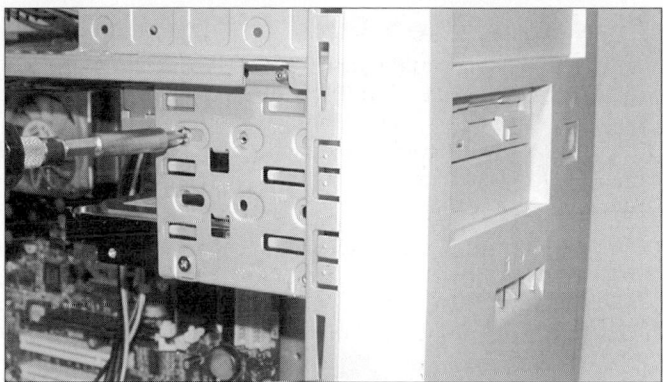

Figure 22.25   Use four screws to secure each drive to the drive bay. If your computer uses a removable drive cage, mount the drives to the drive cage in the same way.

7. If your system has a removable drive cage, slide the drive cage back into the PC and secure it to the chassis using the screws provided with your case (see Figure 22.26).

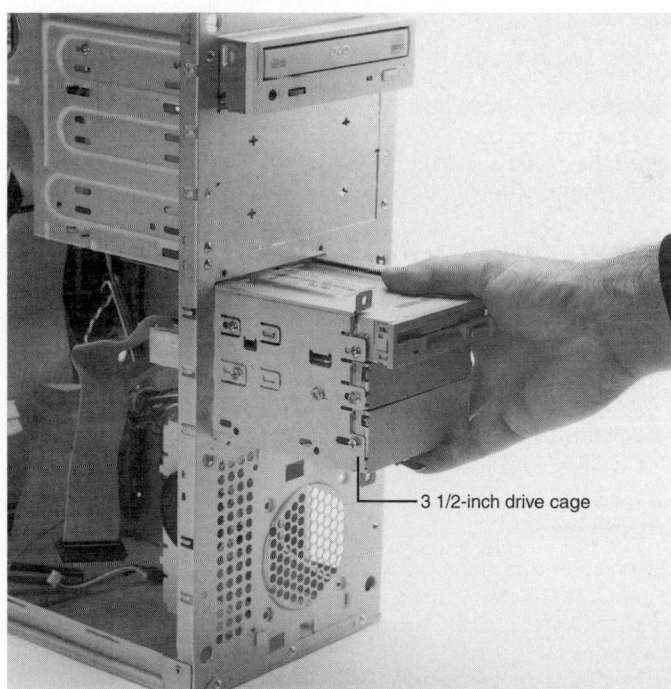

3 1/2-inch drive cage

Figure 22.26   The drive cage inserts into the chassis and is usually held in place by two or four screws. *Chassis courtesy of PC Power & Cooling, Inc. Hard drive supplied by Micro X-Press.*

8. Connect the drive cables to the appropriate locations on your motherboard. See Chapters 7 and 14 for more about jumper settings and cable connections for hard drives and floppy drives.

Removing the Existing Video Card (If Present)

If you are replacing an existing video card (or switching from onboard video to an add-in video card), you should remove the existing installed video driver before powering down to install the new card. This helps prevent the system from improperly identifying the new video card and makes for a smoother upgrade. To do this, open the Device Manager, select the existing Display Adapter, and select Remove or Uninstall. Do not reboot the system if asked; instead you can power down and remove the existing video card.

To physically remove the card, use the following procedure:

1. Shut down and unplug both the system and monitor.
2. Disconnect the video cable running from the monitor to the card.
3. Open the system.
4. If you are not using an ESD ground wire, touch the side of the power supply to avoid ESD damage to your hardware.

◄◄   To learn how to avoid ESD, see "ESD Protection," p. 1228.

5. Remove the screw holding the video card in place.
6. If there are any cables running from your video card to other devices (such as a sound card or DVD decoding board), note their locations and then remove them.
7. Remove the video card from the slot.

In the case of systems that have video card functions built into the motherboard or chipset, usually just installing a new card into an open AGP/PCI slot automatically disables the existing video. In some cases you might have to set a specific jumper on your motherboard to disable any built-in video (refer to your motherboard's documentation). Now you are ready to install a new video card.

Installing the New Video Card and Driver Software

Follow these steps to install a new video card into a system:

1. If necessary, remove the screw and slot cover behind the expansion slot you want to use for the new video card.
2. Slide the video card straight down into the slot where it will be installed.
3. Push the card down into the slot, using a front-to-back rocking motion if necessary to get the edge connector to slide into the slot.
4. Use either the screw you removed during removal of the old card or the screw used in step 1 to fasten the card into place.
5. Attach the video cable from the monitor to the proper connector at the rear of the monitor. If the new card uses a DVI-I connector and the monitor uses the standard 15-pin VGA connector, use a DVI-to-VGA adapter (usually provided with the video card or available separately from stores that stock computer parts).

After the entire system is assembled, when the system boots up, Windows should detect the new video card and automatically begin the driver installation process. At that point, follow the manufacturer's instructions for installing the latest video drivers for the new video card. After the video card drivers are installed, you can use the Windows Display properties to fine-tune its settings for resolution, color depth, or refresh rate if desired.

Note

If you have installed a video card with multiple-monitor support and your existing display still works, you might want to attach it to the secondary display port on your new display card and use it as a second monitor. Dual-display-capable cards are now widely available, using ATI, NVIDIA, and Matrox chipsets. For details, see the section "Multiple Monitors" in Chapter 15.

Installing Additional Expansion Cards

Many systems use additional expansion cards for network interface, Internet connection (modem), sound, and SCSI adapters. These cards are plugged into the bus slots present on the motherboard. To install these cards, follow these steps:

1. Insert each card by holding it carefully by the edges, being sure not to touch the chips and circuitry. Put the bottom-edge finger connector into a slot that fits. Firmly press down on the top of the card, exerting even pressure, until it snaps into place (see Figure 22.27).

2. Secure each card bracket with a screw (see Figure 22.28).

3. Attach any internal cables you might have removed earlier from the cards.

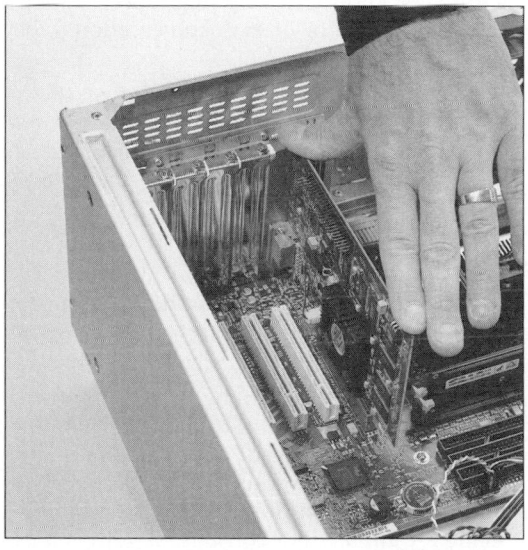

Figure 22.27   This photo shows a video adapter being inserted into the slot. *Motherboard courtesy of Intel Corporation.*

Figure 22.28   Installing the screw to retain the card. *Motherboard courtesy of Intel Corporation.*

Replacing the Cover and Connecting External Cables

Now the system should be nearly assembled. All that remains is installing the cover assembly and connecting any external devices that are cabled to the system. I usually don't like to install the case cover screws until I have tested the system and am sure everything is working properly. Often, I find that a cable has been connected improperly or some jumper setting is not correct, requiring that I remove the cover to repair the problem. Use the following procedure to complete the assembly:

1. Slide the cover onto the case.

2. Before powering up the system, connect any external cables. Most of the connectors are D-shaped and go in only one way.

3. Plug the 15-pin monitor cable into the video card female connector.

4. Attach the phone cord to the modem, if any.

5. Plug the round keyboard cable into the keyboard connector, and plug the mouse into the mouse port or serial port (if you are using a serial mouse).

6. If you have any other external cabling, such as joystick or audio jacks to a sound card, attach them now.

Running the Motherboard BIOS Setup Program (CMOS Setup)

Now that everything is connected, you can power up the system and run the BIOS Setup program. This enables you to configure the motherboard to access the installed devices and set the system date and time. The system also tests itself to determine whether any problems exists. Do the following:

1. Power on the monitor first and then the system unit. Observe the operation via the screen and listen for any beeps from the system speaker.

2. The system should automatically go through a power on self test (POST) consisting of video BIOS checking, a RAM test, and usually an installed component report. If a fatal error occurs during the POST, you might not see anything onscreen and the system might beep several times, indicating a specific problem. Check the motherboard or BIOS documentation to determine what the beep codes mean.

3. If there are no fatal errors, you should see the POST display onscreen. Depending on the type of motherboard BIOS, such as Phoenix, AMI, Award, or others, you have to press a key or series of keys to interrupt the normal boot sequence and get to the Setup program screens that enable you to enter important system information. Normally, the system indicates via the onscreen display which key to press to activate the BIOS Setup program during the POST, but if not, check the motherboard manual for the key(s) to press to enter the BIOS Setup. Common keys used to enter BIOS Setup are F1, F2, F10, Esc, Ins, and Del.

4. After the Setup program is running, use the Setup program menus to enter the current date and time, your hard drive settings, floppy drive types, video cards, keyboard settings, and so on.

5. Entering the hard drive information is most critical when building a new system. Most modern BIOSs feature an autodetect or auto-type setting for the drive; I recommend you choose that if it is available. This causes the BIOS to read the parameters directly from the drive, which eliminates a chance for errors—especially if the builder is less experienced. These parameters include CHS (cylinder head sector) specifications and transfer speed and translation settings such as LBA. Most systems also let you set a *user-definable type*, which means that the cylinder, head, and sector counts for this type were entered manually and are not constant. If you set a user-definable type (not normally recommended unless you don't have "auto" as a choice), it is especially important to write down the exact settings you use if you don't use Auto because this information might be very difficult to figure out if it is ever lost.

Modern ATA drives also have additional configuration items you should record if you set them manually. These include the translation mode and transfer speed setting. With drives larger than 528MB, you should record the translation mode, which is expressed differently in different BIOS versions. Look for settings such as CHS, ECHS (Extended CHS), Large (which equals ECHS), or LBA (logical block addressing). Typically, you set LBA or Large for any drive over 528MB. Whatever you set, it should be recorded because changing this setting after the drive has been formatted can cause problems.

6. After you have checked all the settings in the BIOS Setup, follow the instructions onscreen or in the motherboard manual to save the settings and exit the Setup menu.

◄◄ See "Running or Accessing the CMOS Setup Program," p. 430.

Troubleshooting New Installations

At this point, the system should reset and attempt to boot normally from either a floppy disk or hard disk. With the operating system startup disk in drive A:, the system should boot and either reach an installation menu or an A: prompt. If any problems exist, here are some basic items to check:

- *If the system won't power up at all, check the power cord.* If the cord is plugged into a power strip, make sure the strip is switched on. Usually, a power switch can be found on the front of the case, but some power supplies have a switch on the back as well.

- *Check to see whether the power switch is connected properly inside the case.* There is a connection from the switch to the motherboard; check both ends to ensure that they are connected properly.

- *Check the main power connector from the supply to the board.* Make sure the connectors are seated fully, and if the board is a Baby-AT type, ensure that they are plugged in with the correct orientation and sequence.

- *If the system appears to be running but you don't see anything on the display, check the monitor to ensure that it is plugged in, turned on, and properly and securely connected to the video card.*

- *Check the video card to ensure it is fully seated in the motherboard slot.* Remove and reseat the video card, and possibly try a different slot if it is a PCI card.

- *If the system beeps more than once, the BIOS is reporting a fatal error of some type.* See the BIOS Error code listings in Chapter 5 and on the disc accompanying this book for more information on what these codes mean because they depend on the type and version of BIOS you have. Also, consult your motherboard documentation—look in the BIOS section for a table of beep codes.

- *If the LED on your floppy drive, hard drive, or CD/DVD-ROM drive stays on continuously, the data cable is probably installed backward or is off by some pins.* Check that the stripe on the cable is properly oriented toward pin 1 on both the drive and board connector ends. Also, check the drive jumpers for proper master/slave relationships.

When you are sure the system is up and running successfully, power it off and screw the chassis cover securely to the case. Now your new system should be ready for the operating system installation.

Installing the Operating System

If you are starting with a new drive, you must install the operating system. If you are using a non-Windows operating system, follow the documentation for the installation procedures.

On a newer system in which you are installing an OEM version of Windows 98 or later (which comes on a bootable CD), there isn't really anything you need to do, other than simply booting from the CD (you might have to enable the CD-ROM as a boot device in your BIOS Setup) and following the prompts to install the OS. Windows 98 or later versions automatically recognize that the drive needs to be partitioned and the partitions formatted before the installation can proceed. Additionally, Windows 98 or later versions execute these functions for you, with prompts guiding you along the way. This is the method I recommend for most people because it is relatively simple and straightforward.

If you want to do the partitioning and formatting manually (prior to installing the OS), follow the guidelines in the next few sections.

Partitioning the Drive with DOS and Windows 9x and Me

From the A:> prompt, with the startup disk inserted in the floppy drive, you type the following command:

```
FDISK
```

This command is used to partition your drive. Follow the menus to create either a single partition for the entire drive or multiple partitions. Usually, the first partition must also be made active, which means it will be bootable. I recommend you answer Yes to the prompt Do you wish to enable large disk support (Y/N)?. This enables the partition to be created using the FAT32 or NTFS file system. Then, you can continue accepting default entries for all the prompts to partition the drive as a single bootable partition that covers the entire drive.

Next, exit FDISK; this causes the system to restart.

Note

Using FDISK is covered extensively in Chapter 14.

Formatting the Drive with DOS and Windows 9x and Me

After rebooting on the startup floppy, you need to format each partition you've created. The first partition is formatted using the FORMAT command as follows:

```
FORMAT C:
```

All other partitions are formatted in the same manner: Merely run the command, changing the drive letter for each partition that needs to be formatted.

After the FORMAT command completes on all the drives, you should reboot again from the startup floppy. Now you are ready to install Windows.

Note

Drive formatting is covered extensively in Chapter 10, "Hard Disk Storage." See Chapter 14 for more details on installing and setting up a hard drive.

Preparing the Hard Drive with Windows 2000/XP

If you are using Windows 2000 or Windows XP, the operating system prepares the drive for you during installation if you install the operating system to an empty drive. If unpartitioned space is available on an existing boot drive, you can direct Windows 2000 or Windows XP to use that space and install as a "dual-boot" configuration. This configuration enables you to select your old version or new version of Windows each time you start your computer. You can also replace your existing version of Windows.

If Windows 2000/XP prepares your drive, you can select the file system (FAT32 or NTFS) during the process. After Windows has partitioned and formatted the drive, it completes the installation process.

Loading the CD-ROM Driver

If your system supports booting from the CD and you are installing a version of Windows that comes on a bootable CD, you can disregard this section because the CD-ROM drivers automatically are loaded as you boot from the CD. You can then either proceed with the installation from the CD or copy the OS files from the CD to the hard drive and install from the hard drive instead.

If you must first boot from a floppy (because your system can't boot from a CD or your version of Windows isn't bootable), you must make sure your startup floppy disk is properly configured to support the CD/DVD drive in your system. This requires that real-mode (DOS-based) drivers be installed on the disk that is compatible with your drive. The easiest solution is to use a Windows 98 or later startup floppy disk because it is already prepared with the proper drivers for 99% of all systems on the market. Even if you are installing Windows 95, you can still use the Windows 98 or later startup disk to start the process.

If you are using a Windows 95 startup disk and you don't have the CD-ROM drivers on it, you should look for a CD-ROM driver disk that usually comes with your drive. It should have a driver installation batch file on it which, if run, will copy the drivers to your startup disk and create the appropriate CONFIG.SYS and AUTOEXEC.BAT files to enable CD-ROM support. If the driver is called CDROM.SYS, that file—along with the following line (or something similar)—should be added to the CONFIG.SYS file on your Windows 95 startup disk:

```
device=CDROM.SYS /D:oemcd001
```

This causes the CDROM.SYS driver to be loaded and assigns it an in-memory driver designation of oemcd001. Any designation can be used here, but it should be eight characters or fewer and must match a similar designation in the next step.

Next, you must load the Microsoft CD-ROM extensions driver in your AUTOEXEC.BAT file. This driver is called MSCDEX.EXE and is already included on the Windows 95 startup disk. If you used the designation I listed in the previous step, add the following line to the AUTOEXEC.BAT file on the Windows 95 startup disk:

```
LH MSCDEX.EXE /D:oemcd001
```

This loads the MSCDEX.EXE driver (in upper memory via the LH or LoadHigh command if possible) and looks to attach to the CD-ROM driver loaded earlier via the driver designation oemcd001 in this case.

After these statements are added to the CONFIG.SYS and AUTOEXEC.BAT files, you should reboot on the startup floppy. Now you also should be able to access your CD-ROM drive. It will appear one drive letter after your last drive partition. If your hard disk partitions are C: and D:, the CD-ROM drive will be E:.

Note that these procedures require that you find your CD-ROM driver and copy it onto the startup disk. If you can't find the driver or have a SCSI hard disk (which uses different types of drivers), I recommend you borrow a copy of a Windows 98 or later version startup disk. These startup disks already include a series of drivers that work with virtually any CD-ROM drive on the market, even SCSI versions.

After you have successfully created a startup disk with the CD-ROM drivers (or have the Win98 startup disk), insert the Windows CD-ROM in your CD/DVD drive. After booting from the startup floppy, change to the CD/DVD drive letter. Then at that prompt, run the SETUP command. This starts the Windows installation program. From here, you can follow the prompts to install Windows as you see fit. This procedure can be somewhat lengthy, so be prepared to spend some time. You will be installing not only Windows, but also the drivers for any hardware detected during the installation process.

Whether you are booting from floppy or CD, I recommend copying the Windows files to your hard disk and actually running the installation from the hard disk and not the CD. This is helpful in the future should you want to reinstall or install any additional parts of Windows because it will then work directly from the hard disk and you won't be asked to insert the CD.

To do this, first check the CD for the directory containing the *.CAB files and copy them to the hard disk. For example, using Windows 98 it would go something like this:

```
copy E:\WIN98\*.* C:\WIN98 /S
```

This copies all the files from the WIN98 directory on the CD-ROM (E: drive in this example) to the hard disk and places them in a directory called WIN98. Then, you can remove the CD (it is no longer needed) and run the installation directly from the hard disk by entering the following commands:

```
C:
CD\
C:\WIN98\SETUP
```

These commands change you to drive C:, place you in the root directory, and then run the Windows SETUP program to start the installation. From there, the menu-driven Windows installation routines guide you. If you are using a different version of Windows, merely change the directories used in the previous example to the appropriate directories for your version of Windows.

Note

If you want to create a bootable CD containing your Windows installation files, see Chapter 13, "Optical Storage." For more information about installing CD/DVD drives, see Chapter 14.

After Windows is installed, you can install any additional drivers or application programs you want. At this point, your system should be fully operational.

Note

If you prefer to install a version of Linux or other non-Windows operating system, follow the instructions given for the particular distribution you are using.

Installing Important Drivers

After installing the operating system, the first thing you need to do is install drivers for devices where drivers were not found on the Windows CD. This often includes things such as chipset drivers for your motherboard, drivers for newer video cards, USB 2.0 drivers, and more. Of these, the motherboard chipset drivers are the most critical and should be installed first. A CD containing these drivers should have been included with your motherboard; insert this disc and follow the prompts to install the chipset drivers. Then install other drivers, such as video, network, modem, and so on.

Disassembly/Upgrading Preparation

After you've built your system, you probably will have to open it again sometime to perform a repair or an upgrade. Before you power off the system for the last time and begin to open the case, you should learn and record several things about your computer. Often, when working on a system, you intentionally or accidentally wipe out the CMOS Setup information. Most systems use a special battery-powered CMOS clock and a data chip that is used to store the system's configuration information. If the battery is disconnected, or if certain pins are accidentally shorted, you can discharge the CMOS memory and lose the setup. The CMOS memory in most systems is used to store simple things such as how many and what type of floppy drives are connected, how much memory is in the system, and the date and time.

A critical piece of information is the hard disk–type settings. Most modern BIOSs have an autodetect feature that reads the type information directly from the drive. I recommend you set the drive type to Auto, which automatically sets all the necessary parameters for you. With older BIOSs you must explicitly tell the system the parameters of the attached hard disk. Therefore, you need to know the current settings for cylinders, heads, and sectors per track.

If you do not enter the correct hard disk–type information in the CMOS Setup program, you will not be able to access the data on the hard disk. I know of several people who lost some or all of their data because they did not enter the correct type information when they reconfigured their systems. If this information is incorrect, the usual results are a missing operating system error message when the system starts and the inability to access the C: drive.

Some people think that it's possible to figure out the parameters by looking up the particular hard disk in a table. (I have included a table of popular hard disk drive parameters in the Technical Reference on the disc. This table has proven to be useful to me time and time again.) Unfortunately, this method works only if the person who set up the system originally entered the correct parameters. I have encountered a large number of systems in which the hard disk parameters were not entered correctly; the only way to regain access to the data is to determine, and then use, the same incorrect parameters that were used originally. As you can see, no matter what, you should record the hard disk information from your setup program.

Most systems have the setup program built right into the ROM BIOS software. These built-in setup programs are activated by a key sequence usually entered during the POST. Most systems show a prompt on the screen during the POST indicating which key to press to enter the BIOS Setup.

The major vendors have standardized on these following keystrokes to enter the BIOS Setup:

- *AMI BIOS.* Press Del during POST.
- *Phoenix BIOS.* Press F2 during POST.
- *Award BIOS.* Press Del or Ctrl+Alt+Esc during POST.
- *Microid Research BIOS.* Press Esc during POST.

If your system does not respond to one of these common keystroke settings, you might have to contact the manufacturer or read the system documentation to find the correct keystrokes to enter setup.

Some unique ones I have encountered are as follows:

- *IBM Aptiva/Valuepoint.* Press F1 during POST.
- *Older Phoenix BIOS.* Boot to a safe mode DOS command prompt, and then press Ctrl+Alt+Esc or Ctrl+Alt+S.
- *Compaq.* Press F10 during POST (does not apply to all Compaq models).

◄◄ See "Running or Accessing the CMOS Setup Program," p. 430.

After you're in the BIOS Setup main screen, you'll usually find a main menu allowing access to other menus and submenus offering various sections or screens. When you get the setup program running, record all the settings. The easiest way to do this is to print it. If a printer is connected, press Shift+Print Screen; a copy of the screen display will be sent to the printer. Some setup programs have several pages of information, so you should record the information on each page.

Many setup programs allow for specialized control of the particular chipset used in the motherboard. These complicated settings can take up to several screens of information—all should be recorded. Most systems return these settings to a BIOS default if the CMOS battery is removed, and you lose any customized settings you might have changed. See Chapter 5 for more information on the BIOS settings.

CHAPTER 23

Extreme Modifications: Overclocking, Cooling, and Chassis Upgrades

Modifying, or *modding*, computer systems has been going on since even before the advent of the PC. In fact, because most of the early personal computers were either made from kits or entirely home built, custom modifications were the norm. And because of that, few systems were exactly alike. Even when fully functional personal computers and, more specifically, PCs came rolling off assembly lines in mass-produced fashion, people still found ways to make their own system different from all the others.

Computer modifications are usually designed to increase or improve performance or functionality in some way, but they can also be purely cosmetic in nature, or some combination of both. Because I am definitely more into function than form, I emphasize performance- or functionality-enhancing modifications in this chapter.

One of the primary modifications you can perform on a system is to make it run faster, which is usually called *overclocking*. When chips run faster, they run hotter, so cooling upgrades and modifications usually go hand-in-hand with overclocking. Systems that run cool tend to be more stable and more reliable, so even if you don't overclock your system, ensuring that it runs cool is essential for trouble-free operation. Anytime overclocking is discussed, cooling is certain to be involved because increasing the speed of a system also increases the cooling requirements. Many systems are not properly configured for good cooling even at their standard speeds, much less when overclocked.

New interfaces bring new connectors to the PC, and many of these are more useful on the front of the system rather than in the back. Bringing modern interfaces to the front panel; adapting newer drives for different form factors; and adding windows, vents, and fans are all modifications that can be made to a chassis or case to improve or update it to handle the latest hardware.

Finally, you can perform purely cosmetic modifications, such as custom painting or internal lighting, which can make your system stand out from the rest. I cover the functional modifications in this chapter, with sound engineering principles applied such that you can either modify an existing system correctly or purchase new components with the desired features already integrated.

Overclocking

One of the most popular performance-enhancing modifications of all time is overclocking, which can be defined as running all or part of the system faster than it was originally rated or intended to run. Overclocking is usually applied to the processor, but it can also be applied to other components in the system, including memory, video cards, bus speeds, and more.

Overclocking PCs dates all the way back to the original 4.77MHz IBM PC and 6MHz AT systems of the early 1980s. In fact, IBM made overclocking the AT easy because the quartz crystal that controlled the speed of the processor was socketed. You could obtain a faster replacement for about a dollar and easily plug it in. The first several editions of this book covered how to perform this modification in detail, resulting in a system that was up to 1.5 times faster than it started out. Modern systems allow overclocking without replacing any parts by virtue of simple and easy-to-change BIOS Setup options.

Quartz Crystals

To understand overclocking, you need to know how computer system speeds are controlled. The main component controlling speed in a computer is a quartz crystal. Quartz is silicon dioxide (SiO_2) in crystalline form. Oxygen and silicon are the most common elements on earth (sand and rock are mostly silicon dioxide), and computer chips are made mainly from silicon. Quartz is a hard, transparent material with a density of 2649 kg/m³ (1.531 oz/in³) and a melting point of 1750° C (3182° F). Quartz is brittle but with a little bit of elasticity, which is perhaps its most useful attribute.

In crystalline form, quartz can be used to generate regular and consistent signal pulses to regulate electronic circuits, similar to the way a metronome can be used to regulate music. Quartz crystals are used because they are *piezoelectric*, which is defined as having a property that generates a voltage when subjected to mechanical stress and that also generates mechanical stress when subjected to a voltage. Piezoelectricity was first discovered by Pierre and Jacques Curie in 1880, and it is the essential feature of quartz that makes it useful in electronic circuits.

The key to piezoelectricity is that when you twist, bend, deform, or simply apply pressure or stress to a quartz crystal, a small voltage is generated. This property is commonly used in sensors or transducers to detect pressure or sound waves. For example, the knock sensors used in virtually all modern automobile engines are based on quartz crystals that are sensitive to the vibrations produced in the engine block when detonation (uncontrolled burning of fuel) occurs. Because detonation can rapidly damage an engine, the engine management computer uses input from one or more knock sensors to retard the ignition timing, thus preventing engine damage. Some microphones and phonograph pickup devices also use quartz crystals for converting sound waves or the motion of the needle in the groove into a voltage.

Piezoelectricity works two ways, meaning that if a voltage is generated when you bend a crystal, likewise if you apply voltage to a crystal it bends (contracts, expands, or twists) in a similar fashion. Although the crystal is mostly brittle in nature, it is still somewhat elastic, such that any deformation tends to snap back and then occur again, resonating at a natural frequency as long as the voltage is present. Much like a tuning fork or the pipe in an organ, the natural resonant frequency depends on the size and shape of the crystal. In general, the smaller and thinner it is, the faster it vibrates.

The actual movement is exceedingly small, on the order of 68 nanometers (billionths of a meter) per centimeter, which in a normal crystal is only a few atoms in length. Although the movement is very small, it is also quite rapid, which means tremendous forces can be generated. For example, the surface acceleration of a 50MHz crystal can exceed five million times the force of gravity.

Crystal resonators are made from slabs of quartz sawed from raw quartz crystal stock. Although the stock can come from natural quartz, most crystals are made from synthetically grown quartz. The raw stock slabs are cut into squares, rounded, and ground into flat discs called *blanks*. The thinner the disc, the higher the resonant frequency; however, there are limits as to how thin the discs can be made before they break. The upper limit for fundamental mode resonators is approximately 50MHz. At that frequency, the discs are paper thin and are generally too fragile to withstand further grinding. Still, higher-frequency crystals can be achieved by using harmonics of the fundamental frequency, resulting in crystals of up to 200MHz or more. Even higher frequencies can be achieved by using frequency synthesizer circuits, which use a base crystal-generated frequency fed to a circuit that then generates multiples of frequency that can extend well into the gigahertz or terahertz range. In fact, crystal-based frequency synthesizer circuits are used to generate the high operating speeds of modern PCs.

The crystal packages, as well as the shape of the actual quartz crystals inside the packages, can vary. The packages are usually a metal can that is either cylindrical or oblong in shape, but they can also have other shapes or be constructed of plastic or other materials (see Figure 23.1).

The sliver of quartz inside the package is normally disc shaped, but it is shaped like a tuning fork in some examples. Figure 23.2 shows a cylindrical crystal package with the cover removed, exposing the tuning fork–shaped sliver of quartz inside.

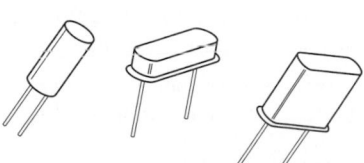

Figure 23.1 Crystal packages of varying shapes.

Figure 23.2 Crystal interior showing the quartz tuning fork.

Most crystals use a disc-shaped sliver of quartz as a resonator. The disc is contained in a hermetically sealed evacuated enclosure.

Figure 23.3 shows the interior view of a typical crystal with a disc-shaped resonator inside.

The quartz disc inside has electrodes on each side, allowing a voltage to be applied to the disc. The details are shown in Figure 23.4.

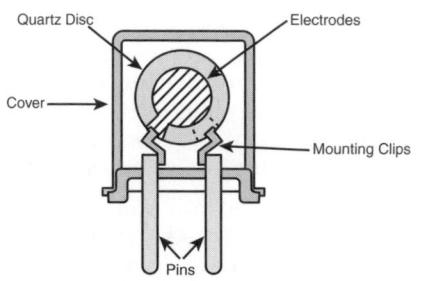

Figure 23.3 Crystal interior showing disc-shaped quartz resonator.

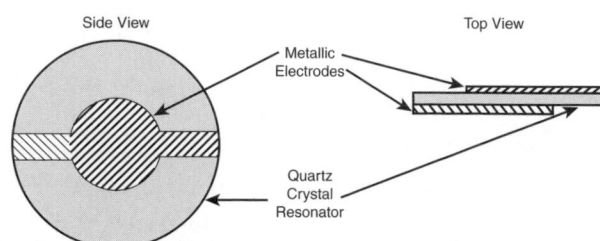

Figure 23.4 Disc-shaped quartz resonator details.

Walter G. Cady was the first to use a quartz crystal to control an electronic oscillator circuit in 1921. He published his results in 1922, which led to the development of the first crystal-controlled clock by Warren A. Marrison in 1927. Today, all modern computers have multiple internal oscillators and clocks, some for controlling bus and processor speeds and at least one for a standard time of day clock.

Overclocking History

Overclocking has been around since the beginning of computing. As long as there have been computers, there have been people trying to make them run faster. I began overclocking PCs back in the early 1980s, using a variety of devices on the market. The easiest system to overclock was the original IBM AT, which used a socketed crystal to run the processor. Two versions of the XT were available—one that used a 12MHz crystal and one that used a 16MHz crystal. The timer chip divided the crystal speed by 2, resulting in processor speeds of 6MHz and 8MHz.

A popular trick at the time was to pop the 12MHz or 16MHz crystals out of their sockets and replace them with 18MHz or 20MHz crystals, which sped up the systems to 9MHz or 10MHz. Back in 1984, I was able to purchase crystals for as little as $1 each from RadioShack, and they could be changed in seconds. In my 6MHz system, I was able to use an 18MHz crystal to get the system to run at 9MHz. That was a 50% increase in speed for about $1! I had tried a 20MHz crystal (10MHz speed), but the system would not boot up at that speed, so I had to drop back to the 18MHz (9MHz speed) crystal instead.

Taking this further, some companies released variable frequency oscillators, which basically amounted to a variable speed crystal you could use to replace the fixed stock crystal. A control panel was then mounted on the back of the system, which had an adjustment knob you could use to change the system speed. The most sophisticated of these was the XCELX, which allowed you to adjust the original IBM AT from 6.5MHz to 12.7MHz. Figure 23.5 shows the XCELX, which dated from 1985.

The instructions told you to turn up the throttle until the system crashed and then back down a notch or two. How fast a given system would run depended on all the specific components contained within.

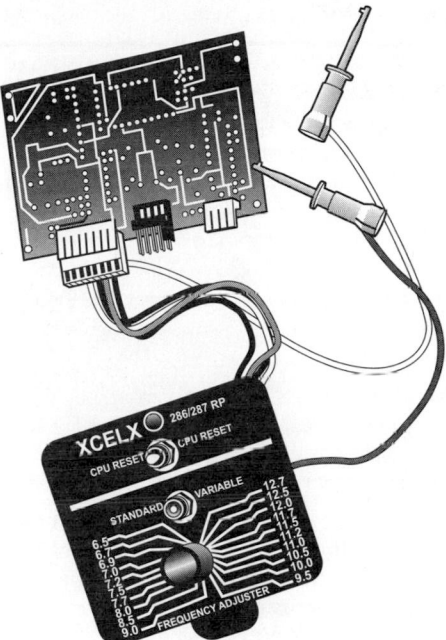

Figure 23.5 The XCELX frequency adjuster, a "throttle" that could be used to speed up the IBM AT.

Tip

One problem in the vintage IBM AT and XT-286 systems was that the clock speed was checked during the Power On Self Test (POST). This caused problems if you replaced the socketed clock crystal in these systems for a cheap and easy speed-up. In IBM AT and XT-286 systems, the POST checked the system refresh rate (clock speed) to ensure that it was 6MHz or 8MHz, depending on which system you had. A marginally faster or slower rate caused the test to fail and resulted in a POST error of one long and one short beep, followed by a halt (**HLT**) instruction.

To eliminate the test and enable a faster-than-normal clock rate, you had to patch the instruction at the proper location from a 73h (JAE—Jump if Above or Equal) to an EBh (JMP—Jump unconditionally). When this instruction was changed, the test never fell into the error routine, no matter how fast the rate. The JAE instruction occurred at F000:05BC in IBM AT systems with the 06/10/85 or 11/15/85 ROM BIOS versions and at F000:05C0 in XT-286 systems. Note that the original IBM AT system with the 01/10/84 BIOS did not have this test. By creating a new set of ROM chips with this instruction changed by an EPROM programmer, you could eliminate this speed check and enable faster clock rates.

Few people are interested in overclocking systems that are more than 20 years old, but it is interesting to see that hotrodding PCs has been around for as long as PCs themselves have existed!

Modern PC Clocks

A modern PC has at least two crystals on the motherboard; the main crystal is used to control the speed of the motherboard and motherboard circuitry, and the other is used to control the real time clock (RTC). The main crystal is always 14.31818MHz (it might be abbreviated as 14.318 or just 14.3), and the RTC crystal is always 32.768KHz.

Why 14.31818MHz?

The original 1981 vintage IBM PC ran at 4.77MHz, a speed derived by taking a 14.31818MHz crystal and using a divider circuit to divide the frequency by 3 to get 4.77MHz. The same 14.31818MHz crystal was also divided by 4 to get 3.58MHz, which is the exact frequency needed for the NTSC color video modulation signal required to be compatible with color TV. Another circuit divided the crystal frequency by 12 to get 1.193182MHz, which was used by an 8253 programmable three-channel 16-bit interval timer/counter chip. Each channel could be used to take an input clock signal and produce an output signal by dividing by an arbitrary 16-bit number. Channel 0 was used to make the time of day clock ticks. It was programmed by the BIOS to call INT 08h every 65,536 ticks, which was about 18.2 times per second (or about every 55 milliseconds). The software routines linked to INT 08h caused the time of day clock to be updated and could also chain to any other activities that needed to be done periodically. Channel 1 was used to tell the DMA to refresh the dynamic RAM every 72 cycles (about 15 microseconds), and channel 2 was used to make an audio signal for the speaker (beeps)—different tones could be made by changing the divisor.

As a testament to computer evolution, all modern PCs are still controlled by a 14.318MHz crystal! The crystal, in conjunction with a frequency timing generator chip, is used to derive virtually all the frequencies used on a modern motherboard by the CPU bus, PCI bus, AGP bus, memory bus, and USB.

PCs don't run at 14.318MHz, so how can a crystal of that speed be used to control their speed? And what happens when you install a different processor? How does the system adjust the bus and other speeds to accommodate the new chip? The answer is that a special chip called a frequency timing generator (FTG) or frequency synthesizer is used in conjunction with the crystal to derive the actual speeds of the system. Figure 23.6 shows a portion of a motherboard with an FTG chip with a 14.318MHz crystal below it.

Figure 23.6   Frequency synthesizer chip with a 14.318MHz crystal.

The RTC uses its own separate 32.768KHz crystal to count time independent from the speed of the system. Figure 23.7 shows a 32.768KHz crystal next to a chipset South Bridge or I/O controller hub, which contains the RTC circuitry and CMOS RAM.

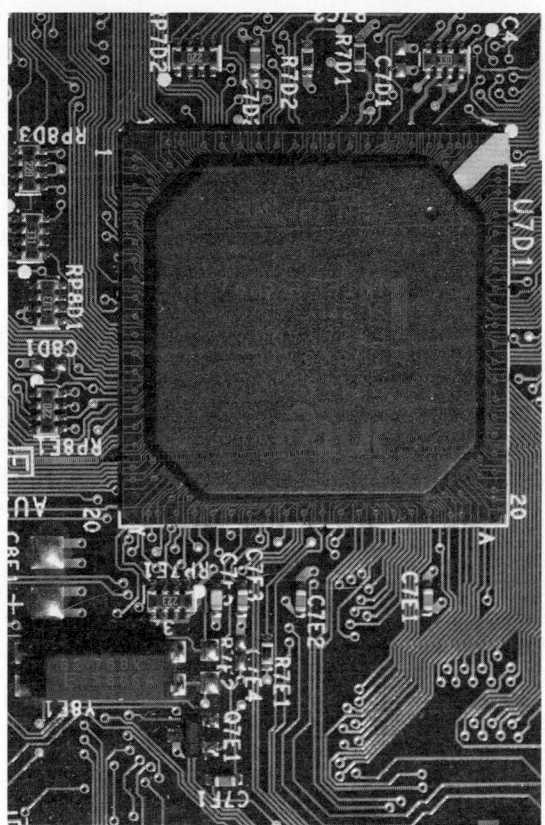

Figure 23.7 Chipset South Bridge (I/O controller hub) incorporating an RTC, along with the 32.768KHz clock crystal.

Most frequency synthesizer chips used on PC motherboards are made by Integrated Circuit Systems (www.icst.com) or Cypress Semiconductor (www.cypress.com; formerly International Microcircuits Inc [IMI]). These chips use phased locked loop (PLL) circuitry to generate synchronized processor, PCI, AGP, and other bus timing signals that are all derived from a single 14.318MHz crystal. The crystal and frequency synthesizer chip are usually situated near the processor and main chipset component of the motherboard.

The amazing thing about these chips is that most of them are programmable and adjustable, so they can change their frequency outputs via software, which results in the system running at different speeds. Because all CPUs are based on the speed of the CPU bus, when you change the CPU bus speed generated by the frequency synthesizer chip, you can change the speed of your processor. Because the PCI, AGP, and memory buses are often synchronized with the speed of the processor bus, when you change the processor bus speed by a given percentage, you also change the speed of those other buses by the same percentage. The software to accomplish this is built in to the BIOS Setup menus of most modern motherboards.

Overclocking Tips

Most modern motherboards automatically read the CPU and memory components to determine their proper speed, timing, and voltage settings. Originally, these settings were controlled by jumpers and switches on 486 and Pentium boards, but in most modern boards you can enter the BIOS Setup to change these settings to manual and then use the menu options in the BIOS Setup to alter the speed of the system. Because such alterations can make the system unstable, most systems are designed to boot into the BIOS Setup at a default low speed so you are not locked out from making changes in the future. This makes overclocking as simple as changing a few menu options and then rebooting to test the selections you've made.

The concept for overclocking is simple: You change the settings to increase the speed of the processor, memory, buses, and so on until the system becomes unstable. Then you can go back in and reduce the settings until it is stable again. In this manner, you find the maximum sustainable speed for a system. Because each processor is different, even ones with the same ratings can end up allowing different maximum stable speeds.

This is made possible by how processors and other components are actually manufactured. For example, the current Prescott version of the Pentium 4 is a chip that is 112 square mm and made on 300mm wafers, resulting in a maximum of 631 chips per die. Many of those chips won't pass testing, but let's say that 80% (or 504 chips) do. Intel currently sells the Prescott version at speeds from 2.4GHz through 3.4GHz. This means that all the 500+ chips coming off the wafer are potentially 3.4GHz (or faster) chips. They are tested after manufacture and sorted into bins by how fast they run. Early in manufacturing a given processor design, they have more running at the lower speeds and fewer ones achieving the maximum settings. This is why the fastest chips are the most expensive—generally fewer of them pass the testing at that speed. Eventually, however, as they tweak the manufacturing processes and chip design, more and more of the finished chips pass the higher speed tests. But lower-speed chips are priced less and sell more, so Intel might have to dip into the faster bins and mark those chips at the lower speeds to fill the larger number of orders. Essentially what I'm saying is that Intel sets out to make all the chips on the wafer identically and tries to make them so they will all run at the highest speed. If you purchase one of the lesser-rated chips, you really have the same chip as the higher-rated versions; the difference is the higher-rated ones are guaranteed to run at the higher speeds, whereas the lower-rated ones are not. That is where overclockers come in. They purchase lower-rated chips and essentially do their own testing to try to run them at the higher speeds. They can also start with the highest-rated chips and see whether they can run them even faster, but success there is much more limited. The most successful overclocking is always with the lowest-rated speed of a given design, and those chips are also sold for the lowest price. In other words, statistically you might be able to find many of the lowest-speed grade chips that are capable of running at the highest-speed grade (because they are essentially identical during manufacture); however, if you start with the highest-speed grade, you might be able to increase the speed only a very small percentage.

The key to remember is that a difference exists between the rated speed of a chip and the actual maximum speed at which it runs. Manufacturers such as Intel and AMD have to be conservative when they rate chips, so a chip of a given rating is always capable of running at least some margin of speed faster than the rating—the question is how much faster? The only way to know that is by testing chips individually.

Bus Speeds and Multipliers

Because modern processors run at a multiple of the motherboard speed and the selected multiple is locked within the processor, all you can do to change speeds is to change the processor bus speed settings. The processor bus is also called the CPU bus, front side bus (FSB), or processor side bus (PSB), all of which are interchangeable terms.

For example, I built a system that uses an Intel Pentium 4 3.2E processor, which typically runs at 3200MHz on an 800MHz CPU bus. Thus, the processor is locked to run at four times the speed of the CPU bus. I was able to increase the CPU bus speed from 800MHz to 832MHz, which meant the processor speed increased from 3200MHz to 3328MHz, which is 128MHz faster than the rating. This took all of about 60 seconds to reboot, enter the BIOS Setup, make the changes in the menu, save, and reboot again. This was only a 4% increase in overall speed, but it didn't cost a penny and the system seemed to be just as stable as it was before.

Many motherboards allow changes in speed of up to 50% or more, but a processor rarely sustains speeds that far above its rating without locking up or crashing. Also note that, by increasing the speed of the processor bus, you are increasing the speed of the memory bus, PCI bus, and AGP bus by the same percentage. Therefore, if your memory is unstable at the higher speed, the system will still crash, even though the processor might have been capable of sustaining it. The lowest common denominator prevails, which means your system will run faster only if all the components are up to the challenge.

Many motherboards allow voltage changes to be made for components such as processors, memory, and video cards. Be careful when making these changes because you can damage a component with improper voltage. Still, many overclockers have found that by tweaking the voltage up or down a tenth or so at a time, they can get a system to run more stable than had otherwise been possible.

Cooling

Heat can be a problem in any high-performance system. The higher-speed processors consume more power and therefore generate more heat. The processor is usually the single most power-hungry chip in a system, and in most situations, the fan inside your computer case is incapable of handling the load without some help.

Heatsinks

At one time, a *heatsink*, a special attachment for a chip that draws heat away from the chip, was needed only in systems in which processor heat was a problem. However, starting with the faster Pentium processors in the early 1990s, heatsinks have been a necessity for every processor since.

A heatsink works like the radiator in your car, pulling heat away from the engine. In a similar fashion, the heatsink conducts heat away from the processor so it can be vented out of the system. It does this by using a thermal conductor (usually metal) to carry heat away from the processor into fins that expose a high amount of surface area to moving air. This enables the air to be heated, thus cooling the heatsink and the processor as well. Just like the radiator in your car, the heatsink depends on airflow. With no moving air, a heatsink is incapable of radiating the heat away. To keep the engine in your car from overheating when the car is not moving, auto engineers incorporate a fan. Likewise, a fan is always incorporated somewhere inside your PC to help move air across the heatsink and vent it out of the system. In some name-brand systems, the fan included in the power supply is enough when combined with a special heatsink design; in most cases, though, an additional fan must be attached directly over the processor to provide the necessary levels of cooling. Case fans are also typical in recent systems to assist in moving the hot air out of the system and replacing it with cooler air from the outside.

The heatsink is clipped or, rarely today, glued to the processor. A variety of heatsinks and attachment methods exist. Figure 23.8 shows various passive heatsinks and attachment methods.

Tip

According to data from Intel, heatsink clips are the number-two destroyer of motherboards (screwdrivers are number one). When installing or removing a heatsink that is clipped on, be sure you don't scrape the surface of the motherboard. In most cases, the clips hook over protrusions in the socket and, when installing or removing the clips, scratching or scraping the surface of the board right below where the clip ends attach is very easy. I like to place a thin sheet of plastic underneath the edge of the clip while I work, especially if board traces that can be scratched are in the vicinity.

Heatsinks are rated for their cooling performances. Typically, the ratings are expressed as a resistance to heat transfer in degrees centigrade per watt (°C/W), where lower is better. Note that the resistance varies according to the airflow across the heatsink.

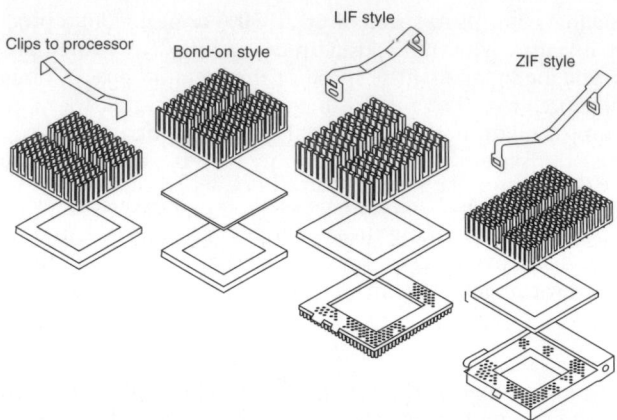

Figure 23.8   Passive heatsinks for socketed processors showing various attachment methods.

Active Heatsinks

To ensure a constant flow of air and more consistent performance, many heatsinks incorporate fans so they don't have to rely on the airflow within the system. Heatsinks with fans are referred to as *active* heatsinks (see Figure 23.9). Active heatsinks have a power connection. Older ones often used a spare disk drive power connector, but most recent heatsinks plug in to dedicated heatsink power connections found on the newer motherboards.

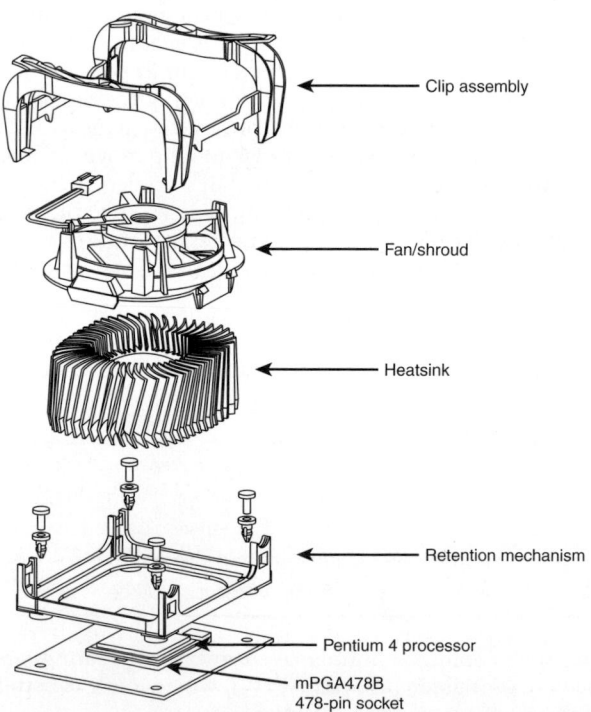

Figure 23.9   Active heatsink suitable for a Pentium 4 processor using Socket 478.

The Pentium 4 design uses two cams to engage the heatsink clips and place the system under tension. The force generated is 75 lbs., which produces a noticeable bow in the motherboard underneath the processor. This bow is normal, and the motherboards are designed to accommodate it. The high amount of force is necessary to prevent the heavier heatsinks from pulling up on the processor during movement or shipment of the system, and it ensures a good bond for the thermal interface material (thermal grease).

Figure 23.10 shows the design used on most Athlon 64 and 64 FX processors, featuring a cam and clip assembly on one side. Similar to the Pentium 4 double-cam assembly shown earlier, this design puts 75 lbs. of force between the heatsink and the processor. Bowing of the motherboard is prevented in this design by the use of a special stiffening plate underneath the motherboard. The heatsink retention frame actually attaches to this plate through the board. The stiffening plate and retention frame normally come with the motherboard, but the heatsink with fan and the clip and cam assembly all come with the processor.

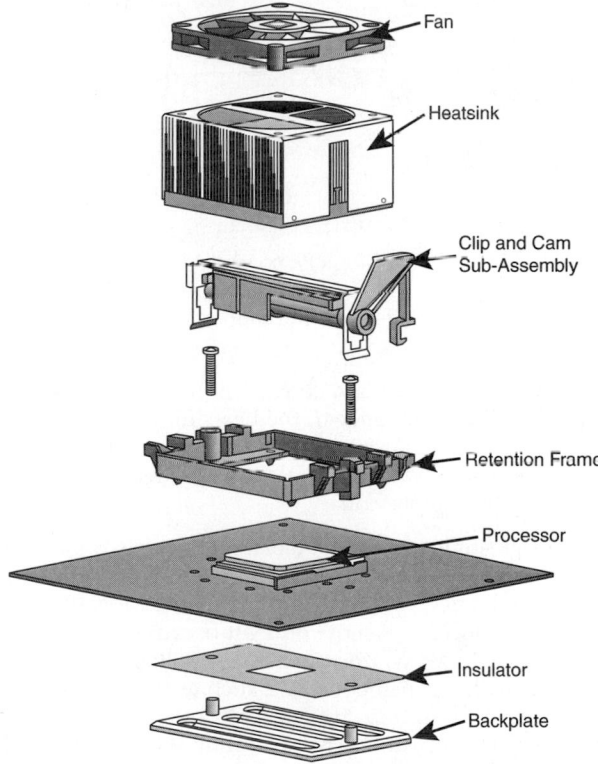

Fan

Heatsink

Clip and Cam Sub-Assembly

Retention Frame

Processor

Insulator

Backplate

Figure 23.10   Active heatsink suitable for an Athlon 64, Athlon 64 FX, or Opteron processor using Socket 754.

Tip

One of the best reasons to use the motherboard-based power connectors for the fan is that most recent system BIOS setup programs can display the fan performance and report it to a system monitoring program. Because some processors— particularly older Athlon processors—can be destroyed in a few moments by a malfunctioning processor heatsink fan, this feature can help prevent a disaster inside your system.

Active heatsinks use a fan or other electric cooling device that requires power to run. Active heatsinks also require power and usually plug in to the motherboard CPU fan connector (or, in older systems, a disk drive power connector). If you do get a fan-type heatsink, be aware that some on the market are of very poor quality. The bad ones have motors that use sleeve bearings, which freeze up after a very short life. I recommend only fans with ball-bearing motors, which last about 10 times longer than the sleeve-bearing types. Of course, they cost more—but only about twice as much, so you'll save money in the long run. Expect to pay anywhere from $15 to $25 for a high-quality active fan heatsink, unless you purchase a "boxed" processor that includes a factory-supplied, high-quality active heatsink in the box with the chip.

Figure 23.11 shows an active heatsink arrangement on a Pentium II/III processor. The Slot A–based Athlon processors use a similar arrangement.

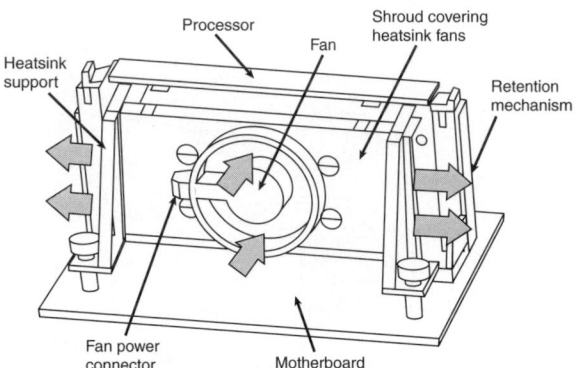

Figure 23.11   An active (fan-powered) heatsink and supports used with cartridge-type Pentium II/III processors.

With the wide variety of processor speeds and construction on the market today, you also need to match the processor speed to the speed range of the heatsink you plan to use. Heatsinks made for faster processors have a larger cooling area, and an increasing number of them use a copper conducting plate or are made of solid copper rather than less-conductive aluminum. Figure 23.12 compares two heatsinks made for Athlon XP processors.

Passive heatsinks are basically aluminum-finned radiators that rely on airflow from an external source. Passive heatsinks don't work well unless there is some airflow across the fins, usually provided by a chassis-mounted fan that sometimes features a duct to direct airflow directly through the fins on the heatsink. Integrating a passive heatsink is more difficult because you must ensure that the airflow comes from some other source; however, this can be more reliable and very cost effective if done correctly. This is why many of the larger name systems, such as those from Dell and Gateway, often use passive heatsinks with a ducted chassis fan. Systems built by individuals or smaller companies that don't have the ability to engineer a custom passive cooling solution should instead rely on an active heatsink with a built-in fan. An active heatsink provides a more certain cooling solution regardless of other airflow characteristics in the system.

Processors sold as boxed or retail versions from Intel and AMD include high-quality active heatsinks designed to work under the worst possible ambient conditions (see Figure 23.13). One of the main reasons I recommend purchasing boxed processors is that you are guaranteed to get a high-quality heatsink with the processor, one that is designed to cool the processor under the worst conditions and which should last the life of the system.

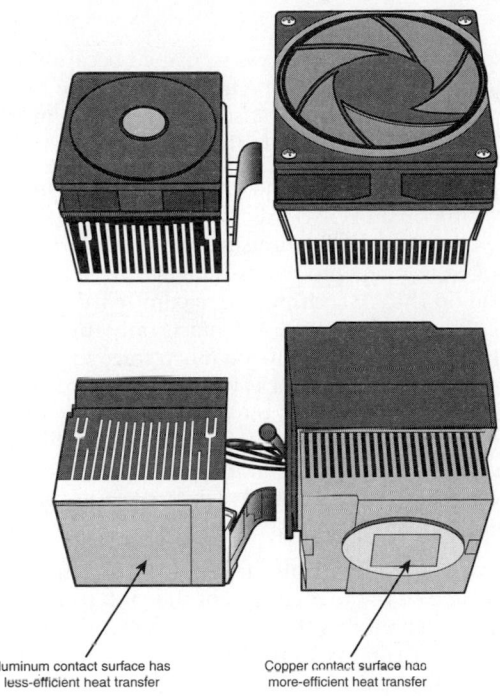

Aluminum contact surface has
less-efficient heat transfer

Copper contact surface has
more-efficient heat transfer

Figure 23.12   An all-aluminum active heatsink (left) is designed for slower processors than the copper/aluminum model at right.

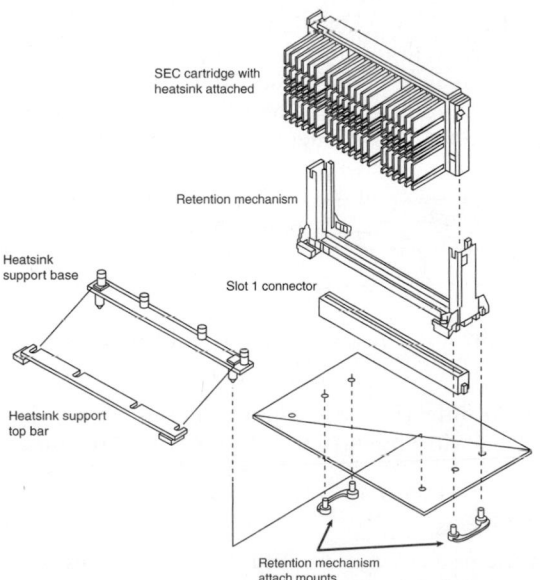

SEC cartridge with
heatsink attached

Retention mechanism

Heatsink
support base

Slot 1 connector

Heatsink support
top bar

Retention mechanism
attach mounts

Figure 23.13   A passive heatsink and supports used with Pentium II/III–SECC processors.

Heatsink Clamping Force

The FC-PGA packaging used by some processors is so named because the raw processor die is placed upside down on top of the chip. This enables the heatsink to come in direct or near-direct contact with the die, resulting in the maximum heat transfer to the sink. Unfortunately, some problems have occurred that have forced chip makers to modify their designs.

The main problem is one of force—too much and unevenly applied. Intel specifies a moderate 20-pound static load force for the heatsink on an FC-PGA die, whereas AMD specified a higher 30-pound static loading force for the spring clip to attach the heatsink on the Athlon, Duron, and Athlon XP processors. This has unfortunately resulted in many processors being damaged during heatsink installation. The reason for the higher static load on the AMD chips is to maximize the thermal transfer. Because the die rises up from the surface of the chip, the heatsink contacts only the die itself and overhangs in all directions. If, while installing the heatsink, you apply too much force to one corner or edge of the heatsink, you place an uneven force on the die and it cracks with a loud snap. This, of course, destroys the chip, and such damage is normally not warranted by the chip manufacturer because it is considered improper handling and not a manufacturer defect. Although this cracking problem affected both AMD and Intel processors, it was much more of a problem with the AMD chips due to the higher force from the heatsink clip specified by AMD. These problems have caused many vendors to provide a warranty for the processor only if it is sold with a motherboard and preinstalled by the vendor.

To correct these problems, AMD and Intel both have come up with solutions. AMD first began installing rubber pads near each of the four corners of the chip to help support the overhanging parts of the heatsink and prevent uneven forces that result in cracking. Unfortunately, even with these pads, you can still crack the die if you install the heatsink in a tilted or cockeyed position. To avoid damage, the Athlon 64 uses a different heatsink mounting method that secures the heatsink to the motherboard with a clip that is screwed into place.

Intel and AMD now install a metal cap called an integrated heat spreader (IHS) over the die of its newer processors. This protects the die from direct force and helps spread out the thermal contact point between the processor and heatsink. Most of the IHS-equipped chips allow up to a 100-pound static force from the heatsink and are virtually immune to the cracking problems related to improper heatsink installation. Intel's current heatsink designs for processors with integrated heat spreaders use a clamping force of 75 lbs. nominal on the processor. All Pentium 4, Celeron 4, Pentium III/Celeron Tualatin (0.13-micron), and AMD Athlon 64 and 64 FX processors include this (see Figure 23.14). In general, FC-PGA with the integrated heat spreader is called FC-PGA2.

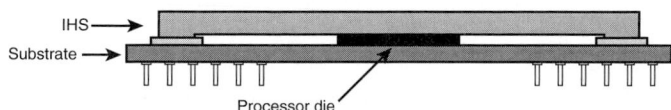

Figure 23.14   Side view of an FC-PGA2 processor showing the integrated heat spreader mounted on top of the die.

If you are installing an AMD or Intel processor that does not use an IHS metal cap, be extra careful to keep the heatsink flat and level with the surface of the die while attaching or removing the heatsink clip.

Heatsink Ratings and Calculations

When cooling a processor, the heatsink transfers heat from the processor to the air. This capability is expressed in a figure known as *thermal resistance*, which is measured in degrees Celsius per watt (C/W). The lower the figure, the lower the thermal resistance and the more heat the heatsink can remove from the CPU.

To calculate the heatsink required for your processor, a formula can be used:

$$R_{total} = T_{case} - T_{inlet}/P_{power}$$

T_{case} is the maximum allowable CPU case temperature, T_{inlet} is the maximum allowable inlet temperature to the CPU heatsink, and P_{power} is the maximum power dissipation of the processor. For example, the Pentium 4 3.4E (Prescott) processor is rated for a maximum operating temperature of 73° C and a maximum heatsink inlet temperature of 38° C, and it has a maximum thermal output of 103 watts. This means the heatsink required to properly cool this chip needs to be rated 73° C – 38° C / 103 W = 0.34° C/W. This figure includes the resistance of both the thermal interface material (thermal grease) as well as the heatsink itself, so if you used a thermal grease with a known resistance of 0.01° C/W, the heatsink would need to be rated at 0.33° C/W or less.

Another useful formula can be used to describe processor power:

$$P_{power} = C \times V^2 \times F$$

P_{power} is the maximum power output of the processor, C is the capacitance, V^2 is the voltage squared, and F is the frequency. From this you can see that if you double the frequency of a processor, it will consume twice as much power, and if you double the voltage, it will consume four times as much power. Consequently, if you lower the voltage by half, it will consume only one fourth the power. These relationships are important to consider if you are overclocking your processor because a small increase in voltage will have a much more dramatic effect than a similar increase in speed.

In general, increasing the speed of a processor by 5% increases the power consumption by only the same amount. Using the previous heatsink calculation, if the processor speed was increased by 5%, the 103W processor would now draw 108.15W and the required heatsink rating would go from 0.34° C/W to 0.32° C/W, a proportional change. In most cases, unless you are overclocking to the extreme, the existing heatsink should work. As a compromise, you can try setting the voltage on manual and dropping it a small amount to compensate, thereby reducing the power consumption. Of course, by dropping the voltage, the CPU might become unstable, so this is something that needs to be tested. As you can see, changing all these settings in the interest of overclocking can take a lot of time when you consider all the testing required to ensure everything is working properly. You have to decide whether the rewards are worth the time and energy spent on setting it up and verifying the functionality.

Note that most professional heatsink manufacturers publish their °C/W ratings, whereas many of what I call the "boutique" heatsink vendors do not. In many cases the manufacturers of many of the more extreme heatsinks don't do the testing that the professional manufacturers do and are more interested in the looks than the actual performance.

Installing a Heatsink

To have the best possible transfer of heat from the processor to the heatsink, most heatsink manufacturers specify some type of thermal interface material to be placed between the processor and heatsink. This typically consists of a ceramic, alumina, or silver-based grease but can also be in the form of a special pad or even a type of double-stick tape. Some are called *phase-change* material because they change viscosity (become thinner) above certain temperatures, enabling them to better flow into minute gaps between the chip and heatsink. In general, thermal greases offer higher performance than phase-change materials, but because they always have a lower viscosity, they flow more easily, can be messy to apply, and (if too much is used) can spill from the sides onto the socket and motherboard.

No matter what type you use, a thermal interface aid such as thermal grease or phase-change material can improve heatsink performance dramatically compared to installing the heatsink dry. Thermal interface materials are rated by thermal conductance (in which case higher is better) or thermal resistance (in which case lower is better). Unfortunately, several industry-standard rating scales are used to measure performance, often making product comparisons difficult. Some measure the thermal conductivity; others measure the thermal resistance; and the scales used can vary greatly. The most commonly reported specification is thermal resistance in degrees centigrade per watt (°C/W) for an interface layer 0.001" thick and 1 square inch in size. For a given material, the thinner the interface layer or the larger the area, the lower the resistance. In addition, due to other variables such as surface roughness and pressure, it is often impossible to directly compare different materials even if they appear to use the same ratings scale.

As a means of offering some sort of comparison, let's look at the effect on processor temperatures by using thermal interface materials of different specifications. Currently, the highest thermal output processor is the Pentium 4 3.4E, which is rated at 103W thermal output with a surface area on the heat spreader of 1.5 square inches. Using thermal interface materials of different C/W specifications, Table 23.1 shows the rise in temperature that will result.

Table 23.1   Thermal Interface Material Resistance Versus CPU Temperature Rise for a 103W Pentium 4 Processor

Thermal Rating (°C/W)	Temperature Rise (°C)	Thermal Rating (°C/W)	Temperature Rise (°C)
0.000	0.00	0.050	3.43
0.005	0.34	0.060	4.12
0.010	0.69	0.070	4.81
0.020	1.37	0.080	5.49
0.030	2.06	0.090	6.18
0.040	2.75	0.100	6.87

Most of the better thermal greases are rated from 0.005 to 0.02 C/W per square inch, which would result in a rise of between 0.34° and 1.37° C. Even if there was a "perfect" thermal grease available, you would reduce the CPU temperature by only less than 2° over most of the products currently on the market. I've seen actual tests of multiple brands of thermal greases, and in most cases the differences in temperature readings between different brands are insignificant. For that reason, I generally don't get too excited about different brands of thermal grease; most of the premium products on the market have surprisingly similar performance.

You can purchase thermal grease in small single-use tubes or larger versions that can service multiple processor installations. Most of the recommended thermal greases include alumina or silver, which offer the lowest thermal resistances. Silver is generally the best but is significantly more expensive with real-world differences that are very slight. One brand (Arctic Silver) has even developed a following sufficient to cause others to counterfeit the product and name. The important thing to note is that, based on calculations as well as in tests I've seen, there has been only a couple of degrees difference in CPU temperature under full load when substituting one brand of thermal grease for another. If you want the best, choose a compound with embedded silver. The next best option is alumina and then the less expensive (and somewhat less effective) ceramic-based greases.

Figure 23.15 shows the thermal interface pad or grease positioned between the processor and heatsink.

Most systems on the market today use improved motherboard form factors (shapes) called ATX or BTX. Systems made from these types of motherboards and cases allow for improved cooling of the processor because the processor is repositioned in the case and room is provided for a chassis fan or even a duct to direct airflow over the processor. Most of these cases also feature one or more secondary fans to further assist in cooling. The larger case-mounted fans, especially those with ducts mounted directly over the processor, add to the cooling capability of the system.

◄◄   See "ATX" p. 210.

◄◄   See "BTX" p. 224.

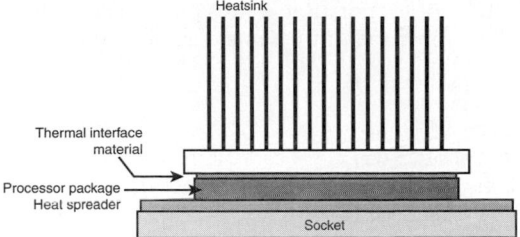

Figure 23.15 Thermal interface material helps transfer heat from the processor die to the heatsink.

Liquid Cooling

One of the more extreme methods for cooling a PC is to use a form of liquid cooling. Liquids have a much greater thermal carrying capacity than air, and as processors run hotter and hotter, it can be advantageous or even necessary in some situations to use a form of liquid cooling to dissipate the extreme levels of heat generated, especially in smaller or more confined spaces.

Several forms of liquid cooling are available, including

- Heat pipes
- Water cooling
- Refrigeration

Each of these uses a liquid or vapor to absorb the heat of the processor or other components and take that heat to a heat exchanger where it must eventually be dispersed to the air. So, all liquid cooling involves air cooling as well; it just removes the exchange of heat to the air to a remote place. Also, the heat exchanger (radiator) used can be much larger than what would fit directly on the processor or other chips, which is another reason liquid cooling offers much greater cooling capacity.

Of all the types of liquid cooling available, heat pipes are the only type that is practical and cost-effective in production-level PCs. Water cooling and especially refrigeration are limited to those who are pursuing extreme overclocking and are willing to pay the extreme price and put up with all the drawbacks and disadvantages that come with these two options.

Heat Pipes

Heat pipes were invented by George Grover at the Los Alamos National Laboratory in 1963. In simplest terms, a *heat pipe* is a thermal conductor designed to efficiently move heat from one place to another.

A typical heat pipe consists of a hermetically sealed tube incorporating a fine wick structure lining the inner walls, with a hollow core in the center. When constructed, the tube is first completely evacuated of air, then partially filled with a special fluid, and then sealed. The type of fluid and remaining vacuum inside allow the fluid to boil at relatively low temperatures. When the pipe is heated at one end, the fluid changes phase from liquid to vapor, absorbing a tremendous amount of heat in the process. The vapor then travels through the hollow core to the other end of the heat pipe where it condenses, changing phase again back into a liquid and releasing a tremendous amount of heat in the process. The liquid then travels back to the original end through the wick structure via capillary action (see Figure 23.16).

Heat pipes work by causing a liquid to change phase into a gas to absorb heat and then by causing the gas to change phase back into a liquid to release heat. The energy required to change phase is called the *latent heat of evaporation*. For example, the latent heat of evaporation for water is about 540 cal/g. Most heat pipes use water, ammonia, and methanol. The specific liquid is selected based on the temperature range at which the pipe will work. Water normally boils at 100° C (212° F); however, inside a heat pipe, the pressure is reduced by a partial vacuum such that the boiling point is at room temperature. Because of the heat of evaporation, a heat pipe is generally 10–10,000 times more thermally conductive than a solid copper rod of the same diameter and length.

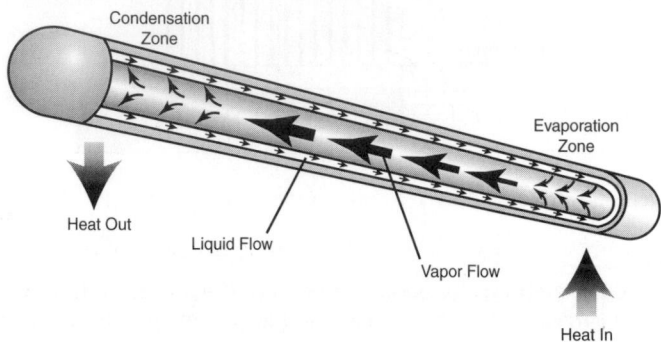

Figure 23.16 Heat pipe interior structure and function.

Heat pipes cannot work alone. They need to be attached to the processor or other heat producing device at one end, and they must have some way of getting rid of the heat at the other end. Usually the condensing end is attached to a conventional heatsink, often with a fan. Figure 23.17 shows one of the heat pipe–based heatsinks used in the Shuttle line of small form factor systems.

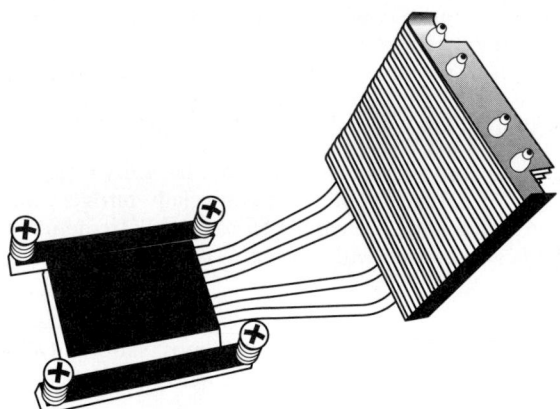

Figure 23.17 Heat pipe system with four pipes for cooling a processor.

In this example, a fan would be mounted on the back panel blowing through the fins attached to the ends of the heat pipes.

Heat pipes have many advantages. Because they are sealed and have no moving parts, they don't require any maintenance and don't wear out. If properly designed, they can even withstand freezing, although they won't work properly until the liquid inside is thawed. Heat pipes are also very compact and are ideal for small form factor system designs. This is one reason almost all laptop computers have been cooled by heat pipes since the early 1990s.

Heat pipes are not only useful as a specific cooling solution, but can also be used to enhance conventional heatsinks. By embedding heat pipes inside a conventional heatsink, the thermal distribution within the heatsink is dramatically improved. Figure 23.18 shows a heatsink with two heat pipes allowing for greater transfer of heat from the bottom to the top of the sink.

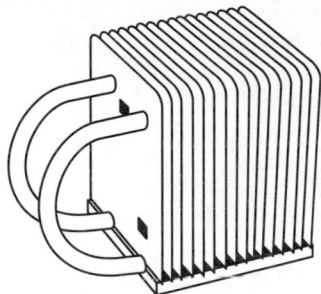

Figure 23.18   Heatsink with heat pipes for improved thermal distribution and performance.

Of all of the liquid cooling mechanisms, heat pipes have the most promise for future use in desktop computers.

Water Cooling

Water cooling is simple in concept but more complicated in reality. The idea is to circulate water over the processor or other components, thereby keeping them cool. The reality is a bit more difficult, making water cooling expensive, difficult to implement, and suitable only for extreme situations.

Water cooling involves several main components:

- *Water blocks.* Mounted on the processor and sometimes on the video card or chipset North Bridge, these are mostly blocks of metal with internal water passages and fittings to connect hoses.
- *Hoses and fittings.* These are used to interconnect all the components in the system.
- *Reservoir.* These are used to provide a sufficient amount of water to cool the components, as well as to cool the water for recirculation.
- *Pump.* A device used to move the water through the system.
- *Coolant.* The fluid, usually water, which is pumped through the system.

A diagram of a water cooling system using an external reservoir and pump is shown in Figure 23.19.

Some systems use pumps and reservoirs that are internal to the PC or that are mounted on the top, sides, or back. Placing the pump and reservoir inside can be difficult because these components require additional room.

Although water cooling systems can provide a tremendous amount of cooling capacity, they can be troublesome to use and maintain. Their primary disadvantages are that they require a pump to move the water and, if the pump fails, the system overheats. In addition, the water tends to cause corrosion in the pump, water blocks, and reservoirs and can even be subject to problems such as algae growth or other contamination. Finally, every fitting is the source of a potential leak and, if water leaks inside the system, it can cause the entire system to short out and fail. Water cooling systems also have a maintenance drawback: Periodic maintenance is necessary to prevent problems.

Contamination and corrosion have been major problems for water-cooled systems. Many people used plain water in their early designs, which as anybody familiar with automobiles knows allows corrosion and contamination to occur in short order. Using an automotive-style coolant is the best solution for most water cooling systems because the ethylene glycol–based coolants have additives that prevent corrosion and allow for long life. Still, the coolant should be periodically changed, and the water blocks, pump, and reservoir should be inspected for contamination and corrosion. Fittings should also be inspected for leaks periodically.

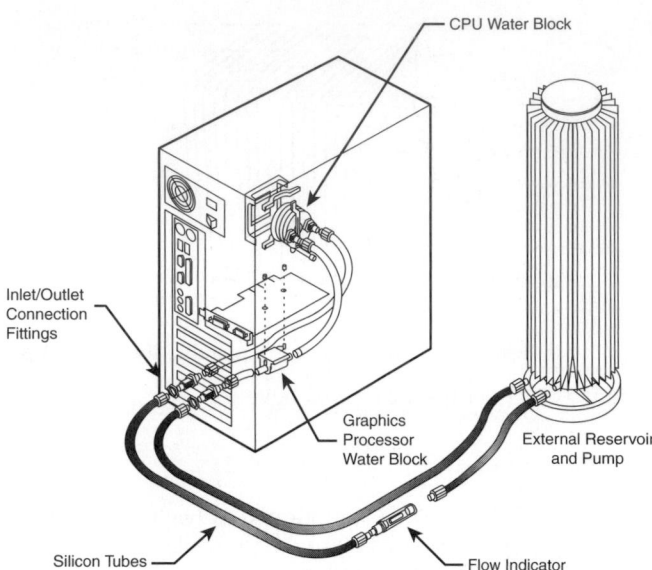

CPU Water Block

Inlet/Outlet
Connection
Fittings

Graphics
Processor
Water Block

External Reservoir
and Pump

Silicon Tubes

Flow Indicator

Figure 23.19   Zalman water cooling system with external reservoir and pump.

A good water cooling system can cost several hundred dollars, much more expensive than air cooling solutions or even heat pipes. They add a lot of visual appeal to a system; many systems use clear hoses and dyes to color the coolant for visual effect.

Due to the expense, maintenance required, potential for failure, and physical size of all the components, water cooling is best used in systems in which extreme overclocking or experimentation is the order. It will probably be a long time before water cooling reaches the point where it is used in commercially produced business or home PCs.

Refrigeration

On the extreme side of cooling, refrigeration enables the processor or other components to be reduced to below room temperature, allowing the extreme limits of overclocking and performance to be tested. When cooled to –40° C (also –40° F), a processor can be run at 33%–100% faster than rated. Unfortunately, this speed comes at a price—the refrigeration equipment is very expensive.

Because of the cost and expense, only a few companies have ever offered refrigerated chassis, mainly KryoTech and nVENTIV. In 1996, KryoTech (www.kryotech.com) introduced the first commercially available refrigerated PC. Unfortunately, due to costs and business concerns, it discontinued its chassis in 2002. nVENTIV (www.nventiv.com) was founded in 2000 as Chip-con and also introduced refrigerated chassis; today it has several models available. A cutaway view of the Mach II GT chassis and cooling module is shown in Figure 23.20.

The key to refrigerated cooling at –40° is the CPU block, which not only has to cool the chip, but also has to prevent condensation from forming. Special insulation and sealing are key to making this work. The nVENTIV CPU block is shown in Figure 23.21.

You can purchase an entire chassis or just the lower cooling unit, which can be used to adapt any system to refrigerated cooling. These cooling solutions sell from about $800 to $1,200, so this is not an inexpensive proposition. Still, if you must have the absolute fastest system on the block and you live for the ultimate in overclocking, the only way to go is refrigerated cooling.

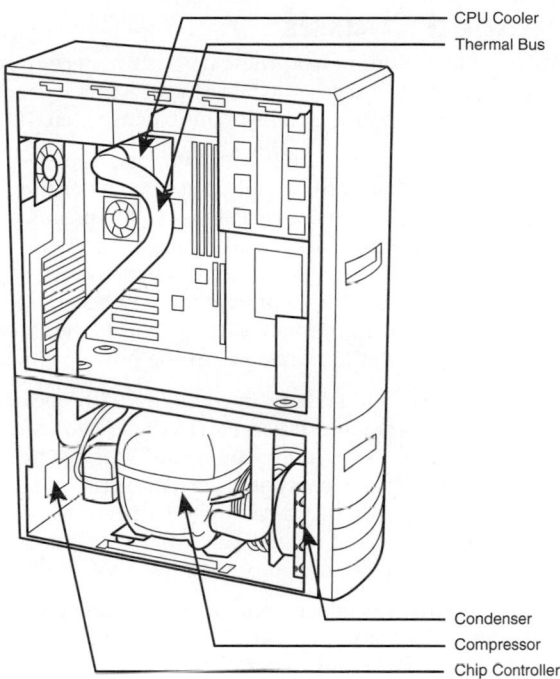

Figure 23.20   nVENTIV refrigerated cooling system cutaway.

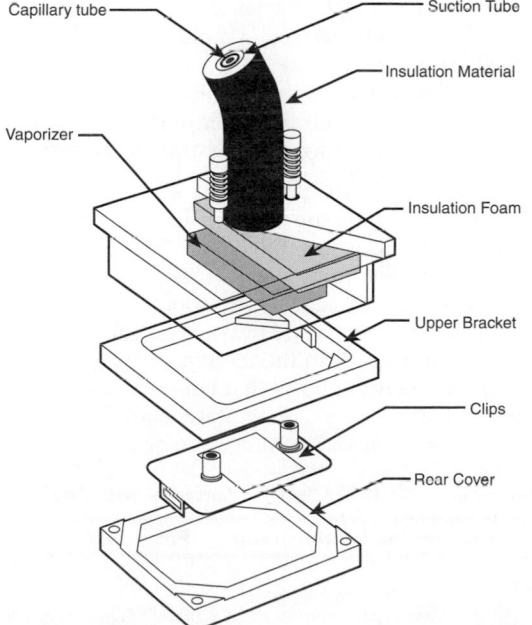

Figure 23.21   nVENTIV refrigerated processor block.

Thermally Advantaged Chassis

With processors generating more and more heat these days, some recent breakthroughs in chassis engineering and design have allowed for even the fastest processors to be properly cooled, without spending a fortune on an excessive amount of fans or an expensive cooling solution.

PC power supplies have always contained a fan. For many years, that single fan in the power supply bore the responsibility of cooling not only the supply, but also the entire system and even the processor. In fact, PCs prior to the 486 didn't even use heatsinks on the processor because they generated only a couple of watts of heat. Passive heatsinks first became a standard fixture on processors with the 486DX2 in 1992, which used up to 5.7W of power. Active heatsinks first appeared on the retail Pentium processors from Intel (called Overdrive processors) and became a standard fixture on boxed or retail Pentium II and III and AMD Athlon models in 1997 and later. Most chassis up until that time did not incorporate a cooling fan, except for what was in the power supply.

Chassis fans first became popular in OEM systems in the mid-1990s because they usually used less expensive passive heatsinks on the processor. It was more efficient to use a single chassis fan to cool both the chassis and the processor and save money by using a passive heatsink (without a fan) on the processor. By 2000, with the Pentium 4, many systems began using both an active processor heatsink (with a fan) and a chassis fan. Most modern systems include three fans—one in the power supply, one in the active heatsink on the processor, and one for the rear of the chassis. Some systems have additional fans, but three is the most common and most cost-effective design.

Unfortunately, with the most recently introduced processors reaching and even exceeding the 100W power level, it has become impossible for a standard chassis design to cool the system without resorting to adding more fans or using more exotic (and expensive) liquid cooling setups. A minor breakthrough in chassis design has occurred that can allow even processors consuming more than 100W to be adequately cooled in a three-fan system, without employing exotic solutions or even adding any fans.

As we know from the formula earlier in this chapter, processor power consumption is proportional to speed and is proportional to the square of the voltage it consumes. Even though processor voltages have been decreasing, speeds have been increasing at a much more rapid pace, such that power consumption is reaching all-time high levels beyond 100W. To combat this heat, heatsink manufacturers have increased the efficiency of processor heatsinks significantly over the past 10–15 years. Heatsinks are available today with thermal resistances on the order of 0.33° C/W or less. Unfortunately, conventional air-cooled heatsinks are fast approaching limits of the technology.

One cost-effective method of improving heatsink performance is to reduce the ambient temperature around the processor, which means lowering the temperature of air entering the heatsink. To ensure proper cooling for their boxed (retail) processors, Intel and AMD specify maximum temperature limits for the air that enters the heatsink fan assembly. If the air temperature entering the heatsink goes over that amount, the heatsink will not be able to adequately cool the processor. Because they must account for extreme circumstances, all modern systems and heatsinks are designed to operate properly if the external environmental ambient temperature in the room is 35° C (95° F). This means that, in general, PCs are designed to work in environments of up to that temperature. To operate in environments with higher temperatures than that, more specialized designs are required. Table 23.2 shows the maximum heatsink air inlet temperatures allowed for various processors with factory-installed heatsinks.

Table 23.2   Maximum Heatsink Inlet Temperatures for Various Processors

Environmental Temp.	Max. Heatsink Inlet Temp.	Processor Type
35° C (95° F)	45° C (113° F)	AMD K6, Pentium I, II, III
35° C (95° F)	42° C (107.6° F)	AMD Athlon, XP, 64, 64 FX
35° C (95° F)	40° C (104° F)	Pentium 4 Willamette, Northwood
35° C (95° F)	38° C (100.4° F)	Pentium 4 Northwood 3GHz+, Prescott 2.4GHz+

As you can see, newer, hotter processors are making more demands on system cooling. The most demanding processors today require that the internal chassis temperature remain at or below 38° C (100.4° F), even if the system is running in a room temperature of 35° C (95° F). The internal temperature rise, or preheating of air inside the system, is typically caused by heat from components such as motherboard chipsets, graphics cards, memory, voltage regulators, disk drives, and other heat-generating components (including the processor itself). Even with all these devices producing heat, the specifications for many newer processors require that the air temperature inside the chassis at the heatsink can rise only to 3° C (5.4° F) over ambient. This places extreme demands on the chassis cooling.

Conventional chassis are incapable of maintaining that low of a differential between the chassis interior and ambient temperatures. The only way to achieve that has been by adding an excessive amount of fans to the system, which unfortunately adds cost and significantly adds to the noise level. Many systems with multiple fans on the front, rear, and sides are still incapable of maintaining only 3° C (5.4° F) over ambient at the processor heatsink. Fortunately, a simple solution was derived that not only solves the problem, but also adds no fans and very little cost to a system. The best part is that this new design can be added to most existing chassis for under $10 in parts and has an easy installation.

Both Intel and AMD have been releasing documents describing the thermal attributes of their processors and guides showing ideas for cooling systems and chassis designs that can adequately cool the system. Chassis that have been specifically designed to improve cooling for the processor by maintaining a temperature of 38° C or less at the processor heatsink inlet are often referred to as *thermally advantaged chassis*. Using a thermally advantaged chassis both allows the processor to remain cool even under extreme environmental conditions and helps reduce noise. Most modern processors and chassis incorporate cooling systems that can adjust the speeds of the fans. If the temperatures remain below specific limits, the fans run at lower speeds, thus reducing the noise level. If temperatures rise, so do fan speeds and noise. In general, thermally advantaged chassis enable fan speeds to remain lower, resulting in quieter operation.

To meet the thermally advantaged chassis requirements, the following specifications are recommended:

- Accepts an industry-standard ATX, MicroATX, or FlexATX motherboard
- Accepts an industry-standard ATX, SFX, or TFX power supply with integral exhaust fan
- Uses a removable side cover with an adjustable processor duct and adapter card vent
- Provides a primary chassis rear exhaust fan of 92mm or larger and an optional front-mounted 80mm fan (excluding any fans in the power supply)

Because a thermally advantaged chassis is much better at cooling for very little extra cost, I highly recommend you look for these features on the next system you buy or build.

Processor Duct

The latest advancement in chassis design is the addition of a duct or air guide directly over the processor. This is called a *processor duct* or *chassis air guide*, and it essentially enables the processor heatsink to draw air directly from outside the chassis, greatly improving the thermal performance of the processor heatsink and easily meeting the requirement for a 38° C or lower heatsink inlet temperature. The specifications for this duct, and for an additional vent in the side cover for adapter cards such as graphics boards, can be found in an official standard called the Chassis Air Guide design guide, which was initially published in May 2002 and revised in September 2003. This guide details the dimensions and locations of the processor duct, as well as other attributes of the design. Figure 23.22 shows a typical tower chassis with the processor duct installed in the side cover.

The processor duct is essentially a tube positioned directly over the processor heatsink, allowing it to pull cool air from outside the chassis. When viewed from the side, the duct is usually covered by a grille or vent cover. Figure 23.23 shows the processor duct and adapter card vents as viewed from the side.

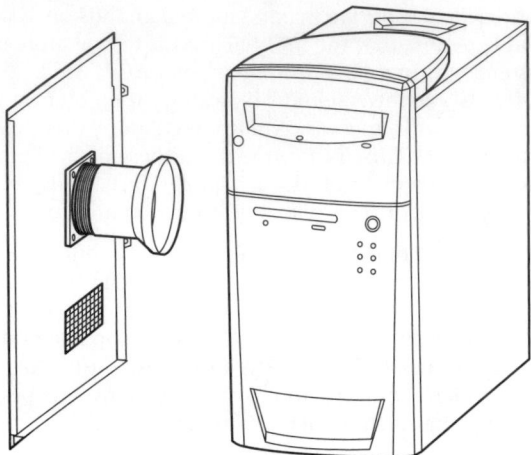

Figure 23.22   Thermally advantaged chassis featuring a processor air duct and adapter card vent in the side cover.

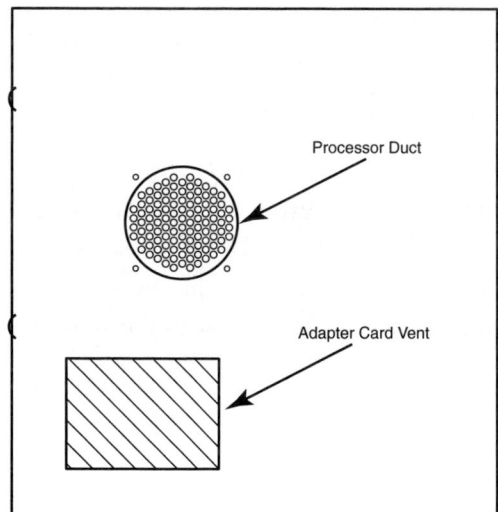

Figure 23.23   Thermally advantaged chassis processor duct and adapter card vent as viewed from the side.

The processor duct is the most important part of the thermally advantaged chassis design, and the placement of the duct is critical to its performance. The duct must be centered over the processor heatsink, and it must be positioned such that the end of the duct is spaced 12mm–20mm from the top of the heatsink. This ensures that the processor heatsink ingests only cool air from outside the chassis and enables some air to spill over to cool other parts of the system. Figure 23.24 shows the duct placement in relation to the top of the processor heatsink.

Because chassis can vary in size, shape, and dimension, the Chassis Air Guide standard details the placement of the processor duct and adapter card vent in relation to an industry-standard ATX motherboard.

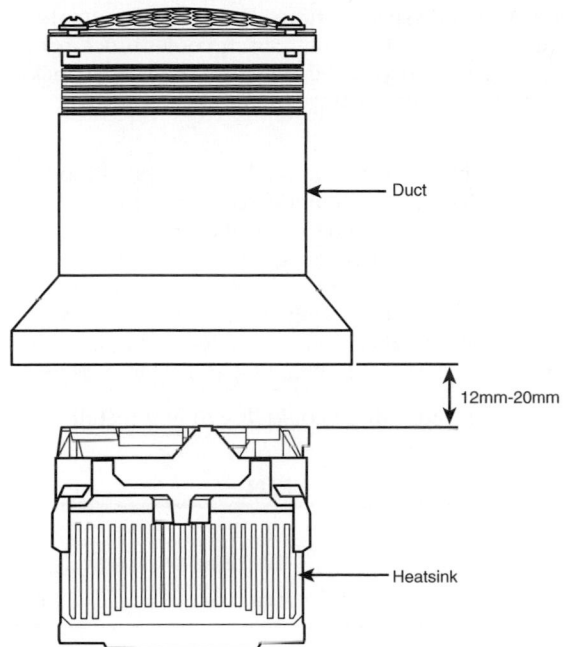

Figure 23.24   Processor air duct placement in relation to the processor heatsink.

The effect of the processor duct is quite noticeable in system operation. In a study done by Intel, it tested a system running Windows XP with a 3GHz Pentium 4 processor, a D865PERL motherboard, a GeForce4 video card, DDR400 memory, a hard drive, a CD-ROM drive, a sound card, and both rear- and front-mounted 80mm fans. The system was running in a 25° C (77° F) room, and the test results were as follows:

	Without CPU Duct	**With CPU Duct**
CPU inlet temp.	35° C (95° F)	28° C (82.4° F)
CPU fan speed	4050rpm	2810rpm
Sound level	39.8 Dba	29.9 Dba

As you can see, adding the duct dropped the temperature of the processor by 7° C (12.6° F), even while allowing the heatsink fan speed to drop to the lowest setting. The result is a processor that runs cooler, a fan that lasts longer, and less noise. As you can see, even with dual chassis fans already in the system, the processor duct makes a huge difference.

By selecting a thermally advantaged chassis, you ensure that your processor remains cool under the most extreme environmental conditions, not to mention that you extend the life of the heatsink fan and cause your system to be much quieter overall.

Functional Chassis Mod: Adding a Processor Duct

Now that you know to look for a thermally advantaged chassis with a processor duct for your next system, what about the systems you already have? Fortunately, this is one modification that is extremely easy to perform to an existing system. Unlike purely cosmetic modifications, this mod benefits your system tremendously and is much more about function and performance than it is about looks.

After studying the Chassis Air Guide specifications, I thought this would be a perfect mod to perform to one of my existing systems. The benefits are obvious: A cooler processor is a happier processor, and the rest of the system is happier as well. If you had thoughts about overclocking, this modification will improve the cooling capability of your existing heatsink such that you won't need to replace it even in an overclocking situation.

After searching the local home improvement and hardware stores, I found the perfect solution for adding a processor duct to an existing system in the plumbing section! As I was looking over various fittings and parts to see what I could make work in the most efficient and least costly manner, I heard the inevitable "Can I help you?" from one of the store attendants. I thought to myself, "How am I going to answer? I mean, I can't really tell him I'm looking for parts to modify my computer! Ahh, what the heck," I thought. So, I said, "Okay, maybe you can help. I'm looking for parts that I can use to add a processor duct to my computer, which conforms to the official Chassis Air Guide 1.1 standard, thus making it a thermally advantaged chassis." "Um, never mind…" was all he could say in response, as he walked away shaking his head.

After checking everything out, I found that I could design and install the modification using only two parts as follows:

Item	P/N	Price
2" no-caulk shower drain (PVC)	30171	$5.97
4" flexible downspout connector (rubber)	PDSC 43	$2.99
	Total	$8.96

I purchased these parts at Menards; however, any decent home improvement or hardware store should have them. The parts are shown in Figure 23.25.

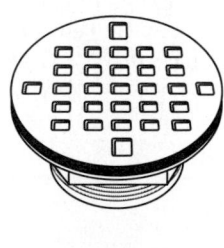

Figure 23.25   2" no-caulk shower drain (for processor duct) and a 4" rubber flexible downspout connector (for processor duct).

The duct is exceedingly simple; it merely consists of the two pieces mated. The rubber downspout connector slips over the threaded end of the PVC shower drain and can be adjusted or even trimmed to get the precise distance from the top of the CPU heatsink.

To install the duct, follow these directions:

1. Remove the chassis side cover. Place a layer of masking tape completely covering the outer skin of the side cover to protect the paint from scratches when you are cutting the hole.

2. Looking at the cover as it would be positioned on the chassis, make a mark directly over the center position of the processor heatsink.

3. Using a hole saw, jigsaw, or other tools, cut a 3.25" (82.5mm) hole in the side cover, using the mark you made as the center point. The hole does not have to be cosmetically perfect or precise because the flange on the PVC shower drain will cover about a quarter of an inch of material beyond the hole.

4. Take the PVC shower drain and pull off the stainless steel strainer (it snaps off); then remove and discard the internal locknut, locknut spinner, and no-caulk gasket.

5. Unscrew the outer locknut, remove the paper and rubber gaskets, and discard the paper gasket.

6. Slide the PVC drain into the hole in the side cover, with the flange on the outside and the threaded portion on the inside.

7. Slip the rubber gasket over the threaded portion, and then screw on the outer locknut and tighten it down.

8. Take the rubber flexible downspout connector and slide the narrow portion over the threads on the PVC shower drain.

9. Place the cover and duct assembly back on the system for a trial fitting, look through the open duct, and measure the distance between the end of the rubber downspout connector and the top of the processor (see Figure 23.26).

Figure 23.26   Peering through the duct to measure the clearance between the duct and processor heatsink.

10. Remove the side cover and duct assembly; then trim the rubber downspout connector with a knife or razor blade as necessary, so the distance from the end of the connector and the top of the CPU heatsink is between 12mm and 20mm (approx. 0.47"–0.79"). You might need to refit the cover several times when measuring and trimming.

11. Finally, snap the stainless steel strainer into place on the duct, and reinstall the side cover and duct assembly on the system (see Figure 23.27).

As you can see, the instructions are simple. The most difficult part is cutting the hole in the side cover. But even that isn't terribly hard, mainly because the flange of the drain covers an additional quarter of an inch of the cover, hiding the fact that the hole might be out of round or have rough edges.

Figure 23.28 shows the finished product, complete with stainless steel strainer.

Figure 23.27 Side cover with the duct being reinstalled on the chassis.

Figure 23.28 Processor duct and adapter card vent locations in relation to an ATX motherboard.

The system I used already had a vent for the adapter card area. Plus, it used a 92mm rear fan, so with the addition of the processor duct, it now fully meets the thermally advantaged chassis with Chassis Air Guide standards. Not only is it functional, but it actually looks pretty good, too. The stainless steel strainer adds an "industrial" look to the mod, adding a little form to the function.

Upon powering up the system with the duct in place, I immediately noticed that the processor was pulling air through the duct, allowing it to run noticeably cooler. Not bad for under $9 and about 15 minutes to cut the hole!

Front Panel I/O and Accessories

One of the features found in most new chassis is that they have front panel connectors for things like USB, FireWire, and audio connections such as microphone and headphone connectors. Many newer motherboards feature connections for USB and FireWire front-panel connectors built in to the motherboard. Most boards have these connections on the back panel, but they also provide additional ports via pin-header connectors on the board, which are designed for cables to plug in for front-panel connections. If you have a newer chassis, all you have to do is plug in the connectors from the chassis to the motherboard to enable the ports. What if you are upgrading your system to a new motherboard with integrated USB and maybe FireWire and sound, or you have a FireWire card and sound card and want to run connections for all these ports out the front of the system?

There are several solutions to this problem. One of the most amazing is the FrontX system of completely configurable front panel connectors, which install into a standard 5.25" bay or which you can custom install into any available flat surface on the front panel of your chassis.

Other front panel solutions come in the form of devices that have the same form factor as a 3.5" floppy drive and use the second 3.5" bay found on most systems. Because many newer systems don't even come with floppy drives, and even older systems came with only one drive, there is undoubtedly a free 3.5" bay waiting to be used.

The FrontX System

One of the most interesting, useful, and (most importantly) configurable case accessories is the line of front panel ports available from FrontX (www.frontx.com).

FrontX is a unique system that starts with a special front casing that fits into a 5.25" external drive bay. The casing contains several bays that can hold a maximum of eight ports of your choosing. If eight ports isn't enough, you can add a second casing and eight more ports. The ports are sold separately and include virtually every connector type you would want to use. An exceptional feature is that the front casing and all the ports are available in black, gray, or ivory to fit the color scheme of almost any system you might have.

An example of a FrontX casing with a serial port, microphone, speaker, headphone, USB and game port connector is shown in Figure 23.29.

Figure 23.29 FrontX 5.25" bay casing with several ports installed. *Photo courtesy FrontX.com.*

In this example, there is still room for another small port to be added. Currently, FrontX has the following ports available:

- Headphone port
- Audio-In port
- Microphone port
- Game/MIDI port

- USB type A
- Dual USB type A
- IEEE 1394 (FireWire/i.LINK)

- S-Video
- RCA (composite) video
- Serial port (9 pin)
- PS2 (keyboard/mouse) port

All these ports are available with internal or external connections. For example, if your motherboard has a USB pin-header connector for front-panel USB ports, you can use the FrontX internal version. If your motherboard doesn't have a pin-header connector but has only the standard connectors on the rear panel, you can use the FrontX external port version that connects to the external port on the back and then routes the cable through a special bracket back into the chassis, where it can then be mounted in the FrontX panel.

In addition to making both external and internal port connector versions of all the ports available, FrontX also has all types of extra cables, connectors, terminals, or any other special hardware you might need for installation. It even has guides for installing the FrontX ports directly into your front panel, something these ports are ideal for. If you want a custom case with every type of connector, that can be placed where you want it, and comes in the color you want, I highly recommend you check out these products. There is currently nothing else quite like them on the market.

Alternative Drive Bay Front-Panel Devices

One of the most popular devices you can install fits into a 3.5" bay and has USB, FireWire, and microphone/headphone connections, as well as an 8-in-1 digital card reader supporting CompactFlash I/II, MicroDrive, Secure Digital Card/Multimedia Card, Memory Stick/Memory Stick Pro, SmartMedia, and XD Picture Card. One example is the In-Win CR-I530 shown in Figure 23.30, which is available in both beige and black versions.

Figure 23.30   In-Win CR-I530 3.5" bay USB/FireWire/audio plus digital card reader. *Photo courtesy NewEgg.com.*

Another alternative is to combine a floppy drive with a USB digital card reader. Companies such as Mitsumi and Y.E. Data make combo floppy/card reader devices that fit into 3.5" bays. If you don't have a 3.5" external bay available but do have a 5.25" bay, you can use something like the Bytecc 5.25" front-panel device, which includes USB, FireWire, and audio connections plus a 7-in-1 digital card reader.

Another similar unit is the Galaxy 5.25" Multi Adapter Panel and Temperature controller. This device fits into a standard 5.25" bay and includes USB, FireWire, and audio ports as in the previous devices. However, instead of a digital card reader, it has a built-in temperature monitor and display and can control the speeds of up to four internal fans. The fan speeds are adjusted automatically according to the internal temperature, which is sensed via two sensors you can attach anywhere inside the system.

This is great if you have front- and rear-mounted fans you want to control to run the system more quietly when possible or at full speed when playing games or other processor-intensive applications.

If you use several USB devices, normally you have one or more hubs connected to the USB ports on your system, expanding the total number of ports you have. Whereas many newer motherboards have six or eight integrated USB ports, many older motherboards have only two or four, making a hub even more of a necessity. Rather than having one dangling around, you can add a built-in USB 2.0 hub to your system via one of the 3.5" drive bays using something like the Heisei 4-Port USB 2.0 front-panel hub.

If you are into something that adds an industrial or nostalgic look to your system while adding a little functionality as well, you can add a device such as the Cooler Master Musketeer controller panel (see Figure 23.31). This panel is designed to display the fan voltage; audio sound level; and temperature of the included thermal sensor, which you can position anywhere inside the chassis. Two slider controls let you adjust fan speeds and volume. I'm a fan of old radios and equipment and really like the industrial look with analog meters.

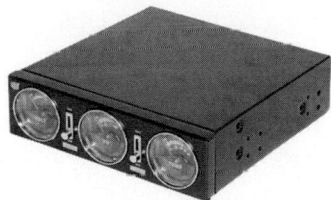

Figure 23.31   Cooler Master 5.25" bay LLC-U01 Musketeer controller panel. *Photo courtesy NewEgg.com.*

All these devices are available from online retailers such as NewEgg (www.newegg.com).

CHAPTER 24

PC Diagnostics, Testing, and Maintenance

PC Diagnostics

No matter how well built your PC is and how well written its software, something is eventually going to go wrong, and you might not always have a support system available to resolve the problem. Diagnostic software can be vitally important to you anytime your computer malfunctions or you are in the process of upgrading a system component or especially building an entirely new system from scratch. This chapter examines the types of diagnostics software available, and particularly those utilities you might already own because they are included with common operating systems and hardware products.

You also might find that your system problems are caused by a hardware malfunction and that you must open the computer case to perform repairs. This chapter also examines the tools and testers used to upgrade and repair PCs—both the basic items every user should own and some of the more advanced devices.

Of course, the best way to deal with a problem is to prevent it from occurring in the first place. The preventive maintenance sections of this chapter describe the procedures you should perform on a regular basis to keep your system in good working order. This chapter describes several levels of diagnostic software that are either included with your system or available from your system manufacturer and third parties. This chapter describes how you can get the most from this software. It also details the various ROM BIOS audio codes and error codes and examines aftermarket diagnostics and public-domain diagnostic software.

Diagnostics Software

Several types of diagnostic software are available for PCs. Some diagnostic functions are integrated into the PC hardware or into peripheral devices, such as expansion cards, whereas others take the form of operating system utilities or separate software products. This software, some of which is included with the system when purchased, assists users in identifying many problems that can occur with a computer's components. In many cases, these programs can do most of the work in determining which PC component is defective or malfunctioning. The types of diagnostic software are as follows:

- *POST.* The power on self test operates whenever any PC is powered up (switched on). These routines are contained within the motherboard ROM as well as ROMs on expansion cards.

- *Manufacturer-supplied diagnostics software.* Many of the larger manufacturers—especially high-end, name-brand manufacturers such as IBM, Hewlett-Packard, Dell, and others—make special diagnostics software expressly designed for their systems. This manufacturer-specific software normally consists of a suite of tests that thoroughly examines the system. In some cases, these utilities are included with the system, or you can download these diagnostics from the manufacturer's online services at no charge; otherwise, you might have to purchase them. Many vendors include a limited version of one of the aftermarket packages that has been customized for use with their systems. In some older IBM and Compaq systems, the diagnostic software is installed on a special partition on the hard drive and can be accessed during startup. This was a convenient way for those system manufacturers to ensure that users always had diagnostics available.

- *Peripheral diagnostics software.* Many hardware devices ship with specialized diagnostics software designed to test their particular functions. Adaptec SCSI host adapters, for example, include diagnostic functions in the card's ROM BIOS that you can access with a keystroke (Ctrl+A) at boot time. Sound cards normally include a diagnostic program on a disk along with the drivers, which test and verify all the card's functions. Network adapters usually include a diagnostic specific to that adapter on a disk, also normally with the drivers. Other devices or adapters also might provide a diagnostic program or disk, usually included with the drivers for the device.

- *Operating system diagnostics software.* Operating systems, such as Windows 9x/Me and Windows NT/2000/XP, include a variety of diagnostic software utilities designed to identify and monitor the performance of various components in the computer.

- *Aftermarket diagnostics software.* A number of manufacturers make general-purpose diagnostics software for PCs. This type of software is often bundled with other system maintenance and repair utilities to form a general PC software toolkit.

The Power On Self Test

When IBM first began shipping the original PC in 1981, it included safety features that had never been seen in a personal computer. These features were the power on self test (POST) and parity-checked memory. Although parity-checked or even error correcting code (ECC) memory is no longer available in most low-end chipsets, every PC still executes a POST when you turn it on. The following sections provide more detail on the POST, a series of program routines buried in the motherboard ROM-BIOS chip that tests all the main system components at power-on time. This series of routines is partially responsible for the delay when you turn on your PC; the computer executes the POST before loading the operating system.

What Is Tested?

Whenever you start up your computer, it automatically performs a series of tests that checks the primary components in your system, such as the CPU, ROM, motherboard support circuitry, memory, and major peripherals such as the expansion chassis. These tests are brief and are designed to catch hard (not intermittent) errors. The POST procedures are not very thorough compared with available disk-based diagnostics. The POST process provides error or warning messages whenever it encounters a faulty component.

Although the diagnostics performed by the system POST are not very thorough, they are the first line of defense, especially when it comes to detecting severe motherboard problems. If the POST encounters a problem severe enough to keep the system from operating properly, it halts the system boot process and generates an error message that often identifies the cause of the problem. These POST-detected problems are sometimes called *fatal errors* because they prevent the system from booting.

How Errors Are Displayed

The POST tests normally provide three types of output messages: audio codes, onscreen text messages, and hexadecimal numeric codes that are sent to an I/O port address.

POST errors can be displayed in the following three ways:

- *Beep codes*. Heard through the speaker attached to the motherboard.
- *POST checkpoint codes*. Hexadecimal checkpoint codes sent to an I/O port address. A special card plugged into either an ISA or a PCI card slot is required to view these codes.
- *Onscreen messages*. Error messages displayed onscreen after the video adapter is initialized.

BIOS POST Beep Codes

Beep codes are used for fatal errors only, which are errors that occur so early in the process that the video card and other devices are not yet functional. Because no display is available, these codes take the form of a series of beeps that identify the faulty component. When your computer is functioning normally, you should hear one short beep when the system starts up at the completion of the POST, although some systems (such as Compaq's) beep twice at the end of a normal POST. If a problem is detected, a different number of beeps sounds, sometimes in a combination of short and long tones.

BIOS POST Checkpoint Codes

POST checkpoint codes are hexadecimal numeric codes written by POST routines to I/O port address 80h as each major step is begun. These are often simply called *POST codes*. These POST codes can be read by only a special adapter card plugged into one of the system slots. These cards originally were designed for system manufacturers to use for burn-in testing of the motherboard. Several companies make these cards available to technicians. Micro 2000, JDR Microdevices, Data Depot, Ultra-X, and Trinitech are just a few manufacturers that market these POST cards. See the vendor list on the accompanying disc for more information about these manufacturers.

POST checkpoint codes can be used to track the system's progress through the boot process from power-on right up to the point at which the bootstrap loader runs (when the operating system load begins). When you plug a POST code reader card into a slot, during the POST you will see two-digit hexadecimal numbers flash on the card's display. If the system stops unexpectedly or hangs, you can identify the test that was in progress during the hang from the two-digit code. This step usually helps to identify the malfunctioning component.

Most older POST reader cards plug into the 8-bit connector that is a part of the ISA or EISA bus. Many systems—even those with PCI slots—still have ISA connectors. In that case, those cards are adequate. However, the motherboards found in most newer PCs have no ISA slots at all, so obviously an ISA POST card won't work. Virtually all the companies that make POST cards also make PCI versions. Micro 2000 has a card called the Post-Probe, which has both ISA and PCI connectors on the same board. PC Certify has a similar card called the PCISA FlipPOST (see Figure 24.1). Both companies also have separate Micro Channel Architecture (MCA) bus adapters that allow POST cards to work in older IBM PS/2 systems with the MCA bus.

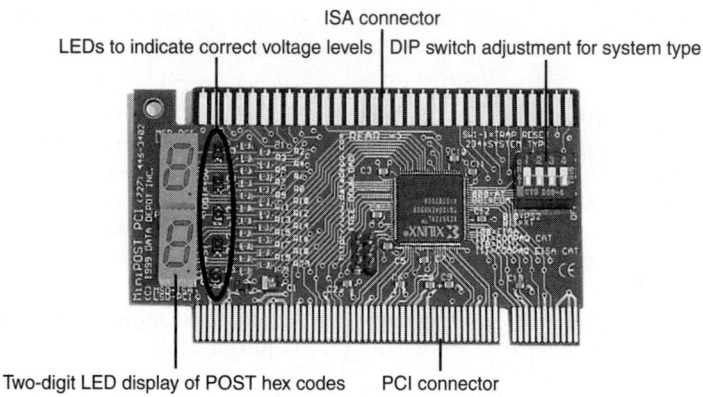

Figure 24.1 The PC Certify PCISA FlipPOST diagnostics card works with both PCI- and ISA-based systems, and it also tests motherboard voltage levels.

No matter what, be sure your POST card works in a PCI slot if you are working on modern PCs. Most newer systems don't have ISA slots, and you will rarely encounter any MicroChannel slots. If you maintain older Compaq or EISA-based systems from any vendor, these systems might use an I/O port address other than port 80. Simpler POST cards monitor only port 80, but more sophisticated cards (such as the PCISA FlipPOST shown in Figure 24.1) have DIP switches or jumper blocks to configure the card to monitor the different I/O port addresses used by Compaq and EISA-based systems.

Note

Listings for additional POST checkpoint codes can be found in the Technical Reference section of the accompanying disc. Also, see Chapter 5, "BIOS," to learn more about working with your BIOS. Remember to consult your motherboard documentation for codes specific to your BIOS version. Also, the documentation included with the various POST cards covers most older as well as newer BIOS versions.

BIOS POST Onscreen Messages

Onscreen messages are brief messages that attempt to indicate a specific failure. These messages can be displayed only after the point at which the video adapter card and display have been initialized.

These different types of error messages are BIOS dependent and vary among BIOS manufacturers, and even in some cases among different BIOSs from the same manufacturer. The following sections list the codes used by the most popular ROM BIOS versions (AMI, Award, Phoenix, and IBM BIOS), but you should consult your motherboard or ROM BIOS manufacturer for the codes specific to your board and BIOS.

Most POST code cards come with documentation listing the POST checkpoint codes for various BIOS versions. If your BIOS is different from what I have listed here, consult the documentation for your BIOS or the information that came with your particular POST card.

Note

I've also included additional BIOS error messages in the Technical Reference section on the disc included with this book.

AMI BIOS POST Error Codes

Table 24.1   AMI BIOS POST Beep Codes

Beeps	Error Description	Action
1	Memory Refresh Error	Clean the memory contacts and reseat the modules. Remove all modules except the first bank. Replace the memory, power supply, and motherboard.
2	Memory Parity Error	Clean the memory contacts and reseat the modules. Remove all modules except the first bank. Replace the memory, power supply, and motherboard.
3	Base 64KB Memory Error	Clean the memory contacts and reseat the modules. Remove all modules except the first bank. Replace the memory, power supply, and motherboard.
4	Timer Error	Check for proper motherboard installation, loose screws, foreign objects causing shorts, and over-tightened screws. Replace the motherboard.
5	Processor Error	Check for proper motherboard installation, loose screws, foreign objects causing shorts, and over-tightened screws. Make sure the processor and heatsink are installed properly; remove and reseat them. Replace the processor. Replace the motherboard.
6	8042 – Gate A20 Error	Check for proper motherboard installation, loose screws, foreign objects causing shorts, and over-tightened screws. Replace the keyboard, motherboard, and processor.
7	Processor Exception Interrupt Error	Make sure the processor and heatsink are installed properly; remove and reseat them. Replace the processor. Replace the motherboard.
8	Display Memory Read/Write Error	Check the video card for proper installation. Try replacing the video card memory, and replace the video card. Replace the motherboard.
9	ROM Checksum Error	Try reseating the motherboard ROM chip. Try reflashing the motherboard ROM. Replace the motherboard.
10	CMOS Shutdown Register Read/Write Error	Replace the CMOS battery. Replace the motherboard.
11	Cache Memory Bad	Make sure cache settings in BIOS Setup are properly configured. Replace the processor. Replace the motherboard.
1 long, 3 short	Conventional/Extended Memory Error	Clean the memory contacts and reseat the modules. Remove all modules except the first bank. Replace the memory, power supply, and motherboard.
1 long, 8 short	Display/Retrace Error	Check the video card for proper installation. Try replacing the video card memory. Replace the video card. Replace the motherboard.

AMI BIOS codes used by permission of American Megatrends, Inc.

If you have a POST card, you can find the AMI BIOS POST checkpoint codes in the Technical Reference section of the disc packaged with this book.

Award BIOS and Phoenix FirstBIOS POST Error Codes

Currently, only one standard beep code exists in the Award BIOS (also known as the Phoenix FirstBIOS). A single long beep followed by two short beeps indicates that a video error has occurred and that the BIOS cannot initialize the video screen to display any additional information. If multiple or continuous beeps occur with an Award BIOS, this usually indicates problems with the power supply or memory.

Table 24.2   Award BIOS/Phoenix FirstBIOS POST Beep Codes

Beeps	Error Description	Action
1 long, 2 short	Video Card Error	Check the video card for proper installation. Try replacing the video card memory, and replace the video card. Replace the motherboard.
1 long, 3 short	Video Card Error	Check the video card for proper installation. Try replacing the video card memory, and replace the video card. Replace the motherboard.
Continuous beeps	Memory Error	Clean the memory contacts, and reseat the modules. Remove all modules except the first bank. Replace the memory, power supply, and motherboard.

If you have a POST card, you can find the Award BIOS and Phoenix FirstBIOS POST checkpoint codes in the Technical Reference section of the disc packaged with this book.

Table 24.3   Award BIOS POST Onscreen Error Messages

Message	Description
BIOS ROM checksum error - System halted	The checksum of the BIOS code in the BIOS chip is incorrect, indicating the BIOS code might have become corrupt. Contact your system dealer to replace the BIOS.
CMOS battery failed	The CMOS battery is no longer functional. Contact your system dealer for a replacement battery.
CMOS checksum error - Defaults loaded	Checksum of CMOS is incorrect, so the system loads the default equipment configuration. A checksum error can indicate that CMOS has become corrupt. This error might have been caused by a weak battery. Check the battery and replace if necessary.
CPU at *nnnn*	Displays the running speed of the CPU.
Display switch is set incorrectly	The display switch on the motherboard can be set to either monochrome or color. This message indicates the switch is set to a different setting than indicated in Setup. Determine which setting is correct, and then either turn off the system and change the jumper or enter Setup and change the VIDEO selection.
Press ESC to skip memory test	The user can press Esc to skip the full memory test.
Floppy disk(s) fail	Can't find or initialize the floppy drive controller or the drive. Make sure the controller is installed correctly. If no floppy drives are installed, be sure the Diskette Drive selection in Setup is set to NONE or AUTO.
HARD DISK initializing. Please wait amoment	Some hard drives require extra time to initialize.
HARD DISK INSTALL FAILURE	Can't find or initialize the hard drive controller or the drive. Make sure the controller is installed correctly. If no hard drives are installed, be sure the Hard Drive selection in Setup is set to NONE.
Hard disk(s) diagnosis fail	The system might run specific disk diagnostic routines. This message appears if one or more hard disks return an error when the diagnostics run.
Keyboard error or no keyboard present	Can't initialize the keyboard. Make sure the keyboard is attached correctly and no keys are pressed during POST. To purposely configure the system without a keyboard, set the error halt condition in Setup to HALT ON ALL, BUT KEYBOARD. The BIOS then ignores the missing keyboard during POST.
Keyboard is locked out - Unlock the key	This message usually indicates that one or more keys have been pressed during the keyboard tests. Be sure no objects are resting on the keyboard.

Table 24.3   Continued

Message	Description
Memory Test:	This message displays during a full memory test, counting down the memory areas being tested.
Memory test fail	If POST detects an error during memory testing, additional information appears giving specifics about the type and location of the memory error.
Override enabled - Defaults loaded	If the system can't boot using the current CMOS configuration, the BIOS can override the current configuration with a set of BIOS defaults designed for the most stable, minimal-performance system operations.
Press TAB to show POST screen	System OEMs might replace Phoenix Technologies' AwardBIOS POST display with their own proprietary displays. Including this message in the OEM display permits the operator to switch between the OEM display and the default POST display.
Primary master hard disk fail	POST detects an error in the primary master IDE hard drive.
Primary slave hard disk fail	POST detects an error in the secondary master IDE hard drive.
Resuming from disk, Press TAB to showPOST screen	Phoenix Technologies offers a save-to-disk feature for notebook computers. This message might appear when the operator restarts the system after a save-to-disk shutdown.
Secondary master hard disk fail	POST detects an error in the primary slave IDE hard drive.
Secondary slave	POST detects an error in the secondary slave IDE hard hard disk fail drive.

Phoenix BIOS POST Error Codes

The following codes are for the Phoenix BIOS, version 4.

Table 24.4   Phoenix BIOS 5.x and Earlier POST Beep Codes

Beeps	Error Description	Action
1-2	Video Card Error	Check the video card for proper installation. Try replacing the video card memory, and replace the video card. Replace the motherboard.
1-3	CMOS RAM Read/ Write Error	Replace the CMOS battery. Replace the motherboard.
1-1-4	ROM Checksum Error	Try reseating the motherboard ROM chip. Try reflashing the motherboard ROM. Replace the motherboard.
1-2-1	Timer Error	Check for proper motherboard installation, loose screws, foreign objects causing shorts, and over-tightened screws. Replace the motherboard.
1-2-2	DMA Initialization Error	Check for proper motherboard installation, loose screws, foreign objects causing shorts, and over-tightened screws. Replace the motherboard.
1-2-3	DMA Page Register Read/Write Error	Check for proper motherboard installation, loose screws, foreign objects causing shorts, and over-tightened screws. Replace the motherboard.
1-3-1	RAM Refresh Verification Error	Clean the memory contacts, and reseat the modules. Remove all modules except the first bank. Replace the memory. Replace the power supply. Replace the motherboard.
1-3-3	First 64KB RAM Multibit Data Line Error	Clean the memory contacts, and reseat the modules. Remove all modules except the first bank. Replace the memory, power supply, and motherboard.

Table 24.4   Continued

Beeps	Error Description	Action
1-3-4	First 64KB RAM Odd/Even Logic Error	Clean the memory contacts, and reseat the modules. Remove all modules except the first bank. Replace the memory, power supply, and motherboard.
1-4-1	First 64KB RAM Address Line Error	Clean the memory contacts, and reseat the modules. Remove all modules except the first bank. Replace the memory, power supply, and motherboard.
1-4-2	First 64KB RAM Parity Error	Clean the memory contacts, and reseat the modules. Remove all modules except the first bank. Replace the memory. Replace the power supply. Replace the motherboard.
2-x-x*	First 64KB RAM Error	Clean the memory contacts, and reseat the modules. Remove all modules except the first bank. Replace the memory. Replace the power supply. Replace the motherboard.
3-1-1	Slave DMA Register Error	Check for proper motherboard installation, loose screws, foreign objects causing shorts, and over-tightened screws. Replace the motherboard.
3-1-2	Master DMA Register Error	Check for proper motherboard installation, loose screws, foreign objects causing shorts, and over-tightened screws. Replace the motherboard.
3-1-3	Master Interrupt Mask Register Error	Check for proper motherboard installation, loose screws, foreign objects causing shorts, and over-tightened screws. Replace the motherboard.
3-1-4	Slave Interrupt Mask Register Error	Check for proper motherboard installation, loose screws, foreign objects causing shorts, and over-tightened screws. Replace the motherboard.
3-2-4	Keyboard Controller Error	Check for proper motherboard installation, loose screws, foreign objects causing shorts, and over-tightened screws. Replace the keyboard. Replace the motherboard. Replace the processor.
3-3-4	Screen Initialization Error	Check the video card for proper installation. Try replacing the video card memory, and replace the video card. Replace the motherboard.
3-4-1	Screen Retrace Error	Check the video card for proper installation. Try replacing the video card memory, and replace the video card. Replace the motherboard.
3-4-2	Video ROM Error	Check the video card for proper installation. Try replacing the video card memory, and replace the video card. Replace the motherboard.
4-2-1	Timer Interrupt Error	Check for proper motherboard installation, loose screws, foreign objects causing shorts, and over-tightened screws. Replace the motherboard.
4-2-2	Shutdown Error	Check for proper motherboard installation, loose screws, foreign objects causing shorts, and over-tightened screws. Replace the keyboard. Replace the motherboard. Replace the processor.
4-2-3	Gate A20 Error	Check for proper motherboard installation, loose screws, foreign objects causing shorts, and over-tightened screws. Replace the keyboard. Replace the motherboard. Replace the processor.
4-2-4	Unexpected Interrupt In Protected Mode	Check for a bad expansion card. Check for proper motherboard installation, loose screws, foreign objects causing shorts, and over-tightened screws. Replace the motherboard.
4-3-1	RAM Address Error >FFFh	Clean the memory contacts, reseat the modules. Remove all modules except the first bank. Replace the memory. Replace the power supply. Replace the motherboard.
4-3-3	Interval Timer Channel 2 Error	Check for proper motherboard installation, loose screws, foreign objects causing shorts, and over-tightened screws. Replace the motherboard.

Table 24.4   Continued

Beeps	Error Description	Action
4-3-4	Real Time Clock Error	Replace the CMOS battery. Replace the motherboard.
4-4-1	Serial Port Error	Reset the port configuration in BIOS Setup. Disable the port.
4-4-2	Parallel Port Error	Reset the port configuration in BIOS Setup. Disable the port.
4-4-3	Math Coprocessor Error	Check for proper motherboard installation, loose screws, foreign objects causing shorts, and over-tightened screws. Make sure the processor and heatsink are installed properly; remove and reseat them. Replace the processor. Replace the motherboard.
Low 1-1-2	System Board Select Error	Check for proper motherboard installation, loose screws, foreign objects causing shorts, and over-tightened screws. Make sure the processor and heatsink are installed properly; remove and reseat them. Replace the processor. Replace the motherboard.
Low 1-1-3	Extended CMOS RAM Error	Replace the CMOS battery. Replace the motherboard.

Second and third codes can be 1–4 beeps each, indicating different failed bits within the first 64KB of RAM.

Table 24.5   Phoenix BIOS 6.x and Later POST Beep Codes

Beeps	Error Description	Description/Action
1-2-2-3	BIOS ROM Checksum Error	Try reseating the motherboard ROM chip. Try reflashing the motherboard ROM. Replace the motherboard.
1-3-1-1	DRAM Refresh Error	Clean the memory contacts, and reseat the modules. Remove all modules except the first bank. Replace the memory. Replace the power supply. Replace the motherboard.
1-3-1-3	8742 Keyboard Controller Error	Check for proper motherboard installation, loose screws, foreign objects causing shorts, and over-tightened screws. Replace the keyboard. Replace the motherboard. Replace the processor.
1-3-4-1	Memory Address Line Error	Clean the memory contacts, and reseat the modules. Remove all modules except the first bank. Replace the memory. Replace the power supply. Replace the motherboard.
1-3-4-3	Memory Low Byte Data Error	Clean the memory contacts, and reseat the modules. Remove all modules except the first bank. Replace the memory. Replace the power supply. Replace the motherboard.
1-4-1-1	Memory High Byte Data Error	Clean the memory contacts, and reseat the modules. Remove all modules except the first bank. Replace the memory. Replace the power supply. Replace the motherboard.
2-1-2-3	ROM Copyright Error	Try reseating the motherboard ROM chip. Try reflashing the motherboard ROM. Replace the motherboard.
2-2-3-1	Unexpected Interrupts	Check for a bad expansion card. Check for proper motherboard installation, loose screws, foreign objects causing shorts, and over-tightened screws. Replace the motherboard.
1-2	Video Card Error	Check the video card for proper installation. Try replacing the video card memory, and replace the video card. Replace the motherboard.

If you are using a POST card, you can find the Phoenix BIOS POST codes in the Technical Reference section of the disc packaged with this book.

IBM BIOS POST Error Codes

Table 24.6   IBM BIOS Beep Codes

Audio Code	Description
1 short beep	Normal POST—system okay
2 short beeps	POST error—view code on screen
No beep	Power supply, motherboard
Continuous beep	Power supply, motherboard
Repeating short beeps	Power supply, motherboard
1 long, 1 short beep	Motherboard
1 long, 2 short beeps	Video card (MDA/CGA)
1 long, 3 short beeps	Video card (EGA/VGA)
3 long beeps	3270 keyboard card

IBM BIOS beep and alphanumeric error codes used by permission of IBM.

Table 24.7   IBM BIOS POST/Diagnostics Display Error Codes

Code	Description
1xx	System board errors
2xx	Memory (RAM) errors
3xx	Keyboard errors
4xx	Monochrome Display Adapter (MDA) errors
4xx	PS/2 system board parallel port errors
5xx	Color Graphics Adapter (CGA) errors
6xx	Floppy drive/controller errors
7xx	Math Coprocessor errors
9xx	Parallel printer adapter errors
10xx	Alternate parallel printer adapter errors
11xx	Primary Async Communications (Serial COM1:) errors
12xx	Alternate Async Communications (Serial COM2:, COM3:, and COM4:) errors
13xx	Game control adapter errors
14xx	Matrix printer errors
15xx	Synchronous Data Link Control (SDLC) Communications adapter errors
16xx	Display Station Emulation Adapter (DSEA) errors (5520, 525x)
17xx	ST-506/412 fixed disk and controller errors
18xx	I/O expansion unit errors
19xx	3270 PC attachment card errors
20xx	Binary Synchronous Communications (BSC) adapter errors
21xx	Alternate Binary Synchronous Communications (BSC) adapter errors
22xx	Cluster adapter errors

Table 24.7   Continued

Code	Description
23xx	Plasma monitor adapter errors
24xx	Enhanced graphics adapter (EGA) or video graphics array (VGA) errors
25xx	Alternate Enhanced Graphics Adapter (EGA) errors
26xx	XT or AT/370 370-M (memory) and 370-P (processor) adapter errors
27xx	XT or AT/370 3277-EM (emulation) adapter errors
28xx	3278/79 emulation adapter or 3270 connection adapter errors
29xx	Color/graphics printer errors
30xx	Primary PC network adapter errors
31xx	Secondary PC network adapter errors
32xx	3270 PC or AT display and programmed symbols adapter errors
33xx	Compact printer errors
35xx	Enhanced display station emulation adapter (EDSEA) errors
36xx	General-purpose interface bus (GPIB) adapter errors
37xx	System board SCSI controller errors
38xx	Data acquisition adapter errors
39xx	Professional graphics adapter (PGA) errors
44xx	5278 display attachment unit and 5279 display errors
45xx	IEEE interface adapter (IEEE 488) errors
46xx	A real-time interface coprocessor (ARTIC) multiport/2 adapter errors
48xx	Internal modem errors
49xx	Alternate internal modem errors
50xx	PC-convertible LCD errors
51xx	PC-convertible portable printer errors
56xx	Financial communication system errors
70xx	Phoenix BIOS/chipset unique error codes
71xx	Voice communications adapter (VCA) errors
73xx	3 1/2" external disk drive errors
74xx	IBM PS/2 display adapter (VGA Card) errors
74xx	8514/A display adapter errors
76xx	4216 PagePrinter adapter errors
84xx	PS/2 speech adapter errors
85xx	2MB XMA memory adapter or XMA adapter/A errors
86xx	PS/2 pointing device (mouse) errors
89xx	Musical Instrument Digital Interface (MIDI) adapter errors
91xx	IBM 3363 write-once read multiple (WORM) optical drive/adapter errors
96xx	SCSI adapter with cache (32-bit) errors
100xx	Multiprotocol adapter/A errors
101xx	300/1200bps internal modem/A errors

Table 24.7   Continued

Code	Description
104xx	ESDI or MCA IDE fixed disk or adapter errors
107xx	5 1/4" external disk drive or adapter errors
112xx	SCSI adapter (16-bit without cache) errors
113xx	System board SCSI adapter (16-bit) errors
129xx	Processor complex (CPU board) errors
149xx	P70/P75 plasma display and adapter errors
152xx	XGA display adapter/A errors
164xx	120MB internal tape drive errors
165xx	6157 streaming tape drive or tape attachment adapter errors
166xx	Primary Token-Ring network adapter errors
167xx	Alternate Token-Ring network adapter errors
180xx	PS/2 wizard adapter errors
185xx	DBCS Japanese display adapter/A errors
194xx	80286 memory-expansion option memory-module errors
200xx	Image adapter/A errors
208xx	Unknown SCSI device errors
209xx	SCSI removable disk errors
210xx	SCSI fixed disk errors
211xx	SCSI tape drive errors
212xx	SCSI printer errors
213xx	SCSI processor errors
214xx	SCSI write-once read multiple (WORM) drive errors
215xx	SCSI CD-ROM drive errors
216xx	SCSI scanner errors
217xx	SCSI magneto optical drive errors
218xx	SCSI jukebox changer errors
219xx	SCSI communications errors
243xxxx	XGA-2 adapter/A errors
I998xxxx	Dynamic configuration select (DCS) information codes
I99900xx	Initial microcode load (IML) error
I99903xx	No bootable device, initial program load (IPL) errors
I99904xx	IML-to-system mismatch
I99906xx	IML (boot) errors

IBM BIOS beep and alphanumeric error codes used by permission of IBM.

POST Memory Count

On some PCs, the POST also displays the results of its system memory test on the monitor. The last number displayed is the amount of memory that tested successfully. For example, a system might display the following message:

```
32768 KB OK
```

The number displayed by the memory test should agree with the total amount of memory installed on the system motherboard. Some older systems display a slightly lower total because they deduct part or all of the 384KB of UMA (upper memory area) from the count. On old systems that use expanded memory cards, the memory on the card is not tested by the POST and does not count in the numbers reported. Also, this memory test is performed before any system software loads, so many memory managers or device drivers you might have installed do not affect the results of the test. If the POST memory test stops short of the expected total, the number displayed can indicate how far into the system memory array a memory error lies. This number can help you identify the exact module that is at fault and can be a valuable troubleshooting aid in itself.

Peripheral Diagnostics

Many types of diagnostic software are used with specific hardware products. This software can be integrated into the hardware, included with the hardware purchase, or sold as a separate product. The following sections examine several types of hardware-specific diagnostics.

SCSI Diagnostics

Unlike the IDE drive support that is built into the system BIOS of virtually every PC, SCSI is an add-on technology, and most SCSI host adapters contain their own BIOS that enables you to boot the system from a SCSI hard drive. In some cases, the SCSI BIOS also contains configuration software for the adapter's various features, and diagnostics software as well.

The most popular manufacturer of SCSI host adapters is Adaptec, and most of its host adapters contain these features. An Adaptec SCSI adapter normally includes a BIOS that can be enabled or disabled. When the BIOS is activated, you see a message on the monitor as the system boots, identifying the model of the adapter and the revision number of the BIOS. The message also instructs you to press Ctrl+A to access what Adaptec calls its SCSISelect utility.

The SCSISelect utility identifies the Adaptec host adapters installed in the system and, if more than one exists, enables you to choose the adapter you want to work with by selecting its port address. After you do this, you are presented with a menu of the functions built into the adapter's BIOS. Every adapter BIOS contains a configuration program and a SCSI Disk Utilities feature that scans the SCSI bus, identifying the devices connected to it. For each hard disk drive connected to the bus, you can perform a low-level disk format or scan the disk for defects, remapping any bad blocks that are found.

For SCSI adapters that use direct memory access (DMA), a Host Adapter Diagnostics feature is also available, which tests the communication between the adapter and the main system memory array by performing a series of DMA transfers. If this test fails, you are instructed how to configure the adapter to use a lower DMA transfer rate.

Network Interface Diagnostics

As with SCSI adapters, many network interface adapters are equipped with their own diagnostics, designed to test their own specialized functions. Depending on the network adapter, these tests might require you to boot with a DOS disk, or they might function within Windows.

The DIAG program included with all Linksys network interface cards, for example, performs the following internal tests on the Linksys EtherFast 10/100 Ethernet adapter:

- Configuration test
- I/O test
- ID test
- Internal Loopback test
- Link Status test
- Interrupt test
- Network Function test

The Network Function test sequence requires that you have another node installed on the same network with a Linksys adapter. By running the Diag software on both computers, you can configure one adapter to send data and the other to be the receiver. The sender transmits test messages to the receiver, which echoes the same messages back again. If the adapters and network are functioning properly, the messages should return to the sending system in exactly the same form as they were transmitted.

Other network adapters have similar testing capabilities, although the names of the tests might not be exactly the same.

If you do not have the driver or diagnostics files for your network adapter, you can normally download them free of charge from the manufacturers' respective Web sites.

General-Purpose Diagnostics Programs

A large number of professional third-party diagnostics programs are available for PC systems. These are commercial programs that are used by technicians to perform testing of new systems (often called burn-in testing) or testing of existing systems either in the shop or in the field.

Most of the commercial PC diagnostics can test all your PC's key components. In addition, specific programs are available to test memory, floppy drives, hard disks, video adapters, and most other areas of the system. Some of the programs I recommend most highly include

- *AMIDiag Suite.* See www.ami.com for more information.
- *MicroScope.* See www.micro2000.com for more information.
- *QA+FE.* See www.eurosoft-us.com for more information.

Tip

Before trying a commercial diagnostic program to solve your problem, look in your operating system. Most operating systems today provide at least some of the diagnostic functions that diagnostic programs do. You might be able to save some time and money.

Unfortunately, no clear leader exists in the area of diagnostic software. Each program has unique advantages, and as a result, no program is universally better than another. When deciding which diagnostic programs to include in your arsenal, look for the features you need.

One of the most popular is AMIDiag from AMI. This program runs on virtually any PC and tests most of the hardware in the system. AMIDiag is available in a native Windows version that also supports third-party diagnostics modules or in a DOS version that can be used to test hardware, regardless of the operating system, by using a DOS boot disk to start the system.

Note

The disc included with this book contains a breakdown of some of the PC diagnostics software available today. See the Technical Reference section of the disc.

Operating System Diagnostics

In many cases, it might not be necessary to purchase third-party diagnostic software because your operating system has all the diagnostic tools you need. Windows 9x/Me and NT/2000/XP include a large selection of programs that enable you to view, monitor, and troubleshoot the hardware in your system.

Windows XP has numerous tools, utilities, and error-reporting features that can be useful in helping you determine the cause of problems. The most serious problems can be caused by corrupt files or buggy software on the system, as well as defective or incorrectly configured hardware, and will often result in a STOP or "blue-screen" error, causing Windows to enter a special debugging mode. When this happens, Windows XP is normally configured to save a dump of the error in a memory dump file, which can be useful if it is a software bug you are going to report to Microsoft. Still, it is always a good idea to write down the error for future reference.

The Hardware Boot Process

The term *boot* comes from the word bootstrap and describes the method by which the PC becomes operational. Just as you pull on a large boot by the small strap attached to the back, a PC loads a large operating system by first loading a small program that can then pull the operating system into memory. The chain of events begins with the application of power and finally results in a fully functional computer system with software loaded and running. Each event is triggered by the event before it and initiates the event after it.

Tracing the system boot process might help you find the location of a problem if you examine the error messages the system displays when the problem occurs. If you see an error message that is displayed by only a particular program, you can be sure the program in question was at least loaded and partially running. Combine this information with the knowledge of the boot sequence, and you can at least tell how far the system's startup procedure had progressed before the problem occurred. You usually should look at whichever files or disk areas were being accessed during the failure in the boot process. Error messages displayed during the boot process and those displayed during normal system operation can be hard to decipher. However, the first step in decoding an error message is knowing where the message came from—which program actually generated or displayed it. The following programs are capable of displaying error messages during the boot process:

OS Independent:

- Motherboard ROM BIOS
- Adapter card ROM BIOS extensions
- Master (partition) boot record
- Volume boot record

OS Dependent

- System files
- Device drivers (loaded through `CONFIG.SYS` or the Win Registry `SYSTEM.DAT`)
- Programs run by `AUTOEXEC.BAT`, the Windows Startup group, and the Registry

The first portion of the startup sequence is *operating system independent*, which means these steps are the same for all PCs no matter which operating system is installed. The latter portion of the boot sequence is *operating system dependent*, which means those steps can vary depending on which operating system is installed or being loaded. The following sections examine both the operating-system-independent startup sequence and the operating-system-dependent startup process for various operating systems. These sections provide a detailed account of many of the error messages that might occur during the boot process.

The Boot Process: Operating System Independent

If you have a problem with your system during startup and can determine where in this sequence of events your system has stalled, you know which events have occurred and probably can eliminate each of them as a cause of the problem. The following steps occur in a typical system startup regardless of which operating system you are loading:

1. You switch on electrical power to the system.

2. The power supply performs a self-test (known as the POST). When all voltages and current levels are acceptable, the supply indicates that the power is stable and sends the Power_Good signal to the motherboard. The time from switch-on to Power_Good is normally between .1 and .5 seconds.

3. The microprocessor timer chip receives the Power_Good signal, which causes it to stop generating a reset signal to the microprocessor.

◀◀ See "The Power_Good Signal," p. 1154.

4. The microprocessor begins executing the ROM BIOS code, starting at memory address FFFF:0000. Because this location is only 16 bytes from the very end of the available ROM space, it contains a JMP (jump) instruction to the actual ROM BIOS starting address.

◀◀ See "Motherboard BIOS," p. 402.

5. The ROM BIOS performs a test of the central hardware to verify basic system functionality. Any errors that occur are indicated by audio "beep" codes because the video system has not yet been initialized. If the BIOS is Plug and Play (PnP), the following steps are executed; if not, skip to step 10.

6. The Plug and Play BIOS checks nonvolatile random access memory (RAM) for input/output (I/O) port addresses, interrupt request lines (IRQs), direct memory access (DMA) channels, and other settings necessary to configure PnP devices on the computer.

7. All Plug and Play devices found by the Plug and Play BIOS are disabled to eliminate potential conflicts.

8. A map of used and unused resources is created.

9. The Plug and Play devices are configured and reenabled, one at a time. If your computer does not have a Plug and Play BIOS, PnP devices are initialized using their default settings. These devices can be reconfigured dynamically when Windows starts. At that point, Windows queries the Plug and Play BIOS for device information and then queries each Plug and Play device for its configuration.

10. The BIOS performs a video ROM scan of memory locations C000:0000–C780:0000 looking for video adapter ROM BIOS programs contained on a video adapter found either on a card plugged into a slot or integrated into the motherboard. If the scan locates a video ROM BIOS, it is tested by a checksum procedure. If the video BIOS passes the checksum test, the ROM is executed; then the video ROM code initializes the video adapter and a cursor appears onscreen. If the checksum test fails, the following message appears:

`C000 ROM Error`

11. If the BIOS finds no video adapter ROM, it uses the motherboard ROM video drivers to initialize the video display hardware, and a cursor appears onscreen.

12. The motherboard ROM BIOS scans memory locations C800:0000–DF80:0000 in 2KB increments for any other ROMs located on any other adapter cards (such as SCSI adapters). If any ROMs are found, they are checksum-tested and executed. These adapter ROMs can alter existing BIOS routines and establish new ones.

13. Failure of a checksum test for any of these ROM modules causes this message to appear:

`XXXX ROM Error`

where the address *XXXX* indicates the segment address of the failed ROM module.

14. The ROM BIOS checks the word value at memory location 0000:0472 to see whether this start is a cold start or a warm start. A word value of 1234h in this location is a flag that indicates a warm start, which causes the BIOS to skip the memory test portion of the POST. Any other word value in this location indicates a cold start, and the BIOS performs the full POST procedure. Some system BIOSs let you control various aspects of the POST procedure, making it possible to skip the memory test, for example, which can be lengthy on a system with a lot of RAM.

15. If this is a cold start, the full POST executes; if this is a warm start, a mini-POST executes, minus the RAM test. Any errors found during the POST are reported by a combination of audio and displayed error messages. Successful completion of the POST is indicated by a single beep (with the exception of some Compaq computers, which beep twice).

16. The ROM BIOS searches for a boot record at cylinder 0, head 0, sector 1 (the very first sector) on the default boot drive. At one time, the default boot drive was always the first floppy disk, or A: drive. However, the BIOSs on today's systems often enable you to select the default boot device and the order in which the BIOS will look for other devices to boot from if necessary, using a floppy disk, hard disk, or even a CD-ROM drive in any order you choose. This sector is loaded into memory at 0000:7C00 and tested.

If a disk is in the drive but the sector can't be read, or if no disk is present, the BIOS continues with step 19.

Booting from CD-ROM or Floppy

If you do want to boot from a CD-ROM, be sure the CD-ROM drive is listed before the hard disk in the boot devices menu in your BIOS setup. To ensure that you can boot from an emergency CD or floppy disk, I recommend setting the CD-ROM as the first and the floppy drive as the second boot device. A hard disk containing your operating system should be the third device in the boot device list. This enables you to always be ready for an emergency. So long as you do not start up the system with a floppy or bootable CD loaded, the BIOS bypasses both the CD and floppy disk drives and boots from the hard drive.

Note that not all operating system CDs are bootable. Windows 95 CDs are not bootable; however, with Windows 98, Microsoft made the operating system CD bootable, but only for OEM (original equipment manufacturer) versions. This does not extend to retail versions of these Windows CDs. Windows NT 4.0 and later, including Windows 2000 and XP, are shipped on bootable CDs. See Chapter 13, "Optical Storage," for information on how to make a bootable CD.

17. If you are booting from a floppy disk and the first byte of the volume boot record is less than 06h, or if the first byte is greater than or equal to 06h and the first nine words contain the same data pattern, this error message appears and the system stops:

```
602-Diskette Boot Record Error
```

18. If the volume boot record can't find or load the system files, or if a problem was encountered loading them, one of the following messages appears:

```
Non-System disk or disk error
Replace and strike any key when ready
```

```
Non-System disk or disk error
Replace and press any key when ready
```

```
Invalid system disk_
Replace the disk, and then press any key
```

```
Disk Boot failure
```

```
Disk I/O Error
```

All these messages originate in the volume boot record (VBR) and relate to VBR or system file problems.

19. If no boot record can be read from drive A: (such as when no disk is in the drive), the BIOS then looks for a master boot record (MBR) at cylinder 0, head 0, sector 1 (the very first sector) of the first hard disk. If this sector is found, it is loaded into memory address 0000:7C00 and tested for a signature.

20. If the last two (signature) bytes of the MBR are not equal to 55AAh, software interrupt 18h (Int 18h) is invoked on most systems. This causes the BIOS to display an error message that can vary for different BIOS manufacturers, but which is often similar to one of the following messages, depending on which BIOS you have:

IBM BIOS:

```
The IBM Personal Computer Basic_
Version C1.10 Copyright IBM Corp 1981
62940 Bytes free_
Ok_
```

Most IBM computers since 1987 display a strange character graphic depicting the front of a floppy drive, a 3 1/2" disk, and arrows prompting you to insert a disk in the drive and press the F1 key to proceed.

AMI BIOS:

```
NO ROM BASIC - SYSTEM HALTED
```

Compaq BIOS:

```
Non-System disk or disk error
replace and strike any key when ready
```

Award BIOS:

```
DISK BOOT FAILURE, INSERT SYSTEM DISK AND PRESS ENTER
```

Phoenix BIOS:

```
No boot device available -
strike F1 to retry boot, F2 for setup utility
```

or

```
No boot sector on fixed disk -
strike F1 to retry boot, F2 for setup utility
```

Although the messages vary from BIOS to BIOS, the cause for each relates to specific bytes in the MBR, which is the first sector of a hard disk at the physical location cylinder 0, head 0, sector 1.

The problem involves a disk that either has never been partitioned or has had the Master Boot Sector corrupted. During the boot process, the BIOS checks the last two bytes in the MBR (first sector of the drive) for a signature value of 55AAh. If the last two bytes are not 55AAh, an Interrupt 18h is invoked, which calls the subroutine that displays one of the error messages just shown, which basically instructs the user to insert a bootable floppy to proceed.

The MBR (including the signature bytes) is written to the hard disk by the FDISK or DISKPART programs. Immediately after a hard disk is low-level formatted, all the sectors are initialized with a pattern of bytes, and the first sector does not contain the 55AAh signature. In other words, these ROM error messages are exactly what you see if you attempt to boot from a hard disk that has been freshly low-level formatted, but has not yet been partitioned.

21. The MBR searches its built-in partition table entries for a boot indicator byte marking an active partition entry.

22. If none of the partitions are marked active (bootable), the BIOS invokes software interrupt 18h, which displays an error message (refer to step 20).

23. If any boot indicator byte in the MBR partition table is invalid, or if more than one indicates an active partition, the following message is displayed and the system stops:

    ```
    Invalid partition table
    ```

24. If an active partition is found in the MBR, the partition boot record from the active partition is loaded and tested.

25. If the partition boot record can't be read successfully from the active partition within five retries because of read errors, the following message is displayed and the system stops:

    ```
    Error loading operating system
    ```

26. The hard disk's partition boot record is tested for a signature. If it does not contain a valid signature of 55AAh as the last two bytes in the sector, the following message is displayed and the system stops:

    ```
    Missing operating system
    ```

27. The volume boot record is executed as a program. This program looks for and loads the operating system kernel or system files. If the volume boot record can't find or load the system files, or if a problem was encountered loading them, one of the following messages appears:

    ```
    Non-System disk or disk error
    Replace and strike any key when ready
    ```

    ```
    Non-System disk or disk error
    Replace and press any key when ready
    ```

    ```
    Invalid system disk_
    Replace the disk, and then press any key
    ```

    ```
    Disk Boot failure
    ```

    ```
    Disk I/O Error
    ```

    All these messages originate in the volume boot record (VBR) and relate to VBR or system file problems.

From this point forward, what happens depends on which operating system you have. The operating-system-dependent boot procedures are discussed in the next several sections.

The DOS Boot Process

1. The initial system file (called IO.SYS or IBMBIO.COM) is executed.

2. The initialization code in IO.SYS/IBMBIO.COM copies itself into the highest region of contiguous DOS memory and transfers control to the copy. The initialization code copy then relocates MSDOS.SYS over the portion of IO.SYS in low memory that contains the initialization code because the initialization code no longer needs to be in that location.

3. The initialization code executes MSDOS.SYS (or IBMDOS.COM), which initializes the base device drivers, determines equipment status, resets the disk system, resets and initializes attached devices, and sets the system default parameters.

4. The full DOS file system is active, and control is returned to the IO.SYS initialization code.

5. The IO.SYS initialization code reads the CONFIG.SYS file multiple times.

6. When loading CONFIG.SYS, the DEVICE statements are first processed in the order in which they appear. Any device driver files named in those DEVICE statements are loaded and executed. Then, any INSTALL statements are processed in the order in which they appear; the programs named are loaded and executed. The SHELL statement is processed and loads the specified command processor with the specified parameters. If the CONFIG.SYS file contains no SHELL statement, the default

\COMMAND.COM processor is loaded with default parameters. Loading the command processor overwrites the initialization code in memory (because the job of the initialization code is finished).

During the final reads of CONFIG.SYS, all the remaining statements are read and processed in a predetermined order. Thus, the order of appearance for statements other than DEVICE, INSTALL, and SHELL in CONFIG.SYS is of no significance.

7. If AUTOEXEC.BAT is present, COMMAND.COM loads and runs AUTOEXEC.BAT. After the commands in AUTOEXEC.BAT have been executed, the DOS prompt appears (unless AUTOEXEC.BAT calls an application program or shell of some kind, in which case the user might operate the system without ever seeing a DOS prompt).

8. If no AUTOEXEC.BAT file is present, COMMAND.COM executes the internal DATE and TIME commands, displays a copyright message, and displays the DOS prompt.

Some minor variations from this scenario are possible, such as those introduced by other ROM programs in the various adapters that might be plugged into an expansion slot. Also, depending on the exact ROM BIOS programs involved, some of the error messages and sequences can vary. Generally, however, a computer follows this chain of events while "coming to life."

You can modify the system startup procedures by altering the CONFIG.SYS and AUTOEXEC.BAT files. These files control the configuration of DOS and allow special startup programs to be executed every time the system starts.

The Windows 9x/Me Boot Process

Knowing exactly how Windows 9x and Millennium Edition (Me) load and start can be helpful when troubleshooting startup problems. The Windows 9x boot process can be broken into three phases:

■ The IO.SYS file is loaded and run. (Windows 9x's IO.SYS combines the functions of DOS's IO.SYS and MSDOS.SYS.)

■ Real-mode configuration takes place.

■ The WIN.COM file is loaded and run.

Phase 1—Loading and Running the IO.SYS File

1. The initialization code initializes the base device drivers, determines equipment status, resets the disk system, resets and initializes attached devices, and sets the system default parameters.

2. The file system is activated, and control is returned to the IO.SYS initialization code.

3. The Starting Windows message is displayed for <n> seconds, or until you press a Windows function key. The amount of time the message is displayed is determined by the BootDelay=<n> line in the MSDOS.SYS file; the default is 2 seconds.

4. The IO.SYS initialization code reads the MSDOS.SYS configuration file. If you have multiple hardware profiles, you receive the following message and must choose a hardware configuration to use:

Windows cannot determine what configuration your computer is in.

5. The LOGO.SYS file is loaded and displays a startup image onscreen.

6. If the DRVSPACE.INI or DBLSPACE.INI file exists, it is loaded into memory. IO.SYS also automatically loads HIMEM.SYS, IFSHLP.SYS, and SETVER.EXE.

7. The IO.SYS file checks the system Registry files (SYSTEM.DAT and USER.DAT) for valid data.

8. IO.SYS opens the SYSTEM.DAT file. If the SYSTEM.DAT file is not found, the SYSTEM.DA0 file is used for startup. If Windows 9x/Me starts successfully, the SYSTEM.DA0 file is copied to the SYSTEM.DAT file.

9. The DBLBUFF.SYS file is loaded if the DoubleBuffer=1 is in the MSDOS.SYS file or if double buffering is enabled under the following Registry key:

   HKLM\System\CurrentControlSet\Control\WinBoot\DoubleBuffer

Note

Windows 9x Setup automatically enables double buffering if it detects that it is required.

10. If you have multiple hardware profiles, the hardware profile you chose is loaded from the Registry.

11. In Windows 9x/Me, the system looks in the Registry's Hkey_Local_Machine\System\CurrentControlSet key to load the device drivers and other parameters specified there before executing the CONFIG.SYS file.

Phase 2—Real-Mode Configuration

Some older hardware devices and programs require that drivers or files be loaded in real mode (16-bit mode) for them to work properly. To ensure backward compatibility, Windows 9x processes the CONFIG.SYS and AUTOEXEC.BAT files if they exist:

1. The CONFIG.SYS file is read if it exists, and the statements within are processed, including the loading of drivers into memory. If the CONFIG.SYS file does not exist, the IO.SYS file loads the following required drivers:

   IFSHLP.SYS

   HIMEM.SYS

   SETVER.EXE

   IO.SYS obtains the location of these files from the WinBootDir= line of the MSDOS.SYS file and must be on the hard disk.

2. Windows reserves all global upper memory blocks (UMBs) for Windows 9x operating system use or for expanded memory support (EMS).

3. The AUTOEXEC.BAT file is processed if present, and any terminate-and-stay resident (TSR) programs listed within are loaded into memory.

Phase 3—Loading and Running the WIN.COM File

1. The WIN.COM file is loaded and run.

2. The WIN.COM file accesses the VMM32.VXD file. If enough RAM is available, the VMM32.VXD file loads into memory; otherwise, it is accessed from the hard disk (resulting in a slower startup time).

3. The real-mode virtual device driver loader checks for duplicate virtual device drivers (VxDs) in the WINDOWS\SYSTEM\VMM32 folder and the VMM32.VXD file. If a VxD exists in both the WINDOWS\SYSTEM\VMM32 folder and the VMM32.VXD file, the duplicate VxD is "marked" in the VMM32.VXD file so that it is not loaded.

4. VxDs not already loaded by the VMM32.VXD file are loaded from the [386 Enh] section of the WINDOWS\SYSTEM.INI file.

Required VxDs

Some VxDs are required for Windows to run properly. These required VxDs are loaded automatically and do not require a Registry entry. Windows 9x requires the following VxDs:

*BIOSXLAT	*CONFIGMG	*DYNAPAGE	*DOSMGR
*EBIOS	*IFSMGR	*INT13	*IOS
*PAGESWAP	*SHELL	*V86MMGR	*VCD
*VCACHE	*VCOMM	*VCOND	*VDD
*VDMAD	*VFAT*VKD	*VMCPD	*VPICD
*VTD	*VTDAPI	*VWIN32	*VXDLDR

5. The real-mode virtual device driver loader checks that all required VxDs loaded successfully. If not, it attempts to load the drivers again.

6. After the real-mode virtual device driver loading is logged, driver initialization occurs. If any VxDs require real-mode initialization, they begin their processes in real mode.

7. VMM32 switches the computer's processor from real mode to protected mode.

8. A three-phase VxD initialization process occurs in which the drivers are loaded according to their InitDevice instead of the order in which they are loaded into memory.

9. After all the VxDs are loaded, the KRNL32.DLL, GDI.EXE, USER.EXE, and EXPLORER.EXE (the default Windows 9x GUI shell) files are loaded.

10. If a network is specified, load the network environment and multiuser profiles. The user is prompted to log on to the installed network. Windows 9x/Me enables multiple users to save their custom desktop settings. When a user logs on to Windows, her desktop settings are loaded from the Registry. If the user does not log on, the desktop configuration uses a default desktop.

11. Programs in the StartUp group and the RunOnce Registry key are run during the last phase of the startup process. After each program in the RunOnce Registry key is started, the program is removed from the key.

Windows NT/2000/XP Startup

When you start a Windows NT, 2000, or XP system (which are all based on the same set of integral code), the boot process is different from that of a DOS or Windows 9x/Me system. Instead of the IO.SYS and MSDOS.SYS files used by 9x/Me, Windows NT/2000/XP use an OS loader program called Ntldr.

The basic Windows NT/2000/XP startup process is described in the following step-by-step procedures:

1. *The partition boot sector loads Ntldr (NT Loader).* It then switches the processor to protected mode, starts the file system, and reads the contents of Boot.ini. The information in Boot.ini determines the startup options and initial boot menu selections (dual-booting, for example). If dual-booting is enabled, and a non-NT/2000/XP OS is chosen, Bootsec.dos is loaded. If SCSI drives are present, Ntbootdd.sys is loaded, which contains the SCSI boot drivers.

2. Ntdetect.com *gathers hardware configuration data and passes this information to Ntldr.* If more than one hardware profile exists, Windows uses the correct one for the current configuration. If the ROM BIOS is ACPI compliant, Windows uses ACPI to enumerate and initialize devices.

3. *The kernel loads.* Ntldr passes information collected by Ntdetect.com to Ntoskrnl.exe. Ntoskrnl then loads the kernel, Hardware Abstraction Layer (Hal.dll), and Registry information. An indicator near the bottom of the screen details progress.

4. *Drivers load and the user logs on.* Networking-related components (for example, TCP/IP) load simultaneously with other services and the Begin Logon prompt appears onscreen. After a user logs on successfully, Windows updates the Last Known Good Configuration information to reflect the current configuration state.

5. *Plug and Play detects and configures new devices.* If new devices are detected, they are assigned resources. Windows extracts the necessary driver files from Driver.cab. If the driver files are not found, the user is prompted to provide them. Device detection occurs simultaneously with the operating system logon process.

The following files are processed during Windows NT/2000/XP startup:

- Ntldr
- Boot.ini
- Bootsect.dos (multiple-boot systems only)
- Ntbootdd.sys (loaded only for SCSI drives)
- Ntdetect.com
- Ntoskrnl.exe
- Hal.dll
- Files in systemroot\System32\Config (Registry)
- Files in systemroot\System32\Drivers (drivers)

PC Maintenance Tools

To troubleshoot and repair PC systems properly, you need a few basic tools. If you intend to troubleshoot and repair PCs professionally, there are many more specialized tools you will want to purchase. These advanced tools enable you to more accurately diagnose problems and make jobs easier and faster. The basic tools that should be in every troubleshooter's toolbox are as follows:

- Simple hand tools for basic disassembly and reassembly procedures, including a flat blade and Phillips screwdrivers (both medium and small sizes), tweezers, an IC extraction tool, and a parts grabber or hemostat. Most of these items are included in $10–$20 starter toolkits found at most computer stores.

- Diagnostics software and hardware for testing components in a system.

- A multimeter that provides accurate measurements of voltage and resistance, as well as a continuity checker for testing cables and switches.

- Chemicals, such as contact cleaners; component freeze sprays; and compressed air for cleaning the system.

- Foam swabs, or lint-free cotton swabs if foam isn't available.

- Small nylon wire ties for "dressing" or organizing wires.

Some environments also might have the resources to purchase the following devices, although they're not required for most work:

- Memory-testing machines, used to evaluate the operation of single inline memory modules (SIMMs), dual inline memory modules (DIMMs), Rambus inline memory modules (RIMMs), or double data rate (DDR) DIMMs

- Serial and parallel loopback (or wrap) plugs to test serial and parallel ports

- A network cable scanner (if you work with networked PCs)

- A serial breakout box (if you use systems that operate over serial cables, such as Unix dumb terminals)

- A POST card (if you work with computers running DOS or other non-Windows operating systems, you might prefer to get a POST card that can also display IRQs and DMAs in use)

In addition, an experienced troubleshooter will probably want to have soldering and desoldering tools to fix bad serial cables. These tools are discussed in more detail in the following sections.

Hand Tools

When you work with PC systems, the tools required for nearly all service operations are simple and inexpensive. You can carry most of the required tools in a small pouch. Even a top-of-the-line "master mechanics" set fits inside a briefcase-sized container. The cost of these toolkits ranges from about $20 for a small service kit to $500 for one of the briefcase-sized deluxe kits. Compare these costs with what might be necessary for an automotive technician. An automotive service technician would have to spend $5,000–$10,000 or more for a complete set of tools. Not only are PC tools much less expensive, but I can tell you from experience that you don't get nearly as dirty working on computers as you do working on cars.

In this section, you learn about the tools required to assemble a kit that is capable of performing basic, board-level service on PC systems. One of the best ways to start such a set of tools is to purchase a small kit sold especially for servicing PCs.

Figure 24.2 shows some of the basic tools you can use to work on PCs. Many of these tools can be found in one of the small PC toolkits that sell for about $20.

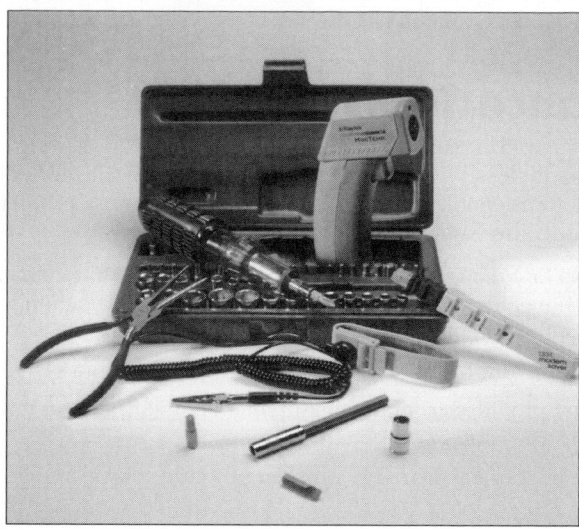

Figure 24.2   The basic tools you need to work on your PC are shown here.

Note

Some tools aren't recommended because they are of limited use. However, they normally come with these types of kits.

You use nut drivers to remove the hexagonal-headed screws that secure the system-unit covers, adapter boards, disk drives, and power supplies in most systems. The nut drivers work much better than conventional screwdrivers.

Because some manufacturers have substituted Phillips-head screws for the more standard hexagonal-head screws, standard screwdrivers can be used for those systems. If slotted screws are used, they should be removed and replaced with Torx (preferred), hex, or Phillips-head screws that capture the driver tool and prevent it from slipping off the head of the screw. It is especially important never to allow slotted screws to be used on or near a motherboard because a flat-bladed screwdriver can very easily slip and damage the board.

Caution

When working in a cramped environment such as the inside of a computer case, screwdrivers with magnetic tips can be a real convenience, especially for retrieving that screw you dropped into the case. However, although I have used these types of screwdrivers many times with no problems, you should be aware of the damage a magnetic field can cause to magnetic storage devices such as floppy disks. Laying the screwdriver down on or near a floppy can damage the data on the disk. Fortunately, floppy disks aren't used that much anymore. Hard drives are shielded by a metal case; CD/DVD drives are not affected because they work optically; and memory and other chips are not affected by magnetic fields (unless they are magnitudes stronger than what you'll see in a hand tool).

Chip-extraction and insertion tools are rarely needed these days because memory chips are mounted on SIMMs, RIMMs, or DIMMs and processors use zero insertion force (ZIF) sockets or other user-friendly connectors. The ZIF socket has a lever that, when raised, releases the grip on the pins of the processor, enabling you to easily lift it out with your fingers.

◄◄   See "Zero Insertion Force," p. 90.

However, if you work with older systems, you can use a chip extractor to install or remove memory chips (or other smaller chips) without bending any pins on the chip (see Figure 24.3). Usually, you pry out larger chips, such as microprocessors or ROMs, with the small screwdriver. Larger processors up through the 486 might require a chip extractor if they are mounted in the older low insertion force (LIF) socket. These chips have so many pins on them that a large amount of force is required to remove them, despite the fact that they call the socket "low insertion force." If you use a screwdriver on a large physical-size chip such as a 486, you risk cracking the case of the chip and permanently damaging it. The chip extractor tool for removing these chips has a very wide end with tines that fit between the pins on the chip to distribute the force evenly along the chip's underside. This minimizes the likelihood of breakage. Most of these types of extraction tools must be purchased specially for the chip you're trying to remove.

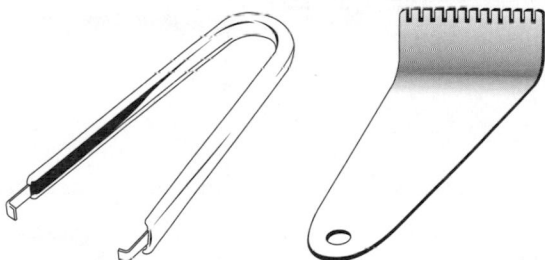

Figure 24.3   The chip extractor (left) is used to remove an individual RAM or ROM chip from a socket, but it would not be useful for a larger processor chip. Use an extractor such as the one on the right for extracting socketed processors—if the processor does not use a ZIF socket.

Tip

The older-style chip extractor shown on the left in Figure 24.3 does have another use as a keycap extractor. In fact, for this role it works quite well. By placing the tool over a keycap on a keyboard and squeezing the tool so the hooks grab under the keycap on opposite sides, you can cleanly and effectively remove the keycap from the keyboard without damage. This works much better than trying to pry off the caps with a screwdriver, which often results in damaging them or sending them flying across the room.

The tweezers and parts grabber can be used to hold any small screws or jumper blocks that are difficult to hold in your hand. The parts grabber is especially useful when you drop a small part into the interior of a system; usually, you can remove the part without completely disassembling the system (see Figure 24.4).

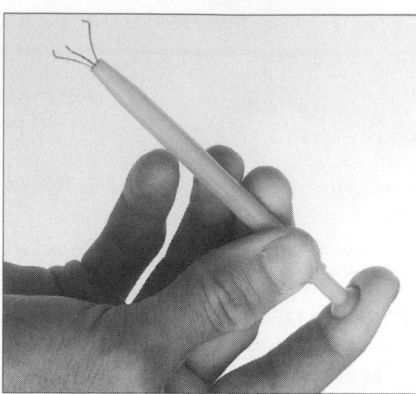

Figure 24.4 The parts grabber has three small metal prongs that can be extended to grab a part.

Finally, the Torx driver is a star-shaped driver that matches the special screws found in most systems (see Figure 24.5). Torx screws are vastly superior to other types of screws for computers because they offer greater grip and the tool is much less likely to slip. The most common cause of new motherboard failures is the use of slotted screwdrivers that slip off the screw head, scratching (and damaging) the motherboard. I never allow slotted screws or a standard flat-bladed screwdriver anywhere near the interior of my systems. You also can purchase tamperproof Torx drivers that can remove Torx screws with the tamper-resistant pin in the center of the screw. A tamperproof Torx driver has a hole drilled in it to allow clearance for the pin. Torx drivers come in a number of sizes, the most common being the T-10 and T-15.

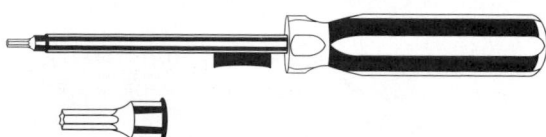

Figure 24.5 A Torx driver and bit.

Although this basic set is useful, you should supplement it with some other basic tools, such as

- *Electrostatic discharge (ESD) protection kit.* This includes a wrist strap and mat (such as those from Radio Shack or Jensen Tools) and prevents static damage to the components on which you are working. These kits consist of a wrist strap with a ground wire and a specially conductive mat with its own ground wire. You also can get just the wrist strap or the antistatic mat separately. In areas or times of the season when there is low humidity, static charges are much more likely to build up as you move, increasing the need for ESD protection. A wrist strap is shown in Figure 24.6.

- *Needle-nose pliers and hemostats (curved and straight).* These are great for gripping small items and jumpers, straightening bent pins, and so on.

- *Electric screwdriver.* Combined with hex, Phillips, standard, and Torx bit sets, this tool really speeds up repetitive disassembly/assembly. Black and Decker offers the VersaPak VP730 (www.blackanddecker.com).

- *Flashlight.* You should preferably use a high-tech LED unit such as those from Lightwave (www.longlight.com), which enable you to see inside dark systems and are easy on batteries.

- *Wire cutter or stripper.* This is useful for making or repairing cables or wiring. For example, you'd need this (along with a crimping tool) to make 10BASE-T Ethernet cables using UTP cable and RJ-45 connectors (see Chapter 20, "Local Area Networking").

- *Vise or clamp.* This is used to install connectors on cables, crimp cables to the shape you want, and hold parts during delicate operations. In addition to the vise, Radio Shack sells a nifty "extra hands" device that has two movable arms with alligator clips on the end. This type of device is very useful for making cables or for other delicate operations during which an extra set of hands to hold something might be useful.

- *Metal file.* This is used to smooth rough metal edges on cases and chassis and to trim the face-plates on disk drives for a perfect fit.

- *Markers, pens, and notepads.* Use these for taking notes, marking cables, and so on.

- *Windows 98 startup floppy.* This has DOS 7.0 and real-mode CD-ROM/DVD drivers, which can be used to boot test the system and possibly load other software.

- *Windows 2000/XP original (bootable) CD.* This can be used to boot test the system from a CD-ROM/DVD drive, attempt system recovery, OS installation, or to run other software.

- *Diagnostics software.* This commercial, shareware, or freeware software can be used for PC hardware verification and testing.

- *Power on self test (POST) card such as the Post Probe from* www.micro2000.com. This is used for displaying POST diagnostics codes on systems with fatal errors.

- *Nylon cable-ties.* These are used to help in routing and securing cables; neatly routed cables help to improve airflow in the system.

- *Digital pocket multimeter (such as those from Radio Shack).* This is used for checking power supply voltages, connectors, and cables for continuity.

- *Cleaning swabs, canned air (dust blower), and contact cleaner chemicals.* These are used for cleaning, lubricating, and enhancing contacts on circuit boards and cable connections. Products include those from www.chemtronics.com, as well as contact enhancer chemicals such as Stabilant 22a (www.stabilant.com).

- *Spare CR-2032 lithium coin cell batteries.* These are used as the CMOS RAM batteries in most systems, so it is a good idea to have a replacement or two on hand.

Safety

Before working on a system, there are certain safety procedures that should be followed. Some are to protect you, whereas others are to protect the system on which you are working.

From a personal safety point of view, there really isn't that much danger in working on a PC. Even if it is open with the power on, PCs run on only 3.3, 5, and 12 volts, meaning no dangerous, life-threatening voltages are present. However, dangerous voltages do exist inside the power supply and monitor. Most power supplies have 400 volts present at some points internally, and color displays have between 50,000 and 100,000 volts on the CRT! Normally, I treat the power supply and monitor as components that are replaced and not repaired, and I do not recommend you open either of them unless you really know what you are doing around high voltages.

Before working on a PC, you should unplug it from the wall. This is not really to protect you so much as it is to protect the system. A modern ATX form factor system is always partially running—that is, as long as the system is plugged in. So, even if it is off, standby voltages are present. To prevent damage to the motherboard, video card, and other cards, the system should be completely unplugged. If you accidentally turn the system all the way on, and plug in or remove a card, you can fry the card or motherboard.

Electrostatic discharge protection is another issue. While working on a PC, you should wear an ESD wrist strap that is clipped to the chassis of the machine (see Figure 24.6). This ensures that you and the system remain at the same electrical potential and prevents static electricity from damaging the system as you touch it. Some people feel that the system should be plugged in to provide an earth ground. That is not a good idea at all, as I previously mentioned. No "earth" ground is necessary;

all that is important is that you and the system remain at the same electrical potential, which is accomplished via the strap. Another issue for personal safety is the use of a commercially available wrist strap, rather than making your own. Commercially made wrist straps feature an internal 1-meg ohm resistor designed to protect you. The resistor ensures that you are not the best path to ground should you touch any "hot" wire.

When you remove components from the system, they should be placed on a special conductive antistatic mat, which is also a part of any good ESD protection kit. The mat is also connected via a wire and clip to the system chassis. Any components removed from the system, especially items such as the processor, the motherboard, adapter cards, disk drives, and so on, should be placed on the mat. The connection between you, the mat, and the chassis will prevent any static discharges from damaging the components.

Note

It is possible (but not recommended) to work without an ESD protection kit if you're disciplined and careful about working on systems. If you don't have an ESD kit available, you can discharge yourself by touching any exposed metal on the chassis or case.

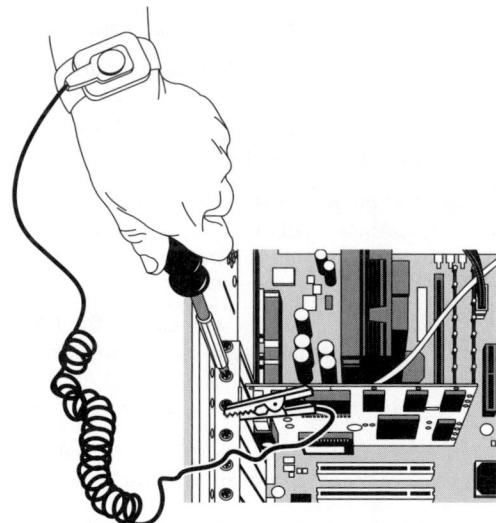

Figure 24.6   A typical ESD wrist strap clipped to a nonpainted surface in the case chassis.

The ESD kits, as well as all the other tools and much more, are available from a variety of tool vendors. Specialized Products Company and Jensen Tools are two of the most popular vendors of computer and electronic tools and service equipment. Their catalogs show an extensive selection of very high-quality tools. (These companies and several others are listed in the Vendor List on the accompanying disc.) With a simple set of hand tools, you will be equipped for nearly every PC repair or installation situation. The total cost of these tools should be less than $150, which is not much considering the capabilities they provide.

A Word About Hardware

This section discusses some problems you might encounter with the hardware (screws, nuts, bolts, and so on) used in assembling a system.

Types of Hardware

One of the biggest aggravations you encounter in dealing with various systems is the different hardware types and designs that hold the units together.

For example, most systems use screws that fit 1/4-inch or 3/16-inch hexagonal nut drivers. IBM used these screws in all its original PC, XT, and AT systems, and most other system manufacturers use this standard hardware as well. Some manufacturers use different hardware, however. Compaq, for example, uses Torx screws extensively in many of its systems. A Torx screw has a star-shaped hole driven by the correct-size Torx driver. These drivers carry size designations such as T-8, T-9, T-10, T-15, T-20, T-25, T-30, and T-40.

A variation on the Torx screw is the tamperproof Torx screw found in power supplies, monitors, hard drives, and other assemblies. These screws are identical to the regular Torx screws, except that a pin sticks up from the middle of the star-shape hole in the screw. This pin prevents the standard Torx driver from entering the hole to grip the screw; a special tamperproof driver with a corresponding hole for the pin is required. An alternative is to use a small chisel to knock out the pin in the screw. Usually, a device sealed with these types of screws is considered to be a replaceable unit that rarely, if ever, needs to be opened.

Caution

Note that devices sealed with tamperproof Torx screws generally have high voltages or other dangers waiting inside, so being able to bypass these screws doesn't mean it's always a good idea. Be sure you know what you are doing before disassembling devices such as monitors and power supplies.

Many manufacturers also use the more standard slotted-head and Phillips-head screws. Slotted-head screws should *never* be used in a computer because the screwdriver can very easily slip and damage a board. Using tools on these screws is relatively easy, but tools do not grip these fasteners as well as hexagonal head or Torx screws do. In addition, the heads can be stripped more easily than the other types. Extremely cheap versions tend to lose bits of metal as they're turned with a driver, and the metal bits can fall onto the motherboard. Stay away from cheap fasteners whenever possible; the headaches of dealing with stripped screws aren't worth it.

Some system manufacturers now use cases that snap together or use thumb screws. These are usually advertised as "no-tool" cases because you literally do not need any tools to remove the cover and access the major assemblies.

To make an existing case tool-free, you can replace the normal case screws with metal or plastic thumbscrews. However, you still should always use metal screws to install internal components, such as adapter cards, disk drives, power supplies, and the motherboard, because the metal screws provide a ground point for these devices.

English Versus Metric

Another area of aggravation with hardware is the fact that two types of thread systems exist: English and metric. IBM used mostly English-threaded fasteners in its original line of systems, but many other manufacturers used metric-threaded fasteners.

The difference between the two becomes especially apparent with disk drives. American-manufactured drives typically use English fasteners, whereas drives made in Japan, Taiwan, and other Pacific Rim countries (where most disk drives are now made) typically use metric. Whenever you replace a floppy drive in an older PC, you encounter this problem. Try to buy the correct screws and any other hardware, such as brackets, with the drive because they might be difficult to find as separate items. Many drive manufacturers offer retail drive kits that include all the required mounting components. The OEM's drive manual lists the correct data about a specific drive's hole locations and thread size.

Tip

Before you discard an obsolete computer, remove the screws and other reusable parts, such as cover plates, jumper blocks, and so on. Label the bag or container with the name and model of the computer to help you more easily determine where else you can use the parts later.

Hard disks can use either English or metric fasteners; check your particular drive to see which type it uses. Most drives today use metric hardware.

Caution

Some screws in a system can be length-critical, especially screws used to retain hard disk drives. You can destroy some hard disks by using a mounting screw that's too long; the screw can puncture or dent the sealed disk chamber when you install the drive and fully tighten the screw. When you install a new drive in a system, always make a trial fit of the hardware to see how far the screws can be inserted into the drive before they interfere with its internal components. When in doubt, the drive manufacturer's OEM documentation will tell you precisely which screws are required and how long they should be. Most drives sold at retail include correct-length mounting screws, but OEM drives usually don't include screws or other hardware.

Test Equipment

In some cases, you must use specialized devices to test a system board or component. This test equipment is not expensive or difficult to use, but it can add much to your troubleshooting abilities.

Electrical Testing Equipment

I consider a voltmeter to be required gear for proper system testing. A multimeter can serve many purposes, including checking for voltage signals at various points in a system, testing the output of the power supply, and checking for continuity in a circuit or cable. An outlet tester is an invaluable accessory that can check the electrical outlet for proper wiring. This capability is useful if you believe the problem lies outside the computer system.

Loopback Connectors (Wrap Plugs)

For diagnosing serial- and parallel-port problems, you need loopback connectors (also called wrap plugs), which are used to circulate, or wrap, signals (see Figure 24.7). The plugs enable the serial or parallel port to send data to itself for diagnostic purposes.

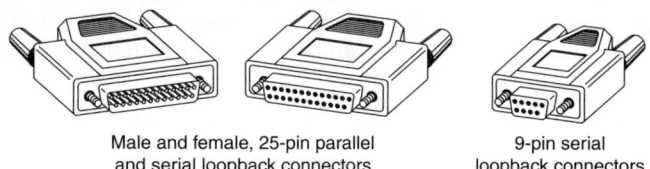

Male and female, 25-pin parallel
and serial loopback connectors

9-pin serial
loopback connectors

Figure 24.7 Typical wrap plugs, including 25-pin and 9-pin serial and 25-pin parallel versions.

Various types of loopback connectors are available. To accommodate all the ports you might encounter, you need one for the 25-pin serial port, one for the 9-pin serial port, and one for the 25-pin parallel port. Many companies, including IBM, sell the plugs separately, but be aware that you also need diagnostic software that can use them. Some diagnostic software products, such as Micro 2000's Micro-Scope, include loopback connectors with the product, or you can purchase them as an option for about $30 a set. Note that there are some variations on how loopback connectors can be made, and not all versions work properly with all diagnostics software. You should therefore use the loopback connectors recommended by the diagnostics software you will be using.

IBM sells a special combination plug that includes all three connector types in one compact unit. The device costs about the same as a normal set of wrap plugs. If you're handy, you can even make your own wrap plugs for testing. I include wiring diagrams for the three types of wrap plugs in

Chapter 17, "I/O Interfaces from Serial and Parallel to IEEE 1394 and USB." In that chapter, you also will find a detailed discussion of serial and parallel ports.

Besides simple loopback connectors, you also might want to have a breakout box for your toolkit. A breakout box is a DB25 connector device that enables you to make custom temporary cables or even to monitor signals on a cable. For most PC troubleshooting uses, a "mini" breakout box works well and is inexpensive.

Meters

Some troubleshooting procedures require that you measure voltage and resistance. You take these measurements by using a handheld Digital Multi-Meter (DMM). The meter can be an analog device (using an actual meter) or a digital-readout device. The DMM has a pair of wires called test leads or probes. The test leads make the connections so that you can take readings. Depending on the meter's setting, the probes measure electrical resistance, direct-current (DC) voltage, or alternating-current (AC) voltage. Figure 24.8 shows a typical DMM being used to test the +12V circuit on an ATX motherboard.

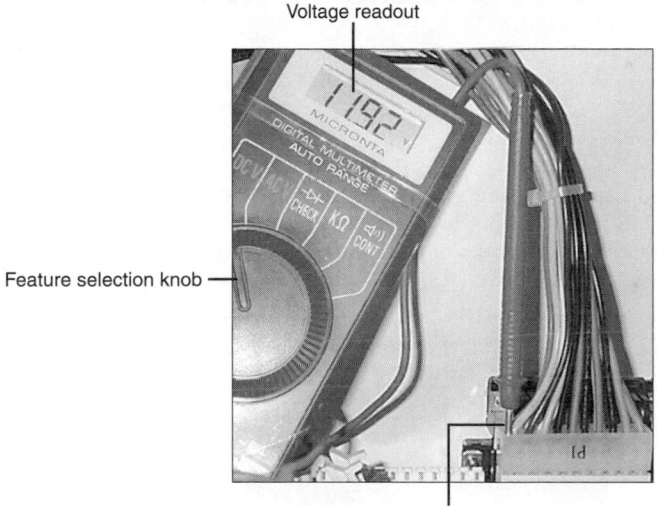

Voltage readout

Feature selection knob

Red lead inserted into ATX power connector

Figure 24.8   A typical digital multimeter tests a motherboard's +12V circuit.

Usually, each system-unit measurement setting has several ranges of operation. DC voltage, for example, usually can be read in several scales, to a maximum of 200 millivolts (mV), 2V, 20V, 200V, and 1,000V. Because computers use both +5V and +12V for various operations, you should use the 20V maximum scale for making your measurements. Making these measurements on the 200mV or 2V scale could "peg the meter" and possibly damage it because the voltage would be much higher than expected. Using the 200V or 1,000V scale works, but the readings at 5V and 12V are so small in proportion to the maximum that accuracy is low.

If you are taking a measurement and are unsure of the actual voltage, start at the highest scale and work your way down. Most of the better meters have autoranging capability—the meter automatically selects the best range for any measurement. This type of meter is much easier to operate. You simply set the meter to the type of reading you want, such as DC volts, and attach the probes to the signal source. The meter selects the correct voltage range and displays the value. Because of their design, these types of meters always have a digital display rather than a meter needle.

Caution

Whenever you are using a multimeter to test any voltage that could potentially be 50V or above (such as AC wall socket voltage), always use one hand to do the testing, not two. Either clip one lead to one of the sources and probe with the other or hold both leads in one hand.

If you hold a lead in each hand and accidentally slip, you can very easily become a circuit, allowing power to conduct or flow through you. When power flows from arm to arm, the path of the current is directly across the heart. The heart muscle tends to quit working when subjected to high voltages. They're funny that way.

I prefer the small digital meters; you can buy them for only slightly more than the analog style, and they're extremely accurate and much safer for digital circuits. Some of these meters are not much bigger than a cassette tape; they fit in a shirt pocket. Radio Shack sells a good unit in the $25 price range; the meter (refer to Figure 24.8) is a half-inch thick, weighs 3 1/2 ounces, and is digital and autoranging, as well. This type of meter works well for most, if not all, PC troubleshooting and test uses.

Caution

You should be aware that many analog meters can be dangerous to digital circuits. These meters use a 9V battery to power the meter for resistance measurements. If you use this type of meter to measure resistance on some digital circuits, you can damage the electronics because you essentially are injecting 9V into the circuit. The digital meters universally run on 3V–5V or less.

Logic Probes and Logic Pulsers

A logic probe can be useful for diagnosing problems in digital circuits (see Figure 24.9). In a digital circuit, a signal is represented as either high (+5V) or low (0V). Because these signals are present for only a short time (measured in millionths of a second) or oscillate (switch on and off) rapidly, a simple voltmeter is useless. A logic probe is designed to display these signal conditions easily.

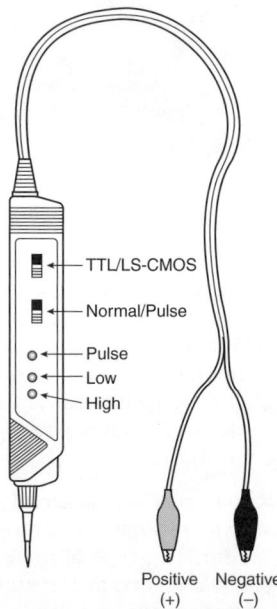

Figure 24.9   A typical logic probe.

Logic probes are especially useful for troubleshooting a dead system. By using the probe, you can determine whether the basic clock circuitry is operating and whether other signals necessary for system operation are present. In some cases, a probe can help you cross-check the signals at each pin on an integrated circuit chip. You can compare the signals present at each pin with the signals a known-good chip of the same type would show—a comparison that is helpful in isolating a failed component. Logic probes also can be useful for troubleshooting some disk drive problems by enabling you to test the signals present on the interface cable or drive-logic board.

A companion tool to the probe is the logic pulser. A *pulser* is designed to test circuit reaction by delivering a logical high (+5V) pulse into a circuit, usually lasting from 1 1/2 to 10 millionths of a second. Compare the reaction with that of a known-functional circuit. This type of device normally is used much less frequently than a logic probe, but in some cases it can be helpful for testing a circuit.

Outlet Testers

Outlet testers are very useful test tools. These simple, inexpensive devices, sold in hardware stores, test electrical outlets. You simply plug in the device, and three LEDs light up in various combinations, indicating whether the outlet is wired correctly (see Figure 24.10).

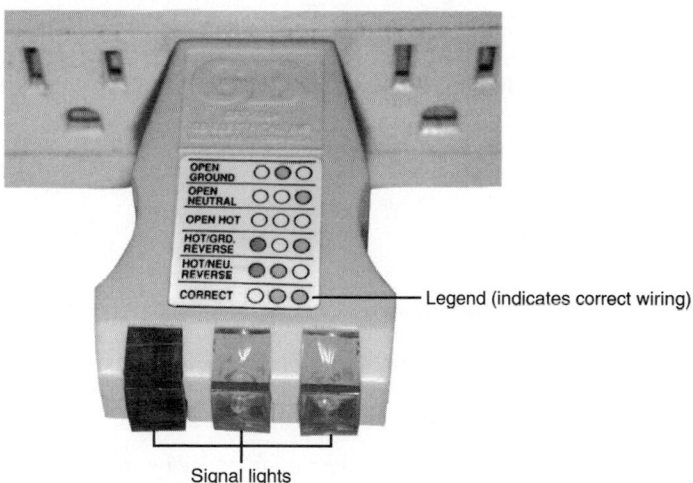

Figure 24.10 A typical outlet tester.

Although you might think that badly wired outlets would be a rare problem, I have seen a large number of installations in which the outlets were wired incorrectly. Most of the time, the problem is in the ground wire. An improperly wired outlet can result in unstable system operation, such as random parity checks and lockups. With an improper ground circuit, currents can begin flowing on the electrical ground circuits in the system. Because the system uses the voltage on the ground circuits as a comparative signal to determine whether bits are 0 or 1, a floating ground can cause data errors in the system.

Caution

Even if you use a surge protector, it will not protect your system from an improperly wired outlet. Therefore, you still should use an outlet tester to ensure your outlet is computer friendly.

Once, while running one of my PC troubleshooting seminars, I used a system that I literally could not approach without locking it up. Whenever I walked past the system, the electrostatic field generated by my body interfered with the system and the PC locked up, displaying a parity-check error message. The problem was that the hotel at which I was giving the seminar was very old and had no grounded outlets in the room. The only way I could prevent the system from locking up was to run the class in my stocking feet because my leather-soled shoes were generating the static charge.

Other symptoms of bad ground wiring in electrical outlets are continual electrical shocks when you touch the case or chassis of the system. These shocks indicate that voltages are flowing where they should not be. This problem also can be caused by bad or improper grounds within the system. By using the simple outlet tester, you can quickly determine whether the outlet is at fault.

If you just walk up to a system and receive an initial shock, it's probably only static electricity. Touch the chassis again without moving your feet. If you receive another shock, something is very wrong. In this case, the ground wire actually has voltage applied to it. You should have a professional electrician check the outlet immediately.

If you don't like being a human rat in an electrical experiment, you can test the outlets with your multimeter. First, remember to hold both leads in one hand. Test from one blade hole to another. This should read between 110V and 125V, depending on the electrical service in the area. Then, check from each blade to the ground (the round hole). One blade hole, the smaller one, should show a voltage almost identical to the one you got from the blade-hole–to–blade-hole test. The larger blade hole when measured to ground should show less than 0.5V.

Because ground and neutral are supposed to be tied together at the electrical panel, a large difference in these readings indicates that they are not tied together. However, small differences can be accounted for by current from other outlets down the line flowing on the neutral, when there isn't any on the ground.

If you don't get the results you expect, call an electrician to test the outlets for you. More weird computer problems are caused by improper grounding and other power problems than people like to believe.

Memory Testers

I now consider a memory test machine an all-but-mandatory piece of equipment for anyone serious about performing PC troubleshooting and repair as a profession. The tester is a small device designed to evaluate SIMMs, DIMMs, RIMMs, and other types of memory modules, including individual chips such as those used as cache memory. These testers can be somewhat expensive, costing upward of $1,000–$2,500 or more, but these machines are the only truly accurate way to test memory.

Without one of these testers, you are reduced to testing memory by running a diagnostic program on the PC and testing the memory as it is installed. This can be very problematic because the memory diagnostic program can do only two things to the memory: write and read. A SIMM/DIMM/RIMM tester can do many things a memory diagnostic running in a PC can't do, such as

- Identify the type of memory
- Identify the memory speed
- Identify whether the memory has parity or is using bogus parity emulation
- Vary the refresh timing and access speed timing

- Locate single bit failures
- Detect power- and noise-related failures
- Detect solder opens and shorts
- Isolate timing-related failures
- Detect data retention errors

No conventional memory diagnostic software can do these things because it must rely on the fixed access parameters set up by the memory controller hardware in the motherboard chipset. This prevents the software from being capable of altering the timing and methods used to access the memory. You might have memory that fails in one system and works in another when the chips are actually bad. This type of intermittent problem is almost impossible to detect with diagnostic software.

The bottom line is that there is no way you can test memory with true accuracy while it is installed in a PC; a memory tester is required for comprehensive and accurate testing. The price of a memory tester can be justified very easily in a shop environment where a lot of PCs are tested because many software and hardware upgrades today require the addition of new memory. With the large increases in the amount of memory in today's systems and the stricter timing requirements of newer motherboard designs, it has become even more important to be able to identify or rule out memory as a cause of system failure. One company manufacturing memory testers I recommend is Tanisys Technology; its Darkhorse Systems line of memory testers can handle virtually every type of memory on the market. See the Vendor List on this book's disc for more information. Also, see Chapter 6, "Memory," for more information on memory in general.

Special Tools for the Enthusiast

All the tools described so far are commonly used by most technicians. However, a few additional tools do exist that a true PC enthusiast might want to have.

Electric Screwdriver

Perhaps the most useful tool I use is an electric screwdriver. It enables me to disassemble and reassemble a PC in record time and makes the job not only faster but easier as well. I like the type with a clutch you can use to set how tight it will make the screws before slipping; such a clutch makes it even faster to use. If you use the driver frequently, it makes sense to use the type with replaceable, rechargeable batteries, so when one battery dies you can quickly replace it with a fresh one.

Caution

Note that using an electric screwdriver when installing a motherboard can be dangerous because the bit can easily slip off the screw and damage the board. A telltale series of swirling scratches near the screw holes on the board can be the result, for which most manufacturers rightfully deny a warranty claim. Be especially careful if your motherboard is retained with Phillips-head screws because they are extremely easy for the bit to slip out of. Normally, I recommend using only Torx-head or hex-head screws to retain the motherboard because they are far more resistant to having the bit slip out and cause damage.

With the electric screwdriver, I recommend getting a complete set of English and metric nut driver tips as well as various sizes of Torx, flat-head, and Phillips-head screwdriver tips.

Tamperproof Torx Bits

Any devices such as power supplies and monitors are held together with tamperproof Torx screws. Tamperproof Torx driver sets are available from any good electronics tool supplier.

Temperature Probe

Determining the interior temperature of a PC is often useful when diagnosing whether heat-related issues are causing problems. This requires some way of measuring the temperature inside the PC, as well as the ambient temperature outside the system. The simplest and best tool I've found for the job is the digital thermometers sold at most auto parts stores for automobile use. They are designed to read the temperature inside and outside the car and normally come with an internal sensor, as well as one at the end of a length of wire.

With this type of probe, you can run the wired sensor inside the case (if it is metal, make sure it does not directly touch the motherboard or other exposed circuits where it might cause a short) with the wires slipped through a crack in the case or out one of the drive bays. Then, with the system running you can take the internal temperature as well as read the room's ambient temperature. Normally, the maximum limit for internal temperature should be 110°F (43°C) or less. If your system is running near or above that temperature, problems can be expected. You also can position the probe in the system to be near any heat producing devices, such as the processor, video card, and so on, to see the effect of the device. Probing the temperature with a device such as this enables you to determine whether additional cooling is necessary (that is, adding more cooling fans to the case) and enables you to check to see whether the added fans are helping.

Infrared Thermometer

Another useful temperature tool is a noncontact infrared (IR) thermometer, which is a special type of sensor that can measure the temperature of an object without physically touching it (see Figure 24.11). You can take the temperature reading of an object in seconds by merely pointing the handheld device at the object you want to measure and pulling a trigger.

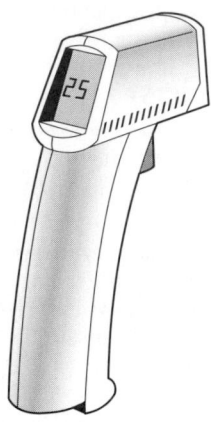

Figure 24.11   A noncontact infrared thermometer.

An IR thermometer works by capturing the infrared energy naturally emitted from all objects warmer than absolute zero (0° Kelvin). Infrared energy is a part of the electromagnetic spectrum with a frequency below that of visible light, which means it is invisible to the human eye. Infrared wavelengths are between 0.7 microns and 1,000 microns (millionths of a meter), although infrared thermometers typically measure radiation in the range 0.7–14 microns.

Because IR thermometers can measure the temperature of objects without touching them, they are ideal for measuring chip temperatures in a running system—especially the temperature of the CPU heatsink. By merely pointing the device at the top of the CPU and pulling the trigger, you can get a very accurate measurement in about 1 second. To enable more accuracy in positioning, many IR thermometers incorporate a laser pointer, which is used to aim the device.

IR thermometers are designed to measure IR radiation from a device; they can't be used to measure air temperature. The sensors are specifically designed so that the air between the sensor and target does not affect the temperature measurement.

Although several IR thermometers are available on the market, I use and recommend the Raytek (www.raytek.com) MiniTemp series, which consists of the MT2 and MT4. Both units are identical, but the MT4 includes a laser pointer for aiming. The MT2 and MT4 are capable of measuring temperatures between 0° and 500°F (-18°–260°C) in one half of a second with an accuracy of about plus or minus 3°F (2°C). They cost $80–$100 and are available from NAPA auto parts stores (these devices have many uses in automotive testing as well) and other tool outlets.

Large Claw-Type Parts Grabber

One of the more useful tools in my toolbox is a large claw-type parts grabber, normally sold in stores that carry automotive tools. Having one of these around has saved many hours of frustration digging back into a system or behind a desk for a loose or dropped screw.

These grabbers are very similar to the small claw-type grabber included with most PC toolkits, except they are much larger—normally two feet or so in length. They can be useful if you drop a screw down inside a tower case, or even on the floor under or behind a desk or cabinet. Although magnetic parts grabbers are also available, I normally recommend the claw-type because using a powerful magnet near a computer can cause problems with any disk storage media you have about, or even the hard disk or CRT-type display.

Preventive Maintenance

Preventive maintenance is the key to obtaining years of trouble-free service from your computer system. A properly administered preventive maintenance program pays for itself by reducing problem behavior, data loss, and component failure and by ensuring a long life for your system. In several cases, I have "repaired" an ailing system with nothing more than a preventive maintenance session. Preventive maintenance also can increase your system's resale value because it will look and run better.

Developing a preventive maintenance program is important to everyone who uses or manages personal computer systems. The two types of preventive maintenance procedures are active and passive.

An *active* preventive maintenance program includes procedures that promote a longer, trouble-free life for your PC. This type of preventive maintenance primarily involves the periodic cleaning of the system and its components. The following sections describe several active preventive maintenance procedures, including cleaning and lubricating all major components, reseating chips and connectors, and reformatting hard disks.

Passive preventive maintenance includes steps you can take to protect a system from the environment, such as using power-protection devices; ensuring a clean, temperature-controlled environment; and preventing excessive vibration. In other words, passive preventive maintenance means treating your system well.

Active Preventive Maintenance Procedures

How often you should perform active preventive maintenance procedures depends on the system's environment and the quality of the system's components. If your system is in a dirty environment, such as a machine shop floor or a gas station service area, you might need to clean your system every three months or less. For normal office environments, cleaning a system every few months to a year is usually fine. However, if you open your system after one year and find dust bunnies inside, you should probably shorten the cleaning interval.

Other hard disk preventive maintenance procedures include making periodic backups of your data and critical areas, such as boot sectors, file allocation tables (FATs), and directory structures on the disk. Also, you should defragment hard disks at least once a month to maintain disk efficiency and speed.

The following is a sample weekly disk maintenance checklist:

- Back up any data or important files.
- Delete all temporary files, such as
  - *.tmp (files with a .tmp extension)
  - *.* (files beginning with a tilde (~))
  - *.chk (files with a .chk extension)
  - Web browser history and temporary Internet files
- Empty the Recycle Bin.
- Check for and install antivirus software updates. If you have a broadband Internet connection, you might prefer to configure your antivirus software program to check automatically for updates daily.
- Run the defragmenting program.

The following are some monthly maintenance procedures you should perform:

- Create an operating system startup disk.
- Check for and install any updated drivers for video cards, sound cards, modems, and other devices.
- Check for and install any operating system updates.
- Clean the system, including the monitor screen, keyboard, CD/DVD drives, floppy drive, mouse, and so on.
- Check that all system fans are operating properly, including the CPU heatsink, power supply, and any chassis fans. You can use the system BIOS readout of fan speeds to perform a quick check. Open the system to examine any fans that aren't working or are running more slowly than normal.

System Backups

One of the most important preventive maintenance procedures is the performance of regular system backups. A sad reality in the computer repair and servicing world is that hardware can always be repaired or replaced, but data cannot. Many hard disk troubleshooting and service procedures, for example, require that you repartition or reformat the disk, which overwrites all existing data.

The hard disk drive capacity in a typical PC has grown far beyond the point at which floppy disks are a viable backup solution. Backup solutions that employ floppy disk drives, such as DOS backup software, are insufficient and too costly for hard disk backups in today's systems. Table 24.8 shows the number of units of various types of media required to back up the 80GB drive in my current notebook/laptop system.

Table 24.8   Amounts and Costs of Various Media Required to Back Up a Full 80GB Drive

Media Type	Number Required	Unit Cost	Net Cost
1.44M floppy disks	54,883	$0.15	$8,232
48X 80-minute/700MB CD-R discs	109	$0.25	$27
4X DVD+/-R discs	18	$1.50	$27
DAT DDS-4 tapes (native)	4	$15	$60
DAT DDS-4 tapes (compressed)	2	$15	$30

Assuming the drive were full, it would take 54,883 1.44MB floppy disks, for example, to back up the 80GB hard disk in my current notebook/laptop system! That would cost more than $8,232 in disks, not to mention the time involved. As you can see, even CD-R would be miserable, requiring 109 discs to back up the entire drive. DVD+/-R, on the other hand, would require only 18 discs, which still wouldn't be much fun but would be adequate in a pinch. Tape, however, really shines here because it would require only two DAT DDS-4 tapes to back up the entire drive, meaning I would have to switch tapes in the drive only once. Although the media cost is a little higher with the tape as compared to CD/DVD, the time savings are enormous. Imagine trying to back up a full 300GB drive in a desktop system—that would require 64 DVD+/-R discs but only eight DAT DDS-4 tapes.

The best form of backup has traditionally been magnetic tape. The two main standards are Travan and DAT (digital audio tape). Travan drives are generally slower and hold less than the newest DAT drives, but both are available in relatively competitive versions. The latest Travan tape drives store 20GB/40GB (raw/compressed) on a single tape, whereas DAT DDS-4 drives store 20GB/40GB per tape.

These tapes typically cost $15 or less. If you use larger drives, new versions of DAT and other technologies can be used to back up your drive.

Tape is generally the fastest and safest form of backup, especially considering you can make multiple backups to different tapes, and even move some of the backups offsite in case of theft or fire. Still, the initial cost of the drive has been an impediment to many. The increasing popularity of writable CD-RW drives presents an alternative, although backing up an entire drive requires multiple CDs. In the previous 80GB example, you would need as many as 109 700MB CDs to perform a single backup. Although the media cost is only about $27, the time involved is still considerable. Recordable DVDs offer 4.7GB of storage per disc, so that would reduce the number of discs needed dramatically, to only 18 in our 80GB example.

Although a tape drive can cost up to $500 or more, the media costs are really far more significant than the cost of the drive. If you perform responsible backups, you should have at least three sets of media for each system you are backing up. You should use each media set on a rotating basis, and store one of them offsite at all times, in case of fire or theft. You also should introduce new media to the rotation after approximately a year to prevent excessive wear. If you are backing up multiple systems, these media costs can add up quickly. In addition, you should factor in the cost of your time. If a backup requires manual intervention to change the media during the job, as with any technology except high-capacity tape or external hard drives, I don't recommend it. A backup system should be capable of fitting a complete backup on a single tape or drive so you can schedule the job to run unattended. If someone has to hang around to switch tapes or media every so often, backups become a real chore and are more likely to be overlooked. Also, every time a media change occurs, the likelihood of errors and problems you might not see until you attempt to perform a restore operation substantially increases. Backups are far more important than most people realize, and spending a little more on a quality piece of hardware such as a Travan, DAT, or other high-capacity tape drive will pay off in the long run with greater reliability, lower media costs, higher performance, and unattended backups that contain the entire system file structure. As a second choice for immediate backups, I recommend an external hard drive, although you should still determine how you plan to store the data you want to keep permanently.

With the increasing popularity of removable bulk storage media such as cartridge drives, including Iomega's Zip, and rewritable CDs (CD-RWs), many people are using these devices to perform system backups. In most cases, however, although these drives are excellent for storing backup copies of selected data, they are impractical solutions for regular system backups. This can be due to both the capacity of the media in relation to today's hard disk drives and the cost of the media. You should use multiple sets of media with a CD-RW drive, just as you would with a tape backup.

Although the media for a CD-RW drive are quite inexpensive, it would take several discs to back up a multigigabyte hard drive, adding a measure of inconvenience to the backup process that makes it far less likely to be performed on a regular basis. Rewritable DVD drives can store 4.7GB (uncompressed) on a single DVD, and media costs drop to around $1.50 per disc in quantities. A rewritable DVD drive has about the same overall media costs for a backup as compared to a CD-RW drive, but reduces the amount of media required considerably. However, it still requires the operator to swap backup media periodically when more than 4.7GB of data must be backed up, and it requires you to use multiple sets of media. Another alternative for backup is to install a second hard drive of equal (or larger) capacity and simply copy from one drive to another. With the low cost of drives these days, this is an economical, fast, and efficient method; however, if a disaster occurs, such as theft or fire, you'll still lose everything. Also, with only one backup, if your backup goes bad when you depend on it, you'll be without any other alternatives. An ATA RAID 1 array automatically mirrors the contents of one drive to another (see Chapter 7, "The ATA/IDE Interface," for details); many motherboards now have built-in ATA or SATA RAID adapters.

What I like to do is use a second hard disk to make complete backups of my entire drive weekly, followed by monthly backups to tape. This enables me to not only back up quickly and efficiently, but I also can easily swap my backup slave drive for a failed master and be up and running again in minutes. The tape backup then becomes more of an insurance policy. You can perform hard disk–based backups for more than one system with an external hard drive. External hard disks are available in capacities up to 300GB and don't require media swapping. Some models even offer one-button backups. However, you might eventually want to move the data on the external drive over to CD, DVD, or tape media for permanent storage. Although the upfront cost of an external hard drive can be significant (around $400 for a 200GB model, $300 for a 120GB model, or under $200 for an 80GB model), there is no additional media cost until you want to move some data to permanent tape, CD, or DVD storage.

Tip

No matter which backup solution you use, the entire exercise is pointless if you cannot restore your data from the storage medium. You should test your backup system by performing random file restores at regular intervals to ensure the viability of your data.

If your backup supports disaster recovery, be sure to test this feature as well by installing an empty drive and using the disaster recovery feature to rebuild the operating system and restore the data.

Cleaning a System

One of the most important operations in a good preventive maintenance program is regular and thorough cleaning of the system. Dust buildup on the internal components can lead to several problems. One is that the dust acts as a thermal insulator, which prevents proper system cooling. Excessive heat shortens the life of system components and adds to the thermal stress problem caused by greater temperature changes between the system's power-on and power-off states. Additionally, the dust can contain conductive elements that can cause partial short circuits in a system. Other elements in dust and dirt can accelerate corrosion of electrical contacts, resulting in improper connections. In all, the regular removal of any layer of dust and debris from within a computer system benefits that system in the long run.

Tip

Cigarette smoke contains chemicals that can conduct electricity and cause corrosion of computer parts. The smoke residue can infiltrate the entire system, causing corrosion and contamination of electrical contacts and sensitive components, such as floppy drive read/write heads and optical drive lens assemblies. You should avoid smoking near computer equipment and encourage your company to develop and enforce a similar policy.

Floppy disk drives are particularly vulnerable to the effects of dirt and dust. A floppy drive is essentially a large "hole" in the system case through which air continuously flows. Therefore, these drives accumulate a large amount of dust and chemical buildup within a short time. Hard disk drives, on the other hand, do not present quite the same problem. Because the head disk assembly (HDA) in a hard disk is a sealed unit with a single barometric vent, no dust or dirt can enter without passing through the barometric vent filter. This filter ensures that contaminating dust and particles cannot enter the interior of the HDA. Thus, cleaning a hard disk requires blowing off the dust and dirt from outside the drive. No internal cleaning is required.

Disassembly and Cleaning Tools

Properly cleaning the system and all the boards inside requires certain supplies and tools. In addition to the tools required to disassemble the unit, you should have these items:

- Contact cleaning solution
- Canned air
- A small brush
- Lint-free foam cleaning swabs
- Antistatic wrist-grounding strap

You also might want to acquire these optional items:

- Foam tape
- Low-volatile room-temperature vulcanizing (RTV) sealer
- Silicone-type lubricant
- Computer vacuum cleaner

These simple cleaning tools and chemical solutions enable you to perform most common preventive maintenance tasks.

Chemicals

Chemicals can be used to help clean, troubleshoot, and even repair a system. You can use several types of cleaning solutions with computers and electronic assemblies. Most fall into the following categories:

- Standard cleaners
- Contact cleaner/lubricants
- Dusters

Tip

The makeup of many of the chemicals used for cleaning electronic components has been changing because many of the chemicals originally used are now considered environmentally unsafe. They have been attributed to damaging the earth's ozone layer. Chlorine atoms from chlorofluorocarbons (CFCs) and chlorinated solvents attach themselves to ozone molecules and destroy them. Many of these chemicals are now strictly regulated by federal and international agencies in an effort to preserve the ozone layer. Most of the companies that produce chemicals used for system cleaning and maintenance have had to introduce environmentally safe replacements. The only drawback is that many of these safer chemicals cost more and usually do not work as well as those they've replaced.

Standard Cleaners

For the most basic function—cleaning components, electrical connectors, and contacts—one of the most useful chemicals is 1,1,1 trichloroethane. This substance is an effective cleaner that was at one time used to clean electrical contacts and components because it does not damage most plastics and board materials. In fact, trichloroethane is very useful for cleaning stains on the system case and keyboard as well. Unfortunately, trichloroethane is now being regulated as a chlorinated solvent, along with CFCs (chlorofluorocarbons) such as Freon, but electronic chemical-supply companies are offering several replacements.

Alternative cleaning solutions are available in a variety of types and configurations. You can use pure isopropyl alcohol, acetone, Freon, trichloroethane, or a variety of other chemicals. Most board manufacturers and service shops are now leaning toward alcohol, acetone, or other chemicals that do not cause ozone depletion and comply with government regulations and environmental safety.

Recently, new biodegradable cleaners described as "citrus-based cleaners" have become popular in the industry, and in many cases are more effective and more economical for circuit board and contact cleaning. These cleaners are commonly known as d-limonene or citrus terpenes and are derived from orange peels, which gives them a strong (but pleasant) citric odor. Another type of terpene is called a-pinene, and is derived from pine trees. You must exercise care when using these cleaners, however, because they can cause swelling of some plastics, especially silicone rubber and PVC.

You should make sure your cleaning solution is designed to clean computers or electronic assemblies. In most cases, this means that the solution should be chemically pure and free from contaminants or other unwanted substances. You should not, for example, use drugstore rubbing alcohol for cleaning electronic parts or contacts because it is not pure and could contain water or perfumes. The material must be moisture-free and residue-free. The solutions should be in liquid form, not a spray. Sprays can be wasteful, and you almost never spray the solution directly on components. Instead, wet a foam or chamois swab used for wiping the component. These electronic-component cleaning solutions are available at any good electronics parts store.

Contact Cleaner/Lubricants

These chemicals are similar to the standard cleaners but include a lubricating component. The lubricant eases the force required when plugging and unplugging cables and connectors, reducing strain on the devices. The lubricant coating also acts as a conductive protectant that insulates the contacts from corrosion. These chemicals can greatly prolong the life of a system by preventing intermittent contacts in the future.

A unique type of contact enhancer and lubricant called Stabilant 22 is currently on the market. This chemical, which you apply to electrical contacts, greatly enhances the connection and lubricates the contact point; it is much more effective than conventional contact cleaners or lubricants.

Stabilant 22 is a liquid-polymer semiconductor; it behaves like liquid metal and conducts electricity in the presence of an electric current. The substance also fills the air gaps between the mating surfaces of two items that are in contact, making the surface area of the contact larger and also keeping out oxygen and other contaminants that can corrode the contact point.

This chemical is available in several forms. Stabilant 22 is the concentrated version, whereas Stabilant 22a is a version diluted with isopropanol in a 4:1 ratio. An even more diluted 8:1-ratio version is sold in many high-end stereo and audio shops under the name Tweek. Just 15ml of Stabilant 22a sells for about $40; a liter of the concentrate costs about $4,000!

As you can plainly see, Stabilant 22 is fairly expensive, but little is required in an application, and nothing else has been found to be as effective in preserving electrical contacts. (NASA uses the chemical on spacecraft electronics.) An application of Stabilant can provide protection for up to 16 years, according to its manufacturer, D.W. Electrochemicals. You will find the company's address and phone number in the Vendor List on the accompanying disc.

Stabilant is especially effective on I/O slot connectors, adapter-card edge and pin connectors, disk drive connectors, power-supply connectors, and virtually any connector in the PC. In addition to enhancing the contact and preventing corrosion, an application of Stabilant lubricates the contacts, making insertion and removal of the connector easier.

Dusters

Compressed gas often is used as an aid in system cleaning. You use the compressed gas as a blower to remove dust and debris from a system or component. Originally, these dusters used CFCs (chlorofluorocarbons) such as Freon, whereas modern dusters use either HFCs (hydrofluorocarbons such as difluoroethane) or carbon dioxide, neither of which is known to damage the ozone layer. Be careful when you use these devices because some of them can generate a static charge when the compressed gas leaves the nozzle of the can. Be sure you are using the type approved for cleaning or dusting off computer equipment, and consider wearing a static grounding strap as a precaution. The type of compressed-air cans used for cleaning camera equipment can sometimes differ from the type used for cleaning static-sensitive computer components.

When using these compressed air products, be sure you hold the can upright so that only gas is ejected from the nozzle. If you tip the can, the raw propellant will come out as a cold liquid, which not only is wasteful but can damage or discolor plastics. You should use compressed gas only on equipment that is powered off, to minimize any chance of damage through short circuits.

Closely related to compressed-air products are chemical-freeze sprays. These sprays are used to quickly cool down a suspected failing component, which often temporarily restores it to normal operation.

These substances are not used to repair a device, but to confirm that you have found a failed device. Often, a component's failure is heat-related, and cooling it temporarily restores it to normal operation. If the circuit begins operating normally, the device you are cooling is the suspect device.

Vacuum Cleaners

Some people prefer to use a vacuum cleaner instead of canned gas dusters for cleaning a system. Canned gas is usually better for cleaning in small areas. A vacuum cleaner is more useful when you are cleaning a system loaded with dust and dirt. You can use the vacuum cleaner to suck out the dust and debris instead of simply blowing it around on the other components, which sometimes happens with canned air. For onsite servicing (when you are going to the location of the equipment instead of the equipment coming to you), canned air is easier to carry in a toolkit than a small vacuum cleaner. Tiny vacuum cleaners also are available for system cleaning. These small units are easy to carry and can serve as an alternative to compressed air cans.

Some special vacuum cleaners are specifically designed for use on and around electronic components; they are designed to minimize electrostatic discharge (ESD) while in use. If you are using a regular vacuum cleaner and not one specifically designed with ESD protection, you should take precautions, such as wearing a grounding wrist strap. Also, if the cleaner has a metal nozzle, be careful not to touch it to the circuit boards or components you are cleaning.

Brushes and Swabs

You can use a small makeup, photographic, or paint brush to carefully loosen the accumulated dirt and dust inside a PC before spraying it with canned air or using the vacuum cleaner. Be careful about generating static electricity, however. In most cases, you should not use a brush directly on circuit boards, but only on the case interior and other parts, such as fan blades, air vents, and keyboards. Wear a grounded wrist strap if you are brushing on or near any circuit boards, and brush slowly and lightly to prevent static discharges from occurring.

Use cleaning swabs to wipe off electrical contacts and connectors, disk drive heads, and other sensitive areas. The swabs should be made of foam or synthetic chamois material that does not leave lint or dust residue. Unfortunately, proper foam or chamois cleaning swabs are more expensive than typical cotton swabs. Do not use cotton swabs because they leave cotton fibers on everything they touch. Cotton fibers are conductive in some situations and can remain on drive heads, which can scratch disks. Foam or chamois swabs can be purchased at most electronics supply stores.

Caution

One item to avoid is an eraser for cleaning contacts. Many people (including me) have recommended using a soft pencil-type eraser for cleaning circuit-board contacts. Testing has proven this to be bad advice for several reasons. One reason is that any such abrasive wiping on electrical contacts generates friction and an ESD. This ESD can be damaging to boards and components, especially the newer low-voltage devices. These devices are especially static sensitive, and cleaning the contacts without a proper liquid solution is not recommended. Also, the eraser will wear off the gold coating on many contacts, exposing the tin contact underneath, which rapidly corrodes when exposed to air.

Some companies sell premoistened contact cleaning pads soaked in a proper contact cleaner and lubricant. These pads are safe to wipe on conductors and contacts with no likelihood of ESD damage or abrasion of the gold plating.

Silicone Lubricants

You can use a silicone lubricant such as WD-40 to lubricate the door mechanisms on floppy disk drives and any other part of the system that might require clean, nonoily lubrication. Other items you can lubricate are the disk-drive–head slider rails and even printer-head slider rails, to provide smoother operation.

Using silicone instead of conventional oils is important because silicone does not gum up and collect dust and other debris. Always use the silicone sparingly. Do not spray it anywhere near the equipment because it tends to migrate and will end up where it doesn't belong (such as on drive heads). Instead, apply a small amount to a toothpick or foam swab and dab the silicone lubricant on the components where needed. You can use a lint-free cleaning stick soaked in silicone to lubricate the metal print-head rails in a printer.

Obtaining Required Tools and Accessories

You can obtain most of the cleaning chemicals and tools discussed in this chapter from an electronics supply house, or even your local Radio Shack. A company called Chemtronics specializes in chemicals for the computer and electronics industry. These and other companies that supply tools, chemicals, and other computer and electronic cleaning supplies are listed in the Vendor List on the accompanying disc. With all these items on hand, you should be equipped for most preventive maintenance operations.

Disassembling and Cleaning Procedures

To properly clean your system, you must at least partially disassemble it. Some people go as far as to remove the motherboard. Removing the motherboard results in the best possible access to other areas of the system; but in the interest of saving time, you probably need to disassemble the system only to the point at which the motherboard is completely visible.

To do this, remove all the system's plug-in adapter cards and the disk drives. Complete system disassembly and reassembly procedures are listed in Chapter 22, "Building or Upgrading Systems." Although you can clean the heads of a floppy drive with a cleaning disk without opening the system unit's cover, you probably will want to do more thorough cleaning. In addition to the drive heads, you should clean and lubricate the door mechanism and clean any logic boards and connectors on the drive. This procedure usually requires removing the drive.

Next, do the same thing with the hard disk drives: Clean the logic boards and connectors, and lubricate the grounding strap. To do this, you must remove the hard disk assembly. As a precaution, be sure your data is backed up first.

Reseating Socketed Chips

To learn how to reseat socketed chips, such as the ROM BIOS on some older systems, see the Technical Reference section on the disc packaged with this book.

Cleaning Boards

After reseating any socketed devices that might have crept out of their sockets (see the Technical Reference on the disc for details), the next step is to clean the boards and all connectors in the system. For this step, use the cleaning solutions and the lint-free swabs mentioned earlier.

First, clean the dust and debris off the board and then clean any connectors on the board. To clean the boards, using a vacuum cleaner designed for electronic assemblies and circuit boards or a duster can of compressed gas is usually best. The dusters are especially effective at blasting any dust and dirt off the boards.

Also, blow any dust out of the power supply, especially around the fan intake and exhaust areas. You do not need to disassemble the power supply to do this; simply use a duster can and blast the compressed air into the supply through the fan exhaust port. This will blow the dust out of the supply and clean off the fan blades and grill, which will help with system airflow.

Caution

Be careful with ESD, which can cause damage when you are cleaning electronic components. Take extra precautions in the dead of winter or in extremely dry, high-static environments. You can apply antistatic sprays and treatments to the work area to reduce the likelihood of ESD damage.

An antistatic wrist-grounding strap is recommended (refer to Figure 24.6 earlier in this chapter). This should be connected to a ground on the card or board you are wiping. This strap ensures that no electrical discharge occurs between you and the board. An alternative method is to keep a finger or thumb on the ground of the motherboard or card as you wipe it off.

Cleaning Connectors and Contacts

Cleaning the connectors and contacts in a system promotes reliable connections between devices. On a motherboard, you should clean the slot connectors, power supply connectors, keyboard and mouse connectors, and speaker connector. For most plug-in cards, you should clean the edge connectors that plug in to slots on the motherboard and any other connectors, such as external ones mounted on the card bracket.

Submerge the lint-free swabs in the liquid cleaning solution. If you are using the spray, hold the swab away from the system and spray a small amount on the foam end until the solution starts to drip. Then, use the soaked foam swab to wipe the connectors on the boards. Presoaked wipes are the easiest to use—simply wipe them along the contacts to remove any accumulated dirt and leave a protective coating behind.

On the motherboard, pay special attention to the slot connectors. Be liberal with the liquid; resoak the foam swab repeatedly, and vigorously clean the connectors. Don't worry if some of the liquid drips on the surface of the motherboard. These solutions are entirely safe for the whole board and will not damage the components.

Use the solution to wash the dirt off the gold contacts in the slot connectors, and then clean any other connectors on the board. Clean the keyboard and mouse connectors, the grounding positions where screws ground the board to the system chassis, the power-supply connectors, the speaker connectors, and the battery connectors.

If you are cleaning a plug-in board, pay special attention to the edge connector that mates with the slot connector on the motherboard. When people handle plug-in cards, they often touch the gold contacts on these connectors. Touching the gold contacts coats them with oils and debris, which prevents proper contact with the slot connector when the board is installed. Make sure these gold contacts are free of all finger oils and residue. It is a good idea to use one of the contact cleaners that has a conductive lubricant, which makes it easier to push the adapter into the slot and also protects the contacts from corrosion.

You also should use the swab and solution to clean the ends of ribbon cables or other types of cables or connectors in a system. Clean the floppy drive cables and connectors, the hard disk cables and connectors, and any others you find. Don't forget to clean the edge connectors that are on the disk drive logic boards, as well as the power connectors to the drives.

Cleaning the Keyboard and Mouse

Keyboards and mice are notorious for picking up dirt and garbage. If you ever open up an older keyboard, you will be amazed at the junk you find in there.

To prevent problems, you should periodically clean the keyboard with a vacuum cleaner. An alternative method is to turn the keyboard upside down and shoot it with a can of compressed air. This blows out the dirt and debris that has accumulated inside the keyboard and possibly prevents future problems with sticking keys or dirty keyswitches.

If a particular key is stuck or making intermittent contact, you can soak or spray that switch with contact cleaner. The best way to do this is to first remove the keycap and then spray the cleaner into the switch. This usually does not require complete disassembly of the keyboard. Periodic vacuuming or compressed gas cleaning prevents more serious problems with sticking keys and keyswitches.

Most mice are easy to clean. In most cases, a twist-off locking retainer keeps the mouse ball retained in the body of the mouse. By removing the retainer, the ball drops out. After removing the ball, you should clean it with one of the electronic cleaners. I recommend a pure cleaner instead of a contact cleaner with lubricant because you do not want any lubricant on the mouse ball. Then, wipe off the rollers in the body of the mouse with the cleaner and some swabs.

Monthly cleaning of a mouse in this manner eliminates or prevents skipping or erratic movement. I also recommend a mouse pad for most ball-type mice because the pad prevents the mouse ball from picking up debris from your desk.

Other pointing devices requiring little or no maintenance are the IBM-designed TrackPoint and similar systems introduced by other manufacturers, such as the Glidepoint by Alps. These devices are totally sealed and use pressure transducers to control pointer movement. Optical mice that don't use a ball or roller mechanism also require little or no maintenance. Because they are sealed, cleaning need only be performed externally and is as simple as wiping off the device with a mild cleaning solution to remove oils and other deposits that have accumulated from handling them.

Hard Disk Maintenance

Certain preventive maintenance procedures protect your data and ensure that your hard disk works efficiently. Some of these procedures actually minimize wear and tear on your drive, which prolongs its life. Additionally, a high level of data protection can be implemented by performing some simple commands periodically. These commands provide methods for backing up (and possibly later restoring) critical areas of the hard disk that, if damaged, would disable access to all your files.

Defragmenting Files

Over time, as you delete and save files to a hard disk, the files become fragmented. This means they are split into many noncontiguous areas on the disk. One of the best ways to protect both your hard disk and the data on it is to periodically defragment the files on the disk. This serves two purposes. One is that by ensuring that all the files are stored in contiguous sectors on the disk, head movement and drive wear and tear is minimized. This has the added benefit of improving the speed at which the drive retrieves files by reducing the head thrashing that occurs every time it accesses a fragmented file.

The second major benefit, and in my estimation the more important of the two, is that in the case of a disaster in which the file system is severely damaged, the data on the drive can usually be recovered if the files are contiguous. On the other hand, if the files are split up in many pieces across the drive, figuring out which pieces belong to which files is virtually impossible without an intact file system. For the purposes of data integrity and protection, I recommend defragmenting your hard disk drives on a monthly basis.

The three main functions in most defragmentation programs are as follows:

- File defragmentation
- File packing (free space consolidation)
- File sorting

Defragmentation is the basic function, but most other programs also add file packing. Packing the files is optional on some programs because it usually takes additional time to perform. This function packs the files at the beginning of the disk so all free space is consolidated at the end of the disk. This feature minimizes future file fragmentation by eliminating any empty holes on the disk. Because all free space is consolidated into one large area, any new files written to the disk are capable of being written in a contiguous manner with no fragmentation.

The last function, file sorting (sometimes called disk optimizing), is not usually necessary and is performed as an option by many defragmenting programs. This function adds a tremendous amount of time to the operation and has little or no effect on the speed at which information is accessed. It can be somewhat beneficial for disaster recovery purposes because you will have an idea of which files came before or after other files if a disaster occurs. Not all defragmenting programs offer file sorting, and the extra time it takes is probably not worth any benefits you will receive. Other programs can sort the order that files are listed in directories, which is a quick and easy operation compared to sorting the file ordering the disk.

Windows 9x/Me/2000/XP include a disk defragmentation program with the operating system, which you can use on any file system the OS supports. For older DOS, Windows 3.x, and some versions of NT, you must purchase a third-party defragmentation program. Norton Utilities includes a disk defragmenter, as do many other utility packages. If you elect to use a third-party product on a Windows 9x/Me/2000/XP system, be certain that it supports the file system you use on your drives. Running a FAT16 defragmentation program on a FAT32 drive can cause severe problems. An excellent third-party defrag program that works on all systems is VOPT by Golden Bow. See the Vendor List on the accompanying disc for more information on these programs.

Before you defragment your disks, you should run a disk repair program, such as ScanDisk or Norton Disk Doctor, even if you are not experiencing any problems. This ensures that your drives are in good working order before you begin the defragmentation process.

Windows Maintenance Wizard

Windows 98 and above include a Task Scheduler program that enables you to schedule programs for automatic execution at specified times. The Maintenance Wizard walks you through the steps of scheduling regular disk defragmentations, disk error scans, and deletions of unnecessary files. You can schedule these processes to execute during nonworking hours, so regular system activities are not disturbed.

Virus Checking

Viruses and spyware are dangers to any system, and making scans with an antivirus program a regular part of your preventive maintenance program is a good idea. Many aftermarket utility packages are available that scan for and remove viruses and spyware. No matter which of these programs you use, you should perform a scan for virus and spyware programs periodically, especially before making hard disk backups. This helps ensure that you catch any potential problem before it spreads and becomes a major catastrophe. In addition, selecting antivirus and antispyware products from vendors that provide regular updates is important. The updates include signatures that determine which virus or spyware programs the software can detect and cure, and because new virus and spyware programs are constantly being introduced, these updates are essential.

Tip

Because viruses are more dangerous and numerous than ever, turn on the firewall feature in your operating system and enable the automatic update feature found in most recent antivirus programs to keep your protection up to date. Even with a dialup connection, it takes only a few minutes a day to get downloads. If you have a broadband connection, the latest protection is downloaded in just a few moments. Using the firewall will help prevent many types of virus and other software exploits from attacking your system.

Passive Preventive Maintenance Procedures

Passive preventive maintenance involves taking care of the system by providing the best possible environment—both physical and electrical—for the system. Physical concerns are conditions such as ambient temperature, thermal stress from power cycling, dust and smoke contamination, and disturbances such as shock and vibration. Electrical concerns are items such as ESD, power-line noise, and radio-frequency interference. Each of these environmental concerns is discussed in the following sections.

Examining the Operating Environment

Oddly enough, one of the most overlooked aspects of microcomputer preventive maintenance is protecting the hardware—and the sizable financial investment it represents—from environmental abuse. Computers are relatively forgiving, and they are generally safe in an environment that is comfortable for people. Computers, however, are often treated with no more respect than desktop calculators. The result of this type of abuse is many system failures.

Before you set up a new PC, prepare a proper location for it that is free of airborne contaminants such as smoke or other pollution. Do not place your system in front of a window; the computer should not be exposed to direct sunlight or temperature variations. The environmental temperature should be as constant as possible. Power should be provided through properly grounded outlets and should be stable and free from electrical noise and interference. Keep your system away from radio transmitters or other sources of radio frequency energy.

Note

I also don't recommend using computer desks that place the system unit in a sealed cabinet; this is a good way to promote overheating.

Heating and Cooling

Thermal expansion and contraction from ambient temperature changes place stress on a computer system. Therefore, keeping the temperature in your office or room relatively constant is important to the successful operation of your computer system.

Temperature variations can lead to serious problems. You might encounter excessive chip creep, for example. If extreme variations occur over a short period, signal traces on circuit boards can crack and separate, solder joints can break, and contacts in the system can undergo accelerated corrosion. Solid-state components such as chips can be damaged also, and a host of other problems can develop.

Temperature variations can wreak havoc with hard disk drives, too. On some drives, writing to a disk at different ambient temperatures can cause data to be written at different locations relative to the track centers. This can cause read and write problems at a later time.

To ensure that your system operates in the correct ambient temperature, you must first determine your system's specified functional range. Most manufacturers provide data about the correct operating temperature range for their systems. Two temperature specifications might be available, one indicating allowable temperatures during operation and another indicating allowable temperatures under nonoperating conditions. IBM, for example, indicates the following temperature ranges as acceptable for most of its systems:

System on: 60–90° Fahrenheit

System off: 50–110° Fahrenheit

For the safety of the disk and the data it contains, avoid rapid changes in ambient temperatures. If rapid temperature changes occur—for example, when a new drive is shipped to a location during the winter and then brought indoors—let the drive acclimate to room temperature before turning it on. In extreme cases, condensation can form on the platters inside the drive head-disk assembly (HDA), which is disastrous for the drive if you turn it on before the condensation has a chance to evaporate. Most drive manufacturers specify a timetable to use as a guide in acclimating a drive to room temperature before operating it. You usually must wait several hours to a day before a drive is ready to use after it has been shipped or stored in a cold environment. Manufacturers normally advise that you leave the drive in its packing until it is acclimated. Removing the drive from a shipping carton when extremely cold increases the likelihood of condensation forming as the drive warms up.

Most office environments provide a stable temperature in which to operate a computer system, but some do not. Be sure to give some consideration to the placement of your equipment.

Power Cycling (On/Off)

As you have just learned, the temperature variations a system encounters greatly stress the system's physical components. The largest temperature variations a system encounters, however, are those that occur during the warm-up period right after you turn on the computer. Powering on a cold system subjects it to the greatest possible internal temperature variations. If you want a system to have the longest and most trouble-free life possible, you should limit the temperature variations in its environment. You can limit the extreme temperature cycling in two simple ways during a cold startup: Leave the system off all the time or leave it on all the time. Of these two possibilities, of course, you probably will want to choose the latter option. Leaving the power on is the best way I know to promote system reliability. If your only concern is system longevity, the simple recommendation is to keep the system unit powered on (or off!) continuously. In the real world, however, there are more variables to consider, such as the cost of electricity, the potential fire hazard of unattended running equipment, and other concerns, as well.

If you think about the way light bulbs typically fail, you can begin to understand how thermal cycling can be dangerous. Light bulbs burn out most often when you first turn them on because the filament must endure incredible thermal stress as it changes temperature, in less than one second, from ambient to several thousands of degrees. A bulb that remains on continuously lasts longer than one that is turned on and off repeatedly.

The place where problems are most likely to occur immediately at power-on is in the power supply. The startup current draw for the system during the first few seconds of operation is very high compared to the normal operating-current draw. Because the current must come from the power supply, the supply has an extremely demanding load to carry for the first few seconds of operation, especially if several disk drives must be started. Motors have an extremely high power-on current draw. This demand often overloads a marginal circuit or component in the supply and causes it to burn or break with a "snap." I have seen several power supplies die the instant a system was powered up. To enable your equipment to have the longest possible life, try to keep the temperature of solid-state components relatively constant, and limit the number of startups on the power supply. The only way I know to do this is to leave the system on.

Although it sounds like I am telling you to leave all your computer equipment on 24 hours a day, 7 days a week, I no longer recommend this type of operation. A couple of concerns have tempered my urge to leave everything running continuously. One is that an unattended system that is powered on represents a fire hazard. I have seen monitors catch fire after internally shorting and systems whose cooling fans have frozen, causing the power supply and the entire system to overheat. I do not leave any system running in an unattended building. Another problem is wasted electrical power. Many companies have adopted austerity programs that involve turning off lights and other items when not in use. The power consumption of some of today's high-powered systems and accessories is not trivial. Also, an unattended operating system is more of a security risk than one that is powered off and locked.

Realities—such as the fire hazard of unattended systems running during night or weekend hours, security problems, and power-consumption issues—might prevent you from leaving your system on all the time. Therefore, you must compromise. Power on the system only one time daily. Don't power the system on and off several times every day. This good advice is often ignored, especially when several users share systems. Each user powers on the system to perform work on the PC and then powers off the system. These systems tend to have many more problems with component failures.

If you are in a building with a programmable thermostat, you have another reason to be concerned about temperatures and disk drives. Some buildings have thermostats programmed to turn off the heat overnight or over the weekend. These thermostats are programmed also to quickly raise the temperature just before business hours every day. In Chicago, for example, outside temperatures in the winter can dip to –20° (excluding the windchill factor). An office building's interior temperature can drop to as low as 50° during the weekend. When you arrive Monday morning, the heat has been on for only an hour or so, but the hard disk platters might not yet have reached even 60° when you turn on the system. During the first 20 minutes of operation, the disk platters rapidly rise in temperature to 120° or more. If you still have an inexpensive stepper motor hard disk and begin writing to the disk at these low temperatures, you are setting yourself up for trouble.

Tip

If you do not leave a system on continuously, at least give it 15 minutes or more to warm up after a cold start before writing to the hard disk. This practice does wonders for the reliability of the data on your disk.

If you do leave your system on for long periods of time, make sure the screen is blank or displays a random image if the system is not in use. The phosphor on the picture tube can burn if a stationary image is left onscreen continuously. Higher-persistence phosphor monochrome screens are most susceptible, and the color displays with low-persistence phosphors are the least susceptible. Most of the monitors used with today's PCs will not show the effect of a screen burn. If you ever have seen a monochrome display with the image of some program permanently burned in—even with the display off—you know what I mean. Look at the monitors that display flight information at the airport; they usually show some of the effects of phosphor burn.

Most modern displays that have power-saving features can automatically enter a standby mode on command by the system. If your system has these power-saving functions, enable them because they help reduce energy costs and preserve the monitor.

Static Electricity

Static electricity or electrostatic discharge (ESD) can cause numerous problems within a system. The problems usually appear during the winter months when humidity is low or in extremely dry climates where the humidity is low year-round. In these cases, you might need to take special precautions to ensure that your PC is not damaged. See Chapter 21, "Power Supply and Chassis/Case," and Chapter 22 for more information on ESD.

Static discharges outside a system-unit chassis are rarely a source of permanent problems within the system. Usually, the worst possible effect of a static discharge to the case, keyboard, or even a location near the computer is a parity check (memory) error or a system lockup. In some cases, I have been able to cause parity checks or system lockups by simply walking past a PC. Most static-sensitivity problems are caused by improper grounding of the system power. Be sure you always use a three-prong, grounded power cord plugged in to a properly grounded outlet. If you are unsure about the outlet, you can buy an outlet tester, such as those described earlier in this chapter, at most electronics supply or hardware stores for only a few dollars.

Whenever you open a system unit or handle circuits removed from the system, you must be much more careful with static. You can permanently damage a component with a static discharge if the charge is not routed to a ground. I usually recommend handling boards and adapters first by a grounding point such as the bracket to minimize the potential for static damage.

An easy way to prevent static problems is with good power-line grounding, which is extremely important for computer equipment. A poorly designed power-line grounding system is one of the primary causes of poor computer design. The best way to prevent static damage is to prevent the static charge from getting into the computer in the first place. The chassis ground in a properly designed system serves as a static guard for the computer and redirects the static charge safely to the ground. For this ground to be complete, therefore, the system must be plugged in to a properly grounded three-wire outlet.

If the static problem is extreme, you can resort to other measures. One is to use a grounded static mat underneath the computer. Touch the mat first before you touch the computer to ensure that any static charges are routed to ground and away from the system unit's internal parts. If problems still persist, you might want to check out the building's electrical ground. I have seen installations that had three-wire outlets that were rendered useless by the building's ungrounded electrical service.

Power-Line Noise

To run properly, a computer system requires a steady supply of clean, noise-free power. In some installations, however, the power line serving the computer also serves heavy equipment, and the voltage variations resulting from the on/off cycling of this equipment can cause problems for the computer. Certain types of equipment on the same power line also can cause voltage spikes—short, transient signals of sometimes 1,000V or more—that can physically damage a computer. Although these spikes are rare, they can be crippling. Even a dedicated electrical circuit used by only a single computer can experience spikes and transients, depending on the quality of the power supplied to the building or circuit.

During the site-preparation phase of a system installation, you should be aware of these factors to ensure a steady supply of clean power:

- If possible, the computer system should be on its own circuit with its own circuit breaker. This setup does not guarantee freedom from interference, but it helps.

- The circuit should be checked for a good, low-resistance ground, proper line voltage, freedom from interference, and freedom from brownouts (voltage dips).

- A three-wire circuit is a must, but some people substitute grounding-plug adapters to adapt a grounded plug to a two-wire socket. This setup is not recommended; the ground is there for a reason.

- Power-line noise problems increase with the resistance of the circuit, which is a function of wire size and length. So, to decrease resistance, avoid extension cords unless absolutely necessary, and then use only heavy-duty extension cords.

- Inevitably, you will want to plug in other equipment later. Plan ahead to avoid the temptation to connect too many items to a single outlet. If possible, provide a separate power circuit for non–computer-related devices.

Air conditioners, coffee makers, copy machines, laser printers, space heaters, vacuum cleaners, and power tools are some of the worst corrupters of a PC system's power. Any of these items can draw an excessive amount of current and wreak havoc with a PC system on the same electrical circuit. I've seen offices in which all the computers begin to crash at about 9:05 a.m. daily, which is when all the coffee makers are turned on!

Also, try to ensure that copy machines and laser printers do not share a circuit with other computer equipment. These devices draw a large amount of power.

Another major problem in some companies is partitioned offices. Many of these partitions are prewired with their own electrical outlets and are plugged in to one another in a sort of power-line daisy-chain, similar to chaining power strips together. I pity the person in the cubicle at the end of the electrical daisy-chain, who is likely to have very erratic power!

As a real-world example of too many devices sharing a single circuit, I can describe several instances in which a personal computer had a repeating parity check problem. All efforts to repair the system had been unsuccessful. The reported error locations from the parity-check message were inconsistent, which normally indicates a problem with power. The problem could have been the power supply in the system unit or the external power supplied from the wall outlet. This problem was solved one day as I stood watching the system. The parity check message was displayed at the same instant that someone two cubicles away turned on a copy machine. Placing the computers on a separate line solved the problem.

By following the guidelines in this section, you can create the proper power environment for your systems and help ensure trouble-free operation.

Radio-Frequency Interference

Radio-frequency interference (RFI) is easily overlooked as a problem factor. The interference is caused by any source of radio transmissions near a computer system. Living next door to a 50,000-watt commercial radio station is one sure way to get RFI problems, but less-powerful transmitters can cause problems, too. I know of many instances in which cordless telephones have caused sporadic random keystrokes to appear, as though an invisible entity were typing on the keyboard. I also have seen RFI cause a system to lock up. Solutions to RFI problems are more difficult to state because every case must be handled differently. Sometimes, simply moving the system eliminates the problem because radio signals can be directional in nature. At other times, you must invest in specially shielded cables for external devices, such as the keyboard and the monitor.

One type of solution to an RFI noise problem with cables is to pass the cable through a toroidal iron core, a doughnut-shaped piece of iron placed around a cable to suppress both the reception and transmission of electromagnetic interference (EMI). Many monitors include a toroid (sometimes spelled *torroid*) on the cable that connects to the computer. If you can isolate an RFI noise problem in a particular cable, you often can solve the problem by passing the cable through a toroidal core. Because the cable must pass through the center hole of the core, it often is difficult, if not impossible, to add a toroid to a cable that already has end connectors installed.

Radio Shack sells a special snap-together toroid designed specifically to be added to cables already in use. This toroid looks like a thick-walled tube that has been sliced in half. You simply lay the cable in the center of one of the halves, and snap the other half over the first. This type of construction makes adding the noise-suppression features of a toroid to virtually any existing cable easy.

The best, if not the easiest, way to eliminate an RFI problem is to correct it at the source. It is unlikely that you'll be able to convince the commercial radio station near your office to shut down, but if you are dealing with a small radio transmitter that is generating RFI, sometimes you can add a filter to the transmitter that suppresses spurious emissions. Unfortunately, problems sometimes persist until the transmitter is either switched off or moved some distance away from the affected computer.

Dust and Pollutants

Dirt, smoke, dust, and other pollutants are bad for your system. The power-supply fan carries airborne particles through your system, and they collect inside. If your system is used in an extremely harsh environment, you might want to investigate some of the industrial systems on the market designed for harsh conditions.

Many companies make special hardened versions of their systems for harsh environments. Industrial systems typically use a different cooling system from the one used in regular PCs. A large cooling fan is used to pressurize the case rather than depressurize it. The air pumped into the case passes through a filter unit that must be cleaned and changed periodically. The system is pressurized so that no contaminated air can flow into it; air flows only outward. The only way air can enter is through the fan and filter system.

These systems also might have special keyboards impervious to liquids and dirt. Some flat-membrane keyboards are difficult to type on, but are extremely rugged; others resemble the standard types of keyboards but have a thin, plastic membrane that covers all the keys. You can add this membrane to normal types of keyboards to seal them from the environment.

A relatively new breed of humidifier can cause problems with computer equipment. This type of humidifier uses ultrasonics to generate a mist of water sprayed into the air. The extra humidity helps cure problems with static electricity resulting from a dry climate, but the airborne water contaminants can cause many problems. If you use one of these systems, you might notice a white, ash-like deposit forming on components. The deposit is the result of abrasive and corrosive minerals suspended in the vaporized water. If these deposits collect on the system components, they can cause all kinds of problems. The only safe way to run one of these ultrasonic humidifiers is to use distilled water. If you use a humidifier, be sure it does not generate these deposits.

If you do your best to keep the environment for your computer equipment clean, your system will run better and last longer. Also, you will not have to open up your unit as often for complete preventive maintenance cleaning.

Troubleshooting Tips and Techniques

Troubleshooting PC hardware problems can seem daunting to the uninitiated, but in reality it is much simpler than it seems. Most problems can be diagnosed and corrected using few, if any, special tools and can be accomplished by anybody who can apply simple deductive reasoning and logical thinking. PCs have become more complicated and yet simpler all at the same time. More and more complex internal circuits mean that there are potentially more things that can go wrong—more ways the system can fail. On the other hand, today's complex circuits are embedded into fewer boards, with fewer chips on each board and more serial interconnections using fewer pins (fewer wires). The internal consolidation means that isolating which replaceable component has failed is in many ways simpler than ever before. An understanding of the basics of how PCs work, combined with some very simple tools, some basic troubleshooting tips, and logical thinking and common sense, will enable you to effectively diagnose and repair your own systems, saving a tremendous amount of money over taking it to a shop. In some cases, you can save enough money to practically pay for an entire new system. The bottom line with troubleshooting PC problems is that a solution exists for every problem, and through simple practices combined with deductive reasoning, that solution can easily be found.

Note

This section lists basic and general system troubleshooting procedures and guidelines. For specific procedures for troubleshooting a component in the system, use Appendix C, "Troubleshooting Index," as a quick reference for finding the chapter or section dedicated to that part of the PC.

Modern PCs—More Complicated and More Reliable

Consider this: The modern PC is an incredible collection of hardware and software. Focusing specifically on the hardware, between 50 and more than 400 million transistors exist in modern processors (see the following note). In addition, nearly 4.3 billion transistors are in 512MB of RAM; hundreds of millions of transistors exist in the motherboard chipset, video processor, and video RAM; and millions more are in the other adapter cards or logic boards in the system. Each of these billions of interconnected transistors must not only function properly, but also operate in an orderly fashion within strictly enforced timing windows, some of which are measured in picoseconds (trillionths of a second). When you realize that your PC will lock up or crash if any one of these transistors fails to operate properly and on time—and/or any one of the billions of circuit paths and interconnections between the transistors or devices containing them fails in any way—it is a wonder that PCs work at all!

Note

There are currently 178 million transistors in the Pentium 4 Extreme Edition Northwood, 144 million in the Pentium M Dothan, 125 million in the Pentium 4 Prescott, and nearly 106 million in the latest Athlon 64 Clawhammer and 64FX Sledgehammer. In the high-end server/workstation processor market, the 100-million-transistor mark was breached by a single-die CPU on May 22, 2000, when Intel introduced a 700MHz version of the Pentium III Xeon (code named Cascades) with 2MB of on-die L2 cache and 140 million transistors. This chip was built using older 0.18-micron technology and utilized an enormous die of 385 sq.mm. That's more than 19.6mm on each side, or nearly three and a half times the size of the Pentium 4 Prescott die of 112 sq.mm.

The Itanium 2 McKinley processor was introduced on July 8, 2002, and includes 32KB L1, 256KB L2, and up to 3MB of L3 cache integrated into a die containing a whopping 221 million transistors. This chip also uses older 0.18-micron technology and is the biggest I've ever heard of for a processor at 421 sq.mm (more than 20.5mm square), which is more than 3.75 times the size of the Pentium 4 Prescott.

Finally, the Itanium 2 Madison was introduced on July 30, 2003 with 6MB of integrated L3 cache, including an incredible 410 million transistors on a 374 sq.mm (more than 19.3mm square) die using newer 0.13-micron technology. Madison has established new records for transistor count as well as the amount of on-die cache.

Although these server/workstation processors are extreme, the technology used in them eventually filters down to the desktop and mobile processors. We will likely see the 1-billion-transistor mark breached by the follow-ons to these higher-end server chips during the current 90-nanometer process or next-generation 65-nanometer lifecycle.

Every time I turn on one of my systems and watch it boot up, I think about the billions upon billions of components and trillions upon trillions of machine/program steps and sequences that have to function properly to get there. As you can now see, many opportunities exist for problems to arise.

Although modern PCs are exponentially more complicated than their predecessors, from another point of view they have become simpler and more reliable. When you consider the complexity of the modern PC, it is not surprising that problems occasionally do arise. However, modern design and manufacturing techniques have made PCs more reliable and easier to service despite their ever-increasing internal complexity. Today's systems have fewer and fewer replaceable components and individual parts, which is a bit of a paradox. The truth is that, as PCs have become more complex, they have also become simpler and easier to service in many ways.

Industry-Standard Replaceable Components

The use of industry-standard components is one of the key features of a PC. This means that virtually all the parts that make up a system are interchangeable with other systems in some manner. This also means that the parts are plentiful, inexpensive, and generally very easy to install. A typical PC contains the following replaceable components, most of which are made to industry standards for design and form factor:

- Motherboard
- Processor
- CPU heatsink/fan
- RAM
- CMOS battery
- Chassis with optional fan
- Power supply

- Video card*
- Monitor
- Sound card*
- Speakers
- Network card*
- Hard drive
- CD-ROM/RW drive

- DVD-ROM/+RW drive
- Floppy drive
- Drive cables
- Keyboard
- Mouse

May be integrated into the motherboard in some systems.

Although some of the more well-optioned systems might have even more components than listed here, you can see that most PCs have fewer than 20 replaceable "parts." Some can have as few as 10–15, depending on how many options are present and how they are integrated. From a hardware troubleshooting or repair perspective, one of these components is either improperly installed (configured) or defective. If it's improperly installed or configured, the component can be repaired by merely reinstalling it or configuring it properly. If it's truly defective, the component must simply be replaced. When a PC is broken down to the basic replacable parts, you can see that it really isn't that complicated, which is why I've spent my career helping people to easily perform their own repairs or upgrades and even build entire systems from scratch.

Reinstall or Replace?

When dealing with hardware problems, the first simple truth to understand is that you do not usally *repair* anything—you *reinstall* or *replace* it instead. You reinstall because the majority of PC hardware problems are caused by a particular component being improperly installed or configured. I remember hearing from IBM many years ago that it had found that 60% or more of the problems handled by its service technicians were due to improper installation or configuration, meaning the hardware was not actually defective. This was, in fact, the major impetus behind the plug-and-play revolution, which has eliminated the need to manually configure jumpers and switches on most hardware devices. This has thus minimized the expertise necessary to install hardware properly and has also minimized installation, configuration, and resource conflict problems. Still, plug and play has sometimes been called *plug and pray* because it does not always work perfectly, sometimes requiring manual intervention to make it work properly.

You replace because of the economics of the situation with computer hardware. The bottom line is that it financially is much cheaper to replace a failed circuit board with a new one than to repair it. For example, you can purchase a new, state-of-the-art motherboard for around $100, but repairing an existing board normally costs much more than that. Modern boards use surface-mounted chips that have pin spacings measured in hundredths of an inch, requiring sophisticated and expensive equipment to attach and solder the chip. Even if you could figure out which chip had failed and had the equipment to replace it, the chips themselves are usually sold in quantities of thousands and obsolete chips are usually not available. The net effect of all of this is that the replacable components in your PC have become disposable technology. Even a component as large and comprehensive as the motherboard is replaced rather than repaired.

Troubleshooting by Replacing Parts

You can troubleshoot a PC in several ways, but in the end it often comes down to simply reinstalling or replacing parts. That is why I normally use a simple "known-good spare" technique that requires very little in the way of special tools or sophisticated diagnostics. In its simplest form, say you have two identical PCs sitting side by side. One of them has a hardware problem; in this example let's say the memory module (DIMM) is defective. Depending on how and where the defect lies, this could manifest itself in symptoms ranging from a completely dead system to one that boots up normally but crashes when running Windows or software applications. You observe that the system on the left has the problem but the system on the right works perfectly—they are otherwise identical. The simplest technique for finding the problem would be to swap parts from one system to another, one at a time, retesting after each swap. At the point when the DIMMs were swapped, upon powering up and testing (in this case testing is nothing more than allowing the system to boot up and run some of the installed applications), the problem has now moved from one system to the other. Knowing that the last item swapped over was the DIMM, you have just identified the source of the problem! This did not require an expensive ($2,000 or more) DIMM test machine or any diagnostics software. Because components such as DIMMs are not economical to repair, replacing the defective DIMM would be the final solution.

Although this is very simplistic, it is often the quickest and easiest way to identify a problem component as opposed to specifically testing each item with diagnostics. Instead of having an identical system standing by to borrow parts from, most technicians have an inventory of what they call "known-good spare" parts. These are parts that have been previously used, are known to be functional, and can be used to replace a suspicious part in a problem machine. However, this is different from new replacement parts because, when you open a box containing a new component, you really can't be 100% sure that it works. I've been in situations in which I've had a defective component and replaced it with another (unknown to me) defective *new* component and the problem remained. Not knowing that the new part I just installed was also defective, I wasted a lot of time checking other parts that were not the problem. This technique is also effective because so few parts are needed to make up a PC and the known-good parts don't always have to be the same (for example, a lower-end video card can be substituted in a system to verify that the original card had failed).

Troubleshooting by the Bootstrap Approach

Another variation on this theme is the "bootstrap approach," which is especially good for what seems to be a dead system. In this approach, you take the system apart to strip it down to the bare minimum necessary, functional components and test it to see whether it works. For example, you might strip down a system to the chassis/power supply, bare motherboard, CPU (with heatsink), one bank of RAM, and a video card with display and then power it up to see whether it works. In that stripped configuration, you should see the POST or splash (logo) screen on the display, verifying that the motherboard, CPU, RAM, video card, and display are functional. If a keyboard is connected, you should see the three LEDs (capslock, scrlock, and numlock) flash within a few seconds after powering on. This indicates that the CPU and motherboard are functioning because the POST routines are testing the keyboard. After you get the system to a minimum of components that are functional, you should reinstall or add one part at a time, testing the system each time you make a change to verify it still works and that the part you added or changed is not the cause of a problem. Essentially, you are rebuilding the system from scratch using the existing parts, but doing it one step at a time.

Many times problems are caused by corrosion on contacts or connectors, so the mere act of disassembling and reassembling a PC will "magically" repair it. Over the years, I've disassembled, tested, and reassembled many systems only to find no problems after the reassembly. How can merely taking it apart and reassembling repair a problem? Although it might seem that nothing was changed and everything is installed exactly like it was before, in reality simply unplugging and replugging renews all the slot and cable connections between devices, which is often all the system needs. Some useful troubleshooting tips include

- Eliminate unnecessary variables or components that are not pertinent to the problem.
- Reinstall, reconfigure, or replace only one component at a time.
- Test after each change you make.
- Keep a detailed record (write it down) of each step you take.
- Don't give up! Every problem has a solution.
- If you hit a roadblock, take a break or work on another problem. A fresh approach the next day often reveals things you overlooked.
- Don't overlook the simple or obvious. Double- and triple-check the installation and configuration of each component.
- Keep in mind that the power supply is one of the most failure-prone parts in a PC, as well as one of the most overlooked components. A high-output "known-good" spare power supply is highly recommended to use for testing suspect systems.
- Cables and connections are also a major cause of problems, so keep replacements of all types on hand.

Before starting any system troubleshooting, a few basic steps should be performed to ensure a consistent starting point and to enable isolating the failed component:

1. Turn off the system and any peripheral devices. Disconnect all external peripherals from the system, except for the keyboard and video display.

2. Make sure the system is plugged in to a properly grounded power outlet.

3. Make sure the keyboard and video displays are connected to the system. Turn on the video display, and turn up the brightness and contrast controls to at least two-thirds of the maximum. Some displays have onscreen controls that might not be intuitive. Consult the display documentation for more information on how to adjust these settings. If you can't get any video display but the system seems to be working, try moving the card to a different slot (not possible with AGP adapters) or try a different video card or monitor.

4. To enable the system to boot from a hard disk, make sure no floppy disk is in the floppy drive. Or put a known-good bootable floppy with DOS or diagnostics on it in the floppy drive for testing.

5. Turn on the system. Observe the power supply, chassis fans (if any), and lights on either the system front panel or power supply. If the fans don't spin and the lights don't light, the power supply or motherboard might be defective.

6. Observe the power on self test (POST). If no errors are detected, the system beeps once and boots up. Errors that display onscreen (*nonfatal* errors) and that do not lock up the system display a text message that varies according to BIOS type and version. Record any errors that occur and refer to the disc accompanying this book for a list of BIOS error codes for more information on any specific codes you see. Errors that lock up the system (*fatal* errors) are indicated by a series of audible beeps. Refer to the disc for a list of beep error codes.

7. Confirm that the operating system loads successfully.

Note

The Technical Reference section of the disc accompanying this book contains an exhaustive listing of BIOS error codes, error messages, and beep codes for BIOSs from Phoenix, AMI, Award, Microid Research, and IBM.

Problems During the POST

Problems that occur during the POST are usually caused by incorrect hardware configuration or installation. Actual hardware failure is a far less-frequent cause. If you have a POST error, check the following:

1. Are all cables correctly connected and secured?
2. Are the configuration settings correct in Setup for the devices you have installed? In particular, ensure the processor, memory, and hard drive settings are correct.
3. Are all drivers properly installed?
4. Are switches and jumpers on the baseboard correct, if changed from the default settings?
5. Are all resource settings on add-in boards and peripheral devices set so that no conflicts exist— for example, two add-in boards sharing the same interrupt?
6. Is the power supply set to the proper input voltage (110V–120V or 220V–240V)?
7. Are adapter boards and disk drives installed correctly?
8. Is a keyboard attached?
9. Is a bootable hard disk (properly partitioned and formatted) installed?
10. Does the BIOS support the drive you have installed, and if so, are the parameters entered correctly?
11. Is a bootable floppy disk installed in drive A:?
12. Are all memory SIMMs or DIMMs installed correctly? Try reseating them.
13. Is the operating system properly installed?

Hardware Problems After Booting

If problems occur after the system has been running, and without having made any hardware or software changes, a hardware fault possibly has occurred. Here is a list of items to check in that case:

1. Try reinstalling the software that has crashed or refuses to run.
2. Try clearing CMOS RAM and running Setup.
3. Check for loose cables, a marginal power supply, or other random component failures.
4. A transient voltage spike, power outage, or brownout might have occurred. Symptoms of voltage spikes include a flickering video display, unexpected system reboots, and the system not responding to user commands. Reload the software and try again.
5. Try reseating the memory modules (SIMMs, DIMMs, or RIMMs).

Problems Running Software

Problems running application software (especially new software) are usually caused by or related to the software itself, or are due to the fact that the software is incompatible with the system. Here is a list of items to check in that case:

1. Does the system meet the minimum hardware requirements for the software? Check the software documentation to be sure.
2. Check to see that the software is correctly installed. Reinstall if necessary.

3. Check to see that the latest drivers are installed.

4. Scan the system for viruses using the latest antivirus software.

Problems with Adapter Cards

Problems related to add-in boards are usually related to improper board installation or resource (interrupt, DMA, or I/O address) conflicts. Chapter 4, "Motherboards and Buses," has a detailed discussion of these system resources, what they are, how to configure them, and how to troubleshoot them. Also be sure to check drivers for the latest versions and ensure that the card is compatible with your system and the operating system version you are using.

Sometimes adapter cards can be picky about which slot they are running in. Despite the fact that, technically, a PCI or ISA adapter should be able to run in any of the slots, minor timing or signal variations sometimes occur from slot to slot. I have found on numerous occasions that simply moving a card from one slot to another can make a failing card begin to work properly. Sometimes moving a card works just by the inadvertent cleaning (wiping) of the contacts that takes place when removing and reinstalling the card, but in other cases I can duplicate the problem by inserting the card back into its original slot. When all else fails, try moving the cards around! Because some motherboards share a single IRQ between two PCI slots or between a PCI and an AGP slot, changing one of the PCI cards to another slot can resolve conflicts.

Caution

Note that PCI cards become slot specific after their drivers are installed. By this I mean that if you move the card to another slot, the plug-and-play resource manager sees it as if you have removed one card and installed a new one. You therefore must install the drivers all over again for that card. Don't move a PCI card to a different slot unless you are prepared with all the drivers at hand to perform the driver installation. ISA cards don't share this quirk because the system is not aware of which slot an ISA card is in.

Top Troubleshooting Problems

These are some of the most frequently asked troubleshooting questions I receive.

When I power the system on, I see the power LED light and hear the fans spin, but nothing else ever happens.

The fact that the LEDs illuminate and fans spin indicates that the power supply is partially working, but that does not exclude it from being defective. This is a classic "dead" system, which can be caused by almost any defective hardware component. In my experiences I've had more problems with power supplies than most other components, so I recommend immediately using a multimeter to measure the outputs at the power supply connectors and ensure they are within the proper 5% tolerances of their rated voltages. Even if the voltage measurements checked out, you should swap in a high-quality, high-power, known-good spare supply and retest. If that doesn't solve the problem, you should revert to the bootstrap approach I mentioned earlier, which is to strip the system down to just the chassis/power supply, motherboard, CPU (with heatsink), one bank of RAM (one DIMM), and a video card and display. If the motherboard now starts, begin adding the components you removed one at a time, retesting after each change. If the symptoms remain, use a POST card (if you have one) to see whether the board is partially functional and where it stops. Also, try replacing the video card, RAM, CPU, and then finally the motherboard, and verify the CPU and (especially) the heatsink installation.

The system beeps when I turn it on, but there is nothing on the screen.

The beep indicates a failure detected by the ROM POST routines. Look up the beep code in the table corresponding to the ROM version in your motherboard. This can typically be found in the motherboard manual; however, you can also find the beep codes for the most popular AMI, Award, and Phoenix BIOS earlier in this chapter.

I see a STOP or STOP ERROR in Windows NT/2000/XP.

Many things, including corrupted files, viruses, incorrectly configured hardware, and failing hardware, can cause Windows STOP errors. The most valuable resource for handling any error message displayed by Windows is the Microsoft Knowledgebase (MSKB), an online compendium of more than 250,000 articles covering all Microsoft products. You can visit the MSKB at support.microsoft.com, and from there you can use the search tool to retrieve information specific to your problem. For example, say you are receiving Stop 0x0000007B errors in Windows XP. In this case, you should visit the MSKB and enter the error message in the search box. In this case, I typed stop 7B error Windows XP in the box, and it returned two articles, one of which was Microsoft Knowledgebase Article number 324103, titled, "HOW TO: Troubleshoot "Stop 0x0000007B" Errors in Windows XP." Upon this link, I was taken to the article at support.microsoft.com/default.aspx?scid=kb;en-us;324103, which has a complete description of the problem and solutions. The article states that this error could be caused by the following:

- Boot-sector viruses
- Device driver issues
- Hardware issues
- Other issues

The article explains each issue and solution in detail. All things considered, the MSKB is a valuable resource when dealing with any problems related to or reported by any version of Windows or any other Microsoft software.

I see Fatal Exception errors in Windows 95/98/Me.

This is the equivalent of the STOP error in Windows NT/2000/XP. As indicated in the previous answer, this can be caused by both hardware and software problems, and the best place to check for specific solutions is in the Microsoft Knowledgebase (MSKB) at support.microsoft.com.

The system won't shut down in Windows.

This is another example where the MSKB comes to the rescue. For example, by searching for shutdown problems Windows XP, (substitute the version of Windows you are using), you will quickly find several articles that can help you troubleshoot this type of problem. This problem has been caused by bugs in motherboard ROM (try upgrading your motherboard ROM to the latest version), bugs in the various Windows versions (visit www.windowsupdate.com and install the latest fixes, patches, and service packs), or in some cases configuration or hardware problems. I'll defer to the MSKB articles for more complete explanations of the Windows issues.

The power button won't turn off the system.

Desktop PCs built since 1996 mostly use the ATX form factor, which incorporates a special power supply design such that the power switch is connected to the motherboard and not the power supply directly. This enables the motherboard and operating system to control system shutdown, preventing an unexpected loss of power that can cause data loss or file system corruption. However, if the system experiences a problem and becomes frozen or locked up in some way, the motherboard might not respond to the power button, meaning it will not send a shutdown signal to the power supply. It might seem that you will have to pull the plug to power off the system, but fortunately a forced shutdown override is provided. Merely press and hold down the system power button (usually on the front of the chassis) for a minimum of 4 seconds, and the system should power off. The only drawback is that, because this type of shutdown is forced and under the control of the motherboard or operating system, unsaved data can be lost and some file system corruption can result. You should therefore run ScanDisk (found in the Windows Accessories, System Tools folder) in Windows 95/98/Me/NT/2000 or Chkdsk in Windows XP to check and correct any file-system issues after a forced shutdown.

The modem doesn't work.

First verify that the phone line is good and that you have a dial tone. Then check and, if necessary, replace the phone cable from the modem to the wall outlet. If the modem is integrated into the motherboard, check the BIOS Setup to ensure that the modem is enabled. Try clearing the Enhanced System Configuration Data (ESCD) in the BIOS Setup. This forcees the plug-and-play routines to reconfigure the system, which can resolve any conflicts. If the modem is internal and you aren't using the COM1/COM2 serial ports integrated into the motherboard (as for an external modem), try disabling the serial ports to free up additional system resources. Also, try removing and reinstalling the modem drivers, ensuring that you are using the most recent drivers from the modem manufacturer. If that doesn't help, try physically removing and reinstalling the modem. If the modem is internal, install it in a different slot. Or, if the modem is external, make sure it has power and is properly connected to the serial or USB port on the PC. Try replacing the external modem power brick and the serial/USB cable. Finally, if you get this far and it still doesn't work, try replacing the modem and finally the motherboard.

Note that modems are very susceptible to damage from nearby lightning strikes. Consider adding lighting arrestors or surge suppressors on the phone line running to the modem, and unplug the modem during storms. If the modem has failed after a storm, you can be almost certain that it has been damaged by lightning. The strike might have damaged the serial port or motherboard, in addition to the modem. Any items damaged by lightning will most likely need to be replaced.

The keyboard doesn't work.

The two primary ways to connect a keyboard to a PC are either via the standard keyboard port (usually called a PS/2 port) or via USB. One problem is that many older systems that have USB ports cannot use a USB keyboard because USB support is provided by the operating system—for instance, if the motherboard has a USB port but does not include what is called USB Legacy Support in the BIOS. This support is specifically for USB keyboards (and mice) and was not common in systems until 1998 or later. Many systems that had such support in the BIOS still had problems with the implementation; in other words, they had bugs in the code that prevented the USB keyboard from working properly. If you are having problems with a USB keyboard, check to ensure that USB Legacy Support is enabled in the BIOS. If you are still having problems, make sure you have installed the latest BIOS for your motherboard and any Windows updates from Microsoft. Some older systems never could properly use a USB keyboard, in which case they should change to a PS/2 keyboard instead. Some keyboards feature both USB and PS/2 interfaces, which offer the flexibility to connect to almost any system.

If the keyboard is a PS/2 type and is having problems, the quickest way to verify whether it is the keyboard or the motherboard is to replace the keyboard with a known-good spare. In other words, borrow a working keyboard from another system and try it. If it still doesn't work, the keyboard controller on the motherboard is most likely defective, meaning the entire board must be replaced. My favorite replacement keyboards come from the PC Keyboard Co. (www.pckeyboard.com), which makes the legendary buckling spring design used by IBM. The company even offers versions with the Trackpoint pointing device built in.

I can't hear any sound from the speakers.

This can often be as simple as the speakers being unplugged or powered off, so don't overlook the obvious and check to be sure! Also check the volume controls in Windows or your application to see that they are turned up and not muted. When you are sure the volume is turned up and the speakers have power and are plugged in, you need to verify whether the problem is with the speakers or the sound card. To do this most efficiently, you merely connect different known-good speakers and see whether they work. If they don't, clearly the issue is in the sound card—possibly the configuration of the card is incorrect or the card itself is defective. The first thing to try is clearing the ESCD in the BIOS Setup. This essentially forces the plug-and-play routines to reconfigure the system, which can resolve any conflicts. If this doesn't help, try removing and reinstalling the sound card drivers. Finally, if that doesn't help, physically remove and replace the card from the system. You might try replacing it first in the same slot and then in a different slot because timing issues can sometimes exist from one slot to the next. If that doesn't work, you must try replacing the card. If the sound "card" really isn't a card but is integrated into the motherboard, first try the ESCD reset and driver reinstallation. Then, if that doesn't work, you have to try disabling the integrated sound and perhaps installing a replacement card or replacement motherboard.

If your problem is only with playing audio CDs, check for a cable between the sound card and the drive. If there is no cable, check the properties for the drive in the Device Manager in Windows to see whether the Digital CD Audio option is checked (enabled). If it's not, enable it. If your system will not allow digital CD audio to be enabled, it is not supported and you must install an analog cable connected between the sound card and the drive.

The monitor appears completely garbled or unreadable.

A completely garbled screen is most often due to improper, incorrect, or unsupported settings for the refresh rate, resolution, or color depth. Using incorrect drivers can also cause this. To check the configuration of the card, the first step is to power on the system and verify whether you can see the POST or the system splash screen and enter the BIOS Setup. If the screen looks fine during the POST but goes crazy after Windows starts to load, the problem is almost certainly due to an incorrect setting or configuration of the card. To resolve this, boot the system in Windows Safe mode (hold down the F8 function key as Windows starts to load). This bypasses the current video driver and settings and places the system in the default VGA mode supported by the BIOS on the video card. When the Windows desktop appears, you can right-click the desktop, select Properties, and then either reconfigure the video settings or change drivers as necessary.

If the problem occurs from the moment you turn on the system—and even if you boot to a DOS floppy (such as a Windows 98 startup floppy)—a hardware problem definitely exists with the video card, cable, or monitor. First, replace the monitor with another one; if the cable is detachable, replace that, too. If replacing the monitor and cable does not solve the problem, the video card is probably defective. Either replace the card or, if it is a PCI-based card, move it to a different slot. If the video is integrated into the motherboard, you must add a separate card instead or replace the motherboard.

The image on the display is distorted (bent), shaking, or wavering.

This can often be caused by problems with the power line, such as an electric motor, an air conditioner, a refrigerator, and so on causing interference. Try replacing the power cord, plugging the monitor and/or the system into a different outlet, or moving it to a different location entirely. I've also seen this problem caused by local radio transmitters such as a nearby radio or television station or two-way radios being operated in the vicinity of the system. If the monitor image is bent and discolored, it could be due to the shadow mask being magnetized. Turn the monitor on and off repeatedly; this causes the built-in degaussing coil around the perimeter of the tube to activate in an attempt to demagnetize the shadow mask. If this seems to work partially but not completely, you might need to obtain a professional degaussing coil from an electronics or TV service shop to demagnetize the mask. Next, replace the monitor cable, try a different (known-good) monitor, and finally replace the video card.

I purchased an upgraded AGP video card, and it won't fit in the slot.

Most newer AGP video cards are designed to conform to the AGP 4X or AGP 8X specification, both of which run on only 1.5 volts. Most older motherboards with AGP 2X slots are designed to accept only 3.3V cards. If you were to plug a 1.5V card into a 3.3V slot, both the card and motherboard could be damaged. Special keys have therefore been incorporated into the AGP specification to prevent such disasters. Typically, the slots and cards are keyed such that 1.5V cards fit only in 1.5V sockets and 3.3V cards fit only in 3.3V sockets. Additionally, universal sockets are available that accept either 1.5V or 3.3V cards. The keying for the AGP cards and connectors is dictated by the AGP standard as shown in Figure 24.12.

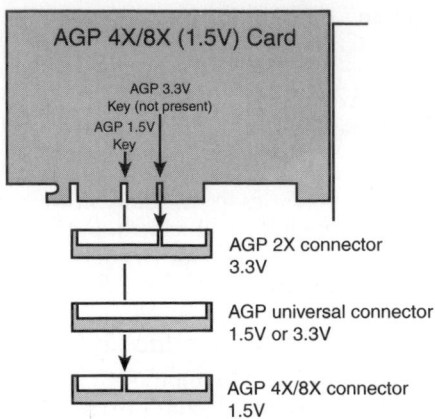

Figure 24.12 AGP 4X/8X (1.5V) card and how it relates to 3.3V, universal, and 1.5V AGP slots.

As you can see from Figure 24.12, AGP 4X or 8X (1.5V) cards fit only in 1.5V or universal (3.3V or 1.5V) slots. Due to the design of the connector and card keys, a 1.5V card cannot be inserted into a 3.3V slot. So, if your new AGP card won't fit in the AGP slot in your existing motherboard, consider that a good thing because, if you were able to plug it in, you would have fried both the card and the board! In a case such as this, you have to either return the 4X/8X card or get a new motherboard that supports 4X/8X (1.5V) cards.

I installed an upgraded processor, but it won't work.

First, make sure the motherboard supports the processor that is installed. Also make sure you are using the latest BIOS for your motherboard; check with the motherboard manufacturer to see whether any updates are available for download, and install them if any are available. Check the jumper settings (older boards) or BIOS Setup screens to verify that the processor is properly identified and set properly with respect to the FSB (or CPU bus) speed, clock multiplier, and voltage settings. Make sure the processor is set to run at its rated speed and is not overclocked. If any of the CPU settings in the BIOS Setup are on manual override, set them to automatic instead. Then reseat the processor in the socket. Next, make sure the heatsink is properly installed and you are using thermal interface material (that is, thermal grease) at the mating junction between the CPU and heatsink.

Just because a processor fits in the socket (or slot) on your motherboard does not mean it will work. For a processor to work in a system, the following things are required:

- *The CPU must fit in the socket.* Most Pentium 4 and newer Celeron processors use Socket 478; Pentium III and older Celerons use Socket 370; and Athlon/Duron processors use Socket 462 (also called Socket A).

- *The motherboard must support the voltage required by the CPU.* Modern motherboards set voltages by reading voltage ID (VID) pins on the processor and then setting the onboard voltage regulator module (VRM) to the appropriate settings. Older boards might not support the generally lower voltage requirements of newer processors.

- *The motherboard ROM BIOS must support the CPU.* Modern boards also read the CPU to determine the proper FSB (or CPU bus) speed settings as well as the clock multiplier settings for the CPU. Many CPUs have different requirements for cache settings and initialization, as well as for bug fixes and workarounds.

- *The motherboard chipset must support the CPU.* In some cases, specific chipset models or revisions might be required to support certain processors.

Before purchasing an upgraded processor for your system, you should first check with the motherboard manufacturer to see whether your board supports the processor. If so, it will meet all the requirements listed previously. Often, BIOS updates are available that enable newer processors to be supported in older boards, beyond what was originally listed in the manual when you purchased the board. The only way to know for sure is to check with the motherboard manufacturer for updated information regarding supported processors for a particular board.

As a specific example, newer versions of the Pentium 4 support hyper threading (HT) technology (one processor acts as if it were two processors, increasing performance). It would be great to purchase one of these new processors as an upgrade for an existing Pentium 4 system. Unfortunately, many existing boards do not accept these new processors. If you are considering replacing an existing Pentium 4 with a new HT technology version, you need to verify that the motherboard supports this processor. Specifically, the board must have one of the more recent chipsets, support the 533MHz or 800MHz FSB speed required by the chip, and incorporate a setting in the BIOS Setup to enable or disable the HT technology. Some preexisting boards might be capable of doing this with only a BIOS upgrade, but other boards do not meet the chipset and FSB requirements. In that case, you need a new processor and motherboard together to upgrade.

The system runs fine for a few minutes but then freezes or locks up.

This is the classic symptom of a system that is overheating. Most likely the CPU is overheating, but other components such as the video card or motherboard chipset can also be overheating. If the system is new or custom built, the design might be insufficient for proper cooling, and bigger heatsinks, more fans, or other solutions might be required. If the system was working fine but now is exhibiting this problem, check to see whether the problem started after any recent changes were made. If so, then whatever change was made could be the cause of the problem. If no changes were made, most likely something such as a cooling fan is either failed or starting to fail.

Modern systems should have several fans, one inside the power supply, one on the CPU (or positioned to blow on the CPU), and optionally others for the chassis. Verify that any and all fans are properly installed and spinning. They should not be making grinding or growling noises, which usually indicates bearing failure. Many newer systems have thermostatically controlled fans; in these systems it is normal for the fan speeds to change with the temperature. Make sure that the chassis is several inches from walls and that the fan ports are unobstructed. Try removing and reseating the processor; then reinstall the CPU heatsink with new thermal interface material. Check the power supply and verify that it is rated sufficiently to power the system (most should be 300 watts or more). Use a digital multimeter to verify the voltage outputs of the power supply, which should be within +/–5% of the rated voltage at each pin. Try replacing the power supply with a high-quality replacement or known-good spare.

I am experiencing intermittent problems with the hard drive(s).

Most systems use ATA (AT-Attachment, commonly called IDE) interface drives, which consist of a drive and integrated controller, a ribbon cable, and a host adapter circuit in the motherboard. Typically, intermittent problems are found with the cable and the drive—it is far more rare that the host adapter fails or exhibits problems. Many problems occur with the cables. ATA drives use either 40-conductor or 80-conductor cables, with one 40-pin connector at either end and optionally one in the middle. Drives supporting transfer rates higher than ATA-33 (33MBps or Ultra DMA Mode 2) must use 80-conductor cables. Check the cable to ensure that it is not cut or damaged; then try unplugging and replugging it into the drive and motherboard. Check to see that the cable is not more than 18" (46cm) in length because that is the maximum allowed by the ATA specification. This is especially important when you are using the faster ATA-100 or ATA-133 transfer rates. Try replacing the cable with a new 80-conductor 18" version.

If replacing the cable does not help, replace the drive with a spare, install an OS, and test it to see whether the problem remains. If the problem does remain, the problem is with the motherboard, which will most likely need to be replaced. If the problem does not remain, the problem is most likely with your original drive. You can simply replace it or try testing, formatting, and reinstalling to see whether the drive can be repaired. To do this, you need the low-level format or test software provided by the drive manufacturer. You can find out more about where to get this for various makes of drives in Chapter 14, "Physical Drive Installation and Configuration."

The system won't boot up; it says `Missing operating system` on the screen.

When your system boots, it reads the first sector from the hard disk—called the master boot record (MBR)—and runs the code contained in that sector. The MBR code then reads the partition table (also contained in the MBR) to determine which partition is bootable and where it starts. Then it loads the first sector of the bootable partition—called the volume boot record (VBR)—which contains the operating-system-specific boot code. However, before executing the VBR, the MBR checks to ensure that the VBR ends with the signature bytes 55AAh. The `Missing operating system` message is displayed by the MBR if it finds that the first sector of the bootable partition (the VBR) does not end in 55AAh.

Several things can cause this to occur, including these:

- *The drive parameters entered in the BIOS Setup are incorrect or corrupted.* These are the parameters defining your drive that you entered in the BIOS Setup, and they're stored in a CMOS RAM chip powered by a battery on your motherboard. Incorrect parameters cause the MBR program to translate differently and read the wrong VBR sector, thus displaying the `Missing operating system` message. A dead CMOS battery can also cause this because it loses or corrupts the stored drive translation and transfer mode parameters. In fact, in my experience, a dead battery is one of the more likely causes. To repair, check, and replace the CMOS battery, run the BIOS Setup, go to the hard drive parameter screen, and enter the correct drive parameters. Note that most drive parameters should be set to auto or autodetect.

- *The drive is not yet partitioned and formatted on this system.* This is a normal error if you try to boot the system from the hard disk before the OS installation is complete. Boot to an OS startup disk (floppy or CD), and run the SETUP program, which will prompt you through the partitioning and formatting process during the OS installation.

- *The MBR and/or partition tables are corrupt.* This can be caused by boot sector viruses, among other things. To repair this, *cold* boot (power off, then on) from a known, noninfected, write-protected floppy or bootable CD containing the FDISK program (preferably Win98 or later). Enter **FDISK/MBR** at the command prompt, which recopies the MBR code but doesn't alter the partition table. Then reboot. If the message persists, and you need to recover the data on the drive, you then must either rebuild the partition tables from scratch using a third-party utility such as the DISKEDIT program included with the Symantec Norton Utilities or hire a data recovery specialist who can do this for you. If you don't need to recover the data on the drive, simply reinstall the OS from scratch, which will prompt you through partitioning and formatting the drive.

- *The VBR is corrupt.* To repair with Windows 95/98/Me, secure a bootable floppy that was created by the same OS version as is on the hard disk and that contains the SYS command from that OS. Run SYS C:, which recopies a good VBR and system files to the volume. For Windows NT/2000/XP, you can use the Recovery Console or DiskProbe utilities (found on the bootable operating system CD).

The system is experiencing intermittent memory errors.

If the memory was recently added or some other change was made to the system, you should undo that addition/change to see whether it is the cause. If it's not, remove and reseat all memory modules. If the contacts look corroded, clean them with contact cleaner and then apply contact enhancer for protection. Check the memory settings in the BIOS Setup; generally, all settings should be on automatic. Next, upgrade to the latest BIOS for your motherboard, and remove all memory except one bank. Then run only one bank of memory, but in the second or third bank position. A socket can develop a problem, and most motherboards do not require that the sockets be filled in numerical order. Also, replace the remaining module with one of the others that was removed, a new module, or a known-good spare.

If you get this far, the problem is most likely either the motherboard or the power supply—or possibly some other component in the system. Remove other components from the system to see whether they are causing problems. Reseat the CPU, and replace the power supply with a high-quality new unit or a known-good spare. Finally, try replacing the motherboard.

The system locks up frequently and sometimes reboots on its own.

This is one of the classic symptoms of a power supply problem. The power supply is designed to send a special Power_Good signal to the motherboard when it has passed its own internal tests and outputs are stable. If this signal is dropped, even for an instant, the system resets. Problems with the power good circuit cause lockups and spontaneous rebooting. This can also be caused if the power at the wall outlet is not correct. Verify the power supply output with a digital multimeter—all outputs should be within +/–5% of the rated voltages. Use a tester for the wall outlet to ensure that it is properly wired, and verify that the voltage is near 120V. Replace the power cord or power strip between the power supply and wall outlet.

Unfortunately, the intermittent nature makes this problem hard to solve. If the problem is not with the wall outlet power, the best recourse is to replace the power supply with a high-quality new unit or a known-good spare of sufficient rating to handle the system (300 watts or higher recommended). If this doesn't help, reseat the CPU and reinstall the heatsink with new thermal interface material. Then reseat the memory modules, run only one bank of memory, and finally replace the motherboard.

I installed a 60GB drive in my system, but it is recognizing only 8.4GB.

Motherboard ROM BIOSs have been updated throughout the years to support larger and larger drives. BIOSs older than August 1994 are typically limited to drives of up to 528MB, whereas BIOSs older than January 1998 are limited to 8.4GB. Most BIOSs dated 1998 or newer support drives up to 137GB, and those dated September 2002 or newer should support drives larger than 137GB. These are only general guidelines; to accurately determine this for a specific system, you should check with your motherboard manufacturer. You can also use the BIOS Wizard utility from www.unicore.com/bioswiz/index2.html. It tells you the BIOS date from your system and specifically whether your system supports the Enhanced Hard Disk Drive specification, which means drives larger than 8.4GB.

If your BIOS does not support EDD (drives larger than 8.4GB), the three possible solutions are as follows:

- Upgrade your motherboard BIOS upgrade to a 1998 or newer version that supports >8.4GB.
- Install a BIOS upgrade card, such as the ATA Pro Flash from www.firmware.com or the Ultra ATA 133 PCI card from www.maxtordirect.com.
- Install a software patch to add >8.4GB support.

Of these, the first one is the most desirable because it is usually free. Visit your motherboard manufacturer's Web site to see whether it has any newer BIOSs available for your motherboard that will support large drives. If it doesn't, the next best thing is to use a card such as the ATA Pro Flash from MicroFirmware or the Ultra ATA 133 PCI card from Maxtor. I almost never recommend the software patch solution because it merely installs a special driver in the boot sector area of the hard drive, which can result in numerous problems when booting from different drives, installing new drives, or recovering data.

The 137GB barrier is a bit more complicated because, in addition to BIOS issues, operating system and chipset-based ATA host adapter driver issues are involved. Drives larger than 137GB are accessed using 48-bit logical block address (LBA) numbers, which require BIOS support, chipset driver support, and operating system support. Generally, you need a BIOS with 48-bit LBA support (normally dated September 2002 or newer), the latest chipset driver such as the Intel Application Accelerator (for motherboards using Intel chipsets, at www.intel.com/support/chipsets/iaa), and Windows XP with Service Pack 1 (or later) installed. If your motherboard BIOS does not provide the necessary support, the Maxtor Ultra ATA 133 PCI card listed earlier adds this support to your system. The original version of XP, as well as Windows 2000/NT or Windows 95/98/Me, does not currently provide native support for hard drives larger than 137GB.

If you have a system without BIOS support, check with your motherboard manufacturer for an update (or you can use a card with onboard BIOS, such as the Ultra ATA 133 PCI card from Maxtor). If your motherboard uses a non-Intel chipset, check with the motherboard or chipset manufacturer for driver updates to enable 48-bit LBA support.

My CD-ROM/DVD drive doesn't work.

CD and DVD drives are some of the more failure-prone components in a PC. It is not uncommon for one to suddenly fail after a year or so of use.

If you are having problems with a drive that was newly installed, check the installation and configuration of the drive. Check the jumper settings on the drive. If you're using an 80-conductor cable, the drive should be jumpered to Cable Select; if you're using a 40-conductor cable, the drive should be set to either master or slave (depending on whether it is the only drive on the cable). Check the cable to ensure that it is not nicked or cut and is a maximum of 18" long (the maximum allowed by the ATA specification). Replace the cable with a new one or a known-good spare, preferably using an 80-conductor cable. Make sure the drive power is connected, and verify that power is available at the connector using a digital multimeter. Also make sure the BIOS Setup is set properly for the drive, and verify that the drive is detected during the boot process. Finally, try replacing the drive and, if necessary, the motherboard.

If the drive had already been installed and was working before, first read different discs, preferably commercial-stamped discs rather than writeable or rewriteable ones. Then try the steps listed previously.

My USB port or device doesn't work.

Make sure you have enabled the USB ports in the BIOS Setup. Make sure your operating system supports USB—Windows 95 and NT do not, whereas Windows 98 and later do have USB support. Then remove any hubs and plug the device directly into the root hub connections on your system. Replace the cable. Many USB devices require additional power, so ensure that your device has an eternal power supply connected if one is required. Replace the power supply.

I installed an additional memory module, but the system doesn't recognize it.

Verify that the memory is compatible with your motherboard. Many subtle variations exist on memory types that can appear to be identical on the surface. Just because it fits in the slot does not mean the memory will work properly with your system. Check your motherboard manual for the specific type of memory your system requires, and possibly for a list of supported modules. You can visit www.crucial.com and use its memory selector to determine the exact type of memory for a specific system or motherboard. Also note that all motherboards have limits to the amount of memory they support, and many boards today support only up to 512MB or 1GB. Again, consult the motherboard manual or manufacturer for information on the limits for your board.

If you are sure you have the correct type of memory, follow the memory troubleshooting steps listed previously for intermittent memory problems.

I installed a new drive, but it doesn't work and the drive LED remains lit.

This is the classic symptom for a cable plugged in backward. Both ATA and floppy drives are designed to use cables with keyed connectors; however, some cables are available that lack this keying, which means they can easily be installed backward. When the cable is installed backward into either the motherboard or the drive, the LED on the drive remains lit and the drive does not function. In some cases, this can also cause the entire system to freeze. Check the cables to ensure that they are plugged in properly at both ends; the stripe on the cable indicates pin-1 orientation. On the drive, pin-1 typically is oriented toward the power connector. On the motherboard, look for orientation marks silk-screened on the board or observe the orientation of the other cables plugged in (all cables follow the same orientation).

While I was updating my BIOS, the system froze and now the system is dead!

This can occur when a flash ROM upgrade goes awry. Fortunately, most motherboards have a recovery routine that can be enabled via a jumper on the board. When enabled, the recovery routine causes the system to look for a floppy with the BIOS update program on it. If you haven't done so already, you need to download an updated BIOS from the motherboard manufacturer and follow its directions for placing the BIOS update program on a bootable floppy. Then set BIOS recovery mode via the jumper on the motherboard, power on the system, and wait until the procedure completes. It usually take up to 5 minutes, and you might hear beeping to indicate the start and end of the procedure. When the recovery is complete, turn off the system and restore the recovery jumper to the original (normal) settings.

If your motherboard does not feature BIOS recovery capability, you might have to send the board to the manufacturer for repair.

I installed a new motherboard in an older Dell system, and nothing works.

Many older Dell Dimension systems (Dimension 4100, 8100, or older systems) do not fully conform to the ATX specification with respect to their power supplies and the power connectors on their motherboards. If you replace one of these nonstandard Dell power supplies with a standard ATX type, or replace the nonstandard Dell motherboard with a standard ATX type, you risk frying both the power supply and the motherboard. The older Dell systems can be upgraded only by replacing both the motherboard and the power supply at the same time.

Starting in 2001, Dell converted to using industry-standard ATX power supplies and motherboard power connectors for its systems, so this should not be a problem for the Dimension 4200, 8200, and later machines.

I installed a PCI video card in an older system with PCI slots, and it doesn't work.

The PCI bus has gone through several revisions; most older slots are "2.0" type, and most newer cards need "2.1" or later PCI slots. The version of PCI your system has is dictated by the motherboard chipset. If you install a newer video or other PCI card that requires 2.1 slots in a system with 2.0 slots, often the system won't boot up or operate at all.

If you check the chipset reference information in Chapter 4, you might be able to determine which revision of PCI slots your motherboard has by knowing which chipset it has. If this is your problem, the only solution is to change either the card or motherboard so that they are both compatible.

CHAPTER 25

File Systems and Data Recovery

Boot Sectors

To manage a disk and enable all applications to see a consistent interface to the file system no matter what type of storage hardware is being used, the operating system creates several structures on the disk. The most important of these are the boot sectors (also called *boot records*). There two main types of boot sectors are called master boot records (MBRs) and volume boot records (VBRs).

Only one MBR exists on a physical disk, and it is always found at the beginning of the disk. A single disk can contain multiple partitions (also called *volumes*), and a VBR can be found at the start of each volume. The structure of the MBR is consistent among different operating systems and file systems; however, the VBR depends mainly on the type of file system used on the volume. The following section examines the structure and design of both MBRs and VBRs.

Figure 25.1 is a simple diagram showing the relative locations of the MBR and VBR on an 8.4GB disk with a single FAT partition.

Note

Some removable cartridge drives, such as the SuperDisk (LS-120 and LS-240) and Iomega Zip drive, function like high-capacity floppy disk drives. They lack a master boot record and diagnostic cylinder and can't be partitioned like hard disk drives. Other higher-capacity removable drives, such as the legacy Iomega Jaz and Castlewood Orb, can be partitioned like a hard disk drive.

All PC hard drives using the FAT16 file system are similar.

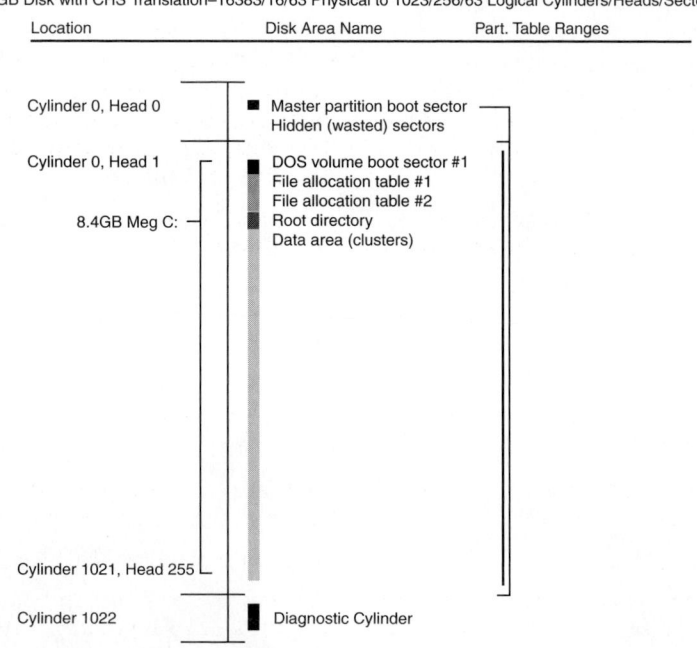

Figure 25.1 FAT16 file-management structures on a typical 8.4GB drive.

Each disk area has a purpose and a function. If one of these special areas is damaged, serious consequences can result. Damage to one of these sensitive structures usually causes a domino effect, limiting access to other areas of the disk or causing further problems in using the disk. For example, the OS normally can't access a drive at all if the MBR is corrupted. Therefore, you should understand these data structures well enough to be able to repair them when necessary. Rebuilding these special tables and areas of the disk is essential to the art of data recovery.

Master Boot Record

The first PC OS to support hard disks—DOS 2.0 (released on March 8, 1983)—was also the first to introduce the capability to partition a drive. *Partitioning* is basically dividing the drive into multiple volumes. One commonly misunderstood concept is that all drives that *can* be partitioned *must* be partitioned; that is, you have to partition the drive even if you are going to set it up with only one partition. Another name for a partition is a *logical volume* because the partition shows up as an additional drive letter or volume to the OS.

Although the primary use for partitioning today is to divide a single drive into multiple volumes for use by the same OS, originally it was intended to allow multiple OSs, each with different file systems, to coexist on a single drive. This multi-OS capability still exists today; however, additional aftermarket utilities often are required to manage and boot from multiple OSs on a single machine.

Tip

If you want to dual-boot Windows 9x/Me with Windows 2000/XP without purchasing aftermarket boot managers, install Windows 9x or Me first and then install Windows 2000 or XP either on the unused space on the first hard disk or in a primary partition on an additional hard disk. Windows 2000 or XP will set up a boot manager for you.

To use a hard disk with different operating systems, you can create partitions to logically divide the disk. You can, for example, create one or more FAT or NTFS partitions for use with Windows and leave the rest of the disk storage area for use by another OS's file system, such as Linux. Each of the FAT or NTFS partitions appear to an OS that supports it as a separate drive letter. For example, Windows 9x/Me ignores the unused or non-FAT partitions, whereas Windows 2000/XP sees both FAT and NTFS partitions but ignores others such as Linux and OS/2 HPFS.

Even though Windows NT, 2000, and XP have a command-line disk partitioning program called DISKPART, disk partitions are usually prepared with the GUI-based Disk Management tool (2000/XP) or Disk Administrator (NT).

◀◀ For more information about creating and formatting partitions with any of these operating systems, see Chapter 14, "Physical Drive Installation and Configuration," p. 831.

Information about each of the partitions on the disk is stored in a partition (or volume) boot record at the beginning of each partition. Additionally, a main table lists the partitions embedded in the master boot record.

The MBR, which is also sometimes called the master boot sector, is always located in the first physical sector of a disk (cylinder 0, head 0, sector 1) and consists of the following structures:

- *Bootstrap code.* The instructions used to locate and load the VBR from the active (bootable) partition.

- *Master partition table.* A table consisting of four 16-byte entries for up to four primary partitions, or three primary partitions and one extended partition. Each primary partition defines a logical drive, and an extended partition can be further partitioned into multiple logical drives. A given partition entry indicates which type of partition it is, whether it is bootable, where it is located physically on the disk, and how many sectors it occupies.

- *Signature bytes.* A 2-byte signature (55AAh) used by the motherboard ROM and other code to validate the sector.

Primary and Extended Partitions

Most OSs are designed to support up to 24 volumes on a single hard disk drive (represented by the drive letters C:–Z:), but the partition table in the master boot record (MBR) can have a maximum of only four entries. This is handled by using a single primary partition, which is seen as the first logical drive (C:), and an extended partition, which is then further partitioned into additional logical drives (D:, E:, F:, and so on).

Note

Although Windows NT uses Disk Administrator and Windows 2000 and XP use Disk Management to create disk partitions instead of FDISK, the following discussion refers to FDISK for simplicity's sake.

An *extended* partition is listed in the master partition table the same as a primary partition, but it differs in that you can use its disk space to create multiple logical partitions, or *volumes*. You can create only one extended partition on a single drive, meaning that typically there will never be more than two entries in the master partition table, one primary and one extended.

The logical volumes you create in the extended partition appear as separate drive letters to the operating system, but they are not listed in the master partition table. Volumes in the extended partition are not bootable. You can create up to 23 volumes out of a single extended partition (assuming that you have already created a primary partition, which brings the total number of volumes to 24).

Each of the subpartitions in an extended partition includes an extended partition table located in the first sector of the subpartition. The first sector of the extended partition contains an extended partition table that points to the first subpartition and, optionally, another extended partition. The first sector of that extended partition has another extended partition table that can reference another volume as well as an additional extended partition. This chain of references continues, linking all the volumes in the extended partition to the master partition table. It is important to note that, if the entry for the extended partition in the MBR is lost or damaged, the chain will be broken at the start and all volumes contained within will be inaccessible—essentially meaning that they will disappear.

Few people have any reason to create 24 partitions on a single disk drive, but the extended partition can create a chain of linked partitions on the disk that makes it possible to exceed the four-entry limitation of the master partition table.

Because the master boot record contains the first program loaded from disk that the system executes when you boot a PC, it is frequently a target for creators of computer viruses. A virus that infects or destroys the MBR can make it impossible for the BIOS to find the active partition, thus preventing the operating system from loading. Because the MBR contains the first program executed by the system, a virus stored there loads before any antivirus code can be loaded to detect it. To remove an MBR virus, you must first boot the system from a clean, uninfected disk, such as a floppy, bootable CD/DVD, or USB drive, and then run an antivirus program to test and possibly repair or restore the MBR.

Each partition on a disk contains a volume boot record starting in the first sector. With the FDISK or DISKPART utilities, you can designate a primary partition as active (or bootable). The master boot record bootstrap code causes the VBR from the active primary partition to receive control whenever the system is started.

Although FAT12, FAT16, FAT32, or NTFS partitions are mainly used when running Windows, you can also create additional disk partitions for Linux, Novell NetWare, OS/2's HPFS, AIX (Unix), XENIX, or other file systems or operating systems by using disk utilities provided with the alternative OS or in some cases a third-party disk partitioning tool such as Symantec's PartitionMagic. A partition that is not recognized by a particular operating system is simply ignored. If you install multiple operating systems on a single drive, a boot manager program (which might be included with the operating systems or installed separately) can be used to allow you to select which partition to make active each time you boot the system. As another alternative, you could install different operating systems in different primary partitions and then use FDISK, DISKPART, or some other partitioning program to change the one you want to boot as active.

Table 25.1 shows the format of the master boot record and its partition tables. The table lists the fields in each of the master partition table's four entries, the location on the disk where each field begins (the offset), and its length.

Table 25.1   Master Boot Record Format

Offset (Hex)	Offset (Dec)	Name	Length	Description
000h	0	Boot Code	446 bytes	Bootstrap code; loads the VBR from the active partition.

Partition Table Entry #1

Offset (Hex)	Offset (Dec)	Name	Length	Description
1BEh	446	Boot Indicator	1 byte	Boot status; 80h = active (bootable). Otherwise, it's 00h.
1BFh	447	Starting Head	1 byte	Starting head (or side) of partition in CHS mode.
1C0h	448	Starting Cylinder/Sector	16 bits	Starting cylinder (10 bits) and sector (6 bits) in CHS mode.
1C2h	450	System Indicator	1 byte	Partition type/file system.
1C3h	451	Ending Head	1 byte	Ending head (or side) of partition in CHS mode.
1C4h	452	Ending Cylinder/Sector	16 bits	Ending cylinder (10 bits) and sector (6 bits) in CHS mode.
1C6h	454	Relative Sector	4 bytes	Count of sectors before partition, which is the starting sector of the partition in LBA mode.
1CAh	458	Total Sectors	4 bytes	Total number of partition sectors in LBA mode.

Partition Table Entry #2

Offset (Hex)	Offset (Dec)	Description	Length	Description
1CEh	462	Boot Indicator	1 byte	Boot status; 80h = active (bootable). Otherwise, it's 00h.
1CFh	463	Starting Head	1 byte	Starting head (or side) of partition in CHS mode.
1D0h	464	Starting Cylinder/Sector	16 bits	Starting cylinder (10 bits) and sector (6 bits) in CHS mode.
1D2h	466	System Indicator	1 byte	Partition type/file system.
1D3h	467	Ending Head	1 byte	Ending head (or side) of partition in CHS mode.
1D4h	468	Ending Cylinder/Sector	16 bits	Ending cylinder (10 bits) and sector (6 bits) in CHS mode.
1D6h	470	Relative Sector	4 bytes	Count of sectors before partition, which is the starting sector of the partition in LBA mode.
1DAh	474	Total Sectors	4 bytes	Total number of partition sectors in LBA mode.

Partition Table Entry #3

Offset (Hex)	Offset (Dec)	Description	Length	Description
1DEh	478	Boot Indicator	1 byte	Boot status; 80h = active (bootable). Otherwise, it's 00h.
1DFh	479	Starting Head	1 byte	Starting head (or side) of partition in CHS mode.
1E0h	480	Starting Cylinder/Sector	16 bits	Starting cylinder (10 bits) and sector (6 bits) in CHS mode.
1E2h	482	System Indicator	1 byte	Partition type/file system.
1E3h	483	Ending Head	1 byte	Ending head (or side) of partition in CHS mode.
1E4h	484	Ending Cylinder/Sector	16 bits	Ending cylinder (10 bits) and sector (6 bits) in CHS mode.
1E6h	486	Relative Sector	4 bytes	Count of sectors before partition, which is the starting sector of partition in LBA mode.
1EAh	490	Total Sectors	4 bytes	Total number of partition sectors in LBA mode.

Table 25.1 Continued

Offset (Hex)	Offset (Dec)	Description	Length	Description
			Partition Table Entry #4	
1EEh	494	Boot Indicator	1 byte	Boot status; 80h = active (bootable). Otherwise, it's 00h.
1EFh	495	Starting Head	1 byte	Starting head (or side) of partition in CHS mode.
1F0h	496	Starting Cylinder/Sector	16 bits	Starting cylinder (10 bits) and sector (6 bits) in CHS mode.
1F2h	498	System Indicator	1 byte	Partition type/file system.
1F3h	499	Ending Head	1 byte	Ending head (or side) of partition in CHS mode.
1F4h	500	Ending Cylinder/Sector	16 bits	Ending cylinder (10 bits) and sector (6 bits) in CHS mode.
1F6h	502	Relative Sector	4 bytes	Count of sectors before partition, which is the starting sector of partition in LBA mode.
1FAh	506	Total Sectors	4 bytes	Total number of partition sectors in LBA mode.

Offset (Hex)	Offset (Dec)	Description	Length	Description
			Signature Bytes	
1FEh	510	Signature	2 bytes	Boot sector signature; it must be 55AAh.

CHS = Cylinder head sector
LBA = Logical block address

The data in the partition table entries tells the system where each partition starts and ends on the drive, how big it is, whether it is bootable, and which type of file system is contained in the partition. The starting cylinder, head, and sector values are used only by systems running in CHS mode, which is standard for all drives of 8.4GB or less. CHS values do not work past 8.4GB and therefore cannot represent partitions on drives larger than that. Drives larger than 8.4GB can be fully addressed only in LBA mode. In that case, the starting cylinder, head, and sector values in the table are ignored, and only the Relative Sector and Total Sectors fields are used. The Relative Sector field indicates the precise LBA where the partition begins, and the Total Sectors field indicates the length, which is always contiguous. Thus, from those two values the system can know exactly where a partition is physically located on a disk.

Note

The processors on which the PC is based have a design characteristic that is important to know for anybody editing or interpreting boot sectors. Numbers larger than 1 byte are actually read backward! This is called *little endian format* (as in reading the number from the little end first) or *reverse-byte ordering*. People typically read numbers in *big endian format*, which means from left to right, from the big end first. However, because PC processors read in little endian format, most numeric values larger than 1 byte are stored so that the least significant byte appears first and the most significant byte appears last. For example, the value for the Relative Sector field in the MBR for the first partition is usually 63, which is 3Fh in hex, or 0000003Fh (4 bytes long) in standard big endian hexadecimal format. However, the same number stored in little endian format would appear as 3F000000h. As another example, if a partition had 23,567,292 total sectors (about 12GB), which is 01679BBCh in hexadecimal, the number would be stored in the MBR partition table Total Sectors field in reverse-byte/little endian format as BC9B6701h.

As an aside, the use of reverse-byte order numbers stems from the way processors evolved from 8-bit (1 byte) designs to 16-bit (2 byte), 32-bit (4 byte) designs and beyond. The way the internal registers are organized and implemented dictates how a processor deals with numbers. Many processors, such as the Motorola PowerPC chips used in Macintosh systems, read numbers in big endian format. PC processors, on the other hand, are all based on Intel designs dating back to the original Intel 8088 processor used in the first IBM PC. Of course, how a particular processor reads numbers doesn't make any difference to those using a system. In the PC, the only people who have to deal with reverse-byte order or little endian numbers directly are machine or assembly language programmers—and those who want to edit or interpret raw boot sectors!

Each partition table entry contains a system indicator byte that identifies the type of partition and file system used in the partition referenced by that entry. Table 25.2 shows the standard values and meanings of the system indicator bytes, and Table 25.3 lists the nonstandard values.

Table 25.2   Standard System Indicator Byte Values

Value	Partition Type	Address Mode	Partition Size
00h	None	—	—
01h	Primary FAT12	CHS	0–16MiB
04h	Primary FAT16	CHS	16MiB–32MiB
05h	Extended	CHS	0–2GiB
06h	Primary FAT16	CHS	32MiB–2GiB
07h	NTFS/HPFS	All	All
0Bh	Primary FAT32	CHS	512MiB–2TiB
0Ch	Primary FAT32	LBA	512MiB–2TiB
0Eh	Primary FAT16	LBA	32MiB–2GiB
0Fh	Extended	LBA	2GiB–2TiB

CHS = Cylinder head sector
LBA = Logical block address

Table 25.3   Nonstandard System Indicator Byte Values

Value	Partition Type	Value	Partition Type
02h	MS-XENIX Root	75h	IBM PC/IX
03h	MS-XENIX usr	80h	Minix v.1.1–v1.4a
08h	AIX File System Boot	81h	Minix v1.4b-up or Linux
09h	AIX Data	82h	Linux swap file
0Ah	OS/2 Bootmanager	83h	Linux native file system
12h	Compaq diagnostics	93h	Amoeba file system
40h	ENIX 80286	94h	Amoeba bad block table
50h	Ontrack Disk Manager read-only DOS	B7h	BSDI file system (secondary swap)
51h	Ontrack Disk Manager read/write DOS	B8h	BSDI file system (secondary file system)
52h	CP/M or Microport System V/386	DBh	DR Concurrent DOS/CPM-86/CTOS
54h	Ontrack Disk Manager non-DOS	DEh	Dell system restore (hidden)
55h	Micro House EZ-Drive non-DOS	E1h	SpeedStor 12-bit FAT extended
56h	Golden Bow Vfeature Deluxe	E4h	SpeedStor 16-bit FAT extended
61h	Storage Dimensions SpeedStor	F2h	DOS 3.3+secondary
63h	IBM 386/ix or Unix System V/386	F4h	SpeedStor primary
64h	Novell NetWare 286	FEh	LANstep
65h	Novell NetWare 386	FFh	Unix/Xenix Bad Block Table Partition

These values can be useful for somebody trying to manually repair a partition table using a disk editor such as the Disk Edit program included with Norton Utilities (now part of Norton SystemWorks).

Undocumented FDISK

FDISK is a very powerful program. In DOS 5 and later versions, including Windows 9x/Me, it gained some additional capabilities (Windows NT uses Disk Administrator, whereas Windows 2000/XP use Disk Management or the DISKPART program to perform the functions of FDISK). Unfortunately, these capabilities were never documented in any of the Microsoft documentation for Windows or DOS. The most important undocumented parameter in FDISK is the /MBR (master boot record) parameter, which causes FDISK to rewrite the master boot record code area, leaving the partition table area intact.

The /MBR parameter is tailor-made for eliminating boot sector virus programs that infect the master boot record (located at cylinder 0, head 0, sector 1) of a hard disk. To use this feature, enter the following:

```
FDISK /MBR
```

FDISK then rewrites the boot record code, leaving the partition tables intact. This should not cause any problems on a normally functioning system, but just in case, I recommend backing up the partition table information to floppy disk before trying it. You can do this by using a third-party product such as Norton Utilities.

Be aware that using FDISK with the /MBR switch overwrites the partition tables if the two signature bytes at the end of the sector (55AAh) are damaged. This situation is highly unlikely, however. In fact, if these signature bytes were damaged, you would know—the system would not boot and would act as though there were no partitions at all. If you are unable to access your hard disk after booting from a clean floppy or removable-media drive, your system might be infected with a boot sector virus. You should scan for viruses with an up-to-date antivirus program and use it to guide repair.

Caution

Also note that **FDISK** **/MBR** should be used only on systems using the normal master boot record structure. If a disk-management program such as Disk Manager, Disc Wizard, EZ-Drive, MaxBlast, Data Lifeguard Tools, or similar is being used to allow your system to access the drive's full capacity, do not use **FDISK** **/MBR** because these programs use a modified MBR for disk access. Using **FDISK** **/MBR** will wipe out the changes they made to your drive and could make your data inaccessible.

The equivalent Windows NT/2000/XP Recovery Console feature to DOS/Windows 9x/Me's FDISK /MBR is called FIXMBR. The Recovery Console equivalent to FDISK is DISKPART. For details on the use of these commands, type HELP after loading the Recovery Console.

Volume Boot Records

The volume boot record starts in the first sector on any area of a drive addressed as a volume, including primary partitions or logical volumes inside an extended partition. On a floppy disk or removable cartridge (such as a Zip disk), for example, the volume boot record starts at the physical beginning of the disk because the disk is recognized as a volume without the need for partitioning. On a hard disk, the volume boot record is located as the first sectors within any disk area allocated as a primary partition, or as a logical drive (volume) inside an extended partition. Refer to Figure 25.1 for an idea of the physical relationship between this volume boot record and the other data structures on a disk. The volume boot record resembles the master boot record in that it contains the following elements:

- *Jump Instruction to Boot Code.* A 3-byte Intel x86 unconditional branch (or jump) instruction that jumps to the start of the operating system bootstrap code within the sector.
- *BIOS Parameter Block.* Contains specific information about the volume, such as its size, the number of disk sectors it uses, the size of its clusters, and the volume label name. Used by the file system driver to determine the type and status of the media. Varies according to the type of file system on the media.

- *Boot Code.* The instructions used to locate and load the initial operating system kernel or startup file, usually either IO.SYS or NTLDR.

- *Signature Bytes.* A two-byte signature (55AAh) used by the motherboard ROM and other code to validate the boot sector.

Either the motherboard ROM or the master boot record on a hard disk loads the volume boot record of the active partition on a disk. The program code in the volume boot record is given control of the system; it performs some tests and then attempts to load the first operating system file (in DOS/Windows 9x/Me the file is IO.SYS and in Windows NT/2000/XP the file is NTLDR). The volume boot record, similar to the master boot record, is transparent to the running system; it is outside the data area of the disk on which files are stored.

Note

Many of today's systems are capable of booting from drives other than standard floppy disk and hard disk drives. In these cases, the system BIOS must specifically support the boot drive. For example, some BIOS products enable you to select an ATAPI CD-ROM (or DVD) as a boot device, in addition to the floppy and hard disk drives. Many can also boot from drives connected to USB ports, adding even more flexibility to the system.

Other types of removable media, such as Zip cartridges and LS-120 disks, can also be made bootable. When the BIOS properly supports it, an LS-120 drive can replace the existing floppy disk drive as drive A:. Check the setup screens in your system BIOS to determine which types of drives can be used to start your system.

The VBR is typically created on a volume when the volume is high-level formatted. This can be done with the FORMAT command included with DOS and Windows, or you can also use Windows NT's Disk Administrator and Windows 2000/XP's Disk Management programs to perform this task after partitioning the disk. All volumes have a VBR starting in the first sector of the volume.

The VBR contains both program code and data. The single data table in this sector is called the media parameter block or disk parameter block. The operating system needs the information this table contains to verify the capacity of the disk volume as well as the location of important structures, such as the FATs on FAT volumes or the Master File Table on NTFS volumes. The format of this data is very specific.

Although all VBRs contain boot code in addition to the BIOS parameter block (BPB) and other structures, only the boot code from the VBR in the bootable volume is executed. The others are read by the operating system during startup to determine the volume parameters.

The VBR on FAT12 and FAT16 volumes is 1 sector long and contains the jump instruction, the main BPB, bootstrap code, and signature bytes. Table 25.4 shows the format and layout of the FAT12/16 VBR.

Table 25.4   FAT12/16 Volume Boot Record Format

Offset (Hex)	Offset (Dec)	Name	Length (Bytes)	Description
000h	0	BS_jmpBoot	3	Jump instruction to boot code, usually EB3C90h.
003h	3	BS_OEMName	8	OEM ID. Indicates which system formatted the volume. Typically, it's MSWIN4.1. Not used by the OS after formatting.
00Bh	11	BPB_BytsPerSec	2	Bytes per sector; normally 512.
00Dh	13	BPB_SecPerClus	1	Sectors per cluster. It must be a power of 2 greater than 0; typically 1, 2, 4, 8, 16, 32, or 64.

Table 25.4 Continued

Offset (Hex)	Offset (Dec)	Name	Length (Bytes)	Description
00Eh	14	BPB_RsvdSecCnt	2	Number of sectors reserved for the boot record(s); it should be 1 on FAT12/16 volumes.
010h	16	BPB_NumFATs	1	Count of FAT structures on the volume; usually 2.
011h	17	BPB_RootEntCnt	2	Count of 32-byte directory entries in the root directory of FAT12 and FAT16 volumes; it should be 512 on FAT12/16 volumes.
013h	19	BPB_TotSec16	2	16-bit total count of sectors on volumes with less than 65,536 sectors. If 0, then BPB_TotSec32 contains the count.
015h	21	BPB_Media	1	Media descriptor byte; normally F8h on all nonremovable media, and F0h on most removable media.
016h	22	BPB_FATSz16	2	FAT12/16 16-bit count of sectors occupied by one FAT.
018h	24	BPB_SecPerTrk	2	Sectors per track geometry value for interrupt 13h; it's usually 63 on hard disks.
01Ah	26	BPB_NumHeads	2	Number of heads for interrupt 13h; it's usually 255 on hard disks.
01Ch	28	BPB_HiddSec	4	Count of hidden sectors preceding the partition that contains this volume; it's usually 63 for the first volume.
020h	32	BPB_TotSec32	4	32-bit total count of sectors on volumes with 65,536 or more sectors. If 0, then BPB_TotSec16 contains the count.
024h	36	BS_DrvNum	1	Int 13h drive number; it's usually 00h for floppy disks or 80h for hard disks.
025h	37	BS_Reserved1	1	Reserved (used by Windows NT); it should be 0.
026h	38	BS_BootSig	1	Extended boot signature; it should be 29h if the following three fields are present. Otherwise, it's 00h.
027h	39	BS_VolID	4	Volume serial number; used with BS_VolLab to support volume tracking on removable media. Normally generated using the date and time as a seed when the volume is formatted.
02Bh	43	BS_VolLab	11	Volume label. Matches the 11-byte volume label recorded in the root directory; it should be set to NO NAME if there is no volume label.
036h	54	BS_FilSysType	8	Should be FAT12, FAT16, or FAT. Not used by the OS after formatting.
03Eh	62	BS_BootCode	448	Bootstrap program code.
1FEh	510	BS_Signature	2	Signature bytes; should be 55AAh.

The VBR on a FAT32 volume is 3 sectors long, although 32 sectors are reserved at the beginning of the volume for the default and backup VBRs. The default VBR is in sectors 0, 1, and 2, and the backup VBR is in sectors 6, 7, and 8. These are all created at the time the volume is formatted and do not change during normal use. The first sector contains a jump instruction, the BPB, initial bootstrap code, and signature bytes. The second sector is called the FSInfo (file system information) sector and contains signature bytes and information used to assist the file system software; the third sector contains only additional bootstrap code and signature bytes. Table 25.5 shows the format and layout of the first sector of the 3-sector long FAT32 VBR.

Table 25.5   FAT32 VBR Format, BPB Sector 0

Offset (Hex)	Offset (Dec)	Name	Length (Bytes)	Description
000h	0	BS_jmpBoot	3	Jump instruction to boot code; it's usually EB5890h.
003h	3	BS_OEMName	8	OEM ID; indicates which system formatted the volume. It's typically MSWIN4.1. Not used by the OS after formatting.
00Bh	11	BPB_BytsPerSec	2	Bytes per sector; normally 512.
00Dh	13	BPB_SecPerClus	1	Sectors per cluster; it must be a power of 2 greater than 0. It's normally 1, 2, 4, 8, 16, 32, or 64.
00Eh	14	BPB_RsvdSecCnt	2	Number of sectors reserved for the boot record(s); it should be 32 on FAT32 volumes.
010h	16	BPB_NumFATs	1	Count of FAT structures on the volume; usually 2.
011h	17	BPB_RootEntCnt	2	Count of 32-byte directory entries in the root directory of FAT12 and FAT16 volumes; should be 0 on FAT32 volumes.
013h	19	BPB_TotSec16	2	16-bit total count of sectors on volumes with less than 65,536 sectors. If 0, then BPB_TotSec32 contains the count. Must be 0 for FAT32 volumes.
015h	21	BPB_Media	1	Media descriptor byte, normally F8h on all nonremovable media, F0h on most removable media.
016h	22	BPB_FATSz16	2	FAT12/16 16-bit count of sectors occupied by one FAT; it should be 0 on FAT32 volumes, and BPB_FATSz32 contains the FAT size count.
018h	24	BPB_SecPerTrk	2	Sectors per track geometry value for interrupt 13h; usually 63 on hard disks.
01Ah	26	BPB_NumHeads	2	Number of heads for interrupt 13h; usually 255 on hard disks.
01Ch	28	BPB_HiddSec	4	Count of hidden sectors preceding the partition that contains this volume; usually 63 for the first volume.
020h	32	BPB_TotSec32	4	32-bit total count of sectors on volumes with 65,536 or more sectors. If 0, then BPB_TotSec16 contains the count. Must be non-zero on FAT32 volumes.
024h	36	BPB_FATSz32	4	FAT32 32-bit count of sectors occupied by one FAT. BPB_FATSz16 must be 0.
028h	40	BPB_ExtFlags	2	FAT32 only: Bits 0–3. Zero-based number of active FAT. Valid only if mirroring is disabled (bit 7 = 1). Bits 4–6. Reserved. Bit 7. 0 indicates FAT is mirrored; 1 indicates only the FAT referenced in bits 0–3 is active. Bits 8–15. Reserved.
02Ah	42	BPB_FSVer	2	Version number of the FAT32 volume. A high byte is a major revision number; a low byte is a minor revision number. It should be 00h:00h.
02Ch	44	BPB_RootClus	4	Cluster number of the first cluster of the root directory; usually 2.
030h	48	BPB_FSInfo	2	Sector number of extended FSInfo boot sector structure in the reserved area of the FAT32 volume; usually 1.
032h	50	BPB_BkBootSec	2	Sector number of the backup copy of the boot record; it's usually 6.

Table 25.5 Continued

Offset (Hex)	Offset (Dec)	Name	Length (Bytes)	Description
034h	52	BPB_Reserved	12	Reserved; should be 0.
040h	64	BS_DrvNum	1	Int 13h drive number; it's usually 00h for floppy disks or 80h for hard disks.
041h	65	BS_Reserved1	1	Reserved (used by Windows NT); it should be 0.
042h	66	BS_BootSig	1	Extended boot signature; it should be 29h if the following three fields are present. Otherwise, it's 00h.
043h	67	BS_VolID	4	Volume serial number; used with BS_VolLab to support volume tracking on removable media. Normally generated using the date and time as a seed when the volume is formatted.
047h	71	BS_VolLab	11	Volume label. Matches the 11-byte volume label recorded in the root directory, should be NO NAME if there is no volume label.
052h	82	BS_FilSysType	8	Should be FAT32. Not used by the OS after formatting.
05Ah	90	BS_BootCode	420	Bootstrap program code.
1FEh	510	BS_Signature	2	Signature bytes; it should be 55Aah.

Table 25.6 shows the format and layout of the FAT32 FSInfo sector, which is the second sector of the 3-sector-long FAT32 volume boot record.

Table 25.6 FAT32 VBR Format, FSInfo Sector 1

Offset (Hex)	Offset (Dec)	Name	Length (Bytes)	Description
000h	0	FSI_LeadSig	4	Lead signature, validates sector; it should be 52526141h.
004h	4	FSI_Reserved1	480	Reserved; it should be 0.
1E4h	484	FSI_StrucSig	4	Structure signature; it validates sector and should be 72724161h.
1E8h	488	FSI_Free_Count	4	Last known free cluster count on the volume. If FFFFFFFFh, the free count is unknown and must be recalculated by the OS.
1ECh	492	FSI_Nxt_Free	4	Next free cluster; it indicates where the system should start looking for free clusters. Usually set to the last cluster number allocated. If the value is FFFFFFFFh, the system should start looking at cluster 2.
1F0h	496	FSI_Reserved2	12	Reserved; it should be 0.
1FCh	508	FSI_TrailSig	4	Trailing signature; it should be 000055AAh.

Table 25.7 shows the format and layout of the FAT32 Boot Code sector, which is the third and final sector of the 3-sector-long FAT32 volume boot record.

Table 25.7   FAT32 VBR Format, Boot Code Sector 2

Offset (Hex)	Offset (Dec)	Name	Length (Bytes)	Description
000h	0	BS_BootCode	510	Boot program code
1FEh	510	BS_Signature	2	Signature bytes; should be 55AAh

It is interesting to note that this third sector has no system-specific information in it, which means the contents are the same from system to system. Thus, if this sector (and its backup at LBA 8) were damaged on one system, you could obtain a copy of this sector from any other FAT32 volume and use it to restore the damaged sector.

The VBR on NTFS volumes is 7 sectors long, although 16 sectors are reserved at the beginning of the disk for the VBR. A backup of the 16-sector VBR area is reserved at the end of the volume, which contains a backup VBR. The first sector of the 7 is the BPB sector, and it contains a jump instruction, the BPB, and signature bytes. Sectors 2–7 contain only additional boot code, with no signature bytes or any other structures. Because the boot code is not system specific, all but the first VBR sector should be the same on any NTFS volume. Table 25.8 shows the format and layout of the first sector of the 7-sector-long NTFS VBR.

Table 25.8   NTFS VBR Format, BPB Sector 0

Offset (Hex)	Offset (Dec)	Name	Length (Bytes)	Description
000h	0	BS_jmpBoot	3	Jump instruction to boot code; it's usually EB5290h.
003h	3	BS_OEMName	8	OEM ID; indicates which system formatted the volume. Typically, it's NTFS. Not used by the OS after formatting.
00Bh	11	BPB_BytsPerSec	2	Bytes per sector; it's usually 512.
00Dh	13	BPB_SecPerClus	1	Sectors per cluster; must be a power of 2 greater than 0. It's normally 1, 2, 4, or 8.
00Eh	14	BPB_RsvdSecCnt	2	Reserved sectors before the VBR; the value must be 0 or NTFS fails to mount the volume.
010h	16	BPB_Reserved	3	Value must be 0 or NTFS fails to mount the volume.
013h	19	BPB_Reserved	2	Value must be 0 or NTFS fails to mount the volume.
015h	21	BPB_Media	1	Media descriptor byte; it's normally F8h on all non-removable media and F0h on most removable media.
016h	22	BPB_Reserved	2	Value must be 0 or NTFS fails to mount the volume.
018h	24	BPB_SecPerTrk	2	Sectors per track geometry value for interrupt 13h; usually 63 on hard disks.
01Ah	26	BPB_NumHeads	2	Number of heads for interrupt 13h; usually 255 on hard disks.
01Ch	28	BPB_HiddSec	4	Count of hidden sectors preceding the partition that contains this volume; normally 63 for the first volume.
020h	32	BPB_Reserved	4	Value must be 0 or NTFS fails to mount the volume.
024h	36	Reserved	4	Not used or checked by NTFS; it's normally 80008000h.
028h	40	BPB_TotSec64	8	Total count of sectors on the volume.
030h	48	BPB_MftClus	8	Logical cluster number for the start of the $MFT file.
038h	56	BPB_MirClus	8	Logical cluster number for the start of the $MFTMirr file.
040h	64	BPB_ClusPerMft	1	Clusters per MFT file/folder record. If this number is positive (00h–7Fh), it represents clusters per MFT record. If the number is negative (80h–FFh), the size of the record is 2 raised to the absolute value of this number.

Table 25.8 Continued

Offset (Hex)	Offset (Dec)	Name	Length (Bytes)	Description
041h	65	Reserved	3	Not used by NTFS.
044h	68	BPB_ClusPerIndx	1	Clusters per index buffer; it's used to allocate space for directories. If this number is positive (00h–7Fh), it represents clusters per MFT record. If the number is negative (80h–FFh), the size of the record is 2 raised to the absolute value of this number.
045h	69	Reserved	3	Not used by NTFS.
048h	72	BS_VolID	8	Volume serial number; used to support volume tracking on removable media. Normally generated using the date and time as a seed when the volume is formatted.
050h	80	Reserved	4	Not used by NTFS.
054h	84	BS_BootCode	426	Bootstrap program code.
1FEh	510	BS_Signature	2	Signature bytes; should be 55AAh.

The Data Area

The data area of a partition is the place after the VBR where the actual files are stored. It is the area of the disk that is divided into clusters and managed by the file system.

Diagnostic Read-and-Write Cylinder

On drives accessed via CHS addressing (drives smaller than 8.4GB), partitioning programs such as FDISK reserve the last cylinder of a hard disk for use as a special diagnostic test cylinder. Because this cylinder is reserved, FDISK might report fewer total cylinders than the drive manufacturer states are available. If present, operating systems do not use this cylinder for any normal purpose because it lies outside the partitioned area of the disk.

◄◄ See "Disk Formatting," p. 651.

On systems using a host protected area (HPA), the system can reserve space on the end of a drive for system recovery or restoration software, diagnostics, and other utilities. This situation can account for additional discrepancies between the total capacity reported by FDISK and the drive manufacturer's reported capacity.

The diagnostics area enables software such as a manufacturer-supplied diagnostics disk to perform read-and-write tests on a hard disk without corrupting any user data. Many of these programs also swap spare cylinders for damaged cylinders if damaged cylinders are detected during testing.

File Systems

Physically, the hard disks and other media provide the basic technology for storing data. Logically, however, the file system provides the hierarchical structure of volumes and directories in which you store individual files and the organizational model that enables the system to locate data anywhere on a given disk or drive. File systems typically are an integrated part of an operating system (OS), and many of the newer OSs provide support for several file systems from which you can choose.

Several file systems are available from which to choose in a modern PC. Each file system has specific limitations, advantages, and disadvantages, and which ones you use can also be limited by the operating system you choose. Not all operating systems support all the file systems.

The primary file systems to choose from today include

■ File allocation table (FAT), which includes FAT12, FAT16, and FAT32

■ New Technology File System (NTFS)

Although other file systems, such as OS/2's High Performance File System (HPFS), are in use on PCs, these are the two you're most likely to find on a Windows-based PC. Consequently, this chapter focuses mainly on FAT and NTFS.

Clusters (Allocation Units)

File systems store data in *clusters*, which are often called *allocation units*. The term *allocation unit* is appropriate because a single cluster is the smallest unit of the disk that the operating system can handle when it writes or reads a file. A cluster is equal to one or more 512-byte sectors, in a power of 2. Although a cluster can be a single disk sector, it is usually more than one. Having more than one sector per cluster reduces the size and processing overhead and enables the operating system to run faster because it has fewer individual units to manage. The trade-off is in wasted disk space. Because operating systems manage space only in full-cluster units, every file consumes space on the disk in increments of one cluster.

Because the operating system can allocate only whole clusters, inevitably a certain amount of wasted storage space results. File sizes rarely fall on cluster boundaries, so the last cluster allocated to a particular file is rarely filled completely. The extra space left over between the actual end of the file and the end of the cluster is called *slack*. A partition with large clusters has more slack space, whereas smaller clusters generate less slack.

The effect of larger cluster sizes on disk utilization can be substantial. A 2GiB partition containing about 5,000 files, with average slack of one-half of the last 32KiB cluster used for each file, wastes more than 78MB (5000 × [.5 × 32] KiB) of file space. When files smaller than 32KiB are stored on a drive with a 32KiB allocation unit, waste (slack) factors can approach 40% of the drive's capacity. Newer file systems such as FAT32 and NTFS allow the use of smaller clusters, which use space on the disk more efficiently. For example, the same 2GiB partition with 5,000 files on it would use 4KiB clusters with either NTFS or FAT32 instead of 32KiB clusters with FAT16. Assuming the same amount of slack for each file, the smaller cluster size reduces the average amount of wasted space on that partition from more than 78MB to less than 10MB.

Note

How much space does your current cluster size waste? To find out, you can download a free Windows utility called Karen's Disk Slack Checker from Karen Kenworthy's Web site. Go to `http://www.karenware.com/powertools/ptslack.asp`.

File Allocation Table Types

Until the release of Windows XP, the most commonly used file systems were based on a file allocation table (FAT), which keeps track of the data stored in each cluster on a disk. FAT is still the most universally understood file system, meaning it is recognized by virtually every operating system that runs on PCs, and even non-PCs. For example, FAT is even recognizable on Apple Mac systems. For this reason, although NTFS (covered later in this chapter) is usually recommended with Windows XP, for greater compatibility across systems and platforms, most external hard disks and removable-media drives use FAT as their native file systems. Also, if you want to dual-boot Windows XP and Windows 9x/Me, you need to use FAT-based file systems even on your main drives.

Three main varieties of the FAT system exist, called FAT12, FAT16, and FAT32—all of which are differentiated by the number of digits used in the allocation table numbers. In other words, FAT16 uses 16-bit numbers to keep track of data clusters, FAT32 uses 32-bit numbers, and so on. The various FAT systems are used as follows:

- *FAT12.* Used on all volumes smaller than 16MiB (for example, floppy disks).

- *FAT16.* Used on volumes from 16MiB through 2GiB by MS-DOS 3.0 and most versions of Windows. Windows NT, Windows 2000, and Windows XP support FAT16 volumes as large as 4GiB. However, FAT16 volumes larger than 2GiB cannot be used by MS-DOS or Windows 9x/Me.

- *FAT32.* Optionally used on volumes from 512MiB through 2GiB, and required on all FAT volumes over 2GiB, starting with Windows 95B (OSR 2.x) and subsequent versions.

FAT12 and FAT16 are the file systems originally used by DOS and Windows and are supported by every other PC operating system from past to present. An add-on to the FAT file systems called VFAT is found in Windows 95 and newer. VFAT is a driver in Windows that adds the capability to use long filenames on existing FAT systems. When running Windows 95 or newer, VFAT is automatically enabled for all FAT volumes.

Although all PC operating systems support FAT12 and FAT16, Windows 2000 and XP also have support for FAT32 as well as non-FAT file systems such as NTFS.

FAT12

FAT12 was the first file system used in the PC when it was released on August 12, 1981, and it is still used today on all floppy disks and FAT volumes less than 16MiB. FAT12 uses a table of 12-bit numbers to manage the clusters (also called *allocation units*) on a disk. A *cluster* is the storage unit in the data area of the disk where files are stored. Each file uses a minimum of one cluster, and files that are larger than one cluster use additional space in cluster increments. FAT12 cluster sizes are shown in Table 25.9.

Table 25.9   FAT12 Cluster Sizes

Media Type	Volume Size	Sectors per Cluster	Cluster Size
5 1/4" DD floppy disk	360K	2	1KiB
3 1/2" DD floppy disk	720K	2	1KiB
5 1/4" HD floppy disk	1.2MB	1	0.5KiB
3 1/2" HD floppy disk	1.44MB	1	0.5KiB
3 1/2" ED floppy disk	2.88MB	2	1KiB
Other media	0–15.9MiB	8	4KiB

DD = Double density   KiB = Kibibyte = 1,024 bytes
HD = High density   MiB = Mebibyte = 1,048,576 bytes
ED = Extra-high density

Each cluster on a FAT12 volume is typically 8 sectors in size, except on floppy disks, where the size varies according to the particular floppy type. 12-bit cluster numbers range from 000h to FFFh (hexadecimal), which is 0–4,095 in decimal. This theoretically allows 4,096 total clusters; however, 11 of the cluster numbers are reserved and cannot be assigned to actual clusters on a disk. Cluster numbers start at 2 (0 and 1 are reserved), number FF7h is reserved to indicate a bad cluster, and numbers FF8h–FFFh indicate an end-of-chain in the FAT, leaving 4,085 clusters (4,096 – 11 = 4,085). Microsoft subtracts 1 from this to eliminate boundary problems, allowing up to exactly 4,084 clusters maximum in a FAT12 volume.

FAT12 volumes include 1 sector for the boot record and BPB (BIOS parameter block), two copies of the FAT (up to 12 sectors long each), up to 32 sectors for the root directory (less only on floppy disk media), and a data area with up to 4,084 clusters. Because each FAT12 cluster is 8 sectors (except on floppy disks), FAT12 volumes are limited to a maximum size of 32,729 sectors (1 sector for the boot record + 12 sectors per FAT × 2 FATs + 32 sectors for the root directory + 4084 clusters × 8 sectors per cluster). This equals 16.76MB or 15.98MiB. FAT12 volume limits are detailed in Table 25.10.

Table 25.10   FAT12 Volume Limits

Volume Limit	Clusters	Sectors per Cluster	Total Volume Sectors	Volume Size (Decimal)	Volume Size (Binary)
Maximum size	4,084	8	32,729	16.76MB	15.98MiB

MB = Megabyte = 1,000,000 bytes   MiB = Mebibyte = 1,048,576 bytes

PC/MS-DOS 1.x and 2.x use FAT12 exclusively, and all later versions of DOS and all Windows versions automatically create a FAT12 file system on any disks or partitions that are 32,729 sectors or less

(16.76MB) in size. Anything larger than that is automatically formatted as FAT16, FAT32, or NTFS. Characteristics of FAT12 include the following:

- Is used on all floppy disks
- Has a default format on FAT volumes of 16.76MB (15.98MiB) or less
- Is supported by all versions of DOS and Windows
- Is supported by all operating systems capable of reading PC disks

FAT12 is still used in PCs today on very small media because the 12-bit tables are smaller than those for FAT16 and FAT32, which preserves the most space for data.

FAT16

FAT16 is similar to FAT12 except it uses 16-bit numbers to manage the clusters on a disk. FAT16 was introduced on August 14, 1984, along with PC/MS-DOS 3.0, with the intention of supporting larger hard drives. FAT16 picked up where FAT12 left off and was used on media or partitions larger than 32,729 sectors (15.98MiB or 16.76MB). FAT16 could theoretically support drives of up to 2GiB or 4GiB. However, even with FAT16, DOS 3.3 and earlier were still limited to a maximum partition size of 32MiB (33.55MB) because DOS 3.3 and earlier used only 16-bit sector addressing internally and in the BPB (BIOS parameter block, stored in the volume boot sector, which is the first logical sector in a FAT partition). The use of 16-bit sector values limited DOS 3.3 and earlier to supporting drives of up to 65,535 sectors of 512 bytes, which is 32MiB (33.55MB).

As a temporary way to address drives larger than 32MiB, PC/MS-DOS 3.3 (released on April 2, 1987) introduced the extended partition, which could internally support up to 23 subpartitions (logical drives) of up to 32MiB each. Combined with the primary partition on a disk, this allowed for a total of 24 partitions of up to 32MiB each, which would be seen by the operating system as logical drives C–Z.

To take full advantage of FAT16 and allow for larger drives and partition sizes, Microsoft collaborated with Compaq, who introduced Compaq DOS 3.31 in November 1987. It was the first OS to use 32-bit sector addressing internally and in the BPB. Then the rest of the PC world followed suit on July 19, 1988, when Microsoft and IBM released PC/MS-DOS 4.0. This enabled FAT16 to handle partition sizes up to 2GiB using 64 sectors per cluster.

Each cluster in a FAT16 volume is up to 64 sectors in size. 16-bit cluster numbers range from 0000h to FFFFh, which is 0–65,535 in decimal. This theoretically allows 65,536 total clusters. However, 11 of the cluster numbers are reserved and cannot be assigned to actual clusters on a disk. Cluster numbers start at 2 (0 and 1 are reserved), number FFF7h is reserved to indicate a bad cluster, and numbers FFF8h–FFFFh indicate an end of chain in the FAT, leaving 65,525 clusters (65,536 – 11 = 65,525). Microsoft subtracts 1 from this to eliminate boundary problems, allowing up to 65,524 clusters maximum in a FAT16 volume. FAT16 cluster sizes are shown in Table 25.11.

Table 25.11   FAT16 Cluster Sizes

Volume Size	Sectors per Cluster	Cluster Size
4.1MiB–15.96MiB[1]	2	1KiB
>15.96MiB–128MiB	4	2KiB
>128MiB–256MiB	8	4KiB
>256MiB–512MiB	16	8KiB
>512MiB–1GiB	32	16KiB
>1GiB–2GiB	64	32KiB
>2GiB–4GiB[2]	128	64KiB

1. Volumes smaller than 16MiB default to FAT12; however, FAT32 can be forced by altering the format parameters.
2. Volumes larger than 2GiB are supported only by Windows NT/2000/XP and are not recommended.

MB = Megabyte = 1,000,000 bytes
KiB = Kibibyte = 1,024 bytes
MiB = Mebibyte = 1,024KiB = 1,048,576 bytes
GiB = Gibibyte = 1,024MiB = 1,073,741,824 bytes

FAT16 volumes include 1 sector for the boot record and BPB, two copies of the FAT (default and backup) up to 256 sectors long each, 32 sectors for the root directory, and a data area with up to 65,524 clusters. Each FAT16 cluster can be up to 64 sectors (32KiB) in size, meaning FAT16 volumes are limited to a maximum size of 4,194,081 sectors (1 sector for the boot record + 256 sectors per FAT × 2 FATs + 32 sectors for the root directory + 65,524 clusters × 64 sectors per cluster). This equals a maximum capacity of 2.15GB or 2GiB. FAT16 volume limits are shown in Table 25.12.

Note

Windows NT/2000/XP can optionally create FAT16 volumes that use 128 sectors per cluster (64KiB) in size, bringing the maximum volume size to 4.29GB or 4GiB. However, any volumes formatted in that manner are not readable in virtually any other OS. Additionally, 64KiB clusters cause many disk utilities to fail. For maximum compatibility, FAT16 volumes should be limited to 32KiB clusters and 2.15GB/2GiB in size.

Table 25.12   FAT16 Volume Limits

Volume Limit	Clusters	Sectors per Cluster	Total Volume Sectors	Volume Size (Decimal)	Volume Size (Binary)
Minimum size	4,167	2	8,401	4.3MB	4.1MiB
DOS 3.0-3.3 max.	16,343	4	65,533	33.55MB	32MiB
Win9x/Me max.	65,524	64	4,194,081	2.15GB	2GiB
NT/2000/XP max.	65,524	128	8,387,617	4.29GB	4GiB

MB = Megabyte = 1,000,000 bytes   MiB = Mebibyte = 1,048,576 bytes
GB = Gigabyte = 1,000 bytes   GiB = Gibibyte = 1,024MiB = 1,073,741,824 bytes
MB = 1,000,000,000 bytes

Some notable characteristics and features of FAT16 include

- FAT16 is fully supported by MS-DOS 3.31 and higher, all versions of Windows, and some Unix operating systems.

- FAT16 is fast and efficient on volumes smaller than 256MiB but relatively inefficient on larger volumes because the cluster size becomes much larger than with FAT32 and NTFS.

- The boot sector information is not automatically backed up, and if damaged or destroyed, access to the volume is lost.

- If case of a problem, you can boot the system using any MS-DOS bootable floppy to troubleshoot the problem and if necessary, repair the volume. Many third-party software tools can repair or recover data from FAT16 volumes.

- The root directory (folder) can handle up to a maximum of 512 entries, which is further reduced if any root entries use long filenames.

- FAT16 has no built-in security, encryption, or compression capability.

- File sizes on a FAT16 volume are limited only by the size of the volume. Because each file takes a minimum of one cluster, FAT16 volumes cannot have more than 65,524 total files.

VFAT and Long Filenames

The original Windows 95 release uses what is essentially the same FAT file system as DOS, except for a few important enhancements. Like much of the rest of Windows 95, the operating system support for the FAT file system was rewritten using 32-bit code and called a *virtual file allocation table (VFAT)*. VFAT works in combination with the 32-bit protected mode VCACHE (which replaces the 16-bit real mode SMARTDrive cache used in DOS and Windows 3.1) to provide better file system performance. However, the most obvious improvement in VFAT is its support for long filenames. DOS and Windows 3.1 had been encumbered by the standard 8.3 filenaming convention for many years, and adding long filename support was a high priority in Windows 95—particularly in light of the fact that Macintosh and OS/2 users had long enjoyed this capability.

The problem for the Windows 95 designers, as is often the case in the PC industry, was backward compatibility. It is no great feat to make long filenames possible when you are designing a new file system from scratch, as Microsoft did years before with Windows NT's NTFS. However, the Windows 95 developers wanted to add long filenames to the existing FAT file system and still make it possible to store those names on existing DOS volumes and for previous versions of DOS and Windows to access the files.

VFAT provides the capability to assign file and directory names that are up to 255 characters in length (including the length of the path). The three-character extension is maintained because, like previous Windows versions, Windows 9x relies on the extensions to associate file types with specific applications. VFAT's long filenames can also include spaces, as well as the following characters, which standard DOS 8.3 names can't: +,;=[ ].

The first problem when implementing the long filenames was how to make them usable to previous versions of DOS and 16-bit Windows applications that support only 8.3 names. The resolution to this problem was to give each file two names: a long filename and an alias that uses the traditional 8.3 naming convention. When you create a file with a long filename in Windows 9x/Me, VFAT uses the following process to create an equivalent 8.3 alias name:

1. The first three characters after the last dot in the long filename become the extension of the alias.

2. The first six characters of the long filename (excluding spaces, which are ignored) are converted into uppercase and become the first six characters of the alias filename. If any of these six characters is illegal under the standard 8.3 naming rules (that is, +,;=[ ]), VFAT converts those characters into underscores.

3. VFAT adds the two characters ~1 as the seventh and eighth characters of the alias filename, unless this will result in a name conflict, in which case it uses ~2, ~3, and so on, as necessary.

Aliasing in Windows NT/2000/XP

Note that Windows NT/2000/XP creates aliases differently than Windows 9x/Me (as shown later).

NT/2000/XP begins by taking the first six legal characters in the LFN and following them with a tilde and number. If the first six characters are unique, a number 1 follows the tilde.

If the first six characters aren't unique, a number 2 is added. NT/2000/XP uses the first three legal characters following the last period in the LFN for a file extension.

At the fifth iteration of this process, NT/2000/XP takes only the first two legal characters, performs a hash on the filename to produce four hexadecimal characters, places the four hex characters after the first two legal characters, and appends a ~5. The ~5 remains for all subsequent aliases; only the hex numbers change.

Tip

You can modify the behavior of the VFAT filename truncation mechanism to make it use the first eight characters of the long filename instead of the first six characters plus ~1. To do this, you must add a new binary value to the `HKEY_LOCAL_MACHINE\System\CurrentControlSet\control\FileSystem` Registry key called `NameNumericTail`, with a value of `0`. Changing the value to `1` returns the truncation process to its original state.

Although this Registry change creates "friendly" alias names, it causes many programs working with alias names to fail and is not recommended.

VFAT stores this alias filename in the standard name field of the file's directory entry. Any version of DOS or 16-bit Windows can therefore access the file using the alias name. The big problem that still remains, however, is where to store the long filenames. Clearly, storing a 255-character filename in a 32-byte directory entry is impossible (because each character requires 1 byte). However, modifying the structure of the directory entry would make the files unusable by previous DOS versions.

The developers of VFAT resolved this problem by using additional directory entries to store the long filenames. Each of the directory entries is still 32 bytes long, so up to 8 might be required for each long name, depending on its length. To ensure that these additional directory entries are not misinterpreted by earlier DOS versions, VFAT flags them with a combination of attributes that is not possible for a normal file: read-only, hidden, system, and volume label. These attributes cause DOS to ignore the long filename entries, while preventing them from being mistakenly overwritten.

Caution

When using long filenames on a standard FAT12 or FAT16 partition, you should avoid storing them in the root directory. Files with long names that take up multiple directory entries can more easily use up the limited number of entries allotted to the root directory than files with 8.3 names. On FAT32 drives, this is not a problem because the root directory has an unlimited number of entries.

In an experiment, I created a small (1KiB) text file on a floppy disk and gave it a 135-character long filename using Windows 98. I copied the file and pasted it repeatedly into the root directory of a floppy disk using Windows Explorer. Before I could make 20 copies of the file, the system displayed a **File copying** error. The disk could not accept any more files because the extremely long filename had used up all the root directory entries.

This solution for implementing backward-compatible long filenames in Windows 9x is ingenious, but it is not without its problems. Most of these problems stem from the use of applications that can access only the 8.3 alias names assigned to files. In some cases, if you open a file with a long name using one of these programs and save it again, the connection to the additional directory entries containing the long name is severed and the long name is lost.

This is especially true for older versions of disk utilities, such as Norton Disk Doctor for MS-DOS, that are not designed to support VFAT. Most older applications ignore the additional directory entries because of the combination of attributes assigned to them, but disk repair utilities usually are designed to detect and "correct" discrepancies of this type. The result is that running an old version of Norton Disk Doctor on a partition with long filenames results in the loss of all the long names. In the same way, backup utilities not designed for use with VFAT can strip off the long filenames from a partition.

Note

When using VFAT's long filename capabilities, you definitely should use disk and backup utilities that are intended to support VFAT. Windows 9x includes VFAT-compatible disk repair, defragmentation, and backup programs. If, however, you are for some reason inclined to use an older program that does not support VFAT, Windows 9x includes a clumsy, but effective, solution.

A program is included on the Windows 9x CD-ROM called LFNBK.EXE. It doesn't install with the operating system, but you can use it to strip the long filenames from a VFAT volume and store them in a text file called **LFNBK.DAT**. You can then work with the files on the volume as though they were standard 8.3 FAT files. Afterward, you can use LFNBK.EXE to restore the long filenames to their original places (assuming the file and directory structure has not changed). This is not a convenient solution, nor is it recommended for use in anything but extraordinary circumstances, but the capability is there if needed. Some backup programs designed for disaster recovery (which enable you to reconstruct the contents of the hard drive without reloading Windows first) have used this feature to enable restoration of a Windows drive with long filenames from a DOS prompt (where only 8.3 alias names usually are supported).

Another problem with VFAT's long filenames involves the process by which the file system creates the 8.3 alias names. VFAT creates a new alias every time you create or copy a file into a new directory; therefore, the alias can change. For example, you might have a file called Expenses-January04.doc stored in a directory with the alias EXPENS~1.DOC. If you use Windows 9x Explorer to copy this file to a directory that already contains a file called Expenses-December03.doc, you are likely to find that this existing file is already using the alias EXPENS~1.DOC. In this case, VFAT assigns EXPENS~2.DOC as the alias of the newly copied file, with no warning to the user. This is not a problem for applications that support VFAT because the long filenames are unchanged, but a user running an older application might open the EXPENS~1.DOC file expecting to find the list of January 2004 expenses and see the December 2003 expenses list instead.

FAT32

FAT32 is an enhanced version of the FAT file system first supported by Windows 95B (also known as OEM Service Release 2, released in August 1996). FAT32 is also supported in Windows 98/Me and Windows 2000/XP. FAT32 is not supported in the original release of Windows 95 or in any release of Windows NT.

FAT32 works just like FAT16; the only difference is that it uses numbers with more digits, so it can manage more clusters on a disk. Unlike VFAT, which is a Windows 9x innovation that uses existing file system structures, FAT32 is an enhancement of the FAT file system itself. In other words, whereas VFAT is implemented as part of the Windows 9x Virtual Machine Manager (Vmm.vxd), FAT32 is implemented by the FDISK program before the Windows GUI is even loaded. FAT32 was first included in the Windows 95 OEM Service Release 2 (OSR2, also known as Windows 95B) and is also part of Windows 98/Me, Windows 2000, and Windows XP operating systems.

Note

Because the FDISK utility can implement the FAT32 file system when you partition the drive, you can't use FAT32 on a floppy disk or any removable cartridge that does not use a partition table. However, any medium you can partition with FDISK can use FAT32.

One of the main reasons for creating FAT32 was to use disk space more efficiently. FAT32 uses smaller clusters (4KiB clusters for drives up to 8GiB in size), resulting in a 10%–15% more efficient use of disk space relative to large FAT16 drives. FAT32 also supports partitions of up to 2TiB in size, much larger than the 2GiB limit of FAT16. FAT32 cluster sizes are shown in Table 25.13.

Table 25.13   FAT32 Cluster Sizes

Volume Size	Sectors per Cluster	Cluster Size
32.52MiB–260MiB[1]	1	0.5KiB
>260MiB–8GiB	8	4KiB
>8GiB–16GiB	16	8KiB
>16GiB–32GiB	32	16KiB
>32GiB–2TiB[2]	64	32KiB

1. Volumes smaller than 512MiB will default to FAT16, although FAT32 can be forced by altering the format parameters.
2. Windows 2000 and XP format FAT32 volumes only up to 32GiB; however, they support existing FAT32 volumes up to 2TiB.

MB = Megabyte = 1,000,000 bytes
GB = Gigabyte = 1,000MB = 1,000,000,000 bytes
TB = Terabyte = 1,000GB = 1,000,000,000,000 bytes
KiB = Kibibytes = 1,024 bytes
MiB = Mebibyte = 1,024KiB = 1,048,576 bytes
GiB = Gibibyte = 1,024MiB = 1,073,741,824 bytes
TiB = Tebibytes = 1,024GiB = 1,099,511,627,776 bytes

Although the name implies that FAT32 uses 32-bit numbers to manage clusters (allocation units) on a disk, FAT32 actually uses only the first 28 bits of each 32-bit entry, leaving the high 4 bits reserved. The only time the high 4 bits are changed is when the volume is formatted, at which time the whole 32-bit entry is zeroed (including the high 4 bits). The high 4 bits are subsequently ignored when reading or writing FAT32 cluster entries; therefore, if those bits are non-zero, they are preserved. Microsoft has never indicated any purpose for them other than simply being reserved.

So, although the entries are technically 32-bit numbers, FAT32 really uses 28-bit numbers to manage the clusters on a disk. Each cluster on a FAT32 volume is from 1 sector (512 bytes) to 64 sectors (32KiB) in size. 28-bit cluster numbers range from 0000000h to FFFFFFFh, which is 0–268,435,455 in decimal. This theoretically allows for 268,435,456 total clusters. However, 11 of the numbers are reserved and cannot be assigned to actual clusters on a disk. Cluster numbers start at 2 (0 and 1 are reserved), the number FFFFFF7h is reserved to indicate a bad cluster, and numbers FFFFFF8h–FFFFFFFh indicate an end of chain in the FAT, leaving exactly 268,435,445 clusters maximum (268,435,456 – 11 = 268,435,445).

FAT32 volumes reserve the first 32 sectors for the boot record, which includes both the default boot record (3 sectors long, starting at logical sector 0) and a backup boot record (also 3 sectors long, but starting at logical sector 6). The remaining sectors in that area are reserved and filled with 0s. Following the 32 reserved sectors are 2 FATs (default and backup) that can be anywhere from 512 sectors to 2,097,152 sectors in length, with a data area 65,525–268,435,445 clusters.

Each FAT32 cluster is up to 64 sectors (32KiB) in size, so FAT32 disks or partitions could theoretically be up to 17,184,062,816 sectors (32 sectors for the boot record + 2,097,152 sectors per FAT × 2 FATs + 268,435,445 clusters × 64 sectors per cluster), which equals a capacity of 8.8TB or 8TiB. This capacity is theoretical because the 32-bit sector numbering scheme used in the partition tables located in the master boot record (MBR) limits a disk to no more than 4,294,967,295 (2^{32}–1) sectors, which is 2.2TB or 2TiB. Therefore, although FAT32 can in theory handle a volume of up to 8.8TB (terabytes or trillions of bytes), the reality is that we are currently limited by the partition table format of the MBR to only 2.2TB. At the current rate of hard disk capacity growth, single drives of that size will debut between the years 2009 and 2011. Of course, by that time the MBR limitation should be addressed.

Individual files can be up to 1 byte less than 4GiB in size and are limited by the size field in the directory entry, which is 4 bytes long. Because the clusters are numbered using 32-bit values instead of 16-bit ones, the format of the directory entries on a FAT32 partition must be changed slightly. The 2-byte Link to Start Cluster field is increased to 4 bytes, using 2 of the 10 bytes (bytes 12–21) in the directory entry that were reserved for future use.

Note

If you attempt to format a FAT32 volume larger than 32GiB on a system running Windows 2000 or Windows XP, the format fails near the end of the process with the following error:

```
Logical Disk Manager: Volume size too big.
```

This is by design. The format tools included with Windows 2000 and XP will not format a volume larger than 32GiB using the FAT32 file system. Only the format tools are restricted as such; any preexisting volumes up to 2TiB are otherwise fully supported. Microsoft is attempting to force you to use NTFS on any newly created volumes larger than 32GiB. If you are formatting an external USB or FireWire drive that will be moved between various systems, some of which include Windows 98 or Me, you must format the drive on a Windows 98 or Me system.

Windows 95 OSR2 and Windows 98 have additional limitations with FAT32. The ScanDisk tool included with those operating systems is a 16-bit program that has a maximum allocation size for a single memory block of 16MB less 64KB. This means that ScanDisk cannot process volumes using the FAT32 file system that have a FAT larger than 16MB less 64KB in size. Each FAT32 entry uses 4 bytes, so ScanDisk cannot process the FAT on a volume using the FAT32 file system that defines more than 4,177,920 clusters, which after subtracting the two reserved clusters leaves 4,177,918 actual clusters. At 32KiB per cluster—including the boot sector reserved area and the FATs themselves—this results in a maximum volume size of 136.94GB or 127.53GiB. Windows Me and later do not have this limitation.

Table 25.14 lists the volume limits for a FAT32 file system.

Table 25.14   FAT32 Volume Limits

Volume Limit	Clusters	Sectors per Cluster	Total Volume Sectors	Volume Size (Decimal)	Volume Size (Binary)
Minimum size	65,535	1	66,601	34.1MB	32.52MiB
MBR max.	67,092,481	64	4,294,967,266	2.2TB	2TiB
Theoretical max.	268,435,445	64	17,184,062,816	8.8TB	8TiB

MB = Megabyte = 1,000,000 bytes
GB = Gigabyte = 1,000MB = 1,000,000,000 bytes
TB = Terabyte = 1,000GB = 1,000,000,000,000 bytes
KiB = Kibibytes = 1,024 bytes

MiB = Mebibyte = 1,024KiB = 1,048,576 bytes
GiB = Gibibyte = 1,024MiB = 1,073,741,824 bytes
TiB = Tebibytes = 1,024GiB = 1,099,511,627,776 bytes

FAT32 is more robust than FAT12 or FAT16. FAT12/16 uses the first sector of a volume for the volume boot record, which is a critical structure. If the boot sector is damaged or destroyed, access to the entire volume is lost. FAT32 improves on this by creating both a default and a backup volume boot record in the first 32 sectors of the volume, which are reserved for this purpose. Each FAT32 volume boot record is 3 sectors long. The default boot record is in logical sectors 0–2 (the first three sectors) in the partition, and the backup is in sectors 6–8. This feature has saved me on several occasions when the default boot record was damaged and access to the entire volume was lost. In these situations, I was still able to recover the entire volume by manually restoring the volume boot record from the backup by using a sector editor such as Norton Diskedit (included with Norton SystemWorks by Symantec). Because FAT12 and FAT16 do not create a backup boot sector, if the boot sector is destroyed on those volumes, it must be re-created manually from scratch—a much more difficult proposition.

Another important difference in FAT32 partitions is the nature of the root directory. In a FAT32 partition, the root directory does not occupy a fixed position on the disk as in a FAT16 partition. Instead, it can be located anywhere in the partition and expand to any size. This eliminates the preset limit on root directory entries and provides the infrastructure necessary to make FAT32 partitions dynamically resizable. Unfortunately, Microsoft never implemented that feature in Windows, but third-party products such as PowerQuest's PartitionMagic can take advantage of this capability.

As with FAT12/16, FAT32 also maintains two copies of the FAT and automatically switches to the backup FAT if a sector in the default FAT becomes unreadable. The root directory (folder) in a FAT16 system is exactly 32 sectors long and immediately follows the two FAT copies; however, in FAT32 the root directory is actually created as a subdirectory (folder) that is stored as a file, relocatable to anywhere in the partition, and extendable in length. Therefore, a 512-file limit no longer exists in the root directory for FAT32 as there was with FAT12/16.

The main drawback of FAT32 is that it is not compatible with previous versions of DOS and Windows 95. You can't boot to a previous version of DOS or (pre-OSR2) Windows 95 from a FAT32 drive, nor can a system started with an old DOS or Windows 95 boot disk see FAT32 partitions. Most recent distributions of Linux now support FAT32, and even the Mac OS 8.1 and later can read and write FAT32 volumes. For all but the oldest of equipment, FAT32 is the most universally understandable format that supports larger volumes.

Some notable characteristics and features of FAT32 include the following:

■ FAT32 is fully supported by Windows 95B (OSR2), 98, Me, 2000, XP, and later versions.

■ MS-DOS 6.22 and earlier, Windows 95a, and Windows NT do not support FAT32 and cannot read or write FAT32 volumes.

■ Mac OS 8.1 and later support FAT32 drives.

- FAT32 is the ideal format for large, external USB or FireWire drives that will be moved between various PC and Mac systems.

- The root directory (folder) is stored as a subdirectory file that can be located anywhere on the volume. Subdirectories (folders) including the root can handle up to 65,534 entries, which is further reduced if any entries use long filenames.

- FAT32 uses smaller clusters (4KiB for volumes up to 8GiB), so space is allocated much more efficiently than FAT16.

- The critical boot sector is backed up at logical sector 6 on the volume.

- Windows 2000 and XP format FAT32 volumes only up to 32GiB. To format FAT32 volumes larger than 32GiB, you must format the volume on a Windows 98/Me system.

- In case of a boot problem, you must start the system using a bootable disk created using Windows 95B (OSR2), 98, Me, 2000, or XP. A limited number of third-party software tools can repair or recover data from FAT32 volumes.

- FAT32 has no built-in security, encryption, or compression capability.

- File sizes on FAT32 volumes are limited to 4,294,967,295 bytes ($2^{32} - 1$), which is 1 byte less than 4GiB in size.

FAT Mirroring

FAT32 also takes greater advantage of the two copies of the FAT stored on a disk partition. On a FAT16 partition, the first copy of the FAT is always the primary copy and replicates its data to the secondary FAT, sometimes corrupting it in the process. On a FAT32 partition, when the system detects a problem with the primary copy of the FAT, it can switch to the other copy, which then becomes the primary. The system can also disable the FAT mirroring process to prevent the viable FAT from being corrupted by the other copy. This provides a greater degree of fault tolerance to FAT32 partitions, often enabling you to repair a damaged FAT without an immediate system interruption or a loss of table data.

Creating FAT32 Partitions

Despite the substantial changes FAT32 provides, the new file system does have a large effect on the procedures you use to create and manage partitions. You create new FAT32 partitions in Windows 9x/Me using the FDISK utility from the command prompt, just as you would create FAT16 partitions. When you launch FDISK, the program examines your hard disk drives and, if they have a capacity greater than 512MiB, presents the following message:

```
Your computer has a disk larger than 512MB. This version of Windows
includes improved support for large disks, resulting in more efficient
use of disk space on large drives, and allowing disks over 2GB to be
formatted as a single drive.

IMPORTANT: If you enable large disk support and create any new drives on this
disk, you will not be able to access the new drive(s) using other operating
systems, including some versions of Windows 95 and Windows NT, as well as
earlier versions of Windows and MS-DOS. In addition, disk utilities that
were not designed explicitly for the FAT32 file system will not be able
to work with this disk. If you need to access this disk with other operating
systems or older disk utilities, do not enable large drive support.

Do you wish to enable large disk support (Y/N)...........? [N]
```

If you answer Yes to this question, any partitions you create that are larger than 512MiB will be FAT32 partitions. If you want to create partitions larger than 2GiB, you must use FAT32. Otherwise, you can choose which file system you prefer. All the screens following this one are the same as those in previous versions of FDISK.

Normally, the FDISK utility determines the cluster size used when you format the partition, based on the partition's size and the file system used. However, you can override FDISK using an undocumented switch for the FORMAT utility. If you use the command

FORMAT /Z:n

where n multiplied by 512 equals the desired cluster size in bytes, you can create a partition that uses cluster sizes that are larger or smaller than the defaults for the file system.

Caution

The /Z switch does not override the 65,524-cluster limit on FAT16 partitions, so it is recommended that you use it only with FAT32. In addition, you should not use this switch on a production system without extensive testing first. Modifying the cluster size can increase or decrease the amount of slack on the partition, but it also can have a pronounced effect on the performance of the drive. Some disk utilities might not work with nonstandard cluster sizes.

Converting FAT16 to FAT32

If you want to convert an existing FAT16 partition to FAT32, Windows 98 and Me later include a FAT32 Conversion Wizard that enables you to migrate existing partitions in place.

The wizard gathers the information needed to perform the conversion, informs you of the consequences of implementing FAT32, and attempts to prevent data loss and other problems. After you have selected the drive you want to convert, the wizard performs a scan for applications (such as disk utilities) that might not function properly on the converted partition. The wizard gives you the opportunity to remove these and warns you to back up the data on the partition before proceeding with the conversion. Even if you don't use the Microsoft Backup utility the wizard offers, backing up your data is a strongly recommended precaution.

Because the conversion must deal with the existing partition data in addition to creating new volume boot record information, FATs, and clusters, the process can take far longer than partitioning and formatting an empty drive. Depending on the amount of data involved and the new cluster size, the conversion can take several hours to complete.

After you convert a FAT16 partition to FAT32, you can't convert it back with Windows tools, except by destroying the partition and using FDISK to create a new one. Aftermarket partitioning utilities are available that can convert FAT32 back to FAT16 if you want. You should take precautions before beginning the conversion process, such as connecting the system to a UPS. A power failure during the conversion could result in a loss of data.

Third-Party Partitioning Utilities

Windows includes only basic tools for creating FAT32 partitions, but programs such as Partition Commander from VCOM (www.v-com.com) and PartitionMagic from Symantec (which acquired PowerQuest but still maintains a Web page at www.powerquest.com) provide many other partition manipulation features. These programs can easily convert partitions back and forth between FAT16, FAT32, NTFS and other file systems, as well as resize, move, and copy partitions without destroying the data they contain. They also allow changes in cluster sizes beyond what the standard Windows tools create.

File Allocation Table Tutorial

You can think of the FAT as a type of spreadsheet that tracks the allocation of the disk's clusters. Each cell in the spreadsheet corresponds to a single cluster on the disk. The number stored in that cell is a code indicating whether a file uses the cluster and, if so, where the next cluster of the file is located. Thus, to determine which clusters a particular file is using, you start by looking at the first FAT reference in the file's directory entry. When you look up the referenced cluster in the FAT, the table contains a reference to the file's next cluster. Each FAT reference, therefore, points to the next cluster in a

FAT *chain* until you reach the cluster containing the end of the file. Numbers stored in the FAT are hexadecimal numbers that are either 12 or 16 bits long. The 16-bit FAT numbers are easy to follow in a disk sector editor because they take an even 2 bytes of space. The 12-bit numbers are 1 1/2 bytes long, which presents a problem because most disk sector editors show data in byte units. To edit a 12-bit FAT, you must do some hex/binary math to convert the displayed byte units to FAT numbers. Fortunately (unless you are using the DOS DEBUG program), most of the available tools and utility programs have a FAT-editing mode that automatically converts the numbers for you. Most of them also show the FAT numbers in decimal form, which most people find easier to handle.

With FAT16, the cluster numbers are stored as 16-bit entries, from 0000h to FFFFh. The largest value possible is FFFFh, which corresponds to 65,535 in decimal, but several numbers at the beginning and end are reserved for special use. The actual cluster numbers allowed in a FAT16 system range from 0002h to FFF6h, which is 2–65,526 in decimal. All files must be stored in cluster numbers within that range. That leaves only 65,524 valid clusters to use for storing files (cluster numbers below 2 and above 65,526 are reserved), meaning a partition must be broken up into that many clusters or less. A typical file entry under FAT16 might look like Table 25.15.

Table 25.15 FAT16 File Entries

Name	Starting Cluster	Directory Size
USCONST.TXT	1000	4

FAT Cluster #	Value	FAT16 File Allocation Table Meaning
00002	0	First cluster available
...	...	...
00999	0	Cluster available
01000	1001	In use, points to next cluster
01001	1002	In use, points to next cluster
01002	1003	In use, points to next cluster
01003	FFFFh	End of file
01004	0	Cluster available
...	...	...
65526	0	Last cluster available

In this example, the directory entry states that the file starts in cluster number 1000. In the FAT, that cluster has a nonzero value, which indicates it is in use; the specific value indicates where the file using it would continue. In this case, the entry for cluster 1000 is 1001, which means the file continues in cluster 1001. The entry in 1001 points to 1002, and from 1002 the entry points to 1003. The entry for 1003 is FFFFh, which is an indication that the cluster is in use but that the file ends here and uses no additional clusters.

The use of the FAT becomes clearer when you see that files can be fragmented. Let's say that before the USCONST.TXT file was written, another file already occupied clusters 1002 and 1003. If USCONST.TXT was written starting at 1000, it would not have been capable of being completely written before running into the other file. As such, the operating system would skip over the used clusters and continue the file in the next available cluster. The end result is shown in Table 25.16.

Table 25.16   Directory and FAT Relationship (Fragmented File)

	Directory	
Name	**Starting Cluster**	**Size**
PLEDGE.TXT	1002	2
USCONST.TXT	1000	4

	FAT16 File Allocation Table	
FAT Cluster #	**Value**	**Meaning**
00002	0	First cluster available
...	...	...
00999	0	Cluster available
01000	1001	In use, points to next cluster
01001	1004	In use, points to next cluster
01002	1003	In use, points to next cluster

	FAT16 File Allocation Table	
FAT Cluster #	**Value**	**Meaning**
01003	FFFFh	End of file
01004	1005	In use, points to next cluster
01005	FFFFh	End of file
...	...	...
65526	0	Last cluster available

In this example, the PLEDGE.TXT file that was previously written interrupted USCONST.TXT, so those clusters are skipped over, and the pointers in the FAT reflect that. Note that the defrag programs included with DOS and Windows take an example like this and move the files so they are contiguous, one after the other, and update the FAT to indicate the change in cluster use.

The first two entries in the FAT are reserved and contain information about the table itself. All remaining entries correspond to specific clusters on the disk. Most FAT entries consist of a reference to another cluster containing the next part of a particular file. However, some FAT entries contain hexadecimal values with special meanings, as follows:

- *0000h.* Indicates that the cluster is not in use by a file
- *FFF7h.* Indicates that at least one sector in the cluster is damaged and that it should not be used to store data
- *FFF8h–FFFFh.* Indicates that the cluster contains the end of a file and that no reference to another cluster is necessary

To compare FAT16 and FAT32, you can look at how a file would be stored on each. With FAT32, the cluster numbers range from 00000000h to 0FFFFFFFh, which is 0–268,435,455 in decimal. Again, some values at the low and high ends are reserved, and only values between 00000002h and 0FFFFFF6h are valid, which means values 2–268,435,446 are valid. This leaves 268,435,445 valid entries, so the drive must be split into that many clusters or less. Because a drive can be split into so many more clusters, the clusters can be smaller, which conserves disk space. The same file as shown earlier could be stored on a FAT32 system as illustrated in Table 25.17.

Table 25.17   FAT32 File Entries

	Directory	
Name	**Starting Cluster**	**Size**
USCONST.TXT	1000	8

	FAT32 File Allocation Table	
FAT Cluster #	**Value**	**Meaning**
0000000002	0	First cluster available
...	...	...
0000000999	0	Cluster available
0000001000	1001	In use, points to next cluster
0000001001	1002	In use, points to next cluster
0000001002	1003	In use, points to next cluster
0000001003	1004	In use, points to next cluster
0000001004	1005	In use, points to next cluster
0000001005	1006	In use, points to next cluster
0000001006	1007	In use, points to next cluster
0000001007	0FFFFFFFh	End of file
0000001008	0	Cluster available
...	...	...
268,435,446	0	Last cluster available

Because the FAT32 system enables many more clusters to be allocated, the cluster size is usually smaller. So, although files overall use more individual clusters, less wasted space results because the last cluster is, on average, only half filled.

Some additional limitations exist on FAT32 volumes. Volumes less than 512MiB default to FAT16, but FAT32 partitions as small as 32.52MiB can be forced using the proper utilities or commands. Anything smaller than that, however, must be either FAT16 or FAT12.

Using smaller clusters results in many more clusters and more entries in the FAT. A 2GiB partition using FAT32 requires up to 524,288 FAT entries, whereas the same drive needs only 65,536 entries using FAT16. Thus, the size of one copy of the FAT16 table is 128KiB (65,536 entries × 16 bits = 1,048,576 bits/8 = 131,072 bytes/1,024 = 128KiB), whereas the FAT32 table is 2MiB in size.

The size of the FAT has a definite impact on the performance of the file system. Windows 9x/Me uses VCACHE to keep the FAT in memory at all times to improve file system performance. The use of 4KiB clusters for drives up to 8GiB in size is, therefore, a reasonable compromise for the average PC's memory capacity. If the file system were to use clusters equal to one disk sector (1 sector = 512KiB) in an attempt to minimize slack as much as possible, the FAT table for a 2GiB drive would contain 4,194,304 entries and be 16MB in size.

This would monopolize a substantial portion of the memory in the average system, probably resulting in noticeably degraded performance. Although at first it might seem as though even a 2MB FAT is quite large when compared to 128KiB, keep in mind that hard disk drives are a great deal faster now than they were when the FAT file system was originally designed. In practice, FAT32 typically results in a minor (less than 5%) improvement in file system performance. However, systems that perform a great many sequential disk writes might see an equally minor degradation in performance.

The partitioning program generally determines whether a 12-bit, 16-bit, or 32-bit FAT is placed on a disk, even though the FAT isn't written until you perform a high-level format (using the FORMAT utility). On today's systems, usually only floppy disks use 12-bit FATs, but FDISK also creates a 12-bit FAT if you create a hard disk volume that is smaller than 16MiB. On hard disk volumes of more than 16MiB, FDISK creates a 16-bit FAT. On drives larger than 512MiB, the FDISK program included in Windows 95 OSR2, and Windows 98/Me enables you to create 32-bit FATs when you answer Yes to the question Enable Large Disk Support? when you start FDISK. You can also select FAT32 when you prepare a drive with the Windows 2000 or Windows XP Disk Management program (Windows NT doesn't support FAT32).

FAT volumes normally have two copies of the FAT. Each one occupies contiguous sectors on the disk, and the second FAT copy immediately follows the first. Unfortunately, the operating system uses the second FAT copy only if sectors in the first FAT copy become unreadable. If the first FAT copy is corrupted, which is a much more common problem, the operating system does not use the second FAT copy. Even the CHKDSK command does not check or verify the second FAT copy. Moreover, whenever the OS updates the first FAT, it automatically copies large portions of the first FAT to the second FAT. If the first copy was corrupted and subsequently updated by the OS, a large portion of the first FAT is copied over to the second FAT copy, damaging it in the process. After the update, the second copy is usually a mirror image of the first one, complete with any corruption. Two FATs rarely stay out of sync for very long. When they are out of sync and the OS writes to the disk, it updates the first FAT and overwrites the second FAT with the first. This is why disk repair and recovery utilities warn you to stop working as soon as you detect a FAT problem. Programs such as Norton Disk Doctor (included with the Norton Utilities which are a part of Norton SystemWorks) use the second copy of the FAT as a reference to repair the first one, but if the OS has already updated the second FAT, repair might be impossible.

Directories

A *directory* is a simple database containing information about the files stored on a FAT partition. Directories are also called *folders* in Windows.

Each record in a directory is 32 bytes long, with no delimiters or separating characters between the fields or records. A directory stores almost all the information that the operating system knows about a file, including the following:

■ *Filename and extension.* The eight-character name and three-character extension of the file. The dot between the name and the extension is implied but not included in the entry.

Note

To see how Windows 9x/Me extends filenames to allow 255 characters within the 8.3 directory structure, refer to "VFAT and Long Filenames," earlier in this chapter.

■ *File attribute byte.* The byte containing the flags representing the standard DOS file attributes, using the format shown in Table 25.21.

■ *Date/Time of last change.* The date and time that the file was created or last modified.

■ *File size.* The size of the file, in bytes.

■ *Link to start cluster.* The number of the cluster in the partition where the beginning of the file is stored. To learn more about clusters, refer to "Clusters (Allocation Units)," earlier in this chapter.

Other information exists that a directory does not contain about a file. This includes where the rest of its clusters in the partition are located and whether the file is contiguous or fragmented. This information is contained in the FAT.

Two basic types of directories exist: the root directory (also called the root folder) and subdirectories (also called folders). Any given volume can have only one root directory. The root directory is always stored on a disk in a fixed location immediately following the two copies of the FAT. Root directories vary in size because of the different types and capacities of disks, but the root directory of a given disk is fixed. Using the FORMAT command creates a root directory that has a fixed length and can't be extended to hold more entries. The root directory entry limits are shown in Table 25.18. Subdirectories are stored as files in the data area of the disk and can grow in size dynamically; therefore, they have no fixed length limits.

Table 25.18   Root Directory Entry Limits

Drive Type	Maximum Root Directory Entries
Hard disk	512
1.44MB floppy disk	224
2.88MB floppy disk	448
Jaz and Zip	512
LS-120 and LS-240	512

Note

Two advantages of the FAT32 file system are that the root directory can be located anywhere on the disk and it can have an unlimited number of entries. FAT32 is discussed in more detail later in this chapter.

Every directory, whether it is the root directory or a subdirectory, is organized in the same way. Entries in the directory database store important information about individual files and how files are named on the disk. The directory information is linked to the FAT by the starting cluster entry. In fact, if no file on a disk were longer than one single cluster, the FAT would be unnecessary. The directory stores all the information needed by DOS to manage the file, with the exception of the list of clusters the file occupies other than the first one. The FAT stores the remaining information about the other clusters the file occupies.

To trace a file on a disk, use a disk editor, such as the Disk Edit program that comes with the Norton Utilities. Start by looking up the directory entry to get the information about the starting cluster of the file and its size. Then, using the appropriate editor commands, go to the FAT where you can follow the chain of clusters the file occupies until you reach the end of the file. By using the directory and FAT in this manner, you can visit all the clusters on the disk that are occupied by the file. This type of technique can be useful when these entries are corrupted and when you are trying to find missing parts of a file.

FAT directory entries are 32 bytes long and are in the format shown in Table 25.19, which shows the location (or offset) of each field within the entry (in both hexadecimal and decimal form) and the length of each field.

Table 25.19   FAT Directory Format

Offset (Hex)	Offset (Dec)	Field Length	Description
00h	0	8 bytes	Filename
08h	8	3 bytes	File extension
0Bh	11	1 byte	File attributes
0Ch	12	10 bytes	Reserved (00h)
16h	22	1 word	Time of creation
18h	24	1 word	Date of creation
1Ah	26	1 word	Starting cluster
1Ch	28	1 dword	Size in bytes

A word is 2 bytes read in reverse order, and a dword is two words read in reverse order.

Filenames and extensions are left justified and padded with spaces, (which are represented as ASCII 32h bytes). In other words, if your filename is "AL", it is stored as "AL------", where the hyphens are spaces. The first byte of the filename indicates the file status for that directory entry, shown in Table 25.20.

Table 25.20   Directory Entry Status Byte (First Byte)

Hex	File Status
00h	Entry never used; entries past this point not searched.
05h	Indicates that the first character of the filename is actually E5h.
E5h	σ (lowercase sigma). Indicates that the file has been erased.
2Eh	. (period). Indicates that this entry is a directory. If the second byte is also 2Eh, the cluster field contains the cluster number of the parent directory (0000h, if the parent is the root).

Table 25.21 describes the FAT directory file attribute byte. Attributes are 1-bit flags that control specific properties of a file, such as whether it is hidden or designated as read-only. Each flag is individually activated (1) or deactivated (0) by changing the bit value. The combination of the eight bit values can be expressed as a single hexadecimal byte value; for example, 07h translates to 00000111, and the 1 bits in positions 2, 1, and 0 indicate the file is system, hidden, and read-only.

Table 25.21   FAT Directory File Attribute Byte

Bit Positions 7 6 5 4 3 2 1 0	Hex Value	Description
0 0 0 0 0 0 0 1	01h	Read-only file
0 0 0 0 0 0 1 0	02h	Hidden file
0 0 0 0 0 1 0 0	04h	System file
0 0 0 0 1 0 0 0	08h	Volume label
0 0 0 1 0 0 0 0	10h	Subdirectory
0 0 1 0 0 0 0 0	20h	Archive (updated since backup)
0 1 0 0 0 0 0 0	40h	Reserved
1 0 0 0 0 0 0 0	80h	Reserved
Examples		
0 0 0 0 0 1 1 1	07h	System, hidden, read-only
0 0 1 0 0 0 0 1	21h	Read-only, archive
0 0 1 1 0 0 1 0	32h	Hidden, subdirectory, archive
0 0 1 0 0 1 1 1	27h	Read-only, hidden, system, archive

Note

The DOS/Windows command-line **ATTRIB** command can be used to change file attributes. In the Windows GUI, you can use the properties sheet for a file or folder to change the attributes. The archive bit changes automatically when a file is backed up or changed.

FAT File System Errors

File system errors can, of course, occur because of hardware problems, but you are more likely to see them result from software crashes and improper system handling. Turning off a system without shutting down Windows properly, for example, can result in errors that cause clusters to be incorrectly listed as in use when they are not. Some of the most common file system errors that occur on FAT partitions are described in the following sections.

Lost Clusters

Probably the most common file system error, *lost* clusters are clusters the FAT designates as being in use when they actually are not. Most often caused by an interruption of a file system process due to an application crash or a system shutdown, for example, the FAT entry of a lost cluster might contain a reference to a subsequent cluster. However, the FAT chain stemming from the directory entry has been broken somewhere along the line.

Lost clusters appear in the file structure as shown in Table 25.22.

Table 25.22   Lost Clusters in a File Structure

Directory		
Name	**Starting Cluster**	**Size**
(no entry)	0	0

FAT16 File Allocation Table		
FAT Cluster #	**Value**	**Meaning**
00002	0	First cluster available
...	...	...
00999	0	Cluster available
01000	1001	In use, points to next cluster
01001	1002	In use, points to next cluster
01002	1003	In use, points to next cluster
01003	FFFFh	End of file
01004	0	Cluster available
...	...	...
65526	0	Last cluster available

The operating system sees a valid chain of clusters in the FAT but no corresponding directory entry to back it up. Programs that are terminated before they can close their open files typically cause this. The operating system usually modifies the FAT chain as the file is written, and the final step when closing is to create a matching directory entry. If the system is interrupted before the file is closed (such as by shutting down the system improperly), lost clusters are the result. Disk repair programs check for lost clusters by tracing the FAT chain for each file and subdirectory in the partition and building a facsimile of the FAT in memory. After compiling a list of all the FAT entries that indicate properly allocated clusters, the program compares this facsimile with the actual FAT. Any entries denoting allocated clusters in the real FAT that do not appear in the facsimile are lost clusters because they are not part of a valid FAT chain.

The utility typically gives you the opportunity to save the data in the lost clusters as a file before it changes the FAT entries to show them as unallocated clusters. If your system crashed or lost power while you were working with a word processor data file, for example, you might be able to retrieve text from the lost clusters in this way. When left unrepaired, lost clusters are unavailable for use by the system, reducing the storage capacity of your drive.

The typical choices you have for correcting lost clusters are to assign them a made-up name or zero out the FAT entries. If you assign them a name, you can at least look at the entries as a valid file and then delete the file if you find it useless. The CHKDSK and SCANDISK programs are designed to fix lost clusters by assigning them names starting with FILE0001.CHK. If more than one lost chain exists, sequential numbers following the first one are used. The lost clusters shown earlier could be corrected by CHKDSK or SCANDISK as shown in Table 25.23.

Table 25.23   Finding Lost Clusters

Name	Starting Cluster	Size
		Directory
FILE0001.CHK	1000	4

		FAT16 File Allocation Table
FAT Cluster #	**Value**	**Meaning**
00002	0	First cluster available
...	...	...
00999	0	Cluster available
01000	1001	In use, points to next cluster
01001	1002	In use, points to next cluster
01002	1003	In use, points to next cluster
01003	FFFFh	End of file
01004	0	Cluster available
...	...	...
65526	0	Last cluster available

As you can see, a new entry was created to match the FAT entries. The name is made up because there is no way for the repair utility to know what the original name of the file might have been.

Cross-Linked Files

Cross-linked files occur when two directory entries improperly reference the same cluster in their Link to Start Cluster fields. The result is that each file uses the same FAT chain. Because the clusters can store data from only one file, working with one of the two files can inadvertently overwrite the other file's data.

Cross-linked files would appear in the file structure as shown in Table 25.24.

Table 25.24   Cross-Linked Files

Name	Starting Cluster	Size
		Directory
USCONST.TXT	1000	4
PLEDGE.TXT	1002	2

		FAT16 File Allocation Table
FAT Cluster #	**Value**	**Meaning**
00002	0	First cluster available
...	...	...
00999	0	Cluster available
01000	1001	In use, points to next cluster
01001	1002	In use, points to next cluster
01002	1003	In use, points to next cluster
01003	FFFFh	End of file
01004	0	Cluster available
...	...	...
65526	0	Last cluster available

In this case, two files claim ownership of clusters 1002 and 1003, so these files are said to be cross-linked on 1002. When a situation such as this arises, one of the files typically is valid and the other is corrupt, being that only one actual given set of data can occupy a given cluster. The normal repair is to copy both files involved to new names, which duplicates their data separately in another area of the disk, and then delete *all* the cross-linked files. Deleting them all is important because by deleting only one of them, the FAT chain is zeroed, which further damages the other entries. Then, you can examine the files you copied to determine which one is good and which is corrupt.

Detecting cross-linked files is a relatively easy task for a disk repair utility because it must examine only the partition's directory entries and not the file clusters themselves. However, by the time the utility detects the error, the data from one of the two files is probably already lost—although you might be able to recover parts of it from lost clusters.

Invalid Files or Directories

Sometimes the information in a directory entry for a file or subdirectory can be corrupted to the point at which the entry is not just erroneous (as in cross-linked files) but invalid. The entry might have a cluster or date reference that is invalid, or it might violate the rules for the entry format in some other way. In most cases, disk repair software can correct these problems, permitting access to the file.

FAT Errors

As discussed earlier, accessing its duplicate copy can sometimes repair a corrupted FAT. Disk repair utilities typically rely on this technique to restore a damaged FAT to its original state, as long as the mirroring process has not corrupted the copy. FAT32 tables are more likely to be repairable because their more advanced mirroring capabilities make the copy less likely to be corrupted.

An example of a damaged FAT might appear to the operating system as shown in Table 25.25.

Table 25.25   Damaged FAT

Directory		
Name	**Starting Cluster**	**Size**
USCONST.TXT	1000	4
FAT16 File Allocation Table		
FAT Cluster #	**Value**	**Meaning**
00002	0	First cluster available
...	...	...
00999	0	Cluster available
01000	1001	In use, points to next cluster
01001	0	Cluster available
01002	1003	In use, points to next cluster
01003	FFFFh	End of file
01004	0	Cluster available
...	...	...
65526	0	Last cluster available

This single error would cause multiple problems to appear. The file USCONST.TXT would now come up as having an allocation error—in which the size in the directory no longer matches the number of clusters in the FAT chain. The file would end after cluster 1001 in this example, and the rest of the data would be missing if you loaded this file for viewing. Also, two lost clusters would exist; that is, 1002 and 1003 appear to have no directory entry that owns them. When multiple problems such as these appear, a single incident of damage is often the cause. The repair in this case could involve copying the data from the backup FAT back to the primary FAT, but in most cases, the backup is similarly damaged. Normal utilities would truncate the file and create an entry for a second file out of the lost clusters. You would have to figure out yourself that they really belong together. This is where having knowledge in data recovery can help over using automated utilities that can't think for themselves.

NTFS

Windows NT 3.1 (the first version of NT despite the 3.1 designation) was released in August 1993 and introduced the New Technology File System (NTFS), which is unique to NT-based operating systems (including Windows 2000 and Windows XP) and is not supported by Windows 9x/Me. NTFS includes many advanced features not found in the FAT file systems.

NTFS is the native file system of Windows NT, Windows 2000, and Windows XP. Windows 2000 and Windows XP use an enhanced version of NTFS called NTFS 5 or NTFS 2000; Windows NT 4.0 must have Service Pack 4 or above installed to be capable of accessing an NTFS 5/NTFS 2000 disk. Although NT/2000/XP support FAT partitions (and Windows 2000/XP even support FAT32), NTFS provides many advantages over FAT, including long filenames, support for larger files and partitions, extended attributes, and increased security. NTFS, like all of Windows NT, was newly designed from the ground up. Backward compatibility with previous Microsoft operating systems was not a concern because the developers were intent on creating an entirely new 32-bit platform. As a result, no operating systems other than Windows NT and Windows 2000/XP, which are based on Windows NT, can read NTFS partitions.

NTFS supports filenames of up to 255 characters, using spaces, multiple periods, and any other standard characters except the following: *?/\;<>|. Since Windows NT 3.51, NTFS has also supported compression on a file-by-file (or folder-by-folder) basis through each file or folder's properties sheet. No third-party program, such as WinZip or PKZip, is needed to compress or decompress files stored on an NTFS drive. NTFS 5 also supports encryption on a file-by-file or folder-by-folder properties sheet.

Tip

To access advanced file attributes under NTFS such as compression, encryption, and indexing, right-click the file or folder, select Properties, and click the Advanced button to bring up the Advanced properties dialog box.

NTFS supports larger volumes (up to 16TiB), larger files, and more files per volume than FAT. NTFS also uses smaller cluster sizes than even FAT32, resulting in more efficient use of a volume. For example, a 30GiB NTFS volume uses 4KiB clusters, whereas the same size volume formatted with FAT32 uses 16KiB clusters. Smaller clusters reduce wasted space on the volume. NTFS cluster sizes are shown in Table 25.26.

Table 25.26   NTFS Cluster Sizes

Volume Size	Sectors per Cluster	Cluster Size
16MiB–512MiB	1	0.5KiB
>512MiB–1GiB	2	1KiB
>1GiB–2GiB	4	2KiB
>2GiB–2TiB[1]	8	4KiB

1. Larger cluster sizes can be forced by altering the format parameters; however, file compression is disabled if clusters larger than 8 sectors (4KiB) are selected.
MB = Megabyte = 1,000,000 bytes
GB = Gigabyte = 1,000MB = 1,000,000,000 bytes
TB = Terabyte = 1,000GB = 1,000,000,000,000 bytes
KiB = Kibibytes = 1,024 bytes
MiB = Mebibyte = 1,024KiB = 1,048,576 bytes
GiB = Gibibyte = 1,024MiB = 1,073,741,824 bytes
TiB = Tebibytes = 1,024GiB = 1,099,511,627,776 bytes

NTFS uses a special file structure called a master file table (MFT) and metadata files. The MFT is basically a relational database that consists of rows of file records and columns of file attributes. It contains at least one entry for every file on an NTFS volume. NTFS creates file and folder records for each file and folder created on an NTFS volume. These are stored in the MFT and consume 1KiB each. Each file record contains information about the position of the file record in the MFT, as well as file attributes and any other information about the file.

NTFS was designed to manage clusters using up to 64-bit numbers, which is an astronomical amount, but the current implementations use 32-bit numbers instead. Using 32-bit numbers allows for addressing up to 4,294,967,295 clusters, each of which is typically up to 4KiB.

NTFS reserves a total of 32 sectors for a 16-sector-long default volume boot sector and a backup boot sector. The default boot sector is located at the beginning (logical sector 0) of the volume, whereas the backup boot sector is written at the logical center of the volume (if it was formatted using NT 3.51 and earlier) or at the end of the volume (if it was formatted with NT 4.0 or later, including 2000 and XP).

An NTFS volume can therefore comprise up to 34,359,738,392 total sectors (32 sectors reserved for the default and backup boot sectors, plus 4,294,967,295 clusters × 8 sectors), which is 17.59TB or 16.00TiB. The 32-bit sector numbering scheme used in the partition tables located in the MBR limits a single disk to no more than 4,294,967,295 (2^{32}–1) sectors, which is 2.2TB or 2TiB.

Windows 2000 and later versions (including XP Pro) can get around this on nonbootable drives by using a *dynamic disk*. Windows 2000 and XP Professional (but not XP Home) offer two types of storage: basic disks and dynamic disks. *Basic disks* use the same structures as before, with an MBR on the disk containing a partition table limited to four primary partitions per disk, or three primary partitions and one extended partition with unlimited logical drives. Primary partitions and logical drives on basic disks are known as *basic volumes*.

Dynamic disks were first introduced in Windows 2000 and provide the capability to create dynamic volumes that can be simple (using only one drive), spanned (using multiple drives), or striped (using multiple drives simultaneously for increased performance). Dynamic disks use a hidden database (contained in the last megabyte of the disk) to track information about dynamic volumes on the disk and about other dynamic disks in the computer. Because each dynamic disk in a computer stores a replica of the dynamic disk database, a corrupted database on one dynamic disk can be repaired using the database on another. By spanning or striping multiple drives using dynamic disk formats, you can exceed the 2TiB limit of a single MBR-based partition.

Although the 32-bit sector numbering in the partition tables on MBR disks limits NTFS basic disks to 2TiB volumes, you can use dynamic volumes to create NTFS volumes larger than 2TiB by spanning or striping multiple basic disks to create a larger dynamic disk. Because the dynamic volumes are managed in the hidden database, they are not affected by the 2TiB limit imposed by the partition tables in the MBR. In essence, dynamic disks enable Windows 2000 and XP Pro to create NTFS volumes as large as 16TiB. The volume limits for NTFS are listed in Table 25.27.

Table 25.27   NTFS Volume Limits

Volume Limit	Clusters	Sectors per Cluster	Total Volume Sectors	Volume Size (Decimal)	Volume Size (Binary)
Minimum size	32,698	1	32,730	16.76MB	15.98MiB
Basic disk max.	536,870,908	8	4,294,967,295	2.2TB	2TiB
Dynamic disk max.	4,294,967,295	8	34,359,738,392	17.59TB	16TiB

MB = Megabyte = 1,000,000 bytes   *MiB = Mebibyte = 1,024KiB = 1,048,576 bytes*
GB = Gigabyte = 1,000MB = 1,000,000,000 bytes   *GiB = Gibibyte = 1,024MiB = 1,073,741,824 bytes*
TB = Terabyte = 1,000GB = 1,000,000,000,000 bytes   *TiB = Tebibytes = 1,024GiB = 1,099,511,627,776 bytes*
KiB = Kibibytes = 1,024 bytes

Some notable characteristics and features of NTFS include

■ *Files are limited in size to 16TiB less 64KiB or by the size of the volume, whichever is lower.* NTFS supports up to 4,294,967,295 (2^{32}–1) files on a volume.

■ *NTFS is not normally used on removable media because NTFS does not flush data to the disk immediately.* However, it can be used with Zip and Jaz drives. In addition, removing NTFS-formatted media without using the Safe Removal application can result in data loss. For removable media that can be ejected unexpectedly, you should use FAT12, FAT16, or FAT32 instead.

■ *NTFS incorporates transaction logging and recovery techniques.* In the event of a failure, upon reboot NTFS uses its log file and checkpoint information to restore the consistency of the file system.

■ *NTFS dynamically remaps clusters found to contain bad sectors and then marks the defective cluster as bad so it will no longer be used.*

■ *NTFS has built-in security features.* These enable you to set permissions on a file or folder.

■ *NTFS has a built-in encrypting file system (EFS).* This performs dynamic encryption and decryption as you work with encrypted files or folders, while preventing others from doing so.

■ *NTFS enables the setting of disk quotas.* You can track and control space usage for NTFS volumes among various users.

■ *NTFS has built-in dynamic compression, which compresses and decompresses files as you use them.*

NTFS Architecture

Although NTFS partitions are very different from FAT partitions internally, they do comply with the extra-partitional disk structures described earlier in this chapter. NTFS partitions are listed in the master partition table of a disk drive's master boot record, just like FAT partitions, and they have a volume boot record as well, although it is formatted somewhat differently.

When a volume is formatted with NTFS, system files are created in the root directory of the NTFS volume. These system files can be stored at any physical location on the NTFS volume. This means that damage to any specific location on the disk will probably not render the entire partition inaccessible.

Typically, 12 NTFS system files (often referred to as *metadata* files) are created when you format an NTFS volume. Table 25.28 shows the names and descriptions for these files.

Table 25.28   NTFS System Files

Filename	Meaning	Description
$mft	Master file table (MFT)	Contains a record for every file on the NTFS volume in its Data attribute
$mftmirr	Master file table2 (MFT2)	Mirror of the MFT used for recoverability purposes; contains the first four records in $mft or the first cluster of $mft, whichever is larger
$badclus	Bad cluster file	Contains all the bad clusters on the volume
$bitmap	Cluster allocation bitmap	Contains the bitmap for the entire volume, showing which clusters are used
$boot	Boot file	Contains the volume's bootstrap if the volume is bootable
$attrdef	Attribute definitions table	Contains the definition of all system- and user-defined attributes on the volume
$logfile	Log file	Logs file transactions; used for recoverability purposes
$quota	Quota table	Table used to indicate disk quota usage for each user on a volume; used in NTFS 5

Table 25.28   **Continued**

Filename	Meaning	Description
$upcase	Upcase table	Table used for converting uppercase and lowercase characters to the matching uppercase Unicode characters
$volume	Volume	Contains volume information, such as volume name and version
$extend	NTFS extension file	Stores optional extensions, such as quotas, object identifiers, and reparse point data
(no name)	Root filename index	The root folder (directory)

An NTFS partition is based on a structure called the master file table (MFT). The MFT concept expands on that of the FAT. Instead of using a table of cluster references, the MFT contains much more detailed information about the files and directories in the partition. In some cases, it even contains the files and directories themselves.

The first record in the MFT is called the *descriptor*, which contains information about the MFT itself. The volume boot record for an NTFS partition contains a reference that points to the location of this descriptor record. The second record in the MFT is a mirror copy of the descriptor, which provides fault tolerance, should the first copy be damaged.

The third record is the log file record. All NTFS transactions are logged to a file that can be used to restore data in the event of a disk problem. The bulk of the MFT consists of records for the files and directories stored on the partition. NTFS files take the form of objects that have both user- and system-defined attributes. Attributes on NTFS partitions are more comprehensive than the few simple flags used on FAT partitions. All the information on an NTFS file is stored as attributes of that file. In fact, even the file data itself is an attribute. Unlike FAT files, the attributes of NTFS files are part of the file itself; they are not listed separately in a directory entry. Directories exist as MFT records as well, but they consist mainly of indexes listing the files in the directory—they do not contain the size, date, time, and other information about the individual files.

Thus, an NTFS drive's MFT is much more than a cluster list, like a FAT; it is actually the primary data storage structure on the partition. If a file or directory is relatively small (less than approximately 1,500 bytes), the entire file or directory might even be stored in the MFT. For larger amounts of storage, the MFT record for a file or directory contains pointers to external clusters in the partition. These external clusters are called *extents*. All the records in the MFT, including the descriptors and the log file, are capable of using extents for storage of additional attributes. The attributes of a file that are part of the MFT record are called *resident* attributes, whereas those stored in extents are called *nonresident* attributes.

NTFS 5 (NTFS 2000)

Along with Windows 2000 came a new variation of NTFS called NTFS 5 (also called NTFS 2000); NTFS 5 is also used by Windows XP. This update of the NT file system includes several new features that are exploited and even required by Windows 2000 and Windows XP. Because of this, when you install Windows 2000 or Windows XP, any existing NTFS volumes automatically are upgraded to NTFS 5 (there is no way to override this option). If you also run Windows NT versions earlier than Windows NT 4 Service Pack 4 (SP4), NT 4 is no longer capable of accessing the NTFS 5 volumes. If you want to run both NT 4 and Windows 2000 or Windows XP on the same system (as in a dual-boot configuration), you must upgrade NT 4 by installing Service Pack 4 or later. An updated NTFS.SYS driver in Service Pack 4 enables NT 4 to read from and write to NTFS 5 volumes.

New features of the NTFS 5 file system include:

■ *Disk quotas.* System administrators can limit the amount of disk space users can consume on a per-volume basis. The three quota levels are Off, Tracking, and Enforced.

- *Encryption.* NTFS 5 can automatically encrypt and decrypt files as they are read from and written to the disk (not available in Windows XP Home Edition).

- *Reparse points.* Programs can trap open operations against objects in the file system and run their own code before returning file data. This can be used to extend file system features such as mount points, which you can use to redirect data read and written from a folder to another volume or physical disk.

- *Sparse files.* This feature enables programs to create very large files as placeholders but to consume disk space by adding to the files only as necessary.

- *USN (Update Sequence Number) Journal.* Provides a log of all changes made to files on the volume.

- *Mounted drives.* You can attach volumes including drives and folders to an empty folder stored on an NTFS drive. For example, you can create a folder on one drive that allows you to access content stored on another drive.

Because these features—especially the USN Journal—are required for Windows 2000 to run, a Win2000/Server 2003 domain controller must use an NTFS 5 partition as the system volume.

NTFS Changes in Windows XP

The location of the MFT has changed in Windows XP versus Windows 2000 and Windows NT. In Windows 2000 and Windows NT, the MFT is typically located at the start of the disk space used by the NTFS file system. In Windows XP, the $logfile and $bitmap metadata files are located 3GB from the start of the disk space used by NTFS. As a result, system performance has been increased by 5%–8% in Windows XP over Windows 2000 or Windows NT.

Another improvement in Windows XP's implementation of NTFS is the amount of MFT information read into memory. During bootup, Windows XP reads only a few hundred kilobytes of MFT information if all drives are formatted with NTFS. However, if some or all of the drives are formatted with FAT32, many megabytes of information (the amount varies by the number of drives and the size of the drives) must be read during bootup. Thus, using NTFS utilizes system memory more efficiently.

NTFS Compatibility

Although NTFS partitions are not directly accessible by DOS and other operating systems, Windows NT/2000 is designed for network use, so other operating systems are expected to be capable of accessing NTFS files via the network. For this reason, NTFS continues to support the standard DOS file attributes and the 8.3 FAT naming convention.

One of the main reasons for using NTFS is the security it provides for its files and directories. NTFS security attributes are called *permissions* and are designed to enable system administrators to control access to files and directories by granting specific rights to users and groups. This is a much more granular approach than the FAT file system attributes, which apply to all users.

However, you can still set the FAT-style attributes on NTFS files using the standard Windows NT/2000 file management tools, including Windows NT/2000 Explorer and even the command-prompt ATTRIB command. When you copy FAT files to an NTFS drive over the network, the FAT-style attributes remain in place until you explicitly remove them. This can be an important consideration because the FAT-style attributes take precedence over the NTFS permissions. A file on an NTFS drive that is flagged with the FAT read-only attribute, for example, can't be deleted by a Windows NT/2000 user, even if that user has NTFS permissions that grant her full access.

To enable DOS and 16-bit Windows systems to access files on NTFS partitions over a network, the file system maintains an 8.3 alias name for every file and directory on the partition. The algorithm for deriving the alias from the long filename is the same as that used by Windows 95's VFAT. Windows NT/2000 also provides its FAT partitions with the same type of long filename support used by VFAT, allocating additional directory entries to store the long filenames as necessary.

Creating NTFS Drives

NTFS is for use on hard disk drives. You can't create an NTFS floppy disk (although you can format some removable media, such as Iomega Zip and Jaz cartridges to use NTFS). Three basic ways to create an NTFS disk partition are as follows:

- Create a new NTFS volume out of unpartitioned disk space during the Windows NT/2000 installation process or after the installation with the Disk Administrator utility.

- Format an existing partition to NTFS (destroying its data in the process), using the Windows NT Format dialog box (accessible from Windows NT Explorer or Disk Administrator) or the FORMAT command (with the /fs:ntfs switch) from the command prompt.

- Convert an existing FAT partition to NTFS (preserving its data) during the Windows NT/2000 installation process or after the installation with the command-line CONVERT utility.

NTFS Tools

Because it uses a fundamentally different architecture, virtually none of the troubleshooting techniques outlined earlier in this chapter are applicable when dealing with NTFS partitions, nor can the disk utilities intended for use on FAT partitions address them. Windows NT has a rudimentary capability to check a disk for file system errors and bad sectors with its own version of CHKDSK, but apart from that, the operating system contains no other disk repair or defragmentation utilities. Windows 2000 and Windows XP include a command-line and GUI version of CHKDSK and also include a defragmenting tool that is run from the Windows Explorer GUI. Windows XP Professional also includes DSKPROBE, a direct disk sector editor, in its Windows Support Tools (the Windows 2000 Resource Kit also contains DSKPROBE).

One difference between Windows 2000/XP's CHKDSK and Windows 9x/Me's SCANDISK is that CHKDSK cannot fix file system errors if it is run within the Windows GUI. If you run CHKDSK and select the Automatically Fix File System Errors option, you must schedule CHKDSK to run at the next system startup. You can run CHKDSK without this option to find file system problems; you can also run CHKDSK within the Windows GUI to look for and attempt to fix bad sectors.

Tip

You can use the **FSUTIL** command-line program in Windows 2000 and Windows XP to learn more about a particular drive's file system, including whether you need to run CHKDSK or a third-party disk repair tool. For example, to determine whether drive D: is *dirty* (has file system errors requiring repair), you would open a Windows 2000/XP command prompt and enter this command:

FSUTIL DIRTY QUERY D:

For more examples of **FSUTIL** commands and syntax, enter **FSUTIL** with no options at a Windows 2000/XP command prompt.

The NTFS file system, however, does have its own automatic disk repair capabilities. In addition to Windows NT/2000/XP's fault-tolerance features, such as disk mirroring (maintaining the same data on two separate drives) and disk striping with parity (splitting data across several drives with parity information for data reconstruction), the OS has two features to help improve reliability:

- Transaction management
- Cluster remapping

NTFS can roll back any *transaction* (its term for a change to a file stored on an NTFS volume) if it isn't completed properly due to disk errors, running out of memory, or errors such as removing media or disconnecting a device before the transaction process is complete. Each transaction has five steps:

1. NTFS creates a log file of the metadata operations of the transaction (file updates, erasure, and so on) and caches the file in system memory.

2. NTFS stores the actual metadata operations in memory.

3. NTFS marks the transaction record in the log file as committed.

4. NTFS saves the log file to disk after the transaction is complete.

5. NTFS saves the actual metadata operations to disk after the transaction is complete.

This process is designed to prevent random data (lost clusters) on NTFS drives.

With cluster remapping, when Windows (NT/2000/XP) detects a bad sector on an NTFS partition, it automatically remaps the data in that cluster to another cluster. If the drive is part of a fault-tolerant drive array, any lost data is reconstructed from the duplicate data on the other drives.

Despite these features, however, there is still a real need for third-party disk repair and defragmentation utilities for Windows NT/2000/XP. These were scarce when Windows NT was first released, but third-party utilities that can repair and defragment NTFS drives are now widely available. One I recommend is Norton Utilities 2004 (also included in Norton SystemWorks 2004) by Symantec, which works with Windows 98, Windows Me, Windows 2000, and Windows XP. Earlier versions work with Windows NT 4.0 and Windows 95. If you are looking for even faster defragmentation, Golden Bow's VoptXP (which also supports Windows 9x, Me, and 2000) is a longtime favorite.

High Performance File System

The High Performance File System (HPFS) was first introduced in OS/2 version 1.2 and included many additional features over the existing FAT16 system available at the time. HPFS was also supported in Windows NT 3.x versions but not any later versions. In many ways, HPFS was the predecessor to the NTFS that later debuted in Windows NT.

For more information about HPFS, see the Technical Reference section of the disc packaged with this book.

File System Utilities

The CHKDSK, RECOVER, and SCANDISK commands are the DOS damaged-disk recovery team. These commands are crude, and their actions sometimes are drastic, but at times they are all that is available or necessary. RECOVER is best known for its function as a data recovery program, and CHKDSK typically is used for inspection of the file structure. Many users are unaware that CHKDSK can implement repairs to a damaged file structure. DEBUG, a crude, manually controlled program, can help in the case of a disk disaster—if you know exactly what you are doing.

SCANDISK is a safer, more automated, more powerful replacement for CHKDSK and RECOVER in Windows 9x/Me. Windows 2000 and XP do not include SCANDISK and instead have beefed up CHKDSK to handle NTFS.

If you are using MS-DOS 5.0 or older, the only disk testing utilities supplied with your version of MS-DOS are CHKDSK and RECOVER. To learn more about how CHKDSK works, see *Upgrading and Repairing PCs, 11th Edition*, included in electronic form on the disc packaged with this book.

The RECOVER Command

The DOS RECOVER command is designed to mark clusters as bad in the FAT when the clusters can't be read properly. When the system can't read a file because of a problem with a sector on the disk going bad, the RECOVER command can mark the FAT so another file does not use those clusters. When used improperly, this program is highly dangerous. The RECOVER utility has not been included in DOS since version 5 and is not supplied in Windows 9x/Me because its functionality has been replaced by SCANDISK.

Caution

Be very careful when you use **RECOVER**. Used improperly, it can do severe damage to your files and the FAT. If you enter the **RECOVER** command without a filename for it to work on, the program assumes you want every file on the disk recovered and operates on every file and subdirectory on the disk. It converts all subdirectories to files, places all filenames in the root directory, and gives them new names (**FILE0000.REC**, **FILE0001.REC**, and so on). This process essentially wipes out the file system on the entire disk. Do not use **RECOVER** without providing a filename for it to work on. This program should be considered as dangerous as the **FORMAT** command. **RECOVER** is so notorious for this behavior that older versions of the Norton Utilities had a Recover from DOS RECOVER option that could sometimes undo the damage caused by improper use of **RECOVER**.

An improved version of RECOVER that recovers data from a specified file is only one of the command-line programs provided with Windows NT, 2000, and XP. To use this version of RECOVER, which works with both FAT and NTFS file systems, open a command prompt and enter the command as shown here:

```
RECOVER (drive\folder\filename)
```

For example, to recover all readable sectors from a file called Mynovel.txt stored in C:\My Documents\Writings, you would enter the following command:

```
RECOVER C:\My Documents\Writings\Mynovel.txt
```

Because the NT/2000/XP version of RECOVER requires you to specify a filename and path, it cannot destroy a file system the way the DOS RECOVER command could. However, you should not use wildcards with the NT/2000/XP version of RECOVER. Instead, specify a single filename as shown in this example, or use a third-party tool such as Norton Disk Doctor to check the drive and attempt data recovery from damaged files.

SCANDISK

You should check your FAT partitions regularly for the problems discussed in this chapter and any other difficulties that might arise. By far an easier and more effective solution for disk diagnosis and repair than CHKDSK and RECOVER is the SCANDISK utility, included with DOS 6 and higher versions, as well as with Windows 9x/Me. This program is more thorough and comprehensive than CHKDSK or RECOVER and can perform the functions of both of them—and a great deal more.

Note

The equivalent of **SCANDISK** in Windows NT/2000 and Windows XP is called **CHKDSK**, but it is far more powerful than the old MS-DOS **CHKDSK** program. For more information on the old MS-DOS **CHKDSK** program, see *Upgrading and Repairing PCs, 12th Edition*, included in its entirety on the disc accompanying this book.

SCANDISK is similar to a scaled-down version of third-party disk repair programs such as Norton Disk Doctor, and it can verify both file structure and disk sector integrity. If SCANDISK finds problems, it can repair directories and FATs. If the program finds bad sectors in the middle of a file, it marks the clusters (allocation units) containing the bad sectors as bad in the FAT and attempts to read the file data by rerouting around the defect.

Windows 9x includes both DOS and Windows versions of SCANDISK, which are named SCANDISK.EXE and SCANDSKW.EXE, respectively. Windows scans your drives at the beginning of the operating system installation process and automatically loads the DOS version of SCANDISK whenever you restart your system after turning it off without completing the proper shutdown procedure. You can also launch SCANDISK.EXE from a DOS prompt or from a batch file using the following syntax:

```
Scandisk x: [/a] [/n] [/p] [dblspace.nnn/drvspace.nnn]
x: - designator of the drive that you want to scan
/a - scans all local fixed hard disks
/n - noninteractive mode; requires no user input
```

```
/p - scans only, without correcting errors
/custom - runs Scandisk with the options configured in the
➥[CUSTOM] section of the Scandisk.ini file
dblspace.nnn or drvspace.nnn - scans a compressed volume file,
➥where nnn is replaced by the file extension (such as 001)
```

The SCANDISK.INI file, located in the C:\WINDOWS\COMMAND directory on a Windows system by default, contains extensive and well-documented parameters you can use to control the behavior of SCANDISK.EXE. Note that the options in the SCANDISK.INI file are applied only to the DOS version of the utility and have no effect on the Windows GUI version.

You also can run the GUI version of the utility by opening the Start menu and selecting Programs, Accessories, System Tools. Both versions scan and repair the FAT and the directory and file structures, repair problems with long filenames, and scan volumes that have been compressed with DriveSpace or DoubleSpace.

SCANDISK provides two basic testing options: Standard and Thorough. The difference between the two is that the Thorough option causes the program to scan the entire surface of the disk for errors in addition to the items just mentioned. You also can select whether to run the program interactively or let it automatically repair any errors it finds.

The DOS and Windows versions of SCANDISK also test the FAT in different ways. The DOS version scans and, if necessary, repairs the primary copy of the file allocation table. After this, it copies the repaired version of the primary to the backup copy. The Windows version, however, scans both copies of the FAT. If the program finds discrepancies between the two copies, it uses the data from the copy that it judges to be correct and reassembles the primary FAT using the best data from both copies. If the FAT information is not reconstructed correctly, some or all of your data might become inaccessible.

SCANDISK also has an Advanced Options dialog box that enables you to set the following parameters:

- Whether the program should display a summary of its findings
- Whether the program should log its findings
- How the program should repair cross-linked files (two directory entries pointing to the same cluster)
- How the program should repair lost file fragments
- Whether to check files for invalid names, dates, and times

Although SCANDISK is good, and is certainly a vast improvement over the old DOS CHKDSK, I recommend using one of the commercial packages, such as the Norton Utilities (included with Norton SystemWorks), for any major disk problems. These utilities go far beyond what is included in DOS or Windows.

Disk Defragmentation

The entire premise of the FAT file systems is based on the storage of data in clusters that can be located anywhere on the disk. This enables the computer to store a file of nearly any size at any time. The process of following a FAT chain to locate all the clusters holding the data for a particular file can force the hard disk drive to access many locations on the disk. Because of the physical work involved in moving the disk drive heads, reading a file that is heavily fragmented in this way is slower than reading one that is stored on consecutive clusters.

As you regularly add, move, and delete files on a disk over a period of time, the files become increasingly fragmented, which can slow down disk performance. You can relieve this problem by periodically running a disk defragmentation utility on your drives, such as the one included with Windows 9x. When you run Disk Defragmenter, the program reads each of the files in the disk, using the FAT table to access its clusters, wherever they might be located.

The program then writes the file to a series of contiguous clusters and deletes the original. By progressively reading, erasing, and writing files, the program eventually leaves the disk in a state where all its files exist on contiguous clusters. As a result, the drive is capable of reading any file on the disk with a minimum of head movement, thus providing what is often a noticeable performance increase.

The Windows Defragmentation utility provides this basic defragmenting function. It also enables you to select whether you want to arrange the files on the disk to consolidate the empty clusters into one contiguous free space (which takes longer). The Windows 98/Me version adds a feature that examines the files on the disk and arranges them with the most frequently used program files grouped together at the front of the disk, which can make programs load more quickly.

To show how defragmenting works, see the example of a fragmented file shown in Table 25.29.

Table 25.29   Fragmented File

Directory		
Name	**Starting Cluster**	**Size**
PLEDGE.TXT	1002	2
USCONST.TXT	1000	4

FAT16 File Allocation Table		
FAT Cluster #	**Value**	**Meaning**
00002	0	First cluster available
...	...	...
00999	0	Cluster available
01000	1001	In use, points to next cluster
01001	1004	In use, points to next cluster
01002	1003	In use, points to next cluster
01003	FFFFh	End of file
01004	1005	In use, points to next cluster
01005	FFFFh	End of file
...	...	...
65526	0	Last cluster available

In the preceding example, the file USCONST.TXT is fragmented in two pieces. If you ran a defragmenting program, the files would be read off the disk and rewritten in a contiguous fashion. One possible outcome is shown in Table 25.30.

Table 25.30   Defragmented File

Directory		
Name	**Starting Cluster**	**Size**
PLEDGE.TXT	1004	2
USCONST.TXT	1000	4

Table 25.30   Continued

	FAT16 File Allocation Table	
FAT Cluster #	**Value**	**Meaning**
00002	0	First cluster available
...	...	...
00999	0	Cluster available
01000	1001	In use, points to next cluster
01001	1002	In use, points to next cluster
01002	1003	In use, points to next cluster
01003	FFFFh	End of file
01004	1005	In use, points to next cluster
01005	FFFFh	End of file
...	...	...
65526	0	Last cluster available

Although it doesn't look like much was changed, you can see that now both files are in one piece, stored one right after the other. Because defragmenting involves reading and rewriting a possibly large number of files on your drive, it can take a long time, especially if you have a large drive with a lot of fragmented files and not very much free working space on the drive.

Third-party defragmentation utilities, such as the Speed Disk program included in the Norton Utilities, provide additional features, such as the capability to select specific files that should be moved to the front of the disk. Speed Disk also can defragment the Windows swap file and files that are flagged with the system and hidden attributes, which Disk Defragmenter will not touch.

Caution

Although the disk-defragmentation utilities included with Windows and third-party products are usually quite safe, you should always be aware that defragmenting a disk is an inherently dangerous procedure. The program reads, erases, and rewrites every file on the disk and has the potential to cause damage to your data when interrupted improperly. Although I have never seen a problem result from the process, an unforeseen event—such as a power failure—during a defragmentation procedure can conceivably be disastrous. I strongly recommend that you always run a disk-repair utility, such as SCANDISK, on your drives before defragmenting them and have a current backup ready.

Windows NT 4.0 does not include a defragmentation utility, but Windows 2000 and Windows XP do include such a utility. Note that third-party defragmentation utilities available for recent and current versions of Windows, such as Golden Bow Systems's VoptXP (www.vopt.com), are often faster and offer more features than Windows's own defragmentation programs.

Third-Party Programs

When you get a Sector not found error reading drive C:, the best course of action is to use one of the third-party disk-repair utilities on the market, rather than DOS's RECOVER or even SCANDISK. The Norton Utilities by Symantec (also included in Norton SystemWorks) stands as perhaps the premier data recovery package on the market today. This package is comprehensive and automatically repairs most types of disk problems.

Norton Utilities and Norton SystemWorks

Programs such as Norton Disk Doctor can perform much more detailed repairs with a greater amount of safety. Disk Doctor preserves as much of the data in the file as possible and can mark the FAT so the bad sectors or clusters of the disk are not used again. These programs also save Undo information, enabling you to reverse any data recovery operation.

Disk Doctor is part of Symantec's Norton Utilities package, which includes a great many other useful tools. For example, Norton Utilities has an excellent sector editor (Norton Disk Editor) that enables you to view and edit any part of a disk, including the master and volume boot records, FATs, and other areas that fall outside the disk's normal data area. Currently, no other program is as comprehensive or as capable of editing disks at the sector level. The disk editor included with Norton Utilities can give the professional PC troubleshooter or repairperson the ability to work directly with any sector on the disk, but this does require extensive knowledge of sector formats and disk structures. The documentation with the package is excellent and can be very helpful if you are learning data recovery on your own.

Note

Data recovery is a lucrative service that the more advanced technician can provide. People are willing to pay much more to get their data back than to replace a hard drive.

You also can create a rescue disk for restarting your system and testing the drive in case of emergencies, unerase accidentally deleted files (even if the Recycle Bin was bypassed), and unformat accidentally formatted drives.

Norton Utilities is now available in version 2004 as part of Norton SystemWorks 2004 (for Windows 98/Me/NT/2000/XP). SystemWorks 2004 also includes Norton Anti-Virus and Norton CleanSweep Uninstaller; the Professional version also includes Norton Ghost disk imaging software. Some of the programs provided with Norton Utilities are designed to be run from the command line or from a DOS prompt, such as the following:

- Norton Disk Doctor (NDD.EXE)
- Disk Editor (DISKEDIT.EXE)
- UnErase (UNERASE.EXE)
- UnFormat (UNFORMAT.EXE)
- Rescue Restore (RESCUE.EXE)

Most Norton Utilities programs are designed to be run from within the Windows GUI, and several of the utilities include both Windows and command-prompt versions. You should be careful when using older versions of Norton Utilities, such as version 8.0 (designed for Windows 3.1 and MS-DOS), with 32-bit versions of Windows because of the possibility of data loss due to a lack of support for long filenames and large drives.

File Systems and Third-Party Disk Utilities

The most important consideration when you purchase third-party disk utilities is to choose products that support your file system. For example, Norton Utilities supports both FAT (including FAT32) and NTFS files systems. On the other hand, SpinRite 5 supports all FAT file systems but not NTFS. Never use a disk utility not designed for your file system, and never use an out-of-date disk utility (designed for an earlier operating system) on your disk. In both cases, you could cause irreparable damage to the data on your drive.

Data Recovery

Recovering lost data can be as simple as opening the Windows Recycle Bin, or it might require spending hundreds of dollars on specialized data recovery software or services. In the worst-case scenario, you might even need to send your drive to a data recovery center. Several factors affect the degree of difficulty you can have in recovering your data, including

- How the data was deleted
- Which file system was used by the drive on which the data was stored
- Whether the drive uses magnetic, optical, magneto-optical, or flash memory to store data
- Which version of Windows or other OS you use
- Whether you already have data-protection software installed on your system
- Whether the drive has suffered physical damage to heads, platters, or its circuit board

The Windows Recycle Bin and File Deletion

The simplest data recovery of all takes place when you send files to the Windows Recycle Bin (a standard part of Windows since Windows 95). Pressing the Delete key when you have a file or group of files highlighted in Windows Explorer or My Computer or clicking the Delete button sends files to the Recycle Bin. Although a file sent to the Recycle Bin is no longer listed in its normal location by Windows Explorer, the file is actually protected from being overwritten. By default, Windows 95 and above reserve 10% of the disk space on each hard disk for the Recycle Bin (removable-media drives don't have a Recycle Bin). Thus, a 10GB drive reserves about 1GB for its Recycle Bin. In this example, as long as less than 1GB of files has been sent to the Recycle Bin, a so-called deleted file is protected by Windows. However, after more than 1GB of files has been sent to the Recycle Bin, Windows allows the oldest files to be overwritten. Thus, the quicker you realize that a file has been sent to the Recycle Bin, the more likely it is you can retrieve it.

To retrieve a file from the Recycle Bin, open the Recycle Bin, select the file, right-click it, and select Restore. Windows lists the file in its original location and removes it from the Recycle Bin.

If you hold down the Shift key when you select Delete or press the Delete key, the Recycle Bin is bypassed. Retrieving lost data at this point requires third-party data recovery software.

Recovering Files That Are Not in the Recycle Bin

The Recycle Bin is a useful first line of defense against data loss, but it is quite limited. As you learned in the previous section, it can be bypassed when you select files for deletion, and files stored in the Recycle Bin are eventually kicked out by newer deleted files. Also, the Recycle Bin isn't used for files deleted from a command prompt or when an older version of a file is replaced by a newer version.

Products such as Norton UnErase (part of the Norton Utilities and Norton SystemWorks) are necessary if you want to retrieve files not in the Recycle Bin. However, the effectiveness of Norton UnErase and how you should use it depends on the version of Windows you use and the file system used by your drives.

Norton UnErase and Norton Protected Recycle Bin—Win9x/Me

With Windows 9x/Me, which use the FAT file system, retrieving data from a drive that doesn't have Norton Utilities installed isn't difficult. However, installing Norton Utilities before you start to delete files that you might want to retrieve makes it even easier. You can run Norton UnErase from the bootable CD included in current versions and run UnErase as a command-prompt program if you don't have it already installed and need to retrieve erased data. You will need to provide the first letter of each file you want to unerase.

Caution

Do *not* install data recovery software to a drive you are attempting to retrieve data from because you might overwrite the data you are attempting to retrieve. If you are trying to recover data from your Windows startup drive, install another hard disk into your system, configure it as a boot drive in the system BIOS, install a working copy of Windows on it, boot from that drive, and install your data recovery software to that drive. If possible, install a drive large enough (at least 10GB or larger) so that you have several GB of free space on it for storing recovered data.

However, if you have already installed Norton Utilities, you probably have the Norton Protected Recycle Bin on your desktop in place of the regular Recycle Bin. Compared to the Windows standard-model Recycle Bin, the Norton Protected Recycle Bin protects files that have been replaced with newer versions and files that were deleted from a command prompt. To retrieve a file stored in the Norton Protected Recycle Bin, open the Recycle Bin, select the file you want to retrieve, right-click it, and select Retrieve to put it back in its original location.

Alternatively, you can start the Norton UnErase Wizard from the Norton Utilities menu. You can search for recently deleted files (these files are stored in the Recycle Bin), all protected files on local drives (also stored in the Recycle Bin), and any recoverable files on local drives. When you select the last option, you can narrow down the search with wildcards or file types and specify which drives to search. You must supply the first letter of the filename for files that were not stored in the Recycle Bin; you can also see which files were deleted by a particular program. To undelete a file with the UnErase Wizard, select the file, provide the first letter of the filename if necessary, click Quick View to view the file (if your file viewer supports the file format), and click Recover to restore the file to its original location.

With Windows 9x/Me, you can search both hard and removable-media (floppy, flash memory) drives for lost files, although the Recycle Bin works only for hard drives.

Norton UnErase and Norton Protected Recycle Bin—Win 2000/XP

Norton UnErase and Norton Protected Recycle Bin work in a similar fashion with Windows 2000/XP as with Windows 9x/Me, but with a significant exception: The UnErase Wizard can search only hard drives. Removable-media drives are not supported.

Tip

If you want to use Norton UnErase Wizard to retrieve data from a floppy drive and don't have Windows 9x/Me installed on your system, start your computer with the Norton bootable CD and run UnErase from the CD startup menu.

If you have a dual-boot system that can run Windows 9x/Me and Windows 2000/XP and you also want to use Norton UnErase Wizard with Zip, USB, and flash memory devices, start the computer with Windows 9x/Me, install Norton Utilities or SystemWorks under Windows 9x/Me, and start your computer with Windows 9x/Me if you need to search removable media drives for lost data.

Alternatives to Norton UnErase

VCOM's System Suite 4.0 (previously sold by Ontrack) is an integrated utility suite that offers an undelete feature similar in many ways to Norton UnErase. However, System Suite's FileUndeleter works with removable-media drives as well as hard drives under all supported versions of Windows, including Windows XP.

Although it's not an automatic tool, you can use Norton's Disk Editor (DISKEDIT.COM) to retrieve lost data from hard, floppy, and most types of removable-media drives under any file system and most operating systems, including Linux. See the section "Using the Norton Disk Editor" later in this chapter.

Undeleting Files in NTFS

Because the file structure of NTFS is much more complex than any FAT file system version and some files might be compressed using NTFS's built-in compression, you should use an NTFS-specific file undeletion program to attempt to recover deleted files from an NTFS drive. For example, you should use a version of Norton Utilities or Norton SystemWorks compatible with NTFS, such as the 2002 or later versions. Also, you should enable the Norton Protection feature, which stores deleted files for a specified period of time before purging them from the system. Using Norton Protection will greatly enhance Norton UnErase's capability to recover deleted files.

If you need to recover deleted files and have not already installed an undelete program such as Norton Utilities or Norton SystemWorks's Norton UnErase, you should consider a standalone file recovery program, such as

- *Active Undelete.* This series of products also works with flash memory cards; more information and a free demo are available from http://www.active-undelete.com.

- *Restorer 2000.* Available in FAT, NTFS, and Professional versions; more information and a free demo are available from http://www.bitmart.net/r2k.shtml.

- *Ontrack EasyRecovery.* More information and a free demo are available from http://www.ontrack.com.

Tip

Some file-undelete products for NTFS can undelete only files created by the currently logged-in user, whereas others require the administrator to be logged in. Check the documentation for details, particularly if you are trying to undelete files from a system with more than one user.

Retrieving Data from Partitioned and Formatted Drives

When a hard disk, floppy disk, or removable-media drive has been formatted, its file allocation table, which is used by programs such as Norton UnErase or VCOM System Suite's FileUndeleter to determine the location of files, is lost. If a hard drive has been repartitioned with FDISK or another partitioning program (such as Windows 2000/XP's Disk Management), the original file system and partition information is lost (as is the FAT).

In such cases, more powerful data-recovery tools must be used to retrieve data. To retrieve data from an accidentally formatted drive, you have two options:

- Use a program that can unformat the drive.

- Use a program that can bypass the newly created FAT and read disk sectors directly to discover and retrieve data.

To retrieve data from a drive that has been partitioned, you must use a program that can read disk sectors directly.

Norton Unformat and Its Limitations

Norton Utilities and Norton SystemWorks offer Norton Unformat, which can be launched from the bootable CD to unformat an accidentally formatted FAT drive. However, Norton Unformat has significant limitations with today's file systems and drive types, including the following:

- *Norton Unformat doesn't support NTFS drives.* This means many Windows 2000– and XP-based systems can't use it for data recovery.

- *Norton Unformat cannot be used with drives that require device drivers to function, such as removable-media drives.*

- *Norton Unformat works best if the Norton Image program has been used to create a copy of the FATs and root directory.* If the image file is out-of-date, Unformat might fail; if the image file is not present, Unformat cannot restore the root directory and the actual names of folders in the root directory will be replaced by sequentially numbered folder names.

- *Norton Unformat cannot copy restored files to another drive or folder.* It restores data back to the same drive and partition. If Unformat uses an out-of-date file created by Norton Image to determine where data is located, it could overwrite valid data on the drive being unformatted.

For these reasons, Norton Unformat is not the most desirable method for unformatting a drive. You can use the powerful, but completely manual, Norton Disk Editor (DISKEDIT) to unformat a drive or retrieve data from a formatted drive, but other alternatives are simpler.

Retrieving Lost Data to Another Drive

Many products on the market can retrieve lost data to another drive, whether the data loss was due to accidental formatting or disk partitioning. One of the best and most comprehensive products is the EasyRecovery product line from Ontrack DataRecovery Services, a division of Kroll Ontrack, Inc. The EasyRecovery product line includes the following products:

- *EasyRecovery DataRecovery.* Recovers data from accidentally formatted or deleted hard, floppy, and removable-media drives and repairs damaged or corrupted Zip and Microsoft Word files. Local and network folders can be used for recovered files.

- *EasyRecovery FileRepair.* Repairs and recovers data from damaged or corrupted Zip and Microsoft Office (Word, Excel, Access, PowerPoint, and Outlook) files. Local and network folders can be used for recovered files.

- *EasyRecovery Professional.* Combines the features of DataRecovery and FileRecovery and adds features such as file type search, RawRecovery, and user-defined partition parameters to help recover data from more severe forms of file system corruption and accidental partitioning. A free trial version displays files that can be recovered (and repairs and recovers Zip files at no charge); it can be downloaded from the Ontrack Web site (http://www.ontrack.com).

An earlier version of EasyRecovery Data Recovery Lite can recover up to 50 files and is included as part of VCOM's System Suite (previously sold by Ontrack).

When you start EasyRecovery Professional, you can choose from several recovery methods, including these:

- *DeletedRecovery.* Recovers deleted files

- *FormatRecovery.* Recovers files from accidentally formatted drives

- *RawRecovery.* Recovers files with direct sector reads using file-signature matching technology

- *AdvancedRecovery.* Recovers data from deleted or corrupted partitions

In each case, you need to specify another drive to receive the retrieved data. This read-only method preserves the contents of the original drive and enables you to use a different data-recovery method if the first method doesn't recover the desired files.

Which options are best for data recovery? Table 25.31 shows the results of various data-loss scenarios and recovery options when EasyRecovery Professional was used to recover data from a 19GB logical drive formatted with the NTFS file system under Windows XP.

Table 25.31   Data Recovery Options and Results with EasyRecovery Professional

Type of Data Loss	Data Recovery Method	Data Recoverable?	Details	Notes
Deleted folder	DeletedRecovery	Yes	All files recovered.	All long file and folder names preserved.
Formatted drive (full format)	FormatRecovery	Yes	All files recovered.	New folders created to store recovered files; long filenames preserved for files and folders beneath root folder level.
Logical drive deleted with Disk Management	AdvancedRecovery	Yes	All files and folders recovered.	All long file and folder names preserved.
Formatted drive with new data copied to it	FormatRecovery	Partial	Files and folders that were not overwritten were recovered.	Long filenames and folders preserved.

Table 25.31   Continued

Type of Data Loss	Data Recovery Method	Data Recoverable?	Details	Notes
Formatted, repartitioned drive reformatted as FAT32 (117MB Disk 1)	AdvancedRecovery	No	Could not locate any files to recover.	
	RawRecovery	Partial	Nonfragmented files recovered.	Original directory structure and filenames lost; each file type stored in a separate folder and files numbered sequentially.
Formatted, repartitioned drive formatted as NTFS (18.8GB Disk 2)	AdvancedRecovery	No	Could not locate any files to recover.	
	RawRecovery	Partial	Nonfragmented files recovered.	Original directory structure and filenames lost; each file type stored in a separate folder and files numbered sequentially.

As Table 25.31 makes clear, as long as the data areas of a drive are not overwritten, complete data recovery is usually possible—even if the drive has been formatted or repartitioned. Thus, it's critical that you react quickly if you suspect you have partitioned or formatted a drive containing valuable data. The longer you wait to recover data, the less data will be available for recovery. In addition, if you must use a sector-by-sector search for data (a process called RawRecovery by Ontrack), your original folder structure and long filenames will not be saved. You will therefore need to re-create the desired directory structure and rename files after you recover them—a very tedious process.

Tip

If you use EasyRecovery Professional or EasyRecovery DataRecovery to repair damaged Zip or Microsoft Office files, use the Properties menu to select a location for repaired files (the original location or another drive or folder). By default, repaired Outlook files are copied to a different folder, whereas other file types are repaired in place unless you specify a different location.

As you can see from this example, dedicated data-recovery programs such as Ontrack EasyRecovery Professional are very powerful. However, they are also very expensive. If you have Norton Utilities or Norton SystemWorks and don't mind taking some time to learn about disk structures, you can perform data recovery with the Norton Disk Editor.

Using the Norton Disk Editor

In my PC Hardware (Upgrading and Repairing) and Data Recovery/Computer Forensics seminars, I frequently use the Norton Disk Editor—an often-neglected program that's part of the Norton Utilities and Norton SystemWorks—to explore drives. I also use Disk Editor to retrieve lost data. Because Disk Editor is a manual tool, it can sometimes be useful even when friendlier automatic programs don't work correctly or are unavailable. For example, in physical sector mode, Disk Editor can be used with any drive regardless of what file system was used, since at that level it is working underneath the OS. Additionally, because Disk Editor displays the structure of your drive in a way other programs don't, it's a perfect tool for learning more about disk drive structures as well as recovering lost data. This section discusses two of the simpler procedures you can perform with Disk Editor:

- Undeleting a file on a floppy disk
- Copying a deleted file on a hard disk to a different drive

If you have Norton SystemWorks, SystemWorks Professional, or Norton Utilities for Windows, you have Norton Disk Editor. To determine whether it's installed on your system, look in the Norton Utilities folder under the Program Files folder for the following files: DISKEDIT.EXE and DISKEDIT.HLP.

If you don't find these files on your hard disk, you can run them directly from the Norton installation CD. If you have SystemWorks or SystemWorks Professional, look for the CD folder called \NU to locate these files.

Disk Edit is a command-prompt program designed primarily to access FAT-based file systems such as FAT12 (floppy disks), FAT16 (MS-DOS and early Windows 95 hard disks), and FAT32 (Windows 95B/Windows 98/Me hard disks). You can use Disk Edit with Windows NT, Windows 2000, and Windows XP if you prepared the hard disks with the FAT16 or FAT32 file systems. Disk Edit will also work on NTFS volumes; however, in that case it can only be used in physical sector mode.

I strongly recommend that you first use Disk Editor with floppy disks you have prepared with noncritical files before you use it with a hard disk or vital files. Because Disk Editor is a completely manual program, the opportunities for error are high.

The Disk Edit files can easily fit on a floppy disk, but if you are new to the program, you might want to put them on a different drive from one you will be examining or repairing. *Never* copy Disk Edit files (or any other data recovery program) to a drive that contains data you are trying to recover because the files might overwrite the data area and destroy the files you want to retrieve. For example, if you are planning to examine or repair floppy disks, create a folder on your hard disk called Disk Edit and copy the files to that folder.

You can use Disk Editor without a mouse by using keyboard commands, but if you want to use it with a mouse, you can do so if your mouse attaches to the serial or PS/2 mouse ports (USB mice generally don't work from the command prompt, but if your USB mouse has a PS/2 mouse port adapter, you can use it by plugging the mouse and adapter into the PS/2 port). You must load an MS-DOS mouse driver (usually MOUSE.COM) for your mouse before you start Disk Editor. If you have a Logitech mouse, you can download an MS-DOS mouse driver from the Logitech Web site. If you have a Microsoft mouse, Microsoft doesn't provide MS-DOS drivers you can download, but you can get them from the following Web site:

http://www.bootdisk.com/readme.htm#mouse

For other mice, try the Microsoft or Logitech drivers, or contact the vendor for drivers. Keep in mind that scroll wheels and other buttons won't work with an MS-DOS driver.

I recommend you copy your mouse driver to the same folder in which Disk Editor is located.

Using Disk Editor to Examine a Drive

To start the program, do the following:

1. Boot the computer to a command prompt (not Windows); Disk Editor needs exclusive access to the drives you plan to examine. If you use Windows 9x, press F8 or Ctrl to bring up the startup menu and select Safe Mode Command Prompt, or use the Windows 9x/Me Emergency Startup disk (make one with Add/Remove Programs). If you use Windows 2000 or XP, insert a blank floppy disk into drive A:, right-click drive A: in My Computer, and select Format. Select the Create an MS-DOS Startup Disk option and use this disk to start your computer.

2. Change to the folder containing your mouse driver and Disk Editor.

3. Type **MOUSE** (if your mouse driver is called MOUSE.COM or MOUSE.EXE; otherwise, substitute the correct name if it's called something else). Then press Enter to load the mouse driver.

4. Type **DISKEDIT** and press Enter to start the program. If you don't specify a drive, Disk Editor scans the drive on which it's installed. If you are using it to work with a floppy disk, enter the command **DISKEDIT A:** to direct it to scan your floppy disk. Disk Editor scans your drive to determine the location of files and folders on the disk.

5. The first time you run Disk Editor, a prompt appears to remind you that Disk Editor runs in read-only mode until you change its configuration through the Tools menu. Click OK to continue.

After Disk Editor has started, you can switch to the drive you want to examine or recover data from. To change to a different drive, follow these steps:

1. Press Alt+O to open the Object menu.

2. Select Drive.

3. Select the drive you want to examine from the Logical Disks menu.

4. The disk structure is scanned and displayed in the Disk Editor window.

Disk Editor normally starts in Directory mode, but you can change it to other modes with the View menu. When you view a drive containing data in Directory mode, you will see a listing similar to the one shown in Figure 25.2.

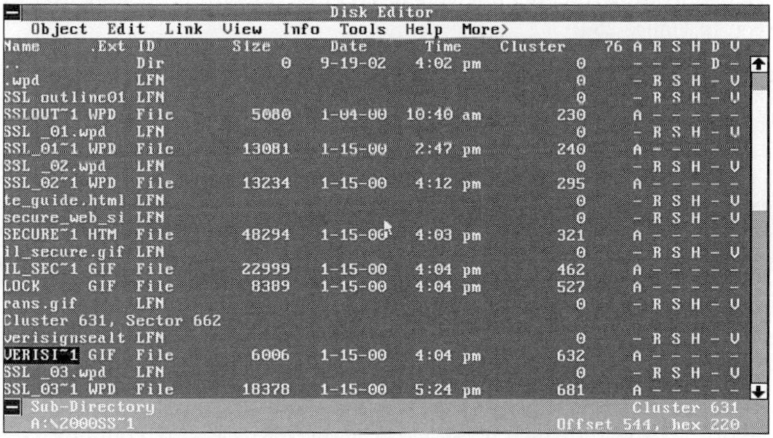

Figure 25.2 The Norton Disk Editor directory view of a typical floppy disk.

The Name column lists the names of the directory entries, and the .EXT column lists the file/folder extensions (if any). The ID column lists the type of directory entry, including

- *Dir.* A directory (folder).
- *File.* A data file.
- *LFN.* A portion of a Windows long filename. Windows stores the start of the LFN before the actual filename. If the LFN is longer than 13 characters, one or more additional directory entries is used to store the rest of the LFN. The next three columns list the file size, date, and time.

The Cluster column indicates the cluster in which the first portion of the file is located. Drives are divided into clusters or allocation units when they are formatted, and a *cluster* (allocation unit) is the smallest unit that can be used to store a file. Cluster sizes vary with the size of the drive and the file system used to format the drive.

The letters *A*, *R*, *S*, *H*, *D*, and *V* refer to attributes for each directory entry. *A* (archive) means the file hasn't been backed up since it was last modified. *R* is used to indicate that the directory entry is read-only, and *S* indicates that the directory entry has the System attribute. *H* indicates that the directory entry has the Hidden attribute, whereas *D* indicates that the entry is a directory. Finally, *V* is the attribute for an LFN entry.

The file VERISI~1.GIF (highlighted in black near the bottom of Figure 25.2) is interesting for several reasons. The tilde (~) and number at the end of the filename indicate that the file was created with a 32-bit version of Windows. 32-bit versions of Windows (Windows 9x/Me, 2000, and XP) allow the user to save a file with a long (more than eight characters) filename (plus the three-character file extension such as .EXE, .BMP, or .GIF). In addition, long filenames can have spaces and other characters not allowed by earlier versions of Windows and MS-DOS. The process used by various versions of Windows to create LFN entries is discussed earlier in this chapter in the section called "VFAT and Long Filenames."

When you view the file in Windows Explorer or My Computer, you see the long filename. To see the DOS alias name within the Windows GUI, right-click the file and select Properties from My Computer or Windows Explorer. Or, you can use the DIR command in a command-prompt window. The LFN is stored as one or more separate directory entries just before the DOS alias name. Because the actual long name for VERISI~1.GIF (Verisignsealtrans.gif) is 21 characters, two additional directory entries are required to store the long filename (each directory entry can store up to 13 characters of an LFN), as seen in Figure 25.2.

Determining the Number of Clusters Used by a File

As discussed earlier in this chapter, an area of the disk called the file allocation table stores the starting location of the file and each additional cluster used to store the file. VERISI~1.GIF starts at cluster 632. Clusters are the smallest disk structures used to store files, and they vary in size depending on the file system used to create the disk on which the files are stored and on the size of the drive. In this case, the file is stored on a 1.44MB floppy disk, which has a cluster size of 512 bytes (one sector). The cluster size of the drive is very important to know if you want to retrieve data using Disk Editor.

To determine the cluster size of a drive, you can open a command-prompt window and run CHKDSK C: to display the allocation unit size (cluster size) and other statistics about the specified drive. You can also look up the information in Tables 25.1, 25.3, 25.5, and 25.7 in this chapter.

To determine how many clusters are used to store a file, look at the size of the file and compare it to the cluster size of the drive on which it's stored. The file VERISI~1.GIF contains 6,006 bytes. Because this file is stored on a floppy disk that has a cluster size of 512 bytes, the file must occupy several clusters. How many clusters does it occupy? To determine this, divide the file size by the number of clusters and round the result up to the next whole number. The math is shown in Table 25.32.

Table 25.32   Determining the Number of Clusters Used by a File

File Size (FS) of VERISI~1.GIF	Cluster Size (CS)	Result of (FS) Divided by (CS) Equals (CR)	(CR) Rounded Up to Next Whole Number
6,006	512	11.73046875	12

From these calculations, you can see that VERISI~1.GIF uses 12 clusters on the floppy disk; it would use fewer clusters on a FAT16 or FAT32 hard disk (the exact number depends on the file system and size of the hard disk). The more clusters a file contains, the greater the risk is that some of its data area could be overwritten by newer data if the file is deleted. Consequently, if you need to undelete a file that was not sent to the Windows Recycle Bin or was deleted from a removable-media drive or floppy drive (these types of drives don't support the Recycle Bin), the sooner you attempt to undelete the file, the more likely it is that you can retrieve the data.

The normal directory display in Norton Disk Editor shows the starting cluster (632) for VERISI~1.GIF. If a file is stored on a drive with a lot of empty space, the remainder of the clusters will probably immediately follow the first two—a badly fragmented drive might use noncontiguous clusters to store the rest of the file. Because performing data recovery when the clusters are contiguous is much easier, I strongly recommend that you defragment your drives frequently.

To see the remainder of the clusters used by a file, move the cursor to the file, press Alt+L or click the Link menu, and select Cluster Chain (FAT); you can also press Ctrl+T to go directly to this view. The screen changes to show the clusters as listed in the FAT for this file, as shown in Figure 25.3. The clusters used by the file are highlighted in red, and the filename is shown at the bottom of the screen. The symbol <EOF> stands for *end of file*, indicating the last cluster in the file.

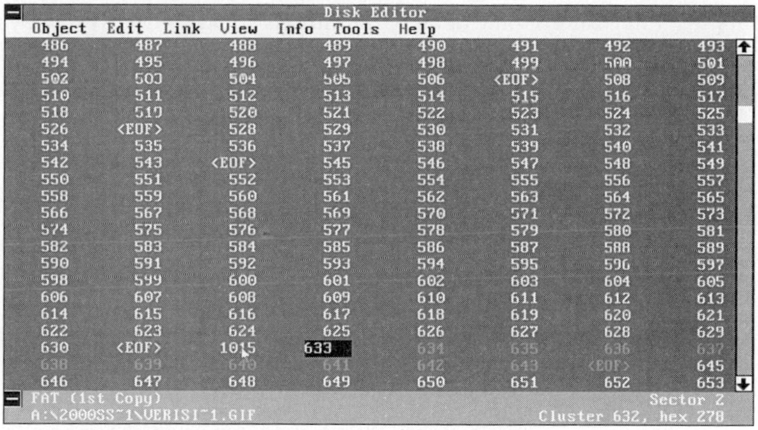

Figure 25.3   The FAT view of VERISI~1.GIF. All its clusters are contiguous.

How the Operating System Marks a File When It Is Deleted

If a file (VERISI~1.GIF, in this example) is deleted, the following changes happen to the disk where the file is stored, as shown in Figure 25.4:

- The default directory view shows that the first character of the filename (V) has been replaced with a σ (lowercase sigma) character.

- There are now two new types of entries in the ID column for this file and its associated LFN:
  - Erased. An erased file
  - *Del LFN.* An LFN belonging to an erased file

Note also that the beginning cluster (632) is still shown in the Cluster column.

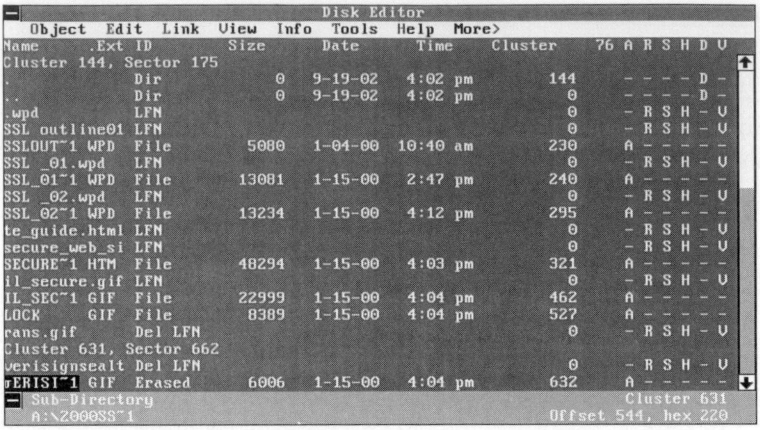

Figure 25.4 The Directory view after `VERISI~1.GIF` has been deleted.

Zeroes have also replaced the entries for the cluster locations after the beginning cluster in the FAT. This indicates to the operating system that these clusters are now available for reuse. Thus, if an undelete process is not started immediately, some or all of the clusters could be overwritten by new data. Because the file in question is a GIF graphics file, the loss of even one cluster will destroy the file.

As you can see from analyzing the file-deletion process, the undelete process involves four steps:

■ Restoring the original filename

■ Locating the clusters used by the file

■ Re-creating the FAT entries for the file

■ Relinking the LFN entries for the file to the file

Of these four, the most critical are locating the clusters used by the file and re-creating the FAT entries for the file. However, if the file is a program file, restoring the original name is a must for proper program operation (assuming the program can't be reloaded), and restoring the LFN entries enables a Windows user accustomed to long filenames to more easily use the file.

If you want to make these changes to the original disk, Disk Editor must be configured to work in Read-Write mode.

To change to Read-Write mode, follow these steps:

1. Press Alt+T to open the Tools menu.

2. Press N to open the Configuration dialog box.

3. Press the spacebar to clear the check mark in the Read Only option box.

4. Press the Tab key until the Save box is highlighted.

5. Press Enter to save the changes and return to the main display.

Caution

As a precaution, I recommend that you use DISKCOPY to make an exact sector-by-sector copy of a floppy disk before you perform data recovery on it, and you should work with the copy of the disk, not the original. By working with a copy, you keep the original safe from any problems you might have; plus, you can make another copy if you need to.

After you change to Read-Write mode, Disk Editor stays in this mode and uses Read-Write mode every time you use it. To change back to Read-Only mode, repeat the previously listed steps but check the Read-Only box. If you are using Disk Editor in Read-Write mode, you will see the message Drive x is Locked when you scan a drive.

Undeleting an Erased File

After you have configured Disk Editor to work in Read-Write mode, you can use it to undelete a file.

To recover an erased file, follow this procedure:

1. To change to the folder containing the erased file, highlight the folder containing the erased file and press Enter. In this example, you will recover the erased file VERISI~1.GIF.

2. Place the cursor under the lowercase sigma symbol and enter the letter you want to use to rename the file.

3. If the keyboard is in Insert mode, the lowercase sigma will move to the right; press the Delete key to delete this symbol.

4. This restores the filename, but even though the ID changes from Erased to File, this does *not* complete the file-retrieval process. You must now find the rest of the clusters used by the file. To the right of the filename, the first cluster used by the file is listed.

5. To go to the next cluster used by the file, press Ctrl+T to open the Cluster Chain command. Because you changed the name of the file, you are prompted to write the changes to the disk before you can continue. Press W or click Write to save the changes and continue.

6. Disk Editor moves to the first cluster used by the deleted file. Instead of cluster numbers, as seen earlier in Figure 25.3, each cluster contains a zero (0). Because this file uses 12 clusters, there should be 12 contiguous clusters that have been zeroed out if the file is unfragmented.

7. To determine whether these are the correct clusters for the file, press Alt+O or click Object to open the Object menu. Type **c** to open the Cluster dialog box (or press Alt+C to go to the Cluster dialog box). Enter the starting cluster number (**632** in this example) and the ending cluster number (**644** in this example). Click OK to display these clusters.

   Disk Editor automatically switches to the best view for the specified object, and in this case, the best view is the Hex view (see Figure 25.5). Note that the first entry in cluster 632 is GIF89a (as shown in the right column). Because the deleted file is a GIF file, this is what we expected. Also, a GIF file is a binary graphics file, so the rest of the information in the specified sectors should not be human-readable. Note that the end of the file is indicated by a series of 0s in several disk sectors before another file starts.

   Because the area occupied by the empty clusters (632–644) contains binary data starting with GIF89a, you can feel confident that these clusters contain the data you need.

8. To return to the FAT to fill in the cluster numbers for the file, open the Object menu and select Directory. The current directory is selected, so click OK.

9. Move the cursor down to the entry for VERISI~1.GIF, open the Link menu, and click Cluster Chain (FAT). The Cluster Chain refers to the clusters after the initial cluster (632); enter **633** in the first empty field, and continue until you enter **643** and place the cursor in the last empty field. This field needs to have the <EOF> marker placed in it to indicate the end of the file. Press Alt+E to open the Edit menu and select Mark (or press Ctrl+B). Open the Edit menu again and select Fill. Then, select End of File from the menu and click OK. Refer to Figure 25.3 to see how the FAT looks after these changes have been made.

10. To save the changes to the FAT, open the Edit menu again and select Write. When prompted to save the changes, click Write; then click Rescan the Disk.

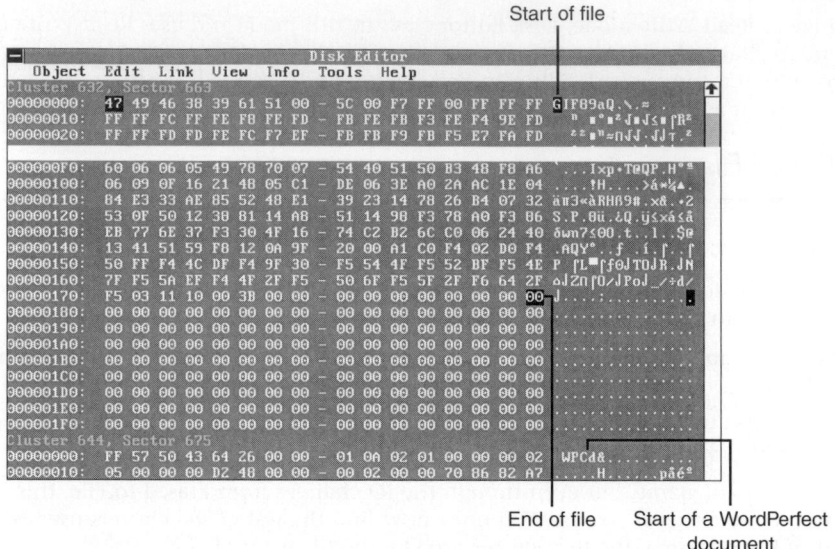

Figure 25.5   The start and end of the file VERISI~1.GIF.

11. To return to Directory view, open the Object menu and select Directory. Click OK.

12. The LFN entries directly above the VERISI~1.GIF file are still listed as Del LFN. To reconnect them to VERISI~1.GIF, select the first one (verisignsealt), open the Tools menu (press Alt+T), and select Attach LFN. Click Yes when prompted. Repeat the process for rans.gif.

13. To verify that the file has been undeleted successfully, exit Disk Editor and open the file in a compatible program. If you have correctly located the clusters and linked them, the file will open.

As you can see, this is a long process, but it is essentially the same process that a program such as Norton UnErase performs automatically. However, Disk Editor can perform these tasks on all types of disks that use FAT file systems, including those that use non-DOS operating systems; it's a favorite of advanced Linux users.

Retrieving a File from a Hard Disk or Flash Memory Card

What should you do if you need to retrieve an erased file from the hard disk or a flash memory card? It's safer to write the retrieved file to another disk (preferably a floppy disk if the file is small enough) or to a different drive letter on the hard disk. You can also perform this task with Disk Editor.

Tip

If you want to recover data from a hard disk and copy the data to another location, set Disk Editor back to its default Read-Only mode to avoid making any accidental changes to the hard disk. If you use Disk Editor in a multitasking environment such as Windows, it defaults to Read-Only mode.

The process of locating the file is the same as that described earlier:

1. Determine the cluster (allocation unit) size of the drive on which the file is located.

2. Run Disk Editor to view the name of the erased file and determine which clusters contain the file data.

However, you don't need to restore the filename because you will be copying the file to another drive.

The clusters will be copied to another file, so it's helpful to use the Object menu to look at the clusters and ensure that they contain the necessary data. To view the data stored in the cluster range, open the Object menu, select Cluster, and enter the range of clusters that the cluster chain command indicates should contain the data. In some cases, the first cluster of a particular file indicates the file type. For example, a GIF file has GIF89a at the start of the file, whereas a WordPerfect document has WPC at the start of the file.

Tip

Use Norton Disk Editor to view the starting and ending clusters of various types of files you create before you try to recover those types of files. This is particularly important if you want to recover files from formatted media. You might consider creating a database of the hex characters found at the beginning and ending of the major file types you want to recover.

If you are trying to recover a file that contains text, such as a Microsoft Word or WordPerfect file, you can switch Disk Edit into different view modes. To see text, press F3 to switch to Text view. However, to determine where a file starts or ends, use Hex mode (press F2 to switch to this mode). Figure 25.6 shows the start of a Microsoft Word file in Text format and the end of the file in Hex format.

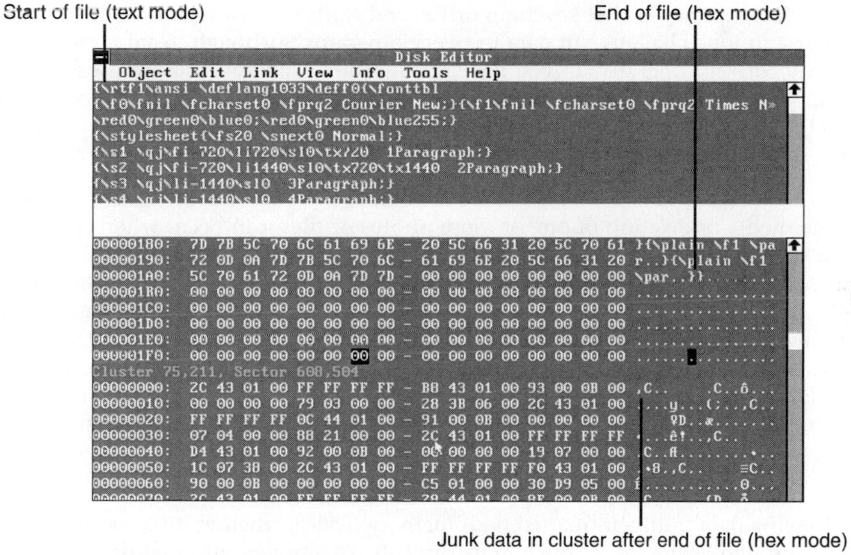

Figure 25.6 Scrolling through an erased file with Disk Editor.

To copy the contents of these clusters to a file safely, you should specify the sectors that contain the file. The top of the Disk Editor display shows the sector number as well as the cluster number. For example, the file shown in Figure 25.6 starts at cluster 75207, which is also sector 608470. The end of the file is located in sector 608503.

To write these sectors to a new file, do the following:

1. Open the Object menu.
2. Select Sector.
3. Specify the starting and ending sectors.
4. Click OK.
5. Scroll through the sectors to verify that they contain the correct data.
6. Open the Tools menu.

7. Click Write Object to.

8. Click To a File.

9. Click the drive on which you want to write the data.

10. Specify a DOS-type filename (eight characters plus a three-character extension); you can rename the file to a long filename after you exit Disk Edit.

11. Click OK, and then click Yes to write the file. A status bar appears as the sectors are copied to the file.

12. Exit Disk Edit and open the file in a compatible program. If the file contains the correct data, you're finished. If not, you might have specified incorrect sectors or the file might be fragmented.

Norton Disk Editor is a powerful tool you can use to explore drives and retrieve lost data. However, your best data recovery technique is to avoid the need for data recovery. Think before you delete files or format a drive, and make backups of important files. That way, you won't need to recover lost data very often.

Data Recovery from Flash Memory Devices

Flash memory devices such as USB keychain drives and cards used in digital cameras and digital music players present a unique challenge to data recovery programs. Although, from a user standpoint, these devices emulate conventional disk drives, have file allocation tables similar to those found on floppy disks, and can usually be formatted through the Windows Explorer, many data recovery programs that work well with conventional drives cannot be used to recover data from flash memory devices—especially when the device has been formatted.

Under several conditions, data loss can occur with a flash memory device. Some of them, such as formatting of the media or deletion of one or more photos or files, can occur when the device is connected to the computer through a card reader or when the flash memory device is inserted into a digital camera. When photos are deleted, the file locations and name listings in the file allocation tables are changed in the same way as when files are deleted from magnetic media: The first character of the filename is changed to a lowercase sigma (refer to Table 25.19), indicating the file has been erased. Just as with magnetic media, undelete programs that support removable-media drives and the Norton Disk Editor can be used to retrieve deleted files on flash memory devices in the same way that they retrieve deleted files from magnetic media. Note that Disk Editor must be run in read-only mode and works best on systems running Windows 9x/Me. Data files can also be damaged if the flash memory card is removed from a device before the data-writing process is complete.

However, retrieving data from a formatted flash memory device, whether it has been formatted by a digital camera or through Windows, is much more difficult. Traditional unformat programs such as the command-line Norton Unformat program provided with Norton Utilities and Norton SystemWorks can't be used because flash memory devices are accessible only from within the Windows GUI and command-line programs are designed to work with BIOS-compatible devices such as hard and floppy drives.

Note

When a digital camera formats a flash memory card, it usually creates a folder in which photos are stored. Some cameras might also create another folder for storing drivers or other information.

If you need to recover data from a formatted flash memory device, the following programs work extremely well:

- *Ontrack EasyRecovery Professional Edition*; free evaluation and more information are available from http://www.ontrack.com

- *PhotoRescue*; free evaluation and more information are available from http://www.datarescue.com/photorescue/

Norton Disk Editor (incorporated into Norton SystemWorks, and Norton SystemWorks Pro) can also be used to recover data if you can determine the starting and ending clusters used by the data stored on the device.

To recover data from a formatted flash memory card with EasyRecovery Professional Edition, the RawRecovery option (which recovers data on a sector-by-sector basis) must be used. This option bypasses the file system and can be used on all supported media types. A built-in file viewer enables you to determine whether the recovered data is readable.

PhotoRescue, which works only with standard photo image types such as JPG, BMP, and TIF, can access the media in either logical drive mode (which worked quite well in our tests) or physical drive mode. Physical mode uses a sector-by-sector recovery method somewhat similar to that used by EasyRecovery Professional Edition. PhotoRescue also displays recovered photos in a built-in viewer.

With both products, you might recover data from not just the most recent use before format, but also leftover data from previous uses. As long as the data area used by a particular file hasn't been overwritten, the data can be recovered— even if the device has been formatted more than once.

Table 25.33 provides an overview of our results when trying to recover data from two common types of flash memory devices: a Compact Flash card used in digital cameras and a USB keychain storage device.

Table 25.33   Retrieving Lost Data from Flash Memory Devices

| | | | Results by Data-Recovery Program | | |
Device	Cause of Data Loss	Norton Utilities	Ontrack/Vcom System Suite	DataRescue Photo Rescue	Ontrack EasyRecovery Professional
Compact Flash 64MB	Deleted selected files in camera	Recovered data back to device when used with Windows 9x/ Me only.[1, 2]	Recovered data to user-specified folder.[1, 3]	Recovered data from most recent format and from previous card uses to specified folder.[3, 4]	RawRecovery recovered deleted files from current and previous uses; refer to Table 24.35 for limitations.[3, 4]
Compact Flash 64MB	Deleted selected files with Windows Explorer	Recovered data back to device when used with Windows 9x/ Me only.[1,2]	Recovered data to specified folder when used with any supported version of Windows.[3]	Recovered data from most recent format and from previous card uses to specified folder (files and folders renamed).	DeletedRecovery recovered deleted data from current use (first character of file/folder name lost).
Compact Flash 64MB	Format in camera	Drive could not be unformatted; Disk Edit could retrieve data from current and previous uses to user-specified folder.[3, 5, 6]	Could not locate data. No data was recovered.	Recovered data from most recent format and from previous card uses to user-specified folder.[3, 4]	RawRecovery recovered all readable data, including data from previous card uses to user-specified folder.[3, 4]
Compact Flash 64MB	Format in card reader	Drive could not be unformatted; Disk Edit could retrieve data from current and previous uses.[5, 6]	Could not locate data. No data was recovered.	Recovered data from most recent format and from previous card uses to user-specified folder.[4]	RawRecovery recovered all readable data, including data from previous card uses to user-specified folder.[4]

Table 25.33   Continued

| | | | Results by Data-Recovery Program | | |
| | Cause of | | Ontrack/Vcom | DataRescue | Ontrack EasyRecovery |
Device	Data Loss	Norton Utilities	System Suite	Photo Rescue	Professional
USB keychain drive (128MB)	Deleted folder with My Computer	Disk Edit can retrieve data from current use.[3, 6]	Partial success: Recovered some files.[3]	We recovered photo files only.[3, 4]	RawRecovery retrieved most files.[3, 4]
USB keychain drive (128MB)	Formatted by Windows Explorer	Disk Edit can retrieve data from current use.[3, 6]	Partial success: Recovered some files (folder names and structure lost).[3]	Recovered photo files only.[3, 4]	RawRecovery retrieved most files.[3, 4]

1. *User supplied first letter of filename during undelete process.*
2. *Norton UnErase doesn't support removable-media drives in Windows NT/2000/XP.*
3. *Program operates in read-only mode on the drive containing the lost data.*
4. *Original file and folder names were not retained; files are numbered sequentially and might need to be renamed after recovery.*
5. *Windows must be used to access flash memory devices, and Norton Unformat can't be used in a multitasking environment such as Windows.*
6. *Disk Edit requires the user to manually locate the starting and ending sectors of each file and write the sectors to another drive with a user-defined filename.*

Common Drive Error Messages and Solutions

Several common error messages are associated with problems in the file system or drives. This section covers the common ones, listing their causes and possible solutions.

Some of the most common file system errors are as follows:

- Missing Operating System
- NO ROM BASIC - SYSTEM HALTED
- Boot Error Press F1 to Retry

- Invalid Drive Specification
- Invalid Media Type
- Hard Disk Controller Failure

These usually occur when booting the system or when trying to log in to or access a drive. The following sections describe each of these errors and offer possible solutions.

Missing Operating System

This error indicates problems in the master boot record or partition table entries. The partition table entries might be pointing to a sector that is not the actual beginning of a partition. This can also be caused by invalid BIOS settings, in some cases resulting from a dead or dying battery. In fact, in my experience, corrupt or improper BIOS settings—such as incorrect geometry (cylinder/head/sector) or LBA mode settings—are the leading cause of this problem. Another cause can be virus damage to the MBR. This error also can occur if no active partition is defined in the partition table.

The normal solution is to correct the invalid BIOS settings. The BIOS settings for drive parameters and LBA translation must be set to the same values as when the drive was partitioned and formatted to read the drive correctly. If the MBR on a FAT drive is damaged or virus infected, you can try FDISK /MBR to repair it. Use FIXMBR with an NTFS drive. Other types of damage require more sophisticated use of a disk editor utility or repartitioning and reformatting the drive to start over.

NO ROM BASIC - SYSTEM HALTED

This error is generated by the AMI BIOS when the boot sector or master boot record of the boot drive is damaged or missing. This error also can occur if the boot device has been improperly configured or is not configured at all in the BIOS. In this case, data in the partition might be valid and undamaged, but no bootable partition exists.

IBM systems in this situation used to drop into a built-in BIOS version of BASIC, but most non-IBM BIOS manufacturers did not license this code from Microsoft. So, instead of dropping into BASIC, they displayed this cryptic message. Because the most common cause of this type of error is a failure to set at least one partition as active (bootable), the typical solution is to run FDISK and set the primary partition as active. If this is not the problem, the solution is to repair the damaged MBR or correct the improper BIOS settings.

Other possible problems include corrupted or missing drive parameters in the BIOS Setup.

Boot Error Press F1 to Retry

This error is generated by the Phoenix BIOS when the hard disk is missing a master boot record or boot sector or when there is a problem accessing the boot drive. This has the same meaning as NO ROM BASIC does on an AMI BIOS. The most common cause of this message is having no partitions defined as active (bootable). See the previous section for more information.

Invalid Drive Specification

This error occurs when you attempt to log in to a drive that has not been partitioned or for which the partition table entry has been damaged or is incorrect. Use FDISK to partition the drive or to check out the existing partitions. If they are damaged, you probably should use a data recovery utility such as the Norton Utilities to correct the problem. Such correction might require manual editing of the partition table with the Disk Edit program included with the Norton Utilities. Another solution is to repartition the drive from scratch, but this causes any existing data on the drive to be overwritten.

Invalid Media Type

This indicates the partition table is valid, but the volume boot sector, directory, or file allocation tables are corrupt, damaged, or not yet initialized. For example, this is the standard error you would receive if you tried to access a drive that had been partitioned but not yet formatted. The FORMAT command is what creates the volume boot record (VBR), file allocation tables, and directories on the disk.

The repair typically involves using a data recovery utility, such as the Norton Utilities Disk Doctor, or redoing the high-level format on the drive. Because high-level formatting does not actually destroy the data, one technique to recover is to high-level format (OS Format) the volume and then immediately unformat it using the unformat utility included with the Norton Utilities.

Hard Disk Controller Failure

This message indicates the hard disk controller has failed, the hard disk controller is not set up properly in the BIOS, or the controller can't communicate with the attached drives (such as with cable problems).

The solution is to check out the drive installation and ensure that the cables to the drive are properly installed, the drive is receiving power, it is spinning, and the BIOS Setup definitions are correct. If all these are correct, the drive, cable, or controller might be physically damaged. Replace them with known-good spares one at a time until the problem is solved.

General File System Troubleshooting for MS-DOS, Windows 9x, and Windows Me

Here are some general procedures to follow for troubleshooting drive access, file system, or boot problems:

1. Start the system using a Windows startup disk, or any bootable MS-DOS disk that contains FDISK.EXE, FORMAT.COM, SYS.COM, and SCANDISK.EXE (Windows 95B or later versions preferred).

2. If your system can't boot from the floppy, you might have more serious problems with your hardware. Check the floppy drive and the motherboard for proper installation and configuration. On some systems, the BIOS configuration doesn't list the floppy as a boot device or puts it after the hard disk. Reset the BIOS configuration to make the floppy disk the first boot device if necessary and restart your computer.

3. Run FDISK from the Windows startup disk. Select option 4 (Display Partition Information).

4. If the partitions are listed, make sure that the bootable partition (usually the primary partition) is defined as active (look for an uppercase *A* in the Status column).

5. If no partitions are listed and you do not want to recover any of the data existing on the drive now, use FDISK to create new partitions, and then use FORMAT to format the partitions. This overwrites any previously existing data on the drive.

6. If you want to recover the data on the drive and no partitions are being shown, you must use a data recovery program, such as the Norton Utilities by Symantec or Lost and Found (also by Symantec; formerly PowerQuest), to recover the data.

7. If all the partitions appear in FDISK.EXE and one is defined as active, run the SYS command as follows to restore the system files to the hard disk:

   SYS C:

8. For this to work properly, it is important that the disk you boot from be a startup disk from the same operating system (or version of Windows) you have on your hard disk.

9. You should receive the message System Transferred if the command works properly. Remove the disk from drive A:, and restart the system. If you still have the same error after you restart your computer, your drive might be improperly configured or damaged.

10. Run SCANDISK from the Windows startup disk or an aftermarket data-recovery utility, such as the Norton Utilities, to check for problems with the hard disk.

11. Using SCANDISK, perform a surface scan. If SCANDISK reports any physically damaged sectors on the hard disk, the drive might need to be replaced.

General File System Troubleshooting for Windows 2000/XP

The process for file system troubleshooting with Windows 2000/XP is similar to that used for Windows 9x. The major difference is the use of the Windows 2000/XP Recovery Console, which is clarified here:

■ If the Recovery Console was added to the boot menu, start the system normally, log in as Administrator if prompted, and select the Recovery Console.

■ If the Recovery Console was not previously added to the boot menu, start the system using the Windows CD-ROM or the Windows Setup disks. Select Repair from the Welcome to Setup menu, and then press C to start the Recovery Console when prompted.

If your system can't boot from CD-ROM or the floppy, you might have more serious problems with your hardware. Check your drives, BIOS configuration, and motherboard for proper installation and configuration. Set the floppy disk as the first boot device and the CD-ROM as the second boot device and restart the system.

After you start the Recovery Console, do the following:

1. Type **HELP** for a list of Recovery Console commands and assistance.

2. Run DISKPART to examine your disk partitions.

3. If the partitions are listed, make sure that the bootable partition (usually the primary partition) is defined as active.

4. If no partitions are listed and you do not want to recover any of the data existing on the drive now, use FDISK to create new partitions, and then use FORMAT to format the partitions. This overwrites any previously existing data on the drive.

5. If you want to recover the data on the drive and no partitions are being shown, you must use a data recovery program, such as Norton Utilities by Symantec or Lost and Found by Symantec, to recover the data.

6. If all the partitions appear in DISKPART and one is defined as active, run the FIXBOOT command as follows to restore the system files to the hard disk:

   FIXBOOT

7. Type **EXIT** to restart your system. Remove the disk from drive A: or the Windows 2000 or XP CD-ROM from the CD-ROM drive.

8. If you still have the same error after you restart your computer, your drive might be improperly configured or damaged.

9. Restart the Recovery Console and run CHKDSK to check for problems with the hard disk.

This glossary contains computer and electronics terms that are applicable to the subject matter in this book. The glossary is meant to be as comprehensive as possible on the subject of upgrading and repairing PCs. Many terms correspond to the latest technology in disk interfaces, modems, video and display equipment, and standards that govern the PC industry. Although a glossary is a resource not designed to be read from beginning to end, you should find that scanning through this one is interesting, if not enlightening, with respect to some of the newer PC technology.

The computer industry is filled with abbreviations used as shorthand for a number of terms. This glossary defines many abbreviations, as well as the terms on which the abbreviations are based. The definition of an abbreviation usually is included under the acronym. For example, *video graphics array* is defined under the abbreviation *VGA* rather than under *video graphics array*. This organization makes looking up a term easier—*IDE*, for example—even if you do not know in advance what it stands for (*integrated drive electronics*).

These Web sites can also help you with terms not included in this glossary:

    webservices.cnet.com/cgi/Glossary.asp

    www.webopedia.com

    whatis.techtarget.com

1–50X CD-ROM maximum speeds in relation to the speed of a music CD (1X = 150KBps). At speeds of 16X or above, most drives are CAV and reach their rated speeds only on the outer edges of the disc. See also *CLV* and *CAV*.

3GIO The original name for PCI Express, a forthcoming replacement for existing PCI connections. See also *PCI Express*.

10BASE-2 IEEE standard for baseband Ethernet at 10Mbps over RG-58 coaxial cable to a maximum distance of 185 meters. Also known as Thin Ethernet (Thinnet) or IEEE 802.3.

10BASE-5 IEEE standard for baseband Ethernet at 10Mbps over thick coaxial cable to a maximum distance of 500 meters. Also known as Thick Ethernet or Thicknet.

10BASE-T A 10Mbps CSMA/CD Ethernet LAN that works on Category 3 or better twisted-pair wiring, which is very similar to standard telephone cabling. 10BASE-T Ethernet LANs work on a "star" configuration, in which the wire from each workstation routes directly to a 10BASE-T hub. Hubs can be joined together. 10BASE-T has a maximum distance of 100 meters between each workstation and the hub.

24x7 Refers to continuous 24 hours a day, 7 days a week computer or services operation.

56K The generic term for modems that can receive data at a maximum rate of 56Kbps. See also *V.90*, *V.92*, *X2*, *K56flex*.

64-bit processor A processor that has 64-bit registers. The Intel Itanium and Itanium 2 processors for workstations and servers, which can also emulate 32-bit Intel processors; the AMD Athlon 64 desktop processor, which also emulates 32-bit x86 Intel and AMD processors; and the AMD Opteron, designed for use in server and workstation tasks, are some of the 64-bit processors now available.

100BASE-T A 100Mbps CSMA/CD Ethernet local area network (LAN) that works on Category 5 twisted-pair wiring. 100BASE-T Ethernet LANs work on a "star" configuration in which the wire from each workstation routes directly to a central 100BASE-T hub. This is the current standard for 100Mbps Ethernet, replacing 100BASE-VG.

100BASE-VG The joint Hewlett-Packard–AT&T proposal for Fast Ethernet running at 100Mbps. It uses four pairs of Category 5 cable using the 10BASE-T twisted-pair wiring scheme to transmit or receive. 100BASE-VG splits the signal across the four wire pairs at 25MHz each. This standard has not found favor with corporations and has been almost totally replaced by 100BASE-T.

286 See *80286*.

386 See *80386DX*.

404 Web site error code indicating the specified page is not found. Some Web sites display a customized error message instead of the standard 404 code.

486 See *80486DX*.

586 A generic term used to refer to fifth-generation processors similar to the Intel Pentium, such as the AMD K6 series and the VIA Cyrix MII.

640KB barrier The limit imposed by the PC-compatible memory model using DOS mode. DOS programs can address only 1MB total memory, and PC compatibility generally requires the top 384KB to be reserved for the system, leaving only the lower 640KB for DOS or other real-mode applications.

802.11 The family name for various wireless Ethernet standards. See also *IEEE 802.11 family*.

1000BASE-T A 1,000Mbps Ethernet local area network (LAN) that runs over four pairs of Category 5 cable. Popularly known as Gigabit Ethernet, 1000BASE-T can be used as an upgrade to a properly wired 100BASE-T network because the same cable and distance limitations (100 meters) apply.

1394 See *FireWire*.

8086 An Intel microprocessor with 16-bit registers, a 16-bit data bus, and a 20-bit address bus. This processor can operate only in real mode.

8087 An Intel math coprocessor designed to perform floating-point math with much greater speed and precision than the main CPU. The 8087 can be installed in most 8086- and 8088-based systems and adds more than 50 new instructions to those available in the primary CPU alone.

8088 An Intel microprocessor with 16-bit registers, an 8-bit data bus, and a 20-bit address bus. This processor can operate only in real mode and was designed as a low-cost version of the 8086.

8514/A An analog video display adapter from IBM for the PS/2 line of personal computers. Compared to previous display adapters, such as EGA and VGA, it provides a high resolution of 1,024×768 pixels with as many as 256 colors or 64 shades of gray. It provides a video coprocessor that performs two-dimensional graphics functions internally, thus relieving the CPU of graphics tasks. It uses an interlaced monitor and scans every other line every time the screen is refreshed.

80286 An Intel microprocessor with 16-bit registers, a 16-bit data bus, and a 24-bit address bus. It can operate in both real and protected virtual modes.

80287   An Intel math coprocessor designed to perform floating-point math with much greater speed and precision than the main CPU. The 80287 can be installed in most 286- and some 386DX-based systems, and it adds more than 50 new instructions to what is available in the primary CPU alone.

80386   See *80386DX*.

80386DX   An Intel microprocessor with 32-bit registers, a 32-bit data bus, and a 32-bit address bus. This processor can operate in real, protected virtual, and virtual real modes.

80386SX   An Intel microprocessor with 32-bit registers, a 16-bit data bus, and a 24-bit address bus. This processor, designed as a low-cost version of the 386DX, can operate in real, protected virtual, and virtual real modes.

80387DX   An Intel math coprocessor designed to perform floating-point math with much greater speed and precision than the main CPU. The 80387DX can be installed in most 386DX-based systems and adds more than 50 new instructions to those available in the primary CPU alone.

80387SX   An Intel math coprocessor designed to perform floating-point math with much greater speed and precision than the main CPU. The 80387SX can be installed in most 386SX-based systems and adds more than 50 new instructions to those available in the primary CPU alone.

80486   See *80486DX*.

80486DX   An Intel microprocessor with 32-bit registers, a 32-bit data bus, and a 32-bit address bus. The 486DX has a built-in cache controller with 8KB of cache memory as well as a built-in math coprocessor equivalent to a 387DX. The 486DX can operate in real, protected virtual, and virtual real modes.

80486DX2   A version of the 486DX with an internal clock-doubling circuit that causes the chip to run at twice the motherboard clock speed. If the motherboard clock is 33MHz, the DX2 chip will run at 66MHz. The DX2 designation applies to chips sold through the OEM market, whereas a retail version of the DX2 sold by Intel and designed for use as an upgrade was sold as an Overdrive processor.

80486DX4   A version of the 486DX with an internal clock-tripling circuit that causes the chip to run at three times the motherboard clock speed. If the motherboard clock is 33.33MHz, the DX4 chip will run at 100MHz.

80486SX   An Intel microprocessor with 32-bit registers, a 32-bit data bus, and a 32-bit address bus. The 486SX is the same as the 486DX, except that it lacks the built-in math coprocessor function and was designed as a low-cost version of the 486DX. The 486SX can operate in real, protected virtual, and virtual real modes.

80487SX   An Intel microprocessor with 32-bit registers, a 32-bit data bus, and a 32-bit address bus. Although the name implies that the 80487SX adds floating-point math capabilities, in reality the 487SX is the same as the 486DX, except that it uses a modified pinout and must be installed in a special 80487SX socket. When installed, the 80487SX replaces the 80486SX for all processing tasks. The 487SX can operate in real, protected virtual, and virtual real modes.

A+   Refers to the CompTIA A+ Certification, a vendor-neutral certification for computer hardware technicians. A+ Certification exams test knowledge of basic hardware and software skills. The A+ Certification can be used as part of the exam requirements for the Microsoft Certified System Administrator (MCSA) credential.

abend   Short for *abnormal end*. A condition occurring when the execution of a program or task is terminated unexpectedly because of a bug or crash.

absolute address   An explicit identification of a memory location, device, or location within a device.

AC (alternating current)   The frequency is measured in cycles per seconds (cps) or hertz (Hz). The standard value running through the wall outlet is 120 volts at 60Hz through a fuse or circuit breaker that usually can handle about 15 or 20 amps.

accelerated graphics port   See *AGP*.

Accelerated Hub Architecture (AHA)   An Intel technology used on its 800-series chipsets to transfer data between the memory controller hub (MCH), which is equivalent to the North Bridge, and the input/output controller hub (ICH), which is equivalent to the South Bridge. AHA transfers data at 266MBps, twice the speed of the PCI bus previously used.

accelerator board   An add-in board replacing the computer's CPU with circuitry that enables the system to run more quickly. See also *graphics accelerator*.

access light   The LED on the front of a drive or other device (or on the front panel of the system) that indicates the computer is reading or writing data on the device.

access mechanism   See *actuator*.

access time   The time that elapses from the instant information is requested to the point that delivery is completed. It's usually described in nanoseconds (ns) for memory chips and in milliseconds (ms) for disk drives. Most manufacturers rate average access time on a hard disk as the time required for a seek across one third of the total number of cylinders plus one-half the time for a single revolution of the disk platters (latency).

accumulator   A register (temporary storage) in which the result of an operation is formed.

acoustic coupler A device used to connect a computer modem to a phone line by connecting to the handset of a standard AT&T-style phone. The audible sounds to and from the modem are transmitted to the handset through the coupler while the handset is resting in the coupler. Although often thought of as obsolete, an acoustic coupler can be used to ensure the availability of a modem connection when traveling and access to an RJ-11 jack is unavailable.

ACPI (Advanced Configuration and Power Interface) A standard developed by Intel, Microsoft, and Toshiba that is designed to implement power management functions in the operating system. ACPI is a replacement for APM. See also *APM*.

ACR Short for Advanced Communication Riser, an alternative to CNR advocated by the ACR Special Interest Group (www.acrsig.org). ACR, like CNR, is designed to allow motherboard designers to add low-cost network capabilities to motherboards but uses the same PCI connector used by PCI expansion cards.

Acrobat Refers to the Adobe Acrobat program for creating and reading cross-platform documents created in Adobe's Portable Document Format (PDF) file format. Many computer and component manuals are available online in Acrobat format. The Acrobat Reader can be downloaded free from Adobe's Web site.

active high Designates a digital signal that must go to a high value to be true. Synonymous with positive.

active low Designates a digital signal that must go to a low value to be true. Synonymous with negative.

active matrix A type of LCD screen that contains at least one transistor for every pixel on the screen. Color active matrix screens use three transistors for each pixel—one each for the red, green, and blue dots. The transistors are arranged on a grid of conductive material, with each connected to a horizontal and a vertical member. See also *TFT*.

active partition Any partition marked as bootable in the partition table. See also *boot manager*.

actuator The device that moves a disk drive's read/write heads across the platter surfaces. Also known as an access mechanism.

adapter The device that serves as an interface between the system unit and the devices attached to it. It's often synonymous with circuit board, circuit card, or card, but it also can refer to a connector or cable adapter that changes one type of connector to another.

adapter description files (ADF) Refers to the setup and configuration files and drivers necessary to install an adapter card, such as a network adapter card. Primarily used with Micro Channel Architecture (MCA) bus cards.

add-in board See *expansion card*.

address Refers to where a particular piece of data or other information is found in the computer. Also can refer to the location of a set of instructions.

address bus One or more electrical conductors used to carry the binary-coded address from the microprocessor throughout the rest of the system.

ADSL (asymmetric digital subscriber line) A high-speed transmission technology originally developed by Bellcore and now standardized by ANSI as T1.413. ADSL uses existing UTP copper wires to communicate digitally at high speed between the telephone company central office (CO) and the subscriber. ADSL sends information asymmetrically, meaning it is faster one way than the other. The original ADSL speed was T-1 (1.536Mbps) downstream from the carrier to the subscriber's premises and 16Kbps upstream. However, ADSL is available in a variety of configurations and speeds. See also *DSL*.

AGP (accelerated graphics port) Developed by Intel, AGP is a fast, dedicated interface between the video adapter or chipset and the motherboard chipset North Bridge. AGP is 32 bits wide; runs at 66MHz base speed; and can transfer 1, 2, 4, or 8 bits per cycle (1x, 2x, 4x, or 8x modes) for a throughput of up to 2132MBps.

aliasing Undesirable visual effects (sometimes called artifacts) in computer-generated images caused by inadequate sampling techniques. The most common effect is jagged edges along diagonal or curved object boundaries. See also *antialiasing*.

allocation unit See *cluster*.

alphanumeric characters A character set that contains only letters (A–Z) and digits (0–9). Other characters, such as punctuation marks, also might be allowed.

AMD Short for Advanced Micro Devices, the number-two PC processor maker. AMD makes the popular K6, Athlon, Opteron, and Duron series of processors, as well as chipsets and flash memory devices.

ampere The basic unit for measuring electrical current. Also called amp.

AMR Short for Audio/Modem Riser, it's an Intel-developed specification for packaging modem I/O ports and a codec chip into a small card that can be installed into an AMR slot on a motherboard. Although many motherboards have AMR slots, AMR risers have not been popular, and the CNR specification has largely replaced AMR. See also *CNR*.

analog The representation of numerical values by physical variables such as voltage, current, and so on; continuously variable quantities whose values correspond to the quantitative magnitude of the variables.

analog loopback   A modem self-test in which data from the keyboard is sent to the modem's transmitter, modulated into analog form, looped back to the receiver, demodulated into digital form, and returned to the screen for verification.

analog signals   Continuously variable signals. Analog circuits are more subject to distortion and noise than are digital circuits but are capable of handling complex signals with relatively simple circuitry. See also *digital signals*.

analog-to-digital converter   An electronic device that converts analog signals to digital form.

AND   A logic operator having the property that if P is a statement, Q is a statement, R is a statement..., then the AND of P, Q, R... is true if all statements are true and is false if any statement is false.

AND gate   A logic gate in which the output is 1 only if all inputs are 1.

animation   The process of displaying a sequential series of still images to achieve a motion effect.

ANSI (American National Standards Institute)   A nongovernmental organization founded in 1918 to propose, modify, approve, and publish data processing standards for voluntary use in the United States. It's also the U.S. representative to the International Standards Organization (ISO) in Paris and the International Electrotechnical Commission (IEC). For more information, see the Vendor List on the disc packaged with this book. Contact ANSI, 1430 Broadway, New York, NY 10018.

answer mode   A state in which the modem transmits at the predefined high frequency of the communications channel and receives at the low frequency. The transmit/receive frequencies are the reverse of the calling modem, which is in originate mode. See also *originate mode*.

antialiasing   Software adjustment to make diagonal or curved lines appear smooth and continuous in computer-generated images. See also *aliasing*.

antistatic mat   A pad placed next to a computer upon which components are placed while servicing the system to prevent static damage. Also can refer to a larger-sized mat below an entire computer desk and chair to discharge static from a user before he touches the computer.

antivirus   Software that prevents files containing viruses from running on a computer or software that detects, repairs, cleans, or removes virus-infected files.

APA (all points addressable)   A mode in which all points of a displayable image can be controlled by the user or a program.

aperture grille   A type of shadow mask used in CRTs. The most common is used in Sony's Trinitron monitors, which use vertical phosphor stripes and vertical slots in the mask, compared to the traditional shadow mask that uses phosphor dots and round holes in the mask. See also *shadow mask*.

API (application program interface)   A system call (routine) that gives programmers access to the services provided by the operating system. In IBM-compatible systems, the ROM BIOS and DOS together present an API that a programmer can use to control the system hardware.

APM (Advanced Power Management)   A specification sponsored by Intel and Microsoft originally proposed to extend the life of batteries in battery-powered computers. It is now used in desktop computers as well. APM enables application programs, the system BIOS, and the hardware to work together to reduce power consumption. An APM-compliant BIOS provides built-in power-management services to the operating system. The application software communicates power-saving data via predefined APM interfaces. Replaced in newer systems by ACPI. See also *ACPI*.

application   End-user–oriented software, such as a word processor, spreadsheet, database, graphics editor, game, or Web browser.

Application Layer   See *OSI*.

arbitration   A method by which multiple devices attached to a single bus can bid or arbitrate to get control of that bus.

archive bit   The bit in a file's attribute byte that sets the archive attribute. Tells whether the file has been changed since it last was backed up.

archive file   A collection of files that has been stored (often in a compressed format) within a single file. Zip and CAB files are the most common types of archive file formats used with Windows-based PCs. See also *Zip file* and *CAB file*.

archive medium   A storage medium (floppy disk, tape cartridge, or removable cartridge) to hold files that need not be accessible instantly.

ARCnet (Attached Resource Computer Network)   A baseband, token-passing LAN technology offering a flexible bus/star topology for connecting personal computers. Operating at 2.5Mbps, it is one of the oldest LAN systems and was popular in low-cost networks. It was originally developed by John Murphy of Datapoint Corporation. Although ARCnet (www.arcnet.com) is no longer used for office networking, it is still a popular choice for networking embedded systems, such as heating and air conditioning systems.

areal density   A calculation of the bit density (bits per inch, or BPI) multiplied by the track density (tracks per inch, or TPI), which results in a figure indicating how many bits per square inch are present on the disk surface.

ARQ (automatic repeat request)   A general term for error-control protocols that feature error detection and automatic retransmission of defective blocks of data.

ASCII (American Standard Code for Information Interchange)   A standard 7-bit code created in 1965 by Robert W. Bemer to achieve compatibility among various types of data processing equipment. The standard ASCII character set consists of 128 decimal numbers ranging from 0 to 127, which are assigned to letters, numbers, punctuation marks, and the most common special characters. In 1981, IBM introduced the extended ASCII character set with the IBM PC, extending the code to 8 bits and adding characters from 128 to 255 to represent additional special mathematical, graphics, and foreign characters.

ASCII character   A 1-byte character from the ASCII character set, including alphabetic and numeric characters, punctuation symbols, and various graphics characters.

ASME (American Society of Mechanical Engineers; www.asme.org)   ASME International has nearly 600 codes and standards in print, and its many committees involve more than 3,000 individuals, mostly engineers but not necessarily members of the society. The standards are used in more than 90 countries throughout the world.

aspect ratio   The measurement of a film or television viewing area in terms of relative height and width. The aspect ratio of most modern motion pictures varies from 5:3 to as large as 16:9, which creates a problem when a wide-format motion picture is transferred to the more square-shaped television screen or monitor, with its aspect ratio of 4:3. See also *letterbox*.

assemble   The act of translating a program expressed in an assembler language into a computer machine language.

assembler language   A computer-oriented language whose instructions are usually in one-to-one correspondence with machine language instructions.

asymmetrical modulation   A duplex transmission technique that splits the communications channel into one high-speed channel and one slower channel. During a call under asymmetrical modulation, the modem with the greater amount of data to transmit is allocated the high-speed channel. The modem with less data is allocated the slow, or back, channel. The modems dynamically reverse the channels during a call if the volume of data transfer changes.

asynchronous communication   Data transmission in which the length of time between transmitted characters can vary. Timing depends on the actual time for the transfer to take place, as opposed to synchronous communication, which is timed rigidly by an external clock signal. Because the receiving modem must be signaled about when the data bits of a character begin and end, start and stop bits are added to each character. See also *synchronous communication*.

asynchronous memory   Memory that runs using a timing or clock rate different from (usually slower than) the motherboard speed.

AT clock   Refers to the Motorola 146818 real-time clock (RTC) and CMOS RAM chip, which first debuted in the IBM AT and whose function has been present in all PC-compatible systems since. Keeps track of the time of day and makes this data available to the operating system or other software.

ATA (AT Attachment Interface)   An IDE disk interface standard introduced in March 1989 that defines a compatible register set, a 40-pin connector, and its associated signals. See also *IDE* and *SATA*.

ATA-2   The second-generation AT Attachment Interface specification, approved in 1996. This version defines faster transfer modes and logical block addressing schemes to allow high-performance, large-capacity drives. Also called Fast ATA, Fast ATA-2, and enhanced IDE (EIDE).

ATA-3   Published in 1997, ATA-3 defines 8-bit DMA transfers and SMART support for drive failure prediction.

ATA/ATAPI-4   The fourth-generation ATA specification was published in 1998. ATA/ATAPI-4 incorporates ATAPI and adds Ultra DMA/33 (33MBps) transfer mode; APM support; an optional 80-wire, 40-pin cable; support for Compact Flash memory devices; and enhanced BIOS support for larger drives.

ATA/ATAPI-5   Approved in 2000, ATA/ATAPI-5 includes UDMA/66 support, mandates the 80-wire cable for UDMA/66, detects the cable type, and allows UDMA/66 or faster speeds only if the 80-wire cable is present.

ATA/ATAPI-6   The latest draft standard, ATA/ATAPI-6 includes UDMA/100 (100MBps) support and increases the ATA drive size limit to 144.12PB (petabytes). See also *petabyte*.

ATAPI (AT Attachment Packet Interface)   A specification that defines device-side characteristics for an IDE-connected peripheral, such as a CD-ROM or tape drive. ATAPI is essentially an adaptation of the SCSI command set to the IDE interface. ATA-4 and newer ATA standards include ATAPI standards.

Athlon An AMD sixth-generation processor family roughly comparable to the Intel Pentium III and Pentium 4. Later models (beginning with the Thunderbird core) include on-die L2 cache running at full core speed. It includes MMX and AMD 3DNow! instructions for multimedia performance. Originally available in a Slot-A cartridge package, all Athlons are now available only in the Socket-A (462-pin) package. The Mobile Athlon XP, which replaced the Athlon 4, is designed for mobile applications, the Athlon MP is designed for workstation/server multiprocessor configurations, and the Athlon XP is designed mainly for single processor applications. All three use the improved Thoroughbred core and 3DNow! Professional multimedia extensions. The Athlon XP processors include AMD's new QuantiSpeed design for faster internal operation and are rated by their performances relative to the Intel Pentium 4, rather than by their clock speeds. For example, the Athlon XP 2600+, which performs comparably to the Pentium 4 2.6GHz processor, runs at a clock speed of about 2.1GHz.

Athlon 64 An AMD processor (code-named Clawhammer) that uses a 64-bit internal design. The Athlon 64 also emulates 32-bit x86 processors from Intel and AMD. It uses a new ball grid array socket called Socket 754; an integrated DDR memory controller (instead of using the North Bridge for memory connections); an improved version of the AMD-developed HyperTransport connection to AGP, PCI, and other components; and an improved heatsink-mounting solution. It supports MMX and AMD 3dNow! Instructions for multimedia and uses a performance-rating system similar to that used by 32-bit Athlon processors. See also *Athlon*.

ATM (asynchronous transfer mode) A high-bandwidth, low-delay, packet-like switching and multiplexing technique. Usable capacity is segmented into fixed-size cells consisting of header and information fields, allocated to services on demand.

attribute byte A byte of information, held in the directory entry of any file or folder, that describes various attributes of the file or folder, such as whether it is read-only or has been backed up since it last was changed. Attributes can be set by the DOS ATTRIB command or with Windows Explorer.

ATX A motherboard and power supply form factor standard designed by Intel and introduced in 1995. It is characterized by a double row of rear external I/O connectors on the motherboard, a single keyed power supply connector, memory and processor locations that are designed not to interfere with the installation of adapter cards, and an improved cooling flow. The current specification—ATX 2.0—was introduced in December 1996.

audio A signal that can be heard, such as through the speaker of the PC. Many PC diagnostic tests use both visual (onscreen) codes and audio signals.

audio frequencies Frequencies that can be heard by the human ear (approximately 20Hz–20,000Hz).

auto-answer A setting in modems enabling them to answer incoming calls over the phone lines automatically.

auto-dial A feature in modems enabling them to dial phone numbers without human intervention.

auto-disconnect A modem feature that enables a modem to hang up the telephone line when the modem at the other end hangs up.

auto-redial A modem or software feature that automatically redials the last number dialed if the number is busy or does not answer.

AUTOEXEC.BAT A special batch file DOS and Windows 9x execute at startup. Contains any number of DOS commands that are executed automatically, including the capability to start programs at startup. See also *batch file*.

automatic head parking Disk drive head parking performed whenever the drive is powered off. Found in all modern hard disk drives with a voice-coil actuator.

available memory Memory currently not in use by the operating system, drivers, or applications, which can be used to load additional software.

average access time The average time it takes a disk drive to begin reading any data placed anywhere on the drive. This includes the average seek time, which is when the heads are moved, as well as the latency, which is the average amount of time required for any given data sector to pass underneath the heads. Together, these factors make up the average access time. See also *average seek time* and *latency*.

average latency The average time required for any byte of data stored on a disk to rotate under the disk drive's read/write head. Equal to one-half the time required for a single rotation of a platter.

average seek time The average amount of time it takes to move the heads from one random cylinder location to another, usually including any head settling time. In many cases, the average seek time is defined as the seek time across one-third of the total number of cylinders.

AVI (audio video interleave) A storage technique developed by Microsoft for its Video for Windows product that combines audio and video into a single frame or track, saving valuable disk space and keeping audio in synchronization with the corresponding video. AVI files are widely supported by media players and video production programs.

AWG American Wire Gauge, a U.S. standard for measuring the thickness of copper and aluminum wire for electrical and data-transmission use. Thinner wire is used to save space and for short distances, but thicker wire has less resistance and is better for long wire runs.

B Channel The bearer channel in an ISDN network, it's used to carry data at a rate of 64KBps. See also *BRI*.

backbone The portion of the Internet or wide area network (WAN) transmission wiring that connects the main Internet/WAN servers and routers and is responsible for carrying the bulk of the Internet/WAN data.

backplane A rarely used motherboard design in which the components typically found on a motherboard are instead located on an expansion adapter card plugged into a slot. In these systems, the board with the slots is the backplane. The PCI Industrial Computer Manufacturers Group (PICMG) single-board computer designs for rackmount systems are the primary users of backplane designs today.

backup The process of duplicating a file or library onto a separate piece of media. It's good insurance against the loss of an original. Depending on how the backup was made, the data might need to be restored with a special program before reuse.

backup disk Contains information copied from another disk. Used to ensure that original information is not destroyed or altered.

backward compatibility The design of software and hardware to work with previous versions of the same software or hardware.

bad sector A disk sector that can't hold data reliably because of a media flaw or damaged format markings.

bad track table A label affixed to the casing of an ST412/506 or ESDI hard disk drive that tells which tracks are flawed and incapable of holding data. The listing is entered into the low-level formatting program. Modern ATA (IDE) and SCSI drives are low-level formatted during manufacture and don't have (or need) a bad track table.

balanced signal Refers to signals consisting of equal currents moving in opposite directions. When balanced or nearly balanced signals pass through twisted-pair lines, the electromagnetic interference effects—such as crosstalk caused by the two opposite currents—largely cancel each other out. Differential signaling (used by some types of SCSI interfaces) is a method that uses balanced signals.

balun Short for balanced/unbalanced. A type of transformer that enables balanced cables to be joined with unbalanced cables. Twisted-pair (balanced) cables, for example, can be joined with coaxial (unbalanced) cables if the proper balun transformer is used.

bandwidth 1) Generally, the measure of the range of frequencies within a radiation band required to transmit a particular signal. The difference between the lowest and highest signal frequencies. The bandwidth of a computer monitor is a measure of the rate at which a monitor can handle information from the display adapter. The wider the bandwidth, the more information the monitor can carry and the greater the resolution. 2) Used to describe the data-carrying capacity of a given communications circuit or pathway. The bandwidth of a circuit is a measure of the rate at which information can be passed.

bank The collection of memory chips or modules that make up a block of memory readable or writeable by the processor in a single cycle. This block, therefore, must be as large as the data bus of the particular microprocessor. In PC systems, the processor data bus (and therefore the bank size) is usually 8, 16, 32, or 64 bits wide. Optionally, some systems also incorporate an additional parity or ECC bit for each 8 data bits, resulting in a total of 9, 18, 36, or 72 bits (respectively) for each bank. Memory in a PC always must be added or removed in full-bank increments. The number of memory chips or modules that make up a bank varies with the width of the memory in bits and the size of the processor's data bus. For example, a K6-2 processor has a data bus that is 64 bits wide. If the motherboard uses 72-pin SIMMs (which are 32 data bits wide), a bank is two SIMMs. However, if the motherboard uses DIMMs, which are 64 data bits wide, a bank is one DIMM.

bar code The code used on consumer products and inventory parts for identification purposes. Consists of bars of varying thickness that represent characters and numerals that are read with an optical reader. The most common version is called the universal product code (UPC).

base-2 Refers to the computer numbering system that consists of two numerals: 0 and 1. Also called binary.

base address Starting location for a consecutive string of memory or I/O addresses/ports.

base memory The amount of memory available to the operating system or application programs within the first megabyte, accessible in the processor's real mode.

baseband transmission The transmission of digital signals over a limited distance. ARCnet and Ethernet local area networks use baseband signaling. Contrasts with broadband transmission, which refers to the transmission of analog signals over a greater distance.

BASIC (Beginner's All-purpose Symbolic Instruction Code)   A popular computer programming language originally developed by John Kemeny and Thomas Kurtz in the mid-1960s at Dartmouth College. Normally, BASIC is an interpretive language, meaning that each statement is translated and executed as it is encountered, but it can be a compiled language, in which all the program statements are compiled before execution. Microsoft Visual Basic, a popular development environment for Windows, is not related to BASIC.

batch file   A set of commands stored in a disk file for execution by the operating system. A special batch file called AUTOEXEC.BAT is executed by DOS each time the system is started. All DOS and Windows batch files have a .BAT file extension.

baud   A unit of signaling speed denoting the number of discrete signal elements that can be transmitted per second. The word baud is derived from the name of J.M.E. Baudot (1845–1903), a French pioneer in the field of printing telegraphy and the inventor of Baudot code. Although technically inaccurate, baud rate commonly is used to mean bit rate. Because each signal element or baud can translate into many individual bits, bits per second (bps) usually differs from baud rate. A rate of 2,400 baud means that 2,400 frequency or signal changes per second are being sent, but each frequency change can signal several bits of information. For example, 33.6Kbps modems actually transmit at only 2,400 baud.

Baudot code   A 5-bit code used in many types of data communications, including teletype (TTY), radio teletype (RTTY), and telecommunications devices for the deaf (TDD). Baudot code has been revised and extended several times. See also *baud*.

bay   An opening in a computer case or chassis that holds disk drives.

BBS (bulletin board system)   A computer that operates with a program and a modem to enable other computers with modems to communicate with it, often on a round-the-clock basis. Although BBSs were once the primary means of distributing information and software, the Internet has almost completely replaced BBSs.

benchmark   A test or set of tests designed to compare the performance of hardware or software. A popular set of benchmarks for PC hardware is the *PC Magazine* benchmarks, such as Business Winstone, WinBench, and others. You can order CDs or download selected benchmarks from www.veritest.com/benchmarks/pcmbmk.asp.

bezel   A cosmetic panel that covers the face of a drive or some other device.

Bézier curve   A mathematical method for describing a curve, often used in illustration and CAD programs to draw complex shapes.

BGA (ball grid array)   A packaging technology used by Socket 478 Pentium 4 and Celeron processors, as well as many recent motherboard chipsets and video card memory chips. BGA uses small solder balls instead of pin connectors to enable more signaling paths to exist in a smaller space and improve signal accuracy.

bidirectional   1) Refers to lines over which data can move in two directions, such as a data bus or telephone line. 2) Refers to the capability of a printer to print from right to left and from left to right alternately.

binary   See *base-2*.

BIOS (basic input/output system)   The part of an operating system that handles the communications between the computer and its peripherals. Often burned into read-only memory (ROM) chips or rewritable flash (EEPROM) memory chips found on motherboards and expansion cards, such as video cards and SCSI and ATA/IDE host adapters. See also *firmware*.

bipolar   A category of semiconductor circuit design that was used to create the first transistor and the first integrated circuit. Bipolar and CMOS are the two major transistor technologies. Almost all personal computers use CMOS technology chips. CMOS uses far less energy than bipolar.

bisynchronous (binary synchronous control)   An earlier protocol developed by IBM for software applications and communicating devices operating in synchronous environments. The protocol defines operations at the link level of communications—for example, the format of data frames exchanged between modems over a phone line.

bit binary digit   Represented logically by 0 or 1 and electrically by 0 volts and (typically) 5 volts. Other methods are used to represent binary digits physically (tones, different voltages, lights, and so on), but the logic is always the same.

bit density   Expressed as bits per inch (BPI). Defines how many bits can be written onto one linear inch of a track. Sometimes also called linear density.

bit depth   The number of bits used to describe the color of each pixel on a computer display. For example, a bit depth of two (2^2) means the monitor can display only black and white pixels; a bit depth of four (2^4) means the monitor can display 16 different colors; a bit depth of eight (2^8) allows for 256 colors; and so on.

bitmap   A method of storing graphics information in memory, in which a bit devoted to each pixel (picture element) onscreen indicates whether that pixel is on or off. A bitmap contains a bit for each point or dot on a video display screen and enables fine resolution because any point or pixel onscreen can be addressed. A greater number of bits can be used to describe each pixel's color, intensity, and other display characteristics.

blank or blanking interval A period in which no video signal is received by a monitor while the videodisc or digital video player searches for the next video segment or frame to display.

block A string of records, words, or characters formed for technical or logic reasons and to be treated as an entity.

block diagram The logical structure or layout of a system in graphics form. Does not necessarily match the physical layout and does not specify all the components and their interconnections.

Blue Book The standard for enhanced CDs (CD-E). CD-E media contains both music (for play on standard CD players) and computer content. Developed by Philips and Sony in 1995.

blue screen of death A system crash in Windows that replaces the normal desktop with a blue screen with white text reporting the problem and locks up the system. Also referred to as a BSOD, this condition can be triggered by defective memory, file system errors, and other system problems.

Bluetooth An emerging short-range networking standard, Bluetooth is designed to enable PCs, mobile phones, input devices, and PDAs to exchange data with each other. Bluetooth uses the same 2.4GHz frequency range used by some types of wireless phones and by the IEEE 802.11b Wi-Fi wireless Ethernet network. Bluetooth has a speed of 1Mbps or 2Mbps, depending on the version.

BMP A Windows graphics format that can be device dependent or independent. Device-independent BMP files (DIB) are coded for translation to a wide variety of displays and printers.

BNC (Bayonet-Neill-Concelman) Also known as British-Naval-Connector, Baby-N-Connector, or Bayonet-Nut-Coupler, this bayonet-locking connector is noted for its excellent shielding and impedance-matching characteristics, resulting in low noise and minimal signal loss at any frequency up to 4GHz. It is used in Ethernet 10BASE-2 networks (also known as IEEE 802.3 or Thinnet) to terminate coaxial cables. It is also used for some high-end video monitors. BNC is named for its connection type (bayonet) and its co-developers.

bonding In ISDN, joining two 64Kbps B channels to achieve 128Kbps speed. Bonding can also be used with analog modems that use the Multilink Point-to-Point protocol that is supported by Windows 98 and newer versions but by only a few ISPs.

Boolean operation Any operation in which each of the operands and the result take one of two values. A Boolean search can be performed with many search engines used on Web sites and help files using operators such as AND, OR, and NOT.

boot To load a program into the computer. The term comes from the phrase "pulling a boot on by the bootstrap."

boot manager A program that enables you to select which active partition to boot from. Often supplied with aftermarket disk-partitioning programs, such as PartitionMagic, or installed by default when you install a Windows upgrade into a separate disk partition instead of replacing your old version. See also *active partition*.

boot record The first sector on a disk or partition that contains disk parameter information for the BIOS and operating system as well as bootstrap loader code that instructs the system how to load the operating system files into memory, thus beginning the initial boot sequence to boot the machine.

boot sector See *boot record*.

boot sector virus A virus designed to occupy the boot sector of a disk. Any attempt to start or boot a system from this disk transfers the virus to the hard disk, after which it subsequently is loaded every time the system is started. Many older PC viruses, particularly those spread by infected floppy disks, are boot sector viruses.

bootstrap A technique or device designed to bring itself into a desired state by means of its own action. The term is used to describe the process by which a device such as a PC goes from its initial power-on condition to a running condition without human intervention. See also *boot*.

boule Purified, cylindrical silicon crystals from which semiconducting electronic chips, including microprocessors, memory, and other chips, in a PC are manufactured. Also called an ingot.

bps (bits per second) The number of binary digits, or bits, transmitted per second. Sometimes confused with baud.

branch prediction A feature of fifth-generation (Pentium and higher) processors that attempts to predict whether a program branch will be taken and then fetches the appropriate following instructions.

BRI Short for basic rate interface, it's a form of ISDN used in home and small business applications. A 2B+1D BRI service has two B channels and a single D channel for signaling and control uses.

bridge In local area networks, an interconnection between two similar networks. Also the hardware equipment used to establish such an interconnection.

broadband transmission A term used to describe analog transmission. Requires modems for connecting terminals and computers to the network. Using frequency division multiplexing, many signals or sets of data can be transmitted simultaneously. The alternative transmission scheme is baseband, or digital, transmission.

brownout An AC supply voltage drop in which the power does not shut off entirely but continues to be supplied at lower-than-normal levels.

BSOD See *blue screen of death*.

bubble memory A special type of nonvolatile read/write memory introduced by Intel in which magnetic regions are suspended in crystal film and data is maintained when the power is off. A typical bubble memory chip contains about 512KB, or more than four million bubbles. Bubble memory failed to catch on because of slow access times measured in several milliseconds. It has, however, found a niche use as solid-state "disk" emulators in environments in which conventional drives are unacceptable, such as in military or factory use.

buffer A block of memory used as a holding tank to store data temporarily. Often positioned between a slower peripheral device and the faster computer. All data moving between the peripheral and the computer passes through the buffer. A buffer enables the data to be read from or written to the peripheral in larger chunks, which improves performance. A buffer that is *x* bytes in size usually holds the last *x* bytes of data that moved between the peripheral and CPU. This method contrasts with that of a cache, which adds intelligence to the buffer so that the most often accessed data, rather than the last accessed data, remains in the buffer (cache). A cache can improve performance greatly over a plain buffer.

bug An error or a defect in a program; it can be corrected through program patches (for applications or operating systems) or firmware updates (for BIOS chips).

burn-in The operation of a circuit or equipment to establish that its components are stable and to screen out defective ports or assemblies.

BURN-Proof Short for buffer underrun error-proof, it's a technology developed by Sanyo to prevent buffer underruns during the creation of CD-Rs. BURN-Proof, which has been licensed to many CD-RW drive makers, enables a drive to pause the burning process and continue after sufficient data is available in the drive's buffer. The drive and CD-mastering software must both support BURN-Proof for this feature to work. Ricoh's JustLink works in a similar fashion. See also *lossless linking*.

burst mode A memory-cycling technology that takes advantage of the fact that most memory accesses are consecutive in nature. After setting up the row and column addresses for a given access, using burst mode can then access the next three adjacent addresses with no additional latency.

Burst Static RAMs (BSRAMs) Short for Pipeline Burst SRAM, BSRAMs are a common type of static RAM chip used for memory caches where access to subsequent memory locations after the first byte is accessed takes fewer machine cycles.

bus A linear electrical signal pathway over which power, data, and other signals travel. It is capable of connecting to three or more attachments. A bus is generally considered to be distinct from radial or point-to-point signal connections. The term comes from the Latin *omnibus*, meaning "for all." When used to describe a topology, bus always implies a linear structure.

bus mouse An obsolete type of mouse used in the 1980s that plugs into a special mouse expansion board (occasionally incorporated into a video card) instead of a serial port or motherboard mouse port. The bus mouse connector looks similar to a motherboard mouse (sometimes called PS/2 mouse) connector, but the pin configurations are different and not compatible.

busmaster An intelligent device that, when attached to the Micro Channel, EISA, VLB, or PCI bus, can bid for and gain control of the bus to perform its specific task without processor intervention. Most recent motherboards incorporate busmastering ATA/IDE host adapters, but this feature must be enabled in both the BIOS and through the installation of Windows drivers to be effective.

byte A collection of bits that makes up a character or other designation. Generally, a byte is 8 data bits. When referring to system RAM, an additional parity (error-checking) bit is also stored (see *parity*), making the total 9 bits.

C A high-level computer programming language. A programming language frequently used on mainframes, minis, and PC computer systems. C++ is a popular variant.

C3 A Socket 370-compatible processor developed by VIA Technology from the Cyrix "Joshua" after VIA purchased Cyrix from National Semiconductor. The C3 is noted for its very small die size and cool operation, making it a suitable choice for portable computers and embedded computers.

CAB file Short for cabinet file, the archive file type used by Microsoft to distribute recent versions of Windows and applications. Some recent versions of WinZip can be used to manually extract files from a .CAB file; you can also open .CAB files within Windows Explorer with Windows 98 after you install the Windows 98 Plus! package and with Windows Explorer in Windows 2000, Windows Me, and Windows XP.

cable modem   A broadband Internet device that receives data through the cable TV system. The cable modem can be a one-way device (using a conventional analog modem for dialing and uploading) or a two-way device.

CableLabs Certified Cable Modem   A cable modem that meets the Data or Cable Service Interface Specifications (DOCSIS) standards for modulation and protocols. Various brands and models of modems meet this standard on cable networks that also meet this standard. DOCSIS/CableLabs Certified Cable Modems can be purchased as well as leased.

cache   An intelligent buffer. By using an intelligent algorithm, a cache contains the data accessed most often between a slower peripheral device and the faster CPU. See also *L1 cache, L2 cache*, and *disk cache*.

caddy   A cartridge designed to hold a CD or DVD disc. Some CD drives use caddies, particularly in harsh or industrial environments. DVD-RAM drives also use a caddy to protect the disc.

CAM (Common Access Method)   A committee formed in 1988 that consists of several computer peripheral suppliers and is dedicated to developing standards for a common software interface between SCSI peripherals and host adapters.

candela   Abbreviated cd, a candela is the standard unit of measurement for luminosity. The brightness of LCDs and other types of displays is sometimes measured in cd units.

capacitor   A device consisting of two plates separated by insulating material and designed to store an electrical charge.

card   A printed circuit board containing electronic components that form an entire circuit, usually designed to plug into a connector or slot. Sometimes also called an adapter.

card edge connector   See *edge connector*.

CardBus   A PC Card (PCMCIA) specification for a 32-bit interface that runs at 33MHz and provides 32-bit data paths to the computer's I/O and memory systems, as well as a new shielded connector that prevents CardBus devices from being inserted into slots that do not support the latest version of the PC Card (PCMCIA) standard. CardBus slots can also be used with normal 16-bit PC Card (PCMCIA) devices.

carpal tunnel syndrome   A painful hand injury that gets its name from the narrow tunnel in the wrist that connects ligament and bone. When undue pressure is put on the tendons, they can swell and compress the median nerve, which carries impulses from the brain to the hand, causing numbness, weakness, tingling, and burning in the fingers and hands. Computer users get carpal tunnel syndrome primarily from improper keyboard ergonomics that result in undue strain on the wrist and hand.

carrier   A continuous frequency signal capable of being either modulated or impressed with another information-carrying signal. The reference signal used for the transmission or reception of data. The most common use of this signal with computers involves modem communications over phone lines. The carrier is used as a signal on which the information is superimposed.

carrier detect signal   A modem interface signal that indicates to the attached data terminal equipment (DTE) that it is receiving a signal from the distant modem. Defined in the RS-232 specification. Same as the received line-signal detector.

CAT   Short for category, it describes the ANSI/EIA 568 wiring standards used for data transmission. The most common CAT standards include CAT 3 (16Mbps maximum data rate, suitable for 10BASE-T Ethernet) and CAT 5 (used for 100BASE-T Fast Ethernet or 1000BASE-T Gigabit Ethernet).

cathode ray tube (CRT)   A device that contains electrodes surrounded by a glass sphere or cylinder and displays information by creating a beam of electrons that strike a phosphor coating inside the display unit. This device is most commonly used in computer monitors and terminals.

CAV (constant angular velocity)   An optical disk recording format in which the data is recorded on the disk in concentric circles. CAV disks are rotated at a constant speed. This is similar to the recording technique used on floppy disk drives. CAV limits the total recorded capacity compared to CLV (constant linear velocity), which also is used in optical recording. See also *CLV*.

CCITT   An acronym for the Comité Consultatif International de Télégraphique et Téléphonique (in English, the International Telegraph and Telephone Consultative Committee or the Consultative Committee for International Telegraph and Telephone). Renamed ITU (International Telecommunications Union). See also *ITU*.

CCS (common command set)   A set of SCSI commands specified in the ANSI SCSI-1 Standard X3.131-1986 Addendum 4.B. All SCSI devices must be capable of using the CCS to be fully compatible with the ANSI SCSI-1 standard.

CD (compact disc or compact audio disc)   A 4.75" (12cm) optical disc that contains information encoded digitally in the constant linear velocity (CLV) format. This popular format for high-fidelity music offers 90 decibels signal/noise ratio, 74 minutes of digital sound, and no degradation of quality from playback. The standards for this format (developed by NV Philips and Sony Corporation) are known as the Red Book. The official (and rarely used) designation for the audio-only format is CD-DA (compact disc-digital audio). The simple audio format is also known as CD-A (compact disc-audio). A smaller (3") version of the CD is known as CD-3.

CD burner Refers to either a CD-R or CD-RW drive. See also *DVD burner*.

CD+G (Compact Disc+Graphics) A CD format that includes extended graphics capabilities as written into the original CD-ROM specifications. Includes limited video graphics encoded into the CD subcode area. Originally developed and marketed by Warner New Media (later Time Warner Interactive), it's a popular choice for self-contained karaoke systems.

CD-I (Compact Disc-Interactive) A compact disc format released in October 1991 that provides audio, digital data, still graphics, and motion video. The standards for this format (developed by NV Philips and Sony Corporation) are known as the Green Book. CD-I did not catch on with consumers and is now considered obsolete.

CD+MIDI (Compact Disc+Musical Instrument Digital Interface) A CD format that adds to the CD+G format digital audio, graphics information, and musical instrument digital interface (MIDI) specifications and capabilities. Originally developed and marketed by Warner New Media (later Time Warner Interactive).

CD-R (Compact Disc-Recordable, sometimes called CD-writable) CD-R discs are compact discs that can be recorded and read as many times as desired. CD-R is part of the Orange Book standard defined by ISO. CD-R technology is used for mass production of multimedia applications. CD-R discs can be compatible with CD-ROM, CD-ROM XA, and CD audio. Orange Book specifies multisession capabilities, which enable data recording on the disc at various times in several recording sessions. Multisession capability enables data such as digital photos, digital music, or other types of data files to be added to a single disc on different occasions. The original capacity of CD-R media was 650MB (74 minutes), but most recent CD-ROM and compatible optical drives support the larger 700MB (80-minute) media.

CD-ROM (compact disc-read-only memory) A 4.75" laser-encoded optical memory storage medium with the same constant linear velocity (CLV) spiral format as audio CDs and some videodiscs. CD-ROMs can hold about 650MB of data and require more error-correction information than the standard prerecorded compact audio discs. The standards for this format (developed by NV Philips and Sony Corporation) are known as the Yellow Book. See also *CD-ROM XA*.

CD-ROM drive A device that retrieves data from a CD-ROM disc; it differs from a standard audio CD player by the incorporation of additional error-correction circuitry. CD-ROM drives usually can also play music from audio CDs.

CD-ROM XA (compact disc-read-only memory extended architecture) The XA standard was developed jointly by Sony, Philips, and Microsoft in 1988 and is now part of the Yellow Book standard. XA is a built-in feature of newer CD-ROM drives and supports simultaneous sound playback with data transfer. Non-XA drives support either sound playback or data transfer, but not both simultaneously. XA also enables data compression right on the disk, which also can increase data transfer rates.

CD-RW (compact disc-rewritable) A type of rewritable CD-ROM technology defined in Part III of the Orange Book standard that uses a different type of disc, which the drive can rewrite at least 1,000 times. CD-RW drives also can be used to write CD-R discs, and they can read CD-ROMs. CD-RWs have a lower reflectivity than standard CD-ROMs, and CD-ROM drives must be of the newer multiread variety to read them. CD-RW was initially known as CD-E (for CD-erasable).

CD Video A CD format introduced in 1987 that combines 20 minutes of digital audio and 6 minutes of analog video on a standard 4.75" CD. Upon introduction, many firms renamed 8" and 12" videodiscs CDV in an attempt to capitalize on the consumer popularity of the audio CD. The term fell out of use in 1990 and was replaced in some part by "laser disc" and, more recently, "DVD." See also *video-on-CD*.

CD-WO (compact disc-write once) A variant on CD-ROM that can be written to once and read many times; developed by NV Philips and Sony Corporation. Also known as CD-WORM (CD-write once/read many), CD-recordable, or CD-writable. Standards for this format are known as the Orange Book.

CD-WORM See *CD-WO*.

CDMA Short for code division multiple access, a popular family of wireless protocols used in cellular phones for Internet and email access.

Celeron A family of processors that are low-cost versions of the Pentium II, Pentium III, and Pentium 4 processors. The major differences include a smaller amount of L2 cache and lower clock speeds.

Centronics connector Refers to one of two types of cable connectors used with either parallel (36-pin edge connector) or SCSI (50-pin edge connector) devices.

ceramic substrate A thin, flat, fired-ceramic part used to hold an IC chip (usually made of beryllium oxide or aluminum oxide).

CERN (Conseil Européen pour la Recherche Nucléaire; The European Laboratory for Particle Physics) The site in Geneva where the World Wide Web was created in 1989.

CGA (color graphics adapter) A type of PC video display adapter introduced by IBM on August 12, 1981, which supports text and graphics. Text is supported at a maximum resolution of 80×25 characters in 16 colors with a character box of 8×8 pixels. Graphics are supported at a maximum resolution of 320×200 pixels in 16 colors or 640×200 pixels in 2 colors. The CGA outputs a TTL (digital) signal with a horizontal scanning frequency of 15.75KHz and supports TTL color or NTSC composite displays.

channel 1) Any path along which signals can be sent. 2) In ISDN, data bandwidth is divided into two B-channels that bear data and one D-channel that carries information about the call.

character A representation—coded in binary digits—of a letter, number, or other symbol.

character set All the letters, numbers, and characters a computer can use to represent data. The ASCII standard has 256 characters, each represented by a binary number from 1 to 256. The ASCII set includes all the letters in the alphabet, numbers, most punctuation marks, some mathematical symbols, and other characters.

charge coupled device A light-sensing and storage device used in scanners and digital cameras to capture the pixels.

check bit See *parity*.

checksum Short for *summation check*, a technique for determining whether a package of data is valid. The package, a string of binary digits, is added up and compared with the expected number.

chip Another name for an IC, or integrated circuit. Housed in a plastic or ceramic carrier device with pins for making electrical connections.

chip carrier A ceramic or plastic package that carries an integrated circuit.

chipset A single chip or pair of chips that integrates into the clock generator, bus controller, system timer, interrupt controller, DMA controller, CMOS RAM/clock, and keyboard controller. See also *North Bridge* and *South Bridge*.

CHS (cylinder head sector) The term used to describe the nontranslating scheme used by the BIOS to access IDE drives that are less than or equal to 528MB in capacity. See also *LBA*.

CIF (common image format) The standard sample structure that represents the picture information of a single frame in digital HDTV, independent of frame rate and sync/blank structure. The uncompressed bit rate for transmitting CIF at 29.97 frames/sec is 36.45Mbps.

circuit A complete electronic path.

circuit board The collection of circuits gathered on a sheet of plastic, usually with all contacts made through a strip of pins. The circuit board usually is made by chemically etching metal-coated plastic.

CISC (complex instruction set computer) Refers to traditional computers that operate with large sets of processor instructions. Most modern computers, including the Intel 80xxx processors, are in this category. CISC processors have expanded instruction sets that are complex in nature and require several to many execution cycles to complete. This structure contrasts with RISC (reduced instruction set computer) processors, which have far fewer instructions that execute quickly.

clean room 1) A dust-free room in which certain electronic components (such as chips or hard disk drives) must be manufactured and serviced to prevent contamination. Rooms are rated by Class numbers. A Class 100 clean room must have fewer than 100 particles larger than 0.5 microns per cubic foot of space. 2) A legal approach to copying software or hardware in which one team analyzes the product and writes a detailed description, followed by a second team who reads the description written by the first and then develops a compatible version of the product. When done correctly, such a design methodology will survive a legal attack.

client/server A type of network in which every computer is either a server with a defined role of sharing resources with clients or a client that can access the resources on the server.

clock The source of a computer's timing signals. It synchronizes every operation of the CPU.

clock multiplier A processor feature where the internal core runs at a higher speed than the motherboard or processor bus. See also *overclocking*.

clock speed A measurement of the rate at which the clock signal for a device oscillates, usually expressed in millions of cycles per second (MHz).

clone Originally referred to an IBM-compatible computer system that physically as well as electrically emulates the design of one of IBM's personal computer systems. More currently, it refers to any PC system running an Intel or compatible processor in the 80x86 family.

cluster Also called *allocation unit*. A group of one or more sectors on a disk that forms a fundamental unit of storage to the operating system. Cluster, or allocation unit, size is determined by the operating system when the disk is formatted. Larger clusters generally offer faster system performance but waste disk space.

CLV (constant linear velocity) An optical recording format in which the spacing of data is consistent throughout the disk and the rotational speed of the disk varies depending on which track is being read. Additionally, more sectors of data are placed on the outer tracks compared to the inner tracks of the disk, which is similar to zone recording on hard drives. CLV drives adjust the rotational speed to maintain a constant track velocity as the diameter of the track changes. CLV drives also rotate more quickly near the center of the disk and more slowly toward the edge. Rotational adjustment maximizes the amount of data that can be stored on a disk. CD audio and CD-ROM use CLV recording. See also *CAV*.

CMOS (complementary metal-oxide semiconductor) A type of chip design that requires little power to operate. In PCs, a battery-powered CMOS memory and clock chip is used to store and maintain the clock setting and system configuration information.

CMYK (cyan magenta yellow black) The standard four-color model used for printing.

CNR Short for Communications and Networking Riser, it was developed by Intel as a replacement for the AMR. CNR enables motherboard makers to offer low-cost modem, networking, and audio features through a special expansion slot. Unlike AMR, a CNR slot can be built as a shared slot with a PCI slot. See also *AMR*.

coated media Hard disk platters coated with a reddish iron-oxide medium on which data is recorded.

coaxial cable Also called *coax cable*. A data-transmission medium noted for its wide bandwidth, immunity to interference, and high cost compared to other types of cable. Signals are transmitted inside a fully shielded environment, in which an inner conductor is surrounded by a solid insulating material and then an outer conductor or shield. Used in many local area network systems, such as Ethernet and ARCnet.

COBOL (Common Business-Oriented Language) A high-level computer programming language used primarily by some larger companies. It has never achieved popularity on personal and small business computers.

code page A table used in DOS 3.3 and later that sets up the keyboard and display characters for various foreign languages.

code page switching A DOS feature in versions 3.3 and later that changes the characters displayed onscreen or printed on an output device. Primarily used to support foreign-language characters. Requires an EGA or better video system and an IBM-compatible graphics printer.

CODEC (coder-decoder) A device that converts voice signals from their analog form to digital signals acceptable to more modern digital PBXs and digital transmission systems. It then converts those digital signals back to analog so you can hear and understand what the other party is saying. Also refers to compression/decompression software used in the creation of digital audio and video files, such as MP3 and MPEG, and for videophone programs.

coercivity A measurement in units of oersteds of the amount of magnetic energy to switch or "coerce" the flux change in the magnetic recording media. High-coercivity disk media require a stronger write current.

cold boot The act of starting or restarting a computer from a powered-off state. If the system is on, this requires cycling the power off and then back on. A cold boot causes all RAM to be forcibly cleared. See also *warm boot*.

collision In a LAN, if two computers transmit a packet of data at the same time on the network, the data can become garbled, which is known as a collision.

collision detection/avoidance A process used on a LAN to prevent data packets from interfering with each other and to determine whether data packets have encountered a collision and initiate a resend of the affected packets.

color graphics adapter See *CGA*.

color palette The colors available to a graphics adapter for display.

COM port A serial port on a PC that conforms to the RS-232 standard. See also *RS-232*.

COMDEX The largest international computer trade show and conference in the world. COMDEX/Fall is held in Las Vegas during October, and COMDEX/Spring usually is held in Chicago or Atlanta during April.

command An instruction that tells the computer to start, stop, or continue an operation.

COMMAND.COM An operating system file that is loaded last when the computer is booted. The command interpreter or user interface and program-loader portion of DOS.

command interpreter The operating system program that controls a computer's shell or user interface. The command interpreter for MS-DOS (and the command-line sessions in Windows 9x/Me) is COMMAND.COM; the command interpreter for the graphical shell in Windows versions through 9x/Me is WIN.COM; the command interpreter for NT-based versions of Windows (including Windows 2000 and Windows XP) is CMD.COM.

common The ground or return path for an electrical signal. If it's a wire, it usually is colored black.

common mode noise Noise or electrical disturbances that can be measured between a current- or signal-carrying line and its associated ground. Common mode noise is frequently introduced to signals between separate computer equipment components through the power distribution circuits. It can be a problem when single-ended signals are used to connect different equipment or components that are powered by different circuits.

CompactFlash An ATA flash memory card physical format approximately one third the size of a standard PC Card. Often abbreviated CF or CF+, CompactFlash cards are identical in function to standard ATA Flash PC Cards (PCMCIA) but use 50 pin connectors instead of 68. ATA flash cards contain built-in disk controller circuitry to enable the card to function as a solid-state disk drive. CF cards can plug into a CompactFlash socket or with an adapter into a standard Type I or II PC Card (PCMCIA) slot. CF cards are used by many types of digital cameras.

compatible 1) In the early days of the PC industry when IBM dominated the market, a term used to refer to computers from other manufacturers that had the same features as a given IBM model. 2) In general, software or hardware that conforms to industry standards or other de facto standards so that it can be used in conjunction with or in lieu of other versions of software or hardware from other vendors in a like manner.

compiler A program that translates a program written in a high-level language into its equivalent machine language. The output from a compiler is called an object program.

complete backup A backup of all information on a hard disk, including the directory tree structure.

composite video Television picture information and sync pulses combined. The complete wave form of the color video signal composed of chrominance and luminance picture information; blanking pedestal; field, line, and color-sync pulses; and field-equalizing pulses. Some video cards have an RCA jack that outputs a composite video signal. See also *RGB*.

compressed file A file that has been reduced in size via one or more compression techniques. See also *archive file*.

computer Device capable of accepting data, applying prescribed processes to this data, and displaying the results or information produced.

computer-based training (CBT) The use of a computer to deliver instruction or training; also known as computer-aided (or assisted) instruction (CAI), computer-aided learning (CAL), computer-based instruction (CBI), and computer-based learning (CBL).

CONFIG.SYS A file that can be created to tell DOS how to configure itself when the machine starts up. It can load device drivers, set the number of DOS buffers, and so on.

configuration file A file kept by application software to record various aspects of the software's configuration, such as the printer it uses. Windows uses .INI files and the Windows Registry to control its configuration.

console The unit, such as a terminal or a keyboard, in your system with which you communicate with the computer.

contiguous Touching or joined at the edge or boundary, in one piece.

continuity In electronics, an unbroken pathway. Testing for continuity usually means testing to determine whether a wire or other conductor is complete and unbroken (by measuring 0 ohms). A broken wire shows infinite resistance (or infinite ohms).

control cable The wider of the two cables that connect an ST-506/412 or ESDI hard disk drive to a controller card. A 34-pin cable that carries commands and acknowledgments between the drive and controller.

controller The electronics that control a device, such as a hard disk drive, and intermediate the passage of data between the device and computer.

controller card An adapter holding the control electronics for one or more devices, such as hard disks. Ordinarily occupies one of the computer's slots.

conventional memory The first megabyte or first 640KB of system memory accessible by an Intel processor in real mode. Sometimes called base memory.

convergence Describes the capability of a color monitor to focus the three colored electron beams on a single point. Poor convergence causes the characters onscreen to appear fuzzy and can cause headaches and eyestrain.

coprocessor An additional computer processing unit designed to handle specific tasks in conjunction with the main or central processing unit.

copy protection A hardware or software scheme to prohibit making illegal copies of a program.

core An old-fashioned term for computer memory.

core speed   The internal speed of a processor. With all modern processors, this speed is faster than the system bus speed, and that speed relationship is regulated by the clock multiplier in the processor.

CP/M (Control Program for Microcomputers, originally Control Program/Monitor)   An operating system created by Gary Kildall, the founder of Digital Research. Created for the old 8-bit microcomputers that used the 8080, 8085, and Z-80 microprocessors. It was the dominant operating system in the late 1970s and early 1980s for small computers used in business environments.

cps (characters per second)   A data transfer rate generally estimated from the bit rate and character length. At 2,400bps, for example, 8-bit characters with start and stop bits (for a total of 10 bits per character) are transmitted at a rate of approximately 240cps. Some protocols, such as V.42 and MNP, employ advanced techniques such as longer transmission frames and data compression to increase characters per second.

CPU (central processing unit)   The computer's microprocessor chip; the brains of the outfit. Typically, an IC using VLSI (very-large-scale integration) technology to pack several functions into a tiny area. The most common electronic device in the CPU is the transistor, of which several thousand to several million or more are found.

crash   A malfunction that brings work to a halt. A system crash usually is caused by a software malfunction, and ordinarily you can restart the system by rebooting the machine. A head crash, however, entails physical damage to a disk and probable data loss.

CRC (cyclic redundancy checking)   An error-detection technique consisting of a cyclic algorithm performed on each block or frame of data by both sending and receiving modems. The sending modem inserts the results of its computation in each data block in the form of a CRC code. The receiving modem compares its results with the received CRC code and responds with either a positive or negative acknowledgment. In the ARQ protocol implemented in high-speed modems, the receiving modem accepts no more data until a defective block is received correctly.

crosstalk   The electromagnetic coupling of a signal on one line with another nearby signal line. Crosstalk is caused by electromagnetic induction, where a signal traveling through a wire creates a magnetic field that induces a current in other nearby wires. Various methods including twisting wire pairs and placing ground wires between data wires are used to combat crosstalk and create more reliable data communications.

CRT (cathode-ray tube)   A term used to describe a television or monitor screen tube.

current   The flow of electrons, measured in amperes, or amps.

cursor   The small, flashing hyphen that appears onscreen to indicate the point at which any input from the keyboard will be placed.

cycle   Time for a signal to transition from one leading edge to the next leading edge.

cyclic redundancy checking   See *CRC*.

cylinder   The set of tracks on a disk that are on each side of all the disk platters in a stack and are the same distance from the center of the disk. The total number of tracks that can be read without moving the heads. A floppy drive with two heads usually has 160 tracks, which are accessible as 80 cylinders. A typical 120GB hard disk will physically have about 56,000 cylinders, 6 heads (3 platters), and an average of about 700 sectors per track, for a total of about 235,200,000 sectors (120.4GB).

Cyrix   Originally a Texas-based maker of Intel-compatible math coprocessor chips, Cyrix later developed low-cost, plug-compatible 6x86 and 6x86MX Pentium-class processors that were manufactured by IBM and other fabricators. Cyrix also developed the first chipsets with integrated audio and video (the MediaGX series). Cyrix was later absorbed into National Semiconductor, which retained the MediaGX technology when it sold Cyrix to VIA Technologies. VIA formerly developed and sold the VIA Cyrix MII, a low-cost Super Socket 7 processor, and currently sells and develops the C3, developed from the Cyrix "Joshua" processor. See also *C3* and *VIA Technologies*.

D/A converter (DAC)   A device that converts digital signals to analog form. See also *RAMDAC*.

D-channel   In ISDN, a 16Kbps channel used to transmit control data about a connection.

daisy-chain   Stringing up components in such a manner that the signals move serially from one to the other. Most microcomputer multiple disk drive systems are daisy-chained. The SCSI bus system is a daisy-chain arrangement, in which the signals move from computer to disk drives to tape units, and so on. USB and IEEE-1394 devices also use the daisy-chain arrangement when hubs are used.

daisywheel printer   An impact printer that prints fully formed characters one at a time by rotating a circular print element composed of a series of individual spokes, each containing two characters that radiate from a center hub. Produces letter-quality output but has long been replaced by laser and LED printers.

DAT (digital audio tape) A small cassette containing 4mm-wide tape used for storing large amounts of digital information. DAT technology emerged in Europe and Japan in 1986 as a way to produce high-quality, digital audio recordings and was modified in 1988 to conform to the digital data storage (DDS) standard for storing computer data. Raw/compressed capacities for a single tape are 2/4GB for DDS, 4/8GB for DDS-2, 12/24GB for DDS-3, and 20/40GB for DDS-4.

data 1) Groups of facts processed into information. A graphic or textural representation of facts, concepts, numbers, letters, symbols, or instructions used for communication or processing. 2) An android from the twenty-fourth century with a processing speed of 60 trillion operations per second and a storage capacity of 800 quadrillion bits, and who serves on the USS Enterprise NCC-1701-D with the rank of lieutenant commander.

data bus The connection that transmits data between the processor and the rest of the system. The width of the data bus defines the number of data bits that can be moved into or out of the processor in one cycle.

data cable Generically, a cable that carries data. Specific to HD connections, the narrower (20-pin) of two cables that connects an ST-506/412 or ESDI hard disk drive to a controller card.

data communications A type of communication in which computers and terminals can exchange data over an electronic medium.

data compression A technique in which mathematical algorithms are applied to the data in a file to eliminate redundancies and therefore reduce the size of the file. See also *lossless compression* and *lossy compression*.

Data Link Layer In networking, the layer of the OSI reference model that controls how the electrical impulses enter or leave the network cable. Ethernet and Token-Ring are the two most common examples of Data Link Layer protocols. See also *OSI*.

data separator A device that separates data and clock signals from a single encoded signal pattern. Usually, the same device performs both data separation and combination and is sometimes called an endec, or encoder/decoder.

data transfer rate The maximum rate at which data can be transferred from one device to another.

daughterboard Add-on board to increase functionality and/or memory. Attaches to the existing board.

DB-9 9-pin D-shell connector, primarily used for PC serial ports.

DB-25 25-pin D-shell connector, primarily used for PC parallel ports.

DC Direct current, such as that provided by a power supply or batteries.

DC-600 (Data Cartridge 600) A data-storage medium invented by 3M in 1971 that uses a 1/4"-wide tape 600 feet in length.

DCE (data communications equipment) The hardware that performs communication—usually a dialup modem that establishes and controls the data link through the telephone network. See also *DTE*.

DDE (dynamic data exchange) A form of inter-process communications used by Microsoft Windows to support the exchange of commands and data between two applications running simultaneously. This capability has been enhanced further with object linking and embedding (OLE).

DDoS (distributed denial of service) Refers to a type of denial-of-service attack that uses multiple computers that have been taken over by an intruder to attack a targeted system. See also *DoS*.

DDR (double data rate) A type of SDRAM that allows two accesses per clock cycle, doubling the effective speed of the memory. The most common types of DDR include PC2100 (also known as DDR 266MHz), PC2700 (also known as DDR 333MHz) and PC3200 (also known as DDR 400MHz). See also *SDRAM*.

DDR2 (double data rate 2) A type of SDRAM that enables two accesses per clock cycle, doubling the effective speed of the memory. DDR2 has more robust signaling and is faster than conventional DDR. The most common types of DDR2 include PC2-3200 (also known as DDR2-400MHz), PC2-4300 (also known as DDR2-533MHz), PC2-5400 (also known as DDR2-667MHz), and PC2-6400 (also known as DDR2-800MHz). See also *DDR* and *SDRAM*.

de facto standard A software or hardware technology not officially made a standard by any recognized standards organization but that is used as a reference for consumers and vendors because of its dominance in the marketplace.

DEBUG The name of a utility program included with DOS and used for specialized purposes, such as altering memory locations, tracing program execution, patching programs and disk sectors, and performing other low-level tasks.

decibel (dB) A logarithmic measure of the ratio between two powers, voltages, currents, sound intensities, and so on. Signal-to-noise ratios are expressed in decibels.

dedicated line A user-installed telephone line that connects a specified number of computers or terminals within a limited area, such as a single building. The line is a cable rather than a public-access telephone line. The communications channel also can be referred to as nonswitched because calls do not go through telephone company switching equipment.

dedicated servo surface In voice-coil–actuated hard disk drives, one side of one platter given over to servo data that is used to guide and position the read/write heads.

default Any setting assumed at startup or reset by the computer's software and attached devices and operational until changed by the user. An assumption the computer makes when no other parameters are specified. When you type DIR without specifying the drive to search, for example, the computer assumes you want it to search the default drive. The term is used in software to describe any action the computer or program takes on its own with embedded values.

defect map A list of unusable sectors and tracks coded onto a drive during the low-level format process.

defragmentation The process of rearranging disk sectors so files are stored on consecutive sectors in adjacent tracks.

degauss 1) To remove magnetic charges or to erase magnetic images. Normal applications include CRT monitors and disks or tapes. Most monitors incorporate a degaussing coil, which surrounds the CRT, and automatically energize this coil for a few seconds when powered up to remove color or image-distorting magnetic fields from the metal mask inside the tube. Some monitors include a button or control that can be used for additional applications of this coil to remove more stubborn magnetic traces. 2) Also the act of erasing or demagnetizing a magnetic disk or tape using a special tool called a degaussing coil.

density The amount of data that can be packed into a certain area on a specific storage media.

desktop A personal computer that sits on a desk.

device driver Originally, a memory-resident program loaded by CONFIG.SYS that controls an unusual device, such as an expanded memory board. Windows also uses device drivers, but they are loaded through the Windows Registry or .INI files.

DHCP (Dynamic Host Configuration Protocol) A protocol for assigning dynamic IP addresses to devices on a network. With dynamic addressing, a device can have a different IP address every time it connects to the network. Routers, gateways, and broadband modems can function as DHCP hosts to provide IP addresses to other computers and devices on the network.

Dhrystone A benchmark program used as a standard figure of merit indicating aspects of a computer system's performance in areas other than floating-point math performance. Because the program does not use any floating-point operations, performs no I/O, and makes no operating system calls, it is most useful for measuring the processor performance of a system. The original Dhrystone program was developed in 1984 and was written in Ada, although the C and Pascal versions became more popular by 1989.

DHTML (Dynamic HTML) A collective term for cascading style sheets, layering, dynamic fonts, and other features encompassed in standard HTML 4.0, Netscape Navigator 4.x and above, and Internet Explorer 4.x and above. Because of differences in how browsers interpret particular DHTML features, many developers incorporate browser-checking code into their Web pages to enable or disable certain features depending on the browser being used to view the page.

diagnostics Programs used to check the operation of a computer system. These programs enable the operator to check the entire system for any problems and indicate in which area the problems lie.

dialup adapter In Windows, a software program that uses a modem to emulate a network interface card for networking. Most commonly used to connect to an Internet service provider or a dialup server for remote access to a LAN.

die An individual chip (processor, RAM, or other integrated circuit) cut from a finished silicon chip wafer and built into the physical package that connects it to the rest of the PC or a circuit board.

differential An electrical signaling method in which a pair of lines are used for each signal in "push-pull" fashion. In most cases, differential signals are balanced so that the same current flows on each line in opposite directions. This is unlike single-ended signals, which use only one line per signal referenced to a single ground. Differential signals have a large tolerance for common-mode noise and little crosstalk when used with twisted-pair wires even in long cables. Differential signaling is expensive because two pins are required for each signal.

digital camera A type of camera that uses a sensor and internal or removable flash memory in place of film to record still images. Digital cameras' picture quality is usually rated in megapixels. See also *megapixel*.

digital loopback A test that checks the modem's RS-232 interface and the cable that connects the terminal or computer and the modem. The modem receives data (in the form of digital signals) from the computer or terminal and immediately returns the data to the screen for verification.

digital signals Discrete, uniform signals. In this book, the term refers to the binary digits 0 and 1.

digital signature An electronic identifier used to authenticate a message or the contents of a file. Windows 98 and above are designed to prefer digitally signed device drivers (drivers approved by the Windows Hardware Quality Labs) and will warn you if you try to install an unsigned device driver.

digital-to-analog converter (DAC) A device for converting digital signals to analog signals. VGA-based displays are analog, so video cards that connect to them include a DAC to convert the signals to analog to drive the display.

digitize To transform an analog wave to a digital signal a computer can store. Conversion to digital data and back is performed by a D/A converter (DAC), often a single-chip device. How closely a digitized sample represents an analog wave depends on the number of times the amplitude of a wave is measured and recorded (the rate of digitization), as well as the number of levels that can be specified at each instance. The number of possible signal levels is dictated by the resolution in bits.

DIMM (dual inline memory module) A series of memory modules used in Pentium and newer PCs. They are available in many different versions, including those with SDRAM, DDR or DDR2, 3.3V, 2.5V or 1.8V, buffered, unbuffered or registered, and in 64-bit (non-ECC/parity) or 72-bit (ECC/parity) form. See also *DDR*, *DDR2*, and *SDRAM*.

DIP (dual inline package) A family of rectangular, integrated-circuit flat packages that have leads on the two longer sides. Package material is plastic or ceramic.

DIP switch A tiny switch (or group of switches) on a circuit board. Named for the form factor of the carrier device in which the switch is housed.

direct memory access (DMA) A process by which data moves between a disk drive (or other device) and system memory without direct control of the central processing unit, thus freeing it up for other tasks.

Direct Rambus DRAM See *RDRAM*.

directory An area of a disk that stores the titles given to the files saved on the disk and serves as a table of contents for those files. Contains data that identifies the name of a file, the size, the attributes (system, hidden, read-only, and so on), the date and time of creation, and a pointer to the location of the file. Each entry in a directory is 32 bytes long. Windows refers to subdirectories (directories beneath the root directory) as folders.

DirectX A set of graphics-related drivers and APIs that translates generic hardware commands into specific commands for particular pieces of hardware. Developed by Microsoft, DirectX lets graphical or multimedia applications take advantage of specific features supported by various graphics accelerators.

disc Flat, circular, rotating medium that can store various types of information, both analog and digital. *Disc* is often used in reference to optical storage media, whereas *disk* refers to magnetic storage media. *Disc* also is often used as a short form for videodisc or compact audio disc (CD).

disk Alternative spelling for disc that generally refers to magnetic storage medium on which information can be accessed at random. Floppy disks and hard disks are examples.

disk access time See *access time*.

disk cache A portion of memory on the PC motherboard or on a drive interface card or controller used to store frequently accessed information from the drive (such as the file allocation table [FAT] or directory structure) to speed up disk access. With a larger disk cache, additional data from the data portion of a drive can be cached as well. See also *cache*, *L1 cache*, and *L2 cache*.

disk partition See *partition*.

display A device used for viewing information generated by a computer.

display adapter The interface between the computer and the monitor that transmits the signals which appear as images on the display. This can take the form of an expansion card or a chip built into the motherboard.

dithering The process of creating more colors and shades from a given color palette. In monochrome displays or printers, dithering varies the black-and-white dot patterns to simulate shades of gray. Grayscale dithering is used to produce different shades of gray when the device can produce only limited levels of black or white outputs. Color screens or printers use dithering to create additional colors by mixing and varying the dot sizing and spacing. For example, when converting from 24-bit color to 8-bit color (an 8-bit palette has only 256 colors compared to the 24-bit palette's millions), dithering adds pixels of different colors to simulate the original color. Error diffusion is a type of dithering best suited for photographs.

DLC (Data Link Control) Refers to the Data Link Layer in the OSI model. Every network interface card (NIC) has a unique DLC address or DLC identifier (DLCI) that identifies the node on the network. For Ethernet networks, the DLC address is usually called the Media Access Control (MAC) address.

DLL (Dynamic Link Library) An executable driver program module for Microsoft Windows that can be loaded on demand, linked in at runtime, and subsequently unloaded when the driver is no longer needed.

DMA See *direct memory access*.

DMI (Desktop Management Interface) DMI is an operating-system– and protocol-independent standard developed by the Desktop Management Task Force (DMTF) for managing desktop systems and servers. DMI provides a bidirectional path to interrogate all the hardware and software components within a PC, enabling hardware and software configurations to be monitored from a central station in a network.

DNS (domain name system or service) An Internet service that translates domain names into numeric IP addresses. Every time you use a domain name, a DNS server must translate the name into the corresponding IP address.

docking station Equipment that enables a laptop or notebook computer to use peripherals and accessories normally associated with desktop systems.

DOCSIS See *CableLabs Certified Cable Modem*.

doping Adding chemical impurities to silicon (which is naturally a nonconductor) to create a material with semiconductor properties that is then used in the manufacturing of electronic chips.

DoS (denial of service) An Internet attack on a resource that prevents users from accessing email, Web sites, or other services. It usually exploits security shortcomings in email or Web servers. See also *DDoS*.

DOS (Disk Operating System) A collection of programs stored on the DOS disk that contain routines enabling the system and user to manage information and the hardware resources of the computer. DOS must be loaded into the computer before other programs can be started.

dot pitch A measurement of the width of the dots that make up a pixel. The smaller the dot pitch, the sharper the image.

dot-matrix printer An impact printer that prints characters composed of dots. Characters are printed one at a time by pressing the ends of selected wires against an inked ribbon and paper.

double density (DD) An indication of the storage capacity of a floppy drive or disk in which eight or nine sectors per track are recorded using MFM encoding. See also *MFM encoding*.

download The process of receiving files from another computer.

downtime Operating time lost because of a computer malfunction.

DPMI (DOS Protected Mode Interface) An industry-standard interface that allows DOS applications to execute program code in the protected mode of the 286 or later Intel processor. The DPMI specification is available from Intel.

DPMS (Display Power Management Signaling) A VESA standard for signaling a monitor or display to switch into energy conservation mode. DPMS provides for two low-energy modes: standby and suspend.

DRAM (dynamic random access memory) The most common type of computer memory, DRAM can be manufactured very inexpensively compared to other types of memory. DRAM chips are small and inexpensive because they normally require only one transistor and a capacitor to represent each bit. The capacitors must be energized every 15ms or so (hundreds of times per second) to maintain their charges. DRAM is volatile, meaning it loses data with no power or without regular refresh cycles.

drive A mechanical device that manipulates data storage media.

driver A program designed to interface a particular piece of hardware to an operating system or other standard software.

drum The cylindrical photoreceptor in a laser printer that receives the document image from the laser and applies it to the page as it slowly rotates.

DSL (digital subscriber line) A high-speed digital modem technology. DSL is either symmetric or asymmetric. Asymmetric provides faster downstream speeds, which is suited for Internet usage and video on demand. Symmetric provides the same rate coming and going. See also *ADSL*.

DSM (digital storage media) A digital storage or transmission device or system.

DSP (digital signal processor) Dedicated, limited-function processor often found in modems, sound cards, cellular phones, and so on.

DTE (data terminal [or terminating] equipment) The device, usually a computer or terminal, that generates or is the final destination of data. See also *DCE*.

dual cavity pin grid array Chip packaging designed by Intel for use with the Pentium Pro processor that houses the processor die in one cavity of the package and the L2 cache memory in a second cavity within the same package.

dual independent bus (DIB) architecture A processor technology with the existence of two independent buses on the processor—the L2 cache bus and the processor-to-main memory system bus. The processor can use both buses simultaneously, thus getting as much as two times more data into and out of the processor than a single bus architecture processor. The Intel Pentium Pro, Pentium II, and newer processors from Intel and AMD (such as the AMD Athlon and Duron) have DIB architecture.

dual scan display   A lower-quality but economical type of LCD color display that has an array of transistors running down the x and y axes of two sides of the screen. The number of transistors determines the screen's resolution.

dumb terminal   A screen and keyboard device with no inherent processing power connected to a computer that is usually remotely located.

duplex   Indicates a communications channel capable of carrying signals in both directions.

Duron   A low-cost version of the Athlon processor with less L2 cache. Available in the Socket A (462-pin) chip package.

DVD (digital versatile disc)   Originally called digital video disc. A new type of high-capacity CD-ROM disc and drive format with up to 28 times the capacity of a standard CD-ROM. The disc is the same diameter as a CD-ROM but can be recorded on both sides and on two layers for each side. Each side holds 4.7GB on a single layer disc, whereas dual-layer versions hold 8.5GB per side, for a maximum of 17GB total if both sides and both layers are used, which is the equivalent of 28 CD-ROMs. DVD drives can read standard audio CDs and CD-ROMs.

DVD burner   Popular term for a rewritable DVD drive, particularly one that uses DVD-R/RW or DVD+R/RW media.

DVD-A   A DVD format designed to support high-quality music and audio. DVD-A uses 24-bit sampling at 96KHz, significantly better than CD audio (16-bit at 44.1KHz). Unlike DVD, DVD-A discs can be played on conventional CD players but produce the highest quality only when played on DVD-A players.

DVD-R   A writeable DVD format compatible with standalone DVD players and DVD-ROM drives. DVD-R was introduced by Pioneer and was released to the DVD Forum (www.dvdforum.org) in July 1997. It uses a wobbled-groove recording process to store 4.7GB of data and is optimized for sequential data access. See also *DVD-RW*.

DVD+R   A writeable DVD format compatible with standalone DVD players and DVD-ROM drives. DVD+R was developed by the DVD+RW Alliance (www.dvdrw.com), whose members include Microsoft, Sony, HP, and Dell. In addition, it is supported by second-generation DVD+RW drives and holds 4.7GB of data. DVD+R/RW are the only recordable DVD formats that fully support the Mt. Rainier (also called EasyWrite) standard coming in Windows Longhorn (in 2005). This enables discs to be used right out of the box with automatic background formatting and no additional packet-writing software required. DVD+R/RW are the most compatible, fastest, most capable, and most popular of all the recordable DVD formats. See also *DVD+RW*.

DVD-RAM   A rewritable DVD format developed by Panasonic, Toshiba, and Hitachi and supported by the DVD Forum. DVD-RAM is the oldest DVD rewritable format, but because the media uses a caddy and has a lower reflectivity than normal DVD media, DVD-RAM discs are not compatible with other types of DVD drives or with standalone DVD players.

DVD-RW   A rewritable DVD format developed by Pioneer and released to the DVD Forum in November 1999. It uses a phase-change technology similar to CD-RW. As with most CD-RW media and drives, the entire disc must be formatted before it can be used. Its write speed is also lower than DVD+RW, and the entire disc must be erased before it can be used to store new data. See also *DVD-R*.

DVD+RW   A rewritable DVD format developed by the DVD+RW Alliance; the first DVD+RW drives were released in 2001. DVD+RW uses a phase-change technology similar to CD-RW and DVD-RW. DVD+R/RW are the only recordable DVD formats that fully support the Mt. Rainier (EasyWrite) standard coming in Windows Longhorn (in 2005). This enables discs to be used right out of the box with automatic background formatting and no additional packet-writing software required. DVD+R/RW are the most compatible, fastest, most capable, and most popular of all the recordable DVD formats. See also *DVD+R*.

DVI (Digital Video Interactive)   A standard that was originally developed at RCA Laboratories and sold to Intel in 1988. DVI integrates digital motion, still video, sound, graphics, and special effects in a compressed format. DVI is a highly sophisticated hardware compression technique used in interactive multimedia applications.

DVI (Digital Visual Interface)   The current de facto standard for LCD displays developed by the Digital Display Working Group in April 1999. DVI-D provides digital signals only, whereas DVI-I (which is more common) provides both digital and analog signals. A DVI-I connector can be converted to VGA with an external adapter.

Dvorak keyboard   A keyboard design by August Dvorak that was patented in 1936 and approved by ANSI in 1982. Provides increased speed and comfort and reduces the rate of errors by placing the most frequently used letters in the center for use by the strongest fingers. Finger motions and awkward strokes are reduced by more than 90% in comparison with the familiar QWERTY keyboard. The Dvorak keyboard has the five vowel keys, AOEUI, together under the left hand in the center row and the five most frequently used consonants, DHTNS, under the fingers of the right hand.

dynamic execution A processing technique that enables the processor to dynamically predict the order of instructions and execute them out of order internally if necessary for an improvement in speed. Uses these three techniques: Multiple Branch Prediction, Data Flow Analysis, and Speculative Execution.

E2000 Also called Energy 2000, this is a Swiss-developed standard for power management that calls for computer monitors to use only 5 watts of power when in standby mode.

EBCDIC (Extended Binary Coded Decimal Interchange Code) An IBM-developed, 8-bit code for the representation of characters. It allows 256 possible character combinations within a single byte. EBCDIC is the standard code on IBM minicomputers and mainframes, but not on the IBM microcomputers, where ASCII is used instead.

ECC (error correcting code) A type of system memory or cache that is capable of detecting and correcting some types of memory errors without interrupting processing.

ECP (enhanced capabilities port) A type of high-speed parallel port jointly developed by Microsoft and Hewlett-Packard that offers improved performance for the parallel port and requires special hardware logic. ECP ports use both an IRQ and a DMA channel. See also *IEEE 1284*.

edge connector The part of a circuit board containing a series of printed contacts that is inserted into an expansion slot or a connector.

EDO (extended data out) RAM A type of RAM chip that enables a timing overlap between successive accesses, thus improving memory cycle time.

EEPROM (electrically erasable programmable read-only memory) A type of nonvolatile memory chip used to store semipermanent information in a computer, such as the BIOS. An EEPROM can be erased and reprogrammed directly in the host system without special equipment. This is used so manufacturers can upgrade the ROM code in a system by supplying a special program that erases and reprograms the EEPROM chip with the new code. Also called flash ROM.

EGA (enhanced graphics adapter) A type of PC video display adapter first introduced by IBM on September 10, 1984, that supports text and graphics. Text is supported at a maximum resolution of 80×25 characters in 16 colors with a character box of 8×14 pixels. Graphics are supported at a maximum resolution of 640×350 pixels in 16 (from a palette of 64) colors. The EGA outputs a TTL (digital) signal with a horizontal scanning frequency of 15.75KHz, 18.432KHz, or 21.85KHz, and it supports TTL color or TTL monochrome displays.

EIA (Electronic Industries Association) An organization that defines electronic standards in the United States.

EIDE (Enhanced Integrated Drive Electronics) A specific Western Digital implementation of the ATA-2 specification. See also *ATA-2*.

EISA (Extended Industry Standard Architecture) An extension of the Industry Standard Architecture (ISA) bus developed by IBM for the AT. The EISA design was led by Compaq Corporation. Later, eight other manufacturers (AST, Epson, Hewlett-Packard, NEC, Olivetti, Tandy, Wyse, and Zenith) joined Compaq in a consortium founded September 13, 1988. This group became known as the "gang of nine." The EISA design was patterned largely after IBM's Micro Channel Architecture (MCA) in the PS/2 systems, but unlike MCA, EISA enables backward compatibility with older plug-in adapters. EISA products became obsolete after the development of the PCI slot architecture. See also *PCI*.

electronic mail (email) A method of transferring messages from one computer to another.

electrostatic discharge (ESD) The grounding of static electricity. A sudden flow of electricity between two objects at different electrical potentials. ESD is a primary cause of integrated circuit damage or failure.

ELF (extremely low frequency) A very low-frequency electromagnetic radiation generated by common electrical appliances, including computer monitors. The Swedish MPR II standard governs this and other emissions. Also called VLF (very low frequency).

embedded controller In disk drives, a controller built into the same physical unit that houses the drive rather than on a separate adapter card. IDE and SCSI drives both use embedded controllers.

embedded servo data Magnetic markings embedded between or inside tracks on disk drives that use voice-coil actuators. These markings enable the actuator to fine-tune the position of the read/write heads.

EMM (expanded memory manager) A driver that provides a software interface to expanded memory. EMMs were originally created for expanded memory boards but also can use the memory management capabilities of the 386 or later processors to emulate an expanded memory board. EMM386.EXE is an example of an EMM that comes with DOS and Windows 9x.

EMS (Expanded Memory Specification)
Sometimes also called the LIM spec because it was developed by Lotus, Intel, and Microsoft. Provides a way for microcomputers running under DOS to access additional memory. EMS memory management provides access to a maximum of 32MB of expanded memory through a small (usually 64KB) window in conventional memory. EMS is a cumbersome access scheme designed primarily for pre-286 systems that could not access extended memory.

emulator A piece of test apparatus that emulates or imitates the function of a particular chip.

encoding The protocol by which data is carried or stored by a medium.

encryption The translation of data into unreadable codes to maintain security.

endec (encoder/decoder) A device that takes data and clock signals and combines or encodes them using a particular encoding scheme into a single signal for transmission or storage. The same device also later separates or decodes the data and clock signals during a receive or read operation. Sometimes called a data separator.

Energy Star A certification program started by the Environmental Protection Agency. Energy Star–certified computers and peripherals are designed to draw less than 30 watts of electrical energy from a standard 110-volt AC outlet during periods of inactivity. Also called Green PCs. See also *E2000*.

Enhanced CD (CD-E) See *Blue Book*.

enhanced graphics adapter See *EGA*.

enhanced small device interface See *ESDI*.

EPP (enhanced parallel port) A type of parallel port developed by Intel, Xircom, and Zenith Data Systems that operates at almost ISA bus speed and offers a tenfold increase in the raw throughput capability over a conventional parallel port. EPP is especially designed for parallel port peripherals, such as LAN adapters, disk drives, and tape backups. See also *IEEE 1284*.

EPROM (erasable programmable read-only memory) A type of read-only memory (ROM) in which the data pattern can be erased to allow a new pattern. EPROM usually is erased by ultraviolet light and recorded by a higher-than-normal voltage programming signal.

equalization A compensation circuit designed into modems to counteract certain distortions introduced by the telephone channel. Two types are used: fixed (compromise) equalizers and those that adapt to channel conditions (adaptive). Good-quality modems use adaptive equalization.

error control Various techniques that check the reliability of characters (parity) or blocks of data. V.42, MNP, and HST error-control protocols use error detection (CRC) and retransmission of error frames (ARQ).

error message A word or combination of words to indicate to the user that an error has occurred somewhere in the program.

ESCD (extended system configuration data) Area in CMOS or Flash/NVRAM where plug-and-play information is stored.

ESDI (Enhanced Small Device Interface) A hardware standard developed by Maxtor and standardized by a consortium of 22 disk drive manufacturers on January 26, 1983. A group of 27 manufacturers formed the ESDI steering committee on September 15, 1986, to enhance and improve the specification. A high-performance interface used primarily with hard disks, ESDI enables a maximum data transfer rate to and from a hard disk of between 10Mbps and 24Mbps. ESDI was replaced by IDE and SCSI interfaces. ESDI drives use the same 34-pin and 20-pin cables used by ST412/ST506 drives.

Ethernet A type of network protocol developed in the late 1970s by Bob Metcalf at Xerox Corporation and endorsed by the IEEE. One of the oldest LAN communications protocols in the personal computing industry, Ethernet networks use a collision-detection protocol to manage contention. Ethernet is defined by the IEEE 802.3 standard. See also *10BASE-T*.

expanded memory Otherwise known as EMS memory, this is memory that conforms to the EMS specification. Requires a special device driver and conforms to a standard developed by Lotus, Intel, and Microsoft.

expansion card An integrated circuit card that plugs into an expansion slot on a motherboard to provide access to additional peripherals or features not built into the motherboard. Also referred to as an add-in board.

expansion slot A slot on the motherboard that physically and electrically connects an expansion card to the motherboard and the system buses.

extended graphics array See *XGA*.

extended memory Direct processor-addressable memory addressed by an Intel (or compatible) 286 or more advanced processor in the region beyond the first megabyte. Addressable only in the processor's protected mode of operation.

extended partition A nonbootable DOS partition (also supported by Windows) containing DOS volumes. Starting with DOS v3.3, the FDISK program can create two partitions that serve DOS: an ordinary, bootable partition (called the primary partition) and an extended partition, which can contain as many as 23 volumes from D: to Z:.

external device A peripheral installed outside the system case.

extra-high density (ED) An indication of the storage capacity of a floppy drive or disk in which 36 sectors per track are recorded using a vertical recording technique with MFM encoding.

FAQ (frequently asked questions) Name for a list of popular questions and answers covering any particular subject.

Fast Ethernet Popular term for 100BASE-T and other 100Mbps versions of Ethernet. Fast Ethernet uses CAT 5 cable.

Fast Page Mode RAM A type of RAM that improves on standard DRAM speed by enabling faster access to all the data within a given row of memory by keeping the row address the same and changing only the column.

Fast-ATA (fast AT attachment interface) Also called Fast ATA-2, these are specific Seagate and Quantum implementations of the ATA-2 interface. See also *ATA-2*.

FAT (file allocation table) A table held near the outer edge of a disk that tells which sectors are allocated to each file and in what order.

FAT32 A disk file allocation system from Microsoft that uses 32-bit values for FAT entries instead of the 16-bit values used by the original FAT system, enabling partition sizes up to 2TB (terabytes). Although the entries are 32-bits, 4-bits are reserved and only 28-bits are used. FAT32 first appeared in Windows 95B and is also supported by Windows 98, Windows Me, Windows 2000, and Windows XP.

fault tolerance The capability of a computer to withstand a failure. Many levels of fault tolerance exist, and fault tolerance can be applied to several components or systems in the computer. For example, ECC (error correcting code) memory is considered fault tolerant because it is typically capable of automatically identifying and correcting single bit errors.

fax/modem A peripheral that integrates the capabilities of a fax machine and a modem in one expansion card or external unit. Almost all 14.4Kbps and faster modems sold for use in desktop or portable PCs include fax capabilities.

FC-PGA (flip-chip pin grid array) A type of chip packaging first used in the Socket PGA370 version of the Pentium III where the raw processor die has bumped contacts spaced on the face of the die and is mounted facedown to a pin grid array carrier. The heatsink is then directly attached to the back of the raw silicon die surface.

FDISK The name of the disk-partitioning program under several operating systems, including DOS and Windows 9x/Me, to create the master boot record and allocate partitions for the operating system's use.

feature connector On a video adapter, a connector that enables an additional video feature card, such as a separate 3D accelerator, video capture card, or MPEG decoder, to be connected to the main video adapter and display.

fiber optic A type of cable or connection using strands or threads of glass to guide a beam of modulated light. Allows for very high-speed signaling and multiplexing as well as the combining of many data streams along a single cable.

FIFO (first-in, first-out) A method of storing and retrieving items from a list, table, or stack so that the first element stored is the first one retrieved.

file A collection of information kept somewhere other than in random-access memory.

file attribute Information held in the attribute byte of a file's directory entry.

file compression See *compressed file*.

filename The name given to the disk file. For DOS, it must be from one to eight characters long and can be followed by a filename extension, which can be from one to three characters long. Windows 9x and above ease these constraints by allowing filenames of up to 255 characters including the directory path.

firewall A hardware or software system designed to prevent unauthorized access to or from a private network.

FireWire Also called IEEE 1394 or i.Link. A serial I/O interface standard that is extremely fast, with data transfer rates up to 400MBps, 800MBps, or 3.2GBps, depending on the version of standard used. Most current implementations use the 400MBps IEEE 1394a version.

firmware Software contained in a read-only memory (ROM) device. A cross between hardware and software, firmware can be easily updated if stored in an EEPROM or flash ROM chip. See also *EEPROM* and *flash ROM*.

fixed disk Also called a hard disk, it's a disk that can't be removed from its controlling hardware or housing. Made of rigid material with a magnetic coating and used for the mass storage and retrieval of data.

flash ROM A type of EEPROM developed by Intel that can be erased and reprogrammed in the host system. See also *EEPROM*.

flicker A monitor condition caused by refresh rates that are too low, in which the display flashes visibly. This can cause eyestrain or more severe physical problems.

floating-point unit (FPU) Sometimes called the math coprocessor; handles the more complex calculations of the processing cycle.

floppy disk A removable disk using flexible magnetic media enclosed in a semirigid or rigid plastic case.

floppy disk controller The logic and interface that connects a floppy disk drive to the system.

floppy tape A tape standard that uses drives connecting to an ordinary floppy disk controller, such as QIC-80 or Travan-1.

floptical drive A special type of high-capacity removable disk drive that uses an optical mechanism to properly position the drive read/write heads over the data tracks on the disk. This enables more precise control of the read/write positioning and therefore narrower track spacing and more data packed into a smaller area than traditional floppy disks. The LS-120 and LS-240 SuperDisk drives are recent examples of floptical drives.

flow control A mechanism that compensates for differences in the flow of data input to and output from a modem or other device.

FM encoding Frequency modulation encoding. An outdated method of encoding data on the disk surface that uses up half the disk space with timing signals.

FM synthesis An audio technology that uses one sine wave operator to modify another and create an artificial sound that mimics an instrument.

folder In a graphical user interface, a simulated file folder that holds documents (text, data, or graphics), applications, and other folders. A folder is similar to a DOS subdirectory.

footprint Describes the shape of something. See also *form factor.*

form factor The physical dimensions of a device. Two devices with the same form factor are physically interchangeable. The IBM PC, XT, and XT Model 286, for example, all use power supplies that are internally different but have exactly the same form factor.

FORMAT The DOS/Windows format program that performs both low- and high-level formatting on floppy disks but only high-level formatting on hard disks.

formatted capacity The total number of bytes of data that can fit on a formatted disk. The unformatted capacity is higher because space is lost defining the boundaries between sectors.

formatting Preparing a disk so the computer can read or write to it. Checks the disk for defects and constructs an organizational system to manage information on the disk.

FORTRAN (formula translator) A high-level programming language developed in 1954 by John Backus at IBM primarily for programs dealing with mathematical formulas and expressions similar to algebra and used primarily in scientific and technical applications.

fragmentation The state of having a file scattered around a disk in pieces rather than existing in one contiguous area of the disk. Fragmented files are slower to read than files stored in contiguous areas and can be more difficult to recover if the FAT or a directory becomes damaged.

frame 1) A data communications term for a block of data with header and trailer information attached. The added information usually includes a frame number, block size data, error-check codes, and start/end indicators. 2) A single, complete picture in a video or film recording. A video frame consists of two interlaced fields of either 525 lines (NTSC) or 625 lines (PAL/SECAM), running at 30 frames per second (NTSC) or 25 frames per second (PAL/SECAM).

frame buffer A memory device that stores, pixel by pixel, the contents of an image. Frame buffers are used to refresh a raster image. Sometimes they incorporate local processing capability. The "depth" of the frame buffer is the number of bits per pixel, which determines the number of colors or intensities that can be displayed.

frame rate The speed at which video frames are scanned or displayed: 30 frames per second for NTSC and 25 frames per second for PAL/SECAM.

FTP (File Transfer Protocol) A method of transferring files over the Internet. FTP can be used to transfer files between two machines on which the user has accounts. Anonymous FTP can be used to retrieve a file from a server without having an account on that server.

full duplex Signal flow in both directions at the same time. In microcomputer communications, it also can refer to the suppression of the online local echo. 100BASE-TX network cards capable of full-duplex operations can run at an effective speed of 200Mbps when full-duplex operation is enabled.

full-height drive A drive unit that is 3 1/4" high, 5 1/4" wide, and 8" deep. Equal to two half-height drive bays.

full-motion video A video sequence displayed at full television standard resolutions and frame rates. In the U.S., this equates to NTSC video at 30 frames per second.

function keys Special-purpose keys that can be programmed to perform various operations. They serve many functions, depending on the program being used.

G.lite A popular form of ADSL, G.lite can be self-installed by the user. Also referred to as the G.992.2 standard.

gas-plasma display Commonly used in portable systems, it's a type of display that operates by exciting a gas—usually neon or an argon-neon mixture—through the application of a voltage. When sufficient voltage is applied at the intersection of two electrodes, the gas glows an orange-red. Because gas-plasma displays generate light, they require no backlighting.

gateway Officially, an application-to-application conversion program or system. For example, an email gateway converts from SMTP (Internet) email format to MHS (Novell) email format. The term gateway is also used as a slang term for router. See also *router*.

gender When describing connectors for PCs, connectors are described as male if they have pins or female if they have receptacles designed to accept the pins of a male connector.

genlocking The process of aligning the data rate of a video image with that of a digital device to digitize the image and enter it into computer memory. The machine that performs this function is known as a genlock.

Ghost Popular utility program sold by Symantec that can be used to create a compressed version of a drive's contents and clone it to one or more PCs over a network or via CD storage.

gibi A multiplier equal to 1,073,741,824.

gibibyte (Gi) A unit of information storage equal to 1,073,741,824 bytes (1,024×1,024×1,024 equals a Gi). Formerly known as a binary gigabyte. See also *gigabyte* and *kilobyte*.

GIF (Graphics Interchange Format) A popular raster graphics file format developed by CompuServe that handles 8-bit color (256 colors) and uses the LZW method to achieve compression ratios of approximately 1.5:1 to 2:1. You can reduce the size of a GIF file even more by dropping unused colors from the file.

giga A multiplier indicating one billion (1,000,000,000) of some unit. Abbreviated as g or G. The binary giga (1,073,741,824) is now referred to as a gibi. See also *gibi*.

gigabyte (GB) A unit of information storage equal to 1,000,000,000 bytes. The value formerly called a binary GB (1,073,741,824 bytes) is now called a gibibyte. See also *gibibyte*.

gigahertz GHz is used to measure the clock frequency of high-performance processors. The first 1GHz desktop processor was introduced by AMD (a 1GHz Athlon) in March 2000.

GPU (graphics processing unit) A 3D graphics chip that contains advanced 3D rendering features such as hardware, vertex, and pixel shaders. NVIDIA's GeForce 3 and GeForce 4 Ti series; the ATI Radeon 7xxx, 8xxx, and 9xxx series; and the Matrox Parhelia series are typical GPUs. See also *hardware shader*, *pixel shader*, and *vertex shader*.

graphics accelerator A video processor or chipset specially designed to speed the display and rendering of graphical objects onscreen. Originally, accelerators were optimized for 2D or 3D operations, but all current graphics accelerators, such as NVIDIA's GeForce and ATI's RADEON series, accelerate both types of data.

graphics adapter See *video adapter*.

Green Book The standard for Compact Disc-Interactive (CD-I). Philips developed CD-I technology for the consumer market to be connected to a television instead of a computer monitor. CD-I is not a computer system but a consumer device that made a small splash in the market and disappeared. CD-I discs require special code and are not compatible with standard CD-ROMs. A CD-ROM can't be played on the CD-I machine, but Red Book audio can be played on it.

GUI (graphical user interface) A type of program interface that enables users to choose commands and functions by pointing to a graphical icon using either a keyboard or pointing device, such as a mouse. Windows is the most popular GUI available for PC systems.

half duplex Signal flow in both directions but only one way at a time. In microcomputer communications, half duplex can refer to activation of the online local echo, which causes the modem to send a copy of the transmitted data to the screen of the sending computer.

half-height drive A drive unit that is 1.625" high, 5 1/4" wide, and 8" deep.

halftoning A process that uses dithering to simulate a continuous tone image, such as a photograph or shaded drawing, using various sizes of dots. Newspapers, magazines, and many books use halftoning. The human eye merges the dots to give the impression of gray shades.

handshaking The process of exchanging information about speeds and protocols between analog modems to establish a dialup connection. If your modem volume is high enough, you can hear handshaking as a series of distinct tones at the start of a modem-to-modem call.

hard disk A high-capacity disk storage unit characterized by a normally nonremovable rigid substrate medium. The platters in a hard disk usually are constructed of aluminum or glass/ceramic. Also sometimes called a fixed disk.

hard error An error in reading or writing data caused by damaged hardware.

hard reset Resetting a system via the hardware, usually by pressing a dedicated reset button wired to the motherboard/processor reset circuitry. Does not clear memory like a cold boot does. See also *cold boot.*

hardware Physical components that make up a microcomputer, monitor, printer, and so on.

hardware shader A general term describing the processing of vertex or pixel shading in a GPU's hardware. GPUs such as the ATI 8xxx and 9xxx series or the NVIDIA GeForce 3 and GeForce 4 Ti-series GPU chips have hardware shaders compatible with DirectX 8 and above.

HDLC (High-Level Data Link Control) A standard protocol developed by the ISO for software applications and communicating devices operating in synchronous environments. Defines operations at the link level of communications—for example, the format of data frames exchanged between modems over a phone line.

head A small electromagnetic device inside a drive that reads, records, and erases data on the media.

head actuator The device that moves read/write heads across a disk drive's platters. Most drives use a stepper-motor or voice-coil actuator.

head crash A (usually) rare occurrence in which a read/write head strikes a platter surface with sufficient force to damage the magnetic medium.

head parking A procedure in which a disk drive's read/write heads are moved to an unused track so they will not damage data in the event of a head crash or other failure.

head seek The movement of a drive's read/write heads to a particular track.

heatsink A mass of metal attached to a chip carrier or socket for the purpose of dissipating heat. Some heatsinks are passive (relying on existing air currents only), but most heatsinks on processors are active (including a fan). Many video card accelerator chips and motherboard North Bridge chips are also fitted with heatsinks today.

helical scan A type of recording technology that has vastly increased the capacity of tape drives. Invented for use in broadcast systems and now used in VCRs. Conventional longitudinal recording records a track of data straight across the width of a single-track tape. Helical scan recording packs more data on the tape by positioning the tape at an angle to the recording heads. The heads spin to record diagonal stripes of information on the tape. Helical scan is used by DAT/DDS, Exabyte, and AIT drives.

hexadecimal number A number encoded in base-16, such that digits include the letters A–F and the numerals 0–9 (for example, 8BF3, which equals 35,827 in base-10).

hidden file A file not displayed in DOS directory listings because the file's attribute byte holds a special setting.

high density (HD) An indication of the storage capacity of a floppy drive or disk, in which 15 or 18 sectors per track are recorded using MFM encoding.

High Sierra format A standard format for placing files and directories on CD-ROMs, proposed by an ad hoc committee of computer vendors, software developers, and CD-ROM system integrators. (Work on the format proposal began at the High Sierra Hotel in Lake Tahoe, Nevada.) A revised version of the format was adopted by the ISO as ISO 9660. Use the ISO 9660 format to create cross-platform CD-R recordings.

high-definition television (HDTV) Video formats offering greater visual accuracy (or resolution) than current NTSC, PAL, or SECAM broadcast standards. HDTV formats generally range in resolution from 655 to 2,125 scanning lines, having an aspect ratio of 5:3 (or 1.67:1) and a video bandwidth of 30MHz–50MHz (5+ times greater than the NTSC standard). Digital HDTV has a bandwidth of 300MHz. HDTV is subjectively comparable to 35mm film.

high-level formatting Formatting performed by the DOS FORMAT program. Among other things, it creates the root directory and FATs.

history file A file created by utility software to keep track of earlier use of the software. Many backup programs, for example, keep history files describing earlier backup sessions.

hit ratio In describing the efficiency of a disk or memory cache, the hit ratio is the ratio of the number of times the data is found in the cache to the total number of data requests. 1:1 is a perfect hit ratio, meaning that every data request was found in the cache. The closer to 1:1 the ratio is, the more efficient the cache.

HMA (high memory area) The first 64KB of extended memory, which typically is controlled by the HIMEM.SYS device driver. Real-mode programs can be loaded into the HMA to conserve conventional memory. Normally, DOS 5.0 and later use the HMA exclusively to reduce the DOS conventional memory footprint.

HomePNA A home networking standard using existing home or office telephone wiring to obtain speeds up to 11Mbps.

HomeRF A wireless home network using radio waves to obtain speeds up to 11Mbps.

horizontal scan rate   In monitors, the speed at which the electron beam moves laterally across the screen. It's normally expressed as a frequency; typical monitors range from 31.5KHz to 90KHz, with the higher frequencies being more desirable.

host   The main device when two or more devices are connected. When two or more systems are connected, the system that contains the data is typically called the host, whereas the other is called the guest or user.

hotfix   A software patch for a Microsoft application or operating system. Hotfixes can be downloaded individually from the Windows Update Web site or as a service pack. Microsoft also calls them quick fix engineering (QFE) files.

HPT (high-pressure tin)   A PLCC socket that promotes high forces between socket contacts and PLCC contacts for a good connection.

HST (High-Speed Technology)   The now-obsolete U.S. Robotics proprietary high-speed modem-signaling scheme, developed as an interim protocol until the V.32 protocol could be implemented in a cost-effective manner.

HT technology   See *hyper-threading technology*.

HTML (Hypertext Markup Language)   A language used to describe and format plain-text files on the Web. HTML is based on pairs of tags that enable the user to mix graphics with text, change the appearance of text, and create hypertext documents with links to other documents. See also *DHTML*.

HTTP (Hypertext Transfer Protocol)   The protocol that describes the rules a browser and server use to communicate over the World Wide Web. HTTP allows a Web browser to request HTML documents from a Web server. See also *hypertext*.

hub   A common connection point for multiple devices in a network. A hub contains a number of ports to connect several segments of a LAN together. When a packet arrives at one of the ports on the hub, it is copied to all the other ports so all the segments of the LAN can see all the packets. A hub can be passive, intelligent (allowing remote management, including traffic monitoring and port configuration), or switching. A switching hub is also called a switch. See also *switch*.

Huffman coding   A technique that minimizes the average number of bytes required to represent the characters in a text. Huffman coding works for a given character distribution by assigning short codes to frequently occurring characters and longer codes to infrequently occurring characters.

hybrid fiber coaxial (HFC)   A network (such as that used by digital cable TV and two-way cable modems) that uses fiber-optic cabling for its backbone with coaxial cable connections to each individual computer or TV.

hyper-threading technology   A method (also called HT technology) developed by Intel for running two different instruction streams through a processor at the same time. Introduced in 2002, HT technology was first used in the Intel Xeon processor with hyper-threading technology, with speeds starting at 2.8GHz; the first HT technology–enabled desktop processor was the 3.06GHz Pentium 4.

hypertext   A technology that enables quick and easy navigation between and within large documents. Hypertext links are pointers to other sections within the same document; other documents; or other resources, such as FTP sites, images, or sounds.

HyperTransport   AMD's high-speed technology for connecting the North Bridge and South Bridge or equivalent chips on a motherboard. HyperTransport runs at six times the speed of the PCI bus (800MBps versus 133MBps for PCI). The original name was Lightning Data Transport (LDT). Several chipset makers, including AMD and NVIDIA, use HyperTransport.

Hz   An abbreviation for hertz—a frequency measurement unit used internationally to indicate one cycle per second.

i.Link   Sony's term for IEEE 1394/FireWire port. See also *FireWire*.

I/O (input/output)   A circuit path that enables independent communication between the processor and external devices.

I/O controller hub   See *ICH*.

I/O port (input/output port)   Used to communicate to and from another device, such as a printer or disk.

IA-64   Intel's 64-bit processor architecture, first used in the Itanium processor for servers.

IBMBIO.COM   One of the DOS system files required to boot the machine in older versions of PC-DOS (IBM's version of MS-DOS). The first file loaded from disk during the boot, it contains extensions to the ROM BIOS.

IBMDOS.COM   One of the DOS system files required to boot the machine in older versions of PC-DOS (IBM's version of MS-DOS). Contains the primary DOS routines. Loaded by IBMBIO.COM, it in turn loads COMMAND.COM.

IC (integrated circuit)   A complete electronic circuit contained on a single chip. It can consist of only a few or thousands of transistors, capacitors, diodes, or resistors, and it generally is classified according to the complexity of the circuitry and the approximate number of circuits on the chip. SSI (small-scale integration) equals 2–10 circuits; MSI (medium-scale integration) equals 10–100 circuits. LSI (large-scale integration) equals 100–1,000 circuits, and VLSI (very-large-scale integration) equals 1,000–10,000 circuits. Finally, ULSI (ultra-large-scale integration) equals more than 10,000 circuits.

ICH (I/O controller hub) Intel's term for the chip used in its 8xx chipsets to interface with lower-speed devices such as PCI slots, USB ports, ATA drives, and other devices traditionally controlled by the South Bridge chip. ICH chips connect with the memory controller hub (the 8xx chipsets' replacement for the North Bridge) through a high-speed hub interface. Current ICH chips used by Intel 8xx–series chipsets include the ICH2 and ICH4. See also *MCH*.

IDE (Integrated Drive Electronics) Describes a hard disk with the disk controller circuitry integrated within it. The first IDE drives commonly were called hard cards. Also refers to the ATA interface standard—the standard for attaching hard disk drives to ISA bus IBM-compatible computers. IDE drives typically operate as though they are standard ST-506/412 drives. See also *ATA*.

IEEE 802.3 See *10BASE-2*.

IEEE 802.11 family A family of wireless network standards commonly known as wireless Ethernet, the most popular of which include 802.11a (54Mbps using 5GHz signaling) and 802.11b (11Mbps using 2.4GHz signaling). 802.11b is frequently called Wi-Fi. See also *Wi-Fi*.

IEEE 1284 A series of standards for parallel ports. IEEE 1284 includes EPP and ECP configurations as well as the older bidirectional and 4-bit compatible parallel port modes. Printer cables that can work with all modes are referred to as IEEE 1284–compliant cables. See also *EPP* and *ECP*.

IEEE 1394 See *FireWire*.

illegal operation A command sent to Windows or the processor that can't be performed. Illegal operations can be triggered by software bugs or conflicts between programs in memory; although the name is reminiscent of a penalty in football, an illegal operation is hardly ever caused by the computer user. In most cases, you can continue to work and might even be able to restart the program without rebooting.

impedance The total opposition a circuit offers to the flow of alternating current, measured in ohms.

incremental backup A backup of all the files that have changed since the last backup.

inductive A property in which energy can be transferred from one device to another via the magnetic field generated by the device, even though no direct electrical connection is established between the two.

.INF file A Windows driver and device information file used to install new drivers or services.

ingot See *boule*.

initiator A device attached to the SCSI bus that sends a command to another device (the target) on the SCSI bus. The SCSI host adapter plugged into the system bus is an example of a SCSI initiator.

inkjet printer A type of printer that sprays one or more colors of ink on the paper; it can produce output with quality approaching that of a laser printer at a lower cost.

input Data sent to the computer from the keyboard, the telephone, a video camera, another computer, paddles, joysticks, and so on.

InstallShield A popular program used to create installation and uninstallation routines for Windows-based programs.

instruction Program step that tells the computer what to do for a single operation.

integrated circuit See *IC*.

interface A communications device or protocol that enables one device to communicate with another. Matches the output of one device to the input of the other device.

interlacing A method of scanning alternate lines of pixels on a display screen. The odd lines are scanned first from top to bottom and left to right. The electron gun goes back to the top and makes a second pass, scanning the even lines. Interlacing requires two scan passes to construct a single image. Because of this additional scanning, interlaced screens often seem to flicker unless a long-persistence phosphor is used in the display. Interlaced monitors were used with the IBM 8514/A display card but are now obsolete for desktop computers.

interleave ratio The number of sectors that pass beneath the read/write heads before the "next" numbered sector arrives. When the interleave ratio is 3:1, for example, a sector is read, two pass by, and then the next is read. A proper interleave ratio, laid down during low-level formatting, enables the disk to transfer information without excessive revolutions due to missed sectors. All modern IDE and SCSI drives have a 1:1 interleave ratio.

interleaved memory The process of alternating access between two banks of memory to overlap accesses, thus speeding up data retrieval. Systems that require only one memory module per bank to operate can work more quickly when two are installed if the system supports interleaved memory.

internal command In DOS, a command contained in COMMAND.COM so that no other file must be loaded to perform the command. DIR and COPY are two examples of internal commands.

internal device   A peripheral device installed inside the main system case in either an expansion slot or a drive bay.

internal drive   A disk or tape drive mounted inside one of a computer's disk drive bays (or a hard disk card, which is installed in one of the computer's slots).

Internet   A computer network that joins many government, university, and private computers together over phone lines. The Internet traces its origins to a network set up in 1969 by the Department of Defense. You can connect to the Internet through many online services, such as CompuServe and America Online, or you can connect through local Internet service providers (ISPs). Internet computers use the TCP/IP communications protocol. Several million hosts exist on the Internet; a host is a mainframe, mini, or workstation that directly supports the Internet protocol (the IP in TCP/IP).

Internet Explorer (IE)   Microsoft's line of Web browsers for Windows and Macintosh computers. Most Web sites are optimized to display best on systems running recent versions of IE.

interpreter   A program for a high-level language that translates and executes the program at the same time. The program statements that are interpreted remain in their original source language, the way the programmer wrote them—that is, the program does not need to be compiled before execution. Interpreted programs run more slowly than compiled programs and always must be run with the interpreter loaded in memory.

interrupt   A suspension of a process, such as the execution of a computer program, caused by an event external to that process and performed in such a way that the process can be resumed. An interrupt can be caused by internal or external conditions, such as a signal indicating that a device or program has completed a transfer of data. Hardware interrupts (also called IRQs) are used by devices, whereas software interrupts are used by programs. See also *IRQ*.

interrupt vector   A pointer in a table that gives the location of a set of instructions the computer should execute when a particular interrupt occurs.

IO.SYS   One of the DOS/Windows 9x system files required to boot the machine. The first file loaded from disk during the boot, it contains extensions to the ROM BIOS.

IP address   An identifier for a computer or device on a TCP/IP network. The format of an IP address is a 32-bit numeric address written as four numbers separated by periods, in which each number can be 0–255. The TCP/IP protocol routes messages based on the IP address of the destination.

IPv6   A new version of the IP protocol that expands the range of IP addresses from 32 bits to 128 bits, which relieves the strain on the current universe of IP addresses. IPv6 is backward compatible with IPv4 to allow its gradual adoption.

IPX (internetwork packet exchange)   Novell NetWare's native LAN communications protocol (primarily in versions 4.x and earlier) used to move data between server and/or workstation programs running on different network nodes. IPX packets are encapsulated and carried by the packets used in Ethernet and the similar frames used in Token-Ring networks.

IrDA   An infrared communications standard established by the Infrared Data Association in 1993. IrDA is currently used primarily for data transfer between portable computers or to allow portable computers to print to a printer with an IrDA port.

IRQ (interrupt request)   Physical connections between external hardware devices and the interrupt controllers. When a device such as a floppy controller or a printer needs the attention of the CPU, an IRQ line is used to get the attention of the system to perform a task. On PC and XT IBM-compatible systems, eight IRQ lines are included, numbered IRQ0–IRQ7. On the AT and PS/2 systems, 16 IRQ lines are numbered IRQ0–IRQ15. IRQ lines must be used by only a single adapter in the ISA bus systems, but Micro Channel Architecture (MCA) adapters and most PCI-based systems can share interrupts. IRQ sharing with modern systems requires a system with PCI cards and Windows 95B or above. Windows 2000/XP are better at sharing IRQs than Windows 9x/Me.

ISA (Industry Standard Architecture)   The bus architecture introduced as an 8-bit bus with the original IBM PC in 1981 and later expanded to 16 bits with the IBM PC/AT in 1984. ISA slots are occasionally found in PC systems today, but the latest chipsets have eliminated them.

ISA bus clock   Clock that normally operates the ISA bus at 8.33MHz.

ISDN (Integrated Services Digital Network)   An international telecommunications standard that enables a communications channel to carry digital data simultaneously with voice and video information.

ISO (International Standards Organization)   The ISO, based in Paris, develops standards for international and national data communications. The U.S. representative to the ISO is the American National Standards Institute (ANSI). See also *High Sierra format*.

ISO 9660   An international standard that defines file systems for CD-ROM discs, independent of the operating system. ISO (International Standards Organization) 9660 has two levels. Level one provides for DOS file system compatibility, whereas level two allows filenames of up to 32 characters. See also *High Sierra format*.

ISP (Internet service provider)   A company that provides Internet access to computer users. Most ISPs originally provided dialup analog modem service only, but many ISPs now provide various types of broadband support for DSL, cable modem, or fixed wireless Internet devices. Some ISPs, such as America Online (AOL), also provide proprietary content.

Itanium   An Intel eighth-generation processor, code-named Merced, it is the first 64-bit instruction PC processor from Intel. It features a new Explicitly Parallel Instruction Computing (EPIC) architecture for more performance when running optimized code. Also, it features internal L1/L2 and L3 error correcting code (ECC) caches to improve throughput and reliability. It was designed initially for the server or high-end workstation market. The improved Itanium 2 processor offers faster clock speeds and faster cache memory. See also *L3 cache*.

ITU (International Telecommunications Union)   Formerly called CCITT. An international committee organized by the United Nations to set international communications recommendations—which frequently are adopted as standards—and to develop interface, modem, and data network recommendations. The Bell 212A standard for 1,200bps communication in North America, for example, is observed internationally as CCITT V.22. For 2,400bps communication, most U.S. manufacturers observe V.22bis, whereas V.32, V.32bis, V34, and V34+ are standards for 9,600bps, 14,400bps, 28,800bps, and 33,600bps, respectively. The V.90 standard recently was defined for 56Kbps modems.

J-lead   J-shaped leads on chip carriers, which can be surface-mounted on a PC board or plugged into a socket that then is mounted on a PC board, usually on .050" centers.

jabber   An error condition on an Ethernet-based network in which a defective network card or outside interference is constantly sending data, preventing the rest of the network from working.

Java   An object-oriented programming language and environment similar to C or C++. Java was developed by Sun Microsystems and is used to create network-based applications.

JavaScript   A scripting language developed by Netscape for Web browsers. JavaScript can perform calculations and mouse rollovers, but it doesn't require the Web browser to download additional files, as with Java.

Jaz drive   A proprietary type of removable media drive with a magnetic hard disk platter in a rigid plastic case. Developed by Iomega, Jaz drives were discontinued in 2002, but media is still available for both 1GB and 2GB versions of the drive.

JEDEC (Joint Electron Devices Engineering Council)   A group that establishes standards for the electronics industry. JEDEC established the original PC66 SDRAM standard.

Joliet   Microsoft extension of the ISO 9660 standard for recordable/rewritable CDs. Joliet is designed for use with 32-bit Windows versions that support long filenames, but it supports file/folder names up to 128 bytes (128 European or 64 Unicode characters) only. Some very long folder/filenames might need to be truncated when stored on a Joliet-format CD.

joule   The standard unit of electrical energy, it's frequently used to measure the effectiveness of surge suppressors.

joystick   An input device generally used for game software, usually consisting of a central upright stick that controls horizontal and vertical motion and one or more buttons to control discrete events, such as firing guns. More complex models can resemble flight yokes and steering wheels or incorporate tactile feedback.

JPEG (Joint Photographic Experts Group)   The international consortium of hardware, software, and publishing interests which—under the auspices of the ISO—has defined a universal standard for digital compression and decompression of still images for use in computer systems. JPEG compresses at about a 20:1 ratio before visible image degradation occurs. A lossy data compression standard that was originally designed for still images but also can compress real-time video (30 frames per second) and animation. Lossy compression permanently discards unnecessary data, resulting in some loss of precision. Files stored in the JPEG format have the extension `.jpg` or `.jpeg`.

JScript   Microsoft's equivalent to JavaScript. See also *JavaScript*.

jukebox   A type of CD-ROM drive that enables several CD-ROM discs to be in the drive at the same time. The drive itself determines which disc is needed by the system and loads the discs into the reading mechanism as needed.

jumper block   A small, plastic-covered metal clip that slips over two pins protruding from a circuit board. Sometimes also called a shunt. When in place, the jumper block connects the pins electrically and closes the circuit. By doing so, it connects the two terminals of a switch, turning it "on." Jumper blocks are commonly used to configure internal hard drives and motherboard settings.

K6   The popular line of Socket 7 and Super Socket 7 processors developed by AMD. Members included the K6, K6-2, and K6-III.

K56flex   A proprietary standard for 56Kbps modem transmissions developed by Rockwell and implemented in modems from a variety of vendors. Superseded by the official V.90 standard for 56Kbps modems. See also *X2*, *V.90*, and *V.92*.

Kermit   A protocol designed for transferring files between microcomputers and mainframes. Developed by Frank DaCruz and Bill Catchings at Columbia University (and named after the talking frog on *The Muppet Show*), Kermit was widely accepted in the academic world before the advent of the Internet.

kernel   Operating system core component.

key disk   In software copy protection schemes popular during the 1980s, a distribution floppy disk that must be present in a floppy disk drive for an application program to run.

keyboard   The primary input device for most computers, consisting of keys with letters of the alphabet, digits, punctuation, and function control keys.

keyboard macro   A series of keystrokes automatically input when a single key is pressed.

keychain drive   A popular term for small solid-state devices using flash memory that connect to a PC through the USB port. Such devices are recognized as drive letters and have typical capacities ranging from 32MB to 128MB. Most have a fixed capacity, but some have provision for upgradeable memory with SD or other small-form-factor flash memory. Also known as *thumb* drives.

keylock   Physical locking mechanism to prevent internal access to the system unit or peripherals.

kibi   A multiplier indicating 1,024 of some unit. Abbreviated as Ki. See also *gibi*.

kilo   A multiplier indicating one thousand (1,000) of some unit. Abbreviated as k or K. When used to indicate a number of bytes of memory storage, the multiplier definition changes to 1,024. One kilobit, for example, equals 1,000 bits, whereas one kilobyte equals 1,024 bytes.

kilobyte (KB)   A unit of information storage equal to 1,000 bytes (decimal) or 1,024 bytes (binary). Binary KB are now called kibibytes. See also *kibi*.

kludge   An inelegant but workable solution for a software or hardware problem.

L1 cache (level one)   A memory cache built into the CPU core of 486 and later generation processors. See also *cache* and *disk cache*.

L2 cache (level two)   A second-level memory cache external to the processor core, usually larger and slower than L1. Normally found on the motherboards of 386, 486, and Pentium systems and inside the processor packages or modules in Pentium Pro and later Intel processors, AMD K6-III processors, and Athlon and Duron processors. Cartridge-based caches used in the Pentium II, early Celeron, Pentium III, and Athlon processors run faster than motherboard cache but at speeds up to only one-half the CPU speed. Modern Socket 370, Socket A, and other socket-based processors contain the L2 cache inside the CPU die, enabling the L2 cache to work at the full speed of the processor. See also *SEC*, *cache*, and *disk cache*.

L3 cache (level three)   A third-level memory cache external to the processor core. The only current Intel-compatible processors to include L3 cache are the Itanium and Itanium 2 processors from Intel. Depending on the model, these contain 2MB or 4MB of L3 cache that runs at full processor speed. If a motherboard provides L2 cache, such as many Super Socket 7 motherboards made for Pentium and Pentium-compatible processors, L2 cache becomes L3 cache if a processor with integrated L3 cache, such as the AMD K6-III, is used. Motherboard-based cache modules run at FSB speeds, which are much slower than on-chip or on-die processor speeds. See also *cache* and *disk cache*.

LAN   Local area network; a network contained within a building. Both home and office networks are considered LANs. Ethernet, Fast Ethernet, Gigabit Ethernet, and Wireless Ethernet are used in office LANs, whereas home LANs might use Ethernet, Fast Ethernet, HomePNA, HomeRF, or Wi-Fi Wireless Ethernet.

landing zone   An unused track on a disk surface on which the read/write heads can land when power is shut off. The place a parking program or a drive with an autopark mechanism parks the heads.

LAPM (link-access procedure for modems)   An error-control protocol incorporated in CCITT Recommendation V.42. Similar to the MNP and HST protocols, it uses cyclic redundancy checking (CRC) and retransmission of corrupted data (ARQ) to ensure data reliability.

laptop computer   A computer system smaller than a briefcase but larger than a notebook that usually has a clamshell design in which the keyboard and display are on separate halves of the system, which are hinged together. These systems normally run on battery power. Many vendors use the terms notebook and laptop computer interchangeably.

large mode   A translation scheme used by the Award BIOS to translate the cylinder, head, and sector specifications of an IDE drive to those usable by an enhanced BIOS. It doesn't produce the same translated values as LBA mode and is not recommended because it is not supported by other BIOS vendors.

large-scale integration   See *IC*.

laser printer A type of printer that is a combination of an electrostatic copying machine and a computer printer. The output data from the computer is converted by an interface into a raster feed, similar to the impulses a TV picture tube receives. The impulses cause the laser beam to scan a small drum that carries a positive electrical charge. Where the laser hits, the drum is discharged. A toner, which also carries a positive charge, is then applied to the drum. This toner—a fine, black powder—sticks to only the areas of the drum that have been discharged electrically. As it rotates, the drum deposits the toner on a negatively charged sheet of paper. Another roller then heats and bonds the toner to the page. See also *LED printer*.

latency 1) The amount of time required for a disk drive to rotate half a revolution. Represents the average amount of time to locate a specific sector after the heads have arrived at a specific track. Latency is part of the average access time for a drive. 2) The initial setup time required for a memory transfer in DRAM to select the row and column addresses for the memory to be read/written.

LBA (logical block addressing) A method used with SCSI and IDE drives to translate the cylinder, head, and sector specifications of the drive to those usable by an enhanced BIOS. LBA is used with drives that are larger than 528MB and causes the BIOS to translate the drive's logical parameters to those usable by the system BIOS.

LCC (leadless chip carrier) A type of integrated circuit package that has input and output pads rather than leads on its perimeter.

LCD (liquid crystal display) A display that uses liquid crystal sealed between two pieces of polarized glass. The polarity of the liquid crystal is changed by an electric current to vary the amount of light that can pass through. Because LCD displays do not generate light, they depend on either the reflection of ambient light or backlighting the screen. The best type of LCD, the active-matrix or thin-film transistor (TFT) LCD, offers fast screen updates and true color capability.

LED (light-emitting diode) A semiconductor diode that emits light when a current is passed through it.

LED printer A printer that uses an LED instead of a laser beam to discharge the drum.

legacy port I/O ports used on systems before the development of the multipurpose USB port. Serial, parallel, keyboard, and PS/2 mouse ports are legacy ports.

letterbox Refers to how wide-screen movies are displayed on TV or monitor screens with normal aspect rations of 4:3. Because wide-screen movies have aspect ratios as high as 16:9, the wide-screen image leaves blank areas at the top and bottom of the screen. This area is sometimes used for displaying subtitles on foreign-language films. See also *aspect ratio*.

LIF (low insertion force) A type of socket that requires only a minimum of force to insert a chip carrier.

light pen A handheld input device with a light-sensitive probe or stylus connected to the computer's graphics adapter board by a cable. Used for writing or sketching onscreen or as a pointing device for making selections. Unlike mice, it's not widely supported by software applications.

line voltage The AC voltage available at a standard wall outlet, nominally 110V–120V in North America and 220V–230V in Europe and Japan.

linear tape-open (LTO) An open standard for tape backups whose first products were introduced in mid-2000. LTO was jointly developed by Seagate, IBM, and Hewlett-Packard. Ultrium format products have capacities of up to 100GB, whereas the faster Accelis products have capacities of up to 25GB.

lithium-ion A portable system battery type that is longer-lived than either NiCad or NiMH technologies, can't be overcharged, and holds a charge well when not in use. Lithium-ion batteries are also lighter weight than the NiCad and NiMH technologies. Because of these superior features, Li-ion batteries have come to be used in all but the very low end of the portable system market.

local area network (LAN) The connection of two or more computers, usually via a network adapter card or NIC.

local bus A generic term used to describe a bus directly attached to a processor that operates at the processor's speed and data-transfer width.

local echo A modem feature that enables the modem to send copies of keyboard commands and transmitted data to the screen. When the modem is in command mode (not online to another system), the local echo usually is invoked through an ATE1 command, which causes the modem to display the user's typed commands. When the modem is online to another system, the local echo is invoked by an ATF0 command, which causes the modem to display the data it transmits to the remote system.

logical drive A drive as named by a DOS drive specifier, such as C: or D:. Under DOS 3.3 or later, a single physical drive can act as several logical drives, each with its own specifier. A primary partition can contain only one logical drive; an extended partition can contain one or more logical drives. See also *extended partition* and *primary partition*.

logical unit number See *LUN*.

lossless compression   A compression technique that preserves all the original information in an image or other data structures. PKZIP and Microsoft CAB files are popular applications of lossless compression.

lossless linking   A technique used by DVD+RW drives to enable the DVD+RW video writing process to pause and continue as data is available. Lossless linking enables DVD+RW video media to be read by standalone DVD video players and DVD-ROM drives.

lossy compression   A compression technique that achieves optimal data reduction by discarding redundant and unnecessary information in an image. MP3, MPEG, and JPEG are popular examples of lossy compression.

lost clusters   Clusters that have been marked accidentally as "unavailable" in the FAT even though they don't belong to any file listed in a directory. See also *cluster*.

low-level formatting   Formatting that divides tracks into sectors on the platter surfaces. Places sector-identifying information before and after each sector and fills each sector with null data (usually hex F6). Specifies the sector interleave and marks defective tracks by placing invalid checksum figures in each sector on a defective track.

LPT port   Line printer port, a common system abbreviation for a parallel printer port. Common LPT port numbers range from LPT1 to LPT3.

LPX   A semiproprietary motherboard design used in many Low Profile or Slimline case systems. Because no formal standard exists, these typically are not interchangeable between vendors and are often difficult to find replacement parts for or upgrade.

luminance   Measure of brightness usually used in specifying monitor brightness.

LUN (logical unit number)   A number given to a device (a logical unit) attached to a SCSI physical unit and not directly to the SCSI bus. Although as many as eight logical units can be attached to a single physical unit, a single logical unit typically is a built-in part of a single physical unit. A SCSI hard disk, for example, has a built-in SCSI bus adapter that is assigned a physical unit number or SCSI ID, and the controller and drive portions of the hard disk are assigned a LUN (usually 0). See also *PUN*.

LZW (Lempel Zev Welch)   A lossless compression scheme used in the GIF and TIFF graphic formats, named after its co-creators, Abraham Lempel, Jacob Ziv, and Terry Welch.

MAC address   Short for Media Access Control address, this is a unique hardware number assigned to network hardware, such as NICs and routers. The MAC address assigned to the WAN side of some broadband Internet routers can be changed to equal the MAC address of the NIC previously used to attach to a broadband device, such as a cable modem.

machine address   A hexadecimal (hex) location in memory.

machine language   Hexadecimal program code a computer can understand and execute. It can be output from the assembler or compiler.

macro   A series of commands in an application that can be stored and played back on demand. Many applications from various vendors support Microsoft Visual Basic for Applications as their macro language.

macro virus   A computer virus that uses a scripting language to infect Microsoft Word document templates or email systems.

magnetic domain   A tiny segment of a track just large enough to hold one of the magnetic flux reversals that encode data on a disk surface.

magneto-optical recording   An erasable optical disk recording technique that uses a laser beam to heat pits on the disk surface to the point at which a magnet can make flux changes.

magneto-resistive   A technology originally developed by IBM and commonly used for the read element of a read/write head on a high-density magnetic disk. Based on the principle that the resistance to electricity changes in a material when brought into contact with a magnetic field, in this case, the read element material and the magnetic bit. Such drives use a magneto-resistive read sensor for reading and a standard inductive element for writing. A magneto-resistive read head is more sensitive to magnetic fields than inductive read heads. Giant magneto-resistive heads are an improved version that store more data in the same space.

mainframe   A somewhat vague distinction that identifies any large computer system normally capable of supporting many users and programs simultaneously.

mask   A photographic map of the circuits for a particular layer of a semiconductor chip used in manufacturing the chip.

master boot record (MBR)   On hard disks, a one-sector-long record that contains the master boot program as well as the master partition table containing up to four partition entries. The master boot program reads the master partition table to determine which of the four entries is active (bootable) and then loads the first sector of that partition, called the volume boot record. The master boot program tests the volume boot record for a 55AAh signature at offset 510; if it's present, program execution is transferred to the volume boot sector, which typically contains a program designed to load the operating system files. The MBR is always the first physical sector of the disk, at Cylinder 0, Head 0, Sector 1. Also called master boot sector.

math coprocessor A processing chip designed to quickly handle complex arithmetic computations involving floating-point arithmetic, offloading these from the main processor. Originally contained in a separate coprocessor chip, starting with the 486 family of processors. Intel now has incorporated the math coprocessor into the main processors in what is called the floating-point unit.

MCA (Micro Channel Architecture) Developed by IBM for the PS/2 line of computers and introduced on April 2, 1987. Features include a 16- or 32-bit bus width and multiple master control. By allowing several processors to arbitrate for resources on a single bus, the MCA is optimized for multitasking, multiprocessor systems. Offers switchless configuration of adapters, which eliminates one of the biggest headaches of installing older adapters. MCA systems became obsolete after the development of the PCI bus.

MCGA (multicolor graphics array) A type of PC video display circuit introduced by IBM on April 2, 1987, which supports text and graphics. Text is supported at a maximum resolution of 80×25 characters in 16 colors with a character box of 8×16 pixels. Graphics are supported at a maximum resolution of 320×200 pixels in 256 (from a palette of 262,144) colors or 640×480 pixels in two colors. The MCGA outputs an analog signal with a horizontal scanning frequency of 31.5KHz and supports analog color or analog monochrome displays.

MCH (memory controller hub) Intel's term for the chip used in its 8xx-series chipsets to connect the processor with high-bandwidth devices such as memory, video, and the system bus, replacing the North Bridge chip. MCH chips connect with the I/O controller hub (the 8xx chipsets' replacement for the South Bridge) through a high-speed hub interface. See also *ICH*.

MCI (media control interface) A device-independent specification for controlling multimedia devices and files. MCI is a part of the multimedia extensions and offers a standard interface set of device control commands. MCI commands are used for audio recording and playback and animation playback. Device types include CD audio, digital audio tape players, scanners, MIDI sequencers, videotape players or recorders, and audio devices that play digitized waveform files.

MDA (monochrome display adapter; also, MGA—mono graphics adapter) A type of PC video display adapter introduced by IBM on August 12, 1981, that supports text only. Text is supported at a maximum resolution of 80×25 characters in four colors with a character box of 9×14 pixels. Colors, in this case, indicate black, white, bright white, and underlined. Graphics modes are not supported. The MDA outputs a digital signal with a horizontal scanning frequency of 18.432KHz and supports TTL monochrome displays. The IBM MDA card also includes a parallel printer port.

mean time between failure See *MTBF*.

mean time to repair See *MTTR*.

mebi A multiplier indicating 1,048,576 of a unit of measurement.

mebibyte (Mi) A unit of information storage equal to 1,048,576 bytes (1,024×1,024 equals 1Mi). This value was previously called a binary megabyte. See also *megabyte* and *kilobyte*.

medium The magnetic coating or plating that covers a disk or tape.

mega A multiplier indicating one million (1,000,000) of some unit. Abbreviated as m or M. Traditionally, mega has also been defined as 1,048,576 (1,024 kilobytes, where kilobyte equals 1,024) in applications such as memory sizing or disk storage (as defined by many BIOSs and by FDISK and other disk preparation programs). The term mebi is now used for 1,048,576. See also *mebi*.

megabyte (MB) A unit of information storage equal to 1,000,000 bytes. Also called a decimal megabyte. The value 1,048,576 bytes has been called a binary megabyte but is now known as a mebibyte. See also *mebibyte*.

megapixel A unit of digital camera resolution equal to approximately 1,000,000 pixels. A one-megapixel camera has a resolution of approximately 1,152×864; a two-megapixel camera has a resolution of approximately 1,760×1,168. Finally, a three-megapixel camera has a resolution of approximately 2,160×1,440. One-megapixel or lower-resolution cameras are suitable for 4"×6" or smaller snapshots only, whereas two-megapixel cameras produce excellent 5"×7" enlargements and acceptable 8"×10" enlargements. Three-megapixel or higher-resolution cameras produce excellent 8"×10" and 11"×14" enlargements. The higher the megapixel rating, the more flash memory space is used by each picture and the longer it takes each picture to be recorded to flash memory.

memory Any component in a computer system that stores information for future use.

memory caching A service provided by extremely fast memory chips that keeps copies of the most recent memory accesses. When the CPU makes a subsequent access, the value is supplied by the fast memory rather than by the relatively slow system memory. L1 and L2 caches are memory caches found on most recent processors. See also *L1 cache*, *L2 cache*, and *L3 cache*.

Memory Stick A Sony-developed flash memory device that's about the size of a stick of gum. It is used by digital cameras, camcorders, digital music players, and voice recorders—primarily those made by Sony.

memory-resident program A program that remains in memory after it has been loaded, consuming memory that otherwise might be used by application software.

menu software Utility software that makes a computer running DOS easier to use by replacing DOS commands with a series of menu selections.

MFM encoding (modified frequency modulation encoding) A method of encoding data on the surface of a disk. The coding of a bit of data varies by the coding of the preceding bit to preserve clocking information. Used only by floppy drives today because it stores less data than other types of encoding such as RLL. See also *RLL*.

MHz An abbreviation for megahertz, a unit of measurement indicating the frequency of one million cycles per second. One hertz (Hz) is equal to one cycle per second. Named after Heinrich R. Hertz, a German physicist who first detected electromagnetic waves in 1883.

MI/MIC (mode indicate/mode indicate common) Also called forced or manual originate. Provided for installations in which equipment other than the modem does the dialing. In such installations, the modem operates in dumb mode (no auto-dial capability), yet must go off-hook in originate mode to connect with answering modems.

micro (μ) A prefix indicating one millionth (1/1,000,000 or .000001) of some unit.

micron A unit of measurement equaling one millionth of a meter. Often used in measuring the size of circuits in chip manufacturing processes. Current state-of-the-art chip fabrication builds chips with 0.13 to 0.15-micron circuits.

microprocessor A solid-state central processing unit much like a computer on a chip. An integrated circuit that accepts coded instructions for execution.

microsecond (μs) A unit of time equal to one millionth (1/1,000,000 or .000001) of a second.

MIDI (musical instrument digital interface) An interface and file format standard for connecting a musical instrument to a microcomputer and storing musical instrument data. Multiple musical instruments can be daisy-chained and played simultaneously with the help of the computer and related software. The various operations of the instruments can be captured, saved, edited, and played back. A MIDI file contains note information, timing (how long a note is held), volume, and instrument type for as many as 16 channels. Sequencer programs are used to control MIDI

functions such as recording, playback, and editing. MIDI files store only note instructions and not actual sound data. MIDI files can be played back by virtually all sound cards, but old sound cards might use FM synthesis to imitate the musical instruments called for in the MIDI file. Recent sound cards use stored musical instrument samples for more realistic MIDI playback.

MII A Socket 7–compatible processor originally developed by Cyrix and now sold by VIA Technologies as the VIA Cyrix MII.

milli (m) A prefix indicating one thousandth (1/1,000 or .001) of some unit.

millisecond (ms) A unit of time equal to one thousandth (1/1,000 or .001) of a second.

MIME (Multipurpose Internet Mail Extensions) Allows Internet and email services to exchange binary files and select the proper program to open the file after it's received.

minitower A type of PC system case that is shorter than a full- or mid-sized tower. Most low-cost computers sold at retail stores use the minitower case combined with a Micro-ATX motherboard.

MIPS (million instructions per second) Refers to the average number of machine-language instructions a computer can perform or execute in one second. Because various processors can perform different functions in a single instruction, MIPS should be used only as a general measure of performance among various types of computers.

MMX An Intel processor enhancement that adds 57 new instructions designed to improve multimedia performance. MMX also implies a doubling of the internal L1 processor cache on Pentium MMX processors compared to non-MMX Pentium processors. Later processors also include MMX along with other multimedia instructions.

mnemonic An abbreviated name for something used in a manner similar to an acronym. Computer processor instructions are often abbreviated with a mnemonic, such as JMP (jump), CLR (clear), STO (store), and INIT (initialize). A mnemonic name for an instruction or an operation makes it easy to remember and convenient to use.

MNP (Microcom Networking Protocol) Asynchronous error-control and data-compression protocols developed by Microcom, Inc., and now in the public domain. They ensure error-free transmission through error detection (CRC) and retransmission of erred frames. MNP Levels 1–4 cover error control and have been incorporated into CCITT Recommendation V.42. MNP Level 5 includes data compression but is eclipsed in superiority by V.42bis—an international standard that is more efficient. Most high-speed modems connect with MNP Level 5 if V.42bis is unavailable. MNP Level 10 provides error correction for impaired lines and adjusts to the fastest possible speed during connection. MNP Level 10EC is an improved version of MNP Level 10, adding more reliability and support for cellular phone hand-offs.

MO (magneto-optical) MO drives use both magnetic and optical storage properties. MO technology is erasable and recordable, as opposed to CD-ROM (read-only) and WORM (write-once) drives. MO uses laser and magnetic field technology to record and erase data.

mobile module (MMO) A type of processor packing from Intel for mobile computers consisting of a Pentium or newer processor mounted on a small daughterboard along with the processor voltage regulator, system's L2 cache memory, and North Bridge part of the motherboard chipset.

modem (modulator/demodulator) A device that converts electrical signals from a computer into an audio form transmittable over telephone lines, or vice versa. It modulates, or transforms, digital signals from a computer into the analog form that can be carried successfully on a phone line; it also demodulates signals received from the phone line back to digital signals before passing them to the receiving computer. To avoid confusion with other types of Internet connection devices such as cable modems, modems are often called analog modems or dialup modems.

modulation The process of modifying some characteristic of a carrier wave or signal so that it varies in step with the changes of another signal, thus carrying the information of the other signal.

module An assembly that contains a complete circuit or subcircuit.

monitor See *display*.

monochrome display adapter See *MDA*.

MOS (metal-oxide semiconductor) Refers to the three layers used in forming the gate structure of a field-effect transistor (FET). MOS circuits offer low-power dissipation and enable transistors to be jammed closely together before a critical heat problem arises. PMOS, the oldest type of MOS circuit, is a silicon-gate P-channel MOS process that uses currents made up of positive charges. NMOS is a silicon-gate N-channel MOS process that uses currents made up of negative charges and is at least twice as fast as PMOS. CMOS, complementary MOS, is nearly immune to noise, runs off almost any power supply, and is an extremely low-power circuit technique.

motherboard The main circuit board in the computer. Also called planar, system board, or backplane.

mouse An input device invented by Douglas Engelbart of Stanford Research Center in 1963 and popularized by Xerox in the 1970s. A mechanical mouse consists of a roller ball and a tracking mechanism on the underside that relays the mouse's horizontal and vertical position to the computer, allowing precise control of the pointer location onscreen. The top side features two or three buttons and possibly a small wheel used to select or click items onscreen. Old-style optical mice sold in the 1980s used a single optical sensor and a grid-marked pad as an alternative to the roller ball. The latest optical mice use two optical sensors and can be moved across virtually any nonmirrored surface.

MPC A trademarked abbreviation for Multimedia Personal Computer. The original MPC specification was developed by Tandy Corporation and Microsoft as the minimum platform capable of running multimedia software. In the summer of 1995, the MPC Marketing Council introduced an upgraded MPC 3 standard. The MPC 1 Specification defines the following minimum standard requirements: a 386SX or 486 CPU; 2MB RAM; 30MB hard disk; VGA video display; 8-bit digital audio subsystem; CD-ROM drive; and systems software compatible with the applications programming interfaces (APIs) of Microsoft Windows version 3.1 or later. The MPC 2 specification defines the following minimum standard requirements: 25MHz 486SX with 4MB RAM; 160MB hard disk; 16-bit sound card; 65,536-color video display; double-speed CD-ROM drive; and systems software compatible with the APIs of Microsoft Windows version 3.1 or later. The MPC 3 Specification defines the following minimum standard requirements: 75MHz Pentium with 8MB RAM; 540MB hard disk; 16-bit sound card; 65,536-color video display; quad-speed CD-ROM drive; OM-1–compliant MPEG-1 video, and systems software compatible with the APIs of Microsoft Windows version 3.1 and DOS 6.0 or later. Virtually all computers sold since 1995 exceed MPC 3 standards.

MPEG (Motion Picture Experts Group) A working ISO committee that has defined standards for lossy digital compression and decompression of motion video/audio for use in computer systems. The MPEG-1 standard delivers decompression data at 1.2Mbps–1.5Mbps, enabling CD players to play full-motion color movies at 30 frames per second. MPEG-1 compresses at about a 50:1 ratio before image degradation occurs, but compression ratios as high as 200:1 are attainable. MPEG-2 extends to the higher data rates (2Mbps–15Mbps) necessary for signals delivered from remote sources (such as broadcast, cable, or satellite). MPEG-2 is designed to support a range of picture aspect ratios, including 4:3 and 16:9. MPEG compression produces about a 50% volume reduction in file size. MP3 (the audio layer portion of the MPEG-1 standard) provides a wide range of compression ratios and file sizes for digital music storage, making it the de facto standard for exchanging digital music through sites such as Napster and its many rivals. See also *lossy compression*.

MPR The Swedish government standard for maximum video terminal radiation. The current version is called MPR II, but most monitors also comply with the newer and more restrictive TCO standards. See also *TCO*.

MSDOS.SYS One of the DOS/Windows 9x system files required to boot the machine. Contains the primary DOS routines. Loaded by IO.SYS, it in turn loads COMMAND.COM.

Mt. Rainier An emerging standard for CD-RW and DVD+RW drives that provides for native operating system support of CD-RW and rewriteable DVD media. Drives and operating systems that support the Mt. Rainier standard (www.mt-rainier.org) can read or write Mt. Rainier–formatted CD-R/RW or DVD+R/RW media without the need for proprietary packet-reading software such as Roxio's UDF Volume Reader for DirectCD-formatted media (www.roxio.com).

MTBF (mean time between failure) A statistically derived measure of the probable time a device will continue to operate before a hardware failure occurs, usually given in hours. Because no standard technique exists for measuring MTBF, a device from one manufacturer can be significantly more or significantly less reliable than a device with the same MTBF rating from another manufacturer.

MTTR (mean time to repair) A measure of the probable time it will take a technician to service or repair a specific device, usually given in hours.

Multichannel Multipoint Distribution Service (MMDS) The most common form of so-called "wireless cable TV," MMDS is also used for two-way wireless Internet service. One of the leading MMDS technology manufacturers is Navini Networks (www.navini.com).

multicolor graphics array See *MCGA*.

multimedia The integration of sound, graphic images, animation, motion video, and text in one environment on a computer. It is a set of hardware and software technologies that is rapidly changing and enhancing the computing environment.

multisession A term used in CD-ROM recording to describe a recording event. Multisession capabilities allow data recording on the disk at various times in several recording sessions. Kodak's Photo CD is an example of multisession CD-R technology. See also *session (single or multisession)*.

multitask To run several programs simultaneously.

multithread To concurrently process more than one message by an application program. OS/2 and 32-bit versions of Windows are examples of multi-threaded operating systems. Each program can start two or more threads, which carry out various interrelated tasks with less overhead than two separate programs would require.

multiuser system A system in which several computer terminals share the same central processing unit (CPU).

nano (n) A prefix indicating one billionth (1/1,000,000,000 or .000000001) of some unit.

nanosecond (ns) A unit of time equal to one billionth (1/1,000,000,000 or .000000001) of a second.

NetBEUI (NetBIOS Extended User Interface) A network protocol used primarily by Windows NT and Windows 9x and most suitable for small peer-to-peer networks. NetBEUI is not supported by Microsoft in Windows XP and above but can still be manually installed for use in troubleshooting computers.

NetBIOS (Network Basic Input/Output System) A commonly used network protocol originally developed by IBM and Sytek for PC local area networks. NetBIOS provides session and transport services (Layers 4 and 5 of the OSI model).

NetWare Novell's server-based network for large businesses. NetWare 5 and NetWare 6 are designed to work well with IP-based networks.

network A system in which several independent computers are linked to share data and peripherals, such as hard disks and printers.

network interface card (NIC) An adapter that connects a PC to a network.

Network Layer In the OSI reference model, the layer that switches and routes the packets as necessary to get them to their destinations. This layer is responsible for addressing and delivering message packets. See also *OSI*.

NiCad The oldest of the three battery technologies used in portable systems, nickel cadmium batteries are rarely used in portable systems today because of their shorter life and sensitivity to improper charging and discharging. See also *NiMH* and *lithium-ion*.

NiMH A battery technology used in portable systems. Nickel metal-hydride batteries have approximately a 30% longer life than NiCads, are less sensitive to the memory effect caused by improper charging and discharging, and do not use the environmentally dangerous substances found in NiCads. Newer lithium-ion (Li-ion) batteries are far superior. NiMH batteries can sometimes be used in place of NiCads.

NLX A new low-profile motherboard form factor standard that is basically an improved version of the semiproprietary LPX design. It's designed to accommodate larger processor and memory form factors and incorporate newer bus technologies, such as AGP and USB. Besides design improvements, it is fully standardized, which means you should be able to replace one NLX board with another from a different manufacturer—something that was not normally possible with LPX.

node A device on a network. Also any junction point at which two or more items meet.

noise Any unwanted disturbance in an electrical or mechanical system.

noninterlaced monitor A desirable monitor design in which the electron beam sweeps the screen in lines from top to bottom, one line after the other, completing the entire screen in one pass. Virtually all CRTs sold recently for desktop use are noninterlaced.

nonvolatile memory (NVRAM) Random-access memory whose data is retained when power is turned off. ROM/EPROM/EEPROM (flash) memory are examples of nonvolatile memory. Sometimes NVRAM is retained without any power whatsoever, as in EEPROM or flash memory devices. In other cases, the memory is maintained by a small battery. NVRAM that is battery maintained is sometimes also called CMOS memory (although CMOS RAM technically is volatile). CMOS NVRAM is used in IBM-compatible systems to store configuration information. True NVRAM often is used in intelligent modems to store a user-defined default configuration loaded into normal modem RAM at power-up.

nonvolatile RAM disk A RAM disk powered by a battery supply so that it continues to hold its data during a power outage.

North Bridge The Intel term for the main portion of the motherboard chipset that incorporates the interface between the processor and the rest of the motherboard. The North Bridge contains the cache, main memory, and AGP controllers, as well as the interface between the high-speed (normally 66MHz or 100MHz) processor bus and the 33MHz PCI (peripheral component interconnect) or 66MHz AGP (accelerated graphics port) buses. The functional equivalent of the North Bridge on the latest 8xx-series chipsets from Intel is the MCH. See also *chipset, ICH, MCH,* and *South Bridge.*

notebook computer A very small personal computer approximately the size of a notebook.

NTSC The National Television Standards Committee, which governs the standard for television and video playback and recording in the United States. The NTSC was originally organized in 1941 when TV broadcasting first began on a wide scale in black and white, and the format was revised in 1953 for color. The NTSC format has 525 scan lines, a field frequency of 60Hz, a broadcast bandwidth of 4MHz, a line frequency of 15.75KHz, a frame frequency of 1/30 of a second, and a color subcarrier frequency of 3.58MHz. It is an interlaced signal, which means it scans every other line each time the screen is refreshed. The signal is generated as a composite of red, green, and blue signals for color and includes an FM frequency for audio and a signal for stereo. See also *PAL* and *SECAM,* which are incompatible systems used in Europe. NTSC is also called composite video.

null modem A serial cable wired so that two data terminal equipment (DTE) devices, such as personal computers, or two data communication equipment (DCE) devices, such as modems or mice, can be connected. Also sometimes called a modem-eliminator or a LapLink cable. To make a null-modem cable with DB-25 connectors, you wire these pins together: 1-1, 2-3, 3-2, 4-5, 5-4, 6-8-20, 20-8-6, and 7-7.

numeric coprocessor See *math coprocessor.*

NVRAM (nonvolatile random access memory) Memory that retains data without power. Flash memory and battery-backed CMOS RAM are examples of NVRAM.

object hierarchy Occurs in a graphical program when two or more objects are linked and one object's movement is dependent on the other object. This is known as a parent-child hierarchy. In an example using a human figure, the fingers would be child objects to the hand, which is a child object to the arm, which is a child to the shoulder, and so on. Object hierarchy provides much control for an animator in moving complex figures.

OC (optical carrier) rates Various data rates for optical fiber used in Internet backbones, based on the OC-1 rate of 51.84Mbps. Multiply the OC rate by 51.84Mbps to derive the data rate. For example, OC-12 is 622.08Mbps (51.84×12).

Occam's Razor Also spelled Ockham's Razor; popular name for the principle that the simplest explanation is usually the correct one—a very useful principle in computer troubleshooting.

OCR (optical character recognition) An information-processing technology that converts human-readable text into computer data. Usually a scanner is used to read the text on a page, and OCR software converts the images to characters. Advanced OCR programs, such as OmniPage, can also match fonts, re-create page layouts, and scan graphics into machine-readable form.

ODI (Open Data-link Interface)   A device driver standard from Novell that enables multiple protocols to run on the same network adapter card. ODI adds functionality to Novell's NetWare and network computing environments by supporting multiple protocols and drivers.

OEM (original equipment manufacturer)   Any manufacturer who sells its product to a reseller. Usually refers to the original manufacturer of a particular device or component. Most HP hard disks, for example, are made by Seagate Technologies, who is considered the OEM. OEM products often differ in features from retail products and can have very short warranty periods if purchased separately from their intended use.

OLE (object linking and embedding)   An enhancement to the original Dynamic Data Exchange (DDE) protocol that enables the user to embed or link data created in one application to a document created in another application and subsequently edit that data directly from the final document.

online fallback   A feature that enables high-speed error-control modems to monitor line quality and fall back to the next lower speed if line quality degrades. Some modems fall forward as line quality improves.

open architecture   A system design in which the specifications are made public to encourage third-party vendors to develop add-on products. The PC is a true open architecture system, but the Macintosh is proprietary.

operating system (OS)   A collection of programs for operating the computer. Operating systems perform housekeeping tasks, such as input and output between the computer and peripherals and accepting and interpreting information from the keyboard. Windows XP and MacOS X are examples of popular OSs.

optical disk   A disk that encodes data as a series of reflective pits that are read (and sometimes written) by a laser beam.

Orange Book   The standards for recordable (CD-R) and rewritable (CD-RW) compact discs.

originate mode   A state in which the modem transmits at the predefined low frequency of the communications channel and receives at the high frequency. The transmit/receive frequencies are the reverse of the called modem, which is in answer mode. See also *answer mode*.

OS/2   An operating system originally developed through a joint effort by IBM and Microsoft Corporation and later by IBM alone. Originally released in 1987, OS/2 is a 32-bit operating system designed to run on computers using the Intel 386 or later microprocessors. The OS/2 Workplace Shell, an integral part of the system, is a graphical interface similar to Microsoft Windows and the Apple Macintosh system. OS/2 Warp 4 is the most recent one and is used primarily as a server or in back-office functions today.

OSI (Open Systems Interconnection)   A reference model developed by the International Organization for Standardization (ISO) in the 1980s, the OSI model splits a computer's networking stack into seven discrete layers. Each layer provides specific services to the layers above and below it. From the top down, the Application Layer is responsible for program-to-program communication; the Presentation Layer manages data representation conversions. Next, the Session Layer is responsible for establishing and maintaining communications channels, and the Transport Layer is responsible for the integrity of data transmission. The Network Layer routes data from one node to another, the Data Link Layer is responsible for physically passing data from one node to another, and finally, the Physical Layer is responsible for moving data on and off the network media.

output   Information processed by the computer or the act of sending that information to a mass storage device, such as a video display, printer, or modem.

overclocking   The process of running a processor or video card at a speed faster than the officially marked speed by using a higher clock multiplier, faster bus speed, or faster core clock speed. Not recommended or endorsed by processor or video card manufacturers. See also *clock multiplier*.

OverDrive   An Intel trademark name for its line of upgrade processors for 486, Pentium, and Pentium Pro systems. Although Intel no longer sells OverDrive processors, similar products are available from Evergreen Technologies and PowerLeap Products, Inc., for these processors plus Pentium II, Pentium III, Pentium 4, and Celeron-based systems.

overlay   Part of a program loaded into memory only when it is required.

overrun   A situation in which data moves from one device more quickly than a second device can accept it.

overscanning   A technique used in consumer display products that extends the deflection of a CRT's electron beam beyond the physical boundaries of the screen to ensure that images always fill the display area.

overwrite   To write data on top of existing data, thus erasing the existing data.

package   A device that includes a chip mounted on a carrier and sealed.

packet   A message sent over a network that contains data and a destination address.

packet writing   A recording technique that sends data to a CD-R or CD-RW disc in multiple blocks, enabling normal writing processes in Windows Explorer to be used instead of a CD-mastering program. Compatible packet-reading software, such as Roxio's UDF Reader for DirectCD, must be used on systems that don't have a CD-R or CD-RW drive to enable the media to be read. See also *Mt. Rainier*.

pairing   Combining processor instructions for optimal execution on superscalar processors.

PAL   1) Phase Alternating Line system. Invented in 1961, a system of TV broadcasting used in England and other European countries (except France). PAL's image format is 4:3, 625 lines, 50Hz, and 4MHz video bandwidth with a total 8MHz of video channel width. With its 625-line picture delivered at 25 frames per second, PAL provides a better image and an improved color transmission over the NTSC system used in North America. As a consequence, PAL and NTSC video tapes aren't interchangeable. 2) Programmable array logic, a type of chip that has logic gates specified by a device programmer.

palmtop computer   A computer system smaller than a notebook that is designed so it can be held in one hand while being operated by the other. Many are now called PDAs or personal digital assistants.

parallel   A method of transferring data characters in which the bits travel down parallel electrical paths simultaneously—for example, eight paths for 8-bit characters. Data is stored in computers in parallel form but can be converted to serial form for certain operations.

parity   A method of error checking in which an extra bit is sent to the receiving device to indicate whether an even or odd number of binary 1 bits was transmitted. The receiving unit compares the received information with this bit and can obtain a reasonable judgment about the validity of the character. The same type of parity (even or odd) must be used by two communicating computers, or both may omit parity. When parity is used, a parity bit is added to each transmitted character. The bit's value is 0 or 1, to make the total number of 1s in the character even or odd, depending on which type of parity is used. Parity checking isn't widely supported on recent systems, but memory with parity bits can be used as ECC memory on systems with ECC-compatible chipsets. See also *ECC*.

park program   A program that executes a seek to the highest cylinder or just past the highest cylinder of a drive so the potential of data loss is minimized if the drive is moved. Park programs are not interchangeable between drives and are no longer required on most drives 40MB and above because these drives self-park their heads for safety.

partition   A section of a hard disk devoted to a particular operating system. Most hard disks have only one partition, devoted to DOS. A hard disk can have as many as four partitions, each occupied by a different operating system. DOS v3.3 or later can occupy two of these four partitions. A boot manager enables you to select the partition occupied by the operating system you want to start if you have multiple operating systems installed in different partitions. See also *boot manager*.

Pascal   A high-level programming language named for the French mathematician Blaise Pascal (1623–1662). Developed in the early 1970s by Niklaus Wirth for teaching programming and designed to support the concepts of structured programming.

passive matrix   Another name for dual-scan, display-type LCDs.

PC Card (PCMCIA—Personal Computer Memory Card International Association)   A credit card–sized expansion adapter for notebook and laptop PCs. PC Card is the official PCMCIA trademark; however, both PC Card and PCMCIA card are used to refer to these standards. PCMCIA cards are removable modules that can hold numerous types of devices, including memory, modems, fax/modems, radio transceivers, network adapters, solid state disks, hard disks, and flash memory adapters.

PCI (Peripheral Component Interconnect)   A standard bus specification initially developed by Intel in 1992 that bypasses the standard ISA I/O bus and uses the system bus to increase the bus clock speed and take full advantage of the CPU's data path. The most common form of PCI is 32 bits wide running at 33MHz, but 66MHz and 64-bit wide versions of PCI are frequently used on servers.

PCI Express   A high-speed serial I/O interconnect standard being developed by the PCI-SIG (www.pcisig.com) as an eventual replacement for the original PCI standard. The initial version of PCI Express supports 0.8V signaling at 2.5GHz.

PCL (Printer Control Language)   Developed by Hewlett-Packard in 1984 as a language for the HP LaserJet printer. PCL is now the de facto industry standard for PC printing. PCL defines a standard set of commands, enabling applications to communicate with HP or HP-compatible printers and is supported by virtually all printer manufacturers. Various levels of PCL are supported by HP and other brands of laser and inkjet printers.

PCM (pulse code modulation)   A technique for digitizing analog signals by sampling the signal and converting each sample into a binary number. Also stands for powertrain control module, which is what the computer in most modern automobiles is called.

PDA (personal digital assistant) A handheld, palm-sized computer that functions primarily as a personal organizer and can be combined with a cellular phone or pager. Leading examples include the Palm series, Windows–based PalmPCs, and the Handspring (which also runs the Palm OS).

PDF (portable document format) Files with this extension can be read with the Adobe Acrobat Reader. See also *Acrobat*.

peer-to-peer A type of network in which any computer can act as both a server (by providing access to its resources to other computers) and a client (by accessing shared resources from other computers).

pel See *pixel*.

Pentium An Intel microprocessor with 32-bit registers, a 64-bit data bus, and a 32-bit address bus. The Pentium has a built-in L1 cache segmented into a separate 8KB cache for code and another 8KB cache for data. The Pentium includes an FPU or math coprocessor. It is backward compatible with the 486 and can operate in real, protected virtual, and virtual real modes. The MMX Pentium has a 16KB cache for code, has a 16KB cache for data, and adds the MMX instruction set.

Pentium II An Intel sixth-generation processor similar to the Pentium Pro but with MMX capabilities and SEC cartridge packaging technology. Includes L2 cache running at half-core speed.

Pentium III An Intel sixth-generation processor similar to the Pentium II but with SSE (Streaming SIMD Extensions) added. Later PIII models (codenamed Coppermine) include on-die L2 cache running at full core speed. It's available in both cartridge (Slot 1) and chip package (Socket 370) versions.

Pentium 4 The first Intel seventh-generation processor, it's based on a new 32-bit microarchitecture that operates at higher clock speeds because of hyper pipelined technology, a rapid execution engine, a 400MHz system bus, and an execution trace cache. The 400MHz system bus is a quad-pumped bus running off a 100MHz system clock, making 3.2GBps data transfer rates possible. The advanced transfer cache is a 256KB, on-die Level 2 cache with increased bandwidth over previous microarchitectures. The floating-point and multimedia units have been improved by making the registers 128 bits wide and adding a separate register for data movement. Finally, SSE2 adds 144 new instructions for double-precision floating-point, SIMD integer, and memory management. The original version for Socket 423 was codenamed Willamette, whereas the latest Socket 478 version was codenamed Northwood.

Pentium Pro An Intel sixth-generation (P6) processor with 32-bit registers, a 64-bit data bus, and a 36-bit address bus. The Pentium Pro has the same segmented Level 1 cache as the Pentium but also includes a 256KB, 512KB, or 1MB of L2 cache on a separate die inside the processor package. The Pentium Pro includes an FPU or math coprocessor. It is backward compatible with the Pentium and can operate in real, protected, and virtual real modes. The Pentium Pro fits into Socket 8.

peripheral Any piece of equipment used in computer systems that is an attachment to the computer. Disk drives, terminals, and printers are all examples of peripherals.

persistence In a monitor, the quality of the phosphor chemical that indicates how long the glow caused by the electrons striking the phosphor will remain onscreen.

petabyte (P) A measure of disk capacity equaling 1,000,000,000,000,000 bytes.

PGA 1) Pin grid array. A chip package that has a large number of pins on the bottom designed for socket mounting. 2) Professional graphics adapter. A limited-production, high-resolution graphics card for XT and AT systems from IBM.

phosphor A layer of electroluminescent material applied to the inside face of a cathode-ray tube (CRT). When bombarded by electrons, the material fluoresces, and after the bombardment stops it phosphoresces.

phosphorescence The emission of light from a substance after the source of excitation has been removed.

Photo CD A technology developed by Eastman Kodak and Philips that stores photographic images on a CD-R recordable compact disc. Images stored on the Photo CD can have resolutions as high as 2,048×3,072 pixels. Up to 100 true-color images (24-bit color) can be stored on one disc. Photo CD images are created by scanning film and digitally recording the images on compact discs. The digitized images are indexed (given a 4-digit code), and thumbnails of each image on the disc are shown on the front of the case along with its index number. Multisession capability enables several rolls of film to be added to a single disc on different occasions.

photolithography The photographic process used in electronic chip manufacturing that creates transistors and circuit and signal pathways in semiconductors by depositing different layers of various materials on the chip.

photoresist A chemical used to coat a silicon wafer in the semiconductor manufacturing process that makes the silicon sensitive to light for photolithography.

physical drive A single disk drive. DOS defines logical drives, which are given a specifier, such as C: or D:. A single physical drive can be divided into multiple logical drives. Conversely, special software can span a single logical drive across two physical drives.

Physical Layer See *OSI*.

physical unit number See *PUN*.

Picture CD A simplified version of Photo CD that stores scanned images from a single roll of film on a CD-R disc. Images on Picture CDs, unlike those on Photo CDs, are stored in the industry-standard JPEG file format and can be opened with most photo-editing programs.

PIF (program information file) A file that contains information about a non-Windows application specifying optimum settings for running the program under Windows 3.x. These are called property sheets in 32-bit Windows.

pin 1) The lead on a connector, chip, module, or device. 2) Personal identification number. A personal password used for identification purposes.

pin compatible Chips having the same pinout functions. For example, a VIA C3 processor is pin compatible with an Intel Celeron (Socket 370 version).

pinout A listing of which pins have which functions on a chip, socket, slot, or other connector.

PIO mode (programmed input/output mode) The standard data transfer modes used by IDE drives that use the processor's registers for data transfer. This is in contrast with DMA modes, which transfer data directly between main memory and the device. The slowest PIO mode is 0, and the fastest PIO mode is mode 4 (16.66MBps). Faster modes use Ultra DMA transfers. See also *Ultra DMA*.

pipeline A path for instructions or data to follow.

pixel A mnemonic term meaning picture element. Any of the tiny elements that form a picture on a video display screen. Also called a pel.

pixel shader A small program that controls the appearance of individual pixels in a 3D image. Most recent mid-range and high-end GPUs such as NVIDIA's GeForce 3 and GeForce 4 Ti series and the ATI 8xxx and 9xxx series have built-in pixel shaders. See also *GPU*, *hardware shader*, and *vertex shader*.

PKZIP The original ZIP-format compression/decompression program developed by the late Phil Katz. His company, PKWARE, continues to develop PKZIP for popular operating systems, including Windows.

planar board A term equivalent to motherboard, used by IBM in some of its literature.

plasma display A display technology that uses plasma (electrically charged gas) to illuminate each pixel. Plasma displays are much thinner than conventional CRT displays but are much more expensive than CRTs or LCD displays. Several vendors now sell HDTV plasma displays that can also be connected to computers with VGA or DVI video connectors.

plated media Hard disk platters plated with a form of thin metal film medium on which data is recorded.

platter A disk contained in a hard disk drive. Most drives have two or more platters, each with data recorded on both sides.

PLCC (plastic leaded-chip carrier) A chip-carrier package with J-leads around the perimeter of the package.

Plug and Play (PnP) A hardware and software specification developed by Intel that enables a PnP system and PnP adapter cards to automatically configure themselves. PnP cards are free from switches and jumpers and are configured via the PnP BIOS in the host system, or via supplied programs for non-PnP systems. PnP also allows the system to detect and configure external devices, such as monitors, modems, and devices attached to USB or IEEE-1394 ports. Windows 9x, Me, 2000, and XP all support PnP devices.

polling A communications technique that determines when a device is ready to send data. The system continually interrogates polled devices in a round-robin sequence. If a device has data to send, it sends back an acknowledgment and the transmission begins. Contrasts with interrupt-driven communications, in which the device generates a signal to interrupt the system when it has data to send. Polling enables two devices that would normally have an IRQ conflict to coexist because the IRQ is not used for flow control.

port Plug or socket that enables an external device, such as a printer, to be attached to the adapter card in the computer. Also a logical address used by a microprocessor for communication between it and various devices.

port address One of a system of addresses used by the computer to access devices such as disk drives or printer ports. You might need to specify an unused port address when installing any adapter boards in a system unit.

port replicator For mobile computers, a device that plugs into the laptop and provides all the ports for connecting external devices. The advantage of using a port replicator is that the external devices can be left connected to the replicator and the mobile computer connected to them all at once by connecting to the replicator, rather than connecting to each individual device. A port replicator differs from a docking station in that the latter can provide additional drive bays and expansion slots not found in port replicators. Traditionally, port replicators have plugged into a proprietary bus on the rear of a portable computer, but so-called universal models might attach to the PC Card (PCMCIA) slot or to a USB port.

portable computer A computer system smaller than a transportable system but larger than a laptop system. Very few systems in this form factor are sold today, but companies such as Dolch still produce them. Most portable systems conform to the lunchbox style popularized by Compaq or the briefcase style popularized by IBM, each with a fold-down (removable) keyboard and built-in display. These systems characteristically run on AC power and not on batteries, include several expansion slots, and can be as powerful as full desktop systems.

POS (Programmable Option Select) The Micro Channel Architecture's POS eliminates switches and jumpers from the system board and adapters by replacing them with programmable registers. Automatic configuration routines store the POS data in a battery-powered CMOS memory for system configuration and operations. The configuration utilities rely on adapter description files (ADF) that contain the setup data for each card.

POST (power on self test) A series of tests run by the computer at power-on. Most computers scan and test many of their circuits and sound a beep from the internal speaker if this initial test indicates proper system performance.

PostScript A page-description language developed primarily by John Warnock of Adobe Systems for converting and moving data to the laser-printed page. Instead of using the standard method of transmitting graphics or character information to a printer and telling it where to place dots one by one on a page, PostScript provides a way for the laser printer to interpret mathematically a full page of shapes and curves. Adobe Acrobat converts PostScript output files into files that can be read by users with varying operating systems. See also *Acrobat*.

POTS (plain old telephone service) Standard analog telephone service.

power management Systems used initially in mobile computers (and now also used in desktop systems) to decrease power consumption by turning off or slowing down devices during periods of inactivity. See also *APM*.

power supply An electrical/electronic circuit that supplies all operating voltage and current to the computer system.

PPGA (plastic pin grid array) A chip-packaging form factor used by Intel as an alternative to traditional ceramic packaging.

PPP (Point-to-Point Protocol) A protocol that enables a computer to use the Internet with a standard telephone line and high-speed modem. PPP has largely replaced the Serial Line Internet Protocol (SLIP) because it supports line sharing and error detection.

precompensation A data write modification required by some older drives on the inner cylinders to compensate for the higher density of data on the (smaller) inner cylinders.

Presentation Layer See *OSI*.

primary partition An ordinary, single-volume bootable partition. See also *extended partition*.

printer A device that records information visually on paper or other material.

processor See *microprocessor*.

processor speed The clock rate at which a microprocessor processes data. A typical Pentium 4 processor, for example, operates at 2GHz (2 billion cycles per second).

program A set of instructions or steps telling the computer how to handle a problem or task.

PROM (programmable read-only memory) A type of memory chip that can be programmed to store information permanently—information that can't be erased. Also referred to as OTP for one-time programmable.

proprietary Anything invented by one company and that uses components available from only that one company. Especially applies to cases in which the inventing company goes to lengths to hide the specifications of the new invention or to prevent other manufacturers from making similar or compatible items. The opposite of standard or open architecture. Computers with nonstandard components that are available from only the original manufacturer, such as Apple Macintosh systems, are known as proprietary.

protected mode A mode available in all Intel and compatible processors except the first-generation 8086 and 8088. In this mode, memory addressing is extended beyond the 1MB limits of the 8088 and real mode and restricted protection levels can be set to trap software crashes and control the system.

protocol   A system of rules and procedures governing communications between two or more devices. Protocols vary, but communicating devices must follow the same protocol to exchange data. The data format, readiness to receive or send, error detection, and error correction are some of the operations that can be defined in protocols.

proxy server   A computer that acts as a gateway between the computers on a network and the Internet and also provides page caching and optional content filtering and firewall services to the network. Some home network software solutions for Internet sharing, such as WinProxy, use a proxy server.

PS/2 mouse   A mouse designed to plug into a dedicated mouse port (a round, 6-pin DIN connector) on the motherboard, rather than plugging into a serial port. The name comes from the fact that this port was first introduced on the IBM PS/2 systems.

PUN (physical unit number)   A term used to describe a device attached directly to the SCSI bus. Also known as a SCSI ID. As many as eight SCSI devices can be attached to a single SCSI bus, and each must have a unique PUN or ID assigned from 7 to 0. Normally, the SCSI host adapter is assigned the highest-priority ID, which is 7. A bootable hard disk is assigned an ID of 0, and other nonbootable drives are assigned higher priorities.

QAM (quadrature amplitude modulation)   A modulation technique used by high-speed modems that combines both phase and amplitude modulation. This technique enables multiple bits to be encoded in a single time interval.

QDR (quad data rate)   A high-speed SDRAM technology (www.qdrsram.com) that uses separate input and output ports with a DDR interface to enable four pieces of data to be processed at the same time. See also *DDR*.

QIC (Quarter-Inch Committee)   An industry association that sets hardware and software standards for tape-backup units that use quarter-inch–wide tapes. QIC, QIC-Wide, Travan, and Travan NS drives are all based on QIC standards.

Quantum   Formerly a major maker of hard disk drives and now a major maker of attached network storage devices. Quantum-brand disk drives are now sold and supported by Maxtor.

QWERTY keyboard   The standard typewriter or computer keyboard, with the characters Q, W, E, R, T, and Y on the top row of alpha keys. Because of the haphazard placement of characters, this keyboard can hinder fast typing.

RAID (redundant array of independent or inexpensive disks)   A storage unit that employs two or more drives in combination for fault tolerance and greater performance, used mostly in file server applications. Originally used only with SCSI drives and host adapters, many motherboards now feature IDE RAID implementations.

rails   Plastic or metal strips attached to the sides of disk drives mounted in IBM ATs and compatibles so that the drives can slide into place. These rails fit into channels in the side of each disk drive bay position and might be held in position with screws or snap into place.

RAM (random-access memory)   All memory accessible at any instant (randomly) by a microprocessor.

RAM disk   A "phantom disk drive" in which a section of system memory (RAM) is set aside to hold data, just as though it were a number of disk sectors. To an operating system, a RAM disk looks and functions like any other drive.

RAMBUS Dynamic RAM   See *RDRAM*.

RAMDAC (random-access memory digital-to-analog converter)   A special type of DAC found on video cards. RAMDACs use a trio of DACs—one each for red, green, and yellow—to convert image data into a picture. RAMDACs were formerly separate chips but are now integrated into the 3D accelerator chips on most recent video cards.

random-access file   A file in which all data elements (or records) are of equal length and written in the file end to end, without delimiting characters between. Any element (or record) in the file can be found directly by calculating the record's offset in the file.

random-access memory   See *RAM*.

raster   A pattern of horizontal scanning lines normally on a computer monitor. An electromagnetic field causes the beam of the monitor's tube to illuminate the correct dots to produce the required characters.

raster graphics   A technique for representing a picture image as a matrix of dots. It is the digital counterpart of the analog method used in TV. Several raster graphics standards exist, including PCX, TIFF, BMP, JPEG, and GIF.

RCA jack   Also called a phono connector. A plug and socket for a two-wire coaxial cable used to connect audio and video components. The plug is a 1/8" thick prong that sticks out 5/16" from the middle of a cylinder.

RDRAM (Rambus DRAM)   A high-speed dynamic RAM technology developed by Rambus, Inc., which is supported by Intel's 1999 and later motherboard chipsets. RDRAM transfers data at 1GBps or faster, which is significantly faster than SDRAM and other technologies and which is capable of keeping up with future-generation high-speed processors. Memory modules with RDRAM chips are called RIMMs (Rambus inline memory modules). Rambus licenses its technology to other semiconductor companies, who manufacture the chips and RIMMs. RDRAMs are used by some of Intel's mid-range and high-end chipsets for the Pentium III and Pentium 4 desktop processors and their server counterparts.

read-only file   A file whose attribute setting in the file's directory entry tells DOS not to allow software to write into or over the file.

read-only memory   See *ROM*.

read/write head   A tiny magnet that reads and writes data on a disk track.

real mode   A mode available in all Intel 8086–compatible processors that enables compatibility with the original 8086. In this mode, memory addressing is limited to 1MB.

real-time   The actual time in which a program or an event takes place. In computing, real-time refers to an operating mode under which data is received and processed and the results returned so quickly that the process appears instantaneous to the user. The term also is used to describe the process of simultaneous digitization and compression of audio and video information.

reboot   The process of restarting a computer and reloading the operating system.

Red Book   More commonly known as Compact Disc-Digital Audio (CD-DA), one of four compact disc standards. Red Book got its name from the color of the manual used to describe the CD-Audio specifications. The Red Book audio standard requires that digital audio be sampled at a 44.1KHz sample rate using 16 bits for each sample. This is the standard used by audio CDs and many CD-ROMs.

refresh cycle   A cycle in which the computer accesses all memory locations stored by DRAM chips so that the information remains intact. DRAM chips must be accessed several times per second; otherwise, the information fades.

refresh rate   Another term for the vertical scan frequency of monitors.

register   Storage area in memory having a specified storage capacity—such as a bit, byte, or computer word—and intended for a special purpose.

Registry   The system configuration files used by Windows 9x, Windows Me, Windows NT, Windows 2000, and Windows XP to store settings about installed hardware and drivers, user preferences, installed software, and other settings required to keep Windows running properly. Replaces the WIN.INI and SYSTEM.INI files from Windows 3.x. The Registry structure varies between Windows versions.

remote digital loopback   A test that checks the phone link and a remote modem's transmitter and receiver. Data entered from the keyboard is transmitted from the initiating modem, received by the remote modem's receiver, looped through its transmitter, and returned to the local screen for verification.

remote echo   A copy of the data received by the remote system, returned to the sending system, and displayed onscreen. A function of the remote system.

rendering   Generating a 3D image that incorporates the simulation of lighting effects, such as shadows and reflection.

resolution   1) A reference to the size of the pixels used in graphics. In medium-resolution graphics, pixels are large. In high-resolution graphics, pixels are small. 2) A measure of the number of horizontal and vertical pixels that can be displayed by a video adapter and monitor.

reverse engineering   The act of duplicating a hardware or software component by studying the functions of the component and designing a different one that has the same functions.

RFI (radio frequency interference)   A high-frequency signal radiated by improperly shielded conductors, particularly when signal path lengths are comparable to or longer than the signal wavelengths. The FCC now regulates RFI in computer equipment sold in the U.S. under FCC Regulations, Part 15, Subpart J.

RGB (red green blue)   A type of computer color display output signal comprised of separately controllable red, green, and blue signals; as opposed to composite video, in which signals are combined prior to output. RGB monitors offer much higher resolution and sharper pictures than composite monitors.

ribbon cable   Flat cable with wires running in parallel, such as those used for internal IDE or SCSI.

Rich Text Format (RTF)   A universal file format suitable for exchanging formatted text files between different word processing and page layout programs.

RIMM (Rambus inline memory module)   A type of memory module made using RDRAM chips. See also *RDRAM*. *

RISC (reduced instruction set computer)
Differentiated from CISC, the complex instruction set computer. RISC processors have simple instruction sets requiring only one or a few execution cycles. These simple instructions can be used more effectively than CISC systems with appropriately designed software, resulting in faster operations. See also *CISC*.

RJ-11 The standard two-wire connector type used for single-line telephone connections.

RJ-14 The standard four-wire connector type used for two-line telephone connections.

RJ-45 A standard connector type used in networking with twisted-pair cabling. Resembles an RJ-11/14 telephone jack, but RJ-45 is larger with more wires.

RLL (run-length limited) A type of encoding that derives its name from the fact that the techniques used limit the distance (run length) between magnetic flux reversals on the disk platter. Several types of RLL encoding techniques exist, although only two are commonly used. (1,7) RLL encoding increases storage capacity by about 30% over MFM encoding and is most popular in the very highest capacity drives due to a better window margin, whereas (2,7) RLL encoding increases storage capacity by 50% over MFM encoding and is used in the majority of RLL implementations. Most IDE, ESDI, and SCSI hard disks use one of these forms of RLL encoding.

RMA number (return-merchandise authorization number) A number given to you by a vendor when you arrange to return an item for repairs. Used to track the item and the repair.

ROM (read-only memory) A type of memory that has values permanently or semipermanently burned in. These locations are used to hold important programs or data that must be available to the computer when the power initially is turned on.

ROM BIOS (read-only memory basic input/output system) A BIOS encoded in a form of read-only memory for protection.

root directory The main directory of any hard or floppy disk. It has a fixed size and location for a particular disk volume and can't be resized dynamically the way subdirectories can.

router A device that is used to connect various networks, intelligently routing information between them. It is used to internetwork similar and dissimilar networks and can select the most expedient route based on traffic load, line speeds, costs, and network failures. Routers use forwarding tables to determine which packets should be forwarded between the connected networks. A cable or DSL modem is an example of a simple router that connects the Internet to your own network. Many routers include firewall capability to block suspect packets from being transmitted between networks.

routine Set of frequently used instructions. It can be considered as a subdivision of a program with two or more instructions that are related functionally.

RS-232 An interface introduced in August 1969 by the Electronic Industries Association. The RS-232 interface standard provides an electrical description for connecting peripheral devices to computers. Originally, RS-232 (serial) ports on computers used a 25-pin interface, but starting with the IBM AT, most use a 9-pin interface.

RTC (real-time clock) A battery-powered clock included on the motherboard of 286-class and newer computers. The contents of the RTC are read at startup time to provide the time display in the operating system's clock. It's often part of the NVRAM chip.

S/PDIF (Sony Philips Digital Interface) Provides digital I/O on high-end sound cards and multimedia-capable video cards. Might use either an RCA jack or optical jack; some devices support both types of S/PDIF connectors.

S-Video (Y/C) Type of video signal used in the Hi8 and S-VHS videotape formats in which the luminance and chrominance (Y/C) components are kept separate, providing greater control and quality of each image. S-video transmits luminance and color portions separately, thus avoiding the NTSC encoding process and its inevitable loss of picture quality.

SATA (Serial ATA) A high-speed serial interface designed to replace the current parallel ATA and UltraATA drive interface standards. Serial ATA 1.0 uses a seven-wire data/ground cable and supports direct point-to-point connections to host adapters at initial speeds of up to 150MBps, which is faster than UltraATA-133. Serial ATA II is a version of the SATA standard designed for servers. See also *Ultra DMA*.

scan codes The hexadecimal codes actually sent by the keyboard to the motherboard when a key is pressed.

scan lines The parallel lines across a video screen, along which the scanning spot travels in painting the video information that makes up a monitor picture. NTSC systems use 525 scan lines to a screen; PAL systems use 625.

ScanDisk The default Windows 9x/Me drive-testing program; might be referred to as error checking in the Drive properties screen. Windows NT, Windows 2000, and Windows XP use CHKDSK to test drives.

scanner A device that reads an image and converts it into computer data.

scanning frequency A monitor measurement that specifies how often the image is refreshed. See also *vertical scan frequency*.

scratch disk   A disk that contains no useful information and can be used as a test disk. IBM has a routine on the Advanced Diagnostics disks that creates a specially formatted scratch disk to be used for testing floppy drives.

SCSI (small computer system interface)   A standard originally developed by Shugart Associates (then called SASI for Shugart Associates System Interface) and later approved by ANSI in 1986. SCSI-2 (now called SPI-2) was approved in 1994, and SCSI-3 (now called SPI-3) began the approval process in 1995. Ultra SCSI-4 (now called SPI-4) is currently in the development process. 8-bit (narrow) versions of SCSI typically use a 50-pin connector and permit multiple devices (up to 8 including the host) to be connected in daisy-chain fashion. Some low-cost narrow SCSI devices might use a 25-pin connector. Wide and Ultra Wide versions of SCSI use a 68-pin connector and can support up to 16 devices including the host.

SDLC (Synchronous Data Link Control)   A protocol developed by IBM for software applications and communicating devices operation in IBM's Systems Network Architecture (SNA). Defines operations at the link level of communications—for example, the format of data frames exchanged between modems over a phone line.

SDRAM (synchronous DRAM)   RAM that runs at the same speed as the main system bus.

SEC (single edge contact)   An Intel processor packaging design in which the processor and optional L2 cache chips are mounted on a small circuit board (much like an oversized memory SIMM), which might be sealed in a metal and plastic cartridge. The cartridge is then plugged into the motherboard through an edge connector called Slot 1 or Slot 2, which looks similar to an adapter card slot. Several variations to the SEC cartridge form factor exist: The single edge contact cartridge (SECC) has a cover and a thermal plate; the single edge contact cartridge 2 (SECC2) has a cover, but no thermal plate; and the single edge processor package (SEPP, which is used only with Celeron processors) has no cover or thermal plate. In implementations with no thermal plate, the heatsink is attached directly to the processor package or die.

SECAM   Sequential Couleur A Mémoire (sequential color with memory), the French color TV system also adopted in Russia. The basis of operation is the sequential recording of primary colors in alternate lines. The image format is 4:3, 625 lines, 50Hz, and 6MHz video bandwidth with a total 8MHz of video channel width.

SECC (single edge contact cartridge)   See *SEC*.

SECC2 (single edge contact cartridge 2)   See *SEC*.

sector   A section of one track defined with identification markings and an identification number. Most sectors hold 512 bytes of data.

security software   Utility software that uses a system of passwords and other devices to restrict an individual's access to subdirectories and files.

seek time   The amount of time required for a disk drive to move the heads across one-third of the total number of cylinders. Represents the average time it takes to move the heads from one cylinder to another randomly selected cylinder. Seek time is a part of the average access time for a drive.

self-extracting file   An archive file that contains its own extraction program. Open it in a file manager, such as Windows Explorer, to uncompress the files it contains. Because all types of files, including trojans, can be distributed as .exe files (the extension also used by self-extracting files), consider using a program such as WinZip to examine the contents of an .exe file before you open it.

semiconductor   A substance, such as germanium or silicon, whose conductivity is poor at low temperatures but is improved by minute additions of certain substances or by the application of heat, light, or voltage. Depending on the temperature and pressure, a semiconductor can control a flow of electricity. Semiconductors are the basis of modern electronic-circuit technology.

SEPP (single edge processor package)   See *SEC*.

sequencer   A software program that controls MIDI file messages and keeps track of music timing. Because MIDI files store note instructions instead of actual sounds, a sequencer is needed to play, record, and edit MIDI sounds. Sequencer programs enable recording and playback of MIDI files by storing the instrument, note pitch (frequency), duration (in real-time) that each note is held, and loudness (amplitude) of each musical or sound-effect note.

sequential file   A file in which varying-length data elements are recorded end to end, with delimiting characters placed between each element. To find a particular element, you must read the whole file up to that element.

serial   The transfer of data characters one bit at a time, sequentially, using a single electrical path.

Serial ATA   See *SATA*.

serial mouse   A mouse designed to connect to a computer's serial port.

serial port   An I/O connector used to connect to serial devices. See also *RS-232*.

server   A computer in a network that enables resources such as files and printers to be shared by multiple users.

servo The mechanism in a drive that enables the head positioner to adjust continuously so that it is precisely placed above a given cylinder in the drive.

servo data Magnetic markings written on disk platters to guide the read/write heads in drives that use voice-coil actuators.

session (single or multisession) A term used in CD-ROM recording to describe a recording event. In a single session, data is recorded on a CD-ROM and an index is created. If additional space is left on the disc, another session can be used to record additional files along with another index. Some older CD-ROM drives do not expect additional recording sessions and therefore are incapable of reading the additional session data on the disc. The advent of Kodak's Photo CD propelled the desire for multisession CD-ROM XA (extended architecture) drives.

Session Layer See *OSI*.

settling time The time required for read/write heads to stop vibrating after they have been moved to a new track.

shadow mask A thin screen full of holes that adheres to the inside of a color CRT. The electron beam is aimed through the holes in the mask onto the phosphor dots. See also *aperture grille*.

shadow RAM A copy of a system's slower-access ROM BIOS placed in faster-access RAM, usually during the startup or boot procedure. This setup enables the system to access BIOS code without the penalty of additional wait states required by the slower ROM chips. Also called shadow ROM or ROM shadowing.

shell The generic name of any user interface software. COMMAND.COM is the standard shell for DOS; 32-bit Windows uses the Windows Explorer as a graphical shell and either COMMAND.COM (Windows 9x/Me) or CMD.EXE (Windows NT/2000/XP) as the command-line shell.

shielded twisted-pair (STP) Unshielded twisted-pair (UTP) network cabling with a metal sheath or braid around it to reduce interference, usually used in Token-Ring networks.

shock rating A rating (usually expressed in G force units) of how much shock a disk drive can sustain without damage. Usually two specifications exist for a drive powered on or off.

signal-to-noise (S/N) ratio The strength of a video or an audio signal in relation to interference (noise). The higher the S/N ratio, the better the quality of the signal. The latest high-end sound cards have an S/N ratio of 100:1.

silicon The base material for computer chips. An element, silicon (symbol Si) is contained in the majority of rock and sand on earth and is the second most abundant element on the planet next to oxygen.

SIMD (single instruction multiple data) The term used to describe the MMX and SSE instructions added to the Intel processors. These instructions can process matrixes consisting of multiple data elements with only a single instruction, enabling more efficient processing of graphics and sound data.

SIMM (single inline memory module) An array of memory chips on a small PC board with a single row of I/O contacts. SIMMs commonly have 30 or 72 connectors.

single-ended An electrical signaling method in which a single line is referenced by a ground path common to other signals. In a single-ended bus intended for moderately long distances, commonly one ground line exists between groups of signal lines to provide some resistance to signal crosstalk. Single-ended signals require only one driver or receiver pin per signal, plus one ground pin per group of signals. Single-ended signals are vulnerable to common mode noise and crosstalk but are much less expensive than differential signaling methods.

SIP (single inline package) A DIP-like package with only one row of leads.

skinny dip Twenty-four– and twenty-eight–position DIP devices with .300" row-to-row centerlines.

sleep See *suspend*.

SLIP (Serial Line Internet Protocol) An Internet protocol that is used to run the Internet Protocol (IP) over serial lines, such as telephone circuits. IP enables a packet to traverse multiple networks on the way to its final destination. Largely replaced by PPP. See also *PPP*.

slot A physical connector on a motherboard to hold an expansion card, SIMMs and DIMMs, or a processor card in place and make contact with the electrical connections.

Slot 1 The motherboard connector designed by Intel to accept its SEC cartridge processor design used by the Pentium II and early Celeron and Pentium III processors.

Slot 2 A motherboard connector for Pentium II and Pentium III Xeon processors intended mainly for file server applications. Slot 2 systems support up to four-way symmetric multiprocessing.

SMART (self-monitoring analysis and reporting technology) An industry standard for advance reporting of imminent hard drive failure. When this feature is enabled in the BIOS and a SMART-compliant hard drive is installed, detected problems can be reported to the computer. This enables the user to replace a drive before it fails. Programs such as Norton System Works and Norton Utilities are compatible with these status messages.

SMBIOS   A BIOS that incorporates system management functions and reporting compatibility with the Desktop Management Interface (DMI).

SMPTE time code   An 80-bit standardized edit time code adopted by SMPTE, the Society of Motion Picture and Television Engineers. The SMPTE time code is a standard used to identify individual video frames in the video-editing process. SMPTE time code controls such functions as play, record, rewind, and forward of video tapes. SMPTE time code displays video in terms of hours, minutes, seconds, and frames for accurate video editing.

snow   A flurry of bright dots that can appear anywhere onscreen on a monitor.

SO-J (small outline J-lead)   A small DIP package with J-shaped leads for surface mounting or socketing.

socket   A receptacle, usually on a motherboard although sometimes also found on expansion cards, into which processors or chips can be plugged.

Socket 1–8   The Intel specifications for eight different sockets to accept various Intel processors in the 486, Pentium, and Pentium Pro families.

Socket 370   A 370-pin socket used by socketed versions of the Celeron and Pentium III and the VIA C3 processors.

Socket 423   The socket used by the initial versions of the Pentium 4.

Socket 462   See *Socket A*.

Socket 478   A 478-pin socket used by the Northwood versions of the Pentium 4.

Socket 603   A 603-pin socket used by Intel Xeon processors based on the Pentium 4 design.

Socket A   A 462-pin socket used by socketed versions of the AMD Athlon and Duron.

SODIMM (small outline dual inline memory module)   An industry-standard 144-pin memory module designed for use primarily in laptop and portable computers.

soft error   An error in reading or writing data that occurs sporadically, usually because of a transient problem, such as a power fluctuation.

software   A series of instructions loaded in the computer's memory that instructs the computer in how to accomplish a problem or task.

sound card   An adapter card with sound-generating capabilities.

South Bridge   The Intel term for the lower-speed component in the chipset that has always been a single individual chip; it has been replaced in the 8xx-series chipsets by the ICH. The South Bridge connects to the 33MHz PCI bus and contains the IDE interface ports and the interface to the 8MHz ISA bus (when present). It also typically contains the USB interface and even the CMOS RAM and real-time clock functions. The South Bridge contains all the components that make up the ISA bus, including the interrupt and DMA controllers. See also *chipset, ICH, MCH,* and *North Bridge.*

SPI (SCSI parallel interface)   Alternative name for common SCSI standards. See also *SCSI.*

spindle   The central post on which a disk drive's platters are mounted.

spindle count   In notebook and laptop computers with interchangeable drives, spindle count refers to how many drives can be installed and used at the same time.

splitter   Used in DSL and cable modem service to separate Internet signals from those used by the existing telephone (DSL) or cable TV service.

SRAM (static random access memory)   A form of high-speed memory. SRAM chips do not require a refresh cycle like DRAM chips and can be made to operate at very high access speeds. SRAM chips are very expensive because they normally require six transistors per bit. This also makes the chips larger than conventional DRAM chips. SRAM is volatile, meaning it will lose data with no power. SRAMs are often used for cache memory.

SSE (streaming SIMD extensions)   The name given by Intel for the 70 new MMX-type instructions added to the Pentium III processor when it was introduced. See also *MMX* and *SIMD.*

ST-506/412   A hard disk interface invented by Seagate Technology and introduced in 1980 with the ST-506 5MB hard drive. IDE drives emulate this disk interface.

stack   An area of memory storage for temporary values that normally are read in the reverse order from which they are written. Also called last-in, first-out (LIFO).

stackable hub or switch   A hub or switch that can be connected to another hub or switch to increase its capacity. The uplink port on the existing hub or switch is used to connect the new hub or switch.

stair-stepping   Jagged raster representation of diagonals or curves; corrected by antialiasing.

standby   Defines an optional operating state of minimal power reduction with the shortest recovery time.

standby power supply   A backup power supply that quickly switches into operation during a power outage.

standoffs   In a motherboard and case design, small nonconductive spacers (usually plastic or nylon) used to keep the underside of the motherboard from contacting the metallic case, therefore preventing short circuits of the motherboard.

start/stop bits The signaling bits attached to a character before and after the character is transmitted during asynchronous transmission.

starting cluster The number of the first cluster occupied by a file. Listed in the directory entry of every file.

stepper motor actuator An assembly that moves disk drive read/write heads across platters by a sequence of small partial turns of a stepper motor. Once common on low-cost hard disk drives of 40MB or less, stepper motor actuators are now confined to floppy disk drives.

stepping The code used to identify the revision of a processor. New masks are introduced to build each successive stepping, incorporating any changes necessary to fix known bugs in prior steppings.

storage Device or medium on or in which data can be entered or held and retrieved at a later time. Synonymous with memory.

streaming In tape backup, a condition in which data is transferred from the hard disk as quickly as the tape drive can record the data so the drive does not start and stop or waste tape.

string A sequence of characters.

subdirectory A directory listed in another directory. Subdirectories themselves exist as files.

subroutine A segment of a program that can be executed by a single call. Also called program module.

superscalar execution The capability of a processor to execute more than one instruction at a time.

surface mount Chip carriers and sockets designed to mount to the surface of a PC board.

surge protector A device in the power line that feeds the computer and provides protection against voltage spikes and other transients.

suspend Refers to a level of power management in which substantial power reduction is achieved by the display or other components. The components can have a longer recovery time from this state than from the standby state.

SVGA (Super VGA) Refers to a video adapter or monitor capable of 800×600 resolution.

SWEDAC (Swedish Board for Technical Accreditation) Regulatory agency establishing standards such as MPR1 and MPR2, which specify maximum values for both alternating electric fields and magnetic fields and provide monitor manufacturers with guidelines in creating low-emission monitors.

switch Also called a switching hub, it's a type of hub that reads the destination address of each packet and then forwards the packet to only the correct port, minimizing traffic on other parts of the network. Unlike a regular hub, which wastes network bandwidth by copying packets to all ports, a switch forwards packets to only their intended recipients, immediately reducing network traffic jams and improving overall efficiency for the entire network. Many switches also support full-duplex service, effectively doubling the speed of full-duplex network cards attached to the switch. See also *hub*.

SXGA (Super XGA) Refers to a video adapter or monitor capable of 1280×1024 or greater resolution.

synchronous communication A form of communication in which blocks of data are sent at strictly timed intervals. Because the timing is uniform, no start or stop bits are required. Compare with asynchronous communication. Some mainframes support only synchronous communication unless a synchronous adapter and appropriate software have been installed. See also *asynchronous communication*.

system crash A situation in which the computer freezes up and refuses to proceed without rebooting. Usually caused by faulty software, it's unlike a hard disk crash—no permanent physical damage occurs.

system files Files with the system attribute. Usually, the hidden files that are used to boot the operating system. The MS-DOS and Windows 9x system files include IO.SYS and MSDOS.SYS; the IBM DOS system files are IBMBIO.COM and IBMDOS.COM.

System Management Mode (SMM) Circuitry integrated into Intel processors that operates independently to control the processor's power use based on its activity level. It enables the user to specify time intervals after which the CPU will be powered down partially or fully and also supports the suspend/resume feature that enables instant power-on and power-off.

tape drive Any data storage drive that uses tape as the storage medium.

target A device attached to a SCSI bus that receives and processes commands sent from another device (the initiator) on the SCSI bus. A SCSI hard disk is an example of a target.

TCM (Trellis-coded modulation) An error-detection and correction technique employed by high-speed modems to enable higher-speed transmissions that are more resistant to line impairments.

TCO 1) Refers to the Swedish Confederation of Professional Employees, which has set stringent standards for devices that emit radiation. See also *MPR*. 2) Total cost of ownership. The cost of using a computer. It includes the cost of the hardware, software, and upgrades as well as the cost of the in-house staff and consultants who provide training and technical support.

TCP (tape carrier package)   A method of packaging processors for use in portable systems that reduces the size, power consumed, and heat generated by the chip. A processor in the TCP form factor is essentially a raw die encased in an oversized piece of polyamide film. The film is laminated with copper foil that is etched to form the leads that will connect the processor to the motherboard.

TCP port number   Logical port numbers used by TCP to communicate between computers—for example, Web browsing (http://) uses TCP port 80. POP3 email uses TCP port 110. Some firewalls require you to manually configure open TCP port numbers to allow certain processes and programs to work.

TCP/IP (Transmission Control Protocol/Internet Protocol)   A set of protocols developed by the U.S. Department of Defense (DoD) to link dissimilar computers across many types of networks. This is the primary protocol used by the Internet.

temporary backup   A second copy of a work file, usually having the extension BAK. Created by application software so you easily can return to a previous version of your work.

temporary file   A file temporarily (and usually invisibly) created by a program for its own use.

tera   A multiplier indicating one trillion (1,000,000,000,000) of some unit. Abbreviated as *t* or *T*. A binary tera (now called a tebi) is 1,099,511,627,776.

terabyte (T)   A unit of information storage equal to 1,000,000,000 bytes.

terminal   A device whose keyboard and display are used for sending and receiving data over a communications link. Differs from a microcomputer in that it has no internal processing capabilities. Used to enter data into or retrieve processed data from a system or network.

terminal mode   An operational mode required for microcomputers to transmit data. In terminal mode, the computer acts as though it were a standard terminal, such as a teletypewriter, rather than a data processor. Keyboard entries go directly to the modem, whether the entry is a modem command or data to be transmitted over the phone lines. Received data is output directly to the screen. The more popular communications software products control terminal mode and enable more complex operations, including file transmission and saving received files.

terminator   Hardware or circuits that must be attached to or enabled at both ends of an electrical bus. Functions to prevent the reflection or echoing of signals that reach the ends of the bus and to ensure

that the correct impedance load is placed on the driver circuits on the bus. Most commonly used with the SCSI bus and Thin Ethernet.

TFT (thin film transistor)   The highest quality and brightest LCD color display type. A method for packaging one–four transistors per pixel within a flexible material that is the same size and shape as the LCD display, which enables the transistors for each pixel to lie directly behind the liquid crystal cells they control.

thick Ethernet   See *10BASE-5*.

thin Ethernet   See *10BASE-2*.

thin-film media   Hard disk platters that have a thin film (usually three-millionths of an inch) of medium deposited on the aluminum substrate through a sputtering or plating process.

Thinnet   See *10BASE-2*.

through-hole   Chip carriers and sockets equipped with leads that extend through holes in a PC board.

throughput   The amount of user data transmitted per second without the overhead of protocol information, such as start and stop bits or frame headers and trailers.

thumb drive   See *keychain drive*.

TIFF (tagged image file format)   A way of storing and exchanging digital image data. Developed by Aldus Corporation, Microsoft Corporation, and major scanner vendors to help link scanned images with the popular desktop publishing applications. Supports three main types of image data: black-and-white data, halftones or dithered data, and grayscale data. Compressed TIFF files are stored using lossless compression.

time code   A frame-by-frame address code time reference recorded on the spare track of a videotape or inserted in the vertical blanking interval. The time code is an eight-digit number encoding time in hours, minutes, seconds, and video frames.

Token-Ring   A type of local area network in which the workstations relay a packet of data called a token in a logical ring configuration. When a station wants to transmit, it takes possession of the token, attaches its data, and then frees the token after the data has made a complete circuit of the electrical ring. Transmits at speeds of 16Mbps. Because of the token-passing scheme, access to the network is controlled, unlike the slower 10BASE-X Ethernet system in which collisions of data can occur, which wastes time. The Token-Ring network uses shielded twisted-pair wiring, which is cheaper than the coaxial cable used by 10BASE-2 and 10BASE-5 Ethernet and ARCnet.

toner   The ultrafine, colored, plastic powder used in laser printers, LED printers, and photocopiers to produce the image on paper.

tower A personal computer that normally sits on the floor and is mounted vertically rather than horizontally.

TPI (tracks per inch) Used as a measurement of magnetic track density. Standard 5 1/4" 360KB floppy disks have a density of 48TPI, and the 1.2MB disks have a 96TPI density. All 3 1/2" disks have a 135.4667TPI density, and hard disks can have densities greater than 3,000TPI.

track One of the many concentric circles that holds data on a disk surface. Consists of a single line of magnetic flux changes and is divided into some number of 512-byte sectors.

track density Expressed as tracks per inch (TPI); defines how many tracks are recorded in 1" of space measured radially from the center of the disk. Sometimes also called radial density.

track-to-track seek time The time required for read/write heads to move between adjacent tracks.

transistor A semiconductor device invented in 1947 at Bell Labs (released in 1948) that is used to amplify a signal or open and close a circuit. In digital computers, it functions as an electronic switch. It is reduced to microscopic size in modern digital integrated circuits containing 100 million or more individual transistors.

Transport Layer In the OSI reference model, when more than one packet is in process at any time, such as when a large file must be split into multiple packets for transmission, this is the layer that controls the sequencing of the message components and regulates inbound traffic flow. See also *OSI*.

transportable computer A computer system larger than a portable system and similar in size and shape to a portable sewing machine. Most transportables conform to a design similar to the original Compaq portable, with a built-in CRT display. These systems are characteristically very heavy and run on only AC power. Because of advances primarily in LCD and plasma-display technology, these systems are obsolete and have been replaced by portable systems.

troubleshooting The task of determining the cause of a problem.

true-color images Also called 24-bit color images because each pixel is represented by 24 bits of data, allowing for 16.7 million colors. The number of colors possible is based on the number of bits used to represent the color. If 8 bits are used, 256 possible color values (2^8) exist. To obtain 16.7 million colors, each of the primary colors (red, green, and blue) is represented by 8 bits per pixel, which enables 256 possible shades for each of the primary red, green, and blue colors or $256 \times 256 \times 256 = 16.7$ million total colors.

TrueType An Apple/Microsoft-developed scalable font technology designed to provide a high-performance alternative to PostScript Type 1 fonts. TrueType fonts are supported by both Windows and MacOS, but a particular TrueType font must either be made in both MacOS and Windows versions or support the cross-platform OpenType font format to be used on both platforms.

TSR (terminate-and-stay-resident) A program that remains in memory after being loaded. Because they remain in memory, TSR programs can be reactivated by a predefined keystroke sequence or other operation while another program is active. Usually called resident programs. TSR programs are often loaded from the AUTOEXEC.BAT file used at startup by DOS and Windows 9x.

TTL (transistor-to-transistor logic) Digital signals often are called TTL signals. A TTL display is a monitor that accepts digital input at standardized signal voltage levels.

TWAIN Imaging standard used to interface scanners and digital cameras to applications such as Photoshop and other image editors. TWAIN enables the user to scan or download pictures without exiting the image-editing program.

TweakUI An unsupported software utility provided by Microsoft for 32-bit Windows users. TweakUI allows users to change the user interface and adjust Registry settings without manual Registry editing.

twisted pair A type of wire in which two small, insulated copper wires are wrapped or twisted around each other to minimize interference from other wires in the cable. Two types of twisted-pair cables are available: unshielded and shielded. Unshielded twisted-pair (UTP) wiring commonly is used in telephone cables and 10BASE-T, 100BASE-TX, and 1000BASE-T networking and provides little protection against interference. Shielded twisted-pair (STP) wiring is used in some networks or any application in which immunity from electrical interference is more important. Twisted-pair wire is much easier to work with than coaxial cable and is cheaper as well.

typematic The keyboard repeatedly sending the keypress code to the motherboard for a key that is held down. The delay before the code begins to repeat and the speed at which it repeats are user adjustable through MODE commands in DOS or the Windows Control Panel.

UART (Universal Asynchronous Receiver Transmitter) A chip device that controls the RS-232 serial port in a PC-compatible system. Originally developed by National Semiconductor, several UART versions are in PC-compatible systems: The 8250B is used in PC- and XT-class systems, and the 16450 and 16550 series are used in AT-class systems. The 16650 and higher UARTs are used for specialized high-speed serial communication cards.

UDF (Universal Disk Format) The disk format used by packet-writing software, such as Adaptec DirectCD. See also *Mt. Rainier* and *packet writing*.

Ultra DMA (UDMA or Ultra ATA) A protocol for transferring data to an ATA interface hard drive. The Ultra DMA/33 protocol transfers data in burst mode at a rate of 33MBps, whereas the even faster Ultra DMA/66 protocol transfers at 66MBps. Ultra DMA/66 also requires the use of a special 80-conductor cable for signal integrity. This cable also is recommended for Ultra DMA/33 and is backward compatible with standard ATA/IDE cables. The fastest UDMA modes are Ultra DMA/100 (supported by most recent chipsets) and Ultra DMA/133 (introduced by Maxtor in 2001).

UltraXGA (UXGA) A screen resolution of 1,600×1,200.

UMB (upper memory block) A block of unused memory in the upper memory area (UMA), which is the 384KB region between 640KB and 1MB of memory space in the PC. BIOS chips and memory buffers on add-on cards must be configured to use empty areas of the UMB; otherwise, they will not work.

unformatted capacity The total number of bytes of data that can fit on a disk. The formatted capacity is lower because space is lost defining the boundaries between sectors. For example, some vendors have referred to the high-density 1.44MB floppy disk as a 2.0MB disk (2.0MB is the unformatted capacity). However, because most media is preformatted today, this issue is fading away.

Unicode A worldwide standard for displaying, interchanging, and processing all types of language texts, including both those based on letters (such as Western European languages) and pictographs (such as Chinese, Japanese, and Korean).

uninterruptible power supply (UPS) A device that supplies power to the computer from batteries so power will not stop, even momentarily, during a power outage. The batteries are recharged constantly from a wall socket.

Universal Asynchronous Receiver Transmitter See *UART*.

unzipping The process of extracting one or more files from a PKZIP or WinZip-compatible archive file.

UPC (universal product code) A 10-digit computer-readable bar code used in labeling retail products. The code in the form of vertical bars includes a five-digit manufacturer identification number and a five-digit product code number.

update To modify information already contained in a file or program with current information.

upper memory area (UMA) The 384KB of memory between 640KB and 1MB. See also *UMB*.

URL (uniform resource locator) The primary naming scheme used to identify a particular site or file on the World Wide Web. URLs combine information about the protocol being used, the address of the site where the resource is located, the subdirectory location at the site, and the name of the particular file (or page) in question.

USB (universal serial bus) USB version 1.1 is a 12Mbps (1.5MBps) interface over a simple four-wire connection. The bus supports up to 127 devices and uses a tiered star topology built on expansion hubs that can reside in the PC, any USB peripheral, or even standalone hub boxes. USB 2.0, also called High-Speed USB, runs at 480Mbps and handles multiple devices better than USB 1.1.

utility A program that carries out routine procedures to make computer use easier.

UTP (unshielded twisted pair) A type of wire often used indoors to connect telephones or computer devices. Comes with two or four wires twisted inside a flexible plastic sheath or conduit and uses modular plugs and phone jacks.

V.21 An ITU standard for modem communications at 300bps. Modems made in the U.S. or Canada follow the Bell 103 standard but can be set to answer V.21 calls from overseas. The actual transmission rate is 300 baud and employs frequency shift keying (FSK) modulation, which encodes a single bit per baud.

V.22 An ITU standard for modem communications at 1,200bps, with an optional fallback to 600bps. V.22 is partially compatible with the Bell 212A standard observed in the U.S. and Canada. The actual transmission rate is 600 baud, using differential-phase shift keying (DPSK) to encode as much as 2 bits per baud.

V.22bis An ITU standard for modem communications at 2,400bps. Includes an automatic link-negotiation fallback to 1,200bps and compatibility with Bell 212A/V.22 modems. The actual transmission rate is 600 baud, using quadrature amplitude modulation (QAM) to encode as much as 4 bits per baud.

V.23 An ITU standard for modem communications at 1,200bps or 600bps with a 75bps back channel. Used in the United Kingdom for some videotext systems.

V.25 An ITU standard for modem communications that specifies an answer tone different from the Bell answer tone used in the U.S. and Canada. Most intelligent modems can be set with an ATB0 command so they use the V.25 2,100Hz tone when answering overseas calls.

V.32   An ITU standard for modem communications at 9,600bps and 4,800bps. V.32 modems fall back to 4,800bps when line quality is impaired and fall forward again to 9,600bps when line quality improves. The actual transmission rate is 2,400 baud using quadrature amplitude modulation (QAM) and optional trellis-coded modulation (TCM) to encode as much as 4 data bits per baud.

V.32bis   An ITU standard that extends the standard V.32 connection range and supports 4,800bps; 7,200bps; 9,600bps; 12,000bps; and 14,400bps transmission rates. V.32bis modems fall back to the next lower speed when line quality is impaired, fall back further as necessary, and fall forward to the next higher speed when line quality improves. The actual transmission rate is 2,400 baud using quadrature amplitude modulation (QAM) and trellis-coded modulation (TCM) to encode as much as 6 data bits per baud.

V.32terbo   A proprietary standard proposed by several modem manufacturers that will be cheaper to implement than the standard V.32 fast protocol but that will support transmission speeds of up to only 18,800bps. Because it is not an industry standard, it is not likely to have widespread industry support.

V.34   An ITU standard that extends the standard V.32bis connection range, supporting 28,800bps transmission rates as well as all the functions and rates of V.32bis. This was called V.32fast or V.fast while under development.

V.34+   An ITU standard that extends the standard V.34 connection range, supporting 33,600bps transmission rates as well as all the functions and rates of V.34.

V.42   An ITU standard for modem communications that defines a two-stage process of detection and negotiation for LAPM error control. Also supports MNP error-control protocol, Levels 1–4.

V.42bis   An extension of CCITT V.42 that defines a specific data-compression scheme for use with V.42 and MNP error control.

V.44   ITU-T designation for a faster data-compression scheme than V.42bis. V.44 can compress data up to 6:1. V.44 is included on most V.92-compliant modems. See also *V.92*.

V.90   ITU-T designation for defining the standard for 56Kbps communication. Supersedes the proprietary X2 schemes from U.S. Robotics (3Com) and K56flex from Rockwell.

V.92   ITU-T designation for an improved version of the V.90 protocol. V.92 allows faster uploading (up to 48Kbps), faster connections, and optional modem-on-hold (enabling you to take calls while online). Most V.92 modems also support V.44 compression. See also *V.44*.

V-Link   A VIA Technologies high-speed (266MBps) bus between the North Bridge and South Bridge chips in VIA chipsets, such as the P4X266 (for Pentium 4) and KT266/266A (for Athlon/Duron). V-Link is twice as fast as the PCI bus and provides a dedicated pathway for data transfer.

vaccine   A type of program used to locate and eradicate virus code from infected programs or systems.

vacuum tube   A device used to amplify or control electronic signals, it contains two major components: a cathode (a filament used to generate electrons) and an anode (a plate that captures electron current after it flows through one or more grids). Largely replaced by the transistor and integrated circuit in most small electronics applications, vacuum tubes in the form of CRTs are still used to make conventional monitors. The Aopen AX4B-533 Tube motherboard uses vacuum tubes for higher-quality integrated sound. See also *CRT*.

VCPI (virtual control program interface)   A 386 and later processor memory management standard created by Phar Lap software in conjunction with other software developers. VCPI provides an interface between applications using DOS extenders and 386 memory managers.

vertex   The corner of a triangle in 3D graphics. The plural of vertex is vertices. See also *vertex shader*.

vertex shader   A graphics processing function built in to recent 3D graphics chips that manipulates vertices by adding color, shading, and texture effects. Recent GPUs such as the NVIDIA GeForce 3 and GeForce Ti and the ATI Radeon series incorporate vertex shaders. See also *GPU*, *hardware shader*, and *pixel shader*.

vertical blanking interval (VBI)   The top and bottom lines in the video field, in which frame numbers, picture stops, chapter stops, white flags, closed captions, and more can be encoded. These lines do not appear on the display screen but maintain image stability and enhance image access.

vertical scan frequency   The rate at which the electron gun in a monitor scans or refreshes the entire screen each second.

very large scale integration   See *IC*.

VESA (Video Electronics Standards Association)   Founded in the late 1980s by NEC Home Electronics and eight other leading video board manufacturers with the main goal to standardize the electrical, timing, and programming issues surrounding 800×600 resolution video displays, commonly known as Super VGA. VESA has also developed the Video Local Bus (VL-Bus) standard for connecting high-speed adapters directly to the local processor bus. The most recent VESA standards involve digital flat-panel displays and display identification.

VFAT (virtual file allocation table) A file system used in Windows for Workgroups and Windows 9x. VFAT provides 32-bit protected mode access for file manipulation and supports long filenames (LFNs)—up to 255 characters in Windows 95 and later. VFAT can also read disks prepared with the standard DOS 16-bit FAT. VFAT was called 32-bit file access in Windows for Workgroups. VFAT is not the same as FAT32.

VGA (video graphics array) A type of PC video display circuit (and adapter) first introduced by IBM on April 2, 1987, which supports text and graphics. Text is supported at a maximum resolution of 80×25 characters in 16 colors with a character box of 9×16 pixels. Graphics are supported at a maximum resolution of 320×200 pixels in 256 (from a palette of 262,144) colors or 640×480 pixels in 16 colors. The VGA outputs an analog signal with a horizontal scanning frequency of 31.5KHz and supports analog color or analog monochrome displays. Also refers generically to any adapter or display capable of 640×480 resolution.

VHS (Video Home System) A popular consumer videotape format developed by Matsushita and JVC.

VIA Technologies A popular vendor of chipsets for AMD Athlon and Intel Pentium 4–based systems; it's also the maker of the VIA C3 processor.

video A system of recording and transmitting primarily visual information by translating moving or still images into electrical signals. The term *video* properly refers to only the picture, but as a generic term, *video* usually embraces audio and other signals that are part of a complete program. Video now includes not only broadcast television but many nonbroadcast applications, such as corporate communications, marketing, home entertainment, games, teletext, security, and even the visual display units of computer-based technology.

Video 8 or 8mm Video Video format based on the 8mm videotapes popularized by Sony for camcorders.

video adapter An expansion card or chipset built into a motherboard that provides the capability to display text and graphics onscreen. If the adapter is part of an expansion card, it also includes the physical connector for the monitor cable. If the chipset is on the motherboard, the video connector is on the motherboard as well.

video graphics array See *VGA*.

video-on-CD or video CD A full-motion digital video format using MPEG video compression and incorporating a variety of VCR-like control capabilities. See also *White Book*.

virtual disk A RAM disk or "phantom disk drive" in which a section of system memory (usually RAM) is set aside to hold data, just as though it were several disk sectors. To DOS, a virtual disk looks and functions like any other "real" drive.

virtual memory A technique by which operating systems such as 32-bit Windows versions load more programs and data into memory than they can hold. Parts of the programs and data are kept on disk and constantly swapped back and forth into system memory. The applications' software programs are unaware of this setup and act as though a large amount of memory is available.

virtual real mode A mode available in all Intel 80386-compatible processors. In this mode, memory addressing is limited to 4,096MB, restricted protection levels can be set to trap software crashes and control the system, and individual real-mode compatible sessions can be set up and maintained separately from one another.

virus A type of resident program designed to replicate itself. Usually at some later time when the virus is running, it causes an undesirable action to take place.

VL-Bus (VESA Local Bus) A standard 32-bit expansion slot bus specification used in 486 PCs, the VL-Bus connector was an extension of the ISA slot; any VL-Bus slot is also an ISA slot. Replaced by the PCI bus, the VL-Bus slot was used on only a very few early Pentium systems.

VMM (Virtual Memory Manager) A facility in Windows enhanced mode that manages the task of swapping data in and out of 386 and later processor virtual real-mode memory space for multiple non-Windows applications running in virtual real mode.

voice-coil actuator A device that moves read/write heads across hard disk platters by magnetic interaction between coils of wire and a magnet. Functions somewhat like an audio speaker, from which the name originated. The standard actuator type on hard drives.

volatile memory Memory that does not hold data without power. Both Dynamic RAM (the main RAM in a computer) and Static RAM (used for cache memory) are considered volatile memory. See also *nonvolatile memory*.

voltage reduction technology An Intel processor technology that enables a processor to draw the standard voltage from the motherboard but run the internal processor core at a lower voltage.

voltage regulator A device that smoothes out voltage irregularities in the power fed to the computer.

volume A portion of a disk signified by a single drive specifier. Under DOS v3.3 and later, a single hard disk can be partitioned into several volumes, each with its own logical drive specifier (C:, D:, E:, and so on).

volume label An identifier or name of up to 11 characters that names a disk.

VPN (virtual private network) A private network operated within a public network. To maintain privacy, VPNs use access control and encryption.

VRAM (video random-access memory) VRAM chips are modified DRAMs on video boards that enable simultaneous access by the host system's processor and the processor on the video board. A large amount of information therefore can be transferred quickly between the video board and system processor. Sometimes also called dual-ported RAM. It has been replaced by SDRAM, SGRAM, and DDR SDRAM on recent high-performance video cards.

VxD (virtual device driver) A special type of Windows driver. VxDs run at the most privileged CPU mode (ring 0) and enable low-level interaction with the hardware and internal Windows functions.

W3C (World Wide Web Consortium) Sets standards for HTML, XML, and the Web.

wafer A thin, circular piece of silicon either 8" (200mm) or 12" (300mm) in diameter from which processors, memory, and other semiconductor electronics are manufactured.

wait states One or more pause cycles added during certain system operations that require the processor to wait until memory or some other system component can respond. Adding wait states enables a high-speed processor to synchronize with lower-cost, slower components. A system that runs with "zero wait states" requires none of these cycles because of the use of faster memory or other components in the system. The widespread use of L1 and L2 memory caches has made the issue of wait states largely irrelevant. See also *L1 cache* and *L2 cache*.

warm boot Rebooting a system by means of a software command rather than turning the power off and back on. See also *cold boot*.

wave table synthesis A method of creating synthetic sound on a sound card that uses actual musical instrument sounds sampled and stored on ROM (or RAM) on the sound card or in system RAM. The sound card then modifies this sample to create any note necessary for that instrument. Produces much better sound quality than FM synthesis.

Webcam An inexpensive (usually under $100) video camera that plugs into a USB or an IEEE 1394/FireWire port for use with video chat, Web sites, or email programs.

Whetstone A benchmark program developed in 1976 and designed to simulate arithmetic-intensive programs used in scientific computing. Remains completely CPU-bound and performs no I/O or system calls. Originally written in ALGOL, although the C and Pascal versions became more popular by the late 1980s. The speed at which a system performs floating-point operations often is measured in units of Whetstones.

White Book A standard specification developed by Philips and JVC in 1993 for storing MPEG standard video on CDs. An extension of the Red Book standard for digital audio, Yellow Book standard for CD-ROM, Green Book standard for CD-I, and Orange Book standard for CD write-once.

Whitney technology A term referring to a magnetic disk design that usually has oxide or thin film media, thin film read/write heads, low floating-height sliders, and low-mass actuator arms that together allow higher bit densities than the older Winchester technology. Whitney technology first was introduced with the IBM 3370 disk drive, circa 1979.

Wi-Fi Name for IEEE 802.11b–compliant network hardware that also meets the interoperability standards of the Wireless Ethernet Compatibility Alliance (WECA). Despite the presence of Wi-Fi approval for various brands of hardware, achieving the simplest setup and operation is still easier if you purchase Wi-Fi/802.11b wireless NICs and access points from the same vendor. See also *802.11*.

wide area network (WAN) A LAN that extends beyond the boundaries of a single building.

Winchester drive Any ordinary, nonremovable (or fixed) hard disk drive. The name originates from a particular IBM drive in the 1960s that had 30MB of fixed and 30MB of removable storage. This 30-30 drive matched the caliber figure for a popular series of rifles made by Winchester, so the slang term *Winchester* was applied to any fixed-platter hard disk.

Winchester technology The term *Winchester* is loosely applied to mean any disk with a fixed or non-removable recording medium. More precisely, the term applies to a ferrite read/write head and slider design with oxide media that was first employed in the IBM 3340 disk drive, circa 1973. Virtually all drives today actually use developments of Whitney technology.

Wintel The common name given to computers running Microsoft Windows using Intel (or compatible) processors. A slang term for the PC standard.

wire frames The most common technique used to construct a 3D object for animation. A wire frame is given coordinates of length, height, and width. Wire frames are then filled with textures, colors, and movement. Transforming a wire frame into a textured object is called rendering.

word length The number of bits in a data character without parity, start, or stop bits.

workstation 1) A somewhat vague term describing any high-performance, single-user computer that usually has been adapted for specialized graphics, computer-aided design, computer-aided engineering, or scientific applications. 2) A computer connected to a server.

World Wide Web (WWW) Also called the Web. A graphical information system based on hypertext that enables a user to easily access documents located on the Internet.

WORM (write-once, read-many or multiple) An optical mass-storage device capable of storing many megabytes of information but that can be written to only once on any given area of the disk. A WORM disk typically holds more than 200MB of data. Because a WORM drive can't write over an old version of a file, new copies of files are made and stored on other parts of the disk whenever a file is revised. WORM disks are used to store information when a history of older versions must be maintained. Recording on a WORM disk is performed by a laser writer that burns pits in a thin metallic film (usually tellurium) embedded in the disk. This burning process is called ablation. WORM drives are frequently used for archiving data. WORM drives have been replaced by CD-R drives, which have a capacity of 650MB–700MB but have similar characteristics.

write precompensation A modification applied to write data by a controller to partially alleviate the problem of bit shift, which causes adjacent 1s written on magnetic media to read as though they were farther apart. When adjacent 1s are sensed by the controller, precompensation is used to write them more closely together on the disk, thus enabling them to be read in the proper bit cell window. Drives with built-in controllers typically handle precompensation automatically. Precompensation usually is required for the inner cylinders of now-obsolete oxide media drives.

write protect Preventing a removable disk or Sony Memory Stick from being overwritten by means of covering a notch or repositioning a sliding switch, depending on the type of media.

X2 A proprietary modem standard developed by U.S. Robotics (since acquired by 3Com) that enables modems to receive data at up to 56Kbps. This has been superseded by the V.90 standard. See also *V.90* and *V.92*.

x86 A generic term referring to Intel and Intel-compatible PC microprocessors. Although the Pentium family processors do not have a numeric designation because of trademark law limitations on trademarking numbers, they are later generations of this family.

Xeon Intel's family name for its server processors derived from the Pentium II, Pentium III, and Pentium 4 desktop processors. The Pentium II Xeon and Pentium III Xeon use Slot 2, whereas Xeon (the Pentium 4 version does not have a numerical designation) uses the new Socket 602. All Xeon processors have larger caches and memory addressing schemes than their desktop counterparts.

XGA (extended graphics array) A type of PC video display circuit (and adapter) first introduced by IBM on October 30, 1990, that supports text and graphics. Text is supported at a maximum resolution of 132×60 characters in 16 colors with a character box of 8×6 pixels. Graphics are supported at a maximum resolution of 1024×768 pixels in 256 (from a palette of 262,144) colors or 640×480 pixels in 65,536 colors. The XGA outputs an analog signal with a horizontal scanning frequency of 31.5KHz or 35.52KHz and supports analog color or analog monochrome displays. Also used to refer generically to any adapter or display capable of 1024×768 resolution.

XML (Extensible Markup Language) A standard for creating and sharing data and data formats over the Internet and other networks. XML, like HTML, uses markup tags to control the page, but XML tags control both appearance and the uses of the data and can be extended with new tags created by any XML user. See also *W3C*.

XMM (extended memory manager) A driver that controls access to extended memory on 286 and later processor systems. HIMEM.SYS is an example of an XMM that comes with DOS and Windows 9x.

XModem A file-transfer protocol—with error checking—developed by Ward Christensen in the mid-1970s and placed in the public domain. Designed to transfer files between machines running the CP/M operating system and using 300bps or 1,200bps modems. Until the late 1980s, because of its simplicity and public-domain status, XModem remained the most widely used microcomputer file-transfer protocol. In standard XModem, the transmitted blocks are 128 bytes. 1KB-XModem is an extension to XModem that increases the block size to 1,024 bytes. Many newer file-transfer protocols that are much faster and more accurate than XModem have been developed, such as YModem and ZModem.

XMS (extended memory specification) A Microsoft-developed standard that provides a way for real-mode applications to access extended memory in a controlled fashion. The XMS standard is available from Microsoft.

XON/XOFF Standard ASCII control characters used to tell an intelligent device to stop or resume transmitting data. In most systems, pressing Ctrl+S sends the XOFF character. Most devices understand Ctrl+Q as XON; others interpret the pressing of any key after Ctrl+S as XON.

Y-connector A Y-shaped splitter cable that divides a source input into two output signals.

Y-mouse A family of adapters from P.I. Engineering that enables a single mouse port to drive two devices. P.I. Engineering also makes the Y-see adapter for dual monitors and the Y-key adapter for dual keyboards.

Yellow Book The standard used by CD-ROM. Multimedia applications most commonly use the Yellow Book standard, which specifies how digital information is to be stored on the CD-ROM and read by a computer. Extended architecture (XA) is currently an extension of the Yellow Book that enables the combination of various data types (audio and video, for example) onto one track in a CD-ROM. Without XA, a CD-ROM can access only one data type at a time. Many CD-ROM drives are now XA capable.

Yellow Book standards See *CD-ROM*.

YModem A file-transfer protocol first released as part of Chuck Forsberg's YAM (yet another modem) program. An extension to XModem designed to overcome some of the limitations of the original. Enables information about the transmitted file, such as the filename and length, to be sent along with the file data and increases the size of a block from 128 bytes to 1,024 bytes. YModem-batch adds the capability to transmit batches, or groups, of files without operator interruption. YModemG is a variation that sends the entire file before waiting for an acknowledgment. If the receiving side detects an error midstream, the transfer is aborted. YModemG is designed for use with modems that have built-in error-correcting capabilities.

Z-buffering A 3D graphics technique used to determine which objects in a 3D scene will be visible to the user and which will be blocked by other objects. Z-buffering displays only the visible pixels in each object.

zero wait states See *wait states*.

ZIF (zero insertion force) Sockets that require no force for the insertion of a chip carrier. Usually accomplished through movable contacts, ZIF sockets are used by 486, Pentium, Pentium Pro, and other socketed processors (including the latest Pentium 4 and AMD Athlon and Duron models).

ZIP (zigzag inline package) A DIP package that has all leads on one edge in a zigzag pattern and mounts in a vertical plane.

Zip drive An external drive manufactured by Iomega that supports 100MB or 250MB magnetic media on a 3 1/2" removable drive.

Zip file A file created using PKZIP, WinZip, or a compatible archiving program.

zipping The process of creating a PKZIP or WinZip-compatible archive file. See also *unzipping*.

ZModem A file-transfer protocol commissioned by Telnet and placed in the public domain. Like YModem, it was designed by Chuck Forsberg and developed as an extension to XModem to overcome the inherent latency when using Send/Ack-based protocols, such as XModem and YModem. It is a streaming, sliding-window protocol.

zoned recording In hard drives, one way to increase the capacity of a hard drive is to format more sectors on the outer cylinders than on the inner ones. Zoned recording splits the cylinders into groups called zones, with each successive zone having more and more sectors per track, moving out from the inner radius of the disk. All the cylinders in a particular zone have the same number of sectors per track.

zoomed video A direct video bus connection between the PC-Card adapter and a mobile system's VGA controller, enabling high-speed video displays for videoconferencing applications and MPEG decoders.

Key Vendor Contact Information

Use this vendor quick reference chart to locate primary contact information for vendors mentioned in this book. Be sure to refer to the vendor database included on the disc accompanying this book. This database contains detailed contact information and descriptions of services and is keyword searchable.

Company	Phone Number	Email	Web Site
3Com Corp.	(800)638-3266		www.3com.com
ABIT Computer	(510)623-0500		www.abit-usa.com
Acer America	(800)733-2237		aac.acer.com
Adaptec	(408)945-8600		www.adaptec.com
Alienware	(305)251-9797		www.alienware.com
Amazon.com	(206)266-1000		www.amazon.com
AMD	(800)538-8450	hw.support@amd.com	www.amd.com
America Online	(800)827-6434		www.aol.com/corp
American Megatrends	(800)828-9264	support@ami.com	www.ami.com
American Power Conversion	(800)788-2208		www.apcc.com
Antec, Inc.	(502)995-0883		www.antec-inc.com
Apple Computer, Inc.	(800)538-9696		www.apple.com
Asus Computer	(502)995-0883		www.asus.com
ATI Technologies, Inc.	(905)882-2600		www.atitech.com
Belden Wire and Cable	(800)235-3361	info@belden.com	bwcecom.belden.com
Black Box Corporation	(724)746-5500	info@blackbox.com	www.blackbox.com
Borland	832-431-1000		www.borland.com
Byte Runner Technologies	(800)274-7897	sdudley@byterunner.com	www.byterunner.com
Cables to Go	(800)293-4970	expert@cablestogo.com	www.cablestogo.com
Canon USA, Inc.	(516)328-5000		www.usa.canon.com
Centon Electronics, Inc.	(800)836-1986		www.centon.com
CompUSA, Inc.	(800)266-7872		www.compusa.com
CompuServe	(800)848-8990		www.compuserve.com
Computer Discount Warehouse	(800)838-4239		www.cdw.com
Corel Systems, Inc.	(800)772-6735		www.corel.com
Creative Labs, Inc.	(800)544-6146		www.creative.com
Crucial Technologies	(800)336-8915		www.crucial.com
D.W. Electrochemicals	(905)508-7500	dwel@stabilant.com	www.stabilant.com
Dell Computer Corp.	(800)915-3355		www.dell.com
D-Link Systems, Inc.	(949)788-0805		www.dlink.com
DTK Computer, Inc.	(909)468-0394		www.dtkcomputer.com
Duracell, Inc.	(800)551-2355		www.duracell.com
Elitegroup Computer Systems	(510)226-7333	info@ecsusa.com	www.ecsusa.com
Epson America, Inc.	(562)981-3840		www.epson.com
Exabyte Corporation	(800)392-2983		www.exabyte.com
Fedco Electronics, Inc.	(800)542-9761		www.fedcoelectronics.com
FIC (First International Computer of America)	(510)252-7777	sales@fica.com	www.fica.com
Gateway, Inc.	(800)846-4208		www.gateway.com
Giga-Byte Technology	(626)854-9338		www.giga-byte.com
Hewlett-Packard	(650)857-1501		www.hp.com

Company	Phone Number	Email	Web Site
Hitachi America Ltd.	(650)244-7601		www.hitachi.com
Hitachi Global Storage Technologies	(800)801-4618		www.hgst.com
IBM Corporation	(800)426-4968		www.ibm.com
Imation Enterprises Corp.	(888)466-3456	info@imation.com	www.imation.com
Infineon Technologies Corporation	(408)501-6000		www.infineon.com
Intel Corp.	(408)765-8080		www.intel.com
Invesys Powerware Division	(919)872-3020		www.powerware.com
Iomega Corp.	(858)795-7000		www.iomega.com
Jameco Computer Products	(800)831-4242		www.jameco.com
JDR Microdevices	(800)538-5000		www.jdr.com
Jensen Tools, Inc.	(800)426-1194		www.jensentools.com
JVC Professional Products Company (USA)	(973)317-5000		pro.jvc.com
KeyTronicEMS	(800)262-6006	info@keytronic.com	www.keytronic.com
Kingston Technology	(877)KINGSTON	tech_support@kingston.com	www.kingston.com
Labtec Enterprises, Inc.	(702)269-3612		www.labtec.com
Lexmark	(800)539-6275		www.lexmark.com
LG Electronics (Goldstar)	(201)816-2127		www.lgeus.com
Linksys	(800)546-5797	support@linksys.com	www.linksys.com
LMS (formerly MaxiSwitch/ Silitek)	(520)294-5450		www.maxiswitch.com
Logitech	(800)231-7717		www.logitech.com
MAG InnoVision	(800)827-3998	tech@maginnovision.com	www.maginnovision.com
Matrox Graphics	(800)361-1408		www.matrox.com/mga
Maxell Corporation of America	(800)533-2836		www.maxell-data.com
Maxtor Corp.	(800)262-9867		www.maxtor.com
McAfee.com Corporation	(408)992-8100		www.mcafee.com
Micro Firmware, Inc.	(800)767-5465		www.firmware.com
Micron PC, LLC	(866)894-5693		www.micronpc.com
Micron Technologies	(208)368-4000		www.micron.com
Microsoft Corp.	(800)426-9400		www.microsoft.com
Mitsumi Electronics Corp.	(972)550-7300		www.mitsumi.com
MSI Computer Corp. (U.S. Division of Micro-Star)	(626)913-0828		www.msicomputer.com
NEC-Mitsubishi Electronics Display of America, Inc.	(888)632-6487		www.necmitsubishi.com
NEC Technologies, Inc.	(800)632-4636		www.nectech.com
Netgear Inc.	(408)907-8000		www.netgear.com
Novell, Inc.	(800)453-1267		www.novell.com
NVIDIA	(408)486-2000	info@nvidia.com	www.nvidia.com
Ontrack Data International	(800)645-3649		www.ontrack.com

Company	Phone Number	Email	Web Site
PC Power and Cooling, Inc.	(800)722-6555		www.pcpowercooling.com
Philips Electronics	(212)536-0500		www.philipsusa.com
Plextor	(800)886-3935	support@plextor.com	www.plextor.com
PNY Technologies	(973)515-9700		www.pny.com
PowerQuest Corporation	(800)379-2566	support@powerquest.com	www.powerquest.com
Proview Technology, Inc. (MAG Innovision U.S. distributor)	(714)799-3899		www.proview.com
Quantum Corp.	(408)944-4000		www.quantum.com
Rambus, Inc.	(650)947-5000		www.rambus.com
Roxio Software	(866)260-7694		www.roxio.com
Samsung Electronics USA	(201)229-4000		www.samsungusa.com
Seagate Technology	(800)732-4283		www.seagate.com
Silicon Image, CMD Storage Systems	(800)426-3832		www.cmd.com
Silicon Integrated Systems Corp. (SiS)	(408)730-5600		www.sis.com
SONICblue	(408)588-8000		www.sonicblue.com
Sony Corporation	(800)326-9551		www.sony.com
SOYO Group, Inc.	(510)226-7696	support@soyousa.com	www.soyousa.com
Supermicro Computer, Inc.	(408)503-8000		www.supermicro.com
Symantec	(800)517-8000		www.symantec.com
Tekram Technologies			www.tekram.com
Toshiba America, Inc.	(800)TOSHIBA		www.csd.toshiba.com
Tripp Lite Manufacturing	(773)869-1111		www.tripplite.com
Tyan Computer Corporation	(510)651-8868	techsupport@tyan.com	www.tyan.com
Ultra-X, Inc.	(800)722-3789		www.uxd.com
U.S. Robotics	(847)874-2000		www.usr.com
Veritas Software	(800)327-2232		www.veritas.com
VIA Technologies, Inc.	(510)683-3300		www.viatech.com
Western Digital Corporation	(800)832-4778		www.westerndigital.com
Zoom Telephonics	(800)666-6191		www.zoomtel.com

Troubleshooting Index

This special index is designed to help you find solutions to problems—*fast*. Whether your system is beeping at startup, you're getting the dreaded blue screen of death, or you can't hear your rocket launcher blasts in your latest Unreal Tournament Deathmatch, this index will help you find solutions, quickly and relatively painlessly.

	Problem		Details About Solution	
Technology	**Symptom**	**Cause**	**Solution**	**Page**
Audio	Your sound card doesn't sound quite right.	Hardware resource conflict.	Use Windows Device Manager to find conflicts and resolve them.	379
Audio	Sound card can't be detected.	Settings already in use by other cards.	Install sound card first.	386
Audio	Can hear music and sounds in Windows but not DOS.	Incorrect settings for Sound Blaster compatibility.	Install emulation settings or run DOS emulation program.	943
Audio	DOS game can't detect sound card correctly.	Inadequate Sound Blaster compliance or missing DOS drivers.	Verify DOS drivers are installed and manually select best emulation.	953
Audio	Game port on sound card conflicts with other game port in system.	Game port uses only a single I/O address range.	Disable sound card's game port or remove other game port from system.	972
Audio	Can't hear any sounds at all.	Various causes, including incorrect connections, mixer setup, power, and so on.	See checklist.	972
Audio	Can hear sound through just one speaker.	Various causes, including incorrect or defective speaker jack/plug, mixer controls, and others.	See checklist.	973
Audio	Volume is low.	Various causes, including mixer controls, volume controls on speakers or sound cards.	See checklist.	974
Audio	Scratchy sound.	Various causes, including interference, ISA sound card, wrong expansion slot.	See checklist.	975
Audio	Computer won't start after installing sound card.	Card might not be installed in slot properly, or Windows IOS might be corrupted.	See checklist.	975
Audio	Speaker or microphone won't work.	Incorrect jacks.	Use correct jack for each device.	979
Audio	Can't use onboard audio.	Audio might be disabled in BIOS.	Enable audio.	437
Battery for CMOS/RTC	System can't maintain correct time when turned off.	Battery is about to fail.	Replace battery.	1207
BIOS	Calendar-related and leap-year bugs.	BIOS is out-of-date.	Upgrade Flash BIOS.	415
BIOS	Can't install Flash BIOS update.	BIOS is write-protected.	Disable write-protection.	420
BIOS	BIOS update fails.	BIOS is corrupted.	Enable Flash Recovery feature and restart update process.	423
CD-ROM	Can't boot from CD-ROM drive.	BIOS is out-of-date.	Upgrade Flash BIOS.	415

	Problem		**Details About Solution**	
Technology	**Symptom**	**Cause**	**Solution**	**Page**
Data recovery	Can't retrieve a particular file stored on a system running Windows NT/2000/XP.	Some sectors of the disk are damaged.	Use NT/2000/XP RECOVER program or third-party tool to retrieve readable data.	1393
Data recovery	Can't locate deleted files in Recycle Bin.	Recycle Bin was bypassed, or files might have been discarded from Recycle Bin.	Use third-party utilities to retrieve files.	1398, 1403
Data recovery	Can't locate files on a FAT disk after it was formatted.	The file allocation tables (FATs) are cleared as part of the format process.	Use third-party utilities to retrieve files.	1398, 1403
Data recovery	Can't locate files on a formatted or erased flash memory card or USB keychain drive.	The file allocation tables (FATs) are cleared as part of the format process.	Use third-party utilities according to type of data loss.	1412
Data recovery	Can't locate files on a partitioned hard disk.	The file allocation tables and partition tables have been cleared and altered.	Use third-party utilities such as Easy Recovery Professional or Norton Disk Editor.	1402, 1403
DirecWAY	Download speeds drop drastically after downloading one or two large files.	DirecPC has enabled FAP (Fair Access Policy) slowdowns on your service.	Download less at one time; take breaks between big downloads, or switch to another service.	1072
DSL	Can't use DSL service after self-install.	Service might not be set up by provider; microfilter might not be installed as needed.	Make sure provider has activated DSL service; make sure all conventional phones and telephony equipment has a microfilter.	1076
DSL	Slower-than-expected service.	Line might be poor quality; RWIN or other Windows Registry settings might not be optimized.	Ask installer to test line; adjust Windows Registry with tools available from DSL Reports.	1070
File transfer	Can't connect two computers with standard parallel cable.	Standard parallel is designed for PC-to-device, not PC-to-PC, connections.	Use a LapLink-compatible parallel cable.	1011
Floppy disk	Can't write data to floppy disk; data can be read.	Floppy disk write protection is enabled in BIOS.	Disable floppy disk write protection.	441
Floppy disk	File Copying Error message when copying files with long filenames to disk.	Long filenames might use multiple directory entries, depending on length of filename.	Create subfolder on floppy disk and store files with long filenames in folder.	1317
Floppy drive	Disk left in floppy drive prevents system bootup.	Floppy drive has higher boot priority than hard drive.	Adjust boot priority in system BIOS.	447
Floppy drive	Contents of all floppy disks viewed appear to be duplicates of the first disk, although the contents of each disk are different.	Changeline support (which detects disk changes) has failed; this problem is also called the "phantom directory."	Verify BIOS setup for drive is correct and that DC jumper (if any) has been set.	698
Floppy drive	Disks placed on top of a TV or monitor have data errors when read.	Magnetic fields generated by the picture tube can corrupt data.	Store disks away from magnetic fields.	702

	Problem		**Details About Solution**	
Technology	**Symptom**	**Cause**	**Solution**	**Page**
Floppy drive	File copying error after copying a few files with long filenames to the floppy disk.	Root directory fills up due to use of multiple directory entries by each long filename.	Create a folder on the floppy disk and copy files with long filenames into the folder.	1370
Floppy drive	Disk access light stays on continuously after system is started.	One end of floppy cable is reversed.	Change reversed end of floppy cable, verifying pin 1 to pin 1.	865
Hard disk	Can't access full capacity of hard drive over 8.4GB.	BIOS is out-of-date.	Upgrade Flash BIOS.	415
Hard disk	Can't access full capacity of hard drive over 8.4GB.	BIOS is out-of-date, and BIOS upgrade is not available.	Install an add-on BIOS card with EDD support.	576
Hard disk	Can't use UDMA drives at full speed.	BIOS is out-of-date.	Upgrade Flash BIOS.	415
Hard disk	IDE drive not ready errors during startup.	Drive not spinning up fast enough at startup.	Enable or increase hard disk predelay time.	439
Hard disk	Can't use drive capacity beyond 528MB.	LBA mode not enabled in BIOS.	Enable LBA mode.	439
Hard disk	Boot section corrupted.	Boot sector virus or other problem.	Use FDISK/MBR (DOS, Windows 9x/Me) or FIXMBR (Windows NT/2000/XP) to restore.	1360
Hard disk	Storing small file uses up a large amount of space on drive.	Files smaller than an allocation unit (cluster) still use an entire allocation unit.	Convert drive to FAT32 or NTFS to be more efficient if possible; remove outdated files from system to save space.	1367
Hard disk	Your 40GB hard disk can't be formatted by Windows 2000 or Windows XP as a single drive with FAT32.	These versions can format up to 32GB only, but can read larger drives.	Prepare drive with third-party utility such as PartitionMagic or use NTFS.	1373
Hard disk	Large numbers of files ending in .CHK are found in root directory of drive.	.CHK files are created by SCANDISK or CHKDSK from lost allocation units.	Shut down system properly to avoid lost allocation units; test drive if problem persists; delete files to free up space.	1384
Hard drive	UDMA/66 or UDMA/100 drive runs at UDMA/33 on systems that support UDMA/66 or UDMA/100.	Incorrect cable might be in use.	Use 80-wire UDMA cable in place of normal 40-wire IDE cable.	540
Hard drive	Can't set IDE drives as master or slave when 80-wire cable is used.	80-wire cable supports cable select, not master/slave.	Install drives at correct locations on cable, and jumper both as Cable Select.	540
Hard drive	Can't read contents of IDE drive over 528MB after moving it to a new system.	Drive geometry or translation not set correctly on new system.	Set correct Cyl-Hd-Sectors setting for drive and LBA or Ext CHS translation.	563
Hard drive	BIOS recognizes full capacity of drive over 8.4GB, but operating system will not.	Some operating systems aren't designed to use drives over 8.4GB.	Upgrade or patch your operating system to achieve compliance.	576

	Problem		Details About Solution	
Technology	**Symptom**	**Cause**	**Solution**	**Page**
Hard drive	Windows 98 FDISK misidentifies the capacity of a drive over 64GB.	FDISK incorrectly reads the disk capacity.	Download an updated version of FDISK from Microsoft's Web site.	675
Hard drive	Can't boot from SCSI hard drive.	SCSI BIOS might not be enabled; system BIOS might not be set properly.	Enable SCSI BIOS and disable booting from IDE drives in system BIOS.	614
Hard drive	`Immediately back up your data and replace your hard disk drive. A failure may be imminent.` error message is seen.	The drive uses SMART to predict back up failures, and the SMART system has detected a serious problem with the drive.	Follow the onscreen instructions to back up your drive.	682
Hard drive	Hard drive letters above C: are pushed higher when second drive is installed.	New drive was prepared with a primary partition, which takes precedence over drive letters in the first drive's extended partition.	Prepare additional drives with an extended partition.	846
Hard drive	New hard disk letters conflict with removable media drives not connected to system in Windows 2000/XP.	Windows 2000/XP doesn't change existing removable-media or optical drive letters when drives are present.	Use Disk Management to adjust existing and new drive letters as necessary.	849
Hard drive	`Invalid Drive Specification` error.	Drive has not been partitioned or high-level formatted, or wrong OS is being used to view drive.	Verify drive is empty with recent Windows versions before running FDISK and FORMAT.	857
Hard drive	`Invalid Media Type` error.	Drive has not been FDISKed, or drive's format is corrupt.	View drive with FDISK's #4 option, and create new partitions as necessary.	857
IDE drives	Can't detect drive with BIOS setup program.	Power cable might be loose or missing.	Reattach power cable.	841
IDE drives	Can't detect drive with BIOS setup program.	Missing or reversed IDE data cable.	Reattach IDE data cable and verify pin 1 to pin 1 at both ends of cable.	841
IDE drives	Can't detect either drive on cable with BIOS setup program.	Both drives might be cabled as master or slave.	Change one drive to master and the other drive to slave.	833
IDE drive	Drive doesn't perform reliably.	IDE cable might be longer than 18".	Switch to 18" cable.	835
IDE drive	Need to install an IDE drive on a system with only Serial ATA connectors.	Serial ATA uses a physically different connector from ATA/IDE.	Use an ATA/IDE drive-to-Serial ATA adapter.	553
IDE drive	Need to install an ATA drive more than 18" from the host adapter.	Ultra-ATA has an 18" limit for reliable performance.	Use a Serial ATA host adapter and drive, or a Serial ATA host adapter and ATA/Serial ATA adapter;Serial ATA cables can be 1 meter long.	553

	Problem		**Details About Solution**	
Technology	**Symptom**	**Cause**	**Solution**	**Page**
Internet	Can't share Internet connection.	Problems with host or client configuration.	See checklist.	1097
IRQ	Conflicts between PCI devices.	PCI IRQ steering not enabled.	Enable PCI IRQ steering.	370
IRQ	Conflicts between COM ports.	IRQs shared between COM1 and 3; between COM2 and 4.	Disable unused COM port or change IRQ if possible.	373
ISA cards	ISA cards have hardware conflicts with PCI cards.	Resources not reserved for ISA cards.	Reserve resources for ISA cards.	444
Keyboard	Num Lock stays off when starting system.	Num Lock shut off in BIOS.	Turn on Num Lock in BIOS.	434
Keyboard	Intermittent keyboard failures.	Keyboard cable or keyboard jack might be defective.	Test keyboard cable or jack with digital multimeter.	1033
Keyboard	Keys are sticking.	Keyboard might have spilled drink or trapped debris under keys.	Remove keytops and clean under keys, or wash out keyboard.	1035
Keyboard	USB keyboard works in Windows but not in DOS or BIOS setup.	USB Legacy mode is not enabled in BIOS or not present.	Connect a standard keyboard (or a keyboard/USB adapter) and enable USB Legacy mode.	1019
Keyboard	Standard keys on keyboard work, but not multimedia or Internet keys.	The keyboard driver is not installed or is defective.	Install the latest driver for your keyboard.	1033
Keyboard	Wireless keyboard doesn't work at some angles relative to the computer.	IR sensors in keyboard and on computer are losing line-of-sight.	Reposition IR sensor connected to computer to maintain line-of-sight.	1053
Keyboard	Wireless keyboard doesn't work at long distances (such as with a Media Center PC and big-screen display).	Conventional wireless devices have a 6-foot range.	Use Bluetooth-enabled keyboard to have a range of up to 30 feet.	1053
Keyboard	Wireless keyboard stops working after you moved the computer.	The receiver might be disconnected from the USB or keyboard port.	Reconnect the receiver and re-synchronize the keyboard and receiver.	1056
LAN	Can't use onboard LAN.	LAN might be disabled in BIOS.	Enable LAN device.	437
Modem	Internal modem locks up system when trying to make a connection.	Modem might be set to same IRQ as the serial port the mouse is attached to.	Disable the unused COM port on the system, and set the modem to use that COM port number.	1005
Modem	Modem works correctly with Internet access, but computer-to-computer terminal emulation produces garbage screens.	Incorrect bps, word length, stop bit, or terminal emulation settings compared to remote system's requirements.	Determine correct values for remote system and set up HyperTerminal or other connection program accordingly.	1080
Modem	56Kbps modem connects at 33.6Kbps or less.	Some telephone lines can't provide greater than 33.6Kbps service.	Switch to a broadband service, or use modem bonding to achieve higher speeds.	1087

	Problem		Details About Solution	
Technology	Symptom	Cause	Solution	Page
Modem	Modem drops calls unexpectedly.	You might have call-waiting enabled, which interrupts the modem carrier signal.	Disable call-waiting (ask phone company for details), or upgrade to modems with call-waiting support.	1092
Modem	Can't dial with analog modem.	Various causes.	See checklist.	1098
Modem	System locks up after installing internal modem.	IRQ conflicts with other ports or devices.	Use Windows Device Manager to find conflicts and resolve them.	379
Modem	Computer can't detect external modem.	Wrong cable, port problems, or power problems.	Check cable, port setup, and power.	1099
Mouse	Mouse doesn't work.	Hardware resource conflict.	Use Windows Device Manager to find conflicts and resolve them.	379
Mouse	Can't use PS/2 mouse.	PS/2 mouse port might be disabled.	Enable PS/2 mouse port.	449
Mouse	Mouse doesn't work when attached via adapter to a different port type.	Mouse might not be hybrid type (designed for various ports).	Use adapters only with hybrid mice; use adapter packaged with mouse.	1043
Mouse	Mouse pointer jerks onscreen.	Mouse ball or rollers are dirty.	Clean mouse mechanism.	1044
Mouse	Mouse works for basic operations, but extra buttons or scroll doesn't work.	Incorrect or outdated mouse driver is being used.	Download and install correct mouse driver from vendor site.	1037
Mouse	Mouse works in Windows, but not when booted to DOS.	DOS driver must be loaded from AUTOEXEC.BAT or CONFIG.SYS.	Install DOS mouse driver, and reference it in startup file(s).	1046
Mouse	Wireless mouse doesn't work at some angles relative to the computer.	IR sensors in mouse and on computer are losing line-of-sight.	Reposition IR sensor connected to the computer to maintain line-of-sight.	1053
Mouse	Wireless mouse doesn't work at long distances (such as with a Media Center PC and big-screen display).	Conventional wireless devices have a range of 6 feet.	Use Bluetooth-enabled mouse to have a range of up to 30 feet.	1053
Mouse	Wireless mouse stops working after you move the computer.	The receiver might be disconnected from the USB or mouse port.	Reconnect the receiver and resynchronize the mouse and receiver.	1056
Network	System locks up after installing network card.	IRQ conflicts with other ports or devices.	Use Windows Device Manager to find conflicts and resolve them.	379
Network	Mouse doesn't work.	Hardware resource conflict.	Use Windows Device Manager to find conflicts and resolve them.	379
Network	Can't connect to other computers on network after installing a new custom-built cable.	Cable might not match prevailing wiring standard on network.	Check wiring of other cables to see which wiring standard is used; build new cable to match.	1123

	Problem		Details About Solution	
Technology	Symptom	Cause	Solution	Page
Network	Distant computer works with 10BASE-T network but not with Fast Ethernet.	Computer might be too far from hub or switch because Fast Ethernet has shorter maximum distance.	Install repeater, or use new switch/hub as repeater.	1126
Network	Can't connect to other users on network, although card diagnostics check out.	Might not have correct network software components installed.	See checklist.	1146
Network	Duplicate computer ID error.	More than one computer has the same name or IP address on the network.	Adjust computer name or IP address with the Network properties sheet.	1148
Network	Users can't see all the computers on the network.	Multiple workgroup names are in use.	Adjust workgroup name (must match for all on network) with Network properties.	1148
Network	Users can't share printers or folders with others.	File/Print sharing might not be installed; folders or printers might not be set to shared.	Install File/Print sharing, and then set shared folders and printers.	1148
Network	Network changes made, but don't work.	Most Windows systems must be rebooted to put network changes into effect.	Reboot system and then try network operations.	1148
Network	One user can't access network, but others can.	User might not have logged on to network.	Log off system and log on; provide name and password when prompted.	1149
Network	One user can't access network, but others can.	Loose cables at computer, hub, switch, or wiring closet.	Check all cable connections.	1149
Network	One user can't access network, but others can.	Password cache might be corrupt or have outdated passwords.	Log on to resources again and give new password when prompted.	1149
Network	Can't access Internet or other TCP/IP-based resources.	Wrong TCP/IP settings.	Open Network properties sheet and adjust TCP/IP settings as needed for your network.	1149
Network	IP Address Conflict error.	Duplicate IP addresses on two or more machines.	Open Network properties sheet and enter correct, unique IP addresses for each system.	1149
Network	Need to create a NetBEUI network using Windows XP.	Can't select NetBEUI as an option.	Install NetBEUI manually from the Windows XP CD-ROM.	1136
Optical drives	Drive slows down when reading CD with a small paper label attached to the label side.	Drive can't run at full speed due to uneven weight distribution and must slow down.	Use full-size labels that cover the entire CD's top surface, or use a marker instead of small labels.	786
Optical drives	CD-ROM drive can't read multiple-session disc.	Drive is not compatible with Orange Book multisession standard (XA standard).	Replace drive with new CD-ROM, CD-RW, or DVD drive.	806
Optical drives	Can't read CD-R or CD-RW disc on a CD-ROM drive, but only on a CD-R/CD-RW drive.	CD probably was created with packet-writing software and not closed before being removed.	Return CD-R or CD-RW disc to original system and close session.	771

	Problem		Details About Solution	
Technology	**Symptom**	**Cause**	**Solution**	**Page**
Optical drives	CD-ROM disc can be read by 32-bit Windows but not by DOS.	CD was created using the UDF (packet-writing) standard.	Use standard mastering software instead of DirectCD to create CDs for use with DOS.	778
Optical drives	Drive runs very slowly or has read errors.	CD lens might be dirty or dusty.	Use a CD lens cleaner, or install a drive with a self-cleaning lens.	798, 826
Optical drives	Can't read CD-RW media on an older drive.	Drives that aren't MultiRead compliant can't read CD-RW media (usually slower than 24x speed).	Replace drive with a MultiRead-compatible CD-ROM or DVD drive or a CD-RW drive.	806
Optical drives	Can't read CD-RW media on MultiRead CD-ROM drive.	Compatible UDF reader might not be installed.	Install UDF reader from CD-RW disc or by downloading reader from software vendor.	826
Optical drives	Can't write to a 10x or faster CD-RW disc in a 4x CD-RW drive.	10x and faster media meets the High-Speed or Ultra-Speed ReWritable standard; not supported by 2x and 4x CD-RW drives.	Use 2x or 4x media for interchange between 10x or faster and 2x/4x CD-RW drives.	806
Optical drives	Can't write to CD-RW or DVD-RW 1x media.	Media might not be formatted.	Format media with UDF packet-writing software before use.	827
Optical drives	Can't write to CD-RW or DVD-RW 1x media.	Media formatted with different UDF program.	Use same UDF packet-writing software to format media and write to media.	827
Optical drives	Can't write to CD-RW or DVD-RW 1x media.	Media might not be correctly identified.	Eject and reinsert media to force redetection.	827
Optical drives	Can't write to CD-RW or DVD-RW 1x media.	UDF packet-writing software might not support drive.	Contact software vendor for an update.	827
Optical drives	Can't write to CD-RW or DVD-RW 1x media.	Disc might have been formatted with Windows XP's own CD-writing software.	Erase media with Windows XP's CD-writing software and reformat with preferred UDF solution.	827
Optical drives	Can't write to CD-RW or DVD-RW 1x media.	Drive firmware might be out-of-date.	Update firmware.	828
Optical drives	Can't read CD-RW media in a CD-ROM drive.	Media might be damaged.	Reinsert media in original drive; repair media if necessary with UDF packet-writing software utilities.	828
Optical drives	CD-RW or rewriteable DVD drive writes to some types of media more slowly than others.	Drive firmware might not be fully compatible with media type in use.	Download and install the latest firmware for the drive.	828
Optical drives	DVD-RW drive is not compatible with 4x DVD-RW media.	Drive firmware was designed before 4x media was introduced.	Download and install the latest firmware for drive and use only 2x media until update is installed.	828
Optical drives	Cannot install new drive firmware.	Drive is being controlled by other software.	Disable CD-writing software before performing firmware update.	830

	Problem		**Details About Solution**	
Technology	**Symptom**	**Cause**	**Solution**	**Page**
Optical drives	Can't read CD-RW media in a DVD.	Drives that aren't MultiRead2 compliant can't read CD-RW or DVD-RAM media.	Replace drive with a MultiRead2 drive.	806
Optical drives	Can't burn a CD-R disc while performing other tasks.	Multitasking operations are causing buffer underruns.	Run only CD-mastering software, slow down burn speed, or upgrade to a drive with buffer underrun protection.	808
Optical drives	Can boot from bootable CD, but can't read contents of CD.	Bootable CD must have CD-ROM driver files and CONFIG.SYS and AUTOEXEC.BAT references to them.	Make sure bootable disk used for creating bootable CD can access CD-ROM.	828
Optical drives	Can't read CD or CD-R discs in a CD-ROM or DVD drive.	Media might not be compatible.	Try different-colored media.	826
Optical drives	Can't read CD-R discs in a CD-ROM or DVD drive.	Media might be written with packet-with packet-x software such as DirectCD.	Reinsert media into original drive, eject media, and select Close to Read on Any Drive.	826
Optical drives	Can't read DVD-RW disc in DVD-ROM drive or DVD player.	DVD-RW media might not be finalized.	Reinsert media into original drive and finalize it before ejecting it.	826
Optical drives	Can't read DVD+RW disc in DVD-ROM drive or DVD player.	DVD+RW media might need to be set to compatibility mode.	Reinsert media into original drive and reset media to compatibility mode.	821
Optical drives	Can't read rewriteable DVD disc in DVD-ROM drive or DVD player.	Disc contains less than 521MB of data.	Add more data to disc beyond 521MB.	826
Optical drives	Can't create writeable DVD.	Incorrect media.	Use +R media in DVD+RW drives; use -R media in DVD-RW drives; either type works in dual-mode drives.	826
Optical drives	Can't create writeable DVD.	Wrong type of project selected in CD/DVD mastering software.	Select DVD project in mastering software.	826
Optical drives	Can't create writeable DVD.	Wrong drive selected.	Select correct drive.	826
Optical drives	Can't create writeable DVD.	Media might be bad.	Try different media.	826
Optical drives	Can't create writeable DVD.	Software might not support recorder.	Get a software update.	826
Optical drives	ATAPI drive runs very slowly, but no read errors.	Wrong cache size.	Adjust cache size in Performance tab of System Properties.	827
Optical drives	ATAPI drive runs very slowly, but no read errors.	CD-ROM drive on same cable as hard drive.	Move CD-ROM drive to secondary cable.	827
Optical drives	ATAPI drive runs very slowly, but no read errors.	UDMA or busmastering drivers might not be installed or enabled.	Install and enable latest UDMA or busmastering drivers.	827

	Problem		Details About Solution	
Technology	**Symptom**	**Cause**	**Solution**	**Page**
Optical drives	ATAPI drive runs very slowly, but no read errors.	Drive might be using MS-DOS Compatibility Mode (BIOS-based) access.	Reinstall drive to use 32-bit Windows drivers.	827
Optical drives	Can't boot from bootable CD.	System might not support bootable CD.	Verify CD-ROM listed as bootable device and listed first in boot.	828
Optical drives	Can't boot from bootable CD.	Wrong disc format (Joliet or other).	Must use ISO 9660 CD format.	828
Optical drives	Can't boot from bootable CD.	SCSI drive and host adapter might not be configured as bootable.	Enable BIOS on SCSI adapter and disable IDE boot devices in system BIOS.	828
Optical	Can't hear music through sound card speakers.	Analog or digital audio cables aren't connected between drive and audio jacks on sound card or motherboard with integrated sound.	Reattach cables to drive and sound card or motherboard; check mixer settings.	944
Parallel port	Can't use onboard parallel port.	Port might be disabled be disabled in BIOS.	Enable port.	437
Parallel port	Conflict between onboard parallel port and other device.	IRQ or I/O port address conflicts with other device.	Adjust IRQ or I/O port address in use, or disable port.	437
Parallel port	Can't use ECP mode.	DMA channel conflicts with another device.	Use alternate DMA channel, or use EPP mode instead.	437
Password	Can't access setup or start system because system prompts for password.	Setup and/or power-on passwords are enabled in BIOS.	Clear password settings.	431
Password	Can't access setup or start system because system prompts for password.	Setup and/or power-on passwords are enabled in BIOS.	Clear password settings.	445
Password	Can't access setup or start system because system prompts for password.	Setup and/or power-on passwords are enabled in BIOS.	Clear CMOS if password settings can't be cleared separately.	445
PCI	IRQ conflicts between PCI cards.	IRQs might be shared between slots.	Move conflicting cards to another PCI slot.	434
PCI	IRQ conflicts between PCI cards.	Auto PCI IRQ Priority might not work for all cards.	Set PCI IRQ priority manually.	434
PnP	Can't install new PnP cards.	PnP/PCI configuration data might be corrupted.	Clear PnP/PCI configuration data and restart system.	434
PnP	Problems with PnP cards and configuration.	BIOS is out-of-date.	Upgrade Flash BIOS.	415
Power management	System can't use power management features.	Power management disabled.	Enable power management.	446
Power management	Can't control power management through Windows.	ACPI power management disabled.	Enable ACPI power management.	446
Power management	Can't use ACPI power management.	BIOS is out-of-date.	Upgrade Flash BIOS.	415

	Problem		Details About Solution	
Technology	Symptom	Cause	Solution	Page
Power management	System locks up or hardware malfunctions when power management is used.	Some older peripherals are not compatible with power management.	Disable APM power management in the system BIOS; disable ACPI power management with Windows' Power properties sheet.	1191
Power supply	System reboots (cold boots with memory check) spontaneously.	Power Good voltage level out of limits.	Check power supply with DMM; replace power supply if defective.	1196
Power supply	Dell power supply fails and replacement has different-colored wires for connectors.	Dell changed to a non-standard version of ATX for systems built September 1998–2000; standard power supplies will not work and will fry!	Buy a Dell-brand or Dell-compatible power supply, or replace motherboard and power supply with standard models.	1171
Power supply	System won't start; power is going to system.	Voltage slider on power supply might be set to wrong voltage.	Set power supply to correct voltage level for local current.	1180
Power supply	Power supply fails after additional components are added to system.	New components require more 5V power than old power supply can provide.	Replace failed unit with a 300-watt or larger unit.	1186
Power supply	Hard disk or fan won't turn.	Defective or overloaded power supply.	Replace failed unit with a 300-watt or larger unit.	1192
Power supply	Electrical shocks on case.	Defective or overloaded power supply.	Replace failed unit with a 300-watt or larger unit.	1192
Power protection	Surge suppressor indicates ground fault.	Outlet lacks ground, or it might use a three-prong-to-two-prong adapter.	Use outlet tester to verify proper wiring in outlets used for computers.	1317
Printer	Parallel printer prints very slowly.	Printer might be attached to non-IEEE or non-ECP parallel port.	Set port to use mode recommended for printer and switch to IEEE-1284 cable if necessary.	1007
Printer	Your printer prints gibberish.	Hardware resource conflict if correct driver used.	Use Windows Device Manager to find conflicts and resolve them.	379
Processor	Can't overclock multiplier.	Multiplier locked on recent AMD, Intel CPUs.	Adjust bus speed instead.	84
Processor	Can't use FC-PGA processor in PGA-370 socket.	Change in voltages and pinout.	Upgrade motherboard or use third-party PGA/FC-PGA adapter.	95
Processor	Can't use PGA or FC-PGA processor in Slot 1.	Wrong form factor.	Use slot-key adapter.	95
Processor	Poor heat transfer from processor to heatsink.	Gaps between processor and heatsink faceplate.	Attach thermal interface pad or grease to processor before attaching heatsink.	1261
Processor	Pentium miscalculates floating-point math.	Errata 23 in Pentium processor.	Have Intel replace affected processor, or use updated processor.	132
Processor	Improper CPU identification during POST.	Old BIOS.	Update BIOS from manufacturer.	198
Processor	Improper CPU identification during POST.	Board is not configured properly.	Check manual, and set board accordingly to proper bus and multiplier settings.	198

	Problem		**Details About Solution**	
Technology	**Symptom**	**Cause**	**Solution**	**Page**
Processor	Can't install newer processors.	BIOS is out-of-date.	Upgrade Flash BIOS.	415
Processor	System won't start after new processor is installed.	Processor not properly installed.	Reseat or remove and reinstall processor and heatsink.	198
Processor	System won't start after new processor is installed.	BIOS doesn't support new processor.	Update BIOS from system or motherboard manufacturer.	198
Processor	System won't start after new processor is installed.	Motherboard can't use a new processor.	Verify motherboard support.	198
RAM	RAM test not detecting any problems and is finishing too quickly.	L1 and L2 memory caches might be enabled.	Disable memory caches before testing memory.	449
RAM	Soft (random) errors occur after adjusting memory timing in BIOS setup.	Refresh rate set incorrectly in BIOS.	Autoconfigure memory timing in BIOS.	435
RAM	Can't determine exact location of bad memory.	Bad memory could be located in any module installed.	Isolate memory defect to find bad module and replace it.	516
RAM	Can't use standard 30-pin or 72-pin SIMMs in some IBM, Compaq, or HP systems.	These systems support non-standard presence detect pins in the SIMMs.	Use SIMMs made especially for the computer model.	483
RAM	Can't insert 168-pin DIMM into the motherboard.	DIMM might be wrong voltage or type for motherboard.	PCs use unbuffered 3.3V DIMMs; others will not fit.	485
RAM	RIMM-based system won't boot up with some RIMM sockets empty.	All RIMM sockets must have memory or continuity module installed.	Install continuity modules into a RIMM socket without memory.	490
RAM	Can't determine speed or type of memory module.	Some memory modules aren't labeled.	Look up memory chip character-istics to determine module speed and type.	493
RAM	Single 72-pin SIMM not recognized on P5-class system.	Memory must be added in banks of 64 bits on P5-class systems; 72-pin SIMM has 32 bits.	Add pair of identical SIMMs as supported by motherboard.	496
RAM	System won't boot after installing new memory.	Memory might be too slow for system.	Install new memory as fast or faster than previous memory.	497
RAM	System locks up; mixed metals (gold/tin) used in sockets and modules.	Corroded memory sockets result from mixing tin sockets/gold memory or vice versa.	Remove memory, clean sockets, and use memory with same metal as sockets.	497
RAM	Soft (random) memory errors.	Power glitches or noise on the line.	Replace power supply if it tests out-of-spec, or install power conditioning equipment.	500
RAM	Soft (random) memory errors.	Incorrect type or speed.	Use memory that matches recommended type and meets or exceeds recommended speed.	500
RAM	Soft (random) memory errors.	RF (Radio Frequency) interference.	Move causes of RF away from system.	500
RAM	Soft (random) memory errors.	ESD (electrostatic discharge).	Use antistatic spray on screen and keyboard and install antistatic mats near system.	510

	Problem		Details About Solution	
Technology	**Symptom**	**Cause**	**Solution**	**Page**
RAM	Memory parity interrupt error message.	Parity checking has detected an error in RAM.	Shut down the system and restart it; remove and reinstall memory.	502
RAM	Out of memory error after upgrading system with AGP card beyond 512MB of RAM.	Windows 9x/Me can't handle memory addresses beyond 512MB along with AGP aperture addresses.	Use no more than 512MB of RAM with Windows 9x/Me and AGP video.	908
Removable media	Can't boot from SuperDisk LS-120 drive.	BIOS is out-of-date.	Upgrade Flash BIOS.	415
Removable-media drive	Can't boot from LS-120 SuperDisk or Zip drive.	ARMD-FDD (ATAPI Removable Device—Floppy), Zip, or LS-120 drive listed after hard drive in boot order.	Adjust boot priority in system BIOS.	447
Removable-media drive	Zip 750 reads and writes to Zip 250 media very slowly.	Drive must adjust read/write speed to use older media.	Use Zip 750 media for full-speed performance.	710
Removable-media drive	Zip 250 reads and writes to Zip 100 media very slowly.	Drive must adjust read/write speed to use older media.	Use Zip 250 media for full-speed performance.	710
SCSI	Data or signaling errors at higher speeds.	Passive termination not suitable for use in faster SCSI versions.	Use other types of terminators at both ends of SCSI daisy-chain.	608
SCSI	Can't use external SCSI device.	External device might have been turned on after system startup.	Turn on external devices first; then boot system.	614
SCSI	Can't detect new SCSI device.	Device might be using a duplicate device ID.	Ensure that each device and the host adapter use a unique device ID.	614
SCSI	PCI SCSI card doesn't work properly.	PCI SCSI cards require a busmastering PCI slot.	Move card to a slot that supports busmastering.	614
Serial ATA drive	System has no Serial ATA ports.	Most systems need a Serial ATA card to enable Serial ATA support.	Install a Serial ATA card into a PCI slot.	839
Serial port	Can't use onboard serial port.	Port might be disabled in BIOS.	Enable port.	437
Serial port	Conflict between onboard serial port and other device.	IRQ or I/O port address conflicts with other device.	Adjust IRQ or I/O port address in use, or disable port.	437
Serial port	COM3 and above work in Windows, but not DOS.	DOS can use only COM1 and COM2 due to BIOS limitations.	Use only COM1 or COM2 for DOS applications.	1003
Startup	System won't start; no error messages onscreen.	Various fatal errors.	Install POST card; restart system to determine error codes and diagnose problem.	453
Startup	System won't start; various error messages indicating system can't boot.	Hard disk might not be connected to system, partitioned, formatted, or set up correctly in BIOS.	Check drive cabling, drive partitions, and BIOS configuration.	454
Startup	Problems during POST.	Various causes.	Use checklist.	1341

	Problem		**Details About Solution**	
Technology	**Symptom**	**Cause**	**Solution**	**Page**
Startup	System beeps several times several times on; doesn't start properly.	Serious or fatal hardware errors.	Count beeps and pattern; determine BIOS used and look up beep code to determine problem.	1287
Startup	System displays error message when turned on; doesn't start properly.	Serious hardware error.	Look up error code in Technical Reference on CD.	1288
Startup	System doesn't start properly; might not beep or display error codes.	Serious or fatal hardware errors.	Install POST diagnostics card and restart system; look up I/O port POST checkpoint code.	1287
Startup	Newly-assembled system won't start.	Various problems.	See checklist.	1247
Startup	System can't boot from hard drive.	Configuration problem with system or drive.	See checklist.	1300
Startup	Missing Operating System error.	Incorrect drive geometry settings, bad CMOS battery, no active partition, bad MBR.	Use checklist.	1414
Startup	NO ROM BASIC - SYSTEM HALTED error.	Incorrect drive geometry settings, bad CMOS battery, no active partition, bad MBR.	Use checklist.	1414
Startup	Boot error Press F1 to retry error.	Incorrect drive geometry settings, bad CMOS battery, no active partition, bad MBR.	Use checklist.	1415
Startup	Invalid drive specification error.	No partition on disk.	Use FDISK or equivalent to partition drive.	1415
Startup	Invalid Media Type error.	No valid format on drive.	Use FORMAT or Norton Disk Doctor.	1415
Startup	Hard Disk Controller Failure error.	Incorrect cabling between drive and host adapter or failed host adapter.	Check cables; then check host adapter.	1415
System	Problems with adapter cards.	Various causes.	Use checklist.	1342
System	System unstable when overclocking.	Incorrect voltage to processor.	Use motherboard that allows fine adjustments to processor voltage.	58
System	System is dead, no beeps, no cursor, no fan.	Power cord failure.	Plug in or replace power cord.	198
System	System is dead, no beeps, no cursor, no fan.	Power supply failure.	Replace power supply with known-good one.	198
System	System is dead, no beeps, no cursor, no fan.	Motherboard failure.	Replace motherboard with known-good one.	198
System	System is dead, no beeps, no cursor, no fan.	Memory failure.	Remove all memory except bank 1 and retest; swap bank 1 if no boot.	198
System	System is dead, no beeps, or locks up before POST begins.	All components either not installed or incorrectly installed.	Check all peripherals, especially memory and graphics adapter. Reseat all boards and socketed components.	198

Problem			Details About Solution	
Technology	Symptom	Cause	Solution	Page
System	System beeps on startup, fan is running, no cursor onscreen. Locks up during or shortly after POST.	Improperly seated or failing graphics adapter.	Reseat or replace graphics adapter. Use known-good spare for testing.	198
System	System beeps on startup, fan is running, no cursor onscreen. Locks up during or shortly after POST.	Poor heat dissipation.	Check CPU heatsink/fan; replace if necessary; use one with higher capacity.	198
System	System beeps on startup, fan is running, no cursor onscreen. Locks up during or shortly after POST.	Improper voltage settings.	Set motherboard for proper core processor voltage.	198
System	System powers up, fan is running, but no beep or cursor.	Processor not properly installed.	Reseat or remove and reinstall processor and heatsink.	198
System	System beeps on startup, fan is running, no cursor onscreen. Locks up during Locks up during after POST.	Wrong motherboard bus speed.	Set motherboard for proper speed.	198
System	System beeps on startup, fan is running, no cursor onscreen. Locks up during or shortly after POST.	Wrong CPU clock multiplier.	Jumper motherboard for proper clock multiplier.	198
System	Device transfers data inaccurately.	Hardware resource conflict.	Use Windows Device Manager to find conflicts and resolve them.	379
System	System frequently locks up.	Hardware resource conflict.	Use Windows Device Manager to find conflicts and resolve them.	379
System	System locks up after running for a time.	Overheating.	Check case and processor fans.	1321
System	System locks up when office equipment such as copiers or microwave ovens nearby are operated.	Corrupted power.	Plug computer into a separate circuit from such devices.	1335
System	POST reports system errors.	Various problems.	See checklist.	1341
System	Some software doesn't run correctly.	Various problems.	See checklist.	1341
System	Hardware and software bugs.	BIOS is out-of-date.	Upgrade Flash BIOS.	415
System	Slow system performance.	System BIOS might not be cached.	Enable caching of system BIOS.	435
System	Memory address conflict between devices.	Two devices are using the same upper memory block.	Move one device to a non-conflicting UMB address.	530
System	Intermittent lockups, memory and drive glitches.	Improperly wired outlets might be providing bad power.	Use an outlet tester to check ground and polarity.	1317

Problem			Details About Solution	
Technology	**Symptom**	**Cause**	**Solution**	**Page**
System	Intermittent lockups, memory and drive glitches.	Other devices on circuit could be causing problems, such as AC units, coffee makers, and so on.	Move computers to their own circuit.	1335
System	Problems after system startup with hardware.	Various causes.	Use checklist.	1341
Tape drives	Can't run tape backup or restore; bad block errors during restore.	Defective tape cartridge, dirty heads, defective cabling, or incorrect software settings.	Replace cartridge, clean heads, check cabling, and rerun confidence test with blank cartridge.	735
USB	Can't use USB ports on system.	USB ports might be disabled, or your system has the wrong Windows version.	Enable USB ports in BIOS, and verify you are using Windows 98, Me, 2000, or XP.	989
USB	USB ports available in BIOS but not visible on system.	USB header cables not installed on motherboard.	Install USB header cables.	989
USB	USB game controller doesn't work with some older games.	USB game controller might not perfectly emulate gameport-based controllers.	Check with software vendor for patches or workarounds.	1052
USB	Can't use USB keyboard and mouse outside of Windows.	USB Legacy support is disabled in BIOS.	Enable USB Legacy support.	437
USB	Can't use USB devices.	USB is disabled or not assigned an IRQ.	Enable USB; assign IRQ to USB.	444
USB	Bus-powered peripherals aren't recognized unless they are removed and reattached.	Power supply might be failing.	Test power supply and replace if voltage levels don't meet specifications.	1192
USB	USB 2.0 ports aren't supporting USB 2.0 devices at top speed.	USB 2.0 ports might not be configured correctly.	Enable USB 2.0 support in system BIOS and install correct drivers.	989
USB	USB keychain drive is not recognized by Windows 98 but is recognized by later versions.	Windows 98 does not have built-in support for USB keychain drives.	Install the correct driver on the Windows 98 system.	716
USB	USB peripherals work when plugged into the computer but not when plugged into a hub.	External hubs that are bus-powered might not provide enough power for some devices.	Use the Power dialog box on the USB hub properties sheet in Device Manager to see the power requirements for a device and the power available.	984
Video	Onscreen icons too small at high resolutions.	High resolutions use more dots onscreen, so each dot takes less screen area and fixed-size icons are smaller.	If you use Windows 98, 2000, or XP, enable Large Icons.	880
Video	Slow video performance with any card type.	Video BIOS might not be cached.	Enable caching of video BIOS.	435
Video	Garbage appears on your video screen for no apparent reason.	Hardware resource conflict.	Use Windows Device Manager to find conflicts and resolve them.	379

	Problem		Details About Solution	
Technology	**Symptom**	**Cause**	**Solution**	**Page**
Video	Can't use AGP card as primary video.	PCI video is set as primary video.	Switch primary video to AGP card.	442
Video	Color depth drops below desired setting when resolution is increased.	Video card doesn't have enough RAM to display the resolution at the same color depth.	Upgrade to a video card with more RAM, or decide whether high resolution or higher color depth is more important.	905
Video	Display is steady at lower resolutions but flickers at higher resolutions.	Higher refresh rates are needed at higher resolutions to avoid flicker.	Adjust display adapter properties to higher refresh rate if supported by monitor.	888
Video	Monitor picture is distorted.	Incorrect geometry adjustments; can vary with resolution.	Use digital picture controls to lock in desired picture quality.	891
Video	Windows can't display more than 256 colors.	Windows might have incorrectly identified the video card chipset.	Manually select the correct chipset with the Advanced option on the Display properties' Adapter section.	905
Video	Mouse pointer problems are visible onscreen.	Buggy video or mouse driver.	Upgrade video and mouse driver software; adjust acceleration one notch down.	910
Video	Frequent screen lockups or invalid page fault errors.	Buggy video driver.	Upgrade video driver or adjust acceleration to None.	910
Video	System chooses wrong adapter as primary in a multiple-monitor configuration.	BIOS controls which PCI slot (or AGP) is for primary video.	Adjust BIOS options for primary video, or change slots if both adapters are PCI.	913
Video	Display works in Safe or VGA mode with Windows XP, but is corrupted in other modes.	A Display, DirectX, or mouse driver might be defective.	Update all drivers.	910
Video	3D acceleration isn't working, but normal business applications work okay.	DirectX drivers might be defective.	Update DirectX.	910
Video	Problems with video capture devices.	Various causes.	See checklist.	935
Video	Monitor picture too dull, bright, dark, or out of focus.	Monitor controls need to be adjusted.	Adjust front, side, or rear controls as needed; focus controls might require a long screwdriver.	936
Video	No picture.	Monitor might be in power-saving mode (flashing or yellow LED), have incorrect contrast or brightness settings (green LED), be receiving no picture data; or be disconnected from power.	Activate system; adjust contrast and brightness; check data and power cables.	938
Video	Jittery picture quality (LCD).	Display not correctly adjusted, or cables might be loose.	Use display-adjustment software to correct problem; check cables.	938
Video	Jittery picture quality (CRT).	Might be caused by incorrect refresh rate settings, loose cable, interference, or bad power supply.	Adjust refresh rate lower, check cables, eliminate sources of interference; tap on monitor (temporary fix only).	938

| **Problem** | | | **Details About Solution** | |
Technology	Symptom	Cause	Solution	Page
Video	Picture displayed in DOS, not Windows.	Wrong video driver or overclocked video card.	Start system in Safe mode, verify correct video driver, or use default setup for video card clock speed.	939
Video	Can't replace built-in video card with add-on PCI video card.	Card might be in wrong slot or not compatible with system, or system might require manual disabling or onboard video.	Check manual for correct procedure for disabling built-in video, or try a different slot.	939
Windows	System running Windows NT 4.0 can't access a drive prepared with Windows 2000 or Windows XP.	If drive is running NTFS 5, Windows NT needs Service Pack 4 or above.	Install Service Pack 4 or above to be compatible with NTFS 5; third-party add-ons must be used for compatibility with FAT32.	1387
Windows	Virus warning triggered when trying to upgrade Windows.	Virus warning feature enabled in system BIOS.	Disable virus warning or boot sector write-protect feature.	449
Windows	Operating system will not boot.	Poor heat dissipation.	Check CPU fan; replace if necessary; might need higher-capacity heatsink.	198
Windows	Operating system will not boot.	Improper voltage settings.	Set motherboard for proper core processor voltage.	198
Windows	Operating system will not boot.	Wrong motherboard bus speed.	Set motherboard for proper speed.	198
Windows	Operating system will not boot.	Wrong CPU clock multiplier.	Jumper motherboard for proper clock multiplier.	198
Windows	Operating system will not boot.	Applications will not install or run.	Improper drivers or incompatible hardware; update drivers and check for compatibility issues.	198
Windows	The PC starts in Safe mode (Windows 9x, Windows Me).	Hardware resource conflict.	Use Windows Device Manager to find conflicts and resolve them.	379
Windows	Problems with operating system or applications.	Various causes.	Use checklist.	1341
Windows	File system problems with Windows 9x/Me or DOS.	Various causes.	See checklist.	1415
Windows	File system problems with Windows 2000/XP.	Various causes.	See checklist.	1416
Wireless input	IR-based wireless mouse or keyboard isn't working.	Direct line-of-sight access to IR receiver might be blocked; batteries might have failed.	Check line-of-sight and move obstacles away from receiver; check and replace batteries as needed.	1056
Wireless input	RF-based wireless mouse or keyboard isn't working.	Batteries might have failed, or interference from other devices might be present.	Check and replace batteries if needed; use different frequencies for nearby RF-based devices.	1056
Wireless network	Wi-Fi 5GHz band device can't connect to other Wi-Fi devices.	Wi-Fi 5GHz is the same as IEEE 802.11a, which is not compatible with other Wi-Fi standards.	Use dual-band devices to connect to all Wi-Fi networks.	1128
Wireless network	Can't connect to network at long distances.	Wireless signals degrade with distance and obstacles.	Add a more powerful antenna to the router or access point.	1132

List of Acronyms and Abbreviations

A

a-Si (hydrogenated amorphour silicon)
ABC (Atanasoff-Berry Computer)
ACL (access control list)
ACPI (Advanced Configuration and Power Interface)
ACR (advanced communications riser)
ADC (analog-to-digital converter)
ADPCM (adaptive differential pulse code modulation)
ADR (advanced digital recording)
ADSL (asymmetric DSL)
AFC (antiferromagnetically coupled)
AGC (automatic gain control)
AGP (Accelerated Graphics Port)
AHA (accelerated hub architecture)
AHRA (Audio Home Recording Act)
AIT (advanced intelligent tape)
ALDC (advanced lossless data compression)
ALi (Acer Laboratories, Inc.)
AMD (Advanced Micro Devices)
AMI (American Megatrends, Inc.)
AMR (anistropic magneto-resistant)
AMR (audio modem riser)
ANSI (American National Standards Institute)
API (application programming interface)
APIC (advanced programmable interrupt controller)
APM (Advanced Power Management)
APS (analog protection system)
ARLL (advanced run length limited)
ASPI (Advanced SCSI Programming Interface)
AT (Advanced Technology)
ATA (AT Attachment)
ATAPI (AT Attachment Packet Interface)
ATF (auto tracking following)
AWG (American Wire Gauge)

B

BASIC (beginner's all-purpose symbolic instruction code)
BBSs (bulletin board systems)
BBUL (bumpless build-up layer)
BEDO RAM (burst extended data out RAM)
BF (bus frequency)

BiCMOS (bipolar complementary metal-oxide semiconductor)
BIOS (basic input/output system)
BLER (block error rate)
BOOTP (bootstrap protocol)
BRI (basic rate interface)
BSOD (blue screen of death)
BTB (branch target buffer)
BURN-Proof (Buffer Under-RuN error Proof)

C

CAB (cabinet file)
CAM (common access method)
CAM ATA (Common Access Method AT Attachment)
CAP (carrierless amplitude/phase)
CAS (column address strobe)
CAT (category)
CATV (community access television)
CCITT (Comite Consultatif International Telephonique et Telegraphique)
CD (compact disc)
CD-DA (compact disc digital audio)
CD-MO (compact disc magneto-optical)
CD-R (compact disc-recordable)
CD-ROM (compact disc read-only memory)
CD-RW (compact disc-rewritable)
CDMA (code-division multiple access)
CDSL (consumer DSL)
CERN (Conseil Européen pour la Recherche Nucléaire, or European Organisation for Nuclear Research)
CF (compact flash)
CFCs (chlorofluorocarbons)
CGA (color graphics adapter)
CHAP (Challenge-Handshake Authentication Protocol)
CHS (cylinder head sector)
CIRC (cross-interleave Reed-Solomon code)
CISC (complex instruction set computer)
CLKMUL (clock multiplier)
CLV (constant linear velocity)
CMYK (cyan magenta yellow black)
CNR (Communications and Networking Riser)

COC (chip on ceramic)
CPU (central processing unit)
CRC (cyclical redundancy checking)
CRT (cathode-ray tube)
CS (cable select)
CS (central switch)
CSA (Canadian Standards Agency)
CSEL (cable select)
CSMA/CD (carrier sense multiple access/collision detect)
CSS (contact start stop)
CSS (content scramble system)
CTFT (color thin film transistor)

D

DAC (digital-to-analog converter)
DAE (digital audio extraction)
DASD (direct access storage device)
DASP (drive action/slave present)
DAT (digital audio tape)
db (decibel)
DBB (dynamic bass boost)
DBR (DOS boot record)
DCC (direct cable connection)
DDMA (Distributed DMA)
DDR SDRAM (double data rate SDRAM)
DDS (digital data storage)
DDWG (Digital Display Working Group)
DFP (digital flat panel)
DFT (drive fitness test)
DIB (dual independent bus)
DIMM (dual inline memory module)
DIN (Deutsches Institut fu[um]r Normung e.V.)
DIP (dual inline package)
DIVX (Digital Video Express)
DLT (digital linear tape)
DMA (direct memory access)
DMM (digital multimeter)
DMT (discrete multitone)
DOCSIS (data over cable service interface specifications)
DOS (disk operating system)
DPMI (DOS protected mode interface)
DPMS (display power-management signaling)
DRAM (dynamic RAM)
DSK (Dvorak simplified keyboard)
DSL (digital subscriber line)
DSLAM (DSL access multiplier)
DSP (digital signal processor)

DSTN (Double-layer SuperTwist Nematic) LCD
DVD (digital versatile disc)
DVD-R (DVD-recordable)
DVD+RW (DVD phase change rewritable)
DVI (Digital Video Interface)

E

EAX (environmental audio extensions)
ECC (error correction code)
ECP (enhanced capabilities port)
EDD (enhanced disk drive)
EDO RAM (extended data out RAM)
EEPROM (electronically erasable programmable ROM)
EFM (eight to fourteen modulation) data encoding
EFS (encrypted file system)
EGA (enhanced graphics adapter)
EIDE (Enhanced IDE)
EISA (Extended Industry Standard Architecture)
ELF (extremely low frequency)
EMI (electromagnetic interference)
ENIAC (Electrical Numerical Integrator and Calculator)
EPIC (explicitly parallel instruction computing)
EPP (Enhanced Parallel Port)
EPROM (erasable programmable ROM)
ESD (electrostatic discharge)

F

FAP (Fair Access Policy)
FAQ (frequently asked questions)
FAT (file allocation table)
FC-PGA (flip-chip pin grid array)
FCC (Federal Communications Commission)
FDDI (Fiber Distributed Data Interface)
FDIV (floating-point divide)
FIC (flex interconnect cable)
FIFO (first in first out)
FM (frequency modulation)
FPM DRAM (Fast Page Mode DRAM)
FPT (forced perfect termination)
FPU (floating point unit)
FSB (front-side bus)
FSK (frequency-shift keying)
FST (flat square tube)
FTP (file transfer protocol)
FUD (fear, uncertainty, and doubt)
FWH (firmware hub)

G

GB (gigabyte)
GHz (gigahertz)
GiB (gigabinary bytes)
GMCH (graphics memory controller hub)
GMR (giant magnetoresistive)
GPA (graphics performance accelerator)

H

HAN (home area network)
HD-ROM (high-density read-only memory)
HDA (head disk assembly)
HDD (hard disk drive)
HDTV (high-definition television)
HER (hard error rate)
HFC (hybrid fiber/coax)
HFS (hierarchical file system)
HID (human interface device)
HLF (high-level formatting)
HMA (high memory area)
HP (Hewlett-Packard)
HPFS (high performance file system)
HRTF (head-related transfer function)
HVD (high voltage differential)
Hz (Hertz)

I

I/O (input/output)
IC (integrated circuit)
ICH (integrated controller hub)
iCOMP (Intel Comparative Microprocessor Performance)
ICS (Internet Connection Sharing)
IDE (Integrated Drive Electronics)
IEC (International Electrotechnical Commission)
IED (ID error detection)
IEEE (Institute of Electrical and Electronic Engineers)
IMA (Interactive Multimedia Association)
IMAPI (image mastering application program interface)
IML (initial microcode load)
INCITS (InterNational Committee on Information Technology Standards)
IOS (input/output supervisor)
IP (Internet Protocol)
IPL (initial program load)
IPS (in-plane switching)
IPX (Internetwork packet exchange)

IR (infrared)
IrDA (infrared data)
IRQ (interrupt request)
ISA (Industry Standard Architecture)
ISDN (Integrated Services Digital Network)
ISO (International Organization for Standardization)
ISP (Internet service provider)
ITU (International Telecommunication Union)

J–K

JPEG (Joint Photographic Experts Group)
Kb (kilobit) 1,000 bits
KB (kilobyte) 1,000 bytes
KHz (kilohertz)
Kib (kibibit) 1,024 bits
KiB (kibibyte) 1,024 bytes
KVAR (kilovolt-amperes-reactive)
KVM (keyboard, video, mouse)
KW/KVA (working power/apparent power)

L

L1 (Level 1)
L2 (Level 2)
LAN (local area network)
LBA (logical block address)
LCD (liquid crystal display)
LED (light-emitting diode)
LIF (Low Insertion Force)
LIM (Lotus Intel Microsoft)
LLF (low-level formatting)
LPT (line printer)
LTO (linear tape-open)
LVD (low voltage differential)

M

MAU (media access unit or media attachment unit)
Mb (megabit) 1,000,000 bits
MB (megabyte) 1,000,000 bytes
MBR (master boot record)
MC (microcartridge)
MCA (MicroChannel Architecture)
MCH (memory controller hub)
MCM (multichip module)
MFM (modified frequency modulation)
MFT (master file table)
MHz (megahertz)
Mib (mebibit) 1,048,576 bits

MiB (mebibyte) 1,048,576 bytes

MIC (memory in cassette)

MIDI (Musical Instrument Digital Interface)

MMC (MultiMediaCard)

MMU (memory management unit)

MMX (multimedia extensions or matrix math extensions)

MNP (Microcom Network Protocol)

MO (magneto-optical)

modem (modulator/demodulator)

MOV (metal-oxide varistor)

MPEG (Motion Picture Experts Group)

MPS (Multiprocessor Specification)

MR (Microid Research)

MRH-R (memory repeater hub RDRAM-based)

MRH-S (memory repeater hub SDRAM-based)

MS (Microsoft)

MS-DOS (Microsoft disk operating system)

MSAU (multistation access unit)

MTBF (mean time between failures)

MTH (memory translator hub)

MTTF (mean time to failure)

MVA (multidomain vertical alignment)

N

NAS (network attached storage)

NDP (numeric data processor)

NEAT (New Enhanced AT)

NetBEUI (NetBIOS Extended User Interface)

NetBIOS (network basic input/output system)

NIC (network interface card)

NiCd (nickel cadmium)

NiFe (nickel ferrite)

NiMH (nickel metal hydride)

NMI (nonmaskable interrupt)

NRTC (National Rural Telecommunications Cooperative)

NRZ (non-return to zero)

NTFS (New Technology File System)

NTSC (National Television System Committee)

NVRAM (nonvolatile RAM)

O

OC (optical carrier)

OCR (optical character recognition)

OD (overdrive)

OEM (original equipment manufacturer)

OLGA (organic land grid array)

OS (operating system)

OSI (open systems interconnection)

OSO (overscan operation)

OSTA (Optical Storage Technology Association)

OTP (one-time programmable)

OTP (opposite track path)

P

p-Si (low-temperature polysilicon)

PAC (PCI/AGP Controller)

PAC (pin array cartridge)

PAL (phase alternate line)

PARD (periodic and random deviation)

PC-DOS (personal computer disk operating system)

PCA (power calibration area)

PCI (Peripheral Component Interconnect)

PCMCIA (Personal Computer Memory Card International Association)

PDF (portable document format)

PFA (predictive failure analysis)

PFC (power factor correction)

PGA (pin grid array)

PH (PCI controller hub)

PI (parity inner)

PIIX (PCI ISA IDE Xcelerator)

PIO (programmed input/output)

PLCC (plastic leaded chip carrier)

PLGA (plastic land grid array)

PMA (power memory area)

PnP (Plug and Play)

PO (parity outer)

PoP (point of presence)

POP3 (Post Office Protocol 3)

POST (power on self test)

POTS (plain old telephone service)

PPD (parallel presence detect)

PPD file (postscript printer description file)

PPGA (plastic pin grid array)

PPI (Programmable Peripheral Interface)

PQFP (plastic quad flat pack)

PRI (primary rate interface)

PRML (Partial-Response Maximum-Likelihood)

PROM (programmable ROM)

PSK (phase-shift keying)

PTP (parallel track path)

Q

QAM (quadrature amplitude modulation)
QEGA (quantum extended graphics array)
QFE (quick fix engineering)
QoS (quality of service)

R

RAB (RAID Advisory Board)
RAID (redundant array of independent disks)
RAM (random access memory)
RAMAC (Random Access Method of Accounting and Control)
RAMDAC (RAM digital-to-analog converter)
RBOC (regional Bell operating company)
RDRAM (Rambus DRAM)
RF (radio frequency)
RFI (radio-frequency interference)
RGB (red green blue)
RIAA (Recording Industry Association of America)
RIMM (Rambus inline memory module)
RISC (reduced instruction set computer)
RLL (run length limited)
RNG (random number generator)
ROM (read-only memory)
RPC (regional playback control)
RRIP (Rock Ridge Interchange Protocol)
RTC (real-time clock)
RTC/NVRAM (real-time clock/nonvolatile memory)

S

SACD (super audio compact disc)
SAL (soft adjacent layer)
SASI (Shugart Associates System Interface)
SATA (Serial ATA)
SCAT (Single Chip AT)
SCMS (serial copy management system)
SCSI (small computer system interface)
SD (super density or secure digital)
SDRAM (synchronous DRAM)
SDSL (symmetrical DSL)
SE (single ended)
SEC (single edge contact)
SEC-DED (single-bit error-correction double-bit error detection)
SECAM (Sequential Couleur Avec Memoire)
SECC (single edge contact cartridge)

SEP (single edge processor)
SER (soft error rate)
SGRAM (synchronous graphics RAM)
SIMM (single inline memory module)
SIPP (single inline pin package)
SiS (Silicon Integrated Systems)
SMART (Self-Monitoring Analysis and Reporting Technology)
SMI (system management interrupt)
SMM (system management mode)
SNR (signal-to-noise ratio)
SPD (serial presence detect)
SPDIF (Sony/Philips Digital Interface)
SPGA (staggered pin grid array)
SPI (SCSI Parallel Interface)
SPS (standby power supply)
SPSYNC (spindle synchronization)
SRAM (static RAM)
SSE (Streaming SIMD Extensions)
STP (shielded twisted pair)
SVGA (Super Video Graphics Array)
SWAP (Shared Wireless Access Protocol)
SXGA (Super Extended Graphics Array)

T

TAD (telephone answering device)
TAO (track-at-once)
TAPI (telephone application programming interface)
TCP (tape carrier packaging)
TCP/IP (Transmission Control Protocol/Internet Protocol)
TDMA (transparent DMA or time-division multiple access)
TFT (thin film transistor)
TIP (Trouble In Paradise)
TLB (translation lookaside buffer)
TPI (tracks per inch)
TSOP (thin small outline package)
TSR (terminate and stay resident)

U

UART (Universal Asynchronous Receiver/Transmitter)
UDF (Universal Disk Format)
UDMA (Ultra-DMA)
UI (user interface)
UL (Underwriters Laboratories)
UMA (unified memory architecture)

UMA (upper memory area)
UMB (upper memory block)
UNIVAC (Universal Automatic Computer)
UPI (Universal Peripheral Interface)
UpnP (Universal Plug and Play)
UPS (uninterruptible power supply)
URL (uniform resource locator)
USB (universal serial bus)
USN (update sequence number)
UTP (unshielded twisted pair)
UXGA (Ultra Extended Graphics Array)

V

VAFC (VESA Advanced Feature Connector)
VBR (volume boot record)
VESA (Video Electronics Standards Association)
VESA VIP (Video Interface Port)
VFAT (virtual file allocation table)
VFC (video feature connector)
VGA (Video Graphics Array)
VID (voltage identification)
VIS (viewable image size)
VLF (very low frequency)
VLSI (very large scale integration)
VM (virtual machine)
VMC (VESA Media Channel)
VoIP (voice over IP)
VRM (voltage regulator module)
VRT (voltage reduction technology)
VxD (virtual device driver)

W–X

W2K (Windows 2000)
WAN (wide area network)
WAP (Wireless Application Protocol)
WBR (wireless broadband router)
WEP (wired equivalent privacy)
Wi-Fi (Wireless Fidelity)
WORM (write once read many)
XA (extended architecture)
XGA (Extended Graphics Array)
XMS (Extended Memory Specification)

Y–Z

Y2K (year 2000)
ZBR (zoned-bit recording)
ZIF (zero insertion force)
ZV (zoomed video)

INDEX

Numbers

More knowledge from the PC hardware master!

For years, Scott Mueller has brought you the most complete, up-to-date information on PC hardware. Now, he has taken that formula for success and written two new books, covering today's hottest topics in the manner you've grown to know and trust. Plus, a new edition of *Upgrading and Repairing Networks* is available now. Don't miss the newest books in the *Upgrading and Repairing* line!

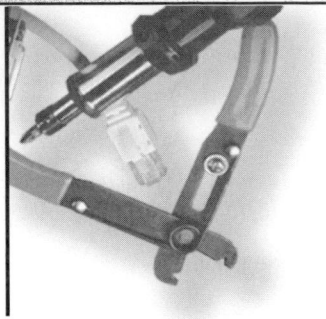

Upgrading and Repairing Laptops
ISBN: 0-7897-2800-1
1008 pp.
$49.99 USD
2nd Edition Coming in 2005!

Upgrading and Repairing Servers
ISBN: 0-7897-2815-X
1408 pp.
$69.99 USD
Coming 2005!

Upgrading and Repairing Networks Fourth Edition
ISBN: 0-7897-2817-6
1312 pp.
$59.99 USD
On shelves now!

Upgrading and Repairing PCs, 16th Edition

Scott Mueller

Thank you for making *Upgrading and Repairing PCs* by Scott Mueller the best-selling PC hardware repair book of all time. Please help us tailor the content of the next edition to best fit your needs by taking a few minutes to answer these questions and returning this self-addressed form. Your opinion counts!

1. Does your job involve upgrading, repairing, building, or troubleshooting PCs on a regular basis?
   - ❑ Yes
   - ❑ No

2. What hardware/peripherals have you upgraded in the past year or intend to upgrade in the next year?
   - ❑ Processor
   - ❑ Motherboard
   - ❑ RAM
   - ❑ Video card
   - ❑ Audio card
   - ❑ Hard disk
   - ❑ CD-ROM or CD-RW drive
   - ❑ DVD-ROM or DVD+/-RW drive
   - ❑ Removable storage
   - ❑ Keyboard or mouse
   - ❑ Wired network card
   - ❑ Wireless network card
   - ❑ Power supply
   - ❑ Case
   - ❑ None of the above
   - ❑ Other _____

3. Have you purchased a previous version of this book?
   - ❑ Yes (list versions) _____
   - ❑ No

4. What convinced you to buy your latest edition of *Upgrading and Repairing PCs*?(Check all that apply.)
   - ❑ Author's reputation
   - ❑ Publisher's reputation
   - ❑ Recommendation
   - ❑ Price
   - ❑ Size
   - ❑ Cover information
   - ❑ Table of contents
   - ❑ Advertisement
   - ❑ Bookstore promotion
   - ❑ Good experience with an earlier edition of the book

5. Where did you buy the most recent edition you own?
   - ❑ Bookstore
   - ❑ Warehouse club
   - ❑ Other _____
   - ❑ Office club
   - ❑ Internet site—Which site? _____
   - ❑ Computer store
   - ❑ Consumer electronics store

6. How often do you refer to *Upgrading and Repairing PCs*?
   - ❑ Daily
   - ❑ Weekly
   - ❑ Monthly
   - ❑ Occasionally
   - ❑ Rarely
   - ❑ Never

7. What's the most frequent reason you refer to *Upgrading and Repairing PCs*?
   - ❑ Add something to my PC
   - ❑ Fix a problem
   - ❑ Improve performance
   - ❑ Enable software
   - ❑ Learn how my PC works
   - ❑ I just bought it and want to see what's new

8. How often do you purchase a revised edition of *Upgrading and Repairing PCs*?
   - ❑ Every year
   - ❑ When I buy a new PC
   - ❑ I won't buy a new edition of this book
   - ❑ Occasionally

9. What are your three favorite and least favorite topics in the book?

Favorite	Least Favorite
_____	_____
_____	_____
_____	_____

10. If you have watched the video content on the disc with this book, how useful did you find it?
    - ❑ Extremely useful
    - ❑ Useful
    - ❑ Not very useful

11. What type of processor is in the computer(s) you currently use? (Check all that apply.)
    - ❑ Intel Pentium 4 (any core)
    - ❑ Intel Pentium M
    - ❑ Intel Pentium 4M
    - ❑ Intel Celeron
    - ❑ Intel Pentium III
    - ❑ Intel Mobile Pentium III
    - ❑ Intel Pentium II
    - ❑ Intel Mobile Pentium II
    - ❑ Intel Pentium/ Pentium MMX or older
    - ❑ Intel Mobile Pentium
    - ❑ AMD Athlon 64/FX
    - ❑ AMD Athlon XP
    - ❑ AMD Athlon
    - ❑ AMD Duron
    - ❑ AMD K6 II or older
    - ❑ Other _____

12. For what purpose do you primarily use your computer(s)?
    - ❑ Personal (non-gaming)
    - ❑ Gaming
    - ❑ Professional

13. Besides *Upgrading and Repairing PCs*, what resources do you use for hardware information? (Check all that apply.)
    - ❑ Web sites—which? _____
    - ❑ Mailing lists
    - ❑ Magazines—which? _____
    - ❑ Colleagues
    - ❑ Other books—which? _____
    - ❑ Other _____

14. Have you pursued or do you plan to pursue any certifications?

	Have Pursued	Plan to Pursue
A+		
MCSE		
Network+		
Cisco(Any)		
Other		
Network+		

Please specify other: _____

15. What types of removable storage media are currently in use in the system(s) you use, upgrade, repair, build, or troubleshoot? (Check all that apply.)

- ❏ 1.44M floppy
- ❏ 2.88M floppy
- ❏ LS-120/240 SuperDisk
- ❏ CD-RW
- ❏ DVD+/-RW
- ❏ Magnetic cartridge media (Zip, Jaz, etc.)
- ❏ Flash memory (Sony Memory Stick, MultiMedia Cards, etc.)
- ❏ Other _____

16. What type of hard drive interfaces are currently in use in the system(s) you use, upgrade, repair, build, or troubleshoot? (Check all that apply.)

- ❏ Parallel ATA (IDE)
- ❏ Serial ATA
- ❏ SCSI (any type)

17. Which operating systems are currently in use in the system(s) you use, upgrade, repair, build, or troubleshoot? (Check all that apply.)

- ❏ MS/PC DOS 6.x or earlier DOS versions
- ❏ Windows 9x or Me
- ❏ Windows NT 4 or older
- ❏ Windows 2000
- ❏ Windows XP
- ❏ Windows Server 2003
- ❏ Linux
- ❏ Other _____

18. Age

- ❏ Under 18
- ❏ 18–25
- ❏ 26–34
- ❏ 35–50
- ❏ 51–65
- ❏ 65+

19. Annual Income

- ❏ Less than $25,000
- ❏ $25,000–$50,000
- ❏ $50,000–$75,000
- ❏ $75,000–$100,000
- ❏ More than $100,000
- ❏ Prefer not to say

20. Job

- ❏ Technician
- ❏ Trainer or teacher
- ❏ Administrator
- ❏ Programmer
- ❏ Computer architect
- ❏ Other _____

If we may contact you for follow-up surveys or questions regarding this book or other Que books, please fill in the following information (otherwise, leave this blank):

Name _____

Address _____

City_____ State _____ ZIP Code _____

Phone number _____ Email address _____

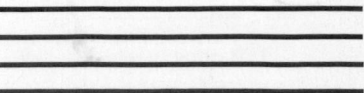

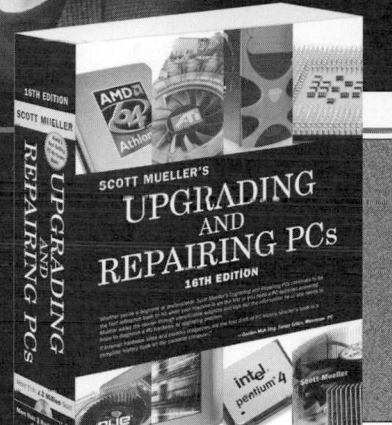

License Agreement

By opening this package, you are agreeing to be bound by the following agreement:

You may not copy or redistribute the entire media as a whole. Copying and redistribution of individual software programs on the media is governed by terms set by individual copyright holders.

The installer and code from the author(s) are copyrighted by the publisher and author(s). Individual programs and other items on the media are copyrighted by their various authors or other copyright holders. Some of the programs included with this product may be governed by an Open Source license, which allows redistribution; see the license information for each product for more information.

Other programs are included on the media by special permission from their authors.

This software is provided as is without warranty of any kind, either expressed or implied, including but not limited to the implied warranties of merchantability and fitness for a particular purpose. Neither the publisher nor its dealers or distributors assume any liability for any alleged or actual damages arising from the use of this program. (Some states do not allow for the exclusion of implied warranties, so the exclusion may not apply to you.)

Installing the DVD

The DVD accompanying this book is playable on both a standalone DVD player (DVD player attached to your television/home theater system) and a DVD drive installed in or connected to your PC.

Standalone DVD Video Players

To play the videos on this DVD, insert the DVD into your standalone DVD video player and navigate the menus using your DVD player's remote, just as you would do with any DVD.

Note

The DVD is region-free. The extra features using Internet (Web) links are not active links; you must enter the specified URLs into your Web browser directly. Extra features and Windows Media Player–formatted videos are also available on Scott's Web site at www.upgradingandrepairingpcs.com.

PC-Based DVD Drives

To play the DVD video content, do the following:

1. Insert the DVD into your PC's DVD drive.
2. Run your previously installed DVD player application and select Play.
3. Navigate the DVD menus as you would any standard DVD video. Any Web links in the DVD Extras section must be manually entered into your browser.

Most DVD drives include a decoder/player application. If you do not currently have a DVD decoder/player installed on your system, you can do one of the following:

- Play the disc in a standard set-top DVD player.
- Use an existing DVD decoder with Windows Media Player 9 or later (visit www.microsoft.com/windows/windowsmedia).
- Purchase a DVD decoder to use with Windows Media Player, such as the plug-in available from Cyberlink (www.gocyberlink.com/winxp_plugin/dvd_se).
- Purchase a complete decoder/player combination, such as PowerDVD by CyberLink (www.gocyberlink.com), WinDVD by Intervideo (www.intervideo.com), or SoftDVD by MGI (www.mgisoft.com).

Here's how to access the Technical Reference files, previous editions of the book, and any other files on the DVD-ROM:

1. Insert the DVD into your PC's DVD drive.
2. Open My Computer.
3. Right-click the icon for the DVD drive containing the disc.
4. Select Explore.
5. Navigate through the folders and files just as if you were viewing files stored on your computer's hard drive.

Note

Many of the documents included in the Extras section of the DVD are in PDF format, which requires Adobe Acrobat to view. Acrobat is included free on the DVD, and updates to Acrobat can be found at www.adobe.com.

System Requirements for DVD-ROM Video

The minimum system configuration is as follows:

- Intel Celeron/Pentium or AMD Duron/Athlon processor, 400MHz
- Windows 98 Second Edition, Me, 2000, or XP
- 64MB of RAM (Windows 2000 and XP require 128MB of RAM)
- 4MB graphics card, 800x600 resolution, 16-bit color
- Direct Sound–compatible sound card
- 4X DVD-ROM drive (UDMA enabled)
- Direct Show–compliant DVD decoder/player software installed
- Direct X 7.0
- Internet Explorer 5.0

Access to DVD Content Without a DVD Player or DVD Drive

If you do not have a set-top DVD player or DVD drive, you can still access all the files included on the DVD-ROM by visiting www.upgradingandrepairingpcs.com. To access these materials on the Web, follow these steps:

1. Remove the DVD from the package insert and note the password on the DVD label.
2. Visit www.upgradingandrepairingpcs.com and follow the DVD link from the home page.
3. Enter your password as included on the DVD label.
4. You can then download any of the files provided there, including Windows Media Player versions of the videos, multiple previous editions in PDF format, a hard drive specification database, a vendor database, and more.